THE YEAR'S WORK 2014

The Year's Work in
English Studies
Volume 95

Covering work published in 2014

Edited by
WILLIAM BAKER
and
KENNETH WOMACK
with associate editors

OLGA FISCHER
A. S. G. EDWARDS
RICHARD WOOD
KIRSTIE BLAIR
MATTHEW CREASY
THERESA SAXON
JAMES GIFFORD
PAUL SHARRAD

Published for
THE ENGLISH ASSOCIATION

by

OXFORD
UNIVERSITY PRESS

OXFORD

UNIVERSITY PRESS

Great Clarendon Street, Oxford OX2 6DP, UK

Oxford University Press is a department of the University of Oxford.
It furthers the University's objective of excellence in research, scholarship,
and education by publishing worldwide in
Oxford New York
Athens Auckland Bangkok Bogotá Buenos Aires Cape Town
Chennai Dar es Salaam Delhi Florence Hong Kong Istanbul Karachi
Kolkata Kuala Lumpur Madrid Melbourne Mexico City Mumbai Nairobi
Paris São Paulo Shanghai Taipei Tokyo Toronto Warsaw

Oxford is a registered trade mark of Oxford University Press
in the UK and in certain other countries
© The English Association 2016

The moral rights of the author have been asserted
Database right Oxford University Press (maker)
First published 2016

British Library Cataloguing in Publication Data
Data available
ISSN 0084-4144
ISBN 9780198801061
1 3 5 7 9 10 8 6 4 2
Typeset by Cenveo publisher services, Bangalore, India
Printed in Great Britain by Bell & Bain, Glasgow

The English Association

The object of The English Association is to promote the knowledge and appreciation of English language and its literatures.

The Association pursues these aims by creating opportunities of co-operation among all those interested in English; by furthering the recognition of English as essential in education; by discussing methods of English teaching; by holding lectures, conferences, and other meetings; by publishing several journals, books, and leaflets; and by forming local branches overseas and at home. English Association Fellowships recognize distinction and achievement in the field of English worldwide.

Publications

The Year's Work in English Studies. An annual narrative bibliography which aims to cover all work of quality in English studies published in a given year. Published by Oxford University Press.

The Year's Work in Critical and Cultural Theory. An annual narrative bibliography which aims to provide comprehensive cover of all work of quality in critical and cultural theory published in a given year. Published by Oxford University Press.

Essays and Studies. A well-established series of annual themed volumes edited each year by a distinguished academic.

English. This internationally-known journal of the Association is aimed at teachers of English in universities and colleges, with articles on all aspects of literature and critical theory, an extensive reviews section and original poetry. Four issues per year. Published by Oxford University Press.

Use of English. The longest-standing journal for English teachers in schools and colleges. Three issues per year.

English 4–11. Designed and developed by primary English specialists to give practical help to primary and middle school teachers. Three issues per year.

English Association Studies. A monograph series published in association with Liverpool University Press.

Issues in English. Occasional pamphlet series.

Membership

Membership information can be found at http://www.le.ac.uk/engassoc or please write to The English Association, University of Leicester, University Road, Leicester LE1 7RH, UK or email: engassoc@le.ac.uk.

The Year's Work
in English Studies

Subscriptions for Volume 95

Institutional (combined rate to both *The Year's Work in English Studies* and *The Year's Work in Critical and Cultural Theory*) print and online: £446.00/$838.00/ €669.00. *Institutional* (*The Year's Work in English Studies* only) print and online: £306.00/$573.00/€461.00.

Please note: £/€ rates apply in Europe, US$ elsewhere. All prices include postage, and for subscribers outside the UK delivery is by Standard Air. There may be other subscription rates available. For a complete listing, please visit www.ywes.oxford journals.org/oup_journals/ywes/access_purchase/price_list.html.

Online Access

For details please email Oxford University Press Journals Customer Services on: jnls.cust.serv@oup.com.

Order Information

Full prepayment, in the correct currency, is required for all orders. Orders are regarded as firm and payments are not refundable. Subscriptions are accepted and entered on a complete volume basis. Claims cannot be considered more than FOUR months after publication or date of order, whichever is later. All subscriptions in Canada are subject to GST. Subscriptions in the EU may be subject to European VAT. If registered, please supply details to avoid unnecessary charges. For subscriptions that include online versions, a proportion of the subscription price may be subject to UK VAT.

Methods of payment. (i) Cheque (payable to Oxford University Press, Cashiers Office, Great Clarendon Street, Oxford OX2 6DP, UK) in GB£ Sterling (drawn on a UK bank), US$ Dollars (drawn on a US bank), or EU€ Euros. (ii) Bank transfer to Barclays Bank Plc, Oxford Group Office, Oxford (bank sort code 20-65-18) (UK), overseas only Swift code BARC GB 22 (GB£ Sterling to account no. 70299332, IBAN GB89BARC20651870299332; US$ Dollars to account no. 66014600, IBAN GB27BARC20651866014600; EU€ Euros to account no. 78923655, IBAN GB16BARC20651878923655). (iii) Credit card (Mastercard, Visa, Switch or American Express).

Back Issues

The current volume plus two back volumes are available from Oxford University Press. Previous volumes can be obtained from the Periodicals Service Company, 11 Main Street, Germantown, NY 12526, USA. Email: psc@periodicals.com; tel: +1 (518) 537 4700; fax: +1 (518) 537 5899.

Further information. Journals Customer Service Department, Oxford University Press, Great Clarendon Street, Oxford OX2 6DP, UK. Email: jnls.cust.serv@oup.com; tel (and answerphone outside normal working hours): +44 (0) 1865 353907; fax: +44 (0) 1865 353485. *In the US, please contact:* Journals Customer Service Department, Oxford University Press, 2001 Evans Road, Cary, NC 27513, USA. Email: jnlorders@oup.com; tel (and answerphone outside normal working hours): 800 852 7323 (toll-free in USA/Canada); fax: 919 677 1714. *In Japan, please contact:* Journals Customer Services, Oxford Journals, Oxford University Press, Tokyo, 4-5-10-8F Shiba, Minato-ku, Tokyo 108-8386, Japan. Email: custserv.jp@oup.com; Tel: +81 3 5444 5858; Fax: +81 3 3454 2929.

The Year's Work in English Studies (ISSN 0084 4144) is published annually by Oxford University Press, Oxford, UK. Annual subscription price is £306.00/$573.00/ €461.00. *The Year's Work in English Studies* is distributed by Mercury International, 365 Blair Road, Avenel, NJ 07001, USA. Periodicals postage paid at Rahway, NJ and at additional entry points.

US Postmaster: send address changes to *The Year's Work in English Studies*, c/o Mercury International, 365 Blair Road, Avenel, NJ 07001, USA.

The Table of Contents email alerting service allows anyone who registers their email address to be notified via email when new content goes online. Details are available at http://ywes.oxfordjournals.org/cgi/alerts/etoc.

Permissions

For permissions requests, please visit www.oxfordjournals.org/permissions.

Advertising

Inquiries about advertising should be sent to Oxford Journals Advertising, Oxford University Press, Great Clarendon Street, Oxford, OX2 6DP, UK. Email: jnlsadvertising@oup.com; tel: +44 (0) 1865 354767; fax: +44 (0) 1865 353774.

Disclaimer

Statements of fact and opinion in the articles in *The Year's Work in English Studies* are those of the respective authors and contributors and not of the English Association or Oxford University Press. Neither Oxford University Press nor the English Association make any representation, express or implied, in respect of the accuracy of the material in this journal and cannot accept any legal responsibility or liability for any errors or omissions that may be made.

Contents

xii   CONTENTS

The University of the West Indies; Tina Steiner, Stellenbosch
University

Abbreviations

1. Journals, Series and Reference Works

19	*Interdisciplinary Studies in the Long Nineteenth Century*
AAR	*African American Review*
AAS	*Australian Aboriginal Studies*
ABäG	*Amsterdamer Beiträge zur Älteren Germanistik*
ABELL	*Annual Bibliography of English Language and Literature*
ABSt	*A/B: Auto/Biography Studies*
AC	*Archeologia Classica*
AcadSF	*Academia Scientiarum Fennica*
ACar	*Analecta Cartusiana*
ACH	*Australian Cultural History*
ACM	*Aligarh Critical Miscellany*
ACR	*Australasian Catholic Record*
ACS	*Australian-Canadian Studies: A Journal for the Humanities and Social Sciences*
ActaS	*Acta Scieniarum: Language and Culture*
ActR	*Action Research*
AdI	*Annali d'Italianistica*
AdLLS	*Advances in Language and Literary Studies*
ADS	*Australasian Drama Studies*
AEnglishes	*Asian Englishes*
AES	*Asian English Studies*
AEQ	*Adult Education Quarterly*
AF	*Anglistische Forschungen*
Affirmations	*Affirmations: Of The Modern*
AfId	*African Identities*
AfricanA	*African Affairs*
AfrSR	*African Studies Review*
AfT	*African Theatre*
AgeJ	*Age of Johnson: A Scholarly Annual*
AH	*Art History*
AHR	*American Historical Review*
AI	*American Imago*
AIQ	*American Indian Quarterly*
AJ	*Art Journal*
AJFS	*Australian Journal of French Studies*
AJHSS	*American Journal of Humanities and Social Sciences*
AJIS	*Australian Journal of Irish Studies*
AJL	*Australian Journal of Linguistics*
AJP	*American Journal of Psychoanalysis*
AJPH	*Australian Journal of Politics and History*
AJS	*American Journal of Semiotics*
AL	*American Literature*

ALA	*African Literature Association Annuals*
ALASH	*Acta Linguistica Academiae Scientiarum Hungaricae*
ALJ	*The Australian Library Journal*
AlexS	*Alexander Shakespeare*
ALH	*Acta Linguistica Hafniensia; International Journal of Linguistics*
Alif	*Journal of Comparative Poetics* (Cairo, Egypt)
ALitASH	*Acta Literaria Academiae Scientiarum Hungaricae*
ALN	*American Literary Nationalism Newsletter*
ALR	*American Literary Realism, 1870–1910*
ALS	*Australian Literary Studies*
ALT	*African Literature Today*
AltMo	*Altre Modernita*
AltT	*alt.theatre:cultural diversity and the stage*
AmasJ	*Amerasian Journal*
AmDram	*American Drama*
AmerP	*American Poetry*
AmerS	*American Studies*
AmLH	*American Literary History*
AmLS	*American Literary Scholarship: An Annual*
AMon	*Atlantic Monthly*
AmPer	*American Periodicals*
Amst	*Amerikastudien/American Studies*
AN	*Acta Neophilologica*
AnBol	*Analecta Bollandiana*
ANCH	*American Nineteenth Century History*
ANF	*Arkiv för Nordisk Filologi*
Anglia	*Anglia: Zeitschrift für Englische Philologie*
Anglica	*Anglica: An International Journal of English Studies*
Anglistik	*Anglistik: Mitteilungen des Verbandes Deutscher Anglisten*
AnH	*Analecta Husserliana*
AnL	*Anthropological Linguistics*
AnM	*Annuale Mediaevale*
Ann	*Annales: Économies, Sociétés, Civilisations*
ANQ	*ANQ: A Quarterly Journal of Short Articles, Notes and Reviews*
AnT	*Anthropology Today*
AntColl	*Antique Collector*
Anthurium	*Anthurium: A Caribbean Studies Journal*
AntigR	*Antigonish Review*
Antipodes	*Antipodes: A North American Journal of Australian Literature*
ANStu	*Anglo-Norman Studies*
ANZSC	*Australian and New Zealand Studies in Canada*
ANZTR	*Australian and New Zealand Theatre Record*
APBR	*Atlantic Provinces Book Review*
APJLE	*Asia Pacific Journal of Education*
APL	*Antwerp Papers in Linguistics*
AppLing	*Applied Linguistics*
AppLiRev	*Applied Linguistics Review*
AppPsycholing	*Applied Psycholinguistics*
APR	*American Poetry Review*
AQ	*American Quarterly*
AR	*Antioch Review*
ArAA	*Arbeiten aus Anglistik und Amerikanistik*
ARAL	*Annual Review of Applied Linguistics*

Arcadia	*Arcadia: Internationale Zeitschrift für Literaturwissenschaft*
Archiv	*Archiv für das Stadium der Neueren Sprachen und Literaturen*
ARCS	*American Review of Canadian Studies*
ArdenS	Arden Shakespeare
Area	*Area: Journal of the Royal Geographical Society*
ArielE	*Ariel: A Review of International English Literature*
Arion	*Arion: A Journal of the Humanities and the Classics*
ArkQ	*Arkansas Quarterly: A Journal of Criticism*
ArkR	*Arkansas Review: A Journal of Criticism*
ArQ	*Arizona Quarterly*
ARS	*Augustan Reprint Society*
Ars&H	*Ars & Humanitas*
ARSR	*Australian Religion Studies Review*
ArtB	*Art Bulletin*
Arth	*Arthuriana*
ArthI	*Arthurian Interpretations*
ArthL	*Arthurian Literature*
Arv	*Arv: Nordic Yearbook of Folklore*
AS	*American Speech*
ASch	*American Scholar*
ASE	*Anglo-Saxon England*
ASInt	*American Studies International*
ASoc	*Arts in Society*
Aspects	*Aspects: Journal of the Language Society* (University of Essex)
AspectsAF	*Aspects of Australian Fiction*
Asp	*Anglais de spécialité*
ASR	*Asian Studies Review*
Assaph	*Assaph: Studies in the Arts (Theatre Studies)*
ATJ	*Asian Theatre Journal*
Atlantis	*Atlantis: A Journal of the Spanish Association for Anglo-American Studies*
ATR	*Anglican Theological Review*
AtS	*Atlantic Studies*
AuBR	*Australian Book Review*
AuFolk	*Australian Folklore*
AuFS	*Australian Feminist Studies*
AuHR	*Australian Humanities Review*
AuJL	*Australian Journal of Linguistics*
Aurealis	*Australian Fantasy and Science Fiction Magazine*
AuS	*Australian Studies*
AuSA	*Australian Studies* (Australia)
AusCan	*Australian-Canadian Studies*
AusPl	*Australian Playwrights*
AustrianS	*Austrian Studies*
AuWBR	*Australian Women's Book Review*
AVSJ	*Australasian Journal of Victorian Studies*
AY	*Arthurian Yearbook*
BAF1900	*British and American Fiction to 1900*
BakhtinN	*Bakhtin Newsletter*
BALF	*Black American Literature Forum*
B&A	*Brain and Language*
BAReview	*British Academy Review*
BARS Bulletin	*British Association for Romantic Studies Bulletin & Review*

BAS	*British and American Studies*
BASAM	*BASA Magazine*
BaylorJ	*Baylor Journal of Theatre and Performance*
BBCS	*Bulletin of the Board of Celtic Studies*
BBCSh	*BBC Shakespeare*
BBN	*British Book News*
BBSIA	*Bulletin Bibliographique de la Société Internationale Arthurienne*
BC	*Book Collector*
BCan	*Books in Canada*
BCMA	*Bulletin of Cleveland Museum of Art*
BCS	*B.C. Studies*
Bell	*Belgian Essays on Language and Literature*
BEPIF	*Bulletin des Itudes Portugaises et Brésiliennes*
BFLS	*Bulletin de la Faculté des Lettres de Strasbourg*
BH	*Book History*
BHI	*British Humanities Index*
BHL	*Bibliotheca Hagiographica Latina Antiquae et Mediae Aetatis*
BHM	*Bulletin of the History of Medicine*
BHR	*Bibliothèque d'Humanisme et Renaissance*
BHS	*Bulletin of Hispanic Studies*
BI	*Books at Iowa*
Bibliotheck	*Bibliotheck: A Scottish Journal of Bibliography and Allied Topics*
Big Muddy	*Big Muddy: A Journal of the Mississippi River*
Biography	*Biography: An Interdisciplinary Quarterly*
BioL	*Biolinguistics*
BJA	*British Journal of Aesthetics*
BJCS	*British Journal of Canadian Studies*
BJDC	*British Journal of Disorders of Communication*
BJECS	*British Journal for Eighteenth-Century Studies*
BJHP	*British Journal for the History of Philosophy*
BJHS	*British Journal for the History of Science*
BJJ	*Ben Jonson Journal*
BJL	*Belgian Journal of Linguistics*
BJPS	*British Journal for the Philosophy of Science*
BJRL	*Bulletin of the John Rylands* (University Library of Manchester)
BJS	*British Journal of Sociology*
Blake	*Blake: An Illustrated Quarterly*
BLC	*Bilingualism: Language and Cognition*
BLE	*Bulletin de Littérature Ecclésiastique*
BLJ	*British Library Journal*
BLR	*Bodleian Library Record*
BN	*Beiträge zur Namenforschung*
BNB	*British National Bibliography*
BoH	*Book History*
Boundary	*Boundary 2: A Journal of Postmodern Literature and Culture*
BP	*Banasthali Patrika*
BPMA	*Bulletin of Philadelphia Museum of Art*
BPN	*Barbara Pym Newsletter*
BRASE	*Basic Readings in Anglo-Saxon England*
BRH	*Bulletin of Research in the Humanities*
Brick	*Brick: A Journal of Reviews*
BRMMLA	*Bulletin of the Rocky Mountain Modern Language Association*
BRN	*Black Renaissance Noire*

BRONZS	*British Review of New Zealand Studies*
BS	*Bronte Studies*
BSE	*Brno Studies in English*
BSJ	*Baker Street Journal: An Irregular Quarterly of Sherlockiana*
BSLP	*Bulletin de la Société de Linguistique de Paris*
BSNotes	*Browning Society Notes*
BSRS	*Bulletin of the Society for Renaissance Studies*
BSSA	*Bulletin de la Société de Stylistique Anglaise*
BST	*Brontë Society Transactions*
BSUF	*Ball State University Forum*
BTHGNewsl	*Book Trade History Group Newsletter*
BTLV	*Bijdragen tot de Taal-, Land- en Volkenhunde*
Bul	*Bulletin* (Australia)
BunyanS	*Bunyan Studies*
BuR	*Bucknell Review*
BurlM	*Burlington Magazine*
BurnsC	*Burns Chronicle*
BWPLL	*Belfast Working Papers in Language and Linguistics*
ByronJ	*Byron Journal*
CABS	*Contemporary Authors Bibliographical Series*
CahiersE	*Cahiers Élisabéthains*
CahiersRMH	*Cahiers de recherches médiévales et humanistes*
CAIEF	*Cahiers de l'Association Internationale des Études Françaises*
CalR	*Calcutta Review*
CamObsc	*Camera Obscura: A Journal of Feminism and Film Theory*
CamR	*Cambridge Review*
CanD	*Canadian Drama/L'Art Dramatique Canadienne*
CanJL	*Canadian Journal of Linguistics*
C&L	*Christianity and Literature*
C&Lang	*Communication and Languages*
C&M	*Classica et Medievalia*
CanL	*Canadian Literature*
CanPo	*Canadian Poetry*
CapR	*Capilano Review*
CARA	*Centre Aixois de Recherches Anglaises*
CaribW	*Caribbean Writer*
CarQ	*Caribbean Quarterly*
CarR	*Caribbean Review*
CASE	*Cambridge Studies in Anglo-Saxon England*
CathHR	*Catholic Historical Review*
CatR	*Catalan Review*
CBEL	*Cambridge Bibliography of English Literature*
CC	*Chimurenga Chronic*
CCL	*Canadian Children's Literature*
CCompCon	*College Composition and Communication*
CCor	*Cardiff Corvey: Reading the Romantic Text*
CCRes	*Cross-Cultural Research*
CCRev	*Comparative Civilizations Review*
CCS	*Comparative Critical Studies*
CCrit	*Comparative Criticism: An Annual Journal*
CCW	*Critical and Creative Wings*
CD	*Comparative Drama*
CDALB	*Concise Dictionary of American Literary Biography*

CDCP	Comparative Drama Conference Papers
CDE	Contemporary Drama in English
CDIL	Cahiers de l'Institut de Linguistique de Louvain
CdL	Cahiers de Lexicologie
CDS	Critical Discourse Studies
CE	College English
CEA	CEA Critic
CEAfr	Cahiers d'Études Africaines
CE&S	Commonwealth Essays and Studies
CEch	Caietele Echinox
CentR	Centennial Review
Centro	Centro: Journal for the Centre for Puerto Rican Studies
CF	Crime Factory
CFM	Canadian Fiction Magazine
CFS	Cahiers Ferdinand de Saussure: Revue de Linguistique Générale
CH	Computers and the Humanities
ChauR	Chaucer Review
ChauY	Chaucer Yearbook
ChE	Changing English
ChildL	Children's Literature: Journal of Children's Literature Studies
ChiR	Chicago Review
ChLB	Charles Lamb Bulletin
CHR	Camden History Review
ChRC	Church History and Religious Culture
CHum	Computers and the Humanities
CI	Critical Idiom
CinJ	Cinema Journal
CIQ	Colby Quarterly
CISh	Contemporary Interpretations of Shakespeare
CJ	Classical Journal
CJE	Cambridge Journal of Education
CJH	Canadian Journal of History
CJL	Canadian Journal of Linguistics
CJPLI	The Cambridge Journal of Postcolonial Literary Inquiry
CJR	Christian–Jewish Relations
CK	Common Knowledge
CL	Comparative Literature (Eugene, OR)
CLAJ	CLA Journal
CLAQ	Children's Literature Association Quarterly
ClassRJ	Classical Receptions Journal
ClassW	Classical World
CLC	Columbia Library Columns
CLCWeb	Comparative Literature and Culture (online)
CLE	Children's Literature in Education
CLet	Confronto Letterario
CLetras	Cadernos de Letras (Faculdade de Letras–UFRJ)
CLIN	Cuadernos de Literatura
CLLT	Corpus Linguistics and Linguistic Theory
CLS	Comparative Literature Studies
Clues	Clues: A Journal of Detection
CMCS	Cambridge Medieval Celtic Studies
CML	Classical and Modern Literature
CN	Chaucer Newsletter

CNIE	Commonwealth Novel in English
CogLing	Cognitive Linguistics
Cog&Em	Cognition and Emotion
CogSem	Journal of Cognitive Studies
ColB	Coleridge Bulletin
ColF	Columbia Forum
CollG	Colloquia Germanica
CollL	College Literature
Colloquy	Colloquy: Text Theory Critique
Com	Commonwealth
Comitatus	Comitatus: A Journal of Medieval and Renaissance Studies
Comparatist	Comparatist: Journal of the Southern Comparative Literature Association
ComparativeCS	Comparative Critical Studies
CompAS	Comparative American Studies
CompD	Comparative Drama
CompLit	Comparative Literature
ComS	Commentary
Concentric	Concentric: Literary and Cultural Studies
ConL	Contemporary Literature
ConLing	Contemporary Linguistics
Connotations	Connotations: A Journal for Critical Debate
ConnR	Connecticut Review
ContempR	Contemporary Review
ConTR	Contemporary Theatre Review
COPAS	Current Objectives of Postgraduate American Studies
Coppertales	Coppertales: A Journal of Rural Arts
Cordite	Cordite Poetry Review
Corp	Corpora
Costume	Journal of the Costume Society
CP	Concerning Poetry
CQ	Cambridge Quarterly
CR	Critical Review
CRev	Chesterton Review
CRevAS	Canadian Review of American Studies
Crit	Critique: Studies in Contemporary Fiction
CritE	The Critical Endeavour
Criterion	The Criterion
CritI	Critical Inquiry
Criticism	Criticism: A Quarterly for Literature and the Arts
CritQ	Critical Quarterly
CritT	Critical Texts: A Review of Theory and Criticism
CrM	Critical Mass
CRJ	Classical Receptions Journal
CS	Critical Survey
CSA	Carlyle Studies Annual
CSASE	Cambridge Studies in Anglo-Saxon England
CSCC	Case Studies in Contemporary Criticism
CSELT	Cambridge Studies in Eighteenth-Century Literature and Thought
CSLT	Cultural Studies and Literary Theory
CSMC	Critical Studies in Media Communication
CSML	Cambridge Studies in Medieval Literature
CSNCLC	Cambridge Studies in Nineteenth-Century Literature and Culture

CSPC	*Cambridge Studies in Paleography and Codicology*
CSR	*Cambridge Studies in Romanticism*
CSRev	*Christian Scholar's Review*
CSSAM	*Comparative Studies of South Asia, Africa and the Middle East*
CStA	*Carlyle Studies Annual* (previously *CAnn*)
CTR	*Canadian Theatre Review*
Cuadernos	*Cuadernos de Literatura Infantil y Juvenil*
CuadHisp	*Cuadernos Hispanoamericanos*
CulA	*Cultural Anthropology*
CulC	*Cultural Critique*
CulS	*Cultural Studies*
CulSR	*Cultural Studies Review*
CUNY	*CUNY English Forum*
Current Writing	*Current Writing: Text and Reception in Southern Africa*
CV2	*Contemporary Verse 2*
CVE	*Cahiers Victoriens et Edouardiens*
CW	*Current Writing: Text and Perception in Southern Africa*
CWS	*Canadian Woman Studies*
CWW	*Contemporary Women's Writing*
DA	*Dictionary of Americanisms*
DAE	*Dictionary of American English*
DAEM	*Deutsches Archiv für Erforschung des Mittelalters*
DAI	*Dissertation Abstracts International*
DAL	*Descriptive and Applied Linguistics*
D&C	*Discourse and Communication*
D&S	*Discourse and Society*
Daphnis	*Daphnis: Zeitschrift für Mittlere Deutsche Literatur*
DC	*Dickens Companions*
DetG	*Dialectologia et Geolinguistica*
DFS	*Dalhousie French Studies*
DHLR	*D.H. Lawrence Review*
DHS	*Dix-huitième Siècle*
Diac	*Diacritics*
Dialogue	*Dialogue: Canadian Philosophical Review*
DiaS	*Diaspora Studies*
DickensM	*Dickens Magazine*
DicS	*Dickinson Studies*
Dictionaries	*Dictionaries: Journal of the Dictionary Society of North America*
DisS	*Discourse Studies*
DJDSNA	*Dictionaries: Journal of the Dictionary of North America*
DJJJ	*Dublin James Joyce Journal*
DLB	*Dictionary of Literary Biography*
DLS	*Doris Lessing Studies*
DM	*Dublin Magazine*
DMT	*Durham Medieval Texts*
DNB	*Dictionary of National Biography*
DOE	*Dictionary of Old English*
DOST	*Dictionary of the Older Scottish Tongue*
DownR	*Downside Review*
DPhil	*Digital Philology*
DPr	*Discourse Processes*
DQ	*Denver Quarterly*
DQR	*Dutch Quarterly Review of Anglo-American Letters*

DQu	Dickens Quarterly
DR	Dalhousie Review
Drama	Drama: The Quarterly Theatre Review
DrS	Dreiser Studies
DS	Deep South
DSA	Dickens Studies Annual
DSCP	Discourse: Studies in the Cultual Politics of Education
DSH	Digital Scholarship in the Humanities
DSNA	DSNA Newsletter
DSQ	Disability Quarterly
EA	Études Anglaises
EAf	English in Africa
EAL	Early American Literature
E&D	Enlightenment and Dissent
E&S	Essays and Studies
E&Soc	Economy and Society
EALCS	Eastern African Literary and Cultural Studies
EARev	English Academy Review
EarT	Early Theatre
EAS	Early American Studies
EASt	Englisch Amerikanische Studien
eBLJ	Electronic British Library Journal
EBST	Edinburgh Bibliographical Society Transactions
EC	Études Celtiques
ECan	Études Canadiennes/Canadian Studies
ECCB	Eighteenth Century: A Current Bibliography
ECent	Eighteenth Century: Theory and Interpretation
ECF	Eighteenth-Century Fiction
ECI	Eighteenth-Century Ireland
ECIntell	Eighteenth-Century Intelligencer
ECLife	Eighteenth-Century Life
ECM	Eighteenth-Century Music
ECN	Eighteenth-Century Novel
ECon	L'Époque Conradienne
ECr	L'Esprit Créateur
ECS	Eighteenth-Century Studies
ECW	Essays on Canadian Writing
EDAMR	Early Drama, Art, and Music Review
EDJ	The Emily Dickinson Journal
EdL	Études de Lettres
EdN	Editors' Notes: Bulletin of the Conference of Editors of Learned Journals
EDSL	Encyclopedic Dictionary of the Sciences of Language
EES	Early English Studies
EF	Études Francaises
EHL	English Historical Linguistics
EHR	English Historical Review
EI	Études Irlandaises (Lille)
EIC	Essays in Criticism
Eiha	Eighth Lamp–Ruskin Studies Today
EinA	English in Africa
EiP	Essays in Poetics
EiR	Essays in Romanticism

EIRC	*Explorations in Renaissance Culture*
Éire	*Éire-Ireland*
EJ	*English Journal*
EJAL	*European Journal of Applied Linguistics*
EJCSt	*European Journal of Cultural Studies*
EJES	*European Journal of English Studies*
EJLP	*European Journal of Language Policy*
EJP	*European Journal of Philosophy*
EL	*Études lawrenciennes*
ELA	*Études Littéraires Africaines*
ELangT	*ELT Journal: An International Journal for Teachers of English to Speakers of Other Languages*
ELet	*Esperienze Letterarie: Rivista Trimestrale di Critica e Cultura*
ELF	*English Language and Literary Forum*
ELH	*English Literary History*
ELing	*English Linguistics*
ELL	*English Language and Linguistics*
ELN	*English Language Notes*
ELR	*English Literary Renaissance*
ELS	*English Literary Studies*
ELT	*English Literature in Transition*
Embl	*Emblematica: An Interdisciplinary Journal of English Studies*
EMD	*European Medieval Drama*
EME	*Early Modern Europe*
EMedE	*Early Medieval Europe* (online)
EMLS	*Early Modern Literary Studies* (online)
EMMS	*Early Modern Manuscript Studies*
EMS	*English Manuscript Studies, 1100–1700*
EMu	*Early Music*
EMW	*Early Modern Englishwomen*
Encult	*Enculturation: Cultural Theories and Rhetorics*
EnginP	*Englishes in Practice*
English	*English: The Journal of the English Association*
EnLT	*English Language Training*
EnT	*English Today: The International Review of the English Language*
EONR	*Eugene O'Neill Review*
EPD	*English Pronouncing Dictionary*
ER	*English Review*
ERLM	*Europe-Revue Littéraire Mensuelle*
ERR	*European Romantic Review*
ERS	*Ethnic and Racial Studies*
ES	*English Studies*
ESA	*English Studies in Africa*
ESC	*English Studies in Canada*
ESLAYb	*EUROSLA Yearbook*
Espéculo	*Espéculo: Revista de Estudios Literarios*
ESPJ	*English for Specific Purposes*
ESQ	*ESQ: A Journal of the American Renaissance*
ESRS	*Emporia State Research Studies*
EssaysMedSt	*Essays in Medieval Studies*
EST	*Eureka Street*
Estudios Ingleses	*Estudios Ingleses de la Universidad Complutense*

ET	Elizabethan Theatre
ETC	English Text Construction
ÉtudesE	Études écossaises
EuLeg	European Legacy
EWhR	Edith Wharton Review
EWN	Evelyn Waugh Newsletter
EWPAL	Edinburgh Working Papers in Applied Linguistics
EWW	English World-Wide
Expl	Explicator
Extrapolation	Extrapolation: A Journal Science Fiction and Fantasy
FC	Feminist Collections: A Quarterly of Women's Studies Resources
FCS	Fifteenth-Century Studies
FDT	Fountainwell Drama Texts
FemF	Feminist Formations
FemR	Feminist Review
FemSEL	Feminist Studies in English Literature
FEMSPEC	FEMSPEC: An Interdisciplinary Feminist Journal Dedicated to Critical and Creative Work in the Realms of Science Fiction, Fantasy, Magical Realism, Surrealism, Myth, Folklore, and Other Supernatural Genres
FemT	Feminist Theory
FFW	Food and Foodways
FG	Fourth Genre: Explorations in Non-Fiction
FH	Die Neue Gesellschaft/Frankfurter Hefte
FilmJ	Film Journal
FilmQ	Film Quarterly
FilmS	Film Studies
FLH	Folia Linguistica Historica
Florilegium	Florilegium: Journal of the Canadian Society of Medievalists
FLS	Foreign Literature Studies / Wai Guo Wen Xue Yan Jie (online)
FMLS	Forum for Modern Language Studies
FoLi	Folia Linguistica
FourthG	Fourth Genre: Explorations in Nonfiction
FranS	Franciscan Studies
FreeA	Free Associations
FrontenacR	Revue Frontenac
Frontiers	Frontiers: A Journal of Women's Studies
FS	French Studies
FSFR	The F. Scott Fitzgerald Review
FSt	Feminist Studies
FT	Fashion Theory
FU	Facta Universitatis
FuL	Functions of Language
FWLS	Forum for World Literature Studies
GAG	Göppinger Arbeiten zur Germanistik
Galaxy	Galaxy: An Open Access Online International Multidisciplinary Research Journal
G&E	Gender & Education
G&H	Gender & History
G&L	Gender & Language
GaR	Georgia Review
GBB	George Borrow Bulletin
GBK	Gengo Bunka Kenkyu: Studies in Language and Culture

GEGHLS	*George Eliot–George Henry Lewes Studies*
GeM	*Genealogists Magazine*
GER	*George Eliot Review*
Gestus	*Gestus: A Quarterly Journal of Brechtian Studies*
GF	*Gender Forum: An Internet Journal for Gender Studies*
GHJ	*George Herbert Journal*
GhJL	*Ghana Journal of Linguistics*
GissingJ	*Gissing Journal*
GJ	*Gutenberg-Jahrbuch*
GL	*General Linguistics*
GL&L	*German Life and Letters*
GlasR	*Glasgow Review*
GlobRev	*Global Review: A Biannual Special Topics Journal*
GLobS	*Global South*
Glossa	*Glossa: An International Journal of Linguistics*
GLS	*Grazer Linguistische Studien*
GPQ	*Great Plains Quarterly*
GR	*Germanic Review*
Gramma	*Gramma: Journal of Theory and Criticism*
GrandS	*Grand Street*
Greyfriar	*Greyfriar Siena Studies in Literature*
GriffithR	*Griffith Review*
GRM	*Germanisch-Romanische Monatsschrift*
Grove	*The Grove: Working Papers on English Studies*
GS	*Gothic Studies*
GSE	*Gothenberg Studies in English*
GSJ	*Gaskell Society Journal*
GSN	*Gaskell Society Newsletter*
HA	*History Australia*
HamS	*Hamlet Studies*
H&T	*History and Theory*
HardyR	*Hardy Review*
Harvard Law Review	*Harvard Law Review*
HatcherR	*Hatcher Review*
HazlittR	*The Hazlitt Review*
HBS	*Henry Bradshaw Society*
HC	*Hollins Critic*
HE	*History of Education*
Hecate	*Hecate: An Interdisciplinary Journal of Women's Liberation*
HEdQ	*History of Education Quarterly*
HEI	*History of European Ideas*
HEL	*Histoire Épistémologie Language*
HEng	*History of the English Language*
Hermathena	*Hermathena: A Trinity College Dublin Review*
Hermes	*Hermes–Journal of Language and Communication in Business*
HeroicA	*Heroic Age: A Journal of Early Medieval Northwestern Europe*
HES	*Helsinki English Studies* (online)
HeyJ	*Heythrop Journal*
HFR	*Hayden Ferry Review*
HistJ	*Historical Journal*
History	*History: The Journal of the Historical Association*
HistR	*Historical Research*
Hitotsubashi	*Hitotsubashi Journal of Arts and Sciences*

HJEAS	*Hungarian Journal of English and American Studies*
HL	*Historiographia Linguistica*
HLB	*Harvard Library Bulletin*
HLQ	*Huntingdon Library Quarterly*
HLSL	*Harvard Law School Library* (online)
HMAS	*Journal of the History of Medicine and Allied Sciences*
HNR	*Harvester New Readings*
HomeCult	*Home Cultures*
HOPE	*History of Political Economy*
HopRev	*Hopkins Review*
HPT	*History of Political Thought*
HQ	*Hopkins Quarterly*
HR	*Harvard Review*
HRB	*Hopkins Research Bulletin*
HSci	*History of Science*
HSE	*Hungarian Studies in English*
HSJ	*Housman Society Journal*
HSL	*University of Hartford Studies in Literature*
HSN	*Hawthorne Society Newsletter*
HSSh	*Hungarian Studies in Shakespeare*
HSSN	*Henry Sweet Society Newsletter*
HT	*History Today*
HTR	*Harvard Theological Review*
HudR	*Hudson Review*
HumeS	*Hume Studies*
HumLov	*Humanistica Lovaniensia: Journal of Neo-Latin Studies*
Humor	*Humor: International Journal of Humor Research*
HUSL	*Hebrew University Studies in Literature and the Arts*
HWJ	*History Workshop*
HWS	*History Workshop Series*
IACS	*Inter-Asia Cultural Studies*
IAFM	*Image: Art, Faith, Mystery*
IAL	*Issues in Applied Linguistics*
IAN	*Izvestiia Akademii Nauk SSSR* (Moscow)
I&C	*Ideology and Consciousness*
I&M	*Immigrants and Minorities*
I&P	*Ideas and Production*
IbéricaR	*Ibérica: Revista de la Asociación Europea de Lenguas para Fines Específicos*
IbsenSt	*Ibsen Studies*
ICAME	*International Computer Archive of Modern and Medieval English*
ICS	*Illinois Classical Studies*
IF	*Indogermanische Forschungen*
IFR	*International Fiction Review*
IGK	*Irland: Gesellschaft and Kultur*
IH	*Interdisciplinarity Humanities*
IHR	*Intellectual History Review*
IJAES	*International Journal of Arabic-English Studies*
IJAL	*International Journal of Applied Linguistics*
IJB	*International Journal of Bilingualism*
IJBC	*International Journal of Business Communication*
IJBEB	*International Journal of Bilingual Education & Bilingualism*
IJCL	*International Journal of Corpus Linguistics*

IJCP	*International Journal of Critical Pedagogy*
IJCS	*International Journal of Canadian Studies*
IJCT	*International Journal of the Classical Tradition*
IJECS	*Indian Journal for Eighteenth-Century Studies*
IJEL	*International Journal of English Linguistics*
IJES	*Indian Journal of English Studies*
IJH	*The International Journal of the Humanities*
IJHSS	*International Journal of Humanities and Social Science*
IJL	*International Journal of Lexicography*
IJMES	*International Journal of Middle East Studies*
IJPR	*International Journal for Philosophy of Religion*
IJSL	*International Journal of the Sociology of Language*
IJSS	*Indian Journal of Shakespeare Studies*
IJWS	*International Journal of Women's Studies*
IlhaD	*Ilha do Desterro: A Journal of Language and Literature*
ILLT	*Innovation in Language Learning and Teaching*
ILR	*Indian Literary Review*
ILS	*Irish Literary Supplement*
ILStud	*Interdisciplinary Literary Studies: A Journal of Criticism and Theory*
Imago	*Imago: New Writing*
IMB	*International Medieval Bibliography*
IndH	*Indian Horizons*
IndL	*Indian Literature*
InG	*In Geardagum: Essays on Old and Middle English Language and Literature*
Inklings	*Inklings: Jahrbuch für Literatur and Ästhetik*
InnR	*Innes Review*
Inquiry	*Inquiry: An Interdisciplinary Journal of Philosophy*
Interactions	*Interactions: Ege Journal of British and American Studies / Ege İngiliz ve Amerikan İncelemeleri Dergisi*
Interlit	*Interlitteraria*
Interventions	*Interventions: The International Journal of Postcolonial Studies*
IntJEL	*International Journal of English and Literature*
IntJSL	*International Journal of Scottish Literature*
IoJCS	*Iowa Journal of Cultural Studies*
IowaR	*Iowa Review*
IPrag	*Intercultural Pragmatics*
IRAL	*IRAL: International Review of Applied Linguistics in Language Teaching*
IRCL	*International Research in Children's Literature*
IRE	*International Review of Education*
Iris	*Iris: A Journal of Theory on Image and Sound*
IRP	*International Review of Pragmatics*
IRWLE	*Indian Review of World Literature in English*
IS	*Italian Studies*
ISh	*Independent Shavian*
Island	*Island Magazine*
Isle	*Interdisciplinary Studies in Literature and Environment*
ISR	*Irish Studies Review*
ITSK	*Interpreting and Translation Studies (Korea)*
ITT	*The Interpreter and Translator Trainer*
IUR	*Irish University Review: A Journal of Irish Studies*

JAAC	*Journal of Aesthetics and Art Criticism*
JAAR	*Journal of the American Academy of Religion*
JAAS	*Journal of Asian American Studies*
JACS	*Journal of African Cultural Studies*
JADT	*Journal of American Drama and Theatre*
JAF	*Journal of American Folklore*
JafM	*Journal of African Marxists*
JAFP	*Journal of Adaptation in Film & Performance*
JAIS	*Journal of Anglo-Italian Studies*
JAL	*Journal of Australian Literature*
JALA	*Journal of the African Literature Association*
JamC	*Journal of American Culture*
JAmH	*Journal of American History*
JAmS	*Journal of American Studies*
JAP	*Journal of Analytical Psychology*
JAPC	*Journal of Asian Pacific Communication*
JAR	*Journal of Anthropological Research*
JArabL	*Journal of Arabic Literature*
JAS	*Journal of Australian Studies*
JASAL	*Journal of the Association for the Study of Australian Literature*
JAStT	*Journal of American Studies of Turkey*
JAW	*Journal of Academic Writing*
JBC	*Journal of Business Communication*
JBeckS	*Journal of Beckett Studies*
JBGU	*Journal of Bunkgo Gakuin University*
JBrowS	*Journal of Browning Studies*
JBS	*Journal of British Studies*
JBTC	*Journal of Business and Technical Communication*
JBuchJ	*John Buchan Journal*
JCanL	*Journal of Canadian Literature*
JCarL	*Journal of Caribbean Literatures*
JCC	*Journal of Canadian Culture*
JCERL	*Journal of Classic and English Renaissance Literature*
JCF	*Journal of Canadian Fiction*
JCGL	*Journal of Comparative Germanic Linguistics*
JChL	*Journal of Child Language*
JChLS	*Journal of Children's Literature Studies*
JCL	*Journal of Commonwealth Literature*
JCLA	*Journal of Comparative Literature and Aesthetics*
JCP	*Journal of Canadian Poetry*
JCPCS	*Journal of Commonwealth and Postcolonial Studies*
JCSJ	*John Clare Society Journal*
JCSR	*Journal of Canadian Studies/Revue d'Études Canadiennes*
JCSt	*Journal of Caribbean Studies*
JCT	*Journal for Contemporary Thought*
JDECU	*Journal of the Department of English* (Calcutta University)
JDHLS	*Journal of D.H. Lawrence Studies*
JDJ	*John Donne Journal*
JDN	*James Dickey Newsletter*
JDS	*Journal of Dracula Studies*
JDTC	*Journal of Dramatic Theory and Criticism*
JEAfS	*Journal of Eastern African Studies*
JEAP	*Journal of English for Academic Purposes*

JEBS	*Journal of the Early Book Society*
JECS	*Journal of Eighteenth-Century British Studies*
JEdBS	*Journal of the Edinburgh Bibliographical Society*
JEH	*Journal of Ecclesiastical History*
JELF	*Journal of English as a Lingua Franca*
JELL	*Journal of English Language and Literature*
JEMCS	*Journal for Early Modern Cultural Studies*
JEMS	*Journal of Early Modern Studies*
JEn	*Journal of English* (Sana'a University)
JEngL	*Journal of English Linguistics*
JENS	*Journal of the Eighteen Nineties Society*
JEP	*Journal of Evolutionary Psychology*
JEPNS	*Journal of the English Place-Name Society*
JES	*Journal of European Studies*
JESR	*Journal of Educational and Social Research*
JETS	*Journal of the Evangelical Theological Society*
Jeunesse	*Jeunesse: Young People, Texts, Cultures*
JFL	*Journal of Faculty of Letters/Edebiyat Fakültesi Dergisi*
JFR	*Journal of Folklore Research*
JGE	*Journal of General Education*
JGenS	*Journal of Gender Studies*
JGH	*Journal of Garden History*
JGL	*Journal of Germanic Linguistics*
JGN	*John Gower Newsletter*
JGSL	*Journal of the Graduate School of Letters*
JH	*Journal of Homosexuality*
JHI	*Journal of the History of Ideas*
JHLP	*Journal of Historical Linguistics and Philology*
JHP	*Journal of the History of Philosophy*
JHPrag	*Journal of Historical Pragmatics*
JHSex	*Journal of the History of Sexuality*
JHu	*Journal of Humanities*
JHuP	*Journal of Humanistic Psychology*
JIAS	*Journal of the International Arthurian Society*
JIEP	*Journal of Indo-European Perspectives*
JIES	*Journal of Indo-European Studies*
JIH	*Journal of Interdisciplinary History*
JIL	*Journal of Irish Literature*
JIPA	*Journal of the International Phonetic Association*
JISR	*Journal of International Social Research*
JIWE	*Journal of Indian Writing in English*
JIWS	*Journal of International Women's Studies*
JJ	*Jamaica Journal*
JJA	*James Joyce Annual*
JJB	*James Joyce Broadsheet*
JJLS	*James Joyce Literary Supplement*
JJQ	*James Joyce Quarterly*
JKS	*Journal of Kentucky Studies*
JL	*Journal of Linguistics*
JLAE	*Journal of Leadership, Accountability & Ethics*
JLCDS	*Journal of Literary and Cultural Disability Studies*
JLG	*Journal of Linguistic Geography*
JLitSc	*Journal of Literature and Science*

JLLC	*Journal of Language, Literature and Culture* (previously AUMLA)
JLLE	*Journal of Language and Literature Education*
JLLI	*Journal of Logic, Language and Information*
JLP	*Journal of Linguistics and Politics*
JLS	*Journal of Literary Semanitcs*
JLST	*Journal of Literary Studies/Tydskrif vir Literatuurwetenskap*
JLSP	*Journal of Language and Social Psychology*
JLVSG	*Journal of the Longborough Victorian Studies Group*
JMBRAS	*Journal of the Malaysian Branch of the Royal Asiatic Society*
JMD	*Journal of Multicultural Discourses*
JMED	*Journal of Modern English Drama*
JMedH	*Journal of Medical Humanities*
JMedL	*Journal of Medieval Latin*
JMemL	*Journal of Memory and Language*
JMEMS	*Journal of Medieval and Early Modern Studies*
JMennS	*Journal of Mennonite Studies*
JMGS	*Journal of Modern Greek Studies*
JMH	*Journal of Medieval History*
JMJS	*Journal of Modern Jewish Studies*
JML	*Journal of Modern Literature*
JMMD	*Journal of Multilingual and Multicultural Development*
JMMLA	*Journal of the Midwest Modern Language Association*
JModH	*Journal of Modern History*
JModPerS	*Journal of Modern Periodical Studies*
JMRC	*Journal of Medieval Religious Cultures* (formerly *MysticsQ*)
JMRS	*Journal of Medieval and Renaissance Studies*
JMS	*Journal of Men's Studies*
JMTP	*Journal of Marketing Theory and Practice*
JNLH	*Journal of Narrative and Life History*
JNPH	*Journal of Newspaper and Periodical History*
JNR	*Journal of the Northern Renaissance*
JNT	*Journal of Narrative Theory* (formerly *Technique*)
JNZL	*Journal of New Zealand Literature*
JNZS	*Journal of New Zealand Studies*
Journeys	*Journeys: The International Journal of Travel and Travel Writing*
Jouvert	*Jouvert: A Journal of Postcolonial Studies*
JoyceSA	*Joyce Studies Annual*
JP	*Journal of Philosophy*
JPC	*Journal of Popular Culture*
JPCL	*Journal of Pidgin and Creole Languages*
JPhon	*Journal of Phonetics*
JPJ	*Journal of Psychology and Judaism*
JPolR	*Journal of Politeness Research: Language, Behavior, and Culture*
JPP	*Journal of Poetry and Poetics*
JPrag	*Journal of Pragmatics*
JPRAS	*Journal of Pre-Raphaelite and Aesthetic Studies*
JPRS	*Journal of Pre-Raphaelite Studies*
JPS	*Journal of Postcolonial Studies*
JPsyR	*Journal of Psycholinguistic Research*
JPW	*Journal of Postcolonial Writing*
JQ	*Journalism Quarterly*
JR	*Journal of Religion*
JRAHS	*Journal of the Royal Australian Historical Society*

JRH	*Journal of Religious History*
JRMA	*Journal of the Royal Musical Association*
JRSA	*Journal of the Royal Society of Arts*
JRT	*Journal of Religion and Theatre*
JRUL	*Journal of the Rutgers University Libraries*
JSA	*Journal of the Society of Archivists*
JSaga	*Journal of the Faculty of Liberal Arts and Science* (Saga University)
JSAS	*Journal of Southern African Studies*
JScholP	*Journal of Scholarly Publishing*
JSem	*Journal of Semantics*
JSoc	*Journal of Sociolinguistics*
JSP	*Journal of Scottish Philosophy*
JSSE	*Journal of the Short Story in English*
JTAS	*Journal of Transnational American Studies*
JTheoS	*Journal of Theological Studies*
JVC	*Journal of Victorian Culture*
JWCI	*Journal of the Warburg and Courtauld Institutes*
JWCP	*Journal of Writing in Creative Practice*
JWH	*Journal of Women's History*
JWIL	*Journal of West Indian Literature*
JWMS	*Journal of the William Morris Society*
JWSL	*Journal of Women's Studies in Literature*
KanE	*Kansas English*
Ka Mate Ka Ora	*Ka Mate Ka Ora: A New Zealand Journal of Poetry and Poetics*
KanQ	*Kansas Quarterly*
KB	*Kavya Bharati*
KCLMS	*King's College London Medieval Series*
KCS	*Kobe College Studies* (Japan)
KDNews	*Kernerman Dictionary News*
KK	*Kritika Kultura*
KJ	*Kipling Journal*
KN	*Kwartalnik Neoflologiczny* (Warsaw)
KompH	*Komparatistische Hefte*
Kotare	*Kotare: New Zealand Notes and Queries*
KPR	*Kentucky Philological Review*
KR	*Kenyon Review*
KS	*Književna Smotra*
KSJ	*Keats-Shelley Journal*
KSMB	*Keats-Shelley Memorial Bulletin*
KSR	*Keats-Shelley Review*
Kuka	*Kuka: Journal of Creative and Critical Writing* (Nigeria)
KWS	*Key-Word Studies in Chaucer*
KYD	*Kill Your Darlings*
LAB	*Linguistic Approaches to Bilingualism*
LabPhon	*Laboratory Phonology*
L&A	*Literature and Aesthetics*
L&B	*Literature and Belief*
L&C	*Language and Communication*
L&E	*Linguistics and Education: An International Research Journal*
Landfall	*Landfall: A New Zealand Quarterly*
L&H	*Literature and History*
L&IC	*Language & Intercultural Communication*
L&L	*Language and Literature*

L&LC	*Literary and Linguistic Computing*
L&M	*Literature and Medicine*
L&P	*Literature and Psychology*
L&S	*Language and Speech*
L&T	*Literature and Theology: An Interdisciplinary Journal of Theory and Criticism*
L&U	*Lion and the Unicorn: A Critical Journal of Children's Literature*
LangAcq	*Language Acquisition*
Lang&S	*Language and Style*
LangAw	*Language Awareness*
LangCog	*Language and Cognition*
LangF	*Language Forum*
LangLearn	*Language Learning: A Journal of Research in Language Studies*
LangM	*Language Matters*
LangQ	*USF Language Quarterly*
LangR	*Language Research*
LangS	*Language Sciences*
Language	*Language* (Linguistic Society of America)
LAQ	*Language Assessment Quarterly*
LASB	*Leeds African Studies Bulletin*
LATCH	*LATCH: A Journal for the Study of the Literary Artefact in Theory, Culture or History*
Latchkey	*The Latchkey: Journal of New Women Studies*
LATR	*Latin American Theatre Review*
LaTrobe	*La Trobe Journal*
LawL	*Law and Literature*
LawLi	*Law and the Literary Imagination*
LB	*Leuvense Bijdragen*
LBR	*Luso-Brazilian Review*
LC&C	*Language, Culture and Curriculum*
LCrit	*Literary Criterion* (Mysore, India)
LCSAW	*Learner Corpus Studies in Asia and the World*
LCUT	*Library Chronicle* (University of Texas at Austin)
LDOCE	*Longman Dictionary of Contemporary English*
LeedsSE	*Leeds Studies in English*
LeF	*Linguistica e Filologia*
Legacy	*Legacy: A Journal of Nineteenth-Century American Women Writers*
L'EpC	*L'Epoque Conradienne*
LeSim	*Le Simplegadi*
LeS	*Lingua e Stile*
LexAsia	*Lexicography: The Journal of AsiaLex*
Lexicographica	*Lexicographica: International Annual for Lexicography*
LFQ	*Literature/Film Quarterly*
LH	*Library History*
LHY	*Literary Half-Yearly*
LI	*Studies in the Literary Imagination*
Library	*The Library*
LibrQ	*Library Quarterly*
Likhaan	*Likhaan: The Journal of Contemporary World Literature*
LIN	*Linguistics in the Netherlands*
LinC	*Languages in Contrast*
LingA	*Linguistic Analysis*

Ling&P	*Linguistics and Philosophy*
Ling&Philol	*Linguistics and Philology*
LingB	*Linguistische Berichte*
LingI	*Linguistic Inquiry*
LingInv	*Lingvisticæ Investigationes*
LingP	*Linguistica Pragensia*
LingRev	*Linguistic Review*
Lingua	*Lingua: International Review of General Linguistics*
LinguistikO	*Lingusitik Online*
Linguistique	*La Linguistique*
LiNQ	*Literature in Northern Queensland*
LIT	*LIT: Literature, Interpretation, Theory*
LitComp	*Literature Compass* (previously *LiteratureC*)
LitH	*Literary Horizons*
LitI	*Literary Imagination: The Review of the Association of Literary Scholars and Critics*
LitLon	*Literary London*
LitR	*Literary Review: An International Journal of Contemporary Writing*
LittPrag	*Litteraria Pragensia: Studies in Literature and Culture*
LLR	*Liverpool Law Review*
LJCS	*London Journal of Canadian Studies*
LJHum	*Lamar Journal of the Humanities*
LLJ	*Language Learning Journal*
LMag	*London Magazine*
LockeN	*Locke Newsletter*
LocusF	*Locus Focus*
Logos	*Logos: A Journal of Catholic Thought and Culture*
LP	*Lingua Posnaniensis*
LPI	*Linguistic and Philosophical Investigations*
LPLD	*Liverpool Papers in Language and Discourse*
LPLP	*Language Problems and Language Planning*
LR	*Les Lettres Romanes*
LRB	*London Review of Books*
LSE	*Lund Studies in English*
LSLD	*Liverpool Studies in Language and Discourse*
LSoc	*Language in Society*
LSp	*Language and Speech*
LST	*Longman Study Texts*
LTeach	*Language Teaching*
LTM	*Leeds Texts and Monographs*
LTP	*LTP: Journal of Literature Teaching Politics*
LTR	*London Theatre Record*
LuK	*Literatur und Kritik*
LVC	*Language Variation and Change*
LW	*Life Writing*
LWU	*Literatur in Wissenschaft und Unterricht*
M&Lang	*Mind and Language*
MÆ	*Medium Ævum*
MAEL	*Macmillan Anthologies of English Literature*
Magistra	*Magistra: A Women's Spirituality in History*
MagL	*Magazine Littéraire*
MAS	*Modern Asian Studies*
M&H	*Medievalia et Humanistica*

M&L	Music and Letters
M&SW	Metaphor and the Social World
M&Sym	Metaphor and Symbol (also Met&Sym)
M&T	Marvels & Tales
MAR	Mid-American Review
Margin	Margin: Life and Letters in Early Australia
MarkhamR	Markham Review
MBL	Modern British Literature
MC&S	Media, Culture and Society
MCI	Modern Critical Interpretations
MCJNews	Milton Centre of Japan News
McNR	McNeese Review
MCRel	Mythes, Croyances et Religions dans le Monde Anglo-Saxon
MCV	Modern Critical Views
MD	Modern Drama
ME	Medieval Encounters
MED	Middle English Dictionary
MedFor	Medieval Forum (online)
MedHis	Media History
MedJ	The Medieval Journal
MedPers	Medieval Perspectives
Meridians	Meridians: Feminsims, Race, Transnationalism
MES	Medieval and Early Modern English Studies
MESN	Mediaeval English Studies Newsletter
MET	Middle English Texts
METh	Medieval English Theatre
MFF	Medieval Feminist Forum
MFRT	Meridiens: Feminism, Race, Transnationalism
MFS	Modern Fiction Studies
MH	Malahat Review
MHJ	Melbourne Historical Journal
MHL	Macmillan History of Literature
MHLS	Mid-Hudson Language Studies
MichA	Michigan Academician
MiltonQ	Milton Quarterly
MiltonS	Milton Studies
MinnR	Minnesota Review
MissQ	Mississippi Quarterly
MissR	Missouri Review
MJLF	Midwestern Journal of Language and Folklore
ML	Music and Letters
MLAIB	Modern Language Association International Bibliography
MLing	Modèles Linguistiques
MLJ	Modern Language Journal
MLQ	Modern Language Quarterly
MLR	Modern Language Review
MLRev	Malcolm Lowry Review
MLS	Modern Language Studies
MMG	Macmillan Master Guides
MMisc	Midwestern Miscellany
MOCS	Magazine of Cultural Studies
ModA	Modern Age: A Quarterly Review
ModCult	Modernist Cultures

ModET	Modern English Teacher
ModM	Modern Masters
ModSp	Moderne Sprachen
Mo/Mo	Modernism/Modernity (previously M/M)
MonSP	Monash Swift Papers
Month	Month: A Review of Christian Thought and World Affairs
MOR	Mount Olive Review
Moreana	Moreana: Bulletin Thomas More (Angers, France)
Mosaic	Mosaic: A Journal for the Interdisciplinary Study of Literature
MoyA	Moyen Age
MP	Modern Philology
MPR	Mervyn Peake Review
MPsych	Media Psychology
MQ	Midwest Quarterly
MQR	Michigan Quarterly Review
MR	Massachusetts Review
MRDE	Medieval and Renaissance Drama in England
MRTS	Medieval and Renaissance Texts and Studies
MS	Mediaeval Studies
MSC	Malone Society Collections
MSE	Massachusetts Studies in English
MSEx	Melville Society Extracts
MSh	Macmillan Shakespeare
MSNH	Mémoires de la Société Néophilologique de Helsinki
MSpr	Moderna Språk
MSR	Malone Society Reprints
MSSN	Medieval Sermon Studies Newsletter
MT	Musical Times
MTJ	Mark Twain Journal
Multilingua	Multilingua: Journal of Cross-Cultural and Interlanguage Communication
MultSh	Multicultural Shakespeare
MusR	Music Review
MW	Muslim World (Hartford, CT)
MWQ	Mid-West Quarterly
NA	Nuova Antologia
NAcad	New Academia: An International Journal of English Language, Literature and Literary Theory
Names	Names: Journal of the American Name Society
NAmR	North American Review
N&Q	Notes and Queries
Narrative	Narrative: Journal of the International Society for the Study of Narrative
NatIds	National Identities
NB	Namn och Bygd
NCaS	New Cambridge Shakespeare
NCBEL	New Cambridge Bibliography of English Literature
NCC	Nineteenth-Century Contexts
NCE	Norton Critical Editions
NCentR	The New Centennial Review
NCFiction	Nineteenth-Century Fiction
NCFS	Nineteenth-Century French Studies
NCGS	Nineteenth Century Gender Studies

NCI	New Critical Idiom
NCL	Nineteenth-Century Literature
NCLE	Nineteenth-Century Literature in English
NConL	Notes on Contemporary Literature
NCP	Nineteenth-Century Prose
NCS	New Clarendon Shakespeare
NCSR	New Chaucer Society Readings
NCSTC	Nineteenth-Century Short Title Catalogue
NCStud	Nineteenth-Century Studies
NCT	Nineteenth-Century Theatre
NCTFilm	Nineteenth-Century Theatre and Film
NDQ	North Dakota Quarterly
NegroD	Negro Digest
NELS	North Eastern Linguistic Society
Neoh	Neohelicon
Neophil	Neophilologus
NEQ	New England Quarterly
NERMS	New England Review
NewA	New African
NewBR	New Beacon Review
NewC	New Criterion
New Casebooks	New Casebooks: Contemporary Critical Essays
NewF	New Formations
NewHibR	New Hibernian Review
NewHR	New Historical Review
NewR	New Republic
NewSt	Newfoundland Studies
NewV	New Voices
Nexus	The International Henry Miller Journal
NF	Neiophilologica Fennica
NfN	News from Nowhere
NF&LS	Newfoundland and Labrador Studies
NFS	Nottingham French Studies
NGC	New German Critique
NGS	New German Studies
NH	Northern History
NHR	Nathaniel Hawthorne Review
NILR	Northern Illinois Law Review
NIS	Nordic Irish Studies
NJES	Nordic Journal of English Studies
NJL	Nordic Journal of Linguistics
NL	Nouvelles Littéraires
NLAN	National Library of Australia News
NL&LT	Natural Language and Linguistic Theory
NLH	New Literary History: A Journal of Theory and Interpretation
NLitsR	New Literatures Review
NLR	New Left Review
NLS	Natural Language Semantics
NLWJ	National Library of Wales Journal
NM	Neuphilologische Mitteilungen
NMAL	NMAL: Notes on Modern American Literature
NMIL	Notes on Modern Irish Literature

NML	*New Medieval Literatures*
NMS	*Nottingham Medieval Studies*
NMW	*Notes on Mississippi Writers*
NN	*Nordiska Namenstudier*
NNER	*Northern New England Review*
NoH	*Northern History*
NoP	*Northern Perspective*
NOR	*New Orleans Review*
Nordlit	*Nordlit: Arbeidstidsskrift i litteratur og kultur*
NorfolkA	*Norfolk Archaeology*
NortonCE	*Norton Critical Edition*
Novel	*Novel: A Forum on Fiction*
NOWELE	*North-Western European Language Evolution*
NPEC	*New Perspectives on the Eighteenth Century*
NPS	*New Penguin Shakespeare*
NR	*Nassau Review*
NRF	*La Nouvelle Revue Française*
NRRS	*Notes and Records of the Royal Society of London*
NS	*Die neuren Sprachen*
NSS	*New Swan Shakespeare*
NTQ	*New Theatre Quarterly*
NTU	*NTU: Studies in Language and Literature* (also *NTUSLL*)
NVS	*Neo-Victorian Studies*
NW	*New Writing: The International Journal for the Practice and Theory of Creative Writing*
NwJ	*Northward Journal*
NWR	*Northwest Review*
NWRev	*New Welsh Review*
NYH	*New York History*
NYLF	*New York Literary Forum*
NYRB	*New York Review of Books*
NYT	*New York Times*
NYTBR	*New York Times Book Review*
NZB	*New Zealand Books*
NZJAS	*New Zealand Journal of Asian Studies*
NZListener	*New Zealand Listener*
OA	*Oxford Authors*
OB	*Ord och Bild*
Obsidian	*Obsidian II: Black Literature in Review*
OED	*Oxford English Dictionary*
OEDNews	*Oxford English Dictionary News*
OENews	*Old English Newsletter*
OELH	*Oxford English Literary History*
OET	*Oxford English Texts*
OH	*Over Here: An American Studies Journal*
OHEL	*Oxford History of English Literature*
OhR	*Ohio Review*
OLR	*Oxford Literary Review*
OnCan	*Onomastica Canadiana*
OPBS	*Occasional Papers of the Bibliographical Society*
OpenGL	*Open Guides to Literature*
OpL	*Open Letter*
OPL	*Oxford Poetry Library*

OPSL	*Occasional Papers in Systemic Linguistics*
OralT	*Oral Tradition*
OrbisLit	*Orbis Litterarum*
OS	*Oxford Shakespeare*
OSci	*Organization Science*
OSE	*Otago Studies in English*
OSS	*Oxford Shakespeare Studies*
OT	*Oral Tradition*
PA	*Présence Africaine*
PacStud	*Pacific Studies*
PAJ	*Performing Art Journal*
P&C	*Pragmatics and Cognition*
P&CT	*Psychoanalysis and Contemporary Thought*
P&L	*Philosophy and Literature*
P&P	*Past and Present*
P&R	*Philosophy and Rhetoric*
P&S	*Pragmatics and Society*
P&SC	*Philosophy and Social Criticism*
PAns	*Partial Answers*
PAPA	*Publications of the Arkansas Philological Association*
Papers	*Papers: Explorations into Children's Literature*
PAPS	*Proceedings of the American Philosophical Society*
PAR	*Performing Arts Resources*
Parabola	*Parabola: The Magazine of Myth and Tradition*
Paragraph	*Paragraph: The Journal of the Modern Critical Theory Group*
Parergon	*Parergon: Bulletin of the Australian and New Zealand Association for Medieval and Renaissance Studies*
ParisR	*Paris Review*
Parnassus	*Parnassus: Poetry in Review*
PastM	*Past Masters*
PaterN	*Pater Newsletter*
PAus	*Poetry Australia*
PBerLS	*Proceedings of the Berkeley Linguistics Society*
PBSA	*Papers of the Bibliographical Society of America*
PBSC	*Papers of the Biographical Society of Canada*
PCL	*Perspectives on Contemporary Literature*
PCP	*Pacific Coast Philology*
PCRev	*Popular Culture Review*
PCS	*Penguin Critical Studies*
PEAN	*Proceedings of the English Association North*
Pedagogy	*Pedagogy: Critical Approaches to Teaching Literarature, Language and Culture*
PEGS	*Publications of the English Goethe Society*
PELL	*Papers on English Language and Literature* (Japan)
PennHist	*Pennsylvania History: A Journal of Mid-Atlantic Studies*
PerfR	*Performance Review*
Peritia	*Peritia: Journal of the Medieval Academy of Ireland*
Perspectives	*Perspectives: Studies in Translatology*
Persuasions	*Persuasions: Journal of the Jane Austen Society of North America*
Persuasions On-Line	*The Jane Austen Journal On-Line*
Philament	*Philament: Online Journal of the Arts and Culture Phonology*
PhilRev	*Philosophical Review: A Quarterly Journal*

PhiN	*Philologie im Netz*
PHist	*Printing History*
Phonetica	*Phonetica: International Journal of Speech Science*
Phonology	*Phonology*
PHOS	*Publishing History Occasional Series*
PhRA	*Philosophical Research Archives*
PhT	*Philosophy Today*
PiL	*Papers in Linguistics*
PIMA	*Proceedings of the Illinois Medieval Association*
PinterR	*Pinter Review*
Pismo	*Pismo: Journal for Linguistics and Literary Studies*
PJCL	*Prairie Journal of Canadian Literature*
PJSS	*Pakistan Journal of Social Sciences*
PJSSH	*Pertanika Journal of Social Sciences & Humanities*
Plat	*Platform*
PLL	*Papers on Language and Literature*
PLoS ONE	*PLoS ONE*
PM	*Penguin Masterstudies*
PMHB	*Pennsylvania Magazine of History and Biography*
PMPA	*Proceedings of the Missouri Philological Association*
PNotes	*Pynchon Notes*
PNR	*Poetry and Nation Review*
PocoS	*Postcolonial Studies*
PocoT	*Postcolonial Text* (online)
PoeS	*Poe Studies*
Poetica	*Poetica: An International Journal of Linguistic-Literary Studies*
Poetics	*Poetics: International Review for the Theory of Literature*
Poétique	*Poétique: Revue de Théorie et d'Analyse Littéraires*
Poetry	*Poetry* (Chicago)
PoetryCR	*Poetry Canada Review*
PoetryNZ	*Poetry New Zealand*
PoetryR	*Poetry Review*
PoetryW	*Poetry Wales*
POMPA	*Publications of the Mississippi Philological Association*
Positions	*positions: asia critique*
PostEng	*Postgraduate English*
Postmed	*Postmedieval: A Journal of Medieval Cultural Studies*
PostS	*Past Script: Essays in Film and the Humanities*
PoT	*Poetics Today*
PP	*Penguin Passnotes*
PP	*Philologica Pragensia*
PPA	*Philosophical Perspectives Annual*
PPR	*Philosophy and Phenomenological Research*
PQ	*Philological Quarterly*
PQM	*Pacific Quarterly* (Moana)
PR	*Partisan Review*
Pragmatics	*Pragmatics: Quarterly Publication of the International Pragmatics Association*
PrairieF	*Prairie Fire*
Praxis	*Praxis: A Journal of Cultural Criticism*
Prépub	*(Pré)publications*
PRev	*Powys Review*
PRIA	*Proceedings of the Royal Irish Academy*

ProfileITP	*Profile: Issues in Teachers' Professional Development*
Prospects	*Prospects: An Annual Journal of American Cultural Studies*
Proteus	*Proteus: A Journal of Ideas*
PRR	*Public Relations Review*
PrS	*Prairie Schooner*
PRSt	*Philip Roth Studies*
PSiCL	*Poznań Studies in Contemporary Linguistics*
PSt	*Prose Studies*
PsyArt	*Psychological Study of the Arts* (hyperlink journal)
PsychR	*Psychological Reports*
PTBI	*Publications of the Sir Thomas Browne Institute*
PubH	*Publishing History*
PULC	*Princeton University Library Chronicle*
PVR	*Platte Valley Review*
PWC	*Pickering's Women's Classics*
PY	*Phonology Yearbook*
QE	*Quarterly Essay*
QI	*Quaderni d'Italianistica*
QJS	*Quarterly Journal of Speech*
QLing	*Quantitative Linguistics*
QQ	*Queen's Quarterly*
QR	*Queensland Review*
QRFV	*Quarterly Review of Film and Video*
QS	*Quebec Studies*
Quadrant	*Quadrant* (Sydney)
Quest	*The Quest*
Quidditas	*Journal of the Rocky Mountain Medieval and Renaissance Association*
Quint	*The Quint: An Interdisciplinary Quarterly from the North*
RadP	*Radical Philosophy*
RAL	*Research in African Literatures*
RALS	*Resources for American Literary Study*
Ramus	*Ramus: Critical Studies in Greek and Roman Literature*
Ranam	*Recherches anglaises et nord-américaines*
R&C	*Race and Class*
R&L	*Religion and Literature*
Raritan	*Raritan: A Quarterly Review*
Rask	*Rask: International tidsskrift for sprog og kommunikation*
RaVoN	*Romanticism and Victorianism on the Net*
RB	*Revue Bénédictine*
RBPH	*Revue Belge de Philologie et d'Histoire*
RBR	*Rare Book Review* (formerly *ABR*)
RCEI	*Revista Canaria de Estudios Ingleses*
RCF	*Review of Contemporary Fiction*
RCPS	*Romantic Circles Praxis Series*
RDE	*Research in Drama Education*
RDN	*Renaissance Drama Newsletter*
RE	*Revue d'Esthétique*
Reader	*Reader: Essays in Reader-Oriented Theory, Criticism, and Pedagogy*
ReAL	*Re: Artes Liberales*
ReAr	*Religion and the Arts*
RecL	*Recovery Literature*

REPCS	Review of Education, Pedagogy and Cultural Studies
RECTR	Restoration and Eighteenth-Century Theatre Research
RedL	Red Letters: A Journal of Cultural Politics
REED	Records of Early English Drama
REEDN	Records of Early English Drama Newsletter
ReFr	Revue Française
REL	Review of English Literature (Kyoto)
Ren&R	Renaissance and Reformation
Renascence	Renascence: Essays on Values in Literature
RenD	Renaissance Drama
Renfor	Renaissance Forum (online)
RenP	Renaissance Papers
RenQ	Renaissance Quarterly
Rep	Representations
RES	Review of English Studies
Restoration	Restoration: Studies in English Literary Culture, 1660–1700
RevAli	Revista Alicantina de Estudios Ingleses
Revels	Revels Plays
RevelsCL	Revels Plays Companion Library
RevelsSE	Revels Student Editions
RevR	Revolution and Romanticism, 1789–1834
Revue/Lisa	Revue/Lisa (e-journal)
RFEA	Revue Française d'Études Américaines
RFR	Robert Frost Review
RG	Revue Générale
RH	Recusant History
Rhetorica	Rhetorica: A Journal of the History of Rhetoric
Rhetorik	Rhetorik: Ein Internationales Jahrbuch
RhetR	Rhetoric Review
RHist	Rural History
RHL	Revue d'Histoire Littéraire de la France
RHT	Revue d'Histoire du Théâtre
RIB	Revista Interamericana de Bibliografia: Inter-American Reviews of Bibliography
Ricardian	Ricardian: Journal of the Richard III Society
RJ	Richard Jefferies Society Newsletter
RJES	Romanian Journal of English Studies
RL	Rereading Literature
RLAn	Romance Languages Annual
RLC	Revue de Littérature Comparée
RL&C	Research on Language and Computation
RLing	Rivista di Linguistica
RLit	Russian Literature
RLMC	Rivista di Letterature Moderne e Comparate
RLT	Russian Literature Triquarterly
RM	Rethinking Marxism
RMR	Rocky Mountain Review of Language and Literature
RM	Renaissance and Modern Studies
RMNews	Retrospective Methods Newsletter
RMSt	Reading Medieval Studies
ROA	Rutgers Optimality Archive
RoCL	Review of Cognitive Linguistics
ROMARD	ROMARD: Research on Medieval and Renaissance Drama

RomN	*Romance Notes*
RomS	*Romance Studies*
RoN	*Romanticism and Victorianism on the Net*
ROO	*Room of One's Own: A Feminist Journal of Literature and Criticism*
RORD	*Research Opportunities in Renaissance Drama*
RPh	*Respectus Philologicus*
RPT	*Russian Poetics in Translation*
RQ	*Riverside Quarterly*
RR	*Romanic Review*
RRDS	*Regents Renaissance Drama Series*
RRestDS	*Regents Restoration Drama Series*
RS	*Renaissance Studies*
RSQ	*Rhetoric Society Quarterly*
RSV	*Rivista di Studi Vittoriani*
RUO	*Revue de l'Université d'Ottawa*
RUSEng	*Rajasthan University Studies in English*
RuskN	*Ruskin Newsletter*
RUUL	*Reports from the Uppsala University Department of Linguistics*
R/WT	*Readerly/Writerly Texts*
SA	*South Asia: Journal of Asian Studies*
SAC	*Studies in the Age of Chaucer*
SBA	*Studies in Bible & Antiquity*
SAD	*Studies in American Drama, 1945–Present*
SAF	*Studies in American Fiction*
Saga-Book	*Saga-Book* (Viking Society for Northern Research)
SAIL	*Studies in American Indian Literatures: The Journal of the Association for the Study of American Indian Literatures*
SAJL	*Studies in American Jewish Literature*
SAJMRS	*South African Journal of Medieval and Renaissance Studies*
Sal	*Salmagundi: A Quarterly of the Humanities and Social Sciences*
SALALS	*Southern African Linguistics and Applied language Studies*
SALCT	*SALCT: Studies in Australian Literature, Culture and Thought*
S&CG	*Social and Cultural Geography*
S&P	*Script and Print*
S&Prag	*Semantics and Pragmatics*
S&S	*Sight and Sound*
Sanglap	*Sanglap: Journal of Literary and Critical Inquiry*
SAntS	*Studia Anthroponymica Scandinavica*
Salt	*Salt: An International Journal of Poetry and Poetics*
SAP	*Studia Anglica Posnaniensia*
SAQ	*South Atlantic Quarterly*
SAR	*Studies in the American Renaissance*
SARB	*South African Review of Books*
SARE	*South Asian Review*
SAsD	*South Asia Diaspora*
SASLC	*Studies in Anglo-Saxon Literature and Culture*
SatR	*Saturday Review*
SB	*Studies in Bibliography*
SC	*Seventeenth Century*
Scan	*Scandinavica: An International Journal of Scandinavian Studies*
ScanS	*Scandinavian Studies*
SCel	*Studia Celtica*

SCER	*Society for Critical Exchange Report*
Scintilla	*Scintilla: Annual Journal of Vaughan Studies and New Poetry*
SCJ	*Sixteenth Century Journal*
SCL	*Studies in Canadian Literature*
ScLJ(S)	*Scottish Literary Journal Supplement*
SCLOP	*Society for Caribbean Linguistics Occasional Papers*
SCN	*Seventeenth-Century News*
ScotL	*Scottish Language*
ScotLR	*Scottish Literary Review*
ScottN	*Scott Newsletter*
SCR	*South Carolina Review*
Screen	*Screen* (London)
SCRev	*South Central Review*
Scripsi	*Scripsi*
Scriptorium	*Scriptorium: International Review of Manuscript Studies*
SCRLL	*Scottish Cultural Review of Language and Literature*
Scru2	*Scrutiny 2*
ScTh	*Scottish Journal of Theology*
SD	*Social Dynamics*
SDR	*South Dakota Review*
SECC	*Studies in Eighteenth-Century Culture*
SECOLR	*SECOL Review: Southeastern Conference on Linguistics*
SED	*Survey of English Dialects*
SEEJ	*Slavic and East European Journal*
SEL	*Studies in English Literature, 1500–1900* (Rice University)
SELing	*Studies in English Linguistics* (Tokyo)
SELit	*Studies in English Literature* (Tokyo)
SELL	*Studies in English Language and Literature*
Sem	*Semiotica: Journal of the International Association for Semiotic Studies*
SEMC	*Studies in Early Medieval Coinage*
Semiosis	*Semiosis: Internationale Zeitschrift für Semiotik und Ästhetik*
SER	*Studien zur Englischen Romantik*
Seven	*Seven: An Anglo-American Literary Review*
SF&R	*Scholars' Facsimiles and Reprints*
SFic	*Science Fiction: A Review of Speculative Literature*
SFNL	*Shakespeare on Film Newsletter*
SFQ	*Southern Folklore Quarterly*
SFR	*Stanford French Review*
SFS	*Science-Fiction Studies*
SH	*Studia Hibernica* (Dublin)
ShakB	*Shakespeare Bulletin*
ShakS	*Shakespeare Studies* (New York)
Sh&Sch	*Shakespeare and Schools*
ShawR	*Shaw: The Annual of Bernard Shaw Studies*
SherHR	*Sherlock Holmes Review*
ShFTP	*Short Fiction in Theory & Practise*
ShIntY	*Shakespeare International Yearbook*
ShJE	*Shakespeare Jahrbuch* (Weimar)
ShJW	*Deutsche Shakespeare-Gesellschaft West Jahrbuch* (Bochum)
ShLR	*Shoin Literary Review*
ShN	*Shakespeare Newsletter*
Shofar	*Shofar: An Interdisciplinary Journal of Jewish Studies*

SHPS	*Studies in the History and Philosophy of Science*
SHR	*Southern Humanities Review*
ShS	*Shakespeare Survey*
ShSA	*Shakespeare in Southern Africa*
ShStud	*Shakespeare Studies* (Tokyo)
SHW	*Studies in Hogg and his World*
ShY	*Shakespeare Yearbook*
SI	*Social Identities: Journal for the Study of Race, Nation and Culture*
SiAF	*Studies in American Fiction*
SiCS	*Sino-Christian Studies: An International Journal of the Bible, Theology, and Philosophy*
SIcon	*Studies in Iconography*
SidJ	*Sidney Journal*
SidN	*Sidney Newsletter and Journal*
Signa	*Signa: Revista de la Asociación Española de Semiótica*
Signs	*Signs: Journal of Women in Culture and Society*
SiHoLS	*Studies in the History of the Language Sciences*
SIL	*Studies in Literature*
SiMed	*Studies in Medievalism*
SIM	*Studies in Music*
Simms	*The Simms Review*
Simplegadi	*Le Simplegadi*
SiP	*Shakespeare in Performance*
SiPr	*Shakespeare in Production*
SiR	*Studies in Romanticism*
SJL	*Southwest Journal of Linguistics*
SL	*Studia Linguistica*
SLang	*Studies in Language*
SLCS	*Studies in Language Companion Series*
SLI	*Studies in the Literary Imagination*
SLJ	*Southern Literary Journal*
SLJH	*Sri Lanka Journal of the Humanities*
SLL	*Studies in Literature and Language*
SLR	*Second Language Research*
SLRev	*Stanford Literature Review*
SLSc	*Studies in the Linguistic Sciences*
SMART	*Studies in Medieval and Renaissance Teaching*
SmAx	*Small Axe: A Caribbean Journal of Criticism*
SMC	*Studies in Medieval Culture*
SMed	*Studi Medievali*
SMELL	*Studies in Medieval English Language and Literature*
SMLit	*Studies in Mystical Literature* (Taiwan)
SMP	*Studia Metrica et Poetica*
SMRH	*Studies in Medieval and Renaissance History*
SMRT	*Studies in Medieval and Renaissance Teaching*
SMS	*Studier i Modern Språkvetenskap*
SMy	*Studia Mystica*
SN	*Studia Neophilologica*
SNNTS	*Studies in the Novel* (North Texas State University)
SO	*Shakespeare Originals*
SOA	*Sydsvenska Ortnamnssällskapets Årsskrift*
SoAR	*South Atlantic Review*

SoC	*Senses of Cinema* (online)
Societies	*Societies*, an open access sociology journal
Sociocrit	*Sociocriticism*
Socioling	*Sociolinguistica*
SociolingS	*Sociolinguistic Studies*
SocN	*Sociolinguistics*
SocSem	*Social Semiotics*
SocT	*Social Text*
SohoB	*Soho Bibliographies*
SoQ	*Southern Quarterly*
SoR	*Southern Review* (Baton Rouge, LA)
SoRA	*Southern Review* (Adelaide)
SoSt	*Southern Studies: An Interdisciplinary Journal of the South*
Soundings	*Soundings: An Interdisciplinary Journal*
Southerly	*Southerly: A Review of Australian Literature*
SoutherlyLP	*Southerly Long Paddock*
SovL	*Soviet Literature*
SP	*Studies in Philology*
SPAN	*SPAN: Newsletter of the South Pacific Association for Commonwealth Literature and Language Studies*
SPAS	*Studies in Puritan American Spirituality*
SpBLC	*Space Between: Literature & Culture, 1914–1945*
SPC	*Studies in Popular Culture*
Speculum	*Speculum: A Journal of Medieval Studies*
SpeechComm	*Speech Communication*
SPELL	*Swiss Papers in English Language and Literature*
Spiritus	*Spiritus: A Journal of Christian Spirituality*
SpM	*Spicilegio Moderno*
SpNL	*Spenser Newsletter*
Sprachwiss	*Sprachwissenschalt*
SpringE	*Spring: The Journal of the e.e. cummings Society*
SPub	*Studies in Publishing*
SQ	*Shakespeare Quarterly*
SR	*Sewanee Review*
SRen	*Studies in the Renaissance*
SSEL	*Stockholm Studies in English*
SSEng	*Sydney Studies in English*
SSF	*Studies in Short Fiction*
SSL	*Studies in Scottish Literature*
SSLA	*Studies in Second Language Acquisition*
SSLLT	*Studies in Second Language Learning and Teaching*
SSOL	*Scientific Study of Literature*
SPap	*Sydney Papers*
SSR	*Scottish Studies Review*
SSt	*Spenser Studies*
SStud	*Swift Studies: The Annual of the Ehrenpreis Center*
Staffrider	*Staffrider*
StaffordS	*Staffordshire Studies*
STAH	*Strange Things Are Happening*
StCH	*Studies in Church History*
STDR	*Sigma Tau Delta Review* (International English Honor Society)
STE	*Studying Teacher Education*
STGM	*Studien und Texte zur Geistegeschichte des Mittelalters*

StHR	*Stanford Historical Review*
StHum	*Studies in the Humanities*
StIn	*Studi Inglesi*
StLF	*Studi di Letteratura Francese*
STP	*Studies in Theatre and Performance*
StQ	*Steinbeck Quarterly*
StrR	*Structuralist Review*
StTCL	*Studies in Twentieth-Century Literature*
StTW	*Studies in Travel Writing*
StudiesAmNaturalism	*Studies in American Naturalism*
StudUBBPhil	*Studia Universitatis Babeş-Bolyai Philologia*
StudWF	*Studies in Weird Fiction*
STUF	*Sprachtypologie und Universalienforschung*
Style	*Style* (De Kalb, IL)
SUAS	*Stratford-upon-Avon Studies*
SubStance	*SubStance: A Review of Theory and Literary Criticism*
SUS	*Susquehanna University Studies*
Suvannabhumi	*Suvannabhumi: Multi-disciplinary Journal of Southeast Asian Studies*
SVEC	*Studies on Voltaire and the Eighteenth Century*
SWPLL	*Sheffield Working Papers in Language and Linguistics*
SWR	*Southwest Review*
SwR	*Swansea Review: A Journal of Criticism*
Symbolism	*Symbolism: An International Journal of Critical Aesthetics*
TA	*Theatre Annual*
Tabu	*Bulletin voor Taalwetenschap, Groningen*
TC	*Textual Cultures: Texts, Contexts, Interpretation*
T&C	*Text and Context*
T&L	*Translation and Literature*
T&P	*Text and Performance*
T&S	*Theology and Sexuality*
T&T	*Text & Talk*
TAnt	*Transforming Anthropology*
TAPS	*Transactions of the American Philosophical Society*
Target	*Target: International Journal on Translation Studies*
TCBH	*Twentieth-Century British History*
TCBS	*Transactions of the Cambridge Bibliographical Society*
TCE	*Texas College English*
TCL	*Twentieth-Century Literature*
TCQ	*Technical Communication Quarterly*
TD	*Themes in Drama*
TDR	*Drama Review*
TEAMS	*Consortium for the Teaching of the Middle Ages*
Telos	*Telos: A Quarterly Journal of Post-Critical Thought*
TennEJ	*Tennessee English Journal*
TennQ	*Tennessee Quarterly*
TennSL	*Tennessee Studies in Literature*
TeReo	*Te Reo: Journal of the Linguistic Society of New Zealand*
TesolQ	*TESOL Quarterly*
Text	*Text: Transactions of the Society for Textual Scholarship*
TextJW	*Text: Journal of Writing and Writing Courses*
TextM	*Text Matters: A Journal of Literature, Theory and Culture*
Textus	*Textus, English Studies in Italy*
TF	*TheatreForum*

TH	Texas Humanist
THA	Thomas Hardy Annual
Thalia	Thalia: Studies in Literary Humor
ThC	Theatre Crafts
TheatreS	Theatre Studies
THEPES	Theory and Practice in English Studies
THES	Times Higher Education Supplement
Thesis	Thesis Eleven
The Victorian	The Victorian
THIC	Theatre History in Canada
THJ	Thomas Hardy Journal
ThN	Thackeray Newsletter
Thought	Thought: A Review of Culture and Ideas
Thph	Theatrephile
ThreR	Threepenny Review
ThS	Theatre Survey: The American Journal of Theatre History
THSJ	Thomas Hardy Society Journal
THSLC	Transactions of the Historic Society of Lancashire and Cheshire
THStud	Theatre History Studies
ThTop	Theatre Topics
THY	Thomas Hardy Yearbook
TIBG	Transactions of the Institute of British Geographers
TiLSM	Trends in Linguistics: Studies and Monographs
Tip	Theory in Practice
TIR	The Irish Review
Tirra Lirra	Tirra Lirra: The Quarterly Magazine for the Yarra Valley
TIS	Translation and Interpreting Studies
TJ	Theatre Journal
TJS	Transactions (Johnson Society)
TkR	Tamkang Review
TL	Theoretical Linguistics
TLJ	The Linguistics Journal
TLR	Linguistic Review
TLS	Times Literary Supplement
TM	Tout Moun: Caribbean Journal of Cultural Studies
TMLT	Toronto Medieval Latin Texts
TN	Theatre Notebook
TP	Terzo Programma
TPLL	Tilbury Papers in Language and Literature
TPLS	Theory and Practice in Language Studies
TPQ	Text and Performance Quarterly
TPr	Textual Practice
TPS	Transactions of the Philological Society
TR	Theatre Record
Traditio	Traditio: Studies in Ancient and Medieval History, Thought, and Religion
TransL	Transnational Literature
TransS	Translation Studies
TRB	Tennyson Research Bulletin
TRHS	Transactions of the Royal Historical Society
TRI	Theatre Research International
TriQ	TriQuarterly
TSAR	Toronto South Asian Review

TSB	*Thoreau Society Bulletin*
TSLang	*Typological Studies in Language*
TSLL	*Texas Studies in Literature and Language*
TStud	*Tolkien Studies*
TSWL	*Tulsa Studies in Women's Literature*
TTR	*Trinidad and Tobago Review*
TUSAS	*Twayne's United States Authors Series*
TvL	*Tydskrif vir Letterkunde*
TWAS	*Twayne's World Authors Series*
TWBR	*Third World Book Review*
TWQ	*Third World Quarterly*
TWR	*Thomas Wolfe Review*
Txt	*Text: An Interdisciplinary Annual of Textual Studies*
TYDS	*Transactions of the Yorkshire Dialect Society*
Typophiles	*Typophiles* (New York)
UCrow	*Upstart Crow*
UCTSE	*University of Cape Town Studies in English*
UCWPL	*UCL Working Papers in Linguistics*
UDR	*University of Drayton Review*
UE	*Use of English*
UEAPL	*UEA Papers in Linguistics*
UES	*Unisa English Studies*
ULR	*University of Leeds Review*
UMSE	*University of Mississippi Studies in English*
UOQ	*University of Ottawa Quarterly*
Upstart	*Upstart: A Journal of English Renaissance Studies*
USSE	*University of Saga Studies in English*
UtopST	*Utopian Studies*
UTQ	*University of Toronto Quarterly*
UWR	*University of Windsor Review*
Var	*Varianta*
VARIENG	*Studies in Variation, Contacts and Change in English* (online)
VCT	*Les Voies de la Création Théâtrale*
VEAW	*Varieties of English around the World*
Verbatim	*Verbatim: The Language Quarterly*
Viator	*Viator: Medieval and Renaissance Studies*
Victo	*Victoriographies*
Views	*Viennese English Working Papers*
VIJ	*Victorians Institute Journal*
VisCom	*Visual Communication*
VJCL	*Victorian Journal of Culture and Literature*
VLC	*Victorian Literature and Culture*
VN	*Victorian Newsletter*
VP	*Victorian Poetry*
VPR	*Victorian Periodicals Review*
VQR	*Virginia Quarterly Review*
VR	*Victorian Review*
VS	*Victorian Studies*
VSB	*Victorian Studies Bulletin*
VWB	*Virginia Woolf Bulletin*
VWM	*Virginia Woolf Miscellany*
WAJ	*Women's Art Journal*
WAL	*Western American Literature*

WAM	*Western American Literature*
W&I	*Word and Image*
W&L	*Women and Literature*
W&Lang	*Women and Language*
Wasafiri	*Wasafiri*
WascanaR	*Wascana Review*
WBEP	*Wiener Beiträge zur Englischen Philologie*
WC	*World's Classics*
WC	*Wordsworth Circle*
WCR	*West Coast Review*
WCWR	*William Carlos Williams Review*
Wellsian	*Wellsian: The Journal of the H.G. Wells Society*
WEn	*World Englishes*
Westerly	*Westerly: An Annual Review*
WestHR	*West Hills Review: A Walt Whitman Journal*
WF	*Western Folklore*
WFE	*Writing from the Edge*
WHASN	*W.H. Auden Society Newsletter*
WHR	*Western Humanities Review*
WI	*Word and Image*
WLA	*Wyndham Lewis Annual*
WLT	*World Literature Today*
WLWE	*World Literature Written in English*
WMQ	*William and Mary Quarterly*
WoHR	*Women's History Review*
Women	*Women: A Cultural Review*
WomGY	*Women in German Yearbook*
WomHR	*Women's History Review*
WORD	*WORD: Journal of the International Linguistic Association*
WPEL	*Working papers in Educational Linguistics*
WPULL	*Working Papers in Urban Language & Literacy*
WPW	*Working Papers on the Web*
WQ	*Wilson Quarterly*
WRB	*Women's Review of Books*
WS	*Women's Studies: An Interdisciplinary Journal*
WSIF	*Women's Studies: International Forum*
WSJour	*Wallace Stevens Journal*
Wstr	*Word Structure*
WSR	*Wicazo Sa Review*
WstA	*Woolf Studies Annual*
WTJ	*Westminster Theological Journal*
WTW	*Writers and their Work*
WUSA	*Working USA*
WVUPP	*West Virginia University Philological Papers*
WW	*Women's Writing*
WWR	*Walt Whitman Quarterly Review*
XR	*Xavier Review*
YCC	*Yearbook of Comparative Criticism*
YeA	*Yeats Annual*
YER	*Yeats Eliot Review*
YES	*Yearbook of English Studies*
YEuS	*Yearbook of European Studies/Annuaire d'Études Européennes*
YFS	*Yale French Studies*

Yiddish	Yiddish/Modern Jewish Studies
YJC	Yale Journal of Criticism: Interpretation in the Humanities
YJLH	Yale Journal of Law and the Humanities
YLS	Yearbook of Langland Studies
YM	Yearbook of Morphology
YNS	York Note Series
YPL	York Papers in Linguistics
YR	Yale Review
YREAL	The Yearbook of Research in English and American Literature
YULG	Yale University Library Gazette
YWES	Year's Work in English Studies

Volume numbers are supplied in the text, as are individual issue numbers for journals that are not continuously paginated through the year.

2. Publishers

A&UA	Allen & Unwin, Sydney, NSW, Australia
AarhusUP	Århus UP, Århus, Denmark
Abbeville	Abbeville Press, New York, NY
AberdeenUP	Aberdeen UP, Aberdeen
Abhinav	Abhinav Publications, New Delhi, India
ABL	Armstrong Browning Library, Waco, TX
Ablex	Ablex Publishing, Norwood, NJ
Åbo	Åbo Akademi, Åbo, Finland
Abrams	Harry N. Abrams, New York, NY
AC	Ayebia Clark, UK
Academia	Academia Press, Melbourne, VIC, Australia
Academic	Academic Press, London and Orlando
Academica	Academica Press, Palo Alta, CA
Academy	Academy Press, Dublin, Eire
AcademyC	Academy Chicago Publishers, Chicago, IL
AcademyE	Academy Editions, London
Acadiensis	Acadiensis Press, Fredericton, NB, Canada
ACarS	Association for Caribbean Studies, Coral Gables, FL
ACC	Antique Collectors' Club, Woodbridge, Suffolk
ACCO	ACCO, Leuven, Belgium
ACP	Another Chicago Press, Chicago, IL
ACS	Association for Canadian Studies, Ottawa, ON, Canada
Adam Hart	Adam Hart Publishers, London
Adam Matthew	Adam Matthew, Suffolk
Addison-Wesley	Addison-Wesley, Wokingham, Berkshire
Adhyayan	Adhyayan Publishers & Distributors, New Delhi, India
Adosa	Adosa, Clermont-Ferrand, France
AEMS	American Early Medieval Studies
AF	Akademisk Forlag, Copenhagen, Denmark
Affiliated	Affiliated East–West Press, New Delhi, India
AfHP	African Heritage Books, London
AFP	Associated Faculty Press, New York, NY
AFWP	Africa World Press, Lawrenceville, NJ
Africana	Africana Publications, New York, NY
Agate	Agate Publishing, Evanston, IL
A–H	Amold-Heinemann, New Delhi, India
Ahriman	Ahriman-Verlag, Freiburg im Breisgau, Germany

Ajanta	Ajanta Publications, Delhi, India
AK	Akadémiai Kiadó, Budapest, Hungary
ALA	ALA Editions, Chicago, IL
Al&Ba	Allen & Bacon, Boston, MA
Albatross	Albatross Books, Sutherland, NSW, Australia
Albion	Albion, Appalachian State University, Boone, NC
Alderman	Alderman Press, London
Aldwych	Aldwych Press, London
AligarhMU	Aligarh Muslim University, Uttar Pradesh, India
Alioth	Alioth Press, Beaverton, OR
Allen	W.H. Allen, London
Allied Publishers	Allied Indian Publishers, Lahore and New Delhi, India
Alma	Alma Books, London
Almond	Almond Press, Sheffield
AM	Aubier Montaigne, Paris, France
AmberL	Amber Lane, Oxford
Amistad	Amistad Press, New York, NY
AMP	Aurora Metro Press, London
AMS	AMS Press, New York, NY
AMU	Adam Mickiewicz University, Posnan, Poland
Anansi	Anansi Press, Toronto, ON, Canada
Anderson-Lovelace	Anderson-Lovelace, Los Altos Hills, CA
Anthem	Anthem Press, London, New York, Delhi
Antipodes	Antipodes Press, Plimmerton, New Zealand
ANUP	ANU (Australia National University) Press, Canberra, Australia
Anvil	Anvil Press Poetry, London
APA	APA, Maarssen, The Netherlands
APH	Associated Publishing House, New Delhi, India
API	API Network, Perth, WA, Australia
APL	American Poetry and Literature Press, Philadelphia, PA
APP	Australian Professional Publications, Mosman, NSW, Australia
Applause	Applause Theatre Book Publishers
APS	American Philosophical Society, Philadelphia, PA
Aquarian	Aquarian Press, Wellingborough, Northants
ArborH	Arbor House Publishing, New York, NY
Arcade	Arcade Publishing, New York, NY
Archon	Archon Books, Hamden, CT
ArchP	Architectural Press Books, Guildford, Surrey
Ardis	Ardis Publishers, Ann Arbor, MI
Ariel	Ariel Press, London
Aristotle	Aristotle University, Thessaloniki, Greece
Ark	Ark Paperbacks, London
Arkona	Arkona Forlaget, Aarhus, Denmark
Arlington	Arlington Books, London
Arnold	Edward Arnold, London
ARP	Australian Reference Publications, North Balwyn, VIC, Australia
Arrow	Arrow Books, London
Artmoves	Artmoves, Parkdale, VIC, Australia
ASchP	Australian Scholarly Publishing, Melbourne, VIC, Australia
Ashfield	Ashfield Press, London
Ashgate	Ashgate, Brookfield, VT
ASLS	Association for Scottish Literary Studies, Aberdeen
ASP	Australian Scholarly Publishing

AStP	Aboriginal Studies Press, Canberra, ACT, Australia
ASU	Arizona State University, Tempe, AZ
Atheneum	Atheneum Publishers, New York, NY
Athlone	Athlone Press, London
Atlantic	Atlantic Publishers, Darya Ganj, New Delhi, India
Atlas	Atlas Press, London
Attic	Attic Press, Dublin, Eire
Atuanui	Atuanui Press, Waikato, New Zealand
AuBC	Australian Book Collector
AucklandUP	Auckland UP, Auckland, New Zealand
AUC Press	American University Press in Cairo, Egypt
AUG	Acta Universitatis Gothoburgensis, Sweden
AUP	Associated University Presses, London and Toronto
AUPG	Academic & University Publishers, London
Aurum	Aurum Press, London
Auslib	Auslib Press, Adelaide, SA, Australia
Austin Macauley	Austin Macauley Publishers Ltd, London
AUU	Acta Universitatis Umensis, Umeå, Sweden
AUUp	Acta Universitatis Upsaliensis, Uppsala, Sweden
Avebury	Avebury Publishing, Aldershot
Avero	Avero Publications, Newcastle upon Tyne
A-V Verlag	A-V Verlag, Franz Fischer, Augsburg, Germany
Axeltree	Axletree Books, New York
BA	British Academy, London
Bagel	August Bagel Verlag, Dusseldorf, Germany
Bahri	Bahri Publications, New Delhi, India
Bamberger	Bamberger Books, Flint, MI
B&B	Boydell & Brewer, Woodbridge, Suffolk
B&J	Barrie & Jenkins, London
B&N	Barnes & Noble, Totowa, NJ
B&O	Burns & Oates, Tunbridge Wells, Kent
Banff	Banff Centre Press, Banff, Canada
BAR	British Archaelogical Reports, Oxford
Barn Owl	Barn Owl Books, Taunton
Barnes	A.S. Barnes, San Diego, CA
Basic Books	Basic Books, New York
Bath UP	Bath UP, Bath
BaylorUP	Baylor University Press, Waco, TX
Bayreuth	Bayreuth African Studies, University of Bayreuth, Germany
BBC	BBC Publications, London
BCP	Bristol Classical Press, Bristol
Beacon	Beacon Press, Boston, MA
Beck	Verlag C.H. Beck oHG, Munich, Germany
Becket	Becket Publications, London
Beckford Society	Beckford Society, UK
Belin	Éditions Belin, Paris, France
Belknap	Belknap Press, Cambridge, MA
Belles Lettres	Société d'Édition les Belles Lettres, Paris, France
Bellew	Bellew Publishing, London
Bellflower	Belflower Press, Case University, Cleveland, OH
Benjamins	John Benjamins, Amsterdam, The Netherlands
BenjaminsNA	John Benjamins North America, Philadelphia, PA
BennC	Bennington College, Bennington, VT

Berg	Berg Publishers, Oxford
Berghahn	Berghahn Books, Oxford and New York, NY
BFI	British Film Institute, London
BibS	Bibliographical Society, London
BilinguaGA	Bilingua GA Editions
Bilingual	Bilingual Press, Arizona State University, Tempe, AZ
Binnacle	Binnacle Press, London
Biografia	Biografia Publishers, London
Birkbeck	Birkbeck College, University of London
Bishopsgate	Bishopsgate Press, Tonbridge, Kent
BL	British Library, London
Black	Adam & Charles Black, London
Black Cat	Black Cat Press, Blackrock, Eire
Black Dog	Black Dog Publishing, London
Blackie	Blackie & Son, Glasgow
Black Swan	Black Swan, Curtin, UT
Blackwell	Basil Blackwell, Oxford
BlackwellR	Blackwell Reference, Oxford
Blackwood	Blackwood, Pillans & Wilson, Edinburgh
Blaue Eule	Verlag die Blaue Eule, Essen, Germany
Bloodaxe	Bloodaxe Books, Newcastle upon Tyne
Bloomsbury	Bloomsbury Publishing, London
BM	Bobbs-Merrill, New York, NY
BMP	British Museum Publications, London
Bodleian	Bodleian Library, Oxford
Bodley	Bodley Head, London
Bogle	Bogle L'Ouverture Publications, London
Böhlau	Böhlau Verlag, Vienna, Austria
BoiseSUP	Boise State UP, Boise, ID
Book Enclave	Book Enclave, Shanti Nagar, Jaipur, India
Book Guild	Book Guild, Lewes
BookplateS	Bookplate Society, Birmingham
Booksplus	Booksplus Nigeria Limited, Lagos, Nigeria
Boombana	Boombana Press, Brisbane, QLD, Australia
Borealis	Borealis Press, Ottawa, ON, Canada
Borgo	Borgo Press, San Bernardino, CA
BostonAL	Boston Athenaeum Library, Boston, MA
Bowker	R.R. Bowker, New Providence, NJ
Boyars	Marion Boyars, London and Boston, MA
Boydell	Boydell Press, Woodbridge, Suffolk
Boyes	Megan Boyes, Allestree, Derbyshire
Bradwell	Books Bradwell Books, Sheffield
Braumüller	Wilhelm Braumüller, Vienna, Austria
Breakwater	Breakwater Books, St John's, NL, Canada
Brentham	Brentham Press, St Albans, Hertfordshire
Brepols	Brepols, Turnhout, Belgium
Brewer	D.S. Brewer, Woodbridge, Suffolk
Brewin	Brewin Books, Studley, Warwicks
Bridge	Bridge Publishing, S. Plainfield, NJ
Brill	E.J. Brill, Leiden, Belgium
BrillA	Brill Academic Publishers
Brilliance	Brilliance Books, London
Broadview	Broadview, London, ON and Lewiston, NY

Brookside	Brookside Press, London
Browne	Sinclair Browne, London
Brownstone	Brownstone Books, Madison, IN
BrownUP	Brown UP, Providence, RI
Brynmill	Brynmill Press, Harleston, Norfolk
BSA	Bibliographical Society of America
BSP	Black Sparrow Press, Santa Barbara, CA
BSU	Ball State University, Muncie, IN
BuckUP	Bucknell UP, Lewisburg, PA
BUP	Birmingham UP, Birmingham
Burnett	Burnett Books, London
Buske	Helmut Buske, Hamburg, Germany
Butterfly	Butterfly Books, San Antonio, TX
CA	Creative Arts Book, Berkeley, CA
Cadmus	Cadmus Editions, Tiburon, CA
Cairns	Francis Cairns, University of Leeds
Calaloux	Calaloux Publications, Ithaca, NY
Calder	John Calder, London
CALLS	Centre for Australian Language and Literature Studies, University of New England, NSW, Australia
Cambria	Cambria Press, Amherst, NY
CambridgeSP	Cambridge Scholars Publishing, Newcastle upon Tyne
Camden	Camden Press, London
CamdenH	Camden House, Rochester, NY
C&W	Chatto & Windus, London
Canongate	Canongate Publishing, Edinburgh
Canterbury	Canterbury Press, Norwich
Canterbury UP	Canterbury University Press, Christchurch, New Zealand
Cape	Jonathan Cape, London
Capra	Capra Press, Santa Barbara, CA
Carcanet	Carcanet New Press, Manchester, Lancashire
CaribB	Caribbean Books, Parkersburg, IA
CarletonUP	Carleton UP, Ottawa, ON, Canada
Carucci	Carucci, Rome, Italy
Cascadilla	Cascadilla Press, Somerville, MA
Cass	Frank Cass, London
Cassell	Cassell, London
Cavaliere Azzurro	Cavaliere Azzurro, Bologna, Italy
Cave	Godfrey Cave Associates, London
CBS	Cambridge Bibliographical Society, Cambridge
CCCP	Critical, Cultural and Communications Press, Nottingham
CDSH	Centre de Documentation Sciences Humaines, Paris, France
CENS	Centre for English Name Studies, University of Nottingham
Century	Century Publishing, London
C–H	Chadwyck–Healey, Cambridge
Chambers	W. & R. Chambers, Edinburgh
Champion	Librairie Honoré Champion, Paris, France
Chand	S. Chand, Madras, India
Chaucer	Chaucer Press
Checkmark Books	Checkmark Books, New York, NY
ChiR	Chicago Review Press, Chicago, IL
Christendom	Christendom Publications, Front Royal, VA
Chronicle	Chronicle Books, London

ChuoUL	Chuo University Library, Tokyo, Japan
Churchman	Churchman Publishing, Worthing, W. Sussex
Cistercian	Cistercian Publications, Kalamazoo, MI
CL	City Lights Books, San Francisco, CA
CLA	Canadian Library Association, Ottawa, ON, Canada
Clarendon	Clarendon Press, Oxford
Claridge	Claridge, St Albans, Hertfordshire
Clarion	Clarion State College, Clarion, PA
Clark	T. & T. Clark, Edinburgh
Clarke	James Clarke, Cambridge
Classical	Classical Publishing, New Delhi, India
ClemsonUP	Clemson University Press, Clemson, SC
CMST	Centre for Medieval Studies, University of Toronto, ON, Canada
Coach House	Coach House Press, Toronto, ON, Canada
Colleagues	Colleagues Press, East Lansing, MI
Collector	Collector, London
College-Hill	College-Hill Press, San Diego, CA
Collins	William Collins, London
CollinsA	William Collins (Australia), Sydney, NSW, Australia
Collins & Brown	Collins & Brown, London
ColUP	Columbia UP, New York, NY
Comedia	Comedia Publishing, London
Comet	Comet Books, London
Connell Guides	Connell Guides, London
Constable	Constable, London
Contemporary	Contemporary Books, Chicago, IL
Continuum	Continuum Publishing, New York, NY
ContinuumL	Continuum, London
Copp	Copp Clark Pitman, Mississauga, ON, Canada
Corgi	Corgi Books, London
CorkUP	Cork UP, Eire
Cornford	Cornford Press, Launceston, TAS, Australia
CornUP	Cornell UP, Ithaca, NY
Cornwallis	Cornwallis Press, Hastings, E. Sussex
Coronado	Coronado Press, Lawrence, KS
Cosmo	Cosmo Publications, New Delhi, India
Coteau	Coteau Books, Regina, SK, Canada
Counterpoint Press	Counterpoint Press, Berkeley, CA
Cowfeather	Cowfeather Press, Middleton, WI
Cowley	Cowley Publications, Cambridge, MA
Cowper	Cowper House, Pacific Grove, CA
CPP	Canadian Poetry Press, London, Ontario, ON, Canada
CQUP	Central Queensland UP, Rockhampton, QLD, Australia
Craftsman House	Craftsman House, The Netherlands
Craig Pottoon	Craig Pottoon Publishing, New Zealand
Crawford	Crawford House Publishing, Hindmarsh, SA
Creag Darach	Creag Durach Publications, Stirling
CreativeB	Creative Books, New Delhi, India
Cresset	Cresset Library, London
Crossing	Crossing Press, Freedom, CA
Crossroad	Crossroad Publishing, New York, NY
Crown	Crown Publishers, New York, NY
Crowood	Crowood Press, Marlborough, Wiltshire

CSP	Canadian Scholars' Press, Toronto, ON, Canada
CSU	Cleveland State University, Cleveland, OH
CULouvain	Catholic University of Louvain, Louvain-la-Neuve, Belgium
CULublin	Catholic University of Lublin, Poland
CUP	Cambridge UP, Cambridge, New York, and Melbourne
Currency	Currency Press, Paddington, NSW, Australia
Currey	James Currey, London
Cushing	Cushing Memorial Library & Archives
CV	Cherry Valley Edition, Rochester, NY
CVK	Cornelson-Velhagen & Klasing, Berlin, Germany
CWU	Carl Winter Universitätsverlag, Heidelberg, Germany
Da Capo	Da Capo Press, New York
Daisy	Daisy Books, Peterborough, Cambridgeshire
D&H	Duncker & Humblot, Berlin, Germany
D&M	Douglas & McIntyre, Vancouver, BC, Canada
D&S	Duffy and Snellgrove, Polts Point, NSW, Australia
Dangaroo	Dangaroo Press, Mundelstrup, Denmark
Daniel	Daniel & Daniel Publishers Inc., McKinleyville, CA
Dawson	Dawson Publishing, Folkestone, Kent
DawsonsPM	Dawsons Pall Mall
DBAP	Daphne Brasell Associates Press
DBP	Drama Book Publishers, New York, NY
Deakin UP	Deakin UP, Geelong, VIC, Australia
De Boeck	De Boeck-Wesmael, Brussels, Belgium
Dee	Ivan R. Dee Publishers, Chicago, IL
De Graaf	De Graaf, Nierwkoup, The Netherlands
Denoël	Denoël S.A.R.L., Paris, France
Dent	J.M. Dent, London
DentA	Dent, Ferntree Gully, VIC, Australia
Depanee	Depanee Printers and Publishers, Nugegoda, Sri Lanka
Deutsch	André Deutsch, London
Didier	Éditions Didier, Paris, France
Diesterweg	Verlag Moritz Diesterweg, Frankfurt am Main, Germany
DLSUP	De La Salle University UP, Manila, Philippines
Doaba	Doaba House, Delhi, India
Dobby	Eric Dobby Publishing, St Albans
Dobson	Dobson Books, Durham
Dolmen	Dolmen Press, Portlaoise, Eire
Donald	John Donald, Edinburgh
Doubleday	Doubleday, London and New York
Dove	Dove, Sydney, NSW, Australia
Dovecote	Dovecote Press, Wimborne, Dorset
Dovehouse	Dovehouse Editions, Canada
Dover	Dover Publications, New York, NY
Drew	Richard Drew, Edinburgh
Droste	Droste Verlag, Düsseldorf, Germany
Droz	Librairie Droz SA, Geneva, Switzerland
DublinUP	Dublin UP, Dublin, Eire
Duckworth	Gerald Duckworth, London
Duculot	J. Duculot, Gembloux, Belgium
DukeUP	Duke UP, Durham, NC
Dundurn	Dundurn Press, Toronto and London, ON, Canada
Duquesne	Duquesne UP, Pittsburgh, PA

Dutton	E.P. Dutton, New York, NY
EA	English Association, London
EAS	English Association Sydney Incorporated
Eason	Eason & Son, Dublin, Eire
East Bay	East Bay Books, Berkeley, CA
Ebony	Ebony Books, Melbourne, SA, Australia
Ecco	Ecco Press, New York, NY
ECW	ECW Press, Downsview, Ontario, ON, Canada
Eden	Eden Press, Montreal and St Albans, VT
EdinUP	Edinburgh UP, Edinburgh
Editoriale Anicia	Editoriale Anicia, Rome, Italy
Educare	Educare, Burnwood, VIC, Australia
Edward Elgar	Edward Elgar, Cheltenham
EEM	East European Monographs, Boulder, CO
Eerdmans	William Eerdmans, Grand Rapids, MI
EETS	Early English Text Society, c/o Exeter College, Oxford
Eihosha	Eihosha, Tokyo, Japan
Elephas	Elephas Books, Kewdale, WA, Australia
Elibank	Elibank Press, Wellington, New Zealand
Elm Tree	Elm Tree Books, London
Ember	Ember Press, Brixham, South Devon
Emerald	Emerald Group Publishing, Bingley, Yorkshire
EMSH	Editions de la Maison des Sciences de l'Homme, Paris, France
Enitharmon	Enitharmon Press, London
Enzyklopädie	Enzyklopädie, Leipzig, Germany
EONF	Eugene O'Neill Foundation, Danville, CA
EPNS	English Place-Name Society, Beeston, Nottingham
epubli	e-book branch of Holzbrinck, Stuttgart, Germany
EPURE	Editions et Presses universitaires de Reims, France
Epworth	Epworth Press, Manchester
Equinox	Equinox Publishing, Sheffield
Eriksson	Paul Eriksson, Middlebury, VT
Erlbaum	Erlbaum Associates, NJ
Erskine	Erskine Press, Harleston, Norfolk
ESI	Edizioni Scientifiche Italiane, Naples, Italy
ESL	Edizioni di Storia e Letteratura, Rome, Italy
EUFS	Editions Universitaires Fribourg Suisse, Switzerland
EUL	Edinburgh University Library, Edinburgh
Europa	Europa Publishers, London
Evans	M. Evans, New York, NY
Exact Change	Exact Change, Boston, MA
Exeter UP	Exeter UP, Devon
Exile	Exile Editions, Toronto, ON, Canada
Eyre	Eyre Methuen, London
FAB	Free Association Books, London
Faber	Faber & Faber, London
FAC	Federation d'Activites Culturelles, Paris, France
FACP	Fremantle Arts Centre Press, Fremantle, WA, Australia
Falcon Books	Falcon Books, Eastbourne
F&F	Fels & Firn Press, San Anselmo, CA
F&S	Feffer & Simons, Amsterdam, The Netherlands
Fantagraphics	Fantagraphics, Seattle, WA
Farrand	Farrand Press, London

Fay	Barbara Fay, Stuttgart, Germany
F–B	Ford–Brown, Houston, TX
FCP	Four Courts Press, Dublin, Eire
FDUP	Fairleigh Dickinson UP, Madison, NJ
FE	Fourth Estate, London
Feminist	Feminist Press, New York, NY
Field Day	Field Day, Derry
Fifth House	Fifth House Publications, Saskatoon, Saskatchewan
Fine	Donald Fine, New York, NY
Fink	Fink Verlag, Munich, Germany
Five Leaves	Five Leaves Publications, Nottingham
Flamingo	Flamingo Publishing, Newark, NJ
Flammarion	Flammarion, Paris, France
Flood	Flood Editions, Chicago, IL
Floris	Floris Books, Edinburgh
FlorSU	Florida State University, Tallahassee, FL
FOF	Facts on File, New York, NY
Folger	Folger Shakespeare Library, Washington, DC
Folio	Folio Press, London
Fontana	Fontana Press, London
Footprint	Footprint Press, Colchester, Essex
FordUP	Fordham UP, New York, NY
Foris	Foris Publications, Dordrecht, The Netherlands
Forsten	Egbert Forsten Publishing, Groningen, The Netherlands
Fortress	Fortress Press, Philadelphia, PA
ForItal	Forum Italicum, Stony Brook University, New York, NY
Francis Boutle	Francis Boutle Publishers, London
Francke	Francke Verlag, Berne, Switzerland
Frank & Timme	Frank & Timme, Berlin, Germany
Franklin	Burt Franklin, New York, NY
FreedomP	Freedom Press, London
FreeP	Free Press, New York, NY
FreeUP	Free UP, Amsterdam, The Netherlands
Freundlich	Freundlich Books, New York, NY
FS&G	Farrar, Straus & Giroux
FSP	Five Seasons Press, Madley, Hereford
FW	Fragments West/Valentine Press, Long Beach, CA
FWA	Fiji Writers' Association, Suva, Fiji
FWP	Falling Wall Press, Bristol
Gale	Gale Research, Detroit, MI
Galilée	Galilée, Paris, France
Gallimard	Gallimard, Paris, France
G&G	Grevatt & Grevatt, Newcastle upon Tyne
G&M	Gill & Macmillan, Dublin, Eire
Garland	Garland Publishing, New York, NY
Gasson	Roy Gasson Associates, Wimbourne, Dorset
Gateway	Gateway Editions, Washington, DC
GE	Greenwich Exchange, UK
Getty	Getty Publications, New York, NY
GIA	GIA Publications, USA
Gininderra	Gininderra Press, Canberra, Australia
Girasole	Edizioni del Girasole, Ravenna, Austria
GlasgowDL	Glasgow District Libraries, Glasgow

Gleerup	Gleerupska, Lund, Sweden
GMSmith	Gibbs M. Smith, Layton, UT
Golden Dog	Golden Dog, Ottawa, ON, Canada
Gollancz	Victor Gollancz, London
Gomer	Gomer Press, Llandysul, Dyfed
GothU	Gothenburg University, Gothenburg, Sweden
Gower	Gower Publishing, Aldershot, Hants
GRAAT	Groupe de Recherches Anglo-Américaines de Tours
Grafton	Grafton Books, London
GranB	Granary Books, New York, NY
Granta	Granta Publications, London
Granville	Granville Publishing, London
Grasset	Grasset & Fasquelle, Paris, France
Grassroots	Grassroots, London
Graywolf	Graywolf Press, St Paul, MI
Greenhalgh	M.J. Greenhalgh, London
Greenhill	Greenhill Books, London
Greenwood	Greenwood Press, Westport, CT
Gregg	Gregg Publishing, Surrey
Greville	Greville Press, Warwick
Greymitre	Greymitre Books, London
GroC	Grolier Club, New York, NY
Groos	Julius Groos Verlag, Heidelberg, Switzerland
Grove	Grove Press, New York, NY
GRP	Greenfield Review Press, New York, NY
Grüner	B.R. Grüner, Amsterdam, The Netherlands
Gruyter	Walter de Gruyter, Berlin, Germany
Guernica	Guernica Editions, Montreal, QC, Canada
Guilford	Guilford, New York, NY
Gulmohar	Gulmohar Press, Islamabad, Pakistan
Hackett	Hackett Publishing Company, Indianapolis, IN
Haggerston	Haggerston Press, London
Hale	Robert Hale, London
Hall	G.K. Hall, Boston, MA
Halstead	Halstead Press, Rushcutters Bay, NSW, Australia
HalsteadP	Halstead Press, c/o J. Wiley & Sons, Chichester, W. Sussex
Hambledon	Hambledon Press, London
HamptonP	Hampton Press, New York, NY
Handel	Handel Books, Nigeria
H&I	Hale & Iremonger, Sydney, NSW, Australia
H&L	Hambledon and London
H&M	Holmes & Meier, London and New York
H&S	Hodder & Stoughton, London
H&SNZ	Hodder & Stoughton, Auckland, New Zealand
H&W	Hill & Wang, New York, NY
Hansib	Hansib Publishing, London
Harbour	Harbour Publishing, Madeira Park, BC
Harman	Harman Publishing House, New Delhi, India
Harper	Harper & Row, New York, NY
Harrap	Harrap, Edinburgh
HarvardUP	Harvard UP, Cambridge, MA
Harvill Secker	Harvill Secker, London
Harwood	Harwood Academic Publishers, Langhorne, PA

Haytee	Haytee Press and Publishing, Ilorin, Nigeria
HBJ	Harcourt Brace Jovanovich, New York and London
HC	HarperCollins, London
HCAus	HarperCollins Australia, Pymble, NSW, Australia
Headline	Headline Book Publishing, London
Heath	D.C. Heath, Lexington, MS
HebrewUMP	Hebrew University Magnes Press
HeidelbergUP	Heidelberg University Press, Germany
Heinemann	William Heinemann, London
HeinemannA	William Heinemann, St Kilda, VIC, Australia
HeinemannC	Heinemann Educational Books, Kingston, Jamaica
HeinemannK	Heinemann Kenya Ltd
HeinemannNg	Heinemann Educational Books, Nigeria
HeinemannNZ	Heinemann Publishers, Auckland (now Heinemann Reed)
HeinemannR	Heinemann Reed, Auckland, New Zealand
Helm	Christopher Helm, London
Herbert	Herbert Press, London
Hermitage	Hermitage Antiquarian Bookshop, Denver, CO
Henry Southeran	Henry Southeran Ltd, London
Hern	Nick Hern Books, London
Hertfordshire	Hertfordshire Publications
Hesperus	Hesperus Press, London
Heyday	Heyday Books, Berkeley, CA
HH	Hamish Hamilton, London
Hilger	Adam Hilger, Bristol
Hippocampus	Hippocampus Press, New York, NY
History Press	History Press, Stroud
HM	Harvey Miller, London
HMSO	HMSO, London
Hodge	A. Hodge, Penzance, Cornwall
Hogarth	Hogarth Press, London
Holmby	Holmby Press, Flyinge, Sweden
HongKongUP	Hong Kong UP, Hong Kong
Horsdal & Schubart	Horsdal & Schubart, Victoria, BC, Canada
Horwood	Ellis Horwood, Hemel Hempstead, Hertfordshire
HoughtonM	Houghton Mifflin, Boston, MA
House of Breathings	House of Breathings, Lansing, MI
Howard	Howard UP, Washington, DC
HRW	Holt, Reinhart & Winston, New York, NY
Hudson	Hudson Hills Press, New York, NY
Hueber	Max Hueber, Ismaning, Germany
HUL	Hutchinson University Library, London
HullUP	Hull UP, University of Hull
Human & Rousseau	Human & Rousseau, Cape Town, South Africa
Humanities	Humanities Press, Atlantic Highlands, NJ
Humming Earth	Kilkerran, Scotland
Huntington	Huntington Library, San Marino, CA
Hurst	C. Hurst, Covent Garden, London
Hutchinson	Hutchinson Books, London
HW	Harvester Wheatsheaf, Hemel Hempstead, Hertfordshire
Hyland House	Hyland House Publishing, VIC, Australia
HyphenP	Hyphen Press, London
IAAS	Indian Institute of Advanced Studies, Lahore and New Delhi

Ian Henry	Ian Henry Publications, Hornchurch, Essex
IAP	Irish Academic Press, Dublin
Ibadan	Ibadan University Press, Ibadan, Nigeria
ICA	Institute of Contemporary Arts, London
Icon	Icon Books, London
IHA	International Hopkins Association, Waterloo, ON, Canada
IJamaica	Institute of Jamaica Publications, Kingston, Jamaica
Imago	Imago Imprint, New York, NY
Imperial CollegeP	Imperial College Press, London
IN	Impressions Nouvelles, Brussels, Belgium
Indigo	Indigo Dreams Publishing
IndUP	Indiana UP, Bloomington, IN
Inkblot	Inkblot Publications, Berkeley, CA
InstEducP	Institute of Education Press, University of London, London
Intellect	Intellect Books, Bristol, and Wilmington, NC
IntUP	International Universities Press, New York, NY
Inventions	Inventions Press, London
IonaC	Iona College, New Rochelle, NY
IowaSUP	Iowa State UP, Ames, IA
Ipswich	Ipswich Press, Ipswich, MA
IrishAP	Irish Academic Press, Dublin, Eire
ISEAS	Institute of Southeast Asian Studies, Singapore
ISI	ISI Press, Philadelphia, PA
Italica	Italica Press, New York, NY
IULC	Indiana University Linguistics Club, Bloomington, IN
IUP	Indiana University of Pennsylvania Press, Indiana, PA
Ivon	Ivon Publishing House, Bombay, India
Jacana	Jacana Media, Johannesburg, South Africa
Jacaranda	Jacaranda Wiley, Milton, QLD, Australia
JadavpurU	Jadavpur University, Calcutta, India
Jesperson	Jesperson Press, St John's, NL, Canada
JHall	James Hall, Leamington Spa, Warwickshire
JHUP	Johns Hopkins UP, Baltimore, MD
JIWE	JIWE Publications, University of Gulbarga, India
JLRC	Jack London Research Center, Glen Ellen, CA
Jonas	Jonas Verlag, Marburg, Germany
Joseph	Michael Joseph, London
JPGM	J. Paul Getty Museum
JT	James Thin, Edinburgh
Junction	Junction Books, London
Junius-Vaughan	Junius-Vaughan Press, Fairview, NJ
Jupiter	Jupiter Press, Lake Bluff, IL
Juvenilia	Juvenilia Press, Sydney, NSW, Australia
JyväskyläU	Jyväskylä University, Jyväskylä, Finland
Kaibunsha	Kaibunsha, Tokyo, Japan
K&N	Königshausen & Neumann, Würzburg, Germany
K&W	Kaye & Ward, London
Kanishka	Kaniksha Publishers & Distributors, Delhi, India
Kansai	Kansai University of Foreign Studies, Osaka, Japan
Kardo	Kardo, Coatbridge, Scotland
Kardoorair	Kardoorair Press, Adelaide, SA, Australia
Karia	Karia Press, London
Karnac	Karnac Books, London

Karnak	Karnak House, London
Karoma	Karoma Publishers, Ann Arbor, MI
Katha	Katha, New Delhi, India
KC	Kyle Cathie, London
KCL	King's College London
KeeleUP	Keele University Press
Kegan Paul	Kegan Paul International, London
Kenkyu	Kenkyu-Sha, Tokyo, Japan
Kennikat	Kennikat Press, Port Washington, NY
KentSUP	Kent State University Press, Kent, OH
KenyaLB	Kenya Literature Bureau, Nairobi, Kenya
Kerosina	Kerosina Publications, Worcester Park, Surrey
Kerr	Charles H. Kerr, Chicago, IL
Kestrel	Viking Kestrel, London
K/H	Kendall/Hunt Publishing, Dubuque, IA
Kingsley	J. Kingsley Publishers, London
Kingston	Kingston Publishers, Kingston, Jamaica
Kinseido	Kinseido, Tokyo, Japan
KITLV	KITLV Press, Leiden, The Netherlands
Klostermann	Vittorio Klostermann, Frankfurt am Main, Germany
Kluwer	Kluwer Academic Publications, Dordrecht, The Netherlands
Knopf	Alfred A. Knopf, New York, NY
Knowledge	Knowledge Industry Publications, White Plains, NY
Köppe	Rüdiger Köppe Verlag, Cologne, Germany
Kraft	Kraft Books, Ibadan, Nigeria
Kraus	Kraus International Publications, White Plains, NY
KSUP	Kent State UP, Kent OH
LA	Library Association, London
Lake View	Lake View Press, Chicago, IL
LAm	Library of America, New York, NY
Lancelot	Lancelot Press, Hantsport, NS
Landesman	Jay Landesman, London
Lane	Allen Lane, London
Lang	Peter D. Lang, Frankfurt, Berne, New York, London
Langaa	Langaa Research and Publishing, Bamenda, Cameroon
LauU	Laurentian University, Greater Sudbury, Ontario, Canada
Lavengro Press	Lavengro Press, Wallingford
Learning Media	Learning Media Ltd, Wellington, New Zealand
Legacy	The Legacy Press, Ann Arbor, MI
Legenda	Legenda, London
LehighUP	Lehigh University Press, Bethlehem, PA
LeicAE	University of Leicester, Department of Adult Education
LeicUP	Leicester UP, Leicester
LeidenUP	Leiden UP, Leiden, The Netherlands
Leopard's Head	Leopard's Head Press, Oxford
Letao	Letao Press, Albury, NSW, Australia
LeuvenUP	Leuven UP, Leuven, Belgium
Levante	Levante editori, Bari, Italy
Lexik	Lexik House, Cold Spring, NY
Lexington	Lexington Publishers
LF	LiberFörlag, Stockholm, Sweden
LH	Lund Humphries Publishers, London
Liberty	Liberty Classics, Indianapolis, IN

Libris	Libris, London
LibrU	Libraries Unlimited, Englewood, CO
Liffey	Liffey Press, Dublin, Eire
Liguori	Liguori, Naples, Italy
Limelight	Limelight Editions, New York, NY
Lime Tree	Lime Tree Press, Octopus Publishing, London
LincolnUP	Lincoln University Press, NB, Canada
LINCOM	LINCOM Europa, Munich, Germany
LIT	Lit Verlag
LITIR	LITIR Database, University of Alberta, AB, Canada
LittleH	Little Hills Press, Burwood, NSW, Australia
LittPrag	Litteraria Pragensia, Prague, Czech Republic
Liveright	Liveright Publishing, New York, NY
LiverUP	Liverpool UP, Liverpool
Livre de Poche	Le Livre de Poche, Paris, France
Llanerch	Llanerch Enterprises, Lampeter, Dyfed
Locust Hill	Locust Hill Press, West Cornwall, CT
Loewenthal	Loewenthal Press, New York, NY
Longman	Pearson Longman Wesley, Harlow, Essex
LongmanC	Longman Caribbean, Harlow, Essex
LongmanF	Longman, France
LongmanNZ	Longman, Auckland, New Zealand
Longspoon	Longspoon Press, University of Alberta, Edmonton, AB, Canada
Lovell	David Lovell Publishing, Brunswick, VIC, Australia
Lowell	Lowell Press, Kansas City, MS
Lowry	Lowry Publishers, Johannesburg, South Africa
LPB	Litteraria Pragensia.Prague, Czech Republic
LSUP	Louisiana State UP, Baton Rouge, LA
LundU	Lund University, Lund, Sweden
LUP	Loyola UP, Chicago, IL
Lymes	Lymes Press, Newcastle, Staffordshire
Lythrum	Lythrum Press, Adelaide, SA, Australia
MAA	Medieval Academy of America, Cambridge, MA
Macleay	Macleay Press, Paddington, NSW, Australia
Macmillan	Macmillan Publishers, London
MacmillanC	Macmillan Caribbean
Madison	Madison Books, Lanham, MD
Madurai	Madurai University, Madurai, India
Maecenas	Maecenas Press, Iowa City, IA
Magabala	Magabala Books, Broome, WA
Magnes	Magnes Press, The Hebrew University, Jerusalem, Israel
Mainstream	Mainstream Publishing, Edinburgh
Maisonneuve	Maisonneuve Press, Washington, DC
Malone	Malone Society, c/o King's College, London
Mambo	Mambo Press, Gweru, Zimbabwe
M&E	Macdonald & Evans, Estover, Plymouth, Devon
M&S	McClelland & Stewart, Toronto, ON, Canada
Maney	W.S. Maney & Sons, Leeds
Mango	Mango Publishing, London, United Kingdom
Manohar	Manohar Publishers, Darya Gan, New Delhi
Mansell	Mansell Publishing, London
Mantra	Mantra Books, New Delhi, India
Manufacture	La Manufacture, Lyons, France

ManUP	Manchester UP, Manchester
Mariner	Mariner Books, Boston, MA
MarquetteUP	Marquette UP, Milwaukee, WI
Marvell	Marvell Press, Calstock, Cornwall
MB	Mitchell Beazley, London
McDougall, Littel	McDougall, Littel, Evanston, IL
McFarland	McFarland, Jefferson, NC
McG-QUP	McGill-Queen's UP, Montreal, QC, Canada
McGraw-Hill	McGraw-Hill, New York, NY
McIndoe	John McIndoe, Dunedin, New Zealand
McPheeG	McPhee Gribble Publishers, Fitzroy, VIC, Australia
McPherson	McPherson, Kingston, NY
MCSU	Maria Curie Skłodowska University, Lublin, Poland
ME	M. Evans, New York, NY
Meany	P.D. Meany Publishing, Port Credit, ON, Canada
Meckler	Meckler Publishing, Westport, CT
MelbourneUP	Melbourne UP, Carlton South, VIC, Australia
Melville	Melville House, New York, NY
Mellen	Edwin Mellen Press, Lewiston, NY
MellenR	Mellen Research UP
Menzies	Menzies Centre for Australian Studies
MercerUP	Mercer UP, Macon, GA
Mercury	Mercury Press, Stratford, ON, Canada
Merlin	Merlin Press, London
Methuen	Methuen, London
MethuenA	Methuen Australia, North Ryde, NSW, Australia
MethuenC	Methuen, Toronto, ON, Canada
Metro	Metro Publishing, Auckland, New Zealand
Metzler	Metzler, Stuttgart, Germany
MGruyter	Mouton de Gruyter, Berlin, New York, and Amsterdam
MH	Michael Haag, London
MHRA	Modern Humanities Research Association, London
MHS	Missouri Historical Society, St Louis, MO
MI	Microforms International, Pergamon Press, Oxford
Micah	Micah Publications, Marblehead, MA
MichSUP	Michigan State UP, East Lansing, MI
Milestone	Milestone Publications, Horndean, Hampshire
Millennium	Millennium Books, E.J. Dwyer, Newtown, Australia
Millstream	Millstream Books, Bath
Milner	Milner, London
MIMBr	Multilingual Matters, Bristol
Minuit	Éditions de Minuit, Paris, France
MIP	Medieval Institute Publications, Western Michigan University, Kalamazoo, MI
MITP	Massachusetts Institute of Technology Press, Cambridge, MA
MLA	Modern Language Association of America, New York, NY
MIM	Multilingual Matters, Clevedon, Avon
MLP	Manchester Literary and Philosophical Society, Manchester
MnaN	Mkuki na Nyota Publishers, Dar es Salaam, Tanzania
Modern Library	Modern Library (Random House), New York, NY
Mohr-Siebeck	Mohr-Siebeck GmbH & Co., Tubingen, Germany
Monarch	Monarch Publications, Sussex
MonashUP	Monash University Publishing, Clayton, VIC, Australia

Moonraker	Moonraker Press, Bradford-on-Avon, Wiltshire
Moorland	Moorland Publishing, Ashbourne, Derby
Moreana	Moreana, Angers, France
MorganSU	Morgan State University, Baltimore, MD
Morrow	William Morrow, New York, NY
Mosaic	Mosaic Press, Oakville, ON, Canada
Motley	Motley Press, Romsey, Hampshire
Mountain	Mountain Press, Cambridge
Mouton	Mouton Publishers, New York and Paris
Mowbray	A.R. Mowbray, Oxford
MR	Martin Robertson, Oxford
MRTS	MRTS, Binghamton, NY
MSUP	Memphis State UP, Memphis, TN
MtAllisonU	Mount Allison University, Sackville, NB, Canada
MTP	Museum Tusculanum Press, University of Copenhagen, Denmark
Mulini	Mulini Press, ACT, Australia
Muller	Frederick Muller, London
MULP	McMaster University Library Press
Murray	John Murray, London
MuseIndia	MuseIndia, Vikrampuri, India
NAL	New American Library, New York, NY
Narr	Gunter Narr Verlag, Tübingen, Germany
Nathan	Fernand Nathan, Paris, France
NBB	New Beacon Books, London
NBCAus	National Book Council of Australia, Melbourne, VIC, Australia
NCP	New Century Press, Durham
ND	New Directions, New York, NY
NDT	Nottingham Drama Texts, c/o University of Nottingham
NEL	New English Library, London
NELM	National English Literary Museum, Grahamstown, S. Africa
Nelson	Nelson Publishers, Melbourne, VIC, Australia
NelsonT	Thomas Nelson, London
New Endeavour	New Endeavour Press
NeWest	NeWest Press, Edmonton, AB, Canada
New Horn	New Horn Press, Ibadan, Nigeria
New Island	New Island Press
NewIssuesP	New Issues Press, Western Michigan University, MI
NH	New Horizon Press, Far Hills, NJ
N-H	Nelson-Hall, Chicago, IL
NHPC	North Holland Publishing, Amsterdam and New York
NIACE	National Institute of Adult Continuing Education
NicV	Nicolaische Verlagsbuchhandlung, Berlin, Germany
NIE	La Nuova Italia Editrice, Florence, Italy
Niemeyer	Max Niemeyer, Tübingen, Germany
Nightwood	Nightwood Editions, Toronto, ON, Canada
NIP	Naval Institute Press, San Diego, CA
NIUP	Northern Illinois UP, De Kalb, IL
NLA	National Library of Australia
NLB	New Left Books, London
NLC	National Library of Canada, Ottawa, ON, Canada
NLP	New London Press, Dallas, TX
NLS	National Library of Scotland, Edinburgh
NLW	National Library of Wales, Aberystwyth, Dyfed

Nodus	Nodus Publikationen, Münster, Germany
Northcote	Northcote House Publishers, Plymouth
NortheastemU	Northeastern University, Boston, MA
NorthwesternUP	Norhwestern UP, Evanston, IL
Norton	W.W. Norton, New York and London
NorUP	Norwegian University Press, Oslo, Norway
Novus	Novus Press, Oslo, Norway
NPF	National Poetry Foundation, Orono, ME
NPG	National Portrait Gallery, London
NPP	North Point Press, Berkeley, CA
NSP	New Statesman Publishing, New Delhi, India
NSU Press	Northern States Universities Press
NSWUP	New South Wales UP, Kensington, NSW, Australia
NT	National Textbook, Lincolnwood, IL
NUC	Nipissing University College, North Bay, ON, Canada
NUP	National University Publications, Millwood, NY
NUSam	National University of Samoa
NUU	New University of Ulster, Coleraine
NWAP	North Waterloo Academic Press, Waterloo, ON, Canada
NWP	New World Perspectives, Montreal, QC, Canada
NYUP	New York UP, New York, NY
OakK	Oak Knoll Press, New Castle, DE
O&B	Oliver & Boyd, Harlow, Essex
Oasis	Oasis Books, London
OBAC	Organization of Black American Culture, Chicago, IL
OberlinCP	Oberlin College Press, Oberlin, OH
Oberon	Oberon Books, London
O'Brien	O'Brien Press, Dublin, Eire
OBS	Oxford Bibliographical Society, Bodleian Library, Oxford
OccP	Occasional Papers, London
Octopus	Octopus Books, London
OdenseUP	Odense UP, Odense, Denmark
OE	Officina Edizioni, Rome, Italy
OEColl	Old English Colloquium, Berkeley, CA
Offord	John Offord Publications, Eastbourne, E. Sussex
OhioUP	Ohio UP, Athens, OH
Oldcastle	Oldcastle Books, Harpenden, Hertfordshire
Olms	Georg Ohms, Hildesheim, Germany
Olschki	Leo S. Olschki, Florence, Italy
O'Mara	Michael O'Mara Books, London
Omnigraphics	Omnigraphics, Detroit, MI
Open Books	Open Books Publishing, Wells, Somerset
Open Court	Open Court Publishing, IL
OpenUP	Open UP, Buckingham and Philadelphia
OPP	Oxford Polytechnic Press, Oxford
Orbis	Orbis Books, London
OregonSUP	Oregon State UP, Corvallis, OR
Oriel	Oriel Press, Stocksfield, Northumberland
Orient Longman	Orient Longman, India
OrientUP	Oriental UP, London
OriginaINZ	Original Books, Wellington, New Zealand
ORP	Ontario Review Press, Princeton, NJ
Ortnamnsarkivet	Ortnamnsarkivet i Uppsala, Sweden

Orwell	Orwell Press, Southwold, Suffolk
Oryx	Oryx Press, Phoenix, AR
OSUP	Ohio State UP, Columbus, OH
Other	Otherland, Kingsbury, VIC, Australia
OTP	Oak Tree Press, London
OUCA	Oxford University Committee for Archaeology, Oxford
OUP	Oxford UP, Oxford
OUPAm	Oxford UP, New York, NY
OUPAus	Oxford UP, Melbourne, VIC, Australia
OUPC	Oxford UP, Toronto, ON, Canada
OUPI	Oxford UP, New Delhi, India
OUPNZ	Oxford UP, Auckland, New Zealand
OUPSA	Oxford UP Southern Africa, Cape Town, South Africa
Outlet	Outlet Book, New York, NY
Outskirts	Outskirts Press, Parker, CO
Overlook	Overlook Press, New York, NY
Owen	Peter Owen, London
OWS	Oscar Wilde Society, London
Pace UP	Pace University Press, New York, NY
Pacifica	Press Pacifica, Kailua, Hawaii, HI
PAJ	PAJ Publications, New York, NY
Paladin	Paladin Books, London
Palgrave	Palgrave, NY
Pan	Pan Books, London
PalMac	Palgrave Macmillan, Hampshire, UK
PanAmU	Pan American University, Edinburg, TX
P&C	Pickering & Chatto, London
Pandanus	Pandanus Press, Canberra, ACT, Australia
Pandion	Pandion Press, Capitola, CA
Pandora	Pandora Press, London
Pan Macmillan	Pan Macmillan Australia, South Yarra, VIC, Australia
Pantheon	Pantheon Books, New York, NY
Paradigm	Paradigm Publishers, Boulder, CO
ParagonH	Paragon House Publishers, New York, NY
Paris	Paris Press Books, Paris, France
Parnassus	Parnassus Imprints, Hyannis, MA
Paternoster	Paternoster Press, Carlisle, Cumbria
Patten	Patten Press, Penzance
Paulist	Paulist Press, Ramsey, NJ
Paupers	Paupers' Press, Nottingham
Pavilion	Pavilion Books, London
PBFA	Provincial Booksellers' Fairs Association, Cambridge
PCP	Playwrights Canada Press, ON, Canada
Peachtree	Peachtree Publishers, Atlanta, GA
Pearson	David Pearson, Huntingdon, Cambridge
Peepal Tree	Peepal Tree Books, Leeds
Peeters	Peeters Publishers and Booksellers, Leuven, Belgium
Pelham	Pelham Books, London
Pembridge	Pembridge Press, London
Pemmican	Pemmican Publications, Winnipeg, MB, Canada
PencraftI	Pencraft International, Ashok Vihar II, Delhi, India
Penguin	Penguin Books, Harmondsworth, Middlesex
PenguinA	Penguin Books, Ringwood, VIC, Australia

PenguinNZ	Penguin Books, Auckland, New Zealand
Penkevill	Penkevill Publishing, Greenwood, FL
Pentland	Pentland Press, Ely, Cambridge
Penumbra	Penumbra Press, Moonbeam, Ontario, ON, Canada
People's	People's Publications, London
Pergamon	Pergamon Press, Oxford
Permanent	Permanent Press, Sag Harbor, NY
Permanent Black	Permanent Black, Delhi, India
Perpetua	Perpetua Press, Oxford
Petton	Petton Books, Oxford
Pevensey	Pevensey Press, Newton Abbot, Devon
PH	Prentice-Hall, Englewood Cliffs, NJ
Phaidon	Phaidon Press, London
PHI	Prentice-Hall International, Hemel Hempstead, Hertfordshire
PhilL	Philosophical Library, New York, NY
Phillimore	Phillimore, Chichester
Piatkus	Piatkus Books, London
PicadorAf	Picador Africa, Johannesburg, South Africa
Pickwick	Pickwick Publications, Allison Park, PA
Pilgrim	Pilgrim Books, Norman, OK
Pinter	Frances Pinter Publishers, London
PLA	Private Libraries Association
Plains	Plains Books, Carlisle
Plenum	Plenum Publishing, London and New York
Plexus	Plexus Publishing, London
Pliegos	Editorial Pliegos, Madrid, Spain
Ploughshares	Ploughshares Books, Watertown, MA
PlovdivUP	Plovdiv University Press, Bulgaria
PML	Pierpont Morgan Library, New York, NY
Polity	Polity Press, Cambridge
Polygon	Polygon, Edinburgh
Polymath	Polymath Press, TAS, Australia
Poolbeg	Poolbeg Press, Swords, Dublin, Eire
Porcepic	Press Porcepic, Victoria, BC, Canada
Porcupine	Porcupine's Quill, ON, Canada
PortN	Port Nicholson Press, Wellington, NZ
Potter	Clarkson N. Potter, New York, NY
Power	Power Publications, University of Sydney, NSW, Australia
PPUBarcelona	Promociones y Publicaciones Universitarias, Barcelona, Spain
Praeger	Praeger, New York, NY
Prakash	Prakash Books, India
Prestel	Prestel Verlag, Germany
PrestigeB	Prestige Books, New Delhi, India
Primavera	Edizioni Primavera, Gunti Publishing, Florence, Italy
Primrose	Primrose Press, Alhambra, CA
PrincetonAP	Princeton Architectural Press, Princeton, NJ
PrincetonUL	Princeton University Library, Princeton, NJ
PrincetonUP	Princeton UP, Princeton, NJ
Printwell	Printwell Publishers, Jaipur, India
Prism	Prism Press, Bridport, Dorset
PRO	Public Record Office, London
Profile	Profile Books, Ascot, Berks
ProgP	Progressive Publishers, Calcutta, India

PSUP	Pennsylvania State UP, University Park, PA
PsychP	Psychology Press (Routledge), New York, NY
PublishNation	PublishNation, London
PUF	Presses Universitaires de France, Paris, France
PULM	Presses Universitaires de la Méditérrannée, Montpellier, France
Punctum	Punctum Books, Brooklyn, New York, NY
PUPV	Publications de l'université Paul-Valéry, Montpellier 3, France
PurdueUP	Purdue UP, Lafayette, IN
Pushcart	Pushcart Press, Wainscott, NY
Pustet	Friedrich Pustet, Regensburg, Germany
Putnam	Putnam Publishing, New York, NY
QED	QED Press, Ann Arbor, MI
Quarry	Quarry Press, Kingston, ON, Canada
Quartet	Quartet Books, London
QUT	Queensland University of Technology, QLD, Australia
RA	Royal Academy of Arts, London
Rainforest	Rainforest Publishing, Faxground, NSW, Australia
R&B	Rosenklide & Bagger, Copenhagen, Denmark
R&L	Rowman & Littlefield, Totowa, NJ
Randle	Ian Randle, Kingston, Jamaica
RandomH	Random House, London and New York
RandomHAus	Random House Australia, VIC, Australia
RandomHNZ	Random House New Zealand Limited, Auckland, New Zealand
Ravan	Ravan Press, Johannesburg, South Africa
Ravette	Ravette, London
Ravi Dayal	Ravi Dayal Publishers, New Delhi, India
Rawat	Rawat Publishing, Jaipur and New Delhi, India
Readworthy	Readworthy Publications, New Delhi, India
Reaktion	Reaktion Books, London
Rebel	Rebel Press, London
Red Kite	Red Kite Press, Guelph, ON, Canada
Red Rooster	Red Rooster Press, Hotham Hill, VIC, Australia
Red Sea	Red Sea Press, NJ
Reed	Reed Books, Port Melbourne, VIC, Australia
Reed NZ	Reed Publishing NZ Ltd., Auckland, New Zealand
Reference	Reference Press, Toronto, ON, Canada
Regents	Regents Press of Kansas, Lawrence, KS
Reichenberger	Roswitha Reichenberger, Kessel, Germany
Reinhardt	Max Reinhardt, London
Remak	Remak, Alblasserdam, The Netherlands
RenI	Renaissance Institute, Sophia University, Tokyo, Japan
Research	Research Publications, Reading
ReScript	ReScript Books, Hastings, Sussex
RETS	Renaissance English Text Society, Chicago, IL
RH	Ramsay Head Press, Edinburgh
RHS	Royal Historical Society, London
RIA	Royal Irish Academy, Dublin, Eire
RiceUP	Rice UP, Houston, TX
Richarz	Hans Richarz, St Augustin, Germany
RITP	Rochester Institute of Technology Press, Rochester, NY
Rivers Oram	Rivers Oram Press, London
Rizzoli	Rizzoli International Publications, New York, NY
Robinson	Robinson Publishing, London

Robson	Robson Books, London
Rockport	Rockport Publishers, Rockport, MA
Rodopi	Rodopi, Amsterdam, The Netherlands
Roebuck	Stuart Roebuck, Suffolk
RoehamptonI	Roehampton Institute London
Ronsdale	Ronsdale Press
Routledge	Routledge, London and New York
Royce	Robert Royce, London
RS	Royal Society, London
RSC	Royal Shakespeare Company, London
RSL	Royal Society of Literature, London
RSVP	Research Society for Victorian Periodicals, University of Leicester
RT	RT Publications, London
Running	Running Press, Philadelphia, PA
Russell	Michael Russell, Norwich
RutgersUP	Rutgers UP, New Brunswick, NJ
Ryan	Ryan Publishing, London
SA	Sahitya Akademi, New Delhi, India
Sage	Sage Publications, London
SageIn	SAGE Publications India, New Delhi, India
SAI	Sociological Abstracts, San Diego, CA
Salamander	Salamander Books, London
Salem	Salem Press, Englewood Cliffs, NJ
S&A	Shukayr and Akasheh, Amman, Jordan
S&D	Stein & Day, Briarcliff Manor, NJ
S&J	Sidgwick & Jackson, London
S&M	Sun & Moon Press, Los Angeles, CA
S&P	Simon & Piere, Toronto, ON, Canada
S&S	Simon & Schuster, New York and London
S&W	Secker & Warburg, London
Sangam	Sangam Books, London
Sangsters	Sangsters Book Stores, Kingston, Jamaica
SAP	Scottish Academic Press, Edinburgh
Saros	Saros International Publishers
Sarup	Sarup & Sons, New Delhi, India
Saur	Bowker-Saur, Sevenoaks, Kent
Savacou	Savacou Publications, Kingston, Jamaica
S-B	Schwann-Bagel, Düsseldorf, Germany
ScanUP	Scandinavian University Presses, Oslo, Norway
Scarecrow	Scarecrow Press, Metuchen, NJ
Schäuble	Schäuble Verlag, Rheinfelden, Germany
Schmidt	Erich Schmidt Verlag, Berlin, Germany
Schneider	Lambert Schneider, Heidelberg, Germany
Schocken	Schocken Books, New York, NY
Scholarly	Scholarly Press, St Clair Shores, MI
ScholarsG	Scholars Press, GA
Schöningh	Ferdinand Schöningh, Paderborn, Germany
Schwinn	Michael Schwinn, Neustadt, Germany
SCJP	Sixteenth-Century Journal Publications
Scolar	Scolar Press, Aldershot, Hampshire
ScotLitInt	Scottish Literature International, Glasgow
SCP	Second Chance Press, Sag Harbor, NY
Scribe	Scribe Publishing, Colchester

Scribner	Charles Scribner, New York, NY
SDSU	Department of English, South Dakota State University, SD
Seafarer	Seafarer Books, London
Seaver	Seaver Books, New York, NY
Segue	Segue, New York, NY
Semiotext(e)	Semiotext(e), Columbia University, New York, NY
Sensations Press	Sensations Press, UK
SePA	Self-Publishing Association
Sequart	Sequart
Seren Books	Seren Books, Bridgend
Serpent's Tail	Serpent's Tail Publishing, London
Sessions	William Sessions, York
Seuil	Éditions du Seuil, Paris, France
7:84 Pubns	7:84 Publications, Glasgow
SH	Somerset House, Teaneck, NJ
Shalabh	Shalabh Book House, Meerut, India
ShAP	Sheffield Academic Press, Sheffield
Shaun Tyas	Paul Watkins Publishing, Donington, Lincolnshire
Shearsman	Shearsman Books, Exeter
Shearwater	Shearwater Press, Lenah Valley, TAS, Australia
Sheba	Sheba Feminist Publishers, London
Sheed&Ward	Sheed & Ward, London
Sheila Markham	Sheila Markham Rare Books
Sheldon	Sheldon Press, London
Shinozaki	Shinozaki Shorin, Tokyo, Japan
Shinshindo	Shinshindo Publishing, Tokyo, Japan
Shire	Shire Publications, Princes Risborough, Buckinghamshire
Shoal Bay Press	Shoal Bay Press, New Zealand
Shoe String	Shoe String Press, Hamden, CT
SIAS	Scandinavian Institute of African Studies, Uppsala, Sweden
SIL	Summer Institute of Linguistics, Academic Publications, Dallas, TX
SIUP	Southern Illinois University Press, IL
Simon King	Simon King Press, Milnthorpe, Cumbria
Sinclair-Stevenson	Sinclair-Stevenson, London
SingaporeUP	Singapore UP, Singapore
SIUP	Southern Illinois UP, Carbondale, IL
SJSU	San Jose State University, San Jose, CA
Skilton	Charles Skilton, London
Slatkine	Éditions Slatkine, Paris, France
Slavica	Slavica Publishers, Columbus, OH
Sleepy Hollow	Sleepy Hollow Press, Tarrytown, NY
Smith Settle	Smith Settle, W. Yorkshire
SMUP	Southern Methodist UP, Dallas, TX
Smythe	Colin Smythe, Gerrards Cross, Buckinghamshire
SNH	Société Néophilologique de Helsinki, Finland
SNLS	Society for New Language Study, Denver, CO
SNTA	Society of Nigerian Theatre Artistes, Lagos, Nigeria
SOA	Society of Authors, London
Soho	Soho Book, London
SohoP	Soho Press, New York, NY
Solaris	Solaris Press, Rochester, MI
SonoNis	Sono Nis Press, Victoria, BC

Sorbonne	Publications de la Sorbonne, Paris, France
Souvenir	Souvenir Press, London
Spaniel	Spaniel Books, Paddington, NSW, Australia
SPCK	SPCK, London
Spectrum	Spectrum Books, Ibadan, Nigeria
Split Pea	Split Pea Press, Edinburgh
Spokesman	Spokesman Books, Nottingham
Spoon River	Spoon River Poetry Press, Granite Falls, MN
Springer	Springer Verlag, Berlin, Germany
SRI	Steinbeck Research Institute, Ball State University, Muncie, IN
SriA	Sri Aurobindo, Pondicherry, India
Sri Satguru	Sri Satguru Publications, Delhi, India
SSA	John Steinbeck Society of America, Muncie, IN
SSAB	Sprakförlaget Skriptor AB, Stockholm, Sweden
SSNS	Scottish Society for Northern Studies, Edinburgh
Stämpfli	Stämpfli Verlag, Bern, Switzerland
StanfordUP	Stanford UP, Stanford, CA
Staple	Staple, Matlock, Derbyshire
Starmont	Starmont House, Mercer Island, WA
Starrhill	Starrhill Press, Washington, DC
Station Hill	Station Hill, Barrytown, NY
Stauffenburg	Stauffenburg Verlag, Tübingen, Germany
StDL	St Deiniol's Library, Hawarden, Clwyd
Steel Rail	Steel Rail Publishing, Ottawa, ON, Canada
Steele Roberts	Steele Roberts Publishing Ltd, Wellington, New Zealand
Steiner	Franz Steiner, Wiesbaden, Germany
Sterling	Sterling Publishing, New York, NY
SterlingND	Sterling Publishers, New Delhi, India
Stichting	Stichtig Neerlandistiek, Amsterdam, The Netherlands
St James	St James Press, Andover, Hampshire
St Martin's	St Martin's Press, New York, NY
StMut	State Mutual Book and Periodical Source, New York, NY
Stockwell	Arthur H. Stockwell, Ilfracombe, Devon
Stoddart	Stoddart Publishing, Don Mills, ON, Canada
StPB	St Paul's Bibliographies, Winchester, Hampshire
STR	Society for Theatre Research, London
Strauch	R.O.U. Strauch, Ludwigsburg, Germany
Streamline	Streamline Creative, Auckland, New Zealand
Stree	Stree/Bhatkal, Kolkata, India
Studio	Studio Editions, London
Stump Cross	Stump Cross Books, Stump Cross, Essex
Sud	Sud, Marseilles, France
Suhrkamp	Suhrkamp Verlag, Frankfurt am Main, Germany
Summa	Summa Publications, Birmingham, AL
SUNYP	State University of New York Press, Albany, NY
SUP	Sydney University Press, NSW, Australia
Surtees	R.S. Surtees Society, Frome, Somerset
SusquehannaUP	Susquehanna UP, Selinsgrove, PA
SussexAP	Sussex Academic Press, Sydney, NSW, Australia
SussexUP	Sussex UP, University of Sussex, Brighton
Sutton	Alan Sutton, Stroud, Gloucester
S–W	Shepheard–Walwyn Publishing, London
Swallow	Swallow Press, Athens, OH

SWG	Saskatchewan Writers Guild, Regina, SK, Canada
Sybylla	Sybylla Feminist Press
SydneyUP	Sydney UP, Sydney, NSW, Australia
SyracuseUP	Syracuse UP, Syracuse, NY
Tabb	Tabb House, Padstow, Cornwall
Taishukan	Taishukan Publishing, Tokyo, Japan
Talonbooks	Talonbooks, Vancouver, BC, Canada
TamilU	Tamil University, Thanjavur, India
T&F	Taylor & Francis Books
T&H	Thames & Hudson, London
Tantivy	Tantivy Press, London
Tarcher	Jeremy P. Tarcher, Los Angeles, CA
Tartarus	Tartarus Press
Tate	Tate Gallery Publications, London
Tavistock	Tavistock Publications, London
Taylor	Taylor Publishing, Bellingham, WA
TaylorCo	Taylor Publishing, Dallas, TX
TCG	Theatre Communications Group, New York, NY
TCP	Three Continents Press, Washington, DC
TCUP	Texas Christian UP, Fort Worth, TX
TEC	Third Eye Centre, Glasgow
Tecumseh	Tecumseh Press, Ottawa, ON, Canada
Telos	Telos Press, St Louis, MO
TempleUP	Temple UP, Philadelphia, PA
Teneo	Teneo Press, Amherst, NY
TennS	Tennyson Society, Lincoln
TexA&MUP	Texas A&MUP, College Station, TX
Text	Text Publishing, Melbourne, VIC, Australia
TextileB	Textile Bridge Press, Clarence Center, NY
The Smith	The Smith, New York, NY
Thimble	Thimble Press, Stroud, Gloucester
Third Millennium	Third Millennium Publishing, London
Thoemmes	Thoemmes Press, Bristol
Thornes	Stanley Thornes, Cheltenham
Thorpe	D.W. Thorpe, Port Melbourne, VIC, Australia
Thorsons	Thorsons Publishers, London
Times	Times of Gloucester Press, Gloucester, ON, Canada
TMP	Thunder's Mouth Press, New York, NY
Totem	Totem Books, Don Mills, ON, Canada
Toucan	Toucan Press, St Peter Port, Guernsey
Touzot	Jean Touzot, Paris, France
TPF	Trianon Press Facsimiles, London
Tragara	Tragara Press, Edinburgh
Transaction	Transaction Publishers, New Brunswick, NJ
Transcendental	Transcendental Books, Hartford, CT
Transcript	Transcript Verlag, Bielefeld, Germany
Transworld	Transworld, London
TrinityUP	Trinity UP, San Antonio, TX
TRP	Texas Review Press, Huntsville, TX
TTUP	Texas Technical University Press, Lubbock, TX
Tuduv	Tuduv, Munich, Germany
TulaneUP	Tulane UP, New Orleans, LA
Tunué	Tunué, Rome, Italy

TurkuU	Turku University, Turku, Finland
Turnstone	Turnstone Press, Winnipeg, MB, Canada
Turtle Island	Turtle Island Foundation, Berkeley, CA
Twayne	Twayne Publishing, Boston, MA
TwoMorrows	TwoMorrows Publishing, Raleigh, NC
UAB	University of Aston, Birmingham
UAdelaide	University of Adelaide, Australia
UAkronP	University of Akron Press, Akron, OH
UAlaP	University of Alabama Press, Tuscaloosa, AL
UAlbertaP	University of Alberta Press, Edmonton, AB, Canada
UAntwerp	University of Antwerp, The Netherlands
UArizP	University of Arizona Press, Tucson, AZ
UArkP	University of Arkansas Press, Fayetteville, AR
UAthens	University of Athens, Greece
UBarcelona	University of Barcelona, Spain
UBCP	University of British Columbia Press, Vancouver, BC, Canada
UBergen	University of Bergen, Norway
UBrno	J.E. Purkyne University of Brno, Czechoslovakia
UBrussels	University of Brussels, Belgium
UBuckP	University of Buckingham Press, Buckingham
UCalgaryP	University of Calgary Press, AB, Canada
UCalP	University of California Press, Berkeley, CA
UCAP	University of Central Arkansas Press, Conway, AR
UCapeT	University of Cape Town Press, South Africa
UChicP	University of Chicago Press, IL
UChesterP	University of Chester Press, Chester. Cheshire
UCDubP	University College Dublin Press, Eire
UCL	University College London Press
UCopenP	University of Copenhagen Press, Denmark
UDelP	University of Delaware Press, Newark, DE
UDijon	University of Dijon, France
UDur	University of Durham, Durham, UK
UEA	University of East Anglia, Norwich
UErlangen-N	University of Erlangen-Nuremberg, Germany
UEssex	University of Essex, Colchester
UExe	University of Exeter, Devon
UFlorence	University of Florence, Italy
UFlorP	University of Florida Press, FL
UFR	Université François Rabelais, Tours, France
UGal	University College, Galway, Eire
UGeoP	University of Georgia Press, Athens, GA
UGhent	University of Ghent, Belgium
UGlasP	University of Glasgow Press
UHawaiiP	University of Hawaii Press, Honolulu, HI
UHertP	University of Hertfordshire Press
UHuelva	Universidad de Huelva Publicaciones, Spain
UIfeP	University of Ife Press, Ile-Ife, Nigeria
UIllp	University of Illinois Press, Champaign, IL
UInnsbruck	University of Innsbruck, Austria
UIowaP	University of Iowa Press, Iowa City, IA
UKanP	University of Kansas Press, Lawrence, KS
UKL	University of Kentucky Libraries, Lexington, KY
ULavalP	Les Presses de l'Université Laval, Quebec, QC, Canada

ULiège	University of Liège, Belgium
ULilleP	Presses Universitaires de Lille, France
ULondon	University of London
Ulster	University of Ulster, Coleraine
U/M	Underwood/Miller, Los Angeles, CA
UMalta	University of Malta, Msida, Malta
UManitobaP	University of Manitoba Press, Winnipeg, MB, Canada
UMassP	University of Massachusetts Press, Amherst, MA
Umeå	Umeå Universitetsbibliotek, Umeå, Sweden
UMichP	University of Michigan Press, Ann Arbor, MI
UMinnP	University of Minnesota Press, Minneapolis, MN
UMirail-ToulouseP	University of Mirail-Toulouse Press, France
UMIRes	UMI Research Press, Ann Arbor, MI
UMissP	University of Missouri Press, Columbia, MO
UMontP	Montpellier University Press, France
UMP	University of Mississippi Press, Lafayette, MS
UMysore	University of Mysore, India
UNancyP	Presses Universitaires de Nancy, France
UNCP	University of North Carolina Press, Chapel Hill, NC
Undena	Undena Publications, Malibu, CA
UNDP	University of Notre Dame Press, Notre Dame, IN
UNebP	University of Nebraska Press, Lincoln, NE
UNethAnt	University of The Netherlands, Antilles
UNevP	University of Nevada Press, Reno, NV
UNewE	University of New England, Armidale, NSW, Australia
UNewH	University of New Hampshire Press, Durham, NH
Ungar	Frederick Ungar, New York, NY
Unicopli	Edizioni Unicopli, Milan, Italy
UnisaP	University of South Africa Press, Muckleneuk, South Africa
Unity	Unity Press, Hull
UnityP	Unity Press Woollahra, NSW, Australia
Universa	Uilgeverij Universa, Wetteren, Belgium
UNMP	University of New Mexico Press, Albuquerque, NM
UNorthTP	University of North Texas Press, TX
UNott	University of Nottingham
UNSW	University of New South Wales, NSW, Australia
Unwin	Unwin Paperbacks, London
Unwin Hyman	Unwin Hyman, London
UOklaP	University of Oklahoma Press, Norman, OK
UOslo	University of Oslo, Norway
UOtagoP	University of Otago Press, Dunedin, New Zealand
UOttawaP	University of Ottawa Press, ON, Canada
UPA	UP of America, Lanham, MD
UParis	University of Paris, France
UPColorado	UP of Colorado, Niwot, CO
UPennP	University of Pennsylvania Press, Philadelphia, PA
UPFlorida	University Press of Florida, FL
UPittP	University of Pittsburgh Press, Pittsburgh, PA
UPKen	University Press of Kentucky, Lexington, KY
UPMissip	UP of Mississippi, Jackson, MS
UPN	Université de Paris Nord, Paris, France
UPNE	UP of New England, Hanover, NH
Uppsala	Uppsala University, Uppsala, Sweden

UProvence	University of Provence, Aix-en-Provence, France
UPSouth	University Press of the South, NO
UPSouthDen	University Press of Southern Denmark
UPValéry	University Paul Valéry, Montpellier, France
UPVirginia	UP of Virginia, Charlottesville, VA
UQP	University of Queensland Press, St Lucia, QLD, Australia
URouen	University of Rouen, Mont St Aignan, France
URP	University of Rochester Press
USalz	Institut für Anglistik and Amerikanstik, University of Salzburg, Austria
USantiago	University of Santiago, Spain
USCP	University of South Carolina Press, Columbia, SC
USFlorP	University of South Florida Press, Florida, FL
USheff	University of Sheffield
Usher	La Casa Usher, Florence, Italy
USydP	University of Sydney Press, Sydney, NSW, Australia
USzeged	University of Szeged, Hungary
UtahSUP	Utah State UP, Logan, UT
UTampereP	University of Tampere Press, Knoxville, TN
UTas	University of Tasmania, Hobart, TAS, Australia
UTennP	University of Tennessee Press, Knoxville, TN
UTexP	University of Texas Press, Austin, TX
UTorP	University of Toronto Press, Toronto, ON, Canada
UTours	Université de Tours, France
UVerm	University of Vermont, Burlington, VT
UVict	University of Victoria, Victoria, BC
UWalesP	University of Wales Press, Cardiff
UWAP	University of Western Australia Press, Nedlands, WA, Australia
UWarwick	University of Warwick, Coventry
UWashP	University of Washington Press, Seattle, WA
UWaterlooP	University of Waterloo Press, Waterloo, ON, Canada
UWI	University of the West Indies, St Augustine, Trinidad
UWIndiesP	University of West Indies Press, Mona, Jamaica
UWiscM	University of Wisconsin, Milwaukee, WI
UWiscP	University of Wisconsin Press, Madison, WI
UWoll	University of Wollongong, NSW, Australia
UYork	University of York, York
Valentine	Valentine Publishing and Drama, Rhinebeck, NY
V&A	Victoria and Albert Museum, London
VanderbiltUP	Vanderbilt UP, Nashville, TE
V&R	Vandenhoeck & Ruprecht, Göttingen, Germany
Van Riebeeck	Van Riebeeck Society, Cape Town, South Africa
Vantage	Vantage Press, New York, NY
Variorum	Variorum, Ashgate Publishing, Hampshire
Vehicule	Vehicule Press, Montreal, QC, Canada
Vendome	Vendome Press, New York, NY
Verdant	Verdant Publications, Chichester
Verso	Verso Editions, London
Victorian Secrets	Victorian Secrets, Brighton, UK
VictUP	Victoria UP, Victoria University of Wellington, New Zealand
Vieweg	Vieweg Braunschweig, Wiesbaden, Germany
Vikas	Vikas Publishing House, New Delhi, India
Viking	Viking Press, New York, NY

VikingNZ	Viking, Auckland, New Zealand
Virago	Virago Press, London
Vision	Vision Press, London
VLB	VLB Éditeur, Montreal, QC, Canada
Voltaire	Voltaire Foundation, Oxford
VP	Vulgar Press, Carlton North, VIC, Australia
VR	Variorum Reprints, London
Vrin	J. Vrin, Paris, France
VUP	Victoria University Press, Wellington, New Zealand
VUUP	Vrije Universiteit UP, Amsterdam, The Netherlands
VWSGB	Virginia Woolf Society of Great Britain
Wadsworth	Wadsworth Cengage Learning, Boston, MA
Wakefield	Wakefield Press
Walker	Walker & Co., New York, NY
W&B	Whiting & Birch, London
W&N	Weidenfeld & Nicolson, London
Water Row	Water Row Press, Sudbury, MA
Watkins	Paul Watkins, Stanford, Lincsolnshire
WB	Wissenschaftliche Buchgesellschaft, Darmstadt, Germany
W/B	Woomer/Brotherson, Revere, PA
Weaver	Weaver Press
Webb&Bower	Webb & Bower, Exeter
Wedgestone	Wedgestone Press, Winfield, KS
Wedgetail	Wedgetail Press, Earlwood, NSW, Australia
WesleyanUP	Wesleyan UP, Middletown, CT
West	West Publishing, St Paul, MN
WestviewP	Westview Press, Boulder, CO
WHA	William Heinemann Australia, Port Melbourne, VIC, Australia
Wheatsheaf	Wheatsheaf Books, Brighton
Whiteknights	Whiteknights Press, University of Reading, Berkshire
White Lion	White Lion Books, Cambridge
Whitston	Whitston Publishing, Troy, NY
Whittington	Whittington Press, Herefordshire
WHP	Warren House Press, Sale, Cheshire
Wiener	Wiener Publishing, New York, NY
Wildwood	Wildwood House, Aldershot, Hampshire
Wiley	(or Wiley-Blackwell) John Wiley, Chichester, New York and Brisbane
Wilmington	Wilmington Square Books, London
Wilson	Philip Wilson, London
Winter	Carl Winter Universitätsverlag, Heidelberg, Germany
Wits	Witwatersrand University Press, Johannesburg, South Africa
WIU	Western Illinois University, Macomb, IL
WL	Ward Lock, London
WLUP	Wilfrid Laurier UP, Waterloo, ON, Canada
WMP	World Microfilms Publications, London
WMU	Western Michigan University, Kalamazoo, MI
Woeli	Woeli Publishing Services
Wolfhound	Wolfhound Press, Dublin, Eire
Wombat	Wombat Press, Wolfville, NS
Wo-No	Wolters-Noordhoff, Groningen, The Netherlands
Woodstock	Woodstock Books, Oxford
Woolf	Cecil Woolf, London

Word Power	Word Power Books, Edinburgh
Words	Words, Framfield, E. Sussex
Worldview	Worldview Publishers, New Delhi and Kolkata, India
WP	Women's Press, London
WPC	Women's Press of Canada, Toronto, ON, Canada
WSUP	Wayne State UP, Detroit, MI
WUO	Wydawnictwo Uniwersytetu Opolskiego, Warsaw, Poland
WUS	Wydawnictwo Uniwersytetu Slaskiego, Katowice, Poland
WVT	Wissenschaftlicher Verlag Trier, Germany
WVUP	West Virginia UP, Morgantown, WV
W-W	Williams-Wallace, Toronto, ON, Canada
WWU	Western Washington University, Bellingham, WA
Xanadu	Xanadu Publications, London
XLibris	XLibris Corporation
YaleUL	Yale University Library Publications, New Haven, CT
YaleUP	Yale UP, New Haven, CO and London
Yamaguchi	Yamaguchi Shoten, Kyoto, Japan
YMP	York Medieval Press
YorkP	York Press, Fredericton, NB, Canada
Younsmere	Younsmere Press, Brighton
Zed	Zed Books, London
Zell	Hans Zell, East Grinstead
Zero	Zero Books

3. Acronyms

AAVE	African-American Vernacular English
AmE	American English
AusE	Australian English
BELF	English as a Lingua Franca in Business
BrE	British English
DP	Determiner Phrase
ECP	Empty Category Principle
EFL	English as a Foreign Language
EIL	English as an International Language
ELFA	English as a Lingua Franca in Academic Settings
ELT	English Language Teaching
eModE	early Modern English
ENL	English as a Native Language
EPNS	English Place-Name Society
ESL	English as a Second Language
ESP	English for Special Purposes
HPSG	Head-driven Phrase Structure Grammar
LF	Logical Form
LFG	Lexical Functional Grammar
ME	Middle English
MED	Middle English Dictionary
MICASE	Michigan Corpus of Academic Spoken English
NZE	New Zealand English
ODan	Old Danish
OE	Old English
OED	Oxford English Dictionary

OF	Old French
ON	Old Norse
OT	Optimality Theory
PDE	Present-Day English
PF	Phonological Form
PhilE	Philippine English
PP	Prepositional Phrase
RP	Received Pronunciation
SABE	South African Black English
SAE	South African English
SingE	Singapore English
TESOL	Teaching English to Speakers of other Languages
TMA	Tense, Mood and Aspect
UG	Universal Grammar
VOICE	Vienna-Oxford International Corpus of English
WE	World Englishes

Preface

The Year's Work in English Studies is a narrative bibliography that records and evaluates scholarly writing on English language and on literatures written in English. It is published by Oxford University Press on behalf of the English Association.

The Editors and the English Association are pleased to announce that this year's Beatrice White Prize has been awarded to Lawrence Warner for *The Myth of Piers Plowman* (2014), published by Cambridge University Press.

The authors of *YWES* attempt to cover all significant contributions to English studies. Writers of articles can assist this process by sending offprints to the journal, and editors of journals that are not readily available in the UK are urged to join the many who send us complete sets of current and back issues. These materials should be addressed to The Editors, *YWES*, The English Association, The University of Leicester, University Road, Leicester LEI 7RH, UK.

Our coverage of articles and books is greatly assisted by the Modern Language Association of America, who annually supply proofs of their *International Bibliography* in advance of the publication of each year's coverage.

The views expressed in *YWES* are those of its individual contributors and are not necessarily shared by the Editors, Associate Editors, the English Association, or Oxford University Press.

We are especially grateful to Kira Condee-Padunova for her superlative work on behalf of this issue. We also wish to thank Michele Kennedy at Penn State Altoona for her kindness, professionalism, and unwavering support.

The Editors

The Year's Work in English Studies, Volume 95 (2016) © *The Author 2016. Published by Oxford University Press on behalf of the English Association. All rights reserved.*
For Permissions, please email: journals.permissions@oup.com
doi:10.1093/ywes/maw020

I

English Language

ROBERT A. CLOUTIER, ANITA AUER,
RADOSŁAW ŚWIĘCIŃSKI, PHILLIP WALLAGE,
GEA DRESCHLER, BEÁTA GYURIS, KATHRYN ALLAN,
MACKENZIE KERBY, LIESELOTTE ANDERWALD,
ALEXANDER KAUTZSCH, MAJA MILIČEVIĆ,
TIHANA KRAŠ, ELIZABETH J. ERLING,
CLAUDIO SCHEKULIN, VERONIKA THIR,
BARBARA SEIDLHOFER, HENRY WIDDOWSON,
CHARLOTTE TAYLOR, AND CHLOE HARRISON

This chapter has fourteen sections: 1. General; 2. History of English Linguistics; 3. Phonetics and Phonology; 4. Morphology; 5. Syntax; 6. Semantics; 7. Lexicography, Lexicology, and Lexical Semantics; 8. Onomastics; 9. Dialectology and Sociolinguistics; 10. New Englishes and Creolistics; 11. Second Language Acquisition; 12. English as a Lingua Franca; 13. Pragmatics and Discourse Analysis; 14. Stylistics. Section 1 is by Robert A. Cloutier; section 2 is by Anita Auer; section 3 is by Radosław Święciński; sections 4 and 5 are by Phillip Wallage and Gea Dreschler; section 6 is by Beáta Gyuris; section 7 is by Kathryn Allan; section 8 is by Mackenzie Kerby; section 9 is by Lieselotte Anderwald; section 10 is by Alexander Kautzsch; section 11 is by Maja Miličević and Tihana Kraš; section 12 is by Elizabeth J. Erling, Claudio Schekulin, Veronika Thir, Barbara Seidlhofer, and Henry Widdowson; section 13 is by Charlotte Taylor; section 14 is by Chloe Harrison.

1. General

The eleven books discussed in this section can be broadly divided into three groups, discussed in the following order: those dealing with aspects of methodology, those focused on theoretical issues, and those targeted at a more general audience.

The Year's Work in English Studies, Volume 95 (2016) © The Author 2016. Published by Oxford University Press on behalf of the English Association. All rights reserved.
For Permissions, please email: journals.permissions@oup.com
doi:10.1093/ywes/maw018

A comprehensive guide to the full-range of linguistic methodology is offered in *Research Methods in Linguistics* edited by Robert Podesva and Devyani Sharma. The chapters are written by leading experts and offer a cursory overview of the given method or methodological issue that, while not always detailed enough to put into practice oneself, offers a sufficient introduction to the topic to better understand research conducted with the particular method or under the conditions discussed in the chapter. For those interested in putting a method into practice, each chapter includes many references that one can consult for more detailed discussion. A useful reference for experienced researchers, this book is also a student-friendly text that is divided into three parts, ordered in successive phases of the research process. Part I ('Data Collection') has ten chapters not only devoted to various methods of collecting data ('Judgment Data', 'Fieldwork for Language Description', 'Surveys and Interviews', 'Sound Recordings: Acoustic and Articulatory Data', 'Ethnography and Recording Interaction', 'Using Historical Texts') but also addressing many ethical and practical issues involved in linguistic research ('Ethics in Linguistic Research', 'Population Samples', 'Experimental Research Design', 'Experimental Paradigms in Psycholinguistics'). The five chapters of Part II ('Data Processing and Statistical Analysis') deal with ways of processing one's data ('Transcription', 'Creating & Using Corpora') and carrying out some of the more common statistical analyses ('Descriptive Statistics', 'Basic Significance Testing', 'Multivariate Statistics'), while Part III ('Foundations for Data Analysis') contains six chapters from the perspective of different sub-fields on developing hypotheses, interpreting one's data and formulating a well-supported argument ('Acoustic Analysis', 'Constructing and Supporting a Linguistic Analysis', 'Modeling in the Language Sciences', 'Variation Analysis', 'Discourse Analysis', 'Studying Language Change Over Time'). A strength of many of the chapters is that they include not only state-of-the-art details of various aspects of the methodology presented but also the debates within the respective fields that have contributed to the development of the accepted methodology.

In contrast to the breadth of the previous book, the following two volumes highlight various aspects of corpus linguistic methodology and research. *Recent Advances in Corpus Linguistics: Developing and Exploiting Corpora*, edited by Lieven Vandelanotte, Kristin Davidse, Caroline Gentens, and Ditte Kimps, is a refereed collection of papers that were presented at the ICAME 33 international conference 'Corpora at the Centre and Crossroads of English Linguistics' in 2012. It contains sixteen articles, including a succinct introduction by the editors that introduces the papers that follow. The book is organized into three parts, each featuring five papers. Those in Part I ('Corpus Development and Corpus Interrogation') explore issues related to constructing corpora (specifically the electronic corpus of *Letters of Artisans and the Labouring Poor (LALP)* (England, *c.*1750–1835) by Anita Auer, Mikko Laitinen, Moragh Gordon, and Tony Fairman and a proposed corpus of eighteenth-century English phonology by Joan Beal and Ranjen Sen) or discuss tools for extracting relevant patterns automatically and processing corpus data. Part II ('Specialist Corpora') is a rather mixed bag of more descriptive corpus-based research: two papers focus on grammatical patterns in World Englishes (relative clauses in Philippine English by Peter Collins, Xinyue Yao, and Ariane Borlongan and the progressive in South and Southeast Asian Englishes by Marco Schilk and Marc Hammel); a paper by Antoinette Renouf develops a new perspective on neology based on a diachronic corpus of *Guardian* news texts; and the final two papers make extensive use of cross-linguistic data (Thomas Egan and Gudrun Rawoens use Norwegian and Swedish translations to gain new insights into the seemingly overlapping prepositions *amid(st)* and *among(st)* in English, and Kerstin Kunz and Ekaterina Lapshinova-Koltunski examine similarities and differences in the use of cohesive connectives in English and German in terms of frequencies and functions). The papers in Part III ('Second Language Acquisition') present research examining ESL/EFL corpus data from various angles: discourse markers used by lecturers, the use of false friends among Spanish learners of English, the use of NLP (Natural Language Processing) tools to uncover unexpected uses of demonstratives by learners of English, and two papers on charting the linguistic development of Dutch students of English over time.

Tommaso Raso and Heliana Mello's edited volume *Spoken Corpora and Linguistic Studies* focuses specifically on issues related to speech-based corpora. The book includes sixteen papers, including the editors' introduction and an appendix, 'Notes on Language into Act Theory (L-AcT)', by Massimo Moneglia and Tommaso Raso, that introduces the most important details of the theory underlying four of the papers in the volume. The main chapters of the book are divided into four sections, the first two of which focus more on methodological issues related to the development of spoken corpora. Section I ('Experiences and Requirements of Spoken Corpora Compilation') features three chapters describing experiences and methodological perspectives from different corpus compilation projects. The three chapters in Section II ('Multilevel Corpus Annotation') address the next step in the process, namely the methodologies and decision-making related to the annotation of corpus data, which can be performed on various levels. Section III ('Prosody and Its Functional Levels') features four chapters that explore how prosody provides information on different phenomena that co-occur in speech activity, for instance, the expression of emotion or stances. The four chapters in the final section ('Syntax and Information Structure') consider the relationships among the diverse levels of the utterance (semantics, information structure, prosody) and how these interact with syntax, criticizing the use of the notion of sentence—especially phrase-structure tree based definitions—as an adequate syntactic unit of reference for spoken corpora and suggesting various alternatives.

A contribution oriented towards theoretically informed pedagogical methodology, *Writing as a Learning Activity*, edited by Perry Klein, Pietro Boscolo, Lori Kirkpatrick, and Carmen Gelati, features studies focused on the changing role of writing in learning. The book includes thirteen articles, including the introduction by the editors that embeds the studies of the volume into the larger discourse of writing pedagogy and highlights three theoretical trends that are having a profound effect on the role of writing in learning: the shift from a domain-general, writing-across-the-curriculum approach towards a domain-specific writing-in-the-disciplines approach; the influence of a writer's cognitive strategies on learning elicited by writing and the extent to which these strategies can be taught, and the shift from a focus on the individual writer towards activity systems of collaborative writing.

The following four books explore various theoretical issues. *Theory and Data in Cognitive Linguistics*, edited by Nikolas Gisborne and Willem Hollmann, grew out of a workshop of the same name held at the Societas Linguistica Europaea meeting in Vilnius in 2010. Including the introduction by the editors, the volume contains nine papers that examine various methodological and theoretical issues in cognitive approaches, with many of the contributions addressing these from a diachronic perspective. Clarifying a number of misunderstandings about collostructional analyses, Stefan Gries defines and demonstrates the method in his article and provides references for its successful application (more on collostructional analysis can be found in Section 5). Jóhanna Barðdal, Thomas Smitherman, Valgerður Bjarnadóttir, Serena Danesi, Gard Jenset, and Barbara McGillivray's innovative research attempts a reconstruction of the syntax and semantics of the dative subject construction in West Indo-European using evidence from various older West Indo-European languages. The contributions by Amanda Patten, Graeme Trousdale, and Willem Hollmann more clearly compare and contrast generative approaches with cognitive approaches to specific linguistic phenomena: Patten examines the history of *it*-clefts; Trousdale focuses on the *what with* construction, and Hollmann considers the representation of word classes. Interestingly, the articles form a continuum with respect to proposing a rapprochement between generative and cognitive linguistics, with Patten stating that constructional approaches are better suited than generative ones to explaining the historical data she examines, whereas Trousdale and Hollmann suggest, to varying degrees, the fruitfulness of combining both theoretical frameworks. The strongest proponent of such collaborations between frameworks, Hollmann, even presents evidence that both sides have failed to acknowledge certain highly relevant facts, which he suggests necessitates the use of insights from both for a more complete understanding of linguistic phenomena. Also taking a diachronic perspective, Nikolas Gisborne's and Sonia Cristofaro's papers differ from the previous three in that they evaluate different approaches within cognitive theory. Gisborne investigates the development of the definite article in English, and Cristofaro discusses several diachronic processes to evaluate various assumptions about psychological mechanisms and speakers' mental representations grounded in synchronic distributional patterns, showing that these diachronic processes do not provide any evidence for these assumptions. Teenie Matlock, David Sparks, Justin Matthews, Jeremy Hunter, and Stephanie Huette shed some interesting light on aspect in an experiment in which they ask participants to describe the events in a video. They found that the aspect used in the question itself ('What happened?' versus 'What was happening?') influenced the way people conceptualize and describe actions, with participants using more motion verbs, reckless language, and iconic gestures in response to the imperfective-framed question than to the perfective-framed one.

The widely held belief among linguists that 'all languages are equally complex' is the topic of investigation in *Measuring Grammatical Complexity* edited by Frederick Newmeyer and Laurel Preston, with the likes of researchers such as John Hawkins, David Gil, Ray Jackendoff, and Peter Culicover, among others, weighing in. As a whole, the volume aims to examine the validity of this widely held belief and the related corollary of complexity trade-offs (the idea that complexity in one part of a language's grammar is balanced out by simplicity in another part) and to develop metrics for measuring relative complexity cross-linguistically. While the contributions examine interesting data and offer some potentially fruitful proposals in determining relative linguistic complexity, the focus of most articles on particular levels of grammar (or, in some cases, even specific aspects within a level of grammar) unfortunately prevents the volume from attaining its perhaps lofty aims. This, however, does not undermine the value of the book; most of the papers offer informative and interesting evaluations and/or proposals of various metrics for measuring complexity, a necessary step in fully evaluating the linguistic complexity question. The editors' introduction summarizes the historical and theoretical background of the linguistic complexity issue before introducing the contributions to the volume. The book features fourteen chapters, including the introduction. Some of the strengths are the various theoretical perspectives (generative grammar, psycholinguistics, neurolinguistics) through which complexity is examined and the linguistic levels (phonology, morphology, syntax, semantics) taken into consideration. It is interesting, though perhaps not surprising, given the differing theoretical perspectives, that the papers offer quite varying ideas on the issue: some argue that there is a continuum of grammatical complexity on which we can place languages (albeit usually with respect to particular linguistic features rather than overall grammatical complexity, thereby softening the claim in the context of the bigger question), others argue the opposite, whereas still others seem to remain agnostic on the issue. These opposing views can largely be related to the differing definitions of linguistic complexity employed by the authors as well as how restrictive the focus of the authors is. Overall, the book contains thought-provoking papers, which contribute an important step towards evaluating the linguistic complexity issue.

Further expounding on some of the ideas in his contribution in the previously discussed volume, John Hawkins's *Cross-Linguistic Variation and Efficiency* is an updating and extension of the general theory presented in his 2004 book *Efficiency and Complexity in Grammars*, with investigations into new areas of grammar and performance from the fields of language processing, linguistic theory, historical linguistics, and typology. In both books, Hawkins presents evidence for the Performance-Grammar Correspondence Hypothesis, which states that 'grammars have conventionalized syntactic structures in proportion to their degree of preference in performance, as evidenced by patterns of selection in corpora and by ease of processing in psycholinguistic experiments' (p. 3). This approach to variation based on efficiency has wide-ranging theoretical consequences for many current issues in linguistics, including the role of processing in language change, the relative strength of competing and co-operating principles, and the notion of ease of processing and how to measure it, among others. One of the strengths of this framework is that it draws from and integrates insights from and advances in numerous linguistic fields and theories.

Showcasing the breadth and inherent interdisciplinarity of the latest research on colour(s), *Colour Studies: A Broad Spectrum*, edited by Wendy Anderson, Carole Biggam, Carole Hough, and Christian Kay, is a collection of papers originally presented at the 2012 conference entitled 'Progress in Colour Studies' held at the University of Glasgow. The volume contains twenty-six papers divided into four sections, in the first of which the keynote talk stands alone, while each of the three other sections includes a short preface introducing the respective section. The first two sections specifically focus on colour and linguistics. Drawing on evidence from linguistics, anthropology, archaeology, art history, and early literature, Carole Biggam, author of the keynote talk in Section I ('Prehistoric Colour Semantics'), suggests that it is possible to draw conclusions about prehistoric colour semantics, proposing that proto-Indo-European had no cool-hue basic colour term. The nine papers in Section II ('Colour and Linguistics') discuss aspects of colour terminology in non-European (Arabic, Aramaic, Himba) as well as European languages (Italian, Portuguese, Finnic, and four papers on English), including the emergence of new colour categories, metaphor and metonymy (the focus of most of the papers on English), the motivation for colour names, and the mapping of colour terms of the Near East. Most of the contributions in Sections III ('Colour Categorization, Naming and Preference') and IV ('Colour and the World') are less linguistically oriented but provide interesting discussion on the relationship between colour and cognition and perception.

The final three books discussed in this review are geared towards or otherwise extremely accessible to linguistics enthusiasts, newcomers to the field of linguistics, and interested laypersons. The second edition of the *Oxford Dictionary of English Grammar* by Bas Aarts, Sylvia Chalker, and Edmund Weiner incorporates a number of improvements: older entries have been revised and updated, and new entries have been added covering recent terminology and the most important English grammars of the twentieth century and beyond. A potential drawback might be the removal of entries on English phonetics, which the authors justify by stating, 'it is very unusual for phonetics to be covered under the heading of "grammar", and this terminology is best dealt with elsewhere' (p. vi). The dictionary includes not only traditional grammatical terms but also numerous terms from various theoretical frameworks that are relevant to English grammar. When a term has different uses in different frameworks, these are also clearly indicated. The dictionary is clearly laid out with visual aids for ease of reading, including the following among others: headwords are in bold; a line space separates each entry from the next; all cross-referenced terms are clearly marked with an asterisk. All of these traits make this a useful tool for people interested in English grammar.

Philip Durkin's *Borrowed Words: A History of Loanwords in English* is a thought-provoking piece of scholarship examining the influx of loanwords into English as well as the many issues involved in such research. The book is divided into six parts, the first giving an introduction to the concepts and data used in the book and the remaining five broadly ordered chronologically with each focusing on particular borrowing situations: Part II covers very early borrowings in Continental Germanic and pre-Old English; Part III examines Latin loanwords in (proto-)Old English; Part IV focuses on Scandinavian influence; Part V is dedicated to French and Latin borrowings in Middle English; and Part VI looks at loanwords after 1500. Not only does the book provide information on the influx of vocabulary items in the history of English, it also offers quite detailed discussion of the techniques and methodology employed in research on loanwords: determining, on the basis of phonological changes, when a borrowing entered the language and the issues involved in deciding whether to consider particular instances of a word as a borrowing or not; for example, Latin borrowings in Old English that always maintain Latin morphology versus those that alternate between Latin and Old English morphology. Though perhaps a bit too technical to maintain the attention of a general audience, the book is quite accessible to non-linguists while still being an invaluable resource for experienced researchers by providing a framework through which one can explore borrowing in any language. (See also Section 5 below.)

Does Spelling Matter? by Simon Horobin outlines the history of English spelling and puts forth the argument that it should remain as it is. His book starts by discussing the evolution of writing systems in general and the complex debate surrounding the relationship between letters and sounds from the Middle Ages up to the present day (and beyond). The subsequent chapters give a chronological sketch of English spelling at its various stages and the various issues and factors that played a role in each stage. Despite its challenges, Horobin argues that English spelling serves not only as a testament to the rich history of the language but also as a way to aid in reading comprehension, which is a side of the argument that typically receives less attention from spelling reformers. The book is very accessible to non-linguists: its use of specialized terminology is minimal, and brief definitions are provided of the terms that are introduced.

2. History of English Linguistics

The year 2014 has once more seen the publication of several studies related to the history of English linguistics. The volume *Norms and Usage in Language History, 1600–1900: A Sociolinguistic and Comparative Perspective*, edited by Gijsbert Rutten, Rik Vosters, and Wim Vandenbussche, which considers the language histories of Dutch, English, French, and German, dedicates three articles to the linguistic history of English. The first of these, 'Norms and Usage in Seventeenth-Century English' (pp. 103–28) by Terttu Nevalainen, discusses diverse processes related to emerging norms, notably those of spelling, lexis, and literary language. This discussion is based on a proposed framework by Bernard Spolsky [2012], which distinguishes 'between actual usage, language attitudes and language management' (p. 103). Selected case studies, notably those of spelling and certain types of vocabulary, reveal that usage, i.e. professional practice and interaction, gave rise to norms, which were then imposed on language users. The second contribution, 'Eighteenth-Century English Normative Grammars and Their Readers' (pp. 129–50) by Ingrid Tieken-Boon van Ostade, aims at answering the question of who the readers of normative grammars were. By analysing the list of subscribers to Richard Postlethwaite's *Grammatical Art Improved* [1795], the study shows that booksellers, teachers, and clergymen, as well as their relatives, and members of the rising middle classes subscribed to these grammars. The author compares Postlethwaite's grammar to that of Robert Lowth [1762] and then continues to discuss the transition from grammars to usage guides. Importantly, she observes that 'a significant part of the reading public of the grammars consisted of other—would-be—grammarians' (p. 147). The third contribution, 'Nineteenth-Century English: Norms and Usage' by Anita Auer, is concerned with grammar writing and grammatical norms during the nineteenth century as well as with actual language usage. Particular attention is paid to the lower social classes, i.e. the language history 'from below', also in the context of schooling and what effect, or lack of it, the scarce opportunities had on actual language usage. A linguistic case study of *you was/you were* in the so-called pauper letters revealed that the stigmatized form *you was* prevailed in lower-class language usage. This may be taken as an indication that the labouring poor were not necessarily familiar with prescriptions/ proscriptions contained in normative grammars. Auer concludes that the nineteenth century, in comparison to previous centuries, still 'deserves a lot more scholarly attention' (p. 151).

Another volume published in 2014 that tries to remedy this lack of research on the nineteenth century is *Late Modern English Syntax*, edited by Marianne Hundt. As regards the history of English linguistics, Lieselotte Anderwald's contribution 'The Decline of the BE-Perfect, Linguistic Relativity and Grammar Writing in the Nineteenth Century' provides some interesting findings. As the title indicates, the paper is concerned with the development of the BE-perfect as reflected in the corpora ARCHER (BrE) and COHA (AmE) as well as the description of the linguistic feature in contemporary grammar books. The corpus study reveals rapid change, i.e. decline (linked to specific verbs) during the nineteenth century, which raises the question 'whether this change was perceived as such in the grammar books of the time, and if so, whether this engendered any positive or negative evaluations' (p. 18). The analysis of the self-compiled 'Collection of Nineteenth-Century Grammars (CNG)' corpus shows that grammar writers found it difficult to comprehend and describe the linguistic feature, partly because of the lack of adequate terminology. In fact, it was possible to determine that the descriptions of British and American grammar writers developed differently over time. Anderwald thus concludes that the close study of grammatical descriptions allows for a 'more nuanced view of grammar writing in the nineteenth century' (p. 35), which is essential to determine the effect of prescriptive comments on actual usage or the lack thereof. In the volume *Contact, Variation and Change in the History of English*, edited by Simone E. Pfenninger, Olga Timofeeva, Anne-Christine Gardner, Alpo Honkapohja, Marianne Hundt, and Daniel Schreier, Lieselotte Anderwald uses the same approach, i.e. grammar comments compared to actual usage, in her paper ' "Pained the Eye and Stunned the Ear": Language Ideology and the Progressive Passive in the Nineteenth Century' (pp. 113–36). Corpus studies on BrE have revealed that the progressive passive rises rapidly in the nineteenth and twentieth centuries. A comparison with North American corpus data shows a different development, namely a lagging behind, which particularly concerns the twentieth century. It can be observed in both varieties of English that the progressive passive is highly text-type sensitive, with newspapers favouring the linguistic features. A close study of prescriptive comments on the progressive passive in 258 grammar books reveals that the use of the linguistic feature, and thereby also its users, was strongly criticized in grammars. Reasons for this particularly negative evaluation of the progressive passive may be its perceived complexity, its rarity overall, and its text-type sensitivity. The corpus of nineteenth-century grammars also serves as the basis of Anderwald's article 'Measuring the Success of Prescriptivism: Quantitative Grammaticography, Corpus Linguistics and the Progressive Passive' (*ELL* 18[2014] 1–21). The research question that is tackled here is 'whether prescriptivism has had any influence on purported differences between British and American English in the rise of the progressive passive' (p. 1). As in the previously discussed paper by Anderwald, text-type sensitivity is considered the determining factor for the occurrence of the progressive passive in both BrE and AmE. Considering the potential effect of prescriptivism, in AmE a sharp decline of the progressive passive can be observed in the 1950s, notably in newspaper language; this development coincides with the publication of William Strunk and E.B. White's guide on style [1959], which advises readers to 'avoid the passive' (p. 14). This may be taken as an indication that prescriptivism has had an influence in this particular case.

Normative grammars also play a role in Tieken-Boon van Ostade's monograph *In Search of Jane Austen: The Language of the Letters*, which may be described as a historical sociolinguistic reconstruction of Jane Austen's language in her letters. The study of Austen's spelling, grammar, and lexicon is discussed in the context of contemporary processes of language standardization. Particularly chapters 5, 'The Language of the Letters: Spelling', and 6, 'The Language of the Letters: Grammar', provide some information on eighteenth-century grammars, notably in relation to spelling rules and to selected morpho-syntactic features. Tieken-Boon van Ostade observes that 'in several linguistic features Jane Austen's usage goes against the trend of the times' (p. 229), which may be exemplified by Austen's preference for preposition stranding over pied piping.

3. Phonetics and Phonology

Some books are like wine—they gain quality with the passage of time. Two such titles have seen ripened and updated editions this year; first, we have a successive (eighth) edition of *Gimson's Pronunciation of English* by Alan Cruttenden, which maintains its strong position as one of the most detailed and comprehensive accounts of BrE pronunciation. The major revision of this work consists in the shift of focus from the description of Received Pronunciation (RP) to a more flexibly defined General British accent. Advocating this change, Cruttenden joins the ongoing academic discussion on the selection of a pronunciation model for teaching and justifies his choice by the fact that RP is perceived as posh, regionally limited, imposed, and outdated, and that General British, apart from being less constrained than RP, has a greater number of speakers than the old standard. Also, the book has a completely rewritten chapter on the history of the English language. The other classic that was thoroughly reviewed and updated is the introductory handbook of phonetics by Peter Ladefoged and Keith Johnson: *A Course in Phonetics*. This extensively illustrated book allows a student without prior linguistic knowledge to learn about speech production, acoustics, and perception, as well as develop practical phonetic skills, including sound production and IPA transcription.

Should one crave entertainment coupled with learning experience, *Sounds Interesting: Observations on English and General Phonetics* by John C. Wells is likely to satisfy the need. This distinguished scholar has selected entries from his phonetic blog and compiled a highly entertaining and, at the same time, deeply insightful and informative book which is filled with anecdotes, reflections, and observations about numerous topics related to general phonetics and the pronunciation of English. The chapters that the entries are grouped into are devoted to such subject areas as English pronunciation, general phonetics, teaching phonetics in English as a foreign language, English intonation, the International Phonetic Alphabet and spelling, accents of English, and the phonetics of languages other than English. The book is a must for those who are fascinated by the oddities of English pronunciation.

Shifting focus from books to research articles, one should mention a study by Adam Lammert, Louis Goldstein, Vikram Ramanarayanan, and Shrikanth Narayanan, who investigated the vowel segment that appears in the regular past tense suffix *-ed* in words such as *fitted* or *needed*, in 'Gestural Control in the English Past-Tense Suffix: An Articulatory Study Using Real-Time MRI' (*Phonetica* 71[2014] 229–48). They argue that the vowel that surfaces after alveolar plosives differs consistently from schwa which is present lexically in comparable consonantal contexts. Acoustic measurements of vowel formants showed that the affix vowel is higher and further forward than lexical schwa, yet lower and more retracted than [I]. These findings were also confirmed by real-time magnetic resonance imaging (rtMRI). Moreover, the MRI analysis of articulatory postures revealed that in the speech of the examined participants there was evidence for articulatory targets in the production of the affix vowel. These novel results compelled the authors to argue against the claim that the vocoid in the suffix is targetless when regarding articulatory gestures.

Another instrumental study of English pronunciation was carried out by Marc Garellek, who set out to establish if word-initial vowels and sonorants become strengthened by means of increased vocal-fold adduction. As described in 'Voice Quality Strengthening and Glottalization' (*JPhon* 45[2014] 106–13), the study consisted in analysing the articulation of proper names with stressed and unstressed initial vocoids, such as *Laura*, *Igor*, or *Annette*. The lexical items were placed in sentence frames in four prosodic positions: utterance-initially (after a breath), IP-initially after a high boundary tone (H%), ip-initially after a high phrase accent (H−), and ip-medially. Utterances, thus prepared, were read out by twelve speakers of AmE and recorded with an electro-glottograph (EGG) and an audio recorder. The subsequent analysis consisted in calculating the vocal-fold contact ratios for the investigated sounds as well as determining the frequencies of the first two harmonics (H1 and H2) and calculating the difference between them to estimate voice quality. The results showed that only initial prominent vowels became strengthened by an increased degree of glottal constriction, which indicates that there occurred word-initial glottalization.

Pre-vocalic glottal stops appear not only in word-initial position. Evidence is provided by Lisa Davidson and Daniel Erker in 'Hiatus Resolution in American English: The Case against Glide Insertion' (*Language* 90[2014] 482–514). Davidson and Erker's investigation focused on examining the way speakers of AmE pronounce vowel hiatuses. To accomplish this task, they recorded passages of text that contained stimuli of three types: word-internal vowel hiatuses (e.g. *nuance*, *kiosk*), phrases with vowel sequences across word boundaries (e.g. *two images*, *she overheard*), and vowel-glide-vowel sequences across word boundaries (e.g. *see yachts*, *knew whiskey*). The first two types of vowel sequence provide contexts for glide insertion ([w] and [j]) as the first vowel is non-high. The vocoids in the test tokens were assessed with regard to voice quality (creak vs. modal phonation), glottal stop insertion, and glottalization. Additionally, extensive acoustic measurements were performed. The results of the experiment are surprising. Contrary to the general assumption that hiatuses are resolved in English by an intervening glide, the findings of the study revealed that the preferred strategy for hiatus resolution across word boundaries is glottal stop insertion. What is more, glide insertion was not attested as a strategy for resolving hiatuses, and in many cases, particularly within words, the hiatuses were not resolved at all.

AmE flaps appear not to be as plain as it may seem at first sight. A number of researchers published articles devoted to this group of sounds in 2014. Aaron Braver, for instance, in his experimental study 'Imperceptible Incomplete Neutralization: Production, Non-Identifiability, and Non-Discriminability in American English Flapping' (*Lingua* 152[2014] 22–44), confirms previous claims that /t/-flaps and /d/-flaps in AmE are not completely neutralized. Having measured the length of vowels, Braver found that those that are followed by /t/-flaps are shorter than the vowels followed by /d/-flaps by 5.69ms, on average. This result seems to reflect the process of pre-fortis clipping that operates in English. The more interesting results of this investigation concern the listeners' perception of the difference between the two types of flap; the participants of the experiment found it difficult to judge correctly the consonants in both identification and two-alternative forced-choice (2AFC) tasks. As a result, the author postulates recognition of two kinds of incomplete neutralization: one that produces segments that can be identified and discriminated between and, on the other hand, incomplete neutralization that renders sounds that evade correct identification and discrimination, such as AmE flaps.

Taps and flaps display variability not only when it comes to the length of preceding vowels. They also differ in the way they are articulated. Donald Derrick and Brian Gick, in 'Accommodation of End-State Comfort Reveals Subphonemic Planning in Speech' (*Phonetica* 71[2014] 183–200), examine the variability of flap/tap realizations in AmE from the perspective of kinematics. With the use of ultrasound imaging, they identify four categorically distinct articulatory variants of the sounds on the basis of the direction of tongue tip/blade movement (alveolar taps, down-flaps, up-flaps, and post-alveolar taps). In a production experiment, Derrick and Gick find indications that particular realizations do not occur randomly; the attested productions display long-distance subphonemic planning that aims at avoiding articulatory conflict. Thus, for instance, if one of the following segments is another tap/flap or a rhotic sound, the selected variant will facilitate the kinematic needs of that segment. The explanation of the phenomenon is grounded in anticipatory co-articulation and end-state comfort effect. Taps/flaps have been found to anticipate upcoming articulations not only within words, but also across syllable, morpheme, and word boundaries, which indicates that the range of this effect is not limited to the immediate lexical context.

It was politicians who came under Valerie Freeman's scrutiny in 'Hyperarticulation as a Signal of Stance' (*JPhon* 45[2014] 1–11). The author analysed a political talk show to verify if the speakers hyperarticulated new information (contrasted with given data) and concepts about which they expressed attitudinal stances. To reach this objective, the concepts reiterated in the recordings at least three times were classified as new or given, and evaluative or neutral. Thus classified tokens were subjected to acoustic analysis to determine if there occurs hyperarticulation in any of the categories. Freeman measured speech-rate over a word/phrase, the fundamental frequency (F0), the frequency of the first two formants (F1 and F2) in the midpoint of stressed vowels within the word or phrase, and vowel duration. The results showed that the speakers hyperarticulated both stance-expressing items and new information. Speech-rate and vowel duration proved to be the most reliable indicators of hyperarticulation in English, whereas pitch did not provide valuable insight.

The issue of the phonological status of affricates in English continues to be a matter of contention. Another scholar to accept the challenge of solving the dilemma is Jeroen van de Weijer, who presents a phonotactics-based account of the problem in 'Affricates in English as a Natural Class' (in Caspers, Chen, Heeren, Pacilly, Schiller, and van Zanten, eds., *Above and Beyond the Segments: Experimental Linguistics and Phonetics*, pp. 350–8). Van de Weijer maintains that the English affricates [tʃ] and [dʒ] constitute a separate natural class of sounds and should be regarded as single underlying units, rather than as phonological sequences. To substantiate this claim, he presents an analysis of their phonotactic restrictions and patterning. The data provided is said to support the Complex Segment Approach to the representation of affricates, in which the phonological specification of the segment includes features that are in common with stops as well as fricatives at the same time.

Finishing this year's section on phonetics and phonology, we review a highly commendable article by Susan Lin, Patrice Speeter Beddor, and Andries W.

Coetzee, who examine the strength of anterior and dorsal constrictions in the English lateral. The results of their study are presented in 'Gestural Reduction, Lexical Frequency, and Sound Change: A Study of Post-Vocalic /l/' (*LabPhon* 5[2014] 9–36). The focus of the paper is on the post-vocalic and pre-consonantal /l/ in AmE, in words such as *help* or *milk*. The primary research question is whether the lexical frequency of occurrence has an effect on the constriction magnitude. To find the answer, the authors employ ultrasound imaging and acoustic analysis. Having scrutinized high- and low-frequency words that contain pre-consonantal /l/, Lin et al. arrive at several interesting conclusions. Firstly, they confirm previous findings that apical and dorsal constrictions characteristic of velarized laterals are most pronounced (least reduced) when an alveolar consonant follows. Secondly, the reduction of alveolar constrictions was greater in high-frequency words. Moreover, acoustic measurements of formant frequencies in the laterals reflected the degree of anterior constriction: F1 and F2 were closer together in tokens with more reduced constrictions.

4. Morphology

Only books and volume chapters will be considered in this section and the following one, covering both 2013 and 2014. One book that appeared on morphology in 2013 is *The Oxford Reference Guide to English Morphology*, written by Laurie Bauer, Rochelle Lieber, and Ingo Plag. This substantial work provides an overview of an extensive range of issues and topics in English morphology. The authors explain that they aim to be theory-neutral in their approach and want to provide 'a thorough, data-rich description of all phenomena of English word-formation' (p. 4). The book opens with a clear definition of central terms, as well as a discussion about methods commonly used in the field. It then provides a very systematic discussion of the basic processes of word-formation: inflection, derivation, and compounding. The book also includes a chapter about the interaction between these processes (such as affix combinations, or combinations of compounding and affixes). The book ends with a chapter on issues of theory and typology of English morphology.

Robert Dixon, in his *Making New Words: Morphological Derivation in English*, provides detailed studies of 200 affixes (ninety prefixes, 110 suffixes) in English that are productive and that change the word class of the word they attach to, i.e. those affixes that create new words. After an explanation of the aims of the book, and a short overview with definitions of central terms, the remaining chapters discuss all 200 affixes in turn. The chapters are organized according to the category of the affix, starting with prefixes (chapters 5 and 6). The next couple of chapters are based on the word class that is the result of the affixation process: affixes making verbs (chapter 7), adjectives (chapter 8), nouns (chapter 9), and finally adverbs (chapter 10). The final chapter before the conclusion discusses combinations of affixes in individual words. Throughout the book, Dixon highlights many differences between affixes in meaning or use, some of them very subtle. He addresses questions such as what determines the choice between the two productive negative prefixes *in-* and *un-*. As Dixon explains, variation can be explained through differences in meaning, phonological factors, historical developments, and, finally, conventions which 'have grown up during the centuries of evolution of Modern English' (p. 15). In the case of *in-* and *un-*, for instance, the answer is that is that *un-* was a Germanic prefix and could attach to all sorts of words, while *in-* is a Romance form in use from roughly 1450, attaching only to Romance words. One theme that recurs at several places in the book is the notion of 'double duty', i.e. words that are used for different functions, not always with a change in form and crucially not with a derivational affix. Some examples are *perfect* (verb and adjective), *abstract* (verb and adjective), and *find* (verb and noun). Dixon concludes that double duty was rare in OE but increased from the ME period onwards, leading not only to possible ambiguity but also to a 'diminishing use (and eventual extinction) of some derivational processes' (p. 398). However, Dixon ends the book with saying that new words, such as those created by derivation, will keep the language 'healthy and active'.

5. Syntax

(a) Modern English
Peter Matthews's *The Positions of Adjectives in English* is a monograph on adjectives in English, focusing on the various positions that adjectives can occupy. Matthews asks two main questions. The first is how much the predicative and attributive uses of adjectives (*The chief is tall* versus *The tall chief*) have diverged throughout the history of English. The second question relates to the first, namely whether this divergence is too great to warrant a categorization of both uses as belonging to one word class of 'adjectives' or not. His answer to the second question is that words that are traditionally classified as adjectives do belong to the class of adjectives although he admits and discusses that there are many problems with the categorization of adjectives. At the beginning of the book, Matthews brings up many general questions with respect to how words should be categorized, pointing out problems with traditional views on word class. For the adjectives, he provides many examples of uneven distribution: some adjectives can only be used predicatively (such as *afraid*) while others can only be used attributively (such as *main* or *utter*). Matthews does not find clear evidence which points to one use being more basic than the other. Another problem for the word class of adjectives is that the words that are generally taken to be adjectives do not seem to have one function that is shared by all adjectives and which is not (often) also a function of words from other classes. However, the most obvious alternative discussed by Matthews, conversion, is not a viable solution, as he discusses in detail. Instead, Matthews argues for what he calls a 'polysystemic' approach, which looks at relations between words from different classes, instead of only looking at the properties of a group of words by themselves. Matthews also considers aspects of the historical development of adjectives, addressing topics such as the increased divergence between the predicative and

attributive use from the end of the Middle Ages onwards, the standardization of the prenominal position, and the acceptability of combining adjectives ('stacking'), which is a more recent development.

Quite a number of books appeared in 2013 and 2014 about CxG: both introductions, reference works and historical studies working within a CxG framework. The first general book is *The Oxford Handbook of Construction Grammar*, edited by Thomas Hoffmann and Graeme Trousdale [2013]. This handbook contains twenty-seven chapters, which cover an extensive range of topics within CxG. The book is divided into five thematic sections: 'Principles and Methods'; 'Constructionist Approaches'; 'Construction: From Morphemes to Clauses and Beyond'; 'Acquisition and Cognition'; 'Language Variation and Change'. The chapters in Section I explain the fundamental principles of CxG, such as the chapter by Adele Goldberg, titled 'Constructionist Approaches' (pp. 15–31) or that by Paul Kay, 'The Limits of (Construction) Grammar' (pp. 32–48). The chapters in Section II describe particular directions within CxG (such as 'Embodied Construction Grammar', by Ben Bergen and Nancy Chang, pp. 168–90). The remaining sections contain chapters which discuss approaches to traditional areas of linguistic investigation through a CxG framework, such as 'Morphology in Construction Grammar' by Geert Booij (pp. 255–73), and 'Construction Grammar and Second Language Acquisition' by Nick Ellis (pp. 365–78). Like all Oxford Handbooks, this volume provides an insightful discussion of current issues, as well as an introduction to some of the basic principles of this model. Although it does not deal specifically with English, many of the discussions and explorations of topics are based on English examples.

For a briefer and more introductory work on CxG readers (and students) can turn to Martin Hilpert's *Construction Grammar and Its Application to English*. This textbook, from the series Edinburgh Textbooks on the English Language, provides an accessible introduction to the principles of CxG. It starts with the basic concepts of CxG: chapter 1 introduces the basic concept of the 'construction', and also devotes quite some space on explaining the argumentation behind the development of CxG and its relation to other linguistic theories. The main argument here is that there are too many idiosyncrasies in the meaning of words and sentences to hold on to the so-called dictionary-and-grammar view; rather, the view is that language consists of form-and-meaning pairs. The fundamental ideas are then elaborated on in the following two chapters: chapter 2 zooms in on one area where constructions play an important role, i.e. argument structure, focusing on valency-increasing and -decreasing constructions; chapter 3 discusses in detail the question whether all constructions are meaningful and 'how speakers' knowledge of language is organized in the construct-i-con' (p. 71). The second part of the book discusses central areas of linguistic enquiry and how CxG deals with them. Chapter 4 discusses the major processes of morphology as they have been discussed and how they are dealt with in CxG. Chapter 5, in turn, addresses information structure. Chapters 6 and 7 are concerned with psycholinguistic evidence for constructions, with chapter 6 focusing on 'comprehension and production' and chapter 7 on language acquisition. The final chapter deals with the issue of language variation and change, which CxG explains by assuming speakers may have different knowledge about particular constructions. Each chapter ends with a list of study questions and suggestions for further reading, directing the student reader to key academic publications in the field.

In addition to these works on CxG, two student-focused works on present-day English grammar published in 2013 will prove to be useful resources for those who teach introductory undergraduate grammar and syntax classes. *Practical Grammar*, by Sara Thorne, discusses all the key concepts for a descriptive introduction to English grammar, comprehensively, clearly, and logically. A pair of chapters deals with each particular level of grammar (words, phrases, clauses, sentences, discourse). The first of each pair introduces topics and concepts. It is followed by a chapter of exercises in which students apply the concepts learned to textual analysis. The text provides a comprehensive introduction, particularly for students engaged in textual or stylistic analysis, but it does not deal with more formal aspects of grammar, for example the representation of constituent structure using syntactic trees. *English Grammar: A Resource Book for Students*, by Roger Berry [2012], is another comprehensive introduction to English grammar, which is structured progressively into sections of increasing complexity and difficulty. The text presents a lot of material that would enhance an introductory grammar course, particularly linguistic questions or problems that students might work on. It also includes reprints of essays by several authors on grammatical topics. These provide useful additional reading for more inquisitive students and also useful discussion points and data for seminar activities.

While Thorne and Berry provide textbooks for undergraduates, *Advanced English Grammar: A Linguistic Approach* by Ilse Depraetere and Chad Langford [2013] is specifically designed as a descriptive grammar for university-level learners of English as an L2. It builds on basic concepts of word classes, phrases, and grammatical functions to explain some of the grammatical idiosyncrasies of English, such as subject–verb inversion, ellipsis, uses of the auxiliary *do*, tag questions, expressions of tense, aspect, and modality, and their use in discourse. Chapters 2 and 3 focus on NPs and VPs, considering complementation and modification patterns, subject–verb agreement, and voice. Chapters 4 and 5 examine aspect and modality in great descriptive detail. Chapter 6 considers discourse-level phenomena such as anaphora and connectives. The final section incorporates a great many exercises to accompany the key points of each chapter.

Finally, *Understanding Language: A Basic Course in Linguistics* (2nd edition), by Elizabeth Winkler, is an overview of the study of linguistics. As such, it would make a good course-book for the kind of introductory surveys of linguistics commonly found on first-year undergraduate linguistics programmes. The chapters on semantics and pragmatics (chapters 8 and 9) seem particularly comprehensive. Unlike some other books of this kind, the introduction to grammar (chapter 6) includes discussion of the advantages and disadvantages of several grammatical frameworks, including phrase-structure grammar and lexical functional grammar. However, the discussion of language variation and change includes very little on quantitative approaches;

it takes a qualitative perspective instead. Chapter 10 discusses the characteristics of computer-mediated communication, and chapter 11 discusses language and gender. The focus of the book is almost exclusively on English, especially AmE, although it does include detailed discussion of several non-standard English varieties.

(b) Early English

In addition to these general works on synchronic CxG, two full-length studies appeared on issues of diachronic syntax from researchers working within a CxG framework. The first of these is Hendrik De Smet's *Spreading Patterns: Diffusional Change in the English System of Complementation* [2013]. After the introduction, De Smet outlines the corpus he has compiled for the current study, expanding on the corpora that are already in general use, such as the Helsinki corpus, especially for the lModE period. Chapter 3 provides a detailed description of the issue of complementation, reviews earlier work on the topic, and includes an explanation of how CxG can deal with these topics and what the advantages of the CxG framework are for this type of study. Chapter 4 has a similar set-up but is concerned with diffusional change, i.e. the spread of a linguistic item, in this case a pattern of complementation, to new environments. The remainder of the book consists of three detailed studies of the development of specific patterns of complementation in the history of English. The first is concerned with *for ... to*-infinitives, as in *It was neither my intention or aim for this to happen* (p. 73), where an NP following *for* is itself followed by a *to*-infinitive. De Smet investigates the spread of this pattern of complementation, asking how the regular PDE system evolved, after the first examples were attested in lME. The second pattern investigated is a 'comparatively unsuccessful' complementation pattern, that of the so-called Integrated Participle Clauses, as in *The receptionist is busy filling a fifth box* (p. 102). This type was introduced around the same time as the *for ... to*-infinitives but never became more than a marginal pattern. Finally, by far the largest part of De Smet's book is devoted to a detailed study of the spread of gerunds as complements, which he calls 'the most dramatic recent change' in the system of complementation. An example is *Would you mind putting Bessie's exercise book back exactly where you found it?* (p. 131), where the gerund functions as the complement of a transitive verb. Throughout the book, De Smet describes in detail the processes and contexts that play a role in the spread of these patterns, such as analogy (based either on semantic considerations, or regularities in a paradigm), the specific 'local' grammatical context for each pattern, and frequency effects. In the conclusion, he also aims to answer the question why diffusion occurs at all. One of the points he makes in this respect is that the synchronic system of complementation, at any given time, is complex and may contain different generalizations at different (abstract) levels. It is this existing potential for variation that often provides the starting point for the spread of particular patterns.

The second study investigating developments in the history of English syntax working within a CxG framework is Peter Petré's *Constructions and*

Environments: Copular, Passive, and Related Constructions in Old and Middle English. Petré investigates three specific developments in copular and passive verbs in OE and ME. The first question he addresses is that of the disappearance of *(ge)weorðan.* OE, like other Germanic languages, had two verbs which could be used to form a passive, but while in other languages, the cognate of *(ge)weorðan* became the standard way of marking the passive, in English this verb was lost entirely. The second question is the merger of *is* and *bið* in the present tense, and to a lesser extent *weseð. Bið* had a specific meaning in OE but this was gradually lost, for instance through the grammaticalization of *shall be.* The final question is the development of two verbs, *becuman* 'become' and *weaxan* 'wax, grow', which became copula verbs over the course of just one or two centuries during the ME period. After the introduction, in which the author also introduces a biological view on language change, chapter 2 first provides a discussion of previous literature on the topics, chapter 3 presents the theoretical framework and the methodology used for the corpus studies, while chapters 4 to 6 discuss the three case studies mentioned above. Central themes in Petré's account of the changes are competition and environmental change, based on the analogy with biology. We will illustrate these concepts with the conclusions drawn from the first case study. The answer to the question why *(ge)weorðan* disappears builds on the notion of competition between the past-tense forms of *(ge)weorðan* and *wesan.* Once the most important distinctions in meaning between these two options were lost, the most frequent item, *wesan,* prevailed. Because competition is not a sufficient explanation in this case, Petré turns to changes in the environment of *(ge)weorðan.* He proposes that *weorðan* was part of a so-called 'bounded' system in OE, a system which was characterized by V2 inversion and 'bounded' time adverbs such as *þa.* Once this system went into decline after V2 inversion was lost, the other features of the system were also lost, including *(ge)weorðan.*

One of the areas of (historical) syntax that has received a considerable amount of attention in recent years is the interaction between syntax and information structure, an aspect of discourse that is concerned with navigating between the hearer's and the speaker's knowledge. *Information Structure and Syntactic Change in Germanic and Romance Languages,* edited by Kristin Bech and Kristine Gunn Eide, addresses the question of this interaction from a diachronic perspective across a variety of languages and with the use of corpora that are newly annotated for the purpose of the current studies. Several of the chapters in the book deal specifically with English. Ann Taylor and Susan Pintzuk's contribution, 'Testing the Theory: Information Structure in Old English' (pp. 53–77), is an attempt to arrive at a clearer understanding of the relevance of certain information-status categories that have been proposed in the literature and used in earlier annotation projects. Using a diagnostic that they developed in earlier work, namely preverbal vs. postverbal occurrence of the object, they test several of these categories. Their results clearly show that certain categories should be considered as separate categories, while other subcategories seem to behave like one group; for instance, discourse-old referents behave differently from the group of accessible referents (generic, general, or situational knowledge), which together behave in roughly the same way. The chapter by Erwin Komen, Rosanne Hebing, Ans van Kemenade, and Bettelou Los, 'Quantifying Information Structure Change in English' (pp. 81–110), investigates several properties of the category 'Subject' which they hypothesize to have changed from OE to PDE as a result of the loss of the V2 constraint. They use an enriched version of the existing corpora of historical English with partially automatically added annotation for information-status categories. Their results provide an interesting outlook on the consequences of the loss of V2 for the subject: the presubject position is less often used for discourse linking, while the subject itself becomes more often inanimate because the subject takes over part of the linking function of the presubject position. In a similar vein, subjects are less often ellipted, presumably because they are less predictable. The chapter by Gea Dreschler, 'Tracing Overlap in Function in Historical Corpora: A Case Study of English Object Fronting and Passivization' (pp. 111–39), also investigates a development in the history of English thought to be connected to the loss of V2. She looks at the function of object fronting and passives in OE and finds that their functions in the corpus overlap to a large extent in that they are both used for 'information-rearranging'. In the second part of the chapter, she provides evidence that the use of passives increases overall after object fronting has been largely lost in eModE, which supports the hypothesis that, as one construction performing a particular function is lost, another construction with the same function increases in use. The chapter by Tamás Eitler and Marit Westergaard, 'Word Order Variation in Late Middle English: The Effect of Information Structure and Audience Design' (pp. 203–31), zooms in on variation in V2 word order at the end of the ME period. The authors analyse four texts by John Capgrave, all written around 1450. They investigate the influence of information structure on word-order variation as well as the influence of the intended audience. They find that the most 'local' text (*Sermon*) has the highest percentage of a syntactic version of V2 (which is least influenced by information structure), while text aimed at a national audience (*Chronicle*) hardly uses this order. Of the four texts, this 'national' text has the most frequent use of non-V2 orders. Eitler and Westergaard also add further details on other topics of V2 variation discussed in the literature, such as the role of verb type (especially auxiliaries and unaccusatives) and of initial adverbs such as *then* on V2 variation. The final chapter to be discussed here is by Kristin Bech and Christine Meklenborg Salvesen, titled 'Preverbal Word Order in Old English and Old French' (pp. 233–70). The authors consider the V2 constraint in OE and OF, stating that while both languages have been described as V2 languages, there are many differences between them; indeed, at the end of the chapter they recommend that the use of the label V2 should be reconsidered. In their study, they focus on clauses in which the subject precedes the verb, investigating the interaction between the subject and other preverbal material. Their main findings are that OF word order is more fixed and the presubject position is more restricted, while OE word order shows more variation, and allows for more types of elements in the presubject position. They conclude that OF is more syntactically driven, while in OE information-structural motivation plays a larger role.

The years 2013–14 saw much interest in OE, particularly in the relationship between OE and other West Germanic languages. In *The Development of Old English*, Don Ringe and Ann Taylor provide a very detailed discussion of Old English in relation to its West Germanic antecedents. Chapters 2 to7 address phonological and morphological developments in West Germanic from proto-West Germanic to the OE period, with chapter 6 in particular focusing on the prehistory of OE and its divergence from other West Germanic languages. Chapter 8 provides a detailed description of OE syntax within a P&P framework. This volume usefully adds to the literature on OE in at least three respects. First, it emphasizes that OE is not uniform by taking a diachronic perspective, arguing that it undergoes syntactic, morphological, and phonological change, and that many of these changes represent the playing out of changes originating in earlier stages of West Germanic. Second, while the discussion of OE sound change covers much of the same ground as standard grammars of OE such as Hogg and Alcorn (discussed below), Ringe and Taylor situate the OE sound changes in the historical West Germanic context in a much more systematic way. Second, the discussion of OE syntax in chapter 8 differs from that in existing reference works by providing a systematic treatment of OE within a current generative syntactic framework, building on and incorporating insights from much recent work in this area. A second volume, discussing OE derivational morphology and the lexicon, is planned. Together, the two volumes will constitute an important reference work on OE.

George Walkden's *Syntactic Reconstruction and Proto-Germanic* also focuses on some specific aspects of the syntax of OE in relation to its West Germanic antecedents. He adopts a state-of-the-art minimalist syntactic framework for his analyses of verbal syntax, the *wh*-system and null arguments in West Germanic. Walkden shows, through a combination of methods, including syntactic and quantitative analysis of early textual data and careful historical reconstruction, that we can trace the development of syntactic properties of OE back into earlier stages of Germanic and reconstruct earlier stages of these changes for which we have little or no textual evidence. He argues that although syntactic reconstruction on the basis of linguistic phylogeny is more problematic than phonological or morphological reconstruction, feature-based minimalist theory may constrain permissible syntactic changes in such a way that reconstruction of certain syntactic properties of proto-Germanic, and even proto-Indo European, might be possible using the methods he proposes.

Two other volumes which take novel approaches to the problems of data in OE and its analysis are Fran Colman's *The Grammar of Names in Anglo-Saxon England: The Linguistics and Culture of the Old English Onomasticon* and *Analysing Older English*, edited by David Denison, Ricardo Bermúdez-Otero, Chris McCully, and Emma Moore. Colman makes a case for names as a source of linguistic data—in the sense that the OE onomasticon exhibits linguistic patterning. She first establishes the categorial status of names within the grammar, and their diachronic and synchronic relationship to common words such as nouns and adjectives. She shows that careful philologically informed study of names provides evidence for the phonological and morphological reconstruction of early OE, which antedates the earliest surviving texts. Colman argues that names differ from other linguistic categories in their semantic and grammatical properties, in ways that need to be understood before names can be used as evidence for linguistic reconstruction. The aim of Colman's research is ambitious in its scope. By necessity, the present book focuses on the place of names within linguistic theory, notably the notional-grammar framework proposed by John M. Anderson. This is rather preliminary to the analysis of names as evidence for the phonology and morphology of early OE, however, and it is clear that the work presented here is only part of a larger story. It will be interesting to see what further insights into OE may emerge from the this onomasticon (for more information on the onomastic aspect of this study, see Section 8 below).

Novel approaches to the analysis of early English data also emerge in Denison et al., eds., *Analysing Older English*. The papers all share a clear empirical focus on the question of what constitutes data in the study of early English. All address the question of how to handle and interpret incomplete historical data, in order to avoid forcing historical data to fit analytical schema or constructs which are based upon the synchronic analyses of present-day languages, notably PDE. Several papers make clear that viewing change from a present-day perspective can mislead us. Consequently, many of the papers are concerned with questions of historical continuities or discontinuities, and with functional rather than formal, theoretically driven explanations of historical phenomena. They challenge and reappraise formally based analyses on the grounds that these analyses provide an inadequate fit to the historical data. The first section focuses on onomastics, for example the processes of name formation. The second section addresses writing practices and the relationship between changes in writing practices and linguistic variation and change, for example micro-variation in spelling patterns as evidence for phonological micro-variation (Roger Lass and Margaret Laing), spelling patterns as evidence for dialect variation in OE (here, R.D. Fulk argues that there are more Anglian spellings in West Saxon texts than has been standardly assumed). Section III concerns itself with dialectal and sociolinguistic variation. April McMahon and Warren Maguire present the results of a new computational method for classifying languages and varieties based on a range of phonological features. This analysis produces a taxonomy in the form of a network, based on degrees of similarity or differences between the varieties. Identifying these relationships might shed light on the historical development of the varieties in question, in a similar way as do phylogenetic approaches to the reconstruction of proto-languages. Section IV focuses on phonological change. Nikolaus Ritt argues that historically recurrent processes of consonant weakening (where weakening is a decrease in perceptibility) and of vowel strengthening (where strengthening is an increase in perceptibility) are both reflexes of English being a stress-timed language rather than a syllable-timed one. The final section comprises two papers on historical syntax by Olga Fischer and by Anthony Warner. Both pursue a strong empirical focus, with both using large-scale historical corpora to identify generalizations and patterns of change. Crucially, both seek to explain change from the perspective of users of the historical varieties themselves, drawing insights from domains of language other than syntax to explain the behaviour of these speakers.

In 2013 a new edition was published of *An Introduction to Old English*, written by the late Professor Richard Hogg and revised by Rhona Alcorn. This has been a most useful reference work for students of OE for some time. The new edition represents some of Richard Hogg's last work, and usefully updates earlier editions by incorporating recent research on OE dialect variation, and the historical and social context in which OE functioned. It remains a comprehensive introduction to OE, suitable for undergraduate students who have mastered basic phonological, morphological, and syntactic concepts. It is more comprehensive than traditional grammars of OE, covering issues of variation in OE (chapter 9), and OE's relationship to later periods of English (chapter 10), as well as providing an accessible and logically structured outline of the grammar of the language. It is also far more accessible than traditional OE grammars. The text has a very student-friendly, direct, and explanatory style throughout, and successfully avoids being either too erudite or too patronizing. Instead, it makes OE interesting by setting it in its historical and linguistic context, and includes well-designed exercises, which can be used both for independent as well as class-directed study.

Turning to other student-focused works, *The History of English* by Stephan Gramley [2013] provides a very student-friendly overview of the history of English from its Germanic origins to the present day. It includes chapters on all the major periods of English. Its focus is on describing the linguistic consequences of external historical events in each period rather than on detailed descriptions of linguistic change (e.g. syntactic changes), or mechanisms of language change (e.g. historical sociolinguistics). Chapters 10–13 discuss the development of American, African, and southern hemisphere varieties of English. Chapter 14 discusses English as a global language. Information is set out clearly in a typical textbook style (including introductory chapter summaries, in-text exercises, discussion of linguistic data, and key-point summaries throughout each chapter). The major advantage of this text, particularly for those teaching or studying the history of English at undergraduate level, is that specific points in the text are supported by extensive and detailed web resources.

Broadening the historical focus yet further, *The History of Languages* by Tore Janson [2013] is a wide-ranging survey of its topic, introducing a breadth of issues rather than pursuing issues in depth. Its aim is to cross the divide between language studies and historical studies. It is accessibly written, and largely descriptive, avoiding linguistic jargon. It provides a useful introduction to language typology (chapter 2), the development of writing systems (chapters 3–5), and the languages of major civilizations, including the Chinese, the Greeks, the Romans, and the Arabs, all of which would provide useful background for students of historical linguistics. Later chapters chart how these early languages develop into the national languages we know today. Throughout the discussion, the focus is on external history, but issues of language emergence, language maintenance, and language death are cogently discussed. The book closes with a discussion of the internationalization of languages like English. Throughout, the book provides a clear introduction to questions and issues which could usefully form the basis of more detailed study.

6. Semantics

At least since the influential work by Richard Montague in the 1960s and 1970s, formal semanticists have been occupied with the task of developing systems for calculating sentence meanings from the meanings of their syntactic constituents compositionally. The Fregean idea that some constituents may denote functions from the denotations of others has been instrumental in this enterprise. A radical generalization of such an approach has been spelled out in detail by Chris Barker and Chung-Shieh Shan in their monograph *Continuations and Natural Language*. Drawing heavily on methods from mathematical logic and computer science, the authors promote the view that certain linguistic expressions may denote functions that take their semantic 'context' as arguments. Such contexts, built from the denotations of the remaining co-constituents, are called 'continuations', as they 'prefigure' the process of semantic derivation. With a particular version of 'order of evaluation' in place—linear left-to-right order being considered a default for incremental interpretation—fully formal and principled accounts of scoping and binding phenomena involving reconstruction, cross-over patterns, and donkey anaphora can be given. Among the many case studies, an analysis of sluicing is provided that identifies the missing semantic part in expressions like *Mary met someone but I don't know who* with a continuation, namely, the meaning of *Mary met*, which can be accessed anaphorically. Barker and Shan go to considerable length to make their theory accessible to readers. This involves carefully chosen notation and graphic representations as well as numerous well-chosen exercises throughout the first half of the book.

Compositional Semantics: An Introduction to the Syntax/Semantics Interface is a new introductory textbook on formal semantics by Pauline Jacobson. The book has a broader coverage than most publications of its kind on the market, particularly the popular textbook by Irene Heim and Angelika Kratzer [1998], and several design features that distinguish it from the latter. For example, the syntactic theory adopted is Categorial Grammar, reference to intensional phenomena and the formal apparatus (possible worlds and times) needed to handle them is introduced early on, whereas the lambda notation itself is introduced relatively late, reflecting a conscious attempt by the author to emphasize the distinction between model-theoretical objects and the convenient notation for representing them. Also somewhat unusually, the book takes the view of Direct Compositionality on the syntax/semantics interface, according to which each syntactic rule is paired with a semantic rule that gives the meaning of the output of the syntactic rule in terms of the meaning(s) of the input expressions to this rule, although analyses of more complex phenomena (from Part III onwards), are presented additionally from the theoretical perspective that relies on the level of LF. The book is divided into four parts. Part I introduces the goals of semantics, fundamental concepts like model, truth conditions, and possible worlds, the notion of compositionality, and the nature of the syntax/semantics interface; it also provides a brief introduction to Categorial Grammar, discusses the interpretations of syntactic categories such as NPs, intransitive and transitive VPs, adjectives, common nouns, and determiners; and finally it presents the semantics of variables and the lambda calculus. Part II introduces generalized quantifiers, type lifting, and generalized conjunction. In Part III, the interpretation of relative clauses, generalized quantifiers in object position, and the interpretation of pronouns are shown in terms of both LF and Direct Compositionality. The final Part IV introduces NPIs, more sophisticated binding phenomena, the semantics of focus, and intensionality-sensitive words within the syntax/semantics interface.

Compositionality issues are also addressed by several contributions to the collection *Approaches to Meaning: Composition, Values, and Interpretation*, edited by Daniel Gutzmann, Jan Köpping, and Cécile Meier. 'Does Context Change?' (pp. 25–44) by Manfred Kupffer provides a comparison of two theoretical frameworks that can handle the case of two syntactic occurrences of the same indexical expression within an utterance referring to different objects, as in *That is the same planet as that* (e.g. when the speaker points to two different photographs of the same planet). Paul Dekker puts forth a new Principle of Compositionality that combines speaker-dependent meanings in 'The Live Principle of Compositionality' (pp. 45–84), and Mats Rooth illustrates two ways of accounting for the semantic equivalence of a sentence and its paraphrase in 'Operators for Definition by Paraphrase' (pp. 85–101).

Syntax–semantics relations also figure centrally in two of the three semantic contributions to the volume *Recursion: Complexity in Cognition*, edited by Tom Roeper and Margaret Speas. Explanatory priority is given to syntax by Wolfram Hinzen, whose chapter 'Recursion and Truth' (pp. 113–37)—among other things—champions the slogan 'Intensionality from Syntax', which is one of the section headings. Taking current Chomskyan minimalist syntax at face value as a model of 'mental computation', the author correlates syntactic encapsulation of subconstituents derived bottom-up (in 'cycles' or 'phases') with pervasive referential opacity of such subconstituents. Some of the more philosophical assumptions of Hinzen's 'anti-realist semantics' are laid out in the remainder. In the chapter 'Recursion, Legibility, Use' (pp. 89–112), Peter Ludlow takes the opposite view and argues that rules of semantic composition are 'prerequisite cognitive abilities' for recursive syntax. From this perspective, semantic rules like predicate modification and abstraction—these are rules that enable unlimited stacking of predicative expressions—filter the kinds of structures that can be interpreted. This supports the traditional conception of language as a collection of form–meaning mappings. Ludlow attempts an additional grounding of the theory within a 'meaning-is-use' approach, designed to replace truth and entities by 'pro-attitudes' and referential intentions of language users. Still on the matter of structural layering but concerned with issues at the semantics–pragmatics interface is Manfred Krifka's contribution entitled 'Embedding Illocutionary Acts' (pp. 59–87). Here it is argued that the Wittgensteinian injunction against confusing representations ('pictures' of states of affairs) and uses thereof (speech acts) can to some extent be defused by developing a proper theory of act denotations. At the core of this proposal is the idea that illocutionary operators like ASSERT change states—'indices', i.e. world-time pairs in the language of formal semantics—such that the commitments of the interlocutors are altered. This allows flexible interaction between these and standard (index-sensitive) denotations like propositions. The resulting formal system is then applied to an analysis of explicit performatives, modification by speech-act adverbials, and indirect speech. In each case, it is shown how speech-act denotations can interact with ordinary semantic operators.

Two collections are concerned with NP reference, that is, the relation between linguistic expressions and entities in the world. *Crosslinguistic Studies on Noun Phrase Structure and Reference*, edited by Patricia Cabredo Hofherr and Anne Zribi-Hertz, contains eleven studies discussing the referential properties of nominal expressions in a wide range of typologically diverse languages or dialectal groups. One group of contributions is concerned with cross-linguistic regularities in NP syntax and semantics, particularly the impact of information structure, countability, and number marking on interpretation. A second group explores the nature and marking of 'definiteness', a heterogeneous concept both from the formal and the interpretational perspective, and one paper, 'When Articles Have Different Meanings: Acquiring the Expression of Genericity in English and Brazilian Portuguese' (pp. 367–97), by Tania Ionin, Elaine Grolla, Silvia Montrul, and Hélade Santos, discusses experimental data on the acquisition of the expression of genericity in a second language. The editors of the collection *Weak Referentiality*, Ana Aguilar-Guevara, Bert Le Bruyn, and Joost Zwarts, see the notion of weak referentiality as 'a kind of cluster concept, covering the different ways in which an indefinite or definite noun phrase can depart from those noun phrases that straightforwardly introduce or pick up an individual referent in the common ground of a discourse' (p. 4). 'Epistemic and Scopal Properties of Some Indefinites' (pp. 45–72) by Tania Ionin discusses the results and theoretical consequences of an experimental study that aimed to compare English *a*- indefinites and *some*-indefinites with regard to scopal versus epistemic specificity, distinguished first by Donka F. Farkas [1994, 2002]. The results show that unstressed and stressed *some*-indefinites are more compatible with scopal specificity than *a*-indefinites, but they are less compatible with epistemic specificity than the latter, stress on *some* playing a major role in both contrasts. In 'How Weak and How Definite are Weak Definites?' (pp. 214–35), Florian Schwarz investigates the possibility of providing a unified semantic analysis for regular definites and the class of weak definites, whose properties include the possible lack of uniqueness, the involvement of semantic enrichment in interpretation, and the fact that they do not support anaphora, as argued by Greg Carlson, Rachel Sussman, Natalie Klein, and Michael Tanenhaus [2006]. Schwarz makes the suggestion that weak definites should be treated as regular definites occurring in VPs that denote kinds of events. Ana Aguilar-Guevara and Maartje Schulpen take a closer look at the adjectives that are acceptable in weak definite constructions in 'Modified Weak Definites' (pp. 237–64). Building on the account of weak definites by Aguilar-Guevara and Zwarts [2010], according to whom these expressions denote kinds, the present authors argue that only adjectives denoting properties of kinds are compatible with weak definites, which is corroborated by their experimental results. 'Functional Frames in the Interpretation of Weak Nominals' (pp. 265–85) by Joost Zwarts puts forth an analysis of weak nominals such as the weak definite in *listen to the radio* and the bare nominal in *watch television*, according to which they refer to certain roles in (mostly functional) frames. This explains the uniqueness properties of weak definites, why only certain nouns can form weak definites, and why they only occur with certain nouns and prepositions. In 'The Indefiniteness of Definiteness' (in Gamerschlag, Gerland, Osswald, and Petersen, eds., *Frames and Concept Types: Applications in Language and Philosophy*, pp. 323–41), Barbara Abbott reviews traditional defining criteria for the definiteness of NPs, in terms of strength, uniqueness, and familiarity, as well as newer ones in terms of principal filters, scope-taking, and occurrence in partitive constructions. After carefully investigating how these approaches fare with respect to universal NPs, partitives, possessive NPs, and specific indefinites the author comes to the conclusion that Bertrand Russell's [1905] proposal in terms of referential uniqueness should be given preference.

Daphna Heller and Lynsey Wolter are also concerned with the referential properties of definites in 'Beyond Demonstratives: Direct Reference in Perceptually Grounded Descriptions' (*JSem* 31[2014] 555–95). The paper focuses on the puzzle of why perceptually grounded definites cannot occur in post-copular position in questions, as in **Who do you think is that guy/the man on the left?*, and why a question with a post-copular name requires a perceptually grounded answer, as in—*Who do you think is Wouter Vossen?*— #*That guy. | The concertmaster of the Brabants Orchestra*. In 'The Polysemy of Measurement' (*Lingua* 143[2014] 242–66), Jessica Rett argues that all individual-denoting DPs have a derived interpretation on which they denote degrees, provided that the salient dimension of measurement is monotonic on the part-whole structure.

Further important studies on the semantics of nominal elements include 'Dependent Plural Pronouns with Skolemized Choice Functions' (*NLS* 22[2014] 265–97) by Yasutada Sudo, which offers a new account of dependent plural pronouns as in *The first-years all think that they are the smartest student*. Alda Mari claims, in 'Each Other, Asymmetry and Reasonable Futures' (*JSem* 31[2014] 209–61), that the variety of interpretations associated with reciprocal sentences can be captured by assuming that they describe a relation that is either actually or possibly strongly reciprocal over the reference set, to the extent that the possibilities are reasonable. Bert Le Bruyn and Henriëtte de Swart propose an analysis of two types of bare co-ordination structure such as *Bride and groom were happy* and *A man and woman are in love* in 'Bare Coordination: The Semantic Shift' (*NL&LT* 32[2014] 1205–46) in terms of intersection between sets of matching pairs, which accords with the lexical semantics and pragmatics of natural co-ordination.

We turn now to studies on DP quantification. Capitalizing on important findings about the differences between so-called comparative versus superlative determiners (such as *more/less than* vs. *at least/at most*) by Bart Geurts and Rick Nouwen [2007], Ariel Cohen and Manfred Krifka offer a new interpretation of the latter, which assumes that they quantify over meta-speech acts: 'Superlative Quantifiers and Meta-Speech Acts' (*Ling&P* 37[2014] 41–90). The authors develop a framework for modelling speech acts and meta-speech acts, the latter of which are taken not to be moves in the conversation but to indicate which moves are possible, modelled in terms of changes of commitment spaces. 'Extensionality in Natural Language Quantification: The Case of *Many* and *Few*' (*Ling&P* 37[2014] 315–51) by Kristen A. Greer wishes to demonstrate that natural language quantification is always purely extensional by providing a single syntactic-semantic structure for the various interpretations of the determiners *many* and *few* (including their proportional, reverse, and cardinal readings) for which intensional analyses have most often been argued in the literature. The account assumes that the semantic arguments of the quantifiers in question are themselves set intersections, and relies on Ariel Cohen's [1999, 2001] proposal that the universe consists of the union of alternatives to the nominal and verbal predicates. 'On the Identification of Quantifiers' Witness Sets: A Study of Multi-Quantifier Sentences' (*JLLI* 23[2014] 53–81) by Livio Robaldo, Jakub Szymanik, and Ben Meijering presents the results of an online questionnaire study that looked at interpretations of so-called Independent Set (IS) readings (aka scopeless readings) of sentences containing multiple quantifiers, such as *Exactly three children ate exactly five pizzas*. The results argue against Barry Schein's [1993] 'global maximization' approach, which assumes that IS readings of multi-quantifier sentences always take into account all individuals in the model: in the presence of certain pragmatic factors, the sentence's meaning is shown to be restricted to subgroups of individuals.

'*No More* Shall We Part: Quantifiers in English Comparatives' (*NLS* 22[2014] 1–53) by Peter Alrenga and Christopher Kennedy puts forth a new account of the interpretation of quantificational expressions in the comparative clause, which relies on the assumption of a silent, comparative clause-internal negative degree quantifier, which interacts with other quantificational expressions to derive the observed range of interpretations. Maria Aloni and Floris Roelofsen look at 'Indefinites in Comparatives' (*NLS* 22[2014] 145–67), aiming to account for their meaning and distribution, with particular attention to the licensing conditions of *any* in comparatives, as in *Michael is taller than (almost) anyone else in his class* (with a universal reading), and to differences in quantificational force between *any* and *some* (cf. *Michael is taller than someone else in his class*, which can only have an existential reading).

'Non-Monotonicity in NPI Licensing' (*NLS* 22[2014] 169–217) by Luka Crnič proposes a new account of the distribution of occurrences of the focus particle *even* that are adjoined at surface structure to an expression entailed by its focus alternatives (such as *even once*). These expressions must occur in a downward-entailing environment, such as in the scope of non-monotone quantifiers, as in *Exactly two congressmen read the constitution even ONCE*. The focus particle *only* is the topic of a paper by Katsuhiko Yabushita, 'A Modal Scalar-Presuppositional Analysis of *Only*' (in McCready, Yabushita, and Yoshimoto, eds., *Formal Approaches to Semantics and Pragmatics: Japanese and Beyond*, pp. 325–41), which takes a fresh look at the difference between positive and negative *only* sentences, as in *Only Mary can speak*

French vs. *Not only Mary can speak French*, according to which only the former is compatible with a continuation *and maybe not even she can* vs. *and maybe he can't*, respectively, that cancels the prejacent, noticed by Manuela Ippolito [2008]. After showing the flaws in Ippolito's account, Yabushita proposes a modal presuppositional account, a modification of the one proposed by Robert van Rooij and Kathrin Schulz [2007]. Elizabeth Coppock and David I. Beaver look at a range of exclusives such as the adverbs *only*, *just*, *exclusively*, *merely*, *purely*, *solely*, *simply*, and the adjectives *only*, *sole*, *pure*, *exclusive*, and *alone* in 'Principles of the Exclusive Muddle' (*JSem* 31[2014] 371–432). They propose a lexical entry schema for these exclusives, according to which they share an at-issue contribution of an upper bound on the viable answers to the current question under discussion, and signal that a lower bound on those answers is taken for granted.

We turn now to the semantics of TAM. Within the collection *Future Times, Future Tenses*, edited by Philippe de Brabanter, Mikhail Kissine, and Saghie Sharifzadeh, Fabio Del Prete addresses an old dilemma in 'The Interpretation of Indefinites in Future Tense Sentences: A Novel Argument for the Modality of Will?' (pp. 44–71). The author suggests that *will* has a temporal semantics, while its modal component is only introduced at a (pragmatic) layer of utterance evaluation. Empirical evidence for the proposal is drawn from certain scopal (non-)interactions between *will* and indefinites—different from what happens with bona fide modals—as well as from the licensing of modal subordination, which *will* shares with standard modals. The analysis is worked out formally, and ways of conceiving of its pragmatic component—e.g. differences from familiar versions of pragmatic enrichment—are addressed. Two further contributions to this collection concern the conceptual under-pinnings of semantics. In 'Talking about the Future: Unsettled Truth and Assertion' (pp. 26–43), Isidora Stojanovic undertakes a systematic formal investigation of four approaches to the problem—familiar since antiquity—of future contingents, that is, 'the problem of specifying the truth conditions for future-tensed sentences in such a way that the resulting semantics remains compatible with the hypothesis of an indeterministic universe' (p. 26). Bridget Copley devotes her chapter 'Causal Chains for Futurates' (pp. 72–86) to arguing for the possibility of direct causation between plans, conceptualized as stative eventualities, and (planned) events. Among other things, this is taken to underlie contrasts like *John is getting married/#sick (tomorrow)* in 'futurate' readings of the present progressive. What makes genuine futures distinct from futurates is that plannability—treated as a presupposition—is not involved in the former. In addition to providing semantic formalization, Copley argues that only minor modifications yield a satisfactory incorporation of 'natural futurates' (*The sun rises/?is rising tomorrow at 6:30*) into the system.

Adeline Patard is concerned with the modal uses of past tenses in 'When Tense and Aspect Convey Modality. Reflections on the Modal Uses of Past Tenses in Romance and Germanic Languages' (*JPrag* 71[2014] 69–97). The unified account of the modal interpretations of past tenses in French, Italian, Spanish, Dutch, English, and German proposed is based on the idea that the different interpretations of past tenses (including the modal ones) reflect specific instantiations of the notion of reference point as 'topic time', 'aspectual vantage point', or 'epistemic evaluation'. 'The Present Tense Is Not Vacuous' (*JSem* 31[2014] 685–747) by Guillaume Thomas argues against Uli Sauerland's [2002] analysis of the present tense, according to which its indexical meaning comes about as a result of a pragmatic competition with the past tense. It also develops an analysis of futurates that derives their temporal orientation from their modal properties. Károly Varasdi, 'Making Progressives: Necessary Conditions are Sufficient' (*JSem* 31[2014]179–207) joins the ranks of recent critics of the standard approach to the truth-conditions of the progressive, proposed by David Dowty [1977, 1979], according to which 'the progressive operator requires that the event be completed in all the inertia worlds assigned to the evaluation index' (p. 180), and argues for the significance of the conditions necessary for the completion of the event. Astrid de Wit and Frank Brisard, 'A Cognitive Grammar Account of the Semantics of the English Present Progressive' (*JLing* 50[2014] 49–90), argue for a unified semantic analysis of the present progressive in terms of 'epistemic contingency or non-necessity in the speaker's conception of current reality' (p. 50), contrasting it to the simple present, which is taken to indicate structural necessity. Susi Wurmbrand, 'Tense and Aspect in English Infinitives' (*LingI* 45[2014] 403–47), proposes a threefold classification of infinitival complements, based on differences in their temporal composition, which allows us to account for selectional restrictions of different infinitive-taking predicates, and phenomena such as SOT and episodic interpretations.

'Fake Tense in Conditional Sentences: A Modal Approach' (*NLS* 22[2014] 117–44), by Kathrin Schulz, proposes that the 'fake' uses of the past tense marker in English conditional sentences indicate a certain kind of ambiguity of the past tense morphology, which can either mark the presence of a temporal operator or a specific modal operator. The latter interpretation is argued to arise through recategorization, in the course of which the simple past develops a second, modal meaning because of structural similarities between the temporal and the modal/epistemic domain. Christian Ebert, Cornelia Ebert, and Stefan Hinterwimmer propose 'A Unified Analysis of Conditionals as Topics' (*Ling&P* 37[2014] 353–408), according to which 'normal indicative conditionals' (NCs) and 'biscuit conditionals' (BCs), both containing fronted antecedents, are to be analysed in terms of aboutness topics and relevance topics, based on their syntactic and semantic similarities to two left-dislocation constructions in German, which have been argued to mark these two types of topicality.

'Enablement and Possibility' (in Leiss and Abraham, eds., *Modes of Modality: Modality, Typology, and Universal Grammar*, pp. 319–51) by Raphael Salkie promotes an 'actualist' approach to modality, eschewing possible worlds. Accordingly, the analysis of *can* is built from an 'enablement' relation, which itself is defined via a fairly abstract interrelation between necessary conditions and the 'actualization' of propositions. In addition to exploring differences between *can* and *may*, Salkie addresses objections to his approach raised earlier by Renaat Declerck. 'Modals and Lexically-Regulated Saturation' (*JPrag* 71[2014] 160–77) by Ilse Depraetere presents a new, three-layered model for the analysis of the meaning of modals, which takes these expressions as essentially polysemous, and consists of a context-independent semantic layer, a context-dependent semantic layer, and a context-dependent pragmatic layer. Ivano Ciardelli, Jeroen Groenendijk, and Floris Roelofsen's study, 'Information, Issues, and Attention' (in Gutzmann et al., eds., pp. 128–66), considers the interpretation of the modal epistemic *might* as in *John might be in London* within Inquisitive Semantics, and argues that it motivates the introduction, in addition to the informative and inquisitive contents of sentences, of a third, 'attentive content', which signifies the sentence's potential to draw attention to certain possibilities. 'Have To, Have Got To, and Must' by Cliff Goddard (in Taboada and Trnavac, eds., *Nonveridicality and Evaluation: Theoretical, Computational and Corpus Approaches*, pp. 50–75) provides Natural Semantic Metalanguage explications for the most important English modals of necessity.

Turning to the semantics of sentence types, Mark Jary and Mikhail Kissine's work *Imperatives*, published in the series Key Topics in Semantics and Pragmatics by Cambridge, provides an informed and systematic survey of the data from a wide range of languages that any serious theory of the semantics/pragmatics of imperatives should be able to account for, as well as a critical discussion of the most influential theories on the market, including the most recent ones. Part I, which reviews the relevant data, is concerned with issues such as the defining criteria for imperative sentences (and their differentiation from other sentence types such as prohibitives or hortatives), the distinction between the imperative verb form and the imperative sentence type, and its impact on the issue whether there are imperative sentences with first- or third-person subjects, the range of uses of the imperative without directive force (as in good wishes, advice, threat, advertising imperatives, permission, audienceless and predetermined cases), and the structure and use of imperative constructions with conditional meaning as a special case of non-directive meaning (as in *Come any closer and I'll shoot*). Part II presents a well-written survey of the main arguments and the critical points of the most significant semantic-pragmatic theories of imperatives in three groups. These include those that view imperatives as encoding directive force, those that treat imperatives as declaratives, and those that see imperatives as representing a distinct semantic type from declaratives, their directive force 'mediated by pragmatic considerations'. The careful argumentation and the presentation of often highly formalized theories in a non-technical fashion makes the volume an accessible first read on the topic. Patrick Georg Grosz's 'Optative Markers as Communicative Cues' (*NLS* 22[2014] 89–115) looks at the apparent obligatoriness of particles such as the English exclusive particles *only*, *just*, and *but* in *if*-optatives in English and German. The author argues that the systematic appearance of optativity cues, which are perceived to be truth-conditionally vacuous, can be explained by postulating a generalized conversational constraint at the semantics/pragmatics interface referred to as 'Utilize Cues': the speaker uses these optativity cues to disambiguate ambiguous structures such as *if*- and *that*-clauses towards optative readings, which have a low frequency or prior probability, which mechanism later becomes automaticized.

'Question Tags and Sentential Negativity' (*Lingua* 145[2014] 173–93), by Adrian Brasoveanu, Karen De Clercq, Donka Farkas, and Floris Roelofsen, argues for the graded nature of sentential negativity. It reports the results of an experimental study trying to quantify the negativity of sentences with the help of a question-tag test. The results show that n-words contribute more negativity than downward-entailing items, and that the strength of negativity induced by both is sensitive to the syntactic position of the negative expression. Regine Eckardt's study of the vocative construction, 'Dear Ede! Semantics and Pragmatics of Vocatives' (in Gutzmann et al., eds., pp. 223–49), is built on the basic observation that it is impossible for vocatives to occur in reported and indirect speech, and claims that 'the vocative not only conveys a property of the addressee of the utterance, but also implicates that the literal content of the utterance is intended as a message by the speaker to that specific addressee' (pp. 223–4), which is trivially satisfied in direct-speech situations, but leads to a mismatch between the message sent and the message commented on in indirect speech.

An exploration of *Lying at the Semantics-Pragmatics Interface* is undertaken by Jörg Meibauer in an attempt to enrich the debate of what is said vs. what is implicated with detailed linguistic studies within the domain of deceptive language use. On the semantic side, this involves revisiting the lexical semantics of the verb *lying*, the vagueness and subjectivity of predicates of taste, the modal and illocutionary semantics of sentence types, the semantics of (varieties of) quotation, including the currently much-discussed phenomenon of 'mixed' quotation (*Ken said that the project 'is hard to understand'*), as well as interpretative aspects of factivity, *verum focus*, and discourse adverbs. The insight gained this way is instrumental in making a case for the idea that false implicatures and presuppositions form part and parcel of deliberate lying. Meibauer successfully demonstrates the viability of an agenda that 'integrates insights from a number of linguistic, philosophical, and psychological areas' and he achieves a commendable level of clarity and systematicity, not the least through condensed presentation of 'difficult' theories and controversies in tabular form. Mixed quotation is also investigated by Emar Meier in 'Mixed Quotation: The Grammar of Apparently Transparent Opacity' (*S&Prag* 7[2014] 1–67), who proposes a compositional account of the construction that handles its simultaneous opacity (meaning that indexicals are 'not adjusted to integrate into the reporting context, and even speech errors or idiolectal variation is preserved', p. 63), and its fully grammatical incorporation into the reporting sentence.

One of the most popular topics at the semantics–pragmatics interface has been the discussion of the origin, classification, processing, and appropriate modelling of scalar implicatures. Salvatore Pistoia Reda, the editor of the collection *Pragmatics, Semantics and the Case of Scalar Implicatures*, isolates three components of scalar implicatures in his introduction, 'Some Remarks on the Scalar Implicatures Debate' (pp. 1–12), namely, the exhaustivity operator, the generation of scalar alternatives, and the 'avoid-contradiction' procedure. In 'The Roots of (Scalar) Implicature' (pp. 13–39), Laurence R. Horn presents a lucid overview of the historical development of the concept that was referred to by H.P. Grice as implicature, and the subtype of the latter that came to be known as scalar implicature in neo-Gricean frameworks. 'Intermediate Scalar Implicatures' by Uli Sauerland (pp. 72–98) compares pragmatic and semantic accounts of scalar implicatures, which differ, crucially, in their treatment of structures where a scalar item occupies a position in the scope of two quantificational operators. The author shows that in these structures the implicature can take scope above one operator but below the other one, which can only be accounted for by a semantic analysis. Bob van Tiel, 'Embedded Scalars and Typicality' (*JSem* 31[2014] 147–77), is interested in the issue of whether scalar terms in embedded structures like *some* in *All the squares are connected with some of the circles* lead to embedded upper-bounded inferences (*some but not all*). He accounts for the fact that his experimental data concerning the relevant types of sentences point towards different conclusions by arguing for the decisive role of typicality effects.

The contributions to the collection *Psycholinguistic Approaches to Meaning and Understanding across Languages*, edited by Barbara Hemforth, Barbara Mertins, and Cathrine Fabricius-Hansen, present further experimental results at the interfaces of syntax, semantics, and pragmatics. Oliver Bott and Fritz Hamm, 'Cross-Linguistic Variation in the Processing of Aspect' (pp. 83–109), found that coercion of simple form accomplishments into an activity reading by means of *for*-modification leads to processing difficulties in self-paced reading experiments in English, but not in German. They account for the English data by claiming that simple form accomplishments, due to competition with the progressive form in this language, automatically receive a perfective interpretation, which leads to a temporary contradiction with the meaning of the *for*-adverbial, which can only be resolved by a complete revision of their meaning. Bergljot Behrens, Barbara Mertins, Barbara Hemforth, and Cathrine Fabricius-Hansen argue, in 'Understanding Coordinate Clauses: A Cross-Linguistic Experimental Approach' (pp. 23–51), on the basis of experimental data from English, Czech, German, and Norwegian, that there is a preference for temporal overlap interpretations of VP co-ordination in contexts that do not force a consequential or resultative interpretation. These findings contradict the predictions of the 'extended script theory' (Robyn Carlson [2002]), according to which the default interpretation of co-ordination is sequential. The preference for temporal overlap interpretations of co-ordinated VPs is also confirmed by Bergljot Behrens, Cathrine Fabricius-Hansen, and Lyn Frazier in 'Pairing Form and Meaning in English and Norwegian: Conjoined VPs or Conjoined Clauses?' (pp. 53–81), which shows that conjoined clauses are even more strongly biased towards simultaneity than conjoined VPs, and this bias is independent of the telicity of the first conjunct. They also illustrate that whenever the second conjunct expresses an adversative or concessive relation, conjoined clauses are preferred to conjoined VPs, but in the absence of adversativity, conjoined VPs are preferred.

Emmanuel Chemla and Lewis Bott, 'Processing Inferences at the Semantics/ Pragmatics Frontier: Disjunctions and Free Choice' (*Cognition* 130[2014] 380–96) report on four experiments that aimed to test whether treating cases of free choice permission, where conjunctive inferences unexpectedly arise from disjunctive sentences (as in *Mary is allowed to eat an ice-cream or a cake*), as second-order scalar implicature is supported by processing data. Graeme Forbes offers 'A Truth-Conditional Account of Free-Choice Disjunction' (in

Gutzmann et al., eds., pp. 167–86), proposing that the apparent conjunctive interpretation of disjunctive *or* in comparative clauses with *than* as in *A is taller than B or C* is to be accounted for by interpreting the comparative clause as a universally quantified identity statement.

Further contributions addressing issues on the semantics–pragmatics interface include 'The Semantics of Sluicing: Beyond Truth Conditions' (*Language* 90[2014] 887–926) by Scott AnderBois, who offers a new perspective on the relationship between the antecedent clause and the elided clause in cases of sluicing, as in *John ate something, but I don't know what ~~John ate~~*. It argues that sluicing is both sensitive to truth-conditional information and the alternative-evoking or issue-raising capacity of the antecedent clause (in the sense of inquisitive semantics), leading to the result that sluicing is licensed only in case the issue introduced by the question in the elided clause has already been introduced by the antecedent clause. 'A Note on the Projection of Appositives' (in McCready et al., eds., pp. 205–22), by Rick Nouwen, looks at the scopal properties of (nominal) appositives, concentrating on cases where appositives occur in the scope of a matrix operator, contradicting traditional descriptive generalizations. The paper claims that certain restrictive interpretations of appositives anchored by indefinites, such as the preferred reading of *If a professor, a famous one, publishes a book, he will make a lot of money*, are to be accounted for in terms of a flexible attachment approach, but also calls attention to the fact that appositives can express different (e.g. inclusive or restrictive) relations to indefinite anchors. Mark Steedman presents 'The Surface-Compositional Semantics of English Intonation' (*Language* 90[2014] 2–57), which assumes that the primitive components of literal meaning are distinguished along four dimensions, such as contrast, information-structural role, claimed presence in (or absence from) the common ground, and claimed speaker/hearer agency, and that other meanings and functions traditionally attributed to the intonational tunes of English (politeness, deixis, affect, commitment, turn-taking, etc.) arise indirectly.

Computational aspects of interpretation are discussed by Henk Zeevat in *Language Production and Interpretation: Linguistics Meets Cognition*. Among the design goals for any cognitively adequate, full-fledged theory, the author identifies compatibility with incrementality in interpretation and the 'well-established psychological hypothesis that interpreting involves simulated production'. One of the core applications concerns definiteness and definite descriptions, for which it is claimed that a particular kind of 'mental representations' can reconcile classical Russellian approaches, the familiarity, and the functional theory. The format in question consists of a 'graph structure of concepts' meant to enrich classical discourse representations. Zeevat's ambitious project combines structural insights from categorial grammar, form-meaning mappings from OT, and interpretation selection procedures in terms of Bayesian probabilism. The contributions to the collection *Computing Meaning*, volume 4, edited by Harry Bunt, Johan Bos, and Stephen Pulman, are concerned with three interrelated issues within computational semantics, namely, the appropriate form of meaning representations, suggestions for modelling natural language inference, and issues related to the construction of semantically annotated corpora and their application in machine learning of meaning computation.

Cross-linguistic differences in what Sapir called the 'formal organization of meaning' are at the heart of Martina Wiltschko's study *The Universal Structure of Categories: Towards a Formal Typology*. The author argues that in order to reconcile such differences with anything like a 'Universal Base Hypothesis', familiar categories like tense and number have to be taken as instantiations of more abstract notions. According to Wiltschko, classification, point of view, anchoring, and (discourse) linking form a hierarchy of deep categories that conforms with (a larger set of) the phrase structures of the languages of the world. They form a 'universal spine' responsible for the make-up of both verbal and nominal projections. In addition to empirical documentation and formal specification of category and feature systems, attention is paid to methodology, drawing among other things on classical language theory such as that laid out by Humboldt and the Port Royal grammarians. The interdisciplinary collection *Frames and Concept Types*, edited by Gamerschlag et al., investigates frames, 'cognitively founded and formally explored devices of representing knowledge about objects and categories by means of attributes and their values' (p. 3) and their relation to concept types in language, philosophy and science, with particular attention to 'emphasiz[ing] the potential richness of frame representations' (p. 4). Sebastian Löbner's background paper 'Evidence for Frames from Human Language' (pp. 23–67) argues for a 'uniform structure of human cognitive representations of linguistic gestures' (p. 65) in terms of recursive attribute-value structures with added constraints (referred to as 'Barsalou frames', cf. Lawrence W. Barsalou [1992, 1999], Barsalou and Christopher R. Hale [1993]). The author argues that certain aspects of grammatical structure, such as constituency, dependency structure, and grammatical function, are in general agreement with representations in terms of frames, and the latter is particularly favoured for representing grammatical features. Similar arguments are made for representing verb case frames, semantic composition, the meaning of argument terms, and the evolution of a vocabulary of abstract attributes. 'Concept Composition in Frames: Focusing on Genitive Constructions' (pp. 243–66) by Wiebke Petersen and Tanja Osswald illustrates the applicability of frame theory to the analysis of genitive constructions.

7. Lexicography, Lexicology, and Lexical Semantics

This section begins with a discussion of publications in the field of lexicography, and goes on to look at work in lexicology and lexical semantics. In each part, the more general publications related to each sub-field will be discussed first, followed by more specialized publications. Research on current synchronic topics will precede historical studies.

The changing landscape of lexicography is reflected this year by a number of publications about the move away from print, and the new formats and methods available. 'Digital Dictionaries: Introduction', by Michael Hancher (*DJDSNA* 35[2014] 272–4), begins a themed collection of three papers and commentary by noting the decline of printed dictionaries, and drawing a parallel between modern 'pop-up' definitions and medieval interlinear glosses. In 'Lexicography 2.0: Reimagining Dictionaries for the Digital Age' (*DJDSNA* 35[2014] 275–86), Ben Zimmer asks 'What is gained and what is lost in the shift from page to pixel?' (p. 276), and argues that the reinvention of dictionaries for the digital medium offers multiple advantages that can make them better informed, more engaging resources. The starting point for Peter Sokolowski's article, 'The Dictionary as Data' (*DJDSNA* 35[2014] 287–98), is the potential that online dictionaries offer for tracking the words people look up. Sokolowski traces the relationship between social and political history, discusses temporary increases in interest in particular words, and considers what people are trying to find out by looking up very familiar words. David Jost surveys the dictionary digitization projects of the publisher Houghton Mifflin, including their encoding of the *American Heritage Dictionary* from the late 1980s onwards (*DJDSNA* 35[2014] 299–302). Finally, Lisa Berglund briefly sketches the educational uses and possibilities of digital dictionaries for students and other users in 'Reflecting on Digital Dictionaries' (*DJDSNA* 35[2014] 303–6).

More in-depth discussions of the interaction between digital-format dictionaries and their users are included in another special issue on the topic, introduced by Marie-Claude L'Homme and Monique C. Cormier's paper 'Dictionaries and the Digital Revolution: A Focus on Users and Lexical Databases' (*IJL* 27[2014] 331–40), which sketches out current themes in this branch of research and concludes that the new formats will rejuvenate the dictionary. In Robert Lew and Gilles-Maurice de Schryver's 'Dictionary Users in the Digital Revolution' (*IJL* 27[2014] 341–59), the authors discuss different methods of user research and the issues these can address; one of their observations is that the traditional divide between dictionaries and other kinds of reference work is breaking down. Christiane Fellbaum looks specifically at 'Large-Scale Lexicography in the Digital Age' (*IJL* 27[2014] 378–95), arguing that the digital revolution has fundamentally changed the potential size of dictionaries, access to databases for professional and non-professional dictionary creators, and the methods by which dictionaries are created. The article looks particularly at the design and evolution of WordNet but also considers other resources 'based on linguistic hypotheses' (p. 388). Marie-Claude L'Homme addresses the question 'Why Lexical Semantics Is Important for E-Lexicography and Why It Is Equally Important to Hide Its Formal Representations from Users of Dictionaries' (*IJL* 27[2014] 360–77), and details a project to convert two specialized lexical multilingual databases, which were created using lexical frameworks, into usable and user-friendly dictionaries.

Dictionary use and users are also the focus of Carolin Müller-Spitzer's edited volume *Using Online Dictionaries*. This includes a number of papers concerned with German lexicographical resources, which will not be reviewed here, but Parts I, 'Basics', and II, 'General Studies on Online Dictionaries', are of interest although they are not restricted to the lexicography of English. After an introduction (pp. 1–10), in which Müller-Spitzer argues that the dominance of the Internet makes this an appropriate locus for this branch of meta-lexicography, Antje Töpel presents a useful and thorough 'Review of Research into the Use of Electronic Dictionaries' (pp. 13–54), which includes individual summaries of important studies from 1993 to 2012. Alexander Koplenig's discussion of 'Empirical Research into Dictionary Use' (pp. 55–76) details the typical process involved in this kind of study with reference to existing work; this is intended for potential researchers, and will be a helpful guide for anyone new to the field. Koplenig and Müller-Spitzer briefly describe 'The First Two International Studies on Online Dictionaries—Background Information' (pp. 79–84), conducted in German and English, which provide data for the remaining four papers in Part II. In 'Empirical Data on Contexts of Dictionary Use' (pp. 85–126), Müller-Spitzer interrogates the results of a survey and concentrates on 'more offbeat circumstances of dictionary use' (p. 90), including use for word games of various kinds; she considers how usage varies with user, making a distinction between 'experts' and 'recreational users' of different kinds. 'General Issues of Online Dictionary Use', jointly authored by Koplenig and Müller-Spitzer (pp. 127–41), looks at the range of dictionaries that users consult and the devices they most commonly use to access online dictionaries. Amongst other findings, the study shows that online dictionary use has marginally overtaken print, and large-screen devices are prevalent; as with the other chapters discussed here, it would be very interesting to compare the results if the survey were replicated now. Müller-Spitzer and Koplenig go on to examine 'Online Dictionaries: Expectations and Demands' (pp. 143–88), and find that survey respondents do not value highly many of the features that a digital format facilitates, such as multimedia content and adaptability; however, a further experiment showed a learning effect where users' ratings of these features were more positive after being presented with their potential applications. Finally, Koplenig and Müller-Spitzer discuss 'Questions of Design' (pp. 189–204), and find that regardless of native language, background, or age, most users prefer online dictionary entries to be presented in a 'tab view' where information on different aspects of word use is presented in different sections.

'Expanding the Notion of Addressing Relations', by Rufus Gouws (*LexAsia* 1[2014] 159–84), considers the links between lemma and article (in his terminology) in a range of dictionaries including the *American Heritage Dictionary* and the *Oxford Advanced Learner's Dictionary* and *OALD*. Gouws proposes a distinction between primary addressing, what is found in traditional 'condensed' entries, and secondary addressing, where entries are written in full sentences that include the lemma. Henning Bergenholtz and Heidi Agerbo propose that 'There Is No Need for the Terms Polysemy and Homonymy' (*Lexikos* 24[2014] 27–35), in a paper that discusses different possible approaches to multiple meanings. They illustrate different ways of presenting the uses of *pigtail* depending on both semantics and grammar, and conclude that electronic formats make it possible to take a new approach which foregrounds grammatical differences and therefore lists more lemmas. Henning Bergenholtz and Rufus Gouws adopt 'A Lexicographical Perspective on the Classification of Multiword Combinations (*IJL* 27[2014] 1–24), informed by a small number of examples from English, Dutch, and Afrikaans and a Danish database. The authors compare how consistently and transparently these expressions are presented across different general and specialized dictionaries, and propose twenty classes that could be used, with a simplified version of the classification for general dictionaries.

In 'Towards Improved Coverage of Southeast Asian Englishes in the *Oxford English Dictionary*' (*LexAsia* 1[2014] 95–108), Danica Salazar describes the *OED*'s changing editorial policies on the inclusion of non-British words, and shows through a number of examples how Southeast Asian lexis has been presented. *OED3* editors are working to improve coverage but face challenges in collecting and labelling data that represents a range of varieties. Lorna Hiles considers ways to adapt existing controlled defining vocabularies for a different variety of English in 'Towards a Southern African English Defining Vocabulary' (*Lexikos* 24[2014] 178–85); a further possibility is to compile an entirely new vocabulary, though Hiles does not endorse either method as more viable. In 'Statistical Methods for Identifying Local Dialectal Terms from GPS-Tagged Documents' (*DJDSNA* 35[2014] 248–71), Paul Cook, Bo Han, and Timothy Baldwin consider the potential of GPS metadata for corpus lexicography. Using a corpus of tweets, they use statistical techniques to examine the usage of known localisms (identified by using the *Dictionary of Regional American*), and to identify expressions with restricted geographical usage that have not previously been recognized as such.

Learners' dictionaries are the focus of Alice Y.W. Chan's paper 'Using LDOCE5 and COBUILD6 for Meaning Determination and Sentence Construction: What Do Learners Prefer? (*IJL* 27[2014] 25–53). She uses tests and questionnaires to compare the usage habits of nine participants; one suggestion is that learners need to be taught to be more critical in their dictionary use, particularly because of difficulties in identifying the relevant sense of a polysemous word. Anna Dziemianko writes 'On the Presentation and Placement of Collocations in Monolingual Learners' Dictionaries: Insights into Encoding and Retention' (*IJL* 27[2014] 259–79), considering differences between the 'Big Five' dictionaries in a study of 358 Polish learners of English and twelve verb + noun collocations. She concludes that the most effective production and retention is achieved by presenting collocations in bold towards the end of an entry and repeating them in examples. 'The Inclusion of Word Formation in OALD8: The Case of Undefined Run-Ons', by Alenka Vrbinc and Marjeta Vrbinc (*Lexikos* 24[2014] 291–309), examines a sample of entries and details the nature of the undefined run-ons, i.e. related forms listed at the end of entries rather than treated separately, and the kind of difficulties that they present to learners. They advocate a more transparent approach, and note that electronic presentation, which is less space-limited, allows more detailed treatment of this kind of lemma. Bartosz Ptasznik and Robert Lew ask 'Do Menus Provide Added Value to Signposts in Print Monolingual Dictionary Entries? An Application of Linear Mixed-Effects Modelling in Dictionary User Research' (*IJL* 27[2014] 241–58), and look at the value of sense-guiding devices for learners of English. An experiment with 118 participants shows an average 20 per cent reduction in access time when signposts are used, but less of an advantage in selecting relevant senses, while combining signposts with menus does not offer additional benefits.

As always, this year there has been a great deal of work on bilingual and multilingual lexicography, and a few examples will be included here. Pádraig Ó Mianáin and Cathal Convery report on the *New English–Irish Dictionary* (*DJDSNA* 35[2014] 318–33), which will be published in print in 2016. The authors set out the lexicographical and socio-historical context for the work and detail its aims and content, before concluding that it is a completely original dictionary that 'has heralded a new dawn for Irish lexicography' (p. 332). In 'Community Engagement in the Revised Chamorro–English Dictionary' (*DJDSNA* 35[2014] 308–17), Sandra Chung and Elizabeth Diaz Rechebei describe ongoing efforts by a group of speakers to preserve their minority language by revising its dictionary; this project is led by a small team of lexicographers but involves non-experts in its design and production. D.J. Prinsloo gives an account of 'Lexicographical Treatment of Kinship Terms in an English/Sedepi–Setswana–Sesotho Dictionary with an Amalgamated Lemmalist' (*Lexikos* 24[2014] 272–90), and concludes that, while amalgamated dictionaries have great potential for African languages, this particular domain challenges lexicographers at the macro- and micro-structural levels. M.A. Petrova's paper 'The Compreno Semantic Model: The Universality Problem' (*IJL* 27[2014] 105–29) looks at data from a range of languages in a multilingual database, and considers the issues and challenges of a semantic model which can accommodate all of these languages.

Specialized dictionaries have also been the focus of some attention, notably Pedro A. Fuertes-Olivera and Sven Tarp's very detailed *Theory and Practice of Specialised Online Dictionaries: Lexicography Versus Terminography*. This begins by asserting that specialized dictionaries merit more attention and a higher status than they have sometimes been afforded, particularly since (according to one study) in 2008–9 they constituted around three-quarters of lexicographical output. In a series of ten chapters, the authors describe and reflect on the theory, practice, and context of this branch of lexicography, devoting a significant portion of the volume to online dictionaries and their particular challenges, and particularly focusing on the Function Theory of Lexicography. Chapter 7 presents 'A Critical View of Terminography', and notes that this varies in different traditions and that it has not excited much interest among native English speakers. Like the rest of the book, this chapter surveys the existing literature in a thorough and comprehensive way. Chapter 8 reviews eighteen online dictionaries of various languages, including monolingual dictionaries such as the *Cambridge Business English Dictionary* and cross-language resources like the *United Nations Multilingual Terminology Database*. The conclusion to the volume advocates collaboration between subject experts and lexicographers, and recognition that specialized lexicography is on a continuum with other branches of lexicography.

Michele F. van der Merwe and Pedro A. Fuertes-Olivera present a study of 'The Influence of the User Needs Paradigm in Specialised Lexicography: Some Reflections in Connection with Two South African Wine Dictionaries' (*IbéricaR* 27[2014] 77–96), comparing dictionaries published forty years apart and the changing needs of their users. The authors propose that subject field labels like those in the 2012 dictionary are particularly valuable for non-experts using specialized dictionaries, and are easier to devise for these works than the word sketches which provide a foundation for non-specialized dictionaries. Sandro Nielsen explores 'Example Sentences in Bilingual Specialised Dictionaries Assisting Communication in a Foreign Language' (*Lexikos* 24[2014] 198–213), giving a thorough survey of the existing literature on the topic and (real and imagined) examples of the different approaches that have been adopted, and comments that online dictionaries offer additional possibilities for access to example sentences.

Shifting the focus to work with a historical perspective, Vincent McCarren's suggestion that OE glosses were a source for an English–Latin bilingual dictionary is questioned by John Considine in 'Old English Glossaries and the *Medulla Grammatice*' (*N&Q* 61[2014] 478–80); he concludes that there is insufficient evidence to prove this kind of relationship. Gabriele Stein's *Sir Thomas Elyot as Lexicographer* looks in detail at the work of an important figure of the sixteenth century, who produced an early Latin–English dictionary as well as several other prose works; his translations and treatises are still well known today, and the dictionary can be seen as influential in English lexicographical history. His reputation as a linguistic innovator is supported by *OED* evidence indicating that he introduced new grammatical terminology. Stein suggests that Elyot's dictionary has not had the scholarly attention it deserves because it is such a complex work, bringing together 'the vast knowledge of the classical world and the scientific thinking of his own day, which he had acquired through his reading and studies, and which he made accessible for his countrymen by using their common tongue, English' (p. 17). The study looks at the historical and linguistic context of Elyot's work, but the main part is devoted to a detailed examination of the dictionary itself, including word list and editorial principles, Elyot's awareness of its readership and the stylistic implications of this, attention to regional variation, and Elyot's approach to headwords, which is compared to that of his predecessors. Chapter 9, 'Elyot's Achievement as a Lexicographer', examines the nature of the *OED* first attestations attributed to Elyot, which show a mixture of borrowings, new formations, and words which must have already existed in the language. In the final chapter, Stein assesses Elyot's impact on subsequent lexicographers, which seems considerable. This is a meticulous study which is useful both in its treatment of Elyot's work and in its critical examination of *OED* evidence.

A very significant work which should be noted here even though it does not deal exclusively with English lexicography is John Considine's study of *Academy Dictionaries 1600–1800*. This presents a unified account of the 'academy tradition' that emerged in Europe in the Renaissance (though Considine is cautious about the use of that phrase (p. 5)), with detailed treatment of the context in which academy dictionaries emerged, including the *Dictionnaire de l'Académie française* and the *Fruchtbringende Gesellschaft*. Most relevant for this publication are the chapters that focus on the period leading up to the publication of Johnson's *Dictionary of the English Language*, which discuss the individuals and societies with interests in such a project, and lead on to an examination of Johnson's work itself. Considine argues that 'Johnson's *Dictionary* towered above works like [Nathan] Bailey's, and this was, first and foremost, because of its place in the academy tradition' (p. 122), and he goes on demonstrate this by comparing Johnson's intentions and practices with those of contemporaries in England and around Europe. The book ends with a consideration of lexicographical projects published or under way in the late eighteenth century, including the Russian dictionary *Slovar' Akademii Rossijskoj*. This is an enormously useful volume which is both erudite and readable, and it is likely to be a standard work in the field for some time to come. The relationship between Johnson's lexicographical work and other writing is explored in Robert DeMaria Jr.'s paper 'Johnson's Editorial Lexicography' (*DJDSNA* 35[2014] 146–61). DeMaria argues that the glosses Johnson includes in editions of works by Thomas Browne and Roger Ascham represent 'hidden acts of lexicography' (p. 146), and these glosses are collected together and presented as addenda to the *Dictionary*.

In 'Linguistics, Lexicography, and the "Early Modern"' (*JEMCS* 14:ii[2014] 94–9), Hannah Crawforth explores the way in which concerns about the relationship between past and present provoked and shaped early English lexicography, and argues that this suggests 'an important pre-history to our own debates about periodization and the concept of the "early modern" that lies within the period itself' (p. 94). A fascinating paper that explores a different aspect of the same period is Lindsay Rose Russell's examination of the nature of women readers in 'Before Ladies and Gentlewomen Were Unskillful: Honorific Invocations of Learned Women in Early Modern Bilingual Dictionaries' (*DJDSNA* 35[2014] 93–120). The involvement of women in some of the lexicographical projects of the period, specifically the bilingual dictionaries that are the focus of this paper, problematizes their representation by many dictionary writers, for example Robert Cawdrey's conflation of 'Ladies, Gentlewomen and any other unskilfull persons' in the title of the *Table Alphabeticall*. John Considine looks at the work of two lexicographers who appear to have independently created models for later historical dictionaries in 'John Jamieson, Franz Passow, and the Double Invention of Lexicography on Historical Principles' (*JHI* 75[2014] 261–81). Neither man seems to have been aware of making a significant methodological breakthrough, perhaps partly because their work grew out of a particular literary and cultural context, but both created milestones in historical lexicography. Ammon Shea revisits the question of Shakespeare's linguistic innovativeness in 'A Sure Uncertainty: On Some Difficulties Using *OED* Online Data to Establish Shakespearian Coinages' (*DJDSNA* 35[2014] 121–45). The number proposed has fallen as new evidence has become available and as different methodologies have been employed; Shea points out that a definitive figure based on *OED* is highly problematic, but equally significant is the difficulty of what it means to invent a word.

John Considine's short paper 'The Deathbed of Herbert Coleridge' (*N&Q* 61[2014] 90–2) uses contemporary sources to reassess the final months of the first editor of *OED*, and concludes that received accounts are not accurate, though Coleridge does appear to have worked on a range of academic projects until the very end of his life. Traci Nagle focuses on a slightly later period of *OED* history in 'The Visible and Invisible Influence of Yule's *Hobson-Jobson* on Murray's *Oxford English Dictionary*' (*IJL* 27[2014] 280–308), and concludes that between 50 and 75 per cent of *OED* entries for South Asian words use material from *Hobson-Jobson*, though without acknowledgement in the early part of the *OED*. In later parts, collaboration between the editors was explicitly signalled by Murray, and letters provide evidence of their discussions.

Michael Adams describes the founding of a recent learned society with its own dictionary in 'The Dictionary Society of North America: A History of the Early Years (Part I)' (*DJDSNA* 35[2014] 1–35). As well as giving a detailed account of the naming of the society and its journal, Adams describes the lexicographical work that took place in the 1960s and 1970s and the various conferences and meetings that led to its founding and early evolution. David Jost traces the varied trends and themes in the articles that make up 'Thirty-Four Years of *Dictionaries*' (*DJDSNA* 35[2014] 36–92), a summary which includes a full bibliography of work published in the journal during this period.

David Scott-Macnab and Kelly-Anne Gilbertson examine a treatise on equine medicine that attests words previously unrecorded in *OED* and *MED*, as well as new senses and antedatings, in 'Unrecorded Middle English Lexical Items in the Fifteenth Century Treatise *Medicines for Horses*: A Preliminary Study' (*N&Q* 61[2014] 344–9). The main part of this article is an annotated wordlist which includes detailed notes on context and use. Javier Ruano-García examines the contribution of a glossary that has previously received little attention in 'Cumbrian Lexis in the *English Dialect Dictionary*: William Nicolson's *Glossarium Brigantinum* (1677) in Focus' (*DJDSNA* 35[2014] 162–86). This work was used by Joseph Wright to illustrate the use of dialect words from both Cumbria and Westmorland, and in a large proportion of cases provided the only evidence for these words.

Turning to lexical semantics, a particularly important and practical publication is *Corpus Methods for Semantics: Quantitative Studies in Polysemy and Synonymy*, edited by Dylan Glynn and Justyna Robinson. The editors note in the opening outline that the aim of the volume is to encourage 'constructive communication' (p. 1) between the methodologies of linguists using corpus data and more traditional approaches involving introspection, and is intended to have both didactic and scientific functions. Section I presents a collection of studies on English and other languages that employ state-of-the-art techniques of corpus analysis, with a focus on cognitive semantics; in Section II, statistical techniques and their uses are described and explained by experts in the field, with chapters on R, frequency tables, collostructional analysis, cluster analysis, correspondence analysis, and logistic regression. The latter will not be discussed further here, but these are clear, well-judged guides that promise to become invaluable to many in the field who lack familiarity or confidence with these approaches. Several papers in Section I are relevant here. Dylan Glynn begins with a discussion of 'Polysemy and Synonymy: Cognitive Theory and Corpus Method' (pp. 7–38), which surveys research in the cognitive semantic tradition and argues that quantitative techniques represent a necessary and logical step forward, one that follows on from introspection-based radial network studies and prototype semantics. In 'Rethinking Constructional Polysemy: The Case of the English Conative Construction' (pp. 61–85), Florent Perek examines a construction which, unlike many others, does not appear to attract a particular kind of verb. He employs a variant of collexeme analysis which focuses on verbs by semantic class, and contends that his findings have implications for the kind of generalizations that can be made about the polysemy of this construction and others. Justyna Robinson discusses the sociolinguistic distribution of the meanings of polysemous adjectives including *awesome*, *gay*, and *wicked* in 'Quantifying Polysemy in Cognitive Sociolinguistics' (pp. 87–115), using survey data from seventy-two speakers, which is analysed via hierarchical agglomerative clustering, decision tree analysis and logistic regression analysis. Her results provide convincing evidence for the 'social grounding of polysemous conceptualisations' (p. 111), and for the marrying of these approaches. Similar interests inform Dylan Glynn's paper 'The Many Uses of *Run*: Corpus Methods and Socio-Cognitive Semantics' (pp. 117–44), which aims to refine the theory, methods, and results of an earlier paper by Stefan Gries by applying a multifactorial usage-feature analysis to corpus data for the verb *run*; the study makes a case for the impact of sociolinguistic factors on semasiological structure. Guillaume Desagulier looks at the conceptual structure of four degree modifiers, and 'attraction' between them, in 'Visualizing Distances in a Set of Near-Synonyms: *Rather*, *Quite*, *Fairly* and *Pretty*' (pp. 145–78). Drawing on several statistical methods and using data from COCA as the basis for collostructional analysis, Desagulier examines the fine semantic differences between these lexemes and the entrenchment of the constructions in which they occur. Sandra C. Deshors and Stefan Th. Gries make 'A Case for the Multifactorial Assessment of Learner Language: The Uses of *May* and *Can* in French–English Interlanguage' (pp. 179–204) by analysing the distribution of morphosyntactic and semantic features with a hierarchical cluster analysis and a logistic regression. Their study suggests that learners build up relatively coherent mental categories which inform their choice of one or other of these verbs but do not always lead to a 'correct' choice. Finally, 'A Diachronic Corpus-Based Multivariate Analysis of "I Think *That*" vs. "I Think Zero"' is presented by Christopher Shank, Koen Pleveots, and Hubert Cuyckens (pp. 279–303), based on spoken and written corpus data from 1560 to 2012; the Corpus of English Dialogues and the Old Bailey Corpus are used to approximate earlier speech. A logistic regression analysis suggests a decrease in zero complementation over time, rather than the increase indicated by previous research. A separate article which is also valuable to lexicographers and lexicologists interested in harnessing (relatively) new technology for research is 'Sketch Engine: Ten Years On' by Adam Kilgarriff, Vít Baisa, Jan Bušta, Miloš Jakubíček, Vojtěch Kovář, Jan Michelfeit, Pavel Rychlý, and Vít Suchomel (*LexAsia* 1[2014] 7–36). This paper reviews the functions, users, and approaches of this ten-year-old corpus tool, traces its revisions and input corpora, and surveys other similar resources; it shows clearly why Sketch Engine is so important in lexicographical research, and why Adam Kilgarriff is such a very great loss to the discipline.

Worth mentioning briefly here although it does not limit its focus to English is Cliff Goddard and Anna Wierzbicka's book *Words and Meaning: Lexical Semantics across Domains, Languages and Cultures*. This builds on the authors' previous work in Natural Semantics Metalanguage (NSM), and examines a number of different categories and domains including words for physical qualities (including *sweet* and *rough*), colour, and pain, and the semantics of proverbs. The first chapter presents a survey of research in semantics and then sets out the principles and methodology of NSM. Subsequent chapters compare the terms found in two or more languages, including English, Russian, Malay, and Polish. Chapter 7 looks solely at English and specifically speech-act verbs, which appear to be more numerous in English than other European languages, and concludes that this large repertoire results from the cultural prominence of writing. Chapter 9 considers the distinction between abstract and concrete nouns and proposes that nouns in the two groups have different semantic structures; this discussion looks particularly interesting for scholars in the field. This is an impressive and thought-provoking book which draws from a very wide range of sources, both very recent and much more established (and in some cases, relatively little-known and neglected). It is unlikely to change anyone's mind about NSM, but even for critics this is a worthwhile read. One study this year which employs NSM is Sandy Habib's 'Dying in the Cause of God: The Semantics of the Christian and Muslim Concepts of Martyr' (*AUJL* 34[2014] 388–98). Habib explicates each in terms of semantic primes and molecules, and notes a fairly high level of similarity between the two concepts, though there is a difference in whether the referent is a combatant or not. Another volume which looks across cultures and languages to explore the relationship between words and concepts is the collection *Emotional Lexicons: Continuity and Change in the Vocabulary of Feeling 1700–2000*, by Ute Frevert, Christian Bailey, Pascal Eitler, Benno Gammerl, Bettina Hitzer, Margrit Perna, Monique Scheer, Anne Schmidt, and Nina Verheyen. It explores one area of vocabulary as represented in German, French, and English encyclopedias. Despite its title, much of the volume focuses on cultural rather than linguistic history, but with more attention to language than is often the case; it may therefore be of interest to linguists interested in terms for emotions in modern times.

A very different perspective is offered by Roy Harris and Christopher Hutton's *Definition in Theory and Practice: Language, Lexicography and the Law*. Harris and Hutton survey the practices and theories of definition that have been employed in the present and the past, and compare lexicographical and legal approaches; they contend that integrating ideas from the two disciplines is valuable, not least because the law is unusual in the way it 'relies overtly upon the possibility of determining verbal meanings' and often refers to dictionaries. They divide their study into three sections. Part I, 'Definition and Theory', is a survey of definition in Western thought, discussing stipulative definition, 'real' definition, which aims to bypass words in favour of concepts, and ostensive definition; chapter 2 also considers 'common usage'. Part II, 'Definition and the Dictionary', looks at the intentions and practices of Johnson and editors of the *OED* and the definitional types that are used in lexicography, and compares definitions and uses of words as diverse as *liberty* and *mahogany*. Part III moves on to 'Definition and the Law', noting the surprising lack of attention to questions of definition; the three chapters present a number of legal cases and the ways in which these dealt with questions of meaning, and look at the question of whether the law can be considered a science. In the concluding chapter, 'Definition, Indeterminacy and Reference', the authors reject pessimistic views that 'see attempts at definition as doomed in advance to failure', and argue for an integrationist approach that privileges first-order linguistic experience.

Julie Coleman's edited volume *Global English Slang: Methodologies and Perspectives* is a collection of eighteen papers on current use by a wide range of speaker groups around the world. These are preceded by an introduction which interrogates the notion of slang itself. As Coleman notes, 'the definition of slang remains unstable to the point that a dozen slang experts happily spent three days circling around this very issue [at the workshop which led to the volume]' (p. 2). A theme of the book is the notion that slang is a product of context and function rather than of any characteristic linguistic features. The papers are presented in four sections. Part I describes 'Contemporary Slang in the United States and England', and includes studies of the slang of hip-hop, inner-city New York, American college students, University of Leicester students, multicultural London, and 'the new canting crew', i.e. English prison inmates and those involved in criminal activities. Like many other papers, the latter considers the origins of a number of expressions, and makes some observations about media attention to this kind of slang. Part II has a broader geographical range, discussing 'Slang in Other English-Speaking Countries', namely Australia, New Zealand, Scotland, Jamaica, and India. Part III looks at 'English Influence on the Slang of Other Languages', and these are Norwegian (specifically Norwegian teenagers), Italian, and Japanese. Finally, Part IV, 'Slang and the Internet', looks at slang in 'new media' including Usenet and Twitter, Urban Dictionary, and gestural slang, and finally considers 'Global English Slang in the Era of Big Data'. A strength of the volume is its varying scope: the inclusion of papers on both very large regional areas and small, narrowly defined groups affords readers some interesting comparisons. The large number of examples that illustrate each chapter make this an informative point of reference for scholars in the field and non-experts, and it looks likely to be a well-used and valued resource.

At the intersection between etymology and lexicology is Philip Durkin's monograph *Borrowed Words: A History of Loanwords in English*. This is an enormously impressive piece of scholarship built on Durkin's research as *OED* deputy chief editor, which incorporates detailed close analysis of individual word histories throughout. Perhaps more importantly, though, it steps back from this data to survey the language in different periods, and explore the impact of borrowing in a methodologically sophisticated way. Part I details the approach of the study, and the nature and challenges of the data. Durkin interrogates the notion of 'the vocabulary of English' and its difficulties: there are lexical differences between regional varieties, but just as significant is variation between the active and passive vocabularies of individual speakers. Because of these differences, 'when we speak about the vocabulary (or lexis) of a language, it can be useful to think of a (not very precisely defined) common core of basic vocabulary' (p. 19). Durkin uses corpora and basic-meaning lists to identify this 'common core', examining the 1,000 and 100 most frequent words in English and considering the proportion of loanwords from different sources. The main part of the book is divided by period and input language, looking first, in Parts II to IV, at OE (and proto-OE) and languages with which it had contact; as in the following sections, there is detailed discussion of the historical context and motivations for borrowing, and the relationship between language change and external history. Part V moves on to ME, focusing on borrowing from Latin and French and the nature of contact between the three languages. Part VI explores the period from 1500 onwards, and moves from Latin and French loanwords to borrowing from a diverse range of European and non-European languages. Finally, Durkin looks at the long-term effects of borrowing and presents general conclusions and a summary of each period. The volume builds on existing research in linguistics and beyond to present an insightful account of the process of borrowing and its effects on English; its careful and transparent handling of the evidence and accessible presentation make it essential for anyone working in this field (more information can be found in Section 1 above).

Sara M. Pons-Sanz's *The Language of Early English Literature: From Caedmon to Milton* is essentially a stylistics textbook, but one which unusually includes chapters on semantics, borrowing, and word-formation (as a means of lexical expansion). Each of these considers the relationship between lexis and its historical and textual context, introduces the topic in a way that makes an eloquent case for its importance to stylistic study, and does not assume detailed linguistic knowledge. The discussion of wordplay in the semantics chapter is a particularly welcome addition to a topic that is relatively under-researched. The historical range of the volume, and the way in which it balances simple, engaging explanation with sophisticated analysis make it a valuable work for students of both literature and linguistics. Another publication at the interface between stylistics and lexicology is 'A Case Analysis of Lexical Features in English Broadsheets and Tabloids', by Yingxia Li, Dongyu Zhang, and Wanyi Du (*IJEL* 4:iv[2014] 115–22). This compares the lexical choices in tabloids and broadsheets from both the US and UK, and finds that fuzzy words are used more frequently in broadsheets, but more numbers can be found in tabloids.

Javier Calle-Martín writes 'On the History of the Intensifier *Wonder* in English' (*AUJL* 34[2014] 399–419), tracing the development of the adverb across the history of the language from OE onwards. The study considers collocational patterns and attitudinal features, and is based on data from a large number of corpora, painstakingly and thoughtfully assembled; it also makes illuminating comparisons with other word histories. The history and treatment of an Anglo-Indian expression which was used in the title of an influential dictionary is the focus for James Lambert's 'A Much Tortured Expression: A New Look at "Hobson-Jobson"' (*IJL* 27[2014] 54–88). The account of this expression given by the editors was not supported by evidence in the dictionary itself and is not wholly accurate; Lambert reassesses the evidence, and presents senses and uses not recorded previously. William Sayers looks beyond the *OED* account and considers the nature of the referents in an eModE phrase which is now obsolete, 'Like Harp and Harrow' (*N&Q* 61[2014] 482–3).

At the more popular end of the market is Jonathon Green's well-informed and entertaining volume *Language! 500 Years of the Vulgar Tongue*. In his conclusion, Green writes that 'Slang is a language of themes' (p. 385), and this is the principle by which the book is organized: most chapters explore a particular area of slang lexis, including the vocabulary of crime and punishment (chapter 4) and gayspeak (chapter 13), while others focus on the slang of a particular region such as Australia (chapter 8) or London (chapter 10). Green weaves examples into a discussion of linguistic and social history which also tells the story of slang lexicography, pausing specifically to describe nineteenth-century slang dictionaries and their writers in chapter 12. Like his other publications, this is a fascinating and highly readable account which has appeal for both linguists and non-linguists. Also published this year is Green's memoir *Odd Job Man: Some Confessions of a Slang Lexicographer*, in which he reflects on his career and its place in the history of slang lexicography. This is a much more personal book, but again it features a colourful range of historical figures and events, and refers to many of the slang words and phrases that Green has collected and catalogued in his career to date. Finally, *Words in Time and Place: Exploring Language through the Historical Thesaurus of the Oxford English Dictionary*, by David Crystal, provides an accessible entrance point for general readers. Fifteen chapters present simplified *HTOED* extracts with commentary on each entry, each with a brief introduction; the sections chosen range from words for 'nose', 'fool', or 'prostitute', to terms of endearment, to oaths and exclamations. The general introduction to the volume is a helpful explanation of how the thesaurus classification works and how the data is presented in the version integrated into the *OED Online*, and is a very gentle beginning for anyone new to *HTOED*.

8. Onomastics

Last year's publications in the field of onomastics were focused on power; this year's selection of publications is similarly thematic. Much of the work cited below concentrates on influence. Of the books and articles published, researchers tended to investigate the formation of names by powerful individuals, such as Christopher Columbus, or they concentrated on the role that names play in various environments (for instance that of a prison yard), or on the concept that names shape identities, like minority names in university settings. Although the studies published in 2014 were sparse, they indicate a profound shift in onomastics. Based on the research mentioned here, it is clear that onomastics will continue to combine multiple academic fields to explore the relationship between names, their creators, and their evolution. It will be interesting to see what future onomastic studies will bring us, what new critical thought will arise with respect to names and their role in our society.

It is a pleasure to announce an important contribution to the formation of names entitled *The Grammar of Names in Anglo-Saxon England: The Linguistics and Culture of the Old English Onomasticon*. Fran Colman reports on the significance between onomastics and the onomasticon in arguing that names as a category, including the lexical parts they are composed of, must be studied by way of the onomasticon. The onomasticon, which includes structural information about the formation of lexical items, paints a fuller picture of their etymology, semantics, and grammatical behaviour. Colman also investigates how names function within OE and compares them with Germanic and non-Germanic naming systems. The book comprises three parts: an introduction and two sections entitled 'On Names' and 'Towards the Old English Onomasticon'. The introduction offers insight into why the onomasticon plays a different and unique role from the study of onomastics alone. Further, it provides information on names' sources and gender. 'On Names' contextualizes names as words and not as nouns. Specifically, the researcher includes chapters entitled 'Names as Words', 'Names Are Not Nouns', and 'A Name Is a Name.' Further chapters in the second part are concerned with 'Old English Personal Name Formation', 'General Lexical Formation', 'Structures of Old English Personal Names', 'On the Role of the Paradigm as a Marker of Lexical-Item Formation', and 'An Old English Onomasticon'. For example, the chapter discussing lexical formation goes into great detail about the differences between lexicon formation and word formation, derivational morphology, and stress assignment, among others. Colman notes that these changes or reductions in word structures have implications even for the present-day English lexicon, which may include 'either *gunwale* or *gunnel*' (p. 189). This thorough exploration of personal names is thought-provoking in its use of the onomasticon and is a nice addition to any onomastics library (for information on the morphosyntactic relevance of this study for OE, see Section 5 above)

Another full-length study published in the field of onomastics is *Christopher Columbus's Naming in the Diarios of the Four Voyages (1492–1504)* written by Evelina Gužauskytė. This book investigates the naming practices used by Christopher Columbus in his travels to the Caribbean Basin. Despite popular belief, Gužauskytė suggests that Columbus's naming practices were not a result of his pride, or of prejudices he may have had. The names chosen by Columbus are, instead, a reflection of the complexities within the European world, the Basin's inhabitants, nature in the area, and the geographical location. The book is divided into six chapters, plus an introduction, conclusion, and a final appendix. The introduction is fairly lengthy; it begins with an interesting account about the 'Capitalaciones de Santa Fe', otherwise known as the contract between the Spanish Crown and Columbus. Gužauskytė notes that the original contract did not mention place names and that this may have served several purposes, including diplomacy, politics, and secrecy. The book continues with chapters entitled ' "Named Incorrectly": The Geographic and Symbolic Functions of Columbian Place Names', 'Words and the World: The Known Corpus of Columbian Place Names', ' "Y Saber Dellos Los Secretos de la Terra": Taino Typonymy and Columbian Naming', 'Heavenly Bodies and Metallurgy in Columbian Typonymy', 'Iguana and Christ', and 'Infernal Imagery: Spirituality and Cosmology in the Final Two Voyages'. On the basis of the title, some may wonder if being a fluent Spanish speaker is necessary for reading this book. While Spanish names are indeed found in it, the book serves as a key text in the onomastic understanding of naming procedures in the Caribbean Basin. The most interesting part of the study is to be found in the appendix, which offers 'A Comprehensive List of Columbian Place Names'. The entries in this list provide a description of the meaning of the place names and when or where they were first noted. The list of nearly thirty pages of place-name entries follows the order in which they were first noted by Columbus in the *diarios*. Remaining names are listed on the basis of the numerous primary sources that Gužauskytė consulted. Gužauskytė even takes the trouble to include alternative spellings and dates first mentioned, where this information is available. In addition, translations are provided for the names.

Finally, a book released in 2014 on the study of place names is *Indigenous and Minority Placenames: Australian and International Perspectives*, edited by Ian D. Clark, Luise Hercus, and Laura Kostanski. This book is the third volume in the series; its focus is on the investigation of place names in Australia, with some toponymic research in other countries such as Canada, Finland, South Africa, New Zealand, and Norway. As with the earlier volumes, the book contains various papers written by different authors, each of which utilizes various disciplines such as anthropology, geography, history, and, of course, linguistics. The vast majority of papers are the product of a conference on place names which took place at the University of Ballarat in 2007. The volume begins with an introduction containing a summary of all the papers included. Each summary includes the general idea, a couple of illustrative examples from the text, and shows where the paper fits into the present context of toponymic studies. Unfortunately, there is no organization or grouping of papers into coherent sections. The individual papers present research on various place names including, but not limited to, the etymologies of place names in Gundungurra and New South Wales, language dissemination via place names, and the use of these names within the language. One of the more interesting chapters is the one entitled 'Doing Things with Toponyms: The Pragmatics of Placenames in Western Arnhem Land' by Murray Garde, who claims that place names are a dense part of the language system within aboriginal cultures that manifest themselves in the frequent use of toponyms in conversation. Garde specifically uses an indexical approach to investigate the pragmatic use of place names in the Bininj Gunwok dialect. The researcher shows that these names are used pragmatically for various roles including the making of mental maps. The volume as a whole should be an interesting read for those interested in the progression of current onomastic research.

In this year's scholarly articles, onomasts investigated several different areas of naming including place names, personal names, and nicknames. Richard Coates attempts to reconcile different interpretations concerning the etymology and meaning of the place name Oundle in 'Oundle, Northamptonshire' (*JEPNS* 46[2014] 40–4). Coates first notes that Oundle is the death-place of both St Wilfrid and St Cett as well as the burial-place of Wulfstan of York, the archbishop. The article continues by showing the various pre-Conquest forms of the name, including 'Undalum', 'undelum', and 'Undele'. Next, Coates briefly summarizes common views of the name from Ekwall, Cox, and Watts, who each argue that the name is tribal. Coates contests that it is unlikely for an 'adjective which is itself derived from a noun then to be morphologically "re-equipped" as a tribal name' (p. 41). Two alternatives are then proposed for the meaning of the original form. The first is that the name is one of topographical importance. The second, and admittedly more plausible, alternative is that the name is a compound noun comprising two elements that together could mean 'shares of divisions made by grant' (p. 42). Even though the article is short, it covers much ground about competing theories of the name's background and meaning and is an excellent representation of onomastic work at its core.

Just as important as the etymologies of place names is the changing and replacing of toponyms. Within onomastics the study of names as commodities and as nationalistic symbols tend to be separated. It is interesting, therefore, that Chris W. Post and Derek H. Alderman combine these two areas of study in '"Wiping New Berlin off the Map": Political Economy and the De-Germanisation of the Toponymic Landscape in First World War USA' (*Area* 46[2014] 83–91). This research focuses on the name of the town New Berlin, Ohio, which was changed to North Canton, Ohio, during the First World War. The onomasts posit that the name change was not simply to de-Germanize the town, as many would suspect. Instead it was a combination of symbolic capital, symbolic annihilation, and rescaling of economic linkages. W.H. Hoover and Hoover Suction Sweeper, two businesses located in the town of New Berlin, viewed the place name as a liability (in terms of profits, customers, and advertisers lost) to their businesses due to its association with Germany. In addition, the name change served as an 'erasure of racial and ethnic histories and identities for the purpose of constructing and selling an exclusive American landscape narrative in which certain social groups are made to appear not to belong or matter' (p. 89). Finally, the renaming of the town allowed for new scalar configurations and associations to be made between the new name North Canton and a nearby city Canton, which was a mecca for large business production. Post and Alderman claim that the name change of New Berlin was not merely a result of a growing nationalistic sentiment against Germany in the US but was also contextualized within a 'wider political economy of local development and employment' (p. 90).

The onomasts in the above-mentioned article demonstrate that place names can represent authority in multiple facets; in a similar way personal names can play a significant role in the shaping and maintaining of one's identity. In an interesting study about the reading of names during convocation ceremonies— 'Reading and Righting the Names at a Convocation Ceremony: Influences of Linguistic Ideologies on Name Usage in an Institutional Interaction' (*Names* 62[2014] 37–48)—Karen Pennesi suggests that the reading and correcting of names is influenced by linguistic ideologies and that this procedure mirrors the use of names in international institutions. In a pilot study, the researcher compared audio recordings of pronunciations of name cards with handwritten notations from two convocation ceremonies in June 2012. The convocations took place at Western University, a Canadian university with a student population of nearly 30,000. A sizeable percentage of these students are international students from about 100 countries. Given the cultural diversity of the students, it is no surprise that a large number of graduating students' names were considered 'unfamiliar' to the Anglo-Canadian orators. In addition, the researcher analysed interviews with four faculty members/orators, five administrative staff, and twenty-one students prior to the convocations. The onomast works from the assumption that the convocation should be seen as a speech event, one which marks the transition from being a student to being a graduate. The speaking of the name is important to several different interlocutors, including the orator, the graduate, the graduate's family, the other convocation personnel, and other spectators. Each of these different groups of people needs to be satisfied by the reading and 'righting' of the graduate's name in order for the speech event to be considered successful. The researcher briefly reviews the protocol for the graduation ceremony indicating that the graduates themselves write comments on the notecards that have their names. From that point, the graduate hands the card to the chief orator, who whispers a proposed pronunciation of the name to the graduate, receives approval from the graduate, and then hands the card to the orator at the microphone, who finally pronounces the graduate's name. In connection with this procedure, it is important for Pennesi to note the competing linguistic ideologies of names. On the one hand, names are considered words that must be pronounced correctly. On the other, names are persons serving a role in the cultural or multicultural identity of the graduate. Pennesi argues that 'subjective experiences play an important role in the development of linguistic ideologies, and these ideologies influence interactions' (p. 43). More simply put, the negotiation of identities between those who are named and those who are saying the name is influenced by the competing linguistic ideologies.

Similarly, nicknames can influence individual identity. The notion that personal names and nicknames have power is not new. However, nicknames in a prison yard may have significantly different power, and this power many manifest itself in different ways. Nicknames in prison yards have been studied before, but Sharon Black, Brad Wilcox, and Brad Platt investigated this phenomenon in a unique way in 'Nicknames in Prison: Meaning and Manipulation in Inmate Monikers' (*Names* 62[2014] 127–36). Black and Wilcox took the suggestion of Holland (cf. *YWES* 68[1990]) of collaborating with a prisoner, in this case Platt, an Arizona State Prison inmate. From this relationship, they were able to collect observations and informal interviews regarding the power of nicknames. Much of the article presents anecdotal evidence for pre-existing research. For example, the use of nicknames to unify a group had already been presented by Holland; however, Platt's observations and informal interviews added real-life testimony to what most researchers do not have access to. Platt's authority in and familiarity with Arizona State Prison allowed for other prisoners to speak more freely in presenting their experiences. Similarly, evidence here substantiated claims that nicknames are a sign of friendship or acceptance, a sign of unacceptance, or a reflection of individuality. They can also be used as a covert form of in-group communication where members who are not in the group are excluded from the conversation based on their lack of nickname awareness. The origin of individual nicknames in prison society was also unique. Nicknames are derived from inmate appearance, personality traits and preferences, and background and experience. As the authors put it, 'the prison yard is a microcosm of humanity under pressure and stress. Considering the phenomenon of prison nicknames can give us all more understanding of the people and conditions they represent' (p. 135).

Just as nicknames serve various purposes in the prison yard setting, monikers also have multiple functions for those outside the prison system. In 'The Adoption of Non-Heritage Names among Chinese Mainlanders' (*Names* 62[2014] 65–75), Peter Sercombe and Tony Young investigate non-heritage names (NHNs) of the mainland Chinese, showing that that NHNs can take on personal, interpersonal, and political uses. The authors are interested in how and why some mainland Chinese students in English-speaking environments assume NHNs. They investigated 156 English linguistic majors, 97.4 per cent of whom had adopted an NHN. The pilot study consisted of two parts, including three days'-worth of informal diary accounts by the researchers and semi-structured interviews with eight subjects. The results show that self-selected or endowed NHNs were used regularly and that the NHN had some sort of connection to a Chinese name or had positive associations such as sounding nice or having a positive meaning. These findings led to the distribution of 156 questionnaires. Even though 97.4 per cent of those surveyed had adopted an NHN, 31.4 per cent indicated that their NHN was less important than their Chinese nickname—suggesting that since their names had been adopted or chosen recently, they could be more easily changed. One of the functions or results of the NHN is to develop a closer relationship between the student and the teacher, with 54 per cent suggesting that the use of the NHN in the classroom increased the closeness in the relationship. Furthermore, 55 per cent indicated that they felt more English and 80 per cent felt less Chinese because of their NHN. The researchers suggest that one of the functions of the NHN is for Chinese students to more easily interact with the non-Chinese. In addition, the use of this NHN enables them to play a part in China's goal of becoming a more globalized country. As stated by Sercombe and Young, 'proficiency in English empowers individuals, suggests a positive image to other Chinese, indicates a degree of cosmopolitanism and reflects China's increasing and desired involvement in the world market' (p. 73).

A relatively unstudied area of onomastics is the relationship between alphabetical name placement and political success. In 'Alphabetical Effects on Political Careers' (*Names* 62[2014] 229–38), R. Urbatsch investigates if 'alphabetically early surnames may promote electoral success' (p. 229). The study makes use of a septemvigesimal system which assigns one number to each letter in the alphabet. Each letter of the names is then assigned a numerical value. Alphabetical distribution of names was calculated for elected officials and for the general population. While these two populations were reviewed, more specific criteria were used to review each research question. Urbatsch sought to discover whether elected officials have alphabetically early names and whether alphabeticism affects leadership positions once elected. In general, Urbatsch found that 'political success is more likely for those whose names appear earlier in the alphabet' (p. 236). This adds credence to recent literature suggesting that alphabetically early names in mock-elections have an advantage (C.R. Bagley [1965]; Andrew J. Johnson and Chris Miles [2011]). More specifically, leadership positions in the House of Representatives are more likely to be filled by members whose names have an early alphabetical position. On the other hand, the Senate does not show this correlation.

With the possibility of names in Congress having a significant impact on political careers, it would be interesting to see how unisex names may shape the future in this respect. Herbert Barry III and Aylene S. Harper investigate unisex names given to infants in 'Unisex Names for Babies Born in Pennsylvania 1990–2010' (*Names* 62[2014] 13–22). Unisex names are names with 'substantial frequency of both genders in the same population in the same year' (p. 13). The authors remind the reader that females are generally given unisex names more frequently than men, as indicated in Herbert Barry III and Aylene S. Harper [1993] and Stanley Lieberson et al. [2001]. To examine this trend more closely, first-name frequencies from 1990, 1995, 2000, 2005, and 2010 were sampled using Pennsylvania birth certificates. These first-name frequencies were evaluated by change of gender preference and consistency of gender preference. In addition, ethnicity was an evaluation criterion, separating names given by 'white mothers' and 'black mothers'. These evaluation criteria created four groups pertaining to unisex names. Statistical analysis was completed using SPSS. Barry and Harper's findings give further support to earlier research that suggests that female babies are more frequently given traditionally male names than vice versa. The researchers posit that this may be due to the fact that male names are more typically associated with status. In addition, the letter 'n' being found in the final position of the name might be an indicator of unisex naming. This is because 'n' as a final letter is highly popular for both male and female names. Given this popularity and the fact that there is a trend of male names being given to baby girls, it is no surprise that 'n' could be a marker of unisex names. In all, Barry and Harper's findings on unisex naming add evidence to the notion that naming in the United States is greatly diverse and that this diversity is due in part to the trend of names becoming appropriate for both genders, the dying out of particular unisex names, and their replacement by new unisex names.

9. Dialectology and Sociolinguistics

In the field of dialectology and sociolinguistics we will start with general works and textbooks, where we note the publication (actually from last year) of John Edwards's *Sociolinguistics: A Very Short Introduction* [2013]. This series is designed for 'anyone wanting a stimulating and accessible way into a new subject' (according to the blurb), and this 'anyone' will be taken on a romp through a very wide range of topics on just over 100 (very small) pages, since Edwards deals with attitudes to variation, prescriptivism, endangered languages and language loss, multilingualism, and, among others, variationist sociolinguistics (well—two of Labov's studies are cited). Wide-ranging, quite readable, this book(let) will give you Edwards's perspective on what is done in the field. Why he feels he has to start with Chomsky, though, beats us. More geared to the (beginning) expert (i.e. student), and more narrow in outlook is Daniel Schreier's *Variation and Change in English: An Introduction*. He sets the scene by explaining that variation is inherent in language (or, perhaps better, societies), introduces variationist sociolinguistics and in particular the socio-linguistic interview as the data-collecting method of choice, and then discusses the data analysis of variation as conditioned by various social processes. This is not as hands-on as some other textbooks, but Schreier does use established studies and talks his readers through them, which makes the way sociolinguists work clear, and should also help students read other studies. Schreier also looks at contact and change (under the headings of creolization, New Englishes, and dialect contact) and ends with the 'million dollar question' (i.e. actuation), to which not much in the way of an answer has been found yet, and which may ultimately turn out to be unresolvable. Altogether, this book is a neat basic introduction to variationist sociolinguistics for undergraduate beginners, which could easily be expanded for a university course by adding more in-depth, original studies. All chapters are followed by questions and suggestions for further reading, making this quite a compact first introduction to the topic.

Much more detailed (and voluminous) is Janet Holmes and Kirk Hazen's edited volume on *Research Methods in Sociolinguistics: A Practical Guide*. Here, more advanced students will learn that there are more methods besides the sociolinguistic interview (which of course also features, in a contribution by Michol Hoffman), such as written surveys and questionnaires (introduced by Erik Schleef), experimental methods (explicated by Katie Drager), or the investigation of computer-mediated discourse (by Jannis Androutsopoulos—more on this topic below). After this first part, with chapters on 'Types of Data and Methods of Data Collection', the remainder of the book presents several 'Methods of Analysis', both more narrowly variationist ones and also some sociocultural ones. Variationist analyses include historical sociolinguis-tics (presented by Terttu Nevalainen), the use of corpus linguistics more generally (Paul Baker), and detailed articles on various levels of analysis, i.e. phonetics (Erik R. Thomas)—although 'sociophonetics', the buzzword of the past few years, is notably absent here; phonology (Paul Kerswill and Kevin Watson, even though phonological analyses are actually only rarely encoun-tered in sociolinguistic work), morphosyntax (Julia Davydova), vocabulary (Michael Adams—with interesting advice on how to construct a sociolinguistic glossary), discourse (Janet Holmes), and an extra (actually very useful) contribution on statistics (Gregory R. Guy). The sociocultural part then adds anthropological analysis, in particular an ethnographic analysis of context and indexicality (Alexandra Jaffe), conversation analysis (Paul Drew), geograph-ical dialectology (David Britain), speech communities and communities of practice (Robin Dodsworth), multilingual contexts (Rajend Mesthrie), style and identity (Nikolas Coupland), and children's acquisition of sociolinguistic competence (Carmel O'Shannessy). All chapters are written from a personal perspective and typically deal with the author's own data. The reader is often directly addressed ('you should measure many tokens of each vowel'), and the more technical discussions are regularly supplemented by sections on 'quagmires and troubleshooting', advice, tips, and project ideas, which make this collection of essays a must-have for young researchers, and also looks helpful if you want to expand your own work into a direction you are not too familiar with yet. Highly recommended!

The Oxford Handbook of Linguistic Fieldwork, edited by Nicholas Thieberger [2012], is now published in paperback. Although this handbook is really geared towards linguistic anthropologists and means 'fieldwork' in the sense of language documentation, it contains some chapters that may also be relevant for sociolinguistics in a narrower sense, especially the chapter on 'Sociolinguistic Fieldwork' (pp. 121–46) by Miriam Meyerhoff, Chie Adachi, Golnaz Nanbakhsh, and Anna Strycharz. Although, as the authors note, sociolinguistics is an extremely heterogeneous field, the extent of the range of fieldwork methods is quite well described by the sociolinguistic interview on the one hand (as we have already seen above), and participant observation on the other. They also helpfully point out that the 'usual' sociolinguistic variables (age, gender, class, ethnicity) 'were never intended to be programmatic' (p. 124), but that sociolinguistics deals (or should deal) with any socially meaningful groups. But in addition, if you are thinking about investigating the 'Language of Food', 'Ethnomathematics' or 'Cultural Astronomy' in a society near you, this handbook may well be worth looking into.

We also note here the publication of what may become a new standard reference work: Raymond Hickey's *A Dictionary of Varieties of English*, a monumental collection of headwords, linguistic detail, and variationist references in the widest sense. Although there is also a short introduction on 'Research Trends in Variety Studies' (pp. 1–7), the bulk of the book is made up of dictionary-style headwords and their entries. In addition, several appendices give an overview of the lexical sets and the phonetic symbols employed, as well as a useful overview of differences between transcription practices (pp. 355–62). The book also contains an extensive 'Reference Guide for Varieties of English' (pp. 363–431), subdivided thematically into regions, roughly following Braj Kachru's concentric circles (although this model is not explicitly used by Hickey). Curiously (given the title), there is also a (short) section on literature of 'Overseas Forms of Spanish' (p. 430)—presumably because of its potential influence on varieties of English overseas (for the same reason, again presumably, some technical Spanish-language terms are found in the entries, such as *seseo*). The dictionary entries themselves include some very basic vocabulary from all levels of linguistics ('phone, phoneme, pharynx, coronal, apocope, sentence, question, imperative, syntagm, synonym, antonym, theme, rheme, aphasia'); some clearly dialectological terms ('apparent time, incipient change, chain shift', including popular non-technical terms like 'brogue, hoi toider, Jafaican, strine', or 'Mockney'), but also some biographical sketches (e.g. of linguists such as Sir Randolph Quirk and Otto Jespersen, creolists such as Hugo Schuchardt and Derek Bickerton, variationist linguists such as Peter Trudgill, William Labov, A.J. Aitken, Hans Kurath, and Ossi Ihalainen, but also of explorers, including Walter Raleigh, James Cook, Thomas Stamford Raffles, and even Christopher Columbus); sketches of varieties and languages, including practically unknown ones (Polari, Shelta); individual linguistic features (e.g. ASK-metathesis, positive *anymore*, CHAIR-CHEER merger, *never* with punctual time reference); geographies (Antigua and Barbuda, Antilles, East Indies); and, finally, corpora (mostly for StE, but the author's own *Corpus of Irish English* is included, as is COLT, FRED, or NECTE). Perhaps unexpected is the inclusion of terms relating to language prescriptivism in the eighteenth and nineteenth centuries (s.v. Samuel Johnson, Bishop Robert Lowth, John Walker, 'prescriptivism, elocution, complaint tradition'), as well as issues of standardization (with entries like 'Inkhorn Controversy', 'Neologizers', 'Archaizers', King James). In other words, 'varieties of English' here has a very wide range, and it might be worth looking up what you're interested in in this volume—we at least haven't found much yet that was missing, perhaps with the exception of the 'Tar Heels' (see below!). Even some comic relief is catered for (s.v. 'pun').

With this dictionary we already move to general publications dealing with English accents and dialects. Some more technical individual contributions have appeared this year. Thus, William A. Kretzschmar, Jr., Ilkka Juuso, and C. Thomas Bailey propose a 'Computer Simulation of Dialect Feature Diffusion' (*JLG* 2[2014] 41–57), where the application of a simple update rule (adopt a variant if two, three, or four neighbours use it, maintain the variant if five or more neighbours use it) in their 'cellular automatons' leads to complex behaviour from which patterns emerge, patterns of the kind we typically see in linguistic atlas data. Vaclav Brezina and Miriam Meyerhoff ask: 'Significant or Random? A Critical Review of Sociolinguistic Generalisations Based on Large Corpora' (*IJCL* 19[2014] 1–28). In fact, they can show nicely that 'by aggregating data we lose track of the individual speaker differences' (p. 10), and random aggregation leads to 'spurious results with very little bearing on social reality' (p. 23). The authors propose that help might be at hand, in the form of the Mann-Whitney U test that can take account of inter-speaker variation, but ultimately researchers should of course know their material, and evaluate their results critically, to obtain meaningful results.

One important general factor that is discussed this year is the role of media, highlighted in a special section of the *Journal of Sociolinguistics* (18:ii[2014]). The bone of contention is Dave Sayers's focus article on 'The Mediated Innovation Model: A Framework for Researching Media Influence in Language Change' (*JSoc* 18[2014] 185–212), where he argues that the mass media (actually, he produces a model for TV, but does not include the Internet) may indeed be a relevant factor in the global spread of linguistic variants, but the audience has to have a high emotional investment and engage with the TV series in question. Traditionally, of course, mass media are taken to be completely irrelevant to language change (except, perhaps, for the diffusion of lexis), as argued by Peter Trudgill in his reply 'Diffusion, Drift, and the Irrelevance of Media Influence' (*JSoc* 18[2014] 214–22), since 'to deny that face-to-face contact is the principal factor in language change would be foolish' (p. 215). Other sociolinguists are not as dogmatic; thus Jannis Androutsopoulos, in his rejoinder 'Beyond "Media Influence"' ' (*JSoc* 18[2014] 242–9), urges researchers to study media-engagement practices, audience design, representation, and style more systematically, but also cautions us that since the English language itself is an important phenomenon of globalization, the anglophone world might be quite untypical in the wider perspective when it comes to media involvement in contact-induced innovation and change. Jane Stuart-Smith, who is one of the few sociolinguists who has actually conducted some of the studies Sayers quotes, claims that potential media influence now is 'No Longer an Elephant in the Room' (*JSoc* 18[2014] 250–61), and calls for more sociolinguists to study this in their speakers, since 'a fundamental problem for any informed discussion is just how little evidence ... there is' (p. 250). This point is elaborated on by Jane Stuart-Smith and Claire Timmins in 'Language and the Influence of the Media: A Scottish Perspective' (in Lawson, ed., *Sociolinguistics in Scotland*, pp. 177–96); they combine variationist sociolinguistic studies of Glasgow innovations with media effects research, based on questionnaires, interviews and participant observation. Overall, only consonantal variants (TH-fronting, L-vocalization and DH-fronting) are influenced by engagement with the (London-based) soap opera *EastEnders*, and media engagement is never the strongest, representing only a contributing factor. This calls for a nuanced understanding of media influence. Finally, Sali A. Tagliamonte, in 'Situating Media Influence in Sociolinguistic Context' (*JSoc* 18[2014] 223–32), points out that in the course of only a few years we have been able to observe rapid shifts in the media, and focusing on only television series and film might already be obsolete. On the other hand, she claims that 'social media do not replace the networks that exist in the real world. Instead, they reinforce them and make them stronger' (p. 230).

Ana Deumert's monograph *Sociolinguistics and Mobile Communication* takes up Jannis Androutsopoulos's call to try and develop a new sociolinguistics of mobile communication. Thankfully, she moves away from the focus on the Western (cultural) world of many earlier works, and writes from a South African perspective; her differentiated analysis of the use of mobile communication especially (but not only) in developing countries makes this contribution particularly relevant. For example, Deumert points out that 'the experience of connectivity in the [global] South is strongly shaped by mobile-centric access' (p. 43) because, for many, computers are unaffordable; this is very different in the global North where resources are plentiful, and 'genres of participation' therefore differ (although there might still be huge internal differences, shaped by gender, class, rurality, ethnicity). Typical genres are 'hanging out', 'messing around' (i.e. learning to do things online), and 'geeking out' (intense media engagement in peer-learning networks, e.g. blogging or gaming), but even inside one country (such as South Africa) there might be huge differences between the haves, the have-less(es), and the have-nots. It is clear that these constraints also shape linguistic practices (e.g. if you cannot afford pictures). Deumert also looks at the Internet as a linguistic landscape, and investigates multilingualism, especially in Wikipedia (in chapter 4), and intertextuality (with remixes, mash-ups) with the example of Barack Obama's slogan 'Yes, we can' (in chapter 5). The most linguistic is chapter 6 ('Bakhtin Goes Mobile'), where she investigates the high linguistic variability in text messaging and argues that rather than use Labov's concept of 'structured heterogeneity', it might be more profitable to think about this in terms of the 'cafeteria principle', which would allow users to pick and choose features to create tensions and harmonies, and be creative in performance and stylization. Going on from this creative use, Deumert also looks at 'Textpl@y As Poetic Language' (chapter 7), where 'skilful' digital writing is analysed. Overall, this is an insightful book that takes the reader on a fascinating journey into areas of the digital world that we perhaps have not explored yet academically, and sets youth practices (which are not confined to 'youth') in a wider frame of sociocultural analysis; as Deumert concludes, 'the digital draws attention to the material aspects of communication and shows intertextuality, heteroglossia, performance and the poetic to be central to meaning-making and sociolinguistic indexicalities' (p. 168).

Away from the media, William Labov argues against micro-analyses (and against generative grammar) in 'The Sociophonetic Orientation of the Language Learner' (in Celata and Calamai, eds., *Advances in Sociophonetics*, pp. 17–29), where he asks: 'What are the data that the child attends to in the process of becoming a native speaker?' (p. 17). He proposes several principles, among others the priority of the community over the individual, and language as a social fact, rather than individual grammars constructed on the basis of some input. In fact, Labov even goes so far as to claim that 'the individual does not exist as a unit of linguistic analysis' (p. 18)—instead, he compares a range of studies that show that children continually compare their parents' dialect with those of their peers, and do not adopt those features of their parents that do not match. This already takes us to more theoretically inclined approaches to variation. In this section, we have deplored the failure to take variation into account in formal analyses. This lacuna is remedied this year by several contributions that have appeared in the volume *Micro-Syntactic Variation in North American English*, edited by Raffaella Zanuttini and Laurence R. Horn (most of which are discussed in the regional sections below). A general problem is taken up by Christina Tortora in 'Addressing the Problem of Intra-Speaker Variation for Parametric Theory' (pp. 294–323). The only possible model (or at least the one Tortora takes as given) seems to be to propose two (or more?) separate grammars in speakers. Tortora also calls for the use of apparent-time scenarios, the investigation of related dialects, and the collection of non-standard corpora in order to identify real instances of language change—probably revolutionary ideas for formal linguists, but quite commonplace in sociolinguistics. On the whole it has to be said for this collection that only a minority of contributors here actually take account of the sociolinguistic work that has already been done on the phenomena discussed, and a true interaction of variationists and formalists thus still seems to be some way away.

From the opposite perspective, Rusty Barrett criticizes (and deconstructs) 'The Emergence of the Unmarked: Queer Theory, Language Ideology, and Formal Linguistics' (pp. 195–223). He proposes that queer theory can have important implications for formal linguistics, which traditionally does not even include questions of gender or sexuality—as Barrett argues, this already 'produces forms of social normativity through performativity' (p. 196). For example, the tenet that language is autonomous and socially neutral 'is itself a form of language ideology that can have serious consequences' (p. 201), e.g. for speakers of marginalized varieties. Example sentences in formalist studies of syntax have long been criticized for reproducing sexism, misogyny, and homophobia, and illustrating 'the' language by examples from standard English only gives a false picture of homogeneity and disregards non-standard dialects—Barrett speaks of the 'flagrant ... illegitimation of a nonstandard variety as something other than English' (p. 203). In addition, the assumption of an essentialist 'universal grammar' equates UG with humanity—meaning that 'exclusion of some humans from that definition always lies just beneath the surface of discussions of whether some feature of UG is found in a given grammar' (p. 209). Finally, the underlying principle of binarity at every level of linguistic description (phonetic features, syllable structure, syntactic trees, parameter setting, etc.) 'erases the variation found across different languages in order to maintain uniformity within the theory. Such an outcome is ... the very basic pattern of normative ideologies of all kinds' (p. 212). Barrett's arguments surely also accord well with the more general desideratum that formal linguistics should pay much more attention to variation, and work in variationist frameworks.

From a different theoretical perspective, Gerard Docherty and Paul Foulkes provide 'An Evaluation of Usage-Based Approaches to the Modelling of Sociophonetic Variability' (*Lingua* 142[2014] 42–56), the most important question perhaps being how to account for 'the production, processing and acquisition of social-indexical information woven into the speech signal' (p. 42). Especially exemplar-based models seem well suited to handle this complexity, because exemplars can be detail-rich, including any association between form and linguistic or non-linguistic factors (and in this respect the exemplar model is a counter-model to Labov's sociolinguistic monitor (see also below), which acts as a separate module). Talking of usage-based linguistics, William A. Kretzschmar, Jr. sketches out the repercussions of employing 'Complex Systems in Aggregated Variation Analyses' (in Szmrecsanyi and Wälchli, eds., *Aggregating Dialectology, Typology, and Register Analysis: Linguistic Variation in Text and Speech*, pp. 150–73). He criticizes much usage-based linguistics for 'trying to align with formal linguistic studies' (p. 150), and for reifying the concepts of grammar and grammaticalization. Instead, usage-based linguistics should take seriously two fundamental properties of language as a complex system, the 'nonlinear distribution of frequencies of a large number of variants' (p. 154), i.e. Kretzschmar's well-known A-curves, and the fact that they appear at every level of analysis, i.e. scalability.

A number of articles have been published this year that focus on methods. Thus, Karen P. Corrigan, Adam Mearns, and Hermann Moisl discuss 'Feature-Based versus Aggregate Analyses of the DECTE Corpus: Phonological and Morphological Variability in Tyneside English' (also in Szmrecsanyi and Wälchli, eds., pp. 113–49). Since feature-based approaches tend to focus on 'well-known shibboleths' (p. 125) to the detriment of most other features, aggregate analyses such as cluster analysis are called for, at least in combination with feature analysis, in order to 'unlock the secrets of variability in languages' (p. 145). In the same collection, one of the editors, Benedikt Szmrecsanyi, provides an introduction to the hows and whys of dialectometry in 'Forest, Trees, Corpora, and Dialect Grammars' (pp. 89–112)—more specifically, he details how a frequency-based analysis of morphosyntactic features that is derived from a corpus (rather than atlas data) provides a more realistic picture of the 'forest', i.e. the 'multitude of features that characterize a given dialect' (p. 91). Jack Grieve offers 'A Comparison of Statistical Methods for the Aggregation of Regional Linguistic Variation' (pp. 53–88), and argues in favour of the new method of multivariate spatial analysis (developed by himself) that allows researchers to 'identify clearer patterns of aggregated regional linguistic variation than the standard approach to dialectometry' (p. 53); this method combines local spatial auto-correlation with factor and cluster analysis.

For Britain, Martijn Wieling, Clive Upton, and Ann Thompson draw on regional information in 'Analyzing the BBC Voices Data: Contemporary English Dialect Areas and Their Characteristic Lexical Variants' (*L&LC* 29[2014] 107–17). Based on the postal-code information provided in this questionnaire study, the authors use methods from dialectometry (hierarchical clustering) to investigate the distribution of the most frequent variants for each of the thirty-eight lexical/conceptual variables included in the questionnaire. The main regional clusters that emerge are Scotland, northern England, and a common area: southern England/Wales/Ireland, but the authors also note that 'characteristic variants for one cluster can appear in another ... distinctiveness of a whole area is thus essentially a relative rather than an absolute attribute' (p. 116), a result that ties in quite nicely with Kretzschmar's A-curves above.

Moving to regionally specific studies, we start with Ireland, and here we have come across a number of historical contributions this year. Thus, Kevin McCafferty says ' "I don't care one cent what [ø] goying on in Great Britten": *Be*-Deletion in Irish English' (*AS* 89[2014] 441–69)—a feature stereotypically associated with AAE, but, as McCafferty shows, also present in the historical letters corpus (CORIECOR) he has compiled for IrE (and, apparently, also attested in Scotland and northern England, if only patchily). However, the pattern of BE-deletion seems to differ from present-day AAE (and creoles); especially NP subjects seem to have favoured BE-deletion in IrE, as did WHAT/IT/THAT/THIS-contexts (much in parallel with Irish Gaelic). McCafferty concludes that 'Irish English is thus unlikely to have exerted much direct influence on BE-deletion in AAE and Caribbean varieties' (p. 441), unless of course the present-day AAE distribution is a more recent development. Based on the same corpus, Kevin McCafferty and Carolina P. Amador-Moreno investigate the claim that ' "[The Irish] Find Much Difficulty in these Auxiliaries ... Putting *Will* for *Shall* with the First Person": The Decline of First-Person *Shall* in Ireland, 1760–1890' (*ELL* 18[2014] 407–29). The authors are able to show that this stereotyped feature of IrE (preferring *will* over *shall*) is actually a relatively recent phenomenon. In the eighteenth century, *shall* was still dominant; in particular, it was 'a variant used primarily by urban writers and in more formal contexts' (p. 409)—perhaps not surprisingly, since the distinction between *shall* and *will* follows 'the kind of rule requiring an arcane and rather arbitrary distinction that is likely not to be acquired ... in informal settings' (p. 410). In shifting to *will*, the more vernacular variant, in the late 1800s in the wake of rising literacy, IrE followed the same trajectory as other varieties of English (e.g. CanE, AmE), but did not drive this change.

For present-day IrE, Alison Henry finds 'Object Shift in Belfast' (in Rhys, Iosad, and Henry, eds., *Minority Languages, Microvariation, Minimalism and Meaning: Proceedings of the Irish Network in Formal Linguistics* [2013], pp. 24–35), a phenomenon otherwise only known from Scandinavian languages, but which she links (in a generative framework) with overt subject imperatives in Belfast English (*Make always you a good effort! Give her you that book!*). This shift is available for pronominal objects (as in the examples), but a subset of speakers even allow full DP objects. In the same collection, Mariachiara Berizzi and Silvia Rossi provide a generative analysis of 'The Syntax of the After Perfect in Hiberno-English' (pp. 53–68), which they analyse in line with spatial PPs. Thus, in their analysis the preposition *after* is the modifier, and the retrospective aspect is encoded in a specific projection of the functional domain. The history of this construction is investigated by Kevin McCafferty in '*I think I will be after making love to one of them*: A Revised Account of Irish English *be after V-ing* and Its Irish Source' (in Haugland, McCafferty, and Rusten, eds., *'Ye Whome the Charms of Grammar Please': Studies in English Language History in Honour of Leiv Egil Breivik*, pp. 197–221). As McCafferty points out, first occurrences of the *after*-perfect in the seventeenth and early eighteenth century were mainly in the future tense (as in the example of the title). Rather than dismiss reports of these early examples as 'Stage Irish', McCafferty argues that both senses were borrowed from the Irish construction, which in earlier times also had future uses. Over the course of the nineteenth century (with the switch from Irish to English), future uses declined, and today the BE-*after*-V-*ing* construction is used in the perfect sense only. Finally for Ireland, Jeffrey L. Kallen discusses 'The Political Border and Linguistic Identities in Ireland: What Can the Linguistic Landscape Tell Us?' (in Watt and Llamas, eds., *Language, Borders and Identity*, pp. 154–68). However, Kallen does not look at varieties of English, but at the use (or non-use) of Irish Gaelic in Northern Ireland as opposed to the Republic of Ireland. Perhaps not wholly unexpectedly, given official bilingualism, Gaelic is regularly encountered in the Republic, but has very different associations with nationalism, Catholicism, and republicanism in the North, and is not found on official signs.

A host of variationist studies on Scotland have appeared this year. Based on the SCOTS corpus, John Corbett broadly re-examines 'Syntactic Variation: Evidence from the Scottish Corpus of Text and Speech' (in Lawson, ed., pp. 258–76). Corbett is able to substantiate some features proposed by Jim Miller (e.g. in 2004; *YWES* 85[2006] 71–2) as typical of Scots (separate negation markers, higher frequency of *never*, a markedly different distribution of modals), but also qualifies some of his claims. For example, Corbett points out that 'some of the features of spoken usage that Miller identifies as "Scottish" are also found in British and American English speech' (p. 272), such as the use of the past tense with *ever* (*were you ever in Memphis?*), or the use of the progressive with stative verbs. Based on the same corpus, Wendy Anderson exclaims, '"But that's dialect, isn't it?": Exploring Geographical Variation in the SCOTS Corpus' (in Bamford, Cavalieri, and Diani, eds., *Variation and Change in Spoken and Written Discourse* [2013], pp. 137–51). Since the 20 per cent of spoken texts in SCOTS come from a large number of varieties, both urban and rural, it is possible to use them to conduct studies, say, on the regional distribution of lexemes. In addition, regional variation is also a topic of discussion, and some qualitative analysis (e.g. on the status of Scots, or on the perception of dialect differences) is therefore also possible.

The Scottish–English border is singled out by a number of publications. Thus, Dominic Watt, Carmen Llamas, Gerard Docherty, Damien Hall, and

Jennifer Nycz investigate 'Language and Identity on the Scottish/English Border' (in Watt and Llamas, eds., pp. 8–26). They look at a feature that is not stereotyped for English/Scottish differences, namely voice-onset timing (VOT), which is generally shorter in Scotland than in England. Although differences are small, they carry social meaning, as the authors find out in their attitudinal study. As for other features investigated, the Scottish–English border seems to be a stronger differentiator in the east than in the west. Chris Montgomery suggests, in 'Perceptual Ideology across the Scottish/English Border' (pp. 118–36), that this asymmetry might in turn be related to commuter patterns (cf. also David Britain below for a similar argument). In addition, his comparison of map-drawing tasks completed by Scottish and English teenagers shows that both groups differentiate the English dialects in quite a similar way, but the English informants have only a rather fuzzy picture of Scottish varieties. Dominic Watt, Carmen Llamas, and Daniel Ezra Johnson also examine another feature, rhoticity, in 'Sociolinguistic Variation on the Scottish–English Border' (in Lawson, ed., pp. 79–102). As noted above, the border seems to play different roles; in the east, rhoticity north of the border seems to be increasing. In the west, on the other hand, there are 'signs of greater linguistic homogeneity among young speakers' (p. 98), and the new (English) labial variant /ʋ/ seems to be gaining ground on both sides of the border. Further north, other developments seem to be under way with respect to /r/. To clarify this, Jane Stuart-Smith, Eleanor Lawson, and James M. Scobbie take the reader on a tour through twentieth-century studies of coda /r/ in 'Derhoticisation in Scottish English: A Sociophonetic Journey' (in Celata and Calamai, eds., pp. 59–96). De-rhoticization (i.e. R-loss) is attested especially in working-class speech (and thus has associations of 'street-smart'), is led by men, and is stronger in the western conurbations (especially Glasgow) than elsewhere. By contrast, in middle-class speakers /r/ is strengthening, to mark a specifically 'Scottish (not UK) middle-class identity', and also as 'differentiation from working-class identity' (p. 65)—a change from above led by women. The authors' careful auditory and acoustic analysis, especially with the new method of UTI (ultrasound tongue imaging) reveals that de-rhoticization arises from differences in timing (a delay in the tongue-tip gesture), and in tongue shape. The same authors (in different order, i.e. Eleanor Lawson, James M. Scobbie, and Jane Stuart-Smith) also provide more detail on the same feature in 'A Socio-Articulatory Study of Scottish Rhoticity' (in Lawson, ed., pp. 53–78), where they point to the fact that acoustic analyses can be misleading, and that speakers obviously produce covert variants that analysts find difficult to analyse, but which nevertheless show clear social stratification, and thus presumably carry social meaning.

Staying with Glasgow, Robert Lawson asks: 'What Can Ethnography Tell Us about Sociolinguistic Variation Over Time? Some Insights from Glasgow' (in Lawson, ed., pp. 197–219). His ethnographic approach to several 'communities of practice' in a Glasgow high school uncovers interesting patterns. In particular, three boys who engage differently with specific groups can be shown to use noticeably different realizations (especially raised and retracted variants) of what Lawson calls the CAT vowel (equivalent to Wells's TRAP, BATH, and PALM vowels). Staying with the same group of informants,

Lawson advises us '"Don't even [θ/f/h]ink aboot it": An Ethnographic Investigation of Social Meaning, Social Identity and (θ) Variation in Glasgow' (*EWW* 35[2014] 68–93). For this variable, [h] is the traditional (working-class) variant, whereas TH-fronting (*fink* for *think*) is the newcomer, surprising because dialectologically it is firmly associated with London (see also Jane Stuart-Smith above on the potential media influence on this change, and Lynn Clark below for another study on this feature). In his adolescent informants, Lawson finds that [f] is increasing in real time at the expense of standard [θ], not the local [h], and that it indexes an 'anti-establishment stance' (p. 86), whereas [h] has remained as a marker of tough masculinity (the stereotypical Glaswegian 'hard man').

Over in Edinburgh, Ole Schützler asks about 'Vowel Variation in Scottish Standard English: Accent-Internal Differentiation or Anglicisation' (in Lawson, ed., pp. 129–52), and finds that in his younger speakers, there is little evidence of diphthongization in the FACE and GOAT vowels (which are monophthongs in SSE, but diphthongs in RP), and thus no anglicization. However, there is a tendency to produce FACE with a more central, and GOAT with a more front vowel, and thus a trend away from the more traditional Scottish variants. Moving north (a little), Lynn Clark tests 'Phonological Repetition Effects in Natural Conversation: Evidence from TH-Fronting in Fife' (in Lawson, ed., pp. 153–76), the same London feature we have already encountered in Glasgow, but that seems to be spreading rapidly elsewhere too (see also below for data from Carlisle). In fact, in Clark's data, over half of her speakers use TH-fronting more than half the time, and TH-fronting thus seems to be very frequent indeed. In addition, Clark can show that the realization of (th) as [f] is subject to priming effects, and is thus the more likely the closer another instance of [f] appears in the context. This is an important insight, because it means that once the priming effect is taken into account, we might get a clear picture of the real innovators in a 'community of practice'.

Thorsten Brato studies 'Accent Variation and Change in North-East Scotland: The Case of (ʍ) in Aberdeen' (in Lawson, ed., pp. 32–52), which is traditionally [f] in Aberdeen, but is increasingly coming under the influence of the Scotland-wide change from [ʍ] to (StE English) [w]. As Brato notes, the traditional [f] (as in *fit* for *what*) 'is now lexically restricted and socially marginalised' (p. 49). Older speakers switch to the supra-local Scottish [ʍ], whereas younger speakers 'bypass this variant' and adopt [w] straight away. An interesting suggestion in Brato's study comes from his observation that teenage working-class boys may be reviving the traditional [f], as an act of dissociation from the standard forms—perhaps a development to look out for in future studies. A relic community not far from Aberdeen is investigated by Robert McColl Millar, with the assistance of Lisa Marie Bonnici and William Barras, in 'Change in the Fisher Dialects of the Scottish East Coast: Peterhead as a Case Study' (in Lawson, ed., pp. 241–57). Perhaps as expected, detailed lexis connected with traditional fishing, but also with local flora and fauna, is eroding, memory is becoming fragmentary, semantic detail is becoming blurred, and as a result, 'gender- and age-mates know different parts of the original lexico-semantic "mosaic"' (p. 255). In this way, what was once community knowledge has individualized, and the dialect (lexis) is slowly dying out. This topic is taken up in more detail by the same authors (McColl Millar, Barras, and Bonnici) in their monograph *Lexical Variation and Attrition in the Scottish Fishing Communities*. Here they present the complete study, which besides Peterborough also includes the old fishing communities of Wick (in the very north-east of the country), Lossiemouth, Anstruther (on the Fife peninsula), and Eyemouth near the border with England. Starting out from an extensive collection of fishing-related dialect words in thesaurus-like fashion culled from general Scots and local dictionaries and a host of individual studies plus archive materials, they devised a questionnaire that was intended to prompt informants to discuss topics with the fieldworker, and in this way elicit dialect lexis, but also knowledge of cultural practices. The results are not completely straightforward, as their detailed studies of fish names, fishing-trade lexis (including typical clothing), words for seaweed and seabirds, sea mammals, and the sea and wind conditions shows. Overall, the northern communities (Wick, Peterborough, and Lossiemouth) have preserved more local words and phrases, perhaps due to their overall isolation from the industrial Scottish south. Generally, an awareness of change seems most prominent in the middle-aged informants, and if they remember local lexis (which cannot have been from work experience) 'there is a powerfully conscious element to these informants' knowledge' (p. 168); some other, younger, informants' knowledge seems to be linked to the heritage industry rather than direct experience and is thus a mediated, second-order relationship that is culturally conditioned. Overall, however, the authors find that 'what evidence we have for counter-currents to lexical attrition are largely confined to individuals' (p. 170). Lexical attrition is visible everywhere (although perhaps not very salient to locals), and local terms have been replaced by non-local (or perhaps supra-local) koineized terms—an early example of 'globalization' in this sense is the word *sou'wester* that is known only under this name everywhere.

Finally, even further out north, Mercedes Durham studies adolescents' attitudes on Shetland in 1983 and 'Thirty Years Later: Real-Time Change and Stability in Attitudes towards the Dialect in Shetland' (in Lawson, ed., pp. 296–318). She finds that 'the proportion of outsiders [i.e. children of parents who came to the islands during the 1980s oil boom] is such that they also influence the local children and they too have begun to use the dialect less' (p. 309); in fact, language use now seems to have reached a tipping point in favour of English, which is increasingly also used within the local community. On the other hand, the written use of dialect has increased, especially in the new media (text messaging and on Facebook), no doubt in order to create a local identity online.

Over in Wales, Bethan Coupland and Nikolas Coupland report on 'The Authenticating Discourses of Mining Heritage Tourism in Cornwall and Wales' (*JSoc* 18[2014] 495–517), based on oral history interviews with tour guides (ex-miners) they conducted at both sites (a Welsh coal mine and a Cornish tin mine). The authors find that these miner-guides 'prove to be sophisticated critical analysts of, and performers of, the multidimensional authenticities of heritage tourism' (p. 501); these multidimensional authenticities refer to material authenticity (the 'realness' of mines as physical spaces, which the ex-miners authenticate with their presence), cultural authenticity (the 'truth' behind mining practices, where the miners serve as interpreters and commentators), performative authenticity (the miner-guides acknowledge that a degree of performance is necessary, but portray themselves as authentic cultural brokers, amongst other things, by using their vernacular accents, which in this context strongly indexes authenticity), and recreational authenticity (since the visitors come as tourists, or 'heritage consumers'). With the ex-miners as meta-cultural agents, Coupland and Coupland claim that rather than de-authenticating heritage-ization, authenticity is 'rationalised and given value' (p. 512) in these different frames. One of the vernacular features of Welsh English the miners are perhaps using more widely is the progressive, and this is investigated by Heli Paulasto in 'Extended Uses of the Progressive Forms in L1 and L2 Englishes' (*EWW* 35[2014] 247–76). Compared with some other varieties, Welsh English is distinctive in using the progressive much more frequently in the extended habitual sense (*my friend is speaking quite a bit of Welsh*), a fact Paulasto puts down to substrate influence.

Moving to England, Sandra Jansen discusses 'Salience Effects in the North-West of England' (*LinguistikO* 66[2014] 91–110), again with respect to TH-fronting, which is also attested in Carlisle and rises steeply in apparent time. There are some intriguing indications that it is not necessarily a recent import from Cockney, but may be of older provenance—surely a suggestion that deserves some more historical investigation. Jansen finds that TH-fronting is preferred by younger, male, working-class speakers, which for her indicates the covert prestige of this variant. By contrast, the discourse markers she also investigates (clause-final *like*, *eh*, and *like eh*) are stereotyped, and openly commented on. Especially clause-final *like* seems to be on the rise again, and is being recycled by the youngest speakers—a development quite different from many other dialect areas.

As is the case for Ireland, a number of studies concentrate on the history of features. Thus, Marcelle Cole traces the Northern Subject Rule (NSR) further back in time in her monograph *Old Northumbrian Verbal Morphosyntax and the (Northern) Subject Rule*. Usually, this complex distributional pattern of verbal *-s* is held to be an early ME development. In her careful study of the interlinear gloss to the Lindisfarne Gospels, Cole uses quantitative statistics to investigate all variables that might influence the shift from *-th* to *-s*, and the establishment of the NSR (with its pronoun and its proximity constraints), and finds that the NP/Pro constraint 'was already a feature of Old Northumbrian' (p. 3), where it (non-categorically) conditioned verb endings, but the same constraints also affected the process of the reduction of verb morphology (*-e, -n* to *-Ø*) in the indicative more generally.

Sylvie Hancil looks at 'The Final Particle *But* in British English: An Instance of Cooptation and Grammaticalization at Work' (in Hancil and König, eds., *Grammaticalization: Theory and Data*, pp. 235–55). This feature is usually documented for IrE (cf. *YWES* 94[2015] 43) with the meaning of EngE 'however', but Hancil does not mention this heritage. Instead, she proposes that this 'relatively recent phenomenon in BrE' (p. 235) (actually—in Tyneside, since she uses the NECTE corpus for her evidence) can be analysed as conveying meanings on a grammaticalization chain from a subordinating conjunction to a final particle with various meta-communicative or metatextual meanings (adversative, intensifier, filler). It is curious, though, that the regional provenance does not play a role here, given the strong historical link of Tyneside with Ireland, nor does Hancil discuss whether the 'new' British instances of clause-final *but* have the same meaning as in IrE, or are a separate development.

Staying with the north, Hilary Prichard provides 'Northern Dialect Evidence for the Chronology of the Great Vowel Shift' (*JLG* 2[2014] 87–102), in particular evidence in favour of the push-chain scenario and of a unitary interpretation. Prichard looks at phonetic realizations of the PRICE, FLEECE, FACE, MOUTH, GOOSE, and GOAT vowels and finds that for the front vowels, there are 'no locales which might be described as having an irregular or incomplete form of the shift' (p. 96), whereas the back vowels 'show far less influence of the GVS' (p. 98), mainly due to the fact that north of the Ribble–Humber line, there were distinct vowel changes (especially ō-fronting, and the lack of an ɔ̄ from OE ā) that prevented the GVS. In addition, she identifies a coherent band of locations in a transition zone with both ō-fronting and ū-diphthongization (so far regarded as 'irregular dialect outcomes') and argues that this geographical distribution is better interpreted as the result of dialect contact, i.e. as the product of diffusion of the shifted ū-forms from the south. For sixteenth-century Yorkshire, Julia Fernández Cuesta listens to 'The Voice of the Dead: Analyzing Sociolinguistic Variation in Early Modern English Wills and Testaments' (*JEngL* 42[2015] 330–58). Fernández Cuesta finds that the three northern linguistic features she analyses (Northern Subject Rule, uninflected genitive, 3pl pronouns) were differently resistant to supra-localization; in particular, urban testators used less dialectal forms than rural ones, and testaments of the high clergy were less dialectal than those of the low clergy. Thus (as could be expected from present-day sociolinguistic insights) both the urban/rural dichotomy and the social rank of the testators already played a role in the supra-localization (standardization) in the north in the first half of the sixteenth century. For a period 300 years later, Paul Cooper claims that '"It Takes a Yorkshireman to Talk Yorkshire": Towards a Framework for the Historical Study of Enregisterment' (in Barysevich, D'Arcy, and Heap, eds., *Proceedings of Methods XIV: Papers from the Fourteenth International Conference on Methods in Dialectology, 2011*, pp. 158–69). In historical texts (mainly dialect literature and literary dialect) from the nineteenth century Cooper finds a consistent feature pool that is used to indicate Yorkshire speech: Definite Article Reduction (DAR), and morphologically variant forms like *sen* (for *self*), *nowt*, *owt*, *mun* (for *must*), or *gan* (for *go*). Rosalind A.M. Temple looks at one other feature of present-day York English, (t,d)-deletion (but that is not specific to this dialect) in 'Where and What Is (t,d)? A Case Study in Taking a Step Back in Order to Advance Sociophonetics' (in Celata and Calamai, eds., pp. 97–136). She suggests that rather than being conditioned by lexical and post-lexical rules (i.e. in Lexical Phonology) (t,d)-deletion is 'a function of common Connected Speech Processes' (p. 99), in parallel with many other processes of lenition, and co-articulation. Extrapolating from synchronic data to the diachronic state of things, Sali A. Tagliamonte, Mercedes Durham, and Jennifer Smith discover

'Grammaticalization at an Early Stage: Future *Be Going To* in Conservative British Dialects' (*ELL* 18[2014] 75–108). A comparison of ten locations across the UK (from the Shetland Islands to Cornwall) shows that some small communities in Scotland and Northern Ireland are the most conservative ones (with *be going to* present only in an incipient stage). Here, the authors discover a strong correlation of *be going to* with questions, in subordinate clauses, and with near-future meanings—environments they analyse as 'trigger environments' for the grammaticalization of *going to*.

The Midlands, in other years often a rather neglected dialect area, also feature this year in a couple of publications. Natalie Braber, in a short essay aimed at lay readers rather than colleagues, reports on 'The Concept of Identity in the East Midlands of England' (*EnT* 30[2014] 3–10). The East Midlands (especially Nottinghamshire, Derbyshire, and Leicestershire) are linguistically often identified as a transition zone with features from both the north and the south. However, many of Braber's (teenage) informants did not identify as either northern or southern, but as specifically Midland, and this may be the start of a new regional identity. Lindsey Bourne contributes a booklet on *Lincolnshire Dialect* also aimed at the general lay reader (and, presumably, local people) that contains an alphabetical list of dialect terms—although it is unclear what the sources used are—and a longer part on local customs, local history, and some local heroes (Isaac Newton, Margaret Thatcher, Alfred Tennyson, and George Boole). Although this is a little book with not much intrinsic linguistic interest, it might be a relevant resource if you are interested in the potentially beginning enregisterment of this variety in the light of Braber's findings above.

The north–south dichotomy is also taken up by David Britain a bit further south, who asks, 'Where North Meets South? Contact, Divergence and the Routinisation of the Fenland Dialect Boundary' (in Watt and Llamas, eds., pp. 27–43). Britain adds another important factor to thinking about geographical and psychological barriers, namely routines. He claims that the dialect boundary of the Fens has survived even after the Fens became passable because 'the boundary effect of the original marshland, and the consequent boundary effects that this engendered—attitudinal, infrastructural, socioeconomic—has shaped people's routine socio-spatial behaviours' (p. 39). One important factor not so far taken into account in dialectology is the obligatory school boroughs that follow administrative districts, which may lead to divergence effects at borders since they affect adolescents in their formative years. In (almost) the same area, Chris Joby reinvestigates 'Third-Person Singular Zero in the Norfolk Dialect: A Re-Assessment' (*FLH* 35[2014] 135–71). This feature is striking because it sets apart East Anglia as a dialect area from the rest of Britain. Peter Trudgill has famously linked the emergence of the complete lack of agreement markers in this part of the world to the Spanish Inquisition, but Joby claims in his detailed historical study that 3sg 'zero-marking was already in use in Norfolk before the arrival of the Strangers' (Dutch immigrants fleeing the Spanish) (p. 145). In addition, there is little evidence of (now StE) 3sg *-s* in written documents from East Anglia before the seventeenth century, whereas Trudgill's argument hinges on a three-way competition between older *-th*, new *-s*, and zero.

Erez Levon and Sue Fox discuss 'Social Salience and the Sociolinguistic Monitor: A Case Study of ING and TH-Fronting in Britain' (*JEngL* 42[2014] 185–217), two variables which they argue differ considerably in social salience (i.e. in the 'relative availability of a form to evoke social meaning', p. 185). In contrast to America (-*ing*) is not as perceptually salient in Britain and does not carry the same strong associations with education or intelligence (vs. casualness, informality of the non-velar variant) that it does in America, possibly due to the fact that [ɪn] was used well into the nineteenth century by the landed gentry, and is still 'a sort of shorthand for upper-class Britishness' (p. 196). TH-fronting, on the other hand, is highly socially and gender-stratified (it is mainly used by working-class men), and enregistered as urban youth language. Nevertheless, in their matched-guise experiment a speaker was not downgraded on the professionalism scale for using either [ɪn] or TH-fronting overall, very different from the logarithmic pattern found by Labov for American variables.

Away from mainland Britain, Anna Rosen investigates a variety only rarely in the focus of variationists in her monograph *Grammatical Variation and Change in Jersey English*. On the basis of interviews with forty speakers, questionnaires, archive material, and some participant observation, Rosen can draw a comprehensive portrait of the grammar of Jersey English, and fill in this gap in the map of varieties. She documents some features rarely documented elsewhere, such as particle *eh* (strongly reminiscent of CanE), FAP ('first verb plus *and* plus plain infinitive', a kind of pseudo-coordination that lacks tense agreement, as in *I went and marry a farmer*), emphatic postposed pronouns (*we were lucky, us*), or adjectival *plenty* (*he's got plenty daughters*), but also old favourites of varieties everywhere, such as the lack of agreement in existentials, relative *what*, or differences in prepositional use. The close-knit, rural, bilingual speakers use the transfer features predominantly, whereas the other features of dialect levelling or supra-localization can be observed in the younger, more mobile speakers. By and large, there does not seem to be much awareness of Jersey English as a separate variety—this is perhaps also due to the fact that the function of identity-constituting variety is taken over by the local variety of (Norman) French, *Jèrriais*. Also, there does not seem to be a movement (yet?) of reviving the local vernacular, or using it for emblematic purposes—surely something to look out for in the future.

And with this study we move further across the Atlantic, where Joe Pater analyses 'Canadian Raising [CR] with Language-Specific Weighted Constraints' (*Language* 90[2014] 230–40), in particular CR before flaps, where the determining factor, voiced vs. voiceless obstruents, is neutralized, but where CR follows the pre-flapped patterns (i.e. *writer* is raised, but *rider* is not). Instead of rule ordering, Pater proposes that 'preflap raised diphthongs are licensed by a language-specific, phonetically arbitrary constraint' (p. 231) in harmonic grammar. This analysis has the advantage of not postulating abstract underlying phonemes and of being learnable by gradual learning algorithms. More sociolinguistic in approach, Charles Boberg gives a general overview of the kinds of 'Borders in North American English' (in Watt and Llamas, eds., pp. 44–54), in particular a history of dialect areas inside the US and the relevance of the political border with Canada. Boberg also distinguishes dialect areas inside Canada, usually held to be homogeneous: the west (British Columbia and the Prairies), Ontario, Quebec, the Maritimes, and Newfoundland. Investigating the internal differentiation of CanE seems to be a trend this year. We will report on regional studies roughly in east-to-west order, starting with Newfoundland. Drawing on materials from Petty Harbour (a small fishing village outside St John's), Becky Childs and Gerard Van Herk observe 'Superstars and Bit Players: Salience and the Fate of Local Dialect Features' (in Barysevich et al., eds., pp. 139–48). Their 'superstars' (salient local features) are verbal -*s* (*I goes*), but also TH-stopping (*dis ting*), which both show U-shaped (curvilinear) trajectories in apparent time as their decline (avoidance) is reversed (revival) due to changes in the local economy, especially the fact that with an increase in tourism today, 'many residents profit ... from demonstrations of traditional ways of life' (p. 141). Other linguistic features, like the local marking of past habituality (by *would* rather than *used to*) or Canadian Raising, show no age effect, and presumably differ in salience. Also for Newfoundland, Sandra Clarke reports on 'Adapting Legacy Regional Language Materials to an Interactive Online Format: The Dialect Atlas of Newfoundland and Labrador English' (in Barysevich et al., eds., pp. 205–14), where interested scholars (and the general public) can now investigate the pronunciation, but also dialect lexis and morphosyntactic features of Newfoundland and Labrador online. On the basis of data from Quebec, Robert Prazeres and Stephen Levey investigate a phenomenon that is surely attested much more widely: 'Between You and I: Case Variation in Coordinate Noun Phrases in Canadian English' (*EWW* 35[2014] 193–224). They note that although generally the accusative is gaining ground (*her and her sister*), the opposite direction (as in the title) is also regularly heard, possibly as a hypercorrect form (they call it the 'polite' pattern) through century-long exposure to prescriptive norms. At least for older speakers, there is a correlation with education (the more education, the more nominative in subject position). This does not hold for the younger speakers, however, who prefer the accusative, leading the authors to confirm also for Quebec English that the accusative 'is increasingly assuming the role of default case in coordinate constructions' (p. 193).

Charles Boberg looks at 'Ethnic Divergence in Montreal English' (*CJL* 59[2014] 55–82), a city where English has clear minority status. His analysis of vowel differences in the major ethnic groups in the anglophone population (British, Jewish, and Italian) shows a huge degree of diversity. Thus, the Italians lag behind in GOOSE-fronting and have less Canadian Raising, Jews have more diphthongal variants in FACE and GOAT, and a variant near /ɔɪ/ in words with (ay) (e.g. *loin* for *line*). Strikingly, these differences do not become less with time (as in other cities), but are becoming more pronounced, and Boberg links this lack of assimilation to the minority status of English in Montreal and the high degree of social and residential segregation; ethnic pride might be another factor (for example, unfronted GOOSE seems to be linked to a popular macho stereotype for Italian men, the 'Italian-American tough guy from Brooklyn', p. 76). In this way, the fact that French is the dominant language has 'preserved a greater degree of diversity among the major ethnic components of the English-speaking community' in Montreal than elsewhere (p. 55).

Sali A. Tagliamonte and Derek Denis move our attention to south-eastern Ontario, where they are 'Expanding the Transmission/Diffusion Dichotomy: Evidence from Canada' (*Language* 90[2014] 90–136), more specifically from Toronto and three locations outside the city. In the diffusion of features from Toronto to these smaller communities (a city, a village, and a hamlet), constraints on the features change, indicating that 'diffusing changes do not perfectly replicate the model system' (p. 90). Specifically, Tagliamonte and Denis look at four variables undergoing change, two with little time depth (the rise of quotative *be like*, and the rise of intensifier *so*), and two that have been changing for longer (the rise of the semi-modal *have to* (over *must*), and the rise of possessive *have* as a full verb). For stative possessive *have*, they find no differences in the constraints, and thus 'a quintessential case of transmission of change in the North American context' (p. 104). For deontic modality, *have to* (despite more internal differences) also 'progressed through parallel transmission' (p. 110) from a common source. The changes in the intensifying system paint a more differentiated picture. Contrary to expectation, intensifying *so* (part of the cyclic renewal of intensifying forms) is a stable form in south-east Ontario, and thus probably 'a takeup of latent tendencies in the extant system' (p. 120), i.e. an instance of drift rather than diffusion. *Be like*, finally, is appropriated as a formulaic chunk, replicating only parts of the Toronto constraints and patterns (especially its high use in the 1sg), and is thus a clear case of imperfect replication in diffusion. Staying with Toronto, Sali A. Tagliamonte and Julian Brooke tell 'A Weird (Language) Tale: Variation and Change in Adjectives of Strangeness' (*AS* 89[2014] 4–41). As the authors show, in this semantic field *strange* is 'quickly moving out of favor' (p. 4), and its place is taken by *weird*—in fact, *weird* is used in 85 per cent of all instances by adolescents—another case of recycling and renewal (in case you were wondering, other alternative terms are *odd, creepy, bizarre, freaky, unusual, eerie, peculiar, whacky,* or *abnormal*, and this shift actually illustrates change across Kretzschmar's A-curves brilliantly, although the authors do not explicitly mention him). Bridget L. Jankowski and Sali A. Tagliamonte are 'On the Genitive's Trail: Data and Method from a Sociolinguistic Perspective' (*ELL* 18[2014] 306–29). In the same Toronto material as for the previous studies, they find for spoken language that the animated possessor seems to be the strongest constraint on the genitive variation (human possessors appear almost categorically with the *s*-genitive, non-human possessors with the *of*-genitive). Elsewhere, the *s*-genitive seems to be coming in in apparent time, especially with short possessors and through names for 'places that are possible locations for humans' (p. 306) (e.g. *Canada's Silicon Valley*). This change is promoted through the speech of working-class speakers.

Still staying with Toronto, Naomi Nagy, Joanna Chociej, and Michol F. Hoffman discuss different ways of 'Analyzing Ethnic Orientation in the Quantitative Sociolinguistic Paradigm' (*L&C* 35:i[2014] 9–26; special issue). They mainly look at the 'heritage language' patterns of Cantonese, Italian, Russian, Ukrainian, and Polish speakers of several generations, although they include some variables in their speakers' English (two vowels involved in the

Canadian Shift, and (t,d)-deletion) as well. Rather than individual correlations, they advocate the use of multivariate analyses because factors may become significant in tandem. Overall, ethnic orientation (i.e. the attitude towards a language and its speakers, differentiated by cross-ethnic comparisons, cross-generational comparisons, cross-linguistic comparisons, and cross-variable comparisons) does not explain all the variation but they do claim that 'it is a key factor in modelling variation in Heritage Language communities' (p. 9), and in fact seems to be more relevant for the use of English than for the use of the heritage languages themselves. Laura Baxter and Jacqueline Peters discuss an ethnic group not yet included in Nagy et al.'s above study, 'Black English in Toronto: A New Dialect?' (in Barysevich et al., eds., pp. 125–38). Most blacks in Toronto are of Caribbean heritage, in particular from Jamaica. Baxter and Peters investigate the rate of (t,d)-deletion, which is extremely high for speakers who reside in an ethnic enclave (Jane and Fitch), compared to non-enclave speakers. This suggests that (in contrast to other ethnic groups in Toronto, like Chinese or Italian Torontonians), 'Black speakers do not ... share a linguistic system with the other ethnic groups in Toronto' (p. 127) but adopt Jamaican features to construct their ethnic identity, in this way creating the new variety of Black Toronto English. Far over in the west, Panayiotis A. Pappas and Meghan Jeffrey investigate 'Raising and Shifting in BC English' (i.e. British Columbia) (in the same collection, pp. 36–47). On the basis of data from Vancouver and Victoria, they find that (despite claims to the contrary) Canadian Raising 'is still a robust phenomenon in BC' (p. 39), and the Canadian Shift is quite advanced, led by women; however, younger men are now 'catching up' (p. 44).

For the US, Robert Urbatsch employs a new resource for studying linguistic variation, 'Historical Regional Variation in Census Occupation Terms' (*AS* 89[2014] 74–88). He uses the 1880 national census to collect data on naming 'workers at drinking establishments' (p. 75) and finds striking regional distributions, such as *barkeepers* (southern) vs. *bartenders* (northern), *bars* vs. *saloons* (both used across the nation) vs. *taverns* (mid-Atlantic states), and the collocations *tending* vs. *attending bar* (also mid-Atlantic states). Urbatsch does not comment on this, but not surprisingly, we also get a 'long tail' of infrequent variants (*public house, drinking house, beer house, dram shop, ale house, tippling house, grog shop*, etc.) as predicted by Kretzschmar's A-curve. Hélène Margerie looks at '*He was angry awful:* Intertwining Paths of Development to New Degree Modifier Constructions in American English' (*AS* 89[2014] 257–87). This is a new (late twentieth-century) construction of AmE where the booster is postposed, and only *terrible, horrible, bad*, and *awful* can appear in this slot. Quite possibly, *He was angry awful* originated in the earlier construction *It scared him awful* with a zero-marked adverb, or through analogy with *He was worried sick* (or both).

We come now to specific regional investigations for the US, again reported on roughly in east-to-west order. James N. Stanford, Nathan A. Severance, and Kenneth P. Baclawski, Jr. uncover 'Multiple Vectors of Unidirectional Dialect Change in Eastern New England [ENE]' (*LVC* 26[2014] 103–40). As we have been reporting over the past few years, studies have shown that traditional eastern New England features are disappearing rapidly in the face of economic and demographic change, and the authors here show that especially young speakers in New Hampshire 'are discarding many traditional ENE pronunciations in favour of levelled, non-regional forms' (p. 103). However, there is a difference in speed (and, presumably, salience), such that some of these features are receding very quickly (non-rhoticity, fronted FATHER, broad-*a* in BATH, unmerged MARY/MARRY/MERRY), whereas for others the change is slower (fronted START, the HOARSE/HORSE distinction), and, as the authors argue, is 'overshadowed' by the fact that /r/ is also present in the same syllable. A dialect feature not discussed before is the topic of Jim Wood's investigation of 'Affirmative Semantics with Negative Morphosyntax: Negative Exclamatives and the New England So AUXn't NP/DP Construction', as in *I play guitar. B: Yes, but so don't I* (meaning: *and so do I*) (in Zanuttini and Horn, eds., pp. 71–114). The geographical distribution seems to centre on western New England, and as Wood's formal analysis shows, both constructions are formally affirmative, despite containing the morphological negative. According to Wood, 'the morphological negation reflects the negative proposition that the speaker wants to reject' (p. 110).

A little further south, we now have the first monograph on *New York City English* (NYCE) since Labov's seminal study more than fifty years ago, this one written by Michael Newman, although with sixteen informants (students) from Queens based on a much narrower range of informants. Newman relates NYCE to its updated 'Geography Demography and Cultural Factors' (chapter 2), where he points out in particular the enormous increase in racial diversity through immigration after 1965. Thus, the number of Latinos has more than doubled, and Asians have very recently emerged as a sizeable community (cf. *YWES* 92[2013] 92 and below for some first studies). The chapters that follow are a (very readable) mix of summaries of earlier studies (starting before Labov, and taking account also of studies that have reproduced, or continued, his work), of reports on his sixteen informants where appropriate, anecdotes and personal memories, and many film and pop-culture references. Newman covers a very comprehensive set of features (in fact many more than Labov originally investigated), both phonetic (the vowel system, the short-*a* split, the low back vowels, the consonants: (r) (th), consonant clusters), morphosyntactic, ethnic variation (AAE, Spanish English, Jewish English), differences in conversational style, and in the lexicon. The most striking result is perhaps the 'prominence of race' (p. 151) that becomes apparent in all the detailed case studies, and as an undercurrent the high stigma that NYCE still carries. For example, the slow increase in rhoticity (reported on in chapter 3) is mainly a white (and Asian) phenomenon, as is GOOSE-fronting, whereas L-vocalization is found much more in AAE speakers, and in Latinos who affiliate closely with African Americans. Despite general trends of supra-localization, NYCE is phonologically still clearly different from other varieties of English, and inside the variety, especially black speakers still use a distinct system of organization. Newman also notes a 'predominant racial split' for morphology (chapter 4, e.g. p. 89) because of the presence of many traditional AAE forms, also promoted through popular culture like hip-hop, and he points out that these forms 'have spread most intensively and systematically into other Black communities and least into

White and East Asian groups' (p. 95). In addition, Newman also reports on Spanish calques and Yiddish contact features, where much more research could surely be done. Differences in conversational style (the topic of chapter 5) include the perception of NY speakers as 'rude', which Newman analyses as a difference in politeness culture (New Yorkers setting more store by positive politeness, which may be interpreted as uncivil, or too direct), AAE discourse practices, and Latino code-switching. For the lexicon (chapter 6) Newman notes that Yiddishisms play a more important role than in other places, as do terms from Italian, but Newman also finds some terms of Dutch origin (*cruller*, *stoop*, or *kill* for a brook or stream), and a long list of terms with a specific NY meaning (or reference). The lexicon is also often racially divided, as the split of the term *neighbourhood* into *nabes* (well-off middle-class residential areas) and *hoods* indicates. Overall, the volume contains a wealth of individual details, a host of reports of other studies, memorable analyses of actors getting the NYC accent wrong (and why), but also a wider view of US society where it differs from New York's. Despite all this commendable academic detail, the book is still a very enjoyable read and should be appreciated by your students as much as your colleagues. In fact, Newman is also very good at pointing out areas where not very many studies have been conducted yet, so anyone looking for a research topic linked to NYCE should have a look at this..

Kara Becker sets out to fill some of these gaps in several studies published this year. In 'Linguistic Repertoire and Ethnic Identity in New York City' (*L&C* 35[2014] 43–54), she provides a detailed case study of one speaker. The three features she analyses (copula absence (a typical AAE feature), BOUGHT-raising (a typical NYCE feature across ethnicities, see also below), and non-rhoticity (potentially a feature of both, see Newman above) are used by the speaker to convey 'intersectional identification practices that go beyond ethnicity and regional identity' (p. 43), e.g. as a young woman, a neighbour-hood housing activist, an authentic Lower East Sider, someone opposed to gentrification, etc. Identity thus has to be construed as a more fluid resource, and 'ethnolinguistic repertoire' is probably a more useful concept than the static 'ethnolect', since linguistic features can now be viewed as 'potential resources for the conveyance of indexical meanings' (p. 50). Becker also examines 'The Social Motivations of Reversal: Raised BOUGHT in New York City English' (*LSoc* 43[2014] 395–420) in her new Lower East Side study. Based on sixty-four informants of various ethnicities, the study finds that the reversal of BOUGHT-raising is 'led by young people, white and Jewish speakers, and the upper and lower middle classes' (p. 396). Her analysis of the indexical meanings of the (traditional raised) variant suggests that it indexes an 'icon of earlier time' (p. 415), a New York character type that is negatively evaluated, namely an older, white ethnic New Yorker from the outer boroughs who is mean and aloof. Another classic marker of NYCE is the subject of another of Becker's studies this year, '(r) We There Yet? The Change to Rhoticity in New York City English' (*LVC* 26[2014] 141–68). This study shows that rhoticity is still increasing, although at a much slower pace than in other localities (such as, say, the American South), and that the change is led by young people, women, middle-class speakers of Chinese, and of Jewish and white ethnicities.

In fact, Becker's informants use postvocalic /r/ in 68 per cent of all cases—quite a high percentage, which also indicates that (in contrast to Labov's 1966 data) postvocalic /r/ in NYC is no longer a feature of formal speech only. On the other hand, non-rhoticity is remarkably stable in African Americans, and they also differ in using linking-r far less. The still comparatively slow speed of this change may be due to the fact that non-rhoticity is not only seen negatively, but also linked to positive values like local authenticity.

A bit further south, in Philadelphia, Suzanne Evans Wagner observes 'Linguistic Correlates of Irish-American and Italian-American Ethnicity in High School and Beyond' (*L&C* 35:i[2014] 75–87) in young women and finds differences in particular in their BOAT vowels (Italian Americans produce a less fronted vowel), their BITE vowels (which is more retracted for Irish Americans in this peer group and indexes 'toughness'; the non-retracted variants on the other hand seem to be linked to 'Italian girls' prissiness', p. 80), and for (*-ing*) (where Irish Americans use more of the non-standard alveolar variant). At least for some of these variants, the ethnic differences disappear after high school, and social differences become more important. Staying with Philadelphia, Suzanne Evans Wagner, Kali Bybel, and Kathryn VerPlanck study general extenders in 'Back and Forth with Classes and That Kind of Thing: A Panel Study of General Extender [GE] Use in Philadelphia' (in Barysevich et al., eds., pp. 337–48). They find that Philadelphian teenagers use *or something*, and *and everything*. GE based on *stuff* seem relatively less frequent (also compared to other places). They also find little evidence of grammaticalization, and conclude that the use of GE is a feature of age-grading. William Labov investigates 'The Role of African Americans in Philadelphia Sound Change' (*LVC* 26[2014] 1–19) and finds evidence of divergence, caused by residential segregation. This is shown in particular by (non-participation in) the traditional Philadelphian short-*a* split, a complex distribution of lexemes across tense and lax *a* that is not acquired faithfully through (adult) diffusion. (To wit: /a/ is tensed before front nasals and voiceless fricatives, before inflectional suffixes, before /d/ in *mad, bad, glad*, but not in irregular verbs, function words, polysyllabic words, or learned words).

Moving to the inland north, quite a well-known phenomenon is exemplified by the title of Elspeth Edelstein's contribution, 'This Syntax Needs Studied' (in Zanuttini and Horn, eds., pp. 242–68). Edelstein calls this the 'alternative embedded passive', and argues that it behaves syntactically differently from the standard construction (*this syntax needs to be studied*), and for that reason cannot be derived from it through ellipsis of *to be*.

Wil Rankinen moves us to 'The Michigan Upper Peninsula English Vowel System in Finnish American Communities in Marquette County' (*AS* 89[2014] 312–47). His study of sixty-nine informants shows that 'younger speakers use variants typically associated with neighbouring Canada' (p. 312), namely the COT-CAUGHT merger, Canadian Shift (CS) and Canadian Raising, rather than features of the substrate Finnish system, or of Michigan Lower Peninsula English (with or without the Northern Cities Shift). Especially in apparent time, the lowering and backing of the lax front vowels (CS) becomes very clear. Just south of the (state) border, Miranda E. Wilkerson, Mark

Livengood, and Joe Salmons examine another ethnic group in 'The Sociohistorical Context of Imposition in Substrate Effects: German-Sourced Features in Wisconsin English' (*JEngL* 42[2015] 284–306). Quite contrary to the belief that, by the third generation, substrate effects completely disappear, the authors can show that in eastern Wisconsin English, where historically (i.e. in the early twentieth century) English was acquired to a large extent from other first-language speakers of German, German 'has left clear structural traces on the local dialects' (p. 286). These structural traces include the final fortition of obstruents (*auslautverhärtung*) and TH-stopping, but also singular forms for *scissors, tweezers, clippers* (which are singular in German), different verbal particles (the stereotyped *come with, go with*), and traces of German modal particles, like the 'softening' *once* (*come here once*), which have become local (rather than German ethnic) features, and (some of them at least) are spreading rather than receding.

For Minnesota, Sara S. Loss discovers 'Iron Range English Reflexive Pronouns' (in Zanuttini and Horn, eds., pp. 215–41) to be a true counter-example to the usual properties of long-distance reflexives. In this dialect, *John thinks that Matt believes in himself* is possible with *himself* referring to *John* (not *Matt*)—at least according to Loss's informants' judgements.

Moving to the American South, Michael Montgomery, Michael Ellis, and Brandon Cooper ask: 'When did Southern American English Really Begin? Testing Bailey's Hypothesis' (in Buschfeld, Hoffmann, Huber, and Kautzsch, eds., *The Evolution of Englishes: The Dynamic Model and Beyond*, pp. 331–48). On the basis of the Corpus of American Civil War Letters, the authors argue that the shift towards what we now know as typical southern forms was a gradual one, and began before the American Civil War, in fact before the 1850s. Their data confirm that *a*-participles, plural verbal *-s*, and *liketa* were already prevalent before 1875, but so were *you all* (with associative meaning), which is actually used by 82 per cent of their letter writers, and *fixin to*, which also seems more widespread—and thus a distinctively southern feature—earlier than supposed. A subset of the material, the North Carolina Civil War letters, also features in a separate publication (actually from last year): Michael Ellis's *North Carolina English, 1861–1865: A Guide and Glossary* [2013]. Six of the letters are also reproduced in facsimile, with transliteration. Ellis provides a very detailed introduction to the material, on the socio-economic background of the letter-writers, and the shape of the letters themselves. The most interesting part of the introduction, however, is an 'Overview of North Carolina English, 1861–1865' (pp. liii–lxix), which contains a regional grammar based on the letters, with extensive quotations from the letters themselves, also including frequency information. Anyone interested in dialect grammar (rather than, say, the lexis) is here saved the cumbersome work of having to go through the extensive glossary that makes up the remainder of the book. Here you will find the early attestations of *you all* that Montgomery et al. discuss above, but also relative *what, at,* or *as,* a host of non-standard verb forms, subordinating *and,* or existential *they* (and of course many more features). A treasure trove that deserves careful exploration, and use in further studies.

The state of North Carolina is also dealt with at length in another publication, this one intended for the wider public, by Walt Wolfram and Jeffrey Reaser, *Talkin' Tar Heel: How Our Voices Tell the Story of North Carolina* (the Tar Heels being people from Carolina, possibly named for the petroleum industry that dominated the state economy). As the authors claim, the 'linguistic richness [of the state has] not been celebrated in the same way as other cultural and historical treasures' (p. 2), and they intend to set right this oversight. They first introduce the various lay terms that are being used to refer to speakers from North Carolina (such as the Tar Heels of the title, but also the more recent North Cackalacky, of dubious etymology) and the attitudes that have surrounded southern speech, and North Carolina speakers more specifically. They then look at 'The Origins of Language Diversity in North Carolina' historically (chapter 2), retelling both its prehistory and its settlement by Europeans (English in the seventeenth century, Scots-Irish, German, Welsh, and French Huguenot settlers in the eighteenth, and of course African slaves since the very end of the seventeenth century). The authors also look at the wide range of the 'Landscaping Dialect: From Manteo to Murphy' (chapter 3), look at urban/rural differences in 'Talkin' Country and City' (chapter 5), and investigate Appalachian English in 'Mountain Talk' (chapter 6). They also look at ethnic varieties. Thus, chapter 7 is dedicated to 'African American Speech in North Carolina', chapters 8 and 9 look at 'The Legacy of American Indian Languages' and more specifically 'Lumbee English: Tar Heel American Indian Dialect', respectively. The most recent arrival on the scene, Latino English, also gets its own chapter: chapter 9 discusses 'Carolina del Norte: Latino Tar Heels'. The final chapter, 10, gives an overall appreciation of 'Celebrating Language Diversity'. As the chapter titles indicate, the intended readers are lay people, but this does not mean that the wealth of materials Wolfram and Reaser can draw on from their own (and many colleagues') fieldwork would be lost on professionals. On the contrary, this is an extremely well-written, readable, yet highly informative work—by all means read it with your smartphone barcode scanner by your side, which will give you immediate access to online videos, audio clips, word lists read out, etc. A wonderful addition to any bookshelf on southern US English.

Talking of Walt Wolfram's colleagues, and of Appalachia, albeit the West Virginia region of it, Kirk Hazen finds 'A New Role for an Ancient Variable in Appalachia: Paradigm Leveling and Standardization in West Virginia' (*LVC* 26[2014] 77–102). In particular, Hazen looks at *was/were*-levelling—a feature in 'direct conflict with social processes of standardization' (p. 77). Perhaps not surprisingly, this feature is in sharp decline across age groups, and levelled *was* is used particularly by speakers with lower social status and less education. However, instead of levelled *was* younger speakers increasingly use a reduced (contracted) variant (*we's late yesterday*) that is 'poised to succeed by concealing a vernacular form from the pressures of standardization' (p. 98). Also dealing with an Appalachian feature, Rafaella Zanuttini and Judy B. Bernstein analyse 'Transitive Expletives in Appalachian English' (in Zanuttini and Horn, eds., pp. 143–77), in particular *they* (or *there*) in combination with a negated finite auxiliary, a quantificational subject, and a transitive verb (e.g. *they can't many people say that*). They provide a formal analysis of *they/there* as an expletive pronoun. The negated auxiliary can raise to a position higher than the subject since informants also allow negative auxiliary inversion, apparently a prerequisite for transitive expletive constructions. Another well-known southern feature is analysed by Corinne Hutchinson and Grant Armstrong in 'The Syntax and Semantics of Personal Datives in Appalachian English' (pp. 178–214). The authors claim that constructions like *I love me some apple pie* are a kind of applicative, more specifically a satisfactive applicative, because 'the direct object matters to the applied argument because the latter is satisfied through the event described by the transitive verb that supplies the third argument of the applicative head' (p. 189). However, the additional meaning is only added as an implicature.

One other distinctive southern feature already mentioned by Montgomery et al. above is discussed in much more detail by Jay L. Myers, '*Fixin' to:* The Emergence of an American Quasi-Modal' (*AS* 89[2014] 42–73). Myers follows the development of the lexical verb *to fix* ('to fasten' > 'to put in order' > 'to get ready' > 'to intend') to the quasi-modal it is used as today. Especially when compared to *be going to*, *be fixin' to* has the added semantic layer of contextual relevance, has 'implications of assessment and commitment' (p. 64) and conveys a sense of 'urgency/immediacy' (p. 65). From quasi-modals to double modals: J. Daniel Hasty claims that 'We Might Should Be Thinking This Way: Theory and Practice in the Study of Syntactic Variation' (in Zanuttini and Horn, eds., pp. 269–93). As the other contributions to this book, Hasty provides a formal analysis of this construction, arguing against an analysis of the first modal as an adverb, but also against an analysis of both modals as just one underlying modal. Instead, he shows that the first modal expresses modality, and the second tense. This contribution is also interesting because Hasty takes sociolinguistic evidence more seriously than the other contributors to this volume, and thus truly attempts to integrate micro-parametric variation and social constraints (and insights).

Moving west (a bit), Michael D. Picone links 'Literary Dialect and the Linguistic Reconstruction of Nineteenth-Century Louisiana' (*AS* 89[2014] 143–69). He takes the use of literary dialect as indicative of nineteenth-century enregisterment of dialect features that helped to construct 'the mystique of the South' (p. 144), and tries to reconstruct from this the actual use of phonological features (such as velar/uvular /r/, or TH-stopping), discourse markers (e.g. right dislocation), dialect lexis, and code-mixing practices between French, Creole, and English.

We have already seen a great interest in the investigation of various ethnic (not necessarily non-white) groups in the regional sections. This trend is also taken up by Lauren Hall-Lew and Malcah Yaeger-Dror, who have edited a special issue of *L&C* on 'New Perspectives on Linguistic Variation and Ethnic Identity in North America' (*L&C* 35:i[2014]). In the introduction (pp. 1–8), they point out that ethnolects are not seen as monolithic anymore but as much more fluid and negotiable, and that incorporating this flexibility into sociolinguistic models complicates them, making them more complex and multidimensional. A paper more methodological in nature is the contribution by Kimberly A. Noels, who discusses three psychological approaches to studying 'Language Variation and Ethnic Identity: A Social Psychological

Perspective' (*L&C* 35:i[2014] 88–96), such as laboratory experiments, questionnaires (especially including hypothetical scenarios), and self-reports. Noels draws attention to the fact that the ethnicity of the investigator might be an important factor, and thus 'researchers should specify whether interviewers are in- or outgroup members *vis-à-vis* the participant, and whether participants perceive them in this manner' (p. 93).

Besides the regional analyses reported on above, relatively little has been published on AAE this year. Marcyliena H. Morgan gives a more general introduction to AAE in her *Speech Communities*. She begins by looking at the historical evolution of the AAE community and its long tradition of communicating in a counter-language and using indirectness, features that also resurface in 'Youth Communities: The Hiphop Nation' (chapter 5)—a chapter that also looks at the emigration of hip-hop artists to Paris, and the local impact there (even on the last French presidential election). Morgan also looks at women's language in 'Voice and Empowerment in Gender and Sexuality' (chapter 6), at online speech communities (chapter 7), AAE in the classroom (chapter 8), and the performance of identity in the speech community (chapter 9). The chapters are quite short and evidently meant for students—thus they contain discussion questions and suggestions for further reading. Their shortness, however, also means that most topics are only dealt with anecdotally, with one or two case studies (often by Morgan herself) cited, with little room for in-depth analysis or controversy—so this monograph gets a mixed review in this respect.

Other contributions on AAE have a strong historical focus this year. Thus, Salikoko S. Mufwene defends 'The English Origins of African American Vernacular English: What Edgar W. Schneider has Taught us' (in Buschfeld et al., eds., pp. 349–64). Based on his ecological approach, Mufwene claims that AAVE and White Southern English shared 'almost two centuries and a half of common social history' (p. 358) and that AAVE only started to diverge after the abolition of slavery and the institutionalization of race segregation. In this sense, Mufwene argues, 'AAVE is an invention of Jim Crow' (p. 358). Ulrich Miethaner looks at data that could support this position in 'Innovation in Pre-World War II African American English? Evidence from BLUR' (pp. 365–85), BLUR being a collection of early twentieth-century blues lyrics. In these texts, Miethaner finds evidence of habitual BE, resultative *be done*, semi-auxiliary *come*, intensifying *steady* and counterfactual *call oneself*—all of them supposed innovations of AAE after the Second World War. Since these constructions were clearly present in the early twentieth century (some of them still in the process of grammaticalization), divergence must have started earlier than posited by Labov, possibly in the nineteenth century, as argued by Mufwene above. John R. Rickford rediscovers 'An Early Study of the Speech of Young Black Children in California: Why It Matters' (*AS* 89[2014] 121–42), conducted in 1971 by Stanley Legum, Carol Pfaff, Gene Tinnie, and Michael Nicholas, that has remained unpublished until today. Rickford contextualizes it and argues that it could provide us with important real-time data on AAE. In addition, these earlier data support the assumption that AAE children's speech becomes more vernacular as they grow older: as the original authors said, 'many nonstandard forms are learned after children enter school'

(p. 123). The California study also lent support to the idea that AAE across the US was relatively uniform grammatically. However, there was also a minority vote by Gene Tinnie, one of the authors, who cautioned that emphasizing the differences of AAE from StE might contribute to racism rather than solve problems, and this might have been one of the reasons why the rest of the material was never analysed in sociolinguistic detail.

Lisa Green moves us to present-day AAE with her insightful formal analysis of 'Force, Focus, and Negation in African American English' (in Zanuttini and Horn, eds., pp. 115–42), where she proposes that negative-auxiliary inversion (NAI) in declaratives (as in *Don't nobody want no tea*) has the function of 'focussing or giving the subject an absolute negation reading' (p. 131), i.e. 'There is not a single person who wants tea', in this way providing emphasis. NAI is also attested in embedded questions and *if*-clauses, although it is not obligatory there.

Sonya Fix looks at the use of one AAE feature, ʟ-vocalization, by white women in her paper 'AAE as a Bounded Ethnolinguistic Resource for White Women with African American Ties' (*L&C* 35:i[2014] 55–74). Fix is particularly interested in women who have 'close interracial contact over decades through long-term intimate partnerships and kinship ties' (p. 56). She uses a complex network and cultural practice index to measure their degree of identification with AA culture and identity and finds that 'the participants with the highest rates of /l/ vocalization ... happen to be the participants with highest current AANSS [network] scores' (p. 66), although of course ultimately speakers are unique persons with their own agency. In this way, they use available (not just linguistic) resources to 'reflect ethnic allegiance and cultural alignment with the African American community' (p. 72). In fiction, the effect seems to be different; thus Qiuana Lopez shows that white girls appropriating hip-hop language are typically portrayed as 'Aggressively Feminine: The Linguistic Appropriation of Sexualized Blackness by White Female Characters in Film' (*G&L* 8[2014] 289–310), since hip-hop and 'coolness' are ideologically associated with (black) masculinity. In the Hollywood films Lopez investigates, the use of hip-hop language allows the (upper-middle-class) female characters 'to gain limited access to communities outside of their ... environment' (p. 307); however, in this portrayal hip-hop culture, gang culture, and street culture are conflated (and identified with being black), and femininity is equated with sexual promiscuity.

Moving to yet another ethnic group, Robert Bayley and Cory Holland uncover 'Variation in Chicano English: The Case of Final (z) Devoicing' (*AS* 89[2014] 385–406). Their investigation of young speakers in south Texas shows that (z) devoicing, a 'stereotypical feature of ChE' (p. 388), is conditioned by phonotactic features, by the morpheme status of (z), the speaker's orientation towards the community, and gender, but not by competence in Spanish: preceding stops and following voiceless segments favour devoicing, as does morpheme status, not wanting to leave the community, and being female—in fact, speakers whose first language is English devoice final (z) more often than speakers of Spanish, and Spanish-language influence thus does not seem to be tenable (at least synchronically). Erik R. Thomas and Janneke Van Hofwegen examine more 'Consonantal

Variation in the English of a Spanish-Substrate Community' in Texas (in Barysevich et al., eds., pp. 48–58), in particular the quality of /l/, /r/, realization of TH, and voice onset time (VOT). For /l/, they find a complex 'boomerang' pattern of change over the four generations investigated, 'from light to dark to light again' (p. 51), quite possibly due to the perception that Chicano speakers experience more power today. TH is realized as a stop frequently, but less frequently assimilated to a preceding consonant. These two variables seem to be ethnically salient. For /r/, the authors document high levels of non-rhoticity, correlating with (lack of) education. VOT similarly seems to be associated with 'standard unmarked, mainstream speech' (p. 57) and correlates with years of education, but not ethnicity. Rosalyn Negrón investigates 'New York City's Latino Ethnolinguistic Repertoire and the Negotiation of Latinidad in Conversation' (*JSoc* 18[2014] 87–118), more specifically in one business conversation. Negrón shows that a variety of features from Spanish and English (in this case, NYC English, AAE, other varieties of English, multiple Spanish dialects and shared ideologies and expectations) belong to the arsenal of the ethnolinguistic repertoire that speakers use flexibly to 'customize their self-presentation to other Latinos' (p. 90), in the process also invoking *latinidad* to 'transcend racial, cultural, and even linguistic differences in the service of imagining a collective past and future for all Latinos' (p. 92).

And finally, Asian Americans have increasingly come to the attention of linguists. Amy Wing-mei Wong and Lauren Hall-Lew link 'Regional Variability and Ethnic Identity: Chinese Americans in New York City and San Francisco' (*L&C* 35[2014] 27–42). In particular, the authors investigate the BOUGHT-vowel (as did Becker above) and find that 'Chinese Americans in the two cities pronounce BOUGHT in ways that are more similar to their respective regional patterns than to one another' (p. 27), i.e. raising in NYC, but merging with BOT (the COT-CAUGHT merger) in San Francisco. Nevertheless, the authors are reluctant to call this assimilation; they suggest instead that regionality and ethnicity intersect here in complex ways, since BOUGHT (formerly also raised in San Francisco) used to be associated with a local 'white' ethnicity (San Francisco's Mission District) but is today presumably only heard as old-fashioned, or indeed as indexing Brooklynese.

Moving to age-related studies, Anna-Brita Stenström discovers a new pragmatic marker, 'The Pragmatic Marker [PM] *Come On* in Teenage Talk' (in Haugland et al., eds., pp. 381–94). OK, the marker may not be new, but it hasn't been investigated before, or had the status of PM conferred upon it. Stenström analyses it as an interpersonal marker with three meanings: it is used as a directive, or as a reactive (both with different degrees of intensity), or as an evaluative (signalling reorientation or emphasis). In addition, Stenström shows that in her teenage speakers, *come on* is used mainly by girls. Stenström has also contributed the (short) monograph *Teenage Talk: From General Characteristics to the Use of Pragmatic Markers in a Contrastive Perspective*, where she contrasts Spanish with English. This small book is more illuminating for the Spanish than for the English analysis, which consists of very short summaries of Stenström's earlier work reported here before (in particular on *anyway*, *come on*, *cos*, *like*, *okay*, *well*, and *you know*), but it may also serve as a striking reminder that in spite of all the differences, teenagers and their pragmatic markers are really quite similar, even across language boundaries. The same point could also be made about Eli-Marie Danbolt Drange, Ingrid Kristine Hasund, and Anna-Brita Stenström, who call attention to striking cross-linguistic parallels involving '"*Your Mum!*" Teenagers' Swearing by Mother in English, Spanish and Norwegian' (*IJCL* 19[2014] 29–59). They distinguish ritual insults, name-calling, expletive interjections, and intensifiers, and find that 'swearing by mother' (SBM) (i.e. offending someone by way of his/her mother) is much more common in Spanish than in English, and least used in Norwegian, presumably linked to the strong Catholic taboos on the concept of the 'whore mother'. The development in English and Norwegian is more recent, and in Norwegian is probably due to loan translations from English. In both languages, SBM mainly has the function of ritual insults, whereas in Spanish it is also used for name-calling, as an expletive, or as an intensifier. Indeed, this material could be used (but isn't by the authors) to make a strong point about cultural transfer that includes not only the linguistic material, but also the cultural practice of, indeed, SBM and that can be clearly linked to African American popular subcultures.

We now come to studies that focus on gender. Starting with rather traditional studies, Frank Herrmann, Stuart P. Cunningham, and Sandra P. Whiteside investigate 'Speaker Sex Effects on Temporal and Spectro-Temporal Measures of Speech' (*JIPA* 44[2014] 59–74). In the thirteen women and eleven men investigated they find evidence for 'lower levels of coarticulation in the speech samples of the women speakers' (p. 60), corroborating earlier studies of women as more careful articulators. However, the authors unfortunately do not say anything about the social meaning of these gender differences, although we would suspect that 'careful speech' is strongly indexed socially. Charlyn M. Laserna, Yi-Tai Seih, and James W. Pennebaker listen to '*Um* . . . Who Like Says *You Know*: Filler Word Use as a Function of Age, Gender, and Personality' (*JLSP* 33[2014] 328–38). As indicated by the title, they investigate the correlation of two 'filled pauses' (*uh* and *um*) and three discourse markers (*I mean*, *you know*, *like*) with age, gender, and personality traits. Indeed the two groups of 'fillers' pattern differently; thus discourse markers are used more by women and young speakers and are associated with the personality trait of 'conscientiousness', whereas filled pauses are used more by older informants. Rosamund Moon looks at adjectives used to describe men vs. women in the Bank of English in 'From *Gorgeous* to *Grumpy*: Adjectives, Age and Gender' (*G&L* 8[2014] 5–41). Moon draws a rather depressing picture of 'cryptotypes' (p. 5), i.e. covert categories that signal age indirectly, from positively evaluated adjectives to do with youth (*gorgeous*, *smooth-skinned*, *strong*, *ambitious*) to negatively evaluated ones covertly linked to age (*frail*, *white-haired*, *dotty*, *grumpy*). In addition, these crypto-types are gendered heteronormatively: 'stereotypically female/feminine characteristics are associated with youth and youthfulness' (p. 16), young men are breadwinners, *middle-aged* is already negative (for women, lacking a partner; for men, referring to being overweight and visibly ageing), and for old age, the collocates indicate isolation, abandonment, widowhood (for women), and ill health, shrunken physique, anger, unhappiness, and decline (for men). This is an interesting study because Moon can show how these adjectives alone transmit 'ageism and sexism ... subtly or subliminally' (p. 36). David Bamman, Jacob Eisenstein, and Tyler Schnoebelen correlate 'Gender Identity and Lexical Variation in Social Media' (*JSoc* 18[2014] 135–60), in particular in a huge corpus of Twitter feeds. Their bottom-up method produces lexical clusters that correlate with (admittedly binary) gender: pronouns, emotion terms (and emoticons), kinship terms, expressive terms (abbreviations, expressive lengthening, exclamation, or question marks etc.), back-channelling and assent terms are all female markers, whereas the language of men is characterized by an absence of these markers, the assent term *yessir*, and swearing or the use of taboo words. Also, men use more content words overall. More interesting is their application to those authors where the gender predictions fail. They can show that these individuals' social networks are less gender-homophilous, or, put the other way around, 'individuals with a greater proportion of same-gender ties make greater use of gender-marked variables' (p. 149). In this way, mainstream gendered language seems to be promoted by gender-homogeneous social networks.

Tommaso M. Milani moves us to everyday (banal) 'Sexed Signs: Queering the Scenery' (*IJSL* 228[2014] 201–25)—an aspect of Linguistic Landscapes (LL) so far not investigated; in fact, Milani goes so far as to claim that LL has erased gender and sexuality. His analysis of an airport newsstand reveals predictable patterns (slim, young, white women and larger, muscular, but also young and white men on the cover of glossy magazines) that reproduce 'the racially short-sighted, ageist ... and fat-obsessed character of contemporary consumer culture' (p. 211) and which are deeply heteronormative. The same can be said about tourist t-shirts that portray men and women as 'opposite but complementary' (p. 214), and even injunctions (Milani's example is from a 'revolutionary' queer cafe) not to be ageist, sexist, homophobic, etc. reproduce the very categories they oppose. William L. Leap looks at 'The *Sex Machine*, the *Full-Body Tattoo*, and the *Hermaphrodite*: Gay Sexual Cinema, Audience Reception, and Fractal Recursivity' (in Zimman, Davis, and Raclaw, eds., *Queer Excursions: Retheorizing Binaries in Language, Gender, and Sexuality*, pp. 129–49) and finds that the audience reception of homoerotic porn movies centres on the construction of 'hypermasculinity' in a way that it can erase, incorporate, or rework racial difference, tattooing, and even hermaphroditism. Throughout all the comments, it becomes clear that they are written from what Leap describes as 'a position of masculine privilege that is grounded in sexual conquest and other forms of achievement' (p. 131), surely an analysis that is relevant beyond gay sexual cinema. Against this rather dominant ('homonormative') position, Jenny L. Davis reports on ' "More Than Just 'Gay Indians' ": Intersecting Articulations of Two-Spirit Gender, Sexuality, and Indigenousness' (pp. 62–80). The indigenous Two-Spirit Americans (who identify as both male and female) in this study place themselves in at least three binary dichotomies: tribal affiliation vs. native/Indian, tribal vs. pan-tribal, and two-spirit vs. queer. Instead of rejecting one of each poles, the speakers used these dualities to 'signal multiple levels of community membership, each of which genuinely represented one part of the speakers' sense of themselves' (p. 78). Still in the same collection, Elijah Adiv Edelman is 'Neither In Nor Out: Taking the "T" Out of the Closet' (pp. 150–69). This rather cryptic title refers to transgender men who practise 'stealth' (i.e. do not make their trans history openly visible), a position that is framed in mainstream lesbian, gay, bi-sexual and transgender (LGBT) discourse as pathological: 'good gay citizens' are out, and 'being out' is equated with a 'personal, social, and political act of self-actualization' (p. 151). Quite to the contrary, Edelman argues, for trans people stealth may actually be the equivalent of coming out because it is 'a resistance to cissexist paradigms where trans disclosure is nonnegotiable' (p. 160).

Becky Childs and Gerard Van Herk call on speakers to 'Work That -s! Drag Queens, Gender, Identity, and Traditional Newfoundland English' (*JSoc* 18[2014] 634–57). The linguistic feature they investigate is verbal -s (*I goes*), which is not only reclaimed (the authors say it is 'upcycled', p. 635) by young urban females (as we have seen above), but is used even more frequently by the local drag queens. The authors give several explanations that may play a role here: in the revival of an obsolescent form, 'drag queens are a step ahead ... they're just cooler ... they are likely to be invested in being at the cutting edge' (p. 649). The old ('Newfoundlandy') meaning may also have become overlaid by the new meanings 'young, urban, female, performed, ironic, playful, in-group' (p. 650), which all seem particularly useful for drag queen performers. Finally, there is also the nationwide use of verbal -s (especially 1sg *Loves it*), with its connotations of 'arch, diva-ish, perhaps slightly ditzy' (p. 650—the authors do explicitly mention Paris Hilton). This 'joke non-standard' use is derived from media representations of non-standard speakers, especially in comedy contexts (Popeye, Cletus (a character from the Simpsons), Talk Like a Pirate) and thus adds more global stylistic associations to the mix. All of these may be relevant, and this 'complexity of ambiguity of intent ... makes the features so appealing for its users' (p. 651).

Finally, Erez Levon links 'Categories, Stereotypes, and the Linguistic Perception of Sexuality' (*LSoc* 43[2014] 539–66). Levon tests this with three linguistic features: higher levels of fundamental pitch, exaggerated pronunci-ation of /s/, and TH-fronting, a typical working-class marker, linked to a careful investigation of informants' stereotypical gender norms. And indeed, listeners' 'affective beliefs about masculinity ... influence whether or not a particular feature is perceived as sounding "gay" ' (p. 554). However, perhaps an even larger role is played by perceptual salience, because especially the presence of sibilance leads to 'contextual nonattention' (p. 557) to less salient cues (such as TH-fronting). Stereotypes thus play a role but do not seem to be the only factor affecting perception.

10. New Englishes and Creolistics

This section presents this year's publications in the above fields. The subsection on New Englishes will proceed from supra-regional contributions to country- and variety-specific studies and from general accounts in book format to articles. In a continuation of last year's survey, countries traditionally categorized in the Expanding Circle will also be covered, especially since the redefinition of the Expanding Circle is among the most thriving areas within the field. The subsection on creolistics will first treat books then articles.

Beginning with publications on New Englishes, we start with two edited volumes which cover several varieties. The first is *The Evolution of Englishes: The Dynamic Model and Beyond*, edited by Sarah Buschfeld, Thomas Hoffmann, Magnus Huber, and Alexander Kautzsch. It contains twenty-seven contributions and was published on the occasion of Edgar W. Schneider's sixtieth birthday to celebrate his contribution to the field as the creator of the widely acclaimed Dynamic Model. After Stephanie Hackert's series editor's preface (pp. ix–x) and the editors' preface, 'The Evolution of Englishes: In Honour of Edgar Schneider on the Occasion of his 60th Birthday' (pp. xi–xviii), the introduction (pp. 1–18) by the editors outlines Schneider's model and the structure of the book and introduces its articles. Eleven papers, which are devoted to applications of the Dynamic Model, are presented in Part I, 'The Dynamic Model'. Part II contains sixteen further articles, which go 'Beyond the Dynamic Model' in taking other 'Empirical and Theoretical Perspectives on World Englishes'.

Part I begins with Bertus van Rooy ('Convergence and Endonormativity at Phase Four of the Dynamic Model', pp. 21–38), who uses AmE and SAE to claim that convergence depends on the nature of contact in a postcolonial setting and that endonormativity is a result of rewritten identities. This ties in with Suzan Coetzee-Van Rooy's 'The Identity Issue in Bi- and Multilingual Repertoires in South Africa: Implications for Schneider's Dynamic Model' (pp. 39–57), in which the author argues that 'being multilingual' is an essential part of South African identities. In 'The Sociophonetic Effects of Event X: Post-Apartheid Black South African English in Multicultural Contact with Other South African Englishes' (pp. 58–69), Rajend Mesthrie asserts that increased contact among the various ethnic groups in South Africa has not led to a more homogeneous SAE. In her contribution 'Beyond Nativization? Philippine English in Schneider's Dynamic Model' (pp. 70–85), Isabel Pefianco Martin claims that a movement for PhilE beyond the nativization phase is unlikely because it 'is not an identity carrier for most Filipinos' (p. 81). In an account of '*T*-Affrication and Relativization in Ghanaian English', Magnus Huber identifies 'Stylistic and Sociolinguistic Variation in Schneider's Nativization Phase' (pp. 86–106), which is actually expected only in Phase 5 of the Dynamic Model. Development in the last phase of Schneider's model is investigated by Pam Peters, who argues that Aboriginal English is 'the most significant aspect' (p. 121) of the 'Differentiation in Australian English' (pp. 107–25). In 'The Evolution of Singlish: Beyond Phase 5?' (pp. 126–41), Lionel Wee identifies 'linguistic sophistication, migration and commodification' (p. 138) as factors that need to be incorporated into the Dynamic Model in the age of globalization. William A. Kretzschmar ('Emergence of "New Varieties" in Speech as a Complex System', pp. 142–59) shows that a complexity science approach to varieties nicely ties in with Schneider's model since it is capable of explaining how several varieties can emerge side by side.

On the basis of Comparative Correlative constructions (*the...*, *the...*), Thomas Hoffmann ('The Cognitive Evolution of Englishes: The Role of Constructions in the Dynamic Model', pp. 160–80) offers a CxG approach to account for differing developments across varieties. Using 'English in Cyprus and Namibia' as cases in point, Sarah Buschfeld presents 'A Critical Approach to Taxonomies and Models of World Englishes and Second Language Acquisition research' (pp. 181–202), arguing that the Dynamic Model is not fully capable of accounting for non-postcolonial Englishes. In a similar vein, Alexander Kautzsch ('English in Germany: Spreading Bilingualism, Retreating Exonormative Orientation and Incipient Nativization?', pp. 203–28) provides empirical data to address the status of English in Germany in view of the Dynamic Model. Among other things, he argues that a redefinition of the settler strand of the model is crucial in applying it to the German context.

The sixteen contributions in Part II are grouped into five 'Focus' sections. In the first, 'Contributions with a Theoretical Focus', Daniel Schreier ('On Cafeterias and New Dialects: The Role of Primary Transmitters', pp. 231–48) shows how in studying new dialect formation it is important to identify 'different types of transmitters', i.e. members of the community who contribute to the spread of dialect features to different extents. Christian Mair ('Does Money Talk, and Do Languages Have Price Tags? Economic Perspectives on English as a Global Language', pp. 249–66) surveys how economists' views of the global role of English can contribute to World Englishes research and how, conversely, the insights of linguists might be useful for econometrics. Ahmar Mahboob's 'Language Variation and Education: A Focus on Pakistan' (pp. 267–81) looks into textbooks in Pakistan and shows how these are used primarily to transmit Islamic culture rather than giving access to the global use of English. The last article in this section, Stephanie Hackert's 'The Evolution of English(es): Notes on the History of an Idea' (pp. 282–300), points to the fact that a discourse-historical approach to language evolution and its link to a hierarchization of varieties is instrumental in understanding present-day ideologies of language. In the second 'Focus' section, 'Cross-Varietal Contributions', Heinrich Ramisch ('At the Crossroads of Variation Studies and Corpus Linguistics: The Analysis of Past Tense and Past Participle Forms', pp. 301–11) argues that variation studies should rely on spoken rather than written material. In his contribution 'Compounding and Suffixation in World Englishes' (pp. 312–30), Thomas Biermeier finds differences in Asian as opposed to African varieties, e.g. that the former have higher type-frequencies than the latter. The third section, 'United States', begins with Michael Montgomery, Michael Ellis, and Brandon Cooper, who ask 'When Did Southern American English Really Begin?' and aim at 'Testing Bailey's Hypothesis' (pp. 331–48). They conclude that this variety emerged well before the Civil War, i.e. much earlier than claimed by Guy Bailey. Salikoko S. Mufwene gives a survey of 'What Edgar W. Schneider Has Taught Us' on 'The English Origins of African American Vernacular English' (pp. 349–64), highlighting the English rather than creole origins of this variety. Ulrich Miethaner's study on 'Innovation in Pre-World War II AAVE?' presents 'Evidence from BLUR' (pp. 365–85) for the beginning of

AAVE in the late nineteenth century. In 'Focus 4: Asia and Africa', Andy Kirkpatrick and Sophiaan Subhan investigate 'The Use of Inflectional Marking for Present and Past Tenses in English as an Asian Lingua Franca' and ask if their findings can be interpreted as 'Non-Standard or New Standards or Errors?' (pp. 386–400). In conclusion, they claim that it is not possible to infer speakers' L1s from the way they mark tense in English. Lisa Lim's contribution 'Yesterday's Founder Population, Today's Englishes' concludes that 'The Role of the Peranakans', a prestigious minority group in Singapore, was crucial 'in the (Continuing) Evolution of Singapore English' (pp. 401–19). David Deterding scrutinizes 'The Evolution of Brunei English' and asks 'How It Is Contributing to the Development of English in the World' (pp. 420–33). His conclusion is that from a global perspective this variety is characterized by comparatively restricted developments. In 'The Evolutionary Trajectory of Cameroonian Creole and its Varying Sociolinguistic Statuses' (pp. 434–47), Aloysius Ngefac evaluates issues of prestige and functions of this contact variety as reflected in its varying labels. The final three papers are grouped under 'Old Varieties, New Perspectives'. Roswitha Fischer's 'Lexical Creativity Reconsidered' investigates the neologisms '*GUI, cyborg, cred, pay-per-view, techno-* and *cyber-*' (pp. 448–69) in *The Guardian*. Clive Upton examines 'The Language of Butchery, the UK's Last Public Craft' (pp. 470–85) from an etymological and lexicographical point of view. The last contribution, Christina Neuland and Florian Schleburg's 'A New Old English?', evaluates 'The Chances of an Anglo-Saxon Revival on the Internet' (pp. 486–504); they come to the conclusion that this 'new' online variety suffers from bad grammar and a large impact of PDE.

The second volume on varieties is *The Variability of Current World Englishes* edited by Eugene Green and Charles F. Meyer. The foreword (pp. v–viii) informs the reader that seven of the ten chapters in this book were presented at the second meeting of the International Society of the Linguistics of English (ISLE) in Boston in 2011. In their introduction (pp. 1–9), the editors set the scene for the investigation of variation 'in a range of new and older varieties' (pp. 2–3) and survey the contributions, which are grouped into two parts: Part I, 'Methodological Issues in Distinguishing Varieties', and Part II, 'Studies of Features in Particular Contexts'. I will only concentrate on the chapters relevant for New Englishes and creolistics. In the methodology part, Caroline R. Wiltshire ('New Englishes and the Emergence of the Unmarked', pp. 13–40) argues that new varieties are more likely to have unmarked as opposed to marked vowels in their repertoire. In 'Globalisation and the Transnational Impact of Non-Standard Varieties' (pp. 65–98), Christian Mair uses data from vernacularized computer-mediated communication in Nigerian Pidgin English, Jamaican Creole, and Camfranglais. He is sceptical about the explanatory power of traditional models as regards the impact of globalization and opts for a turn towards 'complex multilingual settings' (p. 93) in World Englishes research. In his contribution 'The Circle of English: An Exploration of the "Core" and "Periphery" of World Englishes' (pp. 99–124), Gerald Nelson investigates the core vocabulary of ten Inner and Outer Circle varieties of English and claims that World Englishes research might do well to turn its focus on common rather than differing characteristics.

In the first chapter of Part II, Rajend Mesthrie examines 'Contact and Sociolinguistic Factors in the Evolution of a Variety of Black English in Kimberley, South Africa', where he spots 'A Robust, Living Substratum' (pp. 127–47). He shows that it is quite difficult to label the features he studies as either characteristic of this variety or as products of L2 acquisition. Zhiming Bao studies '*Got* in Singapore English' (pp. 147–68) in contexts where it replaces *did* ('I got ask you') and investigates the role of this construction, a transfer feature from Chinese, plays in contact-induced change in SingE. On the basis of four vowels in speakers of JamE and Jamaican Creole who grew up in Canada, Lars Hinrichs examines 'Diasporic Mixing of World Englishes: The Case of Jamaican Creole in Toronto' (pp. 169–98). In general he finds a greater tendency towards CanE vowel realizations. Sali A. Tagliamonte's contribution, 'System and Society in the Evolution of Change: The View from Canada' (pp. 199–238), investigates stative passive *have got* as opposed to *have* and quotative *be like*. She concludes that with respect to these features there is no north–south divide in CanE. For *be like* she found gender differences in the south. In the last chapter, Eugene Green examines 'The Diffusion of *I Need You To* + Infinitive in World Englishes' (pp. 257–84). Quantitative results based on the Corpus of Global Web-Based English reveal that in varieties of English world-wide the occurrence of this pattern is fairly homogeneous, mirroring rapid global diffusion. Due to the lack of sociolinguistic information in the data, a full-fledged analysis of this spread requires other sources. A great benefit of the volume is a 'contextual statement' by the editors placed after each contribution to put each respective chapter in a wider perspective of ongoing research.

This year's third book-length publication is Raymond Hickey's *A Dictionary of Varieties of English*, which covers a wide array of topics pertaining to all varieties of English (dialects as well as New Englishes), ranging from all traditional and some new lexical sets relevant for comparing accents world-wide, via important linguists in the field, to an abundance of varieties. Since the dictionary is extensively discussed in Section 9 above, the reader should turn to that section for more detail.

In addition to the edited volumes and the dictionary, a special issue of the *Journal of English Linguistics* (42:i[2014]), edited by Dirk Noel, Bertus van Rooy, and Johan van der Auwera, presents four articles on 'Diachronic Approaches to Modality in World Englishes', one dealing with White SAE, one with Black SAE and one each with AusE and PhilE. In their 'Introduction to the Special Issue' (*JEngL* (42:i[2014] 3–6), the editors highlight the benefit of a diachronic approach to World Englishes on the basis of corpora especially complied for this purpose, which has been largely neglected so far. The first contribution, by Peter Collins, investigates 'Quasi-Modals and Modals in Australian English Fiction 1800–1999, with Comparisons across British and American English' (*JEngL* (42:i[2014] 7–30) and concludes that AusE is evolving in ways similar to BrE and AmE. Ronel Wasserman and Bertus van Rooy explore 'The Development of Modals of Obligation and Necessity in White South African English through Contact with Afrikaans' (*JEngL* (42:i[2014] 31–50) and claim that through contact with Afrikaans *must* and *should* tend to shift their meanings and become increasingly polysemous. Bertus van Rooy and Ronel Wasserman, 'Do the Modals of Black and White South African English Converge?' (*JEngL* (42:i[2014] 51–67), show that the distance between the two varieties under scrutiny is, in fact, increasing as regards the use of modals. Finally, Peter Collins, Ariane M. Borlongan, and Xinyue Yao present their results of 'A Diachronic Study' of 'Modality in Philippine English' (*JEngL* (42:i[2014] 68–88). They conclude that PhilE is different from both BrE and AmE in general although in some areas of modality it seems to be aligning with AmE. These findings are interpreted as a sign of a stage between endo- and exonormative orientation.

Moving on to general articles and articles on a mix of varieties, Edgar W. Schneider, in 'New Reflections of the Evolutionary Dynamics of World Englishes' (*WEn* 33[2014] 9–32), tests the applicability of his Dynamic Model to Expanding Circle varieties. He concludes that the model is not appropriate for explaining the dynamics in non-postcolonial contexts and introduces the notion of 'transnational attractions' as a more suitable concept to describe situations in which English is used as 'a tool and symbol of modernization, globalization, and economic prosperity' (p. 28). Bertus van Rooy examines 'Progressive Aspect and Stative Verbs in Outer Circle Varieties' (*WEn* 33[2014] 157–72). Based on corpora for spoken and written IndE, KenE, and Black SAE, he concludes that the progressive is not merely expanded to stative verbs, as has been argued by others, but rather to contexts where it captures extended duration. Thomas Brunner investigates 'Structural Nativization, Typology and Complexity' in 'Noun Phrase Structures in British, Kenyan and Singaporean English' (*ELL* 18[2014] 23–48). He finds that NP modification in SingE and KenE differ from BrE in accordance with the typological set-up of the respective substrate languages. In a fairly different but also relevant approach, M. Obaidul Hamid investigates 'World Englishes in International Proficiency Tests' (*WEn* 33[2014] 263–77), reporting that World Englishes-speaking participants in such tests support both StE as the underlying model and 'varietal equality and non-native speakers' right to lexical creativity' (p. 275). As a consequence Hamid demands more awareness-raising on the side of World Englishes research.

Next, we turn to publications dealing with one variety each, starting with Oceania/Australia, with one book appearing on Fiji English and, in addition to Pam Peters's and Peter Collins's contributions mentioned above, eight articles on AusE relevant for the present section in the four issues of the *Australian Journal of Linguistics* (34[2014]).

Lena Zipp's monograph investigates *Educated Fiji English* with respect to *Lexico-Grammar and Variety Status*, intending to analyse and place this type of English within the framework of Schneider's Dynamic Model. After the introduction (pp. 1–4), chapter 2 gives an account of the 'History and the Sociolinguistic Setting' in Fiji (pp. 5–20) and chapter 3 surveys 'Theory, Methodology and Data' (pp. 21–54). The following chapters 4 to 6 are the core of the book, basically treating prepositions in different syntactic contexts, on 'Word Level: Prepositions' (pp. 55–90), 'Phrase Level: Verb-Particle Combinations' (pp. 91–146), and 'Pattern Level: Prepositions and *-ing* Clauses' (pp. 147–86) respectively. In her conclusion (pp. 187–94), Zipp sums up her main results and links her three main hypotheses to her findings.

The linguistic analyses aim at identifying qualitative and quantitative similarities between the use of English by the two ethnic groups in Fiji, i.e. Fijians and Indo-Fijians, as well as testing exonormative influence from IndE or NZE with respect to three theoretical hypotheses, two of which can be tentatively confirmed. The first is that Indo-Fijian English exhibits similarities to IndE, although it is not clear if this results from the 'general similarity of second language phenomena' (p. 188) or from an exonormative orientation towards IndE. The second hypothesis, that Indo-Fijian English and Fijian English display a high degree of similarity, is confirmed by the features under scrutiny, leading Zipp to claim that a national variety might be evolving. Her third hypothesis, that Indo-Fijian English is closer to NZE than to BrE, could not be backed up by empirical evidence.

In a special issue of *AuJL* (34:i[2014]), Pam Peters and Michael Haugh examine 'Speech Styles and Spoken Interaction in the Australian National Corpus' (*AuJL* 34[2014] 1–3), which contains the following two contributions relevant for this section. The first is Kate Burridge and Simon Musgrave's 'It's Speaking Australian English We Are: Irish Features in Nineteenth Century Australia' (*AuJL* 34[2014] 24–49). They find evidence for the influence of several IrE grammatical features in the formation stage of AusE. In the second, Felicity Cox, Sallyanne Palethorpe, and Samantha Bentink have a go at 'Phonetic Archaeology' and examine '50 Years of Change to Australian English /i:/' (*AuJL* 34[2014] 50–75). Focusing on the degree of onglide in /i:/, they report that the 'broadness continuum has contracted' (p. 50).

In another issue of *AuJL*, Jill Vaughan and Jean Mulder, 'The Survival of the Subjunctive in Australian English: Ossification, Indexicality and Stance' (*AuJL* 34[2014] 486–505), attribute the continued use of the mandative and the *were*-subjunctive in AusE to the emergence of certain ossifying frames and the need for indexing certain styles. In 'A Corpus-Based Study', Peter Collins and Xinyue Yao examine 'Grammatical Change in the Verb Phrase in Australian English' (*AuJL* 34[2014] 506–23). With respect to modals, quasi-modals, the progressive, and the present perfect, the authors show that in principle AusE has been changing in ways similar to AmE and BrE, but also point to differences that suggest a certain degree of independence of AusE. Celeste Rodríguez Louro and Marie-Eve Ritz's 'Stories Down Under' examines 'Tense Variation at the Heart of Australian English Narratives' (*AuJL* 34[2014] 549–65). Based on personal narratives by educated speakers of AusE, the authors find evidence for generational differences in the use of tense for foregrounding, and interpret this as change in progress. Ina G. Malcolm, 'A Day in the Park: Emerging Genre for Readers of Aboriginal English' (*AuJL* 34[2014] 566–80), discusses an autobiographical narrative written in Aboriginal English and suggests that a distinct genre is emerging for an Aboriginal English readership. Pam Peters investigates 'Usage Guides and Usage Trends in Australian and British English' (*AuJL* 34[2014] 581–98) with respect to three spelling features. She finds that the differing recommendations in British and Australian usage guides are not mirrored in usage. Kiya Alimoradian, '"Makes Me Feel More Aussie": Ethnic Identity and Vocative *Mate* in Australia' (*AuJL* 34[2014] 599–623), examines the self-reported use of this vocative by Australians whose native language is not English and finds similarities to L1 English Australians, but also a correlation between a less frequent use of *mate* and a stronger heritage orientation.

Moving to South Asia, Marianne Hundt and Devyani Sharma have edited a volume on *English in the Indian Diaspora*, presenting nine contributions on IndE as used outside India. In their introduction (pp. 1–8), the editors outline the rationale behind this volume, i.e. primarily to test if diaspora varieties are different in terms of outcome from non-diaspora varieties and if across diasporic contexts contact features and processes are similar. Glenda Leung and Dagmar Deuber examine 'Indo-Trinidadian Speech' by presenting 'An Investigation into a Popular Stereotype Surrounding Pitch' (pp. 9–27). They conclude that a high pitch is indeed a marker of Indo-Trinidadians but also find that this feature is more prominent in women than men. Farhana Alam and Jane Stuart-Smith's contribution on 'Identity, Ethnicity and Fine Phonetic Detail' provides 'An Acoustic Phonetic Analysis of Syllable-Initial /t/ in Glaswegian Girls of Pakistani Heritage' (pp. 29–53). They find that the girls' articulation of /t/ as either dental or retroflex correlates with their modern or conservative communities of practice. Claudia Rathore studies 'East African Indian Twice Migrants in Britain' by looking into 'Phonological Variation across Generations' (pp. 55–83) with respect to rhoticity. She concludes that, while first-generation migrants continue to be rhotic, second-generation migrants adopt local non-rhoticity. Rajend Mesthrie and Alida Chevalier give a survey of 'Sociophonetics and the Indian Diaspora' and then take a closer look at 'The NURSE Vowel and Other Selected Features in South African Indian English' (pp. 85–104). Their general result is that in Indian SAE stratification by class and gender is setting in. Jakob Leimgruber and Lavanya Sankran investigate 'Imperfectives in Singapore's Indian Community' (pp. 105–30) and find ethnic differentiation between Tamils, Chinese, and Malay. They claim that this is due to subtle differences in the substrate languages of SingE. In 'Zero Articles in Indian Englishes: A Comparison of Primary and Secondary Diaspora Situations' (pp. 131–70), Marianne Hundt studies first-generation Indian migrants to Fiji and Fiji Indian migrants to New Zealand. She concludes that, despite a high degree of fluctuation, article use in the secondary diaspora is closer to metropolitan types of English than in the primary diaspora. Rajend Mesthrie's 'A Lesser Globalisation' provides 'A Sociolexical Study of Indian Englishes in Diaspora, with a Primary Focus on South Africa' (pp. 171–86). He claims that the examination of the Indian diaspora can greatly benefit from analyses of the lexicon, showing both 'cultural retentions from different parts of India' (p. 184) as well as semantic changes due to new contact settings. Lena Zipp ('Indo-Fijian English: Linguistic Diaspora or Endonormative Stabilization?', pp. 187–213) investigates language attitudes and use in Fiji and reports that Fijians and Indo-Fijians are in different phases of Schneider's Dynamic Model. In the last contribution, Devyani Sharma studies 'Transnational Flows, Language Variation, and Ideology' (pp. 215–42). On the basis of the pronunciation of /t/, she shows that the ties of second-generation British Punjabis with India have grown weaker, while at the same time educated IndE has developed into a fairly prestigious variety for this group.

A number of journal contributions also deal with South Asia. Tobias Bernaisch, Stefan Th. Gries, and Joybrato Mukherjee investigate 'The Dative Alternation in South Asian English(es)', i.e. Bangladeshi, Indian, Maldivian, Nepali, Pakistani, and Sri Lankan English, and aim at 'Modelling Predictors and Predicting Prototypes' (EWW 35[2014] 7–31). They find that these varieties display a large degree of similarity with one another and with BrE, the reference variety, as regards the influence of several factors on the occurrence of the two competing dative patterns for the verb give. On the basis of glossaries of IndE features from the 1930s, James Lambert examines the 'Diachronic Stability in Indian English Lexis' (WEn 33[2014] 112–27). He finds an astounding continuity of features over time and posits that endonormativity in IndE has a much longer history than is widely assumed. Finally, Elizabeth J. Erling, Philip Seargeant, and Mike Solly present the results of a survey of attitudes towards 'English in Rural Bangladesh' (EnT 30:iv[2014] 15–21). They report that people's attitudes often mirror unrealistic expectations as regards the benefits of a better knowledge of English. As a result, the authors demand that development programmes take these expectations into account to 'enhance opportunities for economic and social development' (p. 20).

Next are sixteen articles on English in Southeast Asia. In addition to two papers which deal with several varieties, nine contributions are on English in Singapore, six of which are part of a special issue of World Englishes (33:iii[2014]), two are on Malaysia, two on the Philippines, and one on Brunei. Gerhard Leitner, 'Transforming Southeast Asian Language Habits' (WEn 33[2014] 512–25), gives a survey of the history of English in this region, sheds light on unifying and differentiating linguistic developments, and presents some thoughts on educational implications. Cristina Suárez-Gómez examines adnominal 'Relative Clauses in Southeast Asian Englishes' (JEngL 42[2014] 245–68) in Hong Kong, Singapore, and India (with the latter, strictly speaking, belonging to South Asia). Focusing on relativizers, she finds, among other things, that HKE and SingE similarly prefer that, while IndE tends towards wh-words; she interprets this distinction as a reflex of substrate influence.

Turning to the special issue of WEn mentioned above, the editors Kingsley Bolton and Bee Chin Ng's 'The Dynamics of Multilingualism in Contemporary Singapore' (WEn 33:iii[2014] 307–18) serves as an introduction to this symposium and surveys history, educational policy, trends in language acquisition, and language shift in Singapore. The contribution by Ying-Ying Tan, 'English as a "Mother Tongue" in Singapore' (WEn 33[2014] 319–39), uses a questionnaire study on language attitudes and on how English is perceived as an identity marker, finding that English is acquiring the status of a native language. Peter Siemund, Monika Edith Schulz, and Martin Schweinberger's 'Studying the Linguistic Ecology of Singapore: A Comparison of College and University Students' (WEn 33[2014] 340–62) is another questionnaire study on language attitudes and use and finds that Singaporean students are mostly bi- or trilingual and have positive attitudes towards Singlish, English, and their mother tongue. Euvin Loong Jin Chong, and Mark F. Seilhamer investigate 'Young People, Malay and English in Multilingual Singapore' (WEn 33[2014] 363–77). Also using a survey, they confirm the alleged strong status of Malay among L1 Malay-speaking students. Francesco Cavallaro, Bee Chin Ng, and Mark F. Seilhamer examine 'Singapore Colloquial English' (Singlish) with respect to 'Issues of Prestige and Identity' (*WEn* 33[2014] 378–97). Aiming at a reassessment of the widely reported low prestige of Singlish, their matched-guise tests reveal that this non-standard variety, indeed, only has a certain prestige in the private but not the public domain. Despite its title, 'Singlish *Can* and Speech Accommodation in Singapore English' (*WEn* 33[2014] 398–412) by Bee Chin Ng, Francesco Cavallaro, and Daphne Shu Ping Koh, is not about *can* but rather studies how speakers of Singlish and Standard SingE are perceived in salesman–customer dialogues within the framework of accommodation theory. They find that salesmen were rated more positively when they diverged from the language of the customer, while the customers were seen more positively when they converged on the language of the salesmen. Next we turn to the three papers on SingE which are not part of this symposium. In 'Singapore English and Styling the *Ah Beng*' (*WEn* 33[2014] 60–84) David West Brown and Teo Shi Jie study users of English in online forums who style themselves as *Ah Bengs* ('hustlers, gangsters') and find evidence of sociolinguistic variation in SingE with respect to gender, class, and ethnicity. Jakob R.E. Leimgruber investigates 'Singlish as Defined by Young Educated Chinese Singaporeans' (*IJSL* 230[2014] 45–63). On the basis of definitions of Singlish given by Chinese Singaporeans and of attitudinal tests of Hokkien elements, he calls for a redefinition of Singlish as a linguistic repertoire rather than a bundle of features. Ee-Ling Low presents a meta-analysis of many older and recent studies on SingE in 'Research on English in Singapore' (*WEn* 33[2014] 439–57). She concludes that the areas of language use, focusing on variation as well as linguistic features and language education, have been covered widely. As future directions, she suggests more work on language acquisition, language pathology, and classroom discourse. Finally she discusses SingE in the frameworks of Braj B. Kachru's Three Circles and Schneider's Dynamic Model.

Moving on to English in Malaysia, Azirah Hashim examines 'English and the Linguistic Ecology in Malaysia' (*WEn* 33[2014] 458–71), discussing emerging tensions between English, Malay, and other local languages. Ultimately she calls for reactions first and foremost in the domain of education and thus language policy. Toshiko Yamaguchi studies 'The Pronunciation of TH in Word-Initial Position in Malaysian English' (*EnT* 30:iii[2014] 13–21). She finds that a new dental [t] is used by speakers of all ethnicities as an allophone of the voiced and unvoiced dental fricatives. The irregular use of this new [t], however, does not allow a straightforward categorization as a nativized feature. In addition to the two papers mentioned above, PhilE was covered in two further contributions this year. Peter Collins, Ariane M. Borlongan, Joo-Hyuk Lim, and Xinyue Yao provide 'A Diachronic Analysis' of 'The Subjunctive Mood in Philippine English' (in Pfenninger et al., eds., *Contact, Variation, and Change in the History of English*, pp. 250–80). Their analysis confirms a strong connection of PhilE to its 'parent' (p. 259) AmE, but also suggests a certain degree of endonormative stabilization, a result very much in line with Collins et al.'s modality study in *JEngL* (42:i) above. In 'Philippine English Revisited' (*WEn* 33[2014] 50–9) Isabel Pefianco Martin sets out to establish a notion of 'circles within circles' in Kachru's Three Circles model. This seems to be a complement to her discussion of PhilE in the framework of Schneider's Dynamic Model (see above), but she does not cross-reference her two articles, although a combined evaluation would have been welcome. The last paper on Southeast Asia is Noor Azam Haji-Othman and James McLellan's assessment of 'English in Brunei' (*WEn* 33[2014] 486–97). On the basis of a literature review they confirm the previous categorization of Brunei English as a new variety, place it between Phases 3 and 4 of Schneider's Dynamic Model, and call for a closer investigation of sub-varieties and code-mixing in future research.

Moving to East Asia, there is one monograph and one article on South Korea and two articles on HKE. Glenn Hadikin's *Korean English: A Corpus-Driven Study of a New English* contains seven chapters, a reference section, and an index, and aims at establishing the English spoken by Koreans as a variety of English on the basis of analyses of word strings and lexical priming in spoken corpora. In chapter 1, 'Korean English' (pp. 1–18), the author sets the scene with the intention to show that we are not dealing with bad English but a variety of its own. Chapter 2, 'From Phraseology to Lexical Priming' (pp. 19–36), explains the key terms, shows differences between L1 and L2 English phraseology and formulates the objectives of the study. Chapter 3, 'Capturing and Comparing' (pp. 37–48), introduces the methodology: the study used a total of four spoken corpora, two from groups of Korean speakers of English living in Liverpool (83,446 tokens) and Seoul (112,621 tokens), respectively, and two covering spoken UK English, i.e. a selection of data from the BNC (3,945,881 tokens) and a corpus of local Liverpool English (106,562 tokens) collected by a colleague of the author's. Chapters 4 to 6 present the results of the study concerning 'The *of* Environment', a 'Study of *Have a* and *Look*', and a 'Study of the *I* Environment' respectively. The author shows that in all patterns the Korean speakers diverge from the L1 English data in terms of collocations, which the author attributes partly to education material used in Korea. Finally, chapter 7 formulates 'Implications of This Study' (pp. 177–86), again focusing on the 'Emergence of Korean Spoken English', but also critically evaluating variation in the corpora and identifying limitations of this study. Overall, I think Hadikin's claim that we are dealing with an emerging variety is way too strong; it seems more plausible that the divergence of the Korean data from UK English mirrors Korean learner-English. Nevertheless, the collocation-cum-lexical priming approach to World Englishes is innovative and promising. In the article on English in Korea, Sofia Rüdiger also examines—in a much more cautious way than Hadikin—'The Nativization of English in the Korean Context', describing 'Uncharted Territory of World Englishes' (*EnT* 30:iv[2014] 11–14), identifying some lexical and morphosyntactic patterns as potential candidates for structural nativization of English in South Korea.

Next comes Hong Kong. Anna Danielewicz-Betz and David Graddol take a look at 'Varieties of English in the Urban Landscapes of Hong Kong and Shenzhen' (*EnT* 30:iii[2014] 22–32) and provide, mostly on the basis of public signs, an overview of the diverse language landscapes of these two cities. They find that in Hong Kong, English is losing ground while in Shenzen it is becoming more prominent. In both areas the authors note a frequent mixing of BrE and AmE. In the other paper, Stephen Evans, in 'The Evolutionary Dynamics of Postcolonial Englishes: A Hong Kong Case Study' (*JSoc* 18[2014] 571–603), challenges the applicability of Schneider's Dynamic Model to Hong Kong and other Outer Circle Englishes. Using a corpus of primary sources of HKE (e.g. legislative council proceedings and newspapers) spanning the years 1841 to 2012, the author identifies Schneider's test cases based on synchronic data and secondary sources as inadequate, suggests a substantial reorganization of the evolutionary phases of HKE, among other things, and calls for the analysis of primary diachronic data to account for the development of English in Outer Circle countries.

In addition to articles on English in Africa in edited volumes and special issues discussed above, there are four journal contributions, one each on Uganda and South Africa, and two on Namibia. Bebwa Isingoma examines 'Lexical and Grammatical Features of Ugandan English' (*EnT* 30:ii[2014] 51–6). In doing so he counters the widespread practice of subsuming Kenyan, Tanzanian, and Ugandan English under the heading East African English. In her article 'Coconuts and the Middle Class' Kirstin Wilmot investigates 'Identity Change and the Emergence of a New Prestigious English Variety in South Africa' (*EWW* 35[2014] 306–37). On the basis of sociolinguistic interviews and socio-phonetic analyses, she claims that young female speakers educated in elite schools are developing a new social 'deracialized' (p. 335) variety of English. In the first of two contributions on Namibia, Sarah Buschfeld and Alexander Kautzsch, 'English in Namibia: A First Approach' (*EWW* 35[2014] 121–60), introduce the English spoken in Namibia to the field of World Englishes. Namibia is an especially noteworthy case, since it was never a British colony and thus English does not have a long tradition there. Nevertheless, with the 1990 independence, English was introduced as the sole official language. On the basis of a language attitudes and use survey and some tentative candidates for structural nativization, the authors identify clear signals for a shift from foreign to L2 status. Gerald Stell analyses 'Use and Function of English in Namibia's Multiethnic Settings' (*WEn* 33[2014] 223–41). More precisely, he investigates English/local language code-switching patterns in inter- and intra-ethnic communication and highlights the relevance for such an approach in examining the emergence of a new variety.

Moving on to the Caribbean, we find one monograph on English in Jamaica and Trinidad and one article on JamE. Dagmar Deuber examines *English in the Caribbean* focusing on *Variation, Style and Standards in Jamaica and Trinidad*. Using ICE as data source, Deuber aims at describing morphological and syntactic variation with respect to the relationship between standard and creole features in educated speakers. In the introduction (pp. 1–21), the author gives an overview of variation, style, and standard both in Jamaica and Trinidad and in the Caribbean in general and presents the aims and structure of the book. Chapter 2 surveys 'The Background and Context of English in Jamaica and Trinidad' (pp. 22–43) and focuses on the relevant sociolinguistic developments. Chapter 3, 'The Sociolinguistics of Style and the Creole Continuum', presents the book's research context, while chapter 4 gives an

account of 'Data and Methodology' (pp. 67–78). Chapters 5 to 7 are the
empirical core of the book. Here Deuber provides an 'Analysis of
Conversations' with respect to 'Style in Jamaican English' (pp.
79–137), the results of which are used as a starting point for a comparison of JamE to
Trinidadian English in chapter 6, which presents an 'Analysis of Four Text
Categories' going into the details of 'Style and Standard in Trinidadian
English' (pp. 138–201). Chapter 7 investigates what Deuber calls 'the main
question that will be considered in the present study with regard to standards'
(p. 20), i.e. 'The Modal Verbs *Can/Could* and *Will/Would* in Caribbean and
Other Varieties of English' (pp. 202–37). Her main findings, summed up in the
conclusion (pp. 238–54), are as follows. Chapters 5 and 6 show that creole
features (i.e. direct creole influence) are low in terms of overall frequency but
are 'an important feature of style in spoken English in the Caribbean' (p. 238),
ranging from informal to anti-formal. The results of the modal verb analysis in
chapter 7 suggest that indirect creole influence (i.e. English forms with a
particular creole meaning) can range, stylistically speaking, from neutral to
informal in Trinidadian English. These findings lead Deuber to a reinterpretation of the creole continuum (p. 241), incorporating style as a factor more
prominent than social status. In this vein, creole features also contribute to the
identity constructions of educated speakers in marking them as 'professionally
competent yet down-to-earth' (p. 243). With respect to 'Standards in English
in the Caribbean' (p. 244), the author confirms earlier assumptions that the
two varieties under scrutiny are sub-varieties of Caribbean StE. A comparison
of the outcomes with other New Englishes shows that informal Caribbean
varieties cannot clearly be categorized as either ESL, ENL, or creoles, which is
why Deuber suggests employing the rarely used term ESD (English as a second
dialect) for such cases. Finally, the volume is complemented by two appendices
('Markup Symbols' and 'Biodata Form'). In the article on JamE, Ksenija
Bogetić finds 'Linguistic Trajectories of Globalization and Localization' on
the basis of '*Be Like* and the Quotative System of Jamaican English'
(*EnT* 30:iii[2014] 5–12). Further contributions on the Caribbean with a
stronger creolist focus are treated below.

As stated above, the investigation of the nativization of English in non-
postcolonial countries is a hot topic at the moment, especially in European
countries. In addition to a contribution on Germany by Kautzsch (see above),
four papers have touched upon this issue in 2014 with respect to Finland,
Poland, Serbia, and Turkey. Mikko Laitinen, '630 Kilometres by Bicycle:
Observations of English in Urban and Rural Finland' (*IJSL* 228 [2014] 55–77),
takes a linguistic-landscape perspective in surveying the status of English in
Finland. On the basis of a quantitative account of English in signs in rural and
urban areas, he concludes that English is present everywhere, albeit to
different degrees. Aleksandra Kasztalska's article 'English in Contemporary
Poland' (*WEn* 33[2014] 242–62) surveys the history of English in Poland and
the status of English in education, advertising, and the media, provides
examples of the impact of English on Polish, and concludes that English in
Poland has the somewhat ambivalent status of both being 'an economic asset
and a corrupting agent' (p. 242). Tvrtko Prćić's 'English as *the* Nativized
Foreign Language [ENFL] and its Impact on Serbian' (*EnT* 30:i[2014] 13–20)

examines the degree of Anglicization and hybridization of Serbian and concludes that the overwhelming influence of English as a very special foreign language requires sound knowledge of these processes to ensure 'peaceful co-existence' of English and local languages. Beril T. Arik and Engin Arik investigate 'The Role and Status of English in Turkish Higher Education' (*EnT* 30:iv[2014] 5–10). They find that, with about 15 per cent of BA programmes in Turkey being taught exclusively in English, English sees an immense spread in this Expanding Circle country. Interestingly, the subject most frequently taught in English in Turkey is engineering, followed by English-related programmes.

We now turn to the second subsection on creolistics and begin with one edited volume and two monographs. The volume edited by Isabelle Buchstaller, Anders Holmberg, and Mohammad Almoaily investigates *Pidgins and Creoles beyond European Encounters*. Even if this is not about English-lexifier pidgins and creoles, it is included here since it makes an important contribution to the field by going beyond the trodden paths of a European-centred approach to contact languages. This motivation is explicated in the editors' introduction (pp. 1–6), which also briefly sketches the contents of the six papers included. Emanuel J. Drechsel ('Ethnohistory of Speaking: Maritime Polynesian Pidgin in a Trilogy of Historical-Sociolinguistic Attestations', pp. 7–40) examines the methodological problems involved in reconstructing an extinct contact language, in this case a Polynesian-based pidgin used as a means of communication between locals and British and French explorers in the eighteenth century. On the basis of an early text written in pidgin, Anthony P. Grant ('The "Language of Tobi" as Presented in Horace Holden's Narrative: Evidence for Restructuring and Lexical Mixture in a Nuclear Micronesian-Based Pidgin', pp. 41–56) gives an account of the existence of a Micronesian-based pidgin spoken on Tobi Island. Mohammed Almoaily studies 'Language Variation in Gulf Pidgin Arabic' (pp. 57–84) on the basis of morpho-syntactic structures. This pidgin, used by native speakers of Arabic and expatriate workers, is claimed to be largely influenced by universal cognitive processes rather than by the substrates or the superstrate. Rajend Mesthrie asks the question, 'How Non-Indo-European is Fanakalo Pidgin?' and investigates 'Selected Understudied Structures in a Bantu-Lexified Pidgin with Germanic Substrates' (pp. 85–100). He concludes that this pidgin, whose lexicon is 70 per cent Zulu and 30 per cent English and Afrikaans, exhibits a grammar more similar to English than to Zulu but also exhibits structures that result neither from English nor Zulu. Kofi Yakpo and Pieter Muysken tackle 'Language Change in a Multiple Contact Setting' based on 'The Case of Sarnami (Suriname)' (pp. 101–40). This Indian diaspora contact variety seems to have emerged from an interesting mix of koineization and contact with Dutch and Sranan Tongo, the national vernacular of Surinam. Finally, Kees Versteegh examines 'Pidgin Verbs' and asks: are they 'Infinitives or Imperatives?' (pp. 141–70). He claims that foreigner-directed speech is crucial in the emergence of a pidgin, just as child-directed speech has an impact on child speech. On the basis of Arabic foreigner-directed speech, the author shows that the verb-form in Arabic-based pidgins frequently is the

Arabic imperative. The volume is complemented by area, language, and subject indexes.

The first of the two monographs is Claire Lefebvre's *Relabeling in Language Genesis*. The book is made up of nine chapters in which the author elaborates on the concept of relabelling, i.e. relexification, as the driving force behind the creation of contact languages, summarizing and expanding upon her and her associates' previous work on the issue. Unlike earlier work within the framework of Principles and Parameters (P&P), Lefebvre resorts to a CxG approach here, which she deems more appropriate to capture relabelling, a process that 'takes place in the lexical component of the grammar' (p. 5). In her introduction (pp. 1–8) she justifies the need for the book and gives an overview of its structure. Chapter 2, 'Relabeling: A Central Process in Language Contact/Genesis' (pp. 9–30), explains the concept under investigation, noting that other labels that have been used (e.g. relexification, calquing, transfer) might cover the same phenomenon; the chapter also evaluates relabelling in a variety of contexts. Chapter 3 provides an up-to-date version of Lefebvre's 'A Relabeling-Based Theory of Creole Genesis' (pp. 31–102), highlighting the fact that other processes only happen after relabelling. In addition, the author deals with comments and criticism and introduces new data to substantiate her claims. The next two chapters are co-authored with Renée Lambert-Brétière. Chapter 4 investigates 'Relabeling in Two Different Theories of the Lexicon' (pp. 103–38) and concludes that where a P&P approach fails to explain some aspects of relabelling in creole genesis, CxG, more precisely Radical CxG, succeeds. In chapter 5, the two authors examine 'Relabeling and Word Order' from 'A Construction Grammar Perspective' (pp. 139–63) to address the at times ambiguous findings on the influence of substrate and superstrate in creole genesis. Chapter 6, then, elaborates 'On Some Differences between Haitian and Saramaccan', which have Gbe as a common substrate, in order to identify certain 'Relabeling Options' (pp. 164–76) available in creating creoles. Chapter 7, 'Relabeling and the Contribution of the Superstrate Languages to Creoles' (pp. 177–222), explains the necessary, though frequently neglected, investigation of the superstrate in the emergence of creoles. Here the impact of the superstrate is largely attributed to the labels and to word order. 'Relabeling and the Typological Classification of Creoles' (pp. 223–58) is the topic of chapter 8, where it is argued that creoles have typological traits of both substrate and superstrate, depending on which of the two is in operation in the respective area of grammar. The conclusion (chapter 9) claims to establish relabelling as 'A Strong Alternative to the Bioprogram Hypothesis' (pp. 258–71). Here Lefebvre pulls together her findings on relabelling and discusses this process in the light of creole 'Exceptionalism' (pp. 258–60), 'the Principled Contribution of Substrate and Superstrate Languages to Creoles' (pp. 260–1), 'Theories of the Lexicon' (pp. 261–2), 'Types of Morphemes' (pp. 262–4), 'Variation among Creoles' (pp. 264–6), 'Other Approaches to Creole Genesis' (pp. 266–71), most prominently the feature-pool hypothesis, and 'The Relevance of Pidgins and Creoles in the Debate on Language Origins' (p. 271).

In the second monograph, Mareile Schramm examines *The Emergence of Creole Syllable Structure*, providing *A Cross-Linguistic Study* of six Caribbean creoles with Dutch, English, and French as lexifiers, i.e. Berbice Dutch, Negerhollands, Saramaccan, St Kitts, Guiana French Creole, and Trinidad French Creole. In her brief introduction, Schramm justifies the study by asserting that supra-segmentals, such as syllable structure and phonotactic restructuring, have been largely neglected in the description of creoles, and surveys the structure of the book. Chapter 2 discusses the two core issues, 'Creole Genesis and Syllable Structure' (pp. 4–13). In chapter 3, 'Data and Methodology' (pp. 14–44), the author explains which creoles have been selected and why, provides the historical background for the creoles under investigation, surveys her corpora, which consist of the earliest reliable sources available, identifies the main lexifiers, and explains how she coded the data and proceeded in the analysis. Chapters 4 to 6 (pp. 45–231) present the empirical results of the author's analyses of 'Syllable Structure and Phonotactic Restructuring' in the Dutch-, English-, and French-based creoles, respectively. These chapters are structured alike: after an introduction, a review of the literature, and some methodological notes, the results are presented by creole language and are divided into the phenomena under observation: word-initial onsets, word-final codas, and word-internal structures. Chapter 7 (pp. 232–53) then pulls together the findings on the 'Syllable Structure in the Six Creoles' and discusses 'Similarities and Differences', while chapter 8 (pp. 254–308) aims at 'Explaining Creole Phonotactic Restructuring'. In her concluding chapter, Schramm delivers 'A Final Assessment' of 'Creole Syllable Structure'. Schramm's overarching aim is to find out which structures of the lexifier languages are kept intact, which ones are restructured, and which restructuring processes can be observed. The analysis presents evidence for a large degree of variation across creoles, first and foremost in word-final position, both in terms of the structures that are permitted in principle and with respect to preferred repair strategies. In sum, most patterns can be explained in the light of L1 transfer, L2 acquisition, and substrate levelling, basically confirming previous observations that general processes of SLA play a major role in the emergence of phonological patterns of creoles.

Turning to articles published in journals, we start with four contributions with a more general orientation. The first two are by Peter Bakker arguing in favour of the distinctiveness of creoles from non-creoles on the basis of empirical data. In 'Creolistics: Back to Square One?' (*JPCL* 29:i[2014] 177–94), he presents a bitterly ironic account of what non-exceptionalists, i.e. scholars who believe that creoles are in principle not exceptionally different from non-creoles, have contributed to the field, mostly accusing them of using theory and rhetoric—and not data—for their purposes. Even though he does not call himself an exceptionalist, Bakker's aim is to show that creoles 'have an exceptional history, and that creoles therefore are distinctive languages, and distinctive as a group' (p. 188). In his second article, a partly equally ironic guest column in *JPCL*, he reacts to criticism on his and his associates' earlier empirical work on the distinctiveness of creoles and addresses some 'Problems of Sampling and Definition' with respect to 'Creoles and Typology' (*JPCL* 29[2014] 437–55). In a reply to John McWhorter's 'Case Closed? Testing the Feature Pool Hypothesis' (*JPCL* 27[2012] 171–82; cf. *YWES*

93[2014] 96), Salikoko S. Mufwene, 'The Case Was Never Closed: McWhorter Misinterprets the Ecological Approach to the Emergence of Creoles' (*JPCL* 29[2014] 157–71), justifies his 'ecological approach to the emergence of creoles' (p. 157). In the fourth general article, Jeff Siegel, Benedikt Szmrecsanyi, and Bernd Kortmann use data from Tok Pisin, Hawai'i Creole, and some L1 and L2 varieties of English for 'Measuring Analyticity and Syntheticity in Creoles' (*JPCL* 29[2014] 49–85). They find that creoles do not show a higher degree of analyticity than non-creoles but display, in fact, a lower degree of syntheticity.

In addition, the following contributions deal with features in particular pidgins and creoles. In 'A Note on the Haitian Double-Object Construction and the Relabeling-Based Account of Creole Genesis' (*JPCL* 29[2014] 143–56) Claire Lefebvre and Renée Lambert-Brétière aim to substantiate the process of relabelling in Haitian by showing that Haitian has verbs which look as if they were borrowed from French but grammatically behave like verbs from Fongbe, although Fongbe does not have the corresponding verbs. Ahmed-Ibrahim Mousa provides 'A Comparative Study' of broad Jamaican-Creole and Saudi learners of English and finds that with respect to the 'Acquisition of the Labio-Dental Fricative /v/ in English L2 and Jamaican Creole' (*IJEL* 4[2014] 60–9) the two groups under scrutiny resort to the same strategies. Joseph Babasola Osoba examines 'The Use of Nigerian Pidgin in Media Adverts' (*IJEL* 4 [2014] 26–37) from a discourse-pragmatic point of view to show how these advertisements communicate their meaning through presuppositions and implicatures. In the last paper to be discussed in this section, Brett Baker, Rikke Bundgaard-Nielsen, and Simone Graetzer study 'The Obstruent Inventory of Roper Kriol' (*AuJL* 34[2014] 307–44), the major variety of Australian Kriol, and find that its obstruents show traces of both substrate and superstrate influence.

11. Second Language Acquisition

Work dedicated to English as a second or foreign language (ESL/EFL) has been abundant in 2014. All levels of interlanguage grammar have been studied extensively, as have individual learner differences and the role of the learning context. More general topics such as the influence of the first language (L1) on a second language (L2) are also very present; a lot of attention has once again been paid to methodological advancements in the discipline of second language acquisition (SLA). We proceed with our review starting from L2 grammar, moving on towards contextual and individual factors that play a role in L2 acquisition, and finishing with general and methodological works.

The production of papers dedicated to L2 English phonetics and phonology was very rich in 2014, especially as far as journal articles are concerned. In the domain of phonetics, Hyejin Hong, Sunhee Kim, and Minhwa Chung conduct 'A Corpus Based Analysis of English Segments Produced by Korean Learners' (*JPhon* 46[2014] 52–67). The purpose of their analysis, based on manual transcriptions of two large-scale speech corpora, was to compare the patterns of segmental variation produced by L2 learners with those produced by native speakers of English; the results were analysed according to how many corpus segments were realized differently from the canonical dictionary-derived transcriptions (in terms of substitutions, deletions, or insertions). The analysis revealed distinct patterns of variation produced by the two groups of speakers, where for the learners, orthography was found to influence the vocalic variations, while L1 influence was detected in the consonantal ones. Ellenor Shoemaker explores the L2 acquisition of allophonic variation as a word boundary cue in 'The Exploitation of Subphonemic Acoustic Detail in L2 Speech Segmentation' (*SSLA* 36[2014] 709–31). French-speaking L2 learners of English performed a two-alternative forced-choice identification task in which they were required to identify potentially ambiguous phrases in which word boundaries were marked by the word-initial aspiration of plosives (e.g. *Lou spills* vs. *loose pills*) or the presence of prevocalic glottal stops (e.g. *see neither* vs. *seen either*). Participants proved to be more sensitive to the presence of glottal stops than aspiration, suggesting that glottal stops may be a more salient word-boundary cue for learners. The learners were also divided into two groups according to their length of exposure to English; those who had been exposed to English longer identified potentially ambiguous phrases better than those who had been exposed to English for a shorter time.

Dealing with phonetics jointly with grammar, Monika S. Schmid, Steven Gilbers, and Amber Nota tackle the topic of 'Ultimate Attainment in Late Second Language Acquisition: Phonetic and Grammatical Challenges in Advanced Dutch-English Bilingualism' (*SLR* 30[2014] 129–57). Participants in their study were very advanced Dutch-speaking L2 learners of English who were either university students or teachers of English in the Netherlands, and native English speakers living in the Netherlands, who acted as controls; the two groups did not differ in their general proficiency in English. The participants read a word list and did a film retelling task and an acceptability judgement task testing VP ellipsis; their oral productions were subsequently analysed in terms of voice onset time (VOT), vowel discrimination, and perceived foreign accent (using accent ratings performed by native English speakers living in the UK). The L2 learners were shown not to differ from the controls with respect to VOT, but they did differ in vowel discrimination, global nativeness, and acceptability judgements. These results suggest that some phonetic and grammatical properties of the L2 may not be acquired even at the highest level of L2 attainment.

A volume aimed at bringing together research on phonetics/phonology and pronunciation teaching is *Pronunciation in EFL Instruction: A Research-Based Approach* by Jolanta Szpyra-Kozłowska. The book deals with English pronunciation instruction by drawing on the findings of research into EFL learners' acquisition of pronunciation, the efficacy of different teaching approaches, and the usefulness of teaching materials, with empirical findings coming primarily from Polish-speaking EFL learners. The first chapter concerns the issue of choosing an appropriate pronunciation model for EFL teaching, the second the issue of identifying pronunciation priorities for EFL learners, and the third the issue of effective phonetic instruction. In relation to these issues, the author proposes the NELF (Native English as a Lingua Franca) model for EFL teaching, argues that phonetically problematic words

should be given priority in teaching, and proposes a holistic multimodal
approach to pronunciation instruction. Each chapter is divided into two parts:
Part A contains a discussion of a given issue from a theoretical point of view,
and Part B a presentation of some of the author's relevant experimental
studies.

Moving on to phonology, Nan Xu Rattanasone and Katherine Demuth
explore 'The Acquisition of Coda Consonants by Mandarin Early Child L2
Learners of English' (*BLC* 17[2014] 646–59). Three-year-old Mandarin-
speaking children exposed to AusE at preschool took part in an elicited
imitation task, in which the acquisition of coda consonants and phrase-final
lengthening was tested. The children performed well on /t/ and /s/ codas, but
poorly on the phonologically and morphologically more complex /ts/, as well
as on /n/, which is one of the few codas permitted in Mandarin. When
compared to other studies, these results suggest that early child L2 learners
may be a distinct learner group from older child L2 learners, showing
similarities with monolingual children. Also focusing on child L2 learners,
Ellen Simon, Matthias J. Sjerps, and Paula Fikkert investigate 'Phonological
Representations in Children's Native and Non-Native Lexicon' (*BLC* 17[2014]
3–21). They conducted two experiments with Dutch-speaking 9- to 12-year-old
children and adults, who all were L2 learners of English. The task used in the
experiments was a mispronunciation task, in which a vowel within a word was
substituted by another vowel from the same language. The first experiment
was conducted in Dutch and the second in English; the children also
participated in a third experiment, which tested vowel discrimination in
English. The results showed that both learner groups could accurately detect
mispronunciations in Dutch and were more successful (especially children) at
detecting substitutions of native vowels (i.e. those that exist in Dutch) by non-
native vowels than at noticing changes in the opposite direction in English.
Children also proved able to discriminate most of the English vowels. Taken
together, these results suggest that children's perception of English words is
strongly influenced by their L1 phonological categories.

Several papers look at the acquisition of L2 prosody. Candise Y. Lin, Min
Wang, William J. Idsardi, and Yi Xu examine 'Stress Processing in Mandarin
and Korean Second Language Learners of English' (*BLC* 17[2014] 316–46).
Based on the fact that English and Mandarin have lexically contrastive stress
while Korean does not, the study explored whether Mandarin speakers have
better stress perception in English than Korean speakers. The two groups of
L2 learners and a control group of native English speakers took part in a
sequence recall task and a lexical decision task. The former task tested
participants' stress-encoding ability for non-words, while the latter examined
the role of stress in online word recognition. Mandarin speakers outperformed
Korean speakers on both tasks, suggesting that stress-processing in the L2 is
indeed influenced by stress-related properties of the L1. In 'L2 English
Intonation: Relations between Form-Meaning Associations, Access to
Meaning, and L1 Transfer' (*SSLA* 36[2014] 331–53), Marta Ortega-Llebaria
and Laura Colantoni tested the hypothesis that access to contextual meaning
increases the chances of L1 influence on L2 intonation. They assessed the
perception and production of English contrastive sentence focus on the part of

two groups of L2 learners, whose L1s, Mandarin and Spanish, express contrastive focus in a different way, and a native control group. Participants did four tasks in which access to meaning was manipulated by the presence or absence of context. Clearer evidence of L1 transfer was found in the Spanish group than in the Mandarin group. Importantly, L1 transfer effects were stronger in contextualized tasks, supporting the hypothesis that access to meaning increases L1 transfer in the L2 acquisition of focus intonation.

Ulrike Gut and Stefanie Pillai explore 'Prosodic Marking of Information Structure by Malaysian Speakers of English' (*SSLA* 36[2014] 283–302), focusing on the marking of given and new discourse elements. One group of Malay speakers of English read aloud a 179-word story that contained six given and six new words in English, while another group read aloud a 152-word story containing six given and six new words in Malay. Auditory and acoustic analysis was performed on the given-new word pairs, with a focus on pitch accent type, syllable duration, phonetic realization of the rise and pitch peak alignment. The results show that the L2 learners produce longer rises on new than on given words but do not differentiate between the two types of words in terms of pitch accents, syllable duration, pitch peak alignment and steepness of rises, suggesting that they do not mark new and given information in English in a native-like way. Evidence of L1 transfer was found in the average extent and steepness of the rises as well as the pitch peak alignment. Ineke Mennen, Felix Schaeffler, and Catherine Dickie investigate 'Second Language Acquisition of Pitch Range in German Learners of English' (*SSLA* 36[2014] 303–29). German-speaking L2 learners of English of moderate to advanced proficiency and native English speakers read aloud a passage in English; another group of native German speakers read aloud the German translation of the same passage. An acoustic analysis showed that the L2 learners mostly produced target-like pitch range values or their approximations. The approximations of the target and deviations from it proved to be position-sensitive, i.e. the L2 learners adjusted their pitch range differently in earlier compared to later parts of intonational phrases.

Four papers are devoted to L2 rhythm acquisition. Aike Li and Brechtje Post investigate the development of speech rhythm in L2 learners of typologically different L1s in 'L2 Acquisition of Prosodic Properties of Speech Rhythm: Evidence from L1 Mandarin and German Learners of English' (*SSLA* 36[2014] 223–55). Speakers of Mandarin and German with two different proficiency levels in English (lower intermediate and advanced), as well as a control group of native speakers, read aloud twenty English sentences; matching sentences in Mandarin and German were also read by native speakers of these languages. The results of acoustic analysis show that vocalic variability and accentual lengthening develop in a similar way in the two L1 groups. However, the development of the proportion of vocalic material in the utterances is different in the two L1 groups, reflecting L1 influence. These results suggest that L2 rhythm acquisition is influenced by both L1 properties and universal factors. Mikhail Ordin and Leona Polyanskaya look at the 'Development of Timing Patterns in First and Second Languages' (*System* 42[2014] 244–57). In a longitudinal study, they compared rhythmic patterns in the productions of four monolingual English-speaking children at different ages and four adult L2 learners of English (two of whom were native speakers of Italian and two of Punjabi) at different proficiency levels; children's and adults' speech samples were selected from the CHILDES and European Science Foundation (ESF) Second Language databases respectively. The results revealed a progress from more syllable-timed patterns towards more stress-timed patterns in the productions of both groups, suggesting that speech rhythm develops in a similar way in L1 and L2 acquisition.

The aim of the study reported on in 'Elicited Imitation in Search of the Influence of Linguistic Rhythm on Child L2 Acquisition' (*System* 42[2014] 207–19), by Dorota E. Campfield and Victoria A. Murphy, was to determine whether the 'prosodic bootstrapping hypothesis', according to which prosodic cues in the input facilitate lexical and syntactic development in the L1, also holds for L2 acquisition. Polish-speaking children who were beginner classroom L2 learners of English were divided into treatment, comparison, and control groups. Treatment and comparison groups were exposed to a twelve-hour teaching intervention, in which the treatment group was exposed to rhythmically salient input. The effects of the intervention were assessed by means of an elicited imitation task. The results showed that exposure to rhythmically salient input improved the children's ability to repeat longer sentences, confirming the predictions of the 'prosodic bootstrapping hypothesis' in the context of L2 acquisition. In 'Selected Observations on the Effect of Rhythm on Proficiency, Accuracy and Fluency in Non-Native English Speech' (in Szubko-Sitarek, Salski, and Stalmaszczyk, eds., *Language Learning, Discourse and Communication: Studies in Honour of Jan Majer*, pp. 167–91), Ewa Waniek-Klimczak addresses the relationship between the production of elements of the rhythmic structure of English and language proficiency. Speech samples from five Polish-speaking L2 learners of English ranging in proficiency from lower intermediate to near-native were first analysed for their degree of target-like production of selected phonetic variables and then assessed for accuracy and overall language proficiency by experienced Polish-speaking teachers of English. The samples represented fragments of text-reading and semi-spontaneous speech. The results showed that the proficiency ratings corresponded more closely to the elements of rhythm than to segmental articulation. This suggests that the rhythmic organization of speech develops with language proficiency and language experience, while segmental articulation may be subject to fossilization.

Two papers explore the influence of different language-learning experiences on L2 pronunciation. In 'Opening the Window on Comprehensible Pronunciation After 19 Years: A Workplace Training Study' (*LangLearn* 64[2014] 526–48), Tracey M. Derwing, Murray J. Munro, Jennifer A. Foote, Erin Waugh, and Jason Fleming investigate the effects of a pronunciation training programme conducted at the workplace (a factory) with fossilized Vietnamese- and Khmer-speaking L2 learners who had lived in an English-speaking country for an average of nineteen years. A series of perception and production tasks was administered to the participants prior to and following a seventeen-hour intervention; individual interviews were also conducted in the post-test phase. The participants' speech was assessed by native-speaker listeners, and the results revealed significant improvement in the learners' perception, comprehensibility, and intelligibility; however, no improvement was observed in fluency, while accentedness increased in one of the tasks. These results suggest that focused pronunciation instruction can be effective and that accent is partly independent of other speech dimensions. The effects of age and study-abroad experience on the degree of foreign accentedness are examined in 'Study Abroad and Changes in Degree of Foreign Accent in Children and Adults' (*MLJ* 98[2014] 432–49) by Carmen Muñoz and Àngels Llanes. The participants in the study were Catalan-Spanish bilinguals who were learning English as a foreign language; they belonged to two different age groups (children and adults), and learned English in two different contexts (at home and in a study-abroad programme). All participants took part in a semi-structured interview (pre-test and post-test), did a picture-elicited narrative task, and filled out a questionnaire in the post-test. A group of listeners rated the participants' speech samples in terms of the degree of perceived foreign accent. The participants in the study-abroad setting were perceived to have a significantly milder foreign accent in the post-test. The greatest improvement was observed in the group of child participants in the study-abroad setting, even though the effect of age did not prove significant.

Other factors and their influence on the acquisition of L2 phonology are also examined. A volume edited by John M. Levis and Alene Moyer, *Social Dynamics in Second Language Accent*, explores how social factors influence L2 phonological acquisition. Some of the factors considered are attitudes, identity, ethnic group and cultural affiliation, and social contact and networks. The broad question addressed by the volume is why the pronunciation of adult L2 learners is typically non-native-like and how social factors contribute to the observed age effects. The volume comprises chapters devoted to the nature and the learners' views of L2 accent, the teachers' approach to L2 accent, and the social impact of L2 accent; the concluding chapter, by the volume editors, gives some directions for future research and for teaching L2 pronunciation. A different factor, namely L2 proficiency, is addressed by Katy Borodkin and Miriam Faust. They examine 'Native Language Phonological Skills in Low-Proficiency Second Language Learners' (*LangLearn* 64[2014] 132–59) in order to determine whether there is a link between low L2 proficiency and difficulties with L1 phonological processing. Three groups of classroom Hebrew-speaking L2 learners of English (individuals with dyslexia, low-proficiency L2 learners, and high-proficiency L2 learners) did four tasks assessing L1 phonological processing, and an English proficiency test, along with some other tasks. High-proficiency L2 learners outperformed individuals with dyslexia on all four tasks assessing L1 phonological processing, and low-proficiency L2 learners on only two of these tasks: pseudo-word repetition and tip-of-the-tongue naming. These results suggest that both individuals with dyslexia and low-proficiency L2 learners experience difficulties with L1 phonological processing; however, the difficulties experienced by individuals with dyslexia are more pervasive than those experienced by low-proficiency L2 learners.

The role of the learners' conscious, declarative knowledge in the acquisition of L2 phonology is dealt with in two papers. Firstly, Marcin Bergier looks at 'The Influence of Explicit Phonetic Instruction and Production Training

Practice on Awareness Raising in the Realization of Stop Consonant Clusters by Advanced Polish Learners of English' (in Łyda and Szcześniak, eds., *Awareness in Action: The Role of Consciousness in Language Acquisition*, pp. 103–20). In an experimental study participants read English sentences featuring voice-agreeing plosive clusters straddling word boundaries in the context of one intonation unit (e.g. *I can't stop playing my guitar since I got it*). There were two recording sessions, separated by explicit theoretical phonetic instruction and individual production training practice of no release burst in cluster contexts. The results reveal a significant drop in the number of released stops during the second session compared to the first one, suggesting that meta-phonetic awareness facilitates acquisition. Secondly, Ewa Czajka conducted 'An Investigation into the Learners' Awareness of Word-Level Stress' (in Łyda and Szcześniak, eds., pp. 121–9). Upper-intermediate Polish-speaking L2 learners of English completed an oral production test, a written pronunciation test, and a written perception test by means of which their command of English word-stress was assessed. The three different types of pronunciation test were assumed to be related to a different degree to either explicit (declarative) or implicit (procedural) knowledge. The participants also completed a questionnaire aimed at collecting additional information about word-stress learning. An analysis of the relationship between the learners' level of word-stress awareness and their test scores revealed a positive correlation in the case of the written pronunciation test and no correlation in the case of the oral production test; the results were ambiguous in the case of the perception test. Such results point to the need of further investigation into the relationship between the learners' awareness and their pronunciation abilities.

Closely related to the domain of phonology are two studies dedicated to L2 orthography. In 'Reading Russian–English Homographs in Sentence Contexts: Evidence from ERPs' (*BLC* 17[2014] 153–68), Olessia Jouravlev and Debra Jared investigate whether advanced Russian–English bilinguals, born in Russia and living in Canada, activate their knowledge of Russian when reading English sentences. Russian uses Cyrillic script, which shares only a few letters with English but allows for some interlingual homographs (e.g. *MOPE*, meaning 'sea' in Russian). The processing of homographs was studied in a reading task during which event-related potentials were recorded; the focus was on the N400 component, particularly high for semantically incongruent stimuli. Sentences presented to participants contained the English translation of the Russian meaning of a homograph, an interlingual homograph, or a semantically incongruous control word (e.g. *MANY FISH LIVING IN THE OPEN SEA/MOPE/MACE ARE ENDANGERED*). Critical sentences were those in which the Russian meaning of the homographs fitted the context, unlike the English meaning, and it was on these sentences that bilinguals showed a reduction in the N400 component compared to control words, whereas the N400 of monolingual English speakers was of a similar magnitude in the two conditions. This shows that bilinguals automatically activate representations in both of their languages when reading in one of them. Results along similar lines are reported for entirely different scripts in 'Reading English with Japanese in Mind: Effects of Frequency, Phonology, and Meaning in Different-Script Bilinguals' (*BLC* 17[2014] 445–63), where

Koji Miwa, Ton Dijkstra, Patrick Bolger, and R. Harald Baayen present a lexical decision study accompanied by eye-tracking, which examined contributions of frequency, phonology, and meaning of L1 Japanese words on L2 English word lexical decision processes. The response times and eye-fixation durations of late bilinguals were found to depend on L1 Japanese word frequency and cross-language phonological and semantic similarities, but not on a dichotomous factor encoding cognate status. These effects were not observed for native monolinguals; they were explained based on the connectionist model of bilingual interactive activation.

Moving on to the interface between morphology and the lexicon, a topic that continues to receive attention is the role of morphological analysis in reading development and lexical inference. Dongbo Zhang, Keiko Koda, and Xiaoxi Sun, in 'Morphological Awareness in Biliteracy Acquisition: A Study of Young Chinese EFL Readers' (*IJB* 18[2014] 570–85), examine the contribution of morphological awareness to reading comprehension, focusing on 11- and 12-year-old Chinese EFL learners in China, and their reading of both Chinese and English. The learners did a set of tasks that measured compound awareness and reading comprehension in English, and compound awareness, radical awareness, and reading comprehension in Chinese. The results revealed that compound awareness contributed to reading comprehension within both languages; in addition, Chinese compound awareness was found to influence English reading comprehension, but not the other way round. Chinese radical awareness, which is orthography-specific, did not play a role in L2 reading comprehension. The authors conclude that cross-linguistic influence is dependent on typological distance, as well as the learning context. In 'The Role of Morphological and Contextual Information in L2 Lexical Inference' (*MLJ* 98[2014] 992–1005), Megumi Hamada investigates the role of two different types of information that can be used in inferring the meaning of unknown L2 words during reading. Four groups of ESL students from mixed L1 backgrounds, whose proficiency ranged from beginner to advanced, did a pen-and-paper task in which they had to choose the inferred meanings of pseudo-compounds such as *rainfime* from a series of options. The compounds were presented within sentences; in the Morphology Reliable condition, the familiar part of the compounds provided information about the overall meaning, which also matched the context of the sentences, while in the Morphology Unreliable condition, the known word-part did not provide any reliable semantic information nor did it match the context. Proficiency-based differences were found in choosing morphological versus contextual information when the former did not match the context; specifically, in the Morphology Unreliable condition, higher-proficiency learners were able to choose context-based meanings over morphology-based meanings, reaching the correct inference, whereas lower-proficiency learners were more likely to remain faithful to the morphology-based meanings despite divergent contextual information.

Another two studies deal with inferences. 'Lexical Inferencing Strategies: The Case of Successful versus Less Successful Inferencers' (*System* 45[2014] 27–38), by Hsueh-chao Marcella Hu and Hossein Nassaji, is based on a reading task in which the meanings of some words needed to be inferred, and on think-aloud procedures; jointly, these methods are used to tap into the inferencing strategies of advanced Chinese-speaking ESL learners and their successfulness. Twelve types of inferential strategies used by all learners were identified in the think-aloud data. The differences between successful and less successful inferencers were found to pertain to the degree to which they used certain strategies, but also to when and how they used them; some of the salient characteristics of successful inferencers were evaluation and monitoring strategies, a combination of textual and background knowledge, self-awareness, and repeated efforts to infer the target word meanings. Moving the focus into the domain of oral comprehension, 'Lexical Inferencing in First and Second Language Listening' (*MLJ* 98[2014] 1006–21) by Hilde Van Zeeland deals with lexical inferencing success by native and non-native (from different L1 backgrounds) speakers of English. The author explored the effects of contextual clue types, background knowledge, and L2 vocabulary knowledge on inferencing success; native English speakers reached a success rate of 59.6 per cent, while this rate was 35.6 per cent for the non-natives, and success was affected by all three variables under study. The study also measured the L2 learners' ability to notice unknown vocabulary in speech; limited noticing ability was detected, indicating lack of noticing as a potential limiting element for inferencing opportunities and success.

An additional topic related to bilingual lexical processing is language-(non)selectiveness, i.e. the study of whether bilinguals switch off the contextually inappropriate language when the task at hand is clearly unilingual. 'Parallel Language Activation During Word Processing in Bilinguals: Evidence from Word Production in Sentence Context' (*BLC* 17[2014] 258–76), by Peter A. Starreveld, Annette M.B. De Groot, Bart M.M. Rossmark, and Janet G. Van Hell, presents the results of two picture-naming experiments that examined whether bilinguals co-activate the non-target language during word production in the target language. The pictures in this study were shown out of context in one experiment and in visually presented sentence contexts in the other; different participant groups performed the tasks in L1 Dutch and L2 English. Picture names were Dutch–English cognates (e.g. *apple-appel*) or non-cognates (e.g. *bottle-fles*), with the cognate effect serving as the marker of activation of the non-target language; sentence constraint effect was also examined. A cognate effect occurred in both experiments; it was larger in the L2 than in the L1, larger with low-constraint sentences than with high-constraint sentences, and it disappeared in the high-constraint L1 condition. These results point to consistent co-activation of the non-target language in different production situations. Looking at grammatical gender from the perspective of bilingual lexical access, Luis Morales, Daniela Paolieri, Roberto Cubelli, and M. Teresa Bajo, in 'Transfer of Spanish Grammatical Gender to English: Evidence from Immersed and Non-Immersed Bilinguals' (*BLC* 17[2014] 700–8), explore whether the knowledge of grammatical gender in the native language (Spanish) affects speech production in an L2 that lacks gender (English). The bilinguals tested in this study were split in two groups, those immersed in an L1 (in Spain) and those immersed in an L2 context (in the US). Participants did a picture-naming task in which they had to name pictures in the L2 while ignoring distractor words that could be either gender-congruent or gender-incongruent with their Spanish translation. The results revealed that non-immersed participants were slower in naming the pictures in the congruent condition, suggesting that bilinguals are influenced by knowledge about gender in their native language even when producing utterances in a language to which this information does not apply. Similar influence was not observed for immersed bilinguals.

A monograph and an edited volume are entirely devoted to L2 English vocabulary. Xiaoyan Xia's *Categorization and L2 Vocabulary Learning: A Cognitive Linguistic Perspective* relies on the theoretical framework of Cognitive Linguistics and addresses the role of the L1-based concept categorization in L2 vocabulary; the specific stance taken is that of Experientialism, which stresses a motivational relationship between surface linguistic representations and underlying conceptual structures. The author assumes a unitary conceptual model and hypothesizes that the patterns of one's L1-based concept categorization will be present in his or her L2 vocabulary learning as well. The focus is on prototypicality and basic-level effects, related to horizontal and vertical dimensions of categorization respectively: concepts at the basic level are psychologically more salient than concepts at other levels, and prototypical concepts are more salient than marginal concepts. A combination of qualitative and quantitative methods was used in the empirical study: the qualitative data was collected with questionnaires and was used for identifying basic-level and prototypical category members, while the quantitative data came from cued-recall tasks in which the learners were asked to produce L2 words based on cues. The results show that the psychological salience of basic-level and prototypical concepts in one's L1-based conceptual system is related to better retention and faster retrieval of the corresponding L2 words. The author argues that these two effects are dynamic in L2 contexts, being influenced by factors such as the familiarity of a given concept, formal instruction, and exposure to the target culture. A volume dedicated to a specific approach to vocabulary research and vocabulary selection for teaching purposes is *Lexical Availability in English and Spanish as a Second Language*, edited by Rosa María Jiménez Catalán. The studies pertaining to English are collected in Part I ('Lexical Availability in English as L1 and L2'). The volume discusses conceptual and methodological issues related to lexical availability, a vocabulary measure proposed as more relevant for language learners than frequency lists, defined through the ease with which words are generated as members of a given semantic category. All chapters report on studies based on some form of an associative task, in which students are presented with (written) cue words and asked to write down all the words that come to mind in response. Lexical availability indices are calculated on the basis of the position that the words occupy in the list, as well as the frequency with which they occur as associates. As expected, native speakers consistently outperform non-native speakers in the number of words listed in response to the provided cues, and advanced learners outperform lower-level learners.

Among other lexicon-related topics, Xian Zhang and Xiaofei Lu conduct 'A Longitudinal Study of Receptive Vocabulary Breadth Knowledge Growth and

Vocabulary Fluency Development' (*AppLing* 35[2014] 283–304). Their study was based on two versions of the Vocabulary Levels Test, both administered to Chinese-speaking learners of L2 English at three time-points spread over twenty-two months. The first version was administered in paper format and served to estimate participants' vocabulary breadth knowledge, while the second was in computer format and was used to assess vocabulary fluency (operationalized as the speed of meaning recognition). A significant effect of word-frequency level was found on the rate of vocabulary breadth knowledge growth and vocabulary fluency development, as well as a weak relationship between vocabulary breadth knowledge and vocabulary fluency. Findings also suggest that vocabulary fluency development lags behind vocabulary breadth knowledge growth. Paul Booth focuses on yet another aspect of vocabulary acquisition, looking at 'The Variance of Lexical Diversity Profiles and its Relationship to Learning Style' (*IRAL* 52[2014] 357–75). He examines the lexical diversity scores in L2 English texts written by low-proficiency and high-proficiency learners from different L1 backgrounds (mostly Korean, Thai, Mandarin, Japanese, and Arabic). The learners performed two writing tasks, a descriptive and a discursive one; their texts were then analysed using the D-Tools programme, which calculated parameter D, a measure of lexical diversity. The learners also completed two learning-style tests (a visual memory test of paired associates and a test of grammatical sensitivity). The results suggest that learners who are more grammatically sensitive appear to be more likely to restructure their language, i.e. that lexical diversity is to some extent shaped by differences within individuals as well as task conditions.

A number of papers are dedicated to the acquisition of multiword sequences; two corpus-based articles rely on data from the International Corpus of Learner English (ICLE). The first one, on 'The Use of Collocations by Intermediate vs. Advanced Non-Native Writers: A Bigram-Based Study' (*IRAL* 52[2014] 229–52) by Sylviane Granger and Yves Bestgen adopts a usage-based approach to language acquisition and looks at how phraseological competence develops as a function of L2 proficiency. Production data from intermediate and advanced French-, German-, and Spanish-speaking learners of L2 English were analysed and significant differences were detected between collocations at these two proficiency levels; for instance, the intermediate learners were found to over-use high-frequency collocations (such as *hard work*) and under-use strongly associated but less frequent collocations (such as *immortal souls*). A related paper is Magali Paquot's 'Cross-Linguistic Influence and Formulaic Language: Recurrent Word Sequences in French Learner Writing' (*ESLAYb* 14[2014] 240–61). The author investigated transfer effects in French EFL learners' use of recurrent word sequences (lexical bundles) ranging from two to four words in length, using the French component of ICLE as the data source. Different manifestations of L1 influence were detected; many of the learners' idiosyncratic uses of lexical bundles could be traced back to the properties of French word combinations, e.g. their discourse function and frequency of use. The results are in line with a usage-based view of language that assigns an active role to the L1.

Three studies explore the relationship between conventionalized word combinations and the phonological short-term memory (PSTM). Agnieszka Skrzypek and David Singleton look at 'Phonological Short-Term Memory and the Operation of Cross-Linguistic Factors in Elementary and Pre-Intermediate Adult L2 Learners' Collocational Usage' (in Szubko-Sitarek et al., eds., pp. 193–214). The authors test the hypothesis that, when it comes to L2 collocations, L1 transfer may be more operative in learners with lower PSTM than in those with higher PSTM capacity. The participants in the empirical study were elementary and pre-intermediate Polish-speaking adult L2 learners of English who attended a six-month English-language course in Ireland and completed a collocation test at the end of the course. The test consisted of decontextualized multiple-choice questions, collocation accuracy judgement sentences, fill-in-the-blank sentences, and writing tasks. The learners' PSTM capacity was assessed using serial non-word recall and recognition tasks. The results showed that at the elementary level the learners with a lower PSTM capacity tended to produce more cross-linguistic errors, confirming the existence of a link between PSTM capacity and the operation of cross-linguistic influence in the acquisition of L2 collocations. This link, however, did not appear to be strong at the pre-intermediate level. These findings are corroborated by the results of a related study, 'Cross-Linguistic Influence in L2 Writing: The Role of Short-Term Memory' by Agnieszka Skrzypek (in Pawlak and Aronin, eds., *Essential Topics in Applied Linguistics and Multilingualism: Studies in Honor of David Singleton*, pp. 69–88), in which the same hypothesis was tested on the basis of the compositions that the same participants wrote at the end of their English-language course. The results of this study again showed that there is a stronger link between PSTM capacity and the operation of cross-linguistic influence in the acquisition of L2 collocations at the elementary than at the pre-intermediate proficiency level.

Pauline Foster, Cylcia Bolibaugh, and Agnieszka Kotula explore 'Knowledge of Nativelike Selections in an L2' focusing on 'The Influence of Exposure, Memory, Age of Onset, and Motivation in Foreign Language and Immersion Setting' (*SSLA* 36[2014] 101–32). The influence of six variables on the L2 learners' receptive knowledge of conventionalized word combinations is looked at: engagement with the L2 community, motivation to reach a high level of L2 attainment, age of onset (AoA) of L2 acquisition, length of exposure to the L2, phonological short-term memory (PSTM), and the acquisition context (inside vs. outside the L2 community). Two groups of upper-intermediate/advanced Polish-speaking L2 learners of English—resident in the UK and in Poland—and a control group of native English speakers did a native-like selection test, in which they had to underline non-native selections in an authentic text written by a non-native speaker. A questionnaire was also administered, as well as a serial recall task, measuring PSTM. The results indicate that AoA and context of acquisition are the strongest predictors of the ability to detect non-native selections in a text; nativelikeness is guaranteed only for immersion-early starters. PSTM was the only significant predictor in immersion-late starters, but it was insignificant in foreign language learners, suggesting that PSTM and L2 immersion are necessary for the acquisition of native-like selections in the L2.

The acquisition of L2 idioms and metaphors has also been an object of study. 'Getting Your Wires Crossed: Evidence for Fast Processing of L1 Idioms in an L2' (*BLC* 17[2014] 784–97), by Gareth Carrol and Kathy Conklin, reports on a cross-language priming study involving high-proficiency Chinese-speaking L2 learners of English (and a control group of native speakers). The participants did a lexical decision task in which the initial words of English idioms (e.g. *to spill the ...*) and transliterated Chinese idioms (e.g. *draw a snake and add ...*) were shown as primes for the final words (*beans*; *feet*); the goal was to see if in bilinguals cross-language activation would occur for idiomatic sequences in a similar way as for single words. Both native and non-native speakers were the fastest to respond to targets that formed idioms in their L1: bilinguals responded to the target words significantly faster when they completed a Chinese idiom (e.g. *feet*) than when they were presented with a matched control word (e.g. *hair*), while for targets that formed English idioms they were not reliably faster than controls. A dual-route model, based on either a direct lexical or conceptual route, is proposed as a possible explanation for the bilingual performance as well as monolingual access to formulaic language. Jeannette Littlemore, Tina Krennmayr, James Turner, and Sarah Turner also deal with figurative language and conduct in 'An Investigation into Metaphor Use at Different Levels of Second Language Writing' (*AppLing* 35[2014] 117–44). Their study aims to provide a preliminary measure of the amount and distribution of metaphor used by language learners in their writing across different CEFR levels. Essays written by Greek- and German-speaking L2 learners of English are examined for the use of metaphor. The main finding is that the overall density of metaphor increases from CEFR levels A2 to C2; in addition, at lower levels, most of the metaphorical items are closed-class, mainly based on prepositions, while at level B2 and beyond, the majority of metaphorical items become open-class and increasingly sophisticated. The productivity of metaphor use also brings about more errors and more evidence of L1 influence.

A connection between the lexicon and morphosyntax is made in 'Lexical Aspect in the Use of the Present Perfect by Japanese EFL Learners' (*IRAL* 52[2014] 31–57), by Mariko Uno. This study looks at the relationship between tense-aspect morphology and inherent aspectual properties of verb predicates in L2 acquisition, focusing on the use of the English present perfect. Participants in the study were Japanese-speaking learners of L2 English, gathered in a mixed-proficiency group. The participants did a four-passage cloze test, which showed that they associated the present-perfect form with particular semantic aspectual properties of verbs, in particular atelic verbs in contexts with an adverb of duration. Multiple factors are proposed as possible explanations for this finding: perceptual saliency, cognitive processing principles, and prototype formation in the early use of tense-aspect morphology. Verbal aspect and its relation to event conceptualization are dealt with in 'Grammatical Preferences in Aspect Marking in First Language and Second Language: The Case of First Language Dutch, English, and German and First Language Dutch Second Language English, and First Language Dutch Second Language German' (*AppPsycholing* 35[2014] 969–1000) by Béryl

Hilberink-Schulpen, Ulrike Nederstigt, and Marianne Starren. Unlike most related work, which focuses on production, this paper reports on a perception study. Two acceptability judgement experiments were performed, one with native speakers of English, German, and Dutch, and the other with Dutch learners of English and German (at the secondary school diploma proficiency level). The focus of the study was on the relationship between the use of a progressive form and the mentioning of an affected object or endpoint; the participants looked at short videos and judged the accompanying sentences with simple vs. progressive forms and with visible vs. invisible objects. All native speakers demonstrated a preference that corresponded to the inventory of the language they speak, with English speakers choosing the progressive more than the German speakers, and with the Dutch being in between. The learners, on the other hand, treated differently those aspects that are rule-governed (such as progressive marking in English), and those that are a matter of preference. The former were able to overrule the native patterns, whereas the latter were not, and thus proved more problematic for L2 learners.

Among work on syntax, several papers deal with the acquisition of questions. Production of main- and embedded-clause questions is dealt with in 'Second Language Acquisition of English Questions: An Elicited Production Study' (*AppPsycholing* 35[2014] 1055–86), by Lucia Pozzan and Erin Quirk. The authors look at the impact of L1 and L2 syntactic properties on the learners' production of questions in a computerized elicitation task; the focus is on non-target subject-auxiliary inversion patterns. The participants tested in the study were intermediate/advanced Chinese- and Spanish-speaking L2 learners of English; the choice of L1s was motivated by word-order differences between Chinese, Spanish, and English. Yes/no and adjunct and argument *wh*-questions were compared. The results point to some L1 influence, but L2 production was more clearly affected and constrained by the same factors at play in L1 acquisition and dialectal variation, as L2 learners produced higher inversion rates in yes/no than in *wh*-questions in main clauses, and higher non-standard inversion rates in clause-embedded *wh*-questions than in yes/no questions. Interpretation of questions is dealt with in 'Variational Learning in L2: The Transfer of L1 Syntax and Parsing Strategies in the Interpretation of *Wh*-Questions by L1 German Learners of L2 English' (*LAB* 4[2014] 432–61) by Tom Rankin. This study looks at the interaction between L2 processing and grammatical development, and it examines the interpretation of main-clause *wh*-questions in L2 English by upper-intermediate learners whose L1 is Austrian German. German and English share word-order patterns in a range of question forms, but these patterns are derived from different underlying syntactic representations and have distinct semantic interpretations, with German questions being ambiguous, and English questions unambiguous, between subject and object readings. Non-target patterns of interpretation show that learners at high-proficiency levels continue to optionally parse English questions with the head-final VP syntax transferred from the L1; L1 processing cues are also transferred to the L2 in the form of animacy cues for ambiguity resolution. This is interpreted within the Variational Learning framework, which assumes that a set of competing grammars underlies an individual's linguistic performance in both L1 and L2 acquisition, but with the

L1 grammatical representation having a privileged status that continues to parse the L2 input where possible.

A much narrower set of questions is explored by Boping Yuan in ' "*Wh*-on-Earth" in Chinese Speakers' L2 English: Evidence of Dormant Features' (*SLR* 30[2014] 515–49). Assuming that each lexical item is a bundle of phonological, syntactic, and semantic features that are fully transferred from the L1 into the L2, and treating '*wh*-on-earth' questions as polarity items licensed by the question feature, the negation feature, or non-veridical verbs like *wonder*, the study reported on in this article looked at Chinese speakers' L2 acquisition of English '*wh*-on-earth' questions such as *what on earth...* or *who on earth...* . The learners, divided into five proficiency levels from pre-intermediate to very advanced, did an acceptability judgement task, a discourse-completion task, and an interpretation task. The results revealed that they were able to learn the form of '*wh*-on-earth', disallowing its discontinuous use (allowed in their L1), but without fully elaborated features, demonstrating problems, for instance, with semantic features having to do with '*wh*-on-earth' being licensed by non-veridical verbs, and not being linked to discourse entities. To account for these findings, a distinction between active and dormant features in L2 lexicon is posited in the analysis, where it is argued that features transferred from learners' L1 can become dormant if there is no evidence in the target language input to confirm or disconfirm them, which leads to random behaviour in L2 learners' production and interpretation.

A fair amount of work has dealt with the acquisition of the verb *be*. A monograph on the topic is Mable Chan's *Acquisition of* Be *by Cantonese ESL Learners in Hong Kong and Its Pedagogical Implications* [2013]. The book describes the results of an empirical study in which a grammaticality judgement task, a story-writing task, and an acceptability judgement task were administered to Cantonese-speaking L2 learners of English ranging in proficiency from beginner to very advanced. The goal was to examine the role of the L1, developmental stages, and the relationship between morphology and syntax in the learners' acquisition of English *be*; a control group of native English speakers also participated in the study. The results show that the learners' L1 plays an important role in the initial state. Developmental trends were observed in the acquisition of both copula and auxiliary *be* as the learners' knowledge of these verbs increased with proficiency level, converging on the target at the advanced level. The learners' use of tense morphemes contrasted with their knowledge of tense, suggesting that problems with surface morphology do not necessarily indicate lack of knowledge of L2 grammatical properties. On the basis of these findings the author evaluates a number of popular beliefs about the effectiveness of instruction in L2 acquisition and gives some recommendations for the teaching of English grammar. In 'The Functions of the Nontarget *Be* in the Written Interlanguage of Chinese Learners of English' (*LangAcq* 21[2014] 279–303), Suying Yang explores all instances of ungrammatical uses of *be* in written English narratives of Hong Kong students aged between 10 and 19 years and placed at five different proficiency levels from (late) beginner to advanced, taking into consideration the nature of the verb that follows *be*, the syntactic position of *be* + uninflected verb / *be* + inflected verb sequence, as well as the tense marking on *be* and the verb that follows it. The study detects different functions of non-target *be*, with a function shift taking place between lower and higher proficiency levels: at the lowest levels, *be* is largely used as a filler for different functional categories related to inflection; later on, it starts to be used more to mark tense/voice, while at the highest level it only performs the function of marking passive voice of unaccusative verbs. In other words, while problems with mapping abstract functional categories onto surface morphology (which lead to the use of *be* as filler) are temporary and related to lower proficiency levels, over-passivization errors with unaccusatives, due to atypical theme-to-subject mapping of unaccusative verbs, persist into the higher proficiency levels.

Focusing specifically on over-passivization, Taegoo Chung, in 'Multiple Factors in the L2 Acquisition of English Unaccusative Verbs' (*IRAL* 52[2014] 59–87), studies the impact of external causation, animacy, and verb alternation, i.e. factors related to discourse, semantics, and L1 morphological influence. Chinese- and Korean-speaking learners of L2 English at four proficiency levels (elementary to advanced) were tested on a forced-choice elicitation task in which they were asked to read pairs of sentences and choose the grammatical form (active vs. passive) for the second sentence (e.g. *The boy lifted the dog out of the blanket. The dog (appeared / was appeared) slowly.*). The studied factors were found to differ in strength, with the semantics and discourse factors playing significant roles for all L2 learners (the NP semantics factor being overcome earlier). L1 morphological influence in cases of L1/L2 differences was stronger than any other factors, and this influence was the last to overcome.

Also dealing with argument structure are two related papers couched within the framework of CxG and dedicated to verb-argument constructions such as *V against N*. 'Second Language Verb-Argument Constructions Are Sensitive to Form, Function, Frequency, Contingency, and Prototypicality' (*LAB* 4[2014] 405–31), by Nick C. Ellis, Matthew B. O'Donnell, and Ute Römer, reports on a series of free-association tasks used to investigate whether the access to L2 verb-argument constructions is sensitive to statistical patterns of usage in a similar way as is the case in the L1. Verb frequency, verb-construction contingency (showing how faithful verbs are to particular constructions), and verb-construction semantic prototypicality were looked at. Advanced German-, Spanish-, and Czech-speaking L2 learners of English had the task of generating the first word that came to mind in filling the verb slot in frames such as *he __ across the . . .*, *it __ of the . . .*, etc. For each frame, the results were compared with corpus analyses of verb selection preferences and with the semantic network structure of the verbs in these constructions. All learner groups were found to be very similar to native speakers in showing independent effects of frequency, contingency, and prototypicality. To further explore the role of the L1, Römer, Ellis, and O'Donnell also conducted a study on 'Second Language Learner Knowledge of Verb-Argument Constructions: Effects of Language Transfer and Typology' (*MLJ* 98[2014] 952–75). In this paper the authors analyse the same data as in the study described above, focusing on the differences between learners from different L1 backgrounds, in particular with regard to how their L1s express manner and path of motion. All three learner groups relied more than native speakers on general, highly frequent verbs such as *be* or *do*, and produced lower numbers of more specific but less frequent verbs (e.g. *reach* or *crawl*). The results also showed that those learners whose L1 is typologically similar to English in being satellite-framed and encoding manner of motion in the verb, and path in the satellite (Czech and German) produced more target-like verbs than learners whose L1 is verb-framed, i.e. encodes both path and manner in verbs (Spanish). Staying with the cognitive linguistic and usage-based approach to acquisition, Peiwen Li, Søren W. Eskildsen, and Teresa Cadierno write about 'Tracing an L2 Learner's Motion Constructions Over Time: A Usage-Based Classroom Investigation' (*MLJ* 98[2014] 612–28). This article considers how specific motion constructions and their underlying semantic components are expressed and developed over time. The study draws on the Multimedia Adult English Learner Corpus, a longitudinal database of classroom interaction; the development of motion constructions is traced in one Spanish-speaking Mexican L2 learner of English over three and a half years and across four proficiency levels, from beginner to high intermediate. An analysis of the linguistic means used to express Motion, Path, and Ground is conducted, as well as an analysis of patterns with the most widely used verbs *go* and *come*. Overall, the early inventory contained less varied linguistic patterns with a limited number of linguistic resources for the expression of motion, while subsequent use showed the learner moving towards an increasingly productive inventory of motion expressions, with emergent patterns building on previous experience. Constructions with *go* and *come* were initially learned as item-based, and later on showed indication of development into more productive utterance schemas.

Looking at spatial expressions from the perspective of linguistic relativity and the influence of language-specific properties on cognition, Hae In Park and Nicole Ziegler's 'Cognitive Shift in the Bilingual Mind: Spatial Concepts in Korean–English Bilinguals' (*BLC* 17[2014] 410–30) shows that speakers with different native languages perceive spatial relations in different ways and that conceptualization patterns of bilinguals are affected by the concepts of both languages. The paper explores the categorization of spatial concepts in highly advanced adult Korean–English bilinguals. Using similarity judgements (in a triad matching task and a free sort task), a comparison was made between the conceptualization patterns of 'put in' and 'put on' events by Korean–English bilinguals and Korean and English monolinguals, taking into account that Korean distinguishes tight-fitting and loose-fitting events, rather than 'on' and 'in' events. The results revealed significant differences between the monolingual and bilingual groups, demonstrating the process of convergence of the two languages in the bilingual mind. It was also shown that bilinguals' conceptualizations are influenced by additional (non-)linguistic factors, in particular English proficiency and frequency of Korean use. The findings lend support to the claim found in previous research that bilinguals' conceptualization patterns are susceptible to their language experience.

Going back to argument alternations, two papers deal with datives. Within CxG and usage-based approaches to language acquisition, Kim McDonough and Tatiana Nekrasova-Becker 'Compar[e] the Effect of Skewed and Balanced

Input on English as a Foreign Language Learners' Comprehension of the Double-Object Dative Construction' (*AppPsycholing* 35[2014] 419–42). In L1 acquisition the detection of abstract constructions is facilitated when the input is skewed (i.e. when it contains numerous exemplars with a shared lexical item) rather than balanced (i.e. with a small set of lexical verbs occurring an equal number of times). To test whether this also holds for L2 acquisition, the authors looked at the comprehension of the English ditransitive construction in learners exposed to three different input conditions, skewed first, skewed random, and balanced. Over a two-week period, intermediate Thai-speaking EFL learners randomly assigned to different input conditions did a pre-test and a post-test comprehension test, with input treatment in between. The results revealed that balanced input was most effective when transfer of training to new items was required, suggesting that it may promote broader category generalization than skewed input. Taking a different—generative—perspective, Roger Hawkins, Mona Althobaiti, and Yi Ma had two goals in their paper titled 'Eliminating Grammatical Function Assignment from Hierarchical Models of Speech Production: Evidence from the Conceptual Accessibility of Referents' (*AppPsycholing* 35[2014] 677–707). The main goal was to test the effects of the conceptual accessibility of referents (specifically, their animacy) on the production of English dative syntactic frames, and the secondary one to see if learners have difficulty integrating syntactic knowledge where it interfaces with conceptual accessibility. Specifically, the study focused on showing that it is unnecessary to assume assignment of grammatical functions in hierarchical models of speech production, where functions such as subject or direct object are thought to be assigned to noun lemmas in the first stage of production planning, with a conceptually more accessible lemma becoming the subject; conceptual accessibility effects are instead explained through linear ordering. The learners were speakers of Mandarin Chinese and Arabic, at intermediate and advanced levels of English proficiency, and they were tested on a delayed oral sentence recall task. The results point to the effects being related to linear precedence rather than grammatical function assignment, and to advanced learners being qualitatively similar to native speakers.

Using corpus data, *Clausal Complements in Native and Learner Spoken English: A Corpus-Based Study with Lindsei and Vicolse*, by Beatriz Tizón-Couto, compares several groups of English L2 learners and native English speakers, focusing on a complex syntactic phenomenon, and looking separately at complement-taking verbs, adjectives, and nouns. The novel resource introduced in the book is Vicolse, the 100,000-word Vigo Corpus of Learner Spoken English, which contains the production of intermediate-advanced bilingual Spanish-Galician learners. The data from Vicolse are compared to those from the German and Spanish part of Lindsei, as well as the native data from Locnec. Complementation is found to be over-used in all learner corpora (compared to the native corpus), presumably due to the structure of the learners' native languages, which tend to use more complex sentences than English; this tendency was particularly marked for the Spanish-speaking learners. *That*-clauses were also over-used by the learners, especially in Vicolse, compared to zero-complement clauses. However, the overall conclusion is that complementation does not represent a problematic area for intermediate-advanced learners of English.

Two studies look at processing issues in L2 English morphosyntax. Holger Hopp investigates 'Working Memory Effects in the L2 Processing of Ambiguous Relative Clauses' (*LangAcq* 21[2014] 250–78). German-speaking L2 learners of English, ranging in proficiency from mid-intermediate to near-native, and native English controls did an eye-tracking reading experiment and an offline sentence-interpretation task in which their relative-clause attachment preferences were tested in locally ambiguous sentences (e.g. *The director congratulated the instructor of the schoolboys who was writing the reports*) or fully ambiguous sentences (e.g. *The student had liked the secretary of the professor who was killed in the robbery*) respectively. Additionally, their working memory was tested in a reading-span task and their automaticity of basic lexical processing in a lexical decision task. The results revealed native-like relative-clause attachment preferences on the part of the L2 learners who were matched in working-memory capacity to the native speakers as well as similar effects of working memory and lexical automaticity on the attachment preferences of both groups of speakers. These results are interpreted as suggesting that there is continuity between L1 and L2 processing. In 'Real-Time Grammar Processing by Native and Non-Native Speakers: Constructions Unique to the Second Language' (*BLC* 17[2014] 237–57), Danijela Trenkic, Jelena Mirkovic, and Gerry T.M. Altmann look at the online comprehension of English (in)definite articles by intermediate Mandarin-speaking L2 learners, whose L1 does not have articles, and native English speakers, keeping in mind that learners with an L1 Mandarin background have been reported to have persistent difficulties with the production of English articles. The two groups of participants did a visual world eye-tracking experiment testing their comprehension of article usage. The results showed that the L2 learners processed articles in a native-like way: they did not over-rely on lexical and pragmatic information and used different types of information as it became available to resolve reference as soon as possible. To account for the comprehension-production asymmetries with Mandarin speakers' behaviour with English articles, the authors propose that the speakers have multiple meaning-to-form, but consistent form-to-meaning mappings.

Articles have continued to receive attention in other studies as well, as one of the most problematic areas of L2 English due to a lack of a one-to-one form and meaning mapping. Artur Świątek's monograph looks at *The Order of the Acquisition of the English Article System by Polish Learners in Different Proficiency Groups*. The theoretical part of the book discusses the relevant background and previous work related to article acquisition in L1 and L2 English. The use of articles is explained through features on the noun: plus or minus specific referent ([+/– SR]), plus or minus assumed-as-known to the hearer ([+/– HK]), which together define generics ([–SR, +HK]), non-referentials ([–SR, –HK]), first-mention nouns or referential indefinites ([+SR, –HK]), and referential definites ([+SR, +HK]), with idioms and other conventional uses singled out as a separate category (cf. Thorn Huebner [1983]). A set of studies involving Polish (another article-less language) learners of English is presented in the empirical part. Elementary, intermediate, and advanced learners were tested, ranging between 14 and 23 years in age. They performed a task that required the completion of fifty sentences with eighty-seven gaps, comprising obligatory uses of definite, indefinite, and zero articles in different referential contexts. The results indicate that the elementary group had least problems with the indefinite article and most problems with the zero article, the intermediate group had least problems with indefinite articles, but had also acquired zero articles, while the highest-proficiency group no longer had problems with zero articles; in addition, generic nouns (which indicate classes of entities) and idioms were consistently found to be the most problematic contexts, with inconsistent article use, which was acquired last.

In a study of cross-linguistic influence in article use, 'The Role of the Native Language in the Use of the English Nongeneric Definite Article by L2 Learners: A Cross-Linguistic Comparison' (*SLR* 34[2014] 351–79), Anna Chrabaszcz and Nan Jiang examine the effect of the native language on the use of the English non-generic definite article by highly proficient learners with Spanish and Russian as L1 (and a control group of native speakers). Non-generic article uses, those not indicating classes of entities, were divided into five categories: cultural, conventional, situational, textual, and structural; the goal was to look at L1 transfer and its relation to the hierarchy of article difficulty. The learners did an oral elicited imitation task, which was selected instead of a cloze-type task in order to test implicit rather than explicit knowledge of L2 article use. The findings point to a clear L1 influence on participants' reproduction of the definite article; however, various contexts present different levels of difficulty: the Spanish subjects, whose L1 possesses articles that behave in a similar way with regard to non-generic interpretation, performed at a native-like level of accuracy in the grammatical condition, whereas the L1 Russian subjects, whose L1 lacks articles, showed a tendency to omit definite articles. In the ungrammatical condition, Spanish speakers differed from the native speakers in their use of the definite article in conventional and cultural contexts (where there is greater inter-language variability with regard to the use of the article), while Russian participants supplied the definite article significantly less often than both the Spanish participants and the control group along all article categories, showing that they do have the knowledge of the syntactic distribution of articles but experience difficulties with regard to the semantic aspects. Cross-linguistic influence in a different context of article use was studied by Peter Robert Crosthwaite in 'Definite Discourse-New Reference in L1 and L2: A Study of Bridging in Mandarin, Korean, and English' (*LangLearn* 64[2014] 456–92). This study looked at the acquisition of bridging: the use of a definite expression to introduce a new referent into the discourse when its familiarity can be inferred based on pragmatic or general world knowledge shared between speakers and their audience (as in *I was looking at van Gogh's self-portrait. **The** missing ear made me feel sad*). Bridging is different from the typical use of definite expressions for reference maintenance, and is thus expected to pose particular difficulties to L2 learners. Two related experiments are discussed, one to determine native preferences for English, Mandarin, and

Korean, and the other to test the L2 acquisition of bridging in English by speakers of Mandarin and Korean; the learners were selected so that each of the six CEFR levels was represented. The experiment involved a production task based on controlled picture sequences, with neutral, weakly, or strongly inferable referents. It was found that the acquisition of the definite article + noun construction to introduce inferable referents in L2 English occurred at lower CEFR levels for the Mandarin group (A2) than the Korean group (B2), which can be related to positive transfer occurring in Mandarin speakers, as Mandarin—unlike Korean—does make a grammatical distinction between inferable and non-inferable referents.

A different semantics-related topic from the nominal domain is taken up by Shunji Inagaki in 'Syntax-Semantics Mappings as a Source of Difficulty in Japanese Speakers' Acquisition of the Mass–Count Distinction in English' (*BLC* 17[2014] 464–77). The mass–count distinction involves a complex relationship between syntax and semantics. Unlike English, which marks mass vs. count meanings syntactically, through number marking on nouns, Japanese relies solely on the conceptual semantics of words for quantity judgements. The study consisted of three experiments, in which intermediate learners judged whether two large objects/portions are more than six tiny objects/portions or vice versa, with the nouns presented with either mass or count syntactic cues (e.g. *more string* vs. *more strings*); parallel studies were conducted with L1 English and L1 Japanese speakers. Results show that learners correctly base judgements on number for count nouns (judging e.g. that six small cups are more cups than two large cups) and object-mass nouns (e.g. furniture), and on volume for substance-mass nouns (judging that two large portions of mustard are more mustard than six tiny portions); however, for nouns that can be either mass or count in English (e.g. *string(s)*) or cross-linguistically (e.g. *spinach*), they continue to rely on semantics and fail to shift judgements according to the mass-count syntax in which the words appear.

As for studies dedicated to the acquisition of L2 discourse phenomena, Theres Grüter, Hannah Rohde, and Amy J. Schafer explore 'The Role of Discourse-Level Expectations in Non-Native Speakers' Referential Choices' (in Orman and Valleau, eds., *Proceedings of the 38th Annual Boston University Conference on Language Development*, pp. 179–91). Using a story-continuation task, they investigated whether L2 learners make native-like use of available cues in co-reference processing. More precisely, they looked at whether L2 learners create expectations about who will be mentioned next in a discourse on the basis of linguistically encoded information about event structure in the form of grammatical aspect in the preceding context. Participants in the study were Japanese- and Korean-speaking L2 learners of English and native English speakers. The results showed that the L2 learners were less sensitive to the grammatically encoded event structure cue in the previous sentence in their referent choices than the native speakers. By means of an additional, truth-value judgement, task it was ensured that the L2 learners had native-like knowledge of grammatical aspect in English. The authors conclude that L2 learners have reduced ability to generate expectations at the discourse level in the L2. In 'From Spanish Paintings to Murder', Muna Morris-Adams focuses on 'Topic Transitions in Casual Conversations between Native and

Non-Native Speakers of English' (*JPrag* 21[2014] 151–65). Topic transitions are a distinct type of topic shift which do not explicitly signal that a shift is taking place but show a connection to the current or a previous topic. Participants in the study were ten intermediate to advanced L2 learners of English from different L1 backgrounds, who auto-recorded one of their informal conversations with a native English speaker. The analysis of the extracts showed that all conversations flowed smoothly and that L2 learners' topic transitions were skilfully performed. This indicates that L2 learners can successfully master topic management, one of the core components of communicative competence.

Before moving on to pragmatics, and to contextual and individual factors, two studies should be mentioned that concern multiple layers of learner interlanguage grammar. The first is *Learner Corpus Profiles: The Case of Romanian Learners* by Madalina Chitez, which introduces RoCLE, the first learner corpus of English produced by native speakers of Romanian. The corpus is composed of advanced undergraduate student writing (argumentative essays and literary compositions) with a total size of about 200,000 words. The author is interested in creating lexical, grammatical, and lexico-grammatical profiles of the learners' English, focusing on word and part-of-speech frequency distributions, as well as collocations. In addition, articles, prepositions, and the expression of genitive are singled out as phenomena studied in more depth. Some of the particularly interesting findings include a higher verb- and a lower noun-ratio and the more frequent use of certain words and phrases, both of which aspects were rarely or not at all found in LOCNESS, the native corpus used for comparison, an over-use of indefinite versus an under-use of definite articles, and incorrect preposition use following verbs. The notion of fluency is examined from a very broad perspective in a volume edited by Theron Muller, John Adamson, Philip Shigeo Brown, and Steven Herder entitled *Exploring EFL Fluency in Asia*. The editors expand the original understanding of fluency as a property of speaking to all four language skills—speaking, writing, reading, and listening. Understood in such a way, fluency can be defined as 'the smooth, effortless use of any language skill' (p. 2) or 'the ability to process language receptively and productively at a reasonable speed' (Paul Nation, p. 11). The book comprises literature reviews and empirical studies. A number of chapters deal with fluency in one of the four skills; the chapters are grouped according to the skill they are devoted to. The book also contains chapters discussing fluency from a pedagogical perspective; these explore how fluent language skills can be developed in an EFL classroom. Even though the research reported on in the book was conducted in Asia and pedagogical issues discussed in the book apply primarily to Asian contexts, the book is also relevant to contexts beyond these.

In the domain of L2 pragmatics, Carsten Roever, Stanley Wang, and Stephanie Brophy explore the relationship between 'Learner Background Factors and Learning of Second Language Pragmatics' (*IRAL* 52[2014] 377–401). More precisely, they investigate the relative contribution of length of residence, proficiency level, gender, and multilingualism to L2 learners' comprehension of implicature, recognition of routine formulae, and production of speech acts in English. Data were collected by means of a Web-based pragmatics test from learners residing in Germany and the US. The results indicate that proficiency significantly affected all three areas of pragmatics investigated, while multilingualism did not have a significant impact on any area. Length of residence and gender were additional significant factors in the recognition of routine formulae and speech-act production, but their effect was weaker than the effect of proficiency. Soo Jung Youn engaged in 'Measuring Syntactic Complexity in L2 Pragmatic Production' in order to 'Investigat[e] Relationships among Pragmatics, Grammar, and Proficiency' (*System* 45[2014] 270–87). English L2 learners with different L1 backgrounds ranging in proficiency from low-intermediate to advanced performed four written pragmatic assessment tasks, which required them to write texts of different genres. The learners' pragmatic performance was assessed by three trained raters. Additionally, the syntactic complexity of their production was assessed using three measures: global complexity from mean length of T-unit, phrasal-level complexity from mean length of clause, and subordination complexity from mean number of clauses per T-unit. The results show that the learners' pragmatic competence did not always correspond to their proficiency levels. With the exception of phrasal-level complexity, a stronger relationship was found between learners' pragmatic performances and syntactic complexity of their pragmatic production than between their pragmatic performances and proficiency levels. Pragmatically more advanced learners produced longer utterances, more complex structures at the phrasal level, and more subordination, suggesting that syntactic complexity plays an important role in achieving various pragmatic functions.

Hye Yeong Kim looks at 'Learner Investment, Identity, and Resistance to Second Language Pragmatic Norms' (*System* 45[2014] 92–102). The study investigated how English L2 learners' investment in their social identity influences their pragmatic choices, and to what extent the learners resist target-language pragmatic norms by exercising their agency. Korean-speaking L2 learners of English having different ages and different lengths of residence in the US at the time of the study completed questionnaires and discourse-completion tests, and took part in role-plays and individual and open-ended interviews. The analysis of the learners' responses to compliments, requests, and use of titles shows that they made pragmatic choices in a way that enabled them to invest in their social identities. Their pragmatic decisions were influenced by their age and length of stay in the target country, as well as power and social distance, but, above all, by their decisions about which identity to invest in, based on their evaluation of the context. The results suggest that the learners were overall willing to conform to the target-language norms while exercising their agency so as to position and maintain their social identity at the same time.

Two studies deal with speech acts in L2 English. A book-length treatment of the speech act of apologizing is provided in *Towards the Pragmatic Core of English for European Communication: The Speech Act of Apologising in Selected Euro-Englishes* by Agata Klimczak-Pawlak. The volume's central part is an account of an experimental study of the realization of the speech act of apologizing in English by highly proficient non-native speakers from eight European countries (Finland, France, Hungary, Macedonia, Poland,

Slovakia, Spain, and the UK). The participants completed a written discourse completion test that contained sixteen situations, half of which were aimed to elicit apologies with different power and distance settings. The analysis focused on the strategies used by speakers in different countries in four groups of situations characterized by different power and distance constellations. Despite the differences in strategies found between speakers from different countries, some general tendencies in strategy use were discovered across groups in each situation. These represent the pragmatic core for apologizing in Euro-English, and the idea is that they will provide guidance to L2 learners wishing to communicate successfully in Europe. Focusing on the speech act of refusals, Wei Ren conducted 'A Longitudinal Investigation into L2 Learners' Cognitive Processes during Study Abroad' (*AppLing* 35[2014] 575–94). Using retrospective verbal reports (RVRs), the author aimed to gain insight into cognitive processes involved in L2 learners' pragmatic production. Participants in the study were advanced Chinese-speaking L2 learners of English doing a one-year master's degree at one of the universities in the UK. They took part in a multimedia elicitation task eliciting status-equal and status-unequal refusals in English at three different times during their study abroad. The analyses of the RVRs revealed an increase in the amount of attention the learners paid to sociopragmatics in context when they responded to each situation of the task across the three phases. This was accompanied by a decrease in pragmatic difficulties and an increase in pragmatic knowledge reported by the learners. Overall, the results suggest that study abroad influences the cognitive processes involved in L2 learners' pragmatic production.

Study abroad is also the focus of a paper by Julia Jensen and Martin Howard, 'The Effects of Time in the Development of Complexity and Accuracy during Study Abroad' in 'A Study of French and Chinese Learners of English' (*ESLA Yb* 14[2014] 31–64). A longitudinal study was conducted with French- and Chinese-speaking L2 learners of English during their nine-month study at a university in an English-speaking country. The learners participated in three sociolinguistic interviews at intervals of approximately three months. After the second and third interview they also completed a sociolinguistic questionnaire. The interviews were transcribed and analysed in terms of syntactic complexity and accuracy, and the analysis revealed substantial individual variation both within and between individuals: individual learners progressed or regressed in a non-linear fashion over time, and some learners evidenced progress while others did not. The absence of a neat pattern of development either across or within learners points to the complexity of the issue concerning the effect of the duration of the study abroad on L2 development.

A valuable contribution to study-abroad research is a volume edited by Carmen Pérez-Vidal, *Language Acquisition in Study Abroad and Formal Instruction Contexts*. This collection of papers reports on the empirical findings of the longitudinal Study Abroad and Language Acquisition (SALA) project, which investigated the effects of formal instruction (in the country of origin) and study abroad on a group of Catalan–Spanish bilinguals who were advanced L2 learners of English and who participated in a compulsory three-month study-abroad programme in an English-speaking country as part of their translation and interpreting undergraduate degree at a Spanish university. The project examined the short- and long-term impact of these two different learning contexts on the learners' linguistic abilities, their motivation, attitudes, and beliefs regarding foreign language learning, use, and status, and their intercultural awareness. The empirical studies included in the volume reflect these objectives as they look into the learners' phonological, lexical, grammatical, and discourse development, their listening, speaking, and writing skills, their affective characteristics, and intercultural awareness. The volume also includes a chapter explaining the research methodology employed in the project and a chapter describing the design and implementation of the study-abroad programme used. The insights from the volume contribute not only to the understanding of the role of context in L2 acquisition but also to an appreciation of the value of mobility programmes in the education of language specialists.

The relationship between study abroad and affective factors in L2 acquisition is explored by Amy S. Thompson and Junkyu Lee, who examine 'The Impact of Experience Abroad and Language Proficiency on Language Learning Anxiety' (*TesolQ* 48[2014] 252–74). Korean-speaking L2 learners of English completed detailed background questionnaires in which they self-evaluated their English proficiency using a six-point Likert scale, and expressed the amount of their study abroad on a similar scale. They also completed a Korean online version of Foreign Language Classroom Anxiety Scale (FLCAS), assessing four anxiety components: English class performance anxiety, lack of self-confidence in English, confidence with native speakers of English, and fear of ambiguity in English. The results showed that study abroad reduces foreign-language classroom anxiety; however, language proficiency also plays a role. It was also shown that study abroad is crucial for overcoming a fear of ambiguity in language learning. Overall, the results suggest that study abroad has a profound effect on affective factors such as language-learning anxiety.

Moving on to individual learner differences proper, a book by Tammy Gregersen and Peter D. MacIntyre, *Capitalizing on Language Learners' Individuality: From Premise to Practice*, is practical in orientation and broad in scope. The title and the structure of the volume reflect the authors' aim to bridge the gap between theoretical views and research findings about individual learner differences, and classroom application of these notions. Each of the book's seven chapters, devoted to the more prominent learner characteristics (anxiety, beliefs, cognitive abilities, motivation, learning strategies, learning styles, and willingness to communicate) is divided into a theoretical and a practical part. The former summarizes our current state of knowledge and understanding of a given characteristic and explains the relevance of these insights for language learning and teaching; the latter contains hands-on activities for application in the language classroom. Practising language teachers and teachers-in-training can certainly benefit from this book, as can language learners themselves.

Other productions in the field of individual differences focus on individual learner characteristics. In the well-established line of research into motivation, new theoretical and practical insights are provided by *Motivation and Foreign Language Learning: From Theory to Practice*, edited by David Lasagabaster, Aintzane Doiz, and Juan Manuel Sierra. The first part of the book introduces some new theoretical constructs, explores the relationship between motivation and metacognition, contains ideas and evidence on how to improve teachers' and learners' motivation by engaging them in research on their own classroom practices, and offers ideas on how to inspire language teachers' vision. The second part presents empirical studies exploring the relationship between motivation and different language-teaching approaches, with particular emphasis on CLIL (Content and Language Integrated Learning) and the learning of English. An innovative approach to motivation is presented in *Motivational Dynamics in Language Learning*, edited by Zoltán Dörnyei, Peter D. MacIntyre, and Alastair Henry. Theoretical papers (called 'conceptual summaries') and empirical studies included in the volume explore motivation from the perspective of the Complex Dynamic Systems Theory. The originality of this approach lies in viewing motivation as a constantly changing feature rather than a stable learner characteristic, and in directing attention to the individual learner, the learning context, and their interplay. The studies included in the volume are interesting and useful not only for their findings on motivation but also for the methodological solutions adopted in studying it. Following a recent approach to motivation as part of the learner's identity/ self, two volumes focusing on the learner's sense of self make a valuable contribution to research into identity and self-related issues in L2 acquisition: *The Impact of Self-Concept on Language Learning*, edited by Kata Csizér and Michael Magid, and *Multiple Perspectives on the Self in SLA*, edited by Sarah Mercer and Marion Williams. The former explores the influence of self-concept on L2 learning and teaching and includes chapters addressing self-concept from a theoretical point of view, empirical studies into self-related concepts (some of which were conducted from the teachers' perspectives), intervention studies investigating how self-related training improves the students' motivation, as well as an outline of future research directions in this domain. The latter volume provides an overview of different theoretical and methodological approaches to the concept of self in L2 acquisition research. Each approach is presented in a chapter written by a prominent scholar; a particularly useful feature is the presence of annotated bibliographies containing three titles seen as most representative of a given approach.

Moving from affective to cognitive variables, Carmen Muñoz investigates 'The Association between Aptitude Components and Language Skills' (in Pawlak and Aronin, eds., pp. 51–68). The question addressed is whether language-learning aptitude is significantly associated with proficiency in young learners. Ten- to 12-year-old Spanish–Catalan bilingual children who were beginner L2 learners of English were tested on their listening, reading, speaking, and writing skills in English; they also did the Elementary Modern Language Aptitude Test (MLAT-E) in Spanish, measuring their language-learning aptitude. The results indicate that there are significant correlations between aptitude scores and scores on all language skills; correlation with writing was the strongest and with speaking the weakest. Of the different aptitude components, all language skills most strongly correlated with memory abilities; grammatical sensitivity was most closely related to writing. The results suggest that MLAT-E is a good predictor of achievement at beginner proficiency levels and that children rely on memory to a great extent in L2 acquisition. Agnieszka Pietrzykowska explores 'The Relationship between Learning Strategies and Speaking Performance' (in Pawlak, Bielak, and Mystkowska-Wiertelak, eds., *Classroom-Oriented Research: Achievements and Challenges*, pp. 55–68). English L2 learners studying in an English department and ranging in proficiency from intermediate to advanced completed the Strategy Inventory for Language Learning questionnaire, testing the frequency of strategy use. The data from the questionnaire was correlated with the results of the end-of-year examination of different components of speaking: pronunciation, grammatical accuracy, vocabulary use, and fluency. No significant positive correlations were discovered; memory, metacognitive, affective, and social strategies correlated negatively with fluency.

A notion related to learning strategies is learning styles. An overview of research into this concept is given by Patrycja Marta Kamińska in *Learning Styles and Second Language Education*. In the first chapter learning styles are defined, and contrasted with learning strategies. In three subsequent chapters different models of learning styles are presented and grouped according to the number of their components: starting with simple (one-dimensional) models, the author moves on to describe compound (two-dimensional) models, and ends with complex (multi-dimensional) models. The final chapter discusses the pedagogical relevance of research on learning styles and suggests its possible applications in the language classroom, including the option of accommodation and stretching learning styles.

Age is one of the most frequently studied individual variables in L2 acquisition; it is the topic that Carmen Muñoz addresses in 'Contrasting Effects of Starting Age and Input on the Oral Performance of Foreign Language Learners' (*AppLing* 21[2014] 463–82). She investigates, by testing intermediate to advanced Spanish-speaking L2 learners of English, whether early starters outperform late learners in L2 oral performance in instructional settings, as they do in naturalistic contexts. She also examines the effect of four input variables (length of instruction, number of hours of curricular and extracurricular lessons, number of hours spent abroad in an English-speaking setting, and current informal contact with the target language) on the learners' oral performance. Participants filled out an extensive questionnaire and took part in a film-retelling oral narrative task. The narratives were analysed in terms of fluency, lexical diversity, and syntactic complexity. The results show that input is a better predictor of L2 oral performance than starting age, with input quality, contact with native speakers, and cumulative exposure playing a particularly important role. The role of age is also explored by Victoria Murphy in *Second Language Learning in the Early School Years: Trends and Contexts*. The book contains an overview of research into learning more than one language in childhood in five different contexts. After developing a typology of contexts in the introductory chapter, the author discusses in the five chapters that follow research findings on language learning by simultaneous bilinguals, heritage language learners, minority language learners, majority language learners in immersion programmes, and instructed foreign language learners in primary schools. An important feature of these chapters is a subsection containing a discussion of educational implications of the presented research findings. The final chapter summarizes the previously reviewed evidence, and draws some conclusions. Throughout the book, the author stresses that age is not the critical variable in predicting successful outcomes of bilingual development, discussing a variety of contextual factors that contribute to these outcomes. The social and cognitive benefits of bilingualism are also constantly pointed out.

The topic of bilingualism is also taken up by Aneta Pavlenko in her *The Bilingual Mind and What It Tells Us about Language and Thought*. The book discusses the relationship between language and thought (or cognition) by drawing on research on bilingualism, understood in a very wide sense of the term. The starting point is the Sapir-Whorf hypothesis, discussed in the first chapter. The six subsequent chapters examine this hypothesis on the basis of evidence from bilinguals in relation to the categorization of colours, objects, and substances (chapter 2), encoding of number, time, and space (chapter 3), motion categorization and event construal (chapter 4), autobiographical memory and narrative thought (chapter 5), inner speech, interpretative frames, and accomplishment of intersubjectivity (chapter 6), and emotion categorization and affective processing (chapter 7). Directions for future research are given in the concluding chapter. Overall, the book highlights the valuable contributions of bilingualism research to our understanding of the concept of linguistic relativity and the human mind in general.

Before we move to works of general relevance to the field of SLA, we review an interesting book by Mercedes Durham, relevant to the fields of both SLA and sociolinguistics, namely *The Acquisition of Sociolinguistic Competence in a Lingua Franca Context*. The author investigates the extent to which native speakers of French, German, and Italian, who live in Switzerland and use English as a lingua franca (ELF), have native-like sociolinguistic competence in English, or, in other words, to what extent they display the same variation patterns in their language production as native speakers. Two comparable English corpora were compiled; the non-native corpus consisted of e-mails written by Swiss university students who were members of a medical association, while the native corpus was composed of e-mails written by British university students who were members of a sports society. Patterns of variation with respect to four linguistic features were analysed and compared across the two corpora: future tense, relative pronoun choice, complementizer use, and additive adverbial placement. The results show that native-like variation patterns were acquired for relative pronouns and complementizers, but not for the other two features; the influence of the native language was observed with respect to adverbial placement. The results are interpreted by considering feature type, frequency of occurrence, and whether the feature is overtly thought. The author concludes that ELF is a variety of English not so different from the native models.

Among works of general relevance to the field, an important volume is *Interlanguage: Forty Years Later*, edited by ZhaoHong Han and Elaine Tarone. Compiled on the occasion of the fortieth anniversary of the publication of Larry Selinker's seminal 1972 paper 'Interlanguage', the volume contains chapters by distinguished scholars who discuss the relevance of Selinker's paper for past, present, and future SLA research, expanding on or challenging some of the ideas put forth in that paper. A central idea that all scholars agree on is that in the process of L2 acquisition learners do indeed build an independent linguistic system—interlanguage—worth studying in its own right. Christiane Fäcke's, ed., *Manual of Language Acquisition*, is another valuable new resource for all SLA researchers regardless of the language(s) they are dealing with, despite its focus on Romance languages. Of particular relevance to a wider SLA community is the chapter 'Second Language Acquisition' (pp. 179–97) by Alessandro Benati, who offers a general overview of the field and discusses the implications of SLA research for L2 teaching. Also pertaining to a domain wider than L2 English is a thorough treatment of a theoretical framework called MOGUL (Modular-On-line Growth and Use of Language) in *The Multilingual Mind: A Modular Processing Perspective* by Michael Sharwood Smith and John Truscott. The framework is based on Ray Jackendoff's modular view of language and it aims to provide an account of both language development and language processing. The book shows how MOGUL sheds light on some of the key notions in SLA, such as the initial state, ultimate attainment, cross-linguistic influence, optionality, and language-learning anxiety. How MOGUL can be applied to explaining the role of consciousness in L2 acquisition is shown by John Truscott in *Consciousness and Second Language Learning*. The author examines the role of consciousness by looking at how L2 representations are formed in the mind (perception) and how they are modified in the process of memory consolidation and restructuring. An overview of MOGUL is also given in the book, as well as a summary of ideas related to consciousness in SLA.

Three monographs contribute to bridging the divide between SLA theory and the teaching practice. Shawn Loewen, in *Introduction to Instructed Second Language Acquisition*, deals with the L2 classroom setting, assuming that instruction is beneficial for L2 learning and proposing ways to enhance its effectiveness. Among the topics considered we single out a discussion of the types of knowledge (declarative vs. procedural) that L2 instruction can have an impact on, the role of communication and interaction in the classroom (in particular as regards communicative language teaching and task-based language learning), and focus on form. The acquisition of grammar, vocabulary, pronunciation, and pragmatics is examined in the light of how much pedagogical intervention can improve them. Contextual and individual aspects of classroom instruction are looked at as well, as are some specific teaching environments—immersion classes, content-based instruction, and study abroad. Even more pedagogically oriented, *Exploring Language Pedagogy through Second Language Acquisition Research* by Rod Ellis and Natsuko Shintani takes the teaching practice as the starting point, focusing in particular on pedagogical proposals found in teacher guides, and it explores how they are supported by the findings of theoretical research. The core of the book deals with internal and external perspectives on the relationship between theory and practice, including topics such as syllabus design, explicit instruction, and error correction, as well as with individual learner differences. In the concluding part of the book, the authors advocate a 'teaching for learning' approach, not based on deriving often simplified pedagogical implications from the SLA literature, but rather incorporating SLA findings into teacher guides and other pedagogical literature. Somewhat less broad in scope is Mike Long's *Second Language Acquisition and Task-Based Language Teaching*, devoted to an increasingly popular approach to language teaching, which draws on SLA theory and research findings. The book provides an overview of Task-Based Language Teaching (TBLT), as well as a detailed description of how to implement a TBLT programme in practice. The first part outlines the rationale for TBLT, as well as its psycholinguistic and philosophical underpinnings. The second part is more practically oriented and it comprises details pertaining to the six stages of designing, implementing, and evaluating a TBLT programme: needs and means analysis, syllabus design, materials development, choice of methodological principles and pedagogical procedures, student assessment, and programme evaluation. The third part, composed of a single chapter, discusses the future of TBLT and gives directions for further research.

In the reference arena, Vivian Cook and David Singleton's *Key Topics in Second Language Acquisition* is a new introductory textbook to the field. It deals with some of the core issues in SLA in a highly accessible manner. Its novelty lies primarily in an approach that links questions from academic research to very practical issues such as expressing one's feelings in a second language. Eight main questions capture topics from the relationship between different languages in the bilingual mind, the acquisition of L2 lexis, grammar, and writing, to the role of motivation and the relationship between SLA and language teaching. The authors' considerations related to teaching practice are noteworthy. First, it is clearly stated that the critical period hypothesis does not directly apply to the language classroom and that many additional factors on top of biological age need to be considered when assessing the benefits of early language learning in schools. Second, it is shown that the relationship between SLA research and teaching is still a very weak one, and that SLA researchers need to think more about the everyday reality of the language classroom if they are to draw implications for teaching from their theoretical research. Third, it is pointed out that the monolingual native-speaker norm is not only an unnecessary but also an unrealistic target for L2 learners. Another important addition to the general field of SLA is Kirsten M. Hummel's textbook *Introducing Second Language Acquisition: Perspectives and Practices*. The volume provides an introduction to the main concepts, issues, theoretical perspectives, and empirical findings in the field of SLA, as well as brief overviews of the field of first language acquisition (FLA), major L2 teaching approaches, and bilingualism. The topics of language-learning contexts, the age factor, and individual differences in L2 acquisition are treated in separate chapters. Each chapter starts with an outline and overview, and ends with a summary, list of key concepts, self-assessment and discussion questions, exercises and project ideas, suggestions for further reading and viewing, and an extensive list of references. Additional student-friendly features include text boxes on 'language learning in practice' and individual learner experiences, bolded new terms with definitions in the margin, and humorous cartoons interspersed throughout the book.

Published in 2013, the third edition of *Second Language Learning Theories* by Rosamond Mitchell, Florence Myles, and (as of this edition) Emma Marsden, contains an overview of the main theoretical perspectives in the field of SLA, classified as UG-based, cognitive linguistic, interaction-based, meaning-based, sociocultural, and sociolinguistic, each discussed in a separate chapter (or two). Each chapter contains both a description and an evaluation of a given group of theories. The book also includes a chapter introducing key concepts and issues in the field of SLA, as well as one on the recent history of SLA research. In addition to an update on advances in the field since the previous edition (published in 2004), the new edition features a revised and extended treatment of cognitive approaches to SLA, a glossary of key terms, and a timeline of SLA theory development. The year 2013 has also seen the publication of the fourth edition of the highly acclaimed and widely read textbook *Second Language Acquisition: An Introductory Course*, previously by Susan M. Gass and Larry Seliner, and now by Susan M. Gass, Jennifer Behney, and Luke Plonsky. The new edition contains a comprehensive overview of the field of SLA, covering the main concepts, issues, theoretical approaches, methodologies, and research findings in the field, as well as an overview of related disciplines. It has been updated, expanded, and somewhat restructured compared to the previous edition (from 2008), containing new information on learner corpora, linguistic interfaces, gestures, and study abroad, among other things. The new didactic features include text boxes summarizing points to remember, providing suggestions for additional activities, and asking questions about the reader's personal experiences. A companion website contains supplementary material.

Returning to production in 2014, several new books deal with methodology improvement in SLA. *Measuring L2 Proficiency: Perspectives from SLA*, edited by Pascale Leclercq, Amanda Edmonds, and Heather Hilton, presents studies that look at different ways of assessing proficiency in L2 English (and L2 French). The volume is divided into three parts, dealing respectively with general considerations, language processing, and focused assessment instruments. The first part comprises papers looking at oral and written learner production and the ways they can be used to profile different proficiency levels. The second part contains proposals for processing-based proficiency measures and tasks, such as the coefficient of variation in lexical access times. The last part is concerned with verifying the validity and reliability of specific widely used tests. The focus of the book is divided between general proficiency and proficiency in specific L2 domains, and all chapters deal with issues pertaining to validity and reliability. Also related to L2 proficiency is the paper 'Exploring Utterance and Cognitive Fluency of L1 and L2 English Speakers: Temporal Measures and Stimulated Recall' (*LangLearn* 64[2014] 809–54), by Jimin Kahng. Fluency is believed to constitute an essential component of L2 proficiency and the differences between native and non-native speakers' fluency have been a recurring topic in SLA research. The paper investigates utterance fluency and cognitive fluency of native English speakers and Korean-speaking learners of L2 English, where cognitive fluency is defined through the efficiency and automaticity of the processes responsible for the production of utterances, and utterance fluency as those features of utterances that reflect the speaker's cognitive fluency. Quantitative evidence from temporal measures and qualitative evidence from stimulated recall responses was examined; the proficiency of learners, who were divided into a lower-proficiency and a higher-proficiency group, was also taken into account. The L1 and L2 speakers were found to be different in speed, length of run, and silent pauses. In particular, a striking group difference in silent pause rate within a clause was found, consistent with the claim that pauses within clauses reflect processing difficulties in speech production. Stimulated recall responses showed that the lower-proficiency learners remembered more issues regarding L2 declarative knowledge on grammar and vocabulary than the higher-proficiency learners, which is compatible with the declarative/procedural model and studies on automaticity.

Interesting work has been done on CEFR. Brian North's *The CEFR in Practice*, the fourth book in the English Profile Studies series by CUP, deals with the fundamental properties of CEFR and its impact on teaching and assessment. Four core chapters discuss CEFR's role as a common framework, what it implies for teaching, and the assessment of CEFR levels. Some other issues covered are the relation of CEFR to linguistic theory and measurement theory, with an interesting focus on the criticism of the widely used descriptors from an SLA perspective, a major issue being the fact that descriptors were developed from teacher perceptions rather than from actual longitudinal learner data. The conclusion discusses the extent to which CEFR is generating change, the priorities for curriculum development in the future, and how the framework can be further exploited and developed. A paper by Henrik Gyllstad, Jonas Granfeldt, Petra Bernardini, and Marie Källkvist, titled 'Linguistic Correlates to Communicative Proficiency Levels of the CEFR: The Case of Syntactic Complexity in Written L2 English, L3 French and L4 Italian' (*ESLAYb* 14[2014] 1–30), contributes to the study of the linguistic underpinning of the communicatively oriented CEFR levels. It reports on research conducted in Sweden, focusing on English, French, and Italian as foreign languages, examining the relationship between CEFR levels (A1–C2) assigned by experienced raters to learners' written texts and three measures of syntactic complexity (length of T-units, subordinate clauses/T-unit ratio, and mean length of clause). The participants were mostly secondary-school students, between 10 and 19 years old. The data was elicited through two written tasks: a short letter and a narrative. The analysis detected weak to medium-strong positive correlations between the assigned CEFR levels and the three measures of syntactic complexity. Learners at CEFR level A did not vary significantly in syntactic complexity, while at level B differences were found between English and French.

On the purely methodological front, *Research Methods in Second Language Psycholinguistics*, edited by Jill Jegerski and Bill Van Patten, is a valuable collection of papers devoted to the application to SLA of online methods and techniques typically used in the field of psycholinguistics. The central eight chapters describe one method each, discussing the history of the method, the phenomena studied, the stimuli, data-analysis options, and the method's pros and cons. Well-established methods such as self-paced reading and eye-tracking are described, as are several more complex paradigms such as cross-modal priming and visual world eye-tracking; two neurolinguistic techniques—event-related potentials and functional magnetic resonance imaging—are included too. The importance of the volume lies primarily in the focus on behaviourally sensitive measures, often said to be under-represented in SLA research. Aek Phakiti's *Experimental Research Methods in Language Learning* discusses SLA research within the quantitative research paradigm, with a particular focus on statistical analysis. The book aims to provide an accessible step-by-step introduction to the quantitative paradigm as implemented in language acquisition studies. It starts by explaining the central conceptual issues in experimental research, such as variable types and research paradigms; key statistical notions are introduced next, and numerous types of statistical tests frequently used in SLA are explained, alongside the procedures for conducting them in IBM SPSS. The book is unique in being a single-volume guide through experimental research dedicated specifically to SLA. It includes a valuable glossary of key terms in language learning, and a companion website useful for both instructors and students. A different set of methods is dealt with in *Studying Second Language Acquisition from a Qualitative Perspective*, edited by Danuta Gabryś-Barker and Adam Wojtaszek. This collection of fourteen papers elaborates on qualitative and combined quantitative and qualitative methodologies. Qualitative methods are placed in a historical context, within their origins in ethnography, philosophy, sociology, and education, and their appropriateness for language acquisition research is discussed. Studies based on methods such as introspection (including diary-writing, interviews, and biographical narratives) are presented, dealing with a wide range of topics from pronunciation learning strategies to teacher reflection; most papers deal with L2 English as acquired by native speakers of Polish. It is also shown that qualitative and quantitative methods are not mutually exclusive but, rather, complement each other.

12. English as a Lingua Franca

If there were any doubt about it, reasons for including ELF as separate section in *YWES* are made abundantly clear in an entry in the *Routledge Companion to English Studies*, edited by Constant Leung and Brian V. Street, entitled 'English as an International Language/English as a Lingua Franca in Postcolonial and Neomillennial Contexts' by Tope Omoniyi (pp. 100–17). Omoniyi discusses how perspectives on ELF could and should be incorporated into English studies to make it more inclusive, diverse, and appropriate to contemporary realities. Given that English is becoming a language defined by non-native usage, he argues that English studies should not derive solely from the UK and other traditional anglophone countries, but from the English-speaking and English-using world in general. Most of the work on ELF recorded here both endorses and substantiates this view.

The global significance of the phenomenon of ELF continues to be recognized and to engage the intellectual interest of researchers in a number of fields of enquiry. This is evident from the increasing number and extended range of publications in ELF over the years. Some of these are the outcome of particular research projects, like the contributions to the two volumes of *Waseda Working Papers in ELF* edited by Kumiko Murata. Many others take the form of monographs published in the series Developments of English as a Lingua Franca (DELF), published by de Gruyter and edited by Jennifer Jenkins and Will Baker, and appear as articles in the *Journal of English as a Lingua Franca* (*JELF*), edited by Barbara Seidlhofer. Although, as their name indicates, these are dedicated to ELF study, the contributions they contain often relate ELF to a wider context of interdisciplinary research. There are articles in *JELF* which take an explicitly outsider's perspective. One such example is Susan Gal's 'A Linguistic Anthropologist Looks at English as a Lingua Franca' (*JELF* 2[2013] 177–83), in which she identifies the issues of linguistic creativity, standardization, and language ideology that are the common concern of both ELF and linguistic anthropology and which could benefit from collaborative study. Another example is Joseph Lo Bianco's talk, originally presented at one of the annual ELF conferences and printed in *JELF*, entitled 'Dialogue between ELF and the Field of Language Policy and Planning' (*JELF* 3[2014] 197–213). Here Lo Bianco points out that the two areas of study are both involved in language ecology in that both are critically concerned with how languages relate to and compete with each other in different social and communicative contexts. He makes the point that taking a language-planning perspective on ELF can sharpen understanding about its socio-political significance. Socio-political implications of ELF are also addressed in an article by Nora Dorn, Martina Rienzner, Brigitta Busch, and Anita Santner-Wolfartsberger entitled ' "Here I find myself to be judged": ELF/Plurilingual Perspectives on Language Analysis for the Determination of Origin' (*JELF* 3[2014] 409–24). This article challenges the procedure (known as LADO) that is routinely used by immigration authorities in an attempt to determine the country of origin of asylum seekers on the basis of the phonological and other linguistic features of their speech, which in these contexts is often English functioning as a lingua franca. The authors point out that such a procedure presupposes that a language is a fixed entity impervious to variation and change, a presupposition which denies the naturally flexible and adaptive use of language which is evident in the use of ELF.

In view of the increasing recognition of its wider implications, it is not surprising that there has been a good deal of work on ELF-related concerns that has appeared in other books and journals, whose scope nominally extends across other areas of enquiry not specifically concerned with ELF as such. The Italian journal *Textus*, for example, concerned with English studies in general, has a special issue entitled 'Perspectives on English as a Lingua Franca' edited by Maria Grazia Guido and Barbara Seidlhofer (*Textus* 27[2014]). Other work has appeared in journals whose disciplinary field would perhaps seem to be less obviously related to ELF. Khalid Bouti and Rajae Borki, for example, write about ELF in their editorial 'English as a Lingua Franca of Science in Morocco' (*International Journal of Medicine and Surgery* 1:ii[2014] 29–30), raising the question of how far prestige should attach to correct English against the requirement for communicative effectiveness. Another example is Tsedal B. Neeley's paper published in *Organization Science* (*OSci* 24[2013] 476–97), which, under the title 'Language Matters: Status Loss and Achieved

Status Distinctions in Global Organizations', deals with the problem familiar in ELF research of the sense of inadequacy experienced by non-native speakers of English and suggests institutional procedures for countering it. Bringing the concept of ELF into the field of economics and development studies, Elizabeth J. Erling and Philip Seargeant, eds., *English and Development: Policy, Pedagogy and Globalization* [2013], explore the relationship between English and development as this is both promoted in policy and practically realized through education. In this volume, Tom Bartlett's contribution 'Constructing Local Voices through English as a Lingua Franca: A Study from Intercultural Development Discourse' (pp. 163–81) makes a connection between the promotion of participatory approaches in development and ELF by showing how members of a marginalized community in Guyana appropriate English as a means of expressing their local identity and thereby challenge the orthodoxy of the dominant group.

Interest in ELF has also extended to the field of linguistic landscaping, as is evident from the two articles '630 Kilometres by Bicycle: Observations of English in Urban and Rural Finland' by Mikko Laitinen (*IJSL* 228[2014] 55–77) and 'English and Lexical Inventiveness in the Italian Linguistic Landscape' by Paola Vettorel and Valeria Franceschi (*ETC* 6[2013] 238–70). These articles describe the varied and frequently inventive display of English in public notices of different kinds and raise questions about what might motivate such uses. The data here is local. But since ELF is a global means of communication, it is not unexpected to find that there are also studies which deal with its use in globalized digital media of communication such as the Internet. Paola Vettorel's *English as a Lingua Franca in Wider Networking: Blogging Practices* published in the DELF series mentioned earlier, is a case in point. This book is a detailed and closely argued investigation of how ELF users exploit linguistic resources for networking through blogging practices, relating these practices to more general issues concerning language and computer-mediated communication. Another publication that deals with the use of English in computer-mediated communication is Christopher Jenks's article 'Are You an ELF? The Relevance of ELF as an Equitable Social Category in Online Intercultural Communication' (*L&IC* 13[2013] 95–108). Here Jenks looks at the English used in chatrooms but from a very different point of view. He is of the opinion that it is problematic on ethical grounds for researchers to refer to ELF users since to do so puts them into a social category that diminishes their identity. Jenks's concern for how the use of ELF bears on issues of identity is taken up again in his article in the same journal ' "Your Pronunciation and Your Accent is Very Excellent": Orientations of Identity During Compliment Sequences in English as a Lingua Franca' (*L&IC* 13[2013] 165–81). With reference again to chatroom data, Jenks seeks to show how, in the particular case of expressing compliments, ELF users relate to each other in the construction of their identities in the process of their intercultural interaction. These matters are also touched upon in Jenks's book entitled *Social Interactions in Second Language Chat Rooms*.

The issue of how the use of ELF relates to identity raised by Jenks and the articles by Neeley and Bartlett referred to earlier is a recurrent theme in the ELF literature. In their article, 'English as a Lingua Franca: A Source of

Identity for Young Europeans?' (*Multilingua* 33[2013] 437–57), for example, Claus Gnutzmann, Jenny Jakisch, and Frank Rabe explore the perceptions of a selected group of Europeans—1,061 students at the University of Braunschweig, Germany—with regard to the potential role of ELF in the formation of a common European identity. They find positive attitudes towards the idea of ELF as a useful mode of communication, despite adherence to the idea that native-speaker norms are the most legitimate. And while this sample considers plurilingualism to be one of Europe's key underlying concepts, most of them report having only competence in their mother tongue and English. This, the authors argue, calls into question the European ideal of equipping every European with skills in two foreign languages in addition to their mother tongue. Examining another European context, Josep Soler-Carbonell, in his article 'Emerging ELF as an Intercultural Resource: Language Attitudes and Ideologies' (*JELF* 3[2014] 243–68), explores whether English is becoming a language of inter-group communication among speakers of different linguistic backgrounds (i.e. Estonian and Russian) in Estonia. His ethnographically collected data shows that English is only occasionally used (mainly among younger speakers). Focusing on communication rather than on identity, unlike Gnutzmann et al., he finds that both ethno-linguistic groups (Estonians and Russians) continue to learn each other's languages and English, although there is some indication that younger Estonians are more fluent in English than in Russian (as opposed to the older generations). For this reason, the need for English to overcome communicative obstacles does occasionally arise. The author thus suggests that ELF is an extra resource capable of supporting inter-ethnic contacts and facilitating integration. All these publications are concerned with wide communicative networks, but the expression and negotiation of cultural identity are also enacted on a small scale, as is argued and exemplified by two studies of how ELF is used in the dyadic interactions of couples. One of these studies is Svitlana Klötzl's '"Maybe Just Things We Grew Up With": Linguistic and Cultural Hybridity in ELF Couple Talk' (*JELF* 3[2014] 27–48). Klötzl explores how couples use ELF to negotiate a convergence of intercultural identities to maintain intimacy. She shows how in the pragmatic process of hybridization and acculturation they draw upon any available linguistic resources to create their private space. In her article 'ELF Couples and Automatic Code-Switching' (*JELF* 3[2014] 1–26), Kaisa Pietikäinen takes a different approach. Focusing more on the management of communication than the creation of intimacy, and drawing on ideas from the literature on conversational analysis and content analysis, she describes the interaction between multilingual couples as the easy, often automatic, switching from one language code to another.

These two articles, though dealing with particular small-scale interactions, raise critical questions about how ELF as a use of language is to be defined. And there has been much discussion about the nature of ELF, of what kind of linguistic phenomenon it is. Publications on this question vary widely in their generality. We can begin by taking brief notice of summary accounts that characterize it in broad terms. One of these is the entry 'English as a Lingua Franca' by Christiane Meierkord (in Chapelle, ed., *The Encyclopedia of*

Applied Linguistics, pp. 2–7), which discusses ELF with reference to other lingua francas and represents it as different kinds of 'Interaction across Englishes' (pidgins and creoles, second-language and foreign-language Englishes, etc.), some of which are intra- and some inter-national means of communication. Another entry in the same encyclopedia, written by Margie Berns entitled 'Lingua Franca and Language of Wider Communication' (pp. 2–6), is mainly a historical account of different lingua francas and attempts, like that of Basic English and Esperanto, to design an international language. The work of what is referred to as the ELF 'movement' gets only a brief and dismissive mention. Both of these entries describe the general nature of lingua francas with reference to their emergence in the past. Peter Trudgill's article 'Before ELF: GLF from Samarkand to Sfakia' (*JELF* 3[2014] 387–93) explores this topic in rather more detail, drawing parallels between ELF and the lingua franca use of other languages in the past, pointing out that although Latin is usually cited as the main precursor to ELF, Greek was also extensively used as a lingua franca in the ancient world, at times in preference to Latin.

Research on the intrinsic nature of ELF as a use of language, as distinct from these general characterizations, has been both intensive and far-reaching, taking its theoretical bearings from the work of previous years. In focusing on the actual use of English rather than on language as an abstract system, for example, ELF study can be seen as theoretically aligned with recent thinking about usage-based descriptions of language, as is indicated in Cem Aptekin's 'English as a Lingua Franca through a Usage-Based Perspective: Merging the Social and the Cognitive in Language Use' (*LC&C* 26[2013] 197–207). Aptekin criticizes what he sees as the tendency to focus on the functions of ELF to the neglect of form and argues, as have many ELF researchers, for the need to investigate how function and form are related: how the communicative experience of using ELF informs the cognitive development of the language system. Another and related theoretical link is made in an article by Robert Baird, Will Baker, and Mariko Kitazawa entitled 'The Complexity of ELF' (*JELF* 3[2014] 171–96). Here the emphasis is again on actual usage, and the indeterminacy of ELF as performance and practice are seen to exemplify the tenets of complexity theory, which, the authors argue, provide conceptual clarity to observations made elsewhere in the literature about the intrinsic emergent and adaptive character of ELF.

As has been pointed out in the work of previous years, a particular complex feature of ELF is that it not only exploits the encoding potential of English beyond that which becomes conventionally realized in native-speaker contexts, but also draws on whatever other linguistic resources are available and can be appropriately put to adaptive communicative use. The E of ELF, therefore, is essentially variable and can no longer be described in traditional terms as a distinct and bounded linguistic entity. This necessarily calls into question well-established ideas about what it means to be monolingually competent in a language and bi- and multilingually competent in more than one. Suresh Canagarajah addresses this question in his book *Translingual Practice: Global Englishes and Cosmopolitan Relations* [2013]. Here he points out that the assumption that language use is simply a matter of conforming to the norms of monolingual competence disregards the empirical fact that actual communication, as is particularly evident in the use of ELF, is a matter of what he calls 'translingual practice' in that it is enacted by the exploitation of diverse semiotic resources beyond those afforded by a particular language. Canagarajah therefore proposes that it is more appropriate to think in terms of what he calls 'semiodiversity' rather than 'glossodiversity', a terminological distinction that corresponds to the distinction that is seen as crucial in current ELF research between variation and variety and is in accord with complexity theory and with recent sociolinguistic thinking about the essential arbitrariness and indeterminacy of language boundaries.

This view of linguistic communication as involving the use of language as a general resource rather than the performance of a particular and separate language is also expressed in Jens Normann Jørgensen and Janus Spindler Møller's 'Polylingualism and Languaging' (in Leung and Street, eds., pp. 67–83). Here the authors use the term 'polylingualism' to refer to the phenomenon of what Canagarajah calls 'translingual practice', and they propose, as many others have done, that such practice is best described performatively as acts of 'languaging', the latter term one that has frequently been used in the description of ELF interactions. This raises the question of what it means to use, or acquire, linguistic or sociolinguistic competence in contexts of ELF use; this question is considered in Mercedes Durham's book *The Acquisition of Sociolinguistic Competence in a Lingua Franca Context*. This book examines how the differences between the sociolinguistic competences of native speakers (NSs) and non-native speakers (NNSs) are dealt with in ELF interactions. Its focus is not on the mutually adaptive use of language in ELF interactions but on the degree to which the non-natives unilaterally accommodate to the native users by acquiring their patterns of language behaviour and thus approximating to native-speaker sociolinguistic competence.

In its translingual or polylingual functioning, ELF of its nature mediates between speakers of different lingua-cultural backgrounds. This implies that it involves a transcultural as well as a translingual process and so brings into consideration questions about interculturality in linguistic communication in general and in ELF in particular. Will Baker takes up this topic in his chapter 'Interpreting the Culture in Intercultural Rhetoric: A Critical Perspective from English as a Lingua Franca Studies' (in Belcher and Nelson, eds., *Critical and Corpus-Based Approaches to Intercultural Rhetoric* [2013], pp. 22–45), and argues that ELF users, in both spoken and written modes, exploit their cultural resources as they do their linguistic resources in a flexible and adaptable manner in the communicative process.

The question naturally arises as to how this concept of intercultural translingualism relates to multilingualism as conventionally conceived. This question is addressed by Cornelia Hülmbauer and Barbara Seidlhofer in their chapter 'English as a Lingua Franca in European Multilingualism' (in Berthoud, Grin, and Lüdi, eds., *Exploring the Dynamics of Multilingualism: The DYLAN Project* [2013], pp. 387–406), which reports on research on dimensions of multilingualism in Europe carried out in the extensive five-year project 'Language Dynamics and the Management of Diversity' (the DYLAN project). In their chapter, Hülmbauer and Seidlhofer further substantiate the view that ELF is a flexible exploitation of linguistic resources afforded not only by English but by other languages as well, so that ELF is plurilinguistically complex of its very nature. They point out, however, that this flexibility operates not across but beyond demarcated linguistic boundaries, in that elements of the source languages cease to be assignable to separate codes but are functionally fused in the process of use to become plurilinguistic modes of communication in their own right. As such, ELF, it is argued, serves the need for a means of inter-communal communication without undermining the role and status of other languages for intra-communal communication and the expression of sociocultural identity. At the same time, this view of ELF as the exploitation of multiple lingual resources suggests that there is a need to question the traditional conception of multilingualism as the knowledge and use of more than one distinct linguistic system.

Hülmbauer takes up and extends this pluralistic view of ELF in her article 'From Within and Without: The Virtual and the Plurilingual in ELF' (*JELF* 2[2013] 47–73). On the evidence of the ELF data she is concerned with, Hülmbauer demonstrates that ELF users draw on the communicative resources which are virtually available but unrealized in English and other languages. She argues that ELF users draw expediently on these plurilingual resources in the process of 'languaging', of negotiating meaning in response to immediate contextual need.

In spite of all the arguments against it, the view is still widespread that ELF furthers the dominance of English in the interests of its NSs, and so constitutes a threat to multilingual diversity. One way of countering this threat is to propose an alternative means of communication across languages. This is what is proposed by Gerda J. Blees, Willem M. Mak, and Jan D. ten Thije in 'English as a Lingua Franca Versus Lingua Receptiva in Problem-Solving Conversations between Dutch and German Students'(*AppLiRev* 5[2014] 173–93). The idea is that communication is achieved by receptive multilingualism whereby speakers only make productive use of their own languages and need only to understand those of their interlocutors. Thus unlike a lingua franca, such a lingua receptiva (referred to as LaRa) draws on a single linguistic resource, which is identifiable as a distinct language but assumed to be interpretable by its non-speakers. The claim is that such an approach provides for communication across lingua-cultural boundaries while maintaining linguistic diversity. The article reports on empirical research on the relative communicative and cognitive advantages of putting German and Dutch to productive use as a LaRa as against the use of ELF among university students. How ELF relates to the concept of a LaRa is explored in more detail and conceptual depth by Hülmbauer in her article 'A Matter of Reception: ELF and LaRa Compared' (*AppLiRev* 5[2014] 273–95). She points out that a lingua receptiva, unlike ELF, is in its production in conformity with native speaker norms so that the burden of adaptation falls on the recipient and meaning is not interactively negotiated but is a function of recipients' interpretative strategies. Although, she argues, ELF and lingua receptiva can be seen as complementary in that both rely on a sensitivity to and engagement with lingua-cultural similarities and differences, the effectiveness of lingua receptiva is dependent on particular contexts and constellations of participants and so is more restricted in use than ELF.

The notion of a lingua receptiva accords with the concept of a language as a bounded and separate entity, which is at variance with current thinking about ELF that, as noted above, conceives it as a variably adaptable and indeterminate use of linguistic resources. The idea nevertheless persists that ELF is a formal system, a variety of English. In their article 'Linguistic Baptism and the Disintegration of ELF' (*AppLiRev* 4[2013] 343–63) Joseph Sung-Yul Park and Lionel Wee argue the need to shift the direction of ELF research by recognizing that ELF is not a variety definable by its formal features but a dynamic exploitation of variable linguistic resources, apparently unaware that ELF research has long since held this position. Similarly in 'Notes on English used as a Lingua Franca as an Object of Study' (*JELF* 2[2013] 25–46), Janus Mortensen identifies what he sees as a tendency in the ELF literature to reify ELF as a bounded object, an independent language system, and argues the need to shift the focus of enquiry to contextual factors so as to describe ELF encounters in more explicit functional terms as speech events using the SPEAKING frame of reference proposed by Dell Hymes. Another article that takes researchers to task for their supposed reification of ELF is John O'Regan's 'English as a Lingua Franca: An Immanent Critique' (*AppLing* 35[2014] 533–52). Mortensen's article pursues a reasoned argument in support of ELF research by providing it with what he calls a 'conceptual clarification'. In contrast, O'Regan's article is determinedly negative and tendentious, intent on dismissing the study of ELF as theoretically and ideologically misconceived.

Whereas O'Regan takes a philosophical, predominantly Marxist, vantage point in his castigation of ELF study, the perspective taken by Vivian Cook in his much more impartial consideration of ELF is that of a researcher in SLA, as is indicated in the title of his chapter 'ELF: Central or Atypical Second Language Acquisition' (in Singleton, Fishman, Aronin, and Ó Laoire, eds., *Current Multilingualism: A New Linguistic Dispensation* [2013], pp. 27–44). This considers the nature of ELF by raising the question of whether or not it can be defined as a language. Although Cook continually refers to ELF as a variety, he argues that it does not count as a language or kind of English in that it neither constitutes a formal system nor is it the property of a particular community of users. Though Cook seems to be unaware of it, this view corresponds exactly with current thinking in ELF research, but the conclusions drawn from it are very different. From the SLA perspective that Cook takes, the assumption would seem to be that there must be a specific language, a bounded entity, for learners to acquire and so ELF does not qualify as a subject of study. But in the alternative current conceptualization of ELF, as exemplified by publications earlier referred to, ELF is taken to be the strategic use of multiple linguistic resources which are not confined to one language, and from this point of view acquisition can be seen not as the learning of a particular language but as the learning of how to use language in general.

This issue of whether ELF is defined in formal terms as a distinct varietal code, or in functional terms as a variable mode of communication also figures in the following articles. Beyza Björkman, in the (somewhat oddly titled) entry, 'Grammar of English as a Lingua Franca' (in Chapelle, ed., pp. 1–9), describes English grammar usage at a Swedish technical university, observing that 'ELF usage in this instructional setting shows a considerable level of nonstandard grammar that does not interfere with communicative effectiveness' (p. 5) though she later says that these features only occur with low frequencies, thus raising the question how frequent features have to be to qualify as commonalities. Björkman reviews other studies that found commonalities of nonstandard grammar in ELF interactions, emphasizing, however, that research in this area is remarkably scarce. The entry concludes by pointing to overlaps of features in ELF usage with WE, pidgins and creoles, and learner language. The next two papers take up similar issues about the supposed formal properties of ELF but in respect of the relevance of ELF for language pedagogy. In 'English as a Lingua Franca: Ontology and Ideology' (*ELangT* 67[2013] 3–10), Andrew Sewell, like Mortensen (see above), traces a tendency to misrepresent ELF ontologically in essentialist terms as a variety, and this, he suggests, comes about because ELF researchers are ideologically intent on setting ELF in opposition to English as a native language (ENL). He argues that variable and flexible adaptability is a feature of all language use, including ENL, and is not distinctive of ELF. In his reply in the same volume, 'The Distinctiveness of English as a Lingua Franca' (*ELangT* 67[2013] 346–9), Martin Dewey points out that Sewell's non-essentialist views of language are actually in accord with the thinking of ELF researchers and that the distinctiveness of ELF is not that it is a variety or formally different from ENL but that its functional variability and focus on communicative effectiveness reveal the dynamic adaptive process of language use with particular clarity.

The claim that ELF is relevant to English-language teaching is given critical consideration in an article by Michael Swan titled 'ELF and EFL: Are They Really Different?' (*JELF* 1[2012] 379–89). Swan argues that there is no essential difference in that what ELF users produce is simply the approximate version of the language that learners have acquired through their instruction in the standard language. Although he concedes that such versions can be communicatively effective, as has always been the case, they are nevertheless evidence of imperfect learning. Thus he sees the non-conformities that occur in ELF use as essentially learner errors in a different guise. He argues that the acquisition of this approximate competence depends on the learners having an authoritatively described model of competence for learners to approximate to—hence the need for EFL teaching to be based on descriptions of StE and the norms of native-speaker usage. Since descriptions of ELF do not codify it as a variety, as Swan thinks they claim to do, they cannot provide an alternative model and so he concludes that they have little if any pedagogical relevance. Henry Widdowson reacts to this article in 'ELF and EFL: What's the Difference? Comments on Michael Swan' (*JELF* 2[2013] 187–93). He points out that Swan's position is based on the conventional, and conservative, belief that learning English must necessarily be a matter of conformity to what is described and prescribed as the standard language and that this is at odds with the communicatively non-conformist ways in which English, like any language, is actually used as an indeterminate and variable resource. Referring to the distinction that Swan makes between learning English, which requires conformity, and using it, which may not, thereby making use dependent on learning, Widdowson suggests reversing this dependency by focusing not on the linguistic forms of encoded models but on the kind of communicative strategies that characterize the use of ELF. He concludes that although as Swan conceives it, EFL is indeed very different from ELF, in his conception the two can be seen as closely interrelated. Swan reacts in 'A Reply to Henry Widdowson' (*JELF* 2[2013] 391–6) by citing extracts from his article in support of his contention that his argument has been misunderstood and his position misrepresented. This exchange is only one indication of the controversy about the pedagogical relevance of ELF, and the debate is likely to continue.

While the implications of ELF for ELT are often briefly discussed in descriptive works on ELF, a number of publications in 2013 and 2014 have been exclusively concerned with this topic as well as various issues connected with ELF-informed language teaching. Given that Asian speakers nowadays use English primarily as a lingua franca to communicate with other Asians, Andy Kirkpatrick's 'Teaching English in Asia in Non-Anglo Cultural Contexts: Principles of the "Lingua Franca Approach"' (in Marlina and Giri, eds., *The Pedagogy of English as an International Language: Perspectives from Scholars, Teachers, and Students*, pp. 259–86) outlines, as suggested by the title, six principles of a 'Lingua Franca' approach to teaching English in the Asian region. These principles, which challenge a number of widespread assumptions in ELT, are as follows: the goals of teaching are mutual intelligibility and intercultural competence rather than native-like pronunciation, adherence to standard grammar, and knowledge of Anglo-American cultures (principles 1 and 2); not NSs, but 'local multilinguals who are suitably trained' (p. 29) are the most appropriate English-language teachers (principle 3); lingua franca environments rather than NS contexts constitute valuable opportunities to develop learners' linguistic and intercultural competence (principle 4); written language differs from spoken language in that the former is not acquired but needs to be *learned* by both NSs and NNSs and written language norms are largely determined by discipline, genre, and culture (principle 5); assessment needs to be based on 'how successfully [students] can use English in ASEAN settings' (p. 32), not on NS norms (principle 6). The pedagogical principles of ELF-informed teaching as regards the models, methodologies, and teaching materials used, language testing, and the status of NSs and NNSs as teachers and learners of English are also discussed in Nobuyuki Hino's 'Teaching De-Anglo-Americanized English for International Communication' (*JELL* 60[2014] 91–106).

Ian MacKenzie's *English as a Lingua Franca: Theorizing and Teaching English* discusses a number of suggestions that have been made by ELF researchers as to the implications of ELF for ELT, some of which he is more sceptical of than others. This monograph takes a rather critical view of ELF in general. Despite its promising title, however, 'it is hard to see what contribution it makes to the field [of ELF research]' (David Deterding in his review in *JELF* 3[2014] 429–31, p. 431) given that it neither offers new data nor new theoretical ideas.

A number of publications have addressed the status of NS and NNS teachers in connection with ELF. Andy Kirkpatrick, John Patkin, and Wu Jingjing's 'The Multilingual Teacher and the Multicultural Curriculum: An Asian Example for Intercultural Communication in the New Era' (in Sharifian and Jamarani, eds., *Language and Intercultural Communication in the New Era*, pp. 263–85) challenges the privileged position of NS language teachers in Asia. The authors present extracts from the ACE corpus (see below) illustrating the topics discussed by multilingual Asian ELF users, which tend to presuppose familiarity with and knowledge of 'Asian cultures and values' (p. 283). This leads them to conclude that ELF speakers in the region will need to possess cultural knowledge of this kind as well as intercultural competence. These skills will need to be reflected in the local English-language curriculum and, they argue, can best be developed with the help of local multilingual and multicultural teachers with pedagogical training, due to the latter's 'inter-cultural knowledge and skills' (p. 282). In 'Can the Expanding Circle Own English? Comments on Yoo's "Nonnative Teachers in the Expanding Circle and the Ownership of English"' (*AppLing* 35[2014] 208–12), Wei Ren responds to an article by Isaiah Wonho Yoo (*AppLing* 35[2014] 82–6), which disputes the claim of Expanding Circle speakers to the ownership of English. Ren uncovers a number of fallacies in Yoo's work, such as that in maintaining that Expanding Circle speakers 'do not speak English on a daily basis, and [that] there are no separate local varieties of English for them' (p. 3), he fails to take proper account of the widespread use of ELF in the EU and in ASEAN. Ren further argues that NNS teachers from the Expanding Circle will continue to face disadvantages and have their self-confidence undermined if they are required to teach according to NS models. In order for them to be regarded as 'ideal teachers', it will be necessary to acknowledge Expanding Circle speakers' right to the ownership of English, as then 'the linguistic and cultural resources that [local NNS teachers in the Expanding Circle] bring to the classroom will be appreciated' (p. 211). Yet, despite these considerations, the discrimination against NNS teachers in ELT seems to continue, as is evident for instance in Nicola Galloway's '"I Get Paid for My American Accent": The Story of One Multilingual English Teacher (MET) in Japan' (*EnginP* 1[2014] 1–30).

Given the fact that a certain resistance to novel teaching approaches that challenge established ways of thinking, as in the case of ELF, is often observable amongst ELT practitioners, two publications in 2014 were concerned with the necessary measures in teacher education to help teachers incorporate ELF into their actual teaching practice. In 'Pedagogic Criticality and English as a Lingua Franca' (*Atlantis* 36:ii[2014] 11–30), Martin Dewey suggests adopting a sociocultural perspective in teacher education in order to respond to the perceived gap of (ELF) theory and practice so often lamented by teachers. Dewey argues that the convictions about language and pedagogy that teachers hold need to be sufficiently dealt with in teacher education by promoting a critical perspective on teaching practices. He suggests that this might be achieved through narrative enquiry, an approach which consists of teachers recounting their personal experiences, thereby 'becoming compelled to confront how their understanding of teaching came about in the first place'

(p. 24). The importance of engaging with teachers' existing beliefs in order to enable the application of ELF-related findings in ELT is also suggested by Nicos C. Sifakis's 'ELF Awareness as an Opportunity for Change: A Transformative Perspective for ESOL Teacher Education' (*JELF* 3[2014], 317–35). In it, Sifakis argues that, in order for pedagogical change in line with the reality of ELF to take place, teachers need not only to acquire knowledge about ELF and its pedagogical implications, but also to critically revisit their own convictions. He therefore calls for a 'transformative' approach to ELF-aware teacher education which operates in two phases: the first consists of guided readings in the fields of ELF, critical pedagogy, and postmodern applied linguistics, which teachers then reflect on with regard to past experiences and the current circumstances of their teaching. The second phase consists of action research projects during which teachers apply ELF-related matters to their particular teaching context as they see fit. This approach is 'transformative' in that during the entire process, teachers 'engage in a reflective journey that prompts them to become conscious of, challenge, and ultimately transform deeper convictions about ESOL communication and teaching' (p. 328).

The issue of how the perceived gap between ELF theory and the practice of ELT could be closed is also taken up by several publications that examine methods to integrate ELF into the English-language classroom. Enrico Grazzi's monograph *The Sociocultural Dimension of ELF in the English Classroom* reports on a research project on the use of written ELF by Italian high-school students in an Internet-mediated community of practice. After discussing the similarities and differences between ELF and two historical lingua francas (section 1) and a sociocultural approach to ELF rooted in Vygotskian theory (section 2), the author provides a detailed description of the online activities (writing and sharing online book reviews, co-operative writing, and fan fiction) involving the use of ELF by the students participating in the project in section 3 of the book. ELT practitioners who wish to gain an idea of how to provide their own students with similar opportunities for using ELF in natural contexts might find this section particularly useful. The last section presents the results of an ethnographic survey carried out after the project had ended about the students' and their teachers' practices in using ELF online and their views on using ELF in Web-mediated communication, which suggests an overall positive attitude towards the teaching method presented here on the part of both students and teachers. Paola Vettorel's 'ELF in International School Exchanges: Stepping into the Role of ELF Users' (*JELF* 2[2013] 147–73) reports on a similar project, where European primary-school children from different lingua-cultural backgrounds were offered the opportunity to communicate with each other in speech and writing via the Internet using ELF. An analysis of the resulting spoken and written data showed that, although they were beginner learners of English, the pupils 'made all efforts to exploit the (pluri)linguistic resources available to them in their aim to communicate and express their intended meaning' (p. 159), mostly achieving communicative success in the process. Notably, these learners employed a number of linguistic processes and communication strategies attested in other empirical investigations of ELF data (such as grammatical regularization, code-switching, repetition, and asking for clarification or confirmation) when 'stepping into the role of ELF *users*' (p. 165; emphasis original). This encounter with real-world ELF communication, the author argues, 'has allowed [the pupils] to connect their language learning experience with real contexts of use, adding a richer value to both' (p. 169). Vettorel also points to the potential positive effects of such encounters in and with ELF on learners' motivation and self-confidence, an issue which is the focus of I-Chung Ke and Hilda Cahyani's 'Learning to Become Users of English as a Lingua Franca (ELF): How ELF Online Communication Affects Taiwanese Learners' Beliefs of English' (*System* 46[2014] 28–38). This study investigates whether participating in regular ELF online exchanges with Indonesian peers over a two-semester period affected Taiwanese university students' conceptions of and orientation towards English. Ke and Cahyani's findings reveal, amongst other things, 'a significant change in students' acceptance of local accents' (p. 34) and a decrease in the perceived importance of grammatical accuracy in communication with foreigners after the project. However, they also found that 'most students' beliefs about English remain[ed] consistent with the traditional NS-based ELT paradigm' (their abstract).

Another publication reporting on an international writing project is Massimo Verzella and Laura Tommaso's 'Learning to Write for an International Audience through Cross-Cultural Collaboration and Text-Negotiation' (*ChE* 21[2014] 310–21). Notably, the project described in this article recognizes the need to prepare not only NNSs but also NSs of English for international communication, and therefore involves American and Italian university students collaborating with each other. However, in contrast to many other international exchanges, this one turns the tables on the traditional distribution of roles between NS and NNS, in which the NS is regarded as the owner of the English language and assumes the role of the linguistic judge or adviser whereas the NNS assumes the role of the one whose language is being evaluated. Instead, in this project it was the Italian students who gave their American partners feedback with regard to the comprehensibility of their writing. Thus, the American students were able to reflect on the process of accommodating their use of written English to the needs of an international audience.

ELF is also brought to the classroom in Stephanie Ann Houghton and Khalifa Abubaker Al-Asswad's 'An Exploration of the Communication Strategies Used When Culture-Laden Words Are Translated from Japanese to Arabic in ELF Interaction' (*L&E* 28[2014] 28–40), which reports on an English course at a Japanese university with the aim of promoting intercultural communicative competence through the use of ELF. The focus of their article is on the analysis of the communication and translation strategies employed by Japanese students to explain culture-laden Japanese words to a Libyan instructor through ELF. However, the authors also discuss a number of pedagogical implications of their findings, e.g. how the teaching method described can support learners in developing meta-cognitive awareness of the strategies they employ.

Another way of integrating ELF into ELT is suggested by Nicola Galloway and Heath Rose in 'Using Listening Journals to Raise Awareness of Global

Englishes in ELT' (*ELangT* 68[2014] 386–96). In it, the authors describe the use of listening journals to familiarize Japanese university students with different international varieties of English and ELF usage. The activity involved students listening to a particular type of speaker of English or an ELF exchange of their own choice for a minimum of ten minutes per week, recording in their journals the speakers' nationality along with their reasons for choosing the particular speaker(s) or exchange in question and a reflection on the properties of the English they had listened to. The listening journals assumed a dual function, constituting not only a pedagogical tool but also a research instrument that allowed the authors to gain insight into the students' listening preferences and their response to different types of English. The results of the study indicate that students were interested in listening to NNS varieties of English (especially those of neighbouring countries) and that the journals were useful in increasing students' exposure to the latter. However, it seems that the activity was of limited success with regard to raising students' awareness of the nature of ELF communication, as rather than reflecting on the communicative strategies employed by ELF speakers, students tended to concentrate on varieties of English and simply measure NNS English against an NS yardstick in their reflections. The authors conclude that for future implementation, such an activity needs to 'be revised to place more focus on ELF interactions and less on the notion of varieties of English' (p. 394)—an important observation which seems to apply to other ELF- and ELT-related publications as well.

Galloway and Rose's study sheds further light on learners' perspectives on ELF and ELF-related issues in teaching, a theme that is the research focus of several other publications. Another article by Nicola Galloway that addresses this topic is 'Global Englishes and English Language Teaching (ELT): Bridging the Gap between Theory and Practice in a Japanese Context' (*System* 41[2013] 786–803). Galloway employs a mixed-methods approach, using questionnaires and interview data, to investigate the views of Japanese university students on (learning) English and how the latter may have been affected by a Global Englishes class including a module on ELF. Mention also needs to be made of Chit Cheung Matthew Sung, who has published several articles on different aspects of the issue of learner preferences in relation to ELF-informed teaching. His 'Exposure to Multiple Accents of English in the English Language Teaching Classroom: From Second Language Learners' Perspectives' (*ILLT* 8[2014] 1–16) is concerned with learner attitudes towards encountering a range of different accents in the ELT classroom, as is often called for in ELF literature. A particular interest of Sung's is learner (or language user) identities and ELF, especially in connection with pronunciation preferences, as is evident in his papers 'Accent and Identity: Exploring the Perceptions among Bilingual Speakers of English as a Lingua Franca in Hong Kong' (*IJBEB* 17[2014] 544–57), 'I Would Like to Sound Like Heidi Klum': What Do Non-Native Speakers Say about Who They Want to Sound Like?' (*EnT* 29:ii[2013] 17–21), 'English as a Lingua Franca and Global Identities: Perspectives from Four Second Language Learners of English in Hong Kong' (*L&E* 26[2014] 31–9), 'Global, Local or Glocal? Identities of L2 Learners in English as a Lingua Franca Communication' (*LC&C* 27[2014] 43–57), and

'Hong Kong University Students' Perceptions of Their Identities in English as a Lingua Franca Contexts: An Exploratory Study' (*JAPC* 24 2014] 94–112). Sung's concern for the recognition of learner preferences and learner choice with regard to ELF is also explicit in his response to Sewell ([2013], reviewed above), titled 'English as a Lingua Franca and English Language Teaching: A Way Forward' (*ELangT* 67[2013] 350–3).

The learner's perspective is also the focus of Yongyan Zheng's 'An Inquiry into Chinese Learners' English-Learning Motivational Self-Images: ENL Learner or ELF User?' (*JELF* 2[2013] 341–64). Zheng conducted interviews with eight Chinese English majors to investigate their Ought-to and Ideal L2 Selves according to the framework of Zoltan Dörnyei's L2 Motivational Self System. She found that the participants' Ought-to and Ideal L2 Selves were strongly related to NS norms, thereby conflicting with their experiences of and opportunities for using English in their immediate surroundings and thus ultimately leading to demotivation for learning and using English. As a counter-measure, Zheng suggests that teachers could encourage learners to develop more realistic motivational self-images of 'legitimate ELF users' rather than 'perennial ENL learners' (p. 359). A similar yet large-scale study also enquiring into the perspectives of Chinese speakers of English is Ying Wang's 'Non-Conformity to ENL Norms: A Perspective from Chinese English Users' (*JELF* 2[2013] 255–82). Wang's participants were not learners of English, but *users* in that they had a certain degree of linguistic experience with using English (including both university students of different disciplines and English-using professionals). Drawing on questionnaire and interview data from over 760 and 35 participants respectively, her study investigated Chinese speakers' views on non-conformity to ENL norms, for instance as evident in examples from ELF corpus data. Her findings suggest 'a delicate balance between exonormative and endonormative orientations to English' (p. 278) on the part of her participants, who subscribed to the idea of the significance of ENL norms but, at the same time, recognized that non-conformity may have an important communicative and socio-psychological function.

That the distinction between learner and user of English is not always a straightforward one becomes clear when considering studies such as Eda Kaypak and Deniz Ortaçtepe's 'Language Learner Beliefs and Study Abroad: A Study on English as a Lingua Franca (ELF)' (*System* 42[2014] 355–67). This article investigates the impact of an Erasmus-exchange semester spent in an ELF context on Turkish learners' beliefs about learning English. The participants in the study were thus both language learners and ELF users at the same time. The analysis of the questionnaire data suggested that no significant change in the participants' beliefs had taken place during their stay abroad in an ELF context. This finding is in agreement with the ones of a similar study by Bakhtiar Naghdipour, 'Language Learner Beliefs in an English as a Lingua Franca (ELF) Context' (*AdLLS* 5[2014] 22–30). However, the results of Kaypak and Ortaçtepe's qualitative analysis of five student journals indicate that the stay-abroad experience caused students to develop a new perspective on certain aspects of using and learning English, and, moreover, support 'the assumption that language learner beliefs are not homogenous and stable, but contradictory from time to time' (p. 364).

The latter point is stressed by Nicholas Subtirelu in 'What (Do) Learners Want(?): A Re-examination of the Issue of Learner Preferences Regarding the Use of "Native" Speaker Norms in English Language Teaching' (*LangAw* 22[2013] 270–91). This article is noteworthy in that Subtirelu not only presents the results of his own study on learner preferences with regard to traditional and alternative (e.g. ELF-based) models for learning English but also highlights important theoretical and methodological shortcomings of previous studies with a similar focus. On the basis of these considerations, the author opted for a small sample size (eight participants) and an in-depth analysis of longitudinal data (questionnaire responses in conjunction with interview data, both obtained in four sessions over several months). This methodology allowed him, as is evident from his results, to reveal 'the ambivalence, contradiction, or complexity inherent in learners' discussions of their preferences' (p. 286), which, he argues, a one-off questionnaire is unable to capture.

Another important field of interest for ELF researchers has been the impact (or lack thereof) of ELF-related research findings on teaching materials. Studies of teaching materials are of particular interest as the latter seem to be useful indicators of the degree to which novel approaches in ELT might gain ground: as argued by Paola Vettorel and Lucilla Lopriore in 'Is There ELF in ELT Coursebooks?' (*SSLLT* 3[2013] 483–504), 'many innovations in foreign language teaching have been successfully anticipated and diffused mostly thanks to their implementation in teaching materials' (p. 484). In this article, the authors examine whether research findings in the fields of WE and ELF are in any way reflected in the ten most widely sold ELT course-books used in Italian secondary schools. The results of their analysis suggest that the impact of ELF and WE research on the course-books examined is still fairly limited, as course-books are found to lack awareness-raising activities for WE and ELF and suggestions for language use outside school in the students' own local context. They also remain rather conservative in their representation of English speakers and of the contexts in which English is used, with characters being mostly NSs operating in Inner Circle contexts while ELF interactions are apparently not considered a legitimate model. However, the authors observe a shift in perspective as regards the teaching of culture and intercultural awareness, with the relevant course-book sections focusing on different cultures around the world rather than the NS target cultures as they are traditionally conceived.

In 'An Evaluation of the Pronunciation Target in Hong Kong's ELT Curriculum and Materials: Influences from WE and ELF?' (*JELF* 3[2014] 145–70), Jim Chan carries out a qualitative content analysis of the local ELT curriculum, examination papers and ten local textbooks in order to evaluate the pronunciation target in Hong Kong's secondary education with regard to its potential WE and ELF orientation. His findings suggest that, although WE and ELF perspectives seem to be partly discernible in the Hong Kong ELT curriculum, due to the sometimes fairly ambiguous wording it is not quite clear 'which pedagogical ideologies the curriculum conforms to, but it seems to be conceptually still guided by NS norms' (p. 167). Moreover, certain recommendations of the curriculum that could be considered to reflect a WE and/or

ELF perspective (e.g. that learners should be able to understand a range of
different accents) are not sufficiently taken up in the textbooks investigated,
and characteristic features of the local Hong Kong accent are presented as
'errors' in the books' oral tasks. The author also observes 'a clear disjunction
among the language-using situations (e.g., ELF), the identity of speakers (i.e.,
mainly NNSs) and their accents (i.e., mainly RP) in the audio listening
recordings' (p. 167). That is, if recordings include speakers identified as NNSs
who are conversing in ELF contexts, their grammar and pronunciation
generally correspond to NS norms, which 'may give students the impression
that NS pronunciations are the only pedagogical target' (p. 167).

Another study concerned with the analysis of teaching materials from an
ELF perspective is Reiko Takahashi's 'An Analysis of ELF-Oriented Features
in ELT Coursebooks' (*EnT* 30:i[2014] 28–34). This paper investigates the
degree to which sixteen different textbooks used in Japanese high schools
incorporate an ELF perspective to ELT, as indicated by e.g. 'ELF-related
contents/topics' addressed in the course-books (p. 31). The overall trend seems
to be that of a traditional foreign-language perspective, in which a Japanese
speaker uses English to communicate with an NS. Remaining within an Asian
context, Ya-Chen Su's 'The International Status of English for Intercultural
Understanding in Taiwan's High School EFL Textbooks' (*APJLE* [2014] 1–
19) reports that the traditional focus on NS countries and their linguistic
norms persists in the Taiwanese textbooks examined, and although the
cultures of various NS and NNS countries are addressed, 'culturally biased,
superficial, and industry-favoured information prevails' (p. 15).

One field that triggers vibrant discussions in connection with ELF-informed
pedagogy is language testing and assessment. In '30 Years On—Evolution or
Revolution?' (*LAQ* 11[2014] 226–32), Tim McNamara declares that 'communicative language testing is at a point of fundamental change' since 'the
growing awareness of the nature of English as a lingua franca communication
overturns all the givens of the communicative movement as it has developed
over the last 30 or 40 years' (p. 231) and thus calls for a revolution in the field
of language testing. He also critically discusses a particular assessment
framework, the CEFR, lamenting that the latter is nowadays often considered
' "too big to fail" ', which he views as a symptom of 'a general conservatism in
the field of language testing' (p. 229). McNamara criticizes the CEFR for
relying on the traditional opposition between NS and NNS competence,
which, he argues, 'can no longer be sustained' in the light of ELF
communication, concluding that 'a radical reconceptualization of the construct of successful communication that does not depend on this distinction'
(p. 231) is hence necessary. Further criticism on the constructs underlying the
English language-testing industry comes from Christopher Hall in 'Moving
beyond Accuracy: From Tests of English to Tests of "Englishing" ' (*ELangT*
68[2014] 376–85). The author discusses the problems of the dominant
'monolithic ontology of English' (p. 377) in testing, according to which the
language is regarded as a 'singular reified entit[y]' (p. 379) that is associated
with StE and NS usage, from a cognitive and sociolinguistic perspective.
He argues instead for the adoption of a 'plurilithic' approach to testing, which
views English as 'dynamic sets of overlapping phonological, grammatical, and

lexical resources, stored in millions of individual minds, which interact in multiple communities and cultural practices' (p. 379), thereby taking account of the diverse experiences of use made by different types of NSs and NNSs of English in particular localities, as in the case of ELF communication. Thus, the aim of English-language tests would not be to evaluate to what extent a learner's language approximates the norms of StE, but 'a learner's Englishing: what they do with the language in specific situations' (p. 383).

McNamara's article discussed above is not the only publication taking a critical perspective on the CEFR. Jennifer Jenkins and Constant Leung's chapter titled 'English as a Lingua Franca' (in Kunnan, ed., *The Companion to Language Assessment: Abilities, Contexts, and Learners*, pp. 1607–16) critically examines the CEFR and a number of widespread English-language tests, which the authors find to be NS-oriented and '"international" in the sense of being *used* (marketed and administered) internationally rather than in the sense of reflecting international *use*' (p. 1609; emphasis original). They then go on to discuss the implications of empirical ELF research for tests of English, and call for language testing to 'return to its empirical roots' (p. 1614) grounded in the Hymesian view that investigations of actual language use should provide the basis for what is regarded as communicative competence. The chapter concludes with some practical suggestions of how testers could put the implications of ELF for testing English into practice, though the authors stress that it will be necessary to 'devise new approaches altogether to assessing English' (p. 1614) to take account of the inherently flexible and variable nature of ELF.

Another critical examination of the CEFR is Niina Hynninen's 'The Common European Framework of Reference from the Perspective of English as a Lingua Franca: What We Can Learn from a Focus on Language Regulation' (*JELF* 3[2014] 293–316). Drawing on work done for her MA thesis, Hynninen shows that the proficiency level descriptors of the CEFR are centred on NS and target culture norms, which, from the point of view of ELF research, is clearly problematic. She contrasts this with her own research on language regulation in ELF interactions, which suggests that ELF speakers manage their own linguistic and cultural norms rather than consult NSs (even if they are present) for questions of acceptability. Hynninen concludes that 'the CEFR and particularly its descriptors, where the NNS is expected to adapt to the language and culture of the NS, then, is ill-suited to be applied in ELF situations, and it seems clear that we need to develop new descriptors, possibly a new framework altogether, to address the questions raised by lingua franca interaction' (p. 311).

Finally, Constant Leung's 'The "Social" in English Language Teaching: Abstracted Norms Versus Situated Enactments' (*JELF* 2[2013] 283–313) draws on video recordings of classroom discussions at a school and a university in London involving students from diverse ethnic and linguistic backgrounds, for whom English thus constitutes 'a particular case of lingua franca in an English-dominant environment' (p. 296). The extracts presented illustrate the complex negotiation of social norms of language use in a particular communicative situation, which, as shown by the author, the descriptor scales of the CEFR fail to capture. Instead, the 'social' is often depicted as relating to abstract NS conventions and thus as 'stable and predictable' (p. 290) in the CEFR—an observation which also holds true with regard to a number of ELT textbooks examined in this study. Leung hence calls for a reconceptualization of 'the social' in ELT that is based on empirical observations of how speakers exploit their linguistic repertoires in socially acceptable ways in a particular context. All the publications mentioned above are complemented by a rich collection of studies examining a range of implications of ELF for ELT entitled *ELF 5: Proceedings of the Fifth International Conference of English as a Lingua Franca* [2013], edited by Yasemin Bayyurt and Sumru Akcan.

Another area where ELF research has become relevant in educational contexts is that of English-medium instruction (EMI) in higher education. The growth in work exploring EMI within the ELF paradigm is occurring along with the significant increase in the number of universities offering English-medium programmes in ELF settings. This has been driven by powerful economic, technological, and societal forces promoting internationalization, a growing emphasis on research publications and rankings, as well the perceived quality of universities from traditional anglophone countries.

A major contribution to exploring this sub-field is Jennifer Jenkins's book *English as a Lingua Franca in the International University: The Politics of Academic English Language Policy*. By analysing the websites of a large number of universities across the world and investigating staff perceptions of their universities' English-language policies and practices, Jenkins finds that image of English remain firmly rooted in NS ideologies and do not reflect the notion of 'international-ness' that such institutions are striving to present. By conducting interviews with international postgraduate students in an anglophone context, she demonstrates the impact of NS ideologies on international students in terms of their linguistic practices and identities being marginalized within the institution. She also points out (as does Mortensen [2014], discussed below), that a failure to reconceptualize English in line with internationalization policies can result in a dissonance between international and local students, and thus restrict real opportunities for internationalization for both student groups. In another interesting contribution to exploring the role of English in international education, *Desiring TESOL and International Education: Market Abuse and Exploitation*, Raqib Chowdhury and Phan Le Ha analyse how ideals of 'native-speaker' English are perpetuated in the field of TESOL—and the impact this has on students who both resist and appropriate these labels (e.g. through embracing ELF).

Due to the growing number of higher education programmes offered in English there are a number of new studies investigating the role of ELF in national contexts that have been relatively unexplored until now. In their article 'Emerging Culture of English-Medium Instruction in Korea: Experiences of Korean and International Students' (*L&IC* 14[2014] 441–59) Jeongyeon Kim, Bradley Tatar, and Jinsook Choi examine the experiences and perceptions of ELF among local and international students at a Korean university that has an EMI policy. The findings show that the two groups of students have different perceptions of their ownership in English—with the international students more likely to embrace an ELF perspective. This embracing of ELF had a positive impact on their active participation in the classroom (in both English and Korean) and their perceptions of their academic ability to use English as the language of their studies. The study highlights the importance of participants in EMI having a shared perspective of English for successful implementation, as well as the need for policies in support of the use of code-switching to facilitate learning for the local students. There is also a need for support in the national language for international students (as it clearly continues to play an important role in Korean higher education despite policies promoting English), as well as support for using English for all students. Similarly, in 'EFL and ELF College Students' Perceptions toward Englishes' (*JELF* 3[2014] 363–86), Wenli Tsou and Fay Chen compare attitudes to English among Taiwanese English as a foreign language (EFL) and international students on an English-medium MBA programme ('ELF students'). Like Kim et al., they found more acceptance of the idea that English is owned equally by its users regardless of their mother tongue among international students. There was also stronger awareness of the need to develop strategies to facilitate successful communication and skills related to cross-cultural understanding. The EFL students, however, who have little exposure to ELF environments, were more devoted to standard ideals of English. Among both groups, there was little acceptance of localized varieties of English. The study thus suggests the need to reformulate English education in Taiwan so that cross-cultural understanding is fostered through promoting awareness of varieties and English is taught with a view to facilitating international communication.

In the context of Japan, Galloway and Rose's article '"They Envision Going to New York, not Jakarta": The Differing Attitudes Toward ELF of Students, Teaching Assistants, and Instructors in an English-Medium Business Program in Japan' (*JELF* 2[2013] 229–53) examines a bilingual business degree programme in which positive attitudes to ELF are being embraced and students are being prepared for the changing needs of ELF usage in a globalized society. To do so, a system has been developed in which international students are hired to support students in learning business concepts as well as to provide opportunities for real-life ELF use. The findings of the study indicate that both students and student assistants viewed English as a tool of communication in the business world, and had more ELF-oriented perceptions of how they would use and need English in the future than the instructors had realized. They also show how students in the study are surpassing the changes in the curriculum and are meeting the changing demands of ELF head-on.

In 'The Role of English as a Lingua Franca in Academia: The Case of Turkish Postgraduate Students in an Anglophone-Centre Context' (*Procedia* 141[2014] 74–8), Neslihan Onder Ozdemir investigates perceptions of Turkish postgraduate students who have been studying in the UK and US regarding the use of English as the international language of science. Findings indicate that these students believe that the benefits of having English as a universal mode of communication to share research and meet professional needs outweigh its negative aspects. However the majority of the participants felt they were at a disadvantage. This perception is related to the students viewing themselves as foreign-language speakers and not as rightful owners of an international lingua franca.

Beyza Björkman, in 'Peer Assessment of Spoken Lingua Franca English in Tertiary Education in Sweden: Criterion-Referenced Versus Norm-Referenced Assessment' (in Johannesson, Melchers, and Björkman, eds., *Of Butterflies and Birds, of Dialects and Genres: Essays in Honour of Philip Shaw* [2013], pp. 109–22) addresses an issue that spans the concerns of ELF pronunciation, academic ELF, and EMI, in that she investigates peer feedback to oral presentations in a university context. She finds that students rely primarily on norm-referenced assessment, focusing on the importance of native-like pronunciation, and give little attention to criterion-referenced aspects such as intelligibility. Björkman concludes that universities that take their international mission seriously in consequence would need to do more to raise awareness for the dynamics of ELF interaction, for instance by offering workshops across subjects and disciplines, and including both instructors and students. Taken together, all these studies suggest that attitudes about standard language use (particularly with regard to writing) are slow to change, especially among students who study EFL, while students using ELF as part of their studies are more likely to accept the changing ownerships and norms of English.

There are a few new studies which provide detailed insight into how English and other languages are being used in EMI programmes. In his article 'Language Policy from Below: Language Choice in Student Project Groups in a Multilingual University Setting' (*JMMD* 35[2014] 425–42), Janus Mortensen, for example, investigates the patterns of language choice among student project groups in an international study programme in Denmark. He finds that English is the language most commonly used among students; however, the groups demonstrate complex linguistic practices that include Danish as an alternative or supplementary language to English. This shows that the local *de facto* language policies created by the community are much more complex than the university's formal language policy, which promotes the exclusive use of English. This study shows how practising a strict pro-English-language policy may ensure local, short-term inclusion of non-Danish-speakers but could ultimately constrain the potential for multilingual and multicultural development that international university education holds. By not giving them opportunities to use the national language, this policy also inadvertently contributes to the long-term exclusion of international students from the wider society. He thus argues that the use of local languages is a legitimate and indeed desirable part of international education. Another rich picture of classroom discourse comes from the work of Ute Smit's 'Language Affordances in Integrating Content and English as a Lingua Franca ("ICELF"): On an Implicit Approach to English Medium Teaching' (*JAW* 3:i[2013] 15–29). Smit draws on a longitudinal database, comprising classroom interactional and ethnographic data that covers the whole duration of an international, four-semester, English-medium hotel management programme set in Vienna. In spite of the absence of any explicit language-learning aims, she finds evidence of language-learning possibilities within ELF classroom discourse. She calls this 'Implicit Integrating Content and English as a Lingua Franca' (ICELF). She also finds that English was identified and positively evaluated as multifunctional in relation to its relevance for future hospitality careers and its lingua franca function of the participants communicating with each other in the here and now. She suggests, however, that such implicit practices be made more explicit in policy.

All accounts of EMI use, however, are not positive, and the study 'Identifying Academically At-Risk Students in an English-as-a-Lingua-Franca University Setting' (*JEAP* 15[2014] 37–47) by Michael Harrington and Thomas Roche investigates a context in which a large number of students are struggling to follow their university content in English, as is the case in Oman. In this context, where the majority of students and staff have limited proficiency in English and the language has restricted uses in society in general, there are a number of at-risk students. This has negative consequences for the individual student, the institution, and the society as a whole. They thus explore the usefulness of post-enrolment assessment (PELA) for identifying academically at-risk students in an EMI programme in the ELF context of Oman. The study concludes that PELA schemes may be one, but not the only, means of identifying and supporting students without sufficient English proficiency to undertake English-medium education in ELF settings.

Key messages arising from this work are that practice is often ahead of policy in terms of embracing ELF and multilingual practice in EMI programmes. These studies suggest that acceptance of ELF seems to go along with acceptance and promotion of using other languages for learning and communication, as well as a recognition of the need for strategies and intercultural understanding for communication. They also demonstrate a need for more acceptance and promotion of the value of local languages (in the classroom and in academic writing) to promote integration between mixed groups of students (and the long-term integration of 'international' students into national contexts), the quality of national research, and the work against domain loss of national languages.

There is another strand of work in this area, which is exploring whether the dominance of English in academia may be a disadvantage for NNSs: studies suggest that this sense of disadvantage is minimized if conceptions of ELF are embraced. This need for academics to assert ownership and agency over the politics and uses of ELF is put forward by Barbara Seidlhofer in 'Hegemonie oder Handlungsspielraum? Englisch als Lingua Franca in der Wissenschaft' (in Neck, Schmidinger, and Weigelin-Schwiedrzik, eds., *Kommunikation— Objekt und Agens von Wissenschaft* [2013], pp. 178–85). She argues that embracing ELF can give non-anglophone academics some room for man-oeuvre within the global dominance of English as an academic language. Bent Preisler, in 'Lecturing in One's First Language or in English as a Lingua Franca: The Communication of Authenticity' (*ALH* 46[2014] 218–42), explores whether being required to teach in English affects the professional authenticity of Danish academics as reflected in their discourses and interactions with students. The analysis suggests that crucial to teachers' having a sense of authenticity and academic authority are: teachers' ability to authenticate themselves through appropriate communicative strategies, and teachers and students sharing relevant cultural frames of reference.

The issue of disadvantage is a common theme in the growing body of research highlighting the national, institutional, and individual implicit and explicit policies that reinforce the status of English as the global lingua franca of academia, and issues that ELF scholars face when writing for publication in international journals which are invariably in English. Theresa Lillis and Mary Jane Curry, in their article 'English, Scientific Publishing and Participation in the Global Knowledge Economy' (in Erling and Seargeant, eds., pp. 220–42), look at the necessity of participating in scientific knowledge generation and publication in English as part of human development. They point out that necessary resources for publishing in English may often not be present in developing countries, and they show that, even when these circumstances are mitigated, and norms of standard English demanded by journals can be followed, there are further obstacles that face academics from the periphery — including the sites of their research not being deemed significant or representative.

Writing for publication in multilingual contexts is the topic of a special issue of the *Journal of English for Academic Purposes* (13[2014]), edited by Maria Kuteeva and Anna Mauranen, and contributions to this issue both expand the contexts in which such research has been undertaken and provide new insights into the drivers of language choice in writing for publication. In 'English for Research Publication and Dissemination in Bi-/Multiliterate Environments: The Case of Romanian Academics' (*JEAP* 13[2014] 53–64) Laura-Michaela Muresan and Carmen Pérez-Llantada, for example, investigate the research communication practices and attitudes towards the role of English among social science academics in Romania. They find an overwhelmingly positive acceptance of a global academic lingua franca, despite an acknowledgement of the difficulties of writing in English. However, they also demonstrate a continued need for research publication and dissemination in national languages, and recommend providing guidance on language-policy decisions and language-planning interventions to promote multilingualism. A similar study conducted in Turkey, namely Hacer Hande Uysal's 'English Language Spread in Academia: Macro-Level State Policies and Micro-Level Practices of Scholarly Publishing in Turkey' (*LPLP* 38[2014] 265–91), examines macro-level state policies that increasingly promote academic publishing in English and the effects of these policies on academics at two Turkish universities. She finds that academics perceived an advantage of English functioning as the lingua franca of global academia, particularly in the hard sciences, which further endorses the use of English promoted by the government. While these macro- and micro-policies are accompanied by some movements to promote and maintain Turkish as an academic language, she, like Ana Bocanegra-Valle in her article ' "English is My Default Academic Language": Voices from LSP Scholars Publishing in a Multilingual Journal' (*JEAP* 13[2014] 65–77), recognizes the need for policies/practices that will help avoid national-language attrition and raise the standard of non-English published research.

Giving more insight into the process of writing for publication for ELF scholars, Bocanegra-Valle investigates why scholars of Language for Specific Purposes who submit articles to the 'multilingual' journal *Ibérica*, which accepts articles in five European languages, primarily submit articles in

English. She finds that their reasons for doing so include global pressures that articles written in English are of greater quality and credibility—and because they can be more widely accessed. Pilar Mur-Dueñas, in 'Spanish Scholars' Research Article Publishing Process in English-Medium Journals: English Used as a Lingua Franca?' (*JELF* 2[2013] 315–40), investigates the process of writing research articles by a group of Spanish scholars, and reveals the most common type of language revision of manuscripts that are suggested for publication. This provides insight into the extent to which ELF norms are considered acceptable for publication, or whether Anglo-American rhetorical conventions prevail. She finds that these scholars' uses of ELF to communicate the results of their research to the international community initially fail, and they have to change their voice (and thus lose part of their local identity) in order to meet the language and stylistic expectations of the gatekeepers. She thus identifies a need for increasing awareness of ELF across academic publications and among the various stakeholders in journals. These issues are also touched on by Mary Jane Curry and Theresa Lillis, who drew on their research into academic writing and publishing practices (*Academic Writing in a Global Context: The Politics and Practices of Publishing in English* [2010]), to produce *A Scholar's Guide to Getting Published in English: Critical Choices and Practical Strategies* [2013], which aims to help ELF scholars explore the broader social practices, politics, networks, and resources involved in academic publishing and to encourage them to consider how they wish to take part in these practices—as well as to engage in current debates about them.

While EMI has received growing attention, interest in the related yet distinct field of academic ELF has continued to constitute a focal point of ELF research, particularly in Scandinavia. This is not surprising, as in some Nordic countries, such as Iceland, virtually all researchers publish in English on occasion, while a majority publish over 75 per cent of their work in English, according to a survey by Hafdís Ingvarsdóttir and Birna Arnbjörnsdóttir published in 'ELF and Academic Writing: A Perspective from the Expanding Circle' (*JELF* 2[2013] 123–45). The authors argue that, given the pressure to publish in English, the current lack of institutional support for academics needs to be addressed, while also calling for a renewed focus in research on written communication in academic ELF, particularly on the role and impact of 'different cultural and rhetorical styles' (p. 141). Similar concerns are raised by Beyza Björkman in 'Language Ideology or Language Practice? An Analysis of Language Policy Documents at Swedish Universities' (*Multilingua* 33[2013] 335–63). She, too, identifies a lack of 'sufficient guidance as to how students and staff in these university settings are to use English' (p. 335), and a pronounced chasm between policy documents, which tend to underscore the importance of protecting Swedish as an academic language, and actual practice. In their current form, Björkman concludes, these policy documents are therefore only of limited use to their intended target audience, and are unlikely to achieve their proclaimed aims.

One site of research that has received much attention in the past two years is the role of idiomatic language (in the sense of phraseological language more generally, not in the sense of NS idiomaticity) in ELF, particularly in academic settings. In 'Figurative Language and ELF: Idiomaticity in Cross-Cultural Interaction in University Settings' (*JELF* 2[2013] 75–99), Valeria Franceschi builds on earlier work on (re-)metaphorization by Marie-Luise Pitzl and the concept of unilateral idiomaticity by Barbara Seidlhofer, applying them to the analysis of ELFA corpus data. She arrives at the conclusion that, while speakers 'do not appear to shy away from using idiomatic language' (p. 95), they are aware of its markedness and employ strategies such as literalization and flagging of idioms by discourse markers to preclude episodes of misunderstanding. Ray Carey, in 'On the Other Side: Formulaic Organizing Chunks in Spoken and Written Academic ELF' (*JELF* 2[2013] 207–28), investigates both spoken and written sources of academic ELF with a view to potentially different processing mechanisms for high- versus low-frequency idiomatic chunks. His results point towards a higher probability for low-frequency chunks to undergo approximation processes. This pattern holds true for both spoken and written texts (the latter ones unedited, it needs to be pointed out), with the slight differences between these two sets of data not being statistically significant.

Staying with distributional patterns and frequency data in academic ELF, but moving to lexical choices more generally, and cohesive devices in particular, Shin-Mei Kao and Wen-Chun Wang, in 'Lexical and Organizational Features in Novice and Experienced ELF Presentations' (*JELF* 3[2014] 49–79), explore these aspects in three sets of academic ELF data: first, a corpus of presentations by novice users (i.e. undergraduate students); second, a sub-section of the ELFA corpus, as an exemplar of expert usage by academics in a variety of disciplines; and third, the John Swales Conference Corpus (JSCC), to investigate potentially idiosyncratic patterns among scholars of language in particular. A quantitative analysis of lexical variation, richness, and sophistication yields remarkably similar patterns of usage for both groups of experts, with clear differences in the patterns observed for novice users. The picture is similar for cohesive devices, with a stark contrast between novice and expert users, though here small differences between the ELFA and the JSCC scholars can be detected as well. The authors conclude with a discussion of the implications of their findings for the teaching of academic English in international settings, stressing in particular the need for instructors to focus on field-specific academic vocabulary. For two complementary investigations of academic conference presentations from a qualitative perspective, see Anna Mauranen's ' "But Then When I Started to Think ...": Narrative Elements in Conference Presentations' (in Gotti and Guinda, eds., *Narratives in Academic and Professional Genres*, pp. 45–66) and Francisco Javier Fernández-Polo's 'The Role of I Mean in Conference Presentations by ELF Speakers' (*ESPJ* 34[2014] 58–67).

Moving from mostly quantitative, 'traditional' corpus-linguistic work on academic ELF to studies with a partly or exclusively qualitative focus, mention needs to be made of Beyza Björkman's monograph *English as an Academic Lingua Franca: An Investigation of Form and Communicative Effectiveness*, which investigates both form and function, but with an emphasis on the latter. The publication is definitely an important contribution to the field, but as it is largely based on the author's Ph.D. dissertation covered in *YWES* (91[2012]

123), the reader is referred to this earlier discussion (also see Björkman's 'An Analysis of Polyadic English as a Lingua Franca (ELF) Speech: A Communicative Strategies Framework' (*JPrag* 66[2014] 122–38)). Studies that take a purely qualitative, discourse or CA, approach to ELFA data are Anna Mauranen's 'Lingua Franca Discourse in Academic Contexts: Shaped by Complexity' (in Flowerdew, ed., *Discourse in Context*, pp. 225–45), which deals mostly with code-switching and other instances that involve negotiations of language use, and Carmen Maíz-Arévalo's 'Expressing Disagreement in English as a Lingua Franca: Whose Pragmatic Rules?' (*IPrag* 11[2014] 199–224), which analyses a very small, established community of ELF speakers which seems to function differently from more impromptu ELF contexts. Maurizio Gotti's 'Explanatory Strategies in University Courses Taught in ELF' (*JELF* 3[2014] 337–61), on the other hand, arrives at similar conclusions to the previous literature as regards the highly interactive and accommodating nature of interactions in ELF. The phatic element of academic ELF talk is further addressed in Ray Carey's 'A Closer Look at Laughter in Academic Talk: A Reader Response' (*JEAP* 14[2014] 118–23), Karolina Kalocsai's *Communities of Practice and English as a Lingua Franca: A Study of Erasmus Students in a Central European Context* [2013], which takes an in-depth ethnographic look at a small, relatively close-knit community of ELF speakers and the development of their attitudes and linguistic practices over a longer period of time, and Yumi Matsumoto's 'Collaborative Co-Construction of Humorous Interaction among ELF Speakers' (*JELF* 3[2014] 81–107), for which she investigated dyadic interactions using CA methodology, showing that humour can help foster solidarity and minimize potential disagreement among interlocutors. Juliane House, in both 'Developing Pragmatic Competence in English as a Lingua Franca: Using Discourse Markers to Express (Inter)Subjectivity and Connectivity' (*JPrag* 59[2013] 57–67) and 'Managing Academic Institutional Discourse in English as a Lingua Franca' (*FuL* 21[2014] 50–66), investigates ELF office hours with respect to code-switching and the use of discourse markers. Especially the second of these aspects seems noteworthy, as House identifies other uses than those canonically ascribed to them. To conclude this brief review of localized qualitative studies, mention can be made of Maicol Formentelli's 'A Model of Stance for the Management of Interpersonal Relations: Formality, Power, Distance and Respect' (in Kecskés and Romero-Trillo, eds., *Research Trends in Intercultural Pragmatics* [2013], pp. 181–218), which draws on ELFA data to develop its main arguments, though the paper will most likely be of more interest to scholars of CA as a theory and field of study in its own right.

While academic ELF thus continues to be a prolific site of research, corpus studies of ELF are by no means restricted to this context. An important development in this regard has been the release of ACE, the Asian Corpus of English [2014], compiled by a team around project director Andy Kirkpatrick, who summarizes some of the central characteristics of the corpus in 'The Asian Corpus of English: Motivations and Aims' (*LCSAW* 1[2013] 17–30). Developed as a parallel corpus to VOICE, and with the input and support of the development team of the latter, ACE is intended to provide an Asia-centric counterpart to the European-focused VOICE. Like VOICE, the corpus is designed to be rich enough in its presentation of the data to allow for both traditional quantitative corpus linguistic studies and more ethnographic qualitative ones. A first representative example of the former is Andy Kirkpatrick and Sophiaan Subhan's 'Non-Standard or New Standards or Errors? The Use of Inflectional Marking for Present and Past Tenses in English as an Asian Lingua Franca' (in Buschfeld et al., eds., pp. 386–400), which concludes—in line with previous research on ELF in other contexts— that native language transfer is not the prime determiner or reason for non-standard linguistic features, in this case tense marking, in the data they analysed. Two examples of qualitative studies on the data made available in ACE are Ian Walkinshaw and Andy Kirkpatrick's 'Mutual Face Preservation among Asian Speakers of English as a Lingua Franca' (*JELF* 3[2014] 269–91) and Mingyue Gu, John Patkin, and Andy Kirkpatrick's 'The Dynamic Identity Construction in English as Lingua Franca Intercultural Communication: A Positioning Perspective' (*System* 46[2014] 131–42). An extensive study, spanning the quantitative-qualitative divide and ranging from an investigation of pronunciation and lexico-grammar to pragmatic issues such as repairs is David Deterding's *Misunderstandings in English as a Lingua Franca: An Analysis of ELF Interactions in South-East Asia* [2013]. The research was conducted on one of the sub-components of ACE while it was still being compiled, as the author was involved in the data collection for the corpus in Brunei. Given the fact that the vast majority of misunderstandings in Deterding's data can be attributed to phonological and phonetic problems, the book inevitably focuses more on pronunciation than lexis and grammar in ELF interactions. Two other publications are also concerned with the effects of pronunciation-related features on comprehension: Pedro Luis Luchini and Sara Kennedy's 'Exploring Sources of Phonological Unintelligibility in Spontaneous Speech' (*IntJEL* 4:iii[2013] 79–88) aims at providing further empirical evidence to fine-tune Jenkins's [2000] 'Lingua Franca Core' by investigating which pronunciation features lead to loss of intelligibility in an ELF encounter between two Indian speakers and the first author, who acted as a participant researcher. Their findings partly confirm the suggestions of Jenkins's Lingua Franca Core. Despite the small number of participants, this research is valuable in that it does not merely examine the phonological causes of intelligibility problems in ELF in isolation but considers them in conjunction with other factors that might have contributed to loss of intelligibility (e.g. the use of metaphorical expressions, non-familiarity with the interlocutor's accent, or a lack of cultural knowledge). The article also discusses the interlocutors' (in)ability to accommodate receptively and productively to each other by considering their different previous experiences of using English. A methodologically different approach is taken in Hiroko Matsuura, Reiko Chiba, Sean Mahoney, and Sarah Rilling's 'Accent and Speech Rate Effects in English as a Lingua Franca' (*System* 46[2014] 143–50), which investigates the impact of a non-familiar NNS accent and different speech rates on listening comprehension in Japanese university students using an experimental, quantitative approach.

Returning to the ACE corpus, the scope of research that it will ultimately allow is outlined by Andy Kirkpatrick in 'English in Southeast Asia:

Pedagogical and Policy Implications' (*WEn* 33[2014] 426–38). At the same time, the article gives a useful overview of the status and roles of English in the Asian context, which many researchers outside the region might not be familiar with, thus giving them a proper perspective on the data that is being made available in ACE.

Research on ELF in an Asian context is not limited to corpus-linguistic studies, however. Several papers investigate attitudes towards ELF, albeit from different angles and employing different methodologies. For instance, Phanyamon Ploywattanawong and Wannapa Trakulkasemsuk, in 'Attitudes of Thai Graduates Toward English as a Lingua Franca of ASEAN' (*AEnglishes* 16[2014] 141–56), take several recurrent lexico-grammatical features of speakers of Asian ELF as their point of departure, and elicit acceptability ratings with regard to these from their respondents. They arrive at the conclusion that these non-standard features, while not completely accepted, do not receive overly negative judgements from their respondents either, which points towards an ongoing development of norms. A final contribution of note which emerges from studies of ELF in Asia is James D'Angelo's 'Japanese English? Refocusing the Discussion' (*AES* 15[2013] 2–26). D'Angelo revisits some of the conceptual issues which inevitably arise out of the contact between the WE paradigm and ELF research which have already been alluded to. He underlines that these paradigms offer different perspectives on language use, and should thus not be misunderstood to be concerned with necessarily distinct sets of speakers (relatively uncontroversial) or entirely different contexts of use (the author's personal stance).

The release of ACE is surely the most consequential development for research on ELF in Asia. In addition to this new entrant to the scene of ELF corpora, 2013/14 has also been witness to major developments as regards the most 'venerable' of ELF corpora: VOICE. In 2014, the VOICE development team, under the directorship of Barbara Seidlhofer, released two POS-tagged versions of the corpus—VOICE POS Online 2.0 and VOICE POS XML 2.0—continuing the corpus-builders' tradition of providing (novice) users with an easily accessible online interface, yet at the same time making the corpus data available in XML format to allow for more powerful and in-depth analysis by tech-savvy, advanced corpus users. Similarly, just as previous versions, the new POS-tagged corpus comes with extensive and meticulous documentation, both in the form of help files in the corpus interface ('VOICE POS Online. Using VOICE Online'), and a manual published on the project website ('VOICE Part-of-Speech Tagging and Lemmatization Manual'). The key to understanding the relevance and impact of the POS-tagged versions of the corpus is the close interdependence of theory and praxis that characterized the process, well documented in several publications by the central researcher responsible for the genesis of VOICE POS, Ruth Osimk-Teasdale. In 'Applying Existing Tagging Practices to VOICE' (*VARIENG* 13[2013] n.p.), she delineates early conceptual stages of the tagging process, reviews how 'traditional' L1 or L2 error-based tagging schemes were ruled out because they were inadequate for the task at hand, and discusses to what extent a partly automated POS-tagging process can cope with the non-codified forms in VOICE, a paramount question in the annotation of a million-word corpus.

The initial results of the pilot study were promising, at a tagging accuracy of 84.5 per cent (section 5.2), yet also pointed towards the need for an interlaced approach of automated and manual tagging, particularly with regard to non-codified and creative uses of language. Precisely these non-codified items take centre-stage in Osimk-Teasdale's ' "I Just Wanted to Give a Partly Answer": Capturing and Exploring Word Class Variation in ELF Data' (*JELF* 3[2014] 109–43). Here, she discusses how (word-class) conversion and multifunction-ality constitute an essential creative process in ELF data, and how any POS-tagged version of an ELF corpus needs to be designed to reflect this variable nature of linguistic forms and their functions. In line with the exploratory and conceptually critical nature of ELF research more generally, the article does not merely provide a first description of the process of POS-tagging VOICE, but also discusses—and where necessary questions—the underlying theoretical assumptions of such an undertaking. As the earlier, exploratory article by the author foreshadowed, at its heart, POS-tagging—done the traditional way—presupposes an unproblematic and straightforward relationship between linguistic forms and their functions, a premise that ELF data unmasks as precarious, because it is ultimately subject to constant online negotiation and variability. The decision in VOICE POS, therefore, was to present this equivocal association in the tagging format itself, assigning tokens tags for both form *and* function. While in the large majority of cases, these tags converge, the article focuses particularly on incongruent cases, as these are the ones that demonstrate the fluid and adaptable nature of ELF in particular, but also of natural language use more generally. The implications of the study thus go beyond the concerns of ELF research in a narrow sense, and extend to the wider discourse on linguistic categorization and POS-tagging.

It has already been mentioned in this review that scholars have been increasingly exploring the relationships between WE and ELF, and that the role of common cognitive processes based on comparable functional exigencies leads to similar, albeit independently developed, forms and form-function mappings in both of these contexts of English use. It is precisely this hypothesis that is further pursued in Christopher J. Hall, Daniel Schmidtke, and Jamie Vickers's study 'Countability in World Englishes' (*WEn* 32[2013] 1–22), which investigates non-standard uses of mass nouns (*informations*, *one luggage*, etc.) in VOICE and various online (web-as-corpus) sources. Though these forms occur with a frequency that is 'significantly higher ... than IC [Inner Circle] usage' (p. 14), the authors still argue that it is a 'marginal phenomenon' (p. 20), and take issue with 'linguistic descriptions which highlight such peripheral and communicatively inconsequential formal elem-ents on the basis of their contrastiveness' (p. 19). At the very same time, they argue that there has been a 'disproportionate invocation of the count/non-count distinction in prescriptive works for learners' (p. 19), which is grounded neither in its communicative relevance nor in any strong tendency of speakers to diverge from StE usage, but is merely a reflection of its function as a 'shibboleth of the native/non-native dichotomy' (p. 20). Pursuing a similar methodological approach of comparing ELF data to both native and nativized forms of English from around the world, Leah Gilner, in 'An Analysis of ELF Speakers' Lexical Preferences' (*AES* 16[2014] 5–16) and 'High Frequency

Words in Spoken English as a Lingua Franca in Academic Settings' (*JBGU* 14[2014] 1–12), compares the relative proportion of high-frequency words in various ICE corpora and VOICE and ELFA, respectively. In both instances, she finds a remarkable congruence of patterns with regard to these high-frequency words, supporting the view that, far from being isolated varieties bound to diverge on their different trajectories, these manifestations of English are—their differences notwithstanding—still underpinned by a common core. In their article 'How Do "WE" (World Englishes) Make Sense in ELF Communication? Words and Their Meaning Across Cultures' (*JELF* 2[2013] 365–88), Zhichang Xu and Thuy Ngoc Dinh explore how new meanings are attached to existing English words in ELF communication and whether WE speakers from different cultures share identical meanings of the same English lexical item. Drawing on theoretical concepts from lexical semantics, cultural linguistics, WE, and ELF to analyse the data, they use a 'free-response word association task' with ten informants from different cultural backgrounds to explore their instantaneous reactions to twelve English lexical items. They find that it is not always the case that words share identical meanings, that meanings of English words change and vary in accordance with EFL contexts, and that WE speakers expand the connotations of English words and their associated idiomatic expressions and metaphors in different cultural contexts. They therefore suggest that ELF be seen as 'a heterogeneous entity involving lexical semantic transfer and variation, and nativized forms and meanings through translanguaging across cultures and varieties of English' (p. 369). They conclude by considering the implications of this for ELF communication and English vocabulary teaching, recommending that English learners be reminded of the fluidity and variation of ELF lexical meaning, and that they be encouraged to take note of the significant role of context and culture in communication. Finally, Heiko Motschenbacher, in 'A Typologically Based View on Relativisation in English as a European Lingua Franca' (*EJAL* 1[2013] 103–38) and *New Perspectives on English as a European Lingua Franca* [2013] (the former in essence one topical excerpt from the monograph) likewise draws on, compares, and contrasts the discourses of expanding-circle variety studies ('Euro-English'), ELF, and related paradigms. His data is fascinating in that it represents a truly (i.e. ideologically) European context, viz. the Eurovision Song Contest. However, the empirical analysis of internal variation ultimately underlines the fact that a variety-based framework is probably not the one best suited to an explanation of variability in ELF, as it fails to account for the fluidity of the data. So, their overlaps and points of contact notwithstanding, it can be concluded that the ELF and WE paradigms are, in the end, underpinned by somewhat different conceptualizations of variation in language, and that they are suited to the analysis of distinct contexts.

Concluding this discussion of corpus-linguistic work, the 'big three' in the world of (spoken) ELF corpora as of 2014 are VOICE, ELFA, and ACE—ordered here by date of release/availability. The impact of these resources within the field of ELF research is inestimable, yet they might still be only partly familiar to the linguistic community at large. In 'Speaking Professionally in an L2: Issues of Corpus Methodology' (in Bamford,

Cavalieri, and Diani, eds., pp. 5–32) Anna Mauranen therefore reviews some of the central desiderata in the compilation of the ELFA corpus for a wider audience. Similarly, Barbara Seidlhofer, in 'Corpus Analysis of English as a Lingua Franca' (in Chapelle, ed., pp. 2–5), summarizes the essential characteristics of all three major ELF corpora for those outside the field, and illustrates the kind of research they permit. She concludes with a brief appraisal of how ELF corpus research already has, and will continue to generate, findings of relevance on important issues in applied linguistics such as intercultural communication, language testing, the development of peda-gogical prescriptions in ELT, or translation and interpreting. Though these issues of applied linguistics are arguably at the forefront of much of the discourse around ELF, Ana Pirc demonstrates that ELF data can and should equally be a fertile ground for questions of a more formal-linguistic nature. In 'Construction Grammar and "Non-Native Discourse"' (*THEPES* 6[2013] 55–73), she draws on ELF data (VOICE and ELFA) as an empirical basis against which to re-evaluate some tenets of 'theoretical general linguistics' (p. 56). The limitations of approaches to language which focus exclusively on an idealized NS have been discussed at length by scholars both within and outside the field of ELF. However, Pirc breaks new ground in suggesting that there are, in fact, formal theoretical models that have the potential to accommodate the more variable nature of ELF and non-native discourse more generally, a prime example being CxG. Most of the author's work is dedicated to an exploration of how features that have been identified as characteristic of ELF can be accounted for by CxG principles. A prime example is the fundamental assumption of CxG that linguistic constructions are not fixed and immutable entities, but constitute a network that is 'restructured in the course of ... linguistic experience' (p. 58). It is easy to see how well this matches up with the widely recognized fluidity and creativity of ELF discourse. At the same time, Pirc demonstrates how ELF research and data have much to offer to other branches of linguistics and vice versa, so it can be hoped that these implications will be explored further in the years to come.

One of the main domains in which ELF research continues to grow is that of business and workplace communication. This research features a number of workplace domains including multinational corporations, banks, small and medium-sized enterprises, the maritime industry, and engineering. Although the contexts explored in this research are also starting to expand (to Asia and the Middle East), much of it continues to focus on European contexts. In 'Multilingualism in European Workplaces' (*Multilingua* 33[2014] 11–33), Britt-Louise Gunnarsson provides an overview of research in this area, which includes ELF studies. She highlights the main reasons for the upsurge in this research (e.g. the expansion of the EU, migration, developments in technol-ogy); distinguishes key themes (e.g. positive or problem-based accounts); introduces a model which allows for analysis of the complex and dynamic interplay between workplace discourse and its various contextual frames; and identifies areas for future research. Also focusing on multilingualism, Anne Kankaanranta and Leena Louhiala-Salminen's article 'What Language Does Global Business Speak? The Concept and Development of BELF' (*IbéricaR* 26[2013] 17–34) traces the development of the concept of Business

English as Lingua Franca (BELF) and how their own empirical studies on language use in internationally operating organizations has influenced their views on the development of this concept. The findings of this research show that, for BELF speakers, the genre knowledge of the domain of business, and particularly awareness of its goal-oriented nature, is far more important than grammatical correctness in workplace communication. They therefore argue that in discussing workplace communication, emphasis should be placed on the domain of use rather than the type of English used. Thus, they propose that the referent term for BELF should shift to 'English as Business Lingua Franca'. Jo Angouri and Marlene Miglbauer provide further detailed insight into the dynamic and diverse linguistic ecology of modern multinational workplaces in ' "And Then We Summarise in English for the Others": The Lived Experience of the Multilingual Workplace' (*Multilingua* 33[2014] 147–72). Drawing on interview data with forty employees in senior and junior management posts in twelve companies situated in six European countries where English is the official corporate language, they find that employees draw on a range of linguistic resources in order to manage their work-related interactions, with a constant interplay between ELF and local languages. Participants also reported code-switching as a common practice, but often saw it as a new skill superimposed upon them in an already demanding work reality. While these employees see their multilingualism as an aspect of cosmopolitanism, an identity the participants readily ascribe to, dominant ideologies about NS English still prevail. In another contribution, 'Local Languages and Communication Challenges in the Multinational Workplace', Angouri and Miglbauer (in Sharifian and Jamarani, eds., pp. 225–44) discuss the role of local languages in intercultural communication and the perceived communication challenges that employees face when switching out of their local language. In line with findings of ELF research, employees reported various strategies that they use to enhance intercultural communication, including interactional cooperation; tolerance in pragmatic ambiguity; politeness; and switching from oral to written communication (or vice versa) to ensure understanding. Key messages from this research are that, despite a clear need for and use of ELF in various domains, local languages remain very commonly used in multinational workplaces.

Further studies on the role of local languages in multinational workplaces and the drivers of language choice include Leilarna Kingsley's 'Language Choice in Multilingual Encounters in Transnational Workplaces' (*JMMD* 34[2013] 533–48). She explores the explicit official language policy as well as employees' practices and beliefs (i.e. the implicit policy) in three international Luxembourg banks. The study reveals that while English is the language most frequently used, a number of other languages were used in meetings, informal communication, e-mails, and presentations. Language choices were determined by employees' linguistic repertoire; transactional goals (e.g. arguing and negotiating one's case, communicating information accurately); and relational goals (e.g. maintaining and enhancing rapport, solidarity, and collegiality with colleagues). In particular, the goals of inclusion and fairness drove participants' choice of English. In ' "It's Pretty Simple and in Greek ...": Global and Local Languages in the Greek Corporate Setting'

(*Multilingua* 33[2014] 117–46), Ifigenia Mahili investigates the interplay between global and local languages in private businesses in Greece and finds that English is used in higher-ranking posts and Greek, the local language, in lower-ranking posts; this was due to the need of employees with more responsibility for accountability and transparency and communication with parties outside Greece. Use of English was also associated with higher levels of professional expertise: English was used to talk about complex and key business issues while Greek was restricted to simple and informal routine communication. The analysis also shows that language skills are perceived as a commodity related to employees' job retention and progression, and thus become increasingly relevant during times of economic crisis. Taken together, these studies suggest that any suggestions for language policy in international business contexts be localized, multilingual, and sensitive to the social context.

Several studies make use of discourse-analytic methods to provide detailed insight into ELF workplace communication. Key issues explored include whether convergence is occurring with regard to communication patterns. This is explored in Anne Kankaanranta and Wei Lu's article 'The Evolution of English as the Business Lingua Franca: Sings of Conference in Chinese and Finnish Professional Communication' (*JBTC* 27[2013] 288–307). They examine the characteristics of communication between Chinese and Finnish business professionals in international Finnish companies based in China. As Chinese oral communication has been traditionally described as indirect, the study focuses in particular on how Chinese and Finnish business professionals perceive Chinese BELF communication in relation to directness. They found that there was general agreement that clarity and directness contribute to the effectiveness of the communication needed in business to get the work done. The Chinese employees perceived their own communication as more open and direct when they used BELF, particularly the younger employees, while Finns perceived themselves to be less direct than they would be in Finnish. This suggests that Chinese and Finnish BELF communication may be converging, reflecting speakers' attempts to adjust. However, the Finnish employees still perceive the Chinese BELF communication as indirect, seeing it as bearing national characteristics. However, when exploring BELF in another domain, Geneviève Tréguer-Felten's article 'Can a Lingua Franca Bridge the Communication Gap Between Corporations Set in Different Cultures?' (in Kecskés and Romero-Trillo, eds., pp. 263–82) finds no evidence of convergence. Undertaking a discourse analysis of ELF communication between Chinese and French corporations via corporate brochures or website self-presentations, she concludes that the ELF discourse used to attract a 'foreign' audience displayed widely different qualities, which seem to be deeply embedded in the corporations' respective national cultures. She thus concludes that communication in this context is largely unsuccessful and points to a communication gap not likely to be bridged by ELF use alone. Dissonance in these findings suggest a need for further work in this area.

Building on research which explores how organizations communicate with their consumers by using English, Catherine Nickerson and Belinda Crawford Camiciottoli's article 'Business English as a Lingua Franca in Advertising Texts in the Arabian Gulf: Analyzing the Attitudes of the Emirati Community'

(*JBTC* 27[2013] 329–52) presents the results of a survey of the attitudes of consumers towards the use of English in advertising texts in the United Arab Emirates (UAE). Despite the fact that Middle Eastern economies are among those with the highest spending power in the world, this has been until now unmapped territory for BELF research. These authors explored whether consumers were able to comprehend the English in advertising texts and whether the language used influenced their attitudes towards the product and their intention to buy it. They found that most of the participants either had no preference for the language used in advertising or preferred Arabic rather than English, and that the language used in the advertising text did not significantly influence participants' attitudes towards the ad. There was one exception: the language of the text did influence whether the participants viewed the product as basic or advanced, with Arabic being perceived as marking something more advanced. Finally, there was concern expressed about preserving the Arabic language and cultural identity. This study suggests that English is viewed less neutrally in the Middle East than in other parts of the world and therefore the efficacy of its use in advertising should be considered.

The number of domains in which BELF is being explored is growing, not only including advertising texts (discussed above), but also e-mail exchanges and business meetings. In many of these studies, discourse-analytic methods drawing on corpora are being applied to provide detailed insight into communicative strategies. Many of these studies explore how community and consensus is achieved in multicultural professional communication, as well as the instances in which communication fails. In 'Managing Discourse in Intercultural Business Email Interactions: A Case Study of a British and Italian Business Transaction' (*JMMD* 34[2013] 515–32), for example, Ersilia Incelli investigates a ten-month e-mail exchange between a medium-sized British company and a small Italian company to account for the salient features of business e-mail communication in the setting of intercultural interaction, e.g. requesting and providing information/clarification, negotiating payment terms, quoting prices, and organizing delivery. The findings reveal how accommodation strategies facilitate understanding; however, there is also evidence of how low levels of language competence and low cross-cultural awareness can lead to miscommunication, putting a business transaction at risk. Patricia Pullin considers the linguistic markers used to 'Achiev[e] Comity'—solidarity and cooperation—in BELF discourse with respect to 'The Role of Linguistic Stance in Business English as a Lingua Franca (BELF) Meetings' (*JELF* 2[2013] 1–23). She applies a fine-grained pragmatic analysis to authentic audio-recorded BELF interaction in meetings, focusing on the use of 'stance markers' (e.g. hedges like *perhaps, might, sort of* and boosters like *clearly, excellent*) used to express opinions, evaluation, and affect, and how they contribute to nurturing and maintaining comity. She also found that common ground with regard to business knowledge and conventions, in addition to the role and power of the meeting chair, were important to achieving comity, highlighting—as other studies have—the social as well as linguistic factors important for creating consensus and community in international business communication. Using a sociolinguistic discourse-analytic perspective, Tiina Räisänen investigates a Finnish engineer's repertoire to give detailed insight into linguistic practices in a multilingual meeting in 'Processes and Practices of Enregisterment of Business English, Participation and Power in a Multilingual Workplace' (*SociolingS* 6[2012] 309–31). She also finds, similarly to Pullin [2013] (see above), that the achievement of shared understanding in business is not a matter of overall proficiency in English but of an overall competence to use particular, context-specific bits of a communicative repertoire, which consists of language, gestures, and other resources.

Providing an Asian perspective on the interplay of discourse, language and business practices, Hiromasa Tanaka looks at 'Lying in Intra-Asian Business Discourse in an ELF Setting' (*IJBC* 51[2014] 58–71). He examines naturally occurring business interaction between Japanese and Indian small business owners, and lies told and detected by the interlocutors. Highlighting differences in business practices, language proficiency, and situated identities, the analysis illustrates how Indian and Japanese ELF speakers tried to coconstruct meaning and how they dealt with issues emerging from behaviours marked with a certain degree of deception. He thus shows how lying is used strategically to avoid conflict, and thus maintain cross-cultural business relationships. Also investigating an Asian context, Keiko Tsuchiya and Michael Handford's 'A Corpus-Driven Analysis of Repair in a Professional ELF Meeting: Not "Letting It Pass"' (*JPrag* 64[2014] 117–31) examines turn-taking in a multiparty professional ELF meeting from a bridge-building project in South Asia, using a corpus-assisted discourse analysis. In contrast to previous research that shows that 'letting it pass' is a widely used practice in BELF communication (e.g. Alan Firth, 'The Discursive Accomplishment of Normality: On "Lingua Franca" English and Conversation Analysis' (*JPrag* 26[1996] 237–59)), the results of this study show that the chair regularly cut into the conversation, giving corrections or suggestions— something the authors call 'not letting it pass'. Through post-meeting interviews they found that this strategy was used to ensure comprehension of the audience. The study thus suggests that in this field of construction engineering, less emphasis is placed on face-saving strategies like 'letting it pass' because of the need to ensure understanding and focus on safety.

There are further studies that consider the pedagogical applications of BELF research, and the process of developing research-informed curricula. In the context of Germany, where higher education is being asked to answer the need of industry for a highly trained workforce, Claudia Böttger, Juliane House, and Roman Stachowicz describe how they used research on different pragmatic uses in ELF interaction to inform the design of a practice-oriented English course that prepares employees for communicating more effectively. This is the focus of their chapter 'Knowledge Transfer on English as a *Lingua Franca* in Written Multilingual Business Communication' (in Bührig and Meyer, eds., *Transferring Linguistic Know-How into Institutional Practice* [2013], pp. 117–36). Given the need for companies to improve their employees' language and intercultural skills, joint industry–university knowledge-transfer schemes such as the one described here have been proven (through rigorous monitoring and evaluation) to help fulfil employees' and organizations' communicative needs, thus enhancing cost-effectiveness. Patricia Pullin also explores how BELF research has been drawn upon in curriculum development for workplace communication (in domains outside business and economics) in 'From Curriculum to Classroom: Designing and Delivering Courses in Workplace Communication' (*Babylonia* 2[2013] 32–6). With ELF being increasingly used in a number of specific workplace domains, in a number of national and international contexts, such investigation of how the language can be usefully taught to fulfil learners' needs is timely. This bank of research makes clear that there is a continued need for both NSs and NNSs of English to raise their awareness of business communication patterns and intercultural communication strategies.

The number of publications dealing with the implications of the global spread of English for theory and practice of translation and interpreting has risen sharply over the last few years. This is mainly due to the fact that the widespread use of English in international contexts is perceived as threatening the translation and interpreting market by reducing demand and is also putting great strain on translators and interpreters, who are increasingly required to work with source texts produced by NNSs of English, something they have not been prepared for. Indeed, as Stefania Taviano points out in the abstract of 'English as a Lingua Franca and Translation: Implications for Translator and Interpreter Education' (*ITT* 7[2013] 155–67), 'Despite the growth of interest in this field of [ELF] research, however, translation studies has been slow to engage with it.' This is largely true, although there are scholars who have worked in both ELF and translation studies for some time. In 2013 and 2014, Juliane House explicitly examined the relationship between these areas in several papers, asking, 'English as a Global Lingua Franca: A Threat to Multilingual Communication and Translation?' (*LTeach* 47[2014] 363–76). House first clarifies the concept of ELF and then uses insights from her own research projects to argue that the widespread use of ELF is inevitable in the globalized world but that its use in multilingual environments should be recognized as an additional option rather than a replacement for other languages. House's research has shown that the influence on the communicative conventions of German of today's huge volume of translations from English into that language is marginal, and she concludes that fears of the extensive use of a dominant language inhibiting conceptualization in other languages are unfounded. As far as the need for translations is concerned, House argues that due to globalization, not only ELF but also translation will continue to be in great demand (see also her 'English as a Lingua Franca and Translation', in Yves Gambier and Luc van Doorslaer, eds., *Handbook of Translation Studies* [2010], pp. 59–62).

Several members of the translation and interpreting profession have over recent years conducted research into the implications of the vastly increased use of English in settings such as international business, academic conferences, and political meetings, e.g. the institutions of the EU. The titles of Michaela Albl-Mikasa's articles 'The Imaginary Invalid: Conference Interpreters and English as a Lingua Franca' (*IJAL* 24[2014] 293–311) and 'ELF Speakers' Restricted Power of Expression: Implications for Interpreters' Processing' (*TIS* 8[2013] 191–210) (the latter in a special issue on 'Describing Cognitive

Processes in Translation: Acts and Events') give some indication of the degree of unease in the profession due to the increasing amount of non-native English it has to cope with. In both these papers, Albl-Mikasa compares findings of ELF research, which has investigated non-mediated interactions, to the issues reported by (conference) interpreters when confronted with input in L2 English rather than in speakers' L1s, a phenomenon on the rise in many international meetings. The author's studies detail the difficulties interpreters face when having to work with non-native English speakers' conference speeches. Interpreters, she reports, find that the language of these speakers lacks clarity and thus constitutes an enormous cognitive burden for them, which in turn is likely to negatively affect interpretation quality. These mediation situations, in which negotiation of meaning is usually impossible, are of course very different from the interactive translanguaging encounters investigated in most ELF research to date, in which meaning can be negotiated, participants can accommodate to each other, and the linguistic medium is creatively exploited and moulded according to the requirements of specific encounters. This take on ELF communication is a far cry from that of interpreters and translators, who, Albl-Mikasa says 'are trained for full comprehension and detailed meaning recovery' (*IJAL* 24[2014] 306). Nevertheless, the reports of interpreters' difficulties with speeches intended to be made accessible by using ELF constitute a new and welcome contribution to ELF research. In 'Express-Ability in ELF Communication' (*JELF* 2[2013] 101–22) Albl-Mikasa elaborates on interpreters' views, elicited through questionnaires and interviews, on non-native English speakers' 'restricted power of expression' (abstract) and sets these findings in relation both to reports of the perceived limits of their self-expression by ELF speakers in the 'Tübingen English as a Lingua Franca Corpus and Database' (TELF) and to sociocultural and psycholinguistic thinking originating in SLA research. In 'English as a Lingua Franca in International Conferences: Current and Future Developments in Interpreting Studies' (*ITSK* 18:iii[2014] 17–42), Albl-Mikasa summarizes the results of both her own research as outlined above and that of other scholars and presents suggestions for future research, namely 're-consideration of the effectiveness of ELF communication in settings other than informal or semi-formal dialogic interactions, especially in conference settings; re-conceptualization of interpreter training courses; and re-branding of the interpreters' professional status as multilingual communication experts, including the re-definition of their role and self-image as service providers' (p. 31).

Closely related to Albl-Mikasa's themes but based on results obtained through different methods is Karin Reithofer's 'Comparing Modes of Communication: The Effect of English as a Lingua Franca vs. Interpreting' (*Interpreting* 15[2013] 48–73). The author again starts from the observation that the use of ELF is gaining ground in international meetings, particularly in the domains of academia, business, and the institutions of the EU, and is therefore being seen by many interpreters as a threat to their profession. Using a complex method of comprehension testing, Reithofer compared the effect on the audience of a short talk in the area of marketing delivered by an Italian speaker of English with the simultaneous interpretation of this talk into

German. She concludes that in this particular setting 'the interpretation led to a better cognitive end-result in the audience than the original speech in non-native English' (abstract). This article is based on Reithofer's doctoral research, published as *Englisch als Lingua Franca und Dolmetschen: Ein Vergleich zweier Kommunikationsmodi unter dem Aspekt der Wirkungsäquivalenz*. This book allows Reithofer space for a more detailed comparison between the two modes of communication, which she character-izes as complementary rather than competing, depending on setting, purpose, speakers, etc. This longer publication conveys a more balanced picture and emphasizes that the results are valid only for the fairly formal monologic, unidirectional communication situation under investigation, a setting which allows no negotiation of meaning. In her concluding chapter, Reithofer discusses the implications of her findings for interpreter education, inter-preters' professional development, and further interpreting research, high-lighting the importance of developing 'coping strategies' (pp. 260–1).

While most studies relating conference-interpreting to ELF research focus on European contexts, Chia-chien Chang and Michelle Min-chia Wu's 'Non-Native English at International Conferences: Perspectives from Chinese–English Conference Interpreters in Taiwan' (*Interpreting* 16[2014] 169–90) explores the impact of ELF on Chinese–English interpreters in Taiwan. Ten experienced interpreters were interviewed, who reported on the resourceful strategies they developed for coping with challenging non-native English input. These included conscious self-training and studying recordings of speakers from different regions of the world. Accents were a factor these interpreters were particularly wary of, but in general they were found to have a more pragmatic and relaxed attitude than their European counterparts reported on above, accepting ELF situations as 'a fact of life' (p. 187).

A strong indicator of the rising interest in ELF research among translators and interpreters is the fact that 2013 saw the publication of a special issue of *Interpreter and Translator Trainer* (7:ii[2013]) on 'English as a Lingua Franca and Translation: Implications for Translator and Interpreter Education'. Stefania Taviano, the editor, prepares the ground with a very clear and comprehensive overview of the issues that the theory, practice, and pedagogy of translation face due to globalization in general and the current role of ELF in particular. She summarizes the pedagogy-related ELF literature and forcefully argues that it is high time for translation and interpreting curricula to take on board the implications of ELF and to help students 'become aware of and reflect on the rapidly changing nature of their future profession' (abstract). In particular, students need to learn to translate texts written in ELF: this is used as a shorthand term in this issue and elsewhere in the translation and interpreting literature, to refer only to what NNSs of English produce, which is at odds with how the term is used in current ELF research. Taviano does, however, go on to specify that she is referring to the function of ELF, i.e. texts 'produced by international organizations and addressed to international audiences' (abstract). Taviano's introduction also summarizes all articles in this special issue, so anybody who only reads one paper on this topic would be well served by this one. The papers in this special issue all focus on (written) translation. Agnes Pisanski Peterlin examines 'Attitudes towards

English as an Academic Lingua Franca in Translation' (*ITT* 7[2013] 195–216) using semi-structured interviews and questionnaires. She finds that trainee translators and experienced scholars/authors have divergent views on written academic ELF, with the former adhering to NS models and the latter being more assertive regarding their use of English for their own purposes. She concludes that '*Lingua franca* communication does not fit the conventional paradigm according to which a language is embedded in a culture. The findings of the present study suggest that this is something with which trainee translators are not sufficiently familiar' (p. 210), thus indicating the need for translation educators to address 'emancipatory' views on academic ELF in their courses. Along similar lines, Dominic Stewart's 'From Pro Loco to Pro Globo: Translating into English for an International Readership' (*ITT* 7[2013] 217–34) engages with advanced Italian university students' translations of Italian tourist texts for an international readership, thus constituting a move from the local to the global. Like Pisanksi Peterlin, he attributes difficulties that arise with these translations to the fact that students were educated for using Standard BrE appropriate for local consumption but now need to orient to ELF for global purposes. Responding to this challenge proves to be a complex process both for the education of translation students and for assessment. Karen Bennett's 'English as a Lingua Franca in Academia: Combating Epistemicide through Translator Training' (*ITT* 7[2013] 169–93) takes a CDA stance towards the dominance of English in academia that she sees as a danger to the rhetorical norms and scholarly traditions in other languages. She argues that translators unwittingly reinforce this 'slide towards an epistemological monoculture' (p. 189) when translating academic papers into and out of English for international dissemination. As a counter-measure Bennett proposes awareness-raising for translators and students of translation studies combined with training in the reformulation, editing, and critical analysis of texts so as to enable them to resist dominant discourses. Lance Hewson addresses the question 'Is English as a Lingua Franca Translation's Defining Moment?' (*ITT* 7[2013] 257–77), considering the effect the widespread use of ELF is having on the translation market. Though acknowledging recent definitions of ELF as being the communicative medium of choice in any interaction among speakers of different first languages (and so also including native English speakers), Hewson chooses to reduce 'ELF' to the opposite of 'native', arguing that NS and NNS differ with regard to their linguistic and translational competence. He goes on to discuss the difficulties that 'ELF target texts' (p. 265) and 'ELF source texts' (p. 270) pose for the practice, pedagogy, and theory of translation, conceding, however, that 'it can be difficult to say categorically whether [a particular] text is indeed an ELF text' (pp. 263–4). Hewson therefore highlights the unique strengths of translators working into their A language and the difficulties of translating texts produced by non-native writers. Amanda Murphy's article presents a rationale for 'Incorporating Editing into the Training of English Language Students in the Era of English as a Lingua Franca' (*ITT* 7[2013] 235–55). This is done by asking students to engage in reflections on revisions to texts made by expert editors and to use various reference sources before editing documents themselves. The point of this module is to help students arrive at written texts that conform to StE norms and to make them aware of 'the contradiction between English as a Lingua Franca ... in its spoken form and the norms required in international institutions for documents written in English' (her abstract). In the feature article concluding this special issue, Juliane House, in 'English as a Lingua Franca and Translation' (*ITT* 7[2013] 279–98), takes the line that the current widespread use of ELF does not threaten other languages but usefully complements them, a stance that contradicts particularly Bennett's, but also Hewson's and Murphy's in this volume. Of greatest relevance to the theme of this issue is House's discussion of recent developments in translator education that foster students' skills to translate into a language that is not their first. This, she argues, is a widespread practice in many (especially non-European) contexts and entirely appropriate for many areas of the digital economy of today's globalized world. This pragmatic view of contemporary translation realities represents a challenge to traditional assumptions about the superiority of translations relying on native-speaker norms and intuitions.

The increasing number of publications by translation and interpreting scholars that engage with ELF research testifies to the extent of the challenge that the global use of English poses to the profession, resulting in suggestions for rethinking both the education of future translators and interpreters and the nature of the profession itself. It is not surprising that a profession whose existence has always rested on the notion of languages as clearly demarcated, separate entities 'owned' by those that speak them natively will need to make some conceptual adjustments to engage with the current view in ELF research which, as pointed out earlier, represents ELF use in non-segregational terms as an emergent and adaptive process.

13. Pragmatics and Discourse Analysis

The year 2014 proved to be an exciting one for pragmatics and discourse analysis as it was characterized by a series of cross-over initiatives, reaching out beyond the boundaries of the single fields. In pragmatics, this cross-over was seen particularly strongly in the works on corpus pragmatics. While corpus-linguistic methods have become relatively mainstream in discourse analysis, the reach into pragmatics had been quite limited to date. Another continuing area of interdisciplinary development is the increasing attention which prosodic and multimodal factors are gaining in (mainstream) discourse and pragmatic research. The year's work was also characterized by the prominence of evaluation and, connected to this, the continued growth in research into impoliteness. Research into discourse has continued past trends but is increasingly characterized by its responsiveness to current affairs and to the impact agenda that is being set by the British funding councils. Given the very large number of publications in discourse and pragmatics, this review will attempt to address these trends (and only as seen in studies of English) rather than survey the entirety of the excellent research published in 2014.

This year saw the publication of the *Discourse Studies Reader*, edited by Johannes Angermuller, Dominique Maingueneau, and Ruth Wodak, as well as the third edition of the *Discourse Reader*, edited by Adam Jaworski and

Nikolas Coupland. *The Discourse Studies Reader* approaches discourse studies not as a branch of linguistics but as a project 'which runs counter to the division of knowledge into specialized disciplines and sub-disciplines' (p. 1) and the editors explicitly set out to bring together both discourse theory and discourse analysis. This vision is reflected in the broad range of texts, which also represent approaches from different countries. The reader includes seven sections, each of which brings together different viewpoints on discourse. These sections are: 'Theoretical Inspirations: Structuralism versus Pragmatics', 'From Structuralism to Poststructuralism', 'Enunciative Pragmatics', 'Interactionism', 'Sociopragmatics', 'Historical Knowledge', and 'Critical Approaches'. *The Discourse Reader* continues with the same overall approach to discourse as before, but a number of chapters have been deleted and others introduced. The readings in the first section, which examine the roots of discourse, are largely unchanged and mainly draw on the same researchers as those used in the *Discourse Studies Reader*. In the second section, on methods, there has been considerable revision, with chapters on conversation analysis and transcription removed. Part III remains largely the same, while Part IV sees three chapters being cut which, surprisingly, include chapters on politeness and visual interaction, going against the trends identified elsewhere in this review. The fifth section, on 'Identity and Subjectivity', is an aspect which shows very little overlap with the other *Discourse Studies Reader* and has also been substantially revised, with four chapters removed and three new ones introduced (although the topic areas remain broadly the same). The final section, on 'Power, Identity and Control', has dropped texts by Michel Foucault and Judith Butler in favour of more recent texts, including a chapter on corpus-based approaches (by Paul Baker and Tony McEnery).

Moving on to textbooks, 2014 saw the publication of two pragmatics textbooks, both of which go beyond a simple teaching tool by presenting different ways of understanding pragmatics. *Pragmatics and the English Language* by Jonathan Culpeper and Michael Haugh is an important addition to the field; it serves as an introduction both to pragmatics and to a new way of approaching pragmatics: integrative pragmatics. In this approach the authors reject the forced dichotomy of first-order (the view of the researcher) vs. second-order (the view of the participant) perspectives on pragmatics in favour of an approach which acknowledges the importance of both perspectives and focuses on interaction as a way of bridging them. Similarly, they seek to bridge the divide between the North American and European traditions of micro- and macro-pragmatic studies. It is always exciting to see eminent researchers dedicate time to textbooks and the result in this case is a research-driven textbook which is very student-friendly. Each chapter is written in a highly accessible style and combines both theoretical overviews and discussions of case studies. The reflections sections bring in data from a range of Englishes examining variation within and between Englishes and covering both synchronic and diachronic aspects, which is indeed one of the many interesting aspects of the book. The book is positioned explicitly as the pragmatics of English. This is innovative in two ways: first, it acknowledges the plurality of Englishes, and second, it acknowledges the fact that a great deal of pragmatics research is actually English pragmatic research; as they write, 'unlike most introductory pragmatics books which give the impression that the pragmatic phenomena they discuss are general, applicable to many languages and cultures, we call a spade a spade—this is a book about pragmatics and the English language' (p. 12). This awareness and honesty are very much appreciated. The chapters cover both old and new ground, including: familiar referential pragmatics, informational pragmatics, pragmatics meaning, pragmatics acts, interpersonal pragmatics, and meta-pragmatics.

Understanding Pragmatics by Gunter Senft adopts the broad view of pragmatics, conceptualizing it as the 'cultural and social embedding of meaning' (p. 2) and as a 'transdiscipline'. The structure of the book highlights the insights and contributions to pragmatics from a range of disciplines, with each chapter covering one of these. Thus, the following are included: philosophy, psychology, human ethology, ethnology, sociology, and politics. This means that alongside expected topics such as speech-act theory and deixis, which are covered in the first two chapters, the third chapter discusses ritual, which is less frequently covered in such depth in introductory books. In the final chapter, Senft looks to the future of pragmatics and discusses emancipatory pragmatics, which was also the subject of a special edition of the *Journal of Pragmatics* in 2014 (edited by William F. Hanks, Sachiko Ide, and Yasuhiro Katagiri).

Three textbooks which guide students to understanding discourse and the operation of power in texts came out this year, all of which make use of Hallidayan systemic functional linguistics (SFL) to a greater or lesser extent. *Analysing Power in Language: A Practical Guide* by Tom Bartlett puts SFL at the centre of discourse analysis. The goal of the book is presented as enabling readers to produce textual analyses as 'gateways to discourse analysis', that is to say that the methods of SFL are presented to allow for an objective analysis, to support and lead into the interpretation of the meaning in context. The book is written in a personal and accessible style and supported by a number of exercises that make use of a wide range of texts, from the monologues of Winston Churchill and Martin Luther King to Tony Blair and George W. Bush to multi-party interactions from the author's own fieldwork in Guyana. The answers to the exercises are included in an appendix and there is also a glossary, both of which will be appreciated by students. The seven chapters cover topics such as fields of discourse, construing participation, interpersonal meaning, textual meaning, and deixis, thus providing students with a key skills-set for starting to investigate discourse.

Discourse, Grammar and Ideology: Functional and Cognitive Perspectives by Christopher Hart is an introduction to CDA, which entails the investigation of power relations. Hart presents CDA as a set of approaches, each of which has a distinct methodology, but which can be distinguished from other critical approaches by 'its stringent application of linguistics' (p. 6). It is this application of linguistics that can lend the investigation rigour and replicability, which are required for scientifically grounded critical-discourse research. Thus, each of the chapters introduces a set of linguistic tools for casting light on the non-obvious features of discourse. The chapters in the first part introduce more established tools, including those of systemic-functional grammar, the appraisal framework and multimodality. The chapters in the second part cover new ground and bring in recent developments in using cognitive linguistics for CDA, an area in which the author himself has been influential. Topics of the chapters in this section include event structure and spatial point of view, metaphor, and deixis and proximation.

Analysing Political Speeches: Rhetoric, Discourse and Metaphor by Jonathan Charteris-Black similarly aims to show the reader how to analyse and understand discourse and also makes use of SFL (although it is never mentioned in the book). However, it differs from the two previous textbooks in that the focus is on a single discourse type, i.e. political speeches. The book explicitly presents different theoretical approaches to aid triangulation, based on the idea that 'just as we may learn about a sculpture by walking round it, so we may learn about speeches by viewing them from multiple perspectives' (p. xx). These perspectives, the rhetoric, discourse, and metaphor of the title, constitute the three major divisions in the structure of the book. The sections are described as chronological, which presumably refers to when they were first developed rather than the periods in which the approaches are used. The textbook includes a very helpful range of exercises with answers.

Corpus pragmatics, the 'relative newcomer' according to Aijmer and Rühlemann (p. 1) asserted itself strongly in 2014 with three significant edited collections. The first, *Corpus Pragmatics: A Handbook*, edited by Karin Aijmer and Christoph Rühlemann, takes the broad view of pragmatics, arguing that if we consider context to be key to pragmatic interpretation, then data is required. Although not explicitly about English pragmatics, all the chapters use English-language corpora, with two chapters bringing in a cross-linguistic element. In their introduction, they put forward that 'corpus-pragmatic research is more than just pragmatic research and more than just corpus analysis in that it integrates the horizontal (qualitative) methodology typical of pragmatics with the vertical (quantitative) methodology predominant in corpus linguistics' (p. 12). This 'more than the sum of the parts' argument echoes those made in favour of corpus-assisted discourse studies more generally. As they neatly summarize, although research is blossoming in the area of corpus pragmatics, there are currently two dominant patterns of analysis, and in both the researcher starts from the vertical analysis (the quantitative component). In the first, the researcher starts with lexical items, for instance a pragmatic marker such as *well*, and moves from the vertical reading to the horizontal analysis of functions. In the second, the researcher starts with functions and attempts to identify forms. In this case, the search terms cannot relate to form and so are likely to be meta-communicative expressions leading to a discussion of the function that happens to be of interest to the researcher. However, there is another method that is not included in this division and starts instead from the horizontal reading; this concerns research that uses a corpus which has been manually annotated for pragmatic features. In this case, the annotation of the corpus is the first stage of the analysis and is resolutely qualitative. Following the introduction, which provides a thoughtful overview of the methodological integration of corpus pragmatics, there are sixteen chapters, divided into six sections: 'Corpora and Speech Acts', 'Corpora and Pragmatic Principles', 'Corpora and Pragmatics

Markers', 'Corpora and Evaluation', 'Corpora and Reference', and 'Corpora and Turn-Taking'. This range of topics and approaches is one of the strengths of the volume, as is the methodological reflection included in some of the chapters. Of particular interest are the ambitious chapters addressing pragmatic principles. In terms of trends this year, the three chapters on evaluation are also particularly salient. These include a chapter by Bethany Gray and Douglas Biber on stance markers in which they review previous work, noting that analyses of stance typically address overt evaluation before going on to explore methods of identifying less explicit devices. The section titled 'Evaluation' consists of two chapters. In the first, 'Evaluative Prosody', Alan Partington discusses and provides corpus evidence for the properties of evaluative prosody (the phenomenon also referred to as semantic prosody and discourse prosody). The second, 'Tails', by Ivor Timmis, focuses on a specific non-canonical grammatical feature, the tail or right dislocation, and approaches the use of this feature from a sociopragmatic variation perspective. What makes the volume as a whole stand out is the reflection on the methodological processes of doing corpus pragmatics. What is somewhat surprising for a 2014 publication is that none of the chapters discuss written conversation or other forms of computer-mediated communication (CMC), while in fact many of the spoken corpora date back to the 1990s. In many ways this reflects one of the great constraints on corpus pragmatics, which is that building spoken corpora is vastly time-consuming and therefore expensive, meaning that reliance on older corpora will probably continue for English until the new BNC 2014 is released. However, the accessibility of CMC data makes this a marked omission given that the data is available, being used elsewhere, and, more importantly, that this is an integrated part of our daily interactions.

The Yearbook of Corpus Linguistics and Pragmatics is a relatively new series which started in 2013, published by Springer; its very existence neatly illustrates the extent to which corpus pragmatics has established itself. The second volume in the series, edited by Jesús Romero-Trillo, is subtitled *New Empirical and Theoretical Paradigms* and sets out to 'offer novel theoretical and empirical models that can explain language better in itself and in its relation to reality' (p. 1). The book is divided into four sections. In the first, the four chapters challenge existing methodologies, as in Stefan Th. Gries and Allison S. Adelman's chapter, 'Subject Realization in Japanese Conversation by Native and Non-Native Speakers: Exemplifying a New Paradigm for Learner Corpus Research', and also theory, as in Li's 'A Corpus-Based Analysis of Metaphorical Uses of the High Frequency Noun *Time*: Challenges to Conceptual Metaphor Theory'. The second section is grouped by a shared interest in culture, and contains the only corpus study I have come across of Latin in Jacob L. Mey's intriguing chapter, 'Horace, Colors and Pragmatics'. The third section is dedicated to L2 studies, which again shows how corpus pragmatics studies are developing and moving away from the analysis of standard languages. The fourth section contains book reviews (which constitutes an appealing aspect of the series). The chapters in this volume cover seven different languages and include historical, regional, and learner varieties of those languages. The contributors are affiliated with universities in ten different countries and range from emeritus professor to current Ph.D. student. This openness to all scholars means that readers are bound to come across researchers, and therefore ideas and methods, that they have not encountered before, and this is very positive for the field.

The third significant contribution to corpus pragmatics is *Diachronic Corpus Pragmatics* from Benjamins' Pragmatics and Beyond New Series, edited by Irma Taavitsainen, Andreas H. Jucker, and Jukka Tuominen. This collection follows on from a conference panel but is a much more coherent and comprehensive collection than often results from such origins. It sets out to show the usefulness of the combination of the three disciplines of historical linguistics, corpus linguistics, and pragmatics and reflects on the challenges and implications of this combination. In the introduction, 'Diachronic Corpus Pragmatics: Intersection and Interjections', the authors position diachronic corpus linguistics as a branch of historical pragmatics, noting that it is a field still in its infancy (although this book will surely change that). As the authors point out, although corpus pragmatics is somewhat more established as a field, what facilitates diachronic corpus pragmatics more specifically is the fact that corpora have been used in historical pragmatics from its inception in the 1990s. This early combination was the result of a wider shift in pragmatics, the serendipity of the emergence of historical pragmatics at the time corpus resources were developing, and indeed largely a result of Jucker's own previous work in the area. However, the combination is not without its challenges, and these too are addressed in the introductory chapter, with two 'double binds' being identified. The first, common to all corpus pragmatic/ discourse work, is the tension between the drive for larger datasets and the recognition of the importance of rich contextualization. The second is the tension between the desire to maintain the integrity of the original texts and the need to make them retrievable using corpus software. A partial response to these tensions comes, again, in the form of annotation, which will allow for spelling variations to be tagged with a standardized spelling, rather as word forms are matched to lemmas. Similarly, information about speakers and pragmatic features can be added through annotation, maintaining the richness. Another way of increasing the contextualization is the integration of multimodal elements. The authors give the EMENT corpus as an example, which includes images of the original text and so on. There are twelve chapters following the introduction, divided into the areas of 'Words', 'Phrases and Clauses', and 'Utterances and Dialogues'. The first two sections look at analyses which move from form to function, while the last section starts from function. While most of the chapters interpret 'diachronic' as 'historical diachronic', Jucker and Taavitsainen use the free CoHA and CoCA corpora to cover a range from 1820 to 2000, which makes for fascinating reading. One of the interesting features of this collection is that it covers eight languages. However, for the purposes of this review, the most relevant will be the five chapters on English-language data, which cover investigations into degree modifiers (Claudia Claridge and Merja Kytö), multi-adjectival premodification (Jukka Tyrkkö), epistemic/evidential parentheticals (María José López-Couso and Belén Méndez-Naya), complimenting (Andreas H. Jucker and Irma Taavitsainen), and identification of verbal aggression (Dawn Archer).

The last two chapters are especially innovative as they start from functions rather than forms, thus challenging assumptions about the limits of corpus work. Furthermore, each chapter reflects growing trends in other ways. Jucker and Taavitsainen's chapter, like the Culpeper and Haugh textbook, places meta-communicative expressions in a prominent position. Taken together with Garcia McAllister's chapter in the Aijmer and Rühlemann volume mentioned above, we have two new ways of investigating speech acts and dealing with the tensions of precision of recall, in which starting with recognized forms will lead to a high degree of precision in retrieving instances of a particular speech act but will only recall a small number of the potential range. This is also addressed in Archer's chapter, which shows how semantic annotation can be employed in both identifying and theorizing verbal aggression, thus contributing to the burgeoning area of impoliteness studies.

Another major contribution to the integration of corpus linguistics in new areas comes in Paul Baker's *Using Corpora to Analyse Gender*. As he notes in the introduction, 'while discourse analysis has become popular with Gender and Language, this has tended to be based on detailed qualitative studies' (p. 6); he therefore offers corpus linguistics as a complementary approach. Topics cover both the language used by people of different genders and representations of gender and sexuality, and they range from expressing disagreement to changes in discursive representation over time. To show the reader how corpus methods may be integrated into language and gender work, each chapter has a different corpus methodological focus, moving through frequency, collocation, and concordance analysis. Methodological issues are also raised, both regarding the study of gender and the use and interpretation of corpus data.

If the rise of corpus pragmatics represents one important form of 'cross-over' or 'cross-pollination', another highly noticeable one came in the form of many articles pushing for more attention to spoken forms and multimodal aspects of pragmatics and discourse. This included a special issue of *Text & Talk* (34:iii[2014] on 'Multimodality, Meaning-Making, and the Issue of "Text"', edited by Elisabetta Adami and Gunther Kress. In addition, there were stand-alone methodological papers, such as 'Why Do News Values Matter? Towards a New Methodological Framework for Analysing News Discourse in Critical Discourse Analysis and Beyond' (*D&S* 25[2014] 135–58) by Monika Bednarek and Helen Caple, which examines the complete multimodal text to seen how newsworthiness is constructed, and John A. Bateman and Janina Wildfeuer's proposal of 'A Multimodal Discourse Theory of Visual Narrative' (*JPrag* 74[2014] 180–208). Concerning pragmatics, there were papers addressing themes such as impoliteness: Gerard O'Grady's 'The Use of Key in Projecting Face-Threatening Acts in Televised Political Debate' (*T&T* 34 [2014] 685–711); mock-impoliteness: Sean McKinnon and Pilar Prieto's 'The Role of Prosody and Gesture in the Perception of Mock Impoliteness' (*JPolR* 10[2014] 185–219); and turn-taking: Timo Kaukomaa, Anssi Peräkyläb, and Johanna Ruusuvuoric's 'Foreshadowing a Problem: Turn-Opening Frowns in Conversation' (*JPrag* 71[2014] 132–47).

Continuing the theme of 'cross-pollination' in this year's work, the Handbooks of Pragmatics series published by Mouton de Gruyter explicitly brings the two together, conceptualizing discourse as part of pragmatics. *Pragmatics of Discourse*, edited by Klaus Schneider and Anne Barron, is the third volume in this series. Following two introductory chapters which tackle the field of discourse pragmatics and the slippery nature of discourse, the book is structured in three sections. The first, titled 'Approaches to Discourse', covers approaches such as CDA and CA, but also two of the areas of cross-pollination identified in this year's review, in chapters on 'Corpus Linguistics and Discourse Analysis' (Michaela Mahlberg) and 'Multimodal Pragmatics' (Kay O'Halloran, Sabine Tan, and Marissa K.L.E.). The second section surveys discourse structures and again, alongside the familiar topics, we have innovation in the form of Michal Ephratt's chapter on 'Silence'. The third section presents discourse types and domains ranging from medical discourse to legal discourse.

Pragmatic Literary Stylistics, edited by Siobhan Chapman and Billy Clark, also represents a new interdisciplinary area for pragmatic studies (its publication interestingly coincides with the republication of Roger Sell's *Literary Pragmatics* as part of the Routledge Revivals series). The introduction to the volume shows that the rather uncomfortable relationship between the role and contribution of literary stylistics and literary criticism, and interaction between the two, has not been resolved in the time that has elapsed between the first publication of Sell's study and this volume. In this volume, the editors see the primary role of pragmatic literary stylistics as serving to explain 'how different audiences arrive at the understandings they do' (p. 7) and the secondary task as 'developing arguments in support of particular readings' (p. 8). Furthermore, they propose that the application may allow for testing of the pragmatic theoretical frameworks. The ten chapters that follow the introduction present a range of case studies working with pragmatic concepts such as implicature, relevance theory, and face-work. The latter is also addressed in a stylistics context in Derek Bousfield's chapter on 'Stylistics, Speech Acts and Im/politeness Theory' (in Burke, ed., *The Routledge Handbook of Stylistics*, pp. 118–35), which presents a thorough overview of this interaction between pragmatics and stylistics.

The year 2014 saw two weighty contributions from established members of the im/politeness community. The first is by Geoffrey Leech, who was one of the first to theorize politeness, and in so doing shaped the direction of this field (as well as several others). *The Pragmatics of Politeness* reasserts the linguistic origins of im/politeness, the area that Leech refers to as pragma-linguistics (the relationship between pragmatics and linguistic form) as opposed to socio-pragmatics (the relationship between pragmatics and society). The first section (four chapters) presents Leech's view of politeness and explicitly places this within the context of other researchers in the field, which will be very helpful for those coming to the topic for the first time. The second section moves on to analysis and addresses a range of speech acts, from apologies to compliments. In the final chapter in this section he also flips the focus to the intriguing 'opposites' of politeness, of which he identifies four: 'non-politeness', which is the absence of politeness, 'impoliteness', which is the polar opposite of politeness, 'irony or sarcasm', and 'banter'. The last section, titled 'Further

Perspectives', discusses the methods of data collection, interlanguage pragmatics, and the study of politeness in a historical context.

The second volume to make a significant contribution to im/politeness is Michael Haugh's *Im/Politeness Implicatures*. This is a rich and insightful account, which, like Leech's volume, firmly places im/politeness study in a linguistic pragmatic context. It teases out the relationship between two weighty concepts: politeness and implicature. This pair has been theorized in past research, most notably in the neo-Gricean approaches of politeness as implicature. However, this volume takes a fresh approach, in which im/politeness is not seen as an implicature itself, but as an evaluative social practice. Thus, 'the puzzle to be explored … is why it is that implicatures only sometimes give rise to politeness, while in other instances they can give rise to other kinds of evaluations, such as impoliteness, mock politeness, mock impoliteness and shades between' (p. 7). In addressing this question, Haugh calls for a need to situate the analysis with respect to the moral order invoked by participants. This investigation is characterized by a focus on the viewpoints of the participants and the understanding that implicatures may nor reside in a single utterance but emerge over a sequence. Michael Haugh's paper on 'Jocular Mockery as Interactional Practice in Everyday Anglo-Australian Conversation' (*AJL* 34[2014] 76–99) further explores one aspect of im/politeness implicatures, that of banter, one of the impoliteness opposites raised in Leech's volume.

Indirectness also forms the focus of two more papers this year. 'Disentangling Politeness Theory and the Strategic Speaker Approach: Theoretical Considerations and Empirical Predictions' by Jessica Soltys, Marina Terkourafi, and Napoleon Katsos (*IPrag* 11[2014] 31–56) reviews and probes these two accounts of off-record indirect speech. Marcella Bertuccelli Papi's paper investigates 'The Pragmatics of Insinuation' (*IPrag* 11[2014] 1–29), in which insinuation is defined as 'a communicative strategy whereby a speaker intends to make an addressee believe p [proposition], but does not want to be held responsible for communicating p' (p. 2). Although the paper does not explicitly refer to impoliteness, it makes clear that the 'mismatch' strategy used for deception and manipulation is closely associated with other kinds of im/politeness. Impoliteness also received attention from a cross-cultural perspective in 'Expressing Disagreement in English as a Lingua Franca: Whose Pragmatic Rules?' by Carmen Maíz-Arévalo (*IPrag* 11[2014] 199–224), which found that high-proficiency speakers were more likely to formulate the speech act of disagreement using BrE norms of mitigation. Hadar Netz's study of disagreements showed that they were unmarked in a study of children in gifted classes in the US and, as such, not performing impoliteness (*JPrag* 61[2014] 142–60). In Bernie Chun Nam Mak and Hin Leung Chui's study of 'Impoliteness in Facebook Status Updates: Strategic Talk among Colleagues "Outside" the Workplace' (*T&T* 34:ii[2014] 165–85), the use of English itself constitutes one of the strategies and simultaneously helps define the community of speakers. Finally, politeness as a means of investigating community-building was employed in several papers this year, focusing in particular on various forms of informal written conversation. In the study that uses English-language data, Daria Dayer investigates 'Self-Praise in Micro-Blogging' on Twitter (*JPrag* 61[2014] 91–102)

As we have already seen, evaluation has recurred as a theme in many of the pragmatics collections reviewed here; the publication of *Evaluation in Context* by Geoff Thompson and Laura Alba-Juez rightly draws attention to this important concept. The authors state that the volume is designed as a sequel to the influential *Evaluation in Text* [2000] by Susan Hunston and Geoff Thompson. While *Evaluation in Text* brought together the theorists of the major approaches to evaluation at the time and the editors introduced each of these, *Evaluation in Context* is a more traditional edited volume. The eight chapters following the introduction present a more theoretical approach, ranging from revisiting the appraisal model (Geoff Thompson) to evaluation-driven understanding of irony (Laura Alba-Juez and Salvatore Attardo). The last two chapters in this section also deal with prosody and intonation, again signalling the shift to explicitly include these aspects in theorization. The third part of the book consists of ten case studies which illustrate the different contexts in which evaluation may be studied.

14. Stylistics

The publications within stylistics in 2014 are varied and eclectic, with a prevalence of collected volumes and compendium texts. The research published this year demonstrates the sheer versatility and scope of the discipline. This review considers, first, the 'handbooks' of stylistics published in 2014, before moving on to survey the volumes which focus on cognitive applications. The rest of the review is divided thematically and considers the publications which explore reader-response research, the relationship between style and pedagogy, and other cognitive, critical, and corpus-stylistic explorations.

In *The Cambridge Handbook of Stylistics*, edited by Peter Stockwell and Sara Whiteley, Katie Wales ('The Stylistic Tool-Kit: Methods and Sub-Disciplines', pp. 32–45) discusses how stylistics is frequently described as a 'toolkit' for exploring texts; 'a metaphor which appears time and again in definitions and applications of stylistics' (p. 32). This is shown to be true for the two prominent stylistics textbooks published this year, *The Cambridge Handbook of Stylistics* and *The Routledge Handbook of Stylistics*. Both these collected volumes demonstrate the sheer range of what stylistics can offer textual analysis, and show that at the heart of the discipline is the idea that stylistics offers a variety of tools for the excavation of texts.

The Routledge Handbook of Stylistics, edited by Michael Burke, is an accessible textbook, and one which is suitable for a wide audience, from current researchers in the field to those encountering the area for the first time. Featuring contributions from key names in the discipline, the collection is divided into four parts which, when read cumulatively, guide the reader from the origins of the discipline through to the present day and finish with future directions of the field. This volume is centred on the fact that 'Stylistics is a subject to be enjoyed' (p. 7). Part I, 'Historical Perspectives in Stylistics', begins by providing theoretical foundations of stylistics: 'Rhetoric and Poetics: The Classical Heritage of Stylistics' (by Michael Burke, pp. 11–30), 'Formalist Stylistics' (by Michael Burke and Kristy Evers, pp. 31–44); 'Functional Stylistics' (by Patricia Canning, pp. 45–67); and 'Reader Response Criticism and Stylistics' (by Jennifer Riddle Harding, pp. 68–84), the concerns of which are then traced through the rest of the chapters. The second section surveys core issues in the field. Chapter 10, 'Stylistics, Point of View and Modality' (by Clara Neary, pp. 175–90), for example, considers 'one of the most intensively researched areas of stylistic enquiry' (p. 175): point of view. Neary provides a survey of the wider research on point of view, beginning with the four planes of point of view as outlined by Boris Uspensky [1973] (spatial, temporal, psychological, ideological), and considers, in particular, the relationship between modality and point of view. The chapter finishes by recommending future practice, urging readers to 'pay particular attention to the context in which [point of view] shifts take place, thereby facilitating investigation of their potential interpretive effect(s)' (p. 188), and outlines future practice: point of view in drama, reader responses to point of view, point of view in translated texts, and so on. Part III then moves on to explore contemporary topics, such as text-world theory: 'Stylistics and Text-World Theory' (by Ernestine Lahey, pp. 284–96). This chapter traces the three 'main strands of influence' (p. 284) which informed Paul Werth's original research on the text-world model: firstly his reaction to shortcomings of Chomskian generative linguistics; secondly the influence from possible world models, and finally influences from cognitive linguistics (such as Conceptual Metaphor Theory, Prototype Theory, and others). Again, like Neary's chapter, Lahey identifies recommendation for practice by posing some questions in response to a Dan Brown *Angels and Demons* extract. Like Neary, Lahey outlines the importance of context: how are discourse world elements affected in the process of text-world creation? Furthermore, how can text-world theory be used to explore performative contexts? The book finishes by identifying some emerging trends in the field: 'Multimodality and Stylistics (by Nina Norgaard, pp. 471–84), 'Creative Writing and Stylistics' (by Jeremy Scott, pp. 423–39), and 'Stylistics, Emotion and Neuroscience' (by Patrick Colm Hogan, pp. 516–30), amongst others.

The Cambridge Handbook of Stylistics similarly celebrates stylistics' position as an established discipline. This handbook is divided into four sections, and, like the *Routledge Handbook*, the first section situates stylistics in a historical context, drawing out its historical connections with other fields of study as indicated in the chapter titles: 'Stylistics as Rhetoric' (by Craig Hamilton, pp. 63–76); 'Stylistics as Applied Linguistics' (by Ronald Carter, pp. 77–86); and 'Stylistics as Literary Criticism' (by Geoff Hall, pp. 87–100). The first stylistic analyses are included in Part II, a section which focuses on the relationship between stylistics and literary concepts. Jessica Mason's chapter on 'Narrative' (pp. 179–95), for example, examines a new way of accounting for intertextuality in reading, offering a narrative interrelation model to provide a more reader-centred account of what happens when we make connections between texts and other narratives during the reading process. Mason argues that previous definitions of intertextuality make it a text-driven concept, whereas 'narrative interrelation' (as coined by Mason) has a more readerly emphasis. In Part III, 'Techniques of Style', Paul Simpson and Patricia Canning's chapter, 'Action and Event', provides a new application of something which has long been a cornerstone of stylistic analysis: transitivity. This chapter examines the notion of event vs. non-event in texts and discusses the importance of 'narrative gaps' in the representation of narrative events. It argues that, despite its continuing usefulness, transitivity does not account for action which is presented through counterfactuals, dis-narration, and negation. It does not argue that Michael Halliday's transitivity system is not still serviceable for stylistic analysis, but rather that it often cannot offer a holistic sense of action in a text. Part IV, 'The Contextual Experience of Style', contains chapters which consider the position of the reader within the reading experience. For example in her chapter 'Ethics' (pp. 393–407), following the work of Peter Stockwell [2009], Sara Whiteley argues that text-world theory is a useful model through which to consider the ethical experience of reading. Text-world theory concerns situating the reader within the context of reading, and it is this fact—its sensitivity to readerliness—which makes it well suited for exploring the idiosyncratic responses to reading and the relationship between the reader and the text. In this application Whiteley considers the novel *Never Let Me Go* (Ishiguro [2005]). The analysis observes that the text worlds created in the novel establish different narrator and narratee 'roles', and it is seen that readers project themselves into these different narratee roles in order to 'resist' or 'identify with' the protagonist, Kathy. Whiteley further analyses how there are particular stylistic cues that can create clashes which obstruct or confuse this readerly process of projection.

Another article which considers reader response is Lasse Gammelgaard's 'Two Trajectories of Reader Response in Narrative Poetry: Roses and Risings in Keats's "The Eve of St. Agnes"' (*Narrative* 22[2014] 203–18). Gammelgaard builds on Wolfgang Iser's work on 'wandering viewpoints' in reader-response theory and puts forward the argument that reader responses to Keats's narrative poem 'The Eve of St. Agnes' are contingent upon how readers respond, first, to the 'narrative trajectory' and second, to the 'poetic trajectory' of the text. By poetic trajectory Gammelgaard refers to (a) features of style that are unique to poems, and (b) language features which are often seen as foregrounded in poetry but which are not necessarily exclusive to the form (p. 204). In his analysis, Gammelgaard observes that these two trajectories move in different directions: 'As opposed to the narrative's wandering viewpoint, the poetic trajectory mainly works backwards. The reader's discovery of the meaning of this trajectory is retrospective rather than anticipatory' (p. 216). He concludes by suggesting that such a modification of Iser's original model would also potentially be beneficial for the study of prose narratives.

How readers become immersed within a text is something which many cognitive stylisticians question. For example, in María Ángeles Martínez's article 'Storyworld Possible Selves and the Phenomenon of Narrative Immersion: Testing a New Theoretical Construct' (*Narrative* 22[2014] 110–31) considers why some readers undergo a different narrative experience compared to others, and traces these experiences through an analysis using blending theory (Gilles Fauconnier and Mark Turner [2002]) and embodied metaphors: READING IS A JOURNEY; READING IS CONTROL; READING IS INVESMENT (Richard Gerrig [1993]; Peter Stockwell [2009]). Martínez acknowledges that constructs of character have already been discussed in narrative theory, but what about readers' mental constructions of themselves? This paper puts forward the idea that we all have a 'Storyworld possible self': which is 'preliminarily defined as imaginings of the self in story-worlds, formally conceived as blends resulting from matching features across a particular reader's self-concept and a focalizer's character construct' (p. 119). Like Sara Whiteley's discussion of identification mentioned above, Martínez argues that readers can project their story-world possible self 'if, and only if, at least one of the reader's self-schemas or possible selves is activated by narrative cues, that is to say, if the reader is schematic in one or more of the domains in the narration' (p. 119). Martínez argues that this concept may account for differing levels of emotional engagement amongst readers, and also for differences between readers' immersive experiences. The paper concludes by identifying how research into story-world possible selves could be taken forward, and questions how these concepts work in multimodal texts, amongst other potential directions.

The study of literary linguistics often invites scholars to consider how close-text analysis is best taught. Issue 46 of *Style* was a special issue that focused on responses to Peter Rabinowitz and Corrine Bancroft's target essay, 'Euclid at the Core: Recentering Literary Education' (*Style* 48[2014] 1–34), which commented on the challenges of teaching English literature, including when and how to include theory and technical literary language, both at secondary-school level and in the more advanced English classroom in the American school system. They acknowledge early on that in this paper they are not offering a practical guide for how to teach English most effectively but rather that their arguments are centred around one idea: 'we argue that if education doesn't give students the tools to discuss important literary questions (including questions about literature's relationship to the larger world) intelligently, then their education is flawed' (p. 2). In their discussion Rabinowitz and Bancroft put forward the idea that students respond to books with their own 'Kid Knowledge', and that teaching English is about 'Equipping them with language to name their ideas [which] will allow them to develop confidence to create more complicated ideas' (p. 28).

Sheridan Blau's article in this issue, 'Literary Competence and the Experience of Literature' (*Style* 48[2014] 42–7), maps out some of the 'problem spaces' from Bancroft and Rabinowitz's original article. In his response Blau questions how we should equip English students to take on 'intellectually challenging and cognitively difficult texts' (p. 44) and argues that more literary texts are perhaps being neglected while informational texts are given centre stage in the classroom. To address this challenge, Blau offers some practical pedagogical advice and argues that reading and the discussion of reader responses should be a collaborative activity organized in the classroom as 'social workshops' (p. 46). On the other hand Kate Oubre's response, 'Many "Right Answers", Many "Wrong Ones": A Defense of Close Reading in the High School Classroom' (*Style* 48[2014] 66–70), argues that students should become independent readers: 'students need to learn not to mimic me as their teacher or certain literary theorists or critics; rather, they need to learn to analyze on their own by mimicking the process' (p. 67). Oubre discusses how specialist literary terms are useful tools for clarifying and justifying readerly interpretation, but also argues that theory should be taught delicately. In other words, it is useful to allow students the space and independence to research and consider theories in which they are interested but that learning them too early or in the wrong context could be problematic and create barriers to learning. Brian Richardson's offering (*Style* 48[2014] 76–8) also finishes with practical advice: on teaching reader-response theory and on exploring the 'constructedness of fiction' in the classroom. For example, he mentions that a 'good exercise while reading is to have the students guess at what the ending will be, what consequences such an ending has, well before they have finished reading the work' (p. 78). These ideas are of interest to theorists and teachers alike, and will doubtless continue to be discussed along with the changing curriculum.

As acknowledged by Michael Burke in *The Routledge Handbook* and Craig Hamilton in the *Cambridge Handbook* respectively, stylistics has its roots in rhetoric; in Susan and Robert Cockcroft's updated volume of *Persuading People: An Introduction to Rhetoric*, the study of rhetoric is shown to have continuing relevance. This text explores persuasion in spoken and written and literary and non-literary contexts, and encourages readers to both analyse features of rhetoric and to employ rhetorical strategies in their own writing. Following Aristotle, Cockcroft and Cockcroft identify 'three permanent working principles of persuasion', which are: '*ethos* (persuasion through personality and stance); *pathos* (persuasion through the arousal of emotion); and *logos* (persuasion through reasoning)' (pp. 5–6); and these principles provide the foundation for the entire volume. Rather than situating the study of rhetoric as something of the past, the authors argue that, in fact, the art of rhetoric and the stylistic features of persuasion are pervasive in our everyday use of language today. At the end of the volume they identify how cognitive advances in the field 'are prompting new ways of thinking about rhetoric and models of argument' (p. 264).

Cockcroft and Cockcroft's acknowledgement of the usefulness of cognitive models (text-world theory, schema theory, and so on) to inform research into rhetoric signposts how cognitive stylistics continues to develop and expand. Increasingly, cognitive stylistics is beginning to explore the application of cognitive-linguistic models for stylistic analysis. *Cognitive Grammar in Literature*, edited by Chloe Harrison, Louise Nuttall, Peter Stockwell, and Wenjuan Yuan, for example, is the first book of its kind to bring together applications of Ronald Langacker's Cognitive Grammar (CG) as a stylistic model. The book features contributions from academics from a range of backgrounds, applying CG to an equally varied range of texts: from the historical to the contemporary and the postmodern; from poetry to prose and multimodal literature. Ronald Langacker contributes the foreword, where he identifies that the 'comprehensive' nature of CG, which is centred on grammar as an inherently meaningful phenomenon, means that the model is well suited to literary analysis. The volume begins by introducing and defining some of the central CG concepts: namely, 'construal', 'trajector' and 'landmark' alignment, 'image schemas', 'grounding', and 'subjectivity', amongst others. Peter Stockwell's chapter, 'War, Worlds and Cognitive Grammar' (pp. 19–34), opens the 'narrative fiction' section and provides a contrastive analysis of two sections from H.G. Wells's *War of the Worlds* [1898], using a CG consideration to trace the differences between the 'grammar of anticipation' and the 'grammar of action' to analyse the literary texture of the scene. In addition to exploring literary texture, many of the chapters in this volume also explore how attention is directed through language. Chloe Harrison's chapter 'Attentional Windowing in David Foster Wallace's "The Soul Is Not a Smithy"' (pp. 53–68), for example, considers the title's post-postmodern text, 'The Soul Is Not a Smithy', in which the central character recalls a traumatic incident from his childhood. The analysis here shows how a stylistic consideration of which portions of a narrative are windowed, gapped, or spliced successfully provides an indication of a narrator's 'mind style' (Elena Semino [2008]). Arguably, CG as a means of exploring point of view in fiction appears to be one of the more prolific and successful applications in this volume, also discussed by Louise Nuttall ('Constructing a Text World for *The Handmaid's Tale*', pp. 83–100), Elżbieta Tabakowska ('Point of View in Translation: Lewis Carroll's Alice in Grammatical Wonderlands', pp. 101–18), and Michael Pleyer and Christian W. Schneider in a multimodal context ('Construal and Comics: The Multimodal Autobiography of Alison Bechdel's *Fun Home*', pp. 35–52). Overall, this edited collection demonstrates the versatility and flexibility of the CG framework, while putting forward a convincing argument that CG has a lot to offer stylistic analysis. It provides a means of talking about the experiential processes of reading, but it is identified that more work needs to be done to test the boundaries of the model. Are there, indeed, 'limits to what CG can offer literature' (Langacker, p. 14), and where do they lie? These are questions which will hopefully be addressed in future research.

As mentioned, CG traditionally belongs to cognitive linguistics, a discipline which argues that meanings in language are embodied. Put simply, embodiment refers to how our use and understanding of language are shaped by our physical experience in the world. Increasingly, stylistic analyses are beginning to draw on cognitive-linguistic principles in order to strengthen and provide a psychological foundation for the focus on 'readerly' interpretation. Though *The Bloomsbury Companion to Cognitive Linguistics*, edited by Jeannette Littlemore and John R. Taylor, is primarily a compendium of cognitive-linguistic concepts, the text does reference clear points of contact between central cognitive-linguistic ideas and what they can offer stylistics. In chapter 5, 'Cognitive Poetics' (pp. 218–33), for example, Chloe Harrison and Peter Stockwell centre a review of the field on Keith Oatley's [2003] notion of 'writingandreading'. Through this term Oatley ([2003], p. 170) aimed 'to distinguish between general processes of cognitive construction from the discourse structure, and idiosyncratic processes of each reader'. Using reader responses to the book *Naive. Super* (Loe [2005]) from Amazon reviews, Harrison and Stockwell observe how readers use 'enacted metaphors' (Gerrig [1993]; Stockwell [2009]) to review the text. This chapter also draws together some central cognitive-linguistic components—namely, schemas, conceptual metaphors, and attenuation—to consider in more detail how readers frame their own reading experiences. Although not applied in literary contexts elsewhere in the *Companion*, these cognitive-linguistic models are expanded on in other chapters, e.g. 'Lakoff and the Theory of Conceptual Metaphor' (by Dennis Tay, pp. 49–59) and 'Embodied Metaphor' (by Raymond W. Gibbs, pp. 167–84), and certainly provide frameworks which allows stylisticians to explore the more psychological side of reading.

Corpus stylistics continues to be an increasingly popular branch of research in stylistics. In 'Reading Dickens's Characters: Employing Psycholinguistic Methods to Investigate the Cognitive Reality of Patterns in Texts', Michaela Mahlberg, Kathy Conklin, and Marie-Josée Bisson (*L&L* 23[2014] 369–88) combine psycholinguistic methods (eye-tracking (quantitative) and follow-up questionnaires (qualitative)) with corpus-stylistic analysis to explore how readers read 'body language clusters' (repeated language sequences which describe the body language of a particular character) in Dickens's fiction. This article leads on from the research in *Corpus Stylistics and Dickens's Fiction* (Mahlberg [2013]), but the psycholinguistic methods used here offer refreshing new insights into how to explore corpus data. As in Mahlberg, this article acknowledges how characterization is a much-discussed feature in Dickens, and considers, from a psycholinguistic perspective, the role readers play in processing Dickensian characters (i.e. how we draw upon schematic knowledge to help 'fill out' characters). Mahlberg et al. argue that such body-language clusters appear on a cline from more functional (i.e. helping to 'contextualize' the character within the wider scene, which is the focus in the article here) to more 'highlighting' (i.e. more likely to impact on our conceptualization of a character). In the study, participants were required to answer questions about the character in the scene provided, and the results of the study suggested that 'comprehenders remember important character information, but not necessarily the linguistic form in which this information is presented' (p. 383). The eye-tracking part of the study also suggested that some body-language clusters are read more quickly than others, which indicates that we keep such clusters as 'units' in our long-term memory. The paper concludes by arguing that the methods of psycholinguistics and cognitive linguistics can be usefully integrated: Mahlberg et al. argue that 'psycholinguistic methods can add a valuable dimension to the interpretation of corpus stylistic findings' (p. 370), especially since frequently occurring patterns are of interest to both corpus stylisticians and psycholinguists.

Another study that focuses on characterization is Elena Semino's 'Pragmatic Failure, Mind Style and Characterisation in Fiction about Autism' (*L&L* 23[2014] 141–58). In this article Semino identifies a trend in different kinds of fiction to include representations of 'autistic' characters and uses three contemporary novels in which the central character has an autism-spectrum disorder as case studies (*Speed of Dark* by Elizabeth Moon [2002]; *The Curious Incident of the Dog in the Night-Time* by Mark Haddon [2003]; and *The Language of Others* by Clare Morrall [2008]) in order to analyse how the interactional behaviour of these protagonists impacts upon their characterization. Semino observes how a distinctive 'mind style' is signposted through stylistic choices: that unintentional impoliteness is prevalent in the texts; that the maxim of relevance (and levels of informativeness) is frequently broken in dialogue; and finally how the protagonists misunderstand metaphors and figurative language. That we as readers are able to notice these patterns suggests that the novels demonstrate a defamiliarization of everyday conversational exchanges: 'schema refreshment' (Guy Cook [1994]). The paper concludes that all three novels convey a character who has difficulties with communication: protagonists who experience 'pragmatic failure' mostly because they cannot second-guess the intentions of other interlocutors.

Monika Fludernik's article, 'Collective Minds in Fact and Fiction: Intermental Thought and Group Consciousness in Early Modern Narrative' (*PoT* 35[2014] 689–720), similarly considers fictional minds but here within a particular sociocultural context: that of the early modern narrative. Fludernik combines an analysis using New Historicism and cognitive narratology (particularly Alan Palmer's [2004] work on fictional minds) and sets up a comparison between riot scenes in Sir Philip Sidney's classical text *Old Arcadia* [1580], and the 'literary representation of crowds' (p. 693) as depicted in Raphael Holinshed's *Chronicles*.

Although there is perhaps an emphasis within the discipline on focusing on literary texts, stylistic analysis is equally applicable to non-literary texts. A special issue of *Language & Literature*, edited by Marina Lambrou, showcases the versatility of the stylistic toolkit in analysing narrative in many different contexts. In 'Counter Narratives and Controversial Crimes: The Wikipedia Article for the "Murder of Meredith Kercher"' (*L&L* 23[2014] 61–76), for example, Ruth Page 'explores the relationship between macro-level social narratives and micro-level narrative analysis with reference to the counter narratives that emerge in a particular context: the chronicling of non-fictional topics in Wikipedia articles' (p. 62). In particular, Page considers the controversial Wikipedia article which documents the murder of Meredith Kercher and tracks the revisions of its various editors since it was first set up in 2007. In her analysis, Page argues that the presence of multiple tellers works to 'destabilise' (p. 74) the dominant narrative. Similarly, in 'Narrative, Text and Time: Telling the Same Story Twice in the Oral Narrative Reporting of 7/7' (*L&L* 23[2014] 32–48), Marina Lambrou analyses a retelling of the same story: in this instance, a personal narrative of one of the survivors of the 7/7 London terrorist bombings. Lambrou's article discusses how, through storytelling, people are 'able to shape and represent their lives as they (re)construct their experiences—and, in so doing, reconstruct their identity—through stylistic choices' (p. 33). In this study Lambrou focuses in particular on personal narratives as defined in the original work of William Labov and Joshua Waletzky [1967]. The article compares a transcript recording the narrative of a survivor of the 7/7 attacks, Angelo, and then another narrative recorded two and a half years later also spoken by Angelo. Lambrou argues that similarities across both of Angelo's narratives suggest that people have a 'mental story template' (p. 46); she also observes that, interestingly, Angelo 'appears to position himself outside the events as though he is a witness looking in' (p. 47), which may be a stylistic feature of dissociation in such accounts of traumatic experiences. Within this *L&L* issue, it is also demonstrated how reader-response research is an interesting way of examining the narrative effects of particular stylistic choices. Paul Simpson's article 'Just What Is Narrative *Urgency?*' (*L&L* 23[2014] 3–22) observes how readers—or, in this case, viewers—respond to narrative urgency in fiction, which he defines as the process whereby readers identify with characters and their narrative goals. Simpson draws up a general 'checklist' of stylistic features which impact upon a text's narrative urgency. These features include short sentences, the position within the wider narrative hierarchy, and the precedence of material over mental processes, amongst others. Simpson (p. 7) emphasizes that these features are not a 'rigid checklist', but rather 'a constellation of stylistic tendencies'. The paper sets up an experiment with two groups of students and explores how they respond to two different frame sequences from the film *Psycho*—specifically, the scene in which Bates is watching Marion's car sink into the swamp. Group A are shown the original clip, whereas Group B are shown an altered sequence in which the 'Kuleshov Monitor'—the shifts in camera perspective which show Bates's expression—is removed. The participants in the study were given a questionnaire, the key question of which was the final one: 'On a scale of 1–10, how much did you want the car to sink?' (p. 14). The results indicated that the presence of a narrator's facial expression directly impacts upon how readers experience narrative urgency: Group A aligned themselves with the protagonist and wanted the car to sink, whereas the results from Group B clustered around the middle of the scale. This study admits that it is experimental, but the preliminary results here indicate that future empirical research into readerly alignment with narrative urgency would be highly interesting.

Evidently the stylistics toolkit works to excavate non-literary texts as well as multi-modal narratives such as films. Since the very first stylistic analyses, however, poetry has been a mainstay of stylistic analyses. In *Narrative* 22, there was a special issue on the stylistic analysis of poetry. In 'Narrative in Concrete/Concrete in Narrative: Visual Poetry and Narrative Theory' (*Narrative* 22[2014] 234–51), Brian McAllister considers the relationship between form and content in visual poetry in particular. McAllister begins by comparing two visual poems—'ershaffung der eva' ('The Creation of Eve') by Ernst Jandl and 'Silencio' by Eugen Gomringer—which demonstrate different levels of 'narrativity' (Werner Wolf). McAllister considers first how narrativity is built in 'The Creation of Eve' largely through the intertextual link provided in the title (its reference to the biblical text Genesis 2:21–4) and argues that the narrativity in this poem 'arises by negotiating visual and semantic possibilities, balancing movement down the page with the overall shape of the poem, all processed through the title's biblical filter' (p. 238). In contrast, the poem 'Silencio' elicits an '*anti*-narrative schema' (p. 239) and has a much lower level of narrativity. He moves on to consider, amongst other examples by this poet, Ian Hamilton Finlay's 'Tea Kettle Drum Water Lily Cup', which evokes a 'cup of tea' schema, an interpretation that requires 'lots of gap-filling on the part of the reader' (p. 244). McAllister finally considers Finlay's work in context (specifically his poetry displayed in a garden, Little Sparta), and concludes that levels of narrativity are affected by poetic and narrative space. In other words, connections between poems in a situated context such as those in Little Sparta and their print-form counterparts help to 'renegotiate formal features of a text, such as semantic and visual capacities, materiality, political implications, and relationship to surrounding texts and objects' (p. 248).

In *Opposition in Discourse: The Construction of Oppositional Meaning*, Lesley Jeffries studies the semantic phenomenon of opposition, which she also labels 'constructed opposites', 'created opposites', and 'unconventional opposites'. In this volume Jeffries uses case studies to consider, amongst other aims, what 'triggers' unconventional opposites, their function in language, and the relevance of antonymy in the construction of these opposites. The text is divided into five chapters to address these ideas. The first introduces and defines opposites, and the second considers the various types of triggers: structural and lexical. Jeffries argues that such oppositions are prevalent across a variety of text types, and considers how they function in literary contexts (for example, in the poetry of Medbh McGuckian and Carol Ann Duffy, and in prose contexts such as novel openings (chapter 3)), and in non-literary discourse (such as newspaper reporting, magazines (chapter 4)). Chapter 5 looks at constructed opposites from a cognitive-linguistic perspective, and situates opposites as phenomena which are constructed by readers. In other words, Jeffries examines how a reader participates in understanding constructed opposites, and puts forward the idea of an 'opposition image-schema which, if accepted, would be one of the fundamental building-blocks of human existence and understanding' (p. 133).

In the studies reviewed thus far, stylistics has been shown to account for a wide range of texts: literary and non-literary, prose and poetry, mono-modal and multimodal. The application of literary linguistic models can also help us to explore the stylistic features of particular periods or genres. For example, Patricia Canning's monograph *Style in the Renaissance* considers 'the ways in which contemporary stylistics helps us, as readers and thinkers, to realise the meaning potential of historical and literary texts' (p. 1), and questions, in particular, how stylistics representations of ideology indicate the political and theological concerns of early modern England. Canning incorporates both traditional and cognitive stylistic tools, and explores blending in early modern poetry (chapter 1); transitivity and agency in *Macbeth* (chapter 2); representations of world-view in *Macbeth* and *The Changeling* (chapter 3); and metalinguistics and *ekphrasis* in Catholic poetry (chapter 4). Similarly, Daria Tunca's *Style in Nigerian Fiction* demonstrates how a stylistic analysis of a particular fictional genre can shed further light on its literary value. This book begins, for example, by exploring the syntactic arrangements and transitivity in characterization in Adichie's *Purple Hibiscus* [2003], and draws parallels between the patterns in the text and 'the author's awareness of the complexities of her own relationship to postcolonial Nigeria' (p. 63). Like Canning's volume, Tunca's draws upon a range of texts and stylistic frameworks, including ideology in *Half of a Yellow Sun* (Adichie [2006]) (chapter 3); and metaphor in Okri's *The Landscapes Within* [1981] and *Dangerous Love* [1996] (chapter 4), amongst others. At the end of the text Tunca puts forward the idea that a stylistic analysis of African fiction—and postcolonial fiction more generally—is a subdiscipline worth pursuing.

It is clear that stylistics is progressing in new and exciting directions, while demonstrating that the more traditional and core frameworks continue to form the cornerstones of the field. These conventional literary linguistic analyses are positioned alongside emerging applications of the discipline: namely, critical stylistics, cognitive- linguistic extensions, stylistics for pedagogy, and advances in reader-response research, amongst others. It will be interesting to see how these strands are further developed in the research of 2015.

Books Reviewed

Aarts, Bas, Sylvia Chalker, and Edmund Weiner. *The Oxford Dictionary of English Grammar*. 2nd edn. OUP. [2014] pp. x + 453. pb £11.99 ISBN 9 7801 9965 8237.

Aguilar-Guevara, Ana, Bert Le Bruyn, and Joost Zwarts, eds. *Weak Referentiality*. Benjamins. [2014] pp. xii + 390. €105 ($158) ISBN 9 7890 2725 7024.

Aijmer, Karin, and Christoph Rühlemann, eds. *Corpus Pragmatics: A Handbook*. CUP. [2014] pp. 480. £80 ISBN 9 7811 0701 5043.

Anderson, Wendy, Carole P. Biggam, Carole Hough, and Christian Kay, eds. *Colour Studies: A*. Benjamins. [2014] pp. xiv + 417. €105 ($158) ISBN 9 7890 2721 2191.

Angermuller, Johannes, Dominique Maingueneau, and Ruth Wodak, eds. *The Discourse Studies Reader: Main Currents in Theory and Analysis*. Benjamins. [2014] pp. ix + 417. hb €105 ISBN 9 7890 2721 2108, pb €33 ISBN 9 7890 2721 2115.

Baker, Paul. *Using Corpora to Analyse Gender*. Bloomsbury. [2014] pp. 240. pb £24.99 ISBN 9 7814 4110 8777.

Bamford, Julia, Silvia Cavalieri, and Giuliana Diani, eds. *Variation and Change in Spoken and Written Discourse*. Benjamins. [2013] pp. xiii + 290. €95 ISBN 9 7890 2721 0388.

Barker, Chris, and Chung-Shieh Shan. *Continuations and Natural Language*. OUP. [2014] pp. xix + 228. hb £65 ISBN 9 7801 9957 5015, pb £29.99 ISBN 9 7801 9957 5022.

Bartlett, Tom. *Analysing Power in Language: A Practical Guide*. Routledge. [2014] pp. 212. hb £85 ISBN 9 7804 1566 6312, pb £27.99 ISBN 9 7804 1566 6305.

Barysevich, Alena, Alexandra D'Arcy, and David Heap, eds. *Proceedings of Methods XIV: Papers from the Fourteenth International Conference on Methods in Dialectology, 2011*. Lang. [2014] pp. xiv + 348. £45 ISBN 9 7836 3164 3778.

Bauer, Laurie, Rochelle Lieber, and Ingo Plag. *The Oxford Reference Guide to English Morphology*. OUP. [2013] pp. xxvi + 702. hb £90 ISBN 9 7801 9957 9266, pb £35 ISBN 9 7801 9874 7062.

Bayyurt, Yasemin, and Sumru Akcan, eds. *ELF 5: Proceedings of the Fifth International Conference of English as a Lingua Franca.* Boğaziçi University Press. [2013] pp. xii + 424. Price unknown; ISBN unknown.

Bech, Kristin, and Kristine Gunn Eide, eds. *Information Structure and Syntactic Change in Germanic and Romance Languages.* Benjamins. [2014] pp. vii + 421. €105 ISBN 9 7890 2725 5969.

Belcher, Diane, and Gayle Nelson, eds. *Critical and Corpus-Based Approaches to Intercultural Rhetoric.* UMichP. [2013] pp. 264. pb $29.95 ISBN 9 7804 7203 5243.

Berry, Roger. *English Grammar: A Resource Book for Students.* Routledge. [2012] pp. 278. hb £75 ISBN 9 7804 1556 1082, pb £20 ISBN 9 7804 1556 1099.

Berthoud, Anne-Claude, François Grin, and Georges Lüdi, eds. *Exploring the Dynamics of Multilingualism: The DYLAN Project.* Benjamins. [2013] pp. xxi + 440. €99 ($149) ISBN 9 7890 2720 0563.

Björkman, Beyza. *English as an Academic Lingua Franca: An Investigation of Form and Communicative Effectiveness.* MGruyter. [2013] pp. xiv + 264. £82.99 ISBN 9 7831 1027 9146.

Bourne, Lindsey. *Lincolnshire Dialect.* Bradwell Books. [2014] pp. 80. £3.99 ISBN 9 7819 1055 1028.

Buchstaller, Isabelle, Anders Holmberg, and Mohammad Almoaily, eds. *Pidgins and Creoles beyond Africa–European Encounters.* Benjamins. [2014] pp. v + 178. €95 ISBN 9 7890 2725 2708.

Bührig, Kristin, and Bernd Meyer, eds. *Transferring Linguistic Know-How into Institutional Practice.* Benjamins. [2013] pp. vii + 151. €70 ISBN 9 7890 2721 9350.

Bunt, Harry, Johan Bos, and Stephen Pulman, eds. *Computing Meaning, vol. 4.* Springer. [2014] pp. viii + 260. £90 ISBN 9 7894 0077 2830.

Burke, Michael, ed. *The Routledge Handbook of Stylistics.* Routledge. [2014] pp. xviii + 530. £150 ISBN 9 7804 1552 7903.

Buschfeld, Sarah, Thomas Hoffmann, Magnus Huber, and Alexander Kautzsch, eds. *The Evolution of Englishes: The Dynamic Model and Beyond.* Benjamins. [2014] pp. xviii + 513. €105 ($158) ISBN 9 7890 2724 9098.

Cabredo Hofherr, Patricia, and Anne Zribi-Hertz, eds. *Crosslinguistic Studies on Noun Phrase Structure and Reference.* Brill. [2014] pp. xii + 401. €125 ($162) ISBN 9 7890 0426 0825.

Canagarajah, Suresh. *Translingual Practice: Global Englishes and Cosmopolitan Relations.* Routledge. [2013] pp. viii + 216. hb £90 ISBN 9 7804 1568 3982, pb £27.99 ISBN 9 7804 1568 4002.

Canning, Patricia. *Style in the Renaissance.* Bloomsbury. [2014] pp. ix + 209. pb $42.95 ISBN 9 7814 4118 5525.

Caspers, Johanneke, Yiya Chen, Willemijn Heeren, Jos Pacilly, Niels O. Schiller, and Ellen van Zanten, eds. *Above and Beyond the Segments: Experimental Linguistics and Phonetics.* Benjamins. [2014] pp. xii + 363. €105 ISBN 9 7890 2721 2160.

Celata, Chiara, and Silvia Calamai, eds. *Advances in Sociophonetics.* Benjamins. [2014] pp. vi + 207. €99 ISBN 9 7890 2723 4957.

Chan, Mable. *Acquisition of* Be *by Cantonese ESL Learners in Hong Kong and Its Pedagogical Implications*. Lang. [2013] pp. 427. pb £51 ISBN 9 7830 3431 3070.

Chapelle, Carol A., ed. *The Encyclopedia of Applied Linguistics*. Wiley-Blackwell. [2013] pp. 6,582. £1,285 ISBN 9 7814 0519 4730.

Chapman, Siobhan, and Billy Clark, eds. *Pragmatic Literary Stylistics*. Palgrave Studies in Pragmatics, Language and Cognition. PalMac. [2014] pp. 229 £66 ISBN 9 7811 3702 3254.

Charteris-Black, Jonathan. *Analysing Political Speeches: Rhetoric, Discourse and Metaphor*. PalMac. [2014] pp. 296. hb £75 ISBN 9 7802 3027 4389, pb £26.99 ISBN 9 7802 3027 4396.

Chitez, Madalina. *Learner Corpus Profiles: The Case of Romanian Learner English*. Lang. [2014] pp. 244. pb £51 ISBN 9 7830 3431 4107.

Chowdhury, Raqib, and Phan Le Ha. *Desiring TESOL and International Education: Market Abuse and Exploitation*. MIMBr. [2014] pp. xxiv + 262. pb £29.95 ISBN 9 7817 8309 1478.

Clark, Ian D., Luise Hercus, and Laura Kostanski. *Indigenous and Minority Placenames: Australian and International Perspectives*. ANUP. [2014] pp. vii + 398. $33 ISBN 9 7819 2502 1622.

Cockcroft, Robert, and Susan Cockcroft, eds. *Persuading People: An Introduction to Rhetoric*. 3rd edn. PalMac. [2014] pp. xvii + 323. pb £25.99 ISBN 9 7811 3700 3676.

Cole, Marcelle. *Old Northumbrian Verbal Morphosyntax and the (Northern) Subject Rule*. Benjamins. [2014] pp. xvi + 286. €99 ISBN 9 7890 2724 0712.

Coleman, Julie, ed. *Global English Slang: Methodologies and Perspectives*. Routledge. [2014] pp. 256. £105 ISBN 9 7804 1584 2679.

Colman, Fran. *The Grammar of Names in Anglo-Saxon England: The Linguistics and Culture of the Old English Onomasticon*. OUP. [2014] pp. ix + 310. £75 ISBN 9 7801 9870 1675.

Considine, John. *Academy Dictionaries 1600–1800*. CUP. [2014] pp. xi + 259. £65 ISBN 9 7811 0707 1124.

Cook, Vivian, and David Singleton. *Key Topics in Second Language Acquisition*. MlM. [2014] pp. 168. hb £59.95 ISBN 9 7817 8309 1805, pb £17.95 ISBN 9 7817 8309 1799.

Cruttenden, Alan. *Gimson's Pronunciation of English*. 8th edn. Routledge. [2014] pp. 408. hb £100 ISBN 9 7804 1572 1745, pb £32.99 ISBN 9 7814 4418 3092.

Crystal, David. *Words in Time and Place: Exploring Language through the Historical Thesaurus of the Oxford English Dictionary*. OUP. [2014] pp. xvi + 288. £16.99 ISBN 9 7801 9968 0474.

Csizér, Kata, and Michael Magid, eds. *The Impact of Self-Concept on Language Learning*. MlM. [2014] pp. xiv + 407. pb £34.95 ISBN 9 7817 8309 2369.

Culpeper, Jonathan, and Michael Haugh. *Pragmatics and the English Language*. PalMac. [2014] pp. 316. pb £22.99 ISBN 9 7802 3055 1732.

Curry, Mary Jane, and Theresa Lillis. *A Scholar's Guide to Getting Published in English: Critical Choices and Practical Strategies*. MIMBr. [2013] pp. xiv +

173. hb £69.95 ($109.95) ISBN 9 7817 8309 0600, pb £14.95 ($19.95) ISBN 9 7817 8309 0594.

De Brabanter, Philippe, Mikhail Kissine, and Saghie Sharifzadeh, eds. *Future Times, Future Tenses*. OUP. [2014] pp. xiv + 297. £69 ISBN 9 7801 9967 9157.

De Smet, Hendrik. *Spreading Patterns: Diffusional Change in the English System of Complementation*. OUP. [2013] pp. xiv + 279. £53 ISBN 9 7801 9981 2752.

Denison, David, Ricardo Bermúdez-Otero, Chris McCully, and Emma Moore. *Analysing Older English*. CUP. [2014] pp. xiii + 335. hb £62 ISBN 9 7805 2111 2468, pb £30 ISBN 9 7811 0768 1415.

Depraetere, Ilse, and Chad Langford. *Advanced English Grammar: A Linguistic Approach*. Continuum. [2013] pp. 376. hb £80 ISBN 9 7814 4111 0893, pb £26 ISBN 9 7814 4114 9312.

Deterding, David. *Misunderstandings in English as a Lingua Franca: An Analysis of ELF Interactions in South-East Asia*. MGruyter. [2013] pp. x + 208. £82.99 ISBN 9 7831 1028 6519.

Deuber, Dagmar. *English in the Caribbean: Variation, Style and Standards in Jamaica and Trinidad*. CUP. [2014] pp. xiv + 290 £65 ISBN 9 7811 0702 7473.

Deumert, Ana. *Sociolinguistics and Mobile Communication*. EdinUP. [2014] pp. xi + 200. £75 ISBN 9 7807 4865 5731.

Dixon, Robert. *Making New Words: Morphological Derivation in English*. OUP. [2014] pp. xvi + 472. hb £65 ISBN 9 7801 9871 2367, pb £35 ISBN 9 7801 9871 2374.

Dörnyei, Zoltán, Peter D. MacIntyre, and Alastair Henry. *Motivational Dynamics in Language Learning*. MlM. [2014] pp. xix + 429. hb £109.95 ISBN 9 7817 8309 2567, pb £34.95 ISBN 9 7817 8309 2550.

Durham, Mercedes. *The Acquisition of Sociolinguistic Competence in a Lingua Franca Context*. MIMBr. [2014] pp. x + 168. £79.95 ($129.95) ISBN 9 7817 8309 1430.

Durkin, Philip. *Borrowed Words: A History of Loanwords in English*. OUP. [2014] pp. xx + 492. hb £35 ISBN 9 7801 9957 4995, pb £14.24 ISBN 9 7801 9873 6493.

Edwards, John. *Sociolinguistics: A Very Short Introduction*. OUP. [2013] pp. xvii + 133. pb £7.99 ISBN 9 7801 9985 8613.

Ellis, Michael. *North Carolina English, 1861–1865: A Guide and Glossary*. UTennP. [2013] pp. lxxiv + 240. $95 ISBN 9 7816 2190 0023.

Ellis, Rod, and Natsuko Shintani. *Exploring Language Pedagogy through Second Language Acquisition Research*. Routledge/T&F. [2014] pp. 388. hb £95 ISBN 9 7804 1551 9700, pb £28.99 ISBN 9 7804 1551 9731.

Erling, Elizabeth J., and Philip Seargeant, eds. *English and Development: Policy, Pedagogy and Globalization*. MIMBr. [2013] pp. xxiii + 270. hb £99.95 ISBN 9 7818 4769 9466, pb £29.95 ISBN 9 7818 4769 9459.

Fäcke, Christiane, ed. *Manual of Language Acquisition*. MGruyter. [2014] pp. ix + 639. £149.99 ISBN 9 7831 1030 2103.

Flowerdew, John, ed. *Discourse in Context*. Bloomsbury. [2014] pp. ix + 349. pb £29.69 ISBN 9 7816 2356 3011.

Frevert, Ute, Christian Bailey, Pascal Eitler, Benno Gammerl, Bettina Hitzer, Margrit Perna, Monique Scheer, Anne Schmidt, and Nina Verheyen. *Emotional Lexicons: Continuity and Change in the Vocabulary of Feeling 1700–2000*. OUP. [2014] pp. x + 288. £68 ISBN 9 7801 9965 5731.

Fuertes-Olivera, Pedro A., and Sven Tarp. *Theory and Practice of Specialised Online Dictionaries: Lexicography Versus Terminography*. MGruyter. [2014] pp. 282. £99.95 ISBN 9 7831 1034 8835.

Gabryś-Barker, Danuta, and Adam Wojtaszek, eds. *Studying Second Language Acquisition from a Qualitative Perspective*. Springer. [2014] pp. xii + 218. £90 ISBN 9 7833 1908 3520.

Gamerschlag, Thomas, Doris Gerland, Rainer Osswald, and Wiebke Petersen, eds. *Frames and Concept Types: Applications in Language and Philosophy*. Springer. [2014] pp. x + 362. £90 ISBN 9 7833 1901 5415.

Gass, Susan M., Jennifer Behney, and Luke Plonsky. *Second Language Acquisition: An Introductory Course*. 4th edn. Routledge/T&F. [2013] pp. xxiv + 623. hb £100 ISBN 9 7804 1589 4784, pb £38.99 ISBN 9 7804 1589 4951.

Gisborne, Nikolas, and Willem B. Hollman, eds. *Theory and Data in Cognitive Linguistics*. Benjamins. [2014] pp. xi + 262. €95 ($143) ISBN 9 7890 2724 2556.

Glynn, Dylan, and Justyna Robinson. *Corpus Methods for Semantics: Quantitative Studies in Polysemy and Synonymy*. Benjamins. [2014] pp. viii + 545. £88 ISBN 9 7890 2722 3975.

Goddard, Cliff, and Anna Wierzbicka. *Words and Meanings: Lexical Semantics across Domains, Languages and Cultures*. OUP. [2014] pp. 314. £65 ISBN 9 7801 9966 8434.

Gotti, Maurizio, and Carmen Sancho Guinda, eds. *Narratives in Academic and Professional Genres*. Lang. [2013] pp. 511. pb £77 ISBN 9 7830 3431 3711.

Gramley, Stephan. *The History of English*. Routledge. [2013] pp. xxv + 414. hb £90 ISBN 9 7804 1556 6391, pb £25 ISBN 9 7804 1556 6407.

Grazzi, Enrico. *The Sociocultural Dimension of ELF in the English Classroom*. Editoriale Anicia. [2013] pp. 211. pb €22 ISBN 9 7888 6709 1232.

Green, Eugene, and Charles F. Meyer, eds. *The Variability of Current World Englishes*. MGruyter. [2014] pp. viii + 287. €99.95 ISBN 9 7831 1035 2108.

Green, Jonathon. *Language! 500 Years of the Vulgar Tongue*. Atlantic. [2014] pp. 419. £25 ISBN 9 7818 4887 8983.

Green, Jonathon. *Odd Job Man: Some Confessions of a Slang Lexicographer*. Cape. [2014] pp. 330. £17.99 ISBN 9 7802 2409 7581.

Gregersen, Tammy, and Peter D. MacIntyre. *Capitalizing on Language Learners' Individuality: From Premise to Practice*. MlM. [2014] pp. xxvii + 259. pb £29.95 ISBN 9 7817 8309 1195.

Gutzmann, Daniel, Jan Köpping, and Cécile Meier, eds. *Approaches to Meaning: Composition, Values, and Interpretation*. Brill. [2014] pp. xv + 347. €125, $162 ISBN 9 7890 0427 9360.

Gužauskytė, Evelina. *Christopher Columbus's Naming in the Diarios of the Four Voyages (1492–1504): A Discourse of Negotiation*. UTorP. [2014] pp. vii + 276. pb $48.75 ISBN 9 7814 4264 7466.

Hadikin, Glenn. *Korean English: A Corpus-Driven Study of a New English.* Benjamins. [2014] pp. xiv + 192. €90 ISBN 9 7890 2720 3700.

Han, ZhaoHong, and Elaine Tarone. *Interlanguage: Forty Years Later.* Benjamins. [2014] pp. vi + 255. hb €99 ISBN 9 7890 2721 3198, pb €36 ISBN 9 7890 2721 3204.

Hancil, Sylvie, and Ekkehard König, eds. *Grammaticalization: Theory and Data.* Benjamins. [2014] pp. vi + 293. €99 ISBN 9 7890 2725 9271.

Harris, Roy, and Christopher Hutton. *Definition in Theory and Practice: Language, Lexicography and the Law.* Continuum. [2014] pp. 238. £75 ISBN 9 7808 2649 7055.

Harrison, Chloe, Louise Nuttall, Peter Stockwell, and Wenjuan Yuan, eds. *Cognitive Grammar in Literature.* Benjamins. [2014] pp. xiv + 255. hb €99 ISBN 9 7890 2723 4049, pb €36 ISBN 9 7890 2723 4063.

Hart, Christopher. *Discourse, Grammar and Ideology: Functional and Cognitive Perspectives.* Bloomsbury. [2014] pp. 232. £75 ISBN 9 7814 4113 3571.

Haugh, Michael. *Im/Politeness Implicatures.* MGruyter. [2014] pp. xii + 357. €99.95 ISBN 9 7831 1024 0061.

Haugland, Kari E., Kevin McCafferty, and Kristian A. Rusten. *'Ye Whome the Charms of Grammar Please': Studies in English Language History in Honour of Leiv Egil Breivik.* Lang. [2014] pp. xxxiii + 411. pb £50 ISBN 9 7830 3431 7795.

Hawkins, John A. *Cross-Linguistic Variation and Efficiency.* OUP. [2014] pp. xx + 304. hb £ 37 ISBN 9 7801 9966 4993, pb £29.99 ISBN 9 7801 9966 5006.

Hemforth, Barbara, Barbara Mertins, and Cathrine Fabricius-Hansen, eds. *Psycholinguistic Approaches to Meaning and Understanding across Languages.* Springer. [2014] pp. xii + 251. £90 ISBN 9 7833 1905 6753.

Hickey, Raymond. *A Dictionary of Varieties of English.* Wiley-Blackwell. [2014] pp. ix + 456. €90 ISBN 9 7804 7065 6419.

Hilpert, Martin. *Construction Grammar and Its Application to English.* EdinUP. [2014] pp. xii + 220. hb £70 ISBN 9 7807 4867 5845, pb £19.90 9 7807 4867 5852.

Hoffmann, Thomas, and Graeme Trousdale, eds. *The Oxford Handbook of Construction Grammar.* OUP. [2013] pp. 606. £105 ISBN 9 7801 9539 6683.

Hogg, Richard, and Rona Alcorn. *An Introduction to Old English.* 2nd edn. EdinUP. [2013] pp. x + 163. pb £14 ISBN 9 7801 9521 9487.

Holmes, Janet, and Kirk Hazen, eds. *Research Methods in Sociolinguistics: A Practical Guide.* Wiley-Blackwell. [2014] pp. xi + 336. hb £66.95 ISBN 9 7804 7067 3607, pb £30.50 ISBN 9 7804 7167 3614.

Horobin, Simon. *Does Spelling Matter?* OUP. [2014] pp. x + 270. hb £20.99 ISBN 9 7801 9966 5280, pb £12.99 ISBN 9 7801 9872 2984.

Hummel, Kirsten M. *Introducing Second Language Acquisition: Perspectives and Practices.* Wiley-Blackwell. [2014] pp. xii + 274. hb £65 ISBN 9 7804 7065 8031, pb £24.50 ISBN 9 7804 7065 8048.

Hundt, Marianne, ed. *Late Modern English Syntax.* CUP. [2014] pp. xxi + 385. £65 ISBN 9 7811 0703 2798, eBook $79 ISBN 9 7811 3999 0097.

Hundt, Marianne, and Devyani Sharma, eds. *English in the Indian Diaspora.* Benjamins. [2014] pp. ix + 242. €99 ISBN 9 7890 2724 9104.

Jacobson, Pauline. *Compositional Semantics: An Introduction to the Syntax/ Semantics Interface*. OUP. [2014] pp. xx + 427. hb £65 ISBN 9 7801 9967 7146, pb £24.99 9 7801 9967 7153.

Janson, Tore. *The History of Languages*. OUP. [2013] pp. xiii + 280. hb £59 ISBN 9 7801 9960 4289, pb £21 ISBN 9 7801 9960 4296.

Jary, Mark, and Mikhail Kissine. *Imperatives*. CUP. [2014] pp. viii + 326. hb £69.99 ISBN 9 7811 0701 2349, pb £25.99 ISBN 9 7811 0763 2356.

Jaworski, Adam, and Nikolas Coupland, eds. *The Discourse Reader*. 3rd edn. Routledge. [2014] pp. 518. hb £100 ISBN 9 7804 1562 9485, pb £38.99 ISBN 9 7804 1562 9492.

Jeffries, Lesley. *Opposition in Discourse: The Construction of Oppositional Meaning*. Bloomsbury. [2014] pp. viii + 150. pb £14.99 ISBN 9 7814 7252 8384.

Jegerski, Jill, and Bill Van Patten, eds. *Research Methods in Second Language Psycholinguistics*. Routledge /T&F. [2014] pp. 256. hb £100 ISBN 9 7804 1551 8253, pb £36.99 ISBN 9 7804 1551 8260.

Jenkins, Jennifer. *English as a Lingua Franca in the International University: The Politics of Academic English Language Policy*. Routledge. [2014] pp. viii + 243. hb £105 ISBN 9 7804 1568 4637, pb £30 ISBN 9 7804 1568 4644.

Jenks, Christopher. *Social Interaction in Second Language Chat Rooms*. EdinUP. [2014] pp. viii + 176. hb £75 ISBN 9 7807 4864 9495, pb £24.99 ISBN 9 7807 4864 9488.

Jiménez Catalán, Rosa María, ed. *Lexical Availability in English and Spanish as a Second Language*. Springer. [2014] pp. xiv + 205. £90 ISBN 9 7894 0077 1574.

Johannesson Nils-Lennart, Gunnel Melchers, and Beyza Björkman, eds. *Of Butterflies and Birds, of Dialects and Genres: Essays in Honour of Philip Shaw*. Acta Universitatis Stockholmiensis. [2013] pp. 390. pb n.p. ISBN 9 7891 8723 5344. Available online at http://su.diva-portal.org/smash/get/ diva2:629596/FULLTEXT01.

Kalocsai, Karolina. *Communities of Practice and English as a Lingua Franca: A Study of Erasmus Students in a Central European Context*. MGruyter. [2013] pp. viii + 254. £74.99 ($140) ISBN 9 7831 1029 5474.

Kamińska, Patrycja Marta. *Learning Styles and Second Language Education*. CambridgeSP. [2014] pp. viii + 137. £39.99 ISBN 9 7814 4385 4054.

Kecskés, István, and Jesús Romero-Trillo, eds. *Research Trends in Intercultural Pragmatics*. MGruyter. [2013] pp. xiv + 508. €129.95 ISBN 9 7816 1451 5111.

Klein, Perry D., Pietro Boscolo, Lori C. Kirkpatrick, and Carmen Gelati. *Writing as a Learning Activity. Studies in Writing*. Brill. [2014] pp. viii + 388. €125 ISBN 9 7890 0425 9676.

Klimczak-Pawlak, Agata. *Towards the Pragmatic Core of English for European Communication: The Speech Act of Apologising in Selected Euro-Englishes*. Springer. [2014] pp. xi + 140. £90 ISBN 9 7833 1903 5567.

Kunnan, Antony John, ed. *The Companion to Language Assessment: Abilities, Contexts, and Learners*. Wiley-Blackwell. [2014] pp. 2240. £495 ISBN 9 7804 7065 5337.

Ladefoged, Peter, and Keith Johnson. *A Course in Phonetics*. 7th edn. Wadsworth. [2014] pp. 352. £93.99 ISBN 9 7812 8546 3407.

Lasagabaster, David, Aintzane Doiz, and Juan Manuel Sierra. *Motivation and Foreign Language Learning: From Theory to Practice*. Benjamins. [2014] pp. 248. hb £95 ISBN 9 7890 2721 3228, pb £33 ISBN 9 7890 2721 3235.

Lawson, Robert, ed. *Sociolinguistics in Scotland*. PalMac. [2014] pp. xxi + 336. £70 ISBN 9 7811 3703 4700.

Leclercq, Pascale, Amanda Edmonds, and Heather Hilton, eds. *Measuring L2 Proficiency: Perspectives from SLA*. MlM. [2014] pp. 248. hb £99.95 ISBN 9 7817 8309 2284, pb £29.95 ISBN 9 7817 8309 2277.

Leech, Geoffrey. *The Pragmatics of Politeness*. OUP. [2014] pp. 368. hb £68 ISBN 9 7801 9534 1386, pb £27.49 ISBN 9 7801 9534 1355.

Lefebvre, Claire. *Relabeling in Language Genesis*. OUP. [2014] pp. xiv + 328. £64 ISBN 9 7801 9994 5290.

Leiss, Elisabeth, and Werner Abraham, eds. *Modes of Modality: Modality, Typology, and Universal Grammar*. Benjamins. [2014] pp. vi + 511. €105 ($158) ISBN 9 7890 2720 6169.

Leung, Constant, and Brian V. Street, eds. *The Routledge Companion to English Studies*. Routledge. [2014] pp. xxx + 490. £150 ISBN 9 7804 1567 6182.

Levis, John M., and Alene Moyer, eds. *Social Dynamics in Second Language Accent*. MGruyter. [2014] pp. vi + 297. £74.99 ISBN 9 7816 1451 2288.

Littlemore, Jeannette, and John R. Taylor, eds. *The Bloomsbury Companion to Cognitive Linguistics*. Bloomsbury. [2014] pp. xi + 371. £90 ISBN 9 7814 4119 5098.

Loewen, Shawn. *Introduction to Instructed Second Language Acquisition*. Routledge/T&F. [2014] pp. 210. hb £89.99 ISBN 9 7804 1552 9532, pb £32.99 ISBN 9 7804 1552 9549.

Long, Mike. *Second Language Acquisition and Task-Based Language Teaching*. Wiley-Blackwell. [2014] pp. xiii + 439. hb £80.50 ISBN 9 7804 7065 8932, pb £36.95 ISBN 9 7804 7065 8949.

Łyda, Andrzej, and Konrad Szcześniak, eds. *Awareness in Action: The Role of Consciousness in Language Acquisition*. Springer. [2014] pp. xvi + 268. £90 ISBN 9 7833 1900 4600.

MacKenzie, Ian. *English as a Lingua Franca: Theorizing and Teaching English*. Routledge. [2014] pp. x + 204. hb £100 ISBN 9 7804 1580 9900, pb £31.99 ISBN 9 7804 1580 9917.

Marlina, Roby, and Ram Ashish Giri, eds. *The Pedagogy of English as an International Language: Perspectives from Scholars, Teachers, and Students*. Springer. [2014] pp. x + 265. €99.99 ISBN 9 7833 1906 1269.

Matthews, Peter H. *The Positions of Adjectives in English*. OUP. [2014] pp. ix + 190. £60 ISBN 9 7801 9968 1594.

McColl Millar, Robert, William Barras, and Lisa Marie Bonnici. *Lexical Variation and Attrition in the Scottish Fishing Communities*. EdinUP. [2014] pp. v + 194. £70 ISBN 9 7807 4869 1777.

McCready, Eric, Katsuhiko Yabushita, and Kei Yoshimoto, eds. *Formal Approaches to Semantics and Pragmatics: Japanese and Beyond*. Springer. [2014] pp. viii + 374. £117 ISBN 9 7894 0178 8120.

Meibauer, Jörg. *Lying at the Semantics-Pragmatics Interface.* Mouton. [2014] pp. ix + 256. €99.95 ISBN 9 7816 1451 0925.

Mercer, Sarah, and Marion Williams, eds. *Multiple Perspectives on the Self in SLA.* MIM. [2014] pp. xi + 188. pb £24.95 ISBN 9 7817 8309 1348.

Mitchell, Rosamond, Florence Myles, and Emma Marsden. 3rd edn. *Second Language Learning Theories.* Routledge/T&F. [2013] pp. xvii + 379. hb £90 ISBN 9 7804 1582 5832, pb £31.99 ISBN 9 7814 4416 3100.

Morgan, Marcyliena. *Speech Communities.* CUP. [2014] pp. xi + 190. hb £50 ISBN 9 7811 0702 3505, pb £18.99 ISBN 9 7811 0767 8149.

Motschenbacher, Heiko. *New Perspectives on English as a European Lingua Franca.* Benjamins. [2013] pp. xii + 249. €99 ($149) ISBN 9 7890 2721 2078.

Muller, Theron, John Adamson, Philip Shigeo Brown, and Steven Herder, eds. *Exploring EFL Fluency in Asia.* PalMac. [2014] pp. xxii + 331. €99.99 ISBN 9 7811 3744 9399.

Müller-Spitzer, Carolin, ed. *Using Online Dictionaries.* MGruyter. [2014] pp. vi + 386. £99.95 ISBN 9 7831 1034 1164.

Murphy, Victoria. *Second Language Learning in the Early School Years: Trends and Contexts.* OUP. [2014] pp. xv + 208. pb £32 ISBN 9 7801 9434 8850.

Neck, Reinhard, Heinrich Schmidinger, and Susanne Weigelin-Schwiedrzik, eds. *Kommunikation—Objekt und Agens von Wissenschaft.* Böhlau. [2013] pp. 198. pb €29.90 ISBN 9 7832 0579 4899.

Newman, Michael. *New York City English.* Mouton. [2014] pp. ix + 181. hb €89.95 ISBN 9 7816 1451 2899, eBook €89.95 ISBN 9 7815 0140 0602.

Newmeyer, Frederick J., and Laurel B. Preston, eds. *Measuring Grammatical Complexity.* OUP. [2014] pp. xvi + 370. £65 ISBN 9 7801 9968 5301.

North, Brian. *The CEFR in Practice.* CUP. [2014] pp. 283. pb £40.10 ISBN 9 7811 0741 4594.

Orman, Will, and Matthew James Valleau. *Proceedings of the 38th Annual Boston University Conference on Language Development.* Cascadilla. [2014] pp. vii + 496 (2-volume set). hb $140 ISBN 9 7815 7473 1958, pb $64 ISBN 9 7815 7473 0951.

Pavlenko, Aneta. *The Bilingual Mind and What It Tells Us about Language and Thought.* CUP. [2014] pp. xv + 382. pb £21.99 ISBN 9 7805 2171 6567.

Pawlak, Mirosław, and Larissa Aronin, eds. *Essential Topics in Applied Linguistics and Multilingualism: Studies in Honor of David Singleton.* Springer. [2014] pp. viii + 305. £117 ISBN 9 7833 1901 4135.

Pawlak, Mirosław, Jakub Bielak, and Anna Mystkowska-Wiertelak, eds. *Classroom-Oriented Research: Achievements and Challenges.* Springer. [2014] pp. xvii + 301. £117 ISBN 9 7833 1900 1876.

Pérez-Vidal, Carmen, ed. *Language Acquisition in Study Abroad and Formal Instruction Contexts.* Benjamins. [2014] pp. vi + 329. €95 ISBN 9 7890 2720 5315.

Petré, Peter. *Constructions and Environments: Copular, Passive, and Related Constructions in Old and Middle English.* OUP. [2014] pp. xvi + 295. £51 ISBN 9 7801 9937 3390.

Pfenninger, Simone E., Olga Timofeeva, Anne-Christine Gardner, Alpo Honkapohja, Marianne Hundt, and Daniel Schreier, eds. *Contact,*

Variation, and Change in the History of English. Studies in Language Companion Series 159. Benjamins. [2014] pp. vi + 326. €99 ($149) ISBN 9 7890 2725 9240, eBook €99 ($149) ISBN 9 7890 2726 9935.

Phakiti, Aek. *Experimental Research Methods in Language Learning*. Bloomsbury. [2014] pp. 384. hb £75 ISBN 9 7814 4112 5873, pb £24.99 ISBN 9 7814 4118 9110.

Pistoia Reda, Salvatore, ed. *Pragmatics, Semantics and the Case of Scalar Implicatures*. Palgrave. [2014] ix + 242. £63 ISBN 9 7811 3733 3278.

Podesva, Robert J., and Devyani Sharma, eds. *Research Methods in Linguistics*. CUP. [2014] pp. xvii + 525. hb £69.99 ISBN 9 7811 0701 4336, pb £26.99 ISBN 9 7811 0769 6358.

Pons-Sanz, Sara M. *The Language of Early English Literature: From Caedmon to Milton*. Palgrave. [2014] pp. xviii + 278. pb £20.99 ISBN 9 7802 3029 1423.

Raso, Tommaso, and Heliana Mello, eds. *Spoken Corpora and Linguistic Studies*. Benjamins. [2014] pp. vii + 498. €99 ($149) ISBN 9 7890 2720 3694.

Reithofer, Karin. *Englisch als Lingua Franca und Dolmetschen: Ein Vergleich zweier Kommunikationsmodi unter dem Aspekt der Wirkungsäquivalenz*. Narr. [2014] pp. 304. pb €64 ISBN 9 7838 2336 7956.

Rhys, Catrin S., Pavel Iosad, and Alison Henry. *Minority Languages, Microvariation, Minimalism and Meaning: Proceedings of the Irish Network in Formal Linguistics*. CambridgeSP. [2013] pp. xiv + 289. £49.99 ISBN 9 7814 4385 0360.

Ringe, Don, and Ann Taylor *The Development of Old English*. OUP. [2014] pp. xiii + 545. £60 ISBN 9 7801 9920 7848.

Roeper, Tom, and Margaret Speas, eds. *Recursion: Complexity in Cognition*. Springer. [2014] pp. xxi + 267. hb £90 ISBN 9 7833 1905 0850, pb £26.99 ISBN 9 7833 1915 5746.

Romero-Trillo, Jesús. *Yearbook of Corpus Linguistics and Pragmatics 2014: New Empirical and Theoretical Paradigm*. Springer. [2014] pp. vii + 346. $179 ISBN 9 7833 1906 0064.

Rosen, Anna. *Grammatical Variation and Change in Jersey English*. Benjamins. [2014] pp. xii + 237. €99 ISBN 9 7890 2724 9081.

Rutten, Gijsbert, Rik Vosters, and Wim Vandenbussche, eds. *Norms and Usage in Language History, 1600–1900: A Sociolinguistic and Comparative Perspective*. Advances in Historical Sociolinguistics 3. Benjamins. [2014] pp. viii + 334. €99 ($149) ISBN 9 7890 2720 0822, eBook €99 ($149) ISBN 9 7890 2726 8792.

Schneider, Klaus P., and Anne Barron, eds. *Pragmatics of Discourse*. MGruyter. [2014] pp. 628. €199 ISBN 9 7831 1021 4390.

Schramm, Mareile. *The Emergence of Creole Syllable Structure: A Cross-Linguistic Study*. MGruyter. [2014] pp. xii + 416. €99.95 ISBN 9 7831 1033 9567.

Schreier, Daniel. *Variation and Change in English: An Introduction*. Schmidt. [2014] pp. 163. pb €19.95 ISBN 9 7835 0515 5071.

Senft, Gunter. *Understanding Pragmatics*. Routledge. [2014] pp. 222. hb £85 ISBN 9 7804 1584 0569, pb £27.99 ISBN 9 7814 4418 0305.

Sharifian, Farzad, and Maryam Jamarani, eds. *Language and Intercultural Communication in the New Era*. Routledge. [2013] pp. vii + 316. hb £95 ISBN 9 7804 1580 8897, pb £34.99 ISBN 9 7811 3891 0836.

Sharwood Smith, Michael, and John Truscott. *The Multilingual Mind: A Modular Processing Perspective*. CUP. [2014] pp. xvii + 410. £39.99 ISBN 9 7811 0704 0854.

Singleton, David M., Joshua A. Fishman, Larissa Aronin, and Muiris Ó Laoire, eds. *Current Multilingualism: A New Linguistic Dispensation*. MGruyter. [2013] pp. vi + 376. £82.99 ISBN 9 7816 1451 3896.

Stein, Gabriele. *Sir Thomas Elyot as Lexicographer*. OUP. [2014] pp. vii + 439. £75 ISBN 9 7801 9968 3192.

Stenström, Anna-Brita. *Teenage Talk: From General Characteristics to the Use of Pragmatic Markers in a Contrastive Perspective*. PalMac. [2014] pp. ix + 139. £45 ISBN 9 7811 3743 0373.

Stockwell, Peter, and Sara Whiteley, eds. *The Cambridge Handbook of Stylistics*. CUP. [2014] pp. xvi + 689. £105 ISBN 9 7811 0702 8876.

Świątek, Artur. *The Order of the Acquisition of the English Article System by Polish Learners in Different Proficiency Groups*. CambridgeSP. [2014] pp. 185. £39.99 ISBN 9 7814 4385 6294.

Szmrecsanyi, Benedikt, and Bernhard Wälchli, eds. *Aggregating Dialectology, Typology, and Register Analysis: Linguistic Variation in Text and Speech*. Mouton. [2014] pp. vi + 472. €119.95 ISBN 9 7831 1031 7398.

Szpyra-Kozłowska, Jolanta. *Pronunciation in EFL Instruction: A Research-Based Approach*. MlM. [2014] pp. xi + 249. hb £99.95 ISBN 9 7817 8309 2611, pb £24.95 ISBN 9 7817 8309 2604.

Szubko-Sitarek, Weronika, Łukasz Salski, and Piotr Stalmaszczyk, eds. *Language Learning, Discourse and Communication: Studies in Honour of Jan Majer*. Springer. [2014] pp. xv + 272. £90 ISBN 9 7833 1900 4181.

Taavitsainen, Irma, Andreas H. Jucker, and Jukka Tuominen, eds. *Diachronic Corpus Pragmatics*. Pragmatics and Beyond New Series. Benjamins. [2014] pp. viii + 335. €95 ISBN 9 7890 2725 6485.

Taboada, Maite, and Radoslava Trnavac, eds., *Nonveridicality and Evaluation: Theoretical, Computational and Corpus Approaches*. Brill. [2014] pp. vi + 222. €98 ISBN 9 7890 0425 8167.

Thieberger, Nicholas, ed. *The Oxford Handbook of Linguistic Fieldwork*. OUP. [2014] pp. xiv + 545. hb £100 ISBN 9 7801 9957 1888, pb £30 ISBN 9 7801 9968 9811.

Thompson, Geoff, and Laura Alba-Juez. *Evaluation in Context*. Benjamins. [2014] pp. xi + 418. €99 ISBN 9 7890 2725 6478.

Thorne, Sara. *Practical Grammar*. Palgrave. [2012] pp. 336. pb £20 ISBN 9 7802 3054 2907.

Tizón-Couto, Beatriz. *Clausal Complements in Native and Learner Spoken English: A Corpus-Based Study with Lindsei and Vicolse*. Lang. [2014] pp. 349. pb £65 ISBN 9 7830 3431 1847.

Truscott, John. *Consciousness and Second Language Learning*. MlM. [2014] pp. vii + 290. hb £99.95 ISBN 9 7817 8309 2666, pb £29.95 ISBN 9 7817 8309 2659.

Tunca, Daria. *Stylistics Approaches to Nigerian Fiction*. PalMac. [2014] pp. ix + 216. £55 ISBN 9 7811 3726 4404.

van Ostade, Ingrid Tieken-Boon. *In Search of Jane Austen. The Language of the Letters*. [2013] OUP. pp. xii + 304. £44.99. ISBN 9 7801 9994 5115.

Vandelanotte, Lieven, Kristin Davidse, Caroline Gentens, and Ditte Kimps, eds. *Recent Advances in Corpus Linguistics: Developing and Exploiting Corpora*. Brill/Rodopi. [2014] pp. x + 349. €77 ($103) ISBN 9 7890 4203 8714.

Vettorel, Paola. *English as a Lingua Franca in Wider Networking: Blogging Practices*. MGruyter. [2014] pp. xxx + 348. £74.99 ($140) ISBN 9 7831 1032 2859.

Walkden, George. *Syntactic Reconstruction and Proto-Germanic*. OUP. [2014] pp. 296. £65 ISBN 9 7801 9871 2299.

Watt, Dominic, and Carmen Llamas, eds. *Language, Borders and Identity*. EdinUP. [2014] pp. xvii + 268. pb £22.99 ISBN 9 7807 4866 9776.

Wells, John Christopher. *Sounds Interesting: Observations on English and General Phonetics*. CUP. [2014] pp. 217. hb £54.99 ISBN 9 7811 0707 4705, pb £17.99 ISBN 9 7811 0742 7105.

Wiltschko, Martina. *The Universal Structure of Categories: Towards a Formal Typology*. CUP. [2014] pp. xx + 356. £65, $99 ISBN 9 7811 0703 8516.

Winkler, Elizabeth Grace. *Understanding Language: A Basic Course in Linguistics*. 2nd edn. Continuum. [2012] pp. 326. pb $30 ISBN 9 7814 4116 0799.

Wolfram, Walt, and Jeffrey Reaser. *Talkin' Tar Heel: How Our Voices Tell the Story of North Carolina*. UNCP. [2014] pp. xiii + 331. $30 ISBN 9 7814 6961 4366.

Xia, Xiaoyan. *Categorization and L2 Vocabulary Learning: A Cognitive Linguistic Perspective*. Lang. [2014] pp. xvi + 299. £47 ISBN 9 7836 3165 0103.

Zanuttini, Raffaella, and Laurence R. Horn, eds. *Micro-Syntactic Variation in North American English*. OUP. [2014] pp. 365. hb £64 ISBN 9 7801 9936 7221, pb £25.99 ISBN 9 7801 9936 7214.

Zeevat, Henk. *Language Production and Interpretation: Linguistics Meets Cognition*. Brill. [2014] pp. xv + 220. €98, $127 ISBN 9 7890 0425 2899.

Zimman, Lal, Jenny L. Davis, and Joshua Raclaw, eds. *Queer Excursions: Retheorizing Binaries in Language, Gender, and Sexuality*. OUP. [2014] pp. xii + 231. hb £64 ISBN 9 7801 9993 7295, pb £22.99 ISBN 9 7801 9993 7318.

Zipp, Lena. *Educated Fiji English: Lexico-Grammar and Variety Status*. Benjamins. [2014] pp. xviii + 230. €99 ISBN 9 7890 2724 9074.

II

Old English

ERIC LACEY, VICTORIA SYMONS, SIMON THOMSON, AND
CHRISTINE WALLIS

This chapter has ten sections: 1. Bibliography; 2. Manuscript Studies,
Palaeography, and Facsimiles; 3. Cultural and Intellectual Contexts; 4.
Literature: General; 5. The Poems of the Exeter Book; 6. The Poems of the
Vercelli Book; 7. The Poems of the Junius Manuscript; 8. *Beowulf* and the
Beowulf Manuscript; 9. Other Poems; 10. Prose. Sections 1, 4, and 6 are by
Christine Wallis; sections 2, 7, and 8 are by Simon Thomson; sections 3 and 10
are by Eric Lacey; sections 5 and 9 are by Victoria Symons.

1. Bibliography

The *Old English Newsletter* volumes 45:i and 45:iii were published in 2014. The
annual bibliography has been delayed, and so did not appear; however, a
number of subject-specific bibliographies were included: Thomas N. Hall, 'A
Handlist of Anglo-Latin Hagiography, through the Early Twelfth Century
(from Theodore of Tarsus to William of Malmesbury)' (*OENews* 45:i[2014]
1A–23A), as well as S.J. Harris, 'The Library of the Venerable Bede' (*OENews*
45:i[2014] 1B–17B). The sixteenth annual report of the Anglo-Saxon Plant
Name Survey (ASPNS) is supplied by C.P. Biggam (*OENews* 45:iii[2014]
22–4). The *OENews* website also includes a searchable bibliographic database
free to all users who register.

2. Manuscript Studies, Palaeography, and Facsimiles

Two volumes vie to be the most significant publications of 2014 in this
category. Peter Stokes's *English Vernacular Minuscule from Æthelred to
Cnut, circa 990—circa 1035* is an authoritative assessment of the most
important scribal hand in late Anglo-Saxon England, as well as being a major
statement of method. Helmut Gneuss and Michael Lapidge's *Anglo-Saxon
Manuscripts: A Bibliographical Handlist of Manuscripts Written or Owned in
England up to 1100* is an essential reference volume, the culmination of

The Year's Work in English Studies, Volume 95 (2016) © *The Author 2016. Published by Oxford
University Press on behalf of the English Association. All rights reserved.*
For Permissions, please email: journals.permissions@oup.com
doi:10.1093/ywes/maw001

Gneuss's long-running work to catalogue all manuscripts produced or owned in Anglo-Saxon England.

Vernacular minuscule is the hand that became dominant in the eleventh century for writing in English, often called insular minuscule in earlier scholarship. Examples vary quite strongly from one another, and it is no mean feat to control the vast amount of variant data let alone begin to consider implications for regionality and formality of production. Stokes's book provides meticulous descriptions of significant letterforms in an enormous number of manuscripts, grouping around 500 scribal hands by specific shared features with a quasi-mathematical, binary definition of when specific features are present and when they are not. The exhaustive nature of descriptions and comparisons, along with a fine index, makes the book an effective work of reference. The aspiration towards objective descriptions of letterforms and their features, thankfully assisted by a glossary and a few plates, is part of a project to shape the practice of palaeography also demonstrated in the Digipal project, and the terms and processes displayed here will surely become standard palaeographical practice. Stokes's meticulous work extends to discussing scribbles and glosses (important in the early development of the hand). Read continuously, this level of exactitude and detail verges towards the overwhelming, and conclusions about people's behaviours and attitudes towards the texts they worked on risk being obscured by the weight of so many pieces of specific evidence. For the reader, the comparisons between hands and understanding of individual hands becomes more focused on Stokes's categories and classifications than giving any visual sense of the hands themselves. And with all letterforms broken down into so many constituent parts in an attempt to provide objective rather than impressionistic judgements, it becomes impossible for the reader to assess how similar or dissimilar hands actually are. This difficulty is recognized by the author, whose suggestions about provenance and influence are consistently hedged about with uncertainty, identifying possible 'spheres of influence' rather than grouping and circumscribing manuscripts' places and dates of production. This may prove frustrating for some readers, used to a palaeography that provides confident statements about dating and provenance. It is perhaps questionable that, having broken down some existing categorizations, Stokes nonetheless gives some space to describing what particular house styles might have been. The more discursive sections of the book, though, emphasize that 'scribes were human beings, not machines, and so they did not always follow the "rules" rigorously—or at least, not the rules as constructed by modern palaeographers' (p. 198). Stokes's definitions of letters and rejection of impressionistic discussion form the basis of an argument for moving away from pretending that palaeography can construct boundaries or define what individuals were doing and why in particular contexts. A relatively easy criticism of the volume would be that it is overwhelmed by data, with few concrete results. Yet the challenge this methodology and its early results present to palaeography and palaeographical certainties is considerable.

A considerable expansion of the 2001 publication of the same name, Gneuss and Lapidge's *Handlist* lists 1,291 manuscripts and fragments. As in previous iterations, entries give Gneuss number and shelfmark, brief information about date and provenance, followed by contents. The most valuable part of each entry is clearly the bibliography provided for each manuscript, divided into descriptions of the manuscript, art-historical analyses of decoration, reproductions, editions using the manuscript, and other studies. The compression necessary to keep the volume to a reasonable size makes these bibliographies a little challenging to use. Even the subtitles are abbreviated to two, three, or four letters; works are given in undifferentiated form by author and date so it is not always clear when a reference is to a work discussing the manuscript in detail, or merely a broader piece which mentions the manuscript. This is, of course, in itself a mark of the authors' achievement. The *Handlist* is an epic achievement and will be a cornerstone of Anglo-Saxon manuscript studies for the foreseeable future.

Thomas Bredehoft's *The Visible Text: Textual Production and Reproduction from 'Beowulf' to 'Maus'* makes a challenging argument about reading texts in their manuscript context, arguing that we should 'see what is there, rather than reading through it to gain access to an imagined locus of intention' (p. 49). Bredehoft's book is the latest to argue for the validity and value of texts as they appear in their manuscript contexts, as unique 'productions' rather than frequently flawed attempts at 're-productions'. Some detailed attention is paid to the Franks Casket, *Beowulf*, and *The Dream of the Rood* along with some broader discussion of Anglo-Saxon attitudes towards copying texts and interesting discussion of Alfredian texts. Bredehoft discusses manuscripts in relation to comics, arguing for the process of reading as an act of seeing, engaging with manuscript texts as artefacts which do not point towards an ideal or originary text, and do not supply paratexts, but function as individualized instantiations. This leads to some engagingly dramatic statements, such as '*Beowulf* . . . is not a text . . . *Beowulf* should be seen as a unique artefact, rather than a copy of anything at all' (p. 19). There are weaknesses in his discussion. So, for instance, when Bredehoft proposes that because modern definitions we impose on texts are not imposed by manuscripts, 'in their manuscript context, they operate outside of the paratextual definition of text entirely' (p. 46) he overstates his case, given that manuscripts do define their texts, even if their distinctions and divisions are not the ones we would always choose, and that elements such as script size, scribal hand, use of colour, and so on are increasingly regarded as paratextual features that shape interpretation. It is unfortunate, too, that Bredehoft does not discuss attitudes towards the copying process in more detail. Ælfric's concern with being copied accurately, for instance, would have provided a later correlating instance for his discussion of Bede's interest in authority, and there could be more discussion of the attempts to authoritatively reproduce texts in the period. Perhaps the provocative and productive statements he makes could be more readily followed up if the book proposed some form of continuum from productive to reproductive with a discussion of indications that a particular copy inclines one way or another, rather than assigning manuscripts to one category or another. But this is to miss the point of a rhetorically forceful and engaging study, which draws attention to the making of meaning through interactions between readers and manuscripts and gives much room for future study in an engaging, informed, and challenging text.

Thomas Gobbitt examines 'The Manuscript Contexts of the Old English *frið* of Ælfred and Guðrum' (*Manuscripta* 57:i[2013] 29–56). Both Old English copies of the treaty are written by the same scribe in the twelfth-century MS Cambridge, Corpus Christi College, 383. Comparisons of words, graphs, and abbreviations per line in the two versions seem to ascribe more significance to subtle differences than is perhaps warranted, but leads to an interesting proposal that the first copy of Alfred's treaty with Guthrum was deliberately shaped to stand on a page facing the opening of the legal code ascribed to Edward. Gobbitt accumulates detailed observations to produce conclusions of genuine significance for the understanding of the production of manuscripts and meaning-making processes in the period.

In 'The Old English *Promissio Regis*, A Newly Discovered Transcript' (*N&Q* 61[2014] 337–9), Nicholas Sparks transcribes and discusses John Jocelyn's transcription of the *Promissio Regis*, recorded in London, British Library, Cotton MS Tiberius B. IV, on fo. 54ʳ. As Sparks shows, the copy is textually fairly insignificant as Jocelyn probably worked from London, British Library, Cotton MS Cleopatra B. XIII, fos. 56–7. It is, however, of interest that Sparks can reconstruct what Jocelyn was looking at, and identify from annotations that Jocelyn seems to have connected the text with Dunstan's 978 coronation of Æthelred, a reading Sparks follows.

3. Cultural and Intellectual Contexts

Stacey S. Klein, William Schipper, and Shannon Lewis-Simpson, eds., *The Maritime World of the Anglo-Saxons*, contains a number of relevant essays. Juliet Mullins's '*Herimum in Mari:* Anglo-Saxon Attitudes towards *Peregrinatio* and the Ideal of a Desert in the Sea' (pp. 59–73) considers the physical realities of sea-travel and its spiritual significance, particularly the problem that, while the Irish tradition of *peregrinatio* views the sea as a desert apt for spiritual exile, this kind of viewpoint is only alluded to in some Old English poems, and is not appreciably present in Anglo-Latin sources. Mullins surveys the sea-pilgrimage theme in Old English and in Anglo-Latin and argues that the sea stood for something quite different for the Anglo-Saxons: not a desert for spiritual solitude and contemplation, but a metaphor for the tumult of secular problems, and a promotion of dynamic activity in response to this and in their meditation. Gale Owen-Crocker's '". . . *Velis Venti Pleni*. . .": Sea Crossings in the Bayeux Tapestry' (pp. 131–56) returns to the symbolism of sea-crossings, and examines the representation of four voyages depicted on the Bayeux Tapestry (Harold's voyage to France, Harold's return to England, the messenger reporting Harold's accession to William, and William's invasion), and draws attention to their foreshadowing and parallelisms. These, she argues, portray a narrative quite contrary to the common Norman narratives downplaying Harold's legitimacy and competency, and instead set him up as a worthy adversary who is bested by William. Allen Frantzen's '*Be mihtigum mannum:* Power, Penance and Food in Late Anglo-Saxon England' (pp. 157–85) is a fluent negotiation of what both archaeological and literary evidence can tell us about the relationship between social standing, diet, and penance. One novelty here is Frantzen's demonstration that 'the late Anglo-Saxon Church used a new handbook of penance to introduce a commutation related to food practice' (p. 163). Specifically, Frantzen demonstrates that the wealthier members of society were able to atone for their sins materially (whether through alms-giving or freeing slaves) or by passing their fast on to poorer members of society (pp. 164–71), and that atonement in this way could function as a social marker. The other novelty is his systematic dispelling of conceptions that the rise in the consumption of fish in the tenth century was linked to the increasingly prevalent stipulations for fasting (pp. 171–84). Peter Dendle's 'Demons of the Water: Anglo-Saxon Responses to the Gerasene Demoniac' (pp. 187–207) follows, inaugurating a series of more literary-minded chapters. Dendle explores how the exegetical, liturgical, and local connotations of water inform Anglo-Saxon readings of the Gerasene Demoniac, and finds that the image of exorcising water in the episode resonate not only with the purifying nature of baptism, consecration, and redemption, but concepts of watery abodes for evil spirits and perhaps even attitudes towards Scottish foreigners too. His appendix, a parallel text and translation of select passages of Bede's Commentary on Mark (*In Marci Evangelium expositio*, pp. 204–7), is particularly useful for rendering an untranslated Bedan commentary accessible to the non-specialist. Next is Heide Estes's '*Beowulf* and the Sea: An Ecofeminist Reading' (pp. 209–26), which outlines the ecocritical and ecofeminist approaches that have been taken to medieval literature, and highlights the disparity between the attention given to ecocritical readings versus ecofeminist readings of Old English literature. The resulting reading explores interpretative possibilities that arise from such an approach, particularly in relation to framing the relationship between human, animal, and monster and human and nature, and suggests that these unstable relations might help present-day audiences rethink their own constructions of identity and connections with nature. Karl Persson's '*Scip*: A Proposed Solution to Exeter Book Riddle 95' (pp. 227–45) surveys—and points out the problems of—the extant suggestions for the solution of Exeter Riddle 95 (pp. 227–35), before advancing his own reading of *scip* ('ship'). Persson's reading is built upon an interesting combination of allegory and socio-cultural under-standing of ships, and seeks support in Riddle 95's similarity to Riddle 32. His solution neatly aligns Riddle 95 with the other ship-depictions in the Exeter Book in its mediating between spiritual and physical seafaring, though it is by no means definitive, Persson is all too aware of the issues plaguing attempts at solving these riddles. Phyllis Portnoy's 'Verbal Seascapes in Anglo-Saxon Verse' (pp. 247–73) examines the depiction of the biblical Flood in *Beowulf* (pp. 248–56) and *Genesis A* (pp. 256–65), and the sea-crossings in *Exodus* (pp. 266–72) and persuasively argues that they derive from—and draw upon the audience's experience of—biblical art. In the case of *Beowulf* this could have been 'whatever traditions of biblical art may have been at their disposal' (p. 256), whereas for *Genesis A* these images could have been those both within and beyond Junius 11. A tantalizing implication of Portnoy's argument is that the imagery alluded to in these poems derives from Continental models, and that the texts might constitute evidence for Anglo-Saxon contact with Continental art.

Carolin Esser-Miles's '"King of the Children of Pride": Symbolism, Physicality, and the Old English Whale' (pp. 275–301) is a linguistically attentive examination of the whale of the Old English *Physiologus*. It contextualizes the natural historical (pp. 282–6) and exegetical approaches (pp. 286–90) to the whale broadly, and argues that in Anglo-Saxon England and beyond, the biological and exegetical are inextricable and intertwined. This blending of conceptual categories is important, as it grounds spiritual understanding in lived experience, and posits physical experience of whales as contributing to, rather than being separate from, spiritual understanding of the creatures. This inseparability of symbol and creature features in Haruka Momma's 'Ælfric's Fisherman and the *Hronrad*: A Colloquy on the Occupation' (pp. 303–21). Momma focuses on the Fisherman of Ælfric's *Colloquy*, and queries why whales and whaling are so insisted upon within the *magister*'s questions. Momma points out that the whales mentioned in the *Colloquy* are much more naturalistic than any of the others in Old English literature (pp. 311–15), and that the Fisherman, as an independent entrepreneur, does not conform to the Benedictine ideal espoused in the rest of the *Colloquy* (pp. 315–17). She ties his presence in to the growth of fishing, discussed by Frantzen, and argues that the Fisherman reflects the articulation of monastic concern about this new class of money-maker, and that the whaling questions are repeated to force his confession of cowardice, and therefore his unambitious designs which do not threaten the Benedictine ideal.

The Anglo-Saxon world is considered more generally in the fifteen chapters in Gale Owen-Crocker and Brian Schneider's edited collection, *The Anglo-Saxons: The World through Their Eyes*. The first three papers investigate Bede's Christian world-view. Luca Larpi's 'Bede's Use of Gildas: Two Different Chronological Frameworks' (pp. 7–13) interrogates Bede's use of Gildas's *De excidio Britanniae* in two different works. Larpi convincingly shows that Bede, in both his *Chronica Maiora* and *Historia ecclesiastica gentis Anglorum*, tried to organize Gildas's accounts of events of the fifth and sixth centuries into an absolute chronology, but that in the former Bede only altered Gildas's information slightly, while in the latter Bede substantially altered— and challenged—Gildas's narrative in order to stress the Anglo-Saxons' invasion as a dispensation of divine justice. Nicholas Higham's 'Bede's Vision of an English Britain' (pp. 17–21) is less concerned with how Bede's narrative develops than with the motivation for his narrative. In this case, Higham is interested in how Bede describes—and qualifies—the extent of Anglo-Saxon power in Britain. Higham draws attention to nuances in both the *Chronica Maiora* and *Historia ecclesiastica gentis Anglorum* which suggest that, for Bede, while the Anglo-Saxon invasion once led to complete domination of the island of Britain, a series of Northumbrian concessions in the late seventh century had put a question mark over that supremacy, and that for Bede, his admonishment to good Christian behaviour, as seen in his preface of the *Historia*, was the only way continued prosperity could be guaranteed. Christopher Grocock's 'The Sense (or Absence) of Place in Bede' (pp. 23–9) ponders why there is such an absence of geographical detail—particularly relating to those places he would have known well, such as Wearmouth-Jarrow (pp. 26–7). While Grocock's answer to this—namely, that he was adhering to

classical historiographical traditions, that he privileged the spiritual over the
physical, and that he had not travelled very much (pp. 28–9)—is rather what
one would have expected, there is a very convenient catalogue of Bede's
accounts of specific places contained therein. An interesting sideline in
Grocock's argument is the observation that Bede was both familiar with and
able to employ the *locus amoenus* topos, but that he actively avoided doing so
in his prose. Donald Scragg's 'Dwarves, Nosebleeds and a Scurvy Horse:
Some Uses of Manuscripts in Late Anglo-Saxon England' (pp. 55–9)
describes, in some depth, the use of a single manuscript (Oxford, Bodleian
Library, Auct. F.3.6) during the eleventh century. Scragg's tour through the
eclectic accretion of material stresses the roles of individuals interacting with
the manuscript as artefact. We see assorted glosses reflecting varied cultures of
glossing (p. 56), notes of ownership and assorted scribbles—one of which 'it is
just possible' was made by a rider on horseback (p. 58)—and the so-called
'nonsense charms'. Each of these is usefully situated within the wider
framework of Anglo-Saxon manuscripts through Scragg's noting of parallel
occurrences, but it is curious that Scragg does not engage with the potentially
garbled Old Irish in the charm beginning *Gif men ierne blod of nebbe to swiðe*
('If someone has blood running from his nose too heavily', p. 57), as this seems
like a useful point of consideration for the origins of this and its close relative
in *Bald's Leechbook*, which Scragg speculates originated with a Winchester
scribe (p. 58). The section is rounded off by Joyce Hill's 'The Liturgy and the
Laity' (pp. 61–7), which trawls through the available evidence for traces of lay
religious practice. The homilies, pastoral letters, and Old English Martyrology
prove to be useful for insight into the behaviour of congregations, which Hill
reasonably suggests are likely to correspond to observed experiences. Hill
further notes the emphasis on the importance of relics, pilgrimages, and
processions, and how these reveal lay strategies for asserting their ownership
of—and defining their identity by—relics and religious practice.

Jill Frederick's, 'Ships and the Sea in the Exeter Book Riddles' (pp. 79–85)
looks closely at the imagery used in the various riddles which have been solved
as 'ship' (Krapp and Dobbie numbers 19, 32, 36, and 64). She notes that sea-
imagery plays little to no part in these riddles, and that instead they frame the
ship in terms more generally associated with the hall, while at the same time
stressing the ship's logistical rapidity. The associations with the hall point to
ship as sanctuary while stressing its communal activities, and she comes to
similar conclusions about the associations of ships with knowledge as Karl
Persson's '*Scip*: A Proposed Solution to Exeter Book Riddle 95' (above).

Alan Ford confronts a fundamental question of form in the *Wonders of the
East* in his 'Speaking Beyond the Light: Experience and *Auctoritas* in the
Wonders of the East and the *Liber monstrum*' (pp. 129–37). What is it that
grants it authority? The comparable Anglo-Latin *Liber monstrum* draws on the
classical theme of *auctoritas* to justify its information about monsters, while
simultaneously rejecting experience as a possible way of knowing about them
because they no longer exist. Rather different is the *Wonders of the East*, which
does not appeal to *auctoritas*, but instead—at least in the forms we have it—
derives its authority from its manuscript contexts, including BL Cotton
Vitellius A.xv as a piece of vernacular literature; BL, Cotton Tiberius B.v as of

a piece with the observational knowledge of computus; and Bodleian Library, Bodley 614 as part of the Latin mythography of twelfth-century schools.

In the final part of the book is Frank Battaglia's 'Cannibalism in *Beowulf* and Older Germanic Religion' (pp. 141–8). Battaglia endorses a very early dating for *Beowulf* in his discussion of lines 175–88. He connects the shrines mentioned here with Danish sites where fragments of worked human bone and bone-tempered ceramics have been found, which may be evidence for cannibalism. He argues this is *endo*-cannibalism (the consumption of one's own (deceased) people), and in turn connects Grendel's violation of humanity with his *exo*-cannibalism (i.e. the consumption of other people). To this end, he draws on the etymology of OE *eoten* ('giant', < Common Germanic **etuna-* 'eater', 'thing associated with eating') and the usage of *eoten* in the poem. These observations are interesting in themselves and for their insight into the prehistoric past, but his final step in the argument is likely to be too far for most people: namely, that 'an originally pagan poem showed the Danes as reverting, in the face of Grendel's attacks, to observances that in the sixth century were considered ancient fertility-religion practices and were here disparaged' (p. 147). Erin Sebo's 'The Creation Riddle and Anglo-Saxon Cosmology' (pp. 149–56) rounds off the volume. Sebo traces the development of cosmology across four riddles, from Aldhelm's *De Creatura* to Exeter Riddles 40, 66, and 93. Sebo argues that these Exeter riddles reflect various points in the reworking of the Aldhelmian one: Riddle 40 as a close translation, Riddle 66 as a condensation of Riddle 40, and Riddle 93 as the fragment of a further reworking. These refashionings signal shifting priorities and conceptualizations of the universe. Riddle 40, following Aldhelm, emphasizes the universal hierarchy with God superordinate to all creation, whereas Riddle 66 breaks out of this model slightly by accentuating creation's animacy and agency. Finally, Riddle 93 devolves the hierarchy of Aldhelm and Riddle 40 into 'a litany of comparatives' (p. 154).

Christopher A. Jones's 'Furies, Monks, and Folklore in the Earliest *Miracula* of Saint Swithun' (*JEGP* 113[2014] 407–42) centres on an episode which might be revealing in this respect. His objects of study are two closely related Winchester texts of the later tenth century: Lantfred's *Translatio et miracula S. Swithuni* and the derived *Narratio metrica de S. Swithuno* by a monk called Wulfstan. Jones argues that the biblical and classical overtones are symptomatic of Lantfred, a foreigner from Fleury, trying to frame a local superstitious belief in terms of acceptable authorities, leading to the construction of 'a surprisingly roomy imaginative space that accommodates the existence of otherworldly beings without assigning them to fixed categories as human or simply (Christian) demonic' (p. 442). Jones's discussion is valuable not only for its nuanced consideration of the interplay between multiple traditions, but for bringing this curious incident to the notice of other scholars interested in the supernatural denizens of the Anglo-Saxon imagination.

The internal world-view of the Anglo-Saxons is addressed in Alice Jorgensen, Frances McCormack, and Jonathan Wilcox's edited collection *Anglo-Saxon Emotions: Reading the Heart in Old English Language, Literature and Culture*. This collection of essays emerges, as Jorgensen notes in her

introduction, at an exciting moment for the study of emotions (p. 2). There is a
great deal of work on this topic which can be drawn on from other disciplines
(such as psychology, anthropology, and philosophy), and there have been
fruitful ventures into the Old English mind by Antonina Harbus, Leslie
Lockett, and Britt Mize. The chapters may generally be concerned with Old
English linguistic and literary evidence but they engage with theoretical issues
pertinent to other disciplines. Jorgensen's introduction is an example of this:
she outlines the issues and approaches taken to defining and identifying
'emotions' generally (pp. 3–9) before surveying approaches to the topic in Old
English studies (pp. 9–15).

Antonina Harbus's 'Affective Poetics: The Cognitive Basis of Emotion in
Old English Poetry' (pp. 19–34) stresses the need for pursuing cross-
disciplinary studies. She combines cognitive science with literary reading to
make a simple, but important, point: that the mechanisms for emotion do not
change over time. Leslie Lockett's 'The Limited Role of the Brain in Mental
and Emotional Activity According to Anglo-Saxon Medical Learning' (pp.
35–54) queries the origins of the trope of the head–heart dichotomy in English,
and argues that the Anglo-Saxons did not localize the *mod* ('mind') in the
brain. She interrogates both Latin and Old English medical texts and points
out that while they do link an organ to reasoning and perception, the present-
day identification of this with the mind rests on problematic logic. This is
important because it has led to an overstating of the importance of the brain in
the Anglo-Saxon period: it is apparently responsible for some psychological
processes (i.e. processing sensory data), but further ascriptions rest on
anachronistic reasoning.

Daria Izdebska's 'The Curious Case of *TORN*: The Importance of Lexical-
Semantic Approaches to the Study of Emotions in Old English' (pp. 53–74)
proposes a combination of semasiological corpus linguistics, traditional
comparative linguistics, and consideration of medium (whether prose, saint's
life, poetry, or gloss). Stephen Graham's "So What Did the Danes feel?"
Emotions and Litotes in Old English Poetry' (pp. 75–90) argues that litotes
allows elicitation of a variety of contextually appropriate feelings. Jonathan
Wilcox's 'An Embarrassment of Clues: Interpreting Anglo-Saxon Blushes'
(pp. 91–107) is similarly concerned with the potential multivalency of his
subject, though in this case his subject is somatic rather than lexical. His survey
of blushing in the Old English material leads to him posit a methodology for
considering the relationship between emotion and gesture which consists of
close lexical reading, contextual understanding, examining collocating gestures, and considering iconography.

Tahlia Birnbaum's 'Naming Shame: Translating Emotion in Old English
Psalter Glosses' (pp. 109–26) examines the language used to gloss the concept
of 'shame' in the Old English Vespasian, Royal and Lambeth psalter glosses.
Alice Jorgensen's 'Learning about Emotion from the Old English Prose Psalms
of the Paris Psalter' (pp. 127–41) examines the prose psalms of the Paris
Psalter as a source for emotion. Frances McCormack's 'Those Bloody Trees:
The Affectivity of *Christ*' (pp. 143–61) brings together parallels for the use of
bloody tears across Irish, Norse, and Latin works, but finds weeping trees only
in the Exeter *Christ* poems. She argues that the trees here stand metonymically

for the cross, and that they blend feelings of sadness and shame with empathy for Christ's suffering on the cross. Kristen Mills's 'Emotion and Gesture in Hroðgar's Farewell to Beowulf' (pp. 163–75) identifies Hroðgar's tearful embrace of Beowulf (lines 1870–1880a) as conforming to a formula whereby a man embraces, kisses, and weeps for another. Erin Sebo's '*Ne Sorga*: Grief and Revenge in *Beowulf*' (pp. 177–92) surveys four scenes of actual grief in *Beowulf* and finds that they all reflect different ways of reacting to their plight.

Judith Kaup's '*Maxims I:* In the "Mod" for Life' (pp. 193–209) argues that *Maxims I* is an instructive poem oriented around developing an individual's 'mindfulness'. Ronald Ganze's 'The Neurological and Physiological Effects of Emotional Duress on Memory in Two Old English Elegies' (pp. 211–26) applies neurological and cognitive research, particularly in relation to the somatic expression of emotion and on the effects of post-traumatic stress disorder, notably memory dysfunction, to the emotional states of the narrators in *The Wife's Lament* and *The Wanderer*. Finally, Mary Garrison's 'Early Medieval Experiences of Grief and Separation through the Eyes of Alcuin and Others: The Grief and Gratitude of the Oblate' (pp. 227–61) examines expressions for grief in Old English poetry and elsewhere.

Rob Meens's *Penance in Medieval Europe 600–1200* is a convenient synthesis of the extant scholarship on medieval penitentials, and prioritizes this synthesis over novel argumentation (p. 10). Its overarching theme is to stress the multiplicity of practice and to refute the notion that the history of penance was a straightforward transition from public to private. Of particular relevance are Meens's surveys of the development of Irish handbooks in Anglo-Saxon England (pp. 88–100), Willibrord and Boniface's use of these in mission (pp. 102–11), and how Irish and Continental penitential traditions shape the vernacular Old English penitentials (*The Old English Penitential*, the *scrift boc*, and the *Handbook*) in the tenth century (pp. 158–64). This will not supersede Frantzen's *Literature of Penance in Anglo-Saxon England* as much as modify how we view the Old English documents in a European context.

Miranda Wilcox's 'Confessing the Faith in Anglo-Saxon England' (*JEGP* 113[2014] 308–41) is interested in confessions of faith, a practice closely linked with penance. She surveys around fifty different confessions and concludes that the form is 'a ritual discourse that engages with and transmits the tradition of Christian orthodoxy' (p. 309).

The nine chapters in Peter Darby and Faith Wallis's edited collection *Bede and the Future* represent a significant contribution to Bede scholarship, and by virtue of Bede's importance in the development of Anglo-Saxon intellectual culture, a significant contribution to studies of the intellectual milieu of Anglo-Saxon England. Darby and Wallis's introduction, 'The Many Futures of Bede' (pp. 1–21), contains a useful digest of Bede's life and a broad chronological overview of his work. This is not only an introduction to the book, but a handy introduction to Bede generally, that should see use among both students and specialists. The chapters themselves are arranged roughly chronologically, and are introduced within the framework of Darby and Wallis's overview of Bede. The first chapter, 'Why Did Bede Write a Commentary on Revelation?' (pp. 23– 45), by Faith Wallis, argues that Bede's unusual undertaking as a young exegete, around 703, was motivated by contemporary concern about the impending end of the world, and in particular that Bede was anxious to correct misapprehensions about the predictability of its unfolding. Next is Alan Thacker's 'Why Did Heresy Matter to Bede? Present and Future Contexts' (pp. 47–66). Thacker points out that heresy was a very real threat in Bede's day, and he examines the ways in which Bede uses heresy to condemn those teachings and ideas of which he disapproved. Christopher Grocock's 'Separation Anxiety: Bede and Threats to Wearmouth and Jarrow' (pp. 67–92) argues that the *Historia Abbatum* reveals Bede's anxieties about the future of Wearmouth-Jarrow, and that this text was an attempt to consolidate its legacy. Calvin B. Kendall's 'Bede and Islam' (pp. 93–114) sees the 720s as a time when Bede's views of Islam hardened, a change in perspective that is motivated by the contemporary expansion of the Islamic Arab world. Peter Darby's 'Bede's History of the Future' (pp. 115–38) shows how Bede's critical chronologizing tendencies extended beyond his construction of early English history, and examines his construction of a chronology of the events that lead to the Last Judgement. James T. Palmer's 'The Ends and Futures of Bede's *De temporum ratione*' (pp. 139–60) demonstrates how Carolingian scribes silently adapted Bede's polemic to accord more with their own computistical perspectives. Máirín Mac Carron's 'Christology and the Future in Bede's *Annus Domini*' (pp. 161–79) demonstrates that Bede is highly selective in his application of AD dates in his *Historia*. Paul C. Hilliard, in '*Quae res Quem sit Habitura Finem, Posterior Aetas Videbit*: Prosperity, Adversity, and Bede's Hope for the Future of Northumbria' (pp. 181–206), takes the foreboding close of Bede's *Historia* as his starting point (V.23: 'What the result will be, a later generation will discover') and argues that this is not a pessimistic forecast of the future, but rather a commentary on the relative peacefulness of history. The final chapter, Scott DeGregorio's 'Visions of Reform: Bede's Later Writings in Context' (pp. 207–32), closely examines Bede's *Epistola ad Egbertum* and queries why Bede so directly urges reform here when his previous work, as shown in the preceding chapters, had usually been more veiled.

David Pratt's 'Kings and Books in Anglo-Saxon England' (*ASE* 43[2014] 297–377) examines the practices of royal book ownership. This is, as Pratt reminds us, a topic problematized by the chance survival of manuscripts. He notes a change in the culture of royal book ownership in the ninth century: before this there were learned kings collecting books to their particular tastes, but from the reign of Alfred onwards the culture of ownership becomes more interactive in the sense of a variety of different types being circulated for different reasons. Pratt surveys the royal donation of books to churches, the use of books educating royal children, and the circulation of books among the secular aristocracy, and discusses the books of the kings from Æthelred to Cnut in detail. Pratt argues that some royal donations acted as high-status repositories, and that book dissemination could be a political manoeuvre to consolidate royal authority in the ecclesiastical sphere.

Cnut is also the subject of Jacob Hobson's 'National-Ethnic Identities in Eleventh-Century Literary Representations of Cnut' (*ASE* 43 [2014] 267–95). Hobson inspects the portrayal of Cnut in the *Anglo-Saxon Chronicle*, the *Knútsdrápur*, the *Encomium Emmae Reginae*, and the *Translatio Sancti Ælfegi* by Osbern of Canterbury to see how they reconcile Cnut's Viking and English heritage. A different kind of identity is queried in George Molyneaux's 'Did the English Really Think They Were God's Elect in the Anglo-Saxon Period?' (*JEH* 65[2014] 721–37). He questions whether the Anglo-Saxons considered themselves the chosen people of God, specifically in terms of being successors to the Old Testament Israelites. The lack of engagement with vernacular literary depictions of this topos seems to be a major omission in the article.

4. Literature: General

In *Aspects of Anglo-Saxon and Medieval England*, edited by Michiko Ogura, E.G. Stanley, in 'Aldred among the West Saxons: Bamburgh, and What *bebbisca* Might Mean' (pp. 9–24), explores Aldred's colophons in the Lindisfarne Gospels and the Durham Ritual to offer a new interpretation of the adjective *bebbisca*, which Aldred gives as a gloss to the Latin *nazarenus* in the Gospels. He derives the adjective from *Bebba*, the queen after whom the city of Bamburgh is named, suggesting a link in the minds of the Northumbrians between Bamburgh and Nazareth as two important holy cities. In 'The Rewards and Perplexities of Old English Glosses' (pp. 25–30) Fred C. Robinson discusses some of the value of glosses to students of Old English, while also highlighting some pitfalls in their interpretation. He stresses the importance of viewing glosses in context, as the product of an individual scribe, and examines the way in which modern scholars may misinterpret the motivations behind them. In 'Mapping the Anglo-Saxon Intellectual Landscape: The Risks and Rewards of Source Study' (pp. 49–68), Joyce Hill questions the intellectual landscape established through source study of named Anglo-Saxon writers such as Ælfric. While previous editors have looked to the ultimate (often patristic) sources behind existing homiletic and religious works, Hill demonstrates how careful reading can sometimes distinguish works and writers who were only known to individual Anglo-Saxon authors through collections, excerpts, and florilegia. These immediate sources are often omitted by editors, giving a distorted picture of the resources available to writers of the period. Paul E. Szarmach's 'The Old English *Boethius* as a Book of Nature' (pp. 69–92) provides an exploration of the role of nature in the translation of the Latin text. Szarmach argues that the Old English translator demonstrates varying responses to the Latin original, and that he makes nature an important theme of the new translation. Graham D. Caie also concentrates on the theme of nature in his essay, 'Doomsday and Nature in the Old English Poem *Judgement Day II*' (pp. 93–104). Caie compares the opening lines of *Judgement Day II* with its source, Bede's *De die iudicii*, and considers the poem alongside those which follow in MS Cambridge, Corpus Christi College, 201. In doing so, he demonstrates the independent treatment of the poem's opening and makes the case for *Judgement Day II* and its surrounding poems having circulated independently as penitential material.

Dominik Kuhn presents us with an extremely thorough study and edition in his *Der lateinisch-altenglische Libellus Precum in der Handschrift London,*

British Library, Arundel 155. Kuhn's edition is specifically of the Old English glosses to the forty Latin private prayers in this manuscript, with linguistic commentary and palaeographical analysis of the manuscript and a survey of the dissemination of the prayers in Arundel 155, discussions of the dialectal features (pp. 186–90) and word-choices (pp. 190–6).

David Porter's 'Isidore's *Etymologiae* at the School of Canterbury' (*ASE* 43 [2014] 7–44) shows that some 180 of the Old English glosses in the so-called Leiden glossary derive from Isidore's *Etymologiae*. As the glossary can be traced to Theodore and Hadrian's late seventh-century school at Canterbury, this is an important insight into their curriculum. Porter argues, however, that the copy of the *Etymologiae* at Canterbury was not a glossed copy of the complete text, but an abbreviated text—an 'epitome'—parts of which were heavily glossed in Old English, and that this was the direct source of the Isidorean material in the Leiden glossary.

Marcelle Cole's monograph *Old Northumbrian Verbal Morphosyntax and the (Northern) Subject Rule* is predominantly a linguistic study of verb endings and syntax in the Lindisfarne Gospels. Of interest to literature scholars, however, is the way Cole brings her analysis to bear on the question of the authorship of the gospel glosses. Previous palaeographical analysis suggested that, despite minor variations in the quality of the hand, the differences are not sufficient to posit more than one scribe, Aldred. Other analyses have argued that even if the gloss was written entirely by Aldred, the number of linguistic variants suggests that he was working from a number of sources, or from an exemplar which was itself compiled by more than one writer. Cole's analysis reveals significant grammatical changes (such as –ð/-s in third-person present-tense verbs) at around the same points identified by other studies (i.e. at the beginning of Mark, and becoming notably stronger in John). She concludes that 'Matthew stands as a single linguistic unit in contrast to the rest of the text and . . . John may also be considered distinctive' (p. 115), suggesting that Aldred's exemplar had contained a change of hands, or that he had copied his gloss from a variety of sources, incorporating some of his own forms.

Medieval Dress and Textiles in Britain: A Multilingual Sourcebook, edited by Louise M. Sylvester, Mark C. Chambers, and Gale Owen-Crocker, surveys clothing and textiles as they appear in different types of text across the medieval period. The book contains parallel-text excerpts, and covers texts in Old and Middle English, Latin and Anglo-Norman French (including texts which codeswitch), accompanied by modern English translations. Each entry comprises a brief introduction detailing the text's date and manuscript context, as well as notes on the textiles mentioned. The *Sourcebook* covers several types of document, including wills, petitions to the king, wardrobe accounts, moral and satirical works, sumptuary regulations, and poetry. Two of the seven chapters deal with Old English material—chapter 1, 'Wills', and chapter 7, 'Epic and Romance'—and the thematic arrangement of the book is useful in demonstrating what kinds of sources exist for the pre-Conquest period (for example, wardrobe accounts do not appear before the thirteenth century). Chapter 7 includes several excerpts from *Beowulf*, whose vivid descriptions of armour make for good comparison with later Middle English romances, which have a 'precision in the terminology for cloth and clothing' (p. 262). This book also contains useful discussions of some of the specific vocabulary of textiles in the period.

It is always difficult to know where to place works on medievalism, especially works which range across several periods, and so here seems as good as any other. One such work is Heather O'Donoghue's *English Poetry and Old Norse Myth: A History*. O'Donoghue traces the use of Old Norse mythology in English poetry from the very beginnings of English writing until the present day. Key themes are the association of Old Norse with English identity (and nationalism), use and abuse for political expression, and the oscillation between humanizing and abstracting the qualities and representations of the Old Norse gods. The prologue is of particular interest for the Anglo-Saxonist: here O'Donoghue charts the use of Old Norse myth in *Beowulf* (though there is nothing new in these observations), followed by a very cursory nod to its possible presence behind some other Old English material (pp. 24–5).

Similarly concerned with the post-medieval reception of medieval texts is Timothy Graham's 'William Elstob's Planned Edition of the Anglo-Saxon Laws: A Remnant in the Takamiya Collection' (in Horobin and Mooney, eds., *Middle English Texts in Transition*, pp. 268–96) reprints an article that first appeared in *Poetica* 73[2010] that offers discussion of an eighteenth-century transcript of the Anglo-Saxon laws by William Elstob in the Takamiya collection.

5. The Poems of the Exeter Book

The only book-length treatment of the Exeter Book's poetry this year is M.R. Rambaran-Olm's *'John the Baptist's Prayer' or 'The Descent into Hell' from the* Exeter Book*: Text, Translation and Critical Study*. This volume offers an edition, facing-page translation, and extensive commentary on this poem. The introduction runs to more than 140 pages, covering the palaeography and language of the poem, the *descensus* motif, literary analysis (which begins with a further, even more emphatic, rebuttal of the poem's traditional title), and analogous literature. Both the edited text and its accompanying translation are clearly presented. The appendices are an unexpected bonus, providing an index of the *descensus* motif from the first to the twelfth century, various literary analogues to the Old English poem, and a transcription accompanied by digital images of the manuscript.

The Exeter Book riddles elicited some engaging discussion this year, ranging from the shoring up of long-standing solutions to attempts at unearthing entirely new riddles. Regarding the latter, E.G. Stanley makes a case both for a new reading and for a new riddle in 'Exeter Book Riddle 11: Alcohol and Its Effects' (*N&Q* 61[2014] 182–5). This poem, he argues, is actually two riddles. The first of these riddles, Stanley suggests, may have as its subject a garment, a scabbard, or a quiver, whereas the second clearly concerns the effects of alcohol. The second half of the article concerns the problematic crux in line 20 (*heah bringeð*), which Stanley compares to the modern colloquialism 'brings on a high'.

Megan Cavell provides an engaging analysis of literary techniques in 'Sounding the Horn in Exeter Book Riddle 14' (*Expl* 72[2014] 324–7). Weaving together facets of the poem's alliteration, structure, imagery, and manuscript presentation, Cavell demonstrates the ways in which these various elements combine to render the riddle's solution clear.

In 'The "Dark Welsh" as Slaves and Slave Traders in Exeter Book Riddles 52 and 72' (*ES* 95[2014] 235–55), Lynn Brady argues that the 'dark Welsh' figures that appear in both riddles should be understood to refer not only to Welsh slaves, but also to the Welsh slave traders who were 'active raiders of their own people' (p. 235). Brady's review of extant sources demonstrates the extent to which slaves are equated to beasts in both Anglo-Saxon and Welsh literature (pp. 237–8), while the Welsh in the early medieval period were both held as slaves (pp. 238–42) and active participants in slave trading (pp. 242–4). Read in this context, Riddles 52 and 72 can be seen as illustrating a more complex social situation than has previously been recognized, by exploring the 'contradictory roles played by the Welsh as both victims and perpetrators of the slave trade in Anglo-Saxon England' (p. 251).

A rather different approach is taken by Thomas Klein, William F. Klein, and David Delehanty in 'Resolving Exeter Book Riddles 74 and 33: Stormy Allomorphs of Water' (*Quidditas* 35[2014] 29–47). The authors apply the term 'allomorph' to the Exeter Book riddles to refer to 'the alternative forms a riddle object may take in its various real and imaginative environments' (pp. 29–30). The authors apply the concept of allomorphs to two 'transformation' riddles, 33 and 74, both of which they solve as 'water', specifically in the form served up by thunderstorms.

Additionally, three of the Exeter Book riddles are discussed by Allen J. Frantzen in *Food, Eating and Identity in Early Medieval England* (pp. 170, 251, and 167–8 respectively). Each riddle is presented in its original Old English, with an accompanying prose translation, and is discussed in the context of Anglo-Saxon food and its associated material culture. The discussion of the riddles themselves is very brief, no more than a paragraph in each instance, but the broader discussions of which they form a part offer some potentially fruitful insights into the cultural references upon which the riddles themselves draw.

Discussion of the Exeter Book's wisdom poems has largely been in relation to other works this year (see Section 9, Other Poems). However, E.G. Stanley returns to the fray to offer a new interpretation of the cited lines in 'Exeter *Maxims I* lines 181–7: Gambling' (*N&Q* 61[2014] 8–11). These lines are a notable crux in the poem, A detailed close reading provides weight for Stanley's argument that line 185 should be read as 'unless it runs sailingly', with lines 182b and 184 anticipating this nautical turn. Taking the position that the poem is Alfredian, Stanley compares the depiction of Germanic gambling in Tacitus' *Germania* with the 'condemnatory' attitude displayed in *Maxims I*. The moral of these lines, Stanley concludes, is that 'dishonour is at hand' whenever two people meet across a gambling table.

Continuing this linguistic focus, but turning from wisdom to the elegies, Alfred Bammesberger proposes a rereading of a line from *The Seafarer* in 'Old English *eft eadig secg* (*The Seafarer*, line 56a)' (*N&Q* 61[2014] 181–2). Whilst the majority of editors follow Thorpe in emending the opening of this line to *esteadig*, Bammesberger draws attention to the manuscript reading of *eft eadig*. A return to the manuscript, which Bammesberger finds preferable, provides a line with the sense 'the warrior, afterwards (= later in life) a prosperous man . . .' (p. 182).

In 'Wolves' Heads and Wolves' Tales: Women and Exile in *Bisclavret* and *Wulf and Eadwacer*' (*Exemplaria* 26[2014] 328–46), Victoria Blud explores the presentation of gendered exile in the two works. Blud argues that the texts' female characters are depicted in terms as implicitly wolfish as their male counterparts. Although the connection between these two works remains tenuous at best, Blud does identify some intriguing parallels between them, not least their shared suggestion of inherited exile passed from present to future generations.

As 'one of the most ambiguous prosopopoeic poems in the Old English corpus', it is fitting that *The Husband's Message* is chosen as the focus of Miriam Edlich-Muth's study of the technique in 'Prosopopoeia: Sharpening the Anglo-Saxon Toolkit' (*ES* 95[2014] 95–108, at 96). Edlich-Muth reads this challenging poem as one in which three characters involve themselves in 'a complex interplay of absence and textual projection' (p. 98). She argues that it is not up to scholars to find 'ingenious answers' to every apparent contradiction, but rather to 'extend the same poetic licence to Anglo-Saxon poets as we do to more recent writers', by recognizing ambiguity as 'one of the intended literary effects' available to them (p. 108).

In 'Monster, Demon and Warrior: St. Guthlac and the Cultural Landscape of the Anglo-Saxon Fens' (*Comitatus* 45[2014] 105–31), J.T. Noetzel first assesses the historical and imaginative associations of fens from the eighth to the eleventh centuries, taking in Grendel's mere and the *Maxims* poems, before turning to *Guthlac A*, *Guthlac B*, and Felix's *Life of St. Guthlac*. For the Anglo-Saxons, fens presented 'a troubling and hybridized category that disrupts the two-part relationship between land and water' (p. 114). The literature of St Guthlac, Noetzel argues, grounds the metaphor of fenland as a place of 'uncertainty, danger, and monstrosity' (p. 105) by situating it in the historical landscape of the Fens.

The poems of Cynewulf, and in particular the poems' riddling signatures, were also the subject of a number of articles this year. Tom Birkett's 'Runes and *Revelatio*: Cynewulf's Signatures Reconsidered' (*RES* 65[2014] 771–89), presents the signatures at the end of *Christ II*, *Juliana*, *Elene*, and *Fates of the Apostles* as contemplative spaces, with the runic letters acting as a particular focal point. Taking each of the signatures in turn, Birkett demonstrates the complex interplay between the individual and the universal. He rejects any notion of the signatures as acts of exhibition, ostentatiously naming their composer in a poetic landscape of overwhelming anonymity. Instead, he argues, the runic acrostics serve as a focus of contemplation for the reader, situating the individual 'in the context of universal fate' (p. 789).

Discussion of the Cynewulfian signatures continues in Jill Hamilton Clements's 'Reading, Writing and Resurrection: Cynewulf's Runes as a Figure of the Body' (*ASE* 43[2014] 133–54). Although Clements, like Birkett, rejects interpretations of the signatures as simple pleas for prayers, her discussion focuses on the individual poet and his relationship with his work. She firmly grounds the poems in the context of medieval analogies between words and meaning, arguing for an Augustinian interpretation that equates the runic letters of the signatures to the physical body, while their meaning represents the soul. Cynewulf, it is argued, presents his texts as a 'physical remnant of himself in the hands of . . . his readers'; as the reader gives meaning to the runic letters through interpretation and rearrangement of the physical letters, so their prayers bring Cynewulf's soul to the presence of God (p. 154). Clements uses the signatures to make a broader point about the extent to which death and writing are intertwined, with the written word offering both a material presence among the living and an everlasting place in the memory of God.

Cynewulf's signatures, with a particular emphasis on *Elene*, are also discussed in a chapter of *The Arma Christi in Medieval and Early Modern Material Culture: With a Critical Edition of 'O Vernicle'*, edited by Lisa H. Cooper and Andrea Denny-Brown. In 'Figure and Ground: *Elene*'s Nails, Cynewulf's Runes, and Hrabanus Maurus's Painted Poems', Seeta Chaganti presents a reading of *Elene*, both its runic letters and its broader themes, informed by the modern concept of 'figure and ground'. The article itself is an example of the ways in which modern theoretical constructs can provide useful, and appropriate, readings of medieval texts. Like Clements, Chaganti touches on analogies between death and poetry in her discussion of burial and its implications in *Elene* (pp. 60–1). Her conclusion, meanwhile, echoes Birkett's, ultimately arguing that, in *Elene*, Cynewulf uses oscillations between figure and ground to present to the reader a meditative movement between the particular and the universal.

6. The Poems of the Vercelli Book

In *Aspects of Anglo-Saxon and Medieval England*, edited by Michiko Ogura, Jane Roberts uses 'A Context for the Exeter Book: Some Suggestions but No Conclusions' (pp. 31–48) to advocate a reading of the Exeter Book's poems alongside those of the Vercelli Book. Although many previous studies have looked at the Exeter Book in isolation, Roberts detects 'similar themes and interests' (p. 37) in both the prose and the poetry of the Vercelli Book.

Jill Fitzgerald discusses Cynewulf's adaptation of source material in *Elene* in '*Angelus Pacis*: A Liturgical Model for the Masculine "fæle friðowebba" in Cynewulf's *Elene*' (*MÆ* 83[2014] 189–209). Fitzgerald focuses on Cynewulf's modification of the vision of Constantine from its earlier presentation in the *Acta Cyriaci*. Hamilton argues that Cynewulf 'boldly' rewrites poetic tradition, 'first by uniquely incorporating a male peace-weaver . . . and then by aligning the figure with the Christian-Latin tradition' (p. 202). Through this reworking of the past, Cynewulf invests the figure of the peace-weaver with profound meaning; the peace-weaver is equated with the *angelus pacis* who promises victory to Christians against enemies both worldly and spiritual, and so becomes a token of the pledge between God and humanity.

Todd Oakley uses a cognitive linguistic approach to examine the *Dream of the Rood*, in 'Semantic Domains in the *Dream of the Rood*' (*Rask* 40[2014] 331–52) focusing in particular on mental spaces and blending theory. He demonstrates the fruitfulness of a new reading of the poem based on the semantic domains model, and advocates further research using this methodology.

One essay in *Hagiography in Anglo-Saxon England: Adopting and Adapting Saints' Lives into Old English Prose (c.950–1150)*, edited by Loredana Lazzari, Patrizia Lendinara, and Claudia di Sciacca, deals with one of the homilies of the Vercelli Book. In 'The *Decensus ad inferos* in the Old English Prose Life of St Guthlac and Vercelli Homily xxiii' (pp. 229–54), Concetta Giliberto discusses two versions of the Guthlac legend. Both versions descend from a now-lost vernacular translation of Felix's Latin *vita*, and while many classical allusions are absent, the two versions of the story share a number of similarities with other visits to and visions of the underworld (e.g. as depicted in *Vita S. Fursei* and *Vision of Dryhthelm*). However, the narrative as presented in Vercelli Homily xxiii differs markedly in its conclusion, ignoring Guthlac's subsequent life and instead depicting him as ascending directly to heaven with St Bartholomew. Giliberto argues that the two adaptations are important for our understanding of the importance placed by the Anglo-Saxons on the Psalter and on visions of the afterlife.

7. The Poems of the Junius Manuscript

In 'Old English *mægen*: A Note on the Relationship Between *Exodus* and *Daniel* in MS Junius 11' (*ES* 95[2014] 825–48), Carl Kears, noting the general lack of critical interest in the peculiarity of *Exodus* being followed by *Daniel*, makes an argument for the influence of the former on the latter. His suggestion is that the first forty-five lines of *Daniel* repeatedly echo the preceding text and may have been added on to smooth the transition between texts. Kears suggests that 'Whoever was responsible for the composition of *Daniel*'s exordium used poetic words and collocations that were vital to the creation of the interpretive challenge at the heart of *Exodus*' (p. 845).

Scott Thompson Smith's 'Faith and Forfeiture in the Old English *Genesis A*' (*MP* 111[2014] 593–615) is an interesting discussion of ideas in the poem and their relationship with legal practice in the tenth century. He shows that the poem 'models a message about faith and human history that accords with Anglo-Saxon tenurial practice and its enduring demands of loyalty and obligation' (p. 614).

8. *Beowulf* and the *Beowulf* Manuscript

Probably the most eagerly anticipated publication of the year was J.R.R. Tolkien's *'Beowulf': Translation and Commentary, Together with 'Sellic Spell'*, edited by Christopher Tolkien. After the translation is an extensive commentary, produced from what must have been a torturous process of editing lecture notes. It does not cover the whole text, ending with the theft of the cup from the dragon. The translation itself has an antiquated feel, following both vocabulary and syntax of the Old English closely.

Leonard Neidorf's edited volume, *The Dating of 'Beowulf': A Reassessment*, is a more substantial undertaking. It seeks to offer indisputable evidence dating the poem with scientific certainty to the first half of the eighth century. In doing so, it makes claims less about the date of the poem than about the nature of critical discussion and the relative merits of different types of scholarly investigation. Neidorf's book strongly endorses both Robert Fulk's view and his method, expressed most clearly in *A History of Old English Meter*, that the poem was produced in eighth-century Mercia. Neidorf's introduction sets the tone by claiming primacy for linguistic tests.

Most of the chapters in the volume represent significant and productive scholarship on *Beowulf*, and they will be described briefly here. Fulk's '*Beowulf* and Language History' (pp. 19–36) is a restatement of his own views. Neidorf's own chapter is on 'Germanic Legend, Scribal Errors, and Cultural Change' (pp. 37–57). He argues that 'political currency of heroic legend' did not last long beyond Alfred's reign, making a strong argument for a fundamental cultural shift in the concerns of Anglo-Saxon England iterated later in the volume.

Tom Shippey continues with one of Neidorf's themes of 'Names in *Beowulf* and Anglo-Saxon England' (pp. 58–78). Noting that 'There is little or no correlation between frequency of appearance in the poem and record in legend' (p. 72), he asks many valuable questions about the apparent redundancy of names in the poem. Megan E. Hartman attempts to establish 'The Limits of Conservative Composition in Old English Poetry' (pp. 79–96). Using metrical tests, Hartman shows that *Beowulf* is far more consistent in its use of archaic linguistics for metrical formation than *Brunanburh*, *Judith*, and *Maldon*. The argument is that 'tenth-century poets only went so far in their efforts to recreate archaic poetic technique' (p. 95), and that *Beowulf* goes well beyond this 'superficial . . . archaic feel' (p. 82). Thomas Bredehoft's contribution is on a closely related subject: 'The Date of Composition of *Beowulf* and the Evidence of Metrical Evolution' (pp. 97–111) argues that 'the table [of metrical innovations] shows quite clearly a tradition in more or less constant transition, in which innovations happen, and that, when they do, later compositions almost always show evidence of at least some of the earlier innovations' (p. 108).

In '*Beowulf* and the Containment of Scyld in the West Saxon Royal Genealogy' (pp. 112–37), Dennis Cronan examines the motives for the interpolation of Scyld and his relatives in the West Saxon genealogy, and of Æthelweard's motives for excluding them from his copy of the chronicle. His overarching proposal, though, that the claim that Alfred's line was descended from Scyld was provoked by immediate political need, and that this was 'probably stillborn, and had no historical or literary influence' (p. 136), is intriguing.

Frederick Biggs, in 'History and Fiction in the Frisian Raid' (pp. 138–56), suggests that the repetitions of the raid with its variations are carefully constructed by the poet to 'distinguish the historical core of the event from his fictional elaborations and so he can connect both the history and his fictions to the theme of succession' (p. 145). His discussion works its way towards the inevitable but slightly less compelling conclusion that the whole text is an attempt to describe 'a danger in the Christian system [of succession], the lack of a suitable heir, that is less likely to have occurred in the older Germanic way of selecting kings' (p. 156).

Michael Drout's piece, produced with the assistance of Emily Bowman and Phoebe Boyd, on ' "Give the People What They Want": Historiography and Rhetorical History of the Dating of *Beowulf* Controversy' (pp. 157–76), attacks, with neither clarity nor accuracy, work by earlier scholars. It is expressed in purely negative terms and needlessly polemical in tone.

Joseph Harris's 'A Note on the Other Heorot' (pp. 178–90) introduces a site ignored in discussions of the poem: the seventh- and eighth-century Northumbrian monastery twice called *Heruteu* by Bede. He discusses the possible origins of the name, quite reasonably arguing that it is not likely to have come from Denmark given that Lejre is well known in Danish texts and Heorot known only in England. As Harris observes, this is probably more a point of interest than a significant piece of evidence, but he does claim it as 'one additional piece of the puzzle supporting the likelihood of a date in the earlier rather than later Anglo-Saxon period' (p. 189).

Thomas Hill suggests, in '*Beowulf* and Conversion History' (pp. 191–201), that 'if *Beowulf* were composed in the tenth century, the poet was for whatever reason writing about theological concerns appropriate to an earlier age'. As for Cronan, Biggs, and Harris, this cannot lead to a proposed date but broadly continues to lend support to what the volume calls an 'early' *Beowulf*.

Rafael Pascual writes about 'Material Monsters and Semantic Shifts' (pp. 202–18). This is a re-examination of the established idea that later, more certainly Christianized, Old English used words for monsters to mean spiritual rather than physical enemies. The proposal is that 'The pagan characters consistently refer to monsters in spiritually neutral terms' (p. 206).

George Clark provides a final defence of Fulk's argument. His 'Scandals in Toronto: Kaluza's Law and Transliteration Errors' (pp. 219–34) provides a very useful survey of the distribution of verses adhering to Kaluza's law in the poem. Interestingly, this analysis results in Clark remaining open to the possibility that parts of *Beowulf* might have originally been two separate texts, though he finds unity more probable (p. 227). The volume concludes with Allen Frantzen's 'Afterword: *Beowulf* and Everything Else' (pp. 235–48). Here there is an acknowledgement of the vagueness of the concepts of 'early' and 'late'. In a polemic against narcissistic, ahistorical, and theory-led interpretations, the Afterword echoes Fulk's interest in narrowing down possibilities for dating *Beowulf* and the rest of the corpus.

Collectively, there can be no doubt that the book makes a convincing case. Neidorf's volume has clearly been planned to bring a great deal of heat to bear on the dating of the poem which has the unfortunate effect of obscuring some of the light. Much is written about the failings of other research, mostly focused on Roberta Frank, often sounding defensive and aggressive, and frequently leaving a sense that little new is being established even when some interesting arguments are being introduced. Even the strongest chapters have an uncomfortable air of settling scores about them. Tom Shippey, for instance, concludes his lively and convincing study of names in the poem with a rather unnecessary attack on a 2007 Walter Goffart article, and frames the whole piece as an argument with Tolkien, which adds little or nothing to the findings and conclusions of the whole. Almost every chapter in the book assumes a rivalry between 'early' and 'late' daters, with no differentiation made between those scholars who see *Beowulf* as a poem from the ninth century and those who place it in the eleventh. Thus, an argument for 'not late' becomes an argument for early eighth-century Mercia. Presumably an even earlier composition is not an option at all.

Another difficulty with presenting the book as a unified argument is that different chapters do, in fact, engage with different methodologies and approaches to the text. By their nature, it is the more speculative and exploratory pieces that will generate more discussion and interest. There are important suggestions made about broad shifts in culture (Neidorf and others), about the idea of the antique (Cronan), and experimentation in versification (Bredehoft), which risk being overshadowed by the dogmatic tone of the book as a whole. In perhaps the finest piece in an important volume, Bredehoft suggests that 'our understanding of the history of Old English verse may itself have reached a watershed moment' (p. 111). This may be true for the dating of poetry; one hopes it is not for the tone and respect shown in scholarly argumentation. It is also odd that a volume which offers so much to suggest that the poem was first composed in the eighth century does not begin to engage with the question of why anyone wanted to write it down in the eleventh. For all the claims that it was linguistically, metrically, historically, and theologically impossible to have written it by the ninth century, the question of what two men thought they were doing when they wrote it down two hundred years later echoes loud.

Helen Damico's *'Beowulf' and the Grendelkin: Politics and Poetry in Eleventh-Century England* may be the first of a number of responses to Neidorf's volume, or to the conference that preceded it. Damico provocatively pushes the date of the manuscript later than 1035. It is unlikely that many scholars will regard this as plausible. But what the book does do is provide an account of what resonances the poem may have had in eleventh-century England. Damico provides a clear historical narrative, with sensitive and detailed understanding of socio-political and interpersonal relationships, and close poetic analysis.

One more book has relevance to *Beowulf* this year. *Teaching 'Beowulf' in the Twenty-First Century* is a collection of short pieces edited by Howell Chickering, Allen Frantzen, and R.F. Yeager. This is a long-overdue publication, given the growth of interest following on from recent engagements with the text and its world, such as those from Seamus Heaney, Peter Jackson, and Robert Zemeckis. Apart from the introduction, there are twenty-six short pieces on different teaching/interpretative approaches, subdivided into multiple different groupings. The volume is split between 'Materials' and 'Approaches'. 'Materials' covers 'Texts', 'Adaptations', and 'Electronic and Multimedia Resources'. 'Approaches' is further subdivided into 'Course Models' and 'Cultural Models'. The former has groups of pieces on 'Teaching

Beowulf in Old English', 'In Translation', and 'In Writing Courses'. The latter group has 'Traditional' (which here means engaging with Anglo-Saxon history through the poem), 'Interdisciplinary', and 'Contemporary Contexts'. As the introduction by the editors notes, all are focused on 'classroom-tested ways of teaching the poem' (p. 4). The volume is admirably broad, and does not present any form of manifesto for how the text 'should' be taught. Although the editors express a strong preference for the whole poem being engaged with in Old English, many pieces reflect on teaching excerpts and using translations.

In 'The Language of *Beowulf* and the Conditioning of Kaluza's Law' (*Neophil* 98[2014] 657–73) Leonard Neidorf and Rafael Pascual reconsider the evidence for the 'conditioning responsible for the Beowulf poet's apparent awareness of so many archaic length distinctions' (p. 659). Framed as a response to Eric Weiskott's 'A Semantic Replacement for Kaluza's Law in *Beowulf* (*ES* 93[2012] 891–6), the piece is a resolute defence of a phonological explanation for the archaic metrics of the poem.

Alfred Bammesberger writes on '*Fela fricgende*: Royal Entertainment in the Hall Heorot (*Beowulf*, Lines 2105–14)' (*N&Q* 61[2014] 3–8). His proposal is that what is normally printed as *felafricgende* ('knowing of many things') should be separated (as it appears in the manuscript). If accepted, this emendation would turn Hrothgar's singing into a performance delivered 'when (or because) many asked [for it]'. In turn, this episode becomes a particularly special celebration of Beowulf's achievements, where, under the weight of numerous requests, Hrothgar takes up the harp and performs.

Sara Frances Burdoff, in 'Re-reading Grendel's Mother: *Beowulf* and the Anglo-Saxon Metrical Charms' (*Comitatus* 45[2014] 91–103), problematizes the scholarly focus on Grendel's mother's femininity and maternity, arguing that it is reductive to see her only through these lenses, making the case for seeing her in relation to the language of the charms. Burdoff is able to propose explanations for some of the striking specific details in Grendel's mother's narrative, such as the melting sword and sitting on the hero.

Megan Cavell also considers the monsters in 'Constructing the Monstrous Body in *Beowulf*' (*ASE* 43[2014] 155–81). But all of the material here is thoughtful and extremely productive, and this study should influence wider discussions of the idea and purpose of the monstrous in the period as well as being part of readings of *Beowulf*.

Nickolas Haydock has written about 'Film Theory, the Sister Arts Tradition, and the Cinematic *Beowulf*' (*SiMed* 22[2013] 153–80). Haydock reflects on the processes of analysing *Beowulf* and filming it. His wider project is to move medievalism beyond an often narrow focus on the exoticization of source material and creation of the medieval as Other. Haydock provides examples of the kinds of interaction that he sees as more productive, with scholarship and cinema feeding from and into one another in ways that have not always been identified or appreciated by academics keen to place distance between their own work and that of film-makers.

A chapter in Daniel Kline's edited collection, *Digital Gaming Re-imagines the Middle Ages*, also engages with modern media. Candace Barrington and Timothy English's ' "Best and Only Bulwark": How Epic Narrative Redeems

Beowulf: The Game' (pp. 31–42) explores the flaws and absurdities in the game based on Zemeckis's film of *Beowulf*.

Finally, there has been one piece on the works other than *Beowulf* in the manuscript. A philosophical discussion of poetics, primarily focused on *Judith*, is in Manish Sharma's 'Beyond Nostalgia: Formula and Novelty in Old English Literature' (*Exemplaria* 26[2014] 303–27). Sharma gives a brief analysis of Bede's Cædmon narrative as a simultaneously productive and alarming bringing together of different worlds. *Judith* is brought into the same scheme, with Judith herself characterized by a kind of 'molecular fluidity' (p. 317), adapting and shifting in different circumstances.

9. Other Poems

Mary P. Richards's *The Old English Poem 'Seasons for Fasting': A Critical Edition* offers a comprehensive new edition of this late Old English poem. *Seasons for Fasting* was edited as recently as 2012, for inclusion in *Old English Shorter Poems*, volume 1, edited by Christopher Jones, for Dumbarton Oaks Medieval Library, but obviously and by necessity received far briefer treatment in that context than Richards gives it here. The poem itself is something of an oddity, from its stanzaic form to its choice of subject matter. It moves from the proper celebration of the four seasonal ember feasts, the dating of which was a source of contemporary controversy, to a consideration of fasting during Lent, before finishing with an attack on negligent priests. Richards places the poem in its literary contexts, drawing links that range from Wulfstan's alliterative prose, to Ælfric's promotion of teachers as cultural leaders, to the use of sound in *The Battle of Maldon*, and the debates and complaints that would come to characterize later Middle English poetry such as *Piers Plowman* and *Cleanness*. As Richards demonstrates, *The Seasons for Fasting* maintains a connection between poetry and spiritual enlightenment that began with Cædmon, it engages with the complex blurring of prose and poetry that had developed by the end of the Anglo-Saxon period, and it looks forward to Middle English traditions of incorporating preaching into verse. This is 'late poetry', she concludes, but it is not 'debased or quasi-poetry' (p. 83).

Richards's introduction covers the poem, its manuscript and editions, metrical and linguistic features, sources and influences, and style and structure. All of these are presented in measured, straightforward prose that renders even the more obscure aspects of the poem immensely readable, notwithstanding its 'unusual history and obvious flaws' (p. 18). While the introduction is concerned with these broader topics, the rest of the edition focuses primarily on issues of language and editing. Richards takes a conservative approach in her presentation of the text, preferring 'not to obscure possible evidence of dialect and date' through emendation of unexpected forms (p. 83). Readings that differ from previous editions are conscientiously recorded in extensive footnotes on each page. The accompanying commentary is a little brief, and concerned almost entirely with linguistic notes. There is also a very thorough glossary that provides complete line references for every word of the text, up to and including personal pronouns. A translation is included (as is the proviso that it is 'literal' and 'tied to the Glossary', p. 103), but it is slightly awkwardly positioned at the end of the Old English text rather than being presented on facing pages.

Two new anthologies of Old English poetry came out this year. Robert E. Bjork's *Old English Shorter Poems*, volume 2, is the most recent addition to the Dumbarton Oaks Medieval Library series. The volume collects thirty-six poems from the Exeter Book and elsewhere under the theme 'Wisdom and Lyric', and complements Christopher A. Jones's previously published volume of poems 'Religious and Didactic'. Lyric in this instance refers to the elegies, whose expressions of suffering are presented in parallel to the knowledge and experience celebrated in the wisdom poems. Unlike Jones's preceding volume, the poems in this anthology are grouped by source (as 'Poems from *The Exeter Book*' and 'Poems from *The Anglo-Saxon Minor Poems*'), rather than theme. The poems included, and the titles under which they appear, are: *The Wanderer*; *The Gifts of Mortals*; *Precepts*; *The Seafarer*; *Vainglory*; *Widsith*; *The Fortunes of Mortals*; *Maxims I*; *The Order of the World*; *The Rhyming Poem*; *Deor*; *Wulf and Eadwacer*; *The Wife's Lament*; *Resignation (B): An Exile's Lament*; *Pharaoh*; *The Husband's Message*; *The Ruin*; *Durham*; *The Rune Poem*; *Solomon and Saturn*; *Maxims II*; *A Proverb from Winfrid's Time*; *Bede's Death Song*; *Latin-English Proverbs*; and twelve metrical charms.

A number of these poems are also included in R.M. Liuzza's *Old English Poetry: An Anthology*. Beginning with the beginning of Old English poetry, Bede's account of Caedmon, Liuzza presents more than twenty-five poems, grouped together under the themes 'Elegies', 'Wisdom', 'Faith', and 'Fame'. The overlaps with Bjork's edition are felt most strongly in the first two sections, for obvious reasons. It is interesting that both editors include metrical charms in this category. The volume's stated purpose is to demonstrate the range and diversity of Old English poetry, and although the majority of its selection is drawn from the best known and most widely read examples, there are several pleasant surprises included as well. The anthology contains: *The Wanderer*; *The Seafarer*; *Deor*; *Wulf and Eadwacer*; *The Wife's Lament*; *The Ruin*; *The Cotton Maxims*; *The Gifts of Men*; *The Fortunes of Men*; *Vainglory*; *The Order of the World*; Exeter Book Riddles; Old English metrical charms; *Advent (Christ I)*; *Seasons for Fasting*; *Exodus*; *Daniel*; *The Dream of the Rood*; *Andreas*; *The Fates of the Apostles*; *Judith*; *The Battle of Maldon*; *The Battle of Brunanburh*; *The Finnsburh Fragment*; *Widsith*. Unlike the above edition, the poems are here presented only in modern translation. The broad overview of Old English poetry that starts the volume is complemented by more detailed introductions to individual sections, including some suggestions for further reading.

Several of this year's books include brief but pertinent reference to the poems covered in this section. *The Seasons for Fasting* makes an appearance in Allen J. Frantzen's *Food, Eating and Identity in Early Medieval England* (pp. 245–58). Frantzen characterizes the composer of the poem as both an artist and a politician, someone concerned to show the clergy 'what they looked like to . . . the laity they were supposed to teach' (p. 257). Frantzen's primary interest in the poem is, however, incidental to this aim; through a detailed analysis, he draws out the poem's embedded 'glimpses of food culture and the working world'. The first chapter of Stephen Yeager's *From Lawmen to Plowmen: Anglo-Saxon Legal Tradition and the School of Langland* includes a discussion of Old English wisdom literature that touches, albeit briefly, on a wide selection of poems, including those from the Exeter Book, *Maxims II*, the *Durham Proverbs*, *Instructions for Christians*, *Seasons for Fasting*, and the Old English translation of the *Dicts of Cato* (pp. 39–45). These wisdom poems are set in the context of legal-homiletic discourse as creative uses of the sententious forms that similarly underscore, and lend authority to, medieval law codes and charters. *The Battle of Maldon* is discussed, as literary context for the Bayeux Tapestry, in *The Bayeux Tapestry and its Contexts: A Reassessment* by Elizabeth Carson Pastan and Stephen D. White, with Kate Gilbert. Pastan cautions against a false dichotomy that would label these works as 'secular', given that the hanging supposedly commemorating the events of *Maldon* was specifically used to strengthen ties between Byrhtnoth's family and the monastic community. Although the focus of the discussion is on literature regarding the 'Byrhtnoth hanging', this conclusion is equally relevant to *Maldon* itself. Finally, the metrical charm *Wiþ Ymbe* ('For a Swarm of Bees') is included in translation and briefly analysed in *Anglo-Saxon Farms and Farming*, edited by Debby Banham and Rosamond Faith (pp. 104–5), alongside other Old English and Irish literary texts, to provide context for the role of bees in Anglo-Saxon England.

The metrical charms are further discussed in two articles this year. In 'Ploughing through Cotton Caligula A.vii: Reading the Sacred Words of the *Heliand* and the *Æcerbot*' (*RES* 65[2014] 1–17), Ciaran Arthur provides a comparison between the Old English charm and Saxon poem through the context of their shared manuscript. Arthur discusses the ways in which both poems elevate language from ordinary speech into words of power. Steering away from a view of either poem as pagan, Arthur demonstrates the extent to which these texts, when read in the context of the manuscript and in combination with one another, are both fundamentally Christian and reflective of the agendas of the Benedictine reform. An extended analysis of the two poems together identifies many of the themes and wider allusions shared between them. Ultimately, Arthur argues, the Æcerbot was added to Heliand C 'because the latter invested the charm with meaning in its focus on God's Word' (p. 6).

Sara Frances Burdorff, meanwhile, offers a fresh approach to the metrical charms by comparing them to the depiction of Grendel's mother in *Beowulf*, in 'Re-reading Grendel's Mother: *Beowulf* and the Anglo-Saxon Metrical Charms' (*Comitatus* 45[2014] 91–103), discussed above.

In 'Constructing the Old English Solomon and Saturn Dialogues' (*ES* 95[2014] 483–99), Heide Estes argues that the texts of MS Cambridge, Corpus Christi College, 422, poetry and prose both, should be considered a scribally if not authorially single work. Read in this way, the manuscript reflects an increasing trend, beginning towards the end of the ninth century, of uniting prose and poetry. The long-standing separation of the two in modern scholarship is ascribed to the influence of the Anglo-Saxon Poetic Records and Early English Text Society editions, which is reflected not least in the sometimes tricky subdivisions of the present chapter. Estes proposes numerous contemporary analogues that combine poetry and prose in one way or another, with particular reference made to the Alfredian translation of Boethius' *Consolation of Philosophy*, to collections of Old English charms, and to the Vercelli Book and *Beowulf* Codex. Estes emphasizes the value of manuscript evidence.

The Franks Casket has received a healthy share of scholarly attention this year. In 'Use of the Writing Space on the Franks Casket: Editorial and Linguistic Issues' (*Anglica* 23:ii[2014] 113–23), Helena Sobol revisits the textual editing of the casket's inscriptions. Discussion of each of the panels is furnished with an image, transliteration, edition, and translation, along with an account of the engravers' choices of language, alphabet, and layout. The most detailed discussion is reserved for the layout of the front panel's inscription and the change from runic to roman on the back panel, suggesting that the change was necessitated by the narrowness of the writing space available. Sobol's editions of the inscriptions are almost entirely in agreement with those of previous editors. The casket's more problematic or enigmatic features are not discussed; the right-hand panel receives only the briefest of treatments, and the lid is omitted entirely.

Douglas Simms turns his attention to the inscription on the casket's right panel in 'A Thorn in the Right Side of the Franks Casket' (*N&Q* 61[2014] 327). This panel has been widely discussed, not least on account of its use of cryptographic runes, which render an already enigmatic inscription that bit more perplexing to modern scholars. In keeping with current scholarly trends, Simms adopts an approach that requires minimal alteration to the received text. He argues for a redivision of the panel's letters, and a reassessment of its grammar, that renders a quite different reading than the one usually adopted by editors. Although he affirms that this new interpretation 'possesses ambiguities only translatable with difficulty', it nevertheless encourages a valuable fresh look at the casket's thorniest panel.

Thomas Klein discusses the casket as a whole in 'The Non-Coherence of the Franks Casket: Reading Text, Image, and Design on an Early Anglo-Saxon Artifact' (*Viator* 45[2014] 17–54). Klein offers an extended and detailed reading of the casket's imagery, directed by Scott McCloud's *Understanding Comics*. Klein's focus is particularly on the casket's presentation of time and space. He rejects the idea of seeking an overarching programme in the casket's design, preferring instead to approach it as an object that 'strongly resists narrative coherence' in favour of exploring the boundaries and interactions between word and image (p. 44). See also the discussion of Bredehoft in Section 2 above.

The study of genre in Old English poetry is notoriously fraught, but two articles this year boldly tackle the issue. Discussion of *Solomon and Saturn* continues, alongside *Maxims I* and *II*, in Megan E. Hartman's 'The Form and Style of Gnomic Hypermetrics' (*SMP* 1[2014] 68–99). A recognition of the distinct style of these poems allows for the consideration of 'stylistic differences along genre lines' in the Old English poetic corpus (p. 69). Gnomic poems employ hypermetric lines to a greater degree than narrative poems, with such lines frequently identified as particularly irregular by critics.

Hartman compares the style of hypermetric lines in these three poems to that found in the more conservative examples offered by *Beowulf*, *Genesis A*, *Guthlac A*, *Daniel*, and *Exodus*. Through a detailed technical analysis of the structure of hypermetric lines, Hartman demonstrates that such examples in gnomic poetry are not irregular, but instead a 'variant' of traditional hypermetric verse. The prominent use of hypermetric lines in these poems seems designed to add weight and complexity to the texts, in keeping with the individual styles of the poems.

A broader view of poetic genres is taken by Paul Battles in 'Toward a Theory of Old English Poetic Genres: Epic, Elegy, Wisdom Poetry, and the "Traditional Opening"' (*SIP* 111[2014] 1–33). Like Hartman, Battles uses internal characteristics to identify generic conventions, in this case through an examination of the 'traditional opening' of Old English poems. The study first presents an analysis of a substantial number of poems divided into three generic categories: epic, elegy, and wisdom poetry. The approach is staunchly formulaic, and the results at times surprising; according to this model, *Judgement Day II* appears to be as much an elegy as *The Wife's Lament*. The reality, as always, is more complex. Battles argues that 'most' Old English poems are 'generic hybrids' (p. 1), and he makes the case for cross-genre interaction in four specific examples: *Juliana*, *Judgement Day II*, *The Phoenix*, and *The Fates of the Apostles*. The argument presented is necessarily truncated, at times frustratingly so. No reason is given, for instance, for the assurance that *The Wanderer* may still be counted among the elegies in spite of its lack of a traditional opening. Ultimately, Battles emphasizes that generic criteria should not become a measure 'against which poems can be weighed and found wanting', but rather a means by which modern readers can better appreciate the 'tensions between convention and originality' inherent to creative literature (pp. 32–3).

Mark Griffith's 'Old English Poetic Diction Not in Old English Verse or Prose—and the Curious Case of Aldhelm's Five Athletes' (*ASE* 43[2014] 99–131) considers the various manuscripts of Aldhelm's *De Virginitate*. He notes that, although vernacular glosses are spread fairly evenly across *De Virginitate*, a substantial proportion of those that use poetic diction are concentrated in a single paragraph comparing the maidservants of Christ to five athletes. This pattern, Griffith argues, retains the trace of an underlying poetic source for the glossing of the passage.

10. Prose

The most important volume for Old English prose this year is *Hagiography in Anglo-Saxon England: Adopting and Adapting Saints' Lives into Old English Prose (c.950–1150)*, edited by Loredana Lazzari, Patrizia Lendinara, and Claudia di Sciacca. This volume of fourteen essays covers a diverse range of hagiographical writing in the Anglo-Saxon period and beyond, and contains many different methodological approaches. Joyce Hill's 'The Context of Ælfric's Saints' Lives' (pp. 1–28) gives an overview of Ælfric's *sanctorale*, discussing his selection of saints and the sources and models available to him in his writing of each saint's life. Hill discusses the use of Carolingian mixed homiliaries, such as those of Paul the Deacon, Smaragdus, and Haymo of Auxerre, to uncover some of the reasons behind Ælfric's choices. In 'Kingship and Sainthood in Ælfric: Oswald (634–642) and Edmund (840–869)' (pp. 29–66), Loredana Lazzari discusses the tensions between the ideals of a warrior king and a man of God, and discusses how Ælfric successfully blends images of the holy anti-hero (as exemplified by St Martin) with warrior martyrs in the *Lives of Saints*, to emphasize the acceptability of the idea of a just war to lay patrons dealing with the Viking invasions. St Edmund is also discussed at length by Rolf H. Bremmer Jr. in 'Shame and Honour in Anglo-Saxon Hagiography, with Special Reference to Ælfric's *Lives of Saints*' (pp. 95–120). Bremmer argues that, contrary to previous work which detected a move in Anglo-Saxon society from a pre-conversion Germanic honour-shame culture to a Christian-based guilt one, there is ample evidence in late Old English saints' lives for the survival of an honour-shame culture. Indeed, according to Bremmer, values of honour and shame abound in biblical and early hagiographical stories, and it is these notions of shame which are inverted by saints and worn as badges of honour in their martyrdom. Susan Irvine's 'Hanging by a Thread: Ælfric's Saints' Lives and the *Hengen*' (pp. 67–94) explores the formulaic language used by Ælfric as a way of universalizing his saints, while allowing the audience to focus on the differences between different saints' experiences. Irvine focuses on the torture of the *hengen*, and considers the word's collocations to elucidate the nature of the *hengen*. These collocations and alliterative patterns draw attention to the important differences in the martyrdom of individual saints and, Irvine argues, work to alert audiences to the linguistic, narrative, and thematic patterns apparent in the *Lives*.

Claudia di Sciacca looks at the legacy of the Desert Fathers in Anglo-Saxon England in ' "Concupita, Quaesita, ac Petita Solitudinis Secreta": The Desert Ideal in Bede's Prose *Vita S. Cuthberti* and Ælfric's Life of St Cuthbert' (pp. 121–81). In examining the two *Lives* of Cuthbert, Sciacca makes the case for a more positive attitude among Cuthbert's hagiographers towards the eremitic life, and advocates a less polarized understanding of Anglo-Saxon religious life as either eremitic versus coenobitic, or pastoral versus monastic. Winfried Rudolf's 'The Selection and Compilation of the *Verba Seniorum* in Worcester, Cathedral Library, F.48' (pp. 183–228) also considers the impact of the Desert Fathers, in investigating the contents of and rationale behind a collection of ascetic texts in a Worcester manuscript. Rudolf identifies Bishop Wulfstan II of Worcester as the possible instigator and user of the collection.

Giuseppe D. de Bonis's 'The Birth of Saint John the Baptist: A Source Comparison between Blickling Homily xiv and Ælfric's Catholic Homily lxxv' (pp. 255–92), provides a textual analysis of the two homilies to reveal that their authors both relied on a similar variety of Continental sources, although each homily has a different focus. De Bonis argues that the common source material of the Blickling group and Ælfric's homilies means that traditional distinctions between 'orthodox' Ælfrician material and 'heterodox' anonymous homilies are difficult to maintain. Claudio Cataldi's 'St Andrew in the Old English Homiletic Tradition' (pp. 293–308) shows three ways in which the different traditions of St Andrew were reworked for Anglo-Saxon audiences: as a heroic figure in *Andreas*, the Blickling Homily on St Andrew, and in the prose legend found in MS Cambridge, Corpus Christi College, 198; as an example of wisdom in Ælfric's homily on St Andrew, which strips away all the dramatic and marvellous episodes of the story to focus on his martyrdom and re-enactment of Christ's crucifixion; and thirdly in Trinity Homily xxix. In 'An Unfinished Drawing of St Benedict in a Neglected Manuscript of the *Regula S. Benedicti* (Cambridge, Trinity College, O.2.30)' (pp. 309–44), Maria Caterina de Bonis uses manuscript context to explore an illustration identified as St Benedict, which was added to a largely blank page some time after the main text. Despite the manuscript's production at St Augustine's in Canterbury, similarities with Cambridge, Corpus Christi College, 57 suggest that both manuscripts received their glosses at Canterbury, Christ Church, which is the source of other known pictures of St Benedict. Comparison with other manuscripts of the *Rule* of St Benedict indicate that an illustration of the saint was a common accompaniment to the text, and De Bonis speculates that the unfinished drawing in the Trinity manuscript could have been prompted by the lack of such an illustration. Finally, Rosalind Love's 'The Anglo-Saxon Saints of Thorney Abbey and their Hagiographer' (pp. 499–534) and Roberta Bassi's 'St Oswald in Early English Chronicles and Narratives' (pp. 535–56) both explore the post-Conquest life of Anglo-Saxon hagiography, detailing how different saints' lives were rewritten and adapted for new audiences.

The majority of other work on prose this year relates to Ælfric. Brandon W. Hawk's 'Isidorian Influences in Ælfric's Preface to Genesis' (*ES* 95[2014] 357–66) proposes three uses of Isidore's *Etymologiae* in Ælfric's preface: firstly in his unusual rendering of *Genesis* as *gecyndboc*, secondly in a pun in his explanation of Genesis 1:2, and thirdly in his description of baptism shortly afterwards. Hawk also notes that there are thematic parallels between Isidore's work and Ælfric's, particularly along the two dimensions of their concerns for linguistic fidelity and accurate transmission of learning. Edward J. Christie also argues for Isidore influencing Ælfric, in this case in relation to animal lore. Christie's 'The Idea of an Elephant: Ælfric of Eynsham, Epistemology, and the Absent Animals of Anglo-Saxon England' (*Neophil* 98 [2014] 465–479) explores what the Anglo-Saxons could have known about the elephant, both as animal and as symbol. Christie argues that the elephant posed an intellectual conundrum for Ælfric: on the one hand, it was well attested in the learned culture he was steeped in; on the other hand, it stretched credulity to discuss a creature his audience had heard little of—let alone seen. Christie suggests that Ælfric navigated this by following classical precedent and using the elephant as a symbol of the ineffable.

Helen Gittos's 'The Audience for Old English Texts: Ælfric, Rhetoric, and "the Edification of the Simple"' (*ASE* 43[2014] 231–66) is also concerned with the transmission of learning, though she focuses on the choice of medium. Gittos argues that material was not necessarily written in Old English in order to compensate for an audience's lack of Latin. Gittos looks at Jerome's and Gregory's arguments for translating texts, as well as Old High German and visual analogues, to suggest that Old English was used in preference to Latin for multifarious purposes, but that lack of Latinity was not among them.

A different matter of medium is the focus of Rafael J. Pascual's 'Ælfric's Rhythmical Prose and the Study of Old English Metre' (*ES* 95[2014] 803–23). Pascual subjects Ælfric's rhythmical prose to rigid metrical scrutiny, and disputes Thomas Bredehoft's argument that Ælfric's rhythmical prose should be considered poetry. Pascual argues that Bredehoft's tenets are fundamentally unsound, and that the poetic diagnosis of Ælfric's prose stemmed from inadequate definitions of poetic metre.

Less controversial is Richard Shaw's ' "Just as the Books Tell Us": A New Work by Ælfric?' (*N&Q* 61[2014] 328–36). Shaw argues that the prognostic usually called the *Table of Lucky and Unlucky Days* is not a text influenced by Ælfric of Eynsham's homilies, but is, in fact, a text by Ælfric. Shaw's argument really hinges on the use of idiosyncratic phrasing associated with Ælfric, but a case is made for Ælfrician ideas running through the text too. In a similar vein, but not concerned with Ælfric, is Stephen Pelle's 'Newly Recovered Old English Homilies from Cotton Otho A.XIII' (*RES* 65[2014] 193–218). This is an attempt at recovering information about a manuscript nearly destroyed by the 1731 Cotton fire. Pelle trawls through the excerpts recorded by Cotton's cataloguers and early scholars like Humfrey Wanley, and compares these with the extant fragments to attempt to reconstruct the contents and some of the text from this late eleventh-century manuscript.

Two other articles are likewise interested in non-Ælfrician homiletic material. Bill Friesen's 'Legends and Liturgy in the Old English Prose *Andreas*' (*ASE* 43[2014] 209–29) examines liturgical themes running through the prose *Andreas*. Friesen identifies more verbal parallels between the liturgy and the prose *Andreas* than motifs, though part of the difficulty lies in issues of pinpointing precisely what the liturgy was in the mid-eleventh century. He suggests that concerns about authority and orthodoxy might underlie these parallelisms, and he speculates whether such concerns might underlie other Old English texts.

Andreas Lemke's 'Fear-Mongering, Political Shrewdness or Setting the Stage for a "Holy Society"? Wulfstan's *Sermo Lupi ad Anglos*' (*ES* 95[2014] 758–76) argues that the BL Cotton Nero A.i version of the *Sermo Lupi ad Anglos* is both homily and political propaganda, albeit with contradicting messages. As propaganda, it is a rallying flag for resisting Scandinavian invasion; as homily, it prepares its audience for their impending penance under Scandinavian-wrought divine punishment. Lemke shows how the latter is constructed through Gildas's framework of the Anglo-Saxon invasion as divine punishment and Wulfstan's remarks that there are worse among the English, whereas the former is advanced through apocalyptic allusions.

Nicole Marafioti's *The King's Body: Burial and Succession in Late Anglo-Saxon England* is a major contribution to how we read the *Anglo-Saxon Chronicle*. Marafioti surveys the royal burials between the death of Alfred the Great in 899 to just after the accession of William the Conqueror (*c*.1070), and examines the manipulation of site, ceremony, and record to propagate a particular legacy. She demonstrates the *Anglo-Saxon Chronicle*'s increased interest in royal death and burial from 978 onwards, and ties this in with political strategies aimed at securing—or undermining—claims to the throne and the respectability of certain lineages. She also argues that these entries, particularly when they mention the place of burial, were playing up to (and against) national and regional ideas of identity. Of particular interest here are Marafioti's negotiation between the *Anglo-Saxon Chronicle* and the material culture, which she approaches as 'texts' (p. 7), and her discussions paralleling—but also firmly delineating—royal cult and saintly cult.

Debby Banham and Rosamund Faith's *Anglo-Saxon Farms and Farming* also negotiates the material and the textual in pursuit of insight into quotidian life in Anglo-Saxon England, and in doing so advances our understanding of the prose texts *Be gesceadwisan gerefan* ('On the Prudent Reeve', often known as just *Gerefa*), the *Rectitudines singularum personarum* ('The Rights of Different People'), the law-code known as *Dunsætan* ('The Hill-Dwellers'), and Ælfric's *Colloquy*. Banham and Faith illuminate many of the mysterious details of *Gerefa*, such as the identity of the animal called a *hwyorf* (a general beast of burden, p. 84), the value attached to the share and coulter (p. 48), and the meaning of its glut of unusual vocabulary, apparently lifted from glossaries. The *Rectitudines* and Ælfric's *Colloquy* are fruitfully compared with calendar illustrations and archaeological evidence to show how well grounded these texts are in daily life (as opposed to monastic or distanced ideals of it), and this realism is found in even the most unlikely texts, such as *The Wonders of the East* (p. 104). Given that Anglo-Saxon society mostly comprised farmers, this book is a useful reminder of how much the literature is framed by their experiences and annual routines.

Books Reviewed

Banham, Debby, and Rosamond Faith, eds. *Anglo-Saxon Farms and Farming*. OUP [2014]. pp. xvi + 336. £65 ISBN 9 7801 9920 7947.

Bjork, Robert E. *Old English Shorter Poems*, vol. 2: *Wisdom and Lyrics*. Dumbarton Oaks Medieval Library 32. HarvardUP. [2014] pp. 320. £19.95 ISBN 9 7806 7405 3069.

Bredehoft, Thomas. *The Visible Text: Textual Production and Reproduction from 'Beowulf' to 'Maus'*. OUP. [2014] pp. 192. £29 ISBN 9 7801 9960 3152.

Chickering, Howell, Allen J. Frantzen, and R.F. Yeager, eds. *Teaching 'Beowulf' in the Twenty-First Century*. MRTS 449. [2014] pp. 280 £29 ISBN 9 7808 6698 4973.

Cole, Marcelle. *Old Northumbrian Verbal Morphosyntax and the (Northern) Subject Rule*. (NOWELE Supplementary Series 25). Benjamins. [2014] pp. 286. €99 ISBN 9 7890 2724 0712.

Cooper, Lisa H., and Andrea Denny-Brown, eds. *The Arma Christi in Medieval and Early Modern Material Culture: With a Critical Edition of 'O Vernicle'*. Ashgate. [2014] pp. 448. £95 ISBN 9 7814 0945 6766.

Damico, Helen. *'Beowulf' and the Grendelkin: Politics and Poetry in Eleventh-Century England*. Medieval European Studies 16. West Virginia UP. [2014] pp. 378. £34 ISBN 9 7819 3822 8711.

Darby, Peter, and Faith Wallis, eds. *Bede and the Future*. Ashgate. [2014] pp. 269. £95 ISBN 9 7814 0945 6681.

Frantzen, Allen J. *Food, Eating and Identity in Early Medieval England.* Boydell. [2014] pp. 304. £60 ISBN 9 7818 4383 9088.

Gneuss, Helmut, and Michael Lapidge, *Anglo-Saxon Manuscripts: A Bibliographical Handlist of Manuscripts Written or Owned in England up to 1100.* UTorP. [2014] pp. 718. £120 ISBN 9 7814 4264 8234.

Horobin, Simon, and Linne R. Mooney, eds. *Middle English Texts in Transition: A Festschrift Dedicated to Toshiyuki Takamiya on his 70th Birthday.* YMP. [2014] pp. xix + 335. £60 ISBN 9 7819 0315 3536.

Jorgensen, Alice, Frances McCormack, and Jonathan Wilcox, eds. *Anglo-Saxon Emotions: Reading the Heart in Old English Language, Literature and Culture.* Ashgate. [2015] pp. 318. £75 ISBN 9 7814 7242 1715.

Klein, Stacey S., William Schipper, and Shannon Lewis-Simpson, eds., *The Maritime World of the Anglo-Saxons,* Essays in Anglo-Saxon Studies 5. MRTS. [2014] pp. 356. $70 ISBN 9 7808 6698 4966.

Kline, Daniel T., ed. *Digital Gaming Re-imagines the Middle Ages.* Routledge. [2014] pp. 312. £90 ISBN 9 7804 1563 0917.

Kuhn, Dominik. *Der lateinisch-altenglische Libellus Precum in der Handschrift London, British Library, Arundel 155.* Münchener Universitätsschriften Texte und Untersuchungen zur Englischen Philologie 41. Lang. [2014] pp. 387. £55 ISBN 9 7836 3165 4620.

Lazzari, Loredana, Patrizia Lendinara, and Claudia di Sciacca, eds. *Hagiography in Anglo-Saxon England: Adopting and Adapting Saints' Lives into Old English Prose* (c.950–1150). Fédération Internationale des Instituts d'Études Médiévales, Textes et Études du Moyen Âge 73. Brepols. [2014] pp. 590. €65 ISBN 9 8725 0355 1999.

Liuzza, R.M., ed. *Old English Prose: An Anthology.* Broadview. [2014] pp. 240. $17.95 ISBN 9 7815 5481 1571.

Marafioti, N. *The King's Body: Burial and Succession in Late Anglo-Saxon England.* UTorP. [2014] pp. 320. $65 ISBN 9 7814 4264 7589.

Meens, R. *Penance in Medieval Europe 600–1200.* CUP. [2014] pp. 290. £21.99 ISBN 9 7805 2169 3110.

Neidorf, Leonard, ed. *The Dating of 'Beowulf': A Reassessment,* Anglo-Saxon Studies 24. Brewer. [2014] pp. 262. £60 ISBN 9 7818 4384 3870.

Pastan, Elizabeth Carson, and Stephen D. White, with Kate Gilbert, eds. *The Bayeux Tapestry and Its Contexts: A Reassessment.* Boydell. [2014] pp. 476. £60 ISBN 9 7818 4383 9415.

O'Donoghue, Heather. *English Poetry and Old Norse Myth: A History.* OUP. [2014] pp. 242. £55 ISBN 9 7801 9956 2183.

Ogura, Michiko, ed., *Aspects of Anglo-Saxon and Medieval England.* Lang. [2014] pp. 134. £25 ISBN 9 7836 3165 5863.

Owen-Crocker, Gale, and Brian Schneider, eds. *The Anglo-Saxons: The World through Their Eyes.* British Archaeological Reports 595. Archaeopress. [2014] pp. viii + 162. £32 ISBN 9 7814 0731 2620.

Rambaran-Olm, M.R. *'John the Baptist's Prayer' or 'The Descent into Hell' from the Exeter Book: Text, Translation and Critical Study.* Brewer. [2014] pp. 262. £60 ISBN 9 7818 4384 3665.

Richards, Mary P. *The Old English Poem 'Seasons for Fasting': A Critical Edition* Medieval European Studies 15. West Virginia UP. [2014] pp. 220. $44.99 ISBN 9 7819 3822 8438.

Stokes, Peter. *English Vernacular Minuscule from Æthelred to Cnut, circa 990—circa 1035*. Brewer. [2014] pp. 309. £57 ISBN 9 7818 4384 3696.

Sylvester, Louise, Mark C. Chambers, and Gale Owen-Crocker, eds. *Medieval Dress and Textiles in Britain: A Multilingual Sourcebook*. Medieval and Renaissance Clothing and Textiles 2. Boydell. [2014] pp. 412. £60 ISBN 9 7818 4383 9323.

Tolkien, J.R.R. *'Beowulf': Translation and Commentary, Together with 'Sellic Spell'*, ed. Christopher Tolkien. HarperCollins. [2014] pp. 448. £17 ISBN 9 7800 0811 6583.

Yeager, Steven. *From Lawmen to Ploughmen: Anglo-Saxon Legal Tradition and the School of Langland*. UTorP. [2014] pp. 280. $65 ISBN 9 7814 4264 3475.

III

Middle English

KATE ASH-IRISARRI, TAMARA ATKIN, ANNE BADEN-DAINTREE, ALASTAIR BENNETT, DAISY BLACK, MARY C. FLANNERY, CARRIE GRIFFIN, HETTA HOWES, YOSHIKO KOBAYASHI, HOLLY MOYER, MICHELLE M. SAUER, KATIE WALTER, AND WILLIAM ROGERS

This chapter has fifteen sections: 1. General and Miscellaneous; 2. Theory; 3. Manuscript and Textual Studies; 4. Early Middle English; 5. Lyrics and Shorter Poems; 6. *Sir Gawain and the Green Knight, Pearl, Patience, Cleanness*; 7. *Piers Plowman*; 8. Other Alliterative Verse; 9. Verse Romance; 10. Gower; 11. Hoccleve and Lydgate; 12. Secular Prose; 13. Religious Prose; 14. Older Scots; 15. Drama. Sections 1 and 8 are by Anne Baden-Daintree; section 2 is by Katie Walter; section 3 is by Carrie Griffin; section 4 is by Alastair Bennett; section 5 is by Hetta Howes; sections 6 and 13 are by Michelle M. Sauer; sections 7 and 12 are by William Rogers; section 9 is by Holly Moyer; section 10 is by Yoshiko Kobayashi; section 11 is by Mary C. Flannery; section 14 is by Kate Ash-Irisarri; section 15 is by Daisy Black, with the assistance of Tamara Atkin.

1. General and Miscellaneous

Essays on Aesthetics and Medieval Literature in Honour of Howell Chickering, a Festschrift edited by John M. Hill, Bonnie Wheeler, and R.F. Yeager, is nicely focused as a reflection of Chickering's own wide-ranging research interests, and also his practice. As the editors explain, 'Chickering essays usually start as close readings that progress from deeply informed philological word analysis through erudite attention to grammatical and rhetorical variations and build to conclusions about a poem's meanings in terms of aesthetic play and our reading pleasure' (p. 1). This volume contains five essays on various Old English texts, six on Chaucer, and also essays on Gower, Lydgate, and devotional prose and poetry—these are discussed below in other sections—all with an emphasis on the aesthetic qualities of medieval texts, but with some important insights into how such effects are achieved. The final three chapters

The Year's Work in English Studies, Volume 95 (2016) © *The Author 2016. Published by Oxford University Press on behalf of the English Association. All rights reserved. For Permissions, please email: journals.permissions@oup.com*
doi:10.1093/ywes/maw002

offer a reader-focused perspective that extends beyond the Middle Ages. As the final chapter reveals, the question posed by the editors to the various authors was, 'What constitutes "beauty" in medieval English poetry?' (p. 262).

In 'Trawþe and Tresoun: Translating *Sir Gawain and the Green Knight*' (pp. 228–43), Clare Kinney examines the many modern English translations of *Sir Gawain and the Green Knight* in order to establish how the aesthetic of the original poem both invites and resists translation. Her detailed examination of a single stanza in its translations by three contemporary poets (W.S. Merwin, Bernard O'Donoghue, and Simon Armitage) explores the nuances of the Middle English text before comparing the different approaches and their relative merits or drawbacks. Kinney's focus is on textual accuracy, on the effects of adopting a version of alliterative metre (or rejecting this) and of tone, diction, and inappropriate colloquialism. She also provides some nicely judged observations about verse form, and particularly the importance of replicating the effect of the bob and wheel to achieve the changes of pace that shape the narrative drive of the poem. The analysis of the shortcomings of the various translations is based on Kinney's own meticulous close reading of the poem, and she offers some particularly strong insights on the processes of exchange underpinning the narrative, and the problems that the associated vocabulary (particularly *trawþe*) presents when rendered into modern English.

John Ganim's chapter, 'Cosmopolitanism, Medievalism, and Romanticism: The Case of Coleridge' (pp. 244–61), considers the interaction between aesthetics and ethics in the Romantic period in terms of Coleridge's engagement with medieval poetry, and his complex response to the medieval past. Ganim demonstrates that Coleridge's interactions with the medieval at different stages of his literary career were intertwined with contemporary cultural and political contexts, often in a problematic or contradictory manner. He concludes that 'Coleridge's medievalism holds an unstable place in his political and aesthetic system, often complicating the principles he explicitly espoused' (p. 261).

Finally, Nancy Mason Bradbury considers Edward Burne-Jones's illustrations of the *Canterbury Tales* for the 1896 collaboration with William Morris, the *Kelmscott Chaucer*, and the degree to which artistic decisions stem from the aesthetic values of the poems themselves. In this essay, '"A Definite Claim to Beauty": The *Canterbury Tales* in the *Kelmscott Chaucer*' (pp. 262–90), Bradbury re-examines the evidence for the highly selective choice of illustrations, commenting on the aspects of the work left unillustrated (and in some cases even without a decorative border). While romance is clearly privileged over fabliau, many of the more 'serious' tales are also subordinated through lack of illustration, as is the frame narrative—perhaps an indication of reading practices that have been altered by the subsequent critical focus and preferences. The conclusion is about aesthetic preference: that Burne-Jones's preference was for myth and allegory over realism (rather than, as other critics have suggested, a squeamishness about subject matter). Bradbury moves on to analyse aspects of his style (including some illuminating observations about differences between draft designs and the final illustrations). The close reading of the texts concerned is, she argues, fundamental to the mood and symbolism of the illustrations, which reflect an acute engagement with Chaucer's depiction of his characters' subjectivity.

War and Literature, edited by Laura Ashe and Ian Patterson, presents a wide-ranging collection of essays with a strong awareness of the complex moral responsibilities of war writing, underpinned with an awareness that 'Art's idealisation of war and warriors' can be reinforced, 'even when literature seeks directly to condemn conflict' (p. xi). This is complicated by the sense that, particularly in the twentieth century and beyond, there is an urgent need to bear witness and record or represent. Almost half the chapters in this cogently argued collection focus on the medieval period. While some of these have more of a historical than a literary focus, they nonetheless present some thoughtful analysis of the manipulation of language in the context of waging war. In the opening chapter, 'Acts of Vengeance, Acts of Love: Crusading Violence in the Twelfth Century' (pp. 3–20), for example, Susanna A. Throop analyses material such as Latin chronicles, religious treatises, and sermons to identify the precise meaning of 'vengeance' as applied to crusading endeavours, and shows how the violence enacted on the pagan 'other' is seen as reciprocating the violence enacted on Christ.

This close attention to the implications of specific verbal nuances is also a feature of Katie L. Walter's chapter, 'Peril, Flight and the Sad Man: Medieval Theories of the Body in Battle' (pp. 21–40). Walter turns her attention to the various Middle English translations and reworkings of Latinate treatises on war, particularly those of Giles of Rome and Vegetius. The psychology of engagement in war is complex and complicated by a knowledge of the peril faced, yet driven by an urge to fight to the death. An alternative to the reading of medieval battle as driven by sadomasochism is, suggests Walter, to understand that '*sadness* is the necessary counterpart to joy in forming courage in battle' (p. 24). The *tristitia* induced by the expectation of death (as well of bodily suffering) reflects a form of endurance that equates to courage on the battlefield. Walter's examination of the Middle English concept of sadness identifies an interplay of different meanings in vernacular texts involving both grief and constancy or strength. Walter concludes that 'sadness' in Middle English writings on war must be understood in terms of its full semantic range: inuring the knight to the conditions of war and training him appropriately (a preparation she describes as a 'hardening'), but also allowing for the necessity of feeling grief at 'the misery and the senselessness of war' (p. 38).

Catherine A.M. Clarke, in 'Crossing the Rubicon: History, Authority and Civil War in Twelfth-Century England' (pp. 61–83), explores textual engagement with 'the particular horrors of civil war' (p. 62) and employs a wide range of twelfth-century chronicles and histories, in both Latin and Middle English. Her focus then narrows to the ways in which classical models provide a framework for interpretation and expression of the experience of civil war, and those writings which draw on Lucan's *Bellum civile*, particularly Henry of Huntingdon's *Historia Anglorum*. She presents a new reading of the narrative accounts of strange discoveries beneath the earth in William of Newburgh, employing contemporary trauma theory to suggest that 'this may be a further textual expression of the unspeakable horrors of civil conflict' (p. 67). The theme of fracture is explored through the accounts of the damaged earth, the fragmented textual structures, and the narrative voice in the various twelfth-century texts, drawing on the critical response to Lucan, whose text employs a 'fractured' voice to 'express the division and alienation of civil conflict' (p. 71).

Joanna Bellis considers the changes in military practice (and written responses to these) during the reigns of Edward III and Henry V in ' "The Reader myghte lamente": The Sieges of Calais (1346) and Rouen (1418) in Chronicle, Poem and Play' (pp. 84–106). Bellis compares the narration of these two 'strangely similar' sieges, which took place many years apart, 'at either end of the Hundred Years War'. The attempt to map the changing response to these events over time demonstrates a shift in perception which becomes, in the case of Calais, increasingly critical of the practices involved, but with Rouen begins with some reservation but ultimately glorifies the process (and Henry V, its instigator). Analysing a wide range of source materials, including chronicles from contemporary recorders, and those, such as Holinshed, with a historical perspective, eyewitness accounts, and Elizabethan drama, Bellis charts the changes alongside a commentary which identifies the political context and purposes of alterations in bias and emphasis.

Bellis again addresses the narrative accounts of the siege of Rouen in her article, ' "We wanted þe trewe copy þereof" John Page's *The Siege of Rouen*, Text and Transmission' (*MÆ* 83:ii[2014] 210–33). She focuses on the way in which the siege is, in the chronicle history, 'the point at which several continuations within the *Brut* tradition diverge' (p. 211). John Page's (apparently) eyewitness poetic account is embedded within the chronicle, and Bellis's article examines the historical and manuscript context of this poem, revealing much about the processes of textual transmission. The significant differences in the various manuscript witnesses of the poem are, Bellis argues, are neither scribal error (although this also occurs) nor authorial revision, but rather scribal intervention in the form of 'deliberate, dramatic, and interventionist copying' (p. 218). The article concludes with some astute observations on editorial assumptions about textual transmission, and the vulnerability and uncertain status of most Middle English texts.

A collection of essays edited by Amanda Hopkins, Robert Allen Rouse, and Cory James Rushton, *Sexual Culture in the Literature of Medieval Britain*, presents a well-balanced set of studies of individual texts in Middle English (and Scots) with an emphasis on the romance genre. Hopkins and Rushton have previously collaborated on another edited volume, *The Erotic in the Literature of Medieval Britain* [2007], and this new collection extends the range of the earlier volume, including a wider selection of canonical Middle English texts, representing something of the breadth and variety of sexual possibilities, but also engaging more explicitly with definitions of the erotic and of sexuality. The eleven chapters cover a variety of theoretical perspectives, but the collection as a whole considers social controls and expectations regarding sexual behaviours, gendered perspectives on sexuality, and the interaction between sexuality and erotic experience, including the reader's potential for erotic engagement with either text or characters. The introductory essay begins by outlining popular perceptions of medieval culture and sexuality: a long tradition of using 'medieval' as shorthand for barbaric, backward, or misogynistic when delineating the failures of (other) modern cultures. This viewpoint culminates in the popular imagination in the HBO series *Game of Thrones*, which depicts 'a brutal medieval sexuality, a misogynous sexual culture replete with the threat of violent coercion' (p. 1). The essays in this collection, unsurprisingly, represent a more nuanced depiction of modes of sexuality in medieval fictional texts. While the contributions are of a consistently high standard, the range of texts does not stray far from the predictable field of Malory, Chaucer, and popular romance. But there are some less expected texts, and some unexpected directions of desire (the animal and the alchemical, for example). The editors draw attention, as do contributors, to matters of perception, whereby an event might be viewed as fundamentally different by the individual participants. This is related to the distinction they draw between sexuality (connected with self-identity, and the focus of desire) and the erotic: 'sexuality may be inherent or even genetic; the erotic is learned' (p. 4). But the editors are also careful to point out the gulf between modern and pre-modern sexualities (as well as points of connection). Individual chapters are discussed fully below.

While sexual culture and behaviour inform many of the essays in a special issue of *Essays in Medieval Studies*, edited by Elizabeth D. Weber, 'Seduction: The Art of Persuasion in the Medieval World' (*EssaysMedSt* 30[2014] 1–203), 'seduction' is here explored in its widest sense. However, the chapters on Middle English texts do, in fact, deal mainly with sexual relationships. Michelle Sweeney's article, 'Lady as Temptress and Reformer in Medieval Romance' (*EssaysMedSt* 30[2014] 165–78), investigates reversals of gender relationships in *The Knight of the Cart*, *Lanval*, *Sir Gawain and the Green Knight*, and the *Franklin's Tale*. Sweeney proposes that female sexuality, rather than always having a negative effect on a knight's honour (through woman's role as 'temptress') in a romance setting, might conversely be seen as having reforming or salvific power. She analyses scenes of threatened rape and sexual temptation in the four texts, where sexual fulfilment is always underpinned by the threat of violence, and considers such 'emotionally fraught situations' in terms of the outcome for the knight, through the agency (or lack thereof) of the lady.

'Adversarial Relationships between Humans and Weather in Medieval English Literature' (*EssaysMedSt* 30[2014] 67–81) is an essay which engages rather obliquely with the journal's central theme of seduction. Michael W. George takes the opening of the Prologue to the *Canterbury Tales* as a starting point for viewing the 'seductiveness' of the standard springtime opening in terms of its opposites: the actual weather experiences of the fourteenth century, and literary depictions of the hardships of inclement weather conditions. Employing recent scholarship on climate change together with evidence from palaeoclimatology, and historical data on crop yields, George demonstrates that the fourteenth and fifteenth centuries experienced variable temperatures with prolonged periods of increased rainfall. The spring settings of much literature present precisely the opposite: pleasant warm weather, and the understanding that this is an expected recurring situation. When storms and adverse weather appear in fictional texts they have significant narrative agency, and are even figured as 'active antagonist'. George argues that the instability of experienced weather conditions is warded off by the escapism of the idealized spring setting, but further, the 'anomalous period of good weather and harvests' from the mid-1370s to the 1390s may well be reflected in a false optimism in the paradisal landscapes of such poetry.

The natural world delineated in the opening to the General Prologue is also discussed in Louise Westling, ed., *The Cambridge Companion to Literature and the Environment*, in a chapter by Alfred K. Siewers, 'The Green Otherworlds of Early Medieval Literature' (pp. 31–44). Siewers draws on Northrup Frye's concept of 'green world comedy' and extends this to trace a history of 'green worlds' back to an earlier Celtic tradition, examining it through texts including *Tochmarc Étaíne* and the *Mabinogi*. Siewers also finds evidence for their endurance in some canonical Middle English texts, including the *Canterbury Tales*, *Sir Gawain and the Green Knight*, and Malory's *Morte Darthur*. The supernatural Otherworlds of early Welsh and Irish texts (and in the later Arthurian romances) are overlaid and interwoven with the 'actual geography and ecological life on the surface of Earth' (p. 31). The depictions of landscapes in all these texts are, suggests Siewers, informed by a sense of the 'other side' of nature which is beyond human control and understanding.

Analysis of some late medieval texts on the craft of dying is provided by Alison L. Beringer in 'The Death of Christ as a Focus of the Fifteenth-Century *Artes moriendi*' (*JEGP* 113[2014] 497–512), which examines five *Ars moriendi* texts spanning the fifteenth century, in both Latin and English. Much of the focus is on the early fifteenth-century *Speculum* and its later English translations. The variations in these texts demonstrate the different means of employing the Passion to contribute to and shape a dying man's experience of death. Rather than simply encouraging meditation on the events of the Passion, the texts all direct attention towards a confirmation of Christ's death as a means to their salvation. However, Beringer identifies a more affective approach in two of the English texts, in one case explicitly invoking Bernard of Clairvaux's interpretation of the disposition of Christ's body on the cross. And the death of Christ also becomes a model for deathbed behaviour, with, for example, Caxton's *Arte* listing the sequence of Christ's actions on the cross to be imitated by the sick man at the point of death. Finally, drawing also on sermon material with a similar focus, Beringer demonstrates that contemplation of the Passion at the point of death also acts 'as a buffer between the dying person and his enemy, the devil' (p. 512).

Juanita Feros Ruys, in 'Dying 101: Emotion, Experience, and Learning How to Die in the Late Medieval *Artes Moriendi*' (*Parergon* 31:ii[2014] 55–79), also addresses the *Artes moriendi*. However, Ruys's approach is to provide a wide-spanning overview from the early fourteenth to the early sixteenth century, with a focus on the sometimes problematic way in which such texts effect an emotional response in the dying. This article focuses on the German mystic Henry Suso, followed by consideration of texts by three English authors: an anonymous Latin text and Hoccleve's *Series* (both of which draw on Suso), and the early sixteenth-century monastic writings of Richard Whitford. Throughout the tradition the negative emotions of grief and fear can be overcome through appropriate preparation for death which replaces terror of death with the 'beneficial' fear of God, enabling 'new emotions of desire for and joy in death' (p. 62). Heightened emotions (sometimes wrought through description of the physical failings of the dying body) and a reduced focus on procedural advice characterize the fifteenth-century approaches but, as Ruys demonstrates, by the early sixteenth century a new perspective emerges. Fear of death can also be allayed by experiential evidence of sense perception. By drawing on experiences of mystical visions where the separation of body and soul enables a state where no bodily pain is felt, argues Whitford, death should also produce no pain at the point where the soul achieves a sense of liberation from the body. Ruys concludes by outlining Whitford's suggested exercises which bring readers into an imaginative confrontation with death as a form of rehearsal, which operates alongside the formal spiritual preparations.

The article by Ruys appears in a special issue of *Parergon*, 'Medieval and Early Modern Emotional Responses to Death and Dying' (*Parergon* 31:ii[2014]), edited by Rebecca F. McNamara, and Una McIlvenna. This publication aims to present a wide range of case studies from the medieval and early modern periods in order to 'illuminate the variety of premodern affective responses to death and dying' (p. 1). This also draws attention to differences from the present day, but at the same time challenges any 'universalizing notions' about responses to death or dying. The editors provide some helpful contextualizing summary which emphasizes the centrality of death to premodern social and religious practices and culture. Contributors are drawn from several disciplines, and include social and cultural historians and literary scholars, whose frame of reference stretches from the thirteenth to the eighteenth century. Many of the essays in this issue are concerned with post-medieval texts, but the late medieval chronicle tradition is addressed in an article by Alicia Marchant, 'Narratives of Death and Emotional Affect in Late Medieval Chronicles' (*Parergon* 31:ii[2014] 81–98). This cogent analysis of the narrative strategies of the chronicle tradition examines both Latin and English texts in order to demonstrate that, while accounts of deaths are primarily straightforward factual records in accord with the style, structure, and other conventions of the genre, this is not always the case. Marchant provides compelling evidence that, in some accounts of deaths, various techniques were employed which enabled both 'the depiction of emotion and . . . . the manipulation of readers' emotional responses to the narrative' (p. 81). One of the most important of these is the disruption of the chronology of events, either leading to repeated reference to a single event, or a 'collapsing and telescoping of time' (p. 92) to provide suggestive connections between narrative events. This can occur simply through juxtaposition and paratactical structure which invite the reader to make the connection, or similarities of language to connect the events. Marchant demonstrates such techniques through detailed analysis of the various accounts of the execution of Richard Scrope, the archbishop of York, juxtaposed with details of Henry V's subsequent contraction of leprosy. Finally, she provides evidence of embellishment of the narrative through the addition of telling details which affect audience response to the accounts of Scrope's death which have political as well as emotional resonance.

Wendy A. Matlock, in 'Reworking the Household in *The Debate of the Carpenter's Tools*' (*ES* 95:ii[2014] 109–30), demonstrates the degree to which a late fifteenth-century debate poem engages with the process of social change in its redefinition of household and work roles. The central debate (about how hard the anthropomorphized tools should work to ensure prosperity, in the context of a lazy, drunken, and spendthrift master) highlights the underlying tensions between artisanal allegiance to 'patriarchal authority' or to 'a craft or kin group'. The poem dramatizes the situation in a typical household where familial and business relationships intersect in the same domestic setting and produce tensions between different lines of authority at a time when work was becoming increasingly gendered, and guilds were beginning to exclude women, requiring an increased need for the separation of family and workshop.

The relationship between the parallel French and English manuscripts of Charles d'Orléans (BN MS fr. 25458 and BL MS Harley 682) is revisited by Rory G. Critten in a provocative article entitled 'The Political Valence of Charles d'Orléans's English Poetry' (*MP* 111[2014] 339–64). Critten's analysis of specific textual differences leads him to the conclusion that the poet intends to portray quite distinct personae in the two manuscripts. The more coherent and finely realized figure of the lover in the English manuscript is partly due, Critten acknowledges, to the organization, selection, and expansion of material from the French, lending a stronger narrative coherence. But there are also clear translation choices and additional phrases which emphasize the portrayal of the lover as inept and bumbling, with a tone in the English poetry which alternates between dark despair and comedy, in both cases with a clearer erotic bias than the French. Critten then moves on to the (also as yet unresolved but much discussed) issue of why the English verses were written. He re-evaluates biographical evidence to present a picture of a more politically involved and astute Charles than is often presented, with an emphasis on his continued reputation and sense of responsibility during captivity (where traditionally he has been envisaged as being able to 'do little else but write poetry'), and the consequent danger he represented to his captors. While this account is detailed and informative it could have dwelt longer on how the diversionary image-manipulation effected by the duke's poetic presentation might influence our reading of the poems of Harley 682. Comparisons with Hoccleve are tantalizingly raised but not fully explored here.

Elizabeth Harper, in ' "A Tokene and a Book": Reading Images and Building Consensus in *Dives and Pauper*' (*YLS* 28[2014] 173–90), discusses the arguments defending image-worship in this fifteenth-century prose dialogue on the Ten Commandments. Explaining how the text invites an expectation of opposing viewpoints and extreme positions through its dialogic structure, Harper demonstrates that instead it 'seeks to build consensus' between opponents. There are some useful illustrations of Pauper's 'conciliatory approach', which, Harper suggests, underpins the whole enterprise (based on a belief that 'lay people can and should understand scriptural interpretation'). The suggestion that an image might be read as a text is Pauper's response to Dives' clear hostility to images (echoing extreme Lollard positions on image worship). Pauper's persistent use of this metaphor, that an image is 'but a book and a token to þe lewyd peple', encourages a focus on the symbolic qualities of images as a means of building on Lollard preferences in order to establish common ground. This suggests that the text as a whole provides evidence for 'a wider and more interesting variety of "orthodox" stances than has previously been acknowledged', and that Pauper's method is to present 'a form of orthodoxy' that might be acceptable to Lollard sympathizers.

2. Theory

This section divides work broadly into two categories: scholarship on Middle English literary theory, and publications which take up contemporary theoretical approaches to Middle English texts.

While no monographs taking Middle English literary theory as their principal subject were published in 2014, a number of journal articles make notable contributions in this area. In two, Middle English prologues continue to prove a rich source for developing and refining our understanding of literary theory in the vernacular. A.B. Kraebel, 'Middle English Gospel Glosses and the Translation of Exegetical Authority' (*Traditio* 69[2014] 87–123), explores three Middle English translations and commentaries on the gospels of Matthew (extant in two manuscripts, London, BL, MS Egerton 242 and Cambridge, University Library, MS Ii.2.12), Mark, and Luke (both in Cambridge, Corpus Christi College, MS 32). Building on the seminal work of Mary Dove, Kraebel aims to further demonstrate 'the extent to which interest in biblical translation and commentary pervaded Middle English literary culture' (p. 87). Particularly noteworthy are the editions Kraebel provides of the prologues to each of these translations and commentaries, given in three appendices, which will facilitate further work in this area. In the essay itself, in addition to tracing the sources for the commentaries and describing their *mise-en-page*, Kraebel offers a detailed analysis of the prologues. The prologue to the Middle English Matthew commentary is both the most extensive of these and the most interesting for theoretical enquiry: Kraebel notes that it offers 'an account of the commentator's reasons for undertaking this exegetical project, a comparative discussion of the different evangelists . . . and, finally, an account of Matthew's particular authorial intentions and the ways in which he framed his Gospel on the model of earlier Hebrew literature' (p. 99). Kraebel's analysis of the prologues usefully identifies some elements that are drawn from the academic prologue model, but other elements that 'seem to be proper to the vernacular "advocates of translation" genre identified by Dove' (p. 102).

The use of St Anselm's prologue to the *Orationes sive meditationes* in four Middle English manuscripts is the focus of Sarah Noonan's essay, ' "Bycause the redyng shold not turne hem to enoye": Reading, Selectivity, and *Pietatis Affectum* in Late Medieval England' (*NML* 15[2014] 227–56). Noonan situates Anselm's prologue 'within broader theoretical conversations regarding the respective values of indexical and affective modes of reading' (p. 228), and explores 'the textual and codicological contexts' of these Middle English prologues, which are found in manuscripts of the *Manuel de péchés*, *A Talking of the Love of God*, Eleanor Hull's series of meditations, and the *Pseudo-Augustinian Soliloquies*. These contexts all evidence 'a continuous interest in both the devotional and ethical value of reading selectively' on the part of the translators, and the importance of 'paratextual markers' on that of the scribes (p. 231). Noonan frames her argument within a discussion of two medieval theories of knowledge—on the one hand, that gained through reason, and on the other, that gained through an appeal to the affect—and the main reading methods with which they are associated. By exploring the ways in which these prologues and the texts they preface participate in these medieval theories,

Noonan seeks to offer a modification of the traditional understanding that this kind of selective reading 'is geared towards less-learned audiences' not able to engage fully with the texts' intellectual demands (p. 243), stressing instead the affective and ethical value of this kind of reading.

Alan T. Gaylord's essay, 'Devotional Practice in Crafted Mystical Prose and Poetry: A Preliminary Inquiry' (in Hill, Wheeler, and Yeager, eds., pp. 216–27), also contributes to work on theories of reading. Specifically, Gaylord claims for two Middle English texts—Julian of Norwich's *Showings* and *Pearl*—the propaedeutic function of formal beauty, which 'leads the reader to perceive with greater depth, sensitivity, and delight devotional meaning' (p. 217). Gaylord thus imagines contemporary readers of these texts to be engaged 'in a variant of *lectio divinia,* as an exercise of meditation combining both aesthetics and divinity' (p. 219). Central to recognizing this propaedeutic function, Gaylord suggests, is what he terms 'prosodic criticism'—that is, a reading, even for prose, that 'begins with a written text and imagines how it would sound . . . an utterance that rides on a breath, rises and falls with syntactic intonation, and shapes the sounds and stresses of articulation to turn literature into an aural/oral recitation' (p. 219).

Several journal issues appearing in 2014 make theorized approaches to Middle English texts their focus. The *Chaucer Review* issue in memory of Lee Patterson foregrounds and rethinks historicist approaches. Candace Barrington and Emily Steiner, in their introduction to the issue, 'Thinking Historically after Historicism: Essays in Memory of Lee Patterson' (*ChauR* 48:iv[2014] 361–71), highlight Patterson's path-breaking contribution to New Historicism and offer a useful summary of the development of historicist approaches from the 1980s. They also assert the continued importance of the questions New Historicism poses about the category of the literary, and of literature from the past. In summarizing the work of the essays in the issue, Barrington and Steiner assess the contribution New Historicism has made to our understanding of particular Middle English texts and the questions it has prompted to ask of them, and reflect on the future of literary historicism. In this regard Larry Scanlon's contribution, 'Nothing but Change and Variance: The Problem of Hoccleve's Politics' (*ChauR* 48:iv[2014] 504–23), is worth brief mention, although it is treated fully elsewhere. Here, Scanlon identifies the waning of historicism's influence as a particular problem for Hoccleve studies. Raising the scholarly disagreement over ideological affiliations in Hoccleve, Scanlon notes 'this disagreement reaches to the heart of the historicist enterprise for it raises the question: can the poetic impulse itself be historicized? Or does poetry retain some essence that always stands beyond even the most radical forms of historical variation and transformation?' (p. 506). Taking the stance of a believer in an 'ideological Hoccleve', Scanlon offers what he calls an 'aligned' reading of the poet, pointing to the need for and the value of continued engagements with historicism in interpreting Middle English texts.

An issue of *Exemplaria* is devoted to 'Pre-modern Emotions' (26:i[2014] 3–15). In her introduction, Stephanie Trigg evaluates the productiveness of the terms in play—emotion, feelings, passions, affect—for medieval (and early modern) scholarship, and traces something of their recent critical and theoretical lineages. Affect and its 'specialised sense in contemporary theory' receives particular attention, as well as its operation in relation to and against the term 'emotion' (p. 5). Trigg highlights the potential fruitfulness, modelled in the work of Monique Scheer, of Bourdieu's notion of *habitus* in thinking about emotion as practice, and foregrounds both the usefulness and limitations of scholars' own recourse to 'a personal or affective mode in their reading of medieval texts' (p. 10). As Trigg assesses, one contribution these essays collectively make is to emphasize that 'the study of emotion is not just about individual feeling . . . but about the way emotions mediate communities as active agents in social life' (p. 14). Two essays in the issue treat Middle English texts: Rebecca F. McNamara's and Juanita Feros Ruys's 'Unlocking the Silences of the Self-Murdered: Textual Approaches to Suicidal Emotions in the Middle Ages' (*Exemplaria* 26:i[2014] 58–80), and Jessica Rosenfeld's 'Envy and Exemplarity in *The Book of Margery Kempe*' (*Exemplaria* 26:i[2014] 105–21). McNamara and Ruys, drawing on Barbara Rosenwein's concept of 'emotional communities', explore two particular genres: English legal records (in Latin) and what they term 'first-person life records', including *The Book of Margery Kempe* and Thomas Hoccleve's *Series*. In so doing, and building on the concept of emotional communities, they suggest that a genre-based approach is fruitful. Rosenfeld's essay is worth mention here for its engagement with theories of envy in interpreting *The Book of Margery Kempe*. Drawing on Sianne Ngai's recent 'recuperation' of envy enables Rosenfeld to explore 'the way that envy can work as a strategic mode of re-evaluating one's relationship to exemplary ideas' (p. 106). As Rosenfeld explores, Ngai's thinking draws on, but also modifies, Freud's claims for the social function of envy 'as the foundation of all communal feeling' (p. 109), particularly as it concerns the female (or othered) subject, and in its feminist (as well as postcolonial) possibilities. Through this lens, Margery's envy and competitiveness (two aspects of the same emotion) can be understood as tools both for exploring social categories and for representing herself as exemplary. 'Envy is thus well poised', Rosenfeld asserts, 'to make an intervention in the configuration of late medieval hagiographic exemplarity' (p. 110).

Elsewhere, publications in 2014 extend work on Middle English texts in the areas of ecocriticism, disability studies, and phenomenology. Gillian Rudd, in 'Being Green in Late Medieval English Literature' (in Garrard, ed., *The Oxford Handbook of Ecocriticism*, pp. 27–39), makes a detailed reading of the colour green in Middle English texts central to her exploration of the links between medieval literature and the '20th century ecology movement'. While giving sustained attention to *Sir Gawain and the Green Knight*, a number of Chaucer's *Canterbury Tales* (the *Wife of Bath's Tale*, *Friar's Tale*, and *Squire's Tale*), as well as a poem attributed to Chaucer, 'Against Woman Unconstant', are drawn on. Rudd highlights that if 'green' now often is 'good', or is 'the color or ethical and political awareness, equal respect for the human and the nonhuman world', in contrast, in medieval England 'green was the color of falsehood, unreliability, and deception, as well as the color of the natural world and of vigorous new life' (p. 30). Reading 'green' closely in both the *Gawain*-poet and Chaucer leads Rudd to conclude that the colour 'indicates a moment of choice, or of change: a point where things are not fixed and sure, but liable to alter. Moreover, it indicates that whatever choice we make, there will be consequences by which we must abide' (p. 37). Noting both the differences and the continuities between medieval and modern thinking, Rudd suggests that the value of the perspective offered by Middle English texts to ecocritical thinking is thus that it 'can offer alternative patterns of thought, tools that enable us to imagine more fully some of the claims made by ecologists' (p. 37).

Two essays in the 2014 issue of *New Medieval Literatures* make significant contributions to disability studies in relation to Middle English: Tony Vandeventer Pearman's 'Heterosyncracy as a Way of Life: Disability and the Heterosyncratic Community in *Amis and Amiloun*' (*NML* 15[2014] 287–316), and Richard Godden and Jonathan Hsy's 'Analytical Survey: Encountering Disability in the Middle Ages' (*NML* 15[2014] 317–43). In their survey, Godden and Hsy identify the main preoccupations of disability studies—including monstrosity, prosthesis, temporality, and advocacy. They also summarize both the debate over the use of the term disability itself and the dominant models used by scholars to approach disability (for example, the 'cultural', the 'medical', and the 'social', as well as the 'religious'). They give particular space to surveying the theoretical methodologies that draw on the 'scholarship of advocacy' (a means of illuminating 'the marginalization of the other that results from limited perceptions of disability and impairment', p. 322), and on 'crip' theory ('an orientation toward the world that asserts the potential for radical transformation of so-called normative social scripts, desires, and ways of life', p. 322). While the survey takes in the whole range of disciplines and regional and temporal focuses of medieval studies, a number of Middle English texts are focused on: the *Tale of Florent*, the *Wife of Bath's Tale*, *The Weddynge of Sir Gawain and Dame Ragnelle*, and *Amis and Amiloun*. Godden and Hsy conclude that 'what makes disability studies such a thriving and transformative field is precisely its capacity to change and adapt: to invite, accommodate, and sustain concurrent modes of the engagement with the medieval past' (p. 339). In the same issue, Pearman reads the Middle English version of *Amis and Amiloun* through the combined lenses of queer and crip theory. In so doing, Pearman widens attention out from the central friendship of Amis and Amiloun, in which queer readings have posited homoerotic undercurrents, to include a consideration of the men's relationships with women, Belisaunt and Lady Amiloun. Pearman posits that these male–male and male–female relationships establish (taking up Karma Lochrie's term) a 'heterosyncratic' community in the poem. It is, as Pearman understands it, the poem's hybrid genre—a romance with both hagiographical and secular elements—that creates 'a queer/disabled space', in which 'friendships between and among multiple partners become a "way of life"' (p. 290). As such, it is the disabled body of Amiloun on which the poem's heterosyncratic community seems to rely. Michel Foucault's theorizing of 'friendship as a way of life' provides Pearman with the means, in turn, of drawing out the pleasure experienced by and in relation to the disabled body (very often otherwise excluded from discussions of pleasure) within this community.

In 'The Phenomenology of Attention in Julian of Norwich's *A Revelation of Love*' (*Exemplaria* 26:iv[2014] 347–67), Michael Raby foregrounds the debts of the phenomenology—in particular of both Heidegger and Husserl, among others—to medieval thinking. In so doing, he traces the genealogy of critical theories of 'attention' back to Augustine and through medieval ones, giving mystics in general and Julian of Norwich in particular a central place in this genealogy. As Raby notes, for Jean-Luc Marion and Heidegger alike, 'the mystical theologian models a method and a practice that anticipate the phenomenologist's call to return "to the things themselves"' (p. 349). *A Revelation of Love*, Raby argues, raises fundamental questions about attention through two forms in particular: beholding and beseeching. Raby concludes 'her text demands the careful, patient response that she herself models, a way of receiving and keeping its meanings without holding them too tightly, so as to provide space for the text to continue unfolding and deepening' (p. 362).

Nicolette Zeeman's essay, '*Piers Plowman* in Theory' (in Cole and Galloway, eds., *The Cambridge Companion to Piers Plowman*, pp. 214–29), surveys theorized readings of the poem. Noting that 'overtly theorized' readings of the poem are not as common as they are in Chaucer criticism, Zeeman characterizes *Piers Plowman* as a poem rich in complex self-theorization. Zeeman posits the work of two scholars as particularly influential in shaping interpretations of the poem: Anne Middleton's, with its 'formalist underpinnings', and David Aers's, which is both politically and theologically oriented. In addition to political and historicist readings of the poem, Zeeman outlines significant contributions in the areas, among others, of subjectivity, discourse theory, semiotics, psychoanalysis, and gender. She notes that 'these theoretically inflected readings have transformed our understanding of *Piers Plowman*. It is notable that many of them are sensitized not just to the overt articulations of Langland's theory, but also to the complex formal maneuvers by which he articulates it' (p. 27).

3. Manuscript and Textual Studies

There was one volume published for the *Middle English Texts* (*MET*) series in 2014: Francisco Alonso Almedia's *A Middle English Medical Remedy Book*. Almeida edits the collection of popular medicine from Glasgow, University Library MS Hunter 185, the sole extant witness to this particular remedy book, containing texts in French and Latin as well as in Middle English. In fact the edition concerns the whole manuscript, a medical book which consists of a herbal, some Latin notes concerning ingredients and related cures, some items in French, and, the main focus of the edition, a collection of Middle English medical receipts. This section is the most significant in the manuscript, containing over 200 recipes, charms, and prognostications. This section is copied by two scribes, both also responsible for copying the other sections of the manuscript.

Almeida's edition is an important contribution to the study of Middle English remedy books. He concludes that the main audience for this type of manuscript, in particular one that contains trilingual works, would have been physicians; the volume also includes a commentary on the texts and a comprehensive glossary.

The third and final volume of Anne Hudson's *Two Revisions of Rolle's English Psalter Commentary and the Related Canticle* appeared this year. This is a continuation of the volume reviewed for this section in the last issue, and it covers Psalms 116–50 and Canticles 1–12. There are also notes to the psalms and canticles, as well as a glossary, an index of proper names, and a list of biblical references and allusions.

Three Festschrifts were published in 2014 celebrating scholars in the field of Middle English studies. Carol M. Meale and Derek Pearsall have edited a collection of essays in honour of A.S.G. Edwards, *Makers and Users of Medieval Books*. In this volume Orietta da Rold, in 'Codicology, Localization, and Oxford, Bodleian Library, MS Laud Misc. 108' (pp. 48–59), argues for the role that codicological features other than decoration, dialect, and hand can play in the localization of manuscript, features such as the animal skin used, composition of the ink, and other aspects of the physical structure of the book. Her research into these features suggests an Oxford origin for MS Laud Misc. 108. Susanna Fein, in 'The Fillers of the Auchinleck Manuscript' (pp. 60–77), compares two scribes, one the so-called Scribe 1 of Auchinleck, the other the scribe of British Library Harley 2253, in order to better understand a centre of literary production and dissemination active not in London but in the West Midlands.

Lotte Hellinga's 'From Poggio to Caxton: Early Translations of Some of Poggio's Latin *Facetiae*' (pp. 89–104) traces Caxton's intervention in the text, establishing which printed sources he consulted for his translation from the Latin and noting that textual improvements, evident in many of his own translations into the vernacular, may have originated in unidentified originals from which he worked. John Scattergood, in 'Trinity College MS 516: A Clerical Historian's Personal Miscellany' (pp. 121–31), allows us to come closer than is usual to determining when certain texts were acquired by this man—John Benet, vicar of Harlington in Bedfordshire—whose interests were in the main in historical and political texts and events, despite the presence of some utilitarian texts in the volume.

Carol M. Meale considers Katherine de la Pole, Lady Stapleton, as a literary patron and champion of East Anglian manuscript production (pp. 132–49). She argues that two manuscripts, Princeton University Library MS Garrett 141, John Metham's *Amoryus and Cleopes*, and Beinecke Deposit MS Takamiya 38, containing a copy of the *Priuyté of Priuyties* by Johannes de Caritate, are a consequence of Katherine's patronage. In 'Past Ownership: Evidence of Book Ownership by English Merchants in the Later Middle Ages' (pp. 150–77), Kathleen L. Scott records some merchant and craft owners of books. She makes use of two sources: inscriptions in manuscripts and early printed books; and wills, inventories, and indentures. Toshiyuki Takamiya and Richard Linenthal write on early printed Continental books in the Takamiya collection that were owned in England (pp. 178–90). John J. Thompson, in 'Love in the 1530s' (pp. 191–201), examines some of the early modern textual afterlives of Nicholas Love's *Mirror of the Blessed Life of Jesus Christ*. Love's work survives in more than sixty manuscripts and in nine early prints, and Thompson notes that this prolific corpus of material offers an opportunity to examine 'first-, second-, and third-generation texts and versions far removed from the original circumstances in which Love . . . put pen to paper'. Jane Griffiths contributes a chapter on 'Editorial Glossing and Reader Resistance in a Copy of Robert Crowley's *Piers Plowman*' (pp. 202–13), in which she re-examines the paratexts of his 1550 edition, which offer scope for differing interpretations of the poem. She also examines a reader's copy, London, British Library, C.122.d.9, which treats the work as prophetic of the Reformation. The volume closes with an up-to-date list of the publications of A.S.G. Edwards (pp. 224–36).

A Festschrift that celebrates the seventieth birthday of renowned book collector and academic Toshiyuki Takamiya also appeared in 2014. *Middle English Texts in Transition*, edited by Simon Horobin and Linne R. Mooney, acknowledges the scholarship, zeal for collecting, and generosity of this well-known figure in medieval studies. Much of this volume is dedicated to essays that deal with manuscript and/or textual matters. Richard Firth Green's contribution (pp. 1–20) is focused on Adam Pinkhurst, and his connection to the Scrivener's company. Green seeks to work out when Adam Pinkhurst signed his name in the Scrivener's Company Common Paper. Terry Jones (pp. 40–74) examines the manuscripts of Gower's *Confessio Amantis* to establish when the poet rededicated the work before the usurpation of Henry IV. R.F. Yeager (pp. 75–87) argues against the assumption that the little-known French poem *Le Songe Vert* is the work of Gower.

In 'Evidence for the Licensing of Books from Arundel to Cromwell' (pp. 134–58), Susan Powell examines the evidence for the licensing of books in the fifteenth and into the sixteenth century. She deals with Arundel's seventh constitution, which forbids translation of the Scriptures but which also prohibits the reading of anything such that postdates the period prior to Wycliffe. Arundel's constitutions were extremely influential, remaining in place until 1529. Michael G. Sargent also writes in part about Arundel; his essay, 'Bishops, Patrons, Mystics and Manuscripts: Walter Hilton, Nicholas Love, and the Arundel and Holland Connections' (pp. 159–76), uses the evidence of the provenance of the manuscripts of Nicholas Love's *Mirror* and Walter Hilton's *Scale of Perfection* to conclude that the majority of the manuscripts of the *Mirror* were copied in London and not in Yorkshire, and that Walter Hilton did not follow Arundel to the north. Indeed, the manuscript of the *Mirror* owned by Takamiya himself, MS 8, is the one manuscript that was copied in Yorkshire, at Mount Grace, for the widow of its founder. Mary Morse examines (pp. 199–219) Beinecke Deposit Takamiya 56 and its connection to the English birth girdle tradition in other English manuscripts. Carrie Griffin (pp. 220–40) examines the provenance of three of the manuscripts that preserve the Middle English *Wise Book of Philosophy and Astronomy*, including one that has a tentative link to John Dee as well as one that was definitely owned by Samuel Pepys. The volume closes with a bibliography of Toshiyuki Takamiya's writings (pp. 306–17).

The Festschrift dedicated to Derek Pearsall celebrates his discipline-shaping influence on so many areas of medieval studies, and most especially for manuscript studies and textual scholarship. *New Directions in Medieval*

Manuscript Studies and Reading Practices: Essays in Honour of Derek Pearsall, edited by Kathryn Kerby-Fulton, John J. Thompson, and Sarah Baechle, is a substantial volume. Naturally, a good many of the contributions reflect the influence of Pearsall on how we read the medieval manuscript, but several of the essays (which doubtless will be mentioned elsewhere) focus on his attention to close reading and poetics, or what are termed by Kerby-Fulton 'Pearsallian reading practices'. Indeed the volume is interleaved with short forewords to the various sections written by Christopher Cannon, William Marx, John J. Thompson, Siân Echard, Phillipa Hardman, Edward Wheatley, and Nicolette Zeeman, forewords that point up the importance of Pearsall's work and methods for the ways in which we now study texts and manuscripts.

Several of the essays are concerned with the book trade. Carol M. Meale considers the London mercer and bookseller John Colyns, and his inclusion in a list of booksellers summoned to appear before Bishop Tunstall in his second monition of 1526 (pp. 192–206). Colyns was the compiler of London, BL, MS Harley 2252, and Meale finds that the evidence she uses for Colyns's role as a bookseller that is *not* found in Harley 2252 points to a cluster of like-minded individuals around the Stocks Market, important because, as Meale notes, proximity was a key factor in the age of manuscript and print production. A.I. Doyle's 'Books with Marginalia from St. Mark's Hospital, Bristol' (pp. 177–91) is concerned with John Colman, a brother and the last Master of the hospital of St Mark in medieval Bristol who, at the close of the Middle Ages, carefully copied and annotated a group of manuscripts.

The Festschrift devotes a section to papers inspired by the 'New Directions in Later Medieval Manuscript Studies' conference held at Harvard in 1998. Hannah Zdansky, in ' "And fer ouer þe French flod": A Look at Cotton Nero A.x from an International Perspective' (pp. 226–50), asks what the scribe of Cotton Nero A.x, the manuscript that preserves *Pearl, Cleanness, Patience*, and *Sir Gawain and the Green Knight*, might have wanted his book to look like based on what he may have encountered in a multicultural context. She uses evidence of content and script to show that the 'scribe demonstrates the exceptionally multicultural and multilingual situation in the British Isles' (p. 245). Theresa O'Byrne, in 'Manuscript Creation in Dublin: The Scribe of Bodleian e. Museo MS 232 and Longleat MS 29' (pp. 217–91), explores fifteenth-century Irish authors and their texts, focusing on an apprentice clerk Nicholas Bellewe, who shows up in the patent rolls of the Irish Chancery from 1423. O'Byrne argues that Bellewe copied both Warminster, Longleat 29, and Bodleian, e Museo 232 in or near Dublin. Nicole Eddy examines audience in 'The Romance of History: Lambeth Palace MS 491 and Its Young Readers' (pp. 300–23), She argues that some of its early readers were children. Sarah Baechle's 'Chaucer, the Continent, and the Characteristics of Commentary' (pp. 384–405) examines glosses in some manuscripts of the *Canterbury Tales*. In 'The Legacy of John Shirley: Revisiting Houghton MS Eng 530' (pp. 425–45) Stephen Partridge examines the codicological and scribal complexities of this manuscript.

Diverting Authorities: Experimental Glossing Practices in Manuscript and Print, by Jane Griffiths, focuses on glossing practices in manuscript and printed texts. The first two chapters deal with manuscript material in Middle

English. The first chapter, 'Material Processes' (pp. 19–53), addresses glossing practices associated with Lydgate's *Siege of Thebes* and *Fall of Princes*. The second chapter (pp. 54–80) considers 'self-glossing' in two poems, *Reson and Sensuallyte* and Chaucer's *House of Fame*, in Oxford, Bodleian Library, MS Fairfax 16, a well-known collection of vernacular poems that dates from the 1440s. The third chapter is concerned with the glossing of Gavin Douglas's *Eneydos* in manuscript and early print.

Dirk Schultze edits *The Treatise on the Sacrament* extant in Cambridge, St John's College G.25 (*Anglia* 132[2014] 439–72). The text, a translation from Henry Suso's *Horologium sapientiae*, is the first edition of the work from a manuscript with Lollard tendencies. Schultze argues that the manuscript increases understanding of the reception of European mysticism in England, and his edition is comprehensive and careful, including an analysis of the manuscript and the work, and a discussion of the adaptation and translation from Suso and of the work's dialect.

László Sándor Chardonnens, in ' "Thes byne the knoyng off dremys": Mantic Alphabets in Late Medieval English' (*Anglia* 132[2014] 473–505), edits and discusses three Middle English mantic alphabets, works that combine oneiromancy with bibliomancy to aid in the divination of dreams, from fifteenth-century medical miscellanies. In a companion paper, 'Mantic Alphabets in Late Medieval England, Early Modern Europe, and Modern America: The Reception and Afterlife of a Medieval Form of Dream Divination' (*Anglia* 132[2014] 641–75), he sets these texts in a wider historical context.

Teresa M. Tavormina published a major, study on pratical texts in manuscript in 2014: 'Uroscopy in Middle English: A Guide to the Texts and Manuscripts' (*SMRH* 11[2014] 1–154). Uroscopic treatises are extant in large numbers from the later medieval period, largely because of their important to diagnosis in medieval medicine. Tavormina's work surveys between 125 and 150 works. There are also several useful appendices: texts that are often associated with uroscopies (such as the *Tokens of Ipocras*); an index of the manuscripts of uroscopies in Middle English; a listing of works with more than five witnesses; and a list of the three most common token lists (texts describing a series of urinary characteristics).

Susanna Fein and Michael Johnston edited (and contributed to) a collection focused on Robert Thornton and his manuscripts: *Essays on the Lincoln and London Thornton Manuscripts*. Johnston's introduction, 'The Cheese and the Worms and Robert Thornton' (pp. 1–12), calls attention to the amount of detail offered by Thornton's two extant manuscript books that can afford more general insights into scribal and compilation practices; into Latin and vernacular literary culture; and into cultures of, for instance, devotion and medicine, as well as attitudes to literature in a non-centralized context. He advocates using micro-history as way of understanding Thornton and his books, noting at the same time that he was not quite a marginalized figure. But the essays in the volume do put 'Thornton and his two codices under the microscope', since within the context of medieval book production Thornton does not 'fit any of the larger patterns in which most historians of English book production have been interested of late'. The volume approaches

Thornton and his books from five main angles: analysis based on codicology and palaeography; thematic coherence; decoration and appearance of the book; Thornton's social identity; and piety and devotion.

Susanna Fein's essay, 'The Contents of Robert Thornton's Manuscripts' (pp. 13–66), offers an overview and updates the contents of both the Lincoln and London manuscripts, but her contribution also acts as a touchstone for the essays that come after, providing not just a list of contents and a detailed descriptions of the manuscripts but a framework for understanding the substantial library created by Thornton and the ways in which he might have achieved this. The really useful and detailed catalogue is appended with a list of manuscripts that share items with Thornton's. In 'Robert Thornton: Gentleman, Reader and Scribe' (pp. 67–108), George R. Keiser frames the Thorntons as a family sufficiently prosperous to finance a private chapel when Robert was a boy. He argues that this would have required the frequent presence of a clergyman in the Thornton home, most probably also educating the young boy. He goes on to use this fact to show how the manuscripts reflect the kind of education that Robert received by looking at the works derived from monastic spirituality as well as the more practical, medicinal treatises (and the history of scholarly engagement with them as opposed to with the more well-known romances). He moves on to think about how Thornton handled his texts and operated as a scribe in order to understand how he 'extended his influence [on his children] through both his books'. What follows is an extremely detailed reading of the collocation, copying, and choice of texts—as well as a close analysis of several of the literary texts—in both volumes.

In 'The Thornton Manuscripts and Book Production in York' (pp. 109–30) Joel Fredell finds that those general things that might be said about Thornton's manuscripts and literary culture and book production in medieval Britain can be applied more specifically to York, arguing that Thornton's books and that other great witness to Middle English literature, London, British Library, Cotton Nero A.x, share decorative features associated with York at the close of the fourteenth century. Fredell uses evidence of decoration alongside other evidence to identify works that Thornton was probably accessing in booklet form, finding that emerging from this manner of compilation is a 'complex relationship between romance and devotional literature that develops, apparently deliberately, by the arrangements of their scribes'.

Mary Michele Poellinger's essay also centres on the alliterative *Morte*, but she makes her focus the language of violence of the *Morte*, the presence of certain other devotional texts in the Lincoln MS, and, more generally, Thornton's careful attention to genre. ' "The rosselde spere to herte rynnes": Religious Violence in the Alliterative *Morte Arthure* and the Lincoln Thornton Manuscript' (pp. 157–76) examines the devotional works in the manuscript, paying attention to their aesthetic of violence. She then explores the relationship between violence in the *Morte* and the language that is used to describe the Passion in those works, beginning by giving attention, not specifically to the composition of the Lincoln manuscript, but to the arrangement of texts and how that responds to the *Morte*'s use of religious imagery and language, affective piety, and chivalric sacrifice. Michael Johnston's essay, 'Constantinian Christianity in the London Manuscript: The Codicological and Linguistic Evidence of Thornton's Intentions' (pp. 177–204), begins with some thoughts on scribal agency and on scribes as interpreters and creators of meaning, seeing Thornton in this context on occasion as something of a *commentator*. Johnston makes the case for Thornton as an astute reader, interpreter, and compiler, presenting linguistic evidence to demonstrate that, over a sustained period, he drew on a series of exemplars to create a 'Salvation History that posits hard and fast and stable distinctions between Christians and Jews/Muslims', concluding that Thornton himself was wholly responsible for the shape of the sequence. Julie Nelson Couch writes on 'Apocryphal Romance in the London Thornton Manuscript' (pp. 205–34), examining the *Childhood of Christ* poem and how it functions in the context of the manuscript, looking at such matters as how it relates to the narrative of Jesus' childhood found in the *Cursor Mundi*, item 1 in the MS, and also at the romance structure of the poem that foregrounds the role of Mary, and pointing up events that relate to the Passion. She then examines how this correlates with the rest of the manuscript and its preoccupation with both Mary and the Passion. The Afterword (pp. 257–72) to this volume, supplied by Rosalind Field and Dav Smith, focuses on Thornton and place—that place being Stonegrave in Ryedale, north Yorkshire. They bring to life medieval Ryedale, showing how connected it actually was to many of the key political shifts, cultural movements, and centres of devotion of the fourteenth century, moving the discussion into modern times and the restoration of the church at Stonegrave. They also very usefully map the manuscripts and texts that were proximate to Ryedale and circulating in that area.

David Scott-Macnab and Kelly-Anne Gilbertson's article, 'Unrecorded Middle English Lexical Items in the Fifteenth-Century Treatise, *Medicines for Horses*: A Preliminary Study' (*N&Q* 61[2014] 344–9), examines this under-studied tract, which survives in eleven manuscripts, in preparation for a full critical edition. One of the strongest candidates for the base text, a manuscript now in private hands, preserves a version that is lexically interesting, containing certain words that either have limited or no recognition in the *Middle English Dictionary* or that antedate first attestations in the *OED*. Their paper examines some of those words, noting the significance of the lexicon associated with equine medicine and horsemanship, and comparing use and form to the other witnesses to the text.

In 'Reintroducing the English Books of Hours, or "English Primers"' (*Speculum* 89[2014] 693–723), Kathleen E. Kennedy looks at a group of manuscripts that she says pose a 'serious puzzle to modern scholarship on late medieval England'. These English translations provide an excellent way of tracing how a Latin text became English, but since they were sometimes drawn from the Wycliffite Bible, they raise all sorts of questions with respect to audiences for vernacular Scripture and in particular for the Wycliffite Bible's text. Kennedy studies the seventeen extant manuscripts with a view to moving towards a new understanding of fifteenth-century vernacular religion in England. Her article has three sections: a consideration of the Books of Hours in relation to the textual tradition of the Wycliffite Bible; a study of the books as material objects; and the audiences for such texts and books.

Joel Fredell writes on the *Pearl* manuscript (*SAC* 36[2014] 1–39), observing that scholars have learned remarkably little about Cotton Nero A.x as a material object over the years, and he presents evidence that points, not to a Cheshire origin for the volume (in part arrived at by internal geographical readings in *Sir Gawain and the Green Knight*), as had previously been thought, but to the production of the book to York, by comparison with other manuscripts decorated in York in the first two decades of the fifteenth century.

In 'When Scribes Won't Write: Gaps in Middle English Books' (*SAC* 36[2014] 249–78) Daniel Wakelin is interested in why scribes of Middle English leave short gaps mid-line or of a line or less, a phenomenon that is quite common. He conjectures that there are a couple of main reasons for such gaps, one being that the scribe believes there to be text missing from his exemplar and intends to fill this in at a later point. The second is to do with legibility or correctness: a scribe has a complete exemplar, but he either cannot read a word or believes it to be incorrect. Wakelin says that not writing, given the effort involved in letting 'the pen jump forward', must be a 'conscious choice', and his article is both a theoretical consideration of gaps and intentionality and a collection of examples from examined manuscripts.

E.A. Jones (*Library* 15[2014] 421–31) reports on '*A Mirror for Recluses*: A New Manuscript, New Information and Some New Hypotheses'. Hitherto, the sole Middle English version was that extant in London, British Library, MS Harley 2372. Jones notes that a new witness, sold at Christie's in 2014, provides a complete copy of the translation. Deborah E. Thorpe identifies 'British Library, MS Arundel 249: Another Manuscript in the Hand of Ricardus Franciscus (*N&Q* 61[2014] 189–96).

The *Journal of the Early Book Society* was a bumper issue in 2014, containing several essays and short notes that are relevant for this section. Kathryn Kerby-Fulton contributes the first essay; in 'The Clerical Proletariat: The Underemployed Scribe and Vocational Crisis' (*JEBS* 17[2014] 1–34) she turns to the 'unsung heroes of the resurgence of writing in English in the thirteenth and fourteenth centuries': the clergymen who made their living in full or in part as scribes. She argues that they were crucial to the rise of English literature and that their traces can be found in the Middle English texts that they copied as well as in the manuscripts that contain them.

Tania M. Colwell contributes 'The Middle English *Melusine*: Evidence for an Early Edition of the Prose Romance in the Bodleian Library' (*JEBS* 17[2014] 254–82). Victoria Flood, in 'An English *Owain* Prophecy: The Influence of Welsh Prophetic Material in Oxford, All Souls College, MS 33' (*JEBS* 17[2014] 283–92), prints this prophecy. Ralph Hanna identifies bits of Middle English in Merton College 249, a Latin manuscript (dating 1215 to 1230) (*JEBS* 17[2014] 293–301). Merridee L. Bailey, in 'Old Age and Economic Practices: Court of Chancery Cases Involving Richard Pynson, King's Printer' (*JEBS* 17[2014] 302–10), looks at two documents held at the National Archives that supply new detail about the life of Richard Pynson, the early London printer. Finally, Eric Weiskott reports on 'Another New

Fragment of *Speculum Vitae*' (*JEBS* 17[2014] 352–55), found in a printed book in the Beinecke Library.

In 'New Perspectives on the Reception and Revision of *Guy of Warwick* in the Fifteenth Century' (*JEGP* 113[2014] 156–83) Giselle Gos returns to the popular text, originally composed in Anglo-Norman, that is extant in a 'remarkable number' of manuscripts in two verse versions, and translated into Middle English, adapted by Lydgate as well as by various readers and audiences, including the Beauchamp family. Gos examines a series of revisions to the story that can be linked to a late thirteenth-/early fourteenth-century Anglo-Norman manuscript of *Gui*, Wolfenbüttel, Herzog August Bibliothek, Cod. Aug. 87.4.

Janika Bischof's Munster Ph.D. thesis has been published as *Testaments, Donations, and the Values of Books as Gifts: A Study of Records from Medieval England before 1450*. There is some interesting methodology, bringing German and English scholarship together (the former mostly untranslated), making use of Gneuss and Lapidge's work, and deploying numerical analysis to attempt to assess the value of manuscripts outside the limited sphere of the cost of production and to engage with the difficult area of 'the interplay between material and immaterial features of the book' (p. 21). Understandably, given the relative paucity of the evidence, Bischof can make little comment about Anglo-Saxon books, though it is surprising that there is no engagement with work by Heslop and Gameson on the use of books as gifts in Cnut's reign. It is also unhelpful to use 1066 as the key division between different cultural valuations and recording of books, given that the evidence presented suggests a shift in the nature of evidence more either side of 1350.

4. Early Middle English

This year saw the publication of a new collection of essays on Laȝamon's *Brut*, as well as a number of articles on early Middle English sermon literature and new work on hagiography and mystical writing.

Published in 2014 for 2013, *Laȝamon's Brut and Other Medieval Chronicles*, edited by Marie-Françoise Alamichel, presents eleven papers given at the seventh international Laȝamon conference in Paris in 2012, alongside three additional essays by Philip Shaw and Alamichel herself. (Papers from the previous two conferences, at Brown University in 2004 and Bangor University in 2008, are collected in *Reading Laȝamon's Brut*, edited by Rosamund Allen, Jane Roberts, and Carole Weinberg, discussed in this section last year.) In 'Lawman, the Last Old English Poet and the First Middle English Poet' (pp. 11–57), Eric Weiskott argues that Laȝamon's metre is directly related to the metre of Old English and of later Middle English poetry, although unrelated to Ælfric's 'rhythmical alliteration', and asks what can be inferred about the way Laȝamon and his scribes understood the place of the poem's metrical form in literary history. Two appendices offer a diplomatic transcription of fourteen late Old English poems and fragments and the texts of six early Middle English alliterative poems and fragments. Kenneth Tiller links Laȝamon's prosody to the rhythmic alliteration that appears in the post-Conquest entries of the *Anglo-Saxon Chronicles* in 'Laʒamon's *Brut* and the Poetics of the *Peterborough Chronicle*' (pp. 59–79). He argues that Laʒamon echoed the *Chronicle*'s verse forms in those later parts of the *Brut* that depict moments of national crisis. In 'Fictional Truth in Laʒamon's *Brut*' (pp. 81–101), E.G. Stanley explores the complex and various meanings of *treoðe* and its cognates in the *Brut* in the context of some wider reflections on the kinds of fictional and historical 'truth' the poem expresses. Fiona Tolhurst asks 'What Did Laʒamon(s) Do to Geoffrey's Female Figures?' (pp. 103–32). She argues that, in its presentation of Guendoloena, Marcia, and Cordeilla, Geoffrey of Monmouth's *Historia* offered positive models of female kingship, defined partly in contradistinction to bad rule by men, at a time when Empress Matilda was preparing to become England's first female monarch. Because Laʒamon praises behaviour in men that Geoffrey condemns, however, the contrasting virtue of these female figures is harder to recognize in the *Brut*, which also tends to aestheticize violence against women and questions the legitimacy of female rule. Nolwena Monnier also compares these authors' treatment of female characters, along with their presentation by Wace, in 'Arthurian Women from Geoffrey of Monmouth to Laʒamon' (pp. 133–51), focusing in particular on Igraine, Guinevere, and Morgan le Fay, and on the less-studied figures Anna (sister of Arthur) and Helen (niece of Hoel). Charlotte A.T. Wulf compares these authors' treatment of women who lived after Arthur, in 'The Women in the Post-Arthurian Section of Lawman's *Brut*' (pp. 153–67). She counts the references to women in each text, and characterizes the presentation of female characters as active or passive, positive or negative. In 'Letting Be and the Post-Arthurian Section of Lawman's *Brut*' (pp. 169–84), Joseph D. Parry weighs the implications of the poem's final words, 'i-wurðe þet i-wurðe; i-wurðe Godes wille', and asks what they reveal about Laʒamon's attitude towards history. Parry argues for Laʒamon as a 'phenomenologist of history' (p. 183), whose poem stages a situated encounter with the given fact of the past. This encounter involves recognizing the possibilities that have existed at other points in time, particularly for friendship and reconciliation. Gail Ivy Berlin asks how Laʒamon responded to technological innovation, in 'Gadgets and Magic in Laʒamon's *Brut*' (pp. 185–206). Although generally more interested in people than in artefacts, Laʒamon nevertheless recounts several 'technological tales' (including the destruction of Chichester by incendiary sparrows and Bladulf's flight in a *feðer-home*), where he links technology and invention to heathenism, perversity, vanity, and magic. Equally, Laʒamon reveals an interest in contemporary developments in cause-and-effect reasoning in his account of Merlin's challenge to Joram. In 'Brutus and the Trojans: A European (Hi-)story' (pp. 233–66), Alamichel describes the origins and development of the Brutus myth, from Nennius to Milton's 1670 *History of Britain*. In 'The Metrical Chronicle Attributed to Robert of Gloucester and the Textual Transmission of Laʒamon's *Brut*' (pp. 267–92), Philip Shaw discusses two passages from the version of Gloucester's text that circulates with the shorter continuation that may have been interpolated by the author of that continuation, along with a third that shows signs of rewriting. He shows that all three passages draw material from Laʒamon, which supports the view that they are the work of one individual. From the evidence of these passages, he argues that the author of the short continuation may have been based in Malmesbury. In ' "Unum librum qui vocatur Brute": Readers and Owners of the Anglo-Norman *Prose Brut*' (pp. 293–307), Heather Pagan considers the evidence of ownership inscriptions in *Prose Brut* manuscripts, and asks what inferences about ownership can be drawn from the different versions of the text that were copied, and from the manuscript contexts where they appear. Pagan shows that the *Prose Brut* had significant 'cultural capital' in its own time, and was read by clerics and laymen, including merchants as well as aristocrats. Three chapters are in French: Danièle Berton-Charrière's 'Du *Brut* de Laȝamon au *King Lear* de Shakespeare: L'Ellipse ou la "tierce place" ' (pp. 207–31), Frédéric Alchalabi's 'Itinéraire et fortune de la matière troyenne dans l'historiographie castillane (XIIIe–XVe siècles): De la *General Estoria* d'Alphonse X à la *Crónica Sarracina* de Pedro de Corral' (pp. 309–23), and Alamichel's 'Trois versions moyen anglaises des *Grantz Geants*' (pp. 325–53), which presents two Middle English versions of the Albina Prologue to the Anglo-Norman *Prose Brut, Des Grantz Geantz*, with a French translation.

Two articles by Stephen Pelle and one by Pelle and Mark Faulkner throw new light on the early Middle English sermon collections. Pelle identifies partial or complete sources for three early Middle English homilies from Lambeth Palace MS 487, in 'Source Studies in the Lambeth Homilies' (*JEGP* 113[2014] 34–72). He shows that 'Lambeth I' draws its commentary on Christ's entry into Jerusalem from item 55 in the Homiliary of Angers, and 'Lambeth III' draws its image of the eucharistic host as a burning coal for sinful recipients from the *Elucidarium* (which takes the image from the *Vitas Patrum* in turn), while 'Lambeth XIV', a sermon in the 'Sunday List' tradition with a range of Hiberno-Latin connections, derives from the popular Latin sermon 'Veneranda est nobis haec dies sancta', which Pelle presents in full, transcribed from an early manuscript. In 'Newly Recovered English Homilies from Cotton Otho A.XIII' (*RES* 65[2014] 193–218), Pelle attempts to reconstruct some of the late twelfth-century sermons from Cotton Otho A.xiii, which was badly damaged in the Cotton Library fire of 1731. He edits a series of extracts from the Otho homilies from the fifteenth-century transcription by Richard James, along with the incipits and explicits from Humfrey Wanley's 1705 catalogue of 'Saxon' manuscripts in British libraries, and uses related sermons from the Lambeth and Trinity collections to infer the likely content of the missing material. In 'Worcester, Cathedral Library, Q.29, fols. 133–7: An Early Middle English Sermon and Its Context' (*MS* 75[2014 for 2013] 147–76), Pelle and Faulkner discuss an overlooked sermon from Worcester Cathedral Library MS Q.29, first edited in 1961 by E.G. Stanley. The authors demonstrate that the Worcester sermon shares material with a sermon from the Otho A.xiii collection, using James's transcription, and that it derives from a Latin nativity sermon by Geoffrey Babion, and incorporates material from other sermons by him. This proves for the first time that Babion had a direct influence on early Middle English preaching, and raises the possibility that the sermon might be read alongside adaptations from Babion in other vernacular languages. The authors conclude with a discussion of the Latin sermons that appear in the Worcester manuscript, two of which are transcribed as appendices, and a further appendix listing corrections to Stanley's edition.

Ralph Hanna identifies two words of early Middle English in a Latin sermon for Rogation Days from Merton College, Oxford, MS 249, in 'A Blessed Burgh, Fasting, and Filthy Lucre: Middle English Bits from Merton College, MS 249' (*JEBS* 17[2014] 293–301). He argues that this sermon's use of English, just before a reference to Seneca, follows the example of an *ars praedicandi* from the same manuscript—Richard of Thetford's *Ars dilatandi sermones*—which combines classical allusions and bilingual puns in its demonstration of rhetorical dilation. A. Joseph McMullen reads the *Ormulum* as an example of 'vernacular theology', in ' "For þeȝȝre sawle need": The *Ormulum*, Vernacular Theology and a Tradition of Translation in Early England' (*ES* 95[2014] 256–77). For McMullen, Orm's rationale for writing in English and his account of English as a medium of instruction recall the Old English prefaces of Alfred and Ælfric, and anticipate the prologues of later Middle English religious texts. McMullen pays particular attention to the words *wenden* and *turnen*, which describe the activity of translating in Orm's dedication and in earlier and later examples of 'vernacular theology'.

In 'From Wench to Wonder Woman: Lenten Discipline and Miraculous Powers in the *South English Legendary*'s Life of Saint Mary of Egypt' (*EssaysMedSt* 29[2014] 27–41), Christopher Maslanka argues that the account of Mary's penitence in the *South English Legendary* offered a model for laypeople to emulate in their own Lenten observances, and that the text imagines Mary's miracles and her extreme asceticism as heightened versions of laypeople's ordinary religious practice. Where texts like the Lambeth Homilies and *Handlyng Synne* focus on the way that penance expiates past sins, this Life of Mary shows how it could also be productive and empowering for the penitent. Oliver Pickering's essay, 'How Good Is the Outspoken *South English Legendary* Poet? A New Edition of the Prologue to the *Conception of Mary*' (in Kerby-Fulton, Thompson, and Baechle, eds., pp. 34–54), discusses the Prologue to the *temporale* narrative of the *Conception of Mary*, in the *South English Legendary*, extant in three Middle English manuscripts.

Published in 2013, but not included last year in *YWES*, Jenny C. Bledsoe's 'The Cult of St. Margaret of Antioch at Tarrant Crawford: The Saint's Didactic Body and Its Resonance for Religious Women' (*JMRC* 39:ii[2013] 173–206) compares three different versions of St Margaret's *vita* that were available to the religious community at Tarrant Crawford in Dorset: the Katherine Group *Seinte Margarete*, the readings for Margaret's saint's day in a psalter owned by the nunnery, and the sequence of wall paintings representing Margaret's *passio* in the church of St Mary the Virgin. Bledsoe argues that these different versions of the story elaborated a coherent exemplary model for their multiple audiences to emulate, and promised that physical suffering would bring heavenly rewards.

Stephen M. Yeager's *From Lawmen to Plowmen: Anglo-Saxon Legal Tradition and the School of Langland*, argues that Anglo-Saxon charters, sermons, and law codes, which were read and studied after the Norman Conquest, provide an important link between Old English poetry and the later Middle English alliterative tradition; this book is discussed in more detail in

Section 7 below. Readers of this section will be interested in chapter 3, 'Ecclesiastical Anglo-Saxonism in Thirteenth-Century Worcester: *The First Worcester Fragment* and *The Proverbs of Alfred*' (pp. 99–120), and chapter 4, 'Laȝamon's *Brut*: Law, Literature, and the Chronicle-Poem' (pp. 121–49), where Yeager argues that Alfred's *Proverbs* and the *Brut* (alliterative texts attributed to 'law-men') imitate the forms of Anglo-Saxon charters while advancing a critique of contemporary legal innovations.

5. Lyrics and Shorter Poems

One of the most significant 2014 publications for the lyrics and shorter poems section is *The Arma Christi in Early Modern and Medieval Culture*, a collection of essays edited by Lisa H. Cooper and Andrea Denny-Brown, which includes an edition of 'the definitive *arma Christi* poem' (p. 27), 'O Vernicle'. Written in the last quarter of the fourteenth century and copied throughout the fifteenth, 'O Vernicle' is so called because the first object it treats is Veronica's veil. All twenty manuscript witnesses of the Middle English poem have only recently come to light. Despite acknowledgement of its significance, the poem has only been published three times before and never in an edition that takes account of all twenty manuscripts (p. 16). Ann Eljenholm Nichols's edition at the end of the *Arma Christi* volume (pp. 308–92) is therefore a welcome addition to scholarship not only of Middle English lyrics but also of fifteenth-century religious culture more generally. Nichols uses Philadelphia, Redemptorist Archives of the Baltimore Province (*olim* Esopus College) as a base text but includes significant variations from all twenty manuscripts. Major variations are helpfully given on the facing page, and minor variations are given in the critical apparatus at the bottom of the page. Both types of variant are often discussed more fully by Nichols in her commentary at the back of the edition. Such a user-friendly format, always accompanied by clear explanation, really does open up this poem for further study, which can now more easily take account of revealing differences between versions of the poem. Nichols describes her editing style as 'conservative' (p. 346), aiming to preserve the original text as represented by the Esopus roll and emending only when there is substantial evidence for correction. In her brief introduction, Nichols provides a chronological stemma for 'O Vernicle' (p. 313) and identifies two families for the manuscript. She observes a number of structural differences between these two families and also notices the heightened affective piety and intensified personal address of Family II (p. 319). She gives a detailed description of each manuscript witness and shows how both families of the poem were being copied over 'a broad swathe' of the Midlands, commissioned from a wide social spectrum.

Four essays are particularly concerned with the relationship between text and image in witnesses of the poem 'O Vernicle'. In 'Mapping Visual Pilgrimage in an Early Fifteenth-Century *Arma Christi* Roll' (pp. 83–112), Richard G. Newhauser and Arthur J. Russell pay close attention to Edinburgh Scottish Catholic Archives MS GB 0240 CB/57/9 (*olim* Blairs College 9, a prayer roll). It contains twenty-four images and three texts—'O Vernicle', a response prayer beginning 'I thank thee', and a pardon poem beginning 'These arms of Christ'—identified by the authors as a 'set devotional programme' that appears in six other manuscripts, three rolls, and three codices of which Blairs 9, produced around 1400, is among the earliest. Newhauser and Russell make much of the materiality of Blairs 9. They draw attention to how depictions of the *arma Christi* in it are not 'bundled together' in one composite image, unlike on a traditional *arma* page, but are dealt with individually. Because the average user could comfortably view only about 10 inches of the Blairs roll at once, only three to five instruments can be perceived at any given time, thereby imposing a 'preset viewing programme' on the reader, which follows the canonical chronology of the Hours of the Cross (pp. 88–90). They also show how penitential and homiletic imagery in the devotional programme is drawn from sermons on the Passion as well as from vice literature. The final section of the article gives full attention to the idea of 'virtual pilgrimage', using the heightened affective dimension of late medieval pilgrimage to argue that reader-viewers of Blairs 9 are 'transported to the sacred sites depicted in it' (p. 102).

Another essay in this collection which considers 'O Vernicle' and pilgrimage is 'The Footprints of Christ as *Arma Christi*: The Evidence of Morgan B.54' (pp. 113–41), also by Ann Eljenholm Nichols. This essay concentrates on part of a single vellum membrane, which is all that remains of a longer roll written and illustrated in England in the mid-fifteenth century (p. 113). It devotes attention to the central, longest stanza in the poem, the only one during which Christ speaks. The stanza is illustrated in this fragment by a composite image of bloody footprints (*vestigia Christi*), a rare motif not only in illustrations of the *arma Christi* but also in English poetry, and a city gate (linking the gate with the footprints of Christ seems to have been an English innovation, according to Nichols's extensive research).

Ann Astell, in 'Retooling the Instruments of Christ's Passion: Memorial *Technai*, St Thomas the Twin, and British Library Additional MS 22029' (pp. 171–202), also reflects on the confessional and penitential elements of 'O Vernicle'. Paying specific attention to Additional 22029, Astell argues that the poem enables devout readers to take the instruments used on Christ during the Passion and retool them as a means for examining their own consciences, in preparation for confession. Her essay sheds new light on the relationship between text and image.

Finally, Martha Rust argues, in 'The *Arma Christi* and the Ethics of Reckoning' (pp. 143–70), that 'O Vernicle' 'neatly conjoins mundane and spiritual processes of "reckoning"' (p. 143). Her essay considers the *arma Christi* in the poem as three specific kinds of reckoning: firstly as a series of actual existent objects left over from the Passion which function as signs and reminders of its occurrence; secondly as instruments which enable the reader-viewer to recount and meditate upon the discrete events of the Passion; and thirdly as tools which aid estimating or measuring. This intensifies meditation, 'for by attributing to each instrument the power to shield the devout against a specific spiritual peril . . . the poem suggests the possibility of measuring the cost of human sin in itemized and calibrated units of Christ's suffering' (pp. 144–5).

Two of the essays in *Middle English Texts in Transition*, edited by Simon Horobin and Linne R. Mooney, are relevant to this section: 'The Rawlinson Lyrics: Context, Memory and Performance' by John C. Hirsh (pp. 104–55) and 'What Six Unalike Lyrics in British Library MS Harley 2253 Have Alike in Manuscript Layout' by E.G. Stanley (pp. 125–33). Hirsh considers Oxford, Bodleian Library, MS Rawlinson D.913, which contains a collection of loose leaves, unconnected gatherings, bifolia, and fragments. The first leaf (he suggests that to call it a fragment is misleading) contains ten Middle English texts and two French texts, often referred to as the Rawlinson lyrics. Hirsh makes a compelling case for a new understanding of these lyrics as a personal possession, written for and by the same person, most likely a performer.

E.G. Stanley tackles a particularly challenging aspect of six 'unalike' lyrics in London, British Library MS Harley 2253 which are all written in continuous prose, despite the fact that the other poems in the collection (there are just over forty in all that may be considered English) are laid out in stanzas. He offers some hypotheses as to why they were copied in this way. The most persuasive explanation is that the scribe decided to write alliterative poems as if they were prose.

Emily Dolmans edits 'Hunting for Souls: A Newly Discovered Middle English Lyric' (*N&Q* 61[2014] 185–7), a thirteenth-century lyric in Oxford, Bodleian Library, MS Hatton 26, apparently of religious provenance and perhaps intended to be employed in a sermon.

Sarah Noonan uses a late medieval manuscript witness of the 'Short Charter of Christ' to resituate the poem in a more affective light in 'A Translation of Body and Form: Setting the *Short Charter of Christ* to Music in BL Additional MS 5465' (*Viator* 45:ii[2014] 335–56). The Fayrfax manuscript is a song-book that was possibly written by, or under the direction of, the composer Robert Fayrfax (1464–1521). The inclusion of the 'Short Charter' in this manuscript demonstrates the 'enduring interest in late medieval devotional texts' into the sixteenth century (p. 336). Noonan argues that the Fayrfax version of the 'Short Charter', which is usually absent from critical discussion, redefines the poem in order to detextualize Christ's charter and body and to create instead 'an aurally verifiable and devotionally affective performance guaranteeing mankind's salvation' (p. 335). The early modern musical setting deliberately emphasizes the affective, performative aspects of the 'Short Charter'. Manuscript evidence suggests that the Fayrfax version of the poem is likely to have been performed by trained vocalists at the royal court, who could 'aurally re-experience' Christ's body and its suffering by listening to it.

Victoria Flood has published a new transcription of a unique manuscript witness of a late medieval political prophecy: 'An English *Owain* Prophecy: The Influence of Welsh Prophetic Material in Oxford, All Souls College, MS 33' (*JEBS* 17[2014] 283–92). The prophecy appears 'in a late fourteenth-century hand on the final parchment folio of a twelfth-century copy of Malmesbury's *Gesta regum anglorum* with other Latin chronicle material' (p. 283). As Flood carefully illustrates, there are a number of allusions in the uncovered prophecy that 'strongly suggest the acquaintance of its author with Welsh prophetic material mediated through sources other than Geoffrey of

Monmouth', a finding which has wider implications for textual transmission of Welsh material in the later Middle Ages (p. 284).

In 'Unpublished Verse Rubrics in a Middle English *Receptarium* (British Library, MS Sloane 2457/2458)' (*N&Q* 61[2014] 13–15) Jake Walsh Morrisey lists the contents of the manuscript and transcribes five verse rubrics. He draws attention to dense Latin and English marginal glosses and comments in the sections of the manuscript containing verse, which 'attest to users' learned engagement with these so-called "popular" works' (p. 14).

Volume 2 of Susanna Fein's edition of *The Complete Harley 2253 Manuscript* presents each item edited beside a modern English translation on the facing page. Fein argues that this is a particularly appropriate format for a collection that, traditionally, has been treated in parts rather than as a whole largely because of its multilingual complexity. The famous Harley lyric manuscript contains an 'unrivalled collection' of secular lyrics (p. 1) intermingled with contemporary political songs, religious lyrics, and a number of other works from other genres, from fabliaux to saints' lives. It is therefore a difficult manuscript to define. Middle English scholars frequently consider the Middle English lyrics, but much of the French and Latin material has remained unprinted until now and therefore is investigated more rarely. Fein's format makes the manuscript more accessible Her introduction gives a brief overview of the manuscript as a whole, a summary of existing knowledge about the Ludlow scribe himself, and, a consideration of the booklet format of the manuscript, which until recently has not sufficiently informed analysis of Harley's contents. Paying attention to these manuscript divisions, Fein suggests, 'begins to reveal rationales that underlie the Ludlow scribe's anthologizing impulses, showing how he arranged texts with an eye to clustering topics, themes, and/or antithetical arguments inside units smaller than the whole book' (p. 5). In the edition proper, each item is presented very cleanly, with little textual apparatus cluttering the page. However, Fein also provides concise but very helpful introductions to each item at the back of the edition. The volume functions very nicely as a companion piece to the facsimile of the manuscript and the publication of volume one in 2015 is much anticipated.

6. *Sir Gawain and the Green Knight, Pearl, Patience, Cleanness*

Clare R. Kinney, in 'Trawþe and Tresoun: Translating *Sir Gawain and the Green Knight*' (in Hill, Wheeler, and Yeager, eds., pp. 228–43), suggests that the poem provokes constant redactions and retellings because no translation manages to capture its aesthetic. In 'Gawain's Girdle and Joseph's Garment: Tokens of "Vntrawþe"' (*JIAS* 2:i[2014] 46–62), Jana Lyn Gill concentrates on the connections between Arthurian knights and biblical figures as virtuous men. In particular, she examines the congruencies between Gawain's temptation scenes and Potiphar's wife's attempted seduction of Joseph. Lawrence Warner, in 'The Lady, the Goddess, and the Text of *Sir Gawain and the Green Knight*' (*ChauR* 48[2014] 334–51), considers lines 1283 and 2445–55, lines that are often emended. Gillian Rudd's 'Being Green in Late Medieval English

Literature' (in Garrard, ed., pp. 27–39) looks briefly at *Sir Gawain and the Green Knight*, to highlight multiple aspects of ecocriticism. Rudd places the Green Knight on the boundary between human and nature, an otherworldly figure who both merges with the landscape and emerges from it.

Graham Williams, in 'Glossing Over the Lamb: Phonoaesthetic GL- in Middle English and Aural Scepticism in *Pearl*' (*RES* 65[2014] 596–618), addresses phonoaesthetic (sound-semantic) significance in *Pearl*. This approach reveals how sound clusters add to the interpretative meaning. The article demonstrates the idea that 'form follows meaning' in *Pearl*. Claude Willan, in ' "Pearl" and the Flawed Mediation of Grace' (*MP* 112[2014] 56–75), examines *Pearl* as a consolation and a dream vision, with a particular focus on the poem's didacticism. Alan T. Gaylord's 'Devotional Practice in "Crafted" Mystical Prose and Poetry: A Preliminary Inquiry' (in Hill, Wheeler, and Yeager, eds., pp. 216–27) considers *Pearl* in his examination of what happens to devotional texts treated as literature. Andrew Breeze, in 'Pearl and the Plague of 1390–93' (*Neophil* 98[2014] 337–41), considers the dating of *Pearl*. He first presents an overview of twentieth- and twenty-first-century critical discussions regarding dating the poem before arguing that the Maiden may have died of the bubonic plague of 1390–3.

Susanna Fein's 'Of Judges and Jewelers: Pearl and the Life of Saint John' (*SAC* 36[2014] 41–76) examines the authority the jeweller borrows from St John and his associated texts, as well as metaphorical role of the jeweller; thus, the jeweller, applies craft techniques to the vision, especially in his evaluations of the pearl (his treasure) and the Heavenly City. St John, Fein argues, becomes an 'extrasensory exemplar' for the jeweller, especially since he serves as 'God's expert gemologist' (p. 43). Fein goes on to contextualize the jeweller within the Life of St John, relying first on analogous texts, and then turning to the Life itself. She concludes that there are several biblical lessons in play here: certainly the parable of the 'pearl of great price', but also the New Jerusalem of the Apocalypse, drawn both from the Bible and from the Life of St John, the 'supreme appraiser' and judge of true value.

Joshua Easterling, in 'Ascetic Desire and the Enclosed Body in the Middle English *Patience*' (*JMRC* 40[2014] 144–72), examines *Patience*, arguing that in it God's law and human desire become interdependent. This creates a circular, enclosed rhetorical space, one crucial to the fundamental production of the poem.

7. *Piers Plowman*

Lawrence Warner's *The Myth of Piers Plowman: Constructing a Medieval Literary Archive* interrogates the assumptions that undergird the formation of the archive. In the first chapter, Warner discusses evidence that Langland produced *William of Palerne*, and the recognition that if the poem is Langland's, then more connections might be made between the author of *Piers Plowman* and the Beauchamp affinity. Chapter 2 moves to the assumptions of place, where Warner argues for a localization of the C-text to London and a reading of the final version of *Piers Plowman* that connects the poem to the

London riot of 1384. Warner's book continues in this fashion, giving careful readings not only of extant manuscripts but also other documents, linking the poem and poet to a series of events, editors, and, finally, forgers, who give shape and meaning to the archive. *The Myth of Piers Plowman* ultimately makes visible the structure and fabrication of a collection of texts, ideas, and interpretations that constitute the poem.

Andrew Cole and Andrew Galloway's *Cambridge Companion to Piers Plowman* contains twelve essays, organized into four sections. The first section, 'The Poem and Its Traditions', opens with Helen Barr's 'Major Episodes and Moments in *Piers Plowman* B' (pp. 18–32), where she offers detailed explanations of the narrative arc(s) of the B-text, beginning with the appearances of Lady Meed, then moving to a discussion of pilgrimages, pardons, and ploughing. Barr concludes by describing the lines and passus which recount not only the Harrowing of Hell, but also the apocalyptic ending of the B-text. In 'The Version and Revisions of *Piers Plowman*' (pp. 33–49), Ralph Hanna makes clear what is different about *Piers Plowman* as a poem and a text. Central to Hanna's essay here is the argument that readers have to approach *Piers Plowman* differently, not as they might Chaucer, but rather, perhaps, as a series of poems, always in flux. Steven Justice's 'Literary History and *Piers Plowman*' (pp. 50–64) and Jill Mann's 'Allegory and *Piers Plowman*' (pp. 65–82) both employ study of the poem's formal elements, alliteration in the former and personification in the latter, to connect it to wider contexts. Justice's essay begins by situating *Piers Plowman* with its literary ancestors, before turning to the descendants, both indirect and direct. Ending with the end of the *Canterbury Tales*, Justice makes a compelling argument for viewing the Parson and the tale he provides as part of Langland's literary history. Mann's essay likewise touches on formal elements, the nature of Langland's personifications, and the shape of medieval allegories. She notes that Langland's personifications come and go in his text, becoming real as quickly as they lose their embodied nature.

The next section, 'Historical and Intellectual Contexts', opens with Robert Adams's 'The Rokeles: An Index for a "Langland" Family History' (pp. 85–96). Continuing his work tracing the possible aristocratic background of Langland, Adams offers a comprehensive listing of various Rokele relatives, beginning in the eleventh century, along with a description and citations of these figures in various sources. In 'Religious Forms and Institutions in *Piers Plowman*' (pp. 97–114), James Simpson addresses the connection between the self and institutions, noting that liberal ideology often privileges the self over institutions. In 'Political Forms and Institutions in *Piers Plowman*' (pp. 115–35), the essay that follows, Matthew Giancarlo brings to fore the political contexts of the poem. As a companion to Simpson's article, Giancarlo's essay concentrates on how the poem reflects not merely the political events of Langland's day, but also the shape of contemporary political institutions, by offering a reading of the poem's political events, including the marriage and trial of Meed and an extended discussion of 'leaute' in Passus 8–18. Andrew Cole and Andrew Galloway, in 'Christian Philosophy in *Piers Plowman*' (pp. 136–59), examine the extent to which the poem might be influenced by a kind of philosophical background. Noting that it fails to mention any number of expected thinkers or theologians, Cole and Galloway nevertheless maintain that the poem is itself a kind of philosophical model. The authors trace its unending quest for knowledge and philosophical background. The final essay in this section, 'The Non-Christians in *Piers Plowman*' (pp. 160–75), offers a catalogue of sorts for the three types of non-Christian one encounters in Langland's poem. Suzanne Conklin Akbari describes the Jew, Muslim, and 'generic non-Christian' (p. 160) in detail, offering readings of various scenes from the B- and C-texts, as well as showing how Langland's poem thwarts the expectations of the reader in his use of these non-Christians.

In the final section, 'Readers and Responses', Simon Horobin, in 'Manuscripts and Readers of *Piers Plowman*' (pp. 179–97), aims to establish the shape and nature of the poem's audience by an examination of manuscripts and their circulation. Besides listing the various later owners of manuscripts and detailing the dialects of various manuscripts, Horobin also touches on their contents and the frequency with which other texts were copied alongside *Piers*. Lawrence Warner, in 'Plowman Traditions in Late Medieval and Early Modern Writing' (pp. 198–213), gives evidence for the ploughman as a figure of indignation 'against abuses of the age' (p. 199). Beginning with the mention of Piers the Plowman in the rebellion of 1381, Warner moves to the connection of the ploughman to Protestant thought as well as describing ploughman imagery during the reign of Elizabeth II. Finally, in '*Piers Plowman* in Theory' (pp. 214–29), Nicolette Zeeman explores theory inside and outside the poem. Possibly because the poem is already 'self-theorized', scholars have been reluctant to interpret *Piers Plowman* through a specific theoretical bent. The poem, according to Zeeman, makes this work difficult not only because of the compendious knowledge it requires but also because it almost functions as a theory of itself.

Of particular note is a new translation of the B-text by Peter Sutton, a playwright and scholar. The translation itself is preceded by several explanatory sections, including a discussion of the author's identity, a rationale for the choice of text for translation, and a discussion of the poem's major themes.

Stephen M. Yeager's *From Lawmen to Plowmen: Anglo-Saxon Legal Tradition and the School of Langland* traces what would have been for the readers of the poem old, perhaps alien, traditions. Yeager's book primarily takes as central the Anglo-Saxon legal traditions themselves, which he traces in the first three chapters, followed by a chapter on Laȝamon's *Brut* (reviewed elsewhere), followed by two chapters that focus on the *Piers Plowman*-tradition. In 'Defining the *Piers Plowman* Tradition' (pp. 150–82), Yeager traces the development of the Langlandian voice, and connects it to a particular poetic tradition, especially *Richard the Redeless* and *Mum and the Sothsegger*. *Piers Plowman* becomes a kind of catalogue of phrasing and materials for the poem, one which their allegedly shared author uses to maintain this same Langlandian voice. The next chapter, 'Documents, Dreams, and the Langlandian Legacy in *Mum and the Sothsegger*' (pp. 183–204), explores the role of Anglo Saxon legal-homiletic discourse in *Mum and the Sothsegger*, as Yeager analyses the nature of and relationship between text and gloss, as well as the expression of documentary culture with which the poem concludes.

Four Festschrifts contained essays of interest to readers of *Piers Plowman*. In *Makers and Users of Medieval Books: Essays in Honor of A.S.G. Edwards*, edited by Carol M. Meale and Derek Pearsall, J.A. Burrow looks to the debt that Langland might owe the earlier poet of *Wynnere and Wastoure*. In 'Winning and Wasting in *Wynnere and Wastoure* and *Piers Plowman*' (pp. 1–12), Burrow traces Langland's use of personification and of details from contemporary England, concluding that he likely learned to craft particular yet abstract concepts from reading the earlier *Wynnere and Wastoure*. In 'Editorial Glossing and Reader Resistance in a Copy of Robert Crowley's *Piers Plowman*' (pp. 202–13), Jane Griffiths provides a reading of Crowley's view of *Piers Plowman* and its role and value in the Reformation. Resisting earlier readings of Crowley's editing of the poem as purely pro-Reformation, Griffiths looks to the editorial glossing of his first and second editions, as well as the annotations from an early reader who himself resisted Crowley's editorial guidance.

Kerby-Fulton et al., *New Directions in Medieval Manuscript Studies*, offers a number of *Piers Plowman*-related essays. In 'Langlandian Economics in James Yonge's *Gouernaunce*' (pp. 251–70), Hilary E. Fox examines the influence of *Piers Plowman* on James Yonge and his *Gouernaunce of Prynces*. Fox finds frequent echoes of *Piers* in Yonge's handling of good government and its economic effects. In addition, Karrie Fuller, in 'Langland in the Early Modern Household: *Piers Plowman* in Oxford, Bodleian Library MS Digby 145, and Its Scribe-Annotator Dialogues' (pp. 324–41), addresses some of the divergent responses between an owner and annotator of MS Digby 145 and another scribe, Hand B. In examining this conflation of the A- and C-texts, Fuller is sensitive to the topics and lines on which the different annotators disagree.

Finally, a cluster of essays, introduced by Nicolette Zeeman (pp. 447–51), concentrate specifically on Pearsall's 'Langlandian Legacy' (p. 447). First, Jill Mann's 'Was the C-Reviser's Manuscript Really So Corrupt?' (pp. 452–66) supplies the evidence that George Kane's original assertion—that the B-manuscript used for the C-text was corrupt—is not actually supported by readings from the manuscripts. Next, Melinda Nielsen, in 'Emending Oneself: *Compilatio* and *Revisio* in Langland, Usk, and Higden' (pp. 467–88) tracks Thomas Usk's and Langland's 'shared modus operandi of composition and authorship' (p. 467). Throughout the essay, Nielsen makes clear that the revisionary praxis of Langland—a life's work that is also poetic—also defines the work of Usk, whose use of acrostics is key to his compositional practices. The essay concludes by turning to Higden's *Polychronicon* and prose acrostics. Lastly, Kathryn Kerby-Fulton seeks to re-evaluate not only the professional scribes responsible for so much labour in the late medieval world but also the Z-text itself, a project born out of Pearsall's own editorial philosophies in 'Confronting the Scribe–Poet Binary: The Z Text, Writing Office Redaction, and the Oxford Reading Circles' (pp. 489–515). Addressing the tenuously held distinction between professional scribe and author, Kerby-Fulton offers many new clues about the identity of the Z-maker.

Simon Horobin's 'Oxford, Corpus Christi 201 and Its Copy of *Piers Plowman*' (in Horobin and Mooney, eds., pp. 21–39) addresses a particularly important copy of the B-text, important precisely because the manuscript is so vexing to modern editors. Contaminated by readings from both A- and C-texts, the manuscript offers evidence of its redactor in various episodes in the poem, which Horobin catalogues throughout.

Finally, *'Truthe Is the Beste': A Festschrift in Honour of A.V.C. Schmidt*, edited by Nicolas Jacobs and Gerald Morgan, has two essays on *Piers Plowman*. In 'Punctuation in the B Version of *Piers Plowman*' (pp. 5–15), J.A. Burrow writes about various forms of punctuation in the B-version, including paraphs and their function and the variety of punctuation before the caesura in the alliterative line.. Next, in 'Romance Patterns of Naming in *Piers Plowman*' (pp. 37–63), Helen Cooper examines what has been an under-studied connection: the sometimes porous boundary between romance and *Piers Plowman*. While Langland's poem is not a romance, it does share conventions with poems such as *Sir Gawain and the Green Knight*. In 'The Style of Prayer in *Piers Plowman*' (pp. 65–85), Mary Clemente Davlin addresses the number and types of prayers cited and used in *Piers Plowman*, supported by recent work on the penitential psalms, as well as earlier work from Schmidt. Among the types of prayers Davlin catalogues are psalms and verses from the Bible, which constitute the bulk of prayers, as well as smaller interjections and prayers contemporary to the poet. Vincent Gillespie confronts an image in Dame Study's lines in 'Dame Study's Anatomical Curse: A Scatological Parody?' (pp. 95–107). Contextualizing the link between the senses and understanding of the faith and its mysteries with a turn to Guillaume de Deguileville's *Le Pélérinage de la vie humaine*, Gillespie asserts that the poem's judgement on the hierarchy of the senses—hearing is prioritized over sight—is key to Dame Study's mention of *ers* (p. 101) which Gillespie notes should be glossed as 'arse'. Lastly, in '*Aicill* in *Piers Plowman*' (pp. 127–36), Rory McTurk discusses *aicill*, a formal feature of Irish syllabic poetry, and its possible connections to Langland's pararhyme, expanding the original thrust of Schmidt's own argument about Langlandian pararhyme.

Six essays centred on *Piers Plowman* appeared in the 2014 issue of *Yearbook of Langland Studies*, beginning with Marie Turner's 'Guy of Warwick and the Active Life of Historical Romance in *Piers Plowman*' (*YLS* 28[2014] 3–27), which demonstrates how romance 'comes to exert a force on medieval literary culture outside of and apart from its instantiation in individual texts' (p. 7). Turner's essay concentrates on *Guy of Warwick*, tracing how it 'models questions of salvation' (p. 7). Alastair Bennett's 'Covetousness, "Unkyndenesse", and the "Blered" Eye in *Piers Plowman* and "The Canon's Yeoman's Tale"' (*YLS* 28[2014] 29–64) uses the image of the 'blered eye' to show how a lack of charity is presented as unkind in both texts. Bennett includes background about theories of sight and the disorders of the eye, while at the same time connecting Chaucer and Langland through shared motifs and imagery.

Noelle Phillips, in 'Compilational Reading: Richard Osbarn and Huntington Library MS HM 114' (*YLS* 28[2014] 65–104), begins by rehearsing what is known of fifteenth-century scribe Richard Osbarn, before turning to the article's main question: whether Huntington Library MS HM

114 is the result of planning or happenstance, and, further, whether it is meant as a whole book or a series of texts randomly arranged for sale. William Rhodes's 'Medieval Political Ecology: Labour and Agency on the Half Acre' (*YLS* 28[2014] 105–36) utilizes Bruno Latour's notion of 'political ecology' to complicate a tidy understanding of the allegory of the ploughing of the half-acre: in a system where both workers and wasters are inextricably bound, along with institutions, animals, and others, Langland's poetic and agrarian vision reflects the distance between the ideal Christian community and the material conditions of agrarian work.

Jim Knowles's 'Langland's Empty Verbs: Service, Kenosis, and Adventurous Christology in *Piers Plowman*' (*YLS* 28[2014] 191–224) considers the ways in which the poem discusses what counts as and is called serving (pp. 201–2). Jim Knowles and Timothy Stimson have written an overview of the PPEA in 'The *Piers Plowman* Electronic Archive on the Web: An Introduction' (*YLS* 28[2014] 225–38). After describing the nature of the archive, the authors reflect on its importance.

Robert Adams and Thorlac Turville-Petre discuss Aberystwyth, National Library of Wales MS 733B, a conflated text that combines both the A- and C-texts, in 'The London Book-Trade and the Lost History of *Piers Plowman*' (*RES* 65[2014] 219–35). The authors provide evidence of how scribes working in the London book trade might construct such a book. J.A. Burrow's 'The Athlone Edition of "Piers Plowman" B: Stemmatics and the Direct Method' (*N&Q* 61[2014] 339–44) examines the critique of recension that Kane and Donaldson include in their Athlone edition of the B-text. He argues for a place for recension in the creation of critical editions.

Jason Crawford's 'Langland's Allegorical Modernity' (*ES* 95[2014] 597–619) sketches out some of the features of Langland's personification, finding a kind of 'modernity' in the way in which his personifications seem almost incomplete or unstable. Ryan McDermott, in 'Practices of Satisfaction and *Piers Plowman*'s Dynamic Middle' (*SAC* 36[2014] 169–207), recasts *Piers Plowman* as a poem interested in satisfaction, penance, and writing, moving away from a pessimistic view that the poem records the ultimate failure of its apocalyptic ending. McDermott connects his study of *Piers Plowman* to early modern poetry and theology, including Wyatt's paraphrases of the seven penitential psalms.

Part of a special issue of the *Chaucer Review* dedicated to the memory of Lee Patterson, Jennifer L. Sisk's 'Paul's Rapture and Will's Vision: The Problem of Imagination in Langland's Life of Christ' (*ChauR* 48[2014] 395–412) discusses an allusion to St Paul's *visio intellectualis* in *Piers Plowman*, and the distinction this allusion invites between *visio intellectualis*, which is imageless, and the *visio spiritualis*, which Will the dreamer experiences. This distinction allows Sisk to explore the role of imagination in Langland's poetry, as well as the poetry of his contemporaries, including *The Cloud of Unknowing*.

A cluster of essays in *Studies in Medieval and Renaissance Teaching*, introduced and edited by Theodore L. Steinberg, addressed the promise and peril of teaching Langland's poem. Thomas Goodman, in 'Why *Not* Teach Langland?' (*SMRT* 2:i[2014] 7–36), begins by surveying the wealth of editions and materials for *Piers Plowman* now available, a fact that raises the question: why not *Piers Plowman* in lower-level or upper-level courses? He answers that one should teach *Piers Plowman* because, difficult as the poem is, Langland's lines make clear what poetry can do and invite students to consider poetry more fully. Ted Steinberg, in 'I'm Dreaming of *Piers Plowman*' (*SMRT* ??[2014] ??), reviews the place of Langland's poem in an undergraduate curriculum. Louise Bishop, in '*Piers Plowman:* Texts and Contexts' (*SMRT* ??[2014] ??), weighs the nature of anthologies and how to contextualize the poem in lower-level undergraduate courses, including using world literature courses as a context for the poem.

Finally, two works appeared that, while not strictly on *Piers Plowman*, will certainly add to an understanding of the poem and its immediate religious contexts. Kathleen Kennedy's *The Courtly and Commercial Art of the Wycliffite Bible* explores the range of bibles one might designate as a Wycliffite Bible—not all of Kennedy's examples are of complete bibles, and this choice seems wise. At the same time, Kennedy's book treats the range of decorations that one finds in these bibles within a context of Lollard suspicion of iconography, which will of course be useful considering the recent exploration of manuscript illuminations and *Piers Plowman*. Helpful too is Kennedy's inclusion of two appendices, one for digital images and one listing extant manuscripts. Fiona Somerset's *Feeling Like Saints: Lollard Writings after Wyclif* is a compendious undertaking, and one that on its face seems deceptively simple: the best way to arrive at a clear understanding of who the Lollards were and how they practised their beliefs is to look at the extant manuscripts that contain Lollard material. Somerset does precisely this, but also looks at the way in which Lollard writings not only follow Wycliffe, but also, and perhaps more importantly, how they are connected to and written within and against a wider textual culture that includes works that are not Lollard in nature (e.g. *Piers Plowman*). In the third section, for example, in Somerset's discussion of allegory, she notes how 'extensive was the common ground, of both theory and practice, between Lollards and their contemporaries both academic and extramural Lollard and non-Lollard texts, as well as between Lollards and mainstream tradition' (p. 209).

8. Other Alliterative Verse

A number of the most important surviving late medieval alliterative texts were copied by Robert Thornton into his two manuscripts (Lincoln Cathedral MS 91 and BL Additional MS 31042), including the only surviving witness of the alliterative *Morte Arthure*. *Robert Thornton and His Books: Essays on the Lincoln and London Thornton Manuscripts*, edited by Susanna Fein and Michael Johnston (discussed in full in Section 3), is an important study of the compilation of these two manuscripts, with an examination of historical, cultural, and literary contexts, together with an underpinning of detailed palaeographical and textual analysis. The scope of the book is wide (these 'idiosyncratic' manuscripts contain a range of religious, romance, alliterative, lyric, and medical texts), but the following discussion only refers to those chapters concerned specifically with the five alliterative texts (*The Siege of Jerusalem*, *The Parlement of the Thre Ages*, *Wynnere and Wastoure*, *Morte Arthure*, and *The Awntyrs off Arthure*).

In 'Robert Thornton: Gentleman, Reader and Scribe' (pp. 67–108), George R. Keiser's meticulous study of letter forms in the two manuscripts is employed alongside his reassessment of other evidence, such as watermarks, to shed light on Thornton's compilation processes, and the ways in which the organization of material affects our readings of such texts, as with the juxtaposition (and later addition) of the prose *Alexander* with the alliterative *Morte Arthure* in the Lincoln manuscript. This is followed by a study of the thematic and moral consistency of the various texts, demonstrating a unity of purpose on Thornton's part. This includes some useful insights into how the author of the *Awntyrs off Arthure* 'achieved a brilliant thematic union that dramatizes the almost irreconcilable desires of his age and of Robert Thornton's' (p. 90), demonstrating how the poem's two halves appear to reject and then celebrate worldly values. Keiser sees similarly ambivalent conjunctions in the *Parlement of the Thre Ages*. The chapter also includes a detailed discussion and contextual study of the *Siege of Jerusalem*, considering recent revisionist readings, and confirming earlier assessment of the context of the London manuscript as providing a 'Spiritual History' (p. 104), where the other two alliterative poems, *Parlement* and *Wynnere and Wastoure*, may be seen as a unit apart from the main collection of texts, providing a reflective conclusion to the London manuscript.

Ralph Hanna and Thorlac Turville-Petre, in 'The Text of the Alliterative *Morte Arthure*: A Prolegomenon for a Future Edition' (pp. 131–55), argue a compelling case (and invitation) for, as the title suggests, a new edition. While Mary Hamel's 1984 edition is currently the standard modern edition of the text, developments in the understanding of dialects and alliterative metrics since its publication have cast doubt on many of Hamel's editorial decisions. While much of this essay is focused on the detail of Hamel's edition and its shortcomings, it is in the context of demonstrating the value of recent scholarship in informing (in particular) understanding of the poet's employment of alliterative metre, and Thornton's scribal practices, in order to encourage the production of a more authoritative critical edition. Some of the compelling challenges to the text's future editor(s) include a recapitulation of earlier suggestions about geographically determined different metrical rules for alliterative verse, specifically the use of the b-verse to signal the alliterating sound of subsequent lines, whereby seemingly 'irregular' lines may be seen as bridging two 'long leashes of successive lines alliterating on the šame sound' (p. 139). In other words, the many AA | XX lines may actually function as 'anticipating or continuing a multi-line sequence of verses' (p. 140). Hanna and Turville-Petre propose how emendations might be made to irregularly alliterating lines in Thornton's text, based in part on a re-evaluation of surviving alliteration in Malory's prose. The latter part of the chapter is entirely devoted to examining evidence from Malory, and although Hanna and Turville-Petre acknowledge that Hamel does 'pay serious attention to the relationship between the poem and Malory's adaptation' (p. 154), they raise some detailed points of enquiry that need to be addressed by future editors in order to 'establish a more satisfactory text of *Morte Arthure* than any so far published' (p. 155).

In '"The Rosselde Spere to Hid Herte Rynnes"': Religious Violence in the Alliterative *Morte Arthure* and the Lincoln Thornton Manuscript' (pp. 157–75) Mary Michele Poellinger provides a contextual understanding of the violent language and action of the *Morte Arthure*, suggesting that Thornton included the text as a means of highlighting the similarity of descriptive language between secular and affective texts, in particular the *Northern Passion*. Poellinger also provides examples of similar linguistic patterns in other contemporary religious poetry, and in the *Siege of Jerusalem* in Thornton's London manuscript. By identifying and interrogating the 'shared language of violence between genres' (p. 158), Poellinger provides some valuable insights into the moral framework of the *Morte Arthure* through an understanding of the intersections between chivalric violence and the violent language of Passion narratives.

A fuller contextual understanding of the *Siege of Jerusalem* is given in Michael Johnston's chapter, 'Constantinian Christianity in the London Manuscript: The Codicological and Linguistic Evidence of Thornton's Intentions' (pp. 177–204). His focus is on Thornton's scribal behaviour in the London manuscript, beginning with a study of dialects in the opening poems in order to identify the origins of exemplars. His finding that the pairing of the *Northern Passion* and the *Siege of Jerusalem* derives from a single exemplar is borne out by codicological evidence, which suggests that these two texts were originally intended as the opening to the manuscript. However, Johnston also demonstrates that the incipit to the *Siege* 'makes patent the salvation-historical connections between the death of Christ—as narrated in the immediately preceding *Northern Passion*—and the revenge upon the Jews to follow', and thus also confirms Thornton's role as 'literary mediator' (p. 196).

The Siege of Jerusalem is also the subject of an article by Cord Whitaker, 'Ambivalent Violence: Josephus, Rationalist Evangelism, and Defining the Human in the *Siege of Jerusalem*' (*YLS* 28[2014] 137–72), which sets out the case for a reading which views the treatment of the Jews as ambivalent (where it oscillates between the virulent anti-Semitism which troubles many modern readers, and a more sympathetic portrayal of their plight). Whitaker approaches the text through 'the rationalist mode of definition in which opposites such as black and white define one another', ultimately seeing the 'interdependence of religious adversaries' highlighted in the poem through the interactions between Josephus, the Jewish general, and the Romans, Titus and Vespasian, as being key to the text's wider aims.

Critical readings of the *Siege* could also usefully be informed by the arguments of an edition of *Postmedieval*: 'The Holocaust and the Middle Ages' (*Postmed* 5:iii[2014] 269–385), which engages with the problems inherent in reading medieval anti-Semitism in the light of the Holocaust (and of looking for medieval evidence to justify or explain later actions). Of particular relevance are the introductory article by the editors Hannah Johnson and Nina Caputo, 'The Middle Ages and the Holocaust: Medieval Anti-Judaism in the

Crucible of Modern Thought' (*Postmed* 5[2014] 270–7), and the response essay by Fred Evans, 'Ethics and the Voices of the Past' (*Postmed* 5[2014] 359–73).

Adrienne Williams Boyarin has produced the first modern English translation of *The Siege of Jerusalem*, which is clearly aimed at a student readership although, as Boyarin suggests, it might also have some attraction for a wider audience. Clearly indebted to the 2003 EETS edition by Ralph Hanna and David Lawton (and to a lesser extent the editions by Michael Livingston and Thorlac Turville-Petre), and, like these, employing Bodleian Library MS Laud Misc. 656 as the base text, this translation in fact aims to encourage readers to use the modern English version as a means to discovering the Middle English. Boyarin maintains the lineation and section divisions of the most recent editions with the expectation that the translation will be read alongside the original. While Livingston's edition already provides a valuable undergraduate teaching resource with its modernization of spelling and extensive glosses, Boyarin's edition has somewhat different pedagogical aims. This translation is a complement to, rather than a replacement for, the Middle English editions, but it provides a more focused range of supplementary material than these editions, and this is perhaps the greatest strength of her enterprise. The intention is to encourage critical debate amongst readers without the specialized language skills needed to read this text, and the specific ideological focus of her reading contributes to recent critical debate about the moral standpoint of the author (and Thornton's apparent perspective on this in his MS compilation), and the portrayal of the Jews. The contextual material (which includes the expected biblical sources and extracts from the *Golden Legend*), however, is clearly intended to support a discursive and non-prescriptive teaching context, and could usefully encourage socio-historical debate. This material includes other medieval narratives and exempla providing a range of medieval representations of Judaism. The translation itself is very closely allied to the detail and poetic principles of the Middle English text (as Boyarin explains, 'maintenance of the poem's distinctive vocabulary, ambiguities and repetitions; and representation of its original alliterative aesthetic', p. 12), which unfortunately limits its appeal as poetry in its own right. The adherence to the original alliteration and the rather literal translation (generally line by line, if not word for word) leads to some metrical awkwardness, particularly in the opening stanzas, although the poetry seems eventually to bed in to its anachronistic form. Where particular word choices either hide the various nuances of the Middle English term or, conversely, retain archaic or specialist terms, Boyarin provides supplementary information in some substantial explanatory footnotes.

Several articles have been published on other alliterative romances. Kristin L. Bovaird-Abbo sees a more positive reading of Arthur than the critical tradition allows, allied to the political and religious aims of James IV, in *Gologras and Gawane*, in ' "Reirdit on ane riche roche beside ane riveir": Martial Landscape and James IV of Scotland in *The Knightly Tale of Gologros and Gawane*' (*Neophil* 98[2014] 675–88), discussed in detail below in Section 14. Brett Roscoe, in 'Reading the Diptych: *The Awntyrs off Arthure*,

Medium, and Memory' (*Arth* 24:i[2014] 49–65), employs both cognitive psychology and medieval theories of memory to build on A.C. Spearing's description of the poem's structure as a 'diptych'. Through this framework, Roscoe analyses, as does much earlier criticism of this text, the difficulties inherent in reading and understanding the bipartite structure, but ultimately he argues for reading the work as a unified whole. He sees the structure as 'a story of incomplete memory followed by incomplete amnesia' (p. 49). Roscoe also engages with psychoanalytical theory of the uncanny (alongside the *unheimlich* elements of the poem's narrative) to build his argument that the text 'frustrates the reading process' (p. 53) by confusing memorial practices through requiring the reader not only to absorb narrative discontinuities and temporal shifts, but also cryptonymic verbal echoes (although the function and significance of these echoes could usefully have been more clearly elaborated in the discussion).

There were also two articles in 2014 on the alliterative romance *William of Palerne*. Lawrence Warner, in the opening chapter of *The Myth of Piers Plowman* (also discussed in Section 7), considers the 'oddest duck' of Middle English alliterative poetry in terms of authorship and influence. In 'William and the Werewolf: The Problem of *William of Palerne*' (pp. 22–36), Warner revisits the various arguments for and against Langland's authorship of this text. This provocative and engaging essay leaves the reader with the sense that, while there may be no answers, such issues are worth repeated interrogation. Hannah Priest's essay, '"Bogeysliche as a boye": Performing Sexuality in *William of Palerne*' (in Hopkins, Rouse, and Rushton, eds., pp. 85–98), has a somewhat different perspective. Priest investigates aspects of gender and sexuality through the romance's engagement with cross-gender and cross-species disguises. Drawing attention to significant variations from the earlier French version, she finds these transformations to be temporary performances (a form of festivity, 'as with a masked dance or a mumming', p. 98), where social order is restored and reinforced at the end of the narrative.

Other articles on alliterative poetry this year include a chapter by John Burrow, 'Winning and Wasting in *Wynnere and Wastoure* and *Piers Plowman*' (in Meale and Pearsall, eds., pp. 1–12), on the complex moral judgements required by readers of *Wynnere and Wastoure*. Burrow ultimately argues for the possibility of this poem's direct influence on Langland. Beginning with a consideration of the differences of perspective on winning and wasting in *Piers Plowman*, he persuasively builds a body of textual evidence to demonstrate how the moral complexities of the 'alternating speeches of Winner and Waster . . . challenge the reader with a variety of claims and counterclaims' (p. 10). Burrow shows, however, that the greatest ambiguity comes with the unsatisfactory ending, particularly in terms of the King's unwillingness to condemn either behavioural extreme. Finally, he argues that the poem's potential for influence on Langland lies in 'its masterly way with personification', effected through the employment of an array of concrete contemporary details (p. 11).

9. Verse Romance

Two of the books on verse romance this year argue for the recognition of 'gentry romance' and 'crusading romance' as sub-genres of the form. Another preoccupation this year is about the intersections between verse romance and religion, with a variety of articles exploring romance treatments of not only crusading but also pilgrimage, lay piety, and religious others. One book and several articles also examine the roles of women in romance, particularly (but not exclusively) monstrous or dangerous women. Class identity, manuscript studies, and the influence of Middle English romance in the early modern period also receive attention.

In *Romance and the Gentry in Late Medieval England*, Michael Johnston unites literary analysis, historical contextualization, and codicological research (a notable achievement in itself) to argue that a recognizable sub-genre of Middle English romances 'provided the gentry—late medieval England's emergent social class—with a particularly powerful vehicle for expressing and exploring their unique, and emergent, socio-economic identity' (p. 1). Johnston defines and explores the significance of the gentry class in chapter 1, '"A Watered-Down Version of Nobility": The Growth of the Gentry in Late Medieval England'. Chapter 2, 'Gentry Romances: A Literary History', analyses the nine romances that Johnston identifies as, specifically, 'gentry romances': *The Avowing of Arthur, Octavian, Sir Amadace, Sir Cleges, Sir Degrevant, Sir Eglamour of Artois, Sir Gawain and the Carl of Carlisle, Sir Isumbras*, and *Sir Launfal*. Johnston argues that these romances contain five motifs relevant to gentry readers: gentry protagonists; encounters between gentry and aristocracy in which the gentry characters earn the respect of their aristocratic betters; families separated or under threat of extinction (which Johnston links to gentry concerns over procreation and inheritance); knightly characters struggling with largesse, spending, and debt; and finally references to distraint for knighthood, a class marker for the upper echelons of the gentry. In chapter 3, 'Gentry Romances: The Manuscript Evidence', Johnston examines provincial book production practices and manuscripts containing gentry romances from 1350 to 1500 to show that 'that the gentry formed the primary public for these texts: these volumes were produced locally for local readers' (p. 90). The second half of the book contains case studies in which Johnston argues for connections between codicological details, plot points of romances, and the history of families associated with certain manuscripts. Chapter 4, 'Derbyshire Landowners Read Romance', explores the Findern Anthology and the Heege Manuscript. Chapter 5, 'Robert Thornton Reads Romance', examines the two Thornton miscellanies and offers evidence that Thornton perceived the four gentry romances in his collection as a distinct group. Chapter 6, 'The Irelands Read Romance', concludes the book with a study of intersections between gentry life and romance in Princeton University Library, MS Taylor 9, a collection of romances and manorial court documents related to the Ireland family.

Angela Florschuetz's *Marking Maternity in Middle English Romance: Mothers, Identity, and Contamination* places late medieval medical and cultural beliefs and practices involving conception, pregnancy, childbirth and motherhood in dialogue with medieval romances including the Northern *Octavian*, *Sir Gowther*, Chaucer's *Clerk's Tale* and *Man of Law's Tale*, *Richard Coer de Lyon*, and *Melusine*. Florschuetz's discussion ranges among issues of gender, race, nationhood, and identity, with a recurring emphasis on the texts' anxieties about patrilineal inheritance (in biological, psychological, legal, and monetary senses) and 'the permeating influence of the mother's body on her children's identities and thus on her husband's bloodline' (p. xix). Chapter 1, 'Women's Secrets and Men's Interests: Rituals of Childbirth and Northern *Octavian*', explores the traditional all-female space of the lying-in room and argues that masculine intrusion into that space in *Octavian*, out of anxiety over adultery, compromises rather than promotes the family's interests. Chapter 2, '"That moder ever hym fed": Nursing and Other Anthropophagies in *Sir Gowther*', explores medieval medical and Christian discourses about nursing that associate nursing with the Eucharist. Two chapters on the *Canterbury Tales*: '"Youre Owene Thyng": The *Clerk's Tale* and Fantasies of Autonomous Male Reproduction' and '"A mooder he hath, but fader hath he noon". Maternal Transmission and Fatherless Sons: The *Man of Law's Tale*', explore the intersection between genetic and legal inheritance in these two tales. Chapter 5, 'Forgetting Eleanor: *Richard Coer de Lyon* and England's Maternal Aporia', examines the romance's substitution of a demon mother for Richard's historical mother, Eleanor of Aquitaine, and argues that the substitution enables the text to explore the communal fictions and suppressions that go into constructing national identity. Finally, in chapter 6, 'Monstrous Maternity and the Mother-Mark: Melusine as Genealogical Phantom', Florschuetz suggests that *Melusine* pushes the issues *Richard* raises to their extreme, depicting the 'strict model of patrilineal genealogy and the concomitant marginalization of maternal influence' as not only a fiction, but a dangerous one that will inevitably suffer catastrophic collapse, taking family and personal identity with it (p. 155). Throughout her book, Florschuetz argues that these romances present scenarios in which anxieties about preserving the purity of the male bloodline, rather than actual problems with that bloodline, cause the characters' biggest problems.

Inspired by recent historical scholarship that enlarges the definition of crusading activity in the medieval and early modern periods, Lee Manion sets out to expand and deepen the definition of a 'crusading romance' in *Narrating the Crusades: Loss and Recovery in Medieval and Early Modern English Literature*. In his introduction, Manion identifies various generic markers that signal a work's status as 'crusading romance'. In addition to specific motifs, Manion's overarching requirement is that the text exhibit a 'narrative pattern of loss and recovery' (p. 8), corresponding not only to romance's pattern of exile and return but specifically to crusading's rhetoric of reclaiming lost places, people, or relics. Each of the book's subsequent chapters identifies these elements in certain romances while also contextualizing those romances with reference to additional primary texts (treatises and chronicles) and historical background. In chapter 1, 'An Anti-National *Richard Cœur de Lion*: Associational Forms and the English Crusading Romance', Manion borrows David Wallace's and Marion Turner's term 'associational form', to argue that scholars' focus on *Richard*'s nationalistic elements has overlooked its presentation of non-nationalistic associational structures in which Christian crusaders work together across barriers of language or political loyalty. Chapter 2, '*Sir Isumbras*'s "Privy" Recovery: Individual Crusading in the Fourteenth Century', explores *Sir Isumbras* in the context of late medieval English aristocratic practices of joining other countries' wars against non-Christians, engaging in private expeditions, or going on pilgrimages that might or might not involve armed conflict. In chapter 3, 'Fictions of Recovery in Later English Crusading Romances: *Octavian* and *The Sowdane of Babylone*', Manion argues that, by the fourteenth century, crusading was an ideology that could be deployed in service of evangelism and battle in places ranging from the Baltic to North Africa, Iberia to eastern Europe. Both the Southern *Octavian* and *The Sowdane of Babylone* reflect this wider understanding of crusading's geography. The book's final chapter, 'Refiguring Catholic and Turk: Early Modern Literatures of Crusading and the End of the Crusading Romance', suggests that, despite Protestantism's inherent suspicion of Catholic enterprises, the crusade romance maintained a waning but real influence in early modern English poetry and drama. Manion reads James I's *Lepanto*, Book I of Spenser's *The Faerie Queene*, both parts of Marlowe's *Tamburlaine the Great*, Heywood's *The Four Prentices of London, with the Conquest of Jerusalem*, and Shakespeare's *Othello* as evidence of the persistent relevance of the genre beyond the medieval era.

The collection *Sexual Culture in the Literature of Medieval Britain*, edited by Amanda Hopkins, Robert Allen Rouse and Cory James Rushton, contains several articles of interest to scholars of verse romance. Megan G. Leitch's study, 'Enter the Bedroom: Managing Space for the Erotic in Middle English Romance' (pp. 39–53), examines bedroom imagery through a lens of spatial theory in romances including the *Squire of Low Degree, King Horn, Sir Gawain and the Green Knight*, Malory's *Morte Darthur*, and *Melusine*. She argues that 'the scarcity and control of bedrooms and beds' (p. 52) in medieval England adds to the contingent, powerful role these valuable and unstable spaces play in Middle English romance. In 'Fairy Lovers: Sexuality, Order and Narrative in Medieval Romance' (pp. 99–110), Aisling Byrne makes a cogent case that fairy lovers of medieval romance, and especially the taboos they impose on their human partners, allow writers to engage in 'nuanced explorations of ideas of order and disorder and the nature of narrative action' (p. 100). Finally, in 'Invisible Woman: Rape as a Chivalric Necessity in Medieval Romance' (pp. 161–80), Amy N. Vines considers intersections between rape and chivalry by examining the Middle English *Partonope of Blois* as well as Chaucer's *Wife of Bath's Tale* and a relevant section of the Old French *Perceval* continuation. She argues that the commission of rape can be an early stage of a knight's journey to chivalric success.

There are two articles about Middle English romance in *Middle English Texts in Transition*, edited by Simon Horobin and Linne R. Mooney. In 'Bodleian Library, MS Ashmole 33: Thoughts on Reading a Work in Progress' (pp. 88–103), Phillipa Hardman examines the complicated text of *Sir Firumbras* in Ashmole 33, which contains passages suggesting an earlier draft of the work as well as numerous scribal emendations to the fair copy. She urges greater attention to the manuscript's evidence of an 'unending scribal process of interaction with and enrichment of the poem' (p. 99), not only to expand our understanding of *Sir Firumbras* but also to help us more accurately 'discern traces of a lost, possibly still unperfected exemplar behind the apparent imperfections of many another popular romance' (p. 100). In 'Linguistic Boundaries in Multilingual Miscellanies: The Case of Middle English Romance' (pp. 116–24), Gareth Griffith and Ad Putter demonstrate that 'Middle English romances did not on the whole travel in multilingual miscellanies', and they argue that French texts appear with Middle English romances only in exceptional cases.

In the collection *Robert Thornton and His Books: Essays on the Lincoln and London Thornton Manuscripts*, edited by Susanna Fein and Michael Johnston. Julie Nelson Couch examines 'Apocryphal Romance in the London Thornton Manuscript' (pp. 205–34) Julie Nelson Couch examines Thornton's apparent interest in blurring distinctions between romance and Christian religious writing. Thornton labels Couch's major subject text, the *Childhood of Christ*, a 'Romance', leading Couch to explore how this apocryphal tale of Christ's youth not only borrows romance tags and tropes and relates closely to romances such as *Richard Coer de Lyon*, but, more broadly, participates in the manuscript collection's project of linking its romances, sense of history and elements of personal piety to the events of the Passion. Fein and Johnston's book is discussed generally in Section 3. Two chapters on the alliterative *Morte Arthure* are discussed in Section 8.

Links to forms of religious narrative are explored elsewhere. In 'Romancing the City: Margery Kempe in Rome' (*SIP* 111[2014] 680–90), Laura L. Howes connects pilgrimage to romance by suggesting that, in addition to biblical sources and saints' lives, romance narratives from the Emaré and Constance traditions inspired Margery Kempe's description of her visit to Rome, in which she is initially cast out from her Christian housing, wanders destitute, encounters strangers, and finally regains her place in the Christian community, thus following the basic trajectory of a wandering romance heroine. Liliana Sikorska's 'Waiting for the Barbarians: Conceptualizing Fear in Medieval Saracen Romances' (in Bilynsky, ed., *Studies in Middle English: Words, Forms, Senses and Texts*, pp. 47–69) explores Christian fear of the Saracen 'other' in *Sir Isumbras* and *The Sege of Meleyne*. Finally, Marie Turner's multi-layered exploration 'Guy of Warwick and the Active Life of Historical Romance in *Piers Plowman*' (*YLS* 28[2014] 3–27) proposes that, in addition to seeking connections between *Piers Plowman* and specific romances or romance tropes, scholars of both Langland and romance would also benefit from considering romance as 'a mode of thought that Langland harnesses in his attempt to theorize the relationship between the individual subject and the production of history' (p. 7), including penitential history. Turner argues that the stanzaic *Guy of Warwick* and the character of Hawkyn in *Piers* (among others) link the penitential re-narration of the hero's personal history to the commonwealth itself, illustrating how lay piety may be produced and used for individual and common good.

Various articles join Florschuetz's book in a discussion of female characters and femininity in romance. In '*Lybeaus Desconus*: Transformation, Adaptation, and the Monstrous-Feminine' (*Arth* 24:i[2014] 66–85), Eve

Salisbury explores several aspects of this Fair Unknown romance with special emphasis on its hybrid female characters and their monstrous attributes. Salisbury argues that these figures must be either cast out or incorporated into the poem's Arthurian patriarchy. Pinar Taşdelen's 'Angelic Demons and Demonic Angels: Representations of Female Villains in Middle English Metrical Romances' (*JFL* 31:ii[2014] 205–21) collects wrongdoing women from a wide selection of Middle English romances into groupings such as 'domestic' versus 'stranger' and 'pure' versus 'justified'. The article offers an overview of the topic of dangerous womanhood. Finally, in 'Lady as Temptress and Reformer in Medieval Romance' (*EssaysMedSt* 30[2014] 165–78), Michelle Sweeney explores how the sexuality of female characters becomes a source of secular and spiritual reformation for male characters in Chrétien's *Knight of the Cart*, Marie de France's *Lanval*, *Sir Gawain and the Green Knight*, and Chaucer's *Franklin's Tale*.

Nicole Clifton explores 'Early Modern Readers of the Romance *Of Arthour and of Merlin*' (*Arth* 24:ii[2014] 71–91) by analysing early modern marginalia in five manuscript versions (found in the Auchinleck MS, which receives Clifton's most detailed analysis; London, Lincoln Inn MS 150; Oxford, Bodleian Library Douce 236; a 62-line excerpt copied by John Stow that is collected with London, British Library Harley MS 6223; and the Percy Folio). Clifton traces the aspects of the romance that interested these readers, and argues for increased scholarly attention to early modern engagement with Arthurian romance.

In 'Numerological and Structural Symbolism in the Auchinleck Stanzaic *Guy of Warwick*' (*ES* 95[2014] 849–59), Ken Eckert explores how the *Guy of Warwick*-related material in the Auchinleck MS, and particularly the stanzaic *Guy*, deploy theologically significant numbers to enhance meaning. Some of these usages are transparent (the number three evoking the Trinity) and some are more obscure (Eckert speculates about the significance of the oft-repeated number fifteen). Finally, Randy P. Schiff, in 'Reterritorialized Ritual: Classist Violence in *Yvain* and *Ywain and Gawain*' (*TSLL* 56[2014] 227–58), argues that in various ways across both poems, the hero's exile in the forest (and alliance with a lion) naturalizes a feudal sovereignty founded upon legal exception and violence. Within this larger argument, Schiff also explores how the northern English poet of *Ywain and Gawain* adjusts Chrétien's tale for his local audience.

10. Gower

The collection of essays appearing in the tenth volume of the publications of the John Gower Society series, *John Gower in England and Iberia: Manuscripts, Influences, Reception*, edited by Ana Sáez-Hidalgo and R.F. Yeager, illustrates the continuing vigour and widening scope of Gower studies. The volume grew out of papers presented at the second international congress of the John Gower Society, held in Valladolid, Spain, in 2011. Although the most prominent theme running through the collection is Gower's previously under-explored role in Anglo-Iberian literary relations, the individual essays propose a variety of other fresh approaches. The book is divided into five sections under the headings of 'Manuscripts', 'Iberia', 'The Classical Tradition', 'Economy', and 'Reception'. The opening chapter, by Mauricio Herrero Jiménez (pp. 17–31), presents a palaeographic and codicological analysis of the two fifteenth-century manuscripts containing the Portuguese and Castilian translations of the *Confessio Amantis*, in an attempt to shed new light on their production and early ownership. María Luisa López-Vidriero Abelló turns attention to subsequent phases in the ownership history of the Portuguese *Livro do amante*, tracing its acquisition by the first count of Gondomar in the sixteenth century and its passage to the royal library in the first decade of the nineteenth century (pp. 33–49). Shifting the focus to Gower's own Latin glosses on the *Confessio*, Alastair J. Minnis's 'Inglorious Glosses?' (pp. 51–75) maintains that a true understanding of Gower's hermeneutic methodology can only be achieved if he is firmly located within 'a European secular interpretive community' (p. 75). Barbara A. Shailor's essay on the Yale Osborn manuscript of the *Confessio* (Beinecke Osborn MS fa.1) (pp. 77–85) describes the results of the ink and pigment analysis performed on the damaged rubricated sections of the codex and assesses the potential of hyperspectral imaging for the study of late medieval English manuscripts.

The next section, on 'Iberia', opens with David R. Carlson's essay (pp. 89–101), which shows that Gower's unabashedly pro-Lancastrian *Cronica tripertita* finds precedent in the state-sponsored verse propaganda produced in England in the wake of the Black Prince's victory at Nájera in 1367. The battle of Nájera is also the focus of Fernando Galván's essay (pp. 103–17), which offers a detailed account of the political and dynastic factors that linked England to Iberia in the decades leading up to Philippa of Lancaster's marriage to King João I of Portugal. R.F. Yeager centres his discussion around the 'Tale of the Three Questions' at the end of Book I of the *Confessio*, in which Yeager finds possible allusions to Pedro Alfonso's *Disciplina Clericalis* (pp. 119–29). Yeager's analysis of the tale is a call for further investigation into 'what quite possibly is an underestimated Spanish influence on Middle English poetry' (p. 129). The next chapter, by Tiago Viúla de Faria (pp. 131–8), addresses the hitherto unresolved question of how the *Confessio* came into the hands of Philippa of Portugal. His examination of the extant correspondence between Philippa and Henry Despenser leads him to single out the bishop of Norwich as the most likely conduit for the transmission of the *Confessio* to the Iberian peninsula.

Grouped with two other essays under the title of 'The Classical Tradition', Robert R. Edwards's chapter (pp. 141–52) demonstrates how Gower mapped his literary career onto the three-stage Virgilian model, with his minor poems forming a second *cursus* designed to 'renegotiate and reimagine aspects of his major works' (p. 150). Clara Pascual-Argente's discussion of the Castilian *Confesión del amante* (pp. 153–64) examines its self-presentation as a compilation of classical narratives and reads it against the backdrop of the ongoing tension in fifteenth-century Castile between two literary models of antiquity: the old tradition of *roman antique* and newly emerging vernacular humanism. Shifting the focus to Gower's own debt to one of the *romans d'antiquité* in the *Confessio*, Winthrop Wetherbee's essay (pp. 165–79) demonstrates the need to look beyond Genius's infatuation with epic heroism to discern the poet's own attitude towards the epic past, which is, in Wetherbee's view, 'remarkably consistent and in its implications remarkably bleak' (p. 165).

María Bullón-Fernández begins the next section, on 'Economy', with a discussion of 'Goods and the Good in the *Confessio Amantis*' (pp. 183–92). Bullón-Fernández analyses Gower's intense interest in the relation between material things and the self in the *Confessio*, with particular emphasis on the 'Tale of Midas' and the discussion of *gentilesse* in Book IV. In his wide-ranging examination of such diverse but interrelated materials as the record of Gower's acquisition of a chest, the 'Tale of Two Coffers' in the *Confessio*, and the analogous tale in Hoccleve's *Regiment of Princes* (pp. 193–214), Andrew Galloway underlines the significance for later poets of Gower's reflection on the fusion of mercantile and lordly economies, and of the literary model he provided in his poetry to exemplify a poet's political self-commodification. Likening Gower to Balzac due to their shared interest in the representation of 'the present as history', Ethan Knapp's essay (pp. 215–27) shows how Gower's deep ambivalence about the growing commercialization of the English economy led him to create a poetry 'ever attuned to the power and shiftiness of symbolic exchange' (p. 227). The section concludes with Roger A. Ladd's analysis of the linkage between gifts and commerce in the *Confessio* (pp. 229–41), which reveals a decisive shift in Gower's mode of economic critique from the estates satire of his earlier poems to an exploration of the tenuous boundary between royal and mercantile estates.

In the final section, dedicated to the theme of reception, Siân Echard offers close readings of Gower's unduly neglected minor poems (pp. 245–60). She shows that, when read alongside his major works, these poems evince not only his astonishing versatility in handling poetic forms but also the self-reflexive nature of his lifelong exploration of poetic voice. In the following essay (pp. 261–78), T. Matthew N. McCabe puts Gower into dialogue with his younger French contemporary, Alain Chartier, in order to highlight the parallels that exist between their works, such as their obsession with publicity, their universal calls to self-reform, and their articulation of a sense of belonging to an 'international lay culture' (p. 276). A.S.G. Edwards illuminates an important aspect of the twentieth century's reception of Gower by reconstructing the sales history of manuscripts and early printed editions of the *Confessio* (pp. 279–90). Edwards's painstaking recovery of information on their purchase prices demonstrates that, due to their rarity, copies of Caxton's edition have fared better in sales than manuscripts and that there is no necessary correlation between commercial and literary value. Turning back to the issue of Gower's reception in Spain, the final essay, by Alberto Lázaro (pp. 291–8), offers an intriguing account of the long neglect that the *Confessio* suffered during Franco's regime—a silence that was only broken when Juan de Cuenca's Castilian translation of the *Confessio* was republished in a new edition in 1990.

Matthew W. Irvin's *The Poetic Voices of John Gower: Politics and Personae in the Confessio Amantis* is another welcome addition to the publications of the John Gower Society series. The central concern of this book is Gower's use of a fictional authorial persona in the *Confessio* as a means of exploring the proper relationship between prudence and art, two of the five intellectual virtues discussed in Aristotle's moral philosophy. Irvin argues that whereas the persona of Amans is alienated from political reality, and the *fin amour* to which he is bound represents an art severed from moral action, the poetic art created by Gower has the capacity to transform erotic love into an experience productive of political prudence. For, as Irvin cogently demonstrates, it is through the persona of Amans that Gower's readers are drawn into the fictional dialogue between Genius and Amans, at once to experience the pleasures and pains of love and to learn to exercise rational judgement by actively engaging with the exemplary tales narrated by Genius. The tales that receive particular attention in Irvin's analysis are those that raise the issues of *gentilesse*, pity, and labour in such a way as to prompt an understanding of one's proper place in relation to the common good and the hierarchy of rule. For Irvin, what is remarkable about the *Confessio* is its ability to reveal 'even in the pleasures of love poetry, the virtues of political action, and in political action, the pleasures of love' (p. 6).

Gower's authorial personae receive special emphasis in two further studies. In ' "How love and I togedre met": Gower, Amans and the Lessons of Venus in the *Confessio Amantis*' (in Hopkins, Rouse, and Rushton, eds., pp. 69–83), Samantha J. Rayner looks at the question of the *senex amans* in the *Confessio*. Drawing attention to the ways in which Gower insistently describes love as a universal part of human experience, Rayner suggests that the scene of Amans's disclosure as an aged poet plays a crucial role in rendering the lessons of love that the poem offers both timeless and applicable to readers of all ages. Candace Barrington's 'Personas and Performance in Gower's *Confessio Amantis*' (*ChauR* 48[2014] 414–33) argues that the Ricardian version of the *Confessio* moves from didactic allegory to disenchanted prayers as the authorial persona undergoes three stages of transformation: from a sage counsellor into a courtier poet, from a courtier poet into a courtly lover, and finally from Amans into the aged Gower. Barrington claims that the *Confessio* is infused with a sense of opposition to the courtly ethos promoted by Richard II, and that the poet's final prayers acknowledge his failure to instruct an unreceptive king.

Included in the same issue of the *Chaucer Review*, Emma Lipton's 'Exemplary Cases: Marriage as Legal Principle in Gower's *Traitié pour essampler les amantz marietz*' (*ChauR* 48[2014] 480–501) highlights similarities between exemplary narrative and legal logic by showing how the *Traitié* uses exempla to illustrate general principles of marriage and to adjudicate particular cases involving marital transgressions. Lipton argues that in thus modelling itself on a legal treatise, the *Traitié* suggests not only the broad applicability of legal paradigms and vocabulary but also the extent to which law can help to shape moral poetry.

Robert Epstein's 'Dismal Science: Chaucer and Gower on Alchemy and Economy' (*SAC* 36[2014] 209–48) contains an extensive discussion of Gower's view of alchemy as expressed in Book IV of the *Confessio* (pp. 211–32). According to Epstein, Gower endorses alchemy's ability to bring out the innate value of material, which makes wealth created through alchemy seem organic and natural. This view stands in sharp contrast to his condemnation of money in Book V, where, in a way similar to Aristotle's anti-pecuniary critique from the *Politics*, he condemns the qualities of money that enable the creation of wealth *ex nihilo* through exchange and interest.

The main focus of David R. Carlson's 'Gower *Agonistes* and Chaucer on Ovid (and Virgil)' (*MLR* 109[2014] 931–52) is a comparison between Gower and Chaucer in their use of Ovid. The comparison reveals that Gower's deft manipulations of Ovid are based on his intensive study and thorough comprehension of the corpus of Ovidian verse, whereas Chaucer's knowledge of Ovid is less thorough and much mediated by vernacular translation and commentary. Having thus highlighted the difference in the two poets' relations with Ovid, Carlson reads Gower's 'Tale of Ceix and Alceone' in the *Confessio* as an attempt to correct the 'Chaucerian ineptitude' (p. 945) manifest in the use of the same Ovidian story in the earlier *Book of the Duchess*. In 'Stasis and Change: Gower's Gloss on Ovid's Lycaon' (*JELL* 60[2014] 613–32), Robert Newlin also examines Gower's use of Ovid, but his emphasis is less on Gower's direct knowledge of Ovid's oeuvre than on his participation in the tradition of Ovidian exegesis. By juxtaposing the brief passage on Lycaon in Book VII of the *Confessio* with the glosses on the same story found in such medieval commentaries as the *Ovide moralisé* and Thomas Walsingham's *De arcana deorum*, Newlin draws attention to their shared sense of the dynamic between themselves, their times, and their ancient source.

Articles by Lindsay Ann Reid and Serina Patterson focus on the issue of the early modern reception of Gower. Reid's 'Gower's Slothful Aeneas in Batman's *Christall Glasse of Christian Reformation*' (*N&Q* 61[2014] 349–53) uncovers a previously undetected influence of Gower's Middle English tale of Aeneas and Dido on the treatment of sloth in Stephen Batman's polemically motivated work of 1569. Patterson's 'Reading the Medieval in Early Modern Monster Culture' (*SP* 111[2014] 282–311) analyses *A Certaine Relation of the Hog-Faced Gentlewoman called Mistris Tannakin Skinker*, a cheap quarto pamphlet produced in 1640, at the end of which is added a prose translation of Gower's 'Tale of Florent'. Although the medieval poet is here introduced ostensibly to authorize the truthfulness of Tannakin's story, he becomes, in Patterson's view, 'a point of comparison and displacement', by means of which the pamphleteer attempts to 'update Gower's now-antiquated medieval loathly lady' and thereby to 'define an exclusively modern monstrosity' (p. 305).

Reception and reconfiguration of Gower's poem are also addressed by Terry Jones's provocative essay, entitled 'Did John Gower Rededicate his *Confessio Amantis* before Henry IV's Usurpation?' (in Horobin and Mooney, eds., pp. 40–74). Based on a careful examination of what are considered to be pre-usurpation manuscripts of the *Confessio* (San Marino, Henry E. Huntington Library, MS Ellesmere 26 A.17, and Oxford, Bodleian Library, MS Fairfax 3), Jones concludes that there is no reliable evidence to support the standard 'three recension' classification of the *Confessio* manuscripts, nor the widely held proposition that Gower shifted his allegiance from Richard II to Henry IV before the latter came to the throne. Jones claims that the rededication of the *Confessio* to Henry is not an indication of Gower's disillusionment with Richard, but part of a concerted effort on the part of the new Lancastrian regime to 'revise the textual history of the poem' (p. 60). Also included in the volume is R.F. Yeager's 'Le Songe Vert, BL Add. MS 34114 (the Spalding Manuscript), Bibliothèque de la ville de Clermont, MS 249 and John Gower' (pp. 75–87), which examines the content and provenance of the two extant copies of Le Songe Vert, an anonymous dream-vision tentatively ascribed to Gower in 1950. Yeager refutes the attribution on the grounds of the linguistic and stylistic features of the Songe, as well as of the great distance that separated the places of production of the two manuscripts. Yeager speculates that the poem, composed in France, was brought back to England by Henry Despenser, to whom one of the manuscripts originally belonged. Another contribution by Yeager, 'Art for Art's Sake: Aesthetic Decisions in John Gower's Cinkante Balades' (in Hill, Wheeler, and Yeager, eds., pp. 179–93), offers a thoughtful close reading of Gower's French balades. Yeager's interpretation is well attuned to the aesthetic sensibility which makes the Cinkante Balades such an artfully conceived and exquisitely crafted poetic sequence, and elucidates an aspect of Gower's achievement which tends to be obscured by exclusive focus on his self-designated role as social critic and political philosopher.

Misty Schieberle's Feminized Counsel and the Literature of Advice in England, 1380–1500 has a chapter on Gower, entitled 'Women, Counsel, and Marriage Metaphors in John Gower's Confessio Amantis' (pp. 21–60). Schieberle argues that despite its heavy reliance on the tradition of the Mirror for Princes, the Confessio is innovative in its introduction of feminine counsel into the 'overtly masculine and politically-charged genre' (p. 22). Focusing on the 'Tale of Florent' and the 'Tale of the Three Questions', the two exempla that give prominence to women as model counsellors in Book I of the Confessio, Schieberle demonstrates that these women 'represent the necessary subordination of counsellor to king that paradoxically enables authoritative counsel' (p. 27). Schieberle maintains that these two tales combine the image of feminine counsel with marriage metaphors to exemplify an ideal counsellor–advisee relationship in which political advice is perceived by all involved as mutually beneficial and non-threatening.

11. Hoccleve and Lydgate

(a) Hoccleve

David Watt's 2013 book The Making of Thomas Hoccleve's 'Series', was not included in Volume 93. It considers the significance of both the composition of Hoccleve's collection of poems and the collection's physical compilation in manuscript form. Each of his five chapters focuses on a different manuscript: San Marino, Huntington Library, MS HM 111 and MS HM 744; Durham, University Library, MS Cosin V.iii.9; London, British Library, MS Additional 24062; and Oxford, Bodleian Library, MS Selden Supra 53. Watt argues that this approach 'can help us to understand the story that the Series tells about making a book and, more broadly, the way that the making of books might be imagined in the early fifteenth century' (p. 15). In chapter 1, Watt argues that 'Hoccleve invites readers to judge MS HM 111 and the *Series* by inviting one set of readers [fellow clerks of Westminster and London] to measure the distance between what is intended and what is accomplished in the attempt to meet the needs and expectations of other readers' such as Humphrey, duke of Gloucester (p. 22). Watt's second chapter consider the relevance of booklet production (which allowed bookmakers to make decisions about a book's final form at the last possible minute) to MS HM 744 and to the story told by the *Series*, which Watt argues 'depends on its readers' ability to imagine it being made by a narrator who uses booklet production to defer making decisions about its final form as long as possible' (p. 66). The third chapter considers the making of manuscripts such as MS Cosin V.iii.9 in the context of early fifteenth-century anxieties concerning the dangers involved in composing or compiling devotional texts, using the moment when Hoccleve stops translating the source text for 'Learn to Die' as its linchpin. Chapter 4 uses Hoccleve's own formulary, MS Additional 24062, as a lens through which we might understand why Hoccleve's narrator claims to have made the *Series* 'in the hope of re-forming his own character as if he were a child or a young clerk forming it for the first time' (p. 145). In the fifth chapter, Watt turns to MS Selden Supra 53, 'the most authoritative non-autograph manuscript of the *Series*', in order to show how it 'provides evidence that its makers and readers perceived Hoccleve's *Series* as a compilation designed to encourage the kind of contemplation that might lead to personal reform' (p. 186). Overall, Watt aims to show how attention to specific cases of book-'making' (both in the sense of composition and in the sense of physical construction) can contribute to larger narratives about the making and reading of books in the later medieval period.

Two articles focus on Hoccleve's best-known work, the *Regiment of Princes*. Larry Scanlon (*ChauR* 48[2014] 504–23) revisits the issue of Hoccleve's politics in the poem and argues that, 'if anything, ideological readings of Hoccleve have underplayed his royalism' (p. 506). While noting that the historicist approaches that characterized so much of early Hoccleve scholarship are on the wane, Scanlon contends that only 'a forward-looking, critically and theoretically robust historicism' can sufficiently illuminate Hoccleve's political position (p. 505). As Scanlon sees it, the debate concerning Hoccleve's political affiliation is uniquely pertinent to the question of historicism's validity, since it forces us to consider whether poetry and the urge to compose it can ever be historicized in the first place. Scanlon's analysis centres on the figure of Fortune in Hoccleve's *Regiment of Princes*, a figure that, Scanlon argues, Hoccleve takes seriously as he 'articulates his poetic persona into the teeth of a radically unstable political environment that might at any time take a violent turn' (p. 509). After pursuing a reading of Hoccleve's treatment of Fortune that equates her with Sigmund Freud's theory of the 'death wish' (p. 510), Scanlon concludes with a call for medievalists not to put aside the question of the relationship between poetry and ideology.

Hisashi Sugito explores what is termed 'Hoccleve's daydreaming mind' in the *Regiment of Princes* and the *Series* (*ChauR* 49[2014] 244–63). Noting that these two texts have much in common with medieval dream poems (apart from the fact that Hoccleve's narrators do not ever seem to fall asleep), Sugito argues that 'Hoccleve does not need to sleep because he dreams while awake' (p. 246). The article begins with an examination of Hoccleve's references to 'thoght', which Sugito maintains 'puts him in a state of heaviness or dullness, and it is in this state that he achieves the effect of dreaming without actually dreaming a dream' (p. 251). Sugito goes on to consider Hoccleve's depiction of this heavy state of mind in relation to the poet's representation of his professed inability to write; in Hoccleve's poetry, Sugito argues, 'the uncertainty of language is tied to an uncertainty of mind' (p. 259). While noting that an interest in daydreaming is not unique to Hoccleve's works, Sugito concludes that Hoccleve goes further than the authors of medieval dream poems in the way that he 'abandons the setting of dreamworld and stays with reality, describing his mind itself as a dream and thereby rendering dream and reality almost interchangeable' (p. 263).

Peter Brown has published an essay on a manuscript of Hoccleve's *La Male Regle* in a volume in honour of Derek Pearsall (Kerby-Fulton, Thompson, and Baechle, eds.), whose scholarly career has been in large part responsible for the increased attention fifteenth-century poetry has received in recent years. (Other of the volume's contents are reviewed more fully in Section 3.) Brown focuses on the nine stanzas of *La Male Regle* included in Canterbury Cathedral Archives, Register O (fos. 406^v–407^r). Noting that this copy has been neglected by scholars in favour of the version contained in San Marino, Huntington Library MS HM 111, Brown argues that 'the Canterbury *Male Regle*, taken on its own terms rather than as a pale reflection of Hoccleve's "original," is a complete and coherent poem with its own priorities' (p. 408). The version, he continues, in fact bears the title 'Balade', 'as an indication that it is a freestanding composition with a particular purpose and one that, taking its cue from Hoccleve, who wrote many ballades, has improvised its own genre' (p. 408). Brown's analysis of this text includes a transcription of it, which he comes to call 'the Canterbury Balade', and which 'records only those words and letters that are visible to the naked eye either on the parchment or in a magnified digital image' of the manuscript original (p. 412).

Aditi Nafde writes on stanza markers in two manuscripts of the *Regiment of Princes*: London, British Library, MS Arundel 38 and MS Harley 4866 (*N&Q* 61[2014] 5–18). Nafde observes that these two manuscripts, which are among the earliest and most lavishly decorated manuscripts of the *Regiment*, 'have paraphs and initials placed not just at the opening of each stanza but within the body of the stanza itself in a manner quite rare for manuscripts produced in the first quarter of the fifteenth century' (p. 16); however, these mid-stanza and mid-line paraphs are not identically placed across both manuscripts. While conceding that this may simply be the consequence of each scribe using a different exemplar, Nafde suggests that the placement of these paraphs is an indicator of 'careful interaction with the text itself' (p. 16). She concludes by positing that 'if Hoccleve did oversee the production of the presentation manuscripts, the scribes of Arundel 38 and Harley 4866 may have been imitating his concerns' (p. 17). From the minutiae of Hoccleve manuscripts such as these to his place in the literary landscape of late medieval England, the subjects of this year's studies make clear that the rise of Hoccleve scholarship is far from over.

(b) Lydgate

In the last decade of the twentieth century and the first decade of the twenty-first, Lydgate studies largely revolved around research conducted on his more monumental works such as the *Fall of Princes, Troy Book, Siege of Thebes,* and *Life of Our Lady.* Jane Griffiths's *Diverting Authorities: Experimental Glossing Practices in Manuscript and Print* continues this tendency and the related interest in Lydgate's manuscript forms in the examination in its opening chapter of the glosses in the *Fall of Princes* and *Siege of Thebes* in manuscript and early print. She concludes that they may 'have functioned as a locus for discovering and exploring the translator's ownership of his work' (p. 48).

In recent years, Lydgate scholars have turned their attention towards his shorter poems, his mummings and disguisings, and the more curious components of his canon (including his treatise for laundresses). The continuing momentum of this trend is evident in nearly all of the Lydgate studies to appear in 2014, including Claire Sponsler's book on *The Queen's Dumbshows: John Lydgate and the Making of Early Theater,* which considers Lydgate's experiments with various media in the light of theatre history. She focuses on the materiality and context of Lydgate's public poetry in order to 'attend to what we might call situatedness—whether that situatedness is understood as a text's positioning between poets and artisans who together create a drama, its location in an actual performance space such as a city street, its emplacement on a tableau or painted cloth, or its inscription into a chronicle—and to put the lens on audiences and readers as much as on authors and texts' (p. 15). In her first chapter, Sponsler considers how John Shirley's copies of Lydgate's performance pieces both provide information about the circumstances of their performance and also shaped their afterlife. Her second chapter explores how Lydgate's mummings and disguisings 'use the vernacular not as propaganda for court or church but to create a specific image of London' (p. 36), a strategy she describes as 'vernacular cosmopolitanism'. Chapter 3 turns to the poems Lydgate composed for visual display, which Sponsler argues 'point to interactive and performative modes of looking that argue for an understanding of spectatorship as a far from passive engagement with the visual' (p. 68). In her fourth chapter, Sponsler focuses on Lydgate's *Procession of Corpus Christi,* tracing the ways in which the text functions as a kind of interpretative guide for viewers (and readers) of the procession. Chapter 5 considers Lydgate's poem for the royal entry of Henry VI into London on 21 February 1432, examining how 'quotidian (and often ephemeral) writing' (signs, bills, heraldry) works alongside 'durable writing intended to provide an official and permanent account suitable for memorializing an event within chronicles and civic records' in the text (p. 116). Lydgate's most singular text—his verses written to accompany edible 'subtleties' created for Henry VI's coronation banquet—is the subject of Sponsler's sixth chapter, which interprets the eating of the subtleties as the consumption of their 'performance' by spectators at the banquet. In the seventh chapter, Sponsler turns at last to 'the Queen's dumbshows': the *Disguising at Hertford,* the *Mumming at Eltham,* and the *Mumming at*

Windsor, which Sponsler argues 'not only trace [Catherine of Valois's] changing fortunes but also witness the workings of late medieval courtly ceremony, particularly as it attempts to grapple with the problem of what to do with the queen' (p. 168). In the eighth and final chapter of her book, Sponsler turns to *A Mumming of the Seven Philosophers*, contained in Cambridge, Trinity College Library MS R.3.19. As she notes in her Afterword, Sponsler's overall project is to demonstrate how 'vernacular drama in late medieval England is intimately connected to broader cultural processes, so much so that it can be hard to say where a play ends and a poem or picture starts' (p. 213). Joseph Rodriguez's '"With the grace of God at th'entryng of the Brigge": Crown versus Town and the Giant of London Bridge in Lydgate's Triumphal Entry of Henry VI' (in Bennett and Mary Polito, eds., *Performing Environments: Site-Specificity in Medieval and Early Modern English Drama*, pp. 201–21) examines Lydgate's tableaux series that formed part of Henry VI's 1432 entry into London.

Mary C. Flannery's essay on 'Multimedia Lydgate' for the *Oxford Handbooks Online* offers an overview of Lydgate's interest in multimediality in order to examine how he exploits 'the semiotic potential of both poetry *and* image' in his works (p. 2). She begins by situating Lydgate's multimedia works in relation to medieval debates concerning the value—and dangers—of poetry and images, drawing attention to Lydgate's frequent defence of both poetry and 'portreture', 'which he presents not as distractions or empty objects, but as stimuli for "remembraunce"' (p. 5). The second half of her essay concentrates on *The Testament of Dan John Lydgate*, a confessional poem that reflects on the reforming power of the name and image of Jesus. Flannery argues that 'Lydgate's transposition of mixed-media art into a mixed-media poem is indicative of his larger interest in the potential of multimedia literature' (p. 9). While Lydgate is most frequently cited for his prolific output, his writing on behalf of the Lancastrian regime, and his fervent admiration of Chaucer's works, Flannery suggests that he should be granted equal recognition for his innovative multimedia works.

Emma Lipton's article on Lydgate's *Disguising at Hertford* (*JEGP* 113[2014] 342–64) investigates a performance that 'makes the problem of wifely disobedience an issue of royal rule and the occasion for exploring the relationship between sovereign and legal authority' (pp. 342–3). Lipton notes that the *Disguising* presents an ambivalent picture of Lancastrian power and of the power of theatre to promote it, and argues that it 'shows the continuing power of Chaucerian discourse by tying it to the performative power of statutory legal authority at a historical moment when parliamentary authority was growing and the prerogative of kings to embody divine justice was under pressure' (p. 345). Her point is not that Lydgate's disguising is critical of royal power, but that 'it shows kingly justice as ineffective rather than unappealing, reserving its more trenchant criticism for the performative legal language of the Hertford wives' (p. 355). She reads the statements of the wives in the *Disguising at Hertford* as a kind of 'quiting' of the values undergirding Chaucer's *Clerk's Tale*, and argues that Lydgate links this Chaucerian retaliatory dynamic with the citation of legal precedent in a way that draws attention to the limits of the embodied nature of kingly authority.

In her article on Lydgate's *Mumming at Windsor*, Karen Winstead revisits two important aspects of his career: his role as a Lancastrian apologist, and his vacillating treatment of the 'woman question' (*ChauR* 49[2014] 228–43). She begins by surveying Lydgate's career as a poet in the service of the Lancastrian regime, highlighting the uneasiness that so many recent studies have detected behind his supposedly propagandist verse, and remarking that Lydgate was 'not entirely comfortable acting as a spokesperson for Lancastrian interests' (p. 232). The main part of Winstead's article explores Lydgate's depiction of Clothilda, wife of Clovis (the first Christian king of France), in the *Mumming at Windsor*, a depiction she suggests may have been intended to flatter Catherine of Valois (almost certainly present at the mumming's performance), but which contrasts bizarrely with the *Mumming*'s ironic remarks regarding women's famed steadfastness. Winstead wonders, 'was Lydgate also implying criticism of Katherine's conduct—in particular, of her recent remarriage to Owen Tudor in defiance of Parliament?' (p. 241). Whatever his reasons, she argues that, 'by interpolating into the conversion story extended praise of Clothilda and the "joke" at the expense of women which that praise sets up, Lydgate influences the audience's interpretation of the rest of the mumming, which continues with six deadly earnest stanzas that explain the significance of the Holy Ampulla and assert Henry's right to be King of France' (p. 241). She suggests that we might read this as Lydgate's 'faint protest' at his own role in the production of Lancastrian propaganda (p. 243).

Jennifer L. Sisk's article on Lydgate's *Saint Austin at Compton* interweaves Lydgatean criticism with consideration of a subject that is receiving increasing attention from medievalists of late: emotion (*MP* 112:i[2014] 79–96). Sisk takes as her subject 'the logical incompatibility of justice and mercy' (p. 76) that she views as lying at the heart of Lydgate's poem, which narrates the correction by St Augustine of Canterbury of the lord of the village of Compton who is contumaciously refusing to pay his tithes. The lord agrees to pay his fines after witnessing Augustine's miraculous intervention in the case of the resuscitated corpse of a former lord of the village, who was excommunicated for committing the same offence: Augustine persuades the resuscitated corpse of the priest who excommunicated the late lord to grant him a posthumous pardon, which 'brings about a change of heart in the present lord of the village, who not only agrees to pay what he owes but also vows thereafter to follow Austin' (p. 79). Noting that medieval texts do sometimes suggest that emotion has no place in the execution of the law, Sisk argues that Lydgate's poem nevertheless presents the lesson of excommunication and its spiritual consequences 'not doctrinally or through a reasoned explanation of church law but rather dramatically and affectively' (p. 88). She concludes that the poem aims to move its readers towards being 'tretable' (open to positive changes—in this case, the adoption of a more merciful attitude based on a careful reading of the world).

Lydgate studies are brought into conversation with another expanding critical domain—animal studies—by Corey Sparks's article on Lydgate's 'The Churl and the Bird' (*SAC* 36[2014] 77–101). Sparks reads Lydgate's poem as an example of the poet's interest in 'how the space of the medieval prison raises questions about the unsettled (and thus unsettling) boundaries between discipline and desire, between what one may be forced to do and what one wants to do' (p. 78). Sparks situates his analysis in relation to studies of premodern prisons, studies of animals in medieval literature and culture (which have proliferated in recent years), and the hitherto overlooked Bird Cage Inn in Oxfordshire, used as a prison in the medieval period. Sparks argues that 'Thinking through animal figuration—here the caged bird—productively calls attention to the complex imaginative, subjective, and literary resonances specific places of confinement could have in the later Middle Ages' (p. 92). The depiction of the caged bird in Lydgate's poem, he suggests, illustrates and clarifies the distinction between being *compelled* to do something by someone else and doing something compulsively. This interest in compulsion, Sparks notes, is one that also resonates with Lydgate's critical reception, which abounds in metaphors of confinement and limitation. Sparks concludes by arguing that we should use the figure of the wilful jailbird in order to 'take his poem's account of compulsion seriously, locating as it does compulsion within a space cross-cut by natural inclination and literary creation, interiority and exteriority, freedom and confinement' (p. 99).

Misty Schieberle has published an intriguing study of proverbial wisdom in Lydgate's *Order of Fools* (*ChauR* 49[2014] 204–27). As has often been noted, Lydgate displays a tremendous fondness for proverbs throughout his works. Schieberle argues that 'the *Order* is crucial to our understanding of Lydgate's use of proverbs and his ability to critique the aristocracy with subtlety', and that the poem conveys 'an alternate, common mode of understanding the world that is exemplified by Marcolf's cleverness and stands in opposition to Solomon's high-minded sententiousness' as depicted in the *Dialogue of Solomon and Marcolf* (p. 205). Whereas the Latin and French versions of the encounter between Solomon and Marcolf juxtapose the former's aristocratic values and abstract wisdom with the latter's much earthier and down-to-earth point of view, Lydgate's poem effectively 'erases the distinctions between the behaviors of those of "gentyll blood" and the foolish practices of the laborers and peasants that he depicts', using proverbs 'to advise aristocratic readers to reform and embrace commonplace wisdom' (p. 211). Schieberle concludes by identifying Lydgate as 'the only late medieval English poet who both engages Marcolf as the anarchic peasant rival to Solomon's wisdom . . . and forwards Marcolfian proverbs as necessary supplementary wisdom for aristocratic readers' (p. 225).

Appearing in the same volume as Peter Brown's essay on Hoccleve (reviewed above; Kerby-Fulton, Thompson, and Baechle, eds.), A.S.G. Edwards's essay on 'Selling Lydgate Manuscripts in the Twentieth Century' considers the question of how the monetary value of Lydgate manuscripts relates to their cultural value—as he notes, although the prices of manuscripts as they change hands are usually not of interest to scholars, 'prices are an important part of the historical record since they are linked to provenance and the history of a manuscript's ownership and also provide an obvious indicator of both material and cultural value over time' (p. 207). Edwards's study focuses on twentieth-century sales of manuscripts of *The Fall of Princes*, the *Troy Book*, *The Life of Our Lady*, and *The Siege of Thebes* (Lydgate's best-known works, and those that circulated most widely in manuscript form).

Edwards traces the varied fates of Lydgate manuscripts across the twentieth century, from an expensive copy of the *Fall of Princes* (sold to an American dealer for £1,100 in 1924, now San Marino, Huntington Library MS HM 268) to copies of this and other poems that failed to sell at all. The picture presented by this essay's survey suggests that Lydgate manuscripts have not been regular commercial successes, but Edwards's findings raise an intriguing question, which he himself articulates in his conclusion: 'Is there a correlation between the rise in a sense of scholarly significance and increased commercial value?' (p. 216). This is an appropriate question to pose in a volume dedicated to Derek Pearsall, arguably the scholar whose work has done the most to stimulate the recent surge of interest in Lydgate's poetry; doubtless the fate of Lydgate manuscripts in the coming century will begin to provide an answer.

12. Secular Prose

Criticism on and about Malory and *Le Morte d'Artur* dominated scholarship for 2014 for secular prose, although other authors, such as William Caxton and Thomas Usk were represented.

Miriam Edlich-Muth's *Malory and his European Contemporaries: Adapting Late Arthurian Romance* contextualizes Malory's *Morte Darthur* with other adaptations of the Arthurian cycle, comparing works such as *Tavola Ritonda* with Malory's text. Edlich-Muth covers not only the various source materials used in these fourteenth- and fifteenth-century adaptations, but also the various ways in which each adaptation changes its antecedents. Dorsey Armstrong and Kenneth Hodges discuss Malory's geography in *Mapping Malory: Regional Identities and National Geographies in Le Morte Darthur*. This contribution to the study of Malory's text moves from chapters on Cornwall and Wales to chapters that explore Scotland and Lancelot's nationalist identity; apparent in each chapter is the way in which place and its written inscription help to define the borders and boundaries of Malory's Arthurian world.

In *Contested Language in Malory's Morte Darthur: The Politics of Romance in Fifteenth-Century England*, Ruth Lexton explores what she calls 'the contested political language' of Malory's *Morte Darthur* to trace Malory's Arthur, who is neither an ideal nor perfect once and future king, but a monarch as invested in the political struggles of the fifteenth century, like any Lancastrian king. Lexton maps out this imperfect Arthur and his world, moving from Caxton's printing of Malory's text to discussions of individual tales.

Paul Rovang, in *Malory's Anatomy of Chivalry: Characterization in The Morte Darthur* presents a study of various characters in Malory's *Morte Darthur*, interpreting them according to Malory's 'treatment of them as exemplars of virtue and vice, under the wider categories of kinship, knighthood, and womanhood' (p. xiii).

In *'Truthe is the Beste': A Festschrift in Honour of A.V.C. Schmidt*, editors Nicolas Jacobs and Gerald Morgan touch on a crux in Malory's text. P.J.C Field discusses 'Malory's Fyleloly: The Origin and Meaning of a Name' (pp. 87–9) which has no recorded antecedent in Malory's sources. He finds evidence that the name is Old French.

Arthurian Literature contained several essays of interest to readers of Malory's work. Karen Cherewatuk's 'Malory's Thighs and Launcelot's Buttock: Ignoble Wounds and Moral Transgression in the *Morte Darthur*' (*ArthL* 31[2014] 35–59) discusses three wounds which she characterizes as ignoble (p. 36): the self-wounding of Percivale, Gareth's wound to his thigh, and Lancelot's wound in his buttock. K.S. Whetter's 'Weeping, Wounds, and Worshyp in Malory's *Morte Darthur*' (*ArthL* 31[2014] 61–82) assesses combat in Malory, arguing that *worshyp* overshadows wounds and weeping, the other consequences of battle. In 'Sleeping Knights and "Such Maner of Sorow-Makynge": Affect, Ethics and Unconsciousness in Malory's *Morte Darthur*' (*ArthL* 31[2014] 83–99), Megan Leitch explores how sleeping and swooning function not only as states of unconsciousness but also consciousness, as the reader is made fully aware of affect or emotion by this incapacitation. Erin Kissick's 'Mirroring Masculinities: Transformative Female Corpses in Malory's *Morte Darthur*' (*ArthL* 31[2014] 101–30) reflects upon the tales the female dead tell in *Morte Darthur*.

Two chapters on Malory and sexuality appeared in *Sexual Culture in the Literature of Medieval Britain*, edited by Amanda Hopkins, Robert Allen Rouse, and Cory James Rushton. The first, Kristina Hildebrand's '"Open Manslaughter and Bold Bawdry": Male Sexuality as a Cause of Disruption in Malory's *Morte Darthur*' (pp. 13–27), looks at instances in Malory's text where male sexuality places feudal or familial bonds at risk, especially through treason and incestuous desire, implicit and explicit. Hildebrand's examples include both Uther Pendragon's and King Arthur's adulterous unions and resulting offspring and Pellinore's indiscretions, as well as Meleagant's desire for Guinevere. Yvette Kisor's '"Naked as a Nedyll": The Eroticism of Malory's Elaine' (pp. 55–67) discusses the figure of Elaine and the possibility that she is also the maiden Lancelot saves from boiling water in order to compare these figures in Malory's text and the *Lancelot-Grail* cycle (p. 57).

Gender, including studies of femininity, masculinity, and constructions of queer identity, loomed large in the scholarship on Malory in 2014. Megan Arkenberg's '"A Mayde, and Last of Youre Blood": Galahad's Asexuality and Its Significance in *Le Morte Darthur*' (*Arth* 24:iii[2014] 3–22) reads Galahad's virginity as a kind of precursor of a modern sexual identity, that is, as a person and identity opposed to sexual desire. Kristin Bovaird-Abbo's 'Tough Talk or Tough Love: Lynet and the Construction of Feminine Identity in Thomas Malory's "Tale of Sir Gareth"' (*Arth* 24:ii[2014] 126–57) uses the early silence and later absence of Lynet in 'The Tale of Sir Gareth' to see in her silence a challenge to Arthur's authority. Laura Clark, in 'Fashionable Beards and Beards as Fashion: Beard Coats in Thomas Malory's *Morte d'Arthur*' (*Parergon* 31:i[2014] 95–109), contends that beard coats in Malory's text are revised to offer more positive readings of Arthur.

Interiority in Malory's work is the subject of two separate essays. J. Cameron Moore's 'Outward Seeming: Lancelot's Prayer and the Healing of Sir Urry in Malory's *Morte Darthur*' (*Arth* 24:ii[2014] 3–20) compares instances of Lancelot's prayer and its efficacy, along with Lancelot's reaction, in order to connect Lancelot's inner state to his outward emotions. In the healing of Sir Urry, Lancelot's tears are evidence of a conflict between outward faith and inner turmoil. Continuing this investigation into the inner lives of Malory's characters, Meredith Reynolds contends that Malory employs interior monologue to differentiate characters, in her essay 'Interior Monologue in Malory' (*Arth* 24:iii[2014] 79–98).

Caxton's printing of Malory's text is the subject of James Wade's 'The Chapter Headings of the Morte Darthur: Caxton and de Worde' (*MP* 111[2014] 645–67). Wade discusses the nature of Caxton's chapter headings, and their emphasis on the initial events of each chapter. David Eugene Clark concentrates too on layout and reading in Malory in 'Hearing and Reading Narrative Divisions in the *Morte Darthur*' (*Arth* 24:ii[2014] 92–125). In his exploration of the massive Winchester manuscript, Clark distinguishes between visual and aural reception of the manuscript, drawing a distinction between elements like rubrication and layout, on the one hand, and verbal repetition and explicits and colophons on the other. Because these elements often mark the manuscript in ways that are not identical, visual and aural clues also produce different readings (or hearings) of the same manuscript.

Several other authors and textual traditions were the subject of enquiry in 2014. These contributions to our understanding of secular prose include chapters in Bilynsky, ed., *Studies in Middle English*: the first concerns 'twin formulae' in Caxton and Pecock and the second examines the abuse of truth in Ricardian literature. In 'Twin-Formulae and More in Late Middle English: *The Historye of the Patriarks*, Caxton's *Ovid*, and Pecock's *Donet*' (pp. 25–46), Hans Sauer traces the use of 'twin formulae', the linking of two synonymous or 'semantically related' words, in selected texts of the fifteenth century, including Caxton's *Ovid*, Pecock's *Donet*, and *The Historye of the Patriarks*, in order not only to show that these word pairs were frequently used but also to mark out the possible and probable features of the 'twin formulae'. In pinpointing the purpose of these word pairs, Sauer contends that they both served as a 'marked stylistic feature' (p. 44), which could serve as emphasis or clarification for loanwords. In the same volume, Joanna Bukowska and Adam Mickiewicz outline 'the abuse of truth' as a dominant theme in medieval culture, especially *Richard the Redeless* and Thomas Usk's *Testament of Love* (pp. 99–118). The authors catalogue how truth is corrupted—both by a king and his advisers who abuse truth (*Richard the Redeless*) and by a speaker who accuses his contemporaries of corrupting the truth and slandering him.

In 'Dis-orienting the Self: The Uncanny *Travels of John Mandeville*' (in Khanmohamadi, *In Light of Another's Word: European Ethnography in the Middle Ages*, pp. 113–144), Shirin Khanmohamadi examines the first-person narration of the *Travels*. Exploring what she calls 'the special role of the narrator's gaze in boundary-blurring moments of the uncanny' (p. 115), Khanmohamadi locates her study of the 'uncanny' in the 'instability' (p. 116) of the *Travels*' tone and the narrator's seemingly open approach to difference and diversity. Theresa Tinkle, in 'God's Chosen Peoples: Christians and Jews in *The Book of John Mandeville*' (*JEGP* 113[2014] 443–71), offers a rereading of views of Christians and Jews in *The Book of John Mandeville*, which result in 'the interpretive adjustments Mandeville requires of his reader in the process of paging through the work' (p. 446). Katherine Hindley, in '*Mandeville* Rediscovered: Examining Beinecke MS Osborn a.55, the "Lost" Manuscript of *Mandeville's Travels*' (*JEBS* 17[2014] 180–94), describes a manuscript of the Defective Version of *Mandeville's Travels*, purchased by the Beinecke Library, Yale University in 2011.

Jake Walsh Morrissey's 'Anxious Love and Disordered Urine: The Englishing of *Amor Hereos* in Henry Daniel's *Liber uricrisiarum*' (*ChauR* 49[2014] 161–83) traces the porous boundary between medical and literary texts as he compares the depiction of lovesickness in Chaucer's *Canterbury Tales* and Henry Daniel's *Liber uricrisiarum*. Daniel's discussion of *amor hereos* is, according to Morrissey, the lone extant depiction of lovesickness in a Middle English medical text, and Morrissey provides a transcription of the material from *Liber*. Medical prose was also the subject of Julie Orlemanski's 'Thornton's Remedies and the Practices of Medical Reading' (in Fein and Johnston, eds., pp. 235–55). Here, Orlemanski theorizes that the two medical texts in the Lincoln Thornton manuscript, *Liber de Diversis Medicinis* and an incomplete herbal which follows, were copied at different times.

Michael Schmidt's *The Novel: A Biography* does what is perhaps unexpected, and in its first two chapters takes late medieval sources as part of the source tradition of the novel. The first chapter, '"Literature Is Invention": *Mandeville's Travels*, Ranulf Higden's *Polychronicon*, *De Proprietatibus Rerum*' (pp. 17–24), proposes that *Mandeville's Travels* takes prose beyond utilitarian purposes; Schmidt briefly addresses Higden and Trevisa in this chapter as well. The second chapter, 'True Stories: William Caxton, Thomas Malory, Foxe's *Book of Martyrs*' (pp. 26–32) connects Caxton, Malory, and Foxe and their relationship to truth. While the bulk of this chapter deals with Foxe's work, Caxton and Malory figure as important authors whose works highlight the power of fiction to subvert cultural, governmental, or religious institutions.

Several articles examining the prose *Brut* appeared in 2014. Daniel W. Mosser and Linne R. Mooney's 'More Manuscripts by the Beryn Scribe and His Cohort' (*ChauR* 49[2014] 39–76) discusses various scribal activities by the so-called *Beryn* scribe, the copyist of the *Tale of Beryn*. Using various forms of evidence, including the authors argue centrally that Rawlinson C.901, a *Brut* manuscript, which the authors previously designated an affiliated manuscript, was actually copied by the *Beryn* scribe. Julia Boffey, in 'Assessing Manuscript Context: Visible and Invisible Evidence in a Copy of the Middle English *Brut*' (in Kerby-Fulton, Thompson, and Baechle, eds., pp. 165–76), examines San Marino, Henry E. Huntington Library, MS HM 136, a copy of the Middle English *Brut*, and other items to establish 'what can plausibly be said about their collocation and . . . the challenges to definitions of *manuscript context*'.

An issue of *Digital Philology* (*DPhil* 3:ii[2014]) featured essays on the Dartmouth *Brut*, introduced by Michelle R. Warren. In 'Situating Digital Archives' (*DPhil* 3:ii[2014] 169–77) she ties the issue's explorations of the *Brut* manuscript to larger issues in the digital humanities. Deborah Howe and Warren then discuss the steps necessary to conserve the *Brut* in 'The Dartmouth *Brut*: Conservation, Authenticity, Dissemination' (*DPhil* 3:ii[2014]

178–95). Next, Edward Donald Kennedy's '"History Repeats Itself": The Dartmouth *Brut* and Fifteenth-Century Historiography' (*DPhil* 3:ii[2014] 196–214) examines the manuscript in terms of fifteenth-century additions and omissions to address revisions of the manuscript following the death of Henry V. Lister M. Matheson, in 'Contextualizing the Dartmouth *Brut*: From Professional Manuscripts to "The Worst Little Scribbler in Surrey"' (*DPhil* 3:ii[2014] 215–39), situates the Dartmouth *Brut* in the larger context of *Brut* manuscripts, and examines the ownership both of the Dartmouth *Brut* and University of Glasgow MS Hunter 443, along with the characteristics of their respective scribes. In 'Making Histories: Locating the Belfast Fragment of the Middle English Prose Brut' (*DPhil* 3:ii[2014] 240–56), Ryan Perry examines a fragment held by Queen's University's Special Collections. Elizabeth J. Bryan's essay teases out some of the interactions between scribe and illuminator of the Lambeth *Brut* by examining extant instructions to the illuminator (*DPhil* 3:ii[2014] 257–83). Emily Ulrich's 'Echoes in the Margins: Reading the Dartmouth *Brut* in Early Modern England' (*DPhil* 3:ii[2014] 284–303) traces the history of readership of the *Brut* in general before turning to three different annotators of the Dartmouth *Brut*, all of whom annotated the manuscript for diverse reasons. Examining these early modern annotators helps to pinpoint why and how this *Brut* manuscript might have been useful after the fifteenth century. In '"It is to harde for my lernyng": Making Sense of Annotations in Brut Manuscripts' (*DPhil* 3:ii[2014] 304–22), Julia Marvin likewise explores some of the annotations in the Dartmouth *Brut*, arguing that manuscripts with complex and substantial apparatus such as the Dartmouth *Brut* might, in fact, invite annotation as a kind of collaborative act. Annotations, then, might be said to work as a kind of creation that complements the original act of book-making. The last essay, Matthew Fisher's 'Encountering the Dartmouth *Brut* in the Midst of History' (*DPhil* 3:ii[2014] 323–30), links an annotation on folio 79 of the Dartmouth *Brut*, a remembrance of the trial and execution of Thomas of Lancaster by the Despensers, to the type of history that the *Brut* represents.

Two chapters of Lotte Hellinga's *Texts in Transit: Manuscript to Proof and Print in the Fifteenth Century* will prove useful for readers and scholars of secular prose. Chapter 14, 'The *History of Jason*: From Manuscripts for the Burgundian Court to Printed Books for Readers in the Towns of Holland' (pp. 395–409), records the process by which a fifteenth-century imprint of *The Book of St. Albans* became an exemplar for further editions. In keeping with her focus—the movement from manuscript to print at the end of the Middle Ages—this chapter recounts the changes made to this early printed book so that it might produce other editions. The next chapter, 'William Caxton and the Malory Manuscript' (pp. 410–29), takes as its subject the relationship between the Winchester manuscript of Malory and Caxton's printed edition of Malory's work. This chapter revises Hellinga's earlier work on Caxton's possible use of the Winchester manuscript. Throughout the essay, Hellinga treats her earlier article as she does the manuscripts and incunabula she studies, by considering it in flux, and a text open to change.

Death is an appropriate way to end. Two articles appeared in 2014 centred on Caxton's inscription of death, including his *Artes moriendi* and some prose deathbed prayers he printed. A.S.G. Edwards describes the latter in 'Caxton's *Death-Bed Prayers* in Manuscript and Print' (*PBSA* 108[2014] 91–6), where he discusses manuscript versions—perhaps copied post-printing—of Caxton's *Death-Bed Prayers*. Edwards concentrates on a manuscript copy of the *Prayers* and its variants held at Kent State University Special Collections. His article includes a transcription of that copy. Alison L. Beringer compares a group of *Artes moriendi*, all of which emphasize Christ's passion as an exemplar for knowing how to die, in 'The Death of Christ as a Focus of the Fifteenth-Century *Artes moriendi*' (*JEGP* 113[2014] 497–512), on Caxton's *The Arte & Crafte to Know Well to Dye* and the anonymously written, though very similar, *Crafte for to Die* (see Section 1).

13. Religious Prose

Anne E. Mouron edited *The Manere of Good Lyvyng: A Middle English Translation of Pseudo-Bernard's Liber de modo bene vivendi ad sororem*, a work that is particularly relevant to fifteenth-century piety.

Wolfgang Riehle, *The Secret Within: Hermits, Recluses, and Spiritual Outsiders in Medieval England*, focuses on exegesis, allegory, and contemplatio as defining characteristics in covering a wide range of works, including *Ancrene Wisse*, *A Talking of the Love of God*, *The Cloud of Unknowing*, and *The Mirror of Simple Souls* as well as Rolle, Hilton, Margery Kempe, and Julian of Norwich.

Stephen Kelly and Ryan Perry, eds., *Devotional Culture in Late Medieval England and Europe: Diverse Imaginations of Christ's Life*, includes a number of essays on religious works. Denise Despres, 'Adolescence and Interiority in Aelred's Lives of Christ' (pp. 107–26), discusses Aelred's *Rule for a Recluse* and *Jesus at the Age of Twelve*. In 'Out of Egypt, into England: Tales of the Good Thief for Medieval English Audiences' (pp. 147–242), Mary Dzon addresses legends and tales not necessarily from England; however, she does examine Part III of Aelred's *Rule for a Recluse*. Marlene Vallalobos Hennessey's 'The Disappearing Book in *The Revelation of the Hundred Pater Nosters*' (pp. 243–66) argues that the text encourages visualization. Sarah MacMillan similarly argues for imagined participation in Christ's suffering in'þynke ai of criste': Compassionate Thought in *The Prickynge of Love*' (pp. 315–34). Daniel McCann, in 'Health and Heaven: Middle English Devotion to Christ in its Therapeutic Contexts' (pp. 335–62), examines the intersections among 'texts, religious regulation, and conceptualizations of therapeutic practices in premodern cultures' (p. 336).

In 'Living in the Time of Christ: Margery Kempe's "Devoute Ymaginacion"' (pp. 363–84), Elizabeth Scarborough looks at Margery's 'visionary programme' (p. 365). Paul J. Patterson, in 'Translating Access and Authority at Syon Abbey' (pp. 443–60), focuses on translation debates at Syon Abbey which contributed to the development of a reading plan for the nuns, especially since they were 'commanded to put translated texts to use' (p. 445). Katie Ann-Marie Bugyis re-evaluates Love's pastoral intent in 'Through the Looking Glass: Reflections of Christ's "Trewe Louers" in Nicholas Love's *The*

Mirror of the Blessed Life of Jesus Christ' (pp. 461–86). She argues that *The Mirror* 'both responded to the popular piety and ecclesiastical concerns of the day and creatively reworked the theological foundations laid by the writers of scripture' (p. 462).

In 'The Pepysian Version of the Middle English *Meditationes de Passione Christi*' (pp. 487–510), Mayumi Taguchi explores the dissemination of this text. Barbara Zimbalist examines divine speech acts in popular devotional texts in 'Exemplary Speech in *The Life of the Virgin Mary and the Christ*: Trinity College Dublin MS 423' (pp. 511–32). Valerie Allen, in 'Belief and Knowledge in Love's *Mirror*' (pp. 553–72), examines the vocabulary of the text in connection to the discourses in philosophy. Kathryn Kerby-Fulton's 'The Fifteenth Century as the Golden Age of Women's Theology in English: Reflections on the Earliest Reception of Julian of Norwich' (pp. 573–92) examines Julian's Short Text as an extended example of the 'Golden Age of Women's Theology'. Early readers demonstrate awareness of the Short Text as a product of serious theology, if not an enactment of affective imitation. Finally, Sarah James, in '"Hospitable Reading" in a Fifteenth-Century Passion and Eucharistic Meditation' (pp. 593–606), looks at two fifteenth-century sermons that are based on the Latin sermons attributed to Wycliffe. She suggests that this text seems to be comfortable with 'mixed devotional perspectives', which she labels as 'hospitable reading' (p. 604).

Raphaela Sophia Rohrhofer's *Familial Discourses in* The Book of Margery Kempe: "Blyssed be the wombe that the bar and the tetys that yaf the sowkyn" examines familial imagery in Margery's *Book*. In 'Domestic Ideals and Devotional Authority in *The Book of Margery Kempe*' (*JMRC* 40[2014] 1–19), Hwanhee Park considers her *Book* in the context of medieval conduct books. Bryan Van Ginhoven, in 'Margery Kempe and the Legal Status of Defamation' (*JMRC* 40[2014] 20–43), examines *The Book of Margery Kempe* in a secular tradition, that of historical legal cases involving charges of slander. Laura L. Howes, in 'Romancing the City: Margery Kempe in Rome' (*SIP* 111[2014] 680–90), reads Margery as a figure analogous to romance heroines who journey to Rome, such as Constance and Emaré. In 'Envy and Exemplarity in *The Book of Margery Kempe*' (*Exemplaria* 26[2014] 105–21), Jessica Rosenfeld re-examines Margery's conduct as a manifestation of the sin of envy. Juliette Vuille, in ' "I wolde I wer as worthy to ben sekyr of thy lofe as Mary Mawdelyn was": The Magdalene as an Authorizing Tool in the *Book of Margery Kempe*' (in Loewen and Waugh, eds., *Mary Magdalene in Medieval Culture: Conflicted Roles*, pp. 208–25), argues that she tries to present her public emotions as imitations of the Magdalene. Diana Jefferies and Debbie Horsfall, in 'Forged by Fire: Margery Kempe's Account of Postnatal Psychosis' (*L&M* 32:ii[2014] 348–64), discuss the opening of Margery's *Book*, in which she suffers from what medical historians have identified as postnatal psychosis.

Fumiko Yoshikawa's 'The Mapping of Rhetorical Strategies Related to Persuasion in Middle English Religious Prose' (in Bilynsky, ed., pp. 343–60) addresses several works of religious prose, but concentrates on *The Book of Margery Kempe* and Julian of Norwich's *Revelations*, examining them in the light of the ten persuasive strategies outlined in Halmari and Virtanen's

Persuasion Across Genres (John Benjamins [2005]). She concludes that these strategies were most likely employed to make the pieces as persuasively heterodox as possible.

In 'Julian of Norwich and Catherine of Siena: Pain and the Way of Salvation' (*JMRC* 40[2014] 44–74), Anna Minore examines the titular writers' works in regards to their analyses of the causes of pain. Another work that addresses pain in Julian's text is Michael Raby's 'The Phenomenology of Attention in Julian of Norwich's *A Revelation of Love*' (*Exemplaria* 26[2014] 347–67). He claims that Julian develops a 'phenomenology of attention . . . ways in which her focus is turned, sustained, lost, and recovered' (p. 347). Catherine Willits, in 'The Obfuscation of Bodily Sight in the *Showings* of Julian of Norwich' (*JLCDS* 8:i[2014] 81–96), claims that Julian's treatment of bodily sight has important consequences for the construction of blindness as disability in the Middle Ages. Kathleen M. Smith, in 'Language and Authority in Julian of Norwich's *Showings*' (in Fraeters and de Gier, eds., *Mulieres Religiosae: Shaping Female Spiritual Authority in the Medieval and Early Modern Periods*, pp. 169–91), focuses on Julian's phrase *Benedicte dominus* as an 'incantation' that stands in opposition to the English phrase 'all shall be well'. This indicates, she argues, a tradition of constructing Englishness in Julian's language.

Alan T. Gaylord's 'Devotional Practice in "Crafted" Mystical Prose and Poetry: A Preliminary Inquiry' (in Hill, Wheeler, and Yeager, eds., pp. 216–27) looks at what happens when 'a text for devotion is "translated" into 'literature' (p. 216), with the idea of 'craft' as the delineator. Gaylord provides explications of passages as illustrative examples.

John J. Thompson, in 'Love in the 1530s' (in Meale and Pearsall, eds., pp. 191–201), considers Nicholas Love's *Mirror of the Blessed Life of Jesus Christ*, and assesses the reception of the text on the eve of the English Reformation. He suggested that texts like Love's *Mirror* and Walter Hilton's *Scale of Perfection* could be useful in guarding against heretical ideas. In turn, Thompson posits that such 'inward' works became tools of passive resistance.

Courtney E. Rydel, in 'Inventing a Male Writer in Mechtild of Hackeborn's *Booke of Gostlye Grace*' (*JMRC* 40[2014] 192–216), investigates the effect of removing the female (and visionary) from the composition process. The Middle English version of Mechtild's *Book* depicts a single male scribe and narrator instead of the two female scribes of the original. Rydel argues that the translator made a deliberate choice in order to appeal to his fifteenth-century English audience, who expected visionary literature to conform strictly to gender norms.

Lidia Taillefer de Haya and Rosa Munoz-Luna assess translation activities and their effect on gender roles in literary studies in 'Middle English Translation: Discursive Fields According to Social Class and Gender' (*WSIF* 42[2014] 61–7). Although men dominated holistically, women were allowed to develop their own literary voice through translation work, despite being strictly confined by subject matter (e.g. religious literature, under supervision). Laura Saetveit Miles's 'The Origins and Development of the Virgin Mary's Book at the Annunciation' (*Speculum* 89[2014] 632–69) explores Goscelin of Saint-Bertin's *Liber confortatorius*, the *vita* of Christina of Markyate and the

St Albans Psalter, and Aelred of Rievaulx's *De institutione inclusarum*, all of which use the image of the Virgin Mary reading or otherwise engaging with a text, as an 'authorizing model' for their audiences of anchoresses. Mayumi Taguchi, in 'The Choice and Arrangement of Texts in Cambridge, Magdalene College, MS Pepys 2125: A Tentative Narrative about Its Material History' (in Horobin and Mooney, eds., pp. 177–98), examines a late medieval miscellany that contains a number of unique and unpublished religious texts. Taguchi argues that all these texts, including the purported additions, point to a unifying theme of basic texts for private devotion.

14. Older Scots

Ralph Hanna's edition of Richard Holland's *The Buke of the Howlat* is a very welcome addition to the Scottish Text Society series (STS fifth series, 226[2014]). The edition is based on three sixteenth-century witnesses: Chepman and Myllar's 1508 printed copy (Cambridge University Library MS Sel. 1.19, ll. 537–99); the Asloan manuscript (National Library of Scotland MS 16500, fos. 213^r–28^v); and the Bannatyne manuscript (National Library of Scotland MS Advocates 1.1.6, fos. 302^r–10^v). Taking a strong palaeographical focus, Hanna discusses Holland's language and illustrates his distinctive rhyming with corresponding IPA transcriptions. Further introductory material examines the provenance of the poem and evidence of its circulation in the light of recent discoveries in Scottish print history, along with literary and textual sources and biographical information. Hanna uses Asloan as a base for his edition, noting variants from the other two copies. Comprehensive textual notes, along with a glossary, ensure that this is an accessible edition of an important poem of the Older Scots corpus.

In ' "Booke, Go Thy Wayes": The Publication, Reading, and Reception of James VI/I's Early Poetical Works' (*HLQ* 77:ii[2014] 111–31), Sebastiaan Verweij provides a survey of the publicly held extant printed copies of James VI/I's *Essays of a Prentice in the Divine Art of Poesie* and *His Maiesties Poeticall Exercises in Vacant Houres*. In considering the publication, distribution, and circulation of these books, Verweij identifies new owners and readers of the king's works in both Scotland and England, and argues for a wider circulation impact of these texts than has previously been accepted. The article includes transcription and analysis of three previously unknown manuscript poems found in the Lambeth Palace Library copy of the *Essays*.

Covering the period 1450–1660, Katherine Terrell's 'Scots Literature in the Age of the *Makars* and Beyond' (in Demaria, Chang and Zacher, eds., *A Companion to British Literature*, vol. 2: *Early Modern Literature, 1450–1660*, pp. 249–63) provides an overview of the major literary productions of the late medieval and early modern period. The chapter briefly discusses Hary's *Wallace* before examining the major works of Henryson, Dunbar, Douglas, and Lyndsay alongside the Bannatyne Manuscript, the Maitland Folio, and Jacobean court poetry. In outlining the flourishing of pre-Reformation Scots literary culture, Terrell maps what she terms the 'rise and fall of Scottish poetry' from the mid-fifteenth to the mid-seventeenth century (p. 249).

A special issue ('Scottish Renaissances') of the *European Journal of English Studies*, edited by Wolfram R. Keller, J. Derrick McClure, and Kirsten A. Sandrock contains four articles on the intellectual and cultural background of the first Scottish Renaissance (sixteenth to seventeenth centuries). In 'The Scottish Renaissance: A Rough Beast Slouching to be Born?' (*EJES* 18:i[2014] 11–20), Alasdair MacDonald surveys the surviving corpus of literature written in late medieval and early modern Scotland and argues that there is currently an inadequate picture of the first Scottish Renaissance. MacDonald notes several reasons for this, the most pressing being a current critical environment that is too focused on lowland vernacular (particularly to the detriment of neo-Latin) and a 'misguided nationalistic sentiment' (p. 20) that seeks to separate Scottish literary culture from its European context. While not strictly literary in its scope, Joanna Kopaczyk's 'The Language of William Dunbar: Middle Scots or Early Modern Scots?' (*EJES* 18:i[2014] 21–41) will be of interest given the focus on periodization in her linguistic analysis of Dunbar's works. Studying the morphological and phonological features of Dunbar's language, and drawing on Roger Lass's [2000] tests for determining the 'middle' period in Germanic languages, Kopaczyk seeks to reclassify his work as 'Early Modern' rather than 'Middle' Scots. Jane Stevenson reconsiders the circulation of, and engagement with, engravings in late fifteenth-century Scotland as a more widespread part of devotional life than has currently been thought in 'Harley 6919: Word and Image in Renaissance Scotland' (*EJES* 18:i[2014] 42–59). Exploring the ways in which writers such as Dunbar and Henryson demonstrate familiarity with printed images, the majority of Stevenson's article is concerned with a manuscript of William of Touris's *Contemplacyon of Synners* (BL, Harley 6919) in which the rudimentary drawings appear to have been copied from engravings that, Stevenson suggests, were originally pasted into Touris's own manuscript. Donna Heddle's article, 'John Stewart of Baldynneis: Renaissance Scots' Missing Link?' (*EJES* 18:i[2014] 60–72), situates Stewart within the courtly poetic environment cultivated by James VI's desire to make Scotland part of the 'forward-looking Renaissance' (p. 61). In a detailed analysis of the French-inspired neologisms found in Stewart's *Roland Furious*, Heddle suggests that Stewart's distinctive idiolect served a cultural and political agenda that, simultaneously, sought to emphasize Scotland's literary tradition and link this to the linguistic cultural capital of European literature.

In ' "Reirdit on ane riche roche beside ane riveir": Martial Landscape and James IV of Scotland in *The Knightly Tale of Gologros and Gawane*' (*Neophil* 98[2014] 675–88), Kristin L. Bovaird-Abbo reads *Gologros and Gawane* in the light of anxieties created by the expansion of the Ottoman empire following the conquest of Constantinople in 1453. Drawing attention to Arthur's love of tournaments, his desire for international reputation, and his travels to the Holy Land, Bovaird-Abbo proposes that *Gologros and Gawane* encourages Scottish readers to see the parallels between the fictional king and the military interests of their own monarch, James IV, who positioned himself to intervene in the 'larger arena of European diplomacy' (p. 687). Analysing representations of Mary, Queen of Scots' imprisonment in Thomas Wilson's Anglo-Scots translation of George Buchanan's Latin *Detectio*, Danila Sokolov's 'Ane

Dectectioun of Mary Stewart, Queen of Scots, and the Languages of Royal Imprisonment in Medieval and Early Modern England and Scotland' (*JMEMS* 44[2014] 321–44) considers the interplay between eroticism, ethics, and legality in *Ane Detection of the duings of Marie Quene of Scottes*. Sokolov argues that the pamphlet deliberately echoes Boethius, the *Kingis Quair*, and the works of John Fortescue and George Buchanan to imagine Mary as a queen who lacks the skill of self-governance, which results in the loss of her liberty and her kingdom.

In what seems to have been a bumper year for Dunbar studies, William Hepburn offers a historical perspective on Dunbar's work in 'William Dunbar and the Courtmen: Poetry as a Source for the Court of James IV' (*InnR* 65:ii[2014] 95–112). Through a detailed analysis of 'Schir, ye haue mony seruitouris', Hepburn demonstrates how Dunbar creates a virtual court populated by skilled craftsmen who benefited from the Treasury. Such a court, Hepburn suggests, is not entirely at odds with the archival records of this period. In the absence of chronicles and courtly memoirs from the reign of James IV, Hepburn proposes that Dunbar's poetry is a vital resource for enriching our understanding of the late fifteenth-century Scottish court. Using Julia Kristeva's concept of the abject, Anna Caughey provides a compelling examination of Dunbar's positive and negative exploitations of the animality of human subjects in 'Animality, Sexuality and the Abject in Three of Dunbar's Satirical Poems' (in Hopkins, Rouse and Rushton, eds., pp. 127–45). In discussing the ways in which Dunbar tests the boundaries between human and animal, interior and exterior, and the courtly and obscene, Caughey identifies a 'dark *jouissance*' (p. 144) in Dunbar's poetry through which the abject functions as a source of both the erotic and the humorous. Other chapters from this collection are reviewed in Sections 1 and 9. In 'William Dunbar and Colkelbie's Sow: Dogs and Swine' (*N&Q* 61[2014] 481–2), Alasdair MacDonald points to the possibility that Dunbar's reference to the enmity between dogs and swine in the *Testament of Andro Kennedy* might have been influenced by the bestial metaphors in *Colkelbie Sow*. Emily Wingfield analyses both the early sixteenth-century romance *Clariodus* and its manuscript witness in 'Intertextuality in the Older Scots *Clariodus* and Its Manuscript' (*Archiv* 166[2014] 53–69). Wingfield outlines significant additions made to the Scottish poem (a translation of the French *Cleriadus et Meliadice*) that suggest the influence of Henryson, Dunbar, Chaucer, Lydgate, and Gower; she demonstrates that the *Clariodus*-poet was significantly well read in the works of Scottish and English authors of the later Middle Ages. In noting that the decoration and scribal practice of *Clariodus*'s manuscript witness are heavily indebted to Oxford Bodleian Library MS Arch. Selden. B.24, Wingfield reframes how intertextuality might be understood as an aspect of both literary and textual production.

Emily Wingfield's *The Trojan Legend in Medieval Scottish Literature* traces the political, historical, and literary uses of the Matter of Troy in Scotland from the fourteenth to the sixteenth century, particularly as writers engaged with notions of literary authority. She argues that Scottish engagement with the Matter of Troy throughout the Middle Ages shifted from an act of defensive warfare, notably against the English, to one of 'positive revisionism'

(p. 187) and a realization of the advisory potential of this material. In chapter 1, 'Troy in the Older Scots Historical Tradition', Wingfield explicates the Scottish origin myth of Gaythelos and Scota as it is found in Fordun, Bower, Wyntoun, the *Brevis Chronica*, and the *Chronicle of Scotland*. Chapter 2, 'Troy in the Older Scots Romance and Nine Worthies Tradition', considers how the Trojan legend was embedded within romances that did not deal directly with the Matter of Troy. In her analysis of Barbour's *Bruce*, the *Octosyllabic Alexander*, Hay's *Buik of King Alexander the Conquerour*, *Gologros and Gawane*, Hary's *Wallace*, and *Clariodus*, Wingfield assesses the extent to which the Nine Worthies tradition serves an advisory function in Older Scots texts. Chapter 3, '*The Scottish Troy Book*', continues the examination of advisory literature, situating the *Scottish Troy Book* within the 'Advice to Princes' genre that dominated late medieval Scottish literature. Noting that this text 'avoids traditional patriotic affinities' in its representation of Trojan material, Wingfield proposes that its meditations on efficacious private and public governance are 'universally applicable' (p. 119). Chapters 4 and 5 deal with issues of literary authority and the nature of poetic truth, examining the single surviving Scottish witnesses of Chaucer's *Troilus and Criseyde*, Henryson's *Testament of Cresseid* and Douglas's *Eneados*. Wingfield notes that, for Scots writers, Criseyde becomes a 'symbol of the Trojan textual tradition' (p. 122)—she is continually rewritten and reinterpreted—while Douglas's focus on self and public governance demonstrates the relevance and applicability of the Matter of Troy to the late medieval/early modern political climate in Scotland. An appendix includes Wingfield's complete survey of texts that address the Matter of Troy in fifteenth- and sixteenth-century Scotland.

Also examining the nature of literary authority, in ' "Sum Men Sayis…": Literary Gossip and Malicious Intent in Robert Henryson's *Testament of Cresseid*' (*FMLS* 50:ii[2014] 168–81), Mary C. Flannery argues that Henryson's poem interrogates the malicious nature of gossip and the consequences of literary notoriety. Flannery focuses on the intent of writing about Cresseid, which has the potential to transform idle gossip into malicious defamation. In analysing the poem in comparison with late medieval defamation laws, Flannery proposes that Henryson is acutely aware that, in writing the Testament, he is also participating in a form of literary gossip.

In *The Lily and the Thistle: The French Tradition and the Older Literature of Scotland*, William Calin returns to a recently neglected topic of study in order to reassess the influence of French on medieval and early modern Scottish literature. In a wide-ranging survey, Calin deals with high court literature, comic, didactic, and satirical texts, romance, and texts of the Scottish Renaissance. The book is divided into four sections, with each section containing chapters on individual texts. In Part I, 'High Courtly Narrative: The Tale of Love', Calin argues that *The Kingis Quair*, Henryson's *Testament of Cresseid*, Douglas's *Palice of Honour*, Dunbar's *Golden Targe* and *The Thrissill and the Rois*, and Rolland's *Court of Venus* should be read alongside the French *dit amoureux* tradition, a genre that, Calin argues, 'proved to be one of the genres most congenial to the Scots Makars and their public' (p. 13). Part II, 'The Comic, Didactic, and Satiric: A Mode of Clerical Provenance', reads works by Henryson, Dunbar, and Lyndsay, as well as the *Freiris of*

Berwick and *King Hart* as working within a French tradition of satirical didacticism. In Part III, 'Romance', Calin explores the 'belatedness' (p. 176) of romance writing in Scotland that helps to characterize the Renaissance 'moral and political character of some of the Scottish romances' (p. 177). Specific chapters focus on *Fergus, Lancelot of the Laik, Gologros and Gawane, The Taill of Rauf Coilyear*, and *Eger and Grime*. The final section, 'Scots Renaissance: Soundings', considers writings by Mary Queen of Scots, James VI, William Alexander, and William Drummond of Hawthornden. These writers, Calin argues, were 'among the most attached to the French tradition' (p. 222) and their works demonstrate the continued intertextual and international nature of Older Scots literature into the seventeenth century.

Caitlin Flynn and Christy Mitchell's '"It may be verifyit that thy wit is thin": Interpreting Older Scots Flyting through Hip Hop Aesthetics' (*OT* 29:i[2014] 69–86) establishes a common practice of amicable vying for prestige in both the late medieval and early modern flyting tradition and the battle rap of twentieth-century hip hop, in which the act of being insulted functions as a source of recognition. Flynn and Mitchell examine how flyters exploit formal rhetorical devices in ways that parallel emcees' utilization of established forms and style tropes; they argue that, through an understanding of the aesthetics of hip hop we reach the closest approximation of the literary experimentation, skill, and tone of the Older Scots flyting tradition.

15. Drama

One of the most practical books of this year, Philip Butterworth's *Staging Conventions in Medieval English Theatre*, begins by challenging a number of modern assumptions concerning medieval staging processes. Questioning the trend in medieval theatre criticism to adopt post-medieval concepts and terms (such as character, characterization, costume, amateur, professional, stage direction, and special effects), Butterworth's analysis examines staging conventions in medieval theatre through a wide selection of fourteenth- to sixteenth-century English and Cornish plays and supporting texts. Butterworth uses explicit and implicit stage directions alongside contemporary records, reports, and accounts to interrogate the ways in which these practical considerations enabled plays to cultivate relationships between performers and audience through agreed pretence. Each chapter focuses on a different aspect of staging convention, including indoor and outdoor performance; casting and doubling; rehearsing, memorizing, and cuing; coming and going; playing, feigning, and counterfeiting; dressing and disguising; expounding and monitoring; effects; timing and hearing; and seeing and responding. Throughout, Butterworth remains sensitive to the many ambiguities associated with deciphering the physical aspects of medieval staging and their impact on meaning for both performers and audiences.

Characterization is also an important element of Charlotte Steenbrugge's *Staging Vice: A Study of Dramatic Traditions in Medieval and Sixteenth-Century England and the Low Countries*, which offers a detailed analysis of evil characters. Examining the various didactic and theatrical functions performed by the English Vices and the Dutch *sinnekins*, Steenbrugge notes possible mutual influences between Dutch rhetoricians and English playwrights. Each chapter draws the traditions into dialogue with one another and with their own literary cultures; first examining the origins and development of the English Vices and Dutch *sinnekins*; then their respective moral, didactic, and rhetorical functions; and later their theatrical and meta-theatrical properties. The final chapter, 'Historicizing Vice', aligns the moral interludes and *spelen van sinne* with the changes brought by humanism and the Reformation, suggesting that, while these intellectual and religious movements informed popular enthusiasm for the plays, their impact on these negative characters was minimal given that the concept of sin largely remained the same.

Another major theme emerging in this year's work has concerned the importance of objects, in particular their relationship with time. This is the subject matter of Kurt A. Schreyer's book *Shakespeare's Medieval Craft: Remnants of the Mysteries on the London Stage*, which dismantles literary periodization by exploring Shakespeare's connection to the mystery play tradition through a series of medieval stage objects. Beginning with what the first chapter terms 'A Renaissance Culture of Medieval Artefacts', Schreyer identifies several ways in which medieval objects and texts were present in Renaissance theatrical and material cultures via models of exemplarity, palimpsest, and anachronism. This is followed by a detailed study of the Chester Late Banns, with their particular focus on material trappings including props, costumes, and pageant displays as well as their stress on the antiquity of their performance as a means of responding to growing anti-theatrical dissent. Schreyer then proceeds to provide a lively and refreshing reading of some of the often criticized moments of material connection with a medieval 'past' in Shakespeare's plays—including the ass's head worn by Bottom in *A Midsummer Night's Dream*, the troublesome space of Purgatory in *Hamlet*, and the Porter scene of *Macbeth*. In doing so, he argues that objects and places work to re-form and re-member the bonds between medieval object and early modern subject, thus enabling earlier dramatic forms to enjoy a continuing and creative afterlife.

Time and materiality also emerge as concerns in a number of the essays contained in Susan Bennett and Mary Polito, eds., *Performing Environments: Site-Specificity in Medieval and Early Modern English Drama*. Patricia Badir's '"The Whole Past, the Whole Time": Untimely Matter and the Playing Spaces of York' (pp. 17–35) identifies the polychromic performance of three objects through different performance contexts, including the York Mercers' pageant wagon, the Interlude of St Thomas the Apostle, and Sigismund's sword. Again, this analysis unsettles categories of periodization by demonstrating how the untimely properties of artefacts in performance forge links between past and present. In 'John Heywood, Henry and Hampton Court Palace' (pp. 36–55), Elisabeth Dutton examines how secular interludes often 'defer' significant spaces by situating them somewhere other than the halls in which the interludes were played. She also explores the challenges of accommodating the 'presence' of Henry VIII in the performance space raised for the 2009 Hampton Court production of Heywood's *The Play of the Weather*. Kevin Teo's 'Mapping Conflict in the York Passion Plays' (pp. 141–58) argues that the Pinners' *Crucifixion* and Butchers' *Death of Christ* sought to reshape the guilds' relationships with their civic performance spaces through finding referents to their work and tools in the crafting of the suffering body of Christ. The theme of spatial transformation is also present in Clare Wright's 'Body, Site and Memory in the Croxton *Play of the Sacrament*' (pp. 159–79). This identifies the emotional, neurological, and memorial links drawn between performers and audience through the use of playing space. Wright argues that the actors' movement within playing spaces, along with the audience's active participation in the prayers and processions at the end of the Croxton *Play*, generate embodied and emotional memories which colour future interactions with the performance site.

Jacqueline Jenkins and Julie Sanders' collection *Editing, Performance, Texts: New Practices in Medieval and Early Modern English Drama* contains a number of essays on the critical work of editing performance texts. Claire Sponsler's contribution, 'What the *Beauchamp Pageant* Says about Medieval Plays' (pp. 11–26), examines what the illustrated biography of Richard Beauchamp (1382–1439) can tell us about the visual nature of medieval performances and the tendency of dramatic records to use words, not images, to transmit plays. She interrogates the use of dramatic terminology in the *Beauchamp Pageant* (including the words *pagent*, *shewe*, and *processe*), suggesting that the verbal aspects of medieval performances may have mattered less than the visual. In 'The Towneley MS and Performance: Tudor Recycling?' (pp. 49–69), Murray McGillivray provides a reassessment of the Towneley manuscript: its codicology, construction, copying, and marginalia. He questions the relationship the manuscript held with any kind of contemporary performance, suggesting that the manuscript constitutes a compilation made from various parts and sources—potentially as a result of the Marian order to revive the Corpus Christi performances. Mary C. Erler's 'London Commercial Theatre 1500–1576' (pp. 93–106) provides a detailed account of the many kinds of commercial theatrical activity in London prior to the establishment of London's Theatre in 1576. Examining a number of pre-1576 records showing evidence of local plays, pageants, interludes, child musicianship, and choral performance, she reveals the strong commercial involvement from those engaged with the production, space renting, design, and costuming of these activities. Finally, James Purkis's contribution, 'The Revision of MS Drama' (pp. 107–25), looks at how an early modern play might move from draft to final form. He examines two manuscripts of the play *The Humorous Magistrate*, suggesting that the later text is a 'clean copy' of the earlier one.

An increased interest in textual, as well as physical, performances has produced a number of studies re-examining the form and function of the N-Town manuscript. Pamela M. King's contribution to Roger D. Sell, ed., *Literature as Dialogue: Invitations Offered and Negotiated*, engages with the ways plays seek to generate empathetic and bodily responses in their audiences. Focusing on episodes from the N-Town manuscript's *Passion Play II* and *Mary Play*, King's 'Rules of Exchange in Mediaeval Plays and Play Manuscripts' (pp. 177–96) examines the plays' use of dialogue and elements of liturgy, both to provoke complementary response-actions from an audience watching a performance and to engage with the physicality of private devotional reading for those encountering the plays in manuscript form. Gail McMurray Gibson's 'Manuscript as Sacred Object: Robert Hegge's N-Town Plays' (*JMEMS* 44[2014] 503–29) approaches the N-Town manuscript as a material site of contest between past and present religious orthodoxy and examines the ways in which collectors of medieval drama manuscripts inscribed new cultural histories upon them. In 'The Puzzle of the N. Town Manuscript Revisited' (*METh* 36[2014] 104–23), Alexandra F. Johnston persuasively argues that the material was arranged via the scribal rules of *compliatio*—thus following biblical chronology. This, she notes, accounts in part for the disrupted structures of the various plays making up the manuscript.

Gender is the focus in Emma Maggie Solberg's 'Madonna, Whore: Mary's Sexuality in the N-Town Plays' (*CompD* 48:iii[2014], 191–219), which explores the figuring of Mary's sexuality in a wide range of Marian pageants in the N-Town compilation. Heather S. Mitchell-Buck's article, 'Tyrants, Tudors, and the Digby *Mary Magdalen*' (*CompD* 48[2014], 241–59), reflects on the popular development of the tyrant figure and its manifestation in the Digby *Mary Magdalen* play's presentation of Tiberius Caesar, Herod, Pilate, and the King of Marseilles as signifiers of conflicts in political jurisdiction. She also raises questions concerning the efficacy of placing the opposition to tyranny in the hands of a woman 'outside traditional hierarchies of power'.

Cameron Hunt's article, 'Hocus Pocus and the Croxton *Play of the Sacrament*' (*ET* 17:ii[2014] 11–33), explores the intersection of heresy and parody in the play's language and the ways in which the tension this produces is resolved through the play's alignment of transubstantiation with conversion. Similar tensions are identified in Beatrice Groves's article, ' "One man at one time may be in two placys": *Jack Juggler*, Proverbial Wisdom, and Eucharistic Satire' (*MRDE* 27[2014] 40–56), which uses the creative playfulness of the 1553 Marian interlude's doubling narrative to reassert a reading of the play as a satire against Catholic eucharistic doctrine. An article by Erin E. Kelly suggests that medieval religious dramatic forms were being increasingly treated with suspicion. In '*Conflict of Conscience* and Sixteenth-Century Religious Drama' (*ELR* 44[2014] 388–419) Kelly examines the two surviving versions of Nathaniel Woodes's *The Conflict of Conscience* in order to question why Protestant reformers ultimately abandoned drama as a didactic medium with which to propagate religious belief. Connections between medieval religious drama and later plays are further analysed in Catherine Willits's article, 'The Dynamics and Staging of Community in Medieval "Entry into Jerusalem" Plays: Dramatic Resources Influencing Marlowe's *Jew of Malta*' (*MRDE* 27[2014] 78–109). Here, Willits examines two medieval performance traditions—the royal entry and the civic and liturgical performances of the entry of Christ into Jerusalem—as antecedents to the invasion of Malta in the *Jew of Malta*. In doing so, she identifies the strains these entries exposed in the communal unity of the civic space. In 'Sound Vision, and Representation: Pageantry in 1610 Chester' (*ET* 17:i[2014] 137–57), Susan Anderson examines the often overlooked representational roles of non-verbal elements, including music, context, and evidence of audience reception, in the pageant staged on St George's Day in Chester in 1610.

The function of play scripts in the period just before the establishment of London's first commercial theatres is given attention in Tamara Atkin's ' "The Personages that Speake": Playing with Parts in Early Printed Drama' (*METh* 36[2014] 48–69). Here, she examines character lists in a number of manuscript and print interlude and play books in order to show how they may have been used for different markets and readerships. In the same journal, Matthew Sergi offers a reconsideration of the function of play banns in 'Beyond Theatrical Marketing: Play Banns in the Records of Kent, Sussex, and Lincolnshire' (*METh* 36[2014] 3–23). Examining records from these three counties, he argues that banns might be understood less as advertisements for the plays and more as fundraising appeals for help with production costs.

The performance contexts of John Bale's play *The Three Laws* have received attention with James McBain's article 'Recycling Authority: John Bale at Magdalen?' (*METh* 36[2014] 24–47). This evaluates evidence for a 1560–1 performance of the play at Magdalen College, Oxford, and discusses the timeliness of this performance within the developments of Protestant reform. Links to Oxford and aspects of the play's modern performance are further examined in 'Staging and Filming John Bale's *Three Laws*' by Elisabeth Dutton, Maria Sachiko Cecire, and James McBain (*ShakB* 32:i[2014] 65–84). Their account of the EDOX project's contemporary production and documentary film of John Bale's *Three Laws* identifies a fluid sense of time and space within the play and describes the ways in which this was realized both in live performance and through film's own unique relationship to time.

This year's edition of *ROMARD*, 'The Ritual Life of Medieval Europe: Papers by and for C. Clifford Flanigan', edited by Robert L.A. Clark, contains a number of articles from and inspired by the work of Clifford Flanigan. Claire Sponsler's 'Cliffnotes: Performance, Pedagogy, and the Medieval Past' (*ROMARD* 52–3[2014] 27–32) contributes a reflection on Clifford Flanigan's extensive contribution to medieval and Renaissance drama teaching, noting the deeply performance-based nature of his pedagogical practices and their emphasis on the marginal. Clifford Flanigan's three essays focus on the development of the critical methodologies employed in analysing medieval drama. 'The Conflict of Ideology in Late Medieval Urban Drama' (*ROMARD* 52–3[2014] 85–92) promotes ideologically aware readings as points of departure from historicist views of medieval urban drama as primitive; new critical arguments seeking to find an aesthetic unity in the plays; and views of the plays as containing conflicting 'religious' and 'anti-religious' ideologies. 'Localizing the *Visitatio Sepulchri*: Towards a New Orientation of Medieval Drama Studies' (*ROMARD* 52–3[2014] 95–101) aims to encourage readings of the *Visitatio Sepulchri* to (re)place the texts within the 'scripted social drama' of the monastic lives which produced them. The final essay, 'From Popular Performance Genre to Literary Play and Back Again: The Literary Appropriation of Medieval Vernacular Drama' (*ROMARD* 52–3[2014] 103–9) produces an overview of the critical history of medieval plays and their appropriation by elitist and nationalistic critical discourses of literature. Lawrence M. Clopper uses the Towneley Crucifixion play to re-evaluate the extent of clerical participation in civic biblical plays in 'Framing Medieval Drama: The Franciscans and English Drama' (*ROMARD* 52–3[2014] 153–61). Using historical documents to work towards reconstructing the 1461 ceremonial entry of Charles, count of Charolais, Jesse Hurlbut provides an example of the ways in which phenomenological reading processes might convert incidental archival documents 'into a kind of "drama text"', in 'Imagining a Medieval Performance: A Phenomenological Approach' (*ROMARD* 52–3[2014] 179–94).

Books Reviewed

Alamichel, Marie-Françoise, ed. *Laʒamon's Brut and Other Medieval Chronicles: 14 Essays.* L'Harmattan. [2014 for 2013] pp. ii + 358. €37 ISBN 9 7823 4302 0334.

Alonso Almeida, Francisco, ed. *A Middle English Medical Remedy Book. Edited from Glasgow University Library MS Hunter 185. MET 50.* Winter. [2014] pp. 143. €40 ISBN 9 7838 2536 4120.

Archibald, Elizabeth, and David F. Johnson, eds. *Arthurian Literature XXXI.* Brewer. [2014] pp. xii + 208. $90 ISBN 9 7818 4384 3863.

Armstrong, Dorsey, and Kenneth Hodges, eds. *Mapping Malory: Regional Identities and National Geographies in Le Morte Darthur.* Palgrave. [2014] pp. xii + 232. $90 ISBN 9 7811 3703 4854.

Ashe, Laura, and Ian Patterson, eds. *War and Literature.* B&B. [2014] pp. 266. £30 ISBN 9 7818 4384 3818.

Bennett, Susan, and Mary Polito, eds. *Performing Environments: Site-Specificity in Medieval and Early Modern English Drama.* Palgrave. [2014] pp. 271. £60 ISBN 9 7811 3732 0162.

Bilynsky, Michael, ed. *Studies in Middle English: Words, Forms, Senses, and Texts.* Lang. [2014] pp. 367. £49 ($80.95) ISBN 9 7836 3164 4942.

Bischof, Janika. *Testaments, Donations, and the Values of Books as Gifts: A Study of Records from Medieval England before 1450. Münsteraner Monographien zur englischen Literatur 36.* Lang. [2014] pp. 354. £51 ISBN 9 7836 3163 3151.

Butterworth, Philip. *Staging Conventions in Medieval English Theatre.* CUP. [2014] pp. 272. $99.99 ISBN 9 7811 0701 5487.

Calin, William. *The Lily and the Thistle: The French Tradition and the Older Literature of Scotland: Essays in Criticism.* UTorP. [2014] pp. 432. $70 ISBN 9 7814 4264 6650.

Cole, Andrew, and Andrew Galloway, eds. *The Cambridge Companion to Piers Plowman.* CUP. [2014] pp. xviii + 265. £54.99 ISBN 9 7811 0700 9189.

Cooper, Lisa H., and Andrea Denny-Brown, eds. *The Arma Christi in Medieval and Early Modern Material Culture, with a critical edition of 'O Vernicle'.* Ashgate. [2014] pp. xv + 430. £85.50 ISBN 9 7814 0945 6766.

Demaria, Robert Jr., Heesok Chang, and Samantha Zacher, eds. *A Companion to British Literature,* vol. 2: *Early Modern Literature, 1450–1660.* Wiley. [2014] pp. liv + 426. £450 (4-volume set) ISBN 9 7804 7065 6044.

Edlich-Muth, Miriam. *Malory and His European Contemporaries: Adapting Late Arthurian Romance*. Boydell. [2014] pp. ix + 190. $99 ISBN 9 7818 4384 3672.

Fein, Susanna, and Michael Johnston, eds. *Robert Thornton and His Books: Essays on the Lincoln and London Thornton Manuscripts*. YMP. [2014] pp. xii + 310. £60 ISBN 9 7819 0315 3512.

Fein, Susanna, David Raybin, and Jan Ziolkowski, trans. and ed. *The Complete Harley 2253 Manuscript*, vol. 2. TEAMS. MIP. [2014] pp. viii + 518. $24.95 ISBN 9 7815 8044 1988.

Florschuetz, Angela. *Marking Maternity in Middle English Romance: Mothers, Identity, and Contamination*. PalMac. [2014] pp. xxiii + 232. £60 ISBN 9 7811 3734 3482.

Fraeters, Veerle, and Imke de Gier. *Mulieres Religiosae: Shaping Female Spiritual Authority in the Medieval and Early Modern Periods*. Brepols. [2014] pp. xx + 311. €90 ISBN 9 7825 0354 9125.

Garrard, Greg, ed. *The Oxford Handbook of Ecocriticism*. OUP. [2014] pp. xviii + 577. £105 ISBN 9 7801 9974 2929.

Griffiths, Jane. *Diverting Authorities: Experimental Glossing Practices in Manuscript and Print*. OUP. [2014] pp. 256. £60 ISBN 9 7801 9965 4512.

Hanna, Ralph, ed. *Richard Holland: The Buke of the Howlat*. Scottish Text Society. B&B. [2014] pp. 226. £38 ISBN 9 7818 9797 6395.

Hellinga, Lotte. *Texts in Transit: Manuscript to Proof and Print in the Fifteenth Century*. Brill. [2014] pp. xiv + 452. €149 ISBN 9 7890 0427 7168.

Hill, John, Bonnie Wheeler, and R.F. Yeager, eds. *Essays on Aesthetics and Medieval Literature in Honor of Howell Chickering*. PMS 25. Brepols. [2014] pp. viii + 298. $90 ISBN 9 7808 8844 8255.

Hopkins, Amanda, Allen Robert Rouse, and James Cory Rushton, eds. *Sexual Culture in the Literature of Medieval Britain*. B&B. [2014] pp. 186. £50 ISBN 9 7818 4384 3795.

Horobin, Simon, and Linne R. Mooney, eds. *Middle English Texts in Transition: A Festschrift Dedicated to Toshiyuki Takamiya on his 70th Birthday*. YMP. [2014] pp. xix + 335. £60 ISBN 9 7819 0315 3536.

Hudson, Anne, ed. *Two Revisions of Rolle's English Psalter Commentary and the Related Canticle*. EETS 343. OUP. [2014] pp. 600. £65 ISBN 9 7801 9968 8180.

Innes-Parker, Catherine, and Kukita Naoë Yoshikawa, eds. *Anchoritism in the Middle Ages*. UWalesP. [2013] pp. 202. $140 ISBN 9 7807 0832 6015.

Irvin, Matthew W. *The Poetic Voices of John Gower: Politics and Personae in the Confessio Amantis*. Publications of the John Gower Society 9. Brewer. [2014] pp. 328. £60 ISBN 9 7818 4384 3399.

Jacobs, Nicolas, and Gerald Morgan, eds. *'Truthe Is the Beste': A Festschrift in Honour of A.V.C. Schmidt*. Lang. [2014] pp. xxii + 217. £40 ISBN 9 7830 3431 7283.

Jenkins, Jacqueline, and Julie Sanders, eds. *Editing, Performance, Texts: New Practices in Medieval and Early Modern English Drama*. Palgrave. [2014] pp. 264. £50 ISBN 9 7811 3732 0100.

Johnston, Michael. *Romance and the Gentry in Late Medieval England*. OUP. [2014] pp. xiv + 301. £57 ISBN 9 7801 9967 9782.

Kelly, Stephen, and Ryan Perry, eds. *Devotional Culture in Late Medieval England and Europe: Diverse Imaginations of Christ's Life*. Brepols. [2014] pp. xviii + 663. €130 ISBN 9 7825 0354 9354.

Kennedy, Kathleen. *The Courtly and Commercial Art of the Wycliffite Bible*. Brepols. [2014] pp. xiv + 234. €75 ISBN 9 7825 0354 7527.

Kerby-Fulton, Kathryn, John J. Thompson, and Sarah Baechle, eds. *New Directions in Medieval Manuscript Studies and Reading Practices: Essays in Honor of Derek Pearsall*. UNDP. [2014] pp. xv + 551. $66 ISBN 9 7802 6803 3279.

Khanmohamadi, Shirin A. *In Light of Another's Word: European Ethnography in the Middle Ages*. UPennP. [2014] pp. 216. $47.50 ISBN 9 7808 1224 5622.

Lexton, Ruth. *Contested Language in Malory's Morte Darthur: The Politics of Romance in Fifteenth-Century England*. Palgrave. [2014] pp. xii + 252. $90 ISBN 9 7811 3736 4821.

Loewen, Peter V., and Robin Waugh, eds. *Mary Magdalene in Medieval Culture: Conflicted Roles*. Routledge. [2014] pp. xx + 304. $145 ISBN 9 7804 1581 3150.

Manion, Lee. *Narrating the Crusades: Loss and Recovery in Medieval and Early Modern English Literature*. CUP. [2014] pp. ix + 306. £60 ISBN 9 7811 0705 7814.

Meale, Carol M., and Derek Pearsall, eds. *Makers and Users of Medieval Books: Essays in Honour of A.S.G. Edwards*. Boydell. [2014] pp. xvi + 258. £60 ISBN 9 7818 4384 3757.

Mouron, Anne E. *The Manere of Good Lyvyng: A Middle English Translation of Pseudo-Bernard's 'Liber de modo bene vivendi ad sororem'*. Brepols. [2014] pp. x + 586. €110 ISBN 9 7825 0354 5660.

Riehle, Wolfgang. *The Secret Within: Hermits, Recluses, and Spiritual Outsiders in Medieval England*, trans. Charity Scott-Stokes. CornUP. [2014] pp. xviii + 427. $35 ISBN 9 7808 0145 1096.

Rohrhofer, Raphaela Sophia. *Familial Discourses in The Book of Margery Kempe: 'Blyssed be the wombe that the bar and the tetys that yaf the sowkyn'*. Lang. [2014] pp. 175. £30 ISBN 9 7836 3164 1804.

Rovang, Paul, Malory's Anatomy of Chivalry: Characterization in the *Morte Darthur*. FDUP. [2014] xxi + 201. $75 ISBN 9 7816 1147 7788.

Sáez-Hidalgo, Ana, and R.F. Yeager, eds. *John Gower in England and Iberia: Manuscripts, Influences, Reception*. Publications of the John Gower Society 10. Brewer. [2014] pp. 347. £60 ISBN 9 7818 4384 3207.

Schieberle, Misty. *Feminized Counsel and the Literature of Advice in England, 1380–1500*. Brepols. [2014] pp. x + 224. €75 ISBN 9 7825 0355 0121.

Schmidt, Michael. *The Novel: A Biography*. HarvardUP. [2014] pp. xi + 1,172. £29.95 ISBN 9 7806 7472 4730.

Schreyer, Kurt A. *Shakespeare's Medieval Craft: Remnants of the Mysteries on the London Stage*. CornUP. [2014] pp. 280. $49.95 ISBN 9 7808 0145 2901.

Sell, Roger D., ed. *Literature as Dialogue: Invitations Offered and Negotiated*. Benjamins. [2014] pp. 274. $143 ISBN 9 7890 2721 0395.

Somerset, Fiona. *Feeling Like Saints: Lollard Writings after Wyclif*. CornUP. [2014] pp. xiii + 332. $65 ISBN 9 7808 0145 2819.

Sponsler, Claire. *The Queen's Dumbshows: John Lydgate and the Making of Early Theater*. UPennP. [2014] pp. 320. $65 ISBN 9 7808 1224 5950.

Steenbrugge, Charlotte. *Staging Vice: A Study of Dramatic Traditions in Medieval and Sixteenth-Century England and the Low Countries*. Brill. [2014] pp. 264. $75.00 ISBN 9 7890 4203 8455.

Sutton, Peter, trans. *Piers Plowman: A Modern Verse Translation*. McFarland. [2014] pp. vii + 262. $29.99 ISBN 9 7807 8649 5030.

Warner, Lawrence. *The Myth of Piers Plowman: Constructing a Medieval Literary Archive*. CUP. [2014] pp. xiv + 220. $95 ISBN 9 7811 0704 3633.

Watt, David. *The Making of Thomas Hoccleve's 'Series'*. LiverUP. [2013] pp. 272. £75 ISBN 9 7808 5989 8690.

Westling, Louise, ed. *The Cambridge Companion to Literature and the Environment*. CUP. [2014] pp. xiv + 266. £18.99 ISBN 9 7811 0762 8960.

Williams Boyarin, Adrienne, ed. and trans. *The Siege of Jerusalem*. Broadview. [2014] pp. 198. $18.95 ISBN 9 7815 5481 1588.

Wingfield, Emily. *The Trojan Legend in Medieval Scottish Literature*. Brewer. [2014] pp. x + 246. £50 ISBN 9 7818 4384 3641.

Yeager, Stephen. *From Lawmen to Plowmen: Anglo-Saxon Legal Tradition and the School of Langland*. UTorP. [2014] pp. x + 270. $65 ISBN 9 7814 4264 3475.

IV

Chaucer

NATALIE JONES AND BEN PARSONS

This chapter is divided into five sections: 1. General; 2. *The Canterbury Tales*; 3. *Troilus and Criseyde*; 4. Other Works; 5. Reception and Reputation. Sections 1, 3, and 5 are by Ben Parsons; sections 2 and 4 are by Natalie Jones.

1. General

A number of essays have shed valuable light on Chaucer's relationships with his contemporaries, beginning with David R. Carlson's 'Gower *Agonistes* and Chaucer on Ovid (and Virgil)' (*MLR* 109[2014] 931–52). Carlson stresses that, whether or not Chaucer and Gower were friends in reality, their poetry expresses a clear rivalry. A particular flashpoint is the use of Ovid by the two poets. This comes into play in Gower's manifold engagements with the figures of Alcione and Ceix, which relate to Chaucer's treatment of their myth in the *Book of the Duchess*; at other points it is seen in his tendency to draw on Virgil where Chaucer prefers Ovid. Such differences might suggest a proprietary relationship with Ovid on the part of Gower, as well as a sense of friction with his contemporary. Ovid also offers a common focus for understanding Gower and Chaucer in Andrew Galloway's 'Ovid in Chaucer and Gower' (in Miller and Newlands, eds., *A Handbook to the Reception of Ovid*, pp. 187–201). Galloway reviews the points of contact by which the two writers encountered Ovid, such as the grammar school curriculum, the synoptic or moralized commentaries of John of Garland and Pierre Bersuire, and the imitations of Guillaume de Lorris and Jean de Meun. He notes that the two poets made heavy use of exegesis on Ovid, with both adopting personae drawn from medieval commentary on the poet: such material underpins, for instance, Gower's stance as an elderly lover who has outgrown the game of love, and Chaucer's posture as a lover making amends for his crimes against love in the *Legend of Good Women*. For much of Galloway's discussion, however, the use of Ovidian narratives is foregrounded. He finds that Gower leans on Ovid most consistently during the middle part of his career. Chaucer, on the other hand, retains his connection to Ovid throughout his work: Ovid's influence might in fact underpin the various social and generic metamorphoses of the *Canterbury Tales*.

The Year's Work in English Studies, Volume 95 (2016) © *The Author 2016. Published by Oxford University Press on behalf of the English Association. All rights reserved.*
For Permissions, please email: journals.permissions@oup.com
doi:10.1093/ywes/maw003

The relative influence of classical material on Chaucer and Gower continues to be an important basis of comparison in Robert Epstein's 'Dismal Science: Chaucer and Gower on Alchemy and Economy' (*SAC* 36[2014] 209–48). Epstein selects as his theme the treatment of alchemy in the *Confessio Amantis* and *Canterbury Tales*. He notes that the discipline fell both inside and outside institutionalized knowledge in the period, as it could boast 'an ancient lineage and an extensive written tradition', although it 'was never incorporated into the standard curricula of schools' (p. 210). Such ambivalence informs Gower's and Chaucer's views of alchemy. Gower is curiously laudatory of alchemists and their claims: his comments in the fourth book of the *Confessio* ignore the moral and social complaints usually levelled at the subject. He seems aware that alchemy is bounded by natural laws. Chaucer on the other hand sees alchemy as an empty fantasy without results or substance.

George Shuffleton draws connections between Chaucer and another of his contemporaries, discussing the career of 'John Carpenter, Lay Clerk' (*ChauR* 48[2014] 434–56). Carpenter was Common Clerk of London from 1417 to 1438, and is known for his part in compiling the chronicle *Liber albus*, for sponsoring the construction of the Dance of Death at Old St Paul's, and for the extensive library detailed in his will. He also belonged to the same broad social class as Chaucer. His career shows that being a literate non-priest was less an 'uneasy negotiation between well-established social identities' and more 'an empowering combination of secular and sacramental authority', suggesting that clerks could capitalize on their dual role (p. 436). Equally important is the fact that his activities as chronicler and patron show 'the laicization of public memory' in the late Middle Ages, a movement of the power to commemorate from religious to secular hands (p. 456).

Nicolette Zeeman sets Chaucer's work at the meeting-point between art and theology in 'Philosophy in Parts: Jean de Meun, Chaucer, and Lydgate' (in Denery, Ghosh, and Zeeman, eds., *Uncertain Knowledge: Scepticism, Relativism, and Doubt in the Middle Ages*, pp. 213–38). Chaucer participates in a 'recognizable tradition of "literary" and sceptical philosophizing', one which has often escaped the attention of 'historians of medieval philosophy', despite its vitality and importance (p. 234).

A more literal reading of Chaucer's place in his cultural landscape is developed by Laura L. Howes in 'Chaucer's Forests, Parks, and Groves' (*ChauR* 49[2014] 125–33). Howes observes that managed spaces of various kinds, such as woodlands, gardens, and hunting grounds, recur in Chaucer's poetry as sites of aristocratic power. Such sites would have been a part of Chaucer's experience of elevated social circles, from his early service in the households of Elizabeth de Burgh and John of Gaunt, to his later position as Richard's Clerk of Works. They can also be seen in his poetry, as the woodlands of the *Book of the Duchess* and *Parliament of Fowls* are best read as cultivated spaces designed for social interaction; likewise, reference to contemporary land-management can resolve some of the mysteries in his work, such as how Theseus' park can incorporate an amphitheatre, or why gold can be found beneath an oak in the *Pardoner's Tale*. As a result, landscape in Chaucer's hands is not merely a literary resource or series of conventionalized symbols, but is informed by political and practical considerations.

For the past four decades, Jill Mann has herself been a central feature in the landscape of Chaucer criticism. The collection *Life in Words: Essays on Chaucer, the Gawain-Poet and Malory* brings together fifteen of Mann's essays on Middle English, originally published between 1980 and 2009. Eight Chaucerian essays are collected here: 'Troilus' Swoon' (pp. 3–19) argues that Troilus' fainting fit is not a mark of passivity or 'ineffectuality', but a gesture deeply entangled in Chaucer's wider conceptions of love; 'Shakespeare and Chaucer: What Is Criseyde Worth?' (pp. 20–41) explores the themes of value and exchange surrounding the medieval and early modern Criseyde; 'Chance and Destiny in *Troilus and Criseyde* and the *Knight's Tale*' (pp. 42–61) analyses tensions between Fortune and Providence in Chaucer's major reworkings of Boccaccio; 'Chaucerian Themes and Style in the *Franklin's Tale*' (pp. 62–79) emphasizes that patience is a central virtue in the tale, spanning its themes of changeability and *trouthe*; 'Anger and "Glosynge" in the *Canterbury Tales*' (pp. 80–101) meditates on the confluence between deceitful speech and wrath in Chaucer and Langland; 'The Authority of the Audience in Chaucer' (pp. 102–16) considers Chaucer's readerliness and his expectations of his audience; 'Parents and Children in the *Canterbury Tales*' (pp. 117–37) stresses the devotional aspects of childbirth and child-rearing, and the ability of each to stand for surrender to a greater will; and 'Satisfaction and Payment in Middle English Literature' (pp. 138–66) decodes the mercantile language running through the *Clerk's Tale*, *Gawain*, and *Piers Plowman*.

Martin J. Duffell examines Chaucer's versification in 'Chaucer's Pentameter: Linguistics, Statistics, and History' (*ChauR* 49[2014] 135–60). Duffell brings together various strands of linguistic analysis to make sense of Chaucer's metrical innovations, and to identify his precise Continental models, looking to the work of Jakobson and the generative metrics of Halle and Keyser. Duffell's statistical analysis confirms that Chaucer's decasyllabics usually fall into 'the rhythm of canonical iambic pentameters', as 'more than ten times as many stresses fall in even-numbered as in odd-numbered positions' (p. 141). He also shows Chaucer manipulating syntactic subdivisions in order to preserve these patterns, and using monosyllabic words to sustain them. Given the presence of these and other features, it seems most likely that Chaucer's metre is derived from the *endecasillabo* of Petrarch and Boccaccio rather than the French *vers de dix*, as his own rhythmic variety is closest to the Italian poets, who show similar fluidity in their own lines.

A further aspect of Chaucer's language is discussed by Denise Ming-yueh Wang in 'Chaucer's English and Multilingualism' (*MES* 22[2014] 1–27). Wang's essay begins with a potted history of English and its shifting fortunes in legal, literary, and pedagogical discourse after the Conquest, emphasizing the 'poly-linguistic' milieu in which Chaucer was operating; given his family's holdings in the immigrant centre of Vintry Ward, he is likely to have been immersed in multiple languages throughout his life. Wang then moves on to the difficulty of bringing Chaucer's work into contact with other languages in the twenty-first century, drawing on her experiences teaching his poetry in Taiwan. She notes that his work remains 'foreign' even to students specializing in English, a hurdle that might be overcome by calling attention to his own operation in 'a polyglot cultural space' (p. 14), his combination of registers and

traditions, and the traffic of French and Italian material into his own cultural
and linguistic 'world'.

Further guidance on teaching Chaucer is provided by three new handbooks,
Stephen Fender Chippenham's *The Connell Guide to Chaucer's The Canterbury
Tales*, A.J. Minnis's *The Cambridge Introduction to Chaucer*, and Peter W.
Travis and Frank Grady's *Approaches to Teaching Chaucer's Canterbury Tales*.
Each is tailored for a different level of academic audience. The first is aimed at
a pre-university readership, being designed principally for use by GCSE and A-
level students; accordingly, it provides an accessible, affordable, and engagingly written account of Chaucer's foundational status in English literature,
covering such aspects as the tension between rhetoric and reality, and the
extent to which Chaucer offers a panoramic view of fourteenth-century social
order. Minnis's *Introduction*, on the other hand, is written with an undergraduate audience in mind, focusing on the texts most likely to be included on
university curricula: after a brief overview of the key historical and biographical data, *Troilus* and the dream visions receive a chapter each, while two
chapters are dedicated to the *Canterbury Tales*, grouped according to their
common topics. The organizing principle is thematic, as Minnis leads the
reader through important standpoints and strands of critical debate, from
pagan culture and its values in *Troilus* and the *Legend of Good Women*, to
technology and wonders in the *Franklin's Tale* and the *Squire's Tale*, to
femininity in its active and passive voices in the *Wife of Bath's Tale* and the
Man of Law's Tale. Travis and Grady assemble a useful collection of resources
and approaches for instructors, designed to supplant Joseph Gibaldi's 1980
book of the same title. It begins by helping teachers to navigate the formidable
array of scholarship and supplementary material that has built up around
Chaucer, pointing readers towards the authoritative editions, modernizations,
bibliographies, and digital resources, as well as making shrewd suggestions for
student reading. The remainder of the volume is itself formidable in the most
positive sense of the word, bringing together a range of brief essays, including
contributions from Peter Beidler, Larry Scanlon, Kathryn Lynch, and David
Wallace among others. Collectively these pieces touch on every conceivable
aspect of Chaucerian pedagogy. Individual sections, for instance, focus on such
issues as handling Chaucer's Middle English and versification, understanding
his humour and broader legacy, introducing theoretical approaches, and
engaging students in secondary schools or from a non-liberal arts background.
Finally, for specialist researchers, the Annotated Chaucer Bibliography (*SAC*
36[2014] 359–421) offers a reliably detailed overview of scholarship on Chaucer
for 2012, bringing together synopses of 229 articles and listing 42 reviews.

2. The Canterbury Tales

The *General Prologue* to the *Canterbury Tales* has been the subject of a number
of studies this year. *Historians on Chaucer: The General Prologue to the
Canterbury Tales*, edited by Stephen H. Rigby, with the assistance of Alastair
J. Minnis, contains a total of twenty-six essays which, together, provide a
detailed re-examination of all of the character portraits in the *General*

Prologue. Written by medieval historians, these essays examine each portrait in light of the socio-historical context of the late fourteenth century and thus seek to 'demonstrate what historians themselves can contribute to the historical understanding of Chaucer's work' (p. vii). Before turning to the individual descriptions of each of the pilgrims, the volume begins with two introductory chapters. In chapter 1, 'Reading Chaucer: Literature, History, and Ideology' (pp. 1–23), Rigby reflects on the social climate of the late fourteenth century and notes that scholars have typically viewed Chaucer's treatment of social models and hierarchies as either 'conservative', 'sceptical', or 'open-ended' (p. 10). In order to assess the plausibility of these readings, he highlights the value of a historicist approach and asserts that it is a particularly effective tool for examining Chaucer's engagement with social and moral issues. In the second chapter, 'Chaucer the Poet and Chaucer the Pilgrim' (pp. 24–41), Caroline M. Barron considers the possible links between Chaucer the man and his poetic persona in the *Canterbury Tales*, 'Chaucer the pilgrim'. By surveying what we know about Chaucer's early life and the social circles in which he moved, Barron concludes that Chaucer the author and 'Chaucer the pilgrim' share a degree of social aloofness, as both are considered to be 'outsiders, observers rather than participants' (p. 35). Following these two opening chapters, the rest of the collection is devoted to single essays on each of the pilgrims listed in the *General Prologue*; a chapter is also devoted to the Host, Harry Bailly. Although each essay takes its own approach in terms of argument, they all engage with historical context. In his discussion of the Knight's portrait (pp. 42–62), Rigby examines the list of battles and crusades in which the Knight took part. He demonstrates that the surviving historical records suggest that the Knight's conquests would most likely have been seen in a positive light by a contemporary audience. Peter Coss seeks to shed new light on how Chaucer may have understood the Franklin's social standing in the context of the late fourteenth century (pp. 227–46). For Coss, Chaucer is less concerned with the Franklin's actual social position, but is instead using the Franklin's portrait, particularly the attention drawn to the Franklin's own self-presentation, to question the contemporary concern for social mobility and status. He argues that Chaucer intends the description of the Franklin to be read as a 'satire of pretension' (p. 242), which is revealed through the tone of the portrait as well as in the Franklin's rehearsed courtly manners and his tendency towards self-elevation. Rosemary Horrox's essay on the Pardoner (pp. 443–59) further demonstrates the value of approaching a character portrait through its specific historical context. Focusing predominantly on the religious climate of the fourteenth century and the power of the Church as an institution, Horrox argues that the Pardoner's adoption of priestly duties, his preaching, and his false relics all point to his deviant nature and would thus encourage a contemporary audience to regard him as a suspect figure. As a whole, the essays gathered together in *Historians on Chaucer* demonstrate the virtue of approaching the portraits in the *General Prologue* through a historicist lens.

The portraits of the pilgrims in the *General Prologue* also form the subject of Beverly Boyd's monograph, *Chaucer and the Taverners of Ipswich: The Influence of his Paternal Ancestors upon Some Portraits in the General Prologue and upon his Descendants.* Boyd argues that Chaucer's family history, most notably the fact that his paternal ancestors were provincial taverners in Ipswich, was a great source of interest to Chaucer and served as a significant influence on the shaping of some of the portraits in the *General Prologue.* Chaucer's awareness of his family heritage encouraged him to value a simpler way of life, which he placed in contrast to the affectation of courtly behaviour that he was exposed to in London. After recounting Chaucer's ancestry and the history of ownership of his family's Ipswich tavern, Boyd turns to focus on a series of portraits in which Chaucer criticizes courtly affectation. In examining the portraits of the Man of Law, the Merchant, the Prioress, the Monk, and the Friar, Boyd argues that these pilgrims stand in contrast to the 'provincial pilgrims' (the Wife of Bath, the Shipman, the Yeoman, the Franklin, the Miller, the Reeve, the Parson, and the Plowman), who are all 'untouched by the artificiality of courtly behaviour' and thus present a truer reflection of the human condition (p. 91). Boyd argues that the distinction between these two groups of pilgrims is directly informed by Chaucer's knowledge of his paternal ancestry and that this, in turn, made him a 'rather humble' individual (p. 159).

Lawrence Besserman's study, 'Girdles, Belts, and Cords: A Leitmotif in Chaucer's *General Prologue*' (*PLL* 50[2014] 241–4), also draws a distinction within the group of pilgrims, but does so by focusing on dress and clothing. Besserman notes that, while the portraits of such figures as the Yeoman, the Man of Law, and the Franklin all include a description of belts or cords of some sort, the portraits of the religious pilgrims never include such references. He suggests that this distinction is a form of criticism, as during the period it was usual for members of religious orders to wear cords or girdles to signify 'a variety of spiritual and ethical values' (p. 244). Besserman concludes that Chaucer's omission of mention of belts, cords, or girdles in these portraits signals that the religious pilgrims are all 'spiritually lax or corrupt' figures (p. 244).

A consideration of language and syntax in the *General Prologue* is the subject of Norm Klassen's article 'To Seek Distant Shrines: A Syntactical Problem in Chaucer's General Prologue' (*MP* 111[2014] 585–92). Klassen examines lines 12–14 of the *Prologue* and highlights the syntactical difficulty caused by the phrase 'to ferne hawles' (l. 14), frequently glossed as 'to distant shrines'. Klassen argues for a new reading of this line and states that the line as frequently edited contains a syntactical error that has been perpetuated in scholarship. Benjamin S.W. Barootes's 'Whence the *Buf*? Chaucer's Philological Burp' (*Neophil* 98[2014] 495–501) is also concerned with Chaucer's language. Barootes explores the likely etymology and semantic history of the word *buf* (l. 1934) in the *Summoner's Tale* to demonstrate its implications: the etymological roots of *buf* demonstrate that it would be understood as a comic extension of Chaucer's satire, confirming the gluttony and indulgence of the monks being described. Also focusing on language in the *Canterbury Tales* is Agnieszka Wawrzyniak's essay, 'Metaphors, Metonymies and the Coreferentiality in the Conceptualization of Love and Heart in Chaucer's *Canterbury Tales*' (in Bilynsky, ed., *Studies in Middle English: Words, Forms, Senses and Texts*, pp. 311–28). Wawrzyniak identifies and then analyses a total of nine different metaphors and metonymies for love in the *Canterbury Tales*. She argues that 'courtly love' is typically associated with pain and suffering in the *Canterbury Tales*, while marriage is more closely linked to the law and a lack of autonomy.

In 'The "Dialect" of Chaucer's Reeve' (*ChauR* 49[2014] 102–24), Philip Knox reinvestigates the linguistic evidence that Chaucer depicts his Reeve as speaking in a Norfolk dialect. Concentrating particularly on the use of the *ik* pronoun in the Prologue to the *Reeve's Tale*, he concludes that by the later Middle English period scribes in the Norfolk region no longer recognized the *ik* form and typically corrected it. In light of this evidence, Knox asserts that in utilizing the *ik* pronoun Chaucer was not seeking to enhance the verisimilitude of the Reeve but was deliberately employing an archaic form in order to convey a generalized, and rather comic, idea of dialectal difference through speech.

The treatment of sex and gender in the *Canterbury Tales* has been a popular topic of investigation. Drawing upon the concept of queer theory, Tison Pugh's *Chaucer's (Anti-)Eroticisms and the Queer Middle Ages* examines the relationship between the erotic pursuit of love and anti-erotic desire in Chaucer's works. He argues that in the Middle Ages the normative workings of sexual desire are juxtaposed with an anti-eroticism that is encapsulated in the states of virginity, chastity, and widowhood, and is promoted by the medieval Church (p. 4). In the context of Pugh's reading of Chaucer's works, the term 'queer' serves to encapsulate a 'divergent stance vis-à-vis ideological normativity, in matters of gender and sexuality' (p. 3); in light of this, Pugh seeks to highlight the 'queer narrative tensions' that exist 'between eroticism and anti-eroticism' (p. 12) in Chaucer's poetry, and in the *Canterbury Tales* in particular. In chapter 2, 'Mutual Masochism and the Hermaphroditic Courtly Lady in Chaucer's *Franklin's Tale*', Pugh examines the marriage of Arveragus and Dorigen and its refiguring of gender roles to argue that, in spite of the tale's complex web of collective suffering, Dorigen and Arveragus's 'mutual masochism' is what eventually leads to 'their sharing of authority and submission in marriage' (p. 32). Chapter 3, '"For to be sworne bretheren til they deye": Satirizing Queer Brotherhood in the Chaucerian Corpus', examines the depiction of sworn brotherhood in the *Knight's Tale*, *Franklin's Tale*, *Pardoner's Tale*, and *Shipman's Tale*, and argues that these oaths 'carried with them the likely possibility of erotic queerness' (p. 65). In chapter 4, 'Necrotic Erotics in Chaucerian Romance: Loving Women, Loving Death, Destroying Civilization in the *Knight's Tale* and *Troilus and Criseyde*', Pugh asserts that, while for the male characters Emelye and Criseyde are viewed as coveted objects of desire, both women consciously seek to reject this role by aligning themselves with the anti-erotic through their respective chastity and widowhood, thus highlighting the centrality of male narcissism in erotic love. Chapter 5, 'Queer Families in the *Canterbury Tales*: Fathers, Children, and Abusive Erotics', examines the role children play in narratives which focus on male rivalry (such as the *Reeve's Tale*, *Summoner's Tale*, *Clerk's Tale*, and *Physician's Tale*), where they are frequently depicted as the victims of erotic violence. In the final chapter, 'Chaucer's (Anti-)Erotic God', Pugh focuses on Chaucer's treatment of divine love in such narratives as the *Second Nun's Tale*.

Questions of sex and gender are also explored in Amy S. Kaufman's 'Erotic (Subject) Positions in Chaucer's *Merchant's Tale*' (in Hopkins, Rouse, and Rushton, eds., *Sexual Culture in the Literature of Medieval Britain*, pp. 27–38). Here, Kaufman seeks to challenge conventional readings of the *Merchant's Tale* which typically approach the narrative action from the perspective of Januarie and thus render May as a commodity or object (p. 28). She argues that May's erotic agency is, in fact, present in the tale and is communicated to the reader through May's relationship with Damyan; specifically, it is Damyan's role as the conventionally passive courtly lover which allows May the freedom to assert her own erotic identity. In this context, May's craving for pears can be read not only as a latent metaphor for her lust for Damyan, but also as an expression of her desire for agency. Kaufman concludes that, in approaching the action of the tale from the perspective of May rather than that of Januarie, we are able to free May from her role as object and are thus able to 'sympathize with her boredom, her repressed youth' and 'her wasted vitality' (p. 34). Annalese Duprey, in '"Lo, pitee renneth soone in gentil herte": Pity as Moral and Sexual Persuasion in Chaucer' (*EssaysMedSt* 30[2014] 55–66), examines the role of pity in the romantic and sexual relations of the *Merchant's Tale* and the *Franklin's Tale*. Duprey notes that in conventional courtly relationships the exploitation of 'wommanly pitie' is an important means through which the male lover secures the affection of his beloved (p. 55). Although this model of romance is evident in a number of Chaucer's works, Duprey argues that in the *Merchant's Tale* and the *Franklin's Tale* May and Dorigen are able to free themselves from the conventional 'paradigm of pity', and as a result, are able to 'carve out for themselves a position of individual agency' (p. 57). Thus, for Duprey, the pity May feels towards Damyan and his passive love-longing is understood as the vehicle through which she can express her autonomy in their relationship. Dorigen, on the other hand, is able to exploit the paradigm of pity to her own advantage when, at the tale's end, her genuine display of grief prompts Aurelius to release her from her rash promise, thus allowing her to retain her autonomy.

The *Merchant's Tale* also forms the basis of Laura Kendrick's discussion of Chaucer, in her essay 'Medieval Vernacular Versions of Ancient Comedy: Geoffrey Chaucer, Eustace Deschamps, Vitalis of Blois and Plautus' *Amphitryon*' (in Olson and Henderson, eds., *Ancient Comedy and Reception*, pp. 377–96). Here, Kendrick discusses the work of Chaucer and Deschamps, and argues that both writers would have primarily engaged with ancient comedy through medieval Latin adaptations. In her discussion of the *Merchant's Tale*, Kendrick notes that the cuckoldry storyline is not only informed by the twelfth-century Latin comedy *Lidia*, but is also indebted to Vitalis of Blois's *Geta*, which is a rather free adaptation of Plautus's *Amphitryon*. Although *Lidia* has often been recognized as a source for the tale's pear-tree episode, she notes that the tale's comic depiction of the pagan gods 'has its precedent in Vitalis' *Geta* and Plautus' *Amphitryon*' (p. 385). According to Kendrick, the reason this link has been hitherto overlooked is due to Chaucer's 'irreverent attitude' (p. 379) to his sources.

In *Chaucer and Array: Patterns of Costume and Fabric Rhetoric in the Canterbury Tales, Troilus and Criseyde and Other Works*, Laura F. Hodges offers an analysis of Chaucer's 'costume rhetoric' (p. 1). She focuses particularly on costume descriptions and references to textiles and materials, considering their importance within particular texts as well as looking for patterns across Chaucer's works as a whole. Following the introduction, in which Hodges offers an overview of the use of costume rhetoric throughout the *Canterbury Tales*, chapter 1 focuses on the *Knight's Tale* and considers how its use of costume description both fulfils and frustrates an audience's expectation of the romance genre. Although Arcite's funeral adheres to generic convention in its emphasis on the deceased hero being dressed in 'cloth of gold', Hodges notes that the tale does not detail the other main characters' costumes, nor does it include an arming scene, as would be typical in romances. As part of this discussion, Hodges also devotes some attention to the tale's description of the tournament procession and notes that, in many respects, and in particular through its reference to 'cloth of gold', the scene accords with historical accounts of processions in the late fourteenth century. The female undergarment, the smock, forms the subject of chapters 3 and 4, which explore the *Clerk's Tale* and the *Miller's Tale* respectively. Noting that the smock serves as 'an important costume sign representing social status or character' (p. 91), Hodges examines the garment's material and cultural history in order to consider how the smocks worn by Griselda and Alisoun might reflect their character and position. In her discussion of the *Clerk's Tale*, Hodges points to the many clothing transformations that Griselda endures and notes that, in the absence of any detailed descriptions of her costumes, the centrality of Griselda's smocks conveys the changes in her social status. In chapter 4, Hodges examines the description of Alisoun's smock at the beginning of the *Miller's Tale* and notes that the reference to the elaborate embroidery which decorates its collar is particularly unusual. As well as considering the type of embroidery likely to have featured on Alisoun's garment, Hodges also investigates the implications of such decoration, noting that embroidered smock collars, particularly those worn on display as Alisoun's is, would likely have been read as a sign of wantonness and lack of refinement by a contemporary audience. Finally, chapter 5 discusses the place of clothing rhetoric in the *Tale of Sir Thopas*, and considers both the descriptions of Thopas's courtly attire and the arming scene in detail. Hodges notes that, in contrast to his other romances, which are typically lacking in this conventional mode of description, Chaucer devotes considerable space to Thopas's 'comically excessive' (p. 160) dress in order to enhance the parodic nature of this tale.

An interest in dress and clothing also informs John Slefinger's article, 'Two Alisouns: The Miller's Use of Costume and His Seduction of the Wife of Bath' (*EssaysMedSt* 30[2014] 156–64), in which he argues that the *Miller's Tale* can be understood as the Miller's covert attempt to woo the Wife of Bath. Slefinger asserts that the lengthy account of Alisoun's appearance at the beginning of the *Miller's Tale* is intended to resemble the description of the Wife of Bath in the *General Prologue*, as in both instances attention is directed towards the characters' wimples, dress, and social aspirations. He argues that this comparison should be understood as the Miller-narrator's attempt to reframe the Wife of Bath in accordance with his own desires; it reflects his wish to 'control and win the Wife of Bath's sexual attention while undercutting any agency and interiority she may have' (p. 155).

The *Tale of Melibee* has been the subject of several essays this year. Ulrike Graßnick, in ' "This litel tretys": Chaucer's Mirror for Princes in the *Tale of Melibee*' (in Rosenberg and Simon, eds., *Material Moments in Book Cultures: Essays in Honour of Gabriele Müller-Oberhäuser*, pp. 3–15), notes that the *Tale of Melibee* reveals Chaucer's awareness of the Mirror for Princes tradition. Although *Melibee* adheres to a number of conventions allied to this mode of writing, Graßnick asserts that it is a particularly distinctive example due to its emphasis on narrative and the way in which its meaning is affirmed by its broader context in the *Canterbury Tales*. Indeed, she argues that the tale's focus on the dangers of tyrannical rulers is reinforced by the *Monk's Tale*, while Chaucer's interest in female counsellors is confirmed in the *Nun's Priest's Tale* through the character of Pertelote. Stephen Yeager, in 'Chaucer's Prudent Poetics: Allegory, the *Tale of Melibee*, and the Frame Narrative to the *Canterbury Tales*' (*ChauR* 48[2014] 307–21), considers the methods through which Prudence interprets and offers advice. He argues that *Melibee* is concerned with the 'literary mode of moralizing allegory and contingent reading practices' (p. 308) and that her approach is marked by a sensitivity and flexibility that enable her to judge advice rationally and in a manner that is shaped by the immediate circumstances (p. 310). Thus, unlike her husband, Melibee, whose strict adherence to his counsellors' advice prompts him to seek vengeance, Prudence interprets this same advice more freely and in a manner which prioritizes mercy. By juxtaposing Melibee's strict allegorical readings with Prudence's rational and measured understanding, the tale affirms Prudence's role as the personification of practical wisdom and demonstrates that her 'interpretive program' (p. 307), with all of its inconsistencies, allows her to promote a clear argument in favour of mercy. Misty Schieberle also examines the *Tale of Melibee* in the third chapter of her monograph, *Feminized Counsel and the Literature of Advice in England, 1350–1500*. Schieberle devotes the majority of her discussion to an examination of Prudence's counsel, focusing on Prudence's rhetorical skill, the importance of her gender, and her transformation from 'domestic wife to political counsellor' (p. 105). Schieberle argues that although Prudence's rhetorical strategies remain feminized throughout the tale, they can also be understood as 'part of the dramatization of how someone lacking authority develops the authority not only to counsel but also to act as a political agent' (p. 94). Indeed, it is suggested that Prudence serves as an exemplar to the reader and highlights 'how a feminized performance can generate authority' (p. 94).

A number of general, thematic studies have included in their discussions a consideration of Chaucer's works. For example, *Food and the Literary Imagination*, by Jayne Elizabeth Archer, Richard Marggraf Turley, and Howard Thomas, devotes its third chapter to the treatment of food in Chaucer's *Canterbury Tales*. It focuses on how 'questions of food security and anxieties of sustenance help to shape Chaucer's pilgrims, their language and the tales they tell' (pp. 56–7). These concerns are filtered primarily through a consideration of Chaucer's Plowman, who is named in the *General Prologue* but never tells a tale. According to Archer, Turley, and Thomas, the silencing of the Plowman may be an intentional move by Chaucer that both reflects his understanding of the 'heightened tensions surrounding the politics of food supply' (p. 56) and demonstrates his awareness of the contemporary politicization of the Plowman figure in the Peasants' Revolt. In order to demonstrate this, Chaucer's Plowman is considered in relation to the Lollard text *The Complaynte of the Plowman*, which was composed around 1400 and was later attributed to Chaucer himself. It is argued that *The Complaynte* enters into a dialogue with the *Canterbury Tales* through the texts' shared focus on the politics of food and hunger. The chapter ends with a consideration of food and the economics of food supply in the *Reeve's Tale*.

In *Against the Friars: Antifraternalism in Medieval France and England*, Tim Rayborn dedicates a chapter to a consideration of the extent to which English writers of the fourteenth century engaged with antifraternal traditions in their works. Rayborn's discussion of Chaucer focuses specifically on the portrait of the Friar in the *General Prologue* and the *Summoner's Tale*. Rayborn highlights how the portrait of the Friar in the *Prologue* accords to a number of general, antifraternal stereotypes, noting in particular the emphasis on Hubert's greed and arrogance. In the discussion of the *Summoner's Tale*, Rayborn considers the sins of the Friar described in the tale and notes that he most likely serves as 'a kind of "everyman" friar', who is not affiliated with one specific order but shows 'the worst in all of them' (p. 122). Rayborn concludes that while Chaucer's use of antifraternal imagery is informed by popular thought at the time, his depiction of friars in general is imbued with a degree of ambiguity, as Chaucer's attack seems to be directed towards 'hypocrisy in general, not the friars as a singled-out group' (p. 121).

Included in his introductory guide to the Middle English Breton lays, *Reading the Middle English Breton Lays and Chaucer's Franklin's Tale*, Leo Carruthers offers an examination of Chaucer's *Franklin's Tale* and argues that it is a particularly complex and accomplished example of the Breton lay form. Carruthers considers the extent to which the Franklin's story adheres to generic conventions and notes that, in spite of its focus on such themes as the supernatural, love, and loyalty (p. 124), it also plays with expectations by countering these aspects with a gritty edge of realism. Indeed, we are reminded that the clerk who answers Aurelius's requests by making the rocks disappear does so not by any supernatural means, but through his understanding of astrology and astronomical tables. Carruthers concludes that 'Chaucer's intention is not to mock the Breton lay as a genre but to use it as a vehicle for his own purpose'; the function of the *Franklin's Tale* is not merely to entertain, 'but to reflect on human relations in a way much more like serious modern novelists' (p. 131).

Questions surrounding Chaucer's narrative style and structural techniques inform Gerald Morgan's discussion, 'Chaucer's Tellers and Tales and the Design of the *Canterbury Tales*' (in Jacobs and Morgan, eds., *'Truthe is the Beste': A Festschrift in Honour of A.V.C. Schmidt*, pp. 137–68). Morgan explores the structure of the work and considers in detail the relationship between tale and teller. He reminds us of the need to avoid seeing the pilgrim narrators as the 'real tellers' of the tales, pointing to the intentional shaping of the multiple narrative voices contained within the work. Morgan also

examines the 'Fragment Theory' and concludes that although the *Canterbury
Tales* is unfinished it has a sense of completeness; it is 'complete in the sense
that the great organizing ideas of the work . . . have been fully worked out' (p.
164). In the same volume, Nicolas Jacobs's essay, 'Nebuchadnezzar and the
Moral of the Nun's Priest's Tale' (pp. 109–26), considers the thematic
similarities between the *Nun's Priest's Tale* and the *Monk's Tale*. Although
both works seem to have a shared moral point, Jacobs notes that the *Monk's
Tale*, with its relentless focus on man as the victim of Fortune, is ultimately less
successful than the *Nun's Priest's Tale*, which communicates its moral in a
more effective, concise, and sophisticated manner. In noting these distinctions,
Jacobs suggests that the contrast between the two tales can be read as
'Chaucer's light-hearted summary of his own poetic career' (p. 111). He argues
that the juxtaposition of the *Monk's Tale* and the *Nun's Priest's Tale* is
deliberate and demonstrates Chaucer's awareness of his own progression as a
writer: the *Monk's Tale* should be understood as 'Chaucer's little joke at the
expense of his younger self and as an example of how not to address the issue
of fortune', whereas the *Nun's Priest's Tale* serves as 'a sparkling example of
how the mature poet would go about it' (pp. 111–12).

Narrative style is also an important consideration for Michael Murrin in his
examination of the *Squire's Tale* in his monograph, *Trade and Romance*.
Noting that scholars have typically concentrated on the aristocratic focus of
the tale and its teller, Murrin argues that the *Squire's Tale* is intended for a
'mixed audience' (p. 43) and that the narrative works in two social directions:
'upward to the aristocracy and downward to the urban middling sort' (p. 44).
Reflecting on the order of the *Canterbury Tales*, Murrin notes that, in spite of
his courtly aspirations, the Squire is aligned with 'people on the margins
between the upper and middle social levels' (p. 47), such as the Man of Law,
the Merchant, and the Franklin. According to Murrin, this arrangement
encourages us to see a similarity between these pilgrims and prompts us to seek
an 'urban reading' of the tale. Indeed, for Murrin such a reading is affirmed by
the Eastern setting of the *Squire's Tale*, as during the fourteenth century Saraï
was a popular site of trade frequented by many merchants and clerics.

Focusing predominantly on the *Knight's Tale*, Leah Schwebel's 'The Legend
of Thebes and Literary Patricide in Chaucer, Boccaccio, and Statius' (*SAC*
36[2014] 139–68) considers Chaucer's use of sources and his participation in
what she describes as a tradition of 'authorial obfuscation' (p. 141). Schwebel
notes that although Chaucer's failure to cite Boccaccio in the *Knight's Tale* has
typically been read as his attempt to instil the work with greater authority, this
erasure should rather be understood as a literary trope that Chaucer learned
from Boccaccio himself. Indeed, she argues that Boccaccio and Chaucer
purposefully erase their immediate sources in order to 'participate in a tradition
of authorial usurpation practiced by the Latin epicists' (p. 140). In so doing,
both writers are able to acknowledge their debt to the classical tradition, while
also pointing to their own 'preeminence as modern poets writing in a new,
literary language' (p. 140). Yet Schwebel notes that Chaucer does not merely
copy this device in the *Knight's Tale*, but rather reveals 'a further interest in
recovering Boccaccio's silenced source . . . by celebrating Statius as the
predominant authority of Thebes' (p. 153). This manoeuvre is most noticeable at

the beginning of the tale, where Chaucer omits the extra material added by Boccaccio in an effort to return to the original form of the work as written by Statius. By overlooking Boccaccio in favour of naming the ultimate source of his story, Chaucer not only hints at the longstanding literary tradition behind the act of authorial erasure but 'renders this device more conspicuous [and] more metapoetic, than it appeared in previous forms' (p. 156).

Also reflecting on Chaucer's practice as a writer, albeit through the adoption of a biographical approach, is Paul Strohm's *The Poet's Tale: Chaucer and the Year that Made the Canterbury Tales*. Strohm argues that 1386 was a pivotal year for Chaucer and that the events which took place prompted him to write the *Canterbury Tales*. By reflecting on biographical details, Strohm seeks to highlight the connections between Chaucer's 'immersion in ordinary, everyday activities and the separately imagined work of his literary world' (p. 6); he argues that in order to understand the context in which Chaucer conceived the *Canterbury Tales* we must appreciate events in Chaucer's life at that time. The first four chapters of the study are devoted to a consideration of the events that led up to the 1386 crisis. In chapter 1, Strohm asserts that in 1386 it is likely that Chaucer became further estranged from his wife, Philippa; chapter 2 considers the implications of living in Chaucer's lodgings over Aldgate. Chaucer's occupation as Controller of the Customs, including his association with Nicholas Brembre, forms the subject of chapter 3, while chapter 4 examines Chaucer's attendance at the parliamentary sessions in 1386. By charting these events in detail, Strohm demonstrates that, by the end of the year, Chaucer had lost his position as Controller of the Customs and, having been ousted from his Aldgate apartment, had decided to leave London to live in Kent. By considering Chaucer's relationship with literary fame in chapter 6 and the practical implications of his new life in Kent in chapter 7, Strohm asserts that once Chaucer had left London he started to reflect on his role as a writer and decided to begin work on the *Canterbury Tales*. According to Strohm, the form of the *Canterbury Tales* is directly influenced by Chaucer's removal to Kent, as it is argued that without his London audience Chaucer was inspired to create 'an audience of his own invention' (p. 227), that is, the group of Canterbury pilgrims. For Strohm, the creation of this new textual audience is a decisive moment in Chaucer's literary career and reflects his ambition and skill as a writer: 'this expansively imagined Pilgrim band may be taken as an emblem of Chaucer's growing ambition for an enlarged literary public – not as an exact blueprint for the public but as a measure of his increasingly inclusive ambitions' (p. 230). Finally, Strohm concludes his study with an Epilogue, 'Laureate Chaucer', in which he reflects on the rise and influence of Chaucer's works in the fifteenth century, demonstrating that Chaucer's tentative ambition for a wider readership of his poetry was fully realized after his death.

3. Troilus and Criseyde

Foremost among the interesting new readings of *Troilus* is Mary Carruther's 'The Sociable Text of the "*Troilus* Frontispiece": A Different Mode of

Textuality' (*ELH* 81[2014] 423–41). The focus of Carruther's analysis is the famous full-page illustration of Chaucer performing his text before a noble audience, included in Corpus Christi MS 61. What the image presents, with its depiction of a group of hearers gathered before an author, conversing freely as they listen, is a stark contrast to later models of textual engagement, which see reading as 'a solitary activity', performed 'by silent individuals reading something in psychic, if not always actual, solitude' (p. 424). She argues that medieval texts are designed for social consumption above all, as their 'readers' are often active commentators, responding vocally in the company of other consumers, in a moment of collective performance. This element of the *Troilus* also resonates with medieval theories of authorship and reception, as Carruthers observes that physical performance is embedded in such thinking, from the definition of *intentio* as bodily movement, to the sense that narrative is a *ductus* or road on which readers and authors are fellow travellers. Cultures of reception also form a major part of Kara Gaston's ' "Save oure tonges difference": Translation, Literary Histories, and *Troilus and Criseyde*' (*ChauR* 48[2014] 258–83). Gaston takes as her starting point the prologue of Book II, in which Chaucer warns his readers of the historical and cultural distance of the events he is setting out to describe. Chaucer's self-consciousness here asks us to look to the culture from which his own raw material stems, as the development of Italian vernacular poetry offers a way of understanding his own policies as a translator, attempting to convey ancient material in medieval language. Gaston gives a detailed account of the ways in which classical syntax and vocabulary served as a means of bolstering vernacular discourse in Italy, looking principally to Dante's comments in the *Convivio*. Chaucer's treatment of Petrarch in the *canticus Troili* serves as a particular focus for her analysis.

However, most scholarship on *Troilus* has tended to focus on particular characters in the poem, with Pandarus receiving the most sustained attention. Cory James Rushton's essay 'The Awful Passion of Pandarus' (in Hopkins, Rouse, and Rushton, eds., *Sexual Culture in the Literature of Medieval Britain*, pp. 147–58) starts with Donaldson's claim that the (implicitly male) reader is driven to fall in love with Criseyde. This idea drives him to consider Pandarus' conversation with Criseyde in the bed she has recently shared with Troilus (III.1562–82). He argues that the central question here 'is not the lovableness of Criseyde, but her fuckability', and especially the fact that we are invited to view such a quality through the eyes of Pandarus himself (p. 148). A complex pattern of imagery and irony places Criseyde at centre of her uncle's fantasies, from the echoes of Dante's Paolo and Francesca in the eroticized reading Chaucer describes, to his references to traps and bait. Pandarus' function as intermediary affords him both voyeuristic proximity to the lovers and vicarious enjoyment of their coupling; his final profession of hatred for his niece is for his own benefit as much as that of Troilus. Pandarus is also a central concern for Jonathan M. Newman, in 'Dictators of Venus: Clerical Love Letters and Female Subjugation in *Troilus and Criseyde* and the *Rota Veneris*' (*SAC* 36[2014] 103–38). Newman sees Troilus as an erotodidactic text, akin to Ovidian *ars amandi*, although notes that it departs from classical precedent by using Pandarus to embody its discourse. The letters he writes are a key aspect of this function, as they resemble Boncompagno da Signa's *Rota veneris*, a guide to the craft of writing love letters, composed by the leading teacher of rhetoric at Bologna. One particularly suggestive overlap is the slippage of power within this tradition, as the formal love letter is above all a literary game within a 'clerical work culture', serving to showcase its writer's 'prowess' rather than communicate their patron's feelings (p. 113). This in turn registers in Pandarus' own epistolary compositions, as he ceases merely to be a mediator in seduction and is instead able to exert authority over text, body, and voice through his letters. But more important is that Pandarus, unlike Boncampagno or his pupils, is enveloped in a narrative that exceeds his own designs, as he is forced to negotiate with a woman who does not merely exist within manipulable text. The final letter from Criseyde causes the whole string of correspondence to collapse, as her claim that letters convey nothing serves to highlight the ironies of male-authored *ars amandi*, its inability to express what it claims to be asserting.

Priam is the subject of Harold C. Zimmerman's 'Kingship, Fatherhood, and the Abdication of History in Chaucer's *Troilus and Criseyde*' (*Neophil* 98[2014] 129–44). Close analysis of the passages in which Priam appears, which Chaucer takes care to preserve from Boccaccio, shows a general movement away from political vocabulary. The terms Chaucer uses consistently emphasize the king's personal or family relationships rather than his social function, a tendency taken still further by Chaucer's additions to the narrative. Such modifications highlight an important pattern in the poem as a whole, a preference for seeing the events of the Trojan War either in terms of the characters' sense of self or in terms of larger philosophical conceptions, in order to play down the ideological or historical foundation of such ideas. Laura F. Hodges's chapter on 'Sartorial Signs in *Troilus and Criseyde*' (in *Chaucer and Array*, pp. 54–90; adapted from an essay that first appeared in *ChauR* 35[2001]), argues that Chaucer's description of dress is important both symbolically and strategically, as it functions as an index of characterization and to mark important points in the narrative. Thus Criseyde's mourning weeds serve to signpost her simultaneous desirability and deathliness while forming a significant counterpoint to the 'mantel' of Troilus' affection. Richer still is Pandarus' reference to the 'game in myn hood', utilizing a garment likely to signify the boundary between the public and private self in order to drive home connotations of trickery. All of these individual references to apparel draw deeply on the medieval usage of costume as a complex communicative medium. Another pervasive set of symbols in the poem is investigated by Lindsay Ann Reid's 'Virgilian and Ovidian Tree Similes in *Troilus and Criseyde* 2.1373–84' (*Explicator* 72[2014] 158–62). Reid notes a rich seam of arboreal imagery in the text, beginning with Pandarus' reference to Criseyde as a tree that 'bende[s], yet stant on roote' (II.1378). She comments on the classical implications of such terminology, looking to the treatment of the myth of Myrrha in the *Aeneid* and *Metamorphoses* to explain Chaucer's allusions.

4. Other Works

In *Rethinking Chaucer's Legend of Good Women*, Carolyn P. Collette offers a fresh approach to the study of the *Legend* and argues that it should be considered as one of Chaucer's major works. In contrast to earlier studies, which have approached the *Legend of Good Women* through a consideration of its use of sources, Collette argues that the poem is 'best understood within multiple contemporary contexts that frame it as a central text in the development of a major writer's work' (p. 2). By placing the *Legend* in its social, cultural, and literary contexts, Collette seeks to demonstrate that the poem is directly informed by 'major intellectual and artistic developments in late fourteenth century European culture' (p. 155). Collette devotes the central chapters of her study to discrete strands of enquiry, with each chapter engaging with a particular cultural or literary context which, she argues, has had a direct influence on the formation of the poem. In the first chapter, Collette accounts for the Prologue's emphasis on books by reflecting on the context of early English humanism in the court of Edward III. She argues that Chaucer's own passion for books was prominent in the English court and was promoted more widely through the writings of Richard de Bury, author of the *Philobiblon*. By examining each of Chaucer's dream vision poems in turn, Collette asserts that Chaucer's relationship with books culminates in the Prologue to the *Legend of Good Women*, where he celebrates 'books as objects of virtue' (p. 11). Chapter 2 explores the wider literary context of the *Legend*, by examining how the narratives contained within the poem were utilized by other late fourteenth-century writers. Collette devotes attention to the works of Boccaccio, Machaut, Gower, and Christine de Pizan to highlight the range of exemplary purposes the narratives had in the works of Chaucer's near-contemporaries. By surveying how these other writers engaged with the narratives, Collette draws attention to the 'adaptability of the trope of women's fidelity' and how it was repeatedly used to 'exemplify a variety of social and ethical issues' (p. 34). Turning away from a literary context to a philosophical one, chapter 3 argues that the *Legend* is informed by the 'broad influence of Aristotelian thought' (p. 78). Through a consideration of the narratives' collected emphases on social and moral behaviour, Collette asserts that the *Legend* as a whole draws attention to the popular Aristotelian ideas of moderation, temperance, and the importance of the mean. In the final two chapters Collette reflects on the place the *Legend* has within Chaucer's own writing career. In chapter 4, she suggests that the *Legend* was originally a much longer work that was firmly grounded in the tragedy of *Troilus*, while in chapter 5 she reflects on the *Canterbury Tales* and considers how the *Legend* may look forward to this work. By examining the treatment of Dorigen, Griselda, and Cecilia in the *Canterbury Tales*, she argues that Chaucer's conception of women's fidelity had progressed since his writing of the *Legend*.

The Prologue to the *Legend of Good Women* forms the subject of the second chapter in Misty Schieberle's monograph, *Feminized Counsel and the Literature of Advice in England, 1350–1500*. Through a consideration of the depiction of Alceste in the Prologue, Schieberle argues that the strategies Alceste uses to persuade Cupid serve as a model for the dreamer-narrator's own address to the God of Love. Alceste's behaviour teaches the dreamer, Geoffrey, 'not only the necessity of subordinating oneself to a superior but also the paradoxical freedom that comes from embracing a feminized, seemingly powerless position' (p. 63). According to Schieberle, Geoffrey's acceptance of this position directly informs the tone of the legends themselves, as Geoffrey exploits the advantages of this feminized model in order to establish his own authority as poet. Indeed, by replicating 'the submissive but active discourses' of Alceste in the legends, Geoffrey is able 'to continue his critique of love's tyranny and of unwise political behaviours' (p. 77) by adopting the role of the political counsellor who guides and comments on the legends' protagonists.

The *Legend of Good Women* is also considered in Wolfram R. Keller's essay, 'Geoffrey Chaucer's Mind Games: Household Management and Literary Aesthetics in the Prologue to the *Legend of Good Women*' (in Honegger and Vanderbeke, eds., *From Peterborough to Faëry: The Poetics and Mechanics of Secondary Worlds*, pp. 1–24). Grounding his discussion in medieval medical theory, Keller argues that the belief that the brain comprised three interlinked chambers or ventricles serves as a useful model through which to approach the 'poetological journeys' in the *House of Fame* and the Prologue to the *Legend of Good Women*. He claims that in both poems Chaucer not only uses the model of the three ventricles to structure the dreamers' journeys, but also engages with the three mental capacities of imagination, logic, and memory, in order to comment on authorship and literary authority. Although this link is clearly apparent in the *House of Fame*, as evinced through the poem's gradual unveiling of the complicated origins of 'tidings' or narratives, Keller argues that in the Prologue the dreamer-narrator's experience serves as a means through which Chaucer can comment specifically on his own literary works: 'Chaucer replicates the poet's journey through his own noisy mental apparatus, adopting, as it were, a slanted perspective on the judgment of his own works' (p. 3).

The *House of Fame* has been the subject of a number of studies this year, with particular attention being directed towards the presentation of the poem's narrator, Geffrey. Alastair Minnis, in his article 'Chaucer Drinks What He Brews: *The House of Fame*, 1873–82' (*N&Q* 61[2014] 187–9), considers 'Geffrey's' denial that he has come to seek renown in Fame's hall. He explains that lines 1979–80—'For what I drye, or what I thynke, / I wil myselven al hyt drynke'—should be understood as a proverbial expression, evoking the common phrase 'One must drink as one brews' (p. 188). John Burrow's 'Geoffrey's Credo: *House of Fame*, lines 1873–82' (*ChauR* 48[2014] 251–7) considers the same lines. He suggests that line 1882, 'As fer forth as I kan myn art', should be understood as a reflection of 'Geffrey's self-conception as a poet'. Burrow also considers Alexander Pope's *Temple of Fame* (a version of Book III of the *House of Fame*), and observes that Pope sought to include in his poem a concern for reputation and posterity. In light of this, Burrow concludes that reputation and fame seem to be a concern for poets only after the medieval period. An interest in the dreamer-narrator of the *House of Fame* is also shared by Eugene Green in 'Finding Pragmatic Common Ground Between Chaucer's Dreamer and Eagle in *The House of Fame*' (in Bilynsky, ed., pp. 165–83). Green approaches the exchange between the dreamer and the eagle in Book II. He focuses on Chaucer's deployment of pragmatic devices and argues that these linguistic features add veracity to the exchange and shape its development.

In 'Literary Value and the Customs House: The Axiological Logic of the *House of Fame*' (*ChauR* 48[2014] 374–94), Robert J. Meyer-Lee places Chaucer's writing of the *House of Fame* in its socio-economic context, considering how Chaucer's position as Controller of the Customs may have informed the poem's exploration of literary value. He argues that Chaucer's appointment as Controller of the Customs in 1374 may have prompted him to reflect on his standing as a court poet and to rethink the direction of his literary endeavours. He argues that the poem's 'tidings/fame complex' (p. 390), that is, the transmission and treatment of sound from the House of Rumour to the House of Fame, can be understood in direct relation to Chaucer's work in the Customs House. These parallels 'create a socioeconomic framework for what are very much literary concerns' (p. 393).

Finally, in 'Among the Schoolchildren: Joyce's "Night Lesson" and Chaucer's *Treatise on the Astrolabe*' (in Saussy and Gillespie, eds., *Intersections, Interferences, Interdisciplines: Literature with Other Arts*, pp. 35–46), Lucia Boldrini argues that thematic and structural echoes can be found between Chaucer's *Treatise of the Astrolabe* and the 'Night Lesson' chapter in Book II of James Joyce's *Finnegans Wake*. By acknowledging that these works use a shared range of motifs and images, most notably geometrical metaphors to explain language and its circulation, Boldrini argues that Joyce's chapter may have been directly informed by Chaucer's work.

5. Reception and Reputation

Scholarship has continued to show a marked interest in the transformations Chaucer has undergone through various engagements with his work. Beginning with the first generation of his readers, Kathleen L. Scott examines his middle-class audience in 'Past Ownership: Evidence of Book Ownership by English Merchants in the Later Middle Ages' (in Meale and Pearsall, eds., *Makers and Users of Medieval Books: Essays in Honour of A.S.G. Edwards*, pp. 150–77). Scott offers extensive evidence of Chaucer's circulation in the urban, professional locale of the fifteenth century, drawing records from wills, booklists, and manuscript annotations. Chaucer proves to be firmly embedded in the tastes of this particular social stratum: of the manuscripts surveyed, six contain the *Canterbury Tales*, either in its entirety or in extracted form, while four others contain other works by Chaucer; readers of Chaucer include the draper Walter Smyth, the mercer William Fettypace, and the merchant Thomas Heed. As Scott remarks, such popularity shows 'a turn to the indigenous literary culture virtually the moment it developed in an accessible form' (p. 151). Chaucer's links to material culture are also considered in Daniel W. Mosser and Linne R. Mooney's 'More Manuscripts by the *Beryn* Scribe and His Cohort' (*ChauR* 49[2014] 39–76). The article fleshes out the career of a shadowy figure responsible for preserving one of the most idiosyncratic continuations of the *Canterbury Tales*, the *Tale of Beryn*, contained in MS Northumberland MS 455. The *Beryn* copyist is already known to be responsible for several manuscripts of the prose *Brut*, along with copies of the *Prick of Conscience* and *Parliament of Fowls*; here Mosser and

Mooney confirm Simon Horobin's suggestion that he might also have been responsible for the paper sections of the *Canterbury Tales* in MS Princeton University Library MS 100. Going further still, his hand, and the hands of scribes with whom he collaborated, are also seen in Philadelphia, Rosenbach MS 1084/2 and Manchester, Rylands MS English 63, a prose *Brut* in Bodleian Library MS Rawlinson C.901, and Lydgate's *Life of Our Lady* and Hoccleve's *Regiment of Princes* in Cambridge University Library, MS Kk.1.3.

Chaucer's fifteenth-century readers also receive attention in Emma Lipton's 'Law, Chaucer, and Representation in Lydgate's *Disguising at Hertford*' (*JEGP* 113[2014] 342–64). Lipton regards the text as less assertive in its treatment of royal authority than has usually been assumed, locating within it an ambivalent and fractious presentation of monarchical power. At the core of this view is Lydgate's reading of the Wife of Bath, who is evoked as a legal precedent by the rebellious wives of Hertford. Alisoun's simultaneous erosion and appropriation of sovereignty thus comes to inform the text, as Lydgate's wives are shown to locate legal authority in language itself rather than in the speaker from which it originates, shunting the foundation of justice away from the person of the king. Similar concerns are brought into play in Emily Wingfield's 'Chaucer's *Troilus and Criseyde* and Robert Henryson's *Testament of Cresseid*' (in Wingfield, *The Trojan Legend in Medieval Scottish Literature*, pp. 121–49). Although there is little material evidence for Chaucer's Scottish readership, Wingfield notes that his influence is attested by virtually every major poet of the fifteenth and sixteenth centuries, from James I through to Dunbar, Blind Hary, and Lyndsay. She examines two records of this impact: Oxford, Bodleian Library MS Arch. Selden. B.24, a Chaucer manuscript compiled for the Scottish Sinclair family in the last decades of the fifteenth century, and Henryson's *Testament of Cresseid*.

Another fifteenth-century reader representing a different set of sensibilities is considered by Darryl Ellison in ' "Take it as a tale": Reading the *Plowman's Tale* As If It Were' (*ChauR* 49[2014] 77–101). Ellison focuses on the Wycliffite *Plowman's Tale*, accepted as Chaucer's work until Thomas Tyrwhitt's 1775 edition of the *Works*. He reads the tale in terms of the cultural logic that allowed it to be included among Chaucer's authentic works, finding that its attribution to Chaucer was motivated by literary authority as much religious polemic.

One of the most significant contributions to understanding the late medieval and early modern Chaucer is Helen Barr's *Transporting Chaucer*. Barr examines the ways in which Chaucer and his characters have been reprised in later texts. The first chapter, 'The Figure in the Canterbury Stained Glass' (pp. 25–52), considers the continuation of the pilgrimage narrative known variously as the *Beryn Prologue* or *Canterbury Interlude*. The same text is also considered in the following chapter, 'Crossing Borders' (pp. 53–81), along with the supplementary Canterbury tale, *Beryn*, it introduces. 'Chaucer's Hands' (pp. 82–139) is a discussion of the meaning of the hand in medieval culture, focusing on Chaucer's memorialization in manuscript images, which often show him gesturing at his text from its margins. ' "Wrinkled Deep in Time" ' (pp. 140–65) looks to an apparent contradiction in Shakespeare's treatment of Theseus, suggesting that the characters of the *Knight's Tale* and *Two Noble*

Kinsmen are not merely elided from *A Midsummer Night's Dream* but retain a ghost-presence throughout it. 'Bones and Bays' (pp. 166–97) discusses Dryden's *Palamon and Arcite* in the light of William Davenant's earlier modernization of *Two Noble Kinsmen*. 'Reverberate Troy' (pp. 198–245) looks to the interplay between silence, sound, and cacophony in the treatment of Trojan history, dwelling especially on the *House of Fame* and *Troilus and Cressida*.

   William T. Rossiter returns us to the early sixteenth century with the chapter '"In Kent and Christendome": Wyatt In England' (in Rossiter, *Wyatt Abroad: Tudor Diplomacy and the Translation of Power*, pp. 198–224). Rossiter considers Wyatt's simultaneous alertness to tradition and desire for 'new fangilness'. Both of these impulses are conditioned by his knowledge of Chaucer, albeit the Henrician Chaucer of Pynson and Thynne, who provided him with a model for processing Petrarchan material. As a result, Wyatt is shown to be constructing continuities with the English past, rather than initiating a radically new phase in poetry. Renaissance uses of Chaucer also feature in Daniel J. Ransom's 'Chaucerian Echoes in the *Debate betweene Pride and Lowlines*' (*ChauR* 48[2014] 322–33). This paper considers the *Debate betweene Pride and Lowlines*, printed by John Charlwood around 1577, and attributed only to 'F.T.' Although comparatively neglected by contemporary scholarship, the piece was sufficiently popular in the sixteenth century to receive a prose reworking by Robert Greene in 1592. Ransom extracts a range of allusions to Chaucer from the text, as it draws from the *Wife of Bath's Prologue*, the Summoner's portrait in the *General Prologue*, the *Merchants' Tale*, and the *Book of the Duchess*. In the same period, Holly Crocker offers a reading of 'John Foxe's Chaucer: Affecting Form in Post-Historicist Criticism' (*NML* 15[2014] 149–82). She notes that Chaucer is an oddly unfixed, even transcendent, figure in Foxe's *Actes and Monuments*. He is not embedded in the political or religious events of his lifetime to the same extent as Foxe's other witnesses to 'Christes vniversall Church', but instead seems to resonate with other figures beyond his own period, such as Colet and Tyndale.

   Louise D'Arcens takes Chaucer into the Enlightenment in 'Scraping the Rust from the Joking Bard: Chaucer in the Age of Wit' (in D'Arcens, *Comic Medievalism*, pp. 43–67). As D'Arcens writes, this was a particularly important period in consolidating and classifying Chaucer's reputation, producing 'an avalanche of engagement with Chaucer's legacy' which was driven by the need to 'identify a continuous presence of wit in English culture' (p. 45). Thus, in the work of Addison, Hayley, Gay, Pope, and others, Chaucer is seen as a comic author above all, to the extent that these features threaten to obscure other qualities in his work; the vocabulary used to discuss him leans in a decisively comic direction, with the governing terms being such adjectives as 'witty, sprightly, lively, merry, jolly, gleeful, mirthful' and 'genial' (p. 51). Yet at the same time Chaucer is also seen as 'rust'd', requiring 'polish' to be made comprehensible as comedy: in other words, he is seen as both a precursor to modern sophistication and a figure made distant by his primitiveness. Other contradictions also combine in readings of his work, as he is seen as both essentially English and beyond any one culture, while his humour is judged to be simultaneously urbane and crude. As D'Arcens observes, this ambivalence is founded on wider attitudes towards the medieval period itself, its status as an 'other' which was nonetheless integral to modernity's sense of its own identity.

Other work has also analysed the eighteenth-century Chaucer. Thus Simon Horobin examines the career of the Norfolk antiquarian Beaupré Bell (1704–41) in 'Beaupré Bell and the Editing of Chaucer in the Eighteenth Century' (in Meale and Pearsall, eds., pp. 214–23). Bell is known to have written the scattered annotations in two manuscripts of Chaucer now held at Trinity College. Although at first glance Bell's notes might indicate only limited interest in Chaucer, other sources show a much fuller engagement. Horobin identifies his handwriting in a copy of Speght's 1598 Chaucer now held at the Bodleian and a copy of Urry's 1721 *Works* now held at Trinity library. Both of these volumes show Bell paying careful attention to Chaucer, comparing the texts for spelling variants and omitted passages, and showing particular interest in the *Canterbury Tales* and *House of Fame*. Such efforts seem to be part of a wider dissatisfaction among eighteenth-century readers with the texts inherited from the early modern printers, as parallel activities can be attributed to Bell's contemporary, Samuel Pegge. Moving in a similar direction is Barry Sales's 'The Landlord's Tale: An Introduction and Contextualization' (*ECS* 47[2014] 313–20), which looks at an anonymous Ariosto translation dating from 1708. This text shows continued interest in Chaucer in the eighteenth century, as its framework evokes Dryden's imitations of Chaucer from the *Fables*, showing how these two authors continued to mediate Augustan contact with the Middle Ages.

Moving forward in time, A.S.G. Edwards assesses Chaucer's legacy in cold monetary rather than aesthetic terms. In 'What's It Worth? Selling Chaucer's *Canterbury Tales* in the Twentieth Century' (*ChauR* 48[2014] 239–50), Edwards studies the sale of Chaucer manuscripts at auction throughout the twentieth century. Fifteen manuscripts are considered, both complete and fragmentary, sold between 1906 and 1983. Surprisingly, Edwards finds little sense that Chaucer was particularly prized by buyers or sellers. For example, what are now MSS Egerton 2863 and Egerton 2864 fetched less than £200 apiece when auctioned at Sotherby's in 1906; for comparison, a twelfth-century New Testament in the same sale raised nearly three times as much. Other auctions tell a similar story, with the Delamare Chaucer possibly failing to reach its reserve in 1928, and a house in 1975 deliberately exaggerating earlier valuations of another manuscript. Precisely why Chaucer has under-performed at market remains unclear, especially since a copy of Caxton's *Canterbury Tales* sold at Christie's in 1998 for over £5 million, the highest price ever paid for a printed volume. Staying with the twentieth century, Colin Wilcockson looks to visual interpretations of Chaucer in 'Illustrating Chaucer's Canterbury Tales: Eric Gill's Woodcuts for the Golden Cockerel Press' (*Anglistik* 25[2014] 29–43). Building on the work of Holliday and Faulkner, the focus of analysis here is the work of graphic designer Eric Gill, whose selections of images to accompany the 1929–31 *Tales* shows a sensitive and complex engagement with the text.

Chaucer in the twenty-first century receives attention in three essays. Alison Gulley's ' "We wol sleen this false traytor deeth": The Search for Immortality in Chaucer's *Pardoner's Tale* and J.K. Rowling's *The Deathly Hallows*' (in Fugelso, ed., *Ethics and Medievalism*, pp. 189–204) takes as its focus Rowling's story of the 'The Three Brothers', which describes the creation of the three titular artefacts of *Harry Potter and the Deathly Hallows*. Gulley finds that the roots of the story lie in the similar search for Death at the centre of the *Pardoner's Tale*. What binds Rowling and Chaucer together is their mutual interest in the journey as an existential motif, and their emphasis on the inability of human beings to defy death. A more direct kind of adaptation is surveyed in Katrin Rupp, 'Getting Modern on Alisoun's Ass: The BBC and Chaucer's *Miller's Tale*' (*Neophil* 98[2014] 343–52). She offers a reading of the BBC's most recent version of the *Miller's Tale*, that directed by John McKay in 2003 as part of a Bafta-winning series of six of Chaucer's tales. Particular focus falls on the film's negotiation of obscenity, and its attitude towards the exposure of body parts. Although medieval culture did regard the 'privee partes' as disreputable, as sources ranging from Augustine to Bartholomaeus to Chaucer's own Parson can attest, it is the modern adaptation that proves most squeamish about such issues, insulating its audience from the actors' bodies by the judicious use of camera-shots, shadows, and body-stockings. Pop culture also informs Tison Pugh's 'Teaching Chaucer through Convergence Culture: The New Middle Ages as Cross-Cultural Encounter' (in Attar and Shutters, eds., *Teaching Medieval and Early Modern Cross-Cultural Encounters*, pp. 215–28). Pugh asks us to think about the ways in which our own practices as teachers of Chaucer might benefit by looking to contemporary adaptation. He recounts some of his own pedagogical techniques, which employ such material as a means of addressing the complexities of Chaucer's work. In particular, he invites students to consider Chaucer's resistance to such conversion, by viewing either Myerson's ten-minute redaction of the *Knight's Tale* or Pasolini's salacious Wife of Bath. Bryant's *Geoffrey Chaucer Hath a Blog* also features in his teaching, as its self-conscious parody lays bare the processes by which occupants of one set of cultural norms can attempt to make sense of artefacts originating from beyond the limits of their world.

Books Reviewed

Archer, Jayne Elizabeth, Richard Marggraf Turley, and Howard Thomas. *Food and the Literary Imagination*. PalMac. [2014] pp. 248. £55 ISBN 9 7811 3740 6361.

Attar, Karina F., and Lynn Shutters, eds. *Teaching Medieval and Early Modern Cross-Cultural Encounters*. PalMac. [2014] pp. 255. £55 ISBN 9 7811 3748 1337.

Barr, Helen. *Transporting Chaucer*. ManUP. [2014] pp. ix + 276. £70 ISBN 9 7807 1909 1490.

Bilynsky, Michael, ed. *Studies in Middle English: Words, Forms, Senses and Texts*. Lang. [2014] pp. 367. £49 ISBN 9 7836 3164 4942.

Boyd, Beverly. *Chaucer and the Taverners of Ipswich: The Influence of His Paternal Ancestors upon Some Portraits in the General Prologue and upon His Descendants*. Mellen. [2014] pp. 214. £108 ISBN 9 7807 7340 0634.

Carruthers, Leo. *Reading the Middle English Breton Lays and Chaucer's Franklin's Tale*. Atlande. [2013] pp. 189. €19 ISBN 9 7823 5030 2416.

Collette, Carolyn P. *Rethinking Chaucer's Legend of Good Women*. YUP. [2014] pp. xi + 168. £50 ISBN 9 7819 0315 3499.

D'Arcens, Louise. *Comic Medievalism: Laughing at the Middle Ages*. Brewer. [2014] pp. 219. £55 ISBN 9 7818 4384 3801.

Denery, II, Dallas G., Kantik Ghosh, and Nicolette Zeeman, eds. *Uncertain Knowledge: Scepticism, Relativism and Doubt in the Middle Ages*. Brepols. [2014] pp. viii + 195. £90 ISBN 9 7825 0354 7763.

Fender Chippenham, Stephen. *The Connell Guide to Chaucer's The Canterbury Tales*. Connell Guides. [2014] pp. 144. £8.99 ISBN 9 7819 0777 6250.

Fugelso, Karl, ed. *Ethics and Medievalism*. Studies in Medievalism XXIII. Boydell. [2014] pp. 264. £50 ISBN 9 7818 4384 3764.

Hodges, Laura F. *Chaucer and Array: Patterns of Costume and Fabric Rhetoric in the Canterbury Tales, Troilus and Criseyde and Other Works*. Brewer. [2014] pp. xi + 232. £60 ISBN 9 7818 4384 3689.

Honegger, Thomas, and Dirk Vanderbeke, eds. *From Peterborough to Faëry: The Poetics and Mechanics of Secondary Worlds. Essays in Honour of Dr Allen G. Turner's 65th Birthday*. Walking Tree Publications. [2014] pp. 159. £12. ISBN 9 7839 0570 3313.

Hopkins, Amanda, Robert Allen Rouse, and Cory James Rushton, eds. *Sexual Culture in the Literature of Medieval Britain*. B&B. [2014] pp. 192. £50. ISBN 9 7818 4384 3795.

Jacobs, Nicholas, and Gerald Morgan, eds. *'Truthe is the Beste': A Festschrift in Honour of A.V.C. Schmidt*. Lang. [2014] pp. xii+ 217. £40 ISBN 9 7830 3431 7283.

Mann, Jill, *Life in Words: Essays on Chaucer, the Gawain-Poet and Malory*. UTorP. [2014] pp. xxxix + 359. £50 ISBN 9 7814 4264 8654.

Meale, Carol M., and Derek Pearsall, eds. *Makers and Users of Medieval Books: Essays in Honour of A.S.G. Edwards*. Brewer. [2014]. pp. xvi + 258. £60 ISBN 9 7818 4384 3757.

Miller, John F., and Carole E. Newlands, eds. *A Handbook to the Reception of Ovid*. Wiley Blackwell. [2014] pp. 520. £120 ISBN 9 7814 4433 9673.

Minnis, A.J. *The Cambridge Introduction to Chaucer*. CUP. [2014] pp. ix + 167. £12.99 ISBN 9 7811 0769 9908.

Murrin, Michael. *Trade and Romance*. UChicP. [2013] pp. 344. $45 ISBN 9 7802 2607 1572.

Olson, S. Douglas, and Jeffrey Henderson. *Ancient Comedy and Reception*. Gruyter. [2013] pp. xi + 1,086. £168.49 ISBN 9 7816 1451 1663.

Pugh, Tison, *Chaucer's (Anti-)Eroticisms and the Queer Middle Ages*. OSUP. [2014] pp. ix + 242. $64.95 ISBN 9 7808 1421 2646.

Rayborn, Tim. *Against the Friars: Antifraternalism in Medieval France and England*. McFarland. [2014] pp. 256. $39.95 ISBN 9 7807 8646 8317.

Rigby, Stephen H., with the assistance of Alastair J. Minnis. *Historians on Chaucer: The General Prologue to the Canterbury Tales.* OUP. [2014] pp. xx + 503. £65 ISBN 9 7801 9968 9545.

Rosenberg, Simon, and Sandra Simon, eds. *Material Moments in Book Cultures: Essays in Honour of Gabriele Müller-Oberhäuser.* Lang. [2014] pp. xxiv + 286. £45 ISBN 9 7836 3164 7943.

Rossiter, William T. *Wyatt Abroad: Tudor Diplomacy and the Translation of Power.* Brewer. [2014] pp. 258. £60 ISBN 9 7818 4384 3887.

Saussy, Haun, and Gerald Gillespie. *Intersections, Interferences, Interdisciplines: Literature with Other Arts.* Lang. [2014]. pp. 263. £36 ISBN 9 7828 7574 1561.

Schieberle, Misty. *Feminized Counsel and the Literature of Advice in England, 1380–1500.* Brepols. [2014] pp. x + 224. €75 ISBN 9 7825 0355 0121.

Strohm, Paul. *The Poet's Tale. Chaucer and the Year That Made the Canterbury Tales.* Profile. [2014] pp. xiii + 284. £15.99 ISBN 9 7817 8125 0594.

Travis, Peter W., and Frank Grady, eds. *Approaches to Teaching Chaucer's Canterbury Tales.* MLA. [2014] pp. xii + 243. $40 £25.95 ISBN 9 7816 0329 1408.

Wingfield, Emily. *The Trojan Legend in Medieval Scottish Literature.* Brewer. [2014] pp. x + 246. £50 ISBN 9 7818 4384 3641.

V

The Early Sixteenth Century

GAVIN SCHWARTZ-LEEPER AND EDWARD SMITH

This chapter has six sections: 1. General: Prose and Drama; 2. General: Verse; 3. More; 4. Skelton; 5. Surrey; 6. Wyatt. Sections 1 and 2 are by Gavin Schwartz-Leeper and Edward Smith; section 3 is by Gavin Schwartz-Leeper; sections 4, 5 and 6 are by Edward Smith.

1. General: Prose and Drama

There has been a varied crop of studies on early sixteenth-century literature in 2014, with several refreshing publications in the field of prose. Some of these have devoted attention to under-researched writers; others have traversed the traditional medieval–early modern border in topics or areas where such an act of bridging is opportune. Vincent Gillespie and Susan Powell's co-edited collection *A Companion to the Early Printed Book in Britain: 1476–1558* is a paradigm of the second type. Monographs and chapters on Tudor manuscripts have been in the ascendant in recent years; without being strategic perforce, the *Companion* is a high-standard counterweight which gives to the market-place a handsome publication on the history of the printed book and materiality of the text. The collection benefits from the breadth of its time-span, covering the period from the auspicious advent of William Caxton's printing press in England to the dawn of Queen Elizabeth I's reign; and its scope, with chapters sitting in four thematic sections which are organized in judicious fashion. The roll call of contributors is also illustrious, and bears the fruit of an international conference in 2009 which gave rise to the collection. Given its nature as a 'companion', the volume is oriented in no small part to an undergraduate audience fresh to the subject. It therefore follows that the chapters in each section act more as 'overviews' of their chosen subject rather than thesis-statement-driven pieces (with Section IV as a slight exception to this rule). This aim is delivered with aplomb, and justifies the substantial space given below to the collection.

The introduction (pp. 1–9) summarizes the principal areas broached in the book: the nationalistic drivers of print; the significance of learning and the rise of humanism/the New Learning to the book trade; the central role of

The Year's Work in English Studies, Volume 95 (2016) © The Author 2016. Published by Oxford University Press on behalf of the English Association. All rights reserved.
For Permissions, please email: journals.permissions@oup.com
doi:10.1093/ywes/maw004

merchants (who included Caxton among their number) in greasing the wheels of trade; the significance of ecclesiastical markets; and the presence of women as important agents in the economies of print (through their prominent presence in devotional culture in especial). Where the book proper is concerned, Section I, 'The Printed Book Trade', comprises three chapters: Julia Boffey's 'From Manuscript to Print: Continuity to Change' (pp. 13–26); Tamara Atkin and A.S.G. Edwards's co-penned 'Printers, Publishers and Promoters to 1558' (pp. 27–44); and Alan Coates's piece, 'The Latin Book Trade in England and Abroad' (pp. 45–58). Boffey's chapter examines the myriad points of 'contact' (p. 14) between print and manuscript around the start of the sixteenth century, unpacking the nature of their dual existence. Printers and the workmen under them depended on manuscript exemplars as 'setting copies' for their printed copies (evidenced through the survival of such 'marked up' (p. 15) manuscripts). Printing houses were also known to trade in manuscripts and commissioned manual embroidering to their printed material in the form of rubrication, decoration, and binding. Training her gaze on book purchasers, Boffey adduces the affluent merchant Roger Thorney as evidence of the kind of reader who had ready access to both manuscript and printed material, and owned 'hybrid books' (p. 24) assembled together from both media. She ends with a brief consideration of the areas in which manuscript (e.g. diplomatic correspondence) and print (e.g. law books) developed their own spheres or preserves where overlap was minimal. Atkin and Edwards's chapter-length conspectus of printers over the period is broken down into three useful sub-sections. The first, 1476–91, concentrates on Caxton's nascent efforts and the rudeness of English printing paraphernalia in comparison to the Continent at this period, although the focus on printed vernacular material is diagnostic of English practice from the outset. The second sub-section, 1491–1534, gives the limelight to the two major printers who were operational during these years: the King's Printer Richard Pynson and Caxton's successor, Wynkyn de Worde. The discussion here concentrates on their different areas of specialism, as well as those of a cast of smaller-scale printers (such as father–son speculations like that of John and William Rastell). Some attention is also given to the development, and poor faring of, printing centres which developed in the provinces (such as Oxford and York), as well as Scotland, Wales, and Ireland. The final-subsection, 1534–58, examines the consecutive Royal Printers Thomas Berthelet and Richard Grafton, together with others set up around them, highlighting how events after the mid-1530s shaped printers' activities according to the politico-religious currents and controversies of the Reformation. Atkin and Edwards draw the conclusion that print's survival over its first half-century derives from its 'adaptation to swiftly changing political and economic circumstances' (p. 43).

In his welcome third chapter of Section I, Coates delves into the little-studied area of book imports in England, probing 'the kind of books which were being brought in, who was bringing them in, and who was buying or being given them' (p. 45). He covers the 'what' and 'who' in adroit fashion, concentrating on the main importing regions at different times (German-speaking countries, Italy, France), and the companies (such as the Mercers' Company) and institutions (such as Syon Abbey) who were the most promiscuous importers of (largely) Latin material. In one compelling example, Coates sheds light on a book inventory in 1483 which passed through the hands of the Continental printer Johannes de Westfalia, the London-based bookseller Peter Actors, and the Oxford Stationer Thomas Hunt. Coates also addresses the changing profile of printing in the 1520s and 1530s, as successive regulations culminating in the 'Acte for prynters and bynders of bokes' (1534) proscribed the activities of alien printers and gave precedence to native craftsmen. Such a manoeuvre helped to arrest the production of vernacular material on the Continent and ensured that English printers arrogated dominion over this ever more lucrative (if competitive and risk-laden) enterprise.

Moving on from the 'trade' focus of the first section, the subject of Section II is the more mechanical (and too often sidelined) part of the equation: 'The Printed Book as Artefact'. Like the first, it consists of three chapters: Pamela Robinson's 'Paper: Materials and Type' (pp. 61–74), Alexandra Gillespie's 'Bookbinding and Early Printing in England' (pp. 75–94), and Martha W. Driver's 'Woodcuts and Decorative Techniques' (pp. 95–123). Robinson's chapter, punctuated with three instructive illustrations (from Caxton, de Worde, and Pynson editions in turn), offers a salutary reminder about the importance of paper and type to a full consideration of the cultural resonance of printed texts. In the first place, both features can serve as a diagnostic tool. Robinson notes, for instance, that the place of a watermark on printed paper indicates the number of times the paper was folded, and that, in the case of dated works, evidence intimates that the paper stock would have been produced 'three or four years' (p. 63) before being utilized in a printing house. Where type is concerned, the absence of standard sizes can also be exploited: 'determining the body-size of a type can help to distinguish between different specimens' (p. 64). The type used can also point to the cultural 'tone' of a work, as de Worde's more rustic Dutch type for his print of Dame Juliana Berners's *Book of Hawking, Hunting, and Blasing of Arms* testifies. Robinson proceeds to discuss the different types which England's three major printers (Caxton, de Worde, and Pynson) used, observing that the first acquired his from the Low Countries, whereas the two later printers had recourse to types produced in France. The distinct English predilection for bastarda and textura (black-letter) type compared with the modish Roman version popular on the Continent distinguishes England as an 'old-fashioned' typographical practitioner in the first half-century of the moveable type's arrival on these shores.

In a similar vein to Robinson's chapter, Gillespie begins her own illustration-supported piece with an assertion of the significance of binding to a proper appraisal of the printed text: 'To a greater extent than has been previously suggested, the story of the early printed English book is the story about [its] bindings' (p. 75). The narrative Gillespie traces is a technical but fascinating one which unravels the reasons behind the prevalence of 'blind-stamped' binding in English printed texts (that is, binding where no gold is pressed into the metal-stamped patterns). This narrative is a tripartite one. First, looking at the different practices of high-profile printers like Caxton, de Worde, Pynson, and Berthelet in comparison to earlier medieval counterparts, Gillespie concludes that the configuration of the English book trade before and after the advent of printing placed binders (most of whom were of Continental extraction) at an important stage in the chain of production. The second sub-section examines the exponential increase in blind-stamping which accompanied the establishment of the printing press. This marked trend Gillespie attributes in part to the 'international trade in goods and materials' (p. 86), where English craftsmen followed the lead of common Continental exemplars of the style to appeal to a pan-European audience. The stamp could also be exploited as a 'commercial mark' (p. 88), like a printer's device, and aided with business efficiencies as a method of binding on a mass-production scale. Gillespie's third and final part uses blind-stamping as a launchpad to examine the adaptation of other medieval binding technologies (such as 'stab stitching' and the production of hybrid/composite volumes or *Sammelbände*) in the brave new world of print.

Driver's chapter begins with a persuasive appeal to consider woodcuts and other techniques of textual decoration as powerful agents in the 'expanded visual vocabulary' of printed texts with a 'mass-market audience' (p. 95). This contention is supported through the generous provision of images, and a strong focus on three intertwined areas. The first concentrates on the changes which obtained between manuscript and print image. Driver notes that, *contra* manuscript miniatures, printed woodcuts tend to be black and white and therefore secure a 'visual continuity' (p. 97) which yokes image and text. Painting appears to have been an exceptional practice undertaken, for instance, at the behest of a patron. Driver's second section focuses on (French) sources, providing an account of how single woodcuts (factotums) were recycled/recontextualized between texts to instigate a visual dialogue, or connecting of visual syntax, between the source and borrowing text. She uses the instructive case of de Worde's *Nychodemus Gospell* [1511] here, which lifts woodcuts in free-handed fashion from the French publisher Antoine Verard's edition of Terence. The same woodcut in both represents an old man, serving a dramatic purpose as a tableau to complement the main text. Driver also discusses the visual functions fulfilled through banderoles (printed scrolls used for character names and speech), fleurons (floral ornaments), and title pages. The final part of the chapter returns us to Gillespie's terrain of composite volumes. Driver cites Pynson's 1526 edition of Chaucer (among other examples) to demonstrate how woodcuts and other techniques were harnessed to cleave the discrete parts of this *Sammelband* in both senses of the word: to 'indicate conscious linking of the texts' and to serve as a visual marker 'to separate them' (p. 120). The woodcuts thus placed thread the composites into one integral whole and also enable them to be treated—and sold—as separates. This keen insight caps a strong elucidation of the visual language of printed books in the period.

Section III of the *Companion*, 'Patrons, Purchases and Products', considers the dissemination of early printed books. The chapters cover different institutional stakeholders in the chain of book production, and include Anne F. Sutton's 'Merchants' (pp. 127–33), Mary C. Erler's 'The Laity' (pp. 134–49), Susan Powell's 'The Secular Clergy' (pp. 150–275), James G. Clark's 'The Regular Clergy' (pp. 176–206), and James Willoughby's 'Universities, Colleges and Chantries' (pp. 207–24). Sutton's consideration of the mercantile aspects of early and mid-Tudor printing reminds us that this was an industry that transcended cultural, ecumenical, and state borders, especially in its early decades. Sutton also details some aspects of book ownership among English merchants, focusing on Reformist merchant networks. This religious focus dovetails neatly with Erler's essay on the laity's appetite for print. The earliest religious printed texts follow the same patterns as those on the Continent, mainly comprising primers and prayer books, along with more ephemeral texts (including indulgences, almanacs, and proclamations). Erler describes sponsorship, production, and purchases of indulgences up to 1530, before moving on to detail the growth of the production and sale of almanacs and other astrological texts. Erler then discusses book ownership amongst the circle of Margaret Beaufort, which allows for the consideration of non-religious textual production, reception, and dissemination. Erler concludes that comparing Beaufort's circle against lists made by figures like her clerk of the works James Morice and the later Sir William More reveals that the print industry enabled 'substantial private libraries at a level below the aristocratic' (p. 148).

One of the major markets for early printed books was the secular clergy. Susan Powell's chapter begins by examining the market for incunables produced prior to Caxton. These books were often collected by senior ecclesiastics like Thomas Rotherham and Richard Fox, and made their way to the great college libraries at Oxford and Cambridge. Powell shows that, despite this interest in sponsorship and acquisition, authorship by secular clergy was rare (with a few exceptions): 'Priests and the higher clergy did not normally rush into print before the Lutheran threat' (p. 159). The need to disseminate sermons and confutations of Reformist texts created a surge in printed material authored and sponsored by senior clergy, ranging from major treatises to sermons. As the Reformation gathered pace and Reformist clergy began to replace conservative ecclesiastics, the production of vernacular bibles became a central issue; Powell discusses aspects of production through tensions between senior and junior clergy, with a summative section on the role of Thomas Cranmer. Powell concludes with a brief overview of the print industry amid the Marian return to orthodoxy.

Powell's chapter is contrasted by Clark's, which examines the relationship between monastic clergy and the printed text. Clark argues for an initial enthusiastic adoption of the printed book prompting a 'final flowering' of 'academic capacity' in English monasteries, ending around 1500. Despite this, Clark argues that we still know very little about the acquisition and use of print texts in monasteries, a gap due largely to the poor survival rate of monastic texts following the dissolution. Clark tackles this by providing overviews of a number of monastic collections, usually acquired when senior monastics were completing training at university. Clark also marks a disparity between the size of collections held by male monastics as compared with mendicant and female religious communities. This chapter also covers aspects of monastic authorship and printing, concluding that 'it was not print itself that projected the last generation of regulars into public discourse; rather it was a convenient and current medium for an authorial agency already reawakened by the stimulus of reform from within the orders and the rising threat of Reformation from without' (p. 205).

Willoughby's final chapter in Section III looks at the centres of education: universities, colleges, and chantries. He first examines practices of acquisition by the great university libraries at Oxford and Cambridge, but quickly moves on to collegiate institutions beyond the universities, along with collections in hospitals and parish churches. This all-too-brief chapter is of real utility, as it provides a timely reminder that printed books were not confined to London, Oxford, or Cambridge (even if these sites often allowed texts to survive at a higher rate).

Section IV brings together chapters under the umbrella theme 'The Cultural Capital of Print'. It begins with Daniel Wakelin's contribution, 'Humanism and Printing' (pp. 227–47), an excellent and timely consideration of the 'hybrid nationalities of imported books' (p. 228) in the context of the overlapping humanist and print networks. Wakelin examines the mechanisms by which humanist books were imported into England as well as seeking to redefine our understanding of what an 'import' looked like. He cites numerous instances of authors and translators (English and otherwise) producing text—in English, Greek, and Latin—for the English market on Venetian, German, Dutch and French presses: can these texts be said to be 'imports' in the simple sense of commodities produced outside a market? Was Thomas More's *Utopia* an import, as it was partly composed abroad, printed in Louvain, and not printed in England (or in English) for decades after its author's death? Wakelin provides a detailed picture of how these questions demonstrate the complexity of the early modern English import market; he then goes on to discuss their impact on the development of the humanist and vernacular printing trade in England itself, with a focus on educational texts.

Wakelin's discussion of 'translating' printing leads into Brenda M. Hosington's essay on 'Women Translators and the Early Printed Book' (pp. 248–71). Building on the excellent 'Renaissance Cultural Crossroads' project (available at www.hrionline.ac.uk/rcc), Hosington discusses the translations of seven women (Margaret Beaufort, Margaret Roper, Katherine Parr, Mary Tudor, the future Elizabeth I, Anne Cooke, and Mary Basset) to demonstrate that early modern translations by women were not meant to act as private texts (despite contemporary claims), but instead had a substantial public impact increased by the advent of the printing press. Hosington provides a searching look at how a range of women translators interacted within wider print and intellectual networks, their textual influence, and their codicological importance across the early modern period.

No discussion of the early modern print trade can flee the spectre of the Reformation, and Andrew Hope's chapter on 'The Printed Book Trade in Response to Luther' (pp. 272–89) examines the contexts in which English liturgical books were printed abroad. The chapter focuses on Tyndale and the reactions of the Henrician lord chancellors—Wolsey, More, and Cromwell— to reformist literature. The chapter provides a succinct overview of the networks that facilitated the mobility of texts, ideas, technologies, and people, as well as the figures and pressures that resisted that mobilization.

Restricting the mobility of texts is brought more sharply into relief in Thomas Betteridge's subsequent chapter on 'Thomas More, Print, and the Idea of Censorship' (pp. 290–306). This chapter provides an assessment of the manner(s) in which censorship adapted to deal with the printed book as both a material object (which might contain objectionable ideas, and could thus be altered or destroyed) and the objectionable idea itself, which did not need to be read to be problematic. Betteridge surveys modes of censorship from Archbishop Thomas Arundel's 1409 Constitutions to the later years of Henry VIII's reign, largely focusing on the text–metatext relationship between the printed book and the ideas to be found in it. He goes on to discuss the duality of Thomas More's relationship with censorship. More's energies directed towards the maintenance of orthodoxy prior to 1532 consisted both of practical actions (as a key representative of the Henrician government) and ideological ones (as a renowned scholar and lawyer). Following his resignation of the Great Seal, More's relationship with censorship changed as he became a recipient, rather than an arbiter. Betteridge argues that More's attitude towards censorship itself did not change, however, and that More's censoring activities have been overstated amongst his wider conciliar duties. Betteridge shows More's 1529 *Dialogue Concerning Heresies* as an arena for discussing metonymic understandings and applications of censorship, authority, and the printed text—and the responsibility of the reader to understand the metonymic and metatextual aspects of the material book, and to engage with censorship appropriately as a result.

The final essay in this section (and the volume) is Lucy Wooding's 'Catholicism, the Printed Book and the Marian Restoration' (pp. 307–24). This is welcome, as it helps to resist the common notion of the printed text as a reformist technology: as Wooding states, 'the still pervasive conclusion is that the printing press was the foundation of Protestantism, because Protestantism was the religion of the book' (p. 307). The relationship between the press and the reformist shift to *sola scriptura* is hugely important, but it has eclipsed the multifaceted uses of the printed text by Catholics, in England and throughout Europe. Wooding argues persuasively for the printed book to have an 'unusually dominant position within English Catholicism' (p. 308), surveying a large number of key texts: *Assertio Septem Sacramentorum, Golden Legend, De Vera Obedientia, De Unitate, An explication and assertion of the true Catholique faith, A Werke for Housholders, Bouclier of the Catholike fayth,* and the *Acts and Monuments* (among many others). These are set amongst the prominent battles over the creation of vernacular bibles, the revision of liturgy, and the dissemination of sermons and other instructive texts.

As a final note (and one which links well with Griffiths's book below), the *Companion* is supported by a comprehensive and useful paratext. Foremost in this is a substantial index of manuscripts and another of printed books, both organized according to location of production/compilation.

The 2014 addition to the Early English Text Society, Greg Waite's edition of Alexander Barclay's *The famous chronycle of the warre which the Romayns had agaynst Iugurth, usurper of the kyngdome of Numidy* [*c*.1522] provides an exceptionally rich consideration of this important Henrician translation of Sallust's *Bellum Iurgurthinium*. The text of the *Jurgurtha* itself is a meticulous effort to reclaim aspects of Barclay's style lost (or at least muddied) in successive editions; Waite therefore has chosen the first (*c*.1522) edition on which to base this edition (though subsequent substantive variants are noted).

This is a highly functional edition, with detailed and navigable critical apparatus (including a bibliography of relevant primary and secondary texts, glossary, and detailed explanatory endnotes). Waite provides a substantial introduction to the text, broken down into seven sections: an overview of Barclay's life and career; a discussion of the textual effects of his relationship with Richard Pynson (who printed the majority of Barclay's works, including the *Jurgurtha*); a general introduction to Sallust and his works; a list of editions of Sallust (to 1521); coverage of Barclay's sources for his translation; a discussion of Barclay's translation method and style; and a discussion of Waite's editorial methodology. Waite also includes a substantial section that covers the two Pynson editions (*c*.1522 and *c*.1525 in turn) and the third edition of 1557, edited by Thomas Paynell and published by John Walley. This section primarily covers aspects of typography and language, and provides general guides to the changes seen from edition to edition. More information on print runs, critical reception, and readership would have made for a welcome addition, as would the expansion of brief comments about individual editions' intercultural interactions in a pan-European market for neo-Latin translation. Nevertheless, from a codicological standpoint this is a comprehensive introduction and provides an excellent overview of Barclay's sources, methods, and texts. This edition is a useful access point for this under-studied text, and will hopefully prompt further interest in Barclay and his works.

The 1538 publication of another significant printed book, Sir Thomas Elyot's Latin–English dictionary, marked a key moment in early modern English intellectual and linguistic history. This seminal text formed only part of Elyot's monumental contributions to early modern English literature: despite this, there has not yet been a complete edition of Elyot's collected works. This is a rather strange fact, when we consider not just the utility of Elyot's texts to modern scholarship, but also the importance that contemporaries attached to works like the *Dictionary* and *The boke named the Gouernour* [1531]. The lack of accessible editions of Elyot's works has impeded scholarship and risks engendering a lack of awareness of Elyot and his importance to the political, medical, and linguistic cultures of the period.

Gabriele Stein's rich treatment of the *Dictionary* is therefore all the more welcome, as it provides a comprehensive examination of Elyot and his lexicographical practices, the production of the *Dictionary* and its contemporary influence and long-term legacy. This study is broken down into nine sections, preceded by a brief introduction. They cover: 'Compilation, Word Selection, and Presentation'; 'Elyot and His Readers'; 'Early Records of Regional Variation'; 'Linking Lemma and Gloss'; 'Authorial Reference Points'; 'Translating and Explaining Headwords: Elyot's Predecessors'; 'Translating and Explaining Headwords: Elyot's Practice'; 'Elyot's Achievement as a Lexicographer'; and 'Elyot's Dictionary: Impact and Influence'. The size of Stein's study necessitates that this review not be exhaustive, but it is worth observing that the unusual (and unusually rewarding) key feature of this book is that it reads Elyot's *Dictionary* not just as a lexicographical work, but as a complete text; she details how it was created, how it was produced, and how it was read. This has the advantage of showing Elyot and his dictionary within wider contexts of textual production and reception.

However, there remains a distinctly Anglocentric feel to this study: in chapter 7, for example, Stein places Elyot almost exclusively within an English lexicographical context: not a European one. This is a missed opportunity to show Elyot as an internationally known humanist, which he was. As a seasoned diplomat and man of letters, Elyot certainly was not influenced solely by English lexicographical forebears: indeed, much of his *Dictionary* is built on Ambrogio Calepino's *Dictionarium* (which first appeared in 1502, and subsequently in numerous editions). It is not the case that Stein was unaware of Elyot's use of Calepino, but often this use is minimized or cast in a diffuse light as an 'influence'. Greater emphasis on Elyot as translator—not just of Latin, but of the entire project—would have helped reposition him within broader transnational networks of lexicographical and text-production practices.

Despite this missed opportunity, this is a tremendously useful volume and a very welcome addition to Elyot scholarship. The book incorporates a fair amount of Stein's previous work, and while this means some of the insights are not exactly new, they are very well used in this context. As an overview of the *Dictionary* and its English contexts, this book is excellent and will be of real utility not just for lexicographical scholars, but for a wide range of scholars interested in book history, early modern literature, and historical sociolinguistics.

Greg Walker's edited collection *The Oxford Anthology of Tudor Drama* is intended to act as a primary text companion volume to *The Oxford Handbook of Tudor Drama*, edited by Thomas Betteridge and Greg Walker (OUP [2012]), which provides critical considerations of most of the playtexts in this anthology. It functions very well in that respect, but it is also of real—even primary—utility as a standalone volume. Its most initially arresting feature is that Walker has chosen to reproduce the texts with modern English spellings; he has done this to combat the perceived distinction between Shakespeare's plays (so often seen as prescient and accessible, thanks in no small part to the ubiquity of modern English editions) and those of his Tudor peers, which are usually available only in contemporary English versions and accessible primarily to scholars. This anthology, then, is not aimed at scholars of early modern drama, but at students and those potentially unfamiliar with Tudor language. Most importantly, Walker has curated this volume to be of use to actors and directors in order to encourage the performance of these plays. That is not to say that researchers familiar with these plays will not find a use for this volume—the collection is well edited and is a useful companion to the *Handbook*—but its primary use is as an introduction to a broader canon of Tudor dramatic texts.

Walker's introduction to the volume focuses on issues of modernity and innovation: narratives that have characterized assessments of early modern drama for decades. Walker provides a wealth of examples to show that 'evolutionary' tropes in scholarship conform to a teleological march to

Shakespeare, glossing over moments of innovation and beauty throughout the long Tudor century. He concludes that 'the pageant-makers and interluders of the first decades of the Tudor century clearly would have had little to learn from their better-known successors about either formal innovation or ludic audacity'. Walker is quick to point out that he is not arguing for a narrative of decline, but that an evolutionary trope should be understood in a more literal sense: dramatic texts across the century exhibit the gain, loss, and adaptation of features that responded (or failed to respond) to cultural, social, religious, economic, and political factors.

The prefatory materials on each play reflect this argument, eschewing close analysis for contextual information. Broadly speaking, the prefatory materials are broken down into two sections, 'The Playwright' and 'The Play'. Naturally, this structure is adapted for anonymous texts like the York Pageant's *The Fall of the Angels*. Walker discusses the social, religious, economic, and geopolitical contexts of the author's life and works; the genesis of the playtext; and the interactions between actors, audience, setting, and text; and provides a short bibliography to guide further reading. These sections respond to the brief overviews of 'the conditions of performance', 'stage business', 'critics of the drama', and 'religious change and dramatic history' that comprise the volume's introduction (Walker also includes a general justification of the selection of playtexts).

As this is an anthology of 'Tudor' drama, the texts presented within date from prior to 1415 through to *c*.1590. While this section of *YWES* is concerned with texts dating from the first half of the century, it is well worth exploring the entirety of the volume: as Walker argues, to pigeonhole these texts by date alone is to underestimate the complexity of their circulation and leads to the type of compartmentalization that has isolated Shakespeare so firmly from his contemporaries. Excitingly, this does not mean the anthology is heavily weighted towards texts that fall after C.S. Lewis's 'Drab Age', as can be the case with volumes purporting to 'contextualize' Shakespeare's plays: of the sixteen playtexts in the anthology, seven date from before the reign of Elizabeth I. Well-known late medieval texts like *Everyman* are represented, but so too are significantly less-known texts: *The Play of the Weather* (*c*.1533), *Gammer Gurton's Needle* (1550–60), and *Respublica* (1553–4) all appear as well. There is a wide range of genres on display, including the civic pageant (from the York Pageant plays), miracle play (*The Play of the Sacrament*), court pageant (*Respublica*), and the humanist household play (*Fulgens and Lucrece*). Readers with interests ranging beyond 1558 will find public favourites (*Titus Andronicus*, *A Comedy of Errors*, and *Tamburlaine the Great*) alongside classroom staples (*The Spanish Tragedy*) and those deserving a wider audience (*Endymion*, *Thyestes*, and others).

Most refreshingly, Walker manages to introduce these texts without placing them in a teleological framework leading self-evidently to Shakespeare. Instead, he identifies aspects of particular plays that demonstrated change and innovation, and traces how particular features evolved over time (and, yes, how some of them were taken up by Shakespeare and other Elizabethan playwrights). This approach has the effect of tying the plays in the volume to well-known anchor points familiar to most students, and thereby placing the wider corpus of plays in a broader context more complex than a simple 'Shakespeare'/'not Shakespeare' binary. This anthology should become a staple of the undergraduate experience and hopefully will encourage new stage productions of these fascinating and entertaining plays.

The critical move to bring paratextual apparatus out of the margins and to the centre of critical consideration has gathered pace in recent years. Jane Griffiths has been has been a prominent researcher in this field, and caps her work to date with her important monograph, *Divering Authorities: Experimental Glossing Practices in Manuscript and Print*. This is a critical overview of the developments glossing took over the course of the fifteenth and sixteenth centuries, seen through the lens of several representative case studies. While criticism on these purported 'supplements' to a main text are not now cutting-edge, Griffiths's choice of time span is welcome, given that it charts the coexistence of two different media (manuscript and print) and provides the scope to consider different agents (self-glossing authors, reader-emendators, editors, and printers) in the production of paratextual matter. Helpful too is her consistent recourse to reader-response ideas to address how the reader is invited, challenged, and engaged (or not) through the gloss. The 'parodic' function of glossing—its power to (un)settle 'reader expectations about how a gloss is "likely" to behave' (pp. 3–4)—is paramount in Griffiths's interests, and can be traced in her three chapters on earlier Tudor material, two of which take prose as their subject and one verse (for which, see Section 2 below).

Chapter 4, 'Glossing the Spoken Voice' (pp. 103–22), concentrates on the differences in glossing habit between Erasmus's *Moræ Encomium*, printed first in 1521 and several times thereafter, and Sir Thomas Chaloner's 1549 translation of this text, the *Praise of Folie*. These divergences are stark: whereas Erasmus's glosses, like the eponymous speaker Folly, are 'slippery' and involve 'shifting perspectives' (p. 110), Chaloner's serve a much more stabilizing function, being both 'restricted and restrictive' (p. 103) for his readership in seeking to delimit Folly's voice. Writ large, the contrast is one between the 'performative' (Erasmus) and the 'definitive' (Chaloner), and Griffiths devotes the bulk of her chapter to unpicking the niceties of it. Over successive printed editions of the *Morae Encomium*, Erasmus padded out his main text with further marginalia, introducing a parodic version of traditional academic commentary (the Listrius commentary) and an additional 'outer ring' of glosses. The overall effect is a renegotiation of text and supplement to one of 'two linked performances' (p. 111) in which Erasmus's audience are cast as discriminators in the absence of a reliable glossator. Chaloner's glosses, on the other hand, adopt a neutral tone and draw a clear distance between readers, Erasmus the author, and Folly the narrator, where the Latin original flirted with their conflation. Griffiths notes that Chaloner's glosses tend to be succinct (though he does add some additional indexing notes) and, considered apart, read as disconnected and random observations which subvert their apparent purpose of arresting interpretation of a 'potentially heterodox work' (p. 103). In one insightful passage, she demonstrates how Chaloner's treatment of Erasmus's proverbs bears similarities to his handling of glosses: both witness the cessation of *copia* and 'game' in favour of 'earnest' sententiousness.

The chapter ends on a proleptic note, outlining how the different approaches to the gloss in the two texts anticipate future developments of marginalia in the printed medium, as writers grapple with the notions of the 'printed voice' and how a printed text communicates. Griffiths does well to contextualize Chaloner's situation here as an early and somewhat awkward vernacular glossator in print. Another question it would have been useful to probe is the extent to which Chaloner's sententious glosses take their cue from the mid-century Protestant-humanist circles of which he was a part (such as the predilection for 'sayings' and maxims explored in Mary Thomas Crane's seminal *Framing Authority*).

Chapter 5, 'A Broil of Voices' (pp. 123–48), witnesses the bringing together of glossing practice and Reformist conceptions of the authorized text in the works of two Protestant writers: William Baldwin's *Beware the Cat* [1553, printed in 1570] and William Bullein's *Dialogue Against the Fever Pestilence* [1564]. Flipping the theme of the previous chapter, Griffiths argues that, instead of setting out to direct their audiences from the margin in the manner of Chaloner, both writers launch a more radical interrogation of the 'level of authority that should be accorded to the printed word' (p. 123). This aim is bound up with contemporaneous debates over the translation, glossing, and printing of the Bible: Baldwin and Bullein at once espouse the Reformed notion that meaning inheres in the text alone, but also subvert it through their 'unauthorized' and 'wayward glosses' (p. 123) which threaten to dissolve the boundaries between (fictionalized, printed) speech and writing. Where Baldwin is concerned, Griffiths characterizes the (Protestant) narrator G.B. as an inept glossator, whose confidence in written verities is undercut through the inaccurate and inappropriate apparatus he brings to the text of Streamer's words (a figure who prizes the oral and could therefore be construed as more 'Catholic'). Even if G.B.'s diverting glosses serve a satirical thrust (given that Reformers wished to purge the Bible of the *glossa ordinaria* to arrive at an unmediated text), Griffiths sees Baldwin's ultimate aim as the mobilization of discriminating and ethical readers rather than the denigration of 'Catholic' orality. Bullein's wide-ranging and polyvocal *Dialogue* also prompts his audience 'to engage with the text's indirections' (p. 135) as an ethical exercise and example of good (rather than just Reformed) citizenship. Griffiths demonstrates the propensity of the glosses to parrot the words of the heterogeneous cast of characters in the main text and therefore offer a fraught mediation of its content. Pushing further than Baldwin, however, Bullein expresses concern at the glossator's capacity to mislead and withhold (invoking the Catholic practice of biblical gloss), and seems to retreat into a more pared-down method at the conclusion of his *Dialogue* which revives trust in the written word. Griffiths's account of both writers' grappling with speech and writing, and the unstable authority of the gloss against the background of weighty biblical translation questions, is a compelling one which asserts again the paradoxical centrality of the margin in important Tudor texts.

Dante, the high table of Henrician writing, and the proto-Protestant cause seem improbable bedfellows, but form the focus of Nick Havely's chapter 'The "Goodly Maker": Conscripting Dante in Henrician England' (pp. 33–49) in his comprehensive monograph *Dante's British Public: Readers and Texts, from the Fourteenth Century to the Present.* Whereas studies treating the relations between Henrician writers and Petrarch have sometimes verged on an industrial scale, it is somewhat curious that those which obtain between Dante and earlier Tudor intellectuals have hitherto received little critical airing. Conscious of the need to plug a number of gaps, Havely adopts a tripartite structure for his chapter, with each subsection taking up a different (but interlinked) theme. The first part offers an overview of the itineraries through which Dante's texts could have come down to British readers in the period: the burgeoning book trade and fervour for importation which developed in step with the print market; the existence of competing translations of the *Commedia* in Latin and Castilian (John Leland recorded the first in his *Itinerary*, and Catherine of Aragon owned the second) and the appearance of Dantean allusions and verse snippets within manuscripts of Chaucer. Havely notes at the close of this section a literary-historical 'convergence' (p. 36) around the advent of the sixteenth century which witnessed the consolidation of an English triumvirate of poets, consisting of Chaucer, Gower, and Lydgate, to sit alongside the well-established Italian one comprising Dante, Petrarch, and Boccaccio. Skelton, for example, makes much of these triumvirates in *The Garlande of Laurel.* Whereas Gower and Lydgate in the English triumvirate were dropped as the political and religious terrain of Henrician England took shape, the Italian poets remained useful points of reference for writers. This consolidation enabled them to become 'denizened in Henrician England' in a manner that reinforced 'the humanistic bond with Italy and occludes the pre-Reformation English tradition' (p. 42).

Elaborating on Dante's status as a canonical poet for Henrician writers, the second and third parts of Havely's chapter concern the means through which his writing was conscripted into the service of different Henrician 'myths'. A chief one of these is the exploitation of Dante to trumpet Henry VIII's imperial standing and re-creation as a new Augustus via the pens of Richard Morison in *The Remedy of Sedition* [1536], Sir Brian Tuke in his preface to William Thynne's monumental edition of Chaucer [1532], and Henry Parker, tenth Baron Morley, across various of his works. Both Morison and Morley had broad acquaintance with the major works of the Italian Renaissance. Perhaps earlier, however, Dante's anti-papal (though not anti-Catholic) sentiments were spurring English writers to fashion him as a 'witness against Rome' (p. 43) in a similar manner to the appropriation of Petrarch's 'Babylon' sonnets. Havely here adduces *Rede me and be nott wrothe* [1528], the anticlerical invective of the former Observant Franciscans William Roy and Jerome Barlowe (an order with strong historical connections to the Continent), a passage from which perhaps references Dante's *Paradiso.* On a stronger footing is his account of John Bale's use of the *Commedia* and *Monarchia* at the death knell of Henry VIII's reign to construct Dante as a 'witness' who supported reform of the Church. Such a manoeuvre, which takes place in Bale's virulent evangelical text *The Image of Both Churches*, placed him in a continent-wide dialogue with writers like Johannes Oporinus and Matthias Flacius. In covering Dante's textual inroads into Henrician England, both in books and in words which could be harnessed to add heft to major

Henrician causes, Havely accomplishes much in a small compass. It is to be hoped that he has laid the groundwork for future work on the Tudor Dante.

The Festschrift for A.S.G. Edwards which appeared in 2014, *Makers and Users of Medieval Books: Essays in Honour of A.S.G. Edwards*, edited by Carol Meale and Derek Pearsall, features two chapters which pertain to the earlier Tudor period. The first, which focuses on prose, is John J. Thompson's 'Love in the 1530s' (pp. 191–201); the second, on verse, is discussed below. Thompson begins his chapter on a methodological note, stating that his work sprang out of codicological research on Nicholas Love's *Mirror of the Blessed Life of Jesus Christ*, which formed part of a three-year project Thompson supported called 'Geographies of Orthodoxy: Mapping English Pseudo-Bonaventuran Lives of Christ, 1350–1550'. The remit of the project did not allow Thompson and his colleagues to widen their reach to consider other European vestiges of pseudo-Bonaventuran tradition, or the later textual afterlives of these texts as their passage from manuscript to print was completed. This second strand of work is the main subject of Thompson's article, studied through the prism of Love's *Mirror*, which enjoyed promiscuous circulation in manuscript and print (Caxton, Pynson, and de Worde all saw it through the press). It was also pitched into the fierce skirmish over vernacular reading practices which characterized the religious and political ferment of the 1530s. Thompson notes the importance of reader response in the text (a possible lead for developing his work): Love offers his audience a directed series of exercises to experience the 'Gospel narrative of Christ's life on Earth' (p. 194), and later copyists and readers are cast as guardians and promoters of this enterprise. One such was Thomas More, who included the *Mirror* (without an attribution to Love) on an 'approved' reading list during the height of his efforts to proscribe heretical books. Chief among these, of course, were the works of William Tyndale, whose espousal of a 'naked' vernacular text jarred against the conservative preference for a text filtered through Latin tradition. Thompson also notes an additional participant in this battle of reading methodologies: the anonymous writer of the octavo *A Dyurnall: for deuote soules: to ordre them selfe after* [1532?], whose position aligns with More. Within the pages of the book, this author cites Love and promulgates a similar reading practice to him, one contingent upon the choice selection of parts of the book to utilize for devotional meditation. The printer Robert Wyer's mass-production of the *Dyurnall* also evidences for Thompson the readiness with which 'the More–Tyndale controversy was exploited by the sixteenth-century book trade' (p. 200). In contrast to the Dante of Havely's chapter, then, this fascinating chapter ends as a Catholic conscription narrative, with Love's *Mirror* drafted by conservative readers and complicit printers in the 1530s as a model of traditional meditative reading practice which could help stem the 'rising tide of reformism' (p. 201).

Felicity Heal's 2014 monograph, *The Power of Gifts: Gift-Exchange in Early Modern England*, has a more immediate application to the work of historians in the period rather than specialists in literature. Nevertheless, her chapter 'The Politics of Gift-Exchange Under the Tudors' (pp. 87–120) contains incisive accounts of the gift practices which prevailed in Henry VIII's reign and, to a much smaller extent, those of Edward VI and Mary I, which sheds light on the workings of monarchs and court in an important and symbolic sphere of power relations. (Heal also dedicates generous space to Elizabeth I, whose reign lies outside the remit of this chapter.) Opening with a reminder about the central place the gift occupied in binding subjects to the monarch and facilitating patronage relationships, Heal also notes the ritualistic dimensions of gifting, and gives particular attention to two contexts in which 'the script' (p. 92) was most recognizable for the participants: the New Year's exchange of gifts at court and the royal progress. Within her coverage of the former, Heal cites the Great Bible of 1539 as a paradigm of a monarchical gift to the nation, and discusses the surviving gift lists from 1532, 1534, and 1534 in Henry's reign. Throughout the 1530s, gift-giving assumed a political valence, often indicating where royal favour resided. The tireless efforts of Lord Lisle, through his mediator John Husee, to convince Henry of his enduring dedication affords a high-profile example of the politics of gift exchange. Heal also gives some consideration to the single gift list which has passed down from Edward VI's reign (1551–2). In terms of royal progress, Heal points out the lessening of formal visits over the course of Henry's period on the throne. Delving in greater detail into the motivation of subjects' gift-giving, she also adduces the example of William Paget's gift to Edward Seymour, Protector Somerset, in 1549 as an exemplar of the gift-compliment which also fulfilled an exhortatory or counselling function. On the other side of the exchange, she attends to the royal attitude towards gifting, in particular Henry's 'use of tokens to embody favour or assurance' (p. 116). These insights warrant consideration in future literary criticism of the Henrician, Edwardian, and Marian courts and the permutations in their practice relating to the gift.

Of the journal articles on prose subjects which appeared in 2014, Barrett L. Beer's short article, 'John Kyngston and Fabyan's *Chronicle* (1559)' (*Library* 14:ii[2014] 199–207) is a welcome contribution to a rather thin corpus of criticism devoted to mid-Tudor printers and their writerly endeavours. Beer's principal consideration is the continuations that Kyngston added himself to his two 1559 editions of Robert Fabyan's *Chronicle* (printed in 1516, 1532, and 1542), which cover the period 1542 to 1559. Before launching into the specifics of Kyngston's work as continuator, however, Beer outlines Kyngston's earlier career (*fl.* 1553–84), including his association with other printer-chroniclers such as Richard Grafton and John Mychell, the Canterbury Chronicler (the second of whom is an unacknowledged source for some of Kyngston's additions). In a brief but illuminating sweep over the main contents of Kyngston's continuations for the later reign of Henry VIII and those of Edward VI and Mary I, Beer discerns some important consistencies, and ellipses. Like several of his counterparts, Kyngston is interested in recounting martial exploits, but does so at the expense of higher-profile events. In his account of Edward VI, for instance, Kyngston sacrifices detailed content on the Edwardian Reformation and Kett's Rebellion to give attention to the war in Scotland. Likewise, Wyatt's Rebellion in Mary I's reign is given a longer— but still clipped—description. What is perhaps most significant, however, is Kyngston's lack of 'a polemical tone on religious and political issues' (p. 204), evidenced above all in his neutral recapitulation of Mary's religious policy. Beer ends his discussion with an acknowledgement that Kyngston's continuations are best understood in a competitive print market where the currency of content was vital. His commercial acumen also had a literary-cultural benefit, however, keeping 'Fabyan's chronicle before the reading public through the sixteenth century and beyond' (p. 207).

The final item in this section complements Gabriele Stein's work on Sir Thomas Elyot and the role of lexicographer in Tudor England (see above). Hannah Crawforth's short but compelling article, 'Linguistics, Lexicography, and the Early Modern' (*JEMCS* 14:ii[2014] 94–9), takes historical linguistics as its subject and utilizes the prominent humanist Sir John Cheke and his translation of the New Testament as its chief example. Crawforth's point of departure is that early modern dictionary-compilers fall into two categories: the 'prescriptive', who strive at totalizing and static definitions of the language and attempt to delimit usage, often marking out archaic words; and the 'descriptive', whose dictionaries are more 'revisionist and permeable' (p. 94). These contrasting approaches provide models of thinking about periodization and historical linguistics in the period, and Crawforth's central thesis is that writers like Cheke behave much like 'descriptive' practitioners who efface temporal linguistic borders in their theories of language. Wishing to expunge English of its Latinisms and revive and re-coin native Anglo-Saxon words in their stead, Cheke ignores period divisions and 'radically overturns any notion of straightforwardly linear linguistic development by bringing the words of the past back to currency in the present' (p. 97). In this sense, he stands as a paradigm of other early modern linguists in refusing to be trammelled within period-bound restrictions, 'revisit[ing] the language of the past . . . and harnessing its potential for recovery for the future' (p. 97).

2. General: Verse

The principal monograph on earlier Tudor verse (in the main) which issued from an academic press in 2014 is Lindsay Ann Reid's *Ovidian Bibliofictions and the Tudor Book: Metamorphosing Classical Heroines in Late Medieval and Renaissance England*. This uses a panoply of Tudor printed books to provide a rich and searching study of English vernacular uses of Ovid's heroines between Chaucer and Drayton. The early and mid-Tudor periods are well represented, which has the dual effect of bringing under-studied texts more firmly into general awareness and providing a more fluid and convincing sense of continuity between the more widely studied late medieval and late Tudor authors. This book engages closely with the materiality and intertextuality of its corpus. As a result, Reid is able to trace how a range of authors utilized Ovidian characterizations in a fluid, nuanced, and responsive manner that defies persistent scholarly notions of the 'Drab Age'.

The book is divided into five sections, with an appendix detailing the print history of Ovid's works (in Latin) in England from the 1470s to the end of the sixteenth century. The introduction provides overviews of Reid's conceptual uses of intertextuality and the Tudor book; Ovidian intertextuality (in antiquity and in the Tudor period); and Ovid and gender. Two further sections make extensive use of early Tudor laureate John Skelton's *The Boke of Phyllyp*

Sparowe [*c*.1504] and *The Garlande or Chapelet of Laurell* [first printed 1523]: these two sections draw convincing and nuanced connections between the late medieval and early modern through the lens of Skelton's Ovidianism, and merit a chapter-length treatment themselves. Reid's introduction concludes with a brief overview of her thematic and trans-chronological chapters.

Chapter 2 describes Ovidian heroines in English *querelle des femmes* literature from Chaucer to Shakespeare. Reid discusses the relationships between authors, publishers, and readers involved in generating new interpretations of Ovidian feminine tropes and characters in a range of texts, including lesser-known prose pamphlets alongside canonical classics: *The Wife of Bath's Tale*, Gower's *Confessio amantis*, Antony Woodville's *Book Named the Dictes or Sayengis of the Philosophhres* [1477], William Walter's *Spectacle of Louers* [*c*.1533], Thomas Feylde's *Contrauersye Bytwene a Louer and a Iaye* [*c*.1532], Robert Copland's *The Seuen Sorowes that Women Haue When Theyr Husbandes Be Deade* [*c*.1565], Edward Gosynhyll's *Lytle Boke Named the Schole House of Women* [*c*.1541] and *The Prayse of All Women Called Mulierum Pean* [*c*.1542], Robert Burdet's *Dyalogue Defensyue for Women Agaynst Malycyous Dectractours* [1542], Edward More's *Lytle and Bryefe Treatyse Called the Defence of Women Made agaynst the Schole House of* Women [1560], Thomas Wilson's *Arte of Rhetorique*, and *The Taming of the Shrew*. The chapter concludes with an analysis of John Stow's 1561 edition of Chaucer's works and its relationship with Ovidian *querelle des femmes* literature and intertextuality.

Chapter 3 takes a more focused look at Cressida, finding in her a wealth of post-classical developments and concerns with gossip, rumour, and *fama* that cut across the Tudor period. This is particularly bound up in issues of text production, as Reid studies the effects of Cressida's shift to the printed page. Chapter 4 considers the poetry of Isabella Whitney, the 1526 edition of Chaucer's *House of Fame* and the *Heroides* epistolary strand in the *querelle des femmes*. The final chapter examines the evolution of Ovidian (and pseudo-Ovidian) fictive characterizations of Jane Shore, Rosamond Clifford, Elstred, and Matilda Fitzwalter in late Tudor poetry.

There are a few issues that detract from the quality of this volume, though none are problematic enough to disguise its contribution. The book's relationship with specific theoretical frameworks is not made entirely clear in the introduction. It states that this study is not predicated on a feminist critical approach, but many of the examples either adopt or reflect aspects of feminist discourse: the relationship between the author's methodology and these pre-existing frameworks is not entirely clear. The many discursive footnotes are distracting. Finally, the author has missed out on a wealth of recent relevant scholarship: there are only a handful of citations to works published after 2007. While it is no secret that it can take a long time to get a book published (often through no fault of the author), this is a surprising gap nevertheless. It is a particular shame that Reid has not made use of *The Oxford Handbook of Tudor Literature*, edited by Mike Pincombe and Cathy Shrank [2012], or recent work on Churchyard and the *Mirror for Magistrates* by Pincombe, Matthew Woodcock, and Scott Lucas. Despite these lacunae, this is undoubtedly an important book; it makes a substantial contribution to both the study of early and mid-Tudor literature and to our understanding of late medieval and early modern intertextuality. It should be on the shelves of any scholar working on representations of the past in early modern England.

Besides Reid's monograph, a smattering of recent chapters will be of interest to scholars and students of the period. A.S.G. Edwards's chapter 'Beyond the Fifteenth Century' (in Boffey and Edwards, eds., *A Companion to Fifteenth-Century Poetry*, pp. 225–36) foregrounds, in brief space, the most salient features and trends which distinguish poems penned between *c.*1500 and 1547. It therefore serves as an able overview of the period and its preoccupations. Opening with two examples (from *The Great Chronicle of London* and Henry Bradshaw), Edward notes that early sixteenth-century versifiers did not demur from setting contemporaries like Skelton, More, Barclay, and even William Cornysh alongside the lauded poets of the English triumvirate (Chaucer, Gower, Lydgate). Even taking into account the numerous reprints of these founding fathers throughout the Tudor decades, Edwards charts a nascent confidence in the vernacular and a shortening in the 'shadow' (p. 225) of their influence. He touches on the growing importance of the court as a locus of production, and as a context (*inter alia*) in which manuscript production still flourished, fostering a more 'direct' (p. 227) relation between text and audience. Where print was concerned, printers were tardy to tap into the market for verse, but Edwards adduces Hawes, Barclay, and Skelton as poets whose printed output testified to its retail potential. The final discussion of the chapter, on the plenitude of forms in the period and its diagnostic genres, makes some incisive claims about satire as a dominant mode: Barclay, Skelton, Wyatt, and Surrey all dabbled in satirical writing in various guises. The emergence of humanism in the verse of these poets (and others) is also given an 'insular' (p. 233) flavour, as Edwards steers his point to the fact that poets' appropriation of New Learning from the Continent tended not to be direct; rather, it was filtered through 'antecedent native traditions' (p. 234), as in Surrey's translation of Virgil's *Aeneid* through the prism of Gavin Douglas. These are the insights of a critic well versed in the period and the poetic terrain it charted.

Despite his importance as a translator and poet, studies of Gavin Douglas and his vernacular rendering of the *Aeneid* remain sporadic. Jane Griffiths's decision to devote chapter 4 of *Diverting Authorities* (see Section 1 above) to 'Exhortations to the Reader: The Double Glossing of Douglas' *Eneados*' (pp. 81–102) is therefore pleasing. Unlike the texts which form the subjects of chapters 5 and 6, the *Eneados* offers a test case of a text surviving in two different media—the original manuscript (*c.*1513) and William Copland's posthumous printed edition (1553)—and with different agents acting the role of glossator. Painted in broad brushstrokes, Griffiths mounts the persuasive case that Douglas's glosses in Trinity College MS O.3.12 have a 'destabilizing' (p. 81) function through their assertion of the historico-cultural chasm between modern reader and classical author. The *mise-en-page* of the manuscript makes clear that the glosses were integral to Douglas's purpose, continuing and drawing on a wealth of academic commentaries on Virgil. Douglas therefore accessed the *Aeneid* through several layers of mediation, and he takes no pains to disguise the process of transmission and the distortions it entails. Casting himself as a creative interpreter, his glosses do not anchor the text but comment on his own translative choices. At the same time, Douglas's explicit presence in his glosses, coupled with his free-handed use of different commentary traditions, led him to detect a 'self-authorizing strategy' (p. 90) in his practice which readers are invited to supplement. Printing the *Eneados* for a much broader audience, the Copland glossator's preoccupations are different. The edition utilizes glosses to elucidate the text for readers and offer moral instruction through recourse to universalizing (and often misleading and trite) maxims which are not subject to historical flux. For Griffiths, the manuscript and print approaches stem from humanist reading strategies: Douglas's are medieval and Continental, and the Copland glossator's grounded in the importance attached to 'gatherings' and 'sayings' in the Tudor humanist classroom. The chapter ends with a discussion of the peculiar appearance of four glosses from Copland's printed edition in the Trinity manuscript. Griffiths broaches different hypotheses for this occurrence with care, but stresses above all that these glosses could be an act of readerly resistance in Douglas's manuscript text, enlisted to help the reader amidst glosses which otherwise serve the needs of the author.

Griffiths's second sortie into verse and paratextual matter in 2014 (and the final 'general' verse piece reviewed this year) is her chapter in the Festschrift for A.S.G. Edwards: 'Editorial Glossing and Reader Resistance in a Copy of Robert Crowley's *Piers Plowman*' (in Meale and Pearsall, eds., pp. 202–13). In her opening paragraphs, Griffiths signals her departure from John N. King's influential characterization of the edition as a Reformist repurposing of a medieval *Meisterwerk*. Rather, she aligns herself with the more recent criticism on Crowley's *Piers* (citing Rebecca Schoff, Larry Scanlon, and Mike Rodman Jones) that discerns a double purpose of the text: its contribution to the 'plowman' tradition which saw Piers claimed as a Reformist champion in various apocrypha, and its status as an edition within a burgeoning mid-Tudor market for printed medieval 'classics'. The doubleness of Crowley's edition is also diagnostic of both the first and second editions in terms of paratext (both printed in 1550). As in her other chapters considered above, Griffiths's main interest (though she covers other paratextual matters) centres on the glosses of the two editions, which are lighter in the first and more pronounced in the second. Crowley's approach as a glossator is not uniform: some support 'polemical' or 'apocalyptic' readings, while others—in experimental fashion—give biblical citations and therefore put readers to additional work, exhorting them 'to think for themselves' (p. 206) in scurrying after references and devising their own textual interpretations. One interpretation which Crowley is keen to delimit, however, is that *Piers Plowman* is prophetic of the Reformation. Griffiths concludes her chapter with a discussion of one reader's resistance in this regard, evidenced through his(?) copious marginal annotations to the copy of Crowley's second edition which survives as British Library, C.1.22.d.9. A paradigmatic Crowley reader this annotator was not, but the scribblings left—and behind them, Griffiths's chapter—gives compelling insight into how mid-Tudor audiences were both prompted to read *Piers* and to read it for real.

3. More

In examining recent criticism on the works of Sir Thomas More, it is worth acknowledging in brief the appearance of the second edition of Clarence H. Miller's edition of *Utopia*. With useful and accessible prefatory materials and a clear, fluid translation, this affordable paperback edition of *Utopia* should be a student favourite.

Emmanouil Aretoulakis's article, 'The Prefatory/Postscript Letters to St. Thomas More's Utopia: The Culture of "Seeing" as a Reality-Conferring Strategy' (*JEMS* 3[2014] 91–113), discusses the early modern conceptual links between seeing, reading, and knowing through a discussion of the prefatory and postscript letters in Thomas More's *Utopia*. Aretoulakis argues that the letters enhance the verisimilitude of the island of Utopia because they extend the authority of the eyewitness—the central authority of the burgeoning scientific method, the authority of the objective observation—to the reader, who is invited to 'see' Utopia not just through Hythloday's account, but through the framing materials of More and his correspondents. This authority is bolstered by eminent humanists like Guillaume Budé, who are prepared to vouch for the account of Utopia first by virtue of the reputations of the men who have purportedly 'witnessed' Hythloday's descriptions, and second by his own 'investigations'.

Yet the authority of the witness is subverted at a foundational level in Utopia. Budé's testimony links Hythloday and More as 'discoverers' of Utopia, working with More's own letters to 'hopelessly confus[e]' (p. 96) the relationship between the reality of the letter-writers (itself distinct from the tangible world of the reader) and the mimetic world of Utopia, and to unsettle notions of authorship and authority in the observation and interpretation of events and places. Indeed, Giles's additions describe More's written account as providing a more authoritative description of Utopia than Hythloday's own verbal account (at which Giles was present). As Aretoulakis points out, the simulacrum has become more 'real' than the object itself, unsettling notions of the authority of the eyewitness. This article showcases the knowing complexity not just of More's text, but of those colleagues and friends with whom he corresponded to produce the paratextual additions to Hythloday's ostensibly 'authoritative' account.

More remains one of the more enigmatic figures of early modern England; like Shakespeare, he consistently lures scholars to strive to understand who he 'really' was. Travis Curtright's article, 'Thomas More on Humor' (*Logos* 17:i[2014] 13–29), grapples with this Herculean task by tackling the still-contested subject of More's wit: was More's sense of humour evidence of his beatific equanimity and self-awareness, or did it demonstrate a caustic and mocking cynic? Curtright considers this dichotomy by examining More's anecdotes from three critical perspectives: that of modern scholarship (primarily Elton and Marius), early modern assessments (mainly those of Stapleton, Foxe, Erasmus, and Hall), and classical rhetorical advice (Quintilian's and Lucian's in particular). The article is broken down into four overlapping sections: 'Rhetoric and Laughter', 'Minding True Things By Mockery', 'Comedy as Spiritual Combat', and 'Playing the Fool'. These sections discuss aspects and applications of More's wit, from rhetorical, political, disputational, and religious contexts.

Curtright's characterization of More's 'Lucianic combination of censure, reprimand, and wit' (p. 20) depicts a rather different More from the venomous and rather self-involved figure described by scholars like Elton and Marius. Curtright's More is a rhetorician, grounded in the humanist interpretations of Quintilian, Cicero, Aristotle, and Lucian. More's goal is to persuade: not necessarily his opponent, but rather his readership or audience. Curtright argues that 'Mockery . . . need not be considered a vice, a mood, or a consequence of how More's father raised him; it could be a sign of excellent rhetoric' (p. 16). This line of argument distances More, rendering him less culpable and more mysterious; while this does not necessarily provide us with a closer understanding of More himself, it demonstrates persuasively a more nuanced understanding of his self-construction.

The last article under consideration here, Jürgen Meyer's important 'An Unthinkable History of King Richard the Third: Thomas More's Fragment and His Answer to Lucian's Tyrannicide' (*MLR* 109:iii[2014] 629–39), seeks to contextualize Thomas More's fragmentary *History of King Richard the Third* [1513] and its relationship to the great Tudor history-writing projects. The *History* is a complex text, and it has been employed in an overly simplistic narrative of Tudor hegemony (both by modern scholars and by early modern historians). Meyer approaches this problem by placing More's *History* alongside his *Response* [*c*.1506] and John Fortescue's *The Governance of England* [1471]. Meyer argues that all three texts share the same central problem, 'of deciding how a state (whether a smaller 'polis' or a larger 'commonwealth') should respond to one who aspires to liberate those around him from the 'yoke of tyranny' (p. 631). More's *History* presents a complicated picture of tyranny: More's Richard is a tyrant, to be sure, but More struggled to negotiate the constitutional realities of Henry VII's accession to the throne—and therefore the validity of the Tudor dynasty—within the context of Richard's rise to and exercise of monarchical authority. The *Response* instead treats the rise of tyranny within a legalistic framework, in the format of a *controversiae*, which afforded More a greater degree of latitude in describing and discussing the rise of tyrants. Meyer's analysis of all three texts through the lens of Lucian's *Declamation* (which the *Response* was composed against, as More worked with Erasmus to translate Lucian's satires) allows the convolutions of the *History* to be showcased as More's inability (or unwillingness) to square the constitutional implications of Richard's tyranny on the establishment of the Tudor dynasty.

4. Skelton

The landmark publication on John Skelton in 2014 (and one of the most significant in Skelton scholarship to date) is John Scattergood's substantial monograph *John Skelton: The Career of an Early Tudor Poet*. Over a long career as an insightful critic of late medieval and earlier Tudor literature, Scattergood has spilled much ink on Skelton, producing the standard critical edition of this most fascinating and rebarbative of poets (a revised edition of which appeared in 2015), numerous Skelton-themed articles, and the piece on Skelton in the *Oxford Dictionary of National Biography*. The book-length treatment of England's first 'poet lawreat' in *John Skelton* crowns Scattergood's work in this field, splicing original material and free adaptations of his previous criticism to produce the most comprehensive examination of Skelton's life and works to have been published thus far.

Reviewing a book of this scope permits one to touch upon its broader concerns and methodologies but not its niceties. *John Skelton* is amenable in this regard, as Scattergood's *modus operandi* and critical position are clear from the outset. Noting that the details of Skelton's life, like those of most of his Tudor brethren, can be gleaned from the written record alone, Scattergood seeks to locate Skelton both in his own writings and those about him. Rather than grouping together Skelton's works under a series of different themes, he devotes a separate chapter to each poem or collection of shorter poems (such as *Agaynste a Comely Coystrowne*) and moves in chronological fashion through them. The book therefore begins with a consideration of *Upon the Dolorus Dethe . . . of the Mooste Honorable Erle of Northumberlande* [1489] and moves through the likes of *Ware the Hauke* and *Magynfycence* before concluding with *A Replycacyon* [1528]. Interpolated within these poem-centred chapters are short 'contextualizing' ones which pad out the details of Skelton's circumstances at different periods in his life, or concentrate on wider historico-cultural moments. These are 'At the Court of Henry VII (1488–1503): Opportunities and Positions' (chapter 1); 'At Diss (1503–12): "Sedere ad Eurotam"' (chapter 6); 'At the Court of Henry VIII (1512–29): Memorials and Propaganda' (chapter 10); 'The Grammarians' War, 1519–21' (chapter 14); 'Against Wolsey' (chapter 15); and 'For Wolsey' (chapter 19). Scattergood's central thesis, which ties together all of the above, is that Skelton envisioned the poetic vocation as a public-facing rather than an introspective one. Going *ad fontes* to take his cue from Aristotle and classical exemplars, he treated verse as a vehicle to 'praise' or 'blame', utilizing the various public roles of his life (poet laureate—here an academic title—and *orator regius*) to 'deliver moral approbation and censure for the public good' (p. 36). For Scattergood (borrowing a phrase from Judson Boyce Allen), this involved Skelton in the 'ethical poetic' (p. 35) typical of medieval writers, and also ensured that Skelton resorted to bold, bracing, and sometimes downright befuddling strategies to engage his readers. This is a subordinate theme which looms large in Scattergood's discussion of the Wolsey satires in particular.

As other reviewers have commented, Scattergood's structure and approach allow him to make a fruitful marriage of local textual analysis and general observation. Poems are not left uncharted within the *cursus* of Skelton's career; neither does Scattergood isolate them from the major interests of the book or each other, which are obvious pitfalls where poem-specific chapters are concerned. For instance, his characterization of Skelton's little-discussed propaganda poem *A Ballade Agaynst the Scottyshe Kynge* [1513] as 'something of the form of a flyting' (p. 203) provides a neat generic segue into the ensuing chapter 11, which concentrates on Skelton's three most high-profile flytings. Likewise, Scattergood's incisive summation of *Eleanor Rummynge* as a poem 'about the accumulation of wealth and the creation and consolidation of poverty' (p. 228) furnishes a connection with *Magynyfycence*, which transplants this pecuniary focus to the environs of court and the 'proper [financial] management of the royal household' (p. 233). Textual insights are also referred back to the 'praise'/'blame' ethos which compels Skelton's writing, noting that Skelton's satires run the risk of being at cross-purposes in presenting biting criticisms under the guise of (false) acclamation.

Bringing a lifetime of work on Skelton to bear on his book also enables Scattergood to manage the balance of critical voices well when attending to textual analysis. In general, he straddles the line between summarizing the critical tradition of individual poems and amplifying his own voice within this critical chorus with success. It is a slight shame that Scattergood demurs from offering his own insight into one of the more vexed questions in Skelton scholarship—the derivation of the Skeltonic—but his critical overview of this topic in chapter 6 is still instructive. Sharper is Scattergood's contribution to another critical conundrum: the motivation behind Skelton's volte-face from virulent censurer of Thomas, Cardinal Wolsey (a forthright mouthpiece of 'blame') to apparent recipient of his patronage from the mid-1520s to the end of his life in 1529, becoming an instrument of the government in the process. Here, Scattergood sketches in tentative terms how Skelton came to 'some sort of agreement' (p. 353) with Wolsey, and then advances a rationale from the perspective of the cardinal rather than his main subject. It could be that Wolsey drew on historical precedents of 'those who had offended in writing [making] amends in writing' (p. 354), putting Skelton's pen to the service of the state to capitalize on two of his strengths: 'propaganda against the Scots and against the developing threat of heresy' (p. 355). Again, the orientation of Skelton's verse is linked to a public role he occupied and a perceived need to either commend or castigate.

It is fitting, in a series of reviews where paratextual issues have been in the foreground, that the chief gripe about *John Skelton* concerns its additional apparatus. The book contains an index of manuscripts and a general index, but the absence of a bibliographical section is sorely felt. It is difficult to establish whether its omission was Scattergood's decision or that of the publisher, where the rationale would seem to be space-saving. In a book of this range, however, which grapples with a myriad of critical resources on Skelton and historical material on the period at large, it is disappointing that readers are left to shuttle between Scattergood's footnotes for references rather than having a dedicated bibliography to consult. Nevertheless, this one oversight should not detract from what is otherwise a sterling piece of criticism, and one that will doubtless become the standard work on Skelton for new converts and seasoned readers alike.

Moving from the all-encompassing to the specific in terms of critical purview, A.S.G. Edwards contributed two consecutive pieces on Skelton in *Notes & Queries* in 2014. The first, 'John Skelton and "A Lamentable of Kyng Edward the IIII"' (*N&Q* 61[2014] 203–4), adds to the debate over the authorship of the poem bearing that title which survives in three manuscript witnesses and Richard Lant's (1545?) publication of Skelton's works. In his 1969 edition, Robert S. Kinsman categorized the piece as a 'doubtful' one on two grounds: Lant ascribed other material to Skelton where his authorship is under contention, and (supposing Skelton was born in 1465 or thereabouts) he would not have been old enough to compose a poem which appears to date from a short time after Edward IV's death in 1483. Kinsman also cites other critics to assert the point that the poem is not consistent with Skelton's 'style'. Edwards takes issue with each argument. The fact that the elegiac piece is ascribed to Skelton in both Lant's text and the latest manuscript version, which the antiquarian and studied Middle English enthusiast John Stow compiled, leads Edwards to suggest that these attributions could be correct: other Stow ascriptions have been accepted, and 'his knowledge of Middle English manuscripts was considerable' (p. 203). Edwards also notes that Scattergood, Skelton's most recent biographer (see above), postulates that Skelton was born c.1460, and that the exact date is irrecoverable. On the matter of style, Edwards cautions against prescriptive claims, given the range Skelton manifests across his canon and the fact that his 'poetic voice' was not fixed at the formative stage of his career. The place of the Edward IV poem in Skelton's corpus thus remains an open one.

Edwards's second article concentrates on 'Skelton's *Bowge of Court*, Line 186' (*N&Q* 61[2014] 204). This is a vexed line skirted over in existing editorial treatments of the poem (with the exception of Julia Boffey's), and reads in the (1499?) edition which de Worde printed 'Twyst (qd suspecte) goo playe hym I ne reke.' In the later version published c.1510, which de Worde also oversaw, the difficult opening word 'Twyst' is jettisoned for 'Whisht', which Edwards advances (via the *Middle English Dictionary*) as an orthographical variant of the interjection 'Whist', meaning 'Hush!' or 'Be silent!' Comparing the variants between the (1499?) and 1510 printing of the *Bowge* reveals that the later text corrected 'about thirty' (p. 204) typographical errors in the first. Edwards draws the sensible conclusion that the replacement of 'Twyst' with 'Whisht' is one such emendation in a larger 'systematic attempt' (p. 204) to improve the text of the poem, and that 'Twyst' might therefore be a simple corruption.

5. Surrey

The single piece of criticism on Henry Howard, earl of Surrey, in 2014 focuses on one of his most combed-over elegiac poems: Bradley J. Irish's article, 'Rivalrous Emotions in Surrey's "So crewell prison"' (*SEL* 54:i[2014] 1–24), which anticipates a monograph (in progress) on emotions in the Tudor court. From the outset, Irish cuts against the grain of previous scholarship on this poem: this has tended to have either a New Critical slant, unpacking the mnemonic strategies of 'So crewell prison', or, in recent years, an application of Queer Theoretical positions to explore the relationship the fictionalized Surrey and the king's bastard son Henry Fitzroy, duke of Richmond, enjoyed at Windsor. Irish's interest inheres rather in the 'emotional syntax' (p. 1) of the poem. Given what we surmise to be Surrey's character (an archetype of the 'angry young man of privilege' (p. 5)), is it reasonable to suppose he was envious of Richmond, the one young man in the kingdom who was a better-placed scion than him? This is a thought-provoking observation, and Irish is keen for it to act as a 'counterweight' (p. 2) which balances, but does not occlude, foregoing critical commentaries on 'So crewell prison'. Quite apart from the freshness of its insights, Irish's article also draws value from its rigour. He sets his methodological approach within the broader corpus of work being undertaken on early modern emotion, as well as interdisciplinary modern research on the emotions, and proposes his article as a model of how these ideas can be brought to bear on a literary text. It follows that his analysis of the 'darker affective register' (p. 6) of the poem is well informed. Subsection II of the article is given over to comprehensive modern and early modern taxonomies of 'envy' (both comparative discomfort at the success of others, in 'benign' and 'malicious' form', and a more neutral 'emulation'), and sub-section IV to those on 'jealousy' (discomfort at a threat to something possessed or thought to be possessed and a less malicious 'zeal'). Attention to the emotional 'ambivalence' (p. 9) of 'So crewell prison' carries over subsections III and IV. Irish performs some deft close reading here: the conflation of Windsor and Troy in the first quatrain, for instance, both writes Surrey into the Tudor line (an emulous gesture) and fantasizes about aggression towards it (with Surrey as Pyrrhus wreaking death upon Priam and Polites). These dual tensions also colour the several masculine contests which Surrey recalls as mnemonic set-pieces in the poem (including sword-fighting and hunting); the 'jealous', eroticized competition of tennis/courting, where adolescent bonding and sexuality strain against each other; and the conclusion of the poem, where anger and resentment are seen to simmer beneath the plaintive lines. If, in Irish's terms, 'So crewell prison' 'fails as a tool to alleviate [Surrey's] grief' (p. 19), his article succeeds as an examination of the poem's complex emotional contours and as an exemplar of this kind of 'affective' analysis.

A second elegiac poem in Surrey's canon, the much-discussed 'Wyatt resteth here', is the subject of Ryan Hackenbracht's article, 'Mourning the Living: Surrey's "Wyatt Resteth Here," Henrician Funerary Debates, and the Passing of National Virtue' (*Ren&R* 35:ii[2012] 61–82). This article has been overlooked in previous volumes of *YWES*, but adds new life to critical dialogues about the poem and another perspective on the doctrinal affiliations of its author. Whereas critics have focused on religious and political interpretations of the poem, Hackenbracht's argument pushes the significance of its spiritual and ritualistic dimensions. His central argument is that 'Wyatt resteth here' enacts a communal funeral service for the deceased Wyatt and (as the reader unearths in the act of participating) the concomitant passing of national virtue. Given this slant, Surrey's poem contributes to the heated contemporaneous debates about '"the last things"' (p. 63) and Prayers for the Dead. One strength of Hackenbracht's article is his contextualization of this polemic among English intellectuals either side of the divide over three distinct phases in the 1520s (Simon Fish, Thomas More, William Tyndale), 1530s (John Frith), and early 1540s (John Standish, Miles Coverdale, Thomas Becon). His figuring of 'Wyatt resteth here' as a funeral service is also given persuasive clout through his close reading of its structure compared with the Requiem Mass (the invitation to the service, the rumination on the corpus of the deceased). Surrey's one major departure is the 'severed communication' (p. 74) between the living and dead in the final stanza, which signals to

Hackenbracht the work of a Reformist sympathizer. The final part of the article elaborates on the manner in which the reader is left to behold not Wyatt but the 'national crisis' (p. 74) of lost virtue in England which escalates to the abuses of its titular head: Henry VIII. This final gesture also reinforces this view of a 'Protestant' Surrey, insofar as it shuffles the dead from centre stage, mourns the 'gylt'-ridden who remain living, and enjoins them to fulfil their 'obligations . . . toward themselves' (p. 76) in addressing the health of the nation.

6. Wyatt

That Sir Thomas Wyatt was called a 'Reformer' of English verse in the famous words of George Puttenham is well known, as is his role as diplomat for Henry VIII in France, Italy, and Spain for the bulk of his adult life (1526–42). These two facts, one literary-historical and one biographical, are central to William T. Rossiter's impressive monograph *Wyatt Abroad: Tudor Diplomacy and the Translation of Power*, which was the most substantial publication on Wyatt in 2014. For Rossiter, 'reform' and diplomacy lie at the heart of Wyatt's practice as a poet: consolidating what these two notions mean in the context of the book is vital to understanding Rossiter's more granular analysis of Wyatt's poems within his four principal chapters. In the introduction, entitled 'The First Reformer?' (pp. 1–46), Rossiter defines the poetic act of reforming as 'a refashioning of an established source which improves upon that source' (p. 3). In the context of Wyatt in particular, his aim is to mark 'the moment in which late medieval *translatio* meets early modern *imitatio*, where the political meets the poetical, and where the traditional meets the novel' (pp. 2–3). These moments are most visible in Wyatt's translations, most of which were penned during his various embassies to fellow European superpowers. Rossiter considers the diplomatic manoeuvres which coloured Wyatt's professional life as analogous to, even inseparable from, the exchanges required in the act of translation: both enterprises involve the judicious weighing of words, the meeting of different languages and registers, and the shuttling between different authoritative figures. Neither concept ('reform' as poetic refashioning and 'translation-as-diplomacy' (and vice versa) originate with Rossiter perforce, but no previous critical work has applied them with such thoroughness and invention to Wyatt's canon.

Each chapter of *Wyatt Abroad* covers a different diplomatic period in Wyatt's life, and adopts a chronological structure. The increasing convolution of Wyatt's diplomatic missions is contiguous, in Rossiter's analysis, with his development as a translator, as a poet able to cross over from *translatio* to *imitatio*. Chapter 1, '"Sovendra du chaseur": Wyatt in France, French at the English Court' (pp. 47–89), looks at Wyatt's first diplomatic mission to France with Sir Thomas Cheyne in 1526 and his treatment of the French verse he encountered (as well as that he inherited). Rossiter advances the argument that the French influence on Wyatt's verse is much greater than critics (Patricia Thomson in particular) supposed, but that his direct debt to French 'Petrarchans' is small, given that Wyatt's first encounters with Petrarchan ideas (the mid-1520s) pre-date those of his French peers. Rather, his practice around this time fused 'the late medieval French-inflected tradition' (p. 54) familiar to English tradition with his Petrarch sources as a means of 'naturalizing Petrarchism at the English court' (p. 57). In this sense, Wyatt's 'French' and 'Italian' periods, if termed such, are not consecutive but intermingled. Rossiter reads Wyatt's French-inspired poems in the context of his purported romantic involvement with Anne Boleyn, plotting Wyatt's diplomatic activities (real and poetic) alongside his involvement (again, real or otherwise) with Anne. After considering the seven Wyatt poems which have direct French sources (foremost among them 'Ffor to love her' and 'Yf it be so'), Rossiter turns his attention to 'Farewell, Love' and 'If waker care' as paradigms of Wyatt's merging of French influence and Petrarchan sentiment. The second, of course, refers to 'Brunet' (referring to Anne?): Rossiter speculates that Wyatt could be 'subreading' (a recurrent term) Clément Marot here, who addressed a poem at Marguerite of Navarre's court to an unidentified 'Brunette' during Anne's period in France.

Chapter 2, ' "My galy charged": Wyatt in Italy' (pp. 89–122), moves forward to Wyatt's embassy to Italy with Sir John Russell in 1527 (related to his activities in France the year before). Rossiter's main assertion here is that Wyatt's use of Alessandro Vellutello's 1525 edition of Petrarch (*Il Petrarca*), padded out with an extensive commentary, is central to his reception of the Italian poet. It also enabled Wyatt to 'confirm his translative method as being predicated upon the existing medieval method of triangulation between source [Petrarch], commentary [Vellutello] and translation [Wyatt]' (p. 92). Petrarch appealed to Wyatt as his 'paradoxical, antonymic discourse' (p. 94) parallels the diplomatic arts Wyatt was charged to implement, but Wyatt's own encounter with Petrarch's verse, filtered through the mediating Vellutello, is itself a diplomatic exchange. Rossiter unpicks the various influences of *Il Petrarca* on Wyatt, not least of which is his reordering of Petrarch's sequence of poems, which might have some influence on the earlier groupings of lyrics in Wyatt's autograph Egerton Manuscript. Wyatt seems also to have been prompted in his Petrarchan choices via Vellutello's 'cross-referencing system' (p. 117) which links the poem he is annotating with others in the sequence. Particular poems Rossiter discusses vis-à-vis Wyatt's 'diplomatic' contact with Petrarch are *Myne olde dere En'mye*, 'Who so list to hounte', and 'The piller pearisht is'.

Rossiter's chapter 3, ' "So feble is the threde": Wyatt in Spain' (pp. 123–51), focuses on Wyatt's final embassy to the imperial court of Charles V (1537–42). The material is lifted with little substantive alteration from his piece in *Authority and Diplomacy from Dante to Shakespeare*, which was reviewed in last year's chapter and so will not be considered here. Chapter 4, ' "Inward Sion": Wyatt in Jerusalem—The Penitential Psalms and Soteriological Diplomacy' (pp. 152–97), considers Wyatt's paraphrase of the penitential psalms, which Rossiter (following Jason Powell) assigns at least in part to the period of Wyatt's diplomatic residence in Spain. The chapter makes the original insight that Wyatt's version of the psalms depends on his subreading of not just Pietro Aretino, Johannes Campensis, and John Fisher, but also the evangelical Italian writer Antonio Brucioli. Wyatt's handling of the psalms therefore involves the careful fusion of several sources in what is his most sophisticated translative/diplomatic exchange. At the level of the paraphrase proper, Rossiter draws on existing criticism to explore David's interaction with God as a kind of 'soteriological diplomacy' (p. 181) which enacts 'an idealized diplomatic exchange between the penitent sinner and his God' (p. 189). Far removed from the failings of mortal monarchs, God is figured a monarchical ideal, and Wyatt's politicized paraphrase is consistent with the discourse of subjection which prevailed in the Henrician court.

The conclusion, '"In Kent and Christendom": Wyatt in England' (pp. 198–224), returns Wyatt to his native ground, demonstrating how, in addition to the Continental sources Wyatt utilized throughout his poetic career, his medieval English inheritance also supplied a well-stocked store-house. Rossiter in particular picks out Chaucer and Lydgate as developers of an Anglo-Italian tradition which preceded Wyatt, and which Puttenham (returning to the start) effaces in his take on Wyatt as an originary 'reformer'.

The strengths of *Wyatt Abroad* are numerous, and it deserves to be used as a prominent resource in any study of Wyatt which concentrates on his approach as a translator. Rossiter's boldness is commendable: in revising, even dismantling, Puttenham's characterization of Wyatt as trailblazer, Rossiter nuances a critical tradition which has reinforced Wyatt's position as a Tudor innovator. Rossiter does not forbid him this place, but shows how—in important ways—Wyatt is also a medieval practitioner in his use and adaptation of *translatio* and *imitatio*. Rossiter is also the first critic to pick up the gauntlet that Patricia Thomson threw down when she invited her successors to contradict her sense that Wyatt did not draw much from the French poetic tradition. Quite apart from these broader merits, Rossiter's close reading is also intricate, and he handles French, Italian, and Latin sources with equal aplomb. One can (in apt fashion) subread the influence of Thomas Greene's textual analysis of Wyatt in *The Light in Troy* at several junctures over the course of Rossiter's chapters, each of which has a strong thesis and identity tied well to the overall focus on 'reform' and diplomacy. One minor grumble is that the flow of arguments in these individual chapters is sometimes punctuated unduly by the extensive (perhaps over-)use of subheadings, but this does not diminish what is an excellent, though-provoking, and often original monograph on Wyatt.

A poem where Rossiter detects Wyatt's subreading of Ovid, Chaucer, and Lydgate, 'They flee from me', is the focus of Deborah C. Solomon's article, 'Representations of Lyric Intimacy in Manuscript and Print Versions of Wyatt's "They flee from me"' (*MP* 111:iv[2014] 668–82). As the title announces, Solomon's aim is to examine how the *mise-en-page* and typographical features of Wyatt's best-known lyric in manuscript (the Devonshire Manuscript) and print (Tottel's *Songes and Sonettes*) impinge on the 'lyrical intimacy' of the poem (its sense of anonymity/identity, interiority/exteriority, exclusivity/inclusivity). There is much to recommend in Solomon's approach to, and execution of, this thesis. As she mentions, her diplomatic transcription of the Devonshire text of 'They flee from me' is the first full reproduction of this witness to the poem in print (Heale's edition, reviewed in 2013, is modernized; its other appearances have all been as disaggregated textual variants in editions of Wyatt). The Devonshire version of the text also serves Solomon's purpose well in being part of a manuscript whose compilation and use were a communal enterprise. In the first part of the article, Solomon draws the broad contrasts between the experience of reading manuscript and print texts (such as the 'personalization' (p. 671) of script; the 'mechanical neutrality' (p. 673) of print; the propensity of print to democratize its readership); she then discusses how the Devonshire and Tottel copies of the poem in turn conform to these expectations. The second part of the article performs somewhat of a *volta*: unpicking the manuscript and print can (in a fitting manner) act against type. Solomon argues, for instance, that because print witnesses of a text are divorced from a particular scribing individual and occasion, the reading experience is more dislocated and therefore private, despite the 'public' form. This section is compelling, but suffers from being kept in the abstract. Solomon does make some direct application of insights to the poem at hand (such as the manner in which the Devonshire text flirts with the border between secrecy and revelation), but 'They flee from me' seems cosmetic and subordinate to the broader discussion. It is only in her summative paragraph that Solomon offers comments on the 'cautious and circumspect' speaker in Devonshire when juxtaposed with his 'unguarded and unsubtle' (p. 682) counterpart in Tottel. Nevertheless, this is an engaging exploration of how different media can suggest, steer, and even govern how a lyric is communicated to readers.

Wyatt's paraphrase of Psalm 6 is touched upon, amid a host of other early modern versifiers' treatments of the same text (including Sir Philip Sidney, King James VI/I, and John Milton), in Robert Kilgore's wide-ranging article, 'The Politics of King David in Early Modern Verse' (*SIP* 111:iii[2014] 411–41). The thrust of Kilgore's argument is that these poems of David and his sin act 'as a mode of poetical and political analysis' (p. 411). Where Wyatt is concerned (see pp. 428–32 in particular), Kilgore figures his paraphrase as a ' "crafty" performance' (p. 429) which uses the frame narrative to interpose between the reader and the penitent David. This narrator, who serves as the 'figure of the poet' (p. 431), is aware (like David) 'of both their efforts as performances for audiences and the political ramifications of sin' (p. 429). The narrator's depiction of David's penitential gestures is somewhat disingenuous and does not square with the gestures themselves, and Kilgore suggests the Wyatt's paraphrase (and psalms in general) might not just be directed at Henry VIII, but 'enablers' (p. 431) like Jean Mallard (who made Henry's psalter) and Hans Holbein, who are cast in a similar business of public presentation and show.

Books Reviewed

Boffey, Julia, and A.S.G. Edwards, eds. *A Companion to Fifteenth-Century Poetry*. Brewer. [2013] pp. ix + 244. £60 ISBN 9 7818 4384 3535.

Gillespie, Vincent, and Susan Powell, eds. *A Companion to the Early Printed Book in Britain, 1476–1558.* Boydell. [2014] pp. xxviii + 385. £70 ISBN 9 7818 4384 3634.

Griffiths, Jane. *Diverting Authorities: Experimental Glossing Practices in Manuscript and Print.* OUP. [2014] pp. 256. £60 ISBN 9 7801 9965 4512.

Havely, Nick. *Dante's British Public: Readers and Texts, from the Fourteenth Century to the Present.* OUP. [2014] pp. xviii + 355. £65 ISBN 9 7801 9921 2446.

Heal, Felicity. *The Power of Gifts: Gift-Exchange in Early Modern England.* OUP. [2014] pp. xi + 258. £65 ISBN 9 7801 9954 2956.

Meale, Carol M., and Derek Pearsall, eds. *Makers and Users of Medieval Books: Essays in Honour of A.S.G. Edwards.* Brewer. [2014] pp. xvi + 259. £60 ISBN 9 7818 4384 3757.

Miller, Clarence H., ed. *Utopia.* 2nd edn. YaleUP. [2014]. pp. xxv + 232. $8.95 ISBN 9 7803 0018 6109.

Reid, Lindsay Ann. *Ovidian Bibliofictions and the Tudor Book: Metamorphosing Classical Heroines in Late Medieval and Renaissance England.* Ashgate. [2014] pp. xi + 218. £60 ISBN 9 7814 0945 7350.

Rossiter, William T. *Wyatt Abroad: Tudor Diplomacy and the Translation of Power.* Brewer. [2014] pp. x + 246. £60 ISBN 9 7818 4384 3887.

Scattergood, John. *John Skelton: The Career of an Early Tudor Poet.* FCP. [2014] pp. 432. €50 ISBN 9 7818 4682 3374.

Stein, Gabriele. *Sir Thomas Elyot as Lexicographer.* OUP. [2014] pp. xviii + 439. £75 ISBN 9 7801 9968 3192.

Waite, Greg, ed. *Alexander Barclay's Translation of Sallust's Bellum Iurgurthinium.* EETS. [2014]. pp. lxxxix + 361. £65 ISBN 9 7801 9968 8197.

Walker, Greg, ed. *The Oxford Anthology of Tudor Drama.* OUP. [2014] pp. vii + 736. £67 ISBN 9 7801 9968 1129.

VI

The Sixteenth Century: Excluding Drama after 1550

HARRIET ARCHER AND RICHARD WOOD

This chapter has three sections: 1. General; 2. Sidney; 3. Spenser. Section 1 is by Harriet Archer; sections 2 and 3 are by Richard Wood.

1. General

This year's special issue of *Renaissance Studies*, 'The Copious Text: Encyclopaedic Books in Early Modern England', guest-edited by Abigail Shinn and Angus Vine (*RS* 28:ii[2014] 167–332), is a fitting beginning to a review of the year's work. The collection foregrounds the history of a trope which 'defies any kind of totalizing or universal narrative' (p. 174), a defiance which resonates with the year's output in all sorts of ways. Many of the books and articles reviewed in these pages dwell on strangeness and difference, as well as the various forms of codification and control, from fashion to grammar, designed to impose order on the diversity and abundance of late sixteenth-century literary culture. This process is embodied not only by the encyclopedias Shinn and Vine describe, which struggled 'to contain and manage a seemingly overwhelming and chaotic body of knowledge', but also by the ubiquitous 'encyclopaedic thinking' they identify, whereby encyclopedism informs early modern writing of all kinds (p. 176). The volume's subjects range from Erasmus to John Aubrey (discussed in articles by Brian Cummings and Kate Bennett respectively), organized chronologically to delineate a general turn away from copious style, as the exuberant neologizing of the late sixteenth century gave way to a new appreciation for brevity in the rationalizing intellectual culture of later periods. Shinn and Vine's introduction, 'Theorizing Copiousness' (*RS* 28:ii[2014] 167–82), sets out the ways in which the issue builds on Terence Cave's *The Cornucopian Text* [1979], by addressing histories of knowledge not considered in his study of predominantly imaginative literature, in order to reveal the parallel operations of copiousness across texts of apparently diverse genres. Aubrey's manuscript notes, they stress, are an unexpected but appropriate place to conclude a

The Year's Work in English Studies, Volume 95 (2016) © *The Author 2016. Published by Oxford University Press on behalf of the English Association. All rights reserved.*
For Permissions, please email: journals.permissions@oup.com
doi:10.1093/ywes/maw013

narrative which complicates accustomed teleologies of rhetorical and techno-logical development, and foregrounds the collaborative interaction of manu-script and print, of text and its material form. Originating in the classical insistence on matter and words (*res* and *verba*) of corresponding weight, true rhetorical copiousness was perceived to decline in the early 1600s, as the superficial reading encouraged by the practice of commonplacing, and the proliferation of printed copy, were thought to privilege loquacity over the learned deployment of *copia*. Nevertheless, commonplacing and its corollaries led, Shinn and Vine remind us, to the generative reading practices intrinsic to the copiousness of the texts under discussion. Shinn's article, 'Managing Copiousness for Pleasure and Profit: William Painter's *Palace of Pleasure*' (*RS* 28:ii[2014] 205–24), shows how this generative quality was read as a threat: Painter's *Palace*, as invoked in Book II of Edmund Spenser's *Faerie Queene* [1590], for example, metonymically stood for 'wanton or promiscuous reading habits', purveying morally licentious Continental tales to a susceptible English readership in the form of the novella, 'a dangerously fecund genre, capable of energetic and unstoppable reproduction' (p. 208). Shinn argues for the transformative properties of the copious reading experience, in which the work's evocation of the act of commonplacing sets up a dynamic in which both text and reader are invented anew. Painter's *Palace* is able to house its mobile, de-authorized *copia* by maintaining an imprecise boundary between the pleasurable and the profitable. While more could be done to draw out the implications of this dialectic between profit and pleasure, which is repeated throughout the article rather uncritically, its component parts are frequently and productively shown to be ambiguously treated or provocatively inter-dependent. Useful attention is also paid, as throughout this special issue, to paratextual frameworks, and the 'discontinuous reading' they encourage (p. 223). Vine's essay for the collection, 'Copiousness, Conjecture and Collaboration in William Camden's *Britannia*' (*RS* 28:ii[2014] 225–41), foregrounds the ethics of Camden's copiousness, and presents a contrasting vision to Shinn's depiction of an alarming, uncontrollable proliferation in Painter's work. Camden's copious practices rest, Vine argues, on the responsibilities of 'honour and duty' (p. 229) bound up in his restorative project, and the 'moderation and civility' (p. 238) with which he went about his abundant research. *Copia* are deployed in support of an argument, not simply illustratively; in particular, Vine uses Camden's erasure of the British people's genetic difference in support of James I's moves to unification, and his demonstration of the value of historiographical conjecture, to convey a sense of the cumulative arguments put forward. Camden's paratexts are at pains to point out the intellectual labour involved in a copious work of such magnitude, defined by its treatment of inexhaustible subject matter. Far from an 'easy or lazy piling up of words' (p. 230), Camden's practice consistently builds towards a comprehensiveness of content as well as style. Concluding with an opportune reflection on the necessity of generous and collaborative scholarly exchange, Vine's article emphasizes Camden's treat-ment of the vastness and disparity of his project not as sites of tension or difficulty, but as 'part of the point' (p. 241).

Julian Lamb's *Rules of Use: Language and Instruction in Early Modern England* focuses on the work of Camden's sixteenth-century schoolmaster antecedents, reading pedagogical texts by Roger Ascham, George Puttenham, and Richard Mulcaster in turn, before considering the emergence of the monolingual dictionary, to reconstruct the dynamics of linguistic and lexical instruction in the sixteenth and seventeenth centuries. Beginning with the hypothesis that 'the scene of instruction is in some sense paradigmatic of all communication' (p. 5), Lamb focuses on the unbridgeable epistemological gap between teacher and student, and the ensuing misinterpretation and abuse of pedagogical rules. Paying attention to the insistence on, and impossibility of, decorum, Lamb suggests that rather than being deliberately socio-politically exclusive, early modern pedagogy 'is often anxiously aware of its impotence to include' (p. 8). The monograph strives to draw critical discussion of early modern instruction away from the assumption of its basis in elite, coercive power relations and to initiate instead a consideration of what it means to teach and what can be taught; a consideration which, Lamb argues, early modern pedagogical texts explicitly invite. Particularly striking is Lamb's use of moments of perceived failure and insufficiency as starting points for his analysis: Puttenham's failure to define decorum, for example, or Mulcaster's refusal to justify his orthography from first principles. Lamb departs from Victoria Kahn's understanding of Renaissance scepticism as a shift in interest from objective to practical truths, to foreground 'the condition of disappoint-ment and dissatisfaction' resulting from the elusiveness of absolute rules of any kind (p. 16), and much of the book's analysis occupies this negative space, returning to themes of impossibility, contingency, and lack. Chapter 2, 'Using Perfection: Roger Ascham's *Toxophilus* and *The Scholemaster*', opens with Ascham's lack of original creativity, and the problems which arise from the central metaphor of *Toxophilus, the Schole of Shoting*: that the judgement necessary to hit a target in archery is required not only to hit but also to perceive a target in the construction of eloquent speech. Lamb problematizes the 'use' of language, based on the ultimately unknowable character of that use. While Ascham's scepticism does make room for this difficulty, 'at the end of *The Scholemaster*', Lamb suggests, 'he leaves us aiming at examples that are not offered' (p. 57). By contrast chapter 3, 'Decorous Abuse: George Puttenham's *The Art of English Poesy*', defends Puttenham against sceptical critical portraits ranging from the banal to the Machiavellian, which make much of his unwillingness to meet the purported purpose of his tract: to teach the writing of poetry. By adjusting our criteria, and recognizing *The Art of English Poesy*'s 'fidelity to its pedagogical form and intentions' (p. 60), it is possible to recuperate a text whose primary focus is the abuse by poetry of ordinary linguistic rules. Puttenham's courtier 'uses language less as a guise, than as a way of being present in the world', where not only speech but also thought are rhetorical constructs (p. 68). In chapter 4, 'Usual Spelling: Richard Mulcaster's *The First Part of the Elementarie*', Lamb explores the space between 'use' and 'the usual' in terms of orthography, interrogating Mulcaster's redefinition of the customary as a certain grounding for correctness. He suggests that Mulcaster's insistence on the learning of English 'on its own terms' (p. 107) enacted a radical articulation of faith in collective usage rather than elite or private prescription, ultimately concluding that 'reason and custom are mutually grounding' (p. 109), but questions the stability of this pedagogical model. Chapter 5, 'Arts of Use: Early English Dictionaries, 1604–58', proceeds beyond the remit of this review, to assess the residing vulnerability of monolingual dictionaries to sceptical interpretation. Lamb's introduction heads off the potential criticism that its author makes 'only token reference' to early modern England in the work's opening chapters and focuses instead on 'the value of Wittgenstein to early modern scholarship' as 'one of the central contestable issues' with which the book engages (p. 23). But while it is true that chapters 2–5 do offer more localized readings, *Rules of Use* is fundamentally a theoretical work at odds with recent trends in Tudor studies, in its hermeneutic, rather than referential, density. It would be interesting to test to what degree these scenes of instruction really are paradigmatic of a broader spectrum of early modern writing.

Rebecca Wiseman offers an alternative treatment of overlapping subject matter in 'A Poetics of the Natural: Sensation, Decorum, and Bodily Appeal in Puttenham's *Art of English Poesy*' (*RS* 28:i[2014] 33–49). Wiseman explores the intersection of art and nature in early modern thought, and the paradox in Puttenham's treatise which 'ties together sensation and persuasion under the encompassing power of the natural', while rendering 'persuasion alone' as 'the province of human effort' (p. 33). Like Lamb, Wiseman focuses particularly on 'what it means to be a hearer and reader of poetry' (p. 33; cf. Lamb, 'The eye and the ear', p. 74). She also seeks to free critical discussion of the *Art* from the discourse of courtly self-fashioning. Their accounts progress along profoundly different lines, however. Wiseman posits the physical experience of aesthetic pleasure or discomfort as indicative of a poetic work's adherence to a set of natural rules for Puttenham, situating 'poetic making firmly within the bounds of the physiological' (p. 38). For Wiseman, Puttenham's decorum remains uncomfortably entangled with deceit. It is fundamental to Puttenham's project, connecting aesthetic value with social propriety, but ultimately contingent on the customs of a time and place. For Wiseman, unlike Lamb, the Aristotelian notion of *phronesis*, or practical judgement as discussed by Victoria Kahn, remains the key to Puttenham's reconciliation of decorum and natural harmony, and of the poet's local, political role and his claim to universal knowledge. Wiseman resolves the challenges of Puttenham's treatise by advancing a model of 'two registers of decorum, the contingent and the universal', linked by the alignment of art and nature (p. 49)—a far cry from Lamb's portrayal of anxious self-reflexivity.

Catherine Nicholson's substantial and energetic *Uncommon Tongues: Eloquence and Eccentricity in the English Renaissance* also treads some comparable ground, again engaging with humanist pedagogy, rhetoric, and eloquence, and an emerging English poetics. The result is a very rich and very readable contribution to the study of sixteenth-century humanism and nationhood, zeroing in on the vernacular's late sixteenth-century 'turn for the eccentric' (p. 1). Ascham and Puttenham, as well as Thomas Wilson and William Webbe, are brought into play in a series of readings of Lyly, Spenser, Marlowe, and Shakespeare, drawing theory and practice into a welcome dialogue. In the suggestively named introduction, 'Antisocial Orpheus',

Nicholson reads late Elizabethan writing as a challenge to the received association between eloquence and civility and cohesion, arguing that instead estrangement and remoteness were also essential to ancient rhetorical theory. The gathering of a strong society around successful oratory, and disruptive, exilic dispersal, represent two sides of the same rhetorical coin. Thus, in chapter 1, 'Good Space and Time: Humanist Pedagogy and the Uses of Estrangement', Nicholson shows the formative humanist instructors Thomas Elyot and Roger Ascham insisting 'that eloquence both depends and thrives on estrangement' (p. 21). Elyot's foundational text, the *Aeneid*, is a poem 'all about generative displacements' (pp. 26–7), while Ascham's Cicero and Cheke's Sallust are characterized by their adventurous voyaging and exile. Chapter 2, 'The Commonplace and the Far-Fetched: Mapping Eloquence in the English Art of Rhetoric', uses Wilson's *Arte of Rhetorique* [1553] and *The Rule of Reason, Conteinyng the Arte of Logique* [1551] as a way in to the spatial dimension of vernacular oratory, and the negotiation of its dual familiarity and barbarism, in a literary culture which posited 'foreignness as both the antithesis and the epitome of linguistic refinement' (p. 70). Chapter 3, '"A World to See": Euphues's Wayward Style', turns to imaginative literature, rereading Lyly's innovative prose romance, *Euphues: The Anatomy of Wit* [1578], as 'an ironic and insightful critique of the English pursuit of eloquence' (p. 73). Lyly's controversial exploration of the 'pleasures and perils' of copiousness (p. 78) resonates with Shinn's discussion of Painter, detailed above, in terms of the profound danger its use of commonplacing evoked for contemporary readers. Nicholson concludes that the inscrutable ending of *The Anatomy of Wit* gestures towards the emptiness of superfluity, which 'yields only solitude and strangeness' for its principal character (p. 98). Subsequent chapters, 'Pastoral in Exile: Colin Clout and the Poetics of English Alienation', and '"Conquering Feet": Tamburlaine and the Measure of English', and the coda, 'Eccentric Shakespeare', return to more canonical territory, still delivered in Nicholson's witty and inventive style.

In *Barbarous Antiquity: Reorienting the Past in the Poetry of Early Modern England*, Miriam Jacobson foregrounds the neglected vocabulary of East–West exchange which, as she demonstrates, pervades late Elizabethan poetry and literary theory. Beginning with Jonson's translation of Horace's *Ars Poetica* and another 2014 reading of Puttenham's *Arte of English Poesie*, before turning to Shakespeare's and Marlowe's narrative verse, Jacobson describes early modern England's frustrated engagement with a partially vanished classical antiquity as inflected by the search for a new language, which found expression in the adoption of discourses of emerging mercantilism and trade with the Levant. Direct imports from the Ottoman empire, initiated by the 1581 foundation of the Turkey Company (the Levant Company from 1593) led to the import of new words, which Jacobson suggests provided a new lens through which Elizabethan writers and consumers could view their reception of the ancient Middle East, as well as constructing a freely circulating 'poetic currency' (p. 3) with which to define their own relation to fresh commodities. Examining a selection of newly imported terms in the context of specific literary works, Jacobson's fascinating series of case studies reveals the ways in which, unlike the stereotypes of Ottoman identity found in the drama of the period, early modern poetry fosters the associative proliferation of meaning around linguistic merchandise. So, for example, depictions of aesthetic sweetness, previously embellished with references to honey, fruit, or wine, are brought up to date with the presence of the exotic sweetener, sugar, which had just reached the English market. Jacobson suggests that it is sugar's literal malleability which makes it such a valuable metaphorical resource for writers engaged in the definition of poetry's own fantastical generative properties, and notes the use of 'subtlety' specifically to describe both ingenious artistic contrivances and decorative structures crafted in sugar, speaking to the 'vivid material connection between sugar and poetry in the early modern imagination' as powerfully transformative agents. So in chapter 2, 'Shaping Subtlety: Sugar in *The Arte of English Poesie*', Jacobson unpicks Puttenham's dualistic delineation of 'subtlety', a laudable poetic attribute ranked alongside sense and sweetness, on the one hand, and a deceptive mode of dissimulation on the other, united in the 'secret meaning' (p. 70) contained within the emblem, motto, or poetic conceit, and the acceptable dissimulation of literary artifice.

In *The Ovidian Vogue: Literary Fashion and Imitative Practice in Late Elizabethan England*, Daniel D. Moss also engages with late Tudor fashion, and frames 1590s narrative poetry using Shakespeare's engagement with Ovid in *Titus Andronicus* in which, Moss argues, Shakespeare's Lavinia enacts English literary culture's turn away from humanist-approved Virgil towards 'the less stable and less coherent, but more vivid and pliable Ovidian corpus' (p. 6). Moss suggests that 'Ovidianism's functional obsolescence' (p. 7), already in place from the early 1590s, rendered Ovidian allusion a compromised and self-critical mode in which to interrogate allusive and imitative poetic practice. Moss's narrative of serial revision and imitation traces the way in which authors operated within and impacted upon the workings of literary fashion during the decade to create an evolving sense of their own poetic development, in dialogue with shifting fashions for Ovidian tropes. Ovid's celebrity status and provocative reputation during this period gifted his imitators a 'fashionable superstyle' (p. 10), with which Nashe, Shakespeare, Chapman, Spenser, Drayton, and Donne critically interacted. In the graphic and spirited first chapter, 'Impotence and Stillbirth: Nashe, Shakespeare, and the Ovidian Debut', Moss reread's Nashe's explicit *Choice of Valentines* [1593] as a preparatory statement of Ovidian intent, allowing him to tailor his 'unpublishable poem' (p. 25) to the elite tastes of select potential patrons, while offering aesthetic satisfaction to his readers by tempering Ovidian impotence with Chaucerian virility. Chapter 2, 'Shadow and Corpus: The Shifting Figure of Ovid in Chapman's Early Poetry', argues that in order properly to comprehend Chapman's *Ovid's Banquet of Sense* [1595] it must be read in conjunction with his debut, *The Shadow of Night* [1594], a pair of works which articulate radically opposed perspectives on contemporary Ovidian eroticism. Chapter 4, 'The Post-Metamorphic Landscape in Drayton's *Endimion and Phoebe* and *Englands Heroicall Epistles*', similarly reads across its subject's oeuvre to arrive at a new understanding of the intricate chronological contingencies of Ovid's significance. Re-evaluating Elizabethan Ovidianism as a gesture, or sequence of gestures, of contemporaneity rather than retrospection, Moss also sheds useful light on a series of under-studied poems as key actors in this formative period. His 'Ovidian vogue' characterizes not just late Elizabethan poetry but a trend in 2014's criticism, too: Lindsay Ann Reid's *Ovidian Bibliofictions and the Tudor Book: Metamorphosing Classical Heroines in Late Medieval and Renaissance England* [2014], and Susan Wiseman's *Writing Metamorphosis in the English Renaissance: 1550–1700* [2014], also take the perennially attractive poet as a starting point for their studies of sixteenth-century writing.

The alienation concurrent with the transformations of the Elizabethan period is the subject of Mary Thomas Crane's *Losing Touch with Nature: Literature and the New Science in Sixteenth-Century England*. Methodologically, Crane warns, the history of science poses the threat of an ineluctably teleological approach, promoting a reading that places early modern literature on the side of new developments, rather than outmoded perspectives. Sidestepping this dichotomy, Crane asserts her interest in a 'period of ferment, confusion, and angst' (p. 2) as the ancient dictums of Aristotle, Galen, and Ptolemy were supplanted piecemeal during the sixteenth and early seventeenth centuries. In the first chapter, 'Aristotelian Naturalism and Its Discontents', Crane sets out to establish how the knowledge base of 'ordinary educated people' shifted as the sixteenth century radically altered scientific understanding (p. 19). Classical and medieval approaches to understanding the world as essentially 'stable and intelligible' (p. 20) were destabilized by advances in knowledge, threatening the hegemony of Aristotelian ideas; Crane's descriptive account balances the technical treatises of John Dee, Thomas Digges, and Thomas Harriot against those of 'ordinary readers' Gabriel Harvey and Francis Shackleton to demonstrate the impact of scientific discovery on the epistemological questions which explicatory and imaginative literature began to ask. Chapter 3, which shares the monograph's title, further elucidates this epistemological uncertainty. Crane's attention here is dedicated to signs, tokens, and 'secret knowledge', and their legibility—the development of optics, for example, gave early modern investigators a literal new perspective, while the real paradigm shift came in the form of revised astronomical understanding based on that which could not be visibly witnessed. Chapters on Spenser, Shakespeare, and Marlowe are followed by an epilogue whose title asks, 'What about Bacon?' Here, Crane resituates Bacon alongside the theorists of the sixteenth, rather than seventeenth, century, arguing that his primary significance lies in the way in which he 'vehemently attacked' the declining Aristotelian consensus (p. 168). In perceiving this historical moment as an opportunity for progress rather than a loss, Crane suggests, Bacon had a greater impact on the subsequent development of the 'new science' than Dee, Digges, or Harriot, despite their superior scientific contribution.

Confronting the ultimate estrangement, Monica Calabritto and Peter Daly's edited collection *Emblems of Death in the Early Modern Period* takes as its focus the pictorial, allegorical representation of death, paradoxically a figure that often 'stymie[s] the visual imagination' (p. 59), in early modern Europe. The collection impressively complexifies its topic, weaving together these emblems' form, appearance and significance in visual and literary art, the minutiae of their variation in time and space, and the contingencies of context which inform their reception, through chapters which take in German, English, French, Spanish, Hungarian, Italian, Polish, Portuguese, and Swedish practices. This breadth of focus is necessarily sold short by an eclectic and reductive introduction, which belies the richness of its chapters' interpretations: in particular, the volume suffers from its wide scope in forays beyond its stated chronological remit, into the nineteenth and twentieth centuries. By contrast, its synchronic treatment of a large geographical area usefully brings together regions not often considered comparatively, and raises productive questions about the limits of our understanding of 'reading' within and across early modern cultures. Tamara A. Goeglein's chapter, 'Death is in the "I" of the Beholder: Early Modern English Emblems of Death' (pp. 59–95), describes the emblem form as 'inter-artistic', involving 'a deliberate interaction between verbal and visual literacies' (p. 61). Exemplifying the involved Continental heritage of the emblem, Goeglein's discussion of Geffrey Whitney's *Choice of Emblemes* [1586], the 'first emblem book published in English, though not in England' (p. 76), explores the form's impact on the social construction of death, and the role of the 'beholding reader' whose perception is transformed by stepping into the 'I' of the emblem (p. 80). Goeglein's evaluation of the symbolic work done by printed frames, in separating art from 'non-art' on the page, extends to a reading of the book's own performance of a similar function in the world. Goeglein highlights the fact that it is impossible to read Whitney's emblem book, and its arcane and powerful political applications, without an appreciation of its continental European context, and the influence of collections like Claude Paradin's *Devises heroïques* [1551], produced in an English version in 1591, or Hadrianus Junius's *Emblemata* [1565]; a message brought home forcefully by the organization of the volume as a whole.

Helen Hackett also explores the interrelation of text, iconography, and power in 'A New Image of Elizabeth I: The Three Goddesses Theme in Art and Literature' (*HLQ* 77:iii[2014] 225–56), her dense and persuasive discussion of the recently discovered portrait acquired by the National Portrait Gallery, London, in 2013. Hackett reads this new image, a miniature which depicts Elizabeth I encountering Juno, Minerva, and Venus, attributed to Isaac Oliver [*c.*1556–1617], in the context of the earlier painting *Elizabeth I and the Three Goddesses* [1569], and George Peele's court drama *The Araygnement of Paris* [1584]. Beginning with the coronation procession of Anne Boleyn (1533), Hackett follows the deployment of the three goddesses trope in panegyrics which seek to suggest the presence of all three of the goddesses' signature qualities—majesty, wisdom, and beauty—in a single noble figure. Hackett argues that, unlike other classical and biblical allegories which fell in and out of favour, the image was valuable throughout Elizabeth's reign for its pliability: the manuscript record of a 1563 Windsor entertainment overseen by Nicholas Udall is 'consistent with contemporary Protestant polemic that sought to rehabilitate Anne as a champion of the Reformation and to urge her Protestant example upon the new young queen' (p. 235), while the *Three Goddesses* painting of 1569, perhaps painted by Hans Eworth in celebration of the defeat of the Northern Rising, seems to encourage Elizabeth 'to embrace marriage (personified by Juno) and love (personified by Venus) as well as wisdom and martial power (personified by Pallas)' (p. 237). The significance of the frequent literary uses of the motif during the 1570s and 1580s by Gascoigne, Sidney, Gabriel Harvey, and others differed again, helping to 'negotiate the challenge of asserting that she was God's anointed ... while avoiding forms of praise of her sacredness that might smack of idolatry' (p. 240), and creating a useful composite of praiseworthy characteristics to navigate 'the iconographic problem posed by an unmarried woman ruler' (p. 242). Hackett suggests that the new miniature may be best understood as a part of the 'culture of patronage and enforced or ritualized gift exchange' (p. 243) out of which Peele's *Araygnment of Paris* also emerged, metafictionally enacted in the presentation of the golden ball in the mythical scenario to which both works allude. In the performance of Peele's entertainment, Hackett suggests, as in the presentation of the miniature portrait to its subject, 'the invisible screen between image and reality trembled and dissolved' (p. 245), subtly but compellingly announcing its layered subtexts.

Approaching early modern political power through the lens of twentieth-century theory, Victoria Kahn's *The Future of Illusion: Political Theology and Early Modern Texts* provides a masterful and innovative alternative to the dominant mode of historical formalism in this year's reviewed work, framed in the preface as 'a series of conversations: not only between the modern figures and the early moderns who fascinated them, but among the moderns themselves' (p. xii). Pushing methodological discussion and metacritical analysis to the fore, Kahn situates her monograph sceptically amid the contemporary 'religious turn', prompted by identifications of a post-secular crisis of liberal democracy. She argues that the modern and early modern texts addressed 'remind us that poiesis'—the concept that holds up artistic and other forms of making as the only means of understanding—'is the missing third term in both early modern and contemporary debates about politics and religion' (p. 3) when it comes to assessing cultural legitimacy. In contrast to the familiar narrative which posits modern political and aesthetic models as secularized versions of their Christian forerunners, Kahn advances her chosen texts as proponents of 'an entirely immanent account of human nature' (p. 5). The principal, if not single, Tudor author invoked in Kahn's treatise is Shakespeare, alongside later early modern political philosophers, and Machiavelli. But her thesis could have pervasive implications for the way in which all accounts of the intersection of religion and power from the period are read. The first chapter, 'Hamlet or Hecuba: Carl Schmitt's Decision', begins with the author of the seminal *Political Theology* [1922], for whom secularization, in tandem with the degenerative transformation of politics into aesthetics and technology, means that 'the church becomes a theater; the artist takes over the function of the priest' (p. 25); this is a process which he saw at work from the early modern era. The absolutist state of the seventeenth century is, for Schmitt, a man-made product of the technological age, in dialogue with the Hobbesian Leviathan. In his 1956 *Hamlet oder Hecuba*, Schmitt aims to recuperate the 'sublimely barbaric' Shakespeare from aesthetic interpretation, to focus instead on 'a world before poiesis ... in which heroism and tragedy are still possible' (p. 40). On the contrary, Kahn argues that poiesis is precisely the condition of Shakespeare's politics. Chapter 2, 'Sacred Kingship and Political Fiction: Ernst Kantorowicz, Carl Schmitt, Ernst Cassirer, and Walter Benjamin', perceives in Kantorowicz's account of the *King's Two Bodies* a displacement of the body and its replacement by fiction; a vital recourse against the fundamentalist location of power in a particular place. In chapter 3, 'Machiavelli and Modernity: Leo Strauss, Carl Schmitt, and Ernst Cassirer', Kahn contends, in opposition to Schmitt and Strauss, that Machiavelli's civil religion is 'a contested political instrument', capable of both promoting societal cohesion and enforcing oppression (p. 84), while fundamental to 'the secular project of self-assertion' (p. 112). Chapter 4 focuses on the early twentieth-century reception of Spinoza, while chapter 5 turns specifically to 'Freud's Spinoza', and Freud's Renaissance, concluding that, despite Freud's interest in the perceived peeling away of art and science from religion in the sixteenth and seventeenth centuries, Freudian psychoanalysis itself disallows the total overthrow of the religious illusion. Kahn's overarching thesis, and manifesto, maintains that the reintegration of poiesis into modern engagements with political theology enables liberalism to respond to the disintegration of Enlightenment absolutes, not with doubt or self-effacement, but with a renewed awareness of all narratives as competing fictions—a conclusion which indicates why this thought-provoking work has already begun to make its mark in late Tudor scholarship.

Michael Martin's *Literature and the Encounter with God in Post-Reformation England* strikes a quieter note amid a selection of works which tackle poetry as a public-facing engagement with new markets, fashions, and forms, or the negotiation of political power. In an introduction which places the work on something of a defensive footing from the outset, Martin asks that we renew our scholarly focus on 'the more obviously religious elements' (p. 3) of works by John Dee, John Donne, Kenelm Digby, Henry and Thomas Vaughan, and Jane Lead, which, *pace* Kahn, he argues, New Historicism, as well as Marxist and feminist theory, have read as predominantly political or polemical in emphasis. Reading a series of non-religious texts, in addition to sermons and more overtly mystical writings, for their evocation of intimate personal encounters with God, Martin suggests that disorientation, rather than secularization, should characterize our understanding of late sixteenth-century spiritual development, setting his approach up in opposition to Stephen Greenblatt's project 'to subsume the religious into the political' (p. 6). In an age when belief in direct interaction with God was falling out of favour, specifically in Protestant intellectual thought, Martin identifies a seam of attention not to theological understanding, but mystical knowledge. While admitting its 'utter inaccessibility to investigation' (p. 13), Martin takes a contemplative, phenomenological approach to the early modern literature of religious experience, beginning in the first chapter with John Dee via Derrida and Michel de Certeau. Dee's attempts to record the angelic language which might enable him to communicate with God have been, Martin suggests, neglected by comparison with scholarly interest in Dee the magus. Martin argues that this bifurcation may be resolved by paying attention to the intersection of religious and medical understanding in the period, more usually grouped, in the context of Dee's reception, under magic and alchemy. Martin notes the idolatrous potential of the project, which Dee, seemingly 'uncompromised' (p. 27) by the restraints of either Protestant or Catholic doctrine, pursued despite its heretical acceptance of the manifestation of angels, either physical or imaginative. Martin concludes that the apparently antithetical methodologies by which Dee, and the later writers treated in subsequent chapters, attempted to achieve mystical experiences intersect throughout the period covered by his study, to reveal a consistent focus on the personal divine encounter, obscured by prevailing scholarly interests.

Nandra Perry's *Imitatio Christi: The Poetics of Piety in Early Modern England* similarly takes late sixteenth- and seventeenth-century devotional literature as its subject, from Thomas Rogers's 1580 translation of Thomas à Kempis's *Imitatio Christi* through works by Sidney and Elizabeth Cary, to John Milton's *Eikonoklastes* [1649]. Perry argues that the tendency of scholars to adhere to 'rigidly drawn confessional lines' (p. 2) when approaching the writing of the early modern period has promoted a false division between the central secular humanist trope of *imitatio* and the devotional practice of *imitatio Christi*, a division belied by the period's literature. In particular, Perry contends that the neglected relationship between these two forms of imitation is fundamental to the influential poetics of the late Elizabethan era. Indeed, in some lights the two forms are one and the same, but whatever shades differentiate them, their intended goal is always the approach towards perfected Christian virtue. Perry's introduction convincingly situates this argument within an account of the origins of humanist *imitatio*, which concisely sketches out the newly identified representational and existential difficulties which the trope sought to confront. Treading a line between slavish mimicry, denounced as Catholic and superstitious, and unfettered creativity, which connoted Puritan nonconformity, both literary and devotional *imitatio* served to acknowledge the superior authority of a distinct age, voice, or text, but also the irrecoverability of that authority, and the poet or disciple's accompanying interpretative anxiety. Perry situates the study 'within a generously drawn version of the Sidney "circle"', treating Sidney himself in his late Elizabethan context in the first chapter, 'The Church Eloquent: Thomas Rogers, Philip Sidney, and the Reformed Body Visible', followed by a subsequent three chapters on Sidney's seventeenth-century legacy, and 'the pervasiveness of the post-Reformation "incarnational" poetics he so eloquently celebrated' (p. 11). (The monograph might productively be read alongside Robert E. Stillman's robust contemporaneous article, 'Philip Sidney and the Catholics: The Turn from Confessionalism in Early Modern Studies' (*MP* 112:i[2014] 97–129).) Chapter 1, though, also sets out the cleric and translator Rogers's contribution to the dialogue; a near-contemporary of Sidney's, and a fellow-graduate of Christ Church, Oxford, Rogers shared with him 'a career-long preoccupation' with imitation (p. 19). Rogers attempted, through his published translations and adaptations of pre- and counter-Reformation tracts, to bolster the church by promoting the imitation of virtuous models, and set his *Imitation of Christ* explicitly within the context of contemporary anxieties about appropriate modes of literary and devotional imitation in his paratextual commentaries. Further, Perry suggests, for Rogers it was precisely the imitation of sacred texts which offered a form of mediation between the fallen and the divine, a conversation which stretches through time and connects godly readers and writers, and a means of negotiating the fraught question of the hubristic emulation of God's Word and its transformative properties. Perry concludes that, for Rogers at least, 'the dream of Protestant *imitatio*' consists of the 'reciprocal relation between secular "surface" and spiritual "essence"' ' (p. 49), embodied in reformed eloquence, and thrown into relief by Sidney's *Defence of Poesy*. While predominantly falling outside the purview of this account, Perry's *Imitatio Christi* provides a highly valuable backdrop to the concerns of the period, fruitfully interrogating and reinvigorating discussion of the origins of the central Renaissance trope.

In this arena, too, Ovid's *Metamorphoses* still serves as a point of departure. Christina Wald's lucid study, *The Reformation of Romance: This Eucharist, Disguise, and Foreign Fashion in Early Modern Prose Fiction*, treats Renaissance English prose fiction's obsession with foreignness and transformation through the lens of the residual Elizabethan awareness of the doctrine of transubstantiation, reading personal and political transfigurations as modelled conceptually through the prohibited Catholic rite. Wald's monograph joins in the momentum building around disparate Tudor prose writers William Baldwin, John Lyly, George Gascoigne, and Thomas Nashe in contemporary criticism; Baldwin, Gascoigne, and Nashe's prose was also scrutinized this year in Jane Griffiths's *Diverting Authorities: Experimental Glossing Practices in Manuscript and Print* [2014], as well as other studies discussed here. Wald detects in their work an innovative convergence of growing concerns around the malleability of identity, and the suppression of Catholic practices, voiced in both overtly religious and secularized narratives, reflecting the 'cross-fertilization' of religious thought and imaginative literature in the period, and their oscillation between both 'literal and figurative adaptations of theological theorems' (p. 9). Carving out the monograph's interpretative framework in amongst Greenblatt, Helgerson, Duffy, and Maus, and the early modern recognition of subjectivity, the introduction situates its stance against the backdrop of a familiar canon, and the revelation that religion is important to the early modern 'cultural dialogue about selfhood' (p. 28) is unsurprising. However, the ensuing analysis offers a new take on Elizabethan narratives of disguise. The first chapter, 'The Eucharist in Disguise: Theology and Prose Fiction in Early Modern England', discusses Baldwin's satirical work *Beware the Cat* [1570] in the context of a detailed explication of mid-century liturgical reform, in which transubstantiation becomes for Baldwin 'a cipher of fictionality' (p. 58). Chapter 2, 'Disguise and Identity Transformation in Elizabethan Pastoral Romances', assesses the interrogation of inherent characteristics, especially as regards gender and status, in the prose fiction of the late 1580s and early 1590s: Robert Greene's *Pandosto* [1586] and *Menaphon* [1589], Philip Sidney's old and new *Arcadias* [1590 and 1593], and Thomas Lodge's *Rosalynd* [1590] and *A Margarite of America* [1596]. This somewhat hoary assortment of texts works, Wald suggests, because 'they offer a representative variety of aesthetic practices and of the social affiliations of authors and readers' (p. 11). The Elizabethan anxiety with respect to the fluidity of identity is manifested here when disguise and transformations, physical and psychological, conspire to blur certainties about social hierarchies and heredity. The final chapter, 'Foreign Fashion and the Transubstantiation of Englishness', explores the dangers to a sense of English national identity posed by the transformative potential of foreign travel and Continental sartorial styles, elided with the development of a vernacular literature in the fiction of Gascoigne, Lyly, Barnabe Riche, Greene, and Nashe. Wald's book provides a useful take on the perennial concerns of prose romance, which should prove particularly helpful to readers navigating the genre's late sixteenth-century expansion for the first time.

Meanwhile, Christine S. Lee's article 'The Meanings of Romance: Rethinking Early Modern Fiction' (*MP* 112:ii[2014] 287–311) questions the scholarly use of the term as a capacious catch-all expression to signify imaginative prose. She argues that, specifically between 1550 and 1670, the connotations of 'romance' dramatically shifted, as the word itself participated in 'social and historical upheavals of a far greater scale' (p. 288). Despite the novelty and innovativeness in the late sixteenth century of the mode to which it has recently been applied, Lee suggests that the word itself would have felt outdated, and would have referred in any case to narrative verse; Puttenham 'is one of the few to use it, and for him the word is mired in the past' (p. 288). Lee locates in its Italian cognate, *romanzo*, purportedly derived from the Greek *rhōmē*, or 'strength', an association with specifically masculine or martial themes; any nascent sense of the genre is defined by knightly deeds, and excludes pastoral and classical Greek narratives. From this negative starting point, Lee traces the meandering, polyglot history of the romance as we know it, arguing that for those unnamed modes which fell outside the narrow sixteenth-century definition of romance, 'Their lack of a fixed designation suggests a lack of cultural prestige' (p. 298). However, Lee observes, in the seventeenth century the term had become applicable to all fiction, and had acquired a new association with female authors and readers, well documented in recent scholarship. Her article is a timely reminder, amid escalating interest in the late Elizabethan permutations of the genre, that prose fiction was defined until well beyond the Tudor period by the absence of fixity, and that in addition to being concerned with transformations and flexible identities, it was itself a form in flux.

Elsewhere in the study of early modern prose, Tamsin Theresa Badcoe's article ' "As many Ciphers without an I": Self-Reflexive Violence in the Work of Thomas Nashe' (*MP* 111:iii[2014] 384–407) discusses the ways in which Nashe depicts the act of writing through a discourse of self-inflicted physical harm. Focusing on the act of writing by hand, this wide-ranging article shows Nashe engaging with the genesis of text before it reaches the printing house, as well as the new and newly damaging forms taken on by a work once it proliferates in print and is subjected to interpretation beyond the author's control. The interplay between the 'knifelike pen and the inkwell heart' (p. 394) not only lays the author open to self-laceration, but also places him at the mercy of the consuming public, whose appetite for authorial dissection and dissolution vacillates between the redemptive and the grotesque. Reaching into the basic anxieties of textual production, the article sometimes edges into the self-reflexive in its own right, as its own status as a written text is foregrounded by its rhetorical flair, and compelling psychological extrapolations from

Nashe's prose. Like Moss in *The Ovidian Vogue*, considered above, Badcoe draws on the mythical Actaeon as a figure for Nashe, destroyed by his own [Isle of] dogs, but here the parallel signifies deeper wounds than merely those sustained by Nashe's reputation. Badcoe engagingly portrays Nashe's writing as gripped with performative anxiety, and is alert to the humour and lightness of touch required when dealing with late Tudor authorial personae, but also imbues Nashe's work with a metaphysical gravitas, and unexpected grace.

Neither grace nor gravitas are qualities often associated with John Bridges' unwieldy *Defence of the Government Established in the Church of Englande for Ecclesiasticall Matters* [1587], the butt of Martin Marprelate's 'most frequently quoted joke' (p. 3), but Eric D. Vivier begins his reconsideration of this subtle work, 'John Bridges, Martin Marprelate, and the Rhetoric of Satire' (*ELR* 44:i[2014] 3–35), on a conciliatory note. In fact, Vivier argues, Bridges himself was infamous among contemporaries for his comedic rhetorical subversion of his opponents' authority; the article situates the *Defence* as an essential but neglected key to the workings of the Marprelate controversy. Characterized by slow-burning ridicule and tonal playfulness, Bridges' 'patiently deconstructive and wryly condescending prose' (p. 17) works to undermine the interpretative authority which was the linchpin of the Presbyterians' claim to their superior reading of Scripture. Vivier's article seeks to reintegrate Bridges and his deployment of these rhetorical modes into the productive recent evolution of scholarship on the Marprelate tracts. He argues that Martin took the threat Bridges posed to nonconformist authority far more seriously than has been recognized, and read and responded to the *Defence* with care, identifying a series of stylistic features, such as the use of ironic marginal notes, 'conversations with a ventriloquized interlocutor', and 'mock-earnestness' (p. 23)—often held up as innovations of the Marprelate pamphlets—in Bridges' own work. Although Martin 'repeatedly figured Bridges as a fool and a clown' (p. 21), Vivier suggests that it is precisely this vein of mockery which should alert us to Martin's wariness of Bridges' argumentative dexterity. Since it is not, itself, a satirical work, Bridges' *Defence* illuminates 'important continuities between satire and other discourses that rely upon ridicule as a rhetorical strategy' (p. 29). Crucial to this strategy is the acknowledgement of an opponent's potential to undermine one's position's legitimacy, an acknowledgement which brings with it its own form of legitimization. While gesturing towards the wider significance of the late 1580s for the development of satirical forms, Vivier emphasizes the need to read Martin's writings as embedded within a specific historical moment, and their formation as a particular response to this complex negotiation.

2. Sidney

Nandra Perry's book *Imitatio Christi: The Poetics of Piety in Early Modern England*, reviewed in the round in Section 1, contains two sections that deal with the works of Philip Sidney: a subsection of chapter 1 with the title 'The Word Made Flesh: Philip Sidney and the *Defence of Poesy*' (pp. 49–63); and a part of chapter 3 entitled 'Pamela, Charles, and the Royal "Book of Virtue"' (pp. 140–56). In the former, Perry, often in dialogue with Robert Stillman's reading of the *Defence* (*Philip Sidney and the Poetics of Renaissance Cosmopolitanism* [2008]), problematizes Sidney's peculiar vision of poetry's power to 'make[] present to fallen persons, living in fallen times and fallen places, the compelling beauty of the divine essence, which, if it is perfectly embodied in the eloquence of Christ, is also ... embedded in the natural workings of the human heart and mind' (p. 50). In the *Defence*, as Stillman highlights, the controlling metaphor for poetic imitation is the body of Lucretia, painted by a master painter who does not strive for verisimilitude, but seeks to copy 'the outward beauty of such virtue' (*Defence of Poesy*, in *Sir Philip Sidney*, ed. Katherine Duncan-Jones [1989], p. 218). Moreover, the aesthetic that this analogy proffers is designedly anti-tyrannical. Nonetheless, as Perry points out, this aesthetic is also—true to its classical roots— 'profoundly hierarchical, grounding the natural powers of poetry in the natural privileges and the naturally privileged perspectives of aristocracy'. Like the wishes of Thomas Rogers, the subject of another section of Perry's monograph, Sidney's fantasy of 'a beautiful religio-political body, shaped and sustained by good words' remains just that: a fantasy. The bodies Sidney 'strives to "chasten" ... simply won't sit pretty' (pp. 53–6). In the latter section of Perry's book, Pamela's prayer and Pamela herself (or, at least, her 'disciplined royal body') from Sidney's *New Arcadia*, famously appropriated by the *Eikon Basilike*, are employed to 'recover a Protestant genealogy for [Charles's] imitation of Christ, one that privileges the flesh not so much as a vehicle of the Incarnation or the Passion but as a visual analogue for the mediating power of language' (pp. 141–2).

There were two issues of the *Sidney Journal* in 2014. In the first, Joel M. Dodson, in 'Affirming Something: Sidney's *Defence* and the (Dis)Harmony of the Confessions' (*SidJ* 32:i[2014] 39–67), reconsiders Sidney's statement that poetry 'nothing affirms, and therefore never lieth' with respect to credal or doctrinal affirmation in the late sixteenth century. Examining Sidney's *Defence* alongside the similarly conflicted *Harmonia confessionum fidei* of 1581, Dodson elucidates 'the central role of credal confession in problematizing the coherence of English poetics' (p. 39).

Thomas Rist, in '*Astrophil and Stella* Maris: Poetic Ladies, the Virgin Mary and the Culture of Love in Reformation England' (*SidJ* 32:i[2014] 69–92), finds Sidney's sonnet sequence to be derived from a 'Platonically-inflected, Catholic cult of the saints, in which the Virgin was Queen', and 'reveals' Sidney to be a 'religiously conflicted Protestant with deep and literary Catholic sympathies'. In Rist's reading, this aspect of Sidney's sequence was recognized by, and evident in the sonnets of, Samuel Daniel, Bartholomew Griffin, Edmund Spenser, and Barnabe Barnes (p. 69).

Kathryn C. Fore's article, 'Reading and Repentance on the Ister Bank' (*SidJ* 32:i[2014] 93–110), situates the 'Ister Bank' eclogue from Book III of the *Arcadia* within 'competing Calvinist readings of Israel's monarchy' as it is represented in 1 Samuel and Isaiah. Fore reads the eclogue as a peculiarly English response—founded on readings of Calvin's early writings—to the tyrannomachy advocated by the author of *Vindiciae Contra Tyrannos* [1579] and associated with Sidney's mentor, Hubert Languet. In Fore's account, contrary to the putative position of these Continental thinkers, English Calvinists saw the biblical narrative as supporting 'a form of political protest-by-declaration of repentance' (p. 93).

Roger Kuin, in 'This B̶o̶o̶ Writing: A Defence of Sidney's Other Defence' (*SidJ* 32:i[2014] 111–21), uses French 'theory', which he playfully acknowledges might have 'fallen into disuse', to reconsider Sidney's neglected 'Defence of the Earl of Leicester' (p. 111). In defending his uncle's 'name'— conceived here as that which denotes both the individual and his reputation, his honour—Sidney implicitly criticizes himself and removes himself from the category of 'Elizabeth's new men' (p. 116) within which he is so keen to cement Leicester; unlike Leicester, Sidney is neither a Dudley nor a nobleman. Kuin attributes the unease that this text provokes in Sidney scholars to their disavowal of the author it represents, 'a Sidney who in this text exists, if at all, only as a ghost enmeshed in the cobwebs of a crossed text, as a nameless name writing itself in *différance*, deferring the presence of which we were so fond' (p. 120).

In the second issue of the *Sidney Journal* for 2014, Jean R. Brink, in 'Sidney's *A Letter to Queen Elizabeth*: Text and Context' (*SidJ* 32:ii[2014] 1–15), building on the work of Peter Beal and Roger Kuin, reviews the evidence relating to Sidney's *A Letter to Queen Elizabeth*. Brink raises important questions of terminology and interpretation around the so-called scribal publication of the *Letter*. In Brink's view, if there were two versions of *A Letter to Queen Elizabeth*, 'one that was actually presented to the queen and another [represented by the extant copies] that was intended for propaganda purposes and possibly circulated by Leicester and Walsingham', then the less than tactful tone of the extant versions could be explained (p. 7). Such considerations alter what may or may not be safely concluded about the *Letter* and Sidney's relations with Elizabeth.

Brad Tuggle, in 'Riding and Writing: Equine Poetics in Renaissance English Horsemanship Manuals and the Writings of Sir Philip Sidney' (*SidJ* 32:ii[2014] 17–37), highlights the dangers implicit in Sidney's analogy between horseriding and poetics. In Tuggle's lively article, 'the free wills of readers are dangerous for poets if they want interpretive control over their texts'. The poet's anxiety is symbolized by the similarities in orthography and pronunciation between the words *riders* and *readers*. Sidney's puns 'reveal a repressed anxiety about the possible usurpation of the poets' power by their readers' (p. 18).

Roger Kuin, in the first of two notes in this issue, 'Borne High in the Low Countries: Philip Sidney's Cavalry Banner' (*SidJ* 32:ii[2014] 65–72), takes Thomas Lant's engravings of Sir Philip Sidney's funeral procession, or, more specifically, the 'Guidon trayled' in front of the lieutenant of Sidney's cavalry, as his subject. A guidon is a small standard fixed to a lance, and Sidney's bears an image of a fish. Kuin offers a detailed analysis of this *impresa*, symbolic image, depicting a real fish known as an *uranoscopus* ('heaven-gazer'). The significance of this emblem relates, in part, to its origin in a publication of Joachim Camerarius Jr. (1534–98), a physician from Nuremberg, who, along with his father Joachim Sr. and his two brothers Philipp and Ludwig, were close friends of Sidney's mentor Hubert Languet.

The second note, Dana F. Sutton's 'Sir Philip Sidney and the Crown of Poland' (*SidJ* 32:ii[2014] 73–83), revolves around the colourful character Adalbert Łaski, voivode of Siradia, an obscure Polish nobleman who was lavishly entertained on his visit to England in 1583. Though he was a nephew of Jan Łaski the Younger (1499–1560), 'a Reforming theologian who had been personally selected by Archbishop Cranmer to preside over the congregation of Continental Protestant refugees at London during the reign of Edward VI' (p. 73), there are few suggestions why he should have received the sumptuous and extravagant entertainments laid on by the University of Oxford at the government's expense. Sutton's admirable research reveals a possible connection between these events and a 'rumored initiative to place Sidney on the Polish throne' (p. 80). No matter how 'quixotic, if not downright crackpot, [an] ambition' this was, Sutton is persuasive in making the case for its being a plausible explanation for the curious events of 1583 (p. 82).

Julianne Werlin, in an article in *Studies in English Literature, 1500–1900*, 'Providence and Perspective in Philip Sidney's *Old Arcadia*' (*SEL* 54:i[2014] 25–40), reads Sidney's *Old Arcadia* as an attempt to 'to delineate the workings of providence' as they were set out by Philippe Duplessis-Mornay, Huguenot theologian and polemicist, in his *Trewness of the Christian Religion* (published in French in 1581). Contrary to his own suggestion that people who 'desire to haue it proued to them by apparant reasons, that there is a Prouidence which ruleth the world . . . should be answered by a whippe or a hangman, and not by a Philosopher' (*A Woorke concerning the Trewnesse of the Christian Religion*, trans. Philip Sidney and Arthur Golding [1587]), Duplessis-Mornay answered such doubters 'in the manner of a philosopher'. Sidney, using the form of his prose romance, answered them as a poet (p. 25).

Ethan Guagliardo, in 'The Poet, the Skeptic, His Witches, and Their Queen: Political Theology and Poetic Charms in Sidney's *Defence*' (*ELH* 81:iii[2014] 733–56), uses the context of Queen Elizabeth's suppression of idolatry—in part to 'prove[] herself to be an agent of God' (p. 733)—to align Sidney's criticism of prophetic poetry as an illusion with the sceptical views of contemporary Protestants such as Reginald Scot, who tried 'to disenchant the idols and alleviate the iconophobic hysteria destabilizing the nation' (p. 735). Yet, unlike Scot and the sceptics, Sidney embraces the imaginative power of the poetic charm, 'investing the autonomous ordering power of the human mind—not a supernatural order of spirits—with legislative authority in ethical and political matters' (p. 745).

Christopher Baker, in 'Sidney, Religious Syncretism, and *Henry VIII*' (*SN* 86:i[2014] 17–36), shows Shakespeare's indebtedness to Sidney's prose romance *The Arcadia*, going well beyond what others have noted. Reginald Foakes saw the influence of Sidney's *Arcadia* in Wolsey's farewell speech (*King Henry VIII*, 3rd edn. [1957]), but Baker discovers aspects of the same passage that draw upon the final poem of Sidney's *Certain Sonnets*. Baker's most interesting contributions arise from his sensitivity to characterization, such as his observation that a Sidneian context is a useful 'vantage from which to examine . . . the characterization of the queen and the cardinal, which, in their markedly syncretic religious texture, appropriate an outlook similar to

Sidney's, one that remains notably inclusive despite his posthumous fame as a "Calvinist martyr" ' (p. 17).

Robert E. Stillman's article, 'Philip Sidney and the Catholics: The Turn from Confessionalism in Early Modern Studies' (*MP* 112:i[2014] 97–129), is a welcome correction of previous critical assessments of Sidney's piety that have judged him to be either a Calvinist or a crypto-Catholic. Building on his own extensive work on Sidney's place among a cosmopolitan group of Philippists, followers of the great Reformation theologian Philip Melanchthon, Stillman offers a detailed study of Sidney's anticonfessionalism that is thoroughly contextualized within the poet's late sixteenth-century milieu. As Stillman also argues very effectively, the 'religious turn in early modern studies does not require a turn toward confessional identification' (p. 129).

Monika Fludernik, in 'Collective Minds in Fact and Fiction: Intermental Thought and Group Consciousness in Early Modern Narrative' (*PoT* 35:iv[2014] 689–730), examines to what extent collective minds can be traced in two early modern narratives: Sir Philip Sidney's *The Old Arcadia* and Raphael Holinshed's *Chronicles*. Drawing on ideas from cognitive narratology, Fludernik discusses how 'collectivity' and 'intermentality' are represented in the texts' portrayals of riots, offering some conclusions as to how a collective mind is represented, and what insights this gives into subversive thought. An interesting aspect of this study is its use of the riots in *The Old Arcadia* to problematize Greenblatt's containment thesis: for Greenblatt, this literary form, 'as a primary expression of Renaissance power, helps contain "the radical doubts it continually provokes" '; but, in this analysis, 'popular dissent and riot in *The Old Arcadia* do have a reasonable chance of overthrowing the government' (p. 715).

Arthur F. Kinney's note for *Connotations: A Journal for Critical Debate*, 'A Note on Sir Philip Sidney's Art of Blending' (*Connotations* 24:i[2014] 22–6), suggests the art of blending, a cognitive process defined by Gilles Fauconnier and Mark Turner in *The Way We Think: Conceptual Blending and the Mind's Hidden Complexities* [2002], as the means by which readers come to understand certain aspects of literary texts. Kinney cites the example of the character Musidorus, descriptions of whom 'join the epic to the pastoral in a way that requires the reader to redefine the apparent genre to which this novel subscribes'. For Kinney, 'We cannot proceed in our reading without an awareness that Musidorus will be changed by and also shaped by both [epic and pastoral] locales which will remain blended in him' (p. 24).

3. Spenser

Garrett Sullivan's essay, 'Vampirism in the Bower of Bliss' (in Bronfen and Neumeier, eds., *Gothic Renaissance: A Reassessment*, pp. 167–79), discusses the 'critical tradition relating Book 2 of *The Faerie Queene* to the Gothic through the comparison of Acrasia to a vampire', and substantiates and develops the implications of this comparison (p. 167). Employing Kristeva's concept of abjection, Sullivan sees Acrasia as a representation of 'that which is "thrown off" in order to consolidate a "coherent and independent" identity reappearing as a threat to identity'; Acrasia's 'actions have led to Verdant's loss of identity'. Sullivan argues that 'Verdant's self-loss can be attributed to what Spenser sees as the contradiction at the heart of humanness' (p. 168).

Abigail Scherer's essay, 'The "Sweet Toyle" of Blissful Bowers: Arresting Idleness in the English Renaissance' (in Fludernik and Nandi, eds., *Idleness, Indolence and Leisure in English Literature*, pp. 60–85), discusses the tension between the 'moralist's emphasis on virtuous activity and the poet's call to savour the imagination's more sedentary sowings' (p. 60). With reference to the thoughts of Fink, Binswanger, and Agamben on 'the world of play, poetic transcendence, and the poetic stanza as a possessable space', respectively, Scherer 'illumine[s] our understanding of the bower's charismatic qualities' (p. 63).

One chapter in Dennis Austin Britton's book *Becoming Christian: Race, Reformation, and Early Modern English Romance*—'Ovidian Baptism in Book 2 of *The Faerie Queene*' (pp. 59–90)—looks at Spenser. Britton explores an unexplored aspect of the Nymph's well episode in Book II: 'the racial implications of Spenser's treatment of theological controversies'. The Church of England encouraged English Protestants 'to conceive of Christianity as a racial identity, a hereditary or blood trait passed from parents to children'. Book II 'reflects this outlook ... rejecting the infidel-conversion motif and aligning religious identity with concepts of race that were gaining influence in Reformation England' (p. 59).

Patricia Palmer's *The Severed Head and the Grafted Tongue: Literature, Translation and Violence in Early Modern Ireland* contains a chapter, 'Defaced: Allegory, Violence and Romance Recognition in *The Faerie Queene*' (pp. 66–92), in which Book V is considered in the light of Emmanuel Levinas's ideas about the Other, the face, and ethical resistance (*Totality and Infinity* [1969]). With respect to these concepts, Palmer focuses on 'the refusal of recognition' at the centre of what she terms 'colonial romance', a form for which Spenser's Artegall is, in this reading, a noteworthy symbol. The face is the 'site of romance recognition and the locus, for Levinas, of ethical responsibility' (p. 10); Artegall's violent actions in the land of Eirena 'follow the logic ... of defacement' (p. 75). In what is an extensively historicized reading, Palmer sees the 'metaphysical absolutes of allegory ... challenged by the irreducible materiality of their historical analogues': 'the face ... mounts its lonely struggle against the severed head, the marker of unbounded violence' (p. 10).

Stewart Mottram's essay, 'Spenser's Dutch Uncles: The Family of Love and the Four Translations of *A Theatre for Worldlings*' (in Pérez Fernández and Wilson-Lee, eds., *Translation and the Book Trade in Early Modern Europe*, pp. 164–84), restores Spenser's verse translations to 'the commentary they were originally intended to illustrate', as part of the collection of poems, prose commentary, and woodcut illustrations that is *A Theatre for Worldlings*. As well as exploring the four translations 'in relation to their investment in the mythical teachings of the Family of Love', Mottram suggests ways that Familist ideas may have influenced *The Ruines of Time*, and how Spenser's 'treatment of ruin' was affected by Jan van der Noot's response to the same theme in the four *Theatre* volumes (pp. 164–5).

There were two articles published in *Modern Philology* in 2013 that require attention here. The first, Abraham Stoll's 'Spenser's Allegorical Conscience' (*MP* 111:ii[2013] 181–204), highlights the significance of conscience to the 'mechanisms of individual salvation and the politics of public justice' in Books I and V of *The Faerie Queene*. Dividing his article into two parts covering Books I and V respectively, Stoll shows that, in early modern England, 'the Protestant conscience slips into an increasingly psychological mode and that this inward disorder threatens to become an explosive political force' (p. 181). Joe Moshenska, in 'The Forgotten Youth of Allegory: Figures of Old Age in *The Faerie Queene*' (*MP* 110:iii[2013] 389–414), examines old age in Spenser's allegory and finds it to be a 'strategy through which allegorical constriction occurs': old age in allegory is 'a predicate'; it is not 'a transitory or incidental characteristic but an essential and unchanging aspect of the figure in question' (pp. 392, 389–90). With particular reference to female old age, Moshenska highlights those moments when Spenser 'grants its elderly allegorical figures an implicit personal history', only to suppress it: the poem seems to 'guiltily draw[] attention to the very brutality of its own allegorical grasp' (p. 392).

A further article on Spenser appeared in *Modern Philology* in 2014. Andrew Wadoski's 'Spenser, Tasso, and the Ethics of Allegory' (*MP* 111:iii[2014] 365–83) considers the influence of Torquato Tasso's *La Gerusalemme liberata* [1581] on Spenser. Tasso's *Liberata* teaches Spenser 'to think of allegory ... as an ethical act caught up in the ambiguities that attend all social praxis' (p. 365). But, rather than attempt 'to organize and make coherent the fractious worlds of confessional and political difference', as Tasso does, Spenser gives us an allegory that 'is just as corrosive as the error it struggles to correct' (p. 366).

There were two articles on Spenser in *English Literary Renaissance* this year. Galena Hashhozheva's 'The Christian Defense Against Classical Skepticism in Spenser's Legend of Holiness' (*ELR* 44:ii[2014] 193–220), builds on James Nohrnberg's work on Book I of *The Faerie Queene* (*The Analogy of The Faerie Queene* [1976]). In doing so, Hashhozheva rejects the thesis of Harold Skulsky—'Spenser's Despair Episode and the Theology of Doubt' (*MP* 78:iii[1981] 227–42)—in which 'Spenser renounces trust and certainty because "there is ... no infallible defense against such imposture" as that of Duessa or Archimago'. Hashhozheva prefers the more optimistic analysis of Nohrnberg, who 'sees in Book I an extended dramatization of "relations of trust and promise" and a concern with the establishment of the "psychological archetypes" of religious faith'. As such, in this reading—in which the critic recontextualizes *The Faerie Queene* in the scholarship of classical Scepticism and Christian theology (patristic and Reformation)—'Spenser ... places the dignity of a generous trust and a steadfast assurance above the consequences that may arise from their fallibility' (pp. 198–9). Giulio Pertile's article in the same volume, ' "And all his sences stound": The Physiology of Stupefaction in Spenser's *Faerie Queene*' (*ELR* 44:iii[2014] 420–51), examines the moments in Books I and II that Spenser calls 'stounds', when a character is said to be 'in a stound' or 'in an astonishment'. Pertile argues that the stound offers 'a crucial way of mediating between the narrative's demand for motion and change, and an allegory's need for static imagery and meaning'; the stound achieves this 'through its activation of the "spirits," corporeal agents that mediate between body and soul' (p. 420). Pertile makes interesting use of John Donne's 'The Extasie', where the spirits 'bolster [Donne's] argument that the two lovers ought not to refuse their bodies completely in favor of the soul'; 'by inducing Guyon's faint [at the end of Book II, canto vii] the spirits serve a similar (though non-erotic) purpose in Spenser's *Faerie Queene*' (p. 433).

In the first of three articles on Spenser in *Studies in English Literature, 1500–1900*—'Spenser's Poetics of "Transfixion" in the Allegory of Chastity' (*SEL* 54:i[2014] 41–58)—Michael Slater examines Amoret's torture at the hands of Busirane in Book III of *The Faerie Queene*, and builds on previous scholarship (most notably, Gordon Teskey in *Allegory and Violence* [1996]) that regards such violence 'as itself a figure for Spenser's allegory'. Noting that other critics have seen in this episode 'a sexual violence that amounts to rape', Slater situates his argument within this tradition, developing a reading based on 'the figure of "transfixion"—a term that can certainly encompass rape but that does not remain strictly confined to that significance—that exposes the violence implicit in allegory' (pp. 42–3). In this reading, Amoret's transfixion reveals 'the extent to which the allegorical "fixing over"—making a particular body the substance of an abstract concept or form—is also a violent piercing' (p. 48). Joshua Phillips, in his article, 'Monasticism and Idleness in Spenser's Late Poetry' (*SEL* 54:i[2014] 59–79), sees Spenser—particularly in *Colin Clouts Come Home Againe* and Book VI of *The Faerie Queene*—'react[ing] against a Tudor discourse of industry and profit, re-creating in his late poems an *otium honestum*, a state that was not sloth or simply a literary pose or a precise equivalent of contemplation'. For Phillips, Spenser adopts 'idleness as a positive political, religious, and cultural gesture made in opposition to the dominant work ideologies of what Spenser's friend Gabriel Harvey called "an Age of Pollicy, and ... a world of Industry" [*The Works of Gabriel Harvey, D.C.L.*, ed. Alexander B. Grosart [1884], 1:222]' (p. 60). James S. Lambert's article, 'Spenser's *Epithalamion* and the Protestant Expression of Joy' (*SEL* 54:i[2014] 81–103), demonstrates how 'the theological realities of religious and philosophical joy in Spenser's England can yield new insights into how [*Epithalamion*] functions culturally, religiously, and structurally' (p. 82). More particularly, for Lambert, Spenser's *Epithalamion*, as well as reflecting 'communal joy' in its narration of a public celebration of marriage, suggests 'a more private, secret joy that remains ineffable', before, finally, 'bestowing a kind of blessedness, or even grace, upon the listener, much like the practice of reciting the Psalms itself was supposed to do' (pp. 82–3).

The first of two articles on Spenser in *Studies in Philology*—Gillian Hubbard's 'Stoics, Epicureans, and the "Sound Sincerity of the Gospel" in Book 2 of Edmund Spenser's *The Faerie Queene*' (*SIP* 111:ii[2014] 225–54)—finds Spenser, particularly in Sir Guyon's fight with Huddibras and Sansloy in Book II, concerned with a contemporary fight for access to the teaching of the Scriptures: 'the ethical teaching of the church as represented by the model of Christ and the evangelists of the Word' (p. 227). As such, Spenser is in concord with the 'positions ... on preaching and the recruitment and preparation of a preaching clergy taken by Edmund Grindal and Edwin Sandys' (p. 228). Hubbard examines Spenser's presentation of the Aristotelian mean in Book II—in which the poet draws on Platonic and Stoic ideas of temperance—and finds that Spenser overlays the 'Aristotelian perspective' with 'another perspective that surpasses it': 'one more consonant with the Reformed branch of Protestant theology' (pp. 245, 227). Hubbard suggests that, in Spenser's allegory, Guyon's 'righteous zeal to destroy the Bower of Bliss, as well as being 'a straightforward reflection of Protestant reversal of idolatrous practice', may have 'a more contemporary edge ... if it concerns not just Epicurean enervation in general but a self-indulgence that threatens the church' (p. 251). Timothy Duffy's article, ' "The Light of Simple Veritie": Mapping out Spenser's Cosmography in "The Ruines of Time" ' (*SIP* 111:iv[2014] 738–56), considers *The Ruines of Time* alongside William Camden's *Britannia*, and notes the textual mapping evident in both. Duffy tracks the influence of an international community of mapmakers—including the Familists Abraham Ortelius and Jan Van der Noot—on these works, highlighting Camden's and Spenser's debts to this community's 'model for cosmographic work that highlighted spiritual and irenic interests alongside the technical practice of representing space' (p. 738). As Duffy shows, 'Spenser does not translate the act of mapping into poetry; instead, he attempts actually to map with poetry' (p. 743).

There were three articles in *English Literary History* that dealt with Spenser. J.K. Barret's 'Vacant Time in *The Faerie Queene*' (*ELH* 81:i[2014] 1–27) examines Book V, with particular focus on the episode in which Artegall is held in captivity by Radigund and forced to spin flax. In an effort to help Artegall, her beloved, meet his sworn appointment with her, Britomart attempts (without success) to recalculate time. This raises two questions for Barret: 'Why might Spenser provide us such access to a (failed) temporal experiment intended to redress a thwarted schedule? How might we understand this window onto the experience of the passage of time?' (p. 2). Barret notes that 'Britomart's experiment ... calls into question the episode's underlying assumption that time can be carefully plotted, planned and "assynde" [V.vi.3.6]'; and Artegall's lateness is, as one would expect, morally charged: 'going off course results in shameful spinning' (p. 3). Nonetheless, more unexpectedly, Barret manages to 'recover [in Britomart's failed experiment] a recurrent concern about opportunity in *The Faerie Queene* that suggests an embrace of contingency and an engagement with time that operates outside of a providential scheme'. Indeed, Barret goes on to suggest that literature in general 'displaces [to some degree] the notion that time is or can be neatly mapped' (pp. 4–5). Thomas Ward, in his article 'Spenser's Irish Hurrub' (*ELH* 81:iii[2014] 757–86), compares Spenser's *Epithalamion, Colin Clouts Come Home Againe*, and *View of the Present State of Ireland* with respect to their representations of the sound coming from inside and outside; that is, inside and outside the bedchamber, inside and outside England, and inside and outside the Pale. Ward suggests, with reference to a broad range of Spenser's works, including *The Faerie Queene*, that 'the sound of the inside is something the listeners are never in danger of actually having to hear with their corporeal ears, which are too occupied with listening to the clamor from outside' (p. 760). Benedict Robinson's article, 'Disgust c.1600' (*ELH* 81:ii[2014] 553–83), is part of his 'larger project titled "Inventing Emotion," which argues that the seventeenth century elaborated a new concept of emotion that in many ways put pressure on received theories of the passions. In its largest aspect this entailed a shift from an understanding of the passions as forms of thinking with an associated bodily expression to one in which they are primarily bodily events whose relation to thought has become unclear' (p. 555). Spenser's place in this project is as a formative figure, especially for the likes of Ben Jonson. Spenser's legacy is rather equivocal in Robinson's reading, however: on the one hand, Book II of *The Faerie Queene*, in its representation of Duessa, posits a poetics of beauty-as-self-control in which 'bodily hygienics is founded on excretion, in which all that is "fowle and wast" is "close conuaid" by "secret wayes" out the "back-gate" and "throwne out priuily,"' [II.9.32]' (p. 570); but, on the other hand, Book I conceives a 'poetics of ugliness' in which 'Arthur ... strips Duessa to discover "A loathly, wrinckled hag" [I.viii.46]'; 'an apotheosis of male sexual disgust is made to serve a moment of self-recognition: Redcross discovers in Duessa's "secret filth" the history of his own misguided attachments [I.viii.46]' (pp. 569–70).

Drew J. Scheler's article in *Rhetorica: A Journal of the History of Rhetoric*, 'Equitable Poetics and the State of Conflict in Edmund Spenser's *Two Cantos of Mutabilitie*' (*Rhetorica* 32:iv[2014] 362–85) sees Spenser drawing on the tradition of rhetorical argument (including Cicero, Rudolph Agricola, and Philip Sidney) to dramatize the process by which a conflict between general law and particular case can be brought to equitable judgement; 'Spenser ... articulates a poetics that would provisionally stabilize mutability of lived experience for readers, guiding their decisions and actions when moral ideals fall short'; the deliberative context of Spenser's fiction is a site in which 'Extreme conflict can, paradoxically, provoke a certain moral consensus' (pp. 376, 362).

Brenna K. Heffner's article, 'Edmund Spenser's Married Chastity: Ovid, Feminist Coding, and Rhetorical Androgyny in Book III of *The Faerie Queene*' (*LATCH* 7[2014] 112–46), jumps off from Elizabeth's proclamation at Tilbury that she had 'the body ... of a weak and feeble woman; but ... the heart and stomach of a king'. As an example of what Heffner terms 'rhetorical androgyny', Elizabeth's statement provides the basis for a reading of Book III of *The Faerie Queene* in which Spenser, 'rather than asserting his own physical body as a meld of the masculine and feminine ... channels male forms of authority and female forms of communication in an effort to speak to his Early Modern aristocratic female readers'. Spenser's use of Ovid's *Metamorphoses* in Book III, the Legend of Britomart, Knight of Chastity, 'asserts [his] authority to both speak on matters of desire and to moralize on the nature of desire'; he is also able to utilize 'feminist coding strategies designed to allow him to speak to women in ways that only women would notice and understand'—'a desired position for any poet writing under the reign of Elizabeth I' (p. 113).

Rémi Vuillemin, in '"The musical confusion of hounds and echoes in conjunction": Intertextual Friction in Elizabethan Rewritings of the Myth of Actæon' (*Ranam* 47[2014] 175–88), also deals with the subject of Ovidian reception. Vuillemin qualifies Thomas M. Greene's distinction between 'eclectic' and 'heuristic' literary imitations (*The Light in Troy* [1982]). Greene (pp. 40–1) distinguishes between the imitations that combine disparate literary elements that 'only take significance in the new way in which they are used' and the imitations which advertise 'their derivation from the subtexts they carry with them, but having done that, proceed to distance themselves from the subtexts and force us to recognize the poetic distance traversed ... in the language, in sensibility, in cultural context, in world view, and in moral style'. Vuillemin problematizes the process of determining into which of Greene's categories an act of imitation should be placed, and attributes the difficulty of making such judgements to what he terms 'friction': a result of 'the process through which mismatched [literary allusions] are put together creatively' (pp. 175–6). Vuillemin goes on to discuss different interpretations of Spenser's uses of the Myth of Actæon in the *Mutabilitie Cantos*, demonstrating that Greene's theory is wholly appropriate for characterizing Spenser's heuristic imitation of Ovid; other authors' uses of Ovid—such as Drayton's 'Amour 35'—are shown to be less easily categorized using Greene's method.

David Hadbawnik's article, 'The Chaucer-FUNCTION: Spenser's Language Lessons in *The Shepheardes Calender* (*Upstart* [2014] 39 paras.), suggests that Spenser, in *The Shepheardes Calender*, 'takes advantage of lessons learned from Richard Mulcaster and the example of Chaucer to situate himself as a poet furthering the project of language formation in English'. This is achieved with what Hadbawnik calls the 'Chaucer-function'. The Chaucer-function is 'a set of authorial effects built into the poem, [comprising] two components: first, an active process of basing authorship on a "collection of authors" who (using Mulcaster's ideas about language "enfranchisement") bring various linguistic backgrounds into play within a text, and the subsequent, interrelated effect of attribution based on the incorporation of words from those backgrounds into poetic diction' (para. 1). For Hadbawnik, this function 'reveals that the most important author in the text may not even be the anonymous and ephemeral "New Poet," but the various and humble new originals, always singing "in place of" or "like," on whom Spenser's authorial identity is eventually based, and from whom his linguistic ingenuity is ultimately derived' (para. 39).

This year's volume of *Spenser Studies* begins with David Lee Miller's Kathleen Williams Lecture, which is entitled 'The Chastity of Allegory' (*SSt* 29[2014] 1–20). With reference to the work of Maureen Quilligan (*Milton's Spenser* [1983]), Harry Berger Jr. (*Revisionary Play: Studies in the Spenserian Dynamics* [1988]), and Teresa de Lauretis (*Technologies of Gender* [1987]), Miller examines the 'technologies of desire' in Spenser's Legend of Chastity in Book III of *The Faerie Queene*. Miller's focus is on the 'representational apparatuses ... that evoke erotic feeling and shape it as experience', highlighting the 'harm' of 'unchaste discourse'. Spenser's poem offers both a 'utopian fantasy of untrammeled freedom in erotic address' and a 'visionary quest for the *ungesehenmachen* ("making-unhappened") of the amorous discourses dominant in Elizabethan literature, staged as a re-virgination of the culture's erotic imagination'. Beyond the Legend of Chastity, Spenser displays similar concerns in *Amoretti* and *Epithalamion* and the *Faerie Queene* of 1596 (p. 1).

David J. Baker's article, 'Britain Redux' (*SSt* 29[2014] 21–36), asks what influence the development, around the beginning of the twenty-first century, of the 'New British History' had on Spenser studies. Baker finds that, though many advances in scholars' understanding of Spenser were made by this approach, an impasse was reached due to problems of translation and of intercultural exchange.

Talya Meyers's article, 'Saracens in Faeryland' (*SSt* 29[2014] 37–61), focuses on the literary heritage that informs Spenser's Saracens in *The Faerie Queene*, rather than placing them in allegorical or referential contexts, as most other critics do. For Meyers, Spenser's allusions to the death of Turnus from the *Aeneid* offer a new perspective on the narrative organization of Spenser's poem.

Robert Lanier Reid, in his article, 'Sansloy's Double Meaning and the Mystic Design of Spenser's Legend of Holiness' (*SSt* 29[2014] 63–74), examines the significance of the Sans-brothers' absence from the second half of the Legend of Holiness, and interrogates the 'doctrinal import of foy-loy-joy (then again loy)' (p. 63). Whereas Sansfoy's faithlessness and Sansjoy's joylessness are transparent, Reid's decoding of Sansloy offers a useful illumination of Spenser's Christian-Platonic allegory.

Katharine Cleland, in 'English National Identity and the Reformation Problem of Clandestine Marriage in Spenser's *Faerie Queene*, Book I' (*SSt* 29[2014] 75–103), highlights how Roman canon law's sanctioning of clandestine marriage clashed with the Reformed English practice of public uniform marriages. Spenser echoes the Reformed perspective in his portrayal of Redcrosse's union with Duessa, but, as Cleland notes, Spenser's position in Book I is contrary to his portrayal of clandestine marriage in later parts of the poem.

Russ Leo, in his article, 'Medievalism without Nostalgia: Guyon's Swoon and the English Reformation *Descensus ad Inferos*' (*SSt* 29[2014] 105–47), reads the Cave of Mammon episode in *The Faerie Queene* as a novel construal of Christ's descent into hell, often termed the Harrowing of Hell. Although Leo highlights Spenser's recovery of important medieval interpretations of the *descensus*, he sees Spenser as a theological experimenter—reviving indigenous English resources—not as a poet nostalgic for a lost past.

Jerrod Rosenbaum's article, 'Spenser's Merlin Rehabilitated' (*SSt* 29[2014] 149–78), is dedicated to the memory of Darryl James Gless, Distinguished Professor of Renaissance Studies in the Department of English and Comparative Literature at the University of North Carolina, who died on 10 June 2014. Gless's *Interpretation and Theology in Spenser* [1994] was a classic in the field of Spenser studies. Rosenbaum argues that, in Book III, canto iii of *The Faerie Queene*, Merlin's demonic sorcery and position as agent of divine Providence are irreconcilable, and that attempts by other critics to accommodate them in a single figure have been misconceived. Rosenbaum sees Spenser seeking to rehabilitate the sorcerer in line with Protestant beliefs in order that Merlin can participate in the genealogical encomium for Elizabeth, godly magistrate.

Kelly Lehtonen, in 'The Abjection of Malbecco: Forgotten Identity in Spenser's Legend of Chastity' (*SSt* 29[2014] 179–96), suggests that Malbecco's transformation into the abstract concept of 'Gelosy' can be read in terms of the Kristevan abject. Malbecco's abjection—a 'cuckolded old miser ' with an identity crisis—represents 'jealous possession as a vicious, horrifying pathology of Chastity that ruthlessly erodes its sufferer's humanity, yet sustains its sufferer in a hellish state of self-absorption' (p. 179).

Robert W. Tate's article, 'Haunted by Beautified Beauty: Tracking the Images of Spenser's Florimell(s)' (*SSt* 29[2014] 197–218), considers True and False Florimell with a view to mapping an 'ethics of beauty' within the pedagogy of *The Faerie Queene*. Tate places the Florimells' loci among the poem's 'figures of semblance'; and, drawing on Wittgenstein's concept of 'seeing something as something', interrogates the concepts of genuine beauty and derivative beauty. With further theoretical support from Jung, Tate reads False Florimell as an 'anima-ideal': 'a social construct of femininity that men project from within their unconscious upon women' (pp. 197–8).

Jeffrey B. Griswold, in 'Allegorical Consent: *The Faerie Queene* and the Politics of Erotic Subjection' (*SSt* 29[2014] 219–37), studies Spenser's use of erotic subjection as a metaphor for the relationship between conquest and consent. In Book V of *The Faerie Queene*, where Radigund forces Artegall to do women's work while wearing women's clothing, Spenser, in Griswold's reading, shows that 'compliance is not loyalty and violence cannot elicit love' (p. 219).

Matthew Harrison, in 'The Rude Poet Presents Himself: Breton, Spenser, and Bad Poetry' (*SSt* 29[2014] 239–62), looks at the vocabulary of self-deprecation in Edmund Spenser's and Nicholas Breton's poetry, and elucidates the range of functions that it has. For Spenser, 'terms like "rude," "baseness," "rough," and "dischorde" [can be used] to wrestle with style but also poetic identity and purpose: tracing relationships among his archaic diction and colloquial forms, his interpretive difficulty, his plainspoken didacticism, and his sense of the value of poetry' (p. 239). Harrison concludes with a list of the many early readers who sought to revise Spenser's poetry, evidence that 'Spenser's self-deprecation allows for revision and response' (p. 258).

Ruth Kaplan, in 'The Problem of Pity in Spenser's *Ruines of Time* and *Amoretti*' (*SSt* 29[2014] 263–94), interrogates the moral and hermeneutic significance of these works. For Kaplan, the *Ruines of Time* and the *Amoretti* 'stage' a conflict between the Platonic and the (Renaissance interpretation of) Aristotelian understandings of pity as a response to tragedy: a dispute between pity conceived as the revolt of the body against the rule of reason and pity understood as a useful reminder of human mortality.

Jean R. Brink, in her article, 'Publishing Spenser's *View of the Present State of Ireland*: From Matthew Lownes and Thomas Man (1598) to James Ware (1633)' (*SSt* 29[2014] 295–311), offers an explanation for the hiatus between the entry of the *View of the Present State of Ireland* in the Stationers' Register on 14 April 1598 to Matthew Lownes and its belated publication in 1633 by James Ware. Brink shows that MS Bodleian Rawlinson B.478 is linked to the entry in the Stationers' Register, and suggests that this manuscript belonged to Thomas Man, Lownes's father-in-law. If the manuscript remained in the Man family's possession until it was given to Ware, Lownes may never have owned a manuscript of the *View*. Hence, the *View*'s absence from early seventeenth-century folios is explained.

The 'Gleanings' section of *Spenser Studies* contains two entries. Gillian Hubbard, in 'The Folly of Proverbs and the Mammon of Book II of *The Faerie Queene*' (*SSt* 29[2014] 315–24), highlights Spenser's use of the episode from Proverbs 9:13–18 in which a young man, tempted by a woman at the door of her house, eats secret bread and drinks stolen water. In Book II of *The Faerie Queene*, Spenser's Mammon recalls the foolish woman, and Guyon the young man. Whereas in Proverbs Folly is opposed to Wisdom, in *The Faerie Queene* Mammon and Acrasia 'represent alternative antitheses' to Alma (p. 315). Hubbard shows how a close examination of these parallels can uncover the theological depths of this episode from Book II. Rodney Stenning Edgecombe, in 'The Meaning of "Imply" in *The Faerie Queene* III.vi.34' (*SSt* 29[2014] 325–6), suggests that, at this point in his poem, Spenser 'devised a once-off inkhorn coinage of "imply = "fill" . . . basing it upon the Latin verb "implere" '. This devising helps redefine 'imply' to stand for both 'enclose' and 'fill'. As such, as Edgecombe notes, in the Garden of Adonis, 'the plants enclose their own moisture, a fact that enables them to "fill" or irrigate themselves' (pp. 325–6).

There were three contributions of particular significance in *Notes and Queries* this year. Frank Ardolino, in 'Thomas Watson, Shadow Poet of Edmund Spenser' (*N&Q* 61[2014] 225–9), highlights the literary relationship between Watson and Spenser, 'as demonstrated primarily by their public exchange of praise, their Petrarchan sonnet style, the championing of Sir Philip Sidney and Lord Admiral Charles Howard, and . . . by their use of Empedocles'. Ardolino characterizes their association as 'a deliberate literary interaction', marked by 'an alternating pattern of praise of works already published, anticipation of future works, and shared literary styles and methods' (p. 226). David Lee Miller, in 'A Neglected Source for the Mordant and Amavia Episode in *The Faerie Queene*' (*N&Q* 61[2014] 229–31), notes that 'Spenser develops the allegory of this episode directly from Beza's Geneva glosses to Romans chapters 5–7'; Miller shows that 'Recognizing this source enables us to clarify certain points in the allegory' (p. 229). James Doelman's note, 'A Further Note on the Epitaphs in Wigfair 2316' (*N&Q* 61[2014] 404) corrects Andrew Hadfield's note, 'Epitaphs to Spenser and Others in Wigfair 2316' (*N&Q* 59[2012] 522) (see *YWES* 93[2014] 277–94). Contrary to Hadfield's suggestion that the epitaphs on Sidney, Spenser, and Thomas Churchyard were composed by the early eighteenth-century author of the manuscript, who was 'curious about the culture or Elizabethan England and anxious to celebrate its achievements', they were actually written much earlier, and, as Doelman notes, 'frequently appear in early seventeenth-century manuscripts and printed books'.

Books Reviewed

Britton, Dennis Austin. *Becoming Christian: Race, Reformation, and Early Modern English Romance*. FordUP. [2014] pp. 272. $55 ISBN 9 7808 2325 7140.

Bronfen, Elisabeth, and Beate Neumeier, eds. *Gothic Renaissance: A Reassessment*. ManUP. [2014] pp. 272. £70 ISBN 9 7807 1908 8636.

Calabritto, Monica, and Peter Daly, eds. *Emblems of Death in the Early Modern Period*. Droz. [2014] pp. 441. €55.02 ISBN 9 7826 0001 5578.

Crane, Mary Thomas. *Losing Touch with Nature: Literature and the New Science in Sixteenth-Century England*. JHUP. [2014] pp. xi + 227. $49.95 ISBN 9 7814 2141 5314.

Fludernik, Monika, and Miriam Nandi, eds. *Idleness, Indolence and Leisure in English Literature* with an epilogue by Hartmut Rosa. Palgrave. [2014] pp. 328. £63 ISBN 9 7811 3740 3995.

Jacobson, Miriam. *Barbarous Antiquity: Reorienting the Past in the Poetry of Early Modern England*. UPennP. [2014] pp. viii + 286. £39 ISBN 9 7808 1224 6322.

Kahn, Victoria. *The Future of Illusion: Political Theology and Early Modern Texts*. UChicP. [2014] pp. xiii + 246. $45 ISBN 9 7802 2608 3872.

Lamb, Julian. *Rules of Use: Language and Instruction in Early Modern England*. Bloomsbury. [2014] pp. ix + 189. £74.99 ISBN 9 7805 6723 8191.

Martin, Michael. *Literature and the Encounter with God in Post-Reformation England*. Ashgate. [2014] pp. 230. £65 ISBN 9 7814 7243 2667.

Moss, Daniel D. *The Ovidian Vogue: Literary Fashion and Imitative Practice in Late Elizabethan England*. UTorP. [2014] pp. xi + 256. $65 ISBN 9 7814 4264 8685.

Nicholson, Catherine. *Uncommon Tongues: Eloquence and Eccentricity in the English Renaissance*. UPennP. [2014] pp. 218. £36 ISBN 9 7808 1224 5585.

Palmer, Patricia. *The Severed Head and the Grafted Tongue: Literature, Translation and Violence in Early Modern Ireland*. CUP. [2014] pp. 193. £64.99 ISBN 9 7811 0704 1844.

Pérez Fernández, José María, and Edward Wilson-Lee, eds. *Translation and the Book Trade in Early Modern Europe*. CUP. [2014] pp. 284. £60 ISBN 9 7811 0708 0041.

Perry, Nandra. *Imitatio Christi: The Poetics of Piety in Early Modern England*. UNDP. [2014] pp. 288. $32 ISBN 9 7802 6803 8410.

Wald, Christina. *The Reformation of Romance: This Eucharist, Disguise, and Foreign Fashion in Early Modern Prose Fiction*. Gruyter. [2014] pp. £74.99 ISBN 9 7831 1034 3342.

VII

Shakespeare

GABRIEL EGAN, PETER J. SMITH, ELINOR PARSONS,
ELISABETTA TARANTINO, DANIEL CADMAN,
ARUN CHETA, GAVIN SCHWARTZ-LEEPER,
JOHANN GREGORY, SHEILAGH ILONA O'BRIEN, AND
LOUISE GEDDES

This chapter has four sections: 1. Editions and Textual Studies; 2. Shakespeare in the Theatre; 3. Shakespeare on Screen; 4. Criticism. Section 1 is by Gabriel Egan; section 2 is by Peter J. Smith; section 3 is by Elinor Parsons; section 4(a) is by Elisabetta Tarantino; section 4(b) is by Daniel Cadman; section 4(c) is by Arun Cheta; section 4(d) is by Gavin Schwartz-Leeper; section 4(e) is by Johann Gregory; section 4(f) is by Sheilagh Ilona O'Brien; section 4(g) is by Louise Geddes.

1. Editions and Textual Studies

No major critical editions of Shakespeare appeared this year. The only relevant monograph was MacDonald P. Jackson's *Determining the Shakespeare Canon: Arden of Faversham and A Lover's Complaint*, which is an extremely well put together combination of revised versions of previously published articles, joined together with discursive connective tissue and supplemented by fresh writing. The topic is of the highest interest to Shakespearians at all levels, and Jackson's handling of it manages to convey the technical complexity—to satisfy the specialist who is entirely 'up' on the subject—without losing the newcomer to this field. The introduction (pp. 1–6) surveys the history of belief in the Shakespearian authorship of *A Lover's Complaint* and at least part of *Arden of Faversham*, pointing out that if the former is not by Shakespeare then that changes our whole view of *Sonnets* [1609] in which it appeared. For *Arden of Faversham*, Jackson's key claim is that the middle portion—Act 3 in editions that divide it that way—centred upon the Quarrel Scene (scene 8) is by Shakespeare.

Jackson's chapter 1, 'Shakespeare and the Quarrel Scene in *Arden of Faversham*' (pp. 9–39), is substantially the same as his *Shakespeare Quarterly*

The Year's Work in English Studies, Volume 95 (2016) © *The Author 2016. Published by Oxford University Press on behalf of the English Association. All rights reserved.*
For Permissions, please email: journals.permissions@oup.com
doi:10.1093/ywes/maw014

article of the same title reviewed in *YWES* 92[2013], revised lightly to make an excellent introduction to his consideration of the play, beginning with the literary-historical context before moving to his computational method. Jackson's attribution method, now widely known, admired, and emulated, is to search in Literature Online (LION) for phrases and collocations found in the text he is trying to attribute, looking for those that are comparatively rare. In the present case he confined his searches to plays first performed between 1580 and 1600 and threw away all hits that occurred more than five times across LION. What matters is how many such rare links—that is, phrases-in-common—are found between the text to be attributed and each potential author's canon as represented in LION. For the Quarrel Scene in *Arden of Faversham*, twenty-eight plays in LION contain four or more such links, and of those eighteen are by Shakespeare. Even allowing for Shakespeare's canon being larger than anyone else's, that is a compelling predominance of links to Shakespeare, with nearly two-thirds of all the links pointing to this one dramatist.

Chapter 2, 'Reviewing Authorship Studies of Shakespeare and his Contemporaries, and the Case of *Arden of Faversham*' (pp. 40–59), responds to Brian Vickers's *Shakespeare Quarterly* review of Hugh Craig and Arthur F. Kinney's 2009 book *Shakespeare, Computers, and the Mystery of Authorship* (the book was reviewed in *YWES* 90[2011]), which review was also the subject of a brilliant critique by John Burrows in *Shakespeare Quarterly* in 2012 (reviewed in *YWES* 93[2014]). Like Burrows, Jackson here patiently explains where and how Vickers is unjust in his characterizations of the scholarship in Craig and Kinney's book. Then Jackson performs his usual LION search technique, counting how many phrases and collocations are shared between the suspect text and all plays in a certain period, and tabulating those that occur not more than five times; for this the suspect text is Arden's account of his nightmare in scene 6. The vast majority of the links are with Shakespeare plays. Also, Jackson finds a tight cluster of verbal links between the nightmare story and *Venus and Adonis* lines 554–648. In his chapter 3, 'Gentlemen, *Arden of Faversham*, and Shakespeare's Early Collaborations' (pp. 66–84), Jackson notes that Shakespeare's prologue to *Henry V* and his epilogue to *A Midsummer Night's Dream* characterize their audiences as gentle and ask their pardon for his play's shortcomings, and that no other play in the period 1575–1600 besides *Arden of Faversham* does that, according to LION. Jackson goes on to reuse the evidence in Craig and Kinney's book to comment upon his own findings about *Arden of Faversham*, and in particular the links between the part of it that Jackson thinks is by Shakespeare and the parts of several collaboratively written Shakespeare plays that Craig and Kinney think are Shakespeare's; the results are highly convincing. Likewise, Jackson returns to his previous work on compound adjectives in the play (a construction that Shakespeare favoured) and finds that if we separate out scenes 4–9 (that is, Act 3) from the rest of *Arden of Faversham* it has many more of them than the rest of the play (once we normalize for length of sample), and Jackson finds spots of Shakespeare elsewhere in the play too. In sum, as Jackson puts it, 'the old evidence, when revisited, confirms the new' (p. 78). There is a useful additional check in Jackson showing that a number of words and phrases that

Shakespeare almost never uses appear in *Arden of Faversham* but only either side of, not within, the central section that Jackson claims is Shakespeare's. Jackson's chapter 4, 'Parallels and Poetry: Shakespeare, Kyd, and *Arden of Faversham*' (pp. 85–103), is substantially the same as Jackson's 2010 literary-critical article of the same title in *Medieval and Renaissance Drama in England*.

Next comes a wholly newly written chapter on 'Counter-Arguments and Conclusions' to Jackson's claim about *Arden of Faversham* (pp. 104–26). Martin Wiggins reckons that *Arden of Faversham* must be an amateur play because no professional company would demand that a boy actor have so many lines as the heroine does: 588 lines compared to, say, Juliet's 541 in Shakespeare's *Romeo and Juliet*, which is normally considered quite extraordinarily difficult a role for a boy. But as Jackson points out, in the central part of *Arden of Faversham* that is Shakespeare's work, Mistress Arden gets relatively few lines, perhaps because Shakespeare at least could see that overloading the boy would be unwise (p. 105). Wiggins also reckons that the stage directions of *Arden of Faversham* are unprofessional-sounding in using the phrase 'Here enters . . .' and often beginning, like a narrative account, with the word 'Then . . .'. Such stage directions take up the perspective not of the performers but of the audience. Jackson counters that these stage directions might not be authorial but the work of 'a reporter or scribe preparing the script for publication' (p. 105). In any case, Jackson remarks, Thomas Kyd's *Soliman and Perseda*—which, like *Arden of Faversham*, was printed by Edward Allde for Edward White—has similar audience-perspective stage directions using the word 'Then . . .'. Thus Jackson convincingly demolishes Wiggins's claim that the unusual stage directions in *Arden of Faversham* reveal an amateur writer by showing that they can be paralleled with those from the professional drama.

Jackson likewise dismisses the claim that the writer had to know the geographical area around Faversham in Kent, pointing out that the misspellings of several place names tell against it. Regarding the possibility that we are chasing a mirage in author-hunting because the author might be an unknown writer, Jackson lays out the reasons why that is unlikely. In particular, 'The extant plays of 1576–1642 constitute a very large sample (about 700) of all those that were written, and a large sample can, within a slight margin of error, provide trustworthy information about the full population' (p. 117). This means that where we have a play of unknown authorship and find that in various objective tests it matches the works of a known playwright the reason for this is more likely to be that it was written by that known playwright rather than that it was written by someone else we know nothing about.

Chapter 6, '*A Lover's Complaint*: Phrases and Collocations' (pp. 129–40), is partly based on Jackson's 2004 *Shakespeare Studies* article '*A Lover's Complaint* Revisited' reviewed in *YWES* 92[2013]. The first test applied is Jackson's standard one of finding phrases and collocations occurring no more than five times in *A Lover's Complaint* and in LION plays from the period 1590–1610. The result is that links to Shakespeare predominate, even once Jackson normalizes for just how much more Shakespeare writing there is (which, all else being equal, makes a match to Shakespeare more likely). Of the links to Shakespeare plays, the links to plays written 1603–6 predominate, and the links to non-Shakespearian plays also peak around then, so certain phrases seem to have been simply fashionable and widely used.

Jackson then turns to Vickers's ascription of *A Lover's Complaint* to John Davies of Hereford, and starting with John Jowett's demonstration that *A Lover's Complaint* stanza 1 has lots of phrases that Shakespeare used and Davies did not, Jackson extends this approach to consider stanzas 2 to 7, finding the same result. Also, even where the words used to express it differ, particular poetic conceits are shared by *A Lover's Complaint* and Shakespeare. In the new field of computational stylistics there are methodological alternatives within certain practices and we do not yet enjoy a consensus about exactly how to count various phenomena. For example, how much weight should be given to the fact that a single phrase or collocation in the work to be attributed appears multiple times in a work within a known author's canon? Should we count it once for all, or count it once each time it occurs in that known author's canon? When the results of various methods are borderline cases, such questions matter greatly, but as Jackson here demonstrates beyond any doubt, the case of *A Lover's Complaint* is not borderline: 'Whatever mode of reckoning we adopt, the affiliations of *A Lover's Complaint*'s idiolect are with Shakespeare, rather than with Davies' (p. 140).

The next three chapters are essentially the same as previously published essays. Chapter 7, 'Spellings in *A Lover's Complaint* as Evidence of Authorship' (pp. 141–68), reprints Jackson's 2008 essay 'The Authorship of *A Lover's Complaint*: A New Approach to the Problem', published in the *Papers of the Bibliographical Society of America* and reviewed with strong approval in *YWES* 89[2010]. Chapter 8, 'Neologisms and "Non-Shakespearean" Words in *A Lover's Complaint*' (pp. 169–83), is substantially the same as Jackson's 2008 essay of the same title for *Archiv für das Studium der neueren Sprachen und Literaturen*, reviewed with strong approval in *YWES* 89[2010]. And chapter 9, '*A Lover's Complaint, Cymbeline*, and the Shakespeare Canon: Interpreting Shared Vocabulary' (pp. 184–206), is substantially the same as Jackson's 2008 essay of the same title for *Modern Language Review*, reviewed with strong approval in *YWES* 89[2010].

Concluding the second half of the book is the newly written chapter 10, '*A Lover's Complaint*: Counter-Arguments and Conclusions' (pp. 207–18). Marina Tarlinskaja has argued that the verse style of *A Lover's Complaint* is much unlike Shakespeare's verse style, but as Jackson points out, 'we have no way of knowing what metrical characteristics we should expect to find in rhyme-royal stanzas of a narrative poem by Shakespeare that was written in the first decade of the seventeenth century' (p. 207), because aside from this one (if he wrote it) he wrote no others. The only Shakespearian verse writing that uses the same stanzaic form as *A Lover's Complaint* is *The Rape of Lucrece* written more than a decade earlier—and Shakespeare's verse habits of the kind measured by Tarlinskaja demonstrably changed over time—so that we just do not have the right kind of samples to compare with. Next Jackson shows that the conclusion of Ward E.Y. Elliot and Robert J. Valenza that *A Lover's Complaint* is not by Shakespeare was based on flawed tests and misinterpreted results, as he illustrates in a separate article described elsewhere in this review. Lastly Jackson deals with the flaws in Vickers's arguments based on rhyme, that Jackson perceives as vitiated by multiple false assertions and misconceptions about chance. For example, Vickers finds it highly significant that *A Lover's Complaint* and John Davies of Hereford's *Humour's Heaven on Earth* share the triple rhyme *wind/find/mind*, but as Jackson shows this was a common triple rhyme, occurring twenty times in poems from 1593 to 1617 (p. 214).

The book ends with appendices (pp. 219–51) that provide all the data upon which the arguments depend, including extensive lists of phrase-matches from Literature Online.

One book-form collection of essays contains material that is relevant to this review: *Women Making Shakespeare: Text, Reception, Performance*, edited by Gordon McMullan, Lena Cowen Orlin, and Virginia Mason Vaughan as a Festschrift for Ann Thompson. The collection contains many fine essays, but only the few that are relevant to the topic of Shakespeare's texts are noticed here. All the contributors were required to keep to under 3,000 words (including all apparatuses) so the essays do not have the space to go into much detail. In 'Remaking the Texts: Women Editors of Shakespeare, Past and Present' (pp. 57–67), Valerie Wayne notes that the history of women editing Shakespeare starts with Henrietta Bowdler. I would have thought this a rather ignominious beginning since she censored him, but Wayne seems reluctant to condemn her for that. Wayne offers no new evidence in her whistle-stop tour of women editing Shakespeare, just a survey of what is already known, ending in virtually a list of who is active today in editing Shakespeare, and then an actual list of the gender balances of various series and teamwork editions. Surprisingly, Wayne omits Sonia Massai, an editor, textual critic, and historian of the book, even though she contributes to this collection.

In '"To be acknowledged, madam, is o'erpaid": Woman's Role in the Production of Scholarly Editions of Shakespeare' (pp. 69–77), Neil Taylor ponders why women do not edit Shakespeare as much as they teach and write about him. He does not mention the plausible but unfashionable possibility that on average male brains and female brains are attracted to somewhat different activities, so that while there is a considerable overlap—a lot of women do like the work of editing, and like it somewhat more than most men do—there is nonetheless an average difference in the size of the two populations of suitably interested persons. Indeed, given what we know about the evolved differences between male and female brains, the hypothesis of no average difference regarding a task that calls for quite specific cognitive abilities would on the face of it be more implausible than one that posited some difference. The prospect that this possibility raises is that even when all the biases and obstacles are removed there may still not be a 50/50 gender split amongst editors. Perhaps more people believe this than are prepared to say it out loud, for fear of being misunderstood as blaming women for their relative absence from the discipline when of course for most of its history the reason for their absence has been blatantly sexist bias and obstacle-raising.

H.R. Woudhuysen's 'Some Women Editors of Shakespeare: A Preliminary Sketch' (pp. 79–88) is about the biographies of various women editors, not about their work, and 'Bernice Kliman's *Enfolded Hamlet*' (pp. 89–98) by John Lavagnino has some interesting reflections on how user interfaces for digital editions have changed over the past twenty years, but offers nothing substantial on the texts of Shakespeare. In 'Women Making Shakespeare—and Middleton and Jonson' (pp. 99–108), Suzanne Gossett poses the question that the previous essays have avoided regarding inherent (or is it learnt?) gender bias: 'are women editors attracted to the comedies' and so choose to edit them, because of their 'very content' rather than because men are keeping the tragedies and histories to themselves? Gossett does not have an answer (p. 101), but is convinced that men and women have different tastes: 'Conventionally women are assumed to be more interested in fabric and clothes than men are; I have found it so' (p. 102).

Gossett ends with a couple of emendations that she thinks of interest to the feminist editing of Shakespeare. The first is Diana's remark to Bertram: 'I see that men make rope's in such a scarre | That we'll forsake ourselves' (*All's Well That Ends Well* 4.1i.39–40). Gossett finds Gary Taylor's emendation to 'I see that men make toys e'en such a surance . . .' to be incomprehensible, although she then quotes Taylor's careful unpacking of each term and its polysemy. Gossett prefers P.A. Daniels's 'I see that men may rope's [= rope us] in such a snare' and she gives some defence of it against Taylor's objection that it does not lead (as his emendation does) to Diana's sudden demand of a ring from Bertram, arguing that Diana considers herself one of the women (= 'us') who has been so ensnared, so she negotiates for terms.

Next Gossett turns to the problem of some apparently faulty speech prefixes in *Merry Wives of Windsor* 4.1, which Helen Ostovich fixes in the new Norton Shakespeare third edition of the play using a 'specifically feminist justification' (p. 107). Gossett seems to think this goes too far, since 'Even a feminist editor must respect the actual words of a text' (p. 108). Here Gossett comes perilously close to suggesting that the premise of all these essays on feminist editing may be faulty and that so long as editors are not being sexist—and whether that ideal has yet been achieved is an open question—editing has no need of feminist theory. The remainder of the contributions to this collection are about the reception of Shakespeare and hence are of no concern to this review, although they are highly interesting.

This year the theme of the book-form periodical *Shakespeare Survey* was 'Shakespeare's Collaborative Work'. In 'Why Did Shakespeare Collaborate?' (*ShS* 67[2014] 1–17), Gary Taylor observes that we now know that more than one-third of the plays by Shakespeare were collaborative. Shakespeare did not write the beginnings of the plays he collaborated on: he came in at the complicating phase because he was better at characterization (and especially characters experiencing some emerging conflict) than at plot or exposition. In the early 1600s Shakespeare could not alone satisfy the demand for plays about and set in London and he was in general better at comedy (on which he never collaborated) than at history and tragedy (on which he did). Collaboration certainly can produce inconsistency in plays, but it is not at all clear that early audiences and readers minded this: they seem to have valued variety at least as much as unity. And of course, Shakespeare's non-collaborative plays are full of inconsistencies too. Shakespeare collaborated because, in some genres, it made for better plays than he could manage on his own

The second essay is by the present reviewer and is titled 'What Is Not Collaborative about Early Modern Drama in Performance and Print?' (*ShS* 67[2014] 18–28). It argues that recent commentators, especially Tiffany Stern, have overstated the routine alteration and revision of play scripts—the Master of the Revels's licensing fee gave the players a strong disincentive—and have likewise overstated how far printing was an inherently collaborative process. In fact, Egan argues, what got licensed represented pretty well what got performed and what got printed represented pretty well what the printer was given to print. Much in the same vein, Will Sharpe's 'Framing Shakespeare's Collaborative Authorship' (*ShS* 67[2014] 29–43) diagnoses general overstatement of the collaborative nature of dramatic creativity and reasserts the importance of authorship, lone and collaborative. Sharpe sees Shakespeare collaborating to a lesser extent than Taylor does, counting not total plays but lines—initially excluding cases that Taylor considers proven—and finding that more than 90 per cent of Shakespeare's writing went into his sole-authored plays and less than 10 per cent into his collaborative ones. By this method of tallying, Shakespeare could have contributed small parts to many more plays and still put much more (in terms of word counts) into his sole-authored plays than his collaborations. Clearly, we need to be careful how we express ourselves regarding the amount of collaborative writing that Shakespeare undertook.

In 'Collaboration and Proprietary Authorship: Shakespeare *et al.*' (*ShS* 67[2014] 44–59), Trevor Cook takes the opposite line from Egan to argue the poststructuralist position that 'Shakespeare was probably accustomed to definitions of authorship, textual property and the individual very different from our own' because the 'radically collaborative nature of staging a play requires each participant to relinquish his (or her) individual interests' (p. 35). Cook supports Jeffrey Masten's claim that co-authorship was 'a dispersal of authority, rather than a simple doubling of it' (p. 46) and traces the various attempts by authors to assert ownership of, or at least get credit for, their bits of various collaborative works. Cook acknowledges that 'writers at the turn of the seventeenth century could and sometimes did observe proprietary authorship in the context of collaborative working arrangements' (p. 58), but he thinks that inevitably the practice of co-authorship blurs the boundaries of the individual writing stints. Cook repeatedly cites Masten and mocks the folly of scholars who 'are motivated to identify who wrote what in a collaboration so effective that it is difficult, if not impossible, to tell' (p. 59). The next essay, Barry Langston's 'Topical Shakespeare' (*ShS* 67[2014] 60–8), contains readings of topicality in *1 Henry VI* but nothing relevant to this review.

Amongst the highlights of the collection is William W. Weber's essay, 'Shakespeare After All? The Authorship of *Titus Andronicus* 4.1 Reconsidered' (*ShS* 67[2014] 69–84). Ever since scholars have accepted the case for co-authorship of *Titus Andronicus*, Peele has been given scenes 1.1, 2.1, 2.2. and 4.1, and Weber shows that the last of these has not been subject to stringent enough testing. Weber applies MacDonald P. Jackson's technique of looking for near-unique phrase matches in LION, which as remarked above is rapidly becoming the most widely used and trusted method of authorship attribution.

At first sight, though, 4.1 has rather too few feminine endings to be typical
Shakespeare, with just three in its 128 blank-verse lines, but the right number
to be Peele's. But Shakespeare's habitual deviation from his normal rate of
feminine endings is easily broad enough to accommodate one scene having so
few, and counting by acts is more reliable a way of using feminine-ending rates
to attribute authorship.

Weber shows that *Titus Andronicus* 4.1 has tended to be lumped in with the
rest of the Peele contribution to the play even in studies that could have tested
it independently, and since it does not disrupt those studies' general
conclusions of Peele's hand in the play scene 4.1 has remained in the putative
Peele stratum. Only the feminine ending test puts it there. Another test that
might suggest that 4.1 is Peele's rate of use of vocatives, but again, like the rate
of feminine endings, this metric can swing wildly within anybody's scenes,
depending on dramatic content. In particular, 4.1 uses a child actor and it
might well be astute of a dramatist to use a lot of vocatives in such a scene so
that the child has least trouble remembering who is who. Weber uses the handy
checklist of all Shakespeare's child characters given in Kate Chedgzoy,
Suzanne Greenhalgh, and Robert Shaughnessy's collection *Shakespeare and
Childhood* [2007] to see if Shakespeare used vocatives more often in scenes
involving children, and indeed he does: twice as often as in those scenes
without children.

Then comes Weber's application of the Jackson-inspired tests of 4.1. Every
phrase and collocation of the scene—he does not say how distant, for
collocations—was entered into LION and looked for in Peele's and
Shakespeare's canons; this makes for a two-horse race, which in this case is
desirable since no other plausible candidate exists. The phrases and collocation
unique to one canon were recorded as one hit for each unique phrase with the
number of occurrences within each canon not recorded. For this test, the
Shakespeare canon was restricted to *The Comedy of Errors*, *Love's Labour's
Lost*, *Richard II*, *Richard III*, *Romeo and Juliet*, *The Taming of the Shrew*, *The
Two Gentlemen of Verona*, and *Venus and Adonis* to make it as much like
Peele's canon in size and genre-balance as possible; this test is demonstrably
valid for even quite short samples, as 4.1 is. The result is that 25 per cent of
scene 4.1's unique matches to either Peele or restricted-canon Shakespeare are
to Peele and 75 per cent are to Shakespeare. Quite a few of the matches to
Shakespeare are *epizeuxis*, which is supposed to be a Peele trait. Moreover,
looking at individual words there is in 4 just one, *playeth*, that appears in
Peele's canon but not in Shakespeare's canon, and more than a dozen that
appear in Shakespeare's canon and not in Peele's. Turning to subjective
criteria, Weber shows that in 4.1 we see Shakespearian sophistication in its use
of literary and mythical allusions, something Peele was not at all sophisticated
about. The conclusion is the Shakespeare, not Peele, wrote *Titus Andronicus*
4.1.

On the same play, Dennis McCarthy and June Schlueter argue, in 'A
Shakespeare/North Collaboration: *Titus Andronicus* and *Titus and Vespasian*'
(*ShS* 67[2014] 85–101), that the former is an adaptation of the latter, now lost,
which the authors here attribute to Thomas North. The authors search within
the database of the Early English Books Online Text Creation Partnership

(EEBO-TCP) but they mistakenly think that they are searching within the whole of EEBO, so that they unwisely comment of their findings that 'In a database of 128,000 texts, this cannot be coincidence' (p. 92). Depending on which version of the product one has, EEBO-TCP contains no more than about 53,000 texts. More importantly, McCarthy and Schlueter commit what Jackson has identified as the one-horse error in that they use the text-comparison software called Wcopyfind to determine phrases common to *Titus Andronicus* and North's *The Dial of Princes* and only then go looking for these phrases in EEBO-TCP. As Jackson has pointed out, any two substantial texts will have phrases in common that are unique to those two so such a shared link proves nothing.

In 'The Two Authors of *Edward III*' (*ShS* 67[2014] 102–18), Brian Vickers starts with a brief history of authorship-attribution studies about this play—with an in-passing disparagement of the counting of function word frequencies—and confirms the unavoidable conclusion that Shakespeare wrote scenes I.ii, II.i, and II.ii. Vickers contends that Thomas Kyd wrote the remaining sections of *Edward III*. The argument begins with the dramatic convention of 'the narration of an off-stage event, usually a catastrophe, conveyed by a Nuntius' (p. 105) that came from Senecan tragedy. *Edward III* and *The Spanish Tragedy* have this feature and, more unusually, both do it for both sides of a conflict (pp. 108–9).

To explore further the connection, Vickers uses software to find the trigrams—that is, three words in succession—that are common between the non-Shakespearian parts of *Edward III* and *The Spanish Tragedy* and Kyd's translation *Cornelia*, and then eliminates the ones that are found elsewhere in the drama generally, defined as 'plays written for the public theatres before 1596' (p. 111). This way of working is the classic one-horse-race error identified by Jackson, and it is remarkable that Jackson's proof that this method is fatally flawed—first given in a 2008 article in *Research Opportunities in Medieval and Renaissance Drama* (reviewed in *YWES* 90[2011])—has not deterred Vickers and others (such as McCarthy and Schlueter, above) from using it.

In his appendix of what he contends are unique matches between *Edward III* and *The Spanish Tragedy*, Vickers lists 'joynd in one' (p. 116) as such a case, but he overlooks the 1597 quarto of *Romeo and Juliet* (first performed 1594-96) which has 'ioynd ye both in one' (sig. E4v). Likewise Vickers claims that certain single words are found only in *Cornelia* and *Edward III* and nowhere else in pre-1596 drama (pp. 117-8), But for some of his examples this is disputable. The word "engendered" seems not to be rare: it is found in Christopher Marlowe's *Massacre at Paris* (first performed in 1593) and in Thomas Nashe's *Summer's Last Will* and *Testament* (first performed 1592) and *The Merchant of Venice* (first performed in 1596-8) and in other less-well known plays. Or take *coronet*, which again Vickers claims can be found only in *Cornelia* and *Edward III* and no other pre-1596 play. But in fact it appears in John Lyly's *Midas* (first performed in 1589) and in *A Midsummer Night's Dream* (first performed in 1595-96) and in Robert Greene's *Friar Bacon* and *Friar Bungay* (first performed in 1586-90).

Vickers's essay is followed by Francis X. Connor's 'Shakespeare, Poetic Collaboration and *The Passionate Pilgrim*' (*ShS* 67[2014] 119–29). *The Passionate Pilgrim* was published in 1599 by William Jaggard and purported to be by 'W. Shakespeare', but it has only five of his poems in it—three from *Love's Labour's Lost* and two from *Sonnets*—and the rest of the poems are by other people. Connor treats *The Passionate Pilgrim* as a kind of collaboration—in the 'socialized production' sense—although we do not know if Shakespeare had anything to do with it, and Heywood's account of Shakespeare's response to the 1612 edition that put Heywood's work under Shakespeare's name tells us that he was not involved in that edition. Connor reckons that *The Passionate Pilgrim* has its own artistic coherence and he explores first its tangential links to Shakespeare and then its publishing history—what else the Jaggard publishing house was doing and the new market for Shakespeare's books—and how it figures in sammelbands and books of excerpts. Connor wonders why some poems in *The Passionate Pilgrim* are introduced with pilcrows or Aldine leaves, which may be marks showing that the slips of paper holding the poems in *Love's Labour's Lost* were separate from the script of the play and that these marks were the linking devices between the loose sheets and the script.

James P. Bednarz's 'Contextualizing "The Phoenix and Turtle": Shakespeare, Edward Blount and the *Poetical Essays* Group of *Love's Martyr*' (*ShS* 67[2014] 130–48) treats *The Phoenix and the Turtle* as Shakespeare's intentional collaboration in the 1601 book project *Love's Martyr*. This book contains Robert Chester's epic poem *Love's Martyr* followed by twelve 'Poetical Essays' by 'Ignoto', John Marston, George Chapman, Ben Jonson, and *The Phoenix and the Turtle* by Shakespeare. The essay is largely concerned with the ways that the book trade could produce such an innovative collaborative volume and the claim that this is a collaborative work is based on a rereading of the poetical relationship between Shakespeare's poem and Chester's poem to which it responds; so the essay is not of direct relevance to this review.

In 'Shakespeare's Singularity and *Sir Thomas More*' (*ShS* 67[2014] 149–63), James Purkiss reckons that the consensus from W.W. Greg to Gary Taylor is that Shakespeare was not closely involved in the collaborative writing of this play, and Purkiss sets out to show that in fact he was. Purkiss explores what has been discovered about the shares and actions of the various hands in *Sir Thomas More*, emphasizing just how much of this knowledge is speculative. He asserts without justification that a lot of relatively unreliable tests all pointing towards the same conclusion do not themselves add up to a reliable pointer towards that conclusion. In fact they do, and an entire branch of mathematics, much used in medical diagnoses and risk management depends on this principle. Purkiss quotes Michael Hays claiming that 'non palaeographic arguments may reach the same conclusion as palaeographic ones, but they cannot strengthen palaeographic arguments themselves' (p. 153). Is this, indeed, the case?. If the non-palaeographic arguments point strongly to the conclusion that writer X thought up the words in document Y and if document Y has some marked (but non-conclusive) handwriting similarities to document Z that is definitely in the hand of writer X (say, his will), then this non-palaeographic evidence really does strengthen the palaeographic case since the alternative hypotheses become less likely. That is, the field of candidates for whom the palaeographic facts must fit the evidence is thus, by the non-palaeographic evidence, narrowed to those who not only had similar handwriting but were also in a position to copy out the author's words.

Purkiss explores the non-essential point that scholars have disagreed about just how involved Shakespeare was in the writing of *Sir Thomas More*, making a lot of the relatively small differences of opinion about this. Those who think that Shakespeare was disconnected from the writing of the rest of the play complain that the rebels get more cartoonish as they get more rebellious—at the start of the play they are quite dignified and justifiably indignant—and Purkiss explains that this is just what happens to individuated characters when the needs of the drama require it. Hand D seems to pick up from earlier in the play the notion of simplicity in the rebels' action, and that is what Purkiss reckons shows Hand D's close connection with the rest of the play. That is, the representation of the rebels was already turning clownish before Hand D got started and Hand D made it more so. Purkiss revives Gerald Downs's claim (reviewed in *YWES* 88[2009]) that Hand D contains eyeskip errors and so it must be a transcript rather than original composition, in which case, says Purkiss, it might contain a mix of Shakespeare's and others' writing. Indeed, it might, but no one has brought forth anything significant to show that it is and this seems like an attempt by those who would deny Shakespeare's authorship of the crowd-quelling scene to suggest that it might not be wholly his. Purkiss ends by finding a couple of phrases in Hand D that can be found in others' writing, but this kind of non-systematic parallel hunting tells us nothing, as he must know since he reports Jackson's voluminous writing on the strict protocols that need to be followed if such parallels are not to mislead us.

Brean Hammond's contribution to the collection is called '*Double Falsehood*: The Forgery Hypothesis, the "Charles Dickson" Enigma and a "Stern" Rejoinder' (*ShS* 67[2014] 164–78). Like Gary Taylor in 'Sleight of Mind: Cognitive Illusions and Shakespearian Desire' (reviewed in *YWES* 94[2015]), Hammond seeks to show that Tiffany Stern's essay ' "The Forgery of Some Modern Author"? Theobald's Shakespeare and Cardenio's *Double Falsehood*' (reviewed in *YWES* 93[2014]) is quite wrong to suggest that in *Double Falsehood* Theobald passed off his own forgery as Shakespeare's play. Hammond also responds to Stern's other essay on this topic, called ' "Whether one did contrive, the other write, | Or one fram'd the plot, the other did indite": Fletcher and Theobald as Collaborative Writers' (reviewed in *YWES* 93[2014]). Hammond finds a series of factual errors in Stern's account of Theobald's literary activities: she just does not seem to understand that he was not speaking for himself in his regular publication *The Censor* and in general she tries to assassinate his character by implication, for example by observing that he was known for his pantomimes without indicating what a serious genre this was.

Hammond shows that the hypothesized transmission history for *Cardenio* proposed in his Arden3 edition is paralleled in the certain transmission history of the Philip Massinger and Nathan Field play *The Fatal Dowry* that survived in manuscript in the hands of Restoration theatre practitioners and thence reached mid-eighteenth-century performance. There's nothing miraculous or suspicious about this kind of transmission. Thus an eighteenth-century reference to another such manuscript by Francis Beaumont, John Fletcher, and Shakespeare turning up is treated seriously by Hammond and wrongly dismissed as vague by Stern. Hammond notes that Stern ignores the recently discovered allusions to *Cardenio* in pre-Commonwealth performance, and has nothing to say in response to the recent stylometric work that points to Shakespeare's hand in *Double Falsehood*.

The next eleven essays in this volume of *Shakespeare Survey*, fascinating as they are, are unconnected to the topic of this review. Then comes B.J. Sokol's 'John Berryman's Emendation of *King Lear* 4.1.10 and Shakespeare's Scientific Knowledge' (*ShS* 67[2014] 335–44). Some exemplars of Q1 *King Lear* have at 4.1.9–10 the line 'Who's here, my father poorlie, leed' (Q1u) and others '. . . my father parti, eyd' (Q1c) while Q2 and F have '. . . My Father poorely led?' There is no obvious dramatic reason connected to the wider Q/F differences that would explain Q1 and F differing on this reading. There is an attraction to the *poorly led* reading in that Gloucester enters with an old man (who in Q1's stage direction is explicitly leading him) and hence Edgar notices this detail at first before noticing the reason for it. Sokol thinks that the poet John Berryman's emendation to 'My father pearly-ey'd' is correct. Sokol traces the early modern association of pearls with cataracts, referencing his own previous work on Alonso's pearl-eyed blindness in *The Tempest*. For Berryman's reading to be correct, we have to say that Q1u is nearly correct in *poorlie* except that *oo* should be *ea* and that Q1c is entirely correct in *eyd*. How could this happen? Sokol cites personal correspondence from the present reviewer on a similar mix of good and bad readings occurring in a press variant before and after stop-press correction. In such cases the first setting may get some of the letters right while being, at the level of the word, incorrect and unintelligible. Proof correctors care more for overall intelligibility than the percentage of letters correctly set and may alter an entire reading to achieve it, thereby lowering the percentage of letters that are correct. The remainder of this volume of *Shakespeare Survey* is not relevant to this review.

And so to this year's articles. The most significant for our purposes are two by Gary Taylor on the subject of Middleton's adaptation of Shakespeare's *Macbeth*. The first contains a fresh exploitation of Jackson's attribution method described above: Gary Taylor, 'Empirical Middleton: *Macbeth*, Adaptation, and Microauthorship' (*SQ* 65[2014] 239–72). The present reviewer must disclose that he read a pre-publication version of this essay and is acknowledged amongst others for making comments that the author found helpful in revision of it. Once Middleton's *The Witch* was printed in 1778 it became clear that it had influenced *Macbeth* in at least scenes 3.5 and 4.1, but with recent computational approaches both supporting and, in the work of Brian Vickers, denying Middleton's adaptation of *Macbeth*, non-specialists must be tempted to shrug their shoulders and conclude that the matter is undecidable. Naturally, adaptation is harder to spot than collaborative writing because usually an adapter contributes fewer words to the final result than a co-author would. We have ample reason to suspect that 'What? is this so? . . . *Musicke.* | *The Witches Dance, and vanish*' in *Macbeth* (4.1.140–8) is a Middleton interpolation, but it is only sixty-three words in all. This sample seems too small for most methods to test unless we also use bigrams (two words in succession), trigrams (three words in succession), and larger *n*-grams, and also bring in collocations, variant forms, and variant spellings; together these increase the amount of data we have many-fold.

Taylor's method is to go searching for these strings in electronic databases of Shakespeare and Middleton that Oxford University Press now sells as Oxford Scholarly Editions Online. First, a validation stage: does the proposed test find Shakespeare to be the author of a work known to be by Shakespeare? Taylor takes a passage of sixty-three words from *King Lear* that, like the passage from *Macbeth*, is in rhymed tetrameters: 1.3.57–67. The test is whether this passage contains more *n*-grams and collocations from the Shakespeare canon than the Middleton canon, after we discard those that appear in both canons. (It would be interesting to hear of the result for those *n*-grams and collocations from the passage being tested that are found in Shakespeare's and in Middleton's canons: are they found more often in Shakespeare's?) Taylor finds thirteen such parallels with the Shakespeare canon and only two with the Middleton canon counting type-wise, so that if one *n*-gram or collocation matches to two different bits of the Shakespeare canon then it counts only once, and 17:2 counting token-wise, so that one bit of the *King Lear* passage matching two bits of the Shakespeare canon counts twice. Counting either way—13:2 or 17:2 in Shakespeare's favour and against Middleton—the method seems to have correctly identified Shakespeare as much more likely than Middleton to have written the passage from *King Lear*.

Taylor repeats the test with sixty-three words of rhymed tetrameters from undisputed Middleton writing: *A Mad World, My Masters* 4.1.43–51, and again looking only for *n*-grams and collocations that find a match in either the Shakespeare or the Middleton canon but not both. Surprisingly, this comes out at 12:8 in favour of Shakespeare if we count token-wise. Explaining this, Taylor's remarks seem to imply that he has been searching LION as well as OSEO although in his description of the method on page 246 he had mentioned only OSEO; as he rightly observes, Shakespeare is better represented in LION than Middleton is. Also offered as explanations for the failed attribution of *A Mad World, My Masters* are that Shakespeare influenced Middleton (and not vice versa) and that Shakespeare has the bigger canon (about twice the size) and so he has more, as it were, 'opportunity' to match any given *n*-gram or collocation. Other ways to accommodate this surprising failure are to say that this test tells us not to expect much Middleton-like writing in work truly by Shakespeare but to expect Shakespeare-like writing in work truly by Middleton, and that it tells us to count type-wise. (Personally, I would not expect one failed attribution attempt to tell us something so fundamental about the method, variations upon which should emerge only after a lot of randomized tests.)

Counting type-wise instead of token-wise, the present failure to detect Middleton's hand is turned into a marginal success: 6:7 in favour of Middleton. Taylor reckons that the results of this test show that 'collocations are more significant than consecutive word strings' (p. 252) because in this test none of the collocations find matches in Shakespeare and two find matches in

Middleton. (Again, I would counsel that it is too soon to draw any such conclusions about the method from just two validations of it.) Taylor observes that in this test one play, *Hengist, King of Kent*, provides several of the Middleton matches, so we could test 'concentrations in a single work' (p. 253), and that we could also constrain the test by date, so looking for Elizabethan versus Jacobean plays. He notes that if he had applied these constrains to his first validation test on *King Lear*—counting by types, looking only at plays written in the same monarchical reign, looking for concentrations in a single work, and only at collocations—then it would still have pointed to Shakespeare as the author in that case.

Taylor decides to introduce another criterion: overall rarity of the *n*-gram or collocation, as judged by its appearances outside the Shakespeare or Middleton canons in LION. This refinement of dropping those *n*-grams and collocations that also appear in other writers' canons—that is, other than those of Shakespeare and Middleton—makes the test work the way Taylor wants it to: the *King Lear* passage is conclusively Shakespearian, the *Mad World* passage is conclusively Middletonian. Using this newly refined test, Taylor tests the passage from *Macbeth* we started with. He finds: more Middleton than Shakespeare types (8:9) but not tokens (13:11), that Middleton has more Jacobean types (3:9) and tokens (5:11), that Middleton has more unique parallels (1:4 on types, 1:6 on tokens), that Middleton has more unique Jacobean parallels (0:4 on types, 0:6 on tokens), and more concentrations in a single work: 2-types-1-unique for Shakespeare's *Twelfth Night* versus 2-types-2-unique for *The Witch*.

Taylor uses the statistical procedure called Fisher's Exact Test to try to see how likely it is that chance alone would produce the results he has found for the Shakespeare and Middleton parallels to the passage from *Macbeth*. This part of the essay I find least convincing, since his null hypothesis is 'that the Folio *Macbeth* passage was written by Shakespeare' and I am not clear how he thinks Fisher's Exact Test could be used to test that hypothesis. Something is clearly wrong with how Taylor uses Fisher's Exact Test in that he comes to the conclusion that it shows that 'there is a 100 percent probability that the *Mad World* sample and the *Macbeth* sample have the same author' and yet he also asserts that 'This 100 percent probability does not mean there is absolute certainty that they were written by the same author' (p. 256). In fact, as a matter of language, the first claim does entail the second—they are the same claim—and importantly Fisher's Exact Test is not mathematically capable of telling us anything with 100 per cent probability so this application of it must be faulty.

What if someone other than Shakespeare or Middleton wrote the passage? Taylor repeats his searches of *n*-grams and collocations from the *Macbeth* passage in all the Jacobean drama in LION, and finds that the matches come preponderantly from Middleton works: 2:5 by types, 2:9 by tokens. (In fact these are hits he got before, so this is really applying the 'must be Jacobean' constraint and loosening the authorship constraint to be 'by anyone'.) But is it not unfair to look at only Jacobean drama, since Shakespeare had done most of his work by 1603? To meet this hypothetical objection, Taylor relaxes the date constraint to '1576–1642' (for first performance) and finds that

Middleton still predominates. The unavoidable conclusion is that the passage is by Middleton.

After glancing at his own paper on Middleton authoring the five lines between '*"Enter Hecate and the other three witches"* and *"Music and a song"* (4.1.38.1–43.1)' (reviewed below), Taylor turns to *Macbeth* 3.5, where Hecate first appears, which is often claimed to be entirely Middleton's work. It comprises 259 words, almost entirely rhymed tetrameters. For his Shakespeare parallel passage Taylor chooses *Pericles* scene 10 (= 3.0), one of Gower's choruses, from which he picks 259 words. By the same tests as above, Shakespeare predominates in matches to the *Pericles* passage no matter which way you slice it, and Middleton dominates matches to *Macbeth* 3.5. Again, to these entirely convincing results Taylor applies Fisher's Exact Test in ways that are not clearly valid statistically.

To the second edition of Robert S. Miola's Norton Critical Edition of *Macbeth*, Taylor contributes a new essay on the play's authorship in which he takes issue with Brian Vickers's objections to Taylor's claim that Middleton adapted Macbeth ('*Macbeth* and Middleton', in Miola, Robert S., ed. *Macbeth*, Second edition, pp. 296-305). Taylor responds primarily to Vickers's 2010 *Times Literary Supplement* essay called 'Disintegrated: Did Thomas Middleton Really Adapt *Macbeth*?' and the associated files made public on the London Forum for Authorship Studies website (reviewed in *YWES* 91[2012]). Grace Ioppolo wrongly claimed that because the songs in *Macbeth* are merely cued with a few opening words followed by '&c' they were probably not added by an author, since an author would write out the whole song. In fact, as Tiffany Stern showed, such a pointer to the full text of a song held on another piece of paper would be perfectly normal, and authors used them.

In order to argue that Shakespeare might have added the two songs from *The Witch* to *Macbeth*, Vickers had to use an old dating of *The Witch* that assumes that it was written in 1609–16, but in fact the modern dating of the play is late 1615 or 1616. For Vickers to be right, Shakespeare would have had to adapt *Macbeth* in the very last months of his life, which is odd. Taylor reports that Vickers's account of R.V. Holdsworth's work on stage directions that use the present participle *meeting* simply misrepresents Holdsworth's work, and that Holdsworth himself has now declared that it does. Taylor objects (as did this reviewer at the time) that Vickers's use of the evidence of the entrance direction 'Enter Bast[ard] and Curan meeting' from *King Lear* is a red herring because it clearly calls for both men to enter. What is at stake in this discussion is the ambiguity generated by entrances of the form 'Enter A meeting B', not specifying whether B is already on stage, and this is a kind of ambiguity that is common in Middleton and not found in Shakespeare. This ambiguity is found twice in the bits of *Macbeth* that Taylor attributes to Middleton. Shakespeare never used the word *seam* but Middleton used it many times (and *Macbeth* uses it once) to create images of bodies being ripped apart, especially from neck to navel. Jonathan Hope's work on the rates of regulated *do* is not conclusive, but it too points in the direction of Middleton's authorship of *Macbeth* 3.5 and 4.1.

Vickers tries to show that Hecate's rhymed lines are like those of other supernatural characters in Shakespeare, but, as Taylor points out, none of those Shakespearian characters speak in rhymed iambic tetrameters as Hecate does and as lots of Middleton characters, especially supernatural ones, do. Marina Tarlinskaja's analysis of the prosody that Vickers draws upon has now been withdrawn by her because she realizes that she was not grasping exactly which lines Taylor was claiming as Middleton's; once she knew that she decided that there was too little evidence for her approach to work upon. Regarding Vickers's argument based on failing to find certain trigrams from *Macbeth* in the Middleton canon, Taylor reports this reviewer's demonstration (in *YWES* 91[2012]) that they are there and that Vickers simply missed them. Once we search in 'comprehensive, public databases' such as LION, we can find in Middleton many and in Shakespeare few parallels for another excerpt from *Macbeth*, the seven lines from *'Enter Hecat, and the other three Witches'* to *'Musicke and a Song. Blacke Spirits, &c'* (4.1.39–43) that Taylor claims are Middleton's. Taylor here lists them all.

Three articles by Hugh Craig in collaboration with others address the methods by which authorship attribution is currently being carried out. The first, 'An Information Theoretic Clustering Approach for Unveiling Authorship Affinities in Shakespearean Era Plays and Poems' (*PLoS ONE* 9:x[2014] n.p.), shows that, contrary to the assertions of poststructuralism and postmodernism, authorship trumps all other considerations (such as genre and topic) when weighing the likenesses of plays from Shakespeare's time by means of their rates of usage of all words. The authors took 256 plays from Shakespeare's time and used the Intelligent Archive software (described in *YWES* 91[2012]) to regularize their variant spellings and disambiguate (from context and frequency) strings that point to different words, such as the multiple verbs and nouns all represented by the three-character string r-o-w. For the resulting 66,907 unique words in these 256 plays they then counted how many times each word appears in each play, producing a data matrix of $66,907 \times 256$ cells. What followed was the application of an algorithm to see if the rates of usage of these words varied in a way that can be called 'clustering': that a particular set of plays are all alike in their rates of usage (high or low) of particular sets of words. Then they looked to see if the clusters that the algorithm comes up with—and that it was not, as it were, 'informed' of before—align with some known criterion such as author, or genre or date or topic.

The algorithm used was 'Minimum Spanning Tree k-Nearest Neighbour' (MST-kNN), and it was applied after using as the 'distance' between two works the Jensen–Shannon Divergence (JSD) between the frequencies of the words in these two works. Full appreciation of the mathematical formulas in which MST-kNN and JSD are explained is beyond the limit of this reviewer's comprehension. The resulting clusters were clearly dominated by authorship (not genre, not topic) as the most powerful determinant of 'closeness'. As an authorship attribution test this is quite powerful: the authorship of the near neighbours of a work in a cluster is a reliable guide to the authorship of that particular work. The authors talk the reader through the various branches and rings of works in their large cluster-chart, acknowledging the few cases where similarity of genre and topic seem to have shaped the connections. The big conclusion, though, confirms other recent work in this field: authorship is not a post-Romantic principle of categorization and is not subordinate to genre and topic, but really is an objective, detectable facet of the surviving works of this period. Impressively, the authors include their entire raw datasets for others to work on.

In the second of Craig's articles, 'Language Chunking, Data Sparseness, and the Value of a Long Marker List: Explorations with Word N-grams and Authorial Attribution' (*L&LC* 29[2014] 147–63), it is shown that Brian Vickers is wrong to believe that trigrams are inherently better markers of authorship than single words are. The intuition on which this fallacy is based is that *n*-grams where $n > 1$ must be better for authorship attribution than those where $n = 1$ (individual words) because they reflect how the mind uses language. The problem with long strings of words is that there are many different unique instances of them even in quite long texts, with each unique instance being as rare as rare can be. As well as strict *n*-grams (certain words in a certain order), this study uses 'skip *n*-grams' in which 'we find the first instance of one of the listed words, then move to the next of them, ignoring any intervening unlisted words. The second 2-gram begins with the second of these words and adds the third, and so on'. (It is not clear from this description whether or how the number of 'intervening unlisted words' that are skipped might matter here.)

The first corpus tested is 174 English Renaissance sole-authored, well-attributed professional plays in which the old spelling of function words has been modernized and their elisions expanded. The second corpus is 254 articles from Victorian periodicals. In each case the corpus is divided into segments, and finding (even multiple times) or not finding something is counted as a presence or absence for that whole segment. The authors went looking for *n*-grams common or rare or absent in one authorial set compared to others. The key question is what difference it makes when *n* goes from 1 to 5. The authors applied John Burrows's Zeta test that calls one set of text segments (say, an author's) the *base* and another set (say, of other writers') the *counter* and for each *n*-gram gives a number calculated as follows: (number-of-base-segments-containing-this-*n*-gram / number-of-base-segments) + (number-of-counter-segments-lacking-this-*n*-gram / number-of-counter-segments). Thus the Zeta score has a theoretical maximum of 2 for *n*-grams that occur at least once in every base segment and never occur in any counter segment. By repeating this for *n* going from 1 to 5 they were able to see which length of *n*-gram is most distinctive of authorship.

The authors also performed a version of Burrows's Iota test by counting all *n*-grams that appear twice or more in the base set but never in the counter set. Doing this for one author among the Victorian periodical writers and taking the top 500 scoring *n*-grams and plotting how high their Zeta scores are produces a gently sloping downward trend. The top, most authorially distinctive, *n*-gram scores between 1.3 and 1.5 (out of a theoretical maximum 2) and that is true whether the *n*-gram is single words, 2-grams, or 3-grams, but for 4-grams and 5-grams the high score is only around 1.1. Just as interestingly, for the remaining 499 *n*-grams in the 500 top-scoring *n*-grams the rate at which the scores drop off as we go down the list is different for different values of *n*: 1-grams' scores drop off more slowly than 2-grams' scores, 2-grams' scores drop off more slowly than 3-grams' scores, which drop off more slowly than 4-grams' scores, which drop off more slowly than 5-grams' scores. Thus, on average, the lower that n is, the more discriminating of authorship is the n-gram, so 1-grams (individual words) are best.

Next the authors tried to replicate what Vickers's method does: to isolate long n-grams that occur repeatedly in one author and then see if they can reliably attribute one text by that author to that author after they have taken it out of the set and treated it as if it were of unknown authorship. It turns out that 3-grams provided the largest number of markers appearing in more than one work, but 2-grams provided a greater number of markers if we are looking for markers that appear in more than 2, 3, 4, or 5 works. In general then, for this kind of investigation, 2-grams are better than 3-grams. Turning to 'skip n-grams', the authors clarify what this means and it turns out that distance does not count. (Presumably, though, all n of the words have to occur within the same text segment for the skip n-gram to count.)

Because for their skip n-gram test the authors used a pool of predetermined function words, there was no guarantee that the top 500 Zeta-scoring n-grams would be more used by the author in question than in the context set of other authors' writing, and in the event for 1-grams only the top 100 were so used: the other 400 got scores less than 1 (out of a maximum of 2). But for 2-grams to 5-grams the graphs stay above 1 as they peter out, and 2-grams turn out to be best. Just which length of n-gram works best for distinguishing authorship depends on just where you set the threshold for rarity, so that for the author in question, Anne Mozley, 'The 4-grams set yields the largest number of markers appearing in more than one Mozley article, the 3-grams set yields the largest number appearing in more than two, and the 2-grams set provides the single strongest marker: *over.over* does not appear in the articles by others, but appears in four Mozley articles' (pp. 155–6). Thus, contrary to Vickers's assumption, we cannot just say 'look how many works of author X this n-gram appears in without appearing in anybody else's work—this must be beyond coincidence', since in fact the significance of that discovery varies with the length of the n-grams.

When repeating these experiments for other authors and consolidating the results, the outcome is the same: 1-grams are best overall if one is allowing the texts themselves to choose the words (that is, the ones with the highest Zeta score), but if one is using function-word-skip-n-grams then 2-grams are best, and indeed in overall discriminating power the function-word-skip-2-grams are best. With all-word-strict-n-grams, 3-grams are best, and with function-word-strict-n-grams, 4-grams are best. Again, there is no simple rule of thumb for what length of n-gram will be best for authorship attribution. This work was all done with nineteenth-century periodicals, and turning to early modern drama the results are that with all-words-strict-n-grams 1-grams are best and with function-word-skip-n-grams 2-grams are best, and of these two the former are the best for authorship distinction. The authors' conclusion is that 'no one style of n-gram outshines the others in providing authorial markers and that attributionists would be wise to keep an open mind about the usefulness of each' (p. 159). Importantly, function-word-skip-2-grams that do better than 1-grams overall might be getting some of their advantage not because of the particular combination of words but merely because they embody multiple individual function words that are themselves highly discriminatory of authorship. In general, on these results (and contrary to Vickers's assertion) 'rare markers are less useful for attribution than regularly occurring ones' (p. 161).

The third of Craig's three articles, 'Language Individuation and Marker Words: Shakespeare and His Maxwell's Demon' (*PLoS ONE* 8:vi[2013] n.p.), should have been noticed last year but appeared in a publication not normally seen by Shakespearians. The point is essentially the same as that of the article just reviewed—that authorship is detectable in the rates of usage of high-frequency words—but it is pursued here in strict mathematical form. The authors took 168 plays from Shakespeare's time and for each they counted (using the Intelligent Archive) the occurrences of the 55,055 unique words they contain between them. Then the investigators counted using a new metric they have invented, called CM_1, for the rates of usage of these words by John Fletcher, Ben Jonson, Thomas Middleton, and William Shakespeare compared to the other writers. The word choices (for and against each word) are like Maxwell's Demon in the famous gas-physics thought-experiment of the same name, who admits certain highly energetic molecules through his partition by opening it, and shuts it to keep out other, slower molecules.

From the 55,055 unique words found, the ones that are most distinctive of the authorship of Fletcher, Jonson, Middleton, and Shakespeare (that is, four sets of most-distinctive-words) were found using some mathematics of frequency distribution that this reviewer does not fully comprehend. The real advance of this paper appears to be in the mathematical detail of how one processes the frequencies of occurrence of the words to find the words that are most distinctive. Specifically, the authors' newly invented CM_1 score for a word's distinctiveness within the dataset is a refinement of Welch's *t*-test, itself a refinement of Student's *t*-test, to suit a particularly common situation in authorship attribution testing. That situation is where one is comparing a set of plays by a single author with a set of plays known to be by different authors, as in 'Shakespeare versus the Marlowe-Jonson-Middleton set'. The article's authors were able to show that their new CM_1 score beats the usual *t*-test by feeding its results for these 168 plays into the WEKA machine-learning software package, the algorithms of which are not disclosed in this article (although the software is open source), and using 50 of its methods to produce models of authorship based on these data. That is, WEKA was asked to develop tests for authorship based on the frequencies of occurrence of the most distinctive words (as scored by CM_1), which tests were then ranked for how reliably they did in fact detect authorship, and the most effective tests were isolated. The efficiency of these tests (based on CM_1 scoring) was then compared using the same tests based on *t*-test scoring to show that CM_1 is better.

Douglas Bruster and Genevieve Smith, 'A New Chronology for Shakespeare's Plays' (*DSH* [2014] n.p.), offer a new chronology of Shakespeare's plays based on a new analysis of existing verse-style data, and it is largely but not entirely in agreement with the widely accepted chronology. This study uses Ants Oras's pause counts to put the plays in a new order, and other data are brought in to anchor the chronology, such as particular plays' known dates of first performance and the known dates of theatre closure due to plague. (The last of these will, of course, require some assumptions about how Shakespeare reacted to the theatres being closed: did he cease writing plays or carry on regardless?) Oras counted pauses in each syllabic position from 'after 1' to 'after 9' and tabulated the result, using three strengths of pause: A (the weakest) marked by any punctuation, B marked by any punctuation stronger than the weakest punctuation, which is a comma, and C marked by a change of speaker. The use of iambs makes the pauses tend to come after evenly numbered syllables. Early in his career Shakespeare favoured pauses after position 4, but he gradually shifted to favouring position 6, or at least the second half of the line, over his lifetime.

The Oxford *Complete Works* of 1986–7 used Oras's lists to help produce its chronology, but in many cases it insisted on an order that does not quite follow Oras's trends. As Bruster and Smith admit, this sometimes is inevitable since Oras's data put *2 Henry IV* before *1 Henry IV* and *The Tempest* before *Pericles*. (A key point here is that this happens if one assumes that the trend that Oras was tracing drifted consistently in one direction, with no reversals where a new play displays less of the phenomenon than its predecessor; this assumption is not obviously sound.) In an article reviewed in *YWES* 83[2004], MacDonald P. Jackson in 2002 more or less confirmed the Oxford chronology by a new statistical examination of Oras's data, but some anomalies stood out. According to Jackson, *The Merchant of Venice*, *The Merry Wives of Windsor*, and *All's Well That Ends Well* are later than the Oxford *Complete Works'* editors reckoned, and *2 Henry IV*, *Troilus and Cressida*, and *Othello* are earlier.

Oras treated each play as equally important for his work, but of course short plays give less evidence than long ones and should be discounted, and so should plays with a lot of prose (because they have less verse). Bruster and Smith describe the statistical technique of Correspondence Analysis (CA) that they use, and it is like the more familiar Principal Component Analysis (PCA) but suited to categorical rather than continuous data. They acknowledge that plays may have no single date of authorship because they are revised over time, and they decide to exclude from their study Oras's C-pauses because they think that shared verse lines are a different phenomenon altogether. Bruster and Smith are able to also add new data from knowledge of Shakespeare's collaborations that was unavailable to Oras.

Having done the PCA and CA analysis that plots the plays on just two axes (each axis representing a bundle of favoured pause positions), Bruster and Smith explain their 'bootstrap' procedure: they resample by randomly choosing various subsets of datapoints to run the PCA and CA again, which 'affords us some measure of uncertainty for our CA scores' (p. 5). Adding uncertainty sounds undesirable, but what they mean is that the resampling enables them to estimate how much uncertainty attaches to their original results, so they can add what are called 'confidence bars' to the data points. Unfortunately they do not explain why resampling enables this. Presumably if the randomly chosen samples give much the same results as the full dataset then the results are more reliable than if the randomly chosen samples give highly different results. But that is just my guess; it may be wrong, and the principle ought to have been explained by the authors. The '95 per cent confidence intervals' from this resampling 'produce a polygon for each play and trace a gradual arc up and to the right' (p. 5). The authors give no detail on how a confidence interval produces a polygon nor what the arc represents nor why it projects upwards and to the right, but presumably each confidence interval is a one-dimensional value for either CA1 or CA2 so that when CA1 and CA2 are plotted as x/y co-ordinates on a graph the result is a polygon. (I would have guessed that it would be an ellipse, so perhaps this explanation too is wrong.) This does not help us understand the arc unless this simply refers to the drift of the polygons over time as the favoured pause position drifts.

A variant of CA called Constrained Correspondence Analysis (CCA) allows the fixing of certain points when trying to find the seriation (= correct ordering), which is just what we need with the Shakespeare plays. The seriation itself comes entirely from the assumption, not yet made clear by Bruster and Smith, of a continuous one-directional drift in CCA scores with no reversing; this is not necessarily an unreasonable assumption but it does need to be foregrounded. The fixed points used to ground the seriation are *3 Henry VI* being written in late 1591, *Henry V* being written in mid-1599, *Pericles* being written in early 1607, and *The Tempest* being written after 1611. The authors provide a helpful diagram showing how an assumption of one-way and steady drift in CCA score gives a straight line running upwards and to the right on a plot in which the y-axis is CCA score and the x-axis is time. Because we have known CCA scores for certain plays and known dates for those plays, we can fix the x-axis's time-scale and hence allow other plays' dates to be derived from their CCA scores on the y-axis.

This picture enables the generation of an entire chronology, with 95 per cent confidence intervals, although Bruster and Smith also added in further fixed points based on their acceptance of Leeds Barroll's claim that Shakespeare stopped writing plays when the theatres were closed. Moreover, they were able to add in Marina Tarlinskaja's prosodic data, but these are continuous (as percentages) not classes (like Oras's data) so they ran PCA not CA on it. (Just how they combined the results of their analysis of Tarlinskaja's data with the results of their analysis of Oras's data is not made clear.) Bruster and Smith provide a complete listing of their entire Shakespeare chronology and for each play they give a brief discussion of the evidence and how their results compare with those of earlier studies. The especially noteworthy conclusions are that: *Titus Andronicus*, not *The Two Gentlemen of Verona*, is Shakespeare's first play; that *The Two Gentlemen of Verona* comes as late as 1594; and that *As You Like It* is dated 1597, *Troilus and Cressida* 1598, *Measure for Measure* 1602, *Antony and Cleopatra* 1610, *Coriolanus* 1611, and *The Winter's Tale* and *Cymbeline* 1613. (The last two are especially surprising since Simon Forman records seeing the first—and probably the second depending on how we read his account—in 1611.) At the close the authors give the important caveat that their work assumes 'that Shakespeare's verse line developed in one direction, and regularly, without significant deviation' (p. 16). It is notable and comforting that for many of the plays this new analysis more or less confirms the existing chronology derived by quite different means.

Matt Steggle edited Shakespeare's *Measure for Measure* for the third edition
of the Norton Shakespeare, and in a spin-off article, 'The Cruces of *Measure
for Measure* and EEBO-TCP' (*RES* 65[2014] 438–55), he shows how judicious
use of EEBO-TCP can help us make sense of the play's cruces and emend them
where necessary. Steggle gives a technically astute introduction to EEBO-TCP
and its strengths and weaknesses, applauding Jonathan Hope and Michael
Witmore's term 'prosthetic reading' for what we are doing when we use such a
resource. The term is particularly salient when we assert that certain phrasings
are absent from any book, since even the most diligent manual reader could
not be sure of that for thousands of books, although such a reader might be
able to confidently assert the presence of certain phrasings. Steggle rightly
complains that research in textual criticism that uses EEBO-TCP frequently
fails to give enough detail on just how the claimed results were obtained, and
he is scrupulous in this regard.

The first crux considered by Steggle is Escalus's 'Some run from brakes of
Ice' (*Measure for Measure* 2.1.39). A widely adopted emendation is Nicholas
Rowe's '. . . brakes of vice', and although *vice* fits well in the context it is
unclear what a *brake of* it would be. W.W. Skeat objected that a *brake* cannot
be a thicket since nobody ever ran away being chased by one of those. EEBO-
TCP shows no examples of *brakes of ice* or *breaks of ice*, but '*brakes of* OR
breaks of' has seventy-eight hits, 'a small enough number to check one by one'
(p. 444). Steggle found that in devotional literature the notions such as *brakes
of sensuality* and *brakes of vanitie* show that 'the words "brakes of" can
indeed, in writing of this period, be followed by an abstract noun introducing a
metaphorical register' (p. 444) and that the recurrent idea is to avoid them. So,
he supports Rowe's 'brakes of vice' emendation.

The second crux is Angelo's 'Let's write good Angell on the Deuills horne |
'Tis not the Deuills Crest' (*Measure for Measure* 2.4.16–17). Samuel Johnson
read this as conditional: if we write that on the devil's horn, then his horn is no
longer understood to be his crest (= insignia). Bawcutt read it as imperative:
Angelo has discovered that he is no angel, so appearances are deceptive and we
might as well write 'good angel' on the devil's horn since we cannot trust that
his appearance reveals his true nature. Alwin Thaler understood the idea to be
that all sorts of people are now like the devil so his crest no longer exclusively
denotes him. A number of critics have taken the antecedent of *'Tis* to be not
the horns but the inscription 'Good Angel', and others have argued that we
cannot make sense of this crux and emendation is needed, with various, not
terribly widely accepted, proposals.

Steggle points out that a crest does not have to be worn by the person it
denotes but could be carried by, for example, servants on their livery. One
could wear the devil's livery or crest, and indeed in *Measure for Measure*
Isabella goes on to say exactly that about Angelo in 3.1, that he is wearing 'the
cunning Liuerie of hell'. Steggle finds in Richard Braithwaite's work an
occurrence of *devil's crest* meaning his livery (sometimes literalized in fancy
clothes) that we humans wear when we sin. This enables Steggle to gloss
Angelo's lines as saying that 'When the devil looks like the devil, with horns
and so on, you can see him for what he is. His threat is neutralized, then, and
you might as well call him harmless. The real danger is the grave-seeming

person with hidden evil intent. They are the ones wearing the true livery of the devil' (p. 448). This seems rather a lot of meaning to be compressed into the thirteen words of the crux.

The third crux is Angelo's 'Admit no other way to saue his life | (As I subscribe not that, nor any other, | But in the losse of question) that you . . .' (*Measure for Measure* 2.4.88–90). The really tricky bit is 'in the losse of question', which has been glossed a number of unconvincing ways, including 'for the sake of argument' and 'provided that nothing can be said in his defence'. Others have tried emending the words and/or punctuation, for example by moving the closing bracket to after 'other' and reading 'But in the loss of question' as 'when his case is lost'. But Steggle has found in EEBO-TCP that losing the question was a common idiom: in disputes it meant losing the thread and going off-topic, and that suits the context admirably.

The fourth crux is Isabella's characterization of Angelo as one whose grave appearance and pronouncements 'Nips youth i' th' head, and follies doth emmew | As falcon doth the fowl' (*Measure for Measure* 3.1.89–90). The difficulty here is the meaning of 'emmew'. Thomas Keightley's emendation to *enew*, 'the hawking term for a falcon driving a fowl into the water (*en eau*)' (p. 451), has been widely accepted. But Steggle finds that, despite the apparent French etymology, this hawking term was often spelled *emew* and the sense of enclosing (*mewing up*) seems also active. The fifth crux is Angelo's claim that his 'Authority beares of a credent bulke | That . . .' no one will dare dispute his honesty (*Measure for Measure* 2.4.25), where *credent* seems to mean *believable* and *believing* although no one else used it that way, and various emendations have been proposed. EEBO-TCP shows Steggle that this reading is indeed most unusual: a *bulk* can be the direct object of *bear* but not of *bear of*, nor of *bear off* (the currently favoured emendation). Steggle proposes the emendation *bears so far credent bulk* and EEBO-TCP gives plenty of parallel phrasings: belief and disbelief are often conveyed in metaphors of physical distance.

Lukas Erne and Tamsin Badcoe, in 'Shakespeare and the Popularity of Poetry Books in Print, 1583–1622' (*RES* 65[2014] 33–57), show that poetry books consistently enjoyed about twice or thrice the market share of all books that was enjoyed by plays, but reprints were rarer, that Shakespeare's *Venus and Adonis* was the most popular poetry book of its age, that his *The Rape of Lucrece* and *The Passionate Pilgrim* did very well, and that his *Sonnets* was merely typical in not getting a reprint since 80 per cent of such books did not. Erne and Badcoe focus on the popularity of all poetry books published in 1583–1622; as they point out this is companion work to that done by Alan Farmer and Zachary Lesser on the popularity of play books (reviewed in *YWES* 86[2007]). Of necessity they start with some definitions of terms. What makes a book, which may have mixed content, a poetry book? Their answer is that it has to be 'chiefly' verse. What is a book? Answer: not a broadside. What counts as a second edition if the contents change? Answer: they rely on the Short Title Catalogue to make this call. How should we count republication in collections of mixed authorship and miscellanies? Answer: they do it on a case-by-case basis depending on how much of the collection comprises material from the first edition.

Erne and Badcoe's first table shows raw counts for poetry books published each year in 1583–1622, and the average is 17.5 first editions and eight reprints a year. The numbers rise quickly at the beginning of this period before plateauing, and the key transitional year seems to be 1594, which of course is when both Shakespeare's narrative poems were newly out and when playbooks flooded the market too. Political events such as the death of Queen Elizabeth in 1603 and of Prince Henry in 1613 seem to have caused spikes in commemorative poetry books. What about the market share enjoyed by poetry books? We have from Peter W.M. Blayney's work the figures for the total book market size, and it was growing rapidly. Since poetry book sales were largely static after the 1594 jump this means that poetry books had a decreasing share of the market. On average across the period poetry books had about 10 per cent of the market share for all books.

Erne and Badcoe discover that there were always twice or three times as many poetry books on the market as play books, and as demand for one rose or fell so did demand for the other. Of course, numbers of first editions indicate what publishers think will sell, but numbers of reprints indicate what actually did sell. There being more poetry books published than play books, the reprint rate for poetry books was much lower (about half) than that for play books. Perhaps, speculate Erne and Badcoe, the continually renewed publicity for successful plays in the form of theatre revivals kept driving up demand for play reprints. Shakespeare bucks the trend for poetry books generally: he had few published and they were often reprinted. Because there were so many poetry books published, Shakespeare never dominated this market as he did the play-books market if we count first editions. But if we count reprints instead he out-performed the average by a long way. Within that profile, *Venus and Adonis* and *The Rape of Lucrece* were extremely popular (compared to the market average) and even *The Passionate Pilgrim* was well above average. The failure of *Sonnets* to get republished was just normal for this market: as noted, 80 per cent of poetry books were not reprinted. *Venus and Adonis* in particular popularized the heroic sestet verse form as well as the epyllion content concerned with 'youthful eroticism, luxury, and transgression' (p. 49). In 1608 Robert Raworth tried and failed to publish a pirated edition of *Venus and Adonis* (he was caught), which was worth the risk because this was 'the best-selling poetry book of its time, going through more editions than any of the other 701 poetry books first published between 1583 and 1622' (p. 53).

As well as producing his own studies showing that *A Lover's Complaint* is by Shakespeare, MacDonald P. Jackson, in '*A Lover's Complaint* and the Claremont Shakespeare Clinic' (*EMLS* 16:iii[2013] n.p.), is able to show that others' studies that reach the opposite conclusion are flawed. This essay is a critique of the methods by which Ward E.Y. Elliot and Robert J. Valenza of the Claremont Shakespeare Clinic have dismissed *A Lover's Complaint* as non-Shakespearian in an article in *Shakespeare Quarterly* in 1997 and in a collection of essays called *Words That Count* edited as a Festschrift for Jackson in 2004 and reviewed in *YWES* 85[2006]. Their method was to devise a series of counts of various features in the works and then set upper and lower limits for these counts so that as many as possible known-Shakespeare works fall within the boundaries and as many as possible known-non-Shakespeare works fall outside them. Their failure was that they did not hold aside—in the sense of not using them in the determining of their boundaries—some blocks of known-Shakespeare poetry in order to test the validity of their boundaries. The fact that the known-Shakespeare poetry almost all falls within their boundaries is misleading, since that is what those boundaries were set to achieve.

Jackson repeats the Elliott and Valenza method using just *Venus and Adonis* and *The Rape of Lucrece* to set the boundaries and shows that the resulting limits would declare the *Sonnets* to be un-Shakespearian by a greater margin than it declares *A Lover's Complaint* to be un-Shakespearian. (Or rather, he uses their own published data to recalculate the boundaries without actually running their tests again.). Elliott and Valenza's method uses what they call 'handfitting' to determine the upper and lower boundaries: they moved them around manually to include the Shakespearian and exclude the non-Shakespearian. Jackson shows that it is better to use a consistent mathematical procedure to set the boundaries, based on averages and allowing two standard deviations from the average in either direction above and below the average to be the boundaries. Applying this rule with Elliott and Valenza's own results, Jackson is able to show that the tests get better at excluding the non-Shakespeare and that *A Lover's Complaint* now looks Shakespearian.

Jackson has a specific objection to one of Elliott and Valenza's tests, which counts the rates of use of *no* and *not* and divides the occurrences of the former by the occurrences of both. This test is demonstrably incapable of separating Shakespearian from non-Shakespearian poetry, for which the averages on this test are almost identical. Because we are here dealing with comparative rates, a text with lots of *no*s and *not*s can have the same rate as one with hardly any *no*s and *not*s, thereby obscuring the vast difference in absolute terms that makes their figures differently significant. Elliott and Valenza are effectively counting just a small subset of all the function words in a text, and instead the proper way to proceed is to count '*all* those [function words] that occur in Shakespeare's works above a certain level of frequency and compare blocks by principal component analysis'. Jackson has further objections to the counting of averages for features such as *with* being the penultimate word in a sentence where the data's standard deviation is very high; that is, some blocks score highly on this test, some score zero, and the average is not really typical of any one block. Other critiques are that tests derived from plays are demonstrably (Jackson shows it) not reliable for poems and vice versa, and that some of the features they measure, such as rates of feminine endings in verse, were clearly drifting over time. With all these faults, Elliott and Valenza's tests' finding that *A Lover's Complaint* is not by Shakespeare should not be taken as substantial evidence in the matter.

John Jowett, 'Disintegration, 1924' (*Shakespeare* 10[2014] 171–87), traces just why E.K. Chambers chose the word *disintegrators* for those whose approaches to Shakespeare scholarship he vigorously rejected. The rhetorical power of the word *disintegration*, which as Jowett shows still gets used pejoratively about those investigating Shakespeare's co-authorship of plays, comes from Chambers's 1924 talk 'The Disintegration of Shakespeare', which

'encapsulated cultural anxieties flowing from theoretical science and reinforced by inter-war fears among the English elite of weakening social cohesion'
(p. 172). Disintegration was, of course, a modernist concern, with Albert
Einstein breaking up the Newtonian certainties and postwar social cohesion
breaking down. Ernest Rutherford had recently split the atom—named from
a-tome, meaning indivisible—and he used the word *disintegration* in the titles
of several of his works. For Chambers the word especially connoted the social
disintegration warned of in the 1860s in Matthew Arnold's *Culture and
Anarchy*, and for him English literature and especially Shakespeare were
bulwarks against that. Chambers's disintegrators were of two kinds: (1) the
author-attribution specialists giving Shakespeare's works (or parts thereof) to
other authors, and (2) A.W. Pollard and John Dover Wilson for their
particular form of New Bibliography.

As Jowett notes, Chambers was accepting of Wilson's ideas when they
matched his own. Jowett traces the biographies of the two men and their
connected labours in developing the British schools system and their both
being adherents of Matthew Arnold's ideas about the positive social benefits
of education in general and English literature in particular. The early Wilson
thought that Shakespeare's plays were much worked and reworked, coming
originally from other authors, and that the print editions give only the illusion
of 'stability and integrity' (p. 180). Chambers strenuously denied the idea of
endless revision of plays and that this took place in endlessly revised
manuscripts, the 'continuous copy' theory. The manuscript of *Sir Thomas
More* created this impression of endless, untidy revision, and the key question
is how typical one takes this manuscript to be. Jowett sketches the harmful
effect on authorship-attribution scholarship that Chambers's essay had for
decades after its publication. We live now in a age that does not value literary
integrity and coherence, and yet authorship attribution scholarship is not
fashionable, for lingering postmodernism rejects its very model of authorship
as something assignable to a person. Jowett argues that we can think of co-
authorship 'as an articulated conversation or contestation between authors' (p.
182) so that it is both social and individualistic: 'the development of
Shakespeare's drama can be re-animated as a narrative of intersections with
other dramatists and other dramatic styles' (p. 183).

Thomas Merriam, 'Was Munday the Author of *Sir Thomas More*?'
(*Moreana* 151[2014] 245–56), argues that the Original Text of *Sir Thomas
More* looks, on certain tests, rather Shakespearian, so perhaps Shakespeare
worked with Anthony Munday on that as well as the later additions. He starts
by summarizing his own 1987 article that counted 'Five stylometric word
habits' in Munday's *John a Kent and John a Cumber* and Munday's
contributions to the two parts (*Death* and *Downfall*) of *Robert Earl of
Huntingdon*, and *Julius Caesar, Titus Andronicus, Edward III*, and the Original
Text of *Sir Thomas More*. This article claimed that Shakespeare was more
likely than Munday to be the author of the Original Text of *Sir Thomas More*.
Unfortunately, the habits in question are not described in enough detail. For
example, does the habit '*be* followed by *a*' mean followed immediately after or
at some distance? If the former, then why not simply say he counted the
occurrences of the bigram *be a* and if the latter we need to know the maximum

permitted distance. Likewise for the habit '*be* not followed by *a*' are we saying that some other word (other than *a*) had to follow *be* or would it count if *be* were at the end of a sentence, or line, or speech, which are all other ways for *be* to be not followed by *a*? The same kind of uncertainty that could easily have been cleared up applies to all the other habits counted.

Merriam repeats these same tests now with all thirty-six plays in the Folio and plots the resulting data's two principal components for each play— presumably reducing each play's five data points to two—as a scatter-graph. The Shakespeare plays all cluster together with the Original Text of *Sir Thomas More* and *John a Kent* and *John a Cumber*, and the *Robert Earl of Huntingdon* plays cluster together away from this group. But, as Merriam admits, *Edward III* also clusters with the Shakespeare plays despite having only quite a small bit of Shakespeare in it, so Merriam has not proved that this test is good at distinguishing authorship in general. What his test needs is systematic validation by being given randomized samples of plays where the authorship is known and seeing how convincingly it distinguishes plays taken out of that sample and tested as if they were of unknown authorship; this would give an overall reliable rate we could judge. Being right more than 90 per cent of the time would be good.

Rodney Stenning Edgecombe offers some emendations and reinterpret-ations of particular cruces in Shakespeare in 'Five Notes on Shakespeare' (*BJJ* 21[2014] 289–302). Where the Folio text of *1 Henry VI* has 'I: Beauties Princely Maiesty is such, | Confounds the tongue, and makes the senses rough' Edgecombe thinks *rough* needs emendation because senses cannot be made so. He suggests *rush* as it nearly rhymes, and other pairs of lines in this scene rhyme, and elsewhere in Shakespeare the senses, similarly confounded, take flight. In *2 Henry IV* the Lord Chief Justice says that Falstaff lives in 'great infamy' and Falstaff replies 'He that buckles himself in my belt cannot live in less' (1.2.138–40). The joke, according to Edgecombe, is not about Falstaff deliberately pretending that he thinks *infamy* is a cloth he might wear, but that he takes it to be a word meaning hunger (as in *famished*). In Falstaff's claim that 'The young Prince hath misled me. I am the fellow with the great belly, and he my dog' (*2 Henry IV* 1.2.146–7) it is not clear why he calls Hal his dog. Edgecombe reckons that the point is the topsy-turvydom of the dog leading its master, which is what the man-in-the-moon's dog does to him—in one tradition, that dog is really the devil—and Falstaff says elsewhere that he and his crew are minions of the moon (*1 Henry IV* 1.2.26).

The Folio text of *All is True/Henry VIII* has the Duke of Buckingham complain of Wolsey that 'his owne Letter | The Honourable Boord of Councell, out | Must fetch him in, he Papers', which many editors leave unemended. Edgecombe thinks that it makes more sense if the comma in the second line is moved to the end of the line and *he* changed to *the*, giving '. . . The honourable board of council out, | Must fetch him in the papers', which he glosses as meaning that Wolsey puts the king's council out of the picture (circumvents them) and writes letters demanding money from various gentlemen who 'are de facto inscribed in his list or file ("must fetch him in the papers")' (p. 295). I cannot see how 'must fetch him in the papers' means that. When Buckingham says 'my life is spand already: | I am the shadow of

poore Buckingham, | Whose Figure euen this instant Clowd puts on, | By
Darkning my cleere Sunne' the precise meaning is not immediately clear.
Edgecombe suggests that adding a *d* to *figure* solves the problem because then
even clearly means *evening*. Edgecombe does not make explicit what he thinks
the adjective *figured* does in modifying *evening*, but it seems to have the same
meaning as *prefigured*.

Comparing herself to Sylvia, Julia in *The Two Gentlemen of Verona* says
'What should it be that he respects in her, | But I can make respectiue in my
selfe?' Most editors gloss *respective* as *make worthy of respect*, but Edgecombe
thinks that Julia uses the word in the sense of *in respect of* (= regarding) herself
and with a pun on *respicere* (Latin for providence) so he puts a comma after
make. The gloss he gives to the resulting construction seems to me too complex
for the occasion it serves. Sonnet 119 has the lines 'How haue mine eies out of
their Spheares bene fitted | In the distraction of this madding feuer?'
Edgecombe objects to the usual gloss of *fitted* as meaning *convulsively
dislodged* (from *fit* = *seizure*) and reads this as an example of Shakespeare
thinking of one person seeing with another's eyes, so that eyes that are *fitted*
are eyes 'taken out of their spheres and fitted into others'' (p. 300). In a
separate note, 'The "Present Quality of War" Crux in *2 Henry IV* 1.3' (*ShN*
63[2014] 96), Edgecombe attends to Folio *2 Henry IV* having Lord Bardolph
say 'Yes, if this present quality of warre, | Indeed the instant action: a cause on
foot, | Liues so in hope'. Edgecombe proposes turning this into sense by
emending *indeed* > *indued* (in the sense of clothed). That is, if 'Hotspurian
impulsiveness' were clothed with the quality of war—namely foresight, which
Bardolph is about to detail *present*ly—then, yes, a military cause is hopeful.
This is indeed better than the currently accepted emendations of punctuation
only.

An article by Terri Bourus and Gary Taylor, '*Measure for Measure*(s):
Performance-Testing the Adaptation Hypothesis' (*Shakespeare* 10[2014] 363–
401), reports that Bourus directed her university theatre company in two
versions of *Measure for Measure*: one based on the Folio text and one on the
pre-Middleton-adaptation version as constructed by John Jowett's 'genetic
text' for the Oxford Collected Middleton. The practitioners found the aesthetic
effects of the two productions quite different even though the textual variants
are not extensive; a few strategically placed changes can make a lot of
difference. An interesting and previously overlooked point is that the revival of
the play must have opened at the Blackfriars theatre because as John Jowett
showed (in work reviewed in *YWES* 88[2009]) the adaptation occurred
between 6 October 1621, when one of the sources for it became available, and
late March 1622 when Crane's transcript was handed to the Folio printers;
that being winter-time the King's men would be using their indoor theatre. The
Globe performances of the original version of the play in 1604 probably ended
with a jig, which was usual, but these were banned, and the 1621 performances
probably omitted the jig. The remainder of the article has many interesting and
important comments on the performance consequences of the textual
differences between the two versions of the play, but they fall outside the
scope of this review.

Pervez Rizvi, in 'Stemmata for Shakespeare's Texts: A Suggested New Form' (*PBSA* 108[2014] 96–106), proposes a new way of writing editions' stemmata in a tabular form with horizontal rows for individual textual objects (manuscripts, editions), with time running left to right, with boxes in each row denoting the transformations of the object in that row, and with lines between the boxes denoting acts of copying or consultation. One possible objection to this admirable scheme is that it has places for physical objects but not for texts that get stored in actors' heads when they read their parts and that later get expressed in performances. The stemma for *Henry V* in the *Textual Companion* to the Oxford *Complete Works of Shakespeare* has a place for 'performances' and Rizvi objects that 'since a performance is neither a material object nor a change in a material object' (p. 98) it should not be in the stemma. Thus in his stemma for this play there is 'no arrow between the promptbook and the memorially reconstructed text. This shows that the material object called the promptbook was neither copied nor consulted in creating the material object called the memorially reconstructed text' (p. 100). One can see the logic of Rizvi's argument, but if we follow it we lose the link between the authorial papers and the performances they gave rise to. In his stemma the actors seem able to create a memorial reconstruction of something, the script of the play, without there being any connection (any line) between this reconstruction and the thing it reconstructs. How did they do this? If Rizvi could address this objection—perhaps by indicating why it is illusory for the kind of work that stemmata should do or else by making a place for the actors' parts as physical objects—then his plan for a new layout would clearly improve on the existing design.

And so to the round-up from *Notes and Queries*. Karen Britland, 'Psalm 140 and Diana's Crux in *All's Well That Ends Well*' (*N&Q* 61[2014] 241–4), returns to the familiar crux that Suzanne Gossett looked at above. In the Folio *All's Well That Ends Well*, Diana says to Bertram (who is trying to seduce her): 'I see that men make rope's in such a scarre, | That wee'l forsake our selues. Giue me that Ring.' What is meant by 'rope's in such a scarre'? Britland approves of P.A. Daniel's emendation of *scarre* > *snare* that Gary Taylor found impossible because one does not get roped in a snare. The curious *rope's* Britland considers a simple plural with an obsolete apostrophe. (I would have thought that it is far from obsolete and its currency has given it the slang name of a greengrocer's apostrophe.) What about the problem that the image of snaring does not suit well the idea of forsaking oneself? Britland explains this by pointing to Psalm 139 (or 140 according to varying religious opinion) that refers to the ropes and snares by which the innocent are led by the sinful to forsake themselves. (In fact that is not quite what the psalm seems to say, so there is some forcing of the argument to make the allusion seem to fit.)

Thomas Merriam, 'A Phrasal Collocation' (*N&Q* 61[2014] 231–3), ponders in a general and noncommittal way how texts come to use the same strings of words. Charles Forker's edition of *The Troublesome Reign of King John* listed a lot of trigrams (and longer) in common between that play and the plays of George Peele, and Merriam wonders how *n*-grams with a large *n* (such as 7) can come to be in common between two works. He has a particular example in mind: 'the queen and her two sons; And' which appears in Shakespeare's *Titus*

Andronicus and Robert Southwell's *The Epistle of Comfort* (printed perhaps in 1587). Merriam seems to make no more of this than the conclusion that it shows 'the influence of a Jesuit on Shakespeare', which does not seem especially helpful.

Jane Kingsley-Smith, 'A Method Unto Mortification: A New Source for *Love's Labour's Lost*' (*N&Q* 61[2014] 233–6), reckons that *Love's Labour's Lost* was partly inspired by a Protestant theological work about renouncing the vanities of this world. In the play Dumaine says of himself 'Dumaine is mortified', in the sense of having suppressed his appetites. Kingsley-Smith reckons that Shakespeare got the word and the idea from Thomas Rogers's book *A Method of Mortification* (published in 1586), a Protestant theological work based on a Catholic original. The original Catholic author, Diego de Estella, was born in Navarre and, having disapproved of court life there, was forced into a monastery. This biography sounds somewhat like that of the play's Don Armado—Shakespeare's first and most memorable Spanish character—who comes to Navarre's court and considers himself one of those who has signed up for its ascetic life. As Kingsley-Smith shows, the concerns of Rogers's book—just how does one abjure worldly vanities?—are like those of the play, and she traces a number of parallels. Both allude to Ecclesiastes 13:1 on being defiled by touching pitch, both refer to breath being a vapour that is destroyed by sunlight, both refer to stumbling in the darkness of moral ignorance, and both have Judas Maccabeus hurt by idle words.

Chunxiao Wei, ' "Saint Peter's Church" in *Romeo and Juliet*' (*N&Q* 61[2014] 236–8), responds to the claim by Richard Paul Roe in *The Shakespeare Guide to Italy* [2011] to have identified the particular St Peter's Church used by the Capulets in *Romeo and Juliet*. Rather pointlessly, Wei sets out to debunk all this as geographically and historically implausible. It could just as easily be dismissed on literary-historical grounds: we have no reason to think that Shakespeare was using local knowledge since his sources account for everything. Henry Buchanan, '*The Merchant of Venice*, III.ii.99: A Proposed Emendation' (*N&Q* 61[2014] 238–40) has a new solution for the crux in Bassanio's speech about a 'beauteous scarf | Veiling an Indian beauty' (*Merchant of Venice* III.ii.98–9), which has puzzled editors by its notion of beauty hiding beauty. Buchanan reckons that *scarf* is a nautical term for the sails of a ship, which veil its valuable interior or *booty*. (I cannot see that a ship's sails, which go on top, veil its insides.) Buchanan reckons that the line should be emended to refer to the 'beauteous scarf | Veiling an Indian booty', which of course suits the wider maritime-commerce theme of the play.

Leo Daugherty, 'A Previously Unreported Source for Shakespeare's Sonnet 56' (*N&Q* 61[2014] 240–1), reports a new source for one of Shakespeare's poems. Sonnet 56 begins 'Sweet love, renew thy force. Be it not said | Thy edge should blunter be than appetite, | Which but today by feeding is allayed, | Tomorrow sharpened in his former might'. Daugherty hears in this an echo of George Whetstone's sonnet (in *The Rock of Regard* [1576]), 'First loue renue thy force, my ioyes for to consume . . .', for which the context of rekindling lost love with verse is the same. David George, '*Hamlet* and the Southwark Ghost' (*N&Q* 61[2014] 244–6), also has a new source. A ghost story published in 1674 seems to have echoes of Hamlet's father's ghost returning from the dead to talk to him, including the shared detail of an orchard: in *Hamlet* that is where the murder takes place, and in the ghost story the murdered man is buried—and maybe was murdered—in his orchard. Furthermore, in the ghost story, the murderer initially gets away with it, his wife is none the wiser, the ghost walks about in a cellar, and the murdered man has buried wealth, which last detail matches what Horatio speculates is the cause of the ghost's return in *Hamlet*. Also, in the story the ghost says that he must not speak of his experiences after death. When published, the story included accounts of the ghost appearing in Southwark in the 1500s. George points out that the known sources for *Hamlet* lack these details and wonders if Shakespeare heard of this story in Southwark prior to writing the play.

Ingrid Benecke, 'The Shorter Stage Version of Shakespeare's *Macbeth* as Seen through Simon Forman's Eyes' (*N&Q* 61[2014] 246–53), reckons that *Macbeth* as we know it from the Folio was cut before being performed at the Globe in 1611 and seen by Simon Forman, with the omissions being reflected in what Forman omits. Benecke begins with the surprising assertion, for which no reason is given, that Forman's eyewitness account of *Macbeth* at the Globe in 1611 was not influenced by his knowledge of Raphael Holinshed's prose chronicles. (It is commonly thought that Forman's reference to the Weird Sisters as 'feiries or Nimphes' might be such a recollection of Holinshed.) The next sentence is even more confusing as it claims that the play was 'written before 1610/11, most likely between the year 1603 and sometime after spring 1606'. That last clause covers all time from 1606 to the present day, so presumably Benecke means 'in 1606, after its spring'. The next sentence begins 'It therefore . . .' but it is unclear what the antecedent is; the previous sentence began with its own backwards pointer ('That supports . . .'), and the one before that simply asserted that Forman's account is 'closely related' to the Folio text instead of Holinshed's account, which seems to be stating the obvious: Forman primarily recalled the play he saw, not its source. I have no idea what the author is trying to tell us by all this.

Then begins Benecke's account of how Forman's notes differ from the play we have in the Folio, and it wrongly ascribes agency: Forman 'cuts the number of characters down to Duncan, Macbeth and his Lady, Banquo, "Dunkins 2 sonns", and the Macduffs' (p. 247). Surely, no, he simply does not recall or think it worth his trouble to mention the others; this is not cutting in any recognized sense of that term. Because in Forman's notes the main characters are 'flat' and 'far less complex' than in the Folio, Benecke wonders if the psychological subtlety we know from the Folio was not present in what got performed at the Globe in 1611. The simpler explanation would be that it takes many words from a great artist to convey psychological complexity, and brief notes from a physician-spectator cannot be expected to do it.

Benecke rehearses the familiar observation that it is surprising that Forman did not mention the play's explorations of the physical manifestations of mental illness, since that would have been bound to interest him. In places Benecke uses language to describe Shakespeare's play that critics and theatre practitioners might well consider to be highly loaded, for example calling the Weird Sisters 'malevolent hags'. Benecke has a most peculiar notion of the hypothesis that the play was revised between the time Forman saw it and the printing of the Folio—that is, the Middleton adaptation theory—in that she wonders whether 'Hecate and her subservient spirits (III.v, IV.i) were excised' (p. 248) for the show Forman saw, whereas of course the adaptation hypothesis, of which she seems only dimly aware, is that they were added by Middleton after Forman saw the play. Benecke offers many observations and speculations about the play as staged in 1611 based on what Forman does not write, and appears not to appreciate that this is all much too speculative because we do not know why someone might have not recorded something. Some of the writing is particularly awkwardly phrased: 'Macduff meeting Macbeth's enemy in England can be taken to be a traitor to the Scottish throne' (p. 248) and 'He thus centres treasonable evil on Macbeth' (p. 249). In the second half of the article, Benecke gives a second complete summary of how the play looks in Forman's account. According to Benecke, the Forman account represents a coherent cutting of the play and since that cutting is unlikely to have been done by Forman she concludes that what was performed at the Globe was a cut version of the Folio text.

Thomas Merriam, 'A Reply to "*All Is True* or *Henry VIII*: Authors and Ideologies"' (*N&Q* 61[2014] 253–6), reckons that his redistribution of the shares of Shakespeare and Fletcher in *All is True/Henry VIII* is confirmed by a fresh look at some old data. This is a response to MacDonald P. Jackson's article in *Notes and Queries* the previous year (reviewed in *YWES* 94[2015]) in which Jackson showed that the moving of the boundaries of the authorial stints proposed by Merriam would give to Fletcher passages that have Shakespearian (and un-Fletcherian) rates of various verse features and likewise give to Shakespeare passages that have Fletcherian (and un-Shakespearian) rates of various verse features. Merriam responds that 'Metrical and linguistic criteria, of the kind which Jackson carefully summarizes, are not *by themselves* capable of delimiting texts by author' (p. 253).

Merriam offers a cumulative sum (cusum) graph, reprinted from 'page 424 of *Notes and Queries* ccxlviii (December 2003)' (p. 254), which is a cryptic reference: he means it is from his article 'Though This Be Supplementarity, Yet There Is Method In It' (reviewed in *YWES* 84[2005]). But in fact it is not quite a reprint: the picture on page 424 of that article looks quite different from the one reproduced here in the overall shape of the graph and the horizontal axis's labelling. This last point is the clue to why the graphs look different: in the original, the *x*-axis ran from 0 to 3500 (representing sequential lines in the play) and in the present one it runs from 400 to 700. Thus the present graph is about a one-tenth part of the original that has been stretched horizontally by a factor of ten while the *y*-axis (which has no scale in the original or the reproduction) remains unstretched.

A cusum graph like this shows, line by line in the play, the total of all occurrences of a set of words and verbal features: counts of *all, are, conscience, did, 'em*, feminine endings, *find, from, hath, in, is, it, little*, words ending in *-ly, must, now, sure, they, 'tis, too*, and *where/there*. To understand how the graph is made and hence how to read it, one must turn not to Merriam's 2003 article but to the article to which that one refers its reader, in *Literary and Linguistic Computing* from 2000. The method is that for each word or feature the total number of occurrences in the play is counted and divided by the number of lines, which gives us the expected number per line if this word or feature were uniformly distributed across the play. A typical figure might be, say, 0.25 for *and*, meaning that we expect one *and* every four lines. For each line of the play is plotted how many times that feature has occurred up to that point (hence *cumulative* sum), minus the number we would expect to be the sum for that feature up to this point if the feature were uniformly distributed across the play.

Thus if the first *and* occurs in line 3 and there is another in line 4 but none in lines 5 or 6 then the cusum figures for lines 1 to 6 would be –0.25, –0.50, 0.25, 1.0, 0.75, and 0.50. Plotted with line numbers running horizontally and cusum figures running vertically, this means that negative slopes (running north-west to south-east) represent parts of the play where the feature is consistently occurring less often than expected (say because author A wrote those lines), as with our first, second, fifth, and sixth lines having deficits of *and* (none, where 0.25 is expected), and that positive slopes (running south-west to north-east) represent parts of the play where the feature is consistently occurring more often than expected (say because author B wrote those lines), as with our third and fourth lines running a surplus of *and* (one each, where 0.25 each is expected).

Merriam talks the reader through his cusum graph, referring to where the 'breaks' occur, but it is not clear to this reader just what he means by these breaks because there are micro-trends of positive and negative slopes occurring within larger trends that are generally positive or generally negative. In other words, just what counts as an overall positive or negative slope is a function of how closely one looks at the data. But for the present application this is not a serious problem because the passages to be redistributed between Shakespeare and Fletcher occur at known line numbers so Merriam is able to isolate in a separate picture exactly which parts of the graph refer to those passages. As he rightly claims, for the seven passages that he has reallocated from Fletcher to Shakespeare the slopes are clearly positive (indicating Shakespearian authorship). But as he admits, for the two passages that he has reallocated from Shakespeare to Fletcher the slopes are not so clear: 'mostly negative slopes [= Fletcherian] except for their tails' (p. 256).

N.M. Ingebretson, 'A Hound in Shakespeare's Addition to *Sir Thomas More*' (*N&Q* 61[2014] 256–7), spots a crux where one is not usually thought to exist. In the Hand D part of *Sir Thomas More* (by Shakespeare), More refers to the rebels' desire to 'lead the majesty of law in lyam | To slip him like a hound' (6.137–8). The problem is that a *lyam* is a line used to hold a scenting-dog called a lyam-hound (also called a lymer) while greyhounds were held not on a lyam but on a slip. So, this combination of *lyam* and *slip* is a crux. Even if we think *slip* just means *let loose* the problem does not go away, for lyam-hounds were not let loose to chase the quarry but were kept restrained and walked with their handlers behind the pack to pick up the scent again if the pack lost it. Ingebretson offers no solution to this crux, but simply points it out.

For the same play, Regis Augustus Bars Closel, 'The Marginal Latin Tag in the Manuscript of *Sir Thomas More*' (*N&Q* 61[2014] 257–60), has a solution to an old puzzle. In the middle of the rewritten scene of Erasmus meeting More in *Sir Thomas More* there is a strange marginal Latin line '*Et tu Erasmus an diabolus*' (8.191). (It means 'And you are either Erasmus or the devil', which translation Closel neglects to give.) The line comes from anecdotes about More that circulated at the time of the play, and his great-grandson Cresacre More referred to it in his biography of More published around 1631 and possibly in manuscript circulation before then. The line in question is More's response to Erasmus's line, told in the anecdote but not in *Sir Thomas More*, of '*Aut tu es Morus aut nullum*'. (This means 'Either you are More or nobody', and again Closel does not help the reader here.) Closel's suggestion is that both Latin lines were meant to appear in the play as an exchange ('Either you are More . . . And you are either Erasmus . . .') in the midst of their conversation when they recognize one another. Closel is not sure if this exchange was part of the original writing or added during the revisions.

Also on *Sir Thomas More*, Thomas Merriam, 'Determining a Date' (*N&Q* 61[2014] 260–5), reckons that the Original Text was written before the mid-1590s, to judge from its rare-word usage. Different readers of the manuscript of Anthony Munday's *John a Kent and John a Cumber* see different figures in the date written on it, which is not in Munday's hand. Some see 1590, some 1595, and some 1596; most recently, MacDonald P. Jackson, in an article reviewed in *YWES* 92[2013], saw 1596. Fresh examination of the manuscript shows that part of Munday's signature overwrites or is overwritten by part of the date, throwing further doubt on the date because it is not certain which was written on top of which. Since the date of *Sir Thomas More* depends in part on the date of *John a Kent*, this uncertainty spreads to the former play. Jackson has advanced an argument for a late date for *Sir Thomas More* based on various verse features, such as lots of feminine endings, which did not become so common until after 1600. Merriam objects that a couple of late plays (from 1598–1605) also have low rates of feminine endings. Even if true, a couple of such outlier cases would not disprove the overall trend, which is well established.

Merriam turns to Eliot Slater's method of dating plays using their frequencies of rare words, to which he applies the cusum graphing method to show the occurrences in various plays of the rare words collected by Slater. When graphed so that the x-axis is the date and the y-axis is number of occurrences of Slater-rare-words that are common to the play to be dated and various plays for which the date (and hence the y-axis point) is known, the typical cusum pattern is observed. That is, the occurrences in a given play of Slater-rare-words common to various other plays form a rising slope and a falling slope with the peak between the two occurring at the point occupied by the play in the known chronology that has most Slater-rare-words in common with the play to be dated. For *John a Kent* this play is *A Midsummer Night's Dream* of 1595–6, but for the Original Text of *Sir Thomas More* it is *The Comedy of Errors* of 1594, which is rather earlier than Jowett dates the play in his recent edition of it. As a check, Merriam applies the same test to *Sir John Oldcastle* and his method dates it just as we would expect from the external evidence, which is its dependence on *1 Henry IV* and its completion in October 1599 according to Henslowe's Diary.

Adrian Blamires, 'Ben Jonson's Additions to *The Spanish Tragedy* as the Subject of Ridicule' (*N&Q* 61[2014] 265–8), finds evidence of Ben Jonson's dramatic writing not always being appreciated. Edward Alleyn retired from the stage between 1597 and 1600, and during that period the Admiral's men did not play *The Spanish Tragedy*, which they had often performed before. Alleyn returned to the stage in 1601, and the play was revived with Jonson paid to write additions to it, although these seem not to be the additions that survive in the quarto of 1602. The addition of the Painter's Part at least must have existed by 1599 because it is parodied in John Marston's *Antonio and Mellida* of that year. Richard Burbage must have played Hieronimo because *2 Return from Parnassus* mimics him doing it and his famous funeral elegy recalls his performance in the role. Thus the Chamberlain's men must have played *The Spanish Tragedy* during Alleyn's retirement from the stage.

When Alleyn revived the role at the Fortune, he probably felt he had something to prove, and perhaps Jonson's revisions are connected to that. The boys' company play *The First Part of Hieronimo* (published in 1605) is a prequel to *The Spanish Tragedy* and it seems to contain an allusion to Jonson's additions for the revival of *The Spanish Tragedy* when Hieronimo says of the news that Lorenzo is honest 'Go, tell it abroad now; | But see you put no new additions to it'. Blamires reads this as 'evidence that Jonson fulfilled his task, but that his additions did not find favour, at least amongst the Blackfriars cognoscenti' (p. 268). This seems a lot of weight to put on a small allusion, but then Blamires cheerfully admits that indeed it is.

2. Shakespeare in the Theatre

Shakespeare's canonical prominence has tended to augment the profile of the Chamberlain's/King's men at the cost of other acting companies. Moreover, Shakespeare's attachment as writer-in-residence to this single troupe serves to occlude the extent to which, as Lawrence Manley and Sally-Beth MacLean assert, the circumstances surrounding such companies were in flux in the early 1590s. *Lord Strange's Men and Their Plays* demonstrates that, in many ways, Shakespeare is the exception rather than the rule, and the stability associated with his middle and later career wholly atypical. As Manley and MacLean insist in this assiduously researched book, '1589–93 was marked by exceptional fluidity and volatility (as well as artistic ferment) in the theatrical profession'.

At the heart of their project is the repertory and writers associated with Strange's men, including Robert Greene, Thomas Kyd, Thomas Lodge, Christopher Marlowe, Thomas Nashe, and George Peele. In addition, Manley and MacLean argue for the inclusion of plays by Henry Chettle, Anthony Munday, and Shakespeare. Fortunately the Diary of Philip Henslowe is able to assist them here though not without ambiguities and omissions. The arguments in favour of the inclusion of *Sir Thomas More* and *1 Henry VI*, for instance, rely on hypotheses. They date the former play nearly a decade earlier than its latest editor, John Jowett, whose proposal of 1600 postdates the dissolution of the company by seven years, and they assume that Shakespeare authored rather than revised the latter.

Not only were the playwrights hawking their wares about various companies (and in this Shakespeare, in the early days, may have been no exception), but the performers too were willing to forgo fidelity to any one company if the money was right. Edward Alleyn, the star of the Admiral's men, was touring with Strange's men in the early 1590s, and troupes of actors would occasionally fragment and reorganize under new patrons. The central artists of Strange's men eventually became Chamberlain's men. This is a thorough and important book for those interested in the pioneering years of the commercial theatre and the emergence of Shakespeare's subsequent company.

For Andrew James Hartley, *Julius Caesar* is 'so often dismissed as dull, a classroom exercise whose historical roots anchor it to multiple dusty pasts' (p. 241). His vibrant and intelligent book on the play's stage history demonstrates how wide of the mark is such a lazy assumption. In *Julius Caesar: Shakespeare in Performance* Hartley notes the play's 'curious ability to be both historical meditation and urgent contemporary reflection at the same instant' (p. 6). Such an example is Orson Welles's 1937 adaptation, *Caesar: Death of a Dictator*, staged at the Mercury theatre in New York. Hartley's enthusiasm for this production is clear: he calls it 'the most important single production in the play's performance history' (p. 36). Welles (remarkably only 22 years old) read the play as an indictment of the contemporary failure to confront fascism. Hartley not only comments astutely on the production but uncovers the controversies surrounding it, such as Welles's own lacklustre performance: he was more interested in directing, using a stand-in Brutus during rehearsal and stepping into the production at the last minute. The preview was 'a fiasco' (p. 47) with an appalling sound system and an audience who left without applauding. Eventually Welles conceded to Norman Lloyd, who played Cinna the poet, and the scene (having been omitted) was restored. It became 'the emblem of the production' (p. 43). Next, Hartley turns his attention to Joseph Mankiewicz's 1953 film version starring James Mason as Brutus, John Gielgud as Cassius, and Marlon Brando as Mark Antony. The latter's centrality 'announced that Shakespeare could be as much American as he was British' (p. 62). Hartley is fascinating and penetrating on the contextual paranoia surrounding the McCarthy witch-hunts and the way in which Cecil B. DeMille attempted to undermine Mankiewicz in 'a lengthy oration [with] deliberate and obvious parallels to Mark Antony's funeral oration' (p. 71)— illustration, if we needed it, of the play's powerful political discourse. For Hartley, the whole episode, including the film itself, is 'a meditation on the dangers of the new American nationalism' (p. 73).

Closer to home, there are discerning analyses of the play's metamorphoses in the middle of the last century. Lindsay Anderson's 1964 Royal Court version was inflected by the topicality of 'kitchen sink' (p. 88) drama. John Barton's 1968 RSC production confronted the importance of character rather than the heroic scale of the plot, while Trevor Nunn's 1972 RSC production fell victim to an elaborate staging involving complex machinery and technical wizardry which proved intrusive. The BBC version (direct by Herbert Wise in 1979) receives a good kicking—'*Caesar* at its nadir' (p. 131)—as does Peter Hall's 1995 RST production: an 'unmitigated disaster' (p. 156).

The most interesting chapter (to me anyway) was the examination of the ways in which Ron Daniels (RST, 1983), Terry Hands (RST, 1987), and Stephen Pimlott (RST, 1991) responded to the imperious regime of Margaret Thatcher. Pimlott's Caesar, Robert Stephens, for instance, 'glowed with the Iron Lady's certainty, her influence and the dread she inspired in those who had finally mustered the courage to bring her down' (p. 147). Hartley has a thorough sense of the fall-out from the battles pitched between Thatcherite monetarism and cultural investment (and the comprehensive attack on the latter). The hysteria surrounding Howard Brenton's *The Romans in Britain*, directed in 1980 by Michael Bogdanov, intensified questions about the role of the theatre in the undermining of Victorian values, and Hartley concludes glumly that the quietism that characterized Daniels's and Hands's productions was directly the result of the RSC's decision 'to mute the *Romans in Britain* challenge in return for ongoing subsidy' (p. 151). There follow discussions of some of the play's productions in Europe, India, and South Africa as well as the American South (Hartley himself was involved with the 2001 and 2009 productions by the Georgia Shakespeare Festival). This is a terrific book with a real insider's knowledge of the play's Protean potential to reinvent itself according to local (Louisana in the 1930s) and world (9/11) events. It is a model of performance history—a sagacious combination of archive material, historical context, and extrapolation of particular staging decisions.

In ' "Let them use their talents": *Twelfth Night* and the Professional Comedian' (in Findlay and Oakley-Brown, eds., *Twelfth Night: A Critical Reader*, pp. 144–65), Andrew McConnell Stott considers the increasing degree of professionalization surrounding performing and specifically the playing of the jester. Stott notes that Feste is constantly eliciting money from Olivia, Orsino, Viola, and Sebastian: 'Performers are vendors and they need to be paid, the play seems to be saying' (p. 149). This trend takes place against an increasing sense of theatrical entertainment itself as a kind of service industry. One consequence of the development of 'urban labour was the space it created for more clearly defined leisure time, and, as such, the more specialized and commodified leisure market that grew to fill it' (p. 151). Stott details the importance and influence of the livery companies on the emerging theatrical industry. Hemminges, Tarlton, and Armin, for instance, had all completed apprenticeships with one of the livery companies, a position that allowed them 'to bind apprentices to them who studied nothing but playing' (p. 152). In the case of *Twelfth Night* Viola's capacity to 'sing | And speak to [Orsino] in many sorts of music' (I.ii.53–4) puts her in direct professional competition with Feste. But Stott also underlines a fundamental distinction between the two performers—whereas Viola's 'ultimate fate [is] to reconcile appearance and reality, Feste's role is geared towards bringing the contingency of identity more dramatically into relief' (p. 161). Indeed, 'questions of identity are at the root of all the performing services Feste offers' (p. 163). This essay is a useful corrective to the notion that Feste is representative of a festive or carnival spirit; Stott ably demonstrates the ways in which his fooling is part of the new emerging occupation of player.

Three essays, in their different ways, dwell on materiality. The first is Holly Duggan's lively and entertaining essay, ' "As Dirty as Smithfield and as

Stinking Every Whit": The Smell of the Hope Theatre' (in Karim-Cooper and Stern, eds., *Shakespeare's Theatres and The Effects of Performance*, pp. 195–213), in which she argues that 'olfaction is an important aspect and effect of performance' (p. 213). Although her discussion is focused primarily on Jonson's *Bartholomew Fair* and its residence at the Hope theatre ('known for its unique and horrible stench' (p. 197) in part due to its doubling as a bear pit), her insistence on 'the importance of understanding the material conditions of London's theatrical entertainments' (p. 213) holds good for the city's other theatres too. The public theatre, she writes, 'is a space where one can experience, first hand, all the sights, sounds and smells that collectively define London' (p. 208). These might include 'the scent of livestock, pork, leather, tobacco, stale gingerbread, ale, farts, belches, sweat and urine' (p. 204)—hmmm, quite an outing then!

The same volume contains an innovative and ingenious essay by Nathalie Rivere de Carles called 'Performing Materiality: Curtains on the Early Modern Stage' (pp. 51–69). Though theoretically intricate in places, the essay brilliantly discusses the variety of roles curtains can perform in the early modern playhouse by 'unveiling the dramatic and aesthetic role of textile props that have traditionally been seen as nothing other than ornamental fixtures' (p. 55). Colour might indicate the genre of the play—black for tragedy, for instance—but curtains can also be used to reveal characters in the discovery space (Dr Faustus); they can hide characters; conceal or reveal beds and so on. In fact, as de Carles demonstrates, 'stage-hangings possess a significant mobility, they facilitate dynamic movement in other stage proper-ties and actors' (p. 54). The essay is alert to the semiotics of hangings in a sophisticated way. In the case of Faustus, for example, the 'combination of the curtain's initial stasis and its secondary mobility acts as a dynamic pattern for Faustus' performing body' (p. 57). The proximity of curtain and actor is even more pronounced in the case of the hiding Polonius. As de Carles puts it, 'The materiality of the stage-hanging is, in this instance, endowed with a double physicality: it is a reminder of the recently visible performing body of Polonius, and it is a surrogate for his skin: Hamlet will pierce both curtain and man with his dagger' (p. 66). She goes on to note the intriguing textual difference between Q2's and F's 'I'll silence me even here' and Q1's 'I'll shroud myself here'. The latter formulation thus foretells his own demise or, as she puts it, 'Q1 has a greater impact as the arras is truly identified as deadly.' Curtains, she concludes, are not merely passive hangings or ornamental objects, 'they are instruments turning the playwright's language into performance' (p. 69).

Duggan's and de Carles's insistence on materiality is shared by Tiffany Stern. In ' "Fill Thy Purse with Money": Financing Performance in Shakespearean England' (*ShJE* 150[2014] 65–78) she begins by noting the usual penury so conspicuously characteristic of Elizabethan actors and writers before explaining that Shakespeare's affluence stemmed from his status as a sharer ('an investor in his company', p. 66) and a housekeeper ('an investor in the theatres used by his company'). Stern then goes on to examine some of the varied income streams which circulated around the theatre. The selling of ale, nuts, fruit (fresh and dried), tobacco, and prostitutes is well documented, but

Stern also considers the possibility that Shakespeare's company may 'have been involved in one of theatre's other major trades: bookselling' (p. 72). She cites various references within contemporary plays of characters discussing the habit of reading within the playhouse, and she notes that Middleton's 1611 edition of *The Roaring Girl* contains an epistle which trusts the book will 'be allowed . . . Gallery room at the play-house' (p. 73), but I am not sure how convinced I am that a greatly illiterate audience would have been interested in books. To be fair, Stern herself acknowledges that 'This is, of course, speculation' (p. 73). Her further suggestion that the concern in later plays with 'people seemingly unable to see their way through a haze' (p. 74) is due to the build up of tobacco smoke in the indoor theatre is, it seems to me, even more speculative. After all, the 'amazed' lovers of *A Midsummer Night's Dream* are just as lost in the outdoor playhouse. But, in line with Duggan's essay above, Stern is convincing on the olfactory potency of the theatre—here in financial terms: 'Money's look, sound and smell was part of the atmosphere of the playhouse, and everyone who worked for the theatre wanted it' (p. 69).

Tina Krontiris studies the political indifference of postwar Greece to the Nazi destruction of Greek Jews. Her '*The Merchant of Venice* at the National Theatre of Greece [1945] and the Silencing of the Holocaust' (*ShS* 67[2014] 279–98) is a profoundly important if melancholy essay about the circumstances surrounding the production which 'stands symbolically at the beginning of a long series of silences about the Holocaust in Greek history' (p. 298). She demonstrates that the production, directed by Pelos Katselis, was utterly uninterested in the historical events which immediately preceded it: 'the National Theatre's first postwar production of *The Merchant of Venice* expatiated on the play's harmonious theme, downplayed the Jewish-Christian conflict and so it silenced the racial issue' (p. 294). Krontiris explains this peculiarity in terms of a number of postwar circumstances: Greece's desire to treat the Nazi occupation as a crime against Greeks in general (thus not against Jews in particular), the politically fragmented state of postwar Greece, and the government's indifference to Jews returning from the Nazi camps together with their dispossession: 'Reconciliation, mercy, harmony, love— these were the themes stressed in the 1945 performance' (p. 291). This is an important though uncomfortable essay to read: 'Through its choice of an apolitical, escapist interpretation of *Merchant*, the National Theatre's first postwar production participated in the silencing of the Holocaust and the subsequent suppression of the history of Jews in Greece' (p. 280).

In 'Big-Shouldered Shakespeare: Three *Shrews* at the Chicago Shakespeare Theater' (*ShS* 67[2014] 244–64), L. Monique Pittman examines one orthodox and two rather more radical productions of Shakespeare's play. Pittman's attack on CST's artistic director, Barbara Gaines, is puritanical and over-earnest: 'in [Gaines's] understanding of Shakespeare the Humanist, she mystifies the very forces of authority that perpetuate social disequilibrium and injustice' (p. 247). There is also some heavy-handed theoretical posturing: 'The heterogeneous afterlife of the theatre defies monolithic absolutes while the institutional materiality of performance spaces themselves typically represents an elite network of authority that underprops the homogenizing ideology of the dominant class' (p. 245). But once she gets on to discussion of the

productions themselves, the essay sheds this colourlessness. David H. Bell's
2003 production is condemned for having 'channelled a wistful nostalgia and
softened the gender troubles of the play' (p. 248). Apparently, its insipid
aesthetic did little to help: 'a deeply romantic stage design implied the
inevitability of an amorous plot outcome'. Josie Rourke's production of 2010
used an adaptation by Neil LaBute which, frankly, sounds dire. Petruchio's
acceptance of Kate's final submission, 'Now there's a wench', prompted this
response: 'With a grandness of movement, her hands reached up to punctuate
a definitive "Fuck this. We are done here"' (p. 254). Pittman maintains,
apparently seriously, that 'the LaBute-Rourke production questioned, albeit
briefly, the founding and self-constituting assumptions of the Chicago
Shakespeare Theater' (p. 256). Sounds to me more like a case of biting the
hand that feeds you! Finally the Chicago Shakespeare in the Parks festival
production of 2012, directed by Rachel Rockwell, is assessed. Pittman is
rightly sensitive to the implications of taking a 'colour-blind' (p. 261)
production to 'Chicago's segregated neighbourhoods' and, of the casting of a
white Petruchio (Matt Mueller) and a black Katharina (Ericka Ratcliff), she
writes, 'this piece of casting did not appear "blind" unless "blind" is taken to
mean casting without an eye to unintended consequences, namely the visual
implications of a Caucasian man imposing his will on an African-American
woman' (p. 267). This is a powerful and well-made point but elsewhere the
tone of the article is occasionally peevish.

Much more sensitive is 'The Wrathful Dragon versus the Foolish, Fond Old
Man: Duality of Performance and Post-Feminist Affect in the 2013 Oregon
Shakespeare Festival's *King Lear*' (*CahiersE* 86[2014] 63–73). The essay is a
collaboration between Gretchen E. Minton and Kevin A. Quarmby, and its
partnership is appropriate given that the two of them are reviewing Bill
Rauch's production which cast two actors in the key role: 'Like the production
it evaluates, this study bears the hallmark of duality. Neither writer saw the
other's version. Neither communicated their views before committing them to
type. Two actors, two writers, one Shakespeare play' (p. 64). While this casting
decision was perfectly comprehensible in sparing a single actor the physical
demands of playing the role throughout an eight-month season, it also allowed
Rauch to explore the play in an 'expanded' (p. 64) way. Minton saw Jack
Willis in the role while Quarmby attended a performance by Michael Winters.
While Willis played the king as 'the ultimate bullying mob boss' (p. 65),
Winters 'appeared more childlike at [the] moment of regal abdication'.
Accordingly, 'the Winters Lear was bound to elicit more pity, both from
onstage characters and audience' (p. 66). At the closure of I.v, going into the
first interval, 'two respective audiences were left with two very distinct Lear
images: one, a broken old man shuffling into senility; the other, an aggressively
destructive individual, less a danger to himself than to those with whom he
shared the stage' (p. 68). Minton and Quarmby dwell on what they identify as
one of the production's most shocking sequences—the killing of the Fool,
through which the Willis Lear enacted 'his imaginary hatred of his daughters'
(p. 70). For the Winters Lear, however, the moment was all the more shocking
since the audience has watched him 'nonchalantly stroke and pat his Fool on
the head, as if acknowledging a favourite pet'. They go on, 'The accidental

killing of the Fool, not at all surprising with the Willis Lear, was much more unexpected and emotively charged in the hands of Winters.' Finally, the authors show how such an extreme contrast shifted the characterization of Cordelia (played by Sofia Jean Gomez). Winters's Lear, thoroughly destroyed by the storm, had 'declined so completely and realistically that, by the time he was reconciled with his daughter, Cordelia's initial reticence threatened to register as hard-heartedness rather than justifiable self-preservation' (p. 72). Willis's maintenance of a strength and viciousness, by contrast, meant that 'Gomez's equally strong Cordelia could more easily, and with relatively little effort, shine again as the forgiving, loving child of an unworthy parent.' This is an eloquent and insightful essay which integrates wonderfully the two voices of its collaborators and underlines the plurality of performances, even within a single production.

Two very different essays on the reappearance of character as a critical notion appeared this year. In the first, Nick Hutchison, 'a literary scholar' (p. 202), and Donald Jellerson, 'a working performance professional', consider the issues surrounding the critical situation and the realization onstage of character. Their '"I do care for something": *Twelfth Night*'s Feste and the Performance of Character' (*ShakB* 32[2014] 185–206) is first and foremost an attempt to bridge the impasse between theatrical and academic notions of character. For the latter group, they opine, 'asking what characters "want" may seem *passé* or even wrong-headed' (p. 185) while thespians assume that there is an inherent 'character "in" the text that persists as an artifact of language' (p. 188). They rightly note that Shakespeare wrote characters as much as stories 'complete with interior lives, pasts, and possible futures' (pp. 191–2). Unfortunately their resolution is hardly earth-shattering: noting (correctly) that Elizabethan theatre lacked the rehearsal periods of the modern theatre and that the rapidly revolving repertory demanded a new play every day, they conclude: 'Shakespeare must write character not to be "discovered" in a lengthy rehearsal period but to be read and heard in the script itself, both by the actor and the imaginatively active audience' (p. 193). But such implicit stage directions which suggest a character's outlook, mood, or preferences are hardly a new discovery. The remainder of the essay is concerned with Feste's paternalistic care for Olivia, a feature of his character which explains his hostility to Cesario ('in my conscience, sir, I do not care for you', III.i.27) and his contempt for Malvolio. Of course this is entirely feasible as an interpretation, as is the historical evidence that Shakespeare's implicit stage directions addressed the alacrity of new productions but, taken together, they never really add up to constituting the desired rapprochement between gown and greasepaint.

The second essay to deal with character is Edward Pechter's 'Character Criticism, the Cognitive Turn, and the Problem of Shakespeare Studies' (*ShakS* 42[2014] 196–228). Pechter proposes that such interest in character emerges almost as soon as the playwright's earliest commentators: 'Drawn consistently to the facility and intensity with which Shakespeare engages us with different modes of being in the world, the earliest Shakespeareans centered their emergent enterprise on the striking effects of dramatic characterization' (p. 199). Pechter then marches us along the well-trodden paths of Romantic commentators—Coleridge, Keats, Shelley, Hazlitt—and notes the reaction of L.C. Knights not only against Bradley but (less well known and even more intemperate) Ellen Terry who, in Knights's words, 'does not represent critical Authority' (p. 207). Pechter then proposes that the contemporary return to character is not simply a reaction against the dehumanizing thrust of literary theory, but is actually due to the rise of cognitive psychology and evolutionary theories of the mind. Pechter explains, while 'bear attacks are rare these days, the kinds of challenges facing modern humans remain similar to those faced by our earliest ancestors. Whether they entail cooperation . . . or competition . . . they all require attempts to figure out what is in the mind of someone who is trying to figure out what is in ours. Mind reading skills continue to be essential to our success' (p. 211). But Pechter is not satisfied with this explanation and further insists that the category of the literary itself destabilizes it: 'the mixed feelings [cognitivists] struggle with are continuous with the ones that emerged along with the idea of the literary in romantic character criticism' (p. 214). Pechter concludes that such 'mixed feelings' are not, however, necessarily demonstrative of failure: 'Contrary desires do not have to paralyze the will. Even if we cannot move them to a resolution, we can move around within them in critically interesting ways' (p. 222). This is a challenging but exhilarating essay.

Lois Potter claims that Shakespeare 'was too much a man of the theater to be a literary dramatist' (p. 469). In 'Shakespeare and Other Men of the Theater' (*SQ* 65[2014] 455–69) she challenges a number of myths (biographical and theatrical) about the playwright and emphasizes throughout the degree to which he was 'not the sort of writer who felt finished with a play once he had delivered it to his colleagues' (pp. 468–9). In this, he is unlike the purist Ben Jonson, who 'deleted someone else's contribution to *Sejanus* and omitted the collaborative *Eastward Ho!* from the 1616 folio' (p. 457). Potter argues that the paucity of Shakespeare's known collaborations might be due simply to his being unacknowledged rather than the romantically fashionable idea that he was a solo genius. She cites the revivals of *The Spanish Tragedy* [1602] and *Mucedorus* [1610] as productions which might contain what she calls 'invisible contributions' (p. 456). This idea will of course have serious implications for the received wisdom of Shakespeare's canonical centrality: 'there may be some danger in supposing that everything in his work is part of an organic whole, or that this organic whole is his creation rather than ours' (p. 458). Potter goes on to advance two intriguing speculations—the first that Shakespeare was not a bad actor—indeed, she writes, 'I believe that Shakespeare was among [the] very good actors' (p. 462). Again, the evidence is not that he was a poor actor, just that there is none that suggests he was a good one. Burbage is always in the limelight, but as Potter slyly points out, 'Burbage must have been wonderful, but one reason why he always looked like the best actor was that he always had the best parts' (p. 463). The other fascinating possibility Potter comes up with explains Shakespeare's apparent retirement. She postulates that because he is listed second in the players of *Sejanus* he probably played Tiberius, a character who does not figure in the final scene. Therefore Shakespeare 'would have been the logical person to address the audience and ask for its verdict on the play' (p. 465). The fact that the production was greeted with hisses and boos may have contributed to Shakespeare's decision to retire from performing. Of course a lot of this is conjecture, but Potter's detailed historical knowledge and her sound common sense make much in this essay pleasurably convincing.

In a provocative and meticulous study of recent Cressidas, Jami Rogers laments a shift from second-wave to post-feminism. In 'Cressida in Twenty-First Century Performance' (*Shakespeare* 10[2014] 56–71), Rogers considers the performances of Juliet Stevenson and Amanda Root, who took the role for Howard Davies (RSC, 1985), and Sam Mendes (RSC, 1990). In the case of both these productions the Cressidas were more sinned against than sinning— particularly in IV.vi, staged as something approaching a gang rape by the Greek generals. Rogers demonstrates how modest attire, reticence, embarrassment at Pandarus' salacious suggestions and a genuine adoration for Troilus (respectively Anton Lesser and Ralph Fiennes) militated against the portrayal of Cressida as a wanton. In this, both productions 'appeared to be bucking tradition' (p. 61). Rogers goes on to suggest that in spite of the significance of these performances (and productions) 'a less sympathetic view of the character evidently continues to persist elsewhere' (p. 62). Examples include Peter Stein's Edinburgh Festival and RSC production of 2006 in which Annabel Scholey took the role, and Trevor Nunn's National Theatre production of 1999 in which Cressida was played by Sophie Okonedo. These last two Cressidas were sexualized through costume (or in Scholey's case, shedding of costume) and by their lack of interest in Troilus in emotional terms. The argument is generally convincing, though there are a couple of slips along the way. When Rogers talks of the 'feminine ideal' as being 'proscribed by the male gaze' (p. 63), I assume she means the opposite—prescribed—and her description of *The Sun*'s page 3 pictures as a 'steady diet of titillation' (p. 63) is also a (subliminally?) comically counter-productive one. But Rogers has a good eye for detail and, while I did not always agree with her readings of particular production decisions, she neatly extrapolates these to construct significant arguments about the contemporary socio-political position of women—a thoughtful and intelligent article.

Boika Sokolova's 'The Reflective Part of Man: Javor Gardev's Bulgarian Shakespeares' (*CahiersE* 85[2014] 73–83) is a lively account of the work of 'an emblematic name in Bulgarian theatre' (p. 73). Sokolova's analyses of four of Gardev's productions demonstrate her assertion that 'the sound and the fury, the anger and desperation of the Bulgarian post-communist Zeitgeist have found a powerful intellectual expression through a radical performance aesthetic' (p. 73). She examines Gardev's *Bastard*, based on *King John* (Varna, Bulgaria, 2001); *The Tempest* (Adama, Turkey, 2004); *King Lear* (Sofia, Bulgaria, 2006), and *Hamlet* (Sofia, 2012). All of these shows, in their various ways, are characterized by a 'post-Brechtian style [which] challenges illusionist "magic", de-familarises comfortable pre-conceptions about the plays and characters [and] eschews totalising answers' (p. 74). Most radical perhaps was the decision to direct *The Tempest* as a revenge play with the aristocrats 'blown up by Trinculo who was wired up as a suicide bomber, with Caliban operating the remote control. After the explosion, in an emblematic act of self-annihilation, Prospero climbed into a body bag and pulled the zip closed' (p. 76). Here Sokolova identifies a pressing and contemporary political concern: 'in the context of Turkish political reality and Kurdish struggle for independence [the sequence] had powerful political implications in 2004' (p. 78). Other productions are similarly punctuated with symbolic violence. *King Lear* featured a 'profoundly disturbing emblem of the triumph of amorality' (p. 70) by having the body of the hanged Fool 'suspended upstage in his red cloak, like a huge bloody exclamation mark over the action'. Sokolova concludes grimly, 'No easy trips on green fields of memory these [productions], but uncomfortable as they are, they "speak what we feel not what we ought to say"'. While Gardev's aesthetic is clearly a glum reaction to the 'squandered hopes' (p. 75) of post-communist Bulgaria, Sokolova's capacity to capture and explore the productions' aesthetics is both vital and stimulating.

3. Shakespeare on Screen

In 2014 a wide-ranging group of monographs, essay collections, and journal articles focused upon television, film, and Internet-based materials. The distinct approaches of the year's three monographs seem largely to be reflective of the series within which each appears: Oxford University Press's Oxford Shakespeare Topics, Arden Shakespeare's Screen Adaptations, and Palgrave's BFI Film Classics. In the first-mentioned series nearly thirty books have now been published, and Russell Jackson's *Shakespeare and English-Speaking Cinema* is the first screen-focused text. I suggested last year that the spirit of criticism had become one of celebration, and Jackson offers a positive conclusion to his introduction: 'the transgressive, playful dimension of films that profit from Shakespeare . . . is to be valued and celebrated' (p. 15).

His title signals the priority given to textual aspects of the films, and his preference for the term 'cinema' signals the complex contexts within which films exist with an emphasis on an awareness of production, distribution, and audience. Jackson also reminds us that 'the word "film" is an anachronism when applied to work originated and shown by digital means' (p. 6). The six-chapter study has at its heart a consideration of comedy, followed by tragedy. The initial chapters consider 'People' and 'Places' and the penultimate one examines 'Politics in the Shakespeare Films'. The final chapter looks 'Beyond Shakespeare' to consider films which seem, perhaps superficially, to stretch clear-cut identification with Shakespeare's work. Jackson begins his introduction by considering approaches at the core of adaptation studies. His contention that 'the terms "original" and "fidelity". . . remain current in the thinking of those who work on screen (or stage) versions' (p. 2) paves the way for his preference for 'original' to designate 'the play this film starts from' (p. 15). The economy of the term is perhaps necessary in a text with such a huge scope. Support in terms of how commercial pressures function and a premium upon the popular reception of films provides context for Jackson's decision but here, and later in the book, the brevity of engagement with critical debates of this kind might frustrate the reader.

In contrast, the other two monographs focus upon a single play each. Robert N. Watson, in *BFI Film Classics: Throne of Blood*, contextualizes his in-depth study of Kurosawa's film with reference to Shakespearian scholars (including Buchanan, Donaldson, and Hindle), as well as considering its initial reception and the views of film scholars. Particular attention is granted to consideration of the kind of tragedy that is presented, and that approach seems consistent with Watson's broader scholarly interest in both ambition and death in relation to Renaissance texts. One fascinating dimension of the book is the enhanced feature via ClipNotes, a commercially available iPad application devised by one of his UCLA colleagues. The app offers a digest of the book's commentary on the film and enables the film to be watched with the commentary visible. It is not perhaps necessary for a reader familiar with the film who owns the book, but it is useful to reflect on the potential implications for future scholarly approaches. The app allows a critic to sidestep the cost implications of pictorial illustrations in printed texts and, with the use of typed rather than audio commentary, there is less distraction from a film's aural features. Watson's examination of Kurosawa's film is driven by the emphatic idea that '*Throne of Blood* is a profoundly ambivalent exploration of human morality that is at once intensely localised and transhistorical—and is deeply self-conscious about its medium' (p. 15). The BFI Film Classics series accommodates an enviable wealth of illustration, and that pictorial specificity is matched with a rewarding level of detail in an engagement with precise moments in Shakespeare's play. With over 150 volumes of slim texts, the series (which has been running for twenty years) explicitly promotes an author's personal response to the film. Watson expresses in a footnote the hope that his account will show that the reported idea that Kurosawa did not consult the playtext during rehearsals 'cannot have been true' (p. 90).

Samuel Crowl's *Shakespeare's 'Hamlet': The Relationship between Text and Film* is the fourth Shakespearian title in the seven-volume Screen Adaptations series. The series is aimed at students, and so the opening chapter works hard to give a brief introduction to the various ways in which the play has been interpreted. However, the decision to offer, within a four-chapter study, a chapter dedicated to Olivier followed by one focusing on Branagh means that Crowl is able to offer in-depth discussion of both their films. He draws on a range of archival materials from the British Library and the Branagh archives in Belfast. His analysis is also enhanced with materials gleaned from the British Film Institute's recent acquisition of the papers of Helga Cranston, the editor of Olivier's film. Crowl contextualizes the achievements of Olivier and Branagh with some consideration of the treatments by Kozintsev (1964), Richardson (1969), Zeffirelli (1990), Almereyda (2000), Campbell Scott (2001), and Sherwood Hu's *Prince of the Himalayas* (2006).

Under her married name, Helga Cranston's work also features in *Women Making Shakespeare*, edited by Gordon McMullen, Lena Cowen Orlin and Virginia Mason Vaughan. McMullen collates a number of interviews he conducted with her for his article reflecting on her role as film editor for Olivier's *Hamlet* and *Richard III*: 'Editing Olivier's *Hamlet*: An Interview with Helga Keller' (pp. 243–51). The piece usefully unsettles *auteur*-led approaches in film criticism. In other respects, the essay collection falls outside the remit of this review. Whilst over a third of the volume's essays examine women's performance, it is only in the aforementioned interview where film is a focus. Film production remains, largely, a male preserve.

Particular attention has been paid this year to the relationship between theatre and film. In *Shakespeare Bulletin* Susanne Greenhalgh introduces a special performance reviews section examining 'Live Cinema Relays of Shakespearean Performance'. Greenhalgh's introduction (*ShakB* 32:ii[2014] 255–61) offers a valuable survey of the role British Shakespearian productions are playing in the 'live' screenings. Education screenings, encores, and the Globe productions that are filmed on two consecutive evenings give currency to the term 'live'. Greenhalgh draws attention to other labels which further confuse the nomenclature. She suggests that the difficulty agreeing on a term is reflective of the medium's status as a 'hybrid form' and that these reviewers are 'registering and interrogating the significance of this new mode of experiencing Shakespearean performance' (p. 258). Her introductory essay includes some fascinating figures which make explicit the scale of the audiences (around 60,000 for the Donmar Warehouse *King Lear* in 2010) and of the box-office revenue (reportedly well over a million dollars for the RSC's *Richard II* in 2013). Six reviews examine a sample of the output from two key companies: the National Theatre (NT Live) with two productions directed for the screen by Tim van Someren: the Donmar's *Coriolanus* (Rourke, 2014) and the Manchester International Festival's *Macbeth* (Ashford and Branagh, 2014). A further three tragedies were directed for the screen by Robin Lough: *Hamlet* (Hytner, 2010), the Donmar's *King Lear* (Grandage, 2011), and *Othello* (Hytner, 2013). Lough was also the screen director of the Royal Shakespeare Company's first live-to-cinema broadcast: *Richard II* (Doran, 2013). The company has appointed John Wyver as its media consultant. Wyver declares his affiliation in his review of the NT Live *Hamlet* (*ShakB* 32:ii[2014] 261–3). He pays particular attention to the tension between theatrical, televisual, and cinematic languages.

John Wyver shows similar concerns in his essay, ' "All the trimmings?": The Transfer of Theatre to Television in Adaptations of Shakespeare Stagings' (*Adaptation* 7:ii[2014] 104–20). His wide-ranging article leads the journal's special issue, drawing on materials presented at the 'From Theatre to Screen— and Back Again!' conference, held at De Montfort University in Leicester in February 2014. Three of the five articles consider Shakespearian topics. Wyver traces a tradition of live broadcasts, and the subtle changes concomitant with the movement from theatre to television are clearly identified. By noting trends, such as the way live broadcasts in cinemas rather than on television have been dominant in recent years, the article conducts an in-depth analysis of the nuances of cinematic, theatrical, and television styles. He challenges what has become a customarily (and disappointingly) negative critical response.

The desire to offer a corrective to dominant attitudes towards a particular type of screen work is evident in Jacob Boguszak's article, 'The Poetics of Shakespearean Animation' (*ShakB* 32:ii[2014] 159–83). He notes the importance of the engagement because of the increasing use of computer-generated imagery, citing, for example, the CGI sequences in Julie Taymor's *Tempest*

(2010). The approach is logical and he identifies 'five defining aspects of performance in animation: metamorphosis, stillness, space, character, and voice' (p. 161). Boguzak takes the Soyuzmultfilm/S4C *The Animated Tales* two-season series (1992 and 1994) as case studies, and he collates a wealth of persuasive examples from the twelve 25-minute-long adaptations. His discussion of space and voice leads to clear commendation of the series—and indeed of the technique of animation more broadly. In relation to the latter, Boguzak notes the particular meaning that silence acquires 'throwing the (inauthentic, acquired) art of speech into sharp relief' (p. 174) while a heightened awareness of space 'restor[es] the original volatility of meaning on the empty stage' (p. 180).

The annual Shakespeare-focused issue of *Literature/Film Quarterly* is introduced by Elsie Walker, who connects the recent discovery of Richard III's body in Leicester with Kevin Spacey's 'dry wit, rhetorical acumen, indomitable will for power, and capacity for absolute ruthlessness' as Frank Underwood in *House of Cards* (Netflix, 2013–). Walker suggests that both offer reminders of Shakespeare's representation of the king: 'The Body of Richard and the Afterlife of Shakespeare' (*LFQ* 42:ii[2014] 410–13). The five articles include consideration of the various *Romeo and Juliet* references in one episode of the American television show *Cold Case* (CBS, 2003–10), an exploration of the relationship between characterization on television and in the film version of *Strange Brew* (Moranis and Thomas, 1983) alongside analysis of a more mainstream cluster of films: *10 Things I Hate About You* (Junger, 1999), *Anonymous* (Emmerich, 2011), *Coriolanus* (Fiennes, 2011), *Hamlet* (Almereyda, 2000), *Shakespeare in Love* (Madden, 1998), and *The Taming of the Shrew* (Zeffirelli, 1967). *Shrew* adaptations are analysed by Christopher Bertucci in his article on 'Rethinking Binaries by Recovering Bianca in *10 Things I Hate About You* and Zeffirelli's *The Taming of the Shrew*' (*LFQ* 42:ii[2014] 414–22). He offers a useful corrective towards the way scholarship 'fixates' (p. 414) on the play's central couple and, in particular, on the delivery of Katherine's final speech. The argument persuasively rejects a tendency to label screen productions as 'either repressive or progressive' (p. 414) and offers a more nuanced view of the two commercially successful adaptations. Bertucci prompts reassessment of the relationship between Katherine and Bianca, and a detailed analysis of the specific decisions made in each screen version is set alongside the dominant critical views on the films, ensuring that his concluding idea has a secure basis: 'While the sisters never formally organize their resistance against dominant ideologies, they do have moments of dissent and they recognize, to some degree, that they share in many of the same struggles' (p. 423).

The final text for consideration is an essay collection in Palgrave's Reproducing Shakespeare series. Eight essays appear in *Bollywood Shakespeares*, edited by Craig Dionne and Parmita Kapadia. As might be expected, Vishal Bhardwaj's *Omkara* (2006) receives sustained attention from a couple of the contributors and his *Maqbool* (2003) is linked to Gulzar's *Angoor* (1982) and Deepa Mehta's *Bollywood/Hollywood* (2002) and *Water* (2006) to focus upon 'the most provocative adaptations of Shakespeare's plays in contemporary Anglo-Indian, Hindi, and diasporic cinema' (p. 6).

Shakespeare Wallah (Ivory, 1965), *The Last Lear* (Ghosh, 2007), and *Twelfth Night* (Supple, 2003) also feature as case-study texts showing the engagement with the intercultural context of global Shakespeare. The introduction signals a determination to widen the terms of engagement with this scholarly area and the tone is set with probing assessment of the Royal Shakespeare Company's casting and directorial decisions in *Julius Caesar* (Doran, 2012) and *Much Ado About Nothing* (Khan, 2012). Dionne and Kapadia employ the term 'crosshatched' to drive an approach which acknowledges the particularities of different cultural arts forms and their contexts. It provides the 'key to understanding the multivalent textual and political perspectives working in Bollywood appropriations of Shakespeare' (p. 3).

Shakespeare-on-screen scholarship in 2014 seems more disparate than in previous years. There are perhaps strong possibilities for global attention (in relation to the recent experiments in content and form) to the work that is being analysed and to the critical materials themselves. *Literature/Film Quarterly* has recently announced its decision to become an open-access journal. If the shift to greater availability of critical work becomes more widespread, it will be interesting to see whether there is any discernible shift in the style and content of film scholarship.

4. Criticism

(a) General
Shakespeare and the Italian Renaissance: Appropriation, Transformation, Opposition is the latest in a series of important volumes on this subject edited by Michele Marrapodi. The relationship stated in the title is approached in different ways in the eighteen essays divided into three parts that make up this volume. Part I is on 'Appropriations of Poetry and Prose'. In '*Sprezzatura* and Embarrassment in *The Merchant of Venice*', the first of three 'Castiglione' chapters (though the author of *Il cortegiano* also figures at the start of Lawrence Rhu's chapter later in the book), Harry Berger Jr. defines the admittedly anachronistic term 'embarrassment' as the opposite of *sprezzatura*, and then analyses the role of Portia as 'Principal Embarrasser' (p. 23) in *The Merchant of Venice* ('a comedy of embarrassment'), with a couple of added references to *Othello* ('a tragedy of embarrassment', p. 22). Berger tends to overstate 'Portia's war against Antonio' (p. 23), and the Castiglione connection in this chapter is rather tenuous, so much so that the fact that Portia's alias, 'Balthasar', happens to be Castiglione's first name passes without comment. On the other hand, in 'A Niggle of Doubt: Courtliness and Chastity in Shakespeare and Castiglione' John Roe begins by mentioning echoes of *The Courtier* that have been found in Shakespeare's comedies, and later supplements this information by pointing out how, in the passage that has been linked to *Much Ado*, Hoby's translation had created a non-existent female interlocutor. The chapter focuses on 'the activity of the "stage misogynist" whose intention is to slander a woman' (p. 40 n. 3)—a kind of 'courtly' situation that finds an antecedent in Castiglione's dialogues—and

gives us a fine reading of how this affects the characters of Desdemona in *Othello* and Hermione in *The Winter's Tale*. In chapter 3, 'Dramatic Appropriations of Italian Courtliness', Thomas Kullmann explores 'Shakespeare's interest in Italian courtliness' (p. 58), as evidenced first of all by his early plays. Kullmann finds the reason for this interest in the joint attractions of exoticism and of 'the theatrical character of courtliness', including the dramatization of practical jokes (here, in remembering Cardinal Bibbiena's role as recounter of practical jokes in *The Courtier*, Kullmann might also have mentioned his authorship of *La Calandria*, a play with an important 'beffa' component along the lines of Boccaccio). Kullmann's discussion of *Much Ado About Nothing* and *Twelfth Night* (the latter included presumably by virtue of the automatic equation of an aristocratic setting with an Italian locale) is forced to acknowledge the markedly 'uncourtly' character of the jokes in question, but there is an interesting paragraph on Maria's motivation. In an important essay, 'Disowning the Bond: Coriolanus's Forgetful Humanism', Maria Del Sapio Garbero discusses the theme of violated hospitality in *Coriolanus*, drawing on Ovid's *Metamorphoses* and Seneca's *De Beneficiis*. Melissa Walter's chapter is on 'Matteo Bandello's Social Authorship and Paulina as Patroness in *The Winter's Tale*'. Walter sees her title character as performing an 'Italian-coded act of female patronage and artistic creation' (p. 95) in helping to effect Hermione's return, a role that she links back to the representation of women as patrons and active participants in Bandello's *Novelle* and their dedicatory letters. As Walter reminds us, plot-wise Bandello's novella 1.22 has been linked directly to both *Much Ado* and *The Winter's Tale*; however, one is tempted to add, an even more obvious antecedent for such feminine roles can of course be found in Boccaccio's *Decameron* and its framing device. The final essay in Part I, Karen Zyck Galbraith's 'Tracing a Villain: Typological Intertextuality in the Works of Painter, Webster, Cinthio, and Shakespeare', considers *Othello* and *The Duchess of Malfi* in relation to each other and to their respective source novellas in order to show how in these texts 'performativity' is used to reveal 'the "villain" characters' own "muddled" interiority' (p. 109).

Part II deals with 'Transformations of Topoi and Theatregrams', and opens with Keir Elam's chapter on ' "Wanton Pictures": The Baffling of Christopher Sly and the Visual-Verbal Intercourse of Early Modern Erotic Arts'. Quoting several passages in early modern English works, including Ben Jonson's plays, Elam's informative article traces the tradition of linking Elephantis' famed (and no longer extant) sexual drawings with the *Modi* (Erotic Positions), a composite work consisting in Marco Antonio Raimondi's woodcuts from drawings by Giulio Romano (also mentioned in Walter's chapter) to which Pietro Aretino added his lascivious sonnets. Elam's intent is to show that the mention of 'wanton pictures' in the Induction to *The Taming of the Shrew* links Shakespeare's play directly with the original Italian version of its source, Ariosto's *Suppositi*, whose Prologue contains an allusion to this tradition of erotic drawings, while Gascoigne's translation mentions the adjective 'wanton' but no pictures. Elam also suggests that Suetonius' description of Emperor Tiberius may be a source for Shakespeare's Induction too, as it was for the mention of the pictures in *The Alchemist*. Another source adduced here (anticipating Marrapodi's own chapter later in the collection) is Aretino's play *Il marescalco*. However, Elam concludes, the much softer, mythological character of the pictures alluded to in the Induction to *Shrew* aligns them perhaps more closely to another celebrated work by Giulio Romano, the Palazzo Te frescoes in Mantua. In 'Shylock's Venice and the Grammar of the Modern City' Sergio Costola and Michael Saenger analyse the codes that mark Bassanio as native and Shylock as foreign, drawing a parallel with some awkward prepositional usage in John Florio's grammatical works as well as with Florio's own 'foreignness' in London. In the next chapter, Eric Nicholson discusses 'Helen, the Italianate Theatrical Wayfarer of *All's Well That Ends Well*' in terms not so much of derivation from Italian sources as of 'resources in common' (a model he borrows from Richard Andrews) and of 'importable "theatregrams"' (in the wake of Louise George Clubb; p. 165), showing how shared elements with *commedia dell'arte* scenarios modify and augment the Boccaccian storyline. Bruce W. Young's chapter, '"These Times of Woe": The Contraction and Dislocation of Time in Shakespeare's *Romeo and Juliet*', is a thorough discussion of the foreshortening of time in Shakespeare's play compared to previous versions of this story, including how Shakespeare increases the level of anxiety by lowering Juliet's age to 14. These changes shift the focus away from specific Italian cultural features, like duelling and feuding, and make this a tragedy of the misjudgement arising from the compression and misuse of time. Camilla Caporicci's chapter, '"Dark is Light"—From Italy to England: Challenging Tradition through Colours', discusses the rejection of the traditional dark/light opposition in Giordano Bruno, Caravaggio, and Shakespeare. In relation to the playwright, Caporicci draws on the Song of Songs to postulate a new relationship of 'kinship' or derivation of black from white, offering brief but relevant discussions of Shakespeare's black characters and especially of his 'Dark Ladies' (in *Antony and Cleopatra*, *Love's Labour's Lost*, and the sonnets). Part II concludes with Iuliana Tanase's 'The Italian *Commedia* and the Fashioning of the Shakespearean Fool', which strives to link moral categories from Aristotelian theory and Italian comedy to fool-characters in Shakespeare's plays (including Hamlet in his feigned madness).

Part III is devoted to 'Oppositions of Ideologies and Cultures', and opens with Marrapodi's chapter on 'The Aretinean Intertext and the Heterodoxy of *The Taming of the Shrew*', which, complementing Keir Elam's contribution discussed above, focuses on how Aretino's *Il marescalco* can help 'explain the dramatic function of the Induction and its relationship to the rest of [Shakespeare's] play' (p. 236). Lawrence F. Rhu's 'Shakespeare Italianate: Sceptical Crises in Three Kinds of Play' reflects on the 'crises of doubt and jealousy' (p. 260) in *Much Ado About Nothing*, *Othello* and *The Winter's Tale*. Rhu's study focuses on each play in turn and does not take into account any 'external' linking factors, like the fact that the two comedies share the same Italian locale (Messina being actually *in* 'Sicilia'). In her stimulating chapter, 'The Jew and the Justice of Venice', Hanna Scolnicov begins by pointing out how the courtroom scene in *The Merchant of Venice* offers a version of the medieval representation of 'the triumphant *Ecclesia* and the blindfolded *Synagoga*' (p. 275), and then goes on to discuss two other, interlinked, visual allusions in this same scene: Shylock with his knife and scales (a reference, Scolnicov argues, specifically to the representation of Venice as Justice that can be seen all over the city) and Portia/Balthasar dressed up as the law doctor of the *commedia dell'arte*. Thus, Scolnicov concludes, in this scene Shakespeare is both 'imitating and deconstructing the revered notion of the Justice of Venice' (p. 289). Rocco Coronato's chapter, '*Hamlet*, Ortensio Lando, or "To Be or Not To Be" Paradoxically Explained', brings up some striking parallels between Lando's *Paradossi* (partially translated by Anthony Munday in his 1593 *Defence of Contraries*) and Hamlet's counterfeit folly and 'contrarian paradoxes' (p. 296) and, most interestingly of all, 'the emergence of *dulcedo* in the face of adversity and the Stoical anticipation and acceptance of death' (p. 298). Coronato is well aware that the similarities could be part of the general circulation of ideas in the Renaissance, but the comparison with Lando (for instance, on whether it is better to die than to live long and painfully) does indeed seem illuminating. It could also be extended outside *Hamlet*, since Lando's postulation that a fool enjoys more peace of mind than a king (p. 298) could be set beside *2 Henry IV* III.i. Duncan Salkeld's 'Much Ado about Italians in Renaissance London' says a few interesting things about the relationship of *Much Ado About Nothing* with its sources in its first few pages, while the rest of the chapter, with its detailed account of Italian immigrants' dealings with prostitutes in Elizabethan London, taken from the Bridewell Court Minute Book, seems rather less relevant, even though it does include a foreigner by the name of 'Benedick'. Similarly, Anthony R. Guneratne's chapter, 'Shakespeare, Italian Music-Drama, and Contemporary Performance: Space, Time, and the Acoustic Worlds of *Romeo and Juliet* and *The Tempest*', gives a virtuoso discussion of two Shakespeare-based performances at New York's Lincoln Center in 2012, the pastiche opera *The Enchanted Island* and Prokofiev's *Romeo and Juliet* ballet—or at least it does so eventually. Like its title, it goes through quite a lot of things before it gets there: things to do with the two plays in question, music in Shakespeare's plays, theatre history, and the Italian Renaissance in general, though I would query some of its incidental statements. In fact, this whole book could have done with slightly more careful editing, at several levels. However, it is definitely a useful volume, where, to a greater or lesser extent, every essay offers some valuable information or insight.

David Scott Kastan's *A Will to Believe: Shakespeare and Religion* is born out of the 2008 Oxford Wells Shakespeare Lectures, a fact that Kastan elegantly acknowledges by having a quotation from Stanley Wells as epigraph for each of his five chapters. The text has been allowed to maintain a conversational tone, but the book also includes a wealth of relevant notes and bibliographical references. The title, *A Will to Believe*, is drawn from William James and alludes to the notion 'that religion is not a matter of instinct or intuition' (p. 2) but a mixture of personal emotions and social and historical pressures. Throughout the study Kastan steers a middle course: on the one hand he acknowledges, and indeed documents, the centrality of the religious question in Shakespeare's time and how it is reflected in Shakespeare's works; on the other he resists the idea that we should or could infer anything about Shakespeare's own religious position from the available biographical evidence or from a reading of his works. The biographical evidence is discussed in chapter 2, after an introductory first chapter that surveys the state of the question. Chapter 3 deals with the representation of Catholics and Catholicism in the plays, focusing on *Romeo and Juliet*, *Much Ado About Nothing*, and, especially, on *King John* and *Measure for Measure*. Discussion of the two latter plays includes how they were censored at an English college in Valladolid in the mid-1640s—*Measure for Measure* apparently proved too much for the censor, who razored it out altogether. Kastan's position is that 'Shakespeare, although his own faith seems indeterminable, unquestionably reveals an awareness of and perhaps even a sympathy for much of what resisted the reform' (p. 49). What the representation of Catholic elements in these plays undoubtedly tells us is that it was not as controversial as one might expect solely on the basis of contemporary works of religious polemics. In fact, in everyday life people had to adapt to the religious divide, and these plays prove 'that at least at certain moments Catholicism could be represented, especially at a distance, as something more or less neutral' (p. 55). Chapter 4 attempts to inject into this book a 'cosmopolitism' and 'universalism' that in fact it is forced to deny in Shakespeare's own vision, by looking at the representation of Jews and Moors (or of a Jew and a Moor) in *The Merchant of Venice* and *Othello*. Although it may prove a problem in our own reception of the plays, the fact that Shakespeare effectively fails to accommodate Jews and Moors in a universalist vision is simply due to the fact that this is not what the plays are about. Faithful to his premise that he will not look for religious allegory in Shakespeare's plays, Kastan records but does not develop Sir Israel Gollancz's intuition according to which, given that since 1290 there had been no openly practising Jews in England, in the *Merchant of Venice* 'Jewishness . . . can be no more than a metaphor' (p. 89). Finally, in his reading of *Hamlet* in chapter 5, as in the book overall, Kastan moves between accepting and delimiting the importance of the religious issue. Before the appearance of the ghost, Hamlet's problem is his personal grief: theological doubts only come to the fore when he actually sets eyes on the ghost. The ending is again shaped by practical forces, as events precipitate through people's actions, not as a direct consequence of the ghost's injunction. However, the play does throw into relief crucial religious issues: not only the real nature and provenance of ghosts, but the propriety of mourning, and the nature of dying itself. And, as Kastan concludes his elegant and thoughtful study, 'in the space of those uncertainties the play transforms theology into tragedy' (p. 143).

It is worth mentioning, at least briefly, Maurice Charney's *Shakespeare's Style*, even though it is not meant primarily for an academic audience, but rather for the informed reader and spectator—probably more the latter, since it dedicates one short chapter to each of the thirty-four plays ascribed undoubtedly to Shakespeare whereas it does not deal with the poems. It could still, of course, be of interest to academics and especially teachers. Individual chapters would serve well as starting points to stimulate student discussion, as could the book's overall theme: the centrality of 'unresolved dramatic conflict' (p. 177) to Shakespeare's art.

In *Shakespeare's Nature: From Cultivation to Culture* Charlotte Scott effects a thorough reconnaissance of the subject of husbandry and cultivation in early modern England, drawing on a wealth of resources, such as contemporary best-selling manuals by Thomas Tusser and Gervase Markham. This book charts 'the extent to which attitudes to husbandry could reveal a discourse of social relations', and how those attitudes changed as 'ideas of improvement restructured the relationship between the individual and the commonwealth' (p. 221). In terms of readings of Shakespeare's works, the five main chapters deal with the connection between 'the language of husbandry' and 'social approbation' (p. 28) in the sonnets, the politics of peace in *Henry V* (as represented in Burgundy's speech on France as 'this best garden of the world'), the 'emerging distinction between nature and culture' (p. 121) in *Macbeth*, 'the relative values of essential and modified nature' (p. 151) in *The Winter's Tale*, and 'illusory' landscapes (Prospero's masque and Gonzalo's commonwealth) in *The Tempest*. *Timon of Athens* makes an appearance in the Conclusion, where Scott also briefly addresses the controversial question of Shakespeare's unwillingness to intervene in the matter of the Welcombe enclosures (which did not take place anyway).

With Katie Knowles's *Shakespeare's Boys: A Cultural History* we enter into that category of 'hybrid' books that move partly 'inside' and partly 'outside' Shakespeare, since the second part of her study uses aspects of the performance history of Shakespeare's plays in order to examine changes in the representation of boyhood from the long eighteenth century to our own day. Thus, the insights offered in this part of the book relate more to the social history of those periods than to the plays themselves and include, for instance, how 'the Victorian idea of boyhood had become so idealised and specific that . . . the ideal Shakespearean boy was often, for the Victorians, a girl' (p. 9). Part I, on the other hand, offers readings on the plays themselves. It is divided into three chapters, according to the three categories of young boys identified by Knowles as featuring in Shakespeare's plays. Chapter 1 deals with 'noble heirs', who struggle and generally fail to be seen as individual children rather than the representatives of a dynastic line, and meet a brutal end as a consequence (in the history plays, *Macbeth*, and *The Winter's Tale*). Chapter 2 examines the predicament of children who are 'required to stand in for absent male relatives in a context of violence and revenge' (p. 6) in the Roman plays *Titus Andronicus* and *Coriolanus*. Knowles links this to a discussion of 'the complex and often contradictory ways in which boys achieved manhood in early modern England' (p. 65). Her subject is particularly suited to a discussion of *Coriolanus* given, on the one hand, the characterization of the hero by Bate and Rasmussen as 'Peter Pan in full body armour' (cited and rather qualified by Knowles on p. 83) and, on the other, the play's topical link with contemporary portrayals of Henry, Prince of Wales. Chapter 3 refers to the contemporary debate on the merits of an old-style education through apprenticeship or service versus the merits of formal schooling, and links it especially to a discussion of Moth in *Love's Labour's Lost* and Falstaff's Boy in *2 Henry IV* and *Henry V*.

Knowles's book and Deanne Williams's study of *Shakespeare and the Performance of Girlhood* belong to the same Palgrave series, and are thus implicitly packaged, though not explicitly presented, as companion pieces to each other. Indeed Knowles opens the way to Williams's book by stating that 'an examination of "Shakespeare's girls" deserves its own book-length study' (p. 4), but only after potentially undermining such a project in the process of justifying the choice of limiting the subject of her own study to male children: with one exception, 'the girls who appear in Shakespeare's plays are often babies' or 'tend to be young women, of marriageable age . . . the plays' depiction of them as marriageable suggests that they are entering the adult phase of life' (p. 3). Williams does not sufficiently address this issue, i.e. she does not really define what constitutes a 'girl' as opposed to a 'woman' in Shakespeare's plays, unless it is through the recurring argument that girls are defined by the performance of girlhood. There is an interesting initial discussion of the origins and connotations of terms such as 'girl' and 'wench'. In Shakespeare the term 'girl' is applied to self-willed young women (in *The Two Gentlemen of Verona* and *Romeo and Juliet*—see chapter 1), but there is also 'the sense that girlhood is bound up with tears' (p. 67), for instance in *The Taming of the Shrew*. Chapter 2, on 'Isabelle de France', 'recovers' the historical child-bride figure, in opposition to the fact that the Queen in *Richard II* is seen by most readers as an adult. Chapter 3 zooms in on the lute-playing 'Ofelia' in Q1 *Hamlet*. Chapter 4 begins by discussing the girlhood of Elizabeth I both as a historical figure and as portrayed in Thomas Heywood's *If You Know Not Me, You Know Nobody*, and then moves on to the 'lost girls' in *Pericles*, *The Tempest*, and *The Winter's Tale*. (The exception mentioned by Knowles, Clarence's daughter in *Richard III*, does not feature in this study.) Parts II and III are likely to constitute the more original and valuable section of the book, as they move outside Shakespeare's plays to examine, respectively, the shift in Jacobean and Caroline masques, including Milton's *Comus*, where girls were allowed to perform, and seventeenth-century 'writing girls' Lady Rachel Fane and the Cavendish sisters.

Ostensibly an 'outside' book, *Shakespeare and Politics*, edited by Bruce E. Altschuler and Michael A. Genovese, in fact has much to offer in terms of insights into the plays themselves. Its stated purpose is that of using Shakespeare's plays to throw light on contemporary politics, especially those of America (which it does without pulling its punches: see for instance the parallel between Richard III and Richard Nixon on p. 14). The editors are both political scientists, and so are most of the contributors. However, the fast-paced discussions of the plays are illuminating in themselves, and do take into account their multidimensionality. I would love to use this book in a course on Shakespeare—perhaps after doing a bit of editing, as I would not want my students to write about 'Volumina' (pp. 8–9) in their *Coriolanus* essay (that said, there are not really many typos in this unassuming but well-crafted book). This is one of several plays discussed by Michael A. Genovese and Thomas E. Cronin in chapter 1, 'On Shakespeare's Commanders and Kings'. It is worth quoting a passage from this chapter to show why young people who are about to take up their place in the world are likely to appreciate both this book's contents and its style: 'Leaders make choices, good and bad. Where their choices are designed for self-promotion, they often fail; when their choices are made rashly, they often fail; when they decide based on poor or faulty information, they usually fail; where they are too self-absorbed, they usually fail. It is in the choosing that Shakespeare's politics and his morality play out. Fate may play a role, but human intervention—choice—matters most' (p. 3). In chapter 2 Bruce E. Altschuler discusses '*Macbeth* and Political Corruption', demonstrating the play's relevance to a reflection on this evil in our day by looking at a number of modern productions and remakes, from Orson Welles's 1948 *Macbeth* through Barbara Garson's *MacBird!* [1966] to Rupert Goold's 2007–10 production with Patrick Stewart in the title role. In chapter 3, 'A Dionysian Hamlet', Sarah A. Shea takes Nietzsche's definition of Hamlet as a 'Dionysian man' as the starting point for her analysis of this character's journey towards the achievement of 'the necessary intellectual discipline and spiritual fortitude' (p. 48). Shea sees Hamlet as 'Shakespeare's political philosopher par excellence' (pp. 49–50) and points to his eventual acquisition of self-knowledge and coming to terms with his 'unruly drives' (p. 61) as an example to be followed by anyone wanting to take any role in politics, from election candidate to simple voter. Paul A. Cantor's '*Antony and Cleopatra*: Empire, Globalization, and the Clash of Civilizations' draws a parallel between present-day globalization and Shakespeare's reflection on Roman history and politics, while, on the other hand, in discussing another Roman play Philip Abbott, in 'Decisions, Decisions, Decisions: Tyrannicide in *Julius Caesar*', focuses on the assassination of the Roman dictator as a universal example of a crisis situation, in which one decision engenders many others. In his brief chapter on 'Why Iago Is Evil: *Othello* and the American Desire to Understand Corruption', Coyle Neal asserts that 'Americans have a desire to understand *why* that pervades the culture' (p. 99). Neal gives as examples of this the sermon with which John Winthrop sought to justify God-sanctioned inequality in 1630 ('among the first words spoken publicly in colonial America', p. 100) and the way in which the most striking thematic deviation from its Shakespearian original in Tim Blake Nelson's 2001 film *O* is its repeated emphasis on jealousy (in the sense of rivalry) as the single, insisted motivation for the actions of Hugo, its Iago-equivalent. Marlene K. Sokolon's chapter, on 'Richard III, Tyranny, and the Modern Financial Elite', shows how 'Shakespeare's play . . . questions whether democratic peace abolishes the possibility of a Richard in our world' (p. 106) and then depicts a worrying scenario in which the 'financial elite' provides the modern-day environment where such an unscrupulous character might 'plot with fewer legal and constitutional constraints' (p. 107). The remaining chapters (simply listed here because of space constraints) deal with equally and even more substantial issues, such as '*Cymbeline* and the Origins of Modern Liberty' (David Ramsey), 'Shakespeare's *Henry V* and Responsibility for War' (John M. Parrish), '*Troilus and Cressida*: The Value of Reputations and the Corruption of Society' (Lilly J. Goren), 'Deception and Persuasion in *Measure for Measure*' (Carol McNamara), and 'Absurdity and Amateur Hour in the American Political Forest: *A Midsummer Night's Dream* and the Nightmare of Polarization' (Kevan M. Yenerall). From the point of view of what this book tells us about Shakespeare's works in themselves, besides the intrinsic interest of the readings proposed here, there is the fact that by showing how loud and clear Shakespeare puts his political message across this collection supports the view of those who see the plays as actively engaged in the historical and political context of their time, and as addressing important messages to the ruling elite of Elizabethan and Jacobean England.

Kate McLuskie and Kate Rumbold's *Cultural Value in Twenty-First-Century England: The Case of Shakespeare* describes the difficulties intrinsic in the task of defining 'cultural value', even in such a seemingly obvious case as Shakespeare. In this respect, it identifies a 'shift . . . from a view of culture as a special arena of social and intellectual activity to one that dealt with the commonplace, day-to-day leisure activities of the whole population' (pp. 242–3), and how 'the locus of intrinsic value' migrated 'from the product to the audience' (p. 245). (One wonders, however, whether it might not be possible to apply a method similar to that developed by Franco Moretti and his team to 'measure' the canon of the nineteenth-century novel, i.e. a diagram where one axis indicates popular engagement—in Shakespeare's case, for instance, number of spectators, amateur productions, etc.—and the other measures the number of academic studies and editions.) The back cover blurb for this book claims that 'it uniquely uses social policy, anthropology and economics, as well as close readings of Shakespeare's plays'. Though the social study aspect is preponderant, this volume too, therefore, adopts a 'hybrid' approach, as it discusses 'value' both as currently applied to Shakespeare and as represented within a number of Shakespearian plays (on pp. 56–75), particularly *Troilus and Cressida* and *The Merchant of Venice*. There are also references to performance history (for instance, on pp. 130–40), in line with the fact that 'the cultural value of [Shakespeare's] works increasingly depends upon the added value of performance' (p. 247). On the other hand, the final three chapters, mostly the responsibility of Kate Rumbold, are entirely devoted to today's cultural industry and Shakespeare's position within it, as they deal with 'Government and the Values of Culture', 'Value in Shakespeare Institutions', and 'Branding Shakespeare'.

Moving on to the 'Reference' section, Marion Gibson and Jo Ann Esra's *Shakespeare's Demonology* is one of the 2014 additions to what is now the Arden Shakespeare Dictionaries series, an excellent publishing enterprise that has brought us Stuart Gillespie's dictionary of sources, *Shakespeare's Books*, and other useful scholarly tools. The volume is laudably more comprehensive than just a guide to *Macbeth* and Poor Tom's utterances in *King Lear*, though perhaps we would not expect Viola's metaphorical involvement with 'charms' and 'poor monsters' in *Twelfth Night* to earn her six mentions in a dictionary on this subject, as can be gathered from the index that usefully supplements the alphabetical arrangement by keywords (in addition, searchable e-book versions are available for this as for other volumes in the series). The brief introduction draws attention to how 'porous' the boundaries of this subject can in fact be (p. 3), and summarizes the demonology-related sources to which Shakespeare may have had access and the role the subject plays in Shakespeare's works. An especially valuable feature is the seventeen-page up-to-date bibliography.

It may be worth reminding readers that with volume 4, *1598–1602*, Martin Wiggins and Catherine Richardson's *British Drama 1533–1642: A Catalogue* (cf. *YWES* 93[2014] and 94[2015]) has started to reach Shakespeare's major plays. This volume covers *Much Ado About Nothing*, *Henry V*, *Julius Caesar*,

As You Like It, Hamlet, Sir Thomas More, Twelfth Night, and *Troilus and Cressida*, as well as providing an entry for *Love's Labour's Won* and including references to Shakespeare in relation to a variety of other plays from this period. The dating of Shakespeare's (and other early modern) plays was always going to be a contentious issue, but most readers will nonetheless be grateful even for a generic point of reference: in this catalogue the dating is not presented dogmatically, and in the absence of precise evidence we are given both 'Limits' and a 'Best Guess'. The arrangement by best-guess date is in fact invaluable in that it allows us to see at a glance what other less well-known plays were being produced round about the time of the major works of early modern English drama. Entries are meticulous, recording every morsel of available factual evidence on the plays' early textual and performance history, and therefore may offer some neglected fact or source even to experts on a particular play.

In fact, we need to support such large-scale, long-term, labour-intensive projects. Because of its prominence, academic publishing on Shakespeare is liable to showcase any fall in standards. Without wanting to generalize, the temptation to point the finger at a quantity-over-quality, publish-or-perish, quick turnaround regime is strong when one repeatedly comes across certain problems in books issued by major academic publishers: one book gave the title of an early Shakespearian comedy as *Two Gentleman of Verona*—not once or twice, but throughout, including the index; in another, the bibliography showed signs of shockingly poor editing; another's introduction, in summarizing the first chapter, repeated sentences verbatim from it; and in several cases authors had clearly been under pressure to make hyperbolic statements as to the uniqueness of their topic that are then contradicted by the review of previous scholarship in their first pages. We are certainly not the first to call for greater investment of both time and resources to return to academic publishing: so as to enable the sort of care and attention that comes through, for instance, in a book for the general public such as *Shakespeare for Grown-Ups*, by Penguin Random House editors Elizabeth Foley and Beth Coates.

(b) Problem Plays

This year has seen a variety of approaches to all three of Shakespeare's problem plays, covering a range of issues relating to the plays' historical contexts, their sources, and their afterlives on stage. One of the most fruitful topics for discussion on *Measure for Measure* was related to the issues provoked by the Duke's strategies of surveillance in the play. This conceit is at the centre of William M. Hamlin's essay, 'Conscience and the God-Surrogate in Montaigne and *Measure for Measure*' (in Gray and Cox, eds., *Shakespeare and Renaissance Ethics*, pp. 237–60), one of two of this year's essays to consider the problem plays in relation to the influence of Michel de Montaigne. Here, Hamlin places *Measure for Measure* in dialogue with Montaignean scepticism, particularly in relation to the role of conscience; both authors, according to Hamlin, 'think about conscience when conscience fails to function in the ways that their shared cultural inheritance tells them it should' (p. 237). Hamlin argues that Shakespeare consistently responds to the Montaignean view of conscience as a 'scrupulously accurate inward recognition of personal guilt or rectitude' and 'a cognitive state of such extraordinary potency that it consistently finds means to channel itself into outward manifestation' (p. 238). Following on from this view of conscience, Hamlin highlights several occurrences of tropes in Shakespeare's plays that he identifies as 'god-surrogates', which are defined as 'forms of mimetic representation' that 'function to prompt or prod conscience' when it fails 'to carry through with its alleged potential to expose the truth of inward states' (p. 243). One of the most notable instances of this is Hamlet's deployment of the play-within-the-play to expose Claudius's guilt. The Duke's scheme of disguise and surveillance in *Measure for Measure* is seen as a larger-scale replication of the same exercise in order to have Angelo examine his conscience; unlike Claudius, however, Angelo 'has an opportunity to redeem himself by behaving with moral probity' rather than simply revealing his guilty conscience (p. 247). The Duke's treatment of Angelo is based upon the deployment of a variety of 'god-surrogates', including the bed-trick and the need for him to judge Claudio's transgression (both of which are unsuccessful in forcing Angelo to examine his conscience), before capitalizing on a third 'god-surrogate' in the form of Isabella's intervention in the final scene. In spite of being 'pained by his hypocrisy', Angelo does not allow his conscience to spur him into confessing his vices; in this way, he demonstrates that conscience is at work within him, 'though it scarcely functions at anything like the optimistic level imagined by the Duke . . . or by Montaigne in his more positive moments' (p. 255).

Tai-Won Kim's article, 'Pastoral Power and Theatricality: Early Modern Governmentality in Shakespeare's *Measure for Measure*' (*MES* 22:ii[2014] 29–51), begins by emphasizing the play's status as a rare example of one of Shakespeare's comedies that 'enable us to meditate on and discuss the idea of government in early modern England' (p. 29). This focus upon 'the art of government, in both early modern senses of statecraft and governing one's self' helps to reveal how 'the art of government becomes the nodal point of early modern subjectivity' (p. 30). The article considers the Duke's delegation of political authority to Angelo and sees both the Duke's reputation for self-examination and the hypocrisies of Angelo's administration as products of the 'close relationship' Shakespeare establishes 'between political government and the government of one's self' (p. 36). Other focal points in this reading include the Duke's harnessing of theatricality, both in his disguise as the Friar which allows him simultaneously to 'establish his moral superiority and invisible power' while 'keeping a safe distance from the corruption and degradation in Vienna' (p. 38), and in the decidedly theatrical reinstatement of his power at the play's conclusion. The Duke's histrionic reassertion of his power allows him to provide an exemplar of 'respect, admiration, and awe', which serves to address 'an urgent need to find ways to make individuals internalize normative values and ethics' (p. 45). In this reading, then, the Duke's scheme depends not just upon his reassertion of political authority, but also upon inspiring the ability of successful and virtuous self-government in his subjects.

The Duke's governmental strategies are also considered in Benjamin J. Whalen's article, 'Private Conscience, Public Reform, and Disguised Rule in *The Malcontent* and *Measure for Measure*' (*BJJ* 21:i[2014] 73–91). This article considers *Measure for Measure* in the context of the 'disguised duke' genre that enjoyed a brief vogue at the beginning of James's reign and of which John Marston's *The Malcontent* is another notable example. According to Whalen, the plays' similarities go beyond the shared trope of the disguised ruler into more specific themes, including the 'effect of a state's intrusion into the realm of private conscience through the government's adoption of religious authority' and concerns with 'the extensive negative effects of sin upon the community, and the need for repentance to include a sinner's private reconciliation with God and the correction of his relationship with his community' (p. 75). In this sense, both plays show the respective rulers' disguises as means of bringing about broad societal changes through intervention on a personal, microcosmic level. Such endeavours require the rulers to pay particular attention to the spiritual welfare of their subjects; Whalen argues that such concerns on the part of the respective dukes go beyond any 'practical plans or political gains' and are instead rooted in 'an altruistic concern for the spiritual good' of their more recalcitrant subjects (p. 79). This is manifested most specifically in Vincentio's choice of disguise in *Measure for Measure*, with his 'symbolic assumption of the friar's robes' representing 'his essential connection to the spiritual life of the community' (p. 82). This, for Whalen, represents the crucial distinction between the two plays; whilst Marston's Altofronto 'encourages penance in the guise of a malcontent critic', Vincentio's choice of clerical role is a means of 'connecting his physical habit and disguise to the theological language of repentance that he so often invokes' (p. 83). This reading therefore aims to look beyond what are often regarded as cynical governmental strategies adopted by the disguised rulers and to argue for an additional motivation for the disguises based upon pastoral responsibilities to ensure the spiritual health of their commonwealths.

The theological implications of the play were explored in various contributions to scholarly work on *Measure for Measure*. Musa Gurnis's article, '"Most ignorant of what he's most assured": The Hermeneutics of Predestination in *Measure for Measure*' (*ShakS* 42[2014] 141–69), opens by stating that the play 'demonstrates a sustained preoccupation with the central experiential challenge of predestination' and that it 'investigates predestinarian theology and its attendant forms of cultural judgement as an epistemological problem' (p. 141). For Gurnis, such investigations are dependent upon the responses of a theologically diverse audience; the play engages in a 'manipulation of audience and expectation' which 'establishes and then challenges the presumption of a correlation between one's inward predestined condition and external, social status' (pp. 147–8), resulting in a play in which 'souls cannot be slotted into worldly categories' (p. 148). The bulk of the article performs an analysis of Angelo, as a means of representing the play's insistence upon the 'opacity of souls' (p. 158). At his first appearance, Angelo is associated with election in the language employed towards him, before the play gradually unfolds the troubling elements of his character. Through the representation of Angelo, the play initially encourages sympathy and identification with his emotional turmoil before revealing his sinful nature in his attempts at sexually exploiting Isabella. In this way, 'Angelo's cultural identity as a godly man is shown to be an unreliable indicator of the predestined condition of his soul' and, 'instead of revealing his "true state," Angelo's self-diagnosis as one of the damned is itself undermined by the play's comic resolution' (p. 159). By encouraging such mixed responses in the audience, the play therefore engages them in a process that underlines the disjunction between an individual's outward appearance and the condition of their soul, thus highlighting the unreliability of spiritual examination.

The theological issues posed by *Measure for Measure* are also considered in two essays from *Stages of Engagement: Drama and Religion in Post-Reformation England*, edited by James D. Mardock and Kathryn R. McPherson. The first of these is Kathryn R. McPherson's chapter, 'Performing Catechism in *Measure for Measure*' (pp. 155–70), which explores the implications of catechism as a 'pedagogical strategy' (p. 155), particularly in Isabella's first encounter with Angelo. McPherson argues that '*Measure for Measure* offers a fascinating opportunity to explore . . . early modern echoes in the public theaters of the era', as well as to explore the play's emphases upon 'the complexities of reformed faith, gender, and power' and the ways in which it offers a 'critique of how those forces interact' (p. 158). Shakespeare's provision of an opportunity for Isabella to perform catechetical practices, particularly in her interrogation of Angelo, sees the play challenge contemporary tendencies for pedagogy to reinforce gender roles. He thus represents 'an educated, articulate Isabella who, in becoming a sort of catechist to Angelo, resists the very social roles toward which her education had impelled her' (p. 161). Whilst Isabella may engage in catechetical practices, she, and indeed the audience, are left with numerous unanswered questions, and Angelo's failure to learn such premises as 'mercy, moderation, or even honest self-examination' means that Isabella's encounter with him does not ultimately achieve the desired ends of catechism (p. 168). McPherson concludes that this scene reflects the broader development of the play, leaving as it does numerous 'unanswered questions' at its conclusion, which potentially highlight the 'failure of catechetical methods . . . to teach citizens to think through the implications of their faith and judgement' (p. 169).

The same collection also contains Terri Bourus's essay, 'Counterfeiting Faith: Middleton's Theatrical Reformation of *Measure for Measure*' (pp. 195–216). Here, Bourus considers the implications of Thomas Middleton's adaptation of *Measure for Measure* from the early 1620s and emphasizes the need to consider this play as the work of 'two playwrights with markedly different religious profiles' (p. 202). It is also important to consider the fact that the play effectively has two composition dates and that 'the religious climate had significantly changed' by the time Middleton came to revise it, not least because of the impact of the Gunpowder Plot of 1605. The Middletonian revisions respond to this new climate by changing the setting to Vienna, thereby addressing the 'violent religious boundaries' provoked by the Thirty Years War (p. 207). Bourus also makes a number of connections between the Middletonian revisions and his other dramatic works in order to emphasize his preoccupation throughout his career with the representation of Protestantism on stage.

Terri Bourus also collaborated this year with Gary Taylor on *Measure for Measure*(s): Performance-Testing the Adaptation Hypothesis' (*Shakespeare* 10:iv[2014] 363–401) which, like Bourus's other essay this year, considers the implications of the 'genetic text' (p. 363) of *Measure for Measure* produced by John Jowett for the Oxford complete works of Middleton, which aimed both to identify the Middletonian revisions and to reconstruct the original Shakespearian text. This article is an account of the authors' work with the Hoosier Bard company to mount productions of the two distinct texts as a means of experimenting to explore the effects of the adaptation hypothesis. Amongst the issues considered in this article are the effects of Middleton's version being destined to be performed at Blackfriars, the omission of the earlier version's concluding jig, the reappearance of Julietta in the final scene of the revised version, the introduction of various characters (an effect of many of Middleton's revisions clustering around the beginning of scenes and the first appearances of characters), the representation of the female characters, and the changes in public attitudes towards James I that had taken place between the composition of the two versions. Amongst the principal conclusions offered by the article are that the reconstructed earlier version of the play does constitute a coherent, self-contained, and performable dramatic text, as does the revised version, and that the revisions have a significant bearing upon the production as a whole, as 'changes at one point in a character's arc can change the vector of that actor's interpretations' and, because of the interactions and collaborations with the other actors, they 'can have a domino effect on surrounding characters' (p. 394).

The recent performance history of *Measure for Measure* is also considered in Huw Griffiths's article, 'Hotel Rooms and Bodily Fluids in Two Recent Productions of *Measure for Measure*, or, Why Barnardine Is Still Important' (*ShakB* 32:iv[2014] 559–83). Griffiths focuses upon the use of the character of Barnardine in two productions of the play; in spite of his 'relatively marginal position in the narrative', this character is used to tie together a number of the play's key themes in these productions, particularly the position of the individual in relation to the law. The earlier production, staged at the Belvoir theatre, Sydney, in 2010 and directed by Benedict Andrews, contained an extra-textual scene, performed without any dialogue, which takes place in a luxury hotel room and features a naked Barnardine wrecking the room and smearing blood and excrement over the walls. Another production, from the director Thomas Ostermeier, performed the following year at the Schaubühne theatre in Berlin, had Barnardine represented by a pig's carcass which was suspended above the stage and used as a prop in various scenes. The play's head-trick is instigated by having the Provost saw off the pig's head with a chainsaw. Griffiths explores the ways in which these contemporary productions reflected the play's 'oft-noted concerns with justice and surveillance and with forms of personation and substitution' (p. 559), as well as such related issues as torture, physical abjection, and the relationship between the body and the law. Griffiths thus highlights significant continuities between the concerns of these performances and the play's interrogation of the bearings of such issues in the seventeenth century.

Alongside Hamlin's essay, Montaigne also figures in this year's scholarship on *All's Well That Ends Well*. Arthur Kirsch's article, 'The Bitter and the Sweet of Tragicomedy: Shakespeare's *All's Well That Ends Well* and Montaigne' (*YR* 102:ii[2014] 63–84), considers Shakespeare's turn towards the tragicomic genre in the 'problem' comedies of the early 1600s, and particularly the genre's potential for 'exploring the actual texture of human experience', thereby associating itself directly with the methods employed for self-examination in Montaigne's *Essays* (p. 66). Montaigne's influence upon Shakespeare's turn towards tragicomedy, Kirsch argues, can be discerned particularly through the shared emphases on sexuality, with Shakespeare 'drawing upon Montaigne's sense of his embodied being, and most especially his sexual being' (p. 68). Kirsch outlines a number of parallels between *All's Well* and Montaigne's essay 'Upon Some Verses of Virgil', including their shared sense of the disjunction between noble birth and virtue, and highlights *All's Well* as 'a reflection of Montaigne's tragicomic way of thinking about sexuality', particularly the decline of youthful sexual prowess (p. 69). Kirsch also explores how the two texts meditate upon the often vexed relationship between love and sexuality, and concludes by considering how *All's Well* anticipates the engagement with Montaigne in Shakespeare's late romances.

Also considering the European influences upon *All's Well That Ends Well* is Eric Nicholson's essay, 'Helen, the Italianate Theatrical Wayfarer in *All's Well That Ends Well*' (in Marrapodi, ed., pp. 163–79), which proposes a series of Italianate influences upon the play which go beyond what is often acknowledged to be its principal source, the tale of Giletta di Narbona from the third day of Giovanni Boccaccio's *Decameron* cycle. Nicholson bases his analysis upon a model of 'resources in common' which follows the premise that 'professional theatre practitioners of early modern Europe developed a working method of assimilating and transforming, each in their own way, a common pool of gags, poetic tropes, character types, plot-lines, and narrative devices' (p. 165), meaning that Shakespeare's engagement with his sources was in fact part of a more complex method of cultural appropriation than 'the kind of one-way "influence" or even competitive imitation postulated by traditional literary histories' (p. 165). According to Nicholson, the adaptation would have involved, in part, a collaborative endeavour between Shakespeare and his players which would have entailed 'trying out, mixing and matching, cutting and pasting, as it were, a heterogeneous variety of theatrically oriented devices, some of them Italianate and made available by travelling actors' and audiences' reports' (p. 165). Such premises provide a framework for analysing a number of tropes drawn from Italianate theatrical tradition, including Helena's association with the figure of the *prima donna innamorata*, and Paroles' similarities to the Capitano figure. Nicholson therefore argues that *All's Well*'s response to Italianate culture is in fact the product of an engagement with a variety of theatrical tropes, practices, and conventions, rather than a response to an individual narrative template. Such engagement also lends the play a sense of self-conscious theatricality, conveyed especially through the representation of Helena.

The year's scholarship on *All's Well* also includes a short note by Karen Britland. In 'Psalm 140 and Diana's Crux in *All's Well That Ends Well*' (*N&Q* 61[2014] 241–4), Britland examines one of the most puzzling cruces in the Shakespearian canon. Diana's lines in response to Bertram's wooing in IV.ii ('I see that make rope's in such a scarre') have been the subject of considerable editorial debate and, relatively recently, provoked a radical emendation by Gary Taylor for the Oxford edition of the play. Britland contests Taylor's emendation of the line to 'I see that make toys e'en such a surance' by instead arguing for a lighter emendation to 'I see that men may rope's in such a snare'. This emendation is based largely upon verbal parallels with the fifth verse of Psalm 140 in various translations as well as the two texts' common emphases upon 'the ways in which the evil speakers lay traps for the unwary' (p. 213).

Two of the three essays on *Troilus and Cressida* from this year both focus, coincidentally, on the effect of musical cues in the play. Russell West-Pavlov's article, 'Trumpets and Strumpets: Time, Space, Emulation and Violence in Shakespeare's *Troilus and Cressida*' (*Anglia* 131:i[2014] 1–22), examines the effects and resonances of a number of trumpet calls that take place throughout the play. West-Pavlov highlights the numerous bearings that this 'theatrical sign' has upon the 'semiotic structure of the drama', particularly in terms of the representation of the scenario (in the midst of war), the place (a military camp), and the time ('the threshold to combat') (p. 2). Trumpet calls also relate closely to the principal themes of the play and the representation of a 'masculine ethos of warlike bravour which depends upon ongoing conflict to reinforce its warlike identity' (p. 3). Such concerns are complemented by the trumpet call's contribution to a 'self-reflexive turn which, by addressing the problem of imitation', relates its self-conscious theatricality to questions of masculine emulation (p. 3). The various trumpet calls, signalling, by turns, prompts to demonstrations of masculine prowess, the exchange of women, and the performative and emulative properties of chivalry, therefore combine to participate in the play's inscription of 'the Trojan War narrative and its Shakespearean deconstruction within a new economy of entertainment as entrepreneurial exchange' (p. 16). Such commodification highlights the theatre's own situation within an emergent consumer culture; as a result, the kinds of 'spiralling processes of violence' dramatized by the play were experienced 'as a brake upon the development of an increasingly hegemonic economic system of wealth- rather than rank-based competition' (p. 19).

The relationship between temporality and musical devices also figures in Erin Minear's essay, 'Music for Helen: The Fitful Changes of *Troilus and Cressida*' (in Dunn and Larson, eds., *Gender and Song in Early Modern England*, pp. 153–68), which argues that it is a work in which 'the treatment of music, by playing on the tension between philosophical harmony and sonic experience, provides a new—even inverted—perspective that confers value on change and the ephemeral' (p. 154), with music also serving to undermine the association between sound and motion. The chapter begins by examining III.i, a scene dominated by musical metaphors and culminating in a song by Pandarus. This follows Paris' mocking of Pandarus' 'emptily repetitive language' with a further implication that the song to follow will be identical to the 'fits' for which he is criticized—'empty hiccups of sound' (p. 155)—and, indeed, with its 'relentless repetition of the word "love"', the resultant song 'enacts the progress of sexual desire and finally devolves into meaningless, if suggestive, syllables' (p. 156). The prominence of this song during the only scene to feature Helen, the subject of the conflict, is one example of the ways in which the play 'insistently breaks down the cherished distinction between the virtuous "harmony" of war and the effeminate music of love. Both kinds of music are marked by an exaggerated emphasis on materiality and meaning-lessness' (pp. 157–8). Pandarus' song is also reflective of how 'the play's narrative struggles to unfold in time, but cannot since all the plot develop-ments are not only inevitable, but already present, "couched" in the current instant' (p. 162), meaning that the characters in the play are unable to escape from the historical figures they are destined to become; this results in a situation in which 'the future is superimposed over the present' (pp. 161–2). Pandarus' song also comes to reflect 'this static reality, functioning emblematically as the kind of song such a man would sing' (p. 163). Such points are brought to bear by Minear upon the play's representation of Cressida and the inevitability that she will forever be characterized by her sexuality and ability to 'sing any man at first sight'.

The recent performance history of *Troilus and Cressida* is also covered in this year's scholarship by Aneta Mancewicz's article, 'Looking Back at the Audience: The RSC & the Wooster Group's *Troilus and Cressida* (2012)' (*MultSh* 11:xxvi[2014] 65–79), which examines the critically unsuccessful collaborative production of the play by the British and American companies. The two groups worked largely independently with distinct staging and conceptual choices (the RSC took on the roles of the Greek characters, while the New York-based Wooster Group presented the Trojans). For Mancewicz, the controversial reception of this venture 'exposed differences in the staging of Shakespeare between the UK and the US, as well as between classical and avant-garde theatre'; in this way, the production offers us an 'insight into the nature of Shakespearean staging and spectating in Anglophone culture' (p. 66). Mancewicz draws on the experience of seeing the production in performance, alongside a selection of reviews and critical responses to it, in order to outline how such responses brought to the fore a number of preoccupations with Shakespearian performance in Britain, including 'the perception of the text as an autonomous universe governed by realistic rules, psychological principles, and immediate political concerns'; as a result, the production was particularly notable for how it provided a reflection of its audience and the ways in which it 'powerfully exposed their assumptions and preferences' (p. 76).

(c) Poetry

In 2013 a major publication with focus on Shakespeare's poetry was produced. *The Oxford Handbook of Shakespeare's Poetry*, edited by Jonathan F.S. Post, contains thirty-eight essays each focusing on different aspects of Shakespeare's poetry. Despite the title, the majority of the book contains essays which are not specifically about Shakespeare's poems as such, but engage with a number of his dramatic works. The book is divided into seven parts, grouping between three and ten essays in each. Part I, 'Style and Language', contains five essays. The first of these, 'Shakespeare's Styles' by Gordon Teskey, focuses on the changing of Shakespeare's writing style over the course of his life, with Teskey noting, 'Over the course of his approximately twenty-year career, Shakespeare's style quite naturally changed, so that we may speak of him writing in a succession of styles' (p. 3). Teskey examines the Shakespeare canon as a whole, engaging with a number of the plays, but spends significant time on *Hamlet* and the 'To be, or not to be' soliloquy. There is a similar focus on later passages both in this play and also a number of others to bolster his position. Chapter 2 is 'Shakespeare's Style in the 1590's' by Goran Stanivukovic, in which the author argues that the final decade of the sixteenth century saw greater importance being placed on language than on stories and characters. Stanivukovic frames his argument in three subsections and engages with critics from both Renaissance and modern times. Chapter 3, 'Shakespeare's Late Style' by A.R. Braunmuller, continues the focus begun by Stanivukovic but looks in more depth at Shakespeare's later activity. Braunmuller engages with a number of plays, with particular focus on the comparatively early *Macbeth* and ending his essay with an examination of *The Winter's Tale*. As with Stanivukovic's essay there is also reference to older critics; Braunmuller makes specific reference to John Dryden and discusses Shakespeare's work in the terms framed by this author. Chapter 4 is 'Shakespeare and the Arts of Cognition' by Sophie Read, and begins with a brief discussion of *Hamlet* and *Macbeth*. Read compares the two, noting 'If *Hamlet* drags in the most fascinating of ways until its high-speed ending, *Macbeth* traces the reverse trajectory of temporal extremes', noting that the difference in tempo in the two plays can be ascribed to the mental state of the eponymous characters. Read moves on to engage with the sonnets, and again notes the differing cadence throughout the sequence and discusses what may be gleaned from this. Margaret Ferguson's 'Fatal Cleopatras and Golden Apples', which forms chapter 5 and closes Part I, is primarily engaged with Shakespeare's use of wordplay and puns. Ferguson looks at a number of the plays and unsurprisingly spends some time focusing on Sonnet 135, with its frequent repetition of the word 'will'. Ferguson discusses other interpretations of this and other sonnets as well as presenting her own theories.

Part II, 'Inheritance and Invention', contains eight chapters and is headed by Colin Burrow's essay 'Classical Influences'. This piece discusses the classical styles that can be read within Shakespeare's work and begins by examining Shakespeare's knowledge of the classics. Burrow notes that Shakespeare would have been aware of such authors as Ovid and Virgil and points out that *Venus and Adonis* is based on part of Ovid's *Metamorphoses*. Burrow continues by engaging with other Shakespeare works, including *The Rape of Lucrece*, before focusing on the sonnets. Here he notes that 'Shakespeare's debts to classical poetry are elusive and diffusive' (p. 110), and then examines some examples of this debt. Ovid's *Metamorphoses* is also discussed in chapter 7, Anthony Mortimer's essay 'Shakespeare and Italian Poetry', which focuses heavily on Italian poetry of the sixteenth century and how this influenced Shakespeare. Mortimer looks at poets such as Agostini, dell'Anguillara, and Dolce, who all completed Italian translations of Ovid's work, and then examines Shakespeare's continuation of this work with *Venus and Adonis*. Of course any discussion of Italian Renaissance poetry would be incomplete without reference to Petrarch, and Mortimer looks at this author as well as, to a lesser extent, Dante, to add weight to his argument. Mortimer ends his piece by examining in some depth Petrarch's *Canzoniere* and examining the influences found within Shakespeare's sonnets. In chapter 8 Anne Lake Prescott discusses Shakespeare and the French author Joachim Du Bellay in her piece 'Du Bellay and Shakespeare's Sonnets'. Prescott argues that Shakespeare would have read Du Bellay, and that his sonnets were influenced by this author. She also makes the point that Shakespeare was equally influenced by Spenser's *Ruines of Rome* and notes that 'Ruinish'—a term she and the Hieatt brothers have coined to describe 'a lexical force-field made of walls, *tempus edax*, bloody foundations, civil broils, "ruinate", "injurious", "of yore", prideful self-containment, giants, maps, "wear", "outworn", "map", and more' (p. 135)—not only appears frequently in the works of Shakespeare and Spenser but also in numerous other works. Continuing to make reference to 'Ruinish', Prescott moves on to examine Du Bellay's *Antiquitez*, before considering anti-Petrarchism and concluding her essay with a brief discussion of *Titus Andronicus*. Chapter 9, Linda Gregerson's 'Open Voicing: Wyatt and Shakespeare', discusses Thomas Wyatt's translation of Petrarch's *Rime sparse* and the influence this had on Shakespeare. Gregerson begins by noting that Wyatt's translation is much less rhetorical than those that preceded it; she writes that this version is 'Grounded, demotic, shot through with grievance and insinuation' (p. 153), giving a much different impression than the previous versions. Gregerson continues by using her analysis of Wyatt to discuss Shakespeare's works; she engages with a number of the sonnets, as well as the plays, with specific focus on 'a comedy (*Twelfth Night*), a history play (*1 Henry IV*), and a tragedy (*Othello*)' (p. 163). Chapter 10 is '"Grammar Rules" in the Sonnets: Sidney and Shakespeare' by Alysia Kolentsis, in which the author discusses the development of the English language with specific focus on the works of Sidney and Shakespeare. Kolentsis looks in depth at *Astrophel and Stella* and compares Sidney's grammatical usage with that of Shakespeare in a number of sonnets. Chapter 11, Catherine Nicholson's 'Commonplace Shakespeare: Value, Vulgarity and the Poetics of Increase in *Shake-Speares Sonnets* and *Troilus and Cressida*', begins by comparing these two George Eld-produced 1609 editions of Shakespeare's works, noting the varied reception of the works both at the time and by modern scholars. Nicholson continues to discuss the idea of value within both editions as well as touching upon other themes that the works share. Chapter 12, Marion Wells's 'Philomela's Marks: Ekphrasis and Gender in Shakespeare's Poems and Plays', traces the impact of Ovid's version of the classical tale on Shakespeare, focusing on four of his works, including *Lucrece*. Wells discusses the motif of rape that exists within her four chosen texts and draws interesting parallels between the more violent tales of *Lucrece* and *Titus Andronicus* and the 'softer' comedy *The Winter's Tale*. This section is concluded by John Kerrigan's 'Shakespeare, Elegy and Epitaph', which discusses epitaphs written by Shakespeare, including the poet's own. To further his argument Kerrigan engages with a number of the sonnets as well as the less well-known *Phoenix and the Turtle*. The essay also contains a discussion of epitaphs written for Shakespeare by other authors, including John Milton.

Part III, 'Songs, Lyrics and Ballads', contains only two chapters: 'Song in Shakespeare: Rhetoric, Identity and Agency' by Gavin Alexander and 'Shakespeare's Popular Songs and the Great Temptations of Lesser Lyric' by Steve Newman. Both of these essays focus on poetical language within Shakespeare's plays rather than any of the poems themselves; Alexander writes about how we are to respond to the lyric poems within such works as *As You Like It* and *Othello*, while Newman continues this theme with this focus on the songs that appear in some of Shakespeare's more well-known plays including *Hamlet* and *A Midsummer Night's Dream*.

Chapter 16, Abigail Rokison's 'Shakespeare's Dramatic Verse Line', begins Part IV, 'Speaking on Stage'. Like the preceding two chapters, this focuses more on poetical styles within Shakespeare's prose than on his poetry *per se*. Rokison discusses Shakespeare's use of various techniques, including his employment of blank verse, in an attempt to 'consider the potential dramatic function of these various forms' (p. 285). This approach is echoed in chapter 17, 'Shakespeare's Word Music', with Paul Edmondson beginning his essay with a series of passages from a number of plays describing the sound of Shakespeare's poetry as 'music'. The essay continues with an analysis of Viola's speech from *Twelfth Night* before moving the focus to Lady Macbeth's dialogue with the Doctor and Gentlewoman from Act V, scene i of *Macbeth*. Bruce R. Smith's essay, 'Finding Your Footing in Shakespeare's Verse', also addresses poetical styles within Shakespeare's dramatic work. Smith gives the reader advice on how best to understand and appreciate the rhyme and metre of Shakespeare's words, giving examples from many of his plays before briefly engaging with the sonnets to conclude the chapter. Chapter 19, 'From Bad to Verse: Poetry and Spectacle on the Modern Shakespearean Stage' by Jeremy Lopez, asks, 'Is it possible to hear blank pentameter verse during a theatrical performance?' (p. 340). Lopez engages with a number of critics and theatrical personae to find an answer. The final chapter of Part IV is ' "Make My Image but an Alehouse Sign": The Poetry of Women in Shakespeare's Dramatic Verse' by Alison Findlay, and focuses on the symbolism within speeches by female characters within the plays. Beginning with Catherine's English lesson in *Henry V*, Findlay also discusses the poetic voices of Cleopatra and Lady Macbeth, amongst others, to show how the use of language offers different meanings based on the speaker's gender.

Part V, 'Reading Shakespeare's Poems', is the first section that focuses exclusively on Shakespeare's poetry. The ten essays here feature criticism on most of Shakespeare's poetic works, ranging from chapters on the sonnets to an essay on *The Phoenix and the Turtle*. The first of these, ' "To Show and So to Publish": Reading, Writing, and Performing in the Narrative Poems' by Charlotte Scott, examines both *The Rape of Lucrece* and *Venus and Adonis* and how these pieces work effectively as dramatic forms. In chapter 22, Subha Mukherji also looks at *Venus and Adonis* in 'Outgrowing Adonis, Outgrowing Ovid: The Disorienting Nature of *Venus and Adonis*'; the author uses this

poem, and to a lesser extent *Lucrece*, to interrogate Shakespeare's relationship
with Ovid. Joshua Scodel's 'Shame, Love, Fear, and Pride in *The Rape of
Lucrece*' focuses on the manner in which these emotions are portrayed in the
poem. Scodel not only comments on the way Lucrece's emotions are
represented, but also discusses the same elements with regard to Tarquin
and Brutus, before concluding his piece with an examination of shame within
the Golden Age. The next five chapters primarily engage with the sonnets.
Chapter 24, 'The Sonnets in the Classroom: Student, Teacher, Editor-
Annotator(s), and Cruxes' by David Sofield, looks at the difficulties
encountered when teaching the sonnets and offers some analysis of a
number of them. This is followed by L.E. Semler's essay, ' "Fortify Yourself
in Your Decay": Sounding Rhyme and Rhyming Effects in Shakespeare's
Sonnets', which examines the rhyming patterns found within the sequence and
what effect the use of different forms has. Chapter 26 is David Schalkwyk's
'The Conceptual Investigation of Shakespeare's Sonnets', wherein the author
looks at the voices present in these works and the manner in which they are
represented throughout the sequence. Chapter 27, Russ McDonald's ' "Pretty
Rooms": Shakespeare's Sonnets, Elizabethan Architecture and Early Modern
Visual Design', examines a different element of these works, with the author
proposing 'a new context for examining the Sonnets' (p. 486), that of visual
design in the sixteenth century. McDonald examines the poems and suggests
that Shakespeare's use of style and pattern can be linked with similar patterns
found in architecture of the era. In chapter 28, 'The Poetics of Feminine
Subjectivity in Shakespeare's Sonnets and *A Lover's Complaint*', Melissa E.
Sanchez addresses what she feels is a neglected aspect of these two works,
conceding that 'the dark lady is indeed promiscuous', but then asking: '*and so
what if she is?*' (p. 507). Sanchez illustrates her point by discussing the female
perspective in *A Lover's Complaint* before also analysing a small number of the
sonnets. Chapter 29 also engages with *A Lover's Complaint*, with Katherine A.
Craik's 'Poetry and Compassion in Shakespeare's *A Lover Complaint*'. Craik
examines this poem in depth, discussing examples of compassion within the
work, while also engaging with a number of critics of both the Renaissance
and the modern era to express her views. The final chapter of this part, John
Kerrigan's 'Reading *The Phoenix and Turtle*', focuses on one of Shakespeare's
less frequently examined poems. Kerrigan provides the reader with an
examination of the text, discussing a number of themes and interpretations of
the work.

Part VI, 'Later Reflections', contains five essays which are concerned with
Shakespeare's reception in post-Renaissance times. The first of these is
'Shakespearean Poetry and the Romantics' by Michael O'Neill, which
examines the manner in which the Romantic poets responded to
Shakespeare. O'Neill discusses the reaction of poets such as Wordsworth
and Byron, and how Shakespeare's poetry affected these poets in different
ways. In chapter 32, Herbert F. Tucker continues to bring Shakespeare more
up to date in his essay 'Shakespearean Being: The Victorian Bard'. Like
O'Neill in the previous chapter, Tucker looks at the reception of Shakespeare
in this era. Peter Robinson, in chapter 33, 'Shakespeare's Loose Ends and the
Contemporary Poet', carries out a similar exercise with relation to modern

poets, including Ted Hughes, John Ashbery, and Elizabeth Bishop, noting that a number of these poets created poems in direct response to Shakespeare's works. Unlike the previous two essays, the major point of focus for Robinson's piece is the plays rather than the poetry with which O'Neill and Tucker primarily engage. James Longenbach, in 'The Sound of Shakespeare Thinking', takes a slightly different approach. Beginning with a discussion of key scenes in *The Tempest* and *3 Henry VI*, Longenbach notes how 'Thinking in Shakespeare is what turns us, changes us, makes us move.' The author proceeds to discuss some of the Romantic poets before concluding his chapter with a brief discussion of Shakespeare in relation to Woolf's *Mrs Dalloway*. Judith Hall's 'Melted in American Air' concludes Part VI and discusses the reception of Shakespeare in the United States. Hall examines the reaction of a number of American figures and does not limit herself to those involved solely in the written media, discussing the likes of Cole Porter alongside more traditional subjects such as Walt Whitman.

The final part of the book, Part VII, 'Translating Shakespeare', contains three essays all concerned with the issues faced when translating the poetry of Shakespeare into a different language. The first of these, 'Yves Bonnefoy and Shakespeare as a French Poet' by Efrain Kristal, examines the manner in which Bonnefoy, a celebrated poet in his own right, translated a number of Shakespeare's works, including *Venus and Adonis*, *Lucrece*, and the complete sonnets. Kristal also briefly discusses alternative translations before concluding his piece with an examination of Bonnefoy's translations of a number of the plays. Chapter 37, 'Glocal Shakespeare: Shakespeare's Poems in Germany' by Christa Jansohn, discusses how Shakespeare's poetry is as well received by the German audience as his plays. Jansohn examines a number of theatrical productions of the narrative poems before discussing why there has not been a well-received translation of the sonnets. The book concludes with Belén Bistué's 'Negotiating the Universal: Translations of Shakespeare's Poetry In (Between) Spain and Spanish America'. In this essay Bistué discusses the unique challenges faced by those who wish to translate Shakespeare's poetry into Spanish considering the historical enmity between the British and Spanish empires.

Changing focus to articles published on this subject, it is notable that there has been a relative dearth of material written over the last year. Of the nine articles discussed here three were published in the latter half of 2013 with only six new articles written in 2014. The majority of these articles focus on the sonnets. Mike Ingham discusses the challenges faced in adapting the sonnets into musical form in his essay 'The True Concord of Well-Tuned Sounds": Musical Adaptions of Shakespeare's Sonnets' (*Shakespeare* 9:ii[2013] 220–40), citing examples from artists like Rufus Wainwright and Ladysmith Black Mambazo. Suzanne M. Tartamella compares the 'Dark Lady Sonnets' (Sonnets 127–52) with elements of Shakespeare's dramatic work in her article 'Reinventing the Poet and Dark Lady: Theatricality and Artistic Control in Shakespeare's *Taming of the Shrew*' (*ELR* 43:iii[2013] 446–77), arguing that there is value in discussing the play in relation to these specific sonnets. In contrast, Fenghua Ma engages with the first 126 sonnets in her paper 'The Tragic Vision in the Fair Youth Group in Shakespeare's Sonnets' (*TPLS*

4:v[2014] 941–8), looking at the 'Fair Youth' in relation to such concepts as friendship and betrayal. In the essay 'Anatomies of Imagination in Shakespeare's Sonnets' (*SEL* 54:i[2014] 105–24), Suparna Roychoudhury discusses the relationship between love, poetry, and the body before engaging with the sonnets and giving examples of where this occurs in Shakespeare's work.

Jonathan P.A. Sell's essay, 'Terminal Aposiopesis and Sublime Communication: Shakespeare's *Sonnet 126* and Keats's *To Autumn*' (in Sell, Borch, and Lindgren, eds., *Ethics of Literary Communication: Genuineness, Directness, Indirectness*, pp. 167–88), discusses the use of this technique in literature through the years, while also specifically engaging with Shakespeare's and Keats's works. Also focusing on only one of Shakespeare's sonnets is Leo Daugherty, who has written a brief note discussing 'A Previously Unreported Source for Shakespeare's *Sonnet 56*' (*N&Q* 61[2014] 240–1).

Two articles focus on *Venus and Adonis*. The first of these, Ernest P Rufleth's 'Courting Disaster: Hunting and Wooing in Shakespeare's *Venus and Adonis*' (*Poetica* 81[2014] 33–58), discusses these two concepts as they appear within the poem, noting the disparity in the amount Shakespeare wrote about each subject. As seems to be *de rigueur*, Rufleth also compares Shakespeare's version of the poem with its source material, Ovid's *Metamorphoses*, noting the differences between the two and offering theories as to why these differences occur. Sofie Kluge, in her essay 'Adonis at the Crossroads: Two (Three) Early Modern Versions of the Venus and Adonis Myth' (*MLN* 129:v[2014] 1149–69), discusses Shakespeare's version of the myth in relation to Pedro Soto De Rojas's *Fragmentos de Adonis* with specific focus on the interpretation of Adonis in both works.

Lukas Erne and Tamsin Badcoe have chosen not to focus on any one element of Shakespeare's poetry, but instead look at the reception of his works at the time of their initial publication in their article 'Shakespeare and the Popularity of Poetry Books in Print, 1583–1622' (*RES* 65[2014] 33–57). Erne and Badcoe do not focus solely on Shakespeare, but also note the popularity or otherwise of other writers and their works.

(d) Histories

This year provided a number of interesting items dealing with or touching on Shakespeare's history plays, ranging from the politics of food to the physical landscape and the metaphysical self. Marisa R. Cull's *Shakespeare's Princes of Wales: English Identity and the Welsh Connection* examines the 'Welshness' of Shakespeare's princes of Wales, arguing for a paradoxical Wales that, for contemporary audiences, was both familiar and alien; an ally and a rebel; the foundation of the commonweal's mythic past and a perpetual reminder of the altogether more ancient claims to rulership of the island's original inhabitants. In Cull's introduction, she points to Fluellen as a neat encapsulation of the paradoxical view of the Welsh: he is at once both a comic rustic and a shrewd, 'barbed' (p. 3) observer of the English. Taking Pocock's articulation of early modern British political identity as a starting point, Cull's study provides a nuanced and insightful reading of Shakespeare's history plays to reveal this fundamental paradox; crucially, Cull also situates Shakespeare's works within the wider developmental context of the humanist history play, discussing a broad range of sixteenth- and seventeenth-century historical and dramatic works to illuminate the centrality of 'Welshness'.

Perhaps the most fraught aspect of this paradox is the repeated English 'staging' of Wales at moments of crisis in the succession (most pertinently for Shakespeare's audience, in the establishment of the Stuart dynasty). Cull shows how the English co-opting of Welsh identity was brought out to the public in precisely these moments of communal uncertainty in order to manage and promote particular readings of the Anglo-Welsh past. This paradox is eminently visible, perhaps most so in the Henriad. The 'fetishized' (p. 53) Prince Hal is constructed emphatically and repeatedly as the Prince of Wales, in continual tension with his role as English heir: in *1* and *2 Henry IV*, he is focused largely on asserting his independence from his father (both as his literal father and as the paterfamilias of the kingdom: a timely distinction in Jacobean England).

The first chapter provides a contextual assessment of the political uses of the literal principality and title, demonstrating a changing attitude towards the uses of the title, Wales, and Welsh identity throughout the sixteenth and seventeenth centuries. Cull focuses on demonstrating how successive English monarchs used the Welsh principality and its attendant title to 'stage' claims about bloodlines, borders, and rights. The subsequent chapters focus on the symbolic value of Wales and its princes, and it is here that we find the most valuable contributions from Cull as she provides comprehensive analyses of well-chosen illustrative texts ranging from well-known to less well-known writers from across the late sixteenth and seventeenth centuries. Though the title of the book makes a Shakespearian focus clear, Cull does an admirable job of integrating texts by a range of authors alongside Shakespeare's histories.

One of the most successful sections of this book is chapter 2, which considers the symbolic roles of the principality and its title amid anxieties about the tensions and connections between Welsh and English identity (both cultural and royal). Despite the popular identification of Prince Hal as Shakespeare's most visible Prince of Wales, Cull puts great emphasis on reminding us that Hal is not Shakespeare's only Prince of Wales; indeed, he is not even the only Prince of Wales in the Henriad. Chapter 2 therefore focuses largely on the 'shadowed princes' (p. 12) in *1* and *2 Henry IV*: Owen Glendower and Edmund Mortimer. Cull identifies a Jacobean anxiety about the uncertain importance of a direct, bloodline-based claim to the throne (in relation to other justifications), and points to both a sense of the 'unfulfilled potential' (p. 55) of Wales, and a contemporary concern with how to harness that potential for English gain. Cull discusses the apparent lack of 'capable princes' in Shakespeare's histories in this context, and more specifically, in relation to the issues raised by the Tudors' Welsh connections and the transition of the crown to the Stuarts.

Chapter 3 focuses specifically on the preoccupation of the 1590s English stage with dramatized attempts to absorb a specifically Welsh history of martial and monarchical authority. Cull uses George Peele's *Edward I* and Shakespeare's *Henry V* to examine the implications of these two texts' negotiations over the English co-opting of (historically Welsh) 'British' mythic history, from Brutus to Arthur and beyond. The 'Brutus' founding myth that the Tudor monarchs promoted so energetically exemplifies the manner in which early modern English monarchs recognized the authority of the ancient Britons, and its use demonstrates the negotiations (cultural, political, and religious) required to harness that authority for a post-1066 ruling class.

Chapter 4 marks a shift from examinations of how the English Crown appropriated Welsh identity as a corollary to English power in moments of crisis to a consideration of the staging of the Jacobean 'British' union effort. Read through the investiture of Henry Frederick as Prince of Wales in 1610— which united the traditional titles of the Scottish and English heirs apparent for the first time—Cull shows how Shakespeare's *Cymbeline* (written for the King's men) and R.A.'s *The Valiant Welshman* (written for the Prince of Wales' men) stage the role(s) of the Prince of Wales in line with their patrons' conflicted relationship.

The final chapter looks at the aftermath of the death of James Frederick and the run up to the English Civil War, concluding that there was a significant decline in the 'use value and the symbolic value of the princedom of Wales' (p. 14). Among other texts (including Ben Jonson's *For the Honour of Wales, King and Queene's Entertainment at Richmond*, and Thomas Nabbe's birthday masque for the future Charles II), Cull uses Milton's *A Maske at Ludlow Castle* to show how the decades preceding the Civil War mark a lack of attention and use of the symbolic value of Wales: both the principality and the title itself. This, Cull argues, led in no small part to the literal neglect of the unifying power of the Welsh 'other', and contributed to the rise of divisions within the English polity.

Shakespeare's Princes of Wales concludes with an unusual brief epilogue that leaps to the 1969 investiture of the current Prince of Wales, Charles Windsor. This is not a criticism; too often the early modern past is made to feel more like a foreign country than it perhaps is. This epilogue showcasing the politically sensitive and utilitarian investiture of Charles provides a point of contact between our worlds that, if not a mirror image, reminds us that there are useful analogies to be found between our sense of spectacle and that of the early modern world.

There has been a great deal of attention paid to Shakespeare's boy actors over the past thirty years, but as Katie Knowles's impressive first monograph *Shakespeare's Boys: A Cultural History* shows, we have not yet understood Shakespeare's children as well as one might have assumed. Knowles's study seeks to participate in the relatively recent development of interdisciplinary 'childhood studies' to understand the cultural contexts of Shakespeare's boy characters from the early modern period through to the present day. This monograph incorporates aspects of performance, gender, and cultural studies, but retains a tight focus on performances in British contexts. It is not a criticism of this volume to suggest that more work is required—clearly—on

SHAKESPEARE   463

non-British contexts, but rather is a compliment: Knowles has made clear how much is yet to be done on this rich and important topic.

As this book covers a very long chronological range, it is divided into two parts. Part I covers the early modern period to the Restoration, with Part II discussing the eighteenth century to the present day. Chapter 1 focuses on the aristocracy in the first tetralogy, *King John*, *Macbeth*, and *The Winter's Tale*, considering how youthful heirs are subject to the often impossible (indeed, often fatal) pressures of maintaining a dual sense of self as individual leader and as dynastic representative-in-waiting; of being both a vulnerable child and the moral (and legal) superior of often proud lords. This chapter will therefore have a particular pull for readers interested primarily in Shakespeare's history plays. Knowles presents these readings through a sociolinguistic lens, arguing that the transitional early modern usage of 'imp' parallels similar changes in contemporary attitudes towards the individuality of aristocratic children.

Chapter 2 examines two of the Roman plays—*Titus Andronicus* and *Coriolanus*—through the 'hyper-masculinity' of these early modern depictions of martial Rome. Knowles shows how the 'little men' who are required to stand in for their fathers demonstrate a complex attitude towards the transition to adulthood in this intensely masculine environment. While chapter 2 depicts boys imitating men, one of the most interesting aspects of chapter 3 looks at men imitating boys. The chapter looks at aspects of education in early modern England, contrasting the 'new style' grammar schools—and their focus on the cultivation of values and skills—with the older forms of apprenticeship (including the page system). While readers primarily interested in the history plays will enjoy Knowles's examination of Falstaff's Boy in *2 Henry IV* and *Henry V*, it is Knowles's analysis of the lords of Navarre in *Love's Labour's Lost* and the links between their scholasticism and cultivated boyhood that demonstrate the value of this approach most neatly.

Chapter 4 marks the beginning of Part II, and surveys the Restoration and eighteenth-century adaptations of Shakespeare's works with a particular focus on the increased use of pathos in reworked versions of the histories and tragedies. Knowles argues that the increased sentimentality of the boy characters marks a process of simplification and 'coherence', which would lead to the reactionary rise of 'Bardolatry' in the later eighteenth century. Chapter 5 follows this sentimental trend into the Victorian era, considering a continuing process of idealization for children that created a context where violence against children was anathematized. Not only did this require the significant alteration of particular plays or characters (or the complete removal of particular plays from production), but it also created a vogue for female actors to play boy roles (including young girl actors as well as women), as it was felt that boy actors could not communicate the vulnerability of the child characters.

The final chapter brings the study up to the modern day, considering a range of filmic productions alongside those on stage. Knowles characterizes these productions as developing a tension between the 'innocent' and the 'culpable' child. Knowles also examines the breaking down of barriers between the 'child' and 'adult' characters, demonstrating a fluidity between 'immature' adults and 'uncomfortably adult' children in line with developing modern conceptions of the psychological role of childhood events and pressures in shaping the adult.

Knowles's chronological sweep inevitably means that a very tight thematic focus must be maintained to avoid an endless series of digressions, and as such, it would not be fair to critique this book for not providing extensive coverage of each concept or period it touches. Knowles makes clear that there is a wealth of scholarship on early modern children that she is not attempting to ignore or replicate; despite this, a closer relationship between contemporary works and Knowles's impressive close readings would have provided a fruitful context that otherwise is left to the reader. Nevertheless, this is a very useful and well-written book that merits close attention and is sure to refresh critical interest in Shakespeare's children.

This has been a good year for scholarship on Shakespeare's children: along with Knowles's monograph on boys we have also been given Deanne Williams's *Shakespeare and the Performance of Girlhood*. In a wide-ranging but well-organized study, Williams provides convincing and searching analyses read through a feminist lens; this book is about the self-conscious performance of girlhood not as an abstract point of interest for abstruse scholarship on the past, but as a conscious and continuous process that unites us with that not-always-distant past. The introduction makes this abundantly clear by connecting Williams's own past with formal and informal performances of girlhood from the past four centuries, moving through aspects of gender history, performance studies, cultural studies, critical theory, and film studies.

Divided into three sections, this book provides an overview of performances of girlhood that will be of interest to scholars of gender, theatre, performance, history, and literature. Part I looks at the characters described as or called 'girl' in Shakespeare's plays. This section shows how Shakespeare appropriated contemporary discourses of girlhood and adapted them onstage: in some ways a virtue of necessity, when we consider the male world of the Elizabethan playhouse; in others, an(other) opportunity for the playwright to call attention to aspects of cultural understanding. The first chapter, 'Peevish and Perverse', begins by considering the relationships between girlhood and morality, first through Joan La Pucelle in *1 Henry VI* and subsequently through *The Two Gentlemen of Verona*, *The Taming of the Shrew*, and *Romeo and Juliet*. The second chapter will be of particular interest for readers of this section, as it examines Queen Isabelle in *Richard II*, encompassing Isabelle's status as conflated first and second wife, as girl/woman, and as Anglo-French Elizabethan symbol. The third chapter takes an equally nuanced look at Ophelia and representations of girlhood and madness in *Hamlet*.

Part II moves forward in time to examine the more complex attitudes to the performance of girlhood found in Stuart masques. These attitudes are more 'complex' because of the increasing opportunities for girls and women to perform on Stuart stages, which allowed for an additional reflective layer to historical roles previously played by boys; this in turn helped fuel a rise in the number of parts written for female actors themselves.

Part III completes this trajectory by examining female writers and performers themselves, and considering how previous material and contemporary contexts were adapted by (or responded to) by these writers and actors.

Though the content covered in this section falls outside the remit of this review, it is well worth reading; it draws the material of the previous two sections together into a fascinating set of case studies that merit close attention. This volume is a necessity for anyone interested not just in Shakespeare's girls, but also in a wide range of themes and topics touching on childhood, gender, power, and performance. If its breadth was the only thing this book contributed, it would still be worth reading; beyond that, its excellent style and interesting methodology make it clear that it is a very important addition to early modern studies.

Michael Saenger's new monograph *Shakespeare and the French Borders of English* brings together linguistic, political, and performative boundaries to examine Anglo-French relationships and their importance in Shakespeare. Building on recent work on the interplay between language, literature, law, and performance, Saenger provides us with a study of the physical and intangible borders—and thus the identity—of Shakespeare's England. This book thus engages with aspects of political history, historical linguistics, translation studies, and performance studies, in addition to material that will be of interest to literary critics and historians of a broader stripe. It should be emphasized that this is not a book about French influence on early modern English Shakespeare, nor a book about English depictions of France, but rather a study of how 'Shakespeare uses the idea of France to explore language and identity' (p. 6). In this, Saenger fits within a group of recent scholarship on the historical sociolinguistics of political and cultural identity (though this study is not an exclusively linguistic one by any means), and makes a valuable contribution to this group.

The first two chapters of the book deal largely with theory and methodology. Chapter 1 provides a theoretical background and framing for the subsequent chapters, arguing that postcolonial discourses have, in some ways, impeded Anglo-French studies; Saenger instead reads his texts through feminist and queer theoretical lenses. Chapter 2 provides a solid grounding in the historical sociolinguistic aspects of the study through case studies incorporating German and classical Greek linguistic concepts of 'foreignness' and the self. Saenger utilizes these case studies to demonstrate similar issues in a range of Anglo-French texts. There is much to recommend these two chapters, not least that they (Chapter 2 in particular) place the most emphasis on contextualizing Shakespeare's representations.

The second section focuses on genre studies, considering selected texts from Shakespeare's histories, comedies, and tragedies in turn. Chapters 3 and 4 will be of the greatest interest to readers looking for criticism on Shakespeare's histories; they discuss representations—or, as Saenger neatly describes it, 'a version of the memory of France'—of Anglo-French history in *Richard II* and *Henry V* (though there are a number of references to other Shakespearian plays as well) (p. 105). These are not surprising choices, dealing as they do with the loss and reconquest of France for an age concerned quite seriously with both insular and continental geopolitical borders and identities in general, along with the relatively recent memory of the Henrician French incursions. While they are not surprising (either in terms of playtext choice or critical insights), these two chapters provide clear and convincing connections to a range of contemporary texts, ranging from the well-known *Mirror for Magistrates* to less well-known texts such as Thomas Cooper's 1549 *Chronicle of the World*. These two chapters are highly useful in this respect. It is a shame that this book must have been in the final stages of production at the same time as *The Oxford Handbook of Holinshed's Chronicles*: chapter 3, 'Anterior Design: Presenting the Past in *Richard II*', in particular presents a number of excellent opportunities to engage with that rich resource. That is, of course, no fault of the author's and does not imply a criticism of the book; however, future studies might benefit from reading these texts together. This study is highly recommended for readers interested in aspects of cultural exchange, memory, and language.

Our next item is Charlotte Scott's *Shakespeare's Nature: From Cultivation to Culture*. This study looks at agrarian Shakespeare: the links between the natural world and its representation in Shakespeare's plays and in Shakespeare's wider cultural contexts. Scott argues that the values of late Tudor and early Stuart England were shaped by the 'terms and practices of husbandry', in that the cultivation of the self was a form of 'self-mastery' that lay at the heart of early modern moral discourse (p. 2). These practices are consistently expressed through agrarian metaphors and display a fundamental concern with the establishment of order and consistency. Scott provides an extended introduction to provide a nuanced look at early modern agrarian cultural influence and importance, which helps this book connect to a developing body of scholarship on the cultural importance of early modern landscapes. While its conclusions often confirm what many scholars will already have felt, it is a valuable addition to this fruitful field of study.

This book encompasses a range of Shakespeare's works, and readers of this section may choose to limit their attention to chapter 3, '*Henry V*: Humanity and Husbandry' (though the entire book is well worth reading). This chapter focuses primarily on the Duke of Burgundy's lengthy speech in V.ii (found in the First Folio edition of the play, but not the 1600 quarto) as exemplifying the agrarian tropic associations between virtue, peace, and husbandry. Scott focuses in particular on the associations between the plough, the practice of ploughing, and morality (specifically, Christian morality). Through the war with France, England is left 'wild' and unmanaged: indeed, both countries are devastated, and the destruction of the physical farmland reflects the misdirection of resources and management into war instead of peace. Burgundy's speech seeks to remind both monarchs that 'peace is commensurate with good management' (p. 94).

The relationship between England and France is a complex one, and Scott argues that Burgundy's positioning as mediator is central to the play's conceptual development of France as a 'new England', a 'space of alterity' (p. 100) that allows for observation of the empirical results of war. The landscape itself is a form of social discourse, and the social, cultural, and environmental pressures that shape that discourse help to mark France as a kind of ethical nexus, a way for Henry V and Shakespeare's early modern audiences to think through the management of the commonweal.

As mentioned above, this study's utility lies in its drawing together of primary texts (dramatic, poetic, legal, and otherwise) with modern scholarship on language, literature, and landscapes. The extensive footnotes provide a very rich network of critical connections for the reader to explore, though the discursive aspects of the footnotes can be a bit distracting. There are occasional lapses in critical assessment—the frequent mention of 'Christian' morality would have benefited from analysis more sensitive to the confessional complexities of the period—but that does not detract too seriously from what is a book that is sure to help further encourage the bringing together of literary, historical, and landscape studies.

Moving from the physical to the philosophical, 2014 has also seen the publication of an excellent essay collection, *Shakespeare and Continental Philosophy*. Edited by Jennifer Ann Bates and Richard Wilson, this collection represents an attempt to revisit aspects of poststructuralist thinking in Shakespeare studies by placing at the centre of this field the 'rift' between the aesthetic anglophone critical and philosophical approaches to Shakespeare and the positivist-flavoured European readings of England's national symbol. These essays invite us to solve this puzzle through the pairing of particular philosophers (e.g. Nietzsche, Lacan, Aristotle) with selected plays, reading the plays through philosophical lenses that renew the emphasis on the imaginative power of the texts rather than on the historicist 'spaces, places, people, and things' that have become dominant in Shakespeare studies.

Most relevant to this section in *Shakespeare and Continental Philosophy* is James A. Knapp's chapter, 'Richard II's Silent, Tortured Soul' (pp. 94–120). Starting with Richard's musings on the mirror and interiority in IV.i, Knapp examines the tensions between Richard's material world and the internal self through the lens of Nietzsche's understanding, in *The Birth of Tragedy*, of the productive tensions between 'Apollonian and Dionysian forces'. Using aspects of Cartesian phenomenology and Jean-Luc Marion's 'givenness', Knapp characterizes *Richard II* as a tragedy through Richard's inability to 'know' his metaphysical, interior self; it is thus not Richard's political failures that characterize the play and king, but his philosophical failures. This is a useful and provocative volume, but one feature will be applauded unanimously by all readers: it has appeared simultaneously in hardback and wallet-friendly paperback versions.

The final book to be highlighted here is David Scott Kastan's *A Will to Believe: Shakespeare and Religion*. Kastan's previous works are important enough that any of his publications will draw considerable attention; this review would be incomplete without at least a brief mention of the aspects of his latest book that are relevant to the histories. The book itself does an excellent job of tackling some of the perennial questions faced by Shakespeare scholars: What did Shakespeare believe? How did his beliefs affect his plays? To what extent do his plays reveal aspects of early modern belief? These are perennial questions because they are impossible to answer with any certainty (beyond the certain knowledge that scholarly attempts to answer them almost invariably reveal more about the critic than Shakespeare). Kastan mitigates this by telling us that 'Shakespeare declines to tell us what to believe, or what he believed. But . . . he shows us that human beings do believe and in their various and variant beliefs, they discover and create complex relations to their pasts and their futures' (p. 7). Kastan describes Shakespeare's plays operating in a religious world that was largely unconcerned with dogma, even in an age of intense confessional conflict. In this, Kastan follows historians like Eamon Duffy by arguing that the plays deal with the broad strokes of Christianity, which was what most people were concerned with. The plays do not engage with complicated aspects of theology; instead, Kastan identifies psychological factors as provoking most of the plays' crises. Kastan's closest engagement with doctrinal issues of interest to historicist readers comes in chapter 3, 'All Roads Leads to Rome', and most of his mentions of the history plays come in this section.

There have been a number of noteworthy articles published in 2014, foremost of which is the 2014 volume of *Shakespeare Studies*, which is concerned with food studies and Shakespeare. Of the essays within, three merit particular attention in this section, dealing as they do with a selection of history plays. The first of these is Rebecca Laroche and Jennifer Munroe, 'On a Bank of Rue; or, Material Ecofeminist Inquiry and the Garden of *Richard II*' (*ShakS* 42[2014] 42–50). Laroche and Munroe argue that the garden scene in *Richard II* benefits from a materialist reading—rather than a metaphorical one—to reveal the gendered aspects of the garden, scene, and characters. Laroche and Munroe argue that the Gardener is not linking the garden to England through metaphors about monarchical rule, but is suggesting practical methodologies for the maintenance of the kingdom. This essay urges scholars to think about how we incorporate the material turn into considerations of early modern food studies, and responds to several of the issues regarding the materiality of literary landscapes raised in Scott's *Shakespeare's Nature*.

The second of our essays in this volume considers the politics of hunger in *2 Henry VI* and the English market for sack (as read through Falstaff in *1* and *2 Henry IV*). In 'Revolting Diets: Jack Cade's "Sallet" and the Politics of Hunger in *2 Henry VI*' (*ShakS* 42[2014] 51–62) Hillary Eklund provides a view of food politics in Shakespeare from the bottom up. Eklund's reading of this play demonstrates the interplay between hunger, poverty, criminality, and sedition, and challenges traditional associations between these forces. This essay reads food inequalities as informing political positions: the excesses of the nobility fuel 'internecine' battling—and further waste—while the hunger of the 'lower' people forces searches for new modes of resource distribution.

The last of our three essays in this volume looks at sack. In '"More Natural to the Nation": Situating Shakespeare in the "Querelle de Canary"' (*ShakS* 42[2014] 106–21), Barbara Sebek reads the role(s) of sack in early modern England through Falstaff in *1* and *2 Henry IV*. Tracing the production and exchange networks that brought the extremely popular sweet wine to England and making use of the seventeenth-century epistolary travel accounts of James Howell, Sebek examines the literature of alcohol manufacture, purchase, and consumption. These networks and debates are framed through larger concerns about consumption, identity, and the body politic.

There are a number of other essays in this collection that deal with issues relevant to the study of the histories, even if they do not necessarily mention the histories themselves. Among these is Diane Purkiss's 'The Masque of Food: Staging and Banqueting in Shakespeare's England' (*ShakS* 42[2014]

91–105). This wide-ranging article brings *Timon of Athens* and *Titus Andronicus* together with a range of early modern texts including the *Hypnerotomachia Poliphili* [1499], Robert May's *The Accomplisht Cook* [1660], Thomas Dawson's *The Good Huswifes Jewell* [1596], Dekker's *The Shoemakers Holiday* [1600] and *If It Be Not Good, the Diuel Is in It* [1612], *A Warning for Fair Women* [1599], William Davenant's *The Cruell Brother* [1630], Thomas Goffe's *Orestes* [1633], Heywood and Brome's *The Witches of Lancashire* [1634], *The Wisdome of Doctor Dodypoll* [1600], George Chapman's *The Tragedy of Alphonsus Emperour of Germany* [1654], Ben Jonson's *A Masque of the Metamorphos'd Gypsies* [*c*.1621], the 1597 *Daemonologie* of James I, and others. This is an exceptionally rich reading of the staging of banqueting and performative consumption, and would benefit readers examining aspects of political performance in Shakespeare and other early modern texts.

In '"What More Remains?"': Messianic Performance in *Richard II'* (*SQ* 65:i[2014] 22–48), Dominic Sherman discusses *Richard II* as a performative and political laboratory, wherein objects, people, and concepts are tested and discarded. Drawing on a range of theoretical propositions and proponents, Sherman argues that criticism of *Richard II* has settled into a binary state, using as an example David Scott Kastan's statement that Richard's theatricality is empowered through its superficiality: 'The "lye" of the theater demystifies the idealization of the social order that the ideology of degree demanded' (quoted p. 24). Sherman counteracts this characterization of the 'lye' as impotent by arguing that a binary structure oversimplifies the nature of performative political power. For Sherman, *Richard II* paradoxically 'defines the theatre as a specifically executed set of actions that depend on materiality to disconnect signification and to make themselves impotent, incapable, and ultimately *im*material by design' (p. 26; emphasis in original). Richard's subsequent deposition marks the failure of this theatricality: however, this is an *active* failure, a failure that cannot be achieved without the paradoxical power of its own performativity. Sherman calls this 'messianic performance': actions that require failed actions in a self-defeating paradox. Sherman reads this as a Pauline trope for the 'material texture of the stage', with a messianic Richard revealing the artifice and superficiality of performance as 'an alternative to ideological structures of meaning-making' (p. 26) in line with Paul's dissection of the self in 1 Corinthians. Paul describes himself as neither a Jew nor *not* a Jew, but rather a third thing in between: this too is Richard's place as king/not-king. This important article thus cuts against Richard as Žižek's 'zero at the center of the crown', and sees Richard as both zero *and* crown (and something beyond either), and merits close attention not just from those concerned with Shakespeare's kings, but for all early modern scholars who consider early modern representations of the past and their uses.

Moving from 'nothing' to the absence of memory, Jonathan Baldo's wide-ranging 'Shakespeare's Art of Distraction' (*Shakespeare* 10:ii[2014] 138–57) covers a significant swathe of Shakespeare's plays to demonstrate succinctly how Shakespeare uses distraction and forgetfulness as a key aspect of his stagecraft. As with so many aspects of his works, Shakespeare's use of distraction interrogates the nature of that which is distracted in a self-knowing way: the plays are themselves entertainments, and consciously seek to manipulate the attention and the sense of self of those in the audience. Baldo touches on many plays outside the remit of this section, but one particularly trenchant example falls in *Henry V*: Baldo characterizes the play as a complex game of distraction whereby the characters seek to distract each other, and Henry seeks to distract the audience most of all. Henry is pushed to war by the Church prelates who hope he will forget his efforts to appropriate Church wealth; for his part, Henry endeavours that we will all forget that he executes Bardolph for stealing from the Church—the Church that Henry himself was so assiduously working to appropriate, only forestalled by payments and the war with France. Shakespeare too is grappling with distraction: Baldo argues that the second tetralogy shows a fragmented land, so distracted as to 'forget' itself; Shakespeare's Britain too is distracted, unable to reconcile official ecumenical positions with a similarly fragmented population. Baldo's movement through the canon is deft and convincing, and elucidates with clear examples the interplay between memory and distraction in Shakespeare.

A final essay that readers of this section may find interesting is Lucy Munro's '"Nemp your sexes!": Anachronistic Aesthetics in *Hengist, King of Kent* and the Jacobean "Anglo-Saxon" Play' (*MP* 111:iv[2014] 734–61). Though it does not cover Shakespeare's history plays, it provides a useful reminder about the historiographical pressures that helped shape Shakespeare's sense of English history. While this article's consideration of the early modern senses of the Saxon/British 'other' is most relevant to plays like *Coriolanus* and *King Lear*, it also is applicable to the issues raised by Marisa Cull in her treatment of *Henry V*. Munro's consideration of the 'performative' past also has clear importance for spectacle-rich plays like *Henry VIII*, and is well worth the attention of readers interested in a range of early modern history plays.

(e) Tragedies

One of the most important monographs in this section is Simon Palfrey's *Poor Tom: Living 'King Lear'*. This book explores the role of Edgar, who has more lines than anyone except the king but who is relatively ignored by critics. It argues that by attending to Edgar, and especially his role as poor Tom, we can understand how 'He irrupts in the middle of the Edgar-role, somehow its totem, in some obscure way almost the role's cause, at once patchwork of the already lived and previously spoken, and an image of pure potentiality' (p. 9). It is Palfrey's attentiveness to *King Lear*, and especially Tom, which is so compelling. The book is made up of twenty-eight short chapters, each with twelve 'scenes' with twelve 'interludes', a prelude, introduction, conclusion, and a brief afterword. With the exception of the prelude and the afterword, the book does not tend to offer the personal memoir seen in some other experimental literary criticism on Shakespeare recently.

However, there is something experimental about the monograph; as Palfrey explains in the afterword, 'This book has a twin sister, called *Shakespeare's*

Possible Worlds, published by Cambridge University Press, bigger and better-mannered than *Poor Tom*' (p. 257). The 'scenes' tend to work through the play, paying particular attention to the role of Edgar/Tom. The 'interludes' offer slightly more reflective responses to issues raised in the 'scenes': for example, Edgar's duel with his brother discussed in scene 11 is followed by an interlude entitled 'Jacob and Esau', which Palfrey argues offers a 'tantalizing precursor of the story of *Lear*'s brothers' (p. 225). In some senses Palfrey's work here offers a collage of methodological frameworks, showing a range of different kinds of attention to the text and philosophical, spiritual, and theatrical possibilities; concerns about the animal and vegetable, cue-scripts, and spectres, are synthesized with thinkers such as Simone Weil, Emmanuel Levinas, and Maurice Blanchot. This range is disorienting at times, but ultimately it rewards patient reading. The final sections on the echoes of Tom in the closing moments of the play are particularly thought-provoking: '*King Lear* is a play that in a profound sense happens at the deposition, in the lapsed space between one covenant and the next: between death and life, extinction and recovery, participation and eradication. And as ever, the ultimate figure for this tantalized condition is Tom' (p. 249). As well as championing the one-play Shakespeare monograph, the book offers an understanding and feeling reading of *King Lear* that, at heart, challenges the status quo of much Shakespeare criticism.

Another, more explicitly, critical-creative book is *Tales from Shakespeare: Creative Collisions* by Graham Holderness. Holderness sets out his manifesto thus: '"Creative criticism" mingles criticism and creativity together in a promiscuously hybrid discourse. Its arguments operate, as do the creative works it studies, as much by metaphor as by logical argument. And it penetrates into areas where criticism normally dares not go, deep into the subjectivity of the critic and reader. It proposes, in short, a new and fundamentally reorientated relationship between criticism and creativity' (p. xiv). Following an introduction concerning the question of 'appropriation' in relation to *Hamlet* and the idea of 'collision' taken from particle physics, Holderness's book consists of four parts. Each part is split into two sections: the first is more recognizably 'critical', while the second is 'creative', although, of course, Holderness is working to show how porous this boundary can be. Two parts are particularly relevant to this section. The first part considers the story of a performance of *Hamlet* (and *Richard II*), which is said to have been performed on board the *Red Dragon* off the coast of what is now Sierra Leone in 1607. This chapter is not out to prove the account's authenticity, but considers it as a cultural collision that can tell us something about our view of Shakespeare; the next section is followed by a 'creative-critical' (p. 35) commentary on the narrative, although this is focused on *Richard II*. The other relevant part is Part III, on *Coriolanus*, which investigates the collision between the play and Ralph Fiennes's film version. He suggests provocatively that 'in order to deepen our sense of what Shakespeare's *Coriolanus* has to offer us, we need to take the hero out of the play altogether'; that is, we need to try 'searching contemporary culture not just for signs of Shakespeare's *Coriolanus*, but also for examples of the Coriolanus figure, reproduced as a kind of contemporary folk-hero and cultural mythos' (p. 90): Holderness offers Kathryn Bigelow's *The Hurt Locker* and Sam Mendes's James Bond film, *Skyfall*. The second section of this part offers a creative response to *Coriolanus* in the form of a spy-thriller narrative, which will be of interest to those working in adaptation studies and creative writing to start with. However, the book clearly has a larger axe to grind; that is, thinking through the 'continual reciprocal traffic of exchange and transformation' (p. 225) between 'Shakespeare' and 'not Shakespeare', as well as investigating our narration of Shakespeare and the Shakespearian tales that we carry on.

Nicole E. Miller's *Violence and Grace: Exceptional Life between Shakespeare and Modernity* represents an important study in the seemingly ever-expanding field of studies in political theology, and one of the most important when it comes to early modern English studies. The first half of the book, entitled 'States of Affliction', focuses particularly on early modern drama in relation to the modern thinkers Hannah Arendt, Ernst Kantorowicz, and Carl Schmitt. As Miller explains, her 'primary goal is not only to demonstrate the ways the playwrights explore the febrile political tensions of the period, but also to show how their works illuminate modern political phenomena originating in medieval and Renaissance political theology (p.3). The second half of the book, 'States of Grace', includes two chapters relevant to this section. Chapter 3, 'Sacred Life and Sacrificial Economy: Coriolanus in No-Man's-Land', explores how in *Coriolanus* 'Shakespeare captures the state of exception coupled to the transition from monarchy (*Regnum Romanum*) to fledgling Republic (*Res Publica Romanum*), a moment of crisis never really subsumed in the reordering of civic affiliation at the play's close' (p. 102). Typical of the theoretical dexterity shown in this book, the chapter touches on 'the peculiar tensions inhabited by the modern citizen-soldier, thinking of these tensions in terms of the economy of the gift, its exploitations, impossibilities, and doublings' (p. 103), before reading the play in relation to Agamben's concept of 'bare life' and Walter Benjamin on violence. Thinking through the economy of the gift in the play, Miller ends by suggesting that 'What Coriolanus represents, finally, remains a *suspended* grace, a token withheld, a sign never fully either inscribed or understood, even as we are called upon to "assist" in his remembrance' (p. 132). Chapter 4, 'The Aesthetic of Messianic Time: Gravity and Grace in *King Lear*', responds particularly to the writing of Simone Weil. As Miller explains, 'For Weil, "affliction" (*malheur*) provides the most insistent sense of materiality, the reminder of our fleshly presence in the world; yet, paradoxically, affliction also bears within itself the capacity to draw us toward grace. Like Paul's "now", Weil's *malheur* incorporates both a sense of fate, or doom—of that which is to come—and also folds itself around the *heur*, the punctual sense of a specific time, a now' (pp. 135–6). Miller's chapter, which, like the rest of her monograph, is hard to do justice to here, explores how *King Lear* confronts the aesthetics of suffering. The monograph ends with a short epilogue which reflects on the stakes of reading and political life by way of the last words of the protagonist of *Timon of Athens*.

Janet Clare's *Shakespeare's Stage Traffic: Imitation, Borrowing and Competition in Renaissance Theatre* is an important reassessment of the way we consider Shakespeare's plays in relation to those of his contemporaries, and the relationship between stage and page. Clare explains that she uses the term '"theatre traffic" as a simultaneously competitive and interactive process, illustrated through attention to the plays that variously interlock' (p. 2). Chapter 6, entitled '*Hamlet* and the Humour of Children', reads *Hamlet* alongside such plays as *The Spanish Tragedy*, *Antonio and Mellida*, *Antonio's Revenge*, *The Malcontent*, and *The First Part of Jeronimo*, but her reading is especially alert to the different published versions of *Hamlet*. 'Poised at a crucial moment of theatrical and literary production, the textual history of *Hamlet* offers', she argues, 'a striking instance of the way plays were shaped or re-shaped to take cognizance of each other' (pp. 166–7). 'More than any other play by Shakespeare, although perhaps not more than any other play of its time, *Hamlet* is explicitly embroiled in theatrical fashion, and this intrudes into the script' (p. 192). She ends by suggesting that 'the publication of Q2 [*Hamlet*] could have been something of a riposte to the generic inventiveness of *Antonio's Revenge*: a literary makeover of a popular play in response to the former's de-construction of the genre' (p. 194). The point of this chapter, however, is not to prove the priority of one version of a play over another, but to explore how *Hamlet* was not created in isolation but as part of a conversation, in print and on the stage, about theatre and revenge tragedy.

Forensic Shakespeare by Quentin Skinner is a major study of Shakespeare's use of judicial rhetoric as a method of argument in a number of his plays, especially the tragedies. In his introduction Skinner explains that 'By focusing on the theory of judicial rhetoric we can hope in the first place to help explain why certain of Shakespeare's scenes have a particular shape, and why a number of individual speeches conform to a recurrent pattern and arrange-ment' (p. 2). The chapters of the book do not focus on individual plays, but draw on a range of scenes from 'several in which the dramaturgy is extensively drawn from classical and Renaissance treatises on judicial rhetoric' (p. 1). *Hamlet* features as a key text: Skinner is particularly interested in the way in which characters in the plays are called upon to act as judges, 'hearing, assessing, and delivering a verdict on the truth of what they are told' (p. 73). Skinner also focuses on the role of rhetoric in the speeches by Brutus and Antony following the death of Caesar in *Julius Caesar*, and Alcibiades' defence of Timon in Act III of *Timon of Athens*. In *Othello*, Iago 'illustrates the age-old anxiety voiced by Plato in the Gorgias about the morality of the rhetorical arts' (p. 251). Iago is an adept rhetorician who 'shows himself acutely aware of the rhetorical rules for ensuring that a fabricated *confirmatio* can be made to sound like the truth' (p. 252). In response to a *confirmatio* may come the defence, or *refutatio*; this Skinner explores in the closing scene of *Romeo and Juliet*, where the actions of Friar Lawrence and Balthasar are questioned, stating that 'the enquiry that Shakespeare goes on to dramatize has no parallel in Arthur Brooke's *Romeus and Juliet*, but it closely follows the analysis in the *Ad Herennium*' (p. 271), the classical book on rhetoric. The *Rhetorica ad Herennium* is in fact an important text in Skinner's argument, which goes some way to showing how we have often overlooked rhetorical manuals such as this one in our assessment of Shakespeare's books and learning and his construction of certain scenes, especially in the tragedies.

Bridget Escolme's *Emotional Excess on the Shakespearean Stage: Passion's Slaves* does play out its argument through an analysis of modern theatre and film productions; however, it also has relevant chapters to this section. The first chapter ' "A brain that leads my use of anger': Choler and the Politics of Spatial Production', reads *Coriolanus* in relation to anger and writers such as Plutarch, Seneca, and Montaigne on this emotion, as well as touching on Žižek's reading of the Ralph Fiennes's film of *Coriolanus*. Escolme pays particular attention to the way in which the emotion of anger seems to put characters in motion in different historical and performance settings. *Hamlet* is briefly considered in the chapter ' "Stop your sobbing": Grief, Melancholy and Moderation', but the other main chapter relevant to this section is ' "Give me excess of it": Love, Virtue and Excessive Pleasure in *All's Well That Ends Well* and *Antony and Cleopatra*'. Escolme suggests that in early modern drama love is 'un-self-ish because it undoes the self' (p. xxxvii). She argues that '*Antony and Cleopatra* places love in precisely the contradictory position in which it, and the passions more generally, appear in early modern philosophical treatises: though they cause violence, sickness and distress, life would be bland and humans "brutish" without them' (p. 142). The synthesis of historical and performance studies makes this study particularly valuable.

Shakespeare's Staged Spaces and Playgoers' Perceptions by Darlene Farabee includes two central chapters on the tragedies. As Farabee explains in the introduction, each 'of the following chapters focuses on an individual play to explore how stage mechanics and stage-illusion interact to produce effects for playgoers and readers' (p. 12). In 'Narrative and Spatial Movement in *Hamlet*: "To find his way" ', Farabee explores how the characters' special interactions establish positions for playgoers. She shows how playgoers remain with 'a non-moving Hamlet' (p. 92) as narrative events hurry forward. The chapter, 'Place, Perception, and Disorientation in *Macbeth*: "A walking shadow" ', investigates how 'the relentless forward movement of the narrative sweeps playgoers along with Macbeth himself' (p. 98). Darlene Farabee's work will be of interest to those working on stage space and the affective potential of scenic apparatus on playgoers, but another key benefit is to offer a model for close reading which is sensitive to the plays and the early modern stage spaces they were performed in.

Violence, Trauma, and Virtus in Shakespeare's Roman Poems and Plays: Transforming Ovid, by Lisa S. Starks-Estes, traces the predominant myth of Ovid's Philomela in Shakespeare's works, particularly those based on Roman history or myth and legend. She argues that Shakespeare 'turns to Ovid for the means to articulate the unspeakable, to examine the erotics of aggression, and to investigate the tragic effects of violence—of trauma' (p. 2). As might be expected, there are a number of chapters on the tragedies. 'Shakespeare's Perverse Astraea, Martyr'd Philomel and Lamenting Hecuba: Ovid, Sadomasochism, and Trauma in *Titus Andronicus*', which deals with a sadomasochistic Tamora and the Philomela-like Lavinia, argues that Shakespeare responds to Marlowe's *Dido and Aeneas* by creating 'an Ovidian revenge play' (p. 97). 'Dido and Aeneas "Metamorphis'd": Ovid, Marlowe, and the Masochistic Scenario in *Antony and Cleopatra*' continues this Marlovian interest exploring how Shakespeare 'out-Ovids' (p. 112) Marlowe and Ovid by creating, in *Antony and Cleopatra*, an anti-epic heroism. These chapters are in Part I, 'Love's Wound: Violence, Trauma, and Ovidian

Transformation in Shakespeare's Roman Poems and Plays'. Part II deals with 'Transforming Bodies: Trauma, *Virtus*, and the Limits of Neo-Stoicism in Shakespeare's Roman Poems and Plays'. Two essays in this section deal with the body and an Ovidian poetics of transformation: 'Bleeding Martyrs: The Body of the Tyrant/Saint, the Limits of "Constancy", and the Extremity of the Passions in *Julius Caesar*'; and ' "One whole wound"': *Virtus*, Vulnerability, and the Emblazoned in *Coriolanus*'. Shakespeare emerges here as 'an anti-Augustan, Ovidian poet-playwright' (p. 144). The book is concerned with sources and politics in the early modern period; however, its other psycho-analytical approaches mean that it also has much to offer on the way in which violence and trauma are represented.

Hospitality and Treachery in Western Literature, by James A.W. Heffernan, is a wide-ranging monograph, as the title suggests, but it contains a useful chapter on Shakespeare. Following chapters on classical and biblical hospi-tality, as well as one on *Beowulf* and *Gawain*, chapter 4, 'Staging Hospitality: Shakespeare', has sections on *Timon of Athens*, *King Lear*, *Macbeth*, and also *The Winter's Tale*. His essay explores a historical shift in emphasis, when 'the word *hospitality* came to mean not sustenance for the poor but entertainment, often lavish entertainment of the rich and influential' (p. 119); thus, this 'turns hospitality into showmanship' (p. 119). Perhaps predictably, 'Timon is virtually devoured by his guests' (p. 121), while *King Lear* 'exemplifies the violation of Christian hospitality' (p. 122) and *Macbeth* the 'subversion of hospitality' (p. 129). And yet putting the plays in the larger context of hospitality in literature helps to identify how Shakespeare's plays 'test the very meaning of hospitality in his own time' (p. 148).

Christopher Warley's *Reading Class through Shakespeare, Donne and Milton* includes a chapter entitled 'Just Horatio'; this chapter revises the article published as 'Specters of Horatio' (*ELH* 75[2008] 1023–5). For Warley, 'the social position of Horatio remains tantalizingly unclarified' and thus 'The specter of Horatio presiding over *Hamlet* becomes the name and the means for class criticism generally' (p. 70). He suggests, following Harold Bloom, that 'reading or viewing *Hamlet* requires identifying, one way or another, with Horatio (p. 48). Warley's approach is thus particularly concerned with the act of interpretation and hesitation. The monograph includes this chapter in the context of a reading of Shakespeare, Donne, and Milton with a close reading which is lightly inflected by thinkers such as Adorno, Bourdieu, and Derrida.

Another book attuned to modern thinkers is *All for Nothing: Hamlet's Negativity* by Andrew Cutrofello, which is published in the Short Circuits series edited by Slavoj Žižek. He examines how, 'For the past four hundred years, Hamlet has been lurking . . . in the space of philosophical positions' (p. 14): 'What the figure of the Sophist represented for Plato, Hamlet has represented for modern philosophers' (back cover). The five chapters are centred on five forms of Hamlet's negativity: 'his melancholy, negative faith, nihilism, tarrying, and non-existence' (p. 13); his 'non-existence' can refer to his death or his status as a fictional character. According to Cutrofello, these forms roughly correspond to the five stages of the play, although not quite the five acts. *All for Nothing* is an extraordinarily learned work which deals with a large range of thinkers from Descartes and Deleuze to Schopenhauer and

Schmitt, as well as taking in nearly all of Shakespeare's plays at one point or other. This is a book as much about these, mostly Continental, thinkers as it is about Shakespeare, but it deserves to be read by those working on *Hamlet*, and on Shakespeare in relation to philosophy.

Leon Harold Craig's *Philosophy and the Puzzles of Hamlet: A Study of Shakespeare's Method* will be regarded by many working in English studies as something of a curiosity. Working in the traditions of analytic philosophy, it argues that, with *Hamlet*, 'the most oft-cited problems and criticisms are actually solvable puzzles' (back cover). Craig comments of recent *Hamlet* criticism that, 'if I suspect that a particular piece of criticism would be practically unintelligible to Shakespeare, it's of little use to me' (p. 14); Craig argues that this is because he is trying to 'understand Shakespeare's plays as he most likely understood them himself' (p. 14). However, Craig's enterprise tends to see *Hamlet* as literature to be read, and furthermore as a 'consummate work of *reason*' (p. 189; emphasis in original). There is good evidence to suggest that early modern people did imagine Shakespearian drama as being literature, but Craig hardly touches on the similarities and differences between theatre audiences and readers. Thus, the book's argument tends to put puzzle-reading philosophers on the one hand, and 'non-philosophical readers' (p. 4) and theatre-goers on the other: 'the pursuit of an answer to a recognizable puzzle will lead a thoughtful student of the play to notice other curious features which are easily overlooked in a performance, or in initial and superficial readings' (p. 6). Nevertheless, those perplexed by the questions of *Hamlet*, such as the protagonist's madness, or 'the relationship between acting and actual life' (p. 85), will find in this book a whole range of insights on these questions.

Shakespeare's 'Whores': Erotics, Politics and Poetics, by Kay Stanton, includes a chapter on 'The Heroic Tragedy of Cleopatra: The "Prostitute Queen"'. An earlier version of this chapter appeared as an essay in 2002 in *The Female Tragic Hero in English Renaissance Drama*, edited by Naomi Conn Lieble, but was not reviewed then. She argues that 'Cleopatra's deserved status as tragic hero can be recovered by focusing less on what is demonstrably repressive and misogynistic Aristotelian tradition and more on the roots and psychic functions of tragedy' (p. 71). The chapter features in Stanton's monograph among a series of chapters examining female sexuality in the context of the word 'whore' in Shakespeare.

Alex Schulman's *Rethinking Shakespeare's Political Philosophy: From Lear to Leviathan* is the first monograph in the Edinburgh Critical Studies in Shakespeare and Philosophy series edited by Kevin Curran. The book is split into two parts: 'Shakespearean Antiquity' and 'Shakespearean Modernity'. Relevant chapters include 'Pagan Christs: Politics in the Roman Plays', in the first part, and '*King Lear* and the State of Nature', in the second. In the first of these, Schulman pays attention to the concept of civic virtue, arguing that '*Coriolanus*, *Julius Caesar* and *Antony and Cleopatra* depict differing concep-tions of the person, refracted through shifting regimes: not only political regimes, the classical-monarchy-aristocracy-democracy model that set the terms for Aristotle's heirs, but philosophical and psychological regimes, regimes of individual and collective self-understanding in transition between

Paganism and Christianity' (p. 56). Rather than moving though the plays in the chronology of authorship, he moves through Roman history, 'covering the decline of the republic and coming of empire, and of Christianity in *Julius Caesar* and *Antony and Cleopatra*' (p. 57). Schulman reads *King Lear* in relation to modern social contract theory; in *The Secular Contract: The Politics of Enlightenment* [2011], Schulman argued that social contract theory was intertwined with secularization, 'dethroning the timeless *Theos* of scriptural revelation to enable free collective reconstruction politics' (p. 24). The second half of his book on Shakespeare explores how 'The social contract represents a second birth into political maturity, modern liberal democracy's supersession (or *ersatz*) of the older rites of rebirth anchoring tribal ritual and religious conversion. This trope unites Hobbes' *Leviathan*, Spinoza's *Tractus*, Locke's *Second Treatise on Civil Government*, Rousseau's *Du contrat social*, and Kant's political essays' (p. 24). Schulman suggests '*King Lear* as a dramatic prototype for a construction (story? fable?) subsequently influential in early modern political theory: the state of nature prompting a social contract' (p. 123). Those already familiar with the history of political philosophy will find this book most useful as it ventures speedily from Plato and Aristotle right across, via Shakespeare, to Hobbes and Kant.

Kurt A. Schreyer's *Shakespeare's Medieval Craft: Remnants of the Mysteries on the London Stage* explores the synergies of medieval theatrical traditions and Shakespearian drama. The monograph includes an opening chapter, 'Toward a Renaissance Culture of Medieval Artifacts', and one on the Chester Banns, before chapters on individual Shakespeare plays next to medieval ones; these explore how Shakespeare's plays recollect mystery plays, even as they reinscribe medieval elements with new significance. ' "Then Is Doomsday Near": *Hamlet*, the *Last Judgement*, and the Place of Purgatory' focus on the space under the stage: Hamlet seeks not only to murder his father's killer but, like the stage devils of the *Last Judgement*, to send his soul off to Hell' (p. 129). The final chapter is entitled ' "Here's a Knocking Indeed!": *Macbeth* and the *Harrowing of Hell*'. Schreyer argues that Hell also had 'an "aural scene" that Shakespeare's audience would readily have recognized from its experience of provincial mystery drama' (p. 151). So, an audience at the Globe might hear knocking but they could also remember the 'aura of Hell from the mysteries' (p. 152). The extent to which early modern audiences *did* remember medieval drama at such times is difficult to ascertain, but Schreyer's study will be of use to those working on early modern material culture in the theatre and examining the medieval remains in Shakespearian drama.

Shakespeare in London is a volume co-authored by Hannah Crawforth, Sarah Dustagheer, and Jennifer Young that features several chapters on the tragedies. Each chapter pairs one Shakespearian text with a place, street, or institution in London, working chronologically from *Titus Andronicus* in 1594 to *Henry VIII* in 1613, and, as if that was not clever enough, the chapters move geographically from west to east London. In addition, each chapter has a topic, such as violence, politics, or class; so the first chapter is entitled 'Violence in Shakespeare's London: *Titus Andronicus* (1594) and Tyburn'. Other relevant chapters include 'Class in Shakespeare's London: *Romeo and Juliet* (1595–6) and the Strand', 'Religion in Shakespeare's London (1600–1) and St Paul's', 'Medicine in Shakespeare's London: *King Lear* (1605–6) and Bedlam', and 'Economics in Shakespeare's London: *Timon of Athens* (1607) and the King's Bench Prison, Southwark'. This is a dexterous undertaking which pays off in terms of introducing students to a cultural materialist and historically savvy approach to the plays which does not lose sight of Shakespeare's language: as the authors explain in the acknowledgements, this book originates in a course on 'Shakespeare's London' at King's College, London. The book will be particularly helpful for students of Shakespeare, but scholars interested in the representation of London will also want to consult it.

Arden Shakespeare published a number of student-focused guides to Shakespeare in 2014. Laurie Maguire's *Othello: Language and Writing*, in the Arden Student Skills: Language and Writing series, follows in the footsteps of Emma Smith's *Macbeth: Language and Writing*, reviewed last year. The *Othello* volume contains chapters on 'Language and Narrative', 'Language and Genre', 'Language and Boundaries', and, as usual, 'Writing Tips and Topics'. The section on 'Language and Genre' contains more on performance history and Shakespeare's contemporaries than the *Macbeth* volume, but it maintains the series' focus on Shakespeare's language. This series is clearly one of the most useful of its kind.

Moving to edited collections, this year also saw the publication of two volumes concerned with the tragedies in the Arden Shakespeare State of Play series. This series acts as a helpful parallel to the Arden Student Skills series but offers a range of essays by different contributors on the play in question; not all of these essays are aimed simply at students, but offer new research as well. *Macbeth: The State of Play*, edited by Ann Thompson, is split into four parts. Part I, 'The Text and its Status', contains a piece by Anthony B. Dawson on 'Notes and Queries Concerning the Text of *Macbeth*' and one by Brett Gamboa on 'Dwelling "in doubtful joy": *Macbeth* and the Aesthetics of Disappointment', which works from the impression that 'No other play by Shakespeare has so extensive a history of disappointing audiences' (p. 31) and goes on to think through how the play might be structured to create this effect. Part II deals with 'History and Topicality' and contains three essays: Dermot Cavanagh's on 'Politic Bodies in *Macbeth*', Debapriya Sarkar on '"To crown my thoughts with acts": Prophecy and Prescription in *Macbeth*', and Kevin A. Quarmby on 'Lady Macbeth, First Ladies and the Arab Spring: The Performance of Power on the Twenty-First-Century Stage'; the first two essays deal with early modern history, while the third considers modern performance and the media's construction of Hillary Clinton as a Lady Macbeth figure. Part III contains 'Critical Approaches and Close Reading': Darlene Farabee on '"A walking shadow": Place, Perception and Disorientation in *Macbeth*' discusses how 'Macbeth's moral and psychological deterioration manifests itself through his inability accurately to perceive his location and direction' (p. 138), and contrasts this with Banquo; the other essays include Geraldo U. de Sousa on 'Cookery and Witchcraft in *Macbeth*', and Jonathan Hope and Michael Witmore on 'The Language of *Macbeth*'. The final part is entitled 'Adaptation and Afterlife': Sandra Clark examines evidence concerning the text used in *Macbeth* productions in 'The Shapes of *Macbeth*: The Staged Text'; Philippa Sheppard writes on 'Raising the Violence while Lowering the Stakes: Geoffrey Wright's Screen Adaptation of *Macbeth*', a film on drug gangs set in present-day Melbourne; and the final essay is by Ramona Wray on 'The Butcher and the Text: Adaptation, Theatrically and the "Shakespea(Re)-Told" *Macbeth*', which considers the 2005 adaptation of *Macbeth* in the BBC's Shakespeare(Re)-Told season.

Othello: The State of Play, edited by Lena Cowen Orlin, is not divided into parts. It includes ten essays on various topics: Laurie Maguire on '*Othello*, Theatre Boundaries, and Audience Cognition'; Lois Potter on ' "All's One": Cinthio, *Othello* and *A Yorkshire Tragedy*'; Robert Hornback on ' "Speak[ing] Parrot" and Ovidian Echoes in *Othello*: Recontextualizing Black Speech in the Global Renaissance'; Ian Smith on 'Othello's Black Handkerchief' (this appeared as a journal article, reviewed last year); Ambereen Dadabhoy on 'Two Faced: The Problem of Othello's Visage', which explores 'Shakespeare's ambivalent construction of Othello through a re-*turn* to the geographic, cultural, and imperial hegemonies of the eastern Mediterranean' (pp. 122–3); Lynn Enterline on 'Eloquent Barbarians: *Othello* and the Critical Potential of Passionate Character', where she argues that '*Othello* both uses and interrogates the grammar school's language, curriculum, and disciplinary methods for achieving eloquence by giving classically inflected methods for achieving eloquence to precisely those characters its rhetorical training was designed to exclude: women and "barbarians" ' (p. 154); James Siemon on 'Making Ambition Virtue? *Othello*, Small Wars, and Martial Profession', which explores 'Shakespeare's first post-war tragedy' (p. 178); David Schalkwyk on 'Othello's Consummation', which reads the play in relation to Lucretian accounts of love and desire; Robert N. Watson on the linking of neologisms and synonyms in 'Othello's Double Diction'; and, finally, Colleen Ruth Rosenfeld on 'Shakespeare's Nobody', which considers the issue of who or what is knocking in Act IV, scene iii, and its repercussions for our understanding of the play. Like the *Macbeth* volume, this book will be useful for undergraduates, but it will also be valuable to scholars writing on the play.

Shakespeare and Renaissance Ethics, edited by Patrick Gray and John D. Cox, is a particularly powerful volume. The editors' contextualizing intro-duction suggests that 'the pendulum of critical momentum, having swung too far in the direction of abstract theorizing, may now be at risk of swinging too far in the opposite direction, that of materialist detail . . . One purpose of an anthology such as the present one is to help the field recover some sort of equilibrium' (p. 11). The essays in this volume, then, unashamedly address such issues as 'ideas', 'thinking', and 'human moral choice' (p. 13), but with an awareness of past critical disputes. Part I is entitled 'Shakespeare and Classical Ethics'. It starts with Gordon Braden's essay on 'Fame, Eternity and Shakespeare's Romans', which reads suicide in *Julius Caesar* and *Antony and Cleopatra* in relation to classical and Christian views on the subject, and early modern representations of suicide: 'When Shakespeare does dramatize an unmistakably Roman suicide, he displays a scrupulousness that his fellow dramatists do not always show. The scruple has to do with what the imminent suicide imagines will happen next' (p. 42). So, in *Julius Caesar*, Brutus does not anticipate a heavenly afterlife, as he appears to in North's translation of Plutarch's *Lives*. Similarly, Braden argues that Antony and Cleopatra are not represented as seriously considering that they will exist in a heavenly afterlife following their deaths. In defiance of Christian retrospective interpretations, the imagined afterlife for Shakespeare's Romans is resolutely of this world, and their suicides very much a 'worldly endgame' (p. 53).

Part II of the book, 'Shakespeare and Christian Ethics', includes a chapter on 'Shakespeare's Prayers', which deals in part with Claudius's prayer in *Hamlet* and 'the distinction between "contrition" and "attrition"'' (p. 129) in Christian theology. 'The Morality of Milk: Shakespeare and the Ethics of Nursing', by Beatrice Groves, is also in this second part of the book. She writes that an 'aphorism of the early modern period stated that milk could transmit morals and that a child might be infected by the weak principles of the woman who nursed him: "he sucked evil from the dug"' (p. 139). Her essay includes subsections on *Romeo and Juliet* and *Coriolanus* that explore some of the times that Shakespeare alludes to this aphorism; however, she finds that Shakespeare's wet-nurses do not follow this convention: Groves argues that nursing is 'an apt symbol for Christian ethics . . . Shakespeare's nuancing of these fears and prejudices can be read as an ethical position celebrating the nonblood ties that bind communities together and a redemption of the female, lower-class "other"' (p. 154). Also in this part, Russel M. Hiller writes on 'Hamlet the Rough-Hewer: Moral Agency and the Consolation of Reformation Thought'. He argues that 'Hamlet's antic disposition throughout the tragedy's long middle is his active response to the problematic world of Elsinore, his method of "rough-hewing" his way until he is morally satisfied to face his destiny as revenger' (p. 168). Hamlet, in this view, is not stuck in an 'ultra-Calvinist, predestined prison' (p. 161): he is a 'moral dynamo' (p. 177).

The final part of the book is entitled 'Shakespeare and the Ethical Thinking of Montaigne': the essays in this section compare and contrast the two 'thinkers' because, 'Like Shakespeare, Montaigne engaged closely with a wide range of both classical and Christian reflections on ethics' (p. 21). Patrick Gray's '"HIDE THY SELFE": Montaigne, Hamlet, and Epicurean Ethics' suggests that Montaigne followed the 'Epicurean principle "*lathe biosas*" (live unnoticed)' (p. 213) and that *Hamlet*, and particularly Hamlet's behaviour, can be seen as a critique of this principle, and perhaps implicitly of Montaigne himself. The other relevant essay in this section is 'Madness, Proverbial Wisdom, and Philosophy in *King Lear*' by Peter Mack. Mack works from the fact that informal moral philosophy was part of the grammar-school curriculum, and was read and collected in the form of aphorisms in particular. He argues that both Shakespeare and Montaigne 'used narratives to reflect on the truth and applicability of moral *sententiae*': 'where the proverbs and axioms summarise established moral teaching on different sides of a question, Lear's wild perceptions and the bleak narrative of the play offer the audience new ways of thinking about these issues' (p. 284). This essay's focus on humans and animals via Montaigne could also make it productive to be read alongside Laurie Shannon's *The Accommodated Animal*, reviewed last year, which this essay does not mention. Overall, this volume may strike some as being very old-school, but the baby should not be thrown out with the bathwater: there is a great deal of high-calibre thinking at work here.

The Return of Theory in Early Modern English Studies, volume 2, edited by Paul Cefalu, Gary Kuchar, and Bryan Reynolds, follows on from a volume in 2010 edited by Reynolds and Cefalu. In Part I, on 'Posthumanism', Joseph Campana's essay on 'The Bee and the Sovereign (II): Segments, Swarms, and the Shakespearean Multitude' will be of particular interest to researchers in animal studies and political theology, as it responds to work in these fields in a reading of *Coriolanus*. As well as drawing out the political ramifications of the language of bees in relation to sovereignty and the multitude, the essay argues that 'The value of a new wave of work on early modern creatures is that this first wave of work that primarily treats a restricted range of creatures and that primarily revolves around the problem of human exceptionalism might be expanded not merely for the sake of greater inclusivity but so as to encourage greater complexity in how we frame life in its many forms in the Renaissance' (p. 63).

Part III, on 'Historical Phenomenology', includes two relevant essays. In 'Shakespearean Softscapes: Hospitality, Phenomenology, Design', Julia Reinhard Lupton continues her work exploring the affinities between design theory and Shakespearian drama, ending by analysing the 'hostile softscape' of Birnam Wood in *Macbeth*: 'What the softscape paradigm allows us to apprehend is the extent to which environments of entertainment, including their battlefield inversions, are composed indifferently of both living and fashioned stuff (foliage, flags, banners, drums, trumpets, blood, breath), fluid entities whose phenomenal effects (sound, color, motion, smell and their mutual melding) course among natural and media ecologies, eroding their distinctions by creating alternative rivulets of meaning and agency and becoming figures for the shifts and feints of consciousness itself' (pp. 156–7).

Also in Part III is 'Describing the Sense of Confession in *Hamlet*' by Matthew J. Smith; he proposes that early modern drama can be read as a form of phenomenological description. Focusing on Claudius's confession scene, he argues that 'the scene's sense of confessionality is less a direct and simple effect of Claudius's speech than it is a diffusion of the penitent's interior struggle into its perceptual environment' (p. 167). Shakespearian drama, Smith suggests, 'enacts phenomenological description by presenting actions like confession—actions typically understood as only secondarily perceptible—in their distinct inaccessibilities' (p. 180). Those working on Shakespeare cannot be expected to include reference to every relevant article in their work, but this essay could be read fruitfully alongside Joseph Sterrett's 'Confessing Claudius: Sovereignty, Fraternity and Isolation at the Heart of Hamlet' (*TPr* 23:v[2009] 739–61).

Gothic Renaissance: A Reassessment, edited by Elisabeth Bronfen and Beate Neumeier, follows from a conference in Cologne on the English Renaissance and the Gothic. The first part, entitled 'Shakespearean Hauntings', includes two chapters on *Hamlet*. In 'Yorick's Skull', John Drakakis starts by considering the skull used in the David Tennant *Hamlet* at the RSC. He asks: 'how might the strange case of André Tchaikowsky's skull, and his wish that it should be used in modern performance of *Hamlet*, help to illuminate a "Gothic" strain in Shakespeare's *Hamlet* that we might even wish to extend to Renaissance writing generally?' (p. 26). In an answer that takes in Freud,

Bataille, Derrida, and a number of other early modern playwrights and eighteenth- and nineteenth-century writers, Drakakis suggests that it 'is the question whether we can consider Shakespeare and his contemporaries as "Gothic" writers in *their* culturally specific engagement with "history" that intertextual events such as the re-animation of André Tchaikowsky's skull as the dead jester Yorick, bring into focus for us' (p. 29).

The essay by Drakakis is followed by Catherine Belsey's 'Beyond Reason: *Hamlet* and Early Modern Stage Ghosts'. This essay considers the evidence for the idea that *Hamlet* had a hand in the development of the Gothic genre. Belsey reads the ghost in *Hamlet* in the context of classical drama and popular storytelling, suggesting that 'Shakespeare's uncanny apparition represents a new departure in early modern drama' and that 'the fascination of what exceeds mortal understanding was eagerly taken up by some of the dramatist's own contemporaries' (p. 32). Belsey suggests that the fascination with undecidability in *Hamlet* can be seen translated in the later Gothic novel, 'as it continued to permit in fiction the return of an undecidability Enlightenment science longed to dispel' (p. 50). Her contribution is both theoretically informed and historically aware, and shares Janet Clare's attention to intertexuality in her monograph, reviewed above. Part IV, entitled 'Persistence of the Gothic', includes an essay on 'Shakespeare, Ossian and the Problem of "Scottish Gothic" ', which discusses how '*Macbeth* frequently served as the lens through which "Gothic" Scotland was perceived and represented' in the eighteenth and nineteenth centuries (p. 239); it can be fruitfully read alongside *Macbeth: A Critical Reader*, edited by John Drakakis and Dale Townshend, reviewed last year.

Edited by Jennifer Ann Bates and Richard Wilson, with an introduction by the latter, *Shakespeare and Continental Philosophy* is touted as 'the first collection to explore the interface between continental thinking and Shakespeare's plays' (back cover). A number of essays touch on Shakespeare's tragedies, but four are especially relevant. Jennifer Ann Bates's essay, 'Hamlet and Kierkegaard on Outwitting Recollection', reads *Hamlet* next to Kierkegaard's pseudonymously authored *Concluding Unscientific Postscript to Philosophical Fragments*. She reads these 'two Danish melancholics' as people who both see themselves 'as having to set right the joint of time' (p. 40). She argues that the 'central image in *Hamlet* and *Postscript* is . . . that of a grave out of which and into which things rise and fall back. The task for Hamlet and [Kierkegaard's pseudonymous author] Climacus is to make the plot into a moment of genuine embodiment that becomes, has actual, forward movement' (p. 41). Author of *Hegel and Shakespeare on Moral Imagination* [2010], Bates focuses on the oaths of *Hamlet* and the graveyard scene depicted in *Postscript* to reflect on theatre, existentialism, and 'the ghostly call to remember' (p. 46).

'Is Othello Jealous? Coleridge and Russell contra Wittgenstein and Cavell', by Andrew Cutrofello, explores the relationship between jealousy and scepticism. Following Coleridge, Cutrofello suggests that Othello is not prone to suspicion and jealousy, as Leontes is in *The Winter's Tale*; rather, Othello is a sceptic. It is Iago who transforms 'Othello's scepticism into something like jealousy by allegedly warning him against it' (p. 127). Besides taking in thinkers who have read *Othello* and considering Descartes's own scepticism, the essay is a philosophical reflection on the nature of jealousy: 'something like scepticism underlies Othello's jealousy, while something like jealousy underlies Descartes' scepticism' (p. 123). As the final footnote explains, a different version of some of this material appears in *All for Nothing*, reviewed above.

Edward S. Casey's 'Hamlet on the Edge' works from the premise that borders are often more fixed and determined, whereas a boundary is 'a comparatively porous edge' (p. 136). As Casey concedes, 'the distinction between "border" and "boundary" is mostly [his], but the argument that death is a land whose edge is boundary-like is Hamlet's' (pp. 136–7). Casey reads Shakespeare alongside Heidegger and Merleau-Ponty in a consideration of the boundary states in *Hamlet*, especially sleeping, dreaming, Hamlet's madness, and 'the intermediacy [sic] of mirrors' (p. 139); his essay is a good example of thinking *with* Shakespeare, because Casey goes on to consider the repercussions of the play and these boundary states for the understanding of our own existence: 'we are "beings of the between" who live from one intermediacy to another, all the while remaining in the *metaxu* of our life as a whole' (p. 144).

'"No" as Affirmation: A Continental-Philosophical Reading of *Coriolanus*', by Bernard Freydberg, works from Mary Beard's suggestion that 'the study of the classics is the study of what happens in the gap between antiquity and us' (quoted p. 236). Freydberg focuses on the character of Coriolanus's wife, Virgilia. He argues that in Act I, scene iii, when Volumnia insists that her daughter-in-law should spend time with her, and Virgilia responds 'No, good madam, I will not out of doors' (I.iii.72), her ' "No" is affirmative in every essential sense' (p. 242). Her 'No' affirms her independence and her fearlessness in the face of ridicule, but Freydberg also suggests that her 'No' is the 'only means of self-assertion available to her' (p. 243). He goes on to draw parallels between the natures of Virgilia and Coriolanus, and ends by affirming that in their difference 'the perhaps untimely theme of *Coriolanus* emerges: the awesome power of human marital love'. Freydberg's argument is not always entirely convincing, but his attention to Virgilia is valuable.

Turning to journal articles, Arthur F. Kinney's 'Recognizing Shakespearian Tragedy' (*ShS* 67[2014] 221–34) responds to the writing influenced by cognitive science, such as that of Daniel Gardner in *The Science of Fear* [2009], to suggest that Shakespeare's own tragedies are frequently structured via fear: 'Galen taught Shakespeare that the primal passion of fear alone lay at the heart of tragedy for the characters in the play' (p. 224). After briefly considering the shaping of fear in Shakespeare's comedies and histories, Kinney goes on to explore the role of fear in *Macbeth*, *Hamlet*, *Othello*, and *King Lear*. A footnote explains that this article is a companion piece to 'Recognizing Leontes' (*ShS* 63[2010] 326–37). His article also offers a useful insight into early modern writing on the passions, such as those by Thomas Wright and Robert Burton, with a view to understanding how Shakespeare's first audiences might have interpreted the characters' supposed emotional states.

Other particularly relevant essays in *Shakespeare Survey* that may be of interest include: '*Othello* Across Borders: On an Interlocal and Intermedial

Exercise' (*ShS* 67[2014] 327–34) by Rui Carvalho Homem, on '*Bandanna* (1999), an opera by Daron Aric Hagen with a libretto by the Irish poet Paul Muldoon, [which] dislocates the plot of *Othello* to the fraught setting of a town on the border of the US and Mexico in the internationally momentous year of 1968'; B.J. Sokol's 'John Berryman's Emendation of *King Lear* 4.1.10 and Shakespeare's Scientific Knowledge' (*ShS* 67[2014] 335–44); and 'Spectacle, Representation and Lineage in *Macbeth* 4.1' (*ShS* 67[2014] 345–71) by William C. Carroll.

In 'Classical Quotation in *Titus Andronicus*' (*ELH* 81:iii[2014] 787–810) Pramit Chaudhuri explores the four Latin quotations in the play, suggesting that 'their notorious garbling reflects the thematic concerns of the play as a whole' (p. 787). Chaudhuri follows Brian Vickers's attribution, which would assign the two Senecan quotations to George Peele, and argues that 'Peele's advanced training in Latin suggests that the wording of the two Senecan quotations was not an error of language or memory, but rather a deliberate adaptation' (p. 788). Chaudhuri shows how the theme of mutilation in the play 'extends to the very atomic level of Latin citations' (p. 802).

Lori Schroeder's 'The Only Witness a Tongueless Child: Hearing and Reading the Silent Babes of *Titus Andronicus* and *The Winter's Tale*' (*MRDE* 27[2014] 221–47) begins by analysing a story of child murder reported in various early modern broadside accounts; a child witness loses her tongue at the murder scene. Schroeder argues that the accounts point towards 'a keen desire for closure that is both aesthetically and socio-politically reassuring' (p. 222). Paying particular attention to Lavinia and the silent Lucius and infant at the end of the play, she suggests that, in 'an attempt to close down anxiety, [*Titus Andronicus*] in many ways only opens up its own nervousness, essentially doubling and compounding it' (p. 237).

J.K. Barret's 'Chained Allusion, Patterned Futures, and the Dangers of Interpretation in *Titus Andronicus*' (*ELR* 44:iii[2014] 454–85) examines how *Titus Andronicus* 'constructs its present tense on literary historical terms: not only is the play overwhelmingly devoted to classical allusion and imitation, but its characters also constantly and overtly refer to these texts' (p. 453). Shakespeare's characters act out scenes from Ovid's *Metamorphoses* without an awareness of the consequences. Barret's work is focused on temporality and interpretation; characters live out and interpret events via textual models, which foreclose the future.

John McGee had two articles published on *Romeo and Juliet* this year. 'Piloted by Desire: The Nautical theme in *Romeo and Juliet*' (*ES* 95:iv[2014] 392–409) picks out the conceit of Cupid as a suicidal ships' pilot, a god who pilots Romeo. McGee examines the nautical theme in relation to the source, Arthur Brooke's *Romeus and Juliet*: in Brooke 'the maritime imagery powerfully conveys the lovers' subjugation to forces beyond their control' (pp. 397–8); in Shakespeare they 'convey wilful self-endangerment' (p. 398). This essay clearly complements Laurence Publicover's essay on 'Shakespeare at Sea', reviewed below. 'A Set of Wit Well-Played in *Romeo and Juliet* Act 2, Scene3?' (*Shakespeare* 10:i[2014] 1–22), by John McGee, examines the contest of wit between Romeo and Mercutio, arguing that, far from there being friendly banter between them, an unchanging Romeo is thoroughly outwitted by a satirical Mercutio.

In 'Tragic Proportions: The Art of Tyranny and the Politics of the Soul in *Hamlet*' (*ELR* 44:i[2014] 78–107) Katherine Bootle Attie suggests that, 'Like Plato in *The Republic*, Shakespeare in *Hamlet* aestheticizes tyranny as a misperception of size, scale, and proportion' (p. 80). Key figures in her argument include Hamlet, Claudius, Laertes, Pyrrhus, and Fortinbras, but the article also focuses on the concept of audience. The idea of a tyrannically clapping audience in the play, she argues, comes from Plato's *Republic*, where 'Socrates reasons that tyranny can happen to anybody because it is as much a moral state as a political one' (p. 79). Both tyranny and tragedy display an 'art of disproportion' (p. 84).

András Kiséry's '"I Lack Advancement": Public Rhetoric, Private Prudence, and the Political Agent in *Hamlet*, 1561–1609' (*ELH* 81:i[2014] 29–60) explores the politics of *Hamlet* in relation to earlier stories of Hamlet, or Amlethus. He argues that, rather than representing the conflict between Claudius and Hamlet as one of public politics or the commonwealth, as it is in source texts, Shakespeare's *Hamlet* 'carefully and consciously confines itself to an exploration of political actions from the perspective of prudence and of personal loyalties' (p. 31). Kiséry's thesis is that this shift marks a change in the history of Hamlet and of English drama. Like Attie's piece, this one pays special attention to the representation of tyranny, but Kiséry also goes on to address the representation of the political network of agents bound to a patron in relation to early modern political culture.

Seth Lerer, in 'Hamlet's Poem to Ophelia and the Theatre of the Letter' (*ELH* 81:iii[2014] 841–63), argues that 'Among the most dramatically and typographically enigmatic of the play's scenes is the one of Hamlet's love letter to Ophelia' (p. 842). He explores the different representations and printings of the scene in Q1, Q2, the First Folio, and later editions such as Rowe's, arguing that they display 'not garbled versions of a Shakespeare original, but rather various performance practices in flux' (p. 843); these include different ways of performing interiority. He goes on to suggest that, as Act II progresses, 'the play builds a pervasive sense of the already-quotedness of life' (p. 857).

Robert I. Lubin's '"Apparel oft proclaims the man": Visualizing *Hamlet* on the Early Modern Stage' (*ShakB* 32:iv[2014] 629–47) will be of interest to those working on early modern costuming or visual culture. Lubin argues that we can learn much about the way costume signifies in *Hamlet* by paying attention to references to clothing in the play's language. Key figures include Hamlet, the Ghost, Horatio, Claudius, and Fortinbras: the military apparel of Fortinbras makes him the most appropriate leader, following the representation of the armoured Ghost, whereas Hamlet's funeral weeds associate him with the black-gowned scholar Horatio.

In 'Relation and Responsibility: A Levinasian Reading of *King Lear*' (*MP* 111:iii[2014] 485–509) Kent R. Lehnhof provides a philosophical reading of *King Lear* via the thinking of Emmanuel Levinas, who once commented that 'It sometimes seems to me that the whole of philosophy is only a meditation of Shakespeare' (p. 486). Lehnhof employs Levinas's concern with intersubjectivity to consider how the play 'explores what it means to be in relation to the other and to be responsible for the other' (p. 488), as well as thinking through the repercussions for how we respond to *King Lear* as audience members and literary critics. This article could profitably be read alongside Howard Caygill, 'Levinas and Shakespeare' (in Bates and Wilson, eds., *Shakespeare and Continental Philosophy*, reviewed above).

A miniature version of Simon Palfrey's monograph on *Poor Tom* is available through his article 'Attending to Tom' (*SQ* 65:i[2014] 1–21), which is adapted from the book, reviewed above.

John Baxter's 'Tying the Knot in *Othello*' (*EIC* 64[2014] 266–92) begins by investigating what happens 'outside the "acted action" of the play' (p. 267), with special focus on the marriage of Desdemona and Othello and some attention to that of Emilia and Iago. Baxter goes on to suggest that the 'handkerchief clinches the "tying" of *Othello*'s plot, but because it brings Emilia into the action, it also inaugurates the "untying"' (p. 278); this is because, according to Baxter, Emilia discovers a new understanding of marriage and intervenes at the play's conclusion. Baxter examines the different attitudes to marriage voiced in the play, as well as historical sources such as writing on marriage in the Book of Common Prayer, to argue that 'the tying of the knot in the play is completed as a kind of double knot, winding from the completion or fulfilment of the marriage knot between Othello and Desdemona back through the marriage ceremony to a snarl of attitudes and behaviours hostile to marriage' (p. 288).

Responding to Keith Thomas's monograph, *Religion and the Decline of Magic* [1971], in 'Distracting Othello: Tragedy and the Rise of Magic' (*PMLA* 129:iv[2014] 649–71) Donald Hedrick explores a magic associated with sleights of hand and deception; he designates the supernatural kind as 'magic1' and the stage magic as 'magic2'. Although attention to the first kind of magic may have declined during the early modern period, Hedrick argues that the second kind 'informs the distinctive tragedy of Shakespeare's *Othello*' (p. 649). Hedrick examines this stage magic in the context of Theodor Adorno's work on distraction.

Antony and Cleopatra features heavily in Laurence Publicover's 'Shakespeare at Sea' (*EIC* 64[2014] 138–57). In an essay which historicizes the early modern sea, as well as paying close attention to Shakespeare's language, Publicover argues that 'Across a number of plays, but mostly consistently in *Antony and Cleopatra*, sea imagery allows Shakespeare to explore characters' desire to unanchor themselves from the worlds that have formed them' (p. 140). Publicover suggests that this sea has a different resonance from Romantic and post-Romantic ones; 'Antony's dissolution is an act of negation rather than a creative process' (p. 153). Publicover shows how the sea works in Shakespeare not just as a metaphor for chaos and disorder, but also as a 'rich and complex symbol for a form of selfhood that is at the same time a rejection of selfhood' (p. 153).

One of the few articles on *Coriolanus* this year is Anny Crunelle-Vanrigh's '"Seeking (the) mean(s)": Aristotle's *Ethics* and Shakespeare's *Coriolanus*' (*CahiersE* 86:ii[2014], 23–44). Crunelle-Vanrigh reads the play in relation to Aristotle's understanding of *virtus* in the *Nicomachean Ethics*, as well as Machiavelli's *virtù* in *The Prince*; she argues that the play is influenced by

Aristotle's *Ethics* in ways that go beyond the simple identification of Martius as a magnanimous man but inform the play's 'dialectic of excess and defect' (p. 24). The article focuses especially on how Coriolanus's quarrel with Aufidius 'harbours a battle of doctrines that nearly turns their single combat into a political allegory, the friction of *virtus* and *virtù*' (p. 37).

The *Shakespeare Jahrbuch* this year focused on 'Money and Power' and included an article by Katherine A. Gillen on ' "What he speaks is all in debt": Credit, Representation and Theatrical Critique in *Timon of Athens*' (*ShJE* 150[2014] 94–109). The article explores the play's critique of the patronage system in relation to its 'broader interrogation of the ways in which proto-capitalist credit practices destabilize understandings of value and representation, artistic as well as monetary' (p. 94). It is the play's reflections on credit practices which make it resonate with twentieth-century audiences. Noting the lack of receptive audiences in the play itself, Gillen speculates that Shakespeare and Middleton may have used theatre in this play 'to shock a public that is imagined as self-interested and apathetic' (p. 108).

(f) Late Plays

The Tempest, as always, remains the most popular critical focus amongst Shakespeare's late plays, followed closely by *The Winter's Tale*. *Cymbeline* likewise produced work of note, but neither *Two Noble Kinsman* nor *Pericles, Prince of Tyre* did. Transformation and classical texts are two themes that seem to stand out in this year's works.

Themes of colonialism, race, and the body continue to dominate discussion of *The Tempest*. John Kunat's article, ' "Play Me False": Rape, Race, and Conquest in *The Tempest*' (*SQ* 65:iii[2014] 307–27), begins by pointing to the inherent contradiction of the golden-age scene as foregrounding the contrast between nature and civilization (pp. 307–8). For Kunat '*The Tempest* is not so much an historical allegory as an imaginary reconstruction of the mode through which sovereign authority may have been instituted' (p. 324).

The contrast between the natural and the civilized in the play is represented primarily—for Kunat—through the character Caliban. For Kunat, Caliban is presented on the one hand by his 'civilized' master as a diabolic beast, humanity at its most natural and base. On the other hand Kunat argues that it can be read 'that Caliban's socialization was circumscribed by a particular view of human nature, one associated in the play with the corrupt world of Italian politics' (p. 308).

Kunat ably argues that the rape in the play should not be reduced to simple dichotomies, but that the full 'discursive complexity of sexual violation' in early modern England must first be brought to bear on the act itself. Kunat also warns against readings of the rape as solely a 'colonialist fantasy' to justify Caliban's enslavement, although he acknowledges that from the modern perspective this reading is immediately apparent (pp. 309–10).

Instead Kunat ties the possession or 'conquest' of Miranda to the framing of the play: Alonso's daughter 'Claribel's marriage to the King of Tunis' (p. 311). Kunat pursues 'the parallel between Ferdinand and Caliban in their drive to possess Miranda, with the King of Tunis positioned as the anomalous figure who undermines what otherwise appears as an absolute distinction between them and the different worlds they represent'. Kunat suggests the family on the island, in which both African and European coexist, is written large in the political family at the end of the play: 'the presumptive family that Prospero attempted to create on the island is transposed to the political realm, in which Africa and Europe are now bound to one another through marriage, collapsing the sexual and social contracts into one another in a way that belies their mutual origin in forms of consensual domination' (p. 327).

Kunat's well-argued and thoughtful paper takes a traditional reading of race, politics, and colonialism in *The Tempest* and transforms it. Kunat does this by pointing to the thematic and discursive links between Miranda's potential conquistadors, and to the return to the framing of the play at its end by Gonzalo, who reminds the audience that 'In one voyage | Did Claribel her husband find at Tunis' just as 'Ferdinand, her brother, found a wife' (5.1.208–10)' (p. 326). This reading moves the play firmly away from colonization as it relates to the New World, and views it within its stated Mediterranean context, although I would quibble with the emphasis on Caliban as an African rather than as the 'Black man' or 'black boy' who often represented a demonic figure in early modern Europe. Yet there are many well-made points in Kunat's work, not least in his emphasis on the interaction between the framing of the play and its main themes.

Race and the Mediterranean context in *The Tempest* are also central to Irina Kantarbaeva-Bill's discussion of Anglo-Ottoman anxieties in the play: 'Anglo-Ottoman Anxieties in the *Tempest*: From Displacement to Exclusion' (*Caliban* 52[2014] n.p.). Rather than focusing on the nature/civilization, African/ European, and male/female dialectics of Kunat, Kantarbaeva-Bill urges us to move away from the traditional interpretation of the play as a 'metaphor of colonization, either of the New World or of Ireland', and notes that '*The Tempest*'s pervasive setting on an island in the Mediterranean serves to illuminate how each English reference to the Ottomans depends upon Shakespeare's choice of displacement'. In this reading Tunis is interpreted within its historical context as a part of the Ottoman empire, and as the heir to ancient Carthage. The framing of the play through Claribel's marriage is likewise foregrounded, though in this case as a site of European contention with Ottoman power. Likewise Sycorax and Caliban's island are the site of conflict between Ottoman and European territory, with the island as Ottoman soil captured and held by Prospero.

This reading does not disregard the colonial context that so many have read into the play, but resituates it within the actual Mediterranean, and within the real geopolitical circumstances of the period. Like Kunat, Kantarbaeva-Bill is emphasizing both the actual context of the play and how Shakespeare's framing establishes that context.

Jasmine Lellock's work on alchemy and language in *The Tempest*, 'Boiled Brains, "Inward Pinches", and Alchemical Tempering in *The Tempest*' (in Hopkins and Ostovich, eds., *Magical Transformations on the Early Modern English Stage*, pp. 123–37), moves us away from Shakespeare's framing of the play. Lellock delves into the question of what kind of magic or alchemy

Prospero uses, and how this influences our understanding of both the nature of his magic and his character. Lellock engages with a variety of early modern texts on alchemy and magic, and draws connections between their conceptions and Shakespeare's representation of Prospero. The form of magic, and the ends for which it is used, was a major source of contention in early modern Europe, and this contention and the uncertainty it creates around Prospero serve as a narrative in which transformation plays a central role. Of course this transformation is neither simple nor easy: suffering serves as a trial to temper both characters and narrative, transforming them as alchemy and conjury were purported to be able to magically transform the ordinary into the extraordinary. For Lellock the play itself as a whole 'seems to posit that theatre itself is a philosopher's stone that can lead to transformation' (p. 137).

Shannon Kelley's study of the symbolic role of coral in *The Tempest*, 'The King's Coral Body: A Natural History of Coral and the Post-Tragic Ecology of *The Tempest*' (*JEMCS* 14:i[2014] 115–42), also deals with the extraordinary and transformation, but in relation to ecological history. Kelley examines how the study of how natural history had conceived of coral influenced Shakespeare's use of it as a metaphor for resurrection. The understanding of coral itself was as a wondrous substance, of unknown taxonomy: coral was neither plant nor animal but a synthesis of both to Linnaeus and Aristotle. It was a shrub to Pliny, even a 'vegetal mineral' in Theophrastus. Coral was considered a remedy for illness by Pliny, was used in funerary rituals, and 'occupies a liminal space between death and resurrection' (p. 123). Alonso is symbolically reimagined by Shakespeare (via Ariel) as 'poetic vision' of a 'non-decomposed coral and pearl corpse' (p. 130). For Kelley the transformation or 'changes in its physiological structure create a provocative metaphor for the body politic' (p. 134).

R. Allen Shoaf's discussion of *The Tempest* in chapter 5 (pp. 69–84) of his *Lucretius and Shakespeare on the Nature of Things* suggests that it was Shakespeare's familiarity with Lucretius and Epicurus that led to *The Tempest*'s title. This is therefore—for Shoaf—an examination of the opposing desires in the tempestuous mind of the protagonist and a desire for *ataraxia*, a state of calm. For Shoaf, *The Tempest* is the mature work of a poet exploring the boundaries of his own power, and the power of mankind more generally in the face of natural power. In this reading of the play Prospero is the authorial avatar who is interacting with a reading of Lucretius on the power of man and nature. The possibility of transformation, of change, is bound up in Prospero's tempestuous desires and the need to be able to control them and the future through his predictions. These ideas themselves are not wholly new, but the connection to a philosophical framework leads to some intriguing conclusions about Prospero's temperament and its relationship to the play at large: 'As long as Prospero seeks vengeance, as long as he incants in anger, as long as he craves total control, he is in the tempest and (far more destructive) the tempest is in him' (pp. 80–1).

Studies of *Cymbeline* this year venture away from nationalist themes. Benjamin V. Beier's study of persuasive language in *Cymbeline*, 'The Art of Persuasion and Shakespeare's Two Iagos' (*SIP* 111:i[2014] 34–64), compares Imogen's ability to overcome Iachimo with the linguistic dominance of Iago in

Othello. Beier argues that Shakespeare rarely wrote characters that were as able as the sharp-sighted Imogen to perceive and combat the villain's sophistry. Or, as Beier argues, 'In Cymbeline, Imogen suggests that apt and ethical rhetoric is at least equal to, if not more powerful than sophistical speech' (p. 62). Imogen's instrument for persuasion, her 'art', is not only her use of language, but at a key moment of the play her voice itself. Beier argues that in *Cymbeline* Shakespeare shows that the natural, intuitive knowledge of Imogen and other characters allows the story to be turned aside from the tragedy of *Othello*.

Questions of personal liberty, law, and the socio-legal structures of early modern England as reflected in Shakespeare's plays are discussed in Camilla R. Barker's 'Shackles in Shakespeare: On the Falsity of Personal Liberty in Renaissance England' (*LLR* 35:i[2014] 25–42). The question of how developments in law and their underlying principles impacted representation of society in early modern literature is a field certainly worthy of more discussion—as the recent discussion of oral contracts and law in Christopher Marlowe's *Faustus* by Laura Levine in *Magical Transformations on the Early Modern English Stage* deftly showed. However, Barker's grip on the historical context of Shakespeare's plays lets down the framework within which she is working. For example, in discussing the crisis the loss of Cymbeline's children creates, she references Henry VIII's succession laws, not the late Elizabethan succession crisis. However, Barker's discussion of Prospero's power and the lack of personal liberty amongst the 'subjects' of the island in *The Tempest* shows the potential of the thematic discussion of freedom in early modern drama from a socio-legal perspective.

Cymbeline is also briefly discussed in Lisa S. Starks-Estes's *Violence, Trauma, and Virtus in Shakespeare's Roman Poems and Plays*. In the coda to her book, Starks-Estes discusses Shakespeare's engagement with Ovid in the trauma and masochism of *A Midsummer Night's Dream* and *Cymbeline*. She argues that *Cymbeline* was 'composed at a time when attitudes toward the Roman poet had begun to shift' and the play therefore 'voiced Shakespeare's defence of and rededication to Ovid' (p. 162). The coda points to Shakespeare's use of the nightingale 'to establish himself as an Ovidian poet-playwright', and to signal 'his multi-layered borrowings from Ovid', in particular, from the tragic story of Philomela (p. 162). For example, when Imogen finds Cloten's headless body (although a case of mistaken identity), Shakespeare's heroine imitates Ovid's Hecuba (as his Venus had earlier done) by smearing her face with her dead loved-one's blood. For Starks-Estes this moment of Ovidian tragedy 'becomes a vivid representation of traumatic grief' which builds upon her melancholy, becoming a state of near-insanity (p. 178). Starks-Estes' discussion of tragedy and trauma, on the one hand, and Roman *virtus*, on the other, is embodied by Imogen's two brothers, who, in and through their relationship with her as the boy Fidele, display their own *virtus* and experience Ovidian tragedy.

Discussions of religious themes come to the fore in this year's works on *The Winter's Tale*. Jill Delsigne's examination of the play, 'Hermetic Miracles in *The Winter's Tale*' (in Hopkins and Ostovich, eds., pp. 91–108), contrasts Shakespeare's positive depiction of Paulina's transformation of Hermione

from statue to woman with the negative depiction of magic-wielding friars in
Friar Bacon and Friar Bungay. Unlike Friar Bacon in the earlier play,
Hermione denies she is using evil spirits to achieve her ends, and instead
humbly describes herself as merely a conduit for God's miracle. Delsigne
argues that the transformation of the statue in *The Winter's Tale* is a positive
use of the Roman Catholic hermetic tradition of animating statues of saints
and martyrs. She draws upon Lodovico Lazzarelli's 'synthesis of Catholicism
with hermeticism' to 'provide a model' for Paulina's animation of Hermione
(p. 108). For Delsigne the repentance of Leontes leads to Paulina's act of
reconciliation, her restoration of Leontes' lost family. But Friar Bacon's
repentance comes only at the end of the play, when his own attempt at
animating a brass head has failed. Unlike Paulina's quasi-sacramental act of
reconciliation following Leontes' extended penitence, Friar Bacon's act of
magic uses 'ghastly fiends' and 'devils' in schemes which usually had
unforeseen and tragic consequences.

   Robert Appelbaum examines the same moment in *The Winter's Tale* in
'"Lawful as Eating": Art, Life, and Magic in The Winter's Tale' (*ShakS*
42[2014] 32–41), but focuses on the analogy of Leontes between the lawfulness
of eating and the restoration of Hermione through the art of magic.
Appelbaum examines the inherent problems in the words used by Leontes in
his injunction, the relationship between poor diet and Leontes' behaviour in
the play to this point, the power of kingship to make magic 'as lawful as
eating', and the problem of whether any actual magic occurs at this point in
the play, and if it did, whether it was 'white' or 'black' magic. Appelbaum
concludes that in making his statement 'If this be magic, let it be an art lawful
as eating' Leontes is condoning the act, whatever its origins, and that in his
association 'Leontes wishfully demystifies the magic he apprehends' (p. 39).
But this act also re-mystifies eating for Appelbaum, who argues in his
conclusion that 'Eating, as he alludes to it, embodies the right to life, a right
that it behoves a king and a nation to protect. And he implies that this activity
and the right to life that warrants it should be as wonderful— though perhaps
also as contentious—as the magic that has awakened his faith' (p. 40).
Appelbaum ably engages with texts on magic, food, and early modern drama
as well as his source in this brief but engaging piece of scholarship.

   The final article to focus on the moment of the statue's transformation is by
Hannah Chapelle Wojciehowski: 'Statues that Move: Vitality Effects in *The
Winter's Tale*' (*L&T* 28[2014] 299–315). In her examination of Hermione's
return, Wojciehowski draws upon 'insights from the fields of psychology and
cognitive neuroscience to aesthetic experience' (p. 300). She suggests that
shared understandings of embodied cognition are also influenced by how the
world around us conceives of them. She ties together modern understandings
of cognition with early modern conceptions of sight and hearing, and argues
that 'post-Reformation loss' of art and affect in religious contexts caused the
'theatrical recuperation' of visual modes of inducing affect (p. 311). The role of
viewing in the effect of vitality seen in the transformation of Hermione from
statue to woman is therefore part of a 'Watershed moment', the Protestant
Reformation, which was 'a collective rethinking of beliefs and practices on a
monumental scale' (p. 312). This monumental shift therefore allows 'today's

cognitive cultural historians . . . the occasion to theorise how the neural imaginations of individuals and groups may have been gradually rewired in response to massive ideological and technological changes' (p. 312). Without Appelbaum's political emphasis, Wojciehowski also points to Leontes' statement on magic as 'an art as lawful as eating', but for Wojciehowski this is 'the experience of vitality' through which 'we feel and reaffirm our attachments to each other and to life itself' (p. 312).

Julia Reinhard Lupton's article, 'Judging Forgiveness: Hannah Arendt, W.H. Auden, and *The Winter's Tale*' (*NLH* 45:iv[2014] 641–63), likewise focuses on Hermione's return in Act V, but unlike Delsigne and Appelbaum, she focuses on Hermione herself rather than on either Paulina or Leontes. Reinhard Lupton engages with the opposing views of W.H. Auden and Hannah Arendt on forgiveness as an act or forgiving as 'an action that always involves the speech and comportment of a plurality of persons' (p. 641). These form the basis for Reinhard Lupton's questioning of the extent to which Hermione forgives her husband Leontes for his role in the deaths and losses incurred during the play on her return to him. As Lupton argues, Hermione is aware of Leontes' responsibility for the events of the play and this needs to 'be considered in any tallying of the play's final settlements' (p. 642). By engaging with different understandings of forgiveness, Lupton aims at—and succeeds in—deepening our understanding of the actions of Hermione once she is restored to her family (p. 657). Lupton points out the two opposing views of forgiveness presented by these two authors suggest both common and divergent heritages, suggesting that how we interpret Hermione's actions at the end of the play might rely on how we ourselves view forgiveness and reconciliation based on the social constructs within which we act (p. 642).

The role of social mores, or theological upbringing, in influencing conceptions of sin, repentance, and forgiveness in *The Winter's Tale* is also the central theme of Paul D. Stegner's work on the gendered construction of penitence in the play: 'Masculine and Feminine Penitence in *The Winter's Tale*' (*Renascence* 66:iii[2014] 189–202). Stegner immediately sets the tone of his article by stating that 'Shakespeare's theological vision in the play is rooted in a modified form of traditional penitential practices' (p. 189). In Leontes' exchange with Camillo in Act I, Stegner sees evidence of Shakespeare's understanding of Catholic doctrine on sacramental confession. This establishes a tripartite, formulaic, and defined mode for penitence and forgiveness. Stegner contrasts this 'masculine' forgiveness, with Paulina's later counselling of Leontes. Following the death of Mamilius, and the apparent loss of both Hermione and Perdita, Paulina claims that the scope of his crimes demands a perpetual penitence, which Leontes' extreme guilt induces him to comply with. These two opposing priest-like figures, Camillo and Paulina, are then discussed within a framework that shows how medieval and early modern writers conceptualized penitence and forgiveness as gendered behaviours. Paulina uses the language of feminine deference, Stegner shows, to manipulate Leontes into his penitence, sustain it, and bring it to an end. However Paulina herself, in ending Leontes' sorrow, Stegner argues, is brought back under male control through matrimony. Stegner suggests that in ordering the marriage of his two opposing priest-figures Leontes not only revokes Paulina's permission to speak—'O peace, Paulina'—but 'reasserts masculine governmental authority' (p. 199).

The Winter's Tale and The Tempest are only briefly discussed in Susan Wiseman's work on metamorphosis in Writing Metamorphoses in the English Renaissance. But it is her discussion of The Winter's Tale and contemporary tales of children found in the wild that I wish to highlight here. The loss and return of Leontes' family are often discussed within the terms of redemptive religion, but Wiseman's focus is on how these ideas reflected popular literature about children left or lost in the wild. It is in the context of losing a child to the wild that Wiseman discusses the thematic meaning of the bear that ensures Perdita's anonymity by killing Antigonus. For Wiseman, 'the interplay of stories of "lost" and "found" ' in the play gives the audience 'a bravura, interrogative reworking of ready-made, pre-known stories about these events' (p. 185). Wiseman is here referring to tales of children lost after wild natural violence, such as attacks by wild animals, or weather events such as the storm in which these events occur: 'the bear's arrival before the audience links the stories of lost and found children' in Jacobean England to Shakespeare's tale (p. 186). But the wild in this story is less wild than at first glance. Wiseman points to the bear garden of London's South Bank, and the semi-tameness of the pastoral landscape Perdita actually finds herself in. For Wiseman, 'Perdita's story, then, is of a child saved from the wild lodged in a play deeply immersed in, and interrogating the social basis of, stories of wild children' (p. 190). The interaction between ballads and broadsides about wild children, and the framing of Perdita's loss are only an aside in Wiseman's work, but nonetheless rich and thought-provoking. And Wiseman's discussion of bears, bear-baiting, and their relevance for tales of metamorphosis, such as Perdita's, is as intriguing and informative as the rest of her work, brief though it may be.

As always, The Tempest has been the most studied of the late plays. It seems to be a continuing site of scholarship, along with The Winter's Tale, while works like Pericles, Prince of Tyre and Two Noble Kinsman are not represented at all. However, there is an overwhelming, if unintended, theme to the works this year. They are either investigating transformation or are taking the existing scholarship and using a close examination of detail, transforming how we might have thought about concepts, for example colonialism and imperialism in The Tempest, and bringing greater depth to those plays as a result. Emphasizing the framing of a play such as The Tempest shows Shakespeare's intended Mediterranean context, and opens up new areas of study, for example the Ottoman connections of the King of Tunis and how these might impact on our interpretation of the island's inhabitants.

Most of the work this year has focused on the minutiae of the plays in question, challenging our preconceptions by returning to details of character, context, and language. There was little this year, in comparison to previous years, to challenge the genre of the late plays. Instead some of the richest work was to be found in brief examinations of Shakespeare's use of wider ideas, such as Kelley's ecological history of coral, or Wiseman's examination of Perdita's loss.

(g) Comedies

Michael Collins's collection of essays honouring Stephen Booth, *Reading What's There: Essays on Shakespeare in Honor of Stephen Booth*, is, unsurprisingly, a selection of new critical readings of the texts themselves which, amid some of the other methodologies on offer this year, feels underdeveloped and somewhat dated. Michael Goldman's essay, 'On the Final Songs in *Love's Labour's Lost*' (pp. 41–9), offers an analysis of how the closing songs of *Love's Labour's Lost* meaningfully conclude a process of 'playing through to reality' (p. 45), where 'theatrical and festive activities become ways of touching the universe of death and adult limitation and becoming adequate to it' (p. 45). The figurative and syntactical simplicity of the songs, Goldman contends, returns us to an 'almost abstractly conventional festivity' (p. 46), offering a closure to the news of death, and culmination of the twelve-month test, opening the reader to the new values advanced by the end of this play. Goldman's lightly bardolatrous essay invokes (but does not fully utilize) pastoralism as a means of arguing for the songs as a conscious 'advance in style' (p. 46) for Shakespeare. Goldman's essay, for the 'serious mind' (p. 48) ponders a slightly out-of-date concern as to whether the closing songs are 'a final poignant aporia of the poet or the intrusion of an actor tidying up', insisting on the absolute binary between play and reality that characterizes the literary rejection of the theatrical.

Margaret Maurer's contribution to the volume, 'Leonato and Beatrice in Act 5, Scene 5, Line 97 of *Much Ado About Nothing*' (pp. 89–98), is a consideration of the last scene of *Much Ado* that attempts to strip away the editorial intervention that sees Beatrice passed from Leonato to Benedick for a kiss, as editors of the line 'peace, I will stop your mouth' (V.iv.97) often construct it. Instead of acknowledging these bonds between men, Maurer looks to the silent presence of Innogen, mother of Hero, in the first quarto, as evidence of a demonstration of 'a silent woman as the pretext of a man taunting another man with the possibility of cuckoldry', in retaliation for the Act I, scene i, insulting of Leonato by Benedick, which Maurer imagines could have been in the presence of the unspeaking Innogen. The homosocial connotations of the situation are passed over in favour of a short précis of 'a pervasive series of unobtrusive imprecisions in the play' (p. 94) centred on familial connections that raise questions of Beatrice's fatherless condition, in this maddeningly brief and speculative essay.

Craig Dionne and Parmita Kapadia's collection, *Bollywood Shakespeares*, is an important contribution to the field of globalized Shakespeares, recognizing the tradition of Indian Shakespeare and specifically locating that tradition in the vibrant Bollywood industry. The book covers a wide range of adaptations, but for our purposes, Richard Allen's study, 'Comedies of Errors: Shakespeare, Indian Cinema, and the Poetics of Mistaken Identity' (pp. 165—92), is of interest. Allen suggests that the motif of mistaken twins in *The Comedy of Errors* is a popular trope in Bollywood cinema, and proposes studying the history of this trope in the cinema, to underscore 'the relationship between knowledge and sight precisely by confounding that relationship' (p. 166). Allen draws two lines of Shakespearian influence on the

Indian cinema—the first through the Bengali literary and cultural tradition that is inherently colonial, and the second of Parsi theatre, which had an 'irreverent, appropriative relationship' (p. 167) to Shakespeare. Citing the first Indian translation of the play, in 1869, into *Bhrantibilas* (the play of errors), Allen argues that the Bengali tradition offers an 'Indianization' of the characters that allows for relative fidelity to the plot, and that subsequently produced the first cinematic rendition of the play in Bengali, *Bhranti Bilash* [1963], which was followed by *Angoor* [1982], and more recently, *Do Dooni Char* [2010]. These films, Allen contends, contrast strikingly with the British adaptive history of the play, choosing to play up sensuality over romance, proposing that 'familial closeness breeds a relationship of playful intimacy that could quickly slide into something else' (p. 174).

Allen goes on to tentatively suggest 'an indirect influence through the profound impact that Shakespeare's plots had on the Parsi theatre of Bombay' (p. 181) that was a determining factor in the shape of popular Hindi cinema. Parsi's bold and aggressive rewrites allowed melodrama to penetrate the trope of fraternal twins and mistaken identity, a hybridity which renders *The Comedy of Errors* appealing to celebrity actors looking to display range. Allen traces the narrative through several examples, including *Afsana* [1951], *Chinatown* [1962], *Haseena Maan Jayegi* [1968], *Kishen Kanhaiya* [1990], and *Bade Miyan* [1998], which, somewhat intriguingly, conflates Shakespeare's play with Michael Bay's 1995 Hollywood blockbuster, *Bad Boys*. Allen closes his fascinating précis of *The Comedy of Errors*' Bollywood history with the suggestion that if this play 'had not existed, it would have to have been invented by Bollywood' (p. 189).

Next up is Patrick Gray and John D. Cox's collection, *Shakespeare and Renaissance Ethics*. Indira Ghose's essay, 'Shakespeare and the Ethics of Laughter' (pp. 56–75), examines the various ethics of laughter, throughout the comedies, arguing that Shakespeare exhibits a discomfort with purely derisory laughter, instead, seeing out alternative sources of the comic. Thankfully, she chooses to take on *Twelfth Night*, the exception to her rule that 'scapegoat figures in his comedies are rarely humiliated in a devastating manner' (p. 66), to illustrate this point. Ghose makes the contestable claim that the increased popularity in classical ideas of decorum 'led to the emergence of a divide between elite and popular culture in the early modern period' (p. 67), and turns to Malvolio as the example of a joke that goes too far, outlining how the prank opens with an ostensible satire on a social climber, and ends with 'a sense of unease' (p. 70) at Malvolio's degradation.

Jane Kingsley-Smith's essay, 'Aristotelian Shame and Christian Mortification in *Love's Labour's Lost*' (pp. 76–97), attempts to re-evaluate the impact of Aristotle's *Rhetoric* on early modern literary accounts of shame, turning her attention to *Love's Labour's Lost* as a 'labour of mortification and repentance' (p. 95), that ultimately achieves very little. Kingsley-Smith creates a comparative structure that pits the more sensitive Shakespeare against the shamelessness of Montaigne, by suggesting that, for Shakespeare, the self-mortification of shame 'produces a defensive reaction that hides the self from the self' (p. 83). To that end, she situates the men of Navarre's vows within a discourse of mortification that they make no attempt to redress, instead reinventing themselves as lovers, as Armado does in the face of his lust for Jaquenetta. Kingsley-Smith asserts the importance of Aristotle's *Rhetoric*, which 'judges the moral efficacy of shame from a perspective of something like disappointment' (p. 89), and which characterizes the play.

Ruben Espinosa and David Ruiter's collection, *Shakespeare and Immigration*, is an important, book, not only because of its timely content, but for its inclusion of convincing, modern scholarship that intersects past and present in a rigorous, academic manner. Eric Griffin's essay, 'Shakespeare, Marlowe, and the Stranger Crisis of 1590' (pp. 13–36), which opens the volume, examines the role of theatre during the 'stranger crisis' of the late sixteenth century, examining, among other texts, *The Comedy of Errors*' place as a site of the ambivalent domestic attitude towards Elizabeth's open immigration policy. Griffin's brief consideration outlines an Ephesus that is analogous to early modern England through its ambivalence towards the precarious balance of traditional and contemporary religious and nationalist identity. This is manifest in the Latinate literary references of *The Comedy of Errors* routinely being 'subordinated to an earlier Greek heritage that is constructed, both in national and spiritual terms, as more pure than its universal successor' (p. 16). However, the play's attitude to the status of England as a refuge for immigrants is more ambivalent; its elevation of English financial and social concerns manifest in a reticence towards strangers jars with more nationalist discourses found in pamphlets such as *A Fig for the Spaniard or Spanish Spirits*. The essay goes on to stand *The Comedy of Errors* alongside *Sir Thomas More* and, as would be expected, *The Jew of Malta* and *Titus Andronicus*, arguing, that these plays, by reflecting the widespread ambivalence regarding large-scale immigration, operated as a locus for public dissatisfaction with London's sudden influx of foreign and domestic immigrants.

In his essay 'My Hopes Abroad: The Global/Local Nexus in *The Merchant of Venice*' (pp. 37–58), Geraldo U. deSousa argues that the play's portrayal of sites of cross-cultural and transnational encounters articulates an anxiety about Venice's participation in a global marketplace. The globalization that Antonio embodies, deSousa argues, destabilizes the notion of home and creates a character who demonstrates a 'demarcation between exterior and interior space' (p. 43), who cannot articulate, or even interrogate, the source of his unhappiness. Antonio's self-alienation stands in contrast to Portia, who represents a robust defence of Venetian ideals, particularly in the courtroom, where she underscores the 'boundaries between Venetian and the alien' (p. 44). Through her late father's will, Portia has been thrust into a global marketplace, creating a paradox between the secure home that the intentionality of the will envisions and the 'casino for foreigners' (p. 45) Belmont has become. Yet the marriage to a Venetian man allows a clear establishment of ownership over her house that frees Portia to be able to leave her home and save her husband. DeSousa makes an effective contrast of Belmont to Shylock's home, in the argument that Shylock's abode delineates the plight of many transnational migrants and the ways in which the security of the house may contrast with a profound sense of cultural alienation. The juxtaposition, unfortunately, omits an examination of Jessica's migration from one 'home' to the other, in favour of a comparison with Barabas's home in *The Jew of Malta*, ending with the idea of Shylock as a refugee in his own house.

Kathryn Vomero Santos's contribution is an essay entitled 'Hosting Language: Immigration and Translation in *The Merry Wives of Windsor*' (pp. 59–72), and uses the discrepancies between Evans's Welsh and Caius's French accents to explore the ways in which the play demonstrates an English that 'serves as a host that is as hospitable as it is hostile to its strange guests' (p. 60). In particular, she argues, Shakespeare's dialogic drama stages the hospitality of the English language that simultaneously absorbs difference and demonstrates a resistance to complete assimilation for the foreign-born immigrant. Relying on the metaphor of translation that characterizes Falstaff's wooing of Mistresses Page and Quickly, Santos argues that the 'out-of-into' translation from the source language to a target language is analogous to a process of crossing borders, and can often leave the immigrant in a liminal space.

Santos takes her conceit further, arguing for the English language as an arena of linguistic play, even as it 'acknowledges that the host language is vulnerable to violation' (p. 67) by the natives who also fail to master appropriate English grammar and vocabulary. At this point, the Host becomes central, both as an organizing principle of the play's dramaturgy, caught between the two foreigners, and as an emblem of the linguistic metaphor, as he 'emphatically declares his possession of the English language at the expense of Evans and Caius and becomes a figure for English as a host language that both makes room and denies entry at the proverbial inn' (p. 67), and in spite of the Host's own fears of being cozened due to verbal slippage, the play affirms a difference that maintains the boundaries that incomplete language demarcates.

Elizabeth Acosta Valdez's excellent essay, 'Open Doors, Secure Borders: The Paradoxical Immigration Policy of Belmont in *The Merchant of Venice*' (pp. 177–98), is a presentist study that frames the play in the context of the current American Diversity Visa Immigration programme (also known as the green card lottery), in particular, emphasizing the institutional advantage given to those with a clear proficiency in English, noting that, for both would-be American citizens and suitors to Portia's hand, 'winners are not chosen based on random luck, but rather through calculated measures, in which the criterion is similitude' (p. 184). Bassanio, who carries all of the traits of the undesirable immigrant, is able to overcome the flawed lottery thanks to the vulnerability of the casket test to manipulation, highlighting the failure of the system. Yet, Acosta Valdez argues, we should not view Portia's interest in Bassanio as any less self-interested than his in her. Portia's manipulation of the casket lottery secures her a husband 'who can be manipulated in a way that allows Portia to have that agency and ownership she desires' (p. 189) and he is selected for precisely the qualities that her late father sought to exclude. This exclusion of more worthy candidates brings Acosta Valdez's reading back to the present, under the guise of contemporary audience response; the audience can use the casket scene of *The Merchant of Venice* to meditate on the resistance to, and manipulation of, the system against valid candidates for permanent residency who are seen as less ideologically desirable: foreigners who are 'too foreign' (p. 192). Acosta Valdez's powerful essay ends on the acknowledgement that both systems 'seem to promote discrimination and racial prejudice (p. 194).

Frances E. Dolan's student-centric guide *Twelfth Night: Language and Writing* is an informally written, pop-culture-referencing introduction to the play that opens with the suggestion that the reader 'use the play as a starting point—as evidence in itself—rather than turning first to the work of historians and critics to explain it' (pp. 5–6). Dolan pushes students to ask questions of their own, historicizing the play by discussions of boy actors, Elizabeth I, and Puritanism. The book also offers a wealth of strategies for thinking and writing about the play, asking the reader questions to prompt further thought, and suggesting sources such as the Open Source Shakespeare concordance as a place to seek out language patterns. As the book works through formal elements, such as patterns of imagery, the role of the blazon, tropes, and verse forms, it regularly pauses to offer writing strategies, including checklists and rhetorical devices to ensure that an essay engages the reader. Dolan's book is dense in content, but accessible to its intended audience, and thorough to a point that exceeds Shakespeare analysis. It is full of good writing advice, and carefully works through a concise reading of the play.

Alison Findlay and Liz Oakley-Brown's *Twelfth Night: A Critical Reader*, Arden's second critical companion to *Twelfth Night*, offers an introductory overview of critical approaches to the play, beginning with a critical and performance history, moving through 'new directions' for the text, and closing with a short essay on pedagogical resources for those using the play in a classroom setting. Unlike the Norton critical editions that offer a wide variety of topics in abridged form, Arden's critical reader includes an overview of the play's reception, and four lengthy 'new directions' essays that constitute the bulk of the book. Keir Elam's essay, ' "Ready to distrust mine eyes": Optics and Graphics in *Twelfth Night*' (pp. 99–122), historicizes the play's' optical illusions, contextualizing its 'veritable catalogue of visual images' (p. 107) through a discussion of other early modern art. Randall Martin's contribution, 'Shipwreck and the Hermeneutics of Transience in *Twelfth Night*' (pp. 123–43), frames the shipwreck as part of a greater exploration of how 'eschatological and diachronic time and knowledge, and their related hermeneutic tendencies . . . illuminate respective shipwreck and holiday epistemologies' (p. 126) in the play, creating a positive portrayal of 'open subjective potential' (p. 126). Andrew McConnell Stott's ' "Let them use their talents": *Twelfth Night* and the Professional Comedian' (pp. 144–65) uses both textual study and theatre history to suggest reading Feste as a paid fool, one whose relationship to festivity 'belongs more to his ability to evoke sentimental longing for it rather than being its inherent, fully embodied representative' (p. 147). Finally, Tiffany Stern's essay, 'Inverted Commas around the "Fun": Music in *Twelfth Night*' (pp. 166–88), examines the music of *Twelfth Night*, arguing for music as not only a part of characterization but 'a site of comedy' (p. 180) that enacts a progression that is parallel to the central narrative. The essays that comprise the book seem to be original and diverse pieces of scholarship, which left me puzzled as to the anticipated readership: they seem too long and too niche for an undergraduate audience, and a little ambitious to work as a teaching aid.

Turning to Robert Henke and Eric Nicholson's collection, *Transnational Mobilities in Early Modern Theatre*, Henke's essay, '*The Taming of the Shrew*, Italian Intertexts, and Cultural Mobility' (pp. 23–36), is a source study that affirms the values of Shakespeare's Italian connections by identifying the transnational and transcultural roots of *The Taming of the Shrew* as a site of exploration, as opposed to nationalist anxiety. In particular, Henke traces the explicit allusions to *commedia dell'arte* to suggest that the implicit homage present in Shakespeare's play illustrates an easy cultural mobility between England and Italy. The dramaturgical mobility that Henke argues is demonstrative of a transnational aesthetic circulation is also reflected in the play itself, as it meditates on 'the questions of mobility, border-crossing and identity formation' (p. 32). Frustratingly, Henke only begins to deeply connect with *The Taming of the Shrew* at the very end of his essay, pointing out Gremio's dependence on foreign commodities that would immobilize Bianca and categorizing Gremio's acquisitiveness as 'rapine, rather than true cultural mobility' (p. 36); and he declines to offer an substantive alternative from the play.

Susanne Wofford, in the most pithy essay of the collection, 'Hymen and the Gods on Stage in Shakespeare's *As You Like It* and Italian Pastoral' (pp. 69–92), aligns Rosalind with the 'mago' (or in this case, 'maga') figure of the Italian pastoral tradition, and suggests that the play goes further in its use of its transnational counterpart by the representation of the god Hymen on stage. Using the notion of 'theatregram' that has been adopted as a key methodology in the book in which the essay appears, Wofford aligns Hymen with the 'dichotomous experience of eros' (p. 76), that characterizes late sixteenth-century Italian pastoral, sorting carefully through both art history and pastoral literature to explore the implications of Hymen's double gender, of the male god representing female physiognomy. This intertheatricality, Wofford argues, is further enhanced by the presence of the Italian madrigal in English culture. Wofford uses this extensive contextualization to suggest that, in *As You Like It*, Hymen becomes a symbolic figure of power and authority, albeit theatrical, and not religious, achieved through the potency of its metaphorical value. In the Italian pastoral, Hymen and Cupid become theatregrams that allow for generic closure of a text. Hymen, Wofford contends, must be embodied as a Roman god to become a performative authority for the marriages that Rosalind arranges, and to create a space to validate the results of her transgressions. Furthermore, Hymen arranges a conditional closure of the play, which allows for the marriages even as it leaves open-ended the gendered roles of husband and wife in Rosalind and Orlando's union. Wofford evokes the notion of theatrical faith, which elides religious commitment through its recognition of its own theatricality, rightly insisting on a valuation of the aesthetic over the spiritual.

Schalkwyk's essay, 'Shakespeare's Untranslatability' (pp. 229–44), is a robust defence of transposing Shakespeare's plays into new cultural artefacts through the act of translation, and uses Uys Krige's *Twaalfde Nag*, an Afrikaans translation of *Twelfth Night*, as his central example of the values of transcribing the play linguistically. Schalkwyk makes a brief and well-worn defence of the adaptive processes before embarking on his main topic: why

Twaalfde Nag might, in fact, be a better play than *Twelfth Night*. Schalkwyk uses his own experience of directing a bilingual (English and Afrikaans) production of the play. He argues that translation allowed for the Afrikaans dialect to be used to flesh out, and make relevant (and funny), the largely flat dialogue between Feste and Sir Andrew in II.iii which is, he rightly argues, 'within, not beyond, the ethics of translation' (p. 237), through a loyalty, not only to the spirit of the text, but to Shakespeare's own theatrical practice. While Schalkwyk acknowledges the limitations of translation in particular instances, he defends the poetical reconfiguration on the grounds that it places the audience in the same position as its early modern counterpart, receiving the words 'with surprise, delight, and wonder at their powerful newness' (p. 240).

Melissa Walter's essay, '"Are You a Comedian?": The Trunk in *Twelfth Night* and the Intertheatrical Construction of Character' (pp. 53–66), uses the trope of the trunk to argue for a relationship between the novella and dramatic form that is 'interactive and reciprocal' (p. 53). White suggests Barnabie Riche's tale 'Of Apollonius and Silla' as a possible source for *Twelfth Night*, before focusing on the extensively used trope of a trunk as conveyer of bodies (both dead and alive). Walter's argument, however, hangs on the presence of a trunk indicated in Trevor Nunn's 1995 film instead of Shakespeare's text, and she tackles this absence of the trunk in the play itself by explaining that its presence is indicated by Viola's ability to change clothing. If, Walter argues, Viola's clothes come out of a trunk at the beginning of the drama, and the trunk is staged, 'the image of the trunk as a limited material thing, which contains varied narrative and symbolic possibilities, like the human body itself, is also staged' (p. 64).

As with many books on adaptation, Alexa Huang and Elizabeth Rivlin's collection *Shakespeare and the Ethics of Appropriation* is less concerned with textual exegesis than methodology. Courtney Lehmann's challenging and occasionally difficult essay, 'Double Jeopardy: Shakespeare and Prison Theatre' (pp. 89–106), argues for an ethical interrogation of pedagogical performance projects in prisons, and uses her own experience of a production of *Measure for Measure*, performed at Kentucky's Luther Luckett penitentiary, to examine the complex issues of oppressive heteronormativity, silence, and retributive justice that such close interaction with Shakespeare's text might elicit. Lehmann's claim that Shakespeare 'can be appropriated as a powerful source of resistance to the warehousing of social identity in prison' (p. 101) is particularly illustrated in the exploration of the clowns, Pompey and Lucio, whose masks allow the actors, a cop-killer and paedophile respectively, the opportunity to 'perform alternative relationships to centralized power' (p. 101), offering these men a moral strength to see through the facades of authority, rendering Shakespeare 'a broker of transparency' (p. 101). Lehmann's suggestion that Shakespeare performance is potentially 'a spur to their self-transformation' (p. 102) is ideologically contentious, but nonetheless this essay is an important evaluation of the impact that Shakespeare study and performance can have outside academe.

Jessica Dell's New Historicist contribution, '"A witch, a quean, an old cozening quean!": Image Magic and Shakespeare's *The Merry Wives of Windsor*' (in Hopkins and Ostovich, eds., pp. 185–202), uses local history of witchcraft to suggest that the play exposes and exorcises 'largely misogynistic views of woman and magic through laughter' (p. 186). Dell structures her argument around Ford's ongoing conflation of witchcraft and sexual immorality, which, at the close of the play, allows the people of Windsor to abandon their false and destructive superstitions in favour of celebrating the true magic of female virtue' (p. 193). By localizing her discussion of witchcraft to Windsor, Dell is able to posit a successful female confrontation with ignorance and bigotry, connecting history to the communitas in the play. Mother Pratt, the absent witch, becomes crucial to this argument, embodying both Ford's anxieties about the homosocial bonds of women and his wife's experience of the same. It is Mother Pratt's absence from the play, Dell argues, that empties the threat of such a figure by allowing Falstaff to impersonate her, and renders Ford's attempted witch hunt comically impotent. Moreover, Dell trades on the traditional notion of the witch as socially impotent to suggest that the childless local curiosity, Mistress Ford, embraces the negative associations of the figure of the witch to 'gain access to the supposed magical arsenal attributed to her witch-counterpart ' (p. 196) and harness the power of superstition for her own benefit, enacting transformations and tricks on the watered-down Ford substitute, Falstaff. Once empowered, Dell argues, the two wives use their moral authority to create a queen, and use the hunting imagery throughout not only to legitimize Falstaff as prey, but to exceed their association with a queen, Elizabeth, by invoking a goddess, Diana, who punishes the men on behalf of the women of Windsor.

In Laurie Johnson, John Sutton, and Evelyn Tribble's collection *Embodied Cognition and Shakespeare's Theatre: The Early Modern Body-Mind*, James Knapp's essay, 'Mental Bodies in *Much Ado About Nothing*' (pp. 86–103), uses Claudio's rejection of Hero as a starting point to consider the 'relationship between Hero's outward appearance and her immaterial character' (p. 87). Knapp focuses on a pre-Cartesian moment of uncertainty as to the mind/body divide as a means of understanding the play's preoccupation with 'nothing', found in its thematic emphasis on the gap between the material and immaterial. Knapp uses Ambroise Paré's theory of the three mental faculties—imagination, reasoning, and memory—as key to navigating the space between the mind and body to suggest that the scenes of both recognition and misrecognition that characterize *Much Ado About Nothing* are constructed through a process of comparing memory and imagination. The human capacity for cognition, Knapp argues, relies on a dependable relationship between material and mental bodies, and confusion arises 'when the characters are invited to compare mental bodies derived from the imagination's ability to create false images in the mind without any immediate external stimulus' (p. 96). That is to say, the fictions offered to a character reconstruct the memory of a mental body by endowing it with the characteristics imagined. This draws Knapp to the altar scene, in which Claudio's imaginings allow him to misread Hero's blush as a mark of her shame, a notion further complicated by the fact that an audience would likely only recognize the blush through its narrated description. Ultimately, Knapp argues, *Much Ado About Nothing* fails to resolve the 'more troubling implications of the mysterious interplay between the material body, corporeal spirit (thought), and immaterial soul' (p. 100).

Peter Kishore Saval's book *Reading Shakespeare through Philosophy* is an attempt to imagine Shakespearian drama as philosophical praxis, and is in large part, extraordinary, although the structural imbalance between the chapters is occasionally frustrating. Too brief is his eloquent and convincing chapter, 'A Philosophy of History in *Love's Labour's Lost*', which attempts to view the play as a 'cerebral puzzle' (p. 50), as a means of countering the 'anemic character of the play itself' (p. 50). Saval suggests a preposterous reading that envisions the play as an 'ass-backwards' (p. 50) riddle of history, envisioning a historicized reading that takes the delayed marriage of Henry of Navarre to Queen Margot as the beginning of a chain of events that leads to the St Bartholomew's Day Massacre. To do so, he reimagines the play as a comic history, in that 'it fulfils historical time by putting it off, and presents a history of what was never written and what did not take place' (p. 51). Comedy, therefore, Saval argues, becomes redemptive up to its foregone conclusion, 'because it delivers redemption from the dead time of history' (p. 55). This anamorphosis of history manifests itself in a play that is continually confounding generic expectation, blending light and dark, humour and melancholy.

Potentially a book in itself, the chapter 'Primordial Debt, Communism, and *The Merchant of Venice*' makes up the bulk of this slim volume. The essay is an attempt to frame *The Merchant of Venice* as part of 'a vision of human life that stretches from the individual to the cosmos' (p. 59), challenging 'our liberal ideas about the connection between subjective autonomy and human freedom' (p. 59). The chapter drives slowly towards *The Merchant of Venice* because of the need to unpack disparate philosophies, which is one of the failings of this otherwise excellent book. Saval frames his discussion of the play with a lengthy exposition of anthropologist David Graeber's *Debt*, which argues that money arose as a result of debt, that fulfilled 'a general sense of social obligation that exists in every human society' (p. 60), identifying 'primordial debt' as the myth of obligation that is impressed upon humans operating within a society, government, or faith. After making the appropriate nod towards Mauss's study of the gift, Graeber proposes that the myth of primordial debt constitutes a 'form of baseline communism' (p. 61) that creates a system of social obligations without accounting for them, as a means of encouraging social bonds. Communism, here, means not a political practice but a basic human sociability that resists the notion of indebtedness—something that the criminalization of debt pollutes.

Saval uses his carefully unpacked theory as a means of suggesting that the development of coinage is something that 'uproots individuals from their complex relationships and therefore promotes the very individual isolation with which its ideology colludes' (pp. 71–2). He begins with the etymology of *basanos* and how its connection with the torture of slaves 'reveals how the confusion of human and commercial values intersects with the whole of the military-coinage-slavery complex of the ancient world' (p. 88). When he finally reaches *The Merchant of Venice*, Saval connects 'the material form of money to an entire argument about the very character of human relationships' (p. 92), as well as to the Eucharist, as a means of foreshadowing a Nietzschean tragedy in Portia's narrative. He suggests that the crux at the heart of *The Merchant of Venice* is the characters' inability to distinguish between that which should be kept and that which can be contracted. Unfortunately, Saval's enthusiasm for his methodology leaves little time for Shylock, intriguingly suggesting at the end of the lengthy essay that the court's decision 'is not a *rejection* of that logic of usury and debt, but an act in support of it', overriding 'his claim that there are certain human desires . . . that cannot be monetized' (p. 102).

In his chapter 'The Being of the Future in *Twelfth Night*', Saval revisits an idea he alludes to throughout the book, that 'we require new metaphysical ideas to make sense of this idea of time' (p. 125). He does so by looking to Aristotle's *De Interpretatione*, to suggest that the challenge of verbalizing the indeterminate character of the future is linked to 'the affections of the soul in time, whose limits are the limits of anxiety about what can be spoken and what's to come' (p. 128), and suggests that *Twelfth Night* 'starts to look as though it promises to reveal a solution' (p. 128) to the discursive tension between a character and fate. *Twelfth Night*, he contends, continuously presents a sense of betrayal that represents itself as excessive, hallucinatory to the point of madness, 'that must grasp itself in the relinquishment of its own proper territory' (p. 137). 'The porosity of this discourse' (p. 137) manifests itself in a multivalent voice that affirms and silences, finding equivocal character in multiple spaces, such as the Captain's silence or Olivia's letters. Consistent throughout his book is the insistence on the value of genre. Saval closes by noting that, similarly to his position on *Love's Labour's Lost*, in *Twelfth Night*, 'comedy presents the openness to a principle of unity neither as the one, nor the all, but singularity as an unaccountable difference' (p. 142).

The New Kitteridge Shakespeare *The Two Gentlemen of Verona*, edited by Matthew Kozusko, situates the text in a performance context, offering the student and casual reader discussion topics, a brief essay on reading Shakespeare as performance, and a filmography. As part of its dedication to the series' founder, George Kitteridge, the text follows Kitteridge's 1903 edition, with annotations by Kozusko. Most interestingly, the closing essay establishes parameters for reading the play visually, offering help with the recognition of performance choices, discouraging the reader from leaning on Shakespeare's intentions as a dramatist, and offering a pithy defence of reading against the authority of the playwright, which should empower the reader to move past performance and into critical thinking.

In Michele Marrapodi's collection *Shakespeare and the Italian Renaissance: Appropriation, Transformation, Opposition*, Sergio Costola and Michael Saenger's essay, 'Shylock's Venice and the Grammar of the Modern City' (pp. 147–62), attempts to link Shylock and John Florio, through idiomatic language, to suggest an Italian intertextuality that marks Shylock out as Other, both in London and Venice. Costola and Saenger historicize the London–Venice relationship to suggest that the Shakespearian audience would have expected a 'complex balance of Englishness and foreignness' (p. 148) in their representation. Costola and Saenger make a similar argument to Valdez Acosta, although they more speculatively assign Bassanio's success at the casket test to his Protestant ideology, which guides the choice; this also allows them to view Shylock as a double alien, which is revealed not only in his faith, but also in his language. The essay takes pains to note that what the play offers is 'not an implicit contrast between any religion and any other, but rather a linguistically marked contrast in the way in which such distinctions are made socially' (p. 161).

John Florio's connections to Shakespeare have been well documented, but Costola and Saenger draw attention to the way in which Florio 'wrestled with his relationship to an English society that was at turns expansively multilingual and spasmodically xenophobic' (p. 154), ultimately marketing his Italianate identity as something both awkward and flamboyant. In particular, Costola and Saenger home in on a problem with prepositions that marks Shylock as a Florio-esque outsider to Venice, allowing Portia the opportunity to distinguish between the merchant and the Jew once he begins to talk.

Hanna Scolnicov's essay, 'The Jew and the Justice of Venice' (pp. 275–90), argues that although 'ideological confrontation between the messages of the Old and of the New Testaments, between the defeated Synagoga and the triumphant Ecclesia' (p. 276) dominates the play, the relocation of this debate to a 'civil and Venetian framework' (p. 276) destabilizes the certainty of the outcome. Scolnicov builds her argument on an attempt to visually reconstruct the courtroom scene, using Shylock's probable stage props of knife and scales as a 'bitter parody' (p. 280) of the figure of Justice, and by extension of Venetian justice. Scolnicov uses this mockery to build a case for Shakespeare's familiarity with Venice's intense identification with the figure of Justice, manifest in art across the city. Scolnicov focuses on these tenuous authorial connections over a deeper interrogation of the claim that 'Shylock cuts a grotesque figure, a parody of Justice', in opposition to Portia, whose virginity enshrines her as the 'true representative of Justice' (p. 286), even as her cross-dressing marks her as part of the more 'farcical' (p. 287), tension-relieving tradition of *commedia dell' arte*.

Duncan Salkeld's essay, 'Much Ado About Italians in Renaissance London' (pp. 305–16), argues for a conflation of Italy and contemporary London as a source of anxiety, because of the way the tropes of genre are awkwardly juxtaposed against a seedier reality that looks to the city beyond the playhouse walls. As is consistent with Marrapodi's collection, Salkeld spends some time outlining the analogous Italian text—in this case, Ariosto's *Orlando Furioso*, whose fifth canto not only adheres to *Much Ado*'s Hero subplot, but, Salkeld contends, mirrored a practice of hiding away women in early modern London.

Salkeld seeks to draw a parallel between *Much Ado About Nothing* and a late 1570s prostitution ring, through the evidence that many of the men prosecuted for keeping prostitutes were Italian and a more generalized reputation of Italians in London for sexual deception and licentiousness. Likewise, Salkeld attempts to build a case for potential sources, or at least cultural overlap, on the 1601/2 case of the propositioning (or abduction—the distinction is deliberately left vague in the essay) of Mary Copeland, by the French 'Master Benedick'. Like many of the essays in this collection, the lack of distinct methodology allows for little more than raising an interesting coincidence that is rarely fully tethered to a reading of the text.

Marrapodi's book shares many topics and methodologies with Henke and Nicholson's *Transnational Mobilities*, including the concept of theatregrams. In ' "Wanton Pictures": The Baffling of Christopher Sly and the Visual-Verbal Intercourse of Early Modern Erotic Arts' (pp. 123–46), Keir Elam argues for the trans-cultural value of the erotic art promised to Christopher Sly at the beginning of the play, tracing the Italian connection from the Prologue's admonition to the audience not to expect a 'wanton Suppose', which, Elam argues, looks to Ariosto's *I Suppositi*'s own references to erotic art, as well as Aretino and Raimondi's infamous illustrated sonnets, which, Elam argues, enjoyed a presence on the early modern English stage. In particular, Jonson's extensive referencing of the illustrations of the Aretino validates not only the assumption that the texts were known by dramatists and audiences alike, but that at the heart of 'this early modern English tradition of citations are not the sonnets but the "pictures", as they are almost invariably called, often attributed directly, as we have seen, to Aretino' (p. 133).

Elam moves back towards *The Taming of the Shrew* through Aretino's own play, *Il Marescalco*, which through the homosocial trope of a man marrying a boy in disguise, offers its audience a 'double Aretinian pedigree' through allusions to the sonnets and dramatic similarities to his plays. Unfortunately, Elam does not fully unpack the implications for *Taming of the Shrew*'s gender politics when he points out the passive ventriloquism of the women in Aretino's sonnets, which he acknowledges as misogynistic, instead maintaining a textual focus on the ekphrasis of trans-cultural references throughout the induction.

In David McInnis and Matthew Steggle's collection *Lost Plays in Shakespeare's England*, Christi Spain-Savage's chapter, 'Reimagining Gillian: *The Merry Wives of Windsor* and the Lost "Friar Fox and Gillian of Brentford" ' (pp. 229–52), argues that the archetype of the Witch of Brentford, based on history, and most notably presented in the lost Admiral's men's play *Friar Fox and Gillian of Brentford*, validates the recent critical trend that sees *The Merry Wives of Windsor* as revised between the 1602 quarto and 1623 First Folio. Spain-Savage notes that the revisions between the quarto and Folio versions of the play refine Falstaff's comedy in the scene from a broad physical endeavour to a more topical resonance of Mother Prat, which looked towards the recent representation of Gillian of Brentford by the Admiral's men. Spain-Savage traces the literary evolution of Gillian from a tavern hostess and bawd into a cunning woman, suggesting that the shift, from a bawd to the witch that Falstaff alludes to, occurs in the lost play *Friar Fox and Gillian of Brentford*; Spain-Savage offers the conjecture that Gillian's association with a comically mystical religious figure might have marked her out with the potential for necromancy that informed Shakespeare's appropriation, which shifts from 'Gillian of Brentford' in 1602, to 'the witch of Brentford' in 1623. Moreover, Spain-Savage suggests that the desexualization of the woman of Brentford speaks more to the public identification of Gillian as a cunning woman than as a bawd, further supporting Spain-Savage's case for the influential presence of *Friar Fox and Gillian of Brentford* in *The Merry Wives of Windsor*.

Lindsay Ann Reid's brief treatment of *The Taming of the Shrew* as part of her larger study of Ovid's place in the culture of the Tudor book, *Ovidian Bibliofictions and the Tudor Book: Metamorphosing Classical Heroines in Late Medieval and Renaissance England*, treats the play as an exemplum that saw women in literature 'collected, glossed, and represented in a series of new and ever-changing textual permutations' (p. 40). Reid argues that *The Taming of the Shrew* is deeply 'invested in exploring the persuasive power of the Tudor rhetor and in dramatizing the labile nature of exempla in the *querelle des femmes*' (p. 58), particularly through Bianca's schooling. The ironic invocation of Ovid in Bianca's courtship pedagogy creates an intertextual identity for women, employing both literary and rhetorical strategies as a means of shaping or contextualizing character. In particular, Reid argues, the concept of the good and bad sister is constructed so as to allow the most skilled orator 'to render shrewish women and worthy women virtually interchangeable' (p. 60). Petruchio's rhetorical ability is consecrated in the final act, where he is able to dominate other men in the game of exemplary wives, staging the 'persuasive ability of the rhetor to argue in utramque partem' (p. 63).

Kurt Schreyer's book *Shakespeare's Medieval Craft: Remnants of the Mysteries on the London Stage* is an insightful analysis of the heritage of medieval mystery plays on Shakespeare's stage. In the chapter 'Balaam to Bottom: A Sixteenth-Century Translation', -Schreyer proposes to elide the Ovidian allusions, and instead read Bottom's ass's head in the context of 'the drama, liturgy festival, and polemic of the sixteenth century' (p. 74). He foregrounds the materiality of the craftsmen, and builds an argument for a parallel between the popular Chester Cycle play *Moses and the Law: Balaack and Balaam*, in which the unwitting Balaam falls into an argument with his ass, which has stopped on the road to prostrate itself in the presence of an angel. Schreyer trades on the well-established artisanal nature of medieval drama to suggest the quality of the ass's costume that might indicate the play's popularity, which extended into the seventeenth century and, more significantly, to suggest that Shakespeare was 'keenly aware of the centrality of craft to mystery playing, and the Pyramus and Thisbe scenes in *Dream* comically exploit it' (p. 78).

Schreyer uses the Chester Cycle to launch a brief history of the ass-headed man, moving through Scot's *Discoverie of Witchcraft* in 1584, into Protestant anti-papal tracts, including John Barthlet's *The Pedegrewe of Heretiques* [1566] and Pierre Boaistuau's 1569 *Certaine Secrete Wonders of Nature*, suggesting a metamorphosis (pun intended) of the image between generations of viewers of the Chester Cycle. This multifaceted figure of the popish ass, Schreyer contends, could simultaneously represent Rome's spiritual greed, beastly appetites, and vicarious sexuality, and a theatrical nostalgia to the people who witnessed the image in the late sixteenth century. Schreyer then uses the textual references of the materiality of the head, combined with properties accounts, to speculate that an impoverished craft guild might have sold the head to London players. More engagingly, he builds on this speculation to propose a transformation of the object of the ass's head from feminized devotional parody to a more secular sexualized object. This conflation, he contends, looks backward rather than forwards, and 'brings the religious history of the ass into closer proximity by retaining previous cultural affinities' (p. 95), before satirizing the archaic dramatic forms that the presence of the ass's head would invoke, through Pyramus and Thisbe.

Mary Villeponteaux's book *The Queen's Mercy: Gender and Judgment in Representations of Elizabeth I* is a historicist exercise to identify Elizabeth as an influence on a variety of early modern texts. In her chapter, '"A Goodly Musicke In Her Regiment": Elusive Justice in *The Merchant of Venice*', Villeponteaux argues that Portia represents an Elizabeth figure who is historicized as Protestant by the burden she bears, not only to show mercy, but to impose a rigorous punishment on the religious others who would threaten her realm. Villeponteaux cleaves a little too much to the Portia/Elizabeth analogy, eschewing a more layered argument of representation in favour of historical analogies, arguing that Portia 'most fully embodies the conflicting fantasies of Elizabeth as a judge who can act both as a tender, merciful queen and rigorous scourge of religious enemies' (p. 112). That said, there is value in the shift away from a Marian figure of Elizabeth in the analysis of Portia's implementation of punishment. Portia's calculated distance from the final judgement of Shylock, Villeponteaux claims, elides the charge of severity in much the same way that Elizabeth disavowed responsibility for Mary Stuart's execution, and the end of the chapter's inclusion of *Endymion* begins a more effective dialogue about the ways in which Elizabeth's (and thereby Portia's) rule continues to be subject to the pressures of a largely male court.

'"Pardon Is Still the Nurse of Second Woe": *Measure for Measure* and the Transition from Elizabeth to James', registers the play as a product of a liminal time in between two rulers, asserting that the text is subsequently an anticipation of 'a more absolutist ideology' (p. 134) that would be inherently less merciful than its predecessor's. Villeponteaux aligns Elizabeth with the Duke Vincentio, whose leniency has seen the kingdom fall into disarray, yet resists the execution of strict justice for fear of tarnishing his image. In *Measure for Measure*, Villeponteaux contends, 'mercy is repeatedly aligned with sexuality, the fruits of pardon with the fruits of intercourse' (p. 141). In the wake of such contamination, Isabel's plea for clemency is undermined by the sordid reality of what such mercy could unleash—a concern realized when the appeal to Angelo's empathy awakens his desire for Isabel. Villeponteaux brings this argument back to James I by arguing that the quality of mercy is dictated by the privacy of the decision-making process, where the unruly passions of the individual may run free. By contrast, she argues, the final scene, in which mercy is meted out in the public sphere, removes the danger of unbounded, subjective mercy—something that she argues James I stage-managed throughout his monarchy.

Unsurprisingly, Susan Wiseman's exploration of metamorphosis as a literary device, *Writing Metamorphosis in the English Renaissance 1550–1700*, begins with a discussion of *A Midsummer Night's Dream*, offering the play up as 'a test case in the transformations undergone by classical metamorphosis' (p. 15). Metamorphosis, for Wiseman, is thematized, both through the intertextual character that defines the play's construction, and through theatrical discourse, for example in the doubling of mechanicals with fairies. Her thesis leads into a brief précis of the various source materials that

Shakespeare stitches together in the play, and the various transformations within the narrative. Wiseman suggests that the transformation accrues valuable layers onto the original baseline, and leaves a residue that propels forward, which, she argues, pits 'the constant and true against the changed and wandering' (p. 25), both textually and thematically. The chapter juggles the discussion of source material and the shape of the content, to suggest 'a dense saturation of metaphoric material which is in varying degrees likely to be present to auditors' (p. 27). Wiseman's book covers an enormous breadth of material, and passes through our subject texts briefly. The book's later discussion of transformed nature in *The Tempest* proposes the play as a cabinet of curiosities that appeals to the curiosity of seventeenth-century audience members. More pithy than the *Midsummer Night's Dream* exegesis, Wiseman's discussion of *The Tempest* proposes that metamorphosis is addressed under the topic of generation, posing 'the conundrum of the monster alongside the magical resolution of the problem of inheritance in the main plot' (p. 116), through Caliban's desire to people the isle with his own progeny. The 'generation and uses of monsters' (p. 116) is filtered through an analysis of Trinculo, who envisions an adoption, and use, for the monstrous progeny of the island. The constant shifting of genre in the play reinforces the navigation of the borders between human, natural, supernatural, and monstrous, and these movements are classified as metamorphic 'in either Aristotelian or Baconian formations' (p. 124).

Amid a sea of productions, Magdalena Adamczyk's 'Interactional Aspects of Language Based Humour in Shakespeare's Comedies: The Dynamics of Punning by Ladies in Waiting' (*Atlantis* 36:i[2014] 11–30) is the lone article on *The Two Gentlemen of Verona* in 2014. Building a comparative study that also includes *Twelfth Night* and *Much Ado About Nothing*, Adamczyk suggests that among ladies in waiting punning becomes an attempt to assert dominance over interlocutors. Adamczyk's article is data-driven, creating a word-to-pun ratio to establish a gender division that sees servant women out-punning their male counterparts. She notes a 'socially asymmetric all-female participant frame-work' for puns that empower the serving women, most commonly over their mistresses' pretentious expectations, observing that, for example, Lucetta's punning delays the handover of Julia's letter. Punning, therefore, allows women to interact and redress aspects of social imbalance.

Ryan Farrar, in his essay, '*As You Like It*: The Thin Line Between Legitimate Utopia and Compensatory Vacation' (*UtopST* 25:ii[2014] 359–83), contends that *As You Like It* recognizes the inconsistency of personal utopias, and as a result creates, in the Forest of Arden, 'a space in which social fantasy uncharacteristic of Elizabethan society can blossom' (p. 366). The conflict between the courtly visions and enactment of utopian values and Jaques' more complicated and realistic response is enacted to complicate the Duke's creation of a pastoral Arcadia. Farrar uses canonical scholars, including Harold Bloom, to make broad assertions about the Romantic nature of the Forest of Arden, suggesting that the subjective moods create a conflicting pack of attitudes that 'may disrupt and taint the forest's natural order' (p. 370). Most interestingly, Farrar suggests that the duality present in the play, in particular Orlando's dystopian experience, permits an ambivalent appeal to two entirely different audiences (p. 372), creating a play the ending to which is both 'tidy and subversive' (p. 380).

Leah Marcus's far-reaching discussion of implicit colonialism as a characteristic of *As You Like It*'s reception history, 'Anti-Conquest and *As You Like It*' (*ShakS* 42[2014] 170–95), doesn't entirely fulfil its promise to examine 'the paratextual means by which editors have intensified a fascinating process of provincialization in editing the play' (p. 171), instead, offering a deep, if occasionally digressive, reading of gendered animal imagery in the play, suggesting that the animal–human interactions within the play are analogous to colonialism. Marcus's labyrinthine argument begins with the suggestion that Shakespeare's excision of the French elements of *Rosalynde* creates a more thoroughly English narrative, which establishes a bias in the play's central characters against the foreign. This isolates Jaques through his continual association with 'strange rituals that have come over the years to carry strong colonial resonances' (p. 173), and requires his removal from the play, in order to remove 'the threat of nebulous difference that might otherwise taint Rosalind, Orlando, and the rest of the "inland bred"' (p. 174). From there, Marcus goes on to suggest Jaques' sympathetic, yet nonetheless colonial, association with the deer of the forest, which she convincingly argues by tracing the Latin roots of Jaques' exclamation 'ducdame!' (II.v.54), translating it as 'Lead, O deer!' (p. 186). The threat of human and animal melding that occurs when Orlando imagines himself a doe to Adam's fawn, and the general gender instability, contribute to a threat of contamination to the sacred provincialism in the Forest of Arden that is contained by Jaques' isolation at the end of the play.

All of this is well and good, but Marcus rests her editorial argument on the claim that Rosalind is sufficiently preferred to warrant insulation from the contaminative threat of the outsider. Marcus rests this on the argument that 'editors have chivalrously protected Rosalind against references that point to her underlying male identity', such as instances of 'hee' in the Folio text and the assumption that the Folio's final '*Exit*' of the play is an '*Exeunt*', taking all of the characters offstage for Rosalind's epilogue, thus denying them the opportunity to engage with the gender confusion that Rosalind's declaration of female identity would elicit, and preventing entirely any challenge to the well-ordered ending (pp. 189–90). Unfortunately, Marcus does not convincingly connect this to the editorial agency she claims drives the essay, leaving unsubstantiated the claim that the 1986 Oxford Shakespeare 'encountered considerable resistance' (p. 172) to its suggestion that the forest at the heart of the text was the French Ardennes; and, moreover, Marcus follows this with nineteenth- and early twentieth-century stage history to reinforce the argument. This is a pity, because otherwise the essay overall is well crafted and its complex trajectory carefully worked out.

Matthieu A. Chapman's essay, 'The Appearance of Blacks on the Early Modern Stage: *Love's Labour's Lost*'s African Connections to Court' (*EarT* 17:ii[2014] 77–94), is an attempt to redress the 'continual erasure of actual blacks from English theatrical history in favour of white men in blackface' (p. 80). Chapman's important essay also attempts to undo the perceived academic binary that suggests a prevailing fascination with black bodies that permits only revulsion and fascination, challenging the assumptions of critics such as Dympna Callaghan and Ayanna Thompson. Chapman does so by arguing for the presence of 'actual blacks on commercial and court stages', going as far as to suggest the possibility 'that Shakespeare wrote the blackamoor musicians into *Love's Labour's Lost* to make use of actual blackamoor musicians available at court' (p. 80) as a demonstration of cultural and economic power. Chapman uses the scant evidence available to suggest that the exploitation of the performative skills of black Africans was commodified by the nobility at court to 'enhance their own social status' (p. 81). From there, it is a reasonable assumption that the commercial stages followed suit, and Chapman suggests that there was an exploitation at play through 'staging the exoticism of othered races for commercial purposes' (p. 81), using a selection of texts, including Marlowe's *Tamburlaine*, Lodge's *Wounds of Civil War*, George Peele's *Battle of Alcazar*, and Beaumont and Fletcher's *Island Princess*, as well as Shakespeare's own *The Merchant of Venice* and *Titus Andronicus*, as evidence. Moreover, Chapman synthesizes the textual examples with the practical argument that it was simply more affordable and easier to hire a black actor rather than pay for cosmetics that would eliminate the ability for an actor to play both a black and a white character in the same production.

Chapman concludes his argument by speculating that Shakespeare wrote the blackamoor musicians into his play 'to garner favour by allowing the Elizabethan court an opportunity to place actual black Africans on the stage as a display of status and power' (p. 88). Although Chapman freely acknowledges the likelihood that his is an argument 'of possibility rather than probability' (p. 89), the 1605 performance of *Love's Labour's Lost* at Whitehall, which occurred the day before Jonson presented *The Masque of Blackness*, speaks to a fetishization that encourages the assumption that the court interest in black Africans created social sanctions that allowed a space for black performers.

As its title suggests, Tara and Philip Collington's article, ' "The Time When ... The Place Where": Chronotopes and Chronologies in *Love's Labour's Lost*' (*SP* 11:iv[2014] 786–820), examines the way in which Bakhtin's chronotope can be used to illustrate three concurrent temporo-spatial frames in the play that 'affect[] thematic coherence' (p. 789) throughout the text. The article argues for three frameworks. The chronotope of the retreat is signified by the three-year withdrawal from sexual contact, in which 'physical space is rigidly demarcated (inside vs. outside), and distances are precisely measured into zones' (p. 796). The invasion of the men's isolated space brings the chronotope of the embassy into play, the public nature of which collapses a clear distinction between time and space, and, more importantly, brings the chronotope into direct collision with that of the retreat, which is invoked in the play by the vaguely militaristic presence of the French tents and humorous siege mentality. These two chronotopes interact in such a way that blurs the consistency of the timeline in the play, which is the chronotope of the comic idyll, which 'preserves space as an idealized natural setting for courtship but accelerates temporality to a fever pitch' (p. 809) to satisfy the Aristotelian unity of time, and complement the notion of love's frenzy. This final chronotope is deeply invested in the pastoral, existing in a space that accelerates temporal change, both by the association with the changing seasons and the insistence that, to the lovers, '*every second counts*' (p. 811)—an idea that is later complicated by the intrusion of real life as the play concludes. Collington and Collington's article suggests that the play's ostensibly unsatisfactory ending can occur because of the braiding together of these three distinct chronotopes, which continue to operate on their individual spatio-temporal prerogatives, ultimately resulting in 'an audacious medley' (p. 820) of experimental forms.

Maurice Hunt's brief essay, 'Thomas Nashe, *The Vnfortvn ate Traveller*, and *Love's Labour's Lost*' (*SEL* 54:ii[2014] 297–314), is an argument for Nashe's *The Vnfortvnate Traveller* as influential on the diction, imagery, and satirical nature of Shakespeare's *Love's Labour's Lost*. In particular, Hunt notes that the 'repetition of parallel clauses and phrases within an elaborate sentence; the similar structure of colorful, often hyperbolic rhetoric; the huddling of utterance in a nonstop statement; the preference for cumulative sentences bursting with imaginative metaphors' (p. 297) links Moth's Act III speech to Nashe's prose style. Linguistic similarities abound, including the likening of the King of Navarre's love sonnet to Surrey's poems in Nashe, as well as dramaturgical common ground, including *Love's Labour's Lost*'s staging of the Nine Worthies, a vision that is presented to Charles V in Nashe's prose picaresque. Hunt acknowledges that his case is not new, seeking to add to Douglas Bruster's recent critical analysis of Nashe's influence. Hunt suggests that, in this case, the value of association lies in the character of Moth, who, by association, Hunt suggests, makes Nashe's Juvenalian excess 'more attractive' (p. 310), repaying a compliment to Nashe in response to the defence of plays that exists in *Pierce Penilesse*.

In 'Antonio's (Happy) Ending: Queer Closure in All-Male *Twelfth Night*' (*CompD* 48:iii[2014] 221–40) Chad Allen Thomas argues that the recent history of post-millennial all-male productions of *As You Like It* creates 'a cross-gendered Shakespearean aesthetic that is sexy, provocative, queer, and often emphasizes homoerotic attraction' (p. 223). Thomas argues for a 'more explicit, textual homoeroticism' (p. 224) that modern productions, in conversation with one another, can yield, moving away from an examination of how such eroticism was manifest in early modern staging. As Thomas acknowledges, such productions spring from an ideological choice to queer Shakespeare, eschewing the recent trend for 'original practice' productions. Thomas uses cross-gender casting to challenge the argument of Northrop Frye's 1957 model of comedy, which suggests that end-of-play coupling satisfies audience expectations. The suggestion that 'cross-gender casting can reveal a stage production's attitude towards sexual and gender identity in ways that we can otherwise only intuit' (p. 229), because of corporeal embodiment, does not seem to permeate deeper than the assumption that performance denotes gender, and as a result, offers more of a survey of increased acceptance by recent audiences than a more carefully theorized assessment of the value of eroticized male bodies on the modern stage. Thomas's affirmative case for the ways in which 'Queer Shakespeare offers lesbian and gay audience members the opportunity to feel as if they belong' (p. 237) would also have benefited from being contextualized by a broader queer history of Shakespeare on stage.

Ellen M. Caldwell's essay, 'Opportunistic Portia as Fortuna in *The Merchant of Venice*' (*SEL* 54:ii[2014] 349–73), presents Portia as the emblem of the Renaissance figure of the fickle Fortuna, who creates 'rewards and punishments as determined by her desire' (p. 349). As a result, Caldwell states, the play becomes a study not of justice and mercy, but 'of how opportunistic entrepreneurs operate in marriage and the market place' (p. 350). After a cursory nod towards Shakespeare's correct and incorrect use of emblems scattered across his plays, Caldwell jumps into a close reading of the emblematic imagery in the first scene of Act IV, to make a case for reading the scene iconographically. Moving from Shylock's scale-wielding parody of justice to Justice's own representation as a legal scholar in the 1758–60 *Iconologia*, Caldwell goes on to more carefully parse the play to suggest that 'Portia dons the blindfold of male disguise that allows her to use the law's impartiality to exercise her obvious partiality in this legal dispute' (p. 352). To define Portia as Fortuna not only undermines any semblance of justice in the play, but also speaks to an early modern conflation of Fortuna and Occasio that allows for Caldwell's description of Portia as an entrepreneur, pragmatically taking advantage of 'unlooked for and undeserved' (p. 364) changes in circumstances that she can manipulate to her advantage.

David Goldstein's essay, 'Jews, Scots, and Pigs in *The Merchant of Venice*' (*SEL* 54:ii[2014] 315–48), is a historicist reading that situates the obsession with similitude in *The Merchant of Venice* as part of a greater topical anxiety between England and Scotland that emerged during the 1590s. In particular, Goldstein's lengthy meditation on *kashrut*, a practice, he notes, that is omitted from *The Jew of Malta* and *The Three Ladies of London*, argues that the practice was positively viewed as analogous to the Christian sacrifice of generosity in early modern culture. Goldstein makes this argument to reinforce the extant critical connection between Jews and Puritans in early modern culture, before noting that there was another prominent group which was associated with 'religious radicalism, usury, miserliness, greed, cruelty, hypocrisy, falsehood, jealousy, Old Testament literalness, outright Judaizing, persecution by the Spanish inquisition, and all round otherness' (p. 320)—the Scots. The post-Scottish Reformation transferral of Puritan stereotypes onto the Scots, Goldstein argues, centralizes gluttony, and by introducing Shylock with his rejection of pork, Shakespeare plays on the popular contemporary myth of the Scottish aversion to pork, further tracking swine-Scottish punning to James I's family name, which is derived from 'sty ward' or pig-keeper (p. 324), to convincingly suggest that the expectations of a stage Scot are 'paradoxically embodied in the person of a Venetian Jew' (p. 326).

To argue for the Scottish contextual reading rejects traditional notions of *The Merchant of Venice* as engaging with the Lopez controversy, or the larger issue of Puritan radicalism, and by doing so, suggests a complex engagement with the notion of the union of two crowns, which is manifest in the Bassanio–Portia and Jessica–Lorenzo pairings, in which 'the principle of parity struggles, mostly unsuccessfully, within a hierarchy of dominance' (p. 329). To do so requires analogizing Bassanio as the Scot and Portia as an avatar of Elizabeth, which is manifest in Portia's attempt to sever Bassanio from his divided duty between her and the implicitly French Antonio. Likewise, the anxiety surrounding Jessica's conversion and assimilation suggests an uneasy alliance between the two nations.

Harriet Phillips's essay, 'Late Falstaff, the Merry World, and *The Merry Wives of Windsor*' (*Shakespeare* 10:ii[2014] 111–37), attempts to redress the critical disappointment in Falstaff's representation in the play by suggesting that nostalgia for his past comedic glory drives the nature of comedy in the play. *Merry Wives of Windsor* 'explores the pressures of accommodating the past in early modern England' (p. 113) through the carnivalesque Sir John, exposing the impossibility of nostalgia's continued existence in the present. Philips unpacks the outdated nature of the merry world topos to Elizabethan culture, suggesting that traditional merriment becomes increasingly suspect during the Puritan Reformation. The emphasis on Falstaff's age, his downward spiral, from the Henriad into *Merry Wives of Windsor*, and the contemporary nature of Shakespeare's Windsor all contribute to the portrayal of a man out of date. Philips chooses not to discuss Anne Page and the generational disparity in the play, instead arguing for an evolution of the wives' humour that ultimately leaves Falstaff 'an old comic adrift in a new form' (p. 126).

Jason Gleckman's convincing essay ' "I know a bank. . .": *A Midsummer Night's Dream*, Fairies, and the Erotic History of England' (*Shakespeare* 10:i[2014] 23–45), uses literary history, specifically Spenser's *The Faerie Queene*, as a means of interrogating the evolving value of marital eroticism in Protestant England through 'those erotic beings native to the English countryside: the fairies' (p. 23). Gleckman argues for seeing the transition between Egeus' ancient privilege to dispose of Hermia as he wishes and Theseus' slightly more modern amelioration as analogous to the early modern transferral of nuns' authority—derived from the Virgin Mary—to the virginal queen, Elizabeth I. It is 'in such ways, [that] the opening of *A Midsummer Night's Dream* offers a concise imaginary history of the erotic' (p. 25). Linking Lysander's English gifts of 'knacks, trifles, nosegays, sweetmeats' (I.i.34) with the environment that houses the fairies, Gleckman creates a space for the uninhibited erotic, and argues that by looking to Spenser we might see how the intensity of these erotic, sexual desires might be channelled towards the Protestant faith.

Unsurprisingly, Gleckman moves to Book III, and Britomart, to make his case, arguing that she becomes Shakespeare's 'template for womanhood, the embodiment of an erotic *virtù* that produces, among other things, a female insistence on marrying the man of her choice' (p. 30). Gleckman uses ecocriticism to elucidate the eroticized female autonomy that links Spenser's women and Shakespeare's, using Spenser's own acknowledgement of the sensual forest and garden to create a reflection in *A Midsummer Night's Dream*, one that absorbs Spenser's own belief in concupiscence, which allows God to work through the flesh as deeply as through the spirit, turning 'the heart of stone into one of flesh' (p. 35). If Bottom, as Gleckman argues, is 'capable of receiving the intense gift' (p. 36) of fairy-generated sexual power, there is hope for us all.

Peter Herman's essay, 'Equity and the Problem of Theseus in *A Midsummer Night's Dream*; or, The Ancient Constitution in Ancient Athens' (*JEMCS*

14:i[2014] 4–31), argues a simple yet significant premise: that Theseus, by using his equity to overrule Egeus' demands for Hermia's death, pushes up against tyranny, achieving 'the right result, but for the wrong reasons' (p. 4). This presents a potentially darker vision of Theseus that is more in accord with the 'threatening atmosphere that hangs over' (p. 23) Pyramus and Thisbe and the resolutions of the play as a whole. Athens, Herman argues, was a 'nation of laws, not people' (p. 7), created by Theseus, and aspirationally recognized by an early modern England and monarch who 'embraced their subservience to the law' (p. 8). Herman delves deeply into sixteenth-century judicial debates that circulated around the extent of monarchical equity, not surprisingly finding his wealth of material produced in the 1520s, in response to Thomas Wolsey's declaration that the king 'ought of his royal dignity and prerogative to mitigate the rigor of the law where conscience hath the most force' (quoted in Herman, p. 12). Theseus' own impatience for his wedding, Herman suggests, is an acquiescence in the rule of law, and his first-act amelioration of Egeus' demands is as far as he might reasonably go without circumventing the law, even in the face of what an early modern audience would have recognized as a 'monstrous' (p. 17) patriarchal privilege. This matters, Herman contends, because as well as undermining the Ancient Constitution, it also violates the English coronation oath, and looks forward to Theseus' own overthrow and expulsion from Athens.

Gitanjali Shahani's essay, 'The Spicèd Indian Air in Early Modern England' (*ShakS* 42[2014] 122–37), is a splendid New Historicist treatment of *A Midsummer Night's Dream* that argues that there is a manifestation of the ambivalence about 'cultural corporeal boundaries' (p. 123) that the spice trade provoked in Titania's preoccupation with her Indian boy. Shahani examines both anti-spice pamphlets and recipe books to suggest a concern with the contamination of the natural body that specifically implicated women, by the domestic source of such contamination. That the dangers of 'heterogeneous mixing' (p. 127) of spices in the kitchen were offset by female medical and culinary expertise emerges in *A Midsummer Night's Dream*, where 'we see early articulations of a justificatory logic that would inform later narratives of colonial plunder' (p. 129), drawn together by Robin Goodfellow's participation in an 'indigenous domestic economy' (p. 130).

Shahani argues that the pre-colonial vision of a 'part mythical, part mercantile' (p. 131) India, which Titania's obsession with the changeling boy indicates, is a manifestation of the 'growing female fascination with Indian novelties' (p. 131) that was causing consternation in the domestic English household. As a result of this credible, well-argued historical assessment, Shahani's reading of Oberon's attempt to curtail the 'female obsession with foreign merchandise' (p. 133) is persuasive. This is further compounded by the article's efficient examination of Bottom as a mulatto, which calls attention to Titania's troublesome obsession with the 'implicit monstrosity of the Indian boy' (p. 134).

Paul Innes's article, 'Sensory Confusion and the Generation Gap in *Much Ado About Nothing*' (*CS* 26:ii[2014] 1–20), offers a careful and well-argued close reading of how the play 'plays with spectatorship, hearing and audience perspectives' (p. 4). In particular, Innes argues, acknowledging our current placement in a very visual culture will allow us to look back more carefully at the Renaissance stage, which thrived on verbal representation, the uncertainty of which is key to *Much Ado About Nothing*. To abandon a search for character psychology, Innes argues, not only affords a closer understanding of Renaissance dramaturgy, but will reveal a difference between generations that underpins the play. The dramatic narrative schema that divides character groups by generational differences is founded on the Renaissance notion of utility—that is to say that age, like gender, 'is another "nothing" that is rope for dramatic exploration' (p. 13). In *Much Ado About Nothing*, Innes contends, age and experience are able to circumvent the ongoing miscommunications that characterize the play, and that, ultimately, 'Leonato functions as the leader of a group of characters that will re-assert patriarchal control over the women and the younger men of the play' (p. 15). Leonato's reconstitution of patriarchy at the end of the play, embodied when he stops Beatrice's mouth by giving her to Benedick, renders *Much Ado About Nothing* more akin to the late plays, such as *The Tempest* or, more obviously, *The Winter's Tale*, which engage with generational anxieties.

Jonathan Burton's essay, 'Christopher Sly's Arabian Night: Shakespeare's *The Taming of the Shrew* as World Literature' (*JEMCS* 14:iii[2014] 3–30), on *The Taming of the Shrew* seeks to consider the influence of non-Western narrative traditions on Shakespeare's imagination, arguing that *The Taming of the Shrew*'s lord-for-a-day Christopher Sly narrative finds commonality in *The Arabian Nights*, which also draws on the dream-conceit. Burton's analysis is tilted towards the pedagogical goal of 'crossing cultural and disciplinary borders in a moment when East and West continue to be seen in terms of their allegedly irreconcilable traditions and values' (p. 7).

Kerry Gilbert-Cooke's effective essay, 'Addressing the Addressee: Shakespeare and Early Modern Epistolary Theory' (*JEMS* 3[2014] 243–63), makes the argument that epistolary theory manifests itself in Shakespeare through the concern of appropriate superscription. Gilbert-Cook specifically examines comedies in this context, because of the 'vertical communication' (p. 245) that is exclusive to the comedies, as characters reach out to their social superiors. The article uses the historiography of epistolary writing to argue for an under-theorization of the formal elements of the letter, in particular, the role of the addressee. In Shakespeare, Gilbert-Cooke contends, attention is drawn to the formal elements of the letter to reinforce the contents of the text, conveying especially eroticism, allowing for reading to reciprocate 'the desire that writing conveyed' (p. 255). For example, Malvolio's act of reading Maria's letter crystallizes his fantasy of social advancement, that, following the perusal of the letter, manifests itself in lust for Olivia. The social deference indicated by the formal elements of Maria's letter makes explicit the social opportunity at the heart of the letter, which is what Malvolio seizes upon. At the other end of the spectrum, the lack of care and attention to the details of Falstaff's letters to Mistresses Page and Ford, identical in all but name, communicate the disrespect that spurs their revenge—more so than the impetus behind their composition.

Nick Hutchison and Donald Jellerson's analysis, in '"I do care for something": *Twelfth Night*'s Feste and the Performance of Character' (*ShakB*

32:ii[2014] 185–206), of Feste's character attempts to work 'at the intersection of performance practice and literary analysis' (p. 186), foregrounding the interdisciplinary methodology as a means of debating character. Proposing a 'strategic essentialism' (p. 188) that is born out of historical stage practice, literary analysis, and actor preparation, Hutchison and Jellerson use the type of character exploration that is typical of the modern rehearsal room as a means of discovering the mysterious 'something' that Feste claims to care for in III.i of *Twelfth Night*, referring several times to the rehearsal processes of unnamed actors. The collaborative work between the performance practitioner and literary scholar yields an admirable close reading, although I suspect the main value of such an article is pedagogical, as it indeed does rely on a textual essentialism that can only work in a more traditional production context; that is, assuming that no directorial concept reconfigures the balance of characters, their relationship to one another, and the setting. Even if the stability of such a practice feels somewhat overstated, this well-researched and diligent essay makes a salient case for academic investment in the 'emotional life' (p. 191) of characters.

In a careful close reading, 'What they Will: Comic Grammar in *Twelfth Night*' (*Shakespeare* 10:ii[2014] 158–70), Rikita Tyson argues that the use of modal auxiliary verbs, particularly 'will', suggests that the play ultimately rests 'hope' on the active use of 'will'. Tyson resists the urge to unpack all instances of 'I will' in *Twelfth Night*, carefully choosing instances that illustrate the verb's association with wish and desire. This modal utterance, which she links with 'can', 'may', 'must', and 'might', 'bring a being into being, demonstrating the thinking, evaluating, and judging that characters are always doing by means of these declarations' (p. 160), locating activity in *Twelfth Night* in small verbal choices made by various characters. Viola's language, for example, posits her will that her brother will survive the shipwreck, creating hope 'through an act of will and wordplay' (p. 163). Hope, in turn, creates the will to seek out the opportunity that leads Viola to Orsino. Tyson carefully traces out the interplay of assertion of, and submission to, the wills of the self and others, to outline how these utterances create a space for action. Ultimately, she argues that Viola's 'actions show us the paradox of will suggested by the fluidity of modal meanings: obligation and volition, inference and demand, can be revealed by, compressed into, and even enacted by these pinpricks of words in the smallest of sentences' (p. 167); this sort of paradox shapes the comic energies of the play, and gives direction to the desires of the characters.

Books Reviewed

Altschuler, Bruce E., and Michael A. Genovese, eds. *Shakespeare and Politics*. Routledge. [2014] pp. x + 202. hb £90 ISBN 9 7816 1205 1581, pb £27.99 ISBN 9 7816 1205 1598.
Bates, Jennifer Ann, and Richard Wilson, eds. *Shakespeare and Continental Philosophy*. EdinUP. [2014] pp. xiii + 303. £90 ISBN 9 7807 4869 4945.

Bronfen, Elisabeth, and Beate Neumeier, eds. *Gothic Renaissance: A Reassessment*. ManUP. [2014] pp. xi + 272. £70 ISBN 9 7807 1908 8636.

Cefalu, Paul, Gary Kuchar, and Bryan Reynolds, eds. *The Return of Theory in Early Modern English Studies*, vol. 2. PalMac. [2014] pp. xi + 310. £60 ISBN 9 7811 3735 1043.

Charney, Maurice. *Shakespeare's Style*. FDUP. [2014] pp. xxii + 184. $70 ISBN 9 7816 1147 7641.

Clare, Janet. *Shakespeare's Stage Traffic: Imitation, Borrowing and Competition in Renaissance Theatre*. CUP. [2014] pp. xi + 305. £65 ISBN 9 7811 0704 0038.

Collins, Michael, ed. *Reading What's There: Essays on Shakespeare in Honor of Stephen Booth*. UDelP. [2014] pp. vii + 179. $70 ISBN 9 7816 1149 5072.

Craig, Leon Harold. *Philosophy and the Puzzles of Hamlet: At Study of Shakespeare's Method*. Bloomsbury. [2014] pp. ix + 281. £74 ISBN 9 7816 2892 0475.

Crawforth, Hannah, Sarah Dustagheer, and Jennifer Young. *Shakespeare in London*. Bloomsbury. [2014] pp. xvii + 262. £50 ISBN 9 7814 7257 3728.

Crowl, Samuel. *Shakespeare's 'Hamlet': The Relationship between Text and Film*. ArdenS. Bloomsbury. [2014] pp. 176. £45 ISBN 9 7814 7253 8918.

Cull, Marisa R. *Shakespeare's Princes of Wales: English Identity and the Welsh Connection*. OUP. [2014] pp. x + 203. £55 ISBN 9 7801 9871 6198.

Cutrofello, Andrew. *All for Nothing: Hamlet's Negativity*. MITP. [2014] pp. xiii + 226. pb £15.95 ISBN 9 7802 6252 6340.

Dionne, Craig, and Parmita Kapadia, eds. *Bollywood Shakespeares*. PalMac. [2014] pp. 224. £55 ISBN 9 7811 3738 6120.

Dolan, Frances E. *Twelfth Night: Language and Writing*. ArdenS. [2014] pp. 188. £9.99 ISBN 9 7814 7251 8323.

Dunn, Leslie C., and Katherine R. Larson, eds. *Gender and Song in Early Modern England*. Ashgate. [2014] pp. 236. £65 ISBN 9 7814 7244 3410.

Escolme, Bridget. *Emotional Excess on the Shakespearean Stage: Passion's Slaves*. Bloomsbury. [2014] pp. xxxix + 302. £60 ISBN 9 7814 0817 9666.

Espinosa, Ruben, and David Ruiter, eds. *Shakespeare and Immigration*. Ashgate. [2014] pp. viii + 217. £95 ISBN 9 7814 0941 1000.

Farabee, Darlene. *Shakespeare's Staged Spaces and Playgoers' Perceptions*. PalMac. [2014] pp. xi + 180. £55 ISBN 9 7811 3742 7144.

Findlay, Alison, and Liz Oakley-Brown, eds. *Twelfth Night: A Critical Reader*. ArdenS. [2014] pp. 300. £17.99 ISBN 9 7814 7250 3312.

Foley, E., and B. Coates. *Shakespeare for Grown-Ups: Everything You Need to Know about the Bard*. Square Peg. [2014] pp. 326. £12.99 ISBN 9 7802 2409 8557.

Gibson, Marion, and Jo Ann Esra. *Shakespeare's Demonology: A Dictionary*. ArdenS Dictionaries. Bloomsbury. [2014] pp. x + 238. £100 ISBN 9 7808 2649 8342.

Gray, Patrick, and John D. Cox, eds. *Shakespeare and Renaissance Ethics*. CUP. [2014] pp. x + 309. £60 ISBN 9 7811 0707 1933.

Hartley, Andrew James. *Julius Caesar: Shakespeare in Performance*. ManUP. [2014] pp. xi + 258. £70 ISBN 9 7807 1907 9191.

Heffernan, James A.W. *Hospitality and Treachery in Western Literature*. YaleUP. [2014] pp. x + 426. $65 ISBN 9 7803 0019 5583.

Henke, Robert, and Eric Nicholson, eds. *Transnational Mobilities in Early Modern Theatre*. Ashgate. [2014] pp. 320. £70 ISBN 9 7814 0946 8295.

Holderness, Graham. *Tales from Shakespeare: Creative Collisions*. CUP. [2014] pp. xv + 245. £25 ISBN 9 7811 0707 1292.

Hopkins, Lisa, and Helen Ostovich, eds. *Magical Transformations on the Early Modern English Stage*. Ashgate. [2014] pp. 265. £70 ISBN 9 7814 7243 2865.

Huang, Alexa, and Elizabeth Rivlin, eds. *Shakespeare and the Ethics of Appropriation*. Palgrave. [2014] pp. vi + 274. $95 ISBN 9 7811 3737 5766.

Jackson, MacDonald P. *Determining the Shakespeare Canon: Arden of Faversham and A Lover's Complaint*. OUP. [2014] pp. 288. £49.50 ISBN 9 7801 9870 4416.

Jackson, Russell. *Shakespeare and the English-Speaking Cinema*. OUP. [2014] pp. 208. £45 ISBN 9 7801 9965 9470.

Johnson, Laurie, John Sutton, and Evelyn Tribble, eds. *Embodied Cognition and Shakespeare's Theatre: The Early Modern Body-Mind*. Routledge. [2014] pp. vii + 268. £90 ISBN 9 7811 3800 0759.

Karim-Cooper, Farah, and Tiffany Stern, eds. *Shakespeare's Theatres and the Effects of Performance*. Bloomsbury. [2014] pp. xix + 296. £60 ISBN 9 7814 0814 6927.

Kastan, David Scott. *A Will to Believe: Shakespeare and Religion*. OUP. [2014] pp. xii + 156. £25 ISBN 9 7801 9957 2892.

Knowles, Katie. *Shakespeare's Boys: A Cultural History*. Palgrave. [2014] pp. x + 258. £55 ISBN 9 7811 3700 5366.

Kozusko, Matthew, ed. *The Two Gentlemen of Verona (New Kittredge Shakespeare)*. Hackett. [2014] pp. 120. £7.50 ISBN 9 7815 8510 2938.

Maguire, Laurie. *Othello: Language and Writing*. Bloomsbury. [2014] pp. xvii + 208. £30 ISBN 9 7814 7251 8293.

Manley, Lawrence, and Sally-Beth MacLean. *Lord Strange's Men and Their Plays*. YaleUP. [2014] pp. 475. £35 ISBN 9 7803 0019 1998.

Mardock, James D., and Kathryn R. McPherson, eds. *Stages of Engagement: Drama and Religion in Post-Reformation England*. Duquesne. [2014] pp. 360. $58 ISBN 9 7808 2070 4739.

Marrapodi, Michele, ed. *Shakespeare and the Italian Renaissance: Appropriation, Transformation, Opposition*. Ashgate. [2014] pp. 388. £80 ISBN 9 7814 7244 8392.

McInnis, David, and Matthew Steggle, eds. *Lost Plays in Shakespeare's England*. Palgrave. [2014] pp. 312. £63 ISBN 9 7811 3740 3964.

McLuskie, Kate, and Kate Rumbold. *Cultural Value in Twenty-First-Century England: The Case of Shakespeare*. ManUP. [2014] pp. viii + 264. £70 ISBN 9 7807 1908 9848.

McMullan, Gordon, Lena Cowen Orlin, and Virginia Mason Vaughan, eds. *Women Making Shakespeare: Text, Reception, Performance*. ArdenS. [2014] pp. 384. £16.99 ISBN 9 7814 0818 5230.

Miller, Nicole E. *Violence and Grace: Exceptional Life between Shakespeare and Modernity*. NorthwesternUP. [2014] pp. x + 245. $79.95 ISBN 9 7808 1013 0142.

Miola, Robert S., ed. *Macbeth*. 2nd edn. Norton. [2014] pp. 416. £7.95 ISBN 9 7803 9392 3261.

Orlin, Lena Cowen, ed. *Othello: The State of Play*. Bloomsbury. [2014] pp. xi + 289. £50 ISBN 9 7814 0818 4776.

Palfrey, Simon. *Poor Tom: Living 'King Lear'*. UChicP. [2014] pp. ix + 272. $35 ISBN 9 7802 2615 0642.

Post, Jonathan F.S., ed. *The Oxford Handbook of Shakespeare's Poetry*. OUP. [2013] pp. 784. £105 ISBN 9 7801 9960 7747.

Reid, Lindsay Ann. *Ovidian Bibliofictions and the Tudor Book: Metamorphosing Classical Heroines in Late Medieval and Renaissance England*. Ashgate. [2014] pp. 230. £95 ISBN 9 7814 0945 7350.

Saenger, Michael. *Shakespeare and the French Borders of English*. Palgrave. [2013] pp. xvi + 238. £58 ISBN 9 7811 3732 7826.

Saval, Peter Kishore. *Reading Shakespeare through Philosophy*. Routledge. [2014] pp. vii + 182. £90 ISBN 9 7804 1570 9026.

Schreyer, Kurt A. *Shakespeare's Medieval Craft: Remnants of the Mysteries on the London Stage*. CornUP. [2014] pp. 280. £30.95 ISBN 9 7808 0145 2901.

Schulman, Alex. *Rethinking Shakespeare's Political Philosophy: From Lear to Leviathan*. EdinUP. [2014] pp. x + 231. £70 ISBN 9 7807 4868 2416.

Scott, Charlotte. *Shakespeare's Nature: From Cultivation to Culture*. OUP. [2014] pp. x + 258. £52 ISBN 9 7801 9968 5080.

Sell, Roger D., Adam Borch, and Inna Lindgren, eds *Ethics of Literary Communication: Genuineness, Directness, Indirectness*. John Benjamins Publishing Company. [2013] pp. 283. £70 ISBN 9 7890 2721 0364.

Shoaf, R. Allen. *Lucretius and Shakespeare on the Nature of Things*. CambridgeSP. [2014] pp. 165. £41.99 ISBN 9 7814 4386 5319.

Skinner, Quentin. *Forensic Shakespeare*. OUP [2014] pp. xii + 356. £20 ISBN 9 7801 9955 8247.

Stanton, Kay. *Shakespeare's 'Whores': Erotics, Politics, and Poetics*. PalMac. [2014] pp. x + 191. £55 ISBN 9 7811 3702 6323.

Starks-Estes, Lisa S. *Violence, Trauma, and Virtus in Shakespeare's Roman Poems and Plays: Transforming Ovid*. PalMac. [2014] pp. viii + 236. £55 ISBN 9 7811 3734 9910.

Thompson, Ann, ed. *Macbeth: The State of Play*. Bloomsbury. [2014] pp. xii + 293. £50 ISBN 9 7814 7250 3206.

Villeponteaux, Mary. *The Queen's Mercy: Gender and Judgment in Representations of Elizabeth I*. Palgrave. [2014] pp. xi + 227. £60 ISBN 9 7811 3737 1744.

Warley, Christopher. *Reading Class through Shakespeare, Donne, and Milton*. CUP. [2014] pp. viii + 211. £55 ISBN 9 7811 0705 2925.

Watson, Robert N. *BFI Film Classics: Throne of Blood*. PalMac. [2014] pp. 96. pb £12.99 ISBN 9 7818 4457 6647.

Wiggins, Martin, with Catherine Richardson. *British Drama 1533–1642: A Catalogue*, vol. 4: *1598–1602*. OUP. [2014] pp. xiv + 474. £100 ISBN 9 7801 9926 5749.

Williams, Deanne. *Shakespeare and the Performance of Girlhood*. Palgrave. [2014] pp. xii + 278. £55 ISBN 9 7811 3702 4756.

Wiseman, Susan. *Writing Metamorphosis in the English Renaissance 1550–1700*. CUP. [2014] pp. 254. $99.99 ISBN 9 7811 0704 1653.

VIII

Renaissance Drama: Excluding Shakespeare

EOIN PRICE, ELIZABETH SHARRETT, HELEN F. SMITH, PER SIVEFORS, AND CLARE WHITEHEAD

This chapter has three sections: 1. Editions and Textual Matters; 2. Theatre History; 3. Criticism. Section 1 is by Eoin Price; section 2 is by Elizabeth Sharrett; section 3(a) is by Helen F. Smith; section 3(b) is by Per Sivefors; section 3(c) is by Clare Whitehead.

1. Editions and Textual Matters

The year 2013 was a significant one for *The Spanish Tragedy*: it appeared as a single edition in the Arden Early Modern Drama series and as part of the RSC's *William Shakespeare and Others: Collaborative Plays*. Another edition was added to that list in 2014: Michael Neill's Norton Critical Edition. The Norton format, designed with the student reader in mind, combines the expected ingredients—text, annotations, and introduction—with useful supplementary material—secondary sources; extracts from influential critical essays—so the edition comfortably differentiates itself from either of last year's offerings. Neill, one of the most accomplished and experienced editors of early modern plays, has produced a typically fine edition that offers an excellent introduction to this important play.

The Norton advertising blurb promises an 'authoritative text' but, of course, the matter is rather more complicated than that, as Neill's 'Textual Note' attests. Neill's base text is the British Library's 1592 quarto-form octavo and this has been collated with the same library's 1602 version, in which, famously, a number of new scenes were introduced. Neill treats the 1602 text with scepticism: he says the revisions have been 'inexpertly grafted on to the play' and claims 'it is highly unlikely' that they were ever performed on the stage (p. xxxix). Even so, Neill prefers to include the additions—signalled by a change of typeface—as they appeared in the 1602 version, rather than relegating them to an appendix. This approach was also used by the Arden and RSC *Collaborative Plays* editions, and Neill explains the benefits: it aids the

The Year's Work in English Studies, Volume 95 (2016) © *The Author 2016. Published by Oxford University Press on behalf of the English Association. All rights reserved.*
For Permissions, please email: journals.permissions@oup.com
doi:10.1093/ywes/maw006

reader to appreciate the 'dramatic function' of the scenes and offers 'a reminder of the fluid nature of early modern playscripts' (p. xl). The text itself is smartly but unobtrusively annotated, and collation lines—perhaps of less immediate interest to the student reader—are listed at the end of the edition rather than alongside the text. While the glosses are, necessarily, much less detailed than in the Arden edition, they are nonetheless helpful on a range of matters, from Renaissance staging practice to the translation of Latin speeches. Neill's richly historicized and generously illustrated introduction is also commendable: it covers a lot of ground in a small amount of space, although it is perhaps unfortunate that it makes no mention of the play's more recent theatrical afterlife.

The great value of the Norton format is the inclusion of the secondary sources, and these have been well chosen. The section marked 'Contexts' is split into three smaller sections: 'Sources and Biography', 'Revenge', and 'Contemporary Reception'. The first of these contains an English translation of Virgil's *Aeneid* VI, lines 268–901, translated by A.S. Kline. The passage provides an important context for Don Andrea's lengthy opening speech. It also features a passage from Jacques Yver's *A Courtly Controversy of Cupid's Cautels*, translated by Sir Henry Wotton and published in 1578. This passage offers useful context for the *Soliman and Perseda* play-within-the-play. Next, Neill provides a section from the anonymously authored libel *Leicester's Commonwealth* [1584] which attacked Queen Elizabeth's unpopular favourite, Robert Dudley, the earl of Leicester. The details from this passage chime well with Lorenzo's machinations in Kyd's play. Finally, Neill provides an extract from Thomas Nashe's preface to Robert Greene's *Menaphon*, in which Kyd—'the kid in Aesop'—is satirized. This is certainly a useful context, although it might equally have appeared in the 'Contemporary Reception' section.

The section on 'Revenge' provides an extended passage from the Anglican homily 'An Exhortation Concerning Good Order and Obedience', as well as shorter extracts from Michel de Montaigne's essays 'Of Cruelty' and 'Cowardice, the Mother of Cruelty', and Francis Bacon's famous discussion of 'wild justice' in 'Of Revenge'. Taken together, the extracts attest to conflicting attitudes to revenge. They complement Neill's introduction and, especially, his discussion of the Darnley Memorial revenge painting (p. xxx). The final context—contemporary reception—is illustrated by a single example: the anonymous *Spanish Tragedy* ballad, printed in 1620. This is a wonderful accompaniment to the main text, which gestures towards the wider cultural landscape, and serves as one example of the kind of afterlife *The Spanish Tragedy* enjoyed, but I would have welcomed further examples. *The Spanish Tragedy* may well be the play most commonly quoted, misquoted, and referenced by other Renaissance dramatists. Indeed, much later, lines from the play were also used near the end of T.S. Eliot's *The Waste Land*. It is impossible to do justice to the range of ways in which the play was received in its own time, but a slightly bulkier 'Reception' section might have driven home the cultural cachet the play held in the Renaissance. The edition closes with selected passages from a number of seminal essays, from G.K. Hunter's 'Ironies of Justice in *The Spanish Tragedy*' (*RenD* 8[1965] 61–74) to Lorna Hutson's *The Invention of Suspicion* (OUP [2007]). Each essay is given its own thematic subheading—'Stagecraft', 'The Language of the Play', 'Metadramatic Readings', 'Justice and Revenge', 'Violence and Death', 'Politics and Subversion', 'The Play of Opposites', and 'Iconography'. These essay extracts are augmented by a helpful, up-to-date bibliography which includes last year's Arden edition among its list of useful editions.

The spate of recent *Spanish Tragedy* editions raises questions about whether the play is due another major theatrical production. The Globe and RSC have shown some commitment to performing non-Shakespearian Renaissance plays: this has involved some revivals of famous and relatively frequently performed plays—Marlowe's *Doctor Faustus* (RSC, 2016); Ford's *'Tis Pity She's a Whore* (Globe, 2014)—alongside less frequently performed plays— Dekker's *The Shoemaker's Holiday* (RSC, 2015); Marston's *The Malcontent* (Globe, 2014); Ford's *The Broken Heart* (Globe, 2015)—and some plays that have not had professional productions for centuries, such as Ford's *Love's Sacrifice* (RSC, 2015). As yet, however, there has been no big revival of *The Spanish Tragedy*: the play has not received anything like the attention afforded to Marlowe's contemporaneous *Doctor Faustus. The Spanish Tragedy* was last performed at the RSC in 1997 and at the National in 1984; it may be that it is now due a major twenty-first-century production. The plethora of recent editions certainly provides compelling evidence of the play's continued appeal.

After last year's edition of *The Spanish Tragedy*, Arden Early Modern Drama has this year turned attention towards a less widely known play: Richard Brome's *A Jovial Crew*, edited by Tiffany Stern. Arden has alternated between editing well-known texts—Webster's *The Duchess of Malfi* [2009]; Ford's *'Tis Pity She's a Whore* [2011]—and rarely edited texts such as Massinger's *The Renegado* [2010] and Fletcher's *The Island Princess* [2012]. Although *A Jovial Crew* was last edited in 2010 by Eleanor Lowe, Helen Ostovich, and Richard Cave, as part of the *Richard Brome Online* project, Stern's edition is the first scholarly text in print for over forty years. The earlier online edition has a wider scope—it provides modern spelling, old spelling, and dual-text editions as well as useful videos of stage readings of selected scenes—but this new print edition offers a valuable introduction and contains useful appendices, a glossary of cant terms, and Brome's biography. It also represents a significant improvement on previous print editions by taking into account the important recent scholarship by Matthew Steggle, Julie Sanders, and others. Indeed, Anne Haaker's Regents Renaissance Drama series edition [1968] is now out of print.

In an illuminating introduction, Stern makes a strong case for the importance of the play both to 'the history of theatre' and 'the history of England' (p. 2) without reducing the play to the status of historical document. One of the advantages of the Arden series—in contrast to the Revels series, for example—is that, following the Arden Shakespeare format, introductions begin with critical discussion and end with textual, bibliographical, and editorial matters. It would be a disservice to the study of bibliography to suggest it is less interesting or important than critical, interpretative, contextual, or performative matters, but detailed discussion of textual cruces can be intimidating and bewildering to student readers, especially when they are confronted with an unfamiliar play. It is a good decision to begin, as this edition does, with a lively analysis of the play's title and mood: it is an appealing way of offering this relatively little-known play to a wider readership.

The textual matters are, in any case, not especially problematic. The text is 'clean', and Stern suggests that 'Brome himself had prepared the text for printing' (p. 51). Indeed, Stern goes further, claiming that he also designed the title page, which links *A Jovial Crew* with other Brome plays. The title-page motto, taken from Martial, is also used on the title pages of *The Northern Lass* and *The Sparagus Garden*, as well as *The Court Beggar* and *The Novella*. The latter two were printed after Brome's death, but Stern suggests they may have been used on his behalf or, intriguingly, they may have been included in the manuscript which went to press. The motto's emphasis on laughter suggests that Brome 'may have wanted to be known for "laughing" literature' in the way that Jonson was known for ' "humorous" writing' (p. 52). However, the lack of variance between printed texts makes the decision to print the title page and paratextual material under the heading 'Quarto Paratext' a little confusing. Although the play had a rich afterlife in ballad form and was printed as a 'ballad opera' (p. 65) in 1731, the four earliest versions of the play (including the two collated for this edition) were quartos. The play itself, despite deriving from a quarto text, is simply labelled 'A Jovial Crew, or The Merry Beggars', so it is strange that the paratexts are labelled in this way when the main text is not. The effect is to estrange the paratext from the play, as if they were not parts of the same material object. The reasons for this separation are not fully clear, to this reader at least. Stern writes interestingly about the topicality of the paratexts, which reflect 'Brome's new, 1650s view' (p. 47) on a play he had written a decade earlier: are the paratexts marked as 'Quarto' to emphasize the difference between work composed in the 1650s and work composed when the play was written, in the 1640s? If so, this is not made clear and is undercut by Stern's intriguing suggestion that it is possible that 'the new material of 1652 is not confined simply to the paratext' (p. 49). A quick perusal of other Arden Early Modern Drama series editions suggests this might be a house style, but I am not sure, in this instance, that the distinction between paratext and playtext is particularly helpful. But this is a small quibble indeed: this is a fine edition of a fascinating play and a worthy addition to an important series.

The year's other major new edition is electronic and appears as part of the Digital Renaissance Editions project (http://digitalrenaissance.uvic.ca/). It is, in fact, not one edition, but several. Joost Daalder, with the help of Brett D. Hirsch, has produced editions of *The Honest Whore, Part 1* (by Dekker and Middleton) and *The Honest Whore, Part 2* (by Dekker alone). Daalder provides modernized texts of both plays, but he also offers original-spelling editions of Q1 and Q2 *1 Honest Whore*—both were printed in 1604, but they vary significantly, as explained in the Textual Introduction to the two parts— and of Q1 [1630] *2 Honest Whore*. Furthermore, facsimiles of all of these texts are provided, with the permission of the Folger Shakespeare Library (for Q1 *1 Honest Whore*) and the National Library of Scotland (for Q2 *1 Honest Whore* and Q1 *2 Honest Whore*). The plays have been edited before, but never so fully. The last time either play was edited was in 2007, when Paul Mulholland edited the first part for the *Thomas Middleton: The Collected Works* under the title *The Patient Man and the Honest Whore*. The two plays were edited together by Nick de Somogyi in his 1998 Globe Quartos edition, but Daalder's edition far exceeds that, and, indeed, all other editions of the plays. If anything, there is *too* much information here. Online editions allow for more space and are able to do things beyond the scope of print (as the *Richard Brome Online* project shows) but there are times when brevity might be best. One of the appeals of the Arden Early Modern Drama series is its relative slightness; correspondingly, one of the drawbacks of the Arden Shakespeare 3 series is the size of the editions: at times, they feel bloated. The level of detail provided by Daalder is impressive, but it would be a shame if the sheer size of the introductory material put off prospective readers, especially since, as an open-access resource, Digital Renaissance Editions can pitch themselves towards a wider, non-academic audience. In all, though, this is a really impressive and important project which has made available two significant plays. It is customary for me to hope that each edition I review inspires future theatrical performance, but it should be emphasized that the *Honest Whore* plays are especially ripe for revival. It is a shame that their most recent professional performance (at the Globe, in 1998) conflated the two texts in a way which seems greatly to have obscured the quality of the two plays. Daalder's edition allows a wider audience to experience and enjoy these plays. It, and the wider Digital Renaissance Editions project, are to be applauded.

The year was also notable for a high number of revised editions issued by New Mermaids: this included two single editions and two collections. Stephen Guy-Bray was tasked with writing a new introduction to the 1997 edition of *Edward II* edited by Martin Wiggins and Robert Lindsey. This admirable introduction challenges received views of the play. Guy-Bray argues that 'the almost unanimous consensus among contemporary critics that Edward is a weak king is simply bizarre' (p. xxiii), but dominant prejudices of the day have come to be accepted without challenge. Guy-Bray will not stand for this, and his deft and illuminating essay keeps the reader critically alert. The revised introduction places a much greater emphasis on the representation of sexuality in the play than the Wiggins introduction, and it is also able to refer to more recent criticism. It is therefore an excellent guide to the play. New Mermaids also reissued Brian Gibbons's edition of *The Duchess of Malfi*. This is now the fifth edition of that famous play, published thirteen years after the fourth edition. It remains a good student edition of the play, but now has the advantage of including some of the most recent major productions. *The Duchess of Malfi* has proven to be particularly popular in the last few years, and a number of significant productions are addressed in this revised edition. Laurie Sampson's outstanding 2010 production at the Royal and Derngate Theatre in Northampton is accurately described as 'intelligent, [and] highly imaginative' (p. xx), the immersive *Malfi*, produced in 2010 by the English National Opera and Punchdrunk, is also given a paragraph, as is the Old Vic's 2012 production. The edition came too late to make mention of the *Malfi* that opened the Globe's Sam Wanamaker Playhouse in 2014. These new production details are appreciated: if anything, there might have been more of them, although the interested reader can always seek out new information, if they choose.

New Mermaids also included the text of the older, fourth, edition of Gibbons's *Malfi* as part of a new anthology of four plays collected under the title *Women on the Early Modern Stage*. The other play texts included are Heywood's *A Woman Killed with Kindness*, edited by Frances E. Dolan in 2012, John Fletcher's *The Tamer Tamed*, edited by Lucy Munro in 2010, and Rowley, Dekker, and Ford's *The Witch of Edmonton*, edited by Arthur F. Kinney in 1998. Each of the single editions of these plays contains an essay by the editor, but for the purposes of this anthology those introductions have been replaced by a single, newly commissioned introduction by Emma Smith. Smith's sharp and lively piece begins with a concise discussion of early modern women and leads into a series of short, two-page introductions on each of the plays in the volume. A final paragraph addresses the issue of the plays today. The introduction does a fine job of providing key information, and the anthology brings together, in a more affordable edition, a number of important plays. It may therefore be of interest to students and teachers looking to expand their knowledge of early modern drama. Similarly, New Mermaids commissioned Robert N. Watson to write a similar introduction to a new anthology of four Ben Jonson plays. This anthology contains the texts of Watson's own *Volpone*, edited in 2003, Roger Holdsworth's *Epicæne or The Silent Woman*, edited in 1979, Elizabeth Cook's *The Alchemist*, edited in 2010, and G.R. Hibbard's *Bartholomew Fair*, edited in 2007. It is unusual, perhaps, to see an edition from 1979 alongside three much more recently edited texts, but the edition serves its purpose. Watson's introduction offers a useful biographical sketch and introduction to Jonsonian comedy, before delving into short introductions to each of the plays. It will be interesting to gauge the success of this anthology enterprise, but there ought to be a place in the market for such collected editions if they allow easier access to a greater variety of plays. Pairing more well-known texts such as *Volpone* alongside less widely read/staged plays like *Epicæne* may indeed be a good way of broadening the horizons of students and general readers.

The single editions and anthologies produced this year by Norton, Arden, Digital Renaissance Editions, and New Mermaids are complemented by a major study of the editing of performance texts. Jacqueline Jenkins and Julie Sanders are the editors of *Editing, Performance, Texts: New Practices in Medieval and Early Modern English Drama*, a collection of essays addressing manuscripts, archives, and the process of editing through performance. One of the volume's strengths is its resistance to the restrictions of standard periodization: it is refreshing to see medievalists and early modernists sharing insights into textual editing. Accordingly, the volume resists the tendency in so much early modern scholarship to privilege Shakespeare. J. Gavin Paul's excellent chapter on reading and performance in the archives takes Shakespeare as its subject, but even those chapters which feature Shakespeare prominently, such as Christie Carson's discussion of the relationship between page and stage, analyse non-Shakespearian Renaissance drama too. Carson discusses the Records of Early English Drama, the Queen's Men and Their Plays project, and the Early

Modern London Theatre Database alongside *The Cambridge King Lear CD-ROM*.

Essays on a range of different kinds of Renaissance plays—for example, Lynette Hunter and Peter Litchenfels detail the intriguing case of *The Humorous Magistrate*; Richard Cave, Eleanor Lowe, and Brian Woolland recount the challenges of editing Richard Brome online; James Purkiss discusses manuscript drama; Mary C. Erler addresses the under-studied case of London commercial drama pre-1574—sit happily alongside chapters on medieval plays. For example, Claire Sponsler analyses the *Beauchamp Pageant* within the wider context of medieval drama; Boyda Johnstone considers the illustrated *Abbey of the Holy Ghost*; and Murray McGillivray addresses the Towneley manuscript. The essays, taken together, do indeed offer evidence of the new practices promised by the title but I wonder if more might have been made of what is surely the next step for textual editing: digital editions. Electronic texts are discussed, of course, but only two of the essays do so thoroughly. The two essays which deal with the subject (those of Carson, and of Cave, Lowe, and Woolland) appear at the end of the book, and this might appropriately gesture towards the future: digital editions surely offer the best way of disseminating medieval and Renaissance texts to a wider audience (even if that wider audience is composed of students and academics). Cave, Lowe, and Wolland give important insights into the process of editing through performance and, in turn, the challenges, and the values, of editing online.

2. Theatre History

June Schlueter explores the provenance of two pieces of theatrical evidence that significantly inform our understanding of the Renaissance theatre—the Swan and Peacham sketches—through an examination of their materiality in her article, 'Drawing in a Theatre: Peacham, De Witt, and the Table-Book' (*TN* 68:ii[2014] 69–86). In her discussion of their origins, Schlueter analyses the drawing habits of the artists associated with the images, on the basis of the surviving miscellany of their writings and drawings. In doing so, she makes a compelling argument that a 'table-book', or 'writing-table', may have been the means by which Henry Peacham and Johannes de Witt made their initial drawings. The pages of these pocket-sized objects, which could be carried easily and discreetly, were covered in wax, allowing their users to make impressions upon each leaf with a metal-point stylus. The image could then be transferred onto paper, either by hand or by rubbing, meaning that if such a tool was used in the making of the Swan sketch, for instance, the document we have today by Aernout van Buchell is at the very least a copy of a copy. The wax impression could then be cleared away from the page with a fingertip, rendering impossible any chance of recovering a lost 'original' of the two sketches.

Table-books were popularly and commonly used, as demonstrated by Schlueter's search for the objects on the Early English Books Online database, resulting in nearly 500 hits. John Downame's 1604 *The Christian Warfare*, for instance, makes reference to using table-books to write sermons, and Edward

Topsell's *The Historie of the Foure-Footed Beasts* [1607] describes cleaning the pages with either a sponge or a cloth. John Aubrey records that Sir Philip Sidney used one to 'write down his notions' while writing *Arcadia*. Perhaps most familiar to Renaissance drama scholars is Hamlet's mention of them when he remarks, 'My Tables, my Tables; meet it is I set it downe' (I.v.108). Schlueter proposes that, if De Witt and Peacham used these books to create their sketches, their portability may have allowed the artists to do so within the theatre, and not necessarily from memory, as has been suggested by some scholars. Her article is extremely useful for the ways in which it re-examines these familiar pieces of evidence by drawing upon the documents' material features. Additionally, it reconsiders how audience members such as De Witt and Peacham may have experienced the drama depicted in their images. While Schlueter concedes that ultimately it is impossible to tell whether the artists did use table-books or whether they drew them from within their respective theatres, she calls attention to the value of revisiting such familiar documents of the field to question whether our current narratives need amending, in the hope that such re-examination will provide a greater understanding of the workings of the early modern theatre.

Siobhan Keenan contributes to the field of repertory studies in her monograph *Acting Companies and Their Plays in Shakespeare's London*, which unpacks the variety of elements that went into the making of plays in the English Renaissance theatre, and is particularly concerned with the impact companies had on this creative process. The study considers how various factors, such as needs, practices, resources, and pressures on acting companies and playwrights informed both the performance and publication of drama from this period, as well as the writing practices of playwrights. Through a series of cases studies in each chapter that draw on an impressive range of theatrical evidence, Keenan challenges the assumption that playwrights were the sole force behind the creation of plays. She demonstrates that it was in fact a collaborative endeavour in which playwrights, acting companies, and individual actors, audiences, patrons, and material conditions all played a role in shaping dramatic texts. While the success of companies, she argues, was directly tied to their ability to secure a permanent venue, there remained a need for plays to be portable and transferable across venues such as playhouses, halls, private homes, and, most desirably, at court.

Gabriel Egan provides insights into what the 'official' closure of the theatres in 1642 at the start of the English Civil War meant for Caroline society, and in particular what it meant for those involved in the theatre industry, in his article 'The Closure of the Theatres' (*YES* 44[2014] 103–19). Drawing on the work of multiple theatre historians, Egan begins by charting the process of revision which the traditional narrative of how the theatres closed has undergone over the past thirty years; that it was not simply that the monarch loved drama and that the Puritans hated it. Indeed, as Egan demonstrates, not all Puritans were anti-theatricalists, and not all actors, who were effectively servants of the royal household, supported the king. Furthermore, though the theatres were officially closed, there is evidence to suggest that royalists continued to enjoy dramatic performances during the war. Thus, Egan recognizes that just as there is no common consensus on whether it was primarily economic or religious factors which led to the outbreak of the Civil War, theatre historians are unable to agree on why Parliamentarians 'officially' put an end to performances in commercial venues. A series of short case studies explore the experiences of those involved in the industry, such as Eyllaerdt Swanston, who, though a well-known actor of the King's men, was unique amongst his colleagues for his Parliamentarian sympathies. As Egan asserts, it is not his intention to reject the wider historical narratives that seek to define these major events, but, rather, to better understand the various parts by which they were made.

Responding to the emerging critical interest in the history of emotions in the early modern period, Allison P. Hobgood seeks to recover the audience's embodied experience of playgoing in her carefully researched monograph *Passionate Playgoing in Early Modern England*. While many scholars have shied away from what they have perceived to be an irrecoverable and subjective endeavour, Hobgood maintains that a lack of direct evidence of audiences' reaction to plays should not dissuade scholars from investigating this significant yet overlooked aspect of Renaissance theatre history. The book cautiously, though convincingly, negotiates the difficult task of recovering this experience through an interdisciplinary methodological approach, which unites performance studies with cultural criticism and theatre history. It draws on an array of evidence, including humoral theory, philosophical and medical treatises, pro- as well as anti-theatrical literature, and drama which, Hobgood asserts, when analysed together, 'contain a productive narrative' (p. 9) about what early modern theatre-goers may have felt and experienced when attending plays. For instance, in her study of Thomas Heywood's *A Woman Killed With Kindness*, she suggests that the dramatist utilized the potential fear and shame of his audience to help create emotional impact, inviting them to check the extent of their own indulgence in emotional excess. Thus, though dramatists drew emotional responses from their audiences, Hobgood effectively demonstrates that playwright and playgoer alike worked to mutually shape drama.

The contributions to Andrew Gurr and Farah Karim-Cooper's edited collection, *Moving Shakespeare Indoors: Performance and Repertoire in the Jacobean Playhouse*, bring together examination of the theatre history of the English Renaissance, as well as the appropriation of that history through contemporary practice-based performance research at the Globe's reconstructed Jacobean indoor theatre—the Sam Wanamaker Playhouse. The book primarily concerns the King's Men's move into the Second Blackfriars in 1608, which made them the first adult professional company to secure a permanent commercial indoor playing venue. The rich variety of contributions consider what prompted this shift, and what impact it had on both the plays written for the new space and the experience of theatre-goers. In their introduction, Gurr and Karim-Cooper explain that the design for the reproduction theatre was based on the Worcester College drawings by John Webb, once thought to be the Cockpit, which they note served as a 'spatial map' when designing the building which 'Shakespeare might recognize' (p. 1).

The book is divided into three parts, the first of which focuses on the hard evidence that was used to construct the Wanamaker, including discussions of the practical evidence by architectural expert Jon Greenfield and timber craftsman Peter McCurdy, and the documentary evidence related to Burbage's purchase contract of the Blackfriars site by Oliver Jones. Part II considers the material features of these indoor playing spaces, beginning with a chapter by Tiffany Stern on the Blackfriars as a place of nostalgia in Jacobean London, which recalled its past as monastery, the parliament and legatine court, and eventually a theatre. She asks if a yearning for being elsewhere, namely at court, was a characteristic feature that shaped the experience of attending the Blackfriars. Later in the section Sarah Dustagheer considers the acoustic and visual experience at indoor playhouses, proposing that music was a dominant aspect of the dramaturgy of these spaces, and includes an appendix of plays performed at the six longest-running indoor professional playhouses of the period 1575–1642. Paul Menzer then discusses the impact the Blackfriars had on both the open-air amphitheatres of Renaissance London and the nearly 2,000-year-old theatrical tradition of outdoor theatre.

The third part explores the possible influence indoor theatres had on shaping repertory, and includes a chapter by Eleanor Collins in which she explores the figure of the heroic woman in the genres of tragicomedy and romance, genres that were developed and revived on the stage of the Caroline indoor theatres. Finally, Bart van Es puts pressure on the notion that Shakespeare's style changed with the shift of venue, suggesting that, rather, there was a merging of his indoor and outdoor repertories that helped contribute to a style unique to the Blackfriars. The study's essays make a valuable contribution to the field of Renaissance drama for the ways in which they draw on a variety of methodological approaches to recover both a better understanding of the dramaturgical practices of early modern plays performed indoors and the experience of early theatre-goers. By primarily confining the study to the King's Men and the Blackfriars, however, the book overall risks suggesting that its findings about indoor performance are specific to this one company and space. Rather than limit the study in this way, it would have been better served by expanding it to include consideration of other indoor plays, playhouses, and companies.

The fourth instalment of Martin Wiggins's ten-volume catalogue, *British Drama 1533–1642*, surveys the final years of Elizabeth I's reign, covering the period 1598–1602. Included amongst the 310 entries, the volume sees the opening of the Globe theatre, with *Alarum for London* (entry 1191) as the first play in the catalogue associated with the new space, and it follows the Admiral's Men's move from the Rose to the Fortune. More significantly, volume 4 reassigns James Mabbe's *The Spanish Bawd* (entry 1149) from 1631 to 1598, and John Marston's *Histriomastix* (entry 1314) from its traditional date of 1598–9 to 1602. In the case of the latter, Wiggins notes that it has long been assumed that Marston meant the character Chrisoganus (an unsuccessful playwright) to be a flattering representation of Jonson, but that it was instead received as an insult. However, though it was Jonson himself who in 1619 relayed to William Drummond that such an episode had occurred, he did not specify the play and, as E.K. Chambers identifies, it is rather more likely that the character and title in question was Lampatho Doria in *What You Will*. Thus, Wiggins suggests, if *Histriomastix* is later than *What You Will* it 'makes better sense as an attempted apology rather than the original insult' (p. 357), and provides fascinating insight into the relationship between the two playwrights, who eventually collaborated on *Eastward Ho!* (entry 1473). Other major highlights of the volume include the identification of the play recorded in Henslowe's diary as *Albere Galles* and that recorded in Frederic Gerschow's diary as *The Capture of Stuhlweissenburg* (entry 1342), on the duke of Stettin-Pomerania's visit to England in 1602, as one and the same play: *Alba Regalis* by Thomas Heywood and Wentworth Smith. The volume also features the earliest known play at St Omers, *A Brief Dialogue on the Feast of St Thomas of Canterbury, Patron of the English* (entry 1221) of 1599, which survives in manuscript and 'may have been sent to Sir Robert Cecil by an English spy' (p. 181). Finally, entry 1112, *Comedy of the King of England's Son and the King of Scotland's Daughter*, is a play that, intriguingly, is both extant and lost! The lost English original survives in the form of a German translation of the play printed in 1620. Like the rest of his catalogue, Wiggins's fourth volume serves as a remarkable resource, and continues to increase the breadth and depth of our knowledge of the history of the English Renaissance theatre.

Pascale Aebischer makes valuable contributions to the field of film studies and Renaissance theatre history in her monograph *Screening Early Modern Drama Beyond Shakespeare*, in which she explores modern screen adaptations of Jacobean drama, including plays such as *The Changeling* and *The Duchess of Malfi*. The book includes discussion of projects by established and distinguished directors, such as Derek Jarman's *Edward II* and Alex Cox's *Revengers Tragedy*. It also explores works by individuals who are part of the growing grassroots movement online, and who, like Aebischer, are dedicated to extending the canon of screen adaptations beyond Shakespeare through short films and trailers. Collectively these works stand in opposition to the aesthetics, production methods, politics, and funding of 'heritage Shakespeare films' (p. 6), and Aebischer suggests serve to critique the cultural dominance of that industry, which has more or less adopted Hollywood's standards of filmmaking. The study includes an annotated filmography that lists all feature films and online shorts of early modern drama on screen from 1926 to 2012, providing an invaluable resource for future research in this emerging area of Renaissance theatre history. With the exciting increase in the production of non-canonical plays in performance, as evidenced not only by screen adaptations but also by productions from well-funded and independent theatre companies alike, studies such as Aebischer's are vital for understanding, appreciating, and promoting this growing body of work.

Finally, Julie Sanders has created a vital tool for both teachers and scholars of Renaissance drama in her contribution to the Cambridge Introductions to Literature series, *The Cambridge Introduction to Early Modern Drama, 1576–1642*. The book begins by establishing that both the theatres and the companies that emerged in the later decades of the sixteenth century were built upon and grew out of pre-existing theatrical traditions from medieval England, creating continuities that were constantly referenced on stage. These continuities, she explains, crucially formed part of 'the larger nexus of intertexuality that in part . . . defined early modern theatre' (p. 2).

The book's seven chapters are divided by genre, covering tragedy, revenge drama, histories, city comedy, satire, and tragicomedy. Sanders weaves an extensive portfolio of case studies that utilize different critical approaches to explore various companies (adult and boy), dramatic tropes, theatrical venues (including indoor and outdoor), props, costumes, and dumbshows. At the back of the book she provides a chronology of dramatic works that separates the plays by year and title. A third column is devoted to 'Events and Other Publications' and usefully contextualizes for the reader the dramatic work in question in relation to the wider world of early modern history and theatre. This thorough overview makes a valuable contribution to the field of theatre history for the extensive yet accessible ways in which it introduces new readers to the subject.

3. Criticism

(a) General

In 2014 a number of important contributions furthered our knowledge of Renaissance and early modern drama in areas ranging from the performance of economic thought to examinations of clowning and the soul–body dynamic. To start, *Performing Economic Thought: English Drama and Mercantile Writing, 1600–1642* by Bradley D. Ryner is an impressive interdisciplinary work that takes scholarship in a new direction. In his introduction, Ryner points out that English economic thinkers of the late sixteenth and early seventeenth centuries 'published treatises that laid the groundwork for the genre of writing known today as *economics*'. Thus, over the seven chapters of his book, the scholar examines how the economic thought of this period was physically represented in dramatic performances, as well as how the actual ideas of economics were conveyed to the audience. In this endeavour, Ryner consults the physical and material aspects of performance and considers how staged action allowed economic thought to be 'performed differently in the playhouse than in the printed treatise', in order to argue that 'representation techniques available to playwrights could facilitate a more nuanced exploration of economic systems than those available to mercantile writers' (p. 1). The author also makes the interesting observation that 'the stage offered a space for conceptualizing different economic models while fully acknowledging—even emphasizing—that these models were fictional constructions' (p. 5).

The first chapter, which is on the use and function of economic tables in drama, focuses on Walter Mountfort's play *The Launching of the Mary* or *The Seaman's Honest Wife*. Here, Ryner turns his attention to the paraphrasing of Thomas Mun's treatise *A Discourse of Trade* within scenes in which 'members of the East India Company defend the company against customary accusations of squandering English wealth' (p. 16). It is in this respect that the author outlines the unique insight the play is able to provide into the relationship between the stage and mercantile treatises: in order to engage the audience and make his play theatrically effective, the dramatist changes the price of commodities in his staged debate about efficient trade investments. In chapter 2, the author discusses Philip Massinger's *The Emperor of the East* of 1631, and suggests that 'the physical presence of props in the Renaissance playhouse encouraged a different way of thinking about economic circulation than did mercantile treatises' (pp. 50–1). In particular, the author considers an apple that is continually renarrated in the play, causing it to be interpreted variously by different characters and 'according to a number of competing models of royal finance' (p. 51). In the third chapter of his monograph, Ryner examines Thomas Middleton and William Rowley's *The Changeling* of 1622. Here, the scholar is concerned with the different types of characters in dramatic performances, and he explains how 'the tension between conceptualizing the individual as controlling economic transactions and conceptualizing the individual as controlled by impersonal economic forces could be productively thought through on the stage at the level of dramatic character' (p. 78). Chapter 4 examines Shakespeare's *The Merchant of Venice* and *Cymbeline*, and the author considers how the geographical locations presented in drama play a role in its 'commercial metaphors' (p. 107). In the following chapter, Ryner considers how the staged public gossiping in Jonson's *The Staple of News* provides a 'critical interrogation of the techniques of economic representation' (p. 168). This text is studied alongside Thomas Milles's treatise *The Customer's Apology*. In his penultimate chapter, Ryner reflects on genre and economic thought in Richard Brome's *A Jovial Crew* and discusses the characters' awareness of investment and profit. In this chapter, Ryner argues persuasively that 'The convergence of tragicomedy and humours comedy allows Brome to shift between micro- and macro-level explanations of the economic system he stages' (p. 171). The final chapter addresses the performativity of economic models in Thomas Heywood's *If You Know Not Me, You Know Nobody, Part II*, and Philip Massinger's *The Picture*. Overall, *Performing Economic Thought* is an enjoyable, thorough, and intelligent account of the physical and theatrical realization and manifestation of economic thought which provides greater insight into a neglected area of scholarly enquiry.

Ariane M. Bazilet's *Blood and Home in Early Modern Drama: Domestic Identity on the Renaissance Stage* is another significant monograph that explores the fascinating role of blood in domestic environments in early modern drama, since 'blood provided a common vocabulary for analogous power structures of kinship, status, and national identity' in Renaissance England (p. 21). In this important work, Bazilet argues that, 'in response to changing attitudes towards the material home and composition of the family, early modern English drama addressed contemporary debates about domesticity through the language of blood' (p. 20). Over the four chapters of her monograph, Bazilet focuses on different aspects of domestic identity—marriage, adultery, parenthood, and healing. The first chapter concentrates on consummation and the 'Bleeding Bride' in the plays of Shakespeare. Here, the scholar discusses how these plays 'negotiate the significance and implications of the figure of the bleeding bride' (p. 56), in order to present the argument that the image of the bleeding bride 'forged a connection between blood and home built on patriarchal and misogynistic fantasies of sexual and domestic authority' (p. 59). As she turns to the subject of adultery in her second chapter, Bazilet explores cuckoldry and murder in *Arden of Faversham* and *A Warning for Fair Women* through a close reading of the texts. The author pays particular attention to the bleeding, cuckolded husband, 'whose inability to control the sexual desires and behaviors of his wife . . . makes him uniquely susceptible to and deserving of a bloody, violent death', argues Bazilet (p. 114). Chapter 3 looks at the bleeding child in Kyd's *Spanish Tragedy*, and Shakespeare's *Henry VI* and *Titus Andronicus*, as well as in early modern literature and culture. Considering the gendered performance of paternal grief, the scholar examines how 'the exchange of a child's blood for the father's tears represents a masculine assertion of control over the child's vulnerability' (p. 181). The gender of the child also reflects on the presentation of paternal grief, for whereas male children were seen as 'more valuable and cherished vessels of patriarchal blood' female children were 'more fragile and susceptible to corruption' (p. 182). In the final chapter of her book, Bazilet turns to the ideas of the bleeding patient, honour, and bloodline in *The Duchess of Malfi*, *The Maid's Tragedy*, and *El médico de su honra*. In this chapter, the author conducts a fascinating investigation into the ways in which 'the misogynistic fear that bloodline is reproduced through fallible female bodies is mitigated by fantasies of "curing" a tainted bloodline by wounding or murdering women who transgress expectations of sexual honor' (p. 240). In conclusion, Bazilet's *Blood and Home in Early Modern Drama* is an engaging and insightful analysis of 'the intersections of blood and home as expressions of domestic identity' (p. 48).

Heather Hirschfeld's *The End of Satisfaction: Drama and Repentance in the Age of Shakespeare* is an accomplished monograph that addresses how the contemporaries of Shakespeare dramatized the idea of 'satisfaction' in the context of theology and the impact of doctrinal change during the Reformation period. Her first of five chapters provides an introduction to what she terms the 'English Reformation of Repentance' and the progression of ideas of 'satisfaction' in theology and throughout history. Hirschfeld's second chapter is concerned with *Doctor Faustus* and the satisfactions of hell, and poses the question whether it is a contemporary form of the medieval harrowing of hell play. This is an important question in terms of what the play can be seen to represent about the idea of 'satisfaction', since, as Hirschfeld observes, the debate 'over it whether it was *necessary* for Christ to go down to hell or to suffer in his soul . . . rehearses the problem of human satisfaction and redemption . . . as a problem for Christ' (p. 40). In her following chapter, Hirschfeld focuses on the satisfactions of revenge and suggests that Elizabethan revenge tragedy absorbed 'Protestantism's reknitting of the connection between vengeance and repentance, [and] its sanctioning of penitential self-punishment alongside its refusal of penitential satisfaction' (p. 66). In this endeavour, Hirschfeld discusses plays such as Kyd's *Spanish Tragedy*, Shakespeare's *Hamlet*, and Middleton's *Revenger's Tragedy* most of all. In chapter 4, the author examines William Wager's *Enough Is as Good as a Feast* in addition to Shakespeare's *Merchant of Venice*, in order to explore how the mid-Tudor interlude 'literally dramatizes the problem of enough, playing with its elusive, abyssal status as well as with the semantic complication between its economic and penitential values'

(p. 96). Turning to *The Merchant of Venice* she then considers Shylock and the role of the Jewish moneylender in the 'world of Christian repentance' (p. 96). In the fifth and final chapter, the author looks at the satisfactions of marriage in *Othello* and *Love's Pilgrimage*. Here, Hirschfeld uses the playtexts to show that 'The vicissitudes of satisfaction structure early modern accounts of marriage as a sexual, emotional, and communal bond' (p. 121). Hirschfeld's *The End of Satisfaction* provides an effective and enjoyable examination of the complex and various realizations and manifestations of the idea of satisfaction on the Elizabethan and Jacobean stage.

In *Character and the Individual Personality in English Renaissance Drama: Tragedy, History, Tragicomedy* by John E. Curran, the scholar looks at the ways in which plays were sometimes constructed around individual characters and even as 'analyses of character' (p. xi). In the first of his five chapters, Curran addresses different types of stock character. In this endeavour, among discussions of a large number of plays (including the history plays of Shakespeare), Curran considers *The Honest Man's Fortune* from 1613, which, as the author points out, makes reference to a stock character in its title. Whilst the scholar argues that the play 'seems to ground itself on our recognition of a common category of person, who will remain true to the defining principle of honesty' (p. 15), he also, crucially, recognizes that this very character, the honest man, 'emerges as an individual' (p. 15) and explains how that is the case. Inconsistency is the focus of chapter 2, in which Curran discusses Marlowe's *Doctor Faustus*. In particular, regarding the 'transgressing magician' the author observes 'how this character has a singular personality, one which . . . causes tragedy by channeling knowledge and experience no one else has in ways that no one else would' (p. 88). The following chapter makes a further examination of the ways in which dramatists made use of the 'nexus between the moral and the psychiatric to fashion individualistic characters' (p. 140). The fourth chapter explores characters in Renaissance drama that were based on historical identities, such as the Good Duke Humphrey, Cicero, and Perkin Warbeck, and considers how the dimensions and personalities of such characters were shaped, and the implications this entailed. Magnanimity is the subject of the final chapter, in which Curran turns his focus to Shakespeare's Mark Antony in the endeavour to argue that what the character exemplifies is unclear 'because is it Antony, not his meaning, that we're supposed to notice' (p. 293). In conclusion, this is an enjoyable and insightful analysis of character and the individual personality throughout English Renaissance drama, which makes an important contribution to the field.

In 2014, Ashgate's Studies in Performance and Early Modern Drama series published a number of excellent and original new titles with fascinating approaches, angles, and insights into early modern theatre and dramatic performance. Among them, *Staging Women and the Soul–Body Dynamic in Early Modern England* by Sarah E. Johnson is an intelligent and fluid analysis of the web of associations and assumptions around what she refers to as 'the conceptual alignment of women with the body and men with the soul' (p. 12) on the early modern stage. In chapter 1, 'Puppeteer and Puppet', the scholar looks at the character Ursula from Jonson's *Bartholomew Fair* as an exemplification of what she describes as 'female boundlessness and uncontrol'

(p. 13). In this chapter, Johnson argues that in *The Revenger's Tragedy*, as in *Bartholomew Fair*, the puppetry 'presents a misogynistic view of women and yet, in some ways, works to overturn this view' (p. 27). In her second chapter, the scholar argues that in *The Tamer Tamed* Maria's rhetoric 'prompts a reconsideration of gender roles within marriage both through its reliance on a sharp divide between soul and body and through its erasure of that divide in other moments' (p. 72). Her third chapter explores a number of plays with ghosts, such as *The Lady's Tragedy*. Johnson argues that this play 'foregrounds the soul–body dynamic through the Lady by literally bifurcating her into a soul and a body' (p. 105). More broadly, in this chapter she provides an interesting exploration of female ghostliness 'as both defusing and symbolizing female authority' (p. 131). Lastly, the final chapter, which is entitled 'Observer and Spectacle', is interested in the bodily representation of the female soul—particularly since, as Johnson observes, the soul was an entity that was 'most often masculinized through its contradistinction from a feminized body' (p. 133). Overall, *Staging Women and the Soul–Body Dynamic in Early Modern England* is a valuable piece of research that provides a detailed and complex understanding of its subject.

Also published by Ashgate, *Staging England in the Elizabethan History Play: Performing National Identity*, by Ralf Hertel, is a monograph in ten chapters, with two chapters dedicated to each of its five parts. These parts cover territory, history, religion, class, and gender. Hertel uses current political theory in addition to methods established by recent performance studies in a unique approach to the political drama of the late Elizabethan period, which covers new ground on the role of the public theatre in the 'negotiation' of English national identity around the turn of the seventeenth century. In terms of the overall structure of the book, the first chapter of each part concentrates on historical background, followed by a chapter that pays close attention to a particular play. In the first chapter of the first part, 'Plotting England', Hertel explores the transformation of territory into homeland, in recognition of the relevance of territory to manifestations of national identity. He also considers how ideas of territory were staged. In the following section, the scholar puts this background to use in an examination of Shakespeare's *1 Henry IV*. The role of the map, in this play and in *King Lear*, is discussed in this chapter. Moving on to Part II, Hertel's background chapter covers the idea of the national past and how this was staged, posing the question, 'How influential are notions of the past in shaping national identity?' (p. 77). The play discussed in the chapter that follows is *Richard III*, which is examined alongside Polydore Vergil's *Anglica Historia*. Religion is the focus of Part III, which begins with an exploration of ideas of belief (in the context of national identity), and considers how belief was staged. The play Hertel goes on to consider is *King John*, and the scholar begins this discussion by posing the question of whether this is a religious play, and examining a scene of anti-Catholic Protestant rhetoric. Moving on to Part IV, which addresses class, after an exploration of class and national identity on the stage, Hertel then discusses *2 Henry VI*. In the final section, which is on gender, the scholar covers gender and national identity, considering whether nationalism is a 'male phenomenon' (p. 193), and whether the history play is a masculine genre.

In the chapter that follows, Hertel discusses gender in Marlowe's *Edward II* as a play that 'prominently raises the issue of homoerotic love' (p. 213). In this chapter, Hertel asks, 'What does it mean if Gaveston rather than Queen Isabella has access to Edward's body private?' This prompts the further question, 'Does access to the body private imply access to the body politic?' (p. 219). Overall, in this important work Hertel considers the early modern stage as a contested space, within which 'conflicting political positions are played off against each other', and he also considers the impact this had on the 'spectators' collective identity' (p. 1). It is an impressive and thorough contribution to our knowledge of how national identity was constructed and the role theatre had to play in shaping this construction.

In the same series, in *Sensory Experience and the Metropolis on the Jacobean Stage (1603–1625)* Hristomir A. Stanev investigates the five senses upon the Jacobean stage. This includes acts of performance 'in which the body senses and becomes sensed' (p. 3) in addition to the 'idea of the sensory metropolis *on stage*' (p. 3). In his original approach, Stanev argues that, 'Far from dismissing Jonson's dramatization of the senses as an isolated obsession with civic physiology, we should add the names of Shakespeare, Middleton, Dekker, Webster and Fletcher to the list of those early seventeenth-century playwrights who specifically linked the sense to the impact of metropolitan culture' (p. 3). In the first of his seven chapters, Stanev introduces the idea of the sensory metropolis and outlines the structure of the book. Chapter 2 is a study of emerging forms of sensory recognition 'in descriptions and imaginative reconstructions of metropolitan and theatrical environments' (p. 27). In this endeavour, the scholar turns his attention to plays such as Shakespeare's *The Tempest* in addition to Dekker's *The Shoemaker's Holiday* and Haughton's *Englishmen for My Money*, which are discussed alongside contemporary publications such as *A Counterblast to Tobacco* and *The Honesty of This Age*. In his third chapter, Stanev pays particular attention to *Bartholomew Fair* and *The Honest Whore* and observes how the two plays 'use the brothel to stage a peculiar contest between urban and suburban that mirrors the late Elizabethan and Jacobean tendency to depict competitive urbanism in distinctly gustatory terms' (pp. 56–7). *The Puritan* and *Westward Ho* are the focus of chapter 4, in which Stanev explores the 'peculiar relationship between early modern ideas of smell and the dramatic rendition of urban space through its material constituents' (p. 83). In his fifth chapter, the scholar returns to *The Honest Whore*, which he consults alongside *The Pilgrim* with a focus, as the chapter title suggests, on 'Visible Madness and the Invisible Discernment of Charity'. After a discussion of Bedlam, Stanev makes the point that 'Dekker and Middleton ultimately construe seeing as an unstable sensory mode that alludes to certain inconsistencies in the visual and moral fabric of metropolitan experience' (p. 124). In chapter 6, which is entitled 'Invasive City Noise, Alienating Talk, and Troubles of Hearing in *Bartholomew Fair* and *Epicene*', Stanev argues that the plays examine 'the increasingly alienating character of hearing and the diminished value of communication in Jonson's contemporary urban milieu' (p. 135) to a greater extent than has previously been considered, before making a further exploration of this claim. The final chapter, which concerns *Coriolanus* as well as *Timon of Athens*, provides an interesting examination of 'the early modern distrust of touch as a contagious form of contact' (p. 161). In conclusion, *Sensory Experience and the Metropolis on the Jacobean Stage* provides a crucial contribution to an underdeveloped area of research.

Next, *Staging Vice: A Study of Dramatic Traditions in Medieval and Sixteenth-Century England and the Low Countries*, by Charlotte Steenbrugge, is an excellent piece of research which looks at the Dutch influence on English drama, whilst situating the Vice and *sinnekens* 'within their own tradition better to gauge the similarities and differences between the two dramatic types and between their dramatic traditions' (p. 10). As the title suggests, Steenbrugge's impressive monograph focuses on dramatic traditions at the time when the late medieval period transitioned into the early modern, with specific attention to the Low Countries. The author's first chapter focuses on the 'negative' or evil characters and abstractions in both English and Dutch drama. In this chapter, Steenbrugge discusses the Vice and *sinnekens* as distinct dramatic traditions, despite their functioning in a number of similar ways. In the following chapter, the scholar turns to the dramatic functions of the Vice and *sinnekens* and the ways in which they are a figure of temptation for other protagonists, highlighting how the influence of the *sinnekens* is 'normally limited to furthering the demise of an already fallen protagonist' (p. 46). In this regard, Steenbrugge observes that the moral state of the protagonist from the outset of the play is the main factor in how much influence the Vice and *sinnekens* have. In her third chapter, on theatricality, Steenbrugge assesses the theatricality of the early negative characters in addition to the later Vice and *sinnekens*. She also discusses elements of their characterization, such as 'emphasis on physicality, emotions, transgressive language and comedy' (p. 90). In this chapter, Steenbrugge also explores her interesting finding that the 'English Vice seems to be even more theatrical than his forebears whereas the Dutch *sinnekens* are often not as lively and vigorous as the early negative Dutch characters' (p. 90). Chapter 4 then turns to meta-theatricality: the scholar explores and discusses her observation that 'in the earliest surviving English play texts there is an awareness of the presence of an audience that is not found to the same extent in Dutch drama' (p. 159). The final chapter, which is on historicizing vice, considers how historical events such as intellectual and religious movements, and the climates they fostered, impact upon the drama. Overall, *Staging Vice* provides a stimulating and valuable insight into English and Dutch dramatic traditions.

Richard Preiss's *Clowning and Authorship in Early Modern Theatre* is a study of stage clowning in the early modern period, which attempts to 'recover clowning from beyond the margins of printed plays' (p. 7). Preiss outlines that one of the aims of the book is 'to see clowning not as a mere "alternative" authorship, but as its progenitor, part of an ongoing, dialectical exchange in which clowns and authors traded positions, gradually disembodying the one and solidifying the other' (p. 17). In his first chapter, Preiss considers authorship and the axis of reception in discussion of a number of early modern plays. In this chapter, Preiss presents a history of 'how theatre became readable' (p. 59). The second chapter, which is entitled 'Send in the Clown', discusses the evolution of the Vice from Tudor morality to the Elizabethan stage clown, the relationship between country clowns and devils, and also explores clowns as a fusion of the misrule tradition with Jack-a-Lents from popular culture. As Preiss explains, 'Jack-a-Lents were originally effigies at which children threw stones during Lent, a pastime derived from a Shrovetide custom called throwing-at-cocks, in which a tethered rooster was pelted to death' (p. 67). Preiss's third chapter is the first of three case-study chapters. This chapter in particular examines how the Elizabethan stage clown Richard Tarlton 'was strategically converted into an author-figure for a book trade in anonymous popular literature' and how this literature would retroactively 'render Tarlton anonymous' and thus 'expose theatre, like print, as a domain of reproduction rather than production' (p. 110). Chapter 4 focuses on Kemp and his authorship of *Kemps Nine Daies Wonder* [1600] in order to consider the implications his leaving his playing company had for his career and reputation. In his final chapter, the scholar discusses Robert Armin the clown and author, who replaced Kemp as one of the Lord Chamberlain's men. In particular, Preiss examines *Quips Upon Questions* [1600] and makes the argument that it 'pretends to be a theatrical document' but 'collapses into schizophrenic monologue when its constituent voices are represented unintelligibly' (p. 178). Overall, Preiss's *Clowning and Authorship in Early Modern Theatre* is a fascinating and persuasive study of the Elizabethan stage clown.

Passionate Playgoing in Early Modern England, by Allison Hobgood, takes a fascinating look at the emotional experiences and implications of witnessing performances of early modern drama. As Hobgood herself points out, 'few scholars have examined early modern playgoing from the perspective of playgoers themselves' (p. 2), making this research a valuable and insightful contribution to this neglected area of scholarly attention. In her first of five chapters, the author turns her attention to Shakespeare's *Macbeth* in consideration of what she calls the 'mysterious legacy of fear' (p. 34) surrounding the tragedy. In particular she explores how the play confirms Renaissance playgoing 'as a dangerous endeavour that conjured contagiously sickening passions in spectators by employing their knowledge of, as early modern medical philosophies defined it, fear as bodily disease' (p. 35). Thomas Kyd's *Spanish Tragedy* is the focus of chapter 2, which examines the 'emotional afterlives' of ghosts in the play. More specifically, in this chapter Hobgood argues that 'In their constant presence either on the stage proper or in the gallery above, Andrea and Revenge are essential meta-narrative markers of an audience's emotional participation in the ensuing performance' (p. 66). In chapter 3, 'Hazarding Homeopathy in *A Woman Killed with Kindness*', the scholar explores Heywood's domestic tragedy 'as pragmatically staging for early modern spectators illicit and wayward passions as well as the dire consequences of indulgent humoral appetites and failed emotional regulation' (p. 98). Returning to Shakespeare in chapter 4, Hobgood considers *Twelfth Night* and how Malvolio's shame 'is in fact highly contingent upon an audience's emotional collaboration' (p. 129), and presents the interesting argument that *Twelfth Night* 'grappled most keenly with the humiliating dilemma of bodily exposure as it was cultivated cruelly in and by spectators' (p. 129). In the final chapter of the book, which is entitled 'Jonson and the Pleasure Problem', the scholar addresses how Jonson's plays are 'acutely attuned to the reciprocal exchange of feeling in theatre and, more importantly, to the possibility of its failure or, at the very least, its risky unpredictability' (p. 160). In conclusion, *Passionate Playgoing in Early Modern England* is an important and engaging examination of the emotional experience of playgoing in the early modern period.

Moving on to articles published in journals in 2014, Lucy Munro's 'Actors, Plays and Performances in the Indoor Playhouses, 1625–42: Boy Players, Leading Men and the Caroline Ensemble' (*YES* 44[2014] 51–68) effectively explores the repertories of the Caroline indoor playhouses. Munro begins her essay with actor Ezekiel Fenn from Beeston's Boys as he took on his first performance of an adult, rather than a juvenile, male. More specifically, through a textual analysis of the actor's first lines in this role, the scholar raises the question of how the audience would have perceived the masculinity projected by Fenn. In posing such a question, Munro turns her attention to the performances of the indoor playhouses between 1625 and 1642, with a particular focus on 'the impact that company structure and actors' careers had on the shape and content of the repertory' (p. 52). Munro uses evidence such as prologues and epilogues that were tailored around specific actors and their stages of masculinity in support of her claims. Overall, Munro provides critical insight into aspects of dramaturgy that may have been distinctive to theatres such as the Blackfriars, the Cockpit, and the Salisbury Court, as well as their resident companies.

Paul Whitfield White's article, 'The Admiral's Men, Shakespeare, and the Lost Arthurian Plays of Elizabethan England' (*Arth* 24:iv[2014] 33–47), discusses five lost plays mentioned by the diarist Philip Henslowe that relate to King Arthur and the Knights of the Round Table, which, the scholar observes, have never been discussed together. White begins with a discussion of 'Arthurianism' in the Shakespearian drama of this period and the general importance of King Arthur to Tudor royal propaganda. As he turns his attention to the plays, he notes that 'Reconstructing the plots and characters of plays with missing scripts is a daunting and speculate enterprise' (p. 35). However, White makes clever use of evidence in order to get closer to these lost plays: in speculating that the Admiral's men's *The History of Chinon* was based on Christopher Middleton's prose romance, he uses the full title of this work in consideration of the potential narrative of the play. The scholar also discusses (where possible) records of performance, including the dates and number of times the play *Vortiger* was put on. Overall, this is an enjoyable and illuminating article about early modern Arthurian drama.

'Reputation and the Red Bull Theatre, 1625–42' (*YES* 44[2014] 29–50), by Rory Loughnane, is an essay that challenges the idea that the Red Bull theatre was the least reputable of the Jacobean and Caroline theatres in London—an opinion which, as Loughnane points out, 'held sway for much of the twentieth century' (p. 30). Loughnane offers a fresh consideration of the Red Bull theatre, overcoming entrenched scholarly views in an objective examination of the evidence for activities at the Red Bull, ranging from the accession of Charles I up until the closure of the theatres. In particular, he focuses on historical incidents at the Red Bull such as the influence of Nathaniel Tyndale's crime of matricide in 1624 on Ford and Webster's lost play, *A Late*

Murther of the Sonn upon the Mother. The play distastefully exploited this local scandal even down to its marketing, and was licensed 'only days after the prosecution and conviction ha[d] occurred' (p. 33). Whilst this led to a lawsuit against the dramatists, Loughnane points out that 'the Red Bull was not the only theatre that showcased plays exploiting local scandals' (p. 34). This is a thought-provoking essay that highlights a theatre that is worthy of greater study.

Kate Aughterson's 'The Courtesan and the Bed: Successful Tricking in Middleton's *A Mad World, my Masters*' (*MLR* 109:ii[2014] 333–56) poses the question, 'How can a consideration of the play's use of space, the stage property of beds, and femininity enable ways of interpreting both the discourses surrounding theatricality in the play and the courtesan herself?' (p. 334). In this endeavour, the scholar uses a close analysis of Middleton's drama in order to suggest how sexualized, unmarried women are portrayed as the 'source of modern degeneracy', but how, ultimately, binary perceptions of women as either virgins or whores are the catalyst of Folly-wit's 'comic downfall' (p. 352). Overall, in Aughterson's fluent, detailed, and engaging essay, she effectively demonstrates how the bed in Jacobean comedy is a 'rich resource for debating the intersections of gender, identity, and theatricality in early modern drama' (p. 356).

In her article on 'The English Reception of Oldenbarnevelt's Fall' (*HLQ* 77:ii[2014] 157–76), Kimberly J. Hackett examines 'the ways in which the execution of Dutch statesman John van Oldenbarnevelt in 1619 was understood and represented by contemporaries in England' (p. 157), focusing on Philip Massinger and John Fletcher's play *The Tragedy of John van Olden Barnavelt*. In particular, Hackett explores how the events and tension in the Netherlands at this time were represented by the dramatists through classical analogy, thus highlighting the function of the *Tragedy* in what she describes as the 'polarizing political context of late Jacobean England' (p. 157). After a discussion of the historical context of the play in addition to how this was represented in England, the author examines the political commentary evident in readings of Fletcher's play, and also assesses its admonitory function. Hackett's intelligent understanding of *Olden Barnavelt* allows her to show how the voices of the playwrights can be heard 'among others commenting on the same events' (p. 175), suggesting that the play 'asked the audience to look beyond the propaganda' (p. 176).

Gabriel Egan's article on 'The Closure of the Theatres' (*YES* 44[2014] 103–19; also reviewed in Section 2) provides an illuminating reconsideration of the implications of the theatres' closure for Caroline society, as well as for individuals within the theatre industry. First, Egan considers previous coverage of this subject, before he turns to the question of the Civil War and what it meant at the time. Defining his approach, the scholar outlines that 'To take a view on just why the theatres were closed in 1642 requires taking a view on what social function they had served in the preceding decades' (p. 106), and he also explores the impact of the closures on the plays of a number of dramatists. In conclusion, Egan raises a number of interesting questions in this insightful article.

Also on the Civil War, Christopher Matusiak's essay 'Elizabeth Beeston, Sir Lewis Kirke, and the Cockpit's Management during the English Civil Wars' (*MRDE* 27[2014] 161–91) engages with the targeting of the Cockpit in Drury Lane with vigorous confrontation, and asks to what extent 'resistance' in this theatre 'might have distinguished its reputation from those of London's other wartime venues' (p. 162). Starting with Mrs Beeston's playhouse, the author asserts that, 'Had the widow Beeston found commercial theatre distasteful, we can expect her to have liquidated her assets, but instead she retained the Cockpit's lease until its expiration in 1656' (p. 164). Matusiak looks to previous unexamined records of Christopher Beeston's entrepreneurship and 'defiance of the wine drawing ban' (p. 166) and the Cockpit's financial difficulties, raising questions about the implications of business affairs with 'people beyond the theatrical pale' (p. 167). Matusiak also examines Sir Lewis Kirke's involvement with Mrs Beeston and her theatre, which leads to Kirke's ownership of the Cockpit. Kirke's royalist sympathies are also a focus of this essay, which concludes with further questions for study, including whether ideology was 'a factor in William Beeston's negotiations with the Sackvilles and Sir Kenelm Digby to keep the Salisbury Court theatre open after 1649' (p. 182).

In the same publication, Frank Ardolino's essay ' "Author and Actor in This Tragedy": The Influence of Apuleius's *The Golden Ass* on Kyd's *The Spanish Tragedy*' (*MRDE* 27[2014] 110–31) provides insight into Kyd and his use of the 'classical tradition' that, as Ardolino points out himself, has not been previously discussed (p. 110). In this stimulating article, Ardolino argues that 'Kyd is more indebted to the Apuleian tradition of multiple audience perspectives, hermeneutic detection motifs, and the revelation of secrets through initiation into the underworld mysteries of Proserpine/Isis' than has been acknowledged thus far (p. 110). This claim not only has important implications for how we look at Kyd's work but, in turn, for the influence of Kyd upon Elizabethan and Jacobean drama. Ardolino's essay culminates in his argument that the influence of Apuleius on Kyd's work provides further proof that *The Spanish Tragedy* is 'a revenge tragedy with a political-religious subtext' (p. 127).

Finally, 'How To Make Love to the Moon: Intimacy and Erotic Distance in John Lyly's *Endymion*', by Gillian Knoll (*SQ* 65:ii[2014] 164–79), discusses the erotic distance—and its potential implications—involved in loving the moon, and argues that 'Endymion finds fulfillment in what by the end of the play develops into a shared erotic relation with Cynthia' (p. 166). Using a close textual analysis of *Endymion*, Knoll's engaging and fluid article culminates in her conclusion that 'Desire for something infinite and immense, for someone perfect and unattainable, can only ever take the form of imaginative pleasure', and that 'Lyly's *Endymion* insists that this pleasure is profoundly erotic' (p. 179).

(b) Marlowe

The year 2014 saw a slight decrease in the critical output on Marlowe compared to the preceding year. To some extent, the published material also presents a familiar picture: *Doctor Faustus* remains very much the critical focus, while the other plays and the poetry receive varying degrees of attention. However, other, quite interesting, tendencies can also be traced. The author of last year's *YWES* review of Marlowe studies, Chloe Preedy, noted that *Edward II* was a 'surprisingly rare presence in critical discussion' (*YWES 94[2015]* 463). The welcome news from such a perspective is that a significant number of studies were published on this play in 2014, focusing mostly on aspects of politics and gender. Apart from a series of book chapters and journal articles on *Edward II*, a new version of a student edition was released and an issue of *Shakespeare Bulletin* (*ShakB* 32:iii[2014]) was themed 'Derek Jarman and "the Renaissance"' and featured three articles on Jarman's 1991 adaptation of Marlowe's play. Among important themes in Marlowe criticism, Christian and Islamic religious contexts continue to be vital areas of research, with substantial contributions on *Tamburlaine* and *Doctor Faustus*. By contrast Marlowe's poetry received less attention, with the notable exception of M.L. Stapleton's *Marlowe's Ovid: The Elegies in the Marlowe Canon*, the only book-length study to focus on Marlowe exclusively in 2014. Similarly, critical attention to *The Jew of Malta* was relatively limited, with one article discussing the influence on the play of medieval mystery plays, and part of a book chapter that places *The Jew* within the context of foreign politics. *Dido Queene of Carthage* receives treatment in whole, or parts of, articles, while the Ramus scene of *The Massacre at Paris* was subject to wide-ranging contextualization in one essay.

As usual, *Doctor Faustus* was well represented this year, and criticism on the play can be said to continue exploring two well-known critical paths, or intersections between them: on the one hand the aesthetic and literary contexts, and on the other hand how religion and theology inform the play. A distinct example of the first category is Bryan Lowrance's 'Marlowe's Wit: Power, Language, and the Literary in *Tamburlaine* and *Doctor Faustus*' (*MP* 111:iv[2014] 711–33), which charts the concept of 'wit' and how it informs Marlowe's plays. Lowrance's argument is that Marlowe's plays reflect the central meaning of wit (and its closest Latin equivalent, *ingenium*) as the capacity of imagination and linguistic skill to transform into actuality. Wit becomes the process in which Tamburlaine's rhetoric attempts to materialize into an earthly crown and Faustus's intellectual aspiration strives towards material wealth. At the same time, in Marlowe's plays this process is a source of dissatisfaction, even alienation, Lowrance argues, drawing on Freud's discussion of the latter concept. Lowrance's reading locates this alienation in the historical circumstances of Marlowe's own life, but also in the emerging sense of literature as an autonomous discourse in the sixteenth century. Lowrance's study thus places wit in the context of both biography and the Elizabethan system of education, and stresses the extent to which rhetorical and poetic skill were essential for the humanist *vita activa*. Persuasively, Lowrance charts a conflict here between lofty educational ideals and actual employment situation; as is well known, authors like Marlowe became authors precisely because they could not get the positions they were educated for. To Lowrance, Marlowe's understanding of wit arises out of this conflict. While Lowrance's actual readings of *Tamburlaine* and *Doctor Faustus* could have engaged more with existing criticism on closely related topics such as eloquence and aspiration, they also show that wit—both as an actual term and as a practice—is a crucial aspect of the plays. Lowrance justly argues that wit 'emerges as fundamentally ambivalent' (p. 719), but perhaps neglects the full extent of that ambivalence in the humanist understanding of the term; for example, Roger Ascham's distinction between 'hard' and 'quick' wits in *The Scholemaster* [1570] is a case in point which could have shed more light on his argument. Although it is no news that Renaissance rhetoric informed Marlowe's plays, Lowrance's focus on wit together with its anchoring in the specific biographical and educational circumstances of Marlowe's career opens up an extremely rich array of contexts for the plays themselves.

The other tendency—the focus on the theological context of *Doctor Faustus*—is exemplified by James Ross Macdonald's 'Calvinist Theology and "Country Divinity" in Marlowe's *Doctor Faustus*' (*MP* 111:iv[2014] 821–44). This article takes on the role of the devils in the play and claims that they represent diverse or even conflicting religious allegiances. While the A-text of the play has been considered theologically divergent from the B-text in committing itself more obviously to a Calvinist cause, Macdonald sees the A-text as embodying theological contradictions within itself. Particularly, to Macdonald the play veers between staging a devil enclosed by the all-embracing nature of Calvinist providence and the more actively malignant devil represented in Elizabethan popular culture. In setting up this argument, Macdonald's article engages with a vast critical field; the research on the theological and specifically Calvinist implications of *Doctor Faustus* is of course extensive and has even seen an upsurge in the last couple of years, with several publications from 2012 onwards (some of which have been reviewed in previous issues of *YWES*). However, Macdonald shows a solid grasp of this discussion, and the theological contextualization is a particular strength of his analysis, as could be expected from an article on this topic. Of course, the very nature of Macdonald's argument raises the question whether early modern drama was ever theologically 'pure' in its representation of infernal powers. At the same time, his discussion modifies the critical debate on a number of significant points, most notably in his productive insistence on the play (rather than its different textual versions) as a diverse and multidimensional staging of religious beliefs.

A further discussion of the theological aspects of *Doctor Faustus* is in David K. Anderson's *Martyrs and Players in Early Modern England: Religion and Violence on Stage*, which features a chapter (pp. 152–82) that was partly published in 'The Theater of the Damned: Religion and the Audience in the Tragedy of Christopher Marlowe' (*TSLL* 54:i[2012] 79–109; previously reviewed in *YWES* 93[2014] 464). The revised version adds a wider contextual sweep in placing *Doctor Faustus* in a discourse on despair and theology that draws on material such as Thomas Cranmer's biography as well the account of his death in Foxe's *Acts and Monuments*. The argument, however, remains focused on theological tensions and how Marlowe's hero makes impossible an unequivocal condemnation of him by the audience.

The intellectual and theological contexts of *Doctor Faustus*, as well as the later reception history of Marlowe outside English-speaking countries, are the focus of Roy Eriksen's short article 'Carducci Reads Marlowe: Dante and *Doctor Faustus* (B-Text)' (*CahiersE* 85:i[2014] 57–66). His article calls attention to the Italian Nobel laureate Giousé Carducci, who, Eriksen suggests, was the first to connect Marlowe with Dante's *Divina Commedia*, in the *Elegia* XXXII, published in 1882. Such a connection is warranted since links between *Inferno* and *Doctor Faustus* can be found in terms of tone and atmosphere, but also, Eriksen suggests, in more specific parallels between Cantos XVII–XIX and the winged dragon—altered from the *Faustbook*'s flying horse—that Faustus and Mephistopheles ride upon to Rome. Eriksen looks into the theological implications of this intertextual relation, specifically the criticism of the papacy in the *Inferno* and the humiliation of the Pope in *Faustus*. While religion and intertext are clearly at the focus of Eriksen's analysis, his article can in effect be said to suggest two areas of interest: Marlowe's possible use of *Divina Commedia* in *Doctor Faustus* and the way in which Marlowe was construed in nineteenth-century European culture. Although Eriksen's article does not entirely reconcile these two aspects, it provides very rich material for further discussion and research into both.

Another, equally original, take on the issue of religious orthodoxy and intertextual relations in *Doctor Faustus* can be found in Pauline Ruberry-Blanc's chapter '*The Witch of Edmonton*: The Witch Next Door or Faustian Anti-Heroine' (in Hillman and Ruberry-Blanc, eds., *Female Transgression in Early Modern Britain: Literary and Historical Explorations*, pp. 51–70). While Ruberry-Blanc's main interest is focused on her reading of Dekker, Ford, and Rowley's play, she suggests that Elizabeth Sawyer's claims to status register echoes of Faustian aspiration. Beyond the general and obvious parallels between the plays with respect to witchcraft, Ruberry-Blanc detects more specific similarities, for example in their treatment of the association between dogs and devils (such as the character Dog in *The Witch*), and claims that the parallels may have been specifically selected because they would have resonated with audiences that knew *Doctor Faustus*. She also teases out a number of intertextual connections between Marlowe's play, the *Faustbook*, and Greene's *Friar Bacon and Friar Bungay*. Her account, in other words, exemplifies a focus on the intersection of religious and literary contexts, which is—from quite another perspective—reflected in Eriksen's article as well.

More specific discussions of religious aspects continue to inform criticism on *Tamburlaine*, notably in Joel Slotkin's ' "Seeke out another Godhead": Religious Epistemology and Representations of Islam in *Tamburlaine*' (*MP* 111:iii[2014] 408–36). Slotkin locates his argument in the extensive debate on religion, especially in Part 2 of *Tamburlaine*, where the protagonist of course burns the Qur'an. Previous criticism has tended to see the scene as evidence of religious orthodoxy or subversive contempt for religion—with a biographical dimension present in both—and the representation of Islam as primarily a figuration of the political and economic issues in the period. Slotkin's essay attempts to trace Marlowe's play back to the theological context, with *2 Tamburlaine* dramatizing the search for religious knowledge amidst the pervasive religious schisms of Marlowe's time. Specifically two forms of religious scepticism are traceable in *Tamburlaine*, according to Slotkin: the 'Machiavellian', which implies that religion is a form of manipulation, and the 'Pyrrhonic', which instead encourages religious enquiry. Discussing Tamburlaine's own religious inconsistency as an example of such enquiry, Slotkin contends that Marlowe's play 'explores the implications of different forms of belief' (p. 415). Even Muslim belief is not presented in a uniformly negative light, since the play, for example, appears to depict the loss of faith more as a sign of abjection than as an example to follow. Slotkin draws on a wide array of characters in the play, such as Orcanes in Part 1, to support his claim that it dramatizes the quest for religious knowledge, but also sees the protagonist as less one-sided in his intolerance than previous criticism has acknowledged. As Slotkin contends, both Orcanes and Tamburlaine seem to express yearning for 'another Godhead' and hint at the availability of a more transcendent deity. While it remains an open question whether religious tolerance can ever be a significant dimension of Marlowe's play, Slotkin's essay challenges a number of received notions of Islam and Christianity in *Tamburlaine* and thus represents a welcome continuation of critical discussions that are likely to remain high on the agenda for a quite some time.

This year's most significant study on *The Massacre at Paris* is John Guillory's 'Marlowe, Ramus, and the Reformation of Philosophy' (*ELH* 81:iii[2014] 693–732), which focuses on the brief sequence in Marlowe's play where Ramus, the 'Kings Professor of Logick' appears. This is clearly a scene that invites the type of reading Guillory submits, since it stops up the stage action in favour of a surprisingly detailed academic quarrel. Guillory largely eschews the implication of religious overtones (a point frequently made by previous criticism), since the scene itself never refers to theology—'Ramus's Protestant beliefs do not figure in the scene at all' (p. 696), and Marlowe's account focuses entirely on Ramus's attachment to philosophy. Instead Guillory, while acknowledging the virulently anti-Catholic tendency of the play, sets *The Massacre* in the context of contemporary academic debate in and outside Cambridge during Marlowe's time. Gabriel Harvey's Ramist connections are obviously well known, but Guillory introduces a series of debates that have been little discussed in the context of Marlowe's play, such as that involving William Gough, an arts student known to have been 'infatuated' with Ramist doctrine. In this light, the debate in *The Massacre* becomes not so much an expression of religious conflict as 'the sublimated violence of the social form of disputation itself' (p. 703). For Guillory, moreover, *The Massacre* enacts a tendency found in all of Marlowe's plays, a tendency towards 'the pose of philosophical detachment' (p. 710), a 'negation' with an acknowledged relation to the 'will to absolute play' that Stephen Greenblatt once detected in Marlowe. It is the Ramist method, more than any specific religious implication, that sparks off the debate in *The Massacre* and the academic context on which the play draws. Guillory's extensive context-ualization can make the connection to Marlowe's play somewhat thin at times, but as a discussion of the intellectual conditions that shaped early modern Europe, Marlowe's Cambridge, and to some extent *The Massacre*, his article as a whole is quite thought-provoking and full of insights.

Another form of context is suggested by Catherine Willits's 'The Dynamics and Staging of Community in Medieval "Entry into Jerusalem" Plays: Dramatic Resources Influencing Marlowe's *Jew of Malta*' (*MRDE* 27[2014]

78–110). Willits initially suggests that *Tamburlaine* and *Doctor Faustus*, unlike *The Jew of Malta*, have received due attention to their medieval dramatic influences, a claim that perhaps overstates the case somewhat since the medieval aspects of *The Jew of Malta* were subject to extensive treatment in David Bevington's *From 'Mankind' to Marlowe* as early as 1962. That said, her study focuses on a more specific genre, the mystery play, and argues that *The Jew of Malta* draws on the sense of community established in the York, Chester, and N-town entry plays, although Marlowe's play also engages with these texts 'in order to destabilize further the concept of a coherent community' (p. 78). Her contention is that all the three entry plays depict community as irreconcilably heterogeneous, a notion that *The Jew of Malta* draws upon and emphasizes. Willits can be said to make a familiar observation on Marlowe's play—that it depicts a heterogeneous, indeed crumbling, society—but places it within the different context of medieval drama. At the same time, that very heterogeneity opens up the possibility of seeing Barabas, the quintessential outsider, as a paradoxically central figure in a community based on vice and greed. The difference from the mystery plays, according to Willits, is that Marlowe 'forces his audience to see the unsettling ineffaceability of the marginal' (p. 109). Willits's argument rests upon the idea that 'community' as represented in Marlowe's play can be specifically traced back to a medieval literary genre, and although she shows that that genre continued to be influential into the seventeenth century, it is ultimately hard to prove a specific line of influence *on The Jew of Malta*. Despite this, her article is a notable contribution to an area—that of Marlowe and medieval drama—that merits further scholarly work.

Another, much shorter, discussion of *Jew of Malta* can be found in Eric Griffin's 'Shakespeare, Marlowe, and the Stranger Crisis of the Early 1590s' (in Espinosa and Ruiter, eds., *Shakespeare and Immigration*, pp. 13–36) which locates Marlowe's play together with a number of Shakespearian plays in the context of Elizabethan attitudes towards strangers. Griffin uses the pamphlet *A Fig for the Spaniard or Spanish Spirits*, which was sanctioned by the government, as an example of the official propaganda that was spread during the early years of the 1590s, and observes that several Shakespearian plays, which were apparently written during these years, tap into the general atmosphere of social unrest at the time. The Marlovian interest of Griffin's article is in its suggestion that *The Jew of Malta* can be located in the context of the attitudes towards strangers as represented in the Dutch Church Libel and *The Book of Sir Thomas More*, and that Marlowe drew on the general propagandist sentiment in his play. This contextualization is relevant even if Griffin's article features little direct engagement with the text of *The Jew of Malta*.

As for criticism on *Dido Queen of Carthage*, Sheldon Brammall's ' "Sound this angrie message in thine eares": Sympathy and the Translations of the *Aeneid* in Marlowe's *Dido Queene of Carthage*' (*RES* 65[2014] 383–402) discusses the specific textual relationship between Marlowe's play and its principal source. In engaging with previous critical work on the Virgilian connections of *Dido*, Brammall takes the position that Marlowe's play is significant not because it departs from Virgil (a point frequently made) but because it is so close to it, indeed translates directly from it. At the same time, Marlowe avoids incorporating epic elements such as the chorus into his play—according to Brammall a distinct innovation compared to the five previous Continental and English Dido plays he cites. Brammall does not consider theatrical practices as a possible reason for this absence in Marlowe's play but emphasizes the way in which the lack of sympathetic chorus voices creates a discrepancy between, on the one hand, the absence of a unifying commenting voice and, on the other, the presence of Virgilian authority in the form of direct translations. In Brammall's reading, Marlowe's 'stark moments of translation' (p. 402) in the end create an even more poignant presentation than Virgil's of the heroes' thwarted desires. Brammall's distinction between free writing and direct translation is perhaps somewhat too sharp, in the light of the extensive scholarly work that has been done on Renaissance imitation (a concept not much dealt with in his article). But as an exploration of an original critical position and as a rich investigation into the Virgilian context of Marlowe's play, his article has strong merits.

An emphasis on material more than aesthetic conditions informs Chloe Preedy's '(De)Valuing the Crown in *Tamburlaine*, *Dido Queen of Carthage*, and *Edward II*' (*SEL* 54:ii[2014] 259–77), which takes as its starting-point the double meaning of 'crown' in early modern England: the royal diadem and the coin. Claiming basically that the royal diadem is rewritten as a marketable commodity in three Marlovian plays, Preedy's article engages with early modern conceptions of kingship, notably—and justly—the well-known notion of the king's two bodies. While Preedy's close readings of the plays are focused and well founded, they also open up a wide-ranging discussion of early modern monarchy. In *Tamburlaine*, the notion of divine sanction through the crown is questioned, it being hinted instead that 'brute force' (p. 263) is a decisive factor, and Preedy explores a wider context of early modern scepticism on authority through divine right. Dido similarly jeopardizes assumptions about divinely endorsed rule by her strenuous effort to secure the presence of Aeneas in Carthage, and Edward II appears to have the most fully developed sense of the crown as a mere token that could be exchanged at will—in this reading, the king brings the sacred nature of kingship in question and opens up for his barons to take over the crown. Thus, Preedy's Marlowe 'encourage[s] readers and spectators to recognize and question the spiritual concepts of divine-right monarchy that underpin the realities of secular authority, without necessarily condemning their presence' (p. 275), and there is more than a hint of the Machiavellian hero in her contention that 'True power, in Marlowe's drama, belongs to the protagonists who can unflinchingly accept that divine-right rule may be an illusion yet nonetheless exploit the premise to complement their use of secular force' (p. 275). Perhaps the general economic context of Preedy's analysis could have been more consistently explored, especially the Marxist implications of concepts like the oft-repeated 'commodity', although its wide-ranging exploration of the political philosophy at stake in Marlowe's plays represents a most welcome contribution to the field.

As stated, 2014 saw a number of other publications with relevance to *Edward II*. Apart from several critical articles, a revised New Mermaids edition of *Edward II* was published (edited by Martin Wiggins and Robert

Lindsey) with a new introduction by Stephen Guy-Bray (pp. vii–xxviii). *Edward II* is arguably the play by Marlowe that is in most need of such updating, given for example the critical turn towards aspects of sexual politics in the 1990s and onward. Appropriately, Guy-Bray's account is focused on the aspect of sodomy but also on how sodomy shapes the politics and audience sympathies of the play. To Guy-Bray, much subversive potential of Marlowe's play lies in its representation of the monarch not as necessarily 'weak' but as a king who eschews war yet comes across as sympathetic for that very reason. In addition, a short but useful discussion on 'Marlovian aspects' (pp. xxiii–xxvi) considers how *Edward II* relates stylistically and thematically to other plays in the Marlowe canon.

The autumn 2014 issue of *Shakespeare Bulletin* had a focus on Derek Jarman, with three articles on his film version of *Edward II* and the separately published *Queer Edward II* (both from 1991). While Jarman's works certainly have been the topic of numerous academic analyses, the articles have a relevance to Marlowe scholars since they also engage with the theoretical frameworks that have influenced criticism on the play. In ' "To the future": Derek Jarman's *Edward II* in the Archive' (*ShakB* 32:iii[2014] 429–50) Pascale Aebischer usefully traces a textual history, that of the history and development of Jarman's screenplay, from Jarman's first encounter with *Edward II* in a student edition in the 1960s to the rewrites that took place during the shooting of the film. Apart from suggesting the complex political agenda that informed Jarman's work with the film, Aebischer's well-documented account is also of interest because it shows how Jarman gradually distanced himself from his initial close adherence to Marlowe's play and rearranged it into a more episodic structure; in that sense, it raises issues as regards playtext versus contemporary performance. Alexandra Parsons's 'History, Activism, and the Queer Child in Derek Jarman's *Queer Edward II* (1991)' (*ShakB* 32:iii[2014] 413–28) instead focuses on *Queer Edward II*, the text that was published alongside the release of the film. Parsons locates this work in the broad political and theoretical context that informed Jarman's work, noting for example that the *Queer Edward II* was a largely collaborative project and engaged with the text on the level of, for example, physical appearance. Jarman's use of Marlowe, Parsons argues, makes *Queer Edward II* an 'activist text' that stresses 'the continuity of same-sex desire across time' (p. 421). For Jarman, 'intercourse has never occurred in private' and Parsons's discussion elucidates how the personal and the political intermingle in the agenda of *Queer Edward II*. Lee Benjamin Huttner's 'Body Positive: The Vibrant Present of Derek Jarman's *Edward II* (1991)' (*ShakB* 32:iii[2014] 393–412) picks up on the issue of temporal relations and claims that the obvious 'anachronicity' of Jarman's film has less to do with the insertion of contemporary phenomena into a Renaissance play than with its insistence on the present as shaped by the past—and the identification of the body as the site of this conflict. In Huttner's theoretically well-informed account, 'Jarman excavates history to locate scenes of oppression mirroring those of his own present' (p. 409), and the 'queer body positive' hence becomes 'unmoored' (p. 412) as an entity that exists not only in *one* time, but *over* time.

It is perhaps a testimonial to the degree of interest taken in *Edward II* that no fewer than two essays on this play focused in various ways on stage directions. Thomas P. Anderson's 'Surpassing the King's Two Bodies: The Politics of Staging the Royal Effigy in Marlowe's *Edward II*' (*ShakB* 32:iv[2014] 585–611) returns to a well-known theme in criticism on the play: its connection to early modern political theory and monarchic rule. While showing clear awareness of this scholarly context, Anderson looks into aspects of royal funeral ritual and suggests that the hearse that may have been represented on stage would also have had a royal effigy on top. This image of the king, Anderson argues, becomes a 'prosthetic' body that not only represents but renders hollow the idea of royal absolutism. His analysis draws on actual historical circumstances and dramatic practice during Marlowe's time and also considers (as the title suggests) the influential discussion stemming from Kantorowicz's classic *The King's Two Bodies*. In connection with later revisions of Kantorowicz, Anderson contends that the final moments of *Edward II* represent a 'hybrid form of authority' (p. 599) reflecting both the sacred nature of kingship and the idea of the republican commonwealth. In that context the effigy, which according to Anderson could have been embodied by an actor, disrupts the continuity between sovereign and political body. The very theatrical staging of the work, in other words, renders the notion of absolutism problematic. An inevitable problem with this analysis is that it requires considerable speculation as to actual staging, since the play as we have it does not say anything about an effigy (although later editors certainly have had opinions as to the presence of a royal hearse, and the dialogue of the play makes reference to a hearse, at least prior to the final scene). Moreover, audience reception is a dimension that receives relatively scant attention in the essay. Yet Anderson's focus on a specific instance of visual ritual allows for a wide-ranging discussion that encompasses both political context and theatrical practice and creates a productive dialogue between them.

Christopher Shirley's concisely entitled 'Sodomy and Stage Directions in *Edward II*' (*SEL* 54:ii[2014] 279–96) engages with another assumption behind much criticism: the suggestion that Edward is executed by a red-hot spit thrust up his anus, despite the fact that there is no stage direction that says so. In Shirley's argument, it is precisely by omitting this stage direction that the play undercuts the category of 'sodomy' and produces a critique of the legal categorization of Edward and Gaveston as 'sodomites'. Acknowledging both the source for the scene in Holinshed's *Chronicles* (which of course describes the use of the spit in some detail) and the various solutions suggested by modern editors, Shirley claims to identify two tendencies in approaching the sodomy of Marlowe's play: either a buried homophobia that reads the play's supposed misogyny in the light of Marlowe's biography, or a 'salvific' (p. 282) reading that charts a pro-sodomy agenda in Edward and Gaveston's relationship. Shirley's somewhat surprising move is to go back to Alan Bray's classic *Homosexuality in Shakespeare's England* [1982] to emphasize that the indeterminacy of Edward's death as represented in the play also mirrors a general indeterminacy of sodomy as a category. Likewise, the play sets up a sense of indeterminacy of interpretation, reflected not only in the ambiguity of the stage direction but in the entire narrative arc of the play. To Shirley, the play allows for differing generic interpretations, encompassing a 'political history of tyranny' in addition to 'an erotic tragedy of sodomy' (p. 289), depending on the knowledge the audience would have had of either pattern. The printed version's refusal to provide clear knowledge as to Edward's manner of death lays bare the audience's attempt to make sense of the action, thus ultimately revealing sodomy as an indistinct and futile category. Shirley's essay has a strong argumentative thrust even as it tends to pull in different directions; for example, the references to critical bibliography in the first section of the essay remain a relatively underexplored track in the analysis itself. At the same time, by his engagement with established criticism, Shirley shows that the familiar debate on gender, sexuality, and sodomy in Marlowe's play is still capable of taking new and provocative turns.

The final chapter of Ralf Hertel's *Staging England in the Elizabethan History Play* places *Edward II* at the end of a series of readings that consider the role of theatre in shaping political awareness. Hertel's initial suggestion—that criticism has mostly claimed *Edward II* to be about an individual rather than about politics—is somewhat surprising, given the proliferation of contemporary scholarly work from perspectives that parallel his own (needless to say, the many readings that focus on Edward and Gaveston's homoerotic relationship do so because they see a political dimension in it). Hertel's account locates much of the politics of the play in the flaunting of homoeroticism and insists that it is precisely in the public, political sphere that Edward's sodomy becomes problematic, as it parades the lack of unity between king and country, between the bodies of the realm. While part of Hertel's analysis tends to rehearse familiar aspects of criticism on the play, it adds a welcome degree of complexity in its observation that the intermingling of sexuality and politics in the play also has consequences on the level of genre: tragedy and history play are merged (p. 218). Moreover, Hertel traces a series of absences that taken together can be said to represent the overall political core of *Edward II*: the transference of politics from religion and morals to a purely man-made affair '*is* precisely the political message of Marlowe's play' (p. 220). Similar to divine providence, the idea of the nation as 'common weal' is also notably gone from *Edward II*. Gender roles are, furthermore, inverted, with an effeminate king and a manly queen overlapping in their attempts to gain power over the kingdoms. If this bleak drama, then, is 'about' national identity, it rather makes the absence of unifying powers visible. In Hertel's reading, Marlowe's play generates a desire for community and (masculine) stability precisely through its non-representation of such values.

Two more general readings of the Marlowe canon focus on aspects of liminality. Lisa Hopkins's *Renaissance Drama on the Edge* justly assigns an important role to Marlovian drama in her analysis of the preoccupation with borders, both physical and mental, in the theatre. Hopkins emphasizes Marlowe's significance as a playwright unusually fascinated with walls and fortifications, and while this observation is largely familiar in itself, Hopkins teases out a wealth of implications suggesting that physical walls can be a sign of vulnerability as much as a token of safety. But 'edges' also imply borders other than walls, and Hopkins devotes a specific chapter to the aspect of sexuality and borders, with a focus on *Hero and Leander* and its exploration of a liminal territory between Asia and Europe, male and female, human and divine. Similar boundaries are explored—and subverted—in *Edward II*, which of course makes explicit use of *Hero and Leander*, but also in *The Massacre at Paris*, with its troubled staging of porous national and sexual borders. Hopkins's book offers relatively brief but persuasive close readings and locates the theme of boundaries firmly in the wider context of Elizabethan drama, including Shakespeare.

If 'boundaries' can be said to be a familiar theme in Marlowe criticism, related aspects like 'entrapment' and 'enclosure' are no less so. Especially from studies like Marjorie Garber's seminal 1977 essay, ' "Infinite riches in a little room": Closure and Enclosure in Marlowe', it has been a critical common-place to examine how Marlowe's plays explore issues of spatial and temporal liminality. The latest contribution to this critical focus is Julián Jiménez Heffernan's 'Impasse in Marlovian Drama: A Badiou Perspective' (*CompLit* 66:i[2014] 71–94), which prefers another term than the above mentioned ones but builds upon previous theorizations of Marlovian drama. Heffernan's use of Alain Badiou aims to shed light on the peculiar nature of subjectivity in Marlowe's 'splendidly nasty plays' (p. 92): the refusal to comply with exactly the metaphysics of the subject that Heffernan traces in an array of previous readings by, for example, Stephen Greenblatt, Jonathan Dollimore, and Alan Sinfield. In Heffernan's account, Badiou's pessimism about the existence of communal identity is reflected in the 'impasse of clashing disloyalties and the deadlock of overlapping truth-domains' (p. 92) represented by Marlovian drama. While the metacritical and theory-laden discussion of Heffernan's article can almost be said to produce a critical impasse in itself, his readings of Marlowe's plays justly emphasize the political work they do—and their elusiveness to well-meaning categories like 'community' and 'identity'.

Finally, and as stated, it is reassuring to note that the most extensive contribution to Marlowe studies during 2014 dealt not only with expected texts such as *Faustus* or *Tamburlaine* but with Marlowe's poetry, particularly his translations. M.L. Stapleton's *Marlowe's Ovid: The Elegies in the Marlowe Canon* grows out of a long-standing interest in the reception and transform-ation of the *Amores*, as witnessed by his previous *Harmful Eloquence: Ovid's 'Amores' from Antiquity to Shakespeare* (UMichP [1996]), which also discussed *Ovid's Elegies*. The importance of Ovid to Marlowe and his career is a well-trodden path in criticism since the 1990s, with Patrick Cheney's *Marlowe's Counterfeit Profession: Ovid, Spenser, Counter-Nationhood* (UTorP [1997]) as a seminal work. Stapleton is obviously well aware of this context and a substantial part of his introductory discussion is spent in defining his position vis-à-vis Cheney's. What Stapleton suggests is a more moderate claim assuming a less specific order of composition of Marlowe's works than Cheney's. At the same time, a basic tenet underlying Stapleton's discussion is that *Ovid's Elegies* were 'apprentice or student work' that 'functioned as preparation for a career in the theater writing speeches and creating characters' (p. 28). In scrutinizing all of Marlowe's plays as well as *Hero and Leander*, Stapleton considers a series of significant intellectual and aesthetic contexts, such as Erasmian humanist pedagogy and the relation of

Marlowe's translation to the genre of the sonnet sequence. Also notable is Stapleton's comparative examination of the two early editions of Marlowe's translations, *All Ovids Elegies* and the selection found in *Epigrammes and Elegies*. While the comprehensive treatment of Ovid and the specificity of the focus inevitably make for stronger and more persuasive material in some of the chapters, Stapleton's study is a rich contribution to the field that justly stresses Ovid's importance to Marlowe in terms of style and dramatic craftsmanship. In its scope and refreshing focus it also represents, to this reviewer, a most appropriate end to this year's survey of critical work on Marlowe.

(c) Jonson

Critical attention was divided fairly evenly this year across the range of genres in which Jonson wrote, although, as ever, plays and masques proved somewhat more popular subjects of study than poetry. *Epicœne* featured particularly prominently, forming a key part of discussions around both early modern economic thought and conceptions of gender. These issues were further discussed in the context of other plays, including *The Alchemist*, *Bartholomew Fair*, and *The Staple of News*. Questions of interdisciplinarity in the study of the masques received considerable attention, as did Jonson's classical learning, and several essays began to build on the scholarship of the recent Cambridge edition of Jonson's works.

The familiar pairing of Jonson with Shakespeare also surfaced this year, a reminder that Jonson is still sometimes defined not by who he was, but rather by who he was not. *Shakespeare Quarterly* and *Shakespeare Bulletin* both produced special issues under the title 'Not Shakespeare', and both acknowledged the shadow cast by Shakespeare over scholarship on his contemporaries. Both journals sought to interrogate the relationship between Shakespeare and Jonson (among others). *Shakespeare Quarterly* attempted a reversal of the S/~S relationship through essays in which, as Lars Engle, 'Introduction to "Not Shakespeare"' (*SQ* 65:ii[2014] 105–8), notes 'Shakespeare forms the background for the study of other English Renaissance dramatists' (p. 107); whilst *Shakespeare Bulletin* provided at least one essay that used the power dynamic inherent in S/~S as a way in to thinking about the creation of Shakespeare's status in modern media.

In ' "You have no voice!"': Constructing Reputation through Contemporaries in the Shakespeare Biopic' (*SB* 31:i[2014] 11–26), Peter Kirwan examines the presentation of Shakespeare's contemporaries in Roland Emmerich's *Anonymous* and John Madden's *Shakespeare in Love*, as a means of understanding how Shakespeare's reputation is constructed and maintained in contemporary culture. His reading of Ben Jonson, Christopher Marlowe, Thomas Dekker, Thomas Nash, and John Webster, as performed over the two films, is of writers 'used deliberately and systematically to lay the foundations for treatments of Shakespeare as exceptional' (p. 12). Within this group, however, Kirwan draws a distinction: Dekker, Nashe, and Webster become 'fanboy' caricatures for comparison with the 'Romantic genius established for Shakespeare'; Jonson, on the other hand, along with Marlowe, functions in a more sophisticated manner, serving 'to question the nature of memorialization, recognition and connoisseurship in preference to unquestioning fandom' (p. 7). In *Anonymous*, Jonson is still subordinated to Shakespeare (or de Vere) in predictable ways—his play set up as light entertainment against a montage of rapt audiences at spectacular Shakespeare productions—but unlike Dekker and Nashe, who are presented with limited critical faculties, Jonson is positioned as a writer sought out for his appreciative critical thinking. Shakespeare's writing must be read through the lens of Jonson's approval, and so in Kirwan's reading, 'not-Shakespeare' and 'Shakespeare' are indubitably linked: the latter is unable to exist in its modern idealized incarnation without the former, and Jonson comes to serve, in the film, as one of 'the best guides we have to an understanding of Shakespeare's worth' (p. 22).

Bradley D. Ryner is one of several scholars to discuss the intersection of Jonson's writings with early modern ideas of economics. In *Performing Economic Thought: English Drama and Mercantile Writing, 1600–1642* (also discussed in Section 3(a)), he uses the playwright as a case study to demonstrate 'how economic thought during this period was "performed" in the double sense of how it was represented and how it was actually done' (p. 1). Ryner maps 'the representational techniques available to playwrights' onto those available to mercantile writers from the same period and suggests the interpretative freedom available to theatrical writers such as Jonson allowed for 'a more nuanced exploration of economic systems' (p. 1) than mercantile writers could achieve. In the fifth chapter of this book, which elsewhere considers writers such as Philip Massinger, Thomas Middleton, William Shakespeare, and Thomas Heywood, Jonson's writing is paired with that of English customs official Thomas Milles as a means of exploring whether abstract representation was a viable technique for discussions of economic reality in early modern England. Comparing Milles's mercantile treatises with Jonson's *The Staple of News* [1626], Ryner notes the use of allegorical characters in both texts but reveals, through a detailed analysis, that the two casts function differently: in Milles's work, 'allegorical representations are crucial parts . . . that are meant to be credible depictions of systematic economic activity', whereas Jonson's creations 'jarringly shift between appearing as heavy-handed allegories and as quasi-realist characters' (p. 134). Ryner concludes by arguing that Jonson's play highlights the limits of abstraction and allegory as methods of representing the economy, and that this is just one work among several that can establish the early modern English playhouse 'as an extra-cranial technology that afforded diverse ways of conceptualising economic activity' (p. 1).

Chloe Preedy's 'Performance and the "Holy Purse": Ben Jonson's Attack on Puritan Values' (*RenD* 42:ii[2014] 217–42) seeks to reframe the use of contractual and economic imagery in Jonson's plays, moving beyond existing readings of its use as a response to the commercialization of the public theatres, and suggesting instead that Jonson appropriates economic metaphors from contemporary Puritan preaching in order to assert 'the linguistic and performative ascendancy of his theatre by demonstrating its superior ability to generate material and metaphysical profit' (p. 220). Preedy's essay sets out the perceived rivalry between preaching and theatrical performance during the period in which Jonson was writing, and shows how Jonson distinguishes between his own 'entertaining fictions' and 'hypocritical Puritan posturing' by attacking the fictional Puritans of his plays on economic grounds (p. 220). In *The Alchemist* and *Bartholomew Fair*, Puritan characters accumulate wealth but, as the essay demonstrates, the wealth is withheld from circulation, thus encouraging economic stagnation. Preedy contrasts these Puritans with the plays' highly theatrical tricksters, who oppose stagnation by operating a lucrative, speculative, and constantly revolving credit model. The central reading of the essay focuses on the increasingly blurred boundary between material and spiritual profit in Jacobean England, and the idea that Jonson is comparing the respective 'profit' of the religious and theatrical communities in order to expose the threat posed by 'the aggressive separatists values' attributed to Puritanism. Ultimately, Preedy argues, *The Alchemist* and *Bartholomew Fair* demonstrate the value of the theatrical world by 'breaking through separatist boundaries and forcing their Puritan characters back into mainstream commercial, spiritual, and social interaction' (p. 242).

Mark Webster Hall's ' "I am no man, ladies": *Epicene*, Market Forces, and Gender-Occlusion' (*BJJ* 21:i[2014] 17–37) is also concerned with the representation of economic systems in Jonson's work. In this essay, Webster Hall pushes against recent readings of *Epicœne* as a 'plague text' that harks back to London's better times and encourages its characters to occupy the market spaces of the city. Instead, he maps out the staging of movement away from these spaces, and argues that the play 'consistently dramatizes habits of nonconsumption' (p. 17). The author sketches out the physical spaces of the markets in London against the economic landscape of the period, demonstrating how the play foregrounds the economic elements of each character whilst refusing to occupy the literal spaces of financial exchange. The 'patterns of market-avoidance' (p. 21) that Webster Hall identifies in the play are illustrated through detailed analysis of three parties: Morose, the Collegiate ladies, and Dauphine. The essay unites all three under the umbrella of an economic anti-sociability of sorts. The characters are variously engaged with retreat: Morose from city life, the Collegiate ladies from feudal responsibilities in the country, and Dauphine from speech itself 'until speech is deemed profitable' (p. 23). Webster Hall brings the characters further together by reading their attempts to withdraw from the market through the lens of gender. Neither the Collegiate ladies nor Morose and Dauphine fulfil the expectations of gender with regard to their economic involvement in society, and this places their gender status in doubt. As such, the author argues, the characters work 'away from the market and they thereby express the characteristics of both sexes, or (if you will) of neither' (p. 28). Ending with a reading of Epicœne herself, Webster Hall concludes that subjects in the play 'are between one market and another, and this betweenness has dramatic effects on (among other things) their performance of gender' (p. 32).

Valerie Billing's 'Female Spectators and the Erotics of the Diminutive in *Epicœne* and *The Knight of the Burning Pestle*' (*RenD* 42:i[2014] 1–28) demonstrates a similar concern for the instability of gender politics and dynamics as represented in *Epicœne*. Looking at figures within the play and in the early modern audience, Billing considers the way in which small male actors in boy companies of players might be figured as 'diminutive erotic objects' (p. 2) that would appeal to women both on- and off-stage. This is an essay interested in female spectatorship in the early seventeenth century, 'in the politics of women's desire' in a play dominated by a battle of the sexes, and, in particular, in how this desire can 'destabilise both gender order and the supposed teleological force of heterosexuality' (p. 2). Billing's interpretation of the diminutive is not restricted to the 'materially small' but also considers 'how low social rank or economic status might work with physically small stature to enhance the desirability of the diminutive' (p. 5). Her reading therefore shows how women can demonstrate mastery of adult male characters through their diminutive boy proxies. The essay redefines women as subjects rather than objects of desire, and suggests that Lady Haughty of the Collegiate ladies in *Epicæne* need not simply be read through the attitudes of other characters, who see her physical domination of Clerimont's Boy as monstrous. Rather we can think of how she might be 'experienced differently by a female spectator whose desires are aroused by her display of dominance, and who might appreciate this erotic dominance for her own uses outside the theatre' (p. 11).

In 'Jonson's "Italian Riddle": *Epicene* and the Translation of Aretino's Female Speech' (*SQ* 21:ii[2014] 264–80), Andrew S. Keener considers *Epicæne* as a play centrally concerned with 'the early modern period's capacious sense of the word "translation"' (p. 121). He builds on scholarship concerning the influence on educated playwrights of Latin texts from the Renaissance schoolroom, as well as suggestions that Jonson's play owes something to Pietro Aretino's comedy *Il Marescalco*, to argue that 'the erotic discourse of the female Collegiates' can be read as 'another Jonsonian engagement with Aretino' (p. 123). The essay seeks to complicate our understanding of Jonson's sources for *Epicæne*, suggesting that the playwright drew not only on the Italian plot of *Il Marescalco* but also on 'the promiscuous female discourse of the *Ragionamenti*' by Aretino (p. 132). Keener paints Jonson as the translator of Aretino's work (the performance and printing of which was forbidden on the European continent), and the English stage as the unique space for public consumption of this translation. However, as the essay demonstrates, Jonson attempted to mute the Italian provenance of plot and character: he 'obscures and regulates the play's "femall" translation . . . of Aretino's dialogues' and the fact 'that critics and editors have not recognised Aretine echoes in the Collegiates' gossip is a testament to the success of Jonson's effort' (p. 137).

Masques received considerable attention in journal articles this year, with two focusing on the broad spectrum of Jonson's writings in this genre. In 'Archival Principles, Performative Flowerings, and Counterpoint in Ben Jonson's Masques' (*BJJ* 21:i[2014] 38–52), Clarissa Castaneda advocates an interdisciplinary approach to the study of masques, that takes into account 'history, architecture, and design principles, archival practice, anthropology, and music theory [which] each offer their own distinct, refracted lens to the scope of Jonsonian literary analysis' (p. 40). Asserting that Jonson's masques prefigure the collaborative networks that emerged in the creation of opera, and that Jonson's networks of 'professional actors, musicians, choreographers, dancers, artisans' (p. 41), and others are acknowledged in the printed versions of his masques, Castaneda argues that the 'contextual counterpoint between the performed masque and the printed masque' (p. 46) is just one instance of counterpoint in Jonson's masques (others being visual counterpoint via the antemasque and masque contrast, and literary counterpoint through symbolism employed by Jonson). She also suggests that the musical theory of counterpoint can provide a 'vocabulary and method for the interpretation of multivalent symbolism in Jonson masques' (p. 39).

In 'The Language of Looking: Making Senses Speak in Jonsonian Masque' (*RenD* 42:i[2014] 29–55), Amy Rogers displays a similar concern with both textual and theatrical incarnations of the masque form. Her essay interrogates the masque's role 'in articulating and shaping the ways in which seventeenth-century England imagined . . . and represented spectatorship', whilst also tracing 'the developing tendency to represent sight and hearing as separate, even oppositional interpretive activities' (p. 32). She suggests that 'the visual turn' in seventeenth-century entertainment culture—the privileging of the eye over the ear—was not caused by the masque's spectacularity, but actually came first through discourse. By setting out the idea of a 'synesthetic mode' (that is to say, a mode of multiple senses with no inherent division), which was used by writers to describe the ineffable or overwhelming, Rogers is able to map the masque form against this background, and suggest that later masques begin to steer away from this mode and start to distinguish between sights and sounds: 'as playwrights began to conceive of their work as having two potential incarnations (theatrical and textual) they also imagined writing for two different audiences: playgoers and readers' (p. 33). The recurring theme of Jonson's desire for control appears in this essay, as Rogers argues that Jonson tries to create a clearly organized and delineated representation of the senses in his printed masques. The essay suggests that, while his earlier writings in the genre embraced the fluid lines between senses 'to depict experiential excess and linguistic insufficiency', his later masques betray a view of 'language's moments of inarticulateness as something to be feared rather than celebrated' (pp. 39–40). These later works can therefore be read as Jonson's attempt to control the diverse energies of the performed masque and interpret them through a text that feels holistic, rather than diverse.

Moving from the general to the particular, Hannah Smith-Drelich focuses on a single masque in 'Dining at the Devil's Table: Ben Jonson and the Case of Fiendish Indigestion' (*BJJ* 21:ii[2014] 264–80). She proposes a reading of *The Gypsies Metamorphosed* that builds on existing theories that the masque was 'slyly subversive' (p. 264) to George Villiers, the duke of Buckingham, and, in turn, King James, thus challenging the idea of this masque as a conventional entertainment designed to praise royal powers. The essay highlights the historical context of the masque's first performance, detailing Buckingham's reputation at the time as a nepotistic and socially ambitious 'bedchamber favourite' seeking to become 'something more akin to a political favourite' (p. 267). The author's exploration of the masque focuses on 'The Ballad of Cock Lorel', a song that occurs during the 'miraculous transformation' found in masques of the period and functions as 'an anti-masque full of devils, gluttony, and foul wind' (p. 265). Smith-Drelich details the staging of the masque, suggesting that Buckingham's entry onto the stage at the moment when the devil's case of indigestion culminates in an act of flatulence characterizes Buckingham as 'both the hero of the masque and the subsequent product of the Devil's fart' (p. 271). This representation is read against social and political ideas of the period, including the idea that flatulence at the Stuart court could have been received as an expression of defiance, which in this setting could serve as a metaphor for 'the gluttony and excesses of a court and king who were not properly nourishing the body politic' or 'Jonson's opinion of Buckingham, whose greed and anality were polluting the whole of the isle' (pp. 273–4). Smith-Drelich ends the essay by offering a discussion of gypsies as a specifically Scottish problem during the period, and ultimately suggesting that *The Gypsies Metamorphosed* can be read as a comment 'on James's inability to reconcile cultural differences among his subjects' (p. 275), thus transforming the tone of the masque from praise to satire.

Jonson's desire for editorial control emerges for discussion in Francis X. Connor's *Literary Folios and Ideas of the Book in Early Modern England*, which examines the emergence of the literary folio as a distinct and significant format in the 1590s. Eschewing the idea that the folio was simply a practical format for presenting works of great length, Connor uses a series of case studies, ranging from Sidney's *Arcadia*s in the 1590s to the 1647 edition of Beaumont and Fletcher's *Comedies and Tragedies*, to demonstrate that folios' requirements of 'more materials, planning, cost than other formats, [and] sometimes greater risk for publishers' meant that they 'needed to justify themselves as innovative, special books' (p. 13) that showcased bibliographical experimentation. Jonson's *Workes*, published in folio in 1616, sits chronologically at the centre of this study, serving to illustrate the transition from the idea of the book 'as a fundamentally collaborative object that would be expanded, emended and changed by hands other than the author' (p. 14), to a complete work in a finished book. For Connor, Jonson's attempt to present a definitive edition of his work demonstrates the way in which the folio format could be used as a relatively new space to try out various addresses to readers as literary judges and consumers. The chapter reads Jonson in opposition to the practices of English literary culture in the early seventeenth century, which rendered books as cheap and transient objects. His 1616 folio is figured as a key item in the evolving idea of the book during this period, but also as one ultimately undermined, both by the rise of cheap printed ephemera in the decades that followed the *Workes*, and by the ideas of later editors, who believed that publication was not an end in and of itself.

Brian Vickers takes in a spread of both poetry and plays in 'Ben Jonson's Classicism Revisited' (*BJJ* 21:ii[2014] 153–202). The essay, which won this year's Beverly Rogers Literary Award for best essay in the *Ben Jonson Journal*, reflects on Jonson's classical learning and the ways in which it was used, in works from *Poetaster* and *Sejanus* to *Epigrams*, *The Forest*, and *Underwood*. Using the new Cambridge edition of Jonson's works as a backdrop for his argument, Vickers ponders the extent to which Jonson intended his allusions to classical texts to be noticed by his readers. The annotations provided by the new Cambridge editors identify Jonson's extensive use of Greek and Latin sources as models for his own works, and yet without these, Vickers argues, most readers would never notice his borrowings and allusions, such was the way in which they were integrated into the 'verbal fabric' of his writing

(p. 171). These integrations, however, were not universally successful, and the second part of the essay pays particular attention to 'discordant piece[s] of *imitatio*' (p. 173). The majority of the issues arise in his plays, perhaps unsurprisingly, as Vickers argues, since dramatic texts require that borrowed excerpts 'fit the criterion of decorum, fulfilling the expectation that this is what a character in such a situation would say'. Jonson's failure to digest and adapt excerpts is much less frequent 'in the much smaller realm of poetry, since the poet is free to construct a context to match his models' (p. 175). On those rare occasions where Jonson fails to properly integrate his borrowings, it is suggested that he may have fallen foul of the notebook culture fostered by humanist scholars of the period, which encouraged readers to gather notes from their readings in notebooks, often organized under thematic headings. The danger of this practice, according to Vickers, is that 'once an excerpt has been copied out [and] sorted under the appropriate *locus communis*, it loses any relationship to its context', and so Jonson ends up, on occasion, using inappropriate models for his writing (p. 175).

The New Mermaid catalogue of classic plays this year includes *Ben Jonson: Four Plays*, which brings together four of Jonson's most popular and widely studied works in a new anthology edited by Robert Watson (also discussed in Section 1). Focusing on the city comedies for which Jonson is best known today, the volume comprises the most recent single-play versions from the catalogue: Watson's own edition of *Volpone*, Roger Holdsworth's edition of *Epicœne*, Elizabeth Cook's edition of *The Alchemist*, and Alexander Leggatt and G.R. Hibbard's edition of *Bartholomew Fair*. Pitched as an ideal edition for study and classroom use, it includes the series' customary in-depth introductions, further-reading lists, and on-page commentary notes. A few very minor corrections have been made to the individual editions, but otherwise the collection maintains 'the different approaches and emphases of each New Mermaid editor' (p. vi). Watson's major contribution lies in his new introduction, which provides an exploration of the early modern theatrical, cultural, and political contexts vital for understanding a set of 'brilliantly local' plays, 'grounded in the specifics of [Jonson's] time and place' (p. xi). It also promotes study beyond a single text, reaching across the plays to draw out shared characteristics, most importantly 'the rare and wonderful quality' each play has in 'making an audience think not just in between but actually through its laughter' (p. xi).

Finally, the entries in *Notes and Queries* offer a number of subtle interventions in the field this year. Adrian Blamires, in 'Ben Jonson's Additions to *The Spanish Tragedy* as the Subject of Ridicule' (*N&Q* 61[2014] 265–8), argues not only that *The First Part of Hieronimo* can be read as a direct response to the Admiral's men's revival of *The Spanish Tragedy* in the early 1600s, but also that possible digs about Jonson and Edward Alleyn in the play function as textual 'clues' that Jonson fulfilled the task he was paid for in 1601–2 of writing 'new adicyons' for *The Spanish Tragedy*. Hugh Roberts reveals 'Previously Unnoticed Annotations to Jonson's Copy of Rabelais' (*N&Q* 61[2014] 270–3), some of which suggest a continued engagement with the volume by successive early modern readers, while others, if they are taken to be in Jonson's hand, discredit the hypothesis that he stopped deciphering

Œuvres half-way through the first book. Yaoping Zhang, in '*To be a saver in...* and *To save oneself in...* in Ben Jonson' (*N&Q* 61:ii[2014] 268–70), unpicks Herford and Simpson's commentaries on the word 'saver' in IV.i.20 of *Volpone* and III.iii.29 of *Epicæne*, using an eighteenth-century description of 'the theatrical phrase, I never *saved* myself' to reinterpret lines from both these two plays and from *Cynthia's Revels*.

Books Reviewed

Aebischer, Pascale. *Screening Early Modern Drama Beyond Shakespeare.* CUP. [2013] pp. v + 274. £65 ISBN 9 7811 0702 4939.

Anderson, David K. *Martyrs and Players in Early Modern England: Tragedy, Religion and Violence on Stage.* Ashgate. [2014] pp. 252. £65 ISBN 9 7814 7242 8288.

Bazilet, Ariane M. *Blood and Home in Early Modern Drama: Domestic Identity on the Renaissance Stage.* Routledge. [2014] pp. xii + 197. $140 ISBN 0 4157 2065 6.

Connor, Francis X. *Literary Folios and Ideas of the Book in Early Modern England.* PalMac. [2014] pp. x + 236. £60 ISBN 9 7811 3743 8348

Curran, John E. *Character and the Individual Personality in English Renaissance Drama: Tragedy, History, Tragicomedy.* UDelP. [2014] pp. xxiii + 333. $95 ISBN 1 6114 9504 0.

Daalder, Joost, ed., with contributions by Brett D. Hirsch. *The Honest Whore, Part 1.* Digital Renaissance Editions. http://digitalrenaissance.uvic.ca/ Library/Texts/1HW/.

Daalder, Joost, ed., with contributions by Brett D. Hirsch. *The Honest Whore, Part 2.* Digital Renaissance Editions. http://digitalrenaissance.uvic.ca/ Library/Texts/2HW/.

Espinosa, Ruben, and David Ruiter, eds. *Shakespeare and Immigration.* Ashgate. [2014] pp. 228. £95. ISBN 9 7814 0941 1000.

Gibbons, Brian, ed. *The Duchess of Malfi,* by John Webster. New Mermaids. Bloomsbury. [2014] pp. xxvii + 160. £7.99 ISBN 1 4725 2065 3.

Gurr, Andrew, and Farah Karim-Cooper, eds. *Moving Shakespeare Indoors: Performance and Repertoire in the Jacobean Playhouse.* CUP. [2014] pp. v + 284. £65 ISBN 9 7811 0704 0632.

Hertel, Ralf. *Staging England in the Elizabethan History Play: Performing National Identity.* Ashgate. [2014] pp. 282. £95 ISBN 9 7814 7242 0497.

Hillman, Richard, and Pauline Ruberry-Blanc, eds. *Female Transgression in Early Modern Britain: Literary and Historical Explorations.* Ashgate. [2014] pp. 236. £65 ISBN 9 7814 7241 0450.

Hirschfeld, Heather. *The End of Satisfaction: Drama and Repentance in the Age of Shakespeare.* CornUP. [2014]. pp. xi + 239. $55 ISBN 0 8014 5274 0.

Hobgood, Allison. *Passionate Playgoing in Early Modern England.* CUP. [2014] pp. vii + 236. £65 ISBN 9 7811 0704 1288.

Hopkins, Lisa. *Renaissance Drama on the Edge.* Ashgate. [2014] pp. 200. £65 ISBN 9 7814 0943 8199.

Jenkins, Jacqueline, and Julie Sanders, eds. *Editing, Performance, Texts: New Practices in Medieval and Early Modern Drama*. PalMac. [2014] pp. xv + 241. £50 ISBN 1 1373 2010 9.

Johnson, Sarah E. *Staging Women and the Soul-Body Dynamic in Early Modern England*. Ashgate. [2014] pp. 185. £60 ISBN 1 4724 1122 6.

Keenan, Siobhan. *Acting Companies and Their Plays in Shakespeare's London*. Bloomsbury. [2014] pp. 272. £19 ISBN 9 7814 0814 6637.

Neill, Michael, ed. *The Spanish Tragedy*, by Kyd Thomas. Norton Critical Editions. Norton. [2014] pp. xl + 289. £7.95 ISBN 9 7803 9393 4007.

Preiss, Richard. *Clowning and Authorship in Early Modern Theatre*. CUP. [2014] pp. x + 287. £60 ISBN 1 1070 3657 7.

Ryner, Bradley D. *Performing Economic Thought: English Drama and Mercantile Writing, 1600–1642*. EdinUP. [2014] pp. xi + 217. £70 ISBN 0 7486 8465 4.

Sanders, Julie. *The Cambridge Introduction to Early Modern Drama, 1576–1642*. CUP. [2014] pp. vii + 261. £19 ISBN 9 7811 0701 3568.

Smith, Emma, introd. *Women on the Early Modern Stage: A Woman Killed with Kindness; The Tamer Tamed; The Duchess of Malfi; The Witch of Edmonton*. New Mermaids. Bloomsbury. [2014] pp. xxiii + 561. £12.99 ISBN 9 7814 0818 2314.

Stanev, Hristomir A. *Sensory Experience and the Metropolis on the Jacobean Stage*. Ashgate. [2014] pp. x + 213. £60 ISBN 1 4724 2445 X.

Stapleton, M.L. *Marlowe's Ovid: The Elegies in the Marlowe Canon*. Ashgate. [2014] pp. 226. £95 ISBN 9 7814 7242 4945.

Steenbrugge, Charlotte. *Staging Vice: A Study of Dramatic Traditions in Medieval and Sixteenth-Century England and the Low Countries*. Rodopi. [2014] pp. 264. ?56 ($75) ISBN 9 0420 3845 4.

Stern, Tiffany, ed. *A Jovial Crew*, by Richard Brome. Arden Early Modern Drama. Bloomsbury. [2014] pp. xvi + 310. £12.99 ISBN 9 7819 0427 1772.

Watson, Robert N., ed. *Ben Jonson: Four Plays*. New Mermaids. Bloomsbury. [2014] pp. xxvi + 744 . £12.99. ISBN 9 7814 0817 9628.

Wiggins, Martin, and Catherine Richardson. *British Drama 1533–1642: A Catalogue, vol. 4: 1598–1602*. OUP. [2014] pp. viii + 474. £100 ISBN 9 7801 9926 5749.

Wiggins, Martin, ed. *Edward II*. Text edited by Robert Lindsey, revised by Stephen Guy-Bray. New Mermaids. Bloomsbury. [2014] pp. xxiv + 168. £8.99 ISBN 9 7814 7252 0524.

IX

The Earlier Seventeenth Century

AMRITESH SINGH, JOHN R. BURTON, AND
WILLIAM BAKER

This chapter has five sections: 1. Women's Writing; 2. General; 3. Bacon, 4. Browne; 5. Burton. Section 1 is by Amritesh Singh; section 2 is by John R. Burton; sections 3, 4, and 5 are by William Baker.

1. Women's Writing

The most significant studies in seventeenth-century women's writing from 2014 focused on contemporary writing practices and sought to contextualize them within broader literary practices and to examine their effect on immediate socio-political realities. In studying the apologies for her unpolished style that prefaced Margaret Cavendish's published writings, Tina Skouen's article, 'Margaret Cavendish and the Stigma of Haste' (*SIP* 111[2014] 547–70), contributes to the critical discourse that examines the effect of humanist pedagogy on women. Skouen complicates routine understandings of Cavendish as a woman in print by foregrounding an additional 'stigma' that, through Cavendish's numerous, self-reflexive professions, became a distinctive feature of her writings: a hasty and impetuous process of writing that disregarded humanist instruction on writing as a product of careful study and deliberation. Skouen detects a strategic purpose in Cavendish's familiar apologies for the drawbacks of her writing process and argues that Cavendish was attempting to create a new authorial style that ran counter to the established one pursued, amongst others, most notably by Ben Jonson. Skouen illustrates how Cavendish 'constantly draws attention to and even "celebrates" the restless and unregulated movements of her fancy, as if her lack of philosophical method were her biggest strength rather than her weakness' (p. 551). The method-in-madness dictum is appealingly exercised in Skouen's argument and yields, if not always logically, rhetorically convincing readings. While Skouen draws upon the theories propounded by Erasmus, Bacon, and Jonson on practising poesy and traces their classical antecedents as found in Horace to highlight the inventive and ludic quality to Cavendish, her brief engagement with Shakespeare's writing practices reveals that Cavendish

The Year's Work in English Studies, Volume 95 (2016) © *The Author 2016. Published by Oxford University Press on behalf of the English Association. All rights reserved.*
For Permissions, please email: journals.permissions@oup.com
doi:10.1093/ywes/maw005

was not alone in subscribing to a 'hasty' writing process and that it cannot be sufficiently regarded as 'a method of self-distinction' (p. 562). Equally, the extent to which classical humanist traditions and rules held sway in the mid-seventeenth century (which witnessed the proliferation of Cavendish's work) is debatable. Jonson, Skouen's chief point of comparison with Cavendish, was not universally heralded as a pattern for emulation and the laborious pace of his writings, which were characterized by a stilted, classical style, was subject to as much ridicule as reverence. Skouen's argument could be more profitably reorientated to realize how Cavendish was part of a community of writers that was dismissing the final vestiges of an earlier mode of composition than to emphasize her singularity.

John Garrison's *Friendship and Queer Theory in the Renaissance: Gender and Sexuality in Early Modern England* urges a reconsideration of the centrality of the 'couple' as a core unit of sociality. Garrison suggests 'a new approach to assessing early modern social arrangements in order not only to avoid privileging dyadic heterosexuality as normative, but more importantly to ask readers to rethink the model of dyadic sociality itself' (p. xiii). Garrison's argument focuses on moments in early modern texts that stretch the intimacy typically reserved within paired relationships—sexual and/or social—to groups of individuals. Anchored in queer theory, Garrison's analysis attempts to demonstrate 'not only that male and female writers imagined modes of same-sex reproduction but also that their offspring went beyond the textual to include ideas, economic projects, and same-sex households'. Within this broader premise, the semantic capaciousness of the term 'queer' and its plural applications allow Garrison to draw out striking readings from a juxtaposition of Lanyer's *Salve Deus Rex Judaeorum* [1611] with Shakespeare's sonnets [1609]. The chapter on Lanyer and Shakespeare focuses primarily on the economic benefit to be derived from extending one's friendship network: to share amity with more than the one individual is, to extrapolate Montaigne's principles on friendship, to stake a claim on their assets as well. While initially in her volume of poems Lanyer creates multiple selves to assert unique dyadic intimacies with various personages, both living and dead, Garrison shows that she eventually collapses them within a syncretic authorial self to depart from the dyadic ideal and to give birth to a proliferating network of friends. Concurrently, an extension of the standard alliance between writing and paternity in the early modern period allows Garrison to present these multiple same-sex intimacies as offering a unique reproductive possibility that finds fruition in textual parthenogenesis. However, notwithstanding the fresh insight that the work offers into patronage and friendship networks in the early modern period and the manner in which women writers shaped and controlled them, there are moments when the argument takes precedence over textual authority, resulting in wilful misreading. For instance, the analysis of the line 'On your Deserts my Muses doe attend', hinges on reading the word 'deserts' as 'a geographical pun . . . [depicting] Cumberland as either occupying multiple locations or incorporating several locations within her' to portray 'an empty space, waiting to be populated with people or possibility' (p. 86). However, the word 'deserts' here signifies those traits in Cumberland (Lanyer's patroness) which merit a suitable reward that is delivered through the act of writing and reading Lanyer's encomium itself. Lanyer thus skilfully draws Cumberland into a mutual appreciation society that is built on ceaseless and reciprocal gift-giving: patronage and verse-making will be each other's reward. This is not only the obvious meaning here but also, when read in conjunction with cognate verses, likely to be the only one. Such occasional missteps aside, Garrison's theoretical framework that unites queer theory with New Historicism promises richer and riper readings in the ensuing years.

The year also witnessed the publication of *Challenging Orthodoxies: The Social and Cultural Worlds of Early Modern Women*, edited by Sigrun Haude and Melinda S. Zook, which, among its other virtues, foregrounds women's routine engagement with the gunpowder industry and legal and financial discourses. In shedding new light on the material world inhabited by early modern women and their (to us) startling encounters with it, this volume of essays lays new ground for studies in seventeenth-century women's writings.

2. General

As the 21-year-old King Charles II fled for his life after a crushing defeat of his Scottish army at Worcester in 1651, he entrusted the Lesser George medal, symbol of his royal leadership of the Order of the Garter, to one of his colonels, Thomas Blague. Hiding the symbol of royal leadership in a woodpile, Blague was arrested and sent to the Tower. It fell to local Staffordshire royalists to determine how to consign the medal to Blague in London. A calm disposition would be paramount if the medal were to make the journey under the noses of soldiers and guardsmen. For the task, a 58-year-old linen draper born in Stafford who had spent decades in London was chosen. He was unlikely to arouse suspicion, despite being loyal to the royalist cause. The man in question was Izaak Walton, and the fascinating episode of his spiriting the jewel as a secret royal agent appears in the introduction to the latest edition of his enormously successful *The Compleat Angler, or the Contemplative Man's Recreation*, here edited by Marjorie Swann. Almost continuously in print since its first appearance in 1653, the year Cromwell became Lord Protector, Walton's narrative of how a novice urbanite is schooled in the art of fishing is situated by Swann as a response to the question of how one should live in the wake of national conflict and the trauma of personal tragedy (Swann reminds us that the *Angler* was published in the years following the deaths of several of his children and Walton's first wife). The text is presented as a pastoral reflection on human survival, a literary anthology, an inclusive and generous attempt at social reconciliation, an environmental text that positions the natural world both as a reflection of the spiritual creations of God and as a site of wonder, surprise, and endless curious discovery; the stewardship of humankind. The view of nature is given particular attention in Swann's introduction. Walton's Piscator is shown at turns to be captivated by nature and also its captor. Stewardship, conservation, and husbandry do not go without reference to the prime violent ambition of Walton's angling: to kill both bait and fish. However, as Swann reminds us, it is the mutual appreciation of the nature and the simple leisure afforded by the natural environment in the text that forms a centre around which a new post-war social harmony formulates implicitly, gently, and organically. For this edition, Swann elected to use the final edition to appear in print before Walton's death, the 1676 fifth edition, which includes Charles Cotton's treatise on fly-fishing. Indeed, the relationship between Walton, 'the elderly linen-draper who fishes with minnows and maggots', and Cotton, 'the genteel fly-fisherman' (p. xxiv), is cited as a further instance of frontier-crossing solidarity. Since Jonquil Bevan's 1983 edition (reprinted in 1988), scholarly interest in early modern religious thought and practice has intensified, and Swann draws some attention to the apostolic fishermen referenced by Walton, with Douglas Bush's observation of the common etymology of 'angler' and 'Anglican' offering Swann a critical space in which to discuss canon law regarding sports, the fishing clergyman, and the role Walton plays in both the *Angler* and his biographies in forging a new Anglican religious identity. Following her introduction, a select bibliography is usefully divided into critical interests. Swann has also included a chronology of Walton and Cotton, ranging from Walton's birth in 1593 to Cotton's last publication a century later. Four maps of the north London and Derbyshire areas pertinent to the narrative are followed by a facsimile of the 1676 title page and the text itself, adorned with woodcut illustrations of fish, and, as with the Bevan edition, musical notation also appears in facsimile. Fifty pages of explanatory endnotes are followed by a useful glossary of angling terms of the period.

The influence of Italian literary culture upon the English press in the period is not disputed. In 2009 a bibliographical catalogue of Italian books printed in England between 1558 and 1603 appeared, and this year Soko Tomita and Masahiko Tomita have extended the range of the catalogue with *A Bibliographical Catalogue of Italian Books Printed in England 1603–1642*, which includes 187 Italian books which ran to a total of 335 editions. As with the earlier catalogue, each volume lists the author, translator, editor, publisher, printer, and dedicatee, allowing researchers to develop a wider understanding of the literary and publishing networks engaged in the work. Eight appendices follow the catalogue itself, complementing the work with further bibliographical information. Margaret Cavendish's religious views are explored in *God and Nature in the Thought of Margaret Cavendish*, a collection of essays edited by Brandie R. Siegfried and Lisa T. Sarasohn. In their introduction to the collection, the editors demonstrate the breadth of their critical approach by coming to Cavendish initially from the fringes of her works; the first of many fascinating examples of Cavendish's attitude towards religion comes from her reluctance to turn to a customary Christian piety as an apology for publishing as a woman, and from her letters, in which she explores with great intellectual vigour questions about anatomy, physiology, medicine, and natural philosophy, all within the context of a theological framework. Given the complexities involved in defining Cavendish's often ambiguous theological attitudes, the editors have wisely allowed for some disagreement between the contributing scholars, a facet of the volume that serves to demonstrate the liveliness of Cavendish studies.

While several scholars have argued that a variety of impediments render early modern culture an elusive realm to modern readers, Gregory Kneidel centres his attention upon one particular hurdle and one poem: thus far, he argues in his article 'Legal Evidence, Self-Betrayal, and the Case of John Donne's "The Perfume"' (*MP* 112:i[2014] 130–53), readers have denuded the poem of its connections to early modern legal culture. While there is a flourishing field of early modern legal and literary studies, much attention has thus far been focused on drama and romance, and Kneidel's insightful reading will no doubt open up the possibility of future efforts to further reclaim legal culture in literary studies of the period. Claire Jowitt posits that travel poetry of the 1630s was seen at the time as politically nuanced, a feature bolstered by adding an additional layer of imagery—that of the dream or dream vision—in two pieces of Caroline literature, Davenant's poem, 'Madagascar. A Poem Written to Prince Rupert', and Richard Brome's play *The Antipodes*, in her article '"To sleep, perchance to dream": The Politics of Travel in the 1630s' (*YES* 44[2014] 249–64). Both works, she argues, employ the dream as a critique of domestic politics. Another metaphor prevalent in early modern literature is the use of disease and curing disease in relation to religious conversion.

The result of a sustained study of conversion narratives in early modern Europe, funded by an AHRC grant, Helen Smith's 'Metaphor, Cure, and Conversion in Early Modern England' (*RenQ* 67:ii[2014] 473–502), engages with a variety of source material that serves to inform the metaphor and the language of spiritual sickness, which she argues is crucial to the development of the imagined sensation and the relations between bodily and spiritual experiences and feelings in the period. The article will no doubt serve to inform future critical enquiry in the field of religious poetics.

3. Bacon

The years 2013–14 were strong ones for studies of Bacon. Apart from Claire Preston's entry in Andrew Hadfield's comprehensive *Oxford Handbook of English Prose 1500–1640* (*YWES* 94[2015] 1274) and Daniel Derrin's *Rhetoric and the Familiar in Francis Bacon and John Donne* (*YWES* 94[2015] 510–11) mention should be made of Alan Stewart's interesting 'The Case for Bacon' (in Edmondson and Wells, eds., *Shakespeare Beyond Doubt: Evidence, Argument, Controversy*, pp. 16–28). The reasons why Chinese scholars are interested in Bacon may be seen in Xinzhong Yao's comparative analysis, 'Philosophy of Learning in Wang Yangming and Francis Bacon' (*Journal of Chinese Philosophy* 40:iii–iv[2013] 417–35). Wang Yangmin (1472–1529) was a Neo-Confucian philosopher, educationalist, and military general. Yao writes in his abstract that his 'article is a comparative study of the philosophical views on learning and learning methods elaborated by Wang Yangming and Francis Bacon. It argues that as different criteria for the advancement of learning Bacon's empirical learning and Wang's "learning of the heart-mind" represent two different philosophical orientations, and are responsible, at least partially, for laying down the basis for the parting ways of China and Europe at the dawn of the modern era.' Yao in his conclusion observes that 'an appreciation of the mutual complementarity rather than opposition between these two philosophical approaches will be a sign for the new and real advancement of learning' (p. 417). Issues concerning the translation of Bacon into Chinese, amongst others including Arthur Waley and unsurprisingly Ezra Pound, are raised in Zhiqin Wang's 'The Translator's Subjectivity in Literary Translation' (*Comparative Literature: E&W* 19:ii[2013] 96–11). A similar area is treated in Xiangjun Liu and Xiaohu Yang, 'Thematic Progression in English–Chinese Translation of Argumentative Classics: A Quantitative Study of Francis Bacon's "Of Studies" and its 11 Chinese Translations' (*Perspectives* 21:ii[2013] 272–88), which takes a linguistic and quantitative approach,. Two contributions focus on textual and editorial concerns. Karen E Attar gives a detailed and fascinating description in her 'The Cowell Manuscript or the First Baconian: MS294 at the University of London' (*ShS* 65[2013] 323–36). This is complemented by Dana F Sutton, ed. *Sir Francis Bacon, 'Serones Fideles sive Interiora Rerum' (printed 1638): A Hypertext Edition.* A different perspective on Bacon is revealed in Pavneet Aulakh's 'Seeing Things through "Sensible": Emblematic Similitudes and Sensuous Words in Francis Bacon's Natural Philosophy' (*ELH* 81[2014] 1149–72). Aulakh's concern is reflected in his abstract: 'Francis Bacon's views on language are often cited to evidence his break with the past.' Bacon's 'ambition, however, to "collect" a "*Rerum Copiam*" for "constructing true axioms" signals his effort to appropriate specific traditional rhetorical devises discussed, for example, in Erasmus's *De copia*. For instance, his use of fables, which he distilled into emblematic images, demonstrates an attempt to cultivate a hieroglyphic vocabulary capable of conveying "conceits intellectual" through "Images sensible." Moreover, in suggesting parallels that unite disparate disciplines, similitudes offered Bacon an instrument to discover the "*Rerum Copiam*" that constitute his *Philosophia Prima* and thereby advance his scientific project' (p. 1149). By '*Philosophia Prima*', Aulakh explains, Bacon refers to 'an "Originall or vniuersall Philosophie" which he describes as a "*Receptacle for all such profitable obseruations and Axioms, as fall not within the compasse of any of the speciall parts of Philosophie, or Sciences*"' in *The Advancement of Learning* (p. 1164). Guido Giglioni's 'From the Woods of Experience to the Open Fields of Metaphysics: Bacon's Notion of Silva' (*RS* 28:ii[2014] 242–61) argues that 'Bacon's well-known pronouncements on method should be read against the background of his recurrent pleas for a direct experiential involvement with nature' (p. 243). Giglioni concludes that 'the solipsistic and idealistic assumption that thinking activity can do without matter is very distant from Bacon's philosophy. However, while perfectly aware of the importance for a philosopher to be rhetorically savvy, Bacon shares with Plato the view that rhetoric cannot compete with philosophy when matters of truth and discovery are at stake' (p. 261). Allison Machlis Meyer's 'The Politics of Queenship in Francis Bacon's *The History of the Reign of King Henry VII* and John Ford's *Perkin Warbeck*' (*SP* 111:iii[2014] 313–45) demonstrates that 'John Ford's 1634 play *Perkin Warbeck* subtly responds to the view of queenship presented in its key narrative source, Francis Bacon's 1622 *The History of the Reign of King Henry VII*' (p. 313). The eminent Renaissance scholar Andrew Hiscock, in his ' "L'Immortel Chancelier d'Angleterre": Francis Bacon. Memory and Method / "L'Immortel Chancelier d'Angleterre": Francis Bacon, mémoire et méthode' (*Revue/Lisa* e-journal 12:v[2014]) is concerned with the status and functions of memory in the natural philosophy of Francis Bacon. The initial part of Hiscock's article 'reviews the intellectual legacies from antiquity and the medieval centuries which continued to shape learning at the close of the 16th century across Europe.' He then 'considers the ways in which Bacon evaluated the influence of Aristotelian thinking on the educational practices of his time'. An investigation of his writings dating from the first part of the seventeenth century reveals 'how Bacon saw the age's abiding fascination with memory as a significant obstacle to the progress of scientific thinking in Europe'. Hiscock concludes by examining 'how the role of writing (rather than that of memory) is foregrounded in Bacon's writing; and . . . briefly examines the reception of Bacon and his thinking in the 18th and 19th centuries' (http:// lisa.revues.org/6298). A most interesting contribution to Bacon studies is Travis DeCook's 'Francis Bacon's "Jewish Dreams": The Specter of the Millennium in *New Atlantis*' (*SP* 110:i[2013] 115–31). DeCook writes that 'Increasingly, attention is being given to the religious underpinnings of Francis Bacon's project to reform natural philosophy. Within this discussion, however, his vital invocations of Jewish religion and culture have been ignored or represented as largely static and unproblematic, rather than understood in terms of contemporary cultural and theological struggles.' DeCook's focus is Bacon's *New Atlantis*, in which 'Bacon draws on the dynamics of Christian-Jewish relations for several interrelated polemical purposes.' These include the interrelationship of science and religion placed 'against the background of the contemporary upsurge of radical forms of millenarianism and messianism alluded to in *New Atlantis*, which put the relationship between God, nature, and earthly political order under new scrutiny'. Bacon's object in his work is 'to defend his project against a set of vulnerabilities historically associated with natural philosophy's reception by Christianity, vulnerabilities heightened by Bacon's apocalyptic framework and its susceptibility to being paralleled with these disruptive eschatologies' (p. 115). Henry S. Turner, in his 'Francis Bacon's Common Notion' (*JEMCS* 13:iii[2013] 7–32), 'examines the political imaginary of Bacon's philosophy of nature as elaborated in the *Novum Organum*'. Turner argues that Bacon's 'notion of the "common" is in tension with his notion of the "collective"', and suggests some of the ways in which 'Bacon's work can shed light on theories of politics based on a principle of sovereignty'. Turner concludes by 'sketching the outlines of a "compositional" theory of political bodies in Bacon's work' (p. 7).

4. Browne

The year 2013 heralded an important biography of Sir Thomas Browne by Reid Barbour, *Sir Thomas Browne: A Life*, and articles by Kevin Killeen and Claire Preston in Andrew Hadfield's *Oxford Handbook of English Prose 1500–1640* (see *YWES* 94[2015] 500, 1273–5). There was also a note by Reid Barbour in *Notes and Queries*: 'The Parish Church of Sir Thomas Browne's Childhood' (*N&Q* 60[2013] 35–7). Barbour writes that Sir Thomas Browne's 'biographers . . . have assumed through the years that no evidence remains from his childhood parish church, St Michael le Querne. As it turns out this is not the case' (p. 35). A recent author, W.G. Sebald, influenced by Browne's work is the focus of Dawn Morgan's 'The World after Progress: The Thomas Browne of W.G. Sebald' (*ESC* 39:ii–iii[2013] 217–49). In an interesting analysis that illuminates both authors, Morgan, prone as other commentators on Browne to lengthy single sentences, comments that 'Sebald's use of Browne as the model and authority for productively compromising speakers and sources, thematizing and interrogating his own text's means of narrative movement, and opening to fragmentation and laughter that counters rigidity and paralysis in confronting the present apparent lack of alternatives to the historical dead end of progress, unveils a Browne whose works we can now read as themselves unfinished, open-ended, and as sources of ongoing productivity' (p. 245). The year 2014 witnessed the appearance of Kevin Killeen's anthology *Thomas Browne*, in the 21st-Century Oxford Authors series, bringing together under a single cover the vast majority of its subjects printed works without too much omission. However, a notable exception is the exclusion of Browne's *Miscellanies*, published initially in 1712.

Kathryn Murphy's 'The Physician's Religion and *Salus Populi*: The Manuscript Circulation and Print Publication of *Religio Medici*' (*SP* 111:iv[2014] 845–74) is an important addition to our knowledge of the circulation of manuscripts in the pre-Civil War period. Murphy draws upon notation in the diary of the London-based Polish émigré Samuel Hartlib. After his 1626 settlement in England Hartlib 'devoted himself to promoting the advancement of learning and universal reformation, willingly becoming a clearing house for new learning and innovations and a contact point for other individuals interested in such schemes' (p. 848). His diary notes 'constitute the first and hitherto only evidence we have, beyond the extant manuscripts themselves, for the manuscript circulation of Thomas Browne's *Religio Medici*'. Murphy writes: ' the implications of these recently uncovered notes . . . place the manuscript in the milieu of Hartlib, of the Puritan Essex noblewoman Lady Judith Barrington, and of the clergyman John Gauden, and allow consideration of who may have wished to publish *Religio Medici*, and why, and in particular whether, Gauden may have been involved' (p. 845). Another important contribution is found in Claire Preston's '"Meer Nomenclature" and the Description of Order in *The Garden of Cyrus*' (*RS* 28:ii[2014] 298–316), which 'considers the nature of neologism and lexical extension . . . in a range of work by a number of natural philosophers, natural historians, and georgic writers, with special attention to Browne', whom Preston describes as 'perhaps the most fluent scientific neologizer of the early modern period' and '*The Garden of Cyrus* (1658), a work inflected by his natural history and exemplifying some solutions to the terminological needs of early modern science' (p. 298).

5. Burton

Robert Burton, the author of *The Anatomy of Melancholy*, is the subject of several interesting contributions. Stephanie Shirilan's 'Exhilarating the Spirits:

Burtonian Study as a Cure for Scholarly Melancholy' (*SP* 111:iii[2014] 486–520) examines 'the value that Burton not only attributes to study as a cure for melancholy but also induces by prescription'. Her subject's 'seemingly superficial style of survey in *The Anatomy of Melancholy* models an alternative to those grave and ruminating modes of inquiry that Burton deems to be dangerous for the melancholically inclined, instead offering his reader a program for the allegrification of the spirits through the evocation of therapeutic wonder'. For Shirilan 'Burton dispenses his study cure by appealing directly to the transformative powers of the imagination as they were understood by Renaissance Neoplatonists and rhetorical theorists.' These are the subject of the first part of her article. In the second part she turns her attention 'to the complex ironies of Burton's juxtaposed accounts of the institutional causes of scholarly melancholy and the restorative effects of delightful study'. In the third part, which has a message relevant today, Shirilan 'explores the ways that Burton's descriptions of the inexhaustible variety of wonder to be found in studies yet to come and authors yet to be studied induce a sense of futurity and community that militates against the comorbid experiences of alienation and despair to which the melancholic scholar is prone' (p. 486).

An interesting counterpoint to Shirilan's article is found in Stewart Justman's 'The Folly of Systems: The Satiric Tradition and Mental Disorders' (*P&L* 37:ii[2014] 472–85), adopting a psychological approach to satire and melancholy. Justman observes that 'The steep rise in diagnosed depression in the United States was enabled by the use of simplistic checklists of diagnostic criteria as codified in the authoritative Diagnostic and Statistical Manual, which underwent a fundamental change in 1980 and has been revised several times since.' He adds that 'the DSM criteria for depression disregard the traditional distinction between the sadness incident to human life and habitual, excessive melancholy'. Importantly, 'tradition—in particular the satiric tradition, to which Burton's *Anatomy of Melancholy* belongs—not only reminds us that sadness has many shapes, but by the same token cautions against the fallacies of codification as such' (p. 471).

The prolific scholar and critic Kathryn Murphy, in her 'Robert Burton and the Problems of Polymathy' (*RS* 28:ii[2014] 279–97), directs her attention to questions of scholarly erudition and encyclopedism. She writes that 'Robert Burton called his period "this scribling age", in which the copiousness of printed matter and the multitude of authors caused problems both of discernment—how to distinguish true scholars from intellectual quacks?—and of quantity: how can the scholar hope to master the "vast Chaos and confusion of Bookes"?' Burton's questions are no less relevant in our electronic age. Her article 'addresses Burton's engagement with these questions, and examines both his attempt to establish a polymathic persona, and the relationship of the *Anatomy* to other compendious genres of the period'. In the second section of her article Murphy 'compares Burton's versions of polymathy with Johannes Wower's *De polymathia tractatio* [1603], showing how, 'in both the *Anatomy* and his academic play, *Philosophaster*, Burton contrasts the true polymath with the figure of the "polypragmatist", representing a kind of miscellaneous learning which is shallow, deceptive, and mercenary'. In her third section she 'examines Burton's relationship to another model of disciplinary multifariousness: the encyclopaedia, understood by Burton not as a genre, but as an ethos'. In the penultimate section her 'attention turns to polyantheas and other compendious literary genres. Burton's complaints about such short cuts to learning are shown to participate in the controversy over the scholarly method which followed the publication of John Selden's *Historie of Tithes* (1618).' The concluding section of Murphy's learned and fascinating article 'addresses polymathic style: Burton's ambiguous relationship to Erasmian copia, and the struggle to find a voice amid the clamour of citations demanded of the scholar' (p. 279).

Susan Wells's 'Genres as Species and Spaces: Literary and Rhetorical Genre in *The Anatomy of Melancholy*' (*P&R* 47:ii[2014] 113–36) is concerned with epideictic rhetoric, rhetorical theory, satire, and genre classification. Wells writes that 'contemporary genre theory is dominated by metaphors of evolution and speciation; this article proposes alternate metaphors of spatiality and exchange. A spatial understanding of genre permits more productive interactions between literary and rhetorical genre theory. A reading of Robert Burton's *The Anatomy of Melancholy* as a multigenred text suggests some of the potentials of this approach' (p. 113).

Nicolas K. Kiessling's 'The Library of Robert Burton, Addenda et Corrigenda' (*N&Q* 60[2013] 523–6) usefully provides additions and corrections to his '*The Library of Robert Burton*, published by the Oxford Bibliographical Society, N.S. XII, in 1988 . . . There are twenty-three new entries, including a trove of seventeen Frankfurt catalogues, and seven items that were known to be in Burton's library and are now located' (p. 523).

In 'Robert Burton's Poemata' Dana F. Sutton provides an English translation and introduction to Robert Burton's neo-Latin text in *The Philological Museum* (a hypertext edition) [2013]. Finally a more general contextual contribution should not be ignored. Nicholas McDowell's appropriately titled 'Decorum Personae: *The World Turned Upside Down* and the Praise of Folly' (*PSt* 36:iii[2014] 219–33) contrasts Burton's ideas with those of Henry Pinnell, the chaplain of the New Model Army, expressed in his *A Word of Prophesy* [1648]. McDowell writes: 'While Burton conceived of his books as facilitating his writing and of his knowledge of the history of scholarship as granting him authority to write', Pinnell, on the other hand, 'employs his learning against itself and conceives of his satirical method in violently iconoclastic imagery' (p. 226).

Books Reviewed

Edmondson, Paul, and Stanley Wells, eds. *Shakespeare Beyond Doubt: Evidence, Argument, Controversy.* CUP. [2013] pp. 298. £19.99 ISBN 9 7811 0760 3288.
Garrison, John. *Friendship and Queer Theory in the Renaissance: Gender and Sexuality in Early Modern England.* Routledge. [2014] pp. 172. £90. ISBN 9 7804 1571 3221.

Haude, Sigrun, and Melinda S. Zook, eds. *Challenging Orthodoxies: The Social and Cultural Worlds of Early Modern Women*. Ashgate. [2014] pp. 265. £95. ISBN 9 7814 0945 7084.

Killeen, Kevin, ed. *Thomas Browne. 21st-Century Oxford Authors*. OUP. [2014] pp. xlv + 995. £95 ISBN 9 7801 9964 0430.

Siegfried, Brandie R., and Lisa T. Sarasohn, eds. *God and Nature in the Thought of Margaret Cavendish*. Ashgate. [2014] pp. 274. £70. ISBN 9 7814 7243 9611.

Sutton, Dana F., ed. *Sir Francis Bacon, Serones Fideles sive Interiora Rerum (printed 1638): A Hypertext Edition*. The Philological Museum. [2013] http://www.philological.bham.ac.uk/essays/.

Swann, Marjorie, ed. *The Compleat Angler, or the Contemplative Man's Recreation, by Izaak Walton and Charles Cotton*. OUP. [2014] pp. 284 + xxxvi. £14.99. ISBN 9 7801 9965 0743.

Tomita, Soto, and Masahiko Tomita. *A Bibliographical Catalogue of Italian Books Printed in England 1603–1642*. Ashgate. [2014] pp. 602. £76.50. ISBN 9 7814 0942 2891.

X

Milton and Poetry, 1603–1660

WILLIAM BAKER, JAMES DOELMAN, ANNE JAMES, AND MATTHEW MROZ

This chapter has four sections: 1. General; 2. Herbert; 3. Donne; 4.Milton. Section 1 is by William Baker; section 2 is by James Doelman; section 3 is by Anne James; section 4 is by Matthew Mroz.

1. General

With the exception of Donne, Herbert, and Milton, seventeenth-century pre-Restoration poetry has been given short shrift in recent *YWES* discussions. This section will focus upon work published in 2013–14 on Cowley, Crashaw, and Herrick, amongst others. To start with the sole Cowley item that has come to our attention, Nathaniel Stogdill's contribution, ' "Out of Books and Out of Themselves": Invigorating Impartiality in Early Modern England" (in Murphy and Traninger, eds., *The Emergence of Impartiality*, pp. 189–210), looks at Abraham Cowley's prose and poetry to examine the role of impartiality in his work written at a time of traumatic political events.

In his anniversary year, 2013, it is hardly surprising that Richard Crashaw should be given attention. In the first of several contributions, Alex Wong's 'Joseph Beaumont and Richard Crashaw: A Study in Standing-Points' (*English* 62[2013] 316–36) focuses on poetic technique in *Psyche or Love's Mysterie*, Joseph Beaumont's epic poem of 1648, contrasted with Crashaw's work. There are two other contributions of note by Wong: his praise of Crashaw's poetry and importance in 'Crashaw 400: A Quartercentennial Celebration: Part I' (*PNR* 39:v[2013] 60–3); and his assessment of the poet's influence in 'Crashaw 400: A Quartercentennial Celebration: Part II: Legacy' (*PNR* 39:vi[2013] 69–70). Joseph Teller considers the issue of 'Why Crashaw Was Not a Catholic: The Passion and Popular Protestant Devotion' (*ELR* 43:ii[2013] 239–67). Teller observes: 'Crashaw was not a Catholic when he wrote his poetry; he converted to Catholicism only a few years before he died in exile in Rome. Moreover, as the title to his 1646 and 1648 volumes suggests—*Steps to the Temple*, Crashaw perceived himself as an English poet in the tradition of Herbert' (p. 240). Richard Rambuss, in addition to editing

The Year's Work in English Studies, Volume 95 (2016) © *The Author 2016. Published by Oxford University Press on behalf of the English Association. All rights reserved.*
For Permissions, please email: journals.permissions@oup.com
doi:10.1093/ywes/maw007

The English Poems of Richard Crashaw, in his 'Crashaw and the Metaphysical Shudder; or, How To Do Things with Tears' (in McClary, ed., *Structures of Feeling in Seventeenth-Century Cultural Expression*, pp. 253–71), focuses upon the significance of the word 'tears', St Mary Magdalene, and taste in his subject's poetry. Crashaw's poetry also plays an important role in Tesse L Prakas's 'Unimportant Women: The "Sweet Descants" of Mary Sidney and Richard Crashaw' (in Dunn and Larson, eds., *Gender and Song in Early Modern England*, pp. 107–22). As Dunn and Larson explain in their introduction, Prakas interestingly juxtaposes a discussion of the countess of Pembroke's translations with Crashaw, who also 'turns to music and metaphors to explore women's devotional' poetry. However, 'whereas vocal music, especially congregational song, functions as an authorizing mode in Pembroke's experimental verse, Crashaw's musical idiom ultimately works to mitigate the power of women venerated within the Catholic tradition' (p. 13).

Michael Drayton is the subject of several contributions. Rémi Vuillemin, in '"The Musical Confusion of Hounds and Echoes in Conjunction": Intertextual Friction in Elizabethan Rewritings of the Myth of Actæon' (*Ranam* 47[2014] 175–88), writing in a special issue devoted to the subject of 'The Déjà Vu and the Authentic in Anglophone Culture: Contacts, Frictions, Clashes', examines allusion and the influence of Ovid's *Metamorphoses* upon various poets, including Edmund Spenser, Shakespeare, and Michael Drayton. Drayton's response to Shakespeare engages Meghan C. Andrews in 'Michael Drayton, Shakespeare's Shadow' (*SQ* 65:iii[2014] 273–306). Andrews contends that Drayton was acquainted with Shakespeare at the Middle Temple, one of the Inns of Court, and that he was an influential early Shakespearian reader and reworked the Bard's work. Lines from Drayton's *England's Heroicall Epistles* [1597] are found in the Folio texts of *2* and *3 Henry VI* but not in the early quarto and octavo texts of the Henry VI plays. The joint work of Drayton's and his contemporaries, *The Mirror for Magistrates*, reflects Drayton's and Shakespeare's intertextualism in the depiction of history. Drayton's *Poly-Olbion* is considered in Sara Trevisan's 'The Impact of the Netherlandish Landscape Tradition on Poetry and Painting in Early Modern England' (*RenQ* 66:iii[2013] 866–903). For Trevisan, 'Drayton—under the influence of the artistic principles of landscape depiction as explained in' the art murals of Henry Peacham, 'as well as of direct observation of Dutch and Flemish landscape prints and paintings—successfully managed to render pictorial landscapes into poetry' (p. 866).

Robert Herrick is the subject of various contributions. Andrew Lacey, in 'A Possible Echo of Herrick in Shelley's "The Flower That Smiles Today"' (*N&Q* 61[2014] 525–27), writes that 'while "The flower that smiles today" is, in several respects, a typically Shelleyan reflection on transience and death, it also seems to draw upon poetry of the *carpe diem* tradition, particularly Robert Herrick's "To the Virgins, to make much of Time" . . . There are striking parallels in language, theme, and tone between the first stanza of Herrick's poem and the first four lines of Shelley's' (p. 526). A reading of another Herrick poem engages M.W. Brumit in '"Then, then": The Two Poetic Moments of Robert Herrick's "Upon Julia's Clothes"' (*Expl* 72:iv[2014] 282–5). Brumit's focus is on the metaphor of clothing and dress in Herrick's lyric. Martin Corless-Smith's subject is 'Herrick's Wild Civility' (*BJJ* 20:ii[2013] 273–82). Finally, turning to Thomas Traherne, mention should be made of Benjamin J. Barber's 'Syncretism and Idiosyncrasy: The Notion of Act in Thomas Traherne's Contemplative Practice' (*L&T* 28:i[2014] 16–28). Barber's focus is the treatment of contemplation, action, and the poet's relationship to the Divine. For Barber, Traherne supplies his readers 'with instructions on how best to mirror God's act-like nature. Traherne's formulation of God-as-act is expressed in both the *Commentaries of Heaven and Centuries of Meditations*, where his understanding of God draws upon both Neo-Platonic and Aristotelian understandings of "act," while reiterating Christian and biblical conceptions of an ever-creating deity.' In terms of 'method', however, Traherne 'differs from St. Ignatius's *Spiritual Exercises* in its celebration of all creation over any particular object or person. Unlike the Neo-Platonists, Traherne's practice does not seek the ecstatic, but insists on the contemplative's lucidity throughout their spiritual progress' (p. 16).

2. Herbert

The most notable publication of the year is a masterful digital edition of *The Temple*. A 2011 article by Robert Whalen (covered in *YWES* 90[2011]) announced the development of *The Digital Temple*, edited by Robert Whalen and Christopher Hodgkins; 2014—in spite of its 2012 issue date—saw its full launch. Overall, it is an impressive and useful resource and tool for scholars, students, and even general readers of George Herbert. The editors' claims for their text—that it surpasses what has been available in both digital and print form—are largely sustainable. The scope of the project means that both the 1633 printed text of *The Temple* and the two surviving manuscripts can be viewed together (without giving priority to any one of the three), both in facsimile and transcription form. The limitless dimensions of an online 'edition' allow the editors to give *everything*, and with Herbert's *Temple* where there are only two manuscripts and the 1633 printed text, this is feasible and the edition usable. Their ambitious claims also extend to the annotations: they hope that, more than Hutchinson's long-standard edition, their notes and commentary will call into question the image of Herbert as a tranquil representative of the Anglican *via media*. They emphasize the way in which he engaged in major theological, ecclesiastical, and political struggles of the time. In the process, the editors are also careful to note that this project highlights the *orderliness* of design in each of the three witnesses of *The Temple* by allowing for what they call the 'microscopic' searching and analysis possible with it. They also note that in its commentary and notes the *Digital Temple* is much indebted to Helen Wilcox's 2007 edition. While in many ways this is a 'finished' work, there are some suggestions of further developments down the road: 'A more robust encoding—one which includes the tagging of actual rhyming end-words and metrical feet rather than only the larger patterns of rhyme and meter—is planned for a later edition.'

Inge Leimberg's '"Thy words do finde me out": Reading the Last Line of "Affliction (I)"' (*Connotations* 24:i[2014–15] 1–16) revisits the much-discussed paradoxical conclusion ('Let me not love thee [God], if I love thee not') to this most autobiographical of Herbert's poems. However, the article ranges much more broadly, offering an overview of the speaker's encounter with Divine love throughout *The Temple*. That relationship of love, unlike the frustrated desire of the Petrarchan tradition, is insistently mutual. All this sets the stage for Leimberg's reading of the final line of 'Affliction (I)', which argues that other critics have usually treated it as an ellipsis, where other words must be supplied. Instead, Leimberg presents a careful grammatical analysis of the conclusion, focusing in particular on the chiasmic structure of the last six lines, and the grammatical and rhetorical history of 'if' (and the Latin 'si'), concluding that 'if' here is a ' "Si conclusionis" and a synonym of "*Since*"' (p. 6). Leimberg's conclusion is that the final lines present a speaker unable to love God, but still hoping to find a place in his service, dependent upon the *Master's* love.

Helen Wilcox's 'The "Finenesse" of Devotional Poetry: An Collins and the School of Herbert' (in Howard, ed., *An Collins and the Historical Imagination*, pp. 71–85) establishes An Collins as part of a mid-seventeenth-century generation of poets heavily indebted to the model of Herbert. The early pages rehearse the general popularity and influence of Herbert (previously explored by Robert H. Ray, John Shawcross, Sean H. McDowell, Paul Dyck, and Wilcox herself). While the significance of Herbert's work for Henry Vaughan, Richard Crashaw, Christopher Harvey, and Samuel Crossman has long been noted, Wilcox shows how a number of less widely recognized figures—Henry Colman, Julia Palmer, Cardell Goodman, and An Collins—should be considered as part of this ' "school of Herbert" '(p. 72). These poets reflected his poetic structures, plain style, figures of speech, tone, and 'divine conversations' (p. 74). The greatest emphasis is on Collins, who, Wilcox argues, was influenced by *The Temple*'s explicit defence of a plain style and the rooting of devotional poetry in personal experience, particularly suffering. An especially strong influence is found in Collins's adoption of the motif of sweetness to define the experience of Christ. Clearly, Wilcox's deep familiarity with *The Temple* renders her eminently well suited to hear the influence (sometimes subtle, sometimes obvious) of Herbert upon these writers. John Drury's *Music at Midnight: The Life and Poetry of George Herbert*, is a readable introduction to the poet rather than a work that primarily seeks to advance scholarship and criticism in the field; hence it is not covered in detail here.

3. Donne

Broadly related to Donne manuscript studies, Daniel Starza Smith's *John Donne and the Conway Papers: Patronage and Manuscript Circulation in the Early Seventeenth Century* provides a meticulously researched investigation of Donne's presence in the massive collection of Conway Papers that is equally an exploration of the intricacies of Renaissance patronage relations and an exposition of the challenges and opportunities of modern archival research. Smith sets out to 'layer' three puzzles: 'Donne's biography', 'the biography of the Conway family', and 'the history and composition of the Conway Papers' (p. 3). The first part of the book focuses upon the archive itself, a massive and heterogeneous collection subject to both neglect and well-meaning but misguided interventions at various periods in its history, and eventually divided among several repositories. Smith shares both the frustrations and the rewards of this kind of research as he acknowledges new discoveries while identifying inevitable gaps and inconsistencies in the records. The second part of the book turns to the circulation of Donne's works, and in particular to the role Sir Henry Goodere played in this process. It is clear at times, as in the question of whether Jonson was responsible for the scribal copy of *Biathanatos* presented to Edward Herbert (MS è Musaeo 131), as Mark Bland has argued, that Smith wishes the archive to speak more clearly, and is frustrated by its unwillingness to do so. Nevertheless, the evidence he presents, even when inconclusive, suggests that similar studies of other archival collections could, both individually and collectively, yield valuable information about patronage, manuscript circulation, and the lives and works of Donne and his contemporaries.

In 'Stemmatics and Society in Early Modern England'(*SN* 86(supplement)[2014] 29–47), Mark Bland reminds us that a focus upon canonical authors handicaps early modern textual studies because manuscript miscellanies contain works by numerous authors whose texts have been little studied. The restriction of early modern stemmatics to Donne studies prevents us from seeing how information gleaned from one manuscript can inform our understanding of another. As a secondary problem, Bland identifies the difficulty of establishing a history of variants because authors so frequently revised their work. The editors of the Donne Variorum, he claims, have created stemma that 'seem to assume that Donne only ever revised once and so minimise authorial agency, potentially drawing the wrong conclusions from their effort' (p. 33). Bland illustrates these problems by considering the still disputed authorship of 'The Expostulation', which appeared in both Donne's 1633 *Poems*, and Jonson's 1640 *Workes*. Although the Variorum attributes the poem to Donne, in none of the manuscripts consulted is attribution clear. According to Bland, 'The presence of the poem in *1633* without the support of the Group One tradition or the Westmorland manuscript is more of a problem than the *Variorum* editors acknowledge' (p. 43). He argues for eliminating both Donne and Jonson as possible authors and concentrating further stylometric analysis on possible authorship by Sir John Roe or Nicholas Hare, recognizing that 'not all competent seventeenth-century poems need to have been written by authors who are now taught in the higher curriculum' (p. 43).

Christopher Warley, in chapters 4 and 5 of his *Reading Class through Shakespeare, Donne, and Milton*, identifies a broader problem of elitism in our preference for manuscript authors. In his first chapter, 'Ideal Donne', he draws attention, like Bland, to the multiplicity of variants in extant manuscripts, but his point is that Donne's poems, 'upon which modernist aesthetics lavished praise for their formal integrity and authenticity are, actually, a mess' (p. 74). Although Donne's preference for manuscript transmission has been discussed extensively, Warley argues that such discussions have seldom considered class. He argues that the 'stigma of print' influences not only the texts of the poems, but also the modern reading of those texts: 'Donne poems are ineluctably caught up in the politics of modernism, including not only its idealist snobbery but also its fear of the masses, obsession with poetic form, materialist critique, and, consequently, its class politics' (p. 88). In other words, studying Donne is itself an elitist endeavour. In 'Virtuoso Donne', Warley suggests that Donne's poetry fits the definition of virtuosity as both a social activity and one performed for itself rather than to produce something else. Virtuosity assumes class because the very idea of a virtuoso performance assumes inequality. Warley illustrates the paradoxical nature of Donne's position in his love poetry, making 'love an equal-opportunity performance by claiming, at exactly the same time, that the love of his couple is better than everyone else's love' (p. 101), and concludes the chapter with a detailed reading of 'A Valediction: forbidding mourning'.

David Scott Kastan, in his essay 'The Body of the Text' (*ELH* 81:ii[2014] 443–67), joins a number of recent scholars in considering John Marriot's role in the representation of Donne in the earliest editions of his poetry. As the owners of the texts they printed, Kastan argues, early modern publishers generally assumed more responsibility than authors for paratextual elements. Marriot encouraged the reading of the elegies on the author in his 1633 edition of *Poems, by J.D.* as text rather than paratext by taking the unusual steps of placing them after the poems and announcing them in the volume's title. In both style and content, they insist upon Donne's continuing presence after his death, and they identify the author, something no other part of the volume does. By 1633, Donne was known primarily as a preacher rather than a poet, so to enhance the commercial success of his volume Kastan suggests that Marriot deliberately identified the author only by initials, omitted Donne's name from the preliminaries, and included no frontispiece. His purpose was 'not to create anonymity but to undermine the familiar signature of authorship, disclosing, whether by design or not, that it is not an authorial possession but something collaboratively constructed and maintained in the pages of the edition' (p. 461). Kastan concludes that the 'real' Donne is found no more in the printed text than in the body of manuscript witnesses.

Taking as a starting point Thomas Carew's description of Donne banishing Ovidianism with his fresh poetic style, Daniel David Moss, in 'The Brief Ovidian Career of John Donne', chapter 5 of *The Ovidian Vogue: Literary Fashion and Imitative Practice in Late Elizabethan England*, observes that, in both *Metempsychosis* and his elegies, Donne 'colonizes territory previously occupied in the cultural imagination by Ovid and his early modern imitators' (p. 156). He reads *Metempsychosis* 'not as the repudiation of the *Metamorphoses*, but as the epic counterpart to Donne's own erotic elegies— indeed, as their completion or perfection, however incomplete the epic is' (p. 176). Having begun his career 'at the height of the Ovidian vogue in the mid-1590s' (p. 152), Donne later banished Ovid, expressing his scorn by compressing lengthy episodes from the *Metamorphoses* into parodic epigrams, in order to take over his role as teacher in the art of love. Moss argues that Donne's avoidance of Ovidian tropes, however, is not, as others have suggested, anti-Ovidianism, but is more like post-Ovidianism, since his critique is directed less at Ovid than at his own society's revision of the Ovidian tradition. Moss concludes that in later years Donne represented his own story as a metamorphosis, the transformation of secular poet into priest. Carew and others, however, may shoulder the responsibility for our own willingness to accept this narrative.

Ludmila Makuchowska's *Scientific Discourse in John Donne's Eschatological Poetry* seeks to both update and extend outdated discussions of Donne's use of scientific imagery by Charles Coffin (*John Donne and the New Philosophy* [1937]) and Marjorie Hope Nicolson (*The Breaking of the Circle: Studies in the Effect of the 'New Science' upon Seventeenth-Century Poetry* [1950]). The author judiciously limits her topics to cartography, physics, and alchemy and chemistry, while focusing specifically on Donne's references to eschatology in the *Songs and Sonets* and *Divine Poems*. She concludes that Donne juxtaposes Christian doctrine with scientific reasoning, using each to reinforce and to query the other. Donne's references to maps are well known, but Makuchowska connects them to contemporary changes in cartography as the west was displacing the east at the top of maps, replacing a religious orientation of the world with a commercial and imperial one. Donne similarly balances traditional religious imagery, such as the weighing of the soul and human attraction towards good, against his awareness of new discoveries in physics, such as the concept of free fall and the possible existence of the vacuum. Hermeticism, now seen as an important step in the scientific revolution, had made alchemy more acceptable in the Renaissance, and Donne relies in several of his poems upon images of alchemical transformation, including the 'chemical wedding', and introduces tools used by alchemists such as the compass in 'A Valediction: forbidding mourning'. Makuchowska concludes that Donne's 'reliance on both scientific and religious dogmas remains consistent in all poems analyzed here, wherein the two philosophical systems equally reinforce, complement, challenge and invalidate each other' (p. 118). Her short study provides a welcome new look at the scientific contexts of Donne's poetry in the light of early twenty-first-century changes in our understanding of the history of science.

Taking up one area of scientific knowledge deliberately omitted from Makuchowska's study, in her essay 'Milton's and Donne's Stargazing Lovers, Sex, and the New Astronomy' (*SEL* 54:i[2014] 143–71), Catherine Gimelli Martin asserts that Donne's and Milton's early readers would naturally have associated the three topics of her title, given Ficino's Christianization of Plato's ideas about the relationship between the soul and the heavens. William Empson and Charles Coffin popularized the view that Donne favoured the new astronomy; however, Nicolson demonstrated 'that Donne disliked the new astronomy's altered cosmos' (p. 151). Citing 'Love's Growth', *Ignatius, his Conclave*, the epithalamia, and the religious poetry, Martin affirms that Donne preferred the old astronomy. While Donne's lovers are content to be confined or at a still centre surrounded by motion, Milton's explore vast spaces and look outward to the rest of the universe. Both authors, however, envision lovers whose love creates new worlds, neither heavenly nor earthly. Martin concludes that both Donne and Milton are willing to consider the possibility of other worlds; their 'disagreement . . . chiefly lies in how they view these infinite worlds, concentrically rotating around a divine axis, as Donne imagines, or expanding into boundless and still unexplored deeps, as Milton gloriously supposes' (p. 164).

Donne's attitude towards technology, or more particularly its uses, is the subject of Theresa M. DiPasquale's essay, '"A Clock So True": The Chronometry of Virtue in Donne's "Obsequyes upon the Lord Harington"' (*ELR* 44:i[2014] 129–50). DiPasquale reads Donne's use of clock imagery in his 'Obsequyes upon the Lord Harington' as a discreet critique of the interests in mathematics, science, and technology that Harington had shared with the recently deceased Prince Henry. Previous scholars have noted Donne's ambivalence towards the proto-imperialist, religio-political agenda that drove the prince and his friend to value the practical applications of scientific principles, such as cartography and navigation over theoretical speculation. DiPasquale, however, specifically connects Donne's doubts, 'both about the limitless potential of humanity and about the benefits of investing in the technology of time' (p. 136) to the series of clock images at lines 131–54. By first comparing Harington's brief life to one of the short lines of latitude close to the poles in contrast to lengthier lines of longitude that enable navigation, Donne suggests that a longer life would have made Harington more useful in helping his admirers lead virtuous lives. In passing from chronometry to timepieces, however, Donne becomes more critical. Just as erratic pocket watches need to be synchronized with larger, more reliable public clocks, young men like Harington should rely upon the advice of more mature and authoritative men. Harington, however, has imitated the youthful prince. Moreover, the public has been led astray by mistakenly regarding Harington and Henry as reliable authorities. Read in this way, DiPasquale concludes, 'the overarching effect of the clock passage is rather scathing' (p. 142). Finally, she contests the reading of the sundial image as a compliment to Harington, instead suggesting that it may indict Harington for his failure to control the prince rather than simply to follow him, as he established a dangerous course of militant Protestantism. Donne's sceptical attitude to Harington contrasts with the lavish praise heaped upon him by Richard Stock in his funeral sermon, which may explain why Donne felt the need to couch his critique in such ambiguous metaphors.

Helen Wilcox, in 'Donne's "Anatomy" and the Commemoration of Women: "Her Death Hath Taught Us Dearly"', chapter 8 of *1611: Authority, Gender and the Word in Early Modern England*, suggests that the elegiac mood of Donne's 'Anatomy of the World', marking the first anniversary of Elizabeth Drury's death, is in tune with other cultural productions of this year, particularly a number of other commemorations of women. The first of these is Lancelot Langhorne's funeral sermon for Mary Swaine on 17 January 1611. Through a lengthy discourse on the name Mary and its bearers in the New Testament, particularly Mary Magdalene, Langhorne succeeds in 'bring[ing] to life both a biblical text and an ordinary woman of apparently extraordinary virtue' (p. 187). Other commemorations of women in this year, both in prose and in stone, tend towards similarly idealized views of womanhood. Wilcox uses the contemporary interest in alchemy as a metaphor for the transmutation of an actual woman into an idealized version of womanhood through the medium of elegy: 'A woman of flesh and blood—or, in death, of dust and ashes—has risen phoenix-like to a new life, if not in heaven then at least preserved in the words, paper or alabaster of the memorial' (p. 191). Like alchemists, the authors, primarily male, want to turn base metals to gold, but also to play a significant role in that transmutation. The methodology of this study provides a new context for the idealization of Elizabeth Drury that readers, beginning with Ben Jonson, have sometimes considered excessive.

In 'Embracing the Medium: Metaphor and Resistance in John Donne', chapter 3 of *Made Flesh: Sacrament and Poetics in Post-Reformation England*, Kimberly Johnson argues that the elaborate detail in which Donne develops his metaphors creates a sense of presence that overcomes the referentiality of the metaphor. In other words, the metaphor becomes an end in itself rather than simply the medium through which meaning is transmitted. Relating this approach to metaphor to her overarching concern with sacrament, Johnson suggests that Donne saw both language and sacrament as potential methods of incarnation because both 'discompose and disorder perception' (p. 100). Throughout his writing, Donne 'views the sacrament as an interpretively problematic event' (p. 98). His treatment of metaphor suggests a middle path between transubstantiation and memorialization, in which the elaboration of the metaphor itself creates presence. The significance is the metaphor itself rather than what it represents. Johnson traces Donne's literalization of metaphor first through *Death's Duell*, then through several of his religious poems, and finally through 'The Flea' and 'A Valediction of my Name in the Window'.

In Part I 'Rembrandt's Jeremiah: Donne and Learning How to Be a Preacher' of his *Typology and Iconography in Donne, Herbert, and Milton: Fashioning the Self after Jeremiah*, Reuben Sánchez looks at four texts— Donne's translation of *The Lamentations of Jeremy*, 'Good Friday, 1613', a sermon on Lamentations 3:1, and a letter offering consolation to his mother on the death of her daughter—in order to consider how Donne models himself on the figure of Jeremiah. He sees each of these texts structured around the idea of 'convertere': the individual turns from God but turns back as God himself turns toward the individual. In the translation and the poem, the poet seeks consolation for himself, while in the sermon and the letter Donne, now a preacher, has learned to give consolation to others. Donne, in other words, identified with Jeremiah in different ways at different critical times in his life. With the exception of 'Good Friday, 1613', however, the dating of all of these texts remains uncertain. Ultimately, Sánchez argues, Donne models himself on an idea of Jeremiah that is closest to Rembrandt's 1630 painting *The Prophet Jeremiah Lamenting the Destruction of Jerusalem*, in which Sánchez sees the prophet turned partly towards the light that bisects the canvas and partly away from it, both mourning the past and expecting a return in God's time.

In response to recent trends of reading individual Donne sermons in their political contexts, Mark S. Sweetnam, in *John Donne and Religious Authority in the Reformed English Church*, focuses his discussion on three 'issues of theological authority' (p. 9)—the authority of Scripture, the authority of the church, and the authority of the preacher—as they relate to the complete body of Donne's extant sermons. Recognizing that Donne was not an original theologian, Sweetnam nevertheless asserts that he was deeply committed to Protestantism and to the church as a community. Sweetnam follows other recent commentators on Donne's sermons, particularly Jeanne Shami, in arguing that Donne consistently resisted religious labels and sought to promote unity rather than division among Christians, describing a Donne who discouraged his auditors from entering into debate on controversial topics such as the sacrament and predestination, advocated following the English Church in indifferent matters, and generally appealed to as broad a spectrum as possible, drawing a firm line only at Tridentine Catholicism. Sweetnam reiterates Donne's refusal to establish a hierarchical order among preaching, prayer, and the sacrament, but notes that he placed the preaching function of the minister over the sacerdotal role of the priest. A strength of Sweetnam's treatment is his willingness to let Donne speak through lengthy, contextualized quotations from the sermons. Despite his efforts to focus solely upon theology, however, the discussion increasingly demonstrates that Donne's theological thought cannot easily be prised apart from his religio-political context simply because Donne's theology was formed within that context.

Donne's sermons have frequently invited comparison with those of his contemporary, Lancelot Andrewes. In her essay '"The Very, Very Words": (Mis)quoting Scripture in Lancelot Andrewes's and John Donne's Sermons on Job 19:23–27' (*SP* 111:iii[2014] 442–69), Alison Knight performs a detailed comparison of these sermons, leading her to conclude that Donne and Andrewes take contrary approaches to the problem of unstable scriptural language: 'Andrewes seeks to construct polished, performative versions of challenging texts, while Donne argues against the possibility and advisability of such an aim' (p. 464). Knight demonstrates that although carelessness and faulty memory may be responsible for many misquoted texts, the extensive misquotations in these sermons point to deliberate responses to the difficult language of Job. In his Easter 1610 sermon, Andrewes presents his text as an artefact by emending extensively in the epigraph before exchanging his usual practice of examining individual words of the text for a method that acknowledges the slipperiness of the words themselves through misquotation. Despite Job's desire to make his words permanent, Andrewes shows that the Eucharist is the only perfect incarnation of the Word. While Andrewes obscures the imperfections of his text, in his 1620 sermon at Lincoln's Inn on Job 19:26, Donne engages in a variety of paraphrases and misquotations throughout the sermon to demonstrate that while God's Word is everlasting, fallen human language and other human versions of the Word, including church buildings, are subject to corruption. Knight concludes that despite their different approaches, each believes in a 'general project of manifesting or incarnating—not merely explaining—difficult scriptural words to their audience' (p. 447).

The performative dimension of Donne's sermons is explored in Kathleen O'Leary's essay 'Sermon, Salvation, Space: John Donne's Performative Mode and the Politics of Accommodation' (in Kirby and Stanwood, eds., *Paul's Cross and the Culture of Persuasion in England, 1520–1640*, pp. 411–19). In the tradition of Bryan Crockett, O'Leary considers the performative nature of Donne's sermons at Paul's Cross, focusing specifically on his penultimate preaching occasion there on 6 May 1627. Donne, she argues, used both dramatic language and dramatic movement to engage the heterogeneous Paul's Cross audience, most members of which were doubtless attuned to the dynamics of performance not only from the theatre but also from their Catholic past, and to lead them towards spiritual truth. The disruptive atmosphere of the outdoor pulpit (which we can increasingly appreciate as a result of the work of the Virtual Paul's Cross Project, https://vpcp. chass.ncsu. edu/) would have called upon the preacher's ability to make his audience attend, while the physical space, placing the preacher in the centre of a circle, facilitated attentiveness. In his 1627 sermon, Donne actually encourages his auditors to remember their Catholic past in order to lead them to appreciate the transition from such idolatrous experience to one nurtured by God's Word, uniting the group by drawing upon their memories through words rather than images.

In his essay 'Lying in Early Modern Culture' (*TPr* 28:iii[2014] 339–63), Andrew Hadfield argues that if Donne belonged to the Family of Love, as David Wotton has claimed in *Heterodoxy in Early Modern Science and Religion* ([2006] 31–56), he would have had to conceal that fact after 1615. Since evasion or silence did not constitute perjury under early modern law, some theologians distinguished between lying and equivocation to help people to avoid perjuring themselves while maintaining their faith. The Family of Love, popular in England before 1635, was one sect that allowed its members to lie about their faith. Hadfield suggests that, in addition to the sermons and letters Wotton cites, the Holy Sonnet 'At the round earth's imagined corners' might also be read to suggest that Donne was, like the Familists, a mortalist. While Donne may not have lied about his faith in his published works, Hadfield proposes, 'He was certainly economical with the truth' (p. 350). Contrary to a number of recent scholars of Donne's preaching, Hadfield argues that the sermons focus on private than public religion, while Donne's poetry suggests 'a highly individualistic form of religious belief' that may have resulted from his early experiences as a Catholic, particularly the traumatic loss of his brother Henry.

In contrast, in 'A Glass Darkly: John Donne's Negative Approach to God', chapter 2 of *Literature and the Encounter with God in Post-Reformation England*, Michael Martin argues that Donne believed God was accessible to the individual believer only through his or her participation in the body of Christ that is the church, and sought commonality with all Christians rather than emphasizing divisions. Nevertheless, he suggests that Donne approached religion intuitively rather than rationally, through a 'religious aesthetic . . . grounded in humility, the acceptance of God's unfathomable mystery and the human mind's inability to comprehend it' (p. 48), and that scholarship has paid too little attention to the way in which mysticism and negative theology influenced his thought. Although wary of personal mysticism that could lead to pride and idolatry, Donne 'was aware of the conventions of mystical writing, and willing to appropriate them for his own purposes' (p. 60).

While other scholars have suggested that the development of a public sphere in the seventeenth century freed individuals to interpret the act of suicide for themselves rather than having interpretations thrust upon them, James

Kuzner, in his essay 'Donne's *Biathanatos* and the Public Sphere's Vexing Freedom' (*ELH* 81:i[2014] 61–81), concludes that in *Biathanatos* Donne defends this freedom while simultaneously finding it 'vexing rather than enabling or empowering' (p. 61). Donne's text insists, firstly, that no one else has access to a suicide's conscience, and, secondly, that the public lacks the competence to make a judgement on an individual's decision to end his or her own life. Contemporary casuists routinely condemned suicide; however, Donne argued that casuistry cannot settle the suicide question because the potential suicide is the only person who possesses the information to settle the conflict between his or her conscience and God. *Biathanatos* encourages readers to recognize their own freedom to negotiate between themselves and God, but shows that others cannot help them in this difficult process. Kuzner concludes that freedom may ultimately be less empowering, at least in this case, than modern scholars have suggested, since 'As a public text about the freedom to a voluntary death, *Biathanatos* suggests that the utility of the public sphere consists not only in how it advocates and fosters freedoms that enable and empower us . . . [but] the public sphere's utility consists also in showing how freedom brings home our inability to address critical issues with anything like proficiency' (p. 74). Kuzner's argument might be complicated by the textual history of *Biathanatos*, which remained a private rather than a public text throughout Donne's lifetime.

4. Milton

The year 2014 was another banner year in Milton studies, thanks to a group of ten very exciting books and a multitude of scholarly articles covering a wide number of topics related to Milton and his work. Seven monographs were published on Miltonic topics this year, covering seventeenth-century politics and society (Elizabeth Sauer's *Milton, Toleration and Nationhood*, Paul Hammond's *Milton and the People*, and William Walker's *Antiformalist, Unrevolutionary, Illiberal Milton*), Milton's relationship to early modern science (Dennis Danielson's *Paradise Lost and the Cosmological Revolution*), Milton's poetics and connection to classical sources (David Quint's *Inside Paradise Lost* and Jacob Blevins's *Humanism and Classical Crisis*), and the reception of Milton by African American anti-slavery advocates (Reginald A. Wilburn's *Preaching the Gospel of Black Revolt*). Edited collections include Catharine Gray and Erin Murphy's volume of essays utilizing new and exciting approaches to Milton, *Milton Now*, and yet another fantastic group of essays in this year's volume of *Milton Studies*, edited by Laura Lunger Knoppers. Finally, 2014 saw the appearance of Louis Schwartz's *The Cambridge Companion to Paradise Lost*, a wonderful foundational text that will be of interest to many teachers of Milton.

Elizabeth Sauer's *Milton, Toleration and Nationhood* continues recent explorations of the curiously inconsistent attitudes towards religious toleration seen among seventeenth-century writers—even among religious radicals who vigorously defend their own freedom of conscience. Sauer connects early modern debates about whose beliefs are tolerated and under what conditions with concurrent conversations about nationhood, especially *elect* nationhood: about how the political and theological foundations of the English state are imagined and about how *English* nationhood is set apart from other nations. Sauer puts special focus on Milton, arguing that he 'imagines the nation in terms of its embrace of such values as Christian liberty and tolerance, which transcends state power' (p. 2). This embrace, however, is incomplete, according to Sauer, as 'Milton . . . condemns policies on and instances of intolerance without consistently raising toleration to a positive value. His later works oppose a religious settlement and are founded largely on a negatively formulated toleration' (p. 9).

Sauer traces Milton's various stances on toleration in six chapters dealing with different 'feature[s] of nationhood' represented in Milton's work. The first chapter, ' "Temple-worke": Milton's Literary Ecclesiology', explores the relationship among Milton's concern about church governance, his sense of what a Christian nation looks like, and his views on toleration. Sauer works through Milton's early prose (*Of Reformation*, *The Reason of Church-Government*, *Areopagitica*, and others), tracing how the work of reforming the church, 'Temple-worke', in Milton's words, leads him into clashes with English Presbyterians and to a more acute sense of need for toleration within a diverse Christian nation. Chapter 2, 'Reduction: Civilizing Conquests in Ireland', discusses that aspect of nation-building concerned with defining one nation in relation to another by opposition or, in the case of England and Ireland, through conquest. England's campaigns against the Irish under Cromwell allow the 'forging of Englishness' (p. 49), and explicitly Protestant Englishness, in opposition to Irish Catholicism. Sauer, in her consideration of Milton's *Observations upon the Articles of Peace*, argues that, along with Milton's support for Irish subjugation, 'the animus expressed against the Irish became a comment on the troubled status of English toleration and nationhood' (p. 49). Sauer's third chapter, 'Natural Law: Milton's Post-Revolutionary *Defences* of England', examines Milton's defences of the regicide and his other political tracts (*Tenure of Kings and Magistrates*, *Eikonoklastes*, *The Readie and Easie Way*) not in terms of their political ideology, but in terms of Milton's 'privileging . . . the moral disposition of the Protestant nation over its political, republican character' (p. 75). She discusses the ways these texts help audiences (both contemporary and in the latter parts of the seventeenth century) in their evaluation of the revolution. Chapter 4, 'Disestablishment: Divorces of Church and State', examines Milton's later prose (*Treatise of Civil Power*, *Considerations Touching the Likeliest Means to Remove Hirelings Out of the Church*, *Of True Religion*) advocating the end of established religion in Restoration England. Noting that Milton had long agreed that 'religious conformity and the union of church and state are not requisite for the establishment of a civil society or peaceful commonwealth' (p. 95), Sauer argues that within these tracts Milton lays out arguments that reject notions of nationhood bound up in Old Testament theocratic ideas and 'advance an alternative foundation, typological narrative, and conscience for a New Testament nation' (p. 97). In chapters 5 and 6, Sauer turns from an examination of toleration and nationhood as internal discussions within England to a consideration of the topics in regards to the relationships between nations. Chapter 5, 'Geography: Spatial Poetics', treats nationhood 'not as internally defined by principles of natural law, intra-national politics, or church-state relations, but in terms of a global formulation and mapping of place and space' (p. 115). Noting the growing early modern interest in geography and mapping the world's physical and cultural layout, Sauer examines Milton's extensive use of geographical language in his poetry and in his *Brief History of Moscovia*, arguing that these references give us insight into 'the parameters, status, and history as well as the moral character of the nation' (p. 117). Sauer's final chapter, 'Exogamy: "Entercourse" with Philistines', considers *Samson Agonistes* as a 'test' regarding the limits of 'tolerance for ethnic, religious, and national difference' (p. 20). Samson's biblical story stands out because of his transgression of laws guarding ancient Israel against intermixing with the surrounding nations, and Milton uses this aspect of the story to raise questions about 'Israelite chosenness and Philistine reprobation' (p. 20) as well as to 'redefine' the 'terms of inclusion and exclusion' (p. 136). Ultimately, Sauer argues, the poem shows Israelite narratives of nationhood to be vexed and 'at variance with itself' (p. 158).

Sauer's work in this impressive monograph provides deep insights into Milton's religious and political views and contextualizes Milton's views against larger developments in his religious and political milieu. It performs the important work of broadening our often all-too-narrow focus on Milton and local concerns. It also provides means of fully understanding Milton's views on liberty, views that are more situational than modern readers have often taken them, and the complex social forces that informed them.

In *Milton and the People*, Paul Hammond examines Milton's rhetorical use of and shifting attitudes towards the gathered multitudes that formed the commonwealth and church he so often discussed in his writings. In his introductory chapter, 'Who Are the People?', Hammond begins first with terminology, identifying common words that Milton related to 'the people'— democracy, laity, popular, vulgar, plebeian, and others—and traces their Greek or Latin roots in order to display the full range of meanings these words could carry. With this foundation set, he describes his core concerns in the study as understanding 'Milton's struggle with the contradiction between his vision of an ideal people summoned by God to fulfil their historic vocation, and his recognition that many, perhaps most, are incapable of responding to that calling' (pp. 11–12). He argues that such a study reveals that Milton, over time, compresses his own sense of the 'ideal people' into a 'smaller and smaller group' (p. 12). Chapter 2, 'The Young Milton and the Writer's Vocation', discusses Milton's view of himself in relation to the masses in his earliest writing. Hammond describes how Milton's sense of poetic calling leads him into 'a conscious separation from the people, or at least from those who do not share his aims or his abilities' (p. 15). Hammond makes this case by careful examination of Milton's word choices in his Latin school writings and in *A Maske*. Chapter 3, 'The Anti-Prelatical Tracts', considers an aspect of Milton's life and work in which his representation of the people is much more generous: his thoughts on the proper organization of a reformed church. Though Hammond notes tensions within Milton's terminology—he 'uses "the people" in both . . . an Old Testament vision of the whole nation being called to be

God's people, and a New Testament vision of the true believers being called out from the mass of the people' (p. 32)—he also points out that Milton makes great efforts, at least in this context, to argue for the capacity of 'the people' to mind its own spiritual affairs without oversight, despite the fact that such arguments '[sit] awkwardly with Milton's lofty disparagement of the common people elsewhere' (p. 45). 'The Writings on Divorce', discussed in the fourth chapter, demonstrate yet another shift in Milton's account of and relationship with 'the people'. Noting that Milton himself saw his use of English rather than Latin in the first divorce tract as an error that allowed irresponsible reading, Hammond discusses how subsequent tracts are explicitly geared to a more academic and theologically minded (and elite) audience. In addition, he argues that Milton brands the critics of his ideas as coming from 'the lowest of the vulgar' (p. 67).

In chapter 5 of *Milton and the People*, Hammond discusses *Areopagitica* and the 'the role of the enlightened individual who seeks to use his persuasive powers to guide [the people] and to shape the state' (p. 78). Though Milton makes elitist gestures by speaking to a select audience, suggesting that freedom for scholars is necessary to build up the vulgar, and castigating the vulgarity of the licensers, he nonetheless argues for 'the importance of trusting the people to read responsibly and decide wisely' (p. 78). Chapter 6, 'The English Political Writings', notes the intense conflict in seventeenth-century political debates regarding the powers of and attitudes towards 'the people', particularly in regard to the source of regal power and who (the people, the elite, God alone?) has the power to challenge a king. In this chapter, Hammond reviews the political theories of Milton and a number of Milton's contemporaries to trace these conflicts. He suggests that for Milton's part, there is a 'doubleness' (p. 137) to his views of the people, given their immense power 'to put down the mighty, and to demolish idols' (p. 138) but also to be led astray. This leads Milton to shift his vocabulary from talking about 'the people' as they are to his vision of what 'the nation' could be. Between chapters 6 and 7, Hammond includes an 'Excursus' presenting an account of 'Hobbes and the People'. Hammond focuses on Hobbes's efforts to remove the concept of 'the people' as a unified whole from the political equation, apart from their unity within the person of a covenanted sovereign. Apart from the sovereign, there are only individuals in the 'state of nature' (p. 139), and once a sovereign has been empowered there is 'no question of any body—such as a parliament—being thought to represent the people' (p. 141). Failure to understand this relationship between king and subject is, in Hobbes's view, the chief cause of the civil war in England. In chapter 7 Hammond continues his investigation of Milton's work by examining 'The Latin Political Writings'. In his tracts defending the regicide, in which Milton frames arguments as defences of 'the English People', he must consider questions of who the people are and how to understand the actions of some individuals taken in the name of the people. Hammond discusses the difficulty of Milton's task, pointing to the importance of establishing who is empowered to act as a representative of the people, particularly when the issue at hand is the removal of another representative of the people, the king. He also highlights Milton's focus on ennobling the people, 'asserting their . . . right to self-determination' (p. 152) and his strategy of defining the '*populus*' to the exclusion of the '*vulgus*' (p. 179). In chapter 8, 'The Restoration Prose Writings', Hammond focuses on the difficulties Milton faced in *The Readie and Easie Way* as he navigated a changing audience (Parliament in the first edition, the wider electorate in the second), the problematic nature of Parliament as a body as it evolved over the twenty years of civil war and interregnum, and confronted concerns about how a new representative body should be chosen in response to this political moment, particularly given Milton's developing fears of 'the impetuous force of the people' (p. 209). Hammond also considers Milton's 1670 *History of Britain* as an 'oblique commentary on the period through which Milton lived' (pp. 209–10) and the failure of the people 'to achieve that liberty which was within their grasp' (p. 214). Hammond's ninth chapter considers 'The Major Poems: *Paradise Lost*, *Paradise Regained*, and *Samson Agonistes*'. He considers how the Milton's poetic works take up similar questions of 'liberty', 'licence', and 'servitude' (p. 218) as the prose, but in miniature. Adam and Eve are a 'proto-community' (p. 218) that breaks down over the choice of 'licence, the licentiousness of appetite' over 'true liberty' (p. 218), and the fallen angels are a 'rebellious rout' (p. 219) that stands in for the many who similarly fail to embrace liberty. Opposed to these, Hammond argues, are figures like Abdiel, Moses, the Son and Samson, 'a series of images of heroic individuals who submit themselves to, and thereby bear witness to, the will of God' (p. 218).

Hammond's perceptive reading and meticulous scholarship are apparent throughout this significant study. Milton's relationship with 'the people', as Hammond demonstrates, is highly fraught and situationally contingent for Milton as he negotiates his own poetic ambitions and political/religious vision for England. This study is essential for any who are interested in Milton's rhetoric, his ideas about the ideal commonwealth, and Milton's conceptualization of himself in relation to his society.

William Walker's *Antiformalist, Unrevolutionary, Illiberal Milton: Political Prose, 1644–1660* takes on the task of wading into the flood of 'isms' that proliferate in Milton studies today and sorting out the degree to which Milton lives up to the labels applied to him and his work. Drawing on the work of writers like H.M. Höpfl and C.H. George, among others, who raise cautions about the use of anachronistic neologisms to characterize the past in reductive or subjective ways, Walker investigates some key 'isms' that are commonly applied to Milton: 'republicanism, radicalism, and liberalism' (p. 6). Further, in exploring the possibility of an 'antiformalist, unrevolutionary, illiberal' Milton, Walker attempts to seriously consider some parts of Milton's prose that 'we dismiss as *mere* rhetoric' when it 'challenges our assumptions' (p. 7). This study is divided into three sizeable chapters, each focusing on one of the 'isms' Walker aims to reassess.

Chapter 1, 'Antiformalist Milton', makes the argument that Milton's most enduring commitment to the question of the proper form of government is to declining to endorse any in particular. Walker, in a series of constituent arguments, makes the case that Milton hesitates to endorse particular forms of government throughout most of his prose work. Despite having ample opportunity to unequivocally reject monarchy and endorse republicanism, Milton steadfastly does not. The only exception to this pattern is *The Readie and Easie Way*, which, according to Walker, takes an anti-monarchical position in relation to a specific set of political circumstances on the eve of the Restoration. Milton argues against monarchy in order to persuade his countrymen to prevent the re-establishment of the Stuart monarchy in England by whatever rhetorical means necessary. Though Walker finds Milton to be largely anti-formalist, he does find Milton strongly endorsing certain political ideas that are often associated with republicanism: freedom of the people to choose their form of government, freedom of the people to make their own laws, and the ability of the people to control the nation's military power. Walker suggests that any form of government which protected these ideas was acceptable to Milton. In the end, Walker sets out an interesting case that the image of Milton as a committed anti-monarchical republican is an exaggeration. Though no fan of kings, and particularly no fan of Stuart kings, Milton's main political commitments are to meritocracy and the protection of civil liberty, regardless of the form of government.

Walker's second chapter, 'Unrevolutionary Milton', begins with an epigraph from *Tenure of Kings and Magistrates* that sets the tone for the chapter: 'I doe not say it is rebellion, if' (p. 55). Walker begins with definitions of a key term: radicalism is an effort to overthrow something established and replace it with something new. It's about throwing out the old instead of repairing or reforming it. Walker then provides evidence from a variety of potentially radical sites within Milton's oeuvre that seeks to demonstrate that Milton did not describe or conceive of his actions or positions as radical, but rather as mostly conservative, or, in the language of the period, moderate. Walker's collection of arguments is extensive. He describes how Milton and his compatriots rejected the label of rebel for themselves and instead applied it to the king (the one who was in opposition to legitimate authority, as they understood it). The rhetoric of the supporters of Parliament is dissected and shown to be largely affirmative of the office of king even as it fought against the man who held that office. Supporters of Parliament position themselves as acting moderately and in self-defence. Most importantly, the goals of the parliamentarians, both in politics and religion, are cast as restorations of long-standing rights or ancient beliefs. Walker's argument is that, far from being radicals that tear down the old to make way for the new, Milton and the parliamentarians take every opportunity to describe their actions as consistent with the established order. Walker ends this chapter with an examination of several sets of beliefs—Arminianism, antinomianism, and millenarianism—that are sometimes imputed to Milton and that were considered in his day to be heretical. Walker defends Milton (as he represents himself in the prose, 1644–60) against any charge of holding heretical or immoderate versions of any of these beliefs. He argues that Milton's public statements related to these beliefs were largely consistent with orthodox belief of the time.

The final chapter, 'Illiberal Milton', examines whether or not Milton's work supports the notion that his ideas are consistent with modern liberalism, or can even be plausibly seen as foundations of liberalism. Walker argues that though some aspects of Milton's writings are consistent with liberalism, 'there are also fundamental differences between Milton's writings and those by people we now call "liberals", ones which render untenable the view that liberalism is the result of a natural or inevitable development of his ideas' (p. 108). Walker's support for this position spans a wide variety of liberal ideas that are often associated with Milton, ideas such as the equality of all people, affirmation of individual autonomy, the importance of civil liberties, and more. For each of these areas, Walker lays out the arguments for seeing Milton as liberal and evaluating the evidence, sometimes significant evidence, for agreeing. But in each case, Walker points out not only the limits of Milton's liberal ideas, but also the ways in which his larger ideological framework prevents him from moving any further in the liberal direction than he has already gone. For example, with regard to civil liberties, an idea that Milton is often considered to have a unshakeable commitment to, Walker argues that 'Milton is perfectly happy to *deny* a wide range of civil liberties to most men, at least until they live up to his moral and religious standards' (p. 119). The well-known exception to Milton's civil liberty arguments are Catholics. But Walker notes that Catholics are by no means the only ones who are singled out for restriction. He also notes that other key elements of Milton's liberal legacy, freedom of publication, freedom to participate in the political process, freedom of religion, are all explicitly limited in portions of Milton's prose. Finally, Walker observes that, while liberals may draw on Milton for inspiration, Milton's own vision for the future is quite different from that of liberals. To equate liberalism with 'progress or as the fulfillment of Milton's vision . . . is only possible for those whose world view differs profoundly from his' (p. 173).

Walker's study is sure to raise eyebrows among Milton scholars who see Milton as the early modern progenitor of so many modern ideas about liberty and relationships to authority. But regardless of any differing views on the ultimate meaning of Milton's work, Walker's argument in this monograph serves three significant purposes: it reminds us of the importance of examining our own leanings and assumptions as we interpret Milton's work, it asks for precision and care in differentiating Milton's own beliefs or goals from how his words influenced later thinkers, and, above all, it forces us into even closer engagement with Milton's words and contexts. Worthy purposes all.

Paradise Lost and the Cosmological Revolution, by Dennis Danielson, is a fascinating attempt to recapture what he rightly calls 'the magnificence and vibrancy of the cosmic canvas that Milton unfurls in his epic' (p. xiv). Arguing that the cosmological aspects of *Paradise Lost* have been swept up in the 'clichés and generalizations about the shape and meaning of the cosmological revolution' (pp. xiv–xv) that many have made, Danielson aims to restore the seventeenth-century astronomical context—with particular attention given to terminology—that modern readers need to understand the depth of Milton's engagement with the subject. Danielson positions this work as more 'about Milton and his context than about Milton studies' (p. xvii), pointing to John Leonard's recent work *Faithful Labourers* (reviewed in *YWES* 94[2015]) as a resource for those interested in untangling critical responses to this aspect of Milton's work.

Danielson's study spans eight chapters. In chapter 1, 'The Discarded Image', he walks the reader in wonderful detail through the Aristotelian/ Ptolemaic model of the universe and the theory of physics that underpins that model. He allows the reader to see not only the basic features of such a model, but the ways in which that model developed from physical laws as understood in antiquity. The second chapter, 'Multiverse, Chaos, Cosmos', examines first the tendency of Christian thinkers, from St Augustine onward, and particularly in the seventeenth century, to attempt to harmonize pagan understandings of creation and cosmology (especially with regard to concepts like chaos and the source of matter) with teachings from the Bible. Danielson argues, though, that Milton's approach to this concern, his insistence on *creatio ex deo* in place of *creatio ex nihilo*, for example, 'transcends in fresh ways' (p. 33) the attempts of his contemporaries. The chapter concludes with an exposition of Milton's multiverse (a better term for Milton's cosmology than 'world' or 'universe'), its creation, and its cosmography. Next, in 'Copernicus and the Cosmological Bricoleurs', Danielson introduces the changes brought to cosmology by Copernicus and those that follow him. Acknowledging both the innovations and the similarities between the old model and new models, Danielson emphasizes the iterative nature of cosmological theory, calling it 'more a collective achievement of ingenious bricoleurs than is often recognized' (p. 66). Chapter 4, 'Milton and Galileo Revisited (1): "Incredible Delight" ', discusses the contributions of Galileo to cosmological debates—his observations and the philosophical ramifications thereof—as well as considering the response of Milton, who made liberal mention of Galileo's ideas while stopping short of embracing them explicitly, and Bacon, who had less patience than Milton with the lack of a fully understood philosophical system encompassing cosmological innovations. The fifth chapter, 'Milton and Galileo Revisited (2): "What If?" ', sketches a view of seventeenth-century cosmology that was not defined by a binary between Ptolemy and Copernicus, but which encompassed a number of different systems for organizing the heavens—the least accepted of which was the Ptolemaic. Danielson argues cogently that though *Paradise Lost* does not overtly embrace Copernicanism, this fact does not imply that his knowledge of astronomy was deficient or his views on cosmology backward. Instead, Daniel suggests that Milton leans towards a more open-ended engagement with cosmology. Chapter 6, 'The Sun', discusses the role played by our closest star in the cosmological drama Danielson has been unfolding, as well as the significant role it plays in *Paradise Lost*. The shifting of the Sun from planetary status to occupying the centre of the universe was symbolically, even religiously, fraught, as was the discovery of sunspots that marred its bright and seemingly pure face. Danielson draws connections between these astronomical developments and Milton's descriptions of light, creation, and of Satan's considerations of Sun as he approaches Earth. Earth itself is the topic of chapter 7, 'Planet Earth', which examines similar questions of value, nobility, essence, and place regarding the Earth. So many of the difficulties regarding newer systems of cosmology have centred around assumptions that the Earth is the lowest and most ignoble of places, just as similar assumptions of the nobility of the Sun prevented some from accepting that it stood at the centre (or bottom) of this cosmological scheme. Still, others, Danielson notes, saw the rearrangement of the cosmos as an opportunity to assert the nobility of the Earth and the change, growth, and life that are so central to it. Danielson draws parallels between both positions—concerns about the status of the

Earth in relation to other heavenly bodies and this vision of ennobling and extending earthly generation and change into the heavens—with many of the topics discussed by Adam and Raphael in *Paradise Lost*. Danielson's final chapter, as the title suggests, discusses the relationship between this cosmological revolution and 'Space Flight, ET, and Other Worlds'. Copernicus's judgement that the Earth is a planet opens up the possibility that other Earth-like planets may exist amid the vastness of the universe, populated with life. Danielson presents some of the many writers and thinkers, Milton included, who have followed up on such a prospect by considering the existence of other worlds, other places fit for human habitation, the means of travel among them, as well as the possibility of extra-terrestrial life.

Danielson's book is a triumph of scholarship, both in terms of time and energy expended in re-creating for a modern audience the debates over and developments in cosmological theory that occurred through the early modern period and in his careful attention to the breadth and depth of Milton's engagement with and representation of ideas that animated those debates. It promises to engage both science-lovers and Miltonists alike.

David Quint, in *Inside Paradise Lost: Reading the Designs of Milton's Epic*, presents readings of the poem that are, in his words, 'more and less familiar': that it rejects 'war and empire' in exchange for 'Love and Liberty', that Satan's 'lust for power, his institution of monarchy in hell, and his readiness to enslave others' is the foil to the poem's main movement, and that Milton is a 'Christian Humanist' advocating the 'true empowerment of men and women as free moral agents' (p. 1). Quint's main focus, however, is the means by which Milton creates these meanings in his epic: his use of allusion and weaving of deep patterns of word and image for the reader to follow.

Quint presents his argument in eight chapters. Chapter 1, 'Milton's Book of Numbers: Book 1 and Its Catalog', discusses the early portions of *Paradise Lost* as reversal of a scene from the *Iliad*, down to the smallest detail. Instead of gathering to renew their commitment to war, followed by 'Homer's famous catalog of ships' (p. 15), and renewed battle, *Paradise Lost* begins with the catalogue and ends with a discussion of warfare that 'fizzles out' (p. 15). In shaping the poem in this way, Quint argues, Milton reveals the fallen angels' empty and false nature and draws attention to the fact that 'action in this epic will be verbal' (p. 17). In chapter 2, 'Ulysses and the Devils: The Unity of Book 2', Quint argues that the figure of Ulysses and the stories of Ulysses' travels are continually echoed in the second book of *Paradise Lost* and provide thematic unity between the council scene of the early portion of the book and Satan's journey through Chaos at the end. 'Fear of Falling: Icarus, Phaethon, and Lucretius', Quint's third chapter, traces buried connections between Milton's chief focus in the poem—the Fall—and the Ovidean characters of Icarus and Phaethon, connections that only are revealed 'by patient philology from complicated, but coherent and deliberate systems of allusions to earlier epic poetry' (p. 63). Further, Quint argues, Milton uses these images of failed flyers to help him resist Lucretianism by finding 'personal relief or exemption from a fallen condition in the winged elevation of his verse' (p. 85). Chapter 4, 'Light, Vision, and the Unity of Book 3', examines the tension in Book III between the heavenly light that dominates the first half of the book and the solar and stellar light that dominates the second, a tension that asks the reader to examine and reject 'older Platonic analogies and correspondences, particularly between God and the sun' (p. 94). Quint notes that at the demarcation between these two different (but unified) realms of light stands the 'Paradise of Fools', the place for those who cannot rightly see the contrast and fall either 'to idolatry' or 'to godless materialism' (p. 95). Quint further argues that Milton's construction of Book III shows him creating 'a middle ground for poetry to occupy in the era of the New Science' (p. 95): a place where older cosmological ideas can be reused as points of comparison and criticism and as the materials for the making of new art and meaning. 'The Politics of Envy', chapter 5, makes the argument that the motivating force behind the Fall is not pride, as is often thought, but envy. Satan's envy of the Son leads him to his rebellion, and, Quint suggests, to instituting the kind of monarchy in hell that he critiques—falsely, in Quint's view—in heaven. Quint further explores the political dimensions of envy in Milton's historical moment and makes the case that Satan's sinful envy 'is repeated and inverted in the attempts of human conquerors and kings to play God in books 11 and 12' (p. 124). The sixth chapter, 'Getting What You Wish For: A Reading of the Fall', considers the 'double fall' (p. 156)—Eve, then Adam—in *Paradise Lost* and their differing circumstances. Noting that each of the figures corresponds with one of two 'wishes that Milton entertained throughout his writing career'—the wish to be independent and 'self-sufficient' (p. 154) and the wish to be involved with relationship and community, Quint argues that the falls of Eve and Adam function as critiques of each of these wishes in turn, and that 'each seem[s] to tip, to one side or the other, the equilibrium' of the poem. Quint further discusses the reverberation of these wishes and falls in other areas of Milton's oeuvre. Chapter 7, 'Reversing the Fall in Book 10', takes as its subject the after-effects of the fall in Book X. Quint points to an odd moment in the narrative, a logical loop in which Satan seems to be both listening in on Adam and Eve and hurrying back over the bridge to hell to celebrate his victory. He notes that this moment serves as the turning point of the book and of the epic as a whole: the point where the Devil's part in the action ends, stuck as he is in 'this vortex of fallenness' (p. 198), while Adam and Eve move on to reconcile with each other and with God. Quint argues that the construction of Book X demonstrates Milton's reversal of the patterns of the *Aeneid*, which presents the 'incompatibility of marriage and love with the historical mission of its hero', by allowing 'the story of a private couple' to overtake 'the grand all-inclusive history of God and devil' (p. 199). Further, Quint discusses the difficulties of the reconciliation of that couple, due to their consideration of suicide as a solution and to Adam's 'misogynistic' (p. 199) moments, moments, which Quint connects back to a rich library of sources. Lastly, in chapter 8, 'Leaving Eden', Quint considers the linkage (particularly clear in the first edition of the poem) between Book I and Books XI and XII, and the books' common linkage to Milton's *On the Morning of Christ's Nativity*. He argues that Book I's establishment of the devils' stronghold in hell and the account of their future existence as the recipients of idolatrous worship is answered in Books XI and XII in an account of the 'cessation of oracles' as well as the destruction of Eden 'as a possible temple and oracular shrine' (p. 235). He also suggests that Eden, for Milton, stands 'for the poem itself' (p. 235) and that the ending 'depicts the relinquishing of its own imaginative plenitude and riches, the end of epic poetry itself' (p. 236).

Quint's book is a tremendously learned study, displaying his wealth of knowledge of Milton's poem and of the immense body of classical epic literature that Milton draws upon. Not only does he point out the many allusions and connections Milton makes; Quint truly does take us inside the poem's construction to see what Milton *makes* of these materials: the ways these allusions and patterns coalesce into the poem's great themes. And he does all of this with great sensitivity and humour.

In *Preaching the Gospel of Black Revolt: Appropriating Milton in Early African American Literature*, Reginald A. Wilburn takes on the work of not only mapping out the rich presence of Milton within the work of early African American writers, but also theorizing the means by which these authors appropriate Milton for their own ends, the preaching of 'satanic gospels of black revolt . . . for messianic purposes of racial uplift in the cause of liberty and pursuit of freedom' (p. 3). Wilburn presents his argument in seven robust chapters, beginning with his introductory chapter, 'Making "Darkness Visible": Milton and Early African American Literature'. Here, Wilburn begins his work of theorizing by explaining the particular and often contradictory ways in which Milton's work is repurposed for the use of African American writers. He highlights key tropes, such as 'the talking book' (p. 17), from the African American tradition, 'features', he argues, that 'make darkness visible in Milton by calling attention to figures of blackness' (p. 17). He also focuses on the dual relevance for early African American audiences of the Romantic Satan, associated with the 'trope of the Signifying Monkey' (p. 25), and Milton's Eden, arguing that the combination of 'demonic rebellion and Edenic innocence yield[s] a gospel of black revolt that is balanced with a spirit of tempered assertiveness' (p. 35). Wilburn also makes it clear that the writers he considers break down the usual ideological coherences that characterize Milton studies, as they 'are sometimes in dialogue with orthodox interpretive communities and unorthodox ones at other times' (p. 40), the result being an expansion in the interpretative possibilities in Milton's work.

Shifting from the foundation-setting of the first chapter, Wilburn turns to his readings of specific writers in chapter 2, 'Phillis Wheatley's Miltonic Journeys in *Poems on Various Subjects*'. Here, Wilburn discusses Wheatley's engagement with *Paradise Lost*, particularly aspects of Milton's hell, in her *Poems*. He argues that the artistry in Wheatley's poetry is deeply subtextual and intertextual, with 'each successive engagement with Milton' in the poems enriching 'meaning on implied and inferential levels' (p. 58). Her 'journeys' into and out of Milton's hell, Wilburn argues, 'assist her in elevating her people several rungs up the Great Chain of Being' (p. 58) and begins a subversive tradition of African American literary engagement with Milton. Chapter 3, 'Black Audio-Visionaries and the Rise of Miltonic Influence in Colonial America and the Early Republic', turns from Wheatley's poetry to the work of black orators like Olaudah Equiano, Lemuel Haynes, Peter Williams Jr., William Hamilton, and David Walker, who drew on Milton to '[indict] the hell of slavery, often capitalizing on the moment to prophesy

God's imminent wrath' (p. 96). These writers and speakers took Miltonic themes, images, and even patterns of speech for rhetorical use, employing them to move their audiences emotionally and to lead them 'to embrace a spirit of antislavery revolt' (p. 97). The fourth chapter, 'Of Might and Men: Milton, Frederick Douglass, and Resistant Masculinity as Existential Geography', examines the role Milton played in the life and ideas of the great anti-slavery advocate, Frederick Douglass. He discusses Douglass's use of Milton 'as an iconic exemplum of self-made manhood' (p. 151) in his speech 'Self-Made Men', and the deep impression that this example made on Douglass in his other work. Wilburn concludes that 'Milton's literary persona, his use of satanic energy, as well as the Romantics' unorthodox readings of *Paradise Lost* all contribute to Douglass's emphasis on might and manly rhetoric' (p. 188). Wilburn's fifth chapter is 'Breaking New Grounds with Milton in Frances Ellen Watkins Harper's *Moses: A Story of the Nile*', which explores the significant Miltonic influence on Harper's brief epic poem on several levels. Wilburn notes some of the direct connections between Milton and Harper's work: the thematic and structural elements Harper gleaned from Milton's epics and the publication of her epic as a volume of two intertextually linked poems, much like Milton's 1671 volume. But he also notes an echo of Miltonic, demonic transgressiveness in her publication of this poem. Innovating beyond her previous work in the ballad form and the popular tastes of the time, Harper's work demonstrates a ' "wayward" aesthetic' that reworks the ways Milton could be used 'as charted by male writers and orators in the early African American tradition' (p. 195). Chapter 6, 'Miltonic Soundscapes in Anna Julia Cooper's *A Voice from the South*', investigates a fascinating text by the womanist Cooper, a set of eight essays set to music. Wilburn argues that Cooper's work dramatizes the 'indispensability of women and their voices in public discourse' (p. 230), and, further, that Milton plays a key, if subtle, role in this through Cooper's allusions to his work. Drawing on a term from African American musical tradition, 'worrying the line . . . an expressive style of repeating words, phrases, figures, or vocal sounds to exaggerated effect as a means for punctuating meaning' (p. 232), Wilburn holds that Cooper 'worries the line' of the Milton she received 'in order to promote a theme of gendered liberty' (p. 232). Chapter 7, 'Returning to Milton's Hell with Weapons of Perfect Passivity in Sutton E. Griggs's *Imperium in Imperio*', closes Wilburn's consideration of Milton and early African American writers by considering a figure that, he notes, has fallen out of favour in African American literary studies because of his unpopular accommodationist political stance. Wilburn discusses the deeply Miltonic nature of his novel, which presents the conflict between two political leaders, one with 'Satan's militant spirit' and the other a 'new messianic rebel' (p. 279) and which features a 'return to Milton's hell at the site of a black Pandaemonium' (p. 281). Even though Griggs had fallen from prominence within his tradition, Wilburn argues that a full understanding of Griggs's use of Milton will reveal the power of the way he 'privilege[s] the spiritual weaponry of perfect passivity over that of militant strength' (p. 285). Finally, in his epilogue, 'Malcolm X, *Paradise Lost*, and the Twentieth Century Infernal Reader', Wilburn looks ahead into the next century of African

American activism. In his brief discussion of Malcolm X, he notes his double view of Milton's Satan as both a representative of European whiteness and a model for resistance to tyranny such as he saw in America. He suggests that the example of Malcolm X shows how the 'themes, language, and imagery of *Paradise Lost* speak to the 'black consciousness' well into the twentieth century' (p. 333).

Wilburn's book is notable not only for its insightful readings of Milton's influence on the early African American tradition and for his careful theorizing of the ways black authors put Milton to work, but for his insistence that literary critics must attend to and cross the 'color line' (p. 3) of literary studies. Wilburn's willingness to cross that line allows the reader to have a deeper sense of how and what Milton can mean, and also to recognize the ingenuity and rhetorical skill of these writers who, as Wilburn suggests, 'complete and complicate' (p. 58) Milton in their own context.

Also published in 2014 was Jacob Blevins's *Humanism and Classical Crisis: Anxiety, Intertexts, and the Miltonic Memory*. It was not possible in the time available to undertake a full review of this text for the present volume. While this monograph will be revisited in next year's review, I include for the interested reader a listing of Blevins's chapters to give a better sense of the material he covers. Chapter 1 is 'The Convergence of Voice, the Artifacts of Memory: Theoretical Orientations'; chapter 2 is 'The Renaissance, Rom, and Humanism's Classical Crisis'; chapter 3 follows as 'Anxiety and Constructions of the Text: Dialogues with a Classical Past'; chapter 4 presents 'Miltonic Elegy and the Rebirth of a Roman (Split) Subject'; and chapter 5 closes the volume with 'Milton's Heroic Action and Formal Falls'.

We turn now to 2014's edited collections on Milton. *Milton Now: Alternative Approaches and Contexts*, edited by Catharine Gray and Erin Murphy, is a collection of essays aimed at continuing the work of the 1987 collection *Re-membering Milton*, to 'embrace and encourage a more meth-odologically adventurous Milton studies . . . . addressing topics, contexts, and theories rarely broached in the field' (p. 2) with the goal of collecting the most promising new approaches to ongoing critical debates. A secondary goal expressed by the editors is to interrogate the dominance of historicist scholarship in the field. They have organized essays in three sections: 'History and Temporality', which examines both history and time as 'objects of analysis' (p. 4); 'Form and Figures', focusing on formal analysis; and 'Taking Liberties: Reconsidering Miltonic Freedom', which 'emphasizes diversity of topic and approach by offering five very different essays that take up one, central Miltonic concept—liberty.

The first section, 'History and Temporality', opens with ' "Shipwreck is Everywhere": *Lycidas* and the Problems of the Secular' by Sharon Achinstein. Achinstein here offers a reconsideration of the 1638 version of *Lycidas*, the poem without the explanatory heading added in Milton's 1645 collection. This addition, Achinstein suggests, steers the reader towards a prophetic under-standing of the poem and shuts down other avenues of meaning. Achinstein works to recover these other meanings, particularly the relationship between 'questions of divine justice' (p. 29) and 'discourses of commemoration, belief and prophecy' (p. 31), an interplay of sacred and secular concerns. The second

essay in the section, '"What Dost Thou in This World?"' by Jonathan
Goldberg, takes more direct aim at historicist readings of Milton, readings
that attempt to tie poems to particular dates and particular political moments,
by focusing on aspects of *Paradise Regained* that raise questions about timing,
perspective, and the relationship between events and meaning. Beginning with
a spirited critique of critics, such as Laura Lunger Knoppers, who tie *Paradise
Regained* to 1671 and to republican politics (as well as a critique of critics, such
as Stanley Fish, who claim to resist such historicist reductiveness but who
engage in reductions of their own), Goldberg focuses on various 'puzzles'
(p. 55) in the poem: the Son's mission on Earth, his identity, and the meaning
of events like his baptism (represented both in the text and in biblical sources
in different ways and from different perspectives) that resist reductive
readings, that insist on 'non-coincident temporality' (p. 60). The third and
final essay in the first section is Feisal G. Mohamed's 'Milton's Capitalist Son
of God? Temporality and Divine Order in *De Doctrina Christiana*'. Here,
Mohamed discusses the Milton's understanding of time as suggested by his
anti-Trinitarian beliefs, specifically his stance that the Son's creation marks the
beginning of time, and connects these ideas to 'the rationalization of time
taking place in early modern science' (p. 70) and to neo-Marxist discussions of
rational time and capitalism.

The collection's second section, 'Forms and Figures', begins with Ann
Baynes Coiro's 'Sufficient and Free: The Poetry of *Paradise Lost*'. The essay
focuses on the reader's experience in *Paradise Lost*, an experience that is
different from the closed, moralistic one described in Stanley Fish's work. For
Coiro, the experience of the reader in *Paradise Lost* is one of continually
making interpretative choices. These choices, Coiro suggests, are built in to the
poem's verse paragraph form and are what she calls 'unsettling' and
'potentially dangerous', but also 'liberating' (p. 85). The second essay in this
section, Rachel Trubowitz's 'As Jesus Tends to Divinity in *Paradise Regained*:
Mathematical Limits and the Arian Son', takes up the 'figures' theme of the
section in an unusual way for literary studies. Trubowitz notes Milton's
interest in new mathematical developments in the period and applies some of
those concepts in a discussion of Milton's Arianism as it appears in *Paradise
Regained*. She concludes that 'the Arian heresy allows Milton and Newton to
integrate their theological beliefs with the mathematical innovations of their
shared historical moment' (p. 125). The final essay in this section is 'Uncouth
Milton', by Christopher Warley. Warley identifies in Milton's poetry what he
calls an 'uncouth aesthetic' (p. 130), a continuing concern of Milton with the
lowly and anonymous in life as opposed to the noble and exalted one. In his
discussion of *Lycidas*, Warley points to the narrator, the 'uncouth swain'
(p. 129) as a humble character speaking up for another humble character, the
dead Lycidas. He also notes the tensions involved in developing one's poetic
name by standing up for the nameless, as Milton does.

The final section of the collection, 'Taking Liberties: Reconsidering
Miltonic Freedom', is led by Molly Murray's 'The Liberty of the Subject
and the "Pris'ner Samson"'. Murray's key observation regarding *Samson
Agonistes* is that Milton describes Samson not as a slave, but as a prisoner.
Following on from this insight, Murray reconstructs an important context

against which the text might be read: seventeenth-century debates about civil liberties pertaining to imprisonment. She argues that, against this context, *Samson Agonistes* might be read as an effort 'to dramatize and interrogate this domestic strain of prison activism' (p. 152). The next essay, 'What Do Men Want? Satan, the Rake, and Masculine Desire', by Diane Purkiss, takes a radically different approach to the topic of liberty by discussing *Paradise Lost*, and Satan in particular, in relation to the idea of a rake or libertine. Using the poetry of Rochester as a starting point, Purkiss discusses the matrix of liberty, licence, power, and pleasure that underpins libertinism, and the ways in which libertinism connects with Restoration politics in the court of Charles II. She argues that Milton's problematic representations of Satan 'are in part due to its complicated engagement with the chainless, deliquescent rake-libertine' and the 'renewed gender crisis of monarchy' (p. 178). The third essay, Katherine Gillespie's 'Shades of Representation: Lucy Hutchinson's Ghost and the Politics of the Representative', investigates early modern attitudes towards women's liberty by putting Milton into dialogue with the works of Lucy Hutchinson. Working with the political ideas of male writers, like Milton, concerned about excessive political power on the part of rulers, Hutchinson, argues Gillespie, turns these arguments for 'limited dominion' (p. 196) on their head, 'staging a civil war with her own inner tyrant, lamenting that she has become a ghost condemned to purgatory for idolizing her husband' (p. 197), transforming arguments about political liberty into arguments for gender equality. Next, in 'Equiano, Satanism, and Slavery', Mary Nyquist discusses quotations of Milton's Satan in the work of Olaudah Equiano, a freed slave. In the midst of telling his story of escape from slavery, Equiano, a Christian, uses Satan's words describing hell, his views on God's tyranny, and the need for resistance as a means of representing his despair and outrage concerning enslavement. Nyquist's argument draws parallels between Equiano's use of these citations and satanic readings of *Paradise Lost*. The final essay in the volume, Reginald A. Wilburn's 'When Milton Was in Vogue: Cross-Dressing Miltonic Presence and William Craft's Slave Narrative', continues the theme of investigating the use of Milton's words in other texts. Wilburn puts a Miltonic epigraph used by Craft—a protestation of the freedom humans have from the dominion of other humans—into dialogue with a few other curious features of Craft's narrative: a cross-dressing subterfuge by Craft's wife (posing as a wealthy white man and Craft's owner) and Craft's self-assertion in writing the preface to his own narrative. Viewed in the context of these other features, Wilburn argues that 'Craft's use of the Miltonic epigraph is itself a rhetorical framing device that mimics the sartorial function of Ellen's fugitive garb and thus queers the interpretive "grounds of contention" in Milton and African American literary studies' (pp. 248–9).

This year's *Milton Studies*, edited by Laura Lunger Knoppers, once again does not disappoint, bringing readers eight excellent essays on a variety of topics. The first section, 'Medicine and Science', begins with Boyd Brogan's 'The Masque and the Matrix: Alice Egerton, Richard Napier, and Suffocation of the Mother' (*MiltonS* 55[2014] 3–52), a fascinating rethinking of the circumstances behind Milton's *A Maske*. Brogan notes the similarity between the symptoms suffered by the Lady in Milton's drama and a chastity-caused disease called the 'suffocation of the mother'. The correspondence between the symptoms of the disease and the events of the drama suggest the connection; even more compelling is evidence from the files of seventeenth-century physician Richard Napier that Alice Egerton, the woman who played 'the lady', had been treated for this disease a year before the performance. Brogan argues that Milton's writing on this seemingly sensitive topic may have been a result of a commission to celebrate Alice's recovery. Brogan's essay is followed in the volume by ' "His Footstep Trace": The Natural Theology of *Paradise Lost*', by Katherine Calloway (*MiltonS* 55[2014] 53–85). In her essay, Calloway works to free *Paradise Lost* from the Baconian idea that natural theology is a waste of time (p. 55), arguing that in Milton's conception, humans, both fallen and unfallen, should 'apply their reason toward theological ends' (p. 61). However, she notes that human reason is insufficient in itself for a full account of theology and that the poem demonstrates differences between the capabilities of fallen and unfallen humans in this pursuit.

The second section of *Milton Studies* 55, 'Classics for the Contemporary Age', opens with Seth Lobis's 'Milton's Tended Garden and the Georgic Fall' (*MiltonS* 55[2014] 89–111). Lobis's aim in the essay is to investigate georgic elements of the poem in order to correct oversights of previous readings, particularly with regard to Adam and Eve's conversations in Book IX and the fall that follows. Focusing his readings on the word 'tend', Lobis argues that Milton's use of the word draws attention to georgic aspects of the fall and 'invests the georgic with a new ethical and psychological depth' (p. 90). Next in the volume comes Leah Whitington's essay, 'Milton's Poetic of Supplication' (*MiltonS* 55[2014] 113–145). Noting the similarities between Satan's defiance before God and Milton's own republican fervour in his prose tracts, Whitington seeks in this essay a means of understanding supplication, and the refusal to supplicate, that avoids easy and sometimes misleading political conclusions. To this end, Whitington investigates the relationship of the poem to the concept of the suppliant as represented in the larger epic tradition. She argues that attending to this context makes it clear that, far from rejecting supplication outright for political reasons, Milton makes surprising use of it as 'a mechanism for explaining how unequal relationships might be unraveled' (p. 140). John Luke Rodrigue's 'Striking a Miltonic Pose: William Jackson's *Lycidas* and National Musical Identity' (*MiltonS* 55[2014] 147–174) follows. In this piece, Rodrigue discusses eighteenth-century musician William Jackson's adaptation of *Lycidas* and its relationship to the cultural figure Milton had become in that era. Rodrigue notes Milton's growing stature as a national (and nationalist) poet, and he argues that although artistically different from Milton, Jackson uses Milton in order to forward a rather Miltonic project in music: 'reclaiming "ancient liberty" by reviving "national melody" . . . against the ravings of current musical fashions' (p. 160).

At the start of the third section of *Milton Studies* 55, 'History, Politics, and Poetics', is Alison A. Chapman's 'Satan's Pardon: The Forms of Judicial Mercy in *Paradise Lost*' (*MiltonS* 55[2014] 177–206). Chapman takes up a familiar question concerning *Paradise Lost*: is it possible for Satan to receive pardon from God? But instead of examining it theologically, as many have done, she looks to the legal procedures and social conventions regarding judicial pardons in the seventeenth century. Read against the backdrop of this legal and social context, Chapman argues, episodes like Satan's deliberations about the potential for pardon and Adam and Eve's discussion of how to go about seeking pardon both demonstrate the time's 'elaborate cultural discourse' of pardoning, 'with its own forms of address, assumptions, gestures, procedures, preconditions, and contingencies' (p. 179). Next in the section is 'Foreign Policy and the Feast Day: Milton's Poetic Nativity', by Andrea Walkden (*MiltonS* 55[2014] 207–235). In this essay, Walkden establishes a connection between a grouping of three politically themed poems from Milton's Cambridge days and the grouping of religious 'feast day' poems ('Ode on the Morning of Christ's Nativity', 'Passion', and 'Upon the Circumcision'). The earlier group demonstrates, as has been noted, Milton's concern about the religious and political strife in Europe. Walkden works to elucidate aspects of one of these poems, 'In quintum Novembris', by reading it against the backdrop of European religious conflict. But she argues that this poem should also be seen as the first attempt by Milton to write a feast-day poem, and that the earlier group of political poems 'prepared [Milton] to write the English religious odes just a few years later' (p. 210). The last essay in the volume is Michael Komorowski's '"On the New Forcers of Conscience" and Milton's Erastianism' (*MiltonS* 55[2014] 237–268). Komorowski's study takes up questions about Milton's level of commitment to toleration as an absolute principle or whether his position was more pragmatic. In response to some critics who see a common concern about liberty of conscience in both Milton's 1640s poem 'On the New Forcers of Conscience' and his later tract 'Of Civil Power', Komorowski suggests Milton's inclination 'for both intellectual and practical reasons' (p. 239) towards Erastianism. Second, he argues that the poem represents Milton's effort to use poetry to formulate a complex response to his subject, to use it 'for articulating the conflicts and compromises inherent in political activism' (p. 240).

The Cambridge Companion to Paradise Lost, edited by Louis Schwartz, is a very useful volume of essays intended to help the reader unfamiliar with Milton's great epic and its many contexts, 'providing advice and guidance about how to begin thinking about the poem and apprehending what many readers . . . have found so richly compelling about it' (p. xii). The collection is divided into four sections, focusing in turn on characters, contexts, important interpretative issues within the poem, and reception. Given that these texts are meant to be introductory, I won't rehearse the argument of each essay. But to give a sense of the topics covered and the outstanding team of scholars who participated in this collection, I will provide a list of the essays and their contributors. Part I includes Stephen M. Fallon's 'Milton as Narrator in *Paradise Lost*'; 'Satan', by Neil Forsyth; John Rumrich's 'Things of Darkness: Sin, Death, Chaos'; and 'The Problem of God', by Victoria Silver. Part II contains 'Classical Modes', by Maggie Kilgour; Jeffery Shoulson's 'Milton's Bible'; John Creaser's 'The Line in *Paradise Lost*'; 'The Pre-Secular Politics of *Paradise Lost*', by Paul Stevens; and 'Cosmology', by Karen L. Edwards. Part III comprises 'Imagining Eden', by William Shullenberger; Joad Raymond's 'Milton's Angels'; 'Gender', by Shannon Miller; 'Temptation', by W. Gardner

Campbell; and Mary C. Fenton's 'Regeneration in Books 11 and 12'. Lastly, in Part IV is 'Reception', by William Kolbrener. In this volume, Schwartz has succeeded in gathering a great number of important topics concerning *Paradise Lost* and compelling voices within Milton studies. Because of this, his collection will hold immense value for any reader who strives to better understand Milton's masterpiece.

In addition to these books and monographs, the volume and quality of scholarly articles considering Milton in 2014 were impressive. In addition to *Milton Quarterly*'s usual fine assortment of essays, a variety of other journals also published work on Milton. For the convenience of readers, this review groups articles into six thematic categories: seventeenth-century social and political contexts, early modern science, classical and biblical sources, theology, issues of reception and adaptation, and theoretical approaches.

Under the category of articles addressing Milton and seventeenth-century social and political contexts, Thomas N. Corns's 'Christopher Hill on Milton, Bunyan, and Winstanley' (*PSt* 36:iii[2014] 209–18) reviews and reconsiders the influential presence of historian Christopher Hill amongst early modern literary scholarship. Examining Hill's work on Milton, John Bunyan, and Gerrard Winstanley, Corns draws attention to Hill's 'broad strategy' of situating writers 'in a crowded landscape populated with mid-century radicals' (p. 213) and using these webs of connections to solidify arguments for radical themes within the works of these writers. But he also praises Hill as one who gained a uniquely deep understanding of the host of radical ideas proliferating in the mid-seventeenth century, saying that Hill 'had learnt the language of extreme radicalism in early-modern England' (p. 215), enabling him to forge the compelling connections between writers and context that informs the work of so many scholars. Next, Kat Lecky, in 'Naturalization in the *Mirror* and *A Mask*' (*SEL* 54:i[2014] 125–42), examines the relationship between Milton's *A Maske Presented at Ludlow Castle* and John Higgins's *The Firste Parte of the Mirour for Magistrates*. Noting that both texts embrace a 'republican principle of citizenship' (p. 125), a 'naturalized citizenship' based not on birth or background, but on 'political participation' (p. 138), Lecky argues that this points to a new understanding of Milton's early political beliefs that is more republican than has previously been thought. 'Lieuwe van Aitzema and John Milton's *The Doctrine and Discipline of Divorce*: The Marquette Case' (*Dutch Crossing* 38:iii[2014] 235–43), by Paul R. Sellin, presents the account of the translation of Milton's tract *The Doctrine and Discipline of Divorce* into Dutch in the mid-1650s. He situates the publication in relation to the ongoing dispute between Milton and Alexander Morus over Milton's defences of the regicide. Morus, as part of his attack on Milton, made reference to his stance on divorce in order to 'be-smut' (p. 236) Milton (in the words of Aitzema, the publisher of the Dutch translation of *Doctrine*), and in doing so created a 'new and lively market' (p. 238) for Milton's tract and pushed his ideas into Dutch controversies about marriage and divorce. Next, R.V. Young's 'Milton and Solitude' (*BJJ* 21:i[2014] 92–113) explores the theme of solitude in Milton's religious poetry and its relationship to the religious changes brought about by the Protestant Reformation. Noting Milton's 'attraction to the theme of solitude' (p. 98) and the prominent examples of solitary characters—most prominently, Adam and Eve in *Paradise Lost* and the Son in *Paradise Regained*—Young reads Milton's work in relation to similarly themed European poetry. In doing so, he argues that the prevalence of solitude in this poetry is 'evidence for . . . [an] unintended collaboration . . . between the Protestant Reformation and the secularization of Western civilization' (p. 109). Also from the *Ben Jonson Journal* is '*Paradise Lost* and Political Image Wars' (*BJJ* 21:ii[2014] 203–27), by David Loewenstein, which seeks to direct the debate about the political involvements of Milton's *Paradise Lost* away from efforts to make the poem into a political allegory by focusing on Milton's engagement with 'the language and symbolism of political image wars in seventeenth-century England' (p. 203). Noting the historical work of scholars like Kevin Sharpe, who demonstrates that both sides in the English Civil War 'drew on similar vocabularies and symbols of power' (p. 204), Loewenstein argues that Milton is aware of these discourses of power and makes use of them in the poem in order to challenge readers to 'think freshly and skeptically about political image-making' (p. 204). Next, Robert Kilgore's 'The Politics of King David in Early Modern English Verse' (*SP* 111:iii[2014] 411–41) examines the use and treatment of the biblical figure of King David in the politics and poetry of Stuart England to help explain Milton's seeming coolness towards David in his lone appearance in *Paradise Lost*. Though Milton considers David in more detail in his prose works because of David's relevance to biblical discourses of kingship, Kilgore points out the 'politicization of David by the Stuart regime', the usefulness of the biblical poet/king in the hands of early modern writers for 'poetical and political analysis' (p. 413), and Milton's reasons for discomfort concerning David.

Articles concerning Milton and seventeenth-century social and political contexts continue with ' "To due conversation accessible"; or, The Problem of Courtship in Milton's Divorce Tracts and *Paradise Lost*' (*TSLL* 56:i[2014] 43–65), by Lara Dodds, who investigates the problems that underlie Milton's arguments about divorce in his prose tracts. Following the objections of one of Milton's respondents to *Doctrine and Discipline of Divorce*, Dodd explores the connection between Milton's failure with courtship and the problems noted by some with his ideas about marriage and about women in general. Dodds compares Milton's views on 'consent and marriage formation' with other early modern views, she considers the implications of Milton's ideas about divorce and 'his treatment of issues of gender, sexuality and marriage in *Paradise Lost*', and she argues that, within *Paradise Lost*, the twin stories of Adam and Eve's courtship 'allow Milton to revisit the problems posed by courtship in the polemics of the 1640s' (p. 44). Edmund C. White, in ' "Uniform in Virtue": Discipline and Reform in Milton's Doctrine and Discipline of Divorce (1643 and 1644)' (*PSt* 36:ii[2014] 97–116), works to more fully contextualize debates about Milton's two editions of *Doctrine and Discipline of Divorce* within the growing conflict within the Milton's England over church governance and particular questions of how problematic behaviour would be disciplined. Arguing that 'current scholarship . . . either overlooks or misunderstands' the relationship between Milton's work and these conflicts, White seeks to demonstrate the connection between the escalating conflict between Presbyterians and Independents and Milton's revised views in the two editions of the tract. He also highlights the difficulties involved in categorizing Milton's ideas and terminology due to the rhetorical challenges of appealing to the 'widest possible audience' (p. 100) in these debates. Next, John Coffey, in '"The Brand of Gentilism": Milton's Jesus and the Augustinian Critique of Pagan Kingship, 1649–1671' (*MiltonQ* 48:ii[2014] 67–95), considers a very common question within Milton studies: what is the relationship between Milton the political tract writer and Milton the poet? Coffey's answer is that there is a consistency of focus within Milton's work centred on the rejection of 'gentilism' or 'heathenism' and particularly '"the brand of Gentilism upon kingship"' (p. 67). He points to the prose, suggesting that, for Milton, 'The monarchy of Charles I, with its idolatrous claims to "dominion" and "absolute authority", its showy titles and its sycophantic court, was a classic case of "Gentilism"' (p. 71). Coffey then presents arguments describing how each of the great poems placed a special focus exposing, resisting, and overturning these forms of kingship. Next is '"Shot through with Orient Beams": Restoring the Orient to Milton's Paradise' (*MiltonQ* 48:iv[2014] 235–47), in which Jonathan E. Lux proposes a rethinking of Milton's references to the 'orient' in his work. Noting that the concept is most often referenced in conversations about Milton and imperialism, Lux labours to reclaim the idea's connection to imagination, regeneration, and 'new beginnings and creation' (p. 239) through discussions of Milton's references to Asia in his prose works and of uses of the term 'orient' in *Paradise Lost*. Finally, in another essay from *Milton Quarterly*, 'Milton, the *Eikon Basilike*, and Pamela's Prayer: Re-Visiting the Evidence' (*MiltonQ* 48:iv[2014] 225–34), Nicholas McDowell revisits the controversy of Milton's alleged involvement in planting 'Pamela's Prayer' in Charles I's book *Eikon Basilike* in order to make polemical use of it in *Eikonoklastes*. McDowell's purpose is to review the evidence, as it has been reported, of Milton's culpability and to probe it for its accuracy and solidity. He also proposes a 'scenario in which Milton might plausibly have been aware in advance that Pamela's prayer would be published' (p. 227) as part of the king's book, though McDowell has doubts about the plausibility of such a scenario.

This year also brought several excellent articles that considered Milton's engagement with science, beginning with David Thorley's 'Milton and the Microscope' (*ELH* 81:iii[2014] 865–88), which examines Milton's reference to the microscope in *Paradise Regained* and compares the impact of this reference on the work of Marjorie Nicolson, an early twentieth-century critic who argued that Milton's experience with a telescope transformed his appreciation for the scale and grandeur of the heavens. Noting that recent critical engagements with Milton's discussion of science and scientific advances 'often omit to wonder why he should want to stage that discussion at all' (p. 885), Thorley, like Nicolson, presents a reading of Milton's inclusion of the scientific device that is ultimately thematic, not scientific. He argues that, in contrast to the telescope, 'which made the heavens appreciable to man' (p. 886), the microscope used by Satan in *Paradise Regained* 'distorts and magnifies' small things 'out of their natural proportion' (p. 886). Next is 'Milton's Astronomy and the Seasons of Paradise: Queries Motivated by Alastair Fowler's Views' (*Connotations* 24:i[2014] 88–104), by Horace Jeffery Hodges, who here takes up the notion forwarded by Alastair Fowler that the prelapsarian Earth, in Milton's imagination, had only one season, spring, and the Sun remained always in the same constellation of the zodiac, Aries. The text, he notes, refers to multiple seasons, although those seasons 'have no clear agricultural referent for the unfallen earth' (pp. 94–5), and there is evidence from Adam's discourse with Raphael that those seasons can be marked astronomically. Having established the seasonal patterns in the poem, Hodges discusses the astrological consequences of this for the world of *Paradise Lost* in relation to Fowler's claims. In 'The Poetics of Materialism in Cavendish and Milton' (*SEL* 54:i[2014] 173–92), Stephen Hequembourg considers the difficulties faced by 'monist materialist' writers. While, as he notes, most focus on the ways in which these thinkers reconcile their materialism with Christian doctrine, Hequembourg draws attention to the particular problems of poets like Milton and Cavendish as they 'rethink the nature of not only bodies and minds but also that nebulous intermediary, the imagination' (p. 174), and argues that in doing so they create 'an early modern poetics of materialism' that embraces the primacy of matter while retaining the 'exalted role of poetic activity' (p. 175). Catherine Gimelli Martin, in 'Milton's and Donne's Stargazing Lovers, Sex, and the New Astronomy' (*SEL* 54:i[2014] 143–71), discusses the connections in early modern poetry between expressions of romantic/sexual love and 'stargazing' (p. 143). Noting that Plato was the first to make this connection between stars and the souls of lovers, Martin traces the treatment that early modern writers, including Milton and Donne, gave to these Platonic ideas in their work, and she notes the resilience of this common poetic trope in the face of new ideas in astronomy and materialist philosophy. Lastly, in ' "Sad Experiment" in *Paradise Lost*: Epic Knowledge and Evental Poetics' (*Exemplaria* 26:iv[2014] 368–88), Debapriya Sarkar revisits the notion that Eve acts as an empiricist in her encounter with the fruit in Book IX, one seeking knowledge about her world through experimental means. Sarkar rejects this notion, arguing instead that Milton uses what she calls an 'evental poetics' (p. 369) in the poem. Distinguishing common experiences, which are ordinary and predictable, from events, which are extraordinary, unpredictable, and unrepeatable, Sarkar observes just how much of the world of *Paradise Lost*, including the Fall, should be categorized as evental. She argues that, by removing the possibility of experimentation from Eden, Milton is 'raising a philosophical and theological, rather than a scientific, problem: what is the state of being before the Fall?' (p. 371).

Numerous scholars this year also produced work that considered Milton's relationship to his classical and biblical sources. The first article is Stella P. Revard's 'Dalila as Euripidean Heroine' (*PLL* 50:iii–iv[2014] 365–80). In one of her last publications before passing away in 2014, Revard discusses linkages between Milton's Dalila and Euripides' many notable female characters. Though some have seen Milton's treatment of Dalila as evidence of his misogyny, Revard argues that Dalila is every bit as complex and potent as the Euripidean heroines available to Milton as models—and much more complex than the biblical Delilah. Through her, Revard suggests, Milton establishes that he is able to '[use] his female characters to challenge the assumptions of a male-dominated society' (p. 379). Next is 'Digesting Job in *Paradise Lost*'

(*SP* 111:i[2014] 110–31), by Emily A. Ransom, which investigates the connection between the biblical book of Job and Milton's works, not, as is often the case, in relation to Milton's 1671 poems, but in relation to *Paradise Lost*. Though there are obvious Joban connections with the later poetry, Ransom rightly points out that the echoes between Job and *Paradise Lost* are significant: both contain temptation scenes and both are theodicies. It is the aspect of theodicy, the way in which each depicts characters 'who wrestle with God himself', that Ransom focuses on, arguing that 'the Joban reading of *Paradise Lost* may indicate that questioning God activates reason in fallen and unfallen creation alike' (p. 112). Deirdre Derjeantson's 'Milton and the Tradition of Protestant Petrarchism' (*RES* 65[2014] 831–52) considers the influence of Petrarch's sonnets on Milton's developments in the genre. Noting that critics discount the connection between Milton and Petrarch because of conflicts between Milton's religious and political concerns and the tone and ideology of English Petrarchan love poetry, she points to an alternative tradition of Petrarchism, a 'Protestant Petrarch' (p. 837) based on Petrarch's poems considered by Protestants to be critical of the papacy (one of which Milton translates in part in *Of Reformation*). Derjeantson suggests that Milton 'knew Petrarch in all of his guises' and that Petrarch's anti-papal poems had a shaping influence on Milton's own political sonnets. Next, comes Helen Cooper's 'Milton's King Arthur' (*RES* 65[2014] 252–65). Cooper, in this study of Milton's interest in the fabled King Arthur, seeks to expand the scope of enquiry beyond the little we know about Milton's plans to write an English epic focusing on this legendary figure. She builds a case that Milton was drawing on a much wider pool of sources than Geoffrey of Monmouth's history, including romance works like those of Spenser. Understanding Milton's various encounters with Arthur and Arthurian literature, she argues, gives insight into how and why Milton's interest in writing about Arthur waned. In '*Paradise Lost* and the Secret of Lucretian Sufficiency' (*MLQ* 75:iii[2014] 385–409), Sarah Ellenzweig investigates the connection between seventeenth-century physics debates and Milton's *Paradise Lost*. Beginning with the observation that, in his description of Satan's fall through Chaos as potentially endless, Milton 'distanced himself from the orthodoxy of Aristotelian physics' (p. 385) and noting the thematic importance of the Fall to the poem as inviting interplay between considerations of theology and physics, Ellenzweig discusses the influence of Lucretius on Milton's work. Lastly, 'John Milton and Giovanni Boccaccio's *Vita di Dante*' (*MiltonQ* 48:iii[2014] 139–70), by William Poole, describes the discovery of a new book, Boccaccio's *Vita di Dante*, that was once part of Milton's personal library— only the eighth such book still known to exist. He sets out the provenance of the book, beginning with its first owner, Sir Thomas Bodley, and ending 300 years later in the collection of the Bodleian Library he founded, including a detailed account of the evidence pointing to Milton's one-time ownership of the book. Poole then describes the significance of the text to Milton's work and the development of his ideas, particularly on censorship.

Several rich articles considering theological aspects of Milton's poetry and prose appeared this year, beginning with '*De Doctrina Christiana* and Milton's Theology of Liberation' (*SP* 111:iv[2014] 346–74), by Jason A. Kerr. Kerr's essay examines Milton's hermeneutical strategies and theological conclusions in *De Doctrina* as the foundation of a 'theology of a liberated society' (p. 350). He argues that Milton's own liberty in interpreting the Bible, particularly in places where he substitutes words in his quotations of Scripture, along with his non-Trinitarian views on the Father and the Son, point to not only Milton's unique approach to theology, but also to a social framework that is based on 'liberty' and 'charity' that allows great diversity in viewpoint without promoting 'discord' (p. 351). Stephen Hequembourg's 'Milton's "Unoriginal" Voice: Quotation Marks in *Paradise Lost*' (*MP* 112:i[2014] 154–78), makes the case that a textual element as seemingly insignificant as a quotation mark, and the broader textual implications of quotation, can have significant involvement in thematic matters in Milton's poetry, like the question of the roots of the Fall in *Paradise Lost*. Noting the absence of quotation marks in early editions of the poem, Hequembourg sets out strategies for and concerns about noting speech and the speech of others. He argues that there is a connection between how characters approach quotation of others and the origins of sin, that 'the subtle techniques they invent for mimicking each other's voices and attributing speech to absent speakers, all weave themselves inextricably into the story of the fall' (p. 155). Next is Russell M. Hillier's ' "A Happy Rural Seat of Various View": Eve's Mirror Poem and Her Lapse in *Paradise Lost*' (*MiltonQ* 48:i[2014] 1–14), which reconsiders a subtle moment in *Paradise Lost*, Eve's love poem to Adam in Book IV, and a suggestive detail from it: Eve's mention of the word 'tree' in the early part of the poem describing the wonders of Adam's presence in her life and dropping that word in a mirrored second half of the poem describing Eden without Adam in it. This 'lapse' as Hillier calls it, can be understood innocently or as a foreshadowing of Eve's fall to come. However, Hillier argues that the lapse is best viewed in terms of Miltonic freedom in the face of temptation. The inclusion and exclusion of the tree in Eve's poem 'actualizes . . . the potential within unfallen creatures to swerve toward and away from temptation' (p. 9).

Projects considering the reception or adaptation of Milton's work also abounded in 2014. Ian Bickford's ' "Dead Might Not Be Dead": Milton in the Americas and Jamaica Kincaid's Flat World' (*MP* 111:iv[2014] 862–78) continues the investigation of Milton's reception in an American context. Focusing, as earlier scholars have also done, on the work of Jamaica Kincaid, Bickford explores how Kincaid and her work reflect 'something crucial that happens in American readings of Milton' (p. 863). Drawing on a key term from John Shawcross, 'transumption' (p. 864), Bickford argues that in Kincaid we can see the impact of Milton's 'transumption' into an American context and how the American Milton 'encounters, combats, and overtakes' (p. 863) the British Milton. Next, N.K. Sugimura's 'Eve's Reflection and the Passion of Wonder in *Paradise Lost*' (*EIC* 64[2014] 1–28) examines Eve's account of her own creation and her fixation with her watery reflection in relation to some of the earliest eighteenth-century notes and comments on the text. While some readers have dwelt on the possibility of narcissism expressed by the scene, early responses to the poem were drawn more to Eve's sense of wonder, her ' "dwelling in" the experience of the rare and wondrous' as 'a response to . . . the prelapsarian sublime' (p. 2). Sugimura links this sense of wonder, and

Eve's desire to re-create it as expressed in this passage, to her later response to
the appearance of the serpent. If Eve, Sugimura notes, 'had, after the manner
of Narcissus, truly "become so enamoured of her own Face", she would never
have found the serpent at the tree so enticing' (p. 21). Next is Greg M. Colón
Semenza's 'The Ethics of Appropriation: *Samson Agonistes, Inglourious
Basterds*, and the Biblical Samson Tale' (*Adaptation* 7:i[2014] 62–81), which
considers both Milton's *Samson Agonistes* and Tarantino's *Inglourious
Basterds* as adaptations of the story of Samson. He focuses on the ethical
problems posed by all three texts and on how the two adaptations move to
mitigate problematic features of the violent story through self-awareness and
careful selection of the targets of violence. But he also considers the 'moralistic
language' that accompanies these texts as 'born of adaptation's epistemological uniqueness' and also the 'opportunities adaptations offer for considering
fundamental questions about art' (p. 79). Linda Gregerson's 'Milton and the
Tragedy of Nations' (*PMLA* 129:iv[2014] 672–87) discusses Milton's *Samson
Agonistes* and heated discussions of how to view Samson's final violent act.
Gregerson meditates first on Dalila's complex role in the drama as an
unsympathetic truth-teller and her ability to evoke 'readerly self-estrangement'
(p. 674), to 'produce in Milton's reader both recoil and a shock of recognition'
(p. 675). Gregerson then suggests that a similar divided response is needed to
questions of whether Samson's story should be considered 'triumph or
tragedy', arguing that the drama should be considered 'the tragedy of two
nations fighting over a single geographic place' (p. 675). Following Gregerson
is Daniel Shore's 'Milton and Kant?' (*MiltonQ* 48:i[2014] 26–38). In this piece,
Shore reviews and critiques Sanford Budick's book *Kant and Milton*, which
argues that Kant had close knowledge of and was influenced greatly by
Milton's poetry. Shore presents an extended rebuttal of Budick's argument,
contending both that Budick's evidence for Kant's knowledge of Milton is
faulty and that his arguments for Miltonic influence in Kant's work lack basis.
However, Shore suggests that the bringing together of these two figures
reminds us of the commonalities between the two based on similar educational
backgrounds and 'a startlingly similar set of projects and commitments'
(p. 36). Next, 'A Century of Milton Studies in China: Review and Prospect'
(*MiltonQ* 48:ii[2014] 96–109), by Shen Hong, presents a review of the critical
reception of Milton's works in China. Shen divides the reception history into
three distinct periods. First, an early period from the first transmission of
Milton's works into Chinese culture by Western missionaries in 1837 until the
communist revolution in 1949, a period characterized first by Milton being put
to use for 'missionary purposes' (p. 97) and later by attempts by Chinese
scholars to translate works like *Paradise Lost* from the original English.
Second is a thirty-year period following the revolution in which the works were
considered mainly for their 'radical political ideas, revolutionary spirit, and
sharp criticism of the dark side of England's capitalist society' (p. 98). Finally,
there is another thirty-year period, covering the 1980s to the present day, in
which criticism moved from a narrow focus on whether the poem is primarily
revolutionary or religious in nature to expanding to engage with a much wider
range of issues. Lastly, in 'Heroic Demons in *Paradise Lost* and Michael
Madhusudan Datta's *Meghanadavadha kavya*: The Reception of Milton's

Satan in Colonial India' (*MiltonQ* 48:iv[2014] 207–24), Julie Cyzewski expands the conversation regarding Milton and imperialism by pointing to the reception of Milton's Satan as a figure of heroic resistance rather than as a tyrannical colonizing figure, as had previously been argued. Examining conflicted attitudes towards colonialism in both Datta's epic *Meghanadavadha kavya* and *Paradise Lost*, Cyzewski argues that reading the two epics together 'reveals sympathy for anticolonial and anti-imperial actions within each text' (p. 208) and points to the power of the Romantic notion of Milton's Satan within considerations of Milton and imperialism.

Finally, there were several essays this year which considered Milton's work from a strongly theoretical perspective. Peter L. Rudnytsky's 'Freud as Milton's God: Mapping the Patriarchal Cosmos in Psychoanalysis and *Paradise Lost*' (*AI* 71:iii[2014] 253–87) revisits the old debate in Milton studies between critics like C.S. Lewis, who argue for a theologically consistent *Paradise Lost*, and those like Empson, who raise questions about the coherence and theological purpose of the work. Drawing on observations from psychoanalytic theory, Rudnytsky presents a critique of the common theological position that mankind is responsible for its own fall because of free will; he develops a 'psychological profile of God as a narcissist' (p. 273); and he draws parallels between some aspects of the poem, in particular the relationships among the Father, the Son, and Satan, and the development of psychoanalysis. Rudnytsky is followed by Daniel Juan Gil's 'What Does Milton's God Want? Human Nature, Radical Conscience, and the Sovereign Power of the Nation-State' (*L&T* 28:iv[2014] 389–410), which considers Milton's work through the lens of anti-humanist critical theory and questions about the 'transcendental warrant' behind ethical systems, the place from which such systems would seem to proceed: 'either pursue sovereign power or divine revelation' (p. 390). This line of enquiry leads him to Milton and Milton's God. Asking the question, 'What does Milton's God want from humanity?', Gil explores Milton's political and theological thinking and concludes with the interesting notion that 'what Milton's Satan wants and what Milton's God wants are one and the same: for humans to transcend any particular, politically embedded definition of human nature' (pp. 406–7).

It is abundantly clear from these selections of scholarship focused on Milton and his writings that Milton studies is alive and well. Not only is there fresh life in conversations about age-old questions, but there are exciting new fields of enquiry opening up that promise to bring new insights into Milton's poetry and prose and deeper understanding of what and how it means. As these conversations continue to develop, there will be much to look forward to in the year(s) to come.

Books Reviewed

Blevins, Jacob. *Humanism and Classical Crisis: Anxiety, Intertexts and the Miltonic Memory*. OSUP. [2014] pp. x + 172. $62.95 ISBN 9 7808 1421 2417.

Danielson, Dennis. Paradise Lost and the Cosmological Revolution. CUP. [2014] pp. xxiii + 220. $95 ISBN 9 7811 0703 3603.

Drury, John. Music at Midnight: The Life and Poetry of George Herbert. Allen Lane. [2013]. pp. xix +319. ISBN 9 7818 4614 2482.

Dunn, Leslie C, and Larson, Katherine Rebecca, eds. Gender and Song in Early Modern England. Ashgate. [2014] pp.xiv +219. $85.22 ISBN 9 7814 7244 3410.

Gray, Catharine, and Erin Murphy. Milton Now: Alternative Approaches and Contexts. PalMac. [2014] pp. ix + 284. $90 ISBN 9 7811 3738 3099.

Hammond, Paul. Milton and the People. OUP. [2014] pp. xiii + 271. $74 ISBN 9 7801 9968 2379.

Howard, W. Scott, ed. An Collins and the Historical Imagination. Ashgate. [2014]. pp. xi + 255. ISBN 978 1472418470.

Johnson, Kimberly. Made Flesh: Sacrament and Poetics in Post-Reformation England. UPennP [2014] pp. 237. $59.95 ISBN 9 7808 1224 5882.

Kirby, W. J. Torrance, and Stanwood, Paul G., eds. Paul's Cross and the Culture of Persuasion in England. Brill. [2014] pp.502. $199 ISBN 9 7890 00424 2272.

Makuchowska, Ludmila. Scientific Discourse in John Donne's Eschatological Poetry. CambridgeSP [2014] pp. viii +138. £41.99 ISBN 9 7814 4386 5265.

Martin, Michael. Literature and the Encounter with God in Post-Reformation England. Ashgate [2014] pp. 221. $109.95 ISBN 9 7814 7243 2667.

McClary, Susan, ed. Structures of Feeling in Seventeenth-Century Cultural Expression. UTorP. [2012] pp. xiv +400. $80 ISBN 9 7814 4264 0627.

Moss, Daniel David. The Ovidian Vogue: Literary Fashion and Imitative Practice in Late Elizabethan England. UTorP pp. x +256. $65.00 (C) ISBN 9 7814 4264 8685.

Murphy, Kathryn, and Traninger, Anita, eds. The Emergence of Impartiality. Brill [2013] pp. xx +443. $126.77 ISBN 9 7890 0426 0832.

Quint, David. Inside Paradise Lost: Reading the Designs of Milton's Epic. PrincetonUP. [2014] pp. x + 329. $35 ISBN 9 7806 9115 9744.

Sánchez, Reuben. Typology and Iconography in Donne, Herbert, and Milton: Fashioning the Self after Jeremiah. PalMac [2014] x + 275. £57.50 ISBN 9 7811 3739 7799.

Sauer, Elizabeth. Milton, Toleration and Nationhood. CUP. [2014] pp. ix + 223. $99.99 ISBN 9 7811 0704 1943.

Schwartz, Louis. The Cambridge Companion to Paradise Lost. CUP. [2014] pp. xv + 216. $29.99 ISBN 9 7811 0766 4401.

Smith, Daniel Starza. John Donne and the Conway Papers: Patronage and Manuscript Circulation in the Early Seventeenth Century. OUP [2014] pp. xxiii +390. £65 ISBN 9 7801 9967 9133.

Sweetnam, Mark S. John Donne and Religious Authority in the Reformed English Church. Four Courts [2014] pp. 203. €58.50 9 7818 4682 3947.

Walker, William. Antiformalist, Unrevolutionary, Illiberal Milton. Ashgate. [2014] pp. 216. $98.96 ISBN 9 7814 7243 1332.

Warley, Christopher. Reading Class through Shakespeare, Donne, and Milton. CUP [2014] pp. viii + 211. $114.95 (C) ISBN 9 7811 0705 2925.

Whalen, Robert, and Christopher Hodgkins, eds. *The Digital Temple: A Documentary Edition of George Herbert's English Verse.* UPVirginia. [2012] $695 ISBN 9 7808 1393 2521.

Wilburn, Reginald. *Preaching the Gospel of Black Revolt: Appropriating Milton in Early African American Literature.* Duquesne. [2014] pp. xiii + 392. $58 ISBN 9 7808 2070 4715.

Wilcox, Helen. *1611: Authority, Gender and the Word in Early Modern England.* Wiley [2014] xvi +253. £52.99 ISBN 9 7814 0519 3917.

XI

The Later Seventeenth Century

JENNIFER L. AIREY, JAMES OGDEN, ELIZABETH
BRADBURN, AND WILLIAM BAKER

This chapter has five sections: 1. Restoration Drama Excluding Dryden;
2. Dryden; 3. Marvell; 4. Other Poetry; 5. Prose. Section 1 is by Jennifer L.
Airey; section 2 is by James Ogden; section 3 is by Elizabeth Bradburn;
sections 4 and 5 are by William Baker.

1. Restoration Drama Excluding Dryden

The year 2014 was an unusually thin one for criticism of Restoration drama.
Scholars did, however, offer new readings of the political dynamics of the
Restoration playhouse, along with analyses of anti-theatrical discourse and the
biographies of Restoration actors. They also published readings of plays by
authors such as Orrery, Behn, Finch, Lee, and Congreve.

The politics of the Restoration playhouse were the focus of two books
published this year. In *Ravishment of Reason: Governance and the Heroic
Idioms of the Late Stuart Stage, 1660–1690*, Brandon Chua argues that
Restoration heroic drama stood 'at the forefront of a post-war cultural
enterprise to mediate between precedent and experiment, renovation and
revolution, recrimination and oblivion' (pp. 5–6). In the wake of the regicide
and Restoration, British playwrights found themselves torn between support
for traditional concepts of divine monarchy and the desire to redefine the
relationship between subject and monarch. Beginning with an analysis of
William Davenant's theoretical writings, then, Chua traces the often shifting
contours of late seventeenth-century political and theatrical writings, as
playwrights reacted to each new instance of political and social crisis. Early in
the period, Chua argues, playwrights and political theorists alike stressed the
importance of 'public affection' for the monarch (p. 11), thereby differentiating themselves from parliamentarians, who treated affection for the monarch
as a form of 'self-interest or idolatry' (p. 12). By the 1680s, however,
playwrights such as Crowne had begun to question and undermine as 'a series
of hollow conventions' romanticized notions of the subject–monarch relationship (p. 67). In the aftermath of the Glorious Revolution, such doubts

*The Year's Work in English Studies, Volume 95 (2016) © The Author 2016. Published by Oxford
University Press on behalf of the English Association. All rights reserved.
For Permissions, please email: journals.permissions@oup.com
doi:10.1093/ywes/maw008*

would be expressed even more overtly; even loyalist authors such as Behn depicted 'the waning of the values promulgated by the courtly romance' (p. 113). Chua's readings are convincing and his choice of works (including plays by Boyle, Dryden, Crowne, Lee, and Behn) intelligent. Of particular merit is his reading of Lee's complicated, politically ambivalent *Lucius Junius Brutus*. According to Chua, 'While critiquing the excesses of an absolute monarchy in which an unlimited prerogative reduces the public domain to a sovereign's corrupt will, Lee at the same time cultivates and maintains a materialist suspicion toward concepts of civic virtue grounded in a selfless love for the public good' (p. 90). Modern scholars interested in Restoration drama and politics will undoubtedly find this book compelling.

Christopher Loar's *Political Magic: British Fictions of Savagery and Sovereignty* also explores the politics of the playhouse, analysing the relationship between political conceptions of civilized behaviour, 'shifts in British imperial thought and practice, and the much heralded eclipse of belief in magic by a culture of reason' (pp. 1–2). Loar links the growth in technology with the decline in magic belief, arguing that technology (such as guns) replaced the supernatural as a source of magical wonder. Authors and political theorists alike thus turned to displays of 'technological prowess and simulated divinity' in an attempt to 'astonish and instill habits of obedience' both at home and abroad (p. 4). Although much of Loar's book concentrates on works of fiction outside the scope of this section, his second chapter provides an extended reading of Aphra Behn's *The Widdow Ranter* and *The Roundheads*. Reading *The Roundheads* alongside *Oroonoko*, Loar argues that the play is conflicted in its treatment of the relationship between violence and social control. In order to restrain the unruly multitude, rulers and politicians must 'master the soldier's dialect—brute force' (p. 82). At the same time, acts of public violence 'amplif[y] the material fact of violence', and thus they must be channelled into support for a worthy monarch: 'the endpoint of violence must be organized around the hub of the man of quality, who sanctifies this violence and renders it not merely legitimate but even holy' (p. 82). In *The Widdow Ranter* too, lower-class mobs are denigrated and treated as analogous to unruly slaves: 'the rabble is more explicitly connected to the savages they resemble in their violence and unreason' (p. 87). Both plays therefore end with 'a version of sovereign power in which the rabble'—here referring both to the Indians and to rank and file members of the lower class—'is managed by heroic and lawless outsiders, through a deft blend of violence and awe-inspiring performance' (p. 91). While critics such as Paula Backscheider have examined the centrality of spectacle and performance to Restoration conceptions of government, Loar is, to my knowledge, the first to link the decline in magic belief with Restoration political theory and performance. It is an area ripe for analysis, and Loar opens up several important areas for future exploration.

Anne Hermanson turned her attention this year to the 1670s vogue for horror plays, a theatrical sub-genre that features terrible acts of violence, flawed, cowardly heroes, the destruction of family ties, and the lack of a comforting restoration of moral order. In *The Horror Plays of the Restoration*, Hermanson links the success of these plays with a public demand for spectacle and with the arrival of a new generation of playwrights dissatisfied 'with Charles II's leadership' (p. 8). Playwrights, she argues, both capitalized on the power of large-scale display to draw audiences to the theatre and used such shows subtly to criticize the monarch. Violent spectacle also 'threw into relief the very real violence that was a part of everyday life and that was often legitimized with ceremony', including 'state-sponsored torture and death' (p. 22). Hermanson offers readings of plays by Behn, Settle, Dryden, Otway, Lee, Shadwell, and Rochester, concluding that horror plays 'expose underlying skepticism about the existence of moral absolutes' and finally call 'into question the validity of Christian dogma, such as the immortality of the soul' (p. 131).

While many of the plays discussed in the aforementioned books are quite well known, several articles published this year turned their attention to under-studied plays of the period. Thomas Thomason's obscure play *The Life of Mother Shipton* [*c*.1668–71] is the focus of 'Three New Sources for *The Life of Mother Shipton*' (*N&Q* 61[2014] 391–3), Rubén Chaves Tirado's contribution to this year's *Notes and Queries*. Critics such as Gerard Langbaine have identified several sources that Thomason plagiarized (including Massinger's *The City Madam* and Middleton's *A Chaste Maid in Cheapside*), but Tirado identifies several additional source texts, 'all by Sir Aston Cockrain—*The Obstinate Lady* (1657), *Trappolin* (1658), and *The Tragedy of Ovin* (1662)' (p. 391). *The Life of Mother Shipton* has, to date, received scant critical attention, and we can hope that Tirado's note will ignite scholarly interest, both in the play itself, and in 'the study of pastiche techniques in the construction of Restoration drama' (p. 393).

Also under-studied are the works of Roger Boyle, earl of Orrery, which are all too often dismissed as straightforward royalist propaganda. Complicating such readings, Laura R. Rosenthal's 'Rebels for Love: Maternity, Absolutism, and the Earl of Orrery's *Mustapha*' (in Engel and McGirr, eds., *Stage Mothers: Women, Work, and the Theater, 1660–1830*) examines the treatment of maternity in Orrery's *Mustapha*. Long famous as the play that made Elizabeth Barry a star, the play has been mined for its imperial, orientalist, and political contents, but modern critics have generally ignored its nuanced treatment of motherhood. According to Rosenthal, 'Maternal feeling' is 'presumed to cross national and ethnic boundaries', and thus it enables the author to 'explore the presumed tragedy embedded in absolutist monarchy in ways that suggest greater ambivalence than has been recognized' (p. 107). The story of Hurrem, Roxolana's historical counterpart, was well known to Restoration audiences, and her pregnancies were viewed as transgressive; she gave birth to five children in violation of 'the traditional limits placed on concubines, who were only permitted to give birth to one son apiece' (p. 111). By emphasizing Roxolana's motherhood, then, Orrery stages a 'tension between feelings and tradition' (pp. 113–14), while the play's clear sympathy for Roxolana's plight (and Isabella's) problematizes a reading of the play as entirely pro-monarchical. If it 'promotes heroic values', it also 'extends a surprising amount of sympathy to rebels' (p. 117). Rosenthal's article thus foregrounds the importance of female experience to a play most often read for the significance of its male characters.

While Anne Finch has of late been the subject of sustained scholarly critique, she is known today almost exclusively for her poetry. Finch was, however, also a playwright, and thus in 'Anne Finch as Playwright: The Purpose of Manuscripts and Print in Her Pro-Stuart Plays' (*Restoration* 38:i[2014] 19–40), Claudia Kairoff argues that 'a standard critical edition of Finch's writings . . . is urgently needed to advance scholarship on her work, in its political and all other dimensions' (p. 19). Kairoff is very much correct in this assertion, and her nuanced reading of Finch's drama proves how very central Finch's theatrical works should be to understanding her political and aesthetic aims. Focusing on Finch's tragicomedies *The Triumph of Love* and *Innocence* (*c*.1688–90), and her tragedy *Aristomenes* (*c*.1690), Kairoff argues that 'Finch intended her plays to comment on contemporary political events through well-established literary devices and subtle allusions' (p. 19); in her drama, Finch conveys her support first for James II and later for a Stuart restoration. The strength of Kairoff's essay lies in her careful attention to Finch's publication choices; while Finch turned away from the stage in her later years, she did revise *Aristomenes* for her *Miscellany Poems of 1713*, and her changes reflect her continued nostalgia and support for James II's reign. Kairoff concludes that 'a well-annotated and collated edition' of Finch's work, 'showing her revisions as she prepared them for manuscript or print, will enable us to have the same kind of serious, detailed discussion of Finch's writings, poetic persona, and politics that we currently have about contemporaries like Dryden, Behn, and Pope' (p. 34). One hopes that other critics agree.

New perspectives on highly canonical works of the period were also published this year. In 'Sexual Arithmetic: Appetite and Consumption in *The Way of the World*' (*ECS* 47:iii[2014] 261–76), Scott R. MacKenzie examines Congreve's play through the lens of emerging mercantile philosophy, describing the relationship between Milliment and Mirabell as a metaphorical competition between two forms of economic theory. If Mirabell approaches courtship as a 'pre-Williamite regime of gift and obligation' (p. 263), Milliment 'proposes an economy of manufacture and exchange' (p. 263). That is to say, she views romance as a form of 'contractual and transactional social' exchange (p. 263). The conflict between Mirabell and Milliment thus mirrors contemporary efforts to determine which type of consumption—consumption of sex, romantic partners, estates, or goods—will prove dominant in post-Glorious Revolution society. That the play concludes with the taming of libertine desire is not, Mackenzie explains, meant to suggest that Congreve's play 'is in any clear sense proto-feminist' (p. 272). The play does not protest the conflation of women with property, but it does tame rakish desire in ways that enact 'the foundation of something like a consumer model of desire' (p. 272).

Libertine desire is not tamed in the infamous pornographic play *Sodom*, a fact that Derek Shank links with its underlying political message. In '"With drops of sperme pure white & menstrous bloud": *Sodom*'s Smut and the Politics of the Prick' (*Restoration* 38:ii[2014] 21–41), Shank seeks to move beyond questions of attribution to analysis of the play's political philosophy, and he argues that the 'graphic depictions of bodily fluids in the sexual interactions between characters . . . present a critique of some of the central tenets of Hobbes's political philosophy' (p. 21). Unlike prior critics such as Webster and Elias, Shank does not seek to read the play as a direct satire of Charles II's court, but he does link sexual with political activity. The monarchical decree forbidding heterosexual sex 'literalizes the connection between sexuality and politics' (p. 23). It also undermines Hobbes's belief that the pursuit of self-interest and pleasure will result 'in the formation of the commonwealth to the benefit of all' (p. 26), one overseen by a monarch who always acts in the best interests of the state. Instead, the destruction of Sodom occurs because women who desire men cannot challenge the decrees of the body politic, while men indulge the body natural at the expense of communal welfare. Meanwhile, the focus on bodily fluids throughout the play underscores the dissolution of individual identity; fluids intermingle until one partner is indistinguishable from the next, a 'dissolution of the individual subjectivity in which Hobbes's notion of power is founded' (p. 30). While I would not wish to see critics abandon entirely an allegorical reading of the play more specific to its historical moment, Shank's reading is provocative, adding an interesting complication to our understanding of one of the Restoration period's odder artefacts.

Gender and libertine sexuality are also the focus of Kathleen M. Oliver's ' "I will write whore with this penknife in your face": Female Amatory Letters, the Body, and Violence in Wycherley's *The Country Wife*' (*Restoration* 38:i[2014] 41–60). According to Oliver, Wycherley's play stages the era's profound discomfort with female letter-writing, as female-authored letters had the capacity to express inappropriate or threatening desires. This claim is not entirely new—critics have long discussed the relationship between female writing and female desire, and critics such as Sedgwick have discussed at length the play's homosocial rivalries—but it enables Oliver to make an interesting analytical turn. She argues that while Margery's first two attempts at writing firmly link her sexuality with her letter, her third, secret letter undermines that correlation. Since Margery's authorship is never conclusively publicly proven, the letter itself 'cannot be accurately interpreted . . . In other words, a body must be assigned to the letter in order for the letter's true meaning to be understood and revealed' (p. 52). Three different women with three different bodies—Margery, Alithea, and Lucy—are alternately associated with the letter, and as attribution shifts, so, too, does the interpretative meaning of its contents. Letter-writing thus represents a mode of resistance to patriarchal restraint, albeit a temporary one. In the end, Margery will be forced back to the country, where 'no doubt her words will be restricted . . . and her body continually threatened or treated with violence' (p. 55). Through instances of female letter-writing, Wycherley 'inadvertently reveals the toxic byproduct'—domestic violence—'associated with the libertine project of cuckoldry' (p. 55).

Over the past few years, Aphra Behn's *The Widdow Ranter* has received a substantial amount of attention, and it remained a popular subject in 2014. Reading against the critical commonplace that *The Widdow Ranter* encodes its Tory loyalism in its representation of the lower classes, Anita Pacheco's 'Festive Comedy in *The Widdow Ranter*: Behn's Clowns and Falstaff' (*Restoration* 38:ii[2014] 43–61) argues that Behn's allusions to Shakespeare's

Falstaff endow 'her lowly upstarts with a more complex and interesting role than most previous studies of the play have allowed' (p. 44). While the play's representations of Dunce, Whimsey, and Whiff initially imply that honour is an upper-class quality, Behn also acknowledges that honour is 'a luxury that politicians can rarely afford' (p. 45), and she treats the lower-class characters as foils for their betters: 'Like Falstaff, the drunken and cowardly clowns are allowed to play the role of commentators on "respectable" society' (p. 46). Pacheco's argument is convincing; she traces effectively the play's myriad allusions to Shakespeare's Falstaff, pointing out the nuance such allusions lend to the characters at hand. The play's plot structure, too, she suggests, mirrors that of *1 Henry IV* (a play enormously popular with Restoration audiences), insofar as 'the dramatic world of the rebel Bacon . . . corresponds to that of Shakespeare's rebel, Hotspur' (p. 53), and the 'world of the clowns imports into the play the festive liberty of Falstaff' (p. 54). The play thus 'conjures up a society in all its diversity and complexity and . . . rather than peddling a clear-cut partisan message, frustrates the taking of sides' (p. 55). Such an argument offers a useful corrective to the more partisan readings this play has tended to attract.

The year 2014 saw the publication of Kathryn Lowerre's essay collection *The Lively Arts of the London Stage, 1675–1725*, the product of a 2005 conference seeking to deconstruct the scholarly boundaries separating Restoration from eighteenth-century drama. While some of the essays in the collection focus on eighteenth-century materials beyond the scope of this section, it contains several strong offerings on late seventeenth-century theatre. Jennifer Renee Darby's contribution to the volume, 'Burning and Stoic Men: Mad Rants and the Performance of Passionate Pain in the Plays of Nathaniel Lee', examines scenes of male madness in five plays by Nathaniel Lee—*Nero* [1674], *Sophonisba* [1675]. *Gloriana* [1676], *The Rival Queens* [1677], and *Mithridates* [1678]. According to Darby, Lee sought to capitalize on the star power of Michael Mohun and Charles Hart, relying on 'ghosting', audience awareness of an actor's past roles, to attract a viewership: 'Hart and Mohun's onstage performances evoked their earlier work, and helped shape later plays that served to showcase their bankable talent' (p. 193). While some critics have linked Lee's depictions of madness with his own struggles with mental illness, Darby suggests that Lee was first and foremost a businessman trying to sell tickets; he deliberately wrote 'emotionally driven characters that allow the actor to display his or her range' (p. 193). Still, if his focus on madness was commercially prudent, it also enabled him to question constructions of masculinity. As Darby points out, 'Mad heroes, although electrifying on stage, were by cultural definition failing men, because their performance of masculinity was damaged' (p. 198). Darby concludes by arguing that Dryden, too, tapped into the 'vogue for watching Hart perform the mad, emotional, hero consumed by the fire of love contrasted with Mohun's more driven warriors preoccupied with a hyper-discipline of the body' (p. 207), and that he based *All for Love*'s Antony on Lee's *Alexander the Great*. As Darby's article reinforces, to understand fully the dynamics of Restoration drama, we must pay close attention to the strengths of the actors for whom roles were written.

Lowerre's own contribution to *The Lively Arts* volume, ' "Quotation is the sincerest form of . . ."?: Signature Songs as Inter-Theatrical References', examines the use of song quotations in plays of the long eighteenth century. According to Lowerre, 'song quotations are part of a conversation between performers and audiences', and 'part of the dialogue between rival theatre companies' (p. 259). Authors borrowed well-known works to avoid writing new songs, and they expected audiences both to recognize the quoted material and to take pleasure in the act of recognition. While much of Lowerre's discussion concentrates on eighteenth-century materials beyond the scope of this section, she does examine several instances of song quotation in late-century plays, including Motteux's *Love's a Jest* [1695]. Lowerre argues that Motteux used song quotation to pay homage to the late Henry Purcell, who had died several months prior to the play's premiere, and she concludes that musical quotation allowed for 'improvisation and fluidity'. It also 'supports our sense of intensely interactive audience-actor relationships' (p. 278), an important reminder of the ways in which interdisciplinary study of music can inform our understanding of long eighteenth-century theatre.

A third relevant essay in *The Lively Arts*, Timothy Neufeldt's 'Music, Magic, and Morality: Stage Reform and the Pastoral Mode', examines shifting uses of onstage pastoral imagery before and after the Collier controversy. Before the release of Collier's *Short View*, Neufeldt argues, plays 'employing the pastoral mode . . . exploit[ed] it to parody some of the more superficial or immoral conventions endemic to English society' (pp. 133–4). Taking as his central examples Dilke's *The Lover's Luck* [1695], Durfey's *Cinthia and Endimion* [1696], and Settle's *The World in the Moon* [1697], Neufeldt argues that authors use the pastoral mode to satirize such perceived cultural ills as 'the social elite's fashion and cosmetic habits' (p. 134), 'fashionable Beaus' (p. 136), 'ambitions related to courtship and marriage' (p. 138), and 'overly pompous lords and knights' (p. 140). Pastoral dramas after Collier's attack, however, 'display an overwhelming preoccupation with morality' (p. 141). Neufeldt's article adds an additional perspective to the critical debate over the extent of Collier's impact. While critics such as Hume have downplayed Collier's contemporary importance, Neufeldt's reading offers concrete proof of the ways in which authors were indeed 'responding to calls for theatrical reform' (p. 146).

Anti-theatrical controversies in England and on the Continent were also the focus of a two-part special issue published in 2014 by *Restoration and Eighteenth-Century Theatre Research*. The majority of the issue's contents treat later works or works produced in continental Europe beyond the scope of this section, but Clotilde Thouret's 'Between Jest and Earnest: Ironical Defenses of Theatre in Seventeenth-Century England and France' (*RECTR* 29:i[2014] 35–54) analyses seventeenth-century English and French defences of the stage. Ironic defences of the stage have been largely 'disregarded by recent scholars' (p. 37), but Thouret argues that while anti-theatrical polemicists only rarely adopted a mocking tone in their works, satirical defences of the theatre were quite common both in England and on the Continent. Thouret identifies four main types of satire employed in defence of the stage: 'the satire of the opponent, the parody of the polemic, the use of paradoxical arguments, and deceitful vindication' (p. 40). Her article is useful on a number of levels. First, by covering such a broad temporal span—from the late sixteenth to the late eighteenth century—Thouret demonstrates how remarkably static defences of the stage remained in their approach. Secondly, Thouret is correct in arguing that critics have been remiss in their tendency to ignore pro-theatrical polemic, preferring to concentrate their focus on attacks on the stage. Finally, the article offers some interesting commentary on Vanbrugh's pro-theatrical polemic; Vanbrugh, Thouret claims, writes 'falsely orthodox justifications' of his art, 'revealing a playwright who handles provocation with an accomplished wit' (p. 49).

Three 2014 publications by Riki Miyoshi provided insight into the lives and careers of popular Restoration actors. In 'Samuel Sanford and Colley Cibber: Two Players' Acting Techniques and the Rise and Fall of Restoration Villain Tragedy on the London Stage from the 1670s to the 1730s' (*TN* 68:iii[2014] 136–52), Miyoshi considers actor Samuel Sandford's impact on the development of villain tragedy as a genre. As Miyoshi points out, Sandford has to date attracted no substantive critical attention, attracting only passing mention in works by Hume and Wilson. Yet Sandford was an extremely popular actor in his own time; he was ranked fourth among members of the United Company, and his villainous performances were favourites of Charles II. Furthermore, most evil roles in villain tragedy were written specifically for Sandford, and his 'distinctive voice and manner of speaking' may have contributed to the decline in the popularity of rhyme in Restoration tragedy (p. 144). Miyoshi also attributes the decline in the popularity of villain tragedy to Sandford's retirement. Colley Cibber, his successor, did not perform well in villain roles, leading playwrights to abandon the genre. Miyoshi's article makes a welcome contribution to critical studies of the period, restoring to prominence a largely forgotten popular figure. Although modern critics have been generally attentive to the role of individual actors and actresses in the development of English drama, it is clear that Sandford warrants more attention than he has heretofore received.

Miyoshi also contributed two entries on Thomas Killigrew to this year's edition of *Notes and Queries*. Scholars have long been frustrated by the gap in our knowledge of Killigrew's movements between 1643 and 1647, but in 'New Light on Thomas Killigrew's Activities from 1643 to 1647' (*N&Q* 61[2014] 387–8), Miyoshi points out that Henry Neville's *Newes from the New Exchange* places Killigrew in Jersey during that period. After his release from prison, he travelled 'from Jersey to Italy partly on a private mission for Lady Devonshire' (p. 388), rather than sailing to France with Henrietta Maria as previous biographers have surmised. In a second contribution, 'Was Thomas Killigrew a Cripple? An Unpublished Letter from Thomas Killigrew to the Duke of Ormonde' (*N&Q* 61[2014] 388–91), Miyoshi reprints a letter of 6 April 1668 written by Killigrew to James Butler, duke of Ormonde. In this letter, a plea for the life of his cousin who was convicted of the rape of an heiress, Killigrew refers to himself as 'Lame old Tom' (p. 390), inadvertently settling a long-standing modern debate. Some critics have argued that Killigrew's brother (also named Tom) suffered from a physical disability, but Killigrew's reference to himself as 'lame' suggests that he himself 'may have had crooked legs'

(p. 390). Miyoshi's archival work has significantly deepened our understanding of Killigrew's biography.

It has long been a critical commonplace that Shakespeare attained his modern stature in the eighteenth century, and that his reputation during the Restoration was much more tenuous. In 'The Politics of Shakespeare Criticism in the Restoration and Early Eighteenth Century' (*ELH* 81:i[2014] 115–42), Maximillian E. Novak seeks to challenge that view. Restoration literary critics did not exhibit a unified sense of Shakespeare's inferiority; instead, their reactions to Shakespeare's work tended to break down along party lines. 'Those on the side of Whiggish political thought tended to believe in the greatness of Shakespeare; those with Tory beliefs did not' (p. 124). The Tory Thomas Rymer, for instance, criticized Shakespeare for his failure to understand 'the nature of kings, queens and aristocrats', while the Whiggish Lewis Theobald praised unreservedly his understanding of human nature. Novak also links Restoration and early eighteenth-century appreciation for Shakespeare with what he terms the tendency 'to be a Whig in aesthetics as well' (p. 136); that is to say, authors who wanted to reshape English drama along the lines of Greek tragedy tended to dismiss Shakespeare's work. The article makes a welcome contribution to our understanding of Restoration theatrical culture and literary criticism, offering a nuanced analysis of the relationship between aesthetic theory, political philosophy, and early Shakespearian criticism.

A final book published in 2014 was aimed at undergraduate students of Restoration drama. Featuring discussions of Restoration actors and actresses, theatre managers and playwrights, along with an overview of theatrical practice and late seventeenth-century history, David Roberts's *Restoration Plays and Players: An Introduction* provides an accessible and informative overview of the inner workings of the Restoration playhouse. It also provides useful readings of famous plays by authors such as Dryden, Otway, Behn, Lee, Southerne, and Cibber, along with resources for further study. At $75, the book's price point may be prohibitively high, but it would undoubtedly be an extremely useful addition to any undergraduate drama course.

2. Dryden

(a) General

'Much has been said about the worldly Dryden'—so Jack Armistead begins his book, *Otherworldly Dryden: Occult Rhetoric in His Poems and Plays*. Too much, I suppose, about his involvement in political, ecclesiastical, and cultural controversies; not enough, Armistead believes, about his sense of supernatural forces behind earthly phenomena, of more things in heaven and earth than are dreamt of in rationalistic philosophy. He finds in many of the poems and plays an 'occult rhetoric' based on Christian, classical, and non-European sources, and on demonology, astrology and magic generally, although the extent of Dryden's personal occult beliefs cannot be measured. In his early work this rhetoric associates with the revelation of 'Providential design', but from about

1674 his confidence in his power to reveal divine purposes ebbs and flows. It flows in works about devilish Whigs and angelic Tories at the time of the Popish Plot, but ebbs after the death of Charles II: Dryden becomes uncertain about where events are leading England. In *King Arthur* there was some resurgence of confidence, but in *The Secular Masque* there is a little sense of providential design in the seventeenth century, and no power of prophecy about the eighteenth. Armistead takes 'secular' to mean 'non-spiritual' rather than the more likely 'of the century'; Momus dominates, Dryden has certainly not lost his sense of humour, and that may be a sign that he has not lost his faith. Parts of this book have appeared as articles and most have been noticed here: on the poems (*YWES* 58[1979] 326); on the early plays (*YWES* 56[1977] 308–9; 57[1978] 307; 59[1980] 321; and 61[1982] 350) and on *All for Love* (*YWES* 58[1979] 328). Happily retirement has allowed Armistead leisure to complete his portrait of a Dryden seeking, like his old friend Dr Charleton, to reconcile spiritual belief with empirical observation.

I noted two lively essays on Dryden's reputation. Steven N. Zwicker's 'Why Are They Saying These Terrible Things about John Dryden?' (*EIC* 64[2014] 158–79) raises a question that, as a result of the inordinate gossip and scandal surrounding him, occurred to his contemporaries. Zwicker's answer is that Dryden alarmed almost everyone by seeming as 'unfixed in principles and place' as his own Achitophel: he was an experimental poet, playwright and critic, and an apologist by turns for Toryism, Anglicanism, Catholicism, Jacobitism and even Republicanism'. Much gossip, as yet not fully exploited by biographers, is to be found in *The Entring Book of Roger Morrice, 1677–91*, edited in seven volumes by Mark Goldie and others (Woodbridge [2007]). David Hopkins's 'Dr. Leavis's Seventeenth Century' (*EIC* 64[2014] 293–317) argues that Leavis and others have not wholly banished Milton from school and university syllabuses, but Dryden has been 'effectively airbrushed from the record'. Hopkins finds that surprising, as recent scholarly and critical work has emphasized the poet's rich diversity, imaginative range, and expressive vigour; he is much more than the conservative satirist described in earlier criticism. He suggests the source of the problem is 'the fragmentation of the academy'—few academics now have time or inclination to read new work on authors outside their own special fields, so old ideas persist. However, Hopkins must be thinking mainly about Britain, as Dryden is being better served in America (see *YWES* 94[2015] 546–9).

(b) Poetry

Several essays related to Dryden's apologies for the Stuarts. David Parry's 'Sacrilege and the Economics of Empire in Dryden's *Annus Mirabilis*' (*SEL* 54:iii[2014] 531–53) notes that in 1666 an English squadron under Sir Robert Holmes sailed to Terschelling in Holland, plundered a large fleet of merchantmen, and set fire to the ships and the town. In *Annus Mirabilis* stanzas 208–10 Dryden seems to imply that 'Holmes's Bonfire', as it was popularly known, was punished by the Great Fire of London. Parry finds in stanza 208 a previously unnoticed allusion to 1 Samuel 2:12 associating 'our greedy Sea-men' with the sacrilegious 'sons of Belial'. He goes further, and argues for 'a subversive subtext' showing that Dryden whether he knew it or not, had an uneasy conscience about his support for Stuart imperialism; this is an interesting essay. Patricia Gael's 'Kingship and Catholicism in Posthumous Representations of Charles II, 1685–1714' (*SC* 29:ii[2014] 173–96) includes a brief discussion of *Threnodia Augustis*, pointing out that Dryden's poem offers a more than usually detailed description of the deathbed scene. Paul Hammond's 'Dryden's Virgilian Kings' (*SC* 29:ii[2014] 153–71) remarks that in 1689 Dryden and others were asking themselves whether to transfer allegiance from the exiled Catholic James II to the usurping Protestant William III. Dryden's translation of Virgil's *Aeneid* reflects on the kinds of kingship or leadership shown by Aeneas, Evander, Latinus, Mezentius, and Turnus; it is suggested that both the ideal king and the ordinary citizen need qualities of reverence, self-control, and courage. This admirably lucid essay finds that the *Aeneas* is not a straightforwardly Jacobite poem.

This more philosophical Dryden is also found in *Fables Ancient and Modern*. Winifred Ernst's 'Marriage, Force, and Alternatives to Force in John Dryden's *Fables*' (*SP* 111:i[2014] 163–94) is mainly about 'The Wife of Bath, her Tale', 'Cymon and Iphigenia', 'The Twelfth Book of Ovid his Metamorphoses', and 'Theodore and Honoria' in that order. For Ernst these poems present 'startling combinations of rape/force with marriage/persuasion', and so reveal Dryden's thinking about politics and history at the end of his life. He no longer holds one-sided royalist views, but assumes a voice like Ovid's Nestor, 'wise and authoritative', yet self-consciously recognizing 'his own participation in the complex and imperfect world that surrounds him'. Anouska Wilkinson's 'Natural Law in Dryden's Translations of Chaucer and Boccaccio' (*SC* 29:iv[2014] 381–402) makes a determined effort to describe his 'poetic interrogation of the diverging views of natural law that prevailed during the seventeenth century' concentrating on 'Sigismonda and Guiscardo' compared with 'The Wife of Bath, her Tale', and 'Palamon and Arcite' compared with 'Cymon and Iphigenia'. She concludes that Dryden did not assert one view rather than another; characters variously appeal to nature to validate their morality, and 'their perspectives are so numerous that together they query humanity's capacity to interpret natural law'. I was rather surprised to find little or no reference to the ideas of the great German commentator on natural law, Samuel von Pufendorf (1632–94).

To conclude: in '"Vehicles of Prayer" and "Vehicles . . . of Air": *The Hind and the Panther* III. 105–6 and *The Rape of the Lock* I. 50' (N&Q 61:3[2014] 397–8), Kathryn Wells proposes that Dryden's 'vehicles' are 'at the literal level, forms of transport', and as such anticipate the vehicles of Pope's nymphs.

(c) Plays

I found only two essays this year. Joseph F Stephenson's 'Redefining the Dutch: Dryden's Appropriation of National Images from Renaissance Drama in *Amboyna*' (*Restoration* 38:ii[2014] 63–81) argues that *Amboyna* was the first play on the English stage to show the Dutch in a wholly negative light, and a 'remarkably effective' piece of propaganda. It achieved its effect by transferring the Renaissance stage vices of lust, cruelty, and bloodthirstiness from the Spanish to the Dutch. Perhaps more could be said about Dryden's personal dislike of Dutchmen. Geremy Carnes's 'Catholic Conversion and Incest in Dryden's *Don Sebastian*' (*Restoration* 38:ii[2014] 3–19) begins by conceding that the idea that Dryden, himself a Catholic convert, would associate the conversion experience with anything as terrible as incest 'must seem absurd at first glance'. Nevertheless Carnes argues that this play's conclusion 'presents its converts in a highly unsettled state, reflecting the shaken confidence of the Catholic community after the Glorious Revolution'. The innocently incestuous Sebastian and Almeyda go into penitential religious retirement, and the moral is that 'Protestants must allow Catholics to retreat unmolested to the private practice of their criminal faith'. Nothing would induce me to reread *Amboyna*, but in rereading *Don Sebastian* I was struck by Alvarez's remark that if only he'd been told about Sebastian and Almeyda's marriage, he would not have revealed their parentage; Dryden's moral being perhaps that life is just one damn thing after another.

3. Marvell

Criticism on Andrew Marvell sometimes seems to divorce his poetry from his political prose writings. Two essays published in 2014 address this split directly, seeking to pull together Marvell the politician and Marvell the poet. In 'The Dream of a Literal World: Wilkins, Hobbes, Marvell' (*ELH* 81:i[2014] 83–113), Stephen Hequembourg points out that *The Rehearsal Transpros'd* satirizes the late seventeenth-century intellectual movement to purge metaphor from language—the 'dream' of Hequembourg's title. Placing Marvell's political satire in the context of the very different writers John Wilkins and Thomas Hobbes, who nevertheless shared a commitment to literalness, Hequembourg identifies a defence and a theory of figurative language in the prose tract, and he follows with a reading of 'Upon Appleton House' that demonstrates how that poem expresses Marvell's belief in the epistemological necessity of metaphor.

In 'The Chameleon or the Sponge? Marvell, Milton, and the Politics of Literary History' (*SP* 111:i[2014] 132–62), Matthew C. Augustine also seeks to illuminate 'the continuities between Marvell's poetics and his politics' (p. 133), attributing the perceived discontinuity in part to a critical programme, of which Augustine provides a detailed history and analysis, to read Marvell as a kind of political younger brother to Milton. Allowing Marvell the politician to stand apart from Milton, argues Augustine, not only leads to a more nuanced understanding of seventeenth-century politics, but also reveals that the poetics of indeterminacy so evident in his lyrics extended to Marvell's political life as well.

Three more journal articles on Marvell offer readings of individual poems. A.D. Cousins published two essays focusing on the self-conscious and religiously informed contrarieties in Marvell's poetry. 'The Replication and Critique of Libertinism in Andrew Marvell's "To His Coy Mistress"' (*RS* 28:iii[2014] 392–404) identifies in Marvell's most famous lyric a pointed critique of the libertinism that it simultaneously asserts. Revising the *carpe diem* tradition in dialogue with the orthodox Christian opposition to it, Marvell leaves it up to his diverse coterie of readers, Cousins argues, to judge between the two world-views. In another piece, 'Andrew Marvell's "The Coronet": Doubleness, Conversion, and Meditation' (*Parergon* 31:i[2014] 161–74), Cousins traces in one of Marvell's religious lyrics another kind of duality, this one between artistic power and spiritual devotion. Placing these contrasting desires in tense alignment, the poem harmonizes rather than merging them, in the process constructing an Augustinian conversion narrative.

In a different vein, Lauren Shohet's 'Forming History, Inhabiting Form in Marvell's "Upon Appleton House"' (*PoT* 35:iv[2014] 659–88) takes on New Historicism and its critical legacy, particularly its neglect of poetic form. The problems created by this neglect and by an (ironic) collapse of historical distance relate directly to questions Marvell raises in 'Upon Appleton House', a poem that contemplates both historiography and form itself. Shohet demonstrates how reading Marvell's country house poem requires 'an awareness of how forms shape legibility—including the legibility of history' (p. 677). Literary critics and historians should take Marvell's insights to heart. Mention should be made of two intertextual notes on Marvell's poetry that appeared in *Notes and Queries*. Neal Hackler's 'Marvell's Ovidian "Corm'rants"' (*N&Q* 61[2014] 366–9) focuses on 'the fourth and fifth stanzas of Andrew Marvell's "The Unfortunate Lover" and the echoes of Ovid's *Metamorphoses* upon these stanzas'. Takashi Yoshinaka's 'Two Verbal Echoes of John Hall in Marvell's Verse' (*N&Q* 61[2014] 369–71) indicates 'two . . . hitherto undiscovered verbal echoes of Hall in Marvell's verse' (p. 369).

Although 2014 saw no new monographs exclusively on Andrew Marvell, an important interdisciplinary book, Leah Knight's *Reading Green in Early Modern England*, engages with Marvell's poetry and its extended historical contexts throughout, offering an original interpretation of his famous 'green shade' (p. 36) and devoting its final chapter to a fascinating discussion of 'Damon the Mower', linking that poem's theme of 'wounded pride' to a sixteenth-century herbal encyclopedia. Knight knits together a highly diverse group of early modern texts to argue for the fertility of 'reading green', not in the modern, ecocritical sense, but through a shrewdly historicized complex of environmental studies, history of reading, and visual culture. Like many of the other studies treated here, this book renews our sense of Marvell's significance to literary history.

4. Other Poetry

(a) Rochester

It would be misleading to ignore John Wilmot, earl of Rochester. Indeed a very important contribution to our understanding of his work and of late seventeenth-century poetic and dramatic activity is seen in the edition, by Nicholas Fisher and the late Keith Walker, of *John Wilmot, Earl of Rochester: The Poems and Lucina's Rape*. An extensive introduction (pp. xvii–xxvii) is followed by a list of further reading (pp. xxviii–xxxi), and a detailed list of abbreviations (pp. xxxii–xxxiii). The text of the poems includes extensive annotation at the foot of the page (pp. 1–160) and is followed by the text with annotations of Rochester's adaptation of (John) Fletcher's revenge tragedy, *Lucina's Rape or the Tragedy of Vallentinian*, with a text that underscores Rochester's changes (pp. 161–252). There is, too, an index of proper names (pp. 253–6) and an index of titles and first lines (pp. 257–60). Fisher's edition contains the poems in versions contemporary to Rochester and includes the discoveries of the last quarter of a century during which access to previously unavailable manuscripts was allowed.

Women's clothing and Rochester's vocabulary engage Oliver R. Baker in his 'Rochester's "Scotch Fiddle"; or, the Duke's "Scotched Fiddle"?' (*N&Q* 61[2014] 394–5). In a somewhat surprising journal venue, Cynthia Richards, in 'Wit at War: The Poetry of John Wilmot and the Trauma of War' (*ECF* 27:i[2014] 25–54), draws upon Rochester's personal trauma, a result of his own experiences in battle, as the foundation for a reading of his poetry. Richards writes that 'Rochester's reliance on wit means his poetry operates according to principles of association rather than the troubling disassociation connected to trauma. Reading Rochester's poetry as reflecting the trauma of war then complicates its status as poetry that critiques its culture—that names its excesses—rather than poetry which is so compromised by those atrocities as unwittingly to hide them' (p. 25). Movingly she concludes her essay: 'his poetry repetitively and, at times unwittingly, relives the stark inevitability of profound and traumatic loss. He must be read as a wit at war, wounded by battle yet open to life's pleasures. He must be read as a poet deeply, painfully shaped by his age' (p. 54). Nicholas Fisher, the doyen of Rochester critics and scholars, in an important contribution, ' "Damn'd in the Cup": Faith, Poetry, and the Earl of Rochester' (*English* 62[2013] 166–92) vigorously defends Rochester against charges of atheism. Fisher writes that the 'Examination of Rochester's poetry through the lens of faith provides another means by which the unique voice, sensitivity and, above all, honesty of this exceptional poet can be appreciated.' Additionally, 'It also supports the truth of his statement, "I have been guilty of extravagances, but I will assure you I am no atheist"; the personal tragedy of Rochester was that only in his final months did he come to realize, "After a search so painfull and so long | That all his life he hath been in the wrong" (*A Satyr against Mankind*, lines 27–8) and it was not until he was on his death bed that he was able to fill the God-shaped hole that there had been all the time in his spiritual life' (p. 189). Fisher too includes a helpful appendix (pp. 189–92) listing Judaeo-Christian references and classical/pagan references in Rochester's poetry.

(b) Traherne

Another two volumes have been added to Jan Ross's projected eight-volume edition of *The Works of Thomas Traherne*. The first four volumes appeared between 2005 and 2009. The fifth volume contains several texts. A detailed introduction (pp. xiii–xxxvi) is followed by the text based on the Bodleian Library's MS Eng. the. e. 50 (p. xiii) of *Centuries of Meditations* and then textual emendations and notes (pp. 192–249). Ross's introduction encompasses '*The Century* as a Literary Form' (pp. xiii–xvi), 'Literary Form and Purpose' (pp. xvi–xx), 'Description of the Physical Manuscript' (pp. xxi–xxv), and 'Provenance of the Manuscript' (pp. xxvi–xxvii). Ross writes that *Centuries* was 'written perhaps sometime during the late 1660s or early 1670s' and 'although we do not know the identity of Traherne's immediate audience, *Centuries* . . . is specifically addressed to a "friend," who gave him an empty book and asked him to fill it' (p. xvi). The remainder of the fifth volume of Ross's magisterial edition contains the texts of five other Traherne prose works found in manuscript at the Beinecke Library, Yale University Osborn MS b 308. The first of these is *Select Meditations*, 'the remaining portion of a longer work'. The Osborn MS also includes 'two short untitled treatises by Traherne, "Being a Lover of the world," and "The best principle whereby a man can Steer his course in this world," and two very brief works, "A Prayer for Ash Wednesday" and "A Meditation"'. Ross adds that 'neither of [these] is written in Traherne's or the scribe's script; they are not of Traherne's making, and the identity of the author is unknown' (p. xxvii), but they are included in this volume. Her introduction concludes with an account of her general editorial principles (pp. xxxiii–xxxvi). The texts of each of these prose works are also followed by textual emendations and notes (pp. 255–467). There are three appendices. The first contains its then owner 'William T. Brooke's account of the discovery of Thomas Traherne's manuscripts' (pp. 471–4), 'probably written during October, 1910' (p. 471). The second and third appendices contain 'Bodleian MS Eng. the. e.50: Manuscript Foliation' (pp. 475–9) and 'Osborn MS b.308: Manuscript Foliation' (pp. 480–4). Ross also provides a glossary (pp. 487–91).

The sixth volume of *The Works of Thomas Traherne* is devoted to his poetry and 'taken from four manuscripts'. These are at the Bodleian: 'the Dobell Folio, MS Eng. poet. c.42 [containing] thirty-seven autograph poems'; and '"Early Notebook," MS Lat. misc. f.45 [containing] five poems'. There is 'a third manuscript, *Poems of Felicity* . . . Burney MS 392, held at the British Library', containing sixty-two poems. A fourth, '*The Ceremonial Law*', today at the Folger Shakespeare Library, Washington, DC MS V.a.70 (p. xv), 'is an incomplete, autograph narrative poem of 1,748 lines in rhyming couplets' (p. xxx). Ross's introduction (pp. xv–xxxvii) contains descriptions of the physical manuscripts, their provenance, and the general editorial principles (pp. xv–xxxvii) that she uses. There are several appendices, including 'Manuscript Foliation of Poems' (pp. 317–20), a duplication of the first appendix found in the fifth volume, 'William T. Brooke's account . . .' (pp. 321–4), a glossary (pp. 327–8), and an index of titles and first lines (pp. 329–35). Both volumes contain black and white plates illustrating each of the texts transcribed and so superbly edited by Jan Ross. In a general preface Ross writes that 'there has been no attempt to gather all Traherne's extant works into a uniform, printed edition, with the purpose of giving a sense of the manuscripts or printed originals'. This certainly has been achieved. Ross adds: 'the primary purpose of this edition, therefore, is to present a printed text of all of Traherne's known extant works, both published and unpublished' (p. xii). Traherne is one of the most neglected writers of the second half of the seventeenth century, a major reason for this neglect being that most of his work has remained unpublished or unavailable. Ross's edition will be an important factor in redressing this and will hopefully result in a recognition of the qualities of one of the most interesting and 'great poet[s] of the seventeenth century' (p. xxvii).

5. Prose

(a) Hobbes

Writing about the great prose stylist writer and political philosopher Thomas Hobbes should not be ignored. There are several articles of interest to note. Hobbes's rhetoric engages Don Paul Abbott in his ' "Eloquence is Power": Hobbes on the Use and Abuse of Rhetoric' (*Rhetorica* 32:iv[2014] 386–411). Abbott persuasively argues that 'Hobbes's conception of rhetoric displays remarkable consistency. While he rejects the abuses of rhetoric abundant in political oratory he nevertheless embraces the power of eloquence. In *Leviathan* Hobbes reconciles his appreciation of eloquence with his distrust of oratory by refashioning rhetoric into a private, rather than public art, which fulfills many of the traditional duties of rhetoric' (p. 387). A largely neglected area interests Conal Condren. In the intriguingly titled 'The Philosopher Hobbes as the Poet Homer' (*RS* 28:i[2014] 71–89) Condren revisits Hobbes's translation of Homer, produced between 1675 and 1677 when Hobbes was in his old age, 'ill and feeling persecuted . . . written, he said, because he had nothing better to do, and published to distract his critics from his more serious writings'. His translations of the *Iliad* and the *Odyssey* are his 'longest works'. For Condren, 'the translations as a whole are informed by [Hobbes's] conception of philosophy and his sense of the philosopher's responsibility. The oversimplification of his understanding of philosophy has itself helped isolate his Homer from the rest of his work. To recognize that Hobbes's Homeric epics were the work of a philosopher does something to explain the hostility they generated, and the need to translate Homer afresh' (p. 71).

Contributions in books constituted the main bulk of writings on Hobbes during 2013–14. Ryan Hackenbracht's 'Hobbes's Hebraism and the Last Judgement in *Leviathan*' (in Fitsimmons, ed., *Identities in Early Modern English Writing: Religion, Gender, Nation*, pp. 85–115) focuses the areas of eschatology, Hebraisms, the Last Judgement, sovereignty, and national identity in Hobbes's great political/philosophical work. Fabio Raimondi's subject is 'Machiavelli's *Discorsi* and Hobbes's *Leviathan*: Religion as Ideology' (in Arienzo and Petrina, eds., *Machiavellian Encounters in Tudor and Stuart England: Literary and Political Influences from the Reformation to the Restoration*, pp. 173–84). In their introduction the editors of the volume comment that Raimondi's concern is 'with the ideological role of religion in Machiavelli and in . . . Hobbes's theory of the commonwealth, arguing that in both writers religion is a social link that structures and keeps together the various parts of the city and of the commonwealth.' The two differed in their perception of religion: 'while for Machiavelli religion has the aim of supporting the good order of a city promoting political innovation through conflicts, Hobbes, on the contrary, supports the hypothesis that religion must maintain the status quo' (p. 10). Nancy J. Hirschmann's 'Freedom and (Dis)ability in Early Modern Thought' (in Hobgood and Houston Wood, eds., *Recovering Disability in Early Modern England*) finds Hobbes's conceptions of freedom and political citizenship in their essence ignoring those challenged psychologically and/or physically. Paul A. Kottman's contribution, 'Duel' (in Turner, ed., *Early Modern Theatricality*, pp. 402–22), sheds interesting light on Hobbes and our perspectives on him. As Turner indicates in his introductory essay, 'Generalization', 'philosophy from Aristotle to Hobbes to Hegel has always separated a notion of drama from its conditions of performance in the theatre and it has done so in order to idealize a notion of "action" that has been denuded of its concrete and collective embeddedness' (p. 9). Ioannis D. Evrigeni's ' "Not Truth but Image Maketh Passion": Hobbes on Instigation and Appeasing' (in Cummings and Sierhuis, eds., *Passions and Subjectivity in Early Modern Culture*, pp. 165–80), concentrates on Hobbes's use of language with special attention to *Leviathan* and *De Cive*. Hobbes's argumentation and ideas of the implications of the word 'human' engage James Loxley in 'The Claims of a "Civil Science": Hobbes's *Leviathan*' (in Knoppers, ed., *The Oxford Handbook of Literature and the English Revolution*, pp. 394–408).

(b) Bunyan

John Bunyan studies are alive and well. Various articles in journals, many of these in *Bunyan Studies*, appeared on diverse aspects of Bunyan.

Vincent Newey's 'Centring Bunyan: Macaulay, Froude, Hale White' (*BunyanS* 17[2013] 68–97) concentrates upon editions of Bunyan, Robert Southey, and others. Michael Davies's 'When Was Bunyan Elected Pastor? Fixing a Date in the Bedford Church Book' (*BunyanS* 18[2014] 7–41) is a detailed consideration drawing upon historical documents and adopting a historical and biographical approach to Bunyan's role and date of appointment as a pastor within the Congregational Church in Bedford. A different facet of Bunyan is treated by Kathleen Curtin in her 'Identification and Difference in John Bunyan's Reading of Reformation History' (*BunyanS* 18[2014] 42–60). Curtin examines Bunyan's interpretation of important moments in ecclesiastical history, including the rise of Martin Luther and his commentary on Galatians. A similar topic is found in David Parry's 'John Bunyan and Edwin Sandys on Luther's Galatians Commentary' (*N&Q* 61[2014] 377–80).

Margaret Sönser Breen's arrestingly titled 'The Pilgrim's Art of Failure and Belonging—Dialogues between Bunyan and Queer Studies' (*BunyanS* 18[2014] 61–77) treats her subject in a tradition of homosexual writers and homophobia. Adaptation, children's literature, and a bibliography are the subjects of Shannon Murray's 'Playing Pilgrims: Adapting Bunyan for Children' (*BunyanS* 18[2014] 78–106). Finally in this condensation of contributions on Bunyan from the same journal source, Julie Coleman's 'The Manufactured Homespun Style of John Bunyan's Prose' (*BunyanS* 18[2014] 107–37) adopts a linguistic approach to its subject's prose style. The same author writes on

Bunyan in another forum. Her 'Using Dictionary Evidence to Evaluate Authors' Lexis: John Bunyan and the *Oxford English Dictionary*' appears in *Dictionaries* (34[2013] 66–100). Rhetoric, and autobiography with reference to Bunyan and others, concern Peter Burke in his 'The Rhetoric of Autobiography in the Seventeenth Century' (in van der Wal and Rutten, eds., *Touching the Past: Studies in the Historical Sociolinguistics of Ego-Documents* (pp. 149–63). Although Thomas N. Corns's focus is on Gerrard Winstanley in his ' "I Have Writ, I Have Acted, I Have Peace": The Personal and the Political in the Writings of Winstanley and Some Contemporaries' (*PSt* 36:i[2014] 43–51), he has perceptive observations on Bunyan's frequently revised 'most elaborate autobiographical account, *Grace Abounding to the Chief of Sinners*'. For Corns this has 'its share of self-justification, sometimes tailored toward a tacit demonstration of aspects of his Protestant orthodoxy'. The fifth edition, the last Bunyan seems to have revised, 'sees his assertion of the centrality of Bible study and a restatement of a Calvinist soteriology, in the context of renewed anxiety about distinguishing his relatively staid version of dissent from that of Quakers who privilege the spirit within over the revealed word of God and who offer their rather different notion of the extent of free grace' (p. 45). Also placing Bunyan in a wider contemporary context, Jaemin Choi's focus in 'John Bunyan as a Dissenter: A Study of Dissenting Literature in the Restoration' (*MES* 22:i[2014] 121–41) is publishing, authorship, and Dissenters. David Alf is more specific in 'Why No One Can Mend the Slough of Despond' (*EC* 54:iii[2014] 375–92). Alf writes: ' "The Slough of Despond" marks one instance where the seemingly solitary work of spiritual progress is undergirded, interrupted, and complicated by communal obligations. It supplies the aporetic juncture that conditions Christian for a lifetime of tribulations, and the historic evidence to situate such a life in the communities where it would have been lived' (p. 388). A completely different facet of Bunyan is seen in Donal E. Meek's 'John Bunyan in the Kilt: The Influence of Bunyan's Texts on Religious Expression and Experience in the Scottish Highlands and Islands' (*Scottish Studies* 37[2014] 155–63) with its emphasis upon Bunyan's influence, evangelicalism, and Scottish Gaelic translations. Mention should be made of two contributions to essay collections. Nathalie Collé-Bak's '*The Pilgrim's Progress*, Print Culture and the Dissenting Tradition' (in Jung, ed., *British Literature and Print Culture*, pp. 33–57) relates Bunyan's creative masterpiece to image–text relations, print culture, and the study of illustration. 'Changes that are deliberately introduced in the illustrations of *The Pilgrim's Progress* and the interpretative matrix of these' (p. 2) provide the foundation for Collé-Bak's analysis. N.H. Keeble's focus is readership and Puritanism in his contribution, ' "Out of the Spoils Won in Battle": John Bunyan' (in Knoppers, ed., pp. 686–702).

Books Reviewed

Arienzo, Alessandro, and Alessandra Petrina, eds. *Machiavellian Encounters in Tudor and Stuart England: Literary and Political Influences from the*

Reformation to the Restoration. Ashgate. [2013] pp. xiii + 204 pp. $149.95 ISBN 9 7814 0943 6720.

Armistead, Jack M. *Otherworldly John Dryden: Occult Rhetoric in his Poems and Plays*. Ashgate. [2014] pp. x + 187. $149.95 ISBN 9 7814 7242 4976.

Chua, Brandon. *Ravishment of Reason: Governance and the Heroic Idioms of the Late Stuart Stage, 1660–1690*. BuckUP. [2014] pp. 230. $85 ISBN 9 7816 1148 5820.

Cummings, Brian, and Freya Sierhuis, eds. *Passions and Subjectivity in Early Modern Culture*. Ashgate. [2013] pp. x + 317. $149.95 ISBN 9 7814 7241 3642.

Engel, Laura, and Elaine McGirr, eds. *Stage Mothers: Women, Work, and the Theater, 1660–1830*. BuckUP. [2014] pp. 290. $90 ISBN 9 7816 1148 6032.

Fitzsimmons, Lorna, ed. *Identities in Early Modern English Writing: Religion, Gender, Nation*. Brepols. [2014] pp. vi + 206. €75 ISBN 9 7825 0354 2317.

Hermanson, Anne. *The Horror Plays of the Restoration*. Ashgate. [2014] pp. 194. $109.95 ISBN 9 7814 7241 5523.

Hobgood, Allison P., and David Houston Wood, eds. *Recovering Disability in Early Modern England*. OSUP. [2013] pp. viii + 224. $52.95 ISBN 9 7808 1421 2158 .

Jung, Sandro ed. *British Literature and Print Culture*. Brewer. [2013] pp. xiv + 221. $44.85 ISBN 9 7818 4384 3436.

Knight, Leah. *Reading Green in Early Modern England*. Ashgate. [2014] pp. 180. $149.95. ISBN 9 7814 0944 6644.

Knoppers, Laura Lunger, ed. *The Oxford Handbook of Literature and the English Revolution*. OUP. [2012] pp. xxvii + 715. £100 ISBN 9 7801 9956 0608.

Loar, Christopher F. *Political Magic: British Fictions of Savagery and Sovereignty, 1650–1750*. FordUP. [2014] pp. 344. $65 ISBN 9 7808 2325 6914.

Lowerre, Kathryn, ed. *The Lively Arts of the London Stage, 1675–1725*. Ashgate. [2014] pp. 324. $119.95 ISBN 9 7814 0945 5332.

Roberts, David. *Restoration Plays and Players: An Introduction*. CUP. [2014] pp. 260. $75 ISBN 9 7811 0761 7971.

Ross, Jan, ed. *The Works of Thomas Traherne, vol. 5: 'Centuries of Meditations, Select Meditations' with Miscellaneous Works from the Osborn Manuscript*. Brewer. [2013] pp. xxxvi + 492. $130 ISBN 9 7818 4384 3276.

Ross, Jan, ed. *The Works of Thomas Traherne, vol. 6: Poems from the Dobell Folio, 'Poems of Felicity' 'The Ceremonial Law' 'Poems from the Early Notebook'*. Brewer. [2014] pp. xxxviii + 336. $120 ISBN 9 7818 4384 3825.

Turner, Henry S., ed. *Early Modern Theatricality*. OUP. [2013] pp. xiv + 621. £95 ISBN 9 7801 9964 1352.

van der Wal, Marijke J., and Gijsbert Rutten, eds. *Touching the Past: Studies in the Historical Sociolinguistics of Ego-Documents*. Benjamins. [2013] pp. vii + 279. $149 ISBN 9 7890 2720 0808.

Walker, Keith, and Nicholas Fisher, eds. *John Wilmot, Earl of Rochester: The Poems and Lucina's Rape*. Wiley Blackwell. [2013] pp. xxxiii + 260. $41.95 ISBN 9 7811 1843 8794.

XII

The Eighteenth Century

KATHERINE WAKELY-MULRONEY, JAMES SMITH,
KERRI ANDREWS, AND JAMES HARRIMAN-SMITH

This chapter has four sections: 1. General and Prose; 2. The Novel; 3. Poetry; 4. Drama. Section 1 is by Katherine Wakely-Mulroney; section 2 is by James Smith; section 3 is by Kerri Andrews; section 4 is by James Harriman-Smith.

1. General and Prose

It seems appropriate to begin a review of this nature with Manuel Lima's *The Book of Trees: Visualizing Branches of Knowledge*. This lavishly illustrated compendium examines the various methods through which discrete units of information are arranged in comprehensive networks. The tree, Lima explains, 'has been such a successful model for graphically displaying relationships because it pragmatically expresses the materialization of multiplicity (represented by its succession of boughs, branches, twigs, and leaves) out of unity (its central foundational trunk, which is in turn connected to a common root source, or origin)' (pp. 26–7). The majority of the diagrams reproduced in Lima's text are of twentieth- and twenty-first-century origin. Nevertheless, several eighteenth-century examples appear in its introductory sections, among them the famous frontispiece to Denis Diderot and Jean le Rond d'Alembert's 1780 *Encyclopédie*. While Lima's study is not rooted in the eighteenth century *per se*, its attentiveness to the strategies through which knowledge is divided into a series of increasingly specialized categories and sub-categories speaks directly to the task at hand. While this year's publications in eighteenth-century general studies and prose cover a diverse range of subjects, a network of familiar branches emerges in the fields of gender and disability studies, the urban and global Enlightenment, and religion, publishing, and music. There have also been a number of notable author-centric studies on figures such as Edward Gibbon, Jonathan Swift, and Adam Smith. We will begin, however, by examining a series of works which themselves address the problem of taxonomy through their consideration of the literary marketplace and the threat of information overload.

The Year's Work in English Studies, Volume 95 (2016) © *The Author 2016. Published by Oxford University Press on behalf of the English Association. All rights reserved.*
For Permissions, please email: journals.permissions@oup.com
doi:10.1093/ywes/maw009

In *Literature and Encyclopedism in Enlightenment Britain: The Pursuit of Complete Knowledge*, Seth Rudy examines the 'concepts of completeness', both formal and taxonomic, that developed over the course of the seventeenth and eighteenth centuries (p. 1). Completeness, Rudy observes, can refer to either comprehensiveness or cohesiveness. He invites his reader to conceive of these categories in relation to two literary genres: alphabetized encyclopedias, which, in their quest for inclusivity, are continually under revision or expansion, and condensed, selective volumes such as his own study, which rely on carefully chosen examples in order to produce a thematic picture of completeness. These objectives can seem mutually exclusive: as a work becomes more comprehensive, it becomes increasingly difficult to unify its component elements. Rudy therefore concedes that his survey of the systematic characteristics and ideological grounds of encyclopedic projects will inevitably be less than comprehensive ('critical studies too must sacrifice some aspect of completeness in the name of utility', p. 10). The book begins with a consideration of Francis Bacon and John Milton, both of whom expressed the certainty that no one writer or work could hope to comprehend or convey 'complete' knowledge. Nevertheless, over the course of the seventeenth century the network of texts claiming to possess such knowledge was progressively expanding. As Rudy moves into the eighteenth century, his focus shifts from the epic tradition to the encyclopedias and reference texts produced by figures such as John Harris and Ephraim Chambers. He demonstrates that works of this nature became increasingly diverse (and potentially inclusive) over the course of the eighteenth century as the task of the individual editor was divided among 'tens, then hundreds, then thousands of compilers, contributors, publishers, printers, and booksellers' behind any one encyclopedic work (p. 63). In the final chapters, Rudy's focus returns to single-author works, among them the 'comprehensive' novels of the eighteenth century (Henry Fielding promised the reader of *Joseph Andrews* 'a much larger Circle of Incidents, and . . . a greater variety of Characters' (quoted in Rudy pp. 95–6)) and the encyclopedic projects of the Romantic era. During this period, he argues, figures such as Coleridge and Wordsworth located completeness in the poet's ability to 'comprehend anything', rather than everything (p. 125). Rudy's own text, much like many of the works under review, includes a prefatory defence of its unique position in the overcrowded literary marketplace. He proposes that we are currently experiencing a 're-proliferation of print' akin to Enlightenment-era information overload due in part to digitization services such as ECCO and Google Books. The practice of processing and systematizing information is therefore 'a matter of immediate and historical interest across disciplines, both inside and outside academia' (p. 9). In 'The Encyclopaedic Sanctuary: Metaphoric Ambiguity and the *Encyclopédie*' (*ECS* 37[2014] 331–42), Neil Mackay Younger examines the shifting significance of the metaphor of the sanctuary in Diderot's and d'Alembert's work. Mackay Younger argues that our modern notion of the term sanctuary—as a place of refuge and save haven—fails to take into account its sacred meaning as a place of exclusivity and secrecy. Therefore, for Diderot, the encyclopedia safeguarded knowledge in the event of global upheaval, but also from the 'legal and intellectual persecution' he faced personally (p. 336). Thus, the *Encyclopédie* preserves and protects knowledge that is potentially 'inaccessible to the vast majority of humanity' (p. 337).

Several other studies published this year considered the information age, and information overload, in relation to the eighteenth-century book business. In 'Cheese, Stolen Paper, and the London Book Trade' (*ECent* 38[2014] 100–10), William Noblett addresses a particular criminal phenomenon in the mid- to late eighteenth century in which vast swathes of paper—blank and printed, bound and unbound—were stolen in order to be repurposed as food wrappers. Noblett foregrounds the impartial, even democratic, aspect of paper theft: one might find one's Stilton wrapped in pages from a penny pamphlet, Johnson's *Dictionary of the English Language*, or Isaac Watts's *Hymns and Spiritual Songs*. Two publications this year highlighted the relationship between print culture and the dissemination of denominational ideology. In 'Advocacy, Enlightenment, and the Catholic Print Trade in Mathew Carey's Dublin' (*Éire* 49[2014] 244–70), Nicholas Wolf navigates the 'intimate world' of 'printers, engravers, binders, and booksellers' who operated in close proximity to one another in eighteenth-century Dublin (p. 245). This 'close-knit group' was, Wolf stresses, 'bound by shared intellectual networks' as well as 'blocked aspirations' in a predominantly Protestant society (p. 256). Wolf traces the influence of Enlightenment thought (and its supposed denunciation of Catholicism) on Carey's religious identity and on Dublin's Catholic printers more broadly. In *Textual Warfare and the Making of Methodism*, Brett C. McInelly examines the extent to which Methodist identity—its 'religiosity and self-understanding' (p. 10)—was constructed through written responses to public criticism and censure. In a culture where 'anti-Methodist sentiment circulated widely among the eighteenth-century reading public', McInelly stresses that responding to attacks 'became a matter of principle' among believers (p. 3). This was true of high-profile figures such as George Whitefield and John Wesley and of their followers, who responded to critics in published tracts and also privately, in letters and diary entries. Methodism, McInelly argues, 'may have been founded on theological principles, but it was defined and refined by public attacks and defences of those principles' (p. 5). Chapters 1 and 2 establish the significance of print culture to Methodist self-identity and perceptions of Methodism among 'outsiders'. Of particular interest is McInelly's decision to approach Methodism as a 'rhetorical problem', placing argument rather than emotion at the centre of his investigation (p. 62). Chapter 3 explores the fraught relationship between Methodists and the theatre, each 'competing for the authority to "perform" for an impressionable public' (p. 11). While Methodists condemned the playhouse as 'the sink of all profaneness and debauchery' (quoted in McInelly, p. 89), playwrights such as Samuel Foote argued that Methodist preachers were themselves little more than actors. McInelly suggests that scholars such as Henry Abelove, Harry Stout, and John O'Brien unduly replicate anti-Methodist arguments in studies that locate correlations between Methodism and the stage. Yet McInelly risks veering too far in the opposite direction in his own attention to the 'subtle and dramatic ways Methodism and the theatre diverged in both purpose and practice' (p. 92). Chapter 4 transitions from the playbill to the hymnal: while hymn-singing was calculated to stir the practitioner's emotional response, hymns themselves acted as regulatory scripts while also helping to 'externalize and legitimize personal, subjective, "unspeakable" religious experience' (p. 121). Because hymns were charged with the responsibility of 'persuading would-be converts' and also 'sustaining' and 'reassuring believers', McInelly suggests that they too participated in the rhetorical battles waged elsewhere in the pages of apologias and sermons. Chapter 5 investigates the intersection between Methodist spirituality and sexuality (what McInelly terms its 'sexualized spirituality', p. 152). If the charged language of Methodist discourse 'helped forge the close interpersonal relationships that became the hallmark of Methodist societies', it also exposed the church to severe criticism and mockery (p. 12). McInelly also examines the public role of women practitioners, who were particularly subject to charges of sexual enthusiasm and misconduct. The final chapter of this work focuses on Methodist infighting, especially that which occurred between Calvinist and Arminian factions during the Free Grace controversy. The public nature of this dispute, McInelly demonstrates, influenced Methodist doctrine as much as it shaped public perceptions of Methodism. Where Whitefield and Wesley had previously 'utilized the press to defend themselves from anti-Methodist attacks', each now 'depended on the printed word to mount their campaigns against the other' (p. 181). Rather than splinter or diminish Methodist self-understanding, however, incidents of 'internal strife' encouraged believers to rally behind their faith, ultimately 'solidif[ying]' a sense of spiritual community (p. 211).

Two other essays this year explored the rhetorical and social conventions of religious writing. Sarah B. Stein considers the significance of translation to the work of literary critic John Dennis in 'Translating the Bible to Raise the Fallen' (*SECC* 43[2014] 4–27). While scholars have located a tension between neoclassical rules and religious passion in Dennis's critical writing, this essay suggests that Dennis reconciles this opposition in his translation of the Bible into English. Stein argues that, for Dennis, sublime, religious poetry is perfected when poetic rules inherited from the classical tradition are applied by means of translation: 'Religion provides the ideas', she writes, 'but classical poetics, and specifically the rules found in Aristotle and Longinus, provide the form' (p. 13). Jennifer Farooq's 'Preaching for the Queen: Queen Anne and the English Sermon Culture, 1702–1714' (*ECS* 37[2014] 159–69) considers the sociocultural influence of sermons delivered in Anne's court and their afterlife as published texts. By drawing attention to public interest in court sermons during the period (as demonstrated by reactions in the pamphlet press), Farooq reinforces the centrality of religious writing to eighteenth-century reading culture. Farooq's essay, which highlights Anne's patronage of preachers, is part of a special issue of the *Journal for Eighteenth-Century Studies* on 'Queen Anne and British Culture, 1702–1714', introduced by Claudine Van Hensbergen and Stephen Bernard (*ECS* 37[2014] 139–45). Essays in this collection seek to redress the critical tendency to overlook or minimize Anne's participation in the cultural life of her time. In their introduction, Van Hensbergen and Bernard criticize the scholarly tendency to consider Anne through the 'narrow lens' of her correspondence with Sarah Churchill; 'it is hoped' they write, 'that the essays in this collection will make clear the potential breadth of other material available to those wishing to study Anne's life and influence (p. 140).

Brent S. Sirota's *The Christian Monitors: The Church of England and the Age of Benevolence 1680–1730* makes a significant contribution to the field of religious studies in its attention both to the Church and to the socio-cultural context within which it operated at home and abroad. The Anglican revival that took place in the decades surrounding the Glorious Revolution of 1688–9 forms the foundation of Sirota's study. This formative development, he argues, 'was born of a period of religious and political reconstruction, acquired a pronounced political character during an era of revolutionary crisis and partisan struggle, and ultimately achieved normative status in the "age of benevolence" that by the mid-eighteenth century had come to define English public life' (pp. 2–3). Sirota examines the emergence and development of Britain's charitable age through close attention to the Anglican and Protestant ecumenical institutions in the post-revolutionary era, chief among them the Society for Promoting Christian Knowledge (SPCK) and the Society for the Propagation of the Gospel in Foreign Parts (SPG). He observes, with evident frustration, that the legacy of these institutions has been restricted to the 'myopi[c]' interests of historians who happen to be members of the organizations themselves—a criticism that will ring true for many scholars working in the general field of eighteenth-century religious studies (p. 4). This study, Sirota remarks, is not calculated to replace 'the long-prevailing account of the "church in danger" from Catholicism, Nonconformity, irreligion, and enlightenment' (p. 8), but to acknowledge the simultaneity of this narrative with that of an Anglican resurgence—a movement that, as he observes, became increasingly civic-minded and inclusive over the period under review ('Simply put', Sirota writes, 'a program of ecclesiastical renewal continually enlisted what many considered nonecclesiastical instruments and agents', p. 12). The first and second chapters of the text concern the Anglican revival leading up to the revolution of 1688–9 and its aftermath in the 1690s. Readers of this section of *YWES* may be particularly interested in the remaining chapters, which trace these developments in the early decades of the eighteenth century. Chapter 3 explores the origins of the SPCK, which, at an organizational level, embodied the ideological contradictions at the heart of the Anglican revival. If the SPCK 'was obviously an instrument of Anglican renewal . . . its divergent programming reveals the somewhat limited consensus on what such renewal might have entailed' (p. 111). Chapters 4 and 5 examine the Anglican High Church movement in a culture of increasing secularization. Sirota concludes with a study of Anglican voluntary efforts abroad. Chapter 6 proposes that ecclesiastical expansion furthered by the SPCK and SPG be regarded as more than a monolithic imperial enterprise. Sirota reads these efforts as 'the de-territorialization of Anglicanism, a process of rendering the established church less dependent on the political, diocesan, and parochial structures that had proved difficult if not impossible to reproduce abroad' (pp. 224–5).

A significant number of texts published in 2014 approached the eighteenth century from a global perspective. Stacey Sloboda's *Chinoiserie: Commerce and Critical Ornament in Eighteenth-Century Britain* examines the economic and aesthetic significance of imported oriental commodities in eighteenth-century Britain. Sloboda begins her study with a 1755 review of *Les Métamorphoses chinois*, a comic opera featuring opulent chinoiserie backdrops, props, and costumes. The review describes a piece of choreography in which forty-eight 'Chinamen' (English and Swiss performers) 'form eight ranks of dancers, who, by bending down and rising up in succession, give a fair imitation of the waves of the stormy sea' (quoted in Sloboda, p. 1). This dynamic image aptly evokes the sense of disorientation produced by the 'profusion' of chinoiserie goods that reached its height by the mid-eighteenth century, and by the pervasive oriental aesthetic 'deployed in theatre, domestic interiors and architecture, prints, and gardens' during the period. Sloboda is careful, however, to challenge the notion that chinoiserie is an inherently incoherent or illegible style (for example, she critiques critical studies which characterize British interest in oriental commodities as a 'craze', p. 10). Her own study therefore attends to the 'specific qualities' of the objects and interiors under review in relation to their idiosyncratic 'spatial and social contexts' (p. 10). The introductory chapters focus on the production, circulation, and consumption of chinoiserie (particularly porcelain). Chapter 1 focuses on the dialogue between English and Chinese artisans and merchants. Working against the critical assumption that chinoiserie is a predominantly fantastical European construct (and therefore artificial or false) Sloboda examines the trade networks that enabled collaboration between the two cultures so that the exoticism of chinoiserie is figured as a joint production between Chinese and European artists and merchants. Chapter 2 locates chinoiserie 'at the centre' of debates concerning economics and aesthetics, class, and taste. Connections drawn between the materiality of sculptural chinoiserie—its 'focus on circular movement, dramatic extension, and ornamental profusion' (p. 89)—and the fluid dynamism of the marketplace are of particular interest. The remaining chapters and conclusion trace the influence of chinoiserie in increasingly broad spheres: the bedroom, the garden, and the global marketplace. Chapter 3 brings fantasy back to the foreground by highlighting the relationship between the exotic and the erotic. Sloboda uses this context to develop David Porter's suggestion that chinoiserie empowered a 'new arena of aesthetic play' for both sexes (p. 123). The final chapter locates an 'overtly political' iconography in the proliferation of chinoiserie features (among them pagodas and Chinese bridges) in eighteenth-century British gardens (p. 160). By introducing two recognizable and accessible edifices towards the end of her study, the 'Chinese House' at Stowe in Buckinghamshire and Brighton's Royal Pavilion, Sloboda invites twenty-first-century visitors to contemplate possible similarities between their own expectations and impressions of chinoiserie with those of eighteenth-century viewers.

Kristina Kleutghen considers the counterpart to European chinoiserie in 'Chinese Occidenterie: The Diversity of "Western" Objects in Eighteenth-Century China' (*ECS* 47[2014] 117–35). The popularity of European imports during the Qing dynasty led to a surge in the production of domestic occidentarie—material goods which 'disrupt[ed] any agenda inherent to Western imports . . . [and] reflect[ed] what the Chinese did and did not appreciate about the West' (p. 118). Kleutghen's essay is part of a special issue of *Eighteenth-Century Studies* on 'Eighteenth-Century Easts and Wests'. In her introduction to the issue, Chi-ming Yang explains that these locational terms have been pluralized to reflect the heterogeneity of the regions discussed (*ECS* 47[2014] 95–101). Yang positions this collection of essays within 'ongoing efforts across the humanities to decenter the study of empires and traverse the terrain of national, linguistic differences' (p. 96). The varied critical and methodological approaches adopted by each contributor signal, however, that the notion of 'East–West' encounter remains a 'space of disputation' (p. 96). Other contributions include: Matthew W. Mosca, 'The Qing State and Its Awareness of Eurasian Interconnections, 1789–1806' (*ECS* 47[2014] 103–16); Danna Agmon, 'The Currency of Kinship: Trading Families and Trading on Family in Colonial French India' (*ECS* 47[2014] 137–55); Suzanna Marchand, 'Where Does History Begin? J. G. Herder and the Problem of Near Eastern Chronology in the Age of Enlightenment' (*ECS* 47[2014] 157–75); Nabil Matar, 'Christians in the Eighteenth-Century Ottoman Mashriq' (*ECS* 47[2014] 177–94); and Srinivas Aravamudan, 'East–West Fiction as World Literature: The Hayy Problem Reconfigured' (*ECS* 47[2014] 195–231).

Two further essays this year considered eighteenth-century cultures of the Eastern world. Avner Wishnitzer, 'Into the Dark: Power, Light, and Nocturnal Life in 18th-Century Istanbul' (*IJMES* 46[2014] 513–31), examines the shifting, sometimes contradictory, social and political influence of darkness in the early modern Middle East. For the elite and ruling classes, nocturnal darkness provided a backdrop for impressive displays of wealth and prestige, including fireworks and garden parties illuminated by 'thousands of candles and lanterns' (p. 521). But beyond the palace walls and away from city strongholds—'islands of power and light' (p. 517)—nocturnal darkness engendered criminal activity, subversive or stigmatized cultural practice, and political dissent. This study, Wishnitzer suggests, shines its own light on a neglected area of scholarship concerning the nocturnal Middle East prior to the late nineteenth century. Walter N. Hakala looks to Southeast Asia in his essay, 'A Sultan in the Realm of Passion: Coffee in Eighteenth-Century Delhi' (*ECS* 47[2014] 371–88), which examines the phenomenon of coffee-house culture among Delhi's literary elite during the first half of the eighteenth century as demonstrated in contemporaneous Urdu poetry.

Eighteenth-Century Studies demonstrated further commitment to the theme of global Enlightenment in a special issue on 'The Maritime Eighteenth Century'. Essays in this collection exhibit a common interest in the spatial attributes of oceans—their navigability and connective properties, but also, as in Matthew Norton's 'Temporality, Isolation, and Violence in the Early Modern English Maritime World' (*ECS* 48[2014] 37–66), their capacity to preserve distance (Norton's essay discusses the problem of maritime space in relation to piracy and privateering). Prasannan Parthasarathi and Giorgia Riello, 'The Indian Ocean in the Long Eighteenth Century' (*ECS* 48[2014] 1–19), consider the spatial and chronological parameters of the Indian Ocean during the eighteenth century and situate the field of Indian Ocean studies (which often exhibits a Eurocentric bias) within the broader discourse of global history. An essay by Sarah Crabtree, 'Navigating Mobility: Gender, Class, and Space at Sea, 1760–1810' (*ECS* 48[2014] 89–106), considers the on-board diaries composed by Quaker transatlantic ministers. These documents reveal that those on board responded to their new, potentially disorienting, environs by policing the 'spatial orientation and social interaction' between fellow passengers according to gender, class, and race. In so doing, they 'imposed a landed hierarchy on the social geography of the vessel' (p. 91) as though denying the reality that they were no longer on land. Other contributions include Geoff Quilley's 'Art History and Double Consciousness: Visual Culture and Eighteenth-Century Maritime Britain' (*ECS* 48[2014] 21–35) and Christiaan van Bochove's 'Seafarers and Shopkeepers: Credit in Eighteenth-Century Amsterdam' (*ECS* 48[2014] 67–88), which examines the culture of lending between seafarers traversing European and trans-Atlantic routes and merchants in the Dutch Republic prior to urban regulation. Imperialism, empire, and migration are also among the subjects considered in a special issue of *The Eighteenth Century: Theory and Interpretation* on 'The Dispossessed Eighteenth Century' (*ECent* 55[2014])

One of the most wide-ranging studies in terms of geographical scope published in 2014 was *Eighteenth-Century Thing Theory in a Global Context: From Consumerism to Celebrity Culture*, edited by Ileana Baird and Christina Ionescu. This fascinating and diverse collection of essays considers the 'new value invested in things' produced by increasingly extensive international trade networks during the period (p. 2). The emergence of consumer culture is often treated as a *fin-de-siècle* phenomenon; in the first of two introductions, Baird encourages the reader to look back to the eighteenth century and the advent of mass-produced goods, the culture of collections, and the 'it-narrative' in order to locate the origins of this shift (Ionescu's introduction discusses the contributors and their chapters in relation to one another). Baird stresses that this collection makes a unique contribution to the field through its focus on 'the unforeseen relational maps drawn by things in their global peregrinations' (p. 8)—that is, how the meaning of a 'thing' (both material and immaterial) is 'reworked in various cultural contexts' (p. 10). This approach emphasizes the 'trajectory of the object rather than its origin' (p. 15). Each of the first three sections of the book pertains to a specific geographical region. Part I, which focuses on western Europe, begins with a chapter by Christina Jones on chocolate and the invention of the *tasse trembleuse*, a type of serving ware designed especially for drinking chocolate; Kevin Bourque reads Charles Johnstone's it-narrative, *Chrysal, or the Adventures of a Guinea*, in the context of eighteenth-century celebrity culture; and Sophie Thomas examines the afterlife of the feather cloaks James Cook brought back from his exploration of the Hawaiian Islands as they moved from private collections to museums. Finally, Kevin M. McGeough discusses the production and circulation of Egyptian-inspired objects in western Europe. Essays in Part II, which considers Russia, include studies of fashion in the wake 'the radical politicization of sartorial culture' initiated by Peter I in the early eighteenth century (p. 114), the journals and letters of the Anglo-Irish woman Martha Wilmot, who collected gifts and souvenirs during her stay with Princess Ekaterina Romanovna Dashkova in the early nineteenth century, and the printed book—a 'rare object[] and desired commodit[y]' in Russia during the eighteenth century, despite the country's developing literary culture (p. 151). Part III examines Latin America, and begins with a second essay on Charles Johnstone's *Chrysal*—this time in relation to imperial power and the titular guinea's transformation from Peruvian gold to British coinage. In the following chapter, Krystal McMillen writes on the sea turtle—a thing 'at once comestible and material' (p. 24)—in both the public imagination of the eighteenth century and within the pages of Daniel Defoe's *Robinson Crusoe* specifically. Irene Fizer also contributes a chapter on *Robinson Crusoe*, which focuses on the hero's relation to objects on the island, and his umbrella in particular. This section concludes with a chapter on cartographical representation in eighteenth-century Spanish America and the circulation of increasingly accurate maps. The fourth and final section approaches 'things' as collectibles, artefacts, and scientific objects. Laure Marcellesi's chapter on the European gifts brought back to the South Seas by a Polynesian visitor neatly balances Sophie Thomas's essay in Part I. The concluding two chapters examine illustration in Abbé Prévost's *Histoire général des voyages* and the role of souvenirs or relics in *Gulliver's Travels*.

Richard Squibbs's *Urban Enlightenment and the Eighteenth-Century Periodical Essay: Transatlantic Retrospects* considers the circulation of ideas among the urban populace of England, Scotland, and colonial America. Squibbs begins by carefully distinguishing the eighteenth-century periodical from the magazine, a category with which it is often bracketed. He suggests that the fertile interplay between magazine articles and advertisements leads scholars to prioritize commercial aspects over 'the literary-historical developments on the practice of periodical writing' (p. 2). Squibbs takes a deliberate step away from academic trends in order to situate the periodical essay alongside the novel as one of the eighteenth century's pre-eminent literary genres. This counter-movement is replicated (less convincingly) in his decision to present the essay serial as an exclusively male-authored phenomenon. Squibbs contends that the aim of the text is to 'recover the critical discourses surrounding the eighteenth-century essay' rather than impose our present-day standards and expectations concerning inclusivity (p. 14), a practice that 'speak[s] to our current sense that male and female writers should be equally represented in literary histories more than they reflect the circumstances of periodical essay publishing in the eighteenth century' (p. 197 n. 24). Ideally, however, a study of this nature would attempt to satisfy both our modern appetite for equality and our desire for historical accuracy. Chapter 1 explores the literary history of the periodical essay from the early eighteenth century to 1819, while locating the genre's historical origins in antiquity. The following chapters advance this investigation by attributing the 'literary impulse to create urban characters'—a central feature of the periodical essay—to Theophrastus's *Characters*, tracing the influence of this text on essayists' attempts to shape the civic and moral character of their readers. In chapter 4, Squibbs identifies a feeling of futility among mid-century essayists concerning their ability to 'create prominent and sustainable literary publics (p. 81). Because of this, Squibbs argues, the genre began to be conceived of in terms of literary posterity, a decision that led writers to adopt an apolitical cast and develop general moral observations from the particulars of contemporary life. The remaining chapters trace the development of these ideas in Scotland and America in a series of compelling case studies. Here, Squibbs's decision to expand the geographical range of his investigation coincides with a study of the relationship between essay writing and legal training. The periodical press is also considered in James Robert Wood's essay, 'Mr. Spectator's Anecdotes and the Science of Human Nature' (*ECLife* 38[2014] 63–92). Wood reads Joseph Addison and Richard Steele's anecdotes as a form of experimental report. Both genres, he observes, 'produce the illusion of unmediated access to past events' (p. 64). While the early novel exhibits a received understanding of the way in which human ethics are inscribed into the laws of nature, Mr Spectator's anecdotes, like the reports of the Royal Society, were predicated on empirical observation of particular truths that may run contrary to traditional suppositions about the human condition.

A number of journal articles published in 2014 consider urban life in the eighteenth century, whether through the lens of sexuality, consumerism, or the world of letters. Azfar Farid's 'Beastly Sodomites and the Shameless Urban Future' (*ECent* 55 [2014] 391–410) charts shifting cultural conceptions of sodomy in London following the execution of three men after a Holborn molly house was raided in 1726. Arguing that critical discourse surrounding the molly-house phenomenon has focused unduly on effeminacy, Farid's essay investigates the 'beastly urban sodomite' in the public imagination by positioning this figure within its broader socio-cultural context (p. 392). He considers, for example, the moveable boundary between humans and animals during this particular historical period: 1726 was the year in which the 'Wild Boy of Hanover' was brought to London and Mary Toft made the extraordinary claim of having given birth to rabbits. In 'Comfort, the Acceptable Face of Luxury: An Eighteenth-Century Cultural Etymology' (*SEL* 14[2014] 3–21), Marie Odile-Bernez traces a shift in attitude towards consumption indicated by the substitution of the word 'luxury'—a 'negative loaded' term used to connote indulgence (p. 4) for 'comfort', a comparatively virtuous term connected with mental and physical wellbeing. This essay considers the socio-political significations of the word 'comfort' as deployed by novelists and writers on economics, such as Adam Smith and Thomas Malthus. Of especial interest is Odile-Bernez's discussion of comfort as a specifically English phenomenon capable of confounding the French (as illustrated by an amusing episode in Eugène Sue's *Les Mystères de Paris*) (p. 18). In 'The Value of Money in Eighteenth-Century England: Incomes, Prices, Buying Power—and Some Problems in Cultural Economics' (*HLQ* 77 [2014] 373–416), Robert D. Hume investigates the monetary rather than the symbolic value of cultural consumption. This empirical study considers the income levels of the average household across the period in relation to the costs of books, paintings, and theatre, concert, and opera tickets. While only a select number of families could afford 'more than a few shillings a month' on such luxuries (p. 378), this essay takes into account the difference between 'purchase' and 'access' (p. 379). Hume also examines the respective earnings of authors, performers, and artists.

Eric Parisot examines an under-studied aspect of epistolary culture in 'Suicide Notes and Popular Sensibility' (*ECS* 47[2014] 277–91). This essay addresses the vogue, particularly prevalent in the 1770s, for publishing suicide notes in newspapers and magazines. Parisot connects this phenomenon with the rise of sentimentalism, which led readers to view suicide notes as 'opportunities . . . to test their own capacity to feel' (p. 279). For suicidal authors, the possibility of a public audience could awaken 'the competing desires for self-destruction and self-construction' (p. 278). This is evidenced by the self-consciously literary notes Parisot examines, in which the authors imagine their lives as already being in the 'past . . . as attention turns to a legacy founded on a sense of justice and sympathetic humanity' rather than the distressing and potentially violent events in their immediate future (p. 282). Andrew Benjamin Bricker's 'Libel and Satire: The Problem with Naming' (*ELH* 81[2014] 889–921) examines the tendency among eighteenth-century satirists to 'gut' or 'emvowel' the names of their targets (p. 889). Against the critical assumption that this practice protected satirists from the untrained eyes of prosecutors and judges, Bricker argues that the 'real question' was not whether a gutted name could be 'filled in', but whether insinuations against a victim of satire qualified as defamatory. Highlighting the legal and literary significance of a 1713 ruling that determined that deliberately ambiguous names could no longer be relied upon to avert potential prosecutions, Bricker examines the motivations (and misunderstandings) that led some writers to continue the practice of 'strategic naming' in the following decades. Finally, *Social Networks in the Long Eighteenth Century: Clubs, Literary Salons, Textual Coteries* (CambridgeSP), an ambitious collection of essays edited by Ileana Baird that address themes of sociability and public opinion, was unavailable from the publishers or did not arrive in time for review. This work will be discussed next year.

Turning to studies of women's writing during the period, Christina Lupton, 'Gender and Materiality on the Eighteenth-Century Page' (*SEL* 54 [2014] 605–24), challenges the Freudian tendency to view the quill as a phallic object and the blank sheet of paper as symbolic of the receptive female body by reading a series of it-narratives in which instrument and page alike are figured as female. Lupton reveals the inadequacy of these metaphors by focusing on the materiality of the objects under consideration: goose quills cast as women are at the mercy of their male handlers—one claims to have been left 'gaping, in the agonies of ruin, on the ground' after her slit has been unduly widened (quoted in Lupton, p. 612); blank, apparently 'untouched', sheets of paper bore witness to their status as 'recycled and manufactured products' (p. 615). In 'Sarah Fielding's *Lives of Cleopatra and Octavia*: Anecdote and Women's Biographical Histories' (*SECC* 43 [2014] 137–51), April London explores the interplay between anecdote, a genre traditionally used to relay scandalous or salacious material, and exemplary fiction, its unlikely bedfellow. Fielding's work anticipates a generic shift, expressed in successive editions of Johnson's *Dictionary*, in which the anecdote is described first as a secret history and, later, as 'a minute passage of private life' devoid of its earlier, lurid connotations (quoted in London, p. 140). Fielding relies on biographical history to explore the intimate psychology of her protagonists but also to produce a work unapologetically didactic in its aims, exploiting the narrative appeal of historical biography to elicit the reader's sympathy and understanding. London reads Fielding's work as a precursor to later writings by Lucy Aikin, who insisted that biographical anecdote was a successful tool with which to 'mediat[e] for the "great majority of readers" the arcane reaches of gentlemanly and professional historians' (p. 147).

The demarcation of female and male arenas of influence is explored at greater length by Rebecca Davies in *Written Maternal Authority and Eighteenth-Century Education: Educating by the Book*, which charts the 'space of acceptable feminine public intellectualism' produced by women writers during the long eighteenth century (p. 1). Though tightly 'circumscribed in its purely written nature' (p. 2), this space granted female writers access to a discourse otherwise dominated by figures such as John Locke and Jean-Jacques Rousseau. Davies argues that the codification of maternal discipline from the mid-eighteenth century to the early nineteenth century 'disrupts, and largely replaces, patriarchal control of the discourse of knowledge in educational authority in the eighteenth century' (p. 3). Furthermore, if motherhood involves an element of self-negation, Davies observes that certain women writers harnessed the authority of the maternal voice to further privately held political and religious ideologies. This book does much to develop recent work concerning the historical and literary significance of eighteenth-century pedagogical writing and its legacy in present-day discourse. One of the most valuable elements of Davies's study is its inclusion of marginalized women writers such as Ann Martin Taylor (better known as the mother of children's poets Ann and Jane Taylor), alongside prominent figures such as Maria Edgeworth. Davies traces the evolution of written maternal authority from the Enlightenment to the Regency period by focusing on a series of thematically linked (though generically and ideologically diverse) women writers. The book begins, however, with a chapter on *Pamela II* and Samuel Richardson's decision to locate 'ideal maternity' not in the domestic sphere but in Pamela's 'authorship of a written maternal project' (p. 17). This produces a formula, Davies argues, for conceiving of maternal authority in relation to educational discourse rather than the domestic sphere. Chapter 2 explores this notion in relation to Sarah Fielding's *The Governess*, a work that introduces maternal educational authority within the text (in the form of Mrs Teachum, the schoolmistress) and through the voice of its female author. Chapter 3 examines Mary Wollstonecraft's literature for children alongside her overtly political writing in order to elucidate the writer's complex and ultimately pessimistic conception of maternal authority. In chapter 4, Davies discusses Maria Edgeworth's empirical approach to maternal education, one that 'had been closed off by definitive exemplars of maternal education' as presented in works by Richardson and Fielding (p. 87). Chapters 5 and 6 chart the development of maternal authority as a written discipline in the nineteenth century in works by Ann Martin Taylor and Jane Austen, and are further reviewed in Chapter XIII.

In his essay on female education in Frances Burney's *Camilla*, 'Sharp Minds/Twisted Bodies: Intellect, Disability, and Female Education in Frances

Burney's *Camilla*' (*ECent* 55[2014] 1–17), Jason S. Farr contends that the eighteenth century is a neglected period in disability studies. Building on work by scholars such as Felicity Nussbaum and Chris Mounsey, Farr seeks to remedy this oversight by focusing on depictions of disabled figures in literary texts, such as Burney's, as well as the discursive structures that inform notions of disability. The year 2014 witnessed an important contribution to this field in *The Idea of Disability in the Eighteenth Century*, edited by Mounsey. This collection of essays considers what Mounsey terms 'Variability', a concept which rejects the 'reference point of "normal"' in order to communicate 'that every "normal" person [i]s as different (Variable) as every other "normal" person' (p. 17). In his introduction, Mounsey suggests that 'disability studies should follow the typical academic trajectory of a subject area beginning with the general and all-encompassing theory and move toward the specific, local, and personal' (p. 5). Writing candidly of his own experience as a partially sighted person, Mounsey contends—in a statement that may strike some readers as controversial—that 'Disabled people are defined by their disability' and therefore require a history that is distinct from that of able-bodied men and women (p. 6). In so doing, Mounsey presents this collection as a departure from traditional Foucauldian methodology, which focuses more closely on the socio-cultural discourses that produce and enforce otherness than on marginalized figures themselves. Mounsey's introduction includes a brief, instructive case study on poet and politician William Hay, which highlights some of the critical difficulties attending disability studies. Hay authored *Deformity: An Essay* [1754] alongside a range of texts on law and government, and was himself deformed and a dwarf. While 'treat[ing] disabled people as though their disability were marginal to their lives can miss something of great importance', Mounsey observes, 'one wonders whether we ought to read Hay only for his contribution to the way we understand deformity' (p. 10). How, Mounsey asks, do we choose 'to notice people in history' (p. 17)? While several essays in the volume fall outside this section's purview, each of the text's three sections—on methodological, conceptual, and experiential approaches to disability—will be of interest to scholars of eighteenth-century prose. The first section begins with an essay on Margaret Cavendish's natural philosophy, by Holly Faith Nelson and Sharon Akler; Jess Keiser examines John Locke's writing on mental illness; Paul Kelleher approaches 'the rhetoric of deformity in the corpus of British moral philosophy' through Shaftesbury's *Characteristics* (p. 71); and Emile Bojeson examines Scottish philosopher Thomas Reid's criticism of 'the binary of disabled able-bodied' as 'the product of empiricism and skepticism' (p. 21). The second section features only two essays: Anna K. Sagal explores the language of eighteenth-century disability through the character of Uncle Toby in Sterne's *Tristram Shandy*, and Dana Gliserman Kopans examines contemporary periodicals and pamphlets in her study of mental disability and false imprisonment for insanity. Essays in the final section are biographical investigations of 'little-known disabled people, or people who are little known for their disability' (p. 23): Jamie Kingsley examines the devotional poetry of Susanna Harrison, who suffered from chronic pain; Jason Farr suggests that William Hay's and Sarah Scott's writings on disability challenge social bias by suggesting that 'deformity is in

fact a desirable physical condition' (p. 187). In the final two chapters of the
collection, Jess Domanico and Mounsey examine the lives of blind poets
Priscilla Poynton and Thomas Gills.

Scholars continue to concentrate on eighteenth-century literary criticism. In
'The Matter of the Moral Sense: Shaftesbury and the Rhetoric of Tact'
(*MP* 111 [2014] 533–45), Jacob Bodway asserts the joint significance of ethics
and aesthetics to Shaftesbury's conception of moral beauty, arguing that
scholars who fail to recognize the ethical dimension of his aesthetics render 'a
severe disservice to the complexity of his moral theory' (p. 535). In 'Relative
Obscurity: The Emotions of Words, Paint and Sound in Eighteenth-Century
Literary Criticism' (*HEI* 40:v[2014] 644–61), Louise Joy considers the basis on
which literary critics of the period neglected the affections, a category of
emotion carefully distinguished from the passions in eighteenth-century
theology and moral philosophy and actively discussed in other critical
discourses, such as writing on the emotions in music. Two more works
published in 2014 approach eighteenth-century criticism from a distinctly
modern lens. In '*Scrutiny*'s Eighteenth Century' (*EIC* 64[2014] 318–40), J.A.
Smith considers the period as constructed in the pages of F.R. Leavis and L.C.
Knight's literature periodical. The title of James Ley's *The Critic in the Modern
World: Public Criticism from Samuel Johnson to James Wood* suggests that at
least one chapter of the volume will be of interest to eighteenth-century
scholars. Ley begins by countering Northrop Frye's suggestion that the best
criticism is impartial; on the contrary, he writes, criticism at its most engaging
is 'unstable, subjective, [and] presumptuous' (p. 4). Johnson is therefore an
ideal starting point: Ley's portrait highlights the writer's propensity for
absolute judgements ('A Johnsonian aphorism is a cleaver that descends to
sever reason from unreason, true sentiments from false', p. 10) and withering
remarks ('Johnsonian irony . . . comes with a tincture of acid', p. 11). Greater
value is placed on the consistency of Johnson's own critical persona and his
ability to isolate the underlying, universal relevance of any particular subject.
Written with both academic and non-specialist readers in mind, Ley's study is
likely to be of interest to readers of this section for its ability to knit Johnson
into a broader discursive tradition.

While this year saw the publication of three books on music in the
eighteenth century, Catherine Jones's *Literature and Music in the Atlantic
World 1767–1867* fell largely beyond the period boundary of this section, and
Kate Horgan's *The Politics of Song in Eighteenth-Century Britain, 1723–1795*
is discussed in Section 3 below. Roger Matthew Grant's *Beating Time and
Measuring Music in the Early Modern Era* may be of interest to general readers
as well as historians and theorists of music for its discussion of the way in
which the development of a rationalized musical metrical system reflects the
late eighteenth century's broader movement towards standardized units of
measurement. Grant explores the relationship between theories of musical
metre and theories of time. During the eighteenth century, he observes,
musical theorists 'began to express a concern about temporal specificity in
music, worrying that the notation of meter and rhythm no longer
communicated tempo' (p. 2). As a result, they developed a profusion of
metres (some theorists describing 'more than fifty different meter signatures',

p. 2), which had complex relationships with tempo and notation. At the close of the century, a second development took place in which theorists began to understand metre as an absolute measurement divorced from tempo markings and notational practices. These changes coincided with a new understanding of time itself, which natural philosophers had begun to conceive of as separate from the rhythms of the natural world. Grant's study traces the implications of this shift into the early nineteenth century, when Maelzel's metronome (patented in 1815) allowed musical tempo to become a universal language. This study makes an important contribution to the history of music theory; while metre is often considered a 'fairly self-evident' (p. 3) aspect of musical structure, Grant brings it the foreground of musical theory and experience.

Readers of this section may take interest in the introductory part of Sarah Tindal Kareem's *Eighteenth-Century Fiction and the Reinvention of Wonder*, which draws on a variety of prose texts in order to define and theorize 'wonder' during the period under review. Carefully situating her study in relation to affect theory, Kareem challenges the assumption that secularization 'inevitably led to wonder's wane as a significant philosophical and literary sentiment' (p. 2). Wonder did not 'lose its hold' during the eighteenth century, she argues, but became entwined with fictional realism—a phenomenon here termed the 'fictional marvelous' (p. 2). Other studies, as Kareem notes, have found continuities between seventeenth-century 'wonder literature' (whether religious or scientific) and eighteenth-century fiction (p. 66). But where these studies have identified 'similarities of form and content' between the two genres, Kareem focuses on the way in which seventeenth-century descriptions of natural or supernatural prodigies and eighteenth-century fictional narratives seek to inculcate comparable emotional and intellectual responses in their readers. Like consumers of improbable accounts of monstrous births, readers of eighteenth-century novels maintained a complex relationship with the veracity of the texts they encountered: 'moments of strangeness' in either type of composition might indicate either its 'truth' or its 'falsehood'. Over the course of the eighteenth century, however, the marvellous and the fictional were 'established as [separate] literary categories that attempted to elicit different forms of wonderment' (p. 10). Later eighteenth-century fictions could no longer seek to astonish their readers with 'their contested truth value' (p. 13). Instead of producing wonder 'about' or 'at' the remarkable events they described, these texts encourage readers to marvel at the narrative 'artistry that produces the illusion' (p. 14).

Moving to studies of individual authors, Charlotte Roberts's *Edward Gibbon and the Shape of History* offers a close reading of the three instalments of Gibbon's *Decline and Fall*. Roberts's study rests on the observation that Gibbon's work, and subsequent interpretations of his work, exhibit a characteristic hybridity: as 'comprehensive, monumental, and singular', on the one hand, and 'diachronic, iterative . . . and plural' on the other (p. 2). In her assessment of Gibbon scholarship, Roberts remarks that 'The sheer scale and mastery of the *Decline and Fall* make it an object of sublime contemplation, with any attempt to break it down into its constituent parts hampered by the gravitational pull of the work's total identity' (p. 5). Roberts's careful attention to the compositional fabric of *Decline and Fall* is, however, the product of a different—and more defensible—gravitational pull produced by close reading. Chapter 1 examines Gibbon's depiction of character in the work in the wider context of 'historiographical tradition and contemporary thinking on selfhood and identity' (p. 10). Here, Roberts applies her central argument to Gibbon's protagonists, who exhibit the internal divisions and multiplicity characteristic of the work as a whole. Chapters 3 to 5 consider each of the successive instalments of Gibbon's text. Throughout, Roberts 'challenges any progressionist study of Gibbon's work' and suggests that perceptible changes in the author's historiographical outlook and methodological approach are an 'invitation to read backwards as well as forwards, sporadically as well as methodically' (pp. 53–4).

In the field of Samuel Johnson studies, Robert L. Betteridge's essay '"I may perhaps have said this": Samuel Johnson and Newhailes Library' (*ScLJ* 6 [2014] 81–90) considers the Newhailes library room in Edinburgh, which Johnson is supposed to have described as 'the most learned drawing-room in Europe' after a visit in 1773 (p. 81). While the quotation became closely associated with the library room from the mid-twentieth century onwards, it likely derives from George Birkbeck Hill's late nineteenth-century study of Johnson rather than the writer himself. Betteridge considers the collection in relation to Johnson's literary tastes, but also more broadly, as 'an icon of the Scottish Enlightenment' (p. 87). This short essay raises valuable questions concerning the significance of celebrity endorsement through the impact of Johnson's apocryphal remarks on the library's legacy. In 'The Topicality of Samuel Johnson's "Life" of Francis Cheynell' (*RES* 65[2014] 853–65), F.P. Lock explains why Johnson might have been interested in Cheynell, whose life and work had fallen out of public interest by the mid-eighteenth century, and whose political and religious views Johnson strongly opposed. Lock locates a telling correspondence between Cheynell's involvement in the parliamentary attack on Oxford in 1647 and Oxford's aggrieved status in the late 1740s. By 'writ[ing] a life of Cheynell as a kind of parallel history', Lock suggests, Johnson was able to defend Oxford without exhibiting partisanship (p. 865). Regrettably, Howard D. Weinbrot's edited collection *Samuel Johnson: New Contexts for a New Century* (Huntington) did not arrive in time to review and will be discussed next year.

Turning to 2014 Rousseau scholarship, Whitney Arnold addresses the phenomenon of notoriety in her essay 'Rousseau and Reformulating Celebrity' (*ECent* 55[2014] 39–55). Arnold distinguishes between the embodied Rousseau, the textual representation of Rousseau, and 'the public representation of Rousseau that is already implicated in—and serves as an impetus for—the textual representation of Rousseau' (p. 40). Arnold traces Rousseau's increasingly disillusioned attempts to respond to his celebrity in the *Confessions*, the *Dialogues*, and the *Rêveries du promeneur solitaire*, each of which advances a new and different approach to the problem of authenticity and 'public intimacy' (p. 40). Rebecca Dowd Geoffroy-Schwinden's 'Rousseau and the Revolutionary Repertoire' (*SEC* 43[2014] 89–110) considers Rousseau's writing on the place of music in politics and 'the interaction between intellectual and popular musical cultures during the eighteenth century' more broadly (p. 91). This essay suggests that the French republic of the 1790s drew on mid-century musical ideals espoused by Rousseau in the late 1740s. Geoffroy-Schwinden connects Rousseau to the students and scholars accused of circulating disrespectful songs about Madame de Pompadour, the king's mistress. Approached through the lens of performance studies, this incident reflects Rousseau's notion that singing in unison demonstrates a clear political purpose and cultivates a shared emotional response in both performer and listener. Readers of this section may also be interested in Jimmy Casas Klausen's *Fugitive Rousseau: Slavery, Primitivism, and Political Freedom*, which considers Rousseau's political theory in the context of European colonialism and empire.

Mike Hill and Warren Montag's *The Other Adam Smith* begins by discussing the 2008 financial crisis (the same topic, incidentally, is fore-grounded in Jordana Rosen and Chi-Ming Yang's introduction to a special issue of *The Eighteenth Century: Theory and Interpretation* on 'The Dispossessed Eighteenth Century' (*ECent* 55[2014] 137–52)). Hill and Montag consider the failed ideology that perpetuated the crash: the belief that regulation-free markets will reconcile the self-interests of individual agents for the benefit of all. Hill and Montag highlight former chairman of the Federal Reserve Board Alan Greenspan's repeated use of the term 'ideology' to defend his economic policy. 'An ideology is far more expansive than a theory or model', they write; 'It is nothing less than a worldview, which in this case, as in all others, implies not only an economics but also a politics, an ontology, and, finally, a kind of economic theology, if the notion of economy is historically separable from those of theodicy and providence' (pp. 2–3). The authors propose that Greenspan uses the noun 'ideology' in lieu of the proper name Adam Smith. Greenspan's reductive understanding of Smith is representative, they argue, of a tendency to oversimplify the complexities and contradictions inherent to the latter's writing, thereby privileging one persona over another—whether 'the architect of the unrestricted market, who seeks to coordinate individuated self-interest with national wealth' or 'the unwitting social democratic whose work demonstrated the impossibility of market rationality' (p. 5). Efforts to reconcile competing versions of Smith—economic and ethical—in the twentieth and twenty-first centuries tend to reinforce, rather than interrogate, a dualistic approach to his published work. Hill and Montag challenge this binary in their own study by 'widen[ing] the bibliographic frame'—keeping more recently discovered (and often margin-alized) texts in view, and taking into account gaps produced by missing manuscripts on literature, and law and government. Hill and Montag stress that this approach 'does not compel or even allow us to choose one or the other Adam Smith, nor does it require that we begin with the premise that the more recently discovered texts fit unambiguously into the framework of the old based on an assumption of authorial unity' (p. 6). The 'other' Adam Smith is plural, rather than singular.

Finally, 2014 saw an important contribution to the field of Swift studies in Claude Rawson's *Swift's Angers*. Part I, which addresses Swift's prose writings, will be of interest to readers of this section (Parts II and III are concerned with Swift's fiction and poetry). Rawson introduces two funda-mental aspects of Swift's rage from the outset: firstly, even at his most indignant, Swift 'never shows the loss of authorial composure', and secondly, that his anger was, in part, directed inward. Rawson stresses that 'The closeness of Swift's temperament to the things he attacked is a defining feature of his writing' (p. 2). Appropriately, then, the first two chapters of this study examine Swift's fraught relationship with Ireland. Rawson reads works such as *A Tale of a Tub* and *A Modest Proposal* not as evidence of Swift's patriotism but as characteristic of 'the colonial, jealously guarding the interests of the beleaguered settler against the high-handedness of the mother country as well as the savagery of the local population' (p. 16). For example, Rawson challenges Edward Said's reading of the Drapier Letters—that Swift took umbrage at the manner in which Irish natives were being caricatured—when the more likely cause of Swift's outrage was 'the fact that his own people [the Anglo-Irish] [were] being mistaken for the "wild Irish"' (p. 34). Rawson's text has an expository, at times disconnected, feel. With minimal signposting, the argument suffers from a lack of clarity at times. As a result, the reader is left with the strange sensation of having stumbled into the work *in medias res*.

2. The Novel

Work on the eighteenth-century novel this year has ranged from attempts at broad-encompassing new approaches to familiar texts, to attention to under-studied texts, especially by female authors, to titbits of new biographical information about the novelists themselves. We begin with the book likely to have the largest readership and immediate grassroots influence of any examined in this review—and indeed one touched on elsewhere in this volume—the poet and publisher Michael Schmidt's *The Novel: A Biography*. The title is suggestive, for Schmidt offers little in the way of a new theory, history, or means of accounting for the 'rise' of the early novel. Instead it is a creative writer's book, eschewing reference to conventional academic critics in favour of the evaluations and interpretations offered by other novelists—Dickens, Woolf, Joyce, Coetzee for Defoe; Diderot, Jane Austen, D.H. Lawrence for Richardson—and bringing individual tropes and strains together across periods. Thus Defoe is placed alongside Truman Capote, as two authors who conceive of the novel as 'a long piece of reportage' (p. 85), and Patrick O'Brian is illuminated by being read next to Smollett. On *Clarissa*, Schmidt remarks, 'a reader who develops the taste to appreciate it will understand on the pulse what the novel form can be and do' (p. 113). Such occasionally clubbish hints and suggestions are inevitably idiosyncratic, but with the growing influence of creative writing in English departments, any lecturer may at some point be glad of Schmidt's suggestions for how eighteenth-century fiction can be brought together with living questions about the purposes of and approaches to writing today.

In *Eighteenth-Century Fiction and the Reinvention of Wonder*, also discussed above, Sarah Tindal Kareem draws eighteenth-century fiction into a pattern with both Protestant religion and Enlightenment science, as forms which worked to recognize the remarkable, strange, or meaningful in the ordinary or everyday (the experience of 'wonder' in her title). Such work of defamiliarization inside and outside literature—from Coleridge, to Matthew Arnold's 'criticism of life', to Brecht, the Russian Formalists, and contemporary work in theory of mind—is usually thought of as Romantic in origin and modern in tendency. Kareem, however, works to present its literary prehistory in the theorizations of Joseph Addison, David Hume, Adam Smith, and Lord Kames, as well as in such moments in eighteenth-century fiction as Robinson Crusoe's contiguous assessments of the 'sublime terror of the random footprint' he discovers on the beach, and the 'wonder of the sprouting corn' that he has forgotten inadvertently planting (pp. 98–9). In doing so, Kareem joins recent scholars who have aimed to qualify traditional genealogies of the eighteenth-century novel that stress its straightforward empirical realism and Weberian disenchantment. A sense of their shared interest in startling, distantiating wonder also allows Kareem to bring together figures usually opposed or regarded as belonging to contrary cultural currents in the period: thus the Puritan Defoe and the sceptic Hume, or the jovial realists Fielding and Austen and the brooding Gothic writers Walpole and Shelley, can be seen as drawing on common aesthetic resources. It would be interesting to know how either those more resolutely 'everyday' forms such as the it-narrative and the Richardsonian novel in letters, or the more openly fantastic genres such as the oriental tale, might fit into this paradigm; but Kareem has done a service in her interweaving of some surprising eighteenth-century statements on wonder, with some useful readings of the novelistic case studies she does include.

The experience of wonder takes on a more sinister resonance in Christopher F. Loar's *Political Magic: British Fictions of Savagery and Sovereignty, 1650–1750*, here having more in common with what Montaigne—in a phrase that fascinated Jacques Derrida—referred to as the 'mystical foundation of authority' ('Of Experience', in *The Complete Essays* (StanfordUP [1957], p. 821). The question of sovereignty has been a touchstone of critical theory in the twentieth and early twenty-first centuries, incorporating the challenging work of Schmitt, Hayek, Strauss, and Oakeshott on the right, and Benjamin, Bataille, Agamben, Žižek, and the recently published final seminars of Derrida on the left. The paradox common in some way to all these various thinkers—that authority can only be instated on the basis of an exception, some agency that steps outside its strictures in order to license it—is clearly relevant to the political debates around contractual government and divine right, in the thick of which the eighteenth century began. It is gratifying therefore to find a book that registers how preoccupied the fiction of the century after Hobbes was with sovereignty in its irrational, paradoxical aspect. In Loar's analysis, one of the key ways in which eighteenth-century fiction represented the civilizing violence of sovereignty is 'the first gunshot topos' (p. 4): the scene of a supposedly savage or simple indigenous people's first encounter with European mechanized violence, which transforms them from an undifferentiated pre-legal mass into a potentially civilizable polity. Thus the display of making fire with an eyeglass which impresses the Caribs in Aphra Behn's *Oroonoko* [1688], Friday's wonder at, and conversations with, Robinson's gun in Defoe's *Robinson Crusoe* [1719], and Gulliver's introduction of gunpowder to Lilliput and Brobdingnag in Swift's *Gulliver's Travels* [1726] all reveal something about those authors' conceptions of how power is managed within Britain itself.

The texts Loar studies by Cavendish, Behn, Defoe, and Swift are—it so happens—also the subject of another, quite different, monograph this year: *Utopian Geographies and the Early English Novel*, by Jason H. Pearl. For Pearl, the response to travel and discovery in English fiction of this period is precariously placed between sceptical disenchantment and wide-eyed enthusiasm about new possibilities. 'These fictions imagined, questioned, and disproved the existence of utopia but also brought it back to England', he argues; 'they emplaced and debunked utopia, but they also salvaged and reconfigured it as an immediate possibility in the life of the returning traveller' (p. 3). As with Loar's account of these texts' fantasies of sovereignty laid bare in far-flung places, Pearl finds the stress of these novels less on the actuality of utopian places abroad than on the challenge imagining them can present to life at home: 'by virtue of utopia's unreality but also its recuperation as a resilient idea, what was remote became close at hand' (p. 3). This internationally inspired utopianism, Pearl concludes, was eventually both cut off and absorbed by the mid-century domestic turn in the novel. But he contends that, nonetheless, as much as the novel after Richardson constricted the great geographical scope of the earlier tradition his book examines, it also retained something of its performative wish to imagine new and ideal ways of living.

The most theoretically ambitious monograph on the eighteenth-century novel this year is Eva König's *The Orphan in Eighteenth-Century Fiction: The Vicissitudes of the Eighteenth-Century Subject*. Dedicating chapters to seventeen novels built around variations on the orphan figure, König reads the century's changing representation of orphans both as evidencing a textual unconscious concerned with the novel form's own struggles to be accepted as a genre, and—no doubt more controversially—as divisible into the 'three psychic registers' proposed by the psychoanalyst Jacques Lacan: the free-flowing and blissful 'imaginary', the brutally socializing 'symbolic', and the traumatic, incomprehensible 'real' (p. 7). One does not become a Lacanian without expecting to be provocative, but it is exciting to find these familiar texts put to thoughtful uses beyond the reigning historicism of the moment.

Karen Bloom Gevirtz's *Women, the Novel, and Natural Philosophy, 1660–1727* examines seventeenth- and early eighteenth-century debates about identity and the problem of the 'intrinsically detached' subject, summarizing the intellectual situation as one in which 'philosophy countered the potential entropy and chaos of a universe of unattached selves by valuing actions that established a bond with others and that contributed to the well-being of the group' (p. 28). In the midst of what Gevirtz evocatively represents as a scramble to find a proper written form for this predicament, prose fiction becomes peculiarly adept at negotiating the separation between a newly isolated individual and the social reality through which it moves. Because 'questions about the relationship between the self and the community and thus between detachment and morality had a particular resonance for women' (p. 29), women authors are Gevirtz's focus, which has the additional advantage of granting critical attention to the under-studied Jane Barker and Mary Davys, as well as the more familiar Behn and Eliza Haywood.

In Gevirtz's reading, Behn was well aware of the increasing dominance of the autonomous subject as an intellectual paradigm, but resists it in fictions that show the primacy of the body's erotic intersubjectivity. Barker's *Galesia* trilogy [1713–26] pits a rationally knowable internal self against an altogether more chaotic external reality. Haywood's narrators adopt the detachment of Newtonian scientists, while Davys's fictions wrestle with how such detachment can be reconciled with sympathetic moral judgement: a move that, Gevirtz says, 'provides a foundation for literary omniscience' in the modern novel (p. 131).

In *Graphs, Maps, Trees: Abstract Models for a Literary History* [2006], Franco Moretti showed that, whereas worldwide the publication of novels by country had increased year on year since the start of the eighteenth century, the British 1730s were almost unique in representing a decline in the number of novels published. Building on this, Lacy Marschalk, Mallory Anne Porch, and Paula R. Backscheider, in 'The Empty Decade? English Fiction in the 1730s' (*ECF* 26:iii[2014] 375–426), note how many of the big writers of the 1720s—Defoe, Barker, Charles Gildon, Delarivier Manley, and Penelope Aubin—'were recently dead', adding that Davys would die in 1732, Haywood spent the decade in the theatre, and 'no new well-known British novelists rose to fill the void they left' (p. 381). In their examination of the odd range of difficult-to-categorize fictions that *were* published in the decade, a number of surprising points emerge. For one: defying the familiar parallel of the rise of the novel with the rise of the middle class (and with it, the middle-class protagonist), the authors find that 'the middle class is rarely depicted in these works, and, in almost every category, there are two groups of fictions: one polite or even aristocratic and one low or popular' (p. 376).

Returning to the 1720s, the Hillarian circle—the London literary group centred around the writing and amours of Haywood, Aaron Hill, and Martha Fowke—is the subject of Earla Wilputte's *Passion and Language in Eighteenth-Century Literature: The Aesthetic Sublime in the Work of Eliza Haywood, Aaron Hill, and Martha Fowke* (also discussed in Section 3 below). The book is welcome for its situation of—first—Haywood's early fiction in a particular coterie context of collaboration and competition, and—second—of the novels of the 1720s amid other literary forms of that moment, such as poetry, the periodical essay, biblical paraphrase, and letter-writing. In Wilputte's analysis, the Hillarians were trying to find the most effective language in which to articulate what they tend to call 'the passions': those of humanity in the abstract, and their own in particular. As Wilputte's useful series of close readings shows, 'the Hillarian circle . . . all exhibit, in varying degrees, a physically infused, body-oriented, almost medical discourse of blood, veins, atoms, hearts, breasts, and eyes, allied with traditional philosophy's figurative language of floods, storms, and flames in an effort to transcribe the sublime—a unique discourse that would effectively convey the personal passions' (p. 191). This puts Haywood's novels in an interestingly adversarial position, since, as Wilputte notes, 'the coterie regarded poetry as the best vehicle for the sublime' (p. 55). Like much of the literature on this group, Wilputte's book is clearly fascinated by the biographical linkages between these texts and their authors. But perhaps it is more useful for providing some hints on how we might move beyond the scandalmongering those authors deployed so adeptly, and revisit some of their under-read texts on their own terms.

Further attention to Haywood comes in a special issue of the *Journal for Early Modern Cultural Studies*, with papers responding to the recent *Political Biography of Eliza Haywood* [2012] by Kathryn R. King; a book the special issue's editors refer to as 'a significant, watershed moment in the critical reception of Haywood', encouraging 'readers and scholars to consider the ways in which political interests and concerns over what we would today call social justice permeate, and indeed motivate, almost all of her published works' (*JEMCS* 14:iv[2014] 1–8: p. 3). As such, Catherine Ingrassia offers a combative corrective to the 'failure of the historical imagination' that has erased traces of female same-sex eroticism from Haywood's oeuvre, and convincingly advances that 'one reader's "friendship" is another reader's "intimacy"' (*JEMCS* 14:iv[2014] 9–24: p. 11). Sarah Creel builds on recent work on the material appearance of eighteenth-century novels to discuss representations of Haywood herself in the portraits, frontispieces, and printer's emblems that accompanied her writings across her career (*JEMCS* 14:iv[2014] 25–48). Cheryl Nixon considers how Haywood's fiction and periodical writings imply a principled interrogation of family law and the legal status of children (*JEMCS* 14:iv[2014] 49–78). Jenifer Buckley considers the intersections of colonialism, speculative economics, and female sexuality in *Cleomelia; or, The Generous Mistress* [1727] (*JEMCS* 14:iv[2014] 79–100). In their different ways, Rachel Carnell and Eve Tavor Bannet both disrupt our view of Haywood as primarily a novelist by situating her 'secret histories' in the great range of political discourses and metafictional suggestions that resonate in that term (*JEMCS* 14:iv[2014] 101–21, 143–62). Earla Wilputte considers what she calls 'Haywood's Tabloid Journalism', arguing that the relatively unfamiliar novel *Dalinda; or, The Double Marriage* [1749] both cashes in on the well-known public scandal of the bigamous marriage of Thomas Estcourt Cresswell and Elizabeth Scrope and demands her readers take a more critical, interrogative view of what they have been told about it (*JEMCS* 14:iv[2014] 122–42). And finally, King herself offers the case for Haywood's miscellany, *Epistles for the Ladies* [1748–50], which she is here able to consider from perspectives other than the political one that was the emphasis of her biography (*JEMCS* 14:iv[2014] 187–208). In addition, Haywood's neglected but remarkable interrogation of political life in the 1750s, *The Invisible Spy* [1755], appears in a new edition in the admirable P&C Women's Library series this year, edited by Carol Stewart.

On Defoe: Karen Downing's monograph, *Restless Men: Masculinity and Robinson Crusoe, 1788–1840*, is an unusual book and not strictly about the eighteenth-century novel at all. Its focus, moreover, is the construction of masculinity around the start of the nineteenth century; even if statements such as 'men's apparent need for adventure and action has been rewritten, reworked and reinterpreted to speak to the men of any given time' (p. 9) make it sound as if Downing regards the traits of masculinity as a little more fixed and constant than many gender theorists do. Where it is innovative is in organizing its case studies around the evidence of the ongoing readership for Defoe's *Robinson Crusoe*, which beyond its most famous readers in this period—William Cowper, S.T. Coleridge, Charles Dickens—traversed divides of class and nation to become talismanic for many male readers' understanding of their own identity. The book seems to be several things at once. A broad-brush account of statements about masculinity in European culture in this period, an analysis of the culture of the colonization of Australia in particular, and a reception history of Defoe's novel; and these three commitments are not always in view at the same time. Perhaps it is asking for something Downing has not set out to do, but an eighteenth-century novel specialist yearns for a little more comment—even comment on the possibility of making such comment—on the nuances of *how* Defoe was read in this context. Many of the references to Crusoe and his island could have been made—as they often are today—without the speaker having actually read the novel. Downing's period was a great age of cheap magazine editions, illustrated editions, and abridgements, but there is no comment here on what versions of Defoe her Australian colonists might have had available to them. Nor is there reflection on whether there were any specific moments in *Robinson Crusoe* that seemed to lend themselves particularly to citation; and nor do we hear whether these men were interested in Defoe's sequels to *Robinson Crusoe*, the various rip-offs and rewritings the novel was subject to, or indeed in any other novels.

As ever, Defoe is the subject of numerous articles this year. The Crusoe trilogy is Leah Orr's subject in 'Providence and Religion in the Crusoe Trilogy' (*ECLife* 38:ii[2014] 1–24). Orr suggests that the assumption that Robinson's conversion at the end of the first novel straightforwardly reflects Defoe's own religious priorities needs to be qualified by the considerably more complicated representations and attitudes towards conversion in the subsequent instalments. Joshua Gass, in '*Moll Flanders* and the Bastard Birth of Realist Character' (*NLH* 45:i[2014] 111–30), uses genre theory to revisit the question of the 'flatness' of characters in pre-modern narrative. Christopher Peterson provides a brilliant exegesis of Jacques Derrida's interpretation of *Robinson Crusoe* from *The Beast and the Sovereign* [2009–11] in 'The Monolingualism of the Human' (*SubStance* 43:ii[2014] 83–99). And Betty Joseph, in 'The Political Economy of the English Rogue' (*ECent* 55:ii–iii[2014] 175–91), takes Marx's comments on the same novel as a prompt for resituating Defoe's protagonists in the eighteenth-century discourse of the rogue. Also published this year were: Robert Markley's 'Defoe and the Imagined Ecologies of Patagonia' (*PQ* 93[2014] 295–313); Ann Campbell's 'Strictly Business: Marriage, Motherhood, and Surrogate Families as Entrepreneurial Ventures in *Moll Flanders*' (*SECC* 43[2014] 51–68); and Kari Nixon's 'Keep Bleeding: Hemorrhagic Sores, Trade, and the Necessity of Leaky Boundaries in Defoe's *Journal of the Plague Year*' (*JEMCS* 14:ii[2014] 62–81). Katherine Ellison, Kit Kincade, and Holly Faith Nelson have published an edited collection, *Topographies of the Imagination: New Approaches to Daniel Defoe*, with AMS Press, but a copy did not arrive in time for review and will be discussed next year.

New light on Samuel Richardson's novels has come from E. Derek Taylor and Bonnie Latimer, both writing in *Notes and Queries*. Taylor, in 'Samuel Richardson's Printing of Private Bills: Mary Yonge and the Hazards of "Open

Court"' (*N&Q* 61[2014] 331–53) raises the question of why none of Richardson's characters take their antagonists to court. Pamela feels she would be denied justice over B's early affronts because he is himself a justice of the peace, Clarissa goes against the exhortations of friends and family in refusing to seek Lovelace's prosecution, and even Sir Charles Grandison sidesteps the courts in responding to an extortion scheme his cousin has fallen victim to. One answer, Taylor suggests, lies in the many House of Commons private bills that Richardson printed between 1720 and 1761. Focusing on the example of the divorce of William Yonge and Mary Heathcote—the humiliating and unfair details of which Richardson printed in 1725—Taylor suggests that these bills would have provided ample evidence of the doubtfulness of any of his characters' prospective law cases ending positively. In a second article, 'Clementina and the Pope in Richardson's *Sir Charles Grandison*' (*N&Q* 61[2014] 404–9), Taylor considers the enigmatic and rarely noted moment in Richardson's third novel when, during Clementina della Porretta's madness, a visit from 'the Patriarch' is referred to. As Taylor notes, various biographical details of the della Porretta family, as well as hints in the other references to this figure in the novel, make it possible to infer that this figure is no less a personage than Benedict XIV, the then pope: a possibility with fascinating potential for rethinking the already very nuanced relationship of Richardson's third novel to Catholicism. Richardson's engagements with the religious other around the time of *Sir Charles Grandison* are also Latimer's concern in her note, 'Samuel Richardson and Philip Carteret Webb's "Little Paper" on the Jewish Naturalization Act' (*N&Q* 61[2014] 404–6). Richardson seems to have been among the minority who supported the Jewish Naturalization Act immediately after its passing in 1753, and Latimer has noticed the likelihood that he was in fact personally intimate with the lobbyists who pushed the bill through. As Latimer notes, 'this offers us an interesting snapshot of the way in which Richardson's friendship circles—by no means restricted to Tories—may have helped to form his private political opinions, so notoriously difficult to pin down satisfactorily' (p. 406).

The once neglected *Sir Charles Grandison* continues to generate new readings sympathetic to the preoccupations of our own time in James Robert Wood's article, 'Richardson's Hands' (*ECF* 26:iii[2014] 331–53). Wood starts from the uneasiness about manual labour betrayed in *Pamela*, where the kind of work the heroine will fall to should she leave Mr B's employ is both idealized and kept anxiously away from her. By contrast, Wood suggests, by Richardson's third novel, a more sophisticated sense of high life as involving not so much genteel leisure as its own autonomous forms of labour has come together. Wood argues that the compulsion in *Sir Charles Grandison* to map the hard work of producing virtuous social networks onto what the well-heeled characters physically do with their hands is at the heart of this recognition. The article is a valuable addition to recent studies that have stressed the significance of the changing nature of work in eighteenth-century culture, as well as how the novels of the period registered and tried to analyse it.

On *Clarissa* [1747–8] meanwhile, Sarah Nicolazzo, in 'Reading Clarissa's "Conditional Liking": A Queer Philology' (*MP* 112:i[2014] 205–25), reads the heroine's cautious claim to have 'a conditional kind of liking' for Lovelace as 'a tentative linguistic experiment, an attempt to name "something" that had no name before' (pp. 205–6), and so as belonging to a host of half-formed affective terminologies in the early modern period that can now only be approached and reconstructed by way of an avowedly tentative 'queer philology'. Nicolazzo is right to call time on the habit in criticism that treated the phrase as the one 'to quote or allude to if you wanted to unmask Clarissa's desires—whatever you believed those desires to be' (p. 221). In its place, she presents instead a rich account of how, as much as the novel 'dramatizes an emergent form of heterosexuality'—constituted on romantic love inside marriage—'it also dwells on its contradictions, violences, and foreclosed alternatives' (p. 219).

Richardson's personal correspondence is the focus of Donatella Montini's article, 'Language and Letters in Samuel Richardson's Networks' (*JEMS* 3[2014] 173–98), which employs social network theory to investigate the implications of how the novelist and his circles addressed each other. As Richardson's correspondence begins to appear in the Cambridge edition—our review for next year will discuss the publication of the *Correspondence with Sarah Wescomb, Frances Grainger and Laetitia Pilkington* and *Correspondence Primarily on Sir Charles Grandison* (both 2015)—it is good to be reminded of the breadth and nature of those networks. However, as Montini acknowledges, she is forced to 'make the best use of bad data' (p. 181) in her investigations, reliant as she was at the time of writing on the partial and unreliable editions of Anna Barbauld and John Carroll. It will be interesting to see how Montini's researches are qualified by the appearance of a much larger and more reliable dataset as the Cambridge edition proceeds.

Lastly on Richardson, James Fowler has continued his ongoing work of situating Richardson's fiction in the context of its early French reception, with his monograph *Richardson and the Philosophes*. The book is the most sustained examination to date of why Richardson, 'a "counter-Enlightenment" writer' who 'claimed to write religious novels in order to counter anti-Christian tendencies in Britain' (p. 4), should find such a sincere, serious, and even emulative audience in a generation of French intellectuals who 'almost by definition, saw revealed religion as a source of prejudice and superstition' (p. 5). After making the case for Richardson's novels as combative and emphatically contemporary interventions into the religious questions of his own day via his differing treatments of the doctrinally sound Milton and the crypto-deist Pope, Fowler turns successively to the responses they provoked in Voltaire, Rousseau, and Diderot, showing how these writers 'shared the aim of using Richardson's techniques to capture "his" public, but to quite different ends' (p. 171). Voltaire began responding to *Pamela* in a three-act comedy, *Nanine* [1749], which both adapts *Pamela*'s plot and playfully includes the novel itself as reading matter for its heroine. Subsequently, in the collection of his own letters Voltaire occasionally referred to as *Paméla*, the philosopher queerly situates himself in the position of the young girl, with his host at the time of writing, Frederick the Great, positioned as Mr B. After he read *Clarissa*, Fowler finds, Voltaire's engagement with Richardson became more ambivalent: both antagonistic to the tricks Richardson plays to keep his readers enraptured ('seeming always to promise something, but always in the next volume', p. 81), and a most subtle and invested reader of how he does so. Rousseau's *Julie* [1761], in Fowler's analysis, endows *Clarissa* with the very deism that Richardson had set out to discredit, while Diderot—more openly praising, indeed to the point of idolatry, Richardson than Rousseau—nonetheless 'managed the feat of writing a Richardsonian fiction that is . . . fundamentally anti-Christian' (p. 172).

While King's *Political Biography* of Haywood has provoked considerable and wide-ranging engagement this year, J.A. Downie's volume on Fielding in the same series [2009] is responded to in a rather more modest—albeit highly suggestive—contribution on 'Henry Fielding's Proposals for an Internal British Passport System' (*ANQ* 27:iv[2014] 153–7), by Jesper Gulddal. In a few paragraphs of the 1753 pamphlet, *A Proposal for Making an Effectual Provision for the Poor*, Fielding dissents from the long-standing British suspicion of movement-control regimes common on the Continent, proposing what amounts to 'a wholesale criminalisation of vagrancy' (p. 154). Since the 1662 Act of Settlement, itinerant workers and migrants had been obliged to carry a passport-like certificate, and unauthorized paupers could be obliged to return to their home parishes. Fielding's proposed measures go considerably further, however, banning all unauthorized 'wandering' by those who could not prove their employment, ready money, and place of abode, and working innovatively towards standardizing personal identity documents. Fielding's reforms were not enacted, and so belong among his fictions, making it yet more interesting that, in fact, they would seem to foreclose on much of the action of either *Joseph Andrews* or *Tom Jones*. As Gulddal concludes, Fielding 'exploits free mobility for narrative purposes' (p. 157) even as he would legislate against it. But that said, if Fielding's political and novelistic fictions do have something in common here, it is in 'direct(ing) all itineraries toward a final, stabilising endpoint' (p. 157), finally sending all the rogues home.

Also on Fielding: Stephanie Insley Hershinow's article, 'When Experience Matters: *Tom Jones* and "Virtue Rewarded"' (*Novel* 47:iii[2014] 363–82), questions Samuel Johnson's two famous critiques of the novel: first, that Fielding, 'mingl(ing) good and bad qualities' in his characters, improperly prioritizes realism over useful morality; and second, that—in keeping with his maxim that Richardson knows how clocks are made while Fielding merely tells the time—his characters are superficial 'characters of manners' with no deeper understanding of human nature (p. 364). As Hershinow spots, these complaints do not obviously add up, since they make Fielding at once unduly worldly-wise and realistic, and too airily imprecise, when it comes to real people and their morality. We might make the qualification that, for Johnson, morality was not a well-meaning abstraction but the natural order of things, and so there was no necessary contradiction in writing psychologically intricate characters that were also virtuous (thus Richardson). Nonetheless, Hershinow's article helpfully suggests how 'the conceptual interference between these assessments produces a blurrier picture of the Richardson/Fielding debate, and thus of the early novel, than we might expect' (p. 365).

The major event in Sterne studies this year is Melvyn New's magnificent, idiosyncratic, and at times glibly provocative Florida edition of Laurence Sterne's works which is, after four decades, concluded in its ninth volume, 'mirroring Sterne's nine volumes of *Tristram Shandy*' (p. xv). *The Miscellaneous Writings and Sterne's Subscribers, an Identification List* begins with the schematic memoir Sterne wrote for his daughter, which she published in 1775 alongside his letters and the 'Rabelaisian Fragment', also included here. Next is a conservatively attributed selection of political broadsides from the 1741–2 parliamentary elections in York, before—alongside other minor pieces—a very welcome full scholarly edition of the Scriblerian-inflected *Political Romance*. New, ever the Scriblerian in his unwillingness to leave his own preoccupations and squabbles out of his scholarly apparatuses, hopes that his annotations will prove a corrective to 'even the most stubborn of those critics who continue to locate Sterne within the novelistic tradition' (p. xviii), as opposed to his preferred genealogical placing of Sterne in the tradition of the satirical prose of Petronius, Lucian, Rabelais, and Cervantes. In dealing with a period in which long prose fiction was scrambling for its identity, and constantly raiding other discourses and writing approaches across the board, it does not seem clear that we should have to choose.

Yet 'another crucial hinterland' (p. 296) for Sterne's fiction is introduced by the cultural historian Karen Harvey bringing her expertise on the early modern discourse of 'oeconomy'—the ordering of the economic and moral resources of a household—to bear on 'The Manuscript History of *Tristram Shandy*' (*RES* 65[2014] 282–301). As much as Sterne's remarkable novel-object has long been thought of as an event in the history of print culture, Harvey notes that we are invited to imagine Tristram composing his novel surrounded by the manuscripts of his family: his father's pocket-book and writings concerning Tristram's own naming and upbringing and much else, the marriage settlement of Tristram's parents, as well as Yorick's sermon. What follows is an invaluable account of the culture of household manuscript-making, as well as Sterne's own dealings with manuscripts, both in his family life and in his duties as a clergyman. Harvey's aim is 'to restore the domestic manuscript culture in which Sterne practised' as well as to 'root Sterne's novel in the mundane activities of the ordinary lives of middling-sort men', as much as 'the works of Cervantes, Swift or Locke' (p. 296).

Tristram Shandy [1759–67] is also examined in Melanie D. Holm's article, 'Laughter, Skepticism, and the Pleasure of Being Misunderstood in Laurence Sterne's *The Life and Opinions of Tristram Shandy, Gentleman*' (*ECent* 55:iv[2014] 355–75). This makes a welcome analysis of the fascinating claim from the dedication to the novel: that *Tristram Shandy* was written 'to fence against the infirmities of ill health', since 'every time a man smiles,—but much more so, when he laughs, it adds something to this Fragment of Life', which suggests that the function of comedy is to defer death. Holm places this in the context of a range of theories and comments on laughter in the eighteenth century.

Fowler's work on Richardson and Diderot can be read alongside another monograph on the inspiration the *philosophe* took from the English novel, this time in relation to Sterne. Margaux Whiskin's *Narrative Structure and Philosophical Debates in Tristram Shandy and Jacques le fataliste* (written 1765–80), published by the MHRA, analyses Diderot's engagement with Sterne, interpreting both texts as examples of Bakhtinian dialogism. These days, there is a danger of going into autopilot when dealing with Bakhtin and texts within the learned wit tradition, and many of the usual suspects—open-endedness, the collision of high and low, the grotesque body—are indeed in place here. But Whiskin also offers many subtle readings of individual moments in both Sterne and Diderot, as well as some sensitive applications of Bakhtin, not least an ingenious closing comparison with the final 'COCK AND A BULL' (p. 153) passage of *Tristram Shandy* with Bakhtin's analysis of the *coq-à-l'âne* theme in Rabelais.

Sterne is also read through the lens of Bakhtin this year in Jakub Lipski's study, *In Quest of the Self: Masquerade and Travel in the Eighteenth-Century Novel*. Lipski reads *A Sentimental Journey* alongside novels by Fielding and Smollett, arguing that each of these authors brought together travel and the masquerade as convenient metaphors for 'the turmoil over the category of self' (p. 199) at mid-century.

The Shandean continued to bring together a wealth of wide-ranging and international contributions on all aspects of Sterne's work and reception this year. Particularly noteworthy is Marcus Walsh's contribution to the annual, 'Complete Systems and *Tristram Shandy*' (*Shandean* 25[2014] 9–24), which offers a useful genealogy of precursors to Walter Shandy's *Tristopaedia* in a range of early modern discourses.

Paul Goring has continued his ongoing analysis of the minutiae of the Sterne archive in his note, 'Laurence Sterne and Topham Beauclerk: Evidence of an Acquaintanceship' (*N&Q* 61[2014] 436–41). The article assembles new evidence that the antiquary and friend of Samuel Johnson, Beauclerk, was indeed part of Sterne's visiting circle—as his editors have sometimes speculated—at the very end of his life, and that this in turn 'throws light on the type of society that Sterne was seeking out in what turned out to be his final few weeks' (p. 436).

Finally, Claude Rawson's *Swift's Angers*, reviewed above, contains three chapters on Swift's fiction, on mock-editions, the I-narrator, and *Gulliver's Travels*.

3. Poetry

This year saw fewer monographs published on eighteenth-century poetry than has typically been the case recently; this is perhaps a consequence of it being, in Britain at least, the first year of the new REF cycle; interestingly, the majority of the monographs received this year have come from American presses, with Bucknell being particularly active in our field. Whilst the number of monographs might be lower this year, neither the range nor the rigour of the work published in 2014 has suffered, with a pleasing wealth of exciting and innovative works appearing. By most measures 2014 has done well.

Before we turn to 2014, though, a review of a work that did not come to hand in time for the review of works from 2013: Michael Griffin's *Enlightenment in Ruins: the Geographies of Oliver Goldsmith*. A study that examines Goldsmith's oeuvre, it early admits that its subject 'can be difficult to locate' (p. 2), with critics unsure, at times, what to do with Goldsmith. For

Griffin, though, 'there is a consistent set of ideas operating [in his works] which can be isolated and addressed as a manifestation of his Irishness' (p. 3), the importance of which, Griffin suggests, has 'hitherto been ignored as largely incidental to his career' (p. 3). This study sets itself the task of correcting this oversight in Goldsmith scholarship: it 'recuperates the critical potential of his pastoral poetry, and re-evaluates his geographies—imaginative, poetic, scientific, and pseudo-scientific—by studying their oblique relation to the emerging discourses in which he wrote' (p. 3). Griffin sees a reciprocal relationship between Goldsmith's poetry and these discourses, noting that 'Close historical study of eighteenth-century writing nuances post-colonial theory, inflecting it with historical contingency and an awareness of the conflicted experiences of hard-pressed authors operating amidst an emerging, incipiently globalizing modernity' (p. 9). Griffin draws helpful links between Goldsmith and Swift, and Goldsmith and Burke, though a side-effect of this approach is the odd slip into more old-fashioned, biographically inflected criticism. The study focuses on *The Traveller* and *The Deserted Village*, with Goldsmith's prose works being used to 'clarify the politics of the poems, both by contrast *and* continuity' (p. 27). Combining the benefits of a targeted focus with those of a wider-ranging discussion, Griffin's study offers much to any scholar interested in Goldsmith's poetry or its contexts.

Turning now to what was published in 2014, particularly well represented has been Christopher Smart, the subject of an enjoyable monograph by Rosalind Powell and a substantial collection of essays edited by Min Wild and Noel Chevalier. Powell (who also contributes an essay to the edited collection on Smart) offers a reading, in *Christopher Smart's English Lyrics: Translation in the Eighteenth Century*, that sets out to 'recover' the poet's reputation from the ignominy of being largely remembered now for 'a paean to his cat Jeoffry'. Powell asserts that Smart 'would have been horrified' to have been remembered with such a 'monument' (p. 1). Powell's study seeks instead to integrate the many divergent approaches taken to Smart in order to offer a more holistic view of Smart and his work, so as to 'achieve an inclusive reassessment of the poet's writing' (p. 2). Of central interest to Powell, though, is Smart's use of 'translation' (a term used broadly by Powell) throughout his writings. Whilst this is often productive, it does sometimes lead the author astray. Powell asserts, for instance, that 'one need not call upon modern theory in order to reach the conclusion that a poet is always a translator, and it is perfectly reasonable to assume that Smart's own reading may have led him to the idea that even original composition is a form of imitation' (p. 12). Apart from applying undue pressure on readers to accept what they are being told, Powell here offers little evidence in support of her assertions. That said, the book is ambitious and detailed, covering a wealth of Smart's writing, from *Jubilate Agno* to his translations of Horace, and it will undoubtedly make a substantial contribution to the current effort to reassess and re-evaluate Smart's poetics.

In this effort Powell's work is ably supported by the essays included in *Reading Christopher Smart in the Twenty-First Century: 'By Succession of Delight'*, which is efficiently edited and introduced by Wild and Chevalier: their blunt statement of intent in the opening piece sets the tone nicely for the rest of the collection. Arguing that it is about time scholars moved on from fetishizing Smart's 'mad' phases (the echoes of Powell's monograph are perhaps not coincidental—both books emerged from the same conference on Smart), the editors present the collection as being 'both a compendium of current scholarship and a framework for ways of reading Smart in the twenty-first century' (p. 5). It should be noted that while most of this collection is relevant to readers of this section, the segment on Smart's drama is likely to be of less interest.

All the essays in this collection focus on the experiences, identities, and nature of Smart's readers, then and now. The first essay, 'Marginalia in Smart's Horace: The Reader as Critic' by Karina Williamson (pp. 13–25), considers Smart's failure 'to make any impression on the public' (p. 14) in the eighteenth century with his translations of Horace—a concern shared by Powell in her monograph. Williamson's approach enables consideration of wider contexts in relation to Smart, but also extending from him, including queries about the nature of the text and the role of the reader; the result is an intriguing essay.

Min Wild's own essay, 'Christopher Smart, Samuel Taylor Coleridge, and the Tradition of Learned Wit' (pp. 27–44), moves us forward towards the Romantic period, though the parallel reading of Smart and Coleridge justifies including her essay in this section. Wild's argument centres on how Smart and Coleridge 'both found that the vivid, incongruous images offered by the tradition of learned wit could work as an effective mode of attack against . . . Enlightenment philosophers' (p. 39).

Powell reappears as the writer of the third essay in this collection, 'Making an Impression: Christopher Smart's Idea of Writing Well' (pp. 45–61), which proposes 'to conduct an in-depth exploration of what Smart's use of the critical keyword "impression" might entail and to use this tantalizing term to bring us closer to a sense of his poetic theory' (p. 47). Powell's focus here is on *Jubilate Agno* and the translations of Horace, which Powell uses to conduct a wide-ranging and illuminating discussion of the various connotations, for Smart, of being 'impressed'. This topic is also of interest to Fraser Easton in his essay, 'Christopher Smart's Elocution' (pp. 63–84), though the potential connections are flagged in neither Easton's nor Powell's essays, which seems a pity. Easton also looks at 'the themes of reading aloud, hearing, pronunciation, music and sound', offering fruitful connections between 'the secular study of speech' in Smart's poetry (p. 64), and the more religiously minded printed words.

Clement Hawes gives a moving and humane introduction to his essay 'Poised Poesis: Ecstasy in *Jubilate Agno*' (pp. 87–104), where he writes: 'Though Smart is beyond our compassion now, that fellow feeling is another indication of our relative intimacy with him, our camaraderie' (p. 87). For Hawes, acknowledging this fellow-feeling is crucial to bringing Smart 'closer to us' in order to see his 'uncommon poetic originality' (p. 88). While interesting and intelligent, there is perhaps less analysis of Smart's poetry here than might be expected.

For William E. Levine, in 'Keeping, Deflating, and Transcending "the Fool's Conceit": Smart's Hybridization of Satiric and Devotional Modes in his Translations of the Psalms' (pp. 105–22), Smart's 'uncommon poetic originality' is demonstrated through disparities: 'disparities between various registers of poetic diction, breaches of seeming propriety in his low, excessive, irregular or otherwise dissonant style', which enables Smart's work to 'carve its niche' (p. 106). The title might be unwieldy, but the essay is illuminating.

Perhaps the least strong essay in this edited collection is Lori A. Branch's 'The Smallness of Hope, or Reason and the Child: The Case for a Postsecular Christopher Smart' (pp. 143–61), which couples a jargon-heavy style with a self-referentiality which tends to grate. That said, the argument made by Branch that Smart's religiosity operated in a complex social environment is sound and helpful.

The collection is rounded off by a short Afterword from Tom Keymer (pp. 227–32), which looks at the responses of readers to Smart from the 1930s onwards, when *Jubilate Agno* was first returned to scholarship. The intellectual and creative reactions of W.H. Auden, Benjamin Britten, and others are productively examined, as are the changing tastes demonstrated by readers' attitudes to Smart over the past several decades. It is a fitting conclusion to a collection which, as a whole, gestures towards ways for the twenty-first century to (re)assess and (re)value Smart.

Powell flies the banner for Smart again in an article entitled 'Christopher Smart's *Systema Naturae*: Anti-Newtonianism and the Categorical Impulse in *Jubilate Agno*' (*ECS* 37[2014] 361–76), which proposes to explore the increasingly acknowledged relationship between art and science through *Jubilate Agno*, which offers 'a unique contribution to the debate' because of its 'biblical, botanical, geological, animal and personal references' (p. 361).

As in previous years an enjoyable range of writers is considered in the scholarship published in 2014, with lesser-known figures appearing alongside more canonical writers, often with exciting effects. Phillis Wheatley and Anna Laetitia Barbauld both enjoyed coverage in 2014, the former as the subject of a monograph by Paula Loscocco, and the latter as the subject of a substantial collection of essays edited by William McCarthy and Olivia Murphy.

Loscocco's *Phillis Wheatley's Miltonic Poetics* is a Pivot title, so is a deal shorter than more traditional monographs. At 164 pages, though, this is a more substantial Pivot publication than usual, and the study benefits from having the extra elbow room. That said, the Pivot style of presentation still requires work, with strange branding on the pages of the text distracting from the reading experience, and this book features an overwhelming number of abbreviations to add to the reader's woes. The study's explicitly stated aim, what Loscocco terms its 'labor and delight', is 'to encourage modern readers to understand the obscured achievement that is Wheatley's Miltonic poetics' (p. 3). While the 'obscured' is to some extent arguable, this study is welcome for its persistent attentiveness to Wheatley's literary touchstones, and for its sustained attention to the 1773 *Poems*—Loscocco argues persuasively for the importance of looking at the whole volume, stating that 'Understanding Wheatley's *Poems* as a self-contained whole with a single metapoetic narrative makes it possible' to see aspects of the volume that have evaded other studies of Wheatley's poetry (p. 8). There are shortcomings. As well as some unfortunate stylistic infelicities, such as colloquialisms, repetitions, and inelegant sentences (it has to be wondered whether the speedy turnaround of Pivot titles might be to blame), some of the connections made by Loscocco between Wheatley and Milton seem rather tenuous. Abundant evidence is mentioned, but is not presented in the text. Instead, the evidence resides in the references, meaning that readers do not get the opportunity to assess it (and therefore the quality of the argument) properly for themselves. The intended audience for this study is also unclear, given that the language is, on the whole, too informal to be wholly enjoyable to an academic audience, whilst the discussion is likely too detailed for a general readership.

There are few such issues with *Anna Letitia Barbauld: New Perspectives*, which, like Wild and Chevalier's *Christopher Smart in the Twenty-First Century*, was published by Bucknell University Press as part of its Transits series—one to watch, for scholars of the period. And as with the collection of essays on Smart, so this collection on Barbauld seeks to survey the state of scholarship as it currently stands, before suggesting new ways of approaching her poetic oeuvre. This collection is important not least because, as McCarthy notes in his introduction, 'Anna Letitia Barbauld Today' (pp. 1–21), it is 'the first collection of essays by multiple hands devoted exclusively to Barbauld's work' (p. 11); essays are presented 'roughly' in order of 'Barbauld's career chronology' (p. 11), so later essays may have less appeal to readers of this section. That said, McCarthy's urging of researchers to do more to recover the entirety of Barbauld's oeuvre will benefit wider scholarship on eighteenth-century poetry. As McCarthy notes, 'If Barbauld's writing is to remain available to future readers, if new perspectives on it are to remain possible, we must lavish on her the attention our predecessors lavished on the Alexander Popes and the Samuel Coleridges' (p. 21).

McCarthy and Murphy's contributors rally to this battle cry with admirable zeal. Isobel Grundy is given the task of following McCarthy's strident introduction, and does so with panache in ' "Slip-Shod Measure" and "Language of Gods": Barbauld's Stylistic Range' (pp. 22–36). Grundy ranges across Barbauld's poetry and also examines some of the prose, and offers helpful and informative comparisons between the ways in which Barbauld used poetic voices at different points in her career. Grundy hears echoed in Barbauld's poetry the accents of 'other soloists in the great harmony, of Dryden, Addison, Pope, Johnson' and others (p. 34). Barbauld, Grundy suggests, 'responds to other voices and invites poetic response in turn' (p. 34).

Michelle Levy's essay, 'Barbauld's Poetic Career in Script and Print' (pp. 37–58), assesses the state of Barbauld's current critical reception, and offers a comparison with her evaluation by contemporary readers. Levy notes that Barbauld's early fame was built 'upon the print publication of a slim volume of fewer than three dozen poems' (p. 37), but that her continued celebrity depended upon the poet's shrewd use of print, manuscript circulation, and magazines. Levy's argument is revealing of the ways in which Barbauld navigated, and made use of, the literary marketplace.

Sonia Hofkosh centres her discussion, in 'Materiality, Affect, Event: Barbauld's Poetics of the Everyday' (pp. 83–105), on one poem, the beguiling 'Washing-Day', and considers it as representative of a mundane, repeated event. Hofkosh initially asks, 'What can you say about what happened last time you did the wash?' (p. 83), as if anticipating readerly objections to a consideration of this poem, but goes on to argue persuasively that the poem occupies an intriguing middle ground, simultaneously a disruptive event, but one rooted in 'the contingencies of living in a mundane material world' (p. 83). The nuanced discussion is supplemented by some lovely illustrations. Other essays in this volume will likely appeal to any lover of Barbauld's work, but the poetry specialist is best served by the four pieces outlined here.

Another substantial collection of essays likely to appeal to readers of this section is *Eighteenth-Century Poetry and the Rise of the Novel Reconsidered*, edited by Kate Parker and Courtney Weiss Smith and another member of Bucknell's Transits series. Weiss Smith is blunt in her introduction (p. xiii–xxiv) when she asserts that 'We too often let generic divisions organize our teaching and guide our research' (p. xiii). The wayward reader is taken further to task: 'this volume proceeds from a concern that our working assumptions in teaching and research . . . can somewhat obfuscate the . . . habits of eighteenth-century readers' (p. xiii). Weiss Smith urges us instead to consider that poetry and novels 'jostled up alongside' each other physically and in the minds of readers (p. xiii). Whilst the directness is largely enjoyable, Weiss Smith seems at times to be fighting a straw man.

Sophie Gee's essay, 'Heroic Couplets and Eighteenth-Century Heroism: Pope's Complicated Characters' (pp. 3–25), argues that 'Pope steals from a poet to write like a novelist' (p. 3). This is an interesting idea, but the essay is marred by a jarringly informal style and the sense that much of this has been said before. The effect is that what is presented here feels more like an incremental step, rather than the sort of radical rereading promised by the introduction.

Bringing together Eliza Haywood's *The History of Miss Betsy Thoughtless* and Alexander Pope's *The Rape of the Lock*, ' "The Battle Without Killing": Eliza Haywood and the Politics of Attempted Rape' by Kate Parker (pp. 27–48) argues that Haywood's engagement with mock-heroic is deliberate and strategic. Whilst this is a sensible argument to make, it is not necessarily new—Ros Ballaster, who is cited here, has made a similar case. Like Gee's essay, then, this feels incremental rather than particularly new. In addition, the essay does not really examine the intersection of genres—the 'jostling up' of forms—promised by the introduction.

Christina Lupton and Aran Ruth deliver more convincingly on that promise in their essay, 'The Novel's Poem Envy: Mid-Century Fiction and the "Thing Poem" ' (pp. 49–63), which opens with a discussion of a play in order to consider the material relations between novels and poems, and between these and literary circulation. Novels, Lupton and Ruth argue, are represented as inferior because they circulate less freely, less excitingly, and in more circumscribed ways than poems, and so sit outside the chatty and at times ephemeral sociability associated with the exchange of manuscript verse. Novels, they write, 'are more inhibited than [other] kinds of writing when it comes to the energy of their circulation and their ability to affect people as objects' (p. 50). Shelley King's essay, which immediately follows (pp. 65–83), examines the relation between novels and poetry in the context of one writer—Amelia Opie. As it lies outside the period limits of this section, it is only briefly mentioned here.

Sitting more legitimately within the bounds of this section is Wolfram Schmidgen's essay, 'Undividing the Subject of Literary History: from James Thomson's Poetry to Daniel Defoe's Novels' (pp. 87–104). Its style, however, is likely to grate: 'While the beginnings of other genres were irretrievably lost in the mist of ancient time' (p. 87) is one example of the at times hackneyed diction deployed here. More might also have been done to delineate the argument more clearly, though the discussion of how older accounts of the period have tended to stress the importance of differentiation is productive.

Heather Keenleyside, in 'The Rise of the Novel and the Fall of Personification' (pp. 105–33), is stronger, though as with the essays of Gee and Parker it is acknowledged here that the topic under consideration 'is a familiar story' (p. 107). It is unfortunate that so many essays in this collection return to well-trodden ground. That said, there are some nice observations here on Pope's *Eloisa to Abelard* and discussion of Lord Kames and Robert Blair.

David Fairer's contribution, '"Light Electric Touches": Sterne, Poetry, and Empirical Erotics' (pp. 135–60), is the highlight of this collection. Fairer makes some neat links between Sterne's quick-sketch approach in *Tristram Shandy* and Pope's techniques in *Epistle to a Lady*, and argues that Sterne was consciously working within 'an earlier poetic tradition which, unlike the early novel, had responded imaginatively to the erotic implications of empiricism' (p. 138). This is then connected to larger ideas from Newton, Locke, and others at work in the period, an argument which is very well handled. Whilst it does not necessarily offer a new way of reading poetry through novels or the other way round, it instead does a nice job of showing how larger ideas rippled out across modes, disciplines, and genres. It is also beautifully written.

Joshua Swidzinski's essay, '"Great Labour Both of Mind and Tongue": Articulacy and Interiority in Young's *Night Thoughts* and Richardson's *Clarissa*' (pp. 161–86), follows Fairer's lead by also being well written and engaging. Swidzinski proposes asking 'how we might interpret relationships between genres while simultaneously foregrounding the diverse effects produced by generic particularities' (p. 163); he addresses this question by looking back to seventeenth-century debates about interiority and liberty of conscience.

In 'The Art of Attention: Navigating Distraction and Rhythms of Focus in Eighteenth-Century Poetry' (pp. 187–206), Natalie Phillips explores the ways in which poetry sought to claim readers' attention, looking first at Pope's *Epistle to Arbuthnot*, then Gray, Akenside, and forward to the Romantic poets. Phillips's claim that her discussion 'enhances the story we would otherwise tell about attention in the eighteenth-century [*sic*] based on the novel alone' is somewhat undercut by the absence of critics like Margaret Koehler (whose excellent book, *Poetry of Attention in the Eighteenth Century*, was reviewed in this section last year).

The collection of essays is rounded off by a Coda by Margaret Doody (pp. 207–29), which takes an amusing and, at times, a wryly critical view of some of the arguments made in the preceding essays. Doody traces many points of similarity between poetry and fiction in this period, suggesting the fertility inherent in the 'jostling' together of genres in this period.

The blending, and jostling, of genres is also a central concern of Kate Horgan's book, *The Politics of Songs in Eighteenth-Century Britain, 1723–1795*. The opening is somewhat muddled, but the central premise, that the importance of songs to eighteenth-century culture has been overlooked—is ably demonstrated as the book progresses. Horgan traces the meaning of songs from early in the century to the 1790s, which helps to reveal the interconnections, the continuities, between songs and the occasions on which they were sung. Horgan sees 'song' as a genre of considerable 'capaciousness' (p. 11), stating that 'song-forms of this period were malleable and intersected with each other' (p. 11). Horgan's argument is at its strongest when she explores the ways in which songs often overlapped, or were recruited for various, and varying, causes. Whilst there are clear strengths to the argument being made, the presentation of the book itself is not all that might be desired. Apart from several infelicities, in the shape of repetitions of words, which suggest better editing was called for, the writing is often inelegant, with run-on sentences a particular fault. These faults do, at times, undermine the arguments being made.

Also concerned with the intersection of genres is Anne McKee Stapleton's excellent monograph, *Pointed Encounters: Dance in Post-Culloden Scottish Literature*, which is interested in how dance and song became 'a popular shared language' (p. 11) in the aftermath of the 1745 rebellion and the ensuing attempts to 'obliterate Highland culture' (p. 11). McKee Stapleton's focus is on the 'literary significance of representations of dance in . . . poetry, song, dance manuals, and fiction' (p. 11), and the book seeks, intriguingly and interestingly, to 'lessen the theoretical divide between the art of dance and the profession of literature by proposing a cultural history that envelops both' (p. 11). The discussion that ensues is both moving and astute. Of Boswell's description of watching crofters on Skye performing the dance 'America', McKee Stapleton writes that 'the dancers spinning as one unit simulate a community actively resisting, at least temporarily, the political and economic hardships which underlie emigration' (p. 16).

In terms of both topic and time-frame readers of this section are likely to be most interested in chapter 1, which considers representations and uses of the 'Strathspey' dance in poetry and song. McKee Stapleton here argues that 'dance flourished and became allied with imaginative Scottish poetry and song to transgress cultural constraints exerted by England in the eighteenth century', a line pursued through the examination of a range of poetry, song, and dance from this period. The author persuasively maps the interconnections, and inter-reliance, of these forms, and suggests that they all fed into each other in ways that have not been, to date, adequately accounted for. McKee Stapleton attributes this gap in knowledge to the poor scholarly regard in which dance is held, something which this study will surely have done much to challenge. Whilst chapter 1 is most closely connected to poetry of the earlier part of the eighteenth century, reading the whole book is recommended, as it is lucid and engagingly well written, and genuinely illuminates and complicates notions of Scottishness thanks to its truly interdisciplinary approach.

As with previous years, Scottish poetry and related matter were topics considered in a number of studies published in 2014. As well as McKee Stapleton's examination of dance, song, and poetry, this year saw the publication of Richard Holmes's scholarly edition *James Arbuckle: Selected Works*. A contemporary of Allan Ramsay, Arbuckle's best-known poem is probably *Glotta* [1721]—an article by Holmes on this poem published in 2012 was reviewed in this section last year—and it is pleasing to see his wider oeuvre receiving sustained attention here. Holmes includes a range of poetry as well as some of Arbuckle's prose works (Part II), literary essays (Part IV), and translations (Part V) in this edition. Readers, however, might be sceptical about the extent to which this edition enables a fuller recovery of Arbuckle's work. Whilst Arbuckle may not have been the most luminous poetic star of his age, it might be expected that his modern-day editor would have more to say on his account than 'His achievement may be minor', but 'his work may interest many readers as much for the light it sheds on his major contemporaries as for itself' (p. xxxiii)—Holmes's use of the modal verb effectively douses the reader's interest. The stated aims of the edition are similarly low-key: it seeks only 'to provide sufficient contextual information to enable [Arbuckle's] merits to be appreciated' (p. xii). Holmes's modesty, perhaps designed to manage reader expectations, serves rather to dampen the reader's ardour for the subject, not least because Holmes's attention in his introduction is less on his subject than on his subject's contemporaries and associates. Thus we learn, for instance, of the origins of Arbuckle's friends before we learn anything of Arbuckle's own. As a result, a reader new to Arbuckle and eager to learn about this interesting poet is likely to be disappointed, which is a pity. Readers who have greater familiarity with Arbuckle's work might query some of the editorial choices, such as the decision to use chapters (which makes the edition resemble a monograph); the absence of clear breaks between the editorial headnotes and the body of the texts; the presentation of work titles in the same style of text as the preceding editorial sentence; and the lack of line numbers for the poetry. It is undoubtedly beneficial to scholarship that this edition exists, but opportunities to argue more powerfully for Arbuckle's recovery are frustratingly squandered.

'The Long Lost James Beattie: the Rediscovery of "The Grotesquiad"', by Rhona Brown (*RES* 65[2014] 456–73), provides the transcription and first scholarly assessment of a poem which found its way mysteriously into Sir Walter Scott's collection at Abbotsford. It 'uncovers a previously unknown side of Beattie's literary persona while revealing previously obscured lines of influence and generic innovation in the literary landscape of mid-eighteenth-century Scotland and Britain' (p. 456). Brown locates the poem in Beattie's wider oeuvre as well as helpfully contextualizing it.

Dafydd Moore's essay, '"Caledonian Plagiary": The Role and Meaning of Ireland in the Poems of *Ossian*' (in Dew and Price, eds., *Historical Writing in Britain, 1688–1830: Vision of History*, pp. 92–108), explores how the *Ossian* poems conceptualize the relationship between Scottish and Irish culture. Whilst the essay asserts that it takes no issue with the basic premise of much of Ossian criticism, it aims to come at the poems 'from a different angle' (p. 94).

The essay is written in fine style, full of energy as well as information, and is enjoyable to read even if the argument it makes is open to challenge.

One essay in the edited collection *Gender and Space in British Literature, 1660–1820*, edited by Mona Narain and Karen Gevirtz, is likely to appeal to readers of this section. Jeong-Oh Kim's piece, 'Anne Finch's Strategic Retreat into the Country House' (pp. 147–63) argues that Finch's landscape poetry is a means of 'compensating' for the 'loss of power and influence' in the wake of the displacement of 'the Stuart court' (p. 147). Some rather old-fashioned discussion of public and private as entirely 'separate spheres' undermines the argument somewhat, as does the amount of jargon. Some tortuous sentences, too, limit the reader's enjoyment.

The remaining monographs and standalone publications which appeared in 2014 are on a range of subjects. Also discussed above, Earla Wilputte's *Passion and Language in Eighteenth-Century Literature: The Aesthetic Sublime in the Work of Eliza Haywood, Aaron Hill, and Martha Fowke* focuses on a very tight time-frame of just four years, between 1720 and 1724. Whilst it is not exclusively about poetry it uses all three writers' works, including their poetry, as a means to explore how these authors 'attempt to develop a language for the passions that clearly conveys the deepest felt emotions' (p. 2). Wilputte outlines how the relationships between the three 'are collaborative, competitive, and often eroticized' (p. 3). Whilst there are clear theoretical and epistemological grounds for looking at passion and the emotions, the discussion seems equally fascinated by the passions felt and shown *between* coterie members: 'Passion was definitely in the air in the early 1720s circle— passion in our modern sense of the word: volatile, sexually charged emotions' (p. 7). It is unfortunate that Wilputte does not take greater pains to make clear the intellectual grounds for looking at the personal lives of her subjects, as such discussions sometimes come across in this study as salacious rather than scholarly. For instance, Wilputte gives her reasons thus: 'Eliza Haywood and Martha Fowke were both rumoured to have had personal attachments to the married Hill, and both were passionate women and writers' (p. 9), but rumour and generalization fall short of sufficient intellectual reason for this aspect of the study's methodology, especially when, as Wilputte admits, there is little verifiable biographical information with which to confirm or deny these rumours. Readers of this section are most likely to find chapters 3 and 4 of interest, though the latter, which centres on poetic responses to John Dyer's portrait of Fowkes, might disappoint with its tendency to describe, rather than analyse, the poetry under consideration.

Cambridge University Press has again, in 2014, published a number of reissues of early twentieth-century scholarly editions, including W. Murison's edition of *The Traveller* and *The Deserted Village*. Whilst this text is nearly 110 years old, the style is lucid and the biography, plot summary, and discussion of key contexts are all helpful and pithy. There is also a useful chronology of Goldsmith's life placed alongside important contemporary events which will still be of benefit to students. The poem texts themselves are clear and uncluttered, with notes reserved for the back of the book. It certainly makes for clean copy, though it might prove hard work for a reader who regularly needs to consult the notes. And it is likely that readers will want to consult those notes, as they are consistently sensitive to students' likely uncertainty about culture, context, and tone. One example is the note explaining to the reader that, in using 'Dear Sir' to refer to his brother, Goldsmith was just deploying 'the usage of the time' (p. 41), rather than being particularly formal. There are useful cross-references within the text and also to other works by Goldsmith that will help the more ambitious student roam more widely. Even now, then, it would be a high-quality teaching text (and was indeed developed from material 'tested in class-teaching' by the editor with 'several classes of boys' ('Note')), though at £17.99 for 84 pages it might not be students' first choice.

More expensive still is the Cambridge reissue of D.C. Tovey's edition of *Gray's English Poems: Original and Translated from the Norse and Welsh*, which is priced at £20.99, though purchasers do get 294 pages for their money. The edition reproduces thirty-two of Gray's poems, including several of his most famous, such as 'Elegy Written in a Country Churchyard'. The modern student might find this a less genial guide to the poetry—the old-fashioned style and syntax are perhaps a little off-putting. The editor also seems to have had an anti-Johnson axe to grind. That said, the copy-texts are again clean and unfussy, and the reader gets over 200 pages of notes in support of the seventy-nine pages of poetry. These notes are a little over-long at times, and Tovey is much less sympathetic than Murison to any potential ignorance in the edition's readers, offering clipped, highly detailed notes that assume a great deal of learning. It is less clear, therefore, who the modern audience of this text might be.

Cambridge has also reissued the text of Charles Whibley's lecture as *Jonathan Swift: the Leslie Stephen Lecture*, originally delivered in 1917. Unlike the editions of Goldsmith and Gray, there are here no supporting materials published alongside the main text, aside from a very short preface. The book costs £7.99 for just forty-five pages, and there is not even an index. As with Tovey, the imagined audience is unclear. That said, Whibley is an entertaining commentator on Swift, and it is easy to imagine how his words, which have sparkle even when presented dead on a page, would have been enjoyed in the original lecture. A further contribution to Swift studies published by CUP (reviewed in Section 1 above), is Claude Rawson's *Swift's Angers*. Part III deals with Swift's poetry, with chapters on: 'Rage and Raillery and Swift: The Case of Cadenus and Vanessa; 'Vanessa as a Reader of *Gulliver's Travels*'; 'Swift's Poetry: An Overview'; ' "I the lofty stile decline": Vicissitudes of the "Heroick Strain" in Swift's Poems'; and 'Savage Indignation Revisited: Swift, Yeats, and the "Cry" of Liberty'.

A number of journal articles dedicated to eighteenth-century poetry were also published in 2014 on a wide variety of subjects. Erin Parker's essay, ' "Doubt Not an Affectionate Host": Cowper's Hares and the Hospitality of Eighteenth-Century Pet Keeping' (*ECLife* 38[2014] 75–104), takes an unusual, but most productive, approach to Cowper's poetry, using it as a means to explore eighteenth-century attitudes towards animals, and to build links between this and cultural notions associated with guests and guest-right. *The Task* features prominently in the intriguing discussion.

Joshua Crandall, in ' "The Great Measur'd by the Less": The Ethnological Turn in Eighteenth-Century Pastoral' (*ELH* 81[2014] 955–82), looks at the use of comparison in the pastoral form as a way of better understanding the underlying relationship between pastoral and georgic modes. He suggests that, 'Although georgic and pastoral are usually understood by poets and critics alike to be dependent on one another for their meaning', the eighteenth century saw an asymmetrical relationship develop between them (p. 957). Crandall looks at, amongst others, Pope, Gay, and Edward Rushton.

In an essay on a related topic, Sandro Jung argues, in 'William Shenstone's Poetry, The Leasowes and the Intermediality of Reading and Architectural Design' (*ECS* 37[2014] 53–77), that there is a crucial, but often overlooked, relationship between the various works produced by William Shenstone about his estate, The Leasowes, in Halesowen. Jung focuses particularly on a 'largely neglected illustrated manuscript volume' (p. 57) produced by Shenstone in the 1750s, which enables, for Jung, 'a way to facilitate the transition from various states of emotion to moments of reflection, from action to meditation' (p. 57). The article is generously illustrated with images taken from the album.

A pair of essays looking at poetry about Queen Anne appeared in *Eighteenth-Century Studies*. The first, Joseph Hone's 'Politicising Praise: Panegyric and the Accession of Queen Anne' (*ECS* 37[2014] 147–57), argues that the 'outpouring of encomium' that greeted the accession of Anne Stuart 'was not as conventional or straightforward as it may at first seem', and that instead it reveals 'the need for a broader scholarly assessment of the political and cultural significance of the succession' (p. 147). Both Tory and Whig poetry are considered in a wide-ranging article.

Later in the same issue is Juan Christian Pellicer's essay, 'Celebrating Queen Anne and the Union of 1707 in Great Britain's First Georgic' (*ECS* 37[2014] 217–27), which is less successful than Hone's, in part because of the rather didactic tone. John Philip's *Cyder* [1708] is the subject, but the discussion focuses on describing the poem and assessing its politics, rather than analysing it as a work of literature.

Finally comes '*The Landlord's Tale* (1708): An Introduction and Contextualization' by Barry Sales (*ECS* 47[2014] 313–20), which examines potential candidates for authorship of this poem. Ruling out Dryden, William Walker, William Congreve, and others, Sales settles on George Farquhar as the most likely to have written the poem because 'his life and writings . . . seem remarkably compatible with what the author of *The Landlord's Tale* reveals of himself (p. 318). A translation of an episode from canto XXVIII of *Orlando Furioso*, a sixteenth-century Italian narrative poem by Ludovico Ariosto, the poem was originally attributed to Dryden in the period. Sales's article is therefore helpful in setting the scholarly record straight.

4. Drama

This year saw the landmark publication of the *Oxford Handbook of the Georgian Theatre*, an event that placed the field of eighteenth-century theatre research alongside such other, well-developed specialisms as 'Early Modern

Theatre', 'American Drama', or 'Medieval Literature in English'. A review of the *Handbook* will conclude this chapter. The number (and quality) of other publications also published in 2014, however, already offer convincing evidence for the vitality of work in this domain, and it is with these articles and books, loosely organized around three poles of gender, politics, and international circulation, that this overview will begin.

First, gender. Vivian L. Davis analyses Colley Cibber's parodic *Rival Queans* [1690s?] (along with his *Apology* [1740] and acting technique) as typical of the eighteenth-century stage, even in its performance of tragedy, for being more interested in the 'problem of gender broadly conceived' (*ECF* 26[2014] 561) than in masculine–feminine binaries. Such a nuanced approach to the period is also evident in Laura Engel and Elaine McGirr's essay collection, *Stage Mothers: Women, Work, and the Theater, 1660–1830*, which achieves its stated aim of using the figure of the 'stage mother' (either 'performed or performing') to expand 'the discussion of eighteenth-century women's social and dramatic roles by demonstrating the complicated, contradictory and celebratory faces of maternity onstage and on the page' (introduction, p. 2). Of the contributions to this work that concern the stage prior to 1780, two pieces stand out. Laura R. Rosenthal's 'Rebels for Love' (pp. 105–21) offers a historically informed, revisionist reading of the Earl of Orrery's *Mustapha*, which successfully recaptures the work's contemporary 'emotional force' (p. 106). Elaine M. McGirr's ' "Inimitable Sensibility" ' (pp. 63–78) focuses on the career of Susannah Cibber and, wearing its erudition lightly, examines the interplay of fiction and reality in this actress's career to place her performance of Constance (in Colley Cibber's *King John* [1745]) at its apex. Aside from Rosenthal and McGirr's writing, all the other pre-1780 contributions here contain valuable information for the scholar on eighteenth-century motherhood and the theatre, albeit occasionally with too heavy an attachment to historical data or recent cultural theory. The chapters in question are: Helen E.M. Brooks, ' "The Divided Heart of the Actress": Late Eighteenth-Century Actresses and the "Cult of Maternity" ' (pp. 19–42); J.D. Phillipson, 'The Inconvenience of the Female Condition: Anne Oldfield's Pregnancies" (pp. 43–62); Marilyn Francis, 'Rowe's *The Ambitious Stepmother*: Motherhood and the Politics of the Blended Family' (pp. 121–56); and Kathryn Lowerre, 'Staged Virtue: Anastasia Robinson as Ideal Mother in Two Operas of the 1720s' (pp. 137–58).

Like the best chapters of *Stage Mothers*, Fiona Ritchie's *Women and Shakespeare in the Eighteenth Century* also provides a rich yet very readable treatment of its subject, in this case the role played by female critics, playgoers, and actresses in the construction of Shakespeare's reputation from 1660 to the early nineteenth century. In an opening chapter on Catherine (Kitty) Clive and Hannah Pritchard, Ritchie shows, for example, how these actresses, with careful use of their benefit performances, spearheaded new interest in such plays as *The Merchant of Venice* (revived 1741) and *As You Like It* (revived 1740) as part of a 'breeches revival' (p. 95) prior to Garrick's debut. A later section, on the Shakespeare Ladies Club, overcomes a lack of archival evidence to gauge the group's influence through an innovative study of changes to theatrical repertory. While presenting these, and many other, fascinating case studies, Ritchie is also able to connect each of her examples and so sketch out a counter-tradition of women's Shakespeare running through the long eighteenth century, beginning with Elizabeth Pepys and Margaret Cavendish, and stretching down to Dora Jordan and Sarah Siddons, by way of Elizabeth Montagu, Charlotte Lennox, and many more. All these figures, Ritchie shows, paid special attention to Shakespeare's morality, his supposed lack of education, and, most importantly of all, his ability to create supremely complex characters.

Women's cultural contributions are also central to Anne Wohlcke's *The 'Perpetual Fair': Gender, Disorder and Urban Amusement in Eighteenth-Century London*, which offers a clear, if occasionally workmanlike, account of the diversity of entertainment, audiences, and managers at the Southwark, Bartholomew, and May fairs. While principally a historical work, this book's third and fifth chapters provide a useful account of play-booth drama, from the influx of professional players under William Pinkethman in 1698 to the Licensing Act of 1737. Wohlcke's account shows in particular how 'Women were instrumental in the creation of commercialized leisure' (p. 210) generally, and particularly in that available in the play-booths. One of the greatest of these was founded by Anne Mynns in the seventeenth century: Elkanah Settle's *The Siege of Troy* [1701] was commissioned for its stage and Mynns's daughters carried on the business into the eighteenth century, until 1737, when what Wohlcke calls its 'dangerous compound of theatricality and femininity' attracted official constraint.

While *Stage Mothers* and the work of Ritchie and Wohlcke consider the (still neglected) role of women in eighteenth-century drama, Monica Mattfeld's article on the horseback displays of Philip Astley and his son John at Astley's Amphitheatre, '"Undaunted All He Views": The Gibraltar Charger, Astley's Amphitheatre and Masculine Performance' (*ECS* 37[2014] 19–36), is instead concerned with the period's construction of masculinity. Her work shows how equestrian spectacle relied on a powerful, mute rhetoric to offer patriotic displays of gentlemanly values, such as politeness and military chivalry.

Mattfeld's reading of the Astleys and their 'Gibraltar Charger' draws on the work of Joseph Roach, whose influence is discernible elsewhere in the publications of 2014: he is often quoted in *Stage Mothers*, and reprints of his earlier writing make up a substantial proportion of those parts of *European Theatre Performance 1750–1900*, edited by Jim Davis, dealing with the eighteenth century. The other material selected for reproduction here is: Alan S. Downer on acting style (1943), Dene Barnett on ensembles (1972), and James Van Horn Melton on audience (2001).

Roach himself published an article this year, entitled 'Celebrity Culture and the Problem of Biography' (*SQ* 65[2014] 470–81), in which he turns to the discussion of Garrick's Lear in the 1752 correspondence of the Hanbury-Williams family and the sketches of Siddons's Constance made by John Flaxman to argue provocatively that 'stage history . . . is a more illuminating part of [Shakespeare's] proper biography than any extant Elizabethan or Jacobean documents' (pp. 470–1). Both his examples show that, while documentary records of a life 'suggest its evanescence', 'to imagine that same life as sustained by performance is to assert its enduring and continuous presence' (p. 481).

The question of eighteenth-century performance, in its largest, international and political (as well as gendered), sense, is a running theme of Elizabeth Maddock Dillon's *New World Drama: The Performative Commons in the Atlantic World 1649–1849*. Also indebted to Roach (particularly his *Cities of the Dead* [1996]), this volume goes back to the execution of Charles I in 1649, the moment at which popular sovereignty began and the concept of 'commons' acquired new meaning, and ends with the Astor Place Riot 200 years later, which, in tandem with new copyright law, closed the American theatre 'as an institutional site at which a collective—a commons—might legitimately seek to perform itself' (p. 29). Between these two bookends of London and New York, Maddock Dillon takes her reader to Charleston and Kingston to further explore the complexity of circum-Atlantic space, a choice of arena which 'throws into relief the vitality of theatre as a cultural form' (p. 20).

This ambitious book uses the theatre to offer a new understanding of eighteenth-century public life as 'performative commons'. In the course of her work, Maddock Dillon offers substantial critique of her competition in this domain, including Habermas, Foucault, Marx, and Benedict Anderson. There are moments, particularly in the opening chapters of this text, when the author's theoretical manoeuvres make for difficult reading, although later passages amply reward the reader's patience. The work comes alive, for instance, in a chapter entitled 'Transportation', which provides new interpretations of both *The Enchanted Island* [1667] and *The Beggar's Opera* [1728]: the former is seen as 'a play concerned with sexual reproduction in the New World' (p. 105), while the latter 'proposes the performative revivification of the English commons' (p. 117).

Three other articles published in 2014 share with Maddock Dillon an interest in the global, cultural, and political ramifications of eighteenth-century theatre. First, Kevin J. McGinley's 'The 1757 College of Philadelphia Production of *Alfred: A Masque*—Some New Observations' (*HLQ* 77[2014] 37–58) presents a celebrated performance of *Alfred* as not just a gathering of early American cultural and political luminaries, but also 'a representation of the cultural sophistication of the city and even of the American colonies as a whole' (p. 58). On the other side of the Atlantic, and some twenty years later, Sheridan's *The Rivals* [1775] is reread by Daniel O'Quinn in an article entitled 'Navigating Crisis in Sheridan's *The Rivals*' (*ECent* 55[2014] 117–22). Using Lauren Berlant's theorization of crisis, O'Quinn proposes that the 'emergence of laughing comedy in the 1770s . . . is one instance where paradoxically audiences were called on to feel and assess the historical impasse besetting aspects of British polity during the American crisis' (p. 118). Third and finally, Judy A. Hayden's 'Of Windmills and Bubbles: Harlequin Faustus on the Eighteenth-Century Stage' (*HLQ* 77[2014] 1–16) shows how, in the wake of the South Sea Bubble and the Atterbury Plot, both *Harlequin Doctor Faustus* and *The Necromancer* turned to the Faustus narrative in 1723, and so continued a traditional link between this story and political crisis. The two pantomimes, the first by John Thurmond and the second by John Rich, attacked, respectively, Jacobitism and Whig financial policy through, for example, the symbolic, spectacular use of dragons (Thurmond) and windmills (Rich). Such stage effects, however, also guaranteed both works nevertheless enjoyed a wide circulation beyond their immediate political context.

A different kind of circulation, that of musical influence, motivates Vanessa Rogers's article on John Gay's *Polly* [1728] entitled 'John Gay, Ballad Opera and the Théâtre de la Foire' (*ECM* 11[2014] 173–213). Passing over the much-discussed political dimensions of Gay's work, Rogers shows instead how *Polly* recycled specific airs from popular French vaudevilles. Identification of this musical inheritance provides the first concrete evidence for a long-suspected link between ballad operas and the *comédies en vaudeville*. Rogers's lengthy article also contains a wider view of Anglo-French theatrical and musical circulation in the first half of the eighteenth century, including tables summarizing plays and ballad operas with French sources, as well as an appendix enumerating French fair-theatre and plays performed in London from 1718 to 1726: all of which represents a rich mine for future research.

A call for further research and re-evaluation governs Georgina Lock and David Worrall's joint article, 'Cross-Dressed Performance at the Theatrical Margins: Hannah Snell, the Manual Exercise, and the New Wells Spa Theater, 1750' (*HLQ* 77[2014] 17–36). Using a method familiar from Worrall's *British Georgian Theatre as Social Assemblage* [2013], they lay out the social and cultural context of Snell's highly personal performance, including new evidence for locating her 1750 appearance at the New Well's Spa Theatre, under the patronage of the composer and fisheries advocate John Lockman.

From the cross-dressing Hannah Snell to the foppish Colley Cibber by way of stage mothers and female Shakespearians, and from the performative commons of a circum-Atlantic eighteenth century to the political commentary of dragons and windmills, research published in 2014 covers a wide range of topics, expanding the definition of the field of eighteenth-century theatre. Such expansiveness also characterizes the *Oxford Handbook of the Georgian Theatre 1737–1832*, edited by Julia Swindells and David Francis Taylor, which, comprising forty chapters and some 330,000 words, represents an enormous contribution to (not to mention consolidation of) research into drama of the long eighteenth century. In his introduction, Taylor writes of an 'unfortunate irony' whereby the theatre of this time 'laid the foundations for the occlusion of its own complex vitality' (p. 2). Accordingly, the volume aims to recuperate such vitality and, in those chapters concerning the decades from 1700 to 1780 (my focus here), does so successfully.

The *Handbook* is divided into eight sections, covering theatre history, stage legislation, performance culture, 'Spectacles, Sounds, Spaces', genre and form, 'Theatre and the Romantic Canon', women, and race and empire. Three recurring activities (named by Taylor in his introduction) serve to give a general coherence to the volume: a renewed attention to the theatre audience, a reflection on the connection between the eighteenth century and the present, and a demonstration of the place of the theatre in our wider understanding of the period. The successful incorporation of all three of these activities marks the best contributions to this work, although no article ever falls below a high standard of scholarship—something which (along with the inclusion of a select bibliography for each chapter) makes the book as a whole an excellent teaching tool.

Eight chapters, spread across the *Handbook*, deserve particular mention. Angie Sadhu's opening contribution, entitled 'Enlightenment, Exclusion and the Publics of the Georgian Theatre' (pp. 11–30), offers a sense of what is at stake in this domain by arguing that 'studying the Georgian theatre enables us to explore matters of culture from the perspective of the popular rather than the elite' (p. 29). A little later in the same section, Taylor's own piece, on theatre managers and theatre history (pp. 70–88), provides an example of the kind of thing Sadhu believes possible, by rereading eighteenth-century representations of managerial activity in order to reconceptualize the theatre manager as '*nexus*' (p. 74) and encourage others to do likewise, thus overcoming critical biases against 'the enmeshed economic, political and artistic imperatives of the working Georgian playhouse' (p. 88).

Of all the writing here on the political enmeshment of the theatre, that of the volume's other editor, the late Julia Swindells, on the political context of the 1737 Licensing Act (including the passing of the Universities Bill a little before) stands out (pp. 107–22). She shows elegantly how, by the late 1730s, 'theatrical representation had begun to run counter to parliamentary invest-ments' (p. 121), resulting in legislation that stunted 'the development of a generative oppositional political culture' for a 'troublingly long time to come' (p. 122).

A pair of chapters, one on tragedy and the other on comedy, by Misty G. Anderson and Felicity A. Nussbaum, head the most straightforwardly literary section of the *Handbook*. Both contributions manage to combine a clear summary of playwriting in the Georgian era with a compelling argument for its re-evaluation. Nussbaum's piece (pp. 368–89) places women at the conflicted heart of eighteenth-century tragedy (and so reiterates the argument of her article, 'The Unaccountable Pleasures of Eighteenth-Century Tragedy' (*PMLA* 123[2014] 688–707), also published this year), while Anderson delineates the struggle of Georgian dramatists against the ghosts of Restoration comedy (pp. 347–67). A similar accomplishment of synthesis and insight is also found in Bridget Orr's article from later in the collection. Entitled 'Empire, Sentiment and Theatre' (pp. 621–37), its triangulations explain 'the problematics of abolitionism's sentimental rhetoric' with the aid of 'sentiment's . . . theatrical backstory' (p. 636).

The last two contributions I wish to draw attention to are both slightly unusual. The first is an interview with Colin Blumenau on restoration work (both of building and of repertory) undertaken at the Theatre Royal in Bury St Edmunds (pp. 333–43). The second is an article from Marcus Wood on the issues of historical re-enactment in colonial Williamsburg (pp. 706–25). While very different in their content, both chapters offer an alternative (and complementary) approach to the central questions of the *Handbook* as a whole. They show both the rediscovered vitality of Georgian theatre and the challenge it poses to our modern public institutions, whether they be universities, museums, or working theatres.

The three poles of gender, politics, and international circulation, named at the start of this review as central themes of research in 2014, are also present in the *Handbook*. Yet this last volume also suggests an alternative way of encapsulating scholarly work during this year. Almost all the material examined in this overview, whether in the *Handbook* or elsewhere, seeks to redefine the boundaries of its subject. Studies of gender (such as *Stage Mothers*) have stretched unthinking binaries to breaking point; studies of politics (such as Swindells's) have placed theatrical concerns amidst wider governmental issues; and studies of international circulation (such as Maddock Dillons's) continue to elaborate spheres of activity that exceed national frontiers. It seems both that the boundaries of what may be called eighteenth-century drama are expanding and that eighteenth-century drama is itself being used to expand the boundaries of research into other aspects of the eighteenth century. To put this another way, eighteenth-century drama is now becoming more fully connected to the culture of the period as a whole and, beyond this, influential to our own modern critical approaches. The continuation of such rich, connected thinking should, one hopes, be the likely course of research in the years ahead.

Books Reviewed

Baird, Ileana, and Christina Ionescu, eds. *Eighteenth-Century Thing Theory in a Global Context: From Consumerism to Celebrity Culture*. Ashgate. [2014] pp. xiii + 340. £85.50 ISBN 9 7814 7241 3291.

Davies, Rebecca. *Written Maternal Authority and Eighteenth-Century Education in Britain: Educating by the Book*. Ashgate. [2014] pp. xii + 170. £95 ISBN 9 7814 0945 1686.

Davis, Jim, ed. *European Theatre Practice 1750–1900*. Ashgate. [2014] pp. 538. £195 ISBN 9 7814 0941 9129.

Dew, Benjamin, and Fiona Price, eds. *Historical Writing in Britain, 1688–1830*. PalMac. [2014] pp. 240. £55 ISBN 9 7811 3733 2639.

Downing, Karen. *Restless Men: Masculinity and Robinson Crusoe, 1780–1840*. PalMac. [2014] pp. 256. £60 ISBN 9 7811 3734 8944.

Engel, Laura, and Elaine McGirr, eds. *Stage Mothers: Women, Work, and the Theater, 1660–1830*. BuckUP. [2014] pp. 290. $90 ISBN 9 7816 1148 6032.

Fowler, James. *Richardson and the Philosophes*. Legenda. [2014] pp. 195. £55 ISBN 9 7819 0966 2117.

Gevirtz, Karen Bloom. *Women, the Novel, and Natural Philosophy, 1660–1727*. ManUP. [2014] pp. 260. £60 ISBN 9 7811 3738 9206.

Grant, Roger Matthew. *Beating Time and Measuring Music in the Early Modern Era*. OUP. [2014] pp. 328. £30.99 ISBN 9 7801 9936 7283.

Griffin, Michael. *Enlightenment in Ruins: The Geographies of Oliver Goldsmith*. BuckUP. [2013] pp. 226. $85 ISBN 9 7816 1148 5059.

Hill, Mike, and Warren Montag. *The Other Adam Smith*. StanfordUP. [2014] pp. xi + 397. $29.95 ISBN 9 7808 0479 1946.

Holmes, Richard, ed. *James Arbuckle: Selected Works*. BuckUP. [2014] pp. 214. $70 ISBN 9 7816 1148 5530.

Horgan, Kate. *The Politics of Songs in Eighteenth-Century Britain, 1723–1795*. P&C. [2014] pp. 272. £95 ISBN 9 7818 4893 4795.

Kareem, Sarah Tindal. *Eighteenth-Century Fiction and the Reinvention of Wonder*. OUP. [2014] pp. 216. £55 ISBN 9 7801 9968 9101.

Klausen, Jimmy Casas. *Fugitive Rousseau: Slavery, Primitivism, and Political Freedom*. FordUP. [2014] pp. 356. $65 ISBN 9 7808 2325 7294.

König, Eva. *The Orphan in Eighteenth-Century Fiction: The Vicissitudes of the Eighteenth-Century Subject*. PalMac. [2014] pp. 288. £55 ISBN 9 7811 3738 2016.

Ley, James. *The Critic in the Modern World: Public Criticism from Samuel Johnson to James Wood*. Bloomsbury. [2014] pp. 248. $91 ISBN 9 7816 2356 9310.

Lima, Manuel. *The Book of Trees: Visualizing Branches of Knowledge*. PrincetonAP. [2014] pp. 208. $29.95 ISBN 9 7816 1689 2180.

Lipski, Jakub. *In Quest of the Self: Masquerade and Travel in the Eighteenth-Century Novel: Fielding, Smollett, Sterne*. Rodopi. [2014] pp. 223. €48 ISBN 9 7890 4203 8899.

Loar, Christopher F. *Political Magic: Fictions of Savagery and Sovereignty, 1650–1750*. FordUP. [2014] pp. xi + 326. $65 ISBN 9 7808 2325 6914.

Loscocco, Paula. *Phillis Wheatley's Miltonic Poetics*. Palgrave Pivot. [2014] pp. 164. £45 ISBN 9 7811 3747 4773.

Maddock Dillon, Elizabeth. *New World Drama: The Performative Commons in the Atlantic World 1649–1849*. DukeUP. [2014] pp. 368. $94.95 ISBN 9 7808 2235 3416.

McCarthy, William, and Olivia Murphy, eds. *Anna Letitia Barbauld: New Perspectives*. BuckUP. [2014] pp. 404. $95 ISBN 9 7816 1148 5493.

McInelly, Brett C. *Textual Warfare and the Making of Methodism*. OUP. [2014] pp. viii + 245. £53 ISBN 9 7801 9870 8940.

McKee Stapleton, Anne. *Pointed Encounters: Dance in Post-Culloden Scottish Literature*. Rodopi. [2014] pp. 219. $63 ISBN 9 7890 4203 8691.

Mounsey, Chris, ed. *The Idea of Disability in the Eighteenth Century*. BuckUP. [2014] pp. 280. $80 ISBN 9 7816 1148 5592.

Murison, W. *The Traveller and The Deserted Village*. CUP. [2014] pp. 84. £17.99 ISBN 9 7811 0768 2610.

Narain, Mona, and Karen Gevirtz, eds. *Gender and Space in British Literature, 1660–1820*. Ashgate. [2014] pp. 252. £95 ISBN 9 7814 7241 5080.

Parker, Kate, and Courtney Weiss Smith, eds. *Eighteenth-Century Poetry and the Rise of the Novel Reconsidered*. BuckUP. [2014] pp. 280. $80 ISBN 9 7816 1148 4830.

Pearl, Jason H. *Utopian Geographies and the Early English Novel*. UVirginiaP. [2014] pp. 215. $45 ISBN 9 7808 1393 6239.

Powell, Rosalind. *Christopher Smart's English Lyrics*. Ashgate. [2014] pp. 220. £95 ISBN 9 7814 7243 5071.

Rawson, Claude. *Swift's Angers*. CUP. [2014] pp. 314. $44.99 ISBN 9 7811 0761 0101.

Ritchie, Fiona. *Women and Shakespeare in the Eighteenth Century*. CUP. [2014] pp. viii + 256. £64.99 ISBN 9 7811 0704 6306.

Roberts, Charlotte. *Edward Gibbon and the Shape of History*. OUP. [2014] pp. 208. £50 ISBN 9 7801 9870 4836.

Rudy, Seth. *Literature and Encyclopedism in Enlightenment Britain: The Pursuit of Complete Knowledge*. PalMac. [2014] pp. viii + 253. £55 ISBN 9 7811 3741 1531.

Schmidt, Michael. *The Novel: A Biography*. Bellknap. [2014] pp. 1200. £29.95 ISBN 9 7806 7472 4730.

Sirota, Brett S. *The Christian Monitors: The Church of England and the Age of Benevolence, 1680–1730*. YaleUP. [2014] pp. xiii + 360. $65 ISBN 9 7803 0016 7108.

Sloboda, Stacey. *Chinoiserie: Commerce and Critical Ornament in Eighteenth-Century Britain*. ManUP. [2014] pp. xvii + 238. £70 ISBN 9 7807 1908 9459.

Squibbs, Richard. *Urban Enlightenment and the Eighteenth-Century Periodical Essay: Transatlantic Retrospects*. PalMac. [2014] pp. vii + 234. £55 ISBN 9 7811 3737 8231.

Sterne, Laurence. *The Miscellaneous Writings and Sterne's Subscribers, An Identification List*, ed. Melvyn New and W.B. Gerrard. UPFlorida. [2014] pp. 632. $100 ISBN 9 7808 1304 9472.

Stewart, Carol, ed. *The Invisible Spy*, by Eliza Haywood. P&C. [2014] pp. 544. £70 ISBN 9 7818 4893 4412.

Swindells, Julia, and David Francis Taylor, eds. *The Oxford Handbook to the Georgian Theatre 1737–1832*. OUP. [2014] pp. xxv + 758. £110 ISBN 9 7801 9960 0304.

Tovey, D.C. *Gray's English Poems: Original and Translated from the Norse and Welsh*. CUP. [2014] pp. 294. £20.99 ISBN 9 7811 0766 5682.

Whibley, Charles. *Jonathan Swift: The Leslie Stephen Lecture 1917*. CUP. [2014] pp. 45. £7.99 ISBN 9 7811 0768 8360.

Whiskin, Margaux Elizabeth. *Narrative Structure and Philosophical Debates in Tristram Shandy and Jacques le fataliste*. MHRA. [2014] pp. 176. £19.99 ISBN 9 7817 8188 0166.

Wild, Min, and Noel Chevalier, eds. *Reading Christopher Smart in the Twenty-First Century: 'By Succession of Delight'*. BuckUP. [2014] pp. 274. $85 ISBN 9 7816 1148 5196.

Wilputte, Earla. *Passion and Language in Eighteenth-Century Literature: The Aesthetic Sublime in the Work of Eliza Haywood, Aaron Hill, and Martha Fowke*. PalMac. [2014] pp. 256. £57.50 ISBN 9 7811 3744 2048.

Wohlcke, Anne. *The 'Perpetual Fair': Gender, Disorder and Urban Amusement in Eighteenth-Century London*. ManUP. [2014] pp. 256. £70 ISBN 9 7807 1909 0912.

XIII

Literature 1780–1830: The Romantic Period

MAXINE BRANAGH-MISCAMPBELL, ELIZA O'BRIEN, MATTHEW WARD, PAUL WHICKMAN, AND CHRISY DENNIS

This chapter has four sections: 1. General and Prose; 2. The Novel; 3. Poetry; 4. Drama. Section 1 is by Maxine Branagh-Miscampbell; section 2 is by Eliza O'Brien; section 3 is by Matthew Ward and Paul Whickman; section 4 is by Chrisy Dennis.

1. General and Prose

Two of the major themes to come out of the works published in 2014 in the field of Romantic general and prose writing are those of local, national, and global identities, and questions of selfhood. Sarah Houghton-Walker's *Representations of the Gypsy in the Romantic Period* looks at the representation of the gypsy figure in the Romantic period in relation to English identities, among other themes. David Higgins's *Romantic Englishness: Local, National and Global Selves, 1780–1850* examines local English identities in relation to broader conceptions of the self in an increasingly connected national or global context. Two texts also make use of the growing field of Atlantic studies to take a fresh look at travel writing, in the case of Elizabeth A. Bohls's *Slavery and the Politics of Place: Representing the Colonial Caribbean 1770–1833*, and the theme of hospitality in Romantic-period texts in the case of Cynthia Schoolar Williams's *Hospitality and the Transatlantic Imagination, 1815–1835*, which was published as part of Palgrave's The New Urban Atlantic series. I will begin by discussing these texts before moving on to other key publications, which include interesting new insights in the field of women's reading and writing, the study of emotions and feeling, and historical and political writing.

Sarah Houghton-Walker's *Representations of the Gypsy in the Romantic Period* sets out to analyse the 'phenomenon of the gypsy as it was understood by the Romantic Period' (p. 2). She argues that the Romantic fascination with the gypsy-figure grows in partnership with other broader cultural and societal

The Year's Work in English Studies, Volume 95 (2016) © *The Author 2016. Published by Oxford University Press on behalf of the English Association. All rights reserved.*
For Permissions, please email: journals.permissions@oup.com
doi:10.1093/ywes/maw010

changes such as ideas surrounding property, propriety, art, and sympathy. Houghton-Walker situates her subject in relation to the themes of the sublime and English identity. The Romantic-period gypsy, Houghton-Walker argues, is situated between the 'amusing rogues' (p. 12) of the eighteenth century and the 'nostalgic, romanticized gypsy form' (p. 12) of early Victorian literature. She thus sheds new light on the various cultural anxieties represented by the ways in which the gypsy figure was depicted during the Romantic period. She offers a useful overview of the background of the gypsy in eighteenth-century England, and its literary contexts, before going on to analyse the figure in the work of William Cowper and John Clare, Romantic poetry, and Jane Austen's *Emma*, among others, including artists such as Thomas Gainsborough and George Morland. Houghton-Walker situates these close readings in a broader context of literary culture, theories of aestheticism, and questions of class and industry. In so doing, she highlights the importance of the gypsy in the rural Romantic landscape as a significant symbol of Romantic-period anxieties and concerns.

David Higgins's *Romantic Englishness: Local, National and Global Selves, 1780–1850* also deals with identity in English Romantic writing, specifically questioning how localized selfhood is produced in relation to global or national identities and how individuals connect with the national community. Higgins's analysis focuses on autobiographies (including autobiographical poems, personal essays, and letters) written within or about England during the Romantic period, with chapters devoted to focused case studies on William Cowper, Samuel Taylor Coleridge, William Wordsworth, Samuel Bamford, Thomas Bewick and William Cobbett, John Clare, William Hazlitt, Charles Lamb, and Thomas De Quincey. In his work, Higgins re-examines the connection between the local, the national, and the global, and argues that Romantic localism was outward-looking to the national and the global, and was particularly informed by imperialism and colonialism. Higgins aims to bring together two main strands in *Romantic Englishness*, 'an ecocritical account of the relationship between Romantic autobiography and place' and 'an argument for the significance of Englishness in Romantic-period writing' in light of recent critical work on 'Four Nations Romanticism' (p. 12). In his introduction, Higgins admits that, despite its broad scope, *Romantic Englishness* is not definitive in its inclusion of autobiographical writers and focuses on 'analysing Englishness in relation to masculinity' (p. 13). Despite this, the inclusion of labouring-class narratives by Samuel Bamford, Thomas Bewick, and William Cobbett in conjunction with the other writers offers a wide-ranging and fascinating insight into the construction of 'Englishness', and its relationship to place, in Romantic-period autobiography.

Another key publication in 2014 which deals with theories of place and space in relation to Romantic-period writing, focusing specifically on colonial travel and slave narratives, is Elizabeth A. Bohls's *Slavery and the Politics of Place: Representing the Colonial Caribbean 1770–1833*. Bohls argues that the popularity of travel writing during the Romantic period cannot be understood outside the context of colonial expansion. Bohls deals with a variety of writing by planters, scientists, soldiers, politicians, and journalists, and a particular strength of the project is her inclusion of women's narratives in relation to theories of feminist geographies and concepts of home and domestic space. Bohls's analysis does not just focus on the colonial spaces of the Caribbean but also draws on recent scholarship in Atlantic studies to examine the place of Romantic-period writing which covers the spaces between sites of slavery and the imperial centre.

Cynthia Schoolar Williams's *Hospitality and the Transatlantic Imagination, 1815–1835* also draws on recent scholarship in Atlantic studies to examine the discourse of hospitality in the wake of the Napoleonic Wars. Schoolar Williams argues that 'hospitality is an experience and a discourse of paradox. Scenes of welcome evoke, suspend, and defy many of our most powerful binaries' (p. 2). This was particularly important in the 'post-Waterloo' period when questions surrounding national identity were pertinent (p. 177). Each writer Schoolar Williams deals with employs the discourse of hospitality to 'ask a series of questions about displacement and the nation' (p. 3) in a transatlantic, or Anglo-American, context. The book is structured into chapters each dealing with a specific writer: Mary Shelley, James Fenimore Cooper, Washington Irving, and Felicia Hemans. The grouping of this particular set of writers enables Schoolar Williams to draw conclusions surrounding 'the competing imperatives of universal rights, local affiliation, and the global reach of empire' (p. 177).

Brief mention should also be made of Jeffrey N. Cox's *Romanticism in the Shadow of War: Literary Culture in the Napoleonic War Years*, reviewed more fully in Section 3 below. Cox argues for viewing the writing of key Romantic writers not only in the context of the Napoleonic Wars but also in the context of the smaller battles, or 'struggles at the periphery' such as the Russo-Ottoman War, the War of 1812 in North America, and the Latin American Wars of Independence (p. 2). Although his main focus is Romantic poetry and therefore beyond the scope of this section, this text is useful in considering general and prose writing of the Romantic period in light of the various 'moments of expectation turned to disappointment' (p. 23).

Three key publications in the field of women readers and writers were published in 2014. Richard De Ritter's *Imagining Women Readers, 1789–1820: Well-Regulated Minds* is a fascinating addition to the field of the history of reading. De Ritter explores the place of female readers in British culture between 1789 and 1820. Focusing on fictional and idealized representations of readers and evidence of 'actual' reading practices in letters and diaries, this book offers an interesting new insight into the cultural significance of women's reading in the Romantic period, and De Ritter argues that the texts examined 'imagine an alternative identity for novel reading women' (p. 12). Drawing upon recent criticism in the history of reading, and examining work by Hannah More, Mary Hays, Mary Wollstonecraft, Jane West, Maria Edgeworth, and Jane Austen, De Ritter argues that reading was depicted as a form of 'symbolic labour' (p. 11), rather than a dangerous, 'pernicious' (p. 3), or unproductive activity. De Ritter concludes that 'constructions of women readers are . . . shaped by the debates impinging upon British public life' (p. 199) while simultaneously resisting 'stabilising categorisations' (p. 200).

Amy Culley's *British Women's Life Writing, 1760–1840: Friendship, Community and Collaboration* focuses on three main groups of female autobiographers: early Methodist women, late eighteenth-century and Regency courtesans, and British women in Paris during the French Revolution. This structure allows Culley to examine the social networks, exchanges, and friendships between various women during the Romantic period and challenges the traditional view of life-writing as a solitary, private practice. The combination of well-known writers such as Mary Wollstonecraft, Helen Maria Williams, and Mary Robinson, and the introduction of less well-known female contributors to late eighteenth- and early nineteenth-century life-writing is a particular strength of this book and allows the analysis to move beyond the canon of published autobiographies. Culley also examines a wide range of 'women's self-narration', including 'spiritual autobiographies, family memoirs, scandalous memoirs, diaries, journals, biographies, correspondence, travelogues, *romans à clef*, and eye-witness accounts in both print and manuscript sources' (p. 2). This book therefore highlights that life-writing, in all its various forms, played an important role in the female literary culture of the Romantic period and, as Culley argues, 'provides a fuller history of women's literary experiences in the period' (p. 204).

Jeffrey W. Barbeau's *Sara Coleridge: Her Life and Thought* sheds light on the biographical and intellectual history of Samuel Taylor Coleridge's only daughter. The majority of her writing remained unpublished, with the exception of a small collection of children's poetry, a fairy tale, and translations of travel literature. Barbeau's book examines the corpus of Sara Coleridge's unpublished letters and manuscript material, dividing these thematically into writings on beauty, education, dreams, criticism, authority, reason, regeneration, community, and death. Barbeau argues that it was Sara's editing of her father's work which helped her develop 'a thoroughly Coleridgean frame of mind' (p. x). Her writing, he goes on to argue, 'reveals one of the most fascinating and neglected women in nineteenth-century literature, theology, and history' (p. xiv). It is very interesting to see how Sara Coleridge framed and preserved her father's ideas for the Victorian period, while gaining an insight into her as a writer in her own right, and the thematic structure of the book is particularly useful for this.

Three articles printed in *Romanticism* also pay attention to women's writing in the shape of pamphlets by Charlotte Smith and Hannah More. Two articles which deal with Smith's writings were published in 2014: Claire Knowles's 'Hazarding the Press: Charlotte Smith, *The Morning Post* and the Perils of Literary Celebrity' (*Romanticism* 20:i[2014] 30–42) was printed in *Romanticism*'s special issue on celebrity culture, while Carmel Murphy's 'Jacobin History: Charlotte Smith's *Old Manor House* and the French Revolution Debate' (*Romanticism* 20:iii[2014] 271–81) was printed later in the year in 'Unusual Suspects'. Carmel Murphy argues that *Old Manor House* makes use of the tradition of historical writing from the 1770s, which uses history to comment on contemporary political debates. However, she goes on to say that Smith's intentions go beyond this. Murphy argues that Smith's *Old Manor House* is an 'important contribution to the developing French Revolution dialogue' (p. 281). Claire Knowles examines the celebrity culture which grew around female writers as the popular press grew. She examines six poems published by and about Charlotte Smith in *The Morning Post* in order to analyse the way in which the authorial identity which Smith constructs for herself is challenged by the celebrity image created by the popular press. Also appearing in the special issue on celebrity culture was Cato Marks's '"Let Poor Volk Pass": Dialect and Writing the South-West Poor out of Metropolitan Political Life in Hannah More's *Village Poetics*' (*Romanticism* 20:i[2014] 43–59). This article focuses on More's use of language in *Village Poetics* in order to challenge her 'positive contribution to female and labouring-class education' (p. 56). Marks argues that 'through this depiction of the South-West poor, Hannah More attempts to exclude them, and other marginalized peoples she identifies with them, from polite and political debate' (p. 57).

Halina Adams also addresses a woman writer, Helen Maria Williams, and her approach to the French Revolution in *Letters Written in France* [1790]. In 'Imagining the Nation: Transforming the Bastille in Williams's *Letters Written in France* (1790)' (*ERR* 25:vi[2014] 723–41), Adams argues that Williams makes use of 'architectural imagination' to transform the Bastille into 'the ideal site for Williams to interrogate the idea of the nation and nationalism' (p. 723). Her close reading of various passages from the letters reveals 'the enthusiasm and fervor of those heady days' of the Fête de la Fédération (pp. 738–9). Williams instructs her readers on how to read her books, stating that 'if the reader will participate in the creation of the narrative, then her text will be successful' (quoted p. 738), and so Adams argues that 'the real subversive danger of the architectural imagination in *Letters* is that the audience may construct a building, or a nation, one entirely new and completely derived from their own plans' (p. 738).

Randall Sessler's 'Recasting the Revolution: The Media Debate between Edmund Burke, Mary Wollstonecraft, and Thomas Paine' (*ERR* 25:v[2014] 611–26) argues that the debate which emerged from Edmund Burke's *Reflections on the Revolution in France* [1790] can be read as an early form of media debate. Sessler argues that approaching the responses of Burke, Wollstonecraft, and Paine to the French Revolution using a media theory, rather than by only addressing their genre or textuality, enables us to come to different conclusions about the debate (p. 611). Sessler therefore attempts to challenge the idea that the exchange between Burke, Wollstonecraft, and Paine was 'a "struggle to control" the revolution's "textual representation"' by 'maintaining the distinction between genre and media' in order to reveal 'new approaches [to] and readings [of]' the debate (pp. 624–5).

Catherine Packham also addresses Wollstonecraft's response to the French Revolution but focuses on her *Historical and Moral View of the French Revolution* [1794]. In '"The Common Grievance of the Revolution": Bread, the Grain Trade, and Political Economy in Wollstonecraft's *View of the French Revolution*' (*ERR* 25:vi[2014] 705–22), Packham argues that Wollstonecraft's conclusion in *View* 'indicates the difficulties of integrating economic improvement, as envisaged by Smithian political economy, into philosophical history's narrative of human progress' (p. 718). She states that Wollstonecraft foregrounds the bread shortages and the liberation of the grain trade in her portrayal of the march on Versailles in October 1789 while making sure not to 'write a history of revolution founded on the purely economic cause of bead shortages' in order to provide a 'dual representation of the mob as both object of improvement and agents of it' (p. 719).

Remaining in the field of women writers, two articles were also published on Dorothy Wordsworth's writing in 2014, in *European Romantic Review* and *Studies in Romanticism*. Mary Ellen Bellanca's 'After-Life-Writing: Dorothy Wordsworth's Journals in the *Memoirs of William Wordsworth*' (*ERR* 25:ii[2014] 201–18) examines the printing and reception of Dorothy Wordsworth's journal in *Memoirs of William Wordsworth* [1851]. Bellanca aims to 'dispel any lingering impression that her [Dorothy Wordsworth's] prose remained unpublished in her lifetime (she lived until 1855)' (p. 201) with her examination of the ten printed pages of Dorothy's Grasmere journal and forty-five pages from *Recollections of a Tour Made in Scotland, 1803*, both of which were included in the *Memoirs*. Through this it is possible to 'examine what her early readers glimpsed of Dorothy Wordsworth's life writing' and therefore 'recalibrate our narratives of her presence in literary history' (p. 215). Bellanca argues that 'the *Memoirs* interposes her [Dorothy's] voice into its telling of William's life, so that she becomes a distinct autobiographical subject, an agent and a partner as well as witness and source' (p. 202) and furthermore brings a 'more palpable sense of Dorothy Wordsworth as a person, one with an astute, engaged consciousness and a voice' (p. 203). It is the late nineteenth-century editors' dismissal of the importance of the extracts contained in the *Memoirs* which, Bellanca argues, 'obscured the *Memoirs*' exposition of Dorothy Wordsworth's prose and its readership in her life' (p. 202).

Rachel Feder's 'The Experimental Dorothy Wordsworth' (*SiR* 53:iv[2014] 541–59) examines 'Dorothy Wordsworth's commonplace chapbook, a circumscribed collection of poetic "consolations" that occurs within Wordsworth's commonplace book' (p. 542). Feder argues that 'Dorothy Wordsworth's archive survives as a special case of radicalized mixed genres, entextualized or captured in overlapping forms and modes' (p. 543). Her aim in examining this writing is 'to facilitate a reading of Dorothy Wordsworth as an experimental author writing in the literal and figurative margins of a literary history that she is working to construct, and to open up a conversation about how reading the experimental Dorothy Wordsworth might enrich our understanding of the Romantic inheritance' (p. 542).

Two texts which serve to expand our understanding of historical writing in the Romantic period significantly are Ben Dew and Fiona Price's *Historical Writing in Britain, 1688–1830: Visions of History* and Porscha Fermanis and John Regan's *Rethinking British Romantic History, 1770–1845*. Dew and Price's volume covers the long eighteenth century but contains a number of chapters which are relevant to Romantic studies. It deals with the establishment of 'history' as a genre throughout the long eighteenth century, with historians of the period being 'a rather motley collection of philosophers, journalists, historical pamphleteers, churchmen and academics who, with the possible exception of Edward Gibbon, tended to produce works of history while performing other literary and non-literary functions' (p. 2). In their introduction, Dew and Price argue that the end of the eighteenth century saw a shift towards a 'broader conception of history' and 'the emergence of a range of innovative forms of more specialist writing, as sizeable literatures developed around the history of commerce, literature, art, music, natural history, and various scientific disciplines' (p. 6). Historical writing, they argue, is also an important player in the development of other genres. This volume brings together various essays which provide case studies to show how different types of historical writing changed and adapted across the period in line with societal changes. Of particular interest to Romanticists is Dafydd Moore's chapter, 'Caledonian Plagiary: The Role and Meaning of Ireland in the Poems of *Ossian*', in which he argues that his reading of *Ossian* can 'provide a compelling example of recent thinking about the relationship between Enlightenment and Romanticism in Scotland' (p. 104). Sanja Perovic's 'Lyricist in Britain; Empiricist in France: Volney's Divided Legacy' provides an interesting insight into the different receptions of Constantin-François Volney's work in Britain and France in the wake of the French Revolution. Fiona Price's chapter, 'Making History: Social Unrest, Work and the Post-French Revolution Historical Novel', argues that the historical novels of the French Revolution, pre-*Waverley*, 'have a much more immediate sense of the threat of "convulsive metamorphosis"' (p. 158).

Fermanis and Regan's *Rethinking British Romantic History, 1770–1845* also offers a selection of essays dealing with various types of historical writing in the Romantic period. Divided into sections dealing with 'History, Rhetoric, Genre', 'Historical Space and Time', and 'Aesthetics of History', this volume aims to 'rethink three longstanding "narratives" about the nature of British historical writing in its wider European and imperial context from 1770 to 1845', namely, 'the widely held belief that the relationship between history and literature was open and porous', 'the exclusion of literary texts from various accounts of the rise of historicism and the birth of the modern historical method', and 'the widespread characterization of Romantic history as a subjective and emotionally charged reaction to philosophic history and other Enlightenment modes of representing the past' (p. 7). Its selection of essays is successful in complicating these received narratives about historical writing and its crossover into the fiction and poetry of the period.

Also of interest is Sean Franzel's essay, 'Romantic Encyclopedics and the Lecture Form: Schelling, A.W. Schlegel, A. von Humboldt' (*ERR* 25:iii[2014] 347–56). Franzel examines the proliferation of Romantic-era lectures which aimed to be encyclopedic in their scope and subject matter. Franzel's article analyses Friedrich Schelling's 1799 lectures, *Method of Academic Study*, August Wilhelm Schlegel's Berlin lectures, *The Encyclopedia of the Sciences*, and Alexander von Humboldt's 1827/28 *Kosmos* lectures. In so doing, he sheds light on the 'concrete institutional, medial, and formal features of lecturing, including the sequential unfolding of lecture series; the differentiation between disjointed, "historical" information and embodied "living" knowledge; the scene of pedagogical address and the tendency to address a general or so-called "popular" audience; and, in the German case, the underpinnings of scholarly lecturing in the conceptual apparatus of transcendental idealism' (p. 348). Franzel argues that, read 'against the backdrop of earlier projects of Romantic encyclopedics, the lecture comes into view as form that opens a space for experimentation with a de-differential discourse, a discourse that can link different sciences and fields of inquiry to each other' (p. 354).

Two texts which deal with the theme of emotions or feeling in the Romantic period in an innovative way are Joel Faflak and Richard C. Sha's edited volume, *Romanticism and the Emotions*, and Jeremy Davies's *Bodily Pain in Romantic Literature*. *Romanticism and the Emotions* brings together several essays which offer a fascinating insight into the nature of emotion in Romantic literary culture. Dealing not only with the emotions typically associated with the Romantic period, such as trauma and melancholy, but also with 'happiness, humiliation, and various states of peaceful apatheia or affectlessness', the essays in this collection offer scope for new directions in the study of Romantic emotion (p. 4). The chapters provide wide-ranging new insights into how various writers engaged with the emotions, including Adam Smith, Percy Bysshe Shelley, Mary Shelley, Jane Austen, William Wordsworth, Lord Byron, Immanuel Kant, and Thomas De Quincey.

Davies's *Bodily Pain in Romantic Literature* also offers an interesting new argument related to the nature of feeling in Romantic literature. His book discusses four Romantic writers; Jeremy Bentham, the Marquis de Sade, Samuel Taylor Coleridge, and Percy Bysshe Shelley. Each chapter of Davies's book is devoted to one of these writers, who are dealt with in a roughly chronological order, with the study ending with the development of surgical anaesthesia in 1846, the absence of which, Davies argues, is significant in Romantic literary depictions of pain 'as a feeling of being compelled to notice the body's very capacity for feeling' (p. xi). Davies argues that pain should be thought of 'as a reflexive or ironic phenomenon' and that it is 'a demand to attend to the vital sense of sensing that is otherwise diffusely present in the background of experience' (p. 168). The four readings in this volume therefore serve to highlight the significance of literary representations of bodily pain in a pre-anaesthetic era, in relation to broader Romantic concern with 'the full extent of one's powers of feeling' (p. 169).

The remaining texts reviewed in this section are all related to the works of specific political writers: William Cobbett, William Godwin, and William Hazlitt. The second volume of Godwin's letters was released in 2014, and is to be followed by two further volumes. Following on from the first volume, published in 2011 by Oxford University Press, the collection publishes, for the first time, all of Godwin's letters. Edited by Pamela Clemit, it focuses on the years 1798 to 1805 and 'represent[s] a distinct phase in Godwin's life and career' (p. 1). Clemit argues that the letters in this volume show Godwin 'adapting to changes in public mood, seeking compromise in his philosophical commitments, rebuilding his social circles, and remaking himself as the author of novels, plays, biographies, and children's books' (p. 1). The letters in this volume include an eyewitness account of the condition of Ireland on the eve of the 1800 Act of Union and Godwin's search for a new companion in the wake of the death of Mary Wollstonecraft. The letters also provide further insight into Godwin's publishing and social networks at the time.

Stephen Burley's *Hazlitt the Dissenter: Religion, Philosophy, and Politics, 1766–1816* is the first book-length account of Hazlitt's early literary career, and life as a dissenter. Burley aims to provide a fresh reading of Hazlitt's early writings and situates these within the context of eighteenth-century, rather than nineteenth-century, literature. By focusing on Hazlitt's early literary career, Burley hopes to suggest alternative readings of Hazlitt's 'more famous body of work as an essayist and critic in the post-Napoleonic era' (p. 8). The book is structured chronologically and draws on previously unattributed materials. Burley's focus on religion in Hazlitt's writings is a particular strength of the book, and his interdisciplinary approach makes this volume an important contribution, not only to literary studies, but also to the understanding of the 'religious and cultural milieu that frames Hazlitt's writing' (p. 166). Also on Hazlitt, Amanda Louise Johnson's 'William Hazlitt, *Liber Amoris*, and the Imagination' (*ERR* 25:vi[2014] 743–56) examines Hazlitt's *Liber Amoris* [1823], and his erotic memoir and polemic against royalism entitled 'On the Spirit of Monarchy'. Johnson argues that these two texts demonstrate Hazlitt's 'theory of the imagination' (p. 743): 'that the press offers the ideas that mediate the relationship between a subject's private interest and a "common sympathy", both of which exist in the imagination' (p. 753).

James Grande's *William Cobbett, the Press and Rural England: Radicalism and the Fourth Estate, 1792–1835* offers a re-examination of the work of William Cobbett. Grande aims to 'read Cobbett's career as a serious and sustained attempt to think through a set of ideas that had been crystallized in the pamphlet wars of the 1790s' (p. 17). He argues that Cobbett, 'having been the champion of a bellicose, anti-French Britishness', discovers 'an oppositional identity rooted in rural England' (p. 17). The book covers Cobbett's published and unpublished writings to provide a thorough overview of his work and why he came to represent, to Hazlitt, 'a kind of *fourth estate* in the politics of the country' (p. 4).

The key themes and approaches to come out of 2014 criticism in the field of Romantic general and prose writings are largely concerned with different notions of identity: the local, the national, and the global. There is also an increased focus on the political writings of female writers during the pamphlet wars of the 1790s, and a number of publications have made use of new material from canonical writers, and material from less well-known writers, to provide new perspectives on and new directions in political, historical, travel, and life writing, as well as in the broad field of women's writing.

2. The Novel

In Search of Jane Austen: The Language of the Letters, by Ingrid Tieken-Boon Van Ostade, offers a sociolinguistic study of Austen's grammar, vocabulary, and spelling, examining Austen's letters in careful detail. The result is a thorough study not only of Austen's language as letter-writer as opposed to novelist, though there is also a section on Austen's 'Authorial Identity' (pp. 208–24), but of the formulae of letter-writing in Austen's time, the postal system, Austen's correspondents, and the corpus of letters. As Tieken-Boon Van Ostade's study progresses, the importance of her central claim becomes more apparent as an absence in Austen studies to date emerges: why, when

Austen is the subject of so much criticism, parody, and inspiration, has her epistolary language gone almost undiscussed? The author reaches some interesting conclusions about the essentially conservative nature of Austen's language, her brief uses of dialect, and contemporary grammatical correctness. She also argues for the revision of dates for certain undated letters, as well as the dating of *The Watsons* manuscript, based on linguistic evidence rather than anecdote. Though this is a study in sociolinguistics, it contains plenty of information to attract the literary critic.

All varieties of the wonderful online life of Jane Austen are presented in Kylie Mirmohamadi's concise Palgrave Pivot guide to *The Digital Afterlives of Jane Austen: Janeites at the Keyboard*, in which the author sets out not only to trace the proliferation of Austen fans online, but to examine what it is they write, reading it as literary endeavour in its own right while also regarding it as belonging to the wider tradition of publishing Austen's works, reading, and responding to them critically. One of the subjects Mirmohamadi covers is a Canadian online literary community, Wattpad, and its array of Austen-themed fan fiction. Her study of this site shows that such is the familiarity of Austen's work as its own self-referential system in the world of fan fiction that new Austen stories can be produced by readers who have scarcely encountered the original Austen, yet whose works perfectly navigate their online world, revealing the boundless creative potential represented by the *idea* of Austen online, however far from the novels that idea may have travelled.

In *The Hidden Jane Austen*, John Wiltshire offers a counterpoint to the current scholarship on celebrity, cults, and fan fiction in his starting point of rereading. He quotes Richard Cronin and Dorothy McMillan's perceptive argument [2005] about the deliberate crafting of *Emma* as a novel aiming to ' "sacrifice readability" to re-readability' (p. 3), in order to further Austen's claims to be considered a serious writer, rather than the generator of disposable trash. Wiltshire's fascination with the rereadability of Austen's novels is the motivation for his study of the 'hidden' Austen, that is, the 'facets of her writing that might elude the attention of the first-time reader' (p. 4). While Wiltshire is interested in themes of secrecy, silence, and evasion within the novels, he is also an astute reader of Austen's plotting in which the significance of the hidden (a smile, a fear, a lie) comes to be revealed on the first or repeated reading of the novel. His seven chapters address each of Austen's completed novels in turn (*Mansfield Park* gets two chapters) and analyse memory, religion, intimate history, eavesdropping, and how to create a secret where there is none, in *Northanger Abbey*. This study is elegantly written and presents nuanced and persuasive readings of the novels. It exhibits its own readability and rereadability as well as those of Austen.

An excellent new resource is offered in *Approaches to Teaching Austen's Mansfield Park*, edited by Marcia McClintock Folsom and John Wiltshire. Part of the MLA's Approaches to Teaching World Literature series, this is an easy-to-use and thorough teaching aid whose contributors are engagingly subjective and self-reflective in places, are always student-focused, and offer an accessible but scrupulous account of the different aspects of the novel. The study is divided into two parts, 'Materials' and 'Approaches'. Part I contains useful information about the different editions of *Mansfield Park* from its publication date to the present, its critical reception, an account of the three film versions of the novel, and a list of current digital resources, including specialist Austen websites, free sites, and subscription databases. Part II, 'Approaches', begins with an introduction by the editors (pp. 21–49), and its subheadings give a clear indication of its utility: the historical and naval context, religion, the slave trade, introspection, Fanny Price, first-cousin marriage, and the final chapter. The rest of the book consists of four sections. 'Classroom Strategies and Approaches' (pp. 50–104) covers gift theory, the textual scholarship, unexpected locations for the expression of desire, the plausibility of the ending as a happy one, and a discussion (including the rules) of the card game Speculation, which features in the novel when Sir Thomas recommends it as a suitable choice for the family's evening entertainment. Family forms the focus of the second section, 'Thinking about Fanny Price and Families' (pp. 105–42), where sibling relations, a close reading of Fanny's character, Austen's development of interiority from *Pride and Prejudice* to *Mansfield Park*, and the opacity of the Crawfords are discussed. The third section, 'Teaching about *Mansfield Park* in Literary History and Context' (pp. 143–207), covers tragedy, morality, landscape, and a group of essays on readers, reading, and drama. In 'Understanding *Mansfield Park* through the Rehearsals for *Lovers' Vows*' (pp. 155–63), by Penny Gay, we encounter not only Inchbald's play but the descriptions and responses of students who performed it while studying the novel; their awareness of character parallels between *Mansfield Park* and the play, between movement and sociability, and language and desire in Austen's novel is heightened by an understanding of the crucial theatricals. The final section, 'Teaching *Mansfield Park* in the Broader Postcolonial Context' (pp. 208–32), concludes with geography, nationalism and imperialism, and rights. These three essays, by Lynn Voskuil, Lisa Masker, and Paula Loscocco respectively, provide invaluable explanations and practical examples of interpreting the novel in the light of Said's argument about it in *Culture and Imperialism* [1993], which allows the novel to keep its central focus in the classroom discussion by moving beyond the conversation about Antigua between Fanny and Sir Thomas in order to apply Said's views more perceptively and rewardingly.

Marie N. Sørbø's new study *Irony and Idyll: Jane Austen's Pride and Prejudice and Mansfield Park on Screen* provides a very detailed account of each novel and its adaptations. The two sections, each on one novel, each begin with an analysis of the novel in question. *Pride and Prejudice* receives two chapters, and 'Austen's Ironic Voice' (pp. 15–46) sets up an important aspect of Sørbø's later argument relating to the adaptations, in relation to the difficulty of translating Austen's irony on screen. The second chapter is similarly attentive to irony, this time in relation to courtship (pp. 47–78), with four chapters following covering the 1940 Hollywood film, the 1980 BBC TV version, the 1995 BBC TV version, and the 2005 British film, in which the effect of the revision or replacement of Austen's dialogue is considered, from increasing the sentiment, to decreasing the satire, to suggesting an approval of patriarchal culture. The section on *Mansfield Park* is similarly structured, with two chapters on the novel and four on screen versions. The novel chapters address class and patriarchy, and marriage as speculation (again returning to

Sørbø's central interest in irony, here opposed to romance). The four adaptations in question are the 1983 BBC TV series, the 1999 film directed by Patricia Rozema, to which two chapters are given (the most interesting adaptation here in terms of characterization, framing, and narration, and in many ways the version most attuned to the irony in its source-text, as Sørbø argues), and the 2007 ITV film. In a crowded field on Austen adaptation, Sørbø's book provides a clear and coherent path with some persuasive arguments.

Deirdre Le Faye's handsome book, *Jane Austen's Country Life: Uncovering the Rural Backdrop to Her Life, Her Letters and Her Novels*, is packed with colourful nineteenth-century illustrations of rural activities, landscape, and livestock and takes the reader on a pleasant tour through Austen's Hampshire countryside, situating the routine of life in Steventon rectory, as well as at Godmersham and Chawton, within details of a typical rural existence not only for the Austen family but for labourers and landowners too.

Joel Faflak argues that Austen picks up on the early stirrings of a now-dominant cultural trope of happiness as a timeless, affective right, in his analysis of feeling in *Persuasion* and other novels, in 'Jane Austen and the Persuasion of Happiness' (in Faflak and Sha, eds., pp. 98–123; reviewed fully above). In '*Emma*'s Depression' (*SiR* 51[2014] 3–29), Marshall Brown presents a wide-ranging exploration of the conditions of, and possibilities for, happiness in Highbury. Margaret Russett offers a subtle exploration of the media of communication (sentiments, speech, noise, bodies, poetry) in '*Persuasion*, Mediation' (*SiR* 51[2014] 414–77).

The Austen novel explored by *Persuasions* this year is *Mansfield Park*, following on from the Jane Austen Society of North America's AGM title of 'Contexts, Conventions, and Controversies' (*Persuasions* 36[2014]). The volume contains the usual variety of excellent responses to, and interrogations and re-evaluations of, Austen's work, with notable papers on adoption, marriage, noise, morality, editing, habit, and family; its sister journal, *Persuasions On-Line* contains a valuable series of articles on teaching practices for Austen, Gothic parody, and Jane West's novels as a contrast to Austen's (*Persuasions On-Line* 35[2014]). The contexts for engagement with Austen relate to street culture, digitization, and the Austen craze, and the volume also contains a most helpful appendix consisting of the syllabi of the contributors ensuring their good practices can be incorporated and extended.

Elsewhere, Matthew P.M. Kerr explores how new beginnings are figured as repetitions or returns in 'A "First Return to the Sea" in *Persuasion*' (*EIC* 64[2014] 180–201). Shawn Normandin asserts the narratological importance of letters in Austen's completed novels on their own terms, rather than viewing them as having an importance solely in the early epistolary drafts of *Pride and Prejudice* and *Mansfield Park*, in 'Jane Austen's Epistolarity' (*ANQ* 27[2014] 158–65). Kathleen E. Urda provides a thoughtful exploration of the effects which the lack of representation of the much-discussed theatricals have upon interiorization and identity in 'Why the Show Must Not Go On: "Real Character" and the Absence of Theatrical Performances in *Mansfield Park*' (*ECF* 26[2014] 281–302). J.A. Downie turns to time in 'The Chronology of *Mansfield Park*' (*MP* 112[2014] 327–34).

Eric C. Walker analyses *Persuasion* and *Emma* in screen adaptations, in line with the philosophy of Stanley Cavell in relation to marriage and adoption, in a substantial essay, 'Austen and Cavell' (*RCPS* [2014] 36 paras.) Ingrid Tieken-Boon van Ostade examines the familial community surrounding Austen as evinced in her will, in ' "To My Dearest Sister Cassandra": An Analysis of Jane Austen's Will' (*ES* 95[2014] 322–41). Amy Baker attends to character representation in grammatical forms in 'Caught in the Act of Greatness: Jane Austen's Characterization of Elizabeth and Darcy by Sentence Structure in *Pride and Prejudice*' (*Expl* 72[2014] 169–78). Valerie Wainwright explores the tests Austen sets for a range of heroines, including Emma Woodhouse, Elinor Dashwood, Elizabeth Bennet, and Fanny Price, illuminated by recent personality theory, in 'Jane Austen's Challenges, or the Powers of Character and the Understanding' (*P&L* 38[2014] 58–73). In 'What Never Happened: Social Amnesia in *Sense and Sensibility*' (*SEL* 54[2014] 773–91) James O' Rourke offers a detailed rethinking of the narrative structure and focalization techniques employed in the novel which both affirm and destabilize Elinor's perspective. Rebecca Richardson examines the confessional scenes in Austen's novel and locates them in an important formal developmental stage in Austen's writing in 'Dramatizing Intimacy: Confessions and Free Indirect Discourse in *Sense and Sensibility*' (*ELH* 81[2014] 225–44). In 'Feeling Too Much: The Swoon and the (In)Sensible Woman' (*WW* 21[2014] 575–91) Naomi Booth tracks the development of the feminine, erotic spectacle of the swooning subject in *Sense and Sensibility* [1811] from Mackenzie's *The Man of Feeling* [1771].

Susan Spencer provides a good account of the new online resource co-devised by Austen scholar Janine Barchas at http:www.whatjanesaw.org, which seeks to re-create an 1813 exhibition of the paintings of Sir Joshua Reynolds visited by Austen, and also provides other online resources, in 'What Jane Saw' (*ECL* 38[2014] 93–101). In 'Jane Austen and "Banal Shakespeare" ' (*ECF* 27[2014] 105–25) Megan Taylor argues that Austen's few direct quotations from Shakespeare (as opposed to her frequent allusions to and assimilations of his work) in the context of her own works manage to re-energize the recognizable and even the banal. Alessa Johns examines Austen's moral and philosophical debt to a previous woman of letters in 'Jane Austen the Stoic: Channeling Elizabeth Carter and the Bluestocking Ethos' (*WW* 21[2014] 444–63). Nick Bujak considers the shared history of narrative development in fiction and poetry in 'Form and Generic Interrelation in the Romantic Period: Walter Scott's Poetic Influence on Jane Austen' (*Narrative* 22[2014] 45–67).

Olga Volkova rethinks the influence of Scott's novels upon Russian fiction in relation to history, geography, and nation, and traces Gogol's response to Scott, in 'Historicity in *The Bride of Lammermoor* and *Dead Souls*' (*SiR* 51[2014] 149–70). In a welcome analysis of Scott's relatively under-discussed novel of 1828, Katherine Inglis explores the contemporary fascin-ation with blood transfusion in a variety of the novel's reanimation scenes in 'Blood and the Revenant in Walter Scott's *The Fair Maid of Perth*' (in Coyer and Shuttleton, eds., *Scottish Medicine and Literary Culture, 1726–1832*, pp. 196–215). In an exploration of sentiment, sociability, and the threat posed by commercial self-interest to the bonds of community, Natasha Tessone examines Scott's critique of community models past and present in 'Tending to the (National) Household: Walter Scott's *The Antiquary* and "That Happy Commerce" of the Enlightenment' (*ECF* 26[2014] 261–80). Timothy Campbell offers a thoughtful consideration of the ways in which Scott refuses to allow the past to return (in this instance, the old Scottish guillotine) in relation to *The Antiquary*, in 'Pennant's Guillotines and Scott's Antiquary: The Romantic End of the Present' (*RCPS* [2014] 27 paras). Valerie Wallace uncovers the part played by the Reverend Thomas M'Crie, a reviewer for the *Edinburgh Christian Instructor*, and his ally in Nova Scotia, the Reverend Thomas McCulloch, in a dispute over the representation of the Covenanters in Scott's 1816 novel, in 'Fictions of History, Evangelical Whiggism and the Debate over *Old Mortality* in Scotland and Nova Scotia' (in Dew and Price, eds., pp. 182–99; this work is reviewed fully above). L. Levy offers 'A Note on Walter Scott and Irish Literature' (*ScotLR* 6[2014] 91–4). Different forms of transportation, location, and circulation are discussed by Chris Ewers in an analysis of spatial fluidity in 'Roads as Regions, Networks and Flows: *Waverley* and the "Periphery" of Romance' (*JECS* 37[2014] 97–112).

In *A Life with Mary Shelley*, by Barbara Johnson, the late scholar's final study on Mary Shelley is published within a collection of Johnson's earlier essays and some critical and personal tributes to Johnson. The slim volume begins with an introduction by Mary Wilson Carpenter to Johnson's career and publications, her involvement with Shelley criticism from an early stage, and her development as an influential feminist and deconstructionist critic. Johnson's early essays 'The Last Man' [1980], 'My Monster/My Self' [1982], and 'Gender Theory and the Yale School' [1984] are followed by an afterword by Judith Butler, 'Animating Autobiography: Barbara Johnson and Mary Shelley's Monster'. Part II of the volume contains *Mary Shelley and Her Circle* (pp. 51–122), and is in turn followed by an afterword by Shoshana Felman, 'Barbara Johnson's Last Book'. *Mary Shelley and Her Circle* [2009] consists of five chapters on Godwin, Wollstonecraft, Percy Shelley, Byron, and Polidori. As Felman argues in her afterword, the absence of Shelley from this study of her circle is deliberate on Johnson's part, using the structure of absence to explore ideas of marginality and the marginality of Shelley herself, in her writings and her life. The study itself is concise, economical, and has a density of thought that lends it an epigrammatic air at times.

A trio of articles focuses in great depth on one of Mary Shelley's novels in a special volume of *European Romantic Review*. Siobhan Carroll explores Shelley's use of air in *The Last Man* to consider ideas of contagion, global unity, and futurity in 'Mary Shelley's Global Atmosphere' (*ERR* 25[2014] 3–17). In 'A Clandestine Catastrophe: Disciplinary Dissolution in Mary Shelley's *The Last Man*' (*ERR* 25[2014] 19–34) Elizabeth Effinger examines a different type of possibility in the novel, that which is produced when the arts are reduced and almost reduced, and allows for the renewal of music and literature once something of them survives. Ranita Chatterjee turns to Shelley's *Valperga* [1823] as a way of drawing out the relation of the contagion metaphor to biopolitics and the state of the individual's existence within the political, in 'Our Bodies, Our Catastrophes: Biopolitics in Mary Shelley's *The*

Last Man' (*ERR* 25[2014] 35–49). Elsewhere, James P. Carney expands the current scholarly understanding of the effects of classical rhetorical and historical writers on Romanticism in his identification of 'Some Previously Unrecognized References to Classical Historians in Mary Wollstonecraft Shelley's *The Last Man*' (*N&Q* 61[2014] 527–30). Jonas S. Cope argues that an analysis of the character of Winzy in Shelley's short story 'The Mortal Immortal' enables a better understanding of his fellow over-achievers in *Frankenstein* and *Valperga*, in 'The Mortal Immortal: Mary Shelley's "Overreachers" Reconsidered' (*Expl* 72[2014] 122–6). Miranda Burgess reads *Frankenstein* in connection to the overlapping discourses of tropical medicine, epidemiology, and transportation in 'Transporting *Frankenstein*: Mary Shelley's Mobile Figures' (*ERR* 25[2014] 247–65). Anna E. Clark examines the levels of characterization in Shelley's novel to argue that the creature 'is truly unique' because of 'his ability to understand and narrate the perspectives of other characters' (p. 245), in 'Frankenstein; or, The Modern Protagonist' (*ELH* 81[2014] 245–68). Jackson Petsche offers a reading of the vegetarian creature in which he, composed of carcasses, presents a critique of the human consumption of meat, in 'An Already Alienated Animality: *Frankenstein* as a Gothic Narrative of Carnivorism' (*GS* 16[2014] 98–110). Tilottama Rajan's densely argued 'A Peculiar Community: Mary Shelley, Godwin, and the Abyss of Emotion' (in Faflak and Sha, eds., pp. 147–70) reads Shelley's novels as explorations of negativity imbued with the philosophies and attitudes of Byron and Godwin, and existing as an attempt to revisit and revive ideas of community.

Carmel Murphy offers a nuanced consideration of Godwin's intervention in the debate about the uses of history in his 1817 novel *Mandeville* and relates it to his attempt, in the later *History of the Commonwealth in England* [1824–8], to revive republican politics in 'Possibilities of Past and Future: Republican History in William Godwin's *Mandeville* (*KSR* 28[2014] 104–16). In 'Don Quixote and the Sentimental Reader of History in the Works of William Godwin' (in Dew and Price, eds., pp. 162–81) Noelle Gallagher considers the persistence of Godwin's interest in quixotic readers and his approval of sentimental reading practices when reading history as well as fiction, in a chapter that ranges across *Caleb Williams*, 'Of History and Romance', *Thoughts on Man* [1831], *History of the Commonwealth* [1824–8], and *Life of Chaucer* [1803]. Cathy Collett works through Godwin's developing ideas of futurity and the propagation of the human race from *Political Justice* [1793] to *St Leon* [1799] in 'Every Child Left Behind: *St Leon* and William Godwin's Immortal Future' (*ERR* 25[2014] 327–36). Yasmin Solomonescu turns to *Caleb Williams* to test Godwin's attitudes to rhetoric and truth-telling, and whether the two are incompatible or not, in ' "A Plausible Tale": William Godwin's *Things As They Are*' (*ERR* 25[2014] 591–610). Rodney Stenning Edgecombe corrects the provenance of an allusion previously credited to King John, in a discussion of language, parody, and myth-making, in 'Paraphrastic Allusions in *Caleb Williams*' (*N&Q* 61[2014] 502–4). Peter Melville reads Godwin's *St Leon* in the light of Kant's essay 'On a Supposed Right to Lie from Altruistic Motives' [1797] and finds much to say about the complexity of truth-telling in both writers' philosophies, in 'Lying with Godwin and Kant: Truth and Duty in *St Leon*' (*ECent* 55[2014] 19–37).

There was an interesting collection of essays on Mary Wollstonecraft in *Hypatia* this year. Alan M.S.J. Coffee considers the philosophy of independence in a range of Wollstonecraft's writings, including *The Wrongs of Woman*, in 'Freedom as Independence: Mary Wollstonecraft and the Grand Blessing of Life' (*Hypatia* 29[2014] 908–24). Martina Reuter tracks Wollstonecraft's critique of Rousseau's views of nature, sensibility, and women in '"Like a Fanciful Kind of *Half* Being": Mary Wollstonecraft's Criticism of Jean-Jacques Rousseau' (*Hypatia* 29[2014] 925–41), and Lena Hallendius concludes with a searching evaluation of the commodification of rights in *The Wrongs of Woman* in 'Mary Wollstonecraft's Feminist Critique of Property: On Becoming a Thief from Principle' (*Hypatia* 29[2014] 942–57). Diana Edelman-Young examines Wollstonecraft's *A Vindication of the Rights of Woman* in the context of natural and reproductive sciences to suggest that Wollstonecraft uses the language of such sciences to argue explicitly and implicitly for gender equality, in 'Chubby Cheeks and the Bloated Monster: The Politics of Reproduction in Mary Wollstonecraft's *Vindication*' (*ERR* 25[2014] 683–704). Catherine Packham examines another of Wollstonecraft's works in a different context, that of political economy, in her analysis of the representation of bread shortages in '"The Common Grievance of the Revolution": Bread, the Grain Trade, and Political Economy in Wollstonecraft's *View of the French Revolution*' (*ERR* 25[2014] 705–22). Ingrid Horrocks explores the rhythms created in Wollstonecraft's arguments by her idiosyncratic use of dashes (categorizable in three separate ways) in different print editions in '"– –Pugh!": Rereading Punctuation through Wollstonecraft's *Letters Written During a Short Residence*' (*WW* 21[2014] 488–508). In an exploration of rhetoric Inna Volkova argues that examples are used as the starting point for Wollstonecraft's argument, rather than the usual critical view of them as simply a supplement to argument, in '"I Have Looked Steadily around Me": The Power of Examples of Mary Wollstonecraft's *A Vindication of the Rights of Woman*' (*WS* 43[2014] 892–910). A fascinating and almost entirely unknown work of Romantic fiction is presented and examined in '*Selene*: Lady Mount Cashell's Lunar Utopia' (*WW* 21[2014 559–74) by Anne Markey. The three-volume novel dates from 1823 and was never published. Analysing the novel's radical political perspectives and the targets of its utopian satires, Markey makes a compelling case for much greater critical attention to be paid to Mount Cashell's writing, and that she deserves to be known for more than her position on the fringes of the Godwin–Shelley circle and as Mary Wollstonecraft's most famous pupil.

The work of Ann Radcliffe receives several significant re-evaluations in an authoritative and compelling new collection of essays. In *Ann Radcliffe, Romanticism and the Gothic*, Dale Townshend and Angela Wright have gathered some of the most recognizable and influential Gothic critics whose work has done so much to shape the current critical field of Gothic fiction and Romantic Gothic studies more widely; here Radcliffe's central position in the field of Romantic Gothic studies is variously recovered, reappraised, and problematized in the wide-ranging collection of chapters. The collection is divided into three sections. Part I, 'Cultural Contexts', begins with the editors' contribution, 'Gothic and Romantic Engagements: The Critical Reception of Ann Radcliffe, 1789–1850'. It offers a point of orientation for the newcomer to Radcliffe, presenting a useful range of critical responses to her novels, from early dismissals to the blazing celebration of her works by the time of her death in 1823, and provides a helpful overview of the ways in which Radcliffe established a type of novel-writing which produced both astute imitations and critical praise, and doggerel and critical condemnations, which 'Augmented rather than tarnished' the years of silence before Radcliffe's death (p. 14). In the final section the editors examine the views of Radcliffe's skill held by later Romantics such as Hazlitt, Scott, Percy Shelley, and Leigh Hunt, and trace Radcliffe's progression towards the high place she attained in her contemporaries' literary canon. The second chapter, Joe Bray's 'Ann Radcliffe, Precursors and Portraits' takes up the question of Radcliffe's literary qualities and her ability to be at once realistic and fanciful, in Bray's analysis of portrait painting in Radcliffe's fiction and the significance of the discontinuities between the image, or likeness, and the person depicted therein, tracing its potential for emotional affect and the rupturing of reality. The next chapter, 'Ann Radcliffe and Romantic Print Culture' by Edward Jacobs, examines Radcliffe's effects on the form and the status of the novel. Jacobs argues that Radcliffe's fusion of fiction and poetry in her novels 'staged and constructed, to an unprecedented extent' the division between the intensive reading of poetry and the casual reading of popular fiction, leading a new form of mass-market fiction which affected print culture more widely (p. 49). In chapter 4, 'Ann Radcliffe and Politics', James Watt assesses recent critical views of Radcliffe's political position, noting the irony inherent in attempts to construct Radcliffe's views by largely depending on the political opinions held by her husband and other male relatives. Watt carefully negotiates the competing critical claims for conservatism, loyalism, and reformism, and concludes persuasively that it is difficult to trace any engagement with contemporary politics in her work, and that any such claims become more tenuous the more closely we attend to Radcliffe's rhetorical sophistication. Part II, entitled 'Ann Radcliffe's Creative Output', begins with Alison Milbank's 'Ways of Seeing in Ann Radcliffe's Early Fiction: *The Castles of Athlin and Dunbayne* (1789) and *A Sicilian Romance* (1790)'. Here Milbank examines the ways in which Radcliffe adopts the perspective of a 'medieval ballad writer' (p. 85) which, Milbank argues, enables Radcliffe to gain a detached perspective. While this perspective anticipates Romantic poetic vision in certain ways, ultimately it becomes Gothic rather than Romantic, and Milbank offers detailed analysis of the two novels and the double perspective achieved by their melancholic characters and condition. In chapter 6 Diane Long Hoeveler discusses the enormous popularity among readers and influences upon writers, publishers, and the print market of one of Radcliffe's novels throughout the nineteenth century in 'The Heroine, the Abbey, and Popular Romantic Textuality: *The Romance of the Forest* (1791)'. In the next chapter Robert Miles takes as his starting point the old critical opposition of Romanticism to the Gothic (high and low, poetry and prose, irony and sensation) and casts a critical eye over Radcliffe's eligibility to be considered as a Romantic writer by interrogating the concept of Romanticism itself in the light of a new understanding of the popular (low, prosaic, sensational) and its claims on Romanticism, in 'Popular Romanticism and the Problem of Belief: *The Mysteries of Udolpho* (1794)'. In chapter 8, JoEllen DeLucia's 'Transnational Aesthetics in Ann Radcliffe's *A Journey Made in the Summer of 1794 [...]* (1795)', the relationships between Radcliffe's travel writing and contemporary discourses of aesthetics are explored, with DeLucia arguing that in Radcliffe's writing about the wartime Continent and the Lake District in 1794 she uses techniques that often jar or startle the reader, which enable 'spectators to rethink the occlusions and displacements of the picturesque', and that Radcliffe may be considered, with Burke and Paine, as a writer about citizenship, statelessness, and national belonging (p. 145). The next chapter presents Jerrold E. Hogle's contribution, 'Recovering the Walpolean Gothic: *The Italian; or, The Confessional of the Black Penitents* (1796–1797)', in which he reads Radcliffe's *The Italian* as her Dissenting and rational response to Lewis's *The Monk*, which is also informed by, and can be read further as a response to, Walpole's two prefaces to *The Castle of Otranto*, resulting in a novel which exemplifies Radcliffe's contradictory visions of progressive and regressive social history, and which 're-establishes the roots of new "romance" in Walpole's Gothic and thus the grounding of Romanticism in the Gothic's ungrounded mixture of openly incompatible beliefs and styles' (p. 167). Part II concludes with Samuel Baker's chapter, 'Ann Radcliffe Beyond the Grave: *Gaston de Blondeville* (1826) and Its Accompanying Texts', which discusses (via a brief cinematic fantasy) the reasons for the posthumous publication of Radcliffe's novel amid selections from her journals and poetry and the polite critical neglect it has received since. Part III, 'Ann Radcliffe and Romantic Literary Culture', contains the final three chapters. Jane Stabler, in 'Ann Radcliffe's Poetry: The Poetics of Refrain and Inventory', produces a perceptive and rewarding reading of Radcliffe's poetry as poetry in its own right, not simply as poems which interrupt the novels. Stabler's formal attention to the poems published in an unauthorized collection of 1816 demonstrates Radcliffe's technical skill and deliberation in using repetition to explore ideas of creativity, escape, and agency. Sue Chaplin's chapter, 'Ann Radcliffe and Romantic-Era Fiction', discusses Radcliffe's immediate literary effect on contemporary women writers such as Eliza Parsons, Eliza Fenwick, and Maria Regina Roche, her contribution to ideas about literary taste in the period, consumption, and a final comparison drawn between Scott and Radcliffe and the ways in which each writer examines Gothic 'hauntings' (p. 217). The final chapter, chapter 13, comes from Diego Saglia, '"A Portion of the Name": Stage Adaptation of Radcliffe's Fiction, 1794–1806', which is an account of the rapidity with which Radcliffe's novels reached the Romantic stage, how they were reshaped in order to suit it, and the ways in which the stage dealt with Radcliffe's concerns with history and ideology.

Two chapters of Gothic interest appear in *Heteronormativity in Eighteenth-Century Literature and Culture*, edited by Ana De Freitas Boe and Abby Coykendall. Abby Coykendall briefly discusses the reputation of Horace Walpole as a feminine man in 'Queer Counterhistory and the Specter of Effeminacy' (pp. 111–29), and elsewhere in the same volume George E.

Haggerty considers the 'quasi-perfunctory endings' of Radcliffe's *The Mysteries of Udolpho* [1794], Dacre's *Zofloya; or, The Moor* [1806] and Maturin's *Melmoth the Wanderer* [1820], arguing that attempts to re-establish heteronormativity at the conclusion of each are unsuccessful, and that they exemplify the ambivalence at the heart of the Gothic genre, in 'The Failure of Heteronormativity in the Gothic Novel' (pp. 131–49). Scott J. Juengel debates Kantian hospitality with a brief swerve towards Radcliffe's *The Italian* [1797] in 'Late Hospitality: Kant, Radcliffe, and the Assassin at the Gate' (*ERR* 25[2014] 289–98). Peter Otto examines the connections between identity and location in ' "Where Am I, and What?": Architecture, Environment, and the Transformation of Experience in Radcliffe's *The Mysteries of Udolpho*' (*ERR* 25[2014] 299–308).

Irish Gothic continues to gain critical ground, and this year Christina Morin and Niall Gillespie's edited collection *Irish Gothics: Genres, Forms, Modes, and Traditions, 1760–1890* contains some provoking arguments about and reflections upon what that branch of Gothic studies might address. Of relevance here are the following chapters. Diane Long Hoeveler expands the focus of her recent work on anti-Catholicism in Gothic literature to include the popular chapbooks imported and circulated in Ireland in the early nineteenth century, in 'The Irish Protestant Imaginary: The Cultural Contexts for the Gothic Chapbooks Published by Bennett Dugdale, 1800–52' (pp. 34–57), and Niall Gillespie discusses the Gothicization of the Irish political and geographical landscape, as well as popular literature and poetry, in 'Irish Jacobin Gothic, c.1796–1825' (pp. 58–73). Jim Shanahan, in 'Suffering Rebellion: Irish Gothic Fiction, 1799–1830' (pp. 74–93), analyses John Banim's novel *The Boyne Water* and *The Nowlans* [1826], Maturin's *Melmoth the Wanderer* [1820], and *The Milesian Chief* [1812] amidst a consideration of the seeming inseparability of political rebellion and atrocity, and the fraught engagement of Irish Gothic with both silence and screams in the face of suffering in the historical and literary aftermath of the 1798 rebellion. Finally, Richard Haslam examines how Melmoth's 'demonic pact device' (p. 113) is taken up by the writers Banim, Griffin, James Clarence Mangan, and William Carleton and used to incorporate Catholic perspectives into an anti-Catholic mode of writing in their Gothic tales, in 'Maturin's Catholic Heirs: Expanding the Limits of Irish Gothic' (pp. 113–29).

Amy Culley's engaging and detailed study, *British Women's Life Writing, 1760–1840* (reviewed above), contains chapters of particular interest here also. These are the chapters on Mary Robinson and Mary Wollstonecraft. In 'The Literary Family and the "Aristocracy of Genius" in the *Memoirs* of Mary Robinson' (pp. 103–15), Robinson's *Memoirs of the Late Mrs Robinson* [1801] provides Culley with the grounds for a thoughtful examination of the connections between Robinson's complex memoir and her other many and varied literary productions, the still vexed question of Robinson's manipulation of her scandalous reputation, and her support for other women writers. In ' "The Little Hero of Each Tale": Mary Wollstonecraft's Travelogue and Revolutionary Autobiography' (pp. 173–88) Culley turns to *A Short Residence in Sweden, Norway and Denmark* [1796] and views it within the framework of *An Historical and Moral View of the French Revolution* [1794] to demonstrate how 'Wollstonecraft developed personal narrative as a historical mode in the course of her career' (p. 174), suggesting further that in *A Short Residence* Wollstonecraft 'avoids personal confession in favour of a life writing work that is at once secret, intimate, and yet outwardly focused, an effect created in part by correspondence' (p. 179). The chapter continues with a discussion of Godwin's understanding of 'the relational self' in his memoir of Wollstonecraft (p. 185), and concludes with a consideration of how Mary Hays's 'Memoirs of Mary Wollstonecraft' [1800] may be viewed, like Godwin's text, as a means by which Wollstonecraft's revolutionary ideas can be circulated in biographical writing as well as in her own, concluding that 'like Helen Maria Williams, Wollstonecraft moved Romantic autobiography away from solitude, isolation, and introspection in favour of socially engaged and dialogic modes that in turn inspired auto/biographical writing and self-examination in others' (p. 173). Robinson's *Memoirs* are also discussed by Whitney Arnold in 'Mary Robinson's *Memoirs* and the Terrors of Literary Obscurity' (*WS* 43[2014] 733–49) in a reading which takes in Robinson's attack on her contemporary print world and explores the Gothic structure of the *Memoirs* text itself.

A different type of community is uncovered in *British Women Writers and the Asiatic Society of Bengal, 1785–1835: Re-Orienting Anglo-India*. Kathryn S. Freeman delves into a world of scholarly activity in her study of the Asiatic Society of Bengal, whose members studied and translated Sanskrit, wrote poetry, and worked for the British East India Company, making their orientalist studies look more Said's orientalism in practice. Freeman's introduction takes the reader through recent critical history and postcolonial perspectives, and separates women's writing from men's in this period, arguing that they need to be extricated 'from assumptions behind scholarship that represents them as participating in the cultural imperialism that postcolonialism attributes to both the Orientalists and canonical male writers; this inclusiveness has subjected these women authors to a discourse that limits critical engagement with them alongside male writers and the east. My contention is that women's writing connects Orientalism's literalized gendering of east and west in its ambivalence towards nondualism' (pp. 15–16). Arguing that this period of literary history in Anglo-Indian culture is pre-colonial, not colonial or postcolonial, Freeman analyses a range of novels, plays, and poetry by women in the period to uncover their critique of Western dualism, and the binaries relating to reason and emotion, masculinity and femininity, authority and submission, within their encounters with Indian philosophy, culture, and language. Elizabeth Hamilton's *Translation of the Letters of a Hindoo Rajah* [1796] and Sydney Owenson's *The Missionary* [1811] receive fresh and rewarding interpretations here in Freeman's analysis of authorial control and metatextuality, and the ambivalence throughout the sentimental novel of Phebe Gibbes's *Hartly House, Calcutta* [1789] is usefully recovered. Elsewhere, a fascinating account of the development of a discourse surrounding vegetarianism in the midst of British imperial discourse in India is offered by Marguerite M. Regan, who discusses *Hartly House, Calcutta* and *Translations of the Letter of a Hindoo Rajah* in 'Feminism, Vegetarianism, and Colonial Resistance in Eighteenth-Century British

Novels (*SNNTS* 46[2014] 275–92). Elsewhere, 'Empire, Race, and the Debate over the Indian Marriage Market in Elizabeth Hamilton's *Memoirs of Modern Philosophers* (1800)', by John C. Leffel, traces Hamilton's absorption of reproduction of contemporary prejudices regarding the Indian marriage market and female British emigrants in her *Translation of the Letters of a Hindoo Rajah* [1796] as well as her re-evaluation of these prejudices in her next novel (*ECF* 26[2014] 427–54).

A community of maternal authority is explored in Rebecca Davies's well-written and engaging study, also discussed in Chapter XII. *Written Maternal Authority and Eighteenth-Century Education in Britain: Educating by the Book* takes as its starting point the author's claim that women writers' acceptance of the socially approved role of woman as the educator of children allowed them to create a new textual authority as educational writers. From this seemingly simple claim Davies constructs a detailed analysis of the shift from oral or transitory maternal advice to the written authority of educational writers in a variety of genres. Six chapters take us through the writings and authorial development of influential writers: Sarah Fielding, Mary Wollstonecraft, Maria Edgeworth, Jane Austen, and the now obscure Ann Martin Taylor, with a selection of her works from 1814 to 1819. The study opens with a chapter on Samuel Richardson, and from this unexpected beginning Davies argues persuasively that the models for exemplary maternal authority in place at the end of the eighteenth century were absent at the mid-century point, evinced in Richardson's fraught attempts in *Pamela II* [1741] to negotiate existing models of femininity in order to construct a new version of his character as a mother, suggesting that Richardson's solution is to present Pamela as a mother who writes her authority rather than performing it. Through the following five chapters Davies traces the development of this written form of maternal authority and educational discipline in relation to Dissenting culture, empiricism and epistemology, radical politics, and the developing form of the eighteenth-century novel. Despite the writers' successful establishment of a discourse of maternal authority in their texts, such a discourse, as Davies shows, remained stubbornly limited to the written word, and never quite made the leap into the public sphere as a discourse of feminine authority.

Published in 2013 but not reviewed last year is Morgan Rooney's substantial study on *The French Revolution Debate and the British Novel, 1790–1814: The Struggle for History's Authority*. In this Rooney traces the development of the historical novel, ending with the publication of Scott's *Waverley* in 1814 and taking in radical and conservative fiction in the 1790s, the emergence of the national tale, and the many debates on the proper use of historical discourse in writing at the end of the eighteenth century and into the nineteenth. Many of the novels Rooney examines will be familiar to readers of Romantic fiction now, from those by Godwin (*St Leon* [1799]) Edgeworth (*Castle Rackrent* [1800]), and Charlotte Smith (*The Old Manor House* [1793]), to George Walker (*The Vagabond* [1799]), Robert Bisset (*Douglas* [1800]), and Jane West (*A Tale of the Times* [1799]), but rather than arrange these authors on grounds of political opposition (radical versus conservative, Jacobin versus anti-Jacobin) Rooney attends to the ways in which novelists more generally turned to and used history in these decades, writing that 'the literary landscape of the 1790s is populated largely by figures who are operating under an interventionist agenda, and this study examines the (unintended) generic consequences of their interventions' (p. 10). That said, after setting out the debate for history and authority in 1790s political and philosophical writings in his first two chapters (Richard Price, Edmund Burke, James Mackintosh, Mary Wollstonecraft, Thomas Paine) Rooney goes on to devote a chapter to reformist and Jacobin novels, and another chapter to anti-Jacobin and conservative novels. These binaries are hard to shake off, but Rooney's discussion of the novels fills in an important backdrop in the history of generic development, on which Scott so ably capitalized. Mooney claims the work of Sydney Owenson (*The Wild Irish Girl* [1806]) and Jane Porter (*Thaddeus of Warsaw* [1803] and *The Scottish Chiefs* [1810]) as Scott's most active precursors, before concluding with an analysis of *Waverley* itself.

In 'Making History: Social Unrest, Work and the Post-French Revolution Historical Novel' (in Dew and Price, eds., pp. 145–66) Fiona Price brings to light a fascinating range of novels like the anonymous *Charles Dacres: or, the Voluntary Exile, An Historical Novel, Founded on Facts* [1797] and *Lioncel; or, Adventures of an Emigrant* [1803], and E. Cornelia Knight's *Marcus Flaminius* [1792] in a detailed argument about the immediate post-revolutionary origins of the awareness of history as a mass experience which has previously been argued to have occurred much later. In ' "By force, or openly, what could be done?": Godwin, Smith, Wollstonecraft, and the Gagging Acts Novel' (pp. 109–36), John Bugg turns to fiction's engagement with politics in his new study of silence and repression in the 1790s, *Five Long Winters: The Trials of British Romanticism*. Bugg's selection of novels consists of Godwin's *Caleb Williams*, Charlotte Smith's *Marchmont* [1796], and Wollstonecraft's *The Wrongs of Woman, or Maria* [1798], arguing that they respond to political attack in their very form as well as in their content. Throughout his study Bugg examines a variety of 1790s literature illuminated by his central argument of the texts' negotiation of political repression during the revolutionary debates, the Gagging Acts of 1795, and this chapter is an important contribution to our understanding of political fiction and its response in form as well as content to contemporary debates. Bugg writes: 'To trace the arc described by *Caleb Williams*, *Marchmont*, and *The Wrongs of Woman* is to see obfuscation and reticence entering into the conceptual, structural, and even grammatical shape of the novel, as writers discover more sensitive and complex modes for formally registering the trials of the Pitt era' (p. 111).

Anne Frey provides an account of Agnes C. Hall, author of twelve novels written between 1819 and 1834 using the pseudonym Rosalia St Clair, her engagement with the national tale, historical novels, and the literary models provided by Sydney Owenson in 'The National Tale and the Pseudonymous Author: Mobile Identity in the "Rosalia St. Clair" Novels' (*ERR* 25[2014] 181–99). Hall's 'generic incoherence' (p. 182), Frey argues, is what provides a cosmopolitanism lacking in more conventional national tales. Carmel Murphy presents a well-informed reading of Charlotte Smith's engagement with the historical novel to critique government, authority, and Edmund Burke in 'Jacobin History: Charlotte Smith's *Old Manor House* and the French

Revolution Debate' (*Romanticism* 20[2014] 271–81). Smith's early depictions of suburban space, rather than her usual rural scenes, provide the focus for Kate Scarth's interesting exploration of how women occupied and engaged with such locations in 'Elite Metropolitan Culture, Women, and Greater London in Charlotte Smith's *Emmeline* and *Celestina*' (*ERR* 25[2014] 627–48). Roxane Eberle offers a thoughtful account of the ways in which Amelia Opie and her husband John wrote, lived, painted, and debated Romantic creativity in the 1790s, in 'Amelia and John Opie: Conjugal Sociability and Romanticism's Professional Arts' (*SiR* 51[2014] 319–41). John B. Pierce and Shelley King recount the recent discovery of a lost poetry notebook, contrasting its contents to the recent *Collected Poems* and the Oxford edition of Opie's poems, in 'The Rediscovery of Amelia Opie's Cromer Notebook' (*N&Q* 61[2014] 498–501). Matthew J. Rigilano applies Lacanian theory and produces a lucid and engaging analysis of literalization in 'Absorption, Literality, and Feminine Subjectivity in Sophia Lee's *The Recess*' (*ECF* 26[2014] 209–32). Halina Adams looks at the ways in which Helen Maria Williams uses the site of the Bastille in her travel writing as a way to think about past, present, and future in 'Imagining the Nation: Transforming the Bastille in Williams's *Letters Written in France* (1790)' (*ERR* 25[2014] 723–41). An interesting account of Elizabeth Inchbald's farce from 1788 and its connection to French scientific theories about, and against, animal magnetism is offered in Nathaniel Leach's exploration of theatrical and satirical attacks on the discourses of power in 'Gendering Pseudo-Science: Inchbald's *Animal Magnetism*' (*LitComp* 11[2014] 715–23). Another of Inchbald's plays is discussed, this time *A Mogul's Tale*, in an exploration of spectacle by Paula R. Backscheider in 'From *The Emperor of the Moon* to the Sultans' Prison' (*SECC* 43[2014] 219–37).

Some interesting aspects of Romantic fiction in translation are presented by Laura Kirkley's new edition of *Caroline of Lichtfield*, the popular sentimental novel by Isabelle de Montolieu from 1786 which was translated by Thomas Holcroft into English in the same year that it first appeared in French. The introduction sets up the literary and political world of Isabelle de Montolieu, the prolific Swiss writer and translator (including of Austen's novels). Kirkley addresses the surprising popularity that a sentimental romance had among writers like Mary Wollstonecraft, Anna Barbauld, and Holcroft himself, uncovering Montolieu's philosophical inheritance (Rousseau plays a central role here) and her place in Swiss literary circles. The edition is completed by an appendix containing Montolieu's charming songs, substantial editorial notes, and a list of textual variants between the original English text and the editions from 1786 (second edition), 1797, and 1798. Another new edition to note is Ann Yearsley's *The Royal Captives* of 1795 (in *The Collected Works of Ann Yearsley*, reviewed in Section 3 below).

Regina Hewitt argues for a new and rewarding reading of 'Maria Edgeworth's *Harrington* as a Utopian Novel' (*SNNTS* 46[2014] 293–314), suggesting that the novel operates in a more beneficial and socially progressive way when viewed as 'methodologically utopian' (p. 295) in its aims to overcome anti-Semitism, rather than as a novel which concludes with a disappointing and prejudiced dismissal of Judaism. Alex Howard analyses the ways in which the theory and practice of reading from Maria Edgeworth and Richard Lovell Edgeworth's *Practical Education* [1798] are embodied and disrupted in Edgeworth's *Castle Rackrent* [1800], and argues for its connection to contemporary political discourse, in 'The Pains of Attention: Paratextual Reading in *Practical Education* and *Castle Rackrent*' (*NCL* 69[2014] 293–318). In an article about Edgeworth's short stories, Ashley L. Cohen argues persuasively for their shared political concerns relating to 1790s discourses, rather than to the more usual interpretations based on historical practice as represented in the stories, in 'Wage Slavery, Oriental Despotism, and Global Labor Management in Maria Edgeworth's *Popular Tales*' (*ECent* 55[2014] 193–215). Slaney Chadwick Ross examines the metaphorical discussion of English, Scottish, and Irish concerns as interdependent in Edgeworth's little-discussed closet drama from 1817, in 'Maria Edgeworth's *The Rose, Thistle, and Shamrock*: Symbolic Unification, Women's Education, and the Marriage Plot' (*ECent* 55[2014] 377–90). Mary Mullen explores the transhistorical disruptions and discordances in *Castle Rackrent* and their opposition to Edgeworth's ideas of history elsewhere in her work in 'Anachronistic Aesthetics: Maria Edgeworth and the "Uses" of History' (*ECF* 26[2014] 233–59). David Francis Taylor, in 'Edgeworth's *Belinda* and the Gendering of Caricature' (*ECF* 26[2014] 593–624), casts new light on the use of caricature in the novel, and argues for its important relation to the other discourses surrounding women's bodies in the novel. Deborah Weiss turns to another of Edgeworth's relatively neglected writings, *The Parent's Assistant* [1796; 1800], for a discussion of the contribution to capitalist theory made by Edgeworth, in 'Maria Edgeworth's Infant Economics: Capitalist Culture, Good-Will Networks and "Lazy Lawrence"' (*JECS* 37[2014] 395–408). Catherine Craft-Fairchild returns to the fraught portrayal of Anglo-Jewish culture and identity in 'The "Jewish Question" on Both Sides of the Atlantic: *Harrington* and the Correspondence between Maria Edgeworth and Rachel Mordecai Lazarus' (*ECL* 38[2014] 30–63), examining how Edgeworth's inaccurate representation is bound up in her inability to move effectively between lived experience and the solely textual, and her reliance upon previous, prejudiced written accounts.

Peter deGabriele considers the connections between letters and the law in 'The Legal Fiction and Epistolary Form: Frances Burney's *Evelina*' (*JEMS* 14:ii[2014] 22–40). Eleanor C.L. Crouch surveys a wide range of Burney's writings to support an argument about her subtle use of nerve theory in her novels in relation to gender and social behaviour, in 'Nerve Theory and Sensibility: '"Delicacy" in the Work of Fanny Burney' (*LitComp* 11[2014] 206–17). Jason S. Farr explores the difficult position women (unlike men) occupied in the eighteenth century when intellectual brilliance was not matched by physical perfection, in 'Sharp Minds/Twisted Bodies: Intellect, Disability, and Female Education in Frances Burney's *Camilla*' (*ECent* 55[2014] 1–17; also discussed in Chapter XII).

Jacqueline George considers the paradox of individual literary confessions merging with mass-market commodities in 'Confessions of a Mass Public: Reflexive Formations of Subjectivity in Early Nineteenth-Century British Fiction' (*SNNTS* 46[2014] 387–405). George discusses a subgenre of Romantic fiction here, the fictional confession, drawing upon a range of obscure and often outrageous novels from 1814 to 1839 by authors such as Edmund Carrington, John Ainslie, and Thomas Little. Lauren McCoy interrogates histories of the novel which place the *roman-à-clef* as one of the casualties of the novel's progress towards realism, and argues that its continuation invigorated Regency reading practices, in 'Literary Gossip: Caroline Lamb's *Glenarvon* and the *Roman-à-clef*' (*ECF* 27[2014] 127–50). Nicholas M. Williams, in ' "The Liberty Wherewith We Are Made Free": Belief and Liberal Individualism in James Hogg's *Private Memoirs and Confessions of a Justified Sinner*' (*SHW* 24[2014] 32–41) considers the ways in which the structure of belief and the divided structure of the novel work with and against each other, informed by Charles Taylor's arguments in *A Secular Age* [2007].

3. Poetry

In this section, Matthew Ward covers general work on Romantic poetry and work on poets from A to K; Paul Whickman covers poets from L to Z.

The majority of works published on Romantic poetry in 2014 focused on individual authors. But there were several general studies in the field of Romanticism that included discussion of poetry. A number of these works are considered in more detail in the Section 1 of this chapter, and so are only briefly highlighted here. *Bodily Pain in Romantic Literature* by Jeremy Davies includes discussion of Samuel Taylor Coleridge and Percy Shelley amongst its brilliant analysis of feeling in the period. Percy Shelley is also the subject of a chapter in Joel Faflak and Richard C. Sha's edited collection, *Romanticism and the Emotions*, as are Byron and Wordsworth, alongside a number of prose writers. Amidst its socio-cultural interests, Sarah Houghton-Walker's *Representations of the Gypsy in the Romantic Period* finds plenty of room for the role and figuration of the gypsy in John Clare's and William Wordsworth's verse. Though it is more concerned with the prose writing of the period in its valuable charting of a distinct English identity, David Higgins's *Romantic Englishness: Local, National and Global Selves, 1780–1850* also fruitfully explores Clare and Wordsworth, as well as Samuel Taylor Coleridge. Cynthia Schoolar Williams's *Hospitality and the Transatlantic Imagination, 1815–1835* reflects on the shadow cast by the Napoleonic Wars, and offers a chapter on Felicia Hemans in the light of this context. These studies are all discussed in detail above.

Two further important studies were published by Cambridge University Press in 2014. The pervasiveness of conflict in the Romantic period is of central concern to Jeffrey N. Cox in *Romanticism in the Shadow of War: Literary Culture in the Napoleonic War Years*. As he reminds us at the start of his study, 'war is never far from the central works of the Romantic imagination' (p. 1)—whether that be the discharged soldiers or the ruined cottages populating Wordsworth's poetic landscapes, or the romances of the Cockney School that critique and counter the drums of war. Cox congenially redraws the critical field of Romanticism, challenging the monumentalizing turn towards the 'Big Six' as well as the big military and cultural battles of the period. Instead, he argues for the Romantic period as 'an era of small feints, limited campaigns, border raids' (p. 4), both militarily and in the production of its artworks. Cox's nuanced readings of Barbauld, Byron, the Shelleys, and the Cockney School reveal how a range of poets produce 'new forms of art', as they respond to 'moments of crisis' (p. 7). *Romanticism in the Shadow of War* is a superb example of the historicist approach in which Cox has long excelled, and as such it achieves its author's ambition to illustrate that sound historicist readings arise less from a 'hermeneutics of suspicion' (p. 5) than from a celebration of aesthetics amidst awareness of ideological contexts.

The relation between the first- and second-generation Romantic poets is the subject of Andrew Warren's *The Orient and the Young Romantics*. Warren's thought-provoking monograph explores why Byron, Percy Shelley, and Keats so frequently set their works in orientalized settings or Eastern locations. Looking beyond the simple answer, namely that everyone else was doing it at the time too, this fascinating account of canonical poets argues that each writer criticizes the growing imperialism of Europe and the aesthetics as well as the politics of Western expansionism. Warren reads the second-generation Romantic poets as self-conscious and ironic in their handling of the Orient, as they seek creatively to critique the 'Orientalism practised by the eighteenth century and the First Generation Romantics' (p. 3). Indeed, alongside his perceptive close readings that afford fresh insight into well-known poems like *Lamia* and *The Revolt of Islam*, Warren's chief contribution is in noticing the way his young Romantics anticipate key debates within postcolonial studies, not least, as Warren lays out, the fact that the construction of the Orient through the orientalized phantasmagoria of the previous generation is consistently confronted by the second generation through Romantic irony.

This year saw the publication of two large critical editions of two relatively non-canonical abolitionist poets. The first of these, Paul Baines's *The Collected Writings of Edward Rushton*, is a triumph. As well as an abolitionist, Rushton was an accomplished seaman, poet, and bookseller. This is a well-presented scholarly hardback, typical of Liverpool University Press publications, and this first critical edition of Rushton's work is serious without appearing overly formal or dry. Space is given to Rushton's poetry and prose in a manner that allows them to speak for themselves. Baines does not clutter the text with lengthy notes concerning textual variants, history, or glosses, instead confining these to a detailed but concise 'commentary' at the end of the volume. The effect of this is to emphasize the Liverpool-based Rushton as a writer of merit who exceeds his marginal reputation in British Romanticism, and not simply as a figure of regional, historical, or academic interest. Indeed, this edition, containing all his known works, shows Rushton to be a far more prolific writer of poetry than of prose. Not all of Rushton's poems can be labelled 'abolitionist', even if slavery and colonialism are his most common themes and the subjects of his strongest poetry. In this light it is tempting to view Rushton as a transatlantic poet, not only for biographical reasons—his seamanship—but because of the transatlantic themes of much of his writing. His prose, for instance, includes a letter to George Washington admonishing him for 'continuing to be a Proprietor of Slaves' [1797] while his poem 'The Dismember'd Empire' [1782] opens with the Liverpool-based poet reflecting on the seven years of the American War of Independence and the feared 'dismemberment' of the transatlantic empire: 'SEVEN times the globe has made its annual round, / Sublimely rolling thro' the vast profound, / Since Britons first aspir'd to govern slaves, / And hurl'd destruction 'cross th'Atlantic waves' (p. 33, ll. 1–4).

Rushton's relative critical neglect in the nineteenth and twentieth centuries is detailed in Baines's introduction. Although this may partly be due to the nineteenth-century distaste for his radical politics, and the peculiar nature of his posthumous publication, the Popean echoes of this opening passage suggest another reason. Baines sees Rushton's 'splicing of the high diction of Pope and Gray with the populist lyric forms sung by actual sailors in pubs' as 'proto-Romantic' (p. 17). Yet although Rushton engages with themes and forms popular among his Romantic contemporaries, such as poems on the deaths of Chatterton and Burns as well as Wordsworthian echoes in poems such as 'To the Redbreast', much of his work is in the form and style of earlier, eighteenth-century poetry. Could Rushton, therefore, simply have been seen as unfashionable? Nevertheless, he is most certainly a poet worthy of critical attention, and Baines's excellent edition will serve an important role in adding Rushton to the wider Romantic canon.

The other substantial critical edition appearing in 2014 was the three-volume *Collected Works of Ann Yearsley*, edited by Kerri Andrews. Yearsley was a formerly impoverished Bristol poet, playwright, and novelist known far more for her fascinating biographical details, many of which are detailed in Robert Southey's 1831 account, than the actual works that she produced. Although this biographical focus is typical of Romantic-period writers outside the 'Big Six'—though such attention has of course historically overshadowed much of their work too—it is nevertheless more commonly the case for women writers, and Yearsley most particularly. This monumental edition of Yearsley's works from the Pickering Masters series serves to buck the trend.

Of the three volumes of Andrews's edition, only the first contains Yearsley's poetry (as well as letters); the two further volumes contain her play, *Earl Goodwin* (first performed in 1789), and the novel *The Royal Captives* [1795]. Yearsley only produced three volumes of poetry, but Andrews includes her 'Occasional Poems' and, most interestingly, the poems published in various newspapers of the period. This aligns Yearsley's publishing practices with those of contemporary poets such as Coleridge, and such a discovery is evidence of Andrews's impressive scholarship. Elsewhere, Andrews does not allow her research to crowd the poetry and letters by keeping paratextual elements to a minimum. Apart from a few sparse headnotes, Andrews confines details of textual variants, glosses, and contextual information largely to the back of the volume. This is in marked contrast to earlier Pickering Masters editions, such as the editions of Southey's works [2004, 2012] for instance, which include textual variants as footnotes. Southey's frequent revisions and reissues of his works throughout his life, however, necessitate such an approach and this lack of standardization in the series is therefore to be welcomed.

Andrews's concise introduction challenges the narrative that Yearsley's popularity declined from the success of her first volume [1785], which had

1,000 subscribers, to the third [1796], which had far fewer, arguing that this could in fact indicate confidence on the part of her booksellers that Yearsley's work would sell without pre-publication subscription (p. xxvii). Andrews goes on to trace Yearsley's developing poetic style across her three volumes of poetry, highlighting her changed relationship to patronage. Whereas *Poems, on Several Occasions* contained seventeen poems dedicated to one of her two patrons, Hannah More and Elizabeth Montagu, her final volume contained only two such poems to her then patron Frederick Hervey, fourth earl of Bristol. Andrews argues that this book, *The Rural Lyre*, 'is the most adventurous of Yearsley's three volumes' as a result, stating that 'as her career progressed she became less and less reliant on patrons, and therefore had more space in her work—both literally and intellectually—in which to explore other modes' (p. xxx).

It is hoped that Yearsley's relative critical and literary neglect—Duncan Wu's most recent edition of *Romanticism: An Anthology*, published by Wiley Blackwell in 2012, includes only two poems by Yearsley for instance—can begin to be challenged by Andrews's work. A poet of the late eighteenth-century so heavily influenced by the much earlier poetics of Milton, Young, Pope, and Gray, however, is always likely to appear stylistically at odds with her more Romantic contemporaries and, at worst, decidedly unfashionable. Nevertheless, Andrews's thorough scholarship and clear confidence in Yearsley's literary value are very much in evidence in this edition, and at least allow for the debate concerning her merit to take place.

A book published in 2013 but not received in time for review in last year's *YWES* was Kerri Andrews's monograph *Ann Yearsley and Hannah More: Patronage and Poetry*. This is in fact fortunate for our purposes, since the monograph very much works alongside Andrews's edition of Yearsley's poetry, particularly in considering the role of literary patronage as discussed. More and Yearsley are frequently considered as (eventual) antagonists. Indeed, the rivalry was such that in 1788 the publication of Yearsley's *Poem on the Inhumanity of the Slave Trade* was purposefully timed to rival More's *Slavery: A Poem*. Although More was once Yearsley's patron, the two had fallen out following disagreement over the control of the profits the latter had earned from her first volume *Poems, on Several Occasions*. Although this is relatively well-trodden ground, discussed in Donna Landry's *The Muses of Resistance* [2005] and Mary Waldron's *Lactilla, Milkwoman of Clifton* [1996] for instance, Andrews's approach is one that explores the relationship between the two poets throughout their careers. As Andrews puts it, the short-lived literary collaboration of the two has been rather 'well mined' (p. 8). The once collaborative relationship that gave way to rivalry, Andrews argues, was in fact fruitful for both poets. For instance, Andrews not only compares the two abolitionist poems above, but notes how each woman turned to fiction later, and at a similar point in her career (More's *Cœlebs in Search of a Wife* of 1808 and the less successful *The Royal Captives* by Yearsley).

The rivalry between the two poets has often been put down to class antagonisms, politics—More's ultra-conservatism versus Yearsley's relative radicalism—as well as mundane financial matters. Andrews does not necessarily dismiss these; rather, she considers the significance of the complex role played by patronage in the eighteenth century in relation to all the above. In particular, Andrews notes how it was expected that a patronized poet should show gratitude, not only in private, but in print. This is evident in Yearsley's poetry, but not sufficiently so to satisfy More, who herself had been patronized by David Garrick (p. 58). Andrews also considers how the More/Yearsley system of patronage was complicated further by gender, in that the traditional paternal male/female dynamic was of course disrupted. An interesting, and much-needed work, Andrews's monograph is as revealing of the creative processes of writing in the changed, and changing, publishing environment that had become increasingly professionalized as it is of the work of these two female poets. Thoroughly researched and elegantly written, it offers an insight into a creatively beneficial literary relationship, often vexed, between two female Romantic poets beyond the oft-covered male figures of the 'Big Six'.

Hannah More was also the subject of a short article in 2014. Edmund Downey's 'An Unpublished Letter from Hannah More to Ralph Beilby: Radical Connections and Popular Political Literature' (*N&Q* 61[2014] 504–7) is a thorough piece of scholarship that reaffirms, with nuance, the work of Kevin Gilmartin and Olivia Smith. In particular, it reminds us of how the Christian conservative More engaged in similar publishing practices, including even using the same publishers, as radical writers. One example is the Newcastle-based publisher Ralph Beilby, who had previously published the work of the 'ultra-radical' Thomas Spence. Downey includes a full transcription of an unpublished letter between More and Beilby, arguing that this direct correspondence confirms More's conscious and direct interest in securing the services of this particular publisher. A very convincing piece, Downey's argument is that both conservatives and radicals alike were keen to co-opt a plebeian and vernacular mode.

Turning to individual authors, the most important work on Blake from 2014 concerned his religious background. In his seminal 1954 critical work, *Blake: Prophet Against Empire* (reviewed in *YWES* 35[1956]), David Erdman wondered whether Blake's background was Methodist. *Blake and the Methodists*, by Michael Farrell, considers this a very real possibility. Farrell investigates the work of the poet and painter within the context of this important contemporary branch of Christianity, contributing to the continuing and contentious debate surrounding Blake's theology by suggesting his sympathy towards Wesleyan Methodism. As Farrell outlines in his excellent first chapter, Methodism emerges out of the eighteenth-century evangelical revival to become the biggest 'dissenting' religious movement in Blake's lifetime. But there was a large range of dissenting religious groups at this time, and whilst some adhered closely to one single sect, many others saw and appreciated a commonality witnessed between faiths, and held eclectic views. These believers or 'seekers' adopted a 'compound of doctrinal sympathies', Farrell explains, attending various religious meetings but rarely 'subscribing to membership of any particular denomination' (p. 15). Farrell reads Blake as such a seeker, with heterogeneous religious views and practices. Far from being the extreme radical that criticism has tended to paint him as, then, Farrell finds Blake to be much more typical of the syncretic theology of his time. Still, a number of other scholars have comprehensively contextualized Blake's religious views, as Farrell explains. Closest to Farrell's own reading is Robert Ryan's suggestion, in *The Romantic Reformation* (reviewed in *YWES* 77[1999]), that whilst Blake's theology was relatively orthodox for the time, this does not have to be incompatible with religious radicalism. Where Farrell's book is so useful, however, is in developing these issues still further. One of the great strengths of Farrell's argument is its openness to the Blake's ambivalence towards religion. It is a mark of this generous study that Farrell puts forward Blake's wide-ranging theological perspectives even as he convinces us of Methodism's important place in the poet's distinctive vision.

Hazard Adams's *Thinking through Blake* (McFarland) was not received in time for review, and will be covered with material from 2015.

Paul Miner published three essays broadly built around influence and allusion in Blake in *Notes and Queries*. 'Blake and Burke: The Druid Majesty of the Foetus' (*N&Q* 61[2014] 22–7) argues for the poet's adaptation of Burke's conception of the sublime and beautiful. Via a number of perceptive close readings, Miner contends that Blake adopts Burke's dichotomies for 'his own allegorical purposes' (p. 27), particularly in the visionary works. Picking up some of the strands of that essay, 'Blake: The Metaphors of Generation' (*N&Q* 61[2014] 33–8) is a fascinating assessment of Blake's wordplay on 'generation'. Reading Blake's raids on the Bible and Christianity, Miner finds Blakean ambivalence, especially in *Milton* and *Jerusalem*. We know that as well as producing 537 watercolours of Edward Young's *Night Thoughts*, Blake also drew on it for his own enigmatic poetic art. In 'Blake: Thoughts on *Night Thoughts*' (*N&Q* 61[2014] 27–33) Miner explores a number of 'submerged borrowings' in the verse, arguing that these allusions help Blake to 'create a new mythology' (p. 27). I enjoyed the close attention to detail Miner offers throughout these three short essays. Collectively, they illustrate how Blakean allusion contributes to his powerfully compelling mythology.

Since the invaluable publication in 2009 of Robert Bloomfield's letters by *Romantic Circles*, edited by Tim Fulford and Lynda Pratt, a number of scholars have detailed his significance to our understanding of Romantic culture. In 2012, for instance, a special issue of *Romantic Circles*, edited by John Goodridge and Bridget Keegan, offered a range of fruitful impressions of the poet's self-fashioning through his letter-writing, especially his attempts to engage with publishers in London, and Bloomfield also played a part in *Class and the Canon*, edited by Kirstie Blair and Mina Gorji (also 2012). In 2014, Angus Whitehead offered three short pieces in *Notes and Queries* on the labouring-class poet that bring further details of his life and work to the surface. '"I anticipate rather a smile at my adventures": An Unrecorded Letter from Robert Bloomfield to Sir Charles Bunbury' (*N&Q* 61[2014] 73–6) presents a recently discovered letter from Bloomfield in March 1806 to the horse-racing administrator and Whig MP for Suffolk. Whitehead reveals to us the political context in which Bloomfield operated (or perhaps it would be fairer to say in which he tried to operate). As Whitehead explains, the letter to Bunbury shows rather comically the limited progress Bloomfield makes in getting a foothold in, let alone patronage from, Westminster's elite. In '"A relish for hedge-row poetry": A Newly Discovered Letter from Robert

Bloomfield to Sir Samuel Egerton Brydges' (*N&Q* 61[2014] 76–80), meanwhile, Whitehead suggests that Bloomfield's only traced usage of 'hedgerow poetry' implies 'self-deprecation on the labouring-class poet's part' (p. 80). He writes eager to secure both literary support and financial assistance from Brydges— who was a writer, patron of the arts, and founder member of the Roxburghe Club. Finally, ' "Thou Gem of the Ocean, That Smil'st in thy Power": The Full Text of Robert Bloomfield's "Address to the British Channel" ' (*N&Q* 61[2014] 81–3) reflects on the 'chequered textual and reception history' (p. 83) of Bloomfield's widely circulated poem. As Whitehead observes, the questionable state of so much of Bloomfield's work as it has been handed down to us calls out for a reliable and definitive edition, as well as the need for a more comprehensive biography of this notable figure.

In the past five years there have been a number of major editorial undertakings on the collected works of Scottish Romantic writers. Edinburgh University Press will soon be publishing the Edinburgh edition of the poetry of Walter Scott, a project under the stewardship of Alison Lumsden at Aberdeen, and over the next decade or so we will have the fifteen-volume *Oxford Edition of the Works of Robert Burns* from the team at the centre for Burns studies at Glasgow, with Gerard Carruthers as its general editor. The first volume offered as part of this huge undertaking is the *Commonplace Books, Tour Journals, and Miscellaneous Prose*, edited by Nigel Leask. Burns's songs and poetry are justly regarded as some of the most vibrant and evocative of the Romantic period, and his letters afford a valuable example of life-writing. But the prose works presented in this edition have tended to be marginalized by Burns's editors over the years. Indeed, the volume offers the first edited collection of Burns's writing in prose. Leask's *Robert Burns and Pastoral* (reviewed in *YWES* 91[2012]) previously illustrated the critic's deep appreciation of the poet's place in eighteenth-century life and letters. Here, as editor, Leask brings all his vast knowledge to bear in a series of introductory essays for each item in the edition. In command of his sources and a range of scholarship, he neatly conveys the salient issues for modern readers of Burns, especially useful in the context of these less well-known works. Leask provides an uncluttered working text, with the accompanying notes given at the back of the volume. At a little over 100 pages, the notes take up a quarter of the volume. But they are a delight, and both inviting and illuminating. To read them in isolation is to find it confirmed just how knowledgeable Burns was about the history, politics, and literature of the British nation, and to see illuminated his deep love of Shakespeare and Pope in particular. It was also a delight to discover that whimsy was a favourite word of Burns's (p. 318). Since they constitute key periods in Burns's career many readers will probably delve into the three commonplace books reproduced here, at least initially. But even in the 'Prose Fragments' of the final chapter there is much to discover. In just a few pages we are offered a chance to peer into the playful workings of Burns's crafty imagination as he engages with contemporary issues, and mocks literary hacks. Unlike the work of some of those scribblers Burns enjoyed ridiculing, *Commonplace Books, Tour Journals, and Miscellaneous Prose* is a major piece of scholarship, offering ample new material for Romanticists. It is a highly accomplished opening to what promises to be a seminal edition of Burns.

The Reception of Robert Burns in Europe, edited by Murray Pittock, offers fourteen critical essays that trace the cultural impact of Burns's work on the Continent. Often thought of as Scotland's national poet, Burns's appeal has long stretched right across Europe. From the beginning, his verse and song were situated within issues of national identity, celebrated for drawing out and demarcating various cultural memories. As befits a book detailing Burns's transnational influence, Pittock has assembled an international group of scholars and translators that bring with them a broad expanse of knowledge. Each critic helpfully outlines the finer details of a country's historical relation to Burns, something I found extremely helpful. The book opens with Pauline Mackay's very useful timeline which delineates the response to Burns on the Continent between 1795 and 2012 and puts us on a firm footing for the largely historicist readings that lie ahead. Pittock's own introduction nicely highlights that the assimilation of Burns within the complex cultural needs and narratives of European nations had the inevitable effect of removing the poet from his original concerns. Burns initially gained traction on the Continent by way of the German states during the Napoleonic era. As Frauke Reitemeier's chapter, 'Lost in Translation', shows, German reference books published Burns while he was still alive. According to Reitemeier's research, these early translations suggest that what attracted German readers most were the folk-song tradition and the perceived primitivism of Scotland. Burns's progressive politics and linguistic dexterity, in contrast, were of less significance. As Jahn Thon shows in chapter 13, though, these issues were of central importance in Norway as Burns contributed to its growing national fervour.

The reception of Burns in Austria is the subject of Eleoma Bodammer's chapter. As she explains, nineteenth-century Austrian responses to Burns took various forms, and included translations, adaptations, and reviews. Scholars of the German-language reception of Burns have generally overlooked his significance in Austria, however, and Bodammer is effective in explaining the way Austro-German reaction to Burns differs from the better-understood German reception. Rounding off the German-language reception, Silvia Mergenthal considers the impact of Burns in the context of multilingual Switzerland. Dominique Delmaire is keen to 'explore an enigma' (p. 68) in his highly detailed chapter on 'The Critical Reception of Robert Burns in France'. The enigma, as Delmaire understands it, is why Burns's reputation plummeted in France at the start of the twentieth century, when it had been so high and so politically and culturally significant prior to this time. Focusing on Burns's reception in Italy between 1869 and 1972, Francesca Saggini traces the interest of successive generations of Italian critics in the Scottish poet. In contrast to the rather complex cultural landscape that emerges out of Saggini's sketch of Italy, Andrew Monnickendam, in 'Robert Burns and Spanish Letters', argues for only a limited response to Burns in Spain; ultimately Walter Scott's fame appeared to bar any other Scot from getting much of a foothold.

Eastern Europe is pleasingly well represented in this collection by a number of insightful essays. Veronika Ruttkay considers Burns's place amongst popular poetry in nineteenth-century Hungary, while the reception of Burns in all sections of Russian society is well captured by Natalia Kaloh Vid. Martin Procházka, in his chapter on Czech translations of Burns, wonders just how significant a part the poet played in constructing a tenacious national identity, particularly through folk tradition. The impact of Burns on Ukrainian rights is explored by Hanna Dyka, and, much like her impressive charting of Burns as a symbol of liberty to states within the Soviet bloc, Mirosława Modrzewska argues that Burns's relevance to Poland is a particularly contemporary political phenomenon. In chapter 12, Valentina Bold explains that Slovenia's appreciation of Burns began in the nineteenth century, and continues strong today, with Burns primarily understood there as a nature poet and a poet of love (p. 254). The final chapter of the collection, by Kirsteen McCue and Marjorie Rycroft, moves away from the structure of focusing on one nation at a time, and considers the broader theme of 'The Reception of Robert Burns in Music'. This feels a fitting end to a book that details so well the rich migration of Burns. Excepting only 'Happy Birthday', Burns's 'Auld lang syne' is surely the most widely known song around the world. Burns's songs travelled across many continents, in part at least because of Scottish emigration. But his songs were also amongst the earliest recorded music at the beginning of the twentieth century. Focusing on specific historical periods, McCue and Rycroft highlight how European composers and musicians have consistently found Burns to be a personal, political, and musical stimulus. This valuable volume, which combines depth with breadth, illustrates the mixed reputation and continuing importance of Burns in European nations, and is an excellent example of the way reception studies draws attention to the complex interweaving of peoples, periods, and ideas.

Reading Robert Burns, by Carol McGuirk, aims to provide a comprehensive assessment of Burns's poetry and songs. Like other recent studies, McGuirk's book challenges the 'broad brush of myth' (p. 1) that has turned Burns into a cultural icon. McGuirk is keen to re-engage with the elusive and ambiguous elements of his writing. Throughout she saves biographical matters, and political and social contexts, for when she feels they most influence the writing. Her primary attention is given to early manuscripts, Burns's favoured verse forms, and his habits of revision. McGuirk believes that Burns's inventive intertwining of 'vernacular Scots with standard English, changed literary language forever' (p. 4), and she gives a good indication of the importance of his contribution in this field. In her 'Epilogue', McGuirk extends this largely linguistic matter into a discussion of how Burns's distinctive poetic language has become ingrained in what she calls the 'interactive matrix of living cultural exchange', as Burns is 'spoken and sung, or transplanted into new contexts' (p. 190). McGuirk's wide-ranging thesis is most incisive when she reads Burns in relation to other writers, a trend that has become increasingly popular and productive of late. McGuirk naturally feeds off Burns's instinctive openness. Frequently in poetic conversation with others, Burns has also regularly been a poet towards whom others have gravitated for inspiration. William Wordsworth's relation to Burns has long been a subject of critical discussion. But McGuirk finds fresh things to say on the ways in which Wordsworth seeks to emulate and resist Burns's poetic example. A chapter on Burns and other Scots poets, meanwhile, highlights the significance of drinking in Scottish verse, from the eighteenth century to the modernist vernacular of Hugh MacDiarmid. Despite the challenge that such a comprehensive account inevitably creates, McGuirk's is largely a cohesive argument that offers a fruitful reminder of Burns's creativity.

'The Letters of Robert Burns' (*CQ* 43[2014] 97–119) by Grace Egan makes a compelling case for the need to examine the poet's epistles as self-conscious exercises that provide vital insights into the life of a writer. Byron, as so often, might have been speaking of himself when he famously described the 'antithetical mind' possessed by Burns, which was ever 'soaring and grovelling', and mingled 'dirt and deity . . . in that compound of inspired clay' (quoted p. 97). Egan's brilliant essay illustrates that it is in the letters as much as the verse that we find this 'antithetical mind' labouring upon its literary ambitions. For Egan, Burns's 'letters mix together the 'common . . . Clod' and the sentimental to create antithetical writing that is as true to form as it is true to life' (p. 119). 'James Morison, Book Illustration and *The Poems of Robert Burns* (1812)' (*SLR* 6:ii[2014] 25–48), by Sandro Jung, contextualizes an under-evaluated two-volume edition of Burns's verse. Jung details the Morison firm's use of the production of the illustrated book as part of a cultural and patriotic agenda to promote a Scottish canon. In 'The First Publication of Burns's "Tam o'Shanter"' (*SSL* 40:i[2014] 105–15) meanwhile, Bill Dawson examines the early publishing history of the poet's macabre mock-epic.

Byron's place in the cultural landscape of Romanticism has often been directed by a cult of personality, or the politics of celebrity. New Historicists have commonly appropriated Byron as a means by which to critique Romantic ideology as a result of his voice's ironic countering of his Romantic contemporaries, acknowledged by critics such as M.H. Abrams. In recent years, however, there has been a gradual formalist turn, with critics engaging with Byron at the level of the reading experience. Published in 2013, but not received in time for review in last year's *YWES*, *Byron and the Forms of Thought* by Anthony Howe is therefore both timely and appealing in its insistence that the study of poetry must directly engage with its constituent parts, what Howe calls a poem's 'ways of being' (p. 5). For Howe, it is not simply a poet who is thinking in verse, in Simon Jarvis's terms, but any reader attentive to literary form. As Angela Leighton observes in *On Form*, which Howe quotes in his introduction, this formalist method 'stops us in our tracks of thinking, and inserts itself in that moment of stillness. To attend to form is thus to admit some other kind of mental attention, which is not the quick route to a name or the knowledge of an object' (quoted p. 5). Part of Howe's thesis therefore rests on the belief that literary studies affords a dynamic means of unsettling modernity's quantitative analysis in favour of a more capacious and cautious acknowledgement of the complexity of human experience. He thus subtly extends the study of Byronic forms beyond their significance to the Romantic period into questions of the value of literary criticism in modern universities and the wider culture in which they operate. Howe's book is also part of a growing trend to defend Byron as thinker. Emily Bernhard Jackson, in *The Development of Byron's Philosophy of Knowledge: Certain in Uncertainty* [2010], recently offered a reading of Byron as deeply engaged with British empiricism. For Bernhard Jackson this engagement can be traced throughout Byron's writing, and by the time of *Don Juan* has developed into a fully fledged epistemology. Howe shares the belief that Byron's thinking has been underestimated, but he differs in arguing for a more indeterminate and hesitant philosophical stance on Byron's part, and in assuming that it is through the process of composing poetry that Byron is continually engaging with and questioning his thoughts.

Howe divides his book into six essays, and ends with a coda. These essays perhaps necessarily privilege the later works such as *Cain*, but most especially *Don Juan*. In Part I, Howe relates Byron's absorption in philosophical scepticism, and how this leads the poet to believe that verse carries a 'philosophical agency of its own' (p. 8). Part II addresses Byron as literary critic, as he reflects on what poetry might offer ahead of any other compositional practice. In Part III, Howe turns to the poetry in greater detail. He is excellent on Byronic nuance, not least those richly suggestive moments performed by punctuation. Discussing the nihilism in *Don Juan*, canto XVI, for instance, Howe shows Byron's failure to communicate through simile: 'The evaporation of a joyous day' finally leads to his conclusion that it is 'like—like nothing that I know / Except itself'. Suggestively, Howe notes that the dash 'represents a tiny stretch of the infinite quietness predicted by any quest for figurative identity' but that 'it is only through sleight of hand (by using the failure of simile as a simile itself) that the narrator is able to continue at all' (p. 140). For Howe, moments like these reveal Byron's forms of thought; whilst Byron may have found a solution to the 'voiceless thought' in *Childe Harold's Pilgrimage*, the answer is uttered with the 'suspicion that we have merely exchanged despair for textuality' (p. 140).

Eighteenth- and nineteenth-century authors and critics regularly derided publishers as a distasteful feature of literary life. Charles Lamb was not alone in feeling that writers were slaves to the marketization of books propagated by publishers for their own profit. In contrast, Mary O'Connell's *Byron and John Murray: A Poet and His Publisher* suggests publishers can be enablers of literature, and offers a much-needed reappraisal of one of the most profitable associations in book history. As O'Connell notes, a lot of attention has been paid to the rise of the marketplace and its impact on the Romantic period. Much less notice has been given to the influence of a single publishing figure as an arbiter of taste, or as shaper of a literary text, or as facilitator of the complex relationship between writer and reader. O'Connell's choice of Murray is a smart one. As the most significant publisher in the Romantic period, he was also an essential patron of the literary world. His reach extended far beyond Byron to include publishing the *Quarterly Review* and Jane Austen amongst numerous other achievements. No wonder Wordsworth was eager to be taken on, and even Keats flirted with the idea, so successful was Murray in turning a profit for poets as well as for himself. Frequently imagined as antagonistic, and posited as at best a mercenary relationship by Byron scholars, O'Connell convincingly shows that despite their political polarity and 'the difference in class' Byron and Murray 'had fundamentally compatible personalities' (p. 201). For O'Connell, they were friends. At least as Byron defined friends in a letter to Mary Shelley as 'like one's partners in the waltz of this world—not much remembered when the ball is over, though very pleasant for the time' (quoted p. 201). The transitory nature that such a remark suggests also accommodates Byron's pleasure in picking up the dance of friendship at any time. O'Connell's meticulous archival research and thoughtful readings reveal that poet and publisher were frequently in step with each other, and that this presented a personal and creative profit, as well as a financial one. Sensitive yet piercing in its observations, *Byron and John Murray* opens up new pathways in the fields of book-trade history and Byron studies.

The Burning of Byron's Memoirs is an invaluable collection of the late Peter Cochran's essays and papers written over twenty years. An independent scholar, Cochran was a leading authority on Byron for decades, and many of these essays have not been published before or even heard in public. The essays cover various aspects of Byron's life and work, including his complex relationship with friends and family, his conversations with, and allusions to, other writers, and his feelings about men and women. Their range, in keeping with Cochran's capacious interests, is eclectic. Byron's 'dirty jokes' and 'problem with mothers' sit alongside the challenge of being Byron's banker and the poet's relation to nations—especially Scotland and Greece—and to other poets, most notably and insightfully his relation to Shakespeare. The essay from which the book gets its title is a *tour de force* of documentation, detailing the way Byron's *Memoirs* were destroyed days after his death was announced. Each essay in this collection benefits from Cochran's interest in contemporary issues—from geopolitics to sexual politics. Cochran's engagement with these issues is fired by what he feels is Byron's own prescience. As Cochran points out, the 'one thing you can't say about Byron, on most subjects, is that he's out-dated' (p. xii). *The Burning of Byron's Memoirs* affords its readers an insight into the enormous importance of Cochran's work to Byron studies over the years. His website, at https://petercochran. wordpress.com/, has serviced us with accounts of Byron's life and writing, whilst his editorial work and commentary have been priceless. Cochran died in May last year. *The Burning of Byron's Memoirs* articulates how much his voice will be missed.

Byron's sociability is addressed by a number of articles that reflect on his friendships, and relationship to other writers. David Francis Taylor explores Byron's obsession with the oratory of the late eighteenth century in 'Byron, Sheridan, and the Afterlife of Eloquence' (*RES* 65[2014] 474–94). Taylor focuses on a number of speeches by Sheridan from 1787–8, and suggests that Byron self-consciously problematizes any attempt at rendering what was spoken in the past. This thoughtful essay nicely conveys the way Byron's buoyant emulation of Sheridan is also one of inevitable, and necessary, imperfection. 'The Politics of Byron and Alfred de Musset: *Marino Faliero* and *Lorenzaccio*' (*ERR* 25[2014] 757–71), by Joanne Wilkes, shows the importance of Byron's play to the development of Musset's later stage work. While Byron's influence on Musset was immediately recognized on the first publication of the French poet's work in 1829, assessing the overlaps and divergences between the two from a political context reveals Musset's cynicism regarding the chance for any meaningful change, Wilkes argues. This is a skilful essay that combines context with intertextuality.

'The Variants and Transformations of *Fantasmagoriana*: Tracing a Travelling Text to the Byron–Shelley Circle' (*Romanticism* 20[2014] 306–20), by Maximiliaan Van Woudenberg, looks at the infamous ghost-story contest at the Villa Diodati in the summer of 1816. Instead of raking over familiar ground, however, the essay delves into the now little known *Fantasmagoriana*, the French volume of ghost stories, which, according to Mary Shelley later, had been one of the inspirations behind the contest. Van Woudenberg highlights the narrative and genre influence of *Fantasmagoriana* on *Frankenstein* and Byron's ghost story, which would subsequently be adapted by John Polidori as *The Vampyre*. The period after that year without a summer is the subject of 'Byron—Frere—at the Octave' (*ByronJ* 42[2014] 133–43) by N.E. Gayle, which reconsiders the comic creative vista that opened up for Byron in 1817 once he was more familiar with ottava rima. Byron already knew the form in the shape of works by Pulci, Ariosto, and Tasso. For Gayle, however, it is Byron's discovery in 1817 of the humorous English epic, supposedly by the brothers Whistlecraft, but actually by John Hookham Frere, that is of distinct importance to a poet seeking an alternative to the tragic *Tales* and *Manfred*. In 'P. L. Møller: Kierkegaard's Byronic Adversary' (*ByronJ* 42[2014] 35–47), Troy Wellington Smith looks at the philosopher's turn away from the poet via their contemporary Peder Ludvig Møller. Smith discusses how both Byron and Møller serve as models for Kierkegaard's fictional character Johannes the Seducer. In 'Catullus and the Missing Papers' (*ByronJ* 42[2014] 111–22) Timothy Webb reflects on the politically fraught relationship between Byron and Leigh Hunt, and the publisher John Murray. In October 1822, spurred on by Murray's refusal to return *The Vision of Judgement* to Byron, Hunt sent his friend an adaptation of a satirical poem by Catullus. Webb uses this incident to illustrate both Byron's and Hunt's indignation at Murray, and links this to Byron's turn to Leigh's radical brother John in 1823 for the publication of the remainder of *Don Juan*, and *The Vision of Judgement* itself. Webb's insightful essay throws new light on the alliance between Byron and Hunt, who were living near each other near Genoa during this time and collaborating on *The Liberal*.

Ideological as well as literary disputes within publishing history are also the subject of Jason Kolkey's confident and convincing 'Mischievous Effects: Byron and Illegitimate Publication' (*ByronJ* 42[2014] 21–33). Focusing on texts and paratexts, Kolkey shows that the battle between legitimate and 'pirate' booksellers was a pivotal factor in the marketization of books, and details Byron's adroit response to the ever-increasing commodification of his poetics and personality. Paratexts are also of central concern to Ourania Chatsiou's exploration of Byronic irony. In 'Lord Byron: Paratext and Poetics' (*MLR* 109[2014] 640–62) Chatsiou focuses on annotation to illustrate how Byron imaginatively utilizes the opportunity that liminality affords. Delving into Byron's annotations reveals that his notes are not simply an 'undisciplined or calculated authorial self-projection', but also essential to how he seduces and disrupts his readers—what Chatsiou sees as the poetics of Romantic irony, part of a 'total "macro-text" in which everything matters and productively interplays' (p. 642).

A number of critics addressed Byronic travel, broadly conceived, in 2014. In 'Prospects of Europe: The First Iteration of *Childe Harold's Pilgrimage*' (*KSR* 28:i[2014] 37–48) Richard Lansdown offers an analysis of Byron's ambivalent reaction to the history, land, and people of Europe. Lansdown believes that Byron's travels constitute not the 'random series they appear to be' but rather an 'intellectual sequence' that is fashioned from the poet's endeavour to 'understand the present in terms of the past' (p. 38). This excavation of Europe's history in relation to the geopolitical landscape Byron saw all about him is what makes the first two cantos of *Childe Harold's Pilgrimage*, for Lansdown as for many others, the greatest European poem since the *Aeneid*. 'Transformations of Byron in the Literature of British India' (*VLC* 42[2014] 573–93), by Máire ní Fhlathúin, reflects on the reception of, and responses to, Byron's writing by a community of British poets in Romantic-period India. It provides a fascinating account of the dissemination of Byron's work and the personality politics that surrounded the poet. Ní Fhlathúin shows that Indian-based writers also co-opted Byronism into their works via various allusions, adaptations, and imitations, as was also the case with British-based poets in the first half of the nineteenth century. This influence was freighted with political and cultural agency, according to Fhlathúin, as Byron's exoticized vision of the Orient is reconfigured in the context of British India. Paul Giles argues for an important antipodean imaginary in Byron's poetry. 'Romanticism's Antipodean Spectres: *Don Juan* and the Transgression of Space and Time' (*ERR* 25[2014] 365–83) makes a convincing case for reading Romantic poetry via the 'relativism associated with spatial boundaries' (p. 365). For Giles, the 'spectre of antipodes British imperial enterprises' (p. 365) helped to fashion the writing of the Shelleys and Byron. Of particular note in this essay is the way Giles understands this process as at work on a formal level in Byron's verse.

In '"The Controlless Core of Human Hearts": Writing the Self in Byron's *Don Juan*' (*ByronJ* 42[2014] 123–32), by Michael J. Plygawko, Byron's claim to his publisher in April 1817 that 'I hate things *all fiction*' becomes a means of investigating what truth might mean for the poet. Via a series of close readings, Plygawko considers the creative agency at play whenever Byron brings into tension the imagined and the real. '"Our Mix'd Essence": *Manfred*'s Ecological Turn' (*ByronJ* 42[2014] 5–20), by J. Andrew Hubbell, attempts new insight into a well-worn critical field: Byron's radically ambivalent approach to nature. *Manfred* dramatizes the failure of a Wordsworthian faith in nature for Byron, as Hubbell notes. Hubbell's ecocritical stance benefits from recent work by Stephen Cheeke and Timothy Morton, as he acknowledges. But his primary interest lies in pursuing what he sees as Byron's lifelong attention to 'the co-evolutionary interdependence between the natural environment and human society', what Hubbell calls the poet's 'theory of cultural ecology' (p. 6). The brooding Byronic hero is the subject of an article by Gregory Olsen, though with a telling difference. In 'Rewriting the Byronic Hero: "I'll try the firmness of a female hand"' (*ERR* 25[2014] 463–77) Olsen shows in compelling ways how Gulnare in *The Corsair* has many of the characteristics of the Byronic hero. Like Byron's male heroes, Gulnare is 'both Romanticized and demonized' (p. 470) throughout, while her 'crime', for Conrad at least, is her defining feature. 'Energy Like Life: Byron and Ballet' (*ByronJ* 42[2014] 145–56), by Betsy Winakur Tontiplaphol, rehearses the balletic movement of *Don Juan*. Offering a reappraisal of the

Romantic period's response to dance culture by challenging the assumption that Englishmen did not view ballet very highly, Tontiplaphol details the various references to ballet in Byron's writing. Byron's club foot left him rather envious of dancers, and meant he generally refrained from dancing in public. But Tontiplaphol suggests that ballet is the 'non-literary art with which *Don Juan* is most profoundly and productively engaged' (p. 147) and traces the thematic and formal value of the dance to the vim and vigour of his verse. Jonathon Shears's 'Byron's Habits' (*KSR* 28:i[2014] 25–36) delves into the poet's personal peculiarities. Shears's compelling argument is that, even when his actions are apparently desultory, Byron's behaviour might be understood through internal compulsions that the poet was not always conscious of. Using the theory of Pierre Bourdieu and others, Shears provides a fresh approach to that typical Byronic paradox: that the poet is most in control when seemingly surrendering to the loss of it.

Each year John Clare's reputation grows. Yet the criticism that at times his writing focuses too intently on describing the natural world to the detriment of human feeling is one that seems to linger for scholars of his work, despite Jonathan Bate's efforts to reverse this. In *Clare's Lyric: John Clare and Three Modern Poets*, however, Stephanie Kuduk Weiner deftly unearths how Clare 'perceives, feels, and thinks about the world', and how his lyric moments in turn 'invest that world with vividness and immediacy' (p. 3). Her three essays devoted to Clare follow the poet's own practice in being excellent examples of the value of close attention to little details. But Kuduk Weiner also has the capacity of drawing out onto a broader canvas. The first chapter reads Clare as a close listener, and understands the poet's skill at pulling the reader with him in rapt attention to the sounds of the natural world which Clare renders through the soundscape of verse. Kuduk Weiner argues that Clare's use of sound at once admits and looks to overcome the limitations of any verbal mimesis in reading. The second chapter makes a compelling case for reading Clare's hundreds of sonnets as attempts to ward off enclosure by using endings to invite new beginnings. Chapter 3 gives us a fascinating account of Clare's late asylum poems and suggests that he self-consciously uses the medium of poetry to consider 'the linguistic and poetic challenge of representing absence' (p. 87). The second part of the book is concerned with the inspiration poets derive from other poets. Kuduk Weiner explores the impact of Clare's lyrics on Arthur Symons, Edmund Blunden, and John Ashbery. Being, as Kuduk Weiner concedes, 'the foremost theorist of the cosmopolitan, urban, impressionistic aestheticism of the *fin de siècle*' (p. 125), Symons might seem somewhat out of place amidst Clare's creative streams. But Symons's introduction to his 1908 edition of Clare's poems is full of searching insight, and Kuduk Weiner captures the kinship between the two of them well. In chapter 5, Kuduk Weiner finds Clare illuminating Blunden's response to the horrors of the First World War. Her final chapter considers Ashbery's creative and critical responses to Clare as he seeks to 'extract pieces of the world in order 'to re-create reality' within the frame of a work of art' (p. 169). The joy of this book is its framing of Clare's poetics in relation to other artists, asking us to look again at his place in the canon.

The wonderful *John Clare Society Journal* kept up its high standard with a number of admirable essays. 'John Clare's Recollections of Home: The Poetics of Nostalgia' (*JCSJ* 33[2014] 5–19), by Valerie Pedlar, captures the tensions Clare felt and exhibited about being 'at home', not, as she explains, the 'physical attributes' of the place, but the 'fragility and vulnerability of one's relation to oneself, and one's community' (p. 18). Clare's 'nostalgia for home' (p. 18) is expressive of his craving for a time and space before these conflicts existed, Pedlar believes. In a highly suggestive essay, Erin Lafford explores 'the way Clare represents health and madness at the level of sound' (p. 24). 'Clare's Mutterings, Murmuring, and Ramblings: The Sound of Health' (*JCSJ* 33[2014] 24–40) argues that Clare's use of indeterminate, non-linguistic vocal sounds counters the prevailing medical belief at the time that muttering connoted insanity. Employing the work of Gilles Deleuze, Lafford argues that Clare's sounds bring 'health and madness together in the same poetic voice' (p. 25). In 'John Clare and William Hone: A Letter Redated' (*JCSJ* 33[2014] 48–56) Robert Heyes delves into the history of a letter purporting to be from 15 May 1823. It is a letter, Heyes explains, that has always 'puzzled' him (p. 48) because there is no other evidence that Clare was even aware of Hone at this time. Whilst Heyes solves the puzzle simply enough, he uses the mystery to sketch further details of Clare's contact with the literary scene in London, an area, as he says, we still do not know enough about. '*Hic Inde Clare*: Interity, Exocognition, & John Clare's "Proposals for Building a Cottage"' (*JCSJ* 33[2014] 57–72), by Ron Paul Salutsky, offers a neuroscientific approach to Clare's writing, and to art more generally. For Salutsky, a time will soon be upon us when we will be able to read more accurately what occurs in the brain during an aesthetic experience, and not only gain a fuller appreciation of what art means for individual pleasure, but also its therapeutic benefits for our wider community. In 'John Clare's Spenserian Lyric Fragments' (*JCSJ* 33[2014] 73–86), Adam White locates Clare within the tradition of the Romantic fragment poem. Like other exponents of the form, Clare's fragments invoke the idea of a whole. But, White argues, unlike Byron, Shelley, or Keats, Clare's Spenserianism frequently combines its 'interrelations with, and independence from . . . *The Faerie Queene*' (p. 73). This continual construction of Spenserian fragments, White contends, offers a new formal context for thinking of Clare as 'the poet of "little things"' as Mina Gorji has proposed (quoted p. 74).

Two essays found new things to say about the status of enclosure in Clare's thinking. 'The Place of Rhyme in John Clare's Northborough Poems' (*KSR* 28:i[2014] 14–20), by Alex Latter, makes a fine case for the need for greater critical attention to the poetry Clare wrote between 1832 and 1837. In his close readings, Latter skilfully shows how Clare's later use of rhyme was a major innovation in both the sonnet tradition and the eighteenth-century pastoral mode. Essentially, Latter hears the rhyme from this time as a destabilizing impulse redolent of Clare's resistance to all forms of enclosure. In 'John Clare and Biopolitics' (*ERR* 25[2014] 665–82) Chris Washington offers a different spin on ecocritical readings of Clare by considering how enclosure shifts the poet's understanding of the relation between humans and animals. Washington shows how, in Clare's ethical and poetic vision, the consequences of the Enclosure Act transform spaces of human–animal relations once 'consciously and conscientiously respectful' (p. 667) into 'confrontational staging grounds' (p. 666).

The poetry of George Crabbe was given a special issue in *Romanticism* this year. As the editors explain in 'George Crabbe: Times and Spaces' (*Romanticism* 20[2014] 103–5), the essays were originally offered as papers at the 'Crabbe's Tales' conference at Newcastle University in July 2012. This event had celebrated the bicentenary of the publication of the *Tales* by considering Crabbe's place in nineteenth-century poetry and cultural life. Francis Jeffrey felt Crabbe was 'the most original writer who has ever come before us' (quoted p. 103), and the range of articles offered reflect on that originality in a broad but always richly detailed context. Claire Lamont's '"The smallest circumstances of the smallest things": Domestic Interiors in Crabbe's Poems' (*Romanticism* 20[2014] 106–16) delves into the various dwellings described in Crabbe's oeuvre. Throughout, Lamont thoughtfully weaves close reading with valuable nods to Crabbe's inheritance of an eighteenth-century tradition, including that of Goldsmith, who influences Crabbe's *The Village* [1783], and Gray, as well as the many allusions to Burns. Lamont argues for the 'shared spaces' (p. 115) that Crabbe creates—be they poetic, personal, or physical—which, she says, he carefully constructs and sees as so essential to the building of human experience. Lamont is unusual, however, in galloping across Crabbe's published work, from *The Village* [1783] up to *Tales of the Hall* [1819]; the remainder of the essays in the special issue focus in the main on *The Borough* and *Tales*. The latter is the focus of 'Putting Stories Together' (*Romanticism* 20[2014] 185–94) by Gavin Edwards. In a fascinating account, Edwards takes us through the various relations and divergences between the *Tales* and various frame narratives like *A Thousand and One Nights*, the *Canterbury Tales*, and the *Decameron*.

In 'Crabbe's Times' (*Romanticism* 20[2014] 117–27) Michael Rossington is interested in revealing the 'sophistication of Crabbe's historical sensibility' (p. 117), something that few critics have paid much attention to. Rossington reads this sensibility as subtle, with the tales reflecting several narrative and historical perspectives that rarely take priority over each other and so establish tensions between the time of the Napoleonic Wars, when *Tales* was first published, and the periods which the narratives inhabit. For Rossington, the tales therefore invite the reader to identify any political and religious tensions in an English past, while understanding present divisions within that past experience. And while this may provide remedies for repairing social tensions, Rossington argues that it also undermines the very enterprise by suggesting their embedded and repetitive inevitability through history. In 'The "Species in This Genus Known": The Influence of Taxonomy on Crabbe's Tales' (*Romanticism* 20[2014] 128–39) James Bainbridge acknowledges Crabbe's 'love of ambiguity' (p. 139) while arguing for the importance of natural science in the verse. It is the 'tension between the known and unknown' that makes Crabbe's 'poetry unique' (p. 139), according to Bainbridge.

Crabbe's *The Borough*—a series of verse letters that detail the personal lives, events, and buildings of a coastal town—offers a fascinating example of the incongruity at the heart of Crabbe's poetics. It brings into view the specialness of common everyday things so prevalent in much Romantic writing, and in its descriptions anticipates the detail and richness of Victorian novels. Formally, however, it capitalizes on the refinement associated with the heroic couplets of the eighteenth century. This special issue of *Romanticism* reserves a number of its pages for this vital work. In ' "Fences . . . form'd of Wreck": George Crabbe's *The Borough* and the Resources of the Poor' (*Romanticism* 20[2014] 140–50) Matthew Ingleby is interested in the still live issue of the poet's contentious relation to, and description of, the poor. For Hazlitt, after all, Crabbe was incurably conservative, rarely sympathizing with those he depicted, and seemingly unable or unwilling to question the state of the nation. For Fiona Stafford, *The Borough* affords an opportunity to discuss the resonance of the sea, not only as something vital in and of itself, but also as way of evoking the internal movements of Crabbe's thoughts, an 'emblem of my mind', as he was keen on calling it. ' "Of Sea or River": Crabbe's Best Description' (*Romanticism* 20[2014] 162–73) is sensitive to Crabbe's interest in the limitations of language in capturing the world around him, in a way that Stafford feels is comparable to contemporaries like Wordsworth and Coleridge, and would later be explored by Percy Shelley. Andrew Lacey also considers Crabbe in relation to Wordsworth in 'The Epitaphic Poetry of Crabbe and Wordsworth' (*Romanticism* 20[2014] 151–61). Lacey addresses the fact that whilst Romantic epitaphic writing has been the subject of some discussion over the years, Crabbe's place within this tradition is consistently overlooked. As Lacey points out, this is typical of Crabbe's marginal position in Romantic critical discourse, partly because he is associated with an Augustan aesthetic at least as much as a Romantic one. Lacey is right to point out the curiosity of this critical position, since most of the mature work was published after the seminal date (for Romanticists at least) of 1798. Lacey is keen to treat Crabbe as Wordsworth's contemporary, and trace what he calls the 'incongruent treatment of the epitaphic in each poet's oeuvre' (p. 151). Thomas Williams investigates Crabbe's relation to another contemporary poet. In 'George Crabbe and John Clare: Refinement and Reading' (*Romanticism* 20[2014] 174–84) Williams considers both social and subjective identities in poetry. Clare is an interesting poet to bring into comparison with Crabbe, not least because of the former's once marginalized place in the canon and increasing significance for Romantic studies—something that all these essays seek for Crabbe—but more specifically because, as Williams explains, each poet explores how reading provides a means of attaining a curious form of refinement in rural life. As a collection, these essays go a long way in revealing Crabbe's important place in critical discourse, as both Romanticist and witty critic of such a notion. Perhaps the most crucial contribution these essays make to literary criticism is in giving Crabbe an equal footing with more established writers.

Published in 2013, but not received in time for review in last year's *YWES*, Chris Murray's *Tragic Coleridge* details the poet's multitudinous interest in tragedy. The significance of classical precedent to Coleridgean thought is addressed when Murray examines 'On the Prometheus of Aeschylus', a lecture Coleridge wrote late in life. But for Murray its philosophical argument, ahead of any detailed engagement with Aeschylus, suggests that by this stage

Coleridge was unwilling to engage with tragedy (p. 158). Moreover, Murray suggests that Coleridge's reluctance to offer a theory of tragedy might lie in a fear that it might be in conflict with Christian orthodoxy. That is not to say that the tragic did not continue to play an important role in Coleridge's thinking. As Murray neatly shows, it pervades Sibylline Leaves, Biographia Literaria, and The Statesman's Manual. What Murray calls 'tragic Romanticism' (p. 2) is revealed as an idiosyncratic concept for Coleridge, rather than something reducible to classical inheritance or genre. Murray captures the importance of not only London theatre but also Romantic organicism and the fragment in fostering Coleridge's tragic thoughts. He suggests that Coleridge would have been more than capable of advancing tragedy on the stage if there had been more of an opportunity for him to do so. Murray's thesis is a timely contribution to two areas recently given attention. His long section on 'The Daemon', for instance, reveals a parallel with Gregory Leadbetter's Coleridge and the Daimonic Imagination [2011] in its attraction to Coleridge's unease over his own inspiration, perpetually dazzled by daemonic poesis yet fearful of its threat to Reason. Murray's well-argued belief that drama is an essential means of understanding Coleridge's output picks up, as Murray acknowledges, J.C.C. Mays's call for the dramatic mode to be 'incorporated within his writing as a whole' (quoted p. 95). It will be interesting to see how these two strands of Coleridge criticism are taken up further in the years ahead.

Like Tony Howe's Byron and the Forms of Thought reviewed above, Ewan Jones's Coleridge and the Philosophy of Poetic Form is wedded to the idea that poetry is a medium that performs and reveals a particular kind of thinking. In his introduction, Jones notes that focusing on poetic form flies in the face of the current state of Coleridge scholarship. But as he outlines in his 'Coda', recent years have brought something of a turn towards defending literary form as a subject worth critical investigation (and many of the works reviewed here seem to back this assertion up). Throughout, Jones is attentive to verse form, both in his perceptive and original close readings of its constituent parts, and as a broader category that might tell us something significant about artistic thought. This is a revisionary account of Coleridgean poetics and philosophy. In his four chapters Jones unsettles any simplistic summary we might like to believe in, of the best years of Coleridge's verse belonging solely to the energies of his youth. Chapter 3, as well as being full of perceptive observations on the background and practice of the pun, is also admirably focused on Coleridge's late composition 'Limbo'. In the face of Coleridge's own assertions of unproductiveness, Jones proves the significance of Coleridge's post-1800 verse. The established chronology of Coleridge's intellectual development—in broad terms Associationism, to German Idealism, to the 'hermetic idiosyncrasy' (p. 9) of the late Highgate years—is also thoroughly undermined. Rather than detecting a coherent and consistent Coleridgean system, Jones is in agreement with Seamus Perry concerning the 'muddlesomeness of Coleridge's writing' (quoted p. 9). What Jones brings to this notion, however, is the idea that Coleridge philosophized through verse because its form frequently afforded him a particular means of playing with his thoughts. In Jones's hands, very often the turns and returns of Coleridge's verse form are shown to generate unforeseen and unintended consequences for Coleridgean philosophy.

As well as her 2013 essay in *Coleridge, Romanticism and the Orient* on 'The Integral Significance of the 1816 Preface to "Kubla Khan"' (reviewed *YWES* 94[2015]), Heidi Thomson published further material on the poet in *Notes and Queries*. 'Coleridge's "On a Supposed Son" and Friedrich Von Logau's "Auf Ein Zweifelkind"' (*N&Q* 61[2014] 58–61) details the 'private preoccupations' as well as the 'political and economic situation' (p. 59) reflected in the epigram 'On a Supposed Son'. Thomson locates this work partly in the personal context in which Coleridge found himself. As she explains, in the winter of 1800 Coleridge was starting to publicly express his unhappiness over his marriage, and his more insecure feelings over the long-term prospects of fruitful relations with the Wordsworths. Other pieces on Coleridge appeared in *Notes and Queries*. In 'Twenty Untraced Allusions in Coleridge's *Biographia Literaria*' (*N&Q* 61[2014] 61–9) Adam Roberts identifies a number of previously unattributed references in Coleridge's monumental work. As Roberts notes, *Biographia Literaria* is a 'complex web of quotation, reference, allusion, and intertextuality' (p. 61), and trying to account for all of them appears an impossible task. But Roberts seems to have meticulously traced almost all of those either not glossed or not able to be traced in the Princeton edition of 1983, edited by James Engel and W. Jackson Bate. 'Coleridge and *Kurrentschrift*' (*N&Q* 61[2014] 50–4), by Maximiliaan Van Woudenberg, looks at Coleridge's difficulties with reading German characters—the handwritten script today known as *Kurrentschrift*. Despite learning German, Coleridge struggled with *Kurrentschrift* not least because its representation of a number of vowels and consonants is illegible for anyone more used to Latin script. Coleridge portrays his difficulties comically. But the incident 'opens up a new perspective about his reading activities . . . while in Germany' (p. 51). Kathryn Walls, in 'The Wedding Feast as Communion in *The Rime of the Ancient Mariner* (*N&Q* 61[2014] 56–8), offers an interpretation of the final stanzas of the poem based on two religious contexts: Christ's parable of the wedding feast, and the Order for the Administration of the Lord's Supper or Holy Communion as it is offered in the 1662 Book of Common Prayer. As Walls says, this text was the Church of England's standard prayer book at the time Coleridge was composing *The Ancient Mariner*.

Thomas Owens produced two very different yet equally compelling essays on Coleridge. In 'Coleridge, Nitric Acid and the Spectre of Syphilis' (*Romanticism* 20[2014] 282–93) Owens is careful never to state categorically that Coleridge did in fact suffer from syphilis. But he makes a convincing case for his suffering from a 'psychological preoccupation with venereal disease . . . real or imagined' (p. 282). Owens combines knowledge of the medical discourse of the time with a biographical reading of the poet to provide a fascinating insight into Coleridge's own fear that he had the symptoms of the disease, and the sexual experience to have contracted it. In 'Coleridge's Parentheses and the Question of Editing' (*EIC* 64[2014] 373–93), Owens reads Coleridge's punctuation, including his 'mispunctuation', as 'load-bearing', registering 'the absence or presence of strain conceived as mimetic patterns of restraint or exertion' (p. 390). He makes a compelling case for the need for an edition of Coleridge's occasional prose that affords full credence to Coleridgean textual variance, one that does not efface 'Coleridge's mental activity beneath the print' and gives full range to his '"antiphonal voice"' (p. 390).

'"Jealous of the Listening Air"': Silence and Seduction in *Christabel* (*Romanticism* 20[2014] 261–70), by Richard Berkeley, examines the Gothic associations of Coleridge's enigmatic poem. Berkeley sees *Christabel* as offering an 'interesting interpretive problem' (p. 261), not least because it refuses to offer its reader a rationalization of its narrative meaning. Berkeley details the way Coleridge identified himself with Christabel's experience so that what is at stake in the seductiveness of the poem is emblematic of the 'poet's own guilty encounter with gothic literature' (p. 261). Coleridge's engagement with European thought is outlined in detail by James Vigus in 'The Philosophy of Samuel Taylor Coleridge' (in Mander, ed., *The Oxford Handbook of British Philosophy in the Nineteenth Century*, pp. 520–40). As Vigus explains, Coleridge's literary, philosophical, and theological pursuits all make up his 'encyclopaedic quest for unified knowledge' (p. 520). This took the form of a deep engagement with German philosophy, and especially Kantian arguments, so as to pursue a 'rational religion', something that consistently underpins Coleridgean speculation, and which was, Vigus shows, the 'great philosophical challenge of the age' (p. 521).

In 'Coleridge's Disappointment in *The Excursion*' (*WC* 45[2014] 147–51) Seamus Perry shows how frustration was also fruitful for Coleridge. As part of a special issue of *Wordsworth Circle* on *The Excursion*, Perry's essay deftly examines crucial divergences that emerged between Wordsworth and Coleridge that can be perceived in the latter's reaction to *The Excursion*. Examining an imaginative difficulty Coleridge felt was at the heart of Wordsworth's philosophical poetry, Perry explains that the problem 'lies in the relationship between the profound universality of the wisdoms that the poem sets out to enunciate and the highly particularized representation of their contingent spokesman' (p. 148). As Perry shows, this was an issue that stretched back to the two poets' collaborative heyday in the 1790s. 'Coleridge: "Work without Hope"' (*WC* 45[2014] 21–9), by Graham Davidson, examines one poem in subtle and rich detail. Coleridge wrote the first draft of 'Work without Hope' in February 1825. As Davidson explains, on first inspection the poem appears to readers as a pleasingly simple work—displaying the kind of impressions that seemed to form 'themselves into verse instinctively' as J.C.C. Mays has said (quoted p. 22). Davidson nicely weighs up the oddities and ambiguities at play in the poem, however, and their touching import to Coleridge's life.

Sara Coleridge is gradually being accepted as much more than just the preserver of the Coleridge family reputation, or defender of her father's legacy. A number of scholars, perhaps most especially Peter Swaab, have offered us a portrait of her as polymath: a talented poet and prose writer, and a thinker who engaged with politics, philosophy, and theology. Because of this we are slowly appreciating her as one of the leading scholars and artists of the late Romantic and Victorian eras. Jeffrey W. Barbeau's *Sara Coleridge: Her Life and Thought* (also discussed in Section 1 above) adds to this portrait in various ways, skilfully capturing her '*inquiring* spirit' (p. ix). Underpinning this book is a belief in the interrelation between parents and their children. Barbeau understands Sara as 'heir to her father's capacious mind' (p. x), and argues that her intellectual and creative development was fashioned out of her deep knowledge of her father's writing, which produced in her a 'thoroughly Coleridgean frame of mind' (p. x). But at its heart this is a biography of, and critical introduction to, Sara, one that deepens our knowledge of its subject in admirable ways. Barbeau reveals her engagement with the key religious and philosophical debates of her time. As he explains, the issues that concerned her father's generation were well known to her, but she was conscious of the need as a woman to wrestle with new concerns emerging out of an increasingly fast-moving modern world. By the end of this book we better appreciate Sara's independent and energetic intellect, and richly creative voice.

Much good scholarship continues to be published on the evocative verse of Felicia Hemans. Two essays appeared in *Studies in Romanticism* that show the almost limitless ways in which we might read and interpret her poetry. '*England and Spain* and *Domestic Affections*: Felicia Hemans and the Politics of Literature' by Juan Sánchez (*SiR* 53[2014] 399–416) offers a perceptive historicist account of Hemans's engagement with war and imperialism. Sánchez shows how literature becomes a political weapon by which Hemans intervenes in the most charged concerns of her time. Sánchez discerns an ambiguity at the heart of Hemans's response. *England and Spain*, for instance, appears to advance support for Tory policy during the Peninsular War through its invective against Napoleon and patriotic call to arms, yet Hemans can also be heard 'consciously adopting a radical voice' that at times shifts the focus of tyranny from Napoleon and onto England (p. 405).

Image of Dionysian inspiration and Christian sacrifice, of physical pleasure and spiritual healing, the motif of the drinking cup has been ebullient inspiration for numerous Romantic writers. While this theme has regularly focused on a masculine poetic economy, Young-Ok An's 'The Poetics of the "Charmed Cup" in Felicia Hemans and Letitia Elizabeth Landon' (*SiR* 53[2014] 217–38), explores the image in the context of female authorship and power. Hemans and Landon understand the cup and its intoxicating powers as a 'metapoetic device' for analysing the 'intersections of gender, authorship, and life', An argues (p. 218). She proposes that Hemans and Landon 'invert and revise the male-oriented rhetoric of the charmed cup' not only to 'signify their struggles for authorship but also to explore the transformative potential of those struggles' (p. 218). An's intertextual reading is highly suggestive and consistently convincing. These two articles (and the works on Yearsley discussed above) aside, however, there was on the whole too little published on individual female poets, as is further indicated below.

Michael Edson offers us a new way of approaching the retirement poem in the Cockney School of poetry. In 'Leigh Hunt, John Pomfret, and the Politics of Retirement' (*ERR* 25[2014] 423–42) Edson explores how Hunt's turn to this mode 'reflects the rise of a city-bound, middle-class audience for whom retirement was necessarily limited to the reading of retirement poetry' (p. 425). Far from the conservative and conformist response to the pressures of modern life that retirement poetry is sometimes classed as, Edson proposes that Hunt and his contemporaries celebrated the 'pleasure of escaping politics' (p. 425) as a means, paradoxically, of accommodating and realizing reformist principles.

  Byron's problem with Keats, so he said, was that his writing too often displayed signs of a 'sort of mental masturbation—he is always f-gg-g his imagination' (*Byron's Letters and Journals*, ed. Leslie A. Marchand, HarvardUP, 7: 225). For Byron, Keats's 1820 volume of poetry, the extraordinary *Lamia, Isabella, The Eve of St Agnes, and Other Poems*, was the work of an adolescent ('p-ss a bed poetry'), whose sexual immaturity lent his verse an obsessive over-indulgence in sensual desire. The intriguing thing about *Keats, Modesty and Masturbation* is that Rachel Schulkins uses this idea of Keats self-indulgently playing with his quill to suggest that it can be read as offering a form of social utility. Schulkins assumes that the autoeroticism that underscores Keats's verse exists as a 'sexual-political stance' which reveals his criticism of the 'conservative construction of the female as passionless' (p. 3). Like so many other Keats scholars, Schulkins benefits from the brilliant work of Jeffrey Cox and Nicholas Roe, in this case by associating the sensuality of the verse with Keats's liberal politics. Schulkins attempts to move from poetic analysis to wider cultural issues throughout her thesis. Specifically, she proposes that Keats's lines of verse need to be understood within the 'liberal-conservative debate surrounding sexual freedom . . . specifically female sexuality' (p. 3). This is Keats's 'radical eroticism' (p. 43) according to Schulkins, which counters the notion of an asexual woman. Thus female masturbation is read as a performance of 'social revolt against social limitations, pursuing in private that which is publicly prohibited' (p. 5). Schulkins seeks to distinguish her argument from Marjorie Levinson's in *Keats's Life of Allegory* [1988], which, Schulkins suggests, reads Keats's onanistic style with his literary and social insecurities. In contrast, Schulkins identifies masturbation with the 'private sphere of imagination' one where an 'individual seeks his own personal advantage over social good' (p. 4). For Schulkins, this is more typical of the context of the time, which saw masturbation not just as a physical gratification but also indicative of further conditions of the mind.

  In 'Keats, Antiquarianism, and the Picturesque' (*EIC* 64[2014] 119–37), Rosemary Hill offers a lively account of how the poet's sensibility was 'imbued with popular antiquarianism' (p. 120). In tracing this aspect of the Keatsian aesthetic, Hill delves into the philosophical underpinnings of the picturesque, specifically the way landscape painting influences the manner in which the natural world is viewed and how in turn it is re-represented in art. For Hill, Keats is keener on mediated rather than direct experience; and certainly many of his letters and verse back up this idea. Not surprisingly, then, the picturesque, with its 're-echoing between art and life[,] appealed to Keats's temperament' (p. 121). Hill is particularly adept at illustrating how the 'synthetic, the imitative, the second-hand, and sometimes frankly second rate . . . were the ideal subjects for Keats' (p. 121). In 'John Keats and Some Versions of Materiality' (*Romanticism* 20[2014] 233–45) Richard C. Sha seeks in Keats's poetry a Romantic aesthetic that 'refuses to choose between materiality and ideality, substance and event', and seeks out a 'possible ground of synthesis' (p. 241). In a complex but sparklingly communicated argument,

Sha describes what he calls 'Romantic matter', and what this means for an understanding of Keats; how, in moving away from mechanism, writers 'sought to restore volition, attraction, and sympathy to the physical world' conceptualizing things as dynamic, but 'always on the move, in the process of becoming' (p. 238).

For Carmen Faye Mathes, passivity is, paradoxically, a dynamic proposition for Keats. '"Let us not therefore go hurrying about": Towards an Aesthetics of Passivity in Keats's Poetics' (*ERR* 25[2014] 309–18) conjures the staged detachment Keats assumes in order to engage with others, arguing that 'Keatsian passivity invites sociability' (p. 310), opening up mediated lines of discourse to others. As Mathes states, this essay invites us to think through new ways of reading the productivity that emerges out of Keatsian indolence. 'Reading the Heart, Reading the World: Keats's Historiographical Aesthetic' (*ERR* 25[2014] 275–88), by Emily Rohrbach, looks afresh at the relation between William Robertson's *History of America* and Keats's sonnet on Chapman's Homer. Instead of offering another account of the thematic and historicist influence of Robertson's text on Keats's sonnet, however, Rohrbach considers the importance of its mediation through its form. This approach allows Rohrbach to show that Keats's poem 'both critiques Enlightenment causality and progressive historical narration', making available to the 'historical imagination an alternative temporality of surprise that foregrounds the individual subject' (p. 276).

'Keats's Ways: The Dark Passages of Mediation and Why He Gives Up *Hyperion*' (*SiR* 53[2014] 171–93), by Yohei Igarashi, builds on recent work surrounding ideas of media and Romantic poetry. Igarashi is an important figure in this movement, having participated in an MLA roundtable on 'Romantic media studies' in 2013. In this essay, he centres his interest on Keats's fascination with 'imagining communication at a distance' (p. 174). Igarashi attempts, as he says, to take that familiar image of Keats, indoors, absorbed in what he is reading, and 'superimpose upon it an image of Romantic-era Britain enmeshed in increasingly far-reaching domestic and global communication and transportation networks' (p. 174). Where Igarashi is eager to reimagine our impression of Keats via the criss-crossing of international relations of his writing, Scott McEathron, in 'William Hilton's Lost Drawing of Keats' (*KSJ* 63[2014] 58–77), focuses his gaze on a specific portrait of the poet. William Hilton's iconic image from 1822, which is currently sitting at Keats House in Hampstead, is based, as McEathron explains, on a miniature produced by Joseph Severn in 1819. Hilton had depicted Keats in a chalk drawing in 1820, but this has long since vanished—something that has frustrated Keats scholars for years. McEathron, though, has discovered that it survives not only in the known Wass engraving of 1841, but also via an 1865 copy made by George Scharf. This image, reproduced in this essay for the first time, gives us, as McEathron nicely suggests, a contrast to the 'ornate, dark, and almost saddened mien of the Wass engraving', via the more 'open countenance often assigned to the poet'. This valuable essay also makes an important case for giving the rather peripheral figure of Hilton more prominence in Romantic studies.

'*The Narrow Road to the Western Isles*—If Keats Had Journeyed with Basho' (*KSR* 28[2014] 49–57), by Geoffrey Wilkinson, is an imagining of the similarities between Keats and the Japanese poet. As Wilkinson shows, these poets are very different in a number of significant ways. But each shares a sense of himself as a literal and metaphorical traveller at times seeking the anonymity and even annihilation of the self. Christopher Langmuir examines Keats's interest in, and the spiritual nourishment of, travel in 'Keats: The Two and Thirty Palaces Revisited' (*N&Q* 61[2014] 514–15). Keats's letter to Reynolds in February 1818 refers to a place of 'two-and-thirty Palaces', and Langmuir is keen to account for it beyond the orientalist explanations often proposed by editors and critics alike. Langmuir shows that the palaces are the abodes of the winds, something Keats uses to represent the all-encompassing—those 'conceivable points of the compass' (p. 515). As Langmuir explains, this ties in to readings of Keats's thoughts on the capacity of the mind, free to follow its own path, as 'the flight of the imagination radiates in all directions' (p. 515).

Previously reviewed in last year's *YWES*, but reissued in paperback in 2014, was Kathleen Kerr-Koch's *Romancing Fascism: Modernity and Allegory in Benjamin, de Man, Shelley*. One of the early figures associated with deconstruction, and an important critic of Percy Bysshe Shelley, was the sometime controversial figure of Paul de Man. The posthumous discovery of de Man's wartime journalism in 1988, written for occupied Belgium's newspaper *Le Soir*, revealed alleged collaborationist tendencies with the National Socialist occupiers and, most damningly, implicit and explicit anti-Semitism. The fact that de Man has both been tarred by accusations of fascist sympathies and seen as a philosopher and literary theorist with a particular interest in Romanticism is striking; it reminds us of what Kerr-Koch refers to as 'the often presumed antecedent connection between Romanticism and irrationalist ideologies' (p. xii). Whether fascism is necessarily irrational and counter to the Enlightenment project or, in fact, the Enlightenment's apotheosis, is not, however, up for debate.

It is fitting that Kerr-Koch considers de Man alongside Walter Benjamin—a figure who also flirted with anti-Semitism in his life—as readers of Percy Shelley. Kerr-Koch's study is not so much an investigation into the connection between the 'romanticism' of Shelley and the 'fascism' of de Man and Benjamin, as the perhaps misleading title suggests. Rather, Kerr-Koch's interest is in the role played by literary allegory in the works of three writers in the so-called 'age of modernity' of the nineteenth and twentieth centuries. Her study seeks to contest the notion that allegory is somehow ahistorical or depoliticized; its 'process of regraphing' (p. 2) makes it highly appropriate in addressing the vexed issue of 'modernity', perceived as constantly changing, evolving, or advancing. The book essentially turns on considering differing reactions to the Enlightenment legacy that spawned 'modernity'. Benjamin, de Man, and Shelley have, for Kerr-Koch, thought 'about the question of progress in modernity's claim to historical advancement' and 'each has mobilized allegory in the configuration of modern temporality' (p. 9). The fact that these three figures are considered in the same volume, and not in chronological order, can be seen as evidence enough that Kerr-Koch's study offers a challenge to conceptions of a modern, linear, and progressive temporality.

Kerr-Koch's critical and theoretical framework is rigorous and well researched, but her approach would benefit from far more attention to close reading and form. Too often Shelley is not allowed to speak for himself. Formal attention would have aided Kerr-Koch's argument, such as in considering specific examples of Shelley's shifting, unsettled—and unsettling— metaphors. The complexity of the topic cannot be overstated and, generally, Kerr-Koch's prose is clear and accessible (but not always). Nevertheless, this is an ambitious work that rewards close scrutiny and is sure to be of use to scholars of Shelley interested in recontextualizing his approach to allegory and revisiting the history of Shelley criticism.

Two other 2014 articles explore the rich poetic and theoretical legacy of Shelley. Luke Donahue's essay, 'Romantic Survival and Shelley's "Ode to the West Wind"' (*ERR* 25[2014] 219–42), on the (im)possibility of 'ending' in Shelley's poetry, engages with and contests both deconstructive and historicist readings, from Paul de Man to James Chandler. Focusing on 'Ode to the West Wind', Donahue seeks to 'address the *possibility* of the final end of mutability' (p. 220) in a poem that seems to suggest the opposite. What follows is a close reading that is often convincing if not always sufficiently attentive. For instance, the leaves in the opening stanza are not 'ghosts' as Donahue states; rather, they are simply '*like* ghosts' (this is a crucial distinction in Shelley). Similarly, the discussion of the death-to-life movement of the leaves would have been enriched by a consideration of the slipperiness of metaphor in Shelley's poem where the leaves, in fact, are always 'dead', but simply signify or allegorize different things (the poet, his words, his thoughts, etc.). This is nevertheless largely nit-picking of what is a theoretically stimulating piece that adds to, and contests, the wealth of criticism on the poem. Forest Pyle's brief 'Skylark-Image, or the Vitality of Disappearance' (*ERR* 25[2014] 319–25) explores the tension between Shelley's 'vitalism' and, read through Deleuze, his aesthetics of disappearance or absence. Focusing on 'To a Skylark', Pyle compares Deleuze's notion of the time-image with the (non)image of Shelley's bird, which he terms 'Skylark-Image'. Of course, the 'Skylark-Image' is absent or not 'visual', yet this does not mean that the poet does not attempt to figure it with a series of imagistic 'failed' similes. Pyle calls this process an 'untethering'; this disappearing bird is conceived as 'vital', and related to the vitally disturbing effect of the Deleuzean cinematic time-image. An interesting, original, and theoretically thorough article, it is hoped that Pyle will expand this into a larger project and apply this framework to Shelley's poetry more widely.

Cian Duffy produced four short Shelley pieces in *Notes & Queries* that remind us of a number of influences on, and sources for, Shelley's poetry. The first of these, '"Such sweet and bitter pain as mine": Mary Wollstonecraft's *Short Residence* and Percy Shelley's "Lines Written in the Bay of Lerici"' (*N&Q* 61[2014] 515–17), reasserts the clear influence of Wollstonecraft. Not only does Duffy trace the verbal and linguistic echoes of a section of Wollstonecraft's *Short Residence* in Shelley's 'Lines Written in the Bay of Lerici', he also suggests these are '*conceptually* equivalent' (p. 517); both concern the loss of someone loved. Two of his further pieces are concerned with aspects of Shelley's *Hellas*. ' "Less accessible than thou or God": Where *Does* Percy Shelley Locate Ahasuerus in *Hellas*?' (*N&Q* 61[2014] 517–19) considers sources for Shelley's location of the Wandering Jew figure in the poem beside the Bosphorus, and speculates that Shelley's blending of his source material served as a way to dodge the censor. 'Percy Shelley's "Display of Newspaper Erudition" in *Hellas, A Lyrical Drama* (1822)' (*N&Q* 61[2014] 519–23) considers Shelley's use of newspapers, the *Galignani's Messenger* in particular, as sources for an authentic account of the rebellion in Greece. This is strange, however, since the *Galignani's Messenger* was unfavourable to the rebellion, although Duffy demonstrates that Shelley drew on it for what he calls 'matters of fact' (p. 521). Duffy's final piece, ' "Radiant as the Morning Star": A Little-Known Shelley Fragment and its Context' (*N&Q* 61[2014] 523–25), considers a short manuscript fragment of Shelley's that is yet to appear in any scholarly edition of Shelley's poetry. Duffy sets out to contextualize the piece, arguing that it is likely associated with Shelley's relationship with Jane Williams and the 'Fragments of an Unfinished Drama' that Mary Shelley included in *Posthumous Poems of Percy Bysshe Shelley*. This is not simply historical context, however, as Duffy notes thematic echoes. One other Shelley piece that appeared in *Notes & Queries* was Andrew Lacey's 'A Possible Echo of Herrick in Shelley's "The Flower That Smiles Today" ' (*N&Q* 61[2014] 525–7). Lacey suggests that this short poem, originally entitled 'Mutability', echoes the seventeenth-century *carpe diem* tradition of poetry that is evident in Robert Herrick's 'To the Virgins, to make much of time'. A convincing reading, the fact that Shelley's poem was originally entitled 'Mutability' reminds us also of Shelley's other influence, Edmund Spenser and his 'Mutabilitie Cantos', only a generation preceding Herrick.

Stephanie Dumke's 'Rediscovered Keats and Shelley Manuscripts in Kraków' (*KSJ* 63[2014] 39–57) is a fascinating and thoroughly researched article that reminds us not only of the fetishistic nature of nineteenth-century manuscript and holograph collections of Romantic poets, but also the oft-neglected notion of a pan-Continental literary culture in the period (see also Paul Stock's *The Byron-Shelley Circle and the Idea of Europe*, reviewed in *YWES* 91[2012]). Dumke's discovery of manuscript fragments in Kraków, particularly the Shelley pieces, shines a new light on to the vexed relationship between author's fair copy and publisher's printed page. Of particular interest is Dumke's tracing of the differences between a fragment of *Laon and Cythna*, canto I, and the version that made it into print. The fact that this poem was later revised into *The Revolt of Islam*, even though Dumke notes that this particular passage remained unaltered, nevertheless raises interesting questions when attempting to read the *Laon and Cythna/Revolt of Islam* alterations thematically. This article is recommended to scholars of Keats and Shelley if only to remind them that authoritative texts of these two poets may yet be challenged with further manuscript discoveries.

A number of 2014 articles reflected a growing trend in Shelley scholarship to consider Shelley in the context of his readership and the publishing realities of his age. Much of this work is indebted to Neil Fraistat's 'Illegitimate Shelley: Radical Piracy and the Textual Edition as Cultural Performance'

(*PMLA* 94[1994] 409–23). Like his article on Byron (see above), Jason I. Kolkey's 'Venal Interchanges: Shelley's *Queen Mab* and Literary Property' (*ERR* 25[2014] 533–50) argues that the copyright law of the period, largely determined by *Southey v Sherwood* (1817) concerning Southey's *Wat Tyler*, had a profound impact on the readership of Shelley's *Queen Mab* following its 1821 piracy. Not only was this in terms of numbers of readers but, more importantly, in terms of their class. Kolkey illustrates Shelley's contradictory and vexed position on this issue and demonstrates some thorough research into letters, periodicals, statutes, and court proceedings. The reality of this 'democratic' piracy is excellently related to Shelley's own writing; although some close reading of *Queen Mab* itself would have helped to develop an understanding of its attraction to such a readership. Nevertheless, Kolkey is convincing in demonstrating how piracy in the period should make us refigure our conceptions of Romantic authorship and genius.

Similar interests are encountered in Alison Morgan's '"God Save Our Queen!"': Percy Bysshe Shelley and Radical Appropriations of the British National Anthem' (*Romanticism* 20[2014] 60–72). This thoroughly researched article is as much a study of the vexed history of the British National Anthem as it is of the relationship between Shelley's 'A New National Anthem' [1819] and the radical tradition of appropriating 'God Save the King'. Morgan shows how the history of the traditional anthem is itself formed by popular Jacobite tavern singing and the contested rearticulation by English and Welsh citizens. Shelley's radical appropriation—in which 'our Queen' is 'liberty'—is therefore an appropriation of an appropriation. This contextualized reading of Shelley helps us to reconsider the poet alongside not only a 'radical' tradition, but a vernacular culture more widely.

Byoung Chun Min's 'Beyond an Intellectual Bourgeois Public Sphere: Percy Bysshe Shelley's "Hermit of Marlow Pamphlets"' (*KSR* 28:ii[2014] 86–103) is another example, as evidenced by its title, of a work that attempts to reconsider Shelley's relationship with the wider reading public. Min's essay focuses on Shelley's so-called 'Hermit of Marlow' pamphlets—*A Proposal of Putting Reform to the Vote* and *An Address to the People on the Death of the Princess Charlotte*—published in 1817. Min's contention is that these pamphlets mark an increasingly close political relationship with Leigh Hunt, particularly in how the elite intellectual poet could begin to engage the public in wider political discussion. Whereas for Min these pamphlets attempt to construct heterogeneity in political discourse, inculcating a unified and inclusive public sphere, this attempt failed. Instead, the pirating and 'illegitimate publishing' of Shelley's works after his death, making him a champion of radical, working-class causes, 'consolidated class consciousness . . . rather than Shelley's inclusive public sphere open to all classes' (p. 102). An interesting reconsideration of Shelley's relationship to the Habermasian public sphere, Min's contention is that readings of Shelley's radicalism are essentially a misappropriation of his project.

Shelley's relationship with and to the wider population is at stake in Dallin Lewis's 'Prophesying the Present: Shelley's Critique of Malthus in *A Defence of Poetry*' (*ERR* 25[2014] 575–90). Lewis's article details Shelley's nuanced engagement with Malthus, noting, for instance, that 'if Shelley was largely persuaded by Malthus's ratios and principles of population, he was aghast at the social policies he drew from them' (p. 579). Lewis intriguingly and convincingly goes on to consider this in light of *A Defence of Poetry*, indicating that it not only appropriates Malthus's rhetoric of scarcity and excess, but reflects Shelley's anxiety that a Malthusian political economist should usurp the prophet-poet's role as an anticipator of the future.

Charlotte Smith's hugely important role in the Romantic-period sonnet revival is evident in two 2014 articles that focus on these most particularly, offering attentive close reading as well as thorough contextual research. Keith Hasperg's '"Saved by the Historic Page": Charlotte Smith's Arun River Sonnets' (*SiR* 53[2014] 103–29) considers the clear historical and historicizing impulse in Smith's writing, such as in *The Emigrants* [1793] and *Beachy Head* [1807], in relation to the literary history evident in her earlier Arun River sonnets [1786]. Hasperg's opening contention is that Smith's sonnets 'contain the genesis of her unique melding of local history and emotional inflection' (p. 103) that she develops in her later blank-verse poems. As well as noting Smith's invocation of local historical literary figures such as Thomas Otway, Hasperg's most interesting argument is that Smith 'meld[s] a Continental tradition, the Petrarchan sonnet of complaint, with an English strand of loco-descriptive verse' (p. 121). In this engaging piece, Hasperg re-emphasizes Smith's abilities as a sonneteer as well as her complex relationship to tradition and originality. This discussion, and particularly Smith's engagement with Petrarch, is similarly encountered in Mary Anne Myers's article, 'Unsexing Petrarch: Charlotte Smith's Lessons in the Sonnet as a Social Medium' (*SiR* 53[2014] 239–59). Myers traces Smith's varying Petrarchan influence through the different versions of the *Elegiac Sonnets* that first appeared in 1784, noting the various intertextual echoes. While arguing that Petrarch served as Smith's model of poetic immortality, Myers also argues for Smith's originality in radically transforming 'Petrarch into something historical yet modern: a sad sonnet speaker freed from gender constraints' (p. 245). Not only does Myers remind us of Smith's poetic abilities, she also offers an intriguing gendered, or rather non-gendered, reading of her aesthetics arrived at through Petrarchan influence.

Discussions of the relationship of a highbrow Romantic poet to the murky publishing realities of the age were not limited to Shelley in 2014. David Duff's 'Wordsworth's "Prospectus": The Genre' (*WC* 45[2014] 178–84), for instance, does much the same with Wordsworth. Duff relates the 107-line passage from the unfinished first book of *The Recluse*, which Wordsworth had called 'a kind of Prospectus' in his preface to *The Excursion*, to a genre that would have been familiar to many of his readers. A prospectus was not only a manifesto of the literary and philosophical concerns of, say, Wordsworth's poem or of Romanticism more widely, but also, as Duff reminds us, a simple printed advertisement for a future publication in order to attract readers and, most importantly, sales. Not only are we thus reminded of Wordsworth's position within, and negotiation with, the marketplace, but through a thorough consideration of a variety of sources Duff demonstrates how the 'language of the marketplace' frequently also inflects poetic language, for example in the work of Byron and even Keats. In this sense, Wordsworth's prospectus works on a number of levels, and it is of course striking that this prospectus was for a poem that never appeared. This, as Duff reminds us, was not uncommon to the genre. This is an excellent example of New Historicist criticism at its best.

Duff's interest in *The Excursion* was not an isolated example. The year 2014 was, after all, the bicentenary of its publication, and journals, most particularly the special issue of *Wordsworth Circle*, published a large volume of articles and papers on the poem. Famously derided by contemporary critics, a number of bicentenary articles worked not only to salvage the poem from its relative critical neglect, but also to argue for its profound literary merit and its importance within Wordsworth's oeuvre. Some articles, such as Graham Davidson's 'Wordsworth's Wasteland or the Speargrass Redemption' (*Romanticism* 20[2014] 73–83) and Sally Bushell's 'From "The Ruined Cottage" to *The Excursion*: Revision as Re-Reading' (*WC* 45[2014] 75–83), focus on the vexed textual history of the much-revised poem. Both take the first book of *The Excursion*, more commonly anthologized separately as 'The Ruined Cottage', as their starting point. Davidson's piece offers sensitive close reading of the different manuscript versions in which the stories of the Pedlar and Margaret are either separate or 'yoke[d] . . . together' (p. 74). Davidson's argument is that Wordsworth's final decision to combine the two stories is 'a courageous acknowledgment of a conflict in his genius' (p. 74). This conflict is essentially between the mortal, momentary, and earthly suffering of non-poetic everyday life (Margaret) and the visionary, poetic infinite demonstrated by the Wordsworthian poet-figure of the Pedlar. Davidson therefore enables us to see *The Excursion* as a critical poem in the Wordsworth canon that bridges the gap between *Lyrical Ballads* and the more visionary *Prelude*. Bushell's article similarly notes the tensions involved in revision and (writerly) rereading, but uses such theorists as Barthes and Bakhtin to argue for how conceptions of a text's totality and temporality inflect our reading(s) and interpretation(s) of fragments and vice versa. Bushell posits Wordsworth as a 'writerly reader' in this light, and notes how Wordsworth's 'return' to the poem is akin to the Pedlar-cum-Wanderer who guides the reader through 'The Ruined Cottage' and *The Excursion*.

William Galperin's 'The Essential Reality of *The Excursion*' (*WC* 45[2014] 104–18) similarly begins with the revisions made between 'The Ruined Cottage' and Book I. Galperin's convincing argument is that many of the revisions reflect Wordsworth's shifting attitude(s) to the nature of reality and his revised emphasis on 'human life' as opposed to 'Man' and 'Nature' as argued for in the prospectus. The narrative present-tense vignettes in the poem, Galperin argues, serve as a 'memorial to the living'. This article very much functions in dialogue with Jonathan Wordsworth's *The Music of Humanity* (reviewed in *YWES* 50[1971]) and serves as an excellent supplement to this monumental work. A consideration of *The Excursion*'s 'musicality' is the focus of Richard Gravil's 'The Excursion: An Unparalleled "Variety of Musical Effect"' (*WC* 45[2014] 84–92), which not only reminds us of John Thelwall's reading of *The Excursion* (Wordsworth had praised, as Gravil reminds us, Thelwall's good ear) but also offers an overview of Wordsworth's metrical theory. This, excluding Gravil's own work, is barely covered by Wordsworth scholars. Gravil's thorough scansion of passages from *The*

Excursion helps to remind us of the variety of musical effects in the poem, arguing strongly for an aural approach to the text that may help us to discern the different speakers more easily. Gravil also situates Wordsworth's prosody as conversely both within and outside literary tradition, allowing us to reflect on the position of Wordsworth's poetics in literary history. Michael O'Neill's 'Ebb and Flow in *The Excursion*' (*WC* 45[2014] 93–8) similarly makes a very strong case for *The Excursion*'s literary merit, referring to it as a 'masterpiece' that requires no 'self-qualifying apologia' (p. 93) from critics. O'Neill proceeds to justify his claim through his trademark formal attention that shows the poem to be one of sophisticated, intellectual paradox. O'Neill concludes that the poem is one aware of its own 'struggle and difficulty' (p. 98), in ways that later influenced Keats and Shelley.

Jonathan Farina's '*The Excursion* and "The Surface of Things"' (*WC* 45[2014] 99–105) reconsiders Wordsworth's attitude to surfaces and depth in the poem, noting that, despite Wordsworth's accomplishment in a 'depth model of character' (p. 99), surfaces nevertheless remain important to him. Farina suggests in particular that '*The Excursion* exhibits a meaningful superficiality' (p. 99). Highlighting the frequent references to 'things' both in *The Excursion* and in Wordsworth's poetry more widely, Farina's main argument is that these things or objects allow for a 'process of abstraction that produces [a] kind of social connectivity and knowledge' (p. 100). Essentially, surface interest in objects produces an 'epistemological credibility' and serves as a way of determining character through their 'interfac[ing] with the outside world' (p. 105). Tom Clucas's article 'Plutarch's Parallel Lives in *The Excursion*' (*WC* 45[2014] 126–30) shares a similar interest in Wordsworth's characterization but takes a rather different approach. Focusing on the influence of Plutarch, Clucas argues for how Plutarch's view of character shaped Wordsworth's own. In particular, by incorporating 'Essays upon Epitaphs', Clucas discusses the 'Parallel Lives' of Grasmere, ending by demonstrating how 'The "Church-yard Among the Mountains" offers more than Christian solace in *The Excursion*: it serves as a library of human character every bit as replete as Greek and Roman history with exemplary lives' (p. 130). Although Wordsworth's classical inheritance is hardly neglected, as J. Douglas Kneale and Bruce Graver have shown us, Clucas's article nevertheless offers a reading of classical character as fundamental to his poetics.

A number of scholars focused on the religious medieval history in the poem, as opposed to the classical. Ruth Abbott's 'Scholarship, Spontaneity, and *The Excursion* Book IV' (*WC* 45[2014] 119–25) adds a level of nuance to considerations of Wordsworth's epistemology. The detailed accounts of early religious practices outlined by the Wanderer in Book IV are considered as the result of Wordsworth's meticulous scholarship rather than solely spontaneous, poetical inspiration. Abbott's argument is that Wordsworth sees the relationship between scholarship, that is, learning from books, versus inspiration or learning from nature such as in 'The Tables Turned' [1798], as a tense one; nevertheless, it is one that is 'paradoxically co-dependent' (p. 125). The Wanderer's religious history narratives, then, are seen as illustrating how scholastic learning can inform spontaneous inspiration and vice versa. Clare

A. Simmons's 'Medievalism in *The Excursion*' (*WC* 45[2014] 131–7) reads the poem in the light of Gothic medievalism despite its early nineteenth-century 'setting'. Simmons notes how *The Excursion*'s four speakers find something of value in the medieval past which combines to give a Wordsworthian-inflected and 'reformed' medievalism. The medieval past—and the unreformed church—is acknowledged patriotically by the four speakers as part of the past of England and as a pointer towards futurity. The physical church encountered in Book V, often regarded as resembling St Oswald's in Grasmere, is read as a palimpsest in which English and Anglican values are read 'over' the Catholic medievalism that preceded them.

Richard E. Brantley's '*The Excursion*: Wordsworth's Art of Belief' (*WC* 45[2014] 162–70) continues this interest in Wordsworth's theology. Brantley notes the tension between the Anglo-Catholic metaphor of a Gothic church that Wordsworth employs in describing his corpus, and *The Excursion*'s expression of High Church Romanticism. Brantley's reading of the poem, however, is one that reminds us of Wordsworth's engagement with a Low Church dissenting and evangelical tradition as much as, if not more than, Anglicanism. The Wanderer's testimony, for instance, is likened to the teachings of Isaac Watts and John and Charles Wesley. Similarly, the Pastor's story of Ellen is compared to John Wesley's account of Mary Pendavres. Brantley's main contention is that *The Excursion* dramatizes the eighteenth- and nineteenth-century tension between faith and works, or Calvinism and Arminianism, with Wordsworth seeming to settle on the latter. However, this tension is nevertheless poetically fruitful, in that Wordsworth lets the 'theological conundrum of inspiration versus obligation deepen his poetic faith' (p. 170). Brantley helps us to remember that much of the co-opting of Wordsworth as *wholly* Anglican, whatever his public declarations, was more the work of Victorian appropriation. In this sense, Stephen Gill's work still has a very discernible influence. The consideration of Victorian readings of Wordsworth's theology is the subject of Robert M. Ryan's 'Religious Revisioning in *The Excursion*' (*WC* 45[2014] 171–7). Indeed, Ryan's main argument is that 'Wordsworth's poetry, *The Excursion* in particular, figured prominently in theological discussion during what is called the Victorian crisis of faith' (p. 171). Ryan rightly highlights how the poem was claimed by numerous different religious denominations and was seen as fulfilling often opposing spiritual needs. The theological discussions between the four speakers of the poem are seen to offer 'a model of speculative freedom in theology' with various readers seeing Wordsworth's poetry either as 'supplementary to the Bible' or as 'an alternative to scripture'. Ryan's article is itself an excellent supplement to his magisterial *The Romantic Reformation* (reviewed in *YWES* 77[1999]) and is a superb addition to the debates concerning Wordsworth's religion as well as posthumous reception.

This reading of Wordsworth through a Victorian perspective is, at least in part, also found in Kenneth R. Johnston's 'Wordsworth's Excursion: Route and Destination' (*WC* 45[2014] 106–13). Contextualizing the composition of *The Excursion/Recluse* project within the repressive climate of the French Revolutionary Wars, Johnston reads the Solitary as a figure suffering ideological despair following the apparent failure of the ideals of the revolution. Johnston sees Wordsworth's project, then, as one that attempts to revive the Solitary's lost idealism but, unfortunately, results in failure. Intriguingly, Johnston contrasts this to the apparent optimism in Charles Dickens's *A Tale of Two Cities* [1859]. Following attentive close reading of the novel, Johnston argues that it is in the intertextual reading of the two writers that one can observe how the ideals of the French Revolution could still live on in nineteenth-century British culture. Dickens and Wordsworth, then, are seen as writers keen on capturing revolutionary ideals despite the difficult domestic and cultural politics of their respective ages. Revolutionary ideals are also the subject of Stuart Andrews's 'Wordsworth, Southey, Coleridge: Their Iberian Spring' (*WC* 45[2014] 49–3). Andrews's piece is a meticulously researched account of these three poets' reaction to the military and political situation in Spain during the Peninsular Wars as well as their various writings on such issues as the Convention of Cintra. Although Andrews's piece functions more as a historical overview rather than necessarily presenting a rigorous argument, he nevertheless concludes by suggesting that, far from the poets having abandoned their revolutionary ideals by 1810, the location of 'revolution' had simply moved to Spain, as Southey had himself declared in his letters. This article can therefore be read in relation to the work of Diego Saglia, who argues that the Iberian peninsula was seen as a space of British imaginative and revolutionary possibilities.

Reading Wordsworth in relation to, or through the lens of, another writer was the subject of four further articles in 2014. Two of these discussed the co-influential relationship between Wordsworth and Robert Southey in relation to *The Excursion*. Tom Duggett's 'The Dramatic End of *The Excursion*' (*WC* 45[2014] 157–61), for instance, notes how the Wanderer's calls for a 'System of National Education' are not only inspired by the writings of the educational theorist Dr Andrew Bell. We are also reminded, in an echo of Alan Richardson's *Literature, Education and Romanticism* [2004], how Books VIII and IX are heavily indebted to Southey's recent writings in the *Quarterly Review*. Duggett goes on to demonstrate how the debt to Southey is even more pronounced when considering manuscript drafts, and suggests that the seeming endorsement of Bell's theories contains within it the seeds of Wordsworth's later rejection of them by 1838, perhaps influenced by Southey. Quentin Bailey, by contrast, argues in ' "The Ruined Cottage" and Southey's *English Eclogues*' (*WC* 45[2014] 151–7) that Southey's 'English Eclogue VI', known as 'The Ruined Cottage', was heavily influenced by the first version of Wordsworth's poem of the same name. Bailey also compares the protagonist of Southey's poem 'Hannah' to Wordsworth's Margaret. Because of what he sees as Southey's reassertion of class difference, however, the presentation of human suffering is seen as very different in the two poets' work, with Bailey arguing that Southey's depictions result in 'sentimental morality' or 'condescending sympathy' (p. 161). While this is subjective, Bailey's analysis nevertheless helps to reassert the fruitful poetic relationship between the two men, while simultaneously emphasizing their marked differences and individuality.

Robert Stagg's 'Wordsworth, Pope, and Writing after Bathos' (*EIC* 64[2014] 29–44), focuses on a rarely studied element of Wordsworth's poetry through an even rarer literary comparison. Stagg traces Wordsworth's use of bathos in relation to its extensive use by Alexander Pope, who is credited as having brought the word into English in his *Peri Bathous; or, The Art of Sinking in Poetry* [1727]. Whereas Pope generally employed it for satirical effect, Stagg argues for Wordsworth's bathos as working alongside and even enhancing the wonder of the sublime. In order to exalt or to rise, Stagg argues, Wordsworth often has 'to sink' first, meaning that 'wonder emerges from the bathos that initially contains it' (p. 42). This article essentially reveals the Augustan source for a distinctly Romantic effect. Daniel Clay's 'Milton, Mulciber, and *The Prelude*' (*WC* 45[2014] 66–8), on the other hand, revisits and reinterprets *The Prelude*'s Miltonic inheritance and allusions to *Paradise Lost*. Although noting the Miltonic echoes in Wordsworth is not new, indeed, Robin Jarvis, Lucy Newlyn, Jonathan Wordsworth, and Harold Bloom are clear influences on the piece, Clay nevertheless offers an original close reading. Clay notes an allusion in descriptions of Wordsworth's childhood games in both the 1805 and 1850 *Prelude* to the fall of Mulciber in Milton's poem. Such a comparison seems a strange one. Clay's suggestion is that this allusion is perhaps to be considered in the mock-heroic mode, much like Pope's *The Rape of the Lock*. Furthermore, in the light of Harold Bloom, it is perhaps another example of the anxiety of influence.

Two further articles that did not focus on *The Excursion* in 2014 both took original approaches to some key Wordsworthian concepts. James Castell's short article, 'Wordsworth, Silence and the Nonhuman' (*WC* 45[2014] 58–61), turns on two familiar Wordsworthian tropes or themes—his poetry's engagement with animal and other non-human elements, and his paradoxical representation of silence—and considers them through a sophisticated theoretical lens. Not only, then, does Castell's article work within the emerging 'nonhuman turn', it is also far more philosophically and theoretically rigorous, as well as formally attentive, than many pieces that characterize this new literary-critical approach. Considering literature as paradoxically 'silent' and 'breaking the silence', Castell relates this to treatment of the nonhuman, 'when the human noise of language interacts with the natural world' (pp. 58–9). Focusing on 'Yes! Full surely 'twas the Echo' [1807], Castell convincingly demonstrates that 'the relation of animal life to song . . . results in a voiced silence as profound as it is obscure' (p. 61). A stimulating piece, it would be pleasing to see such formal and theoretical rigour applied in a longer article and to a wider body of Wordsworth's poetry.

Although Wordsworth is perhaps most commonly seen as a poet of nature and the nonhuman, it is worth remembering that the city—and London most particularly—plays an important role in much of his writing, whether in simple opposition to Wordsworth's desired 'natural' solitary repose or otherwise. Peter Larkin's complex 'Wordsworth's City Retractions' (*WC* 45[2014] 54–8) considers Wordsworth's ambivalent attitude to London primarily in Books I and VII of *The Prelude* but also the much-anthologized 'Composed upon Westminster Bridge' [1802]. Larkin reads Wordsworth's city as a space that resists easy definition. His discussion of the Bartholomew Fair passage is engaging, although the 'blank confusion' the poet encounters in his endless listing of the 'faces' of the tide of people (as Larkin discusses) could have been read as poetically self-conscious; is this 'blank confusion' a reference to the 'failure' of Wordsworth's blank verse in capturing the ineffable city? Nevertheless, this is a dense, theoretically informed article that rewards attentive reading.

Three articles took a slightly more biographical approach to Wordsworth's poetry, particularly focusing on youth, old age, and death. Peter Swaab's 'Wordsworth's Elegies for John Wordsworth' (*WC* 45[2014] 30–8), for instance, considers a number of elegiac poems Wordsworth wrote following the death of his brother John at sea in 1805. Noting the productive paradox of elegy, in which grief essentially suits the poet's aim, Swaab posits that Wordsworth does not quite seem to fit this pattern. At first, John's death halted Wordsworth's productivity, but ultimately, Swaab argues convincingly through thorough engagement with Wordsworth's letters and poetry, not only do the poems dramatize a struggle to come to terms with grief, they also reflect profound developments in Wordsworth's professional career. Wordsworth's revisionary tendencies throughout his long life, as seen in a number of other articles in 2014, are connected to his interest in the encounters between youth and old age that characterize so much of his poetry. Peter Manning's article 'Wordsworth in Youth and Age' (*ERR* 25[2014] 385–96) takes a multifaceted approach to this issue, considering publication and book history, with images, as well as comparative readings between two 1800 poems and Wordsworth's *To an Octogenarian* [1846]. Whereas the earlier poems are concerned with potentiality, from 'the here' to 'the there' as Manning puts it, *To an Octogenarian* is from the position of 'there' (which is now 'here'), and is more a contemplation of loss and what has passed. Nevertheless, Manning is at pains to stress that potentiality still remains in the later poem, even if this future remains a bleak one. As well as offering up a close reading of a number of less familiar poems, Manning's article encourages us to trace trends and themes in Wordsworth—such as contemplations of youth and age—across his whole career in order to discern both continuation and revision. Returning to a consideration of Wordsworth's youth, Jack Vespa's 'Veiled Movements in "The Vale of Esthwaite"' (*WC* 45[2014] 62–6) follows very much in the wake of the work of David Fairer, in that this early poem of Wordsworth's is read in relation to a Virgilian georgic tradition. Vespa contends, however, that this georgic mode is one approached through seventeenth- and eighteenth-century understandings of Virgil's georgics and that 'The Vale of Esthwaite' demonstrates both an awareness of literary tradition and the promise of the poet that is to come.

Biographical approaches to Wordsworth dominated the monograph publications in 2014. Stephen Gill's 1989 biography, *William Wordsworth: A Life*, is exhaustive, thoroughly researched yet written in an accessible style and thus of use to scholars and more casual readers alike. It is, therefore, rightly considered the go-to critical biography of Wordsworth's life and works and the intersection of the two. In the decades since, numerous other biographies, such as those by Juliet Barker and Lucy Newlyn, have appeared to shed further light on the life of one of the most well-known poets of all time. It would appear then that there is very little space remaining or, indeed, need for, a further biography of Wordsworth. However, 2014 saw the publication of two, admittedly rather different, biographical studies. Of the two, John Worthen's *The Life of William Wordsworth: A Critical Biography* is most similar to Gill's, at least in form, in that it is a single-volume work of exhaustive and highly detailed research into the minutiae of Wordsworth's daily life. What Worthen adds to the wealth of biographical information is an intense attention to Wordsworth's financial situation. Indeed, although it is no secret that Wordsworth's early years were largely spent in poverty, particularly after the death of his father while William was still a child, and then of his brother in 1805, Worthen's study sets out to consider how these financial circumstances in fact affected his creative work as a poet into adulthood and throughout his life. Not only did this situation shape the character of a man Worthen sees as an obstinate, single-minded poet, but we are offered an insight into Wordsworth's publishing practices as allied to his existing economic concerns. Worthen's research is astonishingly attentive to very specific prices and costs and to the mundane realities of a poet's life.

It is this very mundanity, however, that calls into question whether labelling the text a 'Critical Biography' is helpful. Much of Worthen's research does not help in interpreting the poetry, nor do we gain an insight into the creative process; financial minutiae are not exactly thematic concerns for Wordsworth. Connected to this, it is difficult to discern the biography's intended audience; a number of footnotes gloss such things as pre-decimalization currency (p. 11), which would seem to imply an undergraduate readership. It is debatable, however, whether undergraduate students would learn much from, or be interested in, such details of Wordsworth's life. Nevertheless, the level of research is to be commended, and Worthen's book is sure to serve as a valuable resource for future scholars.

Daniel Robinson's *Myself and Some Other Being: Wordsworth and the Life Writing* is an engaging and highly accessible short book that is more than simple literary biography; it turns on the multiplicity of meanings in the phrase 'life-writing'. As well as suggesting Wordsworthian (auto)biography, it also offers up the notion of life-writing as not simply mimetic but life-*creating*, involving a construction of the self as much as it does a simple record. As Robinson himself puts it 'Wordsworth writes *The Prelude* to write that self into existence. This person, the life writing (that is, the living person doing the writing), William Wordsworth, writes his life in the hope of finding words of writing himself as a writer, as *Wordsworth*' (p. 2). This is not to suggest that Robinson—or indeed Wordsworth—somehow sees this life-writing as the solely authentic self since his title, adapted from the second book of *The Prelude*, indicates that writing also creates a 'second self'. Robinson's book then, if implicitly, reminds us not only of Romantic writing's influence on deconstruction but also of Wordsworth's own self-fashioning. It is evident that Andrew Bennett's work on Wordsworth is a strong theoretical influence.

Robinson's further consideration of the term 'life-writing' is one that refers to the vocation in which a life is spent, that is, a 'life [spent] writing', and the continual editing of Wordsworth's poetic autobiography serves to demonstrate that both life and *writerly* life are processes subject to revision. Robinson's main contention is that 'the life writing [is] part of the beginning of the writing life' (p. 3) and we are reminded that *The Prelude* only details the 'growth of a poet's mind' in its earliest years, as a child and a young man. It is indeed the start of, or the prelude to, what is to come, despite its posthumous initial publication. In tracing the life of a writer through his own life-writing, then, it is clever of Robinson to title his own opening chapter 'Prelude'. This charming wit and informal style are evident throughout the book and, even if long-term scholars of Wordsworth may not find much with which they are not familiar, this is a personal and innovative approach that is likely to inform new Wordsworthians as much as it entertains old ones by the manner of its telling.

It is indeed a popular as well as a scholarly pursuit to 'locate' Wordsworth. If one visits the Lake District today one cannot escape the clear Wordsworthian influence on the existing tourist industry. Not all of this is down to the work of the Wordsworth Trust; popular consciousness has led to such a Wordsworthian association with the area that there are at least three Wordsworth Hotels (Cockermouth, Ambleside, and Grasmere) as well as a Daffodils Hotel (Grasmere). Wordsworth himself of course wrote one of the great guidebooks to the region, his *Guide to the Lakes* [1810], which has often led critics to consider him as the Lakes' discoverer. As is evident from the title of her *William Wordsworth and the Invention of Tourism*, Saeko Yoshikawa treads along the same lines. Indeed, she reminds us how the very term 'Lake District' did not come into being until the 1830s, and suggests that this naming was influenced by the 1835 phrase 'the District of the Lakes' that appeared on the title page of the fifth edition of Wordsworth's *Guide* (p. 4). The fact that 'literary tourism' did not quite take off in the region until the Lake District was recognized as a single area, then, essentially implies that Wordsworth created it. Furthermore, Yoshikawa argues, this had a further influence on tourism more widely in the Victorian age. This may seem a bold claim, but Yoshikawa's meticulous research is often convincing. She covers subsequent guides to the Lake District that frequently quoted Wordsworth's poems for picturesque or topographical detail, some of which were even the first instances of the poems in print. In this sense, these guidebooks not only shaped tourists' conceptions of the Lake District but also influenced the Victorian Wordsworth canon. Indeed, the influence of Stephen Gill's work is once again very much in evidence here.

Yoshikawa also details other accounts, such as a book of sketches of Wordsworthian topography from 1850 by an anonymous 'literary pilgrim' in the few weeks after the poet's death. Yoshikawa demonstrates through such attention that, whereas early Wordsworthian tourism was more of the picturesque kind, this developed to become one more associated with poetry and literary pilgrimage; not only to visit the locations associated with the great poet Wordsworth, but also somehow to be imbued by the poetics of the landscape. Fiona Stafford's *Local Attachments: The Province of Poetry* (reviewed in *YWES* 91[2012]) would have helped Yoshikawa to consider the particular poetic resonance of place that draws so many to visit the places associated with great poets, and it is a shame it is not included. Nevertheless, this is an engaging monograph that is exhaustively researched—the bibliography alone will serve as a superb resource for later scholars—and offers a different approach to a relatively well-trodden topic.

Lastly, unfortunately *The Charles Lamb Bulletin* was unavailable through-out the entire writing of this section. Any articles published in that publication relevant to this section will be reviewed as part of 2015.

4. Drama

The texts in this year's review cover a variety of topics including Shakespeare, gender, celebrity, reception, and the theatre itself.

The first text reviewed is the excellent and comprehensive *Oxford Handbook of the Georgian Theatre 1737–1782*, edited by Julia Swindells and David Francis Taylor, also reviewed in Chapter XII. In his introduction, Taylor states that the aim of the *Handbook* is 'to look and listen for the gaps and silences in the narratives we inherit' (p. 2) and this provides the cohesion for the diverse range of topics examined. The *Handbook* is organized into eight sections: 'Theatre, Theory, Historiography', 'Legislating Drama', 'The Changing Cultures of Performance', 'The Whole Show: Spectacles, Sounds, Spaces', 'Genres and Forms', 'Theatre and the Romantic Canon', 'Women and the Stage', and 'Performing Race and Empire'. Sadly, it is not possible in the scope of this piece to review all of the relevant chapters that fall under the heading of Romantic drama; the following is therefore a small representation of the excellent contributions made. Betsy Bolton's engaging chapter 'Theorizing Audience and Spectacle' examines the different approaches that theatre historians and media theorists have used in the past, suggesting that there are a number of 'truisms' which need to be challenged (p. 32), for example the relationship between the actors and the audience. Particularly interesting is Bolton's discussion of the importance of the persona that the celebrity actor has created, particularly when associated with prologues and epilogues that 'are positioned precisely between the intersection between the bourgeoisie public sphere . . . and its "mass cultural public sphere" ' (p. 42). Marvin Carlson's chapter 'Performative Event' also challenges assumptions that have pervaded works about theatre by theatre historians. Carlson demonstrates how changing methodologies in the arts and humanities have opened up new possibilities for examining audience and performance. On a slightly different note, Heather McPherson examines 'the heightened signifi-cance of the actor as cultural icon and artistic commodity' (p. 192). She discusses prints, portraits, and ceramics that represented celebrity actors and actresses playing the roles that they were most associated with. In particular her chapter concentrates on 'how the image of the actor was culturally re-configured, commodified and metamorphosed into porcelain' (p. 193). Paula Backscheider's chapter, 'Retrieving Elizabeth Inchbald', begins with the recognition that Inchbald's dramatic work, until recently, has been neglected. Backscheider suggests that part of the reason for this neglect is because of the 'unorthodox' nature of Inchbald's career, and that 'to understand it requires understanding of many kinds of theatrical practices of the time' (p. 604). In her elucidation of Inchbald's drama, Backscheider examines the relationship between Inchbald and the Haymarket Theatre with Elizabeth Farren as its star and also Inchbald's afterpieces, farces, adaptations, power balances, and 'the

Imperial mind' (p. 616). Backscheider concludes by stating that we are just beginning the work on Inchbald's 'mastery of theatrical practices' (p. 618), and indeed it will be an interesting field of study. All in all, this volume is a considered, coherent, and excellent resource for students and academics in this field.

Fiona Ritchie's chapter 'Jordan and Siddons: Beyond Thalia and Melpomene' is the most relevant chapter for readers of this section in her compelling study, *Women and Shakespeare in the Eighteenth Century*, also reviewed in Chapter XII. Ritchie also challenges some preconceived notions about Shakespeare which concentrate on the page by examining the role of women, critics, actresses, and audiences in the eighteenth century, all of whom were part of the reconfiguration of Shakespeare's reputation across the century. In her examinations of the two actresses, Ritchie states that the identification of Jordan and Siddons as 'rival muses is restrictive rather than productive' (p. 111), and moreover that the 'relationship between Jordan and Shakespeare' has not been so clearly acknowledged (p. 134). Ritchie examines the identification of Siddons as playing tragic heroines and Jordan as playing breeches parts. She also points out that there is little acknowledgement of Jordan's most successful tragic role when she played Ophelia in 1796. This is an important study, and through Ritchie's re-evaluation of their performances we can better understand the careers of these two important eighteenth-century actresses.

Continuing the theme of the importance of women in eighteenth-century theatre is Laura Engel and Elaine McGirr's essay collection *Stage Mothers: Women, Work, and the Theater, 1660–1830*, also considered in Chapter XII. The collection is presented in three sections, 'Actresses, Motherhood, and the Profession of the Stage', 'Representations of Mothers on the Stage', and 'Actresses and Their Children', and examines 'the overlaps and disconnection between representations and realities of maternity' (p. 2). In particular the collection explores the tensions associated with maternity and motherhood for the celebrity actress. McGirr and Engel state that the main aim of the collection is to examine ideas of what it meant to be a woman in the eighteenth century and 'how this shaped female performance' (p. 7). The collection more than achieves its aim. Among the many erudite chapters is Elena Malenas Ledoux's 'Working Mothers on the Romantic Stage', which concentrates on the similarities and differences in the approaches taken by Sarah Siddons and Mary Robinson in order to create their public personas. Moreover, Ledoux examines the ways in which each woman adapted her persona as she responded to 'life-changing events and physical alterations, including child-birth, motherhood, aging and illness' (p. 80). A great strength of this chapter is that Ledoux does not go over old ground with an examination positioned entirely on the personal lives of each woman; rather, she examines the 'enormous amount of slippage between the real and the theatrical . . . and the many layers of performance and intertextuality that they must negotiate to achieve their desired persona' (p. 84). Jade Higa's chapter, 'My Son, My Lover: Gothic Contagion and Maternal Sexuality in *The Mysterious Mother*', examines Horace Walpole's closet drama written in 1786, although not published until 1781. Drawing on Eve Sedgwick's concept of Gothic contagion and the work of Catherine Spooner, Higa examines the maternal sexuality in *The Mysterious Mother* alongside eighteenth-century notions about motherhood. Higa concludes that, in eighteenth-century terms, 'the intertwining of motherhood and sexuality is monstrous and deviant because it has the ability to spread through affect' (p. 192). Other notable essays that are relevant for this section, include Helen E.M. Brooks's ' "The Divided Heart of the Actress: Late Eighteenth-Century Actresses and the "Cult of Maternity" ', Judith Hawley's 'Elizabeth and Keppel Craven and the Domestic Drama of Mother–Son Relations', and Laura Engel's 'Mommy Diva: The Divided Loyalties of Sarah Siddons'.

Texts about Shakespeare endure, and although much of Jean I. Marsden's *The Re-imagined Text: Shakespeare, Adaptation, & Eighteenth-Century Literary Theory* falls outside the remit of this section, the text makes a number of interesting points which are appropriate, not least because of its premise that 'the Restoration and eighteenth century produced one of the most subversive acts in literary history—the rewriting and restructuring of Shakespeare's plays' (p. 1). Moreover Marsden is more interested in the reception of these adaptations rather than a historical examination of the productions. The text is organized in two parts: Part I, 'The Re-imagined Text', which examines adaptations and early criticism of Shakespearian texts and productions, and Part II, 'Refined from the Dross', which examines the decline of adaptation towards the latter part of the eighteenth century. Chapter 5, 'The Search for a Genuine Text', is an interesting examination of the response to Samuel Johnson's 1765 edition of Shakespeare alongside 'the other great Shakespearian phenomenon of the 1760s, Garrick's 1769 Shakespeare Jubilee' (p. 127). Marsden concludes with a discussion of the reasons why so many of the adaptations have disappeared.

The final monograph for this section is one that is slightly off-track, but eminently readable. This is Richard L. Lorenzen's *The History of the Prince of Wales Theatre, London, 1771–1793*. The first two chapters which are relevant to this section, outline the beginnings of the Tottenham Street theatre and its various incarnations until it was renamed the Prince of Wales theatre in 1865; it closed in 1882. The text is meticulously researched and the playbills, engravings, photographs, and caricatures provide an enthralling read about the theatrical activity, audiences, popular taste, and the managers of this now defunct theatre.

The theme of Shakespeare and celebrity is continued in Joseph Roach's 'Celebrity Culture and the Problem of Biography' (*SQ* 65[2014] 470–81), which suggests a correlation between the celebrity status of David Garrick and Sarah Siddons and the 'popular adulation' of Shakespeare (p. 471). Moreover, Roach argues that 'the ongoing collaboration by Shakespeare with celebrated actors and producers expands the idea of what constitutes his "life"—[and] is a more illuminating part of the playwright's proper biography than any of the extant Elizabethan or Jacobean documents or portraits, interesting as they may be as evidence of the period' (p. 471). To support his argument, Roach examines letters between British diplomat Sir Charles Hanbury Williams and his daughters in their discussion of their attendance at theatres and in particular Garrick's portrayal of Lear. Roach also examines a series of sketches by John Flaxman of actors, such as Sarah Siddons, playing Shakespearian roles. Roach concludes his argument by stating that 'a life written in legal documents and real estate transactions is clearly to suggest its evanescence' (p. 481). However, where Shakespeare is concerned, to find the man we should look at the performances of his work.

The final journal article reviewed this year is Slaney Chadwick Ross's 'Maria Edgeworth's *The Rose, Thistle, and Shamrock*: Symbolic Unification, Women's Education, and the Marriage Plot' (*ECent* 55[2014] 377–90). Ross argues that this work, published in Edgeworth's collection *Comic Dramas* [1817], 'is both a re-envisioning of the Irish national tale and a pedagogical treatise for young, upper-class Anglo-Irish women' (p. 377). Moreover Edgeworth's play demonstrates her 'response to a variety of generic influences—from closet drama to the national tale to pedagogical theory' (p. 378). Ross discusses the problematic nature of 'Characteristick Comedy [which] can be at odds with pedagogical performance: the language of contract and moral propriety' (p. 384). Ross concludes with the assertion that although the play is 'a minor representative of Edgeworth's extensive body of work', it is 'a mighty example of Edgeworth's championship of an enlarged sphere of female authority' (p. 387). Finally, it should be noted that the edition of the collected works of Ann Yearsley reviewed in Section 3 above also contains a volume of Yearsley's play, *Earl Goodwin* (first performed in 1789), made available for the first time since the eighteenth century. It is pleasing to see this work in print once again, in this rigorous and intelligently conceived edition.

Books Reviewed

Andrews, Kerri, ed. *The Collected Works of Ann Yearsley*, 3 vols. P&C. [2014] pp. 1,008. £275 ISBN 9 7818 5196 6387.

Andrews, Kerri, Ann Yearsley, and Hannah More. *Patronage and Poetry: The Story of a Literary Friendship*. P&C. [2013] pp. x + 188. £60 ISBN 9 7818 4893 1510.

Baines, Paul, ed. *The Collected Writings of Edward Rushton*. LiverUP. [2014] pp. vii + 348. £75 ISBN 9 7817 8138 1366.

Barbeau, Jeffrey W. *Sara Coleridge: Her Life and Thought*. PalMac. [2014] pp. xx + 227. £57.50 ISBN 9 7811 3732 4979.

Bohls, Elizabeth A. *Slavery and the Politics of Place: Representing the Colonial Caribbean, 1770–1833*. CUP. [2014] pp. 288. £60 ISBN 9 7811 0707 9342.

Bugg, John. *Five Long Winters: The Trials of British Romanticism*. StanfordUP. [2014] pp. xii + 246. $60 ISBN 9 7808 0478 5105.

Burley, Stephen. *Hazlitt the Dissenter: Religion, Philosophy, and Politics, 1766–1816*. PalMac. [2014] pp. 240. £60 ISBN 9 7811 3736 4425.

Clemit, Pamela, ed. *The Letters of William Godwin, vol. 2: 1798–1805*. OUP. [2014] pp. 472. £100 ISBN 9 7801 9956 2626.

Cochran, Peter. *The Burning of Byron's Memoirs*. CambridgeSP. [2014] pp. xiv + 435. £57.99 ISBN 9 7814 4386 8150.

Cox, Jeffrey N. *Romanticism in the Shadow of War: Literary Culture in the Napoleonic War Years*. CUP. [2014] pp. 296. £60 ISBN 9 7811 0707 1940.

Coyer, Megan J, and David E Shuttleton., eds. *Scottish Medicine and Literary Culture, 1726–1832*. Rodopi. [2014] pp. xi + 315. £63 ISBN 9 7890 4203 8912.

Culley, Amy. *British Women's Life Writing, 1760–1840: Friendship, Community and Collaboration*. PalMac. [2014] pp. viii + 270. £55 ISBN 9 7811 3727 4212.

Davies, Jeremy, *Bodily Pain in Romantic Literature*. Routledge. [2014] pp. 228. £90 ISBN: 9 7804 1584 2914.

Davies, Rebecca. *Written Maternal Authority and Eighteenth-Century Education in Britain: Educating by the Book*. Ashgate. [2014] pp. xii + 170. £95 ISBN 9 7814 0945 1686.

De Freitas Boe, Ana, and Abby Coykendall, eds. *Heteronormativity in Eighteenth-Century Literature and Culture*. Ashgate. [2014] pp. xiii + 219. £65 ISBN 9 7814 7243 0175.

De Ritter, Richard. *Imagining Women Readers, 1789–1820: Well-Regulated Minds*. MUP. [2014] pp. 224. £70 ISBN 9 7807 1909 0332.

Dew, Ben, and Fiona Price, eds. *Historical Writing in Britain, 1688–1830: Visions of History*. PalMac. [2014] pp. x + 228. £55 ISBN 9 7811 3733 2639.

Engel, Laura, and Elaine McGirr, eds. *Stage Mothers: Women, Work, and the Theater, 1660–1830*. BuckUP. [2014] pp. 290. $90 ISBN 9 7816 1148 6032.

Faflak, Joel, and Richard C. Sha, eds. *Romanticism and the Emotions*. CUP. [2014] pp. x + 264. $99 ISBN 9 7811 0705 2390.

Farrell, Michael. *Blake and the Methodists*. PalMac. [2014] pp. x + 259. £55 ISBN 9 7811 3745 5499.

Fermanis, Porscha, and John Regan. *Rethinking British Romantic History, 1770–1845*. OUP. [2014] pp. 352. £60 ISBN 9 7801 9968 7084.

Folsom, Marcia McClintock, and John Wiltshire, eds. *Approaches to Teaching Austen's Mansfield Park*. MLA. [2014] pp. 255. $24 (pb) ISBN 9 7816 0329 1989.

Freeman, Kathryn S. *British Women Writers and the Asiatic Society of Bengal, 1785–1835: Re-Orienting Anglo-India*. Ashgate. [2014] pp. viii + 151. £65 ISBN 9 7814 7243 0885.

Grande, James. *William Cobbett, the Press and Rural England: Radicalism and the Fourth Estate, 1792–1835*. PalMac. [2014] pp. 264. £55 ISBN 9 7811 3738 0074.

Higgins, David. *Romantic Englishness: Local, National and Global Selves, 1780–1850*. PalMac. [2014] pp. 240. £55 ISBN 9 7811 3741 1624.

Houghton-Walker, Sarah. *Representations of the Gypsy in the Romantic Period*. OUP. [2014] pp. 304. £60 ISBN 9 7801 9871 9472.

Howe, Anthony. *Byron and the Forms of Thought*. LiverUP. [2013] pp. vii + 195. £70 ISBN 9 7818 4631 9716.

Johnson, Barbara. *A Life with Mary Shelley*. StanfordUP. [2014] pp. xxv + 198. $70 ISBN 9 7808 0479 0529.

Jones, Ewan. *Coleridge and the Philosophy of Poetic Form*. CUP. [2014] pp. xi + 242. £60 ISBN 9 7811 0764 7510.

Kerr-Koch, Kathleen. *Romancing Fascism: Modernity and Allegory in Benjamin, de Man, Shelley.* Bloomsbury. [2014] pp. xii + 219. pb £19.95 ISBN 9 7816 2892 5272.

Kirkley, Laura, ed. *Caroline of Lichtfield, by Isabelle de Montolieu.* Trans. Thomas Holcroft. P&C. [2014] pp. xxxii + 270. £66 ISBN 9 7818 4893 3927.

Kuduk Weiner, Stephanie. *Clare's Lyric: John Clare and Three Modern Poets.* OUP. [2014] pp. xiii + 199. £57 ISBN 9 7801 9968 8029.

Leask, Nigel, ed. *The Oxford Edition of the Works of Robert Burns, vol. 1: Commonplace Books, Tour Journals, and Miscellaneous Prose.* OUP. [2014] pp. xv + 432. £125 ISBN 9 7801 9960 3176.

Le Faye, Deirdre. *Jane Austen's Country Life: Uncovering the Rural Backdrop to Her Life, Her Letters and Her Novels.* Frances Lincoln. [2014] pp. 269. £20 ISBN 9 7807 1123 1580.

Lorenzen, Richard L. *The History of the Prince of Wales's Theatre, London, 1771–1903* UHertP. [2014] pp. viii + 216. £25 ISBN 9 7819 0929 1225.

Mander, W. J., ed. *The Oxford Handbook of British Philosophy in the Nineteenth Century.* OUP. [2014] pp. xii + £95 ISBN 9 7801 9959 4474.

Marsden, Jean I. *The Re-imagined Text: Shakespeare, Adaptation, & Eighteenth-Century Literary Theory.* UKL. [2014] pp. ix + 193. £31.50 ISBN 9 7808 1315 6132.

McGuirk, Carol. *Reading Robert Burns.* P&C. [2014] pp. xx + 255. £95 ISBN 9 7818 4893 5198.

Mirmohamadi, Kylie. *The Digital Afterlives of Jane Austen: Janeites at the Keyboard.* PalMac. [2014] pp. vi + 136. £47 ISBN 9 7811 3740 1328.

Morin, Christina, and Niall Gillespie, eds. *Irish Gothics: Genres, Forms, Modes, and Traditions, 1760–1890.* PalMac. [2014] pp. xi + 215. £55 ISBN 9 7811 3736 6641.

Murray, Chris. *Tragic Coleridge.* Ashgate. [2013] pp. ix + 194. £95 ISBN 9 7814 0944 7542.

O'Connell, Mary. *Byron and John Murray: A Poet and his Publisher.* LiverUP. [2014] pp. ix + 213. £75 ISBN 9 7817 8138 1335.

Pittock, Murray. *The Reception of Robert Burns in Europe.* Bloomsbury. [2014] pp. lxvii + 348. £175 ISBN 9 7814 4117 0316.

Ritchie, Fiona. *Women and Shakespeare in the Eighteenth Century.* CUP. [2014] pp. viii + 256. £64.99 ISBN 9 7811 0704 6306.

Robinson, Daniel. *Myself and Some Other Being: Wordsworth and the Life Writing.* UIowaP. [2014] pp. 134. £15.50 ISBN 9 7816 0938 2322.

Rooney, Morgan. *The French Revolution Debate and the British Novel, 1790–1814: The Struggle for History's Authority.* BuckUP. [2013] pp. viii + 223. $85 ISBN 9 7816 1148 4762.

Schoolar Williams, Cynthia. *Hospitality and the Transatlantic Imagination, 1815–1835.* PalMac. [2014] pp. 244. £53.50 ISBN 9 7811 3734 0047.

Schulkins, Rachel. *Keats, Modesty and Masturbation.* Ashgate. [2014] pp. x + 179. £95 ISBN 9 7814 7241 8791.

Sørbø, Marie N. *Irony and Idyll: Jane Austen's Pride and Prejudice and Mansfield Park on Screen.* Rodopi [2014] pp. ix + 416. pb $120 ISBN 0 7890 4203 8462.

Swindells, Julia, and David Francis Taylor, eds. *The Oxford Handbook of the Georgian Theatre, 1737–1832*. OUP. [2014] pp. i + 758. £115 ISBN 9 7801 9960 0304.

Tieken-Boon Van Ostade, Ingrid. In *Search of Jane Austen: The Language of the Letters*. OUP. [2014] pp. xiv + 282. £44.99 ISBN 9 7801 9994 5115.

Townshend, Dale, and Angela Wright, eds. *Ann Radcliffe, Romanticism and the Gothic*. CUP. [2014] pp. xv + 257. £64.99 ISBN 9 7811 0703 2835.

Warren, Andrew. *The Orient and the Young Romantics*. CUP. [2014] pp. vii + 279. £65. ISBN 9 7811 0707 1902.

Wiltshire, John. *The Hidden Jane Austen*. CUP. [2014] pp. xii + 195. £18.99 (pb) ISBN 9 7811 0706 187.

Worthen, John. *The Life of William Wordsworth: A Critical Biography*. Wiley. [2014] pp. xxi + 500. £80.95 ISBN 9 7804 7065 5443.

Yoshikawa, Saeko. *William Wordsworth and the Invention of Tourism*. Ashgate. [2014] pp. xii + 268. £65 ISBN 9 7814 7242 0138.

XIV

The Victorian Period (1830–1900)

KRISTEN POND, WILLIAM BAKER, ARIANA REILLY,
MICHAEL GILMOUR, CLARA DAWSON, AND
CLARE STAINTHORP

This chapter has three sections: 1. General and Prose; 2. The Novel; 3. Poetry. Section 1 is by Kristen Pond and William Baker; section 2 is by Ariana Reilly, William Baker, and Michael Gilmour; section 3 is by Clara Dawson and Clare Stainthorp.

1. General and Prose

In this section material on George Borrow, Thomas Carlyle, John Jebb, and Charles Ricketts is reviewed by William Baker; all else is reviewed by Kristen Pond.

The year featured some excellent general introductions to Victorian literature, including a new and updated edition of Blackwell's 1999 *A Companion to Victorian Literature*, now entitled *A New Companion to Victorian Literature and Culture* and edited again by Herbert F. Tucker; volume 4 of Wiley-Blackwell's *A Companion to British Literature*, which covers Victorian and twentieth-century literature and is edited by Robert DeMaria, Heesok Chang, and Samantha Zacher; *Twenty-First-Century Perspectives on Victorian Literature* edited by Laurence W. Mazzeno; and finally an interesting volume by Simon Dentith that reflects on the study of Victorian literature.

In the general introduction to the entire four-volume series, *A Companion to British Literature*, DeMaria considers the fraught terms 'British' and 'literature' that make up the title. As his thoughtful introduction makes clear, the editors have carefully assembled essays that provide wide-ranging knowledge without supposing to have all of the answers. In the introduction to volume 4, on Victorian and twentieth-century literature, Heesok Chang muses that if there is one common theme that brings all of the essays together in this volume it is 'irreversible, all-encompassing, and unremitting change of an historically unprecedented kind' (p. xxxii). The social upheavals that begin with the

The Year's Work in English Studies, Volume 95 (2016) © *The Author 2016. Published by Oxford University Press on behalf of the English Association. All rights reserved.*
For Permissions, please email: journals.permissions@oup.com
doi:10.1093/ywes/maw015

Industrial Revolution form the subject, implicitly or explicitly, of the essays. The metropolitan sensibilities, internal divisions, particularities of place and language, and a sense of national progress are just some of the defining characteristics of the Victorian period that these essays address.

The first eight chapters of the twenty-seven in volume 4 focus on Victorian writers and issues. Chapter 1, 'Charles Dickens, Dramatist' by Eileen Gillooly, turns to one of Dickens's 'less-studied roles' as a 'dramatist of everyday life'. From this perspective Gillooly explores how Dickens's novel characters perform multiple roles, his relationship with America, and of course his authorial performances. Chapter 2, 'Becoming George Eliot: Female Authorship in the Nineteenth Century' by Kyriaki Hadjiafxendi, looks to Eliot's early periodical reviews for the values she associates with authorship and then discusses how the critical reception of her own early novels shaped the strategies she herself would use as an author. Chapter 3, 'What Do the Women Do? The Work of Women in the Fiction of the Brontës' by Susan Zlotnick, focuses on the situation of the middle-class woman in the 1830s and 1840s as the workforce changed and began to exclude women. The Brontës explore this problem in their novels and use the figure of the domestic servant to 'draw attention to the soul-destroying narrowness of Victorian women's lives' (p. 37). Chapter 4, 'Evolution and Entropy: Scientific Contexts in the Nineteenth Century' by Suzy Anger, explores the way 'science utterly transformed Victorian culture' (p. 52), adding to a topic of increasing importance in Victorian studies, the interrelation between science and literature in this period. Chapter 5, 'Theatre, Exhibition, and Spectacle in the Nineteenth Century' by Sharon Aronofsky Weltman, rescues the forms of Victorian theatre, melodrama, farce, and extravaganza from the critical neglect due to the modernist devaluation of these dramatic forms. Her essay shows not only how well received these performances were, but just how popular drama was in the period we have understood to be dominated by the novel. Chapter 6, 'Art, Self, and Society: Tennyson and the Brownings, 1830–1857' by Matthew Campbell, explores how Victorian poets faced the changing social contexts in which they composed their poetry and the need for new forms and new directions, represented by the work of Tennyson and the Brownings. Chapter 7, 'Pre-Raphaelite Brothers, Lovers, and the Sister Arts' by Wendy Graham, lays out an introduction to the Pre-Raphaelites as well as an explanation for why they 'shone as beacons of modernity' (p. 107) in their time and continued to have a lasting appeal for the modernists who rejected so much else that was Victorian. Chapter 8, 'Regionalism and Consciousness: Thomas Hardy's Imagined Geographies' by Keith Wilson, presents Hardy as a 'key figure in the democratizing of the subjects and character range of English fiction' (p. 133). A key tension in Hardy's fiction, one that gives his characters enduring importance in readers' minds, is the 'insignificance and vulnerability of their social standing' that exposes the 'bleak contingencies' that govern human lives (p. 133). These essays do just what Chang suggests they do, which is to 'not only inform discussion but also foste[r] dissent' (p. xxxvi). The perspectives offered here at once provide an overview of the period and introduce compelling new scholarship.

Herbert Tucker's *A New Companion to Victorian Literature and Culture* contains heavily revised versions of the previous edition's chapters by the original authors, as well as some chapters by new authors. The sections remain the same as the original: Part I, 'History in Focus', Part II, 'Passages of Life', Part III, 'Walks of Life', Part IV, 'Kinds of Writing', and Part V, 'Borders'. As with the original volume, this volume continues to provide compelling scholarship and informative overviews. The chapter titles are as follows: chapter 1, '1832' by Lawrence Poston; chapter 2, '1851' by Antony H. Harrison; chapter 3, '1870' by Linda K. Hughes; chapter 4, '1897' by Stephen Arata; chapter 5, 'Growing Up: Childhood' by Claudia Nelson; chapter 6, 'Moving Out: Adolescence' by Chris R. Vanden Bossche; chapter 7, 'Growing Old: Age' by Teresa Mangum; chapter 8, 'Passing On: Death' by Gerhard Joseph and Herbert F. Tucker; chapter 9, 'Victorian Sexualities' by James Eli Adams; chapter 10, 'Clerical' by Christine L. Krueger; chapter 11, 'Legal' by Simon Petch and Jan-Melissa Schramm; chapter 12, 'Medical' by Lawrence Rothfield; chapter 13, 'Military' by John R. Reed; chapter 14, 'Educational' by Thomas William Heyck; chapter 15, 'Administrative' by Michael Hunt; chapter 16, 'Financial' by Christina Crosby; chapter 17, 'Industrial' by Herbert Sussman; chapter 18, 'Commercial' by Jennifer Wicke; chapter 19, 'Artistic' by Julie Codell; chapter 20, 'Spectacle' by Joss Marsh; chapter 21, 'Publishing' by Richard D. Altick and James Mussell; chapter 22, 'Poetry' by E. Warwick Slinn; chapter 23, 'Fiction' by Hilary M. Schor; chapter 24, 'Drama' by Alan Fischler; chapter 25, 'Life Writing' by Timothy Peltason; chapter 26, 'Sage Writing' by Linda H. Peterson; chapter 27, 'Historiography' by Edward Adams; chapter 28, 'Literary Criticism' by David E. Latané, Jr.; chapter 29, 'Permeable Protections: The Working Life of Victorian Skin' by Helena Michie; chapter 30, 'On the Parapets of Privacy' by Karen Chase and Michael Levenson; chapter 31, '"Then on the Shore of this Wide World": The Victorian Nation and Its Others' by James Buzard; chapter 32, 'On the Neo-Victorian, Now and Then' by Ann Heilmann and Mark Llewellyn.

Laurence Mazzeno's volume of twelve essays, *Twenty-First Century Perspectives on Victorian Literature*, is suitable for specialists and non-specialists. It provides a sense of how critical commentary on canonical works has changed over the years and introduces some non-canonical works. The introductory essay by Jennifer Cadwallader, 'Victorian Literature: A Cultural and Historical Overview', provides just that; Cadwallader traces a broad picture of the period's defining issues such as industrialization and urban development, 'the woman question', literacy, issues of faith and religious movements, and scientific and technological advances. At eleven pages this is necessarily a brief survey, but it helps orient the reader to the issues that the following essays address in more detail. The chapter devoted to prose writing focuses on Matthew Arnold, a decision that Mazzeno says was driven by how much Arnold's work influenced critical studies in the twentieth century. Clinton Machann, who wrote the essay on Arnold entitled 'Matthew Arnold as a Critic: A Twenty-First Century Perspective', discusses Arnold's influence on twenty-first-century criticism. The other chapters are devoted to novels and poetry, reviewed below. The chapter titles are provided here: chapter 2 by Tamara Sylvia Wagner is entitled '"The Velocity of the Novel-Producing

Apparatus" and "Large Loose Baggy Monsters": The Changing Reputation of the Victorian Novel'; chapter 3 by Chris Louttit is entitled 'Popular Fiction and Social Protest: Dickens in the 1830s'; chapter 4 by Saverio Tomaiuolo is entitled 'Faith and Doubt: Tennyson and Other Victorian Poets'; chapter 5 by Laura Dabundo is entitled 'Victorian Romanticism: The Brontë Sisters, Thomas Carlyle, and the Persistence of Memory'; chapter 6 by Katherine Saunders Nash is entitled 'Overt and Covert Narrative Structure: A Reconsideration of Jane Eyre'; chapter 7 by Barbara Leckie is entitled 'What is a Social Problem Novel?'; chapter 8 by Amy J. Robinson is entitled 'Matrimony, Property, and the "Woman Question" in Anne Brontë and Mary Elizabeth Braddon'; chapter 9 by David Latham is entitled 'A "World of Its Own Creation": Pre-Raphaelite Poetry and the New Paradigm for Art'; chapter 10 by Clinton Machann is entitled 'Matthew Arnold as a Critic: A Twenty-First-Century Perspective'; chapter 11 by Grace Moore is entitled 'Great Expectations, Memories, and Hopes Dashed: Dickens and Late Style'; chapter 12 by Ronald D. Morrison is entitled 'Tragedy and Ecology in the Later Novels of Thomas Hardy'.

While Simon Dentith's book *Nineteenth-Century British Literature Then and Now: Reading with Hindsight* is not an overview of literature in the same way that the above studies are, he nonetheless takes a broad look at our critical practices for reading nineteenth-century texts. Dentith's book is about 'how we read and how we might read', which he explores through the concept of hindsight, both as a reading and critical practice as well as a topic and presence in the texts included in this study. The title of his first chapter, 'The Ambivalence of Hindsight', characterizes the thoughtful way Dentith approaches the concept of hindsight, its influence on our reading practices, and the way he reads the literature in his study. One of the main ambivalences of hindsight is the promise of more enlightened knowledge based on what has been learned in the intervening years, and the threat that knowledge poses to an authentic recuperation of the past.

The first chapter proceeds to explore this tension in the areas of historical method, literary scholarship, and hermeneutics, encompassing both individual and historical hindsight. Chapter 2, 'Reading with Hindsight: The Nineteenth Century and the Twenty-First', explores further the problem of reading across historical distance. Dentith looks at nineteenth-century texts that anticipate future responses to the Victorian period and twenty-first-century memoirs that discuss the relationship between the current century and the nineteenth. The section on nineteenth-century texts moves breezily through Macaulay, John Stuart Mill, Tennyson, and Hardy. Chapters 3 to 5 focus on the novels of Eliot, Dickens, and Trollope, covered in relevant sections below. Chapters 6 and 7 focus on the prose writings of John Ruskin and William Morris. Chapter 6, '"The Things That Lead to Live": Ruskin and Use-Value' looks at *Unto This Last* [1860] as his 'most famous assault on political economy' which from our position of hindsight can be seen as one of the classic statements of the 'inadequacy of the "economic man"' (pp. 101, 103). Chapter 7, 'Utopia Under the Sign of Hindsight', looks at Morris's *News from Nowhere* [1890] and examines the 'continuing value of his utopian thought' which we now read as 'charged with an extraordinary pathos' because of the hopes he placed at the beginning of the socialist upheavals of the twentieth century (p. 123). The final chapter switches from a focus on reading with hindsight to writing with hindsight as Dentith examines twentieth- and twenty-first-century novels set in the nineteenth century for the formal and narrative strategies used to realize or resist hindsight.

Science, medicine, and technology continued to dominate the field of general Victorian studies. Many of these studies focus on evolutionary theory, and while Darwin remains a central figure for critics, a number of works from 2014 also uncover less well-known evolutionary scientists. Kathleen Frederickson's *The Ploy of Instinct: Victorian Sciences of Nature and Sexuality in Liberal Governance* takes an interdisciplinary approach to the sexual sciences, especially as they were influenced by notions of instinct and evolutionary discourse from the 1850s to the beginning of the First World War. Instinct is an important concept for sexuality because instinct, as Frederickson reads it through Foucault, negotiates between the individual and the population, performing a disciplinary and regulatory function. But the relationship between instinct and sexuality also includes desire, and Frederickson claims this relationship offers some important revisions to the Foucauldian thesis. A focus on instinct discourse also revises the emphasis on reason and deliberation in studies of liberalism and shows how 'instinct resolves or produces a problem in the relationship between science and liberal governance' (p. 14).

The first chapter focuses on Charles Darwin's concept of instinct as an influence on the way people act in the face of multiple stimulating objects and how this influenced obscenity legislation. Chapter 2 traces the shift from understanding instinct as opposed to reason to then regarding instinct as inseparable from reason. This chapter takes up Walter Bagehot's *Physics and Politics* [1872] to examine this changing concept of instinct in relation to Victorian liberalism. Chapter 3 looks at the sources Freud used in *Totem and Taboo* to theorize instinct in relation to 'savagery'. As Frederickson shows, Victorian ethnology often used eighteenth-century tropes of instinct to characterize savages. The last chapter looks at the issue of gender and instinct through the suffragette hunger strikes leading up to the First World War. The hunger strikes challenge the binary created between the 'rational citizen' and the 'instinctive woman'. All of these chapters are connected by the movement of instinct as a substitute for reason, on the one hand, and a spur to action on the other. What Fredrickson, and the reader of this book, come to discover is that the savage/civilized binary is not so stable, and that instinct is present in the workings of society just as much as it is in nature.

Reflecting on Darwin, a collection of essays edited by Eckart Voigts, Barbara Schaff, and Monika Pietrzak-Franger, highlights the continued importance of Darwin's influence both inside and outside academia, the 'flooding' rather than 'ebbing' interest in him, as the editors put it in their introduction, 'Cultural Reflections on Darwin and Their Historical Evolution'. The collection pays special attention to the post-millennial trends in the interpretation of Darwin's work and his scientific persona, but the first section of the book, 'The Cultural Evolution of Darwin's Thought', will interest Victorian scholars as they offer reinterpretations of how we have read Darwin's work and his position on key nineteenth-century topics like eugenics. Tracing a transformation in Darwin's reception of Galton's theories, chapter 1, '"I differ widely from you": Darwin, Galton and the Culture of Eugenics' by Angelique Richardson, sheds new light on his scientific thought, thereby deepening our understanding of mid-Victorian environmentalist and hereditarian approaches to human development. Late nineteenth-century literary reception and negotiation of scientific theories of inheritance are the focus of chapter 2, 'Evolution, Heredity and Visuality: Reading Faces with Thomas Hardy' by Susanne Scholz. Chapter 3, '"How like us is that ugly brute, the ape!"': Darwin's "Ape Theory" and Its Traces in Victorian Children's Magazines' by Jochen Petzold, examines the context that limited Darwin's theory to the 'monkey-question' and looks specifically at how this construction of Darwin's claims appears in children's literature. Chapter 4, 'Gender Trouble and Monkey Business: Changing Roles of Simian Characters in Literature and Film between 1870 and 1930' by Julika Griem, focuses primarily on early twentieth-century films and short stories but continues this exploration of how apes were represented in Victorian cultural with particular reference to the affinity between humans and apes. The rest of the chapters trace the cultural implications of Darwin's influence from modernism to the present time, looking at neo-Victorianism, gender, race, and continued misreadings of Darwin.

Part II, 'Darwin's Cultural Resonance Today', includes chapter 5, 'Neo-Victorian Darwin: Representations of the 19th-Century Scientist, Naturalist and Explorer in 21st-Century Women's Writing' by Ann Heilmann; chapter 6 is '(Mis-)representations of Darwin's *Origin* and Evolutionary Master Narratives in *The Sea* (2005) and *The Secret Scripture* (2008) by Felix C.H. Sprang; and chapter 7 is 'Evolution for Better or for Worse? Science Fiction, Literature and Film and the Public Debate on the Future of Humanity' by Angela Schwarz. Part III, 'Darwin as "Pop Star" of Contemporary Theory', includes chapter 8, 'Displacing Humans, Reconfiguring Darwin in Contemporary Culture and Theory by Virginia Richter; chapter 9, 'Ordering Darwin: Evolution and Normativity' by Nils Wilkinson; chapter 10, 'The Limits of Sociobiology: Is There a Sociobiological Explanation of Culture?' by Matthias Gutmann; and chapter 11, '"Survival of the Fittest" in Darwin Metaphysics: Tautology or Testable Theory?' by Momme von Sydow. For another study with evolution and Darwin at its centre, see Piers Hale's *Political Descent: Malthus, Mutualism, and the Politics of Evolution in Victorian England* and his discussion of the politics of evolutionary theory in the section below on politics.

Although Samuel Butler is usually studied in the context of memory or evolutionary thought in the Victorian period, Anna Feuerstein reads him as an important figure for late Victorian notions about the status of animals in her essay 'Chicken Embryos, Headless Frogs, and the Victorian Human–Animal Divide: Samuel Butler's Animal Epistemology' (*JVC* 19[2014] 198–215). The references to animals in Butler's *Life and Habit*, she argues, challenge the 'dominance and legitimacy of empiricism' and instead privilege instinct and common sense (p. 199).

Closely related to evolution but forming its own special interest in the following works, scientific naturalism was the centrepiece of several fine studies in 2014. In their edited collection, *Victorian Scientific Naturalism: Community, Identity, Continuity*, Gowan Dawson and Bernard Lightman attempt to 'reevaluate the place of scientific naturalism in the broader landscape of Victorian Britain' (p. 2). This re-evaluation begins by tracing the history of the term 'scientific naturalism' prior to its traditional association with Huxley beginning in 1892. The introduction proceeds to explain this history, as well as to survey contemporary scholarship and the turn to a history of biology 'from below' (p. 13). The first section of the book, 'Forging Friendships', focuses on the mid-1850s and the creation of a sense of community among scientific naturalists. Chapter 1, '"The Great O. versus the Jermyn St. Pet"': Huxley, Falconer, and Owen on Paleontological Method' by Gowan Dawson, examines the dispute between Huxley, Falconer, and Owen and the way it provided a secular principle that united young emerging scientists. Chapter 2, 'Evolutionary Naturalism on High: The Victorians Sequester the Alps' by Michael S. Reidy, explores the bond created by these scientists' love of mountains. Chapter 3, 'Paradox: The Art of Scientific Naturalism' by George Levine, looks at the philosophical and aesthetic assumptions that created shared bonds.

The second section of the book, 'Institutional Politics', focuses on the 1870s and the metropolitan dining society of the X Club. Chapter 4, 'Huxley and the Devonshire Commission' by Bernard Lightman, focuses on Huxley's attempts to increase state funding for science. Chapter 5, 'Economies of Scales: Evolutionary Naturalists and the Victorian Examination System' by James Elwick, turns to Huxley's work in the educational system and his belief in the importance of exams, a practice that in turn gave cultural authority to scientific naturalism. Chapter 6, 'Odd Man Out: Was Joseph Hooker an Evolutionary Naturalist?' by Jim Enderspy, complicates the conventional understanding of the X Club by emphasizing the class status that sometimes caused Hooker to take an opposing stance to Huxley. This chapter also discusses the connections between naturalism, secularism, and professionalism.

The third section, 'Broader Alliances', returns to the notion of alliances from the first part, but explores the fluid nature of identity and the antagonism between groups. Chapter 7, 'Sunday Lecture Societies: Naturalistic Scientists, Unitarians, and Secularists Unite Against Sabbatarian Legislation' by Ruth Barton, examines the scientific naturalists that were involved in the resistance to legislation that privileged certain religious groups. Chapter 8, 'The Conduct of Belief: Agnosticism, the Metaphysical Society, and the Formation of Intellectual Communities' by Paul White, traces the way scientific naturalists worked with the Metaphysical Society, challenging our notion of scientific naturalists as an exclusive and distinct group of intellectuals. Chapter 9, 'Where Naturalism and Theism Met: The Uniformity of Nature' by Matthew Stanley, uncovers some of the surprising alliances between Christian theists and scientific naturalists.

The final section, 'New Generations', turns to later versions of scientific naturalism and its continuities with and differences from what developed in the 1850s. Chapter 10, 'The Fate of Scientific Naturalism: From Public Sphere to Professional Exclusivity' by Theodore M. Porter, traces the decline of science in general culture with the rise of more technical ideals in science. Chapter 11, 'The Successors to the X Club? Late Victorian Naturalists and Nature, 1869–1900' by Melinda Baldwin, explores the differences in how ideas of the scientific naturalists were disseminated when a second generation decided to use a weekly periodical format as opposed to a monthly one. Chapter 12, 'From Agnosticism to Rationalism: Evolutionary Biologists, the Rationalist Press Association, and Early Twentieth-Century Scientific Naturalism' by Peter Bowler, moves the volume into the early twentieth century as he traces the transition from Huxley's resistance of rationalism to how the second and third generation of scientific naturalists became part of the rationalist movement.

Nineteenth-Century Contexts published a special issue with a focus on science edited by Lynn Voskuil. This collection of essays originated as papers and keynotes for the 2014 annual conference of *Interdisciplinary Nineteenth-Century Studies* in Houston, Texas, around the idea of 'nineteenth-century energies'. In Voskuil's introduction (*NCC* 36[2014] 389–403), she explains how the topics in these collected essays range from harnessing electricity to energies of the individual. The introduction goes on to discusses different scientific developments of energy and how they intersected with nineteenth-century ideologies such as work, labour, and empire. Timothy Morton's essay, 'Victorian Hyperobjects' (*NCC* 36[2014] 489–500), one of the keynote addresses at the conference, locates the concept of hyperobjects and the Anthropocene in the work of nineteenth-century writers like Thomas Hardy and Karl Marx. Morton connects the Victorian mindset and technologies with our own 'object-oriented ontology' that acknowledges the gap between phenomena and objects. The first essay following the introduction, Lynn Badia's '"A Transcendentalism in Mechanics": Henry David Thoreau's Critique of a Free Energy Utopia' (*NCC* 36[2014] 405–19), traces one voice that was against the emerging uses of energy. Thoreau's critique of John Adolphus Etzler's 'free energy' centres on Etzler's mechanistic view of the world. Mayra Botarro's essay, 'Wiring the Body, Wiring the World: Accelerated Times and Telegraphic Obsessions in Nineteenth-Century Latin America' (*NCC* 36[2014] 421–40), examines the development of telegraphy and the way this technology was imagined to place Latin America in the modern world. Jen Hill's essay, 'Whorled: Cyclones, Systems, and the Geographical Imagination' (*NCC* 36[2014] 441–58), focuses on Francis Galton's statistical analysis of weather systems. The 'whorl' is an important image in Galton's scientific work. Hill also traces this image in Conrad's *Typhoon*. Anne O'Neil-Henry, in 'Energy Inefficient: Steam, Petrol, and Automotives at the 1889 World's Fair' (*NCC* 36[2014] 501–15), traces the efforts of one French company, Peugeot, to develop steam and petrol automobiles. In 'Pistolgraphs: Liberal Technoagency and the Nineteenth-Century Camera Gun' (*NCC* 36[2014] 517–34), Jason Puskar examines the agency of the photographer, who pulls the 'trigger' to take a picture. This conception of the liberal subject looks at the collaboration between machines and humans. Elizabeth Coggin Womack's 'Victorian Miser Texts and Potential Energy'

(*NCC* 36[2014] 565–78) looks at another human subject, the miser, as a site for energy renewal. She analyses the miser in Charles Dickens's *Our Mutual Friend* and Thomas Carlyle's *Sartor Resartus*.

Three essays turn more specifically to the human body itself. Ashley Miller, in 'Speech Paralysis: Ingestion, Suffocation, and the Torture of Listening' (*NCC* 36[2014] 473–87), looks at speech as the physiological exchange of energy, focusing on the listener in particular. Adrian Versteegh's essay, also covered in Section 3 below, '"Another Night that London Knew": Dante Gabriel Rossetti's "Jenny" and the Poetics of Urban Insomnia' (*NCC* 36[2014] 551–63), examines the connections made in the nineteenth century between insomnia and urban energy. Lucy Traverse's '*L'Âme Hu(main)e*: Digital Effluvia, Vital Energies, and the Onanistic Occult' (*NCC* 36[2014] 535–50) explores the late-century effluvist belief that the soul was a form of energy. Tom Gunning takes these issues even further in his contribution from the other conference keynote: 'Animating the Nineteenth Century: Bringing Pictures to Life (or Life to Pictures?)' (*NCC* 36[2014] 459–72). His essay connects cinematic images to energy forces explored by effluvists, rather than connecting cinematic techniques to realism. The 'uncanny animation' (p. 462) of cinematic images links this essay to the others in the collection, as they all trace, to some degree, the material object's transference into energy. The interdisciplinary nature of many of these essays demonstrates how we might read science and literature together. The development of energy technologies is also connected to other key events in the period, such as the growth of nation-states and nationalist ideologies.

Several studies this year focused on specific figures in science. In *Reforming Philosophy: A Victorian Debate on Science and Society*, Laura Snyder examines two key intellectual figures of the nineteenth century, John Stuart Mill and William Whewell. Through this comparative study, Snyder re-evaluates both men's cultural heritage by drawing out their similarities rather than pitting them as opponents as most scholars do. The first two chapters each take up these figures individually, with the first focusing on Whewell and reconstructing him as a proponent of inductive methodology rather than deductive methodology. Inductive methodology thus forms one link between the two thinkers, as the second chapter examines Mill's radicalization of induction. Chapter 3 takes on one of the main disagreements between Whewell and Mill, their evaluation of Darwin's theory of evolution and the larger issue of confirmation of scientific theories. Returning to what unites their ideas, chapter 4 shows how both intellectuals rejected Bentham's moral system. Chapter 5 examines Whewell and Mill's relationship to Ricardo and Malthus in order to argue that Mill's views of political economy resembled Whewell's by the end of his career.

Bernard Lightman and Gowan Dawson's collection, *The Age of Scientific Naturalism: Tyndall and His Contemporaries*, traces the role that John Tyndall played in the development of scientific naturalism in the Victorian era. This volume also represents the recovery of Tyndall's place in scholarship reflected in the massive undertaking to transcribe and publish all of his personal correspondence, a work that his wife laboured over for forty-seven years but never completed. This work has created increasing interest in the importance of Tyndall, which this volume attests to. The essays were collected from two conferences organized for this latest research on Tyndall. The first set of essays situates Tyndall's research and public persona within the context of nineteenth-century science. The second set of essays turns to other scientific naturalists usually ignored in favour of Huxley and Darwin. These essays also focus on the physical sciences rather than the human and biological sciences that are normally considered in relation to scientific naturalism. The final grouping of essays explores the communication, such as correspondence and debates within the Metaphysical Society, between these scientists and what this reveals about private versus public knowledge and 'gentlemanly' science.

Joshua Olivier-Mason's '"These Blurred Copies of Himself"': T.H. Huxley, Paul Du Chaillu, and the Reader's Place Among the Apes' (*VLC* 42[2014] 99–122) recontextualizes Huxley's work of anatomy, *Evidence as to Man's Place in Nature*, which is usually read as an extension of Darwin's *Origin of Species*. Olivier-Mason instead reads Huxley's work, especially the first chapter, as a response to Du Chaillu's sensational representation of gorillas based on his eyewitness accounts of gorillas in the wild. Huxley employed novelistic strategies of sympathetic identification, a rhetorical strategy that Olivier-Mason sets against the more detached perspective of the scientist with which Huxley is usually associated.

Onita Vaz-Hooper, in 'Dream Technology: The Mechanization of the De Quinceyan Imagination' (*NCC* 36[2014] 165–77), examines Thomas De Quincey's approach to technology. Although De Quincey often critiques the effects of technology on the human mind, Vaz-Hooper argues that he actually internalizes technological progress, illustrated through his metaphor of the mind as a magic lantern, which is dependent on technology. This essay presents a more complex relationship between De Quincey and technology.

A special issue of *19: Interdisciplinary Studies in the Long Nineteenth Century* demonstrates the body as the focal point in studies of medicine and science. Although recently scholarship has privileged the visual in nineteenth-century studies, this issue contends that the arena of human touch was an important element considered by many nineteenth-century writers, thinkers, and artists. The papers come from a conference in July 2013 in Birkbeck, University of London, on 'The Victorian Tactile Imagination'. The growing interest in the tactile has been encouraged, as Heather Tilley explains in the introduction to this issue, by a 'critique of the visual privileging inherent in structuralist interpretations of material culture studies' and by the move away from Foucauldian critiques in favour of phenomenological approaches. Building on important works such as William Cohen's, these essays examine the relationship between mind and body in the psychophysiological discourses circulating during the nineteenth century.

Roger Smith examines the role of movement in touch perception in 'Kinaesthesia and Touching Reality' (*19* 19[2014]). Using philosophical, scientific, and medical discourses he connects these to the development of modern aesthetics. Alan McNee takes up the issue of embodiment through his focus on mountaineering in 'The Haptic Sublime and the "Cold Stony Reality" of Mountaineering' (*19* 19[2014]). The Victorians, as opposed to the Romantics, emphasized climbing as an end in itself. In tracing the emphasis placed on movement just as much as sight, McNee argues for the emergence of the 'haptic sublime' where transcendence comes through physical exertion and contact. Karen Chase examines one kind of bodily movement, fidgeting, '[E]motion in the Nineteenth Century: A Culture of Fidgets' (*19* 19[2014]). The attention to 'the fidget' demonstrates the nineteenth-century concern with regulating domestic and private life and the concern over how to distinguish between voluntary and involuntary movements. She looks at representations of fidgeting in Charles Dickens's novels. Pamela Gilbert, in 'The Will to Touch: David Copperfield's Hand' (*19* 19[2014]), also looks at the debate over voluntary and involuntary movement in her focus on the hand and the relationship between will and touch in *David Copperfield* [1849–50]. From actual touches to imagined touches, Gillian Beer's essay 'Dream Touch' (*19* 19[2014]) explores the dream touch in literature, beginning with Freud's *Interpretation of Dreams* [1899]. Using examples from poetry, novels, and short stories, Beer examines the way touch can be threatening in dreamscapes. Angela Dunstan in 'Nineteenth-Century Sculpture and the Imprint of Authenticity' (*19* 19[2014]) explores the importance of the artist's touch in the act of sculpting, and how this form of agency was in danger from the development of sculpting machines.

The issue also includes a forum, 'Models for the Blind', of three papers by Lillian Nadar, Jan Eric Olsen, and Vanessa Warne that examine the tactile experience of blind people. Two other forums are also included in this issue, one, 'Objects', on the relationship between objects and touch with essays by Elizabeth Edwards, Kathleen Davidson, and Jenny Pyke, that were inspired by the conference roundtable discussion from Sonia Solicari and Nicola Bown. The final forum, 'Report', by Kara Tennant, Claire Wood, and Angela Loxham, is a survey of the range of papers covered at the conference.

Dominic Janes, in 'Oscar Wilde, Sodomy, and Mental Illness in Late Victorian England' (*JHSex* 23[2014] 79–95), compares the medical records of men who were found not guilty of sodomy by reason of insanity with Wilde's case, in which two of his appeals for release on the grounds of insanity were rejected. In comparing these cases, Janes brings to light not only the legal and medical systems that construct notions of insanity but also the 'personal self-constructions and emotional responses' of those convicted of aberrant sexual behaviour. Another article this year, though not focused on science and medicine, was also focused on Wilde's prison experience. In '"Looking at the Others": Oscar Wilde and the Reading Gaol Archive' (*JVC* 19[2014] 457–80) Peter Stoneley takes a closer look at the 'others' that Oscar Wilde claimed saved him in prison. Using the Reading Gaol archive, Stoneley traces the lives of those who were in prison with Wilde as a way of offering a more nuanced reading of Wilde's prison experience.

The journal *Literature and Medicine* features an engaging essay relevant to Victorian studies by Meegan Kennedy, '"Let Me Die in Your House": Cardiac Distress and Sympathy in Nineteenth-Century British Medicine' (*L&M* 32[2014] 105–32). Against the increasingly clinical practice of medicine in the nineteenth century, Meegan offers the case histories of cardiac disorders as evidence of a continuing Romantic discourse in medical treatises. Three affective elements stand out in these narratives: sensationalism, sentimentalism, and imagined experience. Meegan's essay complicates our notion of the development of medicine in this period, offering a counter-example to our representations of the distancing that took place between patients and physicians.

An interesting connection to the issue of science and medicine is a collection of essays on ageing edited by Katharina Boehm, Anna Farkas, and Anne-Julia Zwierlein entitled *Interdisciplinary Perspectives on Aging in Nineteenth-Century Culture*. One of the main aims and strengths of this collection is the range of essays by literary scholars and social and legal historians, and the range of fields they draw on including performance studies, philosophy, history of science, and periodical studies. The essays are organized around four avenues of exploration: agency, gender and sexuality, place, and narrative and aesthetic form. The volume itself is organized into three parts. Part I, 'Science, Social Reform, and the Aging Body', includes essays that analyse how legal and scientific reforms resulted in 'competing constructions of old age' (p. 10). Lynn Botelho's essay, 'A Respectful Challenge to the Nineteenth-Century's View of Itself: An Argument for the Early Modern Medicalization of Old Age', examines the place of the elderly in the growing professionalization of medicine. Anne-Julia Zwierlein's '"Exhausting the Powers of Life": Aging, Energy and Productivity in Nineteenth-Century Scientific and Literary Discourses', looks at literary responses to scientific theories of bodily attrition and decline. Nigel Goose's 'Gender Perspectives on the Elderly in Town and Countryside in Victorian England' examines ageing in the workforce. Teresa Mangum's essay, 'The Unnatural Youth of the Old "New Woman"', rounds out this section on how evolutionary theories influenced anxieties about the ageing process as manifested in scientific and literary fantasies in which the ageing body is rejuvenated.

Part II, 'Intergenerational Exchanges', begins with an essay by Katharina Boehm, 'Transatlanticism and the Old Indian: Old Age and Cross-Racial Mentorship in Narratives of National Belonging', which examines stories by James Fenimore Cooper and Elizabeth Gaskell and their use of Indian culture to represent 'cross-generational and cross-racial membership' as well as issues of national belonging and cultural heritage (p. 11). 'Freedom of Testation in Victorian England' by Rebecca Probert examines the court of law's attempts to reconcile freedom of testation with ideologies of the married family. Karen Chase's essay, '"Senile" Sexuality', highlights the generational discord figured in vampire narratives around the idea of sexual experience and desire. Jochen Petzold's '"Are You Learning to Grow Old?": "Aging Well" with the Help of *The Girl's Own Paper*, 1880 to 1900', completes this section with an essay that analyses representations of old age in periodical literature for youth. *The Girl's Own Paper*, Petzold finds, supports the idea of intergenerational exchange and dependency.

The third part of this collection 'Transformations and Appropriations of Victorian Old Age', turns to the twentieth century's use of Victorian conceptions of old age. Gordon McMullan's essay, 'Inventing the "Aging" Shakespeare in the Nineteenth Century: A Counterfactual Reading', focuses on Victorian ideas about late-life creativity. David Amigoni's essay, 'Active Aging in the Community: Laughing at/Thinking about Victorian Senescence in Arnold Bennett's *The Old Wives' Tale* and its Theatrical Afterlife', compares Arnold Bennett's novel *The Old Wives' Tale* [1907] with the neo-Victorian 1970s theatrical adaptation to compare how old age was represented differently across these different media and periods. 'Old Age and the Great War: J.M. Barrie's Plays about the British Home Front' by Anna Farkas examines the focus on ageing in Barrie's plays and argues that it 'becomes a lens for an intimate analysis of the challenges faced by a population that was divided along generational lines' (p. 197). Helen Small's essay, 'The Double Standard of Aging: On Missing Stendhal in England', traces the Victorian roots in Susan Sontag's 1972 analysis of ageing and the gendered double standard. Pat Thane's helpful epilogue situates all of these essays within historical and cultural accounts of old age in the nineteenth century.

For additional articles on the topic of medicine, see also Emily Donoho, 'The Madman amongst the Ruins: The Oral History and Folklore of Traditional Insanity Cures in the Scottish Highlands', discussed below with studies on ballad and oral traditions, and Jessica Howell's essay, 'Exploring Victorian Travel Literature: Disease, Race and Climate', discussed below in the travel literature section.

Another subset of studies on science this year involved ecocritical studies. Dewey Hall's *Romantic Naturalists, Early Environmentalists: An Ecocritical Study, 1789–1912* sets out to correct what he views as several misperceptions in current critical work on these writers and on ecology. Such mistaken assumptions, in his view, include the notion that Britain used an American model of national parks, and a critical resistance to linking earlier writers to later ecology movements. Hall describes his aim as developing 'a legacy of environmentalism that includes Wordsworth and Emerson as writers-turned-naturalists who are literary links from White to Muir' (p. 1) The first two chapters discuss White's *Natural History*, one of the foundational texts, Hall argues, for the growing environmental consciousness. He compares a poem White wrote in the *Natural History* with Wordsworth's 'An Evening Walk' and also examines Emerson's interest in White's text. The second chapter turns to focus more exclusively on Wordsworth and how White's influence helped shape Wordsworth as a Romantic naturalist. Chapter 3 returns to Emerson and examines the interrelationships among religion, science, and literature in his lectures. The next chapter continues Hall's argument for recognizing Wordsworth and Emerson as early predecessors of the ecology movement. In this chapter Hall examines what he calls Wordsworth's 'green letters' and Emerson's 'green lectures', both of which indicate an early awareness of environmental concerns. The last chapter will be of most interest to Victorian scholars; here Hall claims that Wordsworth influenced Octavia Hill and therefore the formation of the National Trust. Chapter 6 makes a similar claim in tracing Emerson's influence over Muir and how it led to the creation of the national parks of America. Chapter 7 contains a more extensive look at Muir's writing and aims to identify evidence of Romantic naturalism in it.

Beginning with the more recent trend in ecological science that departs from the classic paradigm of balanced nature to what has been termed chaos ecology, Heidi Scott's *Chaos and Cosmos: Literary Roots of Modern Ecology in the British Nineteenth Century* traces the roots of this view in the Romantic and Victorian periods and claims that 'nineteenth-century literary narratives played a seminal role in sketching out the postmodern view of chaotic nature that would emerge in ecological science of the late twentieth century' (p. 3). In particular, Scott identifies two tropes, the chaotic narrative and the microcosm model, at the point at which literature and ecological theory intersect. Many of the writers themselves traversed the boundaries of author and scientist, such as Dorothy Wordsworth and Charles Darwin. One of the main claims that emerges through each chapter is that scientific understandings of nature have literary origins, especially the literary imaginary that helped to create the theoretical scenarios that inform the science of ecology. The rest of the book is organized around these two tropes, with one part focused on chaos and one part on the microcosm. In each part there is one chapter devoted to Romantic influences, one to Victorian influences, and a third chapter that looks at today's representation of the two tropes. The final section of the book develops a case study using Keats's poetry. While the historical trajectory the book traces will be of interest to Victorian scholars, I discuss the two chapters focused on the Victorian period here. In the section on chaos, the Victorian chapter focuses, as might be expected, on the disruptions of the Industrial Revolution. In the effort to understand the effects of industrialism, Victorian scientists reached a greater understanding of local and global interconnection. The shift from locating chaos in the sublimity of nature to the industry of humans leads the literature of the time to represent the 'common evolutionary origin' humans share with other earthlings. This chapter takes up Richard Jeffries's novel *After London* and H.G. Wells's *The Time Machine*. Jeffries's novel works against the trend of landscape development in the nineteenth century to trace instead a move backwards towards a 'successional recovery of first Nature', but this move, reminiscent of other Victorian writers like William Morris and Samuel Butler, is innovative in the way Jeffries constructs this primary Nature alongside the 'pernicious ghosts of industry past' (p. 53). Wells's novel rejects outright any narrative of Victorian progressivism and he creates a dystopia that places the chaotic source of nature squarely in the hands of humans. The leap in time through eight thousand years provides an evolutionary perspective that pitches species against one another.

The Victorian chapter in the microcosm section of Scott's book looks at early empirical impulses in the work of natural historians including Joseph Priestley, George Sinclair, and Charles Darwin. This context forms the backdrop to Scott's examination of Stephen Forbes's 'The Lake as a Microcosm' in 1887, the first scientific work to openly use the microcosm model. From here, Scott takes us to literary representations of the microcosm in poetry by Matthew Arnold and George Eliot, which she claims had come to represent 'symbolic endangered landscapes' (p. 134). What these chapters, and the others on Romantic influences and current trends, demonstrate is that the insights gained from both the humanities and the sciences can work together to imaginatively envision the future effects of industrialism and pursue better-informed answers to the environmental problems we face today.

To conclude the studies on subjects of science, I turn to those works that consider more generally the important connections between science and literature, or other areas of culture, in the period. Anna Henchman's *The Starry Sky Within: Astronomy and the Reach of the Mind in Victorian Literature* explores not what we see but where we see things from, the 'observer's changing locations in space, and the way the cosmos constantly rearranges itself as a result of that motion' (p. 1). Henchman's study acknowledges the alliance between science and literature quite explicitly as she argues that 'findings in nineteenth-century astronomy helped writers to articulate a set of formal concerns that are central to grand-scale narratives' (p. 1). Her immediate example of this connection is the prevailing astronomical model of a universe with many centres and what Alex Woloch terms the 'polycentric' multiplot novel as the dominant form of fiction. Part I, 'Observers in Motion', focuses on the relation between self and universe. The first chapter in this section offers an overview of astronomy in the period and the ways it connected to broader issues of perception and perspective. In chapter 2, Henchman examines Thomas De Quincey's 1846 essay on astronomy that focuses on the continual motion of both mind and universe. De Quincey's essay ultimately argues that orientation can only be achieved in the observer and not the objective world. Chapter 3 connects the astronomical technique of parallax with the structure of Tennyson's *In Memoriam*. The movement of Tennyson's grief follows the movement through astronomical spaces. Part II, 'Astronomy and the Multiplot Novel', focuses on the novels of Thomas Hardy and George Eliot, and is covered in the relevant sections below.

Laurence Talairach-Vielmas takes us to the land of fairies with *Fairy Tales, Natural History and Victorian Culture*. Talairach-Vielmas extends earlier seminal works on fairies to explore further the particular connections between the new developments in natural history and the literary fairy-tale. The book thus also addresses the larger intersections between literature and science, and many of the writers included in the study were both writers of fairy-tales and naturalists. One of the intersections Talairach-Vielmas is interested in exploring concerns the ways in which natural history borrowed the literary motifs from fairy-tales to define and redefine nature, including the relationship between natural history and gender. One of the most interesting insights the book offers is a Victorian version of science that turns away from empirical methods for methods that made room for 'the invisible or impossible' (p. 6). The first chapters take up the mid-nineteenth-century redefinition of nature sparked by evolutionary theory and examine the efforts of Charles Kingsley and Arabella Buckley to reconcile science and religion through the language and images of wonder. Also included is a discussion of how the urban world and the modern questions raised by industrialization figure into fairy-tales. The three middle chapters of the book more explicitly address gender, women's relationship to nature, and the increasingly common constructions of women as nature. The last two chapters consider beastly and endangered forms of nature. Chapter 6 draws a harsher distinction between a pre-industrial world and the world made cruel through technological develop-ments. The final chapter moves from the themes of an urban, industrialized England to the problem of otherness and imperial expansion represented in Edith Nesbit's *Five Children and It*. Overall, this book helps us to see Victorian strategies for describing a new reality, mediated through the connections between natural history and the fairy-tale.

In *Visions of Science: Books and Readers at the Dawn of the Victorian Age*, James Secord draws our attention to the connection between science and literature by reading seven key works of science as literature; that is, he performs a close reading of them as one might do for novels. The seven works he considers are Humphry Davy's *Consolations in Travel*, Charles Babbage's *Reflections on the Decline of Science*, John Herschel's *Preliminary Discourse on the Study of Natural Philosophy*, Charles Lyell's *Principles of Geology*, Mary Somerville's *Connexion of the Physical Sciences*, George Combe's *Constitution of Man*, and Thomas Carlyle's *Sartor Resartus*. Many of these works are known but seldom studied; thus Secord's book provides new insights into constructions of science in the period.

Nadja Durbach, in '"Skinless Wonders"': Body Worlds and the Victorian Freak Show' (*HMAS* 69[2014] 38–67), examines the exhibitionary culture of the Victorian period and its relationship to science. Her argument is that the scientific and the spectacular are 'symbiotic modes of generating bodily knowledge' (p. 41). Victorian freak shows and more modern versions such as the recent exhibition 'Body Worlds' share a similar dual aim to be both entertaining and educational. This dual aim is important to consider, Durbach contends, in order to see the 'dynamic relationship between popular and professional cultures of the body' (p. 41).

In addition to science, one of the other major areas in Victorian studies in 2014 was colonialism and empire. The range of these studies represents the breadth of this field for Victorian scholars. Several of these books focused on the topic of children in the empire. Ellen Boucher begins *Empire's Children: Child Emigration, Welfare, and the Decline of the British World, 1869–1967* with the fascinating story of Michael Oldfield, child immigrant to Australia at 13. Boucher's captivating writing style makes Oldfield's story come alive, and this feeling follows the reader throughout the book's exploration of child emigration in the settler empire. The book offers new perspectives on the role imperialism played in defining 'Britishness' within the family unit and the nation. Boucher begins this story of child emigration when it became a more organized movement in the late Victorian period and traces it into the later twentieth century when the definitions of Britishness that originally informed child emigration no longer provided a stable sense of identity for either former child emigrants or the nation. Chapters 1 and 2 of the book will be of interest to Victorian scholars as Boucher covers the origin of child emigration policy from the Victorian period to the early 1920s. Chapter 1 examines the construction of settler colonies as safe havens that could rescue poor children from their impoverished conditions in England. Boucher contrasts this narrative with actual stories about the harsh conditions, both physical and psychological, that these children faced. This chapter explores the social and political contexts that made child emigration appear as the best possible solution to the problem of child poverty. The rest of the chapters focus on the growth of this policy in relation to nationalism during the interwar years and then traces its decline from the 1930s to the 1960s, finally showing the effect of changing notions about child welfare and national culture through a comparison to postwar child migrant institutions. Changing theories about the care and nurture of children, alongside evangelical reforming impulses and, of course, imperial ideals about Greater Britain, all influenced the growing trend of child emigration. Despite the failure of some specific child emigration initiatives, such as Barnardo's South African initiative, the 'romanticized imagery of the settler frontier as a space in which ordinary people could start afresh' remained a powerful narrative for those back in Britain (p. 50).

A collection of essays, *Empire Education and Indigenous Childhoods: Nineteenth-Century Missionary Infant Schools in Three British Colonies* edited by Helen May, Baljit Kaur, and Larry Prochner, engages with some of the implications of Enlightenment thinking for the Victorian period, including what enlightenment was, and who was enlightened, and more specifically what this meant for children: 'The various missionary infant school experiments are illustrative of the mix of "enlightened" understandings of childhood, new styles of education, and the evangelical quest to include the poor and the "heathen" as potential civilized citizens in a so-called enlightened society' (p. 1). The book is concerned with 'the relationship between missions and the colonial imperial empires' and how childhood became a space for implementing the Enlightenment notion of progress and British evangelical beliefs (p. 4). The early chapters establish the central background contexts. The introduction lays out the larger contexts of Enlightenment, exploration, and empire. Chapter 1 examines the new ideas about education and how these became integrated with evangelicalism. Chapter 2 explores the better-known history of infant schools in Britain in order to draw comparisons with missionary infant schools. The remaining chapters serve as case studies that engage in a close examination of the missionary infant schools in three different colonial locations: British India, Canada, and New Zealand. These chapters pull together a wealth of undiscovered and overlooked sources about infant schools, such as missionary writings, letters, and government reports, to provide a detailed picture of the theory and daily practice of infant schools. The conclusion demonstrates the significance of this study not only for our understanding of Victorian conceptions of childhood and the intersections between colonial and missionary practices, but also the relevance of this issue for the re-socialization in current programmes that target minority children in schools today.

Finally, Kristine Moruzi and Michelle J. Smith's edited collection *Colonial Girlhood in Literature, Culture and History, 1840–1950* takes up the complex and fraught construction of girlhood in the context of colonialism. They recognize the multiplicity of the term and include women from under 10 to over 70, indigenous girls and colonial girls, fictional and actual girls. The different notions of girlhood under consideration in this collection are linked by imperialism's influence on ideals of femininity. Colonialism and girlhood thus offer two different historical lenses that inform each other in important ways; by exploring them together Moruzi and Smith claim we can understand each more fully. The scope of this collection is wide, covering the Caribbean, India, Canada, Australia, and Ireland, to name just a few of the areas of the empire, and children's literature, history, and anthropology to name just a few of the disciplinary perspectives offered. The book is divided into five parts.

Part I, 'Theorizing the Colonial Girl', focuses on the way in which the category of girlhood can inform our understanding of colonialism. Part II, 'Romance and Marriage', examines the relationship between discourses about marriage and the civilizing mission of colonialism. Part III, 'Race and Class', focuses on fictional representations of girlhood in Australia and New Zealand. Part IV, 'Fictions of Colonial Girlhood', looks at the way non-British authors positioned girls within different realms including education, work, and the nation and empire. Part V, 'Material Culture', explores the construction of girlhood through physical artefacts. This collection presents a complex and comprehensive look at the vexed questions of 'girlhood' and 'colonialism'.

Another group of people affected by imperialism form the focus of *Legacies of British Slave-Ownership: Colonial Slavery and the Formation of Victorian Britain*, an edited collection by Catherine Hall, Nicholas Draper, Keith McClelland, Katie Donington, and Rachel Lang. This book addresses the problem that slave ownership is hidden in plain sight: 'We do not maintain that the slave-owners created modern Britain, but we do not think the making of Victorian Britain can be understood without reference to those slave-owners. This volume is our attempt to accelerate that process of (re)writing slave-ownership back into British history' (p. 27). An online database, *The Legacies of British Slave-Ownership*, is published in parallel with this volume and includes the sources that inform the arguments of the book. The database is described in detail in the appendix. The introduction details some of the more systematic effects of emancipation and takes up some of the key debates surrounding the historical study of slavery and emancipation related to the 'new imperial history', the nineteenth-century colonial state, and family and gender. Eric Williams's controversial *Capitalism and Slavery* is discussed at length in order to clarify and modify his work, as well as work by Cain and Hopkins and William D. Rubinstein. Chapter 2 situates British slave-owners within the British elites of the period and discusses how that position continued post-emancipation. Chapter 3 examines the commercial legacies on a wider scale, moving from the economic impact of emancipation on individual families to the changes in Britain's financial and commercial structure. Chapter 4 traces the connections between men who appear in compensation records and their political positions. The defence of former slave-owner's interests, such as the issue of apprenticeship and the sugar duties controversies, also forms the subject of this chapter. Chapter 5 takes up the writings of the slave-owners themselves and analyses their versions of the history of the aftermath of emancipation. Chapter 6 acts as a case study focused on the Hibbert family. The aim of this book, as described by the authors, is to answer not only 'What happened to the slave owners in Britain after Emancipation?' but also 'How important were the slave-owners in the period after Emancipation?' The volume calls for further work, claiming the book and the database as a baseline for the additional research needed. The database lists 47,000 individuals, but biographical details have been developed for only 3,000 of these thus far.

Hall, Draper, and McClelland also put together an edited collection of papers delivered at University College London on 'Emancipation, Slave-Ownership, and the Remaking of the British Imperial World' in March 2012, organized by the team working on the ERSC-funded project 'Legacies of British Slave-Ownership' from which the above book comes. The collection, entitled *Emancipation and the Remaking of the British Imperial World*, opens with Robin Blackburn's essay, 'The Scope of Accumulation and the Reach of Moral Perception: Slavery Market Revolution, and Atlantic Capitalism', about the relationship between slavery and industrial capitalism. The following two essays engage with the thesis laid out by Eric Williams and Joseph Inikori that slavery was central to industrialization. Pat Hudson modifies this claim to show how it was a necessary but not a sufficient condition, focusing on the way slavery integrated London and provincial money markets. Chris Evans provides counter-examples to the widely used case study of the slave-owning Pennant family in North Wales to show that there were other important industries that developed independent of slavery.

Part II of the book includes three essays that complicate the definitions of 'free labour'. Clare Anderson's chapter places slavery on a continuum of unfree forms of labour that helps to highlight other labour forms such as indenture and convict labour. Anita Rupprecht re-evaluates Adam Smith's argument about whether or not free labour was cheaper within the context of his whole moral and social philosophy. Heather Cateau's essay also troubles easy distinctions between free and unfree labour by showing how some forms of indentureship in the Caribbean were less free than enslavement. Part III of the book turns to the period following emancipation and evaluates the role of the imperial state. Richard Huzzey's essay looks at the arguments about what policies an anti-slavery state should adopt to protect liberties, including the use of military efforts to suppress the international slave trade. Zoë Laidlaw examines how the treatment of settler colonies as self-governing contributed to the dispossession and erasure of Aboriginal people. Part IV takes up the question of history writing. Andrea Stuart evaluates the relationship between family history writing and 'professional' historical accounts arguing for the importance of the fictional imagination in remembering slavery. Mary Chamberlain also evaluates family history for what it might offer that other forms of history lack. In the final section of the book the essays turn to the issue of reparations. Two different debates in two nations, Mauritius and Jamaica, are presented in each chapter. Vijayalakshmi Teelock discusses her time on the Coordination Committee for the Mauritius Truth and Justice Commission, and Verene Shepherd shares her experience as the chairperson of the National Commission on Reparation in Jamaica. Shepherd's essay also traces in detail the historical movement of slaves in Jamaica and the costs of this traffic to the enslaved people. The collection brings together a host of voices and wide-ranging topics to suggest the issues and lines of investigation that need greater attention and require further discussion.

As many of these studies demonstrate, imperialism had a wide-ranging effect on political and cultural ideologies of the period. In *Masculinity and the New Imperialism: Rewriting Manhood in British Popular Literature, 1870–1914* Bradley Deane explores how ideologies of imperialism and masculinity influenced one another. The New Imperialist masculinity emerged largely through the popular genres analysed in this book, pirate stories, military adventures, mummy tales, and lost-world figures. In his discussion of these genres, Deane focuses on the absence of female influence and the presence of foreign men. Deane argues that the colonial other was at times a model for this new masculinity, rather than always used to differentiate British identity. Deane uses sociologist Raewyn Connell's analytic frame of hegemonic masculinity to explain how certain masculine ideologies become more popular than others, and the 'fragility and contingency of a dominant model' (p. 7). Chapters 1 and 2 explore the shift from mid-century conceptions of masculinity, which emphasized personal development, to late-century ideologies based in competition. The first chapter uses Kipling's patriotic poems to explore the conception of honour, and the second chapter examines cultural cross-dressing in the stories of A.E.W. Mason, G.A. Henty, and Kipling. The next chapters turn to the topic of manly development. Chapter 3 looks at the popular stories of the boy who never grows up. The stories Deane explores here involve these forever boys and pirates and emphasize 'competitive play' (p. 17). Chapter 4 focuses on another connection, this time between boys and savages, and shows how the savage boy indicates another type of education, beyond the schoolroom. Here Deane looks at Thomas Hughes's *Tom Brown's School Days* and Kipling's *Stalky & Co.*

The final three chapters trace how these changing ideologies about manhood shaped ideologies on a grander scale beyond the individual. Chapter 5 examines stories of exotic lost worlds by Kipling, H. Rider Haggard, and Conan Doyle that present barbarism as a manly character trait. Chapter 6 takes up mummy stories, whose narrative structure, Deane argues, mirrors the politics of the 'veiled Protectorate'. In the final chapter, Deane examines the futuristic scientific romances of H.G. Wells. Even Wells, who was liberal in outlook, unlike the other writers in this study, cannot imagine a future for masculinity outside the imperialist version of manhood. Deane's book brings together two key issues of the Victorian period, imperialism and masculinity, and shows the important linkage between them.

Settler colonialism, a component of imperialism but distinct in its focus on British citizens who chose to settle, usually permanently, in one of the colonies, was the subject of two studies. *Colonization and the Origins of Humanitarian Governance: Protecting Aborigines across the Nineteenth-Century British Empire* by Alan Lester and Fae Dussart examines the contradiction between the 'humanitarian' government policies between 1815 and 1860 and the violence of settler colonization. One of the main arguments of the book is that the version of British imperialism encompassed by settler colonization established an 'ambivalent foundation for subsequent humanitarian registers of government' (p. 1). While the various humanitarian projects in the colonies from missionaries and charitable societies has been explored, this book focuses specifically on a 'certain register of humanitarian thought and action' in the actual governance of settler colonies. Lester and Dussart thus seek to more fully expose an area of both colonialism and humanitarianism that has largely been neglected as studies tend to focus on missionary organizations rather than the government in the relationship between colonialism and humanitarianism. The introduction goes on to flesh out a thoughtful discussion of the vexed history and definition of humanitarianism, before turning to an explanation of the specific men's lives that form the subject matter of the study. In doing so, Lester and Dussart build from recent theories in several disciplines in order to 'get at this question of the relation between individuals and societies' (p. 26). Chapter 2 focuses on one of the most important shaping influences on shifting policies of the British empire, George Arthur. Arthur's career in colonial governance took him to Jamaica, Honduras, Van Diemen's Land, Canada, and Bombay. In both this chapter and the concluding one of the book, which returns to Arthur, Lester and Dussart argue that his 'personal performances and expressions of colonial government in different sites of empire and through specific episodes of contestation and networks of communication, assisted in the mutability of certain kinds of colonial governmentality considered "humane" around the empire' (p. 30). Chapter 3 examines Thomas Fowell Buxton's work in the Cape Colony to expose British settler abuses through the *Report of the Select Committee on Aborigines* [1837]. Chapter 4 examines the projects of Charles Sievewright and Edward Stone Parker, deputies to the Chief Protector of the Port Phillip Protectorate, and how humanitarian governance did work in positive ways, though limited and vexed as discussed in the chapter, to allow for indigenous agency. Chapter 5 turns to the Protectorates of Aborigines in New Zealand and George Clarke, Chief Protector. This chapter highlights the 'misrepresentations of vulnerability and precariousness that often drove humanitarian action' (p. 33). The essential paradox traced throughout this study, the humane disposition of individuals who were in positions of power over indigenous people, comes to its clearest light in the last chapter, in the figure of George Grey and his policy of amalgamation.

Helen Lucy Blythe's book, *The Victorian Colonial Romance with the Antipodes*, is driven by the question of why middle-class individuals would choose to leave England and travel so far from home, in particular 'Victorian literary perceptions, and how people's metropolitan expectations collided with their colonial experiences' (p. 2). The clash between expectations and reality often produced narratives that destabilized generic and social categories, and it is the formal structure of these narratives that most interests Blythe. For example, Blythe contends that writers who spent time in the far-off lands of the antipodes used a blend of romance and realist conventions in order to make sense of their experiences. The introduction is ambitious and moves along at a clipping pace, covering views of the antipodes from the classical period through the Victorian age, surveying work on settler colonialism, engaging with primary source material that reflects contemporary attitudes about the antipodes, and providing examples of the Romantic discourses used to write about them.

The first three chapters examine the emigrant experience and the attempt in writing to negotiate between the romanticized view gained at a distance and the violence and vulgarity that emerged up close. The ways in which these writers grapple with space invariably influenced the style of their writing, which often focuses on 'journeys of selfhood' (p. 21). The first chapter looks at Tom Arnold's experience in the antipodes, as a self-proclaimed settler who nonetheless left after two years. Blythe looks primarily at his New Zealand letters and *Passages in a Wandering Life*, and highlights the utopian dreaming that often motivated citizens like Arnold to emigrate. Chapter 2 focuses on

Mary Taylor and her correspondence with Charlotte Brontë, and on Taylor's fiction, which emerged from her unplanned fifteen years of settlement running a shop in Wellington. This chapter ends on a theme also addressed in chapter 1, the difficulty these settlers faced when they relocated their literary careers back in England. Having removed themselves from the metropolitan literary field, they continued to remain unseen on their return. Blythe turns to the poet emigrant Alfred Domett and his correspondence and influence on Robert Browning in chapter 3. In keeping with her focus on the infusion of Romantic discourse into writings about that antipodes, Blythe argues here for the 'consolatory function' of the imagination when dealing with friends who emigrated or those left behind in England. Domett's work represents the tension in Victorian literature over the antipodes between the erasure of the colonized and the acceptance of their presence. The final two chapters turn to the novels of Samuel Butler and Anthony Trollope. Blythe explores the significance of 'crossing' borders in Butler's own life, as he transitioned from Cambridge student to colonial sheep farmer, and in his writing. She focuses particularly on the theme of mastery and control in relationships and the dialogism of his novels, which precludes certainty and leaves the reader in the 'in-between' space where settlers often found themselves. The final chapter on Trollope's travel account of Australia and New Zealand and his novel *The Fixed Period* also addresses the 'in-between' space of the antipodes by presenting them as both a mirror and the reverse of England and troubling the dichotomy between civilization and savagery. Trollope's writing is based on brief visits rather than emigration, but he nonetheless works through his only first-person narrator to shrink the distance between the colonized and the English. The significance of Blythe's work, and the thread that links each of the chapters, is the spatial and temporal displacement these various emigrants faced and the way this experience influenced the form of their 'unsettling fictions' (p. 206). As these settlers and writers negotiate between the 'pleasures of distance' and 'horrors of proximity', they combined the textual modes and discourses of romance and realism.

Several studies focus on how empire influenced different areas of writing. In *Melodramatic Imperial Writing from the Sepoy Rebellion to Cecil Rhodes* Neil Hultgren examines the intersection between melodrama and late imperialism, the diverse negotiations melodrama demonstrates in the face of imperialist crises and propaganda. Writers imagined the empire as melodrama using three features of melodrama: its plotting, its emotionality, and its vision of community. Hultgren identifies a rise in melodramatic representations of the empire beginning with the 1857 Sepoy rebellion, and continuing with other conflicts and celebrations. This book has obvious value for studies in imperialism, but because it looks at melodrama beyond plays, including novels, romances, poems, short stories, and journalism, it also has much to add to the conversation about melodrama as a Victorian mode. The first two chapters take up the relationship between empire and melodramatic plotting in short stories and novels by Charles Dickens, Wilkie Collins, H. Rider Haggard, and Marie Corelli. In each of these texts Hultgren explores the connections between history, romance, and melodrama. Chapter 3 turns to the poetry of William Ernest Henley and Rudyard Kipling and the excessive

emotion, usually anger and outrage, that constructs the individual man of
action and the larger representation of this ideal in the military. The fourth
chapter also looks at emotion, but instead of outrage Hultgren explores the
workings of sympathy in Robert Louis Stevenson's 'The Bottle Imp' and his
portrayal of family affections in native Hawaiians. The last chapter focuses on
the fiction of Olive Schreiner, known for her impact on the New Woman
novel, but here examined for her use of melodrama in innovative ways. In the
conclusion, Hultgren offers a brief look at melodrama in the twentieth
century, arguing that the flexibility of the melodramatic mode enabled some of
the experimental art forms produced in the modernist period.

In 'Bombay Graveyards and British Beaches: The Tale of a Victorian
Imperial Scandal' (*JVC* 19[2014] 295–313) Margery Masterson also addresses
melodrama as she reads the trial of Colonel Crawley in both India and then
England in light of the 'fictional and theatrical conventions' of melodrama in
the period. Rather than rely on the strength of evidence, legal trials often relied
instead on melodramatic narratives that echoed popular grievances. Through
this case study, Masterson also demonstrates how the Victorian press worked
with imperial networks to craft 'fiction-infused narratives' and sensationalize
cases.

Padma Rangarajan, in *Imperial Babel: Translation, Exoticism, and the Long
Nineteenth Century*, 'critiques the intellectual discourse of the British Empire
by examining the role of translation in relation to colonial literature and policy
in the nineteenth century' (p. ix). Rangarajan discusses how translation
practices reveal the self-conscious way the English attempted to construct the
empire, as translation 'helped shape the administrative and imaginative course
of the empire' (p. x). Although the book focuses on British orientalists and
authors, Rangarajan still underscores the collaborative nature of translation.
Chapter 1 examines the linguistic theories of the eighteenth century and the
theories of translation that emerged from this context. The second chapter
turns to the translation practices of oriental tales that are in fact fictional texts
that assume 'the guise of real translations' through scholarly paratexts.
Rangarajan includes William Beckford's *Vathek* [1789], Robert Southey's *The
Curse of Kehama* [1810], and Lord Byron's *The Giaour* [1815]. Through an
examination of these texts, Rangarajan traces the rise and fall of Romantic
exoticism. From shorter fiction Rangarajan moves to the oriental novel in
chapter 3, and how interracial romance serves as an allegorical framework to
explore cultural translation in Sydney Owenson's *The Missionary* [1811] and
Phebe Gibbes's *Hartly House, Calcutta* [1789]. The fourth chapter turns to the
actual work of translators, specifically Sir William Jones and Max Müller.
Rangarajan continues to use literature as a way of understanding translation,
arguing, for example, that Jones's poetry provides a way to understand his
seemingly contradictory aesthetics and politics. Rangarajan uses the later
nineteenth-century novels of Rudyard Kipling and F. Anstey in chapter 5 to
examine the unease that emerges in the idea of translation as possible
pollution. This chapter furthers one of the aims of Rangarajan's project, to
illuminate the relationship between early and late nineteenth-century orientalist translation, by setting Elizabeth Hamilton's *The Translation of the
Letters of a Hindoo Rajah* [1798] against Kipling's and Anstey's novels.

This book highlights one of the key shaping influences of colonialism, translation practices, and Rangarajan's study of these practices helps us better understand imperialism in this period.

In a look at another cultural practice with imperial implications, Ann C. Colley's *Wild Animal Skins in Victorian Britain: Zoos, Collections, Portraits, and Maps* examines the practice of collecting and showcasing animals. The book at times necessarily partakes in scholarly discourses about colonialism, but not uncritically, as Colley goes on to claim that the desire to collect and showcase animal skins often revealed the messiness of empire rather than achievements of control and domination. But the book also theorizes skin beyond a colonial context to consider the myriad ways Victorians associated skin with identity. Colley brings together an impressive array of primary sources including literary texts, travel narratives, cartoons, zoo archives, scientific treatises, and portraits, to name just a few. Chapter 1 begins with the zoo in Belle Vue and demonstrates how the two discourses of colonialism and identity intersect through the display and portraiture of animal skins. Chapter 2 turns to natural history collecting to reveal the frustrations and disorder that resulted from attempts to collect specimens from around the empire. Animal taxidermy forms the focus of chapter 3, where Colley follows more closely one writer and photographer, Edward Lear, to show how he critiques the Victorian obsession with surfaces. Chapter 4 explores another obsession related to touch, the Victorian public's propensity to reach through the bars and touch wild animals in their cages. Colley compares the exotic touch to the haptic visuality of gazing at painting that prompt sensations of touch through the eyes. Finally, the book concludes with an exploration of maps inspired by hunters' encounters with wild animals, including the cartographic genre of zoogeography. Colley also examines the work of Hardy and Hopkins as literary examples of how these maps represent certain views of the world. In this chapter, as in the others, Colley shows the breakdown of barriers between human and beast, self and other. In fluid prose, she guides the reader through a myriad of sources and texts, illuminating not only an overlooked but a vital aspect of Victorian culture's obsession with skin, but connecting this also to our understanding of colonialism and identity in the Victorian period.

Julia Kuehn covers a lot of ground in her analysis of representations of the exotic by British women writers and artists in *A Female Poetics of Empire: From Eliot to Woolf*. Kuehn includes novels, travelogues, and paintings, and discusses colonial spaces from India, the Middle East, North Africa, Palestine, and South America. Kuehn situates her study among other attempts to theorize the epistemology of the exotic as a system that moves between difference/relation and representation/aesthetics. Chapter 2 examines closely Eliot's *Daniel Deronda* and the exoticism of the title character as he struggles between the two female characters who offer realist and romantic versions of identity. Chapter 3 shifts genres to Anglo-Indian romances and uses one of the central aspects in theories of exoticism, desire, which Kuehn also maps onto the realist/romantic divide. Chapter 4 turns to painting but continues to explore the blurring of realist/romance ideology. Paintings by Henriette Browne and Elisabeth Jerichau-Baumann employ a documentary realism that normalizes the harem at the same time as they include elements from romance fantasy. Chapter 5 also examines women travellers, but through the medium of travel writing and in the Ottoman regions. Looking at two travel writers and their works, Ellen Miller's *Alone in Syria* and Gertrude Bell's *Persian Pictures, The Desert and the Sown*, and *Amurath to Amurath*, Kuehn examines the tension between conveying information and the more personal affect of these women's experiences of the foreign. Continuing with women's travel writing in chapter 6, Kuehn turns to the category of the picturesque in women's Egyptian travel writing, a category that is a 'combination of a romantic aesthetic with empirical observation' (p. 19). Chapter 7 returns to the genre of the novel, but this time the popular genre of the 'desert romances' by Kathlyn Rhodes and E.M. Hull. In this chapter, Kuehn more fully fleshes out her argument that attaching the exotic to a locality is less helpful than 'analyzing the discursive methods and modalities through which exoticism comes into narrative existence' (p. 20). In the final chapter Kuehn identifies the modernist elements in Victorian exoticism in Woolf's *The Voyage Out*, which positions self-questioning as a voyage into the exotic. Kuehn's book engages with the key issues of colonialism and gender politics through a broad array of texts and writers that span the century.

Several key articles also dealt with the issue of colonialism. *Victorian Literature and Culture* published a special issue on 'Victorian India', co-edited by Mary Ellis Gibson and Melissa Richard. Gibson's editorial introduction meditates on the questions that such a title prompts, such as 'Whose Victorian India?', 'Which Victorian India?', and 'Indian or British subjects?' The essays in this edition of the journal answer these questions in a variety of ways, but they are all clustered around the issues of historiography and epistemology. Gibson's introduction helpfully surveys the major and recent works in postcolonial studies that call into question longstanding truisms about Britain's relationship to India and teleological notions of history. The issue includes a remarkable breadth of topics and issues relevant to India, and the twelve essays cover everything from the epistemology of empire, the historiography of education, ballet, poetry, and missionary tracts, to writers as well known as Kipling and as little known as Bankim Chandra Chatterjee. This range, and the conclusions that each essay reaches, Gibson writes, attest to the growing recognition that Victorian India occupies a central role in Victorian studies, broadening our understanding of the period itself as well as encouraging a scholarly reach beyond canonical texts.

The first essay, Albert D. Pionke's 'The Epistemological Problem of British India in Rudyard Kipling's "The Man Who Would be King"' (*VLC* 42[2014] 335–50), examines Kipling's short story, which Pionke suggests is the best as well as the last story Kipling wrote while in India. Pionke argues that the story does not read as one might expect, as an authoritative summation of empire, but instead maintains a degree of epistemological uncertainty. In '"Not Altogether Unpicturesque": Samuel Bourne and the Landscape of the Victorian Himalaya' (*VLC* 42[2014] 351–68), Sandeep Banerjee examines the photographs taken by Bourne of the Gangotri glacier, the first photographs of the glacier. Banerjee reads the representation of the Ganges mountains alongside the picturesque mode and landscape form which inform Bourne's photographs. Ralph Crane and Lisa Fletcher also focus on images from India in their essay 'Picturing the Indian Tiger: Imperial Iconography in the Nineteenth Century' (*VLC* 42[2014] 369–86), which considers how images of tigers were visual signifiers for India itself. In 'The Squab and the Idler: A Cosmopolitan-Colonial Dialogue in the *Calcutta Star* Between William Thackeray and James Hume' (*VLC* 42[2014] 387–406), Gary Simons clarifies the publishing history of the *Calcutta Star*, including the background of its editor James Hume, and the interchange between Hume and Thackeray through letters and in Thackeray's writings for this journal. In 'When Ditchers and Jack Tars Collide: Benefit Theatricals at the Calcutta Lyric Theatre in the Wake of the Indian Mutiny' (*VLC* 42[2014] 407–23), Mary Isbell uses the reviews in three different English-language periodicals to explore this performance event as an example of the 'fissures within the British community in Calcutta' (p. 408). Kiran Mascarenhas's essay, 'Little Henry's Burdens: Colonization, Civilization, Christianity, and the Child' (*VLC* 42[2014] 425–38), examines how the Evangelical tract *The History of Little Henry and His Bearer* [1814] represents the British dominance expressed through the Charter Act of 1813. In 'Indian Mutiny/English Mutiny: National Governance in Charlotte Yonge's *The Clever Woman of the Family*' (*VLC* 42[2014] 439–55), Kate Lawson argues that Yonge's novel 'foreground(s) the dangers to English national identity and national security posed by the emergent forces of liberalism and feminism' (p. 440).

Sigrid Anderson Cordell's essay, 'Edith Maturin and the *Wide World Magazine*: New Woman Rewritings of Imperial Adventure' (*VLC* 42[2014] 457–74) examines adventure stories, which she calls 'imperial New Woman narratives', for the way they respond to the colonial landscape of India. Sukanya Banerjee's essay, 'Troubling Conjugal Loyalties: The First Indian Novel in English and the Transimperial Framework of Sensation' (*VLC* 42[2014] 475–89), looks at one of Bankim's neglected novels for its presentation of conjugality and what this tells us about a 'transimperial framework' in England and India. In 'Between Two Worlds: Racial Identity in Alice Perrin's *The Stronger Claim*' (*VLC* 42[2014] 491–508), Melissa Edmundson Makala looks at the shifts in thematic concerns of Anglo-Indian domestic novels, represented in the work of Alice Perrin. Molly Engelhardt joins other works that revise Edward Said's conclusions. In her essay, 'The *Real* Bayadère Meets the Ballerina on the Western Stage' (*VLC* 42[2014] 509–34), Engelhardt looks at how 'representations of an imagined India reinforced orientalist ideologies but also challenged the binary necessary for upholding them' (p. 509). In 'Beyond Bengal: Gender, Education, and the Writing of Colonial Indian History' (*VLC* 42[2014] 535–51), Benjamin D. O'Dell examines the presentation of high-caste reform ideals about education in historical literature and argues that such a presentation is an 'inadequate response' to the complex topic of Indian education (p. 535). In 'College English in India: The First Textbook' (*VLC* 42[2014] 553–72), Michael Hancher explores the textbook of David Lester Richardson, *Poetical Selections*, which was 'instrumental in establishing a classroom canon of British poetry in India' before such a curriculum even existed in Great Britain (p. 553). Máire ní Fhlathúin, in 'Transformations of Byron in the Literature of British India' (*VLC* 42[2014] 573–93), looks at the reception of Byron among the poets of the British community in India. Alison Chapman rounds the issue out with her essay, 'Internationalising the Sonnet: Toru Dutt's "Sonnet—Baugmaree"' (*VLC* 42[2014] 595–608) in which she examines what transnationalism and hybridity mean for studies of Victorian poetry, exemplified through Chapman's study of Dutt's poetry.

Lynda Nead, in 'The Secret of England's Greatness' (*JVC* 19[2014] 161–82), considers the complicated pictorial representations of imperialism in two representative works, *The Secret of England's Greatness* by Thomas Jones Barker and *The Toyseller* by William Mulready. Both paintings may at first appear as unambiguous portrayals of colonial Britain, but Nead examines the more complex mystery surrounding these images read in the context of nineteenth-century science and racial identity in the mid-Victorian period.

In 'Kipling, the "Backward" Muslim, and the Ends of Colonial Pedagogy' (*NCC* 36[2014] 251–68) Robert Ivermee builds on the context of recent scholarly interest in Rudyard Kipling's short story 'On the City Wall'. Ivermee sets out to explore the origins of the main character Wali Dad amidst the debate over colonial public instruction and the educational 'backwardness' of Muslim subjects. Ivermee concludes that through the figure of Wali Dad, Kipling objects to the use of colonial education to transform Indian subjects into British men and women.

The *Journal of Victorian Culture* included a digital forum in issue 19:iii that looks specifically at the postcolonial archive. In the introduction to this forum, James Mussell argues that archives can never be neutral and that we must attend to the cultural politics of digitization. Each of the essays considers digitization as a form of cultural production. Adeline Koh, who directs Postcolonial Digital Humanities with Roopika Risam, highlights the way digital archives often reproduce, rather than challenge, canonical approaches. Siobhan Senier looks for ways to improve on traditional approaches to archives by using digitization in her focus on America's indigenous peoples. Finally, Martha Nell Smith looks at the influence an archive can have on the way its contents are interpreted.

One other article that also dealt with digitization and its impact on Victorian research and scholarship was Albert Pionke's 'Excavating Victorian Cuba in the *British Periodicals* Database' (*VPR* 47[2014] 369–97). This essay presents a form of research that utilizes data-mining and concordance analysis to analyse databases. Engaging in this kind of research can reveal aspects of British history and culture otherwise ignored, which is what Pionke reveals in his search for the appearance of Cuba through the *British Periodicals* database and what this can tell us about Cuba in the British imagination.

The publishing industry in the Victorian period was a prominent focus in works published in 2014. Martin Hewitt's *The Dawn of the Cheap Press in Victorian Britain: The End of the 'Taxes on Knowledge', 1849–1869* seeks to amend what he sees as the 'inattention' and 'imprecision and error that [have] led to truncated or inaccurate histories of the repeal of taxes on knowledge' (p. 2). Hewitt examines the impact of the repeal of the taxes on knowledge on the history of the British press. Chapter 1, 'Setting the Scene', provides an overview of the legislation and the state of the press in the 1840s. Chapter 2, 'The Foundations of the Mid-Victorian Campaigns', examines the social and political conditions that led to the campaigns against the taxes. Chapter 3, 'The Association for the Promotion of the Repeal of the Taxes on Knowledge as Pressure Group', looks more closely at the history of the APRTOK, which Hewitt describes as a distinct and innovative 'pressure group'. Chapter 4, 'Repealing the Advertising and Stamp Duties, 1851–5', tells the story of the first steps towards decreasing taxes on print, which included the repeal of advertising duty and then stamp duty. Chapter 5, 'The Paper Duties, 1858–61', marches on to the next project of the campaign, the repeal of paper duty. As Hewitt describes each of these campaign moments, he shows how the newspaper industry and parliament interacted during this period. The later chapters begin to trace the effect of these successful campaigns. In chapter 6, 'The Cheap Press', Hewitt argues that change can be detected not in the existing newspapers but with the creation of new titles, particularly outside London, and the rise of the daily press. The creation of this 'cheap press' led to 'intensified competition and instability in the newspaper market' (p. 127). Chapter 7, 'The *Morning Star*', turns to a case study of one newspaper important for the way in which it would 'illuminate the opportunities and prerequisites for the cheap press in the years after the repeal of the stamp' (p. 128). Chapter 8 turns to the final objective of the campaigns, the removal of the press registration and security system. The concluding chapter assesses the influence of the repeal of the taxes on knowledge on the British press, which changed not only the press itself but also how groups pressured parliament and the growth of Victorian Liberalism.

Nineteenth-Century Transatlantic Reprinting and the Disembodied Book by Jessica DeSpain looks at the ways bookmakers—and she includes here authors, publishers, editors, illustrators, printers, and binders—engaged in discourses of citizenship, embodiment, and national identity. The culture of reprinting helped to destabilize the textuality of books and the role of the body across the practices of reading and citizenship, especially as reading established imagined communities. Her introduction illustrates these linkages through the metaphors used in the copyright debates which equated printing presses with torture machines and authors with martyrs, and saw readers as defiled, fat, idle consumers. DeSpain argues that 'the textual body, physical book, and physical body became interchangeable metaphors of flux' and these 'destabilized bodies inflected issues essential to transatlantic culture' (p. 11). Chapters 2, 3, and 4 focus on the American writers Susan Warner, Fanny Kemble, and Whitman, but chapter 1 will be of especial interest to Victorian scholars in its focus on Charles Dickens's *American Notes for General Circulation*. Dickens's ideas about the relationship between authors' rights and a strong body politic contrasted with America's emphasis on a democratic readership. DeSpain traces the publication and circulation of *American Notes*. The multiplicity of texts that resulted put identity, especially national identity, in flux. DeSpain equates specific moments in Dickens's text, such as his description of the Mississippi, tobacco spittle, and slavery, with the process of consuming reading material. This chapter creates the narrative of a republican America against a tyrannical Britain, in which the diversity of textual reprints performed Americanness.

Sarah Dewis uses her examination of one London couple, John and Jane Loudon, to examine some significant changes to print culture, gardening, and more generally notions of the public and private sphere in *The Loudons and the Gardening Press: A Victorian Cultural Industry*. The Loudons' own printing practices modelled the move by major publishers to print material across multiple forms, and their use of serialization illustrates the democratization of print media. Chapter 1 lays the groundwork for the political implications of their work in gardening as John Loudon casts the gardener as a 'secular saint' in his *Encyclopedia of Gardening* [1822]. This publication provoked debates about the place of working men. Chapters 2 and 3 brings together Dewis's focus on print culture and gardening through her examination of John Loudon's periodical, the *Gardener's Magazine* [1826–44], which was the first to combine science and the design of gardens. Chapter 3 looks more closely at the images included in the periodical and what these illustrations reveal about distribution and audience. Chapter 4 focuses on two more of the Loudon's publications, one an encyclopedia of trees and shrubs and one about cemetery design. Each publication engages with scientific debates of the period, including botany, and the ongoing debates about the disposal of the dead that often took place within religious contexts. Dewis claims that through these publications John Loudon 'reconfigures gardens in the public sphere as a landscape of enlightenment and as a means of social cohesion' (p. 3). Chapter 6 turns to Jane Webb Loudon's brief editorship of the *Ladies' Companion, At Home and Abroad* during a pivotal time for women's journalism. Jane Loudon brings together science and aesthetics to exemplify the Loudons' concern for developing taste in a more accessible way for less elite audiences. Both of the Loudons were criticized for their attempts to democratize taste for both the lower classes and women. Dewis's book incorporates new research through her focus on the Loudons and makes a unique contribution to longstanding conversations about print culture, botany, and the public and private spheres in Victorian culture.

In *Performing Authorship in the Nineteenth-Century Transatlantic Lecture Tour*, Amanda Adams examines a related issue of the publishing industry, the performing author and the need for self-promotion in the face of an increasingly mass audience and growing field of writers. Though deemed necessary, acts of standing in for one's work often made authors uncomfortable, torn between suspicion over the need to perform their role and the desire to remain culturally relevant. Adams argues that the literary tour was a central aspect of nineteenth-century authorship that has been overlooked in scholarship. Adams looks at British and American writers, both successful and otherwise. This book adds much to performance studies, transatlantic studies, and literary celebrity. The introduction helpfully lays out each of these fields and then examines Frederick Douglass as a case study. Chapters then proceed in chronological order and pair a British and an American writer. Chapter 1 looks at Harriet Martineau and Harriet Beecher Stowe. Beginning with the gendered conundrum of a woman performing publicly, Adams illustrates authorial identity as a site of anxiety. Because their opportunity for public performance was minimal, Adams examines the way the 'performance of everyday life', including performances of silence, shaped their authorial identity (p. 34). Chapter 2 looks at Charles Dickens and Mark Twain. Adams argues that the nature of their lectures, the fact that they performed their fictional narratives rather than speaking as 'themselves', helped to make their argument about the author's authority over his text. Their lecture tours thus made an important case for the 'author-as-source' and the 'embodied intimacy' with the published work that fed into arguments for copyright and right to privacy (p. 59).

Chapter 3 takes up a British and an Irish author, Matthew Arnold and Oscar Wilde. Contrary to the authors in the second chapter, Arnold and Wilde emphasized the aesthetic and critical distance that separated the actual person from the public personality. The lecture tour is thus one way of studying the development of a disembodied commodity culture. The final chapter focuses on Henry James. While James embraced the power of performance and was successful on his lecture tours, the actual material of his lectures critiqued celebrity culture. His speeches position the author as an 'elite other' at the same time that they accept and utilize public performance. The conclusion briefly visits the concept of the lecture tour in the twentieth century, tracing its eventual demise with the advent of radio and television. Adams registers this as a loss; no longer can a reading audience witness a singular event that, as she demonstrates throughout the book, was both culturally and personally important to the reader and the author.

A few articles looked at the book collector and book design trade. P.J.M. Marks explores the life of one bookbinder in his essay 'John Jaffray: Victorian Bookbinder, Chartist and Trade Unionist' (*eBLJ* [2014] article 16), available online at http://www.bl.uk/eblj/2014articles/pdf/ebljarticle162014.pdf. This essay provides cultural information about bookbinding as a trade and Jaffray's role in the profession, including his substantial collection of ephemera related to bookbinding.

In 'Holmes's Pipe, Tobacco Papers and the Nineteenth-Century Origins of Media Addiction' (*JVC* 19[2014] 24–42), Susan Zieger reads media addiction through the metaphor of the pipe and the literary character of Sherlock Holmes. She traces the presence of the pipe through stories, novels, and illustrations to show how the pipe becomes an instrument in the cases themselves, but is also central to Holmes's persona and, most importantly, a representation of the reader's own 'addictive media consumption'. While readers may be familiar with Holmes novels and stories, Zieger also includes ephemera related to smoking such as cigarette cards, posters, and smoke-room booklets, which all compare smoking to consuming print.

Heidi Egginton's essay 'Book-Hunters and Book-Huntresses: Gender and Cultures of Antiquarian Book Collecting in Britain, *c.*1880–1900' (*JVC* 19[2014] 346–64) examines representations of the 'book-hunter', a new figure for book-collecting that was used rhetorically to 'venerate "gentlemanly" book-buying' practices. This was set in contrast to feminine forms of book-collecting. The article goes on to interrogate the denigration of female bookbuyers in the periodical press and connects this response to the growing number of female consumers who were able to shape print culture independent of male control.

A. Robin Hoffman's essay 'George Cruikshank's *Comic Alphabet* [1836] and the Audience "À la Mode"' (*NCC* 36[2014] 135–63) examines Cruikshank's *Comic Alphabet*, an illustrated alphabet book complete with puns, satirical references, and comic tableaux. Hoffman argues that this book offers us 'a view of the inevitable intersection between literacy practices, social codes, and book design' (p. 135). Hoffman's study of Cruikshank also informs our understanding of constructions of childhood and education practices in the Victorian period.

The important work in *Victorian Periodicals Review* continues to draw our attention to the essential role that periodicals played in Victorian culture and thus the role they should play in our study of the period. Many of these articles also deal with other elements of Victorian culture, and I have tried to cross-list them where relevant. I list first the essays focused mostly on the print culture of the periodical, the relationship between editors and contributors, or the periodical's place in scholarship today. Linda K. Hughes's essay 'Navigating the Material(ity) of Print Culture' (*VPR* 47[2014] 1–30) offers a new way of thinking about how print culture interacts with other print forms and supplies its own 'discursive web' by moving 'sideways' across genres and texts or literally across pages and issues. Hughes adopts the metaphor of the city rather than the more common one of the body, to explain the materiality and circulation of print. She includes a variety of examples to show the sideways movement of print between genres as novels influenced poetry and vice versa. She also reads Dickens's *Our Mutual Friend* 'sideways' across its serial publication. Jasper Schelstraete, in 'Idle Employment and Dickens's Uncommercial Ruse: The Narratorial Entity in "The Uncommercial Traveller"' (*VPR* 47[2014] 50–65), examines the narratorial and editorial voice adopted by Dickens in the figure of the 'Uncommercial Traveller' in the sketches from 1860 to 1869 in *All the Year Round*. This figure differs in key ways, Schelstraete argues, from Dickens's other narrators by closing the distance between the performance of the author and his audience to focus instead on the commercialized aspect of an author's work.

Lauren Harmsen Kiehna, in 'Sensation and the Fourth Estate: *The Times* and the Yelverton Bigamy Trials' (*VPR* 47[2014] 87–104), examines the interaction between sensational material and the reputable periodical. Her exploration of how *The Times* managed to cover the sensational case involving the Yelverton bigamy trials reveals three distinct strategies that emphasize the legal and institutional implications of the case rather than the sensational elements. Kiehna's essay offers one explanation for how respectable journals attempted to distinguish themselves from the increasing sensationalism of print culture. Fergus Dunne, in 'Centrally Peripheral, Peripherally Central: The "Prout Papers" of Francis Sylvester Mahony' (*VPR* 47[2014] 163–87), examines the peculiar position of one writer, Francis Sylvester Mahony, and his pseudonymous essays in *Fraser's Magazine*. Dunne explores the complex perspectives offered in the essays of this Irish Catholic priest publishing in a pro-Union British Protestant periodical. Kirstie Blair, in '"Let the Nightingales Alone": Correspondence Columns, the Scottish Press, and the Making of the Working-Class Poet' (*VPR* 47[2014] 188–207), argues that the correspondence columns in mid-Victorian Scottish periodicals offer a rich source for witnessing the development of a working-class poetic tradition. Her examination reveals the extent to which editorial commentary shaped newspaper poetry ranging from the satirical to the serious.

Michael D. Lewis, in 'The *Edinburgh* and *Quarterly* Reviews in 1848: Allies against French Revolution and British Democracy' (*VPR* 47[2014] 208–33), traces and compares two journals' reactions to the French revolutions of 1789, 1830, and 1848. Lewis finds that the reviews after the February revolution of 1848 contradict their former positions in their emphasis on Britain's exceptionalism and security. These contradictions reveal how inconsistency in a journal's voice can occur within single essays and not just as a result of editorial changes.

Florence Boos, in '"A Holy Warfare against the Age": Essays and Tales of the *Oxford and Cambridge Magazine*' (*VPR* 47[2014] 344–68), explores the relationship between editors and contributors through a case study of the *Oxford and Cambridge Magazine*, which offers an unusual ratio of reviews and critical articles. This magazine served as an important training ground for writers like Morris, Price, Burne-Jones, and Faulkner. Denise Odello, in 'British Brass Band Periodicals and the Construction of a Movement' (*VPR* 47[2014] 432–53), examines the relationship between editors of brass band periodicals, the bandsmen themselves, and the cultural image of the brass band. While editors worked hard to present brass bands as sophisticated art, bandsmen eventually rejected those efforts in favour of developing a more distinctive brand apart from middle-class art.

Victorian Periodicals Review also published a collection of essays chosen from the Research Society for Victorian Periodicals conference on 'Tradition and the New' held in July 2013. As the editors Natalie M. Houston and Margaret Beetham explain, this theme addresses the way periodicals worked within existing publishing traditions while also creating new ones. Periodicals also had to work with the tension between a consistent format and content while also continually offering something new and enticing to readers. This new and old theme carries through each of the essays chosen for this issue. Charlotte Boman's '"Peculiarly Marked with the Character of our Own Time": Photography and Family Values in Victorian Domestic Journalism' (*VPR* 47[2014] 538–58) examines the new art of photography against the older traditions of portraiture, which reflects changing ideologies about domestic life. In 'Novel Networks: The "Specialité" of the *English Woman's Journal*' (*VPR* 47[2014] 597–612) Teja Pusapati looks at the publishing strategies of one feminist journal. From new publishing strategies in feminist journals, Emma Liggins moves to new ideas of femininity itself in her essay 'Not an Ordinary "Ladies' Paper": Work, Motherhood, and Temperance Rhetoric in the *Woman's Signal*, 1894–1899' (*VPR* 47[2014] 613–30). Changing ideas about femininity are most evident in the mixed content of domestic advertisements alongside political articles. Elizabeth Penner's '"The Squire of Boyhood": G.A. Hutchinson and the *Boy's Own Paper*' (*VPR* 47[2014] 631–47) focuses on a relatively new audience identified by Victorian periodicals, the 'manly boy' or 'boyish man'. Penner looks at the editor, Hutchinson's, efforts to make the paper successful and lasting. Richard Menke takes up one aspect of New Journalism, the extract, in his essay 'Touchstones and Tit-Bits: Extracting

Culture in the 1880s' (*VPR* 47[2014] 559–76). Menke compares older practices of excerpting with those used in *Tit-Bits* and Matthew Arnold's 'The Study of Poetry'. In 'British Solutions to Irish Problems: Representations of Ireland in the British Architectural Press' (*VPR* 47[2014] 577–96), Richard Butler aims to add new material to the discussion about British perceptions of Ireland by focusing on the architectural press such as the periodical the *Builder*.

The following essays from *VPR* demonstrate how attending to periodical literature and essays can broaden our understanding of many areas of Victorian culture as they focus on key issues such as colonialism, gender, religion, and art. Paul Rooney, in 'Home News for India, China, and the Colonies and the Serialization of Arthur Griffiths's Fast and Loose, 1883–84' (*VPR* 47[2014] 31–49), winner of the 2013 VanArsdel Prize Essay, examines the steamship press, using *Home News* as his case study. He argues that this overlooked print form was in fact an important part of print culture for the British empire. Michelle Elleray, in 'Imperial Authority and Passivity in the South Pacific: George Manville Fenn's "The Blackbird Trap"' (*VPR* 47[2014] 319–43), examines the complicated networks between colonialism, settler colonies, and evangelicalism as revealed through the *Boy's Own Paper*, published by the Religious Tract Society. The story 'The Blackbird Trap' exposes the tension between the evangelical mission of the paper and its commercial needs, mirrored in this story's inability to fully account for the violence in its frontier setting.

Dominic Janes, in 'The Role of Visual Appearance in *Punch*'s Early Victorian Satires on Religion' (*VPR* 47[2014] 66–86), examines *Punch* illustrations satirizing different aspects of religious groups in the Victorian period. Janes argues that looking at these images, rather than just satirical text, can lead to a fuller understanding of which particular aspects of religious groups became the target of religious contestation in the Victorian period. Minna Vuohelainen's essay, 'Bernard Heldmann and the *Union Jack*, 1880–83: The Making of a Professional Author' (*VPR* 47[2014] 105–42), follows the life of one author, Bernard Heldmann, as he began his career on staff with the quality boys' weekly *Union Jack* and then became a successful author of crime stories. One of the notable aspects of his career, Vuohelainen suggests, is the way he challenges our assumptions about the content of turn-of-the-century boys' fiction. Heldmann's stories undermined the notion of 'healthy' juvenile fiction and include many elements of emotionality and close male relationships. Marina Cano-Lopez's 'The Outlandish Jane: Austen and Female Identity in Victorian Women's Magazines' (*VPR* 47[2014] 255–73) uses Jane Austen as a case study for the way in which Victorian women's magazines presented the domestic ideology of the Victorian period. Cano-Lopez explores how profiles of Austen in three different magazines reiterate and diverge from the biographical portrait of Austen constructed by her family. The magazine's often contradictory presentations of Austen reveal some of the tensions over definitions of female identity in the domestic ideology of the period.

Melissa Score, in 'Pioneers of Social Progress? Gender and Technology in British Printing Trade Union Journals, 1840–65' (*VPR* 47[2014] 274–95), takes up the larger issue of gendered workplaces by looking at one particular print form, trade union journals, and the way that these periodicals constructed the compositor as a specifically masculine role. Score also shows how these journals function as 'campaigning texts' to protect certain print procedures against mechanization and women's work. Rebecca Mitchell's 'Picturing the "English Roadside": George Meredith's Poetry and *Once a Week*' (*VPR* 47[2014] 234–54), also reviewed in Section 3 below, examines how the illustrated poems in *Once a Week* influenced the reception and interpretation of George Meredith's 1862 volume *Modern Love and Poems of the English Roadside, with Poems and Ballads*. Mitchell's essay provides an interesting look at the interaction of text and image, and what this means for the Victorian period and for our study of it. Christine Kyprianides, in 'Musical Miscellany in Charles Dickens's Journals, 1850–70' (*VPR* 47[2014] 398–431), looks at just how often music-related topics appear in *Household Words* and *All the Year Round*. Her findings suggest the important place of music in the nineteenth century, and the important role that popular journalism, as opposed to just musical references in literature, can play in reconstructing a social history of music.

Amjad Muhsen S. Dajani's essay '*The Islamic World*, 1893–1908' (*VPR* 47[2014] 454–75) aims to draw attention to a major pan-Islamic Victorian periodical. Although the periodical is briefly referenced in discussions of Sheikh Quilliam and British Islam, it has a much broader international focus and circulation that warrant more attention. Troy Gregory offers a corrective to scholarship in his article 'Corrigendum: The Misattribution of R.S. Surtees's *The Richest Commoner in England*' (*VPR* 47[2014] 296–302), which seeks to correctly identify *The Richest Commoner in England* with R.S. Surtee. Finally, it should also be noted that *VPR* 47:iii contains the invaluable RSVP bibliography compiled by Katherine Malone and her team. The bibliography catalogues essays, books, and theses that focus on newspapers and magazines during the Victorian period. This bibliography covers December 2011 to December 2013.

Two other essays not in *VPR* also demonstrate what we gain from a study of periodicals. Kellie Holzer in '"More Ridiculous Than Sad": Editing the Matrimonials in the *London Journal*' (*NCC* 36[2014] 233–49) examines the matrimonials in the *London Journal*, but rather than reading them as miniature romances Holzer attends to the presence of the editor as a kind of narrator shaping these 'compact narratives' beyond the control of the individuals submitting them. Hazel Mackenzie, in 'A Dialogue of Forms: The Display of Thinking in George Eliot's "Poetry and Prose, from the Notebooks of an Eccentric" and *Impressions of Theophrastus Such*' (*PSt* 36[2014] 117–29), argues that Eliot's essays from 'Poetry and Prose, from the Notebooks of an Eccentric' and her *Impressions of Theophrastus Such* are not deviations from the rest of her oeuvre but are instead linked through Eliot's organicist views of form and consciousness. Mackenzie's rereading of these texts posits them as successful works that also provide a fuller understanding of formal problems elsewhere in Eliot's fiction.

A cluster of articles and books from 2014 were concerned with two other forms of literature, the ballad tradition and travel writing. Study of the ballad traditions and oral history are closely linked to the increasing attention to periodicals because these journals were the forum for either printed forms of ballads or for discussions about oral history. A collection by David Atkinson and Steve Roud, *Street Ballads in Nineteenth-Century Britain, Ireland, and North America: The Interface between Print and Oral Traditions*, also reviewed in Section 3 below, focuses on 'street literature' such as broadsides and chapbook ballads. This collection seems written for both those who have a background in folk songs and those who do not. What is meant by 'folk song' is clearly laid out, as well as the oral/written debate that often arises in cultural or literary studies. The editors address the challenges of researching these ballads, particularly in the Victorian and Edwardian period when the 'seemingly chaotic printing trade produced a huge mass of material' (p. 2). The aim of this collection is to provide more quantifiable evidence about folk songs in order to make more informed critical analyses of street literature. The essays cover not only England, the focal point of the folk-song tradition, but also the important locales of Wales, Scotland, Ireland, and across the Atlantic in Newfoundland and the United States. The essays also range from broad surveys of evidence to particular case studies.

The first essay, 'Was There Really a "Mass Extinction of Old Ballads" in the Romantic Period?' by David Atkinson, begins with the Romantic period and traces the history of the ballad. The chapter challenges William St Clair's contention in *The Reading Nation in the Romantic Period* [2004] that there was a 'mass extinction of old ballads', and goes on to show that the production and circulation of ballads were much more dynamic than an 'extinction' theory would suggest. Roy Palmer's chapter, 'Birmingham Broadsides and Oral Tradition', establishes a closer link between printed ballads and oral ballads than scholars have previously allowed for, demonstrating the value of the printed ballad for preserving the oral tradition. In chapter 4, Peter Wood, 'The Newcastle Song Chapbooks', examines what appears to be the absence of a folk-song tradition in the north-east of England by looking at the printing of song chapbooks in Newcastle. This chapter, like Palmer's, takes up the current issue of interest for scholars of street literature about the relationship between different forms of street literature, such as the broadside song and the folk song, or oral versus printed versions of these forms.

Several chapters turn to forms of street literature that have nearly disappeared from scholarly purview. These include Scotland's song tradition, taken up by Chris Wright in chapter 5, 'Forgotten Broadsides and the Song Tradition of the Scots Travellers'. Some nineteenth-century British scholars understood the disappearing tradition of street literature and made efforts to study and preserve it. Martin Graebe's chapter, '"I'd have you to buy it and learn it": Sabine Baring-Gould, his Fellow Collectors, and Street Literature', examines just such folk-song collectors. In 'The Popular Ballad and the Book Trade: "Bateman's Tragedy" versus "The Demon Lover"', David Atkinson takes up Francis James Child's well-known distinction between broadsides and ballads by comparing Child's ballads in order to show the close relationship between ballads and the book trade. Another comparative study in this collection comes from Tom Pettitt's chapter 'Mediating Maria Marten: Comparative and Contextual Studies of the Red Barn Ballads'. His comparison of the many different ballads written about this murder case provides an interesting account of news-ballad composition and the narrative techniques of journalistic song.

Several of the chapters explore key issues of cultural history through ballads, such as chapter 6, 'Welsh Balladry and Literacy' by Ffion Mair Jones, which looks at the effect of the ballad on literacy practices, reflected in both the subject of the ballads themselves and the printing industry. Some chapters examine a specific aspect of ballad production and trade, such as the ballad singers that form the subject of John Moulden's chapter on 'Ballads and Ballad Singers: Samuel Lover's Tour of Dublin in 1830'. Using Samuel Lover's satirical account of his experience with ballad singers, Moulden uncovers some of the practices of a trade that left few traceable footprints. Norm Cohen represents the scope of this edition by turning to America in his chapter 'Henry J. Wehman and Cheap Print in Late Nineteenth-Century America'. Cohen uses Wehman's publishing firm, which dominated the field of American street literature, to explore the development of an American tradition of the form. The final chapter, Anna Kearney Guigné's '"Old Brown's Daughter": Re-contextualizing a "Locally" Composed Newfoundland Folk Song', also represents the range of this collection, not only in her focus on the early twentieth century and Newfoundland, but also in her demonstration of how broadly disseminated street literature influenced current local traditions. She thus establishes a link between popular culture in the past and present-day song and ballad traditions.

19: Interdisciplinary Studies in the Long Nineteenth Century devoted one of its issues this year to the topic of oral culture. The essays collected in this issue were inspired by the thirtieth anniversary of Walter Ong's *Orality and Literacy* and a series of events offered through the London Nineteenth-Century Studies Seminar and the Birkbeck Forum for Nineteenth-Century Studies. Sandra Gustafson's article, 'Orality and Literacy in Transatlantic Perspective' (*19* 18[2014]), opens the issue with an evaluation of the influence of *Orality and Literacy* on nineteenth-century studies. In demonstrating this influence, Gustafson analyses Anthony Trollope's *Phineas Finn* [1869] and Henry Adams's *Democracy* [1880] by focusing on the role of vocal expression. Two essays focus on the important influence of the phonograph. In 'Thomas Edison's Poetry Machine' (*19* 18[2014]), Matthew Rubery argues how replayable words led to innovations in literature. In '"His Father's Voice": Phonographs and Heredity in the Fiction of Samuel Butler' (*19* 18[2014]), Will Abberley explores how the recording of voices influenced views of inheritance, using Samuel Butler's fiction as an example. In 'Spoken Word and Printed Page: G.W.M. Reynolds and the "Charing-Cross Revolution", 1848' (*19* 18[2014]), Mary Shannon examines how Reynolds blurs the oral forms of ballads, chapbooks, and sermons within the textual form of his penny dreadful *The Mysteries of London* [1844–8]. Eliza Cubitt's essay '"The Screaming Streets": Voice and the Spaces of Gossip in *Tales of Mean Streets* (1894) and *Liza of Lambeth* (1897)' (*19* 18[2014]), argues for the power of communal orality in the figure of the gossip. Huston Gilmore's essay '"The Shouts of Vanished Crowds": Literacy, Orality, and Popular Politics in the Campaign to Repeal the Act of Union in Ireland, 1840–1848' (*19* 18[2014]), traces a kind of mass orality as print materials were disseminated in reading rooms. Gilmore's exploration reveals the social hierarchy between those who have a voice and those who do not.

Two other articles focus on oral culture. Rod Hermeston, in 'Indexing Bob Cranky: Social Meaning and the Voices of Pitmen and Keelmen in Early Nineteenth-Century Tyneside Song' (*Victor* 4[2014] 156–80), examines language and dialect in the song culture of the working classes. Hermeston draws a connection between the interpretation of the songs' meanings and the attitudes of audiences about language. Emily Donoho, in 'The Madman amongst the Ruins: The Oral History and Folklore of Traditional Insanity Cures in the Scottish Highlands' (*Folklore* 125[2014] 22–39), looks at the oral culture of medicine and psychiatry in the Highlands through an examination of two sites reputed to heal insanity. Despite the waning hold of supernatural belief systems in this century, Donoho shows the power these locations maintained in Highland culture.

Another important form of literature in the period, travel writing, is closely related to the topic of imperialism reviewed above and was the focus of several studies in 2014. Katarina Gephardt's book *The Idea of Europe in British Travel Narratives, 1789–1914* looks at the clash between identifying as a nation of travellers yet resisting an overarching European identity (signalled more recently in opinions about the European Union). As she describes it, 'the aim of this book is to trace the sources of such attitudes to nineteenth-century imaginative geographies found in fictional and autobiographical narratives of European travel' (p. 4). Added to other discussions about the development of an English or British identity, Gephardt argues that Britain's position in Europe is another contributing factor that should be considered alongside colonial settings and Celtic peripheries. Specifically, Gephardt argues that the internal polarization of Europe, its division between the north-west and the southern and eastern peripheries, was 'integral to the development of the concept of Britishness' (p. 5). Throughout the book, Gephardt traces the main tension in British representations of Europe, which was the impulse to depict Europe as other to express British supremacy and to establish Britain's position within Europe on the basis of identification, what she calls a 'dialectical process that combines identification and differentiation' (p. 10).

One of the strengths of this book is the way Gephardt draws not only on travel narratives but also on the images generated alongside them, whether that is photographs, book covers, or other sources. This is not a study strictly focused on travel narratives, however, as she deliberately blurs the lines between autobiographical and fictional travel narratives as well as between travel writing, fiction, and narrative poetry. Each chapter focuses on a popular writer's well-known work, but looks most closely at the rhetorical strategies used in an embedded travel account or travel subplot. The first chapter investigates shifting ideas about Europe as a result of the French Revolution as seen in Ann Radcliffe's novels. Chapter 2 examines how Byron's rhetorical strategies imagined Europe after the Congress of Vienna in 1815 and the remapping of Europe. Chapter 3 turns to the important role that juxtaposing Britain against Europe played in the social critiques represented in the fiction of Dickens and Giovanni Ruffini set in Italy. In the final chapter, Gephardt turns to the more complicated negotiation between identification and differentiation in two of Stoker's novels, *Dracula* and *The Lady of the Shroud*. Her brief postscript moves into the twentieth century with E.M. Forster and Joseph Conrad in order to show the more explicit critique that emerged along with the suggested need for dialogue to establish a peaceful relationship between Britain and Europe.

Jessica Howell turns to some of the challenges raised by travelling in *Exploring Victorian Travel Literature: Disease, Race and Climate*. Howell examines both colonial travel literature and medical treatises found in colonial illness narratives to examine how the writer's experience of illness sheds light on colonial encounters. Howell also pays close attention to the Victorian connection between climate and health and the way this influenced the perception of tropical climates. Her examination of colonialism through the lens of medical rhetoric allows us to see the ambivalence towards imperialism, as well as the 'disorienting' effects of colonial travel that resist any easy binary between colonizer and colonized. Howell's analysis of illness narratives in travel literature also considers how gender and race affect the representation of illness. This is also valuable as a cross-genre approach that studies both fictional texts and memoirs, treatises, speeches, and diaries.

In chapter 1, 'Mrs Seacole Prescribes Hybridity: Climate and the Victorian Mixed-Race Subject', Howell examines how a mixed-race woman established her authority as a travel writer in contrast to white writers. Howell contends that it is through the language of disease and climate that Seacole stresses white British subjects' incompatibility with the tropics, as opposed to racially mixed subjects. Howell suggests that Seacole intentionally does not align herself with a white readership but instead 'claims their respect and acceptance' (p. 28). Seacole thus combines rhetorical elements from Victorian racial discourse and medical discourse to achieve self-authorization. Chapter 2, 'Mapping Miasma, Containing Fear: Richard Burton in West Africa', examines Richard Burton's conviction that the races must be kept separate to guarantee imperial success. For Burton, therefore, the 'vulnerable white body' was at odds with the colonial impulse. Howell uses Burton's own experience of illness and how he writes about it as an example of the way that focusing on approaches to 'environmental pathology' in travel writing illuminates how imperialist texts 'attempt to depict and then delimit dangers to the white body' (p. 55). Chapter 3, 'Africanus Horton and Climate of African Nationalism', works as a direct counterpart to the previous chapter. James Africanus Beale Horton called Richard Burton 'the most determined African hater', and Horton became known as one of the forefathers of African nationalism. Howell turns to his guides, rather than his more overtly political works, to demonstrate that even in these more neutral texts Horton 'marshals the rhetoric of environmental medicine to promote change' (p. 85). As with the other chapters, Howell pays careful attention in chapter 4, '"Climate Proof": Mary Kingsley and the Health of Women Travellers', to the way Mary Kingsley crafts her travel narratives around the notion of health. Specifically, Kingsley's own strong health and ability to resist disease became a source of authority as she promoted her beliefs about what was best for British colonies in Africa.

Howell turns to fiction in her last chapter, examining Conrad's *Heart of Darkness* as well as his Congo Diaries, in '"Self Rather Seedy": Conrad's Colonial Pathographies'. Howell is attuned to the differences between a novel and a travel narrative; thus she draws attention to the role of Conrad's first-person narrator as opposed to the authorial voices in travel narratives. She ultimately finds that Conrad's characterization of the African climate serves to undermine imperial discourse. Howell's book is of interest to those who study medical discourse in the nineteenth century as well as, of course, colonial studies. The value of the book lies in its combined study of both areas and the valuable insights such an integration yields. Illness narratives give authority to those who write about the illnesses they experience and survive, at the same time as it undermines the authority of Britain's imperializing mission. Howell aptly shows the importance of this focus on illness narratives in colonial discourse as she foregrounds some of the more nuanced and contradictory presentations of colonial experiences.

An essay by Farah Ghaderi and Wan Roselezam Wan Yahya, 'Exoticism in Gertrude Bell's *Persian Pictures* (*VLC* 42[2014] 123–38), looks at the complicated way Bell approaches the issue of exoticism. The authors account for race and gender as key contexts for Bell's construction of the other rather than just a colonial context. Bell had a dual affiliation with Persia and Britain that kept her, the authors argue, from more typical colonial views of Persia and instead enabled a relativistic outlook. One of the aims of this article is to rethink the meanings of exoticism through a focus on gender and Bell's writing more specifically, which adds 'versatility and reciprocity' (p. 123) to exoticism.

Adriana Craciun's essay, 'The Franklin Relics in the Arctic Archive' (*VLC* 42[2014] 1–31), focuses on the material dimension of the famous Franklin expedition, the Franklin relics collected by voyagers searching for Franklin. Craciun analyses the cultural response to these relics within the growing museum culture, or the 'exhibitionary complex' in the period. In the complex responses to these relics, Craciun traces how they came to partake in numerous cultural discourses, scientific, religious, patriotic, and exotic. She looks at three specific hunts for Franklin, led by John Rae (1854), Francis McClintock (1859), and Frederick Schwatka (1880).

A really useful new resource for those interested in Victorian travel writing is Jenny Holt's fully annotated online edition of Isabella Bird's *Unbeaten Tracks in Japan*, which can be accessed through the following link: http://www.kisc.meiji.ac.jp/~jholt/link%20page.htm. The project is ongoing, and encourages further contributions.

Another form of literature important to the period, the short story, is examined by Kate Krueger, who argues for its 'revisionary potential' (p. 2). *British Women Writers and the Short Story, 1850–1930: Reclaiming Social Space* examines women writers whose stories 'begin to establish alternative narratives of occupations' and thus revise dominant narratives of femininity (p. 2). The book includes chapters on Elizabeth Gaskell's 'Cranford' series, the periodical short stories of Mary Elizabeth Braddon and Rhoda Broughton, *Yellow Book* writers George Egerton, Charlotte Mew, and Evelyn Sharp, and stories focused on settler women by Mansfield and Baynton. The conclusion turns to the twentieth century and the stories of Virginia Woolf and Jean

Rhys. The chronological order of these chapters also shapes a history of how the short story developed into a recognized form.

Numerous studies this year draw our attention to other forms of art beyond literature in the Victorian period. In *Victorian Perceptions of Renaissance Architecture*, Katherine Wheeler 'traces changes in the perception and use of the history of Renaissance architecture in these publications along with changes in the architectural profession' (p. 2). Wheeler builds on the work of others who have explored the Victorian interest in the Renaissance by looking specifically at Victorian literature on Renaissance architecture. The choice of adopting Renaissance architectural models influenced the profession itself, Wheeler argues, in terms of the responsibilities of the architect and the role history would play in the design process. She points to the ways in which the style and ideology of the Renaissance suited the new Victorian education system as it transformed from the 'single master approach of apprenticeship and toward the formalized education of larger groups of young men' (p. 6). Each of the subsequent chapters traces changing perceptions of the Renaissance. Chapter 1, 'The Sins of the Renaissance: John Ruskin and the Rise of the Professional Architect', takes up Ruskin's *The Stones of Venice* [1851] as the representative text rejecting Renaissance architecture because he saw Renaissance culture as embodying the alienation that dehumanized the nineteenth-century artisan and worker. Ruskin's publication corresponds with the growing professionalization of the architect, and Wheeler investigates the discomfort with these changes expressed through Ruskin. The second chapter, 'Embracing Decadence: Walter Pater's and John Addington Symonds' Renaissance', discusses the gradual acceptance of Renaissance architecture through Symonds's *Renaissance in Italy* [1875] and Pater's *Studies in the History of the Renaissance* [1873]. Both of these texts refute Ruskin's view of the sins of the Renaissance and instead present it as a source of artful pleasures, signifying the importance of a life focused on the beauty of art and an emphasis on the individual. This chapter also surveys the increasing professionalization of architects, such as the examinations architects had to pass to certify their qualifications. The final three chapters, '"It Is Time To Be Rational": William J. Anderson's *The Architecture of the Renaissance in Italy*', 'The Renaissance as an English Style: J. Alfred Gotch, Reginald Blomfield, and the English Renaissance', and 'Experiencing the Renaissance: Geoffrey Scott's *The Architecture of Humanism*', all trace the shift from interpreting the Renaissance through a historical lens to a theoretical one, and they include authors who were also architects themselves such as William J. Anderson, Reginald Bloomfield, and Geoffrey Scott. What Wheeler aims to show throughout the book's exploration of Victorian views on the Renaissance, interacting with themes of periodization, historical authority, language, and ethnography, is that changing perceptions of the Renaissance were tied to the practice and pedagogy of architecture.

In an article also focused on architecture, 'How the Victorians Un-invented Themselves: Architecture, the Battle of the Styles, and the History of the Term *Victorian*' (*JVC* 19[2014] 1–23), Kelly J. Mays revisits the term 'Victorian' and how it first came into use. Mays argues that the 'battle of the styles' that took place in architecture debates helped to create a distinctively Victorian style that popularized the idea of a Victorian age.

In *Printing and Painting the News in Victorian London: The Graphic and Social Realism, 1869–1891*, Andrea Korda examines three painters, Frank Holl, Hubert Herkomer, and Luke Fildes, whose large-scale exhibition paintings came from their illustrations in the *Graphic* newspaper, to discuss the state of art in an 'age of mechanical reproduction' (p. 1). Unlike their contemporaries, most famously Ruskin who decried the effects of the machine age on art, these men used mechanical mass culture as a means for transforming high art into something more relevant and immediate. The first two chapters following the introduction focus on the illustrated newspaper industry. Chapter 1, '"See for Yourself": Printing the News in Victorian London', focuses on the way the *Illustrated London News* claimed that 'accessible and objective' illustrations could best represent the nation (p. 9). This chapter forms a foil for the comparison with *The Graphic* in chapter 2, 'Ways of Seeing the News: *The Illustrated London News* and *The Graphic*'. *The Graphic*'s approach was distinctive, Korda argues, for maintaining high artistic standards and giving its illustrators great creative freedom. Each of the remaining chapters, 'From Genre Painting to Breaking News: Frank Holl and the Fallen Woman', 'Fallen Men and Strong Pictures: Exhibiting and Collecting Social Realism', and 'Painting the News and Advertising Painting: Hubert Herkomer and the Role of the Artist in the Age of New Media', takes up the individual painters and explores what happens in the translation of these illustrated newspaper paintings to large-scale paintings. The larger implications of Korda's study suggest a new understanding of the development of social realism that takes into account not just its place in modernist art but the influence of nineteenth-century visual culture.

Aleksandra Piasecka's book, *Towards Creative Imagination in Victorian Literature*, traces changing ideas about the creative imagination in the context of shifting beliefs about beauty, attitudes towards nature and society, and the role of religion. The book takes up both theoreticians and practitioners and thus includes critical essays, short stories, and poems. While the chapters cover familiar ground, they also offer moments of keen insight into the Victorian construction of the imagination. Chapter 1, on John Ruskin's *Modern Painters* and *The Stones of Venice*, examines Ruskin's views of beauty, beginning with 'the imaginative faculty', his negative evaluation of the picturesque. Of particular interest is the discussion of how Ruskin reconstructs the role of seeing or observation as Piasecka analyses the description of paintings in *Modern Painters*. Chapter 2 moves to William Morris's short stories 'The Story of the Unknown Church' and *The Hollow Land*, but in relation to Ruskin's aesthetic theories. Piasecka traces the different ways in which Morris's work complements Ruskin's theories and moves past them. Like the second chapter, Chapter 3 begins with an artist's relationship to Ruskin, this time turning to Dante Gabriel Rossetti. After exploring their uneasy relationship, Piasecka traces Rossetti's artistic comments in his letters and poetry, focusing primarily on the role of memory and subjectivity in art. The fourth chapter also begins with the relationship between two artists, focusing on Rossetti and Pater. The rest of this chapter looks at the place of religion in art, art criticism, and the poetic imagination as theorized by Pater. The last chapter focuses on Arthur Symons, beginning with his relationship to Pater and then turning to consider his concept of strangeness and its place in the concepts of beauty and nature as elucidated through his biography, essays, and lyrics. In Piasecka's focus on the imaginative faculties, she articulates both continuities with and breaks from the Romantic tradition of the imagination.

In his *Art's Undoing: In the Wake of a Radical Aestheticism*, Forest Pyle traces what he calls a 'radical aestheticism' across the works of Romantic and Victorian writers, including Shelley, Keats, Dickinson, Hopkins, D.G. Rossetti, and Wilde. Pyle spends the introduction teasing out an explanation of his term, but a definition emerges uneasily through his negations of what it is not. It is clear, however, that Pyle does not mean radical works of art. His emphasis remains on the aesthetic, and the term radical denotes 'a radical engagement with the very processes by which we conceive of the aesthetic' (p. 5). Pyle is therefore looking for art that makes an 'involuntary' and 'obtrusive' claim on us, 'something that approaches the status of an *event*' (p. 10). The final chapter, on Wilde, '"Rings, Pearls, and All": Wilde's Extravagance', departs from the earlier chapters' focus on poetry to consider Wilde's lecture 'The English Renaissance of Art' on his 1882 North American tour. This chapter is also an exploration of whether, or how, a 'radical aestheticism' is present in a text that is expressly about the aesthetic experience. Pyle argues that Wilde's aestheticism is extravagant because he presents it as both a means and an end, as 'the good and the sacred' (p. 212).

Hilary Fraser's ambitious work, *Women Writing Art History in the Nineteenth Century: Looking Like a Woman*, aims to 'correct the partial and distorted view of the emergent discipline of art history, formulated in the nineteenth century and recapitulated in most modern accounts, that art criticism was a masculine intellectual field in which a handful of women played a merely secondary role' (p. 2). Fraser accomplishes this goal by examining both canonical and non-canonical writers, high art and popular cultural forms. Her book also demonstrates the intersection of vision, art, and history as key subjects in writing by women, exploring questions such as: 'was there a specific mode, or spectrum of modes, of looking at art that was specific to women? And, if so, how might we understand the conditions that gave rise to gendered spectatorship? How far, in other words, are aesthetics the product of historically and culturally specific social conditions?' (p. 10).

The first chapter situates several women writers within the emerging discipline of art history. The "pre-disciplinary" stage of art history in Britain at this time made it easier for women to enter this arena professionally. Nonetheless, as chapter 2 demonstrates, it was still considered more acceptable for women writers to focus on art and artists in fiction than in other genres. Fraser turns her attention in this chapter to several women novelists, including Anne Brontë, Mary Elizabeth Braddon, Dinah Craik, George Eliot, and Anne Thackeray Ritchie. From the novel, Fraser moves to consider other genres of art writing including 'Girl Guides' such as travel books, letters, and guidebooks. Many of the women art critics examined in this book began as translators and travel writers, and Fraser gives attention to those beginnings in chapter 3. Fraser also examines more formal examples of art criticism in chapter 4, with Emilia Dilke, Vernon Lee, Anna Jameson, and Julia Cartwright. In this chapter Fraser is particularly interested in tracing how women reconceived the historical periods of the Middle Ages, Renaissance, and the eighteenth century. In the final chapter, Fraser explores women's writing about the so-called 'feminine arts', including the art of the home and dress as well as photography. Rather than suggest that there are categorical differences between the way men and women looked at and wrote about art, Fraser examines how the historical conditions of gender and genre shaped women as art critics and consumers. Most significantly, Fraser brings to the forefront the important voices of women and how they contributed to the development of an art history discipline and to broader aesthetic debates in the Victorian period.

The important late Victorian aesthete Charles Ricketts received some attention this year. Delightfully bound and illustrated with eight colour plates and a plethora of black and white illustrations is Nicholas Frankel's *Charles Ricketts, 'Everything for Art': Selected Writings*. Charles Ricketts (1866–1931) 'established himself as an innovator in the fields of book design, illustration, publishing, and fine printing, and he quickly earned the admiration of leading figures in the literary and art worlds' (p. 19). Frankel's book includes 'Charles Ricketts—A Chronology' (pp. 17–18) and an extensive introduction (pp. 19–73). His selection from Ricketts is divided into four sections: 'Writings on Printing and Book Design' (pp. 77–126); 'Writings on Art' (pp. 129–215); 'Memoirs and Recollections' (pp. 219–60)—these relate to Oscar Wilde and Michael Field—and 'Fiction' (pp. 263–328). There are three appendices of 'Victorian Commentaries' (pp. 331–51) followed by an alphabetically arranged listing of selected reading (pp. 353–4). Frankel's notation throughout this excellent addition to our knowledge of the late Victorian and Edwardian aesthetic world is replete with informative detail.

A special issue of the *Australasian Journal of Victorian Studies*, edited by Paul Watt, focuses on the vocabulary of the arts, especially the aesthetic circumstances that framed literary ideas. The papers were gathered from the annual meeting of the Australasian Victorian Studies Association held in April 2012 at Griffith University. In 'Visualising the Critical: Artistic Convention and Eclecticism in Oscar Wilde's Writings on the Decorative Arts' (*AJVS* 19[2014] 5–19), Deborah van der Plaat offers a new approach to Oscar Wilde's essay 'The Critic as Artist' [1891] by comparing it to the orientalist form. In '"Like an Old Flemish Interior Brought into Action": Victorian Reviews of the Realist Novel and the Appropriation of Visual Arts Vocabulary' (*AJVS* 19[2014] 20–31), Isabel Seidel examines the literary reviews of Geraldine Jewsbury, Margaret Oliphant, and George Eliot and how they use language from the visual arts, what Seidel calls 'word painting', to assess novels. In 'Thomas Woolner's "Bad Times for Sculpture": Framing Victorian Sculpture in Vocabularies of Neglect' (*AJVS* 19[2014] 32–44), Angela Dunstan focuses on the career of Thomas Woolner for the important way he changed the place of sculpture in the Victorian arts by framing it as both a high and popular art form, therefore making sculpture more competitive in a mass market. In the last essay, 'Absolute Music and Ideal Content: Autonomy, Sensation and Experience in Arthur Symons' "Theory of

Musical Aesthetics'" (*AJVS* 19[2014] 45–66), Sarah Collins also looks at the way artists framed their profession, but she focuses on the profession of music. Using Arthur Symons as an example, Collins explores his use of the notion of literary autonomy applied to a musical context.

Music and photography were the subject of a few works from 2014. Owen Clayton begins his book, *Literature and Photography in Transition, 1850–1915*, with a provocative reminder: 'at the time of invention, photography was the most modern method of representation', and as such it attracted the attention of authors in the period (p. 5). He looks at the interaction between literature and photography in the developing years of photograph theories and technologies beginning at mid-century. The main question Clayton pursues throughout is how the literary uses of photography, as metaphor and as mode of literary organization, changed during the period of multiple technological advances. He builds on the important work of Daniel Novak, who argued for a specific Victorian theory of photography; Clayton is interested in assessing the photographic methods and technologies that underlie this theory. In his choice of writers, he selects those who wrote at the key moments when one technology was in the process of replacing another. He includes Mayhew, for example, because he wrote during the time that the daguerreotype was displaced by the wet-plate collodion process. Clayton's first chapter offers a history of photography that emphasizes the different media of photography rather than describing photography as a single entity. After analysing the images in Mayhew's *London Labour and the London Poor* in chapter 2, and especially the way his approach changed in the third volume after he was exposed to wet-plate collodion photography, chapter 3 examines photographic discourse in Robert Louis Stevenson and Amy Levy. In this chapter Clayton connects conceptions of selfhood to photographic methods. He continues to look at photographic discourse in chapter 4 with William Dean Howells, but Clayton's main focus here is on the shift in Howells's work around 1905 when he attempted a new form of literary realism with *London Films*. The final chapter examines Jack London's use of cinematic showmanship in his writings. This book suggests the importance of considering the wide range of media in the Victorian period and the way this influenced the literature of the period.

'The Importance of Cheltenham: Imperialism, Liminality and Gustav Holst' (*JVC* 19[2014] 365–82) by Christopher Scheer makes a case for the importance of Gustav Holst (1874–1934) and his place in the history of British music. It hotography as a single entity was his liminality, Scheer argues, that has limited his influence, but Scheer goes on to describe Holst's interaction with imperialism and evangelicalism in Victorian Cheltenham. This reconsideration of one liminal figure illustrates the way our historical narrative about the Victorian legacy in the twentieth century may need revision.

This year produced some really interesting works on gender, with a notable emphasis on men and masculinity studies. In one of the livelier works, Bridget Walsh explores how murder trials act as a cultural barometer for the social norms of class, gender, and nation in *Domestic Murder in Nineteenth-Century England: Literary and Cultural Representations*. Walsh defines the category of 'domestic murders', as murders of lovers or spouses usually motivated by expediency. These particular cases helped to contest and formulate ideas of domesticity and of masculine identity, as she argues 'the portrayal of domestic murder reflected not a consensus of opinion regarding the domestic space, but rather significant discontent with the cultural and social codes of behavior circulating in society, particularly around the issues of gender and class' (p. 7). Walsh adds important insights to other work on Victorian murder by focusing not just on transgressive women, but also on the way gender was constructed for male perpetrators. Furthermore, she includes a range of evidence such as trial transcripts, novels, broadsides, scientific writing, illustration, and melodrama.

Chapters 1 and 2 begin with what Walsh sees as two of the most important representations of murder, in the press and on the stage. Chapter 1 examines two notorious murder trials as they were represented in several of the major newspapers and broadsides. Walsh highlights in particular the melodramatic representation of good/evil and justice as a way to counteract the destabilizing effect of murder on the sanctity of the home. Chapter 2 compares the 'sanitized' and regulated staging of murder on the official Victorian stage with murder in the 'theatre of the streets'. Chapters 3 to 5 proceed chronologically in order to show shifting representations of murder over time. Chapter 3 takes up the Newgate novel of the 1830s and 1840s, using Dickens's *Oliver Twist* and Thackeray's *Catherine* as examples. Although different in their representations of murder, both of these novels look forward to the psychological realism and sensational villainess that would emerge later in the century. Chapter 4 takes a closer look at the male perpetrator in murder cases and the 'unstable and contested models of masculinity' that emerged in both trial transcripts and novels. Walsh brings together several actual trials as well as several novels, including Collins's *Basil*, Hardy's *Desperate Remedies* and *Far From the Madding Crowd*, and Dickens's *Our Mutual Friend* and *The Mystery of Edwin Drood*. From the male domestic murderer, chapter 5 turns to the portrayals of the female domestic murderer in several trials and novels, including Mona Caird's *The Wing of Azrael* and Thomas Hardy's *Tess of the d'Urbervilles*. Walsh's examination of how murder was represented across several genres and over time adds much to our notions of how Victorians themselves debated the public/private binary and contested prevailing ideologies governing the domestic space and gendered behaviour.

While motherhood is a category often discussed in studies of women, fatherhood is not the first thing associated with men. However, Melissa Jenkins's remarkable book, *Fatherhood, Authority, and British Reading Culture, 1831–1907*, asks us to do just that. Jenkins's interdisciplinary approach to the conflicting constructions of fatherhood in the Victorian period looks not only at fiction but also life writing, conduct books, religious tracts, science writing, and history. While each chapter focuses on a Victorian novelist, Jenkins looks primarily at how these fiction writers construct fatherhood in other genres of writing. In looking back to conduct writing in the eighteenth century, Jenkins shows how the nineteenth century signalled a change in how and when the father's voice appeared in culture. The eighteenth-century conduct book is dominated by the father's voice, but in contrast the majority of conduct literature from the nineteenth century is by and for women. This is a trend echoed in the Victorian novel, in which 'the fictional father's role becomes increasingly difficult to categorize' (p. 3). In her introduction and throughout the book, Jenkins draws insightful connections between the crisis in authority facing both the author and the father. To examine Victorian forms of patriarchal authority, Jenkins draws out three descriptive category pairings from John Stuart Mill's 'The Spirit of the Age' [1831] and Max Weber's *Economy and Society* [1920], a set of categories she describes as suggestive and open to revision, but nonetheless useful as a way towards a kind of taxonomy of fatherhood. Each of the three parts of the book is organized around the three pairings from Mill and Weber. Part I uses Mill's category of 'eminent wisdom and virtue, real or supposed' and Weber's category of 'traditional authority' to track fathers who lose or gain power through their use of conventions. Part II takes up Mill's category of 'the power of addressing mankind' and Weber's 'charismatic authority' and applies these to the power of appeals to sentiment, where 'fatherhood' gains cultural capital by shaping feeling. Part III brings together Mill's category of 'worldly power' and Weber's category of 'legal-rational authority' to reveal how patriarchal figures appropriated other forms of authority as the conventional views of fatherhood waned.

Chapter 1 examines the relationship between Elizabeth Gaskell and Patrick Brontë, and in particular her response to this father's traditional authority, formulated through his requests about how to craft the *Life of Charlotte Brontë*. Jenkins also considers Brontë's fictional iterations of figures of fatherhood, thus weaving together the father's presence as character, author, and editor with which the first section of the book is concerned. The second chapter focuses on the role of father as author in an examination of George Meredith's first and last novels. Jenkins's analysis of the texts written by fathers within these novels sets father–child relationships in the context of textual production and the ambiguous relationship between writers and readers. The third chapter looks at the father's body as a site of authority. Thackeray's representations of fathers preaching and praying locate that authority in theatricality and sentimentality. Jenkins shows how Thackeray's novels intersect with manuals about leading family prayer and religious and sentimental writing. The fourth chapter contrasts the more positive view of paternal authority in George Eliot's nonfiction prose with the more negative vision of paternity in her fictional characters, a transition that Jenkins characterizes as moving from the father's charismatic power to stir his children to moral action to a nostalgic disembodiment that comes from the rise of print as a potential crisis for paternal authority. The fifth chapter examines Samuel Butler's tumultuous relationship to his father (and to his father's writings) and Butler's attempt to separate himself from his father's influence through writing about ancestors and inheritance in the context of science. Chapter 6 also looks at the idea of inheritance and lineage by tracing how Hardy 'uses the history of the family to reconsider history itself' (p. 147). Jenkins illuminates the relationship between material possessions in Hardy's novels and the idea of authorship, ownership, and power as conceived by fatherhood. Jenkins's conclusion is a thoughtful meditation on the issue of categorization as practised by the Victorians and illustrated through their construction of fathers as types. This book provides a refreshing approach to novel study by looking at how constructions of fatherhood in the novel intersect with a host of other cultural writing including biography, conduct books, sermons, and speeches. Her book contributes to our understanding of Victorian notions of fatherhood, operations of the Victorian novel in culture, and the important interchanges between forms of print and cultural discourses.

Another interesting book on fatherhood published this year focuses solely on the novel, but is worth mentioning here because of its combined topics of fatherhood, masculinity, and queer studies. Helena Gurfinkel's *Outlaw Fathers in Victorian and Modern British Literature: Queering Patriarchy* examines the relationship between queer patriarchs, what she calls 'outlaw fathers', and their queer sons. This relationship is based on 'submission and love' rather than 'competition, punishment, and the son's fear, and the father's threat, of castration' (p. 1). Gurfinkel is interested to examine how these queer family ties challenge normative heterosexual models of domesticity and the family. She looks at novels by Trollope, Samuel Butler, Henry James, J.R. Ackerley, E.M. Forster, and Alan Hollinghurst.

Pre-Raphaelite Masculinities: Constructions of Masculinity in Art and Literature, edited by Amelia Yeates and Serena Trowbridge, examines constructions of masculinity in the works of Pre-Raphaelite artists. Despite its apparent obvious association with the 'Brotherhood', the idea of masculinity within the Pre-Raphaelite movement has received little attention, according to the editors. This volume is interdisciplinary as it pulls examples from art, literature, the periodical press, and religious writings. The essays demonstrate the variety of ways in which masculinity was constructed by the Pre-Raphaelites, sometimes challenging and sometimes embracing wider cultural notions of masculinity. The chapters include the following: '"How Grew Such Presence from Man's Shameful Swarm"': Dante Gabriel Rossetti and Victorian Masculinity' by Jay D. Sloan; 'William Morris's *Sigurd the Volsung* and the Parameters of Manliness' by Ingrid Hanson; 'The Hallucination of the Real: Pre-Raphaelite Vision as a Crisis of Romantic Masculinity' by Gavin Budge; 'Health and Manliness in the Reception of Edward Burne-Jones's Work' by Amelia Yeates; 'Marginal Masculinities? Regional and Gender Borders in William Bell Scott's Wallington Scheme' by Rosemary Mitchell; 'Interpreting Masculinity: Pre-Raphaelite Illustration and the Works of Tennyson, Christina Rossetti and Trollope' by Simon Cooke; '"Me, Who Ride Alone"': Male Chastity in Pre-Raphaelite Poetry and Art' by Dinah Roe; 'In Praise of Venus: Victorian Masculinity and Tannhäuser as Aesthetic Hero' by Sally-Anne Huxtable; and finally 'Christianity, Masculinity, Imperialism: The Light of the World and Colonial Contexts of Display' by Eleanor Fraser Stansbie. As Colin Cruise says in the Afterword, the essays in this volume present 'the multiplicity of masculine identities and their performative modes' and the 'range of means by which such representations, both in artistic representation and self-presentation, are made possible' (p. 214).

A special issue of *Nineteenth-Century Contexts*, 'The Male Body in Victorian Literature and Culture' edited by Nadine Muller and Joanne Ella Parsons, aims to address the gap in scholarship on the male body. While there has been much excellent work on the female body in the Victorian period, the editors suggest that the male body can tell us important things about not only gendered identities but other key issues like class, empire, race, nationhood, war, disability, science, and religion. Some of the essays take novels as their subject, but fashion, biography, and science are also included. In 'Eating Englishness and Causing Chaos: Food and the Body of the Fat Man in R.S. Surtees' *Jorrocks's Jaunts and Jollities, Handley Cross,* and *Hillingdon Hall*' (*NCC* 36[2014] 335–46), Joanne Ella Parsons focuses on issues of food consumption and the male body, especially as it intersects with class transgression and the carnivalesque, in three early Victorian novels by Surtees. In 'The Good Soldier: Gilbert Bayes and the Chivalric Statuette' (*NCC* 36[2014] 307–21), Katherine Faulkner examines *fin-de-siècle* chivalric statuettes and Burberry advertisements of men's fashions to assess how the clothes covering the male body figure into national discourses. In '"A Brown Sunburnt Gentleman": Masculinity and the Travelling Body in Dickens's *Bleak House*' (*NCC* 36[2014] 323–34), Charlotte Mathieson focuses on how the sunburnt male body destabilizes categories of race, class, and gender, using *Bleak House* as her example. In 'Noble Lives: Writing Disability and Masculinity in the Late Nineteenth Century' (*NCC* 36[2014] 363–75), Clare Walker Gore focuses on the disabled male body by examining the life of one disabled aristocratic man. Turning to American studies, in '"That Doctor and His Heartless, Bloodless Science!": Disembodied Rational Masculinity in Victorian American Culture' (*NCC* 36[2014] 347–61) Shaun Richards looks at the disembodiment of the male body through the figure of the male scientist in Harold Frederic's *The Damnation of Theron Ware* [1896].

Abigail Joseph's essay '"A Wizard of Silks and Tulle": Charles Worth and the Queer Origins of Couture' (*VS* 56[2014] 251–79) also opens up new ways of thinking about queer Victorian masculinity by suggesting that Charles Worth's fashion production created a relationship to women's clothing based on social and material relations rather than sexual preference or effeminacy. This also provides a new way of looking at the relationships between men and women in the Victorian period as not always directly about bodies and desire but focused on material and aesthetic realms. Joseph's essay examines how the high fashion industry was a 'site where nineteenth-century ideologies of value and gender were both perpetuated and transfigured' (p. 252). Ruth Robbins, in 'Man-Made Fibres? The Split Personalities of Victorian Manliness' (*Victor* 4[2014] 139–55) looks at constructions of 'manliness' in the Victorian period, particularly the contradicting concepts of a man's capacity for violence and the requirement that he be gentlemanly and civilized. An essay by Heather Ellis, '"This Starting, Feverish Heart": Matthew Arnold and the Problem of Manliness' (*CS* 20[2014] 91–115), focuses on Matthew Arnold's influential idea of Christian manliness. Through a close reading of Arnold's school sermons and works that focus on the dangers of boyhood, Ellis highlights the opposition between moral maturity and immoral boyishness that structures Arnold's conception of manliness as well as his educational thought. This essay demonstrates the close connections between Arnold's work on history, manliness, and education.

A helpful review essay in *Victorian Literature and Culture* by Richard A. Kaye entitled 'The New Other Victorians: The Success (and Failure) of Queer

Theory in Nineteenth-Century British Studies' (*VLC* 42[2014] 755–71) discusses the works that have been most exciting in the nexus of Victorian and queer theory over the last two decades.

There were also a number of studies focused on women in 2014. *Picturing Women's Health* is an interesting volume edited by Francesca Scott, Kate Scarth, and Ji Won Chung. This collection of essays explores the construction, representation, and 'picturing' of women's health and bodies. The collection aims to add to existing scholarship on women's health by looking not just at illness but representations of good health as well, and looking not just at 'woman' as a collective but individuated circumstances created by socio-economic status, profession, and lifestyle. The book begins with two essays on novels from the Romantic period by Charlotte Smith and Maria Edgeworth. In the first selection to move into the Victorian period, Sarah Richardson's essay 'Transforming the Body Politic: Food Reform and Feminism in Nineteenth-Century Britain' links dietary and political reform through an examination of two female activists, Anna Kingsford and Annie Cobden-Sanderson. Richardson argues that these women took their traditional authority over domestic concerns like food and used it to gain influence in the political realm by connecting the health of the body politic with the health of the physical body. Alexandra Lewis's essay 'Stagnation of Air and Mind: Picturing Trauma and Miasma in Charlotte Brontë's *Villette*' explores how Brontë moves beyond typical strategies for representing female trauma by using theories of miasma. This essay adds an important area of study for work on the interaction between literature and medicine by incorporating the relationship between atmosphere and affect. Susannah Wilson's essay 'The Iconography of Anorexia Nervosa in the Long Nineteenth Century' focuses on a particular kind of bodily trauma, anorexia nervosa. Wilson considers several cases that made use of illustrations in their study of anorexia and interprets these cases alongside theoretical perspectives of disease and of the gaze. Tabitha Sparks's essay 'Kate Marsden's Leper Project: On Sledge and Horseback with an Outcast Missionary Nurse' analyses the memoir of a missionary nurse and the leper hospital she establishes. Marsden and her memoir come under scrutiny for unreliability, which Sparks reads alongside the 'contradictory values and objectives of professional Victorian nursing' (p. 105). Katherine Ford takes up a more typical topic when thinking about nineteenth-century women's health, female insanity, but her essay, 'Constructs of Female Insanity at the Fin de Siècle: The Lawn Hospital, Lincoln, 1882–1902', incorporates a fresh approach by looking at archival patient records to determine the role that doctors played in the construction of insanity. Claire Brock's essay 'The Fitness of the Female Medical Student, 1895–1910', explores the conditions of female medical students at the London School of Medicine for Women and the tensions that arose between expectations and experiences by analysing student publications and records. The collection ends with an essay by Hilary Marland entitled 'Unstable Adolescence/Unstable Literature? Managing British Girls' Health around 1900' that explores the diverse opinions about girls' health and demonstrates the connections between medicine, education, work, and of course gender ideologies.

A really interesting work on recovering lost women's voices, Anne Schwan's *Convict Voices: Women, Class, and Writing about Prison in Nineteenth-Century England*, focuses on female ex-prisoners. Schwan draws from gallows literature, prison narratives, mid-Victorian novels, prison autobiography, and diaries and letters. By bringing to light female prisoners' perspectives, Schwan hopes to interrogate the broader social issues of gender and class relations. In each of the texts she examines, Schwan is attentive to the tension between giving voice to the marginalized and 'issues of mediation, appropriation, and exploitation' (p. 19). Chapter 1, '"Shame, You Are Not Going to Hang Me!": Women's Voices in Nineteenth-Century Street Literature', offers a history of critical debate about crime and execution broadsides before turning to specific examples. Schwan argues that these texts provided a public space for non-elite female voices. Chapter 2, '"The Lives of which 'There Are No Records Kept'": Convicts and Matrons in the Prison Narratives of Frederick William Robinson', examines the trilogy of prison narratives by Robinson, which Schwan finds to validate women's experiences in prison. Rather than focus on issues of accuracy, Schwan attends to questions of narrative construction, for example the tension between a first-person female narrator and the implied male author. Chapter 3, 'The Limits of Female Reformation: Hidden Stories in George Eliot's *Adam Bede* and Wilkie Collins's *The Moonstone*', argues that the stories of the female convicts in these two novels actually form the core of the narratives through which these authors offer important commentary on the social condition of women. Chapter 4, '"A Clamorous Multitude and a Silent Prisoner": Women's Rights, Spiritualism, and Public Speech in Susan Willis Fletcher's *Twelve Months in an English Prison*', examines a convict memoir by a female prisoner, which presents a contrast to male-authored convict memoirs. Schwan demonstrates how spiritualism and the prison memoir create a platform for female agency and control over the representation of female identity. Chapter 5, 'Adultery, Gender, and the Nation: The Florence Maybrick Case and *Mrs. Maybrick's Own Story*', examines the autobiography of Florence Maybrick, written after her release from fifteen years in prison for murdering her husband. Maybrick's autobiography explicitly calls for legal and prison reform, and critiques the media's representation of criminal cases. Chapter 6, 'Gender and Citizenship in Edwardian Writings from Prison: Kate Gliddon and the Suffragettes at Holloway', examines the symbolic meaning of imprisonment within the suffragettes' first-hand experiences of prison, which often connected the material conditions of women's jails to their ordinary lives. The final chapter, 'Postscript: Rewriting Women's Prison History in Historical Fiction: Margaret Atwood's *Alias Grace* and Sarah Waters's *Affinity*', turns to these two contemporary novelists to explore how the authors imagine these marginalized women's voices from the nineteenth century. The methodology that Schwan follows in this book can provide a template, she hopes, for 'intersectional textual analysis' and can increase our understanding of 'gender and class relations in general and individual and collective responsibilities in the context of women's offending behavior more specifically' (p. 196).

Salome: The Image of a Woman Who Never Was is a book that focuses on the single figure of Salome, but this focus, as the author Rosina Neginsky explains, allows her to examine the process of myth generation, the link between how stories proliferated about Salome and how they do so about women in society in general. Neginsky traces artistic portrayals of Salome from the Bible through the Middle Ages, Renaissance, and nineteenth century, and it is in her chapter on the nineteenth century, 'The Seducer-Destroyer Salome of Nineteenth-Century Art and Literature', that Neginsky articulates the historical conditions in which Salome became 'a symbol of the dangerous and seductive woman who, once allowed to gain social power, would destroy man' (p. 2). Although the nineteenth century makes up only one chapter in this book, anyone interested in the intersections between cultural norms and art or the feminist movement in the period will find that this focus on one particular iteration of mythical woman can add to ongoing conversations about the ideology of Victorian gender.

Jill Lamberton, in '"A Revelation and a Delight": Nineteenth-Century Cambridge Women, Academic Collaboration, and the Cultural Work of Extracurricular Writing' (*CCompCom* 65[2014] 560–87), examines the influence of student writing from the first generation of women to attend Girton and Newnham colleges on the institutional culture for education in middle-class women's lives. Lamberton focuses on extracurricular writing such as letters, diaries, campus periodical articles, and memoirs.

'The "Ungallant Silence of the Historian": Elizabeth Stone, Esther Owen and the Art of Needlework' (*JVC* 19[2014] 261–77), by Kathryn Ledbetter and Renn Edward Wortley, considers the publishing trials of two women authors who wrote needlework books, Elizabeth Stone's *Art of Needlework* [1840] and Esther Owen's *Illuminated Ladies' Book of Useful and Ornamental Needlework* [1844]. These two women's efforts to publish in the face of authorial misattribution and financial mismanagement represent similar issues faced by domestic women artists and the scholars who attempt to study them.

Daisy Hay's essay 'Hair in the Disraeli Papers: A Victorian Harvest' (*JVC* 19[2014] 332–45) asks us to approach archival research differently; rather than reading only those parts of an archive with self-evident documentary value, Hay reads the Disraeli archive holistically. This leads her to an exploration of hair and the collecting habits of Mary Anne Disraeli, and how she enhances our understanding of 'thing culture' in the Victorian period. Hay's article also makes a case for recovering women's voices through archival research that pays attention to silences and absences.

In 'Feminism, Nationalism, Separatism? The Case of Alice Stopford Green' (*JVC* 19[2014] 442–56), Helen Kingstone complicates our views of *fin-de-siècle* women writers through an examination of Alice Stopford Green and the epilogue she wrote in 1915 to her husband's *Short History of the English People* [1874] and a periodical article 'Woman's Place in the World of Letters' [1897]. Kingstone examines the contradictions in Green's work, such as her use of 'woman' as a form of female essentialism at the same time as she insists woman's true nature is never seen. These contradictions are the 'surreptitious means' by which Green voices and subverts English nationalism.

In '"Such a Strong Wish for Wings": *The Life of Charlotte Brontë* and Elizabeth Gaskell's Fallen Angels' (*VLC* 42[2014] 671–90), Meghan Burke Hattaway offers one way of reading Gaskell's handling of Charlotte Brontë's biography by comparing it to the rehabilitation of fallen or public women in Gaskell's fiction, such as *Ruth*. Ultimately Hattaway finds that Gaskell emphasizes Brontë's 'heroic self-discipline' as the quality that makes her an 'Angel in the House' rather than a fallen woman.

Gemma Goodman and Charlotte Mathieson move outside of the typically gendered space of the home to consider literal outside spaces. *Gender and Space in Rural Britain, 1840–1920* is a collection of essays that looks at representations of rural space and those writers who work to show 'a more diverse and complex picture' of rural Britain (p. 1). The book begins at mid-century, when rural spaces were being fundamentally changed by farming practices, railways, and tourism. At the same time, this period saw shifts in gender relations, and this collection takes up the relationship between representations of rural space and representations of femininity and masculinity. Most of the chapters explore texts after 1900, but are nonetheless of interest to Victorian scholars interested in questions of urban and rural identity. Chapter 1, 'Women in the Field', by Roger Ebbatson, examines the representation of women's field labour in the works of Richard Jeffries and Thomas Hardy. Chapter 2, '"Between Two Civilizations": George Sturt's Constructions of Loss and Change in Rural Village Life', by Barry Sloan, looks at themes of loss and change in rural village life in three modernist novels by George Sturt, Alfred Williams, and Flora Thompson. Chapter 3, 'At Work and at Play: Charles Lee's *Cynthia in the West*', by Gemma Goodman, explores the rural space of the coast in Lee's turn-of-the-century novel where traditional gender categories are subverted. Chapter 4, 'Going Out, Going Alone: Modern Subjectivities in Rural Scotland 1900–21', by Samantha Walton, looks at the interaction between town and country in the novels and short stories of two Scottish writers, Mary and Jane Findlater. Chapters 5, 6, and 7 look to Victorian writers, beginning with Lynsey McCulloch's '"Drowned Lands": Charles Kingsley's *Hereward the Wake* and the Masculinization of the English Fens', which attempts to untangle the representation of gender in Kingsley's portrayal of rural spaces. Chapter 6, Charlotte Mathieson's '"Wandering Like a Wild Thing": Rurality, Women, and Walking in George Eliot's *Adam Bede* and *The Mill on the Floss*', examines mobility as a trope of possibility for women in rural settings. Chapter 7, '"I Never Liked Long Walks": Gender, Nature, and Jane Eyre's Rural Wandering' by Katherine F. Montgomery, examines Brontë's rendering of the sublime through her characterization of Jane. Chapter 8 moves from novels to gardening in 'Gertrude Jekyll: Cultivating the Gendered Space of the Victorian Garden for Professional Success' by Christen Ericsson-Penfold, which examines the garden as an acceptable professional space for women. Chapter 9, 'From England to Eden: Gardens, Gender and Knowledge in Virginia Woolf's *The Voyage Out*', begins to move beyond the borders of England in tracing the different effects of rural spaces on the protagonist. The final chapter, Eliza S.K. Leong's 'The Transnational Rural in Alicia Little's *My Diary in a Chinese Farm*', chronicles the life of an English woman on a Chinese farm in the years 1887–1907 and the clash between an English rural identity and a Chinese rural context. This collection thus moves self-consciously beyond British borders to join colonial conversations about the transference of British identity abroad and suggests new areas for the study of rurality.

Goodman's book on rural spaces brings us to another topic of interest in quite a few studies this year: urban environments and their relationship to the changing rural landscape in the Victorian period. Lee Jackson's *Dirty Old London: The Victorian Fight Against Filth* is a look at the sanitary history of Victorian London. The story Jackson skilfully weaves includes the sanitary movement of the 1840s, the fight against typhus by cleansing the slums from the start of the century onwards, the problem of human excrement, mud, and dust (ashes). Each chapter proceeds to explore one specific aspect of 'dirty old London'. Chapter 1, 'The Golden Dustman', examines the dustman, the collector of household refuse. We learn about the average working day of a dustman, his relationship to householders, the economics of their trade business with brickmakers, and the technological advances that helped reform the problem of dust at the same time as it eliminated the need for dustmen. Chapter 2, 'Inglorious Mud', looks at the problem of mud in the streets of London, from the danger posed by slippery streets to horses and people, to the arguments over who was responsible for cleaning pavements, and the politics of the crossing-sweepers, who were often poor children. This chapter also closely traces the story of Charles Cochrane, public health reformer who attempted to rid London of mud. Chapter 3, 'Night Soil', takes up the problem of disposing of human waste, from the early nineteenth century's use of cesspools to the invention of water closets, which would result in new disposal methods like flush toilets. The slow-growing realization of the sanitary problems of human waste, spurred by cholera epidemics, forms part of the subject of this chapter, which helps to illustrate one of the puzzling pieces of London's sanitary history—that 'filth emerged triumphant', largely due to complacent attitudes (p. 7). Chapter 4 traces one victory story over filth, Edwin Chadwick's public health campaign of the 1840s. Despite the short-lived nature of many of his projects—the Metropolitan Sanitary Association lasted only a few years—his work would raise the awareness of pollution issues. Chapter 5 returns to the problem of disposal, but this time the focus is human bodies and bones. Like other waste receptacles, graveyards were not seen as a risk to public health until the problem of cholera induced people to search for better ways to protect the air and water quality of the city. From dead human bodies to living ones, chapter 6 looks at the dirt that clung to the working class, who came to be called 'the great unwashed', the title of this chapter. This problem led to the development of public washing facilities for clothing and public baths for washing the body. Chapter 7, 'The Public Convenience', looks at another public phenomenon, the public toilet, which came with its own sanitary and moral concerns. Chapter 8 examines the connection between fever outbreaks, fever hospitals, and the movement to cleanse the slums. The solutions for sanitizing the slums ranged from demolition to building new and improved housing. This chapter also highlights the debate between the free market and state intervention. The final chapter, 'The Veil of Soot', looks at one of the most ubiquitous sanitary problems, smoke. Two specific campaigns are discussed, one to deal with the 'smoke nuisance' and one to end the sweep's use of child labour. This book also tells the story of politics between centralized government and local parishes in managing the affairs of its people and the politics of class. As Jackson details in his epilogue, as we turn to our own pollution issues in the twenty-first century, the Victorians have left us with their legacy of sanitary reforms, both their successes and their failures.

Eileen Cleere also discusses the issue of cleanliness and urbanization in *The Sanitary Arts: Aesthetic Culture and the Victorian Cleanliness Campaigns*. Cleere examines the connection between the nineteenth-century sanitation reform movement and Victorian aesthetic philosophy: 'taste', she argues, 'as a mechanism of public health and social justice' (p. 9). Cleere aims to reveal a more contested story of sanitation reform than the disciplinary narrative usually circulated in historical accounts of this movement. Rather than focus on how Chadwick's sanitary report restructured the observational habits of Victorians, Cleere focuses on the way the cleanliness campaigns, tied to but larger than Chadwick's reports, created an instinctive sensitivity to filth that shifted cultural taste, importantly challenging the hierarchy of senses that privileged the visual.

The book begins with a key moment in what Cleere calls the 'sanitary aesthetic', the publication of Chadwick's *Sanitary Report* in 1842 and John Ruskin's *Modern Painters* in 1843. Cleere interacts with, sometimes using and sometimes challenging, Foucauldian and structuralist methodologies. Her second chapter focuses on those Victorian novels, represented by Eliot's *Middlemarch* and Gaskell's *North and South*, that combine the teleology of the marriage plot with a sanitary narrative based on social reconciliation. Her third chapter turns to germ theories and their influence on the design of domestic spaces and architecture. Chapter 4 juxtaposes Ruskin's aesthetic theory with Pater's to show the influence of laboratory and surgical science on perceptions of the human body. The last two chapters continue to trace this shift from environmental to what Cleere calls a 'biological phase in cultural history' as she examines the sanitary plot in New Woman fiction. Ward's novel *The Mating of Lydia* represents the transition into a genetic phase in sanitary thinking and ties this to the virtue of feminine responsibility. In her last chapter, Cleere looks at texts that utilize eugenic thinking in the form of 'hygienic breeding', which forms an important ideological force in the New Woman fiction marriage plot. One of the most revealing arguments of Cleere's book is that the aesthetic realm can function to disguise social programmes as natural instincts.

Another kind of anxiety caused by urbanization was energy use. Allen MacDuffie explores this in his book *Victorian Literature, Energy, and the Ecological Imagination*. Victorian writers such as Mill, Ruskin, and Dickens began to recognize humans as a kind of 'environmental force' and the city as representing this 'spiraling energy consumption' (p. 11). MacDuffie explores the various (mis)representations of the relationship between humans and natural resources. Building on the work of literary scholars who have drawn connections between literary and scientific imaginaries, MacDuffie argues that 'the canonical account of energy in Victorian scientific discourse often distorted the ecological significance of the energy concept' (p. 13) usually because Victorian scientists focused on theological concepts of thermodynamics rather than its biological consequences. The first two chapters turn to the Victorian city imagined as a kind of energy system. Chapters 3 to 8 look at specific literary texts that MacDuffie calls 'alternative thermodynamic narratives' for the way they depart from the canonical discourse about thermodynamics. In chapter 1, 'The City and the Sun', MacDuffie explores two opposing energy paradigms based on fossil fuel resources and the way the modern thermodynamic definition obscures this tension. This chapter focuses mainly on Thomas Huxley, Charles Babbage, Tyndall, Carlyle, and a cluster of writers on coal including John Holland, William Armstrong, Edward Hull, and William Stanley Jevons. The first chapter focused on the first law of thermodynamics, and in chapter 2, 'The Heat Death of the Sun at the Dawn of the Anthropocene', MacDuffie focuses on the second law. The cosmological interpretation of the second law illustrates how Victorians attempted to 'construct a social and theological discourse congenial to the expansion and development of industrial motive power' (p. 70). MacDuffie explores this tension in popular thermodynamic works by Tait, Stewart, and Norman Lockyer. In chapter 5, 'John Ruskin's Alternative Energy', MacDuffie turns to what he calls the 'most profound meditation on an emergent energy-intensive culture the Victorian period produced' (p. 137). MacDuffie finds Ruskin so pivotal because of his comprehensive notion of energy as a system that includes the interchange among natural formations, cultural productions, and human environments. Ruskin presents the ecological crisis through his combination of 'rational analysis and imaginative extension' that MacDuffie places as the centrepiece of the chapters on 'alternative thermodynamic narratives'. The rest of the chapters each explore some aspect of thermodynamic discourse in the novel, including 'Energy Systems and Narrative Systems in Charles Dickens's *Bleak House*' (chapter 3), 'The Renewable Energies of *Our Mutual Friend*' (chapter 4), 'Personal Fantasy, Natural Limits: Robert Louis Stevenson's *Dr. Jekyll and Mr. Hyde*' (chapter 6), and 'Evolutionary Energy and the Future: Henry Maudsley and H.G. Wells' (chapter 8).

Several articles also addressed the issue of urbanization. In 'Suburban Identity in Paul Maitland's Paintings of Cheyne Walk' (*JVC* 19[2014] 43–62), Simon Knowles considers the emergence of the modern suburb and how it was defined in relation to urban areas. Looking specifically at Paul Maitland's paintings of Cheyne Walk, Knowles explores how place identity changes over time in response to economic and social structures. Vicky Holmes considers the lives and conditions of lodgers in working-class dwellings in her article 'Accommodating the Lodger: The Domestic Arrangements of Lodgers in Working-Class Dwellings in a Victorian Provincial Town' (*VLC* 19[2014] 314–31). Rather than focus on the dwellings themselves, Holmes puts the lodgers at the forefront of her exploration by using coroners' inquest reports for the town of Ipswich. This article reveals that we can learn much more about the ideology of the Victorian home by focusing on the domestic arrangements of lodgers. Jonathan Cranfield, in 'Sherlock's Slums: The Periodical as an Environmental Form' (*TPr* 28[2014] 215–41), reads late Victorian periodicals, and in particular the *Strand Magazine*, as an environmental form influenced by the development of urban centres. Sarah

Dewis, in *The Loudons and the Gardening Press*, reviewed above, also has some interesting things to say about urbanization.

The politics of space is connected to many of the changes shaping the political landscape at this time. There were several studies devoted to this topic, many of which offered a rereading of the way scholars have constructed the political narratives of the Victorian period. James Vernon constructs one of the most interesting political narratives in the works of 2014 in his book, *Distant Strangers: How Britain Became Modern*. As its title suggests, one of the primary phenomena of modernity is living with strangers, but Vernon also examines the processes that made economic, social, and political relations possible between strangers. At the heart of his argument about modernity in Britain Vernon takes on the definition of modernity itself. He is concerned over the trend in historical studies to see sudden and transformational historical events in terms of longer, uneven processes of change, and while he admits this makes history more democratic it is also a trend that he argues 'evacuates the term modernity of any meaning or analytical utility' (p. xii). Macro-explanations of historical change are part of why history 'still matters and has public value' (p. xv), and his book is an attempt to return to that way of reading history.

In asking the question 'How did Britain become modern?', Vernon provides three answers that structure his book. First, the growth and mobility of the population created a new society of strangers. Secondly, this led to abstract and bureaucratic forms to address how strangers could live and work together. Thirdly, the process of abstraction was dialectical in that it went alongside efforts to 'reembed social, economic, and political life in local and personal relations' (p. 7). The book accumulates evidence through what he calls case studies. Chapter 2 thus takes up the question of Britain's transformation to a modern society through the issue of population, specifically the mobility of Britain's growing population in the nineteenth century. From this exploration of what caused the condition of living with strangers, Vernon turns to how the effects were dealt with. Chapter 3 examines the development of new faceless systems of government that worked at an increasing distance from the people and places it governed. As with chapter 2, which considered the improvements made to transportation systems, chapter 3 examines the advances made in communication technologies that allowed for governing from a distance. In the face of this abstraction and distancing, central organizations, ceremonies, and petitions became a vital part of civil society in what Vernon describes as the formalization of associational culture. He explores this phenomenon in chapter 4, which draws on his argument that modernity was a dialectical process of depersonalization and personalization. Vernon focuses in large part in this chapter on voting practices and electoral procedures as an exemplum of 'the tension between the communal and the individuated form of the political subject' (p. 98). From issues of governance, Vernon turns to economic transformations in chapter 5. Vernon provocatively reverses Adam Smith's contention that the growth of capitalism created a society of strangers to suggest instead that it was the condition of associating with strangers that 'restructured the practice of economic life' (p. 101). As the idea of economy became abstracted from forms of personal exchange, a uniform national economy emerged alongside the emergent discipline of economics.

Vernon's stated aim in this book is to 'rehabilitate modernity as an analytical category' (p. 128) so that it can once again be historically and culturally specific. His case study is really, then, Britain itself. His answer to when and how Britain became modern rejects those typical historical moments of the Enlightenment or the Industrial Revolution and rests instead on the growth and mobility of population. It was this condition of living among strangers that created the changes to political, economic, and social life from face-to-face encounters to systems of abstraction. Vernon holds unswervingly to the idea that this modern transformation took place in the nineteenth century and he is not 'beguiled by attempts' to locate it earlier or later. If Vernon's claims seem audacious to some, he reminds us that he does not have quite the hubris of Virginia Woolf, who claims one very small moment 'on or about December 1910' to mark a transformational historical moment. Vernon at least claims the better part of a century to trace his specific historical moment, and scholars will find his synthesis of research and data a provocative approach to the nineteenth-century historical moment as well as the notion of modernity itself.

Sarah Pickard provides another perspective on behaviour towards others under the conditions of a modern Britain. *Anti-Social Behaviour in Britain: Victorian and Contemporary Perspectives* includes, as the title indicates, later periods than the Victorian, but it begins with the nineteenth century and its attempts to control the conduct of the population, represented in the transformation of the penal system and the numerous acts of legislation that centralized state control. The diverse essays in the collection are united around two key debates: 'what constitutes anti-social behavior among individuals or groups', and 'how and why governments attempted or attempt to deal with anti-social behaviour' (p. xvii). The volume is divided into three parts that each address a specific aspect of anti-social behaviour of individuals and groups and policies developed by the government in response. The first part is entitled 'Anti-Social Behaviour, the Urban Environment and Public Spaces', Part II is entitled 'Anti-Social Behaviour, the Vulnerable and the Marginalized', and Part III is entitled 'Anti-Social Behaviour, Recreation and Leisure'.

Another work that takes types of behaviour as its focus is a collection of essays edited by Monika Fludernik and Miriam Nandi *Idleness, Indolence and Leisure in English Literature*. The volume attempts to do no less than trace a history of idleness in English literature. The introduction proceeds with a word study of 'idleness' and a discussion of its various connotations in different contexts. The essays that will be of interest to Victorian scholars include chapters focused on the stage and works of fiction including 'The Performativity of Idleness: Representations and Stagings of Idleness in the Context of Colonialism' by Monika Fludernik; 'Drama of Idleness: The Comedy of Manners in the Works of Richard Brinsley Sheridan and Oscar Wilde' by Kerstin Fest; 'Idleness and Creativity: Poetic Disquisitions on Idleness in the Eighteenth and Early Nineteenth Centuries' by Richard Adelman; and 'Versions of Working-Class Idleness: Non-Productivity and the Critique of Victorian Workaholism' by Benjamin Kohlmann. Barbara Korte's chapter adds a prose genre to the examination of idleness in 'Against Busyness: Idling in Victorian and Contemporary Travel Writing', which explores the emergence of 'old-fashioned' modes of travelling to counteract the 'haste' of Victorian travel.

Several works in 2014 focused on the issue of class. James Owen re-examines the relationship between the Labour Party and Liberalism, with particular attention to the language used during campaigns, in *Labour and the Caucus: Working Class Radicalism and Organised Liberalism in England, 1868–88*. Chapter 1, 'The Struggle for Political Representation: Labour Candidates and the Liberal Party, 1868–76', analyses the language used during elections and the efforts of working-class candidates to construct their identity in relation to Liberalism. Chapter 2, 'Activism, Identity and Networks: Urban and Rural Working-Class Radicalism, 1868–74', explores early republicanism in London and provincial republican clubs. Owen argues for the importance of 'place' to this movement, particularly for agricultural labourers. Chapter 3, 'Labour's Response to the Caucus: Class, America and Language, 1877–85', explores the Labour Party's reaction to the National Liberal Federation. This chapter also examines the language of elections to analyse how Labour candidates adopted the language of the caucus. Chapter 4, 'Tensions and Fault Lines: The Lib-Lab MPs, the Wider Labour Movement and the Role of Irish Nationalism, 1885–8', explores the shifting definitions of the Labour Party, influenced by the trade union debates, the Irish nationalists, and the deals struck between Lib-Lab MPs and Liberalism in the 1885 general election. Chapter 5, 'Rethinking the "Revival of Socialism": Socialists, Liberals and the Caucus, 1881–8', re-examines the interactions between socialist organizations and Liberalism and analyses the failure of socialists to appeal to working-class liberals.

A critically engaging work in this area is Margaret A. Loose's *The Chartist Imaginary: Literary Form in Working-Class Political Theory and Practice*. In a poetic opening, Loose meditates on why Chartists wrote literature and what role it played in their political aims. For the Chartists she considers, Loose claims that 'art was a site of political debate, a realm in which people could perceive the relations of the world and think about ways of changing them' (p. 3). The very mixture of genres represented in Chartist writing turns Chartists into 'protagonists' in the history and culture of Britain, and Loose argues that studying their literature is vital to understanding the politics of the movement. In each of her chapters, Loose sets out to examine literary techniques and aesthetic form rather than political themes.

The first chapter examines the border-crossing of Ernest Jones. Born in Germany to upper-class parents, Jones nonetheless became the 'poet laureate' of the Chartist movement. Loose is interested to trace the Romantic influence in Jones's poetry and how the lyric 'I' leads to identification with communities beyond national and class boundaries. His work exhibits the kind of internationalism that became important to Chartist literature. Chapter 2 challenges the critical commonplace that Romanticism was the primary poetic ancestor of working-class writing; Loose argues the genealogy was much broader and she focuses particularly on the way three Chartist epics engage with the medieval grotesque, satirical and pastoral conventions, and the epic tradition. Focusing on several works by William James Linton, Thomas Cooper, and Ernest Jones, Loose demonstrates that these writers chose to write in high cultural forms like the epic, and they made these forms work to challenge rather than uphold conservative values. Loose also takes up the hybridity of Chartist writing in chapter 3, where she turns to fiction. Loose asks how working-class writers represent another kind of Victorian response to hybridity, a concept often associated in the period with subversion or a lack of wholeness: she focuses on Alexander Somerville's *Dissuasive Warnings to the People on Street Warfare* [1839], 'Argus''s 'The Revolutionist' [1840], and Thomas Martin Wheeler's *Sunshine and Shadow* [1849–50]. The revolutionary context of each of these texts draws attention to the hybridity of the political and aesthetic elements in Chartist literature. As she does in the other chapters, Loose connects form and politics by concluding that Chartism was a movement that strove to exceed limitations, both formally and politically.

Chapters 4 and 5 take up the issue of gender, examining how Chartist literature converges and departs from Victorian culture's treatment of 'the woman question'. Chapter 4 surveys different responses throughout the Chartist movement before turning to focus on Gerald Massey's poem 'Only a Dream' [1856]. Loose goes on to show that through the poem's complex structure, Massey posits readers as a legislating body and therefore as agents of social change for gender equality rather than mere interpreters of literature. The final chapter examines three women Chartist poets, attending to the themes of memory, imagination, and psychic stress that draw these works together. Loose argues that it was 'precisely through their appeal to the imagination of how things should and might be different' that Chartist poetry fostered personal, intellectual, and political ambition' (p. 172). Loose's careful and insightful readings of Chartist literature, much of it never discussed before, add much to our understanding of the Chartist movement as well as the hybridity and scope of Victorian literature, its form and its aims. This book also introduces us to little-known authors and works, expanding the corpus of writing used to study the Chartist movement, and indeed Victorian literature itself. For another insightful book on Chartism, see Chris Vanden Bossche's *Reform Acts: Chartism, Social Agency, and the Victorian Novel, 1832–1867*, reviewed in the relevant section below.

Gareth Cordery and Joseph S. Meisel also explore the political state of Britain in the nineteenth century through an examination of one key figure, in *The Humours of Parliament: Harry Furniss's View of Late-Victorian Political Culture*. This edition of Furniss's 'The Humours of Parliament' provides an interesting look at political culture in addition to the role of the lecture in British culture. The introduction provides background information on Furniss's career within the context of British cartooning and visual satire, and relevant information on the text, images, and performance of 'Humours'. The introduction also takes a look at two broader contexts, the lecture as a source of entertainment for Victorian audiences and the political developments of the 1880s and 1890s that inform the satire of the 'Humours'. This stated scope is ambitious, but the introduction does indeed deliver on this in a well-organized manner with helpful illustrations and clear section and chapter divisions. While individual topics, such as women or Ireland, do not provide new or specialized information, the value of these historical sections lies in the ways in which the editors put them into conversation with one another and with specific issues related to parliament. The introduction thus makes this edition useful not only for those who may be interested in Harry Furniss himself but also those engaged with the genre of the lecture or the late Victorian political scene. The introduction is followed by the text of Furniss's lecture, including the images that were to accompany it as slides.

In *Political Descent: Malthus, Mutualism, and the Politics of Evolution in Victorian England*, Piers Hale traces the history of evolutionary theory to the nineteenth century in order to show it has been political from its inception. Hale identifies two different political views of evolution that emerged from 1859, one which Hale calls 'Malthusian' and which 'focused upon the adaptation of the individual through struggle as a means to progressive social evolution', and the other an anti-Malthusian strand that came from French naturalist Jean-Baptiste Lamarck and emphasized 'social cohesion as a means to the social evolution of a society' (pp. 6–7). In tracing this history Hale attempts to draw attention to evolutionary political radicals, whose importance has been obscured by the focus on Darwin and 'bona fide' scientists. Hale does focus several of the chapters on Darwin, but offers fresh insights into our constructions of Darwin by reading him in new contexts. The book's first chapter, 'Every Cheating Tradesman: The Political Economy of Natural Selection', begins with Darwin's *Beagle* voyage, but focuses on the 'radical and Lamarckian sentiments' echoed in Darwin's conclusions about the Fuegian social structures. Chapter 2, 'A Very Social Darwinist: Herbert Spencer's Lamarckian Radicalism', positions Herbert Spencer not as a Social Darwinist, but as a philosopher heavily influenced by Godwinian radical ideas. Hale turns to Spencer's early journalism and his first book *Social Statics*. Chapter 3, 'A Liberal Descent: Charles Darwin and the Evolution of Ethics', reads *The Descent of Man* as a confirmation not of individualism but of the progressive Whig politics associated with William Gladstone and John Stuart Mill. Chapter 4, 'Liberals and Socialists: The Politics of Evolution in Victorian England', explores how liberals and socialists borrow from Spencer and Darwin in order to articulate their own versions of evolutionary theory. The context of the 'socialist revival' in the 1880s forms an important backdrop in this chapter. Chapter 5, 'Malthus or Mutualism? Huxley, Kropotkin, and the Moral Meaning of Darwinism', continues to trace different iterations of the debate over the politics of evolution by examining the differences between Thomas Huxley and Peter Kropotkin. Chapter 6, 'Of Mice and Men: Malthus, Weismann, and the Future of Socialism', traces further changes to theories of evolution in the work of German biologist Friedrich Leopold August Weismann, changes that questioned Malthusian political economy as well as undermining the Lamarckian ideas used to articulate an anti-Malthusian stance. Chapter 7, 'Fear of Falling: Evolutionary Degeneration and the Politics of Panmixia', takes up Benjamin Kidd's *Social Evolution* [1894], which positions panmixia as a threat to socialism, and the mathematician Karl Pearson, who came to believe that eugenic measures were necessary to counter panmixia. What Hale's book investigates, and the conclusion further illuminates for us, are the connections between biology and politics.

Anna Kornbluh's *Realizing Capital: Financial and Psychic Economies in Victorian Form* explores the understanding of capital in the Victorian period as it shifted from something fictitious to its own kind of tangible truth, where the fictitious becomes real. The idea of 'fictitious capital' would lead, Kornbluh argues, to the notion that 'subjectivity is fundamentally economic and that the economy is fundamentally psychological' (p. 3). Kornbluh looks particularly at the way that the Victorian novel and journalism depict this transition in thinking about the economy. Her work complements the important work of Mary Poovey, who posits a shift from knowledge of the individual to knowledge of the instrument. Kornbluh suggests a complementary shift which she describes as the 'transition from knowledge of an individual in the particular to knowledge of an individual in general' (p. 10).

Chapter 1, 'Fictitious Capital/Real Psyche: Metalepsis, Psychologism, and the Grounds of Finance', examines the financial press and literary periodicals, particularly the work of Walter Bagehot, founding editor of *The Economist*, and David Morier Evans, a financial journalist. Kornbluh carefully examines the metalepsis used by these writers to turn the effects of financialization into causes of financial events. It was this kind of process that underscores Kornbluh's argument that fictitious capital forms the ground for the construct of psychic economy. In her examination of novels, she does not look for actual bankers or references to economic structures but rather for the formal and aesthetic elements of narrative that expose and reflect fictitious capital, or in the words of her title, that help to 'realize capital'. The middle three chapters each take up a major novel, Dickens's *Great Expectations*, George Eliot's *Middlemarch*, and Anthony Trollope's *The Way We Live Now*. The last two chapters turn to nonfiction. Chapter 5, 'London, Nineteenth Century, Capital of Realism: On Marx's Victorian Novel', reads Marx's first volume of *Capital* as a Victorian novel. His critiques of capital take shape aesthetically, primarily through the tropes of personification and metalepsis. Furthermore, capital itself becomes a character as the psychological subject. Chapter 6, 'Psychic Economy and Its Vicissitudes: Freud's Economic Hypothesis', provocatively situates Freud as heir to Victorian novels rather than Victorian psychology because his idea of economy is metaphorical and figural. By reading Freud's language closely as she has the Victorian novels in her study, Kornbluh aligns psychoanalysis with the Victorian novel's construction of a psychic economy.

Seamus O'Mally's essay 'R.L. Stevenson's "The Beach of Falesá" and the Conjuring-Tricks of Capital' (*ELT* 57[2014] 59–80) examines Stevenson's short story in light of the 'complex attitude toward finance' (p. 61) in the late Victorian period. O'Mally acknowledges the important contexts of colonialism and race in this story, but argues that another key context is the rapidly changing British economic system. This story engages with the debates surrounding banks, currency, and credit.

Religion continues to be a growing interest among Victorian scholars, and, as recent studies make clear, is usually tied in some way to politics. In *An Anglican British World: The Church of England and the Expansion of the Settler Empire, c.1790–1860*, Joseph Hardwick positions the church of England as an imperial institution, and he examines both the ideologies behind this construction and practical issues like staffing and power distribution.

Hardwick's study also traces the important shift towards voluntarism, which arose much more quickly in the colonies than in England, and how this led to certain tensions of authority within the church. Hardwick's book adds to our understanding that the colonial church was not a monolithic institution, but instead of focusing on the tension between Evangelicals, High Churchmen, and Tractarians, which normally inform the diverse religious traditions, Hardwick looks at the Scottish Episcopalians, Irish Evangelicals and Irish High Churchmen.

In each of the chapters Hardwick turns his attention to under-studied groups. The first chapter of the book focuses on recruitment of colonial clergy and the development of the clerical profession, the second chapter looks at the Anglican laity, and the third chapter looks at the newly formed colonial bishoprics. All three of these chapters demonstrate the tensions between different views on church organization and structure. The fourth chapter turns to the domestic networks of support for the colonial church, and the fifth chapter turns from communication between the church in Britain and the colonial church to the ways that colonial churches communicated with one another. The final chapter examines how the church facilitated expressions of English consciousness. Rather than the narrative of a church overwhelmed by the imperial forces that transformed British culture, Hardwick presents a church that was at the forefront of that transformation, both facilitating it and reforming it.

Jamie Gilham tells the story of the first British converts to Islam living on British soil in *Loyal Enemies: British Converts to Islam, 1850–1950*. This story takes place within the context of imperialism and reveals yet another layer to our understanding of this contradictory period in British history. The book explores questions of how and why these people converted and the antipathy they faced. Gilham uses private papers of individuals as well as periodicals, newsletters, bulletins, pamphlets, and books. The first half of the book will be of interest to Victorian scholars as it covers the mid- to late nineteenth century. Chapter 1 looks at the life of the first known British convert, Henry Stanley. Chapter 2 traces the life of W.H. Abdullah Quilliam, who actively propagated Islam in Britain. Chapter 3 looks at the first Muslim missionary organization in Britain, the Liverpool Muslim Institute. An essay by John Wallen, 'Is Burton Still Relevant?' (*The Victorian* 2:1 [2014] 1–12), also focuses on Islam in British culture. Wallen examines the life of Victorian explorer and writer Richard Francis Burton and argues that Burton is an important figure for us to consider today because of his interest in Islam and spiritual truth.

Andrew Atherstone's essay 'Memorializing William Tyndale' (*BJRL* 90[2014] 155–78) explores the reasons behind the Victorian interest in the Bible translator and Reformation martyr. Atherstone focuses on the campaigns to build two monuments for Tyndale, campaigns that downplayed controversies between evangelical theology and Tractarianism in order to present Tyndale as a unifying Protestant figure. Rebecca Styler turns to women and religion in her essay on spiritual autobiographies by women writers, 'Revelations of Romantic Childhood: Anna Jameson, Mary Howitt, and Victorian Women's Spiritual Autobiography' (*LW* 11[2014] 313–30). She examines the use of Romantic childhood images in the autobiographies of

Anna Jameson and Mary Howitt. Through these images, Styler argues, Jameson and Howitt critique dogmatic, formalized religion and instead embrace more feminine forms of spirituality.

The now largely forgotten Sir Richard Jebb (1841–1905) was celebrated in his time. The editor of Sophocles, Professor of Greek at Cambridge from 1889, and MP for the university from 1891 until he died, he became a spokesperson for the humanities. Christopher Stray's *Sophocles' Jebb: A Life in Letters* contains 275 fully annotated and introduced unpublished letters. These letters 'throw a flood of light on Jebb's public and private life, his scholarly work and his friendship and enmities'. Furthermore 'they also illuminate the world of Victorian schools and universities, the realm of clubs and common rooms, of lectures and libraries' (p. 6). Stray's edition concludes with his chronologically arranged 'Richard Claverhouse Jebb: An Annotated Bibliography' (pp. 275–94), an alphabetically arranged annotated listing of archives drawn upon in the edition (p. 295) and a detailed index (pp. 297–304). Literary figures included in the index range from, for instance, George Eliot to Alfred Lord and Hallam Tennyson: it is refreshing to find an index that doesn't include the name of Shakespeare! Another contribution worthy of note concerning Victorian scholars is H.L. Spencer's 'F.J. Furnivall's Last Fling: The Wyclif Society and Anglo-German Scholarly Relations, 1882–1922' (*RES* 65[2014] 790–811). Spencer writes that 'Frederic James Furnivall (1825–1910) is best known, at least to medievalists, as the founder of the Early English Text Society (EETS). But he is a fascinating figure, with much broader literary and social interests; almost an archetypal "Victorian"' (p. 790). Furnivall 'was at the heart of London literary life, a scholar, eccentric, long-time associate of the Working Men's College and the London Philological Society . . . He founded no fewer than seven literary and publishing societies (including the Chaucer and New Shakspere Societies)'. Spencer focuses on 'The Wycliff Society (1882) . . . the last of [his] text societies prompted by the approaching quincentenary of Wyclif's death (1384), and by celebrations commemorating Luther's birth (1483)'. According to Spencer 'The Society testifies to remarkable cultural exchanges and friendship between English- and German-speaking scholars at a time of rising Anglo-German political tension, as well as pressures within the German-speaking and Slav communities in central Europe, Catholic and Protestant. The Society was even briefly revived in 1918 to complete work in progress before war broke out' (p. 792).

Turning to major individual authors, many of the major prose writers from this period, including Arnold, Pater, and Ruskin, have been primarily discussed in the multi-author works reviewed above. George Borrow continues to receive attention from a devoted group of scholars. Accompanied by numerous black and white and colour illustrations, the spring 2014 number of the *George Borrow Bulletin* (*GBB* 8[2014]) begins with two contributions from John Hentges. In the first, 'A Chance Encounter: The Incredible Adventures of Ambrose Gwinnett' (*GBB* 8[2014] 16–27), Hentges relates that Gwinnett (*c.*1689–*c.*1730), pardoned for a murder he probably didn't commit after twenty years in exile and harrowing experiences, returns to England to poverty. He was the subject of a play *Ambrose Gwinnett* [1832], by Douglas Jerrold and was the main reason for the friendship of Borrow and Theodore

Watts-Dutton. Hentges' account is followed by his 'A Word on Douglas Jerrold (1803–1857)' (*GBB* 8[2014] 27–9). Chapters 63 to 67 of Borrow's *Lavengro* refer to 'the author of "works of a serio-comic character"' (*GBB* 8[2014] 29). Mark Mawtus, in his 'Headlong and Crotchet: The Case for Thomas Love Peacock Being the Serio-Comic Author' (*GBB* 8[2014] 29–38), argues that this figure is Peacock. Nine 'Notes and Queries' then follow: first come Ken Barrett and Peter Missler's 'A Tale of Woe: Borrow's Proxy Encounter with the Young Man of Colunga' (*GBB* 8[2014] 39–42); David Mount's 'Alan Hunter's *The Norwich Poems*, A Borrow-Related Item' (*GBB* 8[2014] 42–4); and Mark Mawtus's 'Other Thimblerig References' (*GBB* 8[2014] 44). Ann M. Ridler contributes three notes: 'Borrow's "Songs of Scandinavia" and Prior's "Ancient Danish Ballads"' (*GBB* 8[2014] 45–54); 'Another Illustration from *Look and Learn*' (*GBB* 8[2014] 54); and 'The Yarmouth Bridge Disaster of 1845' (*GBB* 8[2014] 55–6). The final three notes in this issue are Richard Garcia's 'Borrow and the Royal Air Force' (*GBB* 8[2014] 56–7); Anthony Rossi's '*Lavengro* and D'Eterville: Strangers' Hall or Luckett's Court' (*GBB* 8[2014] 59–63); and Michael Rawbone's "Gypsy Music-a note' (*GBB* 8[2014] 63–5).The issue concludes with book reviews and miscellaneous items of interest to students of George Borrow (*GBB* 8[2014] 65–80).

No less interesting is the autumn number (*GBB* 9[2014]), which opens with nine 'Notes and Queries': Charity Scott Stokes's '*Lavengro* at Newnham' (*GBB* 9[2014]) 4–6); David Chandler's 'Carnival and Lent: G.K. Chesterton and Borrow on Selling Novels to Survive' (*GBB* 9[2014]) 6–9); and Ann Farrant's 'George Borrow and Amelia Opie' (*GBB* 9[2014]) 9–14). There follow two notes by Ann M. Ridler: 'A Genealogical Conundrum: Some Afterthoughts on the People Borrow Met in Cornwall' (*GBB* 9[2014] 14–18) and 'The Mysterious Stately' (*GBB* 9[2014]) 18–21). Note six is Tom Bean's 'Reflections on Borrow and on El Greco's *The Burial of the Conde de Orgaz*' (*GBB* 9[2014] 21–3); David Price provides two notes: '*The Church of England* Cat, from Cuttings' (*GBB* 9[2014] 23–6) and '*The Gypsy Parson* by the Rev. George Hall, Rector of Ruckland' (*GBB* 9[2014] 27–33). The final note in this issue is by Ron Fiske, who provided the press-cutting for 'A Postscript on D'Eterville from *Norfolk and Norwich Notes and Queries*, 1902' (*GBB* 9[2014] 33–4). Following book reviews and other miscellaneous items (*GBB* 9[2014] 34–55), there are three main articles. David Nuttall in collaboration with Sharon Floate's 'The 1811 Overture: Being an Account of George Borrow, John Clare, Various Gypsies & a Great Deal of Straw Plait in This Year of the Napoleonic Wars' (*GBB* 9[2014] 56–65); George Hyde's 'Borrowing a Snake' (*GBB* 9[2014] 65–70); and Clive Wilkins-Jones's 'Borrow, Romany Gypsies and the Third Reich' (*GBB* 9[2014] 71–9). The issue concludes with Tony Fielder's 'A Toast to Borrovians the World Over' (*GBB* 9[2014] 80–2). The Lavengro Press, 'established for the purpose of publishing for sale material relating to George Borrow' (p. ii), includes Angus Fraser and Ann M. Ridler, eds., *George Borrow in Cornwall 1853–1854: Notebooks and Correspondence* replete with maps and illustrations. In addition to Ridler's preface (pp. x–xiii) she adds a note on 'Sir Angus Fraser' (1928–2001), 'the pre-eminent Borrovian' (pp. xiii–xiv). Fraser's introduction (pp. xv–xviii) is followed by a detailed chronology (pp. xix–xx), an alphabetical listing with brief biographical details of 'People Encountered during the Expedition' (pp. xxi–xxii), and then the text of 'George Borrow's Cornish Notebooks' (pp. 1–32). Additionally there is 'Correspondence Relating to the Cornish Expedition' (pp. 33–9), followed by 'John Berkeley's Reminiscences' (pp. 39–43) and 'Pollard's Children's Reminiscences' (pp. 43–9). The edition concludes with five appendices (pp. 50–83), an annotated alphabetically arranged bibliography (pp. 84–5), and a most useful extensive double-columned index (pp. 86–8).X

On Carlyle, John Morrow, in 'The Real History of Protestantism: Thomas Carlyle and the Spirit of Reformation' (*BJRL* 90[2014] 305–22), argues that Carlyle's interpretation of the Reformation played a significant role in his own work. Carlyle positioned the Reformation as the main historical event 'that gave the modern world its distinctive ideational, moral and material shape' (p. 306). *Carlyle Studies Annual* (*CStA* 30[2014]) includes an 'Editors' Note' (*CStA* 30[2014]) 1–5) and contains three contributions from David R. Sorenson and one in which he is the joint author: '*Friedrich der Grosse*: An Introduction' (*CStA* 30[2014] 7–9) provides an introduction to '*Friedrich der Grosse*: An Opera', and is jointly written by Sorenson and April Lindner (*CStA* 30[2014] 11–21). They provide a 'synopsis of an opera . . . based upon Carlyle's epic history of the Prussian king' (p. 1). Sorensen also writes on 'Carlyle's *Frederick the Great* and the "Sham-Kings" of the American South' (*CStA* 30[2014] 91–113), in which the focus is 'Carlyle's response to the American Civil War . . . characteristic of a man who courted controversy and reveled in paradox' (p. 91). Sorensen's 'Jean Carlyle Aitken and "Poor Ruskin"' (*CStA* 30[2014] 165–71) is a transcription with annotations and a facsimile reproduction of a letter from Carlyle's sister Jean to her brother, dated 14 April 1867, describing 'an evening that she had spent at Cheyne Row' at which 'John Ruskin with his cousin and ward Joan Agnew (1846–1924)' had been present (*CStA* 30[2014] 165). Other contributions in this issue are no less interesting. Chris R. Vanden Bossche's 'Carlyle's Unpublished "French Republic"' (*CStA* 30[2014] 23–34) is an account with text and collation (pp. 35–58) of the '"French Republic" [that] came close to publication, for it was sent up in print, proofed by Carlyle, and a revised proof was prepared before John Forster, editor of the *Examiner*, decided not to publish it' (p. 23).

Owen Dudley Edwards concentrates on Carlyle in his extensive review essay, 'Mr. Wilson's Victoria' (*CStA* 30[2014] 59–72), of A.N. Wilson's *Victoria: A Life*. Edwards writes that Wilson's 'major source will have to be the letters, as opposed to the pieties of David Alec Wilson and James Anthony Froude. We need to see Carlyle plain' (p. 72). Catherine O'Beirne's '"A cup of tea' as our friends across the Channel say": Marcel Proust Reads *Carlyle intime*' (*CStA* 30[2014] 73–90) 'uncovers enduring affinities between Carlyle and Proust, and shows how the famous scene of Marcel dipping the *madeleine* into tea in the first volume of *À la recherche du temps perdu* [1913–27] may have had its origins in the letters of Thomas and Jane Carlyle'. Indeed for O'Beirne, 'Proust's reading of French translations of Carlyle's letters to his mother and of his portrait of Jane Welsh Carlyle in *Reminiscences* were signal moments in his career as a writer'. Ian Campbell's 'Scott, the Carlyles and

Border Minstrelsy' (*CStA* 30[2014] 115–32), 'in an important reconsideration of Carlyle's relationship with Sir Walter Scott...challenges critical assumptions about the supposed repudiation of the "author of Waverley" by the "Sage of Chelsea"' (p. 2). Abigail Burham Bloom's 'Jane Welsh Carlyle: A Review of Recent Research, 2004–2013' (CStA 30[2014] 133–46) is an extensive narrative account that concludes with an enumerative alphabetical listing of items (pp. 143–6) that even includes a 2004 item broadcast on BBC Radio 4's *Woman's Hour* (p. 146: http://www.bbc.co.uk/radio4/womanshour/2005_18_tue_05.shtml). Three hitherto unpublished letters are the subject of Brent E. Kinser's '"The ugliest stroke that I ever got": An Unpublished Account of the Burning of the *French Revolution* Manuscript' (*CStA* 30[2014] 149–60). Kinser also contributes '*Finding Cassandra*: Alfred Lyttelton's Encounter with Carlyle, 21 July 1878' (*CStA* 30[2014] 172–8). David Southern contributes 'A Newly Discovered Carlyle Letter Donated to the David M. Rubenstein Library at Duke University' (*CStA* 30[2014] 161–4). In another article, Southern's 'The Kindness of Librarians' (*CStA* 30[2014] 179–82), he specifically pays tribute to the assistance of Melvin Schuetz of the Armstrong Browning Library at Baylor University 'for leads to Carlyle letters lately offered for sale or at auction' (p. 179). This most informative issue of the *Carlyle Studies Annual* concludes with four extensive reviews (pp. 185–211).

Some notable articles this year addressed the prose work of Charles Dickens. Jerome Meckier, in 'Dickens and Tocqueville: Chapter 7 of *American Notes*' (*DSA* 45[2014] 113–23), looks at Dickens's well-known critique of Tocqueville, but rather than focusing on *Democracy in America*, Meckier suggests that Dickens also critiqued Tocqueville's earlier treatise *On the Penitentiary System in the United States and Its Application in France* in chapter 7 of Dickens's *American Notes*. Linking the critique to this earlier Tocqueville text, Meckier argues, also helps make sense of the American chapters in *Martin Chuzzlewit*. Another article focused on Dickens's prose, David Parker's 'Pickwick and Reform: Origins' (*DSA* 45[2014] 1–21), argues that Dickens's longstanding interest in reform is evident in this early work, despite his own reference to the first edition as 'a mere series of adventures'. In the preface to a reissue of the papers in 1847, Dickens more explicitly links fiction to reform. Using this preface as well as content from the papers themselves, Parker highlights Dickens's central concern with reform.

Harriet Martineau's prose works attracted two essays this year, the first of which pairs her with Dickens. Iain Crawford's 'Harriet Martineau, Charles Dickens, and the Rise of the Victorian Woman of Letters' (*NCF* 68[2014] 449–83) examines the Dickens–Martineau relationship, and seeks to correct the standing version of the story of their argument over industrial reform which positions Dickens as 'champion of the oppressed' and Martineau as a 'vituperative termagant'. Crawford's rereading of this moment in the lives of two prominent Victorian writers has broader implications for our understanding of the world of the Victorian press and the way that the 'spirit of utilitarianism' exerted a wide influence over much of the cultural history of England. In 'Harriet Martineau and the Impersonality of Pain' (*VS* 56[2014] 675–97), Rachel Ablow examines Harriet Martineau's approach to pain. Ablow argues that Martineau agrees with Bentham's and James Mill's utilitarian approach to pain where all suffering is given equal value. Martineau also makes use of Hartleyan psychology to construct a sufferer who is impartial, who 'frees herself from local attachments' (p. 677). Ablow's exploration offers new ways of thinking about Martineau's political and illness writings together, as well as the distinction between mental and physical pain, or pain and suffering, which Martineau tends to collapse. Ablow's discussion of impersonality also takes us into the arena of the liberal body, where Ablow broadens our assumptions about liberal paradigms and definitions of the normative subject in the nineteenth century as she works to show how Martineau incorporates the female invalid body into a subject position of detachment and objectivity.

Henry Mayhew's prose writings also received notable attention this year. The *Journal of Victorian Culture*'s 'New Agenda' section for this year focused on class and Mayhew, and was edited by Sarah Roddy, Julie-Marie Strange, and Bertrand Taithe. In the introduction, 'Henry Mayhew at 200—the "Other" Victorian Bicentenary' (*JVC* 19[2014] 481–96), the editors urge Victorianists to revisit Henry Mayhew with a 'wider intratextual and intertextual approach' to his works. As an example, the writers explore the complex publishing history of *London Labour and the London Poor*, and then proceed to survey the current scholarship on Mayhew. 'Work, Poverty and Modernity in Mayhew's London' (*JVC* 19[2014] 507–19) by Donna Loftus also reconsiders *London Labour and the London Poor* to argue that it was Mayhew, more than Marx or Booth, who exposed the tensions of capitalism. John Seed's contribution, 'Did the Subaltern Speak? Mayhew and the Coster-Girl' (*JVC* 19[2014] 536–49) looks at one particular interview with a coster-girl in *London Labour and the London Poor* to consider Mayhew's handling of the speaking subject and networks of power. '"What Say You to Free Trade in Literature?": *The Thief* and the Politics of Piracy in the 1830s' (*JVC* 19[2014] 497–506) by Catherine Feely examines the twopenny paper called *The Thief* that was produced by Mayhew from 1832 to 1834. Neil Pemberton's essay, 'The Rat-Catcher's Prank: Interspecies Cunningness and Scavenging in Henry Mayhew's London' (*JVC* 19[2014] 520–35), examines Mayhew's interaction with sanitary discourses and animal welfare through his interviews with rat-catchers and the dog-men of the rat pit. The final article, by Carolyn Steedman, 'Mayhew: On Reading, About Writing' (*JVC* 19[2014] 550–61) considers Mayhew as a writer, using his book *What to Teach and How to Teach It, So That the Child May Become a Wise and Good Man* [1842]. Steedman reads Mayhew's theories of literacy and language in the context of recent turns in history towards empathy and ethics.

In another of the year's works focused on gender and violence, Ingrid Hanson's book *William Morris and the Uses of Violence, 1856–1890* (also discussed elsewhere in this chapter) examines how 'Morris's literary and political constructions of masculinity shape and are shaped by his under-standing of violence' (p. x). This book offers interesting perspectives for scholars interested in Pre-Raphaelite medievalism and the socialism of the *fin de siècle*. Hanson takes up several threads of Victorian discussions surrounding war, labour, and freedom, plus ideas about nobility and manliness. The book traces the myriad influences on Morris's conceptions of violence, from the Oxford Movement to the battle tales of Malory, Scott, and Kingsley, to the Crimean War, Ruskin and Carlyle, and the revival of interest in the Nordic origins of the English language and Viking tales. Hanson offers a closer look at many of Morris's more neglected writings, such as his early romances that make up the subject of chapter 1. Morris's use of violence challenges abstract notions of knowing or being as these short stories celebrate the development of identity through battle. Hanson argues that 'his characters come to an understanding of themselves and the world through the actions of their bodies in combat' (p. 4)

Chapter 2 examines how acts of violence in Morris's first volume of poetry, *The Defence of Guenevere*, serve 'as a means of disrupting power relationships, gender roles and the moral consensus that sustains them' (p. 31). Rather than see a critique of war in these poems, Hanson instead argues that Morris critiques Victorian views of women as domestic and submissive. As Hanson claims in other chapters, Morris neither celebrates nor condemns violence, but instead uses violence to redefine common Victorian cultural tropes, such as femininity. While this chapter's focus on definitions of femininity illustrates that violence was not the sole purview of manliness, chapter 3 turns to focus on how Morris creates a place for violence in communal masculinity in his poem *Sigurd the Volsung and the Fall of the Niblungs* [1876]. Hanson concludes that Morris's conception of violence emphasizes that it consists of more than individual acts of bravery, and is instead a complex expression of a communal identity. Chapter 4 turns to the discourses of imperialism and Marxism. In his Germanic romances, Morris represents unalienated labour as a holy good, but so too does the physical destruction of war become an important kind of pleasurable work. The way Morris uses war in these stories becomes a kind of 'antiwar' that sets communal battle against wars of empire. Morris thus critiques some forms of war while also setting out to define just wars. Chapter 5 continues to examine Morris's socialist positions by turning to his more explicitly socialist writings, including *A Dream of John Ball*, *News from Nowhere*, *Chants for Socialists*, and *The Pilgrims of Hope*. The common argument Hanson traces in each of these works is 'an ideal of communal battle against injustice leading to a communal life without injustice' (p. xx). Hanson illuminates Morris's complicated use of violence, in particular his idea of transformative violence, a concept that offers 'troubling contributions' to past and current ideas of just war theory.

John Henry Newman is the focus of Lawrence Poston's *The Antagonist Principle: John Henry Newman and the Paradox of Personality*. This book, self-described as 'assimilative' of other Newman studies, aims to focus more exclusively on Newman as a 'Victorian writer of multidisciplinary interest' (p. ix). Poston attends to Newman's writing and social relationships that are less likely to be included in theologically or biographically focused studies. In part this book serves as a reassessment of Newman's place in Victorian studies. By tracing the development of Newman's mind revealed through print and private correspondence, Poston accounts for contradictions in Newman's personality, which alternated between self-effacement and aggression through the lens of 'personality', in both its psychological and Christian meanings. Chapter 1 and the epilogue take up some of these contradictions as they create problems in Newman studies, and provide an explanation of how 'personality' raises key epistemological questions about religious belief. Chapters 2 to 8 follow a chronological enquiry into the development of Newman's mind, with chapters 2 to 5 focused on the Anglican Newman and chapters 7 and 8 on the Catholic Newman. Despite this mostly chronological structure, Poston resists a biographical approach and instead uses a textual approach, with chapters clustered around documents and relationships that offer ways of thinking about Newman's own personality as well as his theorizing about the connections between human and divine personality. *The Essay on the Development of Christian Doctrine*, the *Apologia*, and *An Essay in Aid of a Grammar of Assent* are the three major Newman works under consideration. Through this examination of Newman, Poston attempts to 'see Newman steadily and whole' (p. xi) as a 'formidable spiritual presence' and a 'fallible human being' (p. 246).

There were several interesting essays on Walter Pater published in the *Journal of Pre-Raphaelite Studies*. In '"Stirring a Long 'Brain-Wave' Behind It of Perhaps Quite Alien Associations": The Paradoxical Afterlife of Walter Pater's "Consummate Words"' (*JPRS* 23[2014] 37–46), Anne-Florence Gillard-Estrada joins other studies of Pater's careful attention to units in his writing by focusing on the afterlife of the word 'consummate'. Although the word remains associated with disciples of Pre-Raphaelite art, it is often forgotten that the word's popularity originated with Pater. In 'The Authority of Affinity: Walter Pater's Stand Against Decadence in *Plato and Platonism*' (*JPRS* 23[2014] 61–79), Adam Lee builds on other studies of Pater's relationship to Plato to focus on the metaphysical elements of Platonism. Plato's philosophy leads Pater to emphasize authority in the individual soul and artwork, which will result in a balanced, harmonious world. This search for authority is bound up in form, Lee argues, and leads to Pater's emphasis on knowing and representing what is real.

John Ruskin was the subject of an interesting book by Mark Frost, *The Lost Companions and John Ruskin's Guild of St. George*. The main premise of this book is that while scholarship has assumed that we have the complete story of the Guild of St. George, Frost contends this story has been told only from the perspective of Ruskin and his closest allies, resulting in 'more than a century of troubling silence' (p.1). As the title indicates, Frost turns to these lost 'companions', or members, of the Guild to trace their writings and experiences in order to provide a more complete historical picture of the Guild of St. George. Frost looks at the more specific and tangible effects on the lives of the Companions themselves, an effect that often consisted of 'disillusionment, trauma, and poverty' (p.6). Frost accounts for the lack of serious and sustained scholarship on the Guild to its typical inclusion in relation to biography, and usually Ruskin's biography. This creates a focus on the Guild as a theoretical rather than practical enterprise and tends to elide the actual members themselves for the ideas and theories of the Guild.

The chapters proceed in chronological order to examine specific periods of the Guild's history, including the years leading up the Guild's existence, the difficult first four years, the most intensive and successful years between 1875–1877, to the troubling period and demise of the Guild from 1878–1881, and the marginal projects that continued to 1900. Although Ruskin's presence continues to loom large in this book, Frost also incorporates the lost voices of Companions like William Harrison Riley, William Buchan Graham, and John Guy and a closer look at Guild estates like Bewdley, projects that were glossed over by Ruskin or deemed unsuccessful but that in fact have a different history when viewed from a perspective not Ruskin's. In general, this book paints an even darker picture of Ruskin's leadership than has heretofore been recognized, at the same time that it represents a more positive picture of the potential in the Guild's agricultural projects, potential that was unfortunately lost but that nonetheless represents a theoretical and practical interjection in Victorian political, cultural, and aesthetic practices.

Finally, while Ruskin features significantly in many of the works above, Ruskin studies also continue to benefit from the online journal *The Eighth Lamp—Ruskin Studies Today*, edited by Laurence Rousillon-Constantly and Anuradha Chatterjee. Two interesting articles were published this year. The issue begins with helpful information about organizations and conferences relevant to Ruskin and Victorian studies, and a review of books and articles recently published and forthcoming on Ruskin. In '"Swift Visions of Centuries": Langdale Linen, Songs of the Spindle, and the Revolutionary Potential of the Book' (*Eiha* 9[2014] 46- 61), Patrick McDonald discusses the dispute between Albert Fleming and Marian Twelves over the Langdale linen industry's faithfulness to Ruskin's ideals. The tensions between Fleming's and Twelves's ideals are captured perfectly, McDonald argues, in the publication of *Songs of the Spindle*, a Christmas gift book published on Langdale linen with a foreword by Fleming. The book is 'revolutionary' for the way it captures the 'profit-driven Fleming' and the more 'socially conscious Twelves', who represent the conflict between an industrial capitalist system and regressive social movements (p. 61).

In 'John Ruskin and the Characterisation of "Word-Painting" in the Nineteenth Century' (*Eiha* 9[2014] 62–76), Marjorie Cheung explores the definition and usage of the term 'word-painting' in the nineteenth century, and specifically compares Ruskin's early discussions of the term with how it was used by later nineteenth-century periodical writers. Cheung utilizes the British Periodical Database for this study, and discovers that colour is 'one of the defining linguistic characteristics' of Victorian word-painting (p. 62). By comparing Ruskin with periodical writers, Cheung opens up an avenue for further study of Ruskin's influence on the Victorian period.

2. The Novel

In this section, works on Wilkie Collins, George Eliot, and Anthony Trollope are covered by William Baker, and works on Charles Dickens by Michael Gilmour. All other publications are covered by Ariana Reilly.

J. Hillis Miller's deceptively easy style guides us at a leisurely pace through complicated theoretical readings of novelistic community in *Communities of Fiction*, and for the reader who has some time on his or her hands, the journey will be a productive one. Miller begins by identifying a contradiction at the heart of Western notions of identity, illustrated most starkly by Raymond Williams and Heidegger. Miller sees the two theorists as extremes on a continuum of ideas about communities. For Williams, the true community is one that has not been penetrated by the alienating effects of capitalism and where the individual is defined transparently and meaningfully by work done. For Heidegger, such a community would be false, a 'Being-with-one-another' that prevents the unfolding of *Dasein* (p. 9). Only once *Dasein* confronts its 'ownmost potentiality for being' (p. 11) can any authentic community exist. Of course, such a community would be somewhat contradictory, for its authentic unification would rely on its individual members seeing themselves as separate, each moving towards their own individual deaths. These two versions of community, Williams's and Heidegger's, appear irreconcilable, valuing, at least in Miller's reading, completely opposite ways of being in the world. Miller's self-imposed task, then, is to figure out where a selection of novels (Trollope's *Last Chronicle of Barset*, Hardy's *Return of the Native*, Conrad's *Nostromo*, Woolf's *The Waves*, and two shorter narratives by Cervantes and Pynchon) fall on this community continuum and negotiate its necessary contradictions (the chapters on Hardy and Trollope are considered in more detail below). Miller concludes that even when these novels do imagine or gesture towards a community in Williams's sense of the term, they function on the premise that our communities, like Heidegger's, are self-destructive, pushing us away as part of the effort of bringing us in. Throughout the book, Miller hints at the significance of such an understanding of community for our current moment, and in the briefest of codas he leaves us with just that. The inability to take action on global warming, the Patriot Act, and other recent political situations are all taken as examples of self-destructive, even suicidal, models of community.

Henry Staten's superb *Spirit Becomes Matter: The Brontës, George Eliot, Nietzsche* continues the philosophical trend, this time by linking the Victorian interest in psycho-physiology that has received recent interest from critics like Nicholas Dames with Nietzsche's will to power. George Moore's research demonstrating that Nietzsche both read and was influenced by Herbert Spencer allows Staten not only to draw parallels between the thinking of Nietzsche, Brontë, and Eliot, but also to assert that these parallels 'reflect a shared conceptual paradigm' (p. 6). Incidentally, Staten reflects the conceptual paradigm he shares with the current objective turn when he identifies his purpose as 'neither to complete the nineteenth-century theory nor to criticise it for its limitations, but to show how far it is pushed in a certain critical function' by the Brontës and Eliot (p. 12). The primary difference, of course, between Nietzsche and Victorians like Spencer is that where Spencer equates physiological health in the form of energetic discharge with conventional morality, thus strengthening rather than shaking the moral order by finding it a more modern, scientifically appealing ground, Nietzsche rejects any such consonance, calling attention instead to 'the conflict between physiological based values of individual self-assertion and restless striving—the values that were being fostered by the new economic order—and the "herd morality" (as Nietzsche calls it) to which these values were being yoked' (p. 9). Staten gives more credit to the Brontës and Eliot than to Spencer, however. His chapters on *Jane Eyre*, *Middlemarch*, and *Wuthering Heights* (reviewed below) explain how each novelist works through this conflict with her own novelistic, pre-Nietzschean critical moral psychology. While it is not surprising to find Eliot treated in this monograph, the inclusion of the Brontës (as opposed to Hardy, for example) is both less expected and exciting in a critical tradition that frequently allows for only one truly philosophical female novelist. More work could certainly be used in this line.

Patricia McKee's *Reading Constellations: Urban Modernity in Victorian Fiction* applies another theorist, Walter Benjamin, to the significance of the city in nineteenth-century novels by Dickens, Hardy, and James. As the title of the book suggests, McKee is particularly interested in Benjamin's understanding of history in terms of constellations as opposed to forward-moving, progressive lines. These shifting assemblages—where connections appear and disappear as the position of the viewer changes—remind the historian of how much the past depends on his or her position in the present. This interrelation of past and present becomes even deeper for McKee when understood as colportage, another Benjaminian concept for 'when, in present time and space, events appear that occurred there and elsewhere at other times' (p. 4). The city in Victorian novels, McKee asserts, is similarly fragmented, a constantly shifting reassemblage of time and space. What seems to fascinate McKee most about this approach to history and the city is the way that it enables collective identities that are incomplete, unstable, and like no other. Here, disintegration is rearrangement, full of creative potential in contrast to capitalism's 'creative destruction perpetually produc[ing] new improvements that render older products obsolete' (p. 17). Using Benjamin as a lens for the Victorian city is certainly nothing new, but McKee separates herself from previous critics by pointing to her commitment 'to examining how these novels collect together what progressive histories leave out and leave behind: an extensive as well as interruptive reach of identity that the city's anomalous spatial and temporal outlays offer its inhabitants' (p. 5). The individual chapters on Dickens and Hardy are reviewed below.

Stephen Arata's thought-provoking, if open-ended, essay 'Decadent Form' (*ELH* 81[2014] 1007–27) is sure to be a much-cited contribution to studies on decadence and formalism. Discussing the literature and criticism of Arthur Symons, Eliot, Flaubert, and Henry James, Arata circles round what he sees as the central paradox of novelistic form: its simultaneous sloughing away of life's messy excess and excessive stylization of life. Arata links the problem of literary form to the problem of its realization—whether that be, as with Eliot, a conscious refusal to be self-conscious of form or, as with James, an ascetic wastefulness of aesthetic perfection.

A few articles appeared on forms of realism. Valentine Cunningham, in 'Melodrama and Victorian Realist Fiction' (*Anglia* 132[2014] 242–52), argues that, as practised by the Victorians, melodrama was, in fact, 'a mode of realism, a key way of imagining the real' (p. 242). For Hardy, Dickens, and Eliot, melodrama was particularly well suited, in Cunningham's formulation, for dealing with the 'overmuchness' of modern life (p. 243). The nature and limits of realism are also addressed by 'Corelli's Caliban in a Glass: Realism, Antirealism, and *The Sorrows of Satan*' (*ELT* 57[2014] 335–60). Jill Galvan argues that Marie Corelli's engagement with realism is more complicated than is typically acknowledged, asserting that even as Corelli promotes the imagination in what is often taken as an anti-realist pose, her fiction flirts with the realist mode. In fact, Galvan sees Corelli's fiction as an important mediator between the socially motivated realism of new fiction and the apolitical aestheticism of Oscar Wilde. Jacqueline Banerjee's article '"The Conduct of Life" in Walter Besant's *The Ivory Gate* and *The Alabaster Box*' (*ES* 95[2014] 890–906) also complicates our understanding of late-century fiction. Banerjee argues that scholars have been too quick to relegate Besant's fiction to socio-historical rather than literary analysis, arguing that in his later fiction, Besant's use of the kind of didactic realism associated with mid-century social problem fiction was self-conscious and intentional.

Matthew Rubery's *The Novelty of Newspapers: Victorian Fiction after the Invention of the News* is an important contribution to the field in part because of its own merits as a piece of scholarship, but also because it opens up an exciting area for more research. Rubery argues that novels were competing with the news as two 'practice[s] of realistic representation and . . . authoritative form[s] of public knowledge' (p. 4). In order to mount this argument he offers a historical survey of the contemporaneous rise of the novel and the newspaper in the nineteenth century and, through a series of readings, demonstrates how Victorian novelists either made use of newspapers as literary devices or in some cases adapted journalistic techniques for fiction writing. Each of the five chapters in Rubery's study covers a different type of news that was somehow incorporated into the novel. In chapter 1, Rubery notes how the shipping news was picked up by Victorian novelists such as Dickens, Braddon, and Charlotte Yonge in order to reveal the way print participated in the complicated emotional relationships that spanned domestic space and maritime travel. In these texts women read the shipping reports with bated breath, sometimes for news of a loved one's death, sometimes for an account of his daring imperial exploits. Chapter 2 discusses how the front page of nineteenth-century newspapers often displayed what came to be known as the 'agony column' (a blend of personal ads, classifieds, announcements, and miscellaneous complaints) instead of breaking news because the solicitations were frequently so melodramatic. Sensation novelists, Rubery argues, were quick to recognize the potential of such a mechanism for anonymous and unchecked access to the public. In novels such as *Lady Audley's Secret*, advertisements allow individuals to bring a new identity to life by first putting it in print. The third chapter shifts from novels that borrow productively from newspapers to those that take the authority of the newspaper head on. In 'The Leading Article: The Whispering Conscience in Trollope's Palliser Novels' Rubery demonstrates how Trollope in *The Duke's Children* and *Can You Forgive Her?* exposes the editorial 'we' by 'showing the speaker behind the anonymous voice' (p. 17). Chapter 4 discusses not only the public's desire to read interviews, but to give them as well. Rubery interprets James's style as a resistance to this ready disclosure. His fiction, Rubery writes, 'directs attention to people's willingness to share the most intimate details with an unseen audience . . . in a way that ran counter to James's own preference for impersonal narration' (p. 111). Rubery finishes by linking *Heart of Darkness* to the dispatches surrounding Dr Livingstone's disappearance and Conrad's concern about transfer of information within the imperial context.

Beth Palmer also explores the connection between the newspaper and the novel in 'Investigating Charles Reade, the *Pall Mall Gazette* and the "Newspaper Novel"' (*JVC* 19[2014] 183–97), which uses the example of Charles Reade to trouble the often separate historiographies of the novel and the news. For Reade, Palmer argues, the novel and the newspaper were 'partners in enterprises of social reformism and public entertainment', whose forms developed through their mutual interaction (p. 185). Josephine Richstad takes on another novel generic interaction in her 'Genre in Amber: Preserving the Fashionable Novel for a Victorian Decade, Catherine Gore's *Hamiltons* (1834 and 1850)' (*MP* 111[2014] 549–65). Richstad focuses on the repackaging of a fashionable novel of the 1830s as a novel of the 'recent past' in 1850 (p. 550). This repackaging, Richstad argues, 'severs form and content' such that the later edition presents the fashionable novel as 'an artifact within a now-different novel: no longer chronicling the foibles of an age but preserving the mode in which those foibles are achieved' (p. 564).

Chris R. Vanden Bossche's *Reform Acts; Chartism, Social Agency, and the Victorian Novel* seeks to wrest Chartism from the revolutionary politics in which it is often discussed. Vanden Bossche asserts instead that Chartism was, first and foremost, about achieving agency via political representation within the current political system. According to Vanden Bossche such an argument is historical rather than theoretical, a somewhat confusing distinction unless we understand theory to be, specifically, Marxist- and Foucauldian-style historicism. What Vanden Bossche is really reacting against seems to be the impossibility of democratic agency within a theoretical paradigm that assumes all action to be determined by discursive and ideological structures. Vanden Bossche's solution to this problem is to study social agency as the Victorians understood it, which he argues, was as the ability to effect the 'reform of society through possession of the franchise and the power to legislate' (p. 3). For justification, Vanden Bossche briefly references Sharon Marcus's concept of 'just reading' and a handful of other critics suspicious of symptomatic reading. What it would mean to read not just a text, but a social movement, is certainly an interesting question, but Vanden Bossche doesn't provide a clear answer. As a result, what is often a fascinating look at the influence of Chartism in nineteenth-century fiction suffers from some theoretical uncertainty. The book is divided into three parts, each dealing with one ground for Chartist action: moral vs. physical force, land, and unionism. The first chapter in Part I explains how the Chartist press attempted to moralize physical force while maintaining that its authority came from its hesitancy to use force. The next emphasizes how physical force, its morality tenuously maintained, is presented as part of the pathway not to revolution but to legislative reform in Pierce Egan's *Wat Tyler* [1841]. Vanden Bossche then shows how Chartist discourse is mobilized by Harrison Ainsworth in his novel *Guy Fawkes* in order to represent violence as a last resort, and therefore, if not moral, at least ambiguously so. In the final chapter of the first section Vanden Bossche argues that in *Barnaby Rudge* violence is non-agency and demonstrates the aristocratic manipulation of a lower class in sore need of education. The second section explains how the Land Plan replaced moral and physical force as pathways for social agency and is followed by three chapters, on *Coningsby* and *Sybil*, Robert Smith Surtees's comic *Hillingdon Hall*, and Thomas Martin Wheeler's *Sunshine and Shadow* that explore, in different ways, the possible connections between land and social agency. The final section, 'The Social Turn: From Chartism to Cooperation and Trade Unionism, 1848–1855', examines the rise of trade unions in the novels of Kingsley and Gaskell. A coda considers the novels of George Eliot, who, Vanden Bossche argues, situates social agency squarely outside the political, alongside William Howitt's *The Man of the People* [1860], which tries to establish the people's preparedness for the franchise.

Barbara Leckie's essay 'What Is a Social Problem Novel?' (in Mazzeno, ed., *Twenty-First Century Perspectives on Victorian Literature*, pp. 87–109) locates the difficulty in defining the genre of the social problem novel in the instability of the word 'social' itself—an instability amply demonstrated in Vanden Bossche's *Reform Acts*. However, rather than throw up her hands, Leckie sees an opportunity for exploring the very idea of the social by means of this grouping of mid-century texts. As an example, Leckie reveals how problems previously understood as personal, such as housing for the poor, were redefined by the novel as social problems requiring social solutions.

Two articles on Victorian novels appeared in *Nineteenth-Century Context*'s special issue on energy. In 'Victorian Miser Texts and Potential Energy' (*NCC* 36[2014] 565–78), Elizabeth Coggin Womack looks at how the miserly hoard in *London Labour and the London Poor*, *Our Mutual Friend*, and *Sartor Resartus* both obstructs and fuels the circulation of energy through systems of wealth and culture. In the same issue, Timothy Morton declares that we are still in the Victorian era in his essayistic 'Victorian Hyperobjects' (*NCC* 36[2014] 489–500). Drawing on short readings of *The War of the Worlds*, *Tess of the D'Urbervilles*, and *Dracula*, Morton argues that we share with the Victorians a preoccupation with hyperobjects—'entities that are massively distributed in time and space' (p. 489). Capable of being measured but not directly perceived, hyperobjects (like geological time and global warming) are, for Morton, the representational challenge of the inhabitants of the Anthropocene—Victorian, modern, or postmodern as they may be.

Sensation fiction is again the focus of much scholarly attention. Anna Peak's 'Servants and the Victorian Sensation Novel' (*SEL* 54[2014] 835–51) returns to the question of how to classify sensation fiction in the first place. Looking at a variety of sensation novels, Peak convincingly argues that the genre blurs the line between middle- and lower-class reading material—particularly between that of masters and servants. Readers of sensation fiction, Peak contends, take the perspective of servants, thus unsettling the privileges of class, gender, and literacy. A collection of essays edited by Anne-Marie Beller and Tara MacDonald entitled *Rediscovering Victorian Women Sensation Writers* is a case in point. The essays, originally published in a special issue of *Women's Writing* (*WW* 10[2013]) but not previously covered by *YWES*, introduce audiences to sensation writers they may never have heard of and reframe within the genre other authors, such as George Eliot, not typically associated with sensationalism. One of the major takeaways of the collection is just how unstable are the boundaries of the genre. In the first chapter in the collection, 'Sensation Intervention: M.C. Houstoun's *Recommended to Mercy* [1862] and the Novel of Experience', Tabitha Sparks offers an entirely new generic category to solve some of the seeming fluidity of the categories of sensation and realist fiction. Using a little-read novel by M.C. Houstoun as a case in point, Sparks defines the 'novel of experience' as one written between 1860 and 1890 which features 'a socially or romantically experienced' heroine who is reintegrated into society despite her moral ambiguity and which includes both realist and sensational narrative techniques (p. 13). Mary Beth Tegan, in 'Strange Sympathies: George Eliot and the Science of Sensation', complicates Eliot's attitude towards sensation fiction by drawing out the connections between the psycho-physiological realism Eliot deploys in *Romola* and the physiology of sensation central to the popular fiction of lady novelists. 'Sensational Ghosts, Ghostly Sensations' by Nick Freeman discusses the resemblances between sensation fiction and the ghost story, both of which concern unsettling intrusions into domestic life while troubling gendered existence. In 'The False Clues of Innocent Sensations: Aborting Adultery Plots in Rhoda Broughton's *Nancy* (1873)', Tamara S. Wagner analyses a less familiar text by Broughton that, according to Wagner, calls attention to the conventions of sensation fiction by frustrating them. Greta Depledge, in 'Experimental Medicine, Marital Harmony, and Florence Marryat's *An Angel of Pity* (1898)', reads Marryat's novel as not only deeply engaged in the vivisection debate but also as exploring that debate through a love plot so that both medical and romantic narratives are upset. The final two essays both focus on Ouida. Lisa Hager's 'Embodying Agency: Ouida's Sensational Shaping of the British New Woman' links Ouida's *Princess Napraxine* [1884] with her essay 'The New Woman' [1894] in order to argue that sensation fiction provided the language necessary for imagining the future of the New Woman. '"Romans français écrits en anglais": Ouida, the Sensation Novel and *Fin-de-Siècle* Literary Censorship' by Jane Jordan explores how it was that Ouida's novels both scandalized the public and were widely available at lending libraries, and concludes that Ouida self-consciously recategorized her work as a species of French realism by moving her sensational plots out of Britain's domestic spaces and into foreign settings, a rebranding that highlights the stakes of generic categorization.

In 'The Changing Reputation of the Victorian Novel: "The Velocity of the Novel-Producing Apparatus" and "Large Loose Baggy Monsters"' (in Mazzeno, ed., pp. 15–27), Tamara Wagner takes the sensation novel as a prime example of how critical moments determine the reception of fiction, and it would seem that *Rediscovering Victorian Women Sensation Writers* would confirm the trajectory from popular trash to canonical treasure that Wagner charts for the genre. However, Beller and MacDonald admit in their introduction that, so far, the many studies like theirs on neglected authors have often served only 'to demonstrate the canon's extraordinary resilience' (p. 2). While it is true that sensation fiction has become a major field within studies of the Victorian novel, if we think of the canon in terms of what is taught rather than in terms of what receives critical attention, Beller and MacDonald are certainly correct about its resilience. Very few undergraduates are exposed to the authors discussed in the collection, nor are they likely to be any time soon. The gap between criticism and classroom continues to be one in need of theoretical and practical attention.

The related territory covered in Ian Ward's *Sex, Crime, and Literature in Victorian England* is familiar, but his interdisciplinary approach as a scholar of law brings new perspective. Ward reconsiders the woman question in Victorian England by examining the treatment of four crimes—adultery, bigamy, infanticide, and prostitution—in contemporary court cases and in literature. The first half of the book concerns itself with laws and literatures that attempted to either regulate (or expose the regulation of) women within wedlock, while the second half attends to the surveillance and control of women whose sexual crimes took place outside marriage. According to Ward, literature was capable of doing three things lawyers either could not or would not do: 'bring to the court of public opinion incidences of injustice', 'humanise the consequences of this injustice', and 'raise the voices' of marginalized women (pp. 145–6).

Ward's first chapter, 'Criminal Conversations', takes on the crime of adultery, revisiting the debates surrounding Caroline Norton's famously rocky marriage and the Matrimonial Causes Act of 1857 through readings of Ellen Wood's *East Lynne* and Thackeray's *The Newcomes*. Both novels, according to Ward, are novels of 'purpose' about 'the legal consequences of adultery and familial dysfunction' (p. 56). Where Wood uses her legal fiction to prop up the institution of marriage, Thackeray hopes to expose the cruelties that often accompanied lawful wedlock. In chapter 2, 'Fashionable Crimes', Ward focuses on the relationship between the divorce courts and the sensation novel craze, both of which showed an increasing interest in bigamy during the 1850s and 1860s. But the 'real crime' of Braddon and sensation writers like her, Ward contends, 'was the insinuation that their heroines were driven to criminality because the institution of marriage so often causes pain, and the law of marriage is unable, and unwilling, to provide relief' (p. 84). Chapter 3, 'Unnatural Mothers', argues that the Victorian cult of motherhood depended on an 'essentially jurisprudential' (p. 95) definition of the nature of motherhood, a natural mother being one whose children were born within wedlock, and an unnatural one being a mother whose children were born outside it. Frances Trollope's *Jessie Philips*, Eliot's *Adam Bede*, and Gaskell's *Ruth*, Ward asserts, all investigate this legal construction of maternity and its relationship to fallenness. In the final chapter, Ward turns to prostitution and laws such as the Contagious Diseases Act, which burdened England's women with England's sexual sins. According to Ward, Dickens's *Oliver Twist* and Gabriel Rossetti's 'Jenny', despite their many differences, both 'brought to the fore a socially instantiated, and jurisprudentially embedded, injustice' while humanizing prostitutes (p. 144). It is also worth mentioning that Ward's book is notably readable. His conversational style sets *Sex, Crime, and Literature* apart from many other publications for 2014 and makes it an ideal book for assigning as background reading in the undergraduate classroom.

The criminal element is also the concern of Clare Clarke's *Late Victorian Crime Fiction in the Shadows of Sherlock*, a book notable for its interest in expanding the canon of late nineteenth-century detective fiction. Clarke echoes

Anne Humpherys' complaint that critics of detective fiction have focused too exclusively on Dickens, Collins, and Doyle. By answering Humpherys' call, Clarke joins a number of other critics who have attempted in late years to dust off the many neglected works of nineteenth-century detective fiction. In the process, she also calls into question the popular commonplace that early detective fiction was simplistic and overly formulaic—notable only in so far as it established a set of conventions that later practitioners like Raymond Chandler could creatively reconstruct. As Clarke's careful readings demonstrate, early detective fiction was surprisingly complex and varied— particularly in the willingness of these texts to present their detectives as morally ambiguous anti-heroes. Clarke begins her study with a canonical text, Stevenson's *Strange Case of Dr. Jekyll and Mr. Hyde*, arguing that this novel—so often considered in connection with the Gothic—is a pivotal text in the genealogy of detective fiction. Next, Clarke turns to an Australian text, Fergus Hume's *The Mystery of a Hansom Cab*, which she reads as blending local colour writing with familiar representations of the urban, upper-class predator. Chapter 3 attempts to defend the Sherlock Holmes stories from accusations of middle-class conservatism, and the next two chapters, which treat Israel Zangwill's *The Big Bow Mystery* and Arthur Morrison's *Dorrington Deed-Box* respectively, present detective fiction as deeply committed to exposing the material conditions of crime in late Victorian London. The final chapter examines intersections between New Imperialism and detective fiction through a reading of Guy Boothby's *A Prince of Swindlers*.

In the introduction to another monograph that deals heavily in the seedy side of Victorian life, *Street Urchins, Sociopaths, and Degenerates: Orphans of Late-Victorian and Edwardian England*, David Floyd points out that while much has been written about the orphan in the domestic *Bildungsromane* of the early to mid-nineteenth-century, 'the non-traditional, aberrant, at times Gothic orphan of the *fin de siècle* has been largely overlooked' (p. 1). These late-century orphans are the topic of his book, which argues that towards the end of the century orphan narratives cease to be books about domestic promise and become instead stories of 'degeneration, sexual ambiguity, and imperial enterprise' (p. 2). With each chapter focusing on a different type of orphan, Floyd creates an orphanic taxonomy for the *fin de siècle*, beginning with some characters one might not expect to find in a book on orphans. For instance, R.M. Renfield from *Dracula* is the subject of the first chapter where the sycophantic madman becomes a figure for a generation bereft of comforting, accepted traditions. Where Renfield is submissive, the next set of orphans that Floyd treats, including Hyde, Griffin from *The Invisible Man*, and Helen Vaughn from Machen's *The Great God Pan*, are rebellious, out to deliberately corrupt and destroy the social order. Chapter 4 explores the relationship between the orphan and the island in Wells's *The Island of Dr. Moreau* and Stevenson's *Treasure Island* and *Kidnapped*, and chapter 5 compares the fate of British and native orphans in adventure novels by Haggard, Kipling, and Merriman. In the final chapter Floyd argues that Edwardian children's books by J.M. Barrie and Frances Hodgson Burnett offer orphans the possibility of fantastic self-definition while simultaneously undermining that power. Though Floyd's emphasis is on the way orphans reflect the peculiar anxieties of their respective cultural moments, his book is perhaps most interesting for its recognition of an overlooked common thread connecting canonical works of domestic fiction from the mid-century with the genre fiction that flourished at the century's end.

Andrew McCann's *Popular Literature, Authorship, and the Occult in Late Victorian Britain* is sure to prove an important contribution to the recent conversation surrounding late nineteenth-century occultism and enchantment as well as to theories of authorial production. McCann's primary contention in this original study is that popular literature's interest in not only occult themes but, more importantly, occult modes of communication such as automatic writing, trance states, and mediumship, enabled popular writers to complicate the notion of authorial proprietorship that was essential to the monetization of popular literature at the close of the century. To those who had seen the fantastic idea of cross-continent communication become a reality with the telegraph, McCann reminds us, a new technological advance capable of facilitating communications with spirits from the other world might seem none too unlikely. Thus, McCann concludes, we are wrong to focus solely on the ironic dimension of *fin-de-siècle* engagements with the paranormal, a tendency he corrects by focusing on authors who thought of their own writing as a kind of occult practice. Understanding themselves as communicative technologies little different from the telegraph or typewriter, certain of these writers claimed for themselves a literary distinction not based on agency but alterity, and their literature, McCann contends, manifested a democratizing potential at odds with the familiar standardizing model seemingly necessitated by the mass market. Rather, by imagining themselves as the instruments of other, non-commodifiable influences, such authors worked 'towards the insertion of difference into hegemonic systems of signification' (p. 26).

McCann's first chapter focuses on Walter Besant, whose proprietary model of authorship simultaneously valorized the author's relationship with the mass public and denied popular literature's potential for dissent. In chapter 2, McCann argues that George DuMaurier's *Peter Ibbetson*, in addition to offering the kind of fantastic refuge from modern disenchantment discussed by Michel Saler, creates a 'self-reflexivity that invites us to see the compositional process itself as an embodiment of the alienation explored in the novel' (p. 60). In chapter 3, McCann claims that Corelli's belief in the occult nature of her own writing process complicates 'the commercially rationalized model of authorship' to which she also seems to have been tied (p. 113). Next, McCann considers how this decentred model of authorship becomes a way for expatriates like Rosa Praed to open popular literature to non-Western voices, and in chapter 5 he turns to another little-known voice in Victorian fiction, Arthur Machen. Machen's fiction, McCann argues, explored the 'capacity of the body—a locus of both sexual and occult experience—to disrupt and disperse conceptions of authorship tied to the market and its vision of self-possessed subjectivity' (p. 148). Altogether, McCann makes a convincing case for the theoretical sophistication of popular occult literatures that will hopefully encourage a broader reconsideration of other popular genres.

Elaine Freedgood also sees theoretical potential in the occult in her article 'Ghostly Reference' (*ELH* 125[2014] 40–53). Reading ghosts literally and denotatively, Freedgood proposes that the Victorian ghost story sheds light on the formation of the liberal subject. Freedgood observes that this genre has received far less attention than the detective story precisely because it refuses to establish whether or not ghosts exist. For Freedgood, that refusal makes the ghost story 'the perfect liberal form' (p. 46) in so far as it gives the reader the privilege to consider a category that can never be authoritatively resolved.

Those interested in the intersections between visual culture and the novel will welcome David J. Jones's new title in the Palgrave Gothic series, *Sexuality and the Gothic Magic Lantern: Desire, Eroticism, and Literary Visibilities from Byron to Bram Stoker*. Jones argues that the Gothic genre developed in conjunction with the magic lantern show. According to Jones, the phantas-magoria of the eighteenth century pioneered the strange intermingling of the terrifying and the erotic that would become the staple of the Gothic in novels and other literary genres. Drawing on both overt invocations of the magic lantern and unlabelled, but nonetheless phantasmagoric, descriptions and effects, Jones contends that the Gothic novel relied upon recognizable tropes of the horrific and titillating established by this early visual technology. Perhaps most interesting, however, is Jones's assertion that what critics like Grahame Smith, S.S. Prawer, and Sergei Eisenstein have identified as the pre-cinematic cinematicity of some nineteenth-century literature is actually a 'lanternicity' (p. 9). It is not that the novel anticipated film, Jones argues, but that both the novel and film drew upon the illusionary techniques developed by magic lantern shows in the eighteenth and nineteenth centuries. Though it seems like a stretch to accuse such criticism, as Jones does, of an 'intermedial retrospective colonization of literature, an inferring of the agency of proleptic cinematic sensibility', the absence of smoke and mirrors in his own explanation of these apparently anachronistic, cinematographic effects certainly has commonsense appeal (p. 10). The introduction to *Sexuality and the Gothic Magic Lantern* situates Jones's argument within the context of other work on the literary manifestations of magic lanterns and other pre-cinematic technologies while providing a brief overview of how phantasmagoria reflected and produced attitudes towards sex, gender, and the unworldly. His first two chapters detail the pre-Victorian tradition of the magic lantern and lanternicity in works such as Friedrich Schiller's *The Ghost-Seer*, Matthew Lewis's *The Monk*, and Byron's *Manfred* and *Don Juan*. Chapter 3, 'Brontë's *Villette*: Desire and Lanternicity in the Domestic Gothic', explores the spectral nun as both a figure of repressed desire and, more specifically, as a figure from magic lantern shows with which Brontë and her readers would have been familiar. Jones also recognizes the visual effects of the phantasmagoria in the strange, fragmented vision that ends Brontë's most experimental novel. Chapters 4 and 5, 'Le Fanu's *Carmilla*: Lesbian Desire in the Lanternist Novella' and 'Lanternist Codes and Sexuality in *Dracula* and *The Lady of the Shroud*', both treat the role of lanternicity in the rebellious eroticism of the nineteenth-century vampire, particularly in the production of same-sex desire. Finally, in the conclusion, Jones makes his case for how literary criticism has obscured the place of the magic lantern in Gothic literary history by labelling visual effects derived from magic lantern shows as cinematic.

In addition to Jones's book, Palgrave also contributed to the field of eighteenth- and nineteenth-century Gothic studies with *Irish Gothics: Genres, Forms, Modes, and Traditions, 1760–1890*, a collection of essays edited by Christina Morin and Niall Gillespie. In the introduction, Morin and Gillespie readily admit that the 'Irish Gothic' and, indeed, the Gothic more generally, is a vexed category. It is, in fact, this very undefinability that they seem to find most intriguing about the genre. The essays included, they explain, far from delimiting the 'Irish Gothic', seek to open 'up the study of Irish Gothic literature by pushing the terminological limits imposed by restrictive notions of traditions, canons, genres, and even modes, registers, forms, and styles' (p. 6). Only the last four essays deal specifically with Victorian fiction. The chapters on Le Fanu and Stoker are reviewed below.

Transnational and postcolonial concerns were well represented in 2014. The still young University of Adelaide Press, which prints peer-reviewed manuscripts by staff of the university, contributed two titles in this area, *Changing the Victorian Subject*, a collection of essays edited by Maggie Tonkin, Mandy Treagus, Madeleine Seys, and Sharon Crozier-De Rosa, and *Empire Girls: The Colonial Heroine Comes of Age* by Mandy Treagus. Both are well worth investigating. *Changing the Victorian Subject* sets out to broaden our understanding of Victorian literature and its subjects by including colonial fictions within the 'Victorian' umbrella. Writing about people and characters we would normally refer to as colonial subjects as Victorian ones productively decentres the empire in a way that recognizes the relatively of spatial orientation. While the first essay in the volume discusses the legal status of Aboriginal subjects in Victorian Australia, most of the essays concern the novel. 'Identifying with the Frontier: Federation New Woman, Nation, and Empire' by Sharon Crozier-De Rosa, for instance, recovers Catherine Martin's *An Australian Girl* [1890] and, along with it, the position of the New Woman within the Australian frontier. Margaret Allen, in 'A "Tigress" in the Paradise of Dissent: *Kooroona* Critiques the Foundational Colonial Story', argues that Iota's 1871 novel has been neglected because it challenges the progressive narrative of South Australia's colonial history by critiquing the treatment of indigenous peoples. In 'The Making of Barbara Baynton', Rosemary Moore discusses yet another challenge to masculine versions of the bush. By drawing on Freud and Lacan, Moore argues that Barbara Baynton's fiction employed the popular discourse of hysteria in order to expose the abuse of women in the colonies. In her essay 'A Literary Fortune', Megan Brown explores how another Australian woman, Mary Fortune, established her literary identity while exposing the instability of colonial constructions of gender. Dorothy Driver traces the complicated relationships between South American race and gender identity in 'Olive Schreiner's *From Man to Man* and "The Copy Within"'. Ailise Bulfin's 'Guy Boothby's "Bid for Fortune": Constructing an Anglo-Australian Colonial Identity for the *Fin-de-Siècle* London Literary Marketplace' investigates Boothby's performance of hyphenated identity and the double vision created by this non-belonging in his novels. In 'The Scenery and Dresses of Her Dreams: Reading and

Reflecting (on) the Victorian Heroine in M.E. Braddon's *The Doctor's Wife*, Madeleine Seys shifts the focus of the collection to Britain, arguing that Braddon self-consciously rewrites the subject of sensation fiction, thus allowing her heroine to regain respectability. Mandy Treagus's 'The Woman Artist and Narrative Ends in Late-Victorian Writing' is taken from a chapter of *Empire Girls*, reviewed above. Shale Preston's essay on *Little Dorrit* (reviewed below) is followed by a piece by Carolyn Lake on the poetry of Amy Levy. The last essay in the collection returns to the Victorian subject in fiction. 'From "Peter Panic" to Proto-Modernism: The Case of J.M. Barrie' by Maggie Tonkin takes up the final change of the Victorian subject into the modern one while rejecting popular attempts to read *Peter Pan* as psychobiography and pursuing its proto-modern literary style.

In *Empire Girls*, Treagus gives a fresh look at the female *Bildungsroman* by examining its less well-known colonial instantiations. In her introduction she claims that all postcolonial fiction is characterized by ambivalence, though the sources and manifestations of that ambivalence vary wildly. *Empire Girls* examines the particular ambivalence necessitated by the introduction of a female colonial subject into the masculine, imperial genre of the *Bildungsroman*. In her reading of *The Story of an African Farm* [1883], Treagus discusses the doubled male and female *Bildungsromane* in the novel in order to demonstrate how the very aspects of Schreiner's novel that were decried by her critics were actually modelled on similar elements in Goethe's *Wilhelm Meister*. Treagus points out this difference in critical reception in order to explore the significance of gender and nationality for the genre. In the next chapter she reads Sara Jeannette Duncan's *A Daughter of Today* [1894] alongside *The Journal of Marie Bashkirtseff* [1887, 1890] in order to think specifically about the ill-fated *Künstlerroman* of female, colonial subjects. The final chapter, on Henry Handel Richardson's *The Getting of Wisdom* [1910], looks forward to the expanding plots for women in the twentieth century. Treagus reads the colonial boarding school in the novel as a site for the intersection of imperial and patriarchal power but is most interested in the way the novel's heroine gives up on the love plot in order to obtain at least the possibility of achieving the kind of artistic selfhood reserved for heroes in nineteenth-century fiction.

Christine Haskill's 'Valuable Failure as a Unifying Principle in *The Story of an African Farm*' (*ELT* 57[2014] 81–91) also concerns itself with the limited plots available for nineteenth-century women seen through a colonial context. Specifically, Haskill revisits the question of Lyndall's confusingly 'unfeminist' demise in Schreiner's novel (p. 81). After reviewing previous criticism on the ending, Haskill argues that Lyndall's death is a necessary failure or sacrifice and concludes, 'the feminist ideas that previous critics found lacking in *The Story of an African Farm* occur beyond the ending, if readers situate Lyndall's life and death—and especially her perceived failures—as steps in a lengthy process' (p. 82). If regarding Lyndall's death as a sacrifice does not seem particularly original, the fancy formal footwork required to locate the message of a text in a part of the story it does not tell is both intriguing and suggestive for novel theory more broadly.

Two books appeared in 2014 treating fiction specifically from and about Britain's antipodal colonies, Helen Lucy Blythe's *The Victorian Colonial Romance with the Antipodes* and Tamara S. Wagner's edited essay collection, *Domestic Fiction in Colonial Australia and New Zealand*. Blythe's text includes two chapters on novels (the rest is reviewed above). A reading of Mary Taylor's *Miss Miles, or A Tale of Yorkshire Life 60 Years Ago* allows Blythe to explore the cultural resonances of Taylor's decision to displace her discussion of women and artistic labour from the colonies where she sought employment to the British countryside where she was raised. In a chapter on Butler's *Erewhon*, Blythe asserts that Butler was already exploring the dynamics of interpersonal control familiar from *The Way of All Flesh* in the context of colonization in the earlier text. In particular, Blythe suggests that Butler allows for a surprising amount of fluidity in these interactions. Drawing on the anthropological work of Michael Taussig, Blythe argues that the contact zones in Butler's fiction, whether they be between two relatives or the colonizer and the colonized, are marked by mirroring and exchange as well as domination and differentiation.

Each of the eleven essays in *Domestic Fiction in Colonial Australia and New Zealand* asks what happens both ideologically and generically when the domestic spaces of the imperial centre get relocated to the settler colonies in the antipodes. In the opening chapter, Lesa Scholl argues that Harriet Martineau's novel *Homes Abroad* presents the colonies as a kind of second chance where former Britons could build a better England, and yet the novel is riddled with anxieties about the penal history of Australia and the wildness of the bush which expose imperfections in both the imperial and domestic visions. The next two chapters concern Dickens's relationship with imperialism in his novels. Diana C. Archibald looks at the interchanges between the representations of the colonial project in his novels, Urania Cottage, and the letters of Australian settlers that Dickens published in *Household Words*. Jude Piesse pairs *Great Expectations* with serialized settlement novels, locating Dickens's 'preoccupations with home, departure, and nostalgic return' within a larger colonial context (p. 49). Grace Moore also pairs a novel by a canonical author with neglected writing by Australian authors. Alongside the work of Mary Fortune and J.S. Borlase, Anthony Trollope's *Harry Heathcote of Gangoil* can be seen as partaking in a widespread anxiety about arson and colonial vulnerability, an anxiety with both gendered and racial dimensions. In chapter 5, Michelle J. Smith uses the figure of the Australian girl to show how literary culture travelled both ways across the ocean. Visions of Australian girls who display 'physical strength, bravery, horse-riding skills and heroism while dispelling ideas of colonial savagery' poured out of Britain, stories which then had to be addressed in colonial counter-narratives alive to the disconnect between the Australian girl's adventurous and domestic expectations (p. 75). Wagner's own contribution to the collection explores the ambiguous depiction of 'home' in the fiction of Ethel Turner who, Wagner argues, decentres both the metropole and imperialist master-narratives by means of a transoceanic triangulation of Britain with both its colonies and the Americas. Working with the Christian temperance fiction of Maud Jean Franc, Susan K. Martin examines how the narrative of the domestic romance struggles to resolve the sometimes harmonious, sometimes competing, ideologies of imperialism and evangelicalism. Again, domestic fiction becomes the vehicle for transoceanic exchange and cultural negotiation. The next two chapters turn to the figure of the New Woman. Melissa Purdue focuses on the politics surrounding *fin-de-siècle* motherhood in Rosa Praed's *Mrs. Tregakiss*, while Kirby-Jane Hallum investigates the aesthetic movement's colonial iteration. In 'Antipodal Home Economics: International Debt and Settler Domesticity in Clara Chessman's *A Rolling Stone*', Philip Steer makes the case for the domestic novel as interlocutor in matters of transoceanic economics. In the final chapter, Kristine Moffat reads *Ko Meri, or, A Cycle of Cathay: The Story of a New Zealand Life* in order to show how the complicated constructions of home discussed in the previous chapters were built at the expense of indigenous peoples.

Tamara Wagner also edited a special issue of *Women's Writing* entitled 'Girls at the Antipodes: Bush Girlhood and Colonial Women's Writing'. In her introduction (*WW* 21[2014] 139–47), Wagner argues for the importance of studying the colonial girl who, she claims, 'formed a catalyst in the reconceptualization of gender norms that took place in the century's second half...The freedoms enjoyed by the "Bush Girl" fueled debates on gender constraints, on childhood and gender-based upbringing, and on the distinct girl culture that was evolving across and, indeed, through imperial connections' (pp. 139–40). The first contribution to the volume, Mary Orr's '*Adventures in Australia* (1851) by Mrs. R. Lee: Reading for Girls at Home and Abroad' (*WW* 21[2014] 148–65), decries the common practice of thinking about gender in juvenile fiction in terms of genre. Orr points out how *Adventures in Australia*, an adventure story with a female protagonist, troubles this categorization. Kristine Moruzi, in 'The British Empire and Australian Girls' Annuals' (*WW* 21[2014] 166–84), examines the model of girlhood produced by the *Empire Annual for Australian Girls* and the *Australian Girl's Annual*, both of which were distributed in Britain and the colonies with only their titles altered. Michelle J. Smith looks at another periodical for girls in 'Colonial Feminism and Australian Literary Culture in Ethel and Lilian Turner's the *Parthenon* (1889–92)' (*WW* 21[2014] 185–201) in conjunction with the philosophy of 'expediency feminism' as promoted in a women's magazine published by Louisa Lawson, *The Dawn*. Smith argues that the apparently conservative content of the former was part of a larger feminist discourse that negotiated between independence and domestic responsibility. Wagner's own contribution, '"A Little Maid-Errant": Ethel Turner's Suburban Colonial Girl' (*WW* 21[2014] 202–28), looks at Ethel Turner's fiction over the course of her career as responding to models from Britain and the United States as well as the more prevalent bush fiction to which her own domestic novels provided an alternative. Erin Atchison writes about a novel from 1920 in 'The Ideal Colonial Girl and Exiled Modern Woman in Jane Mander's *The Story of A New Zealand River*' (*WW* 21[2014] 229–44). The next essay, '"Knowledge Is No More a Fountain Sealed": Secondary Education for Girls in Colonial New Zealand' (*WW* 21[2014] 245–58), returns to the nineteenth century to discuss the introduction of physical education to the secondary school system as well as Louisa Alice Baker's 1898 novel, *Wheat in the Ear*. The last essay in the issue, 'Colonial Girlhood and the New Girl's Diary' (*WW* 21[2014] 259–74), compares literature about colonial girlhood to the diaries of real colonial girls from 1850 to 1920 and discovers that genre influences the construction of the 'New Girl'.

Andrew Nash has also contributed to the growing field of oceanic studies with his single-author study, *William Clark Russell and the Victorian Nautical Novel: Gender, Genre and the Marketplace*. By examining the neglected career of the once popular Russell, Nash argues, we gain a new perspective on significant moments in the history of the novel, including increasing professionalism in the literary sphere and the replacement of the triple-decker with the single-volume novel. Russell begins his study by familiarizing his reader with the life and major literary trajectory of Russell. Of particular interest is the fact that, before writing maritime fiction, Russell cut his teeth on sensation fiction, sometimes writing under a female sobriquet. These early novels are the subject of Nash's first chapter, which presents Nash's early career as a necessary if original experiment in finding one's own voice. The rest of the book focuses on the nautical fiction for which Russell was known. Readings of *John Holdsworth, Chief Mate* and *The Wreck of the 'Grosvenor'* are followed by chapters on Russell's place within the maritime genre and the role of women and gender in his novels. The final chapters examine two aspects of the novels' material history—their relationship to serialization and their presentation for a wide range of burgeoning mass markets. *William Clark Russell and the Victorian Nautical Novel* is in one sense a recovery project, but it is also a meticulous, archival investigation of the publishing industry that grew up around genre fiction towards the century's end.

The more familiar practitioner of maritime fiction, Frederick Marryat, is the subject of Daniel Wuebben's article, 'Captain Frederick Marryat and *The Floral Telegraph*; or, A Forgotten Coder and His Floral Code' (*VLC* 42[2014] 209–33). Wuebben argues that Marryat was, in fact, the author of a novel titled *The Floral Telegraph*, which marks an interesting moment in the history of long-distance communication.

Giselle Rampaul and Barbara Lalla's *Postscripts: Caribbean Perspectives on the British Canon from Shakespeare to Dickens* offers precisely what the title suggests, an outsider take (specifically a Caribbean outsider take) on canonical British fiction. Two of the essays address Victorian novels. In 'Dickens and Others: Metastance and Remembering', Lalla points out the similarities between the England of Dickens, itself undergoing a process of self-definition, and the developing identity of the Caribbean. As Lalla writes, 'The physical and psychological isolation or strandedness of these texts' central characters who exist on the margins of society or who are at the mercy of power structures and discourses against which they react, the commerce in human flesh, the island sensibility, an ingrained sense of inferiority and taint are all familiar situations to the Caribbean' (p. 4). Also included is an essay by Jak Peake entitled 'Froude, Kingsley and Trollope: Wandering Eyes in a Trinidadian Landscape', which examines how the travel writing of the three novelists participates in the Victorian imperialist project by representing the island's geography as 'tropical picturesque' through loaded ways of '*seeing* or *knowing*' (pp. 108, 99).

Victorian Literature and Culture published a special issue (*VLC* 42:iii) on Victorian India, guest-edited by Mary Ellis Gibson (largely reviewed in Section 1 above) that includes three articles on Victorian novels among its selections. Kate Lawson, in 'Indian Mutiny/English Mutiny: National Governance in Charlotte Yonge's *The Clever Woman of the Family*' (*VLC* 42[2014] 439–55), argues that the Indian Mutiny in this 1860s text acts as 'an object lesson for those acute enough to recognize a looming and analogous "English Mutiny"' in the rebellious causes of liberalism and feminism (p. 440). Sukanya Banerjee's 'Troubling Conjugal Loyalties: The First Indian Novel in English and the Transimperial Framework of Sensation' (*VLC* 42[2014] 475–89) turns our attention to the much-neglected first Indian novel written in English, *Rajmahan's Wife* [1864] by Bankim Chandra Chatterjee. Most famous for his Bengali novels, Banerjee focuses on the conjugal loyalty in the novel and its intersections with changing ideas of bourgeois subjecthood, as well as, metaphorically, imperial power structures. Melissa Edmundson Makala, in 'Between Two Worlds: Racial Identity in Alice Perrin's *The Stronger Claim*' (*VLC* 42[2014] 491–508), also investigates domestic fiction in India. Makala reads the sympathetic love story between a white woman and a man of mixed ethnicity in Alice Perrin's *The Stronger Claim* [1903] as a bold, if complicated, rebuttal to the easy racism of the genre as a whole.

One final postcolonial essay, by Federica Zullo, 'Invading the Metropolis: Thugs and "Oriental Criminals" between Victorian and Postcolonial Stories' (*Textus* 27:ii[2014] 46–66), investigates the 'thug' in literature from the 1830s to Tabish Khair's 2010 *The Thing about Thugs*.

The New Woman did very well this year. For starters, she got a new birthday. In 'A New Date for the Victorian New Woman' (*N&Q* 61[2014] 577–80), William A. Davis calls our attention to an early non-capitalized usage of the term in December of 1889 by Mary Jeune, five years before Ouida supposedly coined it in an 1894 essay. In addition, there were three essays on the New Woman and music. Anna Peak, in 'Music and New Woman Aesthetics in Mona Caird's *The Daughters of Danaus*' (*VR* 40[2014] 135–54), uses Caird's novel to suggest that the aesthetics of New Woman fiction and aestheticism cannot be as easily separated as has been suggested. *The Daughters of Danaus* combines a concern with the material conditions preventing women from becoming great composers with a fascination with music as a pure form. The other two, both by Maura Dunst, treat music in Sarah Grand's *Heavenly Twins*. The first, 'He, Watching over Morningquest: The Chime's Musical Performance in Sarah Grand's *The Heavenly Twins*' (*ILStud* 16[2014] 348–65), argues that the chime that sounds throughout the novel 'acts as a litmus test of the characters' acceptance of patriarchal values' (p. 349). The second, '"Melopoetic Composition": Reading Music in Sarah Grand's *The Heavenly Twins* and George Egerton's *Keynotes and Discords*' (*NCGS* 10[2014]), analyses the musical quality of Grand's and Egerton's writing in order to propose that their prose is melopoetic—neither fully literary nor musical in composition. Identifying a transgressive element in melopoesis, Dunst urges that more attention be given to the interdisciplinary mode in New Woman fiction.

Eileen Cleere's *The Sanitary Arts: Aesthetic Culture and Victorian Cleanliness Campaigns* (reviewed above) contains two chapters on New Woman novels. Having established the ways in which the marriage plot works towards a sanitized artistic vision earlier on in the book, Cleere extends her argument in 'Aesthetic Anachronisms: Mary Ward's *The Mating of Lydia* and the Persistent Plot of Sanitary Fiction' (pp. 110–37) to *fin-de-siècle* fiction— especially that of New Woman—to suggest that 'the biological and reproductive ritual of "mating" is a fundamental component of the new sanitary aesthetic' (p. 113). The following chapter also deals with a New Woman author, Sarah Grand. Looking at two of Grand's later novels, *Adnam's Orchard* [1912] and *Winged Victory* [1916], Cleere explains the ways in which eugenic rhetoric drew on a naturalized version of the sanitary aesthetic.

Sara Jeannette Duncan, Catherine L. Pirkis, Amy Levy, Gissing, George Paston, and Charlotte Riddell also received attention for their New Woman fiction. Cecily Devereux follows the New Woman to the empire in 'An Adventure in Stageland: Sara Jeannette Duncan, Imperial Burlesque, and the Performance of White Femininity in *A Daughter of Today*' (*NCC* 36[2014] 35– 51). A tragic tale about a failed artist/journalist cum female exotic dancer cum autobiographer, *A Daughter of To-Day*, according to Duncan, 'intervene[s] in late-nineteenth-century imperial discourses of gender, race, and class' as the heroine discovers, by performing a burlesque version of her gender in the most public of venues, the 'everyday contractedness' of femininity (p. 36). Duncan's novel was also the focus of a chapter in *Empire Girls* by Mandy Treagus (reviewed above). Katherine Skaris, in 'Affective Labouring in Catherine L. Pirkis' *The Experiences of Loveday Brooke: Lady Detective*' (*The Victorian* 2:ii[2014] 1–14), emphasizes the fact that Pirkis's female protagonist is paid for her labour and solves mysteries using her emotions in addition to other capabilities associated with male detectives. Productively drawing together the work of Deborah Epstein Nord, Gayle Rubin, and Kathy Psomiades, S. Brooke Cameron and Danielle Bird, in 'Sisterly Bonds and Rewriting Urban Gendered Spheres in Amy Levy's *The Romance of a Shop*' (*VR* 40[2014] 77– 96), argue that the kinship bond between the Lorimer sisters enables them to move between domestic and public spheres within the late Victorian city. Finally, in '"The Valley of the Shadow of Books": George Gissing, New Women, and Morbid Literary Detachment' (*NCL* 69[2014] 92–122), Marisa Palacios Knox puts a new spin on the discussion of women's affective response to fiction. Not only were Victorians concerned about women feeling too much, Knox argues, they were also worried about women feeling too little. Knox traces how New Woman fiction by Charlotte Riddel, George Paston, and Gissing promulgated and challenged the idea that 'women's *not* being able to identify with the subjects of literature could be symptomatic of mental or even physical barrenness' (p. 94).

Emma Liggins, in *Odd Women? Spinsters, Lesbians and Widows in British Women's Fiction, 1850s–1930s*, examines the redundant or surplus women of nineteenth-century fiction. Drawing on the queer theory of Judith Butler, Judith Halberstam, and Sharon Marcus, Liggins analyses well-known and obscure texts alongside autobiographies to trace the evolving identities open to women outside marriage in the nineteenth and early twentieth centuries. Liggins does not seek to upend our understanding of singleness, but rather to provide a theoretically informed account of a 'female tradition' something in the style of Ellen Moers or Elaine Showalter. Indeed, Liggins self-consciously chooses only women writers for her study in order to isolate what 'women found "imaginable" as they campaigned for change' (p. 11). In chapter 1, 'Female Redundancy, Widowhood and the Mid-Victorian Heroine', Liggins shows how the discourse surrounding female redundancy at mid-century paved the way for a new kind of heroine and how, in turn, that heroine in novels like *Villette*, *Cranford*, and Charlotte Yonge's *Hopes and Fears* and *The Clever Woman of the Family* 'helped to erode perceptions of redundancy by showing socially useful heroines struggling against the confines of the mid-Victorian marriage plot' (p. 30). In chapter 2, 'Bachelor Girls, Mistresses and the New Woman', Liggins considers the reward reaped by earlier fiction about widows and spinsters: the possibility of young, single heroines living on their own as bachelor girls and New Women. Liggins focuses on the ways in which these women (both real and fictional) protected the spaces they had carved out for themselves, whether by adopting children, as in the fiction of Annie Holdsworth, or by proclaiming a radical celibacy, as in the novels of Ella Hepworth Dixon and Netta Syrett. The last three chapters in the book follow the further evolution of odd women through modernism and into the 1930s.

Several articles also appeared in 2014 dealing with the female body. In 'Pricing Parenthood: The Maternal Body as Commodity in George Moore's *Esther Waters*' (*The Victorian* 2:ii[2014] 1–16), Francesca M. Marinaro 'analyzes Moore's novel to illustrate how viewing the working-class mother exclusively in terms of her commodity value threatens the erasure of the wet nurse's identity as a mother in her own right' (p. 3). Duc Dau's 'The Governess, Her Body, and Thresholds in *The Romance of Lust*' (*VLC* 42[2014] 281–302) argues that the pornographic novel's treatment 'of "dirty" sex, that is "perverse," non-reproductive, and transgressive forms of sexuality, draws attention to the walls of social categories and constructs by the very act of breaking them down' (p. 283). Jane M. Kubiesa revisits the fallen woman plots of *Ruth*, *Adam Bede*, *Tess*, and *Esther Waters* in her article 'The Victorians and Their Fallen Women: Representations of Female Transgressions Nineteenth-Century Genre Literature' (*The Victorian* 2:ii[2014] 1–12).

The male body was the topic of a special edition of *Nineteenth-Century Contexts*, guest-edited by Nadine Muller and Joanne Ella Parsons. Their introduction, 'The Male Body in Victorian Literature and Culture' (*NCC* 36[2014] 303–6), urges readers to fill in the gap left by critics interested in the female body by focusing their attention on masculinity studies. Two of the essays included in the issue concern Victorian novels, including Joanne Ella Parsons's 'Eating Englishness and Causing Chaos: Food and the Body of the Fat Man in R.S. Surtees' *Jorrock's Jaunts and Jollities*, *Handley Cross*, and *Hillingdon Hall*' (*NCC* 36[2014] 335–46). In this essay, Parsons uses the carnivalesque to discuss the class and gender dimensions of both literal and figurative excesses of food. Clare Walker Gore's 'Noble Lives: Writing Disability and Masculinity in the Late Nineteenth-Century' (*NCC* 36[2014] 363–75) looks at three different texts—Dinah Mulock Craik's novel *A Noble*

Life, a biography by Sarah Steele entitled *The Right Honourable Arthur Macmurrough Kavanaugh*, and Lucas Malet's *The History of Sir Richard Calmady*—each of which concerns a disabled male body that is presented as anachronistic to unforgiving late nineteenth-century ideas of masculinity.

Male and female bodies both featured in work on Victorian marriage. As part of a special issue of the *Victorian Review* on 'Victorians and Risk', edited by Daniel Martin, Catherine England's 'Slipping into Marriage: How Heroines Create Desire by Risking their Reputations' (*VR* 40[2014] 109–24) examines the wild speculations that go on in the marriage market. According to England, marriage plots presumed to teach that virtue is rewarded actually suggest with surprising frequency that a slightly damaged reputation may trump a pure one and be worth the risk when playing for husbands. Gretchen Murphy, in 'Revising the Law of the Mother in the Adoption-Marriage Plot' (*NCL* 69[2014] 342–65), argues that more is at stake than bloodlines and inherited class in Victorian novels in which a family member marries an adopted sibling. Drawing on Juliet Mitchell's psychoanalytic theory of sibling relations, she suggests that such plots 'express a kind of wish-fulfillment about a central challenge of democracy: mediating equality and freedom within a legally imposed equality for all [i.e. siblinghood] stands at odds with the freedom to create closed communities of choice' (p. 356). Moving from the adoptive to the consanguineous, Jill Felicity Durey's *Degrees of Intimacy: Cousin Marriage and the Nineteenth-Century Novel* charts the rise and fall of the cousin marriage plot. According to Durey, the key figure in the history of cousin marriage both within and outside literature was Charles Darwin. Though himself married to his first cousin, Darwin's discovery of the importance of variety in species traits led him to the conclusion that the opposite—a large degree of shared traits—might be detrimental. Shortly after Darwin's thoughts on consanguineous marriage became known, Durey asserts, cousin marriage begins to recede from view in nineteenth-century fiction or, instead, to be treated as unfortunate. *Degrees of Intimacy* is organized chronologically, each chapter corresponding to a 'stage' in the treatment of cousin marriage. During the first stage (1800–62), cousin marriage is commonplace and even promoted as a method to preserve property and status. In the second (1862–75), cousin marriage is treated with ambivalence. Fiction from the third stage (1875–82), Durey argues, depicts cousin marriages as hazardous, and fiction from the fourth (1882–1920) either doesn't include it at all or treats it with the utmost contempt. Durey's study is a broad one, covering a total of fifty-four novels and twenty-nine authors whose biographical details form a significant part of the analysis.

Turning to individual authors, several articles appeared on Mary Elizabeth Braddon's *Lady Audley's Secret* and *The Doctor's Wife*, though her other novels were neglected. Elisabetta Marino's '"The Devil in the House": The Character of Lucy in *Lady Audley's Secret* by Mary Elizabeth Braddon' (*BAS* 20[2014] 15–20) discusses how Lucy Graham inverts Patmore's idealized Angel of the House only to be punished for her transgression at the end of the novel. In 'Making the Case: Detection and Confession in *Lady Audley's Secret* and *The Woman in White*' (*VR* 40[2014] 97–116), Anne-Marie Dunbar draws our attention to the final confessions in both texts that seem to confuse as much as they reinforce the damning story pieced together by Robert and Hartwright. The uneasy pairing of these two different epistemological approaches to a mystery (confession and detection), Dunbar argues, 'points to the increasing hegemony of circumstantial evidence and disinterested forms of knowledge, but also to their failure to tell the whole story or to get it right' (p. 99). Building on the work of Pamela Gilbert, Jennifer Conary, in 'Never Great, Only Popular: Mary Elizabeth Braddon's *The Doctor's Wife* and The Literary Marketplace' (*SNNTS* 46[2014] 423–43), contends that Braddon defended sensation fiction by attributing Isabel Gilbert's downfall to reading respectable, artistic poetry and novels. Jennifer Swartz-Levine also examines Isabel's reading material in '*The Doctor's Wife*: Criminal/Justice' (*The Victorian* 2:iii[2014] 1–11), but argues that it is the irreconcilability of legal and literary discourse that results in the character's misery.

The most important contributions to Brontë studies this year are the two chapters—one on *Jane Eyre* and one on *Wuthering Heights*—in Henry Staten's *Spirit Becomes Matter: The Brontës, George Eliot, Nietzsche* (reviewed above), in which he argues that the Brontës and Eliot were early developers of Nietzschean moral neutrality via the nineteenth-century interest in psycho-physiological energy. In the chapter on *Jane Eyre*, 'The Poisoned Gift of Forgiveness' (pp. 31–75), Staten makes the case that Jane does not believe in an afterlife. Though this may seem unlikely, the close reading that brings him to this conclusion is thorough and, if not completely convincing, certainly tempting. On this assertion, Staten is then able to build the argument that Jane's story is primarily one of embracing 'this earth and its earthly loves' (p. 68) and 'resisting the modes of social and personal domination', including the controlling gift of forgiveness, upon which the moral psychology of Christianity depends (p. 68). In the chapter on *Wuthering Heights*, 'The Return to the Heath' (pp. 132–76), Staten relentlessly argues that there is nothing transcendent about Emily Brontë's only novel. Placing considerable emphasis on Catherine's assertion that she belongs on earth and Heathcliff's purely material vision of the two lovers' bodies decaying into the same dust, Staten declares that, through Heathcliff, Brontë 'draws the ultimate spiritual and emotional consequences of biological materialism—consequences Nietzsche for his part was never able to fully accept...and does so in the most heightened dramatic form' (p. 161).

The Brontës outside Britain seem to have been particularly interesting to scholars of late. Helen MacEwan's *The Brontës in Brussels* details the sisters' time in the city while studying at M. Heger's Pensionnat de Desmoiselles and describes the locations they visited with accompanying maps and illustrations. In addition, the book includes excerpts from the novels as well as from letters and essays the sisters wrote while at the school. On a slightly different note, Shouhua Qi and Jacqueline Padgett have compiled an interesting collection of essays on the afterlife of the Brontës in non-Western literatures, *The Brontë Sisters in Other Wor(l)ds*. Taken as a whole, Qi and Padgett write, the essays 'consider the works of the Brontë sisters through a translingual, transnational, and transcultural setting, viewing them as examples of heteroglossia, hybridity, and postcolonial reworkings' (p. 1). Most noteworthy is that many of the primary texts discussed are unfamiliar and take the Brontës to unexpected places. For instance, in 'No Simple Love: The Literary Fortunes of the Brontë Sisters in Post-Mao, Market-Driven China' (pp. 19–49), Qi describes the surge of interest in the Brontë sisters immediately following the end of the cultural revolution, due, Qi argues, to a 'reshuffling' of the literary canon so that works previously considered trivial seemed worthy of consideration. The second essay, 'Rhys's Haunted Minds: Race, Slavery, the Gothic, and Rewriting *Jane Eyre* in the Caribbean' (pp. 51–74) by Suzanne Roszak, returns us to more familiar waters with her reading of *Wide Sargasso Sea*, but her approach is less so. Roszak attends to how Rhys reworks Gothic conventions in ways that offer a more nuanced account of Afro-Caribbean culture than has previously been assumed. In the third chapter, 'On the Migration of Texts: Emily Brontë's *Wuthering Heights, Maryse Condé's La Migration des cœurs*, and Richard Philcox's Translation of Condé's *Windward Heights*' (pp. 75–125), Padgett asks what happens when texts are adapted and translated for new contexts and audiences. Kevin Jack Hagopian's 'The Melodrama of the Hacienda: Luis Buñuel's *Abismos de pasión* as Postcolonial Trans/Plantation' (pp. 127–68) considers another example of what he calls 'transplantation', the process by which a 'canonical source material in one culture is uprooted and relocated to a second culture' (p. 127), this time of *Wuthering Heights* to post-Second World War Mexico. His analysis brings him to the suggestive conclusion that, for Buñuel, 'postcolonialist critique occurs in the space between deterritorialization and resituation' (p. 153). In chapter 5, 'The Undying Light: Yoshida, Bataille, and the Ambivalent Spectrality of Brontë's *Wuthering Heights*' (pp. 169–90), Saviour Catania explores the intersection of Emily Brontë and Bataille through a Japanese film version of her novel. The final essay in the collection, 'Michael Berkeley and David Malouf Rewriting *Jane Eyre*: An Operatic and Literary Palimpsest' (pp. 191–207) by Jean-Philippe Heberlé, examines how the adaptation of *Jane Eyre* for opera both pays tribute to the nineteenth-century text and provides a useful critique. As Heberlé explains, seeing events on the stage adds an immediacy that may be lacking in an individual's private reading of the novel at the same time that the highly conventional nature of opera draws attention to the mechanics of the novel's plot structure that may otherwise go unnoticed. Also of interest to Brontë scholars is Helen Lucy Blythe's chapter on Charlotte's friend Mary Taylor in *The Victorian Colonial Romance with the Antipodes* (reviewed above), which discusses Taylor and Brontë's correspondence in connection with the former's novel *Miss Miles, or A Tale of Yorkshire Life 60 Years Ago*.

Laurence W. Mazzeno includes three chapters on the Brontës in his edited collection, *Twenty-First Century Perspectives on Victorian Literature*. The first of these, 'Victorian Romanticism: The Brontë Sisters, Thomas Carlyle, and the Persistence of Memory' (pp. 63–74) by Laura Dabundo, asserts that Romanticism lived on in the Victorian period in the work of the Brontës and Carlyle in the way they privilege the imagination by emphasizing the subjectivity of narrative. Katherine Saunders Nash, in 'Overt and Covert Narrative Structure: A Reconsideration of *Jane Eyre*' (pp. 75–85), suggests that critical bibliography may offer a fresh way of approaching *Jane Eyre*. Nash believes that introducing the material objects of book production into the classroom would spur students' interest in literature more broadly, and by way of an example of how critical bibliography can inform our interpretations of a work she connects the tension between Jane's *Bildung* and Jane's retrospective with the narrative constraints imposed on Brontë's unified vision by the popularity of the three-volume format. Also in the same collection, Amy J. Robinson, in 'Matrimony, Property, and the "Woman Question" in Anne Brontë and Mary Elizabeth Braddon' (pp. 111–26), pairs *The Tenant of Wildfell Hall* and *Lady Audley's Secret* as novels deeply engaged both with the Gothic and women's rights. Each novel, Robinson concludes, can be read as 'early feminist statements', the final outcomes of which 'are rather conservative because of the way the women's stories are framed by the male perspective' (p. 112).

In 'The Natural History of Thornfield', a chapter from *Spellbound: The Fairy Tale and the Victorians*, Molly Clark Hillard observes how the very structure of *Jane Eyre* draws upon the genre of the natural history in order to blend 'scientific realism and fantastic narrative' (p. 51). For Hillard, Jane's poring over Bewick's natural history, *Birds of Britain*, sets the stage for a novel deeply concerned with the power play between observer and subject. Erik Gray, in 'Metaphors and Marriage Plots: *Jane Eyre*, *The Egoist*, and Metaphoric Dialogue in the Victorian Novel' (*PAns* 12[2014] 267–86), proposes that during the nineteenth century the idea of coverture was replaced by 'an ideal of colloquy' (p. 227), a transition marked by the negotiation (rather than the negation) of difference through shared metaphors during courtship. Brianna Kuhn also discusses matrimony in Brontë's most famous text. In 'Equal Partnerships: Ideal Androgynous Marriages in *Jane Eyre* and *The Woman in White*' (*The Victorian* 2:i[2014] 1–23), Kuhn introduces the concept of an androgynous marriage—one based on equality and in which neither gender reigns uppermost—and concludes that these are the marriages that are shown to be successful in Brontë's and Collins's texts. Alexander L. Barron provides close readings of the symbolic significance of wedding cakes in his article 'Baked Nectar and Frosted Ambrosia: The Unifying Power of Cake in *Great Expectations* and *Jane Eyre*' (*The Victorian* 2:i[2014] 1–11). Tracy Brain's 'Stitching a Life, Telling a Story: Sewing in *Jane Eyre*' (*WW* 21[2014] 464–87) links Jane's success as a narrator to her facility with a needle—two creative outlets that Bertha (the incoherent ripper of wedding veils) emphatically rejects. Antonia Losano takes thing theory and animal studies to *Jane Eyre* in 'Thing Jane: Object and Animals in *Jane Eyre*' (*VJ* 125[2014] 51–75) in order to argue that by aligning Jane with animals and things, 'Brontë privileges the *non*human; she mounts a critique of the human itself, seeing it not as a position of power or strength but one allowing for the abuse of power' (p. 72).

The Connell Guide to Charlotte Brontë's Jane Eyre by Josie Billington, the latest in a series of guides to classic works of literature, also appeared this year. It's a little unclear for whom this book would provide 'all you need to know about the novel in one concise volume' as the cover claims, but the accessible style, engaging format, and frequent illustrations would be suited to high school and college students as well as general enthusiasts. First-time teachers of the novel would probably find the different topics covered, such as 'the governess' and 'Jane the artist', useful, as would students looking for paper topics. Throughout, Billington refers to major criticism of the novel, offering multiple perspectives on each question she covers.

In 'History in the Sickroom: Charlotte Brontë's *Shirley*' (*VJ* 125[2014] 23–45), Kate Lawson argues that 'by linking recovery from illness with recovery of maternal history, *Shirley* suggests that health and the establishment of new "affective ties to this world" are predicated on this painful work of historical discovery' (p. 25). Bethany Dahlstrom, in 'The Forging and Forgery of Identity in G.K. Chesterton's *The Club of Queer Trades* and Charlotte Brontë's *Villette*' (*The Victorian* 2:i[2014] 1–18), considers the malleability of nineteenth-century gender identity by looking at novels where identities are forged in two senses.

In 'Liberal Anguish: *Wuthering Heights* and the Structures of Liberal Thought' (*NCL* 69:i[2014] 1–25), Anat Rosenberg joins the recent academic debate spearheaded in Victorian studies by Amanda Anderson, Lauren Goodlad, and Elaine Hadley. *Wuthering Heights*, Rosenberg argues, offers both a conceptual and an aesthetic contribution to our thinking about complexity in liberalism in its exploration of the incongruity of social and psychic logics in liberal consciousness. Of particular interest to Brontë scholars and enthusiasts alike is *The Annotated Wuthering Heights*, edited by Janet Gezari. Part of a series put out by Harvard University Press, this illustration-filled, coffee-table-size edition is as beautiful as it is instructive. Gezari does a superb job of both explaining obscure details within the text and providing information about cultural references to Brontë's novels, including film adaptations. Anyone writing on *Wuthering Heights* will find Gezari's edition an invaluable resource, and though probably too high for most courses, the price would not be prohibitive for a special topics seminar.

Simon Marsden, in *Emily Brontë and the Religious Imagination*, argues that *Wuthering Heights* and some of Brontë's poetry shows the unresolved tension between spirituality and scepticism that feels postmodern in its interest in religion 'as the excluded other of secular modernity' (p. 2). Though vulnerable to the sense of the post-Enlightenment world's disenchantment, Brontë nevertheless pursued a 'Romantic turn toward subjectivity as the site of religious authority and experience' (p. 145) and sought access to revelation, not within the confines of institutional Christianity, but within nature and the literary imagination. Chapter 1 traces 'the broad cultural shift...from enchantment to disenchantment' (p. 29) that followed the development of Enlightenment rationalism and the Romantic era's discovery of nature as the locus of transcendent apprehension of the divine. Chapter 2 explores 'images of enchantment and disenchantment in Brontë's writing' (p. 27) such as, in an early poem by Brontë, the 'lightening' (p. 34) of the speaker's despondency upon seeing a star and, later in *Wuthering Heights*, Lockwood's apprehension, upon reading Catherine's journal, 'of the enchanted world that threatened the stability of his rationalist orthodoxy' (p. 55). Chapter 3 examines 'the relationship between faith and words' (p. 27) in Brontë's creative repurposing of the narratives of the church to free them from deadening tradition as when Heathcliff 'appropriates biblical language' (p. 84), specifically, Romans 8:58–9, to upbraid Catherine for betraying their love. In the next chapter, Marsden shows that Brontë's writing is littered with scenes of the disarray and fragmentation left in the aftermath of the fall from innocence experienced by every human anew. Chapter 5 explores 'apocalyptic echoes' (p. 142) in Brontë's writing. The longing for 'liberation and renewal' (p. 137), as when Catherine on her deathbed wishes to be outside or a girl again, is constantly qualified by 'moments of *aporia* or fragmentation' (p. 139), evidence that though Brontë's writing 'remains open to redemptive possibility, glimpses in the imaginative re-enchantment of nature and the renewal of encounter with the sacred', the spiritual quest always remains unfinished (p. 147).

Neil Cocks's *The Peripheral Child in Nineteenth-Century Literature and Its Criticism* includes a chapter entitled 'The Child and the Letter: *The Tenant of Wildfell Hall*'. Drawing on Lacan's famous reading of Poe's 'The Purloined Letter', Cocks reads the child as the signifier exchanged between two parties— the parents or, analogically, the letters and diary exchanged between the principal adults in the novel. But, just as in Lacan's essay, the subject positions shift as the letter/child moves between them. Its own meaning unstable, the child is proves a shaky centre on which to ground the rest of the novel.

The first number of *Brontë Studies* this year included a section entitled 'Re-visioning the Brontës', co-edited by Nick Cass and Elizabeth Stainforth. As they explain in their introduction (*BS* 39:i[2014] 3–5), the essays and other contributions to the issue come from a conference of the same name held at the University of Leeds in 2013 in conjunction with two exhibitions, one on artists influenced by the Brontës ('Wildness Between Lines') and the other on their juvenilia ('Visions of Angria'). Each contribution considers some aspect of the Brontë sisters' artistic legacy. The first essay, by Carl Plasa, 'Prefigurements and Afterlives: Bertha Mason's Literary Histories' (*BS* 39:i[2014] 6–13), considers Kate Chopin's refiguring of Bertha in her first novel, *At Fault* [1890]. The second contribution, 'The Brontë Weather Project, 2011–2012' (*BS* 39:i[2014] 14–31), comes from Rebecca Chesney, a visual artist who decided to do a contemporary art project exploring the Brontës' relationship with the weather. An interview (*BS* 39:i[2014] 32–41) between Richard Brown and Blake Morrison, the author of the play *We Are Three Sisters* [2011], is followed by three independent articles and part 6 of the 'Brontë Reading List' (*BS* 39:i[2014] 71–80). According to Ileana Marin in her article 'Charlotte Brontë's Busy Scissors Revising *Villette*' (*BS* 39:i[2014] 42–53), *Villette* shows far more evidence of revision than does either *Jane Eyre* or *Shirley*, suggesting that Brontë was more and more in control of her own work and better able to experiment with novel techniques. A paper by Audrey Hall attempts to identify as Gaskell a woman in a photograph owned by Ellen Nussey (*BS* 39:i[2014] 54–7). The final article in the number, 'The Power of the Spoken Word in *Wuthering Heights*' (*BS* 39:i[2014] 58–70) by Graeme Tytler, discusses the quasi-magical quality of the spoken word in Emily Brontë's only novel.

The second number of *Brontë Studies* (*BS* 39:ii[2014]) included five articles. The first, 'Patrick Brontë: The Man Who Arrived at Cambridge University' (*BS* 39:ii[2014] 93–105) by Brian Wilks, investigates the early life of Patrick Brontë—his reasons for leaving Ireland, his time at Cambridge, and the political climate during his youth—as important factors in understanding the lives and works of his daughters. Going further back in the Brontë family tree, Edward Chitham explores the Brontës' Irish heritage in 'The Brontës' Irish

Background Revisited' (*BS* 39:ii[2014] 106–17). Turning to the novels, Graeme Tytler revisits the character of Hareton Earnshaw in 'The Presentation of Hareton Earnshaw in *Wuthering Heights*' (*BS* 39:ii[2014] 118–29), arguing that he deserves more attention not only because his appearances serve 'specific structural functions, but because he is a kind of touchstone by which we may assess some of the other characters' (p. 119). Looking at Anne Brontë's *The Tenant of Wildfell Hall*, Janina Hornosty's '"Let's Not Have its Bowels Quite so Quickly, Then"': A Response to Maggie Berg' (*BS* 39:ii[2014] 130–40) takes Berg to task for unfairly condemning Gilbert Markham as part of the 'carno-phallogocentric brotherhood' (p. 131) when actually, Hornosty argues, he manages to extricate himself from the dominant symbolic system. Finally, in 'Narrating the Queen in *Jane Eyre*' (*BS* 39:ii[2014] 141–52), Margaret Fain argues that Charlotte Brontë may—consciously or unconsciously—have based plain Jane's progress from much-abused child to happy matriarch on the public image of Queen Victoria's life.

In the third number of *Brontë Studies*, Judith E. Pike takes us back to the early days of the Brontë Society in '"Felicitations to the Brontëites": The 1895 Inaugural Volume of the Brontë Society's Transactions and Other Publications' (*BS* 39:iii[2014] 165–77). Pike pays special attention to how the representation of Elizabeth Gaskell's biography and Yorkshire in the first volume of the society's journal try to repackage the Brontë image. Kristi Sexton, in '*Jane Eyre*: Jane's Spiritual Coming of Age' (*BS* 39:iii[2014] 178–86), refocuses our attention on Jane's spiritual condition in the novel. Also in the third issue, Rodney Stenning Edgecombe provides a few supplementary annotations to *Jane Eyre* about Byron (*BS* 39:iii[2014] 187–90). Graeme Tytler's 'The Presentation of Isabella in *Wuthering Heights*' (*BS* 39:iii[2014] 191–201), a kind of companion piece to his article on Hareton in the previous issue, encourages scholars to recognize the impressive strength Isabella shows considering her privileged upbringing. Magdalen Wing-Chi Ki provides a psychoanalytical reading of the Earnshaw family in 'Family Complexes and Dwelling Plight in *Wuthering Heights*' (*BS* 39:iii[2014] 202–12). The issue also includes Catherine Paula Han's interview with Andrea Galer, a costume designer who worked on the 2006 BBC adaptation of *Jane Eyre* (*BS* 39:iii[2014] 213–24), and an essay by Temma Berg about her experience at 'The Brontë Sisters and Their Work', a conference in Ankara, Turkey (*BS* 39:iii[2014] 225–31). Ian M. Emberson closes the number with his article 'Mr. Lockwood and Mr. Latimer: *Wuthering Heights* and the Ghost of *Redgauntlet*' (*BS* 39:iii[2014] 232–8), which emphasizes the importance of Walter Scott to the Brontës and compares the opening of *Wuthering Heights* with Scott's novel *Redgauntlet*.

For the fourth number, the Brontë Society published a special issue entitled 'Afterlives of the Brontës: Biography, Fiction and Literary Criticism' (*BS* 39:iv[2014]). In their introduction, 'Whose Brontë Is It Anyway?' (*BS* 39:iv[2014] 251–3), Birgit Van Puymbroeck, Olivia Malfait, and Marysa Demoor briefly discuss the evolution of what has come to be known as the 'Brontë Myth'. In 'Lives and Afterlives: *The Brontë Myth* Revisited' (*BS* 39:iv[2014] 254–66), Lucasta Miller reflects on her 2001 book, which demonstrated that the way in which the Brontës have been described at different points in history says as much about the biographer's cultural moment as it does about the Brontës themselves. In this article, Miller turns the same critical eye on her *The Brontë Myth* and suggests that her text should perhaps be understood as a larger interest in metabiography in the early 2000s. 'Beyond *The Brontë Myth*: Jane Eyre, Hannah Cullwick and Subjectivity in Servitude' (*BS* 39:iv[2014] 267–78) by Deirdre D'Albertis reads *Jane Eyre* alongside Hannah Cullwick's diary of her life as a servant. In this excellent, original article, D'Albertis argues that the complicated power dynamics and subject formation of servitude allow us to bypass the binary opposition between ambitious self-creation and feminine self-sacrifice that typifies both the Brontë myth and the sisters' novels. Lesa Scholl, in 'Charlotte Brontë's Polyphonic Voices: Collaboration and Hybrid Authorial Spaces' (*BS* 39:iv[2014] 279–91), takes a Bakhtinian approach to Brontë's novels, arguing that the 'authorial space known as "Charlotte Brontë", or initially, "Currer Bell", was formed out of collaborative processes' and includes the voices of many influences, including the male influences of Branwell Brontë, Constantin Heger, and her publishers (p. 280). In 'Currer Bell, Charlotte Brontë and the Construction of Authorial Identity' (*BS* 39:iv[2014] 292–306), Sandro Jung re-examines the way Brontë separated out her life as a public author and private individual using the penname Currer Bell and how subsequent constructions of 'Charlotte Brontë' have tended to flatten the complex identities she created for herself. Sarah Posman takes a Deleuzean approach in '"Becoming" in *Jane Eyre*: Charlotte Brontë through the Eyes of Gilles Deleuze' (*BS* 39:iv[2014] 307–18). In this interesting essay, she proposes an impersonal approach to Brontë as creative event that would enable us to see how her novels 'create a vision of a different world' (p. 317), a crack in our time as in hers. Birgit Van Puymbroeck's '"The Virgin Soul": Anglo-French Spectres of Emily Brontë, 1880–1920' (*BS* 39:iv[2014] 319–29) examines late nineteenth- and early twentieth-century biographies of Emily Brontë from Belgium, Britain, and France. In 'Standing Alone: Anne Brontë Out of the Shadow' (*BS* 39:iv[2014] 330–40), Marianne Thormählen discusses the reasons for the youngest Brontë sister's long neglect by fans and academics alike and makes the case for the value of her fiction. Finally, Patsy Stoneman's 'Sex, Crimes and Secrets: Invention and Imbroglio in Recent Brontë Biographical Fiction' (*BS* 39:iv[2014] 341–52) looks at over twenty-five recent hypothetical and fictionalized versions of the Brontë biography, connecting these books to a larger, poststructural critical and creative interest in the relationship between fact and fiction, history and imagination.

Scholarship on Samuel Butler was largely concerned with his interest in science and technology. Will Abberley, in '"His Father's Voice": Phonographs and Heredity in the Fiction of Samuel Butler' (*19* 18[2014] 1–23), argues that 'Butler mediated his ideas about heredity, and his complex relationship with his family, through metaphors of phonographic transcription' (p. 1). To make this argument, Abberly draws on several of Butler's works including, most significantly, *The Way of All Flesh*. Looking at Butler's *Life and Habit* rather than one of his novels, Anna Feuerstein suggests that Butler 'challenges Victorian notions of animals precisely through subverting the anthropocentrism that led to hierarchical conceptions of human-animal

difference' (p. 199) in her essay 'Chicken Embryos, Headless Frogs, and the
Victorian Human-Animal Divide: Samuel Butler's Animal Epistemology'
(*JVC* 19[2014] 198–215). In 'Figures of Nineteenth-Century Biopower in
Samuel Butler's *Erewhon*' (*NCC* 36[2014] 53–71), Joshua A Gooch attends to
the deployment of various discourses within the novel in order to demonstrate
how 'imperial global capitalism creates and maintains political consensus'
(p. 53).

Michael Parrish Lee, in his thought-provoking article, 'Eating Things: Food
Animals, and Other Life Forms in Lewis Carroll's Alice Books' (*NCL* 68[2014]
484–512), tries to find common ground between animal studies, actor-network
theory, food studies, and two different strands of thing theory by analysing
forms of biological and social consumption in the Alice books. 'While thing
theory remains rooted in Heidegger's vision of things as "independent" and
"self-supporting"', Lee writes, 'the Alice books give us things in networks, but
networks that supersede, and have utility beyond, the human' (p. 489).

William Baker, Andrew Gasson, Graham Law, and Paul Lewis's 'The
Collected Letters of Wilkie Collins: Addenda and Corrigenda (9)'
(*Wilkie Collins Society* [Dec. 2014] 1–33) contains '39 new letters' and '3266
letters in the sequence to date' (p. 2). There are 'fifteen previously unpublished
letters from Wilkie Collins to' James Steele MacKaye (1842–94), the American
'actor dramatist and theatrical innovator'. Carline Radcliffe observes in her
introduction to them that 'Collins never returned to America nor McKaye to
England but the letters... provide a glimpse of the brief and stimulating
meeting of the two similarly unconventional theatrical creators from opposite
sides of the Atlantic' (p. 5). The Winter 2014 issue of the *Wilkie Collins Society
Newsletter* leads with a notice of the death at the age of 94 of its distinguished
patron, P. D. James (Baroness James of Holland Park; 1920–2014), whose
own work was very much influenced by Wilkie Collins (pp. 1–2). There are a
number of articles on *The Woman in White*. Elizabeth Meadows writes on
'Entropy and the Marriage Plot in *The Woman in White* and *Lady Audley's
Secret*' (*DSA* 45[2014] 311–31). Meadows's concern is with the sensation novel
and its refinements in Collins's novel and Braddon's. She writes that 'the
repetition of sensational thrills that characterizes' these novels 'has paradoxically entropic effects: a state of reduced energy, agency, and volition for
characters and readers alike'. According to Meadows 'Braddon and Collins
make the binding power of conventional plot structures into the subject matter
of plot as their sensation novels portray and enact the loss of energy that
defines entropy'. She demonstrates 'how the entropy plots of' both novels
'theorize the formal requirements of sensation to interrogate the relations
among literary and social conventions and human bodies' (p. 311). S. Brooke
Cameron writes on 'The Resilient Marian Halcombe: On Feminine Feeling
and Wilkie Collins's Debt to Amatory Fiction' in the online journal
Nineteenth-Century Gender Studies (*NCGS* 10:i[2014]). Brianna Kuhn's
'Equal Partnerships: Ideal Androgynous Marriages in *Jane Eyre* and *The
Woman in White*' (*The Victorian* 2:i[2014] 1–23) focuses upon sexual roles and
androgyny. Female sexuality and hysteria are the focus of Camelia
Raghinaru's '(Ir)rationalizing the Female Body in Wilkie Collins's *The
Woman in White*' (*The Victorian* 2:iii[2014] 1–16).

Other articles focus on either the dramatic adaptation of *The Woman in White* or its afterlife. Karen E. Laird, in her '"Paste-and-Scissors Version": The *Woman in White*'s Stage Debut' (*NCC* 36[2014] 179–99), considers James Redding Ware's adaptation. She notes that Collins attacked the copyright laws which meant that 'any scoundrel possessing a pot of paste and a pair of scissors to steal our novels for stage purposes' and comments that 'Ware unapologetically cut and pasted Collins's prose as he repurposed *The Woman in White* for a new form of media, but he also demonstrated considerable skill with his creative use of adaptation techniques that seem more akin to collage than simple papercraft. Although Collins never consented to their union, Ware and Collins were yoked together in a tango of adaptation, eventually merging their ideas about staging *The Woman in White* so intricately that it is hard to see where one's words end and another's begin' (p. 195).

Jessica Cox, in her 'Narratives of Sexual Trauma in Contemporary Adaptations of *The Woman in White*' (in Boehm-Schnitker and Gruss, eds., *Neo-Victorian Literature and Culture: Immersions and Revisitations*, pp. 137–50), concentrates on the themes of trauma in adaptations between 1997 and 2006. Queer theory and the afterlife of *The Woman in White* are the subject of Christine Johns's 'Unconventional Uncles: Queer Father Figures and Avuncular Relationships in Wilkie Collins' *The Woman in White* and Sarah Waters' *Fingersmith*' (*Victorian* 2:ii[2014] 1–15). Other Wilkie Collins novels received critical attention too. Animal and human relations, the grotesque, and Darwinism concern Delphine Cadwallader-Baron in her 'The Grotesque and Darwin's Theory in Charles Dickens's *Great Expectations* and Wilkie Collins's *No Name*' (in Hervouet-Farrar and Vega-Ritter, ed., *The Grotesque in the Fiction of Charles Dickens and Other 19th-Century European Novelists*, pp. 180–91). *The Law and the Lady* is the subject of one book chapter in 2014. Its treatment of privacy, secrecy, collecting and heirlooms, and male homosexuality engages David Ellison in his 'The Ends of Privacy: Dickens, Strange, Collins' (in Huguet and Vanfasse, eds., *Charles Dickens, Modernism, Modernity*, vol., 2, pp. 29–46). Molly Knox Leverenz's illustrated 'Illustrating *The Moonstone* in America: *Harper's Weekly* and Transatlantic Introspection' (*AmPer* 24[2014] 21–44) throws valuable light on the way in which *Harper's Weekly* published *The Moonstone*. According to Leverenz, 'the illustrations demonstrate how *Harper's Weekly*'s engagement with transatlantic discourses is primarily self-reflective. The illustrations do not merely describe England's paranoia objectively, but also seem designed to register America's lingering anxieties after the Civil War; the illustrations not only represent English imperialism, but also America's eye toward expansion.' She concludes that 'in so doing, *Harper's Weekly* informs our understanding of transatlantic crossings and their significance to national identity formation, a topic rich with possibilities for future research' (p. 41).

The two-volume *The Reception of Charles Dickens in Europe* [2013], edited by Michael Hollington, was not received in time for review last year. So many translators, intellectuals and historical events feature in this work that only the most elementary summary can be provided within this space. The first volume contains an introduction (pp. 1–15) by Michael Hollington and launches into 'The Reception of Dickens in Germany' (pp. 17–75). Antje Anderson's

'Dickens in Germany: The Nineteenth Century' (pp. 19–34) surveys review journals such as *Blätter für literarische Unterhaltung* [1818–98] in order to gauge Dickens's translation and reception in Germany and to answer the question: 'What socio-cultural and socio-political factors shaped German readers' response to Dickens?' (p. 19). In 'The Reception of Dickens in Germany, 1900–1945' (pp. 35–50) Norbert Lennartz observes Dickens's 'waning influence on early twentieth-century German literature' (p. 35) and includes an assessment of Dickens's harsher critics, who were anything but objective in a period shaken by war. A discussion of Adorno and his more nuanced critique sheds light on Dickens's ambivalent position within the academy from 1931. Lennartz's conclusion is well put: 'Dickens became marginalized in academic circles, but was widely read elsewhere as a representative of popular culture supplying his German readership with freakish characters and trajectories of oblivion in the face of economic turmoil and the looming horrors of political and humanitarian disaster' (p. 30). With 'Dickens's Reception in Germany after 1945' (pp. 51–68) Stefan Welz provides subsections which summarize the chapter's main areas of focus: 'Cultural Revival and Democratic Reassurance 1945–50' (pp. 51–3), 'Post-War Publication of Dickens's Works' (pp. 53–7), 'The Post-War Academic Reception of Dickens' (pp. 57–60), 'Normalization and Manipulation 1950–70' (pp. 60–4), and 'Theoretical Approaches in Academia and Media Adaptations' (pp. 64–8). Joachim Möller's topic is 'German Illustrations' (pp. 69–75) and their ideological significance at key moments in German history. The second part is 'The Reception of Dickens in Russia' (pp. 77–120). In 'Dickens in Russia: A Survey' (pp. 79–85) Nina Diakonova assesses 'biographical studies; more or less detailed appreciations of the main bulk of his art; and papers on particular novels and stories' (p. 79). The next two chapters—'Dickens in Leo Tolstoy's Universe' (pp. 86–92) by Galina Alekseeva and 'The Underground Passage: Dickens and Dostoevsky' (pp. 93–102) by Michael Hollington—assess Dickens in terms of his links to major Russian novelists. Hollington supplements his study with a 'Note: Did Dickens and Dostoevsky meet in July 1862?' (pp. 101–2). 'Dickens in Twentieth-Century Russia' is the subject of Emily Finer's contribution, which, like others in this section, is indebted to the Soviet Dickensian Igor Katarsky, who died in October 1971 at the age of 52. At the end of this chapter it is noted that a 'narrative whereby Russia is the guardian of Dickens's genius, rather than his culturally alienated homeland, continues with justification, to the present day' (p. 120).

'The Reception of Dickens in France' (pp. 121–66) begins with 'A Historical Survey of French Criticism and Scholarship on Dickens' (pp. 123–41) by Nathalie Vanfasse, who surveys Dickens's reception within French academia and across various theoretical lenses (biography, Foucauldian studies, psychoanalysis). Vanfasse concludes that, in France, Dickens's works were originally popular with a mass audience whilst intellectuals disregarded his writings. Then, with a sea change in critical opinion, 'Dickens became the author read by an educated elite' (p. 141). Christine Huguet's 'Dickens in France: Major Writers' (pp. 142–53) notes that Dickens was consistently grouped with writers such as Dumas, Hugo, and George Sand despite historical factors—'the 1846 dissentions between England and France' (p. 143) for example—that led to 'a genuine Anglophobia' (p. 143). In 'Dickens's Illustrations: France and Other Countries' (pp. 154–66) Gilles Soubigou details that 'Dickens's influence was, if discreet, nonetheless deep. He was important to the development of illustration for literature aimed at the young, and, in the second half of the nineteenth century, he made a major contribution to debates about Realism in art as well as literature' (p. 166). 'The Reception of Dickens in Spain and Portugal' (pp. 167–211) is the title of the third section. In 'The Spanish Dickens: Under Cervantes's Inevitable Shadow' (pp. 169–81) Fernando Galván and Paul Vita are interested in the Dickens–Cervantes connection but most notably discuss translations of Dickens into Spanish and his critical reception. Similarly, in 'Dickens in Catalan Literature' (pp. 182–90) Sílvia Coll-Vinent and Marcel Ortín are interested in translations from the turn of the century to the present day. In particular, the writers analyse 'the role played by one of [Dickens's] translators, Joseph Carner (1884–1970), a poet and prose writer who was also a leader in the formation of public opinion' (p. 183). Jeremy Tambling's 'Dickens and Galdós' (pp. 191–6) turns to a consideration of the Spanish Dickensian. Tambling demonstrates that the 'relationship between Dickens and Benito Pérez Galdós (1843–1920) is both exciting, and also, since Galdós barely referred to Dickens, speculative' (p. 191). Similarities and differences are established. For instance, 'both Dickens and Galdós are intensely interested in social issues, though Galdós's intense reaction to the revolution…makes him a more overtly and immediately political writer than Dickens' (p. 193). With 'Dickens in Portugal' (pp. 197–211) Maria Leonor Machado de Sousa considers 'The Role of the Periodicals' (pp. 197–203), 'The Twentieth Century' (pp. 204–9), and 'The New Media' (pp. 209–10). Overall, the chapter looks into 'how Dickens became known in Portugal through translations, through films and through critical writing and research, academic and otherwise' (p. 210).

Part IV observes 'The Reception of Dickens in Italy' (pp. 213–44). In 'Dickens's Reception in Italy: Criticism' (pp. 215–23) Clotilde de Stasio investigates Dickens's presence in Italian culture, from nineteenth-century reviews by Eugenio Camerini, Erico Nencioni, and others to present-day conferences in Genoa, Verona, and Milan. Next is Alessandro Vescovi's 'The Making of a Classic: A Survey of Italian Translations' (pp. 224–30). Vescovi examines the circulation of Dickens in Italy from 1840, well before unification in 1861, paying particular attention to highbrow and lowbrow editions and the author's wide appeal both within and outside the academic sphere. 'Magic Lantern, Magic Realism: Italian Writers and Dickens from the End of the Nineteenth Century to the 1980s' is by Francesca Orestano. This chapter focuses on the period 'After 1861' (pp. 231–44) and goes on to review 'Dickens and Children's Literature' (pp. 234–6) and 'Dickens and Magic Realism' (pp. 236–44). The latter section treats specifically 'the response to Dickens in the fascist era and beyond it, by significant writers…who experienced marginalization and almost total isolation, as is the case with Giuseppe Tomasi di Lampedusa (1896–1957) in Sicily' (p. 236). Part VI, 'Other German- and French-Speaking National Traditions' (pp. 245–56) contains only

'Dickens in Austria and German-Speaking Switzerland' (pp. 247–56) by Herbert Foltinek. Stage adaptations from the late nineteenth century on are noted here alongside academic criticisms from around 1909. Part VII is entitled 'Other French-Speaking National Traditions' (pp. 257–80). In 'Boz as Tutor: The Reception of Dickens in Francophone Belgium' (pp. 259–71) Carlene A. Adamson explains that Dickens was important to a new country seeking to establish a national identity distinct from French influences. Issues surrounding piracy are considered here as well as the inclusion of Dickens within the Belgian school curriculum. 'Dickens in Francophone Switzerland' (pp. 272–80) sees Neil Forsyth and Martine Hennard Dutheil de la Rochère survey Dickens's stance in Switzerland from 1840. Dickens's 'Impact on Swiss French Writers' (pp. 274) is investigated. Two further subsections deal with the subjects of 'Performance' (pp. 278–9) and 'Academic and Popular Studies in the Twentieth Century' (pp. 279–80). Part VIII, 'Dutch-Speaking National Traditions' (pp. 281–301), contains 'Dickens's Reception in the Netherlands' (pp. 283–94) by Odin Dekkers and 'Dickens's Reception in Flanders' (pp. 295–301) by Walter Verschueren. Dekkers's broad historical sweep ranges from 1837 to the present. Verschueren examines shifting perceptions of Dickens across the pre-war and post-war eras. The bibliography appears at the end (pp. 302–63) and a useful 'Timeline of the European Reception of Charles Dickens, 1833–2013' (pp. xxv–xliii) is provided.

Volume 2 is similarly concerned with the socio-cultural and socio-political implications of Dickens in translation across geographical boundaries, historical periods, and different media. As in the first volume, both academic perspectives and popular perceptions are scrutinized. Two further chapters at the end address how Dickens has been expressed and interpreted on the small and big screens. Part IX, 'Scandinavian National Traditions' (pp. 365–445), contains 'The Reception of Charles Dickens in Denmark from the 1830s to the Present' (pp. 367–87) by Dominic Rainsford; 'Dickens's Reception in Finland' (pp. 388–98) by H.K. Riikonen; 'The Tale and the Toothpick: On Dickens in Iceland' (pp. 399–408) by Astraður Eysteinsson; 'Dickens in Norway' (pp. 409–29) by Tore Rem; and 'Dickens in Sweden' (pp. 430–45) by Ishrat Lindblad. Part X is 'Slavonic National Traditions' (pp. 447–506). This part contains 'An Uninterrupted Journey: Seventeen Decades of Dickens Reception in the Czech Lands' (pp. 449–65) by Zdeněk Beran; 'Dickens in Slovakia' (pp. 466–75) by Soňa Šnircová; 'Dickens in Croatia' (pp. 476–80) by Sintija Culjat; 'Dickens in Poland' (pp. 481–95) by Ewa Kujawska-Lis; and 'Dickens in Bulgaria' (pp. 496–506) by Vladimir Trendafilov. Part XI—'Baltic National Traditions' (pp. 507–28)—includes 'Dickens in Estonia' (pp. 509–14) by Suliko Liiv and Julia Tofantšuk; 'The Reception of Dickens in Latvia' (pp. 515–20) by Inara Peneze; and 'The Great Victorian Realist and Humanist: The Lithuanian Reception of Dickens' (pp. 521–8) by Regina Rudaityte. 'Balkan National Traditions' (pp. 529–59) is the subject of Part XII, which comprises 'Dickens in Romania' (pp. 531–43) by Monica Bottez and 'Exporting Corinthian Currants, Importing Dickensian Stories: The Reception of Dickens in Greece' (pp. 544–59) by Katerina Kitsi-Mitakou and Maria Vara. The only chapter in Part XIII; 'The Hungarian National Tradition' (pp. 561–75), is Géza Maráczi's 'Dickens in Hungary' (pp. 563–75).

The penultimate part is 'The Georgian National Tradition' (pp. 577–86), which consists of Marika Odzeli's 'The Artistic World of Charles Dickens in Georgian Literature' (pp. 579–86). The final part, 'Dickens in European Film and Television' (pp. 587–99), contains 'Dickens in Film' (pp. 589–94) by Grahame Smith and 'Dickens in Television' (pp. 595–9) by Pamela Atzori. An extensive bibliography (pp. 600–79) and an index (pp. 681–703) complete the volume.

   One of the standout 2014 texts is Sean Grass's *Charles Dickens's Our Mutual Friend: A Publishing History*. Grass's stated aim in the introduction, '*Our Mutual Friend*: "The Poorest of Mr. Dickens's Works"' (pp. 1–8), is to provide a 'comprehensive account of how Dickens came to write the novel, what choices he made while writing and revising, when and in what formats the novel first appeared, how it appeared subsequently, how the novel fared financially and critically when it was first published, and how it has fared during the century and a half since' (pp. 3–4). The first chapter, 'The Man from Somewhere: Ellen Ternan, Staplehurst, and the Remaking of Charles Dickens' (pp. 9–36), situates the novel in a biographical context. Chapter 2, 'The Cup and the Lip: Writing *Our Mutual Friend*' (pp. 37–69), is a textual study which takes into consideration Dickens's memoranda book, the number plans, the manuscript, and the surviving proofs. Grass discusses how Dickens underwrote or overwrote instalments and how this affected chapter placement. Also examined at length is a grangerized copy of the novel in the Berg collection. Grass provides here sixteen illuminating plates, including six pages of the manuscript, three pages of proofs, and a page from the first edition. The third chapter, 'Putting a Price Upon a Man's Mind: *Our Mutual Friend* in the Marketplace' (pp. 71–96), asses the commercial impact of the novel. Although *Our Mutual Friend* is often described as a failure, Grass's much more nuanced account hones in on market fluctuations. For example, 'an economic recession caused by the US Civil War . . . injured the publishing industry in England and America' (pp. 6–7). Grass rightly points out that, though Chapman and Hall were disappointed with sales, Dickens the businessman 'made more money than he had earned from a single novel in his life' (p. 94). The two concluding chapters—'A Dismal Swamp? *Our Mutual Friend* and the Victorian Critics' (pp. 97–130) and 'The Voice of Society: *Our Mutual Friend* since 1870' (pp. 131–57)—treat the novel's critical reception from the Victorian period on, taking into account the fact that positive and negative contemporary reviews were often driven by 'value judgements that extend beyond *Our Mutual Friend* to Dickens himself' (p. 100). After this, four appendices are provided: 'Dickens, Ellen Ternan, and Staplehurst' (pp. 159–63), 'The Manuscript, the Proof Sheets, and the Berg Copy' (pp. 165–7), 'Contemporary Reviews of *Our Mutual Friend*' (pp. 169–252), and 'Selected Bibliography of Editions of *Our Mutual Friend*' (pp. 253–6). The first contains items 'related to Dickens's relationship with Ellen Ternan and also to the Staplehurst accident' while the second 'describes the location and condition of . . . three major archival sources' (p. 7). Appendix 3 'contains full transcriptions of all 41 reviews of *Our Mutual Friend* that appeared during or immediately after the novel's serialization' (p. 8). The last 'gives a comprehensive list of editions . . . published in England and the United States during Dickens's lifetime, and a selected list of editions published after 1870' (p. 8). The bulk of this excellent work successfully argues against Henry James's view (that *Our Mutual Friend* is the worst of Dickens's novels) and celebrates this 'most profoundly thoughtful and deliberately artistic book' (p. 2). A bibliography (pp. 257–64) is included as well as a useful index (pp. 265–74).

The Dog in the Dickensian Imagination by Beryl Gray brings Dickens firmly into the grip of the 'animal turn' in literary and cultural studies. Gray seeks to demonstrate that 'Dickens was fascinated by dogs. They were an integral part of his life and his vision of the world; he was entertained and imaginatively stimulated by them throughout his career, and they were vital to his art' (p. 1). The book is made up of two main sections which prove Gray's point: 'A Life with Dogs' (pp. 9–97) and 'Knowing His Place: The Dog in Dickens's Art' (pp. 99–236). There is also a conclusion (pp. 237–40). The first of these contains the chapters 'Dog Fancy' (pp. 11–21), 'A Dog's Life with Dickens: Timber (1842–54)' (pp. 23–33), '"I Have Taken to Dogs Lately": The Great Gad's Hill Dogs' (pp. 35–66), 'Dogs Encountered' (pp. 67–84), and 'Dickens's Dream Dog: Mrs Bouncer' (pp. 85–97). The second section contains 'Man and Dog: *Oliver Twist* and *The Old Curiosity Shop*' (pp. 101–48), 'The Circus Dog and the Whelp: *Hard Times*' (pp. 149–62), 'The Drover's Dog: *Bleak House*' (pp. 163–75), 'The Essential Dog: *Dombey and Son* and *Little Dorrit*' (pp. 177–206), and 'The Defining Dog: *David Copperfield* and *Great Expectations*' (pp. 207–36). The first, biographical, part of the book is an account of the dogs Dickens came into contact with, studied, and wrote about as result of his walks and excursions. 'Dogs are inextricable from Dickens's London', Gray states (p. 4), though she notes that the author was rarely sentimental about them. Some of the dogs Dickens observed appear in the journalism. This section also contains many rare primary texts of interest. For instance, Nelly Ternan's elegy to Bouncer, Dickens's 'dream dog', is reproduced here (p. 95). In the second section, Gray considers, among others, Bull's-eye in *Oliver Twist*, the performing dogs in *The Old Curiosity Shop*, Merrylegs in *Hard Times*, Diogenes in *Dombey and Son*, Henry Gowan's Lion in *Little Dorrit*, and Dickens's 'superlative study of a relationship' (p. 227) between Dora and Jip in *David Copperfield*. (The latter is a subject that forms the basis of Julianne Ruetz's essay in *Dickens Quarterly*, reviewed below.) Gray concludes that, though Dickens could be sympathetic towards dogs, his representations reveal that 'his treatment . . . was not always appropriate, nor was his understanding of them invariably penetrating' (p. 239). Interspersed throughout this highly entertaining and informative study are a number of figures, including 'Charles Dickens and his dog Turk' (p. 35) and 'Mamie Dickens holding Mrs Bouncer and a white kitten' (p. 97). A bibliography (pp. 241–9) and an index (pp. 251–9) are provided at the end.

The latest volume in the Dickens Companion series, the first to emerge in almost a decade, is Trey Philpotts's brilliant *The Companion to Dombey and Son*. An introduction (pp. 1–7) provides a short history of the writing of *Dombey and Son* and identifies some of the main references that appear in the novel. The main text of the companion provides a mine of annotations and information on Victorian culture and history, from journalism on London's street life (Henry Mayhew merits several citations) to the advance of the railroads, a subject Philpotts takes up in his 2014 essay in *Dickens Quarterly*, reviewed below. Philpotts draws upon Dickens's letters, his journalism and his philanthropic projects in order to map the many points made in the book. Intertexts are clearly signalled as Philpotts notes that a number of characters— Captain Cuttle most obviously—borrow from a variety of sources, especially popular song and the Bible. Though designed as a reference source, this superb volume starkly highlights the diversity of the city that inspired Dickens and the art forms that influenced his imagination. A number of illuminating figures and illustrations are dispersed throughout, including the title page from the autograph manuscript. A select bibliography (pp. 527–53) and an index (pp. 554–75) are also included.

Jeremy Clarke's *The Charles Dickens Miscellany* brilliantly illustrates the exuberance of Dickens and his works. There are three sections: 'Living' (pp. 13–68), 'Writing' (pp. 69–144), and 'Reading' (pp. 145–85) and seventeen images, primarily taken from the Rochester Guildhall Museum, many of which are reproduced here for the first time. The first part includes five chapters: 'Growing Up' (pp. 14–24), 'Taking Off' (pp. 25–34), 'Settling Down' (pp. 35–51), 'Abroad' (pp. 52–8), and 'Security and Secrets' (pp. 59–68). An account of Dickens's life is provided and the parameters of the book are established: useful subheadings divide the main concerns and some of the most important facts are highlighted, contained within framed boxes. 'Writing' contains: 'A Guide to the Novels' (pp. 70–97), 'Shorter Fiction' (pp. 98–104), 'Journalism' (pp. 105–14), and 'Subjects & Themes' (pp. 115–44). Each novel is given its own treatment and Clarke offers clear summaries under the headings 'How and When?', 'In a Sentence?', 'Good Things?', 'Disappointments', and 'Read...' in order to give some personal and critical perspectives. The journalism chapter is a welcome addition, illuminating the range of Dickens's writings. Clarke is also interested in how London and the people there conditioned Dickens's imagination: subsections such as 'London as Nourishment' (p. 116), 'London Various' (pp. 117–18), 'Waiters' (pp. 121–2), and 'Cab Drivers' (pp. 125–7) prove that 'London was the cradle of [Dickens's] success' (p. 115). The 'Reading' section includes: 'The Storyteller' (pp. 146–52), 'A Reader's Work' (pp. 153–77), 'Dickens the Reader' (pp. 178–83), and 'Not an End' (pp. 184–5). Printed texts and adaptations are considered here as well as Dickens's reading career. Most interesting are the concluding remarks, where Clarke notes Dickens's presence in the world today: 'Dickens seems embedded in our national life, a living part of our culture' (p. 185) as we appropriate again and again his most famous stories. This is an appropriate conclusion to the volume, opening up a space for further study. 'Places to Visit' (pp. 186–8) and 'Further Reading' (pp. 189–90) are situated at the end.

Also concerned with appropriations is Marc Napolitano's *Oliver! A Dickensian Musical*, winner of The Theatre Book Prize 2014. This monograph is composed of an introduction (pp. 1–8) and seven chapters. Chapter 1 situates the novel within the cultural context of the time and argues that 'Bart's success in adapting Dickens's novel was due in large part to the sense of theatrical and musical experimentation that defined the era in which he wrote' (p. 6). Chapters 2 and 3 treat Bart and his creative team, notably the set designer Sean Kenny and director Peter Coe, who 'helped to ground the project more fully in the Dickensian source, adding the necessary "grit" to balance out the "glitz" that defined Bart's initial conception' (pp. 6–7). While chapter 2 'traces Coe's revisions to the libretto', chapter 3 'gives particular attention to Kenny's contributions, as his groundbreaking scenery helped to define both the narrative and the tone of Bart's adaptation' (p. 7). The fourth chapter surveys the positive critical reception that *Oliver!* received and suggests that the adaptation 'marked a critical chapter in the evolution of the English musical, and likewise in the life stories of the artists associated with the project' (p. 133). To prove this further, in his fifth chapter Napolitano engages in a textual study of the musical. This is no easy task, given those analytical frameworks that drive a boundary between text and performance. Napolitano sensibly surmounts this difficulty by reading four plot threads with an imaginative eye and ear on the business and dynamism of the stage. Chapter 6 contains four main subsections—'*Oliver!* in Japan' (pp. 165–7), '*Oliver!* on Broadway' (pp. 167–73), 'Fidelity Strikes Back: *Oliver!*'s American Reception' (pp. 173–5), and 'The De-semitization of Fagin on Broadway' (pp. 175–80)—which assess the adaptation's extensive international reach and how this came to be at a time when musicals generally failed to break geographical boundaries. In chapter 7 'the big-budget 1968 film adaptation' (p. 7) directed by Carol Reed is examined. It is noted here that 'the film would influence subsequent revivals of the stage property' (p. 7) and indeed the chapter 'concludes with an analysis of the reinvention of this musical, as conducted under the watchful eye of the English impresario Sir Cameron Mackintosh' (p. 7). An epilogue (pp. 207–16) evaluates the success of *Oliver!* along with the status of later Bart musicals, and also fills in Bart's biography, asking 'What Happens When *Oliver!* is Seventy?' (pp. 215–16). Throughout, the study is greatly enhanced by a number of figures and pictures, all of which help to clarify some of the more complex points. There are five appendices, though these are only available online via the OUP website. The notes (pp. 217–63) appear at the end along with the bibliography (pp. 265–79) and the index (pp. 281–7).

Two further books deserve attention here. *Charles Dickens and the Great Jennens Case* by Laurence Ince investigates a legal case that Dickens supposedly borrowed from in *Bleak House*. The case began in 1819 when Dickens was only 7 years old and did not conclude until 1870, the year in which Dickens died. As in Jarndyce and Jarndyce, the lawyers made little effort to settle the case, partly because they continued to make money from it. The case ended when the money involved (used to pay lawyers' fees) ran out. The book charts this history and contains a prologue (pp. 1–3) and eleven chapters. These are 'Charles Dickens—A Brief Biography' (pp. 4–10), '*Bleak House*' (pp. 11–14), 'Charles Dickens and Warwickshire' (pp. 15–18), 'The Origins of the Jennens Fortune' (pp. 19–25), 'Charles Jennens (1700–1773)' (pp. 26–37), 'William Jennens (1701–1798)—The Richest Commoner in England' (pp. 38–47), 'The Aristocratic Heirs' (pp. 48–54), 'New Claimants Appear' (pp. 55–66), 'The Jennens Case: A Global Dimension' (pp. 67–72), 'Jarndyce Versus Jennens' (pp. 73–81), and 'The Final Mystery: The Tale of the Two Williams' (pp. 82–106). The tenth chapter will likely be of most interest to Dickensians as it closely examines affinities between the real-life case and the fictional one represented by Dickens, though differences are clearly noted. In *Walk With Me Charles Dickens* John Costella endeavours to track the walks Dickens would have made around London, using an 1863 street map. In each of his ten walks—through 'The Strand' (pp. 1–32), 'Holborn' (pp. 33–60), 'Southwark' (pp. 63–91), 'Somers Town & St Pancreas' (pp. 93–117), 'Bloomsbury' (pp. 119–50), 'Marylebone (City of Westminster)' (pp. 153–79), 'Chelsea—Knightsbridge—Brompton' (pp. 181–213), 'Clerkenwell' (pp. 215–36), 'Camden Town' (pp. 239–65), and 'Whitechapel & Spitalfields' (pp. 267–98)—Costella hypothesizes how Dickens would have reacted to momentous urban change and social and environmental upheavals. Costella's own pen-and-ink illustrations supplement the text and the author has included a reflective epilogue (pp. 299–301) and a valuable index (pp. 303–10).

A number of 2014 essay collections focus on Dickens's life and work. After the bicentenary celebrations and events, critics began to ponder the reasons behind Dickens's commercial and popular appeal in the twenty-first century. For example, Dickens's links to the modern world were surveyed in the excellent 2012 collection *Dickens and Modernity*, edited by Juliet John. This year, the fascinating two-volume *Charles Dickens, Modernism, Modernity*, edited by Christine Huguet and Nathalie Vanfasse and inspired by 'an all-English Dickens Conference at the château de Cerisy-la-Salle in . . . 2011' (p. 9) contributes to this ongoing project. Volume 1 is split into two sections: 'Urban Modernity' (pp. 45–120) and 'Modernity in/and Motion' (pp. 121–230). An excellent introduction, 'Dickens and the "Wine of Life"' (pp. 19–44) by Huguet and Vanfasse examines Dickens through the lens of the concept of 'modernity', as defined by critics including Charles Baudelaire and Walter Benjamin. In 'Charles Dickens Citoyen de Paris' (pp. 47–69) Michael Hollington's subject is 'the legibility of the city' (p. 48) and he uses Dickens's letters in order to detail 'how intensively and wholeheartedly [Dickens] threw himself into understanding and describing foreign places' (p. 67). One of this chapter's main concerns is to show how Dickens narrates or makes legible an environment which is vast and disorienting and, in this sense, Hollington here expands upon his other studies on Dickens and Europe, which include the many 2014 essays reviewed below, the two-volume edited collection *The Reception of Charles Dickens in Europe* [2013], reviewed above, and *Dickens and Italy: Little Dorrit and Pictures from Italy* [2009], co-edited with Francesca Orestano.

Orestano provides the second essay in volume 1 of *Charles Dickens, Modernism, Modernity*: in 'Two Londoners: Charles Dickens and Virginia Woolf' (pp. 71–93), Orestano states that there has been no sustained analysis of the biographical and literary links between Dickens and Woolf, largely because they are perceived to be polar opposites. Dickens is often described as an entertainer who excels in portraying external realities while Woolf is categorized as a literary modernist who privileges individuality and deep psychological insight. Orestano begins to dismantle tenacious but highly unstable dichotomies (between Dickens and Woolf and, more generally, between Victorianism and modernism) by exploring 'the relationship between two great writers...who were both inspired by London' in ways that show 'the modern mind responding to the...metropolis' (p. 71). In the next chapter, Juliet John provides an insight into 'Longing and the Dickensian City: Place, Popularity and the Past' (pp. 95–120). Spanning the fields of ecocriticism and cultural theory, this is a fascinating account of Dickens's longevity, which 'offers some first reflections on the relationship between Dickens's urban modernity and his popularity, and on the interplay between place and enduring literary appeal' (p. 96). John recognizes that, in Dickens, 'Nature' is often 'man-made Nature' (p. 96); the fog in *Bleak House*, for example, is not a Romantic or natural phenomenon *per se*. With reference to this slippage between 'Nature' and artificiality, John concludes that 'there is after all a kind of organicism in Dickens's writing which co-exists with, and responds to, dislocated representations of urban modernity; it is the interplay of both that informs Dickens's enduring imaginative appeal' (p. 111).

The second section of volume 1 begins with Robert L. Patten's excellent 'Internationalising Dickens: *Little Dorrit* Reconsidered' (pp. 123–50). Shifting the focus away from biographical readings, Patten concentrates on four metaphors that run throughout *Little Dorrit* like a leitmotif—'Sun and shadow...imprisonment...voyaging across distances and climbing upwards and downwards' (pp. 133–4)—with a view to assessing how 'Dickens write[s] Britain all over his known Continent' (p. 133). For Patten, Dickens draws attention to the ways in which the Continent both mirrors *and* diverts from British culture: indeed, 'while Dickens saw Europe through a provincial English lens, he saw...developments of immense European significance' (p. 130). In this sense, *Little Dorrit* can be considered Dickens's modern, international novel par excellence. While Patten details the ways in which Dickens uses foreign locations in his fiction, Vladimir Trendafilov's 'Charles Dickens and Some Urban Legends in Twentieth-Century Bulgaria' (pp. 151–66) looks into how Bulgaria has used or appropriated Dickens. As Trendafilov demonstrates, though Dickens was rarely read in Bulgaria during this period, his image was used as a way to domesticate a foreign celebrity: it was used symbolically, for instance, in surprising places, such as in articles concerned with the supernatural. The next two chapters are, in different ways, concerned with the subject of emotion in relation to Dickens and to modern experience. In 'Mobility and Modernity: Reading *Barnaby Rudge*' (pp. 167–85) Wendy Parkins speculates on the potential responses of two Victorian readers of *Barnaby Rudge* (the working-class Jane Burden and the middle-class William Morris), who were 'Positioned differently in their...relation to the social and economic processes of modernity' (p. 183). She uses these speculations to 'consider how *Barnaby Rudge* evokes varying emotional or affective responses and how such responses may illuminate—or complicate—our interpretation of the text today (p. 169). Signalling a return in Dickens criticism to the dynamism of reader's experience (see, for example, Holly Furneaux's chapter in *Reflections on/of Dickens*, reviewed below), Parkins's essay unearths the ambiguity within modern life and warns 'against assuming a singular or stable reading position, then or now, that could explain away the feeling of reading *Barnaby Rudge*' (p. 183). Gillian Piggott writes on 'Dickens and Chaplin: "The Tramp"' (pp. 187–210). Dickens and Chaplin present two different versions of the tramp. There is the roguish performer or fake who plays on the nativity of the civilized and there is the Romantic tramp who has 'a simplicity of thought and action...that is simultaneously comic and refreshing' (p. 203). By reading Dickens and Chaplin through the lens of both of these versions, 'one can not only identify a great affinity between the two artists, but one can get a sense of the affective and the theatrical contours of city life, and of the act of walking itself' (p. 191). Concluding volume 1 of this collection is Andrew Ballantyne's illustrated 'Dingley Dell: *Pickwick Papers*' Lieu de Mémoire' (pp. 211–30), an account of how nostalgia figures into Dickens's writings. For Ballantyne, Dickens's 'nostalgia was far from being behind-the-times, but...was a harbinger of things to come' (p. 229). Concentrating mainly on Dingley Dell as a place through which old-fashionedness is filtered, Ballantyne states that the 'thing to realise with *Pickwick Papers*' nostalgia and affection with the old-fashioned are that they are symptoms of an awareness of loss...And the change that causes the loss is the change that ushers in modernity. Nostalgia is therefore a symptom of modernity' (p. 226).

Volume 2 of *Charles Dickens, Modernism and Modernity* is composed of four sections: 'The Life of Things' (pp. 9–60), 'Dickens the Thinker' (pp. 61–118), 'Mysteries of the Self' (pp. 119–205), and 'Towards a Modernist Aesthetic?' (pp. 207–63). This volume opens with 'The Topicality of Sketches by Boz' (pp. 11–28) by Paul Schlicke and William F. Long, which shows that 'Dickens's early sketches...were saturated in topical detail, some...instantly recognisable, others...virtually incomprehensible today' (p. 12). Schlicke and Long are particularly strong on Dickens's editorial practice; they identify what the author altered or left out when the sketches were collected together to form *Sketches by Boz* [1836] and note how these alterations impact on meaning. Save for the small error—a 'character named Barnett...whose amputated hand grows back from salamander cells' (p. 13) appears in *The X Files* and not *The X Factor* as stated!—this is a fine opening to the second volume. It exemplifies a renewed focus on Dickens's early texts as critics perceive in them socio-political and reformist significance (see also, for example, essays by David Parker and Galia Benziman in *Dickens Studies Annual*, reviewed below). Next is David Ellison's 'The Ends of Privacy: Dickens, Strange, Collins' (pp. 29–47). This chapter 'consider[s] a number of fictional and non-fictional accounts of privacy *in situ*, of activities unfolding within the notionally protective walls of home' (p. 29). Focusing mainly on *Oliver Twist*, William Strange's controversial *A Descriptive Catalogue of the Royal Victorian and Albert Gallery of Etchings* and Wilkie Collins's neglected *The Law and the Lady* [1875], Ellison goes on to illustrate the various (and unexpected) ways in which privacy can be breached. Unusually, this study refuses to see Oliver as a purely positive or innocent figure. As Ellison argues, he represents a kind of all-seeing force that poses a threat to privacy; indeed, privacy is systematically 'annihilated around Oliver' (p. 36), even when he is not fully awake or conscious. Shifting the focus somewhat in the following chapter, Holly Furneaux continues her excellent work on non-normative (erotic) desire and bonding within Dickens's oeuvre in a study entitled 'Dickens, Sexuality and the Body or, Clock Loving: Master Humphrey's

Queer Objects of Desire' (pp. 47–60). Refreshingly, Furneaux concentrates on one of Dickens's most neglected texts—*Master Humphrey's Clock* [1840–1]— in order to unveil the author's deep-rooted interest in 'the imaginative, emotional and erotic appeal of objects' (p. 47).

Part II, 'Dickens the Thinker', begins with John Bowen's engaging '"The Philosophy of the Thubject": *Hard Times* and the Reasoning Animal' (pp. 63–83). Avoiding 'an essentially self-limiting "historicist" mode' (p. 64), Bowen goes on to show that, in *Hard Times*, 'Both philosophy and animals matter for many reasons, not least because they help us think about the limits of rationality and the "human," in ways that cannot simply be dismissed as "irrationalism" or "anti-humanism"' (p. 66). While critics such as Terry Eagleton have highlighted Dickens's anti-industrial stance in this text, Bowen goes further in his close readings, demonstrating that Dickens was a greater philosopher than traditional criticism would have us believe. Similarly, Lawrence Frank's 'The French Gentleman's Grin: Allusion, Intellectual History, and Narratography in *Our Mutual Friend*' (pp. 85–102) illuminates 'Dickens the thinker' by signposting polyphony in the fiction. Frank seeks to unveil '*how* [Dickens] thought: *how* he intellectually and imaginatively engaged in his novels with Victorian cosmology, psychology, and biology' (p. 85) when staging the tensions between plot and allusion. 'Dickens and the Voices of History' (pp. 103–18), by David Paroissien, turns to a marginal text—*A Child's History of England* [1851–3]—in order to reveal the ways in which Dickens asks his readers to take history seriously. In this text, Dickens ponders questions surrounding power structures, the nature of war, and the monarchy—subjects which render *A Child's History of England* far from politically insignificant or conceptually weak. As Paroissien argues: 'The sad and doleful tales told in *A Child's History of England* reveal a more complicated story than critics have been willing to concede and one that deserves telling (p. 117).

The third part, 'Mysteries of the Self', opens with 'Dickens and the Exploding World: Self and Others in *Great Expectations*' (pp. 121–36), Dominic Rainsford's account of ethical conundrums within Dickens's fiction. For Rainsford, Dickens's 'fictional worlds have room for many different positions, and tend to suggest that it is hopeless to look for any ultimate framework or boundaries for human knowledge and action' (p. 123). In this sense, Dickens relates to topical debates about the expanded or 'exploded' global present and the reach of social and moral responsibility. In 'Dickens and the Post-Modern Self: Fragmentation, Authority and Death' (pp. 137–51) Natalie McKnight argues that Dickens's take on identity is postmodern 'because he frequently underscores the fragmentation, dividedness and incoherence of the self' (p. 137). McKnight implicitly refutes claims that Dickens's characters are one-dimensional; instead, they vivify instabilities and forms of consciousness that depart from everyday experience. Like McKnight, Adina Ciugureanu is interested in liminal psychologies in 'Mania and Melancholia in *David Copperfield*: Dora Spenlow and Uriah Heep' (pp. 153–70). Here, Dickens's tendency to focus on symptoms of insanity is assessed through an analysis of some of the minor characters in *David Copperfield* and *Great Expectations*. In 'Dickens and the Jews / the Jews and

Dickens: The Instability of Identity' (pp. 171–90) Murray Baumgarten describes reversals of Jewish stereotypes in *Our Mutual Friend* and assesses Dickens's place within the history of British literary antisemitism. 'The difficulties Dickens encountered in fashioning Riah . . . indicate the problems he faced in attempting to narrate a Jewish character . . . a figure outside the dominant, hegemonic discourse' Baumgarten suggests. Michal Peled Ginsburg's 'Plotting (in) *Barnaby Rudge*' (pp. 191–205) follows. Focusing on the relationship between fathers and sons, Ginsburg argues that '*Barnaby Rudge* emerges as an unparalleled move away from the plot structure exemplified by *Oliver Twist*' (pp. 192–3) partly because it is the 'least conservative of Dickens's novels' (p. 193). *Barnaby Rudge* sacrifices easy oppositions between good and bad in favour of 'a dynamic of contamination that renders impossible intact innocence and just restoration' (p. 193).

Part IV, 'Towards a Modernist Aesthetic?', begins with 'Dickens and Ambiguity: The Case of *A Tale of Two Cities*' (pp. 209–28) by Matthias Bauer and Angelika Zirker, which suggests that ambiguity 'becomes an appropriate response to an increasingly complex world' (p. 209). In *A Tale of Two Cities* the stylistic device of ambiguity is 'used to criticise the world, to show ways of surviving in it and to suggest, by presenting and inviting constant revaluations of meaning, ways in which an ethical stance may be assumed' (p. 226). With 'Human, Animal, Vegetable, or Mineral? Crossovers between Organic and Inorganic Matter in *Our Mutual Friend*' (pp. 229–47) Valerie Kennedy 'explore[s] some of the most important metaphorical crossovers between the human and the non-human (animal, vegetable, or mineral), and the living and the dead in *Our Mutual Friend*' (p. 230). Concentrating on the novel's first two chapters, Kennedy shows that Dickens constructs two opposing worlds through different types of allusions and metaphors. However, both chapters are said to 'evoke contemporary evolutionary theories and especially the struggle for existence and the survival of the fittest' (p. 244). The last chapter, 'Narrative Closure in *David Copperfield* and *Bleak House*' (pp. 249–63), sees John O. Jordan draw on his excellent monograph *Supposing Bleak House* [2011] in order to argue that 'the endings of [Dickens's] novels are never simple or straightforward, and . . . remain multiple and often ambiguous' (p. 262). Dickens's novels contain multiple endings (the final monthly number, the last illustration, the author's preface, and so on) which can either be read separately or as a whole. This multivalence undercuts attempts to pin down the politics of Dickens's so-called 'happy endings' and leads to a more nuanced understanding of serialization as a publication practice and storytelling strategy.

Another 2014 collection is *Texts, Contexts and Intertextuality: Dickens as a Reader*, edited by Norbert Lennartz and Dieter Koch. Despite its title, this collection largely eschews poststructuralist terminology and abstract theories in order to detail how Dickens's originality lies in his ability to self-consciously borrow from a number of historical materials and art forms. Lennartz details in his introduction, 'Dickens as a Voracious Reader' (pp. 9–16), that 'in all of his novels [Dickens] was eager to draw upon a rich literary and scientific history to make his readers alert to the enormous extent to which his individual talent was embedded in various, mutually inspiring traditions'

(p. 11). One of this book's main strengths is its recognition of the presence of both 'high' and 'low' cultural elements within Dickens's oeuvre. This recognition adds considerable weight to the idea that Dickens was a 'voracious reader' who disregarded cultural hierarchies as a point of ideological principle. For example, Matthias Bauer's opening chapter, 'Dickens and Sir Philip Sidney: Desire, Ethics, and Poetics' (pp. 21–38), can be usefully contrasted with Michael Hollington's second chapter, 'Dickens and the Commedia dell'Arte' (pp. 39–65). While Bauer identifies correlations between Dickens and Sidney throughout his three subsections—'Astrophil and Pip' (pp. 22–5), 'The Sidney Myth' (pp. 25–34), and 'A Poetological Point of Reference' (pp. 34–6)—Hollington explores Dickens's 'passionate commitment to the preservation and dissemination of traditions of popular culture' (p. 42). Although this commitment has been the subject of various full-length studies, this essay is unusual in that it focuses on the French theatrical context (as opposed to British melodrama and pantomime, for example). 'Dickens's fiction has much in common with the *commedia* as a tradition of deeply physical as well as verbal comedy, in which bodily gestures and exploits (*lazzi*) are at least equally essential as vehicles of signification as facial expressions, and violence and even cruelty a regular component of the repertoire of tricks to induce laughter' (pp. 42–3). This oscillation between 'elite' and 'popular' art recurs throughout the collection. Chapter 3 is Wolfgang G. Müller's 'Mr. Pickwick—a New Quixote? Charles Dickens's First Novel in the Tradition of Cervantes' (pp. 67–83). This chapter contains four illustrations and is made up of eight small sections which neatly sum up Müller's area of interest: the connections between *The Pickwick Papers* and *Don Quixote* [1605]. These subsections are: 'A Note on the Cervantes and the Cervantes Tradition' (pp. 67–9), 'Elements in Don Quixote Contributing to Creating a Tradition' (pp. 69–70), 'The Quixotic Tradition before Dickens' (pp. 70–2), 'Quixotic and Not Picaresque' (pp. 72–3), 'From Real to Metaphorical Armour' (pp. 73–8), 'Master and Servant' (p. 78), 'Proverb and Exemplum' (pp. 78–91), and 'Dickens's Reinvention of the Quixotic Novel as a Comic Work' (pp. 81–2). Chapter 4 is similarly concerned with Dickens's links to Cervantes. Paul Vita's 'Conversation and the Comic Novel: *Don Quixote* and *The Pickwick Papers*' (pp. 85–98) is 'interested in comparing the invented dialogues...that contribute to the artistry, significance, and popularity of *Don Quixote* and *The Pickwick Papers*' (p. 85). Vita largely bypasses descriptive passages and Dickens's narrative interjections in order to closely analyse what the *characters* say. In using this method, he is able to demonstrate that both Cervantes and Dickens 'engage in representing through conversations human behaviour and contemporary social realities, rife with economic disparities and class divisions' (p. 86). Like Müller, Vita is partly interested in the master–servant bonds portrayed in *The Pickwick Papers* and in *Don Quixote*: he recognizes that, though characters such as Sam Weller entertain, their words often provide a moral or socio-political judgement.

Chapter 5, Isabel Vila Cabanes's 'Reading the Grotesque in the Works of Charles Dickens and Jonathan Swift' (pp. 99–113), aims to prove that 'Dickens, as an avid reader of Swift, often draws inspiration from Swift in the many grotesque passages of his oeuvre' (p. 99). After defining the grotesque as a multivalent aesthetic category, Vila Cabanes explains that she will focus on three main characteristics: 'the conflict of the comic and the fearful, the estrangement from the familiar world and the use of literary devices which help to create or highlight the grotesque image' (p. 100). She then launches into 'an examination of Dickens's relationship with Swift, by looking at instances of the grotesque in his works' *The Pickwick Papers* [1836], *Oliver Twist* [1838], *American Notes* [1842], *Martin Chuzzlewit* [1843–4], and *Hard Times* [1854], which evince certain affinities with Swift's *Gulliver's Travels* [1726] and 'A Modest Proposal' [1729] (p. 99). Chapter 6, Dieter Koch's 'Dickens and the Tradition of the British Picaresque: Smollet, Dickens and Chance' (pp. 115–27), addresses genre studies and asks to what extent we can fit Dickens into the capacious picaresque tradition. Provided throughout are clarifications and definitions which seek to capture the most important elements of this fictional mode. Ending this section, George Letissier's 'Reading Postmodernity into *Our Mutual Friend*: The World as Text and the Redemption of Reading' (pp. 129–43) is made up of three subsections—'The Experience of Reading Demeaned (pp. 131–5), 'The World as Text—the Vacuity of the Real' (pp. 135–40), and 'The Redemption of Reading (pp. 140–2)—which prove that Dickens's last completed novel is 'concerned with the production of meaning as much as with telling a story' (p. 129). According to Letissier, *Our Mutual Friend* also 'bears witness to a world in which signs and meretricious social protocols are increasingly replacing any direct access to the tangible real' (p. 129).

The next section, 'Dickens as a Reader of Contemporary Literature', begins with Rolf Lessenich's 'Edward Bulwer-Lytton as a Reader of Charles Dickens' (pp. 147–61), which details affinities and differences between two popular authors. Bulwer-Lytton and Dickens were clearly inspired by the same art forms. For example, in their novels, both writers mix popular (theatrical) culture (most obviously melodrama) 'with sombre socio-historical facts' (p. 155) in order to create texts that both entertain and instruct. 'Paradoxically [though], with the warming of friendship between Bulwer and Dickens, the world views of their novels actually diverged more and more' as Dickens became a 'sceptical realist' and Bulwer-Lytton regressed 'to romance and the caring aristocratic conservatism of the Middle Ages' (p. 159). The next chapter is Angelika Zirker's '"To be Taken with a Grain of Salt": Charles Dickens and the Ambiguous Ghost Story' (pp. 163–80). Zirker argues that, in his 1865 Christmas story, 'Dickens outwardly followed the tradition of writing a ghost story ... but at the same time modified the effect of the story by making it ambiguous' (p. 164). Thus, in 'To be Taken with a Grain of Salt', it is clear to Zirker that 'Dickens's focus is not primarily on ghosts but on the creation of an overall ambiguous story' (p. 164). With 'A "Comrade and Friend": The Cultural Work of Charles Dickens's Periodicals' (pp. 181–98), Barbara Korte indicates that Dickens's magazines 'represented their readers' culture for them, voiced their anxieties and desires, and contributed to the formation of the mid-Victorian self' (p. 184). The eclectic mix of the magazines helped in this process: dark pieces were countered by humorous ones and social commentary shared a space with fanciful treatments of urban life. Saverio Tomaiuolo's '"A Pretty Fair Scholar in Dust": Recycling the Sensation Novel in *Our Mutual*

Friend' (pp. 199–213) investigates 'the 'mutual' intertextual dialogue between Dickens and sensationalism, and then... approach[es] *Our Mutual Friend* as a meta-literary reflection on novel writing and plot making' (p. 200). Relying on a central metaphor in the novel, Tomaiuolo describes *Our Mutual Friend* as a text that transforms or 'recycle[s] 'trashy' or 'discarded' sensational pieces, turning them into great works of art' (p. 200). Paul Morris's '*Oliver Twist*, the Perils of Child Identity and the Emergence of the Victorian Child' (pp. 215–31) is an engaging account of the history of the concept of childhood, one which recognizes but complicates the received idea of the innocent Dickensian child. Indeed, Dickens's child characters, notably Oliver, are 'individually shaped— often victimised—by their social environment' (p. 230) in a way that the innocent Romantic child is not.

The final section of this collection, 'Dickens and Non-Fiction', opens with Maria Teresa Chialant's 'Physiognomy, Phrenology and Mesmerism: Dickens and the (Pseudo-)Scientific Discourse' (pp. 235–48). Chialant explores Dickens's knowledge of scientific fields in order to unearth 'to what extent he was familiar with related current literature' (p. 236). She then identifies 'the traces of their influence in his private life, [focusing] on the way he re-used his reading in his own texts' (p. 236). Of concern here are the ways in which weighty topics were made accessible via the medium of fiction. In relation to mesmerism in particular, Chialant concludes that 'Dickens's knowledge and practice of mesmerism... belonged to a period in which the scientific understanding of the phenomena... began to diffuse into popular forms' (p. 246). In '"Animal Spirits: How Human Psychology Drives the Economy"': Dickens as Reader of Victorian Economic Theory?' (pp. 249–62), Nathalie Vanfasse notes that she will 'first study the novelist as a possible reader of Victorian economic theory before showing that his writing can provide a state-of-the-art reader in recent behavioural economics' (p. 249), which dictates that cognitive and emotional factors play a role in economic decisions. Vanfasse here echoes a sentiment that is set out in Aeron Hunt's chapter on Dickens in *Personal Business*: *Character and Commerce in Victorian Literature and Culture* (reviewed below): while Dickens's novels 'may well be fiction... this fiction tells us more than many economic textbooks about how the economy really works' (p. 260). This penultimate chapter on Dickens's economic perceptiveness gives way to the collection's final chapter, Francesca Orestano's fascinating 'Against Reading: Dickens and the Visual Arts' (pp. 263–81), which starts by explicating an apparent gap in Dickens's knowledge. Turning to the visual arts, Orestano pinpoints reasons why Dickens might have refused to be seen as a connoisseur of art, including 'the inherited cultural suspicion aroused by Catholic religious paintings' (p. 265). One particularly convincing explanation is that Dickens recognized issues surrounding reliable expression—he was aware of 'the gap between picture and word, between the truth of visual perception and the language used to encode what is seen' (p. 270). In other words, Dickens seems to grasp issues that would later become a major preoccupation for poststructuralist critics.

Reflections on/of Dickens, edited by Ewa Kujawska-Lis and Anna Krawczyk-Łaskarzewska, is 'inspired by... an event that gathered Dickens researchers and enthusiasts from all over the world at the University of

Warmia and Mazury in Olsztyn, in April 2013' (p. 1). This diverse study seeks to bridge 'the gap between traditional textual analysis and more contextualised readings of the writer's literary output' (p. 1). Part I is entitled 'There is Something Outside the Text' (pp. 5–50). The first chapter is overwhelmingly concerned with historical context and the pressure it exerts on literary texts: Zygmunt Stefan Zalewski's 'Victorian England in the Days of Charles Dickens' (pp. 6–17) surveys the cultural, economic, and socio-political shifts that influenced Dickens's writings. In 'Dickens's "Young Men," *Household Words* and the Development of the Victorian "Special Correspondent"' (pp. 18–31), Catherine Waters argues that '*Household Words* was innovative, combining cheapness of form and price with the serialisation of original fiction, poetry and informational articles on a wide range of topics' (p. 18). She proceeds to reveal that 'a dimension of this newness has not yet received sufficient critical attention...namely, its role in the development of the Victorian special correspondent' (p. 18). Like John Bowen's chapter in *Charles Dickens, Modernism, Modernity*, chapters 3 and 4 of *Reflections on/of Dickens* are concerned with *Hard Times* and Dickens's philosophical standpoint. In 'What Can a Political Philosopher Learn from *Hard Times*?' (pp. 32–41), Agnieszka Czarnecka argues that '*Hard Times* makes us aware of an ancient truth according to which literature is linked with political philosophy' (p. 40). Jacek Mydla reveals, in 'The Utility of Poetry? Rhetoric in Dickens's Quarrel with Utilitarian Philosophers' (pp. 42–50), that 'Dickens the philosopher' (p. 43) plainly illuminates the actions of those who subscribe to utilitarian ideas in order to concretize the abstract. As a method of reacting against utilitarianism, Dickens 'turns *Hard Times* into a circus, eager to demonstrate that language can be freed from its "utilitarian" bondage to encyclopaedic or factual knowledge' (p. 40).

  Part II of the collection, entitled '...And Inside the Text' (pp. 51–92), focuses exclusively on Dickens's short fiction, especially the railway stories, and begins with Wolfgang G. Müller's brilliant 'Innovative Aspects in Dickens's Short Fiction' (pp. 52–66), which posits that 'when we wish to encounter Dickens the innovator we have to look at his short fiction' (p. 53). Müller argues that, in 'Mrs Lirriper's Lodgings' [1863] and 'Mrs Lirriper's Legacy' [1864], Lirriper's 'monologues anticipate elements of the stream-of-consciousness technique, and they belong to the very first examples of you-narration' (p. 63)—that is, 'a kind of narration which is defined by the persistent address of the narrative to an indeterminate "you"' (p. 54). Müller suggests that in 'The Signalman' [1866], Dickens uses 'the ghost story to criticise technological process and its consequences [in a way that] shows superb originality and craftsmanship. The story has a profound ethical substance which is encapsulated in its narrative form' (p. 64). Aesthetically and stylistically then, in his shorter fiction Dickens foregrounds the individual's complex psychological processes—a technique that prefigures the rise of modernism. In 'Coincidence and Causality in "The Signalman" and "The Trial for Murder"' (pp. 67–76) Sławomir Studniarz is similarly interested in Dickens's supernatural tales. According to Studniarz, although both stories feature 'the supernatural in their plot, "The Signalman" and "The Trial for Murder" appear to be wildly divergent...in their respective treatment of the spectral manifestations' (p. 68). For example, 'in "The Signalman" the framework of coincidence is invoked in order to rationalize the sequence of events and thus make them plausible... In "The Trial for Murder" the opposite is at work—the narrator establishes his credentials and his authority early on and the supernatural is never questioned' (p. 76). In 'Redefining Identity through Railway Imagery in "Mugby Junction"' Bożena Depa's objective 'is to investigate Dickens's reworking of the railway motif as a plot device and an organizing principle' (p. 78). It is concluded that 'Dickens succeeds in capturing the hero's psychology through the medium of railway imagery corresponding well with the protagonist's inner dilemmas' (p. 83). At the end of this part, 'Sense of Duty and Sense Deception in Dickens's and Grabiński's Railway Stories' by Małgorzata Nitka assesses how both Dickens and Stefan Grabiński use socio-political and geographical landscapes within their popular railway stories.

Part III, 'Playing with Characters and Themes' (pp. 93–135), ranges from 'Victorian food studies to queer and gender studies' (p. 2) and begins with Anna Grabowska '"A good, contented, well-breakfasted Juryman is a capital thing to get hold of": What Was Eaten for Breakfast in Charles Dickens's Prose' (pp. 94–103). Taking social class and gender issues into account, Grabowska illustrates that 'Dickensian breakfasts are interesting to readers but not only as a backdrop against which the events of the novels take place... the food in Charles Dickens's prose... not only nourishes the characters who eat it, but it also enriches our understanding of these characters' (p. 102). To take one example, immoral characters such as Sir Mulberry Hawk and Lord Verisopht in *Nicholas Nickleby* have breakfast as late as three o'clock in the afternoon—a time which indicates their antisocial or 'negative characters' (p. 95). *Nicholas Nickleby* is the main subject of chapter 10, Marlena Marciniak's 'New Man: *Nicholas Nickleby* as an Example of the Changing Notions of Victorian Masculinity' (pp. 104–12), which considers representations of the nineteenth-century gentleman. She argues that the character of 'Nicholas Nickleby reflects the... redefinition of the concept of masculinity from the stereotypical patriarchal image to a more androgynous model, blending features habitually ascribed to women, such as care-giving, self-sacrifice or sentimentality' (p. 111). For Marciniak, this redefinition signals a potential shift in public attitude at the beginning of the Victorian period: 'The initial success of Dickens's book... may serve as evidence that the Victorians were preparing for a significant reconceptualisation of traditional gender roles' (p. 111). Chapter 11, Aleksandra Kędzierska's 'Pardon for Jacob Marley' (pp. 113–20), shifts the focus onto a character in *A Christmas Carol* who has, for some time, been overshadowed by Scrooge. According to Kędzierska, who assesses 'the confrontation between Marley and Scrooge' (p. 114), 'Marley emerges not only as the true hero of the *Carol* and promoter of Christmas philosophy, but simultaneously one who... has earned and been granted his pardon' (p. 119). Holly Furneaux's excellent '(Re)writing Dickens Queerly: The Correspondence of Katherine Mansfield' (pp. 121–35) follows. Furneaux notes that, in her letters, Mansfield often blurs the boundaries between fiction and reality, identifying 'with a surprising group of Dickens figures: the awkward, the ill, those who resist their positions within their

THE VICTORIAN PERIOD (1830–1900) 861

families' (p. 121). At times, 'reading Dickens was clearly a soothing experience...More often, though, Mansfield references Dickens in order to express feelings of disconnection' (p. 129). For example, by referencing characters such as Mrs Jellyby and Mrs Wilfer, 'Mansfield is able to mobilize Dickens's less likeable figures to assert a sense of identity not based on, indeed at variance with, domestic bliss' (p. 133). Here we discern that, by experiencing a sort of affinity with fictional characters, good or bad, readers are able to make sense of their positioning outside dominant social categories. This phenomenon has not passed in the modern age: as Furneaux details at the end of her study, 'slash fiction and web mashups' (p. 133) provide a space through which minority groups can assert a sense of authority, belonging, and identity, as writers and commenters read homoerotic or non-normative undercurrents into adaptations.

Part IV, entitled 'Intertextual Games' (pp. 137–205), is a comparative section which opens with 'Genre Peculiarity of Dickens's and Nekrasov's Sketches (Comparative Approach)' (pp. 138–45) by Olga Bondaruk. Bondaruk 'trace[s] the thematic and genre peculiarities of Dickens's sketches both within English literature and in comparison with the sketch work of [Nikolay] Nekrasov, the representative of the "natural school" of Russian realism' (p. 138). The Russian realist and Dickens both have an 'aspiration for an authentic description of plain reality' and both make 'use of factual material' (p. 144). However, *Sketches by Boz* also differs from *Physiology of Petersburg* [1845] in its 'moralizing and educational reverberations' (p. 144). The links between Dickens and non-British writers are further explored in Barbara Kowalik's 'Dickens and Prus: A Comparison of *Great Expectations* and "The Sins of Childhood"' (pp. 146–56). Kowalik 'traces the striking parallels between "Grzechy dzieciństwa," a masterpiece of [Bolesław] Prus's short fiction, translated into English by Bill Johnston as "The Sins of Childhood," and Dickens's *Great Expectations*' (p. 146). Though Kowalik admits that it is difficult to determine whether or not the Polish writer self-consciously includes Dickensian aspects within his work, her chapter contains three tables which neatly summarize confluences between the texts under discussion. M.D. Allen's 'George Gissing's *Workers in the Dawn* as a Dickensian Novel' (pp. 157–66) proves that 'Gissing, the first great Dickensian never to have known his predecessor, was steeped in Dickens's novels' (p. 158). Gissing's *Workers in the Dawn* [1880] is assessed alongside *Dombey and Son* and *Bleak House* because the characters within these texts experience similar emotional and financial hardships. Gissing clearly harnesses Dickens's tendency to focus on 'poverty...prostitution and alcoholism' (p. 164). Yet, Gissing's 'indignant and uncompromising tone is his own' (p. 164).

Chapter 16 is Ewa Kujawska-Lis's 'Fathers, Daughters, Sons and Prisons: *Little Dorrit* as the Inspiration for Conrad's *Chance*' (pp. 167–81), in which Dickens's links to 'a forerunner of Modernism' (p. 167) are observed. Like all of the comparative studies in this section, both similarities and diversions are lucidly signposted: while Dickens and Conrad are concerned with the metaphor of (class) imprisonment, for example, and with 'pathological father–daughter relationship[s]' (p. 175), Conrad was also capable of expanding upon Dickens's aesthetic and structural frameworks. For Kujawska-Lis, Conrad is much more preoccupied with 'the psychology of behaviour' and 'social and domestic determinants for an individual's behaviour' (p. 180). Next, Halszka Leleń writes on 'Post-Dickensian Style of Literary Portraiture in the Mimetic Fiction of "a Nawther" H.G. Wells' (pp. 182–94). Noting connections and differences between the characters drawn by Dickens and Wells, Leleń argues that 'The applauded mimetic fiction of H.G. Wells follows in the footsteps of the early writings of Dickens. The very observatory properties of *Sketches by Boz* [1836] are applied by Wells in *The History of Mr. Polly* [1910] and *Kipps* [1905] as well as in other novels and many short stories' (p. 183). Chapter 17 is Aniela Korzeniowska's '*A Christmas Carol* and Its (In)visible Polish Translators' (pp. 195–205). This study 'shows a selected sample of the story's appearance in Poland from the year 1900, illustrating the visibility or invisibility of the given translator, primarily from the point of view of publishing policy' (p. 196). Constituting an important insight into the global reach of *A Christmas Carol* and its adaptations or translations, this chapter will interest those concerned with 'the ethics of translation, publishing policy, and the politics of the times' (p. 203).

The fifth part, 'Intertextual Games Extended—Appropriations', contains many items of interest, including Maria Teresa Chialant's 'Dickens, the Antipodes and the Neo-Victorian Novel: Richard Flanagan's *Wanting*' (pp. 208–21). Though the 'Australia mentioned by the narrators [of Victorian novels] remains outside the texts' (p. 209), the neo-Victorian novel *Wanting* [2008] contains a 'Tasmania plot, consisting of seven chapters, [which] spans the years 1839–49, and [a] London plot, of six chapters, [set in] the 1850s' (p. 212). These plots 'speak to each other . . . and tell two different stories of desire and denial which interact with one another' (p. 212). For Chialant, *Wanting* 'is part of a general critical reassessment of Dickens's work, with the purpose of considering the "other" Dickens: namely, those aspects of his life and work that have been the subject of recent revision, reappraisal, and transformation in contemporary culture' (p. 217). Chapter 20, Barbara Klonowska's '*Great Expectations* a Hundred and Fifty Years Later: Strategies of Appropriation' (pp. 222–34), is a theoretically rigorous work which distinguishes between terms such as 'transposition', 'rewriting', and 'hybridization' in order to explore 'literary techniques aimed at a rejuvenation and readjustment of the canon' (p. 223). Throughout this chapter, Klonowska lucidly argues that appropriations of *Great Expectations*, such as John Fowles's *The Collector* [1963], Peter Carey's *Jack Maggs* [1997], and Lloyd Jones's *Mister Pip* [2006], 'engage with the canonical text, stretching its boundaries to include new ideas' (p. 223). The reinterpretation of Dickens is also the subject of the following chapter. In '"Dickens is one of those authors who are well worth stealing": Evelyn Waugh's *A Handful of Dust* and the Reworking of Dickens' (pp. 235–42) Roksana Zgierska suggests that the allusions to *Little Dorrit*, *Dombey and Son*, *Martin Chuzzlewit*, and *Bleak House* in Waugh's *A Handful of Dust* [1934] 'may actually be seen as the reinterpretation of Dickens's prose' (p. 235). She then claims that 'Dickens is so strongly incorporated into the literary tradition that references to his works provide writers with unlimited possibilities' (p. 241). In particular, Waugh uses Dickens as an avenue into 'highlighting... the criticism of society' and as a way to 'touch upon the topic of how ineffective literature may be in influencing people' (p. 241).

The sixth and final part of *Reflections on/of Dickens*, 'Performing Within and Visualizing Texts' (pp. 243–348), 'focuses on selected visual interpretations and performances of Dickens's novels and characters as well as performances *within* them' (p. 3). Paul Vita's engaging '"Indignation Taking the Form of Nuts": A Reading of Dickens's Audiences' (pp. 244–56), seeks to take a 'closer look at Dickens's representation of his public, especially the rowdy, uncontrollable, and critical audiences in his novels and non-fiction journalism' (p. 244). Focusing on novels as well as on more obscure texts such as 'an article written for the October 4, 1851 issue of *Household Words*, entitled "Shakspeare [*sic*] and Newgate"' (p. 246), Vita illustrates that Dickens's 'comic summaries of contemporary drama offer a... critique of the theatre' and unveil 'the critical, indeed satirical, sensibility all audiences poses' (p. 255). In the following chapter, Michael Hollington continues to provide insights into Dickens and European theatrical genres. 'Dickens and Opera, Italian and Other' (pp. 257–73) demonstrates that Dickens's 'operatic enthusiasms were as intense as his aversions, and can often be read as expressions of radical sympathies' (p. 259). Discussing works as diverse as John Gay's *Beggar's Opera* [1728], Daniel Auber's *La Muette de Portici* [1828], and Dickens's own *The Village Coquettes* [1834], Hollington notes that his aim 'is to begin to suggest that it might be profitable to look at Dickens's novels again through the lens of contemporary opera—how Verdi's fathers and daughters, for instance, have their unmistakable echoes in his work' (p. 271). This chapter will be extremely useful to those who wish to distance themselves from the image of the conservative Dickens; indeed, Dickens draws upon theatrical work that is clearly 'about revolution and insurrection' (p. 261). Chapter 24 is the richly illustrated 'John Leech, Sol Eytinge, Jr., and Fred Barnard: Variations on *A Christmas Carol* (1843 to 1878)' (pp. 274–94). Philip V. Allingham considers 'visual reinterpretations of the novella published by Ticknor and Fields in Boston (1867 and 1868) and by Chapman and Hall in the Household Edition of the *Christmas Books* [1878]' (p. 275). These reinterpretations are 'today relatively unknown, even though their woodcuts, by Sol Eytinge, Jr. and Fred Barnard respectively, conditioned the response to the text by thousands of readers in America and Britain in the nineteenth century' (p. 275). These texts shaped the reading of the source material. For example, while 'Dickens's original illustrators shied away from the inherent socio-political criticisms of the first two Christmas Books... Fred Barnard took a much more socialistic interpretation, dwelling not so much on the joys of the holiday season... as on the grimmer scenes of Scrooge's dream and on the callousness of the governing classes' (p. 292).

The succeeding chapter, 'Picturing Miss Havisham' (pp. 295–16) by Anna Krawczyk-Łaskarzewska, examines 'some of the ways in which [Miss Havisham] has been portrayed across various visual media in the course of the last two and a half centuries' (p. 295). It is suggested that 'contemporary versions of Miss Havisham, whether in the form of illustrations or films, deserve closer examination' because 'they often manage to reflect the spirit of our times, rather than that of the Victorian era' (p. 296). Whereas 'Dickens's Miss Havisham does not seem capable of encouraging emotional identification... some of her pictorial as well as filmic representations have been keen on showing her more redeeming qualities' (p. 313). 'Dickens's Influence on *The Dark Knight Rises*' (pp. 317–32) is the subject of Michał Leliński's following contribution. Using 'the concept of Conceptual Blending, which is the brainchild of two eminent linguists, Gilles Fauconnier and Mark Turner' (p. 317), Leliński illuminates continuities between A *Tale of Two Cities* and a major Hollywood blockbuster. *The Dark Knight Rises*, 'like its literary counterpart... trie[s] to show... socio-political conflict in a fictional plot, referencing real past events, in order to function as a precautionary tale as to where our modern society is heading and how the escalation of this conflict might have terrible repercussions on a city, a country or its people' (p. 330). Isabel Vila Cabanes is similarly concerned with Dickens's presence in today's cultural sphere in the last chapter. In 'Dickens in Popular Culture: Reception and Adaptations of His Works in Contemporary American Adult Animated TV Series' (pp. 333–48), Cabanes considers modern popular shows such as *Beavis and Butt-head* [1993–7, 2001], *South Park* [1997–present], *Futurama* [1999–2003, 2009–present], *Family Guy* [1999–present] and *American Dad!* [2005–present]—which contain echoes and versions of Dickens's best-known texts, namely *Oliver Twist* [1838], *A Christmas Carol* [1843], *David Copperfield* [1849–50], and *Great Expectations* [1860–1] (p. 334). Cabanes notes that 'animated cartoons... can provide valuable insights into the reception of classic literature in present-day society' (p. 344).

Another 2014 collection, *The Grotesque in the Fiction of Charles Dickens and Other 19th-Century European Novelists*, edited by Isabelle Hervouet-Farrar and Max Vega-Ritter, manages to shed some new light on a topic that has been the subject of much discussion since the publication of Michael Hollington's *Dickens and the Grotesque* [1984], which was reprinted in 2014 as part of the Routledge Revivals series. Of the book's sixteen chapters, eleven focus primarily on Dickens; here, I focus on those chapters that will be of immediate interest to Dickensians. The book is split into three parts: 'Influences and Early Forms' (pp. 12–62), 'Expressing 19th-Century Reality: Reason vs. Unreason' (pp. 64–149), and 'Resisting and Negotiating Change' (pp. 152–232). In the introduction, 'The Grotesque in the Nineteenth Century' (pp. 1–10), Hervouet-Farrar notes that the first section 'looks at the fundamental texts and techniques that shaped 19th-century novelists' conception of the grotesque' (p. 8) while the second 'looks into the grotesque as a strategy of representation of 19th-century reality' (p. 8). The third section then examines 'darker facets of the Romantic and Victorian grotesque as symbolic expression of resistance to change' (p. 9). The chapters in Part I are as follows: Dominique Peyrache-Leborgne's '*L'Histoire du roi de Bohême* and *Oliver Twist* under Cruikshank's Patronage: The Dynamics of Text and Image at the Core of the Grotesque in the Novel of the 1830s' (pp. 12–26), Sylvie Jeanneret's 'The Grotesque and the "Drama of the Body" in *Notre-Dame de Paris* and *The Man who Laughs* by Victor Hugo' (pp. 27–36), Anne Rouhette's 'From Smollett to Dickens: Roderick (Random), Barnaby (Rudge), and the

Raven' (pp. 37–50), and Michael Hollington's 'Of Giants and Grotesques: The Dickensian Grotesque and the Return from Italy' (pp. 51–62). In this section, aesthetic considerations come to the fore. For instance, while Peyrache-Leborgne studies the 'close allegiance of text and image' in the 'literary grotesque, highlighting... its essential visual quality' (p. 12), Rouhette turns to the 'ridiculous and the terrible, two elements which... play a major role in the grotesque' (pp. 37–8) as a means of reading *Barnaby Rudge*, its title character and Grip, Barnaby's comical but sinister pet raven. Hollington then conceptualizes the grotesque via reference to strange bodies. He goes on to show 'how the experience of the grotesque in Italy lingered on in Dickens's mind, and is at times directly reflected in the main works that Dickens wrote in the three years following his return from Italy in July 1845—that is to say, in the three Christmas books of 1845, 1846 and 1848 (*The Cricket on the Hearth, The Battle of Life*, and *The Haunted Man*)' (p. 54).

Part II contains Florence Clerc's 'Grotesque Extravagance in the Fictional Worlds of Charles Dickens and Nikolai Gogol from the Perspectives of "Fantastic Realism" and the European Grotesque Tradition' (pp. 64–80), Jacqueline Fromonot's 'Figures of the Grotesque in *The Snobs of England | The Book of Snobs* by William Makepeace Thackeray' (pp. 81–93), Bérangère Chaumont's 'From "Absolute Realism" to Nocturnal Grotesque in Gérard de Nerval's *October Nights*' (pp. 94–107), Isabel Vila-Cabanes's 'The *Flâneur* and the Grotesque Figures of the Metropolis in the Works of Charles Dickens and Charles Baudelaire' (pp. 108–20), Max Véga-Ritter's 'The Construction of the Monstrous in Charles Dickens's Fiction from *The Old Curiosity Shop* to *A Tale of Two Cities*' (pp. 121–32), and Thierry Goater's 'An "Uncanny Revel": The Poetics and Politics of the Grotesque in Thomas Hardy's *The Mayor of Casterbridge*' (pp. 133–49). The chapters in this section highlight the ways in which the grotesque harnesses the strangeness of everyday experience. In her chapter on fantastic realism, for example, Clerc argues that the grotesque emerges as the living and the non-living combine; indeed, both Gogol and Dickens tend 'to single out the incongruous from the ordinary, particularly by conferring on inert objects a life which tends to become exuberant, and thus uncanny' (p. 69). Vila-Cabanes is similarly interested in how the grotesque can be assessed in terms of boundary-crossing: 'The London of Dickens's urban sketches, like the Paris of Baudelaire's poems, is full of liminal figures that lurk around the streets, a space where horror and beauty coexist' (p. 113). Operating as they do within the midst of this confusion, Vila-Cabanes suggests, the *flâneurs* in Dickens's fiction best capture the paradoxes of the modern metropolitan experience. In the next chapter, Véga-Ritter looks at Dickens's monstrous figures (Quilp, Mr Bounderby, and so on) to demonstrate that 'Dickens's grotesque is frequently ambiguous and ambivalent' (p. 131). Quilp, for example, 'may be considered simply as a horrible villain or, conversely, as invested with a semblance of comic weight' (p. 122).

In the third part of this collection, the chapters are: Isabelle Hervouet-Farrar's '"Primitive Elements in a Modern Context": The Grotesque in *The Mystery of Edwin Drood*' (pp. 152–64), Victor Sage's 'Arts of Dismemberment: Anatomy, Articulation, and the Grotesque Body in *Our Mutual Friend*' (pp. 165–79), Delphine Cadwallader-Bouron's 'The Grotesque and Darwin's

Theory in Charles Dickens's *Great Expectations* and Wilkie Collins's *No Name*' (pp. 180–91), Marianne Camus's 'The Female Grotesque in Dickens' (pp. 192–202), Gilbert Pham-Thanh's '*Zuleika Dobson* by Max Beerbohm: The Grotesque of Not Such a Gross Text' (pp. 203–14), Florence Bigo-Renault's 'The Return of Dickens's Grotesques on Screen' (pp. 215–26), and Isabelle Hervouet-Farrar's 'Regeneration and Permanence of the Grotesque' (pp. 227–32) In her essay on *The Mysteries of Edwin Drood*, Hervouet-Farrar assesses the 'grotesque metamorphoses resulting from the unsettling permanence of the past in a modern context, due notably to the characters' rejection of progress' (p. 9). In the next contribution, Victor Sage notes 'a figurative tendency for the Leg to escape the body, the part to be separated from the whole' (p. 166) in Dickens's fiction. While Sage relates Dickens's tendency to focus on separate(d) body parts to his allegiance with Professor Owen, who was 'an anatomist, a bone-man, and a popular national figure' (p. 170), Cadwallader-Bouron assesses the connections between Dickens, Charles Darwin and Owen with a view to better understanding why Dickens and Collins create worlds in which 'all things...form a great continuum, an organic breathing entity in which boundaries are blurred' (p. 181). Camus then draws our attention to gender in relation to the grotesque. Arguing that a 'grotesque, to start with, is...the representation or invention of a creature impossible to find in nature' (p. 192), Camus goes on to suggests 'that Victorian morality or ideology, when it concerns women, is an important element in the construction of nineteenth-century female grotesques' (p. 192). The female grotesque exhibited so-called masculine qualities. Unsurprisingly, then, clear female grotesques such as Mrs Gamp receive attention here. Nevertheless, Camus stresses that characters such as Mrs Boffin in *Our Mutual Friend* reveal that some of Dickens's seemingly grotesque representations are often 'more subtle and less stereo-typical than they might appear to be at first sight' (p. 201). Chapter 16 of this collection takes a rather different turn, dealing as it does with contemporary adaptations. In 'The Return of Dickens' Grotesques on Screen' (pp. 215–26) Bigo-Renault argues that: 'Recent adaptations demonstrate a certain relish in twists and an inflation of deformity which mean that adapted works qualify as entertaining as much as they serve to denounce Victorian defects through the use of gothic or grotesque overtones' (p. 215). Bigo-Renault focuses specifically on adaptations of *Oliver Twist*, *Nicholas Nickleby*, *Bleak House*, *Little Dorrit*, and *Great Expectations*. At the end of her chapter, there is a useful table which outlines viewer numbers and time-slot rating.

A further collection, *Dickens on the Move: Travels and Transformations*, edited by Stefan Welz and Elmar Schenkel, grew out of a Charles Dickens bicentenary conference in Leipzig. This is a shorter collection which contains many items of interest. The editors' preface (pp. vii–xii) notes that 'Dickens seems to continue a British tradition in which dynamism and movement are central' and that this idea is explored 'across classes and countries, characters and texts'. The collection is divided into three sections: 'Geography' (pp. 1–69), 'Adaptation' (pp. 71–118), and 'Reception' (pp. 119–82). The first section contains Elmar Schenkel's 'Moving through the Night: Dickens's Walks in Nocturnal London' (pp. 3–13), which aims to discuss 'Dickens's nightly walks in the context of the culture of night and sleep and to find out which sources he discovered which fed his imagination in this world of Sleep and the City' (p. 3). Next, Stefan Lampadius surveys '*American Notes* and Dickens' Projects of Reform' (pp. 15–38), by discussing how 'Dickens's first American journey in 1842 constitutes an important chapter in his development as a writer and social reformer' (p. 15). Throughout five subsections— 'Introduction—Dickens the Reformer' (pp. 15–18), 'America—The Republic of Imagination' (pp. 18–21) 'Asylums—Education of Heart and Mind?' (pp. 21–6), 'Prisons—Between the Best and Worst' (pp. 26–33), and 'Outlook—Beyond America' (pp. 33–6)—Lampadius argues that 'America strengthened [Dickens's] conviction that change is inevitable and should be guided by people who believe in social progress' (p. 36). In the third chapter, Maria Fleischhack's 'Multilayered Identity and Palimpsest in Charles Dickens' *Little Dorrit*' (pp. 39–55), she argues that, in Dickens's *Little Dorrit*, 'Geography is used to reflect and define characters' while 'buildings correspond to mindsets and behaviour' (p. 55). According to Fleischhack, 'This practice gives several layers to each character and place . . . and adds to the three-dimensionality of the story' (p. 55). Chapter 4, by Stefan Welz, is entitled 'Dickens Goes South: A Gentleman's Perspective' (pp. 57–69). Using *Pictures from Italy* as a case study, Welz 'aims at elucidating some literary and biographical aspects of Dickens's early social and literary self-construction in order to make his unprecedented success understandable from a 21st-century perspective' (p. 57). For Welz, experiences in the south 'made Dickens what he was for the rest of his life: a successful author who knew how to use his literary imagination to put a spell on his readership, to guarantee a lasting success for himself and to promote his social class' (p. 68).

In many ways, the 'Adaptation' section is the linchpin of the collection; after all, this topic has become a major preoccupation in Dickens studies. The Disneyfication of Dickens is the subject of Franziska Burstyn's 'Charles Dickens: A Disney Carol. Disney's Adaptations of Dickens' (pp. 73–86), which explores nineteenth-century children's literature and depiction of poverty, as well as Disney adaptations of *Oliver Twist* (*Oliver and Company* [1988]) and *A Christmas Carol* (*Mickey's Christmas Carol* [1983]) to show how fiction can be transformed to align with 'the expected conventions of . . . family entertainment' (p. 74). *A Christmas Carol* takes precedence in Franziska E. Kohlt's 'Back to the Future: The Time Traveller's Traumatic Jetlag in *A Christmas Carol*' (pp. 87–103). After providing a brief history of 'Christmas and the invention of a tradition' (p. 88), Kohlt argues that *A Christmas Carol* is a time-travel narrative in which 'the immaterial visitors . . . fulfil the function of the time machine, and facilitate a deep psychological and traumatic experience of self-reflection, leading to self-recognition' (p. 101). Like Maria Teresa Chialant's chapter in *Reflections on/of Dickens*, Luise Wolff's following contribution is on a neo-Victorian novel by Richard Flanagan. In '"The World Warped to His Fancy": Charles Dickens in Richard Flanagan's *Wanting*' (pp. 105–18) the central argument is that Flanagan 'tells the story of the forgotten and silenced' by using 'two cross-cutting narratives in which the illustrious and the obscure, London and Tasmania, male and female perspectives are juxtaposed to each other' (p. 105). Flanagan also 'appropriates the Victorian age' (p. 105) by having Charles Dickens as a character who is representative of the nineteenth century.

The first chapter of the 'Reception' section, the third and final part of this collection, is Anna Wille's '"Dickens did not write what the people wanted. Dickens wanted what the people wanted": G.K. Chesterton's Charles Dickens as Character and Critique' (pp. 121–33). Wille demonstrates that, by critiquing Dickensian characters, Chesterton allows them to take on a new life. At the same time, 'the historical Charles Dickens is moved far beyond the original texts he created, to become a character himself' (p. 121). Like D. Allen in *Reflections on/of Dickens*, Wille is also interested in Gissing's responses to Dickens and how these can be employed and understood in our own time. Dickens critics such as George Orwell and Edward Wilson also receive attention here. Next is Marie-Luise Egbert's '"Please, sir, I want some more": Representations of Poverty on the Move' (pp. 135–49), which is concerned with *Oliver Twist* and Vikas Swarup's novel *Q & A* [2005], itself the basis of the Oscar-winning film *Slumdog Millionaire* [2008]. Throughout her subsections— 'Poverty Legislation in Dickens's Day' (pp. 137–8), 'Poor Dickens' (pp. 138–9), 'The How of Narrating Low Life' (pp. 139–42), 'Educating Middle-Class Feeling' (pp. 142–4), and 'Oliver Twist Goes Postcolonial: Vikas Swarup's *Q & A*' (pp. 144–8)—Egbert analyses 'how Dickens's theme of a poor, parentless child has travelled into the present' (p. 136) via a narrative that is set in an Indian context. The penultimate chapter is Dietmar Böhnke's fascinating 'The Lost Leipzig Letters: Charles Dickens, Bernhard Tauchnitz and the German Connection' (pp. 151–67), which discusses the relationship between Dickens and the German publisher Christian Bernhard Tauchnitz, who released a collection of texts by English and American writers. Using some recently discovered letters, Böhnke 'emphasizes the unusual friendship between Dickens and Tauchnitz' (p. 160). After describing the Tauchnitz enterprise and its international significance, Böhnke proceeds to 'describe Dickens's relationship with Germany in more general terms, including the little-known episode of sending his son Charles Dickens Jr . . . to Leipzig for almost two years in 1853–4' (p. 152). Similarly concerned with Dickens's presence beyond Britain is Max Hübner's last chapter, 'Charles Dickens and New Zealand: A Long-Distance Relationship with a Future' (pp. 169–82). Hübner makes his project clear from the start: 'Few critics have discussed how far Dickens's knowledge of New Zealand really went and how much he contributed to the magazine texts about the colony. This paper . . . adds a few points of reference' (p. 170). Historical connections are considered first: New Zealand is referenced in Dickens's journals and letters, for example, and early enthusiasts created a society in Auckland devoted to the collection of the author's work. A second section reveals that 'the works of Dickens [still] attract interest among New Zealand authors' (p, 179). For instance, Lloyd Jones's *Mister Pip* clearly shows that 'Dickens's coming-of-age novels . . . have inspired many postcolonial writers in the Pacific region' (p. 179). Like other studies in this collection, this one spans historical periods and geographical locations, demonstrating that the work as a whole is organized around the literal and metaphorical meanings of travel. This is a bold undertaking which yields some fresh insights. Unfortunately, though, a few errors throughout the book must be noted here. Mrs Gaskell's first name was Elizabeth, not Mary (p. 135). Dickens's father was not 'a naval officer' (p. 138) but a clerk in the navy pay office, and Frances Trollope, not Anthony Trollope, wrote *Michael Armstrong* (p. 141). These minor inaccuracies do not detract from the best of the ideas contained with *Dickens on the Move: Travels and Transformations*.

As expected, the 2014 publication of *Dickens Studies Annual* contains many studies of interest. In '*Pickwick* and Reform: Origins' (*DSA* 45[2014] 1–21) David Parker seeks to demonstrate that Dickens's first extended narrative 'is a book of its era, the Reform era' (p. 18) by assessing the subversive potential of sporting scenes and moments of class conflict within *The Pickwick Papers* [1836–7] and related literature of the period. Next, Dianne F. Sadoff examines many Dickensian adaptations (textual, filmic, pornographic) in an article entitled 'Boz and Beyond: *Oliver Twist* and the Dickens Legacy' (*DSA* 45[2014] 23–44). For Sadoff, *Oliver Twist* [1837–9], with its mixture of disparate genres and modes of representation, is 'appropriate for adaptation, whether on the nineteenth-century page or stage, or on the twentieth- or twenty-first-century screen' (p. 25). Sadoff's astute survey of adaptation theory and its applicability within this context is admirable, though there are some generalizations. Referring to George Rowell's critique in 1956, Sadoff suggests that Victorian 'dramatizations expunged Boz's humour and blunted his observation' (p. 31). In fact, as many critics have noted, social criticism was often embedded within the content and structure of nineteenth-century (re)stagings of Dickens's novels. The following article, Timothy Spurgin's '"Notoriety is the Thing": Modern Celebrity and Early Dickens' (*DSA* 45[2014] 45–62), is an engaging account of the history of literary fame and its negative consequences, as portrayed throughout Dickens's fiction. For Spurgin, 'the interesting question is not whether Dickens got there first. It's what celebrity meant to him and how it figured into his writing' (p. 47). By focusing on early texts, such as *The Pickwick Papers* and *Nicholas Nickleby*, Spurgin is able to examine Dickens's 'own understanding of celebrity culture' (p. 45) at a time long before the reading tours became a popular cultural event. In 'Fatal Extraction: Dickensian Bildungsroman and the Logic of Dependency' (*DSA* 45[2014] 63–94) Aleksandar Stević 'explores the intersections of the Dickensian Bildungsroman and the early and mid-Victorian debates about the sources of poverty' (p. 63). He goes on to examine 'the legitimacy of charitable intervention in alleviating [poverty's] effects' (p. 63). The next article, Galia Benziman's excellent '"Feeble Pictures of an Existing Reality": The Factual Fiction of *Nicholas Nickleby*' (*DSA* 45[2014] 95–112), attends to novels that depict child abuse and child neglect. Like Frances Trollope's *Adventures of Michael Armstrong, the Factory Boy* [1840] and Charlotte Elizabeth Tonna's *Helen Fleetwood* [1841], Dickens's *Nicholas Nickleby* is far from apolitical; in fact, according to Benziman, it is 'a subversive, political power par excellence' (p. 108). As Benziman demonstrates, by limiting his focus to the Yorkshire schools and by exploiting radical humour, Dickens is better able to achieve his aims and assist in paving the way to major institutional reform. Dickens's reformist vision is also the subject of Jerome Meckier's 'Dickens and Tocqueville: Chapter 7 of *American Notes*' (*DSA* 45[2014] 113–23). Meckier suggests 'that the most famous early

Victorian travel writer, who had a life-long interest in prison reform... disagreed thoroughly with [Alexis de] Tocqueville's... treatise *On
the Penitentiary System in the United States and Its Application in France*,
which had been translated in 1833' (p. 113), though this view has been
challenged by many Dickensians, including Michael Slater.

The next two contributions concentrate on *Dombey and Son* [1846–8]: 'How
Dombey and Son Thinks about Masculinities' (*DSA* 45[2014] 125–45) by
Rosemary Coleman and 'Floating Fragments: Some Uses of Nautical Cliché
in *Dombey and Son*' (*DSA* 45[2014] 147–73) by Matthew P. M. Kerr, the
former of which addresses the issue of gender within the novel. Colman argues
that the novel 'embodies a series of unsuccessful experiments in the
theorization of an ideal masculinity—that is, a masculinity capable of both
effective moneymaking and affective caretaking (p. 125). Kerr then shifts the
focus onto imagery in *Dombey and Son*, suggesting that 'the slippery
doubleness of the literary sea is what Dickens finds so appealing' (p, 147).
Kerr constructs his 'discussion around two categories of nautical cliché: those
related to water, and those related to solidity (especially wood)' (p. 147).
'Dickens Goes to War: *David Copperfield* at His Majesty's Theatre, 1914'
(*DSA* 45[2014] 175–203) is the title of Andrew Maunder's illustrated account
of a Beerbohm Tree production. Adapted by Louis Napoleon Parker, the
lavish *The Highway of Life: The Life and Adventures of David Copperfield* was
staged during a period of wartime crisis and was used, according to Maunder,
as a means of 'playing to national opinion and the need for myth-making'
(p. 199), though it did contain a number of social criticisms which prove that
(melodramatic) Dickens adaptations both entertain and instruct. A number of
figures are interspersed throughout. Following is Jennifer Conary's '"Whether
We Like It Or Not": *Bleak House* and the Limits of Liberalism' (*DSA* 45[2014]
205–28). Conary's central argument is clearly stated: 'Decades before any clear
articulation of a theory of "the social" in England, *Bleak House* illustrates the
inadequacy of liberal reform for the widespread systematic problems that
plagued both the nation and the individual' (p. 225). Of interest here is the way
in which Conary draws attention to the restraints placed on individuals and on
communities in Dickens. If the individual is powerless within *Bleak House*, so
too are the groups of people who make change a priority: Dickens was aware
that his social vision had limitations.

With 'Dickens, Disinterestedness, and the Poetics of Clouded Judgment'
(*DSA* 45[2014] 229–45) Zachary Samalin 'argues that, throughout his middle
and later novels, Charles Dickens developed an explicit critique of the ideals of
disinterestedness which continue to dominate discussion of the Victorian
discourse of judgement' (p. 229). Interestingly, Samalin notes that, in *Bleak
House*, Dickens begins to question the role of sight in establishing critical
distance or an objective stance: 'an unceasing onslaught of miasmas and fogs'
limits the 'clear vision required to see the object' (p. 230). Jessica Kuskey goes
on to consider 'Math and the Mechanical Mind: Charles Babbage, Charles
Dickens, and Mental Labor in *Little Dorrit*' (*DSA* 45[2014] 247–74). Babbage
is represented in *Little Dorrit* through the character of Daniel Doyce. Kuskey
posits that the 'novel's representation of mechanized mathematical labor... illuminates the ways Dickens as a novelist and Babbage as an inventor were

simultaneously engaged with contemporary debates about mental labor, intellectual property, and the social utility of the professional' (p. 247). Matthew Heitzman's '"A Long and Constant Fusion of Two Great Nations": Dickens, the Crossing, and *A Tale of Two Cities*' (*DSA* 45[2014] 275–92) follows. Heitzman suggests that *A Tale of Two Cities* 'responds to contemporary Anglo-French political tensions in the wake of the assassination attempt on French Emperor Napoleon III in 1858' (p. 275). Heitzman proceeds to argue that the novel harnesses Dickens's despair over nationalistic rhetoric and cultural boundaries, which set up dangerous social and political divisions and work to perpetuate individual and collective violence, as shown in the text. At the end of *Dickens Studies Annual*, there are two essays which are not directly related to Dickens but are of great interest: Erin D. Chamberlain's 'Servants' Bright Reflections: Advertising the Body in Victorian Literature and Culture' (*DSA* 45[2014] 293–309) and Elizabeth Meadows's 'Entropy and the Marriage Plot in *The Woman in White* and *Lady Audley's Secret*' (*DSA* 45[2014] 311–31). An extensive review section entitled 'Recent Dickens Studies: 2012' (*DSA* 45[2014] 333–98) by Caroline Reitz concludes the volume.

The spring issue of the *Dickensian* contains excellent articles, not least of which is Janet Snowman's opening essay 'John Orlando Parry and Charles Dickens: Some Connections' (*Dickensian* 110[2014] 5–23). Snowman details that the singer, pianist, and amateur artist Parry was 'influenced by the popularity of the characters created by Charles Dickens' (p. 18). Parry is also linked to Dickens 'through social contact with the talented illustrators and artists whom Dickens counted among his circle of friends' (p. 18). This informative article contains fifteen figures, including Parry's detailed *A London Street Scene* 'completed by or after June 1837' (p. 10). William F. Long's 'Defining a Life: Charles's Younger Sister Harriet Ellen Dickens (15 September 1818–19 August 1827)' (*Dickensian* 110[2014] 24–34) follows. Long 'brings together the existing information about the birth and christening dates of the siblings, and the death and burial dates of those dying in childhood' (p. 24). As his title implies, Long primarily 'seeks to resolve the uncertainty about the extent of the short life of Harriet Ellen' (p. 24). David Chandler's 'Singing Dickens: Part III—Musical Theatre Adaptations, 1889–1892' (*Dickensian* 110[2014] 35–44) is a fascinating account of nineteenth-century theatrical adaptations of Dickens's work, especially the operetta *Dolly Varden; or the Riots of the '80 s*. Performed in 1889–90, *Dolly Varden* was 'the only achieved attempt to reimagine a complete Dickens novel as a musical theatre work in the nineteenth-century Anglophone world, and much the fullest exploration of the operetta's capacity to work with Dickensian material' (p. 41). Chandler situates this piece within the context of popular French operettas and notes that it did not depart radically from *Barnaby Rudge*. Moreover, Chandler discusses *Oliver Twist* operettas that have received little to no critical attention: *Bumble. An Incident in Oliver Twist* [1891], written by Frank A. Clement and composed by Oliver Notcutt and *Corney Courted; or the Beadle's Bride* [1892] by Arthur Waugh are given some consideration. In the short article that follows, 'Monks's Medical Condition: A Note' (*Dickensian* 110[2014] 45–7), Nick Cambridge argues that, through Monks,

'Dickens pre-empted doctors [by eighty-nine years] in describing the main features of one medical condition: Sturge-Weber Syndrome' (p. 45). In 'Dickens, Irish Friends, and Family Ties: New Letters to James Emerson Tennent and Lord Dufferin' (*Dickensian* 110[2014] 48–53) Leon Litvack transcribes letters that Dickens wrote to 'three influential Ulstermen: the politician and diplomat Sir James Emerson Tennent (1804–69), the newspaper publisher Francis Dalziel Finlay (1832–1917), and the diplomat Lord Dufferin (1826–1902)' (p. 48). These letters, 'discovered . . . in the Public Record Office for Northern Ireland' reveal 'long and lasting friendships' (p. 48). Finally, in 'Sir John Easthope in Pictures' (*Dickensian* 110[2014] 54–5), Paul Graham reproduces 'two photographic portraits of Easthope as an old man (one of which is the frontispiece to this issue), and a caricature of him and his family, believed to have been executed by an employee' (p. 54). These items, depicting the man who 'employed Dickens as a journalist on his newspaper the *Morning Chronicle* from 1834 to November 1836' (p. 54), were provided by Professor Gianni Lombardi, Easthope's relative.

The summer issue of the *Dickensian* contains 'Charles Dickens's Manager, Thomas Headland' (*Dickensian* 110[2014] 105–12), Sheila Clarke's account of her 'great-great-great-uncle' (p. 105), who was 'assistant to Charles Dickens's manager Arthur Smith' (p. 105) and then 'Readings Manager [from] the Autumn of 1861' (p. 105), after Smith's death. Headland (1806–88) is most often remembered as an incompetent business partner who aggravated Dickens but gained his respect notwithstanding. Clarke seeks to expand the historical record by delineating more positive aspects of Headland's character. Next, Anthony J. Bower and A.J. Pointon focus on 'Pullman and the End of the Mugby Junction Bar?' (*Dickensian* 110[2014] 113–17), noting 'Dickens's unrelenting satire on the English system of railway station refreshment rooms' (p. 113). Two illustrations are produced: 'The first (English) Pullman Dining Car' and 'The Smoking Car' (p. 115). The article ends with a full reproduction of the parodic poem 'THE DINING CAR' [1879] by George Augustus Sala. In 'Ellen Ternan and Charles Dickens: A Re-evaluation of the Evidence' (*Dickensian* 110[2014] 118–30), Brian Ruck analyses the nature of the relationship between Dickens and Ternan and provides 'some alternative explanations that do fit the "evidence" just as well as do the theories of a sexual relationship and pregnancies' (p. 129). Jerome Meckier's '*Martin Chuzzlewit*: Mr Bevan Reconsidered' (*Dickensian* 110[2014] 131–5) comes next. After arguing that, through the character of Bevan, Dickens anticipates 'a literary device later employed by modern utopists' (p. 133), Meckier goes on to suggest that Bevan aims 'to convince us that the America Martin is poised to investigate will not prove to be the ideal republic Dickens had imagined' (p. 133). The next contribution is 'Not the Hero of His Own Life: Amiel, a Swiss Contemporary of Dickens' (*Dickensian* 110[2014] 136–44) by Hennard Dutheil de la Rochère, which looks at *Journal Intime* [1849–81] by the writer and scholar Henri-Frédéric Amiel in order to demonstrate that 'Dicken's novels were widely read a few years after his second stay in French-speaking Switzerland, and their literary qualities, political and moral implications were debated' (p. 143). Amiel was so enthusiastic about Dickens that a 'confusion between life and fiction' (p. 138) emerged. For example, Amiel allowed

Dickens's representation to influence his views on his own life, women and morality. Next, in his excellent 'To Begin With: Justifying Marley in *A Christmas Carol*' (*Dickensian* 110[2014] 145–53), Pete Orford details 'Why *A Christmas Carol* needs Marley *and* the spirits' (p. 146). One of this article's many highlights is Orford's analysis of *A Christmas Carol* through the lens of 'Modern philosophies of counselling and cognitive behaviour therapy (CBT)' (p. 146). This productive framework provides an explanation for the perceived redundancy of the final ghostly visitation: in CBT, the therapist aims to make herself redundant and thus it is not surprising that Scrooge exhibits no resistance when confronted by the final ghost—his 'therapy' is at this point complete.

The winter issue of *The Dickensian* begin with 'Charles Dickens and Franklin Stanwood' (*Dickensian* 110[2014] 201–9), in which James Chance examines a painting called 'Hulk of the Neptune' [1883] or alternatively 'Peggoty's House' by the artist Franklin Stanwood (1852–88). Chance bought this painting at an auction and subsequently discovered links between Dickens and Stanwood, who met on at least one occasion. Filling in Stanwood's biography, Chance speculates on what could have drawn the artist to *David Copperfield*. He provides reproductions of the painting as well as a copy of Hablot Knight Browne's original illustration of Peggoty's home. From visual to verbal art, in the brilliant 'Beginning Dickens: Designing the Opening Sentence of *A Tale of Two Cities*' (*Dickensian* 110[2014] 210–23), Maria K. Bachman and Don Richard Cox illuminate Dickens's editorial practice by paying close attention to one of his most famous sentences. Surveying 'Dickens' approach to fiction' (p. 211), the complex publication history of *A Tale of Two Cities* and the (at times almost incomprehensible) manuscript, Bachman and Cox conclude that 'This sentence . . . was the result of hard work, probably much revision, and careful design' (p. 222). Following is 'Dickens's Presentation Ring of Gold' (*Dickensian* 110[2014] 224–7), in which Anthony J. Bower provides information on a ring (made by Thomas Aston, of Regent's Place) Dickens received from Birmingham Society of Artists on 6 January 1853. Next is 'Where John and Elizabeth Dickens Buried their Children' (*Dickensian* 110[2014] 228–37) by William F. Long and Ruth Richardson. Noting that 'Neither Alfred or Harriet Dickens was buried in the family's home parish graveyard . . . Alfred's grave was in the churchyard of the small inland rural parish of Widley . . . Harriet was buried in the graveyard of St George's Hanover Square (p. 228), Long and Richardson aim to 'consider why John and Elizabeth Dickens chose to bury their children in these less obvious places' (p. 228). 'A Letter from Maria Winter, née Beadnell' (*Dickensian* 110[2014] 238–41) by A.J. Pointon and James Priory examines a letter Dickens received on 9 February 1855 from Maria Beadnell, now Mrs Maria Winter (Dickens's first love). This letter was advertised on e-Bay and Priory bought it, wanting to know whether 'Mrs Winter's written language showed any relation to the vocabulary and verbosity Dickens endowed her with in the role he gave her as Flora Finching in *Little Dorrit*' (p. 238). A transcription is included alongside a reproduction of the autograph letter. More letters are transcribed in Leon Litvack's 'Messages from the Sea: New Dickens Letters to E.E. and W.D. Morgan' (*Dickensian* 110[2014] pp. 242–54). 'Seven new letters from

Dickens to Captain E.E. Morgan [1805–64], and to his son William Dare Morgan (1838–87) . . . are published here for the first time' (p. 242). The letters were 'brought to the attention of the Dickens Letters Project by Robin Morgan Lloyd, a descendant of the captain, who researched Morgan's history in order to inform his work of historical fiction, *Rough Passages to London: A Sea Captain's Tale*, published in 2013' (p. 242). Litvack includes two pictures: one of Elisha Ely Morgan and one of William Dare Morgan. In common with the other numbers of *The Dickensian*, there are book reviews, conference reports, and other matters of interest at the end.

The first issue of *Dickens Quarterly* begins with Joel J. Brattin's '"Notes . . . of Inestimable Value": Dickens's Use (and Abuse) of an Historical Source for *Barnaby Rudge*' (*DQu* 31[2014] 5–16), which assesses the extent to which Dickens borrowed from a Thomas Holcroft pamphlet about the Gordon Riots. By close-reading the manuscript of *Barnaby Rudge*, Brattin manages to reveal 'a surprising number of cases where Dickens borrows Holcroft's words, phrases, and facts, without acknowledgement' (p. 6). At the same time, Brattin makes it clear that this does not constitute a simple case of theft. Dickens manages to fictionalize a factual account with great artistry and skill. In 'Melancholia and Machinery: The Dystopian Landscape and Mindscape in *Hard Times*' (*DQu* 31[2014] 17–32) Darcy Lewis argues that 'In *Hard Times*, Dickens's dystopia is manifested on two axes—the physical landscape of Coketown and the psychic "mindscape" of Louisa Gradgrind—in order to illuminate the effects of industrialization on the environment and the resulting implications of utilitarianism that would reverberate in the individual psyche' (p. 18). This argument is not one-sided: Lewis notes that the dreary and mechanical and the verdant and fertile are fused in Dickens's depictions of the landscape and the mindscape. Jessica A. Campbell's '"Beauty and the Beast" and *Great Expectations*' (*DQu* 31[2014] 32–41) suggests that 'the relationship between *Great Expectations* and "Beauty and the Beast" is deeper than one of simply allusion; rather, the two stories share a concern with learning to shed assumptions and embrace the transformative power of love' (p. 32). 'Overall', Campbell concludes, 'the moral of *Great Expectations* closely resembles the moral of "Beauty and the Beast"' (p. 40). Joanna Robinson's 'Digitalizing Dickens: Adapting Dickens for the Bicentenary' (*DQu* 31[2014] 42–61) surveys the various ways in which Dickens was appropriated during the bicentenary celebrations. BBC and British Council adaptations are considered here, as well as an app released by the Museum of London. Robinson discusses the difficulty in bringing Dickens to a modern (mass) audience and concludes that 'Adaptations were the key to the rediscovery of Dickens in the bicentenary, but ultimately he remains inimitable' (p. 60).

The June issue of *Dickens Quarterly* opens with Robert Stenning Edgecombe 'The Oneiric Vision of *Oliver Twist*' (*DQu* 31]2014] 91–112), in which the dreamscape of *Oliver Twist* is considered. Edgecombe examines 'Dickens's dual imaginative capacity—reconciling the oneiric and the real, the estranging and the reassuring' (p. 98) in order to provide a sophisticated and vivid account of the fluid nature of a novel that is often described as one-dimensional and stiflingly melodramatic. In the excellent 'Genre and the

Counterfactual in *The Old Curiosity Shop*' (*DQu* 31[2014] 113–26), Carra Glatt goes on to 'discuss the question of Little Nell's death in *The Old Curiosity Shop* in terms of Dickens's—and the novel's—ongoing struggle between lingering romanticism and encroaching realism' (p. 115). Nell is out of place in a novel in which romance and realism mix, and in which realism becomes the stronger, if not necessarily always the most dominant, force. As a child of romance Nell is 'remove[d] from her proper sphere into a realism she was never intended to encounter' (p. 118). In 'Making Sense of Place: A Short Walk in Paris with the Uncommercial Traveller' (*DQu* 31[2014] 127–54) John Edmondson invites us to 'follow in my footsteps as I follow in the footsteps of Dickens' (p. 127) through Paris. The 'intention is to suggest the interplay of past, present and future and the individual and cumulative significance of the places we encounter in our psychological and physical movement through urban space' (p. 127). There are sixteen illuminating figures, some of which are in colour. Vladimir Trendafilov, in 'Aesthetizing the Unperceived: Some Attitudes to Beauty in *Oliver Twist*, *David Copperfield*, and *Great Expectations*' (*DQu* 31[2014] 155–64), centres on aesthetic and socio-moral issues within three Dickens novels. For Trendafilov, Dickens does not see beauty as being contained within the 'economic, moral, or communicative' (p. 157) realms. Instead, beauty can be detected in 'Dickens's aesthetic values' (p. 157). Trendafilov argues that 'beauty in Dickens's novels is chiefly categorical, thus belonging to the group comprising Nature, Death, and the rest' (p. 164). At the end of this issue, William F. Long's note on '"Boz": Reinforcement of the Received Wisdom' (*DQu* 31[2014] 165–6) provides details on Dickens's pseudonym and argues against some previous views.

The September issue of *Dickens Quarterly* starts with Nathalie Vanfasse, 'Dickens's *American Notes*: The Literary Invention of a Single Monetary Currency' (*DQu* 31[2014] 189–205). Vanfasse argues that Dickens can 'be considered as the inventor of a single literary currency, namely his *American Notes*, designed to replace an imperfect monetary currency within America, and to be recognized as the world at large as the only valid American currency' (pp. 204–5). Thirteen figures are provided: twelve American banknotes from the period 1830–55 and one illustration by Marcus Stone. In 'Spenlow's Spaniel: Voicing Dissent in *David Copperfield*' (*DQu* 31[2014] 206–15) Julianne Ruetz argues that 'Dora Spenlow's spaniel Jip functions as evidence of the persistent incompatibilities between Dora and David, whether or not David as character or narrator is able to acknowledge them as such' (p. 214). Two illustrations from the novel are included. Next is Brenda Welch, 'Bentham, Illegitimate Children, and "the evil of the law" in *Bleak House*' (*DQu* 31[2014] 216–28). Welch suggests that Ada and Richard's 'wedding ceremony... is unlawful, thus creating problems for Ada and her son... Both... have something to add to Dickens's criticism of the law in that they illustrate his application of Bentham's legal theory as those principles apply to censuring the social and legal sanctions imposed on unwed mothers and illegitimate children' (p. 217). Rodney Stenning Edgecombe, in 'Washington Irving, the "Almighty Dollar" and *Little Dorrit*' (*DQu* 31[2014] 229–34), considers how far Dickens is indebted to Irving's 'A Creole Village' [1837] in *Little Dorrit*, concerned as the latter is with 'a religion of money' (p. 232) and the 'cult of

Merdle' (p. 233). Lastly, William F. Long and Paul Schlicke's '*A Vision of Death's Destruction* and *The Fatalist*: Two Early Dedications to Dickens' (*DQu* 31[2014] 235–58) surveys dedications to Dickens written by John Ouseley and Nicholas Mitchell. These are unusual in that 'very few formal dedications to Dickens . . . unequivocally date from earlier than 1840' (p. 238). Before going on to 'consider how Ouseley's and Mitchell's compositions achieved . . . particular eminence' (p. 239), Long and Schlicke reproduce the dedications and include others, such as one by the notable playwright and Dickens adapter Edward Stirling. An appendix lists thirty-nine previously uncollected texts dedicated to Dickens from the period 1839–69.

December's *Dickens Quarterly* includes Michael Hancher's 'Dickens's First Effusion' (*DQu* 31[2014] 285–97). Hancher notes that Dickens's 'first effusion' was not 'A Dinner at Poplar Walk' [1833] as the author claimed but '"Merry Christmas to You"; or, Wishes not Horses', which 'appeared in print, on January 7, 1832 . . . in the *Athenaeum*' (p. 286). This text has links to *A Christmas Carol* and was plagiarized in a number of places. A full transcription is usefully provided. Shuli Barzilai's '"Scrooge Nouveau": Margaret Atwood Resites *A Christmas Carol*' (*DQu* 31[2014] 298–311) comes next. Atwood's *Payback: Debt and the Shadow Side of Wealth* [2008] is compared to Dickens's *A Christmas Carol*. As Barzilai explains, Atwood's 'is not an adversarial relationship to the text she adapts but, on the contrary, an admiring (albeit free-wheeling) one . . . she pays tribute to, as well as plays with and against, a venerable Original' (pp. 299–300). In the brilliant '*Household Words*, Volume II September 28, 1850–March 22, 1851: Nos. 27–52 312' (*DQu* 31[2014] 312–33) John Drew and Jonathan Buckmaster examine the varied nature of the second volume of *Household Words* under seven subheadings: 'Background' (pp. 312–15), 'Leading Articles' (pp. 315–17), 'Short Fiction' (pp. 317–18), 'Poetry' (pp. 318–20), 'Current Affairs (Social & Cultural; Domestic Politics)' (pp. 320–4), 'Science and Medicine' (pp. 325–7), and 'Editorial Issues' (pp. 327–31). Emerging here is a sense of the eclecticism of Dickens's magazines—an aspect that is touched upon in other 2014 studies. In 'Dickens, the Metropolis and the Railway: Displacement or Progress?' (*DQu* 31[2014] 334–42), Trey Philpotts asks the question: 'what was Dickens's attitude towards metropolitan improvements, particularly those associated with the early years of the railway?' (p. 334). Philpotts challenges the view that Dickens was wholly negative about the railways but ambivalent about urban change as a whole: 'It's not so much that his views are contradictory', he argues, 'but that they evolve in response to a developing discourse of events' (p. 341). As in other issues of *Dickens Quarterly*, there are reviews and notices of interest at the end.

The *Dickens Magazine* returns with its first issue in almost three years. This issue focuses on *A Christmas Carol* and is split into two main parts. Part A is dedicated to a particular novel. Part B looks at the wider Dickens connection and influence. The second issue appeared in April 2015 and will thus be reviewed next year. Part A opens with Tony Williams's 'Beginnings: The Origins of *A Christmas Carol*' (*DickensM* 7:i[2014] 2–3), which discusses such influences as the 'real state of child labour in Britain' (p. 2) and the economic distress of the Irish famines. Robert Heaman's '*A Christmas Carol*: A Synopsis of Staves 1–2' (*DickensM* 7:i[2014] 4) follows. In 'Characters in Focus: The Philanthropists' (*DickensM* 7:i[2014] 5–7) Jacqueline Banerjee argues for the importance of the 'warm-hearted philanthropists who call on Ebenezer Scrooge in his chilly counting-house on Christmas Eve' (p. 5) and provides an account of philanthropy in the Victorian age, focusing on such figures as 'Angela Georgiana Burdett-Coutts (1814–1906), granddaughter of Thomas Coutts, founder of the famous London bank' (p. 6). With 'Victorian Society: Dickens and the "Hungry Forties"' (*DickensM* 7:i[2014] 8–11) Alan Dilnot brings Dickens into conversation with Friedrich Engels and argues that 'because [Dickens] was working with individuals rather than social classes he highlighted different tendencies, and suggested different remedies for abuse' (p. 8). In 'Illustrations: *A Christmas Carol* Illustrations: Part One' (*DickensM* 7:i[2014] 12–15) Philip V. Allingham continues his assessment of the illustrations by John Leech, Sol Eytinge, and E.A. Abbey for various editions of *A Christmas Carol* (see also Allingham's essay on this subject in *Reflections on/of Dickens*, reviewed above). Four illustrations are provided. Next, in 'Historical Background: Ragged Schools' (*DickensM* 7:i[2014] 16–17) a letter Dickens wrote to *The Daily News* on 4 February 1846 on the subject of the 'rise of Ragged Schools' (p. 16) is reprinted. Bert Hornback's 'Characters in Focus: Ghosts in Dickens: Part One—Creatures of the Imagination' (*DickensM* 7:i[2014] 18–20) considers spectral manifestations in a number of Dickens's novels. Although 'Dickens never used ghosts again as he did in *A Christmas Carol* . . . he used the kind of self-examination Scrooge's ghosts provoke in him. And this . . . is what Dickens called his "*Carol* Philosophy"' (p. 20). Isabel Vila Cabanes, in 'Popular Culture: The Place of the *Carol* in Popular Culture' (*DickensM* 7:i[2014] 21–2), looks again at the topic she explores in *Reflections on/of* Dickens—how modern cartoonists appropriate Dickens in contemporary culture and how Dickens is received by contemporary audiences. Alan Dilnot's 'Victorian Culture: Carols and *A Christmas Carol*' (*DickensM* 7:i[2014] 23–4) goes on to explore the history of carol singing and writing from Chaucer to the late nineteenth century. Dilnot also pinpoints references to carols and to carol singers in Dickens's novels, in particular the boy who begins to sing 'God Rest You Merry Gentleman' (*sic*) at Scrooge's counting-house door. In 'Writers in the Dickens Tradition: M.R. James 1862–1936' (*DickensM* 7:i[2014] 25–7) George Gorniak writes on Montague Rhodes James, who 'was an internationally renowned Bible and Church manuscript scholar at King's College Cambridge' (p. 25) and 'was the author of some of the most celebrated ghost stories to be published in the English language' (p. 25). Donald Hawes's 'Contemporary Writer: Thackeray and Christmas' (*DickensM* 7:i[2014] 28–9) attends to Thackeray—a writer who, like Dickens, wrote many Christmas books full of 'confusions, laughter and magic' (p. 29). Lastly, Lucinda Dickens Hawksley provides some biographical details in 'The Dickens Family: The Growing Dickens Family in the 1840s' (*DickensM* 7:i[2014] 30–2), concentrating on a time during which Dickens wrote *A Christmas Carol* and started work on *David Copperfield*.

Also concerned with *A Christmas Carol* is 'Charles Dickens's *A Christmas Carol*: "Such a Noble Meal"' (in Walczuk and Witalisz, eds., *Old Challenges and New Horizons in English and American Studies*, pp. 179–88). Aleksandra

Kędzierska argues against those who describe *A Christmas Carol* as a story about gluttony: '*A Christmas Carol*, despite an occasional focus on sensuality, emphasizing as it does the significance of food and feasting, promotes first and foremost spiritual dimensions of celebration' (p. 186). The didactic potential of the Gothic genre is assessed in Aleksandra Kędzierska's '*A Christmas Carol*— Charles Dickens's Ghostly Academy' (in Kędra-Kardela and Kowalczyk, eds., *Expanding the Gothic Canon: Studies in Literature, Film and New Media*, pp. 87–107). The ghosts that emerge in the text provide valuable lessons, demonstrating 'the success of [the] "Spectral Academy" in reclaiming souls generally considered lost' (p. 88). Interestingly, Kędzierska includes within her chapter a discussion of the ghost of Hamlet's father as he is referenced on the first page of the *Carol*.

Stage adaptations of Dickens's fiction continue to generate interest, as evidenced by Julianne Smith's '*Bleak House* on London's East End Stage, 1853: George Dibdin Pitt and Dickens at the Royal Pavilion Theatre' (*NCTFilm* 41:i[2014] 2–20). Smith argues that *Bleak House; or, The Spectre of the Ghost Walk* (4 June 1853) 'highlights working class participation in the narrative and shapes a critique of Dickens' middle-class activism. Dibdin Pitt disrupts Dickens's portrayal of the poor and working classes by putting these characters centre stage and insisting on their critical participation in Victorian culture' (p. 2). This essay is particularly notable for its recognition of social criticism within nineteenth-century adaptations—a factor that is often denied even in the face of overwhelming evidence. Smith notes that, in Dibdin Pitt, the crossing sweeper Jo is 'a knowing linguist whose speeches feature frequent wordplay' (p. 8). This is a particularly fruitful argument, though it relies on a reading which suggests that, in Dickens, Jo is portrayed as an animal. Some readings of the novel by Sally Ledger in particular present a challenge to these assertions. Marvin Carlson, in 'Dickens and the Invention of the Modern Stage Ghost' (in Luckhurst and Morin, eds., *Theatre and Ghosts: Materiality, Performance and Modernity*, pp. 27–45), notes that he will 'focus literally on stage ghosts, particularly on the stage ghosts of Dickens, their ghostly ancestry and their ghostly progeny' (p. 28). Theatrical adaptations of the Christmas stories are considered here as well as illustrations that portray ghosts (a number of figures are supplied throughout). Carlson goes on to provide an overview of 'The technology of staging ghosts' (pp. 34–7), which includes an extensive discussion of 'Pepper's Ghost' (pp. 27–34)—an innovation in the use of gas, light, and illusion which still appears in commercial films and scientific museums.

A number of essays in the 2014 volume of *Victorian Periodicals Review* focus on Dickens. In 'Idle Employment and Dickens's Uncommercial Ruse: The Narratorial Entity in "The Uncommercial Traveller"' (*VPR* 47[2014] 50–65) Jasper Schelstraete argues 'that the "Uncommercial Traveller" sketches constitute an attempt to reconcile business and pleasure through a self-conscious performance of selling leisure. By eschewing impersonal mass-marketing in favour of a more intimate retail approach, Dickens sought to reinforce a connection to his readership' (p. 51). Schelstraete's discussion also draws upon 'the rivalry between *All the Year Round* and the *Cornhill Magazine*' (p. 51). In 'Musical Miscellany in Charles Dickens's Journals,

1850–70' (*VPR* 47[2014] 398–431) Christine Kyprianides encourages 'scholars to look beyond the intellectual and specialist journals to explore the more mundane coverage of music in family periodicals' (p. 413). In order to explore this rich field, Kyprianides has 'selected over one hundred items on music, musicians, and music-related subjects from the pages of *Household Words* and *All the Year Round* which appeared during Charles Dickens's editorship' (p. 399). In '"Peculiarly Marked with the Character of Our Own Time": Photography and Family Values in Victorian Domestic Journalism' (*VPR* 47[2014] 538–58) Charlotte Bowman suggests that '*Household Words* and *All the Year Round* are especially noteworthy as they generally display limited interest in the intricacies of photography's position in the arts hierarchy and do not dwell on the aesthetic merits of individual images' (p. 538). Dickens here uses the anti-elitist slant of his magazines to make the subject of photography accessible to the widest possible readership. This decision was clearly motivated by both ideological and financial considerations.

In 'Animating Household Gods: Value, Totems, and Kinship in Victorian Anthropology and Dickens's *Dombey and Son*' (*VLC* 42[2014] 33–58) Supritha Rajan argues that 'one way the novel responds to the impact of capitalism on women's economic and political equality is through the relationship Dickens choreographs between Florence, the sacred, and things' (p. 34). Rajan's 'reading of women and sacred things in Dickens's mid-century novel can help us understand why, decades later, Victorian anthropologists became obsessed with the phenomenon of totemism' (p. 34). A following article is similarly concerned with female subjectivity in Dickens. Justine Pizzo's 'Esther's Ether: Atmospheric Character in Charles Dickens's *Bleak House*' (*VLC* 42[2014] 81–98) describes Esther as 'a tentatively embodied subject, one whose affinity with diffuse forms of vapor, mist, and rain punctuates the novel' (p. 81). For Pizzo, Esther's 'atmospheric characterization expresses the difficulty of embodying female subjectivity in narrative form' (p. 95). Though Esther's lack of subjectivity has been the subject of various scholarly works, Pizzo provides fresh insight by linking this problem with interiority to the central theme of immateriality. Tyson Stolte's '"And Graves Give Up Their Dead": *The Old Curiosity Shop*, Victorian Psychology, and the Nature of the Future Life' (*VLC* 42[2014] 187–207) then 'focuses on the interlinked fascinations with the corpse in both *The Old Curiosity Shop* and Victorian mental science, reading Dickens's treatment of death in the novel as his own engagement with—even intervention in—these psychological debates' (p. 188). This is a welcome addition to the study of a novel that is often marginalized because of its apparent lack of interest in the psyche. Margaret J.-M. Sönmez, in 'Authenticity and Non-Standard Speech in *Great Expectations*' (*VLC* 42[2014] 637–69), assesses the ficto-linguistics of *Great Expectations* by discussing 'Victorian attitudes towards non-standard dialects as authentic or inauthentic, and then investigating the speech of Joe Gargery, Abel Magwitch, Mr. Pumblechook and the protagonist/narrator Pip. The issue of narrative authenticity and, ultimately, of the authenticity of the implied author is raised in the conclusion' (p. 637).

English Literary History contains some items of note. In 'Item of Mortality: Lives Led and Unled in *Oliver Twist*' (*ELH* 81[2014] 1225–51), James Buzard engages with recent scholarly debates in Victorian studies focused on the narrative's relationship to the optative mood and on the status of minor characters in fiction. Through a reading of Oliver Twist's minor *alter ego* Dick, Buzard considers the correlation between fictional mode and the possibility of something happening to a character outside what occurs in the text. In 'Pip's Life' (*ELH* 81[2014] 1253–73), Clair Jarvis makes her point clear from the beginning: 'This essay is about the sexual plots that circulate in Charles Dickens's *Great Expectations*. I argue that the novel's emphasis on sexual withholding or delay has consequences not only for how we read characters' development, but also how we read the famously multiple endings of *Great Expectations*' (p. 1253). The subject of sexuality in Dickens is further explored in Shale Preston's 'Miss Wade's Torment: The Perverse Construction of Same-Sex Desire in Little Dorrit' (in Tonkin et al., eds., *Changing the Victorian Subject*, pp. 217–39). Preston suggests that Dickens's representations of same-sex desire are underscored by prejudice. This reading is much less generous than Holly Furneaux's in *Queer Dickens* [2009]. Focusing predominantly on Miss Wade and her negative traits, Preston posits that for Dickens, 'it would seem that it was fine for women to be physically intimate with other women provided that this intimacy was either in full view of men or did not amount to an ongoing orientation that precluded emotional and sexual bonds with men' (p. 235). Nevertheless, Preston does consider some more positive portrayals throughout Dickens's oeuvre, especially in the earlier fiction.

The subject of walking in relation to Dickens received some attention this year. In 'Sleep and Sleep-Watching in Dickens: The Case of *Barnaby Rudge*' (*SNNTS* 46[2014] 1–19) Michael Greaney states his case clearly: 'In his repeated staging of sleep-watching scenes, Dickens assesses the claims that sleepers might have on our attention, and the pleasure or power that we might enjoy at their expense, and he makes this give-and-take between those who watch and those who sleep a principle by which currents of power and meaning are circulated in *Barnaby Rudge*' (p. 8). In his excellent 'The Mystery of Master Humphrey: Dickens, Nightwalking and *The Old Curiosity Shop*' (*RES* 65[2014] 118–36) Matthew Beaumont analyses the complexities of Victorian night travels. Fresh insights are provided throughout. For example, walking pace is said to be conditioned by capitalism: 'Hurried or brisk walking, to polarize rather crudely, marked one's subordination to the industrial system; sauntering or wandering represented an attempt, conscious or unconscious, to escape its labour habits and its time discipline' (p. 123). Taking 'the semiotics of walking' (p. 125) into account, Beaumont proceeds to offer some new perspectives on a relatively neglected character, Master Humphrey, and an under-studied novel, *The Old Curiosity Shop*.

Following in the wake of Michaela Mahlberg's excellent monograph *Corpus Stylistics and Dickens's Fiction* [2013], a number of 2014 studies respond to new, computer-assisted forms of analysis, including 'Reading Dickens's Characters: Employing Psycholinguistic Methods to Investigate the Cognitive Reality of Patterns in Texts' (*L&L* 23[2014] 369–88) by Mahlberg, Kathy Conklin, and Marie-Josée Bisson. This work 'reports the findings of an empirical study that uses eye-tracking and follow-up interviews as methods to investigate how participants read body language clusters in novels by Charles Dickens' (p. 369). The writers further explain their goal: 'The article focuses on the reading of 'clusters', that is, repeated sequences of words. It is set in a research context that brings together observations from both corpus linguistics and psycholinguistics on the processing of repeated patterns' (p. 369). Also notable in this area is Tomoji Tabata's 'Stylometry of Dickens's Language: An Experiment with Random Forests' (in Arthur and Bode, eds., *Advancing Digital Humanities: Research, Methods, Theories*, pp. 28–53). Tabata harnesses the latest complex advances in corpus stylistics and algorithmic analysis to highlight key words and phrases used by Dickens and Collins and to comment on textual choices and issues. A number of useful graphs and tables map these words and their frequency. Also concerned with digital methodologies is Pablo Ruano San Segundo's 'Bridging the Gap between Corpus Linguistics and Literature: A Computational Analysis of Charles Dickens' Ways of Saying in *Dombey and Son*' (in Mármol and Jiménez-Cervantes Arnao, eds., *Studies in Philology: Linguistics, Literature and Cultural Studies in Modern Languages*, pp. 161–72). Segundo uses 'a computational-based approach' to explore 'an aspect that, due to its dispersed nature, has passed unnoticed in [Dickens's] works despite its literary value: speech verbs' (p. 161). Some interesting findings are presented: '*growled* is used just to report men's words, while *whined* introduces female discourse exclusively' (p. 165). Again, there are within this study illuminating tables which chart significant speech acts and speech verbs, particularly those of Mrs Skewton in *Dombey and Son*.

The Dickensian city forms the basis of a number of 2014 studies. In 'The Imperial Metropolis Deconstructed: Dickens's Diverse Views of Victorian London' (*Journal of the Faculty of Letters* (Hacettepe University) 31[2014] 223–29) Himmet Umunç argues that Dickens not only 'brings to the fore the world of London's Othered and underprivileged segments, but also deconstructs it socially and culturally' (p. 224). Similarly concerned with Dickens and the city is Hisup Shin's 'The Prison Unbound: Balzac, Dickens, and William Frith' (*The Korean Society of British and American Fiction* 21[2014] 203–31), which 'examine[s] a selection of novels by Balzac and Dickens and paintings by William Frith, in which the figuration of solitary confinement . . . finds itself merging with . . . types of multiplicity—noises, pedestrians, crowds, vehicles' (pp. 204–5). A chapter in *Forty Ways to Think about Architecture: Architectural History and Theory Today* by Iain Borden, Murray Fraser, and Barbara Penner takes Dickens as its subject, demonstrating how the author can be used to energize a variety of disciplines. Kester Rattenbury's 'Angel Place: A Way In to Dickens's London' (pp. 168–73) explores the links between Dickens and Cedric Price, 'the 20th century's greatest [architectural] designer of near-unthinkable alternatives' (p. 169) and owner of at least fifteen copies of *The Pickwick Papers*. The similarities lie in the way London is conceptualized: 'Dickens, like Price, shows you London in a different way; not to do with how it *looks*, but how it *works*—theatrically, structurally, politically, dramatically, humanly—all around us, every day' (p. 173). An analysis of the Marshalsea as it appears in *Little Dorrit* supports this claim. The Dickensian metropolis likewise emerges in '"Flashes from the Slums":

Aesthetics and Social Justice in Arthur Morrison' (*LitLon* 11:i[2014] 4–21) by Audrey Murfin, which 'places Morrison in conversation with both Charles Dickens's *Oliver Twist* [1838] and with late 19th-century photography, most notably that of American Jacob Riis' (p. 4). Murfin is particularly interested in how Jewishness is represented in *Oliver Twist* and in *A Child of the Jago*.

Online journals continue to provide insights into Dickens and his works. In 'Charles Dickens and the Cat Paw Letter Opener' (*19* 19[2014] 12 paras.), Jenny Pyke considers the sensory expectations surrounding nineteenth-century taxidermy, starting with Dickens's taxidermied cat's paw and moving on to a discussion of *Our Mutual Friend*. In 'Blindness, Prick Writing, and Canonical Waste Paper: Reimagining Dickens in Harriet and Letitia' (*19* 19[2014] 15 paras.) Lillian Nayder discusses the embossed edition of *The Old Curiosity Shop* Dickens made in response to a letter from Dr Samuel Gridley Howe in 1868, taking into account the politics underpinning Dickens's decision, which 'bear on the position of the disabled in the nineteenth century' (para. 2). For Dickens, the 'blind needed to read such works as *The Old Curiosity Shop* to develop the human sympathy that was thought to depend on the faculty of vision—on *seeing* or watching others—and that came readily to the sighted but not to the visually impaired' (para. 3). Nayder's own response to Dickens's position is observable in the fictional portrait of Harriet Dickens, the novelist's blind sister-in-law in *Harriet and Letitia*, her forthcoming novel. Pamela K. Gilbert's brilliant 'The Will to Touch: David Copperfield's Hand' (*19* 19[2014] 17 paras.) contains a history of the study of the senses and goes on to 'focus on Dickens's creative elaboration of a rhetoric of the hand as an expression of the will. In *David Copperfield*, a character's psychological development relates to the way he is able to use his hand' (para. 10). In '[E]motion in the Nineteenth Century: A Culture of Fidgets' (*19* 19[2004] 28 paras.) Karen Chase analyses characters in *The Pickwick Papers*, *Barnaby Rudge*, *Bleak House*, *Little Dorrit*, and *Our Mutual Friend* in terms of what they can tell us about the fidget as a neglected aspect of the sense of touch. For Chase, the 'fidget, in its multiple forms, provides a radical unsettlement of dichotomous structures—voluntary and involuntary, mental and physical, normal and rebellious, individual and social' (para. 27).

This year's *The Victorian* contains notable articles. In 'Victorian Sympathy and the Dickens' Child' (*The Victorian* 2:ii[2014]) Robert McParland looks into the ways in which Dickens generates sympathy for the working-class child. With 'Imposed Identities and Buried Moral Instincts in *Great Expectations*' (*The Victorian* 2:ii[2014]) Erica McCrystal considers imposed and actual selfhoods in one of Dickens's major novels, paying particular attention to how morality dictates identity formation. Alexander L. Barron argues, in 'Baked Nectar and Frosted Ambrosia: The Unifying Power of Cake in *Great Expectations* and *Jane Eyre*' (*The Victorian* 2:ii[2014]), that 'in Brontë, the shared consumption of cake bridges physical, social and spiritual distances between characters, whereas conversely, in Dickens, the unconsumed wedding cake [belonging to Miss Havisham] symbolizes physical, social and spiritual alienation' (para. 3). In 'The Face of the Crowd: Reading Terror Physiognomically in Charles Dickens's *A Tale of Two Cities*' (*The Victorian* 2:iii[2014]), Taylor M. Scanlon examines how Dickens uses the face as a legible text, especially in moments of crisis. Scanlon argues that 'far from attempting to occlude the crowd as a distinct and veiled subject, Dickens reconstructs masses of bodies as a knowable subject by focusing on physiognomically identifiable characters [Monseigneur Evrémonde and Madame Defarge, for example] as signifiers for crowds as a whole' (para. 2).

Dickens and economic matters continue to interest critics. Pauline Reid's 'Specters of Smith: Adam Smith's "Invisible Hand" and Charles Dickens's *Little Dorrit*' (*LIT* 25[2014] 312–33) is an account of capitalist and economic logic within *Little Dorrit*, a novel which critiques the theories of Adam Smith. Reid demonstrates that fiction is immersed in the capitalist system and that capitalism relies on fictions. It is stated that 'the hand of capitalist speculation is everywhere in *Little Dorrit*'s narrative economy' and that the novel acts as 'a recursive criticism of unregulated capitalism' (p. 315). Ben Parker's 'Recognition or Reification? Capitalist Crisis and Subjectivity in *Little Dorrit*' (*NLH* 45[2014] 131–51) explores the issue of transparency within *Little Dorrit* as it pertains to identity formation and to capitalism. Whereas moments of recognition crowd the endings of Dickens's novels, the abstractions of capitalist logic work against recognition to such an extent that in *Little Dorrit* 'the reification of Victorian finance capital [is] isolated in a separate plot' (p. 131). The ungraspable nature of capitalism is here quarantined apart from the neat reconciliations that determine the 'Dickensian family romance' (p. 131)—a separation that further underscores the true nature of the capitalist system. Another study focuses on the mysterious aspect of economic circulation. Keith Clavin's 'Fagin's Coin of Truth: Economic Belief and Representation in *Oliver Twist*' (*Victo* 4[2014] 122–38) centres on counterfeiting in relation to capitalism and characterization. Clavin argues 'that Dickens constructs Fagin in a manner that preys upon anxieties related to the shifting economic paradigms of industrial and financial capitalism, which includes doubts about the dependability of economic networks' (p. 123). As Clavin sees it, 'Fagin reminds us of perhaps the most frightening aspect of urban economics. That is, how easily any of us can be tricked' (p. 135). Zachary Tavlin's 'Market Value and Victorian Hybrids: Dickens and Marx Against Latour' (*Praktyka Teoretyczna* 13:iii[2014] 23–37) is concerned with Dickens and economic theory. Tavlin brings Marx and Dickens (particularly *Our Mutual Friend*) into conversation with Bruno Latour's philosophical writings on the concept of (socio-political) modernity. A number of 2014 book chapters engage in economic readings of Dickens's texts. In 'Investor Ironies in *Great Expectations*' (pp. 45–64), chapter 2 of her *Realizing Capital* (reviewed above), Anna Kornbluh turns to a late Dickens novel concerned with money and the economy. Through a series of brilliant close readings, Kornbluh shows that '*Great Expectations* uses its first-person narration to investigate the logics of personhood in the culture of finance' (p. 46). In contrast to other readings, Kornbluh seeks to reinstate the importance of human agency and human psychology within our conceptions of economic activity in the Victorian era. Aeron Hunt is also concerned with form and Dickens's interest in financial issues in chapter 1 of his *Personal Business* (reviewed above): 'The Trusty Agent: Problems of Confidence in Dickens's Family Firm' (pp. 33–68). Hunt makes his argument apparent as he introduces his research topic: 'By tracing the intersections and divergences between modes of interpretation in different genres—advice manuals, journalism and Dickens's novel of (mis)management, *Dealings with the Firm of Dombey and Son: Wholesale, Retail and for Exportation*—I suggest that the co-implication of representational concerns in commercial and literary practice was very much a live issue, animating and vexing Dickens as he pressed forward his aesthetic and social agendas' (pp. 36–7).

Dickens also features strongly in Noam Yuran's *What Money Wants: An Economy of Desire*, especially in chapter 2, 'Histories: Fantasies of a Capitalist' (pp. 79–124), where Dickens's *Hard Times* is used 'to confront Marx with classical economics' (p. 9). Yuran 'finds in the novel a phenomenological account of money's social ontology, in which the money-object involves real and imagined relations with others' (p. 9). Elsewhere, the topic of Dickens and accountancy comes into focus. In chapter 12 of *The Reckoning: Financial Accountability and the Rise and Fall of Nations*, 'The Dickens Dilemma' (pp. 178–88), Jacob Soll observes that accountancy became a matter of interest for writers such as Dickens, though they rarely looked upon the practice as optimistically as industrialists like Josiah Wedgwood or philosophers such as Jeremy Bentham. A tension arose in the minds of nineteenth-century literary figures: 'Great writers of the nineteenth century would struggle with the dilemma of whether accounting was an instrument of good or of corruption' (p. 178). Sarah E. Skwire's 'Not so *Bleak House:* Business and Entrepreneurship in Dickens' (in Mixon and Cebula, eds., *New Developments in Economic Education*, pp. 97–111) seeks to 'rescue the representation of business . . . in literature written by Charles Dickens' (p. 99). Though Scrooge has led many to believe that Dickens had a negative attitude towards business activity, Skwire pays attention to nuances in representation. Throughout three main subsections—'Dickens and Innovation' (pp. 101–3), 'Dickens and Work' (pp. 103–6), and 'Dickens and Debt' (pp. 106–10)—Skwire argues that, in *David Copperfield*, *Bleak House*, and *Little Dorrit* especially, Dickens shows us that happiness can be obtained through financial security—often a result of hard work and entrepreneurial flair. Patricia McKee's *Reading Constellations* is reviewed above, but two chapters deserve mention here: '*Great Expectations*: The Narrative Winks' (pp. 34–65) and 'London Looking Backward: *Our Mutual Friend*' (pp. 66–99). Using Walter Benjamin's writings on constellations and colportage, McKee explains that the events in each narrative she analyses do not occur linearly and that the characters do not function as wholly autonomous or independent subjects largely because—as we have already seen—the concepts of progression and cohesion are illusions in the disorientating capitalist metropolis. Capitalism alienates and disassembles selfhood to the extent that divided characters such as Pip in *Great Expectations* are compelled to use the matter provided by the city to form a communal identity via the constellation—nonlinear histories of materials and fellow beings.

A number of 2014 essays explore how Dickens received and understood other geographical locations and cultures. In '"Hasten to the Land of Promise": The Influence of Emigrant Letters on Dickens's Life and Literature' (in Wagner, ed., *Domestic Fiction in Colonial Australia and New Zealand*, pp.

37–47) Diana Archibald surveys Dickens's transforming depictions of colonial life and how these shifting perspectives can be attributed to the writings of newly arrived settlers. In '"Ever So Many Partings Welded Together": Serial Settlement and *Great Expectations* (in Wagner, ed., pp. 49–62), Jude Piesse argues that reading *Great Expectations* in conjunction with a number of serialized narratives about settlement emphasizes the novel's preoccupation with empire and uncovers the importance of the tropes of home, departure, nostalgia, and return. Most interestingly, serialization is linked to the dynamics and progress of migration, enacting as it does the 'retrograde movement through memory across long periods of reading time' (p. 55). This link is strengthened throughout the chapter as Piesse identifies images and patterns within *Great Expectations* that are relevant to both migration and to temporality. In '"Irregular Modernization": Charles Dickens and the Crisis of Occidentalism' (pp. 195–232), chapter 6 of *Making England Western: Occidentalism, Race, and Imperial Culture*, Saree Makdisi points out that the 'imperial intensity' (p. 196) of *The Mystery of Edwin Drood* is striking and continues to demonstrate that the 'novel's engagement with questions of empire is far more profound than [any] earlier effort' (p. 196). Dickens does not simply banish characters to foreign lands as a convenient plot device in this text. Instead, he engages openly and intensively with important social and ethical issues of empire. Dickens was not always as astute in his response to other cultures and locations, as is detailed in the first chapter of Giselle Rampaul and Barbara Lalla's edited collection *Postscripts*, reviewed above. Lalla's 'Dickens and Others: Metastance and Re-membering' (pp. 8–26) contains a small account of how, in *Oliver Twist*, 'the West Indies ... serves as a mechanism for establishing distance between persons and situations narrated' (p. 10). After all, this is where Mr Brownlow is dispatched to in the novel, and the news of his absence comes as a great blow to Oliver. Further discussion focuses on characters from novels such as *Barnaby Rudge* and *Little Dorrit*, especially at points where these characters can shed light on the distancing methods used by Dickens in *Oliver Twist*.

From Pompeii: The Afterlife of a Roman Town by Ingrid D. Rowland contains a chapter on 'Charles Dickens and Mark Twain' (pp. 152–67) in which it is noted that the two major literary figures 'were so disconcerted by the foreign setting of Italy that the dead of Pompeii became more manageable for them than the living population of Naples' (p. 153). Chapter 5 of *Early African Entertainments Abroad: From the Hottentot Venus to Africa's First Olympians* by Bernth Lindfors focuses on 'Charles Dickens and the Zulus' (pp. 89–110). After observing that 'The Zulus became one of the most popular shows in London during the summer of 1853' (p. 91) and providing historical reasons for this popularity, Lindfors argues that Dickens's 'The Noble Savage' [1853] was inspired by the 'Zulu Fair Exhibition'—a show that Dickens saw on 26 May 1853. Lindfors then highlights the ideological issues that surround such entertainments, which continued to be performed well after this date. They 'serve to increase the great gulf of misunderstanding between Westerners and Africans and thus perpetuate the pathology of racism' (p. 110). This is something that Dickens demonstrates in his writings as he constructs seemingly insurmountable barriers between two cultures.

From a different angle, Charlotte Mathieson investigates the changes Dickens's characters go through when they return from foreign locations in "'A Brown Sunburnt Gentleman'": Masculinity and the Travelling Body in Dickens's *Bleak House*' (*NCC* 36[2014] 323–34). Focusing on browned or sunburned characters, who re-enter Britain physically altered, Mathieson argues that the transformative influence of the sun on the body opens up a space in which class, ethnic, and gender issues come into focus. For example, in *Bleak House*, the 'sunburnt or tanned male body ... operates in two ways: sunburn both inscribes the ... effects of travel to produce a remodelled masculinity, and it has a further, performative function in producing a body that is read differently, and in turn produces new readings of (white, British) masculinity, through its browned appearance' (p. 332). As we have seen, a number of works look at Dickens and other cultures from the opposite end of the spectrum, illuminating the author's presence and reanimation abroad. To this list can be added 'Rethinking "Global Dickens": The Case of the Cross-Cultural Transfer of *David Copperfield*' (*JVC* 19[2014] 63–78), by Klaudia Hiu Yen Lee, which attends to Chinese translations of *David Copperfield* with a view to exposing 'the difficulty of any wholesale transfer of values in a cross-cultural context and the intricate relationship between the global and the local' (p. 77). In any translation programme a number of variables complicate interpretation: cultural interactions across historical periods most obviously. Thus, when 'Chinese translators made a conscious effort to explore new ideas beyond their own culture, [they] still remained heavily influenced by their own traditions and values' (p. 77). Two further works explored Dickens's international reach, Arne Merilai's 'The Ages of Dickens in Estonian Literature: Some Comparative Perspectives with a Marxist Exposure' (*Interlit* 19[2014] 372–87) and Lydia Wevers's examination of 'Dickens and New Zealand' (*LitComp* 11[2014] 321–7), the latter of which 'examines the social history of the Pickwick Club of New Zealand and its relation to colonialism and Victorian cultural ambitions' (p. 321). Wevers notes that the Pickwick Club was primarily designed to be a convivial enterprise. It 'was clearly intended to be an antidote to some of the less agreeable aspects of colonial settlement, a reminder of civilization and social forms, of charitable intent and class solidarity ... And of course it held its meetings in a pub' (p. 325).

A number of studies focus on Dickens and/in America, particularly in relation to the reading tours. In 'Charles Dickens in Pennsylvania in March 1842: Imagining America' (*PennHist* 81[2014] 51–87), Jane S. Cowden examines Dickens's time in Pennsylvania during his 1842 visit to the US and explores how far this stay contributed to the scathing attacks on America contained within such works as *American Notes* and *Martin Chuzzlewit*. 'Performing Authorship in the Celebrity Sphere: Dickens and the Reading Tours' (*PLL* 50[2014] 115–51) by Whitney Helms argues that Dickens's reading tours or 'capital ventures' (p. 116) can be seen to expose the intersection of commodity discourse and celebrity culture at a pivotal point in the nineteenth century. A chapter in Amanda Adams's *Performing Authorship in the Nineteenth-Century Transatlantic Lecture Tour* (reviewed above)— 'Performing Ownership: Dickens, Twain, and Copyright on the Transatlantic

Stage' (pp. 115–51)—responds to the same topic. Referring to Charles Dickens and Mark Twain, Adams writes about the depoliticization of nineteenth-century reading tours: 'The overt political tenor of ... earlier tours was gone, literary writers were more strictly literary, and entertainment had come to rule the public performance sphere' (p. 58). One chapter in Jessica DeSpain's *Nineteenth-Century Transatlantic Reprinting and the Embodied Book* (reviewed above) focuses on Dickens. The first chapter is entitled '"Here goes Boz—only a shilling!": The Monstrous General Circulation of *American Notes*' (pp. 17–50). Dickens claimed that the American public were victims of the 'disposable reading material ... reprinted in every regional paper across the nation' (p. 12). The circulation of cheap editions of *American Notes* turned this argument inside out. The reprinters declared that they were the upholders of a democratic culture that demanded a plethora of affordable 'high' *and* 'low' texts to reflect the diversity of the citizenry. DeSpain investigates this tension, filtering her sophisticated analysis through the concept of circulation as it relates to the body, to (national) identity, and to material culture. In her fascinating 'Dickens in 1842: Coming to His Senses about America' (*English* 63[2014] 97–114) Nancy Aycock Metz considers 'Charles Dickens's 1842 trip to the United States as visual and auditory experiences' (p. 98). Drawing on material from the letters, from *American Notes*, and from *Martin Chuzzlewit*, Metz goes on to detail that 'Dickens's own writings about the first American trip ... are nowhere more memorable or revealing than when he digresses from events, issues, and controversies to give vivid expression to a more basic and visceral form of perception—to the testimony of his eyes and ears' (p. 99).

There were several further publications on *Our Mutual Friend*, including '"In That Bony Light": The Museum Economy of *Our Mutual Friend*' (*VR* 40[2014] 177–96) by Kayla Kreuger McKinney. She argues that, by reading the novel through the explanatory lens of museum culture and economics, a number of characters and metaphorical allusions come into sharper focus. Heather Tilley examines 'Waste Matters: Charles Dickens's *Our Mutual Friend* and Nineteenth-Century Book Recycling' (in Smyth and Partington, eds., *Book Destruction from the Medieval to the Contemporary*, pp. 152–74). This chapter takes into account 'motifs of book production in Charles Dickens's *Our Mutual Friend*, examining how the formation and deformation of text as a material object in the novel is bound up with the question of authorial identity and literary survival' (p. 153). *Our Mutual Friend* continually emphasizes the fragility of the material world and especially of the paper archive, which links rag-pickers, booksellers, waste-paper men, and authors via a continual process of production, dissemination, and destruction. Dickens's discomfort with this circulating process permeates *Our Mutual Friend* as it explores and questions values connected to the creator and his or her seemingly disposable material. Also concerned with Dickens's last completed novel is the chapter 'The Limits of Authorial License in *Our Mutual Friend*' in Bernard Harrison's monograph *What Is Fiction For? Literary Humanism Restored*. Fairy-tale elements within *Our Mutual Friend* are identified here and Harrison goes on to argue 'that Dickens's work does offer us insight into the human condition and ... that in it authorial license is not entirely unconstrained by something worth calling reality' (p. 272).

Particularly useful is the way in which Harrison revivifies the novel using a methodology that does not rely primarily on heavy contextualization or dense theoretical frameworks.

Bleak House is the subject of 'Metonymy and the Dense Cosmos of *Bleak House*' (*SEL* 54[2014] 793–813) by Benjamin Joseph Bishop, who contributes to the ongoing debate surrounding Dickens's rendering of interiority. Bishop sees 'Esther's narrative, and any intimate interiority that it achieves, to be displaced by Dickens's focus on the "external traits" of other characters and objects' (p. 749). Bishop states that 'though Esther's narrative begins within an interior space, it is nevertheless Dickensian in its propensity to ground itself outside a subjective core' (p. 794). While Esther's character has been said to link with images of fog and vapour, then, Bishop locates her identity in other characters and in material objects. A section in *White Magic: The Age of Paper* by Lothar Müller called 'The Secrets of the Scriveners: Charles Dickens and Mr. Nemo' (pp. 163–8) traces three plot strands in *Bleak House* and argues that the novel turns into a kind of 'paper mythology' (p. 168). Nemo, for instance, is a copyist who fits into 'sinister allegories of modernity' (p. 168).

A number of comparative studies should be of some interest to Dickensians. In 'The Authoring Hero: Perspectives and Limits in Bakhtin's Reading of Dickens' (*The Korean Society for British and American Fiction* 4[2014] 129–49) Fang Li 'explores two passionate but rather surprising affinities: Bakhtin's affinity for Dickens, and Dickens' affinity, in literature and in life, for child-like brides and young actresses' (p. 129). Other comparative studies include 'Comparison Between the Structures of *Wuthering Heights* and *Great Expectations*' (*Socrates* 2:i[2014] 28–32) by Iftikhar Hussain Lone and Shafaq Muzaffer, which assesses Gothic traditions, melodramatic character-ization, and romance plots within two canonical novels. In other comparative works, Dickens and Shakespeare are brought into dialogue. One chapter in W. David Shaw's *The Ghost behind the Masks: The Victorian Poets and Shakespeare* (reviewed below), centres on Dickens. In 'Toils of Fate: Dickens, Hamlet, and Malvolio' (pp. 47–58) Shaw demonstrates that Pip in *Great Expectations* can be read as an amalgamation of Shakespearian characters. Pip can be treated like Hamlet, as a 'helpless victim trapped in the toils of a fate he is powerless to control' (p. 51). Other interpretations are available. Shaw assesses 'how far Pip is able to dupe others in transparently fantastic and funny snares, and how far he is a comic dupe like Malvolio, who walks into traps he might easily have avoided' (p. 51). Daragh Downes traces Dickens's links to Shakespeare in '"I'll drown my book": Travels between the Lines of Shakespeare's *The Tempest* and Dickens's *A Christmas Carol*' (in Sikorska, ed., *Of What Is Past, or Passing, or To Come: Travelling in Time and Space in Literature in English*, pp. 93–105). Downes brings 'Dickens's text into productive comparison with a . . . Shakespearean intertext: the late romance *The Tempest* . . . on specifically characterological grounds, tracing . . . strong lines of contour between the personality, predicament and progression of Prospero and Scrooge' (p. 93).

Also notable in Sikorska's edited collection is Sabina Fazli's '"The token of some great grief, which had been conquered, but not banished": Trauma, Things, and Domestic Interiors in Collins, Dickens and Raabe' (pp. 107–19).

Responding to critical interest in the material, Fazli argues that, in *Great Expectations*, 'Miss Havisham's traumatic experience in the past leads to a particular way of interacting and shaping her material environment in her home' (p. 114). As is the case with Esther, we get a sense of who Havisham is by paying attention to the things dispersed throughout her room and throughout the novel. It is argued here that traumatized interiority in particular is externalized, visible in objects which are described at length within the narrative. Mental states in Dickens's fiction have been observed elsewhere. In 'Anxiety, Symptoms and Containment: A Tale of Two Situations' (*British Journal of Psychotherapy* 30[2014] 106–16) Bernardine Bishop seeks to assess the psychologies of two significant characters in *A Tale of Two Cities*. 'The character of Dr Manette provides an example of the symptomatic personality, and the character of Sidney Carton of the much more modern, personality-disordered individual' (p. 106).

The subject of childhood in Dickens continues to form the basis of outstanding research. *Books for Children, Books for Adults: Age and the Novel from Defoe to James* by Teresa Michals contains a chapter on Dickens entitled 'Educating Dickens: Old Boys, Little Mothers, and School Time' (pp. 137–75). Dickens rarely wrote specifically for a child audience. The exception is *Holiday Romance* [1868], a novella written for the children's monthly *Our Young Folks*. Ironically, though, this was less suitable for children than Dickens's popular novels, which were read by all age groups. Michals traces this diverse readership and then considers representations of the child within Dickens's writings, noting unique qualities. Whereas writer-critics such as George Eliot chart a 'psychological development towards stable adulthood' (p. 138), Dickens's misfits confound this movement towards maturity. Dickens is more concerned with 'the unchanging girl-woman, and... the equally static but often much more troubling boy-man' (pp. 146–7). Dickens unifies his readers in terms of middle-class codes of gender and domesticity instead of dividing them up into age categories. Two chapters in *The Peripheral Child in Nineteenth Century Literature and Its Criticism* by Neil Cocks focus on Dickens: 'The Child and the Thing: *The Mystery of Edwin Drood*' (pp. 83–115) and 'The Queer Child: No Future and "Dickens and the Construction of the Child"' (pp. 119–42). Both engage with the work of Eve Kosofsky Sedgwick, Lee Edelman, and James Kincaid among others in order to afford Dickens's neglected or 'repressed' child characters scholarly attention. Most interesting is Cocks's discussion of 'Deputy', the mysterious child figure in *The Mystery of Edwin Drood*. As Cocks details, 'Deputy' shatters definitions used to discuss the child. He is referred to as a 'thing' and as a 'child' and he is referred to as 'it' throughout the narrative. If other critics have relied on essentialist readings of the child in Dickens, Cocks highlights how the author unsettles the concept of the child by obstructing the way to objective interpretation or definition. In its most extreme and destabilizing tendencies, it is said that *The Mystery of Edwin Drood* goes as far as questioning 'whether certain children are children at all' (p. 114). A chapter on Dickens features in Molly Clark Hillard's *Spellbound* (reviewed above). The second chapter, '*Pickwick Papers* and the End of Miscellany' (pp. 38–49), posits that 'Dickens's picaresque *Pickwick Papers* both anxiously and exuberantly reflects the antiquarian collection'

(p. 8) despite Dickens's best efforts to move from the tale to 'novelty' as publication progressed.

Two important book chapters refer to Dickens's treatment of groups that were marginalized in the Victorian era. 'Reading Dickens: Pleasure and the Play of Bernard Harrison's "Social Practices"' (in Hanna, ed. *Reality and Culture: Essays on the Philosophy of Bernard Harrison*, pp. 49–63) is by Murray Baumgarten. Using the Jews in Dickens's fiction as a starting point, Baumgarten argues that by working 'with Harrison's concept of "social practices," we grasp the range of meanings generated by Dickens's narrative habits, his sociological acuity, and the linguistic choices that produce the characters that people his fiction' (p. 50). This yields some interesting findings: while Dickens sympathized with 'the poor, the downtrodden, the Irish, the colonized' (p. 52), he experienced difficulty when it came to representing the Jew and his psychological state. However, a small factual error should be noted: Chadband appears in *Bleak House* and not *Little Dorrit* as is stated. One chapter in *Illiteracy in Victorian England: 'Shut Out from the World'* by Maxine Burton concentrates on Dickens: 'Charles Dickens and the Realistic Technique' (pp. 63–87). Beginning with 'Henry Mayhew's journalism about the poor' (p. 63), Burton proceeds to 'examine the relationship between the realism of journalism and "realistic" portrayals in novels' (p. 63), especially as they concern the illiterate. Salient points are made. In her analysis of *Bleak House*, Burton pays attention to the illiterate Krook, a character who is often overlooked as critics turn to Jo the crossing sweeper. Although Krook is portrayed as an immoral character, Burton concludes that, while middle-class writers often took literacy for granted, 'Dickens's sympathies cut across the divisions of rich and poor, literate and illiterate' (p. 86).

A number of 2014 studies assess the reception of Dickens in the Victorian period and in modern criticism. In 'Early Reviews of Charles Dickens's Productions of Ben Jonson's *Every Man in His Humour*' (*BJJ* 21[2014] 127–39) Elizabeth D. Woodworth notes that some reviews of Dickens's productions of *Every Man in His Humour* [1598] 'are particularly fascinating since they reveal how the play was produced, acted, and received in the mid- to late nineteenth century' (p. 127). Four reviews are provided as well as five figures depicting such matters as John Leech as Master Matthew and Douglas Jerrold as Master Stephen. The latter is of particular interest, showing how a popular contemporary melodramatist and acquaintance of Dickens appropriated traditional theatrical material. Also of interest is Chris Louttit, '"A Favour on the Million": The Household Edition, the Cheap Reprint, and the Posthumous Illustration and Reception of Charles Dickens (*BH* 17[2014] 321–64). Taking into account, amongst other factors, individual recollections (those of Van Gogh, for example), illustrations, market fluctuations, and music-hall performances, Louttit argues that 'examining the context, reception, and influence of the Household Edition and its illustrations gives us insight into how Dickens's work was understood by many late nineteenth-century readers' (p. 358). Other 2014 works investigate the various ways in which Dickens can be understood today. Louttit also writes on 'Popular Fiction and Social Protest: Dickens in the 1830s' (in Mazzeno, ed., *Twenty-First Century Perspectives on Victorian Literature*, pp. 29–44). Focusing mainly on *Oliver Twist*, Louttit argues that, rather than reading Dickens's early fiction as an entrée to the late masterpieces, we should analyse it in terms of the cultural context of the 1830s. The chapter expands into an assessment of Dickens's literary influences and the nature of popular culture. Some familiar ground is covered here: Dickens's critique of legal sanctions on the poor and his transformation of popular forms such as melodrama. However, it is useful to have a lucid summary of Victorian reviews on *Oliver Twist*, which are placed alongside later assessments by Sergei Eisenstein and others. One chapter in Simon Dentith's *Nineteenth-Century British Literature Then and Now* (reviewed above) focuses on Dickens and *David Copperfield* (pp. 61–80). After discussing the complex generic hybridity of *David Copperfield*, Dentith demonstrates that the novel is full of tensions that complicate interpretation. For instance, the novel questions its own 'Victorianism' even as it subscribes to the aesthetic and ideological parameters associated with this category. For Dentith, it is important to recognize this tension and the consequent possibility of multiple valid readings (those at odds with Foucauldian analysis or New Historicism, for example). In doing so the 'complex and contradictory possibilities of the mid-nineteenth century...can be allowed to speak in surprising ways to our no less complex present' (p. 80). David Rampton's 'Dickens, Chesterton, and the Future of English Studies' (*ChE* 21[2014] 68–78) also focuses on how Dickens can be analysed in our own period. Rampton claims that the work of G.K. Chesterton 'shows how an author-centred approach can bring [Dickens's] central concerns into sharper focus' (p. 68). Rampton does not discredit studies which turn to the social or historical context but seeks to explore the reinvention of more traditional methodologies which align more stringently with textual criticism. Also of interest in this area is '*Great Expectations* and the Complexities of Teacher Development' (*English in Education* 48[2014] 76–92) by Anne Turvey and Jeremy Lloyd, which argues for a more flexible approach to teaching English in the classroom. A case study of *Great Expectations* is included.

   Notes and Queries and *The Explicator* contain some notices of interest on Dickens. In 'Charles Dickens' Jacob Marley and the Gospel of St. Mark' (*N&Q* 61[2014] 547) Song Cho notes that, in *A Christmas Carol*, Dickens 'invites readers to recall a particular biblical passage in which the theme of grace is highlighted' (p. 547). Catherine Wynne's 'Christiana Weller Thompson's Unpublished Journal (1845–6): Sidelights on Dickens' (*N&Q* 61[2014] 548–53) comes next. Wynne 'examines [Thompson's] honeymoon journal...which documents her stay in Genoa between mid-December 1845 and 9 February 1846, and her relationship with Emile and Augusta de La Rue, whom Dickens befriended while treating Augusta with mesmerism for a neurological condition in Italy from December 1844 to May 1845' (p. 548). Rodney Stenning Edgecombe then writes on 'Dickensian and Virgilian Echoes in *Adam Bede*' (*N&Q* 61[2014] 560–1). Edgecombe also argues, in 'Edith Dombey and Thomas Cranmer' (*Expl* 72[2014] 183–4), that, in *Dombey and Son*, Edith Dombey 'finds herself aligned with a pillar of the English reformation, and her moral stature improved in consequence' (p. 184). In '*Great Expectations*: Pip's Name' (*N&Q* 61[2014] 569) Jeremy Tambling considers the reasons why Dickens might have shortened Philip Pirrip to Pip.

Neo-Victorian studies focusing on Dickens continue to proliferate. With 'Coda: The Firm of Charles and Charles-Authorship, Science and Neo-Victorian Masculinities' (in Boehm-Schnitker and Gruss, eds., *Neo-Victorian Literature and Culture: Immersions and Revisitations*, pp. 193–203), Cora Kaplan discusses the ways in which Dickens and Darwin have been domesticated in modern cultural discourse. Kaplan also explores—and cautions against—the critical frameworks used to conceptualize literary celebrities and Victorian history more generally, noting that 'historical change should not be seen as an organic process, even a mediated one, but as an active social, political and cultural force (p. 194). In the third chapter of *Victorians on Screen: The Nineteenth Century on British Television, 1994–2005* by Iris Kleinecke-Bates, 'Real Victorians to Victorian Realities' (p 147–200), there is a discussion of the BBC's *Uncovering the Real Dickens* [2002], in which Kleinecke-Bates analyses 'the factual enquiry into the Victorian age' (p. 149). Included in this chapter are shots from notable productions.

Some other studies of note must be mentioned here. In 'Rebuilding Charles Dickens's *Wreck* and Rethinking the Collaborative' (*SEL* 54[2014] 815–33) Melisa Klimaszewski predominantly focuses on the neglected 'Beguilement in the Boats'—the middle section of *The Wreck*, comprising contributions by Percy Fitzgerald, Harriet Parr, Adelaide Anne Procter, and the Reverend James White and often left out of scholarly editions. Klimaszewski proposes that 'Only by paying attention to this section can we most fully understand *The Wreck*'s thematic concerns and the complicated connections that exist among its narrative parts' (p. 815). In 'Harriet Martineau, Charles Dickens, and the Rise of the Victorian Woman of Letters' (*NCLE* 68[2014] 449–83) Iain Crawford asks the question: 'Why...does what appears to have been a passing spat between two famously intransigent Victorian public figures still matter, and why should we be concerned with it now, so many years after its meaning was apparently settled?' (p. 551). Crawford situates his sophisticated response 'within the context of recent critical readings of Utilitarianism, the experience of industrial society, and the emergence of the professional woman writer' (p. 483). The subject of Dickens and religion has been the cause of much debate in recent years. In 'The Gospel of Amy: Biblical Teaching and Learning in Charles Dickens' *Little Dorrit*' (*C&L* 63[2014] 337–55) Mary Lenard continues to provide insights into this topic. Lenard 'argues that the figure of Amy Dorrit is one intended to engage the reader in addressing the moral and ethical concerns of this world, not to present the ominous shadow of a failed apocalypse. Dickens' work represents not a decline in theology, but the development of a new kind of theology' (p. 337). Belief in theological principles becomes paramount in a text that illuminates economic distress and the dark side of capitalism. *Victorian Literature, Energy, and the Ecological Imagination* by Allen MacDuffie was not received in time by this reviewer but does contain two chapters on Dickens—'Energy Systems and Narrative Systems in *Bleak House*' (pp. 89–133) and 'The Renewable Energies of *Our Mutual Friend*' (pp. 114–36). A full review is provided above.

Readers may be interested to note that Neil Bartlett's scripts have been published in *Charles Dickens: Great Expectations, A Christmas Carol, Oliver Twist*. Bartlett provides an introduction (pp. 5–19) on such issues as production history and theatrical and filmic influences, which extend beyond the twentieth and twenty-first centuries to those melodramas that were performed before the initial publication was even complete. Bartlett notes that his plays are designed to be melodramatic, and in this sense he transforms an aesthetic and dramatic mode that was popularized in the Victorian era and enjoyed by Dickens himself.

The 2014 *George Eliot–George Henry Lewes Studies* is dedicated to the memory of the late Andrew Brown, who edited the Clarendon edition of George Eliot's *Romola* [1993]. In her 'In Memoriam| Andrew Brown (1950–2014)' (*GEGHLS* 66[2014] 1–4), Nancy Henry correctly observes that Andrew Brown 'made his indelible mark as a publisher and scholar. Future generations will continue to value and build upon his research on the works of Bulwer Lytton and George Eliot' (p. 3). Appropriately, the issue is devoted to 'George Eliot's Quarry for *Romola*: An Edition of the Notebook Held in the Morris L. Parrish Collection of Princeton University Library (CO171 [No.69])', edited by Andrew Thompson (*GEGHLS* 66[2014] 5–99). Accompanied by two illustrative figures containing representative pages from the notebook (see pp. 9, 79), Thompson's excellent edition contains acknowledgements (p. 5) and a detailed, helpful introduction (pp. 5–8) in which he explains that he 'present[s] an edition comprising a transcription of the notebook, together with my notes, a list of courses consulted by Eliot while compiling the notebook, and an index' (p. 5). Thompson explains that 'the entries in this notebook are made in English, Italian, French, Latin, and occasionally Greek, and the pages are full of information on the social and political history of the period and in particular on Florence' in the late fifteenth century 'covering many aspects of life in the city, from customs, prices, dress and sumptuary laws, funerals, family names, religious societies, and state offices and officials' (p. 7). There is also a clearly written note on the text (pp. 8–10), which is followed by the transcription of the 'Quarry for *Romola*' (pp. 10–78). An alphabetically arranged, enumerative listing of abbreviations (pp. 79–81) precedes a similarly arranged descriptive index (pp. 81–7) and an extensive notes section of ninety-seven items plus a listing of works cited (pp. 87–99). Thompson's is an invaluable piece of scholarship, a guide to George Eliot's most neglected novel which also provides insight into her creative methodology.

The George Eliot Review for 2014, in addition to essays on other George Eliot novels, also contained material on *Romola*. The issue opened with the annual prize-winning essay in which Milena Schwab-Graham writes on '"In isolation human power is limited, in combustion it is infinite": Tracing Ludwig Feuerbach's *Essence of Christianity* through *Daniel Deronda*' (*GER* 45[2014] 8–15). Schwab-Graham's aim is 'to elucidate Daniel Deronda's Feuerbachian connection, the novel's "vision of [unfamiliar] human claims" on the imagination' (p. 9). In a closely argued essay, she writes: 'Daniel is the principal locus of Eliot's hermeneutics of sympathy, which encompass both the microform of the individual and the macrocosm of society' (p. 12). Barbara Hardy provides a most insightful contribution in her 'Politics and Pastoral in *Silas Marner*' (*GER* 45[2014] 17–21), in which she 'recall[s] and extends' Q.D. Leavis's observation that 'Nancy presses Godfrey's rights on Eppie, who answers the spirit of the insult with a passionate affirmation of class solidarity as well as of loyalty to the only father she has ever known' (p. 17, citing Q.D. Leavis's introduction to the Penguin edition of *Silas Marner* [1967], p. 37). Casaubon's presumed impotence is the subject of Marianne Burton's 'Casaubon's Impotence: A Literary Label?' (*GER* 45[2014] 22–9). Burton 'belong[s] to the anti-impotence camp on the basis of *Middlemarch*'s text' (p. 25): she concludes that 'Eliot is as explicit as she can be that Casaubon fulfills his role "with his unfailing propriety"' ([*Middlemarch*] ch. 20); sex occurs, not blissful sex, but a pragmatic, utilitarian consummation fulfilling legal requirements. How unpleasant that must have been' (p. 28). Burton's essay elicits a vigorous response from Barbara Hardy, whom Burton places in the Casaubon impotence camp (p. 23). At the conclusion of her 'A Response' (*GER* 45[2014] 31–2), Hardy writes that Eliot 'makes it clear that no one, including the reader who accepts the case that the marriage is consummated, will ever know what Dorothea thought of a wedding journey to Rome'. Hardy adds 'this dark joke is moving, strongly guarding Dorothea's reserve, and Casaubon's—but is it not fascinating that apparently no one entertains the possibility that George Eliot left the issue undecided, as a fiction writer can and may?' (pp. 31–2). For Brenda McKay in her 'George Eliot and Psychosomatic Illness: A Footnote to the Biographies' (*GER* 45[2014] 33–41) 'it is truly astonishing that, despite all the psychic disturbances and illnesses she suffered, Eliot was still able to write her marvelous novels' (p. 40). Andrew Sanders gives a subtle reading of *Romola* with close attention to textual detail in his '*Romola* and Politics' (*GER* 45[2014] 42–9) and Leonee Ormond provides useful insight in her 'Frederic Leighton and the Illustrations for *Romola*' (*GER* 45[2014] 50–5). Interesting distinctions are found in Louise Lee's 'Laughter versus Sympathy in *Romola* and *Felix Holt*' (*GER* 45[2014] 56–64). '*Romola*'s Religious Experience' engages Alain Jumeau (*GER* 45[2014] 65–70). In 'Conference Report', A.G. van den Broek gives a clear account of the one-day conference on *Romola* and *Felix Holt* held at the Institute of English Studies in November 2013 (*GER* 45[2014] 71–3). Following book reviews (pp. 74–87), Margaret Harris and Joanne Shattock provide 'In Memoriam' tributes to the late Andrew Brown (*GER* 45[2014] 88–90). This very good issue of the *George Eliot Review* concludes with two notes: Tapan Kumar Mukherjee's 'Oscar Browning's *Life of George Eliot*' (*GER* 45[2014] 91–2) and Rodney Stenning Edgecombe's 'Supplementary Annotations to *Daniel Deronda*' (*GER* 45[2014] 92–5). These are followed by Sheila Woolf's 'George Eliot Birthday Luncheon, 24 November 2013: The Toast to the Immortal Memory' (*GER* 45[2014] 96–8), John Burton's 'Chairman's Annual Report' (*GER* 45[2014] 99–101) and Ayako Tani's 'Japanese Branch Report' (*GER* 45[2014] 102–3) providing a timely reminder of the considerable interest in George Eliot in Japan.

Edgecombe, in the introductory paragraph to his 'Supplementary Annotations to *Daniel Deronda*', writes that 'very little has escaped' the annotations of previous editors of George Eliot's final completed novel (*GER* 45[2014] 92). Graham Handley's excellent Clarendon edition initially appeared in 1984 and four years later as a World's Classics paperback. A new edition with an introduction by K.M. Newton (pp. vii–xxix), an updated select bibliography (pp. xxxi–xxxiv), 'A Chronology of George Eliot' (pp. xxxv–xliv), and revised explanatory notes (pp. 689–713) appeared in 2014. *Daniel Deronda* is a richly intertextual work, and some of the works alluded to or cited from in translation from the German, including authors such as the great Jewish historians Leopold Zunz and Heinrich Graetz or the early medieval Spanish Jewish poet and thinker Judah Halevi, have evaded annotative Newton's attention. Otherwise his is a most valuable and worthwhile updating of Handley's classic edition.

English-educated, Rebecca Mead is a well-known staff writer for the *New Yorker* with a great love for *Middlemarch* and identification with its heroine that she conveys in *My Life in Middlemarch*. She first read the novel when she was 17 in the English seaside town where she grew up. Her book is the recounting of what the novel meant to her and still means: '*Middlemarch* was the one book I had never stopped reading, despite all the distractions of a busy working life' (p. 8). She asks 'what would happen if I stopped to consider how *Middlemarch* has shaped my understanding of my own life? Why did the novel still feel so urgent, after all these years?' (p. 10). Such issues are examined in eight fascinating chapters named after the eightfold division of George Eliot's novel, beginning with '*Prelude*' and 'Miss Brooke' (pp. 1–44) and concluding with 'Sunset and Sunrise', and '*Finale*' (pp. 245–78), with generous, detailed bibliographical notes and acknowledgements (pp. 279–93). Mead's monograph is nicely designed with an intriguing dust-jacket that should be preserved. The computer-generated print is easy on the eyes—this cannot always be said of contemporary books—and *My Life in Middlemarch* is firmly bound.

A number of other studies on George Eliot also appeared in 2014. Judith Wilt, an astute critic of, amongst others Walter Scott, Jane Austen, and George Meredith, has interesting things to say about *Middlemarch* in her *Women Writers and the Hero of Romance*, in which she considers 'the interaction of . . . patterns of hero creation and the feminine imagination' (p. 14). The second chapter of Wilt's book is devoted to '*Middlemarch*: A Romance of Diffusion' (pp. 53–86). Wilt writes: 'convertible as desire, as compulsion, as erotic and anti-erotic, as self and selflessness, the quester and quest object . . . "Will" is both virginal and maternal, shifting . . . between the bright and free (masculine) youth that the girl [Dorothea] covets and the world-trammeled wisdom that the woman seeks. The deck is stacked' (p. 16). George Eliot's late prose work is the subject of S. Pearl Brilmyer's '"The Natural History of My Inward Self": Sensing Character in George Eliot's *Impressions of Theophrastus Such*' (*PMLA* 129[2014] 35–51). For Brilmyer, 'in *Impressions* Eliot invokes the descriptive traditions of natural history and the character sketch to suggest that human beings, like other animals, are conditioned by bodily frameworks and habitual responses that allow them to sense some things and not others'. In addition, 'a meditation also on the history of characterization itself, *Impressions* puts pressure on the modern association of character with individual human psychology' (p. 159). This is a different approach to George Eliot's late prose collection and usefully draws upon her partner George Henry Lewes's work. *Impressions of Theophrastus Such* is the subject too of Hazel Mackenzie's '"A Dialogue of Forms": The

Display of Thinking in George Eliot's Poetry and Prose, from the "Notebooks of an Eccentric" and *Impressions of Theophrastus Such*' (*PSt* 36[2014] 117–29), which, using somewhat convoluted prose, rereads George Eliot's *Impressions of Theophrastus Such* in the light of her early series of journalism 'Poetry and Prose, from the Notebook of an Eccentric'. 'Rather than viewing these texts as experimental deviations', Mackenzie 'casts [them] as part of larger patterns evident in Eliot's canon as a whole'. She argues that 'Eliot, influenced by Ludwig Feuerbach, held to the idea that just as the highest form of organisms was the most complex, so also was the highest form of art the most structurally varied and intricate. From this viewpoint, 'the texts are eminently successful. Moreover, they point the way to achieving a fuller understanding of the apparent problematics of form that have concerned critics in regard to Eliot's better-known fictional works since their original publication' (p. 117). A neglected area of Eliot studies is attention to her style and use of English. According to Sarah Allison in 'Discerning Syntax: George Eliot's Relative Clauses' (*ELH* 81[2014] 1275–97), *Middlemarch*'s 'depiction of . . . the difficulty of perceiving other people—is embedded in the narrative syntax itself'. Consequently she 'traces a peculiar grammatical pattern through *Middlemarch*: clauses that shift from a narrating past to a universalizing presence by means of the relative pronoun "which." These clauses integrate reflection into narrative presentation.' Allison proposes that 'there is an ethics of syntax operating at the level of the clause. Instead of promoting specific values, this "commentative clause" inscribes a process of making judgments, and aims to educate the reader in methods of taking perspective on other people' (p. 1275). In addition, 'present-tense generalizations in this novel are very often tempered by the use of a past-tense narrative statement. I know this', she writes, because she has 'counted them, or at least those occurring in a survey of every third sentence in the novel (4400 sentences)' (p. 1277). In a footnote Allison adds that 'Approximately five percent of the sentences in the survey contained present-tense forms, of which 40 percent were hybrid past-present sentences. Of these 113 sentences, 43 contained commentative clauses (38 percent of all past-present hybrids). Commentative clauses describe moods, moments, and experiences associated with the characters as well as characteristics.' She 'considers commentative clauses throughout the novel.' Allison writes" of the ... commentative clauses [that] describe moods, moments and experience associated with the characters as well as characteristics ... 18 of the 43 commentative clauses are associated with Lydgate's free indirect discourse or describe him directly'; and, additionally, 'the next-closest characters were Rosamond and Casaubon, who were described by five commentative clauses apiece (two of Rosamond's overlap with Lydgate's); and Dorothea was described by four'. Her study 'by looking at hybrid sentences that include both tenses . . . challenges the sharp narratological distinction between present-tense moral commentary and past-tense narration' (pp. 1294–5). This is an important area of analysis that unfortunately doesn't take into consideration Blackwood's compositors' printing house practices or consider the possibility that George Eliot's stylistic structures may be indebted as much to Blackwood's trusted employees as to his authors. Comparison with stylistic devices found in George Eliot's letters and in her prose works not published by

Blackwood's and the employment of tools used in bibliographical study might throw considerably more light on what is undoubtedly an important and, to repeat, a neglected area of George Eliot study.

Other articles on *Middlemarch* include Clinton Machann's 'Teaching *Middlemarch* with a Focus on Theory of Mind' (*ILStud* 16[2014] 75–88). For Machann, 'Mind reading is central to the development of key characters throughout the novel, and readers will recall a variety of encounters in which different characters make accurate and inaccurate assumptions about other people's minds regarding issues important to them.' Further, 'aside from the romantic relationships, there are many important scenes in which the narrator encourages readers to focus on theory of mind in complex ways, including suggestions that they themselves speculate about the consciousness of various characters'. Machann proposes asking 'students to think beyond the plot of the novel and employ their own theory of mind as they speculate about the narrator's complex attitude towards Dorothea in terms of her association with Saint Theresa and the union with Will Ladislaw (controversial with readers through the years), relating biographical information about the historical George Eliot to their construction of the author based on the narrator's commentary' (p. 86). Clearly this is easier said than actually successfully done in the classroom situation: the ideal and the actual realities of teaching will no doubt be in conflict. Doreen Thierauf's highly speculative 'The Hidden Abortion Plot in George Eliot's *Middlemarch*' (*VS* 56[2104] 479–89) argues 'that Rosamond Vincy, George Eliot's paradigm for failed feminine education, intentionally terminates her pregnancy by deciding to go horseback riding and thus illegally assumes control of the Lydgates' family planning'. Furthermore 'by exploring the moral and political consequences of Rosamond's supremely transgressive action', Thierauf 'argues that abortion discourse in Victorian literature not only obscures its own existence to appease hyper-restrictive editorial pressures, but is uniquely suited to showcase the precariousness of middle-class social and biological reproduction'. Missing the opportunity to draw upon books and articles known to have been owned by George Eliot and George Henry Lewes, for Thierauf, 'simultaneously unmentionable and extensively narrated, Rosamond's calculated miscarriage avoids catastrophic revelation when Rosamond manages to make the event appear accidental, reenacting—and reinforcing—a family planning strategy common among middle-class Victorian women' (p. 479). In her 'Dorothea's Boudoir: Dream-Work and Ethical Perception in *Middlemarch*' (*TSLL* 56[2014] 400–27), Annette Federico focuses 'on a particular setting in *Middlemarch*—Dorothea's boudoir at Lowick Manor—to explore intersections among a set of discourses gathering currency in contemporary critical practices: the ethical dimensions of reading literature, the attenuation of ideological or suspicious reading in favor of a return to aesthetic appreciation ("New Formalism"), and the reconsideration of New Historicist approaches to literary texts' (p. 402). Daniel Wright's 'George Eliot's Vagueness' (*VS* 56[2014] 625–48) 'examines George Eliot's preoccupation with the logical problem of vagueness: the idea that our language is riddled with blurry concepts and fuzzy truth-conditions that are impossible to circumscribe with the rigorous precision required by our binary logic'. Wright reads *Middlemarch* 'alongside nineteenth- and twentieth-century work in logic and the philosophy of language (George Boole, John Venn, Gottlob Frege, and Ludwig Wittgenstein)' in order to argue that 'Eliot links the problem of vagueness to both the difficulty and the importance of reasoning about erotic desire and its ethical claims. In the end, the "bad logic" of vagueness provides for Eliot a model of clarity that is ordinary rather than ideal' (p. 625). June Skye Szirotny makes a valuable contribution to the intertextual understanding of *Middlemarch*. In her 'George Eliot's Boy Martyr' (*N&Q* 61[2014] 568–9) she writes that 'in *Middlemarch*, Ladislaw, suspecting that Dorothea wants to become a martyr, tells her she talks as if she had had "a vision of Hades in her childhood, like the boy in the legend"' and convincingly demonstrates that a 'likely source is the figure George Eliot calls "The Boy martyr" in Chaucer's Prioress's Tale' (p. 568).

The second and third chapters of Henry Staten's *Spirit Becomes Matter: The Brontës, George Eliot, Nietzsche* are also devoted to *Middlemarch*. For Staten, the novel 'is a meditation on the nature of ethical consciousness, a meditation that goes far beyond the moral ideology of its time, of its narrator, and of the critics who have been taken in by the narrator's moralism' (p. 76). He concludes a lengthy second chapter (pp. 76–109) by saying that its heroine is 'doomed to fail in her project of self-assertion because of the contradiction internal to her ethic of self-sacrifice'. This is 'the contradiction between [Dorothea's] search for leverage on the external world, and her need to make her internal world immune from the social outside' (p. 109). The third chapter is taken up with a consideration of 'What Things Cost in *Middlemarch*' (pp. 112–31). Staten writes that 'material interests and class conflict are depicted in *Middlemarch* as the background against which Lydgate and Ladislaw are to be understood, and the personal relations between the characters play out against the exigencies generated by political events and economic necessity' (p. 128). Ian Duncan, 'George Eliot's Science Fiction' (*Rep* 125[2014] 15–39), in a convoluted contribution, writes that 'George Eliot's recourse to comparative mythology and biology in *Middlemarch* and *Daniel Deronda* engages a conjectural history of symbolic language shared by the Victorian human and natural sciences. Troubling the formation of scientific knowledge as a progression from figural to literal usage, Eliot's novels activate an oscillation between registers, in which linguistic events of metaphor become narrative events of organic metamorphosis' (p. 15). Both novels also engage Tatiana Kuzmic, in her '"The German, the Sclave, and the Semite": Eastern Europe in the Imagination of George Eliot' (*NCL* 68[2014] 513–41), who 'contributes to George Eliot scholarship by examining the author's interest in Eastern Europe, which spanned the length of her literary career, and its portrayal in her fiction'. Kuzmic 'situates Eliot's Eastern European characters—from the minor ones, such as Countess Czerlaski's late husband in "The Sad Fortunes of the Rev. Amos Barton", to major protagonists, such as Will Ladislaw of *Middlemarch* (1871)—in the context of England's policy towards Poland vis-a-vis Russia during the course of the nineteenth century'. For Kuzmic 'the international political backdrop is especially useful in illuminating the Polish aspect of *Middlemarch* whose publication date and the time period the novel covers (1829–32) happen to coincide with or shortly follow the two major insurrections Poland launched against Russia'. Drawing on Eliot's interactions with Slavic Jews in Germany, Kuzmic 'shows how the creation of Will Ladislaw and his reprisal in the character of Herr Klesmer in *Daniel Deronda* (1876) serves the purposes of Eliot's imagined cure for English insularity' (p. 541).

Studies focusing on *Daniel Deronda* include K.M. Newton's closely argued 'The Otherness of George Eliot' (*TPr* 28[2014] 189–214). According to Newton 'certain assumptions tend to come into play when George Eliot is discussed which significantly influence how she is regarded as an author and how her writing is interpreted. The main assumption is that at the beginning of her writing career she was a rationalist in an Enlightenment tradition, sympathetic to liberal ideas, but later reverted to a more conservative mindset.' For Newton 'This has led to accusations that the decisions she made in her life were incoherent; at the very least she was lukewarm on feminist issues; was opposed to significant political reform; held some objectionable views in relation to class and race.' Newton interestingly argues 'that such views of Eliot do not take into account her otherness as a thinker and intellectual who cannot be accommodated within conventional paradigms, and illustrates that by considering three aspects of her, focusing mainly on her non-fictional writing because it gives more direct access to her thought: the choices she made in her personal life; her social and political thinking; and her position on the Jewish question' (p. 189). In his essay Newton pays especial attention to readings of *Daniel Deronda*. Accompanied by appropriate illustrations, Rebecca Rainoff's 'George Eliot's Screaming Statues, *Laocoon* and the Pre-Raphaelites' (*SEL* 54[2014] 875–99) 'uncovers George Eliot's parodic staging of G.E. Lessing's *Laocoon* in the tableau vivant in *Daniel Deronda*, showing how Lessing's writing scaffolds crucial scenes of ekphrasis in the novel'. Rainoff writes that 'scholars argue that George Eliot aligns herself uncritically with Lessing, but [her] essay offers a new understanding of how she plays with his central binary of visual stasis and narrative movement to reveal Gwendolen Harleth's gradual progress. On a larger level [Rainoff] shows how George Eliot invokes Lessing's distinctions to counter contemporary visual artists who aestheticized tragic female stasis, notably the Pre-Raphaelites and other artists such as Gustave Doré' (p. 875).

John Mazaheri closely reads an exposition of hope, divinity, and love in his 'Hope in the "Sad Fortunes of the Reverend Amos Barton"' (*L&B* 34[2014] 37–53). In a combination of critical acumen and intelligent use of hitherto unused primary materials, Margaret Reynolds's fascinating essay 'After Eliot: Adapting *Adam Bede*' (*English* 63[2014] 198–23), 'considers two nineteenth-century stage adaptations (1862 and 1884)—from manuscripts in the British Library), two silent film versions (1915 and 1918), one stage dramatization (1990), a television film (1991), and a radio adaptation (2001) to consider how these appropriations relate to one another and how they vary in different historical settings'. Reynolds argues that 'the key starting point for Eliot was the story of Mary Voce, a woman executed in 1802 for the murder of her child . . . as the story is transformed in these later remediations, it is the character and fate of Hetty Sorrel that undergo most telling change in performance' (p. 198). *Adam Bede*, and especially the character of Dinah Morris in the context of biblical typology, engage Ryan Marr in 'Dinah

Morris as Second Eve: The Fall and Redemption in *Adam Bede*' (*Logos* 17[2014] 80–102). Rodney Stenning Edgecombe contributes two short essays on the novel. In '*Adam Bede* and *La Sylphide*' (*N&Q* 61[2014] 563–6) he draws attention to parallels between the novel and Adolph Nourrit's ballet, while in 'Dickensian and Virgilian Echoes in *Adam Bede*' (*N&Q* 61[2014] 560–1) he discusses Eliot's use of allusion with especial reference to Hetty and to her trial. Edgecombe's fecundity may also be seen in his 'Poetic "Thickenings" in *The Mill on the Floss*' (*N&Q* 61[2014] 566–8). The late Simon Dentith, in the third chapter '*The Mill on the Floss* and the Social Space of Hindsight' (pp. 41–60) of his *Nineteenth-Century British Literature Then and Now* (also discussed above), uses Bakhtin's notion of dialogue to illuminate Eliot's text: 'the diverse and contradictory valuations that the novel puts into play is by advertising its evidently dialogic qualities, its willingness to put into play competing viewpoints and ideologies' (p. 50). Andrew Elfenbein's 'The United States of Raveloe' (*MLQ* 75[2014] 129–48) sheds an interesting perspective on the post-fictional life of one of Eliot's best-loved works. Elfenbein writes that 'George Eliot's novella *Silas Marner, the Weaver of Raveloe* was central to the high school English curriculum in the United States for much of the twentieth century. Its status had risen during a period of cooperation between high schools and colleges about standards for admission to the latter at the end of the nineteenth century.' He explains that 'even after standardized tests had replaced it as a key to college admissions, *Silas Marner* remained in high schools to furnish an idealized image of education, in which a nonbiological parent successfully replaced unsuitable biological ones. Although the pedagogical moment that enshrined this work has passed, its history raises questions regarding the value of relevance in high school reading, the role of teaching aesthetic judgment, and the connections between high school and college teaching of literature' (p. 129). Jacob Jewusiak, in an interesting but at times unclear article, 'Large-Scale Sympathy and Simultaneity in George Eliot's *Romola*' (*SEL* 54[2014] 853–74), 'argues that George Eliot's *Romola* theorizes large-scale sympathy as a way of ethically engaging large groups of individuals outside one's immediate social ambit'. However, for Jewusiak 'the failed attempts of characters like Savonarola and Tito to imagine the experiences of unknown others suggest that large-scale sympathy estranges the sympathizing subject from the specificity of individual experience'. But there is an important caveat: 'this leads us to see a fault line at the heart of George Eliot's work, whereby the necessity of imagining the simultaneous experience of others is continually brought into conflict with the impossibility—and the danger—of doing so' (p. 853).

Mention should be made of three essays dealing with general topics in George Eliot's work. Maha Jafri's 'Stories We Like to Tell: Gossip in George Eliot's Fiction' (*FMLS* 50[2014] 182–95); Delia da Sousa Correa's 'Voice and Vocation in the Novels of George Eliot' (in Bernhart and Kramer, eds., *On Voice*, pp. 105–16); and Penelope Hone's 'Muted Literary Minds: James Sully, George Eliot and Psychologized Aesthetics in the Nineteenth Century' (in Data and Groth, eds., *Mindful Aesthetics: Literature and the Science of the Mind*, pp. 91–106).

Finally, 2014 witnessed essays focusing as much upon George Henry Lewes as George Eliot. These include Lila Marz Harper's '"That Wondrous Medusa-Face": Goethe's Italian Journey, George Eliot, and George Henry Lewes' (in Ricci, ed., *Travel, Discovery, Transformation*, pp. 135–54): the subjects range from Eliot and Lewes's Italian journey and the impact of Goethe upon them to the use of classical myth. Stefan Waldschmidt writes on 'The Consolation of Physiology: *In Memoriam* in G.H. Lewes's *The Physiology of Common Life*' (*VS* 56[2014] 490–7; also discussed in Section 3 below). Waldschmidt writes, 'In *The Physiology of Common Life* (1859), George Henry Lewes quotes Alfred Tennyson's *In Memoriam* (1850) to explain how an individual comes to recognize one's body as one's own.' For Waldschmidt, in a highly generalized account, 'Lewes and Tennyson are able to appear together in a physiological text because they share the biopolitical assumption that individuals are located in bodies governed by organic laws. In order to make a life subject to organic laws seem liveable, both Tennyson and Lewes will insist that thinking of ourselves organically offers new possibilities for adaptation and consolation that were not available to the sovereign individual of the Enlightenment' (p. 490).

Turning to Elizabeth Gaskell, Elaine Freedgood's tour de force, 'The Novelist and Her Poor' (*Novel* 47[2014] 210–23), examines the use (or lack thereof) of free indirect discourse in *Mary Barton*. The poor in Gaskell's novel are also, Freedgood explains, psychologically poor, in that their subjectivities—lacking the psychic intertextuality of more accomplished readers—cannot blend democratically with that of the narrator. However, this very resistance to FID, Freedgood argues, affords socio-economically impoverished characters free, because unwritten, thoughts. Ending with a meditation on the kinds of invisible omniscience that narrate our own lives, Freedgood retools a familiar text for use in our own historical moment. Looking at the same novel, Amy Coté, in 'Parables and Unitarianism in Elizabeth Gaskell's *Mary Barton*' (*VR* 40[2014] 59–76), arrives at a different but also intriguing conclusion. Reading *Mary Barton* as parable(s) intended to promote open-ended moral contemplation, Coté connects Gaskell's Unitarian faith with her formal choices while challenging Raymond Williams and essays like Freedgood's above which follow him in dismissing the novel's ending as a failure of political imagination. Instead, Coté writes, the narrative succeeds at 'a radical yoking of political and religious discourse in which the implications of a text extend beyond the book and into the readers' lives' (p. 61).

Lindsay Wilhelm's '"Looking South": Envisioning the European South in *North and South*' (*SNNTS* 46[2014] 406–22) expands the title of the novel to include the European south. In *North and South*, as well as in an article for *Household Words*, Wilhelm argues, 'Gaskell constructs a geographic teleology, aligned along a north-south axis, that repositions the south as a preservative echo of the north's past' and 'a figurative site for nostalgia and recollection' (p. 407). At the same time, however, Wilhelm sees such escapism as undermined by Edith and Frederick's complicated returns from the Continent. Ada Sharpe's article, 'Margaret Hale's Books and Flower: *North and South*'s Paratextual Dialogues with Felicia Hemans' (*VR* 40[2014] 197–209), argues that 'Hemans's epigraphs at once underscore and complicate the novel's valuation of women's participation in aesthetic, political, moral, and economic life' by framing Margaret both as a Hemans heroine and as a critical reader of the society that produced such figures (p. 208). In her essay, 'The Ethics of Risk in Elizabeth Gaskell's *North and South*: The Role of Capital in an Industrial Romance' (*VR* 40[2014] 55–71), Eleanor Reeds argues that Gaskell provided an alternative model of financial risk than that based entirely on self-interest with a 'hero and heroine who embrace the intimate and affective aspects of economic decision making' (p. 56).

Talking back to early feminist appraisals of *Cranford* and the 2007 BBC adaptation, Dana Vasiliu argues for more gender-savvy understanding of the novel in 'Challenging the Victorian Patriarchal Ethos: The Role of the Amazons in Elizabeth Gaskell's Cranford' (*The Victorian* 2[2014] 1–11). Christie Allen's 'Trauma in the "Tea-Cup Drama": *Cranford* on the World War II Home Front' (*GSJ* 28[2014] 1–16) looks at the varying reception of the novel in Britain in the Second World War. Michele Cohen, in 'A Mother's Dilemma: Where Best to Educate a Daughter, at Home or at School?' (*GSJ* 28[2014] 35–52), demonstrates how Gaskell's own concern about how to educate her daughter Marianne reflected larger debates about private and public schooling in England. Also, in the same issue, Philip Morey's 'Fiction Illuminated by Reportage: *Mary Barton* and Léon Faucher's *Études sur l'Angleterre*' (*GSJ* 28[2014] 53–71) compares the treatment of working-class life in the nearly contemporaneous texts as well as their reception. Richard Leahy, in 'Fire and Reverie: Domestic Light and the Individual in *Cranford* and *Mary Barton*' (*GSJ* 28[2014] 73–89), uses both nineteenth-century sources and the work of Gaston Bachelard to consider the historical, psychoanalytic, and literary significance of fire and fireside reverie in Gaskell's novels. Looking at the same two texts, Anna Fenton-Hathaway's essay, 'Detours: How *Mary Barton* and *Cranford* Redefined "Redundancy"' (*VLC* 42[2014] 235–50), argues that Gaskell spoke back to W.R. Greg's assertion that England had a surplus of women by creating '*literary* redundancy' (p. 235). Focusing on women and events superfluous to the marriage plot, Gaskell questioned both Greg and the reigning conventions of domestic fiction. Fenton-Hathaway's fresh consideration of the interleaving of social and literary narratives is a welcome addition to Victorian studies. Meghan Healy, in 'Weak-Willed Lovers and Deformed Manliness: Masculinities in *The Scarlet Letter* and *Ruth*' (*GSJ* 28[2014] 17–34), compares models of masculinity in Hawthorne's and Gaskell's fallen woman novels. In '"Such a Strong Wish for Wings": *The Life of Charlotte Brontë* and Elizabeth Gaskell's Fallen Angels' (*VLC* 42[2014] 671–90), Meghan Burke Hattaway provides an original and suggestive analysis of Gaskell's biography. Hattaway argues that Gaskell employs the same strategies she used to soften the fall of her heroine Ruth to make Brontë seem similarly unbruised by her 'fall' from the private to the domestic sphere. Steven Severn draws our attention to a little-discussed novella in 'Narrative Cessation and Professional Culture in Elizabeth Gaskell's *A Dark Night's Work*' (*VR* 40[2014] 155–75). According to Severn, *A Dark Night's Work* exposes the dangers posed by increasing professionalization.

Pat Colling argues, in 'Knowing Your Place: Place and Class in George Gissing's "Slum" Novels, Part 1' (*GissingJ* 50[2014] 3–18), that Gissing's slum novels are not so much about poverty as they are about alienation and class, where the 'slum' symbolizes the permanence and rigidity of classed society. Most of the work on Gissing this year discusses his work in relation to New Woman fiction and is reviewed above.

Rider Haggard also received some attention. In 'Adventures in the Marketplace with H. Rider Haggard: Author–Publisher Relations in *Mr. Meeson's Will*' (*ELT* 57[2014] 497–518), Michelle Allen-Emerson objects to the critical overemphasis on the 'feminization of letters' in the novel which, to Allen-Emerson, has obscured the biographical underpinnings of the text and the related commentary on 'the tension between authors and publishers, the changing conception of literary property, and the emergence of the author as literary celebrity (p. 498). Richard Pearson also takes a biographical approach to Haggard's fiction. In 'Personal and National Trauma in H. Rider Haggard's *Montezuma's Daughter*' (*ELT* 58[2014] 30–53), Pearson argues that at the heart of this dark novel is the traumatic death of Haggard's son while the parents were in Mexico. The 'cyclical narrative structures' repeat rather than overcome Haggard's personal trauma and, by shifting 'the locus of memory onto a subjugated other', complicate the triumphant narrative of the imperial project as well (p. 51).

Perhaps the best contributions to Hardy studies this year are two chapters in Anna Henchman's *The Starry Sky Within* (reviewed above). In the first of these, 'Hardy's Stargazers and the Astronomy of Other Minds' (pp. 129–57), Henchman draws on passages from *Tess of the D'Urbervilles*, *Two on a Tower*, *The Return of the Native*, *A Pair of Blue Eyes*, *Far from the Madding Crowd*, and *The Woodlanders* to explore how Hardy repeatedly, throughout his career, compared observing the heavens and observing other minds, and used scenes of stargazing to illustrate how individuals can temporarily transcend the limitations of fixed, mundane perception. In addition to offering a way to think about the mind, Henchman argues, these celestial scenes provided 'a morally neutral example of the perceptual reasons behind the fact that a person can take up one's entire universe one week and fade into irrelevance the next' (p. 142). The second Hardy chapter, 'Narratives on a Grand Scale: Astronomy and Narrative Space' (pp. 186–230), focuses on Hardy's closet 'epic-drama'. Henchman treats '*The Dynasts* as an antinovel, and its narrating chorus of spirits as an antinarrator to show us a distorted version of narration that makes the norms of the omniscient narrator freshly visible' (p. 196). First showing us how novels by Hardy, Dickens, and Tolstoy create the impression of a stable cosmos with a certain logic and coherence within their pages, Henchman then presents *The Dynasts* as radically upsetting any such order by stepping outside a geocentric view of human life.

Suzanne Keen's *Thomas Hardy's Brains: Psychology, Neurology, and Hardy's Imagination* is another notable contribution to the field of literature and science. As Keen points out in her introduction, Hardy has long been a favourite of critics interested in psychology—especially psychoanalysis—and has also received attention for his interest in the contemporary science of his day, most notably evolutionary science. However, few critics, according to

Keen, seem to be aware of the fact that Hardy also kept abreast of the psychological theories and experiments of his day and incorporated his knowledge into his fiction. Thus, Keen sets out to engage with two (albeit overlapping) areas of recent critical attention—literature and science as well as cognitive theory. Perhaps what Keen best succeeds at is blending the historical specificity common to the former with the theoretical interest of the latter. In her first chapter, Keen meticulously details what Hardy knew about the brain and explains the significance of source texts and writers mentioned in the *Literary Notebooks*, where Hardy kept track of much of his reading. From here, Keen launches into a narratological analysis of Hardy's work in chapter 2, 'The Minds of Hardy's Characters'. What, for Keen, makes Hardy stand out from other nineteenth-century writers interested in the workings of their characters' minds is his preference for psycho-narration or thought report, the practice of relating a character's thoughts from the perspective of a privileged narrator rather than using free indirect discourse. Though this strategy may seem less sophisticated, Keen's contention is that it actually enabled Hardy more accurately to represent a more behaviourist approach to human psychology. Keen's third chapter concerns Hardy's poetry, while the fourth chapter zeros in on the 1880s, which Keen dubs Hardy's 'neurological turn' (p. 130). In *Two on a Tower* and then in *The Woodlanders*, Keen sees Hardy moving from a 'a brain-capacity model to a neurological conception' that is fully realized much later in *The Dynasts*, a key text for Keen as it is for Henchman (p. 10). In the final chapter, 'Empathetic Hardy', Keen draws on her previous book, *Empathy and the Novel* [2007], to explore the use of strategic empathy in Hardy's fiction.

Ken Ireland's *Thomas Hardy, Time and Narrative: A Narratological Approach to his Novels* traces the career-long development of Hardy's narrative technique through formal analyses of each of his fourteen novels. For example, the first chapter, on *Desperate Remedies*, builds on Günther Müller's analysis of the 'micro-rhythms created by the narrative's fragmentation into chapter sections', the transitions between those chapters, and the relative proportion of speech to description (p. 13). *Under the Greenwood Tree* and *A Pair of Blue Eyes* are treated together in the next chapter, which characterizes the former as creating a bucolic pace through smooth transitions and simple plots and the latter as offering a melodramatic experience of time through alternating plot-lines and scale. In chapter 3, Ireland shows how relationships in *Far from the Madding Crowd* are 'subsumed in two essential plot-lines, value systems and attitudes to time: Weatherbury and Troy' (p. 38). Ireland accurately characterizes his work as 'pragmatic and text oriented' (p. 2). However, considering the interweaving of time in his discussions of the novel as both a structural and a thematic element, his assertion that the features he focuses on are 'demonstrably inherent in and constitute the foundations of the work, and as such remain unaffected by changes of critical emphasis or fashion' seems somewhat disingenuous, but that does not necessarily take away from the book (pp. 2–3). What is perhaps most valuable about Ireland's study is its breadth. While his conclusion that Hardy provides a bridge between the Victorians and modernism may not be all that surprising, his painstaking analysis of the manipulation of time in Hardy's novels allows us to see how that bridge was constructed, piece by piece. More accurately, at least from a chronological perspective, we might say that Ireland's book demonstrates the process by which Victorian fiction developed into its modern counterpart.

Jude the Obscure received the most critical attention of any of Hardy's novels this year. One of the best of these studies is Emily Steinlight's 'Hardy's Unnecessary Lives: The Novel as Surplus' (*Novel* 47[2014] 224–41), which returns once again to the question of population in *Jude the Obscure*, but with a novel twist. Turning to Jacques Rancière's political theory of literature, Steinlight argues that what distinguishes Hardy's novels is their recognition of their superfluity, a recognition that drastically undermines the deterministic separation of protagonists from the disposable masses—a deeply political move in Rancière's terms, for it chronicles the 'count of the uncounted' (p. 226). Aaron Matz, in 'Hardy and the Vanity of Procreation' (*VS* 57[2014] 7–32), uses Father Time's murder/suicide as his starting point for an exploration of the connections between Hardy's pessimistic take on procreation and more recent expressions of anti-natalism. In a more historicist vein, Benjamin Cannon's '"The True Meaning of the Word Restoration": Architecture and Obsolescence in *Jude the Obscure*' (*VS* 56[2014] 201–24) situates *Jude* within the craze for church restoration that swept England in the nineteenth century and suggests that, for Hardy, the novel could act as recompense for the lost architectural histories. Patricia McKee's chapter on Hardy in his *Reading Constellations* also focuses on the history of Christminster. In 'Scenes of Reading in *Jude the Obscure*', McKee argues that on awaking in Christminster, Jude realizes that the panoramic vision of the city as the centre of intellectual history is actually only an incomplete assemblage of parts obscuring much of what its very existence requires, including Jude and others like him. If the version of history told by the crumbling buildings fails to offer a meaningful connection to history, work—the act of rebuilding and renovating—may offer an opportunity for colportage. Richard Dellamora, in 'Male Relations in Thomas Hardy's *Jude the Obscure*' (*PLL* 50[2014] 245–68), discusses Hardy's personal life as part of a reading of *Jude the Obscure* in order to consider the importance of class for the overlap of ambitious and erotic desire between men in the nineteenth-century novel. In '*Jude the Obscure* as an Anti-Didactic Novel' (*THJ* 30[2014] 144–60), Rezo D'Agnillo uses Matthew Arnold's principles of Hellenism and Hebraism to discuss Jude's academic and life failures. Abdol Hossein and Sima Ghasemi give a rather simplistic Foucauldian reading of *Jude the Obscure* in 'Hidden Eyes, Invisible Powers: The Panoptic World of Thomas Hardy's *Jude the Obscure*' (*JISR* 7[2014] 127–33). Finally, Faezeh Sivandipour and Rosli Talif's 'Investigating Thomas Hardy's Reaction to Victorian Religious Forces through Reading *Tess of the D'Urbervilles* and *Jude the Obscure*' (*PJSSH* 22[2014] 785–95) identifies Hardy as a meliorist and offers a basic account of the novel and its historical moment broadly defined.

J. Hillis Miller includes a chapter on Hardy, 'Individual and Community in *The Return of the Native*' (in *Communities of Fiction*, pp. 93–138; reviewed above). As in the other readings in the book, Miller tries to place community within *Return of the Native* on a continuum between Raymond Williams and

Heidegger. At first Miller aligns the Egdon community with Williams (idyllic, pre-capitalist), before explaining how the main characters in the novel are cut off by their awareness of themselves as unique, unknowable beings. Eustacia and Clem are, for Miller, confronting *Dasein*. Neither model, Miller concludes, is presented as satisfactory in Hardy's novel. The feeling of being on the outside in Hardy is explored quite literally by Lindsay Gail Gibson in 'Hardy's Lit Interiors' (*THJ* 30[2014] 161–84), which reads a series of scenes in Hardy's fiction where one character standing outside in the dark looks in through a window at another in a well-lit interior. These moments, Gibson argues, 'serve as lyric interpolations in his novels' love plots' (p. 162). The careful lighting and frame enable 'a form of feeling equally incompatible with the daylight constraints of their class identity and with the formal conventions of the novel' (p. 162).

In 'Tess's Boots: Hardy and Van Gogh' (*THJ* 30[2014] 54–65), Roger Ebbatson also draws on Heidegger, this time his discussion of Van Gogh's *A Pair of Shoes*, in order to argue that the boots in *Tess of the D'Urbervilles* and *Under the Greenwood Tree* become sites for the negotiation of utilitarian and erotic being. Barbara Schapiro, by contrast, uses relational psychology to analyse the tense mutual dependence of romantic love, aggression, and idealization in her article, 'Love's Shadow: The Unconscious Underside of Romance in Hardy's *The Woodlanders*' (*Mosaic* 47[2014] 153–67). In an essay for a special issue of *19: Interdisciplinary Studies in the Long Nineteenth-Century*, William A. Cohen turns to Hardy's *The Woodlanders* for help in theorizing the Victorian 'tactile imagination' (p. 2) in his essay 'Arborealities: The Tactile Ecology of Hardy's Woodlanders' (*19* 19[2014] 1–19). Cohen sees Hardy as anticipating recent theorists of affect and the environment in the way that he 'emphasizes the material properties of people and the continuities between them and the world they inhabit' (p. 19).

Two articles appeared on Thomas Hardy and maps of one kind or another. Mary Rimmer's 'Hardy's Culture Maps' (*THJ* 30[2014] 34–53) looks at Hardy's metaphorical mapping—verbal renditions of cultural patterns, associations, and frames of reference that orient individuals (fictional and otherwise) within the world in which they live. Susan E. Cook's 'Mapping Hardy and Brontë' (in Tally, ed., *Literary Cartographies: Spatiality, Representation, and Narrative*, 61–73) presents the creative and satisfying argument that *Tess of the D'Urbervilles* and *Villette* 'mimic cartographic imperialism' (p. 62) by renaming pre-existing locations as part of the process of incorporating them into the fictional world of the novel. However, Cook argues, by centring their novels on characters who feel at sea both socially and geographically, Brontë and Hardy resist the narrative of geopolitical nation-building. Margaret Kolb combines literary plot and mathematical puzzle in her fascinating article, 'Plot Circles: Hardy's Drunkards and Their Walks' (*VS* 56[2014] 595–623), arguing that the structure of Hardy's Wessex novels reflects mathematical theories about the relationship between circularity and causation. In 'Romance Narrative in Hardy's *A Pair of Blue Eyes*' (*VLC* 42[2014] 709–31), John P. Farrell reads Hardy's early novel as a self-conscious layering of two narrative modes—realism and romance—to create a 'sedimentary' text. (p. 717). Carroll Clayton Savant's 'The Sins of the

Grandmother: The Complicated Darwinian Discourse in the Late Victorian Cultural Consciousness and the Role of Behavioral Inheritance in Hardy's *A Pair of Blue Eyes*' (*The Victorian* 2:ii[2014] 1–12) draws parallels between close readings of Darwin's *The Origin of Species* and Hardy's novel while pointing out how the latter engages more broadly with evolutionary theory. For Ronald D. Morrison, Hardy's interest not just in natural science, but in the relationship between humans and the natural world earns him recognition as an early practitioner of ecocriticism in 'Tragedy and Ecology in the Later Novels of Thomas Hardy' (in Mazzeno, ed., *Twenty-First Century Perspectives on Victorian Literature*, pp. 185–201). Rena Jackson's '"Years of Unexpectedness": India and Social Mobility in Hardy's Early Fiction' (*THJ* 30[2014] 121–43) explores how Hardy's early fiction was influenced by key moments in his biography when colonial India collided with his own plans or those of individuals close to him.

Finally, the Hardy enthusiast may be interested in a little book put out by Austin Macauley. Huw Barker Rahane's *Who's Who in Thomas Hardy* includes a section on each of Hardy's novels and collections of short fiction in which one can find an entry for each character appearing in that work with a short description of his or her role in the text. Rahane explains that his object was to provide 'a list of those who *materially* advance or illustrate the plot' that would be 'useful to anyone wishing to find out quickly who Marty South loved in vain or who shot Sergeant Troy' (p. 9). He achieves just that.

In 'Marvelous Plasticity and the Fortunes of Species in *The Water-Babies*' (*P&L* 38[2014] 162–77), Anna Neill writes about the interplay between biological, social, and imaginary forms of evolution and progress in Kingsley's novel.

PMLA published an article on Kipling this year. Allen MacDuffie's '*The Jungle Books*: Rudyard Kipling's Lamarckian Fantasy' (*PMLA* 129[2014] 18–34) labels the evolutionary paradigm of *The Jungle Books* as Lamarckian, part of a late-century reaction to Darwinism that embraced the earlier theorist's outdated logic because it 'emphasized the value of experience, the directive role of culture, and the potential for active self-shaping' (p. 19). *The Kipling Journal* included several articles on Kipling's novels. In '*Kim*, Theosophy, and Two Ethnologists Called Mukherji' (*KJ* 88:cclvii[2014] 30–43), Andrew Huxley explains that 'the political fuel that powered Kipling to write *Kim*' (p. 31) was events that occurred a decade before the novel was written while the young author was working as a journalist reporting on the 'Theosophical Society, the campaign against the Ilbert Bill, and the formation of Indian National Congress' (p. 31). Erin Louttit's article, '"What Profit to Kill Men?": Buddhist Non-Violence in *Kim*' (*KJ* 88:cclvii[2014] 22–9), appears in the same issue and draws our attention to the message of non-violence in the novel. Richard M. Berrong makes an interesting connection between Kipling's fiction and Impressionism in '*Captains Courageous*: The Importance of Impressionist Art in Life' (*KJ* 88:ccliv[2014] 25–39). Kipling, Berrong notes, was very familiar with the work of Whistler and other impressionist painters and often discussed his writing in painterly metaphors. In *Captains Courageous*, Berrong argues, the world of the novel is presented through the perceptions of individuals limited by their own particular vantage point.

Two essays on Le Fanu appeared in Morin and Gillespie, eds., *Irish Gothics: Genres, Forms, Modes, and Traditions, 1760–1890* (reviewed above). Elizabeth Tilley, in 'J.S. Le Fanu, Gothic and the Irish Periodical' (pp. 130–46), examines Le Fanu's roles as the editor of and a contributor to the *Dublin University Magazine* in 1864, the year *Uncle Silas* was published in its pages. Tilley argues that Le Fanu struggled, with mixed success, to separate his own Gothic writings and those published within the *DUM* from the sensation fiction which was fast becoming so popular in Britain. In his essay, '"Whom We Name Not": *The House by the Churchyard* and its Annotation' (pp. 147–67), W.J. McCormack demonstrates through a series of detailed annotations how LeFanu combined Gothic and historical fiction in order to address the complicated, violent politics of the Protestant Ascendancy.

In 'Orthopedic Disability and the Nineteenth Century Novel' (*NCC* 36:i[2014] 1–17), Karen Bourrier argues that orthopaedic disabilities 'gained currency as a visually dramatic way for authors to mark a character as an individual, and to explore how far he could fit into the community, and how psychological suffering could breed sympathy' (p. 3). She provides a brief history of orthopaedic surgery and readings of novels by both George Eliot and Lucas Malet.

Kristen A. Pond contributed a notable article this year entitled 'Harriet Martineau's Epistemology of Gossip' (*NCL* 69[2014] 175–207), in which she situates Martineau's only novel, *Deerbrook*, within the context of the author's other work as an epistemological treatise in its own right. However, where Martineau's non-fiction privileges empiricism, *Deerbrook*, according to Pond, presents the intuitive, speculative gossip of female characters as an important category of knowledge in its own right, one that calls into question what constitutes truth both within and without the fictional world. In 'Martineau's Dissent: Advancing the Dissenters' Cause in *Deerbrook*' (*VJ* 125[2014] 88–107), Michael J. Sobiech argues that *Deerbrook* was an important precursor to Eliot's fiction, which would also portray Dissenters in a positive light. 'If, in the *Illustrations of Political Economy* Martineau wrote in order to spread the gospel of political economy', Sobiech claims, 'in *Deerbrook*, she wrote, in part, to spread the gospel of religious tolerance' (p. 91).

In 'Reading Margaret Oliphant' (*JVC* 19[2014] 232–46), George Levine urges readers to pick up the novels of the long-neglected writer, not for their historical interest but for their literary merit. Paying special attention to *The Ladies Lindores* and *For Love and Life*, Levine credits Oliphant with canny insight into the deep significance in ordinary life. Levine would probably approve, then, of Carrie Dickison's '"[F]or What You May Do with It": The Curate and the Curator in Oliphant's *The Curate in Charge* and *Phoebe Junior*' (*NCC* 36[2014] 217–31). In this article, Dickison reads two of Oliphant's novels as a response to Pater. Oliphant offers 'curatorial labor' with an end beyond itself as an alternative to 'art for art's sake' (p. 229). Though Dickison does not, as Levine would wish, spend much time discussing the aesthetics of Oliphant's own prose, she does at least remind us just how deeply Oliphant was concerned with questions of form and style.

Clare Walker Gore advocates for more attention to another once popular woman writer. In 'Setting Novels at Defiance: Novel Reading and Novelistic Form in Charlotte M. Yonge's *The Heir of Redclyffe*' (*NCGS* 10:i[2014] 1–15), Gore argues for Yonge's generic canniness, highlighting the way she manipulates the boundaries between domestic and Gothic fiction for readerly pleasure. Janet Powney and Jeremy Mitchell introduce readers of *The Victorian* to another little-read author in their article 'A Forgotten Voice: Moral Guidance in the Novels of Mary Gordon (Mrs. Disney Leith), with a Bibliography' (*The Victorian* 2:i[2014] 1–26). Powney and Mitchell's description of Gordon's unobjectionable rural romances calls to mind the fiction of Charlotte Yonge, who in fact published one of Gordon's stories in her magazine.

Several readings of Stevenson's adventure fiction complicate that author's relationship to the imperial project. The empire becomes a casualty of adulthood in Alexandra Valint's 'The Child's Resistance to Adulthood in Robert Louis Stevenson's *Treasure Island*: Refusing to Parrot' (*ELT* 58[2014] 3–29). Valint reads Dr Livesey as 'cruel, greedy, emotionless, and quick to punish those deemed inferior', the representative of an adulthood intent on imperial domination (p. 3). Thus Jim's refusal to grow up, in Valint's reading, 'marks him as being uninterested and opposed' to the maintenance of empire. Daniel Hannah, in 'Queer Wanderings: Transatlantic Piracy and Narrative Seduction in Robert Louis Stevenson's *The Master of Ballantrae*' (*ELT* 57[2014] 184–209), analyses the 'anticipatory structure' of that novel which always gestures outward to what lies beyond and before national and heteronormative discourse (p. 186). In this reading, 'the Atlantic figures forth an uncanny space outside or between nations in which Stevenson's novel probes the queer forms of mastery that order national narratives' (p. 185). Amy R. Wong, in 'The Poetics of Talk in Robert Louis Stevenson's *Treasure Island*' (*SEL* 54[2014] 901–22), draws our attention to Stevenson's privileging of talk. *Treasure Island*, she argues, 'brings special attention to the ways in which talking and adventuring share a heroic, open embrace of the movement at the heart of unpredictable interactions', whether those be with another individual or the environment (p. 902). Looking primarily at *Kidnapped*, *Treasure Island*, and *The Ebb-Tide*, Cannon Schmitt, in 'Technical Maturity in Robert Louis Stevenson' (*Rep* 125[2014] 54–79), argues that Stevenson's *Bildungsromane* require their characters to master a technical language and vocabulary in order to achieve a maturity less fixed than that signalled in the traditional *Bildungsroman* by marriage or assimilation into middle-class society. Allen MacDuffie includes a chapter on *Strange Case of Dr. Jekyll and Mr. Hyde* in his monograph, *Victorian Literature, Energy, and the Ecological Imagination* (reviewed above). In 'Personal Fantasy, Natural Limits: Robert Louis Stevenson's *Dr. Jekyll and Mr. Hyde*' (pp. 170–97), MacDuffie writes about the novel as 'a mythical elaboration of contemporary thermodynamic tropes and an eco-fable about the irreversible depletion of resources' (p. 170). The very plot of the novel, according to MacDuffie, is a carefully engineered yet 'unsustainable narrative', self-consuming and contingent. In 'Women and Sadism in '*Strange Case of Dr. Jekyll and Mr. Hyde*: "City in a Nightmare"' (*ELT* 57[2014] 309–23), Charles Campbell revisits the question of why women occupy such marginal places in *Dr. Jekyll and Mr. Hyde*. Campbell emphasizes the importance of these characters who, for him, 'define the cityscape' which is 'defined at the outset topographically as female' (pp. 310, 320). These women, Campbell argues, serve to remind readers that male sadism erupts when otherwise harmless sexual desire has been repressed.

In honour of the 100-year anniversary of Bram Stoker's death, Four Courts Press has issued *Bram Stoker: Centenary Essays*, edited by Jarlath Killeen. In his introduction, Killeen laments the *Dracula*-centric nature of Stoker criticism, and with some hesitation defends psychoanalytic readings of Stoker's work. Rather than focus on the sexual, however, Killeen recommends that psychoanalytic theory be applied to the intersections between Stoker's technophilia and Irish nationalism. The first three essays focus on Stoker's biography. 'Bram Stoker: The Child That Went with the Fairies' by David J. Skal provides a rather fanciful, loosely psychoanalytic sketch of Stoker's early years when he suffered from a mysterious malady that prevented him from walking. The second essay, 'Bram Stoker: The Facts and the Fictions' by Paul Murray takes former biographers to task for the very kind of speculation that characterizes the preceding essay, i.e. perpetuating misconceptions about Stoker's life. Murray sets out to correct two of these by meticulously working through the material available on Stoker's university years and his death. Elizabeth Miller's 'Bram Stoker: A Man of Notes' looks at Stoker's extant journal in order to demonstrate aspects of Stoker that have been overlooked, such as his sense of humour. Carol A. Senf's essay, 'Bram Stoker: Ireland and Beyond' takes up several of Stoker's less well-known works, including *The Snake's Pass*, *Lady Athlyne*, and *The Shoulder of Shasta*, in which she finds evidence of Stoker's interest in Irish as well as more global politics. Andrew J. Garavel's '*The Shoulder of Shasta*: Bram Stoker's California Romance' locates the gender and racial anxiety so central to *Dracula* in the earlier novel about the American West. William Hughes's '"Rumours of the Great Plague": Medicine, Mythology, and the Memory of the Sligo Cholera in Bram Stoker's *Under the Sunset*' examines medical thought in Stoker's earlier fiction, arguing that Stoker's knowledge of medicine was up to date and his interest in the subject both practical and theoretical. David Floyd contributes an essay entitled '"The Sport of Opposite Forces": Bram Stoker's Generational Anxiety', which considers Stoker's concern for the integrity of the domestic sphere at a time of apparent ideological flux in *Dracula* and a handful of less well-known texts. David Floyd, in '"See How the Bog Can Preserve": Bogs, Snakes, and Irish Stereotypes in *The Snake's Pass*', argues that Stoker's only explicitly Irish text attempts to establish 'the basis for an intra-national and inter-national harmony' (p. 162) for Ireland by imagining a common and unifying past. In '*The Lair of the White Worm*; or, What Became of Bram Stoker?' Darryl Jones takes one of Stoker's 'frankly deranged novels' (p. 164), asserting that its incoherence constitutes its merit for academic study, finding in its use of snake lore an experimental engagement with the Symbolist movement. In the final essay in the collection, Christopher Frayling examines the material traces of Bram Stoker's holiday in Whitby, ultimately suggesting that it is the 'ordinariness' of *Dracula* that makes it such a success.

The authors included in *Bram Stoker: Centenary Essays* were not the only ones interested in Stoker's less recognized fiction. In 'Bram Stoker's *The Lady of the Shroud*: Supernatural Fantasy, Politics, Montenegro and its Double' (*ELT* 57[2014] 519–34), Lisa Hopkins examines possible origins for *The Lady of the Shroud* and draws our attention to the political significance of Stoker's figurative pairing of Montenegro and Scotland. Two essays of Stoker's appeared in Morin and Gillespie, eds., *Irish Gothics* (reviewed above). Jarlath Killeen, in 'Muscling Up: Bram Stoker and Irish Masculinity in *The Snake's Pass*' (pp. 168–87), argues that Stoker translated Ireland's struggle for an independent future into a war between effeminate and muscular masculinities. In '"The Old Far West and the New": Bram Stoker, Race, and Manifest Destiny' (pp. 188–205), Luke Gibbons investigates Stoker's often complicated attitudes towards race and empire in some of his less well-known titles, including *The Mystery of the Sea*, *The Snake's Pass*, and *The Shoulder of Shasta*. Despite all the interest in less well-known Stoker texts, however, *Dracula* still received some attention. In '"The Blood is the Life!"': Victorian Manifestations of Porphyric Anxiety and Bloodlust in Bram Stoker's *Dracula*' (*JDS* 16[2014] 7–22), Ashley Szanter argues that Stoker's most famous novel was influenced by current medical literature on porphyria—a disease causing photosensitivity, redness of the eyes, and trance states—as well as folklore. Marta Miquel-Baldellou suggests that the figure of the vampire in Gothic fiction has important implications for ageing studies, in 'From Pathology to Invisibility: The Discourse of Ageing in Vampire Fiction' (*ET* 12[2014] 95–114). Beginning in the Victorian period with *Camilla* and *Dracula*, and ending with *Twilight* and *Let the Right One In*, Miquel-Baldellou points out that while the ability to survive to an incredibly old age remains a constant in such fiction, the vampire's actual *appearance* has become more youthful, a trend that Miquel-Baldellou reads as part of a larger shift in the treatment of ageing from pathologization to denial. Aubrey L.C. Mishou's article, 'Dearly Departed: The Treatment of the Corpses of Sweethearts' (*The Victorian* 2:iii[2014] 1–10), considers female corpses in Victorian literature, blood-drained and otherwise. In Poe's 'Annabel Lee', Brontë's *Wuthering Heights*, and Stoker's *Dracula*, Mishou argues, the 'sweetheart is valued more dead than alive, and the resulting corpse becomes a catalyst for subversive sexuality, a fetishistic object that legitimizes a fascination with the ultimately vulnerable woman' (p. 3).

William Makepeace Thackeray seems to have fallen completely out of favour, receiving almost no attention in the academic literature from 2014. One exception is Vittoria Rubino's 'The Puppetry and Performance of Society in Thackeray's *Vanity Fair*' (*The Victorian* 2:iii[2014] 1–17). The reading of Thackeray's novel through its own framing metaphor, however, does little to forward scholarship in this area.

A diverse selection of novels by the prolific Anthony Trollope engaged critical attention in 2014 publications. Simon Dentith, in the fifth chapter of his *Nineteenth-Century British Literature Then and Now*, 'Trollope and Political Realism' (pp. 81–100), asks how Trollope's 'fiction, and the historical series in which it participates are illuminated by the subsequent history of parliamentary politics and its attendant scandals'. For Dentith, 'the complex rhetorical economy of Trollope's fiction is disturbed by the subsequent history, and the political and historiographical reflection that it has provoked' (p. 81). Dentith manages to encompass discussion of *Dr. Thorne* (pp. 82–3), *Phineas Finn* (pp. 86–8, 91–6), *Phineas Redux* (pp. 97–9), *The Prime Minister* (p. 98), *Ralph the Heir* (pp. 82–4), and *The Way We Live Now* (p. 98). Dagni Bredersen, in her consideration of widows' mourning customs, 'An Emblem of All the Rest: Wearing the Widow's Cap in Victorian Literature' (in Giorcelli and Rabinowitz, eds., *Fashioning the Nineteenth Century: Habits of Being*, pp. 82–105), includes a discussion of *Barchester Towers*. The fifth chapter, 'Barbarous Benevolence: Anthony Trollope's *The Fixed Period* (1882) and *Australia and New Zealand* (1873)' (pp. 159–96), of Helen Lucy Blythe's *The Victorian Colonial Romance with the Antipodes* discusses these two Trollope novels. Blythe also treats *The New Zealander* [1855–6] much more briefly (pp. 161–2, 215–16). She writes that 'Trollope parodies the utopian rhetoric of colonial settlement in *The Fixed Period*...inspired by travel to New Zealand in the 1870s. His only first-person narrative and futuristic novel, *The Fixed Period* undermines the empirical detachment or critical distance of the author from his narrator and characters' (pp. 6–7). Her discussions of this novel (pp. 159–200), and of *Australia and New Zealand* (pp. 163–71) are extensive.

A critically neglected Trollope novel, the anonymously published *Nina Balatka*, is subjected to extensive treatment in Monica F. Cohen's 'The Paradox of Literary Commercialism in Trollope's *Nina Balatka*' (*Novel* 47[2014] 383–402). Cohen 'seeks to situate Anthony Trollope's short 1866 novel *Nina Balatka* in the context of the market conditions that characterized Victorian literary entertainment'. She argues that '*Nina Balatka*'s failed attempt to assimilate the figure of the Jew into a conventional marriage plot reflects a problem in Trollope's construction of authorship, a problem that inheres in how literary commercialism and literary professionalism might represent mutually exclusive value postulates.' In this most interesting contribution Cohen writes that 'In underscoring the incompatibility of the Jew and the Christian maiden of Prague, *Nina Balatka*'s unconvincing marriage plot uses the same terms that make Trollope's representation of the novelist as both baker and barrister something of a fantasy' (p. 383). Another neglected Trollope novel, *Marion Fay*, is the subject of Frederik Van Dam's '"Wholesome Lessons": Love as Tact between Matthew Arnold and Anthony Trollope' (*PAns* 12[2014] 287–310), which 'argues that the representation of love in Anthony Trollope's *Marion Fay* (1882) is informed by the conceptualization of tact in Matthew Arnold's essays'. However, 'Trollope's thematic exploration of love as tact is mirrored in the novel's style: *Marion Fay* achieves a measure of reserve by framing love within moments that abruptly descend from the exalted to the banal (p. 287).

The neglected novel *Harry Heathcote of Gangoil* [1873] engages Grace Moore in her '"The Heavens Were on Fire": Incendiarism and the Defence of the Settler Home' (in Wagner, ed., *Domestic Fiction in Colonial Australia and New Zealand*, pp. 63–73). Moore is concerned with the fictional treatment of Australian farms and particularly the incendiarism to which they were subject. Denise Lovett, in 'The Socially-Embedded Market and the Future of English Capitalism in Anthony Trollope's *The Way We Live Now*' (*VLC* 42[2014] 691–

707), observes that while it 'is often read as an attack on rampant capitalism, Trollope's novel appears instead to have anticipated a more general acceptance that markets, especially complex financial markets, do not function autonomously, for, by the end of the Victorian period, the very point that Trollope's novel illustrates became common currency'. For Lovett, 'the novel suggests that "the way we live now" requires the conscious and collective structuring of modern capitalist markets to ensure their consistency with English social values and standards of honest commerce' (p. 702). Finally, Patrick Fessenbecker, in his 'Anthony Trollope on Akrasia, Self-Deception, and Ethical Confusion' (*VS* 56[2014] 649–74), draws upon Trollope's fictional and non-fictional work to investigate his 'tendency to reuse a version of the romantic triangle, one where a protagonist is committed to one character, becomes attracted to another, and hence delays fulfillment of the first relationship. This formal feature makes the philosophical problem of akrasia central, as the novels return repeatedly to agents who act against their own best judgment.' Furthermore Fessenbecker argues that 'Trollope's novels reveal a complex array of irrationality, considering how our desires can lead to self-deception and how even judgment unbiased by desire may fail to move an agent. Perhaps most interestingly, Trollope challenges standard assumptions about rational behavior in depicting states of "ethical confusion", where characters act irrationally precisely by acting on their best judgment' (p. 649). The article concludes that 'Trollope offers a moral psychology that complements his view of moral deliberation: the gentleman represents an ideal for moral agency not only because he will be appropriately sensitive to situational particularities, but also because, in minimizing the ethical role of judgment, he will avoid irrationality' (p. 672).

In 'Evolutionary Energy and the Future: Henry Maudsley and H.G. Wells' (pp. 223–51), a chapter in his monograph *Victorian Literature, Energy, and the Ecological Imagination* (reviewed above), Allen MacDuffie explores the way that the discourse surrounding degeneration at the end of the century 'combined evolutionary theory with a concern and waste of energy resources' (p. 225). The discourse of degeneration, according to MacDuffie, 'biologized' the environmentally destructive side effects of industrialism, representing the poor as contaminants rather than as victims. MacDuffie reads *The Time Machine* within this context. The novel ends, MacDuffie claims, with this paradox: 'for productive social reform to happen, the implications of modern scientific thought must be confronted without illusion. But confronting them in all their grim inexorability corrodes the very impetus to reform' (p. 247). Wells receives considerable attention in *Fin de Siècle Fictions, 1890s/1990s: Apocalypse, Technoscience, Empire* by Aristeidis Mousoutzanis. This unusual book moves back and forth between literature of the last decade of each of the past two centuries in order draw attention not so much to similarities as to continuities. Mousoutzanis is particularly interested in the recurrent themes of empire and technoscience that appear in the fiction of both decades, through a rhetoric of shock and trauma. One odd feature of the book is that while the fiction from the 1890s in it is British, the fiction from the 1990s is American. Mousoutzanis asserts that this is the result of space restrictions, but further theorization about the transatlantic nature of the project would be beneficial.

In 'The Hermeneutic Hazards of Hibernicizing Oscar Wilde's *The Picture of Dorian Gray*' (*ELT* 57[2014] 37–58), Richard Haslam takes to task scholars interested in 'Hibernicizing' Wilde, pointing out how tenuous is the nature of many arguments connecting Wilde's work to his Irish background. Haslam urges critics to attend more carefully to the way in which their own biases affect their interpretation of literary texts. In another article published this year, Haslam presumably does just that. His 'Revisiting the "Irish Dimension" in Oscar Wilde's *The Picture of Dorian* Gray' (*VLC* 42[2014] 267–79) again denounces the questionable analogical methodologies of former critics interested in the Irish elements of Wilde's work before launching into an archival consideration of a debate in *Scots Observer* directly following the publication of the novel and the resulting revisions Wilde made to the manuscript. One wonders whether Haslam would take issue with Ellen Scheible's article, 'Imperialism, Aesthetics, and Gothic Confrontation in *The Picture of Dorian Gray*' (*NewHibR* 18[2014] 131–50). Scheible argues that 'England's colonial enterprises in both Ireland and India haunt *Dorian Gray* as repressed subplots that surface sporadically within Wilde's more overt illustration of aesthetic and imperial insatiability' (p. 131). Of particular interest to Gray is the role the Gothic convention in staging submerged confrontations between the colonizer and the colonized.

3. Poetry

In this section Clara Dawson reviews publications on Arnold, Hopkins, Tennyson, Patmore, working-class poets, and poetry from 1870 to 1900. Clare Stainthorp reviews publications on the Rossettis, the Brownings, Swinburne, women poets, and poetry from 1830 to 1870; both contributors review work on periodical poetry.

To begin with general works, E. Warwick Slinn's updated chapter on 'Poetry' (in the reissue of Tucker, ed., *A New Companion to Victorian Literature and Culture*, pp. 331–48) argues that the passive metaphor of reflection does not adequately demonstrate the complexity, dynamism, and disruptive power of Victorian poetry, particularly when it is read alongside Romantic-era poetry. In this inevitably brief but admirably wide-ranging overview Slinn identifies cultural neoformalism as the prevailing trend in scholarship, which 'aligns poetic affectiveness with historical specificity' (p. 336) and draws attention to poetic language's textuality as well as its material production and cultural consumption.

Natalie M. Houston's short essay 'Toward a Computational Analysis of Victorian Poetics' (*VS* 56[2014] 498–510) engages with the new critical possibilities of the digitization of nineteenth-century texts. Houston argues for a definition of digital reading that transcends the binary of close versus distance reading and discusses how three of her current projects (*The Field of Victorian Poetry 1840–1900*, *The Visual Page as Interface*, and *Understanding Victorian Poetic Style*) utilize digital archives of Victorian poems in important new ways, 'mov[ing] beyond human limitations of vision, memory, and attention' (p. 499). This includes mapping the field of poetry publication and 'analysing the graphic codes of Victorian poetry' (p. 504).

John Holmes's chapter 'The Challenge of Evolution in Victorian Poetry' (in Lightman and Zon, eds., *Evolution and Victorian Culture*, pp. 39–63) uses Tennyson to discuss poets' impact on the interpretation of evolution before and after the publication of *On the Origin of Species*. Holmes provides a useful overview of existing critical works, and then covers evolution in poetry before Darwin published his seminal work (arguing that *In Memoriam* is 'one of the most influential mid-century treatments of the idea of evolution' (p. 44)). The second half of the essay considers poetry that engages with the existential implications of evolution and the socio-cultural ramifications of this theory. Referencing a wide range of major and minor poets, Holmes persuasively demonstrates the near-ubiquity of evolutionary themes after *Origin*. He concludes with a litany of future research questions for the study of Victorian poetry and science.

Victorian Irish poetry received considerable attention this year. Matthew Campbell's illuminating book, *Irish Poetry under the Union, 1801–1924*, makes an important contribution to both Victorian studies and Irish studies. Campbell begins by exploring the problems facing the development of Irish poetry in English in the nineteenth century, where 'powerful ideas of rootedness and antiquity met the demands of print culture and performance' (p. 2). The establishment of an Irish poetry confronted the slippage between the authentic and the synthetic, the currents of politics and culture, the relation of Ireland to Victorian England and to the Romantic movement, the translation of Irish songs into English lyrics, and the relation of the Celtic to the Teutonic. The book probes metaphors of cultural union in Irish poetry, but also argues that we must celebrate 'its baggage as synthetic, forged, stolen or mere translation' (p. 8). In chapter 2, 'The Ruptured Ear', Campbell traces the attempt to create poetry which uses or translates Irish sounds or sonic patterns into English, a process he describes as 'conspicuously impure', continuing his focus on the synthetic in Irish poetics. Using Thomas Moore's and Samuel Ferguson's lyric translations from Irish into English, Campbell examines how Irish music, metre, and accent make their way into English verse and explores the political and aesthetic implications therein. The third chapter, 'From Moore to Mahoney: The Transmigration of Intellect', examines two critical positions on Irish poetry in the nineteenth century, one which saw Irish poetry as a union of 'the rudimentary' (p. 48) ballad form with 'the refinement' (p. 48) of modern English, and the other which saw this union as a sentimental veil covering nationalist politics. Campbell has a detailed discussion of the critic Francis Mahoney's essays and poetry to further explore the synthetic nature of Irish nineteenth-century poetry in regard to these polarized positions. In chapter 4, 'Samuel Ferguson's Maudlin Jumble', Campbell traces the complex political context for poetry in the 1830s, with urbanization and growing mass literacy combining with French ideas about republicanism threatening the ascendancy of the Protestant class. Ferguson sought to enable his Protestant audience 'to claim the post-Union Protestant patriotism' he longed for (p. 71) and to create a 'commonality of culture' (p. 72) between Ireland and Great Britain. A chapter on 'Mangan's Golden Years' examines attitudes to history and time, particularly in relation to the catastrophe of the famine. Mangan stands, overall, as an exemplum of the type of Irish writer who found themsel[ves] trapped within circumstances that proved 'too powerful to admit imaginative freedom' (p. 101). The next two chapters reverse the direction of translation and look at English poets writing poems about Ireland, 'Victorian poems that sound ambiguity within themselves' (p. 135). Chapter 6 examines Tennyson's Celtic nostalgia, and in chapter 7, '"Spelt from Sibyl's Leaves": Hopkins, Yeats and the Unravelling of British Poetry', Campbell examines the poetry of Hopkins and Yeats written in Ireland at a historical moment of uncertainty for the Union and argues that Hopkins's poem 'Spelt from Sibyl's Leaves' is an Irish poem which exemplifies the uneasy transplantation of English poetry into 'a place where it should be at home' (p. 167). The final chapter, 'Violence and Measure: Yeats after Union', examines poetry written as the Union was dissolving and focuses on Yeats's 1924 revisions of his earlier poetry, as well as on his war poems.

The second study of Irish poetry was *Essays on James Clarence Mangan: The Man in the Cloak*, edited by Sinéad Sturgeon. It offers a wide-ranging account of Mangan's poetry, prose, and translations, as well as his afterlife in nineteenth- and twentieth-century culture. Sturgeon's introduction emphasizes, and contextualizes, the sheer variety of Mangan's work. The first five chapters consider Mangan as translator, starting with David Lloyd, whose 'Crossing Over: On Mangan's "Spirit's Everywhere"' (pp. 14–32) dwells upon the idea of the spirit of a text and argues that this poem is a 'metacomment on the practice of translation as oversetting' (p. 28). David Wheatley follows with '"Fully Able / To Write in Any Language—I'm a Babel": James Clarence Mangan and the Task of the Translator', exploring the importance of Irish literature and culture to his approach to translation. In '"Antiquity and Futurity" in the Writings of James Clarence Mangan' Joseph Lennon considers Mangan's legacy as 'a man out of time...existing in, or haunted by, ancient Ireland' (p. 53), and how this sits with his visions of a revolutionary future. In 'Cosmopolitan Form: Mangan's Anthologies and the Critique of *Weltliteratur*' Cóilín Parsons asserts that the form in which Mangan's poetry appeared is as worthy of consideration as its content. Parsons argues that 'his anthologies of translations of world literature constitute experimental attempts to represent what Bruce Robbins has called "cosmopolitanism, interrupted"' (p. 85), enabling us to consider Mangan as a product of his time, rather than speaking to another epoch, as is often asserted. Sinéad Sturgeon takes a close-reading approach in 'Night Singer: Mangan Among the Birds', discussing a group of bird poems published during the 1830s; she deftly elucidates the significance of the nightingale, the raven, and the parrot in relation to Mangan's developing poetic voice. In '"The Last of the Bardic Poets": Joyce's Multiple Mangans' John McCourt considers James Joyce's engagement with Mangan's 'proto-post-modern' works (p. 137), highlighting both overt praise and threads of influence. Richard Haslam looks to Mangan's prose works in '"[M]y Mind is Destroying Me": Consciousness, "Psychological Narrative," and Supernaturalist Modes in Mangan's Fiction', as does Anne Jamison in 'The Spiritual "Vastation" of James Clarence Mangan: Magic, Technology, and Identity'. Sean Ryder returns to issues of poetry, translation, and publication contexts in 'Unauthorised Mangan', exploring how the scattering of Mangan's output across periodicals and anthologies during and after his lifetime undermined the possibility of 'present[ing] an authorial identity that would be orderly, unified, permanent' (p. 184). Matthew Campbell has similar concerns in 'Mangan in England' and demonstrates how Mangan might be de-marginalized by analysing his use of poetic and dramatic voice alongside that of his contemporary, Robert Browning. The collection concludes with the evocative 'Afterword: Shades of Mangan', in which Ciaran Carson reflects upon the elusive figure of Mangan within culture and criticism.

In *The Ghost behind the Masks: The Victorian Poets and Shakespeare,* W. David Shaw argues that the Victorian poets 'follow Shakespeare in substituting for the closed dome of belief the unsealed dome of the Pantheon' (p. 1). The book explores themes of death and the afterlife throughout and suggests that Shakespeare's scepticism and visionary imagination can be traced in Victorian poetry. The attentive close readings draw out formal connections between them. The first section, 'Poetic Beginnings', offers a chapter each on Tennyson and Browning. Shaw draws a parallel between the way in which Tennyson matures his craft in *The Princess* and the mock-heroics of *Love's Labour's Lost.* He also suggests that Browning's decision to dramatize historical characters rather than capitalize on the success of his more theatrical monologues, such as 'Porphyria's Lover', mirrors Shakespeare's development of more complex and divided characters such as Richard II and Hamlet. The second section, 'Hamlet's Afterlives', has a chapter on Dickens (reviewed above) and on Tennyson. Shaw here fruitfully compares passages from *Hamlet* and *In Memoriam* which examine man's position in the cosmos. 'Tennyson's grand appraisal of man as paragon and misfit' (p. 63) is, Shaw suggests, echoing Hamlet's reflections on the celestial heavens and man's relation to them. Part III of the book is titled 'Shades of King Lear', and chapter 5 examines the ethics of nature seen through the character of Edmund in *Lear* and Polixenes in *The Winter's Tale.* Shaw explores how Shakespeare's ideas about gardens, nature, and art play out in Victorian poetics and alongside Darwin's theories. A chapter on 'Hardy and the Homilists' demonstrates how Hardy's disappointments mirror the disappointment of hope in *Lear.* In chapter 7, he studies the mockery and raillery in Tennyson's *Idylls of the King* and explores the influence of Lear's Fool. Lear himself upon the heath is the subject of chapter 8, which investigates disillusion in Browning's 'Childe Roland' and 'Caliban upon Setebos'. A fourth and final section, on 'Grace and Death', begins with a chapter on Tennyson and Shakespeare and explores the concept of grace through spiritual and sensual encounters in *Antony and Cleopatra* and *Maud.* Chapter 10 examines how fear of death in three characters, Browning's Cleon, Arnold's Empedocles, and Tennyson's Lucretius, is influenced by a variety of characters in Shakespeare's plays. Chapter 11 returns to Tennyson's *In Memoriam* and reads it alongside Shakespeare's sonnets. The focus in this chapter is 'time the devourer' (p. 193) and Shaw explores how Shakespeare's attitude to the ravages of time was taken up in an age where time was transformed by new geological ideas. The final chapter, 'Oracle Meets Wit: The Promised End', examines literary influence through rhetoric and style as well as direct allusion. Asyndeton and hendiadys in Tennyson, Hopkins, Browning, and Arnold are thoughtfully considered. Throughout, the readings of Victorian poetry are insightful and the book as a whole is illuminating.

Molly Clark Hillard's book *Spellbound: The Fairy Tale and the Victorians*, also discussed above, includes the chapters '"A Perfect Form in Perfect Rest": Tennyson's "Day Dream"', 'The Great Exhibition: Fairy Palace, Goblin Market', and 'Rossetti's Homeopathy' (pp. 92–107, 138–53, and 154–69). Hillard reads Tennyson's 'The Day Dream' in the context of Sleeping Beauty, and in adjacent chapters places it in dialogue with Keats's poem 'Eve of St. Agnes' and Edward Burne-Jones's *Briar Rose* paintings. The young Tennyson, it is argued, participates within the 'circulatory, gestational, and temporal tropes' of contemporary philosophy, science, and literature (pp. 94, 102), calling into question assumptions surrounding both narrative and genre. In the latter two chapters Hillard presents a new interpretation of Christina Rossetti's 'Goblin Market', arguing that it functions as a critique of the Great Exhibition and the literary marketplace. Hillard demonstrates how significant themes in 'Goblin Market'—'fairies, forced fruit, consumptions, contamination' (p. 152)—appeared in images of the Crystal Palace, or 'Fairy Palace' to use its popular nickname, and argues that Rossetti not only comments on commerce and exoticism at the Great Exhibition, but, in this generically and formally hybrid poem, sought to make a statement about the place of women in print media. Published in 2013, but not received in time for review in last year's *YWES*, Forest Pyle's *Art's Undoing: In the Wake of a Radical Aestheticism* includes the chapters 'Hopkins's Sighs' and 'Superficiality: What Is Loving and What Is Dead in Dante Gabriel Rossetti' (pp. 145–70 and 171–208): the wider scope of the book is discussed by Kristen Pond in Section 1 above. Premising that the poetics of the sigh underpins Hopkins's poetry, via interjections, exclamations, and apostrophes, Pyle deftly argues that while Hopkins does not seek radical aestheticism, he arrives at this 'at certain moments of certain poems' (p. 148). Pyle demonstrates how the convergence between aesthetics and theology prompts Hopkins's preoccupation with breaking and buckling, and through his analysis of 'The Windhover' claims that compounding aesthetics and theology 'produces the event of a radical aestheticism' of which 'Christ is the consequence' (p. 169). In the following chapter he argues that 'the genuine significance of Rossetti—and the special form of his acute engagement with a radical aestheticism—is best grasped not in spite of, but by virtue of his *superficiality*' (p. 172; emphasis original), which is to say, his obsession with surfaces. Focusing on the figures of Love and Death throughout, the chapter concludes by highlighting the radically 'superficial demands' that *The House of Life* 'places upon its writer and its readers' (p. 206).

Laurence W. Mazzeno's edited collection of essays on *Twenty-First Century Perspectives on Victorian Literature* contains two chapters on poetry. 'Faith and Doubt: Tennyson and Other Victorian Poets' (pp. 45–62), by Saverio Tomaiuolo, gives a survey of Tennyson's religious concerns from 'Supposed Confessions of a Second-Rate Sensitive Mind' to late poems 'The Ancient Sage' and 'Crossing the Bar'. Tomaiuolo lays out the connections of these poems to contemporary Victorian debates within the fields of science and religion and comments on how Tennyson responded formally to them. David Latham's chapter, 'A "World of Its Own Creation": Pre-Raphaelite Poetry and the New Paradigm for Art' (pp. 127–50), opens with an insightful exploration of Pre-Raphaelite theory. He draws out the contradictions of Pre-Raphaelite practice, the 'jarring conflict of tensions among these three paradoxes—a literary subject within a naturalistic setting with a decorative style' (p. 129) and 'the fusion of opposites' such as 'aesthetics and politics' (p. 133). There are excellent readings of poems, tracing the roots of Pre-Raphaelitism in Keats and Tennyson, and its continuation into the decadence of Yeats at the end of the nineteenth century. Another edited collection of essays published in 2014 is *Victorian Poets: A Critical Reader*, edited by Valentine Cunningham, which compiles a selection of twenty-one previously published articles or book chapters. This book will make an excellent introduction to Victorian poetry, reproducing some of the best work on it in the last few decades, covering a wide range of poets and theoretical approaches.

This year saw the publication of a range of important work on women poets, including Emily Harrington's impressive monograph *Second Person Singular: Late Victorian Women Poets and the Bonds of Verse*. Harrington reconsiders the ethical and aesthetic possibilities of lyric form through insightful readings of (largely non-canonical) women poets' writings, including their verse, essays, diaries, and letters. Focusing on the interaction between 'I' and 'thou', Harrington considers how an interplay between intimacy and distance underlies the numerous bonds written about by late nineteenth-century women, including the maternal, professional, romantic, erotic, and religious. In the introduction and first chapter, '"I, for Thou Callest Such": Christina Rossetti's Heavenly Intimacy', Harrington argues that Rossetti's 'emphasis on silence, restraint, and reserve' (p. 4) orientates many women poets that followed. Through a discussion of Rossetti's lyric poetry and her 'triangulated relationship with God', Harrington concludes that for Rossetti 'lyric intimacy is impersonal', emerging from the dissolution of dramatic subjectivity (pp. 14–15). Harrington's next chapter, '"Appraise Love and Divide": Measuring Love in Augusta Webster's *Mother and Daughter*', considers how the sonnet sequence is used to reveal and articulate maternal love, its infinitude being both desired and doubted. She identifies the significance of (and anxieties surrounding) measuring love through the sonnet form and Webster's repeated metaphors for measurement. The third chapter, 'The Strain of Sympathy: A. Mary F. Robinson, *The New Arcadia*, and Vernon Lee', discusses collaboration and the relationship established between a poem and its readers and subjects, focusing on the implications of the term 'sympathy' and tensions between the aesthetic and the ethical. In '"Be Loved through Thoughts of Mine": Alice Meynell's Intimate Distance' Harrington shows how Meynell's poetry explores the silence required by intimacy, and the distance needed for bonds to form; generative instincts are shown to dominate the rhythms of life and poetry underlining the poetics of motherhood. '"So I Can Wait and Sing": Dollie Radford's Poetics of Waiting' discusses the presentation of lyric as a space for waiting; Harrington argues that the musical settings of Radford's poems speak to incompleteness and the impossibility of establishing longed-for presence. In her conclusion, 'Mary E. Coleridge and the Second Person Plural', Harrington turns to Coleridge's rejection of intimacy and the scope for alternative narratives surrounding lyric and the bonds of verse for late Victorian women.

Simon Marsden's *Emily Brontë and the Religious Imagination*, also reviewed above, reads Brontë's poetry and *Wuthering Heights* alongside theological texts and traditions in order to illuminate the fluidity of religious experience articulated in her writings, concluding that she positions the divine within nature as much as within institutions. This book is impressive for its commitment to ranging across Brontë's body of work, and takes the striking decision to equate her explorations of faith and uncertainty with the postmodern instability between theism and atheism that situates religion in counterpoint to secular modernity. Marsden offers a new reading of 'No coward soul is mine' that finds resonances with James Martineau and other contemporary dissenting theologians, and finds in several of the Gondal poems a space in which Brontë was able to engage with religion outside the bounds of her immediate social context.

Herbert F. Tucker's contribution to the Blackwell *Companion to George Eliot* (edited by Amanda Anderson and Harry E. Shaw, published in 2013, but not received in time for review in last year's *YWES*) is a chapter titled 'Poetry: The Unappreciated Eliot' (pp. 178–91). He highlights the critical failure to consider Eliot's poetry and identifies the opportunity it provides to analyse her work without the lens of canonicity. He suggests ways of approaching these undervalued texts by close-reading excerpts to identify Eliot's performativity and versatility, the heteroglossia inherent in the range of poetic registers and moral sympathy enacted in metre. Wendy S. Williams's ground-breaking *George Eliot, Poetess* goes some way towards addressing the lack of in-depth scholarship on this aspect of Eliot's oeuvre. Working on the premise that poetry was incredibly meaningful to Eliot and an extension of, rather than a departure from, her prose, Williams argues that the 'gender-specific and religiously-motivated poetess role' (p. 8) allowed Eliot to develop a prophetic voice with which to articulate her view that sympathy might replace religion. Chapter 1, 'The Poetess Tradition', analyses Eliot's role as poetess, and Williams finds that Eliot used the conventions of this tradition across a variety of genres, associating herself with femininity in a way that was circumscribed in her novels. The chapter closes with a close reading of the elegy 'Erinna'. In chapter 2, 'Prophet of Sympathy', Williams outlines Eliot's shifting religious views, identifying a doctrine of sympathy as the driving force of her life philosophy. In the early poem 'Mid the Rich Store of Nature's Gifts to Man' Williams finds that Eliot relies on biblical imagery to articulate her loss of faith but continued need for spiritual communion; in the later 'O May I Join the Choir Invisible' Eliot describes a secular heaven founded on sympathy. Chapter 3, 'Sexual Politics in Poetry', examines 'Brother and Sister' and 'How Lisa Loved the King' in the context of Eliot's equivocal attitude to gender and women's rights activism. Williams draws out a more progressive stance on sexual politics than is evident in Eliot's novels, arguing that she interrogates patriarchal assumptions by expressing subversive views while seeming to promote traditional gender roles. In chapter 4, 'Mother to the Nation', Williams finds in the themes of female community and motherhood Eliot's expression of 'the sacred value of sympathy in society' (p. 107). Her readings of *Armgart* and 'Agatha' demonstrate how Eliot sought to guide her readers to comprehend the importance of, and therefore learn to exercise, sympathy for others. A short final chapter looks towards future scholarship on Eliot's poetry, providing suggestions for avenues of research not covered in this impressive study.

Debbie Bark has edited *The Collected Works of Ann Hawkshaw*, publishing Hawkshaw's four volumes of poetry together for the first time, and demonstrating the sheer scope of her poetic output. Bark's 'Biographical Introduction' provides a notably full account of Hawkshaw's life, drawing on two unpublished memoirs (one autobiographical) alongside other family documents. The short editorial introductions to each of Hawkshaw's collections provide both contextual and analytical details, and the presence of other paratextual matter (including contemporary reviews) means that the volume will do much to facilitate future engagement with Hawkshaw in both teaching and research contexts. Cynthia Scheinberg's chapter '"And we are not what they have been": Anglo-Jewish Women Poets, 1839–1923' (in Valman, ed., *Jewish Women Writers in Britain*, pp. 35–65) begins with Celia and Marion Moss's 'bid to define an Anglo-Jewish female poetic identity' (p. 35) in their 1839 volume *Early Efforts*. Scheinberg provides an analysis of the Moss sisters alongside Grace Aguilar and Amy Levy, as well as twentieth-century poets Katie Magnus, Alice Lucas, and Nina Salaman, exploring how they engaged with expectations surrounding Hebrew and English poetic traditions, as well as those arising from gender and class. While Scheinberg's analysis is concise, she nonetheless provides convincing readings of a handful of poems (particularly Levy's 'Sonnet') in establishing their various articulations of Jewishness.

Jessi Snider reviews and builds upon the small amount of existing recuperative critical work on Ingelow in '"A Permanent Place among the English Poets": Recovery, Scholarly Practice, and the Critical Reception of Jean Ingelow' (*VJCL* 125[2014] 33–47). The positive reception of this 'sentimental, domestic verse' (p. 34) upon publication is, Snider argues, a useful indicator of taste, aesthetics, and readership during the 1860s and after. Noting that contemporary reviewers often praised Ingelow through comparisons to eminent poets, Snider asks why she remains hidden from critical view, concluding with an interrogation of modern canon formation and expansion in relation to women writers and tokenism. Christina Richieri Griffin's illuminating essay 'Writing the Rhythms of the Womb: Alice Meynell's Poetics of Pregnancy' (*MP* 112[2014] 226–48) focuses on the lack of sentimentality in poems such as 'Parentage', 'To One Poem in a Silent Time', and 'To the Mother of Christ the Son of Man'. Meynell's surprising ambivalence towards motherhood is, Griffin argues, linked to 'the unmetricality of the children that pregnancy produces' (pp. 230–1) and should be read in the context of late nineteenth- and early twentieth-century debates surrounding pregnancy and childlessness. Cheri Lin Larsen Hoeckley's study of 'The Dynamics of Poetics and Forgiveness in Adelaide Procter's "Homeless"' (*LitComp* 11:ii[2014]

94–106) explores how Procter 'collapses the secular/religious binary' (p. 95) by weaving together different types of forgiveness and the social implications of this act. Hoeckley demonstrates how Procter's conversion to Catholicism underpins the poem's double-voiced attitude to divine mercy, and how the collection *The Chaplet of Verses* is illuminated when one reads the structure as analogous to a rosary.

Stefanie Markovits explores the genre of the verse-novel in 'Adulterated Form: Violet Fane and the Victorian Verse-Novel' (*ELH* 81[2014] 635–61). She links form and content and argues that the hybridity of Fane's *Denzil Place* is intimately connected to its subversive portrayal of an adulterous relationship, that 'verse-novels reveal tensions within the literary modalities of love that correspond to tensions in the social realm' (p. 636). Markovits suggests that verse-novels were better equipped to tackle the delicate subject of adultery than novels across the nineteenth century and also explores in some detail imagery of gardens and rivers in *Denzil Place*. In '"Strong Traivelling": Re-visions of Women's Subjectivity and Female Labor in the Ballad-Work of Elizabeth Siddal' (*VP* 52[2014] 251–76), Jill R. Ehnenn uncovers how 'Siddal establishes a relationship between female selfhood and female labor through her work with ballads, and how the ballad form, itself, contributes to her task' (p. 252). Ehnenn argues that the immediate context of this production necessitated a performance of bourgeois femininity, something Siddal's visual and poetic work sought to problematize through the discourses of embodiment and reverse ekphrasis whereby traditional gender dynamics between verbal and visual representation are challenged. Significant work has also been published on the contribution of women poets (including L.E.L., Violet Fane, and Dora Greenwell) to the sphere of periodical publication, and these are reviewed below.

Steve Roud introduces Atkinson and Roud, eds., *Street Ballads in Nineteenth-Century Britain, Ireland, and North America: The Interface between Print and Oral Traditions* (additionally reviewed in Section 1 above) and comments that it focuses on broadsides and chapbooks as two manifestations of street literature which sold songs to the public and on 'the interplay between the trade in printed songs and the vernacular, primarily oral, singing traditions' (p. 3) which are commonly referred to as folk song. He argues that this field is still developing the tools needed to fully research it and that 'investigation at the micro level is still necessary before medium and higher level theories will become feasible' (p. 2). He summarizes some of the critical debates about the interaction between oral and print culture and the history of research into folk song. The song traditions discussed in the book were discovered by late Victorian and Edwardian enthusiasts and collectors. David Atkinson's chapter, 'Was There Really a "Mass Extinction of Old Ballads" in the Romantic Period?' (pp. 19–36), explores the influence of the print trade on the development of the ballad tradition and questions an accepted view that old ballads were destroyed in the Romantic period. He traces the publishing history in this period and suggests that 'tradition, whatever the value placed on it by contemporaries and by subsequent collectors and investigators, is a consequence of its economic base' (p. 19). 'Birmingham Broadsides and Oral Tradition' (pp. 37–58) by Roy Palmer explores the cultural status and publishing history of the oral ballad and the printed broadside in Birmingham in the nineteenth century. Chapter 4, 'The Newcastle Song Chapbooks' (pp. 59–76), by Peter Wood, points out that Newcastle publications contained very few of the folk songs popular in the south of England and explores this geographical disparity by focusing on Newcastle chapbooks. The fifth chapter, 'Forgotten Broadsides and the Song Tradition of the Scots Travellers' (pp. 77–104) by Chris Wright, argues that Scottish printed broadsides have not been fully considered in histories of Scottish song. These broadsides were seen by nineteenth-century collectors as degrading the tradition of oral balladry, which Wright suggests led to the 'final demise of the Scottish street literature industry' (p. 80).

'Welsh Balladry and Literacy' (pp. 105–26) by Ffion Mair Jones explores the presence of the ballad in Welsh culture, tracing its development through the history of literacy and its implantation from English culture. She examines the creation of a Welsh-language ballad and studies its publishing history. Chapter 7, 'Ballads and Ballad Singers: Samuel Lover's Tour of Dublin in 1830' (pp. 127–46) by John Moulden, examines ballads in their Irish context and focuses on the history of ballad singers and singing in their public context. He examines one account of ballad-singing in Dublin by Samuel Lover, a composer who wrote songs for a middle- and upper-class audience who mocked the street ballad singers. 'Henry J. Wehman and Cheap Print in Late Nineteenth-Century America' (pp. 147–72) by Norm Cohen traces the history of cheap printed chapbooks and broadsides in America, examining printing technology and source materials. In chapter 9, '"I'd have you to buy it and learn it": Sabine Baring-Gould, his Fellow Collectors, and Street Literature' (pp. 173–94), Martin Graebe details the history of the collector Sabine Baring-Gould, who sought to understand the origins of songs from Devon and Cornwall. David Atkinson returns to the fraught hierarchy between oral and printed ballad in 'The Popular Ballad and the Book Trade: "Bateman's Tragedy" versus "The Demon Lover"' (pp. 195–218). He focuses on the history of two ballads named in the chapter title and explores their relation to the book trade. Chapter 11, 'Mediating Maria Marten: Comparative and Contextual Studies of the Red Barn Ballads' (pp. 219–44) by Tom Pettitt, examines a series of broadside ballads inspired by a sensational murder trial in 1827. Pettitt offers a comparative study where he studies the news-ballad alongside prose journalism. The final chapter, '"Old Brown's Daughter": Re-contextualizing a Locally Composed Newfoundland Folk Song' (pp. 245–62) by Anna Kearney Guigné, posits a 'vibrant exchange... between traditional song and popular culture' (p. 245) in Newfoundland. She traces the dissemination of a British ballad, 'Old Brown's Daughter', within Newfoundland.

Working-class song was also the focus of Rod Hermeston's 'Indexing Bob Cranky: Social Meaning and the Voices of Pitmen and Keelmen in Early Nineteenth-Century Tyneside Song' (*Victo* 4[2014] 156–80), which is reviewed in Section 1 above. Another brief article on working-class poetry was written by Kirstie Blair, who examines the poetry of railway poets in 'Inhuman Rhythms: Working-Class Railway Poets and the Measure of Industry' (*VR* 40:i[2014] 35–9). She argues that metre enabled railway poets to engage fully with the opposition of machine time and human time that characterized discourse about railway accidents and that their work engages with a wider concern about how poets respond to an industrialized environment. Her insightful readings of metre in Alexander Anderson's and William Aitken's poems demonstrate 'how [their] rhythm might simultaneously collude with and celebrate the inhuman forces of industry, while also opposing them' (p. 36).

There was an abundance of excellent work on poetry in the periodical press, due in no small part to a special issue of *Victorian Poetry*. In their editorial introduction (*VP* 52[2014] 1–20) Alison Chapman and Caley Ehnes assert that the contributors to this issue argue 'not only why poetry matters to periodical studies, but *why periodical culture matters to Victorian poetry*' (p. 5; emphasis original). They highlight the need for new methodological approaches in poetry scholarship to engage with periodicals (which for the purpose of this issue encompass serial print in all its forms), and conclude with a useful overview of the current state of periodical poetry digitization. This issue offers valuable readings of poems from across the spectrum of periodical publication, and indicates the potential of several new avenues of research. In 'Imagining the Cockney University: Humorous Poetry, the March of Intellect, and the Periodical Press, 1820–1860' (*VP* 52[2014] 21–39), Brian Maidment looks to 'the aesthetically and culturally unambitious verse . . . in the newly proliferating cheap illustrated humorous journals' (p. 21) to provide insights into mass literacy's effect on traditional social characteristics. Maidment argues that serialized song-books play an important role in periodical studies, and demonstrates how these hybrid texts, despite appearing to target and represent the 'literary "low"' (p. 38), were essentially middlebrow. Michele Martinez focuses on a series of poems by Letitia Elizabeth Landon in 'Creating an Audience for a British School: L.E.L.'s *Poetical Catalogue of Pictures* in *The Literary Gazette*' (*VP* 52[2014] 41–63). These striking poems appealed to readers' curiosity and sympathy in order to encourage them to visit the paintings and engravings described in the virtual exhibition. Martinez shows how Landon co-opts features of contemporary art writing, establishing a new function of 1820s periodical poetry and suggesting that this necessitates a reassessment of Landon's poetry more broadly. Andrew Hobbs and Claire Januszewski utilize a large-scale, distance-reading approach in 'How Local Newspapers Came to Dominate Victorian Poetry Publishing' (*VP* 52[2014] 65–87). To develop a sense of trends, contexts, and characteristics Hobbs and Januszewski systematically sampled six newspapers from across the UK every twenty years between 1800 and 1900, logging over 1,000 poems. Preliminary analysis of quantity, sources, identity of poet, and subject is provided, indicating the significance of localism, the popularity of reading and writing poetry across gender, age, and class, and the way local newspapers functioned to encourage engagement with poetry. In '"A Very Poetical Town": Newspaper Poetry and the Working-Class Poet in Victorian Dundee' (*VP* 52[2014] 89–109), Kirstie Blair demonstrates an alternative, smaller-scale method of working with local newspaper poetry. Blair analyses trends in poetry published in three Dundee newspapers between 1858 and 1860, providing close readings and contexts for a small selection. Of particular interest is the importance of poetry competitions in this context, which developed local dialogues and, through commentary on the submissions, guided their working-class readership towards conservative (rather than innovative) approaches to composition.

In '"Making Poetry" in *Good Words*: Why Illustration Matters to Periodical Poetry Studies' (*VP* 52[2014] 111–39), Lorraine Janzen Kooistra argues for 'a visual poetics of everyday life' (p. 113) that arises from pictured poetry in this popular middlebrow periodical. This richly illustrated essay demonstrates the significance of the interaction between verse and woodcut engravings. Through editorial interventions, pairings become single units of composition that, Kooistra argues, make poetry material and shape readers' verbal-visual literacy. The concluding section notes interesting examples of influence and self-referentiality within *Good Words*. Kathryn Ledbetter, in 'Time and the Poetess: Violet Fane and Fin-de-Siècle Poetry in Periodicals' (*VP* 52[2014] 141–59), brings the cyclical form of periodical publication to bear on time in Fane's poetry, which appeared in a range of periodicals, including the short-lived but aptly named *Time*. Ledbetter identifies Fane's concern with seasons, life-cycles, the suspension of time, and, crucially, the dynamism of transatlantic celebrity in conjunction with the specificity of its periodical context. A useful appendix provides a selected list of poetry by Fane in British periodicals. In '"Between Politics and Deer-Stalking": Browning's Periodical Poetry' (*VP* 52[2014] 161–82), Linda K. Hughes notes that it is more abundant than is often assumed (she enumerates the relevant poems in an appendix). Hughes conceptualizes Browning's publication in this context 'as an expression of friendship networks within a gift economy' (p. 162), identifying how each periodical's outlook and editorial policies illuminates these poems' resonances. Of additional interest is the shift in themes before and after Browning's marriage, with earlier poems being primarily about current affairs and later ones registering in various ways his union with Barrett Browning. F. Elizabeth Gray argues, in '"With thrilling interest": Victorian Women Poets Report the News' (*NCGS* 10[2014] 33 paras.) that journalistic poems provided women with the opportunity to engage with news production, often aspiring 'to create dialogues that forwarded their own values ... and to challenge conventional thinking about the authoritative status of texts purporting to offer "a true account"' (para. 1). Gray reads three poems to illustrate this position: 'In the Round Tower at Jhansi, June 8, 1857' (Christina Rossetti), 'Grand Cœur Pour Grande Heure' (Dora Greenwell), and 'A Woman's Wage' (C.A. Dawson).

In '*SIDEWAYS!* Navigating the Material(ity) of Print Culture' (*VPR* 47[2014] 1–30), Linda K. Hughes asks how we are 'to conceptualize this pervasive material presence' (p. 1). Hughes explores some metaphors for conceptualizing Victorian print culture, from the body to the city and the web, and suggests that imagining this massive material body of work as both a city and a web will help to illustrate the 'dynamism of print culture and its relation to multiple audiences' (p. 5). She argues for critical activity which moves laterally and sideways, reading across genre rather than data-mining, in order to illustrate the ways in which genres interact through print culture. One example she gives is the use of advertisements and serial fiction in Dickens's periodical *All the Year Round*, demonstrating that Dickens's novel *Our Mutual*

Friend is 'at once a text, a commodity, and an advertisement' (p. 8). In
'Touchstones and Tit-Bits: Extracting Culture in the 1880s' (*VPR* 47[2014]
559–76), Richard Menke begins with the commitment of the periodical *Tit-
Bits* to reprint 'the best things that have ever been said or written' (p. 559) and
examines its appropriation of Arnold's words. Menke explores the practice of
reprinting or excerpting in periodical culture and argues that Arnold's example
of textual excerpting should lead us to it as a 'late Victorian cultural and
critical practice' (p. 560). He goes on to analyse the excerpt in Arnold's 'A
Study of Poetry' and *Tit-Bits*, an unlikely and illuminating comparison
between what he calls the touchstone and the titbit, where practices of the
periodical press jostle with Arnold's formulations of lasting literary value.

In '"Let the Nightingales Alone": Correspondence Columns, the Scottish
Press, and the Making of the Working-Class Poet' (*VPR* 47[2014] 188–207),
Kirstie Blair argues that correspondence columns in Scottish periodicals were
of fundamental importance in supporting and directing the work of aspiring
working-class poets. Commentaries were offered on appropriate subjects and
the kind of language which should be used in Scottish poetry. Blair examines
both the poetry and the commentary in the poetic community formed through
the correspondence column. Editors tended to advocate the use of simple
forms and recommend that poetry 'should not be too ambitious in subject-
matter, language, and form' (p. 194), but Blair's readings demonstrate that the
complex network created by the correspondence column enabled poetic
experimentation within working-class poetry. Rebecca N. Mitchell examines
nationalist sentiment in George Meredith's early poems in 'Picturing the
"English Roadside": George Meredith's Poetry and *Once a Week*'
(*VPR* 47[2014] 234–54). Meredith later became known for a cosmopolitan
and more nuanced approach to British nationalism, but Mitchell argues that
his earlier poems published in *Once a Week* and the *Examiner* were embedded
in a context of 'nostalgic patriotism' (p. 235) through the choice of publication
and the accompanying illustrations. Mitchell's attentive readings of the
Roadside poems and their illustrations offer an insight into their reception.
She explores how, for example, the 'representation of a verdant, peaceful, and
rural environment' (p. 239) in the illustrations created an impression of an
ideal Englishness which solidified the poems' popularity. Amjad Muhsen S.
Dajani (al-Daoudi) examines the periodical *The Islamic World* in '*The Islamic
World*, 1893–1908' (*VPR* 47[2014] 454–75). It was published by the Liverpool
Muslim Institute and aimed at a global Muslim readership. Dajani offers a full
account of the journal, noted for being an Ottomanist journal 'during a period
of growing hostility towards the Ottoman regime' (p. 454) and read by British
non-Muslims as well as its Muslim audience. The journal posited a global
network of Muslims linked by their faith, and published articles reflecting on
the difference between European and Muslim civilization. It aimed, argues
Dajani, 'to assert Islam's religious superiority over the West' by emphasizing
'the intellectual civilising power of Islam' (p. 456). Dajani traces the circulation
and internationalization of the journal.

There were two articles on Indian poetry in 2014. Tamara Chin describes
her article, 'Anti-Colonial Metrics: Homeric Time in an Indian Prison, ca.
1909' (*ELH* 81[2014] 1029–53), as part of 'a historicist project of critical

prosody' (p. 1029). Chin situates the work of the Indian poet Aurobindo Ghose, a revolutionary educated in England who wrote epic poems in English, within critical debates about metre. She discusses the debates about Homeric translation between Matthew Arnold and F.W. Newman and suggests that, for Ghose too, 'meters had a moral resonance' (p. 1035) and that he uses metre as a way of confronting 'a more complex set of classicisms in British India' (p. 1035). Through a reading of *Ilion: An Epic in Quantitative Hexameters*, the article demonstrates how Ghose's work exposed and employed the politics of the classics in colonial and anti-colonial discourse. Alison Chapman begins her article, 'Internationalising the Sonnet: Toru Dutt's "Sonnet—Baugmaree"' (*VLC* 42[2014] 595–608), with a discussion about where Dutt's poetry fits in Victorian poetry studies, whether in 'an Indian national poetic tradition, or . . . a transnational cosmopolitan poetics' (p. 595). Chapman follows up a growing emphasis on 'the politicized representation of space and place within poetry' (p. 597) in the discipline. Chapman gives a thorough summary of criticism on Dutt, but argues that there 'is a danger of ignoring the uncomfortable and often ironic tensions of her poetry's hybridity' (p. 599) and offers an insightful close reading of 'Sonnet—Baugmaree'. Another international article examined Australian Victorian poetry. Duncan Wu describes Eliza Hamilton Dunlop as 'one of a handful of women willing to confront the bigotry of her age' (p. 888) in 'A Vehicle of Private Malice: Eliza Hamilton Dunlop and the *Sydney Herald*' (*RES* 65[2014] 888–903). Wu takes her poem 'An Aboriginal Mother' and places it in the context of the new periodical media as well as colonial politics in Australia. Wu traces Dunlop's sources in the law and media reports of a trial of white men for the murder of a group of Aboriginals. He details the reception of the poem after it was set to music and the attacks on the poem by the *Sydney Herald*, expanding on how the poem and its reception emerged from contemporary Australian politics.

Articles on late nineteenth-century poetry included those on Thomas Hardy and Lionel Johnson. Laurence Estanove explores the coexistence of Christian and pagan traditions in 'Poetry as Pagan Pilgrimage: The "Animative Impulse" of Thomas Hardy's Verse' (*CVE* 80[2014] 27 paras.), a theme which has been more often explored in Hardy's novels than in his poetry. Estanove attributes the loss and nostalgia in Hardy's verse to his agnostic position and traces an agnostic pilgrimage or quest in the poetry. A reading of 'Aquae Sulis' brings together these ideas and explores the potential reconciliation of Christian and pagan ideas. Jeffrey Blevins begins his article, 'Thomas Hardy's Timing: Poems and Clocks in Late Nineteenth-Century England' (*VP* 52[2014] 591–618), with Hardy's ideas about the looped cycles of history, a 'historical cycle of surges into "complete rationality" and backslides into anti-rational "religion"' (p. 592). He uses these ideas as a basis for an exploration of Hardy's sense of timing in relation to the perception of reality in his poetry. Blevins brings scientific theorists of time and space, Einstein, Comte, and Bergson, to Hardy's poetry, resulting in some interesting readings. In 'Lionel Johnson's Modern Ruins' (*VP* 52[2014] 679–98), Gabriel Lovatt explores Johnson's anxieties about the past, present, and future through the emblem of the ruin in his poetry. He gives a brief summary of the theoretical background to the ruin and argues that 'Johnson's writings often mediate the nostalgia generated by natural ruin with awareness that the turn-of-the-century's volatile social landscape engenders its own devastation' (p. 680). Looking at both the physical body and physical sites of ruins, Lovatt examines both the natural and the historical ruin and suggests that this decadent poet informs the way that modernist writers take up the ruin in their own work.

Turning to individual authors, several of the works above discuss Matthew Arnold, and, as detailed in Section 1 above, he did receive some attention as a critic and intellectual. As a poet, however, he continues to attract limited scholarly attention, though readers might note a short discussion of his and Eliot's poetry in Heidi Scott's *Chaos and Cosmos*, also reviewed in Section 1. While Arnold's star wanes, the Brownings—Barrett Browning in particular—flourish. Josie Billington and Philip Davis's 21st-Century Oxford Authors edition of Elizabeth Barrett Browning's poetry seeks to reorientate approaches to her work by focusing on the poet's development over time. The resultant chronological structure, with considerable space devoted to Barrett Browning's juvenilia and the editors' preservation of the original sequencing in her published works and printing of texts from first editions, provides insights into the progression of her poetic career. The complete text of *Aurora Leigh* and 'Sonnets from the Portuguese' and comprehensive selections from the rest of her corpus are interspersed with extracts from Barrett Browning's courtship correspondence with Robert Browning, as well as illustrations and selections from her diaries and family letters, positioning this as a useful volume for both teaching and research, although the price would be prohibitive for the former. The editors' introduction underlines the largely biographical perspective, outlining the significance of Barrett Browning's poetry at different stages of her life and thus telling the 'Story of a Poet' (p. xi).

The majority of articles published about Barrett Browning in 2014 focused on *Aurora Leigh*. Sheila Cordner has written an account of 'Radical Education in *Aurora Leigh*' (*VR* 40:i[2014] 233–49), a poem often cited by Victorian education reformers as supporting their cause. Cordner highlights the importance of satire in Barrett Browning's descriptions of Aurora's aunt's expectations about the education of women, and the provocative way Barrett Browning contrasts Aurora's emotionally intelligent attitude to learning and Marian's experiential education with Romney's perfunctory Oxbridge experience. It is convincingly argued that Barret Browning encourages readers to share in Aurora's engaged and empathetic mode of reading that transcends gender and class biases, so that they reconsider their position on educational reform. In 'City-Craft as Poetic Process in Elizabeth Barrett Browning's *Aurora Leigh*' (*VP* 52[2014] 619–36) Elizabeth Erbeznik discusses the representation of urban social relations in the poem through Barret Browning's references to the (traditionally feminized) textile industry. The motif of fashion and sewing is 'woven' (p. 621) through *Aurora Leigh* despite the eponymous character's explicit rejection of needle for pen. Erbeznik argues that Aurora's interactions with the working poor entail an empathetic but ultimately restricted view of women's work in an industrialized context; it is only in Aurora's concluding vision that she begins to frankly engage with the ramifications of urban living. Marisa Palacios Knox, in 'Masculine Identification and Marital Dissolution in *Aurora Leigh*' (*VP* 52[2014]

277–300), argues that 'the integrity of her feminine subjectivity' (p. 278) is maintained throughout Aurora's movement across traditional gender boundaries. Knox looks outward to other instances of female identification with male figures through reading in the nineteenth century, contextualizing Aurora's intellectual development and her eventual assimilation into the marriage plot. Knox posits that the recurrent trope of the nosegay, which constitutes a selective process of artificially 'imposing unity through proximity' (p. 290), reflects Barret Browning's intentions for the poem as a whole, particularly in its resistance to androgyny.

Karen Hadley's '"Tulips on Dunghills": Regendering the Georgic in Barrett Browning's *Aurora Leigh*' (*VP* 52[2014] 465–81) focuses on gender and genre, demonstrating how Barrett Browning appropriates the georgic mode to challenge the masculine assumptions of classical history, using Kevis Goodman's *Georgic Modernity and British Romanticism* (CUP [2004]) as a touchstone. Recurring references to soil and cultivation in *Aurora Leigh* strengthen the association between the poet's imaginative labour, agricultural industry, and God's creation of man from earth, enabling Hadley to argue that Aurora's more optimistic view of life and labour, creativity and civilization challenges, feminizes, and modernizes Romney's Virgilian perspective. Michael Tosin Gbogi frames 'Refiguring the Subversive in Elizabeth Barrett Browning's *Aurora Leigh* and Christina Rossetti's "Goblin Market"' (*Neoh* 41[2014] 503–16) as a repositioning of Barrett Browning in relation to her female contemporaries, finding similarities in their subversion of patriarchal assumptions and structures. In addition, published in 2013, but not received in time for review in last year's *YWES*, *Victorian Women Writers, Radical Grandmothers, and the Gendering of God* by Gail Turley Houston, includes the chapter 'Invoking "All the Godheads": Elizabeth Barrett Browning's Polytheistic Aesthetic' (pp. 73–97). Houston argues that 'the rhetorical concept of a female god is important to a number of major, mid-century Victorian women writers who...create alternative mythoi that subversively critique nineteenth-century gender politics' (p. 3). Using Barrett Browning's concept of the 'mother-want' to orientate the book as a whole by connecting it to a 'mother-god-want' (p. 1), Houston finds in *Aurora Leigh* a feminist utopianism that is indebted to polytheism. Houston demonstrates the influence of Greek mythology and Swedenborg, alongside Judaeo-Christian traditions of female divinity, as well as considering whether Barrett Browning tended to ignore the radical voices of her grandmothers in order to amplify her own.

Two articles consider Barrett Browning's wider corpus. John MacNeill Miller, in 'Slavish Poses: Elizabeth Barrett Browning and the Aesthetics of Abolition' (*VP* 52[2014] 637–59), argues that the polarized political readings offered by scholars of 'The Runaway Slave at Pilgrim's Point' are testament to the instability of Barrett Browning's developing politics. He goes on to position 'Hiram Powers' Greek Slave' as her intervention in the fraught connection between gender and abolitionism, and sees Barrett Browning 'turning conservative conventions to ['A Curse for a Nation's] own progressive work' (p. 651). Miller reads these poems as indicative of Barrett Browning's strategic use of the conventions of female body and voice to achieve emancipation, both of American slaves and of the poet from assumptions surrounding the domain of poetess. Sarah Berry's 'Rethinking Intertitles: The Voice and Temporality of Lyric Intertitles in *The Cry of the Children*' (*LFQ* 42[2014] 594–608) is a fascinating account of George Nichols's 1912 film adaptation of Barrett Browning's 'The Cry of the Children'. Berry notes that several of the film's intertitles do not fit the usual classifications of diegetic and non-diegetic, incorporating aspects of both dialogue and exposition by reproducing lines from Barrett Browning's poem. The insertion of the lyric mode into the narrative temporality of film is disruptive, highlighting the contrast between expectations and conventions of (silent) film and lyric poetry.

Volume 21 of the Wedgestone Press's impressive edition of *The Brownings' Correspondence* was published in 2014, edited by Philip Kelley, Scott Lewis, Edward Hagan, Joseph Phelan, and Rhian Williams. It covers November 1854 to November 1855 (Letters 3487–3677), during which period Browning was writing, and then published, *Men and Women* and Barrett Browning was writing *Aurora Leigh*. In addition, the appendices include helpful biographical sketches of correspondents, a list of supporting documents, and contemporary reviews of the Brownings' works.

Robert Browning's corpus was discussed widely in 2014, including two essays on *The Ring and the Book*. Lakshmi Krishnan, in 'Browning and the Intelligent Uses of Anger in *The Ring and the Book*' (*VP* 52[2014] 205–24), deftly builds upon existing scholarship on the representation of hatred in this work. Anger is 'a rhetorical device, tool of revenge, creative force, and, ultimately, instrument of self-definition' (p. 206), refracting Browning's own negative feelings towards critics of his earlier poetry. Krishnan identifies how Browning's fraught relationship with the reading public shapes his poetic voice and aspirations towards truth. Michelle Niemann offers a new approach to the same poem in 'Browning's Critique of Organic Form in *The Ring and the Book*' (*VP* 52[2014] 445–64). Niemann argues that Browning critiques Coleridgean organicism and unity, particularly through the resonances of the much-debated ring metaphor and the organic (specifically vegetative) metaphors used to describe Pompilia, which are shown to echo those used by Coleridge for poetic form. The article shows how Browning finds literary vitality through 'characterizing the interaction between active reader and material text as an enlivening, vivifying one' (pp. 457–8) instead.

In 'Infinite Movement: Robert Browning and the Dramatic Travelogue' (*VP* 52[2014] 185–203) Gregory Tate argues that journeys in Browning's monologues 'enact the relentless mutability of their speakers' minds' (p. 186). Tate identifies the tension between motion and stasis in these poems' formal and narrative concerns, placing them in dialogue with Browning and Barrett Browning's own travel writing. His illuminating readings of 'Clive', 'The Englishman in Italy', 'Childe Roland to the Dark Tower Came', and 'The Last Ride Together' demonstrate how their shared underlying structure in which the speaker aspires to but does not attain a fixed endpoint is indicative of Browning's view of humanity's perpetual wandering.

In 'Unsettled Scores: Meter and Play in Two Music Poems by Browning' (*CritI* 41[2014] 24–52) Herbert F. Tucker offers a prosodic analysis of 'A Toccata of Galuppi's' and 'Master Hugues of Saxe-Gotha' as an intervention into the lack of formal metrical analysis in contemporary criticism. Tucker's hypothesis that 'The meter of a poem is to its rhythm as a composed score is to its performance and also as a text is to its interpretation' (p. 25) serves as a reminder of the utility of such readings in drawing out the complexities of poems in general, and Browning's in particular due to his technical understanding of music. It is an essay that is sure to repay rereading in a teaching context. Richard Gibson's single text study 'Browning's "A Forgiveness": A Grammatical Reading' (*LitComp* 11:ii[2014] 74–83) context-ualizes this poem in relation to the popular lyric and religious texts with which it is in dialogue. Gibson suggests that its 'grammar of forgiveness' is at odds with convention by showing the husband and wife negotiating 'a form of forgiveness rather than relying on established practice' (p. 79). Furthermore, he labels 'A Forgiveness' a dramatic monologue, arguing that the speaker's perspective should not, as other critics have suggested, be equated with Browning's.

Modern Language Quarterly's special issue on the history of academic English yielded three essays on the place of Browning in the development of the discipline during the late nineteenth and early twentieth centuries. In 'Alexander and After: Browning Culture, Natural Method, and National Education, 1889–1914' (*MLQ* 75[2014] 149–70) Heather Murray highlights how Browning underpinned William John Alexander's advocacy of engaging with difficult poems through close textual study, and how this influenced Canadian university teaching. Jennifer McDonell's '"The Fascination of What's Difficult": Browning and MacCallum's Classroom' (*MLQ* 75[2014] 193–214) challenges prevailing views of education and empire by demonstrat-ing how Mungo William MacCallum's promotion of 'the classics and Englishness' (p. 197) and belief in the mental discipline fostered by engaging with literary obscurity led to the prominence of Browning on the University of Sydney's syllabus. Nancy Glazener, in 'The Browning Society in US Public Literary Culture' (*MLQ* 75[2014] 171–91), discusses the positive reception of his poetry after the American Civil War as having grown out of the Shakespeare Clubs of earlier decades; she argues that it is indicative of the public's desire to challenge themselves culturally and socially, and their belief in poetry's transformative properties. Páraic Finnerty also looks to the American reception of Browning, in '"It Does Not Mean Me, But a Supposed Person": Browning, Dickinson, and the Dramatic Lyric' (*CompAS* 12[2014] 264–81). The essay focuses on Dickinson's response to *Men and Women*. In addition Linda K. Hughes has written on Browning's periodical poetry (*VP* 52[2014] 161–82); this is reviewed above with the rest of the special issue of *VP* on periodical poetry.

In 'Long Vacation Pastorals: Clough, Tennyson, and the Poetry of the Liberal University' (*VLC* 42[2014] 251–66), Anna Barton explores 'the inherent materialism of liberal education through the literature of the Victorian university' (p. 252). Barton lays out the debates between conservatives and reformers about the form a liberal education should take. She sets Clough's poem, *The Bothie of Tober-na-Vuolich*, in the context of other undergraduate poems about the long vacation and argues that it shows Clough's 'commit-ment to liberal models of progress' (p. 258). Barton concludes by discussing the liberal aesthetic in Tennyson's *The Princess* and Amy Levy's 'Cambridge in the Long'. *Arthur Hugh Clough: Mari Magno, Dipsychus, and Other Poems*, edited by Anthony Kenny, makes available *Dipsychus* and *Mari Magno* with a few other short poems and sonnets. It is valuable to have a cheaply priced edition available for these less widely read poems of Clough. *Amours de Voyages* and *The Bothie* are the most likely of Clough's poems to appear on undergraduate syllabi; this edition may encourage the teaching of these less canonical works.

The sole publication on Edward FitzGerald this year was 'FitzGerald's Anglo-Persian *Rubáiyát*' by Reza Taher-Kermani (*T&L* 23[2014] 321–35). It seeks to uphold the long-standing, but critically unsupported, claim that FitzGerald demonstrates 'an authentic Persian spirit' (p. 321) through his translation of *Rubáiyát*. Taher-Kermani focuses on translation practices and poetics, showing how FitzGerald maintains several distinctive formal, descriptive, idiomatic, and contextual elements of the original Persian poem.

Publications on Hopkins in 2014 come almost entirely from the *Hopkins Quarterly*. The seventh volume of Hopkins's *Collected Works* was published in 2014, covering *The Dublin Notebook*. The editors Lesley Higgins and Michael F. Suarez S.J. have reproduced a facsimile of the notebook used by Hopkins containing drafts of poems, lecture notes, reading lists, calculations, and musical notations from February 1884 up to the end of December 1885. In 'Hopkins 2014: Five Landmarks for the 125th Anniversary of His Death' (*HQ* 41:i–ii[2014] 3–7), Joseph J. Feeney S.J. gives an overview of five landmark moments in Hopkins's reception across the twentieth century, from his promotion by New Critics to his centennial in 1989 and his continuing fame in 2014. In 'The Coleridges: Notes on a Family Associated with Hopkins' (*HQ* 41:i–ii[2014] 8–18), Tom Zaniello details the genealogy of the Coleridge family (some of whom were friends with Hopkins) and their engagement with the Catholic and Anglo-Catholic theology of the mid-nineteenth century. He explores Hopkins's connections with the Coleridge family and friends through theology and architecture. Ann-Marie Klein begins with Thomas Aquinas's view on human 'capacity to rise above self-interest' and achieve grace (p. 19) in '"Only the Lover Sings": Scotus's Influence on the Will in Hopkins's "Wreck"' (*HQ* 41:i–ii[2014] 19–38). Klein traces these ideas in Hopkins's *The Wreck of the Deutschland* through the thirteenth-century Franciscan philosopher, Duns Scotus. Hopkins reworks Scotus's ideas on will and grace, exploring questions about whether or not human intuition is coerced, the assimilation of the human soul to God, and human liberty. Klein's discussion of these theological debates is interwoven with an attentive reading of the poem.

In '"Cinquefoil Token": Infinitesimal Calculus and "The Wreck of the Deutschland"' (*HQ* 41:i–ii[2014] 39–54), Imogen Forbes-Macphail examines the mathematical principles of Hopkins's poetics. She focuses on the use of infinitesimal calculus and the number five in the *Wreck*, which, she argues, 'encodes Christ's presence into the poem's structure just as Hopkins imagines it to be encoded into the world itself' (p. 39). Forbes-Macphail examines Hopkins's notes and prose writing on mathematics and explores the links between theology and mathematics in the *Wreck*, offering some detailed

mathematical analysis of the poem. In 'A Memoir of "Uncle Gerard": by
Beatrice Handley-Derry' (*HQ* 41:iii–iv[2014] 57–68), Amanda Paxton and
Lesley Higgins explore the biographical background to Beatrice Handley-
Derry's (Hopkins's niece) memoir of Hopkins, which she gave to the
biographer Humphrey House in 1946. Handley-Derry was motivated by
correcting the rather grave image of Hopkins's character, and insisted on his
humour and buoyancy. Noel Barber S.J. examines the intersection of
Hopkins's spirituality and social context in the prose poetry of 1873–4 in
'Hopkins: Jesuit Prose Poet in London, 1873–1874' (*HQ* 41:iii–iv[2014] 69–78).
Barber focuses on Hopkins's relation to the Jesuit milieu he inhabited in
London, 'pursuing an urbane life that could hardly be more congenial' (p. 73)
and he describes some of the personalities with whom Hopkins was living. He
also describes some of the naturalist observations in Hopkins's journals at this
time. Brett Beasley explores Hopkins's attitude to the afterlife in 'Hopkins's
Approach to Mortality and His Innovations in Poetic Form' (*HQ* 41:iii–
iv[2014] 79–100). Beasley demonstrates that Hopkins uses concrete images
rather than abstract conceptions of the afterlife in his poetry. He argues that
Hopkins probes Christian ideas about the afterlife, finding, like Kierkegaard,
'reason to emphasize death's role as an existential horizon' (p. 80). The sonnet
was the form Hopkins turned to in order to explore the tension between an
abstract and a concrete notion of death; Beasley concludes that Hopkins's
formal innovations allowed him to surpass existentialist philosophers in
coming to terms with death. In 'Hopkins, Patmore, and Women' (*HQ* 41:iii–
iv[2014] 101–11), Gerald Roberts explores Hopkins's attitude to women,
beginning with his friendship and correspondence with Coventry Patmore.
Roberts attempts to defend Hopkins against accusations about the lack of
ordinary women in his poems and his insistence on women's obedience by
placing these views in the context of Victorian beliefs.

There was a significant amount of work in 2014 on the Pre-Raphaelites,
which tended to centre upon the poetry of Christina and Dante Gabriel
Rossetti though with some significant research on the wider circle, including
Elizabeth Siddal, Algernon Swinburne, and William Morris. Ingrid Hanson's
persuasive monograph *William Morris and the Uses of Violence, 1856–1890*
spans Morris's corpus in order to explore how war, labour, freedom, and
conceptions of nobility are central to his poetry and prose, showing how
'Morris's literary and political constructions of masculinity shape and are
shaped by his understanding of violence' (p. x). Hanson's first chapter, 'The
Early Romances and the Transformative Touch of Violence', focuses on
Morris's early, rarely discussed short stories. In her discussion of violence as a
form of touch Hanson finds in these 'fragmented' and 'disorientating' tales a
surprising level of physicality, immediacy, and intimacy (pp. 6, 7). Chapter 2,
'Knightly Women and the Imagination of Battle in *The Defence of Guenevere,
and Other Poems*', draws on Morris's first volume of poetry, beginning with a
close reading of the titular poem. She delves into the tension between pain and
passion, the theme of woman as knight, and the intersections between battle
and freedom, sexuality, and corporeality in these early poems. In chapter 3,
'*Sigurd the Volsung* and the Parameters of Manliness', Hanson considers
Morris's saga-derived poem in the context of the relationship between

manliness and nationhood, finding that violence and courage are both male and female traits and come to express 'the character of a people' as well as that of individuals (p. 95). The fourth chapter, 'Crossing the River of Violence: The Germanic Antiwars and the Uncivilized Uses of Work and Play', focuses on the novels *The House of the Wolfings* and *The Roots of the Mountains* and the way in which they demonstrate Morris's problematic 'literary commitment to absolute war' (p. 98). In chapter 5, '"All for the Cause": Fellowship, Sacrifice and Fruitful War', Hanson turns to Morris's explicitly socialist works originally published in *Commonweal*, discussing his prose fiction alongside *The Pilgrims of Hope* and *Chants for Socialists*, which she characterizes as 'invitation[s] into a community of present struggle' (p. 166). She argues that metaphors of violence orientate his propagandistic poems, and that Morris's vision of a peaceful socialist future is inseparable from his commitment to revolutionary warfare.

Amelia Yeates and Serena Trowbridge's impressive edited collection *Pre-Raphaelite Masculinities: Constructions of Masculinity in Art and Literature* sets the tone with a selection of original and wide-ranging accounts of the subject; five of the nine essays cover poetry to some degree. In the editors' introduction Yeates and Trowbridge note that the burgeoning study of Victorian masculinities has thus far largely overlooked the work and reception of the Pre-Raphaelites, a term which is used broadly here to cover the Pre-Raphaelite Brotherhood and 'the second grouping of artists in Oxford around Rossetti, as well as those not formally a part of either group' (p. 1). The introduction provides a helpful contextualizing overview of masculinity studies to date. Jay D. Sloan's essay, '"How Grew Such Presence from Man's Shameful Swarm": Dante Gabriel Rossetti and Victorian Masculinity' (pp. 11–34), focuses on the potential for multiple masculinities and a blurring of the lines between masculine and feminine spheres in D.G. Rossetti's work. Arguing that Rossetti offers commentaries on, rather than identification with, different constructions of masculinity, Sloan provides readings of 'Confessional Man' and 'Pilgrim of Love' that demonstrate ways in which he distances himself from normative Victorian masculinity. Ingrid Hanson's essay, 'William Morris's *Sigurd the Volsung* and the Parameters of Manliness' (pp. 35–53), is substantially the same as the chapter of the same name in Hanson's 2013 monograph reviewed above. In 'Interpreting Masculinity: Pre-Raphaelite Illustration and the Works of Tennyson, Christina Rossetti and Trollope' (pp. 127–49), Simon Cooke considers how illustrators' responses to Tennyson and Christina Rossetti, as well as Anthony Trollope, 'create a mediation of their source material which interprets, interrogates and ultimately creates its own, sometimes contradictory version of the nature of masculinity' (p. 130). Dinah Roe, in '"Me, Who Ride Alone": Male Chastity in Pre-Raphaelite Poetry and Art' (pp. 151–68), argues that there was no single coherent response to the concept of chastity by the PRB, and yet the distinct approaches of Christina Rossetti in 'On Keats', D.G. Rossetti in 'The Staff and the Scrip', and Morris in 'Galahad' draw out the tension between male sexual desire and the creative process. Sally-Anne Huxtable's essay, 'In Praise of Venus: Victorian Masculinity and Tannhäuser as Aesthetic Hero' (pp. 169–87), focuses on retellings of the Tannhäuser myth by Swinburne in

'Laus Veneris' and Burne-Jones in his two paintings (1861 watercolour and 1873–5 oil) bearing the same name, touching also on Morris's 'The Hill of Venus'. Bridging the boundary between Pre-Raphaelitism and aestheticism, Huxtable argues that Swinburne queers masculinity and speaks to the potential for fluidity in masculine identity.

Elizabeth Ludlow's *Christina Rossetti and the Bible: Waiting with the Saints* chronologically documents Rossetti's engagement with the practical theology of Tractarianism through readings of poetry and devotional prose, a recurring theme being how 'an understanding of waiting as expectant hope shapes Rossetti's vision of personhood and remains at the heart of her understanding of what it means to participate with and in the divine line' (p. 2). It is a significant addition to the study of both Christina Rossetti and the field of literature and theology more broadly. Chapter 1, 'Attuned to the Voices of the Saints: Rossetti's Devotional Heritage', outlines important influences upon Rossetti's piety, arising from ancient, medieval, and seventeenth- and nineteenth-century devotional texts. Ludlow is particularly adept at drawing out Rossetti's use of psalms as a model for poetry, focusing on 'Sonnet from the Psalms' and 'After Communion' to demonstrate her lifelong commitment to this devotional and literary tradition. The second chapter, 'Grace, Revelation and Wisdom: Early Poetry Including *Goblin Market and Other Poems* (1862)', considers the themes of contemplation and desire. Ludlow dwells upon Rossetti's contributions to *The Germ*, and concludes with an analysis of her convent poems in the context of medieval and early modern religious texts. Chapter 3, 'Developing a Theology of Purpose: Poetry of the 1860s and Early 1870s, Including *The Prince's Progress and Other Poems* (1866)', considers more closely the significance of publication contexts. Chapter 4, 'Shaping a Poetics of Affect in *A Pageant and Other Poems* (1881)', focuses on Rossetti's poetics of selfhood, and covers how 'the integration of the individual into the Trinitarian community is, for her, what characterises God-given personhood' (p. 160). This chapter includes some of the material in Ludlow's short article 'Christina Rossetti's *Later Life: A Double Sonnet of Sonnets* (1881): Exploring the Fearfulness of Forgiveness' (*LitComp* 11:ii[2014] 84–93), in which she offers a sequential reading of the volume that hinges upon the emptiness of a life that is removed from devotion. Chapter 5, 'Maternity and Vocation: The Devotional Prose', turns to the themes of maternity and vocation in Rossetti's devotional prose writings, particularly in relation to Victorian representations of the Virgin Mary. The closing chapter, '"O Hope Deferred, Hope Still": Shaping the Self through *Verses* (1893)', then traces how Rossetti's sequencing and revision of these lyrics instantiates her later desire to reflect upon lived Christian experiences. Ludlow considers how these poems can be understood as 'liturgical spaces' (p. 213), as well as the importance of visual motifs in defining a divine relationship that is predicated upon waiting for revelation.

Kathleen Anderson and Hannah Thullbery focus on 'Ecofeminism in Christina Rossetti's "Goblin Market"' (*VJCL* 126[2014] 63–87), arguing that the poem 'raises critical and still-relevant questions about the co-inherent roles of women and the environment in a precarious industrialized world' (p. 63). Anderson and Thullbery find in the exploitation and manipulation of nature by the goblin men and the spiritual connection drawn between women and the natural world a cautionary tale about mankind's attempts to dominate both nature and womankind.

Nicholas Frankel announced confirmation of the discovery of 'A New Poem by Christina Rossetti' (N&Q 61[2014] 92–5). Originally published in *The Court and Society Review* Frankel reprints the poem 'New Year, New Love' for the first time since 5 January 1887, noting that alongside the signature 'CGR' it contains several identifiable features of her work, and its publishing context provides additional corroborating evidence. In 'On Christina Rossetti's Correction to the April 25 Entry of *Time Flies*' (*JPRS* 74:i[2014] 9–18) Todd O. Williams describes the significance and implications of a surprising attribution error made by Rossetti in the first edition of *Time Flies*, discussing how it provides an insight into her engagement with religious doubt. In addition, as described above, Emily Harrington's *Second Person Singular: Late Victorian Women Poets and the Bonds of Verse* contains the chapter "'I, for Thou Callest Such": Christina Rossetti's Heavenly Intimacy' (pp. 13–46), and Molly Clark Hillard's *Spellbound: The Fairy Tale and the Victorians* includes two chapters on 'Goblin Market' (pp. 138–69).

José María Mesa Villar's monograph *Women in Dante Gabriel Rossetti's Arthurian Renditions (1854–1867)* offers an analysis of D.G. Rossetti's responses to Arthurian tradition with regard to the content and iconography of his poetry and visual art. The first section of the book is principally concerned with Rossetti's reinterpretation of the themes and female characters in Malory's *Le Morte d'Arthur*, while the second looks to Rossetti's engagement with Tennyson's 'The Lady of Shalott', 'Sir Galahad', and 'The Palace of Art' in relation to unity between genders in particular. The final section discusses the themes of paternalism and rescue in Rossetti's chivalric poems, and also discusses his stained-glass panels depicting St George.

In 'Rossetti's "Portrait(s)": Three New Drafts of a Rossetti Poem' (*JPRS* 74:ii[2014] 5–28) Florence S. Boos and Mark Samuels Lasner describe three previously undocumented draft manuscripts recently acquired by the University of Delaware Library. They reproduce some of the manuscript pages alongside full transcriptions of the poems, and convincingly argue that these drafts bridge the gap between 'On Mary's Portrait' [1847–8] and 'The Portrait' [1869–70], which were previously considered separate poems, offering a potential sequence for all ten extant versions and discussing particularly notable shared, variant, and excised elements across the texts. Adrian Versteegh's "'Another Night that London Knew": Dante Gabriel Rossetti's "Jenny" and the Poetics of Urban Insomnia' (*NCC* 36[2014] 551–63) reads the poem 'within the dual contexts of nineteenth-century sleep medicine and urban energetics' (p. 552) and with an awareness of Rossetti's own experience of insomnia. Drawing upon similarities in how the discourses surrounding sleep disorders and prostitution evolved during the nineteenth century, this essay considers how sleeplessness in the urban setting of 'Jenny' enacts a confrontation between exhaustion through brain-work and body-work.

Charles L. Sligh begins "'Till I Am a Ghost": Dante Rossetti and the Poetic Survival of the Fittest' (*JPRS* 74:ii[2014] 56–73) with a discussion of 'The Blessed Damozel', drawing out Rossetti's 'preoccupation with the limits of mortal knowledge about things immortal' (p. 58). Read in tandem with Walter Deverell's 'The Sight Beyond' (with which it was originally published in *The Germ*) and a selection of other Rossetti poems, Sligh demonstrates his lack of confidence in revelatory answers and preoccupation with his poetic legacy. The question of legacy is also discussed by Jesse Hoffman, who builds upon Isobel Armstrong's interpretation of the 'Willowwood' sequence in *The House of Life* as the development of a photograph (*VP* 48[2010] 461–73) in his richly illustrated essay 'Dante Gabriel Rossetti's Bad Photographs' (*VS* 52[2014] 57–87). Hoffman discusses the place of photography in Victorian elegy, with specific reference to how Elizabeth Siddal's death shaped Rossetti's use of both mediums. The movement between 'selective concealment and exposure of the beloved' (p. 59) is shown to underlie Rossetti's desire to control the image of his beloved, via elegiac sonnet sequence, overpainting of photographs and photographic record of Siddal's drawings and paintings. D.M.R. Bentley discusses 'Dante Gabriel Rossetti's *The Blue Closet* and *The Tune of Seven Towers*: Reception and Significance' (*JPRS* 74:ii[2014] 29–43) with particular reference to Morris's poems of the same name. Bentley seeks to unpick what is a rich but 'at most a tangential relationship' between the poems and the pictures (p. 31), before going on to discuss the reception of Rossetti's paintings.

There was relatively little published on Swinburne in 2014. Małgorzata Łuczyńska-Hołdys employs trauma theory (as per modern psychology and literary studies) in her analysis of the figures of Philomela and Procne in '"For Where Thou Fliest I Shall Not Follow": Memory and Poetic Song in Algernon Charles Swinburne's "Itylus"' (*JPRS* 23:ii[2014] 74–84). Łuczyńska-Hołdys proposes that Swinburne explores trauma through the contrary responses embodied by the two characters' songs: Philomela relives her experiences, her trauma evoked by Swinburne though flashbacks and disjointed images; Procne is in a state of denial, dissociating herself from the violence by embracing the carefree swallow's song. In 'Problematic Genealogies: Algernon Swinburne, Dante Gabriel Rossetti and the Discovery of François Villon' (*VP* 52[2014] 661–78) Claire Pascolini-Campbell seeks to rewrite our critical understanding of Villon within the English canon by showing that Swinburne first uncovered him, rather than Rossetti, who published the first translation. Through documentary evidence Pascolini-Campbell supports her assertion that he was the one to introduce Rossetti to the French poet, concluding with an example of how this new understanding of influence opens up new readings of both poets' translations of Villon. Andrea Henderson considers 'The Physics and Poetry of Analogy' (*VS* 56[2014] 389–97) through a reading of James Clerk Maxwell's scientific prose in parallel with Swinburne's 'Before the Mirror'. Analogy is, Henderson argues, crucial to Victorian natural philosophers' ability to express their discoveries. This 'principle of equivalence' (p. 389) was also an important influence on Swinburne, who asserts through his poetry 'the replacement of metaphor by analogy: [whereby] there is in fact no privileged term, no tenor' (p. 394). While short, this is an important essay that indicates the significance of analogy as a new avenue of study within literature and science.

Broadview Press released two editions of Tennyson's poetry in 2014. An edition of *In Memoriam* is edited by Matthew Rowlinson and contains some useful appendices for teaching, including writings by Arthur Hallam, selections from Paley, Lyell, and Chambers on natural history, selections from Dickens, Mary Russell Mitford, Barrett Browning, and John Keble, contemporary reviews of *In Memoriam*, and an excerpt from Hallam Tennyson's *A Memoir*. Broadview also published *Tennyson: Selected Poetry*, edited by Erik Gray. As well as reprinting *In Memoriam* and *Maud*, the edition contains a good selection of the early poetry and a few selections from his late poetry. The volume also includes a series of visual images: a number of portraits of Tennyson throughout his life, paintings and photographs inspired by his poems, and some photographs of the Crimean War, all of which will be helpful teaching aids. Michelle Geric's 'Reading *Maud*'s Remains: Tennyson, Geological Processes, and Paleontological Reconstructions' (*VLC* 42[2014] 59–79) offers a fascinating reading of remains in *Maud*, using the concept of remains to link geology, narrative, memory, and the past. Geric gives a detailed account of Tennyson's sources in geology and comparative anatomy, including an interesting discussion of the Crystal Palace exhibition. She shows how Tennyson drew on the themes of the Great Exhibition in *Maud*, which depicts 'a terminally materialistic age heading towards a manifestly geological fate' (p. 65). In 'No Second Friend? Perpetual Maidenhood and Second Marriage in *In Memoriam* and "The Conjugial Angel"' (*ELH* 81[2014] 299–323), Mary Jean Corbett suggests that A.S. Byatt 'puts queer and feminist readings of *In Memoriam* into dialogue' in her novella 'The Conjugial Angel'. Taking up this dialogue, Corbett posits a triangular structure within *In Memoriam*, and argues that, rather than the heterosexual and homoerotic being opposed, marriage to a sibling enables the strengthening of homoerotic bonds. Her readings of the poem offer a thorough exploration of this triangular structure and the different expectations for men and women in relation to Victorian family affinities.

In 'The Consolation of Physiology: *In Memoriam* in G.H. Lewes's *The Physiology of Common Life*' (*VS* 56[2014] 490–7), Stefan Waldschmidt explores why Lewes quotes Tennyson's poem in a work on physiology. He argues that they share a common assumption about the body and individuality, that humans live 'a life subject to biology' (p. 492), but that both differ about the ways in which humans can learn to inhabit their bodies. In 'Arthur Hallam's Spirit Photograph and Tennyson's Elegiac Trace' (*VLC* 42[2014] 611–36), Jesse Hoffman explores the relationship between photography and elegy and the connections in the ways in which they trace the afterlife of a subject. The invention of the photograph changes what can remain of the dead and Hoffman traces Tennyson's ambivalence to the photograph. Despite this ambivalence, photography also 'offers a way to connect a physical reality to the imagination' (p. 619) and the article explores Tennyson's portrayal of immortality and spectrality from the 1830s poetry onwards, positing a language of photography in the poetry. Roger Ebbatson focuses on one poem, 'Recollections of the Arabian Nights', in his article, 'Knowing the Orient: The Young Tennyson' (*NCC* 36[2014] 125–34), examining both the notion of commerce with the East and 'the gendered eroticization of the Orient' (p. 126).

Ebbatson draws out the poem's engagement with capitalism and exchange economies, and argues that it imagines the East as a refuge from modern capitalism in the West. He also explores the poem's portrayal of a luxurious female sexuality that destabilizes Western male hegemony. In '"Mighty through Thy Meats and Drinks Am I": The Gendered Politics of Feast and Fast in Tennyson's *Idylls of the King*' (*VP* 52[2014] 225–49), Charlotte Boyce examines the 'gendered ordering of appetite implicit in Victorian culture' (p. 225) and its reproduction in Tennyson's *Idylls*. Boyce explores the medical and religious discourses around the fasting woman and argues that there is some ambiguity to be found in Tennyson's presentation of this cultural phenomenon. She also finds a similar ambiguity around representations of feasting and the portrayal of masculine values. The insightful readings of the poem allow Boyce to reveal a new dimension to the poem's theme of civilization. Benedick Turner's article, 'A Man's Work Must She Do: Female Manliness in Tennyson's *Gareth and Lynette*' (*VP* 52[2014] 483–507), also deals with the complexity of gender in *Idylls of the King*. Turner argues that *Gareth and Lynette* is as much concerned with the notion of women taking on masculine virtues as with the development of Gareth's manhood. Drawing on work on Victorian masculinities, Turner explores the concepts of home, court, and quest to argue that Lynette's development has a much greater significance than previously thought, and that 'she represents the model of manhood that Lancelot at first seems to embody' (p. 486).

Articles in the *Tennyson Research Bulletin* covered a range of topics. In 'Tennyson's Sense of an Ending: The Problem of "Enoch Arden"' (*TRB* 10[2014] 219–36), Norman Page re-examines the ending of 'Enoch Arden' in the context of the poem's reception. He argues that the poem 'has a heavily patterned narrative' (p. 222) and that Enoch's heroism is unconventional, taking 'the form of refraining from action, of self-denial and self-sacrifice' (p. 224). Page compares it to other popular narratives of long-lost sailors and unintended bigamy, suggesting that the ending leaves the poem open to moral and legal questions. Leonée Ormond gives a detailed overview of the background to the writing of 'Akbar's Dream' in '"Akbar's Dream": A Collaboration between Tennyson and Benjamin Jowett' (*TRB* 10[2014] 236–50). Ormond describes the friendship between Jowett and Tennyson, and Jowett's influence on the composition of 'Akbar's Dream', detailing some instances of Victorian religious intolerance as one context for the poem. Ann Kennedy Smith gives a full account of Tennyson's reception in France in 'Tennyson Seen from There: "Enoch Arden's" French Reception' (*TRB* 10[2014] 251–65). She gives examples from reviews and letters by Baudelaire, Milsand, and Taine to demonstrate Tennyson's lacklustre reception in France in the mid-Victorian period. The focus of the article is on the role of 'Enoch Arden' in changing Tennyson's reputation in France, and Smith details the publishing history of Tennyson's British and European editions. In 'King Arthur and Chiasmus in Tennyson's *Idylls of the King*' (*TRB* 10[2014] 266–79), Olivia Loksing Moy engages with debates about the structure of *Idylls of the King*. She intervenes in this debate with a focus on chiasmus, arguing that 'tensions between circularity and idleness, linearity and progress, are all exemplified in the grammatical structure of chiasmus' (p. 266). Moy's attentive readings of chiasmus as both a wider structural principle of Tennyson's epic and on the level of syntax and rhyme offer a reading that, she argues, restores political meaning to the text. In 'Rosa Baring's Birthday Book and an Undiscovered Tennyson Verse' (*TRB* 10[2014] 280–90), Jean Howard details the biographical history of Rosa Baring and the context to Tennyson's private verses to her in the 1830s. Finally, in 'Tennyson, Callimachus and Repetition' (*TRB* 10[2014] 291–2), Peter Pickering notes a connection between repetition in quatrains in the Hellenistic poet Callimachus, and in Tennyson's verse.

Books Reviewed

Adams, Amanda. *Performing Authorship in the Nineteenth-Century Transatlantic Lecture Tour*. Ashgate. [2014] pp. ix + 168. £85 ISBN 9 7814 7241 6643.

Anderson, Amanda, and Harry E. Shaw, eds. *Companion to George Eliot*. Wiley. [2013] pp. xiii + 517. hb £126 ISBN 0 4706 5599 3, pb £27.99 ISBN 1 1190 7247 8.

Arthur, Paul Longley, and Katherine Bode. *Advancing Digital Humanities: Research, Methods, Theory*. PalMac. [2014] pp. xii + 339. £60 ISBN 9 7811 3733 6996.

Atkinson, David, and Steve Roud, eds. *Street Ballads in Nineteenth-Century Britain, Ireland, and North America: The Interface between Print and Oral Traditions*. Ashgate. [2014] pp. 306. £67.50 ISBN 9 7814 7242 7410.

Bark, Debbie, ed. *The Collected Works of Ann Hawkshaw*. Anthem. [2014] pp. xl + 468. hb £60 ISBN 9 7817 8308 0212, pb £25 ISBN 9 7817 8308 4210.

Bartlett, Neil. *Charles Dickens: Great Expectations, A Christmas Carol, Oliver Twist*. Oberon. [2014] pp. 248. £16.99 ISBN 9 7817 8319 0799.

Beller, Anne-Marie, and Tara MacDonald, eds. *Rediscovering Victorian Women Sensation Writers*. Routledge. [2014] pp. x + 125. £90 ISBN 9 7804 1574 5796.

Bernhart, Walter, and Lawrence Kramer, eds. *On Voice*. Rodopi. [2014] pp. xv + 229. $67 ISBN 9 7890 4203 8219.

Billington, Josie. *The Connell Guide to Charlotte Brontë's Jane Eyre*. Connell Guides. [2014] pp. 143. £6.99 ISBN 9 7819 0777 6175.

Billington, Josie, and Philip Davis, eds. *Elizabeth Barrett Browning*. 21st-Century Oxford Authors. OUP. [2014] pp. xxviii + 559. £88 ISBN 9 7801 9960 2889.

Blythe, Helen Lucy, *The Victorian Colonial Romance with the Antipodes*. PalMac. [2014] pp. xii + 243. £57.50 ISBN 9 7811 3739 7829.

Boehm, Katharina, Anna Farkas, and Anne-Julia Zwierlein, eds. *Interdisciplinary Perspectives on Aging in Nineteenth-Century Culture*. Routledge. [2013] pp. 258. $145 ISBN 9 7804 1581 7967.

Boehm-Schnitker, Nadine, and Susanne Gruss, eds. *Neo-Victorian Literature and Culture: Immersions and Revisitations*. Routledge. [2014] pp. vi + 235. $145 ISBN 9 7804 1570 8302.

Borden, Iain, Murray Fraser, and Barbara Penner, eds. *Forty Ways to Think About Architecture: Architectural History and Theory Today*. Wiley. [2014] pp. 280. £24.99 ISBN 9 7811 1882 2616.

Boucher, Ellen. *Empire's Children: Child Emigration, Welfare, and the Decline of the British World, 1869–1967*. CUP. [2014] pp. xi + 292. £60 ISBN 9 7811 0704 1387.

Burton, Maxine. *Illiteracy in Victorian England: 'Shut Out from the World'*. NIACE. [2014] pp. viii + 179. £24.95 ISBN 9 7818 6201 6408.

Campbell, Matthew. *Irish Poetry under the Union, 1801–1924*. OUP. [2014] pp. 264. £64 ISBN 9 7811 0704 4845.

Clarke, Clare. *Late Victorian Crime in the Shadows of Sherlock*. PalMac. [2014] pp. viii + 221. £55 ISBN 9 7802 3039 0539.

Clarke, Jeremy. *The Charles Dickens Miscellany*. History Press. [2014] pp. 190. £9.99 ISBN 9 7807 5249 8881.

Clayton, Owen. *Literature and Photography in Transition, 1850–1915*. PalMac. [2014] pp. 248. $90 ISBN 9 7811 3747 1499.

Cleere, Eileen. *The Sanitary Arts: Aesthetic Culture and the Victorian Cleanliness Campaigns*. OSUP. [2014] pp. xi + 195. $59.95 ISBN 9 7808 1421 2585.

Cocks, Neil. *The Peripheral Child in Nineteenth Century Literature and Its Criticism*. PalMac. [2014] pp. x + 215. £55 ISBN 9 7811 3745 2443.

Colley, Ann C. *Wild Animal Skins in Victorian Britain: Zoos, Collections, Portraits, and Maps*. Ashgate. [2014] pp. xii + 206. £65 ISBN 9 7814 7242 7786.

Cordery, Gareth, and Joseph S. Meisel, eds. *The Humours of Parliament: Harry Furniss's View of Late-Victorian Political Culture*. OSUP. [2014] pp. xxii + 320. $89.95 ISBN 9 7808 1421 2530.

Costella, John. *Walk With Me Charles Dickens*. AuthorHouse. [2014] pp. xviii + 310. £12.95 ISBN 9 7814 9188 9121.

Cunningham, Valentine. *Victorian Poets: A Critical Reader*. Wiley. [2014] pp. 442. hb £80.95 ISBN 9 7806 3119 9137, pb £32.50 ISBN 9 7806 3119 9144.

Data, Chris, and Helen Groth, eds. *Mindful Aesthetics: Literature and the Science of the Mind*. Bloomsbury. [2013] pp. 224. $77 ISBN 9 7814 4110 2867.

Dawson, Gowan, and Bernard Lightman, eds. *Victorian Scientific Naturalism: Community, Identity, Continuity*. UChicP. [2014] pp. 368. $45 ISBN 9 7802 2610 9503.

Deane, Bradley. *Masculinity and the New Imperialism: Rewriting Manhood in British Popular Literature, 1870–1914*. CUP. [2014] pp. viii + 273. $95 ISBN 9 7811 0706 6076.

DeMaria, Robert Jr., Heesok Chang, and Samantha Zacher, eds. *A Companion to British Literature, vol. 4*. Wiley. [2014] pp. 511. £450 (4-volume set) ISBN 9 7804 7065 6044.

Dentith, Simon. *Nineteenth-Century British Literature Then and Now: Reading with Hindsight*. Ashgate. [2014] pp. ix + 182. £60 ISBN 9 7814 7241 8852.

DeSpain, Jessica. *Nineteenth-Century Transatlantic Reprinting and the Disembodied Book*. Ashgate. [2014] pp. xiv + 209. $134.96 ISBN 9 7814 0943 2005.

Dewis, Sarah. *The Loudons and the Gardening Press: A Victorian Cultural Industry*. Ashgate. [2014] pp. xvi + 278. £65 ISBN 9 7814 0946 9223.

Durey, Jill Felicity. *Degrees of Intimacy: Cousin Marriage and the Nineteenth-Century Novel*. Humming Earth. [2014] pp. 286. £35 ISBN 9 7818 4622 0456.

Floyd, David. *Street Urchins, Sociopaths and Degenerates: Orphans of Late-Victorian and Edwardian Fiction*. UWalesP. [2014] pp. 264. £90 ISBN 9 7817 8316 0105.

Fludernik, Monika, and Miriam Nandi, eds. *Idleness, Indolence and Leisure in English Literature*. PalMac. [2014] pp. xi + 309. $95 ISBN 9 7811 3740 3995.

Frankel, Nicholas, ed. *Charles Ricketts, 'Everything for Art': Selected Writings*. Rivendale. [2014] pp. 366. £40 ISBN 9 7819 0420 1229.

Fraser, Angus, and Ann M. Ridler, eds. *George Borrow in Cornwall 1853–1854: Notebooks and Correspondence*. Lavengro Press. [2014] pp. xxiv + 88. £15 ISBN 9 7809 9284 6329.

Fraser, Hilary. *Women Writing Art History in the Nineteenth Century: Looking Like a Woman*. CUP. [2014] pp. 254. £60 ISBN 9 7811 0707 5757.

Frederickson, Kathleen. *The Ploy of Instinct: Victorian Sciences of Nature and Sexuality in Liberal Governance*. FordUP. [2014] pp. xi + 218. $75 ISBN 9 7808 2326 2519.

Frost, Mark. *The Lost Companions and John Ruskin's Guild of St George: A Revisionary History*. Anthem. [2014] pp. 264. £60 ISBN 9 7817 8308 2834.

Gephardt, Katarina. *The Idea of Europe in British Travel Narratives, 1789–1914*. Ashgate. [2014] pp. x + 238. $104.95 ISBN 9 7814 7242 9544.

Gezari, Janet, ed. *The Annotated Wuthering Heights*. HarvardUP. [2014] pp. 454. $35 ISBN 9 7806 7472 4693.

Gilham, Jamie. *Loyal Enemies: British Converts to Islam, 1850–1950*. OUP/Hurst. [2014] pp. 256. $30 ISBN 9 7801 9937 7251.

Giorcelli, Cristina, and Paula Rabinowitz, eds. *Fashioning the Nineteenth Century: Habits of Being*. UMinnP. [2014] pp. xxiii + 289. $75 ISBN 9 7808 1668 7466.

Goodman, Gemma, and Charlotte Mathieson, eds. *Gender and Space in Rural Britain, 1840–1920*. P&C. [2014] pp. 208. $150 ISBN 9 7818 4893 4405.

Grass, Sean. *Charles Dickens's Our Mutual Friend: A Publishing History*. Ashgate. [2014] pp. xiv + 274. £63 ISBN 9 7807 5466 9302.

Gray, Beryl. *The Dog in the Dickensian Imagination*. Ashgate. [2014] pp. xiv + 259. £63 ISBN 9 7814 7243 5293.

Gray, Erik. *Tennyson: Selected Poetry*. Broadview. [2014] pp. 336. $15.95 ISBN 9 7815 5481 2080.

Gurfinkel, Helena. *Outlaw Fathers in Victorian and Modern British Literature: Queering Patriarchy*. FDUP. [2014] pp. 223. $80 ISBN 9 7816 1147 6378.

Hale, Piers. *Political Descent: Malthus, Mutualism, and the Politics of Evolution in Victorian England*. UChicP. [2014] pp. 464. $45 ISBN 9 7802 2610 8490.

Hall, Catherine, Nicholas Draper, and Keith McClelland, eds. *Emancipation and the Remaking of the British Imperial World*. ManUP. [2014] pp. 288. £75 ISBN 9 7807 1909 1834.

Hall, Catherine, Nicholas Draper, Keith McClelland, Katie Donington, and Rachel Lang, eds. *Legacies of British Slave-Ownership: Colonial Slavery and the Formation of Victorian Britain*. CUP. [2014] pp. ix + 327. $99 ISBN 9 7811 0704 0052.

Hall, Dewey W. *Romantic Naturalists, Early Environmentalists: An Ecocritical Study, 1789–1912*. Ashgate. [2014] pp. viii + 232. £60 ISBN 9 7814 0942 2648.

Handley, Graham, ed. *Daniel Deronda, by George Eliot*. Introd. K.M. Newton. OUP. [2014] pp. xliv + 724. £8.99 ISBN 9 7801 9968 2867.

Hanna, Patricia, ed. *Reality and Culture: Essays on the Philosophy of Bernard Harrison*. Rodopi. [2014] pp. xviii + 285. $84 ISBN 9 7890 4203 8196.

Hanson, Ingrid. *William Morris and the Uses of Violence, 1856–1890*. Anthem. [2013] pp. 252. £60 ISBN 9 7808 5728 3191.

Hardwick, Joseph. *An Anglican British World: The Church of England and the Expansion of the Settler Empire, c.1790–1860*. ManUP. [2014] pp. 304. £75 ISBN 9 7807 1908 7226.

Harrington, Emily. *Second Person Singular: Late Victorian Women Poets and the Bonds of Verse*. UPVirginia. [2014] pp. xi + 231. $39.50 ISBN 9 7808 1393 6123.

Harrison, Bernard. *What Is Fiction For? Literary Humanism Restored*. IndUP. [2014] pp. xxvi + 593. $35 ISBN 9 7802 5301 4061.

Henchman, Anna. *The Starry Sky Within: Astronomy and the Reach of the Mind in Victorian Literature*. OUP. [2014] pp. 320. $96 ISBN 9 7801 9968 6964.

Hervouet-Farrar, Isabelle, and Max Vega-Ritter, eds. *The Grotesque in the Fiction of Charles Dickens and Other 19th-Century European Novelists*. CambridgeSP. [2014] pp. vii + 241. £47.99 ISBN 9 7814 4386 7566.

Hewitt, Martin. *The Dawn of the Cheap Press in Victorian Britain: The End of the 'Taxes on Knowledge', 1849–1869*. Bloomsbury. [2014] pp. xv + 309. $100 ISBN 9 7814 7251 1546.

Higgins, Lesley, and Michael F. Suarez, eds. *The Collected Works of Gerard Manley Hopkins*, vol. 7: *The Dublin Notebook*. OUP. [2014] pp. 336. £100 ISBN 9 7801 9953 4029.

Hillard, Molly Clark. *Spellbound: The Fairy Tale and the Victorians*. OSUP. [2014] pp. x + 278. $59.95 ISBN 9 7808 1421 2455.

Hollington, Michael, ed. *The Reception of Charles Dickens in Europe*, vol. 1. Bloomsbury. [2013] pp. xliv + 363. £200 ISBN 9 7818 4706 0969.

Hollington, Michael, ed. The Reception of Charles Dickens in Europe, *vol. 2*. Bloomsbury. [2013] pp. xiv + 703. £200 ISBN 9 7818 4706 0969.

Houston, Gail Turley. *Victorian Women Writers, Radical Grandmothers, and the Gendering of God*. OSUP. [2013] pp. xi + 181. $55.95 ISBN 9 7808 1429 3126.

Howell, Jessica. *Exploring Victorian Travel Literature: Disease, Race and Climate*. EdinUP. [2014] pp. vi + 198. £70 ISBN 9 7807 4869 2958.

Huguet, Christine, and Nathalie Vanfasse, eds. *Charles Dickens, Modernism, Modernity*, vol 1. Editions du Sagittaire. [2014] pp. 230. €20 ISBN 9 7829 1720 2265.

Huguet, Christine, and Nathalie Vanfasse, eds. *Charles Dickens, Modernism, Modernity*, vol 2. Editions du Sagittaire. [2014] pp. 263. €20 ISBN 9 7829 1720 2272.

Hultgren, Neil. *Melodramatic Imperial Writing from the Sepoy Rebellion to Cecil Rhodes*. OhioUP. [2014] pp. xi + 259. £42 ISBN 9 7808 2142 0850.

Hunt, Aeron. *Personal Business: Character and Commerce in Victorian Literature and Culture*. UPVirginia. [2014] pp. xii + 225. $39.50 ISBN 9 7808 1393 6314.

Ince, Laurence. *Charles Dickens and the Great Jennens Case*. PublishNation. [2014] pp. 152. £5.99 ISBN 9 7812 9186 7091.

Ireland, Ken. *Thomas Hardy, Time, and Narrative: A Narratological Approach to His Novels*. PalMac. [2014] pp. 291. $9 ISBN 9 7811 3736 7716.

Jackson, Lee. *Dirty Old London: The Victorian Fight Against Filth*. YaleUP. [2014] pp. 304. $38 ISBN 9 7803 0019 2056.

Jenkins, Melissa Shields. *Fatherhood, Authority, and British Reading Culture, 1831–1907*. Ashgate. [2014] pp. vii + 207. £60 ISBN 9 7814 7241 1617.

Jones, David J. *Sexuality and the Gothic Magic Lantern: Desire, Eroticism, and Literary Visibilities from Byron to Bram Stoker*. PalMac. [2014] pp. x + 254. £50 ISBN 9 7811 3729 8911.

Kędra-Kardela, Anna, and Andrzej Sławomir Kowalczyk, eds. *Expanding the Gothic Canon: Studies in Literature, Film and New Media*. Lang. [2014] pp. 303. £47 ISBN 9 7836 3162 6399.

Keen, Suzanne. *Thomas Hardy's Brains: Psychology, Neurology and Hardy's Imagination*. OSUP. [2014] pp. 236. $64.95 ISBN 9 7808 1421 2493.

Kelley, Philip, Scott Lewis, Edward Hagan, Joseph Phelan, and Rhian Williams, eds. *The Brownings' Correspondence*, vol. 21. Wedgestone. [2014] pp. xvi + 432. $110 ISBN 9 7809 1145 9388.

Kenny, Anthony, ed. *Arthur Hugh Clough: Mari Magno, Dipsychus, and Other Poems*. Carcanet. [2014] pp. 144. £11.65 ISBN 9 7818 4777 2558.

Killeen, Jarlath, ed. *Bram Stoker: Centenary Essays*. FCP. [2014] pp. 206. €40 ISBN 9 7818 4682 4074.

Kleinecke-Bates, Iris. *Victorians on Screen: The Nineteenth Century on British Television, 1994–2005*. PalMac. [2014] pp. x + 233. £60 ISBN 9 7802 3036 3342.

Korda, Andrea. *Printing and Painting the News in Victorian London: The Graphic and Social Realism, 1869–1891*. Ashgate. [2014] pp. 218. $109.95 ISBN 9 7814 7243 2988.

Kornbluh, Anna. *Realizing Capital: Financial and Psychic Economies in Victorian Form*. FordUP. [2014] pp. x + 221 ISBN 9 7808 2325 4972.

Krueger, Kate. *British Women Writers and the Short Story, 1850–1930: Reclaiming Social Space*. Palgrave. [2014] pp. x + 264 $95 ISBN 9 7811 3735 9230.

Kuehn, Julia. *A Female Poetics of Empire: From Eliot to Woolf*. Routledge. [2014] pp. 253. £80 ISBN 9 7804 1571 2415.

Kujawska-Lis, Ewa, and Anna Krawczyk-Łaskarzewska, eds. *Reflections on/ of Dickens*. CambridgeSP. [2014] pp. xii + 362. £49.99 ISBN 9 7814 4386 0086.

Lennartz, Norbert, and Dieter Koch, eds. *Texts, Contexts and Intertextuality: Dickens as Reader*. V&R. [2014] pp. 294. €39.99 ISBN 9 7838 4700 2864.

Lester, Alan, and Fae Dussart. *Colonization and the Origins of Humanitarian Governance: Protecting Aborigines Across the Nineteenth-Century British Empire*. CUP. [2014] pp. 283. $145 ISBN 9 7811 0700 7833.

Liggins, Emma. *Odd Women? Spinsters, Lesbians, and Widows in British Women's Fiction, 1850s–1930s*. ManUP. [2014] pp. viii + 275. £70 ISBN 9 8707 1908 7561.

Lightman, Bernard V., and Michael Reidy, eds. *The Age of Scientific Naturalism: Tyndall and His Contemporaries*. P&C. [2014] pp. xv + 256. £60 ISBN 9 7818 4893 4634.

Lightman, Bernard V., and Bennett Zon, eds. *Evolution and Victorian Culture*. CUP. [2014] pp. xvii + 320. £60 ISBN 9 7811 0702 8425.

Lindfors, Bernth. *Early African Entertainments Abroad: From the Hottentot Venus to Africa's First Olympians*. UWiscP. [2014] pp. xii + 248. $29.95 ISBN 9 7802 9930 1644.

Loose, Margaret. *The Chartist Imaginary: Literary Form in Working-Class Political Theory and Practice*. OSUP. [2014] pp. v + 185. $59.95 ISBN 9 7808 1421 2660.

Luckhurst, Mary, and Emilie Morin, eds. *Theatre and Ghosts: Materiality, Performance and Modernity*. PalMac. [2014] pp. xiv + 228. £60 ISBN 9 7811 3734 5066.

Ludlow, Elizabeth. *Christina Rossetti and the Bible: Waiting with the Saints*. Bloomsbury. [2014] pp. vii + 261. £60 ISBN 9 7814 7251 0952.

MacDuffie, Allen. *Victorian Literature, Energy, and the Ecological Imagination*. CUP. [2014] pp. ix + 305. $95 ISBN 9 7811 0706 4379.

MacEwan, Helen. *The Brontës in Brussels*. Owen. [2014] pp. 218. pb £16.99 ISBN 9 7807 2061 5883.

Makdisi, Saree. *Making England Western: Occidentalism, Race, and Imperial Culture*. UChicP. [2014] pp. xxiii + 295. $90 ISBN 9 7802 2692 3130.

Mármol, Gema Alcaraz, and Mª Mar Jiménez-Cervantes Arnao, eds. *Studies in Philology: Linguistics, Literature and Cultural Studies in Modern Languages*. CambridgeSP. [2014] pp. xiv + 276. £52.99 ISBN 9 7814 4386 2097.

Marsden, Simon. *Emily Brontë and the Religious Imagination*. Bloomsbury. [2014] pp. vii + 183. £60 ISBN 9 7814 4116 6302.

May, Helen. *Empire, Education, and Indigenous Childhoods: Nineteenth-Century Missionary Infant Schools in Three British Colonies*. Ashgate. [2014] pp. + 300. £70 ISBN 9 7814 7240 9607.

Mazzeno, Laurence W., ed. *Twenty-First-Century Perspectives on Victorian Literature*. R&L. [2014] pp. xi + 217. £54.95 ISBN 9 7814 4223 2334.

McCann, Andrew. *Popular Literature, Authorship, and the Occult in Late Victorian Britain*. CUP. [2014] pp. vii + 194. $95 ISBN 9 7811 0706 4423.

McKee, Patricia. *Reading Constellations: Urban Modernity in Victorian Fiction*. OUP. [2014] pp. xii + 184. £44.49 ISBN 9 7801 9933 3905.

Mead, Rebecca. *My Life in Middlemarch*. Crown. [2014] pp. x + 294. $25 ISBN 9 7803 0798 4760.
Mesa Villar, Josér; María. *Women in Dante Gabriel Rossetti's Arthurian Renditions (1854–1867)*. Lang. [2014] pp. 482. pb £74 ISBN 9 7830 3431 2981.
Michals, Teresa. *Books for Children, Books for Adults: Age and the Novel from Defoe to James*. CUP. [2014] pp. ix + 278. £64.99 ISBN 9 7811 0704 8546.
Miller, J. Hillis. *Communities in Fiction*. FordUP. [2014] pp. xiii + 333. hb $95 ISBN 9 7808 2326 3103, pb $30 ISBN 9 7808 2326 3110.
Mixon, Franklin Graves, and Richard J. Cebula, eds. *New Developments in Economic Education*. Edward Elgar. [2014] pp. xvi + 255. £80 ISBN 9 7817 8254 9710.
Morin, Christina, and Niall Gillespie, ed. *Irish Gothics: Genres, Forms, Modes, and Traditions, 1760–1890*. PalMac. [2014] pp. xi + 215. £55 ISBN 9 7811 3736 6641.
Moruzi, Kristine, and Michelle J. Smith, eds. *Colonial Girlhood in Literature, Culture and History, 1840–1950*. PalMac. [2014] pp. 288. $90 ISBN 9 7811 3735 6345.
Mousoutzanis, Aris. *Fin de Siècle Fictions, 1890s–1990s: Apocalypse, Technoscience, Empire*. PalMac. [2014] pp. 272. £55 ISBN 9 7811 3726 3650.
Müller, Lothar. *White Magic: The Age of Paper*. Polity. [2014] pp. xiv + 311. £20 ISBN 9 7807 4567 2533.
Napolitano, Marc. *Oliver! A Dickensian Musical*. OUP. [2014] pp. xiv + 287. £23.49 ISBN 9 7801 9936 4824.
Nash, Andrew. *William Clark Russell and the Victorian Nautical Novel: Gender, Genre and the Marketplace*. T&F. [2014] pp. xi + 231. $150 ISBN 9 7818 4893 3767.
Neginsky, Rosina. *Salome: The Image of a Woman Who Never Was*. CambridgeSP. [2014] pp. 270. £49.99 ISBN 9 7814 4384 6219.
Owen, James. *Labour and the Caucus: Working Class Radicalism and Organised Liberalism in England, 1868–88*. LiverUP. [2014] pp. x + 244. £70 ISBN 9 7818 4631 9440.
Philpotts, Trey. *The Companion to Dombey and Son*. LiverUP. [2014] pp. xiv + 575. £75 ISBN 9 7817 8138 1274.
Piasecka, Aleksandra. *Towards Creative Imagination in Victorian Literature*. CambridgeSP. [2014] pp. 230. £44.99 ISBN 9 7814 4385 7154.
Pickard, Sarah. *Anti-Social Behaviour in Britain: Victorian and Contemporary Perspectives*. PalMac. [2014] pp. xx + 375. £75 ISBN 9 7811 3739 9304.
Poston, Lawrence. *The Antagonist Principle: John Henry Newman and the Paradox of Personality*. UPVirginia. [2014] pp. + 304. $45 ISBN 9 7808 1393 6338.
Pyle, Forest. *Art's Undoing: In the Wake of a Radical Aestheticism*. FordUP. [2013] pp. 328. $32 ISBN 9 7808 2325 1117.
Qi, Shouhua, and Jacqueline Padgett, eds. *The Brontë Sisters in Other Wor(l)ds*. PalMac. [2014] pp. 215. £57.50 ISBN 9 7811 3740 5166.
Rahane, Huw Barker. *Who's Who in Thomas Hardy*. Austin Macauley. [2014] pp. 100. Pb £5.99 ISBN 9 7817 8455 0202.

Rampaul, Giselle, and Barbara Lalla, eds. *Postscripts: Caribbean Perspectives on the British Canon from Shakespeare to Dickens*. UWIndiesP. [2014] pp. 181. $40 ISBN 9 7897 6640 4628.

Rangarajan, Padma. *Imperial Babel: Translation, Exoticism, and the Long Nineteenth Century.* FordUP. [2014] pp. 272. $45 ISBN 9 7808 2326 3615.

Ricci, Gabriel R., ed. *Travel, Discovery, Transformation*. Transaction. [2014] pp. 350. $39.45 ISBN 9 7814 1285 2838.

Rowland, Ingrid D. *From Pompeii: The Afterlife of a Roman Town*. HarvardUP. [2014] pp. vii + 340. £21.95 ISBN 9 7806 7404 7938.

Rowlinson, Matthew. *In Memoriam: Alfred Tennyson*. Broadview. [2014] pp. 216. $16.95 ISBN 9 7815 5481 1434.

Rubery, Matthew. *The Novelty of Newspapers: Victorian Fiction after the Invention of the News*. OUP. [2014] pp. viii + 233. £51 ISBN 9 7801 9536 9267.

Schwan, Anne. *Convict Voices: Women, Class, and Writing about Prison in Nineteenth-Century England*. UPNE. [2014] pp. 304. $85 ISBN 9 7816 1168 6715.

Scott, Francesca, Kate Scarth, and Ji Won Chung, eds. *Picturing Women's Health*. P&C. [2014] pp. vii + 208. £60 ISBN 9 7818 4893 4245.

Scott, Heidi C.M. *Chaos and Cosmos: Literary Roots of Modern Ecology in the British Nineteenth Century*. PSUP. [2014] pp. 224. $64.95 ISBN 9 7802 7106 3836.

Secord, James. *Visions of Science: Books and Readers at the Dawn of the Victorian Age*. OUP. [2014] pp. xiii + 306. £18.99 ISBN 9 7802 2620 3287.

Shaw, David W. *The Ghost behind the Masks: The Victorian Poets and Shakespeare*. UPVirginia. [2014] pp. x + 285. $39.50 ISBN 9 7808 1393 5447.

Sikorska, Liliana, ed. *Of What Is Past, or Passing, or To Come: Travelling in Time and Space in Literature in English*. Lang. [2014] pp. 218. £32 ISBN 9 7836 3164 3860.

Smyth, Adam, and Gill Partington, eds. *Book Destruction from the Medieval to the Contemporary*. PalMac. [2014] pp. xi + 216. £55 ISBN 9 7811 3736 7655.

Snyder, Laura. *Reforming Philosophy: A Victorian Debate on Science and Society*. UChicP. [2014] pp. 386. $59 ISBN 9 7802 2676 7338.

Soll, Jacob. *The Reckoning: Financial Accountability and the Rise and Fall of Nations*. Basic Books. [2014] pp. xvii + 276. $28.99 ISBN 9 7804 6503 1528.

Staten, Henry. *Spirit Becomes Matter: The Brontës, George Eliot, Nietzsche*. EdinUP. [2014] pp. xii + 190. £70 ISBN 9 7807 4869 4587.

Stray, Christopher, ed. *Sophocles' Jebb: A Life in Letters*. Cambridge Philological Society. [2013] pp. x + 306. £45 ISBN 9 7809 5683 8131.

Sturgeon, Sinéad. *Essays on James Clarence Mangan: The Man in the Cloak*. PalMac. [2014] pp. xvi + 242. £55 ISBN 9 7811 3727 3376.

Talairach-Vielmas, Laurence. *Fairy Tales, Natural History and Victorian Culture*. PalMac. [2014] pp. xii + 217. £55 ISBN 9 7811 3734 2393.

Tally, Robert T. Jr., ed. *Literary Cartographies: Spatiality, Representations, and Narrative*. PalMac. [2014] pp. x + 236. £57.50 ISBN 9 7811 3745 6496.

Tonkin, Maggie, Mandy Treagus, Madeleine Seys, and Sharon Crozier-De Rosa, eds. *Changing the Victorian Subject*. UAdelaide. [2014] pp. x + 281. A$44 ISBN 9 7819 2206 4738.

Treagus, Mandy. *Empire Girls: The Colonial Heroine Comes of Age.* UAdelaide. [2014] pp. 280. A$44 ISBN 9 7819 2206 4547.

Tucker, Herbert, ed. *A New Companion to Victorian Literature and Culture.* Wiley. [2014] pp. 584. $200.95 ISBN 9 7811 1862 4487.

Valman, Nadia, ed. *Jewish Women Writers in Britain.* WSUP. [2014] pp. x + 250. $31.99 ISBN 9 7808 1433 2382.

Vanden Bossche, Chris R. *Reform Acts: Chartism, Social Agency, and the Victorian Novel, 1832–1867.* JHUP. [2014] pp. 264. $49.95 ISBN 9 7814 2141 2085.

Vernon, James. *Distant Strangers: How Britain Became Modern.* UCalP. [2014] pp. 184. £16.95 ISBN 9 7805 2028 2049.

Voigts, Eckart, Barbara Schaff, and Monika Pietrzak-Franger, eds. *Reflecting on Darwin.* Ashgate. [2014] pp. 244. $149.95 ISBN 9 7814 7241 4076.

Wagner, Tamara S., ed. *Domestic Fiction in Colonial Australia and New Zealand.* P&C. [2014] pp. xiii + 219. $150 ISBN 9 7818 4893 5167.

Walczuk, Anna, and Władysław Witalisz, eds. *Old Challenges and New Horizons in English and American Studies.* Lang. [2014] pp. 227. £49 ISBN 9 7836 3165 0288.

Walsh, Bridget. *Domestic Murder in Nineteenth-Century England: Literary and Cultural Representations.* Ashgate. [2014] pp. 163. £60 ISBN 9 7814 7242 1036.

Ward, Ian. *Sex, Crime, and Literature in Victorian England.* Hart. [2014] pp. 154. £30 ISBN 9 7818 4946 2945.

Welz, Stefan, and Elmar Schenkel, eds. *Dickens on the Move: Travels and Transformations.* Lang. [2014] pp. xiv + 182. £36 ISBN 9 7836 3164 1583.

Wheeler, Katherine. *Victorian Perceptions of Renaissance Architecture.* Ashgate. [2014] pp. xii + 194. £55.94 ISBN 9 7814 7241 8821.

Williams, Wendy S. *George Eliot, Poetess.* Ashgate. [2014] pp. vii + 161. £65 ISBN 9 7814 7243 7938.

Wilson, A.N. *Victoria: A Life.* Penguin. [2014] pp. xiv + 642. £25 ISBN 9 7815 9420 5996.

Wilt, Judith. *Women Writers and the Hero of Romance.* PalMac. [2014] pp. vii + 220. $95 ISBN 9 7811 3742 6970.

Yeates, Amelia, and Serena Trowbridge, eds. *Pre-Raphaelite Masculinities: Constructions of Masculinity in Art and Literature.* Ashgate. [2014] pp. xi + 251. £60 ISBN 9 7814 0945 5585.

Yuran, Noam. *What Money Wants: An Economy of Desire.* StanfordUP. [2014] pp. xiii + 320. $85. ISBN 9 7808 0478 5938.

XV

Modern Literature

MATTHEW LEVAY, ANDREW RADFORD, MICHAEL
SHALLCROSS, CHRISSIE VAN MIERLO, LUKE FERRETTER,
CLARA JONES, HANNAH TWEED, NICK BENTLEY,
REBECCA D'MONTE, GRAHAM SAUNDERS, NEIL MILES,
MATTHEW CREASY, MATTHEW SPERLING, AND
ADAM HANNA

This chapter has 8 sections 1. General. 2 Pre-1945 Fiction; 3. Post-1945
Fiction; 4. Pre-1950 Drama; 5. Post-1950 Drama; 6. British Poetry pre-1950; 7.
British Poetry post-1950; 8. Irish Poetry. Section 1 is by Matthew Levay; 2(a)
is by Andrew Radford; Section 2(b) is by Michael Shallcross; Section 2(c) is by
Chrissie Van Mierlo; Section 2(d) is by Luke Ferretter; Section 1(e) is by Clara
Jones; Section 3(a) is by Hannah Tweed; Section 3(b) is by Nick Bentley;
Section 4 is by Rebecca D'Monte; Section 5 is by Graham Saunders; Section
6(a) is by Neil Miles Section 6(b) is by Matthew Creasy; Section 7 is by
Matthew Sperling; Section 8 is by Adam Hanna.

1. General

In 2013 and 2014 modernist studies continued to grapple with questions of
periodicity, literary form, media and mass culture, materiality, and the economics
of cultural production—in short, some of most vibrant subjects of the past
decade. And yet, despite their familiarity, these questions were posed in
remarkably original ways, affirming the health of the field overall and suggestive
of multiple avenues for future research. Such vitality largely arises from a
palpable restlessness in contemporary modernist criticism, animated by a desire
to push against established notions of what modernism was (or is), as well as an
increasing willingness to acknowledge and explore the tensions inherent within a
literary period defined by multiplicity. Inspired by the expansiveness of the new
modernist studies—not only its receptivity to the idea of plural modernisms, but
also its interest in the modes of production, institutional patrons, national
literary cultures, and individual readers that shaped the terms by which a concept
like 'modernism' was codified—while remaining appropriately wary of

The Year's Work in English Studies, Volume 95 (2016) © *The Author 2016. Published by Oxford
University Press on behalf of the English Association. All rights reserved.*
For Permissions, please email: journals.permissions@oup.com
doi:10.1093/ywes/maw012

modernism's potential ballooning into something that no longer signifies, scholars today have initiated a thoughtful and thought-provoking conversation regarding these tensions. On the conference circuit, such oppositions took centre stage: the Modernist Studies Association hosted meetings dedicated to 'Everydayness and the Event' in Sussex during 2013 and 'Confluence and Division' in Pittsburgh during 2014, underlining the organization's engagement with the paradoxes at the heart of modernist literature and culture. Other associations, meanwhile, shirked modernist binaries in favour of larger, messier critical concepts: the European Network for Avant-Garde and Modernism Studies hosted its 2014 conference in Helsinki on the theme of 'Utopia', arguably one of the most fraught and divisive notions to carry with it the promise of unity, while the second biannual conference of the Australian Modernist Studies Network, held in Sydney in 2014, explored the well-established but still vital concept of 'Transnational Modernisms', a phrase in which the precise definition of the adjective is only slightly more stable than that of its plural noun. Thus, the major conferences in modernist studies continued to trouble easy accounts of modernism and modernity by thinking through the contradictions and capaciousness that give those concepts their substance.

Published research in modernist studies approached these issues more subtly, but with no less urgency. Indeed, looking through the robust list of books published in the field during these two years, one is immediately struck by the fact that the most exciting modernist scholarship today emerges from a conviction that critics can still do more to expand modernism's formal, temporal, and spatial parameters while still attending to those foundational elements of modernist literature and culture that brought the period its initial renown. Nowhere is that dual attention more pronounced than in Michael North's characteristically magisterial *Novelty: A History of the New*, which takes one of modernism's most familiar features and demonstrates just how little we actually know about it. The book's central aim, North explains, is to 'giv[e] the term *novelty* something more certain to stand for' (p. 1), since 'novelty is not itself by any means new, being one of the very first ideas to trouble the consciousness of humankind, [yet] it seems almost to have no past, as if it arose from nothing every time it occurred' (p. 5). Through his attempt to make a maddeningly abstract concept more concrete, North uncovers a long and varied intellectual history of the new, linking classical philosophy, evolutionary biology, cybernetics, modernist poetry, and visual art in order to show how novelty has appeared for centuries as either the welcome recurrence of established idioms or the recombination of distinct elements into one of several possible new entities.

Novelty begins with a set of foundational chapters that survey the ancient philosophical and later scientific engagements with the concept of novelty, then considers twentieth-century figures like Thomas Kuhn and Norbert Weiner, both of whom illustrate how consistently modern science draws upon older views of the physical world. North's book thus connects a surprising range of material in order to craft an evocative chronicle of the new. Modernism is not the sole player in this long, complex history of novelty. In fact, it is not even the main player, receiving only two dedicated chapters in a book of seven. Nonetheless, North devotes substantial attention to modernism's status as the literary period most associated with the concept, complicating and often debunking traditional perceptions of modernism as either an entirely new phenomenon or a phenomenon primarily dedicated to novelty. His brief history of Pound's famous dictum to 'make it new', traditionally celebrated as the clarion call of modernist aesthetics, offers an instructive example of just how indebted our most fundamental notions of modernism are to a phrase that did not gain its critical lustre until well after its original utterance. As North reminds us, Pound first used the phrase in 1928; when he sought to adopt it as the title of an essay collection in 1934, T.S. Eliot warned Pound that the phrase seemed obscure to the editors at Faber, and would likely confuse the general public. Indeed, 'make it new' did not gain much critical traction until Hugh Kenner interpreted it in 1950 as a sign of Pound's translation efforts, and only became associated with the formal innovations of the modernist avant-garde in the late 1950s and early 1960s, when a host of critics deployed it as the defining statement of experimental poetic practice (pp. 169–70). Here and elsewhere, North demonstrates how a host of assumptions about novelty paved the way for a vision of modernism as an unyielding quest for innovation.

Other monographs also traced the circulation of novelty within modern culture, following a more materialist path towards the kinds of questions for which North's enquiries lay the philosophical and historical groundwork. David Trotter's *Literature in the First Media Age: Britain between the Wars* offers a comprehensive examination of what its author describes as interwar literature's unique ability to register the embedding of everyday experience within new forms of technological communication. Trotter focuses primarily on British literature published between 1927 and 1939, so it might seem hyperbolic to describe as a 'media age' such a short span of time in a relatively small geographical location, but this monograph makes a detailed and convincing case for how the literature of that period was uniquely dedicated to reckoning with those new forms of communication and mediated experience that had become enmeshed within the fabric of daily life, from telephones and televisions to radio and cinema. To differentiate these forms, Trotter begins with a helpful distinction: he labels as 'representational' those technologies, like photography and cinematography, that depend upon the storage of information and then its eventual release; these are distinguished from 'connective' technologies, like the telegraph or telephone, which promise immediate forms of communication carried out at a distance from one's interlocutor. In this way, Trotter emphasizes the density of interwar Britain's media ecology, showing why his book is not only welcome for its attention in minute detail to a significant if under-studied moment in literary history, but also necessary for understanding how and why human behaviour became so conditioned by the multiple forms of technology that had become ubiquitous by the late 1920s and early 1930s.

As with Trotter's previous books, the range of *Literature in the First Media Age* is impressive, in its sweeping view of the period as one of deep technological and cultural ferment. Canonical authors, such as James Joyce, Wyndham Lewis, D.H. Lawrence, Evelyn Waugh, Elizabeth Bowen, and W.H. Auden, are well represented, but the book's attention to the contributions of less frequently studied yet equally important figures is even more significant. Trotter's fourth chapter, for example, considers the function of sound cinema as a builder of collective identity, particularly in relation to literary works of the Popular Front moment. This, he argues 'used the still relatively new experience of cinema to imagine a new representational sociability equal in intensity to, but more democratic and more militant than, the connective sociability encouraged by the steadily increasing popularity of new telecommunications technologies' (p. 169). Here Trotter focuses on the 'collective novel', or those politically driven, leftist fictions whose expansive casts of characters suggest the interconnections of social life that necessarily transcend distinctions based in economic status or individual identity. To demonstrate how the collective novel pursues its goal of 'exposure of and resistance to the class and gender bias of the technological mediation of experience' (p. 199), Trotter turns to novels by Rex Warner, Dot Allan, Henry Green, Harold Heslop, and John Sommerfield, an eclectic assemblage of works that he persuasively ties together as exemplary instances of the collective novel's 'stylized representation of a space for sociability, a space neither wholly private nor wholly public' (p. 203). Other chapters feature similarly diverse sets of texts and, taken together, produce a vibrant history of interwar British literature and its fascination with the mediated life.

Throughout the book, Trotter acknowledges his debt to several influential critics of media and mass culture. These include Lisa Gitelman, whose remarkable new book, *Paper Knowledge: Toward a Media History of Documents* is a fascinating work of cultural history of a brevity which belies the wealth of information it contains. It is also impeccably written, a page-turner about page-turning whose wit enhances the keen, detailed arguments it advances. Beginning with the premise that the document is, despite or perhaps because of its ubiquity in public life, significantly under-theorized, Gitelman sets out to fill a profound gap in our current understanding of print culture, which privileges notions of authorship, readership, and publication that the production of documents openly flouts. As a 'vernacular genre', documents are defined here as 'the recognizable sites and subjects of interpretation across the disciplines and beyond, evidential structures in the long human history of clues' (p. 1). In this account, they function as reproduced traces of fact that exist to provide a concrete basis for affirming and accounting for human knowledge. The document is thus a record, but also a specific, official vehicle for recording; it is recognized in multiple ways by multiple audiences while also signifying its own status as evidence across time and space. By examining in detail multiple modes of producing and reproducing documents, including job printing, mimeographs, microfilm, Xerox machines, and PDFs, Gitelman's study of documentation practices popularized in the United States during and after the late nineteenth century becomes one with profound implications for scholars of modernist print culture. This work will be equally important for scholars interested in the varieties of archiving and informational exchange that became so common in the twentieth century as to escape critical scrutiny.

Gitelman's book is a microhistory of how one of modernity's most common objects is produced, circulated, and consumed. In comparison, Aaron Jaffe's lively new study, *The Way Things Go: An Essay on the Matter of Second Modernism* presents an equally riveting attempt to understand those stages in the life of an object as it makes its way from novelty to waste product. Erudite and stylishly written, Jaffe's lithe volume is perhaps the most formally engaging work in modernist studies of the past two years, beginning with an introductory 'Instruction

Manual' before moving through 100 short, numbered entries, arranged in descending fashion in order to mimic the tracing of our own, contemporary concerns regarding aesthetics and obsolescence back to the dawn of the twentieth century. Despite what might appear like a fairly regimented structure, the book's organizing rubric is actually much looser, and provisionally draws together a series of related attempts to capture the modes through which objects, particularly those mundane items that exist on the margins of utility and waste—the eraser, the urinal, the bar of soap—function in decidedly idiosyncratic, inhuman ways: 'Circling the found object, taking notes on interruptions, staging illuminating crashes and juxtapositions, this book tries to fashion a critical method that resembles a kind of Rube Goldberg apparatus' (p. 13). Quirkily rigorous, the book's tenor is one of energetic intelligence, and Jaffe touches upon a surprising number of modern authors and their objects: beginning with the depressing twenty-first-century phenomenon of the e-book as a professed antidote to the burdensome materiality of the printed book, Jaffe utilizes the work of Walter Benjamin, Charles Baudelaire, and Ulrich Beck, among others, in order to move beyond what he deems the 'poetic materialism' of thing theory (p. 24), chastised as 'insufficiently attuned to the particularities and peculiarities of [things'] traffic', and instead fix upon the uncanny agency of objects within the whirl of modernity (p. 51).

As Jaffe's subtitle indicates, *The Way Things Go* does not offer a single, monochrome account of the modern, but instead posits a modernism characterized by two distinct phases, each wedded to the other. The book's working definition of modernism as 'a particular scene for presenting aesthetic form and accounting for cultural value in the face of a situation in which there is no coherent epistemological account of the whole' subtly characterizes modernism as a process of formation, a continually emerging 'scene' defined by its own contingency (pp. 16–18). Novelty, by these terms, becomes a kind of watchword for ignorance, a way for a burgeoning phenomenon like modernism to profess its prominence by denigrating its forebears, which it cannot fully understand and therefore dismisses as irrelevant. But it is also a concept defined by the temporality of its material, as those novel objects of the present unfailingly become the waste products of the future, carrying with them the potential for future risk. This is where the ideas of 'first' and 'second' come into play, as Jaffe defines first modernism as 'a present with a knowable past', and second, borrowing from Beck's notion of the risk society, as 'hold[ing] an unknowable future determinate of the present' (p. 18). In other words, second modernism is a period of reflexivity, a look back towards the past with a fuller sense of its contingency and capacity for risk; at the same time it comprises an understanding that the future weighs upon the present as a set of risks we cannot yet comprehend. For Jaffe, this backward glance that also projects itself forward is not simply a facile attempt to remove the idea of the postmodern from critical consciousness, but rather proof of 'the unremitting need for continuously returning to the unfinished business of literary history and literary modernity', a history made manifest through those objects that began their lives as novelties, only to end up as emblems of the dangers of waste (p. 19).

Whereas Jaffe is dedicated to a process of defamiliarization, highlighting those aspects of the object that cannot be anthropomorphized or subsumed into tidy narratives of human practice, Andrew Goldstone, in his impressively argued

Fictions of Autonomy: Modernism from Wilde to de Man, sets himself the seemingly unenviable task of resuscitating the familiar concept of autonomy for modernist studies. Derided in virtually every corner of literary scholarship, the idea of autonomy as a conviction of art's fundamental separation from any surroundings or entanglements—its ability to exist in and for itself alone—has borne the brunt of repeated criticism over the past few decades, and its abandonment as an outmoded and politically naive position would seem to make it an irredeemable presence within modernist studies. For Goldstone, however, autonomy entails neither an exclusionary resistance to the social nor a thoroughgoing rejection of historical context. Rather, he argues that 'modernism developed many versions of autonomy, not all of which suppose autonomy to be an essential, axiomatic quality of art' (p. 2). Following Pierre Bourdieu, he demonstrates how autonomy exists for European and American modernist writers as a means of 'setting out—and institutionalizing—their own, independent standards for literary practice', effectively situating themselves within a larger social world in order to find a place in which their work might exist in relative independence (p. 9). In so doing, Goldstone explains, modernist literature and literary criticism often function as 'fictions of autonomy', or texts that grapple with the issue of autonomy as a matter of form and theme in an effort to 'construct real relations between the institutions of art and other fields of social life' (p. 8). His opening example—the treatment of domestic labour in the works of Wilde, Joris-Karl Huysmans, Henry James, and Marcel Proust—is especially illustrative of this phenomenon. Through an illuminating series of close readings, he shows how the domestic servant exemplifies 'the inextricable connection between a "dominant" aesthetic form and social domination'. As such, this figure embodies the fact that modernist autonomy 'is relative and contextual, sensitive to the ways autonomous form carries troubling social entanglements along with it' (p. 25). In this chapter and in those that follow, Goldstone encourages a new and ultimately persuasive response to autonomy in modernist studies, through which the aesthetic and the social are mutually informative rather than at odds.

In very different ways, both Jaffe and Goldstone are interested in disrupting the paths of modernist criticism past and present, either by emphasizing the strangeness of the modernist object or by reinvigorating a seemingly tired theme like autonomy. Other critics approached a similar task by grounding themselves in the fundamentals of archival research and the methodologies of book history. Lise Jaillant's *Modernism, Middlebrow and the Literary Canon: The Modern Library Series, 1917–1955* offers an absorbing account of how one American publisher, in issuing the works of canonical modernists alongside popular science writing, genre fictions, and slightly more middlebrow novels, helped to define modernism's place within a broader literary marketplace during the first half of the twentieth century. Each chapter of the book focuses on a single author: H.G. Wells, Sherwood Anderson, James Joyce, Virginia Woolf, Willa Cather, and William Faulkner. Each serves in this way as a case study supporting Jaillant's larger claim that the Modern Library not only introduced modernism to a wide audience through its commercial clout and its democratic tastes in selecting authors and works, but also played a significant role in developing what became the modern literary canon. According to Jaillant, the Modern Library's eclectic list of titles 'exemplifies the flexibility of cultural categories in the interwar period—a flexibility that was lost in the 1940s and 1950s when critics called for the separation between "high" and "low" cultural forms' (p. 1). Adding to the growing number of monographs devoted to modernist print culture and the history of the book, Jaillant's study, through its evidence of careful research and painstaking work in the archives, offers a fresh perspective on the high/low debate told from the vantage point of one of the century's leading publishers.

For Jaillant, the Modern Library functions as both a vehicle for modernism and an arbiter of cultural value, uniquely positioned to propel modernism into a lively public sphere. By contrast, Sarah Brouillette's penetrating study of the creative economy takes aim at the more insidious convergences between art and commerce. Her *Literature and the Creative Economy* offers a frank assessment of contemporary, neoliberal Britain and its attempt to incorporate the arts into larger social and economic programmes. Focusing on those literary works produced and arts efforts enacted under the New Labour government of 1997–2010, Brouillette offers a fascinating analysis of how the image of the artist as a flexible and self-managing (and, thus, easily exploited) worker, and of the arts as pathways for urban renewal and multicultural inclusion, informed both the policies of New Labour and the literature produced during the height of its power. The first part of the book is devoted to a detailed explication of the concept of the creative economy as the yoking together of creativity discourse and the marketability of ideas, as expressed in neoliberal British policy, neo-Marxism, and mid-century American psychology. The book's second part develops close readings of contemporary fiction and poetry by a diverse range of authors, including Aravind Adiga, Monica Ali, Daljit Nagra, Gautam Malkani, Kazuo Ishiguro, and Ian McEwan, in order to underline the ambivalence with which these writers have addressed their position within economic and governmental models of creativity. Both add up to a bold, insightful study of contemporary British literature that offers a new way of understanding the uses to which art has been put in recent neoliberal practice.

Brouillette's account of the political pressures that inform artistic production in the twentieth and twenty-first centuries is related to Nadine Attewell's *Better Britons: Reproduction, National Identity, and the Afterlife of Empire*. In this book, Attewell offers an enlightening and meticulous interpretation of twentieth-century British and post-imperial literatures, in which issues of intimacy and reproduction are situated within larger questions of nation-building and the politics of race. Focusing on a diverse range of texts and policy documents from Britain, Australia, and New Zealand, Attewell asks how and why reproduction so deeply informed the construction of British and settler identity in the waning years, and, eventually, the afterlife, of empire. She begins with a revealing comparison of Aldous Huxley's *Brave New World* [1932], H.G. Wells's *The Island of Dr. Moreau* [1896], and Australian modernist Eleanor Dark's *Prelude to Christopher* [1934], three novels that experiment with the utopian vision of reproduction as something that can be regulated in order to enact a specific vision of national futurity, typically one that effaces all hints of race. In these novels, Attewell explains, eugenic programmes of reproduction and its regulation participate in broader patterns of utopian thinking, which endeavour to 'insulate the nation from colonial bodies and histories, tethering national futures to the possibility of beginning again, (as if) sui generis' (pp. 25–6). Later chapters follow a similar trajectory, situating literary works by Jean Rhys, F. Tennyson Jesse, Robin Hyde, and John Wyndham, as well as Danny Boyle's popular film *28 Days Later* [2002], alongside policy documents and public debates regarding the links between conceptions of national identity and individual citizens' reproductive capacities. The results are rarely comfortable but always illuminating, and are especially helpful in thinking through the intersections of reproduction, race, and nation in post-imperial Britain.

Attewell's transnational approach is one shared with several new books in modernist studies, indicating that an attention to modernism beyond a traditional Anglo-American framework remains a central concern of recent scholarship. The fascination with modernism's hidden geographies, that is, those locations that were undoubtedly pivotal for modernism yet remain critically underexplored, is precisely what animates Jennifer Scappettone's sweeping monograph *Killing the Moonlight: Modernism in Venice*. Moving deftly between literature, visual art, and architecture, this account of Venice as a city caught between its Romantic past and the pressures of modernity is a kaleidoscope of cultural history, convincing in its arguments and dazzling in its archive. 'My aim', Scappettone declares, 'is to help redraft the geographical and temporal borders of modernist studies, but also to discover and recover a materialist poetics of collective space' (p. 42). She presents Venice as neither a set of tired stereotypes nor a place entirely at ease with its modernization, but rather as a living, built environment whose importance for late nineteenth- and twentieth-century artistic practice arises through its unique blend of the classical and the kitschy, the material and the imaginary. In all its paradoxes, Venice becomes the catalyst for those forms of art whose experimental imperatives gain strength through the material forms of history embedded within the cityscape, which simultaneously attest to the city's progressive decay as well as its appearance of timelessness within the cultural imagination. Written with flair and sharp attention to historical and formal detail, this volume and its 'series of detours from the capitals of modernity' convincingly explains 'why their *passé* urban other remains—in spite of every cliché—a productively estranging place' (p. 42).

The past two years also saw a number of important releases in modernist studies from Cambridge University Press, two of which deserve special mention here for their sizeable contributions to the field (others are featured in later sections of this chapter). Ambitious and tightly conceived, Paul Peppis's *Sciences of Modernism: Ethnography, Sexology, and Psychology* attempts to put to rest the assumption that the modernist interest in science was largely metaphorical. Challenging the idea that science was merely a tool employed by Pound and others to demonstrate the rigorous objectivity and precision with which they approached the craft of poetry, Peppis makes a convincing case for how, 'during this formative, proto-disciplinary moment' of the twentieth century's opening decades, 'both fields labor, simultaneously and often along parallel lines, to articulate and legitimize themselves, regularly informing and being informed by each other's knowledges, languages, genres, and tropes'

(p. 5). Pairing significant scientific texts with contemporaneous fiction and poetry, Peppis demonstrates the myriad ways in which modernism and the human sciences simultaneously came into being through related processes of legitimation, often in relation to the examples of their Victorian predecessors. Many of the literary figures examined in *Sciences of Modernism* are familiar but faint in the history of modernism; they are recognized as integral, early participants in a burgeoning literary phenomenon, but have never been as well known as those more canonical writers of the 1920s. Consequently, each chapter of the book reveals a new dimension of these authors and their relationship to scientific discourse, offering compelling interpretations of Claude McKay's *Constab Ballads*, Mina Loy's *Songs to Joannes*, and Rebecca West's *The Return of the Soldier*. The end result is a volume that methodically and judiciously draws modernism and scientific writing into a mutually productive dialogue, enhancing our view of each as necessarily linked in distinctive patterns of emergence.

While Peppis's book explores the work of authors situated at the margins of modernist literary history, John Whittier-Ferguson's *Mortality and Form in Late Modernist Literature* considers some of the later, less frequently studied, offerings of modernism's seminal figures. Examining those works by Virginia Woolf, T.S. Eliot, Gertrude Stein, and Wyndham Lewis that were composed well after the point of each author's initial renown, this rigorous and impeccably written addition to the growing body of scholarship on late modernism asks how a set of authors who made some of the most essential contributions to modernist literature responded to a host of pressures that all fall under the larger umbrella of 'lateness': the decline of the physical body, the re-examining and reworking of an earlier style, and the impending trauma of a second world war which threatened to rehash the catastrophe of the first on an even broader scale. Of particular note is Whittier-Ferguson's attentiveness to form, as his sensitivity to the late style of these authors makes for consistently absorbing reading. He defends such an approach against the historicism of recent studies of late modernism, noting that 'the details of a text, if attended to with sufficient care, tend to work in more complex, often less coherent and difficult-to-describe ways than had seemed possible when that text was used primarily as a reference point or a landmark for the purposes of charting the terrain in which it appears' (p. 29). Operating from this conviction, *Mortality and Form* does not represent a simple repudiation of historicism, but rather an assertion that aesthetic form enlivens our study of history. Whittier-Ferguson sees form as embodying the means through which prominent modernist authors used their writing to work through the profound transformations of a culture of which they, soon enough, would no longer be a part. In so doing, His study excavates the history of late modernism as an experiment in late style, showing how 'these authors build their later work, in formal and thematic terms, around questions of what it means to be mortal and embodied ... and deeply embedded in historical time' (p. 1).

Speaking of the overlap between history and form, it should escape no one's notice that Fredric Jameson published a new book in 2013, and that that book engages with one of the most vexing issues in modernist studies. Like all of Jameson's work, *The Antinomies of Realism* is a demanding and controversial treatment of the political work of literary form, this time turning Jameson's dialectical method towards realism, a subject he approaches 'as a historical and even evolutionary process in which the negative and the positive are inextricably combined, and whose emergence and development at one and the same time constitute its own inevitable undoing' (p. 6). Realism, by Jameson's formulation, is never a straightforward concept or genre, and instead shuffles between opposite poles that give the realist novel its character. The most significant opposition Jameson posits is that between *récit*—the tale, or narrative, defined by a 'temporality of the chronological, in which, everything having happened already, events succeed each other in what is today loosely called "linear time" '—and affect, or that experience that exists outside time, in which 'the isolated body begins to know more global waves of generalized sensations' (pp. 27–8). For Jameson, realism becomes more understandable when we interpret these and other oppositions in unison, as two distinct yet equally necessary components of a larger category. As with any of Jameson's arguments, this one is uniformly challenging, yet perceptive and pleasurably idiosyncratic in its choice of texts: the usual nineteenth-century novelists get the majority of the attention here, but so too do David Mitchell and Kim Stanley Robinson. It is also highly suggestive for modernist studies, a field that has never entirely come to grips with realism as an aesthetic mode. Jameson claims that modernist novels are 'not at all to be understood as some opposite number of realism but in a very different and incommensurable aesthetic and formal fashion', and such a provocative claim elicits a host of questions that will certainly inform a good deal of future work in modernist criticism (p. 215). What, precisely, is this difference that is not an opposite? How can modernism be considered in relation to realism, and do the two run together in ways that Jameson's conception of them disavows? One looks forward to the projects that will respond to such questions. Whether they align themselves with or against Jameson in their responses, it is certain that these questions will continue to enliven a field that remains eager to engage with some of the most difficult, urgent problems of literary criticism.

2. Pre-1945 Fiction

(a) British Fiction 1900–1930

This year saw the continuing upturn in the critical fortunes of Katherine Mansfield and other interwar women writers, including Mary Butts, Sylvia Townsend Warner, and Dorothy Richardson. Overshadowed and patronized during her lifetime by the media-savvy yet priggish 'Blooms Berries', as Mansfield drolly labelled them in a 1917 letter, the New Zealand author is now the subject of myriad monographs, peer-reviewed articles and cogent surveys aimed at undergraduate audiences, such as Sarah Davison's patiently plotted guide to *Modernist Literatures*.

Gerri Kimber and Angela Smith's *The Poetry and Critical Writings of Katherine Mansfield* is the third volume in the Edinburgh University Press edition of this author's collected works. It is a hugely impressive achievement, which sheds new light on the verse, as well as the full range of Mansfield's aphoristic, parodic, and journalistic narratives. The chronologically arranged and fully annotated book reviews and essays for little magazines are often remarkable for their insight into the imaginative tactics of authors like Joseph Conrad, D.H. Lawrence, and Virginia Woolf. This volume, which also collects Mansfield's translations, should be read alongside Claire Davison's *Translation as Collaboration: Virginia Woolf, Katherine Mansfield and S.S. Koteliansky*.

Edited by Gerri Kimber, Todd Martin, Delia da Sousa Correa, Isobel Maddison, and Alice Kelly, *Katherine Mansfield and World War One* appraises Mansfield's keen imaginative engagement with the First World War and its impact on the formal features and political attitudes woven into her textual fabric, especially her tropes of affective estrangement and repression on the home front. As Vincent O'Sullivan explains, the war was the most devastating public event in Mansfield's lifetime. Her younger brother, Leslie, had journeyed to England to join up with the British army in 1915. That summer he died in a bizarre accident behind the lines. Moreover, Gerri Kimber argues that Mansfield's reaction to the geopolitical strife—as ecological cataclysm; fiscally ruinous endgame; the erasure of a supremely gifted literary generation—is crucial to our grasp of her narrative treatment of privacy, self-perception, and embodiment. As Mansfield stated in a 1919 letter: 'the novel can't just leave the war out ... we have to take it into account and find new expressions, new moulds for our new thoughts'. The most persuasive essays in this volume present a politically shrewd Mansfield, whose 'new expressions'—especially her allusions, indirections, fractured syntax, and disrupted linearity—probe, with hallucinatory power, the dynamics of wartime psychology and the malign influence of government propaganda.

Anna Snaith's *Modernist Voyages: Colonial Women Writers in London, 1890–1945* positions Mansfield as an author who did not simply benefit from the vivid sensations of metropolitan modernity; rather, she decisively contributed to its variegated literary landscape. Snaith's spatial analysis of London poses questions about how the capital's bohemian expatriate cliques generated a transnational modernism. She also canvasses the ways in which the imperial city allowed Mansfield to refine a feminist and formally radical aesthetic—a craft that Virginia Woolf memorably described as 'of the cat kind: alien, composed, always solitary & observant'. Mansfield devotees will be cheered by Snaith's emphasis on the early New Zealand stories which were published in the metropolitan magazines *Rhythm* and the widely influential *New Age*. Snaith also parses Mansfield's *Urewera Notebook*, which documents in telling detail the 1907 journey the author undertook along New Zealand's northern shore.

Gerri Kimber's *Katherine Mansfield and the Art of the Short Story* is an intelligently conceived overview of Mansfield's often torqued and intensely individual fictional idiom. Kimber covers a diverse array of her most famous stories from different scholarly viewpoints. In terms reminiscent of Clare Hanson's *The Gender of Modernism* [1990], Kimber examines Mansfield's abiding themes and mordant economy of phrasing. Mansfield aficionados can ponder how current academic methodologies—especially transnational and postcolonial theories—alter our perception of the topographical specificities and social sympathies described in these tales.

Anne Mounic's *Ah What Is It?—That I Heard: Katherine Mansfield's Wings of Wonder* considers Mansfield in relation to other major modernist figures of the European tradition, including Dorothy Richardson, Woolf, Colette, and Proust. Mansfield also features in Maria DiBattista and Emily O. Wittman's collection, *Modernism and Autobiography*, which furnishes sixteen essays that chart the energetic eccentricity and sheer formal range of modernist memoirs. This volume will be of especial interest to scholars who focus on how Mansfield weaves elements of her life story into the narrative fabric of various texts. Contributors pay close attention to critical issues of confession and encryption, forms of address, self-stylization, and the process of cultivating a brand name in a crowded literary marketplace.

Nicole Rizzuto's 'The Force of the Everyday' (*ConL* 55:ii[2014] 421–9) assesses the narrative depiction of boredom and banality in selected texts by Mansfield. Alex Moffett's 'Hot Sparks and Cold Devils: Katherine Mansfield and Modernist Thermodynamics' (*JML* 37:ii[2014] 59–75) posits that in Mansfield's fiction motifs of temperature are powerfully linked to formal stylistic innovation. Mansfield's correspondence evinces a capacity to exploit the difference between established fictional modes and experimental texts using intriguing metaphors of light and heat. Moffett illustrates how thermal imagery in 'Bliss' and 'At the Bay' contributes to a 'warm modernism', one that Mansfield believes is essential both for portraying bitter post-war civic divisions, and for combating the spiritual malaise that the Great War triggered.

Jane Stafford's '"Simplicity and Art Shades Reign Supreme": Costume, Collectibles, and Aspiration in Katherine Mansfield's New Zealand' (in Gillies and Wussow, eds., *Virginia Woolf and the Common(wealth) Reader*, pp. 78–87) scrutinizes the issue of cross-cultural encounter and especially Mansfield's precise relation to, and opinion of, the Arts and Crafts movement. Stafford presents the 'common(wealth)' as a fabricated entity in Mansfield's fiction and journalism, one that dramatizes competing priorities: between individualist drives and collective responsibility, home-bodies and colonial trespassers, traditional lore and vanguard experiment, rootedness and roaming. Katherine Simpson's 'Wealth in Common: Gifts, Desire, and Colonial Commodities in Woolf and Mansfield' (in Gillies and Wussow, eds., pp. 88–93) addresses Manfield's short story 'A Cup of Tea', and Mary Ann Gillies supplies a shrewdly angled essay entitled 'On a View from the Rims: Katherine Mansfield and Emily Carr' (in Gillies and Wussow, eds., pp. 94–106).

In 2014 the *Journal of New Zealand Literature* devoted a special issue to 'Katherine Mansfield Masked and Unmasked'. Emily Perkins's 'Feeling Things: A Response to Katherine Mansfield's Fiction' (*JNZL* 32:ii[2014] 17–30) extends a lively strand in Mansfield scholarship that weighs the cognitive, affective, and corporeal intersections in modernist 'feeling'. Aimee Gasston demonstrates how 'Phenomenology Begins at Home' by gauging 'The Presence of Things in the Short Fiction of Katherine Mansfield and Virginia Woolf' (*JNZL* 32:ii[2014] 31–51). Tracy Miao canvasses 'Children as Artists: Katherine Mansfield's "Innocent Eye"' (*JNZL* 32:ii[2014] 143–66). In 'Veiling and Unveiling: Mansfield's Modernist Aesthetics' (*JNZL* 32:ii[2014] 203–25), Janet Wilson furnishes a critically adroit response to her subject's narrative evasions, concealments, and allusions.

As Andrew Frayn acknowledges in *Writing Disenchantment: British First World War Prose, 1914–30*, it has become a critical commonplace to note how Great War British fiction, and especially the 'War Books Boom' of 1928–30, dramatizes an experience of bitter disillusionment, with returning combatants unwilling or unable to confront the shock of being immersed in a destructive element. *Writing Disenchantment* argues that non-combatants were just as disaffected as those who fought: indeed, Mansfield produced some of her most psychologically acute work in the immediate aftermath of the conflict. Frayn's percipient account delves deep into previously overlooked archives. The impact of the First World War on the civilian population also looms large in the fiction and polemical journalism of Storm Jameson, who was the subject of a major new biography in 2014: Elizabeth Maslen's *Life in the Writings of Storm Jameson* and Jameson also features in Michael Schmidt's sprawling *The Novel: A Biography*.

E.H. Wright's *Bloomsbury Influences* is an interdisciplinary essay collection that contains a searching essay by Susan Reid on 'Creative Friction: Lawrence, Mansfield and Murry' (pp. 88–109). In the same volume, Sandeep Parmar's 'Crossing the Ritual Bridge: Hope Mirrlees's *The Counterplot* and *Between the Acts*' (pp. 126–40) throws into bolder relief Mirrlees's technically ambitious second novel. Published in 1924 and set in the years immediately following the Great War, *The Counterplot* deserves closer scrutiny given its keen alertness to various aspects of Jane Ellen Harrison's 'tribal ritualism' (p. 130).

In 'Clouds and Power: May Sinclair's War' (*JML* 37:iii[2014] 18–35), Luke Thurston suggests that the challenge posed by Sinclair's wartime writing is that it concentrates for the most part on cathartic release, not the deprivation and bereavement now synonymous with the strife. As the character Nicholas Harrison reflects in Sinclair's *The Tree of Heaven* [1917]: 'when you're up first out of the trench and stand alone on the parapet, it's absolute happiness'. Thurston demonstrates how Sinclair's protagonists are fascinated and attracted by a 'vortex' of primal energy they sense as both destructive and exhilarating, and her narratives 'simultaneously relish and disavow this fantasmatic investment' (pp. 18–19). Thurston concludes that Sinclair's writing provides a salutary lesson about the hazardous 'entanglement' of 'sexual fantasy' and communal brutality. Overall, Thurston's readings offer a thought-provoking lens through which to assess Sinclair's war novels *The Tree of Heaven*, *The Romantic* [1920], and *Far End* [1926]. Daniel Ferrer's 'A Mediated Plunge: From Joyce to Woolf through Richardson and Sinclair' (in Canani and Sara Sullam, eds. *Parallaxes: Virginia Woolf Meets James Joyce*, pp. 25–37) focuses on Sinclair's innovative aesthetic, as does Emma Domínguez-Rué's article 'Pen-Is-Envy: Psychoanalysis, Feminism, Feminism, and the Woman Writer in May Sinclair's *Mary Olivier*' (*JGenS* 22:ii[2014] 152–65).

In *Modernism, Christianity and Apocalypse*, edited by Erik Tonning, Matthew Feldman, and David Addyman, and Tonning's *Modernism and Christianity*, Erik Tonning notes how tropes of numinous vision and religio-scientific discovery in fiction from this era have been largely misconstrued or underestimated. Tonning, and the contributors to the former volume, do an excellent job of redirecting academic attention to the practitioners of what we might call a sacral modernism. Unfortunately, these two projects focus principally on canonical male authors—for example James Joyce, Ezra Pound, David Jones, and Samuel Beckett. Tonning is lucid and lively on the usual suspects (especially Beckett), their mutual influence and associations. But the rather restricted coverage and familiar names remind us that current researchers should follow Elizabeth Anderson's lead in *H.D. and Modernist Religious Imagination* [2013]. Anderson carefully weighs the issue of a gendered approach to spirituality—orthodox and heretical—in modernist cultural production. Indeed, May Sinclair, Sylvia Townsend Warner, Mary Butts, and Hope Mirrlees all treated the scrutiny of religion as a core facet of their adventurously eclectic writings.

Rebekah Lockyer's 'Ford Madox Ford's Musical Legacy: *Parade's End* and Wagner' (*FMLS* 50:iv[2014] 426–52) is part of a special issue concerned with 'Wagner and Literature: New Directions'. Seamus O'Malley's 'Listening for Class in Ford Madox Ford's *Parade's End*' (*Mo/Mo* 21:iii[2014] 689–714) considers how Ford's tetralogy stages 'multiple class conflicts' (p. 689). This article weighs Tietjens's endorsement of eighteenth-century notions of chivalry, power, patronage, and ordered hierarchy. O'Malley also makes an incisive contribution to Ashley Chantler and Rob Hawkes's collection, *Ford Madox Ford's 'Parade's End': The First World War, Culture, and Modernity*, discussing ' "How Much Mud Does a Man Need?": Land and Liquidity in *Parade's End*' (pp. 119–28). In the same collection, Sara Haslam's 'From Conversation to Humiliation: *Parade's End* and the Eighteenth Century' (pp. 36–51) is also of note; Angus Wrenn scrutinizes 'Wagner's Ring Cycle and *Parade's End*' (pp. 67–80), while Rob Spence supplies an insightful account of 'Ford and Lewis: The Attraction of Opposites' (pp. 153–60) and Isabelle Brasme probes 'Articulations of Femininity in *Parade's End*' (pp. 173–85). Mary Maxwell examines Ford's final years of literary creativity in 'Biala and Ford Madox Ford's Buckshee: The Summer at Benfolly' (*YR* 102:iii[2014] 1–30).

Ford's friend and collaborator Joseph Conrad has once again proven to be a powerful draw for textual scholars and cultural historians. Vincent Sherry's *Modernism and the Reinvention of Decadence*, like Marja Härmänmaa and Christopher Nissen's edited collection, *Decadence, Degeneration, and the End: Studies in the European Fin de Siècle*, will appeal strongly to researchers who calibrate novels of London anarchism such as Conrad's *The Secret Agent* and G.K. Chesterton's *The Man Who Was Thursday* in terms of 'exhausted civility' (p. 120) and 'declining times' (p. 60). Sherry's compendious and elegantly crafted enterprise posits that Conrad's modernism shows a deep 'consciousness of decay as the point of its most novel awareness' (p. 98). Sherry sedulously traces the recurrence of the term 'degeneration' in 'several synonyms and cognates' throughout *The Secret Agent* (p. 98). Indeed, Conrad furnishes Sherry with an extended meditation on the experience of 'aftermath' which becomes 'the prime condition of contemporary time' (p. 123). Conrad's aesthetic interest in mapping and tapping this 'aftermath' sensation can be measured against Deleuze's arguments about modernist temporality set forth in Paul Ardoin, S.E. Gontarski, and Laci Mattison's collection, *Understanding Deleuze, Understanding Modernism*, as well as William Vesterman's *Dramatizing Time in Twentieth-Century Literature*. Vesterman offers close readings of both modernist and non-modernist writers such as Wodehouse, Lewis, and Conrad. Vesterman explores how these authors confront and process the mysteries of time and the need for temporal structure in modern fiction—a concern that Katherine Ebury also ponders in *Modernism and Cosmology: Absurd Lights*.

William Freedman's *Joseph Conrad and the Anxiety of Knowledge* is especially strong on *Under Western Eyes* and *The Rescue* as 'indeterminate fables'. Freedman's core chapters are bound together by a confident sense that the lack of a unified analysis in Conrad's fiction is not symptomatic of a weary resignation at the shortcomings of rational language or philosophical credos. Instead, Freedman argues that the bewildering slipperiness of Conrad's narrative fabric is the outcome of a radical ambivalence towards certain modes of knowledge that threaten to simplify discoveries about human affect. Freedman should be read alongside Beci Carver's astute *Granular Modernism*, which positions Conrad as a novelist who relishes the semantic irregularities that make literary tropes resistant to glib explication or brisk summary. In Carver's analysis, Conrad emerges as an author whose 'peculiar responsive sensitiveness . . . to the slightest detail', as Katherine Mansfield famously called it, problematizes our grasp of the interrelation between technical innovation and ideas of history. Conrad also exploits seemingly haphazard or unglamorous everyday events that defy the instincts of conventional historians who seek some ultimate shape in the modern moment. Carver's reading will appeal to scholars who pay special attention to the categories and forms of historical experience that resonate in Conrad's fiction—time as fever-dream; as phantasmagoria; as deadening routine; or as revolutionary rupture.

Johan Adam Warodell's 'Conrad the Doodler' (*CQ* 43:iv[2014] 339–54) postulates that, although 'doodling' furnishes respite from the intellectual struggles of literary production, it is not necessarily a total 'pause' from writing (pp. 339–40), for it is a process that involves thought-adventure. Warodell discusses the ways in which doodling and writing may have intertwined for Conrad. There are, in *The Shadow-Line* [1917] holograph for example, 109 doodles. By shifting his doodles from the edges of the manuscript to the core of scholarly discussion, a visual portrait emerges of an artist for whom 'procrastination' represents a complex mode of affect (pp. 440–1).

Rochelle Rives's 'Face Values: Optics as Ethics in Joseph Conrad's *The Secret Agent*' (*Criticism* 56:i[2014] 89–117) is compelling about the 'thematic importance of legibility in the novel, along with the epistemological uncertainty of the face' (p. 89). G.W. Stephen Brodsky's 'Joseph Conrad: Secular Principles in "Prince Roman"' (*N&Q* 61[2014] 585–6) weighs the representation of Polish aristocrats and political sway in a critically overlooked short story. David Prickett's 'Art Out of Bread-Winning: Conrad and the Question of the Plimsoll Man' (*Conradian* 39:ii[2014] 1–18) scrutinizes the treatment of maritime manners and mores in *The Nigger of the 'Narcissus'* [1897]. Also relevant here is Nicholas Royle's 'Reading Joseph

Conrad: Episodes from the Coast' (*Mosaic* 47:i[2014] 41–67), which provides a deconstructionist approach to various Conrad texts. Douglas Kerr's 'The Secret Secret Sharer' (*Conradian* 39:ii[2014] 19–30) ponders the critical implications of Robert Hampson's recently published monograph *Conrad's Secrets* [2012].

Nidesh Lawtoo's 'Fear of the Dark: Surrealist Shadows in *The Nigger of the 'Narcissus''* (*MFS* 60:ii[2014] 227–50) argues that in *The Nigger of the 'Narcissus'* Conrad lends narrative shape to 'a poetics of darkness' that anticipates surrealist concerns with self-dissolution and loss of civic identity (pp. 227–8). Linking Conrad with Roger Caillois's surrealist account of mimesis, Lawtoo contends that he strives to 'make [us] see' a fear of the dark that has sobering psychological, philosophical, and narratological implications. This perceptive essay contributes to a mimetic line of enquiry in the new modernist studies by suggesting that Conrad's tropes of darkness cast shadows that are more surrealistic than impressionistic.

Beci Dobbin's '"An Elf Wearing a Hat That Makes Him Invisible": Modernism's Shy Irony' (*TPr* 28:iii[2014] 453–71) sheds valuable light on the narrative fabric of Conrad's short story, 'The Informer'. Andrew Purssell's '"The Sense of Primitive Man": Joseph Conrad, W.H.R. Rivers, and Representing the Other in "The End of the Tether"' (*MLR* 109:ii[2014] 357–74) assesses Conrad's ethnographic fascination with and complex representation of Malay culture and its links to colonial discourse. James Purdon's 'Secret Agents, Official Secrets: Joseph Conrad and the Security of the Mail' (*RES* 65[2014] 302–20) provides a compelling account of *The Secret Agent* by flagging thematic obsessions with national security, information flows, and transport networks.

Andrew Glazzard's '"The Shore Gang": *Chance* and the Ethics of Work' (*Conradian* 39:i[2014] 1–16) is a socio-historical assessment of *Chance* [1914], presenting it as an intricately realized meditation on the rituals and ethics of labour. Glazzard's elegantly structured essay is one of a number of critically adroit pieces about Conrad's novel in this specific edition of *The Conradian*, which also includes E.H. Wright's 'The "Girl-Novel": *Chance*, and Woolf's *The Voyage Out*' (*Conradian* 39:i[2014] 80–97) and Helen Chambers's '"Fine-Weather Books": Representations of Readers and Reading in *Chance*' (*Conradian* 39:i[2014] 98–115).

Nisha Manocha's 'The Readable across *Heart of Darkness*' (*Conradian* 39:ii[2014] 31–43) foregrounds the intricacies of narrative voice and anxieties about legibility in Conrad's most famous novella. Annika J. Lindskog's '"It Was Very Quiet There": The Contaminating Soundscapes of *Heart of Darkness*' (*Conradian* 39:ii[2014] 44–60) analyses the treatment of repression and sensory affect in this much-discussed text. Joseph Michael Valente's 'The Accidental Autist: Neurosensory Disorder in *The Secret Agent*' (*JML* 38:i[2014] 20–37) proposes that the discursive construction of 'idiocy' during the modern era shares a basic architecture with theorizations of 'autistic spectrum disorder' today: each masks the rigid scientific demarcations to which it has been nonetheless subjected. Valente argues that the telling overlap in the 'symptomatic profile' of the two cognitive syndromes imbues *The Secret Agent* (pp. 20–1). Valente makes a compelling case for Conrad fashioning the character of Stevie in a manner designed both to underline and to debunk the clinical category of idiocy. This strategy inadvertently lends his protagonist attributes at once consistent with and subversive of the contemporary civic and medical notions of autism. By cannily locating Stevie as the 'opposite' of the idiot he is supposed to be, Conrad presents him, Valente argues, as a silent, austere and watchful authorial 'alter ego' (pp. 22–3).

Kate Armond's 'Wyndham Lewis and the Parables of Expressionist Architecture' (*ModCult* 9:ii[2014] 282–303) assesses *The Caliph's Design* through the critical lens of German Expressionist architectural flair during the years 1918–20. In this postwar text Lewis sees Bruno Taut as the embodiment of a 'single architect with brains', one whose technical gifts might trigger a project of cultural as well as political renovation. Heather Fielding's 'How the Taxi-Cab Driver Reads: Wyndham Lewis, Modernist Aesthetics, and the Novel as Machine' (*JML* 38:i[2014] 128–46) sheds light on that much-misconstrued facet of Lewis's aesthetic theory which packages a certain kind of novel as a textual technology or machine. The merit of Fielding's critical approach is her detailed alertness to how Lewis employs the novel as a means of rethinking civil society's relationship with the technologies of industrial production.

Jill Richards's 'Model Citizens and Millenarian Subjects: Vorticism, Suffrage, and London's Great Unrest' (*JML* 37:iii[2014] 1–17) chronicles Lewis's commentary, in the years before the Great War, on radical suffragette activism. Richards demonstrates that Lewis's polemical and fictional texts transmute the suffragette group into an individual and idealized agent who reacts with insurgent brio to the grievous flaws in England's parliamentary democracy. This searching essay should be read alongside John Whittier-Ferguson's *Mortality and Form in Late Modernist Literature*, which boasts an insightful chapter on Lewis's uncompromising account of geopolitical convulsions (pp. 141–97).

Kevin Rulo's 'Between Old and New: Wyndham Lewis's Modernist "Joint"' (*RES* 65[2014] 495–514) throws into sharper relief a prose work, entitled 'Joint', that Lewis laboured over in the early 1920s before abandoning the text in draft form. For Lewis aficionados who are unaware of the substance of this manuscript, Rulo's nuanced account of the relevant contexts and compositional history will prove invaluable, especially as it reveals his evolving attitude towards the nature and function of modernist satire. Erik M. Bachman's 'How To Misbehave as a Behaviourist (If You're Wyndham Lewis)' (*TPr* 28:iii[2014] 427–51) supplies a theoretically savvy reading of the Lewis short story 'Cantleman's Spring-Mate' in relation to John B. Watson's behavioural psychology.

Elizabeth Pender's 'Mawkishness, or Literary Art: John Rodker's *Adolphe 1920* in Modernism' (*Mo/Mo* 21:ii[2014] 467–85) assesses Rodker's critically neglected novella in relation to Lewis's sprawling and obstreperous satirical novel *The Apes of God* [1930]. *Adolphe 1920* was republished by Carcanet in 1996 and sheds light on Rodker's complex self-positioning within vanguard networking cliques. Pender gauges the novella's contemporary critical reception and how its verbal texture is illuminated given Rodker's frequent contribution of poetry, sketches, and criticism to literary magazines such as *The Egoist* and *The Little Review*.

George M. Johnson's 'Evil Is in the Eye of the Beholder: Threatening Children in Two Edwardian Speculative Satires' (*SFS* 41:i[2014] 26–44) measures the textual representation of children in H.G. Wells's *Food of the Gods* against John Davys Beresford's *The Hampdenshire Wonder* [1911]. Angus Fletcher's 'Another Literary Darwinism' (*CritI* 40:ii[2014] 450–69) canvasses Wells's *The Science of Life* [1929] in terms of its generic features and engagement with the intricacies of evolutionary theory. Fletcher's inventive analysis will be useful to scholars who trace how ideas about genetics were promoted—or contested—by the mainstream media in interwar culture, and what part debates about evolutionary theory played in the popular fascination which family trees, local history, and heredity.

Elizabeth English's *Lesbian Modernism: Censorship, Sexuality and Genre Fiction* not only sheds light on *The Well of Loneliness* trial and consequent ban, but raises questions about the complex histories and ideologies of feminist and lesbian cultural production between the wars. English shows that popular fiction afforded a complex yet under-appreciated framework for lesbian cultural identity. Genre fiction, such as Gothic supernaturalism, historical romance, espionage thrillers, and country-house mysteries, even shaped the artistic vision of canonical and experimental figures such as Mary Butts and Woolf. This is a topic that Matthew Levay elaborates in his essay 'Remaining a Mystery: Gertrude Stein, Crime Fiction and Popular Modernism' (*JML* 36:iv[2013] 1–22), which considers the way in which influential Anglo-American women writers combined a bold artistic imperative with tropes synonymous with commercial genres, thus expanding the technical parameters of and potential audiences for their work.

Radclyffe Hall's narrative strategies in *The Well of Loneliness* also feature in Chase Dimock's article, 'Crafting Hermaphroditism: Gale Wilhelm's Lesbian Modernism in *We Too Are Drifting*' (*CollL* 41:iii[2014] 45–68). Dimock argues that Wilhelm's fiction, in contrast to the striking framework of 'the invert' advanced by Hall's more famous text, portrays the hermaphrodite as a figuration for reassessing lesbian selfhood and desire. Unlike Gertrude Stein or Djuna Barnes, who used idiosyncratic textual modes for portraying dissident felt sensations, Wilhelm achieves this by appealing to middlebrow tastes.

Amy Clukey's 'Enchanting Modernism: Mary Butts, Decadence, and the Ethics of Occultism' (*MFS* 60:i[2014] 78–107) argues that both decadent authors and Mary Butts refined tropes of occultist lore so as to debunk middle-class complacency and narrow-mindedness. Clukey's probing essay focuses well on Butts's short-lived yet intense alliance with Aleister Crowley. The centrepiece of Clukey's article is a methodical examination of Butts's recondite motifs in the cryptic short stories 'Mappa Mundi' and 'Brightness Falls'. Crowley, as author and occultist celebrity, also features in Michael Allis's 'The Diva and the Beast: Susan Strong and the Wagnerism of Aleister Crowley' (*FMLS* 50:iv[2014] 380–404).

This year was noteworthy for an eye-catching array of original analyses of E.M. Forster's fiction. Jonah Corne's 'Queer Fragments: Ruination and Sexuality in E.M. Forster' (*CollL* 41:iii[2014] 27–44) notes that scholars have frequently construed the leitmotif of ruins in Forster's corpus as a byword for hopeless yearning or melancholia. Yet Corne argues that Forster's understanding of environmental decay is more complicated and capacious than critical orthodoxy permits. For Corne, it is solemn yet also leavened with tentative compensations, even muted pleasures, as specific tangible localities become a storehouse of felt sensation. What troubles matters, Corne concludes, is a recurrent association throughout Forster's writing between gaunt dereliction and queer sexuality: a correspondence that emerges in *Howards End* [1910] and *Maurice* [1913–14]. In these texts, Corne demonstrates, a topography of queerly coded ruination reveals otherwise overlooked facets of Forster's depiction of architecture, and especially the operations of memory in an epoch of amnesiac modernity. George E. Haggerty's 'Pan Pipes: Conjugal Friendship in *The Longest Journey*' (*ELT* 57:ii[2014] 155–69) also addresses the queer dynamics of Forster's critically neglected narratives.

The fourth chapter of Helena Gurfinkel's *Outlaw Fathers in Victorian and Modern British Literature: Queering Patriarchy* scrutinizes male domesticity in Forster's posthumously published science-fiction story 'Little Imber' [1961]. Gurfinkel contends that this text rewrites 'the standard sexual encounter between a "gentleman"' and 'a young working-class man, into a political and sexual utopia' (p. 149). 'Little Imber' is a fantastical fragment that continues 'the tradition of its longer, more famous predecessors, *The Longest Journey* and *Maurice*', the two novels that prioritize and affirm 'love (or its possibility) between two men of different social classes in a pastoral setting' (p. 150).

Peter Fifield's '"I often wish you could answer me back: and so perhaps do you!"': E.M. Forster and BBC Radio Broadcasting' (in Feldman, Tonning, and Mead, eds., *Broadcasting in the Modernist Era*, pp. 57–77) considers Forster's lively engagement with the possibilities of radio in the early days of the BBC. Like *Radio Modernism* [2006] and Debra Rae Cohen and Michael Coyle's collection *Broadcasting Modernism* [2009], this essay indicates that the invisible medium of radio triggered numerous developments in the circulation of generic modes. Fifield proposes that Forster embraced radio with relish, developing texts that were to be heard but not read. Forster incorporated the device into his literary narratives, and exploited it to publicize his distinctive craft. He perceived in radio the same restless energy that imbued aesthetic modernism itself.

Suzanne Roszak's 'Social Non-Conformists in Forster's Italy: Otherness and the Enlightened English Tourist' (*ArielE* 45:i–ii[2014] 167–94) acknowledges that recent scholarship has been increasingly attentive to Forster's fascination with problematic notions of here and elsewhere, the endemic and the exotic. This article presents a Forster who was savvy about the textual frameworks that mediated tourism in the early years of the twentieth century: witty fiction-travelogues, illustrated camping manuals, and commercial guidebooks, as well as cartography. Roszak concludes that academic discussion of Forster's Italian fiction has 'lagged behind', with pundits continuing to stress how *Where Angels Fear to Tread* [1905] and *A Room with a View* [1908] variously laud Italian culture and slyly subvert monolithic ideas of English cultural prestige. Roszak contends that while the Italian novels use the trope of the nonconformist to underscore a foreign culture's capacity to prompt reform at home, they also overstate the cultural otherness that separates Italy from England, indulging in primitivist, condescending portraits of Italian communities and *genius loci*. The novels also evince a narrative impulse to sacrifice their Italian characters for the benefit of their English protagonists, depicting the deaths of Italians as a tool for enlightening the obtuse English tourist.

Hedley Twidle's 'Nothing Extraordinary: E.M. Forster and the English Limit' (*EAf* 40:ii[2014] 25–45), like Annabel Patterson's chapter (pp. 23–38) in *The International Novel*, ponders *A Passage to India* [1925] in terms of contested ideologies of Englishness and the workings of the British empire. Philip Gardner's 'E.M. Forster, Surrey and the Golden Fleece' (*RES* 65[2014] 904–21) takes a biographical approach to Forster's narratives. Yangsook Shin's 'A "Condition of England" Novel: A New Historicist Reading of *Howards End*' (*BAF1900* 21:ii[2014] 233–59) pays renewed attention to Forster and the cultural politics of place in this text.

The move to reappraise the spatial and temporal co-ordinates of interwar cultural production which has energized recent Forster scholarship also informs Danielle Price's 'Controlling Nature: Mary Webb and the National Trust' (*CLIO* 43:ii[2014] 225–52). Price positions the regional novels *Gone to Earth* [1917] and *Precious Bane* [1924] as sombre meditations on heritage versus history, individualist aspiration versus tribal togetherness. This astute essay, which illustrates that the bucolic hinterland operates both as shelter from and reflection of the fractures synonymous with industrial modernity, should be read alongside Lucy Thomas's '"Born to a Million Dismemberments": Female Hybridity in the Border Writing of Margiad Evans, Hilda Vaughan and Mary Webb' (in Bohata and Gramich, eds., *Rediscovering Margiad Evans: Marginality, Gender and Illness*, pp. 39–52). Price and Thomas variously grapple with a question that continues to exercise scholars of interwar 'back-to-the-land' fiction, asking how effective the term 'modernism' is as a yardstick of aesthetic worth and as a descriptive framework in relation to rural and regional narratives by overlooked authors such as Leo Walmsley, H.E. Bates, and Sheila Kaye-Smith.

These critical concerns also shape Simon Featherstone's contribution to Monika Fludernik and Miriam Nandi's edited collection, *Idleness, Indolence and Leisure in English Literature* (pp. 235–51). By focusing on the cult of the vagabond in Edwardian narrative, Featherstone says much about the cultural craze for 'rambling' and how it coloured myriad fiction-travelogues and their promotion of localist excursion. Leonie Wanitzek's thoughtful chapter from the same volume, 'Englishness, Summer and the Pastoral of Country Leisure in Twentieth-Century Literature' (pp. 252–72), also examines the symbolism of landscape, especially the role of the bucolic edge-land as a repository of lyric feeling or political desire.

Hazel Sheeky Bird's *Class, Leisure and National Identity in British Children's Literature, 1918–1950* brings ample historical and textual knowledge to the issue of how, in the years following the Great War, children's fiction was 'at the forefront of the literary struggle to control and shape understanding of the countryside as a place of quietude and to ameliorate the effects of mass tourism' (p. 1). This is a nuanced study of 'the camping and tramping genre' that sheds light on what many scholars now call 'modernism in the green'—alluding to an interwar literary landscape marked by spinneys, national parks, ponds, and secret suburban gardens. Moreover, Bird demonstrates a canny grasp of how Arthur Ransome's 'Swallows and Amazons' novels critique the operations of 'the imperial geographic imagination' (pp. 100–1).

Katherine Nash's *Feminist Narrative Ethics: Tacit Persuasion in Modernist Form* forges an intriguing theory of narrative ethics by positioning Forster as an author synonymous with the 'ethics of distance' while John Cowper Powys's published corpus represents an 'ethics of attention'. While offering cogent readings of Forster and Powys, the project also supplies an interdisciplinary framework for combining feminist and rhetorical theory.

James Harker's '"Laura Was Not Thinking": Cognitive Minimalism in Sylvia Townsend Warner's *Lolly Willowes*' (*SNNTS* 46:i[2014] 44–62) indicates that literary and cultural historians have long judged the most arresting facet of *Lolly Willowes* [1926] to be 'the generic shift from realism to fantasy when Laura Willowes becomes a witch and makes a pact with Satan' (pp. 44–5). The most refreshing aspect of Harker's thesis is his focus on Warner's nuanced portrayal of Laura's perceptual habits and verbal mannerisms as an unmarried woman. Exploiting the findings of cognitive science as well as narratology, Harker proposes that Warner's technical daring invites close comparison with contemporaneous modernist depictions of amplified or heightened consciousness.

Laura Marcus and Ankhi Mukherjee's *Concise Companion to Psychoanalysis, Literature, and Culture* traces the tangled history of psychoanalytic theory and its remarkable impact on contemporary literary criticism. Pamela Thurschwell's chapter, on 'Psychoanalysis, Literature, and the "Case" of Adolescence' (pp. 167–89) is revealing in its use of Freudian case studies to reconceptualize literary evocations of the teenager in interwar British fiction. Laura Marcus's *Dreams of Modernity: Psychoanalysis, Cinema, Literature* furnishes an insightful discussion of Dorothy Richardson, covering the period from around 1880 to 1930. She argues that 'modernity' as a form of civic life informed the beginnings of modernism as cultural production, foregrounding Richardson's intricate reactions to the conditions of her own transitional epoch.

Mihai I. Spariosu's *Modernism and Exile: Liminality and the Utopian Imagination* explores exile and utopia as correlated phenomena in the modern movement. The chief merit of this crisp survey is its awareness of exile as a threefold phenomenon: as discursive category, analytical notion, and keenly felt sensation (often of bodily and psychological threat, or ontological emptiness). Spariosu's early chapters scrutinize issues of population mobility and migration, especially their representation in narratives by canonical writers such as Conrad. Spariosu indicates that utopian projects are often refined by an exilic consciousness that attempts to compensate for its displacement or rootlessness by fashioning vivid imaginative domains that limn pathways to self-discovery.

Bridget Chalk's *Modernism and Mobility: The Passport and Cosmopolitan Experience* confronts an intriguing fictional and historical paradox: world-citizenship and restive border-crossing distinguish myriad modernist journals, short stories, and novels. However, the interwar years also reveal increasingly stringent technologies of mobility restriction and monitoring. Labels synonymous with juridical scrutiny and state-managerial power, such as 'alien' or 'émigré' modify interwar demographics through differing lines of affiliation and prerogative. For Chalk, these taxonomic markers prompt reassessment of the causes and outcomes of insider identity, retrenchment, and repatriation. Chalk skilfully employs the emergence of the compulsory passport in the West around 1914 to 'telescope' the shifting parameters of peripatetic 'national identity' (pp. 20–1). This book will be of especial interest to aficionados of overlooked women writers, such as Mary Butts, Rebecca West, and Olive Moore, whose fictions address how nomadic experience is governed by the designation and sedulous policing of nationality, often through documentation such as train-tickets, itineraries, visas, and letters of introduction.

Meghan Marie Hammond's *Empathy and the Psychology of Literary Modernism* shows that *fin-de-siècle* conceptions of empathy are woven into the fabric of literary modernism. Coined in 1909 to combine English 'sympathy' and German *Einfühlung*, 'empathy' is, in Hammond's account, a specifically twentieth-century notion of fellow feeling that seeks to bridge interpersonal distance. Hammond does well to trace the tangled history of empathy, revealing how this multifaceted concept resonates in specific narratives by Dorothy Richardson, Katherine Mansfield, and Ford Madox Ford. The key virtue of this scholarly enterprise is its canny awareness that while these modernist authors strive to render a vivid apprehension of another's thought-processes, they also dramatize the potential for profound disturbance and dislocation in the act of empathy.

Simon Joyce's *Modernism and Naturalism in British and Irish Fiction, 1880–1930* discusses the history of aesthetic modernism and its signal, though often misconstrued, ties to Zola's naturalist credo. Joyce is astute on how the fusion of naturalism and impressionism created a framework for the development of the stream-of-consciousness writing synonymous with Dorothy Richardson.

The opening gambit of Jenelle Troxell's 'Shock and "Perfect Contemplation": Dorothy Richardson's Mystical Cinematic Consciousness' (*Mo/Mo* 21:i[2014] 51–70) ponders Richardson's first contribution to the film journal *Close Up*, in which she recounts her inaugural trip to a picture palace in north London, where she is struck by a profound sense of restorative 'quiet' and by the new kinds of communities forming around the cinema. Richardson's contributions to *Close Up* grew into a regular column, 'Continuous Performance'. As Troxell explains, this title is 'drawn from the early cinematic practice of running movies back to back, continuously' (pp. 51–2). Over the journal's six-year run (1927–33), Richardson resolutely examines cinema's propensity to move viewers into a new realm of consciousness, asserting in her 1931 article 'Narcissus': 'the whole power of the film' resides in 'this single, simple factor': 'the reduction, or elevation of the observer to the condition that is essential to perfect contemplation' (p. 51). Troxell demonstrates that in espousing a contemplative mode of perception, Richardson defends a mode of looking which is denigrated as undiscerning, apolitical, mawkish—in short as 'feminine'—in much historical film criticism. Moreover, by alluding to mystical tenets, in which absorption in the image is cultivated, Richardson succeeds in forging an alternative and enabling model of spectatorship.

Matt Franks's 'Mental Inversion, Modernist Aesthetics, and Disability Exceptionalism in Olive Moore's *Spleen*' (*JML* 38:i[2014] 107–27) proposes that Moore's formally striking 1930 novel *Spleen* explores 'the appropriative relationship between experimental modernism and disability' (pp. 107–8). While the text exploits the aesthetics of broken statues and fractured narratives, it also dramatizes—according to Franks—how modernists proclaim their own exceptional capacity and mobility in ways that buttress eugenic conceptions of disability. Moore shows that feminist and emerging queer politics in the interwar period manipulated disabled aesthetic tropes so as to retool concepts of gendered identity and sexuality through exceptionalism, but did so by reifying disability and race as supposedly fixed categories. Franks's subtle assessment of *Spleen* indicates that modernist studies must process the vexed legacy of appropriating disabled modes of perception and expression.

Chris Brawley's *Nature and the Numinous in Mythopoeic Fantasy Literature* contains a probing chapter on Algernon Blackwood's neo-Romantic pursuit of strange gods in *The Centaur* [1911]. Brawley makes lively links between the scholarly methodologies of ecocriticism and post-humanism and mythopoeic fantasy: texts which often exploit the colonial syncretic as they go in search of the arcane and the miraculous. Making pointed reference to Rudolf Otto's *The Idea of the Holy*, Brawley argues that mythopoeic fantasy seeks to overhaul normative habits of perception to map the esoteric and to refresh notions of the physical world as a locus of spiritual renewal.

Fergal Casey's 'A Celtic Twilight in Little England: G.K. Chesterton and W.B. Yeats' (*ISR* 22:i[2014] 80–90) considers *The Napoleon of Notting Hill* in relation to British imperialism and, most interestingly, the Celtic Revival. Walter Raubicheck's '*The Man Who Was Thursday* and *The Nine Tailors*: All the Evidence Points to God' (*Seven* 31[2014] 95–104) concentrates on figurations of divine providence in one of Chesterton's most formally arresting narratives.

Brian Gibson's *Reading Saki* assesses the whole range of H.H. Munro's often acerbic literary narratives. Gibson's thorough critical re-examination situates this Edwardian author as a deeply vexed—and vexing—commentator on issues of homeland security, anti-suffragist sentiment, class mobility, and the influence of ethnic trespassers.

Lise Jaillant's *Modernism, Middlebrow and the Literary Canon* builds on notable recent research into the varieties of middlebrow fiction in the interwar period by critics such as Melissa Sullivan, Hilary Hinds, and Faye Hammill. Jaillant scrutinizes H.G. Wells's literary and scientific ideas between 1917 and 1930. Well's *The History of Mr Polly* [1910] features in Joseph Wiesenfarth's 'Death in the Waste Land: Ford, Wells and Waugh' (in Chantler and Hawkes, eds., pp. 197–206).

Alexandra Lawrie's *The Beginnings of University English: Extramural Study, 1885–1910* contains a perceptive chapter on Arnold Bennett (pp. 115–48) which discusses his unusual literary reputation. While middlebrow audiences and gifted autodidacts construed Bennett's oeuvre as distinctive and commercially successful 'art', his novels were magisterially rejected by the modernist vanguard in general, and Virginia Woolf in particular, as formally unambitious. Lawrie analyses Bennett's rarely debated literary advice columns for *T.P.'s Weekly*, demonstrating a keen sensitivity to the 'chameleonic' nature of Bennett's professional career. Indeed, Lawrie irradiates Bennett's myriad narrative endeavours to enrich and democratize culture by making aesthetic experience central to, and reflective of, his readers' daily lives.

Angharad Saunders's 'Violating the Domestic: Unmaking the Home in Edwardian Fiction' (*HomeCult* 11:ii[2014] 219–36) considers John Galsworthy's *The Man of Property* [1906] in terms of its complex representation of matrimonial discord and home/land integrity. This special issue, entitled 'Home Unmaking' sheds light on contested definitions of the domestic space in the first three decades of the twentieth century.

Finally, perceptive article-length contributions to John Buchan studies include: Ursula Buchan's 'Fact and Fiction in John Buchan's Great War' (*JBuchJ* 47[2014] 4–14); Michael Haslett's 'Influences on Buchan's Literary Style: A Fresh Look' (*JBuchJ* 47[2014] 32–9); and Michael Redley's 'What Did John Buchan Do in the Great War?' (*JBuchJ* 47[2014] 15–23).

(b) Fiction 1930–1945

As the concept of 'intermodernism' gains critical traction, the range of material produced on the 1930–45 period has expanded accordingly, making 2014 a bumper year for scholarship. The keynote themes of this criticism offer up a heady mixture of trauma, conflict, displacement, affective disturbance, and generational ennui, making Jean Rhys an apt point of departure. Cristina-Georgiana Voicu's *Exploring Cultural Identities in Jean Rhys' Fiction* wrests a positive spin from these perennial themes of Rhys studies, employing a broadly postcolonial perspective to emphasize forms of productive hybridity in Rhys's corpus. Voicu begins with a thorough exposition of the wider political and cultural implications of hybridity in the formation of colonial power structures, before analysing the formal hybridity of the novels. For Voicu, Rhys's dialogic technique 'criticises modernity's tendency to order reality by constructing binary oppositions, which reduce people to homogenous categories', instead positing 'the provisionality of truth and the instability of meaning by employing multi-vocality, irony, parody and images of doubles' (p. 86). Voicu therefore emphasizes the formal 'wordplay', 'satire' and 'call-and-response' techniques through which Rhys invests her texts with a verbal exuberance, to subversively counterpoint her 'themes of betrayal, exploitation, and oppression' (p. 125).

Rebecca Colesworthy's 'Jean Rhys and the Fiction of Failed Reciprocity' (*JML* 37:ii[2014] 92–108) discusses *After Leaving Mr Mackenzie* [1930] as an example of Rhys's 'representation of sexual exchange as an exchange of gifts', viewing the promise of reciprocity as doomed to failure by its location within a wider economic system that conflates all forms of exchange with 'commercial' transaction (p. 93). Recontextualizing Marcel Mauss on the concept of the gift, Colesworthy foregrounds Rhys's depiction of the contamination of interpersonal relations with the logic of the market, resulting in a failure to differentiate 'between gifts and contracts' (p. 102). This ethical category error produces a corresponding 'failure of reciprocity between the sexes', brought about by assumptions of 'a sexual division of labour' (p. 93). Colesworthy argues that failed reciprocity represents a valuable means of rethinking well-established critical interpretations of Rhys's masochism: the 'victimisation of Rhys's male and female characters ... derives not from loss or lack but from an excess, the persistence of an exchange of gifts that exceeds the social system' (p. 105).

A discussion of Rhys's short stories forms the postscript to Kate Krueger's *British Women Writers and the Short Story 1850–1930: Reclaiming Social Space*, which contrasts Rhys with earlier female investigators of social space, from Elizabeth Gaskell to Virginia Woolf, arguing that Rhys's short fiction supplies a 'revisionist' (p. 202) vantage point. For example, while Woolf's characters seem able only to 'observe' the 'shopgirls standing on the other side of the counter ... Rhys has access to different kinds of spaces [and] is consequently presented with the opportunity to tell different narratives' (p. 199). This perspective derives from, and creatively transfigures, the disempowerment of the 'roomlessness [that] actuates her writing' (p. 202), enabling Rhys to identify and critique 'the absences and gaps that these characters often fall through in other narratives' (p. 202).

Rhys's handling of social space is also foregrounded in Tone Selboe's 'Emotional Mapping in *Good Morning Midnight*' (in Lombardo, Sætre, and Zanetta, eds., *Exploring Text and Emotions*, pp. 325–46), which highlights the novel's depiction of characters trapped within a 'hostile' (p. 326) environment, concluding that Rhys's narrative implies 'the necessity of reducing the urban map in order to master or control external and internal emotional pressure' (p. 327). This reading of 'the relation between emotional life and space' (p. 328) leads Selboe to highlight the novel's disturbing 'displacement' (p. 336) of conventional affective tropes from the protagonist to the inanimate world. Rhys presents 'the city itself as a *dramatis persona*' (p. 331) while conversely depicting the acting agent as a bundle of defensive 'masks, caricatures, gestures' (p. 337), resulting in an agonistic stand-off through which 'the notion of *change* is disclosed as an illusion' (p. 340).

Affective disturbances of a temporal, rather than spatial, nature are the primary concern of Erica L. Johnson's 'Haunted: Affective Memory in Jean Rhys's *Good Morning Midnight*' (*Affirmations* 1:ii[2014] 15–38). Conceiving memory as less 'a cognitive than an affective function' (p. 15), Johnson uses the convention of being haunted by shame to demonstrate 'how time itself is short-circuited by the shame affect' in a manner that conflates past with present, and thereby 'restructures memory as haunting' (p. 15). In *Good Morning, Midnight* [1939], 'the overlap of Sasha's past and present' (p. 17) continually conditions her response to events, as illustrated by her 'bodily "experience"' of the shame affect engendered by memory: her 'closed throat and stinging eyes' serve to conjoin the cognitive to the material in a visceral illustration of what Johnson terms the 'collapsed chronotope' (p. 25). For Johnson, Rhys pursues this chronotopic strategy as a means of 'proliferating adjacencies among Sasha's past and present impressions' (p. 31) to demonstrate the temporal entrapment of the shamed subject.

David Punter's *The Literature of Pity*, examines both *Good Morning, Midnight* and *Voyage in the Dark* [1934]. Punter is concerned with the complex connotations of pity as reflected in a wide range of literature, from Shakespeare to the present day, exploring whether pity might signify 'a genuine sharing of feeling', or merely 'an expression of scorn or contempt, which further weakens the other even as it strengthens our own position of assumed superiority' (p. 2). For Punter, *Voyage* illustrates Rhys's 'extraordinary insight into notions of collusion' (p. 119). Rhys's affectless depiction of Anna Morgan 'suspends [the reader's] pity', 'forbid[ding] us from indulging in our most simple, most primitive feelings', while Anna 'continually resists such approaches' (p. 120) on the narrative level. Meanwhile, *Good Morning, Midnight* is conceived in terms of a histrionic exploration of the 'dangerous border with self-pity', with Rhys's scrupulously even-handed portrayal of her heroine corroborating Punter's broader thesis that 'pity ... is at least double-edged' (p. 122). *Voyage in the Dark* also receives sustained attention in Anna Snaith's *Modernist Voyages: Colonial Women Writers in London, 1890–1945*, which highlights Rhys's view of 'the constructedness or performativity of racial categories', centred on a consistent attentiveness to 'the intersection of gender and colonialism' (p. 134). Thus, Snaith foregrounds Anna's 'doubly transgressive position' and consequent 'unease' (p. 135) within London, while using Rhys's biography as background.

Good Morning, Midnight comes back into focus in Bridget T. Chalk's *Modernism and Mobility*, which features a chapter on the traumas of classification in Rhys's interwar fiction. Chalk's study represents an ambitious contribution to recent scholarship on 'the transnational nature of modernism' (p. 9), interpreting this through the prism of the passport, as 'a form of externally determined accounting' (p. 28) of the self, activated when individuals set out to traverse 'metropolitan spaces, ports, and borders' (p. 12). Chalk argues that Rhys consistently 'constructs urban worlds as [an] endless series of border stops', investing her characters with her own sense of vulnerability over '"lacking" a nationality' (p. 119). Turning to *Good Morning, Midnight*, Chalk considers Sasha's subjection to 'an incessant and hostile categorizing gaze' to operate as a social manifestation of deeper psychological anxieties that are articulated formally via the novel's 'anachronic narrative structure' (p. 130). In 'eschewing the traditional narrative dynamics craved by the central character', Rhys 'posits a vision of identity construction that is disordered, incoherent, and out of the individual's control' (p. 121).

Chalk also devotes a chapter to Christopher Isherwood, reading *The Berlin Stories* [1945] as an extended rumination on displacement, here in relation to 'the biopolitical management of the queer individual in itinerancy' (p. 148). For Chalk, Isherwood figures his voluntary displacement from Britain as a liberating performance of 'cosmopolitan identity' (p. 150), while depicting a world in which 'characters are inured to passport regulations and savvy at negotiating them' (p. 149). Again, Chalk demonstrates that this fictional theme arose from bitter personal experience, arguing that humiliating passport difficulties caused by his sexuality merged with his apprehension of the 'coerced movement' (p. 151) practised by Nazi bureaucracy to lend a darker note to his travel narratives, in which subversive 'strateg[ies] of dissemblance' repeatedly prove unequal to 'political forces' (p. 155). Jason M. Coats's 'Sequence and Lyric Narrative in Auden and Isherwood's *Journey to a War*' (*Narrative* 22:ii[2014] 169–84) is also suggestive in this context. While primarily concerned with analysing Auden's contribution to the collaborative text, Coats's broader thesis highlights Isherwood's concern with humanizing the travel narrative form. For Coats, *Journey to a War* [1939] 'exhibits a discontinuous form that jarringly calls attention to its own artifice' (p. 169) in order to defer 'the responsibility of the travel writer to make sense of the specific experience he undertakes' (p. 170).

Tom Ford's adaptation Isherwood's *A Single Man* [1964] from 2009 receives sceptical treatment in two critical interventions. Lee Wallace's 'Tom Ford and His Kind' (*Criticism* 56:i[2014] 21–44) notes that while Isherwood's 'transparent prose and indirect handling of focalization' seem to have arrived 'ready made for cinema's systems of continuous visualisation' (p. 26), other aspects of his prose are not so easily translatable. Specifically, Isherwood's free indirect style positions 'his protagonist within an extremely supple net of personal and impersonal identifications that attract or distance the reader' (p. 25), a litheness that is vitiated by the film's bookending of the action with a 'personal voiceover [that] channels and intensifies spectatorial identification' (p. 26). While this coercive strategy leaves Wallace ambivalent over the merits of the film, Lester C. Colson's contribution to Pat Arneson and Ronald Arnett's collection, *Philosophy of Communication Ethics: Alterity and the Other* (pp. 183–211) is unambiguously hostile, asking 'what does it mean when an apparently well-intentioned homosexual filmmaker does our enemies' work for them by reproducing damaging stereotypes?' (p. 185). Colson feels that the voiceover should be present throughout. While the novel 'invites readers to identify with George's character, to inhabit vicariously his disruptive insights concerning his oppression' (p. 187), Colson argues that Ford's adaptation exchanges interiority for 'handsome surfaces' in an attempt to 'universalize a love story' (p. 205) for the mass market. By way of contrast, he cites a 1990 theatrical adaptation of the novel, which he considers more faithful precisely because it employed a continuous voiceover to maintain contact with 'George's inner life' (p. 195).

Two separate entries in *Notes and Queries* consider Aldous Huxley in relation to D.H. Lawrence. N.S. Boone's note on the correspondences between *Brave New World* [1932] and Lawrence's essay, 'Men Must Work and Women as Well' [1929] (*N&Q* 61[2014] 133–5), draws attention to the essay's rehearsal of several key themes of the novel 'in embryo' (p. 133). In particular, Lawrence discusses the relationship between ennui and freedom from labour, the wider culture impact of Ford's doctrine of industrial mechanization, and the alienating effects of increasing domestic atomization. Rodney Stenning Edgecombe ((*N&Q* 61[2014] 127–9) expands upon this reading in the context of Huxley's own essay-writing, illustrating how the pair arrived at 'similar conclusions ... independently from common points of departure' (p. 128). Citing Huxley's essays on Pascal, Swift, and 'Fashions in Love', collected in

Do What You Will: Essays [1929], Edgecombe finds correspondences between the pair's views on 'discontinuous personae within a compound personality', Swift's 'scatophobia' (p. 128), and the deleterious consequences of the 'bohemian demystification of sex' (p. 129). Meanwhile, Janko Andrijasevic's contribution to Marija Krivokapić-Knežević and Aleksandra Nikčević-Batrićvić's collection, *The Beauty of Convention: Essays in Literature and Culture* (pp. 93–102), considers Aldous Huxley's *Time Must Have a Stop* [1944] as a text preoccupied with 'spiritual convention' (p. 100), in which Huxley challenges the presuppositions of his primarily Western audience by drawing upon alternative metaphysical authorities—in this instance, *The Tibetan Book of the Dead.*

Andrijasevic's view of Huxley as a sceptic who nonetheless 'did not dismiss religions, and ... at times flirted with their dogmatic beliefs' (p. 95) is a characterization few would apply to Samuel Beckett. Nonetheless, Iain Bailey's *Samuel Beckett and the Bible*, offers a fascinating account of the mischievously flirtatious relationship with Christian theology found in Beckett's earliest fiction. Bailey surveys the extraordinary range of Beckett's biblical allusions, from the opening line of *Murphy* [1938], with its Eeyore-ish transposition of Ecclesiastes 1:9, to the blasphemies of *More Pricks Than Kicks* [1934], including the implicit profanity of its titular crib from Acts 9:5, which led to the initial banning of the text in Ireland. Ironic recontextualization is the keynote throughout: in the case of the *More Pricks* ban, no 'blasphemy [was] adduced explicitly in the text'; instead, the issue at stake was Beckett's 'manipulation of biblical material, taking out of context and reinterpreting it, explicitly as part of a series of provocations' (p. 102). Bailey particularly emphasizes Beckett's interest in 'ideas of familiarity and common knowledge' (p. 4), while arguing that his provocations rely symbiotically upon the 'dominant ... communal orthodoxy' (p. 102) to sustain their air of rebellion.

James McNaughton's 'Samuel Beckett's "Echo's Bones": Politics and Entailment in the Irish Free State' (*MFS* 60:ii[2014] 320–44), uses the recent publication of 'Echo's Bones' to explore Beckett's equally sceptical response to the formation of the Irish Free State, expressed once more through theological parody. For McNaughton, Beckett 'makes temporal and historical the language of religious salvation in order to parody contemporary Irish and European politics' (p. 321). In this way, Beckett advertises his fundamental ambivalence towards all narratives of progress: as a 'cosmopolitan Irish intellectual' Beckett 'is completely uninterested in defending a Protestant Ascendancy culture, yet not especially convinced that revolutionary energies have provided a state all that different or worth participating in' (p. 340).

John Pilling's excellent *Samuel Beckett's 'More Pricks than Kicks': In a Strait of Two Wills* explores Beckett's 'brief and none too profitable career as a short story writer' (p. 105) in greater depth. Pilling devotes individual chapters to an account of the collection's origins, a lengthy close analysis of each story, a history of the critical reception, a consideration of the aesthetic difficulties posed by Beckett's project, an exceptionally thorough annotation of the text, and a rebuttal of the critical view that Joyce was an overarching influence upon the collection. His meditation on the problems of Beckett's poetics is especially illuminating. For Pilling, 'each of the stories *seems* to conform to conventional narrative expectations, only to show that this convention *is really of no value*' (p. 135). By ostensibly 'playing the short-story "game"'' (p. 135) while simultaneously subverting its unwritten laws, 'he had shaken up more than a few dormant bones in the short story genre ... a cage that Beckett wanted to rattle, but not with such ferocity as to actually destroy the bars which kept it together' (pp. 139–40).

Sara Jane Bailes and Nicholas Till's *Beckett and Musicality* includes Franz Michael Maier's '"Shades of Lessing": Beckett and the Aesthetics of the Modern Novel' (pp. 9–26), an account of Beckett's early symphonic conception of the modern novel. Maier argues that Beckett's polyphonic interpretation of the form is ironically offset by his depiction of the Smeraldina-Rima in *Dream of Fair to Middling Women* [1932] as 'the archetype of a melodic person' (p. 16). Thomas Mansell's 'Describing Arabesques: Beckett and Dance' (pp. 137–54), explores the 'complex ... unease' (p. 137) of Beckett's relationship with dance. He finds *Dream* an archly satirical rendering of the 'eurythmics' (p. 141) practised at the Schule Dunkelbrau, demonstrative of the novel's wider 'anxiety ... about the body' (p. 142). Regarding *Murphy*, Mansell speculates intriguingly on the possible imaginative correspondence between the triple-M acronym of the Magdalen Mental Mercyseat, Robert Burton's description of music as '"*mentis medicina maestae*" [a roaring-meg against melancholy]', and the 'Margaret Morris Movement' (p. 144), a dance school that featured Lucia Joyce amongst its members.

Richard McGuire's 'Migrant Drifters: Samuel Beckett's *Murphy* and Sam Selvon's *The Lonely Londoners* in a Postcolonial Comparative Context' (*ComparativeCS* 11:ii–iii[2014] 235–48), sets out to 're-evaluate *Murphy* from a postcolonial perspective', considering it primarily as 'a novel of Irish migratory experience in 1930s London' (p. 235). McGuire cites Selvon's tale of anglophone Caribbean migrants to draw attention to *Murphy*'s preoccupation with the plight of displaced individuals whose temperamental vagaries leave them unsuited to the provision of 'unskilled or skilled' (p. 237) migrant labour. This is an interesting, if necessarily partial, way of approaching the much-rehearsed shadow existence of Beckett's protagonist. Murphy's eventual employment at the Magdalen Mental Mercyseat sees him join 'a largely unseen nocturnal migrant workforce', which McGuire compares to the 'Irish London Underground construction and maintenance tunnellers' (p. 247) whose very existence remained opaque to the occupants of daytime London.

Eugene Webb's *Samuel Beckett: A Study of His Novels* devotes an early chapter to a more conventional reading of *Murphy*. Webb's study is 'intended as a guidebook' (p. viii) rather than a theoretical study, and is in some ways the better for its modestly pedagogical aims. Webb proceeds from the view that Beckett's 'various writings constitute a single, coherent presentation of a particular view of life' (p. vii), and specifically that he is 'perhaps the greatest comedian of the grotesque that literature has ever seen' (p. viii). Reading both *Murphy* and *More Pricks Than Kicks* as 'commentaries on Dante's *Purgatorio*' (p. 23), Webb conceives *Murphy* as a bathetic 'parody' (p. 45) of Dante, comically elaborating the protagonist's failed bid to establish an interregnum of stasis within material existence. While this is relatively familiar territory,

Webb produces an interesting account of how Murphy's neuroses impact upon his unstable relationship to the cosmos, in responding to an 'unpredictable ... universe' (p. 48).

This theme is developed in greater detail in Katherine Ebury's excellent *Modernism & Cosmology: Absurd Lights. Murphy* proves an ideal canvas for Ebury's broader aim of articulating 'the completely transformed cosmological model which arose out of [the] crisis in the Newtonian worldview and the effect relativistic cosmology had on modernist literature' (p. 1). Ebury carefully and convincingly delineates the early Beckett's largely overlooked 'interest in contemporary science' (p. 130), discernible in his notes on texts such as James Jeans's *The Universe Around Us* [1929]. Again, Beckett's narratorial irony is foregrounded: 'there are two models of the heavens in *Murphy*, Murphy's own and Beckett's underlying critique of it', with Murphy becoming a figure of narratorial ridicule precisely because his 'model of the heavens is just not daring enough (and too Newtonian)' (p. 137). For Ebury, Beckett's 'quasi-scientific' (p. 136) cosmology is that of 'creative chaos' (p. 137), inimical to the 'structuring impulse' (p. 140) that Murphy manifests in his increasingly unhinged attempts to extrapolate a cosmic meaning for his suffering.

Ebury's introduction cites Flann O'Brien's *The Third Policeman* [1940] as another text in which 'absurdity frequently assumes a cosmological import-ance' (p. 24). This is a timely observation in a year that saw a range of texts dedicated to O'Brien's puckish metaphysical comedies. Maebh Long's *Assembling Flann O'Brien* is a shrewd and authoritative meditation on O'Brien's corpus, which takes the full measure of his 'protean plurality' (p. 2). Long merges critical theory with social historicism to illuminating effect, interpreting the novels as 'a series of fragmentary texts ruptured by a polyphony of voices' (p. 3) that speak to various anxieties of the age. Long's infectious enthusiasm for conveying the co(s)mic absurdity of O'Brien's visions is consistently accompanied by an astute skewering of the near-pathological misogyny that accompanies them. *At Swim-Two-Birds* [1939] emerges as a 'self-obsessed autoerotic fantasy' (p. 34) rendered fertile by a fragmentary aesthetic in which 'vignettes of the self [are] constituted through vignettes of others' (p. 30). Nonetheless, Long notes that the narrator's dream of 'aesthetic reproduction reveals a troubling relation to purity and control' (p. 34), in the wider climate of eugenic propagandizing. Meanwhile, Long's Freudian reading of *The Third Policeman* evokes a Beckettian displacement of erotic and thanatic drives: in this 'modernist hell of nauseating uncertainty ... identity, agency and control are eroded but not destroyed' (p. 57).

Long also features in two essay collections on O'Brien. The first, Ruben Borg, Paul Fagan, and Werner Huber's *Flann O'Brien: Contesting Legacies*, features Tom Walker's compelling essay on '*The Third Policeman* and the Writing of Terror' (pp. 126–42). This posits the novel as a fantastical 'allegory of the aftermath of the War of Independence' (p. 134), which responds to the increase in IRA activity in 1939 by 'centring ... hell in a police barracks' (p. 132), while drawing on the specific murder of a police detective, Timothy O'Sullivan, in 1929, as source material. Ebury's cosmic reading of Beckett is echoed in essays by Ondřej Pilný and Jack Fennell. Pilný (pp. 156–65) suggests possible points of comparison between *The Third Policeman* and Alfred Jarry's mock-scientific concept of 'pataphysics', finding common ground between O'Brien's de Selby and Jarry's Dr Faustroll as eccentric questing figures, satirized by their creators for their 'ambition to master the governing principles of the universe' (p. 160). Meanwhile, Fennell (pp. 33–45) discusses O'Brien's anxieties over 'quantum mechanics' challenge to Newtonian physics' (p. 37) in the context of his ambivalence towards science fiction. Fennell considers O'Brien to have progressed from a light-heartedly comic embrace of 'futuristic narratives' (p. 34) in his early short stories, to a more darkly satirical use of science-fictional tropes in *The Third Policeman*, modifying his earlier 'assumption of inevitable prosperity to one of ontological breakdown' (p. 36).

Ronan McDonald, Sascha Morrell, and Julian Murphet's collection, *Flann O'Brien and Modernism*, explores O'Brien's ludic response to cultural modernity from a wide range of perspectives, including the 'scientific, religious, sexual, linguistic, literary, socio-economic and technological' (p. 8). John Attridge (pp. 27–40) offers an entertaining account of the fine distinction between 'bullshit' and 'sociable lying' (p. 33) in O'Brien's fictional philosophy. Citing O'Brien's departure from earlier modernists' earnest anxieties over the avoidance of rhetorical 'phoniness' (p. 27), Attridge argues that O'Brien developed a sophisticated defence of literary lying. Rónán McDonald explores similar paradoxes of O'Brien's fictional practice in his account of 'Nihilism in *The Third Policeman*' (pp. 135–48). As with McNaughton's reading of Beckett, McDonald identifies an apparent contradiction in O'Brien's targets: he 'mocks the censorious, insular climate of the Irish Free State, and also the liberal intellectuals ... that sought to critique it' (p. 135). For McDonald, O'Brien's stance is one of 'nihilistic comedy' (p. 136).

Stephen Abblitt (pp. 55–67) and Dirk Van Hulle (pp. 107–20) contribute analyses of O'Brien's ambivalent relationship to his closest forebear, Joyce, a theme also developed in the *Cambridge Companion to Irish Modernism*, edited by Joe Cleary, which includes Emer Nolan's 'James Joyce and the Mutations of the Modernist Novel' (pp. 95–110). Nolan recruits both Beckett and O'Brien to explore the 'skeptical investigation of modern Irish society' (p. 95) pursued by Irish writers in Joyce's wake, as a reaction against the sentimentalism of the Irish revival. As with Bailey's account of Beckett, Nolan identifies a strain of 'dissident individualism' ranged against 'collectivist' (p. 95) mentalities, reading *Murphy* as 'an experiment in counter-revivalist comedy' which pursues the notion of exile to a 'radical and impossible' extreme in its solipsistic flight from the 'material reality ... of the body' (p. 107).

Elizabeth Bowen's *The Last September* [1929] also makes a brief appearance in Nolan's survey, and is a key focus in Jessica Gildersleeve's *Elizabeth Bowen and the Writing of Trauma: The Ethics of Survival*, which considers Bowen's work as a 'lifelong project of ethical representation and of understanding the narrative responsibilities of the survivor' (p. 2). Her reading of *The Last September* exemplifies Gildersleeve's central argument that 'the "hauntedness", or the traumatization, of language itself' (p. 5) is a crucial Bowen concern. These uncanny literary traces situate 'the ghost [as] maddeningly "neither presence nor absence"' (p. 45), while Naylor's liminal status operates as a metaphor for the wider political anxieties of the novel: the 'threshold existence of the adolescent girl becomes a figure [for] political uncertainty in 1920s Ireland' (p. 35).

Rhetorical navigation of political turmoil in *The Last September* is also the focus of Siobhan Chapman's contribution to Chapman and Billy Clark's collection, *Pragmatic Literary Stylistics* (pp. 36–54). Chapman employs pragmatic theory to analyse the linguistic ambiguities through which Bowen subtly draws attention to her protagonists' anxieties. Bowen's characters occupy a milieu in which 'what is not talked about is what is most significant' (p. 36), the most important omission being any direct reference to the armed struggle that precipitated the founding of the Irish Free State in 1922. Chapman uses Gricean quantity implicatures to carefully distinguish ' "what is said" [from] "what is implicated" ' as two 'distinct types of meaning' (p. 40), plottable through close analysis of 'characters' selection of ... vocabulary' (p. 46).

Chapman's pragmatic methodology proves an illuminating means of attending to Bowen's manipulation of linguistic conventions as the conduit for an 'indirect handling of her themes' (p. 54). This technique also emerges as key to Clare Connors's 'Free—Indirect—Style (Derrida and Bowen)' (*Parallax* 20:i[2014] 15–28), which reads Bowen's *The Death of the Heart* [1938] in the light of Derrida's *Eperons* [1976]. Connors intriguingly figures the philosopher's 'inimitable and insistent free indirect style' (p. 15) as a complement to the novel form, 'which, from its very bastard origins, has been written by women' (p. 16). She goes on to reveal the ironic intent of this reading, a kind of practical joke against the theorist, since 'never *once*' does Derrida's text quote 'a *single* word from the pen of a woman ... Woman might—conditionally—be taken as a figure *for* writing, but *women's writing* is never read' (p. 22).

Beci Dobbin also explores Bowen's rhetorical practice in her winningly entitled ' "An Elf Wearing a Hat That Makes Him Invisible": Modernism's Shy Irony' (*TPr* 28:iii[2014] 453–71). Contributing to recent critical debates over 'whether irony can have a *purpose*' (p. 456) beyond mere effect, Dobbin lights on the concept of 'shy irony' as a 'mode of literary discretion; a way of being private in public' (p. 468). The texts addressed include Bowen's short story 'Making Arrangements' [1924], which she views as 'a text whose shy irony prompts over-reading' (p. 465), due to Bowen's coy manner, which causes the heavily advertised ironic premise of the narrative to be accompanied by a more subtle authorial 'tight-lipped-ness' (p. 466). For Dobbin, this suggests the double bind of modernist irony: Bowen shares her protagonist's wariness over 'being underestimated', and very much 'wants [her] over-subtlety to be noticed' (p. 468).

In 'At Midcentury: Elizabeth Bowen's *The Heat of the Day*' (*Mo/Mo* 21:i[2014] 125–45), Claire Seiler aims to rethink mid-century writing not as 'either a waning late modernism or a waxing postmodernism' (p. 126), but as a discourse with its own distinct economy of values. To this end, she elaborates the many forms of 'middleness' in the text, particularly its 'deep investment in being in the middle of the century' (p. 126), but also its location in 'the middle of the war, mid-life, [and] the artistic middlebrow' (p. 127). Analysing the unusually tortured gestational process in Bowen's manuscript drafts, Seiler demonstrates that the novel's final emphasis upon middleness emerged late, in the form of changes to setting and characterization.

Lara Feigel's brilliant work of popular scholarship, *The Love Charm of Bombs: Restless Lives in the Second World War*, also hinges upon the contention that as Bowen 'and her century entered their forties together, [she] was determined to take responsibility for her age' (p. 21). Feigel brings Bowen together with contemporaries, including Graham Greene and Henry Green, in a compelling tableau of wartime London seen through the perspective of writers immersed in the war effort, demonstrating that trauma was only one element of the war experience for Bowen and Greene, who worked as ARP wardens, and Green, who worked as an auxiliary fireman. Bowen found her night-time career 'exhilarating' (p. 2) and Greene 'look[ed] forward to the raids' (p. 3) with a kind of suicidal intrepidity, while Green was 'frightened as well as excited' (p. 3) by the blazes that he was sent out to tackle. In Feigel's hands, wartime London becomes an almost carnivalesque space, an interregnum of 'temporal and erotic freedom' (p. 5) in which the 'proximity of death' (p. 31) engenders for Bowen a liberating sense of 'collective community' (p. 30), for Greene 'an irresistible urge to laugh' (p. 31), and for Green a theatrical 'series of roles to play' (p. 44). Feigel's narratorial verve is efficacious in illustrating the rich life experience underpinning *The Heat of the Day*, Greene's *The End of the Affair* [1951], and Green's *Caught* [1943], and passages from the novels are judiciously recruited throughout to illuminate elements of her subjects' biographies.

Greene and Green are also represented elsewhere. James F. Dorrill's 'Allusions at Work in Graham Greene's *A Gun for Sale* and *Brighton Rock*' (*Renascence* 66:iii[2014] 167–88) sets out to 'sharpen the distinction' (p. 167) between Greene's 'entertainments' and his 'serious' literary work, via the context of allusion. Dorrill aims to demonstrate the greater sophistication of the allusive framework of *Brighton Rock* [1938], finding *A Gun for Sale* [1936] concerned merely with 'temporal' rather than 'eternal concerns' (p. 175). While this might seem something of a Leavisian throwback, it does have the advantage of focusing attention on the sheer allusive richness of both texts, encompassing Arnold, Shakespeare, Tennyson, the war poets, and Wordsworth.

In addition to her article on 'shy irony', Beci Dobbin (née Carver, the surname under which she is published here) also published a fine monograph, *Granular Modernism*, adding a second suggestive coinage to the critical lexicon. The central contention of Carver's witty and thought-provoking study is that granular modernism constitutes 'Naturalism's sequel in the Modernist period', but that this development (literally) ingrains a 'malfunction' within photographic naturalism, repackaging the minute delineation of ·sensory experience as modes of 'irrelevance, plotlessness, miscellaneousness, convolution, and confusion … in an attempt to describe a *semi-aware exercise in futility*' (p. 2). Carver devotes a chapter to the effects of this atomistic naturalism in the work of Evelyn Waugh and Henry Green, arguing that *Vile Bodies* [1930] and *Party Going* [1939] consciously set out to turn 'inefficiency into a narrative device' (p. 64). Green's novel is considered as an accumulation of 'thin moments' (p. 101), expressive not only of an interwar sense of generational malaise, but also of 'a new way of thinking about time textually—as bubbles, or vertical shocks' (p. 101). In the case of *Vile Bodies*, the self-described 'cumulative futility' (p. 86) of Waugh's technique is manifested in what Carver terms a 'a scorched earth policy' conceived 'to flatten one opportunity for elaboration after another' (p. 71), thus 'destroying the routes by which the story might continue' (p. 91).

Futility in Green and Waugh, along with Anthony Powell, is also a key theme of Marius Hentea's 'The End of the Party: The Bright Young People in *Vile Bodies*, *Afternoon Men*, and *Party Going*' (*TSLL* 56:i[2014] 90–111). Hentea reads these writers' handling of interwar high-society decadence and 'celebrity culture' through the lens of modernism's ambiguous relationship to class and popular culture, as symbolized by their ironical documentation of 'a social group whose notoriety was due to a combination of snobbery and mass appeal' (p. 91). Hentea cites Powell's portrayal of confusion over the correct approach to tipping in *Afternoon Men* [1931] as evidence not only of discomfort with the dissolution of hierarchical social norms, but also a more fundamental fear that 'what individuals owe to one another in society is not agreed upon any longer' (p. 97). Hentea views Green as more amenable to the flux of social codes, though still preoccupied with the 'inability to maintain the privacy of language' within the protean public sphere, while Waugh emerges as more straightforwardly alarmed by his peers' 'acceptance of social levelling' (p. 95), as manifested linguistically in his upper-class characters' adoption of cockneyisms.

Waugh's attempts to counter these developments are brought to life in Naomi Milthorpe's incisive ' "Too, too shaming": Evelyn Waugh's *Vile Bodies*' (*Affirmations* 1:ii[2014] 75–94), which argues that Waugh deliberately fosters an air of internal vacuity as a means both to deny intimacy and to shame the reader into affective revolt. For Milthorpe, Waugh draws upon the 'centring of shame within the ocular realm' (p. 78) to transmit this 'ugly feeling' (p. 77) outward to the reader. This view of the text as an interrogative agent complements the novel's thematic obsession with physical exposure as a failed catalyst of shame. As Milthorpe explains, Waugh's handling of Agatha Runcible's suspiciously shameless exhibition of her physical 'shaming' is intended to promote what might be termed a shy-making irony: 'by embracing a pose of modernist detachment, the novel paradoxically seeks to provoke the kinds of feelings its characters are apparently unable to access' (p. 81).

Shawna Ross's contribution to Robert Tally's *Literary Cartographies: Spatiality, Representation, and Narrative* (pp. 111–26) draws Waugh's ambivalence over 'publicity' into further productive realms. Waugh's willing-ness to accept 'a free cruise in return for favourable publicity' (p. 114), as documented in *Labels: A Mediterranean Journey* [1930], becomes the pretext for a discussion of his 'career-long engagement with [sea] crossing and cruising' (p. 113). Waugh's self-conscious refiguring of the 'ocean liner ... [as] a discursive phenomenon' (p. 111) resolves itself in a series of self-reflexive analyses of the cruising experience, culminating in his late novella, *The Ordeal of Gilbert Pinfold* [1957]. Ross explores this text as a reflection on modern literary celebrity, within which the protagonist finds himself 'publicised as one of the cruise's main attractions' (p. 120).

A Handful of Dust [1934] is the subject of Roksana Zgierska's essay on Waugh and Dickens in Ewa Kujawska-Lis and Anna Krawczyk-Łaskarzewska's collection, *Reflections on/of Dickens* (pp. 235–43), which argues that Waugh's novel depicts 'a modernized version of Dickensian London' (p. 235). Interpreting *Little Dorrit* [1857] as a neglected urtext, Zgierska highlights the novels' comparable renderings of home and family (or the lack or inadequacy of these elements) and their 'ridiculously passive' (p. 239) male characters. At the same time, she notes significant differences in their endings: while Dickens resolves his tale with an 'optimistic happy ending', Waugh insists upon pursuing 'a vision of society trapped in its bleakness' (p. 241) to the grim end. *A Handful of Dust* is also the focus of Joseph Wiesenfarth's 'Death in the Wasteland: Ford, Wells, and Waugh' (in Chantler and Hawkes, eds., pp. 197–206). Comparing Waugh to Ford's *Parade's End* [1924–8], Wiesenfarth finds him to be preoccupied with a similar conception of the 'irresponsibility' (p. 201) of the age.

Donat Gallagher and Carlos Villar's *In the Picture: The Facts Behind the Fiction in Evelyn Waugh's 'Sword of Honour'* sets out to correct critical misapprehensions about Waugh's biography in relation to the Second World War, including the notorious story of his forced resignation from the Special Service Brigade. This study also attempts 'to place in history' the novels that make up the *Sword of Honour* [1952–61] sequence, considering them as accounts of Waugh's personal 'military experiences and growing disillusion from 1939 to 1945 set against a backdrop of world-scale catastrophes' (p. 3). John Hayward Wilson's 'The Origins of Japanese Interest in Evelyn Waugh, 1948–1963' (*PLL* 50:i[2014] 3–23) details the reception of Waugh's work in Japan via archival research into the A.D. Peters Collection at the University of Texas. While Waugh's projection of cultural superiority limited his popular appeal to the Japanese, Hayward Wilson charts the tenacious propagation of Waugh's work amongst Japanese scholars, leading to a recent spike in interest, despite the absence of any new translations. The continuing interest of Japanese academics in Waugh's work is confirmed to by Fumio Yoshioka's *Reading Short Stories: British, Irish and American Storytellers*, which devotes a chapter to Waugh's short story, 'Mr Loveday's Little Outing' [1936].

The literary meeting of East and West is also the subject of a special issue of *Concentric*, dedicated to 'Orienting Orwell: Asian and Global Perspectives on George Orwell'. Henk Vynckier's foreword, ' "Asia, Your Asia": Reflections on Orwell and Asia' (*Concentric* 40:i[2014] 3–17), highlights Orwell's deep connection to the continent, while using the titular allusion to Orwell's essay, 'England Your England' [1941], to emphasize the ways in which 'My/your knowledge dyads appealed to Orwell's polemical mind' (p. 4). For Vynckier *Down and Out in Paris and London* [1933] and *Nineteen Eighty-Four* [1949] exemplify Orwell's complication of East–West binaries: he sees *Down and Out*'s digression on the oppression of Indian rickshaw pullers as a hint 'that the working poor in both the East and the West . . . are fellow inhabitants of a vast socio-economic underworld' (p. 6). Meanwhile, the triadic totalitarian symmetry of Orwell's final novel is discussed as an analogical comment on global power structures, since 'All three powers have the same geopolitical objectives' (p. 16).

John Rodden's '"A Hanging": George Orwell's Unheralded Literary Breakthrough' (*Concentric* 40:i[2014] 19–33) argues that motifs of textual guilt-expiation and depersonalized state violence that anticipate 'the related, yet broadened, themes of *Nineteen Eighty-Four*' (p. 32) make 'A Hanging' a pivotal text in Orwell's literary development. Douglas Kerr's 'Orwell and Kipling: Global Visions' (*Concentric* 40:i[2014] 35–50) discusses Rudyard Kipling as 'a sort of dialogic partner throughout [Orwell's] life' (p. 37), interpreting this relationship as a 'meeting of opposites in ideology, temperament, and career' (p. 36) which belies a series of more intriguing correspondences, not least their shared status as 'writers of empire' (p. 37). Kerr offers incisive close readings of 'ironic narration' in semi-fictionalized travel narratives by Kipling and Orwell which satirize the authors' 'intensely phobic' responses to contact with the colonial other (p. 40).

Gita V. Pai's 'Orwell's Reflections on Saint Gandhi' (*Concentric* 40:i[2014] 51–77) charts Orwell's reception of the Indian independence leader, culminating in his late essay, 'Reflections on Gandhi' [1949], written contemporaneously with the final revisions of *Nineteen Eighty-Four*. Highlighting Orwell's Indian birth and youthful career in the Imperial Indian Police in Burma, Pai uses this further dialogic tussle as an instructive index of Orwell's 'vacillations regarding pacifism' (p. 61). For Pai, Orwell's early 'cynicism' over Gandhi's 'non-violent tactics' (p. 59) gave way to a realization that Gandhi's tactics had 'accomplished his main political aim in ending British rule peaceably' (p. 64). In 'Against the "Uprush of Modern Progress": Exploring the Dilemma and Dynamics of Modernity in George Orwell's *Burmese Days*' (*Concentric* 40:i[2014] 79–95), Angelia Poon reads Orwell's novel through postcolonial theory, conceiving *Burmese Days* as an example of the colonial voice struggling against 'prejudice and bias [and] yearning for an alternative modernity' (p. 84), only for prejudice to re-emerge in other forms.

Finally, Te-hsing Shan's 'The Reception of George Orwell in Taiwan' (*Concentric* 40:i[2014] 97–125) elaborates the appositely 'Orwellian' aspects of his Taiwanese reception, which reveal 'how the same source text might be differently represented under different conditions of cultural production' (p. 112). As Shan explains, Orwell's enduring popularity in Taiwan is inseparable from translations that 'both affect, and are affected by, the dominant ideology' (p. 100) underlying their production, particularly the 'political antagonism between Taiwan and mainland China during the Cold War era' (p. 102).

The repeated use of *Nineteen Eighty-Four* in these essays as a summative crystallization of Orwell's cultural thought is echoed throughout Orwell scholarship of 2014, as in Firas A.J. Al-Jubouri's *Milestones on the Road to Dystopia*. Al-Jubouri elaborates Orwell's 'self-division', which he sees as arising 'from integrity rather than cynicism and hypocrisy' (p. xii), tracing this trait through the comparative context of both Machiavelli's *The Prince* and Orwell's criticisms of James Burnham's *The Machiavellians* [1943]. Al-Jubouri interprets *Nineteen Eighty-Four* as both a repudiation and a tacit acknowledgement of the force of Machiavellian political strategies.

David J. Lorenzo's *Cities at the End of the World: Using Utopian and Dystopian Stories to Reflect Critically on our Political Beliefs, Communities, and Ways of Life* also uses *Nineteen Eighty-Four* to think critically about real-world political dilemmas. Beginning by comparing and contrasting Orwell's methods with those of Evgenii Zamyatin's *We* [1924], Lorenzo goes on to emphasize the geographical and social immediacy of Orwell's vision, in opposition to readings that see the novel as primarily a critique of overseas communism. For Lorenzo, Orwell is not only concerned with 'human problems generally', but also 'British problems in particular' (p. 157), from the dangers of the state's exploitation of 'the desire for certainty' (p. 158), to a more local 'satire on several types of people Orwell found irksome in contemporary England', including the 'public school hearty' and the 'sandal-wearing, bearded, exercise-bent, hiking-obsessed crank' (p. 171). For Lorenzo, this satirical dimension injects an underexplored 'element of farce' (p. 171) into this most solemnly received of texts.

Keith Elphick's contribution to Susan M. Bernardo's collection, *Environments in Science Fiction: Essays on Alternative Spaces* (pp. 171–90) compares Orwell's dystopian novel to a generic successor, Octavia Butler's *Parable of the Sower* [1993]. Elphick argues that Butler's novel functions as a 'critical dystopia', a subgenre differentiable from the 'despair engulfing ... classic dystopias' such as Orwell's, because it attempts 'to provide answers to the unchallenged problems' of classic dystopias, via characters who 'painstakingly struggle to *adapt* and *better* the problems facing them' (p. 173). Martha C. Carpentier's 'The "Dark Power of Destiny" in George Orwell's *Nineteen Eighty-Four*' (*Mosaic* 47:i[2014] 179–94) contends that the novel's preoccupation with 'dreams [and] the disinterment of archaic memories ... begs for psychoanalytic readings' (p. 179). This approach leads Carpentier to discover a subtly subversive message within Smith's capitulation to Goldstein, arguing that Smith consistently evinces a 'masochism' (p. 183) in relation to the 'paternal imago' (p. 185) of Big Brother, which challenges 'patriarchy via identification with [a] feminized position' (p. 183). While Carpentier's Freudian framework occasionally leads to an excess of veiled phallus spotting, her analysis of the 'masochistic guilt that fuels [Smith's] sadistic punishment' (p. 188) is persuasive.

Patricia Rae's contribution to Mark Levene's collection, *Political Fiction* (pp. 132–52) sets out an original interpretation of *Nineteen Eighty-Four* as a work of 'Late Modernist Imagism'. For Rae, Orwell parades his modernist influences in order to stake out a deliberately ' "*anti*-anti-modernist" position', conceived to challenge the '*anti*-modernist sentiments among Stalinists'. Rae highlights the resemblance of Orwell's precepts in 'Politics and the English Language' [1946] to the 'confident didacticism' and demands for 'concision, concrete sensation, and "freshness" in imagery' found in Imagist manifestos. Rae goes on to cite Orwell's appropriation of Imagist techniques within the novel; she compares Smith's fetishistic obsession with solid objects to Imagist poems and argues convincingly that his mode of thought is imagistic both in its analogical ethos and the characteristically Hulmean similes that it throws forth.

Luc Boltanski's ambitious interdisciplinary monograph, *Mysteries and Conspiracies: Detective Stories, Spy Novels and the Making of Modern Societies*, traces the ways in which 'the thematics of mystery, conspiracy, and inquiry' have informed 'the representation of reality' (p. xiv) in modern literature, as an index of the wider preoccupations of modern society. Drawing material from psychiatry, political science, and sociology, Boltanski also turns to literary texts—including *Nineteen Eighty-Four*—as illustrative case studies. Orwell provides an apt model for his thesis that from the nineteenth century onwards the nation-state became an instrument through which to enact 'the project of organizing and unifying reality . . . for a given population or a given territory' (p. xv).

Steven Ellis's *British Writers and the Approach of World War II* is an erudite and original study of 1939 as a liminal moment in British social and cultural history, in which writers seemed to 'peer backwards into a disabling past and forward into an uncertain future' (p. 13). In a chapter on 'Orwell, Forster and the Role of the Writer' (pp. 147–87), Ellis views Orwell's *Coming Up for Air* [1939] as a text preoccupied with the possibility of escaping to 'the past as a kind of refuge from 1939' (p. 147). Ellis reads the novel against Orwell's near-contemporary essay collection, *Inside the Whale* [1940], identifying a further link to Orwell's debt to literary modernism in the title essay, which suggests a signpost to George Bowling's literary ancestry in figures such as Eliot's Prufrock. As Ellis explains, Bowling establishes a comparable tone of 'constant intimate confiding' (p. 159) with the reader, who is drawn into a compact against the alienating conditions detailed in the narrative. Ellis also projects the text forward, reading Bowling's anxieties as a 'comic anticipation of Winston Smith's circumstances in *Nineteen Eighty-Four*', insofar as 'Hilda and what she represents are a kind of "Big Sister" anticipation of the regime of Orwell's later dystopia' (p. 153).

Ellis's impressively panoramic survey goes on to consider J.B. Priestley's novel, *Let the People Sing* [1939] as an attempt to 'affirm the spirit of the "English People" ' (p. 170). Priestley's wartime activities are also the focus of Richard Dove's contribution to *Vision and Reality: Central Europe after Hitler*, which Dove edited with Ian Wallace. Dove's essay (pp. 195–212) relates the story of a German émigré theatre group's production of Priestley's play, *They Came to a City* [1944]. As with *Let the People Sing*, Dove explains that Priestley's play responds to the war as a 'historical moment of hope', carrying the prospect of 'usher[ing] in a new society' (p. 196). This positive vision not only struck a chord with British audiences, receiving 280 performances over eight months, but also with émigrés fleeing the Nazi regime, who were inspired by the dramatic premise, in which the characters 'confront the question whether to remain in the new city or return to their previous lives' (p. 203). As Dove notes, although Priestley's text subsequently vanished without trace, it might be argued that his utopian vision was realized in more modestly pragmatic form in the social reforms of the postwar Labour government.

Unfortunately, Keith M. Booker's *Brave New World* and Rory MacLean's *Berlin: Portrait of a City through the Centuries* were not made available for review.

(c) James Joyce

David G. Wright's *'Dubliners' and 'Ulysses': Bonds of Character* was published posthumously in 2013 following the author's tragic and untimely death in 2008. Though partly unfinished, and unpolished in places, *Bonds of Character* bears witness to the author's encyclopedic knowledge of the world of Joyce's Dublin: Wright charts each appearance of the characters shared by *Dubliners* and *Ulysses* and collates the data in an appendix. The slender volume is packed with delightful details. For example, Wright's emphasis on the ubiquity of Lenehan in *Ulysses* is telling, and he convincingly argues that the roles played by Lenehan and Corley in *Ulysses* 'closely echo their roles in "Two Gallants"' (p. 89). Wright speculates freely about the rationale underpinning the decision to reuse certain characters, and to dispense with others, and poses a nice question regarding the anonymous boy narrators of the first three short stories in the early collection: 'If they did appear in *Ulysses* in some fashion, how would we know who they were?' (p. 28). He also calls attention to the fact that, despite his appearance as a social outsider, Bloom is familiar with a large number of the characters from *Dubliners*.

Several short chapters trace the particular fortunes of individual characters or groups of characters. In a passage that is dedicated to the fictional afterlife of Bob Doran and Polly Mooney from 'A Boarding House', Wright flags the gendered nature of the manner in which Joyce redeploys figures from *Dubliners*, noting that of around 700 instances where characters from the short story collection are named in *Ulysses*, only twelve cases involve women. He proffers the somewhat tenuous hypothesis that, if the musical women of *Dubliners* had been reused, this would have detracted from Molly's status as a singer (p. 104). Further enjoyable chapters visit topics such as the mystery of Emily Sinico's death, Joe Hynes's politics, and the future fictional lives of the men of 'Grace'. Along with the intrinsic interest to Joyce scholars, owing to Wright's clear, unpretentious prose, the book may also function as an important resource for students: an open invitation to Joyce's world, in all its glorious detail.

Also from 2013, *James Joyce in the Nineteenth Century*, edited by John Nash, stems from a conference at Durham University in 2010. Once a comparatively small corner of Joyce studies, the rise of scholarship attending to 'Joyce and History' dates to the mid-1990s at least, such that the field may now appear somewhat 'overdeveloped'. Accordingly, several essays in this collection explore niche aspects of Joyce's world, but it contains some fine contributions all the same. Luke Gibbons's ' "He Says No, Your Worship": Joyce, Free Indirect Discourse and Vernacular Modernism' (pp. 31–45) begins by returning to Joyce's 1907 article 'Ireland at the Bar' and starts from the particular inflection of the phrase 'your worship' in Joyce's account of an infamous murder trial therein. This may itself owe a debt to the language of the raucous trial that occurs in Dion Boucicault's 1864 play *Arrah-na-Pogue*, a play that is most likely an important source of inspiration for the mock-trial of Shaun-Yawn in chapter III.3 of *Finnegans Wake*. While criticism has, of course, acknowledged Joyce's preoccupation with Irish subject matter, Gibbons emphasizes the importance of Irish literary forms. Ronan

Crowley's superb essay, 'The Queen Is Not a Subject': Victoria's *Leaves from the Journal* in *Ulysses*' (pp. 200–14), functions both as a defence of the often maligned activity of 'source hunting', and an explication of the presence of one source in particular in *Ulysses*: a popular edition of the British monarch's *Leaves from the Journal of Our Life in the Highlands*. Crowley notes that a 2*s*. 6*d*. edition of this work sold 100,000 copies in 1868 alone. Of particular interest to Crowley is Joyce's practice of seamlessly weaving verbiage borrowed from source materials into the fabric of *Ulysses*. As he remarks, 'it is in the novel's covert repetitions—its unmarked and unremarkable cribs— that a rationale for quotation beyond play is most readily discernible' (p. 202).

There were fewer monographs about Joyce in 2014 than is typical, and, broadly speaking, there were comparatively few significant new developments, or gear-shifts, in this corner of English studies. Some recent scholarship has sought to overthrow, or at least refine, the critical assumption that Joyce's Dublin is simply a centre of 'paralysis'. Liam Lanigan's *James Joyce, Urban Planning, and Irish Modernism: Dublins of the Future* approaches the question from a different angle. Lanigan insists that Dublin cannot be understood as the overlooked, provincial backwater that has been portrayed in some of the more reductive criticism, instead arguing that 'the alienation and "paralysis" of the characters in Joyce's early work is, in fact, *produced by*, rather than in spite of, the technological and cultural urbanization of the Dublin they occupy' (p. 3). As he further notes, 'The city's position as a colonial outpost seemingly on the verge of gaining its independence, and one whose existing topography was considered highly problematic by those who inhabited it, made it particularly fertile ground for the spread of planning ideas' (p. 20). Particularly pertinent for an understanding of the nature of the Joycean city is Lanigan's articulation, drawing upon the work of Andrew Kincaid, of the manner in which Irish planning discourse of the era negotiated the disconnect between the rural idealism of certain strands of nationalist rhetoric and the need to forge a modern, urban nation. A further, strong element of Lanigan's argument is his stance against the 'exceptionalism' (p. 1) that so often dominates characterizations of Joyce. We see that Joyce is not alone amongst his contemporaries in renegotiating Dublin as a site of cultural meaning.

The book's focus on urban planning discourse is rather narrow and, perhaps inevitably, the amount of contextual information supplied sometimes surpasses Lanigan's ends. Nonetheless, the idea of planning discourse neatly frames a range of chapters on Joyce-related topics: from a consideration of George Moore's *A Drama in Muslin* and a chapter engaging with Revivalist literature more broadly, through to chapters on *Dubliners* and *A Portrait*. Two moments in *Ulysses* immediately come to mind when the book is considered in the light of ideas associated with the planning and mapping of urban space: the panoramic cityscape of 'Wandering Rocks', and Bloom's vision of the new Bloomusalem in 'Circe'. Lanigan sheds significant light on both, with chapters dedicated to these episodes. It is a shame that *Dublins of the Future* adopts the persistent and regrettable approach of considering Joyce's fiction only up until 1922. The book is forward-looking in other respects, and the epilogue briefly touches upon the ways in which Dublin continues to function as a crucial cultural reference point for writers like Liam O'Flaherty and Maeve Brennan.

Following works like Robert K. Weninger's *The German Joyce* [2012], Arleen Ionescu's *Romanian Joyce: From Hostility to Hospitality* is another case study of Joyce's reception in a single nation. One difference, however, is that, beyond Constantin Brâncuşi's famous spiral portrait, Joyce's Romanian reception is broadly unfamiliar. Chapter 2 traces Joyce's reception in Romania through a dark passage in history: beginning with what Ionescu refers to as the 'Hos(ti)pitalities' of the interwar period, she discusses 'Stalinist and Ceauşist "Schizophrenias"' (p. 97)—a description that gestures towards the disconnect between official political, and broader cultural, reactions to Joyce in the communist era. The final phase of this history is devoted to 'The Turning of the Tide' (p. 128), which Ionescu dates back to 1984. In this year, pre-dating the overthrow of Ceauşescu by half a decade, Mircea Ivănescu's translation of *Ulysses* appeared (an act of translation undertaken in fraught political conditions that Ionescu considers in some detail elsewhere in this study), as well as the first full monograph on Joyce in Romanian. Joyce's global reception also takes centre stage in *TransLatin Joyce: Global Transmissions in Ibero-Latin America*, edited by Brian L. Price, César A. Salgado and John Pedro Schwartz for Palgrave Macmillan's Literatures of the Americas series. Both volumes illustrate Joyce's status as a seemingly eternal source of inspiration for writers emerging from diverse cultural and linguistic traditions.

TransLatin Joyce sets a playful tone from the outset with its polysemous, punning title. The collection opens by revisiting the recent online 'hullabaloo' surrounding Paulo Coehlo's claim in 2012 that *Ulysses* is 'um dos livros que fez esse mal à humanidade' ('one of those books harmful to humanity'). The editors' introduction includes a satisfying take-down of this 'show of smug stardom' by an 'author of vapid parables of mystical self-discovery' (p. ix), and hints at the peculiar threat that a 'glocal' (simultaneously global and local) Joyce might present to a writer like Coehlo. The speculation 'that it becomes possible to argue that Joyce's legacy is at present best valued and understood from the vantage point of postcolonial writing in Spanish and Portuguese' (p. xii) sounds like a step too far, but, as a whole, the volume succeeds in highlighting the profound ways in which hispanophone and lusophone writers have contributed to a global appreciation of Joyce. Contributors approach questions of interpretation, translation, appropriation, and dissemination with reference to a fairly wide range of writers operating within literary cultures that can be deemed 'transLatin' (defined as 'Hispano- and Lusophone modern print cultures and those territories in the Americas where Spanish and Portuguese prevail: the Iberian Peninsula, Mexico, Central America, South America, and the Hispanic Caribbean', p. xii). More obvious candidates for consideration in a Joycean light include the likes of Antonio Marichalar, Jorge Luis Borges, and Carlos Fuentes, and Gayle Rogers's essay on Marichalar's 'Spanish-European Critical Project' (pp. 3–24) draws upon research previously presented in her valuable study, *Modernism and the New Spain* [2012].

John Pedro Schwartz's 'The Geopolitics of Modernist Impersonality: Pessoa's Notes on Joyce' (pp. 25–54) examines Joyce and the 'heteronymic' Fernando Pessoa. Joyce's own employment of Stephen Dedalus as 'alter ego' suggests an immediate point of affinity. The commentary is modelled around four brief lines by Pessoa on Joyce that are contained in the poet's unpublished papers, and which are used as sub-headings by Schwartz: 'The art of James Joyce, like that of Mallarmé, is art preoccupied with method, with how it's made'; 'Even the sensuality of *Ulysses* is a symptom of intermediation'; 'It is hallucinatory delirium—the kind treated by psychiatrists—presented as an end in itself'; 'A literature before dawn'. Schwartz neatly unpacks the first of these in the light of long-standing debates over the structure (or lack thereof) of *Ulysses*. While at times the significance of the brief lines on Joyce is overplayed, Pessoa's words do provide a useful platform for a comparative study, which leads to a fruitful discussion of a shared project of cultural resituation, emanating from two writers born of nations that can be thought 'semi-peripheral' (p. 45). Perhaps inevitably, Schwartz's commentary reveals more about Pessoa than about Joyce, but Schwartz is not unfailingly sympathetic towards the Portuguese poet. Of particular note is his claim that Pessoa 'failed to perceive that he and Joyce shared the broader political program of universalizing a culture marginalized by over a century of imperial decline and three centuries of colonialism, respectively' (p. 48).

Looking beyond the Iberian peninsula, sections dedicated to Argentina, Cuba, and Mexico open up the territory of Joycean reception studies; a reception that has mostly been viewed through a western European or North American lens. Brian L. Price's 'A Portrait of the Mexican Artist as a Young Man' (pp. 181–210) posits a new approach to the ways in which a 'transLatin' author can be thought Joycean by looking beyond connections that have been drawn between the radical linguistic experiments of *Ulysses* and *Finnegans Wake*, and novels by the likes of Fuentes, Julio Cortázar, José Donoso, and Guillermo Cabrera Infante, in order to highlight what Price conceives as the 'Dedalean poetics' of Salvador Elizondo. Particularly enjoyable is Price's account of a prank in which Elizondo was involved in the sixth issue of *S.Nob*: a mock poster and accompanying note for an imaginary film production of *Ulysses*, complete with a false interview from the founder of Paramount Studios that promises a sequel—*Ulysses Strikes Again*.

Situating Joyce rather closer to 'home', *James Joyce and Cultural Memory*, edited by Oona Frawley and Katherine O'Callaghan, is the fourth and final instalment in the Memory Ireland series. It takes a different and more focused approach than earlier volumes in the series, which have a broader, interdisciplinary scope. This volume includes work by a number of 'big names' associated with Joyce studies, and Irish studies in general, including Vincent Cheng, Anne Fogarty, and Declan Kiberd (although Kiberd's essay is in fact a reprint of a chapter from his 2009 work *Ulysses and Us*). Much work on Joyce and memory has focused on the fiction up until 1922, but in his essay ' "Now, just wash and brush up your memoirias": Nation Building, the Historical Record, and Cultural Memory in *Finnegans Wake* 3.3' (pp. 112–24), Len Platt reads the 'Watches of Shaun' in relation to the emergence of Ireland as an independent nation. Platt co-opts elements of the theory of history and memory expressed in Pierre Nora's *Les Lieux de mémoire* for his reading of *Finnegans Wake* as a whole, and the core chapters of Book III in particular. This essay taps into a rich seam when it comes to interpreting chapter III.3, a chronically neglected chapter. The question-and-answer session that dominates the first part of III.3, often articulated in mock-legalese, can easily be understood in the light of the impossible task of comprehending the 'truth' of the past when faced with a flood of partial and contradictory accounts. Platt's discussion of Shaun's 'character', his national and political allegiances, is, however, overly simplistic in places.

Jason King's essay, 'Commemorating *Ulysses*, the Bloomsday Centenary, and the Irish Citizenship Referendum' (pp. 172–86), shifts the topic of conversation from Joyce's Ireland, or the Ireland that he experienced *in absentia* as exile, to the twenty-first century. Homing in on two virtually simultaneous high-profile public events, King crucially emphasizes the way in which the 100th Bloomsday event, designed to celebrate the cultural diversity of modern Ireland, presented a narrative that contrasts starkly with the actual lived experiences of immigrants and asylum-seekers in Ireland. This is exemplified by the outcome of the referendum. He notes that 'in the century between the day of the birth of Mina Purefoy's child and Bloom's celebrated confrontation with the Citizen, and the public commemoration of the Bloomsday Centenary, the definition of Irish nationality had not expanded but constricted' (p. 173). For King, *Ulysses* is less about Bloom's own struggle for recognition than it is about his feelings towards others. Leopold Bloom— with his 'empathy and respect for the cultural identities of others' (p. 186)— can act as exemplar to members of the Irish host society.

Joyceans have often been pioneers of the latest critical trends, but the appearance of *Eco-Joyce: The Environmental Imagination of James Joyce*, edited by Robert Brazeau and Derek Gladwin, represents a relatively late turn to ecocriticism in the field. The volume takes a three-pronged approach to its subject matter, with sections on 'Nature and Environmental Consciousness' (with essays by Fiona Becket, Cheryl Temple Herr, Bonnie Kime Scott, Erin Walsh, and Yi-Peng Lai), and 'Joyce and the Urban Environment' (featuring Margot Norris, Brandon Kershner, Greg Winston, Christine Cusick, and Derek Gladwin). The final section has the niche title 'Joyce, Somatic Ecology and the Body', and features contributions from Eugene O'Brien, Robert Brazeau, James Fairhall, and Garry Leonard. Given its high-profile contributors, the collection will inevitably provoke accusations of 'faddishness': the introduction (however belatedly) of yet another new critical lens through which the work must be reconsidered. The strength of many of the individual readings contained in this volume does, however, bolster the case for an ecocritical approach. This is also true of Katherine O'Callaghan's contribution to the Memory Ireland volume discussed immediately above. In 'Joyce's "Treeless Hills": Deforestation and Its Cultural Resonances' (pp. 95–111), O'Callaghan incorporates an elegant account of the historical and cultural resonances of colonial tree-fellings in Ireland. She looks significantly beyond the moment in 'Cyclops' where a nationalist reaction to the deforestation of Ireland takes centre stage, in order to consider the importance of the theme of deforestation and the potential for environmental renewal in *Finnegans Wake*.

This year also saw the publication of *The Cambridge Companion to 'Ulysses'*, edited by Sean Latham. There is certainly no shortage of 'guidebooks' to Joyce, and the question of whether another Cambridge Companion is strictly necessary at this juncture remains open. But if there is not a need, there is a certainly a desire. The appearance of this volume suggests that such companions continue to be a lucrative prospect for publishers: a consequence of readers' (or prospective readers') enthusiasm for anything that might aid in the daunting task of tackling *Ulysses* for the first time. The companion begins with essays on composition history (pp. 3–18), reception (pp. 19–32), and the book's 'afterlife' (pp. 33–48) by Michael Groden, Joseph Brooker, and Jonathan Goldman, respectively. Some of the material presented here clearly echoes material published elsewhere, for example in Brooker's *Joyce's Critics* [2004]. Nonetheless, these chapters offer a lively introduction to three crucial aspects of the 'biography of the book'. The essays in Part II tackle fundamental issues such as setting and plot, and the third section turns to the episodes of *Ulysses* deemed most challenging for readers: Michael Rubenstein takes on 'Aeolus' and 'Wandering Rocks' (pp. 113–27), Marjorie Howes provides an elegant commentary on memory in 'Sirens' (pp. 128–40), Sean Latham writes on 'Cyclops' and 'Nausicaa' (pp. 140–53), and Cheryl Herr on 'Oxen of the Sun' and 'Circe' (pp. 154–67).

It should be stressed that these chapters do not offer a summary of these difficult later episodes—something so often craved by students of the book— rather, each essay selects a single interpretative frame as its starting point. There are one or two issues here. For example, Herr's claim that in many respects 'Oxen' and 'Circe' can be thought of as 'a single unit of *Ulysses*' (p. 154), feels a little reductive given the distinct technique, and preoccupations, of these two gargantuan experiments in radical prose. The final section selects three aspects of contemporary theory and criticism: R. Brandon Kershner writes on 'Intertextuality' (pp. 171–84), Vike Martina Plock on 'Bodies' (pp. 184–99), and Paul K. Saint-Amour chooses the playful title 'Symbols and Things' (pp. 200–15) for the final chapter of the book. These essays can, of course, only scratch the surface of such an enormous critical field. Kershner, Plock, and Saint-Amour do, however, cover an impressive amount of ground in the short space allotted.

Joyce was included in a number of comparative, multiple-author studies in 2014. Katherine Ebury's *Modernism and Cosmology: Absurd Lights* is a good example. This study begins the enormous task of unravelling the significance of the 'new physics' for Yeats, Joyce, and Beckett. Ebury devotes chapters to 'Yeatsian Cosmology' (in the singular), and 'Joycean Cosmologies'. Such plurality is important as it gestures towards the varied and variable ways in which scientific discourse is present in Joyce's works, especially *Finnegans Wake*—to which Ebury devotes a separate chapter. Elsewhere, Marco Canani and Sara Sullam's collection, *Parallaxes: Virginia Woolf Meets James Joyce* revisits fairly well-trodden ground in bringing together two icons of anglophone literary modernism; and, in *Conspicuous Bodies: Provincial Belief and the Making of Joyce and Rushdie*, Jean Kane visits an (arguably) less obvious, but nonetheless rich, literary relationship. Less strictly academic was Kevin Birmingham's acclaimed work of literary non-fiction, *The Most Dangerous Book: The Battle for James Joyce's 'Ulysses'*, which was named the Sunday Times Literary Non-Fiction Book of the Year for 2014, and received the 2015 PEN New England Award for Non-Fiction. Birmingham is a natural storyteller, and he injects a strong element of fun into the tale he tells. Some of his more imaginative leaps will, inevitably, prove problematic for scholars.

This includes Birmingham's belief (revisiting an old, and by now tired, debate) that Joyce suffered from syphilis.

As ever, journal articles on Joyce appeared in publications emanating from all corners of English studies, and beyond. Margot Norris's lively and entertaining 'The Animals of James Joyce's *Finnegans Wake*' (*MFS* 60:iii[2014] 527–43) can be linked to the blossoming of Joycean ecocriticism, discussed above. At moments, the *Wake* reads like a bestiary, and Norris explores this aspect of the work with characteristic brio. She proposes that a discussion that 'looks at the *Wake*'s animals with an open mind about their status can enrich rather than impoverish their ecological function and significance in the work' (p. 528). Amongst specialist Joyce journals, a highlight of the *Dublin James Joyce Journal* was Clare Hutton's 'The Development of *Ulysses* in Print, 1918–1922' (*DJJJ* 6/7[2013–14] 109–31), which offers some important observations on the features of *Ulysses* as a serial text. Hutton charts the evolution of each chapter from serial publication to 'final' text by calculating the number of words added, which is then expressed as a percentage (this data is presented in a handy table). She proposes a broad model for understanding Joyce's method of revision, suggesting that some episodes (namely, the first three) were only subject to minor or 'micro-revision'; others were revised far more extensively: episodes four to eight, twelve, and thirteen are described as being subject to 'macro-revision'. Naturally, some episodes (namely nine, ten, and eleven) fall somewhere in between the two. Sarah Davison's 'Trenchant Criticism: Joyce's Use of Richard Chenevix Trench's Philological Studies in "Oxen of the Sun" ' (*JoyceSA* [2014] 164–95) supplies the genetic evidence that confirms Joyce did indeed read Trench. This leads to an important discussion of Joyce's response to his reading materials—his 'Trench warfare'.

Unfortunately, it was not possible to obtain copies of Elizabeth M. Bonapfel and Tim Conley's *Joyce and Punctuation* or Patrick Colm Hogan's *'Ulysses' and the Poetics of Cognition* for review.

(d) D.H. Lawrence

Two lifelong D.H. Lawrence scholars, Judith Ruderman and Takeo Iida, published collections of essays in 2014. Judith Ruderman's *Race and Identity in D.H. Lawrence: Indians, Gypsies, and Jews* focuses on Lawrence's construction of the racial other. More than half of the essays are published here for the first time, and the others have been revised, the essay on native Americans substantially so. The value of the book lies in its historical method, in which Ruderman contextualizes Lawrence's writings on American Indians, Gypsies, and Jews within larger currents of European and American discourse. By thinking of Lawrence's work in these contexts, she intends 'both to counteract a common view that he was idiosyncratic in his extreme statements and to suggest some surprising ways in which he deviated from the norms of cultural stereotyping' (p. 3). On the whole, she succeeds in both goals.

The first three chapters deal with Lawrence's writing about Jews. The first deals with his use of anti-Semitic stereotypes—money, littleness, shrewdness—concluding that while Lawrence can be called anti-Semitic, he is a 'most interesting anti-Semite' (p. 44), who is ultimately 'conflicted about Jews' (p. 42). The second sets Lawrence's ideas within wider national debates about the relationship between Jewishness and Englishness. The third sets his thought, especially in *Studies in Classic American Literature*, *Quetzalcoatl*, and *The Boy in the Bush*, in the context of the Zionist movement of which his friend David Eder was a leader. Ruderman argues that Lawrence's longtime fantasy of Rananim, throughout its development, is indebted to his personal and cultural experience of Zionism. Despite a rather tenuous argument about images of milk and honey in the final chapter, these three chapters add up to an important and thorough account of Lawrence's writing about Jews, and are essential reading for any scholar of the subject.

The next two chapters are equally important. In the book's fifth chapter, Ruderman situates Lawrence's writing about American Indians 'in the broader context of Americans' appropriation of "Indianness" to construct personal and national identities' (p. 90), with excellent sections on New Mexico, on Mabel Luhan, and on Indian captivity narratives. In the sixth chapter she does the same historical work with respect to Lawrence's writing about Gypsies, arguing that 'the sum total of [contemporary representations of Gypsies] presented contradictory images that Lawrence both adopted and adapted' (p. 126). The next two chapters address the issue of Lawrence's writing about the racial other obliquely, and therefore slightly less successfully, in investigations which are nevertheless fascinating in themselves, of his representations of clothing and of health.

Takeo Iida's *D.H. Lawrence as Anti-Rationalist: Mysticism, Animism and Cosmic Life in His Works* collects previously published essays. Because of their related thematic concerns, it is very useful to have them in a single volume. The purpose of the volume, as Iida says in his introduction, is 'to demonstrate D.H. Lawrence as a mystic and animistic writer and as a perceiver of cosmic life in his poetry, prose works and paintings' (p. vii). Iida is especially interested in reading Lawrence in the light of Greek, Christian, and Japanese traditions. The first three chapters deal with Lawrence's 'mysticism'. In the first, Iida argues that the motif of the dark sun in Lawrence's work comes not only from Mexican mythology but from a long 'European cultural tradition' (p. 1), from *The Cloud of Unknowing* to John Keble, which also includes the pre-Socratics and the Metaphysical Poets. The second chapter reads 'The Ship of Death' as 'a poem of "spiritual death" and resurrection here on earth', a 'mystic death' like that of Christian mystics such as St John of the Cross (p. 18). The third chapter traces three main influences on Lawrence's idea of 'darkness' in particular—'the Bible, Greek mysticism, and Christian mysticism' (p. 36). Notably, Iida explores the hypothesis that Dean W.R. Inge's *Christian Mysticism*, which Lawrence 'may have read' along with Inge's book on Plotinus (p. 37), is one such influence.

The next five chapters deal with Lawrence's animistic thought. Iida argues that Lawrence 'wants to make people emotionally or intuitively vital by exposing them to the world of nature or the cosmos where the gods dwell' (p. 45), and traces this desire at work throughout the canon of Lawrence's fiction, non-fiction, and poetry. Perhaps *St Mawr* is the most frequently mentioned text. Chapter 6 argues that there is an 'animistic consistency' that unites the two parts of the novella, expressed first in the portrayal of St Mawr and then in the portrayal of the American ranch, in which nature is both 'creative and destructive' (p. 69). In the next chapter, he compares *St Mawr* and *The Escaped Cock* to Rosalie K. Fry's *Child of the Western Isles* insofar as, in all three texts, 'the animistic world is revived in the modern world' (p. 86). In chapter 9, Iida draws a similar comparison between *The Fox* and the work of certain Japanese writers, as well as with animistic elements in European traditions. Chapter 8 addresses one such element: the Green Man, whom Iida sees represented in Lawrence's painting 'Red Willow Trees'. Chapters 10 and 11 compare Lawrence's work to that of two modern Japanese writers, the poet Akiko Yosano and the novelist Sei Ito. Like Lawrence, Iida argues, Akiko is a poet of touch, very unusually at her time in Japanese literary history. Sei Ito, on the other hand, who translated many of Lawrence's works into Japanese, and was 'the most enthusiastic reader of Lawrence' among Japanese novelists (p. 131), diverges from Lawrence in his portrayal of sexuality in several ways, even in his most Lawrentian last novel, *Transformations*. The final chapter is an interesting and informative note on the dust-jacket of *Tortoises*. This is not a Hiroshige print, as previous scholars have asserted, Iida argues, but 'most likely a copy by an unknown illustrator talented enough to deceive both Lawrence and the editors of both the CUP *Letters* and *A Bibliography of D.H. Lawrence*' (p. 143). He provides fascinating details of what the picture in fact represents, contrary to previous interpretations.

Shirley Bricout's *Politics and the Bible in D.H. Lawrence's Leadership Novels* is her own translation of the monograph she published in French in 2008. The book examines Lawrence's uses of the Bible and the political significance of these uses in *Aaron's Rod*, *Kangaroo*, and *The Plumed Serpent*. The first chapter provides a wide survey of intertextual theory, developing from it an account of three main ways in which Lawrence uses the Bible: 'parody', 'pastiche', and 'burlesque travesty'. Bricout sees a political significance within each of them. This chapter includes an impressively thorough table of all Lawrence's references to the Bible in the three leadership novels, which is the most valuable part of the book. One only hopes that Bricout will continue such thorough work on further Lawrence texts.

The second and third chapters are organized according to the different political issues that Bricout argues Lawrence addresses in the leadership novels. The second chapter deals with the Europe that Lawrence's exile characters leave behind, specifically with the questions of religion, the war, and women. The third chapter deals with the new places to which Lawrence's exiles journey, specifically with the questions of language, empire, and community. In each case, Bricout sets out the ways in which Lawrence's borrowings from the Bible articulate his political views. As she puts it, 'The source text, or hypotext, has ... been amplified and transformed for precise semantic needs, in this instance to express a political argument' (p. 49). In the final chapter, she deals with the political theories with which Lawrence interacted, especially fascism and Marxism, 'chartering the mandate assigned to the source text [i.e. the Bible] woven into the narrative fabric' in order to 'show how Lawrence responds to Fascist ideology and [to] Marxism' (p. 229). In discussing Marxism, Bricout delves into the layers of intertextuality that arise from Lawrence's uses of the Bible in response to Marxism, which, she argues, itself has an intertextual relationship to the Bible.

The *D.H. Lawrence Review* published one issue in 2014, entitled 'Ladies of Lawrence'. As Jill Franks explains in her introduction, 'Ecriture Féminine and Women Lawrence Critics' (*DHLR* 39:i[2014] 1–10), the title refers to 'women who read the complexities of this author's work and life as potential material for insight into their own work and life' (p. 2). Seven essays by women critics follow, the political intent of which, Franks writes, 'is to call attention to certain recurring concerns of women critics, and to celebrate ways of writing that integrate lived experience with academic knowledge' (p. 2). The highlight of the collection is Carol Siegel's 'D.H. Lawrence, Mentor' (*DHLR* 39:i[2014] 11–25). Siegel writes that her purpose in the essay is 'to show how Lawrence's work can help us find our way in a life based on affectionate connection to others and devotion to creative expression, while working within English Studies' (p. 11). She does so through a personal reflection on her own background and how Lawrence's 'teachings' (p. 16) allowed her to find in him a source of wisdom for life. She discusses their shared working-class background, his understanding of her experience of racial and gender prejudice, and above all her finding in Lawrence a fellow proponent of 'the centrality of sexuality to the vibrant life' (p. 21). Another direct contribution to the volume's feminist project is Margrét Gunnarsdóttir Champion's ' "To Sift the Vital Fact": Learning, Perception and World-Horizons in D.H. Lawrence's *Sons and Lovers*' (*DHLR* 39:i[2014] 26–39). Drawing on Merleau-Ponty, Champion analyses *Sons and Lovers* as a *Bildungsroman*, but one which explores 'a return to the lived body as an instrument of new knowledge of the configuration "self-other-things" and, in consequence, as an instrument of the potential revision of the hierarchical models of culture' (p. 31). Maturation and learning in the novel, Champion argues, happen through 'feminine intelligence' (p. 38), 'erotic perception' (p. 31), and 'the world of work' (p. 38), the latter being infused with 'femininity, nurture, and good-fellowship' (p. 36).

In 'Caravaggio and D.H. Lawrence: Vulgarity to Sainthood' (*DHLR* 39:i[2014] 51–66), Helen Wussow traces the 'striking' parallels and similarities between the two artists' lives and works (p. 51). Both practise extensive self-portraiture, both use stark contrasts between light and dark; for Wussow, Lawrence's writing often demonstrates a kind of literary chiaroscuro. Both artists evince a 'thoroughgoing sensuality' (p. 62), and both 'challenged society to abandon old ways of seeing for shocking, new interpretations' (p. 63). Even today, she concludes, the works of both are subject to censorship, including by their own admirers. In 'Climbing Down the Alpine Pisgah: Lawrence's Relationships with the Alps' (*DHLR* 39:i[2014] 67–78), Catherine Brown traces Lawrence's shifting views of the Alps throughout his life after he first visited them in 1912, a trajectory she associates with other important 'turns' in Lawrence's life and thought, including his view of God.

Two close textual readings are provided by Violeta Sotirova and Nanette Norris. In 'The Enactment of Feeling: A Stylistic Analysis of Love Scenes in *The Rainbow*' (*DHLR* 39:i[2014] 79–96), Sotirova gives a detailed linguistic analysis of the significance of Lawrence's use of the words 'they' and 'one' for the similarities and differences amongst the three generations of relationships in *The Rainbow*, arguing that 'Lawrence's prose, like that of other Modernists, is particularly iconic and that his language enacts the meaning that his words embody' (p. 80). In 'Two Sides to War: "England, My England" and "Vin Ordinaire"' (*DHLR* 39:i[2014] 97–108), Norris argues that these two stories articulate Lawrence's 'understanding of the impetus to war in the nations of Germany and England' (p. 97). Lawrence sees the two cultures differing in terms of their 'particular emotional character', 'the importance of the male/female balance', and their 'objects of desire', which Norris expounds in the language both of Lacan and of Girard (p. 99). In both stories, 'cultural desire pushes [the protagonists] into war, and personal individualism fails to give them the strength to resist' (p. 106).

Entitled 'D.H. Lawrence and the Discontents of Civilization', the 2014 issue of *Études lawrenciennes* addresses the relationships between Lawrence and Freud, especially Freud's *Civilisation and Its Discontents*. The highlight is Michael Bell's article, 'Myths of Civilization in Freud and Lawrence' (*EL* 45[2014] 9–26), which contrasts two basic forms of world-view, the 'positivist' and the 'aesthetic'. Freud is an example of the former; Lawrence, in a line of thinkers that descends through Schiller and Nietzsche, an example of the latter, although crucially aware of the conflict between the two world-views and exhibiting them artistically in his fiction. For Freud, 'the primordial instincts of man are intrinsically destructive and must be subject to civilized repression and sublimation' (para. 8); Nietzsche, Schiller, and Lawrence, on the other hand, affirm 'a radical trust in the instinctual nature of man' (para. 6). In the former world-view, natural science is the climax of culture; for Lawrence and the modernists, it is a self-aware human fashioning of the world. In these terms, Bell concludes, Lawrence's final triumph is his life, for 'the aesthete is ... the figure who lives most fully within the world' (para. 25). In contrast, Brigitte Macadré-Nguyen's 'Lawrencian Echoes in Freud's *Civilization and Its Discontents*' (*EL* 45[2014] 27–44) compares Freud's text to *Women in Love*. In both, 'civilization is the source of human unhappiness' (para. 7), and both seek similar remedies for humanity's consequent sickness. Both see a reversion to a sexually free and pagan pre-civilized society as a potential answer, Macadré-Nguyen argues, but Freud draws back from taking that path, whereas Lawrence is willing to forge ahead. In 'Redemptions of the Social Body: *Kangaroo* and *The Plumed Serpent*' (*EL* 45[2014] 107–24), Juliette Feyel compares and contrasts the application of Lawrence's and Freud's theories of individual psychology to the political sphere. Through his novels, especially *Kangaroo* and *The Plumed Serpent*, Lawrence is able to 'explore worlds of possibility' and 'experiment with alternative models of society' (para. 6) in response to the crisis that both men see in civilization. Ultimately, Feyel concludes, Lawrence 'redirects his utopian hopes to a smaller community, that of the couple, in which unconscious drives ... can express themselves as long as they counterbalance each other harmoniously' (para. 30). In 'Traumatized by Civilization: Lawrence's and Pat Barker's Characters through the Freudian Lens' (*EL* 45[2014] 161–84), Marina Ragachewskaya compares and contrasts the ways in which Lawrence's *England, My England* stories and Pat Barker's *Regeneration* and *The Ghost Road* relate to Freud's view of civilization. They 'diagnose the same disease in civilization', she argues, 'while offering different therapies' (para. 6). In response to the trauma of the war, Ragachewskaya sees 'Barker professing Freudian therapy, Lawrence preaching for a remembrance of another sort, the memory of the old and bygone civilizations, … of the primitive' (para. 35).

Elise Brault-Dreux provides a fascinating analysis of laughter in *Women in Love* in 'Laughter and Mockery in *Women in Love*: Heterogeneous Symptoms of Discontent' (*EL* 45[2014] 57–76), arguing in the light of *Civilization and Its Discontents* that laughter and mockery in the novel are 'symptoms of discontent' (para. 1), specifically of frustration, of aggressiveness, and of interpersonal crisis. She concludes that laughter in the novel enacts and reveals 'the disintegration of the bonds of society, and therefore the disintegration of civilization in general' (para. 43). In 'The Death Instinct and the Recovery of Psychical Integrity in the Bestiary of *Women in Love*' (*EL* 45[2014] 77–94), Mathilde La Cassagnère examines the 'allotropies' at work in the representation of animals in *Women in Love*, arguing that they represent 'an unwitting prophecy of the theory of instincts delivered by Freud a year later' (para. 3). Stefana Roussenova's 'Lawrence's "Art Speech" and the Malady of Civilization in *Women in Love*' (*EL* 45[2014] 95–106) also analyses the 'Rabbit' chapter of *Women in Love*, drawing 'parallels concerning the role of aggressiveness in love' between Freud and Lawrence (para. 1). In 'The Self and Its Discontents: Ursula's Progress in *The Rainbow*' (*EL* 45[2014] 45–56), Jacqueline Gouirand argues that the arc of Ursula's character-development in the novel is directed towards the ' "happy accommodation" that Freud advises us to find in *Civilization and Its Discontents* … "between the claims of the individual and the mass claims of civilization" ' (para. 5).

The issue also contains two very interesting theoretical readings. Susan Reid's 'Enumerating Difference: Lawrence, Freud, Irigaray and the Ethics of Democracy' (*EL* 45[2014] 125–40) contrasts the ethical thought of the three writers, arguing that while 'all three … begin with the couple, Freud seems unable to progress beyond this point, while for Lawrence and Irigaray the couple is the foundation for all other relationships' (para. 2). Sanatan Bhowal's 'Lawrence and the Question of Gender in Our Times' (*EL* 45[2014] 141–60) argues that, in contrast to Freud, Lawrence's fluid view of gender has substantial shared ground with that of contemporary feminists and gender theorists: 'Lawrence, in his critique of culture, is against all fixed norms, and the norms of gender are no exception' (para. 5).

The *Journal of D.H. Lawrence Studies* opens with two letters of Lawrence, newly annotated with the Cambridge Edition apparatus and published in full. These are 'Further Letters of D.H. Lawrence', edited by John Worthen and Andrew Harrison (*JDHLS* 3:iii[2014] 7–9). The first, dated 16 September 1915, is to Eoa Rainusso, a teacher at Tellaro, expressing Lawrence's deep sympathies for the death of Elide Fiori. He says, 'How sad that land of Tellaro is. It seems to me there is a shadow of death in those steep and narrow streets' (p. 8). There is also an account of Lawrence and Frieda's experience of a Zeppelin dropping bombs on London. The second letter is a postcard, dated 13 October 1924, to Baroness Anna von Richthofen, sent on the way from Taos to Mexico City. Intriguingly the front image (only described, not reproduced, in the Cambridge apparatus) is of a 'Native American woman'

(p. 9): it would be interesting to see which picture postcard Lawrence picked to send to his mother-in-law. This point is picked up in Jonathan Long's excellent and thoughtful, 'The Achievement of the Cambridge Edition of the *Letters* and *Works* of D.H. Lawrence: A First Study' (*JDHLS* 3:iii[2014] 129–51). Long has some criticisms of the *Letters* and *Works*: letters *to* Lawrence are often not included; he laments 'the general policy of not including the sketches, maps, and other pictorial parts of the letters' (p. 134); and he notes changes in policy over the choice of base-texts. But he also sets out the enormous benefits of the edition, which has produced, 'in comparison with most publications of other twentieth-century writers, material unsurpassed in quality and quantity' (p. 142). As he comments in parting, 'How ironical, given Lawrence's view of Cambridge!' (p. 142). Elliott Morsia's 'A Genetic Study of "The Shades of Spring"' (*JDHLS* 3:iii[2014] 153–78) provides an example of the kind of textual criticism facilitated by the Cambridge Edition. Morsia proposes a 'genetic' as opposed to a 'teleological' method in studying the different versions of 'The Shades of Spring', focusing on the creative process rather than on the finished product. He notices that in the later version of the story (published in *The Prussian Officer, and Other Stories*) descriptive scenes and scenery are largely left intact from the first version ('The Harassed Angel'), whereas dialogue undergoes heavy revision. He observes also, against the teleological approach, the significance of the editorial involvement of Edward Garnett, and notes that 'Lawrence's development as a writer was in perennial conflict with his attachment to the past' (p. 176).

Amongst several excellent critical studies in this issue, John Worthen's 'Lawrence and Some Romantic Poets' (*JDHLS* 3:iii[2014] 11–32) studies Shelley's role in Lawrence's thought and work, arguing that Shelley is the example *par excellence* of the 'Male' or 'Spirit' side of the Lawrentian opposition between Male and Female, Spirit and Flesh, Law and Love, etc. Lawrence 'knew that his *own* tendency was toward exactly [this] kind of abstraction and extremity' (p. 24); in this and other ways, Worthen argues, Lawrence ultimately saw in Shelley a kindred spirit. In 'D.H. Lawrence, Philosophy and the Novel: A Nagging Question' (*JDHLS* 3:iii[2014] 51–69), Michael Bell reflects on Lawrence's claim that 'it was the greatest pity in the world when philosophy and fiction got split'. Lawrence compares the proper relationship between the two to a marriage, based like all true relationships on difference. Bell explores this relationship, analysing Lawrence's ability to 'illuminate the specific temperament and life-experience from which a particular set of ideas or attitudes emerges' (p. 54). Arguing that 'if novel and philosophy truly come together it is likely to be at the level of poetry' (p. 57) in the widest sense, Bell finds this kind of coming together in *The Rainbow*, both a portrayal of myths at work and 'a multi-layered, intimate, dynamic example of "modern myth" as a "new way of understanding"' (p. 62). Jane Costin's 'Senses of Touch: Henry Moore, D.H. Lawrence and the First World War' (*JDHLS* 3:iii[2014] 87–109) compares Lawrence and Moore as artists who respond to the war. Both portray people who are out of touch, with themselves and others. Paradoxically, though, along with other war artists, at the same time they represent precisely touch itself, as in 'The Blind Man' or John Singer Sargent's *Gassed*. Ultimately, Costin concludes, both

Lawrence and Moore think of touch as 'a remedy for the even greater
catastrophe they perceived: the fragmentation of the modern world that
instigated the war' (pp. 88–9). In 'Flowers as "Other", then "other", in *The
White Peacock* and *Lady Chatterley's Lover*' (*JDHLS* 3:iii[2014] 71–85), Terry
Gifford offers an ecofeminist reading of Lawrence's last novel, according to
which 'Constance Chatterley's reflections upon her engagements with flowers
are designed ... to bring her into a relationship with nature that parallels that
of Mellors the gamekeeper whose life is already embedded in the woods'
(p. 72). In contrast to *The White Peacock*, Gifford argues, *Lady Chatterley's
Lover* articulates a transition in Lawrence's work in which nature becomes not
'Other', but 'other'; that is, no longer 'alien' but rather a place in which human
beings, as Connie and Mellors do, can 'assume an instinctive at-one-ness with
it: what eco-critics call "inhabitation"'' (pp. 74–5). Finally, Fiona Richards's
'The Streaming of the Sun and the Flowing of the Stars: D.H. Lawrence and
Peter Sculthorpe' (*JDHLS* 3:iii[2014] 33–50) explores the influence of
Lawrence on the Australian composer Peter Sculthorpe.

(e) Virginia Woolf
Amidst the impressive range of Woolf scholarship produced during 2014,
Evelyn Tsz Yan Chan's *Virginia Woolf and the Professions* is a thoroughly
researched and imaginatively argued book, exploring Woolf's complex and
often contradictory attitudes towards the professions. Building on the work of
scholars, including Anna Snaith, who have explored Woolf's interrogation of
notions of public and private spheres, Chan provides careful definitions of her
key terms, drawing out their etymological significance in revealing ways, while
also tracing their development and capacity to take on new and conflicting
meanings in different eras. Each of the book's five chapters offers
contextualized readings of a range of Woolf's texts, focusing primarily on
her later works, *The Years*, *Three Guineas*, and *Between the Acts*, but also
providing rereadings of *Mrs Dalloway* and *To the Lighthouse*.
    Virginia Woolf and the Professions is at its best when Chan considers
Woolf's work alongside historical and contemporary debates about the
professions in institutional publications and newspapers. This approach is
particularly effective in chapter 1, 'The Ethics and Aesthetics of Medicine',
which scrutinizes Woolf's presentation of doctors Bradshaw and Holmes in
Mrs Dalloway in the context of the increasing professionalization of medicine
during the nineteenth century, exemplified in the founding of the General
Medical Council and subsequently the British Medical Association. Chan
finds that Woolf's critique of doctors' desire for money and status and her
championing of 'a more humanistic medicine' (p. 31) is in line with
contemporary accounts of the profession. This chapter is also attentive to
Woolf's aesthetic decisions in the novel, particularly the ways in which her
selective use of 'free indirect thought representation' (p. 50) facilitates her
critique of both doctors. Chapter 2 is interesting about Woolf's understanding
of amateurism and professionalism, offering insights into her own (vexed)
understanding of her status as a writer. Chan's care over socio-historical

contexts is matched by scrupulous attention to draft material. This is especially clear in chapter 4, on *The Years* and *Three Guineas*, in which she compares drafts of *The Years* with the final novel, drawing attention to the 'pregnant emptiness of the published version' (p. 113) and what it can reveal to us about Woolf's ambitions for that novel and its take on professionalism.

Jean Mills's *Virginia Woolf, Jane Ellen Harrison and the Spirit of Modernist Classicism* is a passionately argued monograph that does a wonderful job of rescuing Jane Ellen Harrison's reputation, not only as a classicist, feminist, and public intellectual, but also as a key figure in Woolf's imagination. This book carries on the work of early feminist Woolf scholars in foregrounding the intellectual women in Woolf's life in its efforts to 'locate Woolf not in Bloomsbury ... but within a feminist collective of independent women thinkers' (p. 39). It establishes the relationship between Woolf and Harrison by making—often bold—claims about the 'transpersonal' intellectual and political exchange between these women.

The book opens with a biographical account of Harrison's life as a popular lecturer, drawing on valuable archival research—this section is particularly useful to those not familiar with Harrison's life and work. The next chapter focuses on Woolf's Greek tutor, Janet Case, and suggests that 'Case's methods ... were strategies and techniques developed and inspired by Jane Harrison' (p. 39) in order to support the case for the transpersonal relationship between Woolf and Harrison. Chapter 2 focuses on the relationship between Harrison and Woolf through readings of Woolf's novels and two of her notebooks. (Mills unearths the fascinating fact that Woolf's 'The Libation Bearers Notebook' was attached to a draft of *Mrs Dalloway* (p. 90).) The readings of *A Room of One's Own* and *Three Guineas* alongside writing by Harrison in chapters 3 and 4 highlight the benefits of this study's transpersonal approach. These chapters show this monograph to be an important feminist project and an urgent one too, demonstrating what present-day disciplines such as peace studies can learn from both Woolf and Harrison.

Eric Sandberg's *Virginia Woolf: Experiments in Character* is a thought-provoking investigation of Virginia Woolf's sustained interest in character and experiments with characterization throughout her literary career. This book takes in a range of Woolf's short stories and novels across seven well-researched chapters. In his introduction, Sandberg presents his project as a reclamatory one, outlining the various ideological and linguistic 'attacks on character' since the 1980s. This introduction does an excellent job of explaining why this neglect of character has been especially acute in Woolf scholarship. Sandberg positions his interest in character in terms of a recent ethical turn in literary criticism and argues for the need for character and characterization to be recognized in discussions of Woolf and subjectivity: 'Her experimental representation of self is manifested in experimentation with characterization. It is, consequently, at the juncture of human nature and human character, of the referential and the literary, that Woolf's work operates, exploring different ways of conceiving of human subjectivity and different ways of formulating it within a literary structure' (p. 22).

The first chapter is amongst the most successful in the book, reading Woolf's early reviews and essays on writers including Henry James, Elizabeth

Robins, George Gissing, and Dostoevsky for evidence of her preoccupation with character and her thinking about good characterization and bad. It opens by challenging the critical assumption that Woolf's early reviews were subject to both external and self-censorship and makes a strong case for this early work as instructive in terms of her views on writing and character. Thought-provoking chapters follow on *The Voyage Out*, *Jacob's Room*, *Mrs Dalloway*, *To the Lighthouse*, *The Waves*, and *Between the Acts*, each including thorough and imaginative close readings. Especially convincing is Sandberg's take on the excessive and shifting use of proper names in *Jacob's Room* and his reading of this novel in the context of Woolf's well-known debate with Arnold Bennett.

Barbara Lounsberry's *Becoming Virginia Woolf: Her Early Diaries and the Diaries She Read* is an ambitious monograph concerning Woolf's 1897–1918 diaries. Its seven chapters work chronologically through these diaries, assessing her experimental approach to the form alongside other diarists she read, including Fanny Burney, Walter Scott, Samuel Pepys, James Boswell, and Elizabeth Lady Holland. *Becoming Virginia Woolf* aims to re-emphasize this early, neglected phase in Virginia Stephen's and later Woolf's diary writing; Lounsberry suggests that their formative role in Woolf's development as a writer has been underestimated, especially their influence on Woolf's experimental aesthetics, her love of nature, and her related interest in the lives of women. In early chapters, Lounsberry does a wonderful job of showing just how precocious a reader Virginia Stephen was, and throughout she makes striking parallels between Woolf's journals and those she read. Chapter 1 makes a convincing case for Fanny Burney's role as Woolf's 'Diary Mother', whereas chapter 3 makes the interesting suggestion that Boswell's Hebridean journal 'may have inspired Woolf to start a reading notebook to complement her diary' (p. 70). Chapter 5 discusses William Allingham's diary, which Virginia Stephen read in 1907, and reflects upon her likely response to his character sketch of her father, Leslie Stephen, and his record of Stephen's silent grief upon the death of his first wife, Minnie Thackeray (pp. 104–5).

Frances Spalding's generously illustrated *Virginia Woolf: Art, Life and Vision* accompanied the National Portrait Gallery's blockbuster exhibition of the same title, guest-curated by Spalding. The exhibition included iconic portraits of Woolf painted by her sister, Vanessa Bell, and Duncan Grant, less well-known photographs of Woolf and the Bloomsbury Group, and an array of loaned material, such as Woolf's walking stick. This book presents Woolf's biography through the objects on display in the exhibition, and is attentive to the historical, biographical, and artistic contexts of Woolf's life in each case. Its prologue figures an image of the Woolfs' bomb-damaged house in Tavistock Square, its side ripped off and fireplace panels painted by Vanessa Bell open to view. As a general account of Woolf's life and works, it would have been nice to hear more about her early novels and her political and social commitments. But there is striking material here: Spalding, for example, provides a fascinating account of Woolf's 1915 mental illness, told through extracts from her letters, her sister's concerned reports, and ugly chalk drawings and snide criticism by Woolf on a page of Frances Cornford's book of poetry *Spring Morning*.

Adriana Varga's *Virginia Woolf and Music* is the first edited collection to focus entirely on Woolf's varied engagement with music. The study of Woolf and music has received increasing attention in recent years, notably in Emma Sutton's *Virginia Woolf and Classical Music* [2013]. Varga's far-reaching collection includes biographical essays on the writer's exposure to musical culture and the details of what she listened to when. Rosemary Lloyd's 'Bloomsbury and Music' (pp. 27–45) contextualizes Woolf's listening habits in terms of Bloomsbury's responses to music more generally, showing that philosopher G.E. Moore's influence on the group was musical as well as philosophical and highlighting the important roles both Roger Fry and the less well-known Bloomsbury figure Saxon Sidney-Turner played in guiding the group's musical tastes. Mihalay Szegedy-Mazak's 'Virginia Woolf and Musical Culture' (pp. 46–72) details the concerts Woolf attended but also significant ones she missed, drawing attention to the 'limitations of Virginia's taste' (p. 61), and exploring Woolf's changing attitudes towards Wagner. It is especially pleasing to see work in the Woolfs' archives yielding fresh insights, as we see here in the attention paid to Leonard Woolf's annotated record collection at Sussex.

Other essays in this collection consider the how music figures thematically in Woolf's writing. Jim Stewart's chapter (pp. 110–33) locates a tension in Woolf's engagement with music in her first novel *The Voyage Out*, assessing that text's engagement with the choric song of Sophoclean drama and its wrangling with Nietszchean categories of the Dionysian and the Apollonian. Emma Sutton's contribution (pp. 160–79) explores Woolf's critical engagement with Wagner's anti-Semitic discourses in *Mrs Dalloway*, making a convincing case for the ways in which the Jewish practice of *shivah* is written into this novel. Other essays explore the influence of music at a formal level, considering the degree to which Woolf's writing practices—her use of rhythm and her syntactical decisions—register the influence of music. Sanja Bahun's essay on *Between the Acts* (pp. 229–59) is a striking example of this approach, drawing out the 'historically specific concerns' of this novel in comparison to other 'modernist compositions of the 1930s', including Stravinsky's *The Rite of Spring*, with which Bahun suggests Woolf's novel shares an 'innovative rhythmic structuring' (p. 242). *Virginia Woolf and Music* is a welcome addition to the field, demonstrating a real breadth of approaches and drawing attention to some of Woolf's less widely discussed work, in particular her early novels *The Voyage Out* and *Night and Day*.

Donna Lazenby's *A Mystical Philosophy: Transcendence and Immanence in the Works of Virginia Woolf and Iris Murdoch* traces the mystical content of the novels and philosophical writings of two self-professed atheist writers. Lazenby suggests that Woolf's version of the mystical in her writing—one that rejects artificial ideas of 'unity' (p. 31) or fulfilment but embraces the unknowability and mysteriousness of everyday life—is closer to 'a *mystical* theology' (p. 41), specifically the Christian mystical tradition represented by Plotinus and Pseudo-Dionysus, than to the mystical as it was understood by her contemporaries, including Bertrand Russell. Part I, 'Points of Departure', looks at the limits of existing discussions of mysticism in Woolf's work, suggesting that some scholarship suffers from a misunderstanding of what the mystical is and a tendency to blur the mystic with the visionary. In chapter 4, Lazenby moves on to close readings of Woolf's diaries and *To the Lighthouse*, bringing Woolf into conversation with Plotinus. She focuses on their shared concern with ideas of 'unity, the mystical self, vision, light, love and ecstasy' (p. 127) in order to draw out what she describes as the 'cataphatic' dimensions of Woolf's work. Chapter 6 approaches the other side of the cataphatic–apophatic dialectic which Lazenby sets up in her introduction. This dimension of Woolf's work (identified with anxiety, fragmentation, and her awareness of the problems of artistic expression), although apparently at odds with the embrace of unity we find in the cataphatic in her work, also has its roots in the religious mystical tradition, this time the thought of Psuedo-Dionysus.

Claire Davison's innovative study, *Translation as Collaboration: Virginia Woolf, Katherine Mansfield and S.S. Koteliansky*, aims to show why Mansfield's and Woolf's co-translations with S.S. Koteliansky '*mattered*' (p. 6); what they tell us about their development as modernists, but also the wider significance of the Russians to the modernist project. As such, this is a significant new contribution to our understanding of transnational modernism. Davison states in her introduction that the book aims to foreground the '*poetics* of translation ... arguing that experimenting with style, voice, textual rhythm and editing turned translation into a modernist laboratory, where "exercises in literature" enabled writers to think across traditions, styles and genres' (p. 7). Davison pursues this agenda across five chapters that treat Woolf and Mansfield simultaneously. In the first chapter, Davison considers the different approaches of each co-translator to the task, before closely scrutinizing questions of translation and voice in chapter 2. This includes a fascinating section on Woolf and Koteliansky's joint translation of certain censored passages from Dostoevsky's *The Devils*. Davison shows, through detailed comparison with different translations of the same section, the degree to which the co-translators were faithful to the 'stylistic hybridity' (p. 69) of these passages in their original. Chapter 3 focuses on how Woolf's translation choices show her alertness to 'quelled or irregular voices' (p. 84) and her awareness of the gender politics of the texts she co-translated. Chapter 4 turns to consider how Mansfield and Woolf negotiated the marketplace and challenged existing translation strategies, refusing to 'domesticate' their translations and instead offering the reader 'notes, essays and biographical insights' (p. 112) to guide their reading. Chapter 5, on biographical writing in translation, shows how Russian 'lives' 'inspired the co-translators to try out new methods in their translations, and how ... their own conceptualisations of biography changed' (p. 143) as a result of their readings.

Sanja Bahun's *Modernism and Melancholia: Writing as Countermourning* explores two complicated and contested concepts, modernism and melancholy. Bahun argues that 'the modern "inability to mourn" operates as both a gripping topic and a formal challenge in modernist texts'. Borrowing from anthropologist Peter Homans, she names this 'impossible mourning' in modernist texts 'countermourning' (p. 18). *Modernism and Melancholia* argues that it is in the 'symptomatology of melancholia' (p. 19) that modernist writers found a 'template' for representing and enacting this countermourning. Bahun's claims concerning the historical and social implications of this aesthetic practice are provocative: she suggests that because countermourning suspends or prevents 'acceptance' or 'resignation' it might 'serve as a superior framework to address modernist interventions in the socio-symbolic functioning of society' (p. 18). In her introduction, Bahun promises to query the association of modernism with a melancholic world-view, which results in 'a rejection of social engagement' (p. 4), through chapters considering three case studies of 'countermonument' novels by Andrei Bely, Franz Kafka, and Virginia Woolf.

The chapter on *Between the Acts* is convincingly argued, and the theoretical framework of countermourning allows Bahun to offer fresh takes on familiar themes in Woolf's final novel, including community and the individual, patterning, history, and the tension between politics and aesthetics. This wide-ranging discussion begins by suggesting that the novel's 1939 setting invites us to read it as 'a performance of what Freud deemed a particularly poetic form of melancholia—"anticipatory grief"' (p. 156). It goes on to consider Woolf's search for pattern in the novel, its generic hybridity, and her effort to show through her constant negotiation of external and internal her preoccupation with contemporary history and the degree to which 'non-participation may still present an active work in history' (p. 174). The most convincing example of the novel as enacting the ambivalence crucial to countermourning appears in Bahun's reading of 'unrecorded histories' in the novel. Woolf's efforts to retain 'typological and semantic markers of occlusion' alongside gestures to these '(hi)stories of the obscure' (p. 187), Bahun argues, allow her to avoid appropriating the unrecorded while also hinting at its presence.

Elizabeth Abel's 'Spaces of Time: Virginia Woolf's Life-Writing' (in DiBattista and Wittman, eds., pp. 55–66) explores Woolf's ambivalent attitudes towards the demands of autobiography and her alternative, capacious term proposed in 'A Sketch of the Past', 'life-writing'. Abel offers a subtle comparative reading of Woolf's memoir and *To the Lighthouse*. 'Teasing out the traces of *To the Lighthouse* as a rough guide to the more loosely structured later text', Abel follows 'their shared investment in the early, multisensory space of time whose abrupt termination by the death of Woolf's mother complicates its recovery' (p. 58). This essay also draws attention to the anxieties of Woolf's present-day, writing 'I' about the ensuing Second World War and how these colour her memories of her younger self. This is especially convincing in Abel's reading of 'Woolf's childhood molestation by her brother Gerald' (p. 61).

Victoria Rosner's *Cambridge Companion to the Bloomsbury Group* contains a range of considered essays on the group's origins, politics, and artistic practice, and others that reflect in subtle ways on the history of the group's popular representation and reception. A number of essays will be of particular interest to Woolf scholars. In her appraisal of 'Victorian Bloomsbury' (pp. 19–32), Katherine Mullin offers an account of the 'submerged Victorian influences' (p. 24) discernible in the group's artistic productions and locates Woolf's generous treatment of Victorian life-writing in *Night and Day* as a 'veiled riposte' (p. 28) to Lytton Strachey's *Eminent Victorians*. Morag Shiach's chapter, 'Domestic Bloomsbury' (pp. 57–70), offers insights into the material conditions of Woolf's daily life in London and Sussex, while

Christopher Reed's chapter, 'Bloomsbury as Queer Subculture' (pp. 71–91), explores Woolf's attitudes to homosexuality and offers a lucid critique of the ways in which existing Woolf scholarship has (mis)represented Woolf's relationship to queer Bloomsbury. Helen Southworth's chapter on 'Bloomsbury and Book Art' (pp. 144–61) focuses on Vanessa Bell's covers for her sister's books and Woolf's typesetting for the Hogarth Press. Brenda R. Silver's chapter on 'Intellectual Crossings and Reception' (pp. 198–214) traces Bloomsbury's relationship to Freud before considering the history of Woolf's reception, particularly the transatlantic dimensions of this reception and the important ways in which it has been mediated by class. In the closing chapter of the collection (pp. 183–97), Vesna Goldsworthy explores Bloomsbury's, and particularly Woolf's, distinctive approach to life-writing and assesses its legacies. This collection also contains excellent chapters on 'War, Peace, and Internationalism' by Christine Froula (pp. 93–111) and 'Bloomsbury and Empire' by Gretchen Holbrook Gerzina (pp. 112–29).

In *The Bloomsbury Memoir Club*, eminent literary scholar and cultural historian of the Bloomsbury Group S P. Rosenbaum turns his attention to its relatively underexplored Memoir Club. Published after his death in 2012, the book includes six completed chapters, an appendix on 'Virginia Woolf amongst the Apostles', a list of Memoir Club papers, and a foreword and afterword by the book's assistant editor, James M. Haule. The six chapters focus on papers delivered at the Memoir Club as well as members' relationships to the life-writing genre more broadly, revealing the autobiographical content of work produced in the years of the club's operation but not for presentation at one of its meetings.

Rosenbaum suggests that scholars have often neglected 'the importance of the context in which the Club's memoirs were written' (p. 61). It is likely, however, that his discussion of Woolf's childhood memoir will prove controversial. Presented in the early days of the group, this was later published as '22 Hyde Park Gate' in *Moments of Being*. Rosenbaum suggests it is 'necessary to reclaim the comedy that has virtually disappeared under the mounds of speculation over George Duckworth's incestuous fondlings and cuddlings of his half-sisters' (p. 74). Although this reading of the 'final comic shock of the bedroom scene' is interesting, his recommendation that readers 'put aside all the commentary and controversy that has accumulated over the memoir' (p. 73) is unlikely to succeed. Nevertheless, Rosenbaum's book makes a valuable contribution to Woolf scholarship and it is to be hoped that the second appendix, offering details of materials relating to the club, will prompt further work on this fascinating subject.

Woolf Studies Annual 2014 contributes to our growing understanding of Woolf's engagement with her social and historical moment. Clara Jones's 'Virginia Woolf's 1931 "Cook Sketch"' (*WstA* 20[2014] 1–23) relates the discovery of a previously unpublished sketch by Woolf from 1931, written entirely in the voice of a domestic cook, and includes a transcription and facsimile images of the sketch. Given the increasing attention Woolf's complicated class politics have received in recent years, the class ventriloquism in this sketch makes this a productive discovery for our understanding of Woolf, voice, and class. Also concerned with Woolf's class and gender politics,

Ella Ophir's illuminating '*A Room of One's Own*, Ordinary Life-Writing, and *The Note Books of a Woman Alone*' (*WstA* 20[2014] 25–40) examines the notebooks of Evelyn Wilson, an employment agency clerk, which were edited by M.G. Ostle for publication in 1935. Ophir suggests Ostle's 'political' reading of Wilson's notebooks was influenced by Woolf's argument in *A Room*. This article touches on questions of self-education, life-writing, and work. Ophir is alert to Woolf's ambivalence about the 'value of ordinary life writing from her own time' (p. 28) and the ways in which class contributed to this ambivalence. It is good to hear that Ophir is preparing a digital edition of *The Note Books of a Woman Alone* as this will doubtless advance our understanding of the daily lives of 'common readers' and nuance our understanding of Woolf's take on them.

In another carefully researched and playful contribution, ' "Wretched Sparrows": Protectionists, Suffragettes and the Irish' (*WstA* 20[2014] 41–52), David Bradshaw uses the recurring figure of the sparrow in Woolf's work to explore the Irish themes of *The Years* and Woolf's familiarity with suffrage politics in *Night and Day*. Rod C. Taylor's 'Narrow Gates and Restricted Paths: The Critical Pedagogy of Virginia Woolf' (*WstA* 20[2014] 54–81) argues that Woolf's dialogic theories of education in *A Room of One's Own* and later in *Three Guineas* anticipate the radical philosophies of Paulo Freire. This well-researched work draws attention to the continuing urgency of Woolf's arguments about the relationship between education and militarized society.

The 2014 *Virginia Woolf Miscellany*, edited by Derek Ryan, takes as its subject Woolf and materiality and aims to show the 'multiple modes of materiality that Woolf engages across the span of her writing life' (p. 1). This is illustrated forcefully through short but rigorous essays on subjects ranging from class, to postcards, to waxworks, to X-rays, to mantlepieces. David Bradshaw's 'The Blight of Class: Woolf and the "Lower Orders" ' (*VWM* 85[2014] 11–13) focuses on Woolf's representation of working-class women and includes a meticulous reading of a single episode in *Jacob's Room*, in which Bradshaw discovers evidence of Woolf's engagement with questions of poverty, charity, and coercion. In 'Two Postcards from Skye: Virginia Woolf in the Hebrides' (*VWM* 85[2014] 13–15), Jane Goldman offers an illuminating take on two postcards Woolf wrote to Duncan Grant and Clive Bell during her 1938 trip to the Hebrides; this essay exposes the striking ways in which the form of the postcard and the contents of her truncated messages interact, foregrounding Woolf's visceral responses to the Hebridean landscape. Rachel Crossland's contribution, 'Exposing the Bones of Desire: Virginia Woolf's X-ray Visions' (*VWM* 85[2014] 18–20), makes use of interesting archival material and reflects on the impact Virginia Stephen's chance attendance at a lecture on the subject of X-rays in 1897 may have had on her references to this innovation in her later fiction.

Hermione Lee's '*To Pin Down the Moment with Date and Season*', the fifteenth Annual Virginia Woolf Birthday Lecture, was published by the Virginia Woolf Society of Great Britain in 2014. Lee contemplates Woolf's 'historical precision and her interest in specific dates and seasons', which are sometimes overlooked in favour of her experimental representation of consciousness and 'time-shifts' (p. 5). Opening with the well-known passage from *A Room of One's Own*, from which she borrows her title, Lee demonstrates the degree to which we can 'pin down ... with date and season' the worlds of all of Woolf's novels. Lee playfully notes that the fish delivery, the midday commuter train, and the pageant that occur in *Between the Acts* collectively suggest it is set on a Saturday: 'So the novel, if your interests tend that way, could be dated as 3, 10, 17 or 24 June 1939' (p. 5). Lee moves on to explore how Woolf marked specific dates—of birthdays, marriages, and deaths—in her diaries, concluding that such observances allowed Woolf not only to honour her dead and interrogate her mortality but also, paradoxically, to inhabit and celebrate the 'present moment' (p. 14).

The fall and spring editions of *Modern Fiction Studies* both include articles on Woolf. Valerie Reed Hickman's 'Clarissa and the Coolies' Wives: *Mrs Dalloway* Figuring Transnational Feminism' (*MFS* 60:i[2014)] 52–77) is a thought-provoking article on the figuring of the 'other woman', here the Indian woman in *Mrs Dalloway*, focusing on 'the questions of difference, distance, and ethical encounter with which the whole novel has engaged' (p. 70). This departure from existing discussions, which tend, Hickman argues, to be framed in terms of representation and the limits of Woolf's imagination, finds in her characters' 'catachrestic' invocation of India both problems and possibilities for the continuing project of transnational feminism. Karalyn Kendall-Morwick's 'Mongrel Fiction: Canine *Bildung* and the Feminist Critique of Anthropocentrism in Woolf's *Flush*' (*MFS* 60:iii[2014)] 506–26) contributes to the growing body of scholarship on the subject of Woolf and animals, arguing for the interdependence of Woolf's critiques of patriarchy and of speciesism in her biography *Flush*, which Kenfall-Morwick recasts as canine *Bildung*.

Vicki Tromanhauser's 'Eating Animals and Becoming Meat in Virginia Woolf's *The Waves*' (*JML* 38:i[2014] 73–93) is another example of research conducted at the intersection of animal studies and Woolf studies. This article finds in Woolf's most experimental novel a preoccupation with the 'nonhuman world' (p. 74), arguing that Woolf's 'metaphors of meat and consumption' and the prominence of scenes of eating should be read in the context of Woolf's critique of imperialism and her gender politics. Most thought-provoking is the case Tromanhauser makes for Woolf's exploration of 'the ontology of meat' (p. 83) through the character of Rhoda. This piece is nicely alert to historical and biographical details as well as theoretical contexts, citing, for instance, Woolf's new oil stove in 1929, joints of meat as status symbols, and contemporary experiments in 'tissue-cultured meat' (p. 86).

Woolf studies were well represented in *Modernist Cultures* during 2014. Rebecca Colesworthy's '"The Perfect Hostess": *Mrs Dalloway*, Gift Exchange, and the End of *Laissez-Faire*' (*ModCult* 9:ii[2014] 158–85) reads the role of the gift in this novel through the theories of Mauss and his structuralist heir Lévi-Strauss and offers a thorough account of existing scholarship concerned with Woolf and the marketplace. In 'Rebecca West and the Origins of *A Room of One's Own*' (*ModCult* 9:ii[2014] 186–212), Douglas Mao argues that West's essay 'A Strange Necessity' [1928] is an underexplored intertext for Woolf's feminist polemic published just a year later. Mao presents circumstantial evidence that shows Woolf was familiar with West's essay (she certainly owned it) but also deftly traces the intellectual crossings of these texts and the degree to which Woolf's materialist argument may be read as influenced by West. Anne E. Fernald's engaging 'Taxi! The Modern Taxicab as Feminist Heterotopia' (*ModCult* 9:ii[2014] 213–32) centres on the liminal figure of the taxicab in Woolf's writing. Fernald traces its ambiguous representation as a space of critical observation, as in Helen Ambrose's cab ride at the opening of *The Voyage Out*, and one in which middle-class women can indulge in private thought, as in Eleanor's journey in the 1891 section of *The Years*.

In a 'Facing *Life as We Have Known It:* Virginia Woolf and the Women's Co-operative Guild' (*L&H* 23:ii[2014] 18–34), Alice Wood sets out the details of Virginia and Leonard Woolf's relationship with the Women's Co-operative Guild and its president, Margaret Llewelyn Davies. She then offers a reading of Woolf's 'Introductory Letter' to Llewelyn Davies's edited collection of guildswomen's memoirs published by Hogarth Press in 1931. This letter has polarized critical responses, especially regarding Woolf's treatment of social class. Wood attends to these questions, suggesting that the letter promotes 'scrutiny of middle-class anxieties about social inequality and difference' (p. 31). In an original intervention in this debate, she argues that Woolf may have assumed the 'perspective of an uninformed middle-class narrator' in order to 'foster identification' from the middle-class readership at which the collection was aimed' (p. 27).

Kate McLoughlin's 'Woolf's Crotchets: Textual Cryogenics in *To the Lighthouse*' (*TPr* 28:vi[2014] 949–67) casts fresh light on the most familiar of Woolf's strategies in *To the Lighthouse*: her use of crotchet-style parenthesis on nine occasions during the novel. McLoughlin gives a thorough and useful account of previous readings of these crotchets and offers an imaginative reading of their shape. Identifying the way they 'reach up like arms out of the text' (p. 957), she suggests that they need to be read vertically, rather than horizontally, as open crypts that preserve the memory of the various deaths they record. McLoughlin offers an innovative approach to the novel's commemorative agenda, suggesting that Woolf's crotchets perform not a burial but a preservation: a textual cryogenics (p. 961).

Finally, Jans Ondatje Rolls's *The Bloomsbury Cookbook* is a beautifully produced book of recipes from the personal cookbooks of Helen Anrep, Francis Partridge, and Grace Germany (long-time cook of Vanessa Bell). This book is at its best when recording dinner-table gossip, such as the highly entertaining tales of John Maynard Keynes's greedy table manners and stinginess, which include his attempt to feed eleven guests with three grouse as recorded in a letter from Woolf to Lytton Strachey. The tempting recipes inspired here by the two central meals in *A Room of One's Own* will be of interest to Woolfians and gastronomes alike.

3. Post-1945 Fiction

(a) Fiction 1945–2000

Scholarship on postwar fiction continued to expand during 2014, with surveys of individual decades of literary history featuring amongst the most important work to appear. Thus, within the broad study of contemporary fiction, Bloomsbury's Decades series offers a significant contribution to our understanding of late twentieth-century fiction. The series editors, Nick Hubble, Philip Tew, and Leigh Wilson, suggest that the rapid growth of research into contemporary literature, while dynamic, prevented nuanced assessment and reflection on the field as it emerged. As such, systematic analysis of the creative outputs of individual decades are essential—especially given that the majority of students and young researchers will not have first-hand experience of their cultural and political make-up. Nevertheless, Hubble, Tew, and Wilson are clearly aware this approach may leave them open to charges of arbitrary division: while individual volumes focus on publications from their specific decades, there is also a clear and concerted effort to position the creative and critical outputs of these periods within wider contexts. To this end volumes in the series share a common impetus and structure: a critical introduction to the decade provides the reader with initial contextualization; then a 'Literary History of the Decade', identifies key authors, themes, conflicts, and publishing contexts; two subsequent chapters in each collection respond to key themes of the decade; and the remainder consists of three essays on representative novels and concerns of the relevant decade, followed by two chapters on international reception and contexts of British fiction. This combination of comprehensive socio-political overview and in-depth critical analysis makes this series a supremely useful resource for teaching and researching contemporary fiction.

John Muckle's *Little White Bull: British Fiction in the 50s and 60s* echoes the period-based approach of the series, albeit with less scholarly rigour, presenting the literature of the 1950s and 1960s as 'intensely preoccupied with questions of social class, social mobility ... and "mass society"' (p. 8). Muckle's claim that no other period has been as concerned with class and mobility as the 1950s and 1960s does not always convince, but *Little White Bull* nevertheless offers a wide-ranging introduction to the work of over twenty-five authors publishing during this period, from Alan Sillitoe and Lynn Reid Banks to B.S. Johnson, Angela Carter, and Doris Lessing.

Jayashree Kamblé's *Making Meaning in Popular Romance Fiction: An Epistemology* takes a broader approach to periodization, presenting a coherent analysis of developments in contemporary romance fiction. Kamblé begins with a call for romance fiction to be analysed as more than a set of publishing conventions and stereotypes. Instead, she suggests that romance novels contain a Foucauldian *épistème*, representing the 'discourse of romantic love and marriage under late capitalism' (pp. xiv, 211). Contemporary romance, in Kamblé's definition, comprises narratives where the move from fragmentation to unification is embodied in relationships, where 'romantic attachment is a signifier of sexual, emotional, and economic plenitude' (p. xvii). Kamblé's analysis of republished romances and how changes to key sections of the novels reflect shifting social attitudes to race, gender, and sexuality is particularly compelling. The impressive spread of English-language texts discussed, and the systematic attention to their treatment of capitalism, war, sexuality, race, and religion, makes this monograph a significant development of research into contemporary romance fiction. *Making Meaning in Popular*

Romance Fiction also presents a contrast to the Bloomsbury Decades series, in explicitly focusing on genre-based analysis as a means of engaging with contemporary literature and theory.

In addition to these works focused upon decades, key work in this field on trauma and memory studies appeared during 2014. Natasha Alden's *Reading Behind the Lines: Postmemory in Contemporary British War Fiction* is concerned with how the First World War and the Second World War are re-remembered in British fiction by writers who are one or two generations removed from personal experience of those conflicts. Focusing on the use of historical documentation and source material in contemporary war novels (and their claims to truth and authenticity), Alden asks how collective remembering and Marianne Hirsch's concept of 'postmemory' interact with and develop Linda Hutcheon's theories of historiographic metafiction. Beginning with an analysis of Pat Barker's *Regeneration* trilogy [1991–5], *Reading Behind the Lines* also discusses Graham Swift's *Shuttlecock* [1981], Sarah Waters's *The Night Watch* [2006], and Ian McEwan's *Atonement* [2001]. Alden proposes that these texts are representative of an increasingly historical bias in the British novel, undermining and re-remembering cultural myths, and utilizing historical documentation to reassure the reader of the accuracy of the text. This agenda is particularly obvious in Alden's close reading of Barker's *Regeneration* trilogy: here, Alden challenges critics who have criticized Barker for bringing contemporary biases to her depiction of psychiatry and W.H.R. Rivers's treatments and characterization. Alden offers extensive evidence of the specific changes Barker made to early twentieth-century writing by or about Rivers, Yealland, and Sassoon. Aside from the removal of medical jargon, and dated terms such as 'guffaw' and 'horseplay' (p. 96) which might prevent the reader identifying with the characters, what is striking about Alden's chosen extracts is the overwhelming similarity between Barker's text and the primary material. Alden does not claim strict historical accuracy; rather, she suggests that Barker is myth-building from historical artefacts in *Regeneration*. However, the analysis she provides does offer a counter to historical relativism, demonstrating instead a reading of postmemorial novels rooted in empathy, where 'impasses in representation and historical under-standing do not thwart postmemorial fiction' but create it (p. 205).

Continuing the focus on Barker, Merritt Moseley's *The Fiction of Pat Barker: A Reader's Guide to Essential Criticism* offers a comprehensive overview of Barker's fiction, along with a brief biographical note. The first two chapters focus on Barker's early work: *Union Street* [1982], *Blow Your House Down* [1984], *Liza's England* [1986], and *The Man Who Wasn't There* [1989], discussing 1980s politics, class, gender, and questions of history and authenticity. Chapters 3 to 6 concentrate on the *Regeneration* trilogy, providing an initial contextualization of Barker's use of source material, and exploring key themes of each novel in the trilogy (class divisions, masculinity, mental illness, sexuality, pacifism, and psychiatry). The final chapters evaluate Barker's later work: *Another World* [1998], *Border Crossing* [2001], *Double Vision* [2003], *Life Class* [2007], and *Toby's Room* [2012], continuing the discussion of the use of violence and trauma in Barker's fiction. Moseley summarizes the key themes of Barker's work as gender, sexuality, trauma,

class, history and memory, and therapy, with realism, historiographic
metafiction, and intertextuality as characteristic technical features of her
novels. In the conclusion, Moseley presents a useful overview of monographs
on Pat Barker, alongside two edited collections on her work, providing the
reader with a wide range of further scholarship to consult.

Kazuo Ishiguro also received significant critical attention during 2014. His
work is the focus of Alex Murray's 'The Heritage Industry and
Historiographic Metafiction: Historical Representation in the 1980s' (in
Tew, Horton, and Wilson, eds. *The 1980s: A Decade of Contemporary British
Fiction*, pp. 125–40) and in Yugin Teo's *Kazuo Ishiguro and Memory*, which
explores mourning and remembered grief (both personal and collective) in
Ishiguro's fiction, drawing heavily on Paul Ricoeur's work on memory. Teo
opens the volume with an introduction to contemporary memory studies,
alongside extracts from interviews with Ishiguro, where the latter describes his
interest in memory, as 'the filter through which we read our past ... tinted ...
with self-deception, guilt, pride, nostalgia' (p. 7). Teo distinguishes between
mourning and melancholia in Ishiguro's work, suggesting that the latter term,
with its associations with guilt and 'significant reduction in self-regard' (p. 8),
is more typical in Ishiguro's fiction. The analysis that follows is organized
thematically: Section I, 'Forgetting', examines memory, absence, and trauma
in *A Pale View of Hills* [1982], *The Remains of the Day* [1989], *The Unconsoled*
[1995], and *When We Were Orphans* [2000]. Teo highlights the complexities of
fragmented memory and forgetting, and particularly Ishiguro's characters'
tendency to rewrite their versions of the past. In the central part of the text,
'Remembering', Teo applies Ricoeur's ideas on mutual and self-recognition to
A Pale View of Hills, *An Artist of the Floating World* [1986], *When We Were
Orphans*, and *Never Let Me Go* [2005], stressing common themes of
communication, testimony, and the use of nostalgia as a method for narrating
loss (with particular reference to Hailsham in *Never Let Me Go*). The final
segment, entitled 'Release', explores utopias, wish-fulfilment, and forgiveness
in Ishiguro's oeuvre, and his characters' overwhelming 'desire for relevance or
meaning' (p. 108). Teo concludes by suggesting that Ishiguro's novels highlight
'the possibilities of literature to respond to, and challenge, established theories
of memory, mourning and forgetting' (p. 12), where nostalgia can be a
'testament' (p. 154) and witness to the existence of what was lost. While the
thematic structure of *Kazuo Ishiguro and Memory* occasionally leads to
repetition, this detailed exploration of mourning and remembering presents an
insightful extension to contemporary memory studies and Ishiguro
scholarship.

Emily Horton's *Contemporary Crisis Fiction: Affect and Ethics in the
Modern British Novel* outlines and analyses the 'common aesthetic of crisis'
(p. 1) found in contemporary British fiction. Focusing on the work of Graham
Swift, Ian McEwan, and Kazuo Ishiguro, Horton addresses the concern that,
despite extensive critical work on each of her chosen authors, little has been
written on the 'shared social and ethical dimensions' (p. 1) of their fiction.
Understanding 'contemporary crisis' not as a postmodern disintegration of
signifiers but as 'everyday social anxiety and unease' within a context of
'global neoliberalism' (p. 3), Horton challenges analyses of Swift's work as

postmodern metafiction, instead presenting his writing as responding to distinctly British crises, rooted in reactions to Thatcherism and the historical context of the 1980s. Similarly, Horton suggests that McEwan's deliberate foregrounding of complicated ethical choices indicates the centrality of 'unease', 'crisis' and 'contingency' to his writing. Citing the 'Two Cultures' debate, she proposes that McEwan's novels aim to 'destabilise the public conventions of time, history, memory and desire' (p. 23). Focusing on the merging and distribution of literary and scientific knowledge, Horton positions his work outwith postmodern scepticism. In a final section, Horton's analysis of Ishiguro acknowledges the global reach of his work, but focuses on his representation and critique of human rights, diversity, and ethics, as a writer who is particularly aware of his ethically fraught millennial context.

Shifting from the global to the national, Alasdair Gray also featured heavily in this critical work, with a particular concentration upon his role as spokesperson on Scottish matters. Camille Manfredi's excellent collection, *Alasdair Gray: Ink for Worlds*, presents a detailed analysis of Gray's work as both author and artist. This collection is unique and compelling in the equal weight it gives to Gray's literary and pictorial output. The inclusion, in a final section ('Visions and *Trompe l'œils*'), of attention to the growing amount of archival material on Gray's illustrations, engravings, and paintings is particularly satisfying. Sorcha Dallas's chapter on the Alasdair Gray Foundation is especially noteworthy here (pp. 169–80) and Liliane Louvel's rigorous and original exploration of Gray's paratext in *Poor Things* [1992] is also worth special mention (pp. 181–203), as she highlights Gray's unusual command over elements of the publishing procedure that are typically outwith authorial control (illustrations, typography, prefatory material, cover art) and his subversive use of paratext. The focus on subversion and parody runs throughout the collection, from nationalist concerns to postmodern quest narratives, and adds coherence to an already strongly connected body of essays.

Further analysis of Gray's work appears in Monica Germanà's 'The Awakening of Caledonias? Scottish Literature in the 1980s' (in Tew, Horton and Wilson, eds., pp. 51–74), which presents Gray as part of a group of writers (including Iain Banks, James Kelman, and Janice Galloway) engaged in a 'self-conscious interrogation of the alienated identity and marginalised belonging' (p. 52) of Scottish identity in the 1980s, reacting to Thatcher's politics and the 1979 independence referendum.

In terms of Northern Irish writing between 1945 and 2000, Richard Rankin Russell's new collection, *Bernard MacLaverty: New Critical Readings*, proposes that MacLaverty's prolific literary outputs represent a range of key concerns in Northern Irish literature of the period. Pointing to what he describes as the 'critical neglect' (p. 1) of MacLaverty, Russell introduces this first collection on MacLaverty's work as a defence of his role in British and Northern Irish literature of the late twentieth century. Of particular interest to this review are the chapters on MacLaverty's fiction. Gerry Smyth's interdisciplinary contribution, ' "Join Us": Musical Style and Identity in "My Dear Palestrina" ' (pp. 45–62), unpacks the musical references in

MacLaverty's short story 'My Dear Palestrina', combining cultural and musical history with analysis of political and religious concerns. Stephen Watt's 'MacLaverty's Holocaust: Affect, Memory, and the "Troubles"' (pp. 89–100) ties in with the wider trend towards exploration of trauma and violence in the current critical response to fiction of this period. Presenting MacLaverty's novels *Cal* [1983] and *Grace Notes* [1997] as positioned within a period of 'cultural trauma' (p. 89), Watt suggests that affect theory is a productive lens through which to read MacLaverty's fiction. In doing so, he aligns trauma theory away from its more familiar ground of the First and Second World Wars and the Holocaust, and into more contemporary conflicts. The vast majority of chapters in this collection touch, in some way, upon religious and political identity. In particular, Russell's 'Parabolic Plots in Bernard MacLaverty's *Lamb*' (pp. 27–44) repurposes and explores the parables of the Good Samaritan and the lost sheep. Previous criticism on *Lamb* has presented it as a critique of religion and Catholicism. Russell offers an alternative approach, suggesting that it is Lamb's misreading and neglect of illustrative parables that leads to his degeneration. As such, Russell suggests that *Lamb*, and MacLaverty's fiction more broadly, has an ethical imperative— demanding that readers take moral responsibility for their actions and development.

Martin Ryle and Julia Jordan's collection, *B.S. Johnson and Post-War Literature: Possibilities of the Avant-Garde*, both illustrates the increasing diversity of scholarship on Johnson's work and challenges the statement that Johnson constituted a 'one-man avant garde' (p. 11). Instead, contributors to this collection demonstrate consistent interest in Johnson's relationship to and interaction with his contexts and contemporaries. Contributors compare Johnson's work to that of Samuel Beckett, John Wain, Marc Saporta, James Joyce, and Mark Z. Danielewski, among others, and incorporate a variety of theoretical approaches (modernist, postmodernist, and post-postmodernist). Elsewhere, Philip Tew's 'Turbulent Times: Conflicts, Ideology and the Experimental Novel, 1969–1979' (in Hubble, McLeod, and Tew, eds., *The 1970s: A Decade of Contemporary British Fiction*, pp. 145–80) also discusses B.S. Johnson and his contemporaries, challenging, like Jordan and Ryle's collection, the idea of the singular avant-garde novel—not least by introducing the group-authored *London Consequences* [1972]; and Julia Jordan's '"For Recuperation": Elegy Form and the Aleatory in B.S. Johnson's *The Unfortunates*' (*TPr* 28:v[2014] 745–62) compares Johnson's famous 'book in a box' with Roland Barthes's meditations upon photography and the death of his mother in *Camera Lucida*, offering a compelling reading of form in *The Unfortunates* as a refusal of death's finality.

Also of potential use to scholars working on post-1945 literature are select chapters of Rachel Carroll and Adam Hansen's edited collection *Litpop: Writing and Popular Music*. Rachel Carroll's '"[S]he Loved Him Madly": Music, Mixtapes and Gendered Authorship in Alan Warner's *Morvern Callar*' (pp. 187–200) is a particularly useful example of interdisciplinary work, with a detailed and convincing unpacking of the significance of the musical references in *Morvern Callar*, drawing on a range of gender theory and music history to complement the textual analysis. This interdisciplinary approach is representative of the whole collection, which aims to combine literary criticism with music theory.

A similar interdisciplinary approach can be found in David Bolt's *The Metanarrative of Blindness: A Re-reading of Twentieth-Century Anglophone Writing*, which combines disability studies and literary analysis. Bolt's exploration of the terms 'blind girl' and 'blind man' in novels such as Stephen King's *The Langoliers* [1990] and Rupert Thomson's *The Insult* [1996] reflects on the reductive metanarratives surrounding blindness in the twentieth century, with a particular focus on issues of gender and sexuality. These concerns are continued later in Bolt's text, with a focus on John Wyndham's *The Day of the Triffids* [1951], John Varley's 'The Persistence of Vision' [1978], James Kelman's *How Late It Was, How Late* [1994], and José Saramago's *Blindness* [1995], alongside earlier works involving blindness, such as *Ulysses* [1922] and H.G. Wells's short story 'The Country of the Blind' [1904]. Bolt offers the terms 'ocularcentrism' and 'ocularnormativism' to encompass the 'baseline of assumptions' surrounding sight in literature and culture, and their effect: 'the perpetuation of the conclusion that the supreme means of perception is necessarily visual' (p. 14). Part of an increasingly dynamic body of work on literary and cultural disability studies, *The Metanarrative of Blindness* offers a provocative critical alternative to criticism of these contemporary texts.

(b) Fiction 2000–Present

The allocation of a separate section to twenty-first-century British fiction in this volume reflects a growing body of literary criticism and literary production and acknowledges the distinctive nature of critical writing on contemporary fiction.

This year saw several critical works on writers who might be described as 'black British', although this descriptive category is often put under scrutiny itself. Amongst these, Michael Perfect's *Contemporary Fictions of Multiculturalism: Diversity and the Millennial London Novel* includes seven main chapters, as well as an introduction and coda. In the introduction, Perfect notes that the view of London as a diverse city long precedes the arrival of the *Empire Windrush* in 1948, which is often seen as a symbolic marker for thinking about the advent of a multicultural Britain. However, he also observes that 'while it is crucial to point out that London has *never* been "monocultural", this is *not* the same as saying that it has *always* been "multicultural"', before discussing the difficulty in defining these terms. For the purposes of the book, Perfect takes 'multicultural' to mean 'a form of communal diversity brought about by migration from former British colonies to the former imperial centre following the formal end of Empire' (p. 5), directing attention in this way to writers who have cultural and ethnic links with former colonies of Britain. He also stresses that the focus is not on the ethnicity of the writers, but on works that offer representations of 'ethnic and cultural diversity' (p. 8), arguing that that the former approach has proven unhelpful in readings of certain writers such as Hanif Kureishi and Andrea

Levy. Chapter 1 argues convincingly that Kureishi's identification as a postcolonial writer is inadequate and offers an interesting analysis of *Something To Tell You* [2008] that focuses on the theme of abandonment and the novelist's continued experiment with differing literary modes. By comparison, chapter 2 argues that Andrea Levy should be regarded as a postcolonial writer as opposed to the more usual critical response of placing her as a black British writer. Chapter 3 re-examines Zadie Smith's *White Teeth* [2000]. Starting from previous comparisons between Smith and Salman Rushdie in terms of narratives of contingency and unpredictability in postcolonial contexts, Perfect goes on to argue that, in fact, the model of multiculturalism presented in *White Teeth* is inclusive and moves towards the familiar, rather than the unpredictable or accidental: 'While loudly professing to celebrate a model of multiculturalism premised on chance and contingency, *White Teeth* is ... a very calculated attempt to celebrate a very particular brand of multiculturalism; one that it ultimately seeks to familiarise' (p. 79). The next chapter looks at Monica Ali's London novels, tracing the controversy around her representation of the Sylheti community in east London in *Brick Lane* [2003]. Perfect asks whether the novel's mode should be identified as postmodern or realist, in an attempt to resolve questions about the stereotyping of characters such as Hasina and circumvent 'the tired "authentic" versus "commodified" critical binary' (p. 125). Chapter 5 traces the origins of Gautam Malkani's *Londonstani* [2006], to the author's sociological studies at Cambridge University. Malkani sought, Perfect argues, to investigate the recent trend for young Asian males growing up in London to adopt subcultural codes of behaviour and outlook that are seemingly more akin to African American subcultures and the hyper-masculinity found in some forms of gangsta rap. *Londonstani* draws from ethnographic interviews that dramatize the reasons behind this phenomenon. Chapter 6 discusses two novels addressing asylum and immigration: Chris Cleave's *The Other Hand* [2008]—published in the UK under the title of *Little Bee*—and Brian Chikwava's *Harare North* [2009]. Perfect shows the different ways these novels 'intervene in recent political debates about immigration and multiculturalism in Britain' (p. 158). The final main chapter compares Stephen Kelman's *Pigeon English* [2011] to Malkani's *Londonstani*; and the book ends with a coda speculating on the implications of the continuing interest in London-based novels that address the theme of multiculturalism, set against the fact that the most popular (in terms of both critical reception and commercial success) were produced early in the first decade of the twenty-first century (*White Teeth*, *Brick Lane*, and *Small Island*). A valuable contribution to the increasing interest in the contemporary literature of London that highlights the range and diversity of writing associated with postcolonial, black, and Asian fiction, *Contemporary Fictions of Multiculturalism* also includes a collection of London photographs by Ian Moir.

   Along with Perfect's book, *Andrea Levy: Contemporary Critical Perspectives*, edited by Jeanette Baxter and David James, confirms Levy's positive reception amongst recent writers associated with the label of 'black British fiction'. The editors' introduction (pp. 1–8) addresses Levy's place within the canon of twenty-first-century fiction and the politics of canon formation generally. Following writers like John McLeod, they ask whether the categorization of fiction along ethnic and racial lines can serve to re-ghettoize certain writers within a general field of contemporary literary production. Levy's status, therefore, as a part of this category needs to be scrutinized in a broader context, especially since the comedic qualities of her work mean that it has not been taken as seriously as other work by her contemporaries. Redressing this misrepresentation Baxter and James argue that Levy is seriously concerned to explore the 'relationship between the colonial past and the postcolonial present' and 'reconfigure the narrative of national literary culture by introducing transnational literary forms, voices and influences' (p. 3). In the first chapter, Dave Gunning argues that Levy's first two novels, *Every Light in the House Burnin'* [1994] and *Never Far from Nowhere* [1996], problematize the traditional *Bildungsroman* form by not allowing the central characters a happy resolution to their search for a place within the societies in which they are trying to establish their lives. Matthew Taunton also considers *Never Far from Nowhere*, but concentrates on its location on a council estate in north London. As Taunton argues, in the novel, 'characters are frequently defined by the spaces in which they live' and this allows Levy to examine the class divisions and structures in contemporary Britain (p. 23). This focus allows Taunton to examine Levy's reconsideration of the way in which council estates have garnered a particular set of social and cultural resonances in British fiction and how this opens up broader questions about the politics of the Welfare State. In chapter 3, Michael Perfect considers aspects of literary form in Levy's fiction and in particular the role of narrative memory in her first novel *Every Light in the House Burnin'*. Examining the relationship between memory and trauma, Perfect's close readings shows how Levy's novel exceeds the bounds of realism to reveal how past and present relate to each other through the consciousness of individual characters. This provides an important reading of a novel that has often gone under the radar in Levy criticism and demonstrates that it should in fact be seen as prefiguring similar concerns with past and present in Levy's later and better-known fiction. Next, David James's reading of *Small Island* [2004] moves away from the usual focus on its realist account of the racial and class politics of the Windrush generation and focuses on its inventive play of syntax, diction, and rhythm. As James shows, Levy is able to convey the immediacy of personal actions and experiences while at the same time maintaining the historical long view. Rachel Carroll then offers the first critical reading of the BBC's adaptation of *Small Island*, arguing that significant structural decisions and omissions were intended to make the adaptation more palatable for a 'mass audience' (p. 76). The decision to remove the white character Bernard's racist attitudes, Carroll argues, 'underplays the representation of racist sentiment by ordinary British subjects which is given such a frank and provocative expression in Levy's novel' (p. 76).

In chapter 6, Jeanette Baxter explores Levy's most recent work, reading the *Fruit of the Lemon* [2011] and *The Long Song* [2010] as kinds of 'exquisite corpse' in which an un/folding reveals the relationships between the two novels, and also between the 'complex relations between verbal/written historical accounts and individual /collective acts of individual storytelling'

(p. 79). This innovative approach is not only revealing in relation to these two novels, but also across Levy's writing more generally. Fiona Tolan's contribution considers narrative technique in *The Long Song*: connecting feminist and postcolonial analyses, she places the novel in dialogue with an emerging tradition of the postcolonial *Bildungsroman*. Susan Alice Fischer's chapter discusses *The Long Song*, tracing one source for the novel, a painting Levy saw in Kenwood House: *Dido Elizabeth Belle and Lady Elizabeth Murray*. The illegitimate daughter of Sir John Lindsay, Dido was a woman of African descent, and her costume and Lady Elizabeth's position at the centre of the image allow Fischer to discuss how *The Long Song* repositions the black subject at the centre of the narrative. The book closes with the transcripts of two conversations between Levy and Fischer in 2005 and 2012. Taken as a whole, the book provides an important contribution to and milestone in the development of a critical body of work dedicated to Levy and plays its own part in establishing her in the canon of contemporary British fiction.

Amongst articles focusing on post-2000 British fiction, Laura E. Savu's 'Bearing Wit(h)ness: "Just Emotions" and Ethical Choices in Chris Cleave's *Little Bee*' (*Critique* 55:i[2014] 90–102) draws on theoretical work by Sara Ahmed and Emmanuel Levinas to discuss the ethics of encountering the other in Cleave's novel. Savu offers timely discussion of the experience of the asylum-seeker and refugee, focusing on the eponymous character, a refugee from Nigeria, and her encounter with a British woman, Sarah, after the former flees to Britain. This follows an earlier encounter between Little Bee and Sarah and her husband, Anthony, on a beach in Nigeria just after Little Bee's village has been attacked. By staging this plotline through the dual narrative perspective of the two main female protagonists, Savu argues convincingly that Cleave's novel explores the experience of the refugee by setting it against the normative narrative of the British character, and this is achieved by allowing two narrators' accounts to merge and overlap as the novel progresses. This is a timely and thoughtful reading of a novel that promises to become a staple in the criticism of contemporary fiction.

Addressing a text which has already achieved canonical status, Yugin Teo's 'Testimony and the Affirmation of Memory in Kazuo Ishiguro's *Never Let Me Go*' (*Critique* 55:ii[2014] 127–37) argues that this text marks Ishiguro's return to the consistent tone of narration of *Remains of the Day* [1989], after the more experimental narrative techniques of *The Unconsoled* [1995] and *When We Were Orphans* [2000]. Teo focuses on the importance of memory, drawing on Paul Ricoeur, Susan Rubin Suleiman on the Holocaust, and Susannah Radstone and Katharine Hodgkin's *Regimes of Memory*. Memory, here, comprises the strain between an individual's sense of self and a collective history, the difference between private and public memory and the need for witness in the face of atrocity, which lie at the heart of *Never Let Me Go*.

Discussing the figure of the hacker in contemporary culture, Philip Leonard's 'A Revolution in Code: Hari Kunzru's *Transmission* and the Cultural Politics of Hacking' (*TPr* 28:ii[2014] 267–87) argues that hackers have moved from being seen as either loner computer geniuses out for personal gain or campaigners for the liberty of information to more dangerous figures who may very well threaten national security. Leonard draws on Manuel Castells's emphasis on the differing hierarchies within digital culture and McKenzie Wark's distinction between the hacker and the hacktivist to provide contexts for understanding Kunzru's narrative of transglobal technological workflows. 'In *Transmission*', Leonard concludes, 'the sovereignty of international agents is no longer seen as the source of political action, there are no representatives who have the authority to pronounce on either its illegal or interventionist character, and those who are associated with it neither combine to form an organized hacker movement nor adopt a coherent hacker ethic' (p. 283). Leonard's reading captures the complexities of Kunzru's novel in its engagement with the politics of cosmopolitanism as it is manifest in the economics of contemporary technological systems. A slightly altered version of this article appears in Leonard's *Literature After Globalization: Textuality, Technology and the Nation-State*, which also has chapters on contemporary American fiction.

4. Pre-1950 Drama

Recent publications on early twentieth-century drama include an updated reference resource, an anthology of plays on the First World War, and a couple of works on music and theatre. Syracuse University Press appears to have cornered the market in books on Irish drama, and several books have appeared on pageants, the Abbey Theatre, and women dramatists

J.P. Wearing's epic series of reference books on the London stage has proved an invaluable resource for theatre scholars since it first started to appear in the 1970s. Covering details about productions at every major London theatre from the 1890s to the 1950s, *The London Stage: A Calendar of Plays and Players* eventually spanned sixteen volumes. The indexes have now been republished in two monumental editions, which retain the same chronological divisions into decades (1890-9, 1900-0, etc.) with related material. This new publication also includes four key indexes to aid information-gathering: general, genre, theatre, and title. While there has been the occasional quibble about discrepancies with production figures, Wearing's work remains the most reliable and informative source on plays in London during the first half of the twentieth century, and many will find this two-volume edition of great help.

Given the current interest in the First World War, it is surprising how little of its drama is in print. It was therefore pleasing to hear that Mark Rawlinson, well known for his research on the literature of war, was editing a volume on *First World War Plays*. Rather disappointingly, the choice of seven plays spans 1916 to 2010 rather than being from the period, though the selection is intelligently made, and a useful introduction frames and contextualizes the material. *Night Watches* [1916] by Allan Monkhouse, one of the 'Manchester School' of dramatists, takes the form of a one-act comedy, but its theme is that of trauma and it was one of the first plays to consider the psychological effects of warfare. Rawlinson's introduction provides a helpful analysis of what was then a new scientific branch of study. Alice Dunbar Nelson's *Mine Eyes have Seen* [1918] redresses Ando-centric views of the First World War by providing an African American perspective. It first appeared in *The Crisis*, the official magazine of the National Association for the Advancement of Colored People (NAACP). Hubert Griffith's estimable *Tunnel Trench* [1924] is at the forefront of a wave of plays about the war which appeared in the 1920s and 1930s. Its mixture of realism and symbolism provided the new kind of stage language required for representing the horrors of the battlefield. Noel Coward's *Post-Mortem* [1930] was the dramatist's bitter response to war after acting in R.C. Sherriff's *Journey's End* two years after it first appeared in 1928. Coward was dissatisfied with his play, which he felt he had written too fast and with a lack of critical distance. The anthology is completed by other works, including Theatre Workshop's *Oh What a Lovely War* [1963], Peter Whelan's *The Accrington Pals* [1981], and Abigail Docherty's *Sea and Land and Sky* [2010].

Articles on theatre and the First World War include Tim Crook's 'Vocalizing the Angels of Mons: Audio Dramas as Propaganda in the Great War of 1914 to 1918' (*Societies* 4:ii[2014] 180–221). This provides a fascinating account of an obscure topic: phonograph discs recorded for propaganda reasons and played mainly to potential recruits or serving soldiers. Crook looks at the myth of the Angels of Mons, which revolved around heavenly figures who supposedly appeared to the British Expeditionary Forces on the Western Front in 1914 to aid their victory. This form of sound drama became a small but important part of a modern media machine, designed to 'inform, motivate, comfort and amuse' (p. 215). A special edition of *Shakespeare* about Shakespeare and the Great War included Claire Calvo's 'Celebrating the Tercentenary in Wartime: J.M. Barrie's *Shakespeare's Legacy* and the YWCA in 1916' (*Shakespeare* 10:iii[2014] 261–75). Barrie wrote the one-act *Shakespeare's Legacy* for the Young Women's Christian Association, and his suggestion that the Bard was Scottish 'questions Shakespeare's symbolic value as an Englishman' (p. 272).

In the fulsome *Masques, Mayings and Music-Dramas: Vaughan Williams and the Early Twentieth-Century Stage*, Roger Savage provides an insight into English music-theatre in the early part of the twentieth century. The book describes the revivification of early music, such as that used in May festivals, masques, mumming, and pageants. Its strongest elements are the connections made between artists, places, and ideas. In several essays, the figure of Ralph Vaughan Williams and the locations of Bayreuth, Glastonbury, and Stratford-upon-Avon are very much at the centre. Vaughan Williams associated with Edward Gordon Craig and Sergei Diaghilev and drew upon European traditions, while also championing a pastoral Englishness. The image of the pilgrim-vagabond as filtered through the work of Matthew Arnold and Robert Louis Stevenson became a personal motif for Vaughan Williams, as did the music of Purcell. Savage also considers the revival of the Arts and Crafts movement, feminism, nationalism, and the pursuit of the Wagnerian community festival. All in all, this is an important book which does much to show the richness of music-theatre at this time, and its ability to cross cultural, temporal, and geographical boundaries.

The more commercial form of musical theatre is explored by editors Len Platt, Tobias Becker, and David Linton in *Popular Musical Theatre in London and Berlin: 1890–1939*. This book has a wide remit, concentrating on the 'transnational network' (p. 2) by which cultural exchange took place. This engrossing area of scholarship shows the strong theatrical links that existed at this time between Britain, Europe, and America. The emphasis on London and Berlin counters the notion of Anglo-German hostilities in the early twentieth century. As the editors' introduction (pp. 1–22) states, 'London and Berlin theatre zones become complex sites of fundamental contradiction, not least in the sense that both are deeply inscribed with markers of local and national identity and yet both are representative of a modern cosmopolitan commons' (p. 3). There are three sections: 'The Mechanics of Transfer and Translation', 'Atlantic Traffic', and the enigmatically titled 'Representations in Transition—Cultural Transfer/Stage Others'. Topics include Peter Bailey on the Americanization of the West End revue before the First World War (pp. 135–52) and Viv Gardner on Edwardian music comedy and gender (pp. 202–23). Tobias Becker looks at *The Arcadians* [1909] (pp. 81–101), correctly described as 'the quintessential Edwardian musical play' (p. 83), and shows the process by which this wildly popular work was adapted for other countries; in contrast, Derek B. Scott's chapter (pp. 62–80) shows how German operettas were changed for a British audience. This collection has much to recommend it and is wide-ranging in subject matter, not just focusing on musical theatre but on problems of adaptation as well.

Joan FitzPatrick Dean's *All Dressed Up: Modern Irish Historical Pageantry* is a handsomely illustrated and finely researched work on the history of Irish pageants during the twentieth century. Dean traces the accelerant to this form of participatory spectacle to the 1905 Sherborne Pageant, created by Louis Napoleon Parker and designed to provide a history of this town in Dorset up to the end of the sixteenth century. Anti-modernist and anti-commercial, Parker wrote lists of rules for those wanting to utilize the pageant form, but while it was hugely influential, Dean points to significant differences between the English and Irish pageants: 'Unlike Parker's and other English pageants, Irish historical pageants addressed the emergent or young nation rather than a village or town to suggest a venerable native history that has been long suppressed by a colonial power' (p. 20).

The central premise of *Beyond Realism: Experimental and Unconventional Irish Drama since the Revival*, edited by Dean with José Lanters, is that Irish theatre since the creation of the Abbey Theatre has been dominated by realism. This may be surprising, given the attention already accorded to, for example, the influence of Noh theatre on Yeats, the poeticism of Synge, and the experimentation of O'Casey. However, the essays provide much useful information on Irish theatre during the twentieth century, especially on less well-known works. Amongst the most interesting is Michael Pierse's '*Cock-a-Doodle Dandy*: O'Casey's Total Theatre' (pp. 45–62). This 1949 parable about the attempted religious suppression of Dionysian festivities stands in contrast to the dramatist's realistic Dublin Trilogy but has much to say about liberty and repression, highlighted by the banning of the play by the Catholic Church. Other useful essays include Christopher Collins's ' "This World of Inarticulate Power": J.M. Synge's *Riders to the Sea* and Magical Realism' (pp. 13–37), Fiona Brennan's ' "Magic and Menace": A Re-evaluation of George Fitzmaurice's *The Magic Glasses*' (pp. 38–62), Alexandra Poulain's 'The Passion of Harry Heegan: Sean O'Casey's *The Silver Tassie*' (pp. 63–75), and

Akiko Satake's 'Jack B. Yeats' *In Sand*: An Experiment in the Toy Theatre' (pp. 93–106).

Elizabeth Mannion's *The Urban Plays of the Early Abbey Theatre: Beyond O'Casey*, continues the trend of recuperating the Abbey Theatre's oeuvre. She starts when the theatre was founded in 1904 until 1951 when the original building was burnt down, and also touches on the work of the Gate Theatre, the Theatre of Ireland, the Irish Theatre Company, and the Irish Workers' Dramatic Club. The general view until comparatively recently was that the Abbey Theatre's focus was mainly upon rural drama until the appearance of O'Casey's Dublin Trilogy in the 1920s. Here, Mannion's research in the theatre's archives has unearthed a wide range of over fifty city-based dramas which owe little or nothing to O'Casey. One of the most skilful parts of the book is the reconstruction of a lost work by Matthew Brennan, *A Leprechaun in the Tenement* [1922]. This title is interesting, given that the playing space was a similar size to an average tenement. A subtle argument emerges, suggesting that the Abbey's urban plays subverted the theatre's cultural nationalist premise from within by exposing its problems. As Mannion suggests, given the extreme poverty of the working classes at this time, 'it is not surprising that the dominant social concern is the institutional maintenance of a ghettoized working-class poor. What is unexpected is the extent to which the nationalist movement is portrayed as failing, and in some cases oppressing, the working classes' (pp. 2–3).

Eileen Kearney and Charlotte Headrick, the editors of *Irish Women Dramatists 1908–2001* are both theatre practitioners as well as scholars. They bring the wealth of their experience to the fractious subject of women's near-invisibility in a patriarchal theatre industry. The anthology consists of a long introductory essay which considers the contribution women have made to the English-language Irish theatre from the seventeenth century to Irish drama in the twentieth century. This wide remit means, though, that several fascinating areas are only touched upon. For example, it would have been interesting to hear more about the work of the suffragette Alice Milligan. The main part of the book is taken up with the text of seven plays by women that span the twentieth century. Oddly, while there are only two plays from the earlier part of the period—Lady Gregory's *The Workhouse Ward* [1908] and Teresa Deevy's *The King of Spain's Daughter* [1935]—the remaining five derive from the 1980s onwards. This unexplained historical gap does nothing to dispel the view that women's voices were little heard in early Irish theatre, which is disappointing given the editors' good intentions and wide historical overview. As with Mark Rawlinson's anthology, the trend for publications seems to be towards covering a large time-frame rather than delving in detail into a smaller period. Articles published on Irish drama include Tanya Dean's 'Staging Hibernia: Female Allegories of Ireland in *Cathleen ní Houlihan* and *Dawn*' (*THStud* 33[2014] 71–82), which considers anthropomorphic representations of Ireland as a woman in plays by W.B. Yeats and Augusta Gregory and by Maud Gonne, an ironic contrast with women's sidelining in Irish politics.

5. Post-1950 Drama

Amidst a relatively quiet year for work on postwar drama, 2014 has seen some noteworthy major studies of individual writers. A number of articles have also undertaken welcome re-evaluations of particular dramatists and practitioners. Cristina Delgado-García's 'Dematerialised Political and Theatrical Legacies: Rethinking the Roots and Influences of Tim Crouch's Work' (*Plat* 8:i[2014] 69–84) provides a welcome reassessment of the playwright in terms of the political efficacy in his work, as well as drawing attention to Crouch's early career in the 1980s through his involvement in a recognizable 'political' theatre company, according to common understandings of this term. Delgado-García's also looks at the ideological and aesthetic cross-over in Crouch's work and the relationship this has with conceptual art.

In 'Dealing with Martin Crimp' (*CTR* 24:iii[2014] 309–14), her introduction to a special issue of *Contemporary Theatre Review*, Vicky Angelaki argues that while appearing to be located on the periphery of British playwriting, his work 'is as much part of the Royal Court's narrative as the institution is of Crimp's playwriting' (p. 310). In the same volume, Angelaki's '*Alles Weitere kennen Sie aus dem Kino*: Martin Crimp at the Cutting Edge of Representation' (*CTR* 24:iii[2014] 315–30) examines work produced in 2012 and describes her own experience of seeing Crimp's adaptation of Euripides' *The Phoenician Women* at the Schauspielhaus in Hamburg (so far this production has not been performed in the UK). Angelaki also recounts another German premiere, of *Alles Weitere kennen Sie aus dem Kino*. Aloysia Rosseau's '"Didn't See Anything, Love Sorry": Martin Crimp's Theatre of Denial' (*CTR* 24:iii[2014] 342–52) argues that 'the line which separates denial from repression is a very thin one' (p. 342), listing and analysing a number of strategies that articulate this sense of denial, such as 'displacement, reinterpretation, and concealment' (p. 343). Eléonore Obis's '*Fewer Emergencies* in Paris: Interpreting the "Blank"' (*CTR* 24:iii[2014] 390–5) explores the 2008 Paris premiere of Martin Crimp's trilogy, *Fewer Emergencies* [2005]. In a similar vein, Mireia Aragay, Clara Escoda, and Enric Monforte's 'Martin Crimp at Sala Beckett, Barcelona' (*CTR* 24:iii[2014] 378–89) looks at the reception of Crimp's debut in Spain on the Catalan stage. They observe that Crimp's work as a text-based playwright marks it apart from a theatre culture that seems more comfortable with the devised work of companies such as Els Joglars, Comedians, and La Fura dels Baus. Through this cultural divide, the authors explore *The Country* [2000], *Attempts on Her Life* [1997], and *The City* [2008]. Liz Tomlin's 'Citational Theory in Practice: A Performance Analysis of Characterisation and Identity in Katie Mitchell's Staging of Martin Crimp's Texts' (*CTR* 24:iii[2014] 373–7) considers the notion of identity in a number of works by Crimp. Describing their indeterminate nature, she argues that characters' voices 'regularly interrupt, continue, or contradict each other's narratives, thus preventing any conclusive version of the dramatic reality to settle as definitive' (p. 373). Tomlin explores these ideas by looking in more detail at *The City* and *Attempts on Her Life*, his adaptation of Ferdinand Bruckner's *The Pains of Youth* [2009]. Elizabeth Angel-Perez's 'Martin Crimp's Nomadic Voices' (*CTR* 24:iii[2014] 353–62) visits similar territory to Tomlin, observing that the characters act more as narrators than as actors. Like Tomlin, Angel-Perez concludes that this process 'blurs the contours of the self' (p. 353), concentrating in particular on Crimp's collaborations with composer George Benjamin on *Into the Little Hill* [2006] and *Written on the Skin* [2012], which she identities as post-Beckettian works. Elizabeth Sakellaridou's 'Cruel or Tender? Protocols of Atrocity, New and Old' (*CTR* 24:iii[2014] 363–72) provides comparative analysis of Crimp's classical adaptations. She examines *Cruel and Tender* [2004], his adaptation of Sophocles' *Trachiniae*, alongside another classical Greek tragedy on the King Herakles myth that Crimp consulted, Euripides' *The Madness of Herakles*. Sakallaridou argues that Crimp's attraction to this classical material also follows a pattern in his contemporary plays, namely a fascination with cruelty. Rachel Clements's 'Deconstructive Techniques and Spectral Technologies in Katie Mitchell's *Attempts on Her Life*' (*CTR* 24:iii[2014] 331–41) sees Crimp's plays lending themselves particularly well to Derridean deconstruction, which she believes also marked the approach taken by director Katie Mitchell in her staging of two productions she directed in 1999 and 2007. In the 'Backpages' section of the volume there are also a number of shorter pieces on Crimp's work, including 'Bringing *In the Republic of Happiness* to the Royal Court Stage' (*CTR* 24:iii[2014] 410–11), by Dominic Cooke, former artistic director of the Royal Court. This discusses his involvement as the director of Crimp's latest play in Britain, interpreting it as 'a hilarious and terrifying dissection on the doctrine of individualism' (p. 410). Cooke also provides an informative account of the rehearsal process. Sam Walters's 'Martin Crimp Has Arrived' (*CTR* 24:iii[2014] 412–13) is a recollection from the former founder and artistic director of Orange Tree Theatre in Hampstead, which staged much of Crimp's early work. Walters observes that, even during the first stage of his career, it was apparent that Crimp's work denied easy categorization.

Crimp's one-time contemporary Sarah Kane continues to accrue fresh scholarship. Louise Le Page's 'Rethinking Sarah Kane's Characters: A Human(ist) Form and Politics' (*MD* 57:ii[2014] 252–72) is an admirably thoughtful reassessment of character in Kane's work. Using *Blasted* [1995] as her primary case study, Le Page takes issue with a general critical consensus, that characterization in the play moves from formal naturalism to an animalistic or degraded humanity. Le Page argues that, instead, we should rethink Kane's work through the imagery of collage and conglomerate that Strindberg outlines in his Preface to *Miss Julie* [1881].

Howard Barker, a dramatist who had a profound influence on Kane's work, is the subject of Matthew Roberts's 'From Pain, Poetry: Howard Barker's *Blok/Eko* and the Poetics of Plethoric Theater' (*CD* 48:iii[2014] 261–76), which takes its cue from Barker's prose work *Death, the One and the Art of the Theatre* [2004] and draws attention to the subject of death being 'the very condition that makes poetry possible' (p. 263). The article includes a lengthy close reading of Barker's play *Blok/Eko* [2011] as part of a wider discourse that the play explores through the field of medicine, the individual, and society.

John McGrath's 7:84 theatre company also receives a fresh evaluation in Linda Mackenny's 'The Oppositional Theatre of McGrath and MacLennan in

Scotland, 1989–96' (*NTQ* 30:iv[2014] 352–64). This examines four plays written by McGrath between 1989 and 1996, the period after he resigned as artistic director of 7:84, arguing convincingly that this later work has been relatively neglected due to the reputation of work that the company produced during the 1970s. However, in her analysis of *Border Warfare* [1989], *John Brown's Body* [1989], *The Silver Darlings* [1994], and *A Satire of the Fourth Estate* [1996], Mackenny looks beyond established narratives that often only focus on the demise of the company. K.S. Morgan McKean's 'Into the Darkest Places: Pursuing Politics in the Plays of Phyllis Nagy' (*CTR* 24:i[2014] 66–81) makes the case for understanding Nagy as a political dramatist. This position challenges former interpretations that either placed her as a representative of the 'In Yer Face' drama of the 1990s, or as a postmodern trickster. McKean considers the problems such interpretations bring, as well as looking at how such views have obscured the politics operating in general within many of the plays of the 1990s. These include issues active at the time as well as the prophetic effect that plays such as *Weldon Rising* [1992] and *The Strip* [1995] offered in terms of globalization and the banking crash of 2007.

Charlotte Bell's 'Cultural Practices, Market Disorganization, and Urban Regeneration: Royal Court Theatre Local Peckham and Peckham Space' (*CTR* 24:ii[2014] 192–208) explores two examples of urban regeneration through theatre and discusses the Royal Court's staging of Rachel De-lahay's *The Westbridge* [2011], although the article is critical that such initiatives have been at the expense of older cultural institutions in the area such as the Peckham Settlement.

Bell is also co-author, with Katie Beswick, of 'Authenticity and Representation: Council Estate Plays at the Royal Court' (*NTQ* 30:ii[2014] 120–35), which discusses, amongst others, De-Lahay's *The Westbridge* and Bola Agbaje's *Off the Endz* [2010]. The authors approach these plays through the ways they have been marketed by the theatre for their social authenticity and explore the dangers inherent in this strategy by rendering such drama into what they call 'oppressive imaginings of council estate spaces and residents' (p. 121).

Sara Freeman's 'Gay Sweatshop, Alternative Theatre, and Strategies for New Writing' (*NTQ* 30:ii[2014] 136–53) takes a welcome look at the later history of this influential company, a period which has not received a great amount of scholarly attention to date. Freeman examines the work produced during the tenure of Gay Sweatshop's last artistic director, Lois Weaver, and focuses on events coinciding with the company's tenth-anniversary new play festival in 1985. She argues that this became a marker for policies the company had previously been pursuing through new writing against the new perform-ance-based and -devised work direction in which Weaver wanted to take the company: the article charts how the tensions within these two strands of practice eventually led to the break-up of the company.

Issues of gender are also the subject of Geraldine Harris's 'Post-Feminism? Amelia Bullmore's *Di and Viv and Rose*, April de Angelis's *Jumpy* and Karin Young's *The Awkward Squad*' (*CTR* 24:ii[2014] 177–1). In some ways this article is a continuation of the work Harris produced with her co-author Elaine Aston in their monograph *A Good Night Out for the Girls: Popular*

Feminisms in Theatre and Performance [2013]. Here Harris looks at the position of the three plays in an environment that she identifies as post-feminist, but one where feminism now appears to be 'fashionable' (p. 179), again after a period of what Harris calls 'Feminism fatigue' (p. 180).

Edward Bond's short play *Passion* [1971] is the subject of Tony Coult's forensic performance case study, 'A Passion Play at Ally Pally (*STP* 34:i[2014] 3–37), which is based on his attendance at its inaugural performance at the CND Festival of Life at Alexander Palace in April 1971. The article is also accompanied and completed by a number of photographs of the event taken by the author. Peter Gill directed Bond's *The Fool* at the Royal Court in 1975, and Barney Norris's *To Bodies Gone: The Theatre of Peter Gill* provides an admirable synthesis of the some of the governing philosophical concerns of his diverse output as an actor, director, and playwright. Norris locates Gill's own drama somewhere between a heightened form of naturalism and a process that rejects the form's essential pessimism about the human condition for humanist values. At the same time Norris also identifies an often overlooked radical dimension to the dramatic form that Gill has introduced into his plays that functions below the surface level of meticulous social detail. Examples of this are discussed in monologues such as *Small Change* [1978] and the disrupted chronologies of *Kick for Touch* [1983]. Norris's book also explores the relationship between Gill the director and Gill the dramatist, arguing that the two productively cross-fertilize, particularly when it comes to Gill directing his own work—a practice that has been a notoriously fraught experience for other dramatists. The book's approach also makes informative use of interview material from Gill's colleagues, including Kenneth Cranham, William Gaskill, and Max Stafford Clark. Discussion of directing work inevitably focuses on Gill's celebrated revival of D.H. Lawrence's work at the Royal Court between 1967 and 1968, but also includes a comprehensive assessment of work from *The Sleeper's Den* [1965] to *Versailles* [2014]. Given Gill's roots, the work is also approached by locating it geographically and psychologically within a Welsh context.

In one of the first major studies since Harold Pinter's death in 2008, Mark Taylor-Batty's *The Theatre of Harold Pinter* not only supplies a comprehensive chronological treatment of his prodigious output but also offers a valuable reassessment of his reputation. While the book revisits familiar areas such as gender, time and space, and the family, Taylor-Batty also manages to discover fresh perspectives, including Pinter's excursions into other forms of media such as film, television, and the wireless. The other new strand that the book pursues is Pinter's development as a political dramatist, from the embryonic beginnings in work such *The Birthday Party* [1958] to Pinter's Nobel Prize lecture in 2005. While Taylor-Batty provides most of the text, there also are a number of chapters from other contributors in keeping with the format of this Methuen series: Harry Burton's 'The Curse of Pinter' (pp. 192–214) addresses many aspects of Pinter's stagecraft, including the role of the audience and acting Pinter's characters; Chris Megson's 'Who the Hell's That? Pinter's Memory Plays of the 1970s' (pp. 215–31) makes a fascinating comparison between what some critics have seen as a move towards solipsism and introspection in the 1970s when set against the avowedly socialist turn that

Pinter's contemporaries were pursuing at the time; Ann C. Hall's 'Revisiting Pinter's Women: *One for the Road* (1984), *Mountain Language* (1988) and *Party Time* (1991)' (pp. 232–48) tackles the complex and contentious issue of gender in three plays, identifying their female characters as essentially victims, who somewhat disturbingly are complicit in their victimhood; and Basil Chiasson's 'Pinter's Political Dramas: Staging Neoliberal Discourse and Authoritarianism' (pp. 249–67) returns to the issue of politics, observing that while Pinter avoided any engagement with Thatcherism in his 1980s drama, he did so retrospectively in the 1990s.

R. Darren Gobert's equally impressive collection, *The Theatre of Caryl Churchill*, appeared in the same series. Like Taylor-Batty's volume, Gobert's also achieves a remarkable act of synthesis with another highly prolific and long-established dramatist, while at the same time providing a number of fresh perspectives on a playwright whose work is much discussed and analysed. Gobert primarily adopts an archival and materialist approach, ranging from Churchill's rarely discussed television drama to production files at the Royal Court Theatre, the Manhattan Theatre, and the New York Theatre Workshop and materials contained within the Public Theater in New York. Each chapter contains perceptive close readings of specific plays, often relating them to their production histories. This archival approach often includes analysis of revealing items such as contracts and balance sheets, that Gobert fashions into convincing arguments. He observes, for example, that, within the market-driven world of the theatre, Churchill has been able to plot a career without compromising what he calls 'her collaborative relationships ... to the "cash nexus"' (p. xiii). The materialist focus of the first two chapters shifts a little in the third chapter, 'Identity and the Body', where the plays, *Cloud Nine* [1979], *Ice Cream* [1989], and *Mad Forest* [1990] are examined in terms of the onstage bodies of the actors. Chapter 4 relocates to the rehearsal room and discusses Churchill's collaborative work over the years in *Light Shining in Buckinghamshire* [1976], *Fen* [1983], and *Mad Forest*, work that Gobert sees as ethical and political forms of co-operation. In his final chapter, Gobert examines how a select group of plays, *Traps* [1978], *Blue Heart* [1997], and *Love and Information* [2012], function as theatrical performances. Chapters by other contributors include Elaine Aston's 'The "Picasso" of Modern British Playwrights' (pp. 201–13), which gives a useful overview of Churchill's career in the context of British theatre culture over the past fifty years, while Sian Adiseshiah's '"The Times" of Caryl Churchill's Theatre' (pp. 214–24) develops further some of the arguments from her previous study, *Churchill's Socialism: Political Resistance in the Plays of Cary Churchill* [2009] and brings things up to date with an analysis of Churchill's recent play, *Ding Dong the Wicked* [2012].

William Baker and Jeanette Roberts Shumaker's, *Bernard Kops: Fantasist, London Jew, Apocalyptic Humorist* is the first full-length study of a writer who is perhaps best known for his drama, but has also written poetry and novels. The authors make a convincing argument for reassessing Kops's historical importance within the 1950s 'new wave' drama, seeking to move him out of the peripheral position ascribed to him by most studies of the period. Accordingly Baker and Shumaker go back to one of Kops's best-known early plays, *The Hamlet of Stepney Green* [1957], arguing that the protagonist, David Levy, is representative of a more complex 'angry young man' than John Osborne's Jimmy Porter, perhaps by having more to be angry about. They point to Levy's marginalized position in adapting to a changing postwar East End, as someone haunted by the recent events of the Holocaust. The book provides a fascinating account of Jewish life in London and the various subcultures within London literary life during the 1940s and 1950s. It is arranged in seven thematic chapters which discuss all aspects of Kops's writing simultaneously, while subsections cater for the reader specifically interested in his drama. Kops's less well-known plays are also discussed throughout the volume, but of particular interest is the chapter 'Sex and Politics', which looks at reasons behind the poor reception given to some of his anti-nuclear war plays, including *The Dream of Peter Mann* [1960] as well as Kops's developing political activism during this period.

The contributors to Mireia Aragay and Enric Monforte's collection, *Ethical Speculations in Contemporary British Theatre* expand on what has been described as a recent 'ethical turn' in British drama. The first section, '(Post-)Holocaust Representations', examines the ways memory and dramatic representation operate in the work of several contemporary dramatists. Clara Escoda's 'Violence, Testimony and Ethics in Martin Crimp's *The Country* and *The City*' (pp. 25–41) argues that the shadow of the Holocaust, or the conditions that at least made it possible, continues to haunt the contemporary in both these two plays. Hanna Scolnicov's 'Bearing Witness and Ethical Responsibility in Harold Pinter's *Ashes to Ashes*' (pp. 42–58) and Mark Taylor-Batty's 'How to Mourn: Kane, Pinter and Theatre as Monument to Loss in the 1990s' (pp. 59–78) both look at Pinter's *Ashes to Ashes* [1996]. Scolnicov sees it as directly representative of the Holocaust, even while it makes no direct reference to the event, while Taylor-Batty sees the play as more concerned with issues of representation for the dramatist when confronting this catastrophic event, and also as part of debates from the mid-1990s in art and theatre about the representation of sex and violence. The media's response to Sarah Kane's *Blasted* [1995] is central here and Taylor-Batty perceives *Ashes to Ashes* as a decided response by Pinter to Kane's debut. The next section of the collection, 'Theoretical Speculations', includes Dan Rebellato's 'Two Duologues and the Differend' (pp. 79–5), where he observes that a significant number of new plays since 2000 have used the duologue as dramatic form. Rebellato ascribes this to a resurgence in ethical thinking, as the form encourages 'a fundamental ethical building block of human sociality' (p. 82). Martin Middeke's 'The Undecidable and the Event: Ethics of Unrest in Martin Crimp's *Attempts on Her Life* and debbie tucker green's *truth and reconciliation*' (pp. 96–116) compares the difficulty of interpretation in Crimp's play to the historical enquiries and commissions set up after human rights violations in places such as Rwanda, South Africa, and Bosnia as they are represented in green's play. The third part of the volume, 'Spectatorial Ethics', includes Clare Wallace's 'Playing with Proximity: Precarious Ethics on Stage in the New Millennium' (pp. 117–34), which focuses on Mark Ravenhill's *pool (no water)* [2006], Caryl Churchill's *Seven Jewish Children* [2009], Tim Crouch's *The Author* [2009], and David Greig's *Fragile* [2011] as examples of precarious states. Vicky Angelaki's 'Witness or Accomplice? Unsafe Spectatorship in the Work of

Anthony Neilson and Simon Stephens' (pp. 135–51) looks at *Relocated* [2008] and *Three Kingdoms* [2011]. Like Wallace, she identifies these works as unsettling for their audiences, particularly in regard to the audience's complicity in witnessing acts of women being abducted, tortured, and murdered. Enric Montforte's 'Witnessing, Sexualized Spectatorship and the (De)construction of Queer Identities in *Mother Clap's Molly House, The Pride* and *Cock*' (pp. 152–72) also talks of implicating audiences, although this time through interrogating queer identities. The final section, 'Ethics and Institutions', includes Christine Schlote's 'From Front Page to Front Stage: War Correspondents and Media Ethics in British Theatre' (pp. 173–89), which explores the representation of war reporting and war photography in recent plays, including Stella Feehily's *O Go My Man* [2006], David Hare's *The Vertical Hour* [2008], and Vivienne Franzman's *The Witness* [2012]. Finally, Graham Saunders's 'Kicking Tots and Revolutionary Tots: The English Stage Company Young People's Scheme 1969–1970' (pp. 190–206) argues that, at a time when the Royal Court faced accusations of ignoring fringe theatre, its Young People's Scheme, under the auspices of Jane Howell and Pam Brighton, covertly smuggled the ethics and sensibility of the counterculture into the theatre. This chapter draws extensively on archival sources from the English Stage Company and the Arts Council of Great Britain to look at three significant case studies that played upon fears generated by various moral panics circulating at the time: these include the 'On Violence' workshops to mark the 1969 Edward Bond season; the devised show *Revolution!*, in 1970 where children and adolescents were said to have been instructed in revolutionary techniques aimed at the overthrow of the state; and the revival that same year of Anne Jellicoe's *The Sport of My Mad Mother* for schools, which faced accusations of glamorizing gang violence.

Lastly, Margherita Laera's wide-ranging collection *Theatre and Adaptation: Return, Rewrite, Repeat* is notable for an interview with the dramatist Simon Stephens, who discusses his work in this area, including *The Trial of Ubu* [2012], a translation of Ibsen's *A Doll's House* [2012] and, most well-known, his adaptation of Mark Haddon's novel, *The Curious Incident of the Dog in the Night-Time* [2012].

6. British Poetry 1900–1950

(a) Poetry 1900–1950
While 2014 saw much interesting work in the field of British poetry before the war, this section starts with three works that were unavailable at the time of writing last year. Oliver Tearle's *T.E. Hulme and Modernism* seeks to redress critical emphasis on Hulme's influential theoretical writings at the expense of the poetry itself. Drawing on earlier critics such as C.H. Sisson, who spoke up for the value and achievement of Hulme the poet, Tearle pushes for a more integrated approach to his work, arguing that the poetry is 'a physical manifestation, or enactment, of the theory' (p. 1) rather than a minor afterthought, and thereby looking to challenge the enduring view of Hulme as mere 'ideas man' for modernism. Tearle points to the 'down-to-earth-ness' of

Hulme's poetry, and its sense of man's inherent limitations as a feature of the latter's adherence to 'classical' values (p. 19), while demonstrating how such poems as 'Mana Aboda' and 'Susan Ann and Immortality' incorporate the emotional and intuitive properties of the Romanticism to which such 'values' are ostensibly opposed. In so doing, Tearle gestures towards a proto-poststructuralist dimension to Hulme's work and thought, arguing that he 'inverts the privileged term in the binary pair of romantic/classical, but in doing so he cannot do away with the subordinate term, or romantic attitude altogether' (p. 33). The poetry is thus shown to be of value not least in highlighting those practicalities which the prose writings work to conceal, with attention called to the dual intuitive and intellectual properties of Hulme's work. The poem 'Autumn' is among those read as striking the right balance in this regard, demanding the employment of the intellect just as its imagery defies any such definitive analysis. Rich in insight, Tearle's book reveals a number of hitherto under-discussed literary and intellectual cross-currents, and shows how incomplete is any assessment of Hulme which neglects his poetic practice.

Andrew Webb's *Edward Thomas and World Literary Studies* positions itself against Anglocentrism within British literary studies, drawing on work by theorists such as Pascale Casanova in order to place Thomas's work within the emerging field of world literary space. Addressing Thomas's reception, Webb criticizes, amongst others: Tony Conran, who is upbraided for his portrayal of Thomas as 'a Welshman who effectively becomes English' (p. 53); R.S. Thomas, who is briefly (and, it must be said, unfairly) taken to task for discussing Thomas's poems 'only in relation to the English tradition of "Georgian verse"' (p. 54); and Andrew Motion, who is criticized for having 'no time for serious consideration of Thomas's Welshness' (p. 71). Similar charges are levelled against Matthew Hollis's memorable biography of 2011. In comparison, Webb seeks to 'reclaim Thomas for the Welsh tradition' (p. 77), offering a broader economic and political contextualization of Welsh literature at the turn of the century, before attending to the role of Welsh cultural tradition within Thomas's prose and poetic writings; the latter's interest in Yeats's drama (and associated promotion of writers associated with the Irish revival); and the internal conflict experienced by the poet with regard to his own national affiliation. While this is hardly a book for those new to Thomas's work, it can only help to raise the critical profile of a poet whose work has surely yet to receive its proper due.

Published in anticipation of Thomas's centenary, John Goodby's *The Poetry of Dylan Thomas: Under the Spelling Wall* is underpinned by the belief that Thomas's popular reputation continues to outstrip the critical esteem in which his work has been held. Goodby points to the fact that recurring questions of gender, nationality, and the indeterminate nature of Thomas's 'modernism' have all contributed to his uncertain positioning within the twentieth-century canon. Moreover, Goodby contends that English *and* Welsh neglect of Thomas's work has ensured that 'Thomas criticism is largely innocent of the theory revolution in English studies' (p. xi). Goodby thus embarks on a series of new readings of Thomas's work, with the aim of reappraising him not only in relation to his immediate literary contexts of modernism and the poetry of the 1930s and 1940s, but also, as the Derridean undertones of the title (which contains a quotation from Thomas's poem, 'How shall my animal') suggest, with a view to revising our understanding of Thomas's work in light of subsequent developments in critical theory. Thus, Goodby locates the meaning of such poems as 'A Refusal to Mourn the Death, by Fire, of a Child in London' in a place 'where the limits of language have been made manifest' (p. 354). Meanwhile, attention is drawn to the political dimensions of 'Fern Hill', which is read as helping to give shape to 'the complexity of wartime questionings concerning regression and utopian advance' (p. 360). Overall, this is a study which is challenging yet enlightening, and which undoubtedly represents a necessary step forward in Thomas scholarship.

Turning to work published in 2014, David N. Wells's 'Thomas Hardy's Poetry and International Modernism' (*THJ* 30[2014] 185–9) is concerned with broadening the contexts against which Hardy's poetry is read. Wells argues that, while Hardy's work has generally been closely associated with the English literary tradition (with Hardy having also been claimed as a transitional figure between the nineteenth and twentieth centuries), his poetic sensibility and practice may also be situated in relation to Anglo-American and European modernism. In support of this, Wells points, firstly, to the extent and significance of Hardy's influence on the poets who came after him, drawing attention to his continuing appeal to practising poets (Donald Davie is among those cited), as offering an 'alternative' modernism to that of Eliot or Yeats. Clearly emerging in part from the current vogue for adopting a more 'internationalist' approach to literary studies, Wells invokes Kirsten Blythe Painter's notion of 'tempered' modernism, which derives from attempt by groups including the American Imagists and the Russian Acmeists to overcome the symbolist legacy, extolling instead the virtues of 'clarity, precision, craftsmanship and objectivism'. Wells's claim for Hardy's own modernism thus emphasizes the corresponding metonymic specificity of the verse, which, it is argued, emerges from a 'highly concrete and specific' world-view, and broader 'alignment to the tangible' (p. 189).

In 'Affective Form: Hardy's Poetry and a Sculptural Aesthetic' (*THJ* 30[2014] 66–82), Marion Thain draws upon recent work on metre by Meredith Martin in order to re-examine Hardy's use of form. Thain places Hardy's use of fixed verse forms in context with the use of similar forms by Parnassian French poets and their British counterparts, but concludes by reading Hardy 'through a sculptural aesthetic' (p. 78). The 'spatial discourse' of his poems, combined with their 'typography on the page' (p. 79) renders the presence and absence of the individuals they commemorate.

Guy Cuthbertson's biography of Wilfred Owen begins by noting the thematic importance of the child and childhood within the poetry and observing, with some pathos, that many of those who fought in the First World War were themselves 'barely more than children in uniform.' (p. 4). Subsequent chapters address Owen's early literary interests (Keats features prominently), his private insecurities, and his relationships with his father and mother, before examining his untimely death in 1918 and subsequent literary 'afterlife'. Owen's mother, Susan, is a significant presence, who is, Cuthbertson argues, re-created by Owen as 'the personification of home, childhood, peace and poetry as an alternative to war and sex' (p. 133). In literary terms (as with his personal life) Owen is frequently portrayed as a figure apart; as Cuthbertson argues, 'Owen was *modern* but took a different road from modernism' (p. 138). Among the contemporary figures invoked are D.H. Lawrence, Yeats, and Housman, together with (Edward) Thomas, Brooke, and Sassoon. Cuthbertson posits a particular affinity with Housman, suggesting that Owen saw the latter's poems as 'fragments of his own biography' (p. 156). In terms of Owen's war experience and its effect on his poetry, Cuthbertson suggests that, contrary to previous accounts, his time spent ministering to the sick and dying in Dunsden (where he had been lay assistant to the Reverend Herbert Wigan), along with his military training, ensured that he 'knew about war and death' (p. 161) well before his arrival on the Western Front, and the biography refutes the view that such famous poems as 'Dulce et Decorum Est' accurately capture Owen's own attitude to the war. As well as its emphasis on the formative influences of Owen's early life, then, Cuthbertson's book is undoubtedly valuable for fostering a more refined understanding of the poetry itself.

Further work on the war poets is found in Andrew Scragg's 'Reconsidering a "Neglected Classic" and Widening the Canon of World War I Poetry: *The Song of Tiadatha*' (*ELT* 57:iv[2014] 463–79), which situates Edward Owen Rutter's mock-epic poem within the context of the author's war experiences as a captain in the 7th Battalion Wiltshire Regiment. A parody of Longfellow's *The Song of Hiawatha*, the poem's origin lies in Rutter's discovery of an abandoned copy of the book in a signaller's dugout in Salonica. Scragg maps the development of the resultant poem, which covers the main character's conscription and subsequent experiences in France and then Salonica. Addressing in-jokes and allusions, Scragg points out that the poem's language, in particular its deliberate inclusion of jargon words and phrases used by men in combat, indicates that Rutter produced the poem more for himself and his colleagues in Salonica than for wider circulation. Also noted is the difficulty involved in depicting with levity the commonly accepted brutality and dehumanization of the war: Scragg seeks to resolve this by pointing to the need for humour as a 'survival mechanism' in such circumstances, and maintaining that the poem's associated status as an 'entertainment' by no means justifies the critical neglect it has suffered. Rather, it is argued that re-evaluation of the poem, in part as an alternative to the singular view of Great War literature which is bound up with the lyric vision of such figures as Owen and Sassoon, offers the possibility of 'a wider understanding of the totality of the war' (p. 475).

Much of John Beer's *D.H. Lawrence: Nature, Narrative and Identity* focuses on the prose writings; of relevance here, however, is the chapter entitled 'The Nature of Lawrence's Poetry' (pp. 204–15). The broader aim of the book is towards 'making sense of [Lawrence's] writings as a whole' (p. 1); to this end, Beer's analyses are interwoven throughout with particular events in Lawrence's life, where these are able to further illuminate the work. Arguing for Lawrence's sense of 'the mythological significance of nature' (p. 204), coupled with his experience of nature's harsher realities (Beer cites the death of

Lawrence's mother), this chapter considers Lawrence's search for a poetry capable of expressing both nature's beauty and its violence, and explores the literary forebears (Keats, Tennyson, Coleridge, Whitman—the latter is cited as 'the most important influence', p. 209) to whom Lawrence looked in pursuit of this. In conjunction with this, Beer is attentive to Lawrence's struggle with poetic form, pointing to the latter's search for 'a way of expressing himself straightforwardly in poetry that would not mean abandoning his feeling for life and animation' (p. 213).

Florian Gargaillo's 'Tough Love: W.H. Auden and A.E. Housman' (*CQ* 43:ii[2014] 139–56) offers an interesting and worthwhile discussion of the nature and extent of Housman's influence on Auden's poetry. Pointing to the latter's reluctance to name his 'literary first love', Housman, as a significant influence, Gargaillo astutely observes that such early infatuations nonetheless 'have a way of staying with one beyond the confines of youth, and inflecting the sensibility of maturer years' (p. 140). The article thus identifies a complex relationship pervaded by a 'tough-minded give and take', and going beyond mere adulation or imitation. Among the examples offered is Auden's fourteenth sonnet on the Sino-Japanese war ('Yes, we are going to suffer, now; the sky / Throbs like a feverish forehead; pain is real'), which is read as adopting Housman's 'technique of reduction' (p. 147), so as to avoid the kind of sensationalism which might otherwise accompany a poem dealing with the carnage of military warfare. More generally, Gargaillo persuasively argues that Housman's brand of straightforward artistry was instrumental in creating in Auden's work 'neither a sense of cynicism nor even irony per se, but rather a strong willingness to counterbalance the pretensions of art with hard-nosed realism' (p. 149). To this extent, the article sheds useful new light on the genesis of a number of well-acknowledged traits within Auden's work.

Auden is also the subject of Stewart Cole's 'Love and Other Gods: Personification and Volition in Auden' (*TCL* 60:iii[2014] 367–6), which sets itself at the metaphysical questions surrounding Auden's conception of love within his poetry of the 1930s and 1940s. Cole examines the latter's deployment of a 'personified' love as a means of giving voice to its ambivalences, together with his subsequent bifurcation of love into Eros and Agape (one essentially selfish and the other social in character) as a step in his return to Christianity. Cole notes the tendency to view Auden's use of personification as a symptom of his 'playful and innovatory relationship to poetic tradition' (p. 371), in a way which tends to overlook its ontological implications, and proposes in response an exploration of the 'volitional' struggles in which the poet's personae are engaged. The article also seeks to establish the link between the Auden's turn away from personification and move from England to America in 1939, coupled with his return to the Anglican communion. Thus, whilst 'personification' within Auden's earlier poems serves as an allegorical tool by which he engages the warring forces within, and between, the public and private realms, the 'folded lie' of 'September 1, 1939' is, Cole argues, personification *itself*. Overall, he offers some fresh insight into the elusive character of much of Auden's earlier work, while highlighting the problematic nature of personification within twentieth-century poetry more generally.

A broader account of the literature of the 1930s, Benjamin Kohlmann's *Committed Styles: Modernism, Politics, and Left-Wing Literature in the 1930s* seeks to re-examine literature's adequacy as a vehicle for politics. Kohlmann sees this as exemplified in the politicized writings of the 1930s and assesses the implications for the enduring view of modernism as fundamentally apolitical. Among the chapters of relevance here is 'An Honest Decade: William Empson and the Uses of Poetry' (pp. 53–89), which examines Empson's often uneasy relationship to the ideological conflicts of the period, mapping his early engagement with the critical doctrines of I.A. Richards, in particular with the latter's notion of poetic 'sincerity', and later on with the associated—and even more fraught—concept of 'honesty'; a term which, as the author notes, has been of central importance to the myth of the 1930s. The ambiguities that inhere within Empson's own work are thus read as symptomatic of the difficult task of maintaining 'a precarious distance from the political and aesthetic pressures of the decade without claiming to isolate itself from them' (p. 68). Also of relevance is Kohlmann's third chapter, 'Between Communism and "Purity" of Style: The Revolutions of English Surrealism' (pp. 90–126), which focuses on the work of Thirties poets David Gascoyne and Hugh Sykes Davies, together with examining the links between English Surrealism in the 1930s and the history of French Surrealism (and the formative tensions between the latter and communism). Gascoyne's well-known *Short Survey of Surrealism* is, as Kohlmann notes, generally seen as foundational, though the chapter contends that it is the unpublished notes and occasional essays of the mid-1930s (such as 'Poetry and Reality') which are, in fact, more revealing of the development of the English Surrealist movement, sketching the blueprint for a 'politicized writing that is lodged outside the narrow confines of communist propaganda art' (p. 92). Meanwhile, Sykes Davies's pursuit of stylistic 'purity', as illustrated in his shorter prose poems, is in part seen as counter-productive, having the effect of narrowing down the range of English Surrealism's rhetorical options. Overall, Kohlmann's study offers a valuable new insight into the complex relationship between literature and politics in the 1930s and beyond.

(b) T.S. Eliot

The most significant publications in Eliot studies during 2014 were the first two volumes of his *Complete Prose* under the general editorship of Ronald Schuchard. Drawing heavily on the work of Donald Gallup, they bring together a great number of essays and reviews that Eliot did not republish during his lifetime, adding a wealth of unsigned or unacknowledged items that have been discovered since Gallup's bibliography was published in the 1950s. The first volume, covering the years 1905 to 1918, also reproduces transcriptions of previously unpublished documents, from stories written as a schoolboy to the essays on philosophy Eliot wrote during his studies at Harvard and Oxford. The second volume, covering 1919 to 1926, incorporates the Clarke Lectures previously published by Schuchard as *Varieties of Metaphysical Poetry* [1993].

Readers will pick their own paths through the wealth of material here, all of which is accompanied by extensive and learned annotations as well as lucid and thoughtful introductions to each phase of Eliot's career. The format of these volumes encourages a historically sensitive approach, carefully reproducing texts in the chronological sequence of their composition. Accordingly, in the first volume, Eliot's doctoral thesis on F.H. Bradley is now reproduced alongside his other early student writings, although Eliot didn't publish it until 1964. Read in sequence, lines of development spring out: Eliot's career as a critic began with his philosophical studies and early reviews for journals such as *The Monist* or the *International Journal of Ethics*; his famous theory of 'tradition' first emerges from a defence of his friend Ezra Pound's historical erudition; diagnosing a 'dissociation of sensibility' in 1921, Eliot suggested that the rot 'set in' during the seventeenth century; by 1926, nearly every poet after Dante had become suspicious; and so on.

It is unfortunate that readers will not be able to get their hands on physical copies of these volumes until the series as a whole is complete. Access is currently limited to an online subscription service. The editors hope to publish further ancillary material such as Eliot's notes online. But it is notable that little is done otherwise to take advantage of the edition's current digital format. Still, this is a major scholarly achievement to which all scholars of Eliot's work and intellectual historians of the twentieth century will be indebted.

Vincent Sherry's chapter on Eliot in *Modernism and the Reinvention of Decadence* (pp. 234–79) is an important contribution to ongoing work on the connections between Eliot and the 1890s. In contrast to the emphasis upon direct lines of influence adopted by Ronald Schuchard in *Eliot's Dark Angel* [1999], Sherry conceives of Decadence as a 'literary sensibility' (p. 40) and a 'temporal imaginary' (p. 38), characterized in part by an intimation of crisis: 'this is the age of the secondary and the circumstance of the posthumous' (p. 279). Although this vocabulary may be Lacanian, Sherry's thesis has a historical basis since he roots this intimation of crisis within anxieties about the imminent collapse of 'Britain's fading colonial domain' (p. 247). His approach is also grounded in close reading: Sherry's account of Eliot's early poetry, for example, argues that his apprehension of time registers at an intimate level within its rhythms. Similarly, his detailed scrutiny of the composition of *The Waste Land* discovers 'textual memories and imaginative recesses' (p. 277) within its drafts. *Modernism and the Reinvention of Decadence* is likely to be an influential intervention in Eliot studies.

Martin Lockerd also explores Eliot's links to the *fin de siècle* in ' "A Satirist of Vices and Follies": Beardsley, Eliot and Images of Decadent Catholicism' (*JML* 37:iv[2014] 143–65), which explores the influence of Aubrey Beardsley's poems and line drawings on Eliot's poetry. Lockerd examines the visual and verbal connections Aubrey establishes between Catholicism and the hints of violence and excess in his work, then traces comparable elements within poems such as 'The Love Song of Saint Sebastian' and 'The Lovesong of J. Alfred Prufrock'. Interestingly, although Lockerd also cites Eliot's critical writings from the 1920s on the appeal of damnation in Baudelaire, he doesn't reflect upon the way that these poetic texts precede Eliot's conversion to Anglo-Catholicism by several years.

Amongst the essays in Maria DiBattista and Emily O. Wittman's collection, *Modernism and Autobiography*, Max Saunders's 'T.S. Eliot's Impersonal Correspondence' (pp. 157–69) examines the value of the ongoing and extensive edition of Eliot's letters for our understanding of 'his creative and critical processes' (p. 158). This thoughtful essay maps Eliot's developing theory of poetic impersonality against the demand made upon his nerves by the need to find an appropriate tone and voice in his personal and professional correspondence. Under Saunders' scrutiny, Eliot's letters become simultaneously a figure for and a source of the kind of pained material that he sought to transform into poetry.

Roxana Bîrsanu's *T.S. Eliot's 'The Waste Land' as a Place of Intercultural Exchanges: A Translation Perspective* moves between an account of Eliot's reception in Romania and a history of *The Waste Land* 'as a work of translation' (p. 178). This approach is strongly influenced by recent developments within translation studies, which emphasize the historical and ideological character of translation. Accordingly, Bîrsanu provides information about those Romanian translators who have tackled Eliot's work from 1933 to 2009, providing social and historical background to his reception there. Her account of *The Waste Land* determinedly locates Eliot's poem in a familiar historical narrative about its composition and publication. An interesting chapter describes 'the Modernist approach to translation' (p. 92), concentrating on Eliot's collaboration with St John Perse's *Anabase*; similarly, her account of *The Waste Land* as translation thoughtfully extends this concept beyond Eliot's allusions to texts in other languages to recognize his incorporation of bird song and the verbal representations in the poem of various musical motifs from Wagner and elsewhere.

Beci Carver groups Eliot with Auden as practitioners of what she calls *Granular Modernism* (pp. 102–41). This elusive categorization comprehends 'techniques of irrelevance, plotlessness, miscellaneousness, convolution, and confusion' alongside a self-consciousness of 'futility' within certain modernist texts (p. 2). When it comes to Eliot, his fixation with 'fragments', shored or otherwise, as a means of amassing miscellaneous detail provides Carver with a 'granular' paradigm. This works best when she pulls out and inspects details such as the coughing goat in 'Gerontion' or the outdated 'combinations' of the Typist in *The Waste Land*. Where you might expect her to hold up such details as evidence of a rich imaginative quiddity in these works, her approach is to probe their significance by questioning their relevance. *Granular Modernism* is particularly interesting about the connective syntactical tissues of modernist poetry, especially where they fail to connect or cohere.

Elsewhere, William Viney devotes a chapter to Eliot in *Waste: A Philosophy of Things* (pp. 79–99). Pointing first to the drafts published as *Inventions of the March Hare*, Viney identifies three different approaches to the notion of waste as part of his broader argument about the way that 'things' become waste through narrative. First, he points to the clutter of discarded objects within the landscapes of Eliot's poetry; second, he treats fragments of unpublished poetry as potential waste before observing their role within the 'intratextual' economy of Eliot's later, published poetry; and finally, the interaction of these elements is shown to be symptomatic of a broader, linguistic disquiet about the relationship between meaning and waste.

In his essay on Eliot's career as a radio broadcaster for the BBC, 'T.S. Eliot on the Radio' (in Feldman, Tonning and Mead, eds., *Broadcasting in the Modernist Era*, pp. 99–117), Steven Matthews takes issue with previous accounts of Eliot's broadcasting career, arguing that Eliot's approach shows 'greater flexibility', greater humour, and greater sensitivity to the medium than has previously been acknowledged. In place of a staid, Arnoldian sage, Matthews's reading produces a livelier Eliot, sensitive to difficulties and differences inherent in writing words and reading them aloud over the airwaves.

Benjamin Kohlmann examines Eliot's critical writings in a chapter of *Committed Styles* (pp. 18–52), his account of modernism and politics in the 1930s. This pits Eliot against I.A. Richards on the question of 'belief' in poetry. Eliot's insistence upon the importance and possibility of expressing belief (particularly religious belief) is compared to Richards's doctrine of 'pseudo-statements' in *Practical Criticism*—the irony being that Richards may have modelled his argument about the inability of poetry to make assertions beyond its own verbal limits on Eliot's own practice in *The Waste Land*. Kohlmann then traces the impact of Richards's critical tenets upon contributors to the magazine *Experiment* (including William Empson) during the 1930s. Eliot's debate with Richards had a shaping influence, Kohlmann claims, upon the ways in which critics subsequently debated the relationship between poetry and political commitment.

In 'Listening to Eliot's Thrush' (*PAns* 12:ii[2014] 231–49), Christopher Irmscher traces the 'ornithological genealogy' (p. 232) of the water-dripping song attributed to the hermit thrush in 'What the Thunder Said'. After consulting sources including Frank Michler Chapman's *Handbook of the Birds of Eastern North America*, Irmscher concludes that Eliot valued the sound poetry, symbolic value, and evocative power of this formulation over ornithological accuracy.

In 'Feeling the Elephant: T.S. Eliot's Bolivian Epic' (*JML* 37:iv[2014] 109–29), Loretta Johnson attempts to reconstruct Eliot's account of the adventures of 'King Bolo' and his 'Big Black Queen' from in letters and notebooks in order to counter assertions that these bawdy poems simply reinforce stereotyped ideas of race.

Although it ranges widely, *Ascetic Modernism in the Work of T.S. Eliot and Gustave Flaubert* by Henry Gott does not offer a comprehensive review of Eliot's relationship to the French author. Instead, it focuses upon comparing *The Waste Land* with *La Tentation de Saint Antoine*. Gott's starting point is a shared 'poetics of citation' (p. 17) between these two texts which allowed their authors to bring together and fuse disparate literary, historical, and mythical materials. At the heart of *Ascetic Modernism*, however, lies an argument about the shared symbolic resonance for Eliot and Flaubert of the figures of the desert and the saint. Gott finds a deep structural affinities here, which extend beyond a dissatisfaction with contemporary society towards a sense of personal loss and nostalgia for childhood. In his emphasis upon ascecis, the saintly, and negation, Gott's readings sound very like those critics who address Eliot's later openly Christian poetry. He finds, however, the representation of sainthood in these two texts 'radically inconclusive' (p. 105).

Jim McCue, 'T.S. Eliot, Edgar Lee Masters and Glorious France' (*EiC* 64:i[2014] 45–73), concerns the accretive absorption of allusive material (described, in Eliot's own terms, as 'saturation') in Eliot's work, as much as it traces one particular path of allusive reference. McCue ranges across Eliot's poetic career, identifying debts and points of comparison with Edgar Lee Masters, poet of the *Spoon River Anthology*, but his argument, such as it is, concerns the way that the death of Eliot's friend Jean Verdenal in France during the First World War resonates more generally through the poetry within borrowed images and words, such as 'axeltree'. Masters's work, McCue suggests, belongs to this 'vortex of feelings' (p. 64).

In the same issue of *Essays in Criticism*, Kit Toda pursues one of the same points of allusive reference, in 'Eliot's Cunning Passages: A Note' (*EiC* 64:i[2014] 90–7). Toda re-examines Eliot's borrowing of the word 'axeltree' from George Chapman's *Bussy D'Ambois* in order to suggest that the phrase 'cunning passages' in 'Gerontion' derives from another speech in Act IV, scene i of the same play rather than the misprint of 'cunning axeltree' for 'burning axeltree' in Act V, scene i of the edition that Eliot used. Toda suggests that Bussy's predicament in the play speaks more directly to the atmosphere of backroom machinations in Eliot's poem and his chosen theatrical monologue form.

Omitted from last year's entry in this section, Steven Matthews's *T.S. Eliot and Early Modern Literature* has interests in common with Toda. Matthews moves with agility between Eliot's dramatic, poetic, and critical writings, providing a broader context to Eliot's response to early modern writers such as Chapman, Donne, Andrewes, and Jonson. He investigates contemporary editions of these writers and places Eliot in context with his immediate critical precursors, as a reader of sixteenth- and seventeenth-century literature. Although his general argument that Eliot's 'Early Modern sources ... form a conscious and informing part' of his poetic achievement seems a little obvious, the importance of this book lies in Matthews's close scrutiny of neglected contextual material and in some of the nuanced connections he makes with Eliot's poetic practice. For example, tracking familiar recurrent points of reference, such as Chapman's 'burning axeltree' (discussed by Toda), Matthews also identifies points of allusive contact which do not function as affirmations of the prior text. Rather, they become part of a 'conscious negotiation' (p. 79): in 'Gerontion', Matthews suggests, allusion to Chapman helps signal the speaker's 'lack of consonance with the rhythms of his experience' (p. 80). Amidst the acts of historical recovery in this book, then, there are also some fine readings of Eliot's poetry.

John Whittier-Ferguson begins the chapter on Eliot's later Christian poetry in *Mortality and Form in Late Modernist Literature* (pp. 31–78) by complaining about the current state of the field. Work on Eliot published by major, established university presses tends to favour, he notes, the earlier modernist writings or misunderstands the poetry Eliot published after his conversion to Anglo-Catholicism. The problem lies, according to Whittier-Ferguson, in an imaginative failure to take the question of Eliot's belief seriously. His own study (published by Cambridge University Press) seeks to offer 'an edgy, unsettling, and unsettled Eliot' (p. 31), emphasizing that Eliot's turn to the Church was not a comfortable choice or resignation from the world. Instead, Whittier-Ferguson identifies Eliot's conversion as the start of a difficult path along his 'Christian pilgrimage' (p. 39). This pilgrimage is then traced through readings of *Ash Wednesday*, 'Marina', and Section IV of each of the *Four Quartets*. This focus on the fourth section of each Quartet is informed by Whittier-Ferguson's desire to redeem Eliot's later poetry from accusations of flatness. His dedication to taking Eliot's beliefs seriously produces readings which are passionately sympathetic to the spiritual journey perceived as underlying these poems.

Similarly sympathetic to Eliot's Christian poetry, G. Douglas Atkins published two books on Eliot in 2014, *T.S. Eliot: The Poet as Christian* and *T.S. Eliot's Christmas Poems*. As he notes in the former, 'I have written a good deal about Old Possum recently' (p. vi) and, indeed, Atkins has published two books on Eliot with Palgrave every year since 2012. Inevitably, there is a little overlap: in *Christmas Poems* Atkins devotes a whole chapter to *The Cultivation of Christmas Trees*, identifying its 'essayistic' voice (p. 33) while praising Eliot's capacity to enter into a 'childlike' perspective on the Incarnation, mediated in part through the fate of child-martyr St Lucy, but a chapter on the Christmas poems in *The Poet as Christian* also concludes by examining the role of St Lucy in this poem and its negotiation between childlike wonder and the theology of incarnation. Still, Atkins is an impassioned advocate for Eliot's poetic and theological achievement ('it is a gift to us all', p. 38).

Unfortunately, a copy of Benjamin Lockerd's *T.S. Eliot and Christian Tradition* was not made available for consultation. Such information about this volume of essays as *is* available suggests that it ranges widely, including, amongst others, contributions by William Blisset on Eliot's Anglo-Catholicism, Dominic Manganiello on Eliot's interest in Dante, and John Morgenstein on the influence of the French Catholic revival on Eliot.

David Soud's ' "The Greedy Dialectic of Time and Eternity": Karl Barth, T.S. Eliot, and *Four Quartets*' (*ELH* 81:iv[2014] 1363–91) argues for the influence of the theology of Karl Barth upon T.S. Eliot after his conversion to Anglo-Catholicism. Soud notes differences in theological opinion and temperament between Barth and Eliot regarding mystical experience, but suggests that the central role of moments in and out of time within *Four Quartets* owes much to the 'discourse of dialectical theology' (p. 1372) in Barth's work.

Corey Latta devotes a chapter to Eliot (pp. 115–66) in *When the Eternal Can Be Met*, his study of a Bergsonian theology of time in the work of Eliot, W.H. Auden, and C.S. Lewis. Latta argues that Bergson is not only important to understanding the Christian thought of these writers as individuals, but his philosophical writings about time also provide theological common ground between them that has previously been neglected. Like a doctoral student, Latta is thorough in his discussion of previous critical writing on Eliot and Bergson and keen to establish the distinctive character of his own central claim that Eliot 'poeticises Bergsonian intuition and duration to create a theology of experience in time' (p. 116). In this context, Latta is alert to the difficulties of connecting Bergson's secular writing with Eliot's religious thought and capable of negotiating consequent paradoxes within his readings of the *Four Quartets*. Oddly, however, *When the Eternal Can Be Met* doesn't seem to address Eliot's own rejection of Bergson's epistemology and ontology as a graduate student in the writings that have been transcribed in the new edition of his prose.

In contrast, Matthew Flaherty does look across Eliot's career, linking his postgraduate work on F.H. Bradley to a reading of *Four Quartets* in 'Incommensurable Worlds and "Impossible Union"' (*YER* 30:iii–iv[2013–14] 27–45). Eliot's understanding of 'finite centres' in Bradley's work as delineating the impermeable boundaries between the world of subjective human experience is used by Flaherty to emphasize how *Four Quartets* renders the difficulty of reconciling 'the conflicting assumptions made by other perspectives' (p. 31). Flaherty identifies several differing perspectives or 'windows on experience' (p. 41) within *Four Quartets* in order to argue that there is no unifying force in the work. In this way, he hopes to meet the criticisms of critics, such as Edward Said, hostile to the seemingly reductive influence of Eliot's conversion to Christianity.

David Thatcher also considers Eliot's philosophical training in 'T.S. Eliot's (Dis)appointment with Schopenhauer' (*YER* 30:iii–iv[2013–14] 47–52), where he wonders whether an allusion to life as 'a cheat and a disappointment' within *Murder in the Cathedral* derives from Schopenhauer's *Parerga und Paralipomena* [1851].

Kevin White's 'Accidents and Incidents: A Phenomenologist Reads T.S. Eliot' (*Logos* 17:iv[2014] 169–83) offers a tribute to his philosopher colleague Robert Sokolowski's *Phenomenology of the Human Person* through a reading of the formal structure of *Four Quartets* to illustrate Sokolowski's account of speech as predication and his distinction between accidents, properties, and essences. Most interesting is White's account of Eliot's repeated use of 'the' to refer to situations and images that are simultaneously specific, but resonate with more general symbolic properties. Curiously, he makes no reference to Eliot's own training in philosophy.

Chad Schrock, 'The Passage T.S. Eliot Took' (*EiC* 64:i[2014] 74–90), re-examines the opening lines to 'Burnt Norton' about 'time present and time past', by exploring their origin within a draft speech that Eliot cut from *Murder in the Cathedral*. Schrock reinvests the lines with specific context, giving them 'a local habitation' (p. 79) within the historical and dramatic sequence of Eliot's play and its depiction of the career of Thomas Becket. He also sites them within the personal and theological sequence of Beckett's spiritual dilemma, as represented in the play. Schrock concludes by connecting this textual prehistory to the general concern in *Four Quartets* with 'rewriting' (p. 86) in one form or another.

Anthony Cuda provides a summary account of Eliot's poetic output, concentrating upon the major works, for David Chinitz and Gail Marshall's *Companion to Modernist Poetry* (pp. 450–63). Whilst this contains nothing thing new or contentious, it offers functional information and a useful overview for new readers or students of Eliot's work. Leila Bellour's

'Eroticism versus Mysticism in T.S. Eliot's "The Love Song of St Sebastian" and "Death of St Narcissus"' (*YER* 30:iii–iv[2013–14] 3–26) offers a summary account of two early poems by Eliot along with a digest of critical work on these texts, drawing out common elements of homosexual allusion and misogyny.

Finally, Ghanim Samarrai's' Rejuvenating T.S. Eliot's *The Waste Land* (*CRCL* 41:ii[2014] 112–25) points out the popularity and frequency of Eliot's works in Arabic translations, before exploring the possible debts to *The Waste Land* in Badr Shakir As-Sayâb's *Hymn of Rain* [1954].

7. British Poetry Post-1950

The publication of *Bedouin of the London Evening: Collected Poems and Selected Prose of Rosemary Tonks* by Bloodaxe Books under Neil Astley just months after Tonks's death at the age of 85 was a significant event in 2014. This book went some way to solving 'one of the literary world's most tantalizing mysteries', as Astley puts it in his introduction (p. 9), by bringing the contents of Tonks's two poetry collections, *Notes on Cafés and Bedrooms* [1963] and *Iliad of Broken Sentences* [1967], back into print after almost fifty years. An urbane, cosmopolitan devotee of Baudelaire and Rimbaud who held that 'The main duty of the poet is to excite—to send the senses reeling' (p. 10), Tonks turned her back on literature in the 1970s to embark, in Astley's words, 'on a self-torturing spiritual quest which required her to repudiate her own books' (p. 9). The tortures included 'Taoist eye exercises', such as 'staring for hours at a blank wall, turning the eyes in and looking intensely at bright objects' (p. 22), which left her almost blind for several years. Astley provides a detailed and insightful introduction to Tonks's life and work, reprints the texts of her two collections, scrupulously reproducing the publisher's notes on the books' original dustwrappers, and compiles a selection of her prose. This includes: Tonks's brief statement on her own art for the *Poetry Book Society Bulletin*, describing her 'search for an idiom which is individual, contemporary and musical' (p. 107); her interview with Peter Orr from his 1963 book *The Poet Speaks*; two reviews; and a short story. The influence of Tonks's re-emergence on contemporary poets is being felt already, and this edition will surely provoke renewed interest in her work among scholars. Her six published novels remain in the wilderness.

At 501 pages, *A C.H. Sisson Reader*, edited by Charlie Louth and Patrick McGuinness, is over three times the length of Tonks. This major edition brings together a generous and well-chosen selection of Sisson's poetry, criticism, and writing on social questions. The editors are Oxford Fellows in German and French respectively and bring an appropriately international perspective to a writer who was, in their words, 'one of English poetry's most European-minded' at the same time as he was possessed of a deep 'sense of a specifically English (as distinct from British) cultural inheritance' (p. xiii). The editors' introduction gives a good account of Sisson's paradoxes: the poet who sought 'to align himself with cultural and political order' but who nonetheless— 'because his version of that order, rooted in the seventeenth century, was so against the times'—figured in the literary world as 'radical and oppositional, critical and sceptical' (p. xii). The texts are not annotated except for bibliographical details, but the selection that has been made presents a clear and fascinating path through Sisson's writing and thought.

Sisson receives only one passing mention in Michael Thurston and Nigel Alderman's *Reading Postwar British and Irish Poetry*, amongst a list of British poets published by Carcanet Press (p. 58). The first chapter of this valuable overview begins with a striking juxtaposition of T.S. Eliot writing 'Little Gidding' in London under aerial bombardment in 1942 and Patience Agbabi working as Poet in Residence in a tattoo parlour in 2000, and writing an untitled poem which was 'published' as a tattoo inscribed upon a model's skin (pp. 1–3). This gives some indication both of the range of work the book is interested in and its historical approach. In general, the authors are shy about taking any poem to be more valuable than any other, partly because 'postmodernist poetry ... resists the notions of singularity, greatness, monumentality, and, sometimes, poetry itself'—although if pushed, they admit, they would nominate Edward Kamau Brathwaite, Paul Muldoon, and J.H. Prynne as possible 'great poetic monuments' of postmodernism (p. 8). 'Poems are situated', begins the second chapter, 'A Brief Historical Survey', before expanding on this: 'they are produced, circulated and read in specific historical circumstances' (p. 19). The third chapter refines this for literary purposes by describing the 'specific *institutional* circumstances' (p. 41) in which the creation of poems is fostered. Just as the context of the conflict between Thatcher and the miners is important for understanding Tony Harrison's *V* [1985], so are the contexts of Harrison's grammar-school and red-brick education, the poem's broadcast on Channel Four, and its publication by Bloodaxe and the *Independent* (p. 41). The chapter goes on to describe the place and shape of poetry in relation to schools and universities, to various publishing houses and small presses, and to the Arts Council and Poetry Society. A chapter on form discusses the formations and deformations undergone by sonnet, elegy, and ekphrasis in the period; subsequent chapters discuss place in postwar society, varieties of long poem, and literary groups and anthologies. The book covers an impressively various range of poets in an even-handed manner. The longest entries in the index go to Eavan Boland, Jean 'Binta' Breeze, Edward Kamau Brathwaite, Tony Harrison, Seamus Heaney, Geoffrey Hill, Ted Hughes, Linton Kwesi Johnson, Thomas Kinsella, Philip Larkin, Paul Muldoon, Wendy Mulford, and J.H. Prynne. Relatively few students get the opportunity or make the choice to study postwar poetry from these islands in this sort of broad way, but if they did, this book would be a good place for them to start.

Only part of Basil Bunting's work was done in the postwar period but that part includes the writing of *Briggflatts* [1966], widely seen as his major achievement, and a poem which did much to bridge the gap between high modernism and the younger generation of British poets interested in the possibilities of late modernism who would write in Bunting's wake. In *Basil Bunting* by Julian Stannard, published in Northcote House's valuable Writers and Their Work series, Bunting's story becomes that of 'a poet who kept faith with his muse over half a century' in spite of spending much of that time outside what Auden called 'the tiny jungle' of the literary world (p. 2). Stannard's elegant study moves assuredly through Bunting's rather dramatic life (including being jailed as a schoolboy conscientious objector during the Great War, hanging out with Ezra Pound in Rapallo, and working as a British spy in Persia during the Second World War), before moving on to a detailed study of his poetic oeuvre, with chapters covering his various long poems ('Sonatas') and shorter ones ('Odes') and a separate chapter dedicated to *Briggflatts*; 'All roads lead to Briggflatts', Stannard writes (p. 88). Bunting's work is set in its literary contexts through astute discussions of his influences and principles (Pound and musical structure) and its engagement with mythology and translation. The final two chapters, 'Critical Perspectives' and 'Conclusion', place Bunting's poetry and its reception within a wide range of twentieth-century writing, weighing up his achievement alongside that of his elders—'pegging Bunting's fortunes to the Pound Index', as Stannard wryly puts it (p. 107). *Basil Bunting* also evaluates the poet in the light of influential voices somewhat younger than him, including those of poets associated both with the 'Movement' and with the 'British Poetry Revival' and its associated later iterations of avant-garde energy. Here, Stannard's expert knowledge of Donald Davie's and Charles Tomlinson's work also comes in handy, with Bunting's work playing a key role in Davie's mediation of native and American poetic traditions.

Bunting's relations with Pound also feature in Alex Niven's 'Towards a New Architecture: Basil Bunting's Postwar Reconstruction' (*ELH* 81:i[2014] 351–79), which places 'On the Fly Leaf of Pound's Cantos' in context with the controversy over the award of the Bollingen Prize to Pound for *Pisan Cantos* and with Bunting's disillusionment with the direction of modern poetry. Niven then explores *The Spoils* as a precursor to *Briggflatts* and as symptomatic of Bunting's response to contemporary poetic, material, and historical circumstances.

The Pound Index rose several points in 2014 with the publication of *News from Afar: Ezra Pound and Some Contemporary British Poetries*, edited by Richard Parker. This is the successor to Michael Alexander and James McGonigal's *Sons of Ezra: British Poets and Ezra Pound* [1995], which gathered contributions from the likes of Edwin Morgan, Davie, Tomlinson, Gael Turnbull, and Roy Fisher. The change from 'British Poets' to 'Some British Poetries' between the two books' titles is characteristic: *News from Afar* is focused on poets working in more obscure corners of the plural worlds of contemporary poetry than was its predecessor (though the selection is barely any less male-dominated). The writers under discussion are mainly those whom the editor queasily describes as 'poets that in less testing times might have been termed the avant-garde' (p. 9). Eric Mottram, J.H. Prynne, Veronica Forrest-Thomson, Allen Fisher, and Keston Sutherland loom large. Sometimes the Poundian relevances seem a little far-fetched: Mark Scroggins's essay on John Ruskin, Pound, and Geoffrey Hill is very good, but more substantial on Ruskin and Hill than on Pound (pp. 122–32); Ryan Dobran's essay on Pound and J.H. Prynne's use of Greek sources is likewise more interesting on Prynne's use of Aristeas than Pound's use of Homer (pp. 142–60). Overall, however, the essays richly prove Parker's thesis that 'it is in the fields of political writing, historiography and translation that Pound is most useful for these poets, and in which his experiments have been extrapolated away from his work to the furthest extent' (p. 19).

Several of the contributors respond in creative ways to the brief; the most fruitful of these is 'In Memory of Your Occult Involutions', Keston Sutherland's remarkable four-page compilation of Poundian invective ('Low-brow reader, it shall be you ... shaggy and uncouth marginalians it shall be you') which extracts Pound's blasts and insults as the pith of his didactic critical method (pp. 21–4). Equally, several contributions also discuss or exemplify modes of creative translation—the pick of them is Alex Pestell's learned essay on the Zukofskian (and hence Poundian) versions of Bertran de Born by Michael Kindellan and Reitha Pattison (pp. 303–12).

Matthew Sperling's *Visionary Philology: Geoffrey Hill and the Study of Words* is the first study to draw in a sustained way on the resources of the archive collection of Hill's papers and letters held at the University of Leeds. Working its way backwards chapter by chapter, it traces Hill's reciprocal relationship to the philological scholarship of three editions of the *Oxford English Dictionary*, to Richard Chenevix Trench, to Coleridge, to seventeenth-century empiricism, and to Christian (mainly Augustinian) ideas about language. Along the way, it offers many close readings of Hill's poetry and criticism. Elsewhere, Stefan Hawlin offers a reading of Hill's most recent collection (before the appearance of his *Collected Poems* [2013]), in 'The Argument of Geoffrey Hill's *Odi Barbare*' (*CQ* 43:i[2014] 1–15). The article summarizes Hill's broader preoccupations ('Evil' 'Cultural Memory', etc.) as they occur thematically, providing useful directions towards sources of allusion and recurrent points of reference.

Whereas Hill, in his ninth decade, has now been the subject of more than ten book-length studies, *Don Paterson: Contemporary Critical Essays*, edited by Natalie Pollard, is the first book on its subject, and comes at a time when Paterson is still in mid-career. Pollard's introduction circles around Paterson's multiple and conflicted role within contemporary poetry, focusing on the 'sense of personal and professional self-dividedness' which underwrites his concern with 'the subject of economic patronage and the relationship between the writing of poetry and its reception' (pp. 4–5). The first half of the book, under the heading 'Patterns and Paterson', is primarily concerned with formal and technical questions. It is strongly bookended by Derek Attridge's essay on Paterson's '*Ars Poetica*' (pp. 21–33) and his interview with Paterson on 'Form in Poetry' (pp. 75–82)—although in the absence of a complete published version of Paterson's *Ars Poetica* (apparently forthcoming), Attridge's work is necessarily somewhat piecemeal, and Paterson's introduction of some specialized terms of his own ('conceptual domain', 'isologue', 'literal origo') has yet to prove its usefulness. The second half of the book, 'Poetry in Its Place: Responses and Responsibilities', is a bit more of a rag-bag, but Peter Robinson's essay, 'Punching Yourself in the Face: Don Paterson and His Readers' (pp. 131–44), is a highlight, ranging across Paterson's poems, aphorisms, and criticism to discuss 'Paterson's conflicted ideas of relations with a reader' (p. 140) with a rigorous scepticism towards 'the self-and-other torments of Paterson's public persona' (p. 141) balanced against admiration for his poetic invention. Matthew Sperling contributes an interview with Paterson, who is poetry editor at Picador, on the topic of 'The Publishing of Poetry', to round off the second half of the book (pp. 145–52).

Paterson himself wrote a single-author study which appeared in 2014, about a poet who has not previously been subject of a book-length treatment. *Smith: A Reader's Guide to the Poetry of Michael Donaghy* was published soon after the tenth anniversary of its subject's early death, and is written in the same informal, personal tone as Paterson's *Reading Shakespeare's Sonnets* [2010]. In the course of nimble commentaries on fifty of Donaghy's poems (the poems are printed alongside the commentaries, and include Donaghy's stand-out works along with some more surprising selections), Paterson persuasively shows that Donaghy's poems were like his character, not 'merely elegant, charming and witty' but also 'possessed by fear, guilt, insecurity, paranoia, fatalism and a deeply buried anger', making him a poet who, like Robert Frost, 'sounded light, but read dark' (p. 6).

Finally, 2014 saw publication of two substantial biographies of poets active in this period, *Philip Larkin: Life, Art and Love* by James Booth and *Peter Levi: Oxford Romantic* by Brigid Allen. The profiles of the two subjects could hardly be more different, with Levi's poetry barely in print and his biography appearing modestly from Signal Books, based in the suburbs of Oxford, while Larkin's biography was splashed across the national and international press. Yet Allen's book is the profounder work. Booth advances considerably on the work of his predecessors in Larkin biography in the depth of his knowledge of the archive and the unpublished letters (especially the letters to Larkin's mother and to Monica Jones, his long-time companion), and his detailed analyses of Larkin's major poems are mainly sound and sensitive, but his book is often hamstrung by an unnecessary desire to think well of and defend Larkin in all circumstances—as when he outweighs Larkin's use of racist slurs in his letters with the evidence that he liked jazz music and once had a dream in which he was a black man in fear of being lynched, which Booth interprets as meaning that 'His subconscious was not racist' (p. 10). In comparison, Ryan Hibbert makes a strong case for the conscious and strategic use by Larkin of the 'f-word' within private letters and public poems in 'Philip Larkin, British Culture and Four-Letter Words' (*CQ* 43:ii[2014] 120–38).

Peter Levi was at various times poet, biographer, travel writer, Oxford Professor of Poetry, Jesuit priest, and also 'an unusual kind of academic, much of the interest of whose life lies in the number of borderlines it crossed', in the words of Brigid Allen (p. ix). As a poet he was, as John Fuller insightfully puts it, 'not focused or tempered into originality like Hopkins' but one who 'vigorously adapted a continued eclecticism to the needs of his style, which was pure, narrow, intuitive, symbolic' (quoted on the dustwrapper). Allen's biography begins with novelistic vividness in the London summer of 1976 when Levi, then a Jesuit priest, was visiting IRA prisoners in Brixton gaol while in the grip of his own mid-life crisis; he eventually left his vocation behind, having fallen in love with Deirdre Connolly, the widow of Levi's friend and literary hero, Cyril Connolly. The biography is equally good on Levi's remarkably full life—his scholarly life in Oxford and winters in Greece, his friendship with David Jones and travels with Bruce Chatwin and Patrick Leigh

Fermor—as it is on his poetry and criticism, out of step with many of his English contemporaries in its 'romantic' flair and exuberance, and influenced more by George Seferis and Wallace Stevens than by fashion.

8. Modern Irish Poetry

The unexpected death of Seamus Heaney in August 2013 meant that tributes to him formed a significant portion of the critical writing on modern Irish poetry in 2014. Three appreciations that were, appropriately for their subject, both deeply knowledgeable and personal in their tone, were published in *Eire-Ireland*. Ronald Schuchard's '"Into the Heartland of the Ordinary": Seamus Heaney, Thomas Hardy, and the Divided Traditions of Modern and Contemporary Poetry' (*Éire* 49:iii–iv[2014] 270–300) is a sensitive appreciation of the significance of Hardy in Heaney's poetic life, combining Schuchard's memories of Heaney with criticism of the poet's work. We learn that Heaney 'was not to be diverted by the Troubles from his original poetic: fully half of all his poems are set within ten miles of his birthplace' (p. 286). How many hours of work went into just the second half of that sentence? Terence Brown's 'Seamus Heaney's Tender Yeats' (*Éire* 49:iii–iv[2014] 301–19) is an appreciation of the role the elder poet played in the younger's imagination. As its title suggests, it draws attention to how Heaney fashioned a meliorative and conciliatory predecessor from the varied materials that Yeats left behind. Stephen Regan's '"Things Remembered": Objects of Memory in the Poetry of Seamus Heaney' (*Éire* 49:iii–iv[2014] 320–35) focuses on quotidian and domestic images from Heaney's writings, including 'the pitchfork, the turnip snedder and the harrow pin, [and] also the baking board, the smoothing iron and the clothes horse' (p. 321): items that Heaney's writing has taken from the obscurity of the everyday and made into secular icons. In doing this, Regan draws attention to how Heaney's 'sensuous physical apprehension of the remembered thing' always went alongside a 'soaring imaginative appreciation of its potential symbolic value' (p. 332). Elsewhere, Ben Howard's 'One of the Venerators: Seamus Heaney 1939–2013' (*SR* 122:i[2014] 164–7) emphasizes Heaney's humility, noting that 'though he became a venerable presence in the Republic of Letters, he remained, in his own phrase, "one of the venerators"' (p. 165). Like Howard's tribute, Marianne McDonald's 'In Memoriam: Seamus Heaney: April 13, 1939–August 30, 2013' (*Arion* 21:iii[2014] 151–62) reflects on the poet's work as well as on his unique place in Irish public life.

Though Heaney's life and work prompted many tributes, there was no shortage of other responses from critics. Eugene O'Brien's '"An Art That Knows Its Mind": Prayer, Poetry and Post-Catholic Identity in Seamus Heaney's "Squarings"' (*EI* 39:ii[2014] 127–43) responds to the sublimated Catholicism in the poet's work, seeing in his poetry the replacement of orthodox belief with a form of religious cultural unconscious. Andrew Fitzsimons's '*Mundus et Infans*: The After-Time of the Child in the Poetry of Seamus Heaney' (*JELL* 60:iv[2014] 577–95) also focuses on the ethereal elements of Heaney's work, responding to the mix of earthy realism and spiritual transcendence that characterizes it. Fitzsimons's article is also an exploration of the doubled perspectives of Heaney's work which, in his view, have their origins in 'the context of *mundus et infans*, the world and the child, innocence and experience' (p. 577). Conor Carville's ' "Heaney and the Neighbour": Poetry between Politics and Ethics' (*TPr* 28:iv[2014] 571–92) takes a tripartite view of the poet's work, seeing in it 'an acknowledgment and acceptance of the actual conditions of the moment, the local tensions the narrator has exposed himself to, and an appeal to an alternative space, to the possible suspension of those conditions' (p. 590). Jessica Stephens's 'Death—A Source in Seamus Heaney's Early Autobiographical Poetry' (*EI* 39:i[2014] 155–68) offers a comparison between the attitudes to death that are evinced by Heaney in his early volume, *Death of a Naturalist*, and the elegies to his mother in the sequence 'Clearances'. Finally, Christelle Serée-Chaussinand's 'Actaeon Revisited: Seamus Heaney and Sinéad Morrissey Respond to Titian' (*NewHibR* 18:iv[2014] 119–30) begins with a consideration of the two poets' divergent approaches to Greek myth. The article then becomes a meditation on the meanings of 'translation', with Serée-Chaussinand concluding that the word is not limited to 'rendering or converting a text into another language'. Rather, it includes 'transferring a story from one imagination to another' (p. 130).

The many articles on Heaney's work were complemented by Richard Rankin Russell's lucid and weighty monograph, *Seamus Heaney's Regions*. Unlike the tribute articles that appeared this year, this study was conceived of and completed before the poet's death. Its organizing theme is, as its title suggests, that of the region, a term that Russell understands both literally and figuratively. The literal region is Northern Ireland as historical place, but, from its opening quotation of Heaney's words: 'John Keats once called a poem [of his] "a little region to wander in" ' (p. 1), this monograph pays equal attention to a more dematerialized sense of the word. In particular, Heaney's work is analysed through the lens of the region of an imagined future state, and the region of the spirit realm. The opening chapter discusses the contentious history of Northern Irish regionalism itself; the second pays heed to the fascinating context for Heaney's work for BBC radio at the outset of the Troubles. This chapter draws attention to Heaney's involvement in broad-casting controversies during this period, and is particularly valuable for its engagement with archival material. Heaney's little-known 1968 radio script *Explorations* is brought to light, with its haunting declaration that: 'Your head is a world that contains oceans, continents, the lonely constellations' (p. 80). Subsequent chapters move broadly chronologically through Heaney's poetry, plays, and prose works, paying particular attention to the role of the American civil rights movement in Heaney's imagination; to the presence in his poetry of such precursors as Dante, Yeats, and Eliot; and, relatedly, to his adoption of the tercet form. The last two chapters focus on *Human Chain* [2010], making this the first major monograph on Heaney to include analysis of his final volume of poems. The book is impressive for its knowledge not just of Heaney's work, but of the awesome amount of scholarship that Heaney's work has generated. By focusing on the regional, Russell achieves a task similar to that of its subject: 'the writer', wrote Heaney, 'must re-envisage the region as the original point' (p. 1).

Despite the understandable focus on his work and legacy, Seamus Heaney was just one of several poets from Northern Ireland to receive extended critical attention this year. Stephen Enniss's *After the Titanic: A Life of Derek Mahon*, reminds us that, in the case of Mahon, 'the origin of [his] art lies in suffering' (p. 259). Unlike his more amenable contemporaries, Mahon has mainly chosen to let his work speak for him, and taken the role (to borrow an image from Paul Muldoon) of the hedgehog that shares his secret with no one. This book is therefore valuable for readers of Mahon's work for its wealth of previously unpublished anecdotes, letters, photographs, and other details relating to the poet's life. Poems are negotiations between self-revelation and self-conceal-ment, and this book reveals just how uncertain the border between these two conditions can be. The biographical context provided by this work is entirely fascinating, even if one's sympathy occasionally goes to Mahon for being the subject of such an unremittingly revelatory monograph. This book often casts Mahon in an unflattering light, but also confirms the suspicion that knowledge of the personal failings of a writer cannot detract from the value of what they have written.

The second part of Neil Corcoran's volume of essays on twentieth-century poets, *Poetry & Responsibility*, is entirely devoted to Irish poetry: W.B. Yeats, Seamus Heaney, Louis MacNeice, and Paul Muldoon are all represented, and there is also a very illuminating essay on Irish poetry and visual art. This monograph also contains a chapter on the relationship between the two colossuses of twentieth-century Irish poetry. Its title, 'Question Me Again: Reflections on W.B. Yeats and Seamus Heaney', points up the differences between the interrogatory styles of the two poets, while showing how Heaney made a lifetime's practice of questioning, repurposing, and rewriting the work of his predecessor. The Irish focus of the volume is perhaps unsurprising, given the historic construction of the role of the Irish poet as one that is responsible to and representative of communities beyond his or her readers. There is an excellent essay on Yeats's 'Among School Children', which gives an impressive rundown of the history of clashing readings that this most mysterious of poems has provoked. There is also an insightful essay on the uses of repetition in the poetry of Louis MacNeice, which draws attention to the incantatory and primal functions of this technique. In this piece, Corcoran points out that it is in MacNeice's repetitions that the fugitive emotional centres of his poems can often be glimpsed. Finally, a piece on Paul Muldoon centres around the concept of filiality in the poet's work, and highlights how his poetry has reflected his responsibilities as the progeny of his literary forebear, Seamus Heaney.

Muldoon is also the subject of Christopher K. Coffman's 'Tradition and Critique in Paul Muldoon's "Madoc: A Mystery"' (*ISR* 22:iv[2014] 432–49). This article follows in a long tradition of applying explanatory keys to the work of this most recondite of poets. It interprets the relationship between the Coleridge and Southey characters at the centre of 'Madoc' as a representation of the differing schools of historical interpretation exemplified by the German philosophers Hans-Georg Gadamer and Jürgen Habermas. Pointing out that both philosophers are named in the poem, Coffman argues that 'Madoc' engages with differing views as to the extent that tradition, embodied by language, forms a limit to understanding. This article demonstrates Muldoon's continuing ability to prompt ingenious and inventive readings, and provides further evidence of the mysterious process whereby the methods of poets (which, in Muldoon's case, are highly associative) can be echoed in the work of their critics.

Elsewhere, violence formed the basis of critiques of the work of several poets from Northern Ireland this year. Aidan Tynan's 'A Season in Hell: Paradox and Violence in the Poetry of Padraic Fiacc' (*IUR* 44:ii[2014] 341–56) looks at the intersection of personal and societal tumult that is part of the poetry of its subject. In this article Tynan argues that, to Fiacc, 'the only authentic way to write about violence is to shun the sublimated satisfaction offered by the work of art' (p. 346). Sebastian Owen's "From one April to another": Remembering and Acknowledging the Holocaust in the Poetry of Michael Longley' (*ISR* 22:iii[2014] 358–73) also deals with the ethics of representing violence in poetry, and takes as its starting point the epigraph of *Gorse Fires*: 'Shells I speak and light clouds, and a boat buds in the rain'. These words are from Michael Hamburger's translation of Celan's poem 'Tallow Lamp'. In giving Celan this prominent position in his own work, Owen argues, Longley foregrounds the Holocaust and introduces ideas of Adorno's famous maxim on the barbarity of poetry after Auschwitz. Highlighting how Longley rejects a literal interpretation of Adorno's words, Owen teases out Longley's difficulties in summoning the consolatory power of beauty in the face of atrocity. In an article entitled ' "Second Time Round": Recent Northern Irish History in *For All We Know* and Ciaran Carson's Written Arts' (*NJES* 13:ii[2014] 80–95), Ruben Moi and Annelise Brox Larsen attempt to link the volume to the murderous time and place that is its subject, stating that their aim is to analyse how Carson's work adds 'other disciplinary approaches to the challenges of re-presenting the past' (p. 80). True to this aim, the article provides an array of potted historical sources, and name-checks a number of popular thinkers. However, this is done in a way that, though it has the virtue of being wide-ranging, entirely leaves both the poet and poetry that are ostensibly its reason for being written out of sight for long stretches. Carson was also the subject of Adam Watt's 'Ciaran Carson's *The Alexandrine Plan* and Two Versions of a Fantasy' (*Dix-Neuf* 18:ii[2014] 224–37), which takes the strangeness of the act of translation for its central theme. Among his close analyses of texts by Carson and Patrick McGuinness, Watt pays particular attention to how the unusual word-choices in Carson's translations allow 'the reader [to gain] some kind of purchase on the foreignness of the source-text whilst still following it in her or his "own" language' (p. 227).

Gail McConnell's *Northern Irish Poetry and Theology* contains a welcome new perspective on three of Northern Ireland's most prominent poets—Seamus Heaney, Michael Longley, and Derek Mahon. Near its beginning is this compelling and challenging statement: 'To summarize 30 years of highly polarized literary criticism, critics of contemporary Northern Irish poetry read poets—and even poetic forms—according to the sectarian paradigm by which the Troubles has commonly been understood: Catholic and nationalist versus Protestant and unionist' (p. 3). This detailed study instead takes theology as its focus, arguing that ideas including iconography, sacramentalism, catechism, and iconoclasm all are present in the work of the poets under examination. In taking this original approach, McConnell's monograph offers a salutary revision of the role of religion in Northern Irish poetry, showing it as having a more complex and subtle influence than much existing criticism would suggest.

Elmer Kennedy-Andrews's *Northern Irish Poetry: The American Connection* argues that 'modern globalized culture makes it impossible for literary study to continue operating on traditional nation-based, canonical or exceptionalist models' (p. 2). Looking at the work of a wide range of poets, including John Montague, Seamus Heaney, Derek Mahon, Paul Muldoon, and Ciaran Carson, he demonstrates how America's diverse poetic traditions have both reflected and extended the ideas of poets from Northern Ireland. As Robert Lowell pointed out in 1960, America produced two parallel twentieth-century traditions that he characterized as 'laboriously concocted' recipes and 'gobbets of unseasoned experience', respectively. These 'cooked' and 'raw' poetries have provided Northern Irish poets with Frostian models of formal precision and also with more process-based, postmodern work of the kind presented in *The New American Poetry*. By showing how richly Northern Irish poetry has been infused with both of these divergent traditions, this book does much to question preconceptions of heedless American poetic freewheeling and staid Northern Irish formalism alike.

Anne Kahrio's ' "All this debris of day-to-day experience": The Poet as Rhythmanalyst in the Works of Louis MacNeice, Derek Mahon and Paul Muldoon' (*NJES* 13:ii[2014] 57–79) states at its outset that it employs Henri Lefebvre's 'concept of rhythmanalysis to discuss the rhythmic, repetitive and changing processes of both poetry and the social and phenomenal experience' (p. 57). However, rather than being an exposition of parallels between Lefebvre's writings and those of the poets in question, this article gives a thoughtful account of rhythms and repetitions as subject-matter in the work of the three poets in question. What poets make of the fragmentary and the everyday is also the subject of Erin C. Mitchell's 'Leontia Flynn's Poetic "Museums": Losing, Saving, and Giving Away Belfast's Trash' (*NewHibR* 18:ii[2014] 110–21), which looks at Flynn's work from the point of view of Belfast's postmodern present in which the city's sectarian, industrial past has been repurposed as part of its tourist 'offering'. Mitchell links Flynn's preoccupation with what survives of the past to her poems which centre on her gravely ill father, seeing Flynn's 'museum-poems' as both inventing and chronicling the past (p. 118).

As in previous years, critics forged connections between Northern Ireland and eastern Europe in 2014. Margaret Greaves's ' "Vistas of Simultaneity": Northern Irish Elegies for Yugoslavia' (*NewHibR* 18:iii[2014] 31–51) examines the responses of various Irish poets, including Seamus Heaney, Nuala Ní Dhomhnaill, and Harry Clifton to conflict in the former Yugoslavia. As this list would suggest, the reference in the title to 'Northern Irish Elegies' is slightly misleading, but perhaps justified by the inevitable parallels between Northern Ireland's ethno-sectarian conflict and that of eastern Europe. In the words of Edna Longley, 'Northern Irish people now see themselves in the cracked looking-glass of Yugoslavia' (p. 33). Anne Kahrio also discusses Irish poets' tendency to look east in 'The Familiar and the Foreign: Finnish

Landscapes in Contemporary Irish Poetry' (*EI* 39:i[2014] 183–204), an article in which she discusses work by Tom Paulin, Michael Harnett, and Seamus Heaney. This piece, like Greaves's, points out the parallels to their own country that Irish poets have seen in eastern Europe, calling Finland 'Russia's small Northwestern neighbour' (p. 204).

This year saw the publication of two complementary monographs on the poetry of Medbh McGuckian, *Reading Medbh McGuckian* by Leontia Flynn and *Medbh McGuckian* by Borbála Faragó. Flynn begins with the issue of the perplexity with which McGuckian's work presents the reader, arguing that she is 'testing the generative capacity and nature of poetic language itself' (p. 13). She acknowledges that the identification of source-texts that has been pioneered by Shane Alcobia-Murphy gives the reader one way of thinking about McGuckian's poetry, and adds that another framework within which to see it is provided by the tradition of *écriture féminine*, adding that it is inimical to explication (a topic Flynn explores further in chapter 3). Denying that either approach can provide a final way of reading, Flynn concludes that to read McGuckian's work is to be involved in its creation. Faragó's study, simply entitled *Medbh McGuckian*, centres more on the issue of performance in McGuckian's work. Dealing in a comprehensible manner with some very recondite material, Faragó usefully situates McGuckian's poetry in its divided critical contexts, showing the differing readings that source-hunting 'genetic' criticism, postmodernism, feminism, and sheer exasperation have produced. Five chapters follow the poet's work chronologically, and Faragó focuses on issues that include spirituality, creativity, and death. The final chapter is particularly intriguing for the awareness that Faragó shows of the paradoxical nature of its subject's work. Although McGuckian's poetry has often been characterized as feminist, Faragó writes that 'she reconciles her feminine and national identities by internalizing, rather than critiquing, the gendered myth of Mother Ireland' (p. 180).

Eavan Boland received extended attention in 2014, thanks mainly to the efforts of Jody Allen Randolph, who co-edited a special supplement in the *PN Review* entitled 'A Celebration of Eavan Boland' (*PNR* 41:ii[2014] 43–84) alongside Michael Schmidt. This contains pieces from an array of Boland's contemporaries and admirers. Sandra M. Gilbert combines personal reminiscence and literary critique in a reflection on place-making in the suburbs and poetry-making in the quotidian, noting that 'these realms in which we young mother-poets lived were the suburbs of modernism' (p. 81). Mark Doty's tribute concludes memorably that Boland's task as a poet has been 'to honour the unspeakable and to say what one can' (p. 56). Paula Meehan focuses on the social and economic aspects of Boland's work, calling her Dundrum topos 'haunted by the ghosts of the last wolves, the suburb that by the time ['Making Money'] is written has become the site of a massive development project' (p. 56). A conversation between Shara McCallum and Eavan Boland that rounds off the section underlines the consistency of Boland's concerns across a lifetime of writing poetry: 'I'm always drawn to the work of other women poets', Boland says, 'especially to those ... on the "margins" of empire' (p. 84).

As well as this tribute to Eavan Boland, 2014 saw the first extended study of the poet in a monograph, also by Randolph. *Eavan Boland* gives an insight into Boland's family history, then follows the poet's trajectory from her dislocated childhood in a diplomatic family, to her beginnings as a poet as a student at Trinity College, Dublin, then her life as a suburban housewife, mother, and university teacher. In doing this, Randolph consistently connects these varying backgrounds to the poems themselves, providing a useful biographical context for Boland's work. In particular, this broadly chronological study highlights the sources of Boland's consistent focus on themes of nation, suburb, and the female body. Whilst laudatory in general, Randolph also gives space to some (but not all) of the unfavourable critiques that Boland's work has provoked, quoting Clair Wills's question of whether 'overweening pride, or an accurate sense of her own importance' (p. xviii) is at the root of Boland's sense of her place in the canon. Though Boland's work has provoked highly divergent passions in its readers, this monograph is made necessary by the prominent place she has attained in national life. This position was underscored when Mary Robinson, Boland's contemporary at Trinity College, Dublin, and Ireland's first woman president, said at her inauguration: 'As a woman, I want women who have felt themselves outside history to be written back into history, in the words of Eavan Boland, "finding a voice where they found a vision"' (p. 107).

Cary A. Shay's *Of Mermaids and Others: An Introduction to the Poetry of Nuala Ní Dhomhnaill* seeks to contextualize its subject's writing in Irish poetry, women's writing, and Irish-language writing. The book is divided into four chapters, covering Ní Dhomhnaill's engagement with issues of translation, motherhood, sex, and death, and takes an approach that draws on psychoanalysis. The preface and introduction set out the unusual place Ní Dhomhnaill holds in Irish letters, publishing as she does in Irish but working with translators to produce the English-language versions of her works. The introduction then gives an account of Ní Dhomhnaill's formation as a poet and some of the chief influences on her development, including her moving between English-language and Irish-language environments and her astonishing experience of being declared a ward of court at the age of 19 to prevent her from following her Turkish partner abroad. Though this monograph brings together much interesting material on Ní Dhomhnaill, Shay's approach is perhaps at times unquestioning of some mysterious statements by the poet: for example, Shay paraphrases a statement by Ní Dhomhnaill that Ireland's 'history of conquest and language loss ... must be elevated from a subconscious to a conscious symbol' (p. 12) without going into what this elevation would involve.

Many other contemporary poets with origins in the Republic of Ireland were the focus of critical attention this year. Yeonmin Kim's 'Paul Durcan's Ekphrasis: The Political Aesthetics of Hybridity' (*IUR* 44:ii[2014] 381–97) looks at the poet's ekphrastic poems from the point of view of his generational and socio-political background, seeing him as one of the 'so-called "blank generation," whose members grew up in Ireland between the 1960s and the 1980s, defined by Richard Kearney as a "new breed of urbanized and internationalized youth"' (p. 381). Pilar Villar-Argáiz's edited collection,

Literary Visions of Multicultural Ireland: The Immigrant in Contemporary Irish Literature contains several essays on poetry: one by Villar-Argáiz herself on the immigrant in contemporary Irish poetry, one by Katarzyna Poloczek on representations of 'the new Irish' in contemporary poetry, and one by Michaela Schrage-Früh, which takes Kristevan ideas of 'the foreigner … within' as the starting point for an analysis of poetry written since the turn of the millennium. This volume is especially welcome for including essays on poets who have not yet gained the same volume of critical attention as their more famous peers and predecessors. These poets include Pat Boran, Colette Bryce, Leontia Flynn, Sinéad Morrissey, Mary O'Donnell, Michael O'Loughlin, Mary O'Malley, and David Wheatley. In each of the critical essays the writer considers issues of rootedness, integration, and transculturality. The common note between the essays is that the emergence of Ireland as a multi-ethnic state was simultaneous with its Celtic Tiger period. This volume is therefore particularly interesting as an insight into how poets have responded to the opportunities and inequalities of modern capitalism as it has manifested itself in the Republic. It might also prove to contain new directions for the criticism of Irish poetry in the early twenty-first century.

Michael Thurston and Nigel Alderman's *Reading Postwar British and Irish Poetry* recognizes the political complexities of poetry criticism from its wittily punctuated introduction ('Postwar', 'British', 'Irish', and 'Poetry') onward. The volume gives extended attention to the work of Seamus Heaney, Paul Muldoon, and John Montague, while also making room for the analysis of works by Derek Mahon, Nuala Ní Dhomhnaill, and others. The chapters cover broad thematic headings, including landscape, form, place, and history, and are often divided into shorter essays. The authors 'acknowledge that peculiarly difficult history here by at once including Irish poetry with British and separating Irish poetry from British', before winningly (and ruefully) acknowledging that 'that's a lot of work for the conjunction "and" to do' (p. 14). In practice, the works of Irish poets are sometimes considered alongside the works of poets from elsewhere, and sometimes in separate sections. Given the long history of connections and associations between poetry originating from the neighbouring islands, this seems an entirely reasonable approach.

Work on Yeats included two edited collections and several articles during 2014. Marjorie Howes and Joseph Valente's collection *Yeats and Afterwords* begins with the striking statement that Yeats deliberately positioned himself 'at various historical endpoints—of Romanticism, of the Irish colonial experience, of the Ascendancy, of civilization itself' (p. 1). An excellent set of essays follows on the subject of 'the sense of fatal belatedness that was, still more than Maud Gonne, Yeats's true muse' (p. 3). The book is divided into three parts, the first of which, 'The Last Romantics', focuses on Yeats's relationships with his literary forebears. This section includes an insightful essay by Elizabeth Cullingford on Yeats's repurposing of ancient materials to comment on the new Free State (pp. 42–79). Part II focuses on Yeats's revisions and self-criticisms, and includes a welcome and vastly knowledgeable piece on the differences between the 1925 and 1937 editions of *A Vision* by Margaret Mills Harper (pp. 189–212). The final section, entitled 'Yeats's

Aftertimes', includes essays that examine how the poet's own sense of belatedness influenced writers (including Samuel Beckett, Elizabeth Bowen, and contemporary poets) who engaged with his legacy. Taken together, this collection is a striking affirmation of Wallace Stevens's dictum that it 'is one of the peculiarities of the imagination that it is always at the end of an era'—or, in Yeats's case, several eras.

The *Yeats Annual*, edited by Margaret Mills Harper and Warwick Gould, takes masks as its theme, containing a series of reflections on disguise, theatre, and Yeats's ongoing attempts to find an identity. Highlights include Warwick Gould's 'The Mask before *The Mask*' (*YeA* 19[2014] 3–47), an examination of Yeats's early preoccupations with masks. In this article Gould identifies the years 1908–9 as a crucial period in which long-meditated ideas of the Mask 'suddenly crystallized as an ethical and aesthetic doctrine' (p. 5). In '*A Vision* and Yeats's Late Masks' (*YeA* 19[2014] 147–66), Margaret Mills Harper looks at what happened to the doctrine of the Mask between the publication of Yeats's 1925 and 1937 editions of *A Vision*, tweaking Yeats's line to suggest that 'it is ourselves that we make and remake' (p. 150). Emilie Morin's '"I beg your pardon?": W.B. Yeats, Audibility and Sound Transmission' (*YeA* 19[2014] 191–219) focuses on the radio, taking its title from Yeats's faux-naive question to a wireless set he was having difficulty hearing. Combining archival scholarship with the broadcasting histories of Britain and Ireland, she states that he 'alternately acknowledged and failed to come to terms with the complexities of sound transmission' (p. 218). Michael Cade-Stewart's 'Mask and Robe: Yeats's *Oxford Book of Modern Verse* (1936) and *New Poems* (1938)' (*YeA* 19[2014] 221–58) looks at the effect on Yeats's poetry of his editorship of the *Oxford Book of Modern Verse* [1936], arguing that 'the encumbering robe of office proved less potent than the enabling energies of the new and refurbished masks that accompanied it' (p. 257).

Barry Sheils's 'Poetry in the Modern State: The Example of W.B. Yeats's "Late Style" and "New Fanaticism"' (*NLH* 45:iii[2014] 483–505) explores Yeats's 'fanatical' late political stances in tandem with his intemperate poetic responses to the depredations brought by old age. The psychology of the late Yeats is also at issue in Anne Christine McNeil's short piece, 'Fly or Fall: The Risk of the Remade Self in W.B. Yeats's "An Acre of Grass"' (*Expl* 72:iv[2014] 289–92). In this article, McNeil takes issue with critics who see Yeats's late poem as motivated by a desire for transcendence, emphasizing instead those elements of the poem that communicate the possibility of 'tragic downfall' (p. 291). Yeats's late work is also examined in Daniel Feldman's 'Poetry in Question: The Interrogative Lyric of Yeats's Major Poems' (*PAns*12:i[2014] 87–105), which takes Yeats's 'Among School Children' for its start and end points (though it mistakenly situates the visit that prompted it in Dublin rather than Waterford). In a style that is inflected by Lacan and de Man, on whose work Feldman draws, the article concludes that 'interrogative poetry reveals what we know and, undoubtedly of greater importance, what we do not' (p. 103).

Late Yeats is also the subject of Laura O'Connor's essay, 'W.B. Yeats and Modernist Poetry' (in Cleary, ed., *The Cambridge Companion to Irish Modernism*, pp. 77–94). In it, she makes the arresting point that Yeats's *The Wanderings of Oisin* was published in 1889 and Samuel Beckett's 'Comment

Dire' in 1989, and therefore the publication period of Irish poets associated with the heyday of the modernist movement (often periodized 1890–1939) lasted a century. Yeats's association with the modernists is a more knotted and contested affair than Beckett's but, as O'Connor points out, his transition from Victorian Romanticism to high modernism highlights the continuities that the movement represented, rather than the sense of rupture with which it is typically associated.

Nicholas Meihuizen takes an unusual approach in 'Yeats, Vendler, and Byzantium' (*IUR* 44:ii[2014] 234–53), an article-length act of meta-criticism of Helen Vendler's reading of 'Sailing to Byzantium' in *Our Secret Discipline* [2007]. He first sets out other critical demurrals from her approach, then attacks her sexualized reading of 'Sailing to Byzantium', ultimately accusing her of 'an almost Johnsonian confidence, but also, surely, a lack of subtlety and receptivity' (p. 247). George Bornstein's 'Reading Yeats's "September 1913" in its Contexts' (*SR* 122:ii[2014] 224–35) situates Yeats's poem in its temporal contexts (including the Lane Pictures controversy and the Dublin Lockout), and its textual ones, analysing the 1913 politics of *The Irish Times*, in which it first appeared. Irene Gilsenan Nordin's 'The Place of Writing in the Poetry of W.B. Yeats and Patrick Kavanagh' (*NJES* 13:ii[2014] 43–56) also seeks to place Yeats in his context, contrasting his symbolic style, as others have done before her, with Kavanagh's more 'concrete, emotional and intimate' approach to place (p. 55).

Two essays containing reflections on Yeats are offered in Anne Markey and Anne O'Connor's collection *Folklore and Modern Irish Writing*. Bríona Nic Dhiarmada's '"With a Faery, Hand in Hand": W.B. Yeats, Marina Tsvetayeva, Nuala Ní Dhomhnaill and the Uses of Folklore' (pp. 142–50) opens with indications of the low esteem in which folklore was held in some circles at the end of the nineteenth century, before arguing that both Yeats and Ní Dhomhnaill have used folklore to radical ends: 'Yeats in the making of an Irish modern tradition and Ní Dhomhnaill in giving women a voice denied them in the past' (p. 149). Early Yeats is also the subject of John Dillon's 'Mary Battle and W.B. Yeats—From Folklore to *Gesamtlebenswerk*' (pp. 82–96), which examines the relationship between the poet and the shadowy, second-sighted family servant. Dillon argues that Yeats recognized that 'textual transmission does not do justice to folk culture' (p. 93). Early Yeats was also the subject of Fergal Casey's 'A Celtic Twilight in Little England: G.K. Chesterton and W.B. Yeats' (*ISR* 22:i[2014] 80–90), which shows how ideas of anti-colonialism were not limited to Ireland in the years preceding independence. Taking personal links between Chesterton and Yeats as its starting point, Casey argues that significant elements of Yeats's Revivalist thinking were influential on Chesterton's *The Napoleon of Notting Hill*. Casey points out such shared preoccupations as 'anti-imperialism, mysticism, small-scale economic ingenuity, and parochial patriotism' (p. 88). It is a useful reminder of Edna Longley's assertion that 'The Celtic Twilight fogged up the entire archipelago.'

This year also saw the appearance of Charles I. Armstrong's compelling 'Pub, Parlour, Theatre: Radio in the Imagination of W.B. Yeats' (in Feldman, Tonning, and Mead, eds., pp. 23–37), which begins with a fascinating account of Yeats's distress at the gap between the high-quality effects that actors were able to achieve on the Abbey stage and the 'groans, roars, bellows' (p. 23) that came across on a BBC broadcast in the late 1930s. Armstrong links Yeats's willingness to experiment and innovate on the air with the same qualities in his poetry. This article is a reflection on the nature of radio itself, and its 'paradoxical combination of the solitary and the public' (p. 26). Armstrong also published this year on one of Yeats's little-explored early relationships in his article, 'The "Intimate Enemies": Edward Dowden, W.B. Yeats and the Formation of Character' (*NJES* 13:ii[2014] 80–95), which looks beyond usual analyses of the relationship between Yeats and Dowden, arguing that their famed public antagonism has obscured the ways in which they were in dialogue with each other. Examining ideas of the formation of character in particular, Armstrong argues that an understanding of Yeats's relationship with Dowden is crucial to situating the poet in his Victorian context. Like many of the critics who published on Yeats in 2014, this article shows him in comparative context. There was, however, a particular emphasis on comparisons between Yeats and Heaney, whose relationship was given extended attention by Terence Brown, Neil Corcoran, and Richard Rankin Russell. The willingness of critics to view Yeats and Heaney together not only suggests the profound influence of the former poet on the latter, but also indicates the esteem in which Heaney is held.

Books Reviewed

Alden, Natasha. *Reading Behind the Lines: Postmemory in Contemporary British War Fiction*. ManUP. [2014] pp. 208. £60 ISBN 9 7807 1908 8933.

Al-Jubouri, Firas A.J. *Milestones on the Road to Dystopia: Interpreting George Orwell's Self-Division in an Era of 'Force and Fraud'*. CambridgeSP. [2014] pp. 270. £44.99 ISBN 9 7814 4385 4559.

Allen, Brigid. *Peter Levi: Oxford Romantic*. Signal. [2014] pp. 452. £19.99 ISBN 9 7819 0849 3989.

Aragay, Mireia, and Enric Monforte, eds. *Ethical Speculations in Contemporary British Theatre*. Palgrave. [2014] pp. 240. £49.49 ISBN 9 7811 3729 7563.

Ardoin, Paul, S.E. Gontarski, and Laci Mattison, eds. *Understanding Deleuze, Understanding Modernism*. Bloomsbury. [2014] pp. xiv + 284. £60 ISBN 9 7816 2356 3493.

Arneson, Patricia, and Ronald C. Arnett, eds. *Philosophy of Communication Ethics: Alterity and the Other*. FDUP. [2014] pp. 344. £60 ISBN 9 7816 1147 7078.

Ashe, Laura, and Ian Patterson, eds. *War and Literature*. Brewer. [2014] pp. 266. £30 ISBN 9 7818 4384 3818.

Astley, Neil, ed. *Bedouin of the London Evening: Collected Poems and Selected Prose of Rosemary Tonks*. Bloodaxe. [2014] pp. 153. £12 ISBN 9 7817 8037 2389.

Atkins, G. Douglas *T.S. Eliot: The Poet as Christian*. PalMac. [2014] pp. vii + 110. £45 ISBN 9 7811 3744 6886.

Atkins, G. Douglas *T.S. Eliot's Christmas Poems*. PalMac. [2014] pp. viii + 93. £45 ISBN 9 7811 3748 5700.

Attewell, Nadine. *Better Britons: Reproduction, National Identity, and the Afterlife of Empire*. UTorP. [2014] pp. xi + 324. £45.99 ISBN 9 7814 4264 7022.

Bahun, Sanja. *Modernism and Melancholia: Writing as Countermourning*. OUP. [2014] pp. 256. £45 ISBN 9 7801 9997 7956.

Bailes, Sara Jane, Nicholas Till, eds. *Beckett and Musicality*. Ashgate. [2014] pp. 286. £70 ISBN 9 7814 7240 9638.

Bailey, Iain. *Samuel Beckett and the Bible*. Bloomsbury. [2014] pp. 214. £60 ISBN 9 7817 8093 6888.

Baker, William, and Jeanette Roberts Shumaker. *Bernard Kops: Fantasist, London Jew, Apocalyptic Humorist*. FDUP. [2014] pp. xvii + 149. £44.95 ISBN 9 7816 1147 6569.

Baxter, Jeanette, and David James, eds. *Andrea Levy: Contemporary Critical Perspectives*. Bloomsbury. [2014] pp. xvii + 155. hb £55 ISBN 9 7814 4116 0454, pb £17.99 ISBN 9 7814 4111 3603.

Beer, John. *D.H. Lawrence: Nature, Narrative and Identity*. PalMac. [2014] pp. ix + 243. £55 ISBN 9 7811 3744 1645.

Bernardo, Susan M., ed. *Environments in Science Fiction: Essays on Alternative Spaces*. McFarland. [2014] pp. 277. £36.50 ISBN 9 7807 8647 5797.

Bird, Hazel Sheeky. *Class, Leisure and National Identity in British Children's Literature, 1918–1950*. Palgrave. [2014] pp. x + 208. £60 ISBN 9 7811 3740 7429.

Birmingham, Kevin. *The Most Dangerous Book: The Battle for James Joyce's 'Ulysses'*. Penguin. [2014] pp. 417. £19.69 ISBN 9 7815 9420 3367.

Bîrsanu, Roxana Stefania, *T.S. Eliot's 'The Waste Land' as a Place of Intercultural Exchanges: A Translation Perspective*. CambridgeSP. [2014]. pp. xix + 247. £44.99 ISBN 9 7814 4385 9691.

Bohata, Kirsti, and Katie Gramich, eds. *Rediscovering Margiad Evans: Marginality, Gender and Illness*. UWalesP. [2013] pp. 223. £30 ISBN 9 7807 0832 5605.

Bolt, David. *The Metanarrative of Blindness: A Re-reading of Twentieth-Century Anglophone Writing*. UMichP. [2014] pp. 178. £40 ISBN 9 7804 7202 9587.

Boltanski, Luc. *Mysteries and Conspiracies: Detective Stories, Spy Novels and the Making of Modern Societies*. Polity. [2014] pp. 320. £55 ISBN 9 7807 4566 4040.

Booth, James. *Philip Larkin: Life, Art and Love*. Bloomsbury. [2014] pp. 532. £25 ISBN 9 7814 0885 1661.

Borg, Ruben, Paul Fagan, and Werner Huber, eds. *Flann O'Brien: Contesting Legacies*. CorkUP. [2014] pp. 296. £33.25 ISBN 9 7817 8205 0766.

Brawley, Chris. *Nature and the Numinous in Mythopoeic Fantasy Literature*. McFarland. [2014] pp. ix + 199. £33.95 ISBN 9 7807 8649 4651.

Brazeau, Robert, and Derek Gladwin, eds. *Eco-Joyce: The Environmental Imagination of James Joyce*. CorkUP. [2014] pp. xviii + 329. €39 ISBN 9 7817 8205 0728.

Bricout, Shirley. *Politics and the Bible in D.H. Lawrence's Leadership Novels*. Presses Universitaires de la Méditerranée. [2014] pp. 350. €29 ISBN 9 7823 6781 1048.

Brouillette, Sarah. *Literature and the Creative Economy*. StanfordUP. [2014] pp. ix + 238. £31 ISBN 9 7808 0478 9486.

Canani, Marco, and Sara Sullam, eds. *Parallaxes: Virginia Woolf Meets James Joyce*. CambridgeSP. [2014] pp. xviii + 240. £44.99 ISBN 9 7814 4385 6232.

Carroll, Rachel, and Adam Hansen, eds. *Litpop: Writing and Popular Music*. Ashgate. [2014] pp. 258. £63 ISBN 9 7814 7241 0979.

Carver, Beci. *Granular Modernism*. OUP. [2014] pp. 208. £55 ISBN 9 7801 9870 9923.

Chalk, Bridget T. *Modernism and Mobility: The Passport and Cosmopolitan Experience*. Palgrave. [2014] pp. 256. £60 ISBN 9 7811 3743 9826.

Chan, Evelyn Tsz Yan. *Virginia Woolf and the Professions*. CUP. [2014] pp. 256. £64.99 ISBN 9 7811 0707 0240.

Chantler, Ashley, and Rob Hawkes, eds. *Ford Madox Ford's Parade's End: The First World War, Culture, and Modernity*. Rodopi. [2014] pp. 232. £34 ISBN 9 7890 4203 8639.

Chapman, Siobhan, and Billy Clark, eds. *Pragmatic Literary Stylistics*. Palgrave. [2014] pp. 240. £60.99 ISBN 9 7811 3702 3254.

Chintz, David E., and Gail McDonald, eds. *A Companion to Modernist Poetry*. Blackwell. [2014] pp. 620. £120. ISBN 9 7804 7065 9816.

Cleary, Joe, ed. *The Cambridge Companion to Irish Modernism*. CUP. [2014] pp. 286. £49.49 ISBN 9 7811 0703 1418.

Corcoran, Neil *Poetry & Responsibility*. LiverUP. [2014] pp. ix + 218. £75 ISBN 9 7817 8138 0352.

Cuthbertson, Guy. *Wilfred Owen*. YaleUP. [2014] pp. 346. £25 ISBN 9 7803 0015 3002.

Davison, Claire. *Translation as Collaboration: Virginia Woolf, Katherine Mansfield and S.S. Koteliansky*. EdinUP. [2014] pp. 208. £70 ISBN 9 7807 4868 2812.

Davison, Sarah. *Modernist Literatures: A Reader's Guide to Essential Criticism*. Palgrave. [2014] pp. 248. £17.99 ISBN 9 7802 3028 4012.

Dean, Joan FitzPatrick. *All Dressed Up: Modern Irish Historical Pageantry*. SyracuseUP. [2014] pp. 344. £37.30 ISBN 9 7808 1563 3747.

Dean, Joan FitzPatrick, and José Lanters, ed. *Beyond Realism: Experimental and Unconventional Irish Drama since the Revival*. Rodopi. [2014] pp. 248. £37 ISBN 9 7890 4203 9193.

DiBattista, Maria, and Emily O. Wittman, eds. *Modernism and Autobiography*. CUP. [2014] pp. 318. £60 ISBN 9 7811 0702 5226.

Dove, Richard, and Ian Wallace, eds. *Vision and Reality: Central Europe after Hitler*. Rodopi. [2014] pp. 272. £40 ISBN 9 7890 4203 8158.

Ebury, Katherine. *Modernism and Cosmology: Absurd Lights*. PalMac. [2014] pp. 224. £60 ISBN 9 7811 3739 3746.

Ellis, Steven. *British Writers and the Approach of World War II*. CUP. [2014] pp. 260. £54 ISBN 9 7811 0705 4585.

English, Elizabeth. *Lesbian Modernism: Censorship, Sexuality and Genre Fiction*. EdinUP. [2014] pp. 224. £70 ISBN 9 7807 4869 3733.

Enniss, Stephen. *After the Titanic: A Life of Derek Mahon*. G&M. [2014] pp. xx + 329. £26.99 ISBN 9 7807 1716 4417.

Faragó, Borbála. *Medbh McGuckian*. BuckUP. [2014] pp. xi + 225. £44.95 ISBN 9 7816 1148 5639.

Feigel, Lara. *The Love-Charm of Bombs: Restless Lives in the Second World War*. Bloomsbury. [2014] pp. 528. £25 ISBN 9 7814 0883 0444.

Feldman, Matthew, Erik Tonning, and Henry Mead, eds. *Broadcasting in the Modernist Era*. Bloomsbury. [2014] pp. 296. £60 ISBN 9 7814 7251 2482.

Fludernik, Monika, and Miriam Nandi, eds. *Idleness, Indolence and Leisure in English Literature*. Palgrave. [2014] pp. 328. £60 ISBN 9 7811 3740 3995.

Flynn, Leontia. *Reading Medbh McGuckian*. IAP. [2014] pp. vii + 200. £24.99 ISBN 9 7807 1653 1173.

Frawley, Oona, and Katherine O'Callaghan, eds. *James Joyce and Cultural Memory*. Memory Ireland 4. SyracuseUP. [2014] pp. xi + 234. £37.95 ISBN 9 7808 1563 3525.

Frayn, Andrew. *Writing Disenchantment: British First World War Prose, 1914–30*. ManUP. [2014] pp. x + 259. £70 ISBN 9 7807 1908 9220.

Freedman, William. *Joseph Conrad and the Anxiety of Knowledge*. U of South Carolina P. [2014] pp. 200. £49.95 ISBN 9 7816 1117 3062.

Gallagher, Donat, and Villar, Carlos. *In the Picture: The Facts Behind the Fiction in Evelyn Waugh's 'Sword of Honour'*. Rodopi. [2014] pp. 370. £70 ISBN 9 7890 4203 9001.

Gibson, Brian. *Reading Saki: The Fiction of H.H. Munro*. McFarland. [2014] pp. viii + 287. £43.50 ISBN 9 7807 8647 9498.

Gildersleeve, Jessica. *Elizabeth Bowen and the Writing of Trauma: The Ethics of Survival*. Rodopi. [2014] pp. 250. £38 ISBN 9 7890 4203 7991.

Gillies, Mary Ann, and Helen Wussow, eds. *Virginia Woolf and the Common(wealth) Reader*. ClemsonUP. [2014] pp. 277. £25 ISBN 9 7809 8908 2679.

Gitelman, Lisa. *Paper Knowledge: Toward a Media History of Documents*. DukeUP. [2014] pp. xiii + 210. pb £15.99 ISBN 9 7808 2235 6578.

Gobert, R. Darren. *The Theatre of Caryl Churchill*. Bloomsbury. [2014] pp. 308. pb £16.99 ISBN 9 7814 0815 4526.

Goldstone, Andrew. *Fictions of Autonomy: Modernism from Wilde to de Man*. OUP. [2013] pp. xiv + 204. £41.99 ISBN 9 7801 9986 1125.

Goodby, John. *The Poetry of Dylan Thomas: Under the Spelling Wall*. LiverUP. [2013] pp. xx + 492. £75 ISBN 9 7818 4631 8764.

Gott, Henry Michael. *Ascetic Modernism in the Work of T.S. Eliot and Gustave Flaubert*. P&C. [2013] pp. 240. £95 ISBN 9 7818 4893 4375.

Gurfinkel, Helena. *Outlaw Fathers in Victorian and Modern British Literature: Queering Patriarchy*. FDUP. [2014] pp. xii + 223. £60 ISBN 9 7816 1147 6378.

Hammond, Meghan Marie. *Empathy and the Psychology of Literary Modernism*. EdinUP. [2014] pp. 216. £60 ISBN 9 7807 4869 0985.

Härmänmaa, Marja, and Christopher Nissen, eds. *Decadence, Degeneration, and the End: Studies in the European Fin de Siècle*. Palgrave. [2014] pp. 272. £60 ISBN 9 7811 3747 0881.

Horton, Emily. *Contemporary Crisis Fiction: Affect and Ethics in the Modern British Novel*. Palgrave. [2014] pp. 280. £55 ISBN 9 7811 3735 0190.

Howes, Marjorie, and Joseph Valente, *Yeats and Afterwords*. UNDP. [2014] pp. vii + 348. £30.99 ISBN 9 7802 6801 1208.

Hubble, Nick, John McLeod, and Philip Tew, eds. *The 1970s: A Decade of Contemporary British Fiction*. Bloomsbury. [2014] pp. 288. £52.50 ISBN 9 7814 4113 3915.

Iida, Takeo. *D.H. Lawrence as Anti-Rationalist: Mysticism, Animism and Cosmic Life in His Works*. Melrose. [2014] pp. xii + 175. £9.99 ISBN 9 7819 0975 7165.

Ionescu, Arleen. *Romanian Joyce: From Hostility to Hospitality*. Lang. [2014] pp. 267. £43 ISBN 9 7836 3165 2916.

Jaffe, Aaron. *The Way Things Go: An Essay on the Matter of Second Modernism*. UMinnP. [2014] pp. 159. pb £17 ISBN 9 7808 1669 2033.

Jaillant, Lise. *Modernism, Middlebrow and the Literary Canon: The Modern Library Series 1917–1955*. P&C. [2014] pp. xii + 251. £60 ISBN 9 7818 4893 4931.

Jameson, Fredric. *The Antinomies of Realism*. Verso. [2013] pp. 326. pb £12.99 ISBN 9 7817 8168 8175.

Joyce, Simon. *Modernism and Naturalism in British and Irish Fiction, 1880–1930*. CUP. [2014] pp. 250. £60 ISBN 9 7811 0708 3882.

Kamblé, Jayashree. *Making Meaning in Popular Romance Fiction: An Epistemology*. Palgrave. [2014] pp. 191. HB £56.00. ISBN 9 7811 3739 5047.

Kane, Jean. *Conspicuous Bodies: Provincial Belief and the Making of Joyce and Rushdie*. OSUP. [2014] pp. 209. £38.42 ISBN 9 7808 1421 2608.

Kearney, Eileen, and Charlotte Headrick, eds. *Irish Women Dramatists 1908—2001*. SyracuseUP. [2014] pp. 304. pb £31.50 ISBN 9 7808 1563 3754.

Kennedy-Andrews, Elmer. *Northern Irish Poetry: The American Connection*. PalMac. [2014] pp. 312. £55 ISBN 9 7811 3733 0390.

Kimber, Gerri. *Katherine Mansfield and the Art of the Short Story*. Palgrave. [2014] pp. 114. £45 ISBN 9 7811 3748 3874.

Kimber, Gerri, and Angela Smith, eds. *The Poetry and Critical Writings of Katherine Mansfield: The Edinburgh Edition of the Collected Works*, vol. 3. EdinUP. [2014] pp. 784. £125. ISBN 9 7807 4868 5011.

Kimber, Gerri, Todd Martin, Delia da Sousa Correa, Isobel Maddison, and Alice Kelly, eds. *Katherine Mansfield and World War One*. EdinUP. [2014] pp. x + 194. £45.50 ISBN 9 7807 4869 5348.

Kohlmann, Benjamin. *Committed Styles: Modernism, Politics, and Left-Wing Literature in the 1930s*. OUP. [2014] pp. vi + 223. £60 ISBN 9 7801 9871 5467.

Krivokapić-Knežević, Marija, and Aleksandra Nikčević-Batrićvić, eds. *The Beauty of Convention: Essays in Literature and Culture*. CambridgeSP. [2014] pp. 270. £44.99 ISBN 9 7814 4385 4696.

Krueger, Kate. *British Women Writers and the Short Story, 1850–1930: Reclaiming Social Space*. PalMac. [2014] pp. 264. £50 ISBN 9 7811 3735 9230.

Kujawska-Lis, Ewa, and Anna Krawczyk-Łaskarzewska, eds. *Reflections on/ of Dickens*. CambridgeSP. [2014] pp. 380. £49.99 ISBN 9 7814 4386 0086.

Laera, Margherita. *Theatre and Adaptation: Return, Rewrite and Adaptation*. [2014] pp. viii + 284. pb £22.99 ISBN 9 7814 0818 4721.

Lanigan, Liam. *James Joyce, Urban Planning, and Irish Modernism: Dublins of the Future*. PalMac. [2014] pp. ix + 243. £55 ISBN 9 7811 3737 8194.

Latham, Sean, ed. *The Cambridge Companion to 'Ulysses'*. CUP. [2014] pp. xxv + 229. pb $29.99 ISBN 9 7811 0742 3909.

Latta, Corey. *When the Eternal Can Be Met: The Bergsonian Theology of Time in the Works of C.S. Lewis, T.S. Eliot, and W.H. Auden*. Pickwick. [2014] pp. viii + 226. $20.80 ISBN 9 7807 1889 3606.

Lawrie, Alexandra. *The Beginnings of University English: Extramural Study, 1885–1910*. Palgrave. [2014] pp. ix + 190. £50 ISBN 9 7811 3730 9105 .

Lazenby, Donna. *A Mystical Philosophy: Transcendence and Immanence in the Works of Virginia Woolf and Iris Murdoch*. Bloomsbury. [2014] pp. 344. £65 ISBN 9 7814 7252 2801.

Lee, Hermione. *'To Pin Down the Moment with Date and Season'*. VWSGB. [2014] pp. 16. £5 ISBN 9 7809 5557 1763.

Leonard, Philip. *Literature After Globalization: Textuality, Technology and the Nation-State*. Bloomsbury. [2014] pp. viii + 219. £65 ISBN 9 7814 4119 0710.

Levene, Mark, ed. *Political Fiction*. Salem. [2014] pp. 300. £86.50 ISBN 9 7816 1925 4114.

Lockerd, Benjamin G., ed. *T.S. Eliot and Christian Tradition*. FDUP. [2014] pp. 328. £60. ISBN 9 7816 1147 6125.

Lombardo, Patrizia, Lars Sætre, and Julien Zanetta, eds. *Exploring Text and Emotions*. AarhusUP. [2014] pp. 440. £35 ISBN 9 7887 7934 5584.

Long, Maebh. *Assembling Flann O'Brien*. Bloomsbury. [2014] pp. 256. £60 ISBN 9 7814 4119 0208.

Lorenzo, David J. *Cities at the End of the World: Using Utopian and Dystopian Stories to Reflect Critically on our Political Beliefs, Communities, and Ways of Life*. Bloomsbury. [2014] pp. 240. £65 ISBN 9 7814 4114 1552.

Lounsberry, Barbara. *Becoming Virginia Woolf: Her Early Diaries and the Diaries She Read*. UFlorP. [2014] pp. 272. £67.95 ISBN 9 7808 1304 9915.

Louth, Charlie, and Patrick McGuinness, eds. *A C.H. Sisson Reader*. Carcanet. [2014] pp. 501. £19.95 ISBN 9 7818 4777 2657.

Manfredi, Camille, ed. *Alasdair Gray: Ink for Worlds*. Palgrave. [2014] pp. 240. £55 ISBN 9 7811 3740 1779.

Mannion, Elizabeth. *The Urban Plays of the Early Abbey Theatre: Beyond O'Casey*. SyracuseUP. [2014] pp. 264. £27.95 ISBN 9 7808 1563 3679.

Marcus, Laura. *Dreams of Modernity: Psychoanalysis, Cinema, Literature*. CUP. [2014] pp. 250. £50 ISBN 9 7811 0704 4968.

Marcus, Laura, and Ankhi Mukherjee, eds. *A Concise Companion to Psychoanalysis, Literature, and Culture*. Blackwell. [2014] pp. 450. £79.99 ISBN 9 7814 0518 8609.

Markey, Anne, and Anne O'Connor, eds. *Folklore and Modern Irish Writing*. IAP. [2014]. pp. xi + 250. pb £24.99 ISBN 9 7807 1653 2637.

Maslen, Elizabeth. *Life in the Writings of Storm Jameson: A Biography*. NorthwesternUP. [2014] pp. xix + 556. £35.50 ISBN 9 7808 1016 7674.

Matthews, Steven. *T.S. Eliot and Early Modern Literature*. OUP. [2013] pp. 249. £56 ISBN 9 7801 9957 4773.

McConnell, Gail. *Northern Irish Poetry and Theology*. PalMac. [2014] pp. xi + 261. £50 ISBN 9 7811 3734 3833.

McDonald, Ronan, Sascha Morrell, and Julian Murphet, eds. *Flann O'Brien and Modernism*. Bloomsbury. [2014] pp. 248. £19.99 ISBN 9 7816 2356 8504.

Mills, Jean. *Virginia Woolf, Jane Ellen Harrison and the Spirit of Modernist Classicism*. OSUP. [2014] pp. 224. £26.99 ISBN 9 7808 1421 2523.

Moseley, Merritt. *The Fiction of Pat Barker: A Reader's Guide to Essential Criticism*. Palgrave. [2014] pp. 184. £50 ISBN 9 7802 3029 3304.

Mounic, Anne. *Ah What Is It?—That I Heard: Katherine Mansfield's Wings of Wonder*. Rodopi. [2014] pp. xiii + 245. £50.40 ISBN 9 7890 4203 8646.

Muckle, John. *Little White Bull: British Fiction in the 50s and 60s*. Shearsman. [2014] pp. 342. pb £14.95 ISBN 9 7818 4861 3058.

Nash, John, ed. *James Joyce in the Nineteenth Century*. CUP. [2013] pp. xv + 259. pb £19.99 ISBN 9 7811 0751 4744.

Nash, Katherine Saunders. *Feminist Narrative Ethics: Tacit Persuasion in Modernist Form*. OSUP. [2014] pp. x + 178. £59.95 ISBN 9 7808 1421 2424.

Norris, Barney. *To Bodies Gone: The Theatre of Peter Gill*. Seren Books. [2014] pp. 260. pb £14.99 ISBN 9 7817 8172 1810.

North, Michael. *Novelty: A History of the New*. UChicP. [2013] pp. 258. £18 ISBN 9 7802 2607 7871.

Parker, Richard, ed. *News from Afar: Ezra Pound and Some Contemporary British Poetries*. Shearsman. [2014] pp. 328. £14.95 ISBN 9 7818 4861 3645.

Paterson, Don. *Smith: A Reader's Guide to the Poetry of Michael Donaghy*. Picador. [2014] pp. 272. £9.99 ISBN 9 7814 4728 1979.

Patterson, Annabel. *The International Novel*. YaleUP. [2014] pp. x + 261. £60 ISBN 9 7803 0019 8003.

Peppis, Paul. *Sciences of Modernism: Ethnography, Sexology, and Psychology*. CUP. [2014] pp. xiv + 310. £60 ISBN 9 7811 0704 2643.

Perfect, Michael. *Contemporary Fictions of Multiculturalism: Diversity and the Millennial London Novel*. Palgrave. [2014] pp. xii + 221. £55 ISBN 9 7811 3730 7118.

Pilling, John. *Samuel Beckett's 'More Pricks Than Kicks' In a Strait of Two Wills*. Bloomsbury. [2014] pp. 276. £18.99 ISBN 9 7814 7252 5727.

Platt, Len, Tobias Becker, and David Linton, eds. *Popular Musical Theatre in London and Berlin: 1890–1939*. CUP. [2014] pp. 227. £64.99 ISBN 9 7811 0705 1003.

Pollard, Natalie, ed. *Don Paterson: Contemporary Critical Essays*. EdinUP. [2014] pp. 163. £60 ISBN 9 7807 4866 9417.

Price, Brian L., César A. Salgado, and John Pedro Schwartz, eds. *TransLatin Joyce: Global Transmissions in Ibero-American Literature*. PalMac. [2014] pp. xx + 260. £53.50 ISBN 9 7811 3740 7450.

Punter, David. *The Literature of Pity*. EdinUP. [2014] pp. 256. £70 ISBN 9 7807 4863 9496.

Randolph, Jody Allen. *Eavan Boland*. BuckUP. [2014] pp. xxxi + 249. £42.75 ISBN 9 7816 1148 5363.

Rawlinson, Mark. *First World War Plays: Night Watches, My Eyes Have Seen, Tunnel Trench, Post Mortem, Oh What a Lovely War, The Accrington*

Pals, Sea and Land and Sky. Bloomsbury. [2014] pp. 496. pb £19.99 ISBN 9 7814 7252 9893.

Rolls, Jans Ondatje. *The Bloomsbury Cookbook*. T&H. [2014] pp. 384. £24.95 ISBN 9 7805 0051 7307.

Rosenbaum, S.P. *The Bloomsbury Memoir Club*. PalMac. [2014] pp. 216. £20 ISBN 9 7811 3736 0359.

Rosner, Victoria. *The Cambridge Companion to the Bloomsbury Group*. CUP. [2014] pp. 256. £19.99 ISBN 9 7811 0762 3415.

Ruderman, Judith. *Race and Identity in D.H. Lawrence: Indians, Gypsies, and Jews*. PalMac. [2014] pp. xi + 292. $95 ISBN 9 7811 3739 8826.

Russell, Richard Rankin, ed. *Bernard MacLaverty: New Critical Readings*. Bloomsbury. [2014] pp. 208. £42 ISBN 9 7814 4113 7869.

Russell, Richard Rankin. *Seamus Heaney's Regions*. UNDP. [2014] pp. xiv + 498. pb £46.50 ISBN 9 7802 6804 0369.

Ryle, Martin, and Julia Jordan, eds. *B.S. Johnson and Post-War Literature: Possibilities of the Avant-Garde*. Palgrave. [2014] pp. 232. £55 ISBN 9 7811 3734 9545.

Sandberg, Eric. *Virginia Woolf: Experiments in Character*. Cambria. [2014] pp. 340. £72.99 ISBN 9 7816 0497 8667.

Savage, Roger. *Masques, Mayings and Music-Dramas: Vaughan Williams and the Early Twentieth-Century Stage*. Boydell. [2014] pp. 402. £60 ISBN 9 7818 4383 9194.

Scappettone, Jennifer. *Killing the Moonlight: Modernism in Venice*. ColUP. [2014] pp. xvi + 440. £41.50 ISBN 9 7802 3116 4320.

Schmidt, Michael. *The Novel: A Biography*. HarvardUP. [2014] pp. 1,172. £70 ISBN 9 7806 7472 4730.

Schoenbach, Lisi. *Pragmatic Modernism*. OUP. [2014] pp. 218. £19.99 ISBN 9 7801 9020 7342.

Schuchard, Ronald, and Jewel Spears Brooker, eds. *The Complete Prose of T.S. Eliot: The Critical Edition, vol. 1: Apprentice Years, 1905–1918*. JHUP. [2014] pp 896. ISBN 9 7814 2140 6756. Currently by subscription only.

Schuchard, Ronald, and Anthony Cuda, eds. *The Complete Prose of T.S. Eliot: The Critical Edition, vol. 2: The Perfect Critic, 1919–1926*. JHUP. [2014] pp. 992. ISBN 9 7814 2140 6770. Currently by subscription only.

Shay, Cary A. *Of Mermaids and Others: An Introduction to the Poetry of Nuala Ní Dhomhnaill*. Lang. [2014] pp. xxviii + 258. £55 ISBN 9 7830 3430 8106.

Sherry, Vincent. *Modernism and the Reinvention of Decadence*. CUP. [2014] pp. xi + 333. £60 ISBN 9 7811 0707 9328.

Snaith, Anna. *Modernist Voyages: Colonial Women Writers in London, 1890–1945*. CUP. [2014] pp. 278. £60 ISBN 9 7805 2151 5450.

Spalding, Frances. *Virginia Woolf: Art, Life and Vision*. NPG. [2014] pp. 192. £18.29 ISBN 9 7818 5514 4811.

Spariosu, Mihai I. *Modernism and Exile: Liminality and the Utopian Imagination*. Palgrave. [2014] pp. 224. £55 ISBN 9 7802 3023 1412.

Sperling, Matthew. *Visionary Philology: Geoffrey Hill and the Study of Words*. OUP. [2014] pp. 204. £62 ISBN 9 7801 9870 1088.

Stannard, Julian. *Basil Bunting*. Northcote. [2014] pp. 146. £40 ISBN 9 7807 4631 0489.

Tally, Robert T. Jr., ed. *Literary Cartographies: Spatiality, Representation, and Narrative.* Palgrave. [2014] pp. 252. £57.50 ISBN 9 7811 3745 6496.

Taylor-Batty, Mark. *The Theatre of Harold Pinter.* Bloomsbury. [2014] pp. 305. pb £16.99 ISBN 9 7814 0817 5309.

Tearle, Oliver. *T.E. Hulme and Modernism.* Bloomsbury. [2013] pp. vi + 159. £60 ISBN 9 7814 4115 6655.

Teo, Yugin. *Kazuo Ishiguro and Memory.* Palgrave. [2014] pp. 192. £55 ISBN 9 7811 3733 7184.

Tew, Philip, Emily Horton, and Leigh Wilson, eds. *The 1980s: A Decade of Contemporary British Fiction.* Bloomsbury. [2014] pp. 280. £52.50 ISBN 9 7814 4112 6498.

Thurston, Michael, and Nigel Alderman. *Reading Postwar British and Irish Poetry.* Blackwell. [2014] pp. 342. £70 ISBN 9 7804 7065 7317.

Tonning, Erik. *Modernism and Christianity.* Palgrave. [2014] pp. 172. £18.99 ISBN 9 7802 3024 1770.

Tonning, Erik, Matthew Feldman, and David Addyman, eds. *Modernism, Christianity and Apocalypse.* Brill. [2014] pp. 390. £100 ISBN 9 7890 0427 8264.

Trotter, David. *Literature in the First Media Age: Britain between the Wars.* HarvardUP. [2013] pp. 342. £20 ISBN 9 7806 7407 3159.

Varga, Adriana, ed. *Virginia Woolf and Music.* IndUP. [2014] pp. 348. hb $90 ISBN 9 7802 5301 2555, pb $35 ISBN 9 7802 5301 2463.2

Vesterman, William. *Dramatizing Time in Twentieth-Century Literature.* Routledge. [2014] pp. 206. £85 ISBN 9 7811 3801 5715.

Villar-Argáiz, Pilar, ed. *Literary Visions of Multicultural Ireland: The Immigrant in Contemporary Irish Literature.* ManUP. [2014] pp. xx + 273. £65 ISBN 9 7807 1908 9282.

Viney, William. *Waste: A Philosophy of Things.* Bloomsbury. [2014] pp. xi + 218. £65 ISBN 9 7814 7252 7578.

Voicu, Cristina-Georgiana. *Exploring Cultural Identities in Jean Rhys' Fiction.* Gruyter. [2014] pp. 140. £49.95 ISBN 9 7883 7656 0670.

Wearing, J.P. *The London Stage 1890–1959: Accumulated Indexes.* R&L. [2014] pp. 1,414. £125 ISBN 9 7808 1089 3207.

Webb, Andrew. *Edward Thomas and World Literary Studies.* UWalesP. [2013] pp. xiv + 221. £24.99 ISBN 9 7807 0832 6220.

Webb, Eugene. *Samuel Beckett: A Study of His Novels.* UWashP. [2014] pp. 192. £23.99 ISBN 9 7802 9599 4345.

Whittier-Ferguson, John. *Mortality and Form in Late Modernist Literature.* CUP. [2014] pp. xi + 276. £55 ISBN 9 7811 0706 0012.

Wright, David G. *'Dubliners' and 'Ulysses': Bonds of Character.* Joker. [2013] pp. 163. pb £19 ISBN 9 7888 7536 3222.

Wright, E.H. *Bloomsbury Influences: Papers from the Bloomsbury Adaptations Conference, Bath Spa University, 5–6 May 2011.* CambridgeSP. [2014] pp. xxiii + 249. £60 ISBN 9 7814 4385 4344.

Yoshioka, Fumio. *Reading Short Stories: British, Irish and American Storytellers.* Okayama. [2014] pp. 339. £7 ISSN 2187 4379.

XVI

American Literature to 1900

HELENA GOODWYN, KATIE MCGETTIGAN,
AND REBECCA WHITE

This chapter has two sections: 1 General; 2 American Literature to 1900. Section 1 is by Katie McGettigan; section 2 is by Helena Goodwyn, Katie McGettigan, and Rebecca White.

1. General

The *Journal of American Studies* continues to place nineteenth-century literature in interdisciplinary contexts. Tamara L. Follini's 'Speaking Monuments: Henry James, Walt Whitman and the Civil War Statues of Augustus Saint-Gaudens' (*JAS* 48:i[2014] 25–49) locates James's revaluation of Whitman in the 1890s within James's attempts to confront Civil War trauma. James rejects martial monuments in favour of Whitman's intimate accounts of wounded soldiers' bodies, and Follini reads James's description of New York harbour, in *The American Scene* [1905], as a monument to Whitman. In 'A Chicago Architect in King Arthur's Court: Mark Twain, Daniel Burnham and the Imperialism of Gilded Age Modernity' (*JAS* 48:i[2014] 99–126), Timothy A. Hickman argues that Twain's *Connecticut Yankee* [1889] critiques the modernizing project of US imperialism that Burnham's 1893 World's Fair championed. Although both men understood modernity in spatial terms, Burnham's architecture proposed that the present could recover the past, while Twain argued that such modernization would inevitably lead to destruction. In 'Transcendental Democracy: Ralph Waldo Emerson's Political Thought, the Legacy of Federalism, and the Ironies of America's Democratic Tradition' (*JAS* 48:ii[2014] 481–500), Benjamin E. Park suggests that Emerson's emphasis on education and personal awakening echoes a lingering New England Federalist politics. Park's argument that tensions in Emerson's democratic politics speak to those in the wider antebellum US leaves room for a deeper consideration of Emerson as a representative figure of his political moment. Cynthia Lee Patterson discusses *Godey's Lady's Magazine*'s commentary on contemporary issues in 'Performative Morality: *Godey's* Match Plates, Nineteenth-Century Stage

The Year's Work in English Studies, Volume 95 (2016) © *The Author 2016. Published by Oxford University Press on behalf of the English Association. All rights reserved. For Permissions, please email: journals.permissions@oup.com*
doi:10.1093/ywes/maw016

Practice, and Social/Political/Economic Commentary in America's Popular
Ladies' Magazine' (*JAS* 48:ii [2014] 613–37). Patterson proposes that the
magazine's 'match plate' engravings, which paired virtue and vice, capitalize
on popular stage genres to respond to the economic downturn of the 1850s and
to comment on social problems experienced by the magazine's readers. In
'"Was There Not Reason to Doubt?"': *Wieland* and Its Secular Age' (*JAS*
48:iii[2014] 735–56), Christine Hedlin contextualizes Charles Brockden
Brown's novel within the competing modes of belief that medicine and
religion offered in the early republic. Hedlin argues that Clara is caught
between these discourses, and suggests that Brown ironizes his narrator's final
self-incrimination: in an age of intellectual instability, how can anything be
established beyond doubt? Graham Culbertson uncovers Douglass's interest in
urban environments in 'Frederick Douglass's "Our National Capital":
Updating L'Enfant for an Era of Integration' (*JAS* 48:iv[2014] 911–35).
Comparing Douglass to the architect of Washington DC, Pierre-Charles
L'Enfant, Culbertson analyses how Douglass rebuilds DC in his neglected
speech 'Our National Capital' (1877), in which he argues that for DC to
become a national capital, black labour must drive out Southern indolence.

American Literary History began 2014 with a special issue on 'Literature
and Religion' that expands the canon of American religious texts, as well as
opening these texts to literary methodologies. In 'The Compiler's Art: Hannah
Adams, the *Dictionary of All Religions*, and the Religious World' (*AmLH*
26:i[2014] 28–41), Toni Wall Jaudon demonstrates how Adams's *Dictionary*
[1784–1817] created its detached religious pluralism through the readers'
haptic engagement with the material text. The easily navigable codex
combined with Adams's impartial tone to give readers controllable access to
world religion that would lead them back to Christian truth. Jennifer Graber's
'Religion in Kiowa Ledgers: Expanding the Canon of American Religious
Literature' (*AmLH* 26:i[2014] 42–60) examines how drawings by Southern
Plains Indians express religious belief. Arguing that the Kiowa located sacred
power (*dwdw*) in images of everyday practices, Graber suggests that their
drawings testify to beliefs that endured in a moment of crisis, and provide a
perspective on Native and Christian religions from outside the dominant
Protestant tradition. In 'More Than a Dead American Hero: Washington, the
Improved Order of Red Men, and the Limits of Civil Religion' (*AmLH*
26:i[2014] 61–82), Elaine A. Peña examines the plays and documents of a white
Red Face fraternity, and asks whether their practices constituted 'civil
religion': a public theology that binds individuals through shared nationhood.
Peña suggests the fraternity's performances held particular significance at the
US–Mexico border, acting as communal experience and demonstrating how
powerful fraternity members controlled knowledge production. Another
special forum on the film adaptation of Solomon Northup's *Twelve Years A
Slave* [1853] featured contributions by experts on the literature, visual culture,
and cultural memory of slavery and abolition: John Ernest, John Stauffer,
Miriam Thaggert, Stephanie Li, Andreá N. Williams, Jasmine Nicole Cobb,
Salamishah Tillet, Valerie Smith, and Deborah E. McDowell (*AmLH*
26:ii[2014] 317–84). Approaching both Northup's narrative and Steve
McQueen's film through the lenses of visual studies, gender, sex, authorship,

and memory, these collected short essays critically evaluated the cultural work and representational modes of both the slave narrative and its twenty-first-century descendants.

Elsewhere in the journal, David J. Alworth takes Erving Goffman's frequent recourse to Melville's *White-Jacket* [1850] as a starting point for investigating that novel's exploration of identity, in 'Melville in the Asylum: Literature, Sociology, Reading' (*AmLH* 26:ii[2014] 234–61). Alworth argues that Melville, like Goffman after him, charts how identity develops through relations with both the human and non-human within enclosed, defined settings, and suggests the potential of literary analysis as a sociological tool. David Anthony resurrects a neglected figure in the fascinating and broad-ranging essay, 'Fantasies of Conversion: The Sensational Jewess in Poe and Hawthorne's America' (*AmLH* 26:iii[2014] 431–61). Anthony convincingly argues that the Jewess was a figure of potential conversion, who could represent both sensation and rationality; she embodied America's desire to leave behind financial excess, and became a locus for debates over how to stage sexual excess. Travis M. Foster analyses how the postbellum campus novel stages fantasies of sectional reconciliation and national whiteness in 'Campus Novels and the Nation of Peers' (*AmLH* 26:iii[2014] 461–83). Identifying a genre concerned with idling and extracurricular bonding rather than academic education, Foster argues that its themes of camaraderie and nostalgia trained readers in feelings of citizenship and attempted to heal conflicts in the body politic. In 'Oscar Wilde's Un-American Tour: Aestheticism, Mormonism and Transnational Resonance' (*AmLH* 26:iv[2014] 664–92), Benjamin Morgan rethinks paradigms of transnational study through Wilde's 1882 tour. Proposing that aestheticism and Wilde resisted categorization as British, Morgan suggests that the tour highlights provincial spaces that evade current models of global exchange. Introducing the idea of 'resonance', Morgan argues that transnational studies must incorporate fugitive connections that appear to a future observer—such as the one he posits between Aestheticism and Mormonism.

A variety of essays in *Nineteenth-Century Literature* address American topics. In ' "Universal Mixing" and Interpenetrating Standing: Disability and Community in *Moby-Dick*' (*NCL* 69:i[2014] 26–55), Harriet Hustis argues that it is reductive to view Ahab as the only disabled character in Melville's novel. She suggests that what actually distinguishes Ahab is his response to disability as determinative and othering; through other characters in *Moby-Dick* [1851], Melville presents disability as a familiar condition through which communal bonds can be formed. Kaye Wierzbicki examines how Sarah Orne Jewett's interest in garden design influenced her fiction, in 'The Formal and the Foreign: Sarah Orne Jewett's Garden Fences and the Meaning of Enclosure' (*NCL* 69:i[2014] 56–91). Tracing the changing meanings of fences in Jewett's writing, Wierzbicki proposes that Jewett uses enclosed spaces—including the local colour genre—to incorporate difference into the national body, rather than to exclude it. Caroline Gelmi's ' "The Pleasures of Merely Circulating": Sappho and Early American Newspaper Poetry' (*NCL* 69:ii[2014] 151–74) explores how parodies of Ambrose Philips's 1711 translation of Sappho's fragment 31 mediated political and nationalizing discourses in the early republic. Carefully tracing reprints, Gelmi also shows how American print culture allegorized itself in the figure of Sappho, illuminating a new context for classical reception in the United States. In 'The Sounds and Stages of Emerson's Social Reform' (*NCL* 69:ii[2014] 208–32), Nicole H. Gray brings together Emerson as reformer and as philosopher by rethinking reform as a linguistic process of citation and recontextualizing that itself re-creates the audience as an embodied and active public. Gray's essay skilfully demonstrates how close readings of Emerson's speeches and journals might deepen our understanding of his abolitionist politics and his individual philosophy. Nancy D. Goldfarb reads Melville alongside developments in philanthropy that accompanied the advance of market capitalism, in 'Charity as Purchase: Buying Self-Approval in Melville's "Bartleby the Scrivener"' (*NCL* 69:ii[2014] 233–61). Although Goldfarb illuminates Melville's view that philanthropy distracts from, rather than cures the selfishness of the market, her reading does not radically revise existing debates about the story's critique of capitalism. In '"Pulse for Pulse in Harmony with the Universal Whole": Hearing "Self-Reliance" Anew' (*NCL* 69:iii[2014] 319–41), Prentiss Clark also rethinks a key Emersonian concept, arguing that 'self-reliance' is less about radical, isolated selves than about recognizing one's innumerable and intimate connections with the world, and the accountabilities those connections create. Future work might explore how this reconceptualized 'self-reliance' relates to Emerson's abolitionism, and to the essay and lecture forms. Gretchen Murphy's 'Revising the Law of the Mother in the Adoption-Marriage Plot' (*NCL* 69:iii[2014] 342–65) argues that transatlantic novels in which adoptive siblings choose to marry reject imposed social forms in favour of chosen social contracts. It is debatable whether Murphy's sample is large enough to constitute distant reading, as she claims, but her methodology indicates the potential of historicizing plot elements rather than individual texts. Matthew Flaherty rethinks ethical approaches to James's fiction in 'Henry James at the Ethical Turn: Vivification and Ironization in *The Ambassadors*' (*NCL* 69:iii[2014] 366–93), arguing that James invites the judgement of readers by positioning characters in Hegelian dialectical relations. Flaherty suggests that Maria Gostrey's discriminating thought reveals both the potential and limitation of Lambert Strether's imagination, prompting readers to judge alternative systems of value.

Two strong essays on American literature before 1900 appear in *English Literary History*. In 'Filiation and Affiliation: Kinship and Sentiment in Equiano's *Interesting Narrative*' (*ELH* 81:iii[2014] 923–54), Ramesh Mallipeddi argues that Olaudah Equiano establishes his personhood through ties of sentiment, as well as the acquisition of literacy and property. Mallipeddi analyses how Equiano replaces lost familial and national bonds with sentimental ties that exist alongside the bonds of slavery and with other diasporic Africans, and locates imagined kinship as a means to freedom. Matthew A. Taylor analyses late nineteenth-century ethnographer James Mooney's pathologizing of Native American visionary experience in '"Contagious Emotions" and the Ghost Dance Religion: Mooney's Science, Black Elk's Fever' (*ELH* 81:iii[2014] 1055–82). Taylor shows that Mooney's understanding of the modern self as closed to such infectious beliefs is challenged by Lakota holy man Black Elk, who anticipates new materialisms by suggesting that openness to contagion is essential to being human. As such, the essay fruitfully connects new modes of critical reading with indigenous systems of belief.

2. American Literature to 1900

Published first in Oxford Studies in American Literary History in 2013, Jeffory A. Clymer's *Family Money: Property, Race, and Literature in the Nineteenth Century* is now available in paperback. It asks the challenging question: what were the economic ramifications of intimate interracial relationships in the late antebellum and post-slavery period? To Clymer, such relationships led to not only changes in the language of the American legal system but also to new grounds for literary endeavour. *Family Money* begins with an example from the modern day of a US senator—James Strom Thurmond. Upon Thurmond's death in 2003 his daughter Essie Mae Washington-Williams confirmed the long and loudly whispered rumour that she was indeed Thurmond's kin but made no claim to the property, capital, or other assets willed to his white, legitimate, children. Clymer then argues that had Williams made claims on this inheritance 'she would have violated the strong American notion that emotional and financial ties should be kept separate'. This 'strong American notion' is unsupported by example or evidence and so it is difficult to understand the grounds on which Clymer makes his assertion. The very essence of the American realist and naturalist tradition, as practised by Henry James, Edith Wharton, Theodore Dreiser, and Upton Sinclair, links money, survival, and familial ties in ways that are fundamental to the plots of their novels and to their implied critique of nineteenth-century America. Nevertheless the chapters that follow combine the insights of legal studies, critical race theory, and literary studies to produce some interesting arguments in examination of the works of such authors as Harriet Beecher Stowe, Nathaniel Hawthorne, and Charles Waddell Chesnutt through a framework that sees racial difference as inextricable from other determiners of difference: gender and economic background. In building this framework Clymer draws on the work of legal experts such as Cheryl I. Harris through her 1993 article 'Whiteness as Property'. Adrienne D. Davis's 1999 article, 'The Private Law of Race and Sex: An Antebellum Perspective', which takes as its subject a set of historical case studies that concern wealth and property transfers from white to black citizens, may be thought of as a key text for Clymer's analysis of literary works. In bringing together Stowe's *Dred: A Tale of the Great Dismal Swamp* [1856], Frank J. Webb's *The Garies and Their Friends* [1857], Chesnutt's *The House Behind the Cedars* [1900], and other stories, Clymer allows his readers to observe the ways in which American writers of the late antebellum and post-slavery period could imaginatively address and redress economic injustices that persist today.

In *Suburban Plots: Men at Home in Nineteenth-Century American Print Culture*, Maura D'Amore rethinks literary domesticity by exploring the imaginative potential that the suburban home held for white male authors. Drawing upon architectural pattern books and property adverts, as well as a variety of periodical and literary writings, D'Amore argues that East Coast suburbs provided a space for middle-class authors to construct masculinity away from the debilitating pressures of the city and the heft of rural labour. Unlike the female domestic of sympathy, labour, and sacrifice, this masculine domestic is a space for play, performance, and reverie. Henry David Thoreau and Henry Ward Beecher both use suburban architecture to imagine modes of living that draw generative power from nature. Exploring Donald Grant Mitchell's career beyond *Reveries of a Bachelor* [1850] reveals that he depicted the suburban home as a stage for masculine self-fashioning; D'Amore pairs this performance with a reconsideration of Hawthorne's *The Blithedale Romance* [1852] as a suburban fiction. The strongest chapter imagines Nathaniel Parker Willis as an antebellum Martha Stewart, analysing his creation of an imagined suburban lifestyle community in the readership of the *Home Journal* [1846–67]. D'Amore frequently returns to the lack of closure in these narratives and the gaps that emerge between the real and the ideal, which provide material for humorists and indicate tensions in these masculine fantasies. Yet the problematic ways in which these writers effect and exclude minorities, and diminish the domestic labour of women, might have received deeper consideration. For example, by valorizing domestic disorder and suggesting the benefits of sewing as a male hobby, Beecher diminishes female labour and agency in his fashioning of masculinity. Sustained discussion of problematic aspects of male suburban plots only arises in the coda. Nevertheless, D'Amore's study provides a fruitful spatial remapping of popular and literary writing, and of nineteenth-century masculinity.

Writing in the Kitchen: Essays on Southern Literature and Foodways, edited by David A. Davis and Tara Powell, offers a fascinating and lively discussion of the interplay between cuisine and culture in a range of texts, from novels to cookbooks, from the period of early settlement to the twenty-first century. Born out of a conference panel organized by the Society for the Study of Southern Literature (2010), the volume both recognizes, and embodies, the growing critical attention paid to Southern foodways. As the editors note, reading Southern literature with 'an awareness of food reveals how integral it is', covering 'a complex of microregional and ethnic identities, historical problems and contradictions, and disparities of poverty and plenty', and enabling refreshing analyses of issues such as domesticity, gender and race. The richness of foodways as a mode of inquiry is indeed demonstrated by the diversity of *Writing in the Kitchen*, which, crucially, often recovers and re-evaluates obscure writers and neglected genres. David S. Shields unearths nineteenth-century agricultural periodicals, reasserting the significance of agrarian reading and writing as a field of critical discovery, and illuminating the interrelationship between history, geography, food production and publishing. As Shields explains, the soil crisis of the early nineteenth century led to an explosion of farming magazines, spearheaded by figures such as Thomas Jefferson, in an attempt to fight ecological disaster with scientific knowledge; the plough became led by the pen, as farmers looked to 'print as a means of replenishing the soil, diversifying plantings and constructing a system of practices'. Marcie Cohen Ferris then discusses Southern food as a blend of racial and regional 'conversations', examining various texts (including travel stories, diaries, letters, slave narratives (placing the obscure 'Aunt Delia', who 'spit in the biscuits', alongside Douglass and Jacobs) and accounts written by Northerners). Ferris's engaging essay, coloured by historically illuminating detail, reveals 'an expressive language of food that expands our understanding of race and region in the American South'. Similarly, Sarah Walden interrogates the late nineteenth-century marketing of the 'mammy' figure. Her insightful, yet accessible chapter analyses cookbooks as sites of racial and cultural tension; whereas white female authors performed the 'mammy stereotype' in writing nostalgic cookbooks which celebrated Southern culinary - and, implicitly, class - traditions, African American women published recipes as a means of empowerment. Elizabeth Engelhardt then traces the cookbook's development from the 1870s onwards, retrieving forgotten texts; the retrieval of early poems and songs, centred on food, in African American culture is also taken up by Ruth Salvaggio. Finally, before the volume moves on to a discussion of post-1900 writing, Erica Abrams Locklear presents a thoughtful analysis of food and class in Appalachian literature, recovering minor texts (such as Maria Louise Pool's *In Buncombe County* [1896]) and highlighting both the resurgence of interest in the region's culinary culture and an ongoing tendency to 'other' the 'mountain people'. *Writing in the Kitchen* combines engaging and often entertaining writing with rigorous scholarly analysis and insight, together with cross-disciplinary appeal. It provides, above all, a dynamic lens through which the region's complexity can be better understood, as 'Southern food involves a mass of contradictions ... in which a legacy of racism and exploitation lingers just beneath a veneer of hospitality and nostalgia'. As the authors ultimately show, the written representation of Southern cuisine becomes both celebratory and condemnatory, as the richness of the region's identity is tainted by the bitterness of its troubling past.

In *Nineteenth-Century Transatlantic Reprinting and the Embodied Book*, Jessica DeSpain explores how transatlantic reprinting in Britain and America fashioned and deconstructed national cultural identity by investigating connections between book objects, human bodies, and national bodies. Transatlantic reprinting altered the identity of texts by Charles Dickens, Susan Warner, Fanny Kemble, and Walt Whitman, as an absence of international copyright laws allowed publishers to edit, rearrange, and illustrate texts without the author's permission. Analysing metaphors of bodily defilement that accompanied this reprinting, DeSpain argues that, as well as generating anxiety themselves, reprints also staged concerns about the stability of citizenship, the body politic, and personhood. Chapters skilfully combine attention to the material text with publishing history, biography, and close literary readings. DeSpain demonstrates that Dickens's attacks on reprinting overlay literary and bodily circulation on US geography, creating a wider critique of American democracy that prompted diverse responses from reprint papers and reputable publishers in the US. Studies of the illustrations for and editing of British reprints of *The Wide, Wide World* [1850] and the publication of *Democratic Vistas* [1871] in a British cheap series show that, in repackaging these texts for British audiences, publishers used the material text to defray criticisms of Britain and mute distinctly American forms of identity. Likewise, DeSpain considers how London and Philadelphia editors reconfigured Fanny

Kemble's unmasking of female domesticity in *Journal of a Residence on a Georgia Plantation* [1863], although both editions also materialized contemporary analogies between the slave market and the market for reprinted texts. Concluding that, by the end of the century, international copyright, increasingly globalized economies, and the Arts and Crafts movement's fetishization of the text restricted the disruptive capacity of the transatlantic reprint, DeSpain's engaging monograph makes important strides in bringing together transatlantic studies and book history.

In her fascinating study, *Beyond the Fruited Plain: Food and Agriculture in U.S. Literature, 1850–1905*, Kathryn Cornell Dolan presents an accessible yet scholarly analysis of the link between nineteenth-century literature, agriculture, and US territorial and economic expansion. As with Matthew Wynn Sivils's *American Environmental Fiction* (reviewed below), Dolan's work provides a welcome contribution to the fields of both ecocriticism and American studies, with her examination of Melville, Thoreau, Stowe, and Twain casting new perspectives on these canonical figures, while also retrieving and illuminating the less well-known Frank Norris. Dolan grounds her research within a clearly outlined theoretical framework (following Leo Marx and Raymond Williams) and historical context, yet, moving beyond the typical agrarian study, she discusses agriculture in broader, less idyllic terms. As she maintains, the five authors included in her book are united by their imaginative responses to U.S. culture of the second half of the nineteenth century as well as through their critical reflections on national policies during this period of growth. Dolan also compares her nineteenth-century texts with those written in the twenty-first century, tracing intricate and informative interconnections that help to shed refreshing light on both eras. Chapter 1 focuses on Melville, moving beyond his reputation as a seafaring author and planting him firmly on land; his more obscure works, such as *Pierre*, are retrieved in the process. Dolan's second chapter addresses Thoreau's frequently overlooked attention to agricultural and dietary issues, as a challenge to US agricultural practices. As noted in chapter 3, Stowe expanded upon Thoreau's interest in localized farming; reading beyond her abolitionism, Dolan shows that Stowe explored the interplay between women, domestic reform and US agri-expansion. Dolan subsequently explores Twain's development of nineteenth-century US 'agri-imperialism' as an 'end-of-the-century version of agri-expansion', while she then argues that Norris uses wheat metaphorically, as 'a national corrective against an exploitative U.S. agri-expansion at the beginning of the twentieth century'. Her final section goes on to illustrate connections between nineteenth-century texts and twenty-first-century agri-expansion. Although *Beyond the Fruited Plain* is slightly repetitive at times, it is engaging and insightful, reaffirming George Washington's declaration, in 1796, that 'it will not be doubted that with reference either to individual or national welfare, Agriculture is of primary importance'.

Territories of Empire: U.S. Writing from the Louisiana Purchase to Mexican Independence by Andy Doolen is published in the Oxford Studies in American Literary History series. It begins with a chronology, mapping out the period under discussion: 1787–1835, from the creation of the Northwest Ordinance that provided a model for organizing territory north of the Ohio River to the separation of Texas from Mexico after the so-called 'Texas Revolution'. It complements, to a degree, the work done by Rien Fertel in *Imagining the Creole City: The Rise of Literary Culture in Nineteenth-Century New Orleans* in so far as Doolen charts the successful Americanization of Louisiana whilst Fertel charts attempts at preservation of a Creole resistance. Doolen contributes to debate over the Burr conspiracy, engaging with, amongst other records, the *Western World* newspaper and its part in the controversy. In later pages we are introduced to Zebulon Pike, an explorer whose journals of expedition and discovery were popular enough to be translated into French, German, and Dutch. For Doolen's purposes they are representative of the changing boundaries of the American landscape. 'Opening the Door to Mexico' considers William Davis Robinson's *Memoirs of the Mexican Revolution* [1820], before turning to look at the Monroe Doctrine to connect it with other Anglo-American writings on Latin American independence, such as Timothy Flint's 1826 novel *Francis Berrian; or the Mexican Patriot*. Doolen quotes Frances Trollope, who considered the novel a triumph of 'vigour and freshness', and James Fenimore Cooper's contribution to the articulation of US expansionism and empire through his 'Leatherstocking' novels, *The Pioneers* [1823], *The Last of the Mohicans* [1826], and *The Prairie* [1827]. Doolen challenges scholarship that reads Cooper's novels as 'noxious artifacts of white racism' and argues instead that these works of fiction demonstrate a deep ambivalence, as well as criticism of slavery and expansionism.

Dara Downey's *American Women's Ghost Stories in the Gilded Age* is published in the Palgrave Gothic series edited by Clive Bloom. It consists of six chapters that build together to form a coherent and convincing picture of the ways in which female American authors in the late nineteenth century challenged understandings of the ghostly and the uncanny as predominantly representative of the haunted or hysterical psyche. Downey argues instead that, in the Gothic works of many female authors writing at the end of the nineteenth and beginning of the twentieth century, objects, furnishings, and the trappings of the home were regularly used to grapple with the straining and conflicting ambitions of the age towards greater commodification of the domestic sphere and the codes of moral and religious restraint simultaneously assigned to the female character. This is a study that manages to demonstrate wide-ranging knowledge of the period and its literature while remaining focused on its selected texts and the intricate close reading of them. Downey draws our attention to the common theme in Gothic tales of the period by American women writers of female protagonists who find themselves in sinister situations involving eerie immortalizations of other women as statues or paintings, using Emily Dickinson's poem 510 'It was not Death, for I stood up' [*c*.1862], Edith Wharton's 'Miss Mary Pask' [1925], and Edna Worthley Underwood's 'The Painter of Dead Women' [1910] as examples of this trope, as well as Charlotte Perkins Gilman's 'The Yellow Wall-Paper' [1892], Emma Frances Dawson's 'The Itinerant House' [1896], and stories by Elia W. Peattie, among others, to develop Downey's argument that the spectral in American literature is a dramatization of the problem of visibility, and that to read such stories of uncanny objects as prefiguring Freud's psychoanalytic theory is to overlook the fact that these objects resist the attempts made by female characters to endow them with special meaning. She highlights the critical framework from which her enquiry follows, that of 'thing theory' and the ideas put forth by Bill Brown in his article of the same name. In a brief Afterword we are told that the ghost story is a genre ripe for resurgence in 2014, at a time of patriarchal backlash led by 'Internet trolls' advocating rape culture, and a renewed sense in feminist thought that the female body is anything but free from censorship.

Sari Edelstein's *Between the Novel and the News: The Emergence of American Women's Writing* provides an illuminating account of the relationship between newspapers and women's fiction and non-fiction. Edelstein convincingly argues that female writers located their own work in dialogue with newspapers, often borrowing journalistic techniques at the same time as they criticized modes of representation that the popular press used. She thus shows that female authors anticipated male realist writers in their literary engagement with the mass media. Women's writing operated as a social and epistemological critique of newspapers. Authors like Catharine Maria Sedgwick and Louisa May Alcott questioned and corrected newspapers' representation of women and the working classes, and suggested that sentimental and fictional modes could offer forms of knowledge obscured by sensation and hard facts. But female authors also appropriated the sensational strategies and generic features of newspapers. Edelstein demonstrates that, in *The Hidden Hand* [1859], E.D.E.N. Southworth mirrored the miscellaneous 'story-paper' in which the novel was serialized in its mixed-genre form and its patchwork protagonist. Stretching from Judith Sargent Murray's seduction novel and the Federalist press to yellow journalism and *fin-de-siècle* fiction, Edelstein's study illustrates changes in journalism and shows the breadth of nineteenth-century women's writing with remarkable efficiency and clarity. Particularly striking is her reading of Charlotte Perkins Gilman's 'The Yellow Wall-Paper' as a condemnation of yellow journalism, which provides an exciting new perspective on this much-discussed text. Edelstein also explores ethnic women's writing, showing how African American writers like Elizabeth Keckley and Ida Wells-Barnett, and Chinese American writer Edith Eaton, used the techniques of the press to counter its own privileging of white, male perspectives. Deftly blending the history of the American press with incisive close readings of canonical and non-canonical texts, Edelstein's work will be of great interest to book historians and literary scholars alike.

The Oxford Handbook of the African American Slave Narrative, edited by John Ernest, is an expansive collection of essays. In an introduction that also provides a survey of existing scholarship, Ernest observes that the collection aims to interrogate the continuing unspeakability of slavery rather than imagine it as a resolved problem in American history. Eschewing chapters focused on individual, well-known narratives, the collection is divided into six thematic sections: 'Historical Fractures', 'Layer Testimonies', 'Textual Bindings', 'Experience and Authority', 'Environments and Migration', and 'Echoes and Traces'. Chapters argue for the need to expand scholarship on slave narratives by uncovering forgotten or neglected sources of the testimony of enslaved people, or by applying new methodological approaches to the corpus. Additionally, Eric Gardner and Elizabeth Regosin offer theoretical and practical advice on archival research into slave narratives. Chapters on traditional critical concerns, such as gender and sexuality (Aliyyah I. Abdur-Rahman; DoVeanna S. Fulton), accompany those which productively bring the slave narrative into dialogue with newer subfields, such as ecocriticism (Kimberly K. Smith) and sound studies (Daphne A. Brooks). Others attend to neglected aspects of slave narratives, such as their publishing history (Teresa A. Goddu) and the importance of collaboration (Barbara McCaskill). As well as paying careful attention to celebrated narratives by Douglass, William and Ellen Crafts, Henry Box Brown, and Olaudah Equiano, among others, the collection demonstrates that sources such as legal records, pension files, and the Works Progress Administration interviews are equally useful to literary critics and historians. Scholars expand the genre of the slave narrative geographically and temporally by exploring Caribbean narratives (Nicole N. Aljoe), placing African American narratives in transatlantic and hemispheric contexts (Winfried Siemerling; Helen Thomas), and excavating how the slave narrative functions in post-emancipation writing (William L. Andrews; Joycelyn K. Moody). Ernest has compiled a volume of considerable breadth and depth, and which contains material that will be valuable to researchers and students in a variety of disciplines.

Rien Fertel's *Imagining the Creole City: the Rise of Literary Culture in Nineteenth-Century New Orleans* charts the rise and fall of white Creole print culture in New Orleans. Fertel takes as his framework the lives of five individuals whom he sees as crucial to the creation of the Creole New Orleans identity. We begin with Charles Gayarré, historian, attorney, and politician. He lived from 1805 to 1895 and was engaged in the promotion of Louisiana as a region of special literary romance and significance. In chapter 2 we meet Adrien Rouquette, poet and Catholic priest. He represents, for Fertel, the Catholicism at the heart of the construction of the Creole identity through his poetry and other writings on the divided selfhood of a cosmopolitan Creole elite. The binaries of identification at work here are the national and the local, as well as the American and the French/Spanish. Rouquette himself saw these different pulls of influence as 'political' and 'natural'. America was, for him, representative of the political—nation, state, law—and the French/Spanish allegiance was symbolic of the natural—blood ties, history, language. Chapter 3 introduces us to Alfred Mercier who, amongst other things, ran the French-language publication *Comptes-rendus de l'Athénée Louisianais*. Fertel states that Mercier 'might be' the 'most brilliant of white Creole writers' and calls for a critical examination of his work. Fertel describes Mercier's best-known tale, *L'Habitation Saint-Ybars, ou, Maitres et esclaves en Louisiane* ('The Saint-Ybars Plantation, or, Masters and Slaves in Louisiana'), a text that would not have been out of place in Jeffory Clymer's study of *Family Money* as it deals, in part, with interracial relationships. In this work of fiction, according to Fertel, the complicated elite Creole identity figures as pro-South but antislavery. The importance of place, culture, and blood are, as one might expect, recurring themes throughout this book. In the chapter that considers the works of Grace King, author of histories and tales of Louisiana life, Fertel highlights the phrase 'gold blood': a standard of lineage with which King constructed her narrative of New Orleans history beginning with the Marigny family. In this final chapter Fertel makes clear, if he does not explicitly say so himself, that the work of these early historians of Louisiana and Creole culture did much more to construct such an identity than to preserve a pre-existing and stable selfhood threatened by some insistent drive for the homogenization of the American nation.

Adam Frank's *Transferential Poetics, from Poe to Warhol* considers four artists: Edgar Allan Poe, Henry James, Gertrude Stein, and Andy Warhol. Frank makes the assertion that he has discovered, in each of these four luminaries of their respective times (the book spans the 1840s to the 1980s) and methods, a particular devotion to the 'movement of feeling' between text and reader. To expound his 'transferential' theory Frank refers to the work of Silvan Tomkins on affect theory, as well as the work of Melanie Klein and Wilfred Bion. The author also, the reader is told, relies on Jacques Derrida's 'Freud and the Scene of Writing' in order to think through what he sees as 'theatricalizing' in the writings of the four aforementioned artists. In the chapter on Poe, Frank considers short stories such as 'The Tell-Tale Heart' [1843] alongside Silvan Tomkins's writing on the 'General Images of the affect system' and the taboos of looking. Frank argues that Poe's is a 'shameless' style of composition, and one which mimics the shameless staring that the experience of attending the theatre encourages. 'Maisie's Spasms', the chapter on James, sees the novella *What Maisie Knew*—first published serially in 1897—as an exercise in 'group psychology'. Frank employs Wilfred Bion's *Experiences in Groups*, which he understands as operating in contrast to Freud's theorization of experience as one of personal adaptation, to read James's tale of disappointing parents as an investigation into the relations between individuals and groups. Frank supports his argument with reference to James's plays in which, increasingly, stage directions became abundant and complex in the subtlety of emotion James required his actors to convey. This is why, the author argues, James can be thought of as 'televisual', because the distance at which many of his most intricate stage directions could be interpreted could not have worked for the Victorian stage but translate better to the mediums of film and television.

In *Failure and the American Writer: A Literary History*, Gavin Jones conducts an ambitious, trenchant, and engrossing study of failure as an expressive mode. Beginning by observing that nineteenth-century Americans like Henry Adams experienced failure as a universal condition and an individual problem, Jones argues that, in literature, failure is a 'problem of literary form' rather than just a subject. Authors responded to failure as a lasting state and a means of aesthetic practice, rather than as an isolated period to be overcome on the road to success. Jones analyses how Edgar Allan Poe, Herman Melville, Henry David Thoreau, Stephen Crane, Mark Twain, Sarah Orne Jewett, and Henry James give form to failure, reading each writer's stylistic interventions against their own historical moments and personal relationships with failure itself. For example, Jones reads Poe's hoaxes as part of his wider fixation on interpretative uncertainty and the failure of aesthetic response, and explores how Jewett's sketches fail to become plots and thus find possibility in a refusal to progress that is also a resistance to narratives of decline. Particularly impressive is a chapter that analyses *Pudd'nhead Wilson* [1894] as a text about problems with identity in which identity itself fails; Jones's argument encompasses but also moves beyond readings of the novel as Twain's response to the racial politics of reconstruction. Individual chapters speak strongly to one another, and the book sheds new light on romance and realism by showing how failure is integral to both these genres. This beautifully written book persuasively argues for a uniquely nineteenth-century failure than anticipates failure's modernist incarnation as a mode of critique, but does not itself realize this potential. Proposing that we resist understanding failure as a form of triumph for these writers, Jones himself succeeds in illuminating this complex element of nineteenth-century writing.

The American Novel to 1870, edited by J. Gerald Kennedy and Leland S. Person, forms volume 5 of *The Oxford History of the Novel in English*, a series devoted to adopting a broader understanding of the genre than has been customary in earlier histories. Kennedy and Person's commanding collection draws together the work of thirty-four scholars, and offering impressive scope while maintaining critical depth. The book is organized helpfully into subsections, covering the emergence and early development of the American novel, nation-building, the publishing world, the antebellum period, major novels, cultural influences, and fictional subgenres. Relevant illustrations, a useful bibliography and an expansive index of American novelists are also included (much of the book's value lies in its retrieval of obscure writers). The editors provide an informative and accessible general introduction, placing the development of early US literature within American historical and cultural contexts, while outlining the book's sections. Part of the book's success is born out of its ability to balance comprehensive overviews of established thought with casting new research and original perspectives onto both the traditional canon and more neglected areas of study. Betsy Erkkila, for instance, argues that while the literary exchange between America and England has been widely documented, the artistic interplay between the US and France is less appreciated. Marion Rust revisits Charles Brockden Brown and Susanna Rowson, revising common assumptions about their works (and retrieving their more obscure texts), and reading them in tandem (in contrast to most critical assessments, which juxtapose them). Fiona Robertson reinterprets Walter Scott's legacy, arguing that 'the American historical novelists reputed to have followed him most closely—Cooper, Child, Sedgwick and Simms—constantly questioned and reconfigured his approach and style'. Dana D. Nelson challenges the typical divide between 'savagery' and 'civilization' in her discussion of frontier novels, while Patricia Okker fascinatingly interrogates the (often ignored) influence of periodicals upon novel writing. Shelley Streeby examines the frequently overlooked popularity of cheap sensational fiction, reasserting the significance of female authors of dime novels. Essays on Cooper, Sedgwick, Hawthorne, Melville, and Stowe outline the established reputations of these canonical authors while negotiating their own revisionary readings. The following section then usefully examines major novels by these celebrated writers in greater depth. Further essays move on to consider cultural influences and, finally, fictional subgenres. John Lowe, for example, uncovers minor ethnic novels in interesting detail, while Renée Bergland and

David Leverenz present thought-provoking discussions of gender. G. Murphy expands definitions of travel writing by including slave and captivity narratives, and Scott Peeples provides a colourful account of the city mystery novel. Above all, the sheer scale and diversity of the collection embodies the richness of the American novel, and the dynamism of US literary studies more generally, resolutely dismissing Sydney Smith's infamous exclamation—'In the four quarters of the globe, who reads an American book?'

James D. Lilley's *Common Things: Romance and the Aesthetics of Belonging in Atlantic Modernity* continues critical interest in the commonplace by exploring how the aesthetics of the romance novel interact with forms of belonging that emerged in the late eighteenth century. Lilley suggests that romance and its sister genre, the Gothic, are uniquely able to express modern notions of community that are structured by both inclusion and exception, and in which belonging does not reside in relations between singularities, but exists as a private quality within singularities themselves. This modern logic of community, Lilley proposes, produces a series of 'interrelated (and ultimately illusory) common things ... genre, feeling, race, personhood, property, taste and event' (p. 9): categories that the literature interrogates through its aesthetic form as well as its content. Beginning with a study of how Horace Walpole's *The Castle of Otranto* [1764] examines the relationship between singularity and multiplicity in genre itself, which also critiques twentieth-century genre theory, Lilley analyses how texts engage with and produce these 'common things' within their examinations of community itself. While these critical readings will interest scholars of British and American literature, Lilley's transatlantic scope leans westward. He argues that US writers like Charles Brocken Brown and Robert Montgomery Bird return to the sublime and the Gothic to address how property and personhood function in democracy. He convincingly demonstrates that Washington Irving's 'aesthetics of idling' (p. 125), like the ruined Indians that Irving imagines in *A Tour on the Prairies* [1835], enable, rather than resist, the time and space of the modern colonial nation—an argument that Lilley concludes through repositioning Edgar Allan Poe's 'The Man That Was Used Up' [1839] in the context of the Second Seminole War. Through a careful balance of history and theory, Lilley's study substantially develops our understanding of both community and its literary articulations.

Unsettled States: Nineteenth-Century American Literary Studies, edited by Dana Luciano and Ivy G. Wilson, is a meticulously researched volume which combines rich anecdotal detail with scholarly insight. As the editors note, 'a surge in critical attention to the historical and social production of space and place has begun to denaturalize what constitutes "America"'. Encompassing an impressive array of authors and approaches, the collection seeks 'to consider how this uncertainty might unsettle and remap our critical relations to the field itself'; through appreciating American literature 'in motion', it drives new ways of investigation and interpretation. Much of the value of *Unsettled States* lies in its multi-disciplinary approach, presenting new scholarship within race and ethnic studies, feminist and gender studies, and queer theory. Cross-connections are drawn between the essays, however, lending the book coherence as a whole. As part of the growing momentum in Latino studies, Rodrigo Lazo, in 'Confederates in the Hispanic Attic: The

Archive Against Itself', explores 'the persistence of archival structures as well as the endurance of elements within the archive that challenge the archival sign organizing the content'. Lloyd Pratt then examines the African American archive, while T. Nyong'o considers 'Race, Re-enactment and the "Natural-Born Citizen"'. Shelley Streeby concludes Part I, 'Archives Unbound', by reflecting upon all three essays, noting that they 'take issue with the writing of history as a linear narrative'. Part II, 'States of Exception', commences with David Kazanjian's analysis of early Liberia. While some contributions to the volume are rather densely written, Kazanjian's chapter is especially interesting and accessible, as is Hester Blum's work on polar periodicals. 'The News at the Ends of the Earth' includes fascinating visual images of the magazines, and uncovers the significance of this often overlooked genre. Glenn Hendler's observations about the 1863 New York riots are similarly absorbing, while Jonathan Elmer investigates the significance of Agamben's *State of Exception*, assessing the previous chapters through its theoretical lens. The final section, 'Speculative Sexualities', includes thought-provoking contributions by Kyla Wazana Tompkins and Peter Cariello; most interestingly, Elizabeth Freeman offers new insight into Twain's *A Connecticut Yankee in King Arthur's Court*, reading beyond typical interpretations that focus on class unrest to reveal the novel's perversions.

   The Body of Property: Antebellum American Fiction and the Phenomenology of Possession by Chad Luck is concerned, as the title tells us, with the philosophical questions that attend the ways in which we understand possession. Affect theory is an informing framework here, as it is in Frank's *Transferential Poetics, from Poe to Warhol*: 'embodiment' is the critical term du jour. Luck argues that fiction of the antebellum was engaged in work legal practitioners largely ignored: that is, the metaphysical question of how we come to *own* a thing. The book opens with an engaging historical anecdote of the lawsuit *Pierson vs. Post*—a case of a dead fox—which, the author explains, is in fact one of the most influential rulings of American legal history, concerning a wild animal encountered in what was termed 'waste land', and the claims to ownership on either side of the argument prompted a judicial response that found its intellectual basis in the works of John Locke, Adam Smith, and 'a range of Scottish Enlightenment thinkers'. Luck looks at Charles Brockden Brown's novel *Edgar Huntly* [1799] and argues that in this novel— which is a fictionalized depiction of the Walking Purchase—Brown attempts to 'restore' the bodies of vanished Indians to the history of their dispossession. Nathaniel Hawthorne and Elizabeth Stoddard are explored as being particularly concerned with the relationship between domesticity and ownership, whilst debt and entitlement in the plantation romances feature in works of authors such as William Gilmore Simms. Luck also explores what he names 'theft trope' in George Lippard's sensational novels, in relation to Ann Cvetkovich's 'politics of affect': the repeated use of this figurative device in Lippard's novels forces readers to sympathize with the exploited working class. The Epilogue returns to *Pierson vs. Post* and brings forward a much more recent and bloodier case of hunting rights. Luck reminds his reader that although many years have passed since the 1805 court case America continues to grapple with its understanding of the nature of possession and ownership.

Connecting Detectives: The Influence of 19th-Century Sleuth Fiction on the Early Hard-Boileds is of limited use. Building on a chapter in his previous book, *Cracking the Hard-Boiled Detective: A Critical History from 1920s to the Present*, Lewis D. Moore undertakes to develop comparative readings of nineteenth-century authors Edgar Allan Poe, Charles Dickens, Wilkie Collins, and Arthur Conan Doyle with the works of Carroll John Daly, Dashiell Hammett, Raymond Chandler, Mickey Spillane, and Ross Macdonald (Kenneth Millar). This study is divided into four sections that consider plot, setting, character, themes, language, and form. Although the first chapter considers geography—the cityscape in particular—in its working through of influence passed from the nineteenth-century novel to the 'hard-boileds', there is a strange lack of awareness, here and indeed throughout this book, that with the exception of Poe, Moore is dealing with a transatlantic phenomenon. The nineteenth-century novelists he focuses on are British (again Poe is the exception, but his detective fiction is set in the Old World), and the authors he chooses to focus on as inspired by these nineteenth-century antecedents are all, with no exceptions, North American. Arguments such as 'this mixture of class, gender, and morality has an apparent stability in the nineteenth-century novel' but is 'unsettled in the hard-boiled detective novel' demonstrate a superficial understanding of nineteenth-century detective and sensation fiction. Moore asserts that there is a curious lack of engagement with the British legal system, or only a simplistic criticism of it in the work of Dickens and Collins. He uses *Bleak House* and *The Moonstone* to support this argument, overlooking *The Woman in White*, the plot of which draws repeatedly on Collins's legal training. Trials, lawyers, and the mechanics of the law feature throughout Dickens's novels and are often integral to the plot, even if *Bleak House* is the most obviously negative of his dramatizations of the legal system. In places, chiefly when Moore is analysing the hard-boiled writers with whose fiction he is clearly most intimate, *Connecting Detectives* makes for absorbing reading, but problems occur at the beginning of each chapter when outdated ideas are used to set up the arguments and readings that follow.

In *History Repeating Itself: The Republication of Children's Historical Literature and the Christian Right*, Gregory M. Pfitzer examines nineteenth- and early twentieth-century popular juvenile history texts in two different contexts: their original publication, and their republication as texts for conservative, home-schooling parents. Pfitzer shows how children's histories reflect changing theories of child development in the nineteenth century, as childhood shifted from a vulnerable period to be speedily concluded to a time of innocence to be preserved, and perceptions of children as passive gave way to an emphasis on children's independence. Analysing the growth of juvenile history, Pfitzer suggests that writers including Samuel Goodrich, the Abbott brothers, and Charles Carleton Coffin created a master-narrative of history. Even as each author brought his or her own ideological perspective to historical materials, juvenile histories returned to familiar stories, with a special emphasis on biography. Pfitzer argues that this stable and uncontested past attracts the contemporary Christian Right, who feel threatened by a public school curriculum that emphasizes multiculturalism and history from below. Christian Right publishers claim that nineteenth-century writings give a purer and truer history, unadulterated by ideology. Yet Pfitzer consistently demonstrates that, despite their aversion to revisionism, Christian Right publishers issue revised versions of nineteenth-century histories, and also silently revise these texts themselves. Each study reaches a similar conclusion: publishers contradict the intentions of nineteenth-century authors, who often staunchly supported public schooling, and conceived of their own works as being subject to future revision. Pfitzer openly states his belief that using nineteenth-century popular history to teach twenty-first-century students is misleading and dangerous. Few scholars would disagree. Fluently written, if perhaps overly long, this study illuminates a popular nineteenth-century genre, and temporally extends the culture of reprinting, showing that nineteenth-century history books are far from a thing of the past.

Joan Richardson, in *Pragmatism and American Experience: An Introduction*, presents a welcome sequel to her previous work, *A Natural History of Pragmatism: The Fact of Feeling from Jonathan Edwards to Gertrude Stein* [2007]. As she notes, this earlier volume did not allow her the space to illustrate the 'backstory' of pragmatism; instead, her latest study addresses the need for 'a "re-description" or "re-narration" that will provide a handle with which to grasp the slippery nature of this most protean subject'. Her scholarly, yet accessible, account of the development of pragmatism (from Emerson to Obama) certainly fulfils this central ambition, negotiating and clarifying complex ideas through her commanding knowledge of the subject (meticulous notes accompany the main body of her monograph, alongside the inclusion of a variety of illustrations). Richardson's introduction presents a useful overview of the different ways in which pragmatism can be viewed, incorporating the use of literature (especially poetry) as illustrative of pragmatist thought, and offering a comprehensive survey of critical works in the field. Developing these other scholars, a central thrust of Richardson's study addresses 'the tendency of the Continental and analytic schools to regard pragmatism as a provincial and consequently inferior expression of philosophy's purpose'; as she maintains, the 'Old World attitude completely occludes the importance of William James and his direct inheritance from Emerson'. A key strength of Richardson's book lies in the fact that it embodies in itself much of the methodology outlined by the pragmatists that it explores. Following William James's emphasis upon biography, Richardson provides fascinating and illuminating accounts of her thinkers' lives, placed within their historical contexts. Equally, she offers 'extended samplings of their writing to allow the witnessing of their thinking'. In a similar vein, she repeats 'lines and sections of earlier quoted passages in illustration of the actuality of the ongoing conversation through time that each of the writers discussed here, beginning with Emerson, understood thinking to be: a thread of meaning unwoven from an earlier text, taken up to be rewoven and colour a new fabric of ideas'. Above all, in tracing Barack Obama's indebtedness to earlier pragmatist thinkers, Richardson stresses the timeliness and relevance of pragmatism in the twenty-first-century world.

Augusta Rohrbach's *Thinking Outside the Book* uses five less frequently studied female writers to rethink how we discuss literary production in the light of both twenty-first-century advances in digital dissemination and instances of nineteenth-century authorship that resist dominant critical narratives. Rohrbach argues that terms like literacy, authorship, publication, edition, and editor fail to encompass the fluidity of the book, focusing on what it is rather than what it does. She suggests instead '(re)mediation, memory, history, testimony, and loss' (p. 4), accounting for collaborative and continuous media production in nineteenth-century America and today. Rohrbach examines how the mixed-race Ojibwe poet Jane Johnston Schoolcraft used print to negotiate cultural difference, demanding a place in Anglo-American discourse without capitulating to it. Sojourner Truth's illiteracy does not prevent her from asserting agency through her manipulation of images. Her *Narrative*, which creates memory through collaboration, and remixes print and visual culture, anticipates a Web where all text and images are code. A chapter on Hannah Crafts explores publication's role in history-making by analysing the author's resistance to marketing her novel, alongside Henry Louis Gates's authentication and publication of *The Bondwoman's Narrative* in 2002. The complex publishing history of Augusta Evans's *Macaria* [1864] shows that the novel withstands, rather than relies on, sectional division, with each edition testifying to its historical moment. Attention to the edition continues in the final chapter, on Mary Chesnut's Civil War diary. Revised but unpublished by its author, the diary was issued in multiple twentieth-century editions, in which editors selected according to their own principles, failing to speak to Chesnut's own sense that the printed book was unable to express loss. Intricate close readings limit space for Rohrbach's arguments about the ways in which the Web environment and nineteenth-century print illuminate one another, making them feel somewhat hurried. But Rohrbach successfully illustrates that textual production was a site of agency and resistance, while demonstrating the need to question traditional approaches to authorship and the book.

Martha Schoolman explores the spatial practices of abolitionist writers and argues for critical remapping as an abolitionist project in *Abolitionist Geographies*. She proposes that anti-slavery authors used the negotiation of space as strategy for political dissent. Exploring two historical moments—the emancipation of the British West Indies (1834–8) and the Compromise of 1850—Schoolman analyses how the contentions and contingent geographies of slavery and antislavery intersect with personal spatial orientations in texts by William Ellery Channing, Ralph Waldo Emerson, William Wells Brown, and Harriet Beecher Stowe. Connecting the consumption of sugar and cotton with the travel routes for New England consumptives, Schoolman demonstrates that these two hemispheric geographies interweave in Emerson's lectures, which make the West Indies and New England proximate. Channing and Emerson's August First addresses also use hemispheric geographies and West Indian emancipation to manage the ideological contradictions of the relationship between white antislavery activism and slave rebellion. But for William Wells Brown, the limits of emancipation in the British colonies spawn reflections on the limits of his own transnational mobility, leading him towards a critical mode of cosmopolitanism, centred on Haiti rather than Europe. Stepping forward to 1850, Schoolman maps *Uncle Tom's Cabin* [1852] onto Stowe's own anti-expansionist politics and the intellectual milieu of

Cincinnati, showing the influence of Ohio state politics on the novel's Liberia plot. Finally, spaces of *marronage*—a quiet but radical form of black collective resistance that was associated with isolated rural topographies, and especially the Great Dismal Swamp of *Dred* [1856]—becomes a means for Schoolman to connect Stowe's novel with the more radical writings of James Redpath and Thomas Wentworth Higginson. Schoolman's ambitious chronology compellingly argues for the importance of space to abolitionist thought, and demonstrates that geography is a means to remap established genealogies of the abolition movement, and to rethink its canonical literature.

Matthew Wynn Sivils, in *American Environmental Fiction, 1782–1847*, presents an engagingly written exploration of how the texts produced in the early United States both influenced and reflected the nation's new environmental consciousness. The study is a much-needed addition to the growing field of ecocriticism, as it addresses the comparatively neglected body of literature written prior to the second half of the nineteenth century. While Ralph Waldo Emerson and Henry David Thoreau are often cited as the 'fathers' of American environmental writing, Sivils offers instead a new perspective, which traces the roots of their work back to early republic natural histories, Indian captivity narratives, Gothic novels, and juvenile literature. Although Sivils provides a useful overview of pre-existing critical work, he notes that the established body of research often centres on non-fiction (such as the personal essay). By contrast, his book complements and develops the field by presenting a refreshing focus on *fiction* (including a welcome survey of early environmental writing for children, an area that is comparatively overlooked), balancing insightful analyses of celebrated authors (such as Cooper) with the recovery of more obscure figures (such as William Bartram). Sivils opens by demonstrating the ways in which Crèvecoeur and Bartram created 'an imagined American environment that provided the essential foundation for the environmental fiction that followed', with subsequent chapters tracing the (frequently missed) interconnections between early environmental prose, Indian captivity narratives, and juvenile tales. The second half of the book examines three works by Cooper (*The Pioneers* [1823], *The Prairie* [1827], and *The Crater* [1847]), presenting them as major developments within American environmental fiction while also placing them in dialogue with other contemporary works (including visual art). Like Kathryn Cornell Dolan's *Beyond the Fruited Plain* (reviewed above), Sivils stresses the significance and timeliness of examining literature and the land, noting that at 'the heart of [his] study is the idea that by better appreciating the developments of our culture's ecological consciousness we greatly enrich our present-day understanding of the natural world as a community of interdependence'. Richly illustrated and carefully researched, Sivils's monograph marks a valuable contribution to both American studies and ecocriticism, fulfilling admirably Thoreau's desire to 'speak a word for nature'.

In *The Altar at Home: Sentimental Literature and Nineteenth-Century American Religion*, Claudia Stokes presents an illuminating and revisionary account of the interrelationship between domesticity, gender, and faith. Like Mary McCartin Wearn's *Nineteenth-Century American Women Write Religion* (reviewed below), Stokes seeks to address the neglect of literary

representations of belief, focusing on sentimentalism and, through historicizing this sometimes derided genre, complicating interpretations of it.
Challenging conventional perceptions of sentimentalism as a mode of
conformity, Stokes demonstrates that female sentimental writers 'absorbed
new populist beliefs and sectarian antipathy but moved them indoors, into the
private domestic space'. While Stokes reinvestigates canonical authors (such as
Harriet Beecher Stowe) and recovers those largely forgotten (such as Anna
Warner), she also devotes welcome attention to an array of often overlooked
forms, such as the hymn, the religious revelation, and the spiritual autobiography. *The Altar at Home* starts usefully by outlining the wider religious and
historical contexts that heralded the rise of the religious press and sentimental
literature, exploring sentimentalism within the framework of the Second Great
Awakening and re-establishing the importance and complexity of the hymn.
Stokes also explores mid-century millennialism, developing the common
recognition of its influence upon Stowe by tracing its effect more widely on the
sentimental narrative form. Further sections examine sects, Mormonism, and
Christian Science, with Stokes's thorough, fascinating research casting new
light upon these issues. Her engaging, accessible, and yet scholarly book
ultimately exposes 'the insufficiency of the current sentimental canon, the
corpus of nineteenth-century texts currently studied and taught'. Instead, *The
Altar at Home* demonstrates that 'the sentimental literary archive is more
capacious than we perhaps recognized'. Above all, through her considered
analysis of a number of female sentimentalists, Stokes recovers the complexity,
diversity, and power of Nathaniel Hawthorne's 'damned mob of scribbling
women'.

  *Nineteenth-Century American Women Write Religion: Lived Theologies and
Literature*, edited by Mary McCartin Wearn, offers a comprehensive,
accessibly written overview of the profound influence of religion on shifting
gender roles, as the Second Great Awakening 'authorized' female piety to
move from the private to the public sphere. As nineteenth-century evangelicalism stressed free will, thereby 'creating a new realm of gender autonomy',
Wearn argues that 'religion thus provides an important critical lens through
which to evaluate women's culture of the era'. However, 'sparse critical
attention to religion is particularly problematic in nineteenth-century studies
and has led to a narrowed view of a culture in which faith played so significant
a role'. The volume presents a 'corrective scholarship' that embraces 'the
paradoxes of religion' and articulates 'the proliferation of ways nineteenth-
century women expressed belief'. Commencing with an introductory analysis
of Stowe's *Uncle Tom's Cabin*, the collection also retrieves and illuminates a
range of 'non-canonical' authors from various economic, religious, and
geographical backgrounds. Given the book's scope, it is usefully divided into
sections, with the first three chapters examining women's spiritual autobiography. Nancy F. Sweet, in a meticulously researched and fascinating essay,
outlines Josephine Bunkley's account of her flight from convent abuse. Sweet
reworks previous critical assessments of her tale, arguing that Bunkley
complicates the convent-escape narrative through her challenge to antebellum
conventions regarding female identity and propriety. Joy A.J. Howard then
explores the interrelationship between 'Holiness' and race and gender,

addressing the neglected area of religion in texts composed by African American women, while Rachel Cope interrogates religious memoirs. B.G. Sammons considers agency in Rebecca Harding Davis, and R.L. Tanglen offers a fresh reading of Harriet E. Wilson's *Our Nig*, uncovering the often overlooked religious subplot. Kathryn Crowley likewise reveals new perspectives on Julia Ward Howe's *The Hermaphrodite*, moving beyond the critical focus on gender and sexual politics and highlighting instead the centrality of Swedenborgianism. Valerie D. Levy complicates the figure of the female abolitionist, interrogating the interconnection between race and gender, and balancing well-known and obscure writers. Indeed, while much of the collection's value lies in its discussion of under-researched women (Roxanne Harde showcases Elizabeth Stuart Phelps as a feminist theologian, and Wearn compares Sarah Piatt to Anne Bradstreet), its focus on religion also enables refreshing analyses of the canon; Gregory Eiselein thus remedies the lack of attention devoted to Louisa May Alcott's complex and unconventional religious ideas. While each essay focuses on specific authors and themes, they are also in dialogue with each other; as such, the volume is both meticulously detailed in its case studies and coherent as a whole.

Karen Weingarten's *Abortion in the American Imagination: Before Life and Choice, 1880–1940* traces and interrogates shifts in the literary representation of abortion from the nineteenth to the twentieth century. Her work marks a significant contribution to various fields (including American studies, politics, and feminism), drawing together an encyclopedic knowledge of an array of materials, balancing canonical novels against films, letters, journals, and periodicals. Tracking 'how antiabortion rhetoric was used to delineate the contours of the ideal American citizen, the book constructs a discursive genealogy of one of the most intractable issues in the United States today'. Weingarten's introduction outlines the theoretical framework in which she reads her texts, providing a succinct overview of the complexities of the 'abortion controversy', and its relationship with liberalism, biopolitics, and modernity. Her key argument asserts that 'by studying how the liberal individual serves as a foundational figure in abortion rhetoric, extending from the mid-nineteenth century to today', one can 'deconstruct how the terms are intimately bound to each other and to an American liberalism that upholds individual freedom and rights'. While she follows previous critics (such as Laura Doyle) in analysing how new abortion narratives emerged in the late nineteenth and early twentieth centuries, Weingarten further explores how abortion rhetoric controlled and disciplined women's lives, maintaining that it is 'rooted in political issues that are often defined as "masculine": economy, autonomy, racism and political life'. Although most of the book focuses on the twentieth century, chapter 1 highlights the interplay between abortion and race, as late nineteenth-century anti-abortion laws became infused with anxieties about colour and citizenship (producing a need to discourage relationships between white women and black men). Chapter 2 then outlines Anthony Comstock's polemics, beginning in the 1870s, which moralized against 'obscene acts', and Margaret Sanger's lobbying to legalize contraception; crucially, while much has been written about Sanger's stance on birth control, Weingarten addresses her often neglected thoughts on abortion.

Above all, Weingarten posits that, because the late nineteenth and early twentieth centuries 'marked a formative period for abortion discourse, examining the era's representations of abortion provides insight into how the issue is framed today'. Engagingly written, and incorporating some interesting illustrations (from dime novels to movie posters), *Before Life and Choice* therefore presents important and timely research, not only casting new light on abortion and literature from the past two centuries, but also offering innovative ways of addressing this most heated and relevant of issues in the future.

In the first of the now hugely popular series of Elena Ferranti novels dubbed the 'Neapolitan Novels', *My Brilliant Friend* [2012], the protagonists Lila Cerullo and Elena Greco are, for a time, mesmerized by *Little Women* and reminded of the novel's power throughout their early lives. The novel is given to the fierce and 'brilliant' Lila by her teacher. *My Brilliant Friend* charts, as *Little Women* does, the joys and frustrations of burgeoning womanhood. Early on in the narrative the two friends reach the conclusion that to become an author of fiction might be to become rich and independent and thus to find a way out of the brutal and impoverished neighbourhood of Naples that is their whole world. Without their knowing it, their work ethic and fierce determination to gain some autonomy for themselves mirror not just Jo's turn to the literary as a source of income and freedom but that of Alcott herself. The autobiographical elements of *Little Women* are well documented.

Beverly Lyon Clark's *The Afterlife of Little Women* begins with a quotation from John Frow, and announces the work to be one of reception history. Clark goes on to recall her own childhood relationship with *Little Women* and her later realization that her cherished copy of the text was in fact an abridged version with much of the 'moralizing' removed: she does not comment on whether or not this was an improvement. From here Clark examines responses to the initial publication of Part I of *Little Women* in 1868 and it's continued popularity through to 1900. Chapter 2 charts the critical dismissal of the novel as 'popular' fiction in the following thirty years and its persistent mass approval. In this period the first dramatization of the novel was performed on Broadway in 1912. 'Outwitting Poverty and War, 1930 to 1960' (chapter 3) argues that during this period the arbiters of high culture continued to ignore Alcott's novel but broad readership appeal continued to prevail, and two Hollywood films were made, in 1933 and 1949. Clark argues that the renewed, or rather the unstinting, popularity of *Little Women* in this period can be attributed to the easy relevance and comfort found in its themes. Many readers were drawn to it the author suggests, because it could bring consolation during the Depression, and in opposite circumstances to those of the postwar boom years, its zeal and determined spirit offered energy and inspiration. In the last chapter of her reception study Clark turns to the period after 1960. Second-wave feminism, and the publication of many of Alcott's previously unknown works, have secured her a position, finally, in the academic milieu. As a consequence of this almost universal acceptance of the influence and charm of *Little Women* there has been an increase in the number of creative responses to the text. Thus there has been an explosion of picture books, operas, musicals, poetry, anime, and radical feminist reimaginings. We may be just moments away from 'Little Women and Zombies'.

Published in paperback in 2014 Alexandra Socarides' *Dickinson Unbound: Paper, Process, Poetics* finds, in its focus on the materials and material processes Dickinson used to create her poetry, an inspiring and effective method for reading it. Engaged, as this study is, in an increasingly popular field of critical enquiry that sees attention to material culture (specifically manuscripts here) as in need of reaffirmation, Socarides highlights the debt her research questions owe to Virginia Jackson's 2005 *Dickinson's Misery: A Theory of Lyric Reading*, which won the Modern Language Association Prize for a First Book. Taking *Dickinson's Misery* as a theoretical foundation, Socarides argues that for us to best understand Dickinson's poetry we must have an awareness of the multiple material contexts many of her poems existed in. There is a fundamental relationship, the author argues, between paper, process, and poetics in the poetry of Emily Dickinson, and it is a convincing argument. Socarides agrees with Jackson that the easy identification of Dickinson's poetry as 'lyric' continues to require interrogation. This she then does through the five chapters that make up this poised and stimulating study. Chapter 1 pays close attention to the fascicles of Dickinson's poems and situates them in the context of homemade book-making and scrapbook practices. The author argues persuasively that the 'loose' clusters of poems that Dickinson tied together produce far less coherence than has been latterly read into these arrangements, looking at the relationship between Dickinson's poetry and her correspondence to contend that we should not sever the connection between the rhetorical strategies and formal structural components of either discipline of composition but rather see each as integral to Dickinson's process of revision and communication. Chapter 3 considers the spatial qualities of Dickinson's sewing together of her folded sheets, and chapter 4 extrapolates from these more specific readings of material and its importance, to bring in biographical detail. It is, as *Dickinson Unbound* is throughout, an experiment in reading against categories imposed on Dickinson by scholars whose linguistic choices - in this chapter Socarides questions R. W. Franklin's naming of loose sheets as 'sets' - have become entrenched in ways that the author deems, ultimately 'unhelpful'. Socarides challenges one camp of established scholarly opinion that sees Dickinson's late poetry as a decline in, or disintegration of, the poetic process. Rather, Socarides argues, this apparent dis-composition was instead the result of a heightened awareness of materiality on Dickinson's part and a reluctance to smooth away or hide the poetic process with 'final', neat copies of a poem. Maintaining this 'scrap'piness, the reader is made to understand, might also have been a method for maintaining meaning.

Stephen Matterson's *Melville: Fashioning in Modernity* provides an energetic exploration of the theme of identity across Herman Melville's career. Through close readings of some of Melville's less often studied works, Matterson suggests that Melville uses clothing to imagine his characters' efforts to shape and sustain their identities in the rapid social changes that characterize modernity. Disconnections between their outward-facing identity and their inner sense of self lead characters to suffer alienation and anxiety, which

Melville registers through their discomfort in clothing, or their being wrongly clothed. Furthermore, Matterson argues, these same narratives evidence Melville's self-invention as a writer. Thus, the narrators of *Redburn* [1849] and *White-Jacket* [1850] use clothing to negotiate their individual and social identities, at the same time as Melville navigates a path between accepted forms of writing and fulfilling self-expression. In *Typee* [1846] and *Omoo* [1847], Pacific islanders, Tommo, and Melville use clothing to challenge static binaries in favour of identities based in fluid processes of adaptation and accommodation. An unusually extended study of *Israel Potter* [1856]—including an astute comparison with the slave narrative—argues that it is Melville's most extensive meditation on the self, with Israel's changing dress charting his inability to forge an identity that meets the demands of modernity. Matterson suggests that the uniforms of *Billy Budd* symbolize characters' (dis)comfort in their roles, and especially Vere's inability to reconcile self and duty, but that the novella also acts as Melville's own exercise in self-examination. Matterson draws Melville into dialogue with contemporaries like Thomas Carlyle, Richard H. Dana, and Nathaniel Hawthorne, but also with such eclectic materials as the cartoon *Mr Benn*, and *Down and Out in Paris and London*. Altogether, this lively study demonstrates what can be discovered in the less explored regions of Melville's life and work.

Containing Multitudes: Walt Whitman and the British Literary Tradition, by Gary Schmidgall, is a handsomely presented volume that takes on the task of methodically testing Whitman's claim to have 'resist[ed] much' and 'obey[ed] little' in the works of his transatlantic antecedents. Schmidgall does this by persuasively working through the influence of five major British literary figures upon the poet who would, in later life, come to be affectionately known as the Good Gray Poet, after William Douglas O'Connor's coining of the nickname. These influences are: Shakespeare, Milton, Burns, Blake, and Wordsworth. Scott, Carlyle, Tennyson, Wilde, and Swinburne also receive honourable mention in places. The preface to Schmidgall's study begins with Whitman considering the American landscape, unrepresented, it seems safe to agree, by the works of Shakespeare, Milton, Young, Gray, and Beattie. The author then explores a much later pronouncement by Whitman that Longfellow, Bryant, Emerson, and Whittier deserve placement in the poetic canon written in English. The reader is taken briskly, and playfully, through the various obstacles, or contradictions, that might have prevented the author from undertaking such a comparative work, before we are told that this book wishes to function as a first step, or a doorway through which future scholars will pass to continue the work of establishing Whitman's transatlantic engagements. If there is anxiety here it is short-lived, for what the rest of this study does, in the plainest terms, is deliver a tour de force of dense, sophisticated, encyclopedic Whitman criticism. Of particular nuance and interest is the chapter that focuses on Whitman's affinity with and transformation of much that is present in the works of Shakespeare. Schmidgall is the author of at least three works on Shakespeare— *Shakespeare and Opera*, *Shakespeare and the Courtly Aesthetic*, and *Shakespeare and the Poet's Life*—and thus his insights here are especially articulate and compelling.

Books Reviewed

Clymer, Jeffory A. *Family Money: Property, Race, and Literature in the Nineteenth Century*. OUP. [2014] pp. ix + 204. £20.49 ISBN 9 7801 9022 3878.

D'Amore, Maura. *Suburban Plots: Men at Home in Nineteenth-Century American Print Culture*. UMassP. [2014] pp. 208. hb $80 ISBN 9 7816 2534 0948, pb $22.95 ISBN 9 7816 2534 0955.

Davis, David A., and Tara Powell. *Writing in the Kitchen: Essays on Southern Literature and Foodways*. UMP. [2014] pp. 224. $30 ISBN 9 7814 9680 7977.

DeSpain, Jessica *Nineteenth-Century Transatlantic Reprinting and the Embodied Book*. Ashgate. [2014] pp. 224. £95 ISBN 9 7814 0943 2005.

Dolan, Kathryn Cornell *Beyond the Fruited Plain: Food and Agriculture in U.S. Literature, 1850–1905*. UNebP. [2014] pp. 272. £40 ISBN 9 7808 0324 9882.

Doolen, Andy *Territories of Empire: U.S. Writing from the Louisiana Purchase to Mexican Independence*. OUP. [2014] pp. xiii + 270. £34.49 ISBN 9 7801 9934 8626.

Downey, Dara *American Women's Ghost Stories in the Gilded Age*. PalMac. [2014] pp. viii + 209. £60 ISBN 9 7811 3732 3972.

Edelstein, Sari *Between the Novel and the News: The Emergence of American Women's Writing*. UPVirginia. [2014] pp. 226. hb $59.50 ISBN 9 7808 1393 5898, pb $29.50 ISBN 9 7808 1393 5904.

Ernest, John, ed. *The Oxford Handbook of the African American Slave Narrative*. OUP. [2014] pp. 496. £105 ISBN 9 7801 9973 1480.

Fertel, Rien *Imagining the Creole City: The Rise of Literary Culture in Nineteenth-Century New Orleans*. LSUP. [2014] pp. ix + 203. $39.95 ISBN 9 7808 0715 8234.

Frank, Adam. *Transferential Poetics, from Poe to Warhol*. FordUP. [2014] pp. xiv + 303. $22 ISBN 9 7808 2326 2472.

Jones, Gavin. *Failure and the American Writer: A Literary History*. CUP. [2014] pp. 211. pb $25.99 ISBN 9 7811 0766 2179.

Kennedy, J. Gerald, and Leland S. Person, eds. *The Oxford History of the Novel in English: The American Novel to 1870*. OUP. [2014] pp. 639. £110 ISBN 9 7801 9538 5359.

Lilley, James D. *Common Things: Romance and the Aesthetics of Belongings in Atlantic Modernity*. FordUP. [2014] pp. 256. $50 ISBN 9 7808 2325 5153.

Luciano, Dana, and Ivy G. Wilson, eds. *Unsettled States: Nineteenth-Century American Literary Studies*. NYUP. [2014] pp. 328. £17 ISBN 9 7814 7988 9327.

Luck, Chad. *The Body of Property: Antebellum American Fiction and the Phenomenology of Possession*. FordUP. [2014] pp. ix + 298. $95 ISBN 9 7808 2326 3004.

Lyon Clark, Beverly. *The Afterlife of Little Women*. JHUP. [2014] pp. x + 271. $44.95 ISBN 9 7814 2141 5581.

Matterson, Stephen. *Melville: Fashioning in Modernity*. Bloomsbury. [2014] pp. 240. pb £19.99 ISBN 9 7816 2356 2007.

Moore, Lewis D. *Connecting Detectives: The Influence of 19th-Century Sleuth Fiction on the Early Hard-Boileds*. McFarland. [2014] pp. viii + 201. £35.50 ISBN 9 7807 8647 7715.

Pfitzer, Gregory M. *History Repeating Itself: The Republication of Children's Historical Literature and the Christian Right*. UMassP. [2014] pp. 328. hb $80 ISBN 9 7816 2534 1235, pb $28.95 ISBN 9 7816 2534 1242.

Richardson, Joan. *Pragmatism and American Experience: An Introduction*. CUP. [2014] pp. 276. £20 ISBN 9 7805 2114 5381.

Rohrbach, Augusta. *Thinking Outside the Book*. UMassP. [2014] pp. 180. hb $80 ISBN 9 7816 2534 1259, pb $24.95 ISBN 9 7816 2534 1266.

Schmidgall, Gary. *Containing Multitudes: Walt Whitman and the British Literary Tradition*. OUP. [2014] pp. xxvi + 368. £44.49 ISBN 9 7801 9937 4410.

Schoolman, Martha. *Abolitionist Geographies*. UMinnP. [2014] pp. 240. hb $75 ISBN 9 7808 1668 0740, pb $25 ISBN 9 7808 1668 0757.

Sivils, Matthew Wynn. *American Environmental Fiction, 1782–1847*. Ashgate. [2014] pp. 196. £58.50 ISBN 9 7814 0943 1633.

Socarides, Alexandra. *Dickinson Unbound: Paper, Process, Poetics*. OUP. [2014] pp. xi + 211. £36.49 ISBN 9 7801 9938 0237.

Stokes, Claudia. *The Altar at Home: Sentimental Literature and Nineteenth-Century American Religion*. UPennP. [2014] pp. 281. £39 ISBN 9 7808 1224 6377.

Wearn, Mary McCartin, ed. *Nineteenth-Century American Women Write Religion: Lived Theologies and Literature*. Ashgate. [2014] pp. 200. £85.50 ISBN 9 7814 7241 0429.

Weingarten, Karen. *Abortion in the American Imagination: Before Life and Choice, 1880–1940*. RutgersUP. [2014] pp. 188. £51 ISBN 9 7808 1356 5309.

XVII

American Literature: The Twentieth Century

JAMES GIFFORD, JAMES M. CLAWSON, MARY FOLTZ, ORION USSNER KIDDER, JOLENE ARMSTRONG, AND LINDSAY PARKER

This chapter has seven sections: 1. Poetry; 2. Fiction 1900–1945; 3. Fiction since 1945; 4. Comics; 5. African American Writing; 6. Latino/a, Native, Asian American, and General Ethnic Writing. Section 1 is by James Gifford; section 2 is by James M. Clawson; section 3 is by Mary Foltz; section 4 is by Orion Ussner Kidder; section 5 is by Jolene Armstrong; section 6(a) is by Jolene Armstrong; sections 6(b), (c), and (d) are by James Gifford and Lindsay Parker. The section on drama will recommence in *YWES* 96[2017].

1. Poetry

The completion of the collected writings of Robert Duncan by the addition of two further volumes is the major event of 2014 in American poetry scholarship. Peter Quartermain's edition of *The Collected Early Poems and Plays* (UCalP [2011]; reviewed in *YWES* 93[2014]) is followed now by his excellent edition of *The Collected Later Poems and Plays*, which includes an extensive twenty-seven-page introduction. Quartermain divides Duncan's 'mature' writing from 1958 to 1988 into 'middle' and 'late' periods based on Duncan's 1968 pledge not to publish new work for fifteen years. As Quartermain notes, this is both arbitrary and inevitable, and also not entirely accurate given Duncan's significant small press and private publications from 1968 to 1983. The introduction carefully explicates Duncan's work in relation to his coterie, biography, and historical circumstances while at the same time engaging deeply with the theoretical concepts of importance to Duncan. The editorial apparatus includes an extensive series of explanatory annotations (in endnotes) that also retrace the copy text and variant publications. Included in the annotations are several essay-length analyses and explanations of Duncan's major poems and collections. James Maynard edited the fourth

The Year's Work in English Studies, Volume 95 (2016) © *The Author 2016. Published by Oxford University Press on behalf of the English Association. All rights reserved.*
For Permissions, please email: journals.permissions@oup.com
doi:10.1093/ywes/maw019

volume in the series, *Collected Essays and Other Prose*, which is in many respects a companion to the first volume in the series, *The H.D. Book* (UCalP [2011]; reviewed in *YWES* 91[2012]). Maynard excels here in the kind of detail made possible by his position as curator of the poetry collection at the State University of New York at Buffalo, which houses the Duncan papers. The lengthy introduction is lively and makes important interventions in the critical discourse around Duncan and his influences, revising Ekbert Faas's *Young Robert Duncan: Portrait of the Poet as Homosexual in Society* (BSP [1984]) and adding to Lisa Jarnot's *Robert Duncan, the Ambassador from Venus* (UCalP [2012]; reviewed in *YWES* 93[2014]), the latter of which he had been involved with in his curatorial role. The collection opens auspiciously with Duncan's 1940 review of Henry Miller's *Tropic of Capricorn* (Obelisk [1938]), including the note that Duncan's library includes only the 1952 edition of the novel but with the bookplate dated 1939. This level of care recurs across the annotations and editorial apparatus, checking Duncan's quotations against his own copies of the original materials where possible, and noting variations or errors while providing citations to them. This is particularly productive in relation to Duncan's comments on Ezra Pound and Louis Zukovsky, which may provoke much reconsideration of his work on both. While many scholars have accessed the major essays in the collection, perhaps most notably 'The Homosexual in Society' (pp. 5–18), having ready access to Duncan's critical commentary on figures from Charles Olson, H.D., Robert Creeley, Walt Whitman, and Dante to William Blake, T.S. Eliot, James Joyce, Carl Jung, and Sigmund Freud, is an enormous boon made stronger by a detailed thematic index that attends carefully to Duncan's interests in sexuality, the occult, hermeticism, poetics, politics, and the Great Books tradition. As a whole, the collected writings of Robert Duncan belong in every major research library and anticipate a renewal of critical work on Duncan's corpus, such as Jeffrey Neilson's 'Robert Duncan's Conversion to Poetry' (*ConL* 56:i[2015] 114–44), Scarlett Higgins's 'A Private Public Sphere: Robert Duncan and Jess's Cold War Household' (*ArQ* 70:iv[2014] 109–42), the reviewer's *Personal Modernisms: Anarchist Networks and the Later Avant-Gardes* (UAlbertaP [2014]), Mark Scroggins's *Intricate Thicket: Reading Late Modernist Poetries* (UAlaP [2015]), and Albert Gelpi's *American Poetry after Modernism* (CUP [2015]), all of which quote from these new editions and engage in work made more likely by the care taken in the production of this series.

Other editions from 2014 should appeal to the readers of the collected writings of Robert Duncan. It is remarkable to see the release in the same year of Sharon Thesen and Ralph Maud's *After Completion: The Later Letters of Charles Olson and Frances Boldereff*; Rod Smith, Peter Baker, and Kaplan Harris's *The Selected Letters of Robert Creeley*; and at a bit of a distance Kevin McGuirk's edition of *An Image of Longing: Selected Letters and Journals of A.R. Ammons, 1951–1974. Ommateum to Sphere: The Form of a Motion*. Olson, Creeley, and Duncan all figure in Ammons's letters, although Harold Bloom, Geoffrey Hartman, M.H. Abrams, Josephine Jacobsen, Richard Howard, Josephine Miles, John Logan, and academic editors are more persistent references. Where Whitman appears in Duncan's materials, Ralph Waldo Emerson and Robert Frost are privileged here for Ammons. The argument for renewed work on Ammons is wholly persuasive, and McGuirk's brief introduction is supported by a glossary of names, robust index, and concise footnotes aimed largely at providing citations for unclear references or briefly noting responses from Ammons's interlocutors. Distinct from the practical objectives involved in bringing Ammons's work more attention and providing the critical contextualization his own extended thoughts with colleagues can provide, the book also offers astonishing insight into the institutional life of American poetry in the second half of the twentieth century. Ammons's most important correspondents here are arguably Bloom and Hartman rather than Jacobsen and Miles, pointing to the importance of his post at Cornell University for his poetic work—Abrams is represented less, but this is seemingly due to proximity in the institution rather than by virtue of being a lesser influence (he figures through his discussions with Ammons on his move from Cornell University Press to W.W. Norton & Co., as well as through his responses to critical interpretations of his works). Indeed, the gestures to scholarly publications and critical articles are prevalent across the letters and offer a rare glimpse into the relations among the poet and his critics rather than the discourses between poets or between critics. For both reasons, *An Image of Longing* is excellent, especially in the now expected beauty of ELS Editions' production values. *After Completion* finishes the project begun in *A Modern Correspondence* (WesleyanUP [1999]), also edited by Maud and Thesen and discussed by Andrew Mossin in '"In Thicket": Charles Olson, Frances Boldereff, Robert Creeley and the Crisis of Masculinity at Mid-Century' (*JML* 28:iv[2005] 13–39). The letters in *After Completion* follow after the end of Olson and Boldereff's affair but cover her influence on his development of a projectivist poetics that influenced Duncan deeply and their joint developing interest in Arthur Rimbaud. There is also much to bear out Mossin's arguments about masculinity, such as Olson's lengthy reactions to Boldereff's romantic attachments to others (pp. 19–21, 203–7). The collection is divided into eight sections, each with a brief editorial introduction outlining the major events in their relationship during the period in question, some divisions covering a portion of a year or, later in the collection, periods of up to four years at a time. Olson's letters, particularly those from his time as rector at Black Mountain College, blur the distinction between poetic composition and prose epistolarity by experimenting with the spatial organization of the page. The editorial apparatus is light but provides all essentials for scholars to contextualize the letters, and as a whole the collection will appeal to general readers as well. Among the three, the much-awaited *Selected Letters of Robert Creeley* stands out. While the collection is highly selective, as would be necessary for a correspondent as productive as Creeley (the editors point out that the list of correspondents alone represented in the Stanford Special Collections, among the major repositories of his papers, runs to more than a hundred pages), the book establishes a coherent narrative of his career from his earliest publications corresponding with the 1945 start of his *Collected Poems of Robert Creeley* (UCalP [1982]) to e-mails sent only three weeks before his death in 2005. By drawing representative letters from among Creeley's most important correspondents—such as Duncan, Denise Levertov, Allen Ginsberg, Susan Howe, and Kenneth Rexroth in tandem with his academic interactions with Peter Quartermain, Marjorie Perloff, and even a listserv posting to the University of Buffalo English Department—the editors offer contents useful across Creeley's career and varied interests. An especially helpful part of the process of selection is the book's emphasis on Creeley's professional recommendations to other poets, such as offset printing of a fine press edition for Louis Zukofsky, commenting on the influence of Olson's poetics to William Carlos Williams, or discussing with Kenneth Rexroth the conflicts involved in the production of *The Black Mountain Review* around the reviews of Dylan Thomas and Theodore Roethke. Interspersed are Creeley's drafts for poems (noted in relation to the *Collected Poems* by the editors) as well as remarks on his sometimes overlooked contacts with other writers outside his own generation, such as Robert Graves during his years on Mallorca. The commentary here on James Laughlin also merits attention in relation to the recent projects completed on him, specifically Ian MacNiven's excellent biography, *'Literchoor Is My Beat': A Life of James Laughlin, Publisher of New Directions* (reviewed below), and Peter Glassgold's edition of *The Collected Poems of James Laughlin* (ND [2014]).

Among the editions of 2014, Leonard Diepeveen's *Mock Modernism: An Anthology of Parodies, Travesties, Frauds, 1910–1935* holds a special place. It is by turns charming, hilarious, and deeply informative for the cultural reception of modernist literatures in their time. Louis Untermeyer's mock-poem 'Ezra Pound' from *'—and Other Poets'* (HRW [1916]) seems certain to call out for quotation at conferences: 'It is time we were getting ourselves talked about' (p. 134). The collection is enjoyable in this sense but also has the entirely serious function of showing mass responses to modernism's fragmentation, innovation, and difficulty—that the discomfort with modernist innovation took the form of mockery and satire is both telling and a demonstration of the intensity of the mainstream reactions. Diepeveen manages the delicate balance of allowing the genuinely funny to remain humorous even while annotating its allusions or references, such as translating a quoted passage of Provençal while also noting where it is used by Pound in 'Amrities' (p. 401). While highly enjoyable, the central contention is entirely persuasive: that the discomfort revealed by these 'travesties' (per Diepeveen's subtitle) inform our understanding of the material reception of modernism and how that reception shaped modernism's own sense of elitism and complexity. It is also timely as a remedy for scholarship that may seek out such complexity while overlooking the middlebrow materialist context of modernist works' consumption.

Last among the editions is Bill Morgan's production of *Peter Orlovsky, A Life in Words: Intimate Chronicles of a Beat Writer* with a helpful personal foreword by Ann Charters. The discourse is overtly for the common reader with the aim of bringing Orlovsky's writings and life to a mainstream audience. While Orlovsky is well known in Beat scholarship, both Morgan and Charters lament his general neglect in the popular consciousness of the movement and New American Poetry. The repeated assertion of Orlovsky's heterosexuality (despite his lifelong relationship with Ginsberg after leaving the artist Allen LaVigne) calls out for further discussion and will likely prompt returns to exemplary earlier work such as Raymond-Jean Frontain's 'Peter McGehee and the Erotics of Gay Self-Representation' (*Intertexts* 13:i–ii[2009]

115–51) and Anne Hartman's 'Confessional Counterpublics in Frank O'Hara and Allen Ginsberg' (*JML* 28:iv[2005] 40–56). The project of the book is to present a coherent selection of Orlovsky's unpublished journals, poetry, and correspondence as literary artefacts of their own value distinct from the generally biographical purposes for which he has been used in scholarship. A natural response here would be to critically engage with previous work on life writing and journals among the Beats, such as Jane Falk's 'Journal as Genre and Published Text: Beat Avant-Garde Writing Practices Cover' (*UTQ* 73:iv[2004] 991–1002), Nancy McCampbell Grace and Jennie Skerl's *The Transnational Beat Generation* (Palgrave [2012]), and Skerl's *Reconstructing the Beats* (Palgrave [2004]; reviewed in *YWES* 85[2006]). The text has silently corrected Orlovsky's idiosyncratic misspellings with the aim of 'communicat[ing] the thought and words of Peter Orlovsky to a new readership that might not find his peculiar spellings as charming as Allen did' (p. xxix), although two examples of his poetry in its original state are included.

Daniel Tiffany's study of kitsch is particularly careful in *My Silver Planet: A Secret History of Poetry and Kitsch*. By recuperating the vital role of discussions of kitsch in literary modernism and cultural studies, Tiffany challenges the dismissal of kitsch from modernism by contrasting its lyrical and Romantic elements as they infiltrate modernism through eighteenth through nineteenth century sensibilities. This stands out in the five most pervasive poetic figures in the study: Pound, Ashbery, Thomas Gray, Eliot, and William Wordsworth, in more or less that sequence of importance. The extensive attention to lyric diction, ballads, beauty, banality, and the bogus or counterfeit stands over concerns about the forms of subjectivity and investment in commodified expressions of that subjectivity. The free scope of the book, moving with astonishing agility between the ballad revival to Pound's *Cantos* or Romantic passionate expression and impersonality, and most strikingly across periods and national literatures, provokes the reader to the imaginative potential of the 'secret' of the subtitle. There are many things here to be quibbled over, which would seem inevitable with the necessarily broad gestures, but the core articulation of an entanglement between the poetic tradition and kitsch running from Gray's 'Elegy Written in a Country Churchyard' through to Pound's *Cantos* is irresistible, despite the obvious demands of setting these works and modes together for consideration. The greatest temptation, however, is to read Tiffany's complex (and rewarding) analyses beside the kitsch responses assembled by Diepeveen.

Ian MacNiven's '*Literchoor Is My Beat*': *A Life of James Laughlin, Publisher of New Directions* connects in obvious ways to other recent works of importance: Gregory Barnhisel's *James Laughlin, New Directions, and the Remaking of Ezra Pound* (UMassP [2005]) and his *Cold War Modernists: Art, Literature, and American Cultural Diplomacy* (ColUP [2015]), Loren Glass's *Counter-Culture Colophon: Grove Press, the Evergreen Review, and the Incorporation of the Avant-Garde* (StanfordUP [2013]), and the strategically timed republication of *The Collected Poems of James Laughlin* (ND [2014]). MacNiven has already established his reputation as a biographer with *Lawrence Durrell: A Biography* (Faber [1998]), and this turn to Laughlin follows with the personal engagement with his subject—Laughlin is 'J' just as Durrell was 'Larry', yet this intimacy does not prevent critique or careful attention. That the book completes forty-two chapters with an additional preface and epilogue cues MacNiven's attention to detail, much of which is oriented to the scholar, even while the prose style keeps the engagement of the mainstream reader. The reader opens the book to be told 'Born handsome, brilliant, and rich, all his life James Laughlin courted the art of self-effacement' (p. 3), but it closes with an appendix of authors published by Laughlin through his New Directions, one of the great independent American publishing houses of the twentieth century. This is to say, the book is careful in detail for a scholarly reader interested in Laughlin not so much for his personality and adventures as for the literary talent he nurtured in Ezra Pound, Henry Miller, William Carlos Williams, Robert Duncan, H.D., Jack Kerouac, and a veritable who's who of American literature—yet at the same time, the narrative of the life turns and charms by juxtaposing the quotidian and all too human against the surreal or (on a few occasions) the ridiculous. The very humane approach MacNiven adopts for Laughlin's politics is also helpful, by turns looking to his hesitations over the early stages of European fascism despite Pound's deep influence, or as MacNiven carefully phrases it, 'J would remain, lifelong, a convert to Ezra's economic theories, not at all to his politics' (p. 149). In many respects, Pound is the most pervasive interlocutor in Laughlin's career and dominates the early and middle sections of the book, but the portrait that emerges is utterly convincing in its depiction of Laughlin as a vital influence on his stable of authors even as he turned in ever new directions based on his interactions with them. His critical stance towards T.S. Eliot and Louis Zukofsky may surprise today, but MacNiven integrates the cheeky private correspondence that sits behind Laughlin's critical writings, which deepens the reader's understanding of Pound's shaping influence for both poets—the later 1967 rapprochement between Pound and Allen Ginsberg likewise surprises. It is impossible, after reading MacNiven's account, not to look for Laughlin's influence across American letters from the 1930s onward, reaching for Lawrence Ferlinghetti and Denise Levertov to Thomas Merton, Dylan Thomas, Henry Miller, Kenneth Rexroth, Gertrude Stein, and seemingly near everyone else between. Most tellingly, the book also advocates for Laughlin not only as publisher but as author, which is a thread running across the book.

A late arrival from 2013 follows in the biographical vein. Sandeep Parmar's *Reading Mina Loy's Autobiographies: Myth of the Modern Woman* is a slim volume in Bloomsbury's growing Historicizing Modernism series. The intended audience shifts between undergraduates encountering archival studies afresh and scholars already familiar with Loy's archival state. The descriptions of the archival holdings emphasize how archives accumulate materials, the locations of various holdings, and give an introduction to the nature of archival work and its organization. As Parmar points out, for any archival collection, 'folders organized by subject such as notes on "Jews", "Religion", "Literature", "Metaphysics" and "Art" sometimes gather what appears to be discontinuous musings into a cohesive mould' (p. 5), which is a process that can generate its own form of information even though 'It seems probable that the organization of this array of material into folders is a product of the archivists themselves' (p. 5). This final point is 'reiterated' explicitly as confirmed rather than 'probable' a number of times in the endnotes. This kind of argument has been advanced in detail by Michael O'Driscoll in ' "Dead Catalogues": Ezra Pound's *Guide to Kulchur* and the Archival Consciousness of Modernism' (*GlobRev* 1:i[2013] 1–29) and 'Ezra Pound's *Cantos*: "A Memorial to Archivists and Librarians" ' (*LI* 32:i[1999] 173–89). While Derrida's *Archive Fever: A Freudian Impression* (UChicP [1995]) appears in the bibliography, it does not shape the discussion in the body of the text. The key issue, however, is that these autobiographies cannot be held to a sense of completeness or coherence as published work would be since this is not in the nature of the materials themselves. Provocatively, Parmar's assertion near the end of the project that 'An argument in favour of publishing Mina Loy's autobiographical manuscripts has yet to be made' (p. 165) seems at first to run contrary to the designed influence of the book itself: to bring attention to Loy's prose and revive a readership. Instead, after considering Loy's *Insel* (BSP [1991]) and its consideration for publication by James Laughlin for New Directions (for which there is no new information in MacNiven's biography of this year), Parmar presses for the vitality of the 'unfinished' work as a process the reader may uncover in the archive. The importance of *Insel*'s out-of-print status here, however, changed in the next year with Elizabeth Arnold's edition (Melville [2014]). The contradiction of such an archival experience, however, appears in her difficulty with the nearly exclusively scholarly audience for recuperative projects produced by university presses, such as Bonnie Kime Smith's seminal *The Gender of Modernism: A Critical Anthology* (IndUP [1990]) and *Gender in Modernism: New Geographies, Complex Intersections* (UIllP [1997]; reviewed in *YWES* 76[1998]) and specifically how such editions do not facilitate recuperation in the 'public consciousness' (p. 168)—however, archives, even more than the open stacks of libraries, restrict access to a special elite. An implicit element of Parmar's recuperative project calls back to her excellent *Hope Mirrlees: Collected Poems* (Carcanet [2011]) and the important work of recovering overlooked or censored female modernists. Loy scholarship will have much to respond to here and subsequent work is certain based on Parmar's careful study of Loy's autobiographies.

Amy Moorman Robbins's *American Hybrid Poetics: Gender, Mass Culture, and Form* builds forward from her earlier 'Harryette Mullen's Sleeping with the Dictionary and Race in Language/Writing' (*ConL* 51:ii[2010] 341–70) while extending her interests in contrasting hybrid poetic forms against the avant-garde, particularly the legacy of language poetry. As she described the project in 2010, the productive critical frisson is 'between experimental writing/ poetry that is assumed to explicitly or implicitly contest the viability of any given lyric subject . . . and writing that foregrounds questions and problems of discrete, often racialized selfhood' (p. 341). In short, the central critical problem of *American Hybrid Poetics* is the conflict between identity politics and the prevalence of a materialist conception of subjectivity in the avant-garde that tends to subsume categories of gender or race under class. This leads Robbins to concentrate her early attention on Stephen Burt's work for the journal *Fence* and Cole Swensen and Dave St John's editorial work on

American Hybrid: A Norton Anthology of New Poetry (Norton [2009]), especially Swensen's introduction to the book. The challenge she presents is to interpretations of hybrid poetic forms as a new response to conflicting aesthetic paradigms, to which she instead proposes a much longer ideological conflict between the notions of subjectivity implicit in lyrical forms and their tendency towards the transcendent against the linguistic focus of Olson's projective verse and the Language poets. To this conflict she then adds the complexities of race and gender by looking to the activist potential in the lyrical form bound up with identity politics set in relief against 'two predominantly white anthologies claiming "hybridity" as an aesthetically idiosyncratic and playfully insouciant response to thirty years of poetry wars waged by institutionally secure (mostly white, mostly male) teachers' (p. 8). The polemical tone is frequently presented through quotation or paraphrase, most effectively via Craig Santos Perez's 'Whitewashing American Hybrid Aesthetics' from Mary Biddinger and John Gallaher's collection *Monkey and the Wrench* (UAkronP [2011]), but also in Robbins's blunt contention that such 'mostly white, mostly male' positions of privilege are profoundly troubled since 'Only by erasing the long history of nonconforming aesthetics and excluded middles in American literary history can Swensen claim that hybrid mixings of genre are new' (p. 9). This is certain to elicit responses, both positive and negative (and perhaps especially on how this implicitly positions her project in relation to Susan Howe and Lyn Hejinian), but it gives the project much polemical energy in its assertions, which will be welcome for the reader. The book moves through chapters dedicated successively to Gertrude Stein (with gestures to Kathy Acker), Laura Mullen, Alice Notley, Harryette Mullen, and Claudia Rankine. The chapter on Notley and noir as well as the ubiquity of popular genres or pulp across the project make the focus on exclusively American poetry and poetics a palpable limitation, although this also suggests future work or developments from the project of *American Hybrid Poetics*. Kimmy Beach's *The Last Temptation of Bond* (UAlbertaP [2013]), for instance, would make a natural addition here, and the different uses of the lyric form in British poetry across the twentieth century seem an irresistible addition. The deep conflict in the project may also be productively set in contrast to Stephen Voyce's *Poetic Community: Avant-Garde Activism and Cold War Culture* (UTorP [2013]; reviewed in *YWES* 94[2015]).

Bodies on the Line: Performance and the Sixties Poetry Reading by Raphael Allison encases four chapters successively focused on Frost, Olson, Gwendolyn Brooks, Williams, and Larry Eigner within an opening chapter contextualizing the 1960s scene by contrasting John Ashbery against Ginsberg and a conclusion focused on Sylvia Plath and gender (the chapter on Brooks concentrates on her black subject position). The aural focus here recalls Meta DuEwa Jones's *The Muse Is Music: Jazz Poetry from the Harlem Renaissance to Spoken Word* (UIllP [2011]; reviewed in *YWES* 92[2013]) and Richard Swigg's earlier *Quick, Said the Bird: Williams, Eliot, Moore, and the Spoken Word* (UIowaP [2012]). The contextualizing first chapter sets the critical agenda of the project by adapting work on communications and sociology in the context of performance in the 1960s. Walter Ong's stress on the evanescent nature of the spoken word in *The Presence of the Word* [1967], Lionel Trilling's

Sincerity and Authenticity [1971], Erving Goffman's *The Presentation of Self in Everyday Life* [1959], and Marshall McLuhan's contrasting of the bias of mediums and the communicative contents of style all prepare the reader for Allison's extended discussion of the Civil Rights Movement and the New Left as unavoidable contextualizing facts of the culture of poetry performance in the 1960s. Allison seems strongest when presenting the contrasts among different readings by poets, such as Olson's at the University of California Berkeley and Goddard College, such that his struggle between the possibilities of voice and a logocentrism of the visual text emerges. The discussion of disability in Williams and Eigner is also particularly welcome.

A materialist reading of waste and trash shapes the queer readings in Christopher Schmidt's *The Poetics of Waste: Queer Excess in Stein, Ashbery, Schuyler, and Goldsmith*. Schmidt's project is explicitly Jamesonian in its methodology, looking to economic determinants of superstructural aesthetic responses. The very lack of market value, emphasized in relation to Stein in the book, marks out a poetics of waste insofar as the labour of poetry rebuts a capitalist understanding of value. Pairing this reading of waste with gender and sexuality is effective, and it leads Schmidt to articulate 'a waste management poetics in response to ideologies that phobically associate mass culture—and its "tainting" or corruption of high modernist values—with female and queer bodies' (pp. 4–5). The overlapping position for queer bodies and anti-productive market-poor poetry relates for Schmidt to abjection in relation to the capitalist and industry norms of the period. The unification of materialist and queer theory readings here opens complexities that lie outside the project, such as market forces producing the sexual subjectivities under discussion, but the core lever is entirely persuasive: that the authors under study expose the tensions in commodity capitalism by privileging the abject in waste. The bonding of poetic non-utility to waste also bridges Schmidt's project to potential readings of the Language poets, which he gestures to on several occasions, even while he points to the greater interest in the market for his poetic subjects in contrast to Language's anti-capitalist position. In many respects, Stein anchors the project, and her *Tender Buttons* attracts Schmidt's closest attention. Stein's posthumous *Stanzas in Meditation* only appears in the project through Ashbery's review of the work and certainly merits attention using this methodology, especially with the corrected edition now available (YaleUP [2011]; reviewed in *YWES* 92[2013]). The first two chapters on Stein and Ashbery hold the core articulation of Schmidt's project, and in many respects recall Margueritte Murphy's work in *A Tradition of Subversion* (UMassP [1992]; reviewed in *YWES* 73[1995]), especially given both projects' attention to Stein's *Tender Buttons* and Ashbery's *Three Poems*, although Schmidt gives greater attention to Ashbery's *The Vermont Notebook*.

Janet Boyd and Sharon J. Kirsch's *Primary Stein: Returning to the Writing of Gertrude Stein* fulfils its titular ambitions of sparking a revaluation and rethinking of Stein's accomplishments through greater reference to her texts in published and archival forms while lessening the privileged position often accorded to her personality and coterie. For Boyd and Kirsch, this follows on 'Stein's own efforts throughout her lifetime to shift the focus from her personality to her writing', and as a consequence 'all of the essays take her writing as the core interpretive focus' (p. 2). The attention here to the Stein archives, primarily at Yale but also important collections at the Harry Ransom Center at the University of Texas at Austin and the Donald Gallup Collection at the Southern Methodist University, is rich and concludes with two appendices by Nancy Kuhl and Donald Gallup about the acquisition, scope, and organization of the Stein papers at Yale, running from their deposit (while remaining Stein's property) to their present reorganization in 1996. The individual contributions should have a significant impact on studies of Stein. Rachel Blau DuPlessis returns to her groundbreaking work in 'Woolfenstein' from Ellen G. Friedman's *Breaking the Sequence: Women's Experimental Fiction* (PrincetonUP [1989] pp. 99–114) and *Writing Beyond the Ending: Narrative Strategies of Twentieth Century Women Writers* (IndUP [1985]; reviewed in *YWES* 66[1988]) in the chapter here, 'Woolfenstein, the Sequel' (pp. 37–55). Drawing on Stein's *Tender Buttons*, DuPlessis reopens her juxtaposition of Woolf and Stein, which is more an interweaving than a comparison, closing with the persuasive contention that Woolf's '*The Waves* arguably registers the sub rosa impact of Stein's experimental poetics' (p. 53). The chapter pairs with Rebecca Ariel Porte's comparative project in 'Long Dull Poems: Stein's *Stanzas in Meditation* and Wordsworth's *The Prelude*' (pp. 77–95), in which DuPlessis's reading of Stein in Woolf harmonizes with Porte's of Wordsworth in Stein. The great care given here to Stein's lexical and metrical complexities leads finally to the key intervention in critical discussions. As Porte contends, adeptly, 'It is rather remarkable how Wordsworthian *Stanzas* looks after reading *The Prelude*' (p. 92) and finally 'that *Stanzas* is a poem deeply ambivalent about how Wordsworthian it wants to be' (p. 93). The very productive work with Susannah Hollister and Emily Setina's edition of *Stanzas in Meditation: The Corrected Edition* (mentioned above) indicates the kind of complex reconsiderations that the textual work on Stein is already producing. The project also points to the importance of coming reconsiderations based on Seth Perlow's *Tender Buttons: The Corrected Centennial Edition* (CL [2014]), although most chapters do not use the new edition. Boyd's own contribution turns to Stein's shaping and reshaping of her sense of spatiality and geography's influence on literary form, a complex task made clear by comparing the manuscripts of Stein's lectures. Boyd does so while drawing on Benedict Anderson, Edward Said, and Priscilla Wald for approaches to the nation and territory. A special note should also be made of Adam Frank's 'Radio Free Stein: Rendering Queen and Country', which builds out from his major digital staging of Stein's plays: Radio Free Stein (http://www.radiofreestein.com). Frank's chapter is obviously structured to provoke work and to develop questions, and in this it is sure to elicit a response.

Mark Richardson's *Robert Frost in Context* follows in the style of Jason Harding's *T.S. Eliot in Context* (CUP [2011]; reviewed in *YWES* 92[2013]), John McCourt's *James Joyce in Context* (CUP [2014]), and several other volumes in the series in 2014 and 2015 with many more forthcoming. As with Harding's collection, the individual chapters are excellent, and the project as a whole draws together an enviable range of scholars. Richardson has brought together contributions from Joseph M. Thomas, John Xiros Cooper, Tim

Kendall, Jonathan Levin, Steven Gould Axelrod, and other major scholars as well as work from major artists, including Paul Muldoon, Dana Gioia, Mark Scott, and Jay Parini. It is difficult to conceive of a more authoritative project on Frost, especially appearing as it does in the same year as Donald Sheehy, Richardson, and Robert Faggan's *The Letters of Robert Frost, volume 1: 1886–1920* (Belknap [2014]), all three of whom also contribute to *Robert Frost in Context*: Faggan on Frost's correspondence and Sheehy on rural sociology. Contributors to the volume have written some of the major monographs on Frost from the past twenty years and edited the major editions of Frost's poetry, prose, lectures, and papers—Faggan's *The Cambridge Introduction to Robert Frost* (CUP [2008]; reviewed in *YWES* 90[2011]), Robert Bernard Hass's *Going by Contraries: Robert Frost's Conflict with Science* (UPVirginia [2002]; reviewed in *YWES* 83[2004]), and Earl J. Wilcox and Jonathan N. Barron's *Roads Not Taken: Rereading Robert Frost* (UMissP [2000]; reviewed in *YWES* 81[2002]) all stand as prefiguring and contextualizing the authors' contributions here. Richardson's organizing principle takes on Frost as 'a man of parts' (p. xvii), meaning the sectional divisions of the collection look to Frost's diverse interests in philosophy, religion, politics, the geopolitics that inform his work, gender, psychiatry, style, and so forth. This sectional structure succeeds in stressing Frost's capacious mind and its reflection in his work—it is tempting to see this as a major moment in Frost scholarship with the textual scholarship established and the correspondence now becoming available. Cooper's contribution on Frost and modernism has a polemical call to the New Modernist studies for Frost's inclusion and closer consideration. After two paragraphs sketching the anti-modernist and conservative senti-ments in some responses to Frost, Cooper turns his argument to contend that such opinions 'do not align well with the history of either modernism or Frost's evolution as a poet' and, even more pointedly, 'we find that his difference from the Modernists working in the British capital is not as clear as it became when the literary historians a half-century later got to work on the rewriting and simplifying of history' (p. 85). By detailing Frost's connections to the major American voices of modernist poetry—T.S. Eliot, Ezra Pound, and the Imagists—and their collective familiarity with each other's works, Cooper establishes the importance of a modernist Frost, which he completes through a careful recuperation of the entanglement of Frost's concerns over voice and 'freedom of the material' with core modernist precepts of the everyday speaking voice and impersonality, respectively. It seems impossible not to agree with Cooper's conclusion that 'Frost has not often been included in the roll call of canonical Modernist poets. This is a mistake' (p. 91). Axelrod's contribution on Frost and the Cold War also gives the impression of a major intervention, presenting Frost and Eliot via F.O. Matthiessen's *The Oxford Book of American Verse* as the major figures of twentieth-century American poetry, and Frost in particular as an explicitly leveraged figure in Cold War cultures for the United States Senate and President Kennedy through his poems 'Mending Wall' and 'The Gift Outright'. Axelrod points to the suitability of the other poems in Matthiessen's collection, 'Stopping by Woods on a Snowy Evening' and 'Tree at my Window', to Cold War readings and also Frost's goodwill mission on behalf of the Kennedy administration to the Soviet Union in 1962. In this, Axelrod presents the Bay of Pigs, the Berlin crisis, and the Cuban missile crisis as major contextualizing moments in Frost's late works as well as anachronistic misprisions of Frost's earlier works that were accepted by the poet. Each chapter here is highly readable and generally brief, making the volume particularly suitable for undergraduate use or for recommended readings for any introduction to Frost's poetry.

Two works on Ezra Pound stand out for 2014. Mark Byron's *Ezra Pound's Eriugena* adds to the growing series Historicizing Modernism from Bloomsbury by taking up an archival study of what he establishes as the two major phases of Pound's research on Eriugena (first, from the late 1920s to mid-1930s and, second, from 1939 to *The Pisan Cantos*), with the Trinitarian and predestination controversies mainly tied to the first and Pound's general use and emulation of early medieval sources to the second. Byron's contention that the *Cantos* 'incorporates some of the material aspects of different script traditions' (p. xvii), as with Pound's well-studied use of ideograms, plays out here through early modern materials that are less obvious visually but entirely persuasive in Byron's careful reading. In this, Ziaoming Qian's detailing of Pound's reading ability in Chinese at different moments in time in his *Ezra Pound's Chinese Friends* (OUP [2008]; reviewed in *YWES* 89[2010]) anticipates Byron's outlining of Pound's abilities in Latin. The project builds forward from the critical studies of Neoplatonic thought in Pound's work, particularly Peter Liebregts's *Ezra Pound and Neoplatonism* (FDUP [2004]) as well as A. David Moody's and Peter Bush's work on the *Pisan Cantos*. The closing chapter of *Ezra Pound's Eriugena* focuses closely on Neoplatonism and Bryon's reconfiguration of the existing discourse in Pound scholarship. An entirely different approach to Pound is on offer in Josh Epstein's 'The Antheil Era: Pound, Noise, and Musical Sensation' (*TPr* 28.vi[2014] 989–1014) in which non-linguistic aural experience relates to profit from industrial labour and publicity. By reconceiving Pound and George Antheil's interactions on Pound's *Le Testament de Villon* leading to Pound's *Antheil*, Epstein contends 'Pound considered Antheil's music not just an abstract "form"...but a species of mediated materialist critique' (p. 991). This proves particularly satisfying after Epstein's close attention to the integration of noise in Antheil's *Ballet mécanique* and his demonstration of its importance to Pound and its conceptual links to the Futurists. The unpacking of Antheil's score and its rhythmic peculiarities (p. 1011) as bound up in Pound's 'absolute rhythm' is entirely convincing as an underpinning of temporal manipulation, either in musical rhythm, textual repetitions and so forth, or as patterns unfolding into social diagnosis.

Christina Walter's *Optimal Impersonality: Science, Images, and Literary Modernism* builds on the excellent work on modernism in recent years from Johns Hopkins University Press. She argues that emerging medical models of vision urged a new recombinant sense of relations among the Enlightenment subject, the corporeal experience of perception, and the observed world all in relation to the long-standing modernist concern with impersonality. Ford Madox Ford provides the most persistent example from the introduction, leading to a welcome explication of H.D. and Mina Loy as poets opposed to impersonality in the furtherance of progressive political aims (as with Parmar, the discussion of *Insel* is limited to the 1991 Black Sparrow edition). Following the introduction, Walter offers a theory of optics moving forward from Walter Pater and Michael Fields. This precedes chapters that reconfigure H.D. then Loy, both emphasizing embodiment, followed by a reconceptualization of the importance of scientific discourses to D.H. Lawrence. The culmination of the project is Walter's rethinking of Eliot and impersonality based on her now established approach to optics and vision. By presenting Eliot's theory of impersonality as a deliberate obfuscation to distract the readership from misogyny, racism, anti-Semitism, and fascism, Walter gives herself the polemical position of arguing for a radical form of subjectivity based on cognitive experience, for which vision offers a telling example. Some may resist the characterization of *The Waste Land* as an 'early poem' (p. 217), but the study here of Eliot's contact with J.W.N. Sullivan and his 'Modern Tendencies' as effectively an announcement of 'his own participation in Sullivan's scientific vernacular' (p. 219) and a shaping influence on his essay 'Tradition and the Individual Talent' will surely garner attention. She completes the chapter by moving from the influence of these concepts on *The Waste Land* to a study of his play *The Family Reunion*. The work invites significant rethinking of the scope of modernists reliant on theories of impersonality and the importance of embodied visual experience to their articulation of notions of impersonality. It also implicitly provokes consideration of the overlaps between American poets and British novelists, refuting a clean division between the two based on nation or literary mode.

Granular Modernism, from Beci Carver, takes up several British authors through a conceit from the American novelist Frank Norris's review of the American poet Stephen Crane: the bond between naturalism and an expansive entanglement with the granular expanse of the quotidian. From this, Carver contends that naturalism finds its reconfiguration in modernism through the convolutions and confusions of reproducing the minutiae of everyday life. The absence of Norris's own novel *The Octopus: A Story of California* is striking, offering as it does an American concentration of the same granularity taken here to its conclusion in Beckett's *Watt*. Carver's book is both pithy and adept, sharply contrasting Eliot's poetry from his time as an American and Auden's after his move to America against the French context of Beckett's granularity of waste management (akin to Schmidt's work reviewed above). The implicit topical focus also suggests the book's argument cannot be constrained by a single nationalist focus and instead draws on migratory modernisms.

David Sherman's *In a Strange Room: Modernism's Corpses and Mortal Obligation* continues the substantial Modernist Literature and Culture series from Oxford University Press under Kevin Dettmar and Mark Wollaeger's editorship. Sherman's opening gesture to 'The preternatural beauty of modernist writing about the dead' (p. 1) proves fruitful as an organizing principle, allowing him to move fluidly across American and British writers of prose and poetry. The corpse, eroticism in conjunction with mortality, and mortuary practices in combination with mourning open junctions between James Joyce and William Faulkner, T.S. Eliot and Wallace Stevens, or Djuna Barnes and Virginia Woolf. Readers may recall Sherman's very much akin work 'Is Narrative Fundamental? Beckett's Levinasian Question in *Malone*

Dies' (*JML* 32:iv[2009] 65–81). Like Sherman's discussion of Beckett through Levinas, the arguments of *In a Strange Room* around sexuality in Eliot's elegiac gestures to Jean Verdenal and Barnes's doubling of desire and mortality in *Nightwood* echo those already established but are made more expansive by noting the potentially censorious role of the editor in relation to desire for both authors, Pound for Eliot and Eliot for Barnes. The book's opening gesture to Pound by the series editors (p. ix) is echoed by Sherman's introductory recognition via Pound that 'modernism does find its lost dead, and in surprising ways' (p. 5) by looking to literature as 'a preparation for death' (p. 5). Pound is, despite appearing explicitly only a handful of times in the volume, very much a puppet master here, pulling the strings that guide the articulation of others' anxieties over mortality made especially salient in the destruction of the First World War and the ethical burdens of survivors amidst a transforming world system with new moral and structural pressures. Jacques Lacan, Michel Foucault, Jacques Derrida, and Emmanuel Levinas provide important theoretical frameworks for Sherman's discussion, with further engagement through Simon Critchley's and Judith Butler's more recent work on ethics and mourning, respectively. Important precursors on which Sherman relies are Alan Warren Friedman's *Fictional Death and the Modernist Enterprise* (CUP [1995]), Patricia Rae's collection *Modernism and Mourning* (BuckUP [2007]; reviewed in *YWES* 88[2009]), and Joseph Boone's *Libidinal Currents: Sexuality and the Shaping of Modernism* (UChicP [1998]) as well as the longstanding critical work on the Great War in modernist literatures. Parallel to the literary argument is a wider engagement with the socio-historical responses to mortality and American culture best known through Sandra Gilbert's *Death's Door: Modern Dying and the Ways We Grieve* (Norton [2006]) or the unexpected contemporary popular success of Caitlin Doughty's *Smoke Gets in Your Eyes & Other Lessons from the Crematory* (Norton [2014]). The project also calls for attention to the social sciences' work behind these two projects, such as Ernest Becker's *The Denial of Death* (S&S [1973]) and the more recent Terror Management Theory paradigm in Sheldon Solomon, Jeff Greenberg, and Tom Pyszczynski's *The Worm at the Core: On the Role of Death in Life* (RandomH [2015]).

Melba Cuddy-Kean, Adam Hammond, and Alexandra Peat's *Modernism: Keywords* takes its inspiration from Raymond Williams's *Keywords: A Vocabulary of Culture and Society* (Fontana [1976]; reviewed in *YWES* 56[1977]) but expands to include features and methodologies updated to correspond with the New Modernist studies and digital humanities. A sense of distant reading loosely akin to Franco Moretti's *Distant Reading* (Verso [2013]) based on his 'Conjectures on World Literature' (*NLR*:i[2000] 54–68) is at work across the book but always in combination with the attentiveness of an expert close reader deeply familiar with the period, its movements, and its contexts. The individual chapters or entries in the volume are densely interrelated to other entries with connections and points of convergence articulated explicitly for readers in order to suggest the relational nature of any study of modernism as a movement or period. For example, the entry on 'Shock, Shell Shock' annotates other connections with which readers are quite familiar by now, such as the writings of W.H.R. Rivers, and perhaps the only slightly surprising connections to entries on 'Dada, Surrealism', but also (and perhaps most importantly) the unexpected and highly provocative series of connections to the entry on 'Hygiene'. These unexpected connections among keywords are the most compelling feature of the text apart from its obvious utility as a tertiary work for student use or the undergraduate classroom: the persuasive linking of 'Hygiene' to 'Shock, Shell Shock' provokes rethinking and fresh examinations, and this is but one of many such instances across the forty-one entries.

2. Fiction 1900–1945

Scholarship published in 2014 on American fiction from 1900 to 1945 divides into three distinct varieties. First, studies of networks of modernism approach the literature via aesthetic and political networks. These networks often depict a loose connection among writers and across genres, but they are occasionally tightly constrained, growing from the organization of political action. Second, single-author studies read deeply into literature with little consideration for horizontal connections or networks of collaboration. Third, wide-ranging studies aim for an exhaustive depiction of the literature. While only the first type of scholarship takes it as its aim, literature published in 2014 commonly seeks to build connections among authors, aligning and realigning authors' works into new contexts with each other.

Wesley Beal's *Networks of Modernism: Reorganizing American Narrative* establishes some common framework for a few works on American modernist fiction published this year. Beal's study takes as its focus modernism's 'tension of fragment and whole' (p. 3)—tension that transcends genre and art form and that he argues is best understood as a network. His argument is both convincing and imaginative. Rejecting the tendency to understand the network as a postmodern figure, Beal traces its purchase in the early twentieth century, including radio (pp. 8–10), the rise of corporations (pp. 10–13), and popular culture (pp. 13–15). These connections to extra-literary media have application. For example, Beal demonstrates the network characteristics in visual art of the period, using collage and montage to foreshadow later chapters on the affinity between these techniques and works of literature, including Jean Toomer's *Cane* and John Dos Passos's *U.S.A.* trilogy (pp. 16–17). In the rise of the short-story cycle, too, Beal sees tension between fragment and whole that is emblematic of rising cultural interest in the network form (p. 19); with *Winesburg, Ohio* and *In Our Time*, Sherwood Anderson and Ernest Hemingway 'rely on distributed figuration to represent community and subject—strategies of narration that are only thinkable in the context of the network's emergence throughout the modern period' (p. 21). *Networks of Modernism* may be most impressive in its expansion of the network metaphor to include modernist fiction's aesthetic choices. With Gertrude Stein's *Three Lives*, for instance, Beal finds a turning point for modernism. As a work of fragments, *Three Lives* coheres in the network of connections across the three stories: 'one might read the three stories as creating a disjointed pastiche of the romance . . . in this reading there emerges a new understanding of social space in which the margins become more visible and traditional centers of power are scrutinized, even distributed' (pp. 5–6). Likewise, Jean Toomer's *Cane* refuses the genre conventions of a novel or short-story collection in preference for a network: 'a network of forms—perhaps even as an intensification of the distribution that already informs the short story cycle' (p. 55). Anita Loos's *Gentlemen Prefer Blondes* 'undermine[s] the hierarchies of social class and the gendered norms of public and private spheres' in favour of a 'networked model of community to mediate class stratification and the gendering of public and private' (p. 77). And John Dos Passos's *U.S.A.* trilogy relies on ruptures and fusion to establish a network of American history (pp. 95–6). Nevertheless, in Nathanael West's *The Day of the Locust*, Beal augurs the decline of modernism's network aesthetics; the image of the crowd might suggest the network's tension between fragment and whole, but that tension rejects the productive resolution in other applications and it 'signals a turn away from the utopian zeal for social distribution' (p. 122). In this way, Beal demonstrates the network as more than just a symbol of play; the network becomes simultaneously a symbol of function and distributed understanding.

Beal's use of the network as an idiom for making sense of the tension operating beneath the surface of modernist works is a useful descriptor for modernist aesthetics, but the network might also be explored more widely. Mary Chapman's *Making Noise, Making News: Suffrage Print Culture and U.S. Modernism* is one of two volumes this year showing the effects of political networks on American modernist fiction. Chapman's study places the suffrage movement in a role key to modernism's rise. In short, she argues that the modern suffrage campaign succeeded because 'the print culture it developed was astonishingly innovative and irresistible' (p. 4). That print culture was the rising tide that would lift both suffrage and modernism to success. The study offers something like a response to scholars like Janet Lyon who mark the suffragist influence in British modernism (quoted p. 16). Chapman shows these same elements at work on American shores, where political action motivated the growth of a list of new literary concerns and formal conventions: 'new and varied forms of publicity stunts, spectacle, activism, and design; and a vibrant and complex print culture that experimented with a range of forms and aesthetics' (p. 4). Strikingly, Chapman's connection of the suffrage movement to collectively authored novels like *The Sturdy Oak* (p. 10) resonates with the network aesthetic Beal writes of in *Networks of Modernism*. But Chapman's concerns are more than just formal, and she shows the effects of the movement on content as well, with fiction directly referencing non-fictional events (p. 10). In this way, her study expands the traditional understanding of literature of the modernist oeuvre, which is often imagined as entailing a 'great divide' between art and daily life (p. 16). On the contrary, Chapman's study shows convincing connections, as has been argued in recent years by Irene Gammel's *Baroness Elsa: Gender, Dada, and Everyday Modernity* (MITP [2002]), Bryony Randall's *Modernism, Daily Time, and Everyday Life* (UGlasP [2008]), Liesl Olson's *Modernism and the Ordinary* (OUP [2009]; reviewed in *YWES* 90[2011]), and Siobhan Phillips's *The Poetics of the Everyday* (ColUP [2010]; reviewed in *YWES* 91[2012]). For example, in the story 'Switchboard Suffrage' in Oreola Williams Haskell's *Banner Bearers*, Chapman highlights 'new subjectivities, new collectivities, and, most significantly, new rhetorical strategies' (p. 147). Among other things, works like these helped to drive the shift in fiction from a formal diction to a conversational one (pp. 149–50), and the fictional-but-faithful representation of new technologies like transatlantic telegrams further bridges these divides (p. 151).

Like Chapman's work before it, James Gifford's *Personal Modernisms: Anarchist Networks and the Later Avant-Gardes* traces the nodes of a network connected by political allegiances—though his is almost necessarily one that is less politically activated. In his study, Gifford articulates an impressive understanding of a nearly forgotten generation of writers after Auden, 'a literature and body of work vitally alive, internationally distributed, and developed through a network of mutual support stretching from Shanghai, Cairo, and Athens to London, Paris, New York, and San Francisco' (p. ix)—a network commonly overlooked. The study takes the careful work of outlining its approach to personalism and anti-authoritarianism; the word *personal* in the title qualifies any understanding of the later *anarchist*. For these writers, Gifford employs the term 'personalist' which is 'not socialist, not communist, not liberal and not fascist' (pp. x–xi), and he further explains his choice of adjectives: 'I emphasize the *anti-authoritarian* broad premise rather than a strictly political opposition to government rule as such' (p. xiii). Later, *anarchist* and *personalist* are 'terms that amount to the same thing though with significantly different cultural associations and preconceived biases' (p. 161). After an extensive introduction, the first chapter begins almost cautiously, acknowledging its shape as 'metacritical in many respects' (p. 1), but it does so to fend off confusion of its well-considered stance. For example, Gifford acknowledges both the merits and limits of relying on accounts of authors of the period to explain the prime influencers of the literary scene in the 1930s and 1940s (pp. 3–6), and he returns to primary material to expand previous understanding. Henry Miller's fiction emerges as a keystone to the study, which establishes a context of continuity and connection in writing of this time. With his 1934 *Tropic of Cancer*, for example, Miller drew correspondence from older High Modernists and from the younger generation after Miller, but no response from the Auden group (pp. 61–2). In this way, Gifford shows Miller and writers close to him as distinct from the dominant network of the period while also forging a bridge between older and younger generations. In elaborating the networks that grew from and around Miller's *Tropic of Cancer*, Gifford shows tight connections across literary genres and nationalities (pp. 61–71). His scope and readings prove great, bringing context to American fiction 1900–45 by demonstrating Miller's misunderstood personalist politics in his often overlooked *The Colossus of Maroussi* (pp. 206–10); by recasting the connections of Lawrence Durrell's novel *The Black Book* to Miller's *Tropic of Cancer* to understand Durrell's writing in a wider frame, including T.S. Eliot, Dylan Thomas, and David Gascoyne (pp. 210–23); by linking Elizabeth Smart's *By Grand Central Station I Sat Down and Wept* to Durrell's less well-known fiction (pp. 224–9); and by tying Robert Duncan's poetry to the writing of Durrell and H.D. (pp. 229–34). In this, Gifford is exact in both broad and fine strokes. *Personal Modernisms* augments our understanding of the literary period by uncovering the political mores that helped to shape it in a global setting.

Unlike those that came before them, the next two works take a closer focus on the works of individual authors. With *F. Scott Fitzgerald's Fiction: 'An Almost Theatrical Innocence'*, John T. Irwin offers the third in a critical trilogy on American writers in whose works he sees the influence of Platonic idealism (p. ix). At times more a collection of essays than a unified work on Fitzgerald, Irwin's study nevertheless achieves unity across its offering. Among other things, Irwin infuses his understanding of the texts with personal recollection, connecting his first reading of *The Great Gatsby* to his first reading of *A Tale of Two Cities* (p. 1), connecting his defence of Fitzgerald as a southern writer to a defence of his own southernness (pp. 10, 17), and connecting his own love of popular music of the 1910s–1930s with a similar focus in Fitzgerald's writing (p. 33). Without this shared thematic approach, the study coheres less in its earlier chapters, each of which seems to serve different ends. For example, Irwin's first chapter links Fitzgerald's *The Great Gatsby* to Charles Dickens's *A Tale of Two Cities*, finding a shared romantic idealism in Jay Gatsby and Sydney Carton while showing Fitzgerald's protagonist for his turn to irony (p. 2). Irwin's close readings of the novel find 'symmetry' in that work's 'process of narration and the content of the narrative' (p. 9). The second chapter, meanwhile, argues for Fitzgerald's inclusion in the canon of southern writers—in spite of the author's mixed northern/southern heritage—by distinguishing latitudinal class differences (p. 13) and reading these across a variety of Fitzgerald's fiction: novels *The Great Gatsby* (pp. 17–20) and *Tender Is the Night* (pp. 24, 31–2); short stories 'The Last of the Belles' (pp. 20–1), 'The Ice Palace' (pp. 21–4), 'The Diamond as Big as the Ritz' (pp. 25–8), and 'The Swimmers' (pp. 28–31). The third chapter charts yet another course, suggesting that the changed lyrics of a song recorded by Cole Porter owe their provenance to Fitzgerald's *Tender Is the Night* (p. 35), while the lyrics as they were published show the influence of his *The Great Gatsby* (p. 37); the chapter then turns to Fitzgerald's career as a writer for the stage (pp. 40–6) to remark upon the influence of theatricality in his fiction. In the fourth chapter, Irwin touches upon the Platonic idealism mentioned in his preface; in the theatre of society depicted in Fitzgerald's fiction and drama, Irwin finds connections with the writing of Henry James and Edith Wharton, among others. Chapter 5 connects Fitzgerald's use of myth to that of T.S. Eliot, James Joyce, and the classical Greeks and Romans (pp. 158–78), but Irwin ultimately suggests that the establishment of such a mythic method led to Fitzgerald's writing not growing after the success of *The Great Gatsby* (p. 193). Finally, chapter 6 delivers more fully on the Platonic promises of the preface. While individual chapters at times seem almost independent in their aims, this is to the benefit of the reader whose interest is bound to intersect in specific ways. Ultimately, Irwin's study combines an impressively encyclopedic understanding of Fitzgerald's life and writing with an accessible and personal approach to the works.

Like Irwin's study, Barbara Foley's *Jean Toomer: Race Repression, and Revolution* takes as its interest the work of a single author. In it, Foley offers a keen focus on Toomer's socialist ideologies as they grew at the time he was writing and publishing his first book, *Cane*, in 1923. This focus is intentional and corrective. As Foley explains, this side of Toomer's thought is 'not familiar' to readers of his work (p. 2), but these thoughts are crucial to understanding *Cane*: it 'cannot be understood apart from the upsurge of postwar antiracist political radicalism and its aftermath' (p. 2). Foley explains that any oversight comes in part from reading too much into the romantic elements of Toomer's writings at the time—and by reading the works from the vantage of his later writing (p. 3). Neglecting these political and personal contexts limits any good reading of the novel (p. 6). For example, Foley contends, the novel's form may owe its provenance to the socialist revolution that seemed inevitable after the Russian Revolution (p. 8). And Toomer's reactions to travels and to his genealogical discoveries were both complicit in the author's occasional disengagement from otherwise telling causes (p. 9). Foley offers much to contemporary understanding as her sources are sometimes handwritten, including Toomer's unpublished autobiographies, letters, journals, and journalistic writings (p. 12). As a result, she shows where previous scholarship has fallen short by relying too much on the author's own published accounts, which contradict each other. Toomer's 1931 autobiography, for example, recounts an event in 1919 when he gave up socialism as a 'pipe dream' (p. 21); Foley points out that his 1936 autobiography, on the other hand, suggests that the same event rather strengthened his resolve (p. 26). Similarly, Foley shows that Toomer's supposed distance from other African American writers is commonly miscast. That Beal's study of modernist networks makes passing reference (p. 53) to this understanding, touching on Toomer's rejection of an African American peer network shows just how accepted is the novelist's assumed retreat from the black cause after Waldo Frank publicly 'revealed' his blackness. On the contrary, Foley argues, 'Toomer was a New Negro, albeit one striving to define that identity on his own terms' (p. 52). Ultimately, this study acknowledges the difficulty today in providing an appropriate explication for Toomer: 'the forces producing an arrested historical dialectic in our own time may not be all that different from those with which Toomer grappled in the production of his 1923 masterwork' (p. 256).

Considering neither networks nor specific authors, the final three works published this year aim more generally. The first of these, *American Literature: A History* by Hans Bertens and Theo D'haen, is the least focused. Although the slim volume may occasionally come across as too inclusive, Bertens and D'haen nevertheless do well to keep the study useful to a wide audience. They begin by defining the scope of their study, which is 'the oral and the written literature created in that part of the North American continent that is now the United States of America, with the proviso that those literatures . . . that played no role in the development of American culture and America's self-image will not be considered' (p. 6). And they largely deliver. Of interest in the area of fiction from the period 1900–45, they trace the realism of William Dean Howells, Henry James, and Edith Wharton into the naturalism of Frank Norris and Jack London (pp. 122–3), which recalls Carver's *Granular Modernism* (reviewed above). They find common themes among literature written in devotion to a social cause, whether for employment reform, for women's emancipation and rights, or for the easing of racial tensions and the correction of the depiction of black Americans (pp. 124–32). They point to the introduction of the 'dime novel' in the late nineteenth century as giving an economic opportunity for the rise and spread of popular culture, including the Western and the detective story (pp. 135–6). And with Pauline Hopkins's 'Talma Gordon', which appeared in *The Colored American Magazine* rather than in a dime novel, they show the rise of genre transcending both race and medium (p. 129). In fiction after the First World War, Bertens and D'haen connect writing and political consequences, offering a comprehensive big-picture view of the period that is impressive, though not without political opinion (pp. 141–3). From regionalist fiction, they turn to modernist fiction, assessing many authors by their attitude towards experimentalism: Sherwood Anderson and Gertrude Stein are influential for their experimentalism; Fitzgerald is less successful because he is experimental; Ernest Hemingway is most successful in his works that pushed expectations; John Dos Passos falls from favour when the public loses its taste for experimentalism; William Faulkner chose among new modernist techniques in service of his project to become 'the most important American novelist' of the period; and in African American modernist fiction, Jean Toomer's *Cane* is most notable for its experimentalism (pp. 161–75). In time, these collections of names and influences lose a sense of relation to one another, and the authors' exhaustive treatment highlights one of the limitations of their work: the wide scope discourages depth, and some inclusions feel as if they are satisfying a quota for racial completeness or political exhaustion. For example, a section on social realism between the world wars includes exactly one paragraph on African American writers Richard Wright and William Attaway, exactly one paragraph on Native American writers Joseph Mathews, D'Arcy McNickle, Thomas Whitecloud, and Mourning Dove, and exactly one paragraph on Asian American writers Etsu Sugimoto and Younghill Kang. None would disagree with the inclusion of authors of diverse races and traditions, but grouping authors by their ethnicities in this manner emphasizes the study's shallow approach in order that it may satisfy scope—especially when each of these paragraphs is slimmer than one paragraph devoted entirely to the writing of John Steinbeck on the previous page (pp. 177–8).

Nearly 200 pages longer than the volume by Bertens and D'haen, Lawrence Buell's *The Dream of the Great American Novel* nevertheless takes a tighter focus. In it, although Buell traces the long history of popular interest in the Great American Novel from the mid-nineteenth century into the twenty-first, the lion's share of that pursuit and fascination belongs to the period of American modernism. In fact, while the major works of modernism seem to have contributed both to a decline in enthusiasm for a singularly defining work of fiction and to a rise in certainty that 'U.S. literature no longer had anything to apologize for' (p. 2), these same works are ones later readers hailed as contenders for the title. In following and commenting upon the tradition and works that aspire to it, Buell imagines a plural approach, finding exemplars in Nathaniel Hawthorne's *The Scarlet Letter*; in works about a single individual, such as Fitzgerald's *The Great Gatsby* and Ralph Ellison's *Invisible Man*; in works plotting 'sectional and/or ethnoracial division', including Harriet

Beecher Stowe's *Uncle Tom's Cabin* and Toni Morrison's *Beloved*; and in what he calls 'meganovels', such as Herman Melville's *Moby-Dick*, Dos Passos's *U.S.A.* trilogy, and Thomas Pynchon's *Gravity's Rainbow* (pp. 6–8). In this plural approach, Buell shows the ways certain themes stand out as emblematic of an understood American experience. For instance, in exploring the genre's roots in masculine *Bildungsromane* exploring social mobility, as in Theodore Dreiser's *An American Tragedy* and Fitzgerald's *The Great Gatsby* (pp. 141–50), Buell also acknowledges other 'American'-isms, like 'the dream that was yet to be given the name we now know it by' (p. 139). Likewise, Buell establishes a series of American tensions—'Old World/New World, East/West, North/South; white/red, white/black, white/nonwhite' (p. 218)—to recognize 'cross-currents of allegiance to and entrapment within' respective sides (p. 287), as in William Faulkner's *Absalom, Absalom!* And, in arguing that Dos Passos's less popular *U.S.A.* trilogy is a better representation of the American novel than John Steinbeck's contemporaneous, best-selling *The Grapes of Wrath*, Buell acknowledges the former's importance in what would become a genre of 'monumental American novelistic evocations of social collectives' (p. 421). As much a study of American novels as of readers' and critics' historic approach to an entire field of American novels, Buell's work is itself monumental.

Finally, Priscilla Wald and Michael A. Elliott's study *The American Novel 1870–1940* offers an even tighter scope of time period than that of Buell while besting it by more than a hundred additional pages. In this sixth volume of *The Oxford History of the Novel in English*, Wald and Elliott compile a seemingly exhaustive review of the topic broken into thirty-five chapters across five parts. As they explain in their introduction to the volume, their boundaries acknowledge a desire in post-Civil War America to reimagine the nation through literature (p. xv), then tracing that reimagining across the nation's rise in world power (p. xix). Contributors to the volume trace it in many ways. Many chapters focus on the publication side of literature, tracing these imaginings through its material and physical cultures. For example, changes in copyright law and the publishing industry introduced American audiences to literary celebrities, as Sarah Robbins shows (p. 3), but these changes also introduced authors to the demands and opportunities of celebrity (p. 19), while giving unprecedented influence to editors and reviewers (pp. 12, 14). As Catherine Turner explains, these changes did not always work well for the publishing companies, whose increasing budgets for advertising and author royalties raised the average break-even point of sales to two and a half times their previous amounts from the 1880s into the 1940s (pp. 21–2). And Amy L. Blair documents the rise in readership of the American novel—in new immigrants, newly freed slaves, and new women readers, among others (p. 37)—all of whom contributed to shifting the readership at the end of the nineteenth century in a manner that ultimately broadened access to lower socioeconomic groups in a number of ways (pp. 41–9). Leonard Cassuto's chapter imagines these economic factors taken forth to their most optimistic conclusions, showing that publishers' and authors' search for success was as much a cultural as a financial quest: '"bestseller" is both an American concept and an American word' (p. 323). Other chapters consider the ways that shifts in media consumption gave rise to new authorities. Betsy Klimasmith emphasizes the importance of the newspaper as an artefact, both in the characters' stories and in the novel's composition, while also casting as journalistic the events in works like Dreiser's *Sister Carrie* (pp. 125–7). Patrick Jagoda likewise shows both the influence of Hollywood on literature—as in, for instance, Fitzgerald's incomplete novel about the film industry, *The Love of the Last Tycoon* (p. 501), or the cinematic techniques in Dos Passos's *U.S.A.* trilogy (p. 514)—and the influence of authors on Hollywood, including Faulkner, Nathanael West, and Anzia Yezierska (pp. 508–9). Still other chapters demonstrate the ways to expand traditional understandings of what it was to be American. Orm Øverland, for instance, perforates any assumptions of American literature as monolingual by reading the vibrancy of immigrant languages in American literature, including German, Chinese, Japanese, Norwegian, and Yiddish (pp. 219–23), and Mark Scroggins shows the ways American literature performed on an international stage and absorbed influences from beyond its borders (pp. 392–402). But the volume's intercultural analyses are many. While Ramón Saldívar casts Faulkner's fiction in the context of Latin American issues of coloniality and postcoloniality (p. 469), and Mikko Tuhkanen underscores the ways Richard Wright's *Native Son* expands that novel's typically Western instabilities to include 'the slave trade and the intellectual justifications that its obvious injustice necessitated' (p. 528), Sean Kicummah Teuton returns to North America to show some of these same questions—of marking colonial difference, engaging with the other—at work in novels written by Indigenous authors of the time (pp. 429–35), which recalls his *Red Land, Red Power* (DukeUP [2008]). At the same time, Sonnet Retman and Paul Giles read the novel in the context of the Depression and the period after the First World War, respectively—highlighting, for example, the ways in which uniquely American experiences of these events differentiated American fiction from it British counterpart (p. 436). Still other chapters underscore shifts in style and the emergence of new genres, as Augusta Rohrbach delineating the role of realism in literature after the Civil War, Stephanie Foote charting the Midwestern village novels and the growing influence of the Western, Lee Horsley following the hard-boiled detective novel between world wars, and Gerry Canavan tracking the scene of American science fiction in its serial and other forms.

Such a large volume is necessarily ambitious in its scope, and it may intimidate readers, encouraging them to dip in timidly, approaching only one chapter at a time and never embodying the whole. Wald and Elliott's volume can certainly satisfy those readers having limited interest, but it also offers much more. In crucial ways, the volume's plenitude shows the evolution of a nation reflected in its literature across these critical decades, whether, as in Edlie Wong's contribution showing the influence of the pro-segregationist court case *Plessy v. Ferguson* on works like George Schuyler's satirical *Black No More*, Sutton E. Griggs's *Pointing the Way*, Faulkner's *Light in August*, Charles Chesnutt's *Paul Marchand* and *Marrow of Tradition*, and Pauline Hopkins's *Of One Blood* (pp. 93–7), or, more hopefully, as in Zita Nunes's chapter showing the rise of the Harlem Renaissance contemporaneous to Alain LeRoy Locke's anthology *The New Negro* (p. 453).

Though such a conclusion is beyond the scope or aim of *The American Novel 1870–1940*, Wald and Elliott's collection comes close to suggesting ways of understanding new networks of influence and kinship in American fiction of the time—whether these connections be aesthetic, as shown by Beal, or political, as shown by Chapman and Gifford. Likewise, although single-author studies such as those by Irwin and Foley choose a narrow field of study, these authors' connections inevitably shine through. And inevitably, studies with wide consideration, such as those by Bertens and D'haen, by Buell, and by editors Wald and Elliott, offer opportunities for recognizing the impulses and constraints shared by many authors of the period.

3. Fiction since 1945

During 2014, literary criticism of post-1945 American fiction centred upon three major areas of enquiry: twenty-first-century aesthetic production and the post-9/11 novel, literary cartography of urban and non-urban spaces as well as aesthetic renderings of environmental damage, and fictional engagement with late capitalism. The opening portion of this section of the review will group monographs and collections into these broad areas of focus, even as it also explores connections across such categorizations. The second section turns to discussions of monographs that address representations of sexuality and race with particular attention to literary production from the late 1940s through the 1960s. A third section addresses monographs primarily focused on literary form, including discussion of minimalism, maximalist fiction, and postmodernism, and concludes with a discussion of works that address a few US authors in the context of larger conversations about literary trends beyond a focus on national literary production. The final segment reviews over fifteen monographs and collections focused on single authors.

The most important work on twenty-first-century fiction produced the year under review is Caren Irr's comprehensive and provocative monograph titled *Toward the Geopolitical Novel: U.S. Fiction in the Twenty-First Century*. Covering over 125 novels, Irr succeeds in providing a full account of the re-emergence of the political novel at the turn of the century, which is defined by Irving Howe in *Politics and the Novel* as a genre that explores 'an individual's psychologically rich struggle to articulate political ideas adequate to meet the social concerns of his or her day' (p. 4). According to Irr, a rejection of the political novel occurred later in the twentieth century as writers 'who associated politics with private life often advocated for psychological realism, while pro-postmodernists considered the most challenging experimental works to be the most political' (p. 5). In this way, the political novel celebrated by Howe came to be seen as limited by an 'ideological attitude' or 'authoritarian overkill' (p. 6). Noting the rise of critical calls for aesthetic works that map the 'multinational system' or 'confrontational and socially engaged writing that is attentive to the environment of the present' at the end of the century by thinkers like Fredric Jameson and Walter Benn Michaels, Irr reveals that numerous living authors have responded by returning to the political novel, albeit in ways that expand Howe's previous definition of it. For Irr, the new (geo)political novel 'revisit(s) Howe's focus on the drama of political engagement, even as [it] expand[s] their range beyond local or national questions' (p. 6). As a challenge to 'suburban realism' and 'program fiction', Irr reveals that a wide range of twenty-first-century political fiction 'shatters isolationist myths, updates national narratives, provides points of access for global identifications, and, perhaps most important, allows for reflection on the emerging subjects of consensus (for better or worse) in the United States' (pp. 9, 4). With the aim of providing an overview of the geopolitical novel, Irr divides her study into five genres beneath this larger categorization: 'the migrant novel, the Peace Corps thriller, the national allegory, the revolutionary novel, and the expatriate satire' (p. 10). Each chapter of *Toward the Geopolitical Novel* takes up one of these genres, provides a concise articulation of their larger stakes, and examines a number of fictional case studies.

For example, the first full chapter addresses what Irr calls the 'digital migrant novel', works that move away from the trauma narratives of immigration prevalent in the 1980s and 1990s and towards engagement with 'media systems as figures for transnational cultural exchange' (p. 26). Literary engagement with media systems in recent migrant fictions, in Irr's account, allows for reflection on mass media as a homogenizing force or as a figure for 'political and cultural dogmatism', deep investigation of the 'empowerment approach to ethnic media', and/or exploration of the value of 'dispersed, peer-to-peer media systems' that oppose 'broadcasting or narrowcasting logics' (pp. 26–8). Despite divergent visions of media in a wide variety of digital migrant novels, Irr ultimately argues that most of these works 'borrow the logic of digital-media systems' and '[position] the narrator as a router, filtering and processing an overwhelming multisensory global system' (p. 28). Because of the influence of digital systems, these novels address the challenges and promises of transnational networks with stories of 'mobile subjects who receive and interpret cultural codes while actively transmitting and translating their own information' (p. 29). In this way, the digital migrant novel challenges hegemonic national narratives through exploration of the political import of communal networks to circulate stories that provide counternarratives to limiting understandings of national identity. Situating Edwidge Danticat's *The Dew Breaker*, Junot Díaz's *The Brief Wondrous Life of Oscar Wao*, Jeffrey Eugenides's *Middlesex*, Salvatore Scibona's *The End*, Michael Chabon's *The Amazing Adventures of Kavalier & Clay*, Dinaw Mengestu's *The Beautiful Things That Heaven Bears*, Mohsin Hamid's *The Reluctant Fundamentalist*, and many others within this genre, Irr's formidable analysis and dizzying range in this chapter alone will provide ample spark for future discussion of the geopolitical novel.

The subsequent chapter turns to discussion of twenty-first-century thrillers and Peace Corps novels with particular attention to how this genre 'explores the naïve protagonist's psychological state in order to express its sense that the political unconscious of American development policy is riddled with disturbing repressed elements' and critiques 'liberal humanism' bent on a certain form of progress as well as 'changing the culture of the other' (pp. 68,

67). Referencing a variety of texts including Mark Jacobs's *Stone Cowboy*, Robert Rosenberg's *This is Not Civilization*, Tony D'Souza's *Whiteman*, and Norman Rush's *Mortals*, this chapter provides an exhilarating rendering of current representations of American liberalism and its impact abroad. Chapter 3 examines how 'national allegory has been recast as neoliberal allegory' in a variety of works, and chapter 4 turns to the 'new novel of revolution' with an exploration of how a 'host of authors... revise existing accounts of the revolutionary consciousness, the process by which revolutionary ideas are implemented, and the historical narrative itself' (pp. 103, 143). A final full chapter examines the shifting aims of the expatriate novel infused with a geopolitical consciousness. Each chapter of this impressive work could have been extended to become a single monograph; still, it is fortunate for us that Irr chose instead to construct an overview of how these different genres intersect because of a shared return to and revision of the political novel while simultaneously providing ample nuanced renderings of the aims of specific genres and individual works. As a whole, the monograph is an exhilarating account of twenty-first-century fiction that will inevitably become a foundational text for future studies.

Even as Irr positions the geopolitical novel in opposition to suburban realism, Kathy Knapp's monograph *American Unexceptionalism: The Everyman and the Suburban Novel after 9/11* serves as a challenge to a quick dismissal of the genre as a twenty-first-century shift in tone and content marks new political ambition for such works. Exploring representations of white middle-class men in the suburban novel following 9/11 with analysis of Richard Ford's *The Lay of the Land*, Chang-rae Lee's *Aloft*, Jonathan Franzen's *Freedom*, Philip Roth's *Everyman*, Anne Tyler's *Digging to America*, Gish Jen's *World and Town*, and A.M. Homes's *May We Be Forgiven*, Knapp proposes that authors respond to this tragedy by undermining fantasies of American exceptionalism and presenting a call for increased attention to global economic and political problems. In order to historicize twenty-first-century suburban fiction, Knapp introduces her monograph with a concise discussion of the postwar suburban novel with specific emphasis on the shift in suburban fiction from the 1990s to the present. Drawing on critical works like Catherine Jurca's *White Diaspora: The Suburb and the Twentieth-Century American Novel* (PrincetonUP [2001]) and Andrew Hoberek's *The Twilight of the Middle Class: Post-World War II American Fiction and White-Collar Work* (PrincetonUP [2005]), Knapp provides a brief overview of criticism that identifies what Jurca calls the 'empowering rhetorics of victimization' within mid- to late twentieth-century representations of white suburban men (p. xv). By the 1990s, Knapp argues, the trope of the affluent white male victim plagued by alienation becomes the target of novelists seeking to undermine fantasies of victimization and to show how previous iterations of affluent men's 'resigned disengagement' are 'pathetic smokescreens meant to hide in plain sight his single-minded, childish self-interest and refusal to take responsibility for himself, his family, or the larger world' (p. xviii). Writers publishing suburban novels in the 1990s, like T.C. Boyle, Jeffrey Eugenides, David Gates, and Rick Moody, in other words take the genre of the suburban novel to task in order to discredit 'white male victimization' (p. xx). Still, in

Knapp's argument, even as these novelists create works in which white men are to blame for the 'demise of the family, imperiled youth, ecological ruin, [and] world financial meltdown', they simultaneously 'resurrect this figure by way of an inchoate version of him that deserves the reader's sympathy' (pp. xxii–xxiii). Thus, for Knapp, the suburban novel of the 1990s critiques the solipsism and damaging disengagement from pressing worldly affairs in contemplation of the woes of middle-class life while also positing a needed return of a strong father-figure who might re-establish patriarchal order and conservative family values. In the wake of 9/11, Knapp asserts, critics might expect an intensification of such a trend in literary production, reflecting perhaps political discourse after the fall of the Twin Towers that did affirm the need for a militaristic and paternalistic government to take action to protect citizens from harm. Instead, for her, the post-9/11 suburban novel 'takes its white male protagonist to task for upholding the neoliberal values of individualism, private property ownership, and upward mobility that...have both supported and masked white privilege' (p. xv). In this way, twenty-first-century suburban novels critique both the white, middle-class everyman and his society for their 'predilection for valorizing individual desire, the sole purpose of which is to keep in motion the wheels of production and reproduction upon which our market-driven liberal democracy turns' (p. xxviii). Rather than bemoaning the difficulty of upward mobility or positing a return of a benevolent father-figure that might make the capitalist economy more hospitable for white families trying to make it through recession, the novelists that Knapp examines stage crises within the suburban family in ways that challenge the ideals of neoliberalism and suggest 'new alliances and new modes of being that might overturn this dehumanizing ethos' of late capitalism (p. xxxi).

The first full chapter of the book focuses on Ford's Frank Bascombe novels in order to trace the development of the suburban novel in one canonical author's works. With an opening analysis of *The Sportswriter*, Knapp shows how Bascombe is representative of the self-centred individualism that supplants a commitment to the common good, and of a neoliberal suburban focus on 'the primacy of property ownership' that binds inhabitants together, rather than shared life within community-focused neighbourhoods (p. 6). Frank's unhappiness in the first novel of the trilogy ultimately does not provide a critique of the suburbs that he finds 'stultifying', as his move to Florida at the conclusion of the novel merely reasserts the neoliberal values of individualism, mobility, and property ownership, albeit in a different locale (p. 10). Therefore, his departure for Floridian beaches, meant to signify release in this pre-9/11 suburban novel, reveals the text's indebtedness to neoliberal fantasies that existential woes can be solved by moving to a different, more desirable, location. Turning to *Independence Day*, Knapp charts a development within Ford's forays into suburban life as Frank returns from Florida to his former suburb to become a real-estate broker devoted to developing his community and celebrating 'kumbaya capitalism' (p. 11). In this second work, Frank does undergo a change in his relationship to the suburb in which he celebrates 'a return to old-fashioned community by trumpeting the "Third Way" argument of the Clinton administration that profit and the common good do not have to be mutually exclusive' (p. 13). However, in Knapp's account, this narrative of a committed father-figure returning to make profits while also returning to shape his suburban communities in rituals, like the Fourth of July parade, ultimately reasserts the individualism and market-focused ideology that the novel may have sought to undermine. Despite the protagonist's nostalgic ecstasy in the novel's concluding parade, Frank's role as benevolent real-estate broker and the general celebration of his new-found devotion to community in this second novel merely provide a 'triumphalist narrative' of American exceptionalism, individualism, and Tocquevillian 'self-interest rightly understood' (pp. 14, 12). Addressing *The Lay of the Land*, Knapp argues that this text is influenced by the post-9/11 landscape that gives Ford the opportunity to 'reassess the assumptions that provided the foundation for the previous two novels and [to] consider how these premises might have played a role in leading civilization-as-we-know-it to the brink of the unknown' (p. 15). By critiquing the ideologies that fuelled Frank's previous engagement with suburban life, Knapp powerfully argues that Ford undermines an 'ethos that has reduced freedom to free enterprise and private property' as well as 'neoliberal policies that create poverty' (p. 16). It is through Frank's own experiences of cancer, the loss of his wife, and his witnessing of the damaging impact of profit-driven development on Haddam that he loses his belief in the 'neoliberal argument for personal advancement over the common good' (p. 20). Further, for Knapp, Frank's commitment in the novel to being a mensch by helping others and taking responsibility for his actions points towards an alternative path in which the goal of upward mobility is replaced by a greater desire to connect with unexceptional others also suffering through financial meltdown and the failure of the 'Third Way'.

This astute first chapter creates a strong introduction to future chapters by showcasing how one canonical author's ideas about suburban life have transformed through three major works. With this context, the subsequent chapters focus on how other works of the early twenty-first century also provide a critique of neoliberal ideology and chart an aesthetics of contingency that utilizes the white middle-class everyman's individual suffering as a gateway through which to connect with the suffering of others and to challenge a belief in upward mobility and individualism as the means through which to address such suffering. For example, Knapp provides analysis of Lee's *Aloft* that reveals the novel's critique of triumphalist narratives of American exceptionalism following 9/11 by connecting such narratives to the post-Second World War moment in which returning veterans were seduced into supporting the 'economic interests of the established order' with promises of suburban home ownership, financial security, and upward mobility (p. 29). Still, such commitment to private property and suburban cloistering from worldly affairs with a focus on individual achievement requires characters in the novel to abandon reflection upon the deep history of familial experiences in the Great Depression, as well as the shame and trauma of war. In particular, the novel hints at a suburban forgetting of the United States' use of nuclear weapons in Hiroshima and Nagasaki, the military cover-up of the Tae-Jon massacre during the Korean War, and the loss of American soldiers' lives in the multiple wars of the late twentieth century. Linking suburban 'abundance' to 'military action abroad', the novel suggests that 'in the wake of 9/11, when deadly political violence encroached our boundaries for the first time since Pearl Harbor...the material and psychic consequences of US military and economic policies abroad can no longer be denied' (p. 44). Rather than portray suburbanites who continue to hide away from worldly violence in imagined secure communities, *Aloft* in Knapp's reading 'modestly' illustrates how 'excava[tion] of historical traumas of World War II, the Korean War, the Vietnam War, and the September 11 attacks' by a suburban white everyman marks an opening through which Lee imagines creating a counternarrative to neoliberal ideology in which characters rethink their connections to others both within and beyond the borders of the nation (p. 49).

Subsequent chapters illustrate the critique of suburban values of 'consumerism', 'possessive individualism', and 'fetishization of private property' in Franzen's exploration of gentrification of urban areas based on these values in his novel *Freedom*, and explore the revision of white middle-class masculinity in Roth's *Everyman*, in which identity is not based on 'mastery or individual worth' but instead on 'loss, failure and death' (pp. 52, 109). With full chapters focused on these two authors, Knapp shows how these suburban novels of the twenty-first century focus on masculine figures that abandon desire for individual success and distance from others and worldly events. Instead, facing their own suffering and identifying with the suffering of others, the new suburban everyman opens the door to his own unexceptional status as a bodily being, intimately connected to others. For Knapp, this failed everyman 'modestly' provides a way for novelists to take responsibility for the historic and present-day impact of neoliberal ideologies and policies as well as to imagine alternative ways of forming familial and community networks that might challenge such ideologies. Concluding the monograph with a turn to female-authored middle-class fiction following 9/11, Knapp argues that Tyler, Jen, and Homes depict failed affluent male characters in ways that also critique the neoliberal agenda, which 'works to consolidate white male authority' (p. 112). Further, these novelists explore 'upper-middle-class women and men [who]...put their own problems in perspective as they learn to engage in group projects that seek to build new alliances with those who have been forgotten, ignored, or exploited by the existing social order' (p. 113). As a whole, *American Unexceptionalism* is a provocative and clear examination of recent shifts in the suburban novel following 9/11 that offers astute and cogent close readings of key novels while simultaneously contextualizing such texts within the twentieth-century history of suburban fiction as well as recent events that have fuelled writers' critiques of neoliberalism. Because of both Knapp's insightful close readings of key novels and her smart positioning of such works within the recent financial meltdown and responses to 9/11, this monograph is essential reading for critics examining novelistic attempts to grapple with ways to imagine new alliances beyond those constructed in previous suburban fictions.

Like Knapp's work, editor Kristine A. Miller's collection, titled *Transatlantic Literature and Culture after 9/11: The Wrong Side of Paradise*, includes essays that maintain a focus on aesthetic production that undermines American exceptionalism; however, this collection emphasizes transatlantic literary responses to 9/11 that contextualize and historicize the tragedy and 'represent 9/11 as both a domestic and international difficulty' (p. 12). Countering a trend in studies of post-9/11 fiction either to examine texts through the lens of trauma theory or through poststructuralist accounts of spectacle, both of which focus on the repetition of 'one timeless event', Miller and other writers included in the collection 'look . . . *beyond* our compulsion to repeat this moment of terror, conceiving of 9/11 as both a unique American trauma and a shared piece of local, national and global histories' (p. 3). In order to accomplish this, essays in the collection move past a sole focus on artists' and writers' reflections on United States policy and the impact of 9/11 on the nation and towards artistic representations of the transatlantic impact of this event, thereby eschewing a limited account of domestic trauma. Further, the collection suggests that many artists and writers who reflect on 9/11 call for increased transatlantic conversations about national and international responses to tragedy, especially through examination of empire and the special relationship between the United States and the United Kingdom, as well as the desperate need to examine national responses to the attacks, which have 'amplified their horror' (p. 12) in the 'war on terror'. Essays in the collection explore transatlantic deployment of cultural icons such as James Bond and Sherlock Holmes in the wake of 9/11, John le Carré's post-9/11 novels, Mohsin Hamid's *The Reluctant Fundamentalist*, Gautam Malkani's *Londonstani*, Mahvish Rukhsana Khan's *My Guantánamo Diary*, Joseph O'Neill's *Netherland*, post-9/11 drama, Don DeLillo's *Falling Man*, Colum McCann's *Let the Great World Spin*, Ron English and Fly's engagement with 9/11 in issue 32 of the underground comic *World War 3*, Jess Walter's *The Zero*, Amy Waldman's *The Submission*, and Jennifer Egan's *A Visit from the Goon Squad*. One standout essay in the collection is Matthew Brown's analysis of *Netherland*, which argues that O'Neill utilizes and overlaps the genres of 'trauma narrative, family melodrama, and immigrant fiction . . . to upset rigid ideas of national boundaries by deterritorializing the post-9/11 novel' (p. 116). With a particular focus on the novel's depiction of cricket and the protagonist's reflections on New York City and immigrant status after the attacks, Brown shows how the novel both undermines the 'territorial sentiments of domestic fiction' and explores the possibility for 'extraterritorial identity' that exceeds the boundaries of the nation (p. 125). Still, for Brown, O'Neill's vision of cosmopolitanism is tempered by exploration of how transnational connections and affections like those afforded by networks of New York City's immigrant cricket players can be co-opted to '[reify] national conduct and competitive stereotyping' or put to the service of an 'uneven globalized economy' as evidenced by the cosmopolitanism of the protagonist, who works for a merchant bank with expertise in oil and gas futures (pp. 125–6). Another excellent piece by Graley Herren titled 'Flying Man and Falling Man: Remembering and Forgetting 9/11' juxtaposes two separate iconic images that have been referenced repeatedly in the decade following the attacks—Richard Drew's photograph of a man falling from the towers and Philippe Petit's high-wire performance art between the two towers from 1974—with particular attention to the aforementioned novels by DeLillo and McCann. Crystal Alberts's ' "I'm Only Just Starting to Look": Media, Art and

Literature After 9/11' examines DeLillo's 'Baader-Meinhof' and *Falling Man* by focusing readers' attention on the author's fusion of literary and visual art with reference to Gerhard Richter's *October 18, 1977* and Giorgio Morandi's still-life paintings. Connecting DeLillo's usage of visual art in these two works with English and Fly's graphic narrative of 9/11 and its aftermath that repeatedly alludes to Edvard Munch's *The Scream*, Alberts ultimately argues that these artists use visual art to call readers to 'slowly and conscientiously study [images of 9/11] within a broader historical and cultural context, much as we would a difficult piece of art' (p. 178). Further, references to Richter and Munch challenge American exceptionalism and 'nationalistic myopia' by tying representations of 9/11 to other iconic international visions of violence and responses to it, thereby calling readers to 'move forward into a larger, more global conversation' about 9/11 (p. 179). A final essay that deserves mention here is Laura Frost's 'Archifictions: Constructing September 11', which examines how literary works 'adopt architectural imagery and discourses of building . . . to amplify concerns that were bypassed or minimized in the push toward spatial and economic recovery' in discussions that specifically addressed the rebuilding of lower Manhattan as well as narratives of 'recuperative heroism' and memorialization (p. 201). The collection also includes interviews with O'Neill and Jess Walter that clearly will be of interest to scholars of post-9/11 fiction.

Although not primarily focused on United States fiction produced after 9/11, Amir Eshel's *Futurity: Contemporary Literature and the Quest for the Past* does include analysis of literary works produced after the attacks, including Cormac McCarthy's *The Road* and Paul's Auster's *Oracle Night*. With the larger aim of analysing literary works that '[invoke] our post-1945 age from the perspective of 'modernist events' such as the Sino-Japanese War, the Second World War, the Holocaust, the wars of the Middle East, and the political realities that emerged after the end of the Cold War and after 9/11', Eshel seeks to explore how contemporary German, Jewish Israeli, British, and American writers re-describe historical catastrophes in order both to engage with the factors that produced atrocities and to utilize such engagement to contemplate human action that ultimately may impact the future (p. 4). Countering philosophers like Alain Badiou who argue that contemporary Western cultures exalt in 'instantaneity' and 'a-temporality', Eshel shows how a group of writers are interrogating the past in complex and urgent ways (p. 11). Also challenging work by Russell Jacoby and Fredric Jameson in their arguments about the 'flagging of radical utopian thought' and the 'impoverishment of . . . the Western imagination' in regard to futurity, Eshel claims that many contemporary literary authors are deeply invested in 'ask[ing] if and how we may be able to affect our sociopolitical or ecological conditions by taking political and ethical action' (p. 14). Drawing on Richard Rorty's and Hannah Arendt's theories of how 'poetic language and narrative fiction are capable of reconfiguring our lifeworld' by 'enabl[ing] us to reshape habits, feelings, and even social relations' (p. 7), Eshel's monograph examines the formal strategies that authors use to call readers to contemplate agency and to birth a sense of futurity, despite a pervading sense of doom caused by the continuation of modernity's atrocities into the late twentieth and early twenty-first centuries.

Analysing works like Günter Grass's *The Tin Drum*, Alexander Kluge's *Chronik der Gefühle*, W.G. Sebald's *Austerlitz*, S. Yizhar's *Sipur Khirbet Khizeh*, A.B. Yehoshua's *Facing the Forests*, David Grossman's *See Under: Love*, among many others, Eshel argues that these texts 'signal futurity by focusing on our ability to address our given conditions in actions small and large. The past serves in these works to explore the human ability to address real social, economic, and political conditions—to hold on to the future by asserting human agency' (p. 15).

In terms of Eshel's engagement with post-9/11 novels produced by US authors, he shows how Auster's *Oracle Night* and McCarthy's *The Road* both depict vulnerable or dead children, which 'represent pervasive concerns about contemporary political realities and . . . deep uncertainty about the prospects of humankind's survival' (p. 232). In *Oracle Night*, Eshel argues that a turn to historical catastrophe with reference to Dachau is connected to the deaths of the novel's fictional children and indirectly to 9/11 as a way to trace multiple events in which humans are reduced to what Agamben calls 'bare life', or are seen as disposable base matter. Even as the novel maintains the specificity of historical and more contemporary tragedies, it does seek to undermine the 'conversion of humans into matter' that occurs in each of the texts' referenced events (p. 242). The novel does this both by redescribing the past to showcase this violent conversion in multiple scenarios and by exploring forms of agency in the present that '[allow] us to reflect on what may bring about a new trajectory', a new future (p. 243). Analysis of *The Road* similarly focuses on the endangered son as a sign of a contemporary fear of the end of humankind; still, Eshel reveals that representations of the child's small acts of kindness '[affirm] whatever limited futurity this bleakest of worlds might offer' (p. 239). Further, this apocalyptic tale shows how 'end-time scenarios retain a futural dimension, shocking us into a consideration of how such horrors may not become reality after all' (pp. 238–9). In addition to this analysis, Eshel also examines Philip Roth's *The Plot Against America* and Auster's *Man in the Dark* as exemplary models of 'alternate histories' that 'underscore what traditional historiographic narratives and historical novels often undermine: the role of choice, action, and human agency' (p. 218). Even as the texts clearly do not celebrate unfettered human freedom, their depiction of alternative histories does show how the past could have been otherwise and they thus 'discover that any circumstance is open to human agency', 'any contemporary condition remains open to change' (p. 228). In this way, Eshel argues that both novels open the door to imagining a future that is not already doomed, but instead may be shaped by actions in the present. Because of Eshel's engagement with key debates about post-1945 literary reflection on major catastrophic events of 'modernity' and his thoughtful incorporation and critique of discussions of utopia, futurity, and/or contemporary narrative and aesthetic forms in philosophical and critical works by Badiou, Žižek, and Jameson, among others, *Futurity* will be central to future literary criticism on these topics. In addition, *Futurity* will be important for scholarly investigation of post-9/11 literary production, especially because of its focus on the ways that contemporary authors are contextualizing it within a deeper transnational history of the tragedies of the twentieth century, a focus shared by the editor and essayists of *Transatlantic Literature and Culture after 9/11*.

Beyond substantial treatment of twenty-first-century fiction, a second major critical direction during 2014 was analysis of representations of space, including reflections on aesthetic representations of urban and non-urban environments as well as literary reflections upon environmental crises. One representative monograph of this trend is *Urban Space and Late Twentieth-Century New York Literature: Reformed Geographies* by Catalina Neculai, which provides a theoretically informed, polemical call for interdisciplinary conversations about urban space between literary critics and geographers, with a particular focus on the value of three separate New York novels that depict the city between the 'fiscal crisis of the mid-1970s and the market crash of October 1987' (p. 1). Opening with a discussion of urban geographers' reticence to engage with literary texts as a form of fieldwork into understandings of space because of the ways that representation of urban environments can serve to fetishize space without 'rooting [spatiality] in material social practices and relations' (p. 36), Neculai seeks to show how specific literary texts and literary criticism more broadly can offer fruitful ground for the heterogeneous field of geography. She writes, 'urban narratives—like the ones selected for this project—highlight an aesthetic conjunction between socio-spatial, economic, political, and cultural practices and the formation of a peculiar and singular urban consciousness, which is actualized in, and through, the literary text, and derived from the process of experiencing and interpreting the city as living, historically (re)producing, and transforming matter' (p. 48). While geographers will benefit from thinking through the import of literary studies for research into narratives of urbanity, so, too, literary critics will profit from deeper engagement with debates in urban geography that tie 'spatial metaphors' to their 'material grounding' (p. 49). In sum, Neculai's interdisciplinary monograph explores 'the conceptual correlations between the materiality of space and its metaphoricity in order to give the due cultural dimension to urbanized or spatialized politics and, at the same time, build the essential material grounding for spatial figuration' (pp. 36–7). With exhilarating literary analysis of Don DeLillo's *Great Jones Street*, Joel Rose's *Kill the Poor*, and Jay McInerney's *Brightness Falls* as well as aesthetic 'downtown' works published in *Between C and D* and *The Portable Lower East Side*, Neculai illustrates how 'strands' of urban writing engage critically with the FIRE (finance, insurance, and real estate) economy that was dominating New York City in the period. By combining close readings with detailed historical accounts of the changing city landscape fuelled by the FIRE economy, debates about housing, real estate, and homelessness, and neighbourhood and community organizing, Neculai's monograph shows how these three authors 'refute the mere allegorical transcription of space and seek to produce and socially reproduce urban space in fictional literature' (p. 79).

For example, in a powerful reading of Rose's *Kill the Poor*, she positions the novel within the context of the housing crisis in New York City in the 1980s and reveals how the novel undermines the 'mainstream ideology of redevelopment' and 'corporatist logic of gentrification' (p. 117). The novel succeeds in undermining such logic by mapping the 'macrostructural housing issues such as severe cuts in federal spending on public housing, the pitfalls of homesteading as the DIY solution to the housing crisis, [and] the perils of the "trickle down" ideology of luxury housing development' (p. 117). Still, for Neculai the novel's ability to address larger structural issues occurs through a staging of local and personal bonds and conflicts within a neighbourhood undergoing gentrification by middle-class property owners; thus, the text ultimately showcases the tensions that Reaganite New Federalism, the FIRE industry, and homesteading created on the ground between middle-class 'prospectors' and the underclass within communities designated for redevelopment. Finally, because of the novel's attention to activist critique of FIRE, socio-ethnic conflict, and exclusionary narratives of gentrification that fuel redevelopment, *Kill the Poor* 'emphasizes the role of cultural representation in comprehending the workings of real estate' with a particular desire to '[overwrite] the received script of homesteading' in order to address ' the urgent issues that official accounts of homesteading tendentiously [overlook], such as the antinomies between the commodifying logic of homeownership and the ethos of collective labor' (pp. 150, 132). In other chapters, Neculai continues to provide contextualized analysis that explores 'the incorporation of bohemia into the spatial logic of corporatism and gentrification' in DeLillo's under-studied *Great Jones Street* and 'the finance moment of capital [in the 1980s] and the way in which finance capital...came to condition the functioning of the city' in McInerney's *Brightness Falls* (pp. 98, 171). Because of its nuanced connection of literary analysis to historicized documentation of the FIRE economy's redevelopment of the city, *Urban Space and Late Twentieth-Century New York Literature* is a valuable contribution to interdisciplinary studies of political and aesthetic urban narratives that fuel and counter the 'spatialization of capital' and that have profound consequences, especially for marginalized and impoverished communities (p. 47). Further, Neculai's monograph serves as a model for future literary studies that combine historicized accounts of civic redevelopment, recent work in urban geography, and analysis of literary works in order to provide 'complex critiques of the spatial and socioeconomic transformations' within urban environments and 'profound contemplations of individual and collective roles' within the FIRE economy and beyond it (p. 194).

In addition to Neculai's monograph, *The Cambridge Companion to the City in Literature*, edited by Kevin R. McNamara, includes essays that examine how aesthetic production, which focuses on urban environments, shows that the city's 'creative destruction—the reshaping of the landscape in the pursuit of profits, surveillance, social control, or some other goal—is the ongoing result of social, political, and economic processes' (p. 5). Like Neculai, the editor and essayists read a variety of literary 'city-texts as selectively composing...the known order to stage the process of making sense of the city' as well as the 'interplay between urban environments and human behavior' (p. 5). Because the aim of the collection is to provide a comprehensive overview of the city in literature, it does not maintain a focus on a specific historical period but instead offers essays that address ancient, medieval, and early modern, colonial and postcolonial, modern and postmodern cities. Even as the volume opens with chronological essays that discuss city literature in antiquity, the medieval and early modern period, and eighteenth-century city literature, the later chapters generally eschew a limited focus on a specific historical period in favour of tracing thematic consistencies and developments across such periods. The editor explains the rationale behind this choice by arguing that 'while the scale, spatial extent, and material conditions of cities indeed changed profoundly with the Industrial Revolution's onset, neither the social and spatial changes wrought by industrialism nor the history of the word city erases the social, economic, and cultural continuities between ancient, early modern, and contemporary cities' (p. 3). This is the strength of the collection as chapters like Rob Latham and Jeff Hicks's 'Urban Dystopias' sketch out the 'emergence of urban dystopia' in the late nineteenth century, the dark blossoming of the tradition following the First World War, and shifts in the tradition after the Second World War (p. 163). In this way, Latham and Hicks ground commentary of post-1945 dystopian aesthetics within a deeper history of the tradition that effectively showcases the indebtedness of recent works to literary precursors while simultaneously documenting how more contemporary authors directly respond to changes following the Second World War. For example, they argue that 'from the 1950s to the 1970s' in response to 'the automated butchery of Auschwitz' and 'the atomic flattening of Hiroshima . . . widespread anxieties about looming dangers to civilized life were reflected in a spate of apocalyptic novels and stories depicting vaporized cities, polluted cities, and cities suffering from social breakdown and moral malaise' (p. 168). Addressing works by Kurt Vonnegut, Harry Harrison, John Brunner, J.G. Ballard, John Hersey, Robert Silverberg, and others, this essay skilfully maps the major concerns of dystopian fiction of the three decades following the Second World War before a concluding discussion of cyberpunk and steampunk of the 1980s and 1990s, which references works by William Gibson, Bruce Sterling, and China Miéville, to name just a few of the authors mentioned.

Other authors in the collection use this authorial strategy of tracing developments of city literature across historical periods as well. For example, James R. Giles's 'The Urban Nightspace' works through visions of night from the nineteenth century to the present in works by Émile Zola, Charles Dickens, Stephen Crane, T.S. Eliot, Claude McKay, Norman Mailer, Roberto Bolaño, and John Rechy. So, too, Christophe Den Tandt's 'Masses, Forces, and the Urban Sublime' and Bart Keunen and Luc De Droogh's 'The Socioeconomic Outsider: Labor and the Poor' extend their primary focus on nineteenth- and early twentieth-century literary representations of civic life into the late twentieth century. Still, the two articles that may be of most interest to scholars of post-1945 American literary production are Nick Bentley's 'Postmodern Cities' and Gregory Woods's 'Gay and Lesbian Urbanity'. Bentley provides a clear overview of the larger aims of representations of city life with discussion of the postmodern metropolis 'that metaphorically stands in for the dizzying plurality of contemporary urban living', the city as 'the physical manifestation of consumerist excess', or 'the city as a palimpsest of histories and narratives evoked in the psyche of the observer . . . who attempts to disentangle its multiplicity of texts' (pp. 175–6). Referencing and analysing works by Paul Auster, Orhan Pamuk, Jorge Luis Borges, Italo Calvino, Martin Amis, J.G. Ballard, Bret Easton Ellis, Chuck Palahniuk, Haruki Murakami, Peter Ackroyd, Will Self, Doris Lessing, Angela Carter, and Iain Sinclair, Bentley provides a stellar overview of different and related strands of postmodern visions of the metropolis. Woods's essay tackles the role of the city in fiction that depicts gay and lesbian subculture or homoerotic longing in works by figures such as Auden, Christopher Isherwood, John Rechy, Gore Vidal, Larry Kramer, Audre Lorde, and Rita Mae Brown, to name a few of the many well-known writers that he addresses; still, the unique contribution that this essay offers to studies of LGBT aesthetic works is its transnational turn to evaluate novels like Tahar Ben Jelloun's *Leaving Tangier*, Naguib Mahfouz's *Midaq Alley* and *Sugar Street*, Yukio Mishima's *Forbidden Colors*, Pai Hsien-yung's *Crystal Boys*, and R. Raj Rao's *The Boyfriend*. This transnational view of city literature does not only appear in Woods's essay, but in other chapters as well, such as Seth Graebner's 'Colonial Cities' and Caroline Herbert's 'Postcolonial Cities', which move beyond a familiar comparative approach of European and American literary works to analyse texts produced in and that reflect upon North, West, and South Africa and India. As a whole, the collection provides a stunning overview of the field of literary studies of cities across historical periods and across national borders.

Deep Map Country: Literary Cartography of the Great Plains by Susan Naramore Maher is another study of literary mapping that shares Neculai's focus on works that combine historical, political, economic, social, and geographical narratives to create deeper understandings of place. Still, her focus is on writers of the Great Plains that engage with and undermine triumphalist narratives of westward expansion as well as 'colonization and yeoman ascendancy' fuelled by myths of rugged individualism, and the Jeffersonian grid system that 'desacralizes the landscape and subjects it to material desire, use and exchange' (pp. 4–5). Responding to the environmental devastation of settlement and its impact on diverse species of the bioregion, a desire to document and to recall the historical violence of settlement for indigenous populations and its damaging wake in the present, and the need for new narratives to inform and to shape human interaction with the land, Maher argues that Great Plains writers like Julene Bair, Sharon Butala, Loren Eiseley, Don Gayton, Linda Hasselstrom, William Least Heat-Moon, John Janovy Jr., John McPhee, Kathleen Norris, and Wallace Stegner construct 'deep maps' of the region in their place-based narratives. Building from critical works like Rick Van Noy's *Surveying the Interior: Literary Cartographers and the Sense of Place* (UNevP [2003]), Yi-Fu Tuan's *Topophilia: A Study of Environmental Perception, Attitudes and Values* (ColUP [1990]), and Susan Stanford Friedman's *Mappings: Feminism and the Cultural Geographies of Encounter* (PrincetonUP [1998]), Maher illustrates how primarily non-fictional texts by these authors weave together a variety of narratives about place in order to counter linear accounts of the Great Plains that mimic the Jeffersonian grid. Utilizing Heat-Moon's concept of the 'deep map', Maher argues that deep map writing is distinguished from other place-based narratives because of its 'insistence on capturing a plethora of interconnected stories of a particular location...and framing the landscape within...indeterminate complexity' (pp. 10–11). The authors that she addresses provide cross-sectional narratives that 'articulate scientific perspectives, national as well as personal history and mythology... as well as layers of time both humanly and geologically deep. Steeped in the ironies of loss, [their] deep maps also serve to reestablish worlds that have been lost, to show us ways of honoring the diminished space, and to resist the larger culture's neglect of the rural center of America' (p. 11). Combining geological narratives and natural histories of deep planetary time with a focus on a particular region, cultural geographical accounts of migrations and settlement, biological descriptions of the evolution and adaptation of varieties of species and the larger biome with particular attention to the devastation of settlement, and spiritual or imaginative narration that points towards other ways of understanding and valuing human connection to land, the aforementioned Great Plains writers offer layered, complex, and multivalent works. Ultimately, for Maher, these authors use such deep mapping as a kind of 'protest' against 'our assumptions about land use [and] technology', thereby 'voic[ing]' a place-based environmental ethic' (pp. 21, 12).

One of the many strengths of this monograph is the way in which Maher shows how the narrative strategy of the deep map is shared by literary authors like Stegner, author of *Wolf Willow*, and N. Scott Momaday, author of *The Way to Rainy Mountain*, and science writers like Gayton (*Landscapes of the Interior: Re-Explorations of Nature and the Human Spirit* and *The Wheatgrass Mechanism: Science and the Imagination in the Western Canadian Landscape*) and Janovy (*Keith County Journal, Back in Keith County*, and *Dunwoody Pond: Reflections on the High Plains Wetlands and the Cultivation of Naturalists*). In this way, Maher models a kind of environmental literary criticism grounded in creating interdisciplinary conversation between the sciences and the humanities, following, of course, a group of writers committed to bringing biology, natural history, and cultural geography together. Still, her work shows the import of literary criticism and the study of narrative form for broader conversations about environmental ethics. Since each of the authors that she addresses utilizes deep mapping of place to inspire a rethinking of human impact on bioregions and a revaluing of other species and the unique biome of the Great Plains, they are engaged in exploration of narrative forms that might fuel less damaging kinds of human movement in the region. Although her analysis of Stegner's work clearly will be of interest to scholars of post-1945 literary production, Maher's work on women writers of the Great Plains, including Julene Bair's *One Degree West: Reflections of a Plainsdaughter*, Sharon Butala's *Wild Stone Heart: An Apprentice in the Fields*, and Linda Hasselstrom's *Feels Like Far: A Rancher's Life on the Great Plains*, will also be valuable, especially for feminist critics interested in women writers' memoirs, engagement with patriarchal understandings of working the land and family life, complex personal engagement with their indebtedness to settlement ideologies, and critiques of ways that such ideologies negatively altered the biome and impacted indigenous populations. Analyses of texts by these women writers, as well as Kathleen Norris in *Dakota: A Spiritual Geography*, will be useful for ecofeminists. Still, like most environmental literary criticism, Maher's monograph reflects an interdisciplinary focus, which also will make it useful to scholars of regionalism and Western literature, environmental humanities and science, and life writing and memoir.

Like Maher, Heather Houser attends to contemporary literature that seeks to alter readers' environmental consciousness in her monograph titled *Ecosickness in Contemporary U.S. Fiction: Environment and Affect*. However, her project maps a 'mode' of contemporary environmental writing that she names 'ecosickness fiction': literary texts that 'join experiences of ecological and somatic damage through narrative affect' (p. 2). Analysing works by Jan Zita Grover, David Wojnarowicz, Richard Powers, David Foster Wallace, Marge Piercy, and Leslie Marmon Silko, Houser first identifies a trend in contemporary fiction and memoir that positions illness narratives in relationship to depictions of environmental damage. Registering the impact of increased 'pollution, urbanization, and technologization' on human bodies and the world (p. 5), these authors '[dissolve]... the body-environment boundary through [depictions of] sickness', thereby 'uniting earth and soma through the sickness trope' and 'involv[ing] readers ethically in our collective bodily and environmental futures' (p. 3). Because of Houser's focus on what Arthur Kleinman and others call 'illness narratives', her monograph is a compelling contribution to the medical humanities, especially as she expands from previous work that suggests such contemporary narratives explore illness in relationship to 'economic, institutional and political forces' by insisting upon the import of 'environmental and technological' influences on depictions of sickness (p. 11). Still, Houser's work also powerfully intervenes in ecocriticism and the environmental humanities more broadly because of its emphasis on narrative forms and strategies that inspire ethical contemplation of—and perhaps action on behalf of—the more pressing environmental concerns of our time period, such as 'climate change, species extinction, pervasive toxicity, population growth, capitalist expansion, and technoscientific innovation' (p. 8). Referencing works by Scott Slovic, Lawrence Buell, and Stacy Alaimo, Houser also examines how literary texts 'may affect one's caring for the physical world: make it feel more or less precious or endangered and disposable', as Buell argues in *Writing for an Endangered World* (Belknap [2001], p. 2). Houser's particular take on environmental narratives centres upon engagement with the affective narrative strategies deployed by the aforementioned literary authors. Moving beyond a focus on the pastoral tradition in environmental literary criticism and the familiar terrain of nature writing that promotes 'emotional bonds' between humans and the environment, Houser reveals the surprising affects that appear in and result from reading ecosickness fiction, such as discord and disgust (p. 22). Further, she shows that the 'workhorses of environmental affect such as anxiety and wonder do not function as predictably as we might think', and therefore require greater analysis and theorization (pp. 22–3). In this way, she offers environmental literary critics a more complicated and nuanced rendering of multiple forms of affect that writers explore in works attuned to environmental damage and somatic sickness. Drawing on and at times challenging recent critical studies of affect by Ann Cvetkovich, Charles Altieri, Lauren Berlant, Sara Ahmed, Eve Kosofsky Sedgwick, and Sianne Ngai, Houser effectively argues that ecocritics need to be more attentive to studies of affect as well as the divergent forms of it that appear in literary works because such attention can give insight into the ways that intense emotions 'direct attention, confirm or undermine ethical stances, and spur or stifle political action' (p. 27). Refusing to oversimplify affect's instrumentality or to 'specify the "right" narrative affects for articulating an environmental politics', Houser ultimately shows in close readings of novels and memoirs the 'unique aspects of the literary [that] ignite feelings that draw planet and body into a shared sphere of concern' (p. 27). Because of its interventions in three separate strands of contemporary literary criticism—medical humanities, environmental humanities, and studies of affect—*Ecosickness* is one of this year's most important monographs.

Each of the chapters of *Ecosickness* focuses on a different form of affect. For example, the first full chapter examines discord in Grover's *North Enough: AIDS and Other Clear-Cuts* and Wojnarowicz's *Close to the Knives: A Memoir of Disintegration*, two memoirs of the AIDS epidemic that feature non-urban environments. For Houser, both memoirists explore how 'sickness is a conduit to affective positions that alter environmental perceptions, aesthetics, and ethics such that the fates of soma and planet necessarily intervolve' (p. 38). With analysis *North Enough*, Houser shows how Grover's experiences with those suffering from AIDS impact the way that she understands the landscape that remains after human harvesting of the woodlands of Minnesota and the way that she sees the so-called wastelands of the sub-Arctic zone in Manitoba. Although Grover seeks the healing power of 'nature' in a respite from the disease and death of San Francisco where she served as an AIDS worker, she does not easily find it as her fantasies about nature are confronted with the realities of human impact on land and the 'desolation' that she sees upon visiting the northern tundra. Her feelings of discord, however, do lead in Houser's argument to an environmental and biomedical aesthetic that 'promotes an ethics of resilience and adaptation' (p. 53). Grover's experiences with people living with AIDS as they were denigrated by religious, political, and even medical discourses cause her to connect this violence 'to humans' encroachment on other species and the tendency to decimate "radiant diversity" rather than observe and protect it' (p. 53). In addition, Houser illustrates how Grover's connection between somatic and ecological injury fuels a 'thanatological aesthetic', which both celebrates the persistence of the injured woodland despite damaging human intervention and veers into fetishizing the beauty of destruction and decay (p. 53). In Houser's complex reading of this text, discord both opens up a potential ethics of care for damaged and injured places and also has the potential to become depoliticized when aestheticizing ecological injury takes the place of addressing the causes of it. This brief discussion of Houser's analysis of the connection between ecological and somatic injury in an ecosickness narrative gives just a glimpse of the import that this monograph will have for environmental literary criticism and studies of affect and narrative. With other chapters that address wonder in Powers's *The Echo Maker*, disgust in Wallace's *Infinite Jest*, and anxiety in Silko's *Almanac of the Dead* as well as Piercy's *Woman on the Edge of Time*, Houser continues to dazzle with close readings that provide insight into the surprising ways contemporary authors explore affect as a means to inspire social change and the ways it can promote stasis or detachment from biomedical and environmental dilemmas.

Another contribution to environmental literary criticism is a beautiful collection of essays titled *Green Planets: Ecology and Science Fiction* edited by Gerry Canavan and Kim Stanley Robinson. As the title suggests, the collection focuses upon the ways in which science fiction responds to environmental crises or reflects shifting social understandings of human impact on the planet with utopian or dystopian flair. Following Samuel R. Delany's categorization of ideological positions of modernity in relationship to technological advancement and development, the editors assemble science fiction texts into different camps. First, they identify texts that celebrate a New Jerusalem in which technology and science have resolved all human problems. This kind of utopian vision of the end to human suffering via technology and science contrasts with Arcadian fantasies of a return to oneness with nature in which technology does not interfere with the connection between humans and the environment. These two categories breed their 'dark opposites' as science fiction presents New Jerusalems that become Brave New Worlds in which 'fascist bureaucrats have crushed the soul of the human, machines have replaced work and love, and smog blocks out the stars' (p. 1). So, too, Arcadia imagined as an escape from modernity has its opposite in depictions of 'Lands of the Flies' that show the 'reversal of progress' and a 'return to the nightmare of . . . floods, wars, famine . . . [and] disease' (p. 1). With postmodernity, the editors follow Delany once again by suggesting that new 'ideological forms' arise. In contrast to the celebratory visions of a New Jerusalem, postmodern science fiction offers the 'Junk City': 'the dysfunctional New Jerusalem in slow-motion breakdown' that nevertheless has a 'positive side' in 'visions of improvisational recombinative urban chaos' (p. 3). Beyond the urban, the editors also trace the appearance of toxic rural environments, devastated by human denial of dependence upon the health of the full ecosystem, which Delany calls 'the Culture of the "Afternoon"' (p. 3). In texts of this sort, the editors note that, despite their dark visions of ruination, these texts do offer the 'sublime beauty' of pollution, such as 'the way a sunset, shining splendidly through the smog, glistens off the antifreeze' (p. 3). To Delany's categories of science fiction, the editors add one more position: the Quiet Earth, literary representations of 'a planet . . . devoid of human life entirely' (p. 11). In terms of structure, the editors gather essays together in sections designated by these seven categories: Arcadias, New Jerusalems, Brave New Worlds, Lands of the Flies, Quiet Earths, Junk Cities, and Cultures of the Afternoon. With essays that focus on work by H.G. Wells, Ursula Le Guin, Maggie Gee, Paolo Bacigalupi, and Stanislaw Lem as well as chapters that address literary representations of population growth, apocalyptic and post-apocalyptic fiction, and other forms of aesthetic grappling with ecological futures, the collection is a timely volume with much to offer scholars invested in science fiction and ecocriticism.

This volume's commitment to thinking through science fiction and ecology like Eric C. Otto's *Green Speculations: Science Fiction and Transformative Environmentalism* (OSP [2012]; reviewed in *YWES* 92[2013]) shows an increased investment in the potential of science fiction for the broader field of environmental literary criticism. Still, studies of science fiction released in 2014 also continued to examine posthumanism. Although these volumes do not relate directly to studies of place, it does make sense to mention them briefly here. Elana Gomel's *Science Fiction, Alien Encounters, and the Ethics of Posthumanism: Beyond the Golden Rule* expands from previous evaluations of the alien other by exploring how science fiction texts have the potential to challenge 'anthropocentrism and even ethnocentrism' by embracing a 'posthuman' abandonment of human 'identity' and the 'ideological and moral assumptions' of a particular 'time and place' (p. 28). Even while she acknowledges that science fiction certainly can reflect the ideological assumptions of specific cultures, she is interested in tracing not only the limits of science fiction but also its ability to model 'an ethical response to the radical otherness of the Universe' and to challenge readers to contemplate stepping beyond 'the self-imposed boundaries of our humanity' (p. 28). Exploring the violence of humanism in works by Greg Bear, Housuke Nojiri, and Stephen Wallenfels, the erasure of the Other in Soviet science fiction by Ivan Efremov and the Strugatsky brothers, posthuman subjects in work by Robert Heinlein and Scott Sigler, assimilation in postcolonial science fiction, as well as divergent and vivid representations of transformative encounters with aliens that model posthuman ethics, Gomel's monograph is a rich contribution to global science fiction studies. Victoria Flanagan's *Technology and Identity in Young Adult Fiction: The Posthuman Subject* explores the rise of posthuman issues and themes in twenty-first-century young adult fiction with particular attention to the ways that such texts 'portray technology as empowering for "othered" child[ren] and adolescent subjects' (p. 7). Analysing works from Britain, the United States, Australia, and New Zealand, including Tanith Lee's *The Silver Metal Lover* and *Metallic Love*, Orson Scott Card's *Ender's Game*, Cory Doctorow's *Little Brother* and *Homeland*, and Mary E. Pearson's *The Adoration of Jenna Fox*, Flanagan provides an insightful rendering of a shift within young adult fiction as well as the larger implications of it. Beyond these two works, scholars of science fiction will be interested in Margret Grebowicz and Helen Merrick's *Beyond the Cyborg: Adventures with Donna Haraway*, especially their exploration of feminist sci-fi with reference to Marge Piercy and Le Guin (pp. 112–30). A final introductory volume, Brian Baker's simply titled *Science Fiction*, will be of value for those seeking a guide to major critical evaluations of science fiction or an accessible critical history in connection to major theoretical developments like postmodernism.

A third critical trend in studies of post-1945 aesthetic production is a focus on capitalism, with particular emphasis on capitalist realism and the representation of petrocapitalism. For example, *Reading Capitalist Realism*, edited by Alison Shonkwiler and Leigh Claire La Berge, is a magnificent collection of essays that primarily explores aesthetic and documentarian works produced during the rise of the neoliberal state, the central features of which are 'privatizing wealth, deregulating markets, and reducing social spending', 'supporting the interests of an unfettered global financial system', and 'taking advantage of crises to advance market-based, free-trade oriented, and even financially imperialist agendas' (p. 5). Even as most critics would agree that 'all realism is capitalist' (p. 1), Shonkwiler and La Berge utilize their introduction to the collection to showcase the ways in which realist works produced after the 1970s differ from earlier texts because of a lack of access to imaginable alternatives to capitalism. Following Mark Fisher's *Capitalist Realism* (Zero [2009]), Shonkwiler and La Berge define capitalist realism as a 'general ideological formation in which capitalism is the most real of our horizons, the market-dominant present that forms the limits of our imaginaries' (p. 2). Still, while Fisher claims that capitalist realism is not a 'representational mode or aesthetic' (p. 2), the editors of this collection suggest otherwise and argue that the term can effectively be used to describe documentarian and aesthetic works that 'emphasize the economic while insisting at the same time on the political and representational dimensions of capitalism' (p. 7). To further elucidate their understanding of capitalist realism as a mode, the editors offer three definitional characteristics. First, 'whereas earlier realisms laid claim, however problematically, to a stability of mode and perception, the capitalist realist mode interrupts and disorganizes itself, through incorporation of other genres and through its desire to show the processes of its own commodification' (p. 11). Even as works classified under the term 'capitalist realism' attempt to capture the 'real' of 'economic forms such as the commodity, money, and finance' as well as 'production and consumption', they also highlight how 'realistic' portrayals of such forms 'cannot represent...global capital indexically' (pp. 11, 13). In this way, capitalist realism exhibits both attempts to document circuits of capital and the necessary failure of documentarian and mimetic strategies to do so; thus, capitalist realism turns to melodrama or allegory, for example, thereby marking its own failure to create totalizing narratives that 'expose and make legible the conditions that have been produced by the so-called illegible abstractions of finance capital' (p. 8). Second, capitalist realism, although indebted to nineteenth-century bourgeois fiction and socialist realism, is born of the 'pervasive logic of capitalism in the present' and thus lacks both the naturalization of the 'emergent middle-class subjectivity of capitalism' identified by Nancy Armstrong and the 'opposition to capital' in texts devoted to benefiting the working class (pp. 14–15, 43). Rather than follow Walter Benn Michaels's assertion that neoliberalism is the best term to describe contemporary literary production, Shonkwiler and La Berge argue that, while capitalist realist texts do reflect neoliberal ideologies thereby documenting an inability to imagine alternative economic orders, they also 'constantly seek new avenues' for critique of it, even as they acknowledge 'the limitations of critique' (p. 16). In this way, the editors highlight how capitalist realist texts are more than a simple reflection of neoliberalism because they attempt to map and to critique financial systems. Further, they focus on the difficulty of representing such systems and present the all-encompassing nature of such financial systems in ways that suggest the impossibility of resistance. Third, the editors suggest that contemporary texts in this mode 'repoliticize' realism by 'calling attention to the ways in which capitalism impoverishes our imagination while simultaneously claiming that impoverishment cannot be imagined otherwise' (p. 16). In their account, contemporary texts in this mode challenge previous theorizations of realism within leftist criticism by refusing to grant 'literary realism a naïve authority to demystify capitalist processes of accumulation, or to de-reify the real' (p. 17).

Ultimately, the editors argue that capitalist realist texts show how 'capitalism as a system cannot exist apart from modes of representation, and [that] the realist mode... is invested in an economically situated conception of history' (p. 17). Thus, the political import of contemporary realist texts is their ability to show how historical processes shape aesthetic efforts to capture them, thereby limiting the imaginative presentation of alternatives, while also highlighting how capitalism depends upon certain realist forms of representation to naturalize it.

The essays that follow this introductory tour de force offer exciting analysis of fiction, non-fiction, and film. As a whole, the collection is provocative and rich, as many essays both provide reflections upon the term 'capitalist realism' while also exploring detailed close readings of particular texts. For example, Andrew Hoberek's essay 'Adultery, Crisis, Contract' addresses Jess Walter's *The Financial Lives of Poets* and Lorrie Moore's *A Gate at the Stairs* to explore how adultery is utilized as a 'site... to express anger... at the violation of the contract form putatively central to capitalism but in fact increasingly outmoded within its current incarnation' (p. 48). For Hoberek, in the wake of the subprime mortgage crisis during the first decade of the twenty-first century, discussions of adultery and troubled marriages, both in popular culture and within the aforementioned novels, displace anxiety and fear about the abuses of contractual relationships within capitalism onto a focus on the subject of marriage, 'where contract, its violation, and the resulting fallout seem amenable (unlike in the world of finance) to depiction in a straightforward and easily traceable way' (p. 48). Still, unlike popular accounts of the infidelity of John Edwards, Tiger Woods, Eliot Spitzer, and Jesse James directly following the mortgage crisis, these two novels' engagement with adultery and finance showcases the 'gulf between capitalist theory and capitalist realism as a crisis in realist representation' (p. 49). Other standout articles in the collection are Caren Irr's 'Anti-Capitalism and Anti-Realism in William Vollmann's *Poor People*' and Phillip E. Wegner's 'Things as They Were or Are: On Russell Banks's Global Realisms', which includes a rich discussion of Banks's *The Darling*. As a provocation for increased attention to a shift in the realist mode connected to critical economic changes over the past four decades, *Reading Capitalist Realism* will spark scholarly debate about literary developments after the heyday of postmodernism; the impact of neoliberalism on contemporary fiction, television, film, and non-fiction; and the efficacy of key novelistic engagements with the market-dominant present.

Oil Culture, edited by Ross Barrett and Daniel Worden, similarly engages with representations of capitalism with a particular focus on 'petrocapitalism' or oil capitalism. Acknowledging the dearth of humanistic accounts of oil culture prior to the past two decades, editors introduce their collection by providing an account of the state of the field of oil studies, including discussion of 'industry-centered histories', case studies of 'oil's material development in particular nations', 'studies of energy crisis, war and environmentalism', and cultural studies of 'promotional representations of the American oil [industry]' as well as 'the practices underpinning petroleum-based lifestyles in the United States and other gas-guzzling Western societies' (pp. xxi–xxiii). Building and expanding on previous work in cultural studies, the editors argue for the importance of engagement with aesthetic renderings of oil culture, especially because industry-focused works tend to explore the oil economy with a 'hard-nosed pragmatism' that eschews the import of imagining alternatives to such an economy (p. xxi). Further, studies with a focus on industry can ignore how cultural representations of oil 'worked to accelerate oil capitalism's reorganization of everyday life in North America, Europe, and an expanding array of non-Western nations . . . around the maximally intensive consumption of oil and its chemically engineered derivatives' (p. xxv). Instead of refusing to address representations of oil that serve to bolster petrocapitalism, impact and shape subjects' 'systems of being and belief', or provide alternative imaginings of energy and economics, the editors and essayists analyse 'oil as a cultural material, a force not only in economic and political life but also in everyday experiences and aesthetics' (pp. xxv, xx). This project is imperative not only because peak oil is on the horizon but also because dominant industrial and political discourses of oil continue to fuel processes of extraction that have a devastating environmental impact, to eschew the impact of emissions on climate change, and to inspire military action in the name of sustaining oil-based economies. The editors succinctly argue that 'oil culture . . . has helped to establish oil as a deeply entrenched way of life . . . by tying petroleum use to fundamental sociopolitical assumptions and aspirations, inventing and promoting new forms of social practice premised on cheap energy, refiguring petroconsumption as a self-evidently natural and unassailable category of modern existence, and forestalling critical reconsiderations of oil's social and ecological costs' (p. xxv). To counter a wilful inability to think beyond oil culture and a similarly obstinate lack of engagement with its social and environmental costs, *Oil Culture* provides nuanced, weighty, and polemical accounts of proliferating 'images, narratives, and discourses' that 'have contributed to the formation of an oil spectacle that has sustained industrial and financial commitments to the expanding system of petrocapitalism', following Guy Debord's theorization of 'the society of the spectacle' (p. xxv). With attention to both the 'symbolic forms and practices that enabled the emergence, development, and entrenchment of oil capitalism' and 'symbolic materials' that highlight 'uncertainty, ambivalence, or resistance' to 'oil's ceaseless colonizing expansion' as well as 'alternative perspectives on fossil fuels and the energy economy', the editors and essayists construct a groundbreaking work in oil studies that will provoke future critical conversation about and study of petrocapitalism, cultural representations of oil, and imaginative renderings of a 'post-oil future' (p. xxvi).

In terms of structure, *Oil Culture* opens by grouping essays in sections that trace cultural representations of the early American oil industry (Part I), the mid-century instantiation modern oil capitalism (Part II), and the late twentieth-century global system of oil capitalism (Part III). The two remaining sections address public exhibitions in 'aquariums, art institutions, and science museums' that pressure 'twentieth and twenty-first century imaginings of petroleum' (p. xxix) and aesthetic works that imagine a future beyond oil. Addressing film, television, photography, and novels and providing an account of oil culture from the nineteenth century to the present, the full collection focuses primarily on literary works of the post-1945 period.

Frederick Buell's 'A Short History of Oil Cultures; or, The Marriage of Catastrophe and Exuberance' contextualizes discussion of the oil economy via cultural representations of coal capitalism that revel in 'exuberant' celebration of coal's liberatory power that 'allowed European economies to by-pass the natural limitations of organic energy' (p. 72). While many narratives celebrated the industrial progress ushered in by coal, others, like Frank Norris, Charles Dickens, and Rebecca Harding Davis, constructed narratives of catastrophe that showcased 'machine-made organic nightmares' with depictions of 'miasmic environments to Dickensian oppression of the poor' (pp. 73–4). Buell explores the shift to 'oil-extraction' culture and 'oil-electric-coal capitalism' (p. 74) discussing Ida Tarbell's *History of Standard Oil*, Sinclair Lewis's *Oil!* and the modernist poetics of Hart Crane, Eliot, and Pound. Concluding with a discussion of the re-emergence of fusion between exuberant and catastrophic narratives of the oil economy in the post-1945 period, Buell shows how films and novels celebrate new industries supported by the oil economy and promote catastrophe as a necessary corollary of growth and progress. Even narratives that centre upon the 'myriad environmental, technological, economic, and geopolitical crises' of oil capitalism by staging 'postapocalyptic milieus' seemingly make 'global warming thrilling' or other crises exciting 'thereby injecting exuberance into catastrophe' (p. 83). With particular reference to films like *I Am Legend*, *Terminator*, and *The Day After Tomorrow*, and novels like Bruce Sterling's *Schismatrix*, China Miéville's *Perdido Street Station*, and Gibson's *Neuromancer* as representative of the collapse of narratives of catastrophe and exuberance, Buell also cites works that move beyond this fusion, such as Octavia Butler's *The Parable of the Sower* and Cormac McCarthy's *The Road*, as well as post-oil scenarios like James Howard Kunstler's *World Made By Hand* and Sarah Hall's *The Carhullan Army*.

Another strong essay in the collection, Daniel Worden's 'Fossil-Fuel Futurity: Oil in *Giant*', focuses on representations of oil culture from the 1950s to the present with particular attention to Edna Ferber's *Giant*, the television show *Dallas*, and the film *There Will Be Blood*. He writes, 'Together, these texts map how oil becomes central to the vision of the good life in the post-1945 United States and the ruptures that changes in oil production and availability . . . produce in the vision of the petroleum-consuming family' (p. 110). Beyond astute close readings of scenes, Worden offers the useful concept of 'fossil-fuel futurity', which he defines as a 'narrative device' that dodges the connection between the usage of fuel and its contribution to the establishment of 'normative family life' (p. 110). 'Retrofutures and Petrofutures: Oil, Scarcity, Limit' by Gerry Canavan focuses on mid-century science fiction that posits oil as an energy source to be transcended such that readers 'can see oil's inescapable centrality to twentieth-century liberal capitalism proven precisely through the fantasy of its painless transcendence' (p. 333). While many mid-century works present the surpassing of oil with new and superior resources, Canavan argues that 'the oil shocks of the 1970s' replaced this fantasy of a post-oil future 'with the creeping terror that technological modernity, and its consumer lifestyle, may in fact have no future at all' (p. 333). By documenting shifts in representations of oil culture within science fiction by H.G. Wells,

Isaac Asimov, Laurence Manning, Frank Herbert, Gibson, Kunstler, Paolo Bacigalupi, and others, Canavan creates a powerful account of the contrasting fictional strategies for addressing oil culture inspired by the increased technological growth provided by oil, the crises of the 1970s, and our current movement towards peak oil. Beyond these three essays, *Oil Culture* also includes provocative work by established voices in oil studies, like Imre Szeman, and also by newcomers, thereby serving as an introduction to the field and a glimpse into future directions for transnational and transhistorical accounts of petrocapitalism and cultural representations of it.

Moving past these three trends in studies of post-1945 fiction, two major works were published that extend critical conversations about representations of sexuality and race with a particular focus on works from the late 1940s to the 1960s. *Camp Sites: Sex, Politics, and Academic Style in Postwar America*, a late arrival by Michael Trask, is a stunning contribution to Stanford University Press's Post*45 series; as a study of academic style and liberalism of the 1950s, the New Left's critique of the academy and cultivation of its own oppositional stylistics, and the ways in which camp and the closet queen appear as the antithesis to both forms of stylistics, *Camp Sites* will have broad appeal. Additionally, because Trask traces the homophobic consistencies in both postwar academic and New Left discourses of style in a variety of non-fictional and fictional texts, he provides a fresh and unusual account of the period from 1945 to 1975 that makes strange bedfellows of academic, political, and literary figures not usually grouped together. Two connected questions drive Trask's analysis of multiple works from this period. First, he asks 'What is it about queers that makes them routinely stand in for the abject version of academic style, the instrumental reason or ironic self-fashioning of the liberal intellectual?' (p. 221). In answer to this query, Trask traces the connection between postwar liberalism, 'school culture', and academic style that 'rallied around the hermeneutics of suspicion and its equally powerful fetish of demystification' (p. 21). Exploring interdisciplinary academic style of the 1950s and beyond as a cultivation of 'disaffection from belief', 'detachment', and 'irony', as well as a refusal of 'absolute values or objective truth' (pp. 29–30), Trask highlights how school culture 'parallels' and promotes mid-century liberalism by 'recasting academic freedom from a principle of inclusion to one of insularity . . . and liberalism of the public sphere to a liberalism of private life' (p. 27). The academic style of detachment and ability to see through and map belief systems that shape social relations might open the academic up to a kinship with the gender trouble that camp may provide; yet, as Trask succinctly shows, 'the university offered . . . a competitive version of masculine agency distinguished by the ability to maintain a kind of equilibrium in the maelstrom of propaganda, institutional conflict, and mass hysteria that swept through Cold War America', which contrasts with the fantasized gullibility of the queen (p. 33). In other words, while the masculine and tough academic showcases the inner workings of a variety of social systems and performs his own role within them in an ironic way, the effeminate queer is imagined to believe too much in a performance that she knows is false, to succumb to her own deception. Following the eruption of the abject campy queen or her absent presence in academic discussions of ironic style in work by Leslie

Fiedler and others, Trask shows how mid-century academics erected their masculine style through disavowal of camp and the queer in ways that echoed the liberal establishment's excising of queer people from its administrative ranks.

Because academic masculine style so denigrated camp, it is ironic indeed that the New Left critiqued the detached style of postwar academics by associating them with the assumed inauthenticity of camp. This leads to the second query that guides Trask's monograph, which the majority of his text addresses: 'How is it that queers, so thoroughly reviled by the liberal establishment, could also find themselves so emphatically unwelcome at the revolution?' (p. 221). To answer this question, Trasks begins with an analysis of Ralph Ellison's *The Invisible Man* and argues that this text critiques an academic style that 'detaches the self from society that covets a relief from ambiguity' and delights in the 'dispersal of meaning' because such a stance disavows the realities of Jim Crow America (pp. 42–3). Still, in his reading, Ellison 'retain[s]' the ironic stance of Cold War academics by turning it against them. Trask writes, 'Calling out the academic style in the figure of its abject double, the campy homosexual whose pragmatism lies adjacent to a shameless deviance, Ellison makes that style an erratic mannerist charade, the hallmark of the flaming sissy rather than the tough-minded ironist' (p. 45). This strategy of deriding academic style as queer camp is taken up by figures in the New Left but utilized in a different way. Following Huey P. Newton and other activists, Trask shows how the New Left, like Ellison, critiques academics' denial of 'real-world' certitudes and detachment from addressing injustice, but does so in a way that counters academic style with authenticity, experience, and testimonial speech (p. 86). Highlighting particular sites in which camp or the queer appear in Leftist writing, Trask shows how revolutionary figures imagined academics as flighty queens unable to commit to a righteous cause because of a 'deviant' desire to be topped by powerful men in government and industry. Juxtaposing engagement with texts like Newton's *Revolutionary Suicide* with analysis of Pynchon's *The Crying of Lot 49* and *Gravity's Rainbow*, Norman Mailer's *Armies of Night*, and Doctorow's *The Book of Daniel*, Trask reveals the 'range of opinions on the lavender menace throughout the radical sixties, which tended to see the enemy as combining two queer stereotypes: the soulless authoritarian thug and the flamboyant queens who are unable to resist him' (p. 101).

This brief exploration of Trask's monograph does not do justice to the range of his text nor to the intellectual rush that it provides. Addressing camp sites in campus novels like Mary McCarthy's *The Groves of Academe*, Alison Lurie's *Love and Friendship*, and Nabokov's *Pale Fire*, the suspenseful fiction of Patricia Highsmith, 'deviant ethnographies' like Esther Newton's *Mother Camp*, and novelistic engagement with mid-century feminism in works like Plath's *The Bell Jar* and Erica Jong's *Fear of Flying*, Trask's text covers much ground. While his work will clearly be essential for queer theorists, for scholars of Cold War aesthetic works, and for researchers of mid-century social movements as well as novels that reflect upon them, it also calls for a historicized understanding of academic style that impacts the 'politicized academic in the present' (p. 223). To create a coalition that unites academic and non-academic activists, Trask ultimately argues, 'However academics choose to pursue the politics of representation... that politics seems stubbornly unmindful of the institutional and material roadblocks thrown up at the intersection' (p. 228). Calling for greater examination of the 'difference between the circumstances of academics and the circumstances of those who swim outside the tenure system', Trask concludes his work by discussing how academic styles and outlooks, such as a focus on anti-normativity, relate to institutional privilege (p. 228). His final provocation for continued study of contemporary academic habitus and its historical precursor need not only apply to queer theorists, but can usefully be extended to an interdisciplinary conversation about a larger 'school culture'. It is this focus, in addition to its range, that makes *Camp Sites* a major contribution to the study of post-1945 period.

Desegregating Desire: Race and Sexuality in Cold War American Literature by Tyler T. Schmidt offers a powerful intervention in literary criticism focused on the late 1940s and early 1950s by exploring how eight different authors engage with discourses of desegregation via intimate portrayals of homes and personal lives transformed by cultural shifts during this period. Acknowledging that most studies of 'early histories of the civil rights movement [focus] on interracial political allegiances', Schmidt expands on such studies by showing how novelists and poets maintain a deep interest in private desires that prop up segregationist discourse as well as the ways that interracial and queer desires, 'whether explicitly erotic or a more nebulous form of erotic identification', are 'the catalyst [in literary texts] for many of the personal and social transformations related to race' (pp. 18, 6). Because of multiple diverse authors' turn during this period to literary exploration of private desires and intimate relationships across the colour line, Schmidt traces a 'literature of desegregation' that shows how '"minute and undercover" incidents of racial and sexual encroachments are central to social change and influential in shaping postwar identities' (p. 6). Each chapter pairs two authors together around a key theme in the literature of desegregation. For example, Elizabeth Bishop and Zora Neale Hurston are analysed in the first full chapter with a focus on 'their shared interest in the murky interracial relationships of domestic servitude and the ways that racial ventriloquism—speaking for/as the racial Other—challenges Cold War narratives of domestic containment' (p. 39). Attention to Gwendolyn Brooks's and Edwin Denby's poetry in the second chapter allows Schmidt to analyse their engagement with the desegregation of public spaces and aesthetic renderings of 'social encounters between African American women and gay men in the postwar city, some strained and some affirming' (p. 88). Uniting analysis of William Demby and Ann Petry's representation of interracial and same-sex desire in the third chapter, Schmidt examines their usage of representations of sexuality 'to expose, critique, and at times defend the cultural anxieties regarding racial and sexual integration' (p. 137). The final full chapter addresses works by Jo Sinclair and Carl Offord that 'depict social change less as a reconfiguration of social places... but as moments of psychological transformation, encounters with racial difference in which people develop new forms of social consciousness' (p. 180). With astute contextualization of novels and poetry, attunement to the divergent ways in which authors grapple with desegregation in their works, and a persistent focus on how authors imagine desire to be key to thinking about social transformation, Schmidt's *Desegregating Desire* is a beautiful take on well-known and lesser-known writers. Both Trask's and Schmidt's monographs continue, extend, and deploy queer theoretical insights in new directions in deeply moving and socially engaged ways.

In addition to these works, a number of studies published in the past year address contemporary literary forms, including minimalism, the maximalist novel, and the legacy of postmodernist literary strategies. *American Literary Minimalism* by Robert C. Clark intervenes in debates about literary minimalism by challenging periodizations of the movement that focus primarily on aesthetic production from mid-1970s to the late 1980s without connecting to late nineteenth- and early twentieth-century writers like Hamlin Garland, Ernest Hemingway, and Ezra Pound or without acknowledging the continuation of the movement into the twenty-first century. Beyond creating a deeper literary history that traces influential figures and works that have impacted the construction of contemporary minimalist short stories and novels, Clark also calls for a renewed focus on minimalism as a 'style' or on the formal elements of minimalist prose. This type of critical attention gives readers room to identify the persistence of the movement in works not defined by previous critics' 'generalizations about character types, the perceived role of consumer culture, or domesticity' in such fiction (p. 1). By recognizing that minimalist 'fiction does not reflect a predetermined type of content' and 'is not restricted to a single genre' (p. 2), Clark shows the diversity of the movement, bringing an unusual combination of works together in the full monograph such as Raymond Carver's *Cathedral*, Jay McInerney's *Bright Lights, Big City*, Susan Minot's *Monkeys*, Sandra Cisneros's *Caramelo*, and McCarthy's *The Road*. Clark argues that these works share a commitment to efficient albeit implicative prose and allusiveness, the defining features of minimalism. He writes, 'The language in this type of fiction tends to be simple and direct. Narrators do not often use ornate adjectives and rarely offer effusive descriptions of scenery or extensive detail about characters' backgrounds... Allusion and implication by omission... compensate for limited exposition, to add depth to stories that on the surface may seem superficial or incomplete' (p. 1). Following this succinct definition, Clark provides a history of the movement by exploring the influence of visual Impressionism on Garland in the late 1890s and Pound's understanding of Imagism as both of these movements influence mid- to late twentieth-century minimalism. With analysis of a few short pieces by Garland from 'Chicago Studies', Clark argues that his presentation of the 'sensory nature of human life' in objective reportorial prose that captures 'abbreviated moments of experience' as well as a focus on giving the reader the opportunity to visualize the immediacy of a scene through a self-effacing narrative style, ultimately requires 'readers to 'assemble' images and allusions in order to make a coherent, complete narrative' (p. 13). By setting up this important precursor to contemporary minimalism via discussion of Garland in the context of other literary impressionists like Joseph Conrad, Stephen Crane, Henry James, André Gide, and Anton Chekhov, Clark roots contemporary works in an established literary history. So, too, with discussion of Pound's essay 'Imagisme', Clark shows how the minimalist focus on efficient prose and the direct presentation of objects of study can be 'attributable to Pound, a figure rarely discussed in scholarship on the movement' (p. 14). Having set up a persuasive account of precursors to later twentieth-century minimalism, Clark turns in the following chapters to analysis of individual authors' works with a particular emphasis on recuperating the value of texts by the authors listed above, especially in light of critical commentary by novelists and critics alike who 'scornfully' dismiss the movement because of a perceived lack of depth, 'stylistic richness', or 'sophistication' (p. 20). Indeed, Clark's chapter-long studies of key minimalist works show vividly how allusiveness and implicative prose offer much depth for the careful reader and critic and thereby demand more attention in studies of later twentieth-century work beyond quick dismissal. Clark's *American Literary Minimalism* opens the door for a fresh take on literary history of the post-1945 period by extending critical discussions of minimalism beyond a focus on the 1970s and 1980s by providing both a compelling history of influences and an account of the continuation of the movement into the present day.

In the first chapter following the introduction, Clark turns to a discussion of Hemingway's *In Our Time* and his 'iceberg theory' in order both to provide a detailed account of the key characteristics of minimalism and to lay the groundwork for later examination of Hemingway's influence on Carver, McInerney, and others. With astute close readings of stories like 'Soldier's Home', 'Cat in the Rain', and 'Indian Camp', he argues that Hemingway's key aesthetic minimalist strategies include the 'relaying of sensory details through a non-intrusive' or self-effacing narrator (p. 31), 'allu[ding] to historical events' without providing expository commentary (p. 48), 'generating implication through omission', and 'focus[ing] on images and objects rather than literary abstraction' (p. 25). Clark further showcases how 'sparely written fiction' can achieve 'emotional and intellectual depth' in ways critics acknowledge in relationship to Hemingway but not later minimalists. In this way, Clark leads readers into chapter 2's examination of Carver's *Cathedral* and chapter 3's analysis of McInerney's *Bright Lights, Big City*. The familiar arguments provide powerful extensions of previous criticism by highlighting the 'relationship between perception and epistemic limitation' with prose depicting 'raw sensory experience' that 'supersedes communication of a larger moral or philosophical lesson' (p. 36).

Clark surprises by providing astute readings of *Bright Lights, Big City* that show the influence of Hemingway and Carver and the value of discovering minimalism outside stories of domestic life or a focus on unsophisticated or blue-collar characters associated with the movement. Despite the lack of 'the same degree of sparseness' found in Hemingway and Carver's works, Clark argues that, because 'the book is highly allusive, and important information is implied rather than directly stated', it displays 'techniques central to American literary Minimalism' (p. 70). Further, the non-intrusiveness of the narrator, 'precise' and 'declarative' sentences, and 'sensorial' prose are also signs of such indebtedness (p. 70). Another surprise in this monograph is the inclusion of Sandra Cisneros's long novel *Caramelo* in chapter 5, in which Clark argues that Cisneros's style 'grows from the intersection of South American and US

Minimalism' (p. 113). Tracing the influence of Jorge Luis Borges, Clarice Lispector, and Eduardo Galeano with reference to Hemingway and Carver, Clark shows how Cisneros 'brings a new vitality' to the US minimalist tradition. As with McInerney's novel, this inclusion of *Caramelo* in the minimalist tradition undermines previous critical evaluations of the movement that focus on its apolitical or even nihilistic tone. Utilizing 'simple images' (p. 120), historical and cultural allusion (p. 111), and a focus on the 'beauty that can be found in the mundane' (p. 110), Cisneros's work ultimately shows in Clark's account how minimalism effectively can address 'cultural and political' themes (p. 120). The final full chapter turns to Cormac McCarthy's *The Road*, suggesting that the art of minimalism is alive and well as this novel 'includes no ancillary words or insignificant images, achieving depth through allusion and implication' (p. 122). As with analysis of *Caramelo*, this final full chapter shows how minimalism need not eschew deep engagement with 'acute social commentary' (p. 148). As a whole, Clark's *American Literary Minimalism* is an exciting contribution and compelling account of the literary history and present-day import of the movement.

In contrast to Clark's work, Stefano Ercolino sets out to offer definitional traits of maximalist fiction of the late twentieth century and twenty-first century in *The Maximalist Novel: From Thomas Pynchon's* Gravity's Rainbow *to Roberto Bolaño's* 2666. Countering the arguments that minimalist fiction appears with renewed force at the end of the twentieth century as a challenge to postmodernism or that maximalism is born as a response to American literary minimalism, Ercolino calls for a '*longue durée* perspective' in which the 'two phenomena can be understood as being dialectically coexistent: two elementary possibilities of human expression which have always existed side by side (as in the 1980s and 1990s for example) or alternated (between the twentieth and twenty-first centuries) in determining the aesthetic horizon of a given literary system' (p. 70). Ercolino only briefly takes up the issue of the comparison of twentieth-century minimalist and maximalist fiction, as his primary aim is to detail the latter's characteristics and its relation to modernist works that use the encyclopedic mode, as well as its indebtedness to epic. Expanding on and critiquing key definitions of the contemporary long novel such as Tom LeClair's 'systems novel', Frederick Karl's 'Mega-Novel', and Franco Moretti's 'world text' and 'modern epic', Ercolino identifies 'ten elements' of the maximalist novel, including 'length, encyclopedic mode, dissonant chorality, diegetic exuberance, completeness, narratorial omniscience, paranoid imagination, intersemioticity, ethical commitment, [and] hybrid realism' (pp. xiii–xiv). Each nuanced chapter of the monograph analyses one of these traits with reference to seven primary texts: Pynchon's *Gravity's Rainbow*, Wallace's *Infinite Jest*, DeLillo's *Underworld*, Zadie Smith's *White Teeth*, Franzen's *The Corrections*, Bolaño's *2666*, and Babette Factory's *2005 dopo Cristo*. For example, in his discussion of length as a common trait, Ercolino explores three major reasons for the size of maximalist texts through engagement with *Infinite Jest*. First, maximalist novels require a certain length because it is the 'necessary precondition for . . . the constant and often extreme usage of a series of rhetorical strategies' (p. 21). Second, because the maximalist novel seeks to 'rival the entire world', it 'cannot do so except by assuming the latter's amplitude' (p. 21). Third, turning to the publishing house's campaign prior to the release of Wallace's novel, Ercolino shows how publishers marketed the sheer size of the book as a sign of its import. In this way, he shows that the maximalist novel is beholden, at least in part, to the 'progressive commodification of culture theorized by Fredric Jameson and fully revealed with the advancement of postmodernity and late capitalism' (p. 23). Thus, the successful sales of maximalist novels like *Infinite Jest* point towards 'the assumption that the dimensions of the book constitute an unequivocal sign... of the book's importance', thereby giving the consumer the feeling that 'he is entering into possession of a rather full-bodied synecdoche of "Culture"' (p. 25).

Turning to the encyclopedic mode in the subsequent chapter, Ercolino traces consistencies in the epic and the maximalist novel as both 'respond to a desire to capture the world in one fell swoop' (p. 32). Still, the 'difference between the encyclopedism of the ancient epic and that of the twentieth century does not lie in its nature or function [synthetic representation of totality of the real], but... in the multiplication and the differentiation of the encyclopedia attempts' (p. 31). In his account, the maximalist novel at the end of the twentieth century continues the aims of the ancient epic even as it responds to explosion of data and hypercomplexity of the postmodern world. For Ercolino, the seven representative novels include a variety of different fields of knowledge—'from myth to science, from religion to philosophy, to the entire sphere of the arts'—and attempt to capture 'human learning in its totality which appears to be susceptible to the varying encyclopedic interests of maximalist authors' (p. 45). Thus, he ultimately sees not a single encyclopedism, but 'multiple forms' (p. 45). In this chapter and others, Ercolino usefully elucidates key components of the maximalist novel within larger critical conversations of the relationship between postmodernism and modernism and with reference to the most dominant critical strains of contemporary fiction. This leads to thrilling results, especially in the chapter where he addresses the 'ethical commitment' of such fiction, which he situates 'within a continuity with the best *engagé* literary tradition of the twentieth century and not under the banner of a rupture with the postmodern literary system' (p. 136). Countering critics of postmodern fiction who highlight the frivolous disengagement from ethics, Ercolino considers maximalist novels as part of the postmodern critical tradition, drawing both on its 'aesthetic codes' and its modernist precursor. While in this chapter the maximalist novel is distinguished from postmodern fiction by John Barth, Donald Barthelme, and Umberto Eco, Ercolino is clear that its engagement with themes of 'great historical, political, and social relevance' does connect with the thematic content of the work of other authors identified with postmodernism (p. 136). Thus, acknowledging the maximalist novel's hybridization of postmodernism and modernism might allow for a re-evaluation of the multifaceted ethical engagement of postmodern authors, which analysis of Pynchon's work enables Ercolino to begin. As a whole, *The Maximalist Novel* is an accessible and yet theoretically engaged volume that serves as a strong introduction to debates about late twentieth-century fiction in the encyclopedic mode and a powerful intervention in such debates through concise examination of this kind of narrative's dominant characteristics.

Because Ercolino's connection of maximalist works by Pynchon and Wallace strives to create a bridge between authors identified with postmodernism and those associated with the 'new sincerity' or 'post-postmodernism', his monograph represents a trend in literary criticism of the last decade to make sense of the legacy of postmodernism. So, too, Irmtraud Huber's *Literature after Postmodernism: Reconstructive Fantasies* grapples with lingering postmodern literary strategies and themes as they appear in twenty-first-century novels, including Mark Z. Danielewski's *House of Leaves*, Jonathan Safran Foer's *Everything Is Illuminated*, Michael Chabon's *The Amazing Adventures of Kavalier & Clay*, and David Mitchell's *number9dream*. Still, even as Huber, like Ercolino, refuses to mark a rupture between postmodern and 'post-postmodern' works, she does provide an account of the 'shift of interest'. For her, contemporary works move 'from ontological and epistemological questions to pragmatic ones in an attempt to reclaim fiction as a form of communication that actually manages to convey meaning, however unstable and compromised it may be. In the face of the postmodernist tenets of the inaccessibility of the real, the indeterminacy of meaning, and the impossibility of truth, they explore the ways in which we nonetheless understand reality, construct meaning, and communicate with each other' (p. 15). Like Mary K. Holland's *Succeeding Postmodernism* (Bloomsbury [2013]; reviewed in *YWES* 94[2015]), Huber sees the continuation of some formal and thematic aspects of postmodern fiction in contemporary works that are utilized to promote human connection, communication, affect, and pragmatic engagement with real-world problems. Still, her focus is on the ways in which the aforementioned novels deploy 'fantastic narratives as fictions within fictions, safely embedded in a ... realist frame story' (p. 7). In this way, Huber critiques criticism of twenty-first-century works that focus too heavily upon the re-emergence of realism, which has been called 'dirty realism' or 'neo-realism'. For Huber, the overemphasis on the revival of realism in contemporary works overlooks the ways in which anti-realist fantasies operate within such texts. By tracing the juxtaposition of two different literary stances in contemporary fiction, 'the mimetic and the marvelous', Huber complicates critical narratives of contemporary realism with her exploration of what she calls the 'fantastic mode', a combination of these two stances within a literary text (p. 8). To clarify her definition of this mode, Huber understands the 'marvelous' literary stance as a 'deliberate departure from perceivable reality and a willing suspension of the claim to reflect the extratextual world' (p. 9). A mimetic stance in her account 'pays tribute to that artistic ideal of correspondence to reality' (p. 9). The fantastic mode combines these two stances, allowing a realist narrative frame to rub up against narrative departures from the real. Huber writes, 'While the fantastic mode often leans toward one or the other stance, it derives its main effect and pleasure from exploitation of their basic irreconcilability' (p. 10). The project of her monograph is both to document the fantastic mode and to explore some of the larger implications of it.

To be clear, Huber is not so much countering critical studies of current realism as suggesting that we attune ourselves to the ways in which texts' narrative 'referentiality and mimetic fealty' frame imaginative narrative flights from the real (p. 14). Thus, rather than focus on the use of realism alone, she showcases the play between realism and fantasy in the aforementioned works. In terms of the larger stakes of the 'fantastic mode', the authors she addresses use mimesis and the marvellous in a metafictional gesture 'that foreground[s] the interplay of the real and the imaginative in the fictive, and . . . raise[s] pragmatic questions about its uses and consequences' (p. 14). Her emphasis on the pragmatic is key as she distinguishes the metafictional quality of recent works from postmodern metafiction that 'subvert[s] our sense of reality' (p. 14). Instead, the fantastic mode highlights the 'creative potential of fictions' to shape readers' understanding of ethical 'agency and responsibility' in light of contemporary issues facing our communities and world (pp. 14, 74). Extending the postmodern insight that 'our reality is largely fictive', contemporary novelists in the fantastic mode suggest that 'this makes us responsible for the kinds of fictions that our reality is composed of, and . . . to learn to judge and value' those narratives (p. 75). It is the contrast between the realist and fantastic narratives in these texts that undermines mimetic truth claims, thereby 'offer[ing] . . . scenario[s] of possible narrative choices, interrogating the nature, responsibility and power of narration' (p. 74). Thus, the fantastic mode reveals a commitment to reconstruction rather than deconstruction because this emphasis on the mediation of all narratives, even mimetic ones, leads to an evaluation and construction of narratives with an eye towards their 'creative potential to form and transform the world' (p. 18). Huber's monograph provides a concise articulation of critical studies of the affective and formal shifts after postmodernism in recent novels that nevertheless remain indebted to it; her introduction and first chapter give an effective map of the multiple ways that critics are attempting to define this period and major works within it. Further, in subsequent chapters dedicated to a single primary text from the literary works listed above, she provides a compelling exploration of the fantastic mode in detailed close readings of novels, thereby effectively extending and challenging studies of realism in contemporary works. Finally, her concluding turn towards the 'intriguing prominence of *Bildungsroman* narratives' in contemporary novels opens yet another fruitful way to create an account of works 'after postmodernism' (p. 216).

While a number of monographs published in 2014 address postmodernism's legacy, one monograph maintained a focus on postmodernism and another engaged with the value of theories of decadence for post-1945 literary works. Décio Torres Cruz's *Postmodern Metanarratives:* Blade Runner *and Literature in the Age of Image* provides an extended examination of the film *Blade Runner* in the context of theories of postmodernism, especially the subgenre of cyberpunk and Charles Jencks's understanding of metanarrative: 'a narrative that talks about the process of its own making' and 'inquires about its constituent nature' and its appropriation of and 'similitude with' other narrative forms 'in the pursuit of change' (pp. 36–7). For literary scholars of the post-1945 period, Cruz's engagement with the contemporary fictional texts upon which the movie draws may be of most interest. For example, in chapter

6, 'Collating the Postmodern', Cruz explores the influence of Burroughs's *Blade Runner, a Movie*, Alan Nourse's novel *The Bladerunner*, and Philip K. Dick's *Do Androids Dream of Electric Sheep?*, while charting thematic differences and similarities between literary precursors and the film. *Decadence in Literature and Intellectual Debate since 1945*, edited by Diemo Landgraf, includes a series of chapters that explore the efficacy of theories of decadence for the post-Second World War period. Acknowledging that such theories 'reached their height from the middle of the nineteenth century to the end of the First World War', Landgraf suggests that recent economic and other crises within and across nations have inspired literary and philosophical writers to 'explore reasons for cultural and social decline in their societies' (pp. v–viii). In this way, the collection traces connections between contemporary transatlantic authors' return to concepts of decadence and their aesthetic and theoretical precursors from earlier centuries. Only one chapter in this collection addresses post-1945 American literature: Mario Bosincu's ' "In the very quick of the nightmare": Decadence and Mystics of Wilderness in Henry Miller's Cultural Criticism of Modernity'. With an introductory examination of Whitman, Bosincu examines Whitman's denunciation of 'America's decadence', in which 'calculative rationality' and 'exchange values' trump 'qualitative values' (p. 29). In Bosincu's account, Whitman's critique of the dominance of 'business materialism' and his call for a class of bards in 'Democratic Vistas' to make ' "the pulsations in all matter" perceivable' are taken up once again in the mid-twentieth century by Henry Miller (pp. 30–1). Analysing *The Air-Conditioned Nightmare* [1945], *The Time of the Assassins: A Study of Rimbaud* [1946], *The Cosmological Eye* [1961], and *The Colossus of Maroussi* [1942], Bosincu outlines Miller's polemical stance against the 'decadence of the modern world and of the degeneracy of "civilized man" ' as well as Miller's desire to convert the 'egoic subjectivity' of modern man into an 'earth-bound way of being in the world' (p. 40). The full collection is a compelling provocation to reconsider political, philosophical, and aesthetic theories of decadence for the post-1945 period and brings together articles on diverse aesthetic production from the films of Michelangelo Antonioni to literary works by Mario Vargas Llosa, Alfredo Bryce Echenique, and Michel Houellebecq.

Two final monographs deserve a quick mention before turning to the last section on works focused on single authors. *The Spectral Metaphor: Living Ghosts and the Agency of Invisibility* by Esther Peeren intervenes in criticism of the spectral turn that began in the 1990s, which she defines as 'a loose convergence of interest [within cultural criticism] in the conceptual force of ghosts and haunting' inspired in part by Derrida's *Specters of Marx* (Routledge [1994], p. 9). Arguing that previous cultural criticism has focused primarily upon the haunted rather than the ghosts themselves, or has viewed such spectral presences as signs of repressed history that continues to impact the present, Peeren examines British and American film, fiction, and television series from the late twentieth and early twenty-first centuries that depict living ghosts: 'undocumented migrants, servants or domestic workers, mediums and missing persons' (p. 16). Thus, rather than focus on ghosts as representative of historic traumas, Peeren calls critics to examine the variety of ways that the dispossessed are figured as ghosts of the present in contemporary cultural production. Further, Peeren shows how living ghosts in films including Stephen Frears's *Dirty Pretty Things*, Nick Broomfield's *Ghosts*, Robert Altman's *Gosford Park*, and Alejandro González Iñárritu's *Babel*, as well as in novels such as Sarah Waters's *Affinity*, Hilary Mantel's *Beyond Black*, Ian McEwan's *The Child in Time*, and Bret Easton Ellis's *Lunar Park*, utilize 'spectral agency' to 'challeng[e] the mechanisms that produced them as ghosted' (p. 24). Drawing on Derrida and Antonio Negri's theorizations of 'the ghostly system of capitalist production [that] not only renders labor and its value invisible, but makes workers converge with their labor, so that they can no longer claim a separate existence', Peeren argues that both of these theorists leave a provocative space in their texts for exploited labourers to turn 'the spectralizing system of capitalism against itself' (pp. 21, 23). Instead of countering post-industrial capitalism with a return to the 'reality of exploitation' in an effort to demystify economic systems that produce the dispossessed, she shows how strategic exploitation of their spectrality by living ghosts is depicted in the aforementioned films and novels in order to explore 'individual and collective' strategies to acquire greater agency, albeit an agency still limited by the systems that have made the dispossessed ghosts in the first place (pp. 21, 16). Because of Peeren's expert engagement with theorists of spectrality including Derrida and Negri, as well as theories of spectralized figures like Giorgio Agamben's *homo sacer*, Judith Butler's discussion of 'the ungrievable', and Achille Mbembe's theory of the 'living dead' (p. 15), *The Spectral Metaphor* will be of interest to theoretically inclined literary critics invested in working through the nuances, differences, and congruencies of such theories. In addition, the monograph offers stunning theoretically informed readings of aesthetic production that provide clear delineations of the variety of uses of the spectral metaphor in contemporary texts by showing the differences among representations of living ghosts, which cannot be subsumed under a generalizing theory because of the divergent forms of marginalization that various dispossessed groups experience. For critics of post-1945 American literary production, the final full chapter of the monograph may be of most interest since it offers a compelling interpretation of Bret Easton Ellis's *Lunar Park*. In close readings of scenes from this novel, Peeren explores the ghost of the father who haunts the narrator, named Bret Easton Ellis, in order to provide warnings about the 'difficulty, if not impossibility, of living up to normative ideal[s] of the "man of the house", especially when this ideal has been destabilized by postmodern questionings of identity as a stable, coherent category' (p. 172). Still, this father haunts Bret to call him to contemplate the harm of a kind fatherhood that transmits damaging ideals of masculinity to male children in an effort to help him transform his own relationship with his son, Robby. To counter a kind of paternity that focuses on sons as 'speculative commodities' in need of rearing that transforms their raw potential into right labour for the production of wealth represented by the novel's suburbs, the ghost of the father suggests that the 'economized' parent–child relationship is a legacy that Bret must eschew. As readers of the novel know, Bret cannot disavow this legacy before his son Robby goes missing in an act of what Peeren calls 'self-spectralization'

(p. 174). With analysis of Robby as a missing child, a living ghost who also haunts Bret after his disappearance, Peeren suggests that Robby becomes a 'repudiating [heir]' that 'challenges the notion of succession itself' through his chosen disappearance and flight from paternal grooming into an oppressive economic order (p. 175). Fleeing to 'neverneverland', Robby and other lost boys in the novel create a 'spectral agency' that focuses on a 'new type of sociality that elides the nuclear family and generational competition' (p. 175). In this way, the missing sons go 'from being overlooked and commodified to substantiated and cherished in a non-proprietary mode' (p. 176). By going missing, the living ghosts of Ellis's lost boys haunt paternal figures called to re-evaluate the legacy of capitalism and to ponder new forms of relationality.

While not primarily focused on post-1945 literary production, *The New Literary Middlebrow: Tastemakers and Reading in the Twenty-First Century* by Beth Driscoll will be of value because of its clear definition of middlebrow reading practices and communities through discussion of the contemporary literary marketplace, face-to face reading groups, online and televised reading groups including the Oprah Book Club, literary prizes, and literary festivals. With the primary aim of creating an account of recent book culture, Driscoll argues that 'it is imperative to recognize that the most influential players— prize administrators, TV producers, educators, reviewers, and festival organizers—are descended from the middlebrow institutions of the mid twentieth century, operating in a digital environment with new global reach' (p. 4). Rather than abandon the term because of its derogatory usage meant to distinguish certain literary works from high art or to demean feminized consumers of mass-marketed, accessible literary works, Driscoll both seeks to explore the value of this term for discussion of the contemporary literary marketplace, middle-class readers, and their networks, and to defend the middlebrow from the quick dismissals of academic and other gatekeepers of elite cultural production. Following and expanding upon Pierre Bourdieu's work on literary production as well as his discussion of cultural, social, and symbolic capital translated in the 1980s and 1990s, Driscoll introduces her monograph with the delineation of eight characteristics that she uses to define the middlebrow. In terms of socio-economic class, the new literary middlebrow is 'middle class: the province of the educated and relatively wealthy who nonetheless desire increased status' (p. 43). Because of this positioning, middlebrow literary texts and their consumers can be defined by an 'aspirational' quality that denotes a longing for 'an entrée into the world of elite culture' (p. 43). Association with middle-class consumer patterns and desires can account for some of the pejorative ways in which the term 'middlebrow' is used; still, a third characteristic—'market-oriented distribution networks, [such as] the Book of the Month Club'—is more revealing in that some academic and other critics view the connection between art and commerce as suspect and imagine participants in such clubs as malleable consumers. Indeed, this assertion leads Driscoll to suggest that another aspect of the middlebrow is that it 'relies heavily on cultural intermediaries— salespeople, editors, and critics—'that provide accessible introductions to, advertisements for, and reviews of literary works and participate in shaping contemporary literary consumption and communities' (p. 43). As in previous generations, the middlebrow continues to be 'feminized, not only because its consumers are female, but also because it has been degraded in line with gender inequities that run across the literary field' (p. 43). This point leads Driscoll to identify three final characteristics: the middlebrow is 'emotional', 'recreational', and 'earnest' (pp. 43–4). In this way, middlebrow literary communities value affective responses to literary works as well as book clubs and online forums that foster intimate connections with other readers, celebrate recreational reading as a satisfying pastime that promotes personal growth, and position reading and participation in literary communities with an earnest belief in the connection between literary consumption and 'social responsibility' (p. 44). The full chapters of Driscoll's book are divided into discussions of online and offline books clubs, with a notable emphasis on the Oprah Book Club, analysis of 'Harry Potter and the middlebrow pedagogies of teachers', literary prizes, with a specific emphasis on the Man Booker prize, and literary festivals. For critics of twenty-first-century fiction, the second chapter's discussion of Jonathan Franzen's *The Corrections* and his thoughts on middlebrow readers and texts will be of interest, as will this chapter's discussion of memoir, including James Frey's *A Million Little Pieces* and Cheryl Strayed's *Wild*. While Driscoll does not provide close readings of these texts, this chapter nicely places such works within the phenomenon of Oprah's Book Club as a middlebrow institution that focuses on reading for personal transformation and connection with other earnest readers, as a form of social responsibility, and as a practice that reveres literary works as elevated cultural forms that ultimately inspire individual and perhaps social change. *The New Literary Middlebrow* gives academics the opportunity to reflect upon communities of readers outside institutions of higher education, and as such will be useful for scholars engaged in discussions of popular literary works, their non-academic reception, distribution, and marketing, and powerful forms of literary networks such as book clubs, online forums, and festivals.

The final portion of this section of the review will discuss a number of studies focused on a single author. *Dismembering the American Dream: The Life and Fiction of Richard Yates* by Kate Charlton-Jones is a thorough examination of Yates's oeuvre, including exploration of his stylistic connection to other realist authors of the nineteenth and early to mid-twentieth century, discussion of the major thematic components of his reflections upon 1950s and 1960s America, and illustration of his linkages to other mid-century literary authors. Acknowledging the scant critical and popular attention paid to Yates's work until the recent release of a film version of his *Revolutionary Road*, Charlton-Jones argues that the previous lack of interest in his work revolves around two primary separate phenomena. First, in the 1960s and 1970s, when Yates's published the majority of his work, readers were disinclined to look back to the 1950s, preferring instead to look forward to the possibilities of recent social movements and to celebrate the literary experimentation of writers associated with postmodernism. Compounding this problem for Yates's work is his focus upon characters' 'inertia, self-doubt, and sexual impotence' (p. 5). Charlton-Jones argue that, 'whereas writers such a Philip Roth, John Updike, and Saul Bellow insisted on the intellectual and emotional audacity of their characters, and found readers in great numbers, literary critics seemed to find no such insistence in Yates's fiction' (p. 5). So, too, critical attention from the 1990s to the turn of the century also tended to celebrate postmodern literary strategies and to ignore realist fiction, thereby sidelining realist texts. For Charlton-Jones, the omission of Yates's works from critical discussions is unfortunate because careful study of his novels and stories has much to offer critics interested in how this author and others update realist strategies to address mid-twentieth-century concerns. With depth and nuance, Charlton-Jones addresses this scholarly gap and positions Yates's aesthetic works within a deeper history of American realism while simultaneously maintaining a focus on the unique contributions that Yates offers to this tradition and to a broader understanding of the white middle class in the middle of the century.

This monograph makes three major interventions. First, Charlton-Jones intriguingly situates Yates's characterization and literary exploration of performances of identity within a shift in the social sciences as represented by George Herbert Mead and Erving Goffman. While she does not claim that Yates read works by these authors, Charlton-Jones shows how his work is influenced by the cultural circulation of theorizations of the self that these social scientists promoted, most notably 'the primary role of language in the formation of the self', 'the social bonds that inform personality', and Goffman's 'understanding of the human propensity for social "performance"' (p. 51). Because of Yates's enduring emphasis on how characters utilize idealized notions of self to inform their personal performances in ways that ultimately eschew a focus on an authentic self, she provides numerous close readings of his stories and scenes from novels that show how 'the performative nature of human behavior ... is the ontological starting point for all his work' (pp. 51–2). Even as the focus is on Yates here, this kind of positioning of his characterization within the context of mid-twentieth-century social sciences calls for greater study of realist works of the period and their relationship to thinkers like Goffman. Second, Charlton-Jones situates Yates's work in relation to postmodern authors like Barth and Vonnegut in surprising ways; rather than take for granted the opposition or radical difference of a mid-century realist and his postmodern counterparts, she explores the overlap between some thematic concerns—such as 'the premise that there is no self outside of performance'—even as she clearly illustrates how aesthetic strategies to explore such performance differ greatly as well as Yates's general disdain for postmodern experimentation (p. 86). This kind of scholarship models a way of reading mid-twentieth-century literature thematically to bring realist and postmodern fiction together while maintaining a clear view of the differing formal strategies and impact of specific works. Third, Charlton-Jones recuperates Yates's work by including him in a deeper history of realism in discussions of the influence of Fitzgerald, Henry James, and Hemingway and by comparing his texts to those written by more renowned contemporaries like Cheever, John O'Hara, and Raymond Carver. Always maintaining a focus on the unique accomplishments of Yates, Charlton-Jones nevertheless provides fruitful ground for a larger critical conversation about shifts in the realist endeavour and mid-century representations of the white middle class. In addition to these three interventions, *Dismembering the American Dream* offers commentary on Yates's critique of Hollywood cinema and its romanticized notions of ideal forms of masculinity and femininity, his exploration of how 'men, threated by female ambition, hold back the women they live with', and his critiques of 1950s suburban conformity in postwar America (p. 154). In sum, Charlton-Jones's monograph will inspire fans of Yates's fiction while also provoking critical conversations about realism, discussions of contrasting aesthetic strategies that emerged in mid-twentieth-century American fiction, and debates about representations of gender roles, suburban life, and the middle class following the Second World War.

Each of the authors—Roth, Updike, and Bellow—to whom Charlton-Jones compares Yates received greater critical attention in 2014. For example, Patrick Hayes's *Philip Roth: Fiction and Power* addresses one of Yates's more celebrated contemporaries through a focus on Roth's understanding of literature and power and his engagement with post-1945 theories of aesthetics and ethics. To begin, Hayes shows that Roth's work displays 'a distinctively post-Nietzschean way of valuing literature' that counters critical evaluations of the redemptive power of art to encourage readers to think about the relationships between 'literature, emotion, and ethics' (p. 11). Opposing Roth to Lionel Trilling and Martha Nussbaum, Hayes suggests that his works refuse to pose literature as a site for the formation of the 'right condition of the self' or for the experience of emotions 'that should play a part in . . . ethical decision making' (p. 11). Rather than focus on the 'refinement' of the self or the creation of sympathy within readers for the plights of others, Hayes argues that Roth explores literature's 'power, the way in which it generates compelling forms of intensity and vividness, and thereby [encourages readers] to discover heightened powers of self-creation' (p. 21). Because of this emphasis, Roth is closer to Susan Sontag's and Charles Altieri's renditions of Nietzschean aestheticism, which posits that 'the value of literature lies in its capacity to create awareness of human possibility by generating forms of becoming excessive to, and transgressive of, the depleted range of values established by subject-centered rationality' (p. 22). Still, for Hayes, Roth's work goes beyond these two writers' articulations of literature and power by maintaining a focus on both generating forms of intensity and reflecting upon such forms. Thus, irony becomes important for understanding Roth's work. Hayes argues, 'as "equation with action" the literary text is a performance that establishes value through aesthetic heightening, but as "symbolic action" it sustains a mode of ironic reflection on the nature and consequence of such heightening, rather than aiming to simply enrapture the reader in becoming itself' (p. 24). The aim of the monograph is to follow this insight and to explore with greater nuance Roth's reflection on various critical traditions that seek to define literature's relationship to ethics. As Hayes writes, his monograph tells 'the story of a writer who, distrustful of inherited ways of thinking about his art, starts to explore, with increasing power and audacity, what it means to undomesticate literature from the norms of those institutions and intellectuals who offer to judge and mediate it' (p. 27). In terms of structure, Hayes's first full chapter addresses the influence of 1950s intellectuals and writers associated with New Liberalism on Roth's early work, but later chapters move out to address a significant topic in post-1945 critical discussions of aesthetic value with a particular focus on 'questions about why we value tragedy, how we conceptualize the relationship between art and experience, how we judge the usefulness of literature to life, how the institution of authorship works, and the connection between art and the unconscious' (p. 28). Even as Hayes clearly celebrates Roth's achievements in this work, the monograph also is a fascinating account of shifting postwar debates about what literature does or should do for readers. As such, the monograph is not just a celebration of Roth's genius, but also gives critics the opportunity to reflect upon the past decades' debates about aesthetics, our own positioning within them, and one major author's critical assessment of them.

While Hayes focuses upon Roth's engagement with critical discussion of aesthetics, Laurence W. Mazzeno's *Becoming John Updike: Critical Reception, 1958–2010* attends to critical commentary on Updike's work with a comprehensive presentation of how reviewers and academics responded to specific texts and understood his importance to American letters. Exploring trends in critical reception chronologically through the 'decade of promise and anticipation' (1958–67), the 'breakthrough years' (1968–75), 'years of significant accomplishment' (1981–90), and the turn of the century and the beginning of the twenty-first (pp. 6, 27, 67), Mazzeno carefully maps constellations of critical consensus and divergence, thereby providing a clear account of the evolving assessments of the value of Updike's oeuvre within particular historical moments. The concluding chapters nicely trace competing contemporary evaluations of Updike's legacy, which celebrate him as a 'unique figure in the tradition of Hawthorne, Howells, and Edmund Wilson, dedicated to the task of ... explor[ing] American society and the American psyche', and view his works as displaying the ' "entropic vision" that characterizes modern life', or as an author who will continue to fall out of favour because of his limited focus upon 'white consciousness' (p. 148). Mazzeno's work effectively offers a deep view of the changing critical opinions about Updike while simultaneously exploring a few different directions that studies of his work are beginning to take following his death. Ultimately concluding that exciting studies of Updike will continue to appear despite some critical commentary to the contrary, Mazzeno provides a useful map of current trends and possible future directions.

Gloria L. Cronin and Lee Trepanier's edited collection *A Political Companion to Saul Bellow* addresses Bellow's shifting political allegiances, from his early commitment to Trotskyite communism to his later neoconservatism. Like Wald's *American Night* (reviewed last year in *YWES* 91[2012]), this collection opens with an account of how one author engaged with the literary and political Left, navigated the early years of the Cold War and continued to reflect upon the legacy of the Left even in much later decades of his career. With essayist Judie Newman's introduction to Bellow's Leftist political commitment, early publications in the Socialist Club of the University of Chicago's *Soapbox* as well as the radical student newspaper called *Daily Northwestern*, later publications in the *Partisan Review* and the presence of Trotskyist positions in his novel *Dangling Man* and early drafting of *The Adventures of Augie March*, the collection starts off by showing the substantial indebtedness of Bellow's work to Trotskyism that his 'reputation as a neoconservative has obscured' (p. 9). Still, the collection moves beyond the early years of his literary production to address representations of colonialism, race, gender, and Jewish identity in Bellow's larger oeuvre. For example, Carol R. Smith's powerful essay titled 'The Jewish Atlantic—The Deployment of Blackness in Saul Bellow' draws on Toni Morrison's concept of 'playing in the dark' and Paul Gilroy's theorization of the 'Black Atlantic' to explore how 'Bellow's construction of racial difference operates to reify a positive notion of the Enlightenment as central to assimilated (white) America' (p. 104). Viewing liberal humanism as a way to unite a 'politically divided America of the civil rights period and after', Bellow disavows the way the history of slavery and its legacy undermines a belief in the 'progressive trajectory of the Enlightenment' (pp. 104–5). Analysing 'Looking for Mr. Green', *Henderson the Rain King*, and *Mr. Sammler's Planet*, Smith highlights how Bellow depicts slavery 'as an exceptional aberration' that can be addressed by investing in European liberal humanism in the present, rather than acknowledging how 'the diaspora of Africans...problematiz[es] a belief' in it (pp. 123, 105). The collection concludes with a thorough annotated bibliography of secondary works focused on Bellow's politics compiled by editor Cronin, which serves as an effective resource for critics interested in this aspect of the author's work. With this annotated bibliography and strong essays throughout, editors and essayists surely will achieve their goal of sparking a 'broader conversation about Saul Bellow's political thought' (p. 7).

In addition to Cronin and Trepanier's book, another collection published in the University Press of Kentucky's series Political Companions to Great American Authors also warrants mention. *A Political Companion to Walker Percy*, edited by Peter Augustine Lawler and Brian A. Smith, explores Percy's works with emphasis on his Catholicism, especially his relationship to American Thomism: 'the harmonization of what we know through science and what we know through revelation' (p. 2). Beyond this focus, chapters address Percy's political thoughts on segregation, his engagement with Kierkegaard, Descartes, and Tocqueville, his critique of radical individualism, his grappling with scientism, and his depictions of religion in the South. The collection is an exciting contribution to scholarly studies of the political and philosophical import of Percy's writing, especially in relation to critical accounts of the continued value of religious thinking in major works of the late twentieth century. In this way, the collection echoes the spirit of LeMathieu's *Fictions of Fact and Value* (OUP [2013]; reviewed in *YWES* 94[2015]) because of a shared emphasis upon a need to re-evaluate literary works that engage with 'the postwar crisis of belief', the '"something more" that escapes [scientific] definitions of the human organism', and the 'antinomy between scientific and spiritual commitments' (LeMathieu, p. 67).

Beyond the political context and the critical reception of late twentieth-century authors, Tim Hunt's *The Textuality of Soulwork: Jack Kerouac's Quest for Spontaneous Prose* turns to an exploration of mid-century literary form(s) with a fresh examination of Kerouac's import for understanding the challenges and promises that new technologies posed for writers. To begin, Hunt argues that Kerouac 'sought to write as if language as speaking were primary', thereby 'writing against the grain of a fundamental feature of writing: the way it...transforms language from a process happening in time...into a system operating in and from the space of the page' (p. 178). In this way, Hunt shows how he attempted 'to subvert his era's paradigm for textuality and reinvent the category of literature as an expression of what might be termed secondary literacy' (p. 10). Expanding on Walter J. Ong's *Orality and Literacy: The Technologizing of the Word* (Methuen [1982]), Hunt defines this term as 'a literacy in which writing's committing of language to space has been disrupted by and complicated by the way modern technologies of voice recommit language to time' (p. 181). This dual focus upon Kerouac's desire to counter established ways of understanding writing and to reflect upon how technological developments from the 1880 media revolution through the 1950s created new opportunities and problems for writers provides a compelling framework for re-evaluating this author. Examining the drafting of *On The Road*, Kerouac's journals and letters, his unpublished work journal from the fall of 1951, and his 'magnum opus', *Visions of Cody*, Hunt's monograph clearly will interest scholars of the Beat Generation, but also those invested in studies of mid-century writers' formal experimentation in the context of reflections on technological developments, especially analogue sound recording and radio.

Thomas Pynchon has clearly received more critical attention than the authors discussed above; last year alone three publications were reviewed that focus entirely on his work, and this year the publication of one collection and two monographs will allow this trend to continue. *Pynchon's California*, edited by Scott McClintock and John Miller, is a stellar contribution to Pynchon studies because of its focus on the California novels and its successful effort to show how examination of these supposed 'lesser' texts elucidates the major themes in the longer, critically celebrated works. Expanding from and countering previous criticism that shows how Pynchon's California 'invokes a familiar postmodern dialectic of surface and emptiness', essays in this collection examine the novelist's engagement with the 'myth' of American progress where the 'new is privileged over' engagement with history, and settlement and resettlement involve a process of 'erasure and reconstruction' in which the dispossession of indigenous populations as well as the wilful forgetting of waves of invading prospectors is subsumed under presentist projections of new designs for development and commercial enterprise (pp. 2–4). Still, the collection reveals that alongside a deep engagement with the myth of California as a site for reinvention, which fuels late capitalist mappings of space, lies an equally compelling focus on the local and situated histories of conflict in the state and the possibilities for alternative community structures and countercultures that avoid a total disavowal of the historically and presently dispossessed. In general, essayists 'reject the pessimistic reading of Pynchon's California novels as portraying...any totalizing order of domination by postmodern, late "Capital"' and instead explore 'the significance of feeling, hope, and even transcendence' in Pynchon's depiction of strategies of resistance to such domination (pp. 8–9). In this way, *Pynchon's California* provides fresh readings of *The Crying of Lot 49*, *Vineland*, and *Inherent Vice*, which will spark debate about the novelist's engagement with specific histories of California and his situated discussion of development and

redevelopment in these texts, the import of his representations of counterculture and 'countermemory' as a form of opposition to dominant narratives of
development and its connection to global circuits of capital, his attention to
environmental devastation and textual 'ecological awareness', and his usage of
the noir or detective fiction tradition. This collection will be essential reading
for scholars of Pynchon's work but will also hold the interest of researchers
committed to studying representations of California, its mythic status in the
American imaginary, and literary representations of historical, social,
economic, and political transformation within the state as well as their
connections to related shifts within the larger nation.

A second text moves past a focus on the value of a regional analysis to
examine Pynchon's work in relation to Carlos Fuentes, thereby contributing to
hemispheric American studies and the evaluation of the correlation between
satires of two major authors who both aim to challenge national master-
narratives. *After the Nation: Postnational Satire in the Works of Carlos Fuentes
and Thomas Pynchon* by Pedro García-Caro expands on previous accounts of
postmodern satire to show that these two authors' 'markedly different
aesthetic projects are inflected with a common satirical defiance of official
archives in their ideological function as sacred repositories of national
essences' (p. 20). Drawing on studies of nationalism by Eric Hobsbawm,
Benedict Anderson, Étienne Balibar, and Homi Bhabha, García-Caro
provides an opening discussion of the ways that nationalist discourses create
'the fantasy that the nation is a continuum of affects and practices, as if
cultural history was a result of essentialized static repetitions rather than a
series of conflicts, crises, innovations, and imitations within a shifting
community of individuals and groups over time' (p. 5). While nationalist
history is cleansed of its 'dissident voices ... except in the form of an outside or
defeated "other"', so, too, nationalism as ideology relies on 'a language whose
universal grammar consists of absolute beginnings, perfect preterites, indicative presents, and a manifest future' (p. 5). Narratives of history, the present,
and the future in nationalist discourse ultimately rely on a negation of a
variety of others that might challenge the dominant constitution of fantasies of
national identity and the progressive movement of the nation into a destined
futurity. García-Caro writes, 'In nationalist narratives, the past almost always
prefigures the present as it shoots out into a shared futurity' (p. 7).

This clear theoretical introduction sets the stage for García-Caro's larger
argument that both Fuentes and Pynchon succeed through satire in
challenging nationalist narratives that eschew the conflicts of history and the
present, that disavow the voices of the marginalized, and that confirm the
nation's progressive and destined march into a brighter future. In their
satirical historiographic metafiction, García-Caro shows that they 'fictionalize
history ... not only [to] problematize the access to the archive, [but also to
offer] an alternate, critical, and more ethically productive type of historical
account' that calls readers to undermine 'nationalism's self-evident truths'
about the past, present, and future (pp. 20, 27). Suggesting that such works be
included in the 'emerging postnational canon', García-Caro argues that even
though their texts do not imagine a postnational utopia, they do defy the
'narrative logic of national progressions' and 'the national claims of

exceptionality' and thus provide ways of seeing 'complex fractures and contradictions...on both sides of the imaginary and real line that segregates the continent' (pp. 16, 27, 25). For García-Caro, this process of dismantling hegemonic national narratives through satire and 'exploring the spaces and crevices of resistance' makes both authors key to understanding the contemporary postnational novel (p. 27). In regard to structure, García-Caro divides the monograph into sections that explore the novelists' examination of futurity, the present, and the past as they address national narratives and undermine them with alternative presentations of temporality and spatiality. He examines futurity with primary attention to Fuentes' *La región más transparente* and Pynchon's *V*, the present with a focus on *La muerte de Artemio Cruz*, *Cambio de piel*, and *The Crying of Lot 49*, and history with close readings of *La Campaña* and *Mason & Dixon*. Still, because García-Caro peppers his monograph with references to many other postnational satires and post-1945 works more broadly, the text reaches out to intervene in larger discussions of contemporary literature that challenge fantasies of the nation. In sum, García-Caro's *After the Nation* is an exemplary monograph that reveals the import and analytical power of the transnational turn in American studies and is specifically important as a contribution to Pynchon scholarship because it brings this author into conversation with a key figure in the contemporary Mexican literary canon in ways that show a shared concern with challenging national narratives.

A second monograph on Pynchon's work, Martin Paul Eve's *Pynchon and Philosophy: Wittgenstein, Foucault and Adorno*, is a necessary, erudite, and masterful rendering of the novelist's engagement with key philosophical ideas about ethics, language, and politics in the twentieth century. Rather than focus on a single influence or create a simplified account of Pynchon's critique or support of certain key philosophical concepts, Eve situates extended analysis of novels within nuanced investigation of the novelist's at times critical and, at other moments, complementary relation to discussion of ethics in works by Wittgenstein, Foucault, and Adorno. For example, in analysis of *V*, Eve argues that 'Pynchon is, in his first presentation of Wittgenstein, deeply hostile to logical positivism as a reductive world view that enacts an Adornian transit towards obliteration, at the terminus of which sits the Holocaust' (p. 22). Still, Eve shows that Pynchon's engagement with Wittgenstein is much more complex than vehement dismissal. He argues, 'In Pynchon's work, early Wittgenstein is situated within a framework of totalitarianism, perhaps for its atomizing, logical perspective. Conversely, the late anti-Platonic, anti-Cartesian standpoint in *PI* [*Philosophical Investigations*] certainly resonates with Pynchon's work against such systems' (p. 71). Viewing multiple engagements with Wittgenstein's work—both early and late—in Pynchon's texts, Eve provides an in-depth view of his dismissal of logical positivism, his critique of Romanticism within and beyond Wittgenstein's texts, and Pynchon's complementary critique of a 'Platonic standpoint', 'a commitment to some, if not all, of these totalitarian, non-spatio-temporal abstract[ions]' (p. 69). In this way, Eve charts Pynchon's engagement with mid-century philosophical debates with care, teasing out literary stances that investigate the damaging potentialities for certain understandings of language and ethics as well as promising conceptualizations. With his discussion of Foucault and Pynchon, Eve contrasts the philosopher's and novelist's understanding of and representation of the Enlightenment with a particular emphasis on the novelist's ability to depict 'simultaneous Enlightenment stances... [that] collapse the historical progression that Foucault articulates' in the late 1970s (p. 100). As with the analysis of Wittgenstein's texts, Eve offers readers other accounts of the connection between Foucault and Pynchon by exploring how both thinkers engage with 'resistance and revolution' and ethics as well as the limits and possibilities of self-fashioning (pp. 122–3). The final turn to Adorno and Pynchon in the monograph reads the novelist's work within an Adornian frame, in which 'Pynchon's refusal of synthesis, constellatory mode, refusal of idealism, disdain for logical positivism and (ir)regulative utopia align him with this school of thought' (p. 172). Because of its masterful analysis of both philosophical and literary works and truly fresh insights into Pynchon's engagement with multiple theories of ethics, Eve's *Pynchon and Philosophy* is a major new contribution to Pynchon studies.

In editor Marshall Boswell's collection titled *David Foster Wallace and 'The Long Thing': Essays on the Novels*, he begins by situating Wallace's novels within the context of Edward Mendelson's discussion of Pynchon and the encyclopedic novel. Still, essayists and the editor seek to explore the nuances of Wallace's novels with an eye towards how his long fiction 'epitomize[s] the form but also interrogate[s] and parod[ies] it' (p. viii). Further, essayists explore Wallace's engagement with philosophical thinkers such as Kierkegaard, Wittgenstein, and Derrida. The collection also includes four essays on *The Pale King*, much of which 'originated as papers or keynote addresses delivered at a September 2011 conference held in Antwerp, Belgium' focused on this unfinished novel (p. xii). The collection's essays appeared earlier in two issues of *Studies in the Novel* (*SNNTS* 44:iii[2012]; 44:iv[2012]). Still, Boswell notes that they have been altered for this collection and rearranged to group articles that discuss major trends across the novels with each other and to position articles on a single novel together. As a whole, the collection provides provocative new directions for scholarship on Wallace.

In terms of the publication of monographs focused on single authors, the University of South Carolina Press proved to be a major contributor with six separate monographs in its Understanding Contemporary American Literature series appearing in 2014. *Understanding Dave Eggers* by Timothy W. Galow opens with a narrative summary of the author's literary production, from the publication of *A Heartbreaking Work of Staggering Genius* to *A Hologram for the King*. It also includes a brief account of Eggers's work in film and his philanthropic work with 826 National, a group of literary centres dedicated to helping children improve their writing skills and to fostering creativity, and Voice of Witness, 'a non-profit organization devoted to publishing the stories of people affected by human rights abuses' (p. 6). Following this short ten-page introduction, *Understanding Dave Eggers* provides six chapters, each of which focuses on a single work, and one chapter dedicated to his short-story collections. Chapter 2, simply titled '*A Heartbreaking Work of Staggering Genius*', nicely captures critics' focus on the way that the text challenges 'the conventions of memoir writing and scrutinize[s] the genre's implicit claims to truth' (p. 11). Further, Galow addresses the self-consciousness of the work as well as the way in which the novel 'foregrounds the limitations of individual perspectives' by frequently undermining the narrator's presentation and interpretation of events within the text (p. 15). Yet even as the work displays the self-reflexivity associated with postmodernism, Galow provides an account of this type of authorial strategy that highlights both the impossibility of presenting an accurate reconstruction of past events and the continued desire to 'transcend banality and get at "the core"' of the narrator's experiences of grief and familial love as well as understandings of self (p. 15). Situating the text within 'post-postmodern half irony' identified by critic Lee Siegel, Galow shows how the features identified in earlier postmodern novels are utilized in this work with a sincerity meant to provide an account of the 'emotional struggle' at the 'center of the book' (p. 20). Galow also highlights in this chapter the text's attention to popular culture and 'manufactured sentimentality', fame and the culture of celebrity, and the difficulty of creating art that 'transcends the clichés of contemporary culture' (pp. 22, 25).

Turning to *You Shall Know Our Velocity!* in the next chapter, Galow similarly highlights the novel's self-reflexivity, the narrator's limited perspective, and the tonal mix of 'self-parody' and 'sincerity'. Still, his account of Eggers's second work reveals the greater ambition of this novel in that it combines an 'existential meditation on existence' with an 'allegory about contemporary humanitarian intervention' as well as exploration of 'arrogant Western intervention' (pp. 38–9). For Galow, the major contribution of this work is its ability both to critique certain forms of charity as the main character Will 'struggle[es] to overcome his privilege and to find a new language for encountering the "other"' and to promote the continued engagement with 'moral ambiguities' and 'logical complexities' of action in the world to address social injustice (pp. 39–40). In this way, Galow argues, the novel's satirical engagement with humanitarian efforts does not lead to inaction, but instead calls for an acknowledgement of the ethical complexities of such action while 'blunder[ing] ahead, never leaving the challenges entirely behind but also not letting them stand in the way of a genuine attempt to reach out' (p. 40).

With analysis of Eggers's *What Is the What* and *Zeitoun* in the next two chapters, Galow traces a turn in Eggers's literary production in which he focuses on victims of human rights abuses, creating 'narrative accounts of the tragedies, told from the perspective of particular protagonists (as opposed to . . . works that attempt to document the tragedies from a more removed, historical perspective)' (p. 64). Even as Eggers refers to *What Is the What* as a 'fictionalized autobiography' of Sudanese refugee Valentino Achak Deng and classifies *Zeitoun* as a non-fictional account of the Zeitoun family's experiences during and after Hurricane Katrina, Galow highlights in his analysis how both texts claim 'authenticity' and seek 'to relate larger truths' about the specific experiences of his collaborators (p. 64). Taken together, both works, in Galow's account, utilize 'an accessible human story' to 'frame a larger crisis', either in the Sudan or in the United States (p. 58). Still, there are striking differences between the texts, even as they share this focus. For one, *What Is the What* continues to play with the difficulty of representing individual identity—albeit an identity shaped by the second Sudanese Civil War—and creating narrative representations of events that refuse to over-simplify the war or individual experiences during the conflict. For Galow, this play with representation and truthful narrative provides a 'commentary on the power of narrative more generally' and counters popular media accounts in the United States that focus on 'shocking stories' or remain indifferent to the plight of refugees while simultaneously confronting the 'complex accounts that emerge through the Sudanese government's propaganda' (p. 58). In contrast, *Zeitoun*'s identification as a work of non-fiction 'with multiple references in the paratextual material to fact checking, independent sources, and processes of verification' shows a 'notable' shift in Eggers's rhetorical strategies for addressing violations of human rights (p. 65). Less concerned with revealing the construction of a narrative or highlighting the fictional quality of any single narrative, *Zeitoun* embraces the 'journalistic process', despite the potential for some inaccurate recollection of familial conversations or responses to Hurricane Katrina and its aftermath (p. 65). By sidelining the issue of narrative construction, Eggers can focus on multiple forms of criticism about the nation's response to this tragedy. Galow ultimately argues that the text 'targets the broken system' of government response to natural disaster, 'a system that was quickly fashioned under pressure from hysterical media coverage, the real needs of people trapped in an underwater city, and a vast military apparatus with virtually unchecked powers' (p. 76). With analysis of both of these works, Galow nicely situates close readings within the context of critical reception of the works. With *What Is the What*, Galow highlights how critics explore the ethical implications of the author's utilization of Deng's story as either 'post-colonial arrogance' or thoughtful collaboration (p. 63). With *Zeitoun*, Galow discusses how the divorce of Abdulrahman and Kathy Zeitoun as well as Kathy's charges of domestic abuse have complicated the 'truthfulness' of the narrative that Eggers produced. Other chapters and the afterword in this book address Eggers's short-story collections and films as well as *A Hologram for the King* and *The Circle*. With discussion of these two recent novels, Galow focuses his discussion around Eggers's take on multinational corporations and technological advancement as well as the ethical problems that both of these phenomenon pose for characters.

Another monograph in the series that addresses a post-postmodernist author, *Understanding Michael Chabon* by Joseph Dewey, provides a lively and beautifully written account of Chabon's literary works from his early 'realistic narratives of introspective, creative, nerdy isolates gifted/cursed with energetic imaginations who come to tap...the tonic wonder of community and the tectonic impact of love' to his later invigorating play with 'hoary genres that had long been dismissed by establishment critics as low-octane market-driven entertainments', including novels of fantasy, noir murder mystery, and sci-fi (pp. 18–19). Although this text's primary aim is to provide an overview of Chabon's works, it does connect nicely to recent criticism on a late twentieth- and early twenty-first-century shift from postmodernism. Dewey writes of Chabon and other post-postmodernists that they 'brought together the defining elements of the two principal expressions of the American narrative at mid-century: the formal extravagances of the postmodern era and the compelling consolations of old school storytelling' (p. 2). Arguing that Chabon combines the 'excesses and self-conscious audacity' of writers like Pynchon with the 'psychological realism of John Updike', Dewey still maintains a focus on this author's unique vision that 'treats the anxious tension between escape and engagement, between the sweet, centripetal pull of the redemptive imagination...and the harsh, centrifugal pull of real life' (pp. 2–3, 4). Beyond identifying this theme throughout Chabon's literary works, Dewey also intriguingly positions Chabon's experiments with multiple genres in the first decade of the millennium within the context of post-9/11 fiction, as literary attempts 'to minister to a culture in shock' and the recent *Telegraph Avenue* as a '[narrative] of the Obama era', which 'tap[s] the rich energy of the imagination to transcend entrenched boundaries of race, gender, sexual orientation, and income' (pp. 20–1). This kind of seductive and effective framing of Chabon's work in combination with detailed and exuberant close reading of his novels as well as references to biographical information and critical reception make *Understanding Michael Chabon* an exhilarating contribution to studies of post-postmodernism and one of its major authors.

Understanding Richard Russo by Kathleen Drowne, a third work in this series, offers a nice overview of Russo's work from his first published novel *Mohawk* to *That Old Cape Magic*. The introduction provides a brief biographical sketch of his early years in Glowersville, New York, his enrolment at the University of Arizona as an undergraduate and graduate student, and his ultimate acceptance of various faculty positions. Additionally, the short introductory chapter traces some of Russo's influences, including Dickens, Twain, and Steinbeck, as well as his admiration for his contemporaries, including Richard Yates, Alice Munro, and John Cheever. Still, the primary aim of this piece is to set up the major themes that Drowne identifies in Russo's oeuvre. These include attention to place, especially depictions of 'struggling small towns left behind by the global economy', investigation of socioeconomic class with a particular emphasis on 'the strategies that the working class enacts to survive in environments that offer few options for employment and even fewer opportunities for advancement', exploration of tense relationships between parents and children as well as husbands and wives, illustrations of relationships between working-class white men, and engagement with slapstick and more nuanced comedy (pp. 12–13). In general, each of the following chapters of *Understanding Richard Russo* develops Drowne's overview of these themes in greater depth. For instance, in the second chapter, 'Mohawk', Drowne shows how each of these major themes appears in the text with particular attention to the struggles of a small town with the decline of local industry and the 'toll that environmental contamination takes on the workers at manufacturing plants' (p. 19). Highlighting the text's blue-collar workers' desire for a return to the heyday of tanneries that provided employment opportunities and acknowledgement of the impact of such industries on environmental and human health, Drowne argues that this novel introduces a large theme in Russo's work in which labourers feel 'loyalty for industries that poison their water and yet at the same time provide them with paychecks to feed their families' (p. 23). In this way, Drowne combines analysis of the novel's engagement with socioeconomic class with blue-collar critique of the labour policies of local tanneries and discussion of the regional environmental devastation of such industries that impacts both the health of the full ecosystem and the humans that inhabit it. Despite wider critical dismissal of this first novel, Drowne shows how *Mohawk* remains an important work because it sets the stage for Russo's later and more successful novelistic engagement with socioeconomic class, 'the aspirations of upward mobility, the fears of downward mobility, the tremendous challenges' that working-class labourers and their families face in declining-industry towns (p. 18).

With the third chapter's analysis of *The Risk Pool*, Drowne further traces Russo's exploration of socioeconomic class with a particular focus on how this novel gives a young working-class man—Ned Hall—room to contemplate the financial struggles of his family as well as the wealthier members of the same small-town community as the one depicted in Russo's first novel, *Mohawk*. Highlighting Ned's and other characters' thoughts about economic hardships and fantasies about the lives of the financially secure, Drowne ultimately argues that the novel shows how working-class people 'struggle to make ends meet in their battered little towns, but through lack of imagination, education, employment opportunities, will, or some combination thereof, they seldom succeed at leaving these little towns behind' (p. 37). Even those who do leave the small town of Mohawk, like Ned, find that they continue to be tied to the town left behind, especially because of the vibrant 'community and communal bonds' that exist despite the economic hardships facing declining factory or mill towns (p. 43). With chapter 4, Drowne turns her attention to *Nobody's Fool* by examining the difficulties of relationships between fathers and sons as well as the import of friendships between working-class men in the novel. Chapter 5's close reading of the academic satire *Straight Man* focuses on Russo's effective usage of slapstick and bodily humour as well as his mastery of witty dialogue. Positioning this fourth novel within the context of other works that address academic life such as Mary McCarthy's *The Groves of Academe*, Randall Jarrell's *Pictures from an Institution*, and Kingsley Amis's *Lucky Jim*, Drowne provides important context for this work, even as she ultimately argues that the novel is less about academe than it is about a mid-life crisis of a settled man who longs for the 'unpredictability' of his life before tenure (p. 60). Examinations of *Empire Falls*, *Bridge of Sighs*, and *That Old Cape Magic* in subsequent chapters as well as a final chapter focused on Russo's short-story collections as well as his memoir, *Elsewhere*, and his most recent novella titled *Nate in Venice* continue evaluation of the aforementioned topics. In sum, Drowne's examination of Russo's first four novels effectively maps key overlapping themes with short chapters that could usefully be assigned in the undergraduate classroom.

Thomas Fahy's *Understanding Truman Capote* similarly provides an accessible introduction to Capote's work; still, the stakes of this monograph are substantial as Fahy succeeds in addressing this author's marginalization within queer theory and southern literary studies as well as recuperating the political import of Capote's aesthetic engagement with the 'social anxieties surrounding race relations, gender, sexuality, communism, capitalist culture, the atomic age, poverty, and delinquency in the 1940s and 1950s' (p. 12). Because of Fahy's attention to the 'sociopolitical subtext of Capote's work', he offers a fresh take on it for broader discussions of literary reflections on postwar American culture. For example, in chapter 2's discussion of *A Tree of Night and Other Stories*, Fahy provides close readings of stories to show ways in which the collection as a whole reflects the uncertainty within the nation in the wake of the Second World War. He writes, 'Capotes' collection portrays individuals, like the decade of the 1940s itself, as fragmented—torn between security and fear, communal engagement and isolationism, public and private identity' as a way to highlight 'the tensions characterizing contemporary American culture, which longed to retreat from its global responsibilities as a result of World War II, from the terrifying implications of the atomic age, and from dramatic social changes at home' (pp. 17–18). Further, Fahy argues that the collection critiques this desire for retreat from the terrors of modern life through 'consumer culture and popular entertainment', which serves both as an ineffective balm for contemporary anxieties and as a dangerous escapism that 'encourages greater disengagement from the social and political' (p. 38). With analysis of *Other Voices, Other Rooms*, Fahy provides a deeply moving account of the novel's depiction of the 'brutal inequities at the heart of American society' by 'reject[ing] the silences surrounding violence against black women and homophobia' (p. 45). In Fahy's account, the novel not only explores social marginalization in ways that connect homophobia and racism, but ultimately posits that racism is 'far more insidious than homophobia in America' with depictions of Zoo's rape in the novel (p. 59). Because white gay men have the privilege of their whiteness and because both straight and gay white men 'still rely on the exploitation of black labor', 'racism . . . seems less surmountable than homophobia' (p. 60). In later chapters, Fahy addresses *The Grass Harp* and *The Muses Are Heard* within the context of McCarthyism, *Breakfast at Tiffany's* in connection to Kinsey and the 'sexual conservatism' of the dominant popular culture of the 1950s, and *In Cold Blood* with reference to Cold War fears of invasion, dreams of social mobility, and the realities of mid-century poverty, as well as the texts' reflection upon the Beat writers.

The two remaining volumes published last year in this series are *Understanding Steven Millhauser* by Earl G. Ingersoll and *Understanding Ron Rash* by John Lang. Ingersoll's work opens with a discussion of the dearth of critical attention to Millhauser's literary production, suggesting that this may be due to the author's refusal of self-promotion and disdain for the desire to use biographical information either to construct a public persona or to interpret literary production. Positioning Millhauser as an 'heir' of New Criticism, Ingersoll highlights the author's desire for his art 'to be not interpreted in terms of the author's work, the work's historical context, psychoanalytic theory, and so forth, but only in terms of the works themselves' (p. 1). With each chapter, Ingersoll follows suit, offering thorough close readings of novels, story collections, and novellas. Analysis of Millhauser's early fiction—*Edwin Mullhouse: The Life and Death of an American Writer 1943–1954 by Jeffrey Cartwright* and *Portrait of a Romantic*—centres on Millhauser's depictions of children and young adults, proposing that the author explores the 'genius' of children in their imaginative powers, which the

' "progress" toward adulthood' dulls, thereby 'eradicate[ing]' the 'creativity... that qualifies anyone to become a writer' (p. 12). The chapters on these two novels also explore the novelist's engagement with biography and memoir. For example, readings of *Edwin Mullhouse* investigate the critique of biography in the novel as a practice of 'murder[ing]' the subject, 'turning living monuments into stone' (p. 2) and interrogation of *Portrait* examines the two aspects of the narrator as character and memoirist (p. 27). With discussion of his later work, Ingersoll frequently focuses on Millhauser's combination of realism and fantasy, arguing that he 'ground[s] his narrative in a scrupulously realist world, often with a plethora of details, then subtly move[s] across an imaginary line into the world of fantasy' (p. 5). Ingersoll's close reading of *Martin Dressler*, Millhauser's Pulitzer Prize-winning novel, illustrates this claim by arguing that the author 'push[es] the narrative beyond conventional limits, and demand[s] that his readers follow him into fantasy worlds whose realistic detail support our notion of their "reality" ' (p. 88). Finally, Ingersoll also investigates Millhauser's 'idiosyncratic melding of art and technology' in which he 'resuscitat[es] that tradition of the artist/inventors for a historical period beginning in the nineteenth century and continuing into the twenty-first, a tradition of seeing art and technology not as enemies but companions' (p. 14). As a strong introduction to Millhauser's work, Ingersoll's monograph shows that this author deserves more critical attention and provides multiple inspirational avenues for such future engagement.

Lang's monograph on Ron Rash also provides a nice overview of his short-story collections, poetry, and novels. Situating Rash as a regionalist with universal appeal, Lang traces a variety of influences including Jesse Stuart, Faulkner, Flannery O'Connor, Hemingway, and Wendell Berry. As a part of the Appalachian Renaissance, Lang connects Rash's interest in preserving the region in aesthetic production to a desire to capture the landscape and culture that are changing rapidly due to 'technological and economic changes', to acknowledge and 'commemorate Appalachian history and culture['s]... relevance to fundamental human concerns', and to showcase 'humanity's profound dependence upon the well-being of nature' (pp. 4–5). Each chapter of the book groups a few different texts together. For example, one chapter focuses on three story collections—*The Night the New Jesus Fell to Earth*, *Casualties*, and *Chemistry and Other Stories*—and another pairs his well-known novel *Serena*, recently made into a film, with *The Cove*. In this way, Lang illustrates different moments in Rash's writing life, demarcating shared concerns in works produced during a specific stage of his career, while attending to common themes throughout his oeuvre. Further, Lang offers pertinent information about the publishing history of each text, reviews of individual works, and necessary biographical information, with particular attention to inclusion of Rash's commentary on his life and work as well as its reception and influences.

Three other works appeared in 2014 that deserve mention at the close of this portion of the review. Jonathan R. Eller's *Ray Bradbury Unbound*, the sequel to his *Becoming Ray Bradbury*, offers a comprehensive examination of Bradbury's work during the 1950s and 1960s. Placing Bradbury's more well-known accomplishments from this period 'within the context of other [less celebrated published] writings, his successful media ventures, and the far broader but largely hidden record of his unproduced adaptations and unpublished lectures' (p. 4), Eller's nearly 300-page work will be essential for fans and critics of this author. George Slusser's contribution to the University of Illinois Press's Modern Masters of Science Fiction series titled *Gregory Benford* provides a detailed examination of this major science fiction writer. Acknowledging Benford's status as a 'hard SF writer', Slusser argues that this scientist and novelist believes that his 'task [as a writer] is to present the working scientist as explorer, as seeker of knowledge to be used by humans in what humanists see as the increasingly dehumanized world modern science has created' (p. 3). Beyond focusing on the humanist impulse of his work, Slusser seeks to complicate critical understanding of Benford by positioning him, 'by his dates' as a 'New Wave Writer, the contemporary of Harlan Ellison, Philip K. Dick, and Ursula Le Guin' (p. 4). Attending to Benford's relationship to other science fiction writers as well as the scientific sources from which he draws inspiration for his works and offering detailed readings of specific key novels, Slusser offers rich critical analysis that will interest SF scholars. Finally, *Hemingway, Cuba, and the Cuban Works*, edited by Larry Grimes and Bickford Sylvester, includes essays that address 'Hemingway's place in Cuban history and culture, Cuban evaluations of the man and his work', 'moments in Hemingway's life as an American in Cuba', and analysis of Hemingway's work with 'an explicit Cuban setting' (pp. xi–xii). As this quick overview has shown, 2014 turned out to be an exciting year for monographs and collections focused on single authors, especially because of the attention to less frequently studied authors like Yates, focus on new critical directions in reference to established post-1945 literary figures like Roth and Bellow, and timely consideration of figures of import to the current literary scene, including Chabon and Eggers.

4. Comics

This section opens with reviews of late arrivals from 2013. Ruth Mayer's *Fu Manchu: The Chinese Supervillain and the Spread of Yellow Peril Ideology* explains the character's remarkable popularity from around 1910 to 1970 as well as its almost total disappearance since then. Mayer argues that it is the nature of serials to 'spread' across time, genre, and media, and characters in serials becomes 'figures'. They possess a handful of recognizable features that can be moved from one genre or medium to the next, and this type of figure is, of course, particularly well suited to depicting stereotypes, in this case, one that embodies the Anglo-American fear of Chinese infiltration. Methodologically, Mayer eschews close reading, the tendency to zoom in on exceptional texts with clear boundaries, and instead embraces historiographical and formal aesthetics. The book analyses a collection of moments within the 'spread' of Fu Manchu, specifically moments of retooling and rebooting the figure, many of which moments occur when he appears in a new medium or genre. Mayer's text contains six chapters, the first of which is an extended discussion of seriality theory as it relates to Fu Manchu. The rest of the chapters follow the figure through time while he transitions from one medium to the next. Chapters 2 and 3 look at prose and film, respectively, while Chapter 5 examines comics, arguing that they are a quintessentially serial medium, and that as such they are akin to earthquake detectors, recording minor tremors in the cultural landscape, but in so doing, defining the normal as well as the abnormal in a classic Self–Other relation. Fu Manchu's comic-book appearances include official ones under the original copyright as well as those analogues—figures that retain the original's recognizability—such as Marvel Comics' 'Yellow Claw' or 'The Doctor' in Moore and O'Neill's *League of Extraordinary Gentlemen*. The chapter therefore spends a great deal of time on questions of copyright and audience identification. Finally, chapter 6 answers the question initially asked in chapter 1: why did the figure disappear? While Mayer attributes this partly to growing distaste for its racism, she also notes the rise of Chinese mass-media production, specifically film and television, through which the figure was inverted from an evil mastermind into a mystic and/or master of martial arts.

Karin Kukkonen's relatively slim volume, *Studying Comics and Graphic Novels,* is an introductory textbook designed to help students engage with comics on a critical level. It is also explicitly grounded in cognitive approaches to comics, concerned with bodies as much as minds. The writing style is slightly more casual than that used in critical research, using the second-person 'you' for example, and thus would probably be more approachable for undergraduate students. The introduction also contains what amounts to a brief discussion of the definition of comics, but Kukkonen does it inside out: presenting the elements that people have identified as defining comics without ever asserting one particular definition. This is a very poststructuralist move, one that includes the definitional debate while also sidestepping it. Each of the six chapters contains several subsections, which will surely help readers to navigate the book, but it also potentially encourages them to read discrete sections out of context. The chapters also contain short introductory paragraphs that describe what they hold, a healthy number of visual examples from a variety of kinds of comics, and 'boxed' discussions on discrete topics such as 'Faces, Emotions, and Characters' in chapter 1. Finally, each chapter ends with a checklist of the major ideas in it and a bibliography of recommended readings. In short, it is a textbook that happens to cover comics exclusively. The six chapters cover a variety of topics and work their way from the formalism of the page to the act of writing an essay about comics. Chapter 1, 'What's in a Page', contains four sections and gives the basic concepts and terminology for close analysis of sequential art as an art form. Chapter 2, 'The Way Comics Tell It', is essentially on narratology, and takes the position that all narratives have narrators. Chapter 3, 'Narrating Minds and Bodies', is on autobiographical comics and their embodiedness, and is the only one to focus on one genre exclusively. Chapter 4, 'Novels and Graphic Novels', looks at adaptations of prose novels into comics, comparing the different narrative strategies of the two genres. The absence of a discussion of adaptation *from* comics *to* prose as well as to/from other media (e.g., film, animation, video games) is curious. Sandra Eva Boschenhoff's *Tall Tales in Comic Diction* (WVT [2014]) is a book-length consideration of this very same topic. Chapter 5, 'Comics and Their History', presents an Americentric timeline that essentially starts in Europe, moves to America, and stays there, largely discussing the United States mainstream comic-book industry. Finally, chapter 6, 'The Study and Criticism of Comics', provides specific tools for students to write essays about comics: how to find them, how to find criticism on them, different critical approaches, and then a step-by-step guide to the construction of an actual essay. This last chapter is bound to be the one that students most frequently consult.

Karin Kukkonen's second book of 2013, *Contemporary Comics Storytelling*, takes a narratological/cognitive approach to how three case-study comics have reacted to the postmodernist tendency in American comics of approximately the mid-1980s to the early 2000s. It posits that comics are 'literature' in the sense that they behave like literature, both in terms of their formal complexity and their social function: public debate, canon formation, cultural capital for readers, etc. Thus, the book positions itself at the intersection of formalism, cultural context, and meaning-making (i.e. narratology). The cognitive methodology focuses the discussion on meaning-making and the hybrid nature of comics (word, text, sequence). It is not a systematic approach (e.g. McCloud's *closure* or Groensteen's *arthrology*) but rather a simple accounting for how comics make meaning in readers' minds. Kukkonen argues that comics have previously used postmodernist modes to critique 'high' art's hierarchies because they were taken to be a 'low' art, and thus antagonistic to the 'high', but since comics have been legitimized, they have now started to react against that postmodernist mode, and the book examines three examples of that reaction: *Fables*, *Tom Strong*, and *100 Bullets*. The book contains four chapters in addition to the introduction and conclusion. Chapter 1, 'How to Analyze Storytelling in Comics', in a move that is strongly reminiscent of a dissertation, defines Kukkonen's cognitive methodology: cognitive semantics, discourse psychology, and cognitive narrative studies. It uses *Steve Canyon* as a case study. The remaining three chapters look at *Fables*, *Tom Strong*, and *100 Bullets*, respectively, as three different reactions to postmodernism. Chapter 2, 'Textual Traditions in Comics: *Fables*, Genre, and Intertextuality', argues that Bill Willingham is reacting against the postmodernist fairy tale by reinserting fairy-tale characters into generic narratives, but modern ones such as the hard-boiled detective or spy thriller. Chapter 3, 'Fictionality in Comics: *Tom Strong*, Storyworlds, and the Imagination', argues that, rather than critiquing or deconstructing the master-narrative of the superhero, Alan Moore is reconstructing it through mimesis and 'feel'. Chapter 4, 'Fictional Minds in Comics: *100 Bullets*, Characterization, and Ethics', focuses on fictional minds and how they are constructed through faces and actions in Brian Azzarello's serial narrative in which new characters must face the same moral choice repeatedly. Finally, Kukkonen's conclusion explores the notion of a 'middle range' in enquiry, and argues that her cognitive methodology is readily applicable to comics outside the scope of her book. Finally, her conclusion describes the book as a middle-range study, one that pulls a specific problem from a set of case studies, but a problem that has wider application.

Sandra Eva Boschenhoff's *Tall Tales in Comic Diction, from Literature to Graphic Fiction: An Intermedial Analysis of Comic Adaptations of Literary Texts* is the author's largely unrevised dissertation. It studies adaptations of literary texts to comics as a way of establishing a theory of narratology for comics. Karin Kukkonen's *Studying Comics and Graphic Novels* considers this same topic in its fourth chapter. Boschenhoff posits that such adaptations juxtapose the plots of the original texts with the unique formal requirements of the comic book. She points out the obvious: that in the transition, elements of the original text are lost, just as elements of the comic book are gained. Specifically, comic-book adaptations are conventionally much shorter than the original but also able to compress a great deal of plot into a short space because of their unique representation of time as space and the ability to simultaneously view an entire page of action. The book's table of contents indicates four chapters, including the introduction and conclusion, with the second housing five subsections and the third housing six subsections. It would be more accurate, then, to say that the book contains two *parts* that contain six and five short *chapters* respectively. This meticulously organized structure is very reminiscent of Thierry Groensteen's *System of Comics* [2009], including the fact that both contain a very large penultimate chapter that has the bulk of the theorizing. Thus, chapter 2, 'Theoretical Considerations Concerning Comic Adaptations of Literary Texts', looks at the features of comics as they pertain to adaptation from text. It contains six subsections on two subjects: first, single-image storytelling (with examples), sequential-image storytelling, and image/text storytelling; second, several case studies of adaptation from text to comics. Chapter 3: 'Analyses of Comic Adaptations According to Narratological Categories', the central discussion, looks at comics in terms of five concepts of narratology: temporal phenomena in static images, setting and symbolism, narrators, focalization, and finally poetics and metafiction. Chapter 4 is a traditional conclusion; it restates the book's argument and summarizes the chapters, and it emphasizes the importance of creating a narratological theory of comics.

Kevin Thurman and Julian Darius's short volume, *Voyage in Noise: Warren Ellis and the Demise of Western Civilization,* is half critical articles and half interviews with the author. As such, it is almost literally divided between scholarly work and comics journalism, although it does not contain citations, so is not an academic book per se. The chapters are generally paired with interviews on the same topic, and the result is a dialogue between critic and author. There is a danger that readers might think that the interviews are confirming the criticism, but Ellis is analytical enough that his comments on his own work actually just amount to another form of criticism. The interviews themselves are taken—cannibalized, one could argue—from Thurman and Patrick Meaney's film *Warren Ellis: Captured Ghosts*, so *Voyage in Noise* could be thought of as a convenient way to obtain those interviews in print form. The book has no introduction, the chapters are not numbered, and the interviews are not explicitly connected to their chapters except by virtue of sequence, so readers must navigate the book largely on their own. There are eighteen sections in the book: eleven critical chapters and seven interview excerpts. They proceed in roughly chronological order, except for the first chapter, which is on Ellis and Marek Oleksicki's *Frankenstein's Womb*, a comic book about the creative process itself. Thereafter, *Voyage in Noise* works its way through Ellis's career: his early work at Marvel, an extended period of superhero revisionism, and, of course, the science fiction and horror that he produced in the meantime. The bulk of the book is about superheroes, but the chapters usually talk about how Ellis and his collaborators have used superheroes to comment on other things: terrorism, democracy, religion, and the like. The specific topics and books addressed are *Frankenstein's Womb*, the Marvel 2099 imprint, *Strange Kiss* (and its sequels), *Black Summer* and *No Hero*, analogues of the Fantastic Four, *Nextwave: Agents of H.A.T.E.*, *Supergods*, *Stormwatch*, *The Authority*, and *Transmetropolitan*.

Julian Darius's *The Weirdest Sci-Fi Comic Ever Made: Understanding Jack Kirby's 2001: A Space Odyssey* largely consists of close readings of Kirby's series, initially in juxtaposition to Kubrick's film. The introduction describes the forces that created this unlikely series and its even more unlikely contents. Darius argues that it is a mess but a fascinating one. It appeared eight years after the original novel and film, and unlike the *Star Wars* comics (which had not even happened at that point), *2001* was not part of a franchise, so it did not represent a narrative universe that Marvel could capitalize on in the long term. In the eight years since the film was released, it had become an SF classic and one of Kubrick's most respected creations, so the low status that comics held would not have been nearly as intuitive a connection as the aforementioned *Star Wars* comics would be just one year later; so the marketing was all wrong, but so was the stylistic pairing of Kubrick and Kirby. Kubrick's slow, deliberate planning bears no resemblance to Kirby's feverish output. The film's slow pace and symbolic visuals are the polar opposite of Kirby's bombastic action and cosmic fantasies. Similarly, the film's minimalist dialogue is radically different from Kirby's great volumes of often very purple prose. They are simply nothing alike. Darius emphasizes that it is not the case that Kubrick's work is superior to Kirby's, although many at the time would readily think so. The book's sections are not numbered, but there are effectively three chapters in addition to the introduction. The first section is a close analysis of the first issue of the series, a 'prestige' format book that adapts the entire film. It is largely, although not exclusively, a formal comparison: Kubrick vs. Kirby. Darius argues that Kirby's choices almost consistently clash with Kubrick's, and that the book, while clearly not an adaptation of Clarke's book, is also an odd mixture of the shooting script and the theatrical release. The second section details the first four issues of what then became a series. Here, Darius effectively argues that Kirby went completely off-script—Kubrick's or Clarke's—and turned *2001* into 'a Kirby space adventure comic' (p. 27), although admittedly one that mimics the film's narrative beats. A short subsection also discusses Clarke's sequels—*2010*, *2061*, and *3001*—and reaches the conclusion that while Kirby's comic book followed the existential elements of the original, Clarke followed the more grounded space-travel elements. Darius's last and longest section, taking up nearly half the book, consists of a series of close 'readings' of the rest of Kirby's series, which consists of a satire of superheroes (nos. 5–6), a continuation of the 'star child' narrative hinted at in the film (no. 7), and finally, the story of Mr Machine, who is vaguely connected to the monoliths in the film (nos. 8–10). Darius argues, quite convincingly, that these three issues represent Marvel and/or Kirby giving up on a high-minded science fiction comic book and reverting to the superhero formula.

Alex Romagnoli and Gian Pagnucci's *Enter the Superheroes: American Values, Culture, and the Canon of Superhero Literature* explicitly seeks to legitimize the superhero as a literary figure, which is a bit of a solution in search of a problem considering the large volume of critical work published on superheroes by academic journals and presses on a regular basis. The book also focuses almost entirely on comics from Marvel and DC, the two most-studied publishers in the field, to the exclusion of either those publishers whom Marvel and DC ran out of business or those that have sprung up since the 1980s. The tone of the book is a little less formal than academic, although the work is scholarly in that it uses a consistent citation method. The book contains eleven chapters in addition to an introduction that unfortunately does not contain an explanation of the theoretical or methodological underpinnings of the text. It also outlines the book's chapters, but again, without an explanation for their order. Chapter 1 asserts that superheroes are significant culturally, historically, and academically, and looks at them in a variety of media. Chapter 2 proceeds on the premise that the academy ignores superheroes and looks at how it addresses prominent, non-superhero comics. Chapter 3 focuses on fan reactions to superhero comics as a publicly engaged medium. Chapter 4 looks at 'rebooting' in superhero comics in terms of the relationship between creators and audience. Chapter 5 links superhero aesthetics—bodies, costumes, symbols—to their economic success in American film. Chapter 6 uses the 'Marvel method' of writing in relation to teaching composition as well as the superhero 'origin story'. Chapter 7 looks at superheroes as a children's genre and at moves to shift it to an adult genre. Chapter 8 examines both race and gender in one chapter using two case studies: Ultimate Spider-Man and Catwoman. Chapter 9 addresses superhero deaths: the ones that are always temporary and the ones that are narratively necessary. Chapter 10 looks at how real-world technology influences the depiction of superheroes, and at how superhero technology influences the real world. Chapter 11, finally, uses Harold Bloom's conception of a canon of literature to argue that superheroes and/or comics ought to be in that canon, and that the superhero canon ought to take a certain form.

Nadine Farghaly's *Examining Lois Lane: The Scoop on Superman's Sweetheart* is a collection of essays published in the year of the character's seventy-fifth birthday, and it purports to be the first extended scholarly examination of the character. There is not much by way of theoretical or methodological explanation in the book's introduction, but the majority of chapters are informed by a great deal of feminist theory. The chapters cover the character in a variety of media, which is entirely appropriate given how multi-media the Superman supporting cast has always been: comics, radio, toys, movies, cartoons, television shows, video games, etc. The tone of the writing is generally casual, not quite formal/academic, although the book is ultimately scholarly in that it uses a formal citation method. It must be said, though, that every chapter appears to find it necessary to perform a general introduction to the character and her context, which implicitly assumes an audience that does not already know her: a strange assumption in a work of

American comics scholarship. The bulk of the introduction, however, is taken up by a short essay by Eden Leone on the character's portrayal in *Lois and Clark*, a mid-1990s television series that featured the character, specifically about feminine knowledge-gathering. In addition to the introduction there are fourteen chapters, all of a robust length. Chapter 1, Ryan K. Lindsay's 'Full Disclosure', addresses Morrison and Quitely's *All-Star Superman* 3. Chapter 2, Don Tresca's 'The Evolution of Lois Lane in Film and Television', surveys live-action depictions of the character up to and including Kate Bosworth in *Superman Returns*. Chapter 3, Vibiana Bowman Cvetkovic's 'Feminine Mystique', is on the series *Superman's Girlfriend, Lois Lane* [1958–74]. Chapter 4, Kathleen Rittenhouse's 'Lois and Superman', is a historical and occasionally psychological investigation of Lane's personality. Chapter 5, Bobby James Keuchenmeister and Elizabeth Fleitz Keuchenmeister's 'The Quest of Lois', traces ten years of Lois's character, 1986 to 1996. Chapter 6, Hannah Starke's 'Supermen and Not-So-Super Women', surveys Lane's depiction in comics from the 1940s to the present, including comparisons to epic literature. Chapter 7, Jessica Weiss's 'Sex, the Single Girl, Superman, and the City', performs a feminist analysis of Margot Kidder's portrayal of Lane in the Superman films of the 1970s and 1980s. Chapter 8, Jessica McCall's 'What's Love Got to Do with It?', compares the two versions of *Superman II*, the Lester and Donner cuts. Chapter 9, 'It's a Bird! It's a Plane! It's Lois Lane!', argues that *Lois and Clark* ultimately, by its third season, equally objectifies its two title characters. Chapter 10, 'Woman on Top', once again looks at *Lois and Clark*, but as a postfeminist construction that prioritized a female audience. Chapter 11, 'I Moved On, and So Did the Rest of Us', looks at Lane in *Superman Returns* from a few different perspectives and as an object of focalization for the audience. Chapter 12, '*Smallville*'s Lois Lane', argues that Lane combines several American TV/film types, not necessarily stereotypes. Chapter 13, 'Domesticity Deferred', again looks at *Smallville*'s Lane but this time as a representation of a desire that is always deferred. Finally, Chapter 14, 'Attachment Disorder and *Smallville*', argues that Lane defines her own identity over the course of the series and eventually defines Clark/Superman's at the end.

Shane Densen, Christina Meyer, and Daniel Stein's *Transnational Perspectives on Graphic Narratives: Comics at the Crossroads* is an anthology organized around the call to analyse American comics as intrinsically transnational. It locates their transnationalism in the constant movement of their various elements across borders—texts, creators, capital. This approach is different than, but not envisioned as superior to, national/international analysis, such as Duncan, Smith, and Levitz's *The Power of Comics*. A transnationalist approach, however, focuses on those moments when comics sit on the boundaries between nations and cultures, but for that analysis to be coherent it requires the concept of nation, thus transnationalist approaches do not, in the minds of these editors, render national/international approaches obsolete. Transnational comics being too large a field to cover in one volume, this book focuses on transnationalism in American comics. It also proceeds from the premise that comics inherently lean towards transnationalism because the verbal/visual nature of the medium makes it easier to translate. Further, they argue that the nature of comics is to constantly violate boundaries—between panels, between text and image, etc.—which makes them formally analogous to transnationalism, which is defined by occupying those same boundaries. That said, even if they are, that does not mean that all comics or analyses of comics will automatically be counter-hegemonic, for example, or anti-national. Their formal nature is not deterministic of their ideological content. The book is divided into three sections in order to reflect on the transnationalism in American comics: Part I, 'Politics and Poetics', Part II, 'Transnational and Transcultural Superheroes', and Part III, 'Translations, Transformations, and Migrations'. Part I contains six chapters: 'Transnationalism and Form in Visual Narratives of U.S. Slavery', by M. Chaney; 'Metaphor and Cultural Resonance in Gene Luen Yang's *American Born Chinese*', by E. El Refaie; 'Comics Journalism and Graphic Silence', by G. Banita; 'The Transnational Encounter in Joe Sacco's *Footnotes in Gaza*', by A. Bartley; 'A Transnational Perspective on Hawaii in R. Kikuo Johnson's *Night Fisher*', by I. Laemmerhirt; and 'Transnationalism in the Comics of Warren Craghead III', by D. Wüllner. Part II contains five chapters: 'The Global Appropriation and Distribution of an American Hero', by K. Bieloch and S. Bitar; 'Comic Books and the Translating/Transcreating of American Cultural Narratives', by S. Davé; 'Investigating Manga Versions of Spider-Man', by D. Stein; 'Performing the Transnational Author in the American Comics Mainstream', by J. Ecke; and 'Conceiving the Cosmopolitan Muslim Superhero in *The 99*', by S. Meier. Part III also contains five chapters: 'Narratives of Transcultural Displacement in the Wordless Graphic Novel', by F. Groß; 'Transnational Remediation and the Art of Omission in Frank Miller's *Sin City*', by F. Mehring; 'Jason Lutes's Depiction of Weimar Republic Berlin', by L. Etter; 'The Cultural Crossovers of Bryan Lee O'Malley', by M. Berninger; and 'The North American Reception of *Asterix* and *Tintin*', by J. Gabilliet.

Anthony Mills's *American Theology, Superhero Comics, and Cinema: The Marvel of Stan Lee and the Revolution of a Genre* argues that from approximately 1960 to the present, Marvel's comics and films along with American philosophers and theologians have challenged the concept of humanity that is implied by the so-called 'American monomyth'. This was proposed in *The American Monomyth* by Robert Jewett and John Shelton Lawrence (Doubleday [1977]) as a localized version of Joseph Campbell's notion of the monomyth from his *Hero with a Thousand Faces* (PrincetonUP [1949]). Mills rehearses the not unfamiliar argument that the American monomyth is rooted in both liberal and repressive religious traditions in that nation as well as American notions of independence from Britain and Europe and also the Western genre. In addition to its introduction, the book consists of six chapters, the last of which is a conclusion. Chapter 1, 'The Historical and Theological Background of the Anthropology of the American Monomyth', rehearses the theory of the American monomyth as it appears in literature, comics, and film. Chapter 2, 'The Anthropology of the American Monomyth in Golden Age Superhero Comics (1938–1961)', critiques comics that reproduced the monomyth in the middle of the twentieth century, with heroes who were idealized as rugged (often bigoted) individuals and villains as unambiguously evil (often racist stereotypes). Chapter 3, 'The "Turn to Relationality" in American Theological Anthropology', focuses on five critics who challenge monomythic constructions like those found in American comics over a roughly fifty-year period. Chapter 4, 'The "Turn to Reality" in Silver Age Superhero Comics and Beyond (1961–Present)', looks at how Marvel Comics also challenged the monomyth over that same span of time. Chapter 5, 'Subverting the Anthropology of the American Monomyth in Marvel Comics Superhero Films (1998–2012)', argues that these films continue Marvel's tradition of challenging the monomyth, and the offer alternatives to it. Finally, Chapter 6, 'Conclusion: Anthropological Proposals', synthesizes the previous three chapters into four distinct alternatives to the concept of humanity as implied by the American monomyth.

Chad Nevett's *Shot in the Face: A Savage Journey Into to the Heart of Transmetropolitan* is an anthology of essays on Warren Ellis and Darick Robertson's most famous comic-book series. As a Sequart book, it is analytical and researched but also uses a casual tone and has very short chapters. As is standard with Sequart books, the chapters are not numbered and there is no formal introduction, but the first chapter is the functional introduction. They rest of the book moves from background information about the series, in Brett Williams's 'From Helix to Vertigo', to discussions of journalism. Sean Witze's 'The Future is Inherently a Good Thing' and 'Zero Society' and Chris Murphy's 'Think for Yourself and Question Authority' argue between them that truth is the proper response to oppression, while Ryan K. Lindsay's 'Caffeine in My Fingers' and Patrick Meaney's 'Two Tugs of a Dead Dog's Cock about Truthiness' locate the series relative to real-world American politics. The rest of the book is on a variety of subjects. Chad Nevett's 'Fear and Loathing in the City' argues that Spider Jerusalem is not Hunter S. Thompson but rather a fictionalized adaptation of the character Thompson created for himself. Greg Burgas's 'Supporting Players' asserts that, while they are powerful within the narrative, Yellena and Channon never become fully rounded characters. Sara K. Ellis's 'Manifest Trashscape' points out the motifs of the Western that pepper the series. Julian Darius's 'Grid of Mutilation' demonstrates how the series follows a very specific narrative structure that incorporates serial publication. Johanna Draper Carlson's 'Super-Hero of the Future' argues that Spider is not a superhero. Jason Michelitch's 'The Overlooked Importance of Darick Robertson' highlights Robertson's skills with caricature and the grotesque. Finally, Kevin Thurman's 'Let Us All Drown Screaming' places *Transmetropolitan* within Ellis's oeuvre. However, between Thurman's and Michelitch's chapters is an original interview with Robertson, and the book ends with a similar interview with Ellis, this one assembled from material in Sequart's documentary *Captured Ghosts*.

Tom Shapira's *Curing the Postmodern Blues: Reading Grant Morrison and Chris Weston's* The Filth *in the 21st Century* is a manuscript on a single text, which is quite common for a Sequart book. Also common for Sequart are the somewhat casual tone and introductory nature of the discussion coupled with academic formatting and citation. As with most Sequart books, there is no formal introduction, but the first chapter, 'Beginnings and Explorations', serves as one. In it, Shapira identifies Morrison as an auteur, in the tradition of film studies—because *The Filth* displays Morrison's signature styles and themes—while Weston's art is the filter through which that content reaches the audience. Shapira also establishes that the motifs of *The Filth* are disease and cure, the disease being the postmodern condition, and the cure being *The Filth* itself (i.e. storytelling in general). The book has nine chapters in total, although they are unnumbered, as well as two appendices and three interview transcripts with Grant Morrison, Chris Weston, and Gary Erskine. Interviews with creators are also a regular feature of Sequart books. The chapters (and the appendices) look at postmodernism and cure from various angles: postmodernism as exhaustion, postmodernist influences on Morrison, the immaturity of conspiracy theories, utopia and individuality, metafiction (i.e. 'recursive' narratives), memes, comparison with *The Invisibles*, and finally, Morrison's postmodernism looping back to modernism. The appendices are, in essence, two chapters on other subjects: the Morrison/Alan Moore rivalry and the dark comedy of *The Filth*.

Joseph J. Darowski's *The Ages of Wonder Woman: Essays on the Amazon Princess in Changing Times* is a collection that begins with the familiar claim that the character is both iconic and mysterious, recognizable but hard to understand. Part of the problem is that she has been repeatedly reinterpreted depending on the sensibilities of the era of publication, but the same is true of all long-running superhero characters. The collection contains nineteen short chapters of around twelve pages each. It is worth noting that, going by the authors' names, more than half of these chapters are written or co-written by women, which is, sadly, still a very high proportion for comics scholarship in general and superhero criticism in particular. It does follow, though, that a feminist icon (no matter how ambiguously so) would draw the attention of female critics. The collection is arranged chronologically, spanning from the character's first appearance to 2011, when DC Comics 'rebooted' its internal diegesis, which it has done several times since the mid-1980s. The first two chapters, by Michelle R. Finn and Donna B. Knaff, locate Marston's feminism and contextualize it during and after the Second World War. Craig This describes Frederic Wertham's effects on the character, while Lori Maguire and Joan Ormrod look at Wonder Woman in the Cold War. Francinne Valour explains why the character turned away from romance in the 1960s, and Jason LaTouche, Paul R. Kohl, and Peter W. Lee recontextualize Wonder Woman's feminism in her 'mod' period. Darowski and Ruth McClelland-Nugent then investigate the aftermath of that period, while D.R. Hammontree and Nicole Freim detail her transition into the so-called 'iron age' of American superheroes. Jeffrey K. Johnson analyses two comics that depict Superman and Wonder Woman as a romantic couple, and then Fernando Gabriel Pagnoni Berns and Alison Mandaville study the Wonder Woman comics of Greg Rucka and Gail Simone, respectively. Finally, John Darowski and Virginia Rush look at the 2011 reboot of the character.

New work from 2014 on comics includes Ian Hague's *Comics and the Senses: A Multisensory Approach to Comics and Graphic Novels*, an ambitious book that argues, among many other things, against the notion that comics are an exclusively visual medium, instead addressing all five of the traditional senses as elements of the comic-book viewing/hearing/touching/smelling experience. The book builds on existing comics scholarship and connecting it to existing sensory theories, thus adding new ways of understanding the medium. Furthermore, it argues that all five sense are implicit in most comics and not confined to experimental work. Hague also acknowledges that science has demonstrated that the human body has far more than five senses, biologically speaking, but he structures the book around the five traditional senses because these new-found senses largely fit into the classical ones, and also for simple ease of use. There are six chapters in addition to the introduction and conclusion, and the chapters are structured according to the five senses, with the last being a theoretical discussion and case study on the works of Alan Moore. Chapter 1, 'Eye Like Comics, or, Ocularcentrism in Comics Scholarship', intervenes in two problems of comics studies: the definitional (what the medium *is*) and the mechanical (how it *works*). It argues that an exclusively visual definition of comics is simply insufficient to describe how comics work. The next four chapters cover the five senses. Chapter 2, 'Sight, or, the Ideal Perspective and the Physicality of Seeing', is divided between the idea of comics as an idealized object and the visual as a physical phenomenon. Hague argues that comics are not static, spatially or temporally, and instead change over the course of the reading (or in this case, viewing) process. Chapter 3, 'Hearing, or, Visible Sounds and Seeing with the Ears', distinguishes between imagined and perceived sound in comics, the latter of which has largely been ignored in the criticism. Chapter 4, 'Touch, or, the Taboo/Fetish Character of Comics and Tactile Performance', first discards the characterization of touch as either taboo or fetish, and instead looks at the tactile qualities of comics as objects, both printed and digital. Chapter 5, 'Smell and Taste, or, the Scent of Nostalgia and the Flavour of Advertising', argues that smell and taste pull the audience into memory, unlike the way that sound regulates time. He points out how certain types of comics construct odours, even chemically. Finally, chapter 6, 'Multisensory Aspects of the Comics of Alan Moore', looks at the senses in several of his major works: sound in *V for Vendetta*, touch in *Promethea*, and sight in the use of 3D in *League of Extraordinary Gentlemen: Black Dossier*. Finally, the conclusion returns to the definitional problem, arguing that a reductive definition—one that focuses on what is unique—will inevitably leave out a huge portion of the *performed* experience of comic books.

Carolene Ayaka and Ian Hague's *Representing Multiculturalism in Comics and Graphic Novels* is concerned with determining whether multiculturalism is structurally possible within both comics and comics scholarship, and it makes that determination by looking for patterns in a body of specific examples that must, nevertheless, always be considered in their separate contexts. The editors' introduction provides two very useful guides. As in *Serialization in Popular Culture*, this Routledge book's introduction presents several themes that recur throughout the collection. The first describes a few major themes that appear in specific chapters: national traditions, contact between cultures (transnationalism), children, government/citizenship, and self-expression/self-determination. The second is a detailed bibliography of, and running commentary on, other scholarship on multicultural and/or transnational comics, including Aldama's *Multicultural Comics* (UTexP [2010]) as well as Densen, Meyer, and Stein's *Transnational Perspectives in Graphic Novels* (reviewed above), and several journals and anthologies the contents of which overlap with multiculturalism. The book itself consists of fifteen chapters divided into five sections, in addition to its introduction. Part I, 'Histories and Contexts', places comics that address multiculturalism in a specific time and place: Corey Creekmur on underground comics, Ana Merino on the Hernandez Bros., and Andy Mason on political cartoons in South Africa. Part II, 'Depicting Difference', contains three chapters on the creative tools that depict difference: Simon Grennan on embodiment of creators and audience, Mel Gibson on Bryan Talbot's *Grandville*, and Mihaela Precup on comics created by the Romanian government under Nicolae Ceauşescu. Part III, 'Monstrosity and Otherness', contains three chapters on how society creates/constructs monsters and 'others': Sarah D. Harris on comics under Francisco Franco, Ian Horton on imperialism in British boys' comics of the 1950s, and Jacob Birken on commodification of the 'other'. Part IV, 'Challenging Assumption', has only two chapters, both of which address multiculturalism itself: Maria-Sabina Draga Alexandru on the possibilities of using Tintin to teach positive multiculturalism, and Lily Glasner on children as a cultural group. Finally, Part V, 'Cast Studies', contains four chapters on individuality within multiculturalism: Brenna Clarke Gray and Peter Wilkins on Canadian identity in Bryan Lee O'Malley's *Scott Pilgrim*, Dana Mihăilescu on Jewishness in Leela Corman's *Unterzakhn*, Emma Oki on Asian Americans in Adrian Tomine's *Shortcomings* and *Scenes from an Impending Marriage*, and finally, Alex Link compares Marjane Satrapi's *Persepolis* and Taiyo Matsumoto's *Tekkon Kinkreet*.

Allen Rob and Thijs van den Berg's *Serialization in Popular Culture* addresses four different kinds of serialization: Victorian serial novels, serial films and television, comic books, and finally video games and Wikipedia. As in *Representing Multiculturalism in Comics and Graphic Novels* (reviewed above), the introduction presents several themes that recur throughout the collection. One is that serialization appears to be the single most common, and possibly even necessary, feature of a medium that becomes a *mass* medium even though it is also the product of that medium's individual development. There are other common features of the serial that the collection highlights: the deferral of narrative closure, training the audience members as consumers, the necessarily continuous rhythm of publication, and so-called 'binge watching' (or reading). Serialization is, therefore, not just the result of market logic but a format that does *work* within that logic. The book contains four sections with multiple chapters in each—again, paralleling the structure of *Representing Multiculturalism in Comics and Graphic Novels*—the third of which is on comics. This review focuses on that section's two chapters. Jason Dittmer's 'Serialization and Displacement in Graphic Narrative' suggests three different levels of seriality in comics, from their formal structure on the page to their mode of publication, and uses Moore and Gibbons's *Watchmen* as a case study. Angela Szczepaniak's 'A Series of Thoughts on Seriality in Daniel Clowes' *Eightball*' argues that *Eightball* displays the potential for serialization to resist market logic by using it to critique the comic-book industry and engage the audience rather than being a mere product of that logic and/or doing its work for it.

Tim Hanley's *Wonder Woman Unbound: The Curious History of the World's Most Famous Heroine* is one of three studies on Wonder Woman to appear in the last three years, including *The Ages of Wonder Woman* (reviewed above) and Jill Lepore's *The Secret History of Wonder Woman* (Knopf [2015]). It is a work of popular scholarship that describes the title character's media appearances in chronological order from 1941 to 2014. It is not a strictly chronological work, though, instead presenting essays on concepts or themes from within a given era. The book also places Wonder Woman in constant juxtaposition to other characters, women and men, in superhero comics, which provides valuable context for his descriptions, and thus spends a great deal of time with these other characters. The book contains three sections, arranged according to the so-called 'ages' of American superhero comics—Gold, Silver, and Bronze—as well as two 'interludes'. Part I contains three chapters. Chapter 1, 'The Utopian Alternative', juxtaposes Wonder Woman with the male counterparts of the 1930s/40s. Chapter 2, 'Damsels in Distress', describes how Wonder Woman is designed to subvert gender roles established in other superhero comics. Chapter 3, 'Amazon Princess, Bondage Queen', examines how bondage imagery in Marton's work—not just Wonder Woman comics—expressed his unique form of pseudo-feminism. Interlude 1, 'Wonder Woman's Extra Features', is a fascinating investigation of the other content in these comics, including back-matter and cover art. Part II also contains three chapters. Chapter 4, 'A Herculean Task', describes how, after Marston's early death, later creators transformed her: from an example of a utopian, matriarchal society, she became unique among amazons. Chapter 5, 'Focus on the Family, or Superman Is a Jackass', describes how Wonder Woman's comics were reworked in the 1950s to conform to the preoccupation with marriage. Finally, chapter 6, 'Conforming to the Code', details attempts to eliminate bondage imagery and implications of homosexuality in Wonder Woman comics as a reaction to the accusations of Frederic Wertham. After this chapter are sixteen pages of colour art, most of which is covers and all of which is referenced throughout the book. The second interlude, 'Letters and Advertisements', largely focuses on the demographics of the audience, which can be gleaned from the letters columns. Part III contains four chapters. Chapter 7, 'Wonder Woman No More', and Chapter 8, 'Doin' It for Themselves', describe the ill-fated reworking of the character by Denny O'Neil and Neal Adams in 1968 in which she lost her powers, became obsessed with fashion, and became markedly more violent. Chapter 9, 'Restoration and Re-creation', defines liberal vs. radical feminism in American in the 1970s and their mutual love of amazons, which made Wonder Woman their ideal hero, and arguably influenced DC to give back her powers and persona, and it ends on a brief survey of the character's presentation on film and television. Chapter 10, 'The Mundane Modern Age', essentially argues that the character mostly lurked in the background in the 1980s and 1990s: no iconic stories, television shows, or films. Finally, the conclusion argues that Wonder Woman has become a remarkably recognizable icon of female strength but without necessarily any specific narrative or values behind her.

Joseph J. Darowski's *X-Men and the Mutant Metaphor: Race and Gender in the Comic Books* performs a close reading of *The Uncanny X-Men* comics looking for themes of racial and gendered oppression. The introduction is more of a foreword that defends the legitimacy of studying comics, an unnecessary move given the general acceptance of comics scholarship. The first chapter, then, is the real introduction, but it mostly presents the very well-known history of American superhero comics in general and Marvel/X-Men comics in particular. The rest of the chapters are arranged chronologically, each one covering a span of time (and thus a number of issues), and each chapter follows the same format of subsections: creators, general storyline, characters, and close-reading. This last subsection is largely where the analysis happens. It also must be said that the lion's share of the book's sources are either popular scholarship or the words of comic-book creators, and the text does not foreground a specific methodological reason for this. Indeed, aside from sources on general concepts of oppression, Darowski does not invoke any specific theory or methodology. As a result, the book does not feel connected to academic scholarship in general, and a specific argument is hard to discern. Chapter 2, 'Intriguing Concept, Uneven Execution', covers 1963 to 1970, and largely points out that the seeds of the mutant metaphor were presented in those years without a specific focus. Chapter 3, 'Relaunching and Reimagining' (1975–83), asserts that the series had a more racially diverse cast, and describes the emergence of a trope of powerful women who are both destructive and sexualized. Chapter 4, 'Adding Depth and Exploring Prejudice' (1983–91), argues that the mutants-as-ethnic-group theme had reified, and the series addressed it directly. Chapter 5, 'Broadening the Mutant Metaphor', explains that the powerful/destructive male in *X-Men* comics is not sexualized and that the mutant metaphor was extended to sexual orientation. Chapter 6, 'Reestablishing the Metaphor' (2001–8), describes this period as one of fairly blatant sexual objectification of female characters along with the reassertion of the mutant metaphor as specifically racial. Finally, Chapter 7, 'By the Numbers', presents a series of statistics/graphs of the racial and gendered make-up of the X-Men team, and breaks them down by the same periods as the chapters. It uses *The Official Index of the Marvel Universe: X-Men* for its raw statistics, which is a little dubious, but the raw numbers are potentially very useful to other comics scholars. The very brief conclusion points out a few patterns in the statistics, specifically that, despite the central metaphor of mutation as racial/gendered otherness, the X-Men themselves have been overwhelmingly white and male, and the racial diversity of the series rests on Storm—an African woman—and actually *fell* after 1991, when Chris Claremont left the series.

Matt Yockey's *Batman*, a short volume, is part of Wayne State University Press's TV Milestones series. The tone of the book varies from densely theoretical and abstract to quite literal descriptions of scenes and jokes from the show. It is for academics with a sense of humour, then, and a willingness to enjoy the joke as a joke and then to enjoy dissecting it as a construct. Yockey argues that *Batman*'s satire is a product of self-awareness and a dual sensibility: earnest adventure for kids, campy comedy for adults who can relate to or recall buying into earnest adventure stories when *they* were kids. The self-aware, or metafictional, quality, then, lies in establishing and then crossing the boundary, within the adult viewers' minds, into childhood. This knowing satire is what defines the series as 'camp', in Susan Sontag's sense of the word. It critiques America's faith in a consumerist utopia through a highly consumable product: a highly formulaic television show that has a cliffhanger built into every story. Yockey's book is divided into five chapters plus an introduction, called 'Batman Begins', in which he explains his particular understanding of 'camp' and provides historical context for the series, as well as a conclusion. The chapters are divided by subject. Chapter 1, 'Bat-Civics', highlights the tension between the upright citizenship that the Batman character superficially performs and the show's ironic critique of it. Chapter 2, 'Bat-Difference', concentrates on how the presence of women on the show both addressed and dismissed problems of sexism, specifically Yvonne Cragi's Batgirl and Eartha Kitt's Catwoman, who is doubly different for being a black woman. Chapter 3, 'Bat-Casting', contrasts the casting of the heroes and villains of the series: Burt Ward and Adam West were relative unknowns, so they lived through their characters, whereas the villains were known film stars, whose identities signified more prominently than their characters. Chapter 4, 'Bat-Being', discusses the merchandise produced to capitalize on the show's success, but in terms of the ways it both constructs and destabilizes personal and national identity. Finally, the conclusion, 'Batman Forever', argues that the *Batman* series defines by opposition the darker tone of Batman comics and adaptations that started in the 1970s.

Jason Dittmer's *Comic Book Geographies* is an anthology that claims to, for the first time, marry comics and geography, largely on the basis of their mutual focus on space as a concept and a tool of understanding. Dittmer specifically uses Paul Adams's typology of space/place and context/content to map comic-book practices. 'Place in comics' refers to those places that comics tend to represent, largely based on where comic-book production is located worldwide: America, francophone Europe, and Japan. 'Space in comics' has been thoroughly studied by critics such as Scott McCloud and Thierry Groensteen. On the other hand, 'comics in space' focuses on circulation patterns. Finally, 'comics in place' refers to contexts of reading and production. In addition to Dittmer's introduction, there is a foreword by Daniel Merlin Goodbrey, a practising cartoonist who experiments with multi-linear forms of online comics, partly using what McCloud, in *Reinventing Comics*, calls 'the infinite canvas'. Dittmer references Goodbrey as an example of comics working consciously with space/place and content/context. The body of the volume consists of nine chapters divided into three sections, although Dittmer is quick to point out that these section breaks are quite permeable, that some chapters could have been placed in different sections, which indicates a desire not to categorize but instead to organize. Section 1, 'Representing and Performing Space/Place', focuses on production of spaces within comics. Oliver Dunnett's 'Framing Landscape' describes how depictions of the English countryside in *Dan Dare* comics helped define Britishness after the Second World War. Tony Venezia's '10th April, 1999, Conway Hall,

Red Lion Square' demonstrates 'psychogeography' in comics using Eddie Campbell's *Snakes and Ladders*, an adaptation of Alan Moore's magical performances. Shaun Huston's 'Live/Work' reports on the conditions of comic-book production in Portland in the United States. Section 2, 'Bodies Politic', focuses on how bodies are part of subjectivity formation. Catriona MacLeod's 'From Wandering Women to Fixed Females' compares two *bédé* that represent contexts and spaces through women's bodies. Juliet J. Fall's 'Put Your Body on the Line' demonstrates how autobiographical comics create connections between distant subjects. Edward C. Holland's 'Post-Modern Witness' performs a close reading of Joe Sacco's 'Christmas in Karadzic'. Section 3, 'Space and Comics Theory', directly address space in comics. Julia Round's 'We Share Our Mothers' Health' uses Gothic theory to discuss use of space in *From Hell*, *The Invisibles*, and *The Walking Dead*. Michael Goodrum's 'The Body (Politic) in Pieces' studies the fragmentation of the superhero in post-9/11 Marvel Comics. Finally, Marcus A. Doel's 'Why Comics Is Not a Sequential Art' uses Gilles Deleuze and Chris Ware to argue that comics are defined by 'voiding' as opposed to sequence.

Ann Miller and Bart Beaty's *French Comics Theory Reader* attempts to create, for anglophone comics scholars, a context for the works of French theory that have been translated in the last decade or so (in no small part by the two editors themselves). The introduction describes the major differences between francophone and anglophone comics and comics theory. The former was embraced by the academy some time ago, while the latter was largely critiqued by it until very recently. In the former, theorists are often also cartoonists, while in the latter the two groups have remained largely separate. The academy has tended to locate the former in semiotics, history, and sociology while for the latter it has focused on cultural criticism. The collection itself is made up of texts that are strong examples of specific schools of thought as well as those that have been uniquely influential. It is divided into four sections, each of which contains chapters that are not so much chronological as dialogical; they fall into chronological order most of the time but only by virtue of responding to one another's claims and arguments. Each section also contains a short introduction that briefly summarizes each chapter and, in so doing, ties them together, often pointing out how they are in dialogue with each other. Section 1, 'Origins and Definitions', contains eight chapters that debate where *bande dessinée* came from, both the term and the form, and how exactly to define it. It includes works by Jean-Claude Glasser, Gérard Blanchard, and Francis Lacassin, and then a running debate between Thierry Smolderen, Thierry Groensteen, and Sylvain Bouyer about the defining feature of comics. Section 2, 'Formal Approaches', addresses the development of a collective methodology for francophone comics theory, including some quite pointed internal debates from the Colloque de Cerisy. It includes the work of Pierre Fresnault-Deruelle, Pierre Sterckx, Jacques Samson, and Thierry Groensteen, as well as two chapters co-written by Jan Baetens and Pascal Lefèvre. Section 3, 'French Comics Criticism', contains chapters that offer single-author or single-text analyses, specifically Hergé and Jack Kirby. It includes works by Bruno Lecigne and Jean-Pierre Tamine, Harry Morgan and Manuel Hirtz, Fresnault-Deruelle, Michel Serres, Benoît Peeters, and

Serge Tisseron. Finally, Section 4, 'Reading the French Comics Industry', consists of analyses of the industry itself and how its structure has affected the reception of comics in francophone culture and the development of the art form. It contains chapters by Luc Boltanski, Pascal Ory, Erwin Dejasse, Philippe Capart, Barthélémy Schwartz, and Jean-Christophe Menu.

Andrew Hoberek's *Considering Watchmen: Poetics, Property, Politics* begins with a long introduction, really a chapter, that asks the question 'Is it literature?' but does not seek to answer that question. Instead, it treats it as a prompt to map out the features of the book that are literary—an affiliation with modernist novels, for example—as well as those that belong to it as a comic book: visual/verbal storytelling, creation by committee, corporate production, etc. Hoberek asserts that it *is* a comic book, but one that has distinctly literary qualities that are worth investigating. Specifically, he argues that it has been a major element in the shift towards 'genre' work in the world of fiction. The remainder of the book consists of three chapters and a short discussion, a 'coda', on *After Watchmen*. The chapters do not proceed in a linear fashion, building on one discussion that culminates in a single conclusion, but rather are constantly referential: to themselves, to each other. Chapter 1, 'Poetics', argues that *Watchmen* combines psychological realism (i.e. characters who maintain convincing subjectivities) with formal experimentation in a way that, according to Hoberek, has been the dominant mode of fiction for nearly a century. In so doing, Moore and Gibbons are positioning *Watchmen* to be read as/taken for high art. Chapter 2, 'Property', contends that Ozymandias and Rorschach variously represent the corporate desire to own and profit from intellectual property, the conventional desire for narrative closure, and artistic freedom, and that their shifting symbolism thus references DC Comics and Moore/Gibbons. Chapter 3, 'Politics', argues that *Watchmen*'s critique of statism—represented by Ozymandias's top-down 'solution' to the Cold War and aimed squarely at Margaret Thatcher—is actually intellectually parallel to conservative 'small government' rhetoric (but not the reality), and offers no practical solution. Hoberek does concede that this absence is consistent with Moore's anarchist politics, but he argues that it is also consistent with certain elements of neoliberalism. Finally, the coda describes texts that intersect with *Watchmen*, either influencing it or being influenced by it (e.g. Michael Chabon's *The Amazing Adventures of Cavalier and Klay* or Junot Díaz's *The Brief Wondrous Life of Oscar Wao*), thus arguing by example that *Watchmen* demonstrates that the superhero, while it originated as a power fantasy for children, today provides writers with a convenient source of tropes and imagery for fiction.

Ben Bolling and Matthew J. Smith's *It Happens at Comic-Con: Ethnographic Essays on a Pop Culture Phenomenon* is an anthology written primarily by students who took part in a field-study trip to San Diego Comic-Con in 2007, led by Smith. The individual chapters are revised versions of the students' essays. The collection is not about comics directly but, rather, about the subculture that has formed around comics conventions, specifically Comic-Con, which has become a massive marketing venue for large-scale media properties as well as a social space for the communities that form around them. Matthew Pustz, whose *Fan-Boys and True Believers* (UPMissip [1999]) was a textbook for the field study, writes the foreword and refers to Comic-Con as a laboratory for pop-culture ethnography. As such, the book has a place in the communications/sociology/cultural studies wing of comics scholarship. The collection has thirteen relatively short chapters in addition to a foreword, introduction, and afterword. The chapters are divided into five sections. Part I, 'Identity and Play', contains two essays on *cosplay* and its interactions with superhero/comic books, by Kane Anderson and Catherine Thomas, respectively. Part II, 'Gendered Fandom', contains three chapters about women and queer people living in the very phallocentric space of comic-con: on queer consumers/consumption by Ben Bolling, on feminism and *geek girls* by Lisa H. Kaplan, and on *Twilight* fans by Melissa Miller. Part III, 'Negotiating Fandom through Communicative Practice', contains three chapters: on the social rules of fan talk by Brian Swafford, on panels as image management by Jon Judy and Brad Palmer, and on aggression in geek culture by Chad Wertley. Part IV, 'Technology and Participation', has two chapters on interactive entertainment: *machinema* (using video-game engines to create animated films) by Cameron Catalfu, and Web shows (television shows published online) by Tanya D. Zuk. Part V, 'Attending Con', focuses on the experiences of people at the event: waiting in line by Regina C. Gasser, interaction between fans and pros by Cristian Sager, and volunteering for a for-profit event by Michael J. Tornes. Finally, Randy Duncan and Peter M. Coogan are the co-founders of the Comics Arts Conference, an academic conference that happens essentially within Comic-Con. In that capacity, they write an afterword that describes the development of the CAC and its interaction with Smith's field-study group.

Alex M. Wainer's *Soul of the Dark Knight: Batman as Mythic Figure in Comics and Film* is a manuscript that, while based on the author's dissertation work, significantly expands on it. Where the dissertation examined the mythic qualities of the character in comics, this volume includes adaptation to film. Wainer argues that Batman is rooted in mythopoeia, specifically the character's ability to transform into a creature that is between worlds: the human and the animal. He is different in comics than in film, then, because those two media are formally prone to invoke myth in different ways. The book contains eight article-length chapters. He starts with a survey of myth theory in chapter 1, 'Myth and the Mythic', subdividing it into several schools of thought and finally arriving at modern mass-media representations of it. The second chapter, 'I Shall Become a *Bat!*', establishes the well-known history of Batman, surveying a number of elements of the character and his narrative world, and remarking on his adaptability. The third chapter, 'Mythic Characteristics in Batman', combines the first and second, examining two mythic elements of the character: animal symbolism and duality. The four chapter rounds out the discussion by examining how the form of the comic book is particularly suited to depicting myth through two of Scott McCloud's theories: amplification through simplification and closure. At this point, the book pivots to a three-chapter examination of Batman's adaptation to film. Chapter 5, 'Adapting Batman and the Mythic into Film', examines how film invokes 'myth-like' qualities differently than comics, and uses Tolkien's and Jackson's respective *Lord of the Rings* trilogies to do it. The sixth chapter,

'Batman in Film and Other Media', surveys the character's appearances in film (starting with 1940s serials), television (including live action and cartoons), and prose, as well as briefly touching on video games. Wainer arrives at what feels like the climax of the book in chapter 7, 'Christopher Nolan's Batman Trilogy', which examines all three, in order, focusing to a great degree on the juxtaposition of realism and myth. The last chapter, 'The Comics Medium as a Means of Invoking the Mythic', addresses several issues that arise from Wainer's central argument: other mythic characters in film (including comic-book adaptations) and theories of myth. The book ends with an appendix that juxtaposes theories from McCloud and Frye.

José Alaniz's *Death, Disability, and the Superhero* is a manuscript that argues, broadly speaking, that the superhero invokes the notion of death and dying by resisting it through a hyper-healthy body, usually white and male. It draws on death and disability studies as well as comic scholarship in order to make this argument. The book contains ten chapters, the first of which is an introduction that uses Peter Coogan's four-part definition of the superhero to address elements of the genre: fascism, split identities, and anxiety around masculinity. The middle eight chapters are divided between five on disability and three on death, with the last chapter serving as a conclusion. Chapter 2, 'Disability, Visuality and the Silver Age Superhero', runs parallel to the first by surveying disability theory, focusing on the notion of the 'supercrip' (the high-functioning disabled person) and identifying its comic-book analogue: the disabled superhero. This chapter establishes that the focus of the book will be on Marvel Comics, given their 'flawed hero' formula. Chapter 3, 'Disability, *Daredevil*, and Passing', focuses on the comic in which Matt Murdock/Daredevil masquerades as 'Mike Murdock', using his superpowers to pass as able-bodied. Chapter 4, 'Gender, Race and the "Disabled" Superhero', examines characters whose 'disability' is their superpower, and who thus cannot pass, and focuses on female bodies and bodies of colour. Chapter 5, 'Dismodernism and "The World's Strangest Heroes" ', examines *X-Men* and *Doom Patrol* in terms of the signification of the wheelchair and postmodernism's ability to erase the boundaries between able and disabled bodies but, in so doing, to erase disabled identity. Chapter 6, 'Narrative Prosthetics and *The Human Fly*', analyses Marvel's *Human Fly* and other comics that render disability 'tolerable' to norms of able-bodiedness. This ends the book's examination of disability, and the next chapter, 'The Dismal Trade', begins a study of superheroes and death with the argument that by depicting death as a metaphorical revolving door, superhero comics both invoke its pathos and inevitability as well as denying its very existence. This especially long chapter breaks down various types of deaths as portrayed in superhero comics. Chapter 8, 'Facing Death in *Strikeforce: Morituri*', focuses tightly on a comic book whose premise requires that the protagonists die permanently—no resurrections—thus, in Alaniz's words *deny the denial* of death in superhero comics. Somewhat similarly, the very short chapter 9, 'Death, Bereavement, and the "Funeral for a Friend" ', analyses the spectacle of mourning that occurred in 1992 when DC Comics (briefly) killed Superman. Finally, the book's conclusion equates the denial of disability and death within superhero comics to a denial of history and, thus, of essential humanity.

Joseph Darowski's *The Ages of the Avengers: Essays on the Earth's Mightiest Heroes in Changing Times* is a collection of essays on the Marvel Comics superhero team called 'the Avengers'. It is part of a series of 'The Ages of...' books edited by Darowski, all from McFarland Press, and all organized in basically the same fashion. The book has no introduction (only a very short preface), fifteen (unnumbered) chapters, and no conclusion, and the chapters are arranged chronologically based on the comics that they reference, so there is no explicit theme defining the collection, but the most common methodological approach is historical, such as the Avengers comics either referencing or reflecting a moment in American history: Liam Webb on Sub-Mariner and the Cuban Missile Crisis; Lori Maguire on the Avengers and Vietnam; Paul R. Kohl on the Kree-Skrull War and the Cold War; Nathan Gibbard on religion in the 1970s; Peter W. Lee on Yellow Jacket and Wasp in the Reagan era; Jason LaTouche and John Darowski both write on the Avengers after the Cold War; Morgan O'Rourke on superheroes, social media, and celebrity; and finally, Mark Edlitz and Dyfrig Jones both write on Marvel's *Civil War* and the post-9/11 world on which it comments. The rest of the chapters are either about the publication history of *The Avengers*, in its various incarnations, or close readings of specific episodes: Jason Sacks on the theme of family, Laurie Schwartz on mythology in the 'Korvac Saga', Todd Steven Borroughs on Christopher Priest's depiction of Black Panther, José Alaniz on the Great Lakes Avengers and 'enfreakment', and finally, Darowski (the editor) on dystopian teen fiction.

Joseph Darowski's *The Ages of the X-Men: Essays on the Children of the Atom in Changing Times* is a collection of essays on the Marvel Comics superhero team called 'the X-Men'. It is also part of a series of 'The Ages of...' books edited by Darowski, all from McFarland Press, and all organized in basically the same fashion. The book has only a very short introduction, nineteen (unnumbered) chapters, and no conclusion, and the chapters are arranged chronologically based on the comics they reference, so while there is no explicit theme or logic to the collection, three motifs do emerge: historically grounded readings, readings grounded in identity politics, and finally, a handful of essays about the publication history of the characters. The historically grounded chapters place the X-Men in their moment in American history in some significant way: Brad J. Ricca on popular science of the 1950s, John Darowski (not the editor) on communism and the Cold War, Jean-Philippe Zanco on Xavier's School as hippie commune, Jacob Rennaker on televangelism, Jeff Geers on fears around the millennium, Eric Garneau and Maura Foley on Grant Morrison's post-9/11 X-Men, and Nicolas Labarre on the mass shootings at Columbine. The chapters on identity politics focus on race, gender, and the body: Margaret Galvan on Kitty Pryde and feminism; Clancy Smith on *Days of Future Past* and technological oppression; Nicholaus Pumphrey on Magneto's (retroactive) Jewish backstory; Gerri Mahn on Wolverine and masculinity; Adam Capitanio on celebrity satire in *X-Statix*; Christian Norman and the 'legacy virus' as metaphor for AIDS; Todd Kimball Mack on autism; and finally Morgan and Daniel O'Rourke on mutants as minorities in the Obama era. Finally, there is a small group of chapters on the X-Men themselves: Darowski (the editor) on the 1975 relaunch of the title,

Timothy Elliot and Robert Dennis Watkins on the 1991 launch of *The X-Men*, and David Allan Duncan on the television show *Generation X*.

Joseph F. Berenato's *New Life and New Civilizations: Exploring* Star Trek *Comics* is an essay collection from Sequart, which specializes in work that is both scholarly (rhetorical, researched, cited) and friendly to non-academics: a relaxed tone and a *lot* of summary to catch readers up. The book contains eighteen chapters in addition to a short foreword and an introduction, both of which are largely personal accounts of encountering *Star Trek* and, subsequently, *Star Trek* comic books. The editor, in the introduction, does point out that while most aspects of the franchise have received scholarly attention, the comics, specifically, have not. The subsequent chapters proceed in chronological order by the publishing date of the comics to which they refer, so while the collection has no explicit organizing principle, it is effectively arranged by publisher because the rights have shifted from one to the next since 1967. The result is two blocks of chapters: one on comics published during or soon after the show's initial run, and the other on comics produced after the *Star Trek* films had brought the franchise back into mainstream consciousness. The common theme of the first block of five chapters is that the comics in question bear, at least initially, only superficial resemblance to the show: Scott Tipton and Julian Darius, respectively, on Gold Key's *Star Trek* comics; Alan J. Porter on *City Magazine*'s *Star Trek* strips, contained in its *Joe 90* anthology; Julian Darius on Peter Pan's *Star Trek* audio comics; and finally, Kevin Dilmore on various *Star Trek* colouring books. These last two examples, the audio comics and colouring books, are also remarkable for depicting Lieutenant Uhura, played by the African American actress Nichelle Nichols, as Caucasian. The second block of chapters, on the other hand, covers comics that contain the attention to obscure detail that characterizes *Star Trek* fandom: Rich Handley on the *LA Times* syndicate's *Star Trek* daily strip; Jim Beard on Marvel's first run of *Star Trek* comics; legally bound to expand only on the first film; Colin Smith on the *Mirror Universe Saga* in Marvel's second run; Ian Dawe on feminist elements of DC's *Star Trek*; Robert Greenberger on *The Next Generation* comics, also at DC Comics; Tom Mason on Malibu Comics' Deep Space Nine series; Dayton Ward on 'Marvel Presents: Paramount Comics', which included all incarnations of *Star Trek*; Keith R.A. DeCandido on WildStorm's *Star Trek* comics, designed to be collected for bookstore sales; Mark Martinez on Tokyopop's *Star Trek* manga; WildStorm and IDW's separate *New Frontier* comics, based on a series of novels; Cody Walker on movie tie-in comics; IDW's comics, published after the 2009 'reboot' film; and finally, David A. McIntee on the many crossovers between *Star Trek* and other SF/F properties, including the X-Men (Marvel Comics), the Legion of Super-Heroes (DC Comics), and Doctor Who (the BBC).

Stephen E. Tabachnick's *The Quest for Jewish Belief and Identity in the Graphic Novel* studies a number of graphic novels, including non-fiction and autobiography, by Jewish creators and/or about Jewish identity. The text is very much written from within a Judaic religious perspective as well as from within an American cultural context. It focuses almost exclusively on American comics and treats non-American comics as a special category, and it asks questions that, while not exclusive to Jewish American culture, are central to its particular politics: support for vs. critique of Israel as a state, secularity vs. Jewishness, and the persistence of anti-Semitism. In defining his scope, Tabachnick does uncritically repeat some myths of American comic books—e.g. Max Gaines's self-proclaimed 'invention' of format—and he insists on an ostensibly clear delineation between 'popular' *comics* and 'high-quality' *graphic novels*. One of the implied criteria of *quality graphic novels* also appears to be an adherence to Judaic religious belief and the capacity to convince readers of its ostensible truth. He uses this implied definition to rationalize his choice of primary material rather than focusing exclusively on its significance to Jewish American identity, a much more defensible position. Thus, the book absolutely qualifies as comics scholarship, but it has some strong biases of which readers ought to be aware. In addition to its brief introduction, the book contains eight chapters that are in no explicitly stated order, but appear to start with texts/events that are conventionally definitive to American Jews—the Bible, the Holocaust, immigration—and then look at what would traditionally be outlying phenomena: Jewishness 'abroad', Jewish women, encounters with Israel, and, finally, Orthodoxy. Chapter 1 looks at graphic-novel adaptations of the Bible (Torah, i.e. what Christians call the Old Testament), including Robert Crumb, J.T. Waldman, Basil Wolverton, and Douglas Rushkoff. Chapter 2 focuses exclusively on Art Spiegelman's *Maus*, arguing that Vladek's narration logically implies the existence of God despite Spiegelman's secular-humanist perspective. Chapter 3 looks at many other comics about the Holocaust, including work by Trina Robbins, Joe Kubert, and Alan Moore among others. Chapter 4 examines comics set in Europe and North Africa, both before and after the Holocaust, by Vittorio Giardino, Joann Sfar, James Sturm, and Will Eisner. Chapter 5 flips the perspective and looks at comics about Jewish immigrants to America by Lemelman, Harvey Pekar, and Eisner. While the other chapters are not exclusively about male creators, chapter 6 does look exclusively at Jewish American women's identity as a particular social construction in comics by Sharon Rudahl, Vanessa Davis, Aline Kominsky Crumb, Diane Noomin, and Melissa Lasko-Gross. Chapter 7, which might more logically have been grouped with chapters 4 and 5, examines comics in or about Israel, both from an Israeli perspective—Rutu Modan, Etgar Keret/Asaf Hanuka, Ari Folman/David Polonsky, and Galit Seliktar/Gilad Seliktar—and an American one: Miriam Libicki, Sarah Glidden, and Harvey Pekar/J.T. Waldman. Finally, chapter 8 looks exclusively at comics that reflect positively on Orthodox Judaism by Barry Deutsch, Steve Sheinkin, and James Sturm.

Jeffrey K. Johnson's *Superheroes in Crisis: Adjusting to Social Change in the 1960s and 1970s* argues that, in the 1960s and 1970s, Superman and Batman were revised to both adapt to changing times and remain essentially the same, which is the mode of American superhero comics in general. The characters had already gone through a similar adaptation after the Second World War. Johnson argues that superhero comics have not traditionally had stated political agendas because they were conceived as disposable culture for children: every issue was constructed to be as accessible as possible, and, as a result, cumulatively depicted very little change in, or consequences for, their main characters. Of course, these comics are inherently political or they wouldn't be suitable for the study, so the underlying methodological assumption appears to be that they reflect contemporary American culture rather than commenting on it. It is worth mentioning that the book is the second in RIT's Comics Studies Monograph series, and its design and layout are almost identical to Barbara Postema's *Narrative Structure in Comics: Making Sense of Fragments* (RITP [2013]; reviewed in *YWES* 94[2015]), although it has fewer illustrations and is generally laid out less like an art book. *Superheroes in Crisis* contains four chapters in addition to a short introduction, and they are in chronological order. Chapter 1, 'The Early Years' (1938–59), explains the previous transition that the characters went through, from populist, anti-authoritarian avengers in the 1930s and 1940s, to patriotic soldiers during the Second World War, and finally to patriarchal figures in the 1950s. Johnson does not argue, as many do, that the Comics Code Authority was the prime mover in this transition. Rather, it was America's relative wealth (for some) and cultural conformity that drove the anti-comics movement. Chapter 2, 'Middle-Age Changes' (1960–9), argues that while Superman only changed in minor ways, remaining essentially a 1950s patriarch, Batman shifted from that to gritty detective (although the era was interrupted briefly by the goofiness and camp of the *Batman!* television show). Chapter 3, 'Self-Doubt and Worry' (1970–4), argues that the characters underwent a cultural course correction from the radical change of the 1960s, and Johnson notes that one writer, Denny O'Neil, attempted to 'modernize' both of them by making them more serious and less powerful. Finally, chapter 4, 'Where Do We Go from Here?' (1975–9), argues that America was in a period of social stagnation due to things like Watergate, the war in Vietnam, and a weak economy, and the comics reflected it. Superman stagnated, relying on the same gimmicks and values as those of 1950s, and Batman adapted by fighting against the new social ills. Johnson's argument implies that the Batman has been much more popular than Superman since at least the 1960s, in no small part because Batman can be authority figure or rebel, depending on the era's needs, while Superman's rebelliousness is seemingly no longer accessible, having been beaten out of the character back in the 1930s.

The Origins of Comics: From William Hogarth to Winsor McCay is a translation of Thierry Smolderen's *Naissance de la bande dessinée* (IndUP [2000]) by Bart Beaty and Nick Nguyen, who also translated Thierry Groensteen's *Système de la bande dessinée* (PUF [1999]) as *The System of Comics* (UPMissip [2009]). Like Dunning and Gravett's *Comics Unmasked* (reviewed below) *Origins* presents itself as an art book: it is large-format on slick paper, very few of its pages do not contain images, and at a glance, two-thirds of those images are in colour. It also does not contain a traditional introduction, instead launching into its first chapter with no explanatory remarks by the author or the translator. This could leave readers somewhat adrift, as the chapters are arranged chronologically rather than by subject or concept. However, the writing itself is rich and quite clear, is not laden with complex theory, and makes frequent references in any given chapter to other sequential art/artists (most of the primary material is not 'comics' or *bédé* per se), thus consistently placing the subject of the chapter in a larger historical context. The text is also in continual dialogue with the images, inviting readers to experience the images themselves at least as much as it explicitly analyses those images. As a result, its form emulates the verbal/visual blend of sequential art. There are eight chapters in all, four of which focus on individual creators and the other four on trends or developments in sequential art/*bédé*/ comics. Chapter 1, 'William Hogarth: Readable Images', argues that Hogarth's works—*A Harlot's Progress* etc.—were novels and sequential art, but required a much more visually detailed kind of 'reading' than comics/*bédé* as we know them today. Chapter 2, 'Graffiti and Little Doodle Men', places Rodolphe Töpffer's picture-stories in the larger context of a trend for 'primitive' drawings (caricature, stick figures, etc.), much of which originated in England, and which differentiates his work from Hogarth's painterly detail. Chapter 3, 'The Arabesque Novels of Rodolphe Töpffer', essentially argues that Töpffer's work constituted an ironic rejection of progressive action in favour of the *arabesque*. Chapter 4, 'Go, Little Book', explores the influences of Töpffer's books on later humourists, both English and French, and in terms of form as well as narrative style. Chapter 5, 'The Evolution of the Press', is especially dense with illustrations and wide in its scope, detailing a great many necessary adaptations of Töpffer's style, by then widely accepted and recognized, to periodical formats: newspapers and magazines. These adaptations are the direct precursors of modern comics/*bédé* as we know them. Chapter 6, 'A.B. Frost and the Photographic Revolution', juxtaposes photographic accuracy with the symbolic nature of the picture, and argues that photographs became the default in print culture, thus pushing sequential art to adapt. Chapter 7, 'From the Label to the Balloon', pivots slightly to the development of the word balloon as not just an informative label but an in-the-moment act of speaking. This is the first chapter to spend the bulk of its commentary on an American cartoon: Richard Outcault's *Yellow Kid*. Finally, chapter 8, 'Winsor McCay', argues that *Little Nemo in Slumberland* was a deliberate divergence from the popular comics of the day: visually complex, varied from week to week, resisting formulae at every opportunity, and emulating European work. Smolderen asserts that the artists he examines in the book represent the cartoonist's desire to use sequential art to illustrate the great variety of life itself.

John Dunning and Paul Gravett's *Comics Unmasked: Art and Anarchy in the UK* is the companion piece to an exhibition of the same name at the British Library in the summer of 2014. Like Smolderen's *Origins* (see above), *Comics Unmasked* is an art book: large-format, slick paper, illustrations on two-thirds of its pages, all of them in colour, and commissioned art for the cover. The writing style is much more casual than Smolderen's, however, and while all the images are cited, there is no quotation of secondary sources. The book is seemingly aimed at the general audience that might have attended the show rather than a community of comics scholars. The stated scope is less well-known British comics who have courted controversy and/or challenged conventions rather than those who have achieved mainstream success and/or perpetuated British social norms, although the line between the two is not always that clear. The book contains six chapters in addition to its introduction, which explains the premise of the book and then launches into a short history of comics in Britain: William Hogarth, the Victorian serial press, long-running publications such as *The Beano*, the anti-comics movement, counter-cultural comics, the manga invasion, and finally digital comics. The remaining chapters are organized by broad themes. Chapter 1, 'Mischief and Mayhem', starts with a brief history of *Punch* and focuses largely on the anti-comics movement in Britain that, while ideologically parallel to America's movement, ended up focusing on American comics as the source of the problem. Chapter 2, 'To See Ourselves', looks at comics that reflect on British classism, racism, and attitudes towards immigrants. Chapter 3, 'Politics, Power, and the People', is rooted in the anarchism of the book's title and examines anti-authoritarian comics from George Cruikshank in the early nineteenth century to recent anti-racist and economic-justice comics. Chapter 4, 'Let's Talk about Sex', details comics about sex, from Hogarth's *Harlot's Progress* to more pornographic material such as Alan Moore and Melinda Gebbie's *Lost Girls*, with special attention paid to the legal difficulties of publishing such material given the UK's obscenity laws. Chapter 5, 'Hero with a Thousand Faces', an allusion to Joseph Campbell's book of the same name (Pantheon [1949]), focuses on the adaptation of the American superhero to British concerns: often quite imitative but just as often revisionist and political. Finally, Chapter 6, 'Breakdowns: The Outer Limits of Comics', examines the curious intersection of sex, drugs, magical theory (à la Aleister Crowley), and radical formalism that haunts the fringes of British comics, and is most famous in the work of creators such as Alan Moore, Grant Morrison, and Dave McKean.

Cord A. Scott's *Comics and Conflict: Patriotism and Propaganda from WWII through Operation Iraqi Freedom* is a manuscript from the United States Naval Institute Press, which describes itself as an independent forum for America's maritime soldiers to study the country's national defences. As such, the NIP is not funded by the United States military, but it is ideologically affiliated, and the text shows signs of bias towards American military interests. Nonetheless, it qualifies as a work of comics scholarship given that it is an expanded version of Scott's doctoral dissertation. The argument proceeds from the premise that mass culture is largely controlled by top-down forces, but some of it evades that control and thus reveals the audience's feelings directly. Therefore, *Comics and Conflict* studies how American comics represent war in order to understand how Americans perceive it: heroic, horrific, or both. The book's scope includes major wars fought by America since 1938 (i.e. the first appearance of Superman). As such, it leaves out a great number of covert or less widely known conflicts in which America has taken part. Scott's interest is in the point at which patriotic rallying tips into fascistic or xenophobic propaganda, and his turns of phrase equally praise both those comics that attempted to rally Americans in favour of war and those that critiqued America's involvement. The book contains eight chapters, including a preface that functions as an introduction and a conclusion. The six middle chapters are in chronological order according to America's major conflicts: the Second World War (1939–45), the Cold War (1945–62), the Vietnam War and its cultural impact (1962–91), the end of the Cold War (1991–2001), terrorism post-9/11 (2001–3), and finally the Second Iraq War

(2003–10). Each chapter is further divided into small sections, some only a page long, that describe how comics of a given era depicted war, motifs that developed and carried across different wars, and the necessity for the comics to adapt to an ever-shifting enemy (e.g. from Nazis to communists and eventually to terrorists). These chapters do not make many explicit arguments about America's war comics, choosing instead to report on their contents more than anything else. The last chapter, 'Concepts of War through Comic Books', summarizes the trends that Scott observes. Anti-war comics existed in each era, and while many were limited to simply not depicting combat as horrifying rather than heroic, others, such as the underground comics of the 1960s, were openly critical. Pro-war comics have also existed in every era, especially the Second World War and the Cold War in the 1980s, although many of their creators had never experienced war at first hand. Finally, the book's appendix reprints the Comics Code in its entirety.

A. David Lewis's *American Comics, Literary Theory, and Religion: The Superhero Afterlife* is slim manuscript, written in a clear, approachable tone that makes a complex argument remarkably easy to understand. Lewis proceeds from the premise that afterlives help to define selfhood for audiences and/or the faithful. Put crudely, if our *essence* is all that survives death, then it will, by definition, define what we *essentially* are. He argues that outside superhero comics, a fairly narrow set of signifiers indicate the afterlife for Westerners: e.g. clouds, harps, fluffy wings, etc. However, shared-universe superhero comics, even those created by a single publisher, contain such a variety of depictions of the afterlife that the *superhero* afterlife is rightly a subgenre of afterlife stories. This multiplicity of afterlives parallels the theory of selfhood that Lewis subscribes to, in which all people have multiple internal identities; they contain many different *selves* (rather than the single *self* that a unified afterlife would imply). His short review of afterlife literature makes this argument in historical terms by demonstrating that all conceptions of the afterlife are a product of many beliefs and traditions that continually mutate, and thus are never singular or concrete. In order to have one, more or less consistent, body of comics to work with, Lewis narrows his scope to American superhero comics from 1985 to 2011. He argues that the mid-1980s quite famously saw several landmark comics that shifted the norms of the genre (*Watchmen, The Dark Knight Returns*, and *Secret Wars*), and the industry shifted from selling to newsstands and drug stores to speciality shops: i.e. the direct market. In addition to the introduction and conclusion, the book contains four chapters (of about thirty pages each). Chapter 1, 'The Six Elements of the Superhero Afterlife', argues that the superhero afterlife is made believable by its use of six tropes. Chapter 2, 'The Comic Book Medium's Glimpse of Eternity', makes the argument that the formal qualities of comics—sequential panels, word balloons—are akin to the afterlife. Chapter 3, 'Complexities of Character in *Fantastic Four: Hereafter*', argues that Mark Waid and the late Mike Wieringo's depiction of Heaven depicts characters as *transpersonal* (always in transition), which prompts audiences to think of themselves as transpersonal. Chapter 4, '*Planetary, Promethea* and the Multiplicity of Selfhood', similar to chapter 3, argues that Warren Ellis and John Cassaday as well as Alan Moore and J.H. Williams III use metafiction to reveal that *character* is a fragile literary device, which goes to question the Western conception of selfhood itself. Finally, the conclusion connects all four chapters, arguing that the superhero afterlife creates a model of multiplicity that audiences can use to understand their own multiplicitous selves and to better relate to other people.

Michael Barrier's *Funnybooks: The Improbable Glories of the Best American Comic Books* is a massive though selective history of Dell Comics, from the early 1930s to the mid-1950s. Barrier explicitly states that he selects his examples based on his own sense of quality and preference (e.g. no superheroes), which omits many creators from his survey. In his introduction, he recounts a short history of the American comic book but with several divergences from the conventional narrative, claiming for example that Harry Wildenberg invented the format for Eastman Color Printing. One can infer from M.C. Gaines's relative absence from this story that Barrier is intervening in American comics history to counter Gaines's claim to have invented it, a claim that many historians and scholars have repeated over the decades. Regardless, Barrier's history of comics gradually works its way around to Dell, and it argues that the publisher's ostensibly superior quality resulted from its comics' greater length, which allowed creators to focus on character and story, as well as their best creators' tendency to aim at older and/or more intelligent children. He also implies that using talking animals and children to voice sly commentaries on real life is what the best Dell Comics did: Walt Kelly's *Pogo*, Carl Barks's *Donald Duck*, and John Stanley's *Little Lulu*. The bulk of the book is taken up by an astonishing twenty-seven chapters that, collectively, relate the story of Dell Comics. The subject matter and discourse are much more like those of investigative journalism than academia, which is fitting given that Barrier is not an academic. He describes people's personalities, quotes them at length based on interviews, and goes into the business of comics at great length: licensing deals, sales figures, royalty rates, etc. The narrative starts with Dell's creation as a way to sell colour printing, and ends with its eventual fall due to shifts in the marketplace and loss of the licensing deals with major media companies, Disney and Warner Bros. among them.

Julia Round's *Gothic in Comics and Graphic Novels: A Critical Approach* is a heavily revised and augmented version of her dissertation work and the result of many years of research on the Gothic in comics. Although she argues that the Gothic mode exists in the American tradition at least as much as the British, her book focuses on the 'British invasion' creators of the 1980s and 1990s—e.g. Alan Moore, Neil Gaiman, and others—given that they were influenced by Romantic and Gothic literature to a much greater degree than the American creators, who were, by then, mostly products of the comic-book industry itself (i.e. former fans). The book contains nine chapters and is divided into three sections that are organized around three approaches to the Gothic in comics. Part I, 'History', contains two chapters. The chapters describe a history of British comics, American comics, and the Gothic, noting parallels and divergences, and there is a very short note on comics formalism and Gothic theory. Part II, 'Medium', contains three chapters and five case studies that, collectively, reinterpret comics formalism using Gothic concepts: haunting (page breakdowns), excess (visual/verbal perspectives on the page), and the crypt (aka the gutters as archive). The case studies are *House of Mystery*, *iZombie*, *Sandman*, and *The New Deadwardians*. Finally, Part III, 'Culture and Content', contains four chapters that apply the theories developed in the first two parts. Chapter 6 is on the subculture(s) of comics and the Gothic as well as allegory, and chapter 7 is on literary authenticity in Gothic comics. Finally, chapters 8 and 9 look at modern comic-book presentations of two Gothic figures: the vampire and the zombie. The book ends with a one-page 'Reflection', really an extremely short summary conclusion that simply reviews the major ideas of the argument.

Katherine Roeder's *Wide Awake in Slumberland: Fantasy, Mass Culture, and Modernism in the Art of Winsor McCay* is catalogue-sized (8.5 × 11 inches), full-colour, and contains illustrations on most if not quite all of its spreads, It is a designed book: each chapter begins with a reprint of a key *Nemo* comic, in addition to the internal illustrations. The pages are thick and shiny and each one has wide margins to make extra space for those illustrations. Even the typeface and kerning have been set for maximum visual appeal. In addition to analysing McCay's comic strips for their own meanings, Roeder argues that *Nemo* in particular is an exemplary work of twentieth-century modernism. She makes this argument from within an art-history methodology rather than the predominant literary/cultural approach in American comics scholarship. A large portion of the introduction, for example, cover McCay's biography, placing his working career in the context of turn-of-the-century art education, the printing industry, animation, and vaudeville, where McCay performed *chalk talks* and first showed *Gertie the Dinosaur*, his hand-drawn animation film. The introduction also contains a brief literature review of those few art historians who have examined comic strips as well as noting several works of comics scholarship that have treated them. The book contains six chapters in all, the first of which is the introduction, and a short conclusion. Chapter 2, 'Exploding Boys and Hungry Girls', uses a self-reflexive strip from *Little Sammy Sneeze* to show how McCay both constructed and then violated the form of the comic strip, and Roeder argues that this self-consciousness is one of the prime traits of modernism. Chapter 3, 'Picturing Boyhood', places *Little Nemo in Slumberland* in the context of contemporary visions of childhood as the ultimate creative space, and argues that it fostered consumerist longing. Chapter 4, 'Popular Amusement for All', argues that McCay's use of imagery from circuses, amusement parks, and fairs places viewers in familiar territory so that they can have a safe adventure in Slumberland. Chapter 5, 'Strategies and Techniques of the Advertiser', following on chapter 2, argues that childhood was seen as a creative period but also the perfect time to groom young consumers, and *Nemo* reflects that connection through Christmas and Thanksgiving strips as well as imagery of materialist plenty. Finally, chapter 6, 'The Marriage of Humor and Anxiety', flips the themes of *Nemo* and *Sammy Sneeze* by looking at *Dream of the Rarebit Fiend*, McCay's adult-oriented comic strip that, rather than a fantastical Slumberland, depicts nightmares of violence and loss of identity in the city. Roeder's conclusion takes up the biography that she leaves off from the introduction, briefly describing McCay's under-studied political cartoons, the tail end of his vaudeville career, and his other animated film, *The Sinking of the Lusitania*. She then spends several pages describing how cartoonists who followed (e.g. Frank King, Bill Watterson, Maurice Sendak) were influenced by his work, and she ends by noting that McCay was a product of his time, a synthesizer of many different aesthetics and techniques, rather than a singular genius.

Neil Cohn's *The Visual Language of Comics: Introduction to the Structure and Cognition of Sequential Images* is a book of what Cohn calls 'visual language theory' (p. xv), which describes comics as being written in what he argues is quite literally, and not metaphorically, a language. The book consistently uses linguistics theory and terminology, in keeping with the argument that visual and verbal languages are simply not separate things, which means that it is not a work of semiotics. It has an unusual structure that bears some explanation. The introduction is more of a foreword, and the first chapter is more like a traditional introduction. There are nine chapters in total, divided into two sections, each of which starts with a few pages of introductory text. Chapter 1, 'Introducing Visual Language', explains that Cohn defines comics as divorced from their structural properties (i.e. word/image hybridity, sequential images, dominance of images, verbal/visual blending), but rather as a *structured* system of images, that structure being its morphology, which comics scholars know as visual convention, and its grammar, the narrative as related through a sequence of panels. Section 1, 'Structure of Visual Language', contains chapters 2 to 6. Chapters 2 and 3 both explain 'The Visual Lexicon', morphology in the first case and panel construction in the second. Chapter 4, 'Visual Language Grammar: Narrative Structure', characterizes panels as analogous to sentences rather than words, and presents three kinds of comprehension: linear, promiscuous, and cognitive. Chapter 5, 'Navigation of External Composition Structure', systematically breaks down the viewing sequences of panels. Chapter 6, 'Cognition of Visual Language', compares viewer comprehension with the structure that the previous chapters describe. Section 2, 'Visual Language across the World', contains chapters 7 to 10, and it essentially surveys three kinds of visual language. Chapter 7, 'American Visual Language', looks at three styles in American comics: Kirbyan (after Jack Kirby), Barksian (after Carl Barks), and Independent (from indie comics). Chapter 8, 'Japanese Visual Language', looks at *manga* as essentially one coherent system that has come to influence the rest of the world. Chapter 9, 'Central Australian Visual Language', looks at sand drawing among Central Australian Aboriginal peoples. Finally, chapter 10, 'The Principle of Equivalence', essentially argues that 'we should expect that the mind/brain treats all expressive capacities in similar ways, given modality-specific constraints' (p. 195), an argument that helps explain the book's underlying principles, and would be very useful to read *first*.

Julian Darius's *When Manga Came to America: Super-Hero Revisionism in Mai, the Psychic Girl* is a slim manuscript from Sequart, so it is written in a casual, non-academic tone, and it must be said that some of the writing in this particular book feels a little hurried or off-the-cuff; however, the subject matter is significant and under-studied. The influence of *manga* on Anglo-American comics is hard to overestimate, and *Mai* is one of the very first such comics to be translated into English and published in America through what was a prominent publisher at the time: Eclipse Comics. The book contains three unnumbered chapters in addition to the introduction and an appendix. The introduction contains a brief description of the initial problems of the translation/adaptation of right-to-left *manga* into left-to-right comics, summarizes *Mai*'s plot (which makes some sense given how little known it is), and then offers a qualitative review for reasons that are not clear. The first chapter, 'The Depiction of Superpowers', retells the plot, act by act, commenting on Ryoichi Ikegami's art along the way. The second, '*Mai, the Psychic Girl* and Revisionism', feels like the real heart of the book. Darius places *Mai* in the context of American 'revisionist' comics, which had a watershed year in 1986. Revisionist comics inserted selective elements of realism into superhero stories, and Darius argues that *Mai* specifically parallels Alan Moore and John Totleben's *Miracleman* (as it was known in America). The third chapter, 'Sexuality in *Mai, the Psychic Girl*', describes the series' use of the male gaze and how her powers occasionally come to represent her pubescent sexuality. Finally, the appendix, 'A *Mai* Movie?', briefly reports on the handful of failed attempts to adapt the book into an American film, speculating about what it might have looked like given who was tentatively involved.

Annessa Ann Babic's *Comics as History, Comics as Literature: Roles of the Comic Book in Scholarship, Society, and Entertainment* is an anthology organized around comics as vessels of historical information, and juxtaposes American comics with those from the rest of the world. The introduction does make several questionable assertions in its historical overview though, referring to Rodolphe Töpffer's *Histoire de M. Vieux Bois* by its American title but using the original European publication date, calling Neil Gaiman et al.'s *Sandman* 'manga', and claiming that Will Eisner's *Comics and Sequential Art* was the first academic treatment of comics. These strange claims aside, the book contains several groupings of chapters, the first one containing four of the book's thirteen chapters and focusing on comics outside the United States. The rest are American. The first section focuses on francophone comics: Henri-Simon Blanc-Hoàng on Atlanticism and Marxism; Guillaume de Syon on 1970s French history comics; Annick Pellegrin on the love/hate relationship between America and France; and Melanie Huska on civic-education comics in 1980s Mexico. The second section contains four chapters on war in America: Peter Lee on Wonder Woman as army nurse; Babic (the editor) on Wonder Woman as patriotic icon; and Lynda Goldstein on comic-book representations of 9/11. The third section is on identity politics: Kara M. Kvaran on homosexuality in superhero comics; Micah Rueber on masculinity and Dr Doom; and Christina Dokou on depicting Frank Miller comics in film. Finally, in the last two chapters, Faiz Sheikh discusses hype individuality in *The Walking Dead*, and Beatrice Skordili gives excellent attention to *Logicomix* and logic as a part of human nature.

5. African American Writing

Juda Bennett's critical examination and 'queering' of ghosts in *Toni Morrison and the Queer Pleasure of Ghosts* claims to uncover how Morrison's ghosts are 'already queer' (p. 2), providing a body through which a provocative challenge to heteronormativity can be presented. In her work, Bennett works closely with Judith Halberstam's definition of 'queer' as a site of 'nonnormative logics and organizations' (p. 2), and Bennett expressed her appreciation for the flexibility of the definition to provide a breadth of scope to cover sexual identity, embodiment, desire, and other activities that act as counterpoints to normative enactment. According to Bennett, the queer theory approach enables an 'antiessentialist inquiry into structures of power and identity' (p. 2). Accordingly, the queer approach to reading Morrison's ghosts is used beyond LGBT identity discussions, in a more general way in which the ghosts become a mode through which ethnic women's literature can effectively challenge dominant discourses that tend to want to neutralize language and narrative that speaks from a place of marginality. Bennett asserts that Morrison's ghosts are at the centre of disruption to dominant discourses and histories. Through their apparitions, they provide alternative, counter-discourses and deconstructions of conventional binaries, conventions, and conformations. While the queer effect is used to great advantage as a general disruptor, it also points to the homosexual, lesbian, and bisexual figures in her work. Moreover, Bennett is not unaware of the way in which queer readings can erase race, and assures readers that both black studies and queer theory inform her approach to Morrison's fiction. She asserts that the combination of both queer and black studies, both sharing origins in social and political activism, provides the opportunity for a fruitful 'interanimation' of the two disciplines. Bennett cites the twin themes elucidated by both queerness and ghosts in 'the tension between known and unknown, visible and invisible, familiar and strange' (p. 3). In an effort to avoid an oversimplistic tautology (the uncanny is queer; the queer is uncanny), Bennett points to the necessity of elucidating the space of death by giving it a voice, arguing that Morrison queers the ghost to address 'interlocking forces of racism, sexism, and heteroism' (p. 3). Rather than privileging the supernatural, Bennett draws attention to the opportunity that a ghost's liminality affords as a narrative device: what it means to live between culture, time and space, for instance. Bennett then goes on to reference Sedgwick's definition of queer to point to the opportunity that 'gaps, overlaps, dissonances and resonances, lapses and excesses' (p. 4) when one is trying to communicate something outside the monolithic homogeneity.

Additionally, Bennett's mediation includes Derrida's 'hauntalogy', putting forward the idea that 'readers consider everything as ghost—history, memory, text, and, indeed, the world as we perceive it' (p. 4). Lest readers become concerned that the application, the ghostliness is too glib, and therefore at risk of meaning everything and nothing, Bennett assures us through Derrida that in acknowledging the centrality of ghostliness and its relationship to queerness, the problem of presence and its twin, absence, can be accounted for, since nothing is without 'ghost affects', and it is an application of thought rather than a thing in itself, a lens to filter the experience and the perception of the world around us. In sum, Bennett proposes to 'queer the ghost in Morrison as a way of understanding its relevance to her work and her time' (p. 5). For Bennett, the presence of ghosts is a narrative device through which Morrison's fiction addresses binaries of life/death, presence/absence, and body/spirit and accordingly can be found in many forms that are not strictly the undead. For instance, ghost could be haunting music, a house, a photograph, a voice, a body part, a memory, the colour white, and history itself. In order to ground this approach, Bennett draws upon the Freudian notion of the uncanny, that familiar strangeness that can catch someone off guard, that can alert the reader to a deeper theme or narrative in seemingly un-ghostly things or experiences, and she cites Freud in reminding readers that this experience of the uncanny is a powerful reminder about the 'history of representation at the turn of the twentieth century' (p. 7). Moreover, Bennett argues that the convergence of queer, race, and ghost studies shares a nexus in a certain 'liberationist ethics grounded in the importance of uncovering the repressed in order to release individual and communal potentialities' (p. 7). In short, in Morrison, the ghost 'queers everything but especially Morrison's capacious exploration of love in all its forms and expressions' (p. 7). In order to present her theory and discussion, Bennett presents the literature in pairs of chapters, establishing the relevance of ghosts and queerness not only within single novels, but relationships between various novels, including *Sula*, *Beloved*, *Paradise*, *Love*, *Song of Solomon*, *Jazz*, *Tar Baby*, *A Mercy*, *The Bluest Eye*, and *Home*.

W. Lawrence Hogue's *Postmodernism, Traditional Cultural Forms and African American Narratives* explores the way in which various African American social and political movements, studies, scholars, and cultural and artistic forms have sought to challenge and redefine the way in which African Americans are represented as Other, and often not simply as Other, but as deviant, negative, or binary to whiteness (middle-class, puritan) which is generally privileged as the norm. The central question in the book is how to wrest blackness from a binary that situates blackness as the deviant, primitive, devalued, inferior, negative binary of whiteness. And once freed from the binary, how does the African American assert a different kind of subjectivity; what does it look like? At best, freed black subjectivities have only managed to assert sameness as their puritan white counterparts; sometimes they assert superiority, but they are still caught within the binary and are judged by criteria that see them according to norms rooted in puritan whiteness. Hogue, specifically points to the inherent violence contained within the binaries of Western metaphysics: they reduce and devalue, and the logic of domination of the upper half over the lower half (the opposite of the preferred norm) results in an inherent subordination that is presumed natural and fixed in the binary subjectivity. Hogue's objective is to redefine African American subjectivity outside the binary looks to the notion of difference, as developed by the linguistic school and its descendants, as a way to free itself from binary constructions. Even so, ultimately, the notion of difference, while initially promising liberation, ultimately comes up short in that it is too mysterious, too all-encompassing, too incomplete, in that it is also in process of becoming, but never actually being.

Hogue reviews the various processes through which African Americans have sought to counter the damaging binary they have been caught within since European capture and slavery, post-emancipation and civil rights and beyond. Such attempts have included the racial uplift that middle-class or aspiring middle-class African Americans adopted; however, this action only results in being, even in the most successful cases, as Hélène Cixous articulates it, 'inside without being inside' (p. 7). As a counterpoint to this assimilative approach to subjectivity, other African Americans have adopted a cultural renaissance in which black arts, language, history, and culture are privileged and celebrated. While these efforts, most notably effective in the early twentieth century during the era often referred to as the Harlem Renaissance, or more broadly as the Black Arts Movement, were initially liberating, and had a profound effect on American culture in general, the actual day-to-day rights of African Americans changed little, a realization that gave rise to the civil rights movements of the 1950s and 1960s. However, Hogue argues that despite the liberating potential and effects of the first half of the twentieth century, the organizations at the centre of the movement had 'rigid rules and regulations'; they also 'imposed norms and standards from the top down', and while attaining critical gains politically and citizenship-wise, they achieved this by flipping the binary, adopting middle-class, Christian practices and values: 'they subordinated women, homosexuals, non-Christians, and non-middle class taste and values' (p. 11). In other words, the liberated African American was a middle-class, Christian, heterosexual male. Violent oppression of the subaltern African American had been assumed by middle-class African Americans themselves.

Hogue importantly identifies in Anna Julia Cooper's 1892 text *A Voice From the South* a vision and theorization that would ultimately reappear nearly seventy years later in the postmodern theories of Jean-François Lyotard, Michel Foucault, Gilles Deleuze, and Jacques Derrida: she proposes 'an unregulated freedom or pure difference' (p. 17). In Cooper's under-recognized text, she argues for the 'abandonment of a centralized, rational (grand) narrative; for the abandonment of the whole edifice of patriarchal Euro-American humanism, which has proven incapable of going beyond its own limitations of vision; and for embracing a vision of the world (America) in which multiple incompatible discourse or language games (Wittgenstein) flourish alongside each other' (p. 17). This vision offers the clearest path out of the violent binary bind in which the binaries are 'not separate and equal' but rather a 'violent hierarchy where one has the upper hand and the lower half is defined in a reduced way' (p. 18).

Hogue continues to present the rise of the African American consciousness and liberation from Euro-American humanism and centrism through its troubled history through the civil right era, and through the creation of black studies programmes and departments at American universities, before presenting a series of chapters which offer close readings of six African American texts that all offer alternative representations of African Americans. The close readings include John Edgar Widerman's *Philadelphia Fire*; Percival Everett's *Erasure*; Toni Morrison's *Jazz*; Bonnie Greer's *Hanging by Her Teeth*; Clarence Major's *Reflex and Bone Structure*; and Xam Cartiér's *Muse-Echo Blues*. Accordingly, the focus of these close readings includes privileging of such cultural structures as jazz, the blues, the African American trickster figure, Yoruba gods, African American folk culture, radical democracy, and virtuality, all of which operate outside and distinct from the middle-class puritan American norm.

Marlon Rachquel Moore describes *In the Life and in the Spirit: Homoerotic Spirituality in African American Literature* as a genealogical project to discover who, in the years following James Baldwin's novel *Go Tell It on the Mountain* (Knopf [1953]), wrote about LGBT and its connections to the sacred, and the entanglement of being black, sexually queer, and a Christian. As Moore begins to construct her genealogy, she discovers that Baldwin is not really the beginning of this type of writing: black male homosexuality can be traced to back to 1928 and Richard Bruce Nugent's short story 'Smoke, Lilies, and Jade', and a subsequent publication in 1970 of another of Nugent's stories, 'These Discordant Bells', works to firmly establish him as the origin of queer, black, spiritual fiction. Nugent, along with Hughes, Douglas, Hurston, and Thurman, was firmly rooted in an antithetical stance to Dubois's (and Johnson's and Locke's) New Negro ideology. His extreme and openly gay lifestyle meant that he lost publication opportunities, and it would not be until 2002, and again in 2005 that his work would be collected and published as a restoration of lost manuscripts from the 1920s to the 1940s. For Moore, the troubled publication history works to point to the contentious and buried evidence of a tradition of black queer spirituality. With the aim of answering the question about who and how black writers address the 'intersection of spirituality and same-sex eros' (p. 1), Moore offers critical discussions of a number of texts by queer black writers, including those of Langston Hughes, James Baldwin, Alice Walker, Octavia Butler, Rebecca Cox Jackson, Jewelle Gomez, and Ann Allen Shockley. Her critical discussion is grounded in feminist/womanist discourses, African American literary theory, queer theory, and lesbian/gay studies, and, for what Moore refers to as liberation theology, she looks to the rhetoric of Black Theology. Moore's choice of literature enables her to explore the way in which genre can also afford space for the queer spiritual native to speak, and accordingly her readings also include ex-slave narratives, fantasy, and science fiction genre literature. As a final word on her critical discussions, Moore affirms that within the African American literary tradition, queer spiritual narratives occupy a space that attests to the broad diversity of black writing in the United States.

In Venetria K. Patton's critical study of African American fiction by women, *The Grasp that Reaches Beyond the Grave*, she puts forward the theory of matrifocal fiction: that texts by black women are centred upon the mother–child, or othermother–child relationships because of the unique and central role that women play in family structures. This text seeks to fill what Patton perceives to be a gap in the scholarship on women-centred networks in African American women's writing. Patton cites the attention that scholarship has paid to other familial relations explored in literature, as well as the question of maternity and matrilineality within the African diaspora, as in literature in general. Patton roots her interest in and work on this topic in the womb itself, and also in the particular history of slavery in the slave context of which women are 'natally dead' (p. 3), that slave women are not obligated to fulfil their maternal duties to their children, nor are children obligated to their own parents. Patton cites scholarship that blames the social disconnect that black

Americans have experienced on this missing maternity, a key attribute of the slave's powerlessness, that the 'orphaning' of slaves is key to their complete disempowerment, so that their social existence is contingent on their master. Yet, as Patton and others have observed, elders and ancestral bonds, in particular maternal or mother-figures, persist.

Patton's study extends beyond the scope of the slave narrative but recognizes that to a certain extent the legacy of that history underwrites or informs much African American writing regardless, including works that are roughly contemporary to current times. In light of the revisionist response to slavery during the 1980s under the Reagan administration, which sought to cleanse American history of its close relationship to and residual effects of its slavery past, Patton sees African American women's literature that asserts mother–daughter relationships as providing a counter-narrative to historical amnesia. And Patton explains that the analysis that comprises her book is in dialogue with such works as Nancy J. Peterson's *Against Amnesia: Contemporary Women Writers and the Crises of Historical Memory* (UPennP [2001]) and Gauthier Marni's *Amnesia and Redress in Contemporary American Fiction* (Palgrave [2011]). Like them, Patton is invested in rethinking African Americans' place in American history, ultimately seeking a reconstruction, rather than simply a deconstructive critique of what has been forgotten, left out, and denied. Accordingly, Patton reads these texts as a way women writers can resist the kinlessness that has been viewed as necessitated by slavery by instead asserting a revision that allows the women characters to reclaim their progeny, and in these instances in particular with their daughters who are likely to become mothers themselves. While there is no denying that the family structure is violently disrupted by slavery, emphasis is shifted to the way African Americans responded by positing the family as a key narrative component, celebrating the fluidity of family bonds beyond the typical nuclear family structure, emphasizing instead how the concept of family is open and inclusive (extended family, non-blood relatives, and so forth), rather than closed and exclusive, with special privilege for elders. While the elder is respected for traditional reasons (wisdom and long life), the elder also occupies a sort of liminal position, bridging the natural and supernatural worlds, the place where 'the ancestors and the divine intersect with humans' (p. 8). Therefore the significance of the ancestor figure in African American narrative is culturally specific and references belief systems that position elders as bridging these worlds. The dead are not dead in the western European conception of death, and it is the elders who have access to both the living world and the supernatural world of the ancestors. Moreover, it is the complex kinship system that also provides stability when its core is destabilized by social disruptions such as slavery, acute and systematic poverty and racism, and violent segregation. Patton critically examines this process as it plays out in the works of Julie Dash, Toni Cade Bambara, Paule Marshall, Phyllis Alesia Perry, and Toni Morrison.

Overall, Sarah Gilbreath Ford's book *Tracing Southern Storytelling in Black and White* traces interconnections amongst southern writers from the end of the nineteenth century through the twentieth century, focusing in particular on the use of storytelling in their written texts. Ford achieves this by pairing a black author with a white author in order to demonstrate that the propensity towards oral tradition in written work happens across racial lines, hoping to demonstrate that despite the troubled past, there is a southern culture shared by black and white alike. Ford uses the works of Joel Chandler Harris, Charles Chesnutt, Zora Neale Hurston, William Faulkner, Ralph Ellison, Eudora Welty, Ernest Gaine, and Ellen Douglas. Working with Morrison's call for scholars to acknowledge the considerable contribution of black Americans to the formation of the nation and the nation's literature, Ford's book addressed the interconnectedness of southern black and white culture, focusing particularly on oral culture. However, the affinities between and amongst writers are often tricky to establish, and the relationships are not always viewed as having been friendly or honest. As Ford explains, 'Harris devised a structure to turn the oral stories into written ones', which 'gave Charles Chesnutt ideas about how to record the oral stories he heard as a child, but Harris's use of a black "uncle" to tell stories to a white boy led Alice Walker to complain that her heritage was stolen. Mark Twain picked up the use of dialect from Harris, and Twain's work impacted how Ralph Ellison and William Faulkner used oral storytelling. Twain was also influenced by his exposure to African American culture' (p. 3). So, while the interconnectedness is surely there, the affinity is not always friendly. Nevertheless, examining the literary record as a dialogue provides opportunities for insight into the formation of the southern literary canon. Accordingly, Ford provides discussion on what makes a literature southern, how the South is constructed as an imaginary (following Anderson) community, or as a geographical, cultural entity. Ultimately, Ford sees the South as partly geographical, although not exclusively so; it is also a manner of storytelling—oral—and it is also an imagined, constructed community that shares a particular geography, history, and culture that is both black and white. Finally, the writers chosen by Ford in this study not only share actual connections, they also share an intentional manner of writing that constructs their literature as consciously southern. Ford refers to this construction of southernness, as it is connected to slavery and civil war, shaped by racism and violence as a metanarrative, one that at once feeds into the larger American identity, but is also an 'other' for the nation, differentiated and distinct from the whole American identity. Ford argues that, construction or not, restrictive or not, the conception of the South is borne by the literature as playing into a conception of a South whose identity is directly informed by the slavery/civil war nexus that defines it as 'backward and deviant' (p. 5). Ford establishes a complex relationship between the tendency of southern culture to privilege talking and the confluence of oral features within written texts in southern literature as reflecting cultural practices. This tendency is then extended between and amongst writers to carry out a conversation in a literary style that is not merely organic, but rather intentionally constructed to meet certain ends: a radical discourse that established the conception of the southern as distinct from mainstream America, an extreme form of regional identity that corresponded with extraordinary moments in American history: the Reconstruction era, the Depression and exodus of African Americans from the South, and the civil rights era.

The collection of essays contained in *Racial Blackness and the Discontinuity of Western Modernity* represent the posthumous publication of previously unpublished works by Lindon Barrett which he did not have the opportunity to publish before his death in 2008. Upon discovering that Barrett's laptop with the manuscript on it had been stolen, friends and colleagues reconstructed the manuscript from the versions of chapters that he had shared with them. The book is the result of a considerable amount of reconstructive effort on the part of Barrett's trusted colleagues. As it has been reconstructed, it offers a critical discussion of how 'modern slavery and capitalism developed in conjunction' (p. xii), offering a counter-theory to the traditional view that slavery is a type of feudal institution. Accordingly, Barrett takes the view that modernity has little to do with technological advances and much to do with economic, social, and political pressures in Europe (the consolidation of kingdoms into nation-states, for instance). One technique of effecting the political consolidation of hereditary lands is to forward a theory of ethnic superiority, and its binary, ethnic inferiority. The modern era, according to this view, is defined by the rise of an economic system that distinguishes between rulers and ruled, owners and owned, and capitalists and workers. At the core of Barrett's book is an argument about how capitalism commodifies humans, not always by means of the most visible manner in slavery, but through an economic class system whose disparities are maintained through cultural construction. While Barrett's book tackles modernism as a general concept of culture, the particulars of his arguments and discussion will be of interest to literary studies, as his chapters feature not only salient discussion about American modernity, but specific discussions of slave narratives, cultural writings, and novels by prominent African American writers to illustrate his theories of modernism in the United States.

Trimiko Melancon's book *Unbought and Unbossed: Transgressive Black Women, Sexuality, and Representation* explores the concept of 'sexual citizenship' through the trope of transgressive behaviour and focused on post-1960s black women's texts. While the book takes its name from the political slogan of congresswoman and presidential candidate Shirley Chisholm, the book itself is not about the political arena, but rather about the spirit of transgression that characterizes post-civil rights era literature and culture and the way in which black woman characters are used to transgress heteronormative boundaries of gender and sexuality. Her study includes Toni Morrison, Ann Allen Shockley, Alice Walker, Gayl Jones, and Gloria Naylor and addresses the female characters who transgress the desired and assumed propriety in order to advance sociopolitical aims in postmodern society. Melancon describes her usage of transgressive as 'deliberate "violation" of certain racial, gender, and sexual sociocommunal boundaries' (p. 2), with the intent of destabilizing normative, accepted, and acceptable behaviour. For Melancon, these transgressions hinge on sexuality: 'adultery, promiscuity, interracial sexual intimacy, circumvention of marital sex, sexual violence, same-gender loving, and/or other politics of the intimate' (pp. 2–3). Melancon sees these acts of transgression as arising from a particular socio-historical moment of the 1950s–1970s political and cultural struggles. These characters rebel against stereotypes of black female identity as it is intertwined in racial expectations imposed from within and without black American culture, the script that black women were to follow in order to express their loyalty to black men, and the idealization of marriage and motherhood. Melancon sees these transgressions as ways through which these writers resist essentialist constructions of community, race, and black womanhood in favour of what she describes as a 'progressive black identity' (p. 4) reflective of the sociopolitical moment of their inception. Nevertheless, Melancon acknowledges that despite the seeming empowerment that accompanies the characters' sexual transgression, these women's agency and autonomy are rife with vulnerability that plays out in the form of sexual violence. The violations point to the dangers of silence and the loss that is incurred in the absence of a progressive black sexual politics. While it might seem that the violence overshadows or undermines the aims of the transgressive sexual agencies, Melancon assures us that that is not the case: the vulnerability and transgressive expression free the black women's experience of racial essentialization, and draw attention to the complexity of experience as it is bound up in the sociocultural-historical, political, economic, racial, and gender issues governing black women in the post-civil rights era. In this manner, the transgressions are often accompanied by postmodern techniques of literary narrative and to create a unique ideological and aesthetic narrative to draw attention to diversity as opposed to commonality, as a means by which to counter totalizing feminist and black nationalist discourse and offer instead an intersectional identity and experience. Melancon reads the transgressive actions of the characters studied in this book as a refusal to conform to a particular normativity as inscribed or imposed by fundamental concepts that govern behaviour and desire within a narrow framework of normalcy. These frameworks include conventional (white) feminism, black nationalism, and a then just nascent multi-cultural discourse that consolidates difference as a peculiar sameness of the other, and any other hegemonic, heteronormatizing discourse of identity. And according to the narratives that Melancon discusses in her book, these types of transgression are often dangerous.

Tessa Roynon's book *Toni Morrison and the Classical Tradition: Transforming American Culture*, as part of a series that examines the presence of classical influence on contemporary culture, examines Morrison's engagement with ancient Greek and Roman tradition in her body of work, focusing on the way in which Morrison's works conceives and depicts contemporary experience through the lens of the ancient world, as in dialogue with the ancient past. The main question at the core of the book is to discover why an author such as Morrison, who is deeply committed to African American politics, history, and identity through a clearly European tradition that has likely been to blame for much of the thinking that has led to the legacy of oppression experienced by African Americans from the slavery era on should take this approach. How do invocations of the classical world advance Morrison's objectives to proffer debate about power, identity, and race in her fiction? Roynon contends that Morrison uses the position of the classical tradition as a pillar of Western civilization as well as its subversive potential as a storytelling device to offer an ambivalence towards the classical tradition that becomes a critical and authoritative voice in her oeuvre. In using the same discourse that justified the slave tradition, for instance, Morrison creates a powerful counternarrative that challenges the accepted view of the classical tradition, revealing it as conservative, 'white', and a fabrication of Enlightenment thinking. Morrison uses the classical tradition, its genres and resonances of themes, names, and places, to offer a revisionist writing of America's past that includes the disenfranchised voices of African Americans at various points in their history in America; the classical allusions enable a rewriting of and re-membering of America's past.

By way of introduction to Morrison's work, Roynon points to Morrison's 'minor' in Classics at Howard University, and her study of Latin in high school, and also offers a review of previous scholarship on Morrison's classical allusions, as well as pointing to the gaps in scholarship. In so doing, Roynon offers a series of arguments in her reading of Morrison's oeuvre. Roynon argues that Morrison's use of classical allusions is transnational: Morrison is part of a tradition of diasporic writing that uses classical literature, but importantly, Morrison's use of classically allusive writing suggests that the classical tradition is inherently diasporic. Further, Morrison's use of classical allusions is in line with America's own strategic uses of Greek, Roman, and Egyptian culture and history as a key component of the construction of American histories and identities, and thus her own use should be viewed as political, as a counter-discourse that disrupts the centrality of this usage to bolster Euro-American aims. Finally, rather than viewing Morrison's classical allusions as part of the *classica africana*, or 'black classicism', critics should observe that Morrison asserts a transnationality or pre-nationality to the classical world by transcending classical processes of categorization.

However, Roynon points out that the notion of transformation is often met with scepticism in African American literature: that transformation does not lead unequivocally to political advancement. Accordingly, in chapter 1, Roynon discusses the way in which Morrison addresses European justifications rooted in classical tradition for appropriation of the Americas. In chapter 2, she examines the Latinisms found in *A Mercy* and *Paradise*, wherein Morrison's discourse presents a critique of the 'founding fathers' political and personal identification with the heroes of the ancient world. Roynon argues that Morrison takes particular issue with both the Plutarchan conception of 'representative men' and the notion of the Athenian democracy and Roman republic as models of political representation and governance. In chapter 3, Roynon focuses on Morrison's depictions of slavery, the Civil War, and Reconstruction, taking to task the South's reliance on Graeco-Roman defenders of the Old South, and the way in which these defenders used classical genres of tragedy, epic, and the pastoral to justify slavery, wherein the tragic hero is the downfallen southern man who has lost everything to the ideal of war. In chapter 4 Roynon identifies a period in Morrison's writing in which the practice of scapegoating and Homeric epic are used in her depiction of black experience in the 1920s and 1930s. The journey from south to north, the poverty, and segregation are placed on an equal footing with the heroes and their journeys, trials, and tribulations of ancient times. Chapter 5 looks at Morrison's engagement with the *Oresteia* and its themes of justice in the *Song of Solomon* and *Love*. Roynon identifies Morrison's use of the Greek concept of 'miasma', or pollution, to direct the reader to draw parallels between Morrison's work and the Aeschylean trilogy. The sixth and final chapter focuses on the irony of America's classical inheritance having been inflected by African American meaningfulness, drawing relationships between the influence of Wole Soyinka on Morrison, Morrison's own belief in the 'Sympathetic relationship between classical and West African culture' (p. 27), and the interactions in classical times between North Africa and Greece and Rome. In all, Roynon's book is a comprehensive examination of Morrison's radical use of classical culture and literature in order to effect a counter narrative to Euro-American discourses.

In *Speaking in Tongues and Dancing Diaspora: Black Women Writing and Performing*, Mae Henderson argues that the presence of orality in written texts, at a time when written discourse is privileged, asserts another communicative space, not exclusively oral, nor reliant on textuality, but pointing to the centrality of the oral tradition in informing African American fiction: voice. Henderson points to Hurston's *Their Eyes Were Watching God* as a foundational text as much for its theorization for reading African American literature, as for literature itself. Essentially, Henderson sees that there is a continuum between orality and the oral tradition and textuality in African American writing, and points to the many tropes that have arisen to describe the close and continued relationship between the two: the talking book, speakerly text, and the talking text. Henderson offers her own trope of 'speaking in tongues' as a means by which to capture the oral–textual relationship and 'affirm the power of voice and sonance' (p. 2) in African American literature. These tropes assert a liberation of voice from a group whose members have experienced vocal suppression and self-silencing. The claiming and production of voice are critical to the successful reconstitution of fractured subjectivities, as well as the preservation of communal histories. Henderson's own trope for the communicative strategy, speaking in tongues, is meant to capture the oral tradition and its presence in written text, as well as to invoke the public/private dimension of the tradition of storytelling, as well as to acknowledge the diversity of women speakers in this tradition, to capture the voice of the speaker/writer. Accordingly, Henderson develops and offers an interpretative model that captures the 'interlocutory, dialogic, intertextual, and revisionary character' (p. 2) of black women's writing as performance in literature. Further, she seeks to reclaim a spiritual rite and cultural practice as critical praxis and theoretical trope for critically reading black women's literary performances. Accordingly, Henderson taps into women's roles in the spiritual practices of southern religious traditions which entail speaking in tongues, the interpretation of tongues, the witnessing of spiritual ecstasy, and the moment of ecstasy or revelation and its prevalence as tropes in black women's literature.

Consuela Francis's book *The Critical Reception of James Baldwin, 1962–2010: 'An Honest Man and a Good Writer'* is in part an attempt to address what she perceives as a scholarly gap in work on Baldwin, citing the tendency towards the extremes of critical devotion or neglect with very little thoughtful critical examination in between. Accordingly, Francis seeks to examine how Baldwin is not only significant to the black American literary tradition but remains at the periphery, as a marginal note. Francis cites the fact that critics cannot agree on the central issues presented in his writing. This lack of consensus amongst critics has put him in a marginal position vis-à-vis other important black American writers such as Morrison, Wright, Ellison, and Hurston, to name but a few. Francis points to a number of complexities in Baldwin's work that resist easy categorization, and in this manner looks at each critical period to see how Baldwin's work is perceived. Making critical reception central to the study of Baldwin's work poses a number of challenges to Francis; she cites the large oeuvre, and the numerous and frequent reviews of his work: he had a career span of nearly forty years, making it difficult to ascertain trends in his work and reception. Another challenge that Francis grapples with is the fact that black American writing in general, and Baldwin's writing in particular, has always been subject to multiple levels of discourse, including the critical, political, ideological, and identity-driven, an examin- ation of which reveals intriguing contradictions and controversies in his work. Francis's study of Baldwin's critical reception divides it into three stages: 1963–73, 1974–87, and 1988–2000, giving an overview of trends in each period and in turn placing those trends in a larger historical and critical context. In the second half of the book, Francis spotlights Baldwin's 'Sonny's Blues', looking at the criticism of this, his most famous and most frequently anthologized short story, explaining that because of the unusual amount of attention given to this one story it warrants its own discussion. The final chapter looks at the popular reviews of all of Baldwin's full-length works; Francis argues that it is important to consider the popular reception as well as the academic one in order to gain as full a perspective as possible of Baldwin's critical contribution to black American literature.

In *The Hip-Hop Underground and African American Culture: Beneath the Surface*, James Braxton Peterson traces what he describes as the rhizomatic nature of the black cultural underground, describing the way in which it intersects through time and space with the dimensions of political and artistic movements. Accordingly, Peterson culls his objects of study from music, television, literature, and art. The rhizomatic trope enables Peterson to link African American culture and tradition through its engagement in politics, genealogy, history, language, and music, in particular hip-hop as it manifests in underground cultural movements. Peterson invokes the language of literary studies, as well as ethnographic studies. Peterson's book offers an impressive depth and breadth of critical discussion of black American underground culture, ranging from the times of slavery and the underground railroad to the twenty-first century and the hip-hop culture/movement. Peterson engages in a kind of critical wordplay, engaging in the same linguistic style and cultural discourse in his own theory as those of the subjects he studies. He riffs on the concept of roots, as both an underground system and as a genealogical concept; he plays with the homological linguistics of rhyme (the discourse of hip-hop) and rhizomes; he riffs on roots and routes. So, Peterson's theoretical discourse walks the talk of the very African American cultural phenomenon at the heart of the study. He also chooses the television series *Roots* (based on Alex Haley's novel by the same name), and Baldwin's review in the *New York*

Times of the book in 1976 as an initial example of what he calls a 'sociological rubric' through which the reader/listener can explore underground black culture. All told, this initial discussion wends its way through the concept of roots, Alex Haley's *Roots*, Baldwin's reflections on *Roots*, Frederick Douglass's mystical root, *Invisible Man*'s yam, and the roots of hip-hop lore. Integral to Peterson's argument are the concepts that inform collage, bricolage, sampling, and remixing: discursive repetition with a difference, as he calls it, a nod to Henry Louis Gates's conception of 'signifyin': repetition with a difference. For Peterson, the assemblage of repetition, or creative repurposing, points to an African American underground aesthetic that has roots in collage (visual and aural) as well as in collaboration. While not strictly focused on literature, Peterson's book links literary culture to other artistic manifestations that suggest that they should not be studied in isolation due to the rhizomatic nature of black American art, culture, and history.

Ezra Greenspan's epic tome on the life and work of William Wells Brown, *William Wells Brown: An African American Life*, weighs in at a whopping 600 pages, and covers in awe-inspiring depth the life of Brown (1814–84), reflecting careful and thorough research and an intimacy with its subject matter that is rarely found in contemporary scholarship. Greenspan starts with the question, famously put to DuBois, 'How does it feel to be a problem?', linking the notion of the problematic to Brown's status as mixed race, mixed nationality, neither slave nor free, neither artist nor professional. Brown emblematizes the very heart of the 'problem' of African Americanness and its challenge to dominant histories and discourses. Greenspan traces the unlikely chart of Brown's life as a man fully immersed in the most notorious period in American history. Greenspan discusses the problems he encountered in reconstructing Brown's life, noting that he was a man who wrote non-stop until the day he died, but left behind no diary or personal record of his own life, save for a little correspondence, and does not reveal himself simply even in his own autobiographical writings. Greenspan refers to this as an uncanny ability 'about identity mastered in slavery' (p. 95). Greenspan draws upon the lives and archives of friends and the black American community as a whole. The result is a massive biography that links Brown's life not only to his personal experience as a boy born into slavery in Kentucky, but to that in the works and records of his contemporaries, including the more famous figures in African American literature such as Frederick Douglass, but also such figures as Daniel Boone. In so doing, Greenspan's biography offers a revisionist approach to American nineteenth-century history that integrates the often-times invisible history of blacks with that of whites, reminding readers of their presence despite their erasure from official discourses. No official markers record the presence of a light-skinned slave sometimes referred to as 'Sandy', but here he is, manifest as William Wells Brown, reinserted within the discourse of nineteenth-century American history.

Mary Washington begins her critical examination in *The Other Blacklist: The African American Literary and Cultural Left of the 1950s* by situating her own personal experiences at the beginning and acknowledging the deep vein of anti-civil rights sentiment that underwrote the Cold War, an awareness of which encouraged blacks to be by and large anti-communist, a main target of

Cold War antipathy. For institutions like the Federal Bureau of Investigation, the association between blackness and communist sympathy was strong, and so blacks, even those who stood to benefit most from civil rights actions, assumed an anti-communist stance. Washington explains that anyone who demonstrated strong support for the civil rights movement was automatically assume to possess a weak commitment to anti-communism. Washington cites a commonly asked question at loyalty board hearings in which interviewees were asked whether or not they thought that outspoken support for race equality was an index of favouring communism. Washington argues that despite the fact that nearly every major black writer of the civil rights era was at least moderately influenced by communist or other left-leaning politics, and the fact that the leftist political groups were the most racially diverse and inclusive, the terms of reference for blacklisted, communist, or other left-leaning Americans generally assumes white membership with an absence of black Americans. Washington describes how black Americans came to leftist or communist involvement, citing unions and labour organizations, as well as community and cultural groups that opposed racial segregation. And during the height of McCarthyism, any group that took part in activities that appeared dissenting (including teachers who sought to include Black History Week) were considered subversive, so that any subversive activity was labelled as anti-American and therefore communist. For Washington, however, growing up in the 1950s and 1960s, it was difficult to see how communism would do black people any good when any civil rights work was necessarily viewed as communist. This book is Washington's attempt to examine the radical civil rights movement and its relation to communism, in light of the conspicuous absence of blacks in the history of Cold War politics, and in particular to gain a better appreciation of communist views of race, since, as Washington notes, the Communist Party was the only major American political party to formally oppose racial discrimination, participating and supporting anti-discrimination campaigns and signalling commitment to supporting black liberation from racial segregation laws and practices. For the Communist Party, anti-racism was a major component of the anti-capitalist struggle. Washington seeks to discover the extent to which black civil rights activists who joined the Communist Party did so because of true sympathies with the party or because its stance on racism offered the best opportunities for achieving success in the racial struggle.

Washington begins her interesting study of black literature and culture by marking the conspicuous absence of any mention of communist sympathy in black writers from the 1950s and 1960s, and the very careful way in which black literature from this period is labelled as 'realism, naturalism and modernism', detached from the historical and political environments of the times, enveloped in preoccupations with culture and ethnicity, race as a historical inheritance directly from slavery (omitting the nearly 100 years since the Civil War). Washington questions whether or not aesthetics can be neatly partitioned from the historical/political, especially when the authors of the works in question were known to be active in communist and other left-leaning groups. Further, anthologies such as the much-used *Norton Anthology of African American Literature* denounced Richard Wright's brutal realism as a product of his social protest, at the same time as Ellison, a Marxist, was described as possessing artistic maturity because his novel *Invisible Man* does not contain the sort of brutal realism that Wright uses in his own communist-sympathizing novel *Native Son*. The failure, as a result of this conflict between Cold War interests and civil rights activities, to describe the blacklisted authors and their ordeals as closely connected with communism drained the struggles of writers such as Robeson, DuBois, and Hughes, for instance, of the very real danger and high stakes of their association with 'subversive' groups, all of whom experienced arrest, and/or curtailment of civil liberties. Washington's book proposes a counternarrative that reinserts the black–left presence in Cold War and civil rights history that has by and large been buried, erased, ignored, or censored. Further, she wishes to trace the extent to which many of the black civil rights organizations, clubs, and various advancement organizations of the Cold War era and earlier gained support from the Communist Party. Accordingly, Washington focuses her work on six artists aligned with the left: Lloyd Brown, Julian Mayfield, Charles White, Alice Childress, Gwendolyn Brooks, and Frank London Brown. In so doing, Washington seeks to challenge assumptions about the sources and inspirations for African American writers whose left sympathies have gone largely unacknowledged as a source for aesthetics and cultural production, placing the black literary tradition and the cultural left at the centre of Cold War African American studies for the first time.

Lean'tin L. Bracks and Jessie Carney Smith's edited collected *Black Women of the Harlem Renaissance Era* is an effort to assert the role of women during the Harlem Renaissance in a manner that has not been achieved by previous studies. Generally, the role of women has been downplayed, and even more troubling, the women who have been noted tend to be women of mixed race only. While these women undisputedly made important contributions, the profile is narrow and selective, leaving out the less glamorous contributions of the women whose identities are less captivating, and furthermore ignoring the contribution of white women to the era. The book is organized in an encyclopedia-type format with a breadth and depth of inclusion not generally granted to the women of the era. Bracks and Smith take the widest approach possible in framing the Harlem Renaissance, including women who made a contribution from as early as 1919 and extending to 1945. In particular, Bracks and Smith profile women who worked through traditional channels such as church groups, women's auxiliaries, societies, and national conventions, clubs, and community organizations. At the heart of the encyclopedia are women who, despite systematic racism, harsh economic realities, marginalization, and twofold discrimination based on gender and race, used the resources that they had to advance the rights and position of African American women. Bracks and Smith begin by outlining periods in the early history of the Renaissance in order to contextualize the various efforts of each generation: 1877–1918, 1919, the Harlem Renaissance itself as a phenomenon of the 1920s and 1930s, and 1935–40. This book is an excellent source of information for students and researchers of the topic.

Linda Wagner-Martin, in *Toni Morrison and the Maternal*, cites a longstanding resistance to making statements about the importance of mothering, worried that the act might be sentimentalized or fall into the trap of biological determinism frowned upon by feminist critique. Nevertheless, the maternal is an important topic in Morrison's work, and because of its centrality to her fiction, she rehabilitates the role of mothers and the action of the mother, the maternal, giving them a status worthy of attention and critique. In Morrison, the maternal is complex, diverse, and varied, a testament to its importance, not as a biologically determined role but as a choice, and also as a 'right' of women, what she refers to in interviews as 'ancient properties': ancestors, the legacy of being a woman. Wagner-Martin situates *The Bluest Eye* as a ground-breaking feminist novel in that it puts front and centre mothers 'who had no essential role but to provide that care' (p. 5). It addresses the issue of mothering in the context of feminism, exposing the privilege of white feminist texts to choose the way in which women can assume or avoid the role, juxtaposing the experience of black women in a raw and radical way, and thereby forcing discourse around mothering back into the feminist realm. Wagner-Martin picks up on Marianne Hirsch's assessment that mothers tend to be 'absent, silent or devalued' (p. 7) and asserts that this was the case until Morrison's work emphasized motherhood as complex or represented in multiple ways. Accordingly, Wagner-Martin distinguishes between African American mothering and white mothering, and the presence of the haunting of African American culture by slavery. Wagner-Martin argues that Morrison's centralization of mothers in her body of work culminates in *Beloved*, when maternal love seeks to reclaim lost African American familial structures that were essentially erased during slavery. Wagner-Martin goes on to argue that Morrison's redepiction and centralizing of mothers has effected a change in literary theory, necessitating a change in the way that mothers are treated in theory and criticism.

Jason Frydman begins his study, *Sounding the Break: African American and Caribbean Routes of World Literature*, by tracing the roots of the world literature movement (Goethe's *Weltliteratur*), and surmises that despite the inevitable contacts and networks that formed amongst the literatures of the world, and despite the numerous critical discourses such as postcolonialism, the specific 'nexus' of the African diaspora with world literature has gone unremarked. Nevertheless, despite this consciousness of a world literature, the simultaneous rise of a number of artists of the African diaspora located around the world failed to result in their obtaining a firm foothold on the world literature scene. Hence, African diasporic writing never really becomes part of the world literature category but rather remains regional in its reception and critical examination. Frydman's book rehabilitates W.E.B. DuBois, Zora Neale Hurston, Alejo Carpentier, Derek Walcott, Maryse Condé, and Morrison as world literature authors, as opposed to diasporic regional authors. Central to Frydman's discussion is the way world literature reflects a certain cosmopolitanism; African diasporic writers negotiate their unique voices, often reflecting a vernacularism or New World mannerisms that interface between oral and scribal traditions, blending orality and literacy. Also at the heart of the problem is the tension between local affinities (the South, the Caribbean) and worldly concerns that tend to occupy world literature as topics. Frydman seeks to restore African diasporic literature to the realm of world literature by globalizing the tropes, metaphors, characters, and geographies.

Veronica Watson frames her exploration in *The Souls of White Folk: African American Writers Theorize Whiteness* by citing an early essay by William J. Wilson, writing under the pseudonym of Ethiop in 1860, entitled 'What Shall We Do with the White People?', as well as Malcolm X's essay from just over a hundred years later in 1963, 'God's Judgment', in which both authors question the ability of white Americans to self-govern and maintain citizenship. Both discourses are radical for their times in providing a counter-discourse to white assumptions about black people and their right to citizenship. Watson also cites the coining of the term 'white life novel' in 1995 to designate the abundance of fictional texts written by black authors writing about white characters. Watson seeks to identify and illuminate a tradition of black authors who critically theorize whiteness in their fiction by exploring whiteness as a racialized subjectivity. Watson argues that in these texts are a number of trends that black authors identify and counter: whiteness is presented as universality, a presumption that is largely unchallenged. It is a manner of social organization that is defined by skin colour and the privileges associated with the privileged skin colour. This privileging of whiteness is bound up with other privileges such as gender, class, sexual orientation, and special organization. Watson chooses texts that position whiteness that is problematic for its failure to recognize its narrowness and its tradition of oppression of everything that is non-white. Watson takes the idea of the 'white life novel' and coins a genre term: 'literature of white estrangement'. The core of this study is to examine texts by black authors that challenge whiteness as a social construction, the presumption of whiteness that is unchallenged, the regressive and destructive way in which whiteness constructs a black world. Watson situates this strategy in black writing as a way to reach white readers who might not otherwise engage in critiques of racism, social inequality, and injustice: to reveal whiteness to itself by providing a counternarrative to the presumptions of whiteness. Watson points out that, typically, this literature has been undervalued for three reasons. The first has to do with the way in which African American literature is defined and marketed as separate but equal; this amounts to nothing more than a harking back to segregation, but this time played out on the shelves of bookstores. Secondly, and related to the first reason, is audience reception: white estrangement is difficult for readers, who are accustomed to white assumptions, to understand. The third reason has to do with scholarly treatment of white life novels and the way in which novels about whiteness by black authors have received little if no attention from scholars of colour in literary criticism in America. African American studies and theorists tend to privilege black writers who write about black experiences and black subjects. These three contingencies amount to an exclusion of critical work on theorizing whiteness from the black perspective. Black scholarship itself has been narrow in focusing on protest literature or literature that presents the racial injustices experienced by black Americans. Literature of whiteness has not been viewed as being capable of adding to this discourse of protest or theorization until fairly recently. Critiques of white life literature include the charge that the literature is raceless, that it grows out of an unconscious desire to be white, or displays a revulsion towards black culture. Its transgressive nature and potential has yet to be realized and treated seriously by literary scholarship. Watson's book seeks to conceptualize African American engagement with whiteness as an 'intellectual tradition' in the vast tradition of writing by African Americans from the nineteenth century on, to treat it as a bona fide intellectual strategy of enquiry and resistance. Watson's book looks at non-fictional work, such as essays, letters, journals, sermons, and so forth, as well as fiction in short stories, poetry, and novels.

6. Latino/a, Native, Asian American, and General Ethnic Writing

Fewer books were received for review than is typical for general ethnic writing, and this section will resume its normal length in 2017, reviewing works published in 2015.

(a) Latino/a Writing

Oscar Mireles's edited collection, *I Didn't Know There Were Latinos in Wisconsin: Three Decades of Hispanic Writing*, seeks to bring an otherwise overlooked body of literature to the attention of scholars and society at large: that of the long-standing Latino population of Wisconsin, citing the fact that the Wisconsin community possesses its own unique regional ethnic identity while also sharing much in common with American Latinos in general. Accordingly, the collection features a comprehensive collection of poetry and short stories by Latino and Latina American writers from Wisconsin. Many of the writers in the collection have roots in the labour movement, and are the descendants of the first migrant workers to settle in the area in the 1920s and then again during the Second World War. They are rural and urban, they are subject to similar racist campaigns as Latinos in other states, and they are often over-represented in the demographics by high rates of unemployment and poverty. These concerns and real-life experiences are reflected in the creative writing featured in this collection. The collection is unique in that it features poetry in both Spanish and in English translation and short fiction in English, as well as literature that seeks to capture the linguistic realities of a demographic that speaks primarily in Spanish, despite its long-standing roots in the anglophone United States.

(b) Native Writing

The bilingual anthology of contemporary indigenous writings, *Languages of Our Lands: Indigenous Poems and Stories from Quebec / Langues de Notre Terre: Poèmes et Récits Autochtones du Québec*, brings together writers who contributed to the francophone Aboriginal Emerging Writers programme at the Banff Centre or the subsequent programme in Quebec. All works are presented in French and English with loanwords from the source languages— Wendat, Innu-aimun, Cree, and Algonquin—glossed at the end of the book in a 'Mots/Words' section. This attention to language characterizes several of the works from 2014. The editorial work by Susan Ouriou is strong with an incisive introduction outlining the scope of the project and the challenges of language and indigeneity that it reflects. Christelle Morelli's sensitive work in translation also merits special notice. The range in styles, register, and geography is enormous, yet continuity emerges in concerns over language, land, place, and a remarkably consistent concision in the poetry. Margaret Noodin's *Bawaajimo: A Dialect in Dreams in Anishinaabe Language and Literature* carries forward several of these same concerns in a nuanced linguistic and literary analysis of the importance of indigenous knowledge systems embedded in indigenous mother tongues, even for literature written in English, or as the author poignantly phrases it for Anishinaabe in her preface, 'a language that is wandering wounded into a new century' (p. xi). Noodin points out, in a disruption of the Cartesian *Cogito ergo sum* and Nietzsche's disruption of thought as an articulation of the self in the Enlightenment tradition, that in Anishinaabe 'existence is not tied to thought as much as to connection and direction' (p. xvi). The basis of this contention resides in the linguistic construction that attaches endings to modes of being, which is then reflected forward since 'language can shape narrative and leave traces of that' (p. xvii)—in this, Noodin is utterly convincing. The very careful work on linguistics in relation to a literary tradition with expressly political aims is to be commended here, and the carefulness is a welcome model for future work. While the deliberate focus on Anishinaabe language and culture, or more accurately language-culture, may seem like a limitation in Noodin's project, it also provides a model for other future work. The recurrent theme is that 'language is a source of history and a means of survival ... [that] document[s] the history of Anishinaabe speakers' (p. 15). Based on the propensity of the language to seek out ways 'to communicate what is happening' (p. 16) and develop unity, Noodin comes to the thesis contained in her title's phrasing: 'These are some of the truths of the world where there are words for dreaming (*bwaajige*) and words for storytelling (*dibaajimo*) and nothing to prevent the creation of a new word that implies they might sometimes happen at the very same time ... *bawaajimo*' (p. 17). A similar emphasis on language and storytelling as cultural practice permeates Frederick White's *Emerging From Out of the Margins: Essays on Haida Language, Culture, and History*. Where Noodin struggles with the decline in the number of Anishinaabe speakers despite interventions to promote the language, White confronts the problem directly through matters of classroom teaching, language-acquisition strategies, and how such practices can be transplanted to other indigenous language settings. The book's chapters are divided into two sections: Part I on Haida culture and history with content on mythology, colonization, humour, and oral histories; and Part II specifically focused on Haida language, revitalization strategies, the struggle to transplant ideology from one language to another, and modern technologies in language teaching and linguistics. Each essay is brief and generally written in a jargon-free style that is clearly meant for a broad audience, potentially ranging from scholars to grade-school teachers. The explicit aim to make White's experiences with the Haida language applicable more broadly for others is also very much to the advantage of the book.

Three monographs and one edited collection stand out as signal theoretical projects of the year, and particular note must be given to Glen Sean Coulthard's integration of indigenous studies and Marxist decolonization theory in *Red Skin White Masks: Rejecting the Colonial Politics of Recognition* and Mark Rifkin's continued development of his reading of queer identities in relation to indigenous studies in *Settler Common Sense: Queerness and Everyday Colonialism in the American Renaissance*. Rifkin's work follows on his exceptional pair of monographs *The Erotics of Sovereignty: Queer Native Writing in the Era of Self-Determination* (UMinnP [2012]; reviewed in *YWES* 93[2014]) and *When Did Indians Become Straight? Kinship, the History of Sexuality, and Native Sovereignty* (OUP [2011]; reviewed in *YWES* 93[2014]). The project here is to excavate the procedures of 'settler common sense' as a constructed naturalization to the legacies of displacement by attending to American writers and their often unnoticed displacements of indigeneity. In Rifkin's definition, these everyday expressions of ideology and expropriation 'suggest the ways the legal and political structures that enable non-native access to Indigenous territories come to be lived as given, as simply the unmarked, generic conditions of possibility' (p. xvi). This unfair negotiation of choice in the settler state shapes understandings as well as experiences of place, personhood, and political belonging, such that nineteenth-century American prose writers—Nathaniel Hawthorne, Henry David Thoreau, and Herman Melville—give Rifkin the canonical fodder for expressing the ongoing naturalized inequalities of today. Given the extent of discourses of the everyday in poetry and prose already noted in recent years, the remarkable opportunity here is not for Rifkin to extend discussions of Guy Debord, Henri Lefebvre, and other theorists of the everyday taken up in modernist poetics, but rather for the excellent work already seen to consider Rifkin's critique of what has so far been invisible in those discussions: constructs of the *terra nullius*, place, and absence that also permeate those investigations of the modernist everyday. Rifkin deploys Bruno Latour to great effect here and brings Jack Halberstam's work on queer theory into a disruption of naturalized sovereignty with the pointed reminder that 'the contestation of one set of norms (the heterosexual imaginary of familial order) may be predicated on the unreflexive mobilization of other norms (ordinary modes of settler personhood and placemaking)' (pp. 26–7). The long elaboration of the unconscious modes of settler habitation across the subsequent chapters is careful in extracting recurrent tropes in each of the three canonical authors. This is a study of indigeneity vital to canonical nineteenth-century American prose, current discussions in queer theory, as well as native studies' growth as a critical mode of import beyond native content or creators. By calling for a broader condition of possibility Rifkin has opened a necessary dialogue, which is unsurprising given the already widely recognized excellence of his previous work. Coulthard's *Red Skin White Masks* draws its title from Frantz Fanon and his attendant Sartre-influenced Marxist methodology for articulating the decolonization project during the rapid decolonization of Africa at the mid-century. From Fanon, he specifically draws on the familiar chapters 26–32 of

Marx's *Capital* on primitive accumulation, but refocused here to deal with indigeneity specifically as a relationship with or an ontology built out from land. While Fanon's focus is on negotiating race through discourses of class, Coulthard extends the project to accommodate forms of subjectivity predicated on grounded concepts of indigeneity as belonging in place, which is also presented as anti-capitalist and disruptive to the nation-state. The pressing tension, then, is between these core materialist versus metaphysical understandings. For indigeneity, Coulthard contends, via Vine Deloria Jr., that 'one of the most significant differences that exist between Indigenous and Western metaphysics revolves around the central importance of land to Indigenous modes of being, thought, and ethics' (p. 60). Because of this, indigenous populations privilege place, locality, and embeddedness in place as an ontological framework while the West differs by tending to 'derive meaning from the world in historical/developmental terms, thereby placing *time* as the narrative of central importance' (p. 60). Therefore, 'Place is a way of knowing, of experiencing and relating to the world with others' (p. 61) and hence is always relational; as with Noodin, Coulthard articulates this as embedded in language (Dogrib). He closes by considering the Idle No More movement and indigenous resurgence while offering five theses: first the need for direct action, second the efficacy of anti-capitalist actions as indigenous resistance and affirmation of identity, third dispossession from land driving urbanization as a preface to urban dispossession through gentrification, fourth the vital importance of indigenous feminisms to decolonization and renewal, and fifth a call for scepticism amidst the hegemonic necessity of negotiations within the nation-state apparatus. It is moot to suggest Coulthard's work will provoke meaningful scholarly responses—it already has and is rapidly proving its importance to works as diverse as Lorenzo Veracini's *The Settler Colonial Present* (Palgrave [2015]), Adam J. Barker's ' "A Direct Act of Resurgence, a Direct Act of Sovereignty": Reflections on Idle No More, Indigenous Activism, and Canadian Settler Colonialism' (*Globalizations* 12:i[2015] 43–65), and Geoffrey Brahm Levey's *Authenticity, Autonomy and Multiculturalism* (Routledge [2015]). Dealing with Coulthard's contentions will be unavoidable in future work.

Sam McKegney's edited collection *Masculindians: Conversations about Indigenous Manhood* brings together studies in masculinities and indigeneity, and most specifically the problematic constructed trope of the hypermasculine Indian, through conversations with leading scholars and artists. This structure emphasizes oral discourses, storytelling, and relational knowledge. McKegney's critical work is excellent yet keeps a conversational tone and rapport with his interlocutors throughout, such as his opening explanation of the title's portmanteau originating 'a few years back' and drawing 'attention to the settler North American appetite for depictions of Indigenous men that rehearse hypermasculine stereotypes . . . [and] their ideological progeny' (p. 1). This balance between scholarly rigour and artfully casual discourse is sustained across the collection and is helped by the book's luxurious margins, into which commentary, select excerpts, and annotations are added: marginally rather at the foot of the page. While the contents develop from conversations with major figures, the opportunity to annotate and

McKegney's editorial apparatus incorporates the intellectual roots of the work in previous scholarship without disrupting the colloquial format—these include works such as Rifkin's *When Did Indians Become Straight?* (mentioned above), Cheryl Suzack, Shari Huhndorf, Jeanne Perreault, and Jean Barman's edited collection *Indigenous Women and Feminism: Politics, Activism, Culture* (UBC [2011]), Taiaiake Alfred's *Peace, Power, Righteousness: An Indigenous Manifesto* (OUP [1999]), and Jessica Ball's work on fatherhood as well as the stalwart Gerald Vizenor and Craig Womack. The book opens with a critical introduction and closes with a dialogue on its outcomes with three distinct sections between, each emphasizing one word, in sequence, from the trinity 'wisdom, knowledge, imagination'. Particularly notable conversations include McKegney's discussions with Tomson Highway, Taiaiake Alfred, Jessica Danforth, and Richard Van Camp. The collection will be useful for scholarly work, but seems particularly helpful for the undergraduate classroom where its colloquial introduction of complex concepts rooted in settler colonialism, gender studies and masculinities, and indigenous resurgence will guide junior readers easily through demanding critical thought. The closing bibliography for further readings seems especially suited to such uses. The book will also have a clear appeal to literary scholars at work on the various creative works by the interlocutors, offering as it does a form of interviews not unlike those in the useful series of books on 'conversations' by Earl Ingersoll—*Conversations with Rita Dove* (UPMissip [2003]), *Conversations with Anthony Burgess* (UPMissip [2008]), *Lawrence Durrell: Conversations* (FDUP [1998]; reviewed in *YWES* 79[2001]), and so forth.

Audra Simpson and Andrea Smith's edited collection *Theorizing Native Studies* draws together several of the scholars already mentioned. Coulthard contributes a chapter closely related to *Red Skin White Masks*, 'From Wards of the State to Subjects of Recognition? Marx, Indigenous Peoples, and the Politics of Dispossession in Denedeh', and Mark Rifkin adds 'Making Peoples into Populations: The Racial Limits of Tribal Sovereignty'. Rifkin's chapter turns to Foucault and biopower, connecting nicely with his recent monographs, and Coulthard's chapter encapsulates many of the most crucial arguments from *Red Skin White Masks*, which would function well for classroom work where the summative article's brevity is an advantage over the full project in the book. The introduction from Simpson and Smith is also more than merely an overview of the contents—the editors work systematically through the vital relationship between theory and native studies, moving from a theoretical turn in the discipline running contrary to a more general backlash against theory that they observe in recent years. Only after moving through native studies in relation to Marxism, ethnic studies, postcoloniality, feminism and queer theory, and praxis do they turn to an overview of the book and the ten individual contributors. They also clearly position their project in *Theorizing Native Studies* in relation to recent foundational work, such as Sean Kicummah Teuton's *Red Land, Red Power: Grounding Knowledge in the American Indian Novel* (DukeUP [2008]); Jace Weaver, Craig Womack, and Robert Allen Warrior's *American Indian Literary Nationalism* (UNMP [2006]); and Linda Tuhiwai Smith's *Decolonizing Methodologies* (Zed [1999]). The collection assembles an excellent set of capacious (and differing) approaches to theory in native studies and will also prove helpful for those needing a brief survey of the theoretical state of the field in this moment.

Two editions also merit special notice. The English translation by Peter Frost of Mitiarjuk Nappaaluk's *Sanaaq: An Inuit Novel* offers a rare point of access for English-language readers into Inuit practices and narrative. The book is a bridge translation based on Bernard Saladin d'Anglure's translation into French from the original Inuktitut syllabics—as the introduction points out, this is a novel by an 'illiterate' author who had never read a novel, meaning it was written down in syllabics first as a way of providing a language-learning tool and later to communicate cultural practices and traditional narratives to future generations. While this venue is not suitable for a literary review of the work, the foreword is excellent as a scholarly, biographical, and cultural resource generally, and the book ends with a substantial glossary of Inuktitut words and phrases followed by a bibliography of further reading that draws together essential critical readings. As a novel, the book will delight and startle readers, but as a scholarly resource it is essential—it is difficult to overstate how remarkable this work is and what a great advantage it is to finally have it readily available in an affordable English translation for the general reader, scholars, and classroom use. Also, Sophie McCall has edited Anahareo's *Devil in Deerskins: My Life with Grey Owl*. The book is Anahareo's autobiography up to and through her marriage to Grey Owl, first published in 1972. Although McCall has not annotated the text, the apparatus includes brief forewords by Katherine Swartile and Anne Gaskell and a more substantial closing afterword by McCall, 'Reframing Anahareo's *Devil in Deerskins*'. Again, the book's intention seems overtly oriented to classroom use and teaching as well as to sustain the availability of the autobiography to the general reader.

(c) Asian American Writing

In *Racial Asymmetries: Asian American Fictional Worlds*, Stephen Hong Sohn focuses attention on the relationships among perspective in storytelling and theories of identity based on authorial ancestry and content. This means that conflicts between identity and form resurface across the work, which troubles the easy alignment of character, perspective, and author while retaining the importance of ethnicity and acknowledging the market forces that reduce writing to the native informant paradigm and the 'postracial' aesthetic that has writers presenting narration outside their own racialized identity, much akin to the discussion of 'whiteness' and 'white life writing' in Veronica Watson's *The Souls of White Folk* (reviewed above). He posits the formal innovations of the post-racial aesthetic as a challenge to the 'model minority' model that presents or depicts Asian Americans as a docile, integrated minority. A more radical materialist resistance to this model of interpellation comes in the final chapter dedicated to speculative fiction, which opens with Darko Suvin's concept of cognitive estrangement and radical potentialities from *Metamorphoses of Science Fiction: On the Poetics and History of a Literary Genre* (YaleUP [1979]; reviewed in *YWES* 60[1981]), although this materialist understanding of genre and class-oriented trope of consciousness does not recur in other chapters and the potential lever of Seong-Yu Chu's exclusion from Jameson's major work in the field, *Archaeologies of the Future: The Desire Called Utopia and Other Science Fictions* (Verso [2005]) is undiscussed. This is somewhat surprising given Sohn's prior work on the genre, though it is not the crux of his project. The other chapters focus on single authors but range quite a bit across Asian American literatures. The first takes up the suburb and Chang-rae Lee, the second Sesshu Foster and Chicano identities in California, the third Sigrid Nunez and civil rights, and the fourth Sabina Murray and colonialism followed by the closing chapter on speculative fiction and a 'Coda' rather than a conclusion. The pressure in Sohn's study to radically extend the scope of texts with which Asian American literary studies engages is sure to be treated polemically but is also compelling here and entirely persuasive. The book also follows on his related articles 'Minor Character, Minority Orientalisms, and the Borderlands of Asian America' (*CulC* 82[2012] 151–85) and 'Los Indios Bravos: The Filipino/American Lyric and the Cosmopoetics of Comparative Indigeneity' (*AQ* 62:iii[2010] 547–68)—neither is duplicated in the book, but the projects are very much akin and merit reading together. Readers may also wish to consider the book's subtle developments from his arguments in his co-edited special issue *Theorizing Asian American Fiction* (*MFS* 56:i[2010]).

Dorothy J. Wang's *Thinking Its Presence: Form, Race, and Subjectivity in Contemporary Asian American Poetry* presents itself polemically as primarily a study of poetics that will be read 'topically as a study of Asian American Literature' and forwards the importance of minority poetry's contribution to poetics generally as a contention that 'flies in the face of the reception of ethnic poetry in English' (p. xix) because of the false image of the lyric, prosody, and other categories as racially unmarked. The opening gesture for this position relates to tokenism in syllabuses for the inclusion of African American poets, in her example Langston Hughes, against the presumed universality or racially unmarked status of the high modernists. In this, she contends that while social formations are recognized in form, Language poetry may contend with capitalism, and gender may also play an important role, race has remained either a reductive category or unspeakable. What is perhaps most compelling here is Wang's rhetorical combination of polemic and replication of existing arguments, most strikingly the political nature of avant-garde experimentalism in conflict with racial interpellation and racialized subjectivities. The conversational tone of much of the book, relying on anecdotal accounts of conference sessions and hypothetical syllabuses, is appealing and makes the text easily worked through—at some points the dating of materials reveals its origins in Wang's 1998 dissertation, such as repeated gestures to Bill Moyer's 1995 'The Language of Life' PBS series, but there are several updates and the project is clearly extensively revised and polished. Even a hasty comparison shows the more focused and systematic critical voice at work here. The book closes optimistically with a personal call for critical attention to the vitality of major 'minority poets' in the United States—it is difficult not to ask how the narrative here might compare to other national traditions of Asian poetry and poetics in Canada and the United Kingdom, in which the concerns of tokenism may present differently.

(d) General Ethnic Writing

Carol Fadda-Conrey's *Contemporary Arab-American Literature: Transnational Reconfigurations of Citizenship and Belonging* posits Arab American literature as at a juncture in its history, expanding rapidly with increasing scholarly attention while at the same time confronting bias and popular misconceptions exacerbated by its growth. Theoretically, the book positions its intervention as a balancing between transnational conceptions of literature within the nation and the containing power-strategies built in to diasporic and ethnic conceptualizations. In that productive frisson, Fadda-Conrey asserts a discourse of citizenship belonging to Arab American identities. This allows her to look to trans-Arab solidarities even while privileging the distinctness of the various communities in the United States represented in the book. She looks to Arab immigration to the United States in three phases: the first from 1880 to 1925; from 1925 to 1967, when the Immigration Quota Act limited immigration based on nationality; and from 1967 to the present as following in the wake of the Six-Day War and also in relation to Arab American civil rights movements and associations as well as the problematic identification of Arab minorities as officially 'white'. By opening with Kahlil Gibran and Ameen Rihani as the first voices of the Arab American literary tradition, Fadda-Conrey argues for a solid transnational perspective in their works and articulation of an Arab American identity. Following on an intermediary period of autobiographies that she reads as caught up with shame and nostalgia, this leads, in the 1960s and after, to increasingly complex articulations of transnational identities that complicate notions of nostalgia while shifting from discourses of patriarchy and race to displacement, exile, and dispossession. This last period she regards as inextricably shaped by American foreign policy and conflicts abroad, and hence the persistently transnational conceptualization of Arab American identities in literature. She divides the subsequent sections of the book between 'Reimagining the Ancestral Arab Homeland', 'To the Arab Homeland and Back', 'Translocal Connections between the US and the Arab World', and finally 'Representing Arabs and Muslims in the US after 9/11', followed by a conclusion on these established transnational discourses of identity in relation to the Arab Spring.

Alyosha Goldstein's edited collection *Formations of United States Colonialism* seeks to integrate critical studies of settler colonialism and overseas imperialism by entangling analyses of Native Americans, Puerto Ricans, the Chamorros of Guam, Filipinos, Hawaiians, and Samoans. The book's thirteen chapters are preceded by Goldstein's ambitious introduction, 'Toward a Genealogy of the U.S. Colonial Present'. While the introduction aims to summarize and open the essays of the collection, its turn to Foucauldian genealogy builds from Mark Rifkin's projects noted in Section 6*(b)* above to point to the tensions among territory, jurisdiction, knowledge production, and institutions, contrasting the nationalist interests of imperialism with the potential for non-state pressures such as the UN Declaration on the Rights of Indigenous Peoples from 2007. Parallel to this sense of genealogy is Ann Laura Stoler and Carole McGranahan's 'formation' as a process of dispossession. Hence the project prompts a genealogical method of addressing the formations under scrutiny.

Books Reviewed

Alaniz, José. *Death, Disability, and the Superhero*. UPMissip. [2014] pp. xii + 363. $65 ISBN 9 7816 2846 1176.

Allison, Raphael. *Bodies on the Line: Performance and the Sixties Poetry Reading*. UIowaP. [2014] pp. 236. $49.95 ISBN 9 7816 0938 3039.

Anahareo. *Devil in Deerskins: My Life with Grey Owl*. UManitobaP. [2014] pp. 240. $31.95 ISBN 9 7808 8755 4551.

Ayaka, Carolene, and Ian Hague. *Representing Multiculturalism in Comics and Graphic Novels*. Routledge. [2014] pp. 270. $140 ISBN 9 7811 3802 5158.

Babic, Annessa Ann, ed. *Comics as History, Comics as Literature: Roles of the Comic Book in Scholarship, Society, and Entertainment*. FDUP. [2014] pp. 272. $85 ISBN 9 7816 1147 5562.

Baker, Brian. *Science Fiction*. Palgrave. [2014] pp. 192. $31 ISBN 9 7802 3022 8146.

Barrett, Lindon. *Racial Blackness and the Discontinuity of Western Modernity*. UIllP. [2014] pp. 264. $95 ISBN 9 7802 5203 8006.

Barrett, Ross, and Daniel Worden, eds. *Oil Culture*. UMinnP. [2014] pp. 456. $30 ISBN 9 7808 1668 9743.

Barrier, Michael. *Funnybooks: The Improbable Glories of the Best American Comic Books*. UCalP. [2014] pp. 432. $34.95 ISBN 9 7805 2028 3909.

Beal, Wesley. *Networks of Modernism: Reorganizing American Narrative*. UIowaP. [2014] pp. xiii + 169. $55 ISBN 9 7816 0938 3510.

Bennett, Juda. *Toni Morrison and the Queer Pleasure of Ghosts*. SUNYP. [2014] pp. 215. $80 ISBN 9 7814 3845 3552.

Berenato, Joseph F. New Life and New Civilizations: Exploring *Star Trek Comics*. Sequart. [2014] pp. 298. $16.95 ISBN 9 7819 4058 9053.

Bertens, Hans, and Theo D'haen. *American Literature: A History*. Routledge. [2014] pp. 314. £25 ISBN 9 7804 1556 9989.

Bolling, Ben, and Matthew J. Smith. *It Happens at Comic-Con: Ethnographic Essays on a Pop Culture Phenomenon*. McFarland. [2014] pp. 206. $35 ISBN 9 7807 8647 6947.

Boschenhoff, Sandra Eva. *Tall Tales in Comic Diction, from Literature to Graphic Fiction: An Intermedial Analysis of Comic Adaptations of Literary Texts*. WVT. [2013] pp. 304. €35 ISBN 9 7838 6821 4789.

Boswell, Marshall, ed. *David Foster Wallace and 'The Long Thing': New Essays on the Novels*. Bloomsbury. [2014] pp. 272. $29.95 ISBN 9 7816 2892 4534.

Boyd, Janet, and Sharon J. Kirsch, eds. *Primary Stein: Returning to the Writing of Gertrude Stein*. Lexington. [2014] pp. 320. $95 ISBN 9 7807 3918 3199.

Bracks, Lean'tin L., and Jessie Carney Smith, eds. *Black Women of the Harlem Renaissance Era*. R&L. [2014] pp. 328. $80 ISBN 9 7808 1088 5424.

Buell, Lawrence. *The Dream of the Great American Novel*. Belknap. [2014] pp. xii + 567. £29.95 ISBN 9 7806 7405 1157.

Byron, Mark S. *Ezra Pound's Eriugena*. Continuum. [2014] pp. 224. £60 ISBN 9 7814 4113 9542.

Canavan, Gerry, and Kim Stanley Robinson, eds. *Green Planets: Ecology and Science Fiction*. WesleyanUP. [2014] pp. 312. $27.95 ISBN 9 7808 1957 4275.

Carver, Beci. *Granular Modernism*. OUP. [2015] pp. 208. £55 ISBN 9 7801 9870 9923.

Chapman, Mary. *Making Noise, Making News: Suffrage Print Culture and U.S. Modernism*. OUP. [2014] pp. xii + 273. £42 ISBN 9 7801 9998 8297.

Charlton-Jones, Kate. *Dismembering the American Dream: The Life and Fiction of Richard Yates*. UAlaP. [2014] pp. 296. $49.95 ISBN 9 7808 1731 8253.

Clark, Robert C. *American Literary Minimalism*. UAlaP. [2014] pp. 208. $49.95 ISBN 9 7808 1731 8277.

Cohn, Neil. *The Visual Language of Comics: Introduction to the Structure and Cognition of Sequential Images*. Bloomsbury. [2013] pp. xvii + 221. $42.95 ISBN 9 7814 4118 1459.

Coulthard, Glen Sean. *Red Skin, White Masks: Rejecting the Colonial Politics of Recognition*. UMinnP. [2014] pp. 256. $67.5 ISBN 9 7808 1667 9652.

Cronin, Gloria L., and Lee Tranpanier, eds. *A Political Companion to Saul Bellow*. UPKen. [2013] pp. 296. $40 ISBN 9 7808 1314 1855.

Cruz, Décio Torres. *Postmodern Metanarratives:* Blade Runner *and Literature in the Age of the Image*. Palgrave. [2014] pp. 256. £60 ISBN 9 7811 3743 9727.

Cuddy-Keane, Melba, Adam Hammond, and Alexandra Peat. *Modernism: Keywords*. Wiley. [2014] pp. 288. £65 ISBN 9 7814 0518 6551.

Darius, Julian. *The Weirdest Sci-Fi Comic Ever Made: Understanding Jack Kirby's 2001: A Space Odyssey*. Sequart. [2013] pp. 90. $8.99 ISBN 9 7814 8956 6188.

Darius, Julian. *When Manga Came to America: Super-Hero Revisionism in Mai, the Psychic Girl*. Sequart. [2014] pp. 74. $6.99 ISBN 9 7819 4058 9039.

Darowski, Joseph. *The Ages of the Avengers: Essays on the Earth's Mightiest Heroes in Changing Times*. McFarland. [2014] pp. 204. $40 ISBN 9 7807 8647 4585.

Darowski, Joseph. *The Ages of the X-Men: Essays on the Children of the Atom in Changing Times*. McFarland. [2014] pp. 248. $40 ISBN 9 7807 8647 2192.

Darowski, Joseph J., ed. *The Ages of Wonder Woman: Essays on the Amazon Princess in Changing Times*. McFarland. [2014] pp. 240. $40 ISBN 9 7807 8647 1225.

Darowski, Joseph J. *X-Men and the Mutant Metaphor: Race and Gender in the Comic Books*. R&L. [2014] pp. xiii + 204. $72 ISBN 9 7814 4223 2075.

Densen, Shane, Christina Meyer, and Daniel Stein. *Transnational Perspectives on Graphic Narratives: Comics at the Crossroads*. Bloomsbury. [2013] pp. xvi + 294. $29.95 ISBN 9 7814 7253 5702.

Dewey, Joseph. *Understanding Michael Chabon*. USCP. [2014] pp. 152. $39.95 ISBN 9 7816 1117 3406.

Diepeveen, Leonard. *Mock Modernism: An Anthology of Parodies, Travesties, Frauds, 1910–1935*. UTorP. [2014] pp. 320. $68 ISBN 9 7814 4264 4823.

Dittmer, Jason, ed. *Comic Book Geographies*. Steiner. [2014] pp. 227. €44 ISBN 9 7835 1510 2698.

Driscoll, Beth. *The New Literary Middlebrow: Tastemakers and Reading in the Twenty-First Century*. Palgrave. [2014] pp. 240. £55 ISBN 9 7811 3740 2912.

Drowne, Kathleen. *Understanding Richard Russo*. USCP. [2014] pp. 152. $39.95 ISBN 9 7816 1117 4021.

Duncan, Randy, Matthew J. Smith, and Paul Levitz. *The Power of Comics: History, Form, and Culture*. Bloomsbury. [2013] pp. 445. $29.95 ISBN 9 7814 7253 5702.

Dunning, John, and Paul Gravett. *Comics Unmasked: Art and Anarchy in the UK*. BL. [2014] pp. 192. £25 ISBN 9 7807 1235 7357.

Eller, Jonathan R. *Ray Bradbury Unbound*. UIllP. [2014] pp. 352. $34.95 ISBN 9 7802 5203 8693.

Ercolino, Stefano. *The Maximalist Novel: From Thomas Pynchon's Gravity's Rainbow to Roberto Bolaño's 2666*. Bloomsbury. [2014] pp. 208. £60 ISBN 9 7816 2356 2915.

Eshel, Amir. *Futurity: Contemporary Literature and the Quest for the Past*. UChicP. [2013] pp. 344. $43 ISBN 9 7802 2692 4953.

Eve, Martin Paul. *Pynchon and Philosophy: Wittgenstein, Foucault and Adorno*. Palgrave. [2014] pp. 232. £50 ISBN 9 7811 3740 5494.

Fadda-Conrey, Carol. *Contemporary Arab-American Literature: Transnational Reconfigurations of Citizenship and Belonging*. NYUP. [2014] pp. xi + 272. $75 ISBN 9 7814 7982 6926.

Fahy, Thomas. *Understanding Truman Capote*. USCP. [2014] pp. 184. $39.95 ISBN 9 7816 1117 3413.

Farghaly, Nadine, ed. *Examining Lois Lane: The Scoop on Superman's Sweetheart*. Scarecrow. [2013] pp. xviii + 305. $55 ISBN 9 7808 1089 2361.

Flanagan, Victoria. *Technology and Identity in Young Adult Fiction: The Posthuman Subject*. Palgrave. [2014] pp. 214. £55 ISBN 9 7811 3736 2056.

Foley, Barbara. *Jean Toomer: Race Repression, and Revolution*. UIllP. [2014] pp. xiv + 336. $65 ISBN 9 7802 5203 8440.

Ford, Sarah Gilbreath. *Tracing Southern Storytelling in Black and White*. UAlaP. [2014] pp. 168. $39.95 ISBN 9 7808 1731 8239.

Francis, Consuela. *The Critical Reception of James Baldwin, 1962–2010: 'An Honest Man and a Good Writer'*. CamdenH. [2014] pp. 174. £50 ISBN 9 7815 7113 3250.

Frydman, Jason. *Sounding the Break: African American and Caribbean Routes of World Literature*. UPVirginia. [2014] pp. 192. $55 ISBN 9 7808 1393 5720.

Galow, Timothy W. *Understanding Dave Eggers*. USCP. [2014] pp. 152. $39.95 ISBN 9 7816 1117 4281.

García-Caro, Pedro. *After the Nation: Postnational Satire in the Works of Carlos Fuentes and Thomas Pynchon*. NorthwesternUP. [2014] pp. 304. $39.95 ISBN 9 7808 1013 2153.

Gifford, James. *Personal Modernisms: Anarchist Networks and the Later Avant-Gardes*. UAlbertaP. [2014] pp. xx + 294. £25 ISBN 9 7817 7212 0011.

Goldstein, Alyosha, ed. *Formations of United States Colonialism.* DukeUP. [2014] pp. 432. $99.95 ISBN 9 7808 2235 7964.

Gomel, Elana. *Science Fiction, Alien Encounter, and the Ethics of Posthumanism: Beyond the Golden Rule.* Palgrave. [2014] pp. 248. £55 ISBN 9 7811 3736 7624.

Grebowicz, Margret, and Helen Merrick. *Beyond the Cyborg: Adventures with Donna Haraway.* ColUP. [2013] pp. 208. $30 ISBN 9 7802 3114 9297.

Greenspan, Ezra. *William Wells Brown: An African American Life.* Norton. [2014] pp. 624. $35 ISBN 9 7803 9324 0900.

Grimes, Larry, and Bickford Sylvester, eds. *Hemingway, Cuba, and the Cuban Works.* KentSUP. [2014] pp. 376. $65 ISBN 9 7816 0635 1819.

Hague, Ian. *Comics and the Senses: A Multisensory Approach to Comics and Graphic Novels.* Routledge. [2014] pp. 200. $140 ISBN 9 7804 1571 3979.

Hanley, Tim. *Wonder Woman Unbound: The Curious History of the World's Most Famous Heroine.* ChiR. [2014] pp. xi + 303. $18.95 ISBN 9 7816 1374 9098.

Hayes, Patrick. *Philip Roth: Fiction and Power.* OUP. [2014] pp. 276. £57 ISBN 9 7801 9968 9125.

Henderson, Mae G. *Speaking in Tongues and Dancing Diaspora: Black Women Writing and Performing.* OUP. [2014] pp. 336. £47.99 ISBN 9 7801 9511 6595.

Hoberek, Andrew. *Considering Watchmen: Poetics, Property, Politics.* RutgersUP. [2014] pp. 238. $26.95 ISBN 9 7808 1356 3312.

Hogue, W. Lawrence. *Postmodernism, Traditional Cultural Forms and African American Narratives.* SUNYP. [2013] pp. 340. $27.95 ISBN 9 7814 3844 8343.

Houser, Heather. *Ecosickness in Contemporary U.S. Fiction: Environment and Affect.* ColUP. [2014] pp. 328. $55 ISBN 9 7802 3116 5143.

Huber, Irmtraud. *Literature after Postmodernism: Reconstructive Fantasies.* Palgrave. [2014] pp. 304. £55 ISBN 9 7811 3742 9902.

Hunt, Tim. *The Textuality of Soulwork: Jack Kerouac's Quest for Spontaneous Prose.* UMichP. [2014] pp. 228. $28.95 ISBN 9 7804 7205 2165.

Ingersoll, Earl G. *Understanding Steven Millhauser.* USCP. [2014] pp. 160. $39.95 ISBN 9 7816 1117 3086.

Irr, Caren. *Toward the Geopolitical Novel: U.S. Fiction in the Twenty-First Century.* ColUP. [2014] pp. 280. $32 ISBN 9 7802 3116 4412.

Irwin, John T. F. *Scott Fitzgerald's Fiction: 'An Almost Theatrical Innocence'.* JHUP. [2014] pp. x + 233. $35.60 ISBN 9 7814 2141 2306.

Johnson, Jeffrey K. *Superheroes in Crisis: Adjusting to Social Change in the 1960s and 1970s.* RITP. [2014] pp. 142. $29.95 ISBN 9 7819 3336 0805.

Knapp, Kathy. *American Unexceptionalism: The Everyman and the Suburban Novel after 9/11.* UIowaP. [2014] pp. 228. $45 ISBN 9 7816 0938 2285.

Kukkonen, Karin. *Contemporary Comics Storytelling.* UNebP. [2013] pp ix + 207. $55 ISBN 9 7808 0324 6379.

Kukkonen, Karin. *Studying Comics and Graphic Novels.* Wiley. [2013] pp viii + 182. $17.99 ISBN 9 7811 1849 9924.

Landgraf, Diemo, ed. *Decadence in Literature and Intellectual Debate since 1945.* Palgrave. [2014] pp. 256. £57.50 ISBN 9 7811 3743 1011.

Lang, John. *Understanding Ron Rash*. USCP. [2014] pp. 152. $39.95 ISBN 9 7816 1117 4113.

Lawler, Peter Augustine, and Brain A. Smith, eds. *A Political Companion to Walker Percy*. UPKen. [2013] pp. 272. $40 ISBN 9 7808 1314 1886.

Lewis, A. David. *American Comics, Literary Theory, and Religion: The Superhero Afterlife*. Palgrave. [2014]. pp. 204. $90 ISBN 9 7811 3746 5603.

MacNiven, Ian S. *'Literchoor Is My Beat': A Life of James Laughlin, Publisher of New Directions*. FS&G. [2014] pp. 553. $35 ISBN 9 7803 7429 9392.

Maher, Susan Narramore. *Deep Map Country: Literary Cartography of the Great Plains*. UNebP. [2014] pp. 256. $45 ISBN 9 7808 0324 5020.

Mayer, Ruth. *Fu Manchu: The Chinese Supervillain and the Spread of Yellow Peril Ideology*. TempleUP. [2014] pp. ix + 199. $33.95 ISBN 9 7814 3991 0566.

Maynard, James, ed. *Collected Essays and Other Prose*. UCalP. [2014] pp. 498. $60 ISBN 9 7805 2026 7732.

Mazzeno, Laurence W. *Becoming John Updike: Critical Reception, 1958–2010*. CamdenH. [2013] pp. 270. $34.95 ISBN 9 7815 7113 9375.

McClintock, Scott, and John Miller, eds. *Pynchon's California*. UIowaP. [2014] pp. 228. $45 ISBN 9 7816 0938 2735.

McGuirk, Kevin, ed. *An Image for Longing: Selected Letters and Journals of A.R. Ammons, 1951–1974. Ommateum to Sphere: The Form of a Motion*. ELS. [2014] pp. 452. $40 ISBN 9 7815 5058 4561.

McKegney, Sam, ed. *Masculindians: Conversations about Indigenous Manhood*. UManitobaP. [2014] pp. 248. $34.95 ISBN 9 7808 8755 7620.

McNamara, Kevin R., ed. *The Cambridge Companion to the City in Literature*. CUP. [2014] pp. 320. $29.95 ISBN 9 7811 0760 9150.

Melancon, Trimiko. *Unbought and Unbossed: Transgressive Black Women, Sexuality, and Representation*. TempleUP. [2014] pp. 256. $74.50 ISBN 9 7814 3991 1457.

Miller, Ann, and Bart Beaty, eds. *The French Comics Theory Reader*. LeuvenUP. [2014] pp. 385. €59 ISBN 9 7890 5867 9888.

Miller, Kristine A., ed. *Transatlantic Literature and Culture After 9/11: The Wrong Side of Paradise*. Palgrave. [2014] pp. 280. £55 ISBN 9 7811 3744 3205.

Mills, Anthony. *American Theology, Superhero Comics, and Cinema: The Marvel of Stan Lee and the Revolution of a Genre*. Routledge. [2013] pp. 206. $140 ISBN 9 7804 1584 3584.

Mireles, Oscar, ed. *I Didn't Know There Were Latinos in Wisconsin: Three Decades of Hispanic Writing*. Cowfeather. [2014] pp. 252. $20 ISBN 9 7809 8465 6851.

Moore, Marlon Rachquel. *In the Life and in the Spirit: Homoerotic Spirituality in African American Literature*. SUNYP. [2014] pp. 207. $80 ISBN 9 7814 3845 4078.

Morgan, Bill. *Peter Orlovsky, A Life in Words: Intimate Chronicles of a Beat Writer*. Paradigm. [2014] pp. 352. $29.95 ISBN 9 7816 1205 5824.

Nappaaluk, Mitiarjuk. *Sanaaq: An Inuit Novel*. UManitobaP. [2014] pp. 192. $24.95 ISBN 9 7808 8755 7484.

Neculai, Catalina. *Urban Space and Late Twentieth-Century New York Literature: Reformed Geographies.* Palgrave. [2014] pp. 240. £56 ISBN 9 7811 3734 0191.

Nevett, Chad, ed. *Shot in the Face: A Savage Journey into to the Heart of Transmetropolitan.* Sequart. [2013] pp. 155. $12.99 ISBN 9 7819 4058 9008.

Noodin, Margaret. *Bawaajimo: A Dialect of Dreams in Anishinaabe Language and Literature.* MichSUP. [2014] pp. 234. $29.95 ISBN 9 7816 1186 1051.

Ouriou, Susan, ed. *Languages of Our Land: Indigenous Voices from Quebec / Langues De Notre Terre: Voix Autochtones du Québec.* Banff. [2014] pp. 180. $18.95 ISBN 9 7818 9477 3768.

Parmar, Sandeep. *Reading Mina Loy's Autobiographies: Myth of the Modern Woman.* Bloomsbury. [2014] pp. 208. £18.99 ISBN 9 7814 7259 6505.

Patton, Venetria K. *The Grasp that Reaches Beyond the Grave.* SUNYP. [2014] pp. 226. $28.95 ISBN 9 7814 3844 7360.

Peeren, Esther. *The Spectral Metaphor: Living Ghosts and the Agency of Invisibility.* Palgrave. [2014] pp. 228. £53 ISBN 9 7811 3737 5841.

Peterson, James Braxton. *The Hip-Hop Underground and African American Culture: Beneath the Surface.* Palgrave. [2014] pp. 208. £55 ISBN 9 7811 3730 5244.

Quartermain, Peter, ed. *The Collected Later Poems and Plays.* UCalP. [2014] pp. 931. $49.95 ISBN 9 7805 2025 9294.

Richardson, Mark. *Robert Frost in Context.* CUP. [2014] pp. 418. £65 ISBN 9 7811 0702 2881.

Rifkin, Mark. *Settler Common Sense: Queerness and Everyday Colonialism in the American Renaissance.* UMinnP. [2014] pp. 320. $75 ISBN 9 7808 1669 0572.

Rob, Allen, and Thijs van den Berg. *Serialization in Popular Culture.* Routledge. [2014] pp. 222. $145 ISBN 9 7804 1570 4267.

Robbins, Amy Moorman. *American Hybrid Poetics: Gender, Mass Culture, and Form.* RutgersUP. [2014] pp. 188. $75 ISBN 9 7808 1356 4654.

Roeder, Katherine. *Wide Awake in Slumberland: Fantasy, Mass Culture, and Modernism in the Art of Winsor McCay.* UPMissip. [2014] pp. 222. $60 ISBN 9 7816 1703 9607.

Romagnoli, Alex S., and Gian S. Pagnucci. *Enter the Superheroes: American Values, Culture, and the Canon of Superhero Literature.* Scarecrow. [2013] pp. 246. $72 ISBN 9 7808 1089 1715.

Round, Julia. *Gothic in Comics and Graphic Novels: A Critical Approach.* McFarland. [2014] pp. 268. $40 ISBN 9 7807 8644 9804.

Roynon, Tessa. *Toni Morrison and the Classical Tradition: Transforming American Culture.* OUP. [2014] pp. 240. £53 ISBN 9 7801 9969 8684.

Schmidt, Christopher. *The Poetics of Waste: Queer Excess in Stein, Ashbery, Schuyler, and Goldsmith.* Palgrave. [2014] pp. 224. $95 ISBN 9 7811 3740 2783.

Schmidt, Tyler T. *Desegregating Desire: Race and Sexuality in Cold War American Literature.* UPMissip. [2013] pp. 272. $30 ISBN 9 7814 9680 2637.

Scott, Cord A. *Comics and Conflict: Patriotism and Propaganda from WWII through Operation Iraqi Freedom.* NIP. [2014] pp. 224. $49.95 ISBN 9 7816 1251 4772.

Shapira, Tom. *Curing the Postmodern Bludes: Reading Grant Morrison and Chris Weston's* The Filth *in the 21st Century*. Sequart. [2013] pp. 174. $12.99 ISBN 9 7805 7806 0767.

Sherman, David. *In a Strange Room: Modernism's Corpses and Mortal Obligation*. OUP. [2014] pp. 288. £41.99 ISBN 9 7801 9933 3882.

Shonkwiler, Alison, and Leigh Claire La Berge, eds. *Reading Capitalist Realism*. UIowaP. [2014] pp. 272. $47.50 ISBN 9 7816 0938 2346.

Simpson, Audra, and Andrea Smith, eds. *Theorizing Native Studies*. DukeUP. [2014] pp. 352. $94.95 ISBN 9 7808 2235 6677.

Slusser, George. *Gregory Benford*. UIllP. [2014]. pp. 216. $25 ISBN 9 7802 5207 9801.

Smith, Rod, Peter Baker, and Kaplan Harris, eds. *The Selected Letters of Robert Creeley*. UCalP. [2014] pp. 545. $65 ISBN 9 7805 2024 1602

Smolderen, Thierry. *The Origins of Comics: From William Hogarth to Winsor McCay*, trans. Bart Beaty and Nick Nguyen. UPMissip. [2014] pp. 168. $50 ISBN 9 7816 1703 1496.

Sohn, Stephen Hong. *Racial Asymmetries: Asian American Fictional Worlds*. NYUP. [2014] pp. ix + 289. $85 ISBN 9 7814 7980 0070.

Tabachnick, Stephen E. *The Quest for Jewish Belief and Identity in the Graphic Novel*. UAlaP. [2014] pp. 272. $39.95 ISBN 9 7808 1731 8215.

Thesen, Sharon, and Ralph Maud, eds. *After Completion: The Later Letters of Charles Olson and Frances Boldereff*. Talonbooks. [2014] pp. 304. $24.95 ISBN 9 7808 8922 7064.

Thurman, Kevin, and Julian Darius. *Voyage in Noise: Warren Ellis and the Demise of Western Civilization*. Sequart. [2013] pp. 157. $12.99 ISBN 9 7819 4058 9015.

Tiffany, Daniel. *My Silver Planet: A Secret History of Poetry and Kitsch*. JHUP. [2014] pp. 301. $45 ISBN 9 7814 2141 1453.

Trask, Michael. *Camp Sites: Sex, Politics, and Academic Style in Postwar America*. StanfordUP. [2013] pp. 272. $24.95 ISBN 9 7808 0478 4412.

Wagner-Martin, Linda. *Toni Morrison and the Maternal: From* The Bluest Eye *to* Home. Lang. [2014] pp. 211. £31 ISBN 9 7814 3312 4570.

Wainer, Alex M. *Soul of the Dark Knight: Batman as Mythic Figure in Comics and Film*. McFarland. [2014] pp. 208. $40 ISBN 9 7807 8647 1287.

Wald, Priscilla, and Michael A. Elliott, eds. *The American Novel 1870–1940*. OUP. [2014] pp. xxv + 628. £105 ISBN 9 7801 9538 5342.

Walter, Christina. *Optical Impersonality: Science, Images, and Literary Modernism*. JHUP. [2014] pp. 352. $59.95 ISBN 9 7814 2141 3631.

Wang, Dorothy. *Thinking Its Presence: Form, Race, and Subjectivity in Contemporary Asian American Poetry*. StanfordUP. [2014] pp. xxiv + 416. $50 ISBN 9 7808 0478 3651.

Washington, Mary Helen. *The Other Blacklist: The African American Literary and Cultural Left of the 1950s*. ColUP. [2014] pp. 368. $35 ISBN 9 7802 3115 2709.

Watson, Veronica T. *The Souls of White Folk: African American Writers Theorize Whiteness*. UPMissip. [2013] pp. 176. $55 ISBN 9 7816 1703 8891.

White, Frederick. *Emerging from Out of the Margins: Essays on Haida Language, Culture, and History*. Lang. [2014] pp. 250. $79.95 ISBN 9 7814 3311 6667.

Yockey, Matt. *Batman*. WSUP. [2014] pp. vii + 147. $19.95 ISBN 9 7808 1433 8179.

XVIII

New Literatures

MRIDULA NATH CHAKRABORTY, MARGARET DAYMOND, MICHAEL GRIFFITHS, WEIHSIN GUI, MADHU KRISHNAN, DOUGAL MCNEILL, GRACE MUSILA, IRA RAJA, GISELLE RAMPAUL, PAUL SHARRAD, GERALDINE SKEETE, AND TINA STEINER

This chapter has seven sections: 1. Africa; 2. Australia; 3. Canada; 4. The Caribbean; 5. South Asia; 6. New Zealand & Pacific; 7 Southeast Asia. Section 1 is by Margaret Daymond, Grace Musila, Tina Steiner and Madhu Krishnan; section 2 is by Michael Griffiths and Paul Sharrad; section 3 is by Paul Sharrad; section 4 is by Giselle Rampaul and Geraldine Skeete; section 5 is by Mridula Nath Chakraborty and Ira Raja; section 6 is by Dougal McNeill; section 7 is by Weihsin Gui.

1. Africa

(a) West Africa

This was a particularly productive year for West African literary studies. Unsurprisingly, a key focus was tributes and elegies for Chinua Achebe and Kofi Awoonor, both of whom passed away in 2013. Yaw Asante's 'Tribute: Kofi Awoonor (1935–2013)' (*TvL* 51:i[2014] 74–6) is a thoughtful reflection on a man whose life 'was a commitment and dedication to a country and continent to which he felt deeply attached' (p. 76). In spare prose, Asante foregrounds Awoonor's legacy and the tragedy that he should have been killed in the service of education and knowledge. Elsewhere, *African Literature Today* 32 features a range of retrospectives on, analyses of, and poetic tributes and eulogies to, Awoonor. These items include Kofi Anyidoho's 'Kofi Awoonor: In Retrospect' (*ALT* 32[2014] 121–4); Ghirmai Negash's 'Kofi Awoonor: Poem for a Mentor & Friend' (*ALT* 32[2014] 125–36); Mawuli Adjei's 'Looking Death in the Eye: The Human Condition, Morbidity & Mortality in Kofi Awoonor's Poetry' (*ALT* 32[2014] 137–50); Richard Priebe's 'Eulogy for an Artist, a Statesman, a Teacher & Friend: Kofi

Awoonor' (*ALT* 32[2014] 151–7); Prince K. Adika's 'Postcolonial Trauma & the Poetics of Remembering the Novels of Kofi Awoonor' (*ALT* 32[2014] 158–72); and Kofi Anyidoho's 'Song for Nyidevu' (*ALT* 32[2014] 173). Awoonor's *This Earth, My Brother* is one of two works discussed, along with Amma Darko's *Faceless*, which is read in the concluding chapter of Ato Quayson's masterful study of the production of postcolonial African space, *Oxford Street, Accra*. This must-read book uses the example of a single street in a single district in the titular city to produce an engaging account from the earliest days of empire to the present day, drawing on impressively broad archival research and exploring unexpectedly potent sites for the constitution of spatial precepts, including salsa dancing clubs, fitness studios, and the gym. The study concludes by turning its attention to literary representations of space, particularly representations of movement and traversals of the city. For Quayson, Awoonor's novel is remarkable in the 'peculiar and often unsettling sense of modularity by which the city is experienced' (p. 231), realized through its boldly unconventional, modernist prose.

Awoonor's sudden and tragic murder in Kenya's Westgate massacre of 2013 sent shock waves across the world. Equally potent in its significance was the death in March 2013 of Chinua Achebe, so often thought of as the father of modern African literature. The strength of Achebe's influence is apparent in the sheer volume of tributes and critical engagements with his work throughout 2014. Notable is the tribute in *PMLA* 129:ii[2014], in the issue's 'Theories and Methodologies' section (pp. 237–56), featuring contributions from luminaries of postcolonial and African studies. Elleke Boehmer's contribution, 'Chinua Achebe, a Father of Modern African Literature' (*PMLA* 129:ii[2014] 237–9), begins from the assertion that 'the death of a literary figure bearing a reputation at once local, national, and international invariably raises questions about the writer's legacy and the afterlife of his or her work' (p. 237). Boehmer asserts the strong foundation to Achebe's legacy, both as a critical commentator—notably through his now canonical critique of institutional racism in literary studies via his reading of Conrad—and as an author unto himself. Citing the enduring influence of *Things Fall Apart* as a classic text which 'permanently changed perceptions of African literature on the continent and worldwide' (p. 238), Boehmer makes a compelling case for Achebe's larger importance as an author who found 'success in wresting Africa into non-African frameworks of cognition through the medium of the novel form, yet, importantly, without ever compromising or substantially changing his novels' structures of religious and cultural reference' (p. 239). *Things Fall Apart* is also the starting point for Rhonda Cobham-Sander's 'Chasms and Silences: For Chinua Achebe' (*PMLA* 129:ii[2014] 240–3). The strategic silences embedded within that novel are a means of 'register[ing] possibilities beyond representation' (p. 240), and echo in the aporia underlying the work of resistance and assimilation in Achebe's larger oeuvre. The remainder of the piece traces the many silences and ghosts which haunted Achebe in the wake of Biafra. Achebe's prose style is the subject of the next contribution to the tribute section, Uzoma Esonwanne's '"Restraint... My Style": Deliberate and Mournful' (*PMLA* 129:ii[2014] 243–5). Citing the twin influences of *mbari* and the Igbo masquerade, Esonwanne draws links between the deliberate and measured style of Achebe's fictional writings and his non-fictional prose, making particularly important observations about how authorial control of tone challenges orthodox precepts around late style. The essay's comparison between *Things Fall Apart*, Achebe's first published work, and *There Was A Country*, his last, will be of particular significance for scholars. Harry Garuba, in 'Chinua Achebe and the Struggle for Discursive Authority in the Postcolonial World' (*PMLA* 129:ii[2014] 246–8), moves beyond readings which position Achebe's work within the context of anti-colonial nationalism and cultural colonization in order to excavate his importance for 'this postcolonial present' (p. 246). In so doing, Garuba characterizes Achebe's work as a study in the simultaneous interpellation of the split postcolonial subject by two incompatible discursive orders. Eileen Julien, by contrast, approaches the reading of *Things Fall Apart* from a historical perspective in 'How We Read *Things Fall Apart* Then' (*PMLA* 129:ii[2014] 248–50). Showing the range of reference which gave rise to that work, Julien situates Achebe as an author of the world, 'the exemplar—if not the theorist—of early "postcolonial literature", the one who inaugurated what would be known for fifty years as "African literature"' (p. 249), who, at the time that his first novel was published, was nonetheless read alternately through a teleological vision of African society moving from tradition to modernity or through the lens of 'authenticity'. The penultimate offering in *PMLA*'s tribute to Achebe, James Ogude's 'Reading *No Longer at Ease* as a Text That Performs Local Cosmopolitanism' (*PMLA* 129:ii[2014] 251–3), considers the second published novel, the story of Okonkwo's embattled grandson. Reading the novel as emerging from a period of transition, as the nation-state of Nigeria slowly emerged, the essay traces the movements of two forms of cosmopolitanism in the novel: the idealistic and universal, and the local and situated. For Ogude, the struggle between these two modes is what characterizes Obi Okonkwo's crisis: a desire to transcend not just his Englishness, but the traditional ways of his Igbo people as well. The section ends with Elaine Savory's 'Chinua Achebe's Ecocritical Awareness' (*PMLA* 129:ii[2014] 253–6), which draws a parallel with the loss of the author and the loss of 'the whole earth as habitable space' (p. 253). Reading Achebe's work against the traditional metaphysics of Igbo cosmology, carefully attuned to the earth and environment, Savory concludes with an elegy for a man who 'understood the importance of balance in human and natural ecology' (p. 255) in a manner which has become all too rare.

   Chinua Achebe: Tributes and Reflections, edited by Nana Ayebia Clarke and James Currey, features forty-nine short essays, eulogies, and reflections by a range of international critics and writers, including both rare, previously published texts and newly commissioned work. Beginning with Lyn Innes's tribute to Achebe, published in the *Guardian* as his official obituary, and ending with a reprint of Binyavanga Wainaina's satirical essay, 'How to Write About Africa', the collection as a whole spans ages, generations, and perspectives on Achebe, including personal reminiscences, poetic reflections, and testaments to the author's enduring legacy. Of particular interest to readers will be the hauntingly beautiful prose poem in his praise contributed by Mĩcere Gĩthae Mũgo, and Odia Ofeimun's 'For Chinua Achebe'. Femi Osofisan's 'The Discombobulation of a Rookie Patriot: A Stage Adaptation of Chinua Achebe's *Man of the People*' is another must-read entry. The personal anecdotes are of particular value in humanizing a man who had become a legend.

Rare is a year that does not see critical attention paid to Achebe's oeuvre, irrespective of special commemorations. Taiwo Adetunji Osinubi's essay, 'Cold War Sponsorships: Chinua Achebe and the Dialectics of Collaboration' (*JPW* 50:iv[2014] 410–22) is an important rereading of *Man of the People* not as a study in corruption and failed governance in Nigeria, but rather as part of a class of mid-century works which critique the rhetoric of the Cold War. Osinubi argues that the novel deliberately subordinates its engagement with Cold War geopolitics to localized concerns in the era of decolonization as a means of satirizing the often inflammatory language expressing fear of communism in newly independent nations. By so doing, the novel imagines a world order with space for political engagement outside a post-Second World War East–West binary. A reassessment of Achebe's oeuvre is also the subject of Megan Cole Paustian's ' "A Real Heaven on Their Own Earth": Religious Missions, African Writers, and the Anticolonial Imagination' (*RAL* 45:ii[2014] 1–25), which sets Achebe's memoirs and fiction alongside the work of Ngũgĩ wa Thiong'o to explore the ways in which missionary education, though implicated with colonial domination, served also as a site for radical self-invention via the emancipatory discourses which would drive decolonization. The essay focuses on Achebe's *Education of a British-Protected Child*, *Things Fall Apart*, and *Arrow of God* in order to develop comparative readings of missionary education across genres. This mode of comparative analysis is continued in Aghogho Akpome's 'Ways of Telling: (Re)Writing the Nation in the Novels and Memoir of Chinua Achebe' (*JLST* 30:i[2014] 34–52), which examines the trajectory from Achebe's earlier novelistic output to his final work, the memoir *There Was a Country: A Personal History of Biafra*, in order to argue that his thematization of the postcolonial nation betrays a narrowing of interest from Africa writ large, to the Nigerian nation, and finally to the Igbo ethno-nation. By so doing, Akpome retrospectively radicalizes Achebe's older work. Revisionist reading continues in Oritsegbubemi Oyowe's philosophical essay, 'Fiction, Culture, and the Concept of a Person' (*RAL* 45:ii[2014] 46–62), which revisits Ikuenobe's 2006 reading of *Things Fall Apart* as a study of normative personhood. Oyowe's essay deftly demonstrates that, contrary to the orthodox critical position, Achebe's work cannot be said to make any clear claims about personhood, either metaphysical or normative. Françoise Ugochukwu also turns her attention to *Things Fall Apart* in an absorbing essay that traces the history of film and television adaptations of the novel, notably the highly successful 1987 adaptation as a ten-part miniseries for NTA, in '*Things Fall Apart*: Achebe's Legacy, from Book to Screen' (*RAL* 45:ii[2014] 168–83). Finally, a chapter in Brian May's *Extravagant Postcolonialism: Modernism and Modernity in Anglophone Fiction, 1958–1988*, 'Tradition and the Talent for Individuality', picks up on the theme of the person, reading *Things Fall Apart* and *No Longer At Ease* as studies in the relationship between art and the individual. In both novels, May argues, aesthetics—and particularly beauty—serves as an indication of moral values with a significant political import. This must-read chapter centres on Obi, protagonist of *No Longer At Ease*, positioning his climactic abandonment of his once beloved poetry as the moment in which his ethical and moral quest fails. Drawing on the modernist aesthetic claim to art as weapon, May's readings of both novels situate each as fundamentally about art, beauty, and the power therein.

Achebe is also subject of a chapter in Alexander Täuschel's *World English(es): On the Examples of India and Nigeria*, which focuses on the use of West African English in Nigerian literature through readings of orality in *Things Fall Apart* and *Arrow of God*. Linguistic criticism, particularly stylistic analysis, was a major aspect of Achebe studies in 2014. Isaac Nuokyaa-Ire Mwinlaaru's 'Style, Character and the Theme of Struggle and Change: Chinua Achebe's *Anthills of the Savannah*' (*RAL* 45:ii[2014] 103–21) is a particularly fascinating example of this critical trend, using systemic functional linguistics to explore the narrative and linguistic transformation from fear and powerlessness in the novel to empowerment and bravery. The essay focuses particularly on the relationship between symbolism, narrative situation, and transitivity patternings, on the one hand, and on the other an underlying systemic linguistic analysis of the character of Chris as an exemplar of Achebe's call for an enlightened citizenry to stand up to power and transform society. Aghogho Akpome continues stylistic analysis in 'Dispersal of Narrative Point of View in Chinua Achebe's *Anthills of the Savannah*' (*EARev* 31:i[2014] 19–37), which argues that extant criticism of the novel has been overshadowed by socio-political and thematic readings. Akpome focuses on the narrative and linguistic innovations within the novel, particularly its use of multiple focalizers, emplotment, and temporal non-linearity. Drawing heavily on the narratological work of Jahn and Bal, Akpome convincingly demonstrates the extent to which Achebe creates a panoptic view of African society at the interstices of postcoloniality and postmodernity.

Other 2014 essays on Achebe include Zahra Sadeghi's 'Role of Colonial Subjects in Making Themselves Inferior in Chinua Achebe's *Things Fall Apart*' (*AdLLS* 5:vi[2014] n.p.); Ecevit Bekler's 'The True Face of Pre-Colonial Africa in *Things Fall Apart*' (*RPh* 25:xxx[2014] 96–104); Abubakar Mohammed Sani's 'Literature as Tool for Sustainable Development: A Comparative Literary Analysis of Achebe's *Arrow of God* and Tahir's *The Last Iman*' (*AdLLS* 5:iii[2014]); Arua E. Arua's 'Free Indirect Style in Three Canonical African Novels Written in English' (in Arua, Abioye, and Ayoola, eds., *Language, Literature and Style in Africa*, pp. 2–21), which compares the methods of focalization and style in *Anthills of the Savannah* with Armah's *The Beautyful Ones Are Not Yet Born* and Ngũgĩ's *Petals of Blood*; Aaron Bady's chapter, 'The Thing and the Image: Violence in Chinua Achebe's *Things Fall Apart*' (in Peebles, ed., *Violence in Literature*, pp. 38–53); and Amarjeet Nayak's 'Reading a Culturally Different Text: Meaning Signification Process in Chinua Achebe's Short Stories' (*ShFTP* 4:i[2014] 67–78).

Along with Achebe, Wole Soyinka stands out as a pioneer of West African literary writing, and this distinction did not go unnoticed in 2014. Ivor Agyeman-Duah and Ogochukwu Promise's edited collection, *Essays in Honour of Wole Soyinka at 80*, speaks to the ongoing importance of his literary presence. This volume contains thirty short essays organized over six sections. The first, 'Salutatory Musing for the Master's Tale', features tributes from Ngũgĩ wa Thiong'o, Nadine Gordimer, Sefi Atta, Margaret Busby, Toni Morrison, and Nicholas Westcott. These contributions paint a portrait not just of a literary giant, but of an engaged, kind, and committed individual. Section II, 'The Canvas is Universal: Philosophy, Literature and the Politics of Redemption', comprises three more analytic reflections by Ama Ata Aidoo, Henry Louis Gates Jr., and Ato Quayson, foregrounding the ethico-philosophical dynamics of Soyinka's work. Section III, 'Harvest of Past Seasons: Memoirs, Conversations and Palavers', returns to a more personal idiom, with a broad array of reminiscences and anecdotes by Soyinka's friends and family, including Femi Johnson, Kwame Anthony Appiah, Esi Sutherland-Addy, and Amowi Sutherland Phillips. Section IV, 'The Museum, African Art and Music', surveys Soyinka's legacy, placing his work in the wider landscape of African cultural production through the ages. John Collins and Ivor Agyeman-Duah's take on Soyinka and Fela in 'The Protestants from Abeokuta: Fela Anikulapo-Kuti and His Cousin' is of particular interest, approaching Soyinka through the body of work of the infamous musician. The next section, 'Poetry from the Threshold', includes contributions from luminaries including Derek Walcott and Atukwei Oki. The last section of the volume, 'Tradition and the Modernity of Governance', highlights Soyinka's importance as a political thinker and public figure. It concludes with a reflection by former South African president Thabo Mbeki, who draws connections across Soyinka's engaged intellectualism and the new African renaissance.

Three more essays demonstrate the ongoing literary and political import of Soyinka's work. Solomon Omatsola Azumurana's 'Wole Soyinka's Dystopian/ Utopian Vision in *A Dance of the Forests*' (*TvL* 51:ii[2014] 71–81) reads Soyinka's play through the lens of temporality, arguing that, rather than simply depicting the exigencies of post-independence disillusionment, the work can be read as a linking of a hopeless past to an empty present in order to gesture towards a dystopian future in which atrocities seem inevitable. Paradoxically, however, this fatalistic vision opens the play to the possibility of a utopian future. Based on the premise that only a critical perspective on the past and present can create the space for a hopeful futurity, the essay demonstrates the interweaving of the dystopian and the utopian as a call for engagement. Andrew Barnaby turns his attention to another of Soyinka's plays in his ' "The Purest Mode of Looking": (Post)Colonial Trauma in Wole Soyinka's *Death and the King's Horseman*' (*RAL* 45:i[2014] 125–49), which takes as its starting point Soyinka's statement in his author's note to the play that colonialism is 'a catalytic incident merely'. Drawing on a Freudian analysis of trauma and deferred action, the essay challenges this authorial self-positioning by positioning colonialism as 'an originary missing' of the event itself (p. 127), a kind of not seeing which calls for an ethical project of bearing witness and enables the act of witnessing. Ultimately, Barnaby positions the play as a study in post-memory and responsibility. Mark Mathuray's essay, 'Intimacies between Men: Modernism, African Homosexualities and Masculinist Anxieties in Wole Soyinka's *The Interpreters*' (*JPW* 50:vi[2014] 635–47), addresses what is arguably Soyinka's most famous work of prose fiction. The essay focuses largely on a single, pivotal scene from the novel, in which Biodun Sagoe meets the mixed-race, homosexual American Joe Golder on a dark and stormy night. Mathuray thoroughly explores how the homosexual figure functions within the aesthetics of African high modernism as an ethical challenge to normative discourses of nationalism and tradition. Both marginal and central, the character of Golder destabilizes the hegemonic forms of masculinity and heteronormativity represented by the novel's main characters, who themselves become figures embodying contemporary African nationalist leadership. Finally, a moving and personal reflection on Soyinka rounds out this year's contribution to criticism on the author. In 'Wole Soyinka: "Intellectuel total vs. poète citoyen": An Antitotalitarian Theory of Power' (*BRN* 14:i[2014] 158–63), Alain Ricard ruminates on Soyinka's centrality to his own intellectual formation, reading in his multiple engagements a radical dialogism which threatens totalitarian discourses at their foundation.

Stylistic analyses were not limited to readings of Achebe; other contributions to the developing field of stylistics and West African literature include Godwin Oko Ushie and Idaevbor Bello's 'Umbilical Accord and Symbiosis between Man and the Environment: A Stylistic Analysis of Selected Poems of Joe Ushie's *Hill Songs* and Unima Angrey's *Drought (Ubang)*' (*TPLS* 4:vii[2014] 1327–33) and Edmund Bamiro's 'Stylistic Functions of "Dislocation" in Soyinka's Novels: A Systemic-Functional Analysis' (*TPLS* 4:xii[2014] 2492–7). Most significant in this line of criticism is Daria Tunca's wonderful *Stylistic Approaches to Nigerian Fiction*. Tunca's book begins from the premise that, through a sustained engagement with the principles of stylistic analysis, new meanings and positions may be excavated from the literary text. Tunca is careful to note that this approach is not hostile to 'traditional' literary criticism, but rather serves as an extra set of tools. This stylistic method is outlined in the study's first chapter, 'Towards an "African Stylistics"? Historiographical and Methodological Considerations'. Theory is put into practice in the next chapter, 'Of Palm Oil and Wafers: Characterization in Chimamanda Ngozi Adichie's *Purple Hibiscus*', which convincingly analyses the novel's formal features—particularly its use of proverbs and its recurrent grammatical patterns—to demonstrate protagonist Kambili's awakening throughout the course of the novel. Tunca's deployment of the concepts of mind-style and transitivity are particularly compelling, as is her use of Halliday's systemic-functional grammar. The next chapter retains its focus on Adichie. '"The Other Half of the Sun": Ideology in Chimamanda Ngozi Adichie's *Half of a Yellow Sun*' inspects under-lexicalization, repeated schemas, the use of vocatives, and the use of exemplification to unpack the ideological constructions which undergird the novel. 'Art is a Journey: Metaphor in Ben Okri's *The Landscapes Within* and *Dangerous Love*' compares these two versions of a broadly similar text, identifying the underlying use of conceptual metaphor as a major element in the reconstruction of meaning across each. The final two chapters of the study move to shorter-form fiction, examining the novellas of Chris Abani and Uzodinma Iweala. '"Bi-textual" Poetics Investigating Form in Chris Abani's *Becoming Abigail*' develops a methodical framework for understanding the often contradictory impulses which underlie Abani's prose, creating what is often described as its haunting quality. The concluding chapter to the study,

'Children at War: Language and Representation in Uzodinma Iweala's *Beasts of No Nation* and Chris Abani's *Song for Night*', addresses two difficult novels which engage, in various ways, with the figure of the child soldier and the memory of the Nigerian Civil War. The former text is read through its linguistic inaccuracy, a departure from realism in the text that enables its stylistic range, while the latter text can be described as riddled with ambiguities which result in a split between an empathic and an ironic reading. Tunca closes her study with a call for a reappraisal of the value of stylistics as a form of literary criticism, the value of which is aptly demonstrated throughout the book.

Hamish Dalley's *The Postcolonial Historical Novel: Realism, Allegory, and the Representation of Contested Pasts*, contains two chapters of interest to scholars of West African literature. The first of these, 'Aesthetics of Absent Causality: Chimamanda Ngozi Adichie's *Half of a Yellow Sun*', positions the novel against a larger body of Nigerian Civil War literature, noting the ways in which Adichie's text departs from certain normative features. Dalley argues that, through the use of character and plot, Adichie refuses the imperative to homogenize either victims or perpetrators of violence, instead insisting on 'the inadequacy of historical interpretations that ignore the internal heterogenetic of Nigeria's ethno-religious communities' (p. 126). Citing what he terms the novel's 'aesthetics of absent causality', Dalley uses close readings of the text to demonstrate how, through historical documentation intercut with imaginative elements, Adichie demands an expansion of imaginative horizon beyond the nation-state and its attendant absolutes. In his following chapter, 'Spectres of Civil War Trauma: Chris Abani's *Song for Night*', Dalley turns to another example of war fiction to discuss the significance and applicability of trauma theory in studies of Nigerian Civil War writing. Noting the ambiguities which pepper Abani's novella, Dalley claims that its 'trauma aesthetics' unsettle orthodoxies around history and realism in the postcolonial novel.

Madhu Krishnan's *Contemporary African Literature in English: Global Locations, Postcolonial Identifications* also includes a number of chapters of interest to studies of West African literature. Based upon the premise that the gap between aesthetic and material readings of African texts has led to the constriction of imaginative horizons around the image of Africa, Krishnan's monograph considers case studies by Aminatta Forna, Chimamanda Ngozi Adichie, Chris Abani, and G.A. Agambila. In the second chapter of the study, 'Gender and Representing the Unrepresentable', Krishnan places Forna's *Ancestor Stones* and Adichie's *Half of a Yellow Sun* in conversation with Yvonne Vera's *The Stone Virgins* to examine the intersection of gender and conflict. Both texts subvert the trope of feminization in conflict in order to present alternative visions of engenderment which remain nonetheless under pressure from external material forms. In the following chapter, 'Mythopoetics and Cultural Re-Creation', Krishnan turns to Abani's *GraceLand* as an example of a text which reconfigures traditional and modern mythological narratives to redefine cultural hybridity and liminality. Through its resistance against a collapse into the surreal or arcane, *GraceLand*, Krishnan argues, develops a vision for contemporary Africa which refuses absolutes in favour of an ever-vigilant sense of multiplicity. *GraceLand* and *Half of a Yellow Sun* are again subjects of the study's final chapter, 'Global African Literatures: Strategies of Address and Cultural Constraints', which examines the use of the trope of the book within the book as an unsettling of rhetorical desire and narrative convention. By forcing the reader into a relationship of co-production through the insertion of extra-literary 'texts' within each novel, both subvert absolutist models of cultural identification. The chapter concludes with a discussion of locally published African literature, including Ghanaian politician and writer G.A. Agambila's *Journey*, which chronicles the disillusionment of an educated member of Ghana's burgeoning elite against the background of economic deprivation. *Journey* is another form of African literature beyond that published in the multinational literary market; it draws upon specific localized forms of identification to create a multi-modal narrative structure that points to limits of the 'local' and 'global' in studies of African literature today.

Amongst the most significant publications of 2014 was *Matatu* 45, edited by Ogaga Okuyade. Titled 'Tradition and Change in Contemporary West and East Africa Fiction', the volume deals with authors both canonical and less well-known and features themes of gender, sexuality, diaspora, migration, politics, and space, with a primary focus on writing from the previous decade. Iniobong I. Uko's 'Womanhood, Sexuality, and Work: The Dialectic of Exploitation' (*Matatu* 45[2014] 1–20) sets the writing of Flora Nwapa and Ama Ata Aidoo in dialogue with the work of Nawal El Saadawi to examine the ways in which each author intervenes in the exploitative dynamics of traditional gender relations and opens avenues towards new agendas for African women. That essay is followed by Enajite E. Ojaruega's 'Outgoing and Incoming Africans: Migration and Reverse Migration in Contemporary African Narratives' (*Matatu* 45[2014] 21–34), which reads a number of texts including Adichie's *Purple Hibiscus*, Abani's *GraceLand*, and Tanure Ojaide's *The Activist* to explore the often conflicting sentiments of aspiration through migration and nostalgia through return. Oluwole Coker's 'Development Imperatives and Transnationalism in Third-Generation Nigerian Fiction' (*Matatu* 45[2014] 35–42) addresses two seemingly dissimilar narratives, Okey Ndibe's *Arrows of Rain* and Adaobi Tricia Nwaubani's *I Do Not Come To You By Chance*, in order to discuss the development quest in contemporary Nigerian fiction as the fulcrum of a transnational aesthetic which emerges in these works. Thomas Jay Lynn's 'Postcolonial Encounters Re-envisioned: Kojo Laing's *Woman of the Aeroplanes* as Trickster Narrative' (*Matatu* 45[2014] 153–66) focuses on the Ghanaian author, reading his trickster book as offering an alternative to the historical domination of West Africa through an emphasis on personal and political modes of freedom. Christopher Ouma's 'Countries of the Mind: Space-Time Chronotopes in Adichie's *Purple Hibiscus*' (*Matatu* 45[2014] 167–86) centres on the significance of the university town of Nsukka in Adichie's debut novel. Defining the city as a 'toponym', comprising compounds, houses, and a range of material objects, the essay probes the play of belonging and non-belonging engendered through its trajectories of movement across space and time, ultimately positioning Nsukka as an aesthetic space, a country of the mind, in which a liberating topography is forged. The next essay in the volume, Brian Doherty's 'Writing Back with a

Difference: Chimamanda Ngozi Adichie's "The Headstrong Historian" as a Response to Chinua Achebe's *Things Fall Apart*' (*Matatu* 45[2014] 187–202), reads her short story as an act of literary revision set against Achebe's canonical novel: part homage and part critique. Chitra Thrivikraman Nair's 'Negotiation of Socio-Ethnic Spaces: Chimamanda Ngozi Adichie's *Half of a Yellow Sun* as a *Testimonio* of African National and Ethnic Identity' (*Matatu* 45[2014] 197–209), reads the novel as a negotiated articulation of Biafran and Igbo space within the landscape of twentieth-century geopolitics. Louisa Uchum Egbunike's contribution, 'One-Way Traffic: Renegotiating the "Been-To" Narrative in the Nigerian Novel in the Era of Military Rule' (*Matatu* 45[2014] 217–32), includes Achebe's *No Longer At Ease*, Soyinka's *The Interpreters*, Ekwensi's *Jagua Nana*, Habila's *Waiting for an Angel*, Adichie's *Purple Hibiscus*, and Oguine's *A Squatter's Tale*—its broad historical sweep alone signals its merits. Egbunike's essay makes a compelling case for a rematerialized consideration of 'home' and 'abroad' through close attention to the dynamics of a fundamentally asymmetrical system of exchange. Alexander Greer Hartwiger, 'Strangers in/to the World: The Unhomely in Chris Abani's *GraceLand*' (*Matatu* 45[2014] 233–50), argues that Abani's novel may be read as a reconfiguration of the grounds of world literature through the discourse of the unhomely, as tied to its embodied and spatialized instantiations, ultimately constituting a counter-hegemonic cosmopolitanism. Abani, like Adichie, is one of the better-known contemporary writers from West Africa. Less well known, however, is academic and writer Maik Nwosu, the focus of Ngozi Chuma-Udeh's 'Maik Nwosu's *Invisible Chapters*: Investigating Psychological Fragmentation in Nigerian Literature' (*Matatu* 45[2014] 251–62). The essay is a study of character which seeks to link the ongoing social and political turmoil faced by Nigeria to the psychological fragmentation experienced by Nwosu's characters. James Omuteche's 'The Global Underground and the Illegitimate Diasporas: in Chika Unigwe's *On Black Sisters' Street*' (*Matatu* 45[2014] 263–94) continues the theme of socio-political critique and psychological disorientation. The essay argues that, far from its emancipatory promises, globalization in Unigwe's novel can be linked to the perpetuation of neo-imperial structures of subordination which contribute to the displacement and dislocation of her protagonists, forced instead into exploitation via the submerged and informal channels of global flows and movements. Unigwe's fellow contemporary Nigerian writer is the focus of the next essay in the collection, Owojecho Omoha's 'Fictional Narrative and the Reflective Self in Helon Habila's *Waiting for an Angel*' (*Matatu* 45[2014] 295–314), which turns its attention to narrative style, situating the novel as a self-reflexive manifestation of the author's own experiences as a student in Jos in northern Nigeria. Charles Cliff Feghabo, 'Inverting Otherness in Kaine Agary's *Yellow-Yellow*' (*Matatu* 45[2014] 315–32), redresses the largely ecocritical readings of oil narratives, arguing instead for a more strongly gendered ecofeminist reading of despoliation and exploitation in this body of work. 'Love's Metamorphosis in Third-Generation African Women's Writing: The Example of Lola Shoneyin's *The Secret lives of Baby Segi's Wives*' (*Matatu* 45[2014] 333–64), by Olusegun Adekoya, similarly proposes a feminist reading of contemporary West African writing, reading Shoneyin's debut as an examination of human sexuality in the twenty-first-century African context. The penultimate contribution to the collection, Nmachika Nwokeabia's 'Gender and (Homo)Sexuality in Third-Generation African Writing: A Reading of Unoma Azuah's *Sky-High Flames* and Jude Dibia's *Walking with Shadows*' (*Matatu* 45[2014] 365–80), interrogates the intersectional dynamics of same-sex desire and gendered identifications as a negotiated hierarchy of value. The volume concludes with Shalini Nadaswaran's 'Motif/ ves of Justice in Writings by Third-Generation Nigerian Women' (*Matatu* 45[2014] 381–96), which reads a range of women's writing including Nwaubani's *I Do Not Come to You By Chance*, Abidemi Sanusi's *Eyo*, Akachi Ezeigbo's *Trafficked*, and Sefi Atta's *Swallow* as excavations of Nigeria's socio-political dynamics and the destructive influence of transnational commerce on the ability of Nigerians to attain wellbeing and self-actualization.

Women's writing from West Africa has long held a significant place in criticism, from the foundational work of Flora Nwapa, Buchi Emecheta, and Ama Ata Aidoo to the emergence of twenty-first-century literary stars such as Adichie and Unigwe. In 'Gender-Based Genre Conventions and the Critical Reception of Buchi Emecheta's *Destination Biafra*' (*Literator* 35:i[2014] n.p.), Polo B. Moji studies genre conventions in Nigerian war writing. Arguing that the reception and production of war writing present a stark binary between the feminine home front and masculine war front, Moji questions this orthodoxy. The essay unpacks *Destination Biafra*'s destabilization of gender identities in favour of a radically reoriented vision of gender as fluid and multiple in its instantiation. Emecheta is also the subject of Angela M. Fubara's 'Figures of Pedagogy in Ama Ata Aidoo's *Changes* and Buchi Emecheta's *Double Yoke*' (*TvL* 51:i[2014] 18–28), which takes a comparative perspective on the two novels as studies in feminist teaching. Fubara explores the ways in which each narrative engages with 'strategies that evoke images that go beyond women's disparagement and marginalisation to female empowerment and self-assertion' (p. 19) through the twinned foci of economic independence and education. A final essay on Emecheta, Anegbe Endurance, Abdulhameed A. Majeed, and Gariagan Gift's 'Oppression of the Girl-Child in Buchi Emecheta's *The Bride Price*' (*AdLLS* 5:iv[2014] 163–7), examines the ways in which patriarchal oppression produces a replication of violence across generations in the alienated mother–daughter relationship. While Emecheta and Aidoo remain among the best known of female West African writers, first-published West African woman Flora Nwapa also attracted critical attention in 2014. Part of a special issue of *Research in African Literatures* on 'Africa in the Black Atlantic', Taiwo Adetunji Osinubi's 'Provincializing Slavery: Atlantic Economies in Flora Nwapa's *Efuru*' (*RAL* 45:iii[2014] 1–26) reassesses Nwapa's canonical novel not as a text about women's solidarity, but as part of a 'genealogy of West African fiction on the relations between Atlantic and African slaving networks' (p. 2). Osinubi deftly demonstrates the extent to which the novel engages with a complex and interweaving historical-spatial matrix, mediated by its eponymous character's movements and interactions throughout the text. Readers of *Efuru* often overlook the importance of the Atlantic slave trade to the novel, particularly its connections with the more dominant system of debt bondage. Osinubi's essay provides an important basis for the reappraisal of the novel's politics as well as a keen argument for a critical return to canonical texts from the region. Naomi Nkealah's 'Women's Contribution to the Development of Anglophone Cameroonian Drama: The Plays of Anne Tanyi-Tang' (*RAL* 45:ii[2014] 122–34) similarly makes a convincing call for a return to the writing of earlier generations in its sweeping survey of the work of Tanyi-Tang and her centrality in the development of women's voices and visions in Cameroonian drama.

The new generation of women writers from West Africa was also subject to much critical attention in 2014. Two essays focused on Nigerian British author Helen Oyeyemi. Christopher Ouma's wonderfully rich 'Reading the Diasporic Abiku in Helen Oyeyemi's *The Icarus Girl*' (*RAL* 45:iii[2014] 188–205) proposes a reading of the abiku—the child who dies and is reborn repeatedly—within the context of migration, as a figure through which to 'confront . . . structures of racialized interpretation' (p. 188). Joining readings of the abiku from within its Yoruba tradition with an interpretation based upon psychoanalysis through dissociative identity disorder, Ouma argues that the trope allows the novel to reframe orthodox notions of the African diaspora in a context which moves beyond the overdetermining spectre of the Middle Passage to an African diasporic space of evolution in 'the creative struggle for reconciliation and conjuncture' (p. 196). The second major essay, Aspasia Stephenou's 'Helen Oyeyemi's *White is for Witching* and the Discourse of Consumption' (*Callaloo* 37:v[2014] 1245–59), similarly examines tensions created by the deployment of discrepant traditions in Oyeyemi's work. Stephenou turns her attention to the use of the Caribbean soucoyant myth as a complicating supplement to the vampire narrative in the novel, centring her readings around the discursive potency of consumption as a narrative motif. Linking together the notions of race, history, melancholia, and assimilatory desire, the essay positions the novel as a study in the tension between the past and the present in the constitution of the self via the other.

Chika Unigwe was another main focus of criticism in 2014, particularly centred on her 2009 novel of sex trafficking in Antwerp, *On Black Sisters' Street*. These studies ranged from the more strictly narrative and stylistic, in the vein of Tunca's chapter, described above, to the more sociological. Chielozona Eze's 'Feminism with a Big "F": Ethics and the Rebirth of African Feminism in Chika Unigwe's *On Black Sisters' Street*' (*RAL* 45:iv[2014] 89–103) is a standout in the field, situating the novel as a feminist intervention in the discourse of human rights and the dignities of the bodies of women. Eze highlights the extent to which the novel makes apparent the reduction of women's bodies to their mere use-value for men, as well as how the women unapologetically embrace feminism and women's solidarity in their flight from 'pain and annihilation' (p. 90). Sarah de Mul's 'Becoming Black in Belgium: The Social Construction of Blackness in Chika Unigwe's Authorial Self-Representation and *On Black Sisters' Street*' (*JCL* 49:i[2014] 11–27) sets the novel in dialogue with Unigwe's autobiographical musings on the meaning of ethnic minority writing in Flanders. From the distinctly de Beauvoirian claim that one is not born as African or as black but rather becomes it, de Mul excavates what she terms, following Graham Huggan and Sarah Brouillette, the strategic exoticism at the heart of both Unigwe's non-fictional writing and her novelistic output. Another essay published on Unigwe in 2014 is Rose A. Sackeyfio's 'Black Women's Bodies in a Global Economy: Sex, Lies and Slavery in *Trafficked* and *On Black Sisters' Street*' (in Negash, Frohne, and Zadi, eds., *At the Crossroads: Readings of the Postcolonial and the Global in African Literature and Visual Art*, pp. 199–210), which sets Unigwe's novel in dialogue with Akachi Ezeigbo's *Trafficked*.

No author received as much critical attention in 2014 as Chimamanda Ngozi Adichie. In addition to works already mentioned, Jennifer Rideout, in 'Towards a New Nigerian Womanhood: Woman as Nation in *Half of a Yellow Sun*' (*CE&S* 36:ii[2014] 71–81), demonstrates the ways in which *Half of a Yellow Sun* uses its female characters as archetypes of the nation—defined through the two poles of Mama, who represents traditional practices of community-building bound to the ethno-nation, and Kainene, as a textual manifestation of the 'new', fully modernized Nigerian nation. The essay concludes that it is Olanna, an allegorical female symbol who combines the two discourses, who points to the way forward for the embattled nation-state. Despite an extant critical focus on its individualistic and libidinal dynamics, the novel is also read as a political allegory by Meredith Coffey in '"She is Waiting": Political Allegory and the Spectre of Secession in Chimamanda Ngozi Adichie's *Half of a Yellow Sun*' (*RAL* 45:ii[2014] 63–85). For Coffey, the novel's allegorical potential is demonstrated in its setting of its characters' intimate relationships against the circumstances of history. Reading the novel's end as a refusal of closure, rather than a testament to Biafra's failures, the essay sees the text as a counter-historical discourse that challenges the inevitability of postcolonial disillusionment. Connor Ryan's essay, 'Defining Diaspora in the Words of Women Writers: A Feminist Reading of Chimamanda Ngozi Adichie's *The Thing Around Your Neck* and Dionne Brand's *At the Full and Change of the Moon*' (*Callaloo* 37:v[2014] 1230–44) moves its attention to Adichie's short stories, setting these in dialogue with the work of Canadian writer Brand. Ryan argues that, as studies in migration, the stories collected in *The Thing Around Your Neck* still turn around a fulcrum of gender. Language becomes the site through which the subversion of gendered and racial hierarchies enacted in the diaspora manifests itself, providing a radical reconsideration of 'what it means to be black and female in the diaspora' (p. 1230). Adichie is also mentioned in two essays in a recent special issue of *Transition* on the theme of 'What Is Africa To Me, Now?' Louis Chude-Sokei's 'The Newly Black Americans: African Immigrants and Black America' (*Transition* 113[2014] 52–71), which reads Adichie's short stories and most recent novel, *Americanah*, along with texts by Teju Cole and Chris Abani, as exemplars of the 'new' black American experience; and Madhu Krishnan's 'Negotiating Africa Now' (*Transition* 114[2014] 11–24), which considers Adichie's writerly and media work along with that of writers including Chris Abani in the context of twenty-first-century, trans-national African literary production. A number of other essays which draw on Adichie's work appeared in 2014: Nneka Nora Osakwe's chapter, 'Internationalizing Pedagogy Using African Literature: Teaching Composition Lessons with Chimamanda Adichie's "My Mother, the Crazy

African"' (in Negash et al., eds., pp. 241–56); Leena Hannele Eilittä's '"The World Outside Seemed Mummified into a Sheet of Dead Whiteness": Epiphanic Experience in the Short Stories of Chimamanda Ngozi Adichie' (*ShFTP* 4:i[2014] 79–92); and Londhe Sachin Vaman's '"Families in Crises" in Chimamanda Ngozi Adichie's *Purple Hibiscus*' (*NAcad* 3:ii[2014] 1–4).

Chris Abani has been mentioned several times already, particularly with reference to his critically acclaimed second novel, *GraceLand*. A number of other essays examine the novel as a study in place. Lauren Mason's 'Leaving Lagos: Intertextuality and Images in Chris Abani's *GraceLand*' (*RAL* 45:iii[2014] 206–26) asserts that 'Abani's novel reminds us that the inarticulable elements that constitute diaspora—beyond materiality and shared living conditions—are what written narratives *want* desperately to articulate' (p. 223), and demonstrates how the transnational, cosmopolitan range of extra-literary reference in the novel—from the bright lights of Las Vegas to traditional folklore to Soviet-era cinema—forges, through bricolage, a black identity which exceeds static or orthodox notions of cultural belonging. Cosmopolitan black identity is also explored in John D. Schwetman's 'Leaving Lagos: Diasporic and Cosmopolitan Migrations in Chris Abani's *GraceLand*' (*PCP* 49:ii[2014] 184–202), which reads the failure of Abani's protagonist, Elvis, to find a sense of belonging in Lagos as the instantiation of an earlier moment of diasporic estrangement in his movement from rural Igboland to the Nigerian metropolis. For Schwetman, this narrative move forcibly refuses the essentialization of origins that is so often the foundation of diasporic perspectives in favour of a cosmopolitan narrative of integration and plurality. *GraceLand* was not the only Abani work to receive attention in 2014. In Madhu Krishnan's 'The Storyteller Function in Contemporary Nigerian Narrative' (*JCL* 49:i[2014] 29–45), Abani's 2009 novella *Song for Night* is read against Helon Habila's *Measuring Time*. Krishnan argues that both novels rely upon the intersubjective and collective modes of address more often associated with the spoken word, particularly traditional folklore. Though neither text can be said to be hybridized, in the sense of directly transcribing proverbs or other signifiers of orality, both use a range of techniques to move beyond the strictly linguistic definition of the word in order to transform readers into active co-producers of the text. Alexandra Schultheis Moore and Elizabeth Swanson Goldberg's '"Let Us Begin with a Small Gesture": An Ethos of Human Rights and the Possibilities of Form in Chris Abani's *Song for Night* and *Becoming Abigail*' (*ArielE* 45:iv[2014] 59–87) also reads both works as mediating between an embrace of human rights and a critique of its normative discourses. Both works deliberately craft aesthetic forms which allow a shared ethos to develop between reader and text, exploiting the lacuna which appears at the limits of human rights discourse and law. At the same time, both texts challenge the notion of a universal, shared humanity, instead positing a concept of human rights as a self-reflexive and continuous critique.

Gender Issues in African Literature, edited by Chin Ce and Charles Smith, covers African literatures from across the continent, and includes important essays on Achebe's *No Longer at Ease* and *Anthills of the Savannah*, Akachi Ezeigbo's *Children of the Eagle*, and Buchi Emecheta's *Destination Biafra* in chapters by O. Ojeahere ('Gender and African Modernity', pp. 43–64), J.T.

Tsaaior ('Male Authority, Female Alterity', pp. 90–109), and S.A. Agbor ('Female Writers on War', pp. 65–89), respectively. *Destination Biafra* is the subject, too, of a second chapter by E.N. Ngwang ('Feminist Re-Writing', pp. 110–36). The collection as a whole attempts to examine the ways in which Western discourses around gender and sexuality are countered and challenged in African fiction. In *No Longer at Ease* and *Anthills of the Savannah*, for instance, there is a call for women's solidarity as a means of combating patriarchal norms amplified under colonial modernity; Ezeigbo's novel is read as a study in negotiation, set against the complex terrain of (en)gendered power amongst the Igbo. The two essays on *Destination Biafra*, finally, set it alongside Nadine Gordimer's *None To Accompany Me* and Yvonne Vera's *The Stone Virgins* as an exposé of the particular violence wrought against women in times of war, on the one hand, and as a symbolization of the virtues of a Negritude-inspired female resilience, on the other.

Ce and Smith edited two other volumes, *Counter Discourse in African Literature* and *The Dark Edge of African Literature*. The former volume features chapters on Femi Osofian's *Tegonni: An African Antigone* (A. Van Weyemberg, 'An African Antigone', pp. 43–59), Osonye Tess Onwueme's *The Mission Face* and Ama Ata Aidoo's *The Dilemma of a Ghost* (K. Secovnie, 'Cultural Translation', pp. 61–80), and Chin Ce's *Children of Koloko* (O. Okuyade, 'The Rhetoric of Despair', pp. 95–110). With its heavy focus on drama, the volume will be a particularly valuable resource for theatre scholars at all levels. *The Dark Edge of African Literature* places its emphasis on conflict and violence, featuring chapters on a range of continental African writers, of which essays on Chin Ce and Femi Osofian will be of particular interest. Similarly non-canonical essays can be found in Jessica Munns' chapter, 'Two Oroonokos: Behn's and Bandele's' (in Richards and O'Donnell, eds., *Teaching Behn's Oroonoko* [2013], pp. 162–6; this was missed last year), which draws comparisons between the canonical text and Biyi Bandele-Thomas's revision, and Suzanne Marie Ondrus's chapter 'Childhood Creative Spaces as Survival Spaces in Sade Adeniran's *Imagine This*' (in Yenika-Agbaw and Mhando, eds., *African Youth in Contemporary Literature and Popular Culture: Identity Quest*, pp. 35–52).

Along with its moving tribute to Kofi Awoonor, discussed above, *ALT* 32 includes another article on the abiku: Ikenna Kamalu's 'Abiku in Ben Okri's Imagination of Nationhood: A Metaphorical Interpretation of Colonial-Postcolonial Politics' (*ALT* 32[2014] 20–32) argues that Okri's use of this figure as a cultural metaphor serves the aims of social justice and political reform by foregrounding the once denigrated cultural values of the colonized. Okri's aesthetics of magical realism were also subject of a number of book chapters in 2014: Jennifer Wenzel's 'Petro-Magic-Realism Revisited: Unimagining and Reimagining the Niger Delta' (in Barrett and Worden, eds., *Oil Culture*, pp. 449–64); Durojaiye Owoeye's 'Going Beyond Borders: Rushdie, Okri and the Deconstruction of Realism' (in Arua et al., eds., pp. 22–43); and Stephan Larsen's 'Whose Magic? Whose Realism? Reflections on Magical Realism in Ben Okri's *The Famished Road*' (in Cullhed, Rydholm, and Myrdal, eds., *True Lies Worldwide: Fictionality in Global Contexts*, pp. 275 –87).

ALT 32 also includes an insightful reading by Edward Sackey of a perhaps less well-known text in 'Ayi Kwei Armah's *The Resolutionaries*: Exoteric Fiction, the Common People & Social Change in Post-Colonial Africa—A Critical Review' (*ALT* 32[2014] 47–57), an analysis which unpacks the novel as a socially oriented mode of experimental engagement by a politically engaged author. Deborah L. Klein's '"Manhood" in Isidore Okpewho's *The Last Duty*: Authority or Accountability?' (*ALT* 32[2014] 104–19) considers the novel through the lens of social justice by tracing the tension inherent in conceptions of manhood in times of war, engaging in a careful and methodical character analysis to support her readings.

Genre fiction became a focus of scholarly enquiry in 2014. Terri Ochiagha, in 'The Dangerous Potency of the Crossroads: Colonial Mimicry in Chukwuemeka Ike's *The Bottled Leopard* and Chike Momah's *The Shining Ones: The Umuahia School Days of Obinna Okoye*' (*L&U* 38:i[2014] 86–105), takes a long historical view of children's literature in her examination of two Nigerian boarding-school stories. Drawing on the theoretical work of Homi K. Bhabha, Ochiagha argues that these stories provide an intricate negotiation of identity through colonial mimicry. Both replicating and subverting the generic conventions of the boarding-school novel, these two stories dramatize the simultaneous pull of the colonial school and indigenous collectivities. Moving further back in time is Rebecca Jones's 'Journeys to the Hinterland: Early Twentieth-Century Nigerian Domestic Travel Writing and Domestic Heterogeneity' (*PocoT* 9:iv[2014] 19 pp), which examines Yoruba- and English-language travel writing by I.B. Thomas and E.A. Akintan as a means of rethinking cosmopolitanism through its territorially specific instantiations during the era of amalgamation and nation-formation. Using translocal and regional networks, these travelogues reconfigure the centre/periphery dynamics which have dominated studies of colonialism, exposing the heterogeneity of discrepant cosmopolitan forms. Science fiction is the subject of Matthew Omelsky's '"After the End Time": Postcrisis African Science Fiction' (*CJPLI* 1:i[2014] 33–49), which looks at Efe Okugo's novella *Proposition 23* as a post-Fanonian articulation of revolutionary subjectivity. Okugo's work may be best read as a reconfiguration of biopolitics through its imagination of African futures beyond capital.

(b) Eastern Africa

It was a particularly remarkable year for Eastern African letters as it saw the inaugural issue of the first regional journal dedicated to Eastern African writing—*Eastern African Literary and Cultural Studies*. The journal is additionally unique for being internationally published (through Taylor & Francis), but edited from the University of Nairobi by Kenyan literary scholars Tom Odhiambo and Godwin Siundu. In their introduction to the first issue, they not only emphasize interdisciplinary conversations, with a bias towards literary and cultural studies, but also envision an impact reminiscent of Rajat Neorgy's *Transition* magazine of the 1970s, which offered cutting-edge literary-critical engagement in the region with an alert ear for debates beyond the region's boundaries. They remark that 'there is a need for more space to publish and disseminate research output and knowledge in the literary and cultural studies from eastern Africa' given the growth of the number of universities in the region and the increase in young graduates (*EALCS* 1:i[2014] 1–2).

The first volume offers an exciting range of material. Relevant items are 'Edgy Edgars: The Restless Youth in Suzanna Nelson's *Nightmare along the River Nile: A Story of Twentieth Century Slavery*' by Paul M. Mukundi (*EALCS* 1:i[2014] 17–25), a welcome study of Nelson's novel which has had little critical reception to date. Mukundi reads Nelson's representation of the impact the Lord's Resistance Army on Eastern Africa, specifically on youth, and elucidates some of the key themes: how youth become pawns in a war zone, how abductions happen and but also how resilient strategies of survival are forged in the face of trauma. Mukundi's analysis is followed by Meg Samuelson's insightful paper 'Yvette Christiansë's Oceanic Genealogies and the Colonial Archive: *Castaways* and *Generations* from Eastern Africa to the South Atlantic' (*EALCS* 1:i[2014] 27–38). It traces Christiansë's tropes of dispersal and continuity from Eastern Africa, the Cape, and St Helena. Samuelson carefully shows how Christiansë focuses on subaltern characters who are marginal, displaced, and enslaved to create a narrative tension between ideas of belonging and dispersion, between the desire for home and the impossibility of home. The narratives capture this tension through a cyclical, fragmented, episodic poetics that discloses as well as withholds information and in this way eschews narrative certainty. While Christiansë's novel *Unconfessed* has received sustained critical attention, Samuelson extends her analysis to the author's two poetry collections, *Castaway* [1999] and *Imprehendora* [2009] which are much less well known and which illuminate Christiansë's 'argument with history' (p. 30). Samuelson shows how, rather than offering a counter-history by making her marginal characters speak, Christiansë's key narrative devices create ellipses, track absence, and as a result present the reader with a past that haunts the present. On a different variant of movement and dispersal, Tina Steiner's '"Dwelling in Travel": Of Ships, Trains and Planes in M.G. Vassanji's Fiction' (*EALCS* 1:i[2014] 39–50) explores the networks of travel and how they mediate memory and the formation of migrant subjectivities. Steiner argues that while Vassanji's writing has primarily been read with an emphasis on East African Indians' politics of belonging in the region and the dynamics of migration to the north, an important aspect of this writing relates to travel as a mode of claiming belonging. The ship connects Africa to India, the railway is the reason for indentured Indian presence in the region, and air-travel opens up possibilities of travel and connectivity to the UK and Canada.

Another paper on Vassanji appeared in *JCL*, ' "Since When Has Paper Any Value?": Reading, Materiality, and Meaning in M.G. Vassanji's Fiction' by Ariel Bookman (*JCL* 49:ii[2014] 198–201), focuses on *The Gunny Sack* and *The Book of Secrets* to show that Vassanji's characters, 'both literate and illiterate, engage paper's physical properties to ground their everyday practices of memory, valuation and interpretation' (p. 189). These three categories, memory, value, and interpretation represent the three subsections of this carefully argued piece, to show how paper objects, such as bills, scraps, mildewed diaries, banknotes, letters, posters, and magazines, in their 'thingness' interrupt, complement, and transcend attempts at reading their meaning.

Back with the new journal, M.G. Vassanji's reflective paper 'The New (Asian) African: Politics and Creativity in the 1960s' (*EALCS* 1:i[2014] 51–8) sheds light on an important historical moment in Kenya, Uganda, and Tanzania in the mid-1960s in which the Asian elite creatively asserted an African identity for themselves. Vassanji recalls the post-independence enthusiasm of Asians to embrace Africanity: be it in politics, as demonstrated by the case of K.L. Jhaveri, Sophia Mustafa and Amir Jamal, A.M. Javanjee, Makhan Singh, and Pio Gama Pinto, or in the creative arts, by Rajat Neogy, editor of *Transition*, Bahadur Tejani, Peter Nazareth, Amin Kassam, Yusuf Kassam, Kuldip Sondhi, and Ganesh Bagchi. Vassanji draws a rich canvas of a moment in time when Asian participation flourished and new categories of Asian African identities were tested. The article ends with sketching the end of this historical window and the departure of most East African Asians from the region. Kimani Kaigai offers a nuanced reading of Abdulrazak Gurnah's rather overlooked first novel in 'Sexuality, Power and Transgression: Homophobia in Abdulrazak Gurnah's *Memory of Departure*' (*EALCS* 1:i[2014] 59–70). The paper convincingly suggests that Gurnah's narrative representation of embodied agency offers an insightful optic to read social, political, and economic hierarchies. Kaigai reads the body as 'prime symbol of self, but also of society' (p. 59) in that it is socially constituted and contained. In Gurnah's representation of transgressive bodily behaviour, these categories are questioned yet ultimately the narrative asserts the power of societal control over individual bodies and their classification.

A number of scholars grappled with aspects of life-writing from the region. Jennifer Muchiri's essay, 'The Intersection of the Self and History in Kenyan Autobiographies'' (*EALCS* 1:i[2014] 83–93), as the title suggests, reads a selection of Kenyan autobiographies spanning both colonial and post-independence eras as important sources on the history of the nation over a fifty-year period. Muchiri argues that these life stories reveal 'the unofficial story of a nation in the making' (p. 90). In the same issue of the journal, Ken Walibora Waliaula focuses on Mau Mau veteran and prominent feminist politician Wambui Otieno's 1998 memoir. In 'The Female Condition as Double Incarceration in Wambui Otieno's *Mau Mau's Daughter*' (*EALCS* 1:i[2014] 71–82) Waliaula underlines the importance of this memoir as one of the few—if not the only one at the time of writing—describing a woman's experience of detention in colonial Kenya. In addition to exploring the literal and discursive incarceration as the double burden women prisoners encounter, Waliaula offers a convincing reading of Otieno's autobiography as a classic example of the relational sensibility that informs women's prison writing, as opposed to the emphasis on individual heroism in male prison writing. Otieno emphasizes a familial history of political engagement and resistance to colonial oppression, which she traces all the way back to her great-grandfather, Waiyaki wa Hinga. Waliaula persuasively unpacks the shared patriarchal logics of both the Mau Mau movement and the colonial prison administration in its dealings with women prisoners' bodies; but stresses Wambui Otieno's remarkable strength in manoeuvring around these.

Waliaula's article is usefully complemented by Katherine Bruce-Lockhart's less literary paper ' "Unsound" Minds and Broken Bodies: The Detention of "Hardcore" Mau Mau Women at Kamiti and Gitamayu Detention Camps in Kenya, 1954–1960' (*JEAfS* 8:iv[2014] 590–608). With a particular focus on gender, Bruce-Lockhart investigates how discourses of insanity seek to contain and limit the political agency of female detainees during the final years of the emergency period. This paper is significant as it considers new documentary evidence released from the Hanslope Park Archive since 2011 that sheds light on colonial carceral systems and on women not just affected by the guerrilla-style insurgency but as active participants: 'Initially, the British had not expected women to pose a threat in the rebellion. In part, this myopia stemmed from the government's belief that African women were passive, peaceful, and uninterested in politics, reflecting the androcentric views about violence widely held in colonial Africa' (p. 593). These views also affected the way in which the largely ineffective rehabilitation programmes were implemented in the camps: the women who were resisting their rehabilitation were deemed deviant, as either mad or engaging in witchcraft (p. 596).

It has become something of a tradition to have Ngũgĩ wa Thiong'o feature in speculation about the Nobel Prize in Literature, and 2014 was no exception. While he was not awarded it, his work remains a regular feature in the region's literary studies bibliographies. On this list, two articles offer interesting perspectives on Ngũgĩ's writing: Jairus Omuteche's 'Historification of Kenya's Plural Identities', which appeared in the aforementioned journal (*EALCS* 1:i[2014] 107–16), and Aida Mbowa's 'Between Nationalism and Pan-Africanism: Ngũgĩ wa Thiong'o's Theatre and the Arts and Politics of Modernizing African Culture' (in Bloom, Miescher, and Manuh, eds., *Modernisation as Spectacle in Africa*, pp. 328–48). Omuteche revisits Ngũgĩ's *Weep Not Child* and *Petals of Blood*, arguing that his emphasis on heroism and nationalism, anchored in the Gikuyu ethno-cultural landscape, reiterates the pattern of tribal fragmentation initiated by colonial policy in Kenya and elides the role of plurality in the making of modern Kenya. Aida Mbowa offers a refreshing reading of Ngũgĩ's theatre's contribution to the engendering of the modern subject and a new black aesthetics in Eastern Africa. Her chapter is a welcome rereading of *The Black Hermit* and *The Trial of Dedan Kimathi*, both of which have not received as much critical attention as Ngũgĩ's fiction and memoirs. It explores how his theatre—both onstage and offstage—reflects on modernization 'at the intersection of discourses on liberation, development, socialism, and black aesthetics' (p. 329). Importantly, through her reading of Ngũgĩ the playwright and theatre practitioner, Mbowa underscores cross-cultural conversations between East Africa and the black diaspora on questions of cultural liberation and black/African aesthetics.

'Julius Nyerere, Ujamaa, and Political Morality in Contemporary Tanzania', by Marie-Aude Fouéré (*AfrSR* 57:i[2014] 1–24) is of tangential interest for detailing the iconography and discourse of government and media enshrining Nyerere's legacy to shape ideas of moral political action. In contrast, political parties on the fringe and Zanzibari accounts of the January 1964 revolution contest this iconography in order to draw attention to the fragility of national unity. The article complements 'The Poetry of an Orphaned Nation: Newspaper Poetry and the Death of Nyerere' by Mary Ann Mhina (*JEAfS* 8:iii[2014] 497–514). She analyses her own English translations of Swahili poetry, which appeared during the mourning period in 1999 in *Uhuru*, the paper established by the ruling party. All of the poems offer metaphors and similes that had been used before to describe 'the Father of the nation' and are resuscitated at this time of mourning. While the glorification may be a way to deal with the loss, Mhina also asserts that it foreclosed the possibility of voicing some of the controversies of his legacy (p. 503). However, some of the poets use this platform to make suggestions for the future (p. 505). Kelly Askew's 'Tanzanian Newspaper Poetry: A Commentary in Verse' (*JEAfS* 8:iii[2014] 515–37) argues that although poetry is a genre with deep roots on the East African coastline, the advent of newspapers in Tanzania launched a new avenue for the genre, which enjoyed even greater prominence under the newly independent socialist Tanzania's cultural policy. Askew reads this poetry across colonial and post-independence Tanzania as a form of citizens' assessments of governance broadly, and Nyerere's political career specifically.

Grace A. Musila turns her attention to Kenyan writer and journalist Parselelo Kantai's short fiction and essays, in her chapter 'Archives of the Present in Parselelo Kantai's Writing' (in Newell and Okome, eds., *Popular Culture in Africa: The Episteme of the Everyday*, pp. 244–265). Drawing on Karin Barber's work on popular culture in Africa, the chapter reflects on the network of relations that mediate the ideas, production, and circulation of Kantai's writing. It embodies a complex interface between history, fiction, and autobiography and is an example of the Kwani generation of writers whose work defies simplistic categorization by straddling the canonical-popular divide.

Youth culture and its creative articulations are the focus of Nanna Schneidermann's article '"Mic Power": "Public" Connections through the Hip Hop Nation in Kampala' (*Ethnography* 15:i[2014] 88–105) on the Ugandan rap/hip hop movement Batuuze (meaning 'the people' in Luganda). In contrast to more commercially oriented groups, Batuuze developed a 'vision of a worldwide *conscious movement* of hip hop' (p. 89) giving them a sense of belonging in a global movement that offers, if limited, 'social mobility and experiences of affluence' (p. 102). Rather than producing an alternative public sphere, Batuuze generates connections and opportunities in the lives of the young men affiliated to this movement.

'*Crafting* Forgiveness Accounts after War: Editing for Effect in Northern Uganda' (*AnT* 30.ii[2014] 10–14) is an unusual and fascinating meditation on autobiographical narration in postwar northern Uganda and the dynamics of social repair in an atmosphere deeply poisoned by the betrayals and distrusts of war. The three authors, Lotte Meinert, Juliana A. Obika, and Susan Reynolds Whyte, reflect on their work with a community in war-torn northern Uganda, where, in collaboration with Danish installation artist Tove Nylom, they collected personal voice accounts of trauma and forgiveness and audio-edited them; then presented them to the community as part on an initiative named *Timo Kica*: Voices from Within. Drawing on Hannah Arendt's work on forgiveness, the authors and the artist trace the impact of the editing choices they made—primarily to shorten the accounts and place an accent on immediacy—and the ways in which different stakeholders in the community, including members of the community, academics, and politicians, responded to, and appropriated, the narratives.

African Studies Review features tributes to Ali Mazrui, who passed away a few months after the publication of the journal, in October 2014. Mazrui was a true embodiment of multidisciplinarity, and articles are attentive to this, but for literary scholars, Seifudein Adem's 'Ali A Mazrui, the Postcolonial Theorist' (*AfrSR* 51:i[2014] 135–52) should be of interest. Here, Adem ponders Mazrui's marginality in postcolonial studies, despite his perceptive scholarly contributions to the field; most memorably, his concept of Africans' triple heritage—indigenous cultures, Islam/Christianity, and secular Western culture—which he explored both in his writings and a BBC TV series. Adem suggests that among the reasons behind his marginality is his rejection of a jargon-heavy, theoretically abstract style which was the norm at a certain point, coupled with his prolific writing and mercurial shifts of interest, which make it difficult to quickly distil his core ideas and his propensity for semi-autobiographical writing.

This year saw two landmark studies that have shaped Eastern African scholarship republished: Caroline Elkins's Pulitzer prize-winning *Britain's Gulag: The Brutal End of Empire in Kenya* [2005] and Jan Blommaert's *State Ideology and Language in Tanzania* [1999]. Elkins's detailed study establishes the extent to which Britain's colonial enterprise in Kenya, particularly during the state of emergency in the 1950s, was based on violence, coercion, and torture. She painstakingly compiles historical documents that evidence the human rights violations suffered by the more than one million Kikuyu detainees. It is perhaps no exaggeration to say that this text demolishes any residual complacency regarding the 'civilizing mission' of British colonialism in Kenya and that it offers an important reassessment of the Mau Mau movement. Jan Blommaert's revised and expanded second edition of his book on the historiography of Swahili in postcolonial Tanzania is not only of interest to linguists, but elucidates key points 'in the postcolonial story of languages' (p. ix). Blommaert has included new empirical material and expanded his theoretical framing. At the heart of this path-breaking study lies a paradox: while the Tanzanian example is seen as an exceptional case of successful language planning, with Swahili being spread to all corners of the country, this success has been accompanied by a persistent discourse of its failure. To account for this apparent contradiction, Blommaert shows how Swahili became inextricably intertwined with the political socialist project of *Ujamaa*. When the influence of Tanzanian socialist politics declined, Swahili was regarded similarly as a failed project, contrary to the linguistic evidence so abundantly available. Government was instrumental in the spread of Swahili, but it soon lost control over the language. The book provides significant sociolinguistic evidence to show that Swahili is a diversifying and dynamic language. Of particular interest to literary studies is chapter 5, which focuses specifically on *Ujamaa* literature and the way in which cultural philosophy entered the literary text (pp. 91–105).

Stephen Morton's insightful study, *States of Emergency. Colonialism, Literature and Law* [2013], examines how violent anti-colonial struggles and the legal and military techniques employed by colonial governments to contain them have been imagined in literature. Central to this containment is the suspension of the law during periods of emergency which, rather than the exception, were often the norm in how colonial governments controlled their territories. Morton traces convincingly how such techniques have informed contemporary 'wars on terror'. The book consists of six main chapters framed by an introduction and a conclusion. The case studies in Part I deal with colonial Ireland and colonial India in the late nineteenth century; Part II considers twentieth-century states of emergency in apartheid South Africa, colonial Kenya, and Algeria. Part III, on Israel-Palestine, offers an assessment of the continuities between these colonial states of emergency and how they are reconfigured in the colonial present in Iraq, Afghanistan, and northern Pakistan. Morton compares the legal and bureaucratic rhetoric of colonial statutes and other documents with the narrative structure and imagery of the literature and culture of empire across a range of settings. These rhetorical discursive strategies, in turn, are questioned by the literatures of decolonization. The study argues that 'colonial states of emergency cannot be understood with reference to the law alone' but must engage with the way in which 'colonial stereotypes and narratives have played a significant role in framing anti-colonial insurgents' as the cause of states of emergency (p. 209). Morton's examples are Candler's *Siri Ram Revolutionist*, Ruark's *Something of Value*, and Lartéguy's *Les Centurions*. In contrast, writers like Wicomb, Ngũgĩ, Djebar, and Khoury have 'tried to do justice to the fragmented and often traumatic history of the oppressed' (p. 209). Morton ends the study by considering how stereotypical tropes are replicated in representations of Islam and Muslims in the Western media and some literary works after 9/11. He examines Begg's memoir of his imprisonment at Guantánamo Bay, *Enemy Combatant*, Hamid's novel *The Reluctant Fundamentalist*, and Shamsie's *Burnt Shadows* to conclude that 'if the spatial stories and legal narratives of emergency in Guantánamo Bay, Afghanistan and Iraq help to make sense of the relationship between violence, law and sovereignty in the colonial present, literary and cultural texts can help to shed light on the condition of possibility for justice in these contexts' (p. 224). The book is thus highly relevant and is written in an engaging and readable style.

Historicizing Colonial Nostalgia: European Women's Narratives of Algeria and Kenya 1900–present by Patricia M.E. Lorcin has a comparative focus as well. She analyses novels, memoirs, and letters of women settlers of both colonies in order to identify images and tropes that shape and reshape colonial nostalgia: the 'dislocation in moving from a familiar social environment to an alien one induced them, either consciously or unconsciously, to create an image of the colony that intertwined what they loved best about the social and national spaces they had left behind with what they loved most about the space they had come to inhabit' (p. 195). The needs of the present in which the women find themselves shape their representations and fantasies of the past. Lorcin presents her analysis chronologically and divides her study into three parts. Part I is entitled '1900–1930: Colonial Women and Their Imagined

Selves', and offers an overview of the settler society and the presence of women in Algeria and Kenya, before considering the lives and writing of two iconic women, Isabelle Eberhardt in Algeria and Karen Blixen in Kenya, whose romanticized views of Africa and their place in it reverberate into the postcolonial present. Part II, '1920–1940: Political Realities and Fictional Representations', focuses on the development of the interweaving of narratives of nostalgia and modernity in the works of Elissa Rhaïs, Magali Boisnard, Florence Riddell, and Nora K. Strange. Lorcin argues that 'political tensions marked the interwar period in both colonies' (p. 199) with the consequence that women's narratives reflected a tension between nostalgic fantasies, the local rise of nationalism, and the international loss of confidence in empire, particularly by the end of the Second World War. Part III, 'Imperial Decline and the Reformulation of Nostalgia', considers the period of decolonization and how nostalgia features in the perceptions of self of writers with family histories in Algeria or Kenya: she demonstrates that in the case of Algeria there has developed a veritable industry of *nostalgérie* that is even supported by the French government (p. 203), while nostalgic writing about Kenya is more individualistic, with memoirs like Kuki Gallman's *I Dreamed of Africa* and Mirella Riccardi's photographic record *Vanishing Africa*. Lorcin's study is very accessible and offers a thoughtful analysis of an important topic.

Straddling the boundaries between storytelling, history, and ethnography, Mustafa Kema Mirzeler's riveting book *Remembering Nayeche and the Gray Bull Engiro: African Storytellers of the Karamoja Plateau and the Plains of Turkana* uses the Jie and Turkana myth of origin as a springboard to exploring the place of storytelling in indexing social memory, navigating shifting realities, and articulating ethnic and individual identities. In this myth, Nayeche, a Jie woman, follows the footprints of a grey bull across the East African plateau and eventually sets up the cradle land of the pastoralist community in the Turkana plains. An important concern for the book is the role of a collectively remembered past encoded in storytelling in shaping identity and crafting unity among a community of people, which further mediates the sharing of land resources, as underwritten by shared ancestry.

(c) Southern Africa

Three important firsts and an important historical recovery make up the crop of book-length publications from Southern Africa this year. Mary Lederer has written the first survey of novels written in English by Botswana writers and by others writing about Botswana; the first book-length study of Antjie Krog's writing in English has appeared; and a selection of Olive Schreiner's letters written in the later years of her life has been published. Corinne Sandwith has restored to the record a hitherto forgotten but vital body of left-wing cultural and literary criticism from the very early years of apartheid.

In *Novels of Botswana in English, 1930–2006*, Mary Lederer asks what insiders' novels represent of the understanding that the people of the country have of themselves (i.e. the relationship between ethnicity, ethics, and national identity) and to what extent novels by outsiders that are set in Botswana may or may not confirm that relationship. The stark division between insiders and outsiders appears justified by her survey of the novels: she finds that many recent outsiders' novels simply ignore the people of the country and tend to treat the land as an exotic testing place for their foreign, needy, and/or adventurous protagonists. Achebe's criticisms of Conrad are not mentioned, but they clearly continue to be of concern to Lederer, who says that, as an American who has lived and taught literature in Botswana for many years, 'I have been here long enough to recognize that I hardly know anything' (p. 7). 'Outsider' is perhaps a description which best fits intention rather than origin, for, as Lederer shows, constructive accounts of early Botswana community identity are to be found in *Mhudi* by Sol Plaatje and *A Bewitched Crossroad* by Bessie Head—writers who were both born and raised in South Africa (although Plaatje was ethnically a Tswana). Their novels assess the way that Tswana society faced rapid socio-political change in the past, Plaatje during the time in South Africa of the 'Great Trek and Zulu expansion' (p. 27) in the 1830s but with clear reference to land alienation and erosion of Africans' rights in the early twentieth century, and Head during the time in nineteenth-century Botswana when 'land hunger was pushing British and Afrikaner settlers further north' (p. 30) and the Tswana people feared the loss of their land too. In both cases the Tswana prevailed because their social system was 'more consultative' (p. 28) and therefore had a greater capacity for 'peaceful change' (p. 31). These democratic elements in tradition have become, says Lederer, an important part of the morality which contemporary writers in Botswana present to their readers.

The value of traditional ways is actively, if not didactically, exemplified by writers such as Andrew Sesinyi and Galesiti Baruti, neither of whose work may be known abroad. Sesinyi's first novel, *Love on the Rocks* [1981], was published in the Macmillan Pacesetter series and remains very popular in Botswana. It tells of the trials and success of a poor young man from a rural background who loves and eventually marries (when her family recovers its traditional values) a rich young urban woman. Sesinyi has written two other novels: *Rassie* [1989] and *Carjack* [1999]. Baruti's only novel, *Mr Heartbreaker* [1993], seems to be a lurid account of sex and sin in the city, again written to advocate the 'importance of good old Botswana values' (p. 44). All of these novels reflect the impact on women of social change. A more positive approach to the issue comes from the country's women writers. Unity Dow, a fairly prolific writer whose work was initially published in Australia, shares a later chapter with Bessie Head, but Mositi Torontle, who had published one novel in the period of Lederer's survey, is placed in the chapter with Sesinyi and Baruti. *The Victims* [1993] tells of a young rural woman who understands the importance of an education and who, with a 'strong sense of self-protection and autonomy' (p. 48), will not allow love to turn her from her goals. This novel is one of several that lead Lederer to claim that new writing by women in Botswana is breaking away from the 'prescriptive tendency represented by Sesinyi and Baruti' to 'interrogate how tradition and society will adapt to new ways of understanding the world' (p. 50).

In her following chapters, Lederer first considers writers who spent a period of their lives in Botswana and who, she says, 'illustrate the classic "man versus

nature" plot and conflict, in which the test of the self is played out against
a harsh environment. The fact that other [indigenous] people live in that
same environment and "conquer" it regularly is irrelevant' (p. 52). Naomi
Mitchison's *When We Become Men* [1965] is the one exception in this group,
and this is probably because she enjoyed such deep ties with the BaKgatla
people. Others in the group, which all have foreign protagonists, are Carolyn
Slaughter's *Dreams of the Kalahari* [1981], Caitlin Davies's *Jamestown Blues*
[1996], Anthony Fleischer's *Okavango Gods* [1998], William Duggan's *The
Great Thirst* [1985] and *Lovers of the African Night* [1987], and Norman Rush's
Mating [1991], *Mortals* [2003], and *Whites* [1986]. Rush worked for four years
as director of the Peace Corps office in Botswana. The list could have included
Hilary Mantel, who spent time in Botswana and whose novel *A Change of
Climate* [1994] draws on the Law Reports of Botswana as well as her
observations there. Next come the simpler adventure novels set in Botswana—
what Lederer calls the 'Paper Safari', which can, she says, trace its beginnings
partly back to *Meridiana* [1872] by Jules Verne, in which three Englishmen and
three Russians attempt to cross the Kalahari Desert guided by a 'Bushman',
and partly to the hunting stories of the nineteenth century. Critics such as Dan
Wylie and Stephen Gray have seen this latter genre as 'directly in the service of
imperialism' (Lederer, p. 92). The mythology of the colonial enterprise 'in
which men from England suffer countless hardships . . . [so as] to bring order to
chaotic primitive life in other parts of the world' (p. 96) is the 'unashamed'
basis of Nicholas Monsarrat's two novels, *The Tribe That Lost Its Head* [1956]
and its sequel, *Richer Than All His Tribe* [1968]. They are set in the island of
Pharamaul, a thinly disguised representation of Botswana during the time of
Seretse Khama's marriage to the Englishwoman Ruth Williams. As a member
of the British diplomatic corps in South Africa, Monsarrat had to deal with
many of the problems that arose from resistance to that marriage and
consequently, Lederer suggests, he tended to think of Botswana as always on
the brink of self-destruction. A writer with a similar approach is K.R. Butler,
whose first novel, *A Desert of Salt* [1964], presents the vast desert around the
town of Ghanzi as an 'empty hell' (p. 98), and whose second, *The Evil Damp*
[1966], does much the same for the Okavango Delta. In *The Night of the
Predator* [1991] by Christopher Sherlock, Botswana is a land which the
protagonist dreams could become a vast game reserve, a peaceful alternative to
the horrors of political turmoil in the neighbouring South Africa of the 1980s.
Again it is a dream which ignores the people of the country. British journalist
and satirist Nicholas Luard wrote two novels set in Botswana, *Silverback*
[1996] and *Bloodspoor* [1977]—the latter under the pseudonym James McVean.
Wilbur Smith's *The Sunbird* [1972] concerns a search for the lost city of the
Kalahari. Two novels which depict external forces being brought in to stabilize
Botswana's democracy, conveniently imagined to be fragile, are Steve White's
Battle in Botswana [1982] and Jeff Rovin's *Mission of Honour* [2002].

The great exception to the 'outsider' novelist who ignores the people of
Botswana is of course Alexander McCall Smith, and in his case Lederer has to
grapple with almost the opposite problem: a writer whose books are so
humanly appealing that he is assumed to 'write on behalf of Africa', an
assumption which, she suggests, 'hinders more sensible reception of his books'

(p. 123). What the series, beginning with *The No. 1 Ladies' Detective Agency* [1998] and built around the considerable figure of Mma Precious Ramotswe, does enable Lederer to establish is the people's core moral sense which the protagonist articulates: 'if you knew how a person was feeling, if you could imagine yourself in her position, then surely it would be impossible to inflict further pain' (quoted p. 120). It is a capacity disappearing from modern life. Mma Ramotswe may be a Lady Detective, but she does not solve crimes so much as sort out problems, and novels featuring her do not tackle big issues such as AIDS but they do tackle matters such as the dishonesty that leads both to the spread of the disease and the silence that surrounds those who suffer. McCall Smith's writing about the landscape also leads Lederer to a brief but illuminating comparison with Isak Dinesen on Kenya. A new Botswanan novelist writing crime fiction is Lauri Kubuitsile, who has published two novels to date: *The Fatal Payout* [2005] and *Murder for Profit* [2008]. The latter appeared after Lederer's study went to press, but is listed with other recent novels in an appendix. Her fiction is racy and escapist—the first one was written for serialization in a local newspaper—but reflects many of the issues affecting contemporary Botswana: crime, rampant materialism, sexual abuse, promiscuity, and so on.

Although born in South Africa, Bessie Head lived most of her adult life in Serowe, did most of her writing there, and gradually made it the place through which she understood and represented herself and her immediate and larger worlds. Accordingly she and Unity Dow, the other Botswana writer who is widely known abroad, occupy the culminating chapter of Lederer's study. Both women, she says, wrote from the 'perspective of the underdog' (p. 135) and their cause is that of social justice, leading them to write 'critically [but] hopefully... imagining a Botswana based on what they believe is good about the community' (p. 136). Unity Dow is a human rights activist and a former justice of the High Court of Botswana; Bessie Head lived much of her life in obscurity and poverty. Lederer traces ways in which Head's first novel, *When Rain Clouds Gather* [1968], indicates her own gradual entry into Botswana, the land and its people—a place where she could strive for 'belonging, continuity, a place to be alive' (p. 141)—and, with reference to her other fiction, where she could draw on the past to imagine a society which understood the need for change. Unity Dow's first two novels take up headline issues: *Far and Beyon'* [2000] represents a woman's efforts to help her family acknowledge and cope with the deaths from AIDS of two of their brothers. *The Screaming of the Innocent* [2001] deals with ritual murder and uses a young woman protagonist who is not circumspect or tolerant of patriarchal tradition in her determination to solve a case that the police have allowed government officials to cover up. Dow's third novel, *Juggling Truths* [2004], is anecdotal in its structure and presents a young woman's attempts to balance the truths of modernity which she learns at school with those of custom to which her home gives her access. The fourth novel, *The Heavens May Fall* [2006], is episodic in telling of a young woman lawyer and the difficult cases she encounters; one is of a man, prominent in his community, who has passed as a MoNgwato all his life by hiding the fact that he has a San mother. The protagonist learns just in time that justice would probably not be served were she to reveal the truth. Lederer concludes that the idea of justice in Botswana that inspires both writers is one in which 'morality means not just knowing what is fair and just for all, but applying that knowledge in all aspects of one's life' (p. 160).

Long recognized as a major writer in Afrikaans, Antjie Krog is now receiving sustained attention in English-language literary criticism in South Africa, and *Antjie Krog: An Ethics of Body and Otherness* indicates the level of engagement with her work. It began as a guest-edited issue of *Current Writing* in 2007 and now appears in expanded and more focused form, again edited by Judith Coullie and Andries Visagie. Six of the original essays have been included, with the other seven being specially commissioned. The result covers Krog's writing from 1998 onwards with only *Begging To Be Black* [2009] not drawing an essay of its own. The volume *Skinned: A Selection of Translated Poetry* [2013] is also not studied because it appeared just as this volume was going to press. As the subtitle, *An Ethics of Body and Otherness*, suggests, the primary collective concern is a moral one which focuses particularly on Krog's representation of her own physical body and her powerful personal presence in exploring major events and issues in South Africa's distant and more recent past. 'How do these events and conditions matter *to me*?' seems the most ethical, because the most engaged, approach for her to take. What is also at issue, and which might not be immediately evident from the volume's title, is the question of translation. Exactly what Krog has tried to achieve in undertaking so much translation, and more particularly, why she has felt it so important to try to move between the country's languages, is the subject of several essays. Broadly the reason lies in what the subtitle does denominate— 'otherness'—South Africa's history of racial domination, of enforced separations arising from perceived differences between peoples, and the current need to develop elements of an ethical outlook which might counter the inequalities and distrust consequent on endless divisiveness: tolerance, respect, openness, mutual understanding.

While ethical principles may be general and constant, ethical action needs to be context-specific and, as many of the essays show, Krog's approach to issues through autobiographical narrative and poetry has enabled her to bring this truth to life with great vividness. Louise Viljoen, a distinguished Krog scholar who publishes in Afrikaans as well as English, has two essays in this collection. In ' "I Have Body, Therefore I Am": Grotesque, Monstrous and Abject Bodies in Antjie Krog's Poetry' (pp. 98–132) she establishes a point about Krog's ethics which surfaces in many of the essays: they are usually oppositional and often combative. As Viljoen's epithets suggest, when Krog's topics are at their most transgressive her moral concerns are usually at their most challenging. For example, in discussing a poem which presents a 'breathtaking crudeness of... action' (p. 117) in its last line, Viljoen claims that the poetry both recognizes that an 'aging and menopausal body is indeed an affront to the existing social order' but that it is also 'trying to confront society's negation of the menopausal woman by making this body visible in all its abject specificity' (p. 120). In her second essay, Viljoen takes up a related line of discussion that is also important throughout the volume: autobiographical writing and the ethics of representation. 'The Mother as Pre-text: Autobiographical Writing in Antjie Krog's *A Change of Tongue*' (pp. 133–56) looks at Krog's representations of her relationship to her mother, the Afrikaans writer Dot Serfontein, as a person and as a writer. As it becomes clear that Krog will not replicate her mother's choice to 'rate political loyalty to her Afrikaner heritage higher than loyalty to her writing' (p. 105), but that they share equally in the constant tussle between the claims of family life and writing life, Viljoen touches on Krog's admission (made in a later interview) that in depicting her mother's angry explosion when her daughter objects to being written about she had fictionalized the scene by transferring an incident that occurred between herself and her own daughter onto her mother (pp. 145–6). This leads Viljoen to wonder about the ethics of the means used to ' "lie the truth" [as Krog puts it] or universalise certain experiences' (p. 153). This issue is taken up fully by Kim Rostan in 'The Ethics of Infidelity in *Country of My Skull*' (pp. 24–43). In a sophisticated argument constructed on a series of parallels, Rostan works with Derrida's view that quotation, in shedding its original context, is somewhat paradoxically caught in an 'infidelity at the heart of fidelity'. The transcripted testimonies in Krog's account of the Truth and Reconciliation Commission are similarly unfaithful quotations in which her narrating voice becomes one among many in a new collectivity: a collage of voices. Whereas a family relationship demands 'loyalty', this new, textually created entity demands, like the envisaged new nation, 'justice' (the two concepts and their differentiation are taken from Richard Rorty), and the requirement of justice, of being accountable to an entity larger and newer than the family in the interests of an outcome desired by all, is what Krog's narrator brings as personal experience to the task of encountering so many narratives of atrocity and betrayal.

The sometimes unexpected demands of particularized moral issues and the insights arising from their treatment are explored by Christy Weyer in 'The Ambiguity of the Erotic: Antjie Krog's *Down to My Last Skin*' (pp. 157–83) in which she looks at the poems grouped under the title 'Love Is All I Know'. To illuminate the ethical element in Krog's poetry of the erotic body (which has met with a marked critical silence compared with, for example, the reception of her more political prose writing), Weyer turns to the 'foundational insights' (p. 176) of Simone de Beauvoir, who suggested that 'the erotic experience is the one that most poignantly discloses to human beings the ambiguity of their condition; in it they are aware of themselves as flesh and as spirit [or mind], as the other and as subject' (p. 174). This central ambiguity enables an ethical outlook to flourish, however unlikely that may at times seem. For example when, in Krog's lyric 'marital psalm', the poet-speaker presents her desire for her husband as 'connected to her desire for self-definition' (p. 171) which only his desire for her is able to fulfil, this might seem a retrogressive step in a feminist quest for 'ontogenesis', but as de Beauvoir puts it, 'subjectivity . . . cannot exist without inter-subjectivity'. Weyer adds that this is 'a foundational principle of the Southern African philosophy of *ubuntu*'. She takes this argument further to say that the erotic recognition of the other is ethical both in being reciprocal and in making one vulnerable, for 'to recognise the other as really free is to understand the other as a point of resistance to me' (Bergoffen, quoted p. 175) and it is these boundaries which Krog's poetry seeks to open. The same dynamics, but at work in a very different context, are discussed by Judith Coullie in the last essay in the volume, 'A Question of Ethics in *There Was This Goat: Investigating the Truth*

Commission Testimony of Notrose Nobomvu Konile' (pp. 313–31). Coullie argues explicitly that 'crucial to Krog's ethical project [in all her writing] is the refusal... to take a position and hold it; rather... certainties are rendered fruitfully unstable through the relentless hunting down of ambiguities' (p. 314). The account of their 'pilgrimage' (p. 320, Coullie's term) to visit Mrs Konile in Indwe in the Eastern Cape, which they undertook as part of their effort to comprehend the ambiguities in her TRC testimony, is written by all three investigators who are colleagues at the University of the Western Cape: Nosisi Mpolweni (in the Xhosa Department), Kopano Ratele (in Psychology and Gender Studies) and Antjie Krog (in the Arts Faculty). They combine their trans-disciplinary skills to work on what the official TRC record suggested was an incomprehensible testimony given by the mother of a young man killed by the secret police. Coullie concentrates on Krog's experience of being excluded from the conversation between her Xhosa-speaking colleagues and Mrs Konile, and particularly on her responding to her 'complete marginalisation and effacement with both "delight and anger"' (quoted p. 324). The anger is not difficult to place but the delight is challenging: Coullie sees it primarily as arising from an overturning of the country's old 'racialised hierarchy' (p. 325) and claims that 'like a true pilgrim, Krog has been discomfited and demeaned so as to shed her old identity, to re-enter the community as a changed self, purged, contrite, absolved' (p. 326). Krog's vulnerability, her experience of othering and renewed selfhood, allows Coullie a concluding claim for Krog: 'She admits new truths and finds, for the time being, a new way to be' (p. 327).

As the preceding essays indicate, the matter of cultural as well as linguistic translation pervades the volume, but one or two other topics and writers warrant mention. Anthea Garman has two contributions: the first, 'Antjie Krog and the Accumulation of "Media Meta-Capital"' (pp. 73–97), charts the choices and chances which have allowed Krog to move from being a respected 'Afrikaans woman poet [to a media figure who] enjoy[s] national and international renown' (p. 81). In the second, 'Running with the Jackals: Antjie Krog the Journalist' (pp. 184–214), Garman examines the relationship between Krog's poetry-writing self and her work as a journalist, particularly in her reporting of the TRC hearings. Potentially there is considerable conflict: journalists gather material on an 'intellectual-critical level' providing an objective report of an 'external, public situation' supported by expert opinion, rather than filtering it 'through a person as an affected receiver of the experience' (p. 193), but Krog insists that the truth is realized via 'encounter with the extremes of experience' and brings 'the discomforting contestation' of poetic commitment to her journalism (p. 209). Susan Spearey describes her reasons for teaching *Country of My Skull* to students in Canada and the steps that she took to enable them to engage ethically with the harrowing TRC testimonies. In '*Country of My Skull*, the Transmission of Testimony, and the Democratisation of Pedagogy' (pp. 44–72) she asserts that 'ethics is about how we inhabit uncertainty, together' (p. 45) and expresses the hope that in joining Krog's working 'at affective and embodied—as well as cognitive, socio-political and ideological—levels [we will be enabled] to overcome the constraints upon our capacities as individual and social agents, as witnesses and ethical beings' (p. 67). Also using *Country of My Skull* as case study,

Judith Coullie's other article examines the 'role of memory in the creation of the post-apartheid nation' (p. 1), but takes a less often articulated line on the issue. 'Remembering to Forget: Testimony, Collective Memory and the Genesis of the "New" South African Nation in *Country of My Skull*' (pp. 1–23) attends to several points at which Krog begins to 'negotiate her way out of one kind of [past] nation into another' (p. 8), often by refusing certain of the material that came her way while reporting on the TRC. This kind of forgetting was accompanied by her decisions to foreground other material, for example, the testimony of women. Citing Ricoeur, Coullie concludes that if we are to 'use the past as lessons for future generations... we have a duty to remember and a duty to forget' (pp. 19–20).

In the remaining essays, processes of cultural translation become more specifically linguistic. After a sketch of Bourdieu's ideas in ' "Inhabiting" the Translator's *Habitus*: Antjie Krog as Translator' (pp. 291–312), Frances Vosloo, who works on the sociology of translation, suggests that Krog as a 'self-conscious writer' has made a transition to being a 'self-conscious translator' for healing purposes. In 'Writing the Medea Myth in a New Context: Tom Lanoye, Antjie Krog and *Mamma Medea*' (pp. 241–62), Andries Visagie discusses the decisions made by Krog in translating the Belgian's play into Afrikaans. Lanoye's version of the Medea myth reflects 'the [historical] cultural and linguistic tensions between the Netherlands and Flanders' (p. 244) by using different dialects (as well as metre and register) for the conflicting parties. In translating it, Krog uses different dialects, including 'Engafrikaans', standard Afrikaans, a more colloquial Cape Afrikaans, and Gariep (Namaqualand) Afrikaans. Visagie sees this as making an important political gesture. He notes too that her practice of 'foreignisation' as a translator has always been to counter an embedded resistance to the other, as when she translated Nelson Mandela's autobiography so as to help 'rid [Afrikaans] of the vocabulary of power and retribution' (quoted p. 256).

Dan Wylie writes a subtle assessment, in ' "Now Strangers Walk in That Place": Antjie Krog, Modernity, and the Making of //Kabbo's Story' (pp. 215–40), of the challenge that Krog, like others writing about the painting and story-telling of the San/Bushmen, has faced. She has grappled with dichotomous essentializing of 'Bushman' being and 'Western' knowing in which a Bushman sense of identity and harmonious belonging is seen as an antidote to modernity's 'own perceived lack' (p. 218). Wylie argues that in Krog's *The Stars Say 'Tsau'* (her retranslation into Afrikaans and then into English and versification of selections from the Bleek and Lloyd /Xam manuscripts), 'the two conceptions of identity "co-construct" one another' (p. 218). He turns to Krog's poems in an earlier collection, *Once We Were Hunters: A Journey with Africa's Indigenous People*, to trace the poetic strategies first developed there to create an inner life for an autochthonous community and also allow an interactive expression of her own experience of modernity and its malaise. The resulting voice implies 'that modernity has united [the poet and the indigenous peoples] in their senses of dislocation and uprootedness', largely because their identities are 'analogously threatened' (p. 224). For example, when //Kabbo decided to tell his story to Bleek and Lloyd, to 'embrace literacy as a medium' in an act of resistance rather than an acceptance of domination, he is in a situation very like Krog's as she decides, in writing works such as *Country of My Skull*, to translate herself out of Afrikaans and into a hegemonic English (p. 229). In his assessment of the result of her versification of //Kabbo's stories, Wylie moves with great delicacy, sympathetic to the difficulty of speaking about another, autochthonous, culture and to the tension between reproducing something like a vanished rhetoric while creating one that appeals to a modern reader. He doubts that the results can always have integrity but allows that 'in the [resultant] transculturation, new and potentially fructifying perspectives are opened up' (p. 237).

Taking its title from an article by Ortega y Gasset, 'The Splendour and Misery of Translation: Interview with Antjie Krog' (pp. 263–90) was conducted in 2006 by Ileana Dimitriu. In it Krog explains her long-standing wish to dissociate herself from the power that was vested in Afrikaans and, by using 'same-language translation' (p. 266), to bring back all the 'impure' features that officialdom felt had to be weeded out of the language, as well as to recognize current changes in it. Her choice of English for works such as *Country of My Skull* is not in order to meet English-speaking literary circles, but to reach out to 'the rest of the country . . . my black colleagues (p. 271). The multi-lingual reality of the country also means, she suggests, that when authors use English, they are 'already—at least mentally—translating from their mother tongues. So even if a book appears as a novel in English, it's already a translated text' (p. 277). She has found cultural translation to require 'a complete re-education of myself' (p. 279) and that it has frequently meant encountering the hostility of those who seek security in a monocultural mindset. In the last part of the interview both speakers lament the lack of public understanding of the complexity of the translator's role and consider its various characteristics: missionary/educator; public intellectual; bridge-builder; creator of beauty; interpreter of stylistic challenges; social activist. Krog accepts them all and finally adds poet to the list, seeking in it the 'potential of splendour' (p. 289).

The World's Great Question: Olive Schreiner's South African Letters 1889–1920, edited and introduced by Liz Stanley and Andrea Salter, selects letters written over a thirty-year period after Olive Schreiner returned to South Africa, following nearly a decade in England. There she had become influential after the success of her first novel, *Story of An African Farm* [1883] and had a circle of prominent men and women at home and abroad to whom she could write in her efforts to guide the course of South Africa's development. Thus the editors' decision to focus on her political letters means that a representative self-portrait of this remarkable South African emerges. Mention is made of the edition of Schreiner's letters (heavily and silently amended) published by her husband, Samuel Cronwright Schreiner, shortly after her death in 1920, but nothing is said of another collection edited by Richard Rive, *Olive Schreiner: Letters 1871–99*, published by David Philip in 1987. This is a pity because Schreiner readers and new scholars should be given as much guidance as possible to what of her writing is available. It may be that, as Stanley and Salter have also been responsible for making Schreiner's extant letters—some 5,000 in all—available online at www.oliveschreiner.org, they thought reference to the earlier volume no longer necessary. When she died, 15,000 to 20,000 letters existed, but many were destroyed by her then estranged husband after he had written a biography; the letters that survive today are scattered in archives and private collections around the world, as an appendix shows. The scholarly apparatus in this volume is meticulous, with plentiful information about Schreiner's major correspondents and the events with which she was concerned. The thirty-year span of the letters is divided into ten sections and the editors have written informative introductions to each as well as a general biographical introduction.

The editors say that her letters show Schreiner to have been 'an astute political commentator with an eye for spotting significant developments in political life' and an ambition to see the creation of 'an organised liberal movement cutting across existing territorial, political and "race" divisions' (p. xxv). This was at a time when the country was on the brink of war between British and Boer, and virtually no one in public life gave a thought to the rights of African people. As a woman, Schreiner herself had no political rights and had to seek influence behind the scenes through her letters and her published writing. Her allegory *Trooper Peter Halket of Mashonaland* [1897] is well known as her attack on the exploits of Cecil John Rhodes's British South Africa Company in what would become Southern Rhodesia. It caused a furore, and the letters now offer an opportunity to read how her views on Rhodes developed. He came to be for her the 'symbol of "oppression, injustice & moral degradation"' (letter of 1897, quoted p. 34). Her view is of historical and current interest in the light of the #Rhodesmustfall campaigns. At the same time as she was approaching public figures about Rhodes, Schreiner was warning members of her family not to trust him. Her brother Will, who would become prime minister of the Cape in 1898, was a Rhodes supporter until the Jameson Raid of 1895–6, and her constant fear was that he might have taken insider advice from Rhodes on how to invest his money (a favour which could easily have been called in). Shortly after being assured that this had not happened, she wrote in June 1898 to Will:

> Dear Laddie, don't have more to do with Rhodes than you can help. And the first day he gives you any lawful ground for doing so, <u>cut him openly & forever</u>. There are [*sic*] a certain class of human being . . . with whom the only course is openly & avowedly to declare war against them. I speak from the depths of <u>bitter experience</u> [original emphases] . . .
> I am a one adult one vote man. I believe that every adult inhabiting a land irrespective of race, sex, wealth or poverty should have the vote; & that it is a power more needed by the poor, the weak & feeble than the wealthy or strong. I regard the vote as a small & feeble weapon, but still a weapon by which the weak may be able to defend themselves a little against the exactions of the strong, the poor against the rich,—which I regard as the main purpose of government.

Schreiner called herself a liberal, but as her comments here indicate, her views were very different from those usually labelled 'liberal' in South Africa today, where a weak self-interest seems their main characteristic. This collection of letters, which includes Schreiner's comments on the dangers of capitalism (i.e. great wealth in the hands of a few), demonstrates that liberalism can produce a courageous and principled egalitarianism.

'The World's Great Question' is a phrase Schreiner used at the end of her life when writing to J.C. Smuts, then prime minister, to argue that 'the native question' was not limited to South Africa, but was one for the whole world. In a letter which makes an interesting link with the argument put forward by Dorothy Driver in her essay on *From Man to Man* (reviewed in this section), Schreiner pleaded with Smuts to be far-sighted and to realize that 'We may crush the mass of our fellows in South Africa today, as Russia did for Generations, but today the serf is in the Palace & where is the Czar?' (28 October 1920; p. 368). Her own far-sightedness had led Schreiner to understand oppression in class as much as in racial terms.

Two chapters on Schreiner's fiction also appeared this year. In 'Olive Schreiner: *The Story of an African Farm*', in *Empire Girls: The Colonial Heroine Comes of Age* (pp. 27–108), Mandy Treagus agrees with Rachel Blau Du Plessis that in her first published novel Schreiner rejected nineteenth-century realism because of its 'imbrication with...ideologies of gender' (p. 28). Treagus adds that Schreiner also 'usurped the traditions of the English *Bildungsroman*' and those of the romantic novel because, living 'on the edges of Empire' she could not endorse the 'meritocratic drive' and its promise of 'order, meaning and justice for all' (pp. 28–9) integral to the Victorian novel about successful entry into adult life. Schreiner was, suggests Treagus, much closer to the 'ambivalences and ambiguities [of] the spiritual quest...of the German *Bildungsroman*' (p. 29) but ultimately departed from its distribution of 'rewards and punishments' (p. 31).

As she discusses each aspect of the plot, Treagus reports on the reception then and since of Schreiner's creative decisions, thus giving considerable historical depth to her account of what the genre choices reflect of her world, and of their impact on it. Treagus sees Schreiner shifting from utter rejection of Victorian literary and spiritual values to a profound ambivalence in which the writer is both compliant with and resistant to patriarchy and imperialism. Treagus explores first Waldo's (ultimately rejected) quest story and then the (again, ultimately rejected) romantic story of Lyndall, having placed them as a male-female double protagonist. Waldo's spiritual journey reflects Schreiner's own search for 'models for reading the scriptures' (p. 41) that would take her beyond the views of her Calvinist community. And yet, says Treagus, Calvinist discourses continued to work strongly in Schreiner, as can be seen in the allegorical tale told to Waldo by his Stranger (later published as 'The Hunter' in *Dreams*, and extremely popular in its day), which carries a belief in suffering and self-denial, but also teaches, in its conclusion, the 'abandonment of Christian belief' (p. 52).

The plot of the English *Bildungsroman* 'encapsulates a culture's belief in the certainty of justice' but 'is meaningless in this new [colonial frontier] environment' (p. 56). Protagonists are not rescued via the form's usual devices: 'strangers, vocation, romance or inheritance' (p. 56), although the Waldo–Lyndall story does touch on them when each leaves the farm. At this point, says Treagus, Schreiner's characters cease to stand in contrast to those of Dickens, for example, and move closer to George Eliot, and to *Middlemarch* in particular, with its several failed quests—failures that nevertheless leave the idea of a vocation unquestioned. However, 'growing up as the orphans of Empire in the Karroo . . . vocation becomes impossible, and irrelevant' (p. 62) and Waldo and Lyndall both give up the idea before they reach adulthood.

Nonetheless, Lyndall's story, from its first appearance, was appreciated in England for its representation of 'The Woman Question'. '[Lyndall] begins as a hero but finishes as a heroine, ultimately choosing the role that the romance plot thrusts upon her' (p. 65), is Treagus's summary of Lyndall's loss of faith, and of confidence that she can make a difference in her world. Schreiner's critique of the construction of gender 'remains a masterly piece of analysis [which] had an impact in [its] day' (p. 70), and yet it does not help her to escape the plot for women of her time. When a pregnant Lyndall refuses to marry her Stranger, the story invokes debate on marriage as legalized prostitution and garnered considerable support from women and men reviewers alike, even though current critics have questioned the balance of power in her sexual relationship because it seems so conventional. Treagus suggests that Lyndall is submissive because she has no 'independent labour' available to her, and there are no 'examples of equal heterosexual relationships' in the colony (p. 78). Treagus turns to Lyndall's death and considers the literary precedents on which Schreiner might have drawn (Goethe, for example), its critical interpretation, and the value placed on deathbed scenes in Victorian fiction. Gregory Rose, in his transvestite nursing of the dying Lyndall, is one of the most puzzling features of the novel. Schreiner makes both him and the reader into a voyeur as she 'indulges in the Victorian displacement of sensuality from sex to death' (p. 91). Although many readers will not recognize the connection, Treagus says much can be understood about Gregory Rose by considering his being named after a fourth-century saint, Gregory Nazianzen, who was much concerned with the maintenance of gender boundaries (p. 96). Her other comment, that 'When roles are so limited that there is only one way of being male, and one way of being female, Gregory actually has to assume another gender in order to act out a different role' (p. 99), seems more directly helpful and more closely related to Schreiner's colonial context. In this context, Lyndall 'forgoes repentance in favour of self-reliance' but also dies, leaving the text both resisting and complying with the dominant discourses of the time.

In anticipation of a new edition of Schreiner's unfinished last novel, *From Man to Man*, which she has edited, introduced, and annotated, Dorothy Driver wants her chapter 'Olive Schreiner's *From Man to Man* and "the Copy Within" ' (in Tonkin, Treagus, Seys, and Crozier-De Rosa, eds., *Changing the Victorian Subject*, pp. 123–50) to 'open discussion on . . . the novel's narrative and poetic treatment of what Schreiner saw as the human ideal, and its relation to what [in her novel she] called "the copy within" in the context of evolutionary process' (p. 125). To amplify Schreiner's thinking, Driver draws on her unfinished introduction to Mary Wollstonecraft's *A Vindication of the Rights of Woman*, as well as on Schreiner's reading of Darwin and Plato. From the latter she took her phrase 'the copy within' (a quasi-divine ideal, both origin and end) which allowed her to 'introduce the notion of progress into an evolutionary science that was generally non-teleological' (p. 125).

Driver's discussion of *From Man to Man* rests chiefly on Rebekah, the sister who marries and lives in Cape Town, rather than on Bertie, who is seduced and ends up in prostitution in London. The story of each woman raises issues that were important to Schreiner, but it is through Rebekah that Driver can trace the culmination of Schreiner's thinking about the 'entanglement of gender and racial subordination' (p. 128). Driver traces the maturation of Schreiner's own racial attitudes after *The Story of an African Farm*, both in her writing (the introduction to Wollstonecraft) and her actions (withdrawing from the South African Women's Enfranchisement League, for example, when the majority decided that their demand for the vote for women would not include black women). After noting Schreiner's approving account of an African woman who submitted to her own subordination in the interests of the greater good at that moment in history, Driver suggests that what Schreiner sought was a world in which women could be physically and intellectually powerful *and* retain their deep-rooted sense of social duty without its leading to their subordination.

From Man to Man works with these pointers from the Wollstonecraft essay: 'the restoration of women to a social function beyond the familial; the importance of women's physical and mental labour; the contribution of African culture towards modern civilization; the bringing back to life of the seemingly dead; and the knitting together of vastly disparate times and spaces' (p. 138). Driver discusses the novel's last chapter, in which Rebekah and Drummond, the man to whom Rebekah is drawn but with whom she has refused to conduct a conventional love affair, converse about the creative process. Here 'the copy within' returns as the idea that inspires the artist. It is expressed as Platonic—'the knowledge that the soul attains when in the company of the gods'—and was, Driver says, supported and extended by Schreiner's reading of German literature and philosophy as well as by Darwin, from whom she took the idea that 'the evolutionary history of any organism was retained in that organism and might re-emerge' (p. 142). The essay closes with an account of the imagery which Schreiner threaded through *From Man to Man* in order to draw her reader in to her understanding of the human ideal, recognition of which might 'ward off the disasters consequent on white racism and capitalist greed' (p. 145).

A 'vigorous, non-academic and above all public discussion of literature and culture in pre- and early apartheid South Africa, a tradition that has largely been lost to the historical record' (p. 3) is what Corinne Sandwith sets out to recover and investigate in *World of Letters: Reading Communities and Cultural Debates in Early Apartheid South Africa*. The tradition is that of liberal/left and Marxist oppositional critique conducted largely in periodicals from the 1930s to the 1960s but subsequently forgotten to the extent that when Marxism re-entered the South African academy in the 1970s, those who espoused the ideology wrote without any apparent knowledge of their local forebears. Sandwith gives a subtle, probing, and wide-ranging theoretical analysis of early critical methods which, along the way, reveals its relevance to debates of today. Her work will be invaluable not just to those wanting to know more about the publications and writers she has studied but also to those interested in following the carefully theorized and historically situated analysis of an intellectual movement. The texts and public forums that provide the material with which Sandwith works are magazines from the 1940s such as *South African Opinion* and *Trek*; the forums and publications linked to the Non-European Unity Movement (NEUM); the newspapers and forums that reflect the views of the Communist Party of South Africa (CPSA); a small community news-sheet, *The Voice of Africa*; and a number of 1950s newspapers and magazines that reflect the views of the Congress Alliance. The South African public sphere in the decades covered is presented as a 'discontinuous, fractured terrain of dissonant and contradictory discourses, encompassing a range of parallel or competing circuits of knowledge-production, which co-exist alongside and within the dominant public sphere' and reconfigure the history of South African literary culture (p. 5).

In the connectedness of politics and culture, Sandwith sees her work as complementing Laura Chrisman's *Postcolonial Contraventions* [2003]. In taking up the influence of 'new interpretative communities on the reading and evaluation of texts', she aligns her work with feminist and working-class reappraisals in general and, in the South African/postcolonial context, with the work of Stephanie Newell in *Literary Culture in Colonial Ghana* [2000], Isabel Hofmeyr in *The Portable Bunyan* [2004], and David Attwell in *Rewriting Modernity* [2005]. Her study also draws on book history and the history of reading. Sandwith argues that current work on the 'tensions between political and other kinds of analytical frameworks' has its precedents in the period which she studies, and that what may manifest as a new concern today 'is also, in part, a reinscription' of the 'knots, overlaps and interconnections in what is never a seamless discourse' (p. 13).

In her first two chapters Sandwith reads the late 1930s and early 1940s through *SA Opinion* and *Trek*: 'founding moments in the articulation of leftist cultural discourse in South Africa' (p. 15). *SA Opinion* debated the creation of a South African literature in English, the proper subjects of art, and the social role of the artist. Politically, it took a position between the extremes of international communism and fascism, locally between nationalism (Afrikaner) and jingoistic imperialism; artistically its liberal-Enlightenment values were aligned with 'highbrow' tastes and opposed to crass colonial fare. Sandwith shows that the periodical's sometimes contradictory understanding of its economic context was matched by a similarly strained response to cultural and literary matters. The periodical ceased publication during the war, and when it reappeared its politics had changed in the sense that 'African wage earners... are now positioned outside capitalist-democratic structures in the zone of pure culture' (p. 28) and there was much discussion about preserving 'the native way of life'. The new literary editor was Herman Charles Bosman (now mostly remembered for his short stories), and much attention was given to forging a truly South African culture. For writers in English, this project gradually centred on the concrete particularities of place, and Sandwith gives a brief but fascinating account of what transpired (and what was omitted) in their desire to capture a symbolic landscape. There were some socially conscious, left-leaning critics who objected, in *SA Opinion*, to the occlusion of African modernities from this preoccupation with landscape and the reification of African rural life in painting as in poetry, but their comments were largely ignored by Bosman who, in a time of growing postwar conservatism, was crusading for artistic freedom, autonomy, and individuality.

In the mid-1940s, *Trek*, under the iconoclastic editorship of Jacques Malan, hosted an energetic public discussion of the value of Marxist criticism, the relationship between culture and social justice, and the role of the artist in social change. It became essential reading for South Africa's intelligentsia, black and white, and achieved a wartime circulation of 5,000. Despite this achievement, its role in the country's political and cultural history has, says Sandwith, 'been almost completely overlooked' (p. 49). The Great Depression, followed by the Second World War, turned the public mind to questions of the country's future, and *Trek* radically placed the African proletariat as equals in a common culture. Simultaneously it opposed Stalinism and Hitler's national socialism, and denounced the false wartime promises of 'a better life for all' made by local politicians. Echoing international debates, its cultural criticism diverged from the canons of Soviet socialist realism (p. 66), but 'reflected the energy and inclusiveness of the Popular Front period when left-wing arguments enjoyed a brief legitimacy [and] literary criticism was fashioned as a means of social intervention' (p. 64). Writing from Britain and America received attention, as did the literary left of Europe although literary modernism was not enthusiastically viewed.

Trek also developed its general ideological position in dialogue with social commentary in South Africa, and Sandwith gives particular attention to the debates in its pages between regular contributors and certain academics espousing the literary and cultural approach of F.R. Leavis. Politics again emerges as a nodal point: antagonists saw, for example, a critic's ideological objection to Sarah Gertrude Millin's views on race as an attempt to force on a writer what would today be called political correctness. Leavisites espoused the essential autonomy of a work of art, while others supported art's having explicit political content. Sandwith does not take sides, although her sympathies are clearly left-wing; she indicates the complexity of the positions actually taken as well as their underlying assumptions and values, describing her approach as 'combining appreciation and scepticism (rather than either reverence or repudiation)' (p. 168). *Trek* ended its life shortly after Rand Mines brought a massive libel action against it over two articles about the conditions of employment of African mineworkers. Malan resigned rather than submit to an editorial board of control. A reincarnated *Trek* continued for some time under the editorship of Lily Rabkin (who had been Malan's co-editor) but dropped all political content in 1950.

Dora Taylor, who is the subject of chapter 3, was the most prolific of the contributors to *Trek* during the 1940s. Recently Taylor has become better known in South Africa as a novelist (all posthumously published), a literary journalist (some essays have been republished), and for her role in intellectual political life, but the full contribution that she made to 'a complex and heterogeneous struggle tradition' (p. 87) has yet to be recognized. Her focus on tracing connections between culture and its social roots provoked accusations of 'ideological policing, mistaking literary texts for political pamphlets and applying ready-made formulas to the undecidability of art' (p. 86), but, while there might be some justice in aspects of this reaction, Taylor was influenced not by Stalinism but by Marx himself, Engels and, above all, by Trotsky. Sandwith also gives attention to the similarities of approach between Taylor and Georg Lukács.

On arrival in Cape Town from Scotland, Taylor and her husband joined the city's left-wing intellectual circles, and by 1938 she had become a member of the Workers' Party of South Africa; in the next decade she was deeply involved in the Non-European Unity Movement and collaborated with I.B. Tabata on his projects. Membership of these groups meant that her writing and teaching on cultural and literary matters was done largely at their behest. Facing the threat of fascism and the seduction of the masses by commerce, Taylor emphasized the value of education and the recovery of individual discrimin-ation, but hers was not, argues Sandwith, a reactionary position akin to 'Kulturkritik', for she also turned to a materialist frame in order to understand the forces at work, insisting, with vital importance for her context, on the 'determining influence of entrenched economic inequality' (p. 95). In her literary reviewing, Taylor introduced her readers to the classics of the European, American, and British traditions, using a Trotskyite perspective to indicate their value, and she assessed the writing of South Africans, black and white. Her perspective enabled her to argue that, 'while the economic base is an invaluable and essential guide in tracing the rise of certain ideological concepts, literature at the same time has its own laws of growth, change, assimilation, imitation and revolt . . . The laws of uneven development would seem to hold in literature as well as economics' (*Trek* 1944; quoted, with ellipsis, p. 103).

Olive Schreiner was one of the writers Taylor admired for her unending questioning of received dogma and opposition to the authoritarianism of colonial life. The isolation in which Schreiner conducted her quest for the truth was in stark contrast to the community of ideas (p. 104) that Taylor believed socialism would bring. In espousing literature's truth-telling capacity, Taylor was influenced by nineteenth-century Russian literary criticism, which also led her to espouse a realist aesthetic in order to heighten social consciousness in South Africa. She did not, however, believe that culture could be a weapon in the revolutionary struggle, for that would be to force art to solve problems outside its legitimate sphere (p. 111). Sandwith gives a careful account of Taylor's objections to writers such as Sarah Gertrude Millin, Alan Paton, and Phyllis Altman (*The Law of the Vultures*), and to her assessment of writers such as H.I.E. Dhlomo and R.R.R. Dhlomo; in the latter, 'incipient social critique is undone by an insistent preoccupation with individual morality and Christian themes of sin and repentance' (p. 117). The Dhlomo brothers were mission-educated, and about this time Dora Taylor published, under the pseudonym Nosipho Majeke, *The Role of the Missionaries in Conquest* [1953].

After the narrower focus on Dora Taylor, Sandwith broadens out her discussion again to consider the tensions in the WPSA and the New Era Fellowship (both of which would play a role in NEUM) between demands for citizenship based on merit (i.e. those deemed 'civilized') and political representation as a right accorded to all people. While this debate tended to map onto a class hierarchy in Europe, in South Africa it also had the potential for a racialized hierarchy within the coloured group and a sharp division between coloured and African peoples. Tensions played out in the field of education in particular; when in the early 1940s the government created a separate Department for Coloured Affairs, antagonisms grew and, as a differentiated education was portended, the Teachers' League split. The local press supported the educationalists' argument for merit, and Sandwith records many letters to the editor which expressed the elites' 'enormous sense of (always patronising) responsibility' (p. 141) towards their less fortunate brethren. Younger activists took exception to this moderate position. In *The Torch* the NEUM developed its educational policy of 'nurturing a critical, independent and enlightened black intelligentsia that would act as a vanguard for the developing liberation movement' (p. 147) and, rather than following a 'civilizing' mission, would develop a culture of resistance. Sandwith instances A.C. Jordan's use of *The Tempest* to argue what education should and should not provide, in which he, working with ideas of hybridity, cultural transmission, and affiliation, debunked the idea of exclusivity in white culture. In NEUM circles, people were encouraged to become what would later be termed 'resistant readers', a stance which led to 'vigorous, public political argumentation and critique, in marked contrast to the solitary reading practices of the academic mainstream' (p. 161).

Sandwith next turns her attention to the South African Communist Party and the relationship between politics and culture in its 1940s publications. Again, it is a 'shifting and expansive debate [among] a loose group of individuals around several common themes...protocols of reading...favoured hermeneutic styles and valued texts (pp. 174–5), this time inspired by a Stalinist left. Sandwith gives particular attention to the 'point where Soviet cultural theory encounters the complexities and constraints of semi-colonial and apartheid South Africa' (p. 175). The Left Book Club and the *Guardian* newspaper were two of the chief means by which a favoured ideology and cultural activities were promoted. The former included very little fiction in its lists of recommended reading and, says Sandwith, seems to have held 'an instrumentalist view of writing and a conception of reading as a means of acquiring knowledge and political insight' (p. 184); this mutated into an acceptance of the heroics of Soviet socialist realism and a concern with ' "positive" endings and popular inspiration' (p. 187). Sandwith cites Brian Bunting's disapproval of the short-story collection, *Man Must Live*, by Es'kia Mphahlele: for failing to comply with party criteria, the writer is charged (ironically, in the light of his African nationalist views expressed in *The Voice*, discussed below) with forgetting that he is an African!

After a brief account of attempts to foster a people's theatre in Johannesburg, Sandwith considers the early career of Jack Cope who, some years before he launched and edited the long-running liberal arts journal *Contrast* (still in existence), was a novelist and a vigorous Marxist literary journalist writing chiefly for the *Guardian* and *Trek*. Although never a card-carrying member, styling himself an independent revolutionary, Cope was a presence in party activities as a writer, lecturer, and public speaker; he wrote a biography of veteran trade unionist W.H. Andrews and, after the voluntary dissolution of the party, he continued to be active in the various organizations that took its place. Cope combined, says Sandwith, 'the Romantic-radicalism of the British communists... the aesthetic preoccupations of Soviet socialist realism and the cultural pessimism of the *Scrutiny* school' (p. 200). This aspect of Cope's work has, like the early politico-cultural debates in CPSA circles, unaccountably disappeared from South Africa's broader intellectual history.

To this point, most of the publications and other records that Sandwith has studied are from the Cape, but in her last chapter she turns to Johannesburg, first to a publication from Orlando (now in Soweto) which appeared from September 1949 to June 1952. *The Voice* was an independent, African-owned monthly news-sheet, published on a shoestring and focused on community issues while, in its columns on culture, espousing a distinctive 'energetic African nationalist project in the interests of radical political change' (p. 217). This nationalism was not based on an 'exclusive cultural or ethnic 'family' identity... but rather on the bonds of an oppositional political practice' (p. 225). Its nationalism was more militant than that of the then moderate African National Congress, and its claims to Western cultural access were accompanied by rejection of the 'tribal life' being promoted in the segregation policies of the newly elected white Nationalist government. Among the group of editors and writers who also funded the paper was Es'kia Mphahlele and, although most of the articles and reviews appeared under pseudonyms, Sandwith has been able to identify many of the pieces that he wrote. She shows in some fascinating analysis why Mphahlele's trajectory as a resistant intellectual was different from that outlined by Fanon and why he did not align himself with *negritude*. Satirical parody of English literary classics was a favoured weapon in *The Voice*, and Sandwith outlines all the postcolonial complexity in which 'Western morality is both idealised and contested, Western culture is simultaneously performed and mimicked, inhabited and undermined, claimed and disavowed' (p. 240).

The second Johannesburg focus is on a cluster of publications circulating the views of the Congress Alliance: *Spark*, *Liberation*, and *Fighting Talk* (1942–63). The last was most explicitly engaged with cultural matters (it also published short fiction and poetry), and was for some time edited by Ruth First. Its contributors were concerned with a history of African literary forms and with contemporary writing, with one critic complaining in 1957 that African writers evade 'interpret[ing]African life as it truly obtains today... they have not yet characterised a Mandela, educated, independent and politically victimised' (quoted p. 247). Such a call for a truthful representation of African modernity is linked, says Sandwith, 'to a view of indigenous culture as inherently adaptive, provisional and dynamic' (p. 247). These publications theorized cultural entanglement and the formation of hybridized identities. This was possible in the early years of apartheid when material co-operation and alliances against the divisions of apartheid were still functioning.

Among the journal articles from South Africa this year we have two on the evergreen *Heart of Darkness*. In 'Joseph Conrad in the Popular Imaginary: The Case of *Heart of Darkness*' (*JLS* 30:ii[2014] 17–34) Harry Sewlall revisits Achebe's denunciation of the novel and gives reasons, from close reading of the text, why it should not simply and unthinkingly be perpetuated. In 'Locating the Ambivalence of Colonial Discourse in Joseph Conrad's *Heart of*

Darkness' (*CW* 26:i[2014] 12–17), Feston Kalua concentrates on Marlow 'not only as a metaphor for the ironies and contradictions of the colonial enterprise, but also as challenging all the seeming foundational notions upon which such a markedly flawed edifice was predicated' (p. 13). J.M. Coetzee also continues to feature in South African literary criticism, but in the first instance the focus is on autobiography and philosophical content rather than on any localized reference. 'The Grounds of Cynical Self-Doubt: J.M. Coetzee's *Boyhood, Youth* and *Summertime*' (*JLS* 30:i[2014] 94–112) by Sam Cardoen looks at the trilogy as an extension of Coetzee's writing on secular confession from the mid-1980s. The scepticism in Coetzee's earlier writing is seen to be something that the autobiographies replicate, analyse, and seek to move beyond by setting up as a possibility, but not enacting, writing as a condition of gossip. 'J.M. Coetzee's *The Childhood of Jesus*: A Postmodern Allegory?' by Ileana Dimitriu (*CW* 26:i[2014] 70–81) also has a philosophical emphasis. Dimitriu suggests that Coetzee is exploring the oxymoron of secular spirituality as apt to our uncertain times. Dimitriu, quoting Deborah Madsen, says that 'allegory tends to come into its own during periods of uncertainty about the nature of communications, the reliability of language and the authenticity of culturally important texts [because] allegory is... focused on the complexities and difficulties inherent in the act of interpretation' (p. 75).

Cheryl Stobie's ' "The Devil Slapped on the Genitals": Religion and Spirituality in Queer South Africans' Lives' (*JLS* 30:i[2014] 1–19) examines autobiographical writing in three recently published books: *Reclaiming the L-Word: Sappho's Daughters Out in Africa*, edited by Alleyn Diesel [2011], *Yes I Am! Writing by South African Gay Men*, edited by Robin Malan and Ashraf Johaardien [2010], and *Trans: Transgender Life Stories from South Africa*, edited by Ruth Morgan, Charl Marais, and Joy Rosemary Wellbeloved [2009]. She argues that, while the various forms of religion in South Africa can constrain the rights of sexually nonconforming believers, and while oppression arises from the fact that public opinion lags behind the rights granted in the constitution to individual sexual orientation, these texts also reveal that such believers can establish meaningful spiritual and intimate lives.

' "You Are Suffering from Literary Kwashiorkor": Transculturation at the Confluence of African Literature, Vegetarianism and Indigenous Ritual Practice in Nape'a Motana's *Son-in-Law of the Boere*' (*JLS* 30:i[2014] 53–69), by Dave Nel, argues that Motana's novel should be read as representing the transculturation of three veins of social discourse, a process which arises out of the collision of differentiated civilizations. These veins are: a changed historiography of African literature (the novel is set in a high school where an African teacher attempts to instil a love of writing by Africans in his pupils, and the author uses intertextuality to thicken the implications of this process); becoming a vegetarian as a metaphor for individual change (to abstain from eating meat is a difficult decision for the teacher protagonist as animal slaughter plays a central part in his culture's rituals); and indigenous ritual practice in the context of modernity in South Africa (resolution of this conundrum is presented in the novel in individual physical and psychic terms).

Two accounts of migrants' reception in South Africa are examined by Rebecca Fasselt in ' "Opening Up to the Rest of Africa"? Continental

Connections and Literary (Dis)Continuities in Simão Kikamba's *Going Home* and Jonathan Nkala's *The Crossing*' (*JLS* 30:i[2014] 70–93). The former is a semi-autobiographical novel about a political refugee from Angola and the latter a one-man play about an economic migrant from Zimbabwe. While they join a growing number of texts featuring migrancy to and in South Africa (Fasselt mentions some fifteen titles), they are unusual in presenting matters from the point of view of the migrants themselves. Fasselt considers the potential for this narrative angle to be liberatory and to invoke a spirit of Afropolitanism, but says that on the whole xenophobia continues to divide South Africa from the continent, state functionaries are depicted as still brutal in their exercise of power, and practices of exclusion continue. In Kikamba's novel, music and dance offer one small space in which commonality can be felt.

Tony Voss in 'Notes on Joyce and South Africa: Coincidence and Concordance' (*CW* 26:i[2014] 19–28) traces the knowledge that James Joyce had of the country and events in South Africa, based on *Dubliners*, *Ulysses*, and records from Joyce's life. Working from the early comments of the Afrikaans poet N.P. van Wyk Louw, he also traces the influence of Joyce on South African writers in Afrikaans and English.

Stephen Gray, continuing his articles on writers that he considers unjustly neglected, writes about the once celebrated poet-painter of the 1960s and 1970s, Wopko Jensma in 'Losing His Head: The Poetry of Wopko Jensma and His Reputation' (*CW* 26:i[2014] 29–40). The title is an allusion to the judgement of some that Jensma was deranged, and to the rumour that after his disappearance in the early 1990s he was executed in an unknown spot.

In '"Storytellers, Not Just Case Makers"? A Study of Storytelling in the Essays of Njabulo S. Ndebele' (*CW* 26:i[2014] 41–50), Sara Thackwray revisits the 1991 essay in which Ndebele criticized 1970s black protest writing on the grounds that the short stories in particular were overly diagrammatic in their staging of racial oppression. Tracing his understanding of storytelling to Walter Benjamin's essay 'The Storyteller', she compares Ndebele's views with those of Michael Kirkwood and Michael Vaughan, both also strongly influenced by Benjamin in the 1990s, in order to assess the value of this debate for present literary studies.

Belinda du Plooy takes up Foucault's concepts of 'subjugated' or 'rejected' knowledges in 'A Foucauldian Reading of Power Dynamics in Two Afrikaans Historical Novels: Daleen Matthee's *Fiela's Child* and Micki Pistorius's *Sorg*' (*CW* 26:i[2014] 51–8). The latter title is translated as 'Care'. The novels are set in the latter years of the nineteenth century but reflect the socio-political concerns of the time in which they were written: chiefly the smaller stories of marginalized people. Du Plooy argues that the novels 'unravel ... the practical realities and implications of social control, resistance, power and individual autonomy' (p. 57), both in the fictionalized time and in our own.

In '"Every Place Is Three Places": Bursting Seams in Recent Fiction by Diane Awerbuck and Henrietta Rose-Innes' (*CW* 26:i[2014] 59–69) Ken Barris looks at the creation of a new literary space in which city and nature interpenetrate to form a zone of instability in two short stories: 'Phosphorescence' and 'The Keeper' by Diane Awerbuck, and a novel, *Nineveh*, by Henrietta Rose-Innes.

This interpenetration, or collapse, gives rise to a new genre, the urban pastoral, and, in the short stories, invites the presence of a *flâneur* figure in the Baudelaire or Benjamin mould.

A novel by the Zimbabwean novelist Chenjerai Hove is the subject of Muchativugwa Liberty Hove's 'Reversions and Revisions: Displacement, Heritage and History in Chenjerai Hove's *Ancestors*' (*CW* 26:i[2014] 82–90). He observes that it is a neglected text and argues that it interrogates the position of women—motherhood, forced marriage, girlhood, exile, and voicelessness—silenced under patriarchy. Another article concerning Zimbabwe, but about a much more difficult claim to that identity, is Syned Mthatiwa's 'Subjectivity and Belonging in the Poetry of Bart Wolffe' (*CW* 26:i[2014] 91–106), where the poems of childhood are shown to express a profound and innocent nostalgia, but the later poems, especially those written in exile, reveal a more complex and sometimes self-contradictory sense of identity.

The second issue of *Journal of Literary Studies*, guest-edited by Maurice Taonezvi Vambe and Urther Rwafa, has as its theme 'Violence and Genocide in African Literature and Film'. Nyasha Mboti, in 'Violence in Postcolonial African Film' (*JLS* 30:ii[2014] 38–48), focuses on *Bamako* by the Mauritanian filmmaker Abderrahmane Sissako in order to argue that, for African filmmakers, the vital subject is 'the hidden, hegemonic sinister...form of violence one may call systemic violence...which enables all other violences' (p. 42). Maurice Vambe argues, in 'Violence, Cynicism and the Cinematic Spectacle of (Mis)Representing African Child Soldiers in *Black Hawk Down* and *Blood Diamond*' (*JLS* 30:ii[2014] 49–68) that although in these American-made films child soldiers are superficially depicted as reluctant recruits and victims, they are contextually and symbolically constituted as the enemy, as 'other', and as 'ungrievable', in Butler's term. An approach using Halliday's Systemic Functional Grammar is taken to film by Macaulay Mowarin in 'A Linguistic Reading of the Metaphor of Genocide in *Hotel Rwanda*' (*JLS* 30:ii[2014] 69–85). He analyses the film's representation of lexical choices and syntactic selections made in radio broadcasts in order to inflame the killing in Rwanda of Tutsis by Hutu extremists. He also discusses the protagonist's uses of language in trying to protect those who take refuge in the Sabana hotel, and the role of language in the inertia of the West and its perceptions of the genocide. Urther Rwafa's article 'Playing the Politics of Erasure: (Post)Colonial Film Images and Cultural Genocide in Zimbabwe' (*JLS* 30:ii[2014] 104–14) uses the South African-made film *Strike Back Zimbabwe* as an example of cultural genocide. In 'Rethinking Marikana: Warm and Cold Lenses in Plea for Humanity' (*JLS* 30:ii[2014] 115–34), his consideration of the documentary *The Marikana Massacre: Through the Lens*, Lesibana Rafapa discusses both the 'warm lenses of the eyes of the film-maker, and of the film-viewer [and the material's being] commonly mediated by the cold lens of the camera' (p. 118). After a careful account of the filmic techniques, emphases, and silences, Rafapa concludes that the documentary creates an understanding that all of those involved 'are all human beings irrespective of social, political or economic status and deserve to be treated with humanity at all times' (p. 132). There are two articles on novels in this special issue. One is Tendayi

Sithole's 'Violence: The (Un)real, Power and Excess in Ngũgĩ wa Thiong'o's *Wizard of the Crow*' (*JLS* 30:ii[2014] 86–103) and the other is Ogaga Okuyade's 'Body as Battlefield: Genocide, and the Family in Goretti Kyomuhendo's *Secrets No More*' (*JLS* 30:ii[2014] 135–51). In the latter Okuyade summarizes the ethnicized origins of the Rwanda genocide and then focuses on Kyomuhendo's novel, which uses violence against a particular family, particularly the rape of women, to figure the attempted destruction of a people.

The second number of *Current Writing* in 2014, guest-edited by Margaret Daymond, celebrates the fortieth anniversary of the publication of Bessie Head's novel, *A Question of Power*. Many of the contributors are established Head scholars, some of them pioneers in the field. Among the newer scholars is Grant Lilford, who argues, in 'Madness or Mysticism? The Unconscious Ascetics of Power and Hunger' (*CW* 26:ii[2014] 169–80), that in Head's novel and in *The House of Hunger* by Zimbabwean Dambudzo Marechera, the protagonist's battle is of a psychic rather than a psychological nature. He suggests that from a traditional African perspective and from that of the mystic Desert Fathers of North Africa, the kind of consciousness presented in the novel would not seem strange. He uses Foucault to suggest that a diagnosis of madness should obscure the validity of the critique of power in Head's novel. Another scholar new to the field is Nyasha Mboti who, in 'Questions of Adaptation: Bessie Head's *A Question of Power* and Ingrid Sinclair's *Riches*' (*CW* 26:ii[2014] 181–92), looks at how Sinclair's film creatively reimagines the protagonist's story in Head's novel. Annie Gagiano, 'Topographies of Power and Pain in *A Question of Power*' (*CW* 26:ii[2014] 113–22), focuses on the discourses of outer and inner location in the novel in order to trace the psychic and social journey that the protagonist, Elizabeth, has to undergo. Bessie Head's biographer, Gillian Stead Eilersen, asks herself, in 'Creative Ferment: *A Question of Power* in the 21st Century: Some Thoughts for New Readers' (*CW* 26:ii[2014] 156–61), what advice she would give to readers tackling the novel today. Starting with the idea of a nightmare soul journey, she finds several other signposts, as well as the image of fermentation in which creative and disintegrative elements are inseparably combined, which might act as a guide to the conflict between good and evil that occupies the narrative. Craig MacKenzie, one of Head's editors, reflects on years of reading her fiction in 'A Question of Madness: Re-reading Bessie Head's *A Question of Power*' (*CW* 26:ii[2014] 148–56). After looking at records of her life at the time she was writing the novel, MacKenzie turns to what he considers some of the more perplexing features of the novel and focuses on the protagonist's struggle to distinguish what is 'real' in her life and what belongs in her 'dream' world. This struggle means that the narrative technique cannot be 'a triumph of the ordering power of the individual intellect [but is] one of witness' (p. 151) and it remains a 'landmark work in African fiction' (p. 155). Mary S. Lederer, who has a monograph on Head's fiction forthcoming, considers the requirements for producing an annotated edition of Head's novel in 'Annotating Bessie Head's *A Question of Power*' (*CW* 26:ii[2014] 162–8). Since so much of Head's writing and philosophy involves uncertainty and open-endedness, annotations of her fictional text are particularly important, not least in order to make accurate distinctions between the protagonist's life story and Head's own biography. Annotations could also support Head's claim that the novel represents her Botswana experiences rather than her South African background. Given questions of copyright, Lederer proposes that a reader's companion to the novel would be the best way to provide the necessary assistance to readers. Bessie Head's letters, some published, some collected in the archive in the Khama III Memorial Museum in Serowe, and some still privately owned, form the basis of three articles. Linda Susan Beard, who has edited a comprehensive selection of the letters for publication, writes 'Head on Head, Metacritically Speaking: Bessie Head's Epistolary Critique of *A Question of Power*' (*CW* 26:ii[2014] 123–34). Head was a prolific letter-writer who kept copies of everything; Beard has constructed Head's aesthetic from the correspondence, sets out her commentary on stages of the novel's development, and assembles her account of the narrative methods used, showing the novelist as a considerable literary critic. M.J. Daymond takes Head's letters to the English novelist Paddy Kitchen, to whom Head wrote for nearly twenty years, and with particular intensity during the writing of *A Question of Power*. This correspondence has subsequently been published in *Everyday Matters: Selected Letters of Dora Taylor, Bessie Head and Lilian Ngoyi*, edited by M.J. Daymond [2015]. In ' "I Want to Feel That I Saw and Thought All Those Things for a Purpose": Bessie Head's Letters to Paddy Kitchen about Writing *A Question of Power*' (*CW* 26:ii[2014] 135–47), the letters are used to show that Head worked to turn what might have been inchoate and profoundly disturbing raw experience into a visionary work of art. Stephen Gray, also one of Head's editors, looks at some personal aspects of Head's life, correspondence, and publishing career in 'Some Publishing Personalia Concerning Bessie Head' (*CW* 26:ii[2014] 193–202). He includes several unpublished letters between himself and Head concerning the inclusion of certain of her stories in anthologies, her joy on receiving a copy of Plaatje's novel *Mhudi*, and her going to Iowa City to join the university's International Writing Program.

2. Australia

Australian literary studies in 2014 saw recently popular areas of interest (David Malouf) sustained, older areas (Patrick White) renewed, and a surprising assortment of new approaches moving beyond textual analysis to consideration of theatre-making and varying kinds of print culture, book history, and reception studies.

(a) Books

Colonial Psychosocial: Reading William Lane presents its subject as a 'rabid preacher coughing forth racist bile', a unionist, an 'aspirant dictator' leading Australians to a workers' commune in Paraguay, and a writer of futuristic fiction (p. 7). David Crouch gives us a dramatic sketch of the man and his historical context, treating him as symptomatic of a pathology of white settler colonial utopian dreams and paranoid fears—a 'hypochondria of identity' (p. 15). Claims for Lane's ongoing influence on 'the racially driven violence of subsequent political formations' are perhaps overreaching, though the comments on the Cronulla riot and invasion fiction are of interest. The study is an important corrective to the romance of democratic labour history, with lots of colourful if unedifying scenes of anti-Chinese prejudice in Queensland, partly fuelled by Lane's paper *The Boomerang: The Workingman's Paradise*, written in support of striking shearers in 1891, which envisioned a perfected new society that carried with it 'a pervasive air of disillusionment' (p. 111) linked to mechanized capitalism and city slums. The final chapter shows us what we have not often seen: the 'morbid' prophet working out restless days on a New Zealand newspaper, still spouting 'images of glorified violence' (p. 145).

You can read the first 125 pages of Michael Wilding's 'documentary' *Wild Bleak Bohemia: Marcus Clarke, Adam Lindsay Gordon and Henry Kendall* before hearing mention of what ties them: the founding of Melbourne's Yorick Club. Indeed, if you are looking for an academic study of late nineteenth-century Australian literary bohemia, you won't find it; nor will you find an accessible, prosaic cultural history; the book is meticulously researched. *Wild Bleak Bohemia* feels uncomfortably stuck between the academic and the popular. It forgoes chapter divisions, substituting short sketches, each tied to specific archival and documentary accounts of events (which range from the rollicking to the curious to the banal). It would be a shame, though, for this fascinating book to be ignored. Wilding patiently draws an account of each of its subjects, from expatriate (Clarke), or jockey (Gordon) to the progeny of missionaries (Kendall) and their progress to becoming men of letters. The resulting 'documentary' becomes increasingly layered and (as the reader becomes accustomed to its unusual style) fascinating.

Philip Butterss's *An Unsentimental Bloke: The Life and Work of C.J. Dennis* aims to tell this later story fairly comprehensively, and largely succeeds. From a child born in a pub, coddled by aunties, Dennis wrote his first verses as a boy, before proceeding to a literary apprenticeship writing for and then running such journals as the *Critic* and the *Gadfly*. Butterss's book is an insight into many things: the enduring influence of Kipling on Dennis, his abandoned foray into a dictionary of Australian slang, and the numerous sources for *Songs of a Sentimental Bloke* (though Butterss makes a case for its originality) and much besides.

If Wilding's *Wild Bleak Bohemia* is a documentary in a playful sense, Ken Gelder and Rachael Weaver have compiled a literal documentary in *The Colonial Journals: The Emergence of Australian Literary Culture*. Divided into ten sections, the book provides snapshots of fiction and poetry, reviews, art, and several exemplary 'colonial types' imagined in the press. Canons and taste formation seem to be at the forefront of the authors' sampling of excerpts, as well as the well-argued case that 'the investment in "Australian literature" as an identifiable field of writing happens . . . early on'—as early as the 1860s, in fact.

Igor Maver has read postcolonial literature from his base in Ljubljana, Slovenia. On the one hand, his *Selected Essays on Canadian, Australian and New Zealand Literatures* revisit familiar texts (A.D. Hope's vision of Australia versus Europe in relation to Byron); on the other, it can produce unusual slants and selections. There is an interesting reading of Ouyang Yu's *The Knightsbury Tales*, for example, and the author's interest in diasporic work also has him read Andrew Riemer's *The Hapsburg Café* and catalogue Slovenian writing in Australia (the strongest chapter and important for cataloguing non-English transnational work overlooked in Australia). In addition he looks at poems set in Slovenia by Andrew Taylor and Susan Hampton, and the work of Christopher Koch. These essays often fail to rise above the level of a book review. Many anglophone scholars will, however, find the work of 1920s globetrotter Alma Karlin a revelation, and the Slovenian perspective that shapes the whole book is itself a significant intervention in the field.

As a former student of writer and teacher Margaret Scott, Janet Upcher offers an appreciative thematic reading of the Tasmanian's poetry and prose, emphasizing her migration from England, her feminism, her 'indomitable approach to most things . . . isolation, divorce, bushfire, bereavement, emphysema' (p. 7) mixed with tones of despair and irony, and a juxtaposition of 'the ordinary and the grotesque' (p. 13). *Changing Countries, Bridging Worlds* is a close reading of poems set against biographical information; it points to Scott's handling of sound effects, rhythm, and image as evidence that her verse is more poetic than some critics have allowed (pp. 27–30) and notes her 'emphasis on the regenerative power of memory' (p. 39) and attentiveness to everyday realities. The section on prose takes this icon of regional identity and makes her a universal philosopher, acknowledging her 'fierce social conscience' and historical writings. The book is a good introduction to Scott's work, though a more bracing critical analysis remains to be written.

It is a familiar trope to claim that your favourite writer is not given his or her due by critics, but in Tim Winton's case, it does seem to be true: despite his evident popularity and his work being enshrined in school curricula, he attracts fewer essays than either Carey or Malouf, and those there are, are often attacks on his representations of gender, complaints about lack of attention to Aborigines, or laments about his supposedly conservative Christian outlook. *Tim Winton: Critical Essays*, edited by Lyn McCredden and Nathanael O'Reilly, argues for complexity ('ambivalence' is a common term) and even radical questioning behind the facade of easy-going Aussie norms and romantic stories. The limitation of this is that the familiar themes (realism, masculinity, spirituality, settler colonialism) are again rehearsed. However, most of the chapters provide clear and useful readings of the main texts and a few give interesting extensions to existing critical opinion. Bill Ashcroft ('Water', pp. 16–48) folds Winton into his own interests in *Heimat* and the utopian sublime via a run-through of archetypes (passage to different states of being: epiphany, dream, death, rebirth). Fiona Morrison (' "Bursting with Voice and Doubleness": Vernacular Presence and Visions of Inclusiveness in Tim Winton's *Cloudstreet*', pp. 49–74) makes a good case for the innovative complexity of narration and vernacular idiom. She values the novel's comic mode over its pastoral elegy and emphasizes the centrality of class. In 'Winton's Spectralities or What Haunts *Cloudstreet*?' (pp. 75–95) Michael Griffiths (aided by Derrida) uses the novel's ghosts and some more direct references to Aborigines to show that the author has not ignored the dark colonial past, but echoes Western Australian history so that its haunting of the story's present displays the originary unsettlement of the 'inheritance' in both the novel and settler colonialism, even if it does not envisage Aboriginal land rights. Hannah Schürholz's ' "Over the Cliff and into the Water": Love, Death and Confession in Tim Winton's Fiction' (pp. 96–121) notes that Winton's women tend to suffer self-harm, 'transience and ferocity', and death. Male insecurities (expressed as confessions) are vented or resolved on the bodies of female partners, represented as ambiguous, unknowable others. One foray into statistics and book history (Per Henningsgaard, 'The Editing and Publishing of Tim Winton in the United States', pp. 122–60) uncovers one point of interest: that later American editions which reset all of the novels do not alter Winton's Australian idioms. The point is left hanging, but a bit of historical context would show how Keneally and Carey, film and tourist promotions had prepared the way for such an unusual US tolerance of the foreign. There's some interesting commentary on epigraphs and intertextual debts and some useful US sales figures. Editors often have to take what they can get from contributors, and there are some gaps in this collection: nothing on Winton's two plays or on *An Open Swimmer* or *In the Winter Dark*, and only passing mention of *The Riders*. Nathanael O'Reilly makes good the general emphasis on *Cloudstreet* and *Breath* in 'From Father to Son: Fatherhood and Father–son Relationships in *Scission*' (pp. 161–82), noting the mutual miscommunications founded on feelings of disappointment about children and fear/hero-worship of parents and the search for intimacy and alternative masculinities. Tanya Dalziell covers 'Writing Childhood in Tim Winton's Fiction' (pp. 183–98), reading against a general view of children's literature a story from *Scission*, *Lockie Leonard, Human Torpedo*, and, briefly, the protagonists in *That Eye, The Sky*, and *Breath*. In 'The Cycle of Love and Loss: Melancholic Masculinity in *The Turning*' (pp. 199–220), Bridget Grogan tracks the workings of Winton's sequence of stories to show how 'loss is inherent in character formation' but fragmentation from grief is held in check by 'the cohesive force of love' (pp. 206–7), concluding with a reading of the book's citation of 'Ash Wednesday'. Sissy Helff ('Transcultural Winton: Mnemonic Landscapes of Australia', pp. 221–40) begins with Ricoeur's call for 'translation, exchange of memories and forgiveness' as a way out of Cold War and genocidal hostilities. Winton's popular side (the beach, colourful landscapes) masks a more serious 'oscillation between various temporalities connecting distinct local histories and cross-cultural memories' (p. 223). Romantic Australia is cross-cut with images of industrial modernity and globalization, as in *The Shallows*, in which Queenie is 'the key to a transcultural solidarity that reaches far beyond any given notion of multiculturalism' (p. 229). *The Turning* relies on 'chains of memory' in its structuring and content. Brigid Rooney takes us 'From the Sublime to the Uncanny in Tim Winton's *Breath*' (pp. 221–40). She argues that 'Winton's characters often find themselves unable to resolve or banish the oppositions that divide their world; they can only ward them off or simply survive.' This ambivalence stems from both the author's early experience of Christianity and 'the rootlessness of settler-colonial modernity' (pp. 243–4) and is reflected in the shuttling between sublime surfing and domestic interiors, foreground and background, that produces uncanny repetitions and interruptions, where 'hard work and humble service to what is left of family' sit alongside 'a troubling sense of fatalism' (p. 259). The monotony of repetition, suffocation of the female, and worldly struggle after the sublime are brought together in the most inspiring chapter, Nick Birns's reading of risk in *Breath* sees it as tied to a neoliberal economics that strips bare the prelapsarian idyll, the sublime romance of surfing, sexual adventure, and individual autonomy ('A Not Completely Pointless Beauty: *Breath*, Exceptionality and Neoliberalism', pp. 263–83). A little overreaching but nonetheless interesting as a more nuanced proposition is Hou Fei's connection between *Breath* and the period of change tied with Australia's involvement in Vietnam ('Extreme Games, Hegemony and Narration: An Interpretation of Tim Winton's *Breath*', pp. 283–305), and editor McCredden rounds off the collection with ' "Intolerable Significance": Tim Winton's *Eyrie*" (pp. 306–29). She sees family as a core value in Winton but goes on to consider 'the ability or failure of signs'—of fiction, of art—in his latest work. Kristeva is invoked to point to a reduction to 'intolerable *insignificance* the loss of faith in meaning making and ontological power' (p. 309) and to the novel's play with signs (Scrabble, threatening letters) to posit a 'theology' of humble improvisations of meaning in the face of abject instability.

Shirley Hazzard garners well-deserved attention in a new volume edited by Brigitta Olubas. Like Winton, Hazzard is a successful writer who remains an under-investigated scholarly resource. The opening section of Olubas's *Shirley Hazzard* considers the transition from early works of short fiction to later novels. John Frow identifies *The Evening of the Holiday* as something of a threshold between early short stories and the mature novels, beginning with *The Bay of Noon*, giving an intricate close reading of the temporality of the early work ('Future Anterior: The Evening of the Holiday', pp. 3–11). Fiona Morrison supports Frow's views and goes further, seeing *The Evening of the Holiday* as placing Hazzard amongst poetic pastoral elegists like Robert Lowell and Elizabeth Bishop even as her use of narrative mode suggests a continuity with British novelists like Graham Greene and E.M. Forster (' "This Intricate Lasting Nature": Passage, Pastoral Elegy and the Pedagogy of Loss in *The Evening of a Holiday*', pp. 13–23). Morrison also finds intriguing structural connections with Keats and charts matrilineal inheritance in the text's complex play with aunt-figures. *Shirley Hazzard* devotes two sections of two to three essays each to the major mid-career works of the author—*The Bay of Noon* and *The Transit of Venus*. Lucy Dougan continues the penchant for contextualizing Hazzard through her intertexts and contemporaries, this time in film ('Another Journey to Italy: The Bay of Noon', pp. 27–40). Dougan argues that *The Bay of Noon* [1970] could not escape resonating with Roberto Rossellini's by then canonical *Journey to Italy* [1953]. Intertexts show that the fascist past of Italy must be grappled with, even in a contemporary celebration of its cultural contribution. Thus,

'Hazzard links the long tradition of intertextual exchange and formal transposition in the art romance to a discourse of cultural urgent recovery and rescue' (p. 31). Brigid Rooney continues the emphasis on formal and narratological concerns, building on Olubas's 2012 monograph with a reading of *The Bay of Noon*'s proleptic qualities—qualities that no doubt accrue in *The Transit of Venus* ('"No-One Had Thought of Looking Close to Home": Reading the Province in *The Bay of Noon*', pp. 41–53). Sharon Ouditt remains with regional space: thickly contextualizing it and its place in Hazzard's imaginary ('"Naples Is a Leap": Time, Space and Consciousness in Shirley Hazzard's Naples', pp. 55–61). Gail Jones and Robert Dixon take on *The Transit of Venus*, each with virtuosic, speculative essays. Jones stages a panoply of generic, stylistic, and formal concerns in Hazzard's celebrated novel, limning interiority, Hazzard's modernism (or refusal thereof) and her attachment to the antique, prolepsis (once more), and how they reflect a concern with vision ('Glasses and Speculations: On Hazzard's Transits', pp. 65–76). Dixon also identifies prolepsis as a central formal quality, but his crucial move is to insist on the technique's 'forensic ethical intelligence' (p. 81) in Hazzard's hands ('Returning to the Scene of the Crime: On Re-reading *The Transit of Venus*', pp. 79–93). *The Great Fire* (despite its Miles Franklin Award) does not have a doubled section of its own like *The Transit of Venus* and *The Bay of Noon*. Instead, Claire Seiler's 'The Mid-Century Method of *The Great Fire*' (pp. 97–110) is grouped with Nicholas Birns's 'Does Idealism Preclude Heroism? Shirley Hazzard's United Nations Writings' (pp. 111–20). Seiler positions *The Great Fire* as a strange instance of late style (in Said's sense). Hazzard's final novel (the novelist, still living, has designated it as such) remains concerned with the immediate post-Second World War moment. With such a long-standing focus and centred on a love story unironically narrated, Seiler positions the novel as one that 'performs the kind of benign artistic lateness over which Said passes' (p. 98). Birns's essay claims Hazzard's satirical take on the UN is an idealistic embrace of that organization's cosmopolitan project, one that unexpectedly reflects her identity as an Australian writer who emerges from the end of older imperialisms into the new liberal transnational order. Olubas's book closes with two biographical investigations, one heavily researched, the other drawn from personal reflection. In 'The Transit of Shirley Hazzard' (pp. 123–36), Jan McGuinness draws on interviews with Hazzard and numerous acquaintances to construct a portrait of the writer that sheds light on repeated settings and concerns in her fiction from maternal neurosis in Sydney to vivid recollections of Hiroshima. Martin Stannard's 'Meeting Shirley Hazzard' (pp. 137–43) is a sensitive portrayal of Hazzard and her husband Francis Steegmuller drawn from a meeting in the early 1990s when Stannard was researching Hazzard's friend, British writer Muriel Spark.

If Australian literary figures are under-studied, we might expect popular genre writers to be neglected by scholars also. Nonetheless, we find a book-length study of Australian-born science fiction writer Greg Egan in which his nationality is irrelevant. Instead, it is his place in 'hard SF'—a subgenre that deals in plausible elaborations of physics and the other hard sciences—that matters most. Author Karen Burnham, in *Greg Egan*, says that 'the precision of science has always been an integral part of Egan's worldview' (p. 22).

Burnham is a NASA electrical engineer. She eschews biography in favour of a survey of works according to genre and devotes chapter 4 to assessing the scientific accuracy of Egan's plot devices. However, Burnham often aims at establishing the kind of cohesive world-view one might find in a living subject rather than the contradictory trajectory that can make up a career or oeuvre. This is certainly true of the final chapter, on Egan's relation to the culture wars of the 1990s. The writer's status as an outsider to literary criticism is what makes Burnham's *Greg Egan* fresh and intriguing, even as it is limited by its concern with the empirical.

Like the 2012 conference on Hazzard that led to Olubas's book, the 2012 Association for the Study of Australia in Asia conference, held in India, revisited Patrick White, and generated *Patrick White Centenary: The Legacy of a Prodigal Son*, edited by Cynthia vanden Driesen and Bill Ashcroft. The book is divided into thematic sections. The first, 'Revaluations', is framed by a personal recollection by John Barnes that extends to an overview of White's career ('Australia's Prodigal Son', pp. 2–22). Barnes recalls meeting a frail White when the latter spoke at La Trobe University in the 1980s, complaining that academics seemed only to teach *Voss*. Barnes goes on to distinguish White from such predecessors and contemporaries as Henry Handel Richardson, Martin Boyd, and Christina Stead. White's thematization of Australian history, Barnes contends, is unique because he departs from the form of the historical novel. Bill Ashcroft situates White in theoretical and postcolonial terms ('Horizons of Hope', pp. 22–42). Ashcroft notes that White entered the Australian literary scene when the country was experiencing a resurgence of nationalist valuation of its literature (signalled by the first chair in Australian literature being founded at Sydney University). Yet White's influence seems to have waned after his death even as the study of Australian literature has grown. Ashcroft draws on Foucault's notion of heterotopia and Ernst Bloch's idea of *Heimat* to relate White and homeliness in a similarly paradoxical way, arguing that the acceptance of not being at home is itself the horizon of possibility for a potentially utopian homeliness. Lyn McCredden ('"Splintering and Coalescing": Language and the Sacred in Patrick White's Novels', pp. 43–62) draws on Bataille and Levinas to interrogate the degree to which White's writing—particularly in *The Solid Mandala* and *Riders in the Chariot*—thematizes the limits of language in relation to the sacred. Bridget Grogan continues the section on 'Revaluations' with a critical appraisal of the depiction of corporeality in White's novels, animated by Julia Kristeva's ideas ('Corporeality, Abjection and the Role of Laura Trevelyan in *Voss*', pp. 63–81). Grogan generalizes her account with reference to Elizabeth Hunter in *Eye of the Storm* and Ellen Roxburgh in *A Fringe of Leaves*. John McLaren argues that, while White and his characters are able to escape geographical boundaries, gender remains a solid frame in much of his work ('Patrick White: Crossing the Boundaries', pp. 83–97). Nathanael O'Reilly critiques lingering assumptions that White's novels are anti-suburban, suggesting instead a deep ambivalence about this under-appreciated setting in Australian literature ('The Myth of Patrick White's Anti-Suburbanism', pp. 98–109). O'Reilly's essay expands on his earlier work on the topic by focusing on *Riders in the Chariot*. Satendra Nandan's essay, 'Patrick White: The Quest of the Artist', ties White's vision of artistic inspiration to suffering (pp. 110–24). Pavithra Narayanan's 'Patrick White and Australia: Perspective of an Outsider' connects White's relation to Australia to his activism (pp. 125–40). Like Grogan, Jessica White—who happens to be a relation of the author—foregrounds the role of the body in his fiction ('Inscribing Landscape in Patrick White's Novels', pp. 141–50). Skin and hands, for example, are shown to weather in keeping with a profoundly gradual process of becoming Australian.

The second part of *Patrick White Centenary* is dedicated to 'Genre'. May-Brit Akerholt's '"A Glorious, Terrible Life": The Dual Image in Patrick White's Dramatic Language' (pp. 152–63) reflects on the role of show-specific choices developed from White's language in plays including *The Cheery Soul*, *The Night on Bald Mountain*, and *The Ham Funeral*. Greg Battye looks at portraits and technically reproduced images of White, offering valuable insights into White's friendships with William Yang and Brett Whiteley ('Looking at Patrick White Looking: Portraits in Pain and on Film', pp. 164–80). Sissy Helff draws on Linda Hutcheon's sense of adaptation as innovative in order to show the specificity of one cinematic version of a White novel ('Patrick White-Lite: Fred Schepisi's Filmic Adaptation of *The Eye of the Storm*', pp. 181–95). Glen Phillips closes the section on genre with an intriguing connection: 'The Novelist as Occasional Poet: Patrick White and Katharine Susannah Prichard' (pp. 196–207). As well as reflecting more widely on the role poetry has in the career of novelists, Phillips detects in the poetry of both writers Georgian tendencies, reminding us that these eclipsed such modernist experiments as Imagism in their time.

The third part of vanden Driesen and Ashcroft's book focuses on individual works, though not all the essays are analytic. Indeed, the section opens with an essay by novelist Meira Chand, 'In the Shadow of Patrick White' (pp. 210–21), in which she charts the writing of her historical novel *Brave Sisters* against her reading and interpretation of *A Fringe of Leaves*. Antonella Riem follows with a more conventional essay that nonetheless proceeds from unexpected sources: 'The Spirit of the Creative Word in Patrick White's *Voss*' (pp. 222–40) charts the relation between indigenous and non-indigenous figures through Riane Eisler's *dominator* and *partnership* understanding of cultural paradigms. Another contribution on *Voss* follows from Harish Mehta, who seeks to show how the novel's subversion of the benign affective status of its white characters offers an alternative version of Australian history (' "Violent" Aboriginals and "Benign" White Men', pp. 241–56). Treatment of indigeneity in White most forcefully comes to the fore with Jeanine Leane's 'White's Tribe: Patrick White's Representation of the Australian Aborigine in *A Fringe of Leaves*' (pp. 257–67). For Leane, White's narration moves the novel's protagonist Ellen (and by implication the white reader who identifies with her) from a stereotypical apperception of the savagery of 'the tribe' to a 'transformed consciousness of themselves and where they belong' (p. 266). Nonetheless, Leane notes that this is hardly what Veronica Brady or vanden Driesen have found in the text but instead is an example of white Australian literature's project to normalize white settlement through an imaginary vested in appropriation (p. 257). Elizabeth Webby and Margaret Harris contribute an intriguing and detailed reflection on childhood in an early novel and the posthumously published *The Hanging Garden*, appearing in 2012 in part because of the pair's research grant ('Patrick White's Children: Juvenile Portraits in *Happy Valley* and *The Hanging Garden*', pp. 269–79). Alastair Niven continues with *The Hanging Garden*, suggesting that it is less profitable to think of the text as unfinished than is commonly the case ('*The Hanging Garden*', pp. 280–90). Instead, 'White, whilst realising that it needed major editorial attention, had achieved what he wanted to do with his story' (p. 289). Brian Kiernan nicely rounds out the section with an intriguing thought experiment about the potential reception of White by younger Australia scholars more familiar with Anglo-American New Criticism or Continental theory than with White's earlier work ('Patrick White: Twyborn Moments of Grace', pp. 291–9). *The Twyborn Affair* deploys 'indeterminacy of signifiers, linguistic and sexual, and the indeterminacy of gender itself' to produce a subversive strategy that relies on both proto-postmodernist concerns and a knowledge of the 'old fashioned' canonical (pp. 293, 298). Kiernan closes by noting that the White canon can inspire readings either of the old-fashioned novelist of the *Bildungsroman* and historical novel, or of the self-conscious postmodern writer.

Part IV of the White collection focuses on 'Comparative Studies'. Isabel Alonso-Breto takes issue with Debjani Ganguly's caveats about world literature and reads White's earliest story alongside a novel by a Sri Lankan ('The Shift from Commonwealth to Postcolonial Literatures: Patrick White's "The Twitching Colonel" and Manuka Wijesinghe's *Theravada Man*', pp. 302–18). Gusharan Aurora attempts to connect White's 'religious vision' to traditions beyond the Judaeo-theistic ('The Unity of Being-Synergies between White's Mystic Vision and the Indian Religio-Spiritual Tradition', pp. 319–38). Similarly, Ishmeet Kaur sets up echoes of Sikh religious tradition in White's work ('Establishing a Connection: Resonances in *Guru Granth Sahib* and Works of Patrick White', pp. 339–51). Mark Williams compares White with several New Zealand writers, primarily James K. Baxter and Bill Pearson, on the basis of their depiction of indigenous peoples ('Patrick White and James K. Baxter: Public Intellectuals or Suburban Jeremiahs', pp. 354–67). Julie Mehta focuses on the abject body to compare Alf Dubbo with David Malouf's Gemmy and Velutha in Roy's *The God of Small Things* ('Smelly Martyrs: Patrick White's Dubbo Ushers in Roy's Velutha and Malouf's Gemmy', pp. 368–81).

Part V of this extensive publication is devoted to 'Socio-Political Issues'. It opens with the conference's plenary address by the politician Fred Chaney, a key player in reconciliation politics for a decade or more. Chaney's overview of 'Australia and Its First Peoples' (pp. 384–99) was no doubt intended to cater for mixed levels of expertise, and relates to Patrick White 'only in passing'. Anne de Soyza's 'Aboriginal Progress in the Native Title Era: Truth and Substantive Equality in *Terra Australis*' (pp. 400–12) does link to White, though it is mainly an overview of the process that errs on the side of remedying disadvantage in the vein of Noel Pearson and anthropologist Peter Sutton. Kieran Dolin brings the no doubt necessary legal surveys back to the literary, situating White (following Russell West-Pavlov) in post-Mabo social space and connecting him to Kim Scott's texts, particularly *That Deadman Dance* ('Rewriting Australia's Foundation Narrative: White, Scott and the

Mabo Case', pp. 413–28). Vicki Grieves situates the relation between indigeneity and settler colonialism in even more poignant and particular terms, exposing the history of white male exploitation of indigenous women on the White property 'Belltrees' ('Patrick White, "Belltrees" and the "Station Complex": Some Reflections', pp. 429–42). Keith Truscott connects White, Australia after Mabo, and writers such as Kim Scott through an elemental interpretation of indigenous knowledge ('*Mabo*—Twenty Years On: An Indigenous Perspective', pp. 443–57). Jane Stafford contributes an analysis of the Māori poet Robert Sullivan ('This Poem is a Sea Anchor': Robert Sullivan's Anchor', pp. 458–69). Stephen Alomes reflects on White's legacy and the failure of Australian republicanism ('Flaws in the Glass: Why Australia Did Not Become a Republic...After Patrick White', pp. 470–85). Ameer Ali closes the collection with a consideration of attitudes towards Muslims in Australia, briefly linking this history with Patrick White's account of Australian xenophobia ('Negotiating "Otherness": The Muslim Community in Australia', pp. 486–95).

Marion May Campbell's book *Poetic Revolutionaries: Intertextuality and Subversion* adds to the loose trend in 2014 of reassessing critical orthodoxies. Her concern is to connect questions of avant-garde metafictive, intertextual, and transtextual writing and criticism to Australian literature. Campbell unravels a genealogy linking the *Tel Quel* critics (Derrida, Sollers, Irigaray, etc.) to an eccentric arrangement of post-1980 Australian writers (along with some French and British ones). Chief among these are Kathleen Mary Fallon and Kim Scott. Given that Campbell's book is so concerned with French-inflected experimentation, it is unsurprising that Brian Castro also features. While such a broad reconfiguring of Australian literature should be welcomed, Campbell's omissions ring loudly. For instance, Scott's more humble concern with those 'most local histories' is largely ignored in favour of his trans-meta-intertextualist work. Setting out to prove Fredric Jameson wrong about pastiche and its apolitical nature, Campbell sets up pastiche as something of an end in itself and in doing so perhaps inflates its case. Nonetheless it is an entertaining argument and merits attention.

Owing more to an older-style of literary and feminist work, Mandy Treagus's *Empire Girls: The Colonial Heroine Comes of Age* continues the Victorian studies focus of work over recent years from Adelaide University and echoes the emphasis on women's writing in *Changing the Victorian Subject* (see below), to which Treagus also contributes. Treagus takes the *Bildungsroman* as her particular focus, asking how gender modulates the form, then how it alters when transported to the colonies and to what extent it carries with it structures of empire and patriarchy. Treagus suggests that Henry Handel Richardson's English context has not been as well explored as her European intellectual connections, and echoes other work on white women displaced under colonialism in tracking contradictions and a shared 'ambivalence of voice' (p. 6). Richardson's *The Getting of Wisdom* carries over Victorian attitudes of femininity to an Edwardian colonial girls' school, placing them in conflict with ideas about the New Woman. The author was placed at the edge of British literary society and beyond the bounds of Australian cultural nationalism, and was read in relation to Zola's discomforting realism, though she is able to allow her heroine an open future while still depicting the constraints on her. Treagus seeks to show that HHR's marginal position as a 'proto-modernist' expatriate colonial gave her work a subversive generic edge, but she allows 'ambivalence' to water down definite conclusions. The book's declared focus on the *Bildungsroman* suggests a formalist/structuralist framework that the largely thematic-discursive explication cannot throw more than a diffuse light on, though the argument that HHR was countering the 'sexology' of her day is of interest.

Robert Dixon renews his interest in Alex Miller's work with a monograph, *Alex Miller: The Ruin of Time*, complementing an edited collection of 2012. Dixon insists on Miller's 'high literary seriousness' (p. xviii) and constructs a theory of history and its spatialization. He sees Miller as providing an Australian equivalent to a W.G. Sebald in their shared relation to Benjamin's vision of entropy and ruin. This manifests in Miller's concern with the alienation of the migrant artist, the culpability that the Western subject feels owing to historical genocides, and its Australian localization as the 'failed project of the pastoral settlement in Australia' (pp. 102–3). As with the book on Hazzard, Dixon's scholarly analysis goes some way to build an adequate critical reception of a 'quiet achiever' in Australian fiction.

Drawing on nearly ten years with the Melbourne Theatre Company amidst much other industry experience, Julian Meyrick aims to identify strategies for fostering Australian drama in his Platform Papers essay for drama publisher Currency Press. In *The Retreat of Our National Drama*, Meyrick gives a brief account of Australian theatre history from the late nineteenth century to the emergence of a viable home-grown theatre in the 1970s New Wave. While Meyrick is keen to show via statistics and anecdote that Australian theatre remained commercially viable, he also sees it as disproportionately dominated by classic and recent international adaptations. Although he sees a place for such adaptations, he points to an 'unconscious industry agenda' that refuses to let viable Australian-written plays move from small to large companies (pp. 70–1). Lucid and surprisingly entertaining, Meyrick's account will be as intriguing to those outside the industry as it is potentially controversial for those within it.

Perhaps the most striking book of the year is edited by Vanessa Castejon, Anna Cole, Oliver Haag, and Karen Hughes. *Ngapartji Ngapartji: In Turn in Turn: Ego-Histoire, Europe and Indigenous Australia* takes its title from the Ananga word for mutual reciprocity (p. 9). It brings together ethnographers and historians from indigenous and settler Australian backgrounds as well as from across Europe to address the question of why European scholars of indigenous studies 'are committed to a field so geographically removed from Europe', asking 'could the distance between Europe and Australia also be productive?' (p. 8). Aware of (even self-conscious about) European scholars being accused of exoticization, the editors have invoked Pierre Nora's rubric of *ego-histoire*, which seeks to combine 'a personal history, a broader social history and historiographical reflection' to, in Nora's words, ' "set down one's own story [*histoire*] as one would write someone else's; to try to apply to oneself... the same cool, encompassing and explanatory gaze that one so often directs towards others" ' (p. 22). Bruce Pascoe provides a short preface which pithily warns us:

'Winners write history…but colonists…most often write an excuse' (p. xv). Victoria Greaves describes growing up in northern-central New South Wales as an experience of (re)discovery of her aboriginality, shaped in relation to such key contemporary events as the Freedom Rides ('Ngarranga Barrangang: Self and History, a Contemporary Aboriginal Journey', pp. 25–40). Some stories recall the mission experience of the Stolen Generations, as in Bill Edwards's recollections of Ernabella and beyond ('A Personal Journey with Anangu History', pp. 41–60). Stephen Muecke reflects on the 'Gardiya' or white outsider labelled by a group into which the researcher is partly accepted ('Turning into a Gardiya', pp. 259–70). Contemporary Aboriginal painter Julie Dowling's painting of Noongar hero Yagan enters the frame in Jan Idle's reflection on being a *wadjela* or white person in the south-west of Western Australia ('Yagan, Mrs Dance and Whiteness', pp. 109–25). Jeanine Leane's 'Home Talk' deals with her relationship with being raised by her aunties (pp. 211–25). Yet, while it is rightly the dominant theme, the collection is not only concerned with indigeneity: diaspora comes into the mix as well, with John Docker's account of his research into his own heritage. He connects settler colonial histories in Palestine and questions of the history of partition in South Asia with his own experience as a Jewish Australian (or, 'non-Australian Australian', as he puts it) growing up in Bondi ('Genealogy and Derangement', pp. 173–88). Nora's indirect contribution to indigenous studies produces remarkable reflections though, for better or for worse, it seems unlikely to completely change the field or how it is examined.

(b) Book Chapters
Changing the Victorian Subject, edited by Maggie Tonkin et al., crosses British negotiations of being 'Victorian' with race, gender, and nation concerns at the colonial margins. They join the trend away from narrow cultural nationalism to transnational approaches to Australian literature combined with the 'proximate reading' that Ken Gelder proposes as a complement to 'distant reading'. Amanda Nettlebeck ('Queen Victoria's Aboriginal subjects', pp. 21–35) outlines the 1837 report of the British House of Commons Select Committee on Aboriginal Tribes legislating Crown protection for Aboriginal subjects, relating it to white colonial resistance and the lack of treaty with indigenous Australians, reading a Western Australian trial of frontier murder as a case study. Sharon Crozier-De Rosa ('Identifying with the Frontier: Federation New Woman, Nation and Empire', pp. 37–58) shows how Catherine Martin's novel *An Australian Girl* refused traditional Victorian female domesticity and made both the bush and nation-building places where the New Woman could play an active role. The book contrasts with Francis Adams's popularizing of the Australian Bushman in England and disturbs overly fixed notions of the Australian frontier, blending colonial aspirations to nationhood with mixed views on Aborigines and positive ones about multicultural immigration. Critics complained of Martin's introducing serious matter to the romance form, with British reviewers approving of the 'Girl' and colonial ones favouring the 'Australian'. Margaret Allen also deals with a South Australian writer, showing

how *Kooroona* [1871] contested the image of that state as a liberal home for dissenting Protestants and enlightened in its treatment of Aborigines ('A "Tigress" in the Paradise of Dissent', pp. 59–81). 'Maud Jean Franc' (Matilda Jane Evans) propagated these foundation myths in her novels but 'Iota' (Mrs Mary Meredith), who lived in the mining towns of Moonta and Burra with her surgeon husband, returned to England to write *Kooroona* as a 'high church' critique of lower-class Protestant money-grubbing and of the poor treatment of Aborigines (who unusually are all given indigenous names). Rosemary Moore turns to a better-known figure in considering 'The Making of Barbara Baynton' (pp. 83–103). Acknowledging the 'difficult' aspects of Baynton's work (her fractured narratives plus her challenge to the masculinist bush myth), Moore turns to Freud and biographical uncertainties to account for Baynton's obscuring symbolism and bleak view of human animality. *Human Toll* [1907] reflects anxieties about illegitimacy and fears of male lust. Biblical guilts and trials intersect with infanticide, incest, adultery, and violence, and 'women find in hysterical conversion and the language of the bodily symptom the means of making their feelings known', but reviewers, though impressed, were puzzled (p. 90). *Bush Studies* had a more favourable reception (in Britain more than in Australia) though it deploys the same themes, investing them with the same powerful hysterical indirection. A more popular writer was Mary Fortune, whose forty or so works, mostly serialized and many under pseudonyms, provided a panorama of colonial society, including 'the way women experienced the transition from immigrant to colonist' (p. 106) on the Victorian goldfields (Megan Brown, 'A Literary Fortune', pp. 105–22). Fortune's Victorian woman had to be adaptable, tough-minded, and willing to dispense with old-world convention, as Fortune herself was in carving out a professional writing career. The Australian component of this collection ends with Ailise Bulfin's 'Guy Boothby's "Bid for Fortune": Constructing an Anglo-Australian Colonial Identity for the *Fin-de-Siècle* London Literary Marketplace' (pp. 151–76). Boothby's migration to England and celebrity status there well illustrate claims for the transnational nature of both Australian and Victorian literature. Bulfin places him with Rider Haggard and Kipling as people who use a colonial identity to give them an edge in the metropolitan publishing world. She notes that Boothby's display of cosmopolitan knowledge did not preclude egregious colonial racial stereotypes, and shows his championing of the colonial 'coming man' as opposed to the English gentleman. The collection as a whole will not radically change our view of colonial Australian or general Victorian literature, but it provides interesting embroideries around the edges of the cloths we know.

Since 2014 was on the threshold of the centenary of the event ostensibly consolidating settler Australian national identity—Gallipoli—it is unsurprising that some mention of this appears in Australian literary criticism. We can probably expect more as well. Several articles on Australian First World War representation appear in *The Great War in Post-Memory Literature and Film*, edited by Martin Löschnigg and Marzena Sokołowska-Paryż. Christina Spittel suggests that the post-1970 increase in novels about the war reflects the thick atmosphere of the Vietnam War and its objectors ('Nostalgia for the Nation? The First World War in Australian Novels of the 1970s and 1980s', pp. 255–72). Spittel surveys novels by Thomas Keneally, Roger McDonald, David Malouf, Gwen Kelly, and Geoff Page that come in the wake of histories by Bill Gammage and Patsy Adam-Smith. She also touches on various ANZAC novels by ANZACs themselves, recovered in the 1970s and 1980s from the archives. Claire Rhoden's chapter follows, with a consideration of more recent writing ('Even More Australian: Australian Great War Novels in the Twentieth Century', pp. 273–88)—Peter Yeldham's *Barbed Wire and Roses*, Brenda Walker's *Wing of Night*, and Chris Womersley's *Bereft*.

In the Dramaturgies series issued by Peter Lang, Birgit Däwes and Marc Maufort have edited *Enacting Nature: Ecocritical Perspectives on Indigenous Performance*. The collection, though it includes only one clearly identified indigenous contributor, mostly features scholars and practitioners with a solid history of working with indigenous theatre groups and overtly intends to break down idealized constructions (p. 12), although an insufficiently examined subscription to 'ecospirituality' (p. 14) could well permit the reintroduction of old distortions. The editors' introduction looks for 'interculturally sensitive understandings of specific places' (p. 11) in theatre as a pathway towards ethical and sustainable relationships with the environment. Apart from the US, Canadian, and New Zealand chapters, Australia is represented by Maryrose Casey ('Serving the Living Land. Place and Belonging in Australian Aboriginal Drama', pp. 151–64) and Rachael Swain ('Dance, History and Country: An Uneasy Ecology in Australia', pp. 165–82). Casey reads Wesley Enoch's *The Story of the Miracles at Cookie's Table* and *Black Medea* and David Milroy's *Windmill Baby* to discover what minority writing can bring to the national cultural table (p. 152). She points to Aboriginal writing treating the natural world as an active participant in human drama rather than a passive backdrop to it, and emphasizes 'connection through family to country' (p. 156) as a distinctive indigenous characteristic that comes out in Enoch's figuring of wind and fire as cleansing forces in post-contact disruptions (as in mining) of reciprocal ties between humans and country. Swain takes on a more temporal framework in her focus on how Western history intrudes into indigenous 'dreaming' consciousness (p. 168). Her fascinating composition of multi-modal theatre in dialogue with indigenous peoples in northern Australia and for local audiences mixes historical events and legendary versions of them recorded in dance in a transformation of the tribal 'clever man' role so that theatre might exorcize past trauma. Not exactly an ecocritical project, the account of the plays is compelling, and 'paying attention to country' is clearly an important part of the story. This idea is taken up by Marc Maufort in his comparative study ('Performing the Spirit of the Earth', pp. 235–54), which includes discussion of Andrea James's *Yanagai! Yanagai!*, a play aimed at refuting the white judge who dismissed the Yorta Yorta land claim on the grounds that history had erased any trace of continuous Aboriginal ties to land. Again, on one level a political play about historical claims is not necessarily engaged in ecocritical questions—and magic realism is not a universal ethical solvent—but, like the other plays mentioned, family, land, history, and dreaming coalesce as a cultural ecology of 'country' that is one's being, expressed in unusual mixed-media and poly-stranded storytelling.

Sascha Morell includes an interesting comparative study, 'Soft Drink, Hard Drink and Literary (Re)production in Flann O'Brien and Frank Moorhouse' (in Murphet, McDonald, and Morell, eds., *Flann O'Brien and Modernism*, pp. 175–94). Though there was no direct link between the writers, both Moorhouse (soft-drink manufacture in *The Electrical Experience*) and O'Brien (Guinness) explore connections between commodity culture, literature, and subject formation—and both 'had a close relationship with alcohol' (p. 186). 'Whereas O'Brien tends to apply the language of labour relations to the production of literary art, Moorhouse generally does the opposite, with [character] McDowell conceiving of his business as a kind of artistry' (p. 176). US Coca Cola salesman Becker stresses the 'everyday' nature of his product and himself, while McDowell and advertising offsider Scribner tout the 'poetry' of local manufacture, suggesting pop art as reflected in the magazine design of Moorhouse's book. McDowell, the 'self-made man', sees himself as a worker, but his real workers are invisible and he imbibes Zane Gray's American culture while asserting Australian identity, suggesting a universal commodification of the individual.

Write in Tune: Contemporary Music in Fiction, edited by Erich Hertz and Jeffrey Roessner, contains 'A Novel Idea for a Soundtrack: Tim Winton's *Dirt Music*' by Tanya Dalziell (pp. 43–54). Dalziell notes that although Winton's central character is fleeing north to avoid 'facing the music' of his misdemeanours and also the music that reminds him of a fatal car accident involving his family, the novel has been supplemented with a CD set, *Dirt Music: Music for a Novel*: one disc a compilation of blues-related tunes, another, symphonic pieces, one—Peter Sculthorpe's—derived from Aboriginal music from the northern setting of the book. Originating in the author's untutored enthusiasm for music, the novel and its companion discs are curiously connected in that for the former (unlike the latest e-books that can include soundtracks) one requires no knowledge of the other, though the CDs clearly refer to the novel. Dalziell brings out the book's use of musical topoi connected to affect and memory, showing us aspects of character, and pointing to 'realms of experience beyond the reach of language' (p. 46). Music (and its copying) also generate a theme of authenticity and 'orchestrate' the representation of loss and mourning. A stimulating reading of a work sometimes dismissed as simple formula fiction.

Tamara S. Wagner sets out the complicated but compelling concept of 'home' in settler colonial worlds, especially those in the Antipodes, where 'portable domesticity' had to overcome or adjust to limits of distance, environment, and culture at the same time as colonial literature touted the promise of a new home. Wagner's compilation of essays, *Domestic Fiction in Colonial Australia and New Zealand*, focuses on how women represented this situation. She provides a historical survey of primary and scholarly writing in her introduction, 'Victorian Domestic Fiction Down Under' (pp. 1–20), noting key differences between Australia and New Zealand, shared patterns of migration (around gold rushes, for example), and the intermediary role of North America in imaginative engagement with the new lands.

After some treatment of British writing about the colonies, we find Grace Moore (' "The Heavens Were on Fire': Incendiarism and the Defence of the

Home', pp. 63–73) reading Trollope's *Harry Heathcote of Gangoil* against Melbourne journalism from the increasingly studied Mary Fortune and a short story by J.S. Borlase. Early settlers (as in Trollope's book) were terrified of bushfire, often ignorant of Aboriginal grassland management, and scared of attack, but bush campfires could represent comfort and conviviality and some bushfires were occasions for male bravado. Householders, however, were apprehensive of fire and of high rates of arson (caused by hostile neighbours, or randomly appearing disaffected bush travellers). Mary Fortune, however, allows a female character to use fire as a tool to liberate herself from her father. Borlase allows her female protagonist a romantic rescue from the flames, but leaves her realistically unable to settle back into domestic peace.

Michelle J. Smith considers ' "The Australian Girl" and the Domestic Ideal in Colonial Women's Fiction' (pp. 75–89), reading standard titles by Rosa Praed, Catherine Martin, Ethel Turner, and Miles Franklin. Smith takes up Praed's praise of the squatter's daughter as a 'natural little gentlewoman' regardless of her wild life by British standards, finding in her *An Australian Heroine* and three other colonial novels by Australian women that if British writers used colonial locations to free their women from marriage, Praed, Catherine Martin, Ethel Turner, and Miles Franklin, while celebrating the virtues of bush independence, proved unable 'to accommodate the bracing figure of the Australian Girl (not the New Woman, but a national icon of health and practical abilities), postulating ambiguous or tragic outcomes at best for heroines who deviate from . . . the domestic ideal' (p. 76). The first two authors place their protagonists in unhappy marriages, while Turner kills off her non-conformist, and Franklin allows hers to escape the role of cheerful peasant drudge into an uncertain future in the 'useless' arts.

Tamara Wagner also looks at Turner's less well-known works, *The Wonder Child*, *That Girl*, and *Fugitives from Fortune*, in 'Fugitive Homes: Multiple Migrations in Ethel Turner's Fiction' (pp. 91–110). She points out that despite the author's nationalist sympathies and critics' common focus on the positive aspects of *Seven Little Australians*, Turner's migrants do not always settle in Australia, or they settle but not entirely happily: children often face hardship and squalor. Turner 'writes back to' the British colonial romance, and engages with US New World visions via Louisa May Alcott, such that 'the resulting triangulation of metropole and settler colony with America becomes a means to articulate anxieties about homemaking at a time of unprecedented transoceanic movement' (p. 92).

If we are familiar with the carefree Bush Girl figure, it is worth being reminded of the mass of religious writing in Victorian times, and bracing Christian temperance is discussed by Susan K. Martin in 'Devout Domesticity and Extreme Evangelicalism: The Unsettled Australian Domestic in Maud Jean Franc' (pp. 111–24). Matilda Jane Evans, under her pseudonym, consolidated free-settler Adelaide's reputation as the (Puritan) 'city of churches' and her work circulated for seventy years across Australia, Britain, and North America, but her books did not always end with Christian marriage, even if they aimed to produce a Christian home-making female subject. Franc's ideal home was marked by aesthetic civility, with a garden, distinct from the frontier emphasis on utility and money; evangelical

conversion results in a heart that is ' "swept, garnished, newly furnished" '
(p. 115), but a passion for temperance reform could make the female
protagonist much less of a genteel domestic angel.

Melissa Purdue concludes the Australian section with a reprise on Praed:
' "That's What Children Are—Nought but Leg-Ropes": Motherhood in Rosa
Praed's *Mrs Tregaskiss*' (pp. 125–33). Against a general *fin-de-siècle* background of promoting motherhood as national duty and brake on unbridled
female emancipation, in the outback 'Praed expressed scepticism about the
existence of the maternal instinct and frustration with the expectation that all
women should want to become mothers' (p. 125). Her work countered novels
of emigration in which single women find marriage and happiness in the
colonies. Raised in England, Clare is too refined for the bush, unhappy with
her husband, and fails to nurture her children, who run wild and mix with
Aborigines. The natural landscape offers space for rebellion against domesticity and indulgence in romantic passion, but also threatens (fire, illness) and
finally punishes (taking the eldest child of the failed mother). Complicating
this is the gift Clare receives via an old squatter's bequest to her daughter—a
kind of consolation for chastened return to being a wife and mother with little
prospect of personal happiness.

Andrew Milner, 'The Sea and Summer: *An Australian Apocalypse*' (in
Canavan and Stanley Robinson, eds., *Green Planets: Ecology and Science
Fiction*, pp. 115–26), surveys the long history of utopian and satirical
dystopian writing based on Australia, from Joseph Hall in 1605 to contemporary writers like Greg Egan. Milner singles out Denis Veira and notes
Marx's vision of non-capitalist space in Australia. Nevil Shute's *On the Beach*
and George Turner's *The Sea and Eternal Summer* are modern examples of
nuclear-destruction and global-warming cautionary tales. These function as
'implicitly utopian warnings' rather than anti-utopian critiques (p. 116).
Turner's output and his best-known novel are described, the novel centring on
social stratification under pressure from global bankruptcy and rising oceans.
Turner inherits the 'island nation' trope of Australian and utopian thinking so
that global corporations are ignored.

In Christopher Conti and James Gourley's collection of papers, *Literature
as Translation / Translation as Literature*, Nicholas Jose pursues his interest in
'Australian Literature as Translation' (pp. 1–15). He tracks material
'translated' from one culture into another (European classics into Australian
texts, Aboriginal stories, work by writers of Chinese ancestry) if not also
across languages, in *The Macquarie PEN Anthology of Australian Literature*
[2009] that he co-edited. He points to writing as an ongoing process of
'imitation and adaptation' and translation as 'an index of incommensurability'
provoking fresh inventions. Some writers given more than passing attention
include Ouyang Yu, Chi Vu, John Shaw Neilson, Bill Neidjie, and Alexis
Wright, plus the hoax poet Ern Malley reborn in Peter Carey's *My Life as a
Fake*. Seeing Australian literature as polymorphous but also as resisting
translation, worldly but on the margins of world literature, might be a kind of
'Damage Control' (the chapter's title) against bland universalizing.

Editor Conti adopts a more specific focus in examining 'Mystical
Translation in Patrick White's *Voss*' (pp. 30–46). Humans translate landscape

and are translated by their experience from the mundane to some kind of transcendence: words communicate their inability to express such translation and thereby point via symbols to the spiritual—negation opens space for 'an exchange of souls' (p. 31). Conti usefully analyses critical reactions to *Voss* (praise for mysticism redeeming suburban materialism, criticism for racism and breaking with realism) and asks, 'Does the riddle of the novel hold the secret to the modern search for meaning or clumsily impose the passion play over it?' (p. 33). His answer accuses postcolonial correctness (manifest in Simon During) of sidetracking attention from the central metaphysical concerns of the novel: 'White's intention...is to redeem the mythopoetic relevance of Aboriginal culture, not fictionalise it away', he claims, citing LeMesurier's poems as 'examples of "mystical translation" that bear the potential for intercultural understanding...implying that the Rainbow Serpent and Christ are masks of the same God' (p. 37). Voss 'translates' the Faust myth into a critique of Romanticism, though mirages in and of the text blur any fixed vision, even as such translations become the medium by which we gain some intimation of the foreign and some new view of the familiar.

In the same collection, Joy Wallace ('Flagging Down the *Flâneuse* in Hazel Smith's *City Poems*', pp. 67–80) considers the 'translation' of Baudelaire's *flâneur* into a more contemporary female figure in London and Sydney, arguing that the tradition carries over 'aspects of modernism that will prove impervious to a feminist exploration of being in the city' (p. 68), but finding in 'Returning the Angles' and poems in *Keys Round Her Tongue* a 'tentative interruption' of the city of Baudelaire and Eliot through reconfigured subject–object relations. The female in the city finds a space neither aristocratic nor sterile; she cannot retreat 'behind an allegorising tendency that transmutes sexually disturbing sights into fantasies of genealogy in which [the writer] figures as either absent husband or father' (p. 72) and recoils. Wallace notes Smith's work on Frank O'Hara and her debts to geographer David Harvey and tracks a journey back into Lithuanian and Jewish origins and self-discovery through the father's life and death.

Comparison of poems by Greek Yannis Ritsos and Australian Greek Gail Holst-Warhaft, in the context of modern reworkings of the Homeric myth of return and the figure of Penelope, shows a common suspicion of happy endings, with Holst-Warhaft's *Penelope's Confession* supporting the turn in classical scholarship wherein the wife assumes a more central and problematized role in the sequence of 'recognition' scenes leading to homecoming. Ritsos attributes both surprise and despair to Penelope, leaving us uncertain of our reading of her and the epic's end. Holst-Warhaft gives us access to Penelope's thoughts, but her moments of memory leave us uncertain of her fidelity and conscious of gaps and inconsistencies in her own and other narratives. Play between modern and ancient versions of the woman points to a feminist anchoring of meaning around personal agency: being faithful to one's body and desire, rather than to official/Homeric record. The violent male revenge for 'property damage' and the hanging of the unfaithful maids, and Homer's acceptance of its probity, are questioned by both the contemporary poet and her Penelope, who reweaves her own odyssey, figuring herself as sailor-siren: Victoria Reuter, 'A Penelopean Return: Desire, Recognition, and *Nostos* in the Poems of Yannis Ritsos and Gail Host-Warhaft' (in Gardner and Murnaghan, eds., *Odyssean Identities in Modern Cultures: The Journey Home*, pp. 89–111).

J.M. Coetzee's corpus remains fundamentally South African, and is taught as such, though he himself has been now enthusiastically adopted by literary circles in Australia, his home since 2002. *Approaches to Teaching Coetzee's Disgrace and Other Works*, edited by Laura Wright, Jane Poyner, and Elleke Boehmer, Boehmer includes a chapter on 'Teaching Coetzee and Australia' (pp. 117–22), exploring 'what it is to teach his Australian work and how that work composes…its Australian context' (p. 117). Boehmer sees him as responding to a masculine mainstream in Australian writing, charts some historical parallels between Australia and South Africa, notes that he no longer addresses racial otherness but concentrates on 'the how rather than the what of his representation' and fluctuates in his 'perfunctory' evocation of Australian space 'as a means of both disconnection and affiliation to his new country' (p. 118). Elizabeth Costello does not alter his 'stripped-down, standardized global English', but there is a more definite sense of Australian location than in the South African novels. Coetzee may shift to a more 'heart-based' art, but continues to wrestle with how writing produces truth, and in *Slow Man* he engages with Australia's literary fascination with the fake and, having 'been involved in rounding up the various standard referents of a colonial dystopia…. [he] discards them as inadequate to embody a true Australian reality' (p. 122).

Marc Maufort's chapter, 'Forging Native Idioms: Canadian and Australasian Performances of Indigeneity in an Age of Globalization' (in Moser and Simonis, eds., *Figuren des Globalen: Weltbezug und Welterzeugung in Literatur, Kunst und Medie*, pp. 703–15), with some mention of Jack Davis, deals with Wesley Enoch's *Black Medea* along with New Zealand and Canadian plays by George Miria and Kevin Loring.

(c) Journals

There are several special themed issues and otherwise a variety of topics here such that organizing articles by theme or author discussed would be confusing and inefficient. Entries are therefore listed under their publications, alphabetically by journal title.

Beginning with a problematic distinction between 'Western' and 'post-colonial' writers, based on the notion that the latter are culturally hybrid whereas the former are not, Stephen Rankin considers how a 'Western' writer might represent the cultural other, using Inez Baranay's novel *The Edge of Bali* and a story by Gerson Poyk, 'Kuta, here my love flickers brightly': 'Crossing into the Cultural Other: A Dialogic Reading Strategy' (*ArielE* 45:i–ii[2014] 79–102). Rankin espouses Todorov's 'dialogic' counterpointing of Spanish and Aztec texts, adding, in an idea derived from Bhabha, that the hybridized colonial margins acquire a wider knowledge of cultures than the colonial centre. Whether Poyk (Indonesian but not Balinese) is any more 'postcolonial' or sympathetically hybridized than Baranay (Australian but with lengthy sojourns in PNG and India), and thus more able to 'dialogue' with Balinese society, or whether we are able to do so more through reading of either text is at least open to question.

Australian Literary Studies 29:iii[2014] features a special issue on 'Reading Communities and the Circulation of Print'. Lydia Wevers expands the idea of literary communities beyond formal book clubs and literary societies in 'Reading Dickens' (*ALS* 29:iii[2014] 1–14). Following her 2010 study of reading on a farm in New Zealand in the nineteenth century, she tracks the assertion of social and racial distinctions through reading the popular novelist. Jon Mee draws from arguments made in science studies and book history to shed light on the Philosophical Society of Australasia and the Useful Book Society, which flourished from 1820 to the early 1830s, in '"A Reading People?": Global Knowledge Networks and Two Australian Societies of the 1820s' (*ALS* 29:iii[2014] 74–86). Julieanne Lamond examines what Franco Moretti has called the 'slaughterhouse of literature'—those texts now unread despite their popularity within their era—by mining the archive of a NSW regional library, in 'Forgotten Books and Local Readers: Popular Fiction at the Turn of the Twentieth Century' (*ALS* 29:iii[2014] 87–100). Patrick Buckridge's 'Rescuing Reading: Strategies for Arresting the Decline of Reading in Western Australian Newspapers between the Wars' (*ALS* 29:iii[2014] 101–15) makes an argument for the advantages of researching supposedly marginal print cultures from regional spaces on the basis of their relative manageability, permitting detailed analysis. The flaw here is that small local datasets often do not map tidily onto larger cultural spaces. Nonetheless, the content of Buckridge's article is highly intriguing. Helen Groth tracks the interest in phonographic libraries—books recorded on phonograph records—from their inventor Thomas Edison to Australian newspaper articles of the 1930s. The issue's eclectic new approaches to book history, while fascinating, risk remaining intriguing curiosities until some broad study can integrate their vignettes into a comprehensive panorama.

Susan K. Martin also offers a fascinating piece of book-historical work. She reads colonial women's diaries to see how categories such as the ordinary and the domestic, class, cultural capital, and reading practices are revealed in 'Tracking Reading in Nineteenth-Century Melbourne Diaries' (*AHR* 56[2014] 27–54). Martin insists on the necessity of close reading, echoing Gayatri Spivak, while supporting its conjunction with 'distant reading'. Martin admits that tiny samples of wider phenomena such as diaries 'may not offer the same depth or breadth of data' as Moretti's large-scale digital humanities, but contends that they 'do offer the grain of reading detail' (p. 29). In the same issue, Robert Clarke and Marguerite Nolan offer a reader response analysis of white middle-class reception of novels themed on reconciliation. While they lump Kim Scott's *Benang* (arguably not at all reconciliation-oriented) with more obvious selection such as *The Secret River* or *Journey to the Stone Country*, they do produce some intriguing perceptions about book club readers and their social attitudes: 'Book Clubs and Reconciliation: A Pilot Study on Book Clubs Reading the "Fictions of Reconciliation"' (*AHR* 56[2014] 121–40). In *AHR* 57[2014], Ruth A. Morgan explores the cultural milieu of climate change in the 1980s—reminding us that this was the cultural moment when scientific apperception of greenhouse thinking was taking off: 'Imagining a Greenhouse Future: Scientific and Literary Depictions of Climate Change in 1980s Australia' (*AHR* 57[2014] 43–60). Morgan relates this to, amongst other reference points, George Turner's novel *The Sea and Summer*.

Alyson Miller, 'Stylised Configurations of Trauma: Faking Identity in Holocaust Memoirs' (*Arcadia* 49:ii[2014] 229–53), compares three falsified Holocaust memoirs, including Helen Demidenko's *The Hand That Signed the Paper*. Such memoirs are defended as parodic in terms that draw from postmodern theorists such as Baudrillard.

Kevin Rabelais's 'George Johnston's "*My Brother Jack* at Fifty"' (*ABR* 363[2014] 46–8) is a reflection on the popular text reveals Johnston's craft—the work of an experienced journalist and skilled storyteller. Rabelais predicts continuing appreciation for the work.

In *Australasian Drama Studies* Paul Davies considers the site-specific theatre of Melbourne, largely with attention to the company TheatreWorks, in 'Dramatic Tales Stir the Suburb: Melbourne's Location Theatre Movement 1979–90' (*ADS* 64[2014] 39–70). David Hicks—the Australian Guantánamo Bay detainee—was something of a cultural obsession for the post-9/11 Australian media until his 2007 release. There have been several plays and a documentary directly dramatizing Hicks's story. Russell Fewster considers the most experimental of these—*Honour Bound*—a dance theatre work, which toured Sydney, Melbourne, and Europe while Hicks was still incarcerated, in 'Staging David Hicks' (*ADS* 65[2014] 12–36). In 'Digital Alchemy: The Posthuman Drama of Adam J.A. Cass's *I Love You, Bro*' (*ADS* 65[2014] 37–52), Richard Jordan reconsiders extant definitions of 'digital performance'. For Jordan, there needn't be a direct use of computer technologies in 'delivery forms', but rather, a play like *I Love You, Bro* can be considered digital performance because of its 'construction of identity within a technoscientific narrative' through the 'gradual unravelling into a posthuman subject' of its protagonist (pp. 38, 52). Anyone who takes on the staging of both *Tristram Shandy* and Manning Clark's *History of Australia* is ambitious. Such a person was Tim Robertson, who, with his partner Don Watson, set out to adapt Clark's multiple volumes into a play in the 1980s. Alison Richards, 'Your History: *Manning Clark's History of Australia* and the End of the New Wave' (*ADS* 65[2014] 177–98), considers the work, the Carlton theatre scene, and national theatre history: '*History* can be seen . . . both as an apotheosis of Australian theatre that began in the 1960s, and as a marker of its end' (p. 179). Finally, *ADS* paid tribute to Geoffrey Milne, who passed away in 2013, by publishing his 'chronicle of some of the major developments' of Australian theatre in the 1980s.

Ihab Hassan presents a virtuosic, slightly grandiose panorama of Australian literature in 'Australia Ascending: In the Mirror of David Malouf' (*AR* 72:ii[2014] 235–44). The superlatives in Hassan's essay are thick on the ground: Les Murray is a 'titan of antipodean poets' (p. 236), Malouf 'has set the pace for writers down under' while being also 'a measure of literary value everywhere' (p. 242). Hassan's essay refreshingly pays attention to Malouf's poetry.

Winton, we noted, is popular but not so frequently addressed in academic criticism. This is also true of John Marsden, best known for his young adult 'Tomorrow' series and for his picture book with famed illustrator Shaun Tan, *The Rabbits*. Theodore Scheckels provides a nuanced reading of the discrepancy between these two invasion narratives in 'The Complex Politics and Rhetoric of John Marsden's "Tomorrow" Series' (*Antipodes* 28:ii[2014] 436–49). Where *The Rabbits* operates as an allegory of settler colonial invasion and genocide, Marsden stages his young adult text through an imagined 'Asian invasion'. In the same issue, Dorothy Simmons argues that myth is a mobile narrative mode and provides justification for a comparison of Julian Assange and Ned Kelly, in 'Our Ned: The Makeup of Myth' (*Antipodes* 28:ii[2014] 416–25). Amit Sarwal argues that 'South Asian diaspora family narratives belong to the genre of Australian family histories' (p. 388) in an essay focusing on writers such as Mena Abdullah: 'Beyond Home and into the World: Family in the Short Stories of the South Asian Diaspora in Australia' (*Antipodes* 28:ii[2014] 379–91). Laetitia Nanquette covers under-studied territory in multicultural Australian literature with her 'Iranian Exilic Poetry in Australia: Reinventing the Third Space' (*Antipodes* 28:ii[2014] 393–403). Focusing on Grânâz Moussavi, Nanquette argues that the novelty of this Melbourne-based poet and filmmaker lies in a recalibration of Bhabha's idea of the Third Space 'to preserve the continuity of the Self through nature and belonging to its unchanging world' (p. 401). Michael Wilding is both critic and object of analysis this year as Don Graham engages with a story of Wilding's from the early 1970s in 'Michael Wilding's Texas Story' (*Antipodes* 28:ii[2014] 426–35). Fiona Duthie explores the generic complexity and a key motif of Christopher Koch's fiction in 'Spies in the Shadows: Intelligence and Secret Agents in the Novels of Christopher Koch' (*Antipodes* 28:ii[2014] 456–67). A North American complement to the interest in Hazzard comes from Christine De Vinne, who compares US and UK editions of *The Great Fire* in 'Branded by Fire: Postcolonial Naming in Shirley Hazzard's *The Great Fire*' (*Antipodes* 28:ii[2014] 289–99). Another article advocating a critically unrepresented writer is John Beston's 'Complexity of Thought and Clarity of Expression: The Poetry of Suzanne Edgar' (*Antipodes* 28:ii[2014] 341–50). Beston's close reading illuminates Edgar's unique prosody. Angshuman Kar wisely fore-grounds his speaking position as 'an educated, privileged, upper-caste Indian' 'who teaches Australian Aboriginal poetry to Indian students' (p. 370) in 'Where To? An Indian Perspective on Australian Aboriginal Poetry in English' (*Antipodes* 28:ii[2014] 369–70). Surveying widely from Oodgeroo to Anita Heiss to Jack Davis to Alf Taylor, Kar foregrounds the 'plural affiliations' of Aboriginal poets. *Antipodes* also includes a note on Patrick White by Rodney Stenning Edgecombe. Edgecombe augments previous perceptions of the connection between *The Eye of the Storm* and Stendhal by noting resonances with Victor Hugo's *Les Travailleurs de la mer*. *The Vivisector* is similarly connected to Goethe's *Sorrows of Young Werther* and also to Wordsworth (*Antipodes* 28:ii[2014] 513–17).

Dolores Herrero revisits well-trodden territory in 'Crossing *The Secret River*: From Victim to Perpetrator of the Silent/Dark Side of the Australian Settlement' (*Atlantis* 36:i[2014] 87–105). On the one hand Herrero agrees with critiques of the novel by people like Melissa Lucaschenko and Fiona Probyn-Rapsey, which admonish its complicity with dispossession resulting from sympathy with the protagonist; on the other, Herrero wants to vindicate the novel for acknowledging genocidal aspects of Australian history.

Xavier Pons discusses Steven Carroll's quartet of 'Glenroy' novels, highlighting their interest in temporal in-betweenness and social exclusion, in '"On the Threshold of Change": Liminality and Marginality in Steven Carroll's Fiction' (*CE&S* 37:i[2014] 11–23).

Laura Singeot takes on a rarely analysed text in 'An Odyssey into the "Black Pacific": A Reassessment of Mudrooroo's *The Undying*' (*CE&S* 37:i[2014] 88–99). Singeot somewhat cryptically goes back to DuBois's identification of a double consciousness in the black diaspora in an effort to move discussion of Australian literature away from binaries of black/white, antipodean/European, and relates Mudrooroo's work to 'a tradition of Atlantic writing' and fluid identity construction as mapped by Gilroy and Glissant. The novel reflects questions about what it means to be black arising from Aboriginal links with the US Black Power Movement, and debates over Mudrooroo's genetic origins. Its multiple intertextualities produce a hybrid poetics that backs the formation of a new trans-tribal and transnational black identity.

John Barnes discusses White's vexed relationship with the Australian academy in 'On Reading and Re-Reading Patrick White' (*CQ* 43:iii[2014] 212–30). It is an illuminating supplement to Barnes's recollection in the centenary edited collection. It combines a rich sifting of White's correspondence with a strong articulation of his initially tepid reception by such scholars, and adds insightful comment on his characters as alter egos and Madame Bovary-type doubles.

Other texts long disregarded and recently coming back into the scholarly limelight are by Antigone Kefala. Catalina Ribas Segura considers 'Language and Bilingualism in Antigone Kefala's *Alexia* (1995) and *The Island* (2002)' (*Coolabah* 13[2014] 118–36), canvassing the theories around multilingualism and the cultural politics of migrants' second-language acquisition. The author argues for Kefala having a 'not quite' English style owing to her knowledge of several languages, but attends more to characters' experience of language differences within the works than to stylistic linguistic analysis.

Foreign Literature Studies | Wai Guo Wen Xue Yan Jiu (*FLS*) an online journal from China, carries a wide range of articles of varying length and sophistication. Australian texts feature fairly regularly and issue 36:i[2014] has 'The Problem of Hospitality in J.M. Coetzee's *The Childhood of Jesus*' by Eun Chull Wang (*FLS* 36:i[2014] 35–44) and 'Disoriented and Lonely Dance: Reading Brian Castro's *Shanghai Dancing*' by Ma Lilli and Chen Baozhu (*FLS* 36:i[2014] 163–6). The next issue contains 'Contextualizing Gambling: Why Critics Maligned Frank Hardy's Works' by Danica Cerce (*FLS* 36:ii[2014] 125–35). It is interesting to see Hardy getting some attention, the argument here being that his use of gambling motifs was an unpalatable attack on capitalism. Most interesting, perhaps, is Wang's use of Derrida to suggest that Coetzee is objecting to any distinction between conditional and unconditional hospitality and promoting a return to an unconditional Platonic ideal.

Deleuze and Guattari, via Jaspir Puar, become an anchor for Ellen Smith's argument about Xavier Herbert in 'White Aborigines' (*Interventions* 16:i[2014] 97–116). Many scholars have found the 1930s a perplexing intersection of advocacy for Aboriginal rights, on the one hand, and support for fascistic state controls on the other. Smith looks at this phenomenon within Herbert and related figures from the *Publicist* such as P.R. Stephensen. Herbert and the anthropologist who most influenced him, A.P. Elkin (who goes unmentioned) understood themselves to be liberals but consorted with Stephensen and Miles, who were far more sympathetic to fascism.

The *Journal of the Association for the Study of Australian Literature* published five issues this year. The first, 'DisLocated Readings: Translation and Transnationalism' (*JASAL* 14:i[2014]), addresses the idea of the transnational with a linguistic focus and an emphasis on European receptions of Australian writing. It is co-edited by Leah Gerber and Rita Wilson. The issue opens with a conversation between Alice Pung and Italian academic Adele D'Arcangelo, '*Unpolished Gem/Gemma Impure*: The Journey from Australia to Italy of Alice Pung's Bestselling Novel' (*JASAL* 14:i[2014] 10 pp.). Pung positions her book in relation to Australian ' "migrant" or "ethnic" ' literatures (her terms) and D'Arcangelo makes readers aware of the way it was packaged for and to some degree received by an Italian readership. Colleen Smee gives an account of Amy Witting's writing, focused largely on *Maria's War* [1998], in 'An Exploration of the Transnational Literary Journeys of the Australian Writer Amy Witting and Elena Jonaitis, a Lithuanian Migrant' (*JASAL* 14:i[2014] 10 pp.). Smee uncovers the relation between Witting—a working-class white Australian woman—and the migrants whose lives influenced her own writing and were influenced by her advocacy—notably Jonaitis, inspired by Witting to write her own memoir. In 'Reincarnation: The Orientalist Stereotypes' (*JASAL* 14:i[2014] 10 pp.), Amelberga Vita Astuti uses the US writer Amy Tan's treatment of Orientalism to unpack such Australian writers concerned with similar themes as Lilian Ng and Dewi Anggraeni. Anna Gadd draws from a doctoral thesis on Elizabeth Jolley to make narratological observations about the mode of translation inscribed in *Mr Scobie's Riddle* in 'Space and Language in *Mr Scobie's Riddle*: Translating Displacement into Italian' (*JASAL* 14:i[2014] 13 pp.). For Jean Page, James McAuley does the work of bridging old and new, colonial and metropolitan, postcolonial and transnational, crossing such boundaries via translations of his oeuvre, in 'Writing from the Periphery: The Haunted Landscapes of James McAuley' (*JASAL* 14:i[2014] 14 pp.). Janette Turner Hospital is convincingly annexed to the transnational by Jessica Trevitt in 'Of Frames and Wonders: Translation and Transnationalism in the Work of Janette Turner Hospital' (*JASAL* 14:i[2014] 9 pp.). Nataŝa Kampmark, 'Australian Literature in Serbian Translation' (*JASAL* 14:i[2014] 14 pp.), comments that 'the reception of Australian literature may have been dependent on the efforts of individual enthusiasts and the number of translations may not have been impressive, but those enthusiasts were often distinguished authors, literary scholars and critics, philologists and translators who made sure that what little Australian literature was served to the readers in Yugoslavia/Serbia was fresh, delectable and nutritious' (p. 12). The closing essay in this special issue brings together texts *about* Aboriginal characters with texts *by* Aboriginal authors. In 'Traversing the Unfamiliar: German Translations of Aboriginality in James Vance Marshall's *The Children* and Phillip Gwynne's *Deadly Unna?* and *Nukkin Ya*' (*JASAL* 14:i[2014] 14 pp.), Leah Gerber explores the choices of German translators in rendering Australian colloquialisms and words in Aboriginal languages.

JASAL's second issue for 2014 is a special issue edited by Elaine Lindsay and Michael Griffith stemming from a symposium held the previous year on the occasion of David Malouf's eightieth birthday. Yvonne Smith's 'The Long Breath of a Young Writer' (*JASAL* 14:ii[2014] 11 pp.) opens the issue with close readings of Malouf's early poems to signal elements connected to his beginnings. Dennis Haskell follows with a brief but detailed account of Malouf's under-appreciated forays into essays and poetry, in 'Silence and Poetic Inwardness in the Writings of David Malouf' (*JASAL* 14:ii[2014] 6 pp.). Haskell shows that poetry was not merely an apprenticeship for prose (especially since Malouf has also written a play and libretti). *Harland's Half-Acre* was republished in 2013, fuelling renewed interest, and Carolyn Masel, 'Closure, Completion and Memory in *Harland's Half-Acre*: Phil's Story' (*JASAL* 14:ii[2014] 10 pp.) explicitly contrasts it to Malouf's more studied *Remembering Babylon*. Focusing on voice, she notes that while the latter 'seeks to co-opt us, *Harland's Half-Acre* only requires us to listen to an account' (p. 3). Bill Ashcroft, 'David Malouf and the Poetics of Possibility' (*JASAL* 14:ii[2014] 11 pp.), uses *The Great World*, *An Imaginary Life*, and other novels to foreground how Malouf's novels present 'the ways in which art and literature continually push the boundaries of our understanding, the limits of our ability to imagine a different world'. Ashcroft vigorously insists that this utopian drive is both Malouf's own and, more convincingly, not the pie-in-the-sky idea that many assume it to be. Clare Rhoden, 'Only We Humans Can Know: David Malouf and War' (*JASAL* 14:ii[2014] 10 pp.), tracks the increasingly complex account of war that emerges from *Fly Away, Peter* through to *The Great World* and finally *Ransom*. Nicholas Birns is always novel in his perspective and panoramic in scope. Here he considers 'History as "Precarious Gift": *Harland's Half-Acre* and *The Great World* as Malouf's Not-So-Historical Novels' (*JASAL* 14:ii[2014] 9 pp.), suggesting that the personal always pervades the sweeping arcs of such novels. Both Shirley Hazzard and Malouf are vexed by Australia's place in the wings of a tumultuous world stage: 'the adjective "great" indicates that the small world of Australia can no longer be self-sufficient, that it is inflected and scarred by larger realities' (p. 8). *Remembering Babylon* is accounted for in Clare Archer-Lean's 'David Malouf's *Remembering Babylon* as a Reconsideration of Pastoral Idealisation' (*JASAL* 14:ii[2014] 12 pp.). It is a shame that many readings of Malouf that do address his multiple accounts of gay male desire find 'homoeroticism positioned as apolitical, as placed outside of time and history in a kind of prediscursive and primitive state' (p. 1); in '"As if My Bones Had Been Changed into Clouds": Queer Epiphanies in David Malouf's Fiction' (*JASAL* 14:ii[2014] 10 pp.), Damien Barlow offers a richer alternative, indeed, a reversal. For Barlow, awakenings to same-sex sexuality are political in their conceptual shift: 'Malouf's queer epiphanies posit a different type of epistemology or way of seeing and experiencing life that is not limited by binaries and either/or options' (p. 8). John Scheckter, 'A World of Feeling: David Malouf and the Public Conversation' (*JASAL* 14:ii[2014] 11 pp.), uses Malouf's *The Happy Life*—a recent Quarterly Essay—to debunk the ease with which Australians blame Americans for the world's ills while not thinking of their own growing contribution to them. Kay Ferres rounds out the issue with a reflective account of Malouf's position in the public sphere and the literary communities that foster him. In conferences on Australian literature, you will often hear complaints that there is too much written on certain writers. If Malouf is sometimes mentioned in this way, this issue shows that in his case it is justified.

JASAL's third issue is themed on 'Country' and edited by Brigitta Olubas and David Gilbey. It arises out of the 2013 ASAL conference and ranges from Aboriginal relations to land to ecocritical topics. Kerry Kilner and Peter Minter, 'The BlackWords Symposium: The Past, Present, and Future of Aboriginal and Torres Strait Islander Literature' (*JASAL* 14:iii[2014] 8 pp.), provide a comprehensive perspective on Aboriginal and Torres Strait Islander literature in their article on the BlackWords symposium. The article also analyses the shifting keywords by which scholars have navigated the BlackWords AustLit database. Bruce Pascoe, 'Peek-a Boo Australia' (*JASAL* 14:iii[2014] 5 pp.), provides a playful yet serious preface to the 'Country' issue, drawn from his recent book *Dark Emu*, which challenges the common idea in Australian history that Aboriginal people were nomads lacking technologies of sedentary land custodianship. Jared Thomas, 'Respecting Protocols for Representing Aboriginal cultures' (*JASAL* 14:iii[2014] 13 pp.), surveys the shifting degree to which Aboriginal protocols are being pursued by non-Aboriginal authors before moving to an account of his own novel, *Calypso Summer*, and its construction. Anita Heiss, 'BLACKWORDS: Writers on Identity' (*JASAL* 14:iii[2014] 13 pp.), surveys Aboriginal poetry to foreground the range of responses to white attempts to frame identity. She also highlights the importance of Aboriginal children's writing, theatre (Davis's *Honey Spot*) and the wide range of prose works— often ignored in academia but important in understanding Aboriginal cultural practices of reading and sharing stories. Natalie Harkin's essay 'The Poetics of (Re)Mapping Archives: Memory in the Blood' (*JASAL* 14:iii[2014] 14 pp.) is a stimulating mix of the fictocritical and the analytic, recounting Harkin's own researches into her grandmother's Native Affairs file from the late 1930s and the early 1940s. Harkin effectively draws from Derrida's 'Archive Fever' in a personal vein as well as taking it transnational, through Native America (Kiowa) writer N. Scott Momaday. In 'Writing Forward, Writing Back, Writing Black: Work Process and Work-in-Progress' (*JASAL* 14:iii[2014] 14 pp.), Gus Worby, Simone Ulalka Tur, and Faye Rosas Blanch explore reciprocity in academic collaboration, combining co-authored text with interview-style orthography. Linda McBride-Yuke, in culturally appropriate oral style, shares a personal story which subtly delineates her position as an Aboriginal editor at the State Library of Queensland, in 'Journey of a Lifetime: From the Sticks to the State Library—An Aboriginal Editor's Story' (*JASAL* 14:iii[2014] 8 pp.). Irene Howe similarly provides her 'memoir of an indexer', rounding out the BlackWords symposium section of the 'Country' issue by shedding light on, amidst much else, David Unaipon, in 'The Uniqueness of the BlackWords Resource: Memoir of an Indexer' (*JASAL* 14:iii[2014] 12 pp.).

Jeanine Leane gave the Dorothy Green Memorial Lecture for 2013. This also appears in this issue, and scans with great intellectual agility across settler representations of Aboriginal characters, covering Pritchard, Herbert, White, Malouf, and, briefly, Grenville: 'Tracking Our Country in Settler Literature' (*JASAL* 14:iii[2014] 17 pp.). Leane draws on Heidegger, for whom boundaries are 'spaces not where something ends but where something else begins its presencing' (p. 2). Presence is possible in these writers, but continually thwarted and distorted by racial discourses. Leane takes up Toni Morrison's *Playing in the Dark* as an inspiration.

Alison Ravenscroft opens the regular articles section of the 'Country' issue with an account of travelling to the Warlpiri community of Utopia with two Aboriginal friends from other country than that destination, in 'Sovereign Bodies of Feeling—"Making Sense" of Country' (*JASAL* 14:iii[2014] 17 pp.). Ravenscroft's concern is the different ways in which worlds are made sense of in indigenous country by indigenous or non-indigenous people. She deftly manages the difficult task of balancing theoretical insight with a fictocritical account of experience. Helena Kadmos, in ' "Look What They Done To This Ground Girl!"': Country and Identity in Jeanine Leane's *Purple Threads*' (*JASAL* 14:iii[2014] 11 pp.), argues for the classification of Jeanine Leane's 2012 *Purple Threads* as a 'short-story cycle'—a much-needed category for this form of work and one that might also apply to Tony Birch's *Shadowboxing*. Natalie Quinlivan draws from Kim Scott's paratexts as well as much of the published material on his work in order to position his novels in relation to the wider projects of cultural reclamation in which he is involved, in 'Finding a Place in Story: Kim Scott's Writing and the Wirlomin Noongar Language and Stories Project' (*JASAL* 14:iii[2014] 12 pp.). Clare Hooper's journalistic account *The Tall Man* fascinates many readers today because of its concern with the shocking and brutal death in custody on Palm Island, Queensland, of Moordinyi (or Cameron Doomadgee). Jane Stenning analyses the rhetorical devices employed in Hooper's text in ' "Why Raise Them to Die so Young?"': The Aesthetics of Fatalism in *The Tall Man*' (*JASAL* 14:iii[2014] 11 pp.). She shows how reference to Joseph Conrad and the Bible, for instance, functions to frame specific community concerns in problematically global and canonical ways. Elizabeth Webby speculates on some resonances between nineteenth-century poet Charles Harpur and Dick, the youngest son in Grenville's *The Secret River*, before moving to a fuller reading of early meanings of the trope of 'the bush', in 'Representations of "The Bush" in the Poetry of Charles Harpur' (*JASAL* 14:iii[2014] 8 pp.). Peter Crabb recuperates the work of Charles Edward Augustus de Boos beyond the few texts of his that do the rounds, such as his 1867 *Fifty Years Ago*, in 'Charles Edward Augustus de Boos 1819–1900: His Life, Work, and Writing' (*JASAL* 14:iii[2014] 12 pp.). Susan Sheridan and Emma Maguire survey Nan Chauncy's 1950s children's novels, sketching nascent ecological concerns and asserting their interest in indigenous presence in 'Relationships to the Bush in Nan Chauncy's Early

Novels for Children' (*JASAL* 14:iii[2014] 10 pp.). While others talk of the anxiety of influence that gripped Randolph Stow in relation to Patrick White, Bernadette Brennan, 'Heriot's Ithaka: Soul, Country and the Possibility of Home in *To the Islands*' (*JASAL* 14:iii[2014] 10 pp.), focuses on Stow's depictions of *anima* vis-à-vis White's (mainly in *Voss*) to suggest that they render them proximate to and distinct from each other. Kieran Dolin, 'Place and Property in Post-Mabo Fiction by Dorothy Hewett, Alex Miller and Andrew McGahan' (*JASAL* 14:iii[2014] 12 pp.), expands on his identification of post-Mabo fiction in the aforementioned White Centenary Collection by adding Alex Miller's *Journey to the Stone Country* alongside rethinkings of Dorothy Hewett and Andrew McGahan. Dolin's references are astute in their account of legal cases, drawing from scholars in anthropology and cultural studies—bolstered by the wisdom of Ruby Langford Ginibi—to show the way settler colonial Australia is blind to its own investment in the relation between land and law. Grenville's *Lilian's Story* is clearly overshadowed in academic articles these days by *The Secret River*. Yet, as Laura Deane shows in 'Cannibalism and Colonialism: *Lilian's Story* and (White) Women's Belonging' (*JASAL* 14:iii[2014] 13 pp.), the manner in which Lilian is represented as atavistic racializes her, opening up discourses of disability to those of settler colonialism. Lachlan Brown, '"An Asian Dummy with an Aussie Voice": Ventriloquism and Authenticity in Nam Le's *The Boat* and Tim Winton's *The Turning*' (*JASAL* 14:iii[2014] 9 pp.), provides a nuanced reading of the representation of race as ventriloquism between Nam Le's and Tim Winton's short stories—a reading that playfully and appropriately takes the Turing test as its conjoining metaphor. Stuart Cooke close-reads the cartography of 'Country' in 'Country Escaping Line in the Poetry of Philip Hodgins' (*JASAL* 14:iii[2014] 10 pp.). The poems of contemporary Sydney writer Jill Jones are described by thick layers of irony, not unlike the crud which—according to contributor Caroline Williamson—she punningly associates with former Australian prime minister Rudd, in 'Beyond Generation Green: Jill Jones and the Ecopoetic Process' (*JASAL* 14:iii[2014] 9 pp.). This layering of irony produces an aporia that leads Williamson to seek a stance on the ecopoetic in Jones's work, conscripting Benjamin's readings of revolution, modernity, and the machinal to her cause. In the same issue, Helen Ramoutsaki reflects on her own performative practice in 'A Continuity of Country: Enlivenment in a Live Evocation of Place' (*JASAL* 14:iii[2014] 16 pp.), while Keri Glastonbury ventriloquizes Wiradjuri psychogeography in her 'Lost Wagga Wagga' (*JASAL* 14:iii[2014] 9 pp.). There is unexpected but welcome attention to the long verse text provided by Linda Weste in '"Country" in Australian Contemporary Verse Novels' (*JASAL* 14:iii[2014] 9 pp.), and Heidegger's *Dasein* returns to tarry with Gerald Murnane in Julian Murphy's contribution, 'Being-in-Landscape: A Heideggerian Reading of Landscape in Gerard Murnane's *Inland*' (*JASAL* 14:iii[2014] 11 pp.), which closes the regular articles section of this impressive issue.

Brian Castro's Barry Andrews Lecture, 'Writing Country: Lightning, Agony, and Vertigo' (*JASAL* 14:iii[2014] 11 pp.), is also reproduced in the 2014 *JASAL* 'Country' issue. Castro's tremendously diverse experience contributes to a reflection that characteristically positions Australian literature in relation to transnational examples—from Zadie Smith and Salman Rushdie to J.M. Coetzee to Jeanette Winterson back to Faulkner, who is cited as one in a succession of writers with an imaginative sense of country. Castro's resonances are both erratic and agile, but they are grounded in a characteristically intriguing thesis: 'Australian writers are therefore the most melancholic of writers, turned inward from lack of recognition, not least because of the fear of the difficulty of reception, many of whom eat themselves up from the inside, and in the present era, are supine before sales, overseas notice, and the theodicy of publicity and marketing' (p. 3). He posits that the 'Complexity' that is usually the 'obvious path for a writer of exile' is forestalled by extant cultural positions such as the 'victimage' of the 'little Aussie battler' (p. 9). Castro is provocative as he inserts himself into the company of Adorno and Said. The point, which he knows so well, is that such gestures to transnational exiles as his preferred company are unavoidably silenced in advance by the melancholic inheritance itself.

Laurie Clancy is remembered in the fourth issue of *JASAL* for 2014: 'Man of Many Letters: Essays on Laurie Clancy and His Work'. From his founding association with the short-lived yet lively *Melbourne Partisan* to a remembrance from the legendary literary agent Tim Curnow to recollections by John Barnes and Peter Pierce among others, Clancy's legacy is honoured and, with luck, will spur more academic interest.

JASAL's fifth issue for 2014 is themed on the idea of world literature and continues the conversation from Robert Dixon and Brigid Rooney's *Scenes of Reading* [2013]. Titled 'The Nation or the Globe? Australian Literature and/in the World' Tony Simoes Da Silva's introduction (*JASAL* 14:v[2014] 6 pp.) draws on Philip Mead to point up the irony that the desired end of the nationalist turn in literary studies is voiced by people and in places owing much to structures of nation. Much disagreement ensues about the worldliness of the Nation and the usefulness of the World. Amanda Johnson opens the issue proper with a literary and art-historical account of Tasmania's worldliness, 'Making an Expedition of Herself: Lady Jane Franklin as Queen of the Tasmanian Extinction Narrative' (*JASAL* 14:v[2014] 21 pp.). Several articles concerned with magical realism follow. Richard Flanagan inspires Ben Holgate to argue for magical realism's ironic potential to deal with settler colonial violence in 'Developing Magical Realism's Irony in *Gould's Book of Fish*' (*JASAL* 14:v[2014] 11 pp.). Indigenous catharsis, for Maria Takolander, is also enabled through magical realist irony in 'Magical Realism and Irony's "Edge": Rereading Magical Realism and Kim Scott's *Benang*' (*JASAL* 14:v[2014] 11 pp.). Ken Gelder and Rachael Weaver draw from research for their *Colonial Journals* book to look at the early years of the twentieth century in 'Literary Journals and Literary Aesthetics in Early Post-Federation Australia' (*JASAL* 14:v[2014] 15 pp.). Manoly Lascaris and *Flaws in the Glass* become Shaun Bell's anchor-points in a playful thought experiment about Patrick White's possible literary identity, 'Greece—Patrick White's Country: Is Patrick White a Greek Author?' (*JASAL* 14:v[2014] 14 pp.). Like Bernadette Brennan in the 'Country' issue, Kathleen Steele is interested in the relation between White and Stow in 'Splendid Masculinity: The Wanderer in *Voss* and *To The Islands*' (*JASAL* 14:v[2014] 12 pp.). Guy and Joe Lynch were brothers from New Zealand who, from the 1920s, lived in Sydney and edited *Smith's Weekly*, which Martin Edmond sees as 'in many respects the heir to ephemeral wartime miscellanies like *The Anzac Book*, edited by Charles Bean in a bunker at Gallipoli' (p. 3): 'On Tasman Shores— Guy & Joe Lynch in Australasia' (*JASAL* 14:v[2014] 10 pp.). Edmond also sketches broader patterns of cross-Tasman literary reputation. Robyn Greaves provides a factual account of *Walkabout*, important for culturally significant figures such as Henrietta Drake-Brockman and more popular writers like Ion L. Idriess and Mary Durack, in 'A "Grim And Fascinating" Land of Opportunity: The *Walkabout* Women and Australia' (*JASAL* 14:v[2014] 14 pp.). Contemporary poet Laurie Duggan is given well-deserved attention by Cameron Lowe in his detailed reading focused through an almost psycho-geographic lens, 'Anthropologist of Space: The Poetics of Representation in Laurie Duggan's *Crab & Winkle*' (*JASAL* 14:v[2014] 12 pp.). Cheryl Taylor makes the case for paying more attention to Ronald McKie—she contextualizes him back to the Jindyworobaks and forward to Thea Astley, amongst others in 'Late Retrospectives on Twentieth-Century Catastrophes: The Novels of Ronald McKie' (*JASAL* 14:v[2014] 12 pp.). Theresa Holtby is ambitious in taking on a difficult aspect of Stead's popular novel in 'Hurts So Good: Masochism in Christina Stead's *The Man Who Loved Children*' (*JASAL* 14:v[2014] 12 pp.).

Joseph Cummins attends to one of Australia's favourite sites for positing the existence of regional literatures and continues a long tradition of relating it to its dark colonial past and the Gothic in 'Echoes between Van Diemen's Land and Tasmania: Sound and the Space of the Island in Richard Flanagan's *Death of a River Guide* and Carmel Bird's *Cape Grim*' (*JCL* 49:ii[2014] 257–70). Both novels work with revisionist history and 'embed genealogical narratives' (p. 257), connecting past to present via resonating soundscapes. Deleuze and Guattari's 'refrain' and Paul Carter's 'sound in between' provide a conceptual frame. In the novels, extinction is a common theme: relating to violent Aboriginal–White first contacts and to modern mass murder.

Pilar Baines writes 'Down in Elizabeth Jolley's *The Well*: An Essay on Repression' in what was formerly *AUMLA* and is now the *Journal of Language, Literature and Culture* (*JLLC* 61:i[2014] 46–59). The well is read as a site of female struggle against patriarchy, as a sign of repressed sexuality and the female abject and as 'a place where meanings collapse, forming a metaphor for both oppression and freedom' (p. 46). The Gothic mode helps hold together the novella's social and psychological aspects. Baines sets out archetypal symbolism and textual metaphors of theft and entrapment. Staying close to existing scholarship, she focuses on Hester and her repression of desire, noting how the male closure of the well leaves the mystery and female revolt unresolved.

Bridget Grogan, 'The Decorative Voice of Hidden, Secret Flesh: Corporeal Dynamics in Patrick White's Fiction' (*JLST* 30:ii[2014] 1–16), uses Barthes and Kristeva to examine the way Patrick White presents artistic representation as a bodily force, his style seeking a balance of 'semiotic' and 'symbolic' elements though driven by the former. The article provides examples from author comments, *Voss*, *The Vivisector*, *The Solid Mandala*, *The Twyborn*

Affair, and 'Five-Twenty', a story from *The Cockatoos*, also looking at the use of visual art and music as a means of expressing both the materiality of language and its drive to reach beyond its expressive limits. It is a productive reading, even if Barthes's proposition about the origins of style is dubious.

Hwang, Hoon-sung considers Pledger's play and its adaptation of Kafka's *The Trial* in 'From a Modern Absurd to a Postmodern Absurd Staged in David Pledger's K' (*JMED* 27:ii[2014] 245–66).

In *Kill Your Darlings* Ambelin Kwaymullina, 'Edges, Centres and Futures' (*KYD* 18[2014] 22–33), writes about her work as an Aboriginal writer producing speculative fiction for young adults. She connects with indigenous thinkers from North America and Scandinavia to posit the need to break with standard Western genres, noting pithily that 'Indigenous peoples everywhere are familiar with fantasy because we have long been the subjects of it' (p. 29) and have survived apocalyptic upheavals. She advocates more (equitable) partnerships between indigenous and non-indigenous writers.

In the same issue, Tim Byrne assesses the 'Rise of the Independents: The Rallying of Theatre in Melbourne' (*KYD* 18[2014] 34–45), charting the 'potholed and piecemeal' histories of smaller companies and hailing a new spirit of collaboration from major players (Melbourne Theatre Company, Malthouse) and well attended multi-venue festivals. Byrne gives a quick overview of activity and calls for 'more radical, even revolutionary, staging from independents' (p. 45).

On the international front, Iva Polak has an article (in Croatian) dealing with Archie Weller in the journal *Književna Smotra*(*KS* 46.i[2014] 101–10.

Life Writing 11:i[2014], edited by Stephen Mansfield, focuses on 'writing the father'. In it Bernadette Brennan, 'Kim Cheng Boey's *Between Stations*: "The Architecture of Memory" ' (*LW* 11:i[2014] 39–54), relates the work to ideas of translation and displacement in Rushdie and Heaney to argue that Boey's narrative uses travel to look forwards and backwards, evoking childhood memory and reflecting on writing and reading and creating a life story of mourning and desire. Laura Buzo contributes a personal piece on her father, the playwright Alex Buzo: ' "I Will Go Before You in a Pillar of Fire": Writing the Father. Father the Writer' (*LW* 11:i[2014] 121–6).

Life Writing 11:iv[2014] is a special issue titled 'Displaced Women: Eastern European Post-War Narratives in Australia'. In it eastern Europe seems to spread from Latvia to the Ukraine, and many of the writers included have been overlooked because their narratives were not literary or were not in English. They are increasingly becoming recognized as part of a properly transnational Australian literary history. One novel in English (which also inspired Amy Witting's novel *Maria's War*) is by Elena Jonaitis, and is treated in Sonia Mycak's 'Literary Cultures of Eastern European "Displaced Persons" in Australia: Elena Jonaitis, Helen Boris, Pavla Gruden and Elga Rodze-Kisele' (*LW* 11:vi[2014] 423–35). Another is Maria Lewitt, whose autobiographical fiction prompts Nina Fischer to argue for discussion of Holocaust literature in relation to the specific times and places where it appears: 'Writing a Whole Life: Maria Lewitt's Holocaust/Migration Narratives in "Multicultural" Australia' (*LW* 11:iv[2014] 391–42).

Lyn McCredden continues her work on the sacred in 'Tim Winton's Poetics of Resurrection' (*L&T* [2014] 12 pp.), defending the writer against charges of blindness to race and gender issues owing to his Christian beliefs and arguing that he sees the sacred 'entwined in an earthed, embodied, and material vision of the human' realized by characters testing their limits. Winton is located in a tradition of writers invoking the sacred within and against Australia's dominant secular culture (White, Murray, Hart), and McCredden argues that risk-taking in Winton's fiction is more than a desire to be exceptional, seeking after joy, beauty, and terror as intimations of resurrection.

Literary material in *Meanjin* for 2014 begins with an essay by Paul Genoni and Tanya Dalziell: 'Charmian Clift and George Johnston, Hydra 1960: The "Lost" Photographs of James Burke' (*Meanjin* 73:i[2014] 18–37). Clift's travel books, *Mermaid Singing* and *Peel Me a Lotus*, are 'pictures' of time spent in the Greek islands, also recorded by James Burke, a *Life* magazine photographer. Bio-historical commentary supplements readings of how the photos relate to other accounts of Clift and Johnston. Jim Davidson's 'The Biography as Periscope: Exploring Australian Ambiences' (*Meanjin* 73:i[2014] 94–103) is a personal reflection on writing biographies, including on the two major editors of *Overland* and *Meanjin*, Stephen Murray-Smith and Clem Christesen. Davidson posits ambience/milieu as the key driver of biography and concludes with some gloomy comments on the ambience of literary culture in Australia today. Martin Langford provides an extended review of poetry books by Lisa Gorton, Sarah Day, Chris Wallace-Crabbe, Jacob Zigura, Christopher (Kit) Kelen, and *Contemporary Asian Australian Poets*, edited by Adam Aitken, Kim Cheng Boey, and Michelle Cahill, in 'The Pleasure of Well-Made Rooms: Poetry in Review' (*Meanjin* 73:i[2014] 42–51), including some thoughtful comments on Wallace-Crabbe.

In the next issue, Peter Kirkpatrick continues his entertaining forays into popular culture to show links between Wild West shows and the Bush Balladists, notably Paterson and his 'Man from Snowy River': 'Hellbound for Snowy River' (*Meanjin* 73:ii[2014] 32–41).

Trevor Shearston, 'Head in a Jar' (*Meanjin* 73:iii[2014] 18–28), sketches the historical background to his novel *Dead Birds*, and the subsequent hunt for the actual head of his narrator, taken by explorer Luigi D'Albertis from Papua to Italy.

Meanjin 73:iv[2014] has poet Chris Wallace-Crabbe humorously reflecting on the British culture of his childhood and his gradual incorporation of Australian and European reading. He comments that he has written a lot of poems about food: 'Unemployed at Last, Again' (*Meanjin* 73:iv[2014] 162–7). Cathy Perkins looks into the connections between poet Zora Cross and the First World War, in particular her elegy for her soldier brother, in 'A Spoonful of Blood' (*Meanjin* 73:iv[2014] 18–26).

Jopi Nyman, 'Gillian Mears's *Foal's Bread* as a Postcolonial Pastoral: Land, Humans, and Animals' (*OrbisLit* 69:v[2014] 390–410), not only shows how the novel about horse-jumping and bush life counters positive pastoral myths of nation, it also argues that Mears reshapes relations to the natural environment in accordance with the theoretical trajectory from postcolonial studies to ecocriticism traced by Graham Huggan, Helen Tiffin, and others. Pastoral sceptics (Xavier Herbert, Patrick White, J.M. Coetzee, John Kinsella) frame Mears's ironic exposé of rural sexism, hard slog, and violence, which also confuses human and animal characteristics, thereby suggesting a non-anthropocentric connection to nature. 'By presenting the textual space of the novel as a form of nature, as a space to be ridden and explored, the novel questions the division into culture and nature' (p. 408).

Overland includes an essay by John McLaren, 'Bias Australian' (*Overland* 217[Summer 2014] 86–93), responding to Jim Davidson's account of *Overland*'s editor Stephen Murray-Smith and tracking the conflicts in and around the journal between nationalists and communists. He notes Patrick White's challenge to realism and Dorothy Hewett's break with populism to write her feminist poetry, and the journal's shift from John Morrison and Alan Marshall to writers like Peter Mathers and Gerald Murnane, and concludes that 'the easy image of the Australian is both the strength and the weakness' of the journal's nationalism. The same issue has short personal pieces from Somali Australian Khalid Warsame on finding a position and subject to write about and novelist Kirsten Tranter on her feelings about reviews.

Kate Grenville's *The Secret River* continues to attract analysis. Anouk Lang, 'Going Against the Flow: *The Secret River* and Colonialism's Structuring Oppositions' (*PocoT* 9:i[2014] 16 pp.), picks up Benita Parry's comments on anti-colonial undoing of received narratives to ask what changes have occurred in post-bicentennial Australian fiction. She argues that Grenville succeeds 'in reconfiguring the signifying relations between Australian settlers and the original inhabitants' (p. 2) by reworking national myths of the hard-done-by convict, the battling pioneer, and the first contact story so as to show the untenable racist binaries beneath. Lang usefully connects the book to Canadian theories of 'historiographic metafiction' and provides an intelligent defence of its countering of colonial stereotypes and avoiding an easy humanist blurring of difference.

In the same issue, Christopher Kelen surveys the lyrics of national anthems to investigate how the emergent postcolonial nation-state reproduces colonial tropes: 'Meet the New Boss—Same as the Old' (*PocoT* 9:i[2014] 27 pp.), and Craig Mitchell Smith considers the underwhelming responses to Coetzee's first Australian novel in 'On Not Being Christian: J.M. Coetzee's *Slow Man* and the Ethics of Being (Un)Interesting' (*PocoT* 9:i[2014] 18 pp.), and argues (via contrast with *Diary of a Bad Year*) that the book is intended not to appeal to either activists or those seeking action in a story. The humiliation of being aged and infirm, and Rayment's musing on the slogan 'What would Jesus do?' imply ethical interest, and Costello's exhortations to the passive Rayment (larded with literary references) highlight how active heroes are an expected but not a necessary feature in fiction, so that the novel becomes a provocation to the reader and to secularist society. It is a clear and compelling discussion.

Quadrant has Nicholas Hasluck's launch speech, 'Geoffrey Lehmann's Journey', for the latter's *Poems 1957–2013* (*Quadrant* 59:xi[2014] 72–5). Hasluck recalls the important influence of *The Ilex Tree* [1965], co-authored by Les Murray, Lehmann's undergraduate 'stoush' with Robert Hughes, notes the poet's ability to take on the personae of quirky figures from history, his farmer father-in-law and others, and mentions the poems of travel, domestic life, and ageing, asserting that 'we can sense within the poet's tone unsettling intimations of what lies ahead in changing times, or the real value of what we long for, or have left behind' (p. 75). In the same issue, Jenny Stewart revisits Kate Grenville's *The Secret River* (*Quadrant* 59:xi[2014] 76–9), contrasting it to books that reimagine real historical figures, noting the clash with historians over the author's claim to get beyond raw facts to richer truths, and defending it as the best of the trilogy because of its gripping vicissitudes and troubled characters (unlike their real antecedents, who most likely felt no guilt for their actions). Novelists risk reading the past through the lens of the present, and readers have taken up the book, 'comfortable with being uncomfortable' (p. 79). The final *Quadrant* issue includes the text of Alan Gould's first Axel Clark Memorial Literary Oration, 'Chimaeric David Campbell' (*Quadrant* 58:xii[2014] 88–94). Gould mentions Campbell's long correspondence with his tutor Dr Tillyard. *The Collected Poems* and personal anecdotes are adduced in an attempt to know better the multifaceted writer, whose 'key lay in this acute insight: that mirage was innate to the very fabric of consciousness' (p. 89). Plato and a non-religious quest for grace, painterliness, and humour are some attributes claimed for the work.

In an issue of *Southerly* devoted to ideas on utopia and dystopia, Bill Ashcroft provides an introductory essay, including brief mentions of Banjo Paterson, Henry Kendall, Ada Cambridge, Randolph Stow, Les Murray, Lee Cataldi, Patrick White, and more on David Malouf: 'The Horizon of the Future' (*Southerly* 74:i[2014] 12–35). He asserts via Ricoeur that utopian thinking is not the imagining of perfection but speaking to the present from nowhere, critiquing and offering alternatives (p. 13), and uses Ernst Bloch's *Heimat* and Husserl's notion of the horizon to posit the bounded but open prospects that literature sets forth, disturbing fixed nation-thinking. Lucy Sussex, 'Apocalypse vs Utopia: A Writer's Guide' (*Southerly* 74:i[2014] 90–8), reflects on her own work, with mention of George Turner's *The Sea and Summer*, M. Barnard Eldershaw's *Tomorrow and Tomorrow and Tomorrow*, and, briefly, the work of a few others. Jessica White examines 'Fluid Worlds: Reflecting Climate Change in *The Swan Book* and *The Sunlit Zone*' (*Southerly* 74:i[2014] 142–63). She notes the paucity of fiction about global warming, citing Vance Palmer, George Turner, and Andrew McGahan as Australian exceptions, along with Ian Meadows, James Bradley, and Alexis Wright's *Carpentaria*, with its apocalyptic cyclone. Apocalypse is easier to represent than gradual change, and White looks at how characters respond to the latter in Wright's third novel and Lisa Jacobson's verse novel. While one is about trauma from loss of country, the other deals with genetic modification, loss of species, and echoing absence, and White suggests that speculative climate-change fiction is more effective in raising our awareness than apocalyptic stories. The later work reflects the Australian author's involvement with refugee interests in moving settings to oceans around Indonesia and Iran, and to the Pacific, and imagines 'techno-liberation' as a utopian counter to recognizable geopolitical situations.

It seems that science fiction writer Greg Egan is coming into his own as a subject for scholarly attention. Apart from the book already cited, Darren Jorgensen examines 'Geopolitics in Greg Egan's Science Fiction' (*Southerly*

74:i[2014] 186–98). After a short list of Australian SF writers of note, Jorgensen surveys Egan's 'hard' speculative fiction and its central engagement with quantum physics and 'post-human possibilities' (p. 186). He measures Egan's international reach against Australian aspects of his writing and places him amongst post-cyberpunk subversions of global capitalism: '*Permutation City* is a riposte to the disembodied fantasies of techno-utopianism' manifest in virtual personae uploaded in nano-space (p. 190). Unlike Asimov's human/ machine distinctions, Egan's work merges the opposing terms and engages with the ethics of copies and virtual selves.

Danny Anwar writes of 'The Island Called Utopia in Patrick White's *The Tree of Man*' (*Southerly* 74:i[2014] 217–34). In 'the age of foolishness in the era of late capitalism' (p. 217), rethinking space reflects utopian hope, and White's novel can be read as reimagining Australia to show 'the loss of the universally sacred' as located in the myth of the pioneer. Established readings depict a 'trajectory of the sacred' culminating in Stan Parker's epiphany, but later ones shift transcendence to immanence and future possibility. Anwar might be seen as an instance of Brian Kiernan's new-generation reader of White (see above). Drawing on Jameson, Veronica Brady, Deleuze and Guattari, Benjamin and Lefebvre, Anwar seeks to rethink the melancholy of pastness others find in *The Tree of Man*, tracking a dialectic of spatiality (sacred universal versus profane particular) through which 'a utopian enclave, or island, is given definition' in the last stages of the novel (p. 230). The reading is engaging and ingenious, though the utopian wish of the postmodern critic may be an imposition on the modernist project of White's 'Great Australian Novel' as an island/artwork imaging forth an island/nation.

In the next issue, Michelle Cahill, in 'The Colour of the Dream: Unmasking Whiteness' (*Southerly* 74:ii[2014] 196–211), thinks about whiteness and how it operates to dismiss, contain, or assimilate writing and identities other than those centrally hegemonic. She provides personal 'flashbacks' relating to refugees and migrants and alludes to a range of contemporary 'third space' writing.

J.H. Crone takes up Philip Butterss's call to revalue the verse of C.J. Dennis in the light of its importance amongst soldiers in the First World War, in 'Dreaming Verse: C.J. Dennis and the ANZAC Tradition' (*Southerly* 74:iii[2014] 158–80). Dennis's larrikin figures sound the same populist notes as Prime Minister Howard, who resuscitated old patriotic narratives, while his art harked back to Bernard O'Dowd and Wordsworth in notions of the common man and the bush. Crone attends to poetic technique, claiming post-Adorno reading has neglected this, and that common technique and combative motifs ('stoushing') unify *The Songs of a Sentimental Bloke* and *The Moods of Ginger Mick* (*contra* Butterss and Robin Gerster) and fit with a post-9/11 militarism.

Also in *Southerly*, Anna Poletti and Ali Alizadeh consider 'The Dream of Love in Tsiolkas' *The Slap*' (*Southerly* 74:iii[2014] 212–25). Love and middle-class marriage allow the novelist to dramatize 'ambivalence about the multicultural project of Australian society' (p. 212) and the politics of intimacy. Using Alain Badiou and Lauren Berlant (love as a genre offering both social stability and ambivalence), they inspect character Aisha's conflicted loyalties when her husband slaps the brattish son of friends: formal bindings of family versus (gendered) personal feelings. Tsiolkas shows—in contrasting romance elements with gritty realism—that conflict is never avoidable and that love (cross-cultural/ cross-class marriage) of itself does not solve interpersonal or inter-ethnic tensions.

Jeremy Fisher considers a popular West Australian writer's career in 'A Professional Author: How G.M. Glaskin Earned a Living' (*S&P* 38:i[2014] 39–56). Using papers from both author and publisher, Fisher tracks Glaskin's output and income, concluding that he made his fiction out of his life and (because Glaskin was gay before the term had been coined or the sexuality decriminalized) that his life eventually pushed him out of the literary mainstream. Glaskin was involved in the Fellowship of Australian Writers and kept logbooks of multiple attempts to place stories across the country and overseas and the income derived therefrom. From 1949 he strove to survive solely on his writing, successfully doing so a decade later, then falling back on pensions as his career faded and he returned to Australia. Details of his contracts reveal how he was popular in Germany and Norway as well as selling well in England, courted the French and Dutch markets, and sold best as an adventure romance writer with a touch of the erotic, based on Australian and Southeast Asian settings.

Script & Print continues the work of Katherine Bode and Carol Hetherington in correcting the often distorted picture we have of Australian literature. In 'Retrieving a World of Fiction: Building an Index—and an Archive—of Novels in Australian Newspapers, 1850–1914' (*S&P* 38:iv[2014] 197–211), they take up Elizabeth Morrison's twenty-five-year-old cross-section of Victorian papers from one day in 1891 and her 'drilling down' into Melbourne's *Age*, which produced, respectively, twenty-eight and sixty serialized novels. With the added resource of digitized newspapers in the Trove archive, Bode and Hetherington painstakingly search, cross-check terms, consider the gaps in original materials, and note the chaotic international plundering of copy in which fiction 'as it moved across national borders . . . was often plagiarised and rewritten, re-badged and localised' (p. 203). Comparison of some texts allows attribution of original authorship, though much remains uncertain and the authors note inherent problems in electronic searches. They support Paul Eggert's contention that newspaper fiction is a fluid phenomenon that calls into question the notions of both 'the work' and 'the author' and leaves archival research as always a provisional ongoing process.

In the same issue, Rachel Solomon offers 'Two Studies: Henry Handel Richardson and the Great Extractor' (*S&P* 38:iv[2014] 229–48), an investigation of the author's relationship with the Ulysses Bookshop, which solicited a fine limited edition of her stories. The unexpected success of her final volume of the Mahony trilogy came too late for Richardson to be enthused, but she used the opportunity to reissue old novels and place stories in magazines. Jacob Schwartz obtained two stories and regaled Richardson with presents of rare editions of books and music, receiving signed copies of her work in exchange. Solomon traces the provenance of the stories, the role of agents, and issues over the printing and editing, then tracks the fate of some of the copies.

Schwartz's support and a good review from T.E. Lawrence may have encouraged Richardson eventually to allow publication of her collected stories by Heinemann and Norton in 1934.

Robyn Greaves offers a study of 'Australian Author Marion Halligan—Word Artist' (*TransL* 6:ii[2014] 11 pp.). The novelist's attention to the details of everyday life, dismissed by sexist critics as trivial and female, is appraised in relation to Woolf, and Garry Kinnane's 1998 call for Australian writers to deal with suburban realities. Discussion—ranging across the whole oeuvre—covers Halligan's themes of death, art (painting, photography, tapestry), webs of migration stories, and the need for fiction to give a distancing shaping to memoir.

Apart from Akerholt's article on White mentioned above and the Meyrick piece on theatre, Australian drama features across several journals. Grounded in Bourdieu's work on distinction and taste, 'Reimagining the Wheel: The Implications of Cultural Diversity for Mainstream Theatre Programming in Australia', by Josephine Fleming, Robyn Ewing Michael Anderson and Helen Klieve (*TRI* 39[2014] 133–48), draws on interviews of 726 young people (part of a much larger survey project) asking why they chose to engage or not with theatre. Many were at performances as a school activity and had little idea of what theatre was, had another mother tongue than English, and were part of a popular culture scene that did not include 'formal' staged theatre.

Musing about how neoliberalism's push to efficiencies of system operates against interpersonal communication (voice), Caroline Wake, in 'The Politics and Poetics of Listening: Attending Headphone Verbatim Theatre in Post-Cronulla Australia' (*TRI* 39[2014] 82–100), wonders how theatre can intervene in a mediatized mix of chaos and conservatism without reproducing its structures. She looks at Roslyn Oades's 'headphone verbatim' performance *Stories of Love and Hate*—ordinary voices recounting the 2005 Cronulla race riots—to explore how the medium provokes reflection on how the media produce our communications. Media images of the beach mob violence emphasized the smaller retaliations of Lebanese youth over the large white crowd attacking a few people of Middle Eastern appearance. Oades reduced eighty hours of interviews with both communities to a sixty-five-minute audio script of ten narrative lines and performed to both Bankstown and Cronulla-region audiences. Noting the dangers of 'therapeutic listening' (attending to injury rather than reform in hearing testimonies; sentimental self-validation rather than hearing the other), Wake argues that Oades turns the audience towards 'ethical eavesdropping' where we are visible as listeners to actors listening to people 'talking amongst themselves'. As characters call up radio stations, we also see how stories are processed or left out, and are made aware of how our listening is also part of a media-constructed story and of how we ourselves listen (or not) to events.

Westerly 59:ii[2014] celebrates sixty years of publication. Its contents reflect the mix of Australian and Asian prose and poetry that has characterized the journal since its inception as a student magazine. Descriptive histories of each decade are provided by John Barnes, Elizabeth Webby, Dennis Haskell, Delys Bird, Paul Genoni, and Tony Hughes-d'Aeth, several of these being past editors. They serve up a roll-call of Australian writers of note, marking the effort to extend beyond local names (Randolph Stow, Elizabeth Jolley, Fay

Zwicky, Dorothy Hewett) to cover good writing from across the nation and then the immediate region. The importance of Peter Cowan as editor and critic and the magazine's attention to other art forms (painting, sculpture, theatre, film) from all around the world are some of the main points of interest. Hughes-d'Aeth includes some thought-provoking observations on how contemporary electronic media aggregate and atomize content through mega-repositories, thereby challenging the magazine format, though this can survive as Web pages.

The preceding issue includes review essays on a year of Australian fiction (by Robyn Mundy) and poetry (by John Hawke). What impresses from these is just how many presses (well-established ones, not the covers for self-publishing) continue to publish poetry despite all the laments about their disappearance from the field. Critical articles include a discussion of the 'Anxiety of Reference in *That Deadman Dance*' (*Westerly* 59:i[2014] 70–85) by Rohan Wilson. Following de Man, and the analysis of postcolonialism's intersection with deconstruction by Linda Hutcheon, one historical novelist considers another's (Kim Scott's) use of history and its imaginative reconstruction to rehearse 'ways in which the ethical contract can be made and unmade' in plays between literal and metaphorical textual elements, oral and written record, mimesis and sly mimicry, military drill and Noongar dance. John Burbidge, in 'Gerald Glaskin Revisited' (*Westerly* 59:i[2014] 86–91), provides a version of the preface to his book on G.M. Glaskin in which he discovers the real identity of Neville Jackson, author of a pioneering gay novel, *No End to the Way*, and sets out the questions about Glaskin's career that drove his biography, noting the novelist's unusual early engagement with Asian material. Jane Vaughan investigates 'Form, Artifice and Contemporary Australian Poetics: John Tranter's "The Anaglyph"' (*Westerly* 59:i[2014] 104–22). Tranter's 2010 collection *Starlight* owes much to John Ashbery and showcases experiments with computer-generated verse and recombinations of lines from other poets. Stylistically different from Ashbery's 'Clepsydra', 'The Anaglyph' shares its focus on the process of making poetry and 'the materiality of language and medium' (p. 105). Tranter takes end words from Ashbery's poem as the basis for his own lines, evoking Ern Malley at times and drawing on surrealism and the Oulipo group to challenge 'traditional notions of formal inventiveness' by rejecting ' "heroic" compositional methods' (p. 114).

The interview has been given specific attention in a new journal, *Writers in Conversation* (*WriC*). Australian authors Marion Halligan, Rob Harle, Claire Corbett, Jane Montgomery Griffiths, Hannah Kent, Christos Tsiolkas, and Andrea Goldsmith are included in the two 2014 online issues. Also interviewed by Laurie Glover and Nathaniel Williams are the SF writers Justine Larbalestier and Scott Westerfeld in *Writing on the Edge* (*WE* 24[2014] 96–106).

3. Canada

(a) Theses
There are shortcomings in our supposedly global Web. In this case, two databases listing theses on Canadian literature record only work done in

Canada and the United States, despite there being sites of Canadian literary studies in Britain, across Europe, in India, Australia, and beyond.

The good news is that Canadian writers are strongly represented in postgraduate work in North America. In no particular order, we find Jean Elizabeth O'Hara's queer indigenous studies work 'Up/Staging Two Spirit Plays: Unsettling Sexuality and Gender' (York U, DANS00128); Marrissa McHugh's 'The Invasion of the Home Front: Revisiting, Rewriting and Replaying the First World War in Contemporary Canadian Plays' (U Ottawa DANR98421); Emilia A. Rollie, also working on theatre, 'Women of the Northern Stage: Gender, Nationality and Identity in the Work of Canadian Women Stage Directors' (U Missouri, DA3577976); Jason Woodman Simmonds, 'Aboriginal Shakespeares as Communal Self-Fashioning' (U New Brunswick, DANR95395), along with Rebecca P. Huffman's '*Othello*, Narrative and the Material Construction of Subjectivity in Early Modern British Literature and Postcolonial Adaptations', which includes Djanet Sears's *Harlem Duet* (U Kentucky DA 3579744);

Shirley Anne McDonald examined 'Georgic Ideals and Claims of Entitlement in the Life Writing of Alberta Settlers' (U Alberta, DANR92596), and Josephene Kealey's 'The Mythology of the Small Community in Eight American and Canadian Short Story Cycles' covered Leacock, Duncan Campbell Scott, George Elliott, and Alice Munro (U Ottawa, DANR98206). Kathleen Margaret Patchell looked at 'Faith Fiction and Fame: *Sowing Seeds in Danny* and *Anne of Green Gables*' (U Ottawa, DANR98216), and from the same university Suzanne Bowness submitted 'In Their Own Words: Prefaces and Other Sites of Editorial Interactions in Nineteenth-Century Canadian Magazines' (DANR97996). Continuing the nineteenth-century connection, Abigail Ruth Heiniger wrote on '*Jane Eyre* and Her Transatlantic Literary Descendants: The Heroic Female Bildungsroman and Constructions of National Identity', which also included a reading of *Anne of Green Gables* (Wayne State U, DA3558169).

A more contemporary focus with some Canadian reference comes from Julie Ha Tran, 'Alien Cities: Anxieties about Race, Space, and the Body Politic in the Science Fiction City' (U California, Davis, DA3565566), while other anxieties are rehearsed in theses centred on diasporic writing: Jessica Marisol Brown-Velez, 'Travel, Migration, History, Identity and Place: Four Contemporary Ugandan Playwrights Abroad'—including George Seremba (U Wisconsin, Madison, DA3604289); 'Arab Pluralities and Transnationality: "A Crisis of Conscience" in Arab North American Fiction' by Sylvia Terziman (Wilfred Laurier U, DANR94201); Jeanette Taiyon Coleman includes Nalo Hopkinson in 'Out of the Frying Pan and Into the Fire: Narrative Past-Time as a Temporal Site of Racialized Identity Deconstruction' (U Minnesota, DA3567411) and Jessica Marie Best (U California, Riverside, DA3610895) writes '"Suspended Nameless in the Limbo State": Neoliberalism and Queer Caribbean Diasporas', including Shani Mootoo.

Gender and sexuality provide focus for several works. Lisa Robertson is amongst those discussed by Laurel Peacock in 'The Poetics of Affect in Contemporary Feminist Poetry' (U California, Santa Cruz, DA3589351). Naomi R. Mercer (U Wisconsin, Madison, DA3589098) considers '"Subversive

Feminist Thrusts": Feminist Dystopian Writing and Religious Fundamentalism in Margaret Atwood's *The Handmaid's Tale*, Louise Marley's *The Terrorists of Irustan*, Marge Piercy's *He, She and It*, and Sheri S. Tepper's *Raising the Stones*'. Nicole Lynn Sparling also examines *The Handmaid's Tale* in 'Womb Genealogies: Conceiving the New World' (Pennsylvania State U, DA3577721). Heather Hillsburg widens the scope in 'Furious Females: Women's Writing as an Archive of Anger' (U Ottawa, DANR98515) and Libe García Zarranz (U Alberta, DANS27546) brings together queer, gender, and diasporic elements in 'Queer TransCanadian Women's Writing in the Twenty-First Century: Assembling a New Cross-Border Ethic', reading Dionne Brand, Emma Donoghue, and Hiromi Goto.

Ethics are also at the heart of three quite different works: Jodi Giesbrecht's 'Killing the Beast: Animal Death in Canadian Literature, Hunting, Photography, Taxidermy and Slaughterhouses, 1865–1920' (U Toronto, DANR97007); 'Mourning from a Distance: Traumatic Post-Memory and the Ethics of Engagement' by Dragoslav Momcilovic, who includes treatment of Joy Kogawa's *Obasan* (U Wisconsin, Madison, DA3588525); and Michael Roberson's 'After Language Writing: In Defense of a Provision Poetics' (U Calgary, DANR96765).

(b) Themes and Debates
The major work of recent times comes from the TransCanada project, directed by Smaro Kamboureli. It investigates new directions for Canadian literary studies in the light of social changes and shifts in university systems. Kamboureli and Christl Verduyn have edited the final of three books, *Critical Collaborations: Indigeneity, Diaspora, and Ecology in Canadian Literary Studies*. Kamboureli supplies the introduction (pp. 1–28), moving from Northrop Frye's nation/family-based model of CanLit to a field of epistemic breaks, 'twisted intimacy', and new kinships beyond the filiative/complicit dualities of settler culture. Roy Miki follows with 'Belief as/in Methodology as/in Form: Doing Justice to CanLit Studies' (pp. 29–48). He notes that Frye did not attend to how state processes produced culture, and laments corporatized universities sidelining creative texts. Miki calls for creative critical reading in which the imagination is encountered both in texts and in readers as an unstable, affective whirlpool. The older ethical project of including minority texts in studies becomes a process of 'recognizing conditions producing differential relations from which we benefit or not depending on our access to dominant representational schemata' (p. 41). His analysis of work by Roy Kiyooka demonstrates how CanLit is a provisional and ongoing construction. Julia Emberley ('The Accidental Witness: Indigenous Epistemologies and Spirituality as Resistance in Eden Robinson's *Monkey Beach*', pp. 69–81) considers readers' relation to unsettling testimony narrative, positioning them as 'accidental witnesses' to the violence in both subject and writing in work telling of residential schools trauma. She then teases out underlying patterns of kinship and Haisla spirit canoe journeying to argue for an indigenous psychodrama of healing in contrast to Western theories of unrepresentable trauma. A challenging chapter more closely related to the

institutional questions behind the book is not about literature, but indigenous legal rights to land and nation (Sa'ke'j Henderson, 'Trans-Systemic Constitutionalism: Indigenous Law and Knowledge', pp. 49–68). Marie Battiste provides a more personal reflection on the developments in indigenous activism in 'Ambidextrous Epistemologies: Indigenous Knowledge within the Indigenous Renaissance' (pp. 83–98). These two chapters inform Larissa Lai's search for 'Epistemologies of Respect: A Poetic of Asian/Indigenous Relation' (pp. 99–126). Rejecting any neat apology that closes off history, Lai acknowledges that minority writing often gains acceptance at the expense of indigenous work, and adduces examples from performative collaborations (the 2008 Movement Project, David Khang's *How to Feed a Piano*, and Marie Clements's *Burning Vision*) to show how privilege can be undone, community invoked, and issues of social justice collectively addressed in a messy, open-ended assumption of relation and responsibility. As with many other chapters, Lai draws on Glissant, Lee Maracle, SKY Lee, and Daniel Heath-Justice. Law, politics, and culture come together in environmental studies, and three chapters—Catriona Sandilands, 'Acts of Nature: Literature, Excess and Environmental Politics' (pp. 127–42); Cheryl Lousley, 'Ecocriticism in the Unregulated Zone' (pp. 143–60); and Laurie Ricou, 'Disturbance-Loving Species: Habitat Studies, Ecocritical Pedagogy and Canadian Literature' (pp. 161–74)—look respectively at Dionne Brand's *Land to Light On*, Larissa Lai's *Saltfish Girl*, and a poem, 'Pond', by Don McKay. They posit the expression of a different kind of awe that disrupts universalist ideas of nature, the mix of unregimented hope and chaotic dystopia in which literature is not a barrier but an immersive experience, and attending to locations and linkages from an animal's or plant's perspective. Julie Rak ('Translocal Representation: Chief Buffalo Child Long Lance, Nello "Tex" Vernon-Wood and CanLit', pp. 175–98) crosses cultural studies with literature to examine celebrity figures that cross racial and state boundaries. Problems of belonging and not belonging for people who 'pass' in order to inhabit dominant national spaces lead Rak to reject the transnational in favour of a more nuanced and site-specific translocal. Winfried Siemerling goes translocal by delving into 'Jazz, Diaspora and the History and Writing of Black Anglophone Montreal' (pp. 199–213), citing novels by Callaghan, MacLennan, Gabrielle Roy, Ernest Tucker, Nigel Thomas, and Mairuth Sarsfield. Local, but beyond the anglophone bounds of this review, is François Paré's 'Tradition and Pluralism in Contemporary Acadia' (pp. 215–25). Chrystl Verduyn closes the collection with 'Critical Allegiances' (pp. 227–39), a summation of the TransCanada project and its focus on 'shifts that undiscipline the discipline' and generate 'multiple constituencies' within and beyond the nation construct. The book disappoints in often appearing to merely add on new groups and approaches to the established body of work, but it does set up the parameters for an ongoing questioning and revision of structures.

Contemporary interest in book history and the supporting mechanisms of literary production produces 'Modernism and the Magazines: North America' by Christopher MacGowan (*Mo/Mo* 21:iii[2014] 843–9). This focus is given a gender twist in Michelle Smith's 'Fiction and the Nation: The Construction of Canadian Identity in *Chatelaine* and *Canadian Home Journal* during the 1930s and 1940s' (*BJCS* 27:i[2014] 37–53), while Jody Mason adds a class perspective from a decade earlier: ' "Rebel Woman", "Little Woman" and the Eclectic Print Culture of Protest in *The Woman Worker* 1926–1929' (*CanL* 220[2014] 17–35). This is preceded by Laura Moss's 'distant reading' approach in 'Auditing, Counting, and Tracking CanLit' (*CanL* 220[2014] 6–15). Moss details the 'audit culture' we are all subject to these days at national level and within our institutions. She makes the point that numbers can tell a story and provide a basis for useful knowledge and getting good things done, giving stats on reader patterns in relation to *Canadian Literature* to prove her point, though she also warns that numbers do not tell us how a text affects a reader and are not the full story. Michael Ross in the same issue considers 'Imperial Commerce and the Canadian Muse: The Hudson Bay Company's Poetic Advertising Campaign of 1966–1972' (*CanL* 220[2014] 37–53). More in line with Moss's big picture schema is Anouk Lang's 'Canadian Magazines and Their Spatial Contexts: Digital Possibilities and Practical Realities' (*IJCS* 48[2014] 213–32). Pushing on from the kind of mapping of texts initiated by Franco Moretti, Lang looks at little magazines, mapping the places they come from and the places mentioned in them as imaginative sites, and reflecting on when it is actually useful to spend time digitizing and mapping texts. The critical question behind attention to popular forms of literary dissemination is addressed by Albert Raimundo Braz: 'The Good and the Read: Literary Value and Readership in Canadian Literature' (*CRCL* 41:ii[2014] 174–82).

Literary value is a question driving contemporary attention to the middlebrow. This intersects with book history and cultural studies and is the focus of a special issue of the *International Journal of Canadian Studies* 48[2014], edited by Faye Hammill and Michelle Smith. Wendy Roy looks at 'Home as Middle Ground in Adaptations of *Anne of Green Gables* and *Jalna*' (*IJCS* 48[2014] 9–31), using Homi Bhabha's 'The World and the Home' to reflect on how international screen adaptations of the two middlebrow novels make the homely nation-home into an unhomely imagined middle ground, not quite Canada, not quite anywhere else. Gillian Roberts, '*The Book of Negroes* Illustrated Edition: Circulating African-Canadian History through the Middlebrow' (*IJCS* 48[2014] 53–66) reflects on how the prize-winning novel becomes a medium for pleasurable learning of subaltern history via the Canada Reads programme, a television version, and a 'souvenir edition' laden with photographs. Roberts notes Henry James's scorn of illustrations as relegating novels to middlebrow rank and analyses the complex circulations between historical documents and novel text: how some pictures provide insights into the novel's story, while decorative African pictures make it into a safe 'National Geographic' aestheticized pedagogy. Hannah McGregor and Michelle Smith consider 'Martha Ostenso, Periodical Culture and the Middlebrow' (*IJCS* 48[2014] 67–83), looking at how the 'frame' of *Chatelaine* magazine interacts with the writer's short stories about femininity, national identity, and consumerism. ' "A Sweet Canadian Girl": English-Canadian Actresses' Transatlantic Careers through the Lenses of Canadian Magazines' (*IJCS* 48[2014] 119–35) has Cecilia Morgan assessing how glamour was exchanged between actress and magazine in negotiations between local cultural production and transnational circuits. Marie Vautier reviews English- and French-language Canadian fiction, their interactions and their common 'dialogue' with Europe. She then posits a major shift towards literary engagement with South America, turning from Frances Brooke's *The History of Emily Montague* and *L'Influence d'un livre* by Philippe Aubert de Gaspé *fils* to Nicolas Dickner's *Nikolski* in 'Hemispheric Travel from Europe to las Américas: The Imaginary and the Novel in Québec and Canada' (*IJCS* 48[2014] 191–212).

Jordan Stouck analyses critical practice in 'The Ghosts of Canadian Criticism: History and Social Justice' (*CLIO* 43:iii[2014] 385–95). One revenant ghost is Northrop Frye, summoned forth by Brett David Potter in 'A Word Not Our Own: Northrop Frye and Karl Barth on Revelation and Imagination' (*L&T* 28:iv[2014] 438–56), while Miriam Wallraven also charts connections between literature and history: ' "To Make a History from This Kind of Material is Not Easy": The Narrative Construction of Cultural History in Contemporary Fiction' (*ZAA* 62:ii[2014] 131–48). Her generalized title covers some treatment of Margaret Atwood's *The Handmaid's Tale*. General narrative analysis comes from Heilna du Plooy, who includes a reading of Anne Michaels in 'Between Past and Future: Temporal Thresholds in Narrative Texts' (*JLST* 30:iii[2014] 1–24).

Early Canadian texts don't feature as much as in other years, but from Australia, Mandy Treagus provides two takes on Sara Jeannette Duncan, one a chapter in *Changing the Victorian Subject*, edited by herself, Maggie Tonkin, Madeleine Seys, and Sharon Crozier-de Rosa, the other a section in her own *Empire Girls: The Colonial Heroine Comes of Age*. 'The Woman Artist and Narrative Ends in Late-Victorian Writing' (pp. 201–15) claims that Elfrida in *A Daughter of To-day* [1984] shows none of the 'sense of self-sacrificing duty' common to female protagonists of the time but ambitiously pursues artistic success and derives her assertiveness from *Le Journal de Marie Bashkirtseff* [1887; translated 1890]. The same text and its depiction of the New Woman in a female *Künstlerroman* is the subject of a more detailed and wider-ranging reading in *Empire Girls* (pp. 109–72). Duncan's own position as a Canadian married to an Englishman and living in Calcutta, with experience in journalism, is explored for its complex negotiations of social position, and Elfrida's struggle to be an artist reflects the author's quest to gain recognition as a novelist independent of male standards. Elfrida's suicide is taken as the necessary ultimate expression of female bohemian selfhood prevented from succeeding at either *Bildung* or romance. Duncan's acceptance of ties between nationality and character is offset by her use of ironic exposure of contradictions. The same novel is examined by Cecily Devereux for how it deploys burlesque, in 'An Adventure in Stageland: Sara Jeannette Duncan, Imperial Burlesque, and the Performance of White Femininity in *A Daughter of To-day*' (*NCC* 36:i[2014] 35–51). Women's life writing from Prince Edward Island in the nineteenth and early twentieth century is collected and examined by Mary McDonald-Rissanen in *In the Interval of the Wave*. Cecily Devereux provides the afterword to a reissue of Nellie McClung's 1925 *Painted Fires*, which has a foreword by Benjamin Lefebvre, who also introduces a new edition of Ralph Connor (Charles William Gordon)'s 1909 *The Foreigner: A Tale of Saskatchewan* (afterword from Daniel Coleman). These titles are in Wilfrid Laurier University's Early Canadian Literature series.

Oana Godeanu-Kenworthy, 'Creole Frontiers: Imperial Ambiguities in John Richardson's and James Fenimore Cooper's Fiction' (*EAL* 49:iii[2014] 741–70), invokes settler theory (after Edward Watts) to break from reading these works in a nation-building framework, and open up complexities of negotiation between indigeneity and 'creole' settler relations to land, empire, and whiteness. Cooper is more national and Richardson more colonial. Transnational publishing networks entailed three audiences: European, North American, 'and the new Creole political communities that identified with both' (p. 4). 'Creole' is moved out of a purely racialized understanding to position the two authors in relation to the politics of the time such that, while Cooper uses 'the frontier and the natives to articulate a national form of indigeneity that marks the separation of American culture from its imperial roots, Richardson uses the same material to create a continuous and legitimate imperial past for Canada's colonial present' (p. 9). Richardson also has none of Cooper's nostalgia for a vanishing frontier: nature is a distinct threat; he also values submission to communal civility more than individualist liberty. His Britons are an ethnically and racially diverse group and there is less concern over miscegenation, although crossing the racial divide is avoided.

As departments of comparative literature (and world literature) resist or struggle to accommodate the genuine global variety of writing, new frameworks and pedagogies are sought. The *Canadian Review of Comparative Literature* issued two numbers in 2014 that canvas what is happening and what might happen in Canadian classrooms. There's a lot of 'theorese' peppered throughout and some broad-brush thinking, but how to integrate postcolonial cultural dynamics and indigenous writing into existing structures and practices is a question properly addressed. In volume 41:ii, this issue is tackled by Lindsay R. Parker, and by Pushpa Acharya's advocacy for 'critical regionalism', by Avishek Ray, and by Asma Sayed's 'globalectic reading' of the current situation. '(Non-)Geographical Futures of Comparative Literature', edited by Daniel Fried and Zhang Hui, includes Yulia Pushkarevskaya Naughton's '"In Transit": Taxi Driving as a Mini Paradigm in Gaito Gazdanov's *Night Roads* and Helen Potrebenko's *Taxi!*' (*CRCL* 41:iii[2014] 242–53).

English Studies in Canada in 2014 included a special edition, 'The Dirt on Dirt Today', with an introduction by Mark Simpson taking us through biochemical citizen science to environmental issues, discursive patterns of representation, affect, and so on. 'Feeling dirty' has both social and somatic implications, as Cara Fabre makes clear in her reading of a novel on anorexia, 'This Hunger Is DNA You Cannot Undo: Anorexia and Economically Oriented Subjects in Ibi Kaslik's *Skinny*' (*ESC* [2014] 83–107). Other literary-related articles are Linda Morra's on getting dirty in archives to 'tell the dirt' on our cleaned-up literary canons. She focuses on Marlene NourbeSe Philip's documents and an extraordinary 'shock-jock' attack on her by Michael Coren in 1995 in ' "I'm a Dirty Girl" ' (*ESC* [2014] 5–8). Travis V. Mason, 'Valuing the Devalued, or Dirty Apprehension' (*ESC* [2014] 14–18), looks at poetry by Ken Babstock and Alden Nowlan, starting with the figuring of excess and rubbish dumps versus the representation of nature as 'dirty' by contrast to human civilization. Owing something to Don McKay's 1993 essay on ravens and other ecocritical work, Mason considers poems about gulls (resilient scavengers; mirrors of our own qualities and violence). Cheryl Lousley charts 'Slow Violence and Dirty Mourning' (*ESC* [2014] 31–6) in three versions of the dirty work of coalminers: Sheldon Currie's story, 'The Glace Bay Miners' Museum' [1977], Wendy Lill's 1991 stage version of it, and Mort Ransen's film adaptation, *Margaret's Museum* [1995]. All centre on Margaret's 'dirty' memorializing of dead relatives, preserving body parts for public display to make clear the dirty business of a mining industry that chews up its workers and leaves women to eke out a living in slums. Patrick Lane's novel is the subject of George Grinnell's piece, ' "There Is Another Story, There Always Is" . . . *Red Dog, Red Dog* and the Okanagan' (*ESC* [2014] 109–31). Grinnell notes the despair in the family history in the book and shows how it reveals 'the ways in which memory and grief are attached to the land', revealing a history of environmental degradation and violence behind the tourist facade of the Okanagan valley today. At the same time, the land is romantically figured as an abiding potentially redemptive strength. Playing across looking at and looking away, the novel's uncertainty leads the writer to think about species loss and loss of land in the valley and the dangers of ecological 'improvement'. The article draws upon Timothy Morton's ecological writings. Sarah Wylie Krotz considers the deployment of maps within and around literary texts, noting the turn to 'geocritical' examinations of textual evocations of place, and analysing the exhibition on the Library and Archives Canada website, 'Canada: A Literary Tour'. The 'emplacement' of writers is made problematic in an age of transnational movements (Dionne Brand is cited as an example), but new digital cartographies might provide new ways of remapping literary Canada. This article is fascinating to the non-Canadian reader for the density of attention across time to fixing literary works and writers on the national map. Australian efforts, by contrast, have been mere sporadic sketches.

The First World War has had a lot of attention lately, due in part to the centenary of its beginnings. In *The Great War in Post-Memory and Film*, edited by Martin Löschnigg and Marzena Sokołowska-Paryż, Löschnigg writes ' "Like Dying on Stage": Theatricality and Remembrance in Anglo-Canadian Drama on the First World War' (pp. 153–69); Cherrill Grace is 'Remembering *The Wars*' (pp. 220–37), while Hanna Teichler considers 'Joseph Boyden's *Three Day Road*: Transcultural (Post-)Memory and Identity in Canadian World War I Fiction' (pp. 239–53). In a later section of the book, Alicia Fahey contributes 'Voices from the Edge: De-centering Master Narratives in Jane Urquhart's *The Stone Carvers*' (pp. 411–26). Brigitte Johanna Glaser also provides a comparative study of six novels, including Urquhart's and Frances Itani's *Deafening*, in 'Women and World War I: "Postcolonial" Imaginative rewritings of the Great War' (pp. 425–42).

Löschnigg notes that critical attention to Findley, Hodgkins, and Boyden in fiction has not been matched by work on theatre, and surveys ten or so works that range from tragedy to burlesque, using Nora's *lieu de mémoire* as a framing concept and following Sherrill Grace's identification of a shift towards examining the process of remembering and away from the historical events themselves. The plays depict Canada's 'loss of innocence' while critiquing the legend of the war as a catalyst for national self-realization. Gray and Peterson's music-hall-style *Billy Bishop Goes to War*, Vern Thiessen's *Vimy*, set in a field hospital, two Newfoundland works, David French's *Soldier's Heart* and Kevin Major's *No Man's Land*, and Wendy Lill's *The Fighting Days* depict divisions of ethnicity, region, and gender behind the new collective sense of national identity. Massicotte's *Mary's Wedding*, Vanderhaeghe's *Dancock's Dance*, and Anne Chislett's *Quiet in the Land* variously show the madness of war, and R.H. Thomson's *The Lost Boys*, based on real letters from the Front, shows the lasting traumas of war memory—a theme worked in French and by Vanderhaeghe as well. Presenting the war as theatrical in a theatre context reminds audiences of the constructed drama of war and nation.

Grace presents Findley's 1977 novel as a pioneer of the turn to cultural memory and puts it into biographical context. She sketches critical responses, highlighting Diana Brydon's focus on bearing witness, and discussing the book's mix of biography and fiction: constructed intimacy and documentary distance; varying witness reports of one event; the ethics of remembering/ shaping memory. 'For Findley, nothing is born on the battlefield. It is what we do with the remembering of that obscene past that matters (p. 234).

Teichler considers how Boyden's *Three Day Road* reflects on identity formation, reconstruction, and the nation's process of reconciliation with First Nations people. Anglo-Canada's 'grand narrative' of the birth of a nation hides the involvement of indigenous soldiers in the First World War, and the novel depicts (in its mix of oral forms, indigenous myth, and modernist historical writing) complexities in their negotiation of traditional identities and the machineries of Western conflict, mapping these onto Canada's 'in-between' status as not quite British, not quite independent. For Native soldiers, home turns into another battleground as they struggle to reconnect with both nation and indigenous society. The hope of healing echoes in all returnees and readers remembering wartime loss, as the book's connection with 'mainstream' writing through the shared narratives of war inserts an indigenous story into the national one.

Alicia Fahey looks at Urquhart presenting women telling stories about their village's origins, including some of the battle of Vimy Ridge. Like Findley, Urquhart had absorbed the 'post-memory' of war through family stories and documents and (in line with Lyotard's questioning of grand narratives) inserts multiple marginalized voices into the official national history, interrogating through the image of the monument the way we commemorate war. Urquhart reworks Walter Allward's grand commemorative statue as a more personal work by a woman mourning a lost lover, and concludes by indicating the need to continue memory work and the inability of a fixed monument to preserve the memory of its meanings.

Citing Stewart Hall on the positional nature of all claims, Brigitte Glaser works from postcolonial insistence on local situatedness in relation to world history to look at how marginal colonial sites and marginalized women's voices are deployed to reposition centre/margin dichotomies. Frances Itani's *Deafening* shows how women were kept away from the front but had their domestic peace shattered when they had to become nurses to the traumatized and wounded returnees. Urquhart's Klara, another woman left behind, shows how differences of ethnicity, gender, and individual experience make up the collective story as she shifts attention from battles to memories of loss.

Neta Gordon has produced *Catching the Torch: Contemporary Canadian Literary Responses to World War I*. The introduction rehearses the paradox of Canada's defining itself as a peace-keeping nation by invoking a 'coming of age in battle' myth. Gordon positions her studies around the tropes first worked by John McRae's 'In Flanders Fields' poem, the memory work that attends the Great War, and concepts of sacrifice, nation, commemoration, and unity. Texts show that the national character (quiet duty, tolerance) emerges not *in spite* of reluctance to fight but *as a product* of that reluctance (pp. 5, 15), remarking that few of the texts analysed actually concentrate on battlefield action and none ends in pessimism or in denouncing participation in the war (pp. 21, 79), even while working the 'war is hell' motif. Chapter 1 considers the device of having the dead speak in McRae's poem, the plays *Dancock's Dance* and *Mary's Wedding*, and a novella, *The Deep*. The mask in Vanderhaeghe undoes traditional elegy in which soldiers die so that we might live, substituting a mourning for old values of honour (p. 35); Massicotte shows the irrelevance of elegy in generations separated from the actual deaths and how we are inspired to live through performing memory at a remove. Swan's book is also about how the present makes the dead into what it needs them to be. Chapter 2 deals with concepts of nation in Jack Hodgins's *Broken Ground* and Frances Itani's *Deafening*. Hodgins's early work suggests the war is so morally questionable that it cannot sustain narratives of sacrifice and progress, showing the counter-battle of returned soldiers struggling to conquer their assigned plots of land, whereas Itani allows a national romance based on grief being personal rather than political and community being affirmed through wartime loss. Chapter 3 takes up Dagmar Novak's work on war fiction and her three-stage model in which Findley's *The Wars* is the apex for its presentation of heroism as personal rather than collective and of documentary claims to truth-telling as being unreliable. Alan Cumyn (*The Sojourn, The Famished Lover*) and Jane Urquhart (*The Underpainter, The Stone Carvers*) are less interested in how to use historical record: 'both authors promote the idea that war insiders have a private narrative, one that they either wish to protect from outsiders or forget', whereas outsiders often exploit their narratives for their own purposes (p. 86). There are interesting observations on how Cumyn's novels differ from similar British work and on how he 'willingly rejects the rhetoric of national or ideological sacrifice [but] leaves a space for the type of warfare that a man can still be proud of' (p. 105). Neither Cumyn nor Urquhart is a postmodernist; the latter uses artist figures who try to transcend the details of history but do not deny historical authority. Chapter 4 looks at depictions of war of 'Other Canadians'. If the war forged a national identity, how did First Nations, Québecois, Newfoundland, or German Canadian communities feel about that? Two plays (Vern Thiessen's *Vimy* and Kevin Kerr's *Unity*) and two novels (Joseph Boyden's *Three Day Road* and Daniel Poliquin's *A Secret Between Us / La Kermesse*) are examined here. Gordon claims that Thiessen undermines his interest in diversity and individuals by presenting a fighting unit melded by battle, whereas Kerr (staging a home-front hospital threatened by the Spanish flu—the contagion of war) more critically inspects how unity is constructed. Boyden writes marginalized dysfunction into potentially redemptive living story while Poliquin 'skewers almost every sacred myth' about the war. 'Together what these texts seem to suggest is that even though the national collective is an illusion, it is still—for better or worse—an ideal' (p. 125). There are interesting observations on the 'structural and figurative doublings' in Boyden's book (p. 141) and the problematic connection of sacred time to historical time. Like all the others, Poliquin examines what is worth remembering versus what is chosen to be remembered, and most radically presents an ignoble impersonator in place of the soldier hero. Comments on the function and reception of the translated work suggest further discussion. This is a bare-bones account of a solid set of essays that draw on a wide range of criticism and theory. At times it sounds as though there is an implicit postmodern, post-national standard against which works are found wanting due to some conservative recuperation of a national/communal ideal. The book closes with analysis of the movie *Passchendaele*, contrasting its generic typicality with some of the more complex moves of the plays and novels, and sketching shifts in the national myth following Canada's engagement in Afghanistan.

A book that moves us tidily from McRae's 'In Flanders Fields' to Joseph Boyden and indigenous writing is Cynthia Sugars's *Canadian Gothic: Literature, History and the Spectre of Self-Invention*. Like Neta Gordon, Sugars begins with the dead voices animated by McRae's poem to map out a white settler desire for ghosts to fill the absence of a new world, mixed with fear of the haunting wilderness and native Other. Canadian Gothic, she says, is about settlers being haunted by their relationship to the Gothic itself (p. 75) as an uncanny import used to render homely their unsettled settlement. Sugars looks at the classic works of 'Wilderness Gothic' and charts how French Canadian figures are deployed to anchor an Anglo and European presence. She examines settler representations and appropriations of indigeneity and postcolonial invocations of haunting as both confessions of usurpation and reinscriptions of self in the land and its history (Atwood, Munro, Reaney, Robertson Davies, Findley, and Jane Urquhart are discussed). 'Strangers Within' considers how ethnic minority writers (Brand, Goto, Chariandy, Mayr, Ondaatje) work with 'hauntings of Canadian hauntings' and figures of 'genealogical monstrosity' (p. 180) to disrupt national myths, and ends with a chapter on indigenous writers using 'ghost' figures to teach about the present and undo their own gothicizing by white settler culture. The book carries its theoretical underpinnings lightly and provides a well-structured and clearly argued reading of works mostly familiar by now in Canadian literary studies. Its general propositions are applicable also to other settler nations' writing.

Indigenous studies are well represented in 2014. The main and excitingly important work is *Indigenous Poetics in Canada*, edited by Cree poet Neal McLeod. Arranged in four sections mapping the poetics of memory, performance, place and space, and medicine, the book points to aesthetic practices such as indirect reference, counselling narratives, and the linking together of stories. A second volume will follow. Journals include a philosophical ethics discussion: '"Just Say No": Eden Robinson and Gabor Maté on Moral Luck and Addiction' by Sabrina Reed (*Mosaic* 47:iv[2014] 151–66), and Roshaya Rodness examines the social function of the writer and its media production in 'Thomas King's National Literary Celebrity and the Cultural Ambassadorship of a Native Canadian Writer' (*CanL* 220[2014] 55–72). Identity and performativity frame Laura Beard's 'Playing Indian in the Works of Rebecca Belmore, Marilyn Dumont, and Ray Young Bear' (*AIQ* 38:iv[2014] 492–511). The graphic novel seems to be a particular innovation amongst indigenous Canadian authors and is examined in one manifestation by Miriam Brown Spiers in 'Creating a Haida Manga: The Formline of Social Responsibility in *Red*' (*SAIL* 26:iii[2014] 41–61). Angela Van Essen begins with classroom experience to think through modes of English and storytelling and the cultural politics thereof in 'Circling Stories: Cree Discourse and Narrative Ways of Knowing' (*WE* 25:i[2014] 44–55). Not seen in time for this review, there is 'Games with Kitsch in the Works of Sherman Alexie and Thomas King' by Monika Kocot in Justyna Stępień's collection, *Redefining Kitsch and Camp in Literature and Culture* (pp. 99–122).

Indigenous Perspectives of North America: A Collection of Studies, edited by Enikö Sepsi, Judit Nagy, Miklos Vassányi, and János Kenyeresl, is not a collection of writing by indigenous North Americans but a compendium of essays about them, their writing, and the politics of race relations, mostly from Canadian studies scholars in Europe (and mostly from Hungary). Hartmut Lutz provides a survey of the emergence of indigenous writing in Canada, setting its 'writing back' and 'writing home' against multiculturalism and giving readings of short extracts to illustrate general points. There are also short readings of Daniel David Moses' play *Kyotopolis* (by Martin Kuestler, pp. 102–10), Aboriginal and Métis work read through a postcolonial lens (Cristina-Georgiana Voicu, pp. 125–31), Thomas King's attempt to counter representations of First Nations people and culture in school textbooks in his picture book for children (Fátima Susana Amante, pp. 132–42), Jeannette Armstrong's *Breath Tracks* and land memory (Anna Mongibello, pp. 143–59), Thomas King's *The Truth about Stories* (Éva Zsizsmann, pp. 160–9), *Halfbreed* and *In Search of April Raintree* (Eszter Szenczi, pp. 170–7), and Emily Carr's painting and writing about indigenous subjects (Katalina Kürtosi, pp. 178–8). János Kenyeres looks at non-indigenous attraction to Native culture in art and literature, with some attention to Jack Hodgins (pp. 264–79). The collection does not offer many new insights to scholars familiar with the field, but it will be a useful reference book for anyone starting to study it.

Marc Maufort has produced a chapter, 'Forging Native Idioms: Canadian and Australasian Performances of Indigeneity in an Age of Globalization' (in Moser and Simonis, eds., *Figuren des Globalen*, pp. 703–15). It covers Canadian Kevin Loring's *Where the Blood Mixes*, New Zealander Miria George's *Urban Hymns*, and Australian Wesley Enoch's *Black Medea*.

Lynne Wiltse, Ingrid Johnston, and Kylie Yang, 'Pushing Comfort Zones: Promoting Social Justice through the Teaching of Canadian Literature' (*ChE* 21:iii[2014] 264–77), bring Eden Robinson's *Monkey Beach* and Richard Wagamese's *Keeper 'n Me* together with a 'pedagogy of discomfort' to discuss two instances of classroom interrogation of assumptions and marginalizations in relation to diversity in schools.

Indigenous, mixed-race, and black diasporic studies can become tied together in problematic but productive ways. Petra Fachinger, 'Intersections of Diaspora and Indigeneity: The Standoff at Kahnesatake in Lee Maracle's *Sundogs* and Tessa McWatt's *Out of My Skin*' (*CanL* 220[2014] 74–91), notes how few works there are on the 'Oka uprising' and, in the context of a general shift from considering white appropriation of indigenous work to looking for more complex interactions, invokes solidarities (and differences) between indigenous and diasporic minority groups. Maracle depicts an internal diaspora of the Native to the city and the rebirth of self-assertive community there under female leadership, while McWatt explores new ideas of home that also challenge standard dichotomies of the national imaginary. Both books have their central characters use old myths to anchor themselves and critique media manipulation of the Oka standoff. McWatt's protagonist bonds with another adoptee of indigenous origin, but does not altogether confront diasporic complicity in settler colonialism.

In the same issue, the Caribbean and Canada are linked in Andrea Medovarski's 'Roughing it in Bermuda: Mary Prince, Susanna Strickland Moodie, Dionne Brand, and the Black Diaspora' (*CanL* 220[2014] 94–114). Moodie in England advocated abolition and read Mary Prince. The author uses this detail to reread Moodie as 'diasporic' rather than 'settler' in an effort to open up a conceptual space for a 'black Canada' to emerge. She exposes the (contradictory) racism in *Roughing it in the Bush* as an index to the nation's exclusion of blackness from its narrative, and brings in Dionne Brand's work (*A Map to the Door of No Return* and *Land to Light On*) as rewriting the nation/landscape to show its historical complexities—with some interesting parallels to Moodie.

Brand's work is also examined by Erica L. Johnson in 'Building the Neo-Archive: Dionne Brand's *A Map to the Door of No Return*' (*MFRT* 12:i[2014] 149–71). The central interest is the rich mix of intertextual reference: exploration and slavery-era accounts, contemporary archives of papers and journals, and the 'neo-archive' of postcolonial writers. The interest is in 'how Brand structures something as intimate as personal memory and identity as an intervention in the archive', in part as protest against having to deploy the archive to prove one's humanity (p. 149). Hersch's 'postmemory' is invoked to mark the fusion of individual and collective immersion in history. Affective memory and inspiration from Toni Morrison, Césaire, Naipaul, Coetzee, and others are ways of escaping captivity in the colonialist archive.

Caribbean–Canadian connections are further delineated by Heather Smyth in 'The Black Atlantic Meets the Black Pacific: Multimodality in Kamau Brathwaite and Wayde Compton' (*Callaloo* 37:ii[2014] 389–403). Compton cites Brathwaite as part of a network of connections within black diasporic culture that render black Vancouver life as more than just peripheral to nation and dominant notions of diaspora. Compton shares with Brathwaite a 'mash-up' of language, music, 'turntabling' feedback video-style to bring out multiple meanings and 'tidalectic' flows.

In 'The Transcultural Intertextuality of George Elliott Clarke's African Canadianité: (African) American Models Shaping *George & Rue*' (*AAR* 47:i[2014] 113–28), Ana María Fraile-Marcos attends to the echoes of Richard Wright, Zora Neale Hurston, and William Styron to illustrate Clarke's theory of black Canadian writers having to both repeat and reject not just white

North American but also African American writing in order to discover a complex and different identity.

A different Afro-Canadian identity is worked at by Esi Edugyan in Molly Littlewood McKibbin's 'Subverting the German Volk: Racial and Musical Impurity in Esi Edugyan's *Half-Blood Blues*' (*Callaloo* 37:ii[2014] 413–31). McKibbin traces Nazi constructions of purity in both race and music to then show how Edugyan undoes them in his novel featuring a black German musician 'unhoused' in both France and Germany during the war, who reworks 'Horst Wessel' as a blues tune.

Black diaspora slides over into 'brown' diaspora and the broader category of the 'multicultural'. Alejandra Moreno Álvarez compares two stories, 'Squatter' by Rohinton Mistry, and 'One out of Many' by V.S. Naipaul, in 'Somatic Effects of Migration: R. Mistry and V.S. Naipaul' (in Francisco Fernández and Moreno Alvarez, eds., *A Rich Field Full of Pleasant Surprises: Essays on Contemporary Literature in Honour of Professor Socorro Suárez Lafuente*, pp. 38–49). Both stories feature migrant protagonists crouched on toilets as they move from one country to another; one to Canada only to return to India and find himself doubly displaced, the other to settle in the US. There is mention of *Family Matters* and Rushdie's *Imaginary Homelands*, the focus being on physical discomforts of the body in transit and Bergson's idea of beings in process.

Robert Zacharias examines ambiguities of location in 'In-Between World and Worlds Within: Reading Diasporic Return in Vassanji and Bissoondath' (*CJPLI* 1:ii[2014] 207–21. *The In-Between World of Vikram Lall* and *The Worlds Within Her* show characters escaping the traps of national politics to return at some point either to redeem or exorcize the past. Vassanji's character expects Canada to be an isolated safe haven, but railway history and the Internet link it with his Kenyan origins; Bissoondath's protagonist critiques the ethno-politics of diasporic Indians, but leaves Canada as an 'ontological emptiness' neglecting its own historical and contemporary politics. The readings are of interest, though the critical framework (which faults diaspora studies for not attending to returns and suggests this arises from nation-based methodologies inherited from postcolonial literary studies) seems to forget the body of work on the 'been-to' figure, and to put aside the turn to the 'transnational' that responds to the limitations in recent times of the diaspora model. In the new journal of literary interviews *Writers in Conversation*, Asma Sayed contributes 'Between Nepal and Canada: In Conversation with Pushpa Raj Acharya, Edmonton's 2014–14 Writer-in-Exile' (*WriC* 1:ii[2014] 11 pp.).

Jumana Bayeh's book *The Literature of the Lebanese Diaspora: Representations of Place and National Identity* includes a chapter on Rawi Hage's novel *De Niro's Game* (pp. 101–38) in a section on the city and war. Asserting that the Maronite community has exercised strategic amnesia about its militia's involvement in atrocities, the author reads the opposing attitudes of Hage's two central characters as a challenge to such a tidied-up history and ghettoized view of Beirut. Said, Adorno, and Camus are invoked in the process.

Two book chapters provide thematic readings of texts that are adequately summed up in their titles. Judith Misrahi-Barak looks at 'Rifts and Riffs,

Roots and Routes: Ramabai Espinet's *The Swinging Bridge*' (in Dwivedi, ed., *Tracing the New Indian Diaspora*, pp. 235–51), and Christine Vogt-William charts 'Masculinities Out of Line: Navigating Queerness and Diasporic Identity in Shyam Selvadurai's *Funny Boy* and Shani Mootoo's *Cereus Blooms at Night*' (in Misrahi-Barak and Reynaud, eds., *Diasporas, Cultures of Mobilities, 'Race', I: Diasporas and Cultures of Migrations*, pp. 323–44).

Pluri-culture et écrits migratoires / Pluri-Culture and Migrant Writings, edited by Elizabeth Sabiston and Robert Drummond, includes an interesting assessment by Olga Stein of the dual function of prizes as affecting ethnic minority writing, 'Literary Prizes and Diasporic Writers in Canada: Valorization or Containment' (pp. 315–25).

The most important 2014 work on minority ethnic literary production is Larissa Lai's *Slanting I, Imagining We: Asian Canadian Literary Production in the 1980s and 1990s*, which proposes that Asian Canadian writing and commentary post-1970s, while drawing on older narratives of oppositional heroic emergence, is characterized by ruptures and relationality, informed by poststructuralist theory and works in solidarity with other marginalized cultural groups across paradoxical spaces and different temporalities. Lai provides a strategic genealogy of key moments in literature, film, criticism, and social activism, invoking Foucault, Bhabha, Spivak, Roy Miki, Monika Kin Gagnon, Himani Bannerjee, Smaro Kamboureli, and others to problematize any simplistic understanding of this. Concentrating on the 1980s and 1990s, she mentions ongoing tussles over appropriation that operate across racial lines but also cut across finer lines of nation, class, history, sexuality, and language. Judith Butler's focus on embodiment and iterative sedimentation is applied to these struggles in a careful tracking of how power works, showing how the concept of 'Asian Canadian literature' is an unstable category performing different functions as its contexts of use shift.

Lai's first chapter looks at Wayson Choy and Evelyn Lau 'breaking the silence' around an Asian presence in Canadian culture and the need to retain some 'silence' about subjectivity to escape conscription into the national story. Chapter 2 surveys special 'Asian' issues of journals that are 'exalted in their specialness but debased in the sense that as interruptions to the regular stream . . . they never constitute the regular stream' (p. 33). Chapter 3 considers key anthologies of Asian Canadian writing in the context of state movements from liberal democracy to neoliberal economics. Anthologies enable entry to institutions but thereby run the risk of promoting the containment of political and creative energies and the ossification of the dynamic category of the Asian Canadian. Representational strategies of 'radical carnival' in the major texts of Hiromi Goto are analysed in chapter 4, and chapter 5 presents Rita Wong and jam ismail as working excess to maintain radical edginess in naming and breaking race. In keeping with the idea of Asian Canadian cultural work being relational, the final chapter looks at characters in Atwood's *Oryx and Crake* and Brand's *What We All Long For* and their attempt to escape Enlightenment liberal subjectivity in abjection. Brand offers a glimpse of positive solidarity with those excluded as exceptional by the state, whereas Atwood ends up supporting the status quo. The book is very good at drawing situational complexities in flows of affect and of power. It may be summed up in a passage from the chapter 'queering' anthologies: ' "becoming" is important because it does not require the truth of any essence in order to be productive.... . But if [endpoints] cease to be important, if instead what leads to an open-ended future is the flow between intensities, then liberation resides not in any revolution or any institution, but in the imperfect moment of flow, in the unruly present. What becomes necessary for this kind of liberation is not a polemic, but rather a catalyst' (p. 125). What I would like to suggest here is that the so-called identity-based texts of the late 1980s and early 1990s, that have fallen so out of favour of late, were doing, and continue to do, that catalytic work.

Popular genre scholarship is represented by Adam Glaz writing on alien communication and how we would recognize it at all in a classic SF work and Peter Watt's 2006 novel: 'Rorschach, We Have a Problem! The Linguistics of First Contact in Watt's *Blindsight* and Lem's *His Master's Voice*' (*SFS* 41:ii[2014] 364–91). Lem is rigorously pessimistic about the possibility, and his work shows up some of the shortcuts adopted by Watt in allowing for machine communication, despite the later novel's long list of references on the topic. James Campbell turns to more sensational matters in 'Fear of a Stupid Planet: Sexuality, SF, and Kornbluth's *The Marching Morons*' *Extrapolation* (55:i[2014] 51–71). It contains mention of A.E. Van Vogt's *Slan*. Patricia Gouthro's 'Women of Mystery: Investigating Learning Pathways of Canadian and American Female Crime Fiction Writers' (*AEQ* 64:iv[2014] 356–73) is of interest but not really literary, as indicated by its place of publication: *Adult Education Quarterly*. Sebastian Domsch analyses Dave Sim's graphic novel in 'From Hyper-Make Aardvarks to the Female Void: Gender Politics in *Cerebus*' (in Sedlmayr and Waller, eds., *Politics in Fantasy Media: Essays on Ideology and Gender in Fiction, Film, Television and Games*, pp. 72–84). Lauren J. Lacey has published *The Past That Might Have Been, the Future That May Come: Women Writing Fantastic Fiction, 1960s to the Present*. Chapters deal with revisionary fairy tales, historical fiction in which time is messed with, dystopian fiction, and 'becoming alien in feminist space fiction'. Margaret Atwood is the Canadian discussed. Brett Josef Grubisic, Gisèle M. Baxter, and Tara Lee have edited *Blast, Corrupt, Dismantle, Erase: Contemporary North American Dystopian Literature*. This comprises twenty-five chapters covering Mexico to Canada and includes, along with more general surveys, readings of William Gibson, Margaret Atwood, Larissa Lai, Lisa Robertson, Douglas Coupland, Nalo Hopkinson, and Nicole Brossard.

Jeannette Sloniowski and Marilyn Rose have edited what already looks to be a standard reference: *Detecting Canada: Essays on Canadian Crime Fiction, Television and Film*. The editors provide an introduction and follow with a wide coverage of sub-genres within the print corpus, plus three essays on TV and film. Chapter titles provide a fair indication of the usefulness of the book. Beryl Langer contributes 'Coca-Colonialists Write Back: Localizing the Global in Canadian Crime Fiction'; David Skene-Melvin surveys 'Canadian Crime Writing in English'; and Brian Johnson narrows the focus with 'Canadian Psycho: Genre, Nation, and Colonial Violence in Michael Slade's Gothic RCMP Procedurals'. Single-author studies continue, with Manina Jones's 'Northern Procedures: Policing the Nation in Giles Blunt's *The*

Delicate Storm'; 'Revisioning the Dick: Reading Thomas King's Thumps Dreadfulwater Mysteries' by Jennifer Andrews and Priscilla L. Walton; Jeannette Sloniowski's 'Generic Play and Gender Trouble in Peter Robinson's *In a Dry Season*'; Pamela Bedore's 'A Colder Kind of Gender Politics: Intersections of Feminism and Detection in Gail Bowen's Joanne Kilbourn Series'; Péter Balogh's 'Queer Eye for the Private Eye: Homonationalism and the Regulation of Queer Difference in Anthony Bidulka's Russell Quant Mystery Series'; and Marilyn Rose's 'Under/Cover: Strategies of Detection and Evasion in Margaret Atwood's *Alias Grace*'. The visual media are covered by Sarah A. Matheson, 'Televising Toronto in the 1960s: *Wojeck* and the Urban Crime Genre'; Lindsay Steenberg and Yvonne Tasker, 'North of Quality?' "Quality" Television and the Suburban Crimeworld of *Durham County*'; and Patricia Gruben, 'Mounties and Metaphysics in Canadian Film and Television'.

Interest in women characters in Gail Bowen and Margaret Atwood is continued by K.J. Verwaayen, in 'Ethical Relations, Intertextuality and the Im/possibilities of an "Intersubjective Third" in Margaret Atwood's *The Journals of Susanna Moodie*' (*CWW* 8:iii[2014] 300–18), and by Helen Davies, 'Uncomfortable Questions? Conjoined Sisterhood in Contemporary Women's Writing' (*CWW* 8:iii[2014] 409–27). To this we can add an essay on the online serial by Margaret Atwood and Naomi Alderman, 'Ageing, Disability, and Zombies: *The Happy Zombie Sunrise Home*' by Elizabeth Switaj (*FEMSPEC*14:ii[2014] 27–40). The zombies figure forth a horror of ageing and dementia and close reading of the representations in the story suggests that its feminist aspects are compromised by how age and disability are handled.

Animal studies are becoming a significant aspect of literary scholarship. Canada (once characterized by Atwood by its tales of wild animals and survival—or not—in their territory) is no exception to the rule, Paul Barrett inspecting ' "Animal Tracks in the Margin": Tracing the Absent Referent in Marian Engel's *Bear* and J.M. Coetzee's *The Lives of Animals*' (*ArielE* 45:iii[2014] 123–49).

Children's and young adult writing has always been a feature of Canadian letters, and L.M. Montgomery remains a staple of its scholarship. Paige Gray, ' "Bloom in the Moonshine": Imagination as Liberation in *Anne of Green Gables*' (*ChildL* 42[2014] 169–96), argues against those who see the novel as wholly confirming traditional gender roles, placing its use of imagination centred on Tennyson and Arthurian tales alongside images from suffrage literature and allowing Anne some opening towards the 'new woman' future that Montgomery herself never found.

Heather Snell, 'Outward Bound: Adventures in Cross-Cultural Reading and Global Citizenship in North American Young Adult Literatures' (*CLAQ* 39:ii[2014] 252–74), sees books for young adults responding to multicultural and cosmopolitan impulses arising out of globalization. She follows Tim Brennan in asking 'to *whom* the benefits of particular cosmopolitanisms accrue' (p. 255) and argues that well-meaning promotion of cosmopolitanism relies on a 'rhetoric of deflection' that leaves white, middle-class readers having self-improving adventures in 'othered' spaces that figure as Third World (black) recipients of First World (white) aid. She includes discussion of Beryl Young's *Follow the Elephant* and two titles by Eric Walters: *Alexandria of Africa* and *Beverly Hills Maasai*, neatly labelling them 'diversity conscious but without actually engaging in any critique of how that diversity is constructed, disciplined and manipulated' (p. 261), though Walters does allow some parodic critical humour. By contrast, US writer Kashmira Sheth (*Koyal Dark, Mango Sweet*) provides a more nuanced view of India and diasporic life in America.

'Everything You Do: Young Adult Fiction and Surveillance in an Age of Security' (*IRCL* 7:i[2014] 1–17), by Kerry Mallan, looks at Cory Doctorow's *Little Brother* alongside the American *Hunger Games* and *Article 5* (by Suzanne Collins and Kristen Simmons respectively). Mallan makes the inevitable link to Orwell's *Nineteen Eighty-Four*, but argues that contemporary surveillance methods and global terror threats take stories of intrigue into a new realm, more complex than Cold War espionage fiction, and more blurring of the reality–illusion boundary. This presents ethical challenges to young readers.

In the same issue, Doris Wolf considers 'The Suffering of the Perpetrators: The Ethics of Traumatic German Historicity in Karen Bass's Young Adult World War II Novels' (*IRCL* 7:i[2014] 64–77). She reads *Run Like Jäger* and *Summer of Fire*, which depict German adolescents during the Allied occupation and how their history is used by contemporary youth to build their own identities. What arises is a narrative of victimhood and suffering that slides away from guilt and the ethical challenges of history.

'Going Down the Rabbit-Hole: Teachers' Engagements with "Dialectical Images" in Canadian Children's Literature on Social Justice' (*ChE* 21:i[2014] 79–93), by Teresa Strong-Wilson, Amarou Yoder, and Heather Phipps, studies teaching strategies in elementary school for handling testimonies of trauma by First Nations writers. It draws on Roger Simon's use of Benjamin's concept of the dialectical image, pointing to the classroom as a 'contact zone' between mainstream and marginal and espousing a 'critical nostalgia' approach based on memory and trauma studies.

Mervyn Nicholson examines child–adult relationships as located around work and shaped by class. He covers prose and poetry from Britain, Ireland, the United States, and Canada in 'Class/ic Aggression in Children's Literature' (in Hubler, ed., *Little Red Readings: Historical Materialist Perspectives on Children's Literature*, pp. 3–30). Adrienne Kertzer compares Monique Polak's *What World Is Left?* with other junior reader books by Australian Morris Gleitzman and Irish writer John Boyne in ' "Don't You Know Anything?": Childhood and the Holocaust' (in Adams, ed., *The Bloomsbury Companion to Holocaust Literature*, pp. 121–38).

(c) Author Studies

Author-centred work this year shows some belated attention to Robertson Davies, a predictable bout of Munro fever, and a turn to Anne Carson and Anne Michaels. 'The Last Mythopoet' (*PNR* 41:i[2014] 21–4), by Amanda

Jernigan, examines poetry by Mark Callanan, Jason Guriel, Steven Heighton, Jernigan, Jay McPherson, Peter Sanger, and David West in the light of Northrop Frye's work.

In alphabetical order of subject we find Shahar Bram's 'Postcard Poem, Ekphrastic Delusion: On Margaret Atwood's Poem "Postcard"' (*UTQ* 83:i[2014] 28–38). Also on Atwood, but concentrating on *The Edible Woman*, *Life before Man*, and *The Robber Bride*, K.S. Balaji's 'The Man Haters: The Depiction of Extremist Feminists in the Novels of Margaret Atwood' (*NAcad* 3:iv[2014] 9 pp.), argues that the transgressive women take on masculine oppressive roles and fail to win approval (including Atwood's) as truly feminist figures. This appears in a new online journal, *New Academia*, which claims peer review, but could polish up its English copy-editing. In 'Food for Critical Thought: Teaching the Science Fiction of Margaret Atwood' (*Pedagogy* 14:iii[2014] 475–98) Sean Murray deals with *Oryx and Crake*, *The Year of the Flood*, and *The Edible Woman* as tools for a critical pedagogy around the politics of food, challenging an individualist freedom-of-choice ethic by showing the systemic nature of food production and consumption. Links to other texts are canvassed as the basis for constructing a course on food fiction.

Kym Brindle brings together chapters on a variety of authors as *Epistolary Encounters in New-Victorian Fiction: Diaries and Letters*. She is interested in how and to what purpose contemporary writers present the Victorian era to us through 'fragmented and found material traces' (p. 19) and includes 'A Deviant Device: Diary Dissembling in Margaret Atwood's *Alias Grace*' (pp. 91–117), in which she argues that in the novel Atwood revises her earlier position on Grace Marks. She does not create an actual diary, but simulates one as a diary-like voice, thus avoiding any authoritative textual source. The voice provides commentary on Grace's examiners, who are shown through letters to have an unreliable hold on the truth, and the result is that all are imprisoned in doubt.

Two essays on Atwood were not seen: Louise Nuttall's stylistic analysis 'Constructing a Text World for *The Handmaid's Tale*' (in Harrison, Nuttall, et al., eds., *Cognitive Grammar in Literature*, pp. 83–99), and Karin Höpker's 'A Sense of an Ending—Risk, Catastrophe and Precarious Humanity in Margaret Atwood's *Oryx and Crake*' (in Mayer and Weik von Mossner, eds., *The Anticipation of Catastrophe: Environmental Risk in North American Literature and Culture*, pp. 161–80). Also coming at the literary from a disciplinary tangent, Patrick Colm Hogan, in 'National Identity, Narrative Universals, and Guilt: Margaret Atwood's *Surfacing*' (in Bruhn and Wehrs, eds., *Cognition, Literature and History*, pp. 134–49), uses cognitive theory's ideas of human meaning-making through emplotment of 'narrative prototypes'—heroic, sacrificial, romantic—in order to look at the intersections of nation, race, gender, and white guilt around references to indigenous culture in Atwood's early novel. With a fairly broad brush, Hogan sketches allegorical connections between the narrator's abortion, her emphasis on place, and the 'still-born' hopes for a nation founded on some mix of indigenous and white cultures. He still manages to arrive at a positive reading of the book, envisioning a nation founded not on genocide but on the possibility of such a cultural reconciliation. Suparna Banerjee has produced a comparative study of apocalyptic and dystopian visions based on science and technology, *Science, Gender and History: The Fantastic in Mary Shelley and Margaret Atwood*. She concentrates on *The Handmaid's Tale* and *Oryx and Crake*.

The correspondence of two stalwarts of a generation of Canadian letters has been collected and edited by Nicolas Bradley as *We Go Far Back in Time: The Letters of Earle Birney and Al Purdy*. Bradley supplies a critical introduction. 'Rummagings 15: Thomas Cary's Work for the "Peace and Good Order of a Well-Regulated Society"' (*CanPo* 74[2014] 5–11) is a survey of Cary's journalism and poetry and their engagement with social issues.

Three articles look at Anne Carson's work. Roy Scranton's 'Estranged Pain: Anne Carson's *Red Doc>*' (*ConL* 55:i[2014] 202–14) also considers *Eros the Bittersweet*. Maya Linden's '"Metaphors of War": Desire, Danger and Ambivalence in Anne Carson's Poetic Form' (*WS* 43:ii[2014] 230–45) examines masochistic fixation in self-destructive feminine romantic tragedy, working on *The Glass Essay*, *Plainwater*, and *The Beauty of the Husband*, and asking how Carson's depictions of female passivity escape the distaste such representations usually evoke in feminist critics. Linden argues that theory has often slid across text, life experience, and the political, whereas Carson's historical reach and ironic bricolage insists on the text, sidetracks critics from easy political correctness, and suggests in postmodern poetics ambiguous possibilities for escape from entrapment. Tony Hagland's 'Towards a Postmodern Humanism: Information, Layering and the Composite Poem' (*APR* 43:ii[2014] 37–41) is not dissimilar in its argument and includes a reading of Carson's 'Strange Hour Outcast Hour'.

Robert David Stacey, 'Mad Translation in Leonard Cohen's *Beautiful Losers* and Douglas Glover's *Elle*' (*ESC* 40:ii–iii[2014] 173–97), compares two accounts of destabilizing culture shock in the early phases of colonial contacts via the trope of translation and using R.D. Laing's ideas on schizophrenia. Translation at its extremity generates transformation; across cultures this can manifest as a kind of madness, a breaking through to comprehending otherness that is a breaking down of previous stable forms. Cohen works with translation and prayer (a kind of translation). Glover writes on Cohen and Laing, and takes shamanic transformation as a translation of his transgressive historical character who presents history as a process translating person and culture. We can also note for Cohen fans the publication of *Leonard Cohen on Leonard Cohen: Interviews and Encounters*, edited by Jeff Burger, with a foreword by Suzanne Vega.

George Core writes an overview, 'Revaluation: A Salute to Robertson Davies', equating him with Patrick White and Nobel Prize quality (*SR* 122:iii[2014] 519–21) and John Saumarez Smith provides a narrower biographical focus in 'Robertson Davies and the Introduction Fee' (*BC* 63:i[2104] 103–7).

Another influential figure in Canadian writing is given some attention by Graham H. Jensen. 'An "Architecture of Contradictions": Continuations and the Late Meta-Poetry of Louis Dudek' (*CanPo* 74[2014] 30–59) takes on the three 'Continuations' sequences.

Jinny Huh, 'Detecting Winnifred Eaton' (*MELUS* 39:i[2014] 82–105), puts forwards a case for Winnifred Eaton being a pioneer of Asian American fiction on the basis of her 'Japanese' novels written under the name Onoto Watanna in the early twentieth century. Despite Eaton's Montreal origins, the discussion is entirely in relation to US literature and to the idea of 'passing' narratives in connection with the novelist's mixed Chinese–British background.

Brick 93[2014] 11–18 contains a set of tributes to Mavis Gallant from Michael Helm, Francine Prose, Alison Harris, and Michael Ondaatje.

Capilano Review provides a substantial interview on a contemporary writer: ' "A Portrait of Thinking": Sheila Heti and Thea Bowering on the Phone' (*CapR* 3:xxii[2014] 7–25), while Rachel Sagner Buurma and Laura Heffernan, in 'Notation After the "Reality Effect": Remaking Reference with Roland Barthes and Sheila Heti' (*Representations* 125[2014] 80–102), discuss Heti's 2010 novel *How Should a Person Be?* in relation to Barthes's revision of his pronouncements about realism, moving from a 'solid' conception of its ideological function to a more provisional one. Heti's 'novel of commission' incorporates reference to preparations for the novel-writing to show how the text and the writing process are socially and institutionally shaped.

Leif Sorensen, 'Dubwise into the Future: Versioning Modernity in Nalo Hopkinson' (*AAR* 47:ii–iii[2014] 267–83, 446) looks at *The Midnight Robber* and *The Salt Roads*, suggesting reggae and dub poetry influences on narrative and form in both works, history and futurist visions being flip sides of each other, like the A and B sides of dub versions. Sampling and mixing breaks open the genres of science fiction and historical fiction and talk back to binaries in Donna Haraway's cyborg work.

Allan Weiss examines the politics of cross-cultural experiences in ' "The Culpability of Innocence": The Encounter of Canadian Women in Africa in the Short Stories of Isabel Huggan' (in Sabiston and Drummond, eds., pp. 491–503; not seen for review).

'A Very Fine View of Canada' by Jeffrey Simpson (*QQ* 121:i[2014] 60–71) looks at depictions of the nation in Bruce Hutchinson's *The Unknown Country* [1943] and *The Unfinished Country* [1985].

Another piece in *New Academia* is Shilpa Bhat's 'A Flight of Her Own: Ruminations and Struggles in Margaret Laurence's *The Stone Angel*' (*NAcad* 3:ii[2014] 5 pp.), which tracks Hagar's escape as a battle of the spirit to overcome age and infirmity. It stays very close to the text and thus adds very little to existing scholarship. Clearly the editorial processes are not as rigorously selective as the website suggests.

Susan Knutson has brought back to our attention the work of a major poet. She makes the selections and provides a critical introduction in *Rivering: The Poetry of Daphne Marlatt*. Marlatt follows up the poems with an essay, 'Immediacies of Writing'.

Sarah E. McFarland writes on 'Animal Studies, Literary Animals, and Yann Martel's *Life of Pi*' (in Westling, ed., *The Cambridge Companion to Literature and the Environment*, pp. 152–65). Noting the bio-tech gene manipulations of mosquitoes in the context of disease and the extinction of birds, the author deploys Haraway, Levinas, and Jakob von Uexküll's and

Thomas Nagel's animal-centred phenomenology to reflect on Martel's 'layered narrative that on the one hand defends zoo practices and the study of science but on the other exposes their very flaws, finally privileging imagination over blind fact' (p. 155) by blurring the boundaries between human and animal. The tiger assumes an identity (and his story credibility) when he passes as 'Richard Parker', but remains an animal agent, keeping Pi alive as Pi in turn keeps him alive. The boat is read in terms of zoo politics (protection versus freedom), and the book's ambivalence is resolved as a call to 'shift personhood towards behavior instead of locating it in the human species' (p. 163). Adriana Teodorescu explores 'How a Fantastic Novel Constructs the Enemy Figure: The Untamed Other and the Role of Fantasy in *The Life of Pi*', appearing in the Romanian journal *Caietele Echinox* (*CEch* 26[2014] 181–93).

André Dodeman assesses Scots history in 'Clans and Clashes: Heritage and Authenticity in Alistair McLeod's *No Great Mischief*' (*Ranam* 47[2014] 219–31, 279).

Anne Michaels is interviewed by Sam Solecki: 'A Conversation about Anne Michaels' *Correspondences*' (*CanPo* 74[2014] 60–7), and Mei-yu Tsai finds 'A Poetics of Testimony and Healing in Anne Michaels's *Fugitive Pieces*' (*Shofar* 32:iii[2014] 50–71), drawing on Dori Laub and Marianne Hirsch. Amid a seeming explosion of European attention to Canadian writing, Orlana Palusci, 'Anne Michaels e le ferite di linguaggio' (*AltMo* [2014] 186–99) writes about the 'wounds of language', also reading *Fugitive Pieces* for the work of scientific discourse (geology, meteorology, archaeology) as a means of holding traumatic emotion at bay while pointing to the horrors of technology and history. Palusci opens with a survey of Jewish Canadian writing and some detailing of the narrative strands of the novel, and closes with attention to music and allusions to writing and reading and poetry and translation as ways through suffering. Sabine Strümper-Krobb contributes 'Witnessing, Remembering, Translating: Translation and Translation Figures in Jonathan Safran Foer's *Everything Is Illuminated* and Anne Michael's *Fugitive Pieces*' (in Kaindl and Spitzl, eds., *Transfiction: Research into the Realities of Translation*, pp. 247–59).

Rohinton Mistry is represented this year by two essays, neither of which was available to the reviewer. Uma Jayaraman considers 'Boundary Marking in the Diaspora: An Analysis of Women Characters in Rohinton Mistry's *Family Matters*' (in Dwivedi, ed., pp. 253–70) and the Serbo-Croat journal *Književna Smotra* contains a reading of Rohinton Mistry's short story 'Swimming Lessons' by Vanja Polić: 'Problem multikulturalnosti u noveli "Poduka plivanja" Rohintona Mistryja' (*KS* 46:ii[2014] 65–9).

Alaa Alghamdi adopts a feminist approach to depictions of working-class women, widows, and mourning in 'Different Spheres: Clashing Realities and the Transformative Reprising of "Women's Work" in Lisa Moore's *February*' (*PCP* 49:i[2014] 41–57).

Shani Mootoo is the subject of Catriona Sandilands' 'Violent Affinities: Sex, Gender, and Species in *Cereus Blooms at Night*' (in Westling, ed., pp. 90–103). The novel's mix of violence and *jouissance*, fantasy and reality, asks questions about how we bring together ecocritical politics, feminism, and queer studies to address and even flourish amid endemic violence. Mala's oppressed condition is set against her positive connections with plants and animals, abuse is permeated with empathy, nature brings decay together with beauty. Relationality and becoming matter more than identity, as figured through the cereus plant's role in the narrative, and Mootoo 'points in the direction of a posthumanist performativity, in which different manners of materialization are revealed to be inseparable' (p. 95).

The wheels of the critical Munro industry are turning faster and have produced ' "Deep Deep into the River of Her Mind": "Meneseteung" and the Archival Hysteric' by Katrine Raymond (*ESC* 40:i[2014] 95–122); 'To Be Continued: The Story of Short Story Theory and Other Narrative Theory' (*Narrative* 22:i[2014] 132–49) by Sarah Copland, centred on epiphany in the story 'Passion'; Vanja Polić again, with 'Starost u "Zimskom vrtu" Alice Munro' (*KS* 46:i[2014] 93–9), a reading of 'The Bear Came over the Mountain'; and, on the same text, Sara Jamieson's 'Reading the Spaces of Age in Alice Munro's "The Bear Came over the Mountain"' (*Mosaic* 47:iii[2014] 1–17). Reingard M. Nischik's 'Alice Munro: Nobelpreisgekrönte Maisterin der Short Story aus Kanada' (*ZAA* 62:iv[2014] 359–77) is a descriptive introduction, and Isla Duncan contributes 'Loss and Longing in Alice Munro's "Queenie"' (*BJCS* 27:i[2014] 21–36). Of these, the most noteworthy are Raymond's setting of Munro alongside work by Urquhart and Atwood to 'explore how and why the hysterical mindbody acts as an archive of past emotional traumas and how this might suggest a mode of recovery' (p. 95), though the foundational story is itself made to bear a very heavy superstructure of the medical/feminist archive; also Copland's essay (which responds to five other readings of Munro's story from 2012 and connects with Duncan's narratological approach) opens up short-story analysis to the broader operations of narrative theory and internal focalization without filling in the 'gaps' in the story itself. From a conference in Japan (hence the book title) on region and nation, Marie-Anne Hansen-Pauly's paper on the short story 'Too Much Happiness', 'Regional Voices and Cultural Translation: The Example of Alice Munro', is published in *East Meets West*, edited by J.U. Jacobs, Derrick McLure, and Reiko Aiura (pp. 191–210).

Paolo Javier, 'Some Notes on bpNichol, (Captain) Poetry, and Comics' (in Fink and Haden-Sullivan, eds., *Reading the Difficulties: Dialogues with Contemporary American Innovative Poetry*, pp. 178–87), provides us with a rapid tour of comic-strip art and its ties to contemporary writing, starting with Canadian cartoonist Seth's comments on how comics have a haiku element of structuring and, like much contemporary poetry, involve design as moving shapes around. He charts bpNichol's interest in and use of comics, particularly in *The Martyrology* and *The Captain Poetry Poems*, noting the quest for non-linear modes of communication and the parodic debunking of Canadian poetry's macho aspect.

Michael Ondaatje is the most popular subject in the journals this year. David Babcock, 'Professional Intimacies: Human Rights and Specialized Bodies in Michael Ondaatje's *Anil's Ghost*' (*CulC* 87[2014] 60–83), tracks how disciplinary and personal differences get in the way of UN human rights ideals but also how the embodiment of the professional provides some means of negotiation. Christopher McVey, 'Reclaiming the Past: Michael Ondaatje and the Body of History' (*JML* 37:ii[2014] 141–60), looks at the escapes and returns around the nation in *The English Patient* as registered in relation to the body. In 'Rites of Passage: Moving Hearts and Transforming Memories in Michael Ondaatje's *The Cat's Table*' (*ArielE* 45:i–ii[2014] 35–57), Laura Savu Walker considers two modes of memory work: sensory and affective versus verbal and reflective, showing how they mix in this reprise on autobiography, and how the protagonist's memories becomes linked with stories of others on the voyage to produce an intersubjective identity. Transpersonal relations are also the subject of Shou-Nan Hsu's 'From Sexual Love to Peace: Endless Care and Respect for Strangers in Michael Ondaatje's *Secular Love*' (*CollL* 41:iv[2014] 111–28). Multicultural identity figured in relation to metaphors of ships and journeys is the focus of Lesley Higgins and Marie-Christine Leps's 'Becoming Pluricultural in Ondaatje's Oronsay' (in Sabiston and Drummond, eds., pp. 383–94). They focus on *The Cat's Table* and *Anil's Ghost*. *Anil's Ghost* is also one of the texts discussed in 'The World Novel, Mediated Wars and Exorbitant Witnessing' by Debjani Ganguly (*CJPLI* 1:i[2014] 11–31).

Hung Min-Hsiou employs Deleuze and Guattari to read a poem as 'an artistic model for understanding visual imagery' in 'Autopoiesis in P. K. Page's "Arras": The Peacock Image as a Vision Machine' (*TkR* 44:ii[2014] 123–45). Only the abstract was available, but the typically dense D&G-ese seems to indicate that the article works binaries of new/classical, transformative/machinic, and images of peacock and habit to suggest an 'ecological' revisioning.

Robert G. May considers some aspects of social change and how they affected national symbols in ' "The Selfsame Welkin Ringing": F.R. Scott and the Rewriting of "O Canada" ' (*CanPo* 74[2014] 12–29).

Louis Cabri also deals with poetry in 'Concealment and Disclosure: Nancy Shaw's *Scoptocratic*' (*CapR* 3:xxii[2014] 120–4). This article was not available to the reviewer at the time of writing.

Kate Marantz, 'The Work of Ambiguity: Writerly and Readerly Labor in Carol Shields's *The Stone Diaries*' (*Narrative* 3:xxii[2014] 354–71), details the complexities of fictional autobiography and narrative arrangement and asks, 'What, finally, do these unstable representations and elusive inconsistencies have to do with Shields's writerly project in *The Stone Diaries*, and where do we as readers fit into that project?' (p. 355). She argues that the gaps and inconsistencies force us to consider what it means to work with text, both as writers and readers, and especially in terms of women's work and writing new selves.

Meera Atkinson reads Elizabeth Smart's *By Grand Central Station I Sat Down and Wept* against Marguerite Duras's *L'Amour* in the context of autobiographical novels in 'Strange Body Bedfellows: *Ecriture Feminine* and the Poetics of Trans-Trauma' (*TextJW* 18:i[2014] n.p.).

Ruth Panovsky has laboured extensively to produce *The Collected Poems of Miriam Waddington: A Critical Edition*. Panovsky supplies a critical introduction plus notes on over one thousand pages of Waddington's work in what will evidently be a standard source for scholarship.

In the Laurier Poetry series, Percy Owen has edited and introduced the work of Tom Wayman under the title *The Order in Which We Do Things*. Wayman supplies an afterword entitled 'Work and Silence'—a title interestingly at odds with the poet's public presence as a writer of social change and co-founder of the Vancouver Industrial Writers' Union.

Starting with the writer's defence of small details of text against the depredations of editors, Misao Dean, in 'I Just Love Ethel Wilson: A Reparative Reading of *The Innocent Traveller*' (*ESC* 40:ii-iii[2014] 65–81), sets the alleged loss of literary focus in teaching texts against recovering the joy of the well-crafted sentence in Ethel Wilson's work. Close reading of grammar and style pointing to the tussle between classical realism and modernist disruptions is framed by an engaging personal voice and conceptual underpinning by Sedgwick and Barthes. Dean concludes by saying she cannot teach students to love their texts, but she can 'perform the rituals of care' that Wilson herself exercises in her writing

Dennis Duffy takes a bigger-picture literary-historical approach in his '"The High Priest of Trinity College": Milton Wilson's Role as Canadian Poetry's Gatekeeper, 1957–1968' (*CanL* 220[2014] 198–202). Wilson published a host of poets in *Canadian Forum*, and corresponded with many. His relationship with Irving Layton is a focus.

James Bailey provides us with '"Setting Off Fireworks over a Mysterious City": An Interview with Kathleen Winter' (*WriC* 1:i[2014] 7 pp.).

(d) Drama

Apart from the theses already cited, work on theatre in 2014 covered a variety of topics. Gint Derk countered the apparent loss of visible interest in AIDS by looking at two plays on the subject: 'Queer Embodies Absence: HIV/AIDS and the Creation of Cultural Memory in Gordon Armstrong's *Blue Dragons* and Daniel McIvor's *The Soldier Dreams*' (*JCSR* 48:ii[2014] 122–45), while Ji, Seung-a produced a comparative study of Djanet Sears's reworking of Shakespeare: 'A Ghost Named Othello: Race, Women and Djanet Sears's *Harlem Duet*' (*JMED* 27:i[2014] 93–122). The article is in Korean.

Theatre Survey, despite its subtitle as *The Journal of the American Society for Theatre Research*, contains commentary of Canadian theatre people and plays. Issue 55:ii[2014] includes Joshua Chambers-Letson's 'The Inoperative Iphigenia: Race, Law and Emancipation in Michi Barall's *Rescue Me*' (*ThS* 55:ii[2014] 145–64), Aaron C. Thomas's 'The Queen's Cell: *Fortune and Men's Eyes* and the New Prison Drama' (*ThS* 55:ii[2014] 165–84), and Peter Dickinson's 'Murdered and Missing Women: Performing Indigenous Cultural Memory in British Columbia and Beyond' (*ThS* 55:ii[2014] 202–32). The first deals with how *Rescue Me* [2010], an Asian American reworking of *Iphigenia in Aulis*, inserts contemporary issues of race and identity. The second examines the handling of prison culture, homosexuality, and rape in John Herbert Brundage's 1967 play. The third compares the grim fate of women in George Ryga's *The Ecstasy of Rita Joe* and *The Unnatural and Accidental Woman* by Yvette Nolan and Marie Clements with video art by Rebecca Belmore.

'Ecologies of Dramaturgy' by Beth Blickers (*ThTop* 24:iii[2014] 249–53) assesses the work of Brian Quirt, and Klara Kolinska outlines government policies and the historiography of settler–indigenous conflict as background to a textual reading in ' "Borders to Freedom": Sitting Bull's Precarious Refuge in Sharon Pollack's Play *Walsh*' (*Interactions* 23:i[2014] 161–8).

The journal *alt.theatre* concentrates on community work and in issue 11:ii Will Wiegler discusses theatre work in British Columbia dealing with settler–indigenous reconciliation (*AltT* 11:ii[2014] 10–15), Diane Conrad interviews David Diamond of Theatre for Living about the touring of the interactive piece, *Corporations in Our Heads* (*AltT* 11:ii[2014] 16–20), and Ingrid Hansen looks at the creation of puppet theatre in prisons (*AltT* 11:ii[2014] 21–5).

Canadian Theatre Review 157, in a section on 'alternative globalizations', also canvases plays of social activism, with Susanne Shawyer's 'Occupy Newfoundland and the Dramaturgy of Endurance' (*CTR* 157[2014] 1, 7–11), Barry Freeman's interview with Joe Osawabine and Ron Berti of the Debajehmujig Storytellers, 'On the Road with the Global savages' (*CTR* 157[2014] 1, 12–16), and Matt Jones's 'After Kandahar: Canadian Theatre's Engagement with the War in Afghanistan' (*CTR* 157[2014] 2, 26–9). The two subsequent issues of *Canadian Theatre Review* focus on burlesque and digital performance respectively.

4. The Caribbean

(a) Books

Paule Morgan's monograph *The Terror and the Time: Banal Violence and Trauma in Caribbean Discourse*, which is 'historically grounded and socially situated' (p. 18), is her latest publication related to her interest in trauma theory and Caribbean trauma narratives. Having co-authored the book *Writing Rage: Unmasking Violence in Caribbean Discourse*, co-edited the journal special issue *The Culture of Violence in Trinidad and Tobago*, and co-lectured the course 'Gender Violence and Trauma', Morgan in *The Terror and the Time* continues her examination of how the discourses of literature, print media, popular culture, and personal narrative address the traumatic legacies of migration and colonization experienced by New World peoples in the Caribbean. Morgan investigates, too, how these are discourses not only of suffering, violence, rupture, subjugation, and amnesia but also of resistance, recuperation, empowerment, and creativity. 'Caribbean Narratives of Trauma' (pp. 2–9), the introductory chapter, references seminal texts by Jean Rhys, George Lamming, Derek Walcott, Erna Brodber, V.S. Naipaul, and Harold Sonny Ladoo, and includes work by Opal Palmer Adisa and Shani Mootoo. Her theoretical frameworks draw upon, among others, Paul Crosthwaite, Laurie Vickroy, Jonathan Boulter, Ron Eyerman, Alexandre Dauge-Roth, Stef Craps, Gert Buelen, Michelle Balaev, Michael Rothberg, and Irene Visser.

The Terror and the Time is divided into two parts. There are four chapters in 'Ontologies' which comprise analyses of the slave narrative *Zong* by M. NourbeSe Philip; the short stories 'The View from the Terrace' by Olive Senior and 'Barbados' by Paule Marshall, which centre on the 'persistent personal and institutional legacy of racism and the mechanisms by which it infiltrated and embedded itself in the emerging Caribbean nation' (p. 20); as well as works by V.S. Naipaul that focus on the Indo-Caribbean immigrant and by Derek Walcott which focus on the aftermath of the Middle Passage. In 'Social Issues' myriad topics are addressed: the social impact of poverty; state criminality in fiction by Edwidge Danticat; ageing and Alzheimer's disease in the novels *Cascade* by Barbara Lalla and *Soucouyant* by David Chariandy; childhood trauma, as well as child-shifting as represented in Olive Senior's short story 'Bright Thursdays'; and discourses of alcoholism and death, since the 'pivotal location of rum within Caribbean societies and economies has made it a powerful literary trope' in popular culture, 'particularly calypso and chutney rum lyrics'. Analysis of this last topic is supported by interviews with members of Alcoholics Anonymous and fictional texts 'using phenomeno-logical approaches' (p. 162). In her afterword, Morgan concludes that 'Cultural and creative workers, explored in this text among countless others, have intuitively plumbed the deep-rooted, often irrational traumatizing forces at work within the contemporary social order' (p. 205), yet affirms the existence of a 'restorative process', 'survivors', 'cultural certitude', 'works of faith', and a 'social order of resilient Caribbean nation-states and their diasporic communities' (p. 206).

The language of literature is the primary focus of *Caribbean Literary Discourse: Voice and Cultural Identity in the Anglophone Caribbean* co-authored by Barbara Lalla, Jean D'Costa, and Velma Pollard—all creative writers and well published in the areas of linguistics and literary criticism. The text in two parts—'Fusing Forms and Languages: The Jamaican Experience' and 'Language and Discourse in Caribbean Literary Texts'—draws on essays written individually by the three writers, some having previously been published elsewhere. *Caribbean Literary Discourse* examines the development of vernacular discourses by creative writers within the colonizing context in which official Standard English was used in government, economics, and high culture. Among the authors' major concerns are how language choice and code-switching between Standard English and English-lexicon creole convey nationalist and identity politics, and self-representation; the challenges of teaching code-switching's rhetorical and literary effects in the traditional education system, as well as code-switching's implications for identity in a postcolonial society that is multilingual and multicultural. They also consider intertextual linkages in postcolonial and diasporic literatures and the well-established oral-scribal culture in the region. The five chapters of Part I include two by D'Costa on literature as a survival technique in eighteenth-century Jamaica (pp. 17–41), and the Caribbean novelist's use of language as forming 'A Search for a Literary Medium' (pp. 68–92); two by Lalla on the development phases of Jamaican literary discourse (pp. 42–67), which include ventriloquism, censorship, alternation, and expansion (p. 57), and 'Authority and Identity in the Development of Caribbean Literary Discourse' in terms of the respectability of creole usage (pp. 101–12); and one by Pollard on 'Writing Ourselves into the Literature of the Caribbean' (pp. 93–100).

Part II comprises ten chapters in which D'Costa addresses problems faced in writing children's fiction as they relate to genre, audience, and artistic imagination (pp. 113–21), and language variation in the dialect poetry of famed Jamaican performance poet Louise Bennett (pp. 157–90). Pollard's four chapters deal with 'A Tribute to the Folk' (pp. 122–30), an analysis of the cultural connections in the novel *Praise Song for the Widow* by Paule Marshall, who is of Barbadian ancestry (pp. 143–56); 'Mixing Codes and Mixing Voices' in Trinidadian Earl Lovelace's Commonwealth Prize-winning novel *Salt* (pp. 203–12), and the 'Mothertongue Voices' in the prose and poetic fiction, respectively, of Jamaicans Olive Senior and Lorna Goodison (pp. 221–31). Lalla's chapters examine 'Collapsing Certainty and the Discourse of Re-Memberment' in Trinidadian Merle Hodge's novels *For the Life of Laetitia* and the classic *Bildungsroman, Crick Crack, Monkey* (pp. 131–42), Guyanese poet Martin Carter's 'University of Hunger' as regards 'Conceptual Perspectives on Time and Timelessness' (pp. 191–212), the 'Oral-Scribal Continuum' in Lovelace's *Salt* (pp. 213–20), and 'The Facetiness Factor: Theorizing Caribbean Space in Narrative' (pp. 232–50), which deals primarily with Nalo Hopkinson's speculative fiction *Midnight Robber* and in which the 'Jamaican term, *facetiness*, [is] an essential attitudinal position in Caribbean literature [and] expresses a deep-in-the-bone sense of self that vividly resists any outside inducements to conform because conformity is felt to require a denial of the self' (p. 232).

The anglophone Caribbean has a strong tradition of literary production that creates indelible intertextual linkages between the region's oral and scribal cultures. Carol Bailey's *A Poetics of Performance: The Oral-Scribal Aesthetic in Anglophone Caribbean Fiction* brings together work by literary and cultural theorist Gordon Rohlehr, linguist and literary scholar Barbara Lalla, and others to provide an authoritative work on the subject. It explores the ways in which novels and short stories are impacted by and infused with the region's culture of orature-performance which includes storytelling, calypso, and reggae. These are born of the folk and the urban working-class, and Bailey— working with the terms 'poetics of performance' and 'performing fiction'— demonstrates how they are used as devices which structurally underpin Caribbean prose fiction and how they are grounded in a woman-centred poetics.

The five body chapters are framed by an introduction and afterword. 'Opening Acts: Scholarly and Literary Precursors to Performing Fiction' discusses Samuel Selvon's classic novel of migration *The Lonely Londoners* [1956] and Vic Reid's *New Day* [1949]. Thenceforth, Bailey analyses selected works of Earl Lovelace, Marlon James, Merle Collins, Marie-Elena John, and Colin Channer, namely, *The Wine of Astonishment, The Dragon Can't Dance*, 'Joebell and America', *The Book of Night Women, The Colour of Forgetting, Unburnable*, and 'How to Beat a Child the Right and Proper Way'. Lovelace's three texts are each examined in separate chapters. Collins's and John's novels are studied in '(Re)membering: The Power of Stories', and attention is given to James's novel and Lovelace's *The Wine of Astonishment* in 'Inter-Performance and the Woman-Centred Poetics', while the latter's most popular and canonical novel, *The Dragon Can't Dance*, is addressed in 'Affirming the Female "Subject Person": Rereading Gender Discourses'. Lastly, the concept of the 'Globalizing Yard' in the short stories by Lovelace and Channer is examined.

Of his thirteen chapters in *Caribbean Empire: The Impact of Culture, Literature and History* historian Jerome Teelucksingh dedicates two to a discussion on Caribbean literature and one on the collected essays of a Caribbean-born British writer: 'Spirituality and Superstition in West Indian Novels' (pp. 29–40), 'West Indian Writers and Cultural Chauvinism' (pp. 189–96), and 'Distorted Portrayals in Caryl Phillips's *A New World Order*' (pp. 177–88). In what amounts to a justification for his multidisciplinary book—and for its title *Caribbean Empire*, which may seem oxymoronic—Teelucksingh affirms in his two-page introduction that: 'Culture, activism, academia and religion have not been on separate paths of development. These spheres regularly intersect and have enriched the West Indies' (p. 2); and 'For centuries, the Caribbean (or West Indies) has been a major contributor to global developments and progress' (p. 1). Since religion and spirituality constitute the ethos of all civilizations and empires of the world, Teelucksingh's approach is apropos since 'In the Caribbean there is a widespread belief in superstitions, folklore and myths [and] West Indian novelists have captured some of the superstition and spirituality which is prevalent in the region. The Caribbean society is one of adaptation, acculturation and assimilation. This could explain the mixture of religious beliefs with superstitions and local practices' (p. 29).

Chosen texts in which these elements and processes are depicted are V.S. Naipaul's *A House for Mr. Biswas*, *The Mystic Masseur*, and *A Flag on the Island*; Jan Carew's *Black Midas*; Ismith Khan's *The Jumbie Bird* and *The Obeah Man*; Earl Lovelace's The *Wine of Astonishment*, and Ian McDonald's *The Humming-Bird Tree*. Naipaul and Khan reappear alongside C.L.R. James, Edgar Mittleholzer, Samuel Selvon, Dionne Brand, Lawrence Scott, Roger Mais, and Michael Anthony in Teelucksingh's outlining of the various forms of Caribbean masculinity and male chauvinism portrayed in the literature. It is unsurprising that Teelucksingh devotes an entire chapter to this topic in his exploration of 'empire' since the construction of Caribbean masculinities and chauvinistic behaviour is a legacy of the region's history of slavery, indentureship, and British colonialism. In his chapter on St Kittian-born Phillips, who is 'based outside the Caribbean [and] views the world through a postcolonial lens' (p. 177), Teelucksingh's objective is to offer alternative viewpoints. He begins with the questionable statement that 'Caryl Phillips is not well known among Caribbean readers' (p. 177) and critiques what he sees as the many shortcomings in Phillips's vision for a new world order in terms of 'Race/Ethnicity and Racism', 'Gender, Class and Culture', and 'Pie in the Sky? Practical Solutions?', even though he acknowledges '*A New World Order* skilfully dissects the challenges to the status quo embedded in the mediums of activism, song, literature, ideology and film' (p. 177).

In Jason Frydman's *Sounding the Break: African American and Caribbean Routes to World Literature*, the chapter devoted to Caribbean literature in English is 'Dialectics of World Literature: Derek Walcott between Intimacy and Iconicity' (pp. 82–98). Frydman begins by citing 'Venerable Walcott critic Edward Baugh' as an example of a reader who is exhausted 'with the critical debates that frame' Walcott's work (p. 82). These debates include a focus on 'critical oppositions he dutifully enumerates: Europe and Africa; oral traditions and literary canons; provincialism and cosmopolitanism; poetic myth and positivist history' (p. 82). The chapter then 'tracks how [Walcott] lays bare, as well as fashions his participation in, a commodified field of world literature that constantly threatens to reduce his work to its most exchange-able, emblematic aspects [and how he] recuperates a recalcitrant intimacy in the *longue durée* of world literature, embodied in practices of recitation recursively shuttling, "from hand to mouth," between elite and vernacular idioms and contexts' (pp. 82–3). Frydman argues his point by providing examples of Walcott's poetry, drama, and essays as well as interviews, and by charting his Irish, Greek, Caribbean, and other influences.

An entire chapter is also dedicated to a discussion on Walcott in *The Haitian Revolution in the Literary Imagination: Radical Horizons, Conservative Constraints* by Philip Kaisary. 'The Aesthetics of Cyclical Pessimism: Derek Walcott's *Haitian Trilogy*' (pp. 135–56) examines the plays *Henri Christophe*, *Drums and Colours*, and *The Haitian Earth*, which before their 2002 publication in a single volume 'were largely forgotten works and hard to find' (p. 135). Kaisary examines how these three plays (packaged as 'Revolution as Endless Tyranny and the High Style of *Henri Christophe*', '*Drums and Colours*: The Great Tapestry of Caribbean History', and '*The Haitian Earth*: Independence Discredited') exemplify Walcott's 'reading of Haitian history as an endlessly repeating cycle of tragic violence and tyranny' (p. 135) and his 'profound scepticism about revolution', unlike Aimé Césaire, C.L.R. James, Langston Hughes, and René Depestre, who portrayed the Haitian Revolution as 'open[ing] the gates of black liberation and serv[ing] as an example to anticolonial movements' (p. 137). James's *The Black Jacobins* is analysed in the chapter 'Radical Universalism: The Haitian Revolution, Aimé Césaire and C.L.R. James' (pp. 21–36) as recuperating the revolution, which exemplified agency for black intellectuals and activists engaged in anti-colonial movements and struggles for liberation (p. 36).

The significance of place, space, and geography in Caribbean literature is well established as it relates to notions such as contestation, self-determin-ation, belonging, home, and forced and voluntary migration. *Locating the Destitute: Space and Identity in Caribbean Fiction* by Stanka Radović employs spatial theory to investigate representations of space and place, and the literal and metaphorical meanings of the house in selected texts. Those from the anglophone Caribbean are analysed in the chapters ' "No Admittance": V.S. Naipaul's *A House for Mr. Biswas*' (pp. 77–104) and 'Heterotopia of Old Age in Beryl Gilroy's *Frangipani House*' (pp. 128–53). Preceding chapters are 'Caribbean Spatial Metaphors' (pp. 27–47) and 'A House of One's Own: Individual and Communal Spaces in the Caribbean "Yard Novel" ' (pp. 48–76). Radović explores how representations of Caribbean space in the novels she analyses 'are always "both/and" rather than "either/or" [and how space is] a representative image and...a specific material fact [and] Caribbean discourse, with its persistent focus on its own contested spatiality, opens a unique possibility for reconsidering and broadening the scope of spatial theory'. She adds: 'As they reflect on their region and its history, Caribbean authors and theorists address the inherent complexity of space itself—as image, concept, and experience; projection, utopia, and fact' (p. 27). For her analysis of the 'yard novel', with its destitute, socially disadvantaged characters who live in slum environments, Radović discusses C.L.R. James's seminal *Minty Alley* and necessarily includes his short story 'Triumph' as well; V.S. Naipaul's *A House for Mr. Biswas*, *The Enigma of Arrival*, and *Miguel Street*; Earl Lovelace's *The Dragon Can't Dance*; and Roger Mais's *The Hills Were Joyful Together*. For Beryl Gilroy's *Frangipani House*, focus is placed on the house as an 'exclusionary space' for the aged 'unproductive' and 'isolated' body. The book overall explores heterotopias of space, social reality, and identity.

In *Bodies and Bones: Feminist Rehearsal and Imagining Caribbean Belonging* Tanya L. Shields uses her own methodology, called 'feminist rehearsal'. In 'Reading Caribbean Resistance through Feminist Rehearsal', 'Rehearsing with Ghosts', 'Their Bones Would Reject Yours', 'Hope and Infinity', 'Signs of Sycorax', 'Rehearsing Indigeneity', and 'Rehearsal and Proxy-formance' she draws on sources that include prose, poetry, drama, and the visual arts and on anglophone Caribbean writers like Pauline Melville, Fred D'Aguiar, and Grace Nichols. Privileging 'multiple readings of resistance, rebellion and challenge in the Caribbean context through a feminist analytical lens' (p. 1) that uses the various meanings of 'rehearsal' as repetition, re-examination, revision, and orality/physicality (p. 2), Shields examines the intersectionalities of Caribbean gendered and racialized bodies, particularly those of black women. She claims: 'I invoke bodies and bones as a vivid reminder of the ways in which Caribbean bodies matter; how the tensions that arise in and between those gendered, classed, colored, and sexualized bodies alter, sometimes disappear, and often are reshuffled, lost, and reclaimed' (p. 2).

Rachel L. Mordecai's *Citizenship Under Pressure: The 1970s in Jamaican Literature and Culture* is the first in-depth examination of a definitive period in Jamaican history that saw a stark increase in crime and violence, political and class upheavals, race tensions, black consciousness, emigration by the middle and upper strata of the society, and cultural production. As Curdella Forbes notes in the book's blurb, it is the 'period [that] remains the most significant historical moment in the consciousness of Jamaicans at home and in diaspora'. In providing examples of literary representations of this period, Mordecai discusses Michelle Cliff's novel in 'Exile, Race and Revolution: *No Telephone to Heaven*', Brian Meeks's in 'The Heady Logic of Boundary-Crossing: *Paint the Town Red*', Garfield Ellis's in 'Friends, Fathers, and Tribal Politics: *For Nothing At All*', and devotes an entire chapter to homosexuality and sexual citizenship in 'Sexuality and the Jamaican Citizen'. In one section of this chapter she analyses Patricia Powell's novel under the heading 'Masculinity and Marriage in the 1970s: *A Small Gathering of Bones*', a novel that addresses not only same-sex partnerships, public sex, and homophobia but also HIV/AIDS.

(b) Collections of Essays
The Cross-Dressed Caribbean: Writing, Politics, Sexualities, edited by Maria Cristina Fumagalli, Bénédicte Ledent, and Roberto del Valle Alcalá, studies a

region where the 'politics of clothing have always had a strong symbolic function' (p. 3) and where 'Cross-dressers, hermaphrodites, transgendered people, and transsexuals haunt Caribbean literature' (p. 14). The collection of essays covers all the linguistic blocs of the region. Four essays discuss the literature of the English-speaking Caribbean. In the first section of the text, entitled 'Revolutions in Drag', Chantal Zabus's ' "Cyaan Live Split": Under-Dressing, Over-Performing, Transgendering, and the Uses of Camouflage in Michelle Cliff's *No Telephone to Heaven*' (pp. 57–73) takes a look at how 'nationalism, construed as a resistance to American imperialism, is performed by a "queer" faction, whose bathetic attempts to engender a new nation fail yet augur multiple transfigurations' (p. 57). This is followed by the section ' "Passing" through Time', which includes Lee Easton and Kelly Hewson's ' "Love the Drag... but Your Purse Is on Fire!" ': Cross-Dressings in the Religious Imaginary of *Aelred's Sin*' (pp. 108–26), which examines how the novel 'allows for cross-dressing to be viewed also as a means for repair and redemption, which might counter-balance the forms of hegemonic masculinities that dominate the heteropatriarchal space of the Caribbean' (p. 111). In this section, too, 'Cross-Dressing and the Caribbean Imaginary in Nalo Hopkinson's *Midnight Robber*' by Wendy Knepper (pp. 140–58) investigates how 'Hopkinson's queer fictions not only challenge hegemonic constructions of gender and sexuality but also explore new frontiers for identity formation, citizenship, and community [and how] Hopkinson's narrative employs the motif of nomadic cross-dressing to express alternative constructions of identity and community through a virtualized Caribbean queer imaginary' (pp. 140, 141). Lizabeth Paravisini's 'Helen in Her Yellow Dress: Dressing, Undressing, and Cross-Dressing in the Literature of the Contemporary Caribbean' (p. 220–38), in which Derek Walcott's *Omeros* and Jamaica Kincaid's *The Autobiography of My Mother* are among the texts analysed, is found in the fourth section, 'Symptoms and Detours'. Paravisini cites Christine M.E. Guth when she says that the cross-dressing presented in these texts is a 'creative tool for subverting social and racial stereotypes and creating individual identity' (p. 221).

In Section III, 'Theories in the Flesh', two creative writers offer a fictional piece and an autobiographical essay: Lawrence Scott, whose novel *Aelred's Sin* is mentioned above, writes about young boys' erotic playfulness and crossings-over in 'Tales Told under the San Fernando Hill' (pp. 186–202) and Shani Mootoo reminisces about the 'queer' East Indian experience in 'On Becoming an Indian Starboy' (pp. 167–72). In setting the background for the study, the introduction outlines topics such as 'Caribbean Cross-Dressing and the Politics of Clothing', 'Caribbean Cross-Dressing, Masquerading, and Carnival', 'Caribbean Cross-Dressing, Biopolitics, Mimicry, and Performance', and 'Caribbean Cross-Dressing: Repetition with a Difference'. The book argues that cross-dressing is integrally linked to challenging oppressions arising from the region's history of slavery, indentureship, colonialism, and patriarchy.

Giselle Rampaul and Barbara Lalla's edited publication, *Postscripts: Caribbean Perspectives on the British Canon from Shakespeare to Dickens*, contributes to a growing interest in Caribbean rereadings of British literature.

It follows on from Lalla's *Postcolonialisms: Caribbean Rereading of Medieval English Discourse* and focuses on poetry and prose fiction published by writers such as William Shakespeare, John Donne, Daniel Defoe, Jane Austen, Charlotte Brontë, James Froude, Charles Kingsley, Anthony Trollope, John Edwards Jenkins, Robert Louis Stevenson, J.M. Barrie, Lewis Carroll, and Charles Dickens. *Postscripts* comprises seven chapters preceded by an introduction co-written by the editors in which they argue that, although 'Caribbean re-visioning of British literature is well established in creative works where it expresses itself in rewriting and writing back', *Postscripts* provides a unique and valuable contribution because for 'the most part ... critique of the British canon has been treated as irrelevant to Caribbean literary theory ... [A] Caribbean approach to a range of works in the British canon is yet to be produced [and] little has been done to integrate Caribbean approaches to British literature or any other canon into the body of Caribbean letters' (p. 2).

Lalla's individual chapter is on 'Dickens and Others: Metastance and Remembering' (pp. 8–26), while Rampaul offers two: ' "How Blest Am I ...!": Colonial Desire in Selected Poetry by John Donne' (pp. 27–42) and 'Strange Creatures and Fantastic Worlds: The Other in Selected Nineteenth-Century Children's Texts' (pp. 154–86). Genevieve Ruth Phagoo takes a look at the 'Recovering Nation, Recovering Woman: Shakespeare's Cressida and the Imperial Attic' (pp. 43–76), and Rhonda Kareen Harrison explores 'Far-Off Places and the Invention of Englishness: Rereading *Robinson Crusoe* as Romance' (pp. 79–97). Jak Peake's 'Froude, Kingsley and Trollope: Wandering Eyes in a Trinidadian Landscape' (pp. 98–123) and J. Vijay Maharaj's 'A Study of the Imperial Gaze. Jenkins's Lutchmee and Dilloo: A Study of West Indian Life' (pp. 124–53) are the other essays in the collection. *Postscripts* reveals how Shakespearian to Victorian representations of the Caribbean were part of the British imperialist, nation- and empire-building enterprise. With Caribbean rereadings of these texts as those presented in *Postscripts* scholars are offered 'new critical perspectives on the process and meaning of canon formation, and on early representations of the Caribbean in the British literary tradition' (p. 7).

In *Extravagant Postcolonialism: Modernism and Modernity in Anglophone Fiction 1958–1988*, Brian May challenges the assumption that postcolonial texts fit a certain model. Instead, these texts treat with their protagonists' subjectivities, and they do so by refashioning modernism in individual ways. In chapter 1, 'Memorials to Modernity: Postcolonial Pilgrimage in V.S. Naipaul and Salman Rushdie' (pp. 56–75), May compares the ways in which *An Area of Darkness* and *The Satanic Verses* 'depict contemporary pilgrimages that bring the issue of individuality into sharp relief' giving an opportunity to examine 'the Westernized, modernized self' (p. 58). Chapter 3, 'Modernism Re(d-)dressed: Interrogativity and Individuality in Jean Rhys' (pp. 104–30), moves to an examination of the characters of, and the interactions between, Antoinette and the Rochester in *Wide Sargasso Sea*. May argues that their 'healthy individuality' is the 'fruit of social dialectic—significant personal relations with an authentic and challenging other' (p. 104). He also explores the ways in which two characters from such different backgrounds and world-views react to each other through the medium of dress.

In *What Is a Classic? Postcolonial Rewriting and Invention of the Canon*, Ankhi Mukherjee examines so-called 'classic' texts alongside postcolonial texts directly influenced by them. She shows the ways in which the idea of the 'classic' is formed and perpetuated by its relationships with other texts that eventually contribute to the emergence of another canon. In her chapter 2, 'What Is a Novel? Conrad, Said, Naipaul' (pp. 50–78), Conrad's *Heart of Darkness* is examined alongside Wilson Harris's *Palace of the Peacock* and several of V.S. Naipaul's novels. Chapter 3, ' "Best of the World's Classics": Derek Walcott between Classics and the Classic' (pp. 79–108), Walcott's oeuvre forms the basis of an examination of canonical texts such as *The Odyssey* and *Robinson Crusoe*. In discussing Walcott's allusions to these 'classic' texts, Mukherjee establishes some of the criteria for the establishment of literary canons.

Naipaul is again the subject of Annabel Patterson's chapter, 'V.S. Naipaul, *A Bend in the River*', in *The International Novel* (pp. 111–29). Here, Naipaul's 'nuanced and even sympathetic' (p. 117) construction of the Democratic Republic of the Congo is discussed. His travel novel, Patterson argues, allows for an 'extraordinary mixture of minute observation and broad sociological analysis' (p. 124), even if there is also a certain characteristic pessimism about Africa in Naipaul's writing.

Two chapters on Caribbean literature also appeared in Kinana Hamam's *Confining Spaces, Resistant Subjectivities: Towards a Metachronous Discourse of Literary Mapping and Transformation in Postcolonial Women's Writing*. Chapter 4, 'Erna Brodber's Jane and Louisa Will Soon Come Home' (pp. 48–74), 'focuses on issues of diversity, complexity, and the non-linearity of women's transition' (p. 48). Hamam considers the repressive spaces that women inhabit and the ways in which their attempts at resistance and subversion manifest in complex narratives that move from fragmentation to coherence. Theme and style are revealed to be interrelated in the novel. Chapter 6, 'Jean Rhys's Wide Sargasso Sea' (pp. 104–36), also examines Antoinette's attempts to transcend the confines of her gender and race in a repressive society. Issues of 'female dislocation, hybridity, internal and external colonialism, and preoccupation with liminal identities' (pp. 135–6) are the focus of this chapter.

Susana M. Morris's *Close Kin and Distant Relatives: The Paradox of Respectability in Black Women's Literature* discusses 'family, ambivalence, and notions of respectability' (p. 4) and devotes three chapters to Caribbean writing. In chapter 1, 'A Wide Confraternity: Diaspora and Family in Paula Marshall's *Praisesong for the Widow*' (pp. 17–44), Morris argues for 'an ethic of community' (p. 19) that comes in the form of female familial support and a heritage that grounds the characters despite their move to diasporic spaces and their encounters with 'racism, sexism, and classism in the post-civil rights era' (p. 44). Chapter 2, 'Sins of the Mother? Ambivalence, Agency, and the Family Romance in Jamaica Kincaid's *Annie John*' (pp. 45–73), focuses on family relationships that often result in alienation as much as in affection. Morris explores this through the fraught mother–daughter relationship in Kincaid's semi-autobiographical novel. Finally, chapter 3, 'Daughters of This Land: Genealogies of Resistance in Edwidge Danticat's *Breath, Eyes, Memory*' (pp. 74–102), draws attention to the ways in which 'the cult of virginity' (p. 76) was used to perpetuate dominant and repressive patriarchal structures even in matriarchal families in post-Duvalier Haiti.

There are two chapters on Caribbean literature in *Diasporas, Cultures of Mobilities, 'Race': 1. Diasporas and Cultures of Migrations*, edited by Judith Misrahi-Barak and Claudine Raynaud. Bénédicte Ledent's 'Mind the Gaps: Caryl Phillips's *In the Falling Snow* (2009) and the Generational Approach to the Black Diaspora' (pp. 161–75) uses Phillips's novel to reflect upon and interrogate concepts deployed in diaspora studies such as 'migration, displacement, and unbelonging' (p. 162), especially as they manifest in intergenerational gaps. In 'Masculinities Out of Line: Navigating Queerness and Diasporic Identity in Shyam Selvadurai's *Funny Boy* and Shani Mootoo's *Cereus Blooms at Night* (pp. 323–44), Christine Vogt-William examines the similarities between the Sri Lankan and Trinidadian novels' treatment of queerness in the diasporic context. The marginalization that stems from the politics of inclusion and exclusion, and the movements across boundaries associated with migration, allow for comparisons to be made with the situation of characters who do not conform to heteronormative sexual identities. However, as Vogt-William argues, 'alternative readings of masculinity' can result in 'new forms of agency' and help to shape 'more inclusive and empowering spaces for those heretofore marginalized and disenfranchised' (p. 343).

(c) Journal Articles

The preoccupation with history among Caribbean writers continues to influence scholastic studies. These works often centre on the intersections between writing and memory, as well as the various kinds of discourses that contribute to a sense of self. For example, in 'Building the Neo-Archive: Dionne Brand's *A Map to the Door of No Return*' (*Meridians* 12:i[2014] 149–71), Erica L. Johnson explores the importance of the archives as a gateway to memory in Brand's memoir about her childhood in Trinidad and her move to Canada. By examining the ways in which various types of discourse (including journal entries, missives, newspapers, geographers' logs, popular culture, films, and postcolonial writing) speak to one another, Johnson shows how texts influence and construct not only personal memory, but also colonial historiography. April Shemak's article, 'Re/writing Reconciliation in Merle Collins's *Angel*' (*CarQ* 60:i[2014] 42–60), also examines Collins's rewriting of the Grenada revolution as a 'textual confrontation of trauma and memory' (p. 45). Zetta Elliott's memoir-essay, '"All Land is One Land Under the Sea": Mapping Memory in Canada and the Caribbean' (*CarQ* 60:i[2014] 61–73), is a personal account of the influence of both geographical spaces on her own life and writing.

In her article, 'Writing Possibilities of the Past: Jamaica Kincaid's *Mr Potter*' (*Discourse* 36:i[2014] 71–86), Antonia Purk argues that following the mandate from Edouard Glissant to pursue the colonial past that has not yet been written into history, Kincaid's narrator becomes an author of the text that re-creates her past, her family history, and Antigua's colonial history according to her own terms. Through historiopoesis, the re-creation of a past that has been lost 'produces space for contemporary identity, which bestows a validity on the fictional narrative equal to actual recoveries of the past' (p. 73). Similar arguments are made in another article by Purk, 'Multiplying Perspectives through Text and Time: Jamaica Kincaid's Writing of the Collective' (*COPAS* 15:i[2014] 1–14). In this article, however, a greater range of Kincaid's texts is examined to show how 'narrative repetition and revision' (p. 12) are used as strategies for engaging with the past. In another article, 'What's in a Name? The Resurrection of the Author in Jamaica Kincaid's *The Autobiography of My Mother*' (*CSLT* 12[2014] 44–52), Luciano Cabral also focuses on Kincaid's *Autobiography of My Mother*, drawing attention to the challenges of reading autobiography especially in the face of Roland Barthes's call for the death of the author.

In '"Dead Might Not Be Dead": Milton in the Americas and Jamaica Kincaid's Flat World' (*MP* 111:iv[2014] 862–78), Ian Bickford examines the influence of Milton on Kincaid's writing. Although he argues that Kincaid's understanding of the seventeenth-century poet is shaped by American reception of his work, he also reverses the gaze to examine how Kincaid's writing affects American readings of Milton. Both writers' work can therefore be seen as a 'palimpsest, a writing-over' (p. 878). Also focusing on Kincaid, but comparing her work to that of Toni Morrison, Sam Vásquez, in 'In Her Own Image: Literary and Visual Representations of Girlhood in Toni Morrison's *The Bluest Eye* and Jamaica Kincaid's *Annie John*' (*Meridians* 12:i[2014] 58–87), examines the ways in which these two writers engage in expanding critical discourses on gender, identity, and visual culture in transnational narratives. By comparing the work of an African American writer with that of an Afro-Caribbean one, Vasquez argues that 'both authors demonstrate how black women in different cultural contexts write themselves into visual and historical records' (p. 60).

A 2004 interview with Jamaican poet Lorna Goodison, 'Swaddling: On Lorna Goodison's Womanly Poetics' (*JWIL* 22:ii[2014] 26–41), provides the framework for Christian Campbell's musings on her 'womanly poetics' since, unlike other Caribbean writers who write critical work thereby providing 'a context and a lexicon in which their creative work can be assessed' (p. 26), Goodison only does creative writing.

Issues of national identity, especially in the context of multicultural and multiracial populations, were also the subject of some studies in 2014. In 'Translative and Opaque: Multilingual Caribbean Writing in Derek Walcott and Monchoachi' (*SmAx* 18:iii[2014] 90–106), for example, Kavita Ashana Singh challenges the assumption and widely touted ideal of seamless multiculturalism in the Caribbean by showing how multilingualism and translation expose the problem at the heart of this mixing. Caribbean writers' deployment of creoles in their works demands 'constant translation' (p. 91) by their readers. By comparing the work of Walcott, an anglophone writer, with that of Monchoachi, a francophone writer, Singh shows how the sometimes opaque quality of both writers' literary creoles demands a more rigorous approach to thinking about Caribbean multiculturalism and decolonization.

Tzarina T. Prater focuses on the ways in which Chinese Jamaicans negotiate their identities in the context of Jamaican nationalism in 'Labrish and Mooncakes: The Meeting of Vernaculars in the Work of Easton Lee' (*SmAx* 8:i[2014] 149–60). Taking as its focus the cultural interactions at the Chinese shop, this essay examines the challenges of maintaining individuality while also participating in the wider context of a national identity that participates in 'site-specific orientalis[m]' (p. 150). More specifically, Prater examines Lee's use of rhetorical strategies and vernaculars that reflect and complicate the position of the Chinese diasporic subject in Jamaica.

Child abuse, family violence, and homophobia in Jamaica are put against the backdrop of the nation's colonial past of slavery and colonial violence in Staceyann Chin's memoir. Jocelyn Fenton Stitt, 'Disciplining the Unruly (National) Body in Staceyann Chin's *The Other Side of Paradise*' (*SmAx* 18:iii[2014] 1–17), explores Chin's precarious subject positions of liminality through her biracial heritage and her lesbian identity. The question of where such subjects fit into wider national discourses 'dominated by a larger interconnected system of power and control' (p. 17) is the focus of the article.

Laura Barrio-Vilar, ' "All o' We is One"? Migration, Citizenship, and Black Nativism in the Postcolonial Era' (*Callaloo* 37:i[2014] 89–111), uses the African diaspora as a case study to explore issues of citizenship and belonging in a globalized society founded on migration, naturalization, and blurred cultural and political borders. Focusing on Paule Marshall's *Daughters*, she argues that 'Marshall's story...confronts us with new trends of Black nativism and the urge to develop a diasporic subjectivity that can overcome the challenges of transnational experiences' (p. 89). In 'Caribbean Women Writing: Social Media, Spirituality and the Arts of Solitude in Edwidge Danticat's Haiti' (*CQ* 60:i[2014] 1–22), Curdella Forbes also examines the traumas that arise out of several kinds of 'crossings' (p. 3) associated with globalization. Taking the 2010 Haiti earthquake as her point of departure, Forbes ponders on 'spaces of isolation' and solitude in Danticat's memoir, *Create Dangerously: The Immigrant Artist at Work*.

The relationship between capitalism and the environment was explored in 2014 as well. In 'Spectres in the Forest: Gothic Form and World-Ecology in Edgar Mittelholzer's *My Bones and My Flute*' (*SmAx* 18:ii[2014] 53–68), Michael Niblett extends previous readings of the novel. Mittelholzer's use of 'Euro-American gothic tropes' (p. 54) in his Caribbean novel 'illuminates the particular inflection of capitalist modernity in Guyana' (p. 54) as it reproduces but also challenges stereotypes about the Caribbean. Through its particular engagement with the Guyanese landscape, the political regime of the plantation system, and the sugar industry, the novel also allows for more general observations about how it fits into the world ecological systems of capitalist modernity. Examining representations of the Caribbean landscape in the work of Jamaica Kincaid and Jean Rhys in 'On Representations of Nature and Women in Caribbean Literature' (*Hitotsubashi* 55[2014] 27–33), Midori Saito also argues that 'the workings of capitalism' are responsible for 'the dichotomy between nature and civilization' as much as they are for gender and racial categories (p. 27).

In 'The Clothing Economy of Earl Lovelace's *The Dragon Can't Dance*' (*JCL* 49:i[2014] 81–98), Hella Bloom Cohen focuses on the novel's chapter 3 to explore the significance of the handicraft tradition of Carnival costume-making in the context of a growing capitalist economy. Placing her emphasis on the dragon costume in the novel, Cohen argues that clothing reflects the social condition in its role as symbolic currency where real capital is absent. The dragon costume is read not only as symbol of ancestral memory, but also as a gateway to understanding how issues of production, power, and the global capitalist economy affect the society of Lovelace's novel.

Revisionist readings of early anglophone Caribbean literature also featured in 2014. In 'Amongst the Unbelievable: Race, Faith and Reason in Selected Writings by V.S. Naipaul' (*Literator* 35:i[2014] 1–9), Robert Balfour reconsiders four of the writer's travelogues, arguing that Naipaul's own subject positioning problematizes representations of Islam. For Balfour, Naipaul offers a 'more compassionate perspective on the relationship between faith and political transition in developing societies' (p. 1). The figure of Annie Palmer is revisited in Jennifer Donahue's examination of four textual representations of her: 'The Ghost of Annie Palmer: Giving Voice to Jamaica's "White Witch of Rose Hall"' (*JCL* 49:ii[2014] 243–56). Looking at folklore and obeah as Palmer's instruments of manipulation especially in a context of violence and sexual repression, Donahue argues that she was a symbol of resistance, subversion, and female power.

Jane Bryce's 'Adventures in Form: "Outsider" Fiction in the Caribbean' (*JWIL* 22:ii[2014] 7–25) interrogates the West Indian canon that was formed in the early years of independence and tended to include anti-colonial realist novels. She argues that, with the emergence of new writers and the development and proliferation of other genres of writing (including 'popular' genres such as the romance, crime fiction, and speculative fiction), the canon has to be re-examined and understood, especially in the context of the publishing industry.

A few articles also made connections between Caribbean and Canadian writing in the context of diaspora cultures. In 'The Black Atlantic Meets the Black Pacific: Multimodality in Kamau Brathwaite and Wayde Compton' (*Callaloo* 37:ii[2014] 389–403), Heather Smyth compares the work of a Caribbean and a Canadian poet. She draws attention to the ways in which their similar multimodal approaches (their mixing of the sound, textual, visual, and performative aspects of the work) contribute to 'the ongoing evolution of concepts of "race," culture, and diaspora' (p. 389). The relationship between poetry and sound in Brathwaite's work was also the subject of Andrew Rippeon's article, 'Bebop, Broadcast, Podcast, Audioglyph: Scanning Kamau Brathwaite's Mediated Sounds' (*ConL* 55:ii[2014] 369–401).

The presence and significance of Jews in slave and neo-slave narratives is the subject of Sarah Phillips Casteel's 'Port and Plantation Jews in Contemporary Slave Fiction of the Americas' (*Callaloo* 37:i[2014] 112–29). By comparing the slave experience of victimization and exploitation with that of the Jews who owned them, Casteel adopts a 'multidirectional' (p. 112) approach to understanding the relationship between these two groups in works by Caribbean and Canadian writers.

Taking as her study Michelle Cliff's and Caryl Phillips's 'cross-cultural engagements with the Holocaust' (p. 813), Sarah Phillips Casteel, 'Writing Under the Sign of Anne Frank: Creolized Holocaust Memory in Michelle Cliff and Caryl Phillips' (*MFS* 60:iv[2014] 796–820), also compares the ways in which these Caribbean-born writers' invocations of Anne Frank are localized to Caribbean and diaspora settings (especially as they relate to histories of oppression), but also add to the 'cosmopolitization' (p. 797) of the Holocaust. She also draws attention to 'the deep historical presence of the Sephardic Jews in the Dutch and British Caribbean' (p. 813) as another important frame of reference for her analysis.

The comparative thrust through multimodality continues in Wai Chee Dimock's 'Epic Relays: C.L.R. James, Herman Melville, Frank Stella' (*Comparatist* 38[Oct. 2014] 148–57). Dimock argues that literary texts can be read as 'an open-ended input network' (p. 148). Because texts arise in the context of a literary history and have relationships with other texts, no text is ever complete or discrete, but rather is one phase in a relay. Using the epic as a model through which to link texts by James, Melville, and Stella, Dimock shows how their structures that follow certain patterns of mixed media can allow for intertextual readings.

Also using genre as a way to understand James, Raj G. Chetty, in 'The Tragicomedy of Anticolonial Overcoming: *Toussaint Louverture* and *The Black Jacobins* on Stage' (*Callaloo* 37:i[2014] 69–88), argues that the use of tragicomedy in C.L.R. James's play prevents it from being caught in its context of anti-colonialism. Instead, the play takes on wider relevance even 'in the face of tragic postcolonial failures' (p. 71).

In 'Metafictions of Development: *The Enigma of Arrival*, *You Can't Get Lost in Cape Town*, and the Place of the World in World Literature' (*JCL* 49:i[2014] 63–80), Kara Lee Donnelly compares the work of V.S. Naipaul and Zoë Wicomb, arguing that both writers use the *Bildungsroman* genre and their literary protagonists to reflect their own lives as writers. The literary market reflects global inequalities but still incorporates work from different parts of the globe allowing for a genuine 'World Literature'.

Using Sam Selvon's *The Lonely Londoners* as a 'canonical postcolonial model' (p. 235) through which to examine Samuel Beckett's *Murphy*, Richard McGuire points out the similarities between the two novels, especially in their treatment of migration, in 'Migrant Drifters: Samuel Beckett's *Murphy* and Sam Selvon's *The Lonely Londoners* in a Postcolonial Comparative Context' (*CCS* 11:ii–iii[2014] 235–48). The article thus reveals interesting parallels between the Caribbean and Irish migrant experience in London. Alice Ridout's article, 'Of Pigeons and Expats: Doris Lessing, Sam Selvon, and Zadie Smith' (*DLS* 32[2014] 26–9), compares these three writers' use of the pigeon to also reflect immigrant concerns and their relationship with London.

By examining Caribbean revisionings of Shakespeare's *The Tempest*, Kristin M.S. Bezio draws attention to the ways in which leadership transforms according to time and place. Aimé Césaire's *A Tempest* and Elizabeth Nuñez's *Prospero's Daughter* are the primary texts analysed in 'Bringing Down the Island: Rebellion, Colonial Hierarchy, and Individualized Leadership in Nuñez novel *Prospero's Daughter*' (*JLAE* 11:iii[2014] 126–40).

The interdisciplinary approach of two 'colonial poet-physicians' (p. 300) is the subject of Kelly Wisecup's ' "All Apollo's Arts": Divine Cures, Afro-Caribbean Knowledge, and Healing Poetry in the British West Indies' (*L&M* 32:ii[2014] 299–324). Wisecup draws upon the Greek god of poetry and medicine to explore the connections between the two, especially in the context of colonization in the Caribbean. The work of James Kirkpatrick and James Grainger and their use of 'multiple religious and medical traditions in order to confront the challenges involved in using poetry to heal disease in the Americas' (p. 300) is at the core of this unique study. The tensions between, and intersections of, European and African epistemology made for new ways of thinking about disease and healing in the New World.

In 'Consciousness, the Epistolary Novel and the Anglophone Caribbean Writer: Paulette Ramsay's *Aunt Jen*' (*JWIL* 22:ii[2014] 59–72), Milt Moise examines the ways in which the consciousness of characters is conveyed. By examining a series of letters in the (rare) single-voiced epistolary novel, Moise argues that 'while its focus on the consciousness and voice of the protagonist may initially appear as a limitation, there is ample room to flourish within its spaces' (pp. 70–1). An interview with Paulette Ramsay also appeared in this issue of the *Journal of West Indian Literature*: Carrie J. Walker, 'Out of Many, One Voice: An Interview with Paulette Ramsay' (*JWIL* 22:ii[2014] 42–58).

A few articles also centred on the work of Jean Rhys. In 'Jean Rhys and the Fiction of Failed Reciprocity' (*JML* 37:ii[2014] 92–108), Rebecca Colesworthy, uses theories of the gift to examine Rhys's second novel, *After Leaving Mr McKenzie*. The inequality of gift exchange becomes a way of understanding gender inequalities. In 'The Law of Language and the Law of Structure in the Dominant Masculine Discourse of Jean Rhys's *Wide Sargasso Sea*' (*LPI* 13[2014] 454–60), Cristina-Georgiana Voicu argues that alternative epistemologies and ontologies in the Caribbean challenge the subject position and masculine, colonial discourse of the Rochester character in Rhys's novel. Kristy Butler examines the intertextual relationship between Charlotte Brontë's *Jane Eyre* and Rhys's *Wide Sargasso Sea* using Jacques Derrida's concept of *hauntology* in 'Kristeva, Intertextuality, and Re-imagining "The Madwoman in the Attic" ' (*SLI* 47:i[2014] 129–47). This reading exposes the 'loops' in the narratives as one text 'haunts' the other (p. 130). In 'Victims and Victimizers in the Fiction of Katherine Mansfield and Jean Rhys' (*Antipodes* 28:ii[2014] 315–26), Jane Nardin examines the artistic challenges that 'plagued' (p. 315) women writers in the modernist period and led them to create 'a modernism of their own' (p. 325). Neşe Şenel's 'A Postcolonial Reading of *Wide Sargasso Sea* by Jean Rhys' (*JLLE* 11[2014] 38–45) examines the orientalist perspectives of Caribbean creoles that are exposed in Rhys's novel.

5. South Asia

(a) Books

Perhaps the most interesting book available for review in the last year was Laetitia Zecchini's study of the Indian poet Arun Kolatkar, *Moving Lines:*

Arun Kolatkar and Literary Modernism in India. Zecchini's meticulous framing of Kolatkar's work in its local and international contexts, as well as her astute readings of individual poems, not only compensate for years of critical neglect, but also contribute to widening the debate on literary modernism beyond its recognized locations in England and America. This is an important book, grounded in the belief that modernism and postcoloniality can be read fruitfully in relation to each other, and that literary modernism remains a useful paradigm for reading non-Western literatures, and Kolatkar in particular. Chapter 1 gives a vivid account of the bohemianism and cosmopolitanism characteristic of the anti-establishment community of artists who came together in the cafes of Kala Ghoda, as well as the creative group practice characteristic of the little magazines and small presses that were thriving in the Bombay of the 1960s. While drawing out the cosmopolitan dimension of these publications, demonstrating how the world came to Bombay, Zecchini also carefully pieces together evidence to show how 'Bombay materialized on the global map of modernism' (p. 55).

Kolatkar constituted an influential presence in the underground, anti-commercial, and experimental publications of the time, both in English and Marathi. Together with contemporaries such as Dilip Chitre and Arvind Krishna Mehrotra, he forged a conception of art as defiantly '"little" and lower case' (p. 48), while his context and the city in which he wrote systematically confused the binaries of local vs. cosmopolitan, Indian vs. Western, modern vs. traditional. The poet's bilingualism enabled unorthodoxy. If Marathi was supposedly local, traditional, and authentic, then English was global, modern, and foreign. Kolatkar embodied the give and take between the two—so intense he could not decide which version of a poem was original and which the translation. It is these 'overlapping multilingualities and the transactions' between his two bodies of work in Marathi and English which are the subject of chapter 2. Chapter 3 draws on Kolatkar's diaries, unpublished texts, and some of his best-known works, such as the *Kala Ghoda Poems* and the award-winning *Jejuri*, to make a case for the significance of the poet's visual imagination, and the thematic importance of seeing and sight in his writing. Chapter 4 extends this line of argument to show how the transformation of the ordinary into art is at the centre of Kolatkar's literary practice. As a *flâneur* in Bombay, Kolatkar's domain of vision and exploration remains the city street and that which is literally swept aside or metaphorically abandoned on the wayside of perception. His tendency to ignore the great events of his time to focus instead on the everyday arguably constitutes an alternative lineage for Indian writing in English, which Zecchini identifies as 'definitely modernist' (pp. 92–3). Chapters 5 and 6 deal with the political dimension that lies behind the poetry's deceptively simple surface. As Zecchini observes, the powerful recurrent metaphor of rubbish also stands for the poor, migrants, and literal outcastes who throng the pavements of Bombay. In making filth the subject of his poetry, Kolatkar challenges not only brahminical ideals of purity, characterized by a systematic attitude of repulsion towards what is left over, but also the rhetoric of Hindu nationalism wherein physical pollution is comparable to cultural pollution and in which cleansing space is readable as code for cleansing India of its 'foreign' elements.

Another book that turns its attention to hitherto under-studied Indian English writers is Bruce King's *Rewriting India: Eight Writers*, a collection of essays on Arun Kolatkar, Keki Daruwalla, Amit Chaudhuri, Pankaj Mishra, Upamanyu Chatterjee, Tabish Khair, Susan Visvanathan, and Jeet Thayil. King finds them central to an understanding of how Indian literature has developed over the decades. The volume starts off with a discussion of Kolatkar and Daruwalla, whose poetry laid the foundations for a whole generation of prose writers to come, who form the subject of the next five chapters. The last chapter undertakes an intensive analysis of the writings of Jeet Thayil, whose literary style and thematic preoccupations, as both poet and novelist, allow King to measure the distance that Indian writing in English has travelled since Kolatkar first set the agenda.

Resonating with Zecchini's book, King recounts the 1960s as the period of such counter-culture journals as *Bombay Duck* and *Damn You: A Magazine of the Arts*, and volumes of verse preoccupied not so much with the British, the West, Pakistan, or feudal landlords oppressing peasants, but rather with the writer's immediate context and a self defined against an other comprising, in the first instance, Indians who did not subscribe to the modern secular urban values of the writers themselves. Like Zecchini, King challenges the critical assessment of Kolatkar as an aesthete detached from notions of literature as engagement. Arguing for Kolatkar's poetry to be understood as a cultural statement that is at the same time also political, King draws attention to his defiance of the idealization of traditions, of symbols of official Indian cultural nationalism, and the Hindu revivalist movement with its militant politics, while privileging a poetry of reality, of places and people, of colloquial language and the present (p. 54). Kolatkar's poetry, he argues, pays a unique tribute to the dynamism found on the streets of Bombay as well as in nature, as opposed to a moribund Sanskritic culture that had been used as a basis for social injustice, Hindu extremism, and for a poetic diction that meant little to most people.

The essay on Keki Daruwalla traces the poet's evolution over a lifetime to reveal the struggle that was faced by Indian writing in English before it could develop a voice on the world stage. In the process, his subject matter changed from the observed to the inner self, generalizations about life, and his readings in the literature and history of the world (p. 57). His first three volumes of poetry drew on the world he knew best—his experience as a police officer patrolling a riot-torn city and battling against criminal gangs, his knowledge of Muslim culture, trekking in the far north, and feeling reluctantly distant from peoples and traditions. By contrast, his later work, especially the four volumes of poetry that emerged from the highly productive decade after retirement in 1995, engages with non-Indian subjects that the poet had once feared to approach. These volumes draw upon themes from around the world, especially from history and literature. Often present as the narrative 'I' which sees or imagines, discusses, and pronounces, the later volumes reveal the poet to be familiar with many cultures and feeling part of a poetic community that he can address as an equal (p. 72).

The writings of Amit Chaudhuri, Pankaj Mishra, and Upamanyu Chatterjee reveal a shared set of anxieties about north Indian brahminism being challenged by social change, contemporary mass culture, and the effects of national independence. If Chaudhuri's nostalgia for Bengali high culture was partly the result of his uprooting from Calcutta, Mishra's fiction reveals the frustration of small-town Brahmins who have come down in the world, while the English-speaking Bengali Brahmins of Chatterjee's fiction struggle to make sense of their lives in an India where the power has shifted to governmental organizations, where castes and regions wrestle for social and financial benefits from the state, and where the ideals of patriarchy are being contested by individualism and the nuclear family (p. 136). King rightly observes that, notwithstanding the natural beauty of Chatterjee's prose, it tends to draw too much attention to itself. While part of this self-consciousness may be read as strategic, at least a part may also be read as unwittingly overwrought and exaggerated. Like many satirists, Chatterjee also tends to be a conservative, peddling a vision of India that apparently lacks any sense of shared values, or any consistency of actions and morals (p. 151). Insightful as this account is of Chatterjee's work, King's own observations can sometimes sound rather baldly judgemental. His comments on the characters of Urmila and Shyamanand, for instance ('Like her husband she hoards money; after her death it is revealed that she took and hid in her trunk the silver rattle of a grandson. Like her husband she wants continual attention; she uses the discomforts of age and illness as excuses to bother others', p. 142), do less than justice to the nuanced, individualized, ageing couple who speak to a whole generation after independence brought up on the virtues of thrift, and to a culture where illness in old age has by all accounts a more complex aetiology than suggested by the passing observation about attention-seeking behaviour.

The final chapter, on Jeet Thayil, engages closely with the four volumes of poetry, *Gemini*, *Apocalypso*, *English*, and *These Errors Are Correct*, and the novel *Narcopolis*. As someone who travelled extensively during the formative years of his life, lament for a lost home or the sense of feeling displaced do not figure prominently in Thayil's writing. His powerful and occasionally obscure verse is mostly autobiographical, beginning with the pleasure, pains, and obsessions of decades of drug addiction, then a religious conversion as he cured his addiction, and later the courtship, marriage, and loss of his wife when she was only 27. That Thayil risks obscurity indicates, for King, how far Indian poetry in English has come since the seeming directness of Ezekiel, Daruwalla, Kamala Das, and others, who wrote as if they feared losing the reader (p. 228). While settings are not really significant in Thayil's poetry, his novel focuses on a small area of Bombay: the drug culture of Shuklaji street in the 1970s and 1980s. Whether this makes it an Indian novel, however, remains an open question.

Needless to say, the easy cosmopolitanism of writers like Kolatkar and Thayil is not available to everyone. For the characters of Salman Rushdie's novels from the post-fatwa period, in fact, there is nothing easy about cosmopolitanism. Rushdie's fiction foregrounds a complex response to the very personal and extended experience of persecution by religious fundamentalists opposed to the writer's world-view. Justin Neuman's *Fiction Beyond Secularism* opens with a chapter titled 'Salman Rushdie's Wounded Secularism' (pp. 19–48), in which Neuman explores a range of stories that

Rushdie tells about secularity. Neuman identifies two distinct trajectories that appear to be mutually contradictory: on the one hand, his essays tend to follow a familiar tradition that self-consciously inherits the Enlightenment's rationalism and faith in progress (even as his fiction at the time displays a growing dissatisfaction with the assumption that secularism and pluralism go hand in hand, and that the genealogies of secularism are exclusively Judaeo-Christian); on the other hand, Rushdie tells another set of stories about the way contemporary secularist ideologies produce people who are wounded and vulnerable, shot through with what he calls 'a God-shaped hole'. As a replacement for religion, the literary provides a benign conception of enchantment. Through close readings of *Shalimar the Clown* and *The Enchantress of Florence*, Neuman shows how Rushdie's fiction interrogates some of the most fundamental premises of his secularist commitments, including the assumption that cosmopolitan pluralism and the secularization of the public sphere always go hand in hand. As depicted in *Shalimar the Clown*, the Hindu/Muslim divide and communitarian violence so typical of the subcontinent during decolonization were largely avoided in Muslim-majority Kashmir because of a form of religious cosmopolitanism (*Kashmiriyat*) established not by banishing religion to the private sphere but by actively promoting public religions and nurturing religious attachments. In an insightful analysis of current theories of cosmopolitanism, Neuman notes that, while cosmopolitan ideals were conceived historically in opposition to the nation-state, in recent years they have become increasingly complicit with nationalism and global capital. Beginning with events like the fatwa, religion has come to replace nationalisms as the ideological antithesis of cosmopolitanism. And yet to the extent that some of the most violent flashpoints of the modern world system have less to do with nationalism and more to do with religious and economic differences within and beyond the nation-state, any meaningful understanding of cosmopolitanism must offer a model of inclusivity and universalism that accounts for the substantive differences between religious and non-religious modes of life. The world that Rushdie brings to life in his fiction appears to take on board this criticism of the cosmopolitan as well as to point towards alternative, non-Western ways in which cosmopolitanism has been historically imagined.

Rushdie's critique of the myth of secularism's exclusively Western origins is continued in *The Enchantress of Florence*. Not only does the novel delink humanism from classicism, but by depicting the encounter with fiction through the lens of enchantment it also dissociates secularism from its traditional allies: scepticism, reason, and dispassionate analysis. While the novel shows the cities of Sikri and Florence as being humanist and secular in some limited sense, they are emphatically not places where the retreat of religion corresponds to a fading of the so-called enchanted world of the post-secular imagination. The refusal of militant religiosity in Rushdie's novels does not seem to call for a parallel refusal of magic and credulity. Neither does it imply an epistemological move away from an attitude of faith towards one of scepticism. As Neuman observes, secular humanism in *The Enchantress of Florence* requires and reflects a 'novelistic imagination' that enables the successful storyteller in the novel to 'usurp the prerogative of the gods' in 'the creation of a real life from a dream' (p. 47).

Fiction Beyond Secularism finally puts paid to the critical commonplace that the novel as genre is antithetical to religion. Through a series of engagingly written and rigorously argued chapters on major writers known for their avowedly non-religious orientation, including, apart from Rushdie himself, John Coetzee, Orhan Pamuk, Haruki Murakami, Nadine Gordimer, Don DeLillo, and Ian McEwan, Neuman argues for contemporary fiction to be read for a more systematic, sympathetic, and imaginative response to religion than has been hitherto acknowledged.

The conflict between Western and non-Western modes of knowing and being is also at the heart of Rachel Lee's chapter on Amitav Ghosh's science fiction novel, *The Calcutta Chromosome* in her book *The Exquisite Corpse of Asian America: Biopolitics, Biosociality and Posthuman Ecologies*. Titled 'Everybody's Novel Protist' (pp. 126– 60) Lee's essay shows the novel's clashes between scientific method and counter-science as non-Western belief systems as Ghosh's critique of how Western modernity denigrates Asian and African cosmologies in order to promote its culturally specific science as the most authorized, universal way of knowing. Ghosh's novel counters this 'carved up epistemology' by adopting insights from the life sciences, in particular microbiology. Singling out for attention the parasite responsible for causing malaria (Plasmodium), Ghosh focuses on its multiple migrations of cells, from the intestinal wall of the malarial mosquito to its salivary glands, to the liver and the red blood cells of the vertebrate. As the novel observes, these migrations would not be possible without Plasmodium's ability to transform itself in ways that are designed to identify and enter specific host cells. Lee uses 'this polymorphism', which according to parasite biologists comprises an 'important survival strategy in Plasmodium', to understand the transmission of 'person' across characters inhabiting different spaces and historical times: the mysterious dust sweeper, Mangala, employed in Ronald Ross's malaria research lab in Calcutta *c*.1898, the journalist Urmila Roy living in Calcutta *c*.1995; and the Armenian proprietor Mrs Aratounian, also living in Calcutta *c*.1995. They represent various phases of a single biological entity who in the narrative present appears as Tara, the undocumented nanny living in New York in the late twentieth/early twenty-first centuries.

In an interesting move, Lee uses the multiple embodiments of Plasmodium as a template for comprehending human migration and colonialism, both being suggestive of an encounter between a host body that is relatively static and large-scale and the guest organism which is mobile and microscopic. To the extent that hosting, at both micro and macro levels, raises issues of the entanglement of the natal and the alien, of spatial boundaries that are unclear and involuted (p. 139), it also calls to mind the various kinds of labour that women perform in many cultures, including hosting, caretaking, and reproduction. In contrast to the conventional liberal narrative which equates growth with the leaving behind of obligations of descent and biological dependencies of nurture and care, Lee draws on a feminist framework attentive to caretaking—a form of labour disavowed in the fetishizing of autonomy. The novel's disillusionment with this fragmented world of autonomous individuality further impels Lee to seek the ways in which it extends the meaning of reproduction beyond sexual intercourse, embryogenesis, parturition, and neonatal care to encompass not just the life-cycle of an organism but sometimes the life-cycles of other species as well, finally preparing the protagonists of the novel for crossing over into an 'onto-epistemological realization of collective and cross species enmeshment' (p. 143).

In Adriana Raducanu's *Speaking the Language of the Night: Aspects of the Gothic in Selected Contemporary Novels*, the critique of postcolonial reason evident in the writings of Rushdie and Ghosh is extended to Gothic motifs in non-Western literatures and cultures. The book is written on the premise that the Gothic, although undoubtedly a Western genre, presents characteristics found in literatures produced in historically and geographically remote territories. At least three chapters from this study are relevant here. In 'Tales of the Labyrinths—*The White Tiger* and the Postcolonial Metamorphosis of Gothic' (pp. 25–46), Raducanu looks at how the Gothic is extended beyond its familiar critical domains of psychoanalysis, Marxism, and feminism to engage with postcolonialism. Gothic conventions and postcolonialism share an interest in challenging Enlightenment Reason. To the extent that *The White Tiger* appears to celebrate what is irrational, outside law, and marked by social and cultural dispossession, it lends itself to analysis from the twin perspectives of postcolonialism and the Gothic. The life story of Balram, the novel's protagonist, has obvious similarities to the typical Gothic plots focused on usurpation, intrigue, betrayal, and murder, selfish ambition, and a licentious performance of carnal desire. Raducanu identifies 'a Gothic flavor' in Adiga's disregard of boundaries and his valorization of liminality. Following Julie Hakim Azam's contention about the postcolonial Gothic, Raducanu strives to show how Adiga's novel is less an intertextual writing back to empire than it is a commentary on the politics of home, posing fundamental questions about the relations of personal, family, and public life (p. 40). The second chapter, 'The Sublime of the Intimate Others' (pp. 129–50), offers an altogether less compelling reading of Rushdie's articulation in *Shame* of the various 'dimensions of monstrosity' via the lens of the 'Gothic sublime', while the third, 'Refracting Spaces in Charlotte Brontë's *Jane Eyre* and Anita Desai's *Fire on the Mountain*' (pp. 151–74), focuses on themes and motifs common to the two novels, placing emphasis on how in the Gothic genre the space of the house, shaped by historical, political, social, and psychological co-ordinates, is endowed with a life of its own, establishing a dialectical relationship between interiority and/or entrapment.

(b) Chapters in Edited Volumes

Trauma studies received a fair amount of attention in 2014. Essays in Michelle Balaev's *Contemporary Approaches in Literary Trauma Theory* challenge the classic model of trauma theory, as articulated by Cathy Caruth, wherein trauma is defined as a deferred, recurrent wounding. As Balaev argues in her introduction, the traditional concept of trauma rotates around an assumed paradox: 'that the most direct seeing of a violent event may occur as an absolute inability to know it' (p. 6) Balaev makes a case for moving away from trauma as unrepresentable towards a trauma that finds meaning in the social and cultural specifics of traumatic experience (p. 3). Special mention must be made of Greg Forter's chapter on 'Colonial Trauma, Utopian Carnality, Modernist Form' (pp. 70–105) for its attempt to extend the boundaries of postcolonial and psychoanalytical theories. Through a close comparison of Toni Morrison's *Beloved* and Arundhati Roy's *The God of Small Things*, Forter seeks to show how both novelists employ modernist techniques to convey a concept of trauma in which remembrance does not produce a repetitive foreclosure of knowledge, but rather produces understanding and healing within a modern postcolonial reality. He argues that theoretical attempts to locate trauma at the heart of postcolonial literature have tended to revolve around two opposing poles. On the one hand the therapeutic approach tends towards an over-optimism about 'recovery' that is based on a tacit acceptance of the health of postcolonial modernity. To recover from colonial trauma within this narrative is to accept the cure of identifying one's interests with those of the modern nation-state (pp. 72–5). On the other hand, the anti-therapeutic strand urges readers to challenge this forgetful attachment to the modern. The anti-therapeutic model exhibits excessive pessimism based on a tendency to conflate the historical (and thus remediable) unhealth of colonialism with the original and irremediable 'injuries of subject formation'. A good amount of work in this strand conceptualizes trauma as being so thoroughly grounded in sociality per se that it becomes difficult to see how it might be overcome (p. 73). In both cases the recourse to analogy undermines the effort to redress injuries inflicted by colonialism. Roy's novel by contrast, as Forter shows in his highly productive and original reading, links the social and the psychic dialectically rather than analogically, showing a commitment to the problem of causation, that is, to exploring how trauma is produced and reproduced, induced and transmitted, through the institutions of colonialism and postcolonial societies. In Roy's novel, colonial trauma is comprehensible only through attention to specific bodies and psyches that occupy specific social locations and through a depiction of historically explicable instances of colonial violence. The unrepresentable character of trauma in the novels is not located in its 'originary' status and thus placed beyond history and representation; rather, it has to do with its forcible disjuncture from pre-colonial pasts and the prohibitions against remembrance enforced by particular regimes of power. While this means that these pasts are theoretically recoverable, representable, and narratable, Forter's reading is at the same time equally attentive to the difficulties and ethical challenges of remembrance posed by the novelist (p. 77).

Trauma and representation figure again as categories of analysis in *Narrating 'Precariousness': Modes, Media, Ethics*, a collection of essays edited by Barbara Korte and Frederic Regard. The volume draws on the terms used by Judith Butler in *Precarious Lives* to examine how lives that are insecure, unpredictable, endangered, on the edge, and out of balance, threatened in their corporeal and mental integrity and therefore often bound up in trauma, do not just pose an ethical challenge but also a challenge to representation. A leading question of this volume is how precarious lives can be represented even when their circumstances seem literally and metaphoric-ally unspeakable (p. 7). Ellen Dengel-Janic's 'The Precariousness of Postcolonial Geographies' (pp. 71–84) examines two kinds of spatial precar-iousness in the novels of Amitav Ghosh. Firstly, in *The Shadow Lines*, the image of the map shows the forces of exclusion and danger deriving from borders. If the grandmother's expectation of being able to see a visible line of separation between India and East Pakistan highlights the abstract and arbitrary nature of national borders, the death of Tridib, the experienced citizen of the world, in inter-religious riots serves as a painfully concrete reminder of the border's violent history. In *The Hungry Tide*, precariousness lies both in the socio-political organization and in the natural environment of the Sunderbans. Geographically as well as symbolically the unsettled tide country of the Ganges delta naturally gives rise to stories of struggle, survival, and suffering. At the same time, however, the narrative also takes into account the socio-political impact on this space as a means of underscoring how human existence is always shaped by the complex interrelationships between the geographical and the social aspects of space (p. 78).

In *The Indian Partition in Literature and Films: History, Politics and Aesthetics*, editors Rini Bhattacharya Mehta and Debali Mookerjea-Leonard rightly observe that even as scholarship on Partition and its aftermath has enriched our understanding of how historical trauma, collective memory, and cultural processes are linked, the scope and potential of this work remain constrained by its focus on anglophone writings from the 1980s and 1990s. The present collection attempts to bring together such studies with those on the largely unexplored vernacular works. One chapter of particular interest is Shumona Dasgupta's 'The Extraordinary and the Everyday: Locating Violence in Women's Narratives of the Partition' (pp. 36–51) for its juxtaposition of Amrita Pritam's Punjabi novel *Pinjar* with Shauna Singh Baldwin's anglophone text *What the Body Remembers*. While collective memory of the Partition constructs the aggressors as outsiders, women were sometimes also targeted by men from within their own communities who used the opportunity offered by the chaos to abduct and rape them. Dasgupta's analysis of these two novels strives to resist the tendency to normalize forms of intimate violence enacted against women within the private sphere. By locating women's experience of violence at the crossroads of public and private, personal and political, both Pritam and Baldwin succeed in disrupting the 'othering' of violence. *Pinjar* is a radical feminist text which generates a trenchant critique of the position of women within the institutions of the family and the postcolonial nation. One of the earliest female-authored Partition texts to focus upon the figure of the abducted woman, *Pinjar* underscores the literal and symbolic violence undergirding the female subject's experience of the postcolonial Indian state, and the intimate and interior spaces of the home, paving the way for an ultimate rejection of particular framings of both the home and the nation. Written almost fifty years after Pritam's novella, Baldwin's *What the Body Remembers* revisits the mass deaths of Sikh women during the Partition in the name of saving family and community honour, and juxtaposes these 'suicides' with men bragging about having martyred their women. The extraordinary violence experienced by women during Partition is then tied to the everyday violence experienced by them as a consequence of their desire to be the ideal daughter, wife, and mother. Hence Baldwin also refuses to perpetuate the narrative of women's trauma as a collective, political aggression by 'other men', instead locating the experience of violence firmly within community, and perpetuated by fathers, brothers, husbands, sometimes even by other women. Dasgupta is, however, critical of how the construction of Sikh identity in the texts occurs by opposing self to an 'ethnic' other, perpetuating negative stereotypes about Muslims. For example, the purdah, while it affords Sikh women mobility and safety within the public domain, remains symbolic of the oppression of Muslim women in the novel.

Chetan Deshmane's edited collection *Muses India* includes fifteen essays on a range of writers from India and the Indian diaspora. These include Dean Mahomet, Toru Dutt, Anita Desai, Shashi Deshpande, Arundhati Roy, Suniti Namjoshi, Bharati Mukherjee, Rohinton Mistry, Jhumpa Lahiri, Kiran Desai, and Salman Rushdie. Several essays stand out for their originality and perspective. Anne Paige Rogers's wonderful 'Excessive Desire, Shattered Identities' (pp. 146–63) on Arundhati Roy's *The God of Small Things* argues that, despite the frequency with which resistance is met with violence and loss, the novel nonetheless shows the way for reading transgression as agency. Sukjoo Sohn's 'Suicide and Rebirth of Community in Rohinton Mistry's *A Fine Balance*' (pp. 101–12) makes a similar attempt to read agency in oppression and abjection. Maneck's suicide at the end of the novel, frequently cited as evidence of the novel's bleak perspective on India, shows that what he really wants to achieve is not 'a fine balance' for personal survival; he would like to see a destabilization and subversion of the essentialist hegemonic concept of 'timeless balance'. The argument is interesting, even if Sohn's writing becomes opaque from time to time. Serena Guarracino's 'Identity, Language and Power in Suniti Namjoshi' (pp. 134–45) contends that, although Namjoshi advocates a feminist genealogy for her writing, her perspective is complicated by deep awareness of the falsity of binaries such as male-female and colonizer-colonized. The essay shows how, in works like *Goja*, *Building Babel*, and *Sycorax*, Namjoshi consolidates an anti-canon that hybridizes the English language with all the different traditions that Namjoshi, as a postcolonial writer, can legitimately claim as her own.

(c) Journals

There has been a turn in the last decade towards exploring the role of translation and vernacular writing in South Asian literature. Scholars like Meenakshi Mukherjee have been calling for more comparative work across anglophone and other national languages in India, and the general critical shifts to transnational and world literature formations also suggest a wider base is needed to understand Indian English literature properly. For example, Indian English writing sits uneasily alongside the narrow idea of national culture and the increasing censorship on scholarship under a resurgent Hindu fundamentalism. In a special issue of *South Asia*, Greg Bailey, 'Indology after Hindutva' (*SA* 37:iv[2014] 700–7), teases out the contradictions and uneasy similarities between the attitudes of current political regimes seeking to communicate their own versions of culture and religion to Westerners and insiders alike, and the attempts of subaltern approaches to history and postcolonial theory that also aim to provide an authentic account of Indian culture. Bailey posits a new focus on Indological studies that straddles a fine line between 'objective' knowledge production and an 'indigenous' view of things. The colonial literary interest in race and eugenics is framed anew by Luzia Savary's 'Vernacular Eugenics? *Santati-Sastra* in Popular Hindi Advisory Literature (1900–1940)' (*SA* 37:iii[2014] 381–97). Tracing the emergence of the 'science of progeny' and Indian eugenics to *Ayurveda*, *rati-sastra*, and a single New York-based fringe scientist/practical phrenologist, Orson Squire Fowler (1809–87), Savary presents a fascinating account of the vernacularization of Western science, in the process minting new terminology, and differing from the English-language 'Hindu science' discourses promul-gated mainly by elite nationalists. Within such a narrative, Western 'fringe science' works as an authoritative 'Western' scientific source. Savary calls for more studies of other vernacular public spheres to fully map the process of legitimizing 'science' in colonial times and the role of translation, readapta-tion, and modification of 'foreign' and 'local' content that constitutes South Asian modernity. The article might productively be read alongside Amitav Ghosh's *The Calcutta Chromosome*.

In a masterful essay that breaks out of postcolonial binaries, Sambuddha Sen engages with Ranajit Guha's investment in *Hootum Pyanchar Nakhsa*, a foundational text in the development of Bengali prose. 'Revisioning the Colonial City: Local Autonomy versus the Aesthetics of Intermixtures in the Age of Circulating Print Culture' (*LitComp* 11:i[2014] 26–35) turns from Guha's analysis of the text's handling of time to its use of nineteenth-century visual traditions (building on its citing of Dickens) to show how local writers and artists entered a place of multiple negotiations, of borrowing, erasures, displacements, citations, which unfolded within a mutating field and pushed against the autonomy afforded by traditional practices. This underpinning for work on early anglophone literary production in India is complemented by Robert Phillips, who traces the material history of the shift from a local and located courtly economy to an emergent, proto-national, print-commercial one in 'The Urdu-Language *Khushtar Ramayan*: Verbal- and Visual-Narrative Repertoires and "Sense of Place"' (*SA* 37:iii[2014] 454–73).

Three diverse essays in *Modern Asian Studies* excavate the fascinating history of print culture in the subcontinent. While Brannon D. Ingram teases out tension between the exploitation and suspicion of print's possibilities in 'The Portable Madrasa: Print, Publics and the Authority of the Deobandi "Ulama"' (*MAS* 48:iv[2014] 845–71), Hayden Bellenoit looks at the paper-and record-based mechanisms by which wealth was extracted in the Indian hinterlands in 'Between Qanungos and Clerks: The Cultural and Service-Worlds of Hindustan's Pensmen, c.1750–1850' (*MAS* 48:iv[2014] 872–910). Sarah Waheed locates the courtesan at the centre of moral, ethical, legal, and aesthetic discourses of Muslim respectability, and her invocation in later nationalist and 'progressive' debates, in 'Women of "Ill Repute": Ethics and Urdu Literature in Colonial India' (*MAS* 48:iv[2014] 986–1023). The last has relevance for studies of the several Indian English novels depicting courtesan figures.

In 'Recovering a Demotic Tradition, Challenging Nativism, Fashioning Modernism in Indian Poetry' (*Interventions* 16:ii[2014] 257–76), Laetitia Zecchini reads Arun Kolatkar, Arvind Krishna Mehrotra, and Dilip Chitre for their 'translation' of medieval *bhakti* compositions into a modernist idiom. Creative adaptation is a transgressive and dissident practice for these poets, who bring together the global and the local, folk music and poetry, English and other Indian languages, thereby subverting the quest for territorial origins. *Critical Endeavour* takes up similar issues in K. Satchidanandan's 'Indian Literature or the Tower of Babel: The Role of Translation in Indian Literature' (*CritE* 20[2014] 383–6) and Ravi Nandan Sinha's 'The Theory of Rasa' (*CritE* 20[2014] 368–72). Rositta Joseph Valiyamattam considers the traffic from the other direction in 'Translating Indian Literatures into English: Theory and Praxis' (*Quest* 28:i[2014] 10–32).

Hari M.G. and H.S. Komalesha expand upon 'Inscribing Our Times in an Epic: Arun Kolatkar's *Sarpa Satra*' (*JPP* 2:ix[2014]), on the one hand, and on the other consider the subversive poetics of saint poets and their contemporary reincarnation in 'Sacred Without God: Bhakti in the Poetry of Arun Kolatkar' (*Asiatic* 8:ii[2014] 149–63). This theme finds an echo in a Tamil article with relevance to Ramanujan's and R. Parthasarathy's verse: Vasu Renganathan's 'Being Krsna's Gopi: Songs of Antal, Ritual Practices and the Power Relations between God and Devotee in the Contemporary Tamil Nadu' (*FWLS* 6:iv[2014] 649–74). Vidyan Ravinthran explores stylistic texture as historically expressive in 'Arun Kolatkar's description of India' (*JCL* 49:iii[2014] 359–77). Arvind Krishna Mehrotra, on the other hand, traces the stride of the global in three Indian poet-translators, Toru Dutt, A.K. Ramanujan, and Arun Kolatkar, in 'Translating the Indian Past: The Poets' Experience' (*JCL* 49:iii[2014] 427–39). Mehrotra's rich textual readings prompt the question as to what constitutes the global in the first place: do vernacular transformations bring poetry into the realm of world literature or relegate it to a narrower 'Indian' space?

Contemporary interest in *dalit* writing permeates anglophone Indian scholarship and has to be informed by studies of its vernacular origins. Dominic Vendell grapples with the ethical, eschatological, philosophical, and practical points of difference between the lower-caste Marathi social reformer and educator and his Brahmin critics in 'Jotirao Phule's *Satyashodh* and the Problem of Subaltern Consciousness' (*CSSAM* 34:i[2014] 52–66). Dwaipayan Sen reads Legislative Assembly papers in 'Representation, Education and Agrarian Reform: Jogendranath Mandal and the Nature of Scheduled Caste Politics, 1937–1943' (*MAS* 48[2014] 77–119) and attempts to understand why reforms were frustrated. Alessandro Marino offers a genealogy of Adivasi marginalization in ' "Where's the Time to Sleep?": Orientalism and Citizenship in Mahasweta Devi's Writing' (*JPW* 50:vi[2014] 688–700), while Sadhu Charan Pradhan questions the linearity of 'Time in Autobiographical Fiction: A Note on Maitreyi Devi' (*JCLA* 37:i–ii[2014] 85–8).

In an elegant, erudite, and engaged personalized narrative, Fernando Rosa ponders 'On Not Being Able to Read or Speak Malayalam: Language and Region in Kerala' (*IACS* 15:ii[2014] 214–34). He traces, in a comparative frame with Brazil, intersections of region, nation, and globe (Kerala's Indian Ocean links and the influence of South American writing there), considering the pioneering work of writers like Paremmakkal Tommakattannar, Chandu Menon, C.V. Raman Pillai, Vaikom Muhammed Basheer, and Thakazhi Sivasankara Pillai, who forged a modern regional identity in one of the most syncretic and complex states of India. Pillai's work has influenced anglophone writing, and Kerala is the source of many Indian English texts. Maya Vinai and Jayashree Hazarika examine 'Caste Hegemony versus Communism: The Kerala Society in Anita Nair's Novels' (*Quest* 28:ii[2014] 59–65).

Shital Pravinchandra argues for the centrality and critical importance of the vernacular short story in considerations of the postcolonial anglophone South Asian novel in 'Not Just Prose: *The Calcutta Chromosome*, the South Asian Short Story and the Limitations of Postcolonial Studies' (*Interventions* 16:iii[2014] 424–44). The essay makes the case for locating the non-anglophone regional language short story as the pivotal genre around which postcolonial studies could reinvigorate itself, by providing an unfamiliar literary lens through which to analyse its typical assumptions of imagined nationhoods, hybrid identities, and historical narrativizations. Pravinchandra persuades us that the quintessential project of postcolonialism, that of *re*writing, is thrown into productive disarray by the inscription of vernacular prose forms into the postcolonial narrative, whereby *they* become the master-texts to be rewritten rather than the usual preoccupation with anglophone literature of/from the empire.

Binayak Roy looks at the way in which the ethnographer/historian/writer steps outside the bounds of postmodern diktats even while utilizing their devices, in 'Exploring the Orient from Within: Amitav Ghosh's *River of Smoke*' (*PocoT* 9:i[2014] 21 pp.). Roy applauds Ghosh's sustained efforts to chart an ethical criticism of epistemological divides in his discursive explor-ation of the other, while retaining its ultimate alterity. *The Quest* contains Shivangi Srivastava's 'Language, History and Society: An Assessment of Amitav Ghosh's *The Glass Palace*' (*Quest* 28:ii[2014] 84–90) and Swati Kumari's 'Migration as Subversion of History: Amitav Ghosh's *In an Antique Land*' (*Quest* 28:ii[2014] 116–22), while *Literary Criterion* offers Sujatha S.'s 'Inheritors of Imaginary Homelands: A Study of Amitav Ghosh's fiction' (*LCrit* 40:ii[2014] 131–7).

Following the path-breaking work of Christopher Bayly in excavating the imperial information order, Barbara Watson Andaya offers a nuanced reading of the correspondence of a young British trader in Asia in ' "Gathering 'Knowledge" in the Bay of Bengal: The Letters of John Adolphus Pope (1785–1788)' (*JMBRAS* 87/2:ccvii[2014] 1–19). Published in 1992, these letters are seen as critical cross-cultural communication, and not just trading in orientalism and local information for commercial purposes. James Staples complicates the oversimplified histories of relations between missionaries, converts, and the colonial state in 'Putting Indian Christianities into Context: Biographies of Christian Conversion in a Leprosy Colony' (*MAS* 48:iv[2014]

1134–59). The work provides useful comparisons in reading some early proselytizing novels and contemporary *dalit* Christian narratives.

Aparajita Mukhopadhyay analyses Bengali and Hindi travelogues by Indian railway travellers in the nineteenth and twentieth centuries in 'Colonized Gaze: Guidebooks and Journeying in Colonial India' (*SA* 37:iv[2014] 656–69). The essay demonstrates that despite being influenced by European guidebooks of the period, Indian writers created a distinct and critical narrative tailored to their own envisioning of India. This essay supplements the attention to post/colonial travel literature in English, enhancing its awareness of social contexts and the politics of representation. Swaralipi Nandi also considers vernacular travel narratives in the Western metropolis in 'When the Clown Laughs Back: Nabaneeta Dev Sen's Global Travel and the Dynamics of Humour' (*StTN* 18:iii[2014] 264–78). Nandi sees Dev Sen subverting the 'knowing' and cosmopolitan perspective of the traditional Western traveller in the East by humorously deprecating the naive Bengali traveller in the West who gains awkward, if risible, agency under pressure to be a global citizen.

Sayan Chattopadhyay takes a 'Homeward Journey Abroad: Nirad C. Chaudhuri and the Tradition of Twentieth-Century Indian National Autobiographies' (*JCL* 49:v[2013] 157–72) and demonstrates that 'the unknown Indian's' work deconstructs East/West and village/city binaries by reorienting the conventional spatial directions of an exile's homecoming. Sonali Das ponders 'An Outsider's Inwardness with India: The Case of Ruth Prawer Jhabvala's *Heat and Dust*' (*CritE* 20[2014] 260–72) while Nishtha Saxena examines 'Narrating the Idea of India with Special Reference to Dean Mohamed's *Travels* and Salman Rushdie's Non-Fictional Work' (*LCrit* 40:ii[2014] 99–107).

In 'Anticipatory Anti-Colonial Writing in R.K. Narayan's *Swami and Friends* and Mulk Raj Anand's *Untouchable*' (*JPW* 50:vi[2014] 730–42), Veronica Barnsley valorizes the transnational literary forms and socially committed vision adopted by the latter over the ironic localisms of the former. The former's work is examined by Subismita Lenka in 'Myth, Tradition and the Individual Talent in R K Narayan's *The Guide*' (*CritE* 20[2014] 109–18) and Christina Mahainim in 'Patriarchy and the Predicament of a Woman in R.K. Narayan's *The Dark Room*' (*Quest* 28:i[2014] 97–102). B Parvathi analyses the latter in 'Religiosity and Revolution in Mulk Raj Anand's *The Big Heart*' (*CritE* 20[2014] 83–97).

Andrew Goldstone enters the world of hallucinatory projections in 'Hatterr Abroad: G.V. Desani on the Stage of World Literature' (*ConL* 55:iii[2014] 466–500) and reclaims the 1948 picaresque, satirical novel, *All About H. Hatterr*, as a unique exposé of the cultural machinations of the postwar global anglophone literary field. The essay makes the salutary point that close readings of such hybrid examples of the global novel need to be informed by the histories of publishing, reviewing, and canon-making that constitute the literary circulations of such texts.

Krupa Shandilya explores visions of the apocalyptic in 'The Sacred and the Secular: Spirituality, Aesthetics, and Politics in Rudyard Kipling's *Kim* and Vikram Chandra's *Sacred Games*' (*MFS* 60:ii[2014] 345–65). Shandilya suggests that Chandra's novel subverts the colonial ideology of racial superiority and the exoticized spirituality that underlies Kipling's idea of the Great Game. Rob Ivermee interprets Wali Dad, the central character in the short story 'On the City Wall', as a product of the liberal imperial discourse on English education and as a figure of the religious minority put to use in the writing of the empire in 'Kipling, the "Backward" Muslim and the Ends of Colonial Pedagogy' (*NCC* 36:iii[2014] 251–68).

A special issue looks at 'Literature: The Antidote to Pakistan's Identity Crisis' (*JCL* 49:i[2014]), a theme also invoked elsewhere in Madeline Clements's 'Reframing "Violence", Transforming Impressions: Images in Contemporary Pakistani Visual Art and English-Language Fiction' (*Wasafiri* 29:i[2014] 46–55). Humaira Saeed explores the repression of emotions and the violence of the bureaucratic nation brought into existence by Partition in 'Affecting Phantasm: The Genesis of Pakistan in *The Heart Divided*' (*JPW* 50:v[2014] 535–46). Saeed weighs the implications of reading Mumtaz Shah Nawaz's novel (written 1947–8, but not published until 1957) as Partition fiction by comparing it with Bapsi Sidhwa's *Ice-Candy Man* [1989] and Khushwant Singh's *Train to Pakistan* [1956]. Nazia Akhter offers a historical analysis of intergenerational trauma and haunting memories in 'Rape and the Imprint of Partition in Samina Ali's *Madras on Rainy Days*' (*PocoT* 9:ii[2014] 20 pp.). It addresses the critical role of gendered violence in connecting the personal/individual to the public/collective in postcolonial contexts, and also of the diaspora in shaping alternative narratives of history and memory.

Sarah Illot treads similar ground in the context of the 2002 communal riots in Gujarat, through the lens of interrelated processes of psycho-corporeal and national abjection, in ' "We Are Here to Speak the Unspeakable": Voicing Abjection in Raj Kamal Jha's *Fireproof*' (*JPW* 50:vi[2014] 664–74). K. Nirupa Rani laments 'Paradise Lost on the Shores of *The Sea of Innocence*: Kishwar Desai's Angst about the Victims of Power Politics' (*CritE* 20[2014] 172–81). Vemuri Rupa and C.L.L. Jayaprada look at the 'Deconstruction of Misogynous and Colonial Discourse in Githa Hariharan's *When Dreams Travel*' (*LCrit* 49:i–ii[2014] 51–64), and Nandini Kumari reads Kamala Markandeya's work in 'Rukmani's Identity and Survival in *Nectar in a Sieve*' (*Approaches* 1:i[2014] 122–31).

Cecile Sandston posits that ' "Home Was Always Far Away": Intertextual and Intermedial Poetic Appropriations of Double Consciousness in Sujata Bhatt's *Pure Lizard*' (*SasD* 6:i[2014] 7–18), and Divya Girishkumar analyses 'Celebratory Discourse of the Dispossessed: Diasporic Identities in Meera Syal's *Anita and Me*' (*Quest* 28:ii[2014] 1–7). Cassandra Bausman examines the utopian, liminal, public/private sphere offered by ladies compartments on Indian rail journeys and the limitations of the figurative arrivals into selfhood in ' "Into a Horizon I Will Not Recognize": Female Identity and Transitional Space Aboard Nair's *Ladies Coupé*' (*IoJCS* 15[2014] 56–79).

Rashmi Luthra contends that the creative appropriations of main female characters from the *Ramayana* and the *Mahabharata*, by ordinary women in folk art and literature and by women writers and artists in the feminist domain, articulate a necessary space for postcolonial feminisms while running the risk of unintentional complicity with right-wing conservative projects, in 'Clearing Sacred Ground: Women-Centred Interpretations of the Indian

Epics' (*FemF* 26:ii[2014] 135–61). Shushila Singh weighs 'Moral Dilemma and Lack of Resolutions: Rendering of the *Mahabharata* in Chitra Banerjee Divakaruni's *The Palace of Illusions*' (*CritE* 20[2014] 155–71).

Elsewhere in *The Critical Endeavour*, Bijay Kumar Das considers 'Glocalization and the Eclipse of Postcolonial Theory' (*CritE* 20[2014] 14–25) and P. Balaswamy peruses 'Images of India as Slumdog Millionaire: Trends in Post-Rushdie Indian English Fiction' (*CritE* 20[2014] 83–96). Shymasree Basu writes engagingly on 'Food, Dieting and Questions of Female Self-Esteem: A Comparative Study of Elizabeth Berg's "The Day I Ate Whatever I Wanted" and Bulbul Sharma's "Sweet Nothings"' (*CCW* 1:ii[2014] 27–38).

Isabelle Hesse opens up comparative frames between Jewish and post-colonial identities in 'Colonizing Jewishness? Minority, Exile and Belonging in Anita Desai's *Baumgartner's Bombay* and Caryl Phillips's *The Nature of Blood*' (*TPr* 28:v[2014] 881–99). She argues that, rather than facile tropes of the cosmopolitan Jew, or the Jew as index of universal exile, the figure of the Jew as minority is used by Desai and Philips as a better basis for comparisons of postcolonial (un)belonging. Preserving political and historical specificities is a necessary condition for productive analysis of minority/majority power-plays across postcolonial and Jewish studies.

In another comparative context, Osayimwense Osa challenges the persistent parochialism in contemporary world literature studies, arguing for the inclusion of masterpieces from a variety of literary traditions in a globalized version of the Great Books syllabus, in 'From Spiritual Comfort to Spiritual Combat: Ezeulu in Chinua Achebe's *Arrow of God* and Pranesharcharya in U.R. Ananthamurthy's *Samskara*' (*JCLA* 37:i–ii[2014] 33–48). The latter novel has had some impact on Indian English literary scholarship, and Sharon Pillai takes us 'Back to the Future: Tracking the Moral Imperative in, of and through *Samskara*' (*CollL* 41:ii[2014] 97–119). Also opening up Indian English literary studies, Rashi Rohatgi, 'World Poetry at the Periphery: Poetic Language in Abhimanyu Unnuth and Octavio Paz' (*CCS* electronic supplement [2014] 9–27), gives us a fascinating account of the Hindi Indo-Mauritian writer, whose work *The Teeth of the Cactus* [1982] enjoyed wide circulation in India and shows how little-known local works can sometimes interact in surprising ways with a wider global literary sphere.

Angelia Poon examines the private narratives of postcolonial globalizations in '(In)visible Scripts, Hidden Costs: Narrating the Postcolonial Globe in Kiran Desai's *The Inheritance of Loss*' (*JPW* 50:v[2014] 547–58) and generously concludes that the diminishment of the self of central character Sai to allow room for the narratives of others indicates a political commitment to the world and some small degree of optimism. Ipsita Nayak muses on 'Social Exclusion in the Novels of Arundhati Roy and Kiran Desai' (*CritE* 20[2014] 147–54). In the same issue, Jitendra Narayan Patnaik remembers 'The Tale of Monkey Baba: Reading Kiran Desai's *Hullabaloo in the Guava Orchard*' (*CritE* 20[2014] 130–6). Teresa J. Heloise sheds light on Anita Desai in 'Multicultural Myths in *Journey to Ithaca*' (*Quest* 28:ii[2014] 19–25). Jennifer Randall explores the limits of border-crossing and cultural performativities in hybrid postcolonial texts in 'Jostling with Borders: Anita

Rau Badami's *Can You Hear the Nightbird Call?* (*CE&S* 36:ii[2014] 33–40). She suggests that the generic liminality of the postcolonial novel, blending fact and fiction, comedy and tragedy, idealism and humour, is a sign of modernity's disruption of history.

Joseph Darda harnesses critical global literature to the cause of understanding and coalitions of struggle in 'Precarious World: Rethinking Global Fiction in Mohsin Hamid's *The Reluctant Fundamentalist*' (*Mosaic* 47:iii[2014] 107–22). Using Judith Butler's theorizing of recognizability and the social ontology of inclusion and exclusion, Darda reads Hamid's work as a challenge to the logic of the 'war on terror' and a call for international solidarity. Sarah Illott looks at the way the dramatic monologue and second-person narrative activate discernment in the reader-as-judge in 'Generic Frameworks and Active Readerships in *The Reluctant Fundamentalist*' (*JPW* 50:v[2014] 571–83).

In 'Postcolonial Servitude: Interiority and System in Daniyal Mueenuddin's *In Other Rooms, Other Wonders*' (*ArielE* 45:iii[2014] 33–73), Ambreen Hai shows the Pakistani American writer according centrality and agency to the subaltern figure of the domestic servant in contemporary feudal society while also revealing the intersections of history, class, and gender that keep the underclass under. Krupa Shandilya analyses attempts to recover the voice of the subaltern: 'Writing/Reading the Subaltern Woman: Narrative Voice and Subaltern Agency in Upamanyu Chatterjee's *English August*' (*PocoT* 9:iii[2014] 16 pp.). She suggests that fiction must be read for its elite class position so that we can see how the tribal woman is both rendered subaltern but also has the capacity to act and disturb the political space from which she is otherwise excluded.

Snehal Shingavi, 'Capitalism, Caste and Con-Games in Aravind Adiga's *The White Tiger*' (*PocoT* 9:iii[2014] 16 pp.), takes up the controversy over the linguistic verisimilitude of the novel and the ability of a random individual repertoire to convey the 'condition of India'. Shingavi shows how Adiga shifts the ideology of caste into one of class, and exposes the interplay between innocence and criminality in bourgeois interpretations of poverty, to uncover the limits of slumming and passing in narratives of social transformation. The novel also receives attention in Raj Kumar Sharma's 'A Postmodern Reading of Aravind Adiga's *The White Tiger*' (*Approaches* 1:i[2014] 63–72); C.G. Shyamala's '*The White Tiger*: The Narrative Manoeuvres' (*LCrit* 40:ii[2014] 108–17); and Kavita Arya's 'Irrelevance of Morality: *The White Tiger* and *The 3 Mistakes of My Life*' (*Quest* 28:ii[2014] 54–8).

In ' "A Revolution in Code"? Hari Kunzru's *Transmission* and the Cultural Politics of Hacking' (*TPr* 28:ii[2014] 267–87), Philip Leonard considers hacking as an alternative practice of social intervention involving ethical, political, and personal imperatives whereby 'criminal' activities resist and subvert national and multilateral protocols. Jason D. Price also demands an ethical treatment of subjectivity and the materiality of the non-human. He uses another Kunzru book to take us from Bhabha-derived discussions of hybridity and in-betweenness that lack ethical investment to Deleuze and Guattari's idea of 'becoming animal' in 'Resisting Colonial Mastery: Becoming Animal, Becoming Ethical in *The Impressionist*' (*ArielE* 45:i–ii[2014] 1–34).

Ahmed Mulla examines the complicated texture of diasporic hospitality and denaturalizes the relationship between host and guest in 'Accommodating the Other or the Self: The Illusions of Hospitality in Jhumpa Lahiri's "Hema and Kaushik"' (*CE&S* 36:ii[2014] 41–9). Yun Ling undertakes a predictable examination of hybridity in 'Restorative Nostalgia and Reconstruction of Imaginary Homeland in *The Namesake*' (*SLL* 8:ii[2014] 73–6), while Monica Dahiya offers a comparative analysis in 'Mirroring India: A Cultural Study of Jhumpa Lahiri's *The Namesake* and Bharati Mukherjee's *Jasmine*' (*LCrit* 40[2014] 92–8). Madhurima Chakraborty, 'Adaptation and the Shifting Allegiances of the Indian Diaspora: Jhumpa Lahiri's and Mira Nair's *The Namesake*(s)' (*LFQ* 42:iv[2014] 609–21), compares film version with novel, and much more astutely points out that Nair's interpretation of diasporic/national belonging is not only divergent from, but the reverse of, rootedness in the 'original' culture that Lahiri repudiates.

Melanie Heydari-Malayeri interrogates some of the foundational assumptions of postcolonial belonging which demand an antagonistic negotiation with European cultural legacy in '"Almost the Same, But Not Quite": Masks and Mimicry in Vikram Seth's *An Equal Music*' (*CE&S* 36:ii[2014] 83–92). By virtue of the almost Eurocentric preoccupations of writers like Seth and Ishiguro, she labels them as 'global' or 'international' writers. Sam Knowles credits the nomadic experience and expression of the writer, the entertaining—if limited— authorial performance, with his later literary success in 'The Performing Wanderer: The Travel Writing of Vikram Seth' (*StTW* 18:i[2014] 57–73).

No year can go by without tribute to Rushdie's enduring oeuvre. Rajeshwari Sunder Rajan believes that the novel affords us a singular, defining spirit of the times in 'Zeitgeist and the Literary Text: India, 1947, in Qurratulain Hyder's *My Temples, Too* and Salman Rushdie's *Midnight's Children*' (*CritI* 40:iv[2014] 439–65), and Adrienne D. Vivian thinks time itself becomes a narrative device for postcolonial identity in 'Temporal Spaces in Garcia Marquez's, Salih's and Rushdie's Novels' (*CLCWeb* 16:iii[2014] 1–9). Andrew Gaedtke is interested in delirium and disability in 'Halluci-nation: Mental Illness, Modernity and Metaphoricity in Salman Rushdie's *Midnight's Children*' (*ConL* 55:iv[2014] 701–25), while Madhumita Roy and Anjali Gera Roy draw forth the influences of *One Thousand and One Nights*, *Kathasaritsagar*, *Panchatantra* and Myth in '*Haroun* and *Luka*: A Study of Rushdie's Talismanic Stories' (*JCL* 49:ii[2014] 173–87).

Anna Guttman examines the networks of class hierarchies and caste divisions in 'Loving India: Same-Sex Desire, Hinduism, and the Nation-State in Abha Dawesar's *Babyji*' (*FWLS* 6:iv[2014] 692–707). The essay offers an important corrective to the usual trajectory in contemporary theory and creative writing that privileges the diaspora as the site of emancipatory narratives for South Asian queer voices. Instead, it explores the queering of the Indian nation-state itself both through localized and located reading practices and by reterritorializing South Asian queer discourse in the *Kamasutra*. *Critical Endeavour* 20[2014] gives us Premlata Rout's 'Critiquing Kamala Das's Love Poetry in the Light of Queer Theory' (*CritE* 20[2014] 314–23) and C.N. Srinath's 'Indian Erotic Poetry in English: Kamala Das and After' (*CritE* 20[2014] 387–92).

Poetry is covered well in 2014. Asha Viswas reflects on 'Landscapes of Self: Contemporary Indian Women's Poetry' (*KB* 26[2014] 121–39). Three essays on Sri Aurobindo explore his aesthetics and poetics: A.K. Jha's 'The Petrarchan Sonnet in Sri Aurobindo' (*Approaches* 1:i[2014] 16–19); Haladhar Panda's 'Sri Aurobindo's Critique of English Poetry' (*CritE* 20[2014] 347–67); and Rudrasis Dutta's 'Who Evolves? A Note on Sri Aurobindo's Sonnets on Evolution' (*CCW* 1:i[2014] 8–14). Satyasindhu Ghosh reads 'Nissim Ezekiel's Poetry: Theory and Practice' (*CritE* 20[2014] 299–313) and Sumana Ghosh offers 'Nissim Ezekiel's *Night of the Scorpion*: A Critical Analysis' (*Quest* 28:ii[2014] 91–6). Anita Myles favours 'Gynocentric Leanings in the Poetry of Jayanta Mahapatra' (*Quest* 28:i[2014] 1–9); Gagan Bihari Purohit writes on 'Jayanta Mahapatra's *Land* and the Question of Reader Response' (*CCW* 1:ii[2014] 73–85).

'Tabish Khair in Conversation' (*Wasafiri* 29:i[2014] 33–8) has Imtiaz Dharker drawing out the writer's views on small-town cosmopolitanism, Babu culture, the importance of vernacular languages, the urgency of political literature in the contemporary world, the continuation of a Victorian sensibility in his work, and Muslim societies. 'Against Stenography for the Powerful: An Interview with P Sainath' by Cynthia G. Franklin and S. Shankar (*Biography* 37:i[2014] 300–19) discusses the multiple award-winning documentary journalist's writing in *Everybody Loves a Good Drought* and other works. It addresses the nature, 'personhood', and legal liabilities of corporate entity and contemporary practices of oppression, with acute attention to words and how they get distorted by everyday usage and naturalizing media. 'Manoj Das [is] in Conversation with Bijay Kumar Das' (*LCrit* 49:iii–iv[2014]), while Ruskin Bond is interviewed by S.G. Puri and Arun Kumar Yadav (*Quest* 28:ii[2014] 33–6). Arti Nirmal proffers a reading of 'The Cinematic Translation of Ruskin Bond's *The Blue Umbrella*' (*Quest* 28:i[2014] 42–50). Rajvinder Singh is sure that 'There Is So Much More To Say about Khushwant [Singh]' (*IndLit* 280[2014] 147–51).

Auritro Majumder traces the influence of leftist and Black Power movements on vernacular Indian theatre traditions against the grain of nationalist discourses in 'The Poetics and Politics of Blackness: Literature as a Site of Transnational Contestation in Chanakya Sen's *The Morning After* and Utpal Dutt's *The Rights of Man*' (*JPW* 50:iv[2014] 423–36). Theatre receives further attention in Pravat Kumar Mishra's 'Contextualising Myths, Folklores and Legends in the Plays of Girish Karnad' (*CritE* 20[2014] 260–72) and Kamalakar Bhat's 'Locating the Postcolonial Modern in Girish Karnad's *Tughlaq*' (*LCrit* 40:ii[2014] 74–81). Jnanranjan Padhi considers 'The Ambivalence of Gender in Mahesh Dattani's *Seven Steps Around the Fire*: A Theoretical Approach' (*CritE* 20[2014] 273–80).

English Literature from the north-east is slowly garnering critical respect. The inaugural special issue on 'Terror' of *Sanglap: Journal of Literary and Critical Inquiry* features I. Watitula Longkumer's 'Reading Terror in Literature: Exploring Insurgency in Nagaland through Temsula Ao's *These Hills Called Home: Stories from a War Zone*' (*Sanglap* 1:i[2014] 115–28). Rositta Joseph Valiyamattam interrogates 'Woman as Historian: Personal and National Destinies in Temsula Ao's *These Hills Called Home*' (*Quest* 28:ii[2014] 66–76).

Shanu Shukla and Amarjeet Nayak address 'Splitting of Identity and in Time and Place: An Exploration of North-East Indian Writings through Their Use of Flashbacks and Reminiscences' (*Galaxy* 7[2014]).

The life and writings of Mohandas Karamchand Gandhi have always been studied alongside discussions of Indian English literature. In 'Speaking through Bodies, Exhibiting the Limits: British Colonialism and Gandhian Nationalism' (*FWLS* 6:iv[2014] 675–91), Chandrima Chakraborty presents a nuanced consideration of Gandhi's views on gender that were powerfully influenced and disturbed by the British narrative of India as effeminate, apathetic, and deviant. She argues that Gandhi's experiments with himself and the body disrupt hegemonic histories and present instead a novel, anti-colonial representational practice. In inventing an ascetic discipline in service of the nation, Gandhian methods contest colonialist views of Hindu religion and masculinity and, at the same time, become modes of dominating marginalized castes, classes, genders, and religions. N. Prateebha and G. Baskaran assess the 'Impact of Gandhian Philosophy on the Novels of Nayantara Sahgal' (*Quest* 28:i[2014] 88–94).

Aradhana Sharma argues for the contemporary relevance of the Mahatma in 'Epic Fasts and Shallow Spectacles: the "India against Corruption" Movement, Its Critics, and the Remaking of "Gandhi"' (*SA* 37:iii[2014] 365–80). Siobhan Lambert-Hurley takes up the little-known work of a Muslim disciple of Gandhi in '*The Heart of a Gopi*: Raihana Tyabji's Bhakti Devotionalism as Self-Representation' (*MAS* 48:iii[2014] 569–95), and Shvetal Vyas Pare focuses on the entanglement between personal and political identity in 'Writing Fiction, Living History: Kanhaiyalal Munshi's Historical Trilogy' (*MAS* 48:iii[2014] 596–616), Munshi being a close associate of Gandhi and pre-eminent Gujarati freedom-fighter. J. Daniel Frame scrutinizes the work of the Gadr Party, whose members were dissatisfied with nonviolence and posed a serious threat to the Mahatma's popularity, in 'Echoes of Ghadr: Lala Har Dayal and the Time of Anticolonialism' (*CSSAM* 34:i[2014] 9–23).

Saswat S. Das, Anindya Sekhar Purakayastha, and Sandeep Sarkar attempt a deconstructive intervention in the foundational texts of Indian nationalists like Tagore, Gandhi, Vivekananda, and Nehru in 'Defamiliarising Nationalist Discourses: Performative Ironies of the Normative Indian Episteme' (*Asiatic* 8:ii[2014] 176–94). They argue that these thinkers offered only mythic abstractions and religious normativities, thereby fostering a collective cultural amnesia that saw the birth of a nation both as an intangible site and ominous threat. The writers instead offer Homi Bhabha's conceptualization of Dissemin/Nation as a corrective. Dipesh Chakrabarty provides the historical backdrop to 'Friendship in the Shadow of Empire: Tagore's Reception in Chicago, circa 1913–1932' (*MAS* 48:v[2014] 1161–87) and shows how the theme of 'civilization' influenced the poet's overseas reception.

6. New Zealand and Pacific

This year saw something of a bumper harvest for New Zealand and Pacific English studies, with several important articles treating little-discussed topics or pushing existing work in new directions. Like the El Niño weather patterns the region's farmers work around, these critical gusts of heat seem unpredictable and inexplicable. One attractive crop is Murray Edmond's *Then It Was Now Again*, a selection of forty years' worth of literary critical writing usefully contextualized by the author and Scott Hamilton. Edmond positions himself as part of the 'other tradition' (p. 91) in New Zealand writing, and his interests—in literature and committed politics, and in drama especially—give this collection a set of bearings and a critical assumption quite different, in its partisan, sometimes polemical outlook, to most accounts of postwar writing. All the pieces in *Then It Was Now Again* have previously been published elsewhere, but many were in hard-to-locate small journals and avant-garde periodicals; Atuanui Press is to be congratulated on bringing them accessibly together.

Although it may look more conventional in approach, Helen Lucy Blythe's *The Victorian Colonial Romance with the Antipodes* is, in its way, as unusually ordered and combatively framed as Edmond's collection. Blythe begins with an epigraph from Darwin—'these Antipodes call to one's mind old recollections of childish doubt and wonder' (p. 1)—and proceeds to offer a dialectical account of the doubt and wonder evoked in and produced by European readings of antipodean New Zealand. Victorian colonial imagination takes place, Blythe suggests, in a topsy-turvy world 'characterized by inversion, fancy, impossibility and asymmetry', offering 'a distinctive narrative path for writers, providing a symbolic architecture for investigating the tensions between proximity and distance' (p. 4). Her own study proceeds using similarly imaginative inversions, clashing together biographical studies with close reading, historical contextualization with genre theory, especially by way of conversation with Northrop Frye, and giving subtle attention to the ways in which colonial narratives 'highlighted and destabilized generic as well as social categories' (p. 5). There are thoughtful chapters on Tom Arnold and Mary Taylor. Most refreshing, however, are Blythe's chapters on Alfred Domett's strange epic *Ranolf and Amohia*, its 'lethal Antipodes' read as 'gothic landscape signifying the horror of immanent violence and death in a displacement of the hostilities' of historical struggle with Māori (p. 99), and on Samuel Butler, whose *The Way of All Flesh*, on this reading, develops out of and is facilitated by 'Butler's experiences among settlers and Māori' as they 'highlighted the resemblance of colonial to familial machinations of power' (p. 123). Blythe's intellectually curious and agile book has many virtues; its vice is a tendency to ladle the sauce of 'Theory' so thickly it loses analytical bite. There are also too many simple errors and repetitions, and these ought to have been picked up by Palgrave's copy-editors.

Valérie Baisnée's *'Through the Long Corridor of Distance': Space and Self in Contemporary New Zealand's Women's Autobiographies* offers interesting local readings of Sylvia Ashton-Warner, Barbara Anderson, Fiona Kidman, Lauris Edmond, and Janet Frame. Baisnée's readings are attentive, but readers will need to persevere through quite a bit of theoretical language. The study, Baisnée tells us, 'has sought to skirt the pitfalls of exalting or humiliating the self, or treating it solely as a performance in the narrative' while outlining 'some ethical implications of the hermeneutics of the autobiographical self'

(p. 129). More concrete work is, thankfully, carried out along the way. Elizabeth Hale's collection *Maurice Gee, a Literary Companion: The Fiction for Young Readers*, the first of a projected two-part literary companion, sets out to redress the relative paucity of critical commentary around Gee's substantial body of creative work. Hale's contributors set out to 'show the range and depth of Gee's works for young readers' (p. 22) and, if the collection is never quite sure of its status as a survey, an entrée, or a critical companion, its results are nevertheless engaging. Chapters from Claudia Marquis on the early fantasy novels (pp. 25–54), Diane Hebley on the historical quintet (pp. 55–82) and Elizabeth Hale on *Salt, Gool*, and *The Limping Man* chart Gee's career; other chapters offer more analytical treatment, with Kathryn Walls studying the influence of Lyndhal Gee's writings on her son's novels (pp. 101–21), Louise Clark on his use of the fantasy form (pp. 123–46), and Vivien van Rij (pp. 147–61) on Gee's use of character types. Children's literature is now an established and respectable topic for literary study, and this *Literary Companion* offers resources for further scholarship.

Two contemporary authors, Fiona Kidman and Witi Ihimaera, are discussed in Hamish Dalley's *The Postcolonial Historical Novel: Realism, Allegory, and the Representation of Contested Pasts*, a study suggesting, across chapters covering novels produced in Australia, New Zealand, and Nigeria, that a 'realist imperative shapes the contemporary postcolonial historical novel' (p. 103). Dalley's chapter on Kidman's *The Captive Wife* [2005] (pp. 70–94) and its multiperspectival exploration of the 'limitations of historical knowledge' (p. 70) and the memory of settlement is a competent treatment of an under-discussed text. His argument is twofold. *The Captive Wife*'s 'formal heterogeneity and exploration of events from multiple, sometimes contradictory perspectives' (p. 73) is, Dalley suggests, both a way of engaging 'with public debates about colonial history' by 'foregrounding the putative typicality or representativeness of the documented figures themselves' (p. 70), and thus also an implied commentary on the normative Lukácsian model of realism, and a form of 'allegory in which sex and settlement form two halves of a metaphorical comparison' (p. 71). This formal argument is then linked to a contextual, if sometimes too summary, account of mid-decade controversies over official biculturalism that ran in parallel to the novel's moment of publication. Arguing along similar lines, Doreen D'Cruz's 'Gendering the Colonial Narrative: Fictional Historiography in Fiona Kidman's *The Captive Wife*' (*JPW* 50:iii[2014] 341–53) stresses also the 'reclaimed female historiography' (p. 352) made possible by Kidman's narrative technique. Less successful, and more awkwardly uncertain of its claims, is Dalley's chapter on Ihimaera's *The Trowenna Sea* [2009] (pp. 97–120). Ihimaera's novel has, Dalley claims, 'a vastly expanded spatio-historical frame' (p. 96) compared to Kidman's, and he reads it as a departure, in Ihimaera's oeuvre and in postcolonial literature more generally, opening 'the representation of history to principles not predicated on unity, progressive temporality, or the establishment of continuity between people and places' (p. 99). This argument is detailed, and with a roll-call of familiar critics and theorists produced as sympathetic witnesses; the novel itself, however, is all but kept from the witness box. This may be—although Dalley is too tactful to address the point directly—to do with problems of literary evaluation. A host of carefully indirect and agentless formulations ('disquiet emerged in a magazine review by Jolisa Gracewood', p. 102) half-acknowledge the 'alleged violation' (p. 102) in the text's plagiarisms, but Dalley manages to discuss this text without considering whether it is good enough to support his argument. The chapter shows signs of insufficient editing between composition and publication, too; *The Trowenna Sea* is Ihimaera's 'latest novel' (p. 98) but then a 'subsequent publication' (p. 103) appears. For a book about the historical novel, there's a curious indifference to critical history in Dalley's account, and he makes little of Ihimaera's thirty-year publishing history before *The Trowenna Sea*, and much less again of the rich, contentious archive of postcolonial debates on realism stretching back across the postwar period.

The outstanding publication for 2014 must be, however, Diana Looser's triumphant *Remaking Pacific Pasts: History, Memory and Identity in Contemporary Theater from Oceania*. Bristling with critical insights, sensitive to local material and particular texts, as well as synoptic and synthesizing in its range, Looser's study is multilingual, multi-disciplinary, and hugely ambitious. The number of playtexts and performances *Remaking Pacific Pasts* considers is impressive, reaching from New Zealand to Fiji, Hawai'i to New Caledonia. Looser has read carefully and discerningly across several complex and nationally specific theatre contexts. Her writing is learned, lively, and accessible, and there is a generous provision of illustrations, and a very helpful index of Pacific plays, their year of first performance, and publication date, making this a volume well suited for the advanced undergraduate as much as the scholar and researcher.

Part of the frustration when encountering a work as assured and exacting as *Remaking Pacific Pasts* is to do with the paucity of the critical archive surrounding these texts. Who to argue alongside? Critical controversy and conversation need a body of work for scholars to negotiate their way amongst, and chapters in Birgit Däwes and Marc Beaufort's collection *Enacting Nature: Ecocritical Perspectives on Indigenous Performance* add nutritious topsoil to the scholarly fields. The term ecocritical is, in this collection, as vague and free-floatingly pious as it is elsewhere; the collection's value, however, is in the specific readings and performance contextualizations generated. Hilary Halba's 'Cleansing the Tapu: Nature, Landscape and Transformation in Three Works by Māori Playwrights' (pp. 219–34) surveys political-ecological responses in texts by Witi Ihimaera and Briar Grace-Smith, and posits nature as in a 'sibling' (p. 231) relationship to humanity, rather than as a more traditionally romantic metaphor for the human condition, in the world-view of these two authors. Halba's local readings are careful, but her wider frame— contrasting monolithic Māori and Pākehā world-views as expressive totalities realized in these individual playtexts—can be constricting. Lisa Warrington and David O'Donnell's 'Unfolding the Cloth: Patterns of Landscape and Identity in The Conch's *Masi*' (pp. 199–218), after the inevitable, and tiresome, detour through Homi Bhabha's work, provides a fascinating account of the 'new theatrical language' (p. 200) pioneered by The Conch. Their perform-ances and compositions use cloth, stance, natural materials, translation, and sound to create theatrical works in which the playscript is decentred and ends up one element among many. How, then, ought criticism to conduct itself? The

Conch's work is imaginatively border-crossing in ways literal and figurative, too; a Fijian story in their *Vula* [2002] ended up with Samoan-language elements in performance due to the exigencies of casting and actors' availability, and then this in turn becomes an important element of the work. Warrington and O'Donnell make creative use of Albert Wendt's celebrated discussion of the *'va*, that space between things and concepts so important in Samoan intellectual life, and draw on interviews they conducted with collaborators and performers. Although on francophone Pacific literature and thus not within the realms of English studies, another notable chapter is Diana Looser's 'Je te parle d'harmonie entre les plantes: Ecologies of New Caledonian Nationhood in Pierre Gope's *La Parenthèse*' (pp. 186–98). Using similar comparative theatre studies to Looser, Melissa Kennedy's 'Early Ainu and Māori Postcolonial Theatre: *Postman Heijiro* and *Te Raukura*' (*JPW* 50:iii[2014] 329–40) reads the first Ainu play, performed in 2005, against Harry Dansey's *Te Raukura*, first performed in 1972, in order to find 'thematic and staging similarities between the plays' and 'common motivations, techniques and difficulties for indigenous cultures that wish to iterate resistance' (p. 331). Kennedy concludes her essay with suggestions for further research in Ainu theatre based on the Māori experience: the forty years since Dansey's first production have generated a rich body of work with which to compare and contextualize, whereas *Postman Heijiro* lacks 'a body of Ainu work with which to compare' it (p. 337). Kennedy's essay demonstrates some of the exciting directions this new generation of trans- or internationalizing postcolonial criticism can point towards.

Less successful are two essays on sexuality in contemporary Māori writing. Jana Fedtke's ' "What to Call That Sport, the Neuter Human . . .": Asexual Subjectivity in Keri Hulme's *The Bone People*' (in Cerankowski and Milks, eds., *Asexualities: Feminist and Queer Perspectives*, pp. 329–43) treats Hulme's novel as a 'safe space for asexual identities' (p. 330) rather than as a literary work. Kerewin, Hulme's protagonist, seems, Fedtke worries, 'lonely and does not have anybody around her who feels the way she does or who understands her attitude towards sexuality' (p. 333). She is also, most damagingly of all for her viability as a thinker, a paper being, although Fedtke nowhere acknowledge or considers this. Yanwei Tan in turn scolds Michael, protagonist of Witi Ihimaera's *The Uncle's Story* [2000] for his lack of 'willingness to embrace mutually respectful recognition on an interpersonal basis' (p. 367). Tan's 'Recognition, Political and Interpersonal: Gay Tribalism in Witi Ihimaera's *The Uncle's Tale*' (*MFS* 60:ii[2014] 366–86) is disappointed in poor Michael, with his 'lack of spontaneity in his interpersonal relations and intersubjective exchange' (p. 383), and more disappointed still in his naughty author, Ihimaera, who has 'not come up with an adequate answer to the vexed question of interpersonal relations, both intraracial and interracial' (p. 383). The anti-literary and reductionist drift in criticism is dispiriting.

The situation is not hopeless, however, and three other texts, with their focus on teaching and textuality, show what can be done when Māori writing is approached as a sophisticated and rewarding body of literary work. Julia V. Emberley, in her *The Testimonial Uncanny: Indigenous Storytelling, Knowledge, and Reparative Practices* (pp. 254–88), reads Patricia Grace's

Potiki and *Baby No-Eyes* as examples of the 'indigenous uncanny', a form she sees working in 'a struggle against immobility, stagnation and conservatism' (p. 254). 'Storytelling represents a formation for the transmission of knowledge' (p. 254), Emberley argues, and her political appreciation for Grace's 'Indigenous ethics' (p. 282) is linked throughout the chapter to detailed, attentive readings of her narratives as narratives. Taking up these connections between literary form and ethical and political questions, Matthew Packer's '*E Tu*: On Teaching Patricia Grace's Novel of the Māori Battalion' (*Antipodes* 28:i[2014] 62–73) and Emily R. Johnston's 'Trauma Theory as Activist Pedagogy: Engaging Students as Reader-Witnesses of Colonial Trauma in *Once Were Warriors*' (*Antipodes* 28:i[2014] 5–17) both pleasingly blend practical classroom questions with literary analysis and postcolonial theory. Jane Stafford's ' "This Poem is a Sea Anchor": Robert Sullivan's Anchor' (in vanden Driesen and Ashcroft, eds., *Patrick White Centenary Essays*, pp. 458–69) adds to a growing body of scholarship around Sullivan's important *Star Waka* [1999] sequence, following the lines of his collection as they link together European inheritances reworked for indigenous ends. *Star Waka* is, Stafford contends, one of 'the most significant works of the second generation of Māori Renaissance writers' (p. 460).

As Looser's *Remaking Pacific Pasts* is for criticism, the landmark publication for 2014 in editorial scholarly work must surely be Gerri Kimber and Angela Smith's third volume of the Edinburgh edition of Katherine Mansfield's collected works, *The Poetry and Critical Writings of Katherine Mansfield*. This volume, prepared with the editorial assistance of Anna Plumridge, is bound, along with the Edinburgh edition as a whole, to redefine our sense of Mansfield's achievement and significance in the same way the O'Sullivan and Scott edition of the *Letters* [1984–2008] made new biographical readings thinkable. Kimber and Smith have brought together every piece of non-fiction Mansfield wrote, and include scores of recently discovered items, including poetry, aphorisms, impressions, and translations. Editorial diligence and archival sleuthing bring their rewards here, in a handsome edition both useful and user-friendly as a scholarly resource and pleasing to the eye of the general reader. Claire Davison's substantial introduction to the translations (pp. 141–51) is particularly illuminating, and the opportunity to trace images and motifs across Mansfield's career made all the easier by the bulk of poetry brought together into one volume. With 179 poems, this book contains more than twice the number collected in the last edition [1988] of Mansfield's poetry.

Maurizio Ascari's lively little *Cinema and the Imagination in Katherine Mansfield's Writing*, one of Palgrave's new Pivot series of mini-monographs, usefully supplements the existing literature on Mansfield and cinema by 'using silent cinema as a critical lens' (p. 5) and by paying particular attention to the ways in which Mansfield was 'daring enough to grasp the liberating potential of the narrative syntax of film' (p. 28). Ascari pursues this through both close readings of Mansfield stories in which cinema or cinematic techniques are thematized and accounts of her diary and journalistic entries on cinema, as well as by tracing the development of her circle's approach to cinema from the initially dismissive stance of *Rhythm* and *The Blue Review* through to acceptance and enthusiasm and then into suspicions of mass culture in the age of Chaplin. Ascari's account, delivered across five short and accessible chapters, is, if a little slight, revealing.

'There has been', Alice Kelly suggests in her introduction to this year's edition of *Katherine Mansfield Studies*, edited by Gerri Kimber, Todd Martin, Delia da Sousa Correa, Isobel Martin, and Alice Kelly as *Katherine Mansfield and World War One*, 'a surprising reluctance to view Mansfield as a war writer' (p. 4). Mansfield, after all, lost a close family member and several friends in the war, and saw more of the disruption in France than many of her female contemporaries. The reason for this reluctance, Kelly suggests, may be as much to do with the marginal position of Mansfield's favoured form, the short story, and the novel's associated connection with larger social questions, as with any biographical considerations. The essays collected in the yearbook seek to redress this imbalance, with stimulating results. Josiane Paccaud-Huguet's 'By What Name Are We To Call Death? The Case of "An Indiscreet Journey"' (pp. 13–25) subjects this well-known story to a psychoanalytic reading, treating together the evocations of Eros and Thanatos in its account of a woman's visit to her lover at the front. Paccaud-Huguet wears her Lacanianism lightly, and the result is a sprightly, intellectually stimulating new reading. J. Lawrence Mitchell's informal, almost chatty 'Katherine Mansfield's War' (pp. 27–41) gathers together biographical details in order to challenge the view that Mansfield 'did her best to ignore the 1914–1918 war' (p. 27); in the process, he demonstrates that there are yet further depths into which John Middleton Murry's reputation for 'shameful cravenness' (p. 29) might still plunge. Blending biographical material with close readings of Mansfield's 'Pension Sketches', Isobel Maddison's 'Mansfield's "Writing Game" and World War One' (pp. 42–54) demonstrates how these stories both participated in and, at times, qualified and corrected 'the discourse of anti-invasion' literature (p. 50) popular in the years before the war. Maddison's comparisons of stories as they first appeared in the *New Age* with their later book form is especially intriguing; seemingly minor alterations, made to give the collection coherence, are shown, in her hands, as subtly shifting and making more complex the stories' political positions. Helen Rydstrand's 'Ordinary Discordance: Katherine Mansfield and the First World War' (pp. 55–68) employs a similarly successful combination of biographical and textual approaches, taking the critical commonplace that modernism's 'intensification and illumination of the everyday' was prompted by 'the cataclysm of the war' (p. 55) and looking for examples of this 'radical discontinuity' (p. 55) in Mansfield's immediate responses to the conflict. Alex Moffett, 'Katherine Mansfield's Home Front: Submerging the Martial Metaphors of "The Aloe"' (pp. 69–83), deploys genetic criticism to uncover some of the traces of the war submerged in 'The Aloe', traces written out in subsequent drafts. 'The war moves', Moffett suggests, 'from a metaphorical yet tangible presence in the text, to a seeming and signifying absence' (p. 70). Richard Cappuccio's reading of 'The Aloe', by contrast, looks for martial metaphors and war terms in Kezia's attempts to cope with the disruptive army of Samuel Josephs crowding her out ('War Thoughts and Home: Katherine Mansfield's Model of a Hardened Heart in a Broken World', pp. 84–97). Rounding off the collection,

Erika Baldt's 'Mythology and/of the Great War in Katherine Mansfield's "The Daughters of the Late Colonel"' (pp. 98–112) takes a scene of fly-torturing capriciousness as an intertextual borrowing from *Titus Andronicus*, and proceeds to read Mansfield's story for the way its classical and mythological references both separate and connect readers' historical sense with their understanding of the war's significance. The yearbook taken as a whole is a welcome and fresh account of a curiously under-familiar aspect of this much-read writer.

'Katherine Mansfield Masked and Unmasked', this year's special issue of the *JNZL*, edited by Charles Ferrall, Anna Jackson, Harry Ricketts, Marco Sonzogni and Peter Whiteford, opens with a response to Mansfield's fiction and its 'silent dialogue between author and reader' (p. 26) from the acclaimed novelist Emily Perkins. Other articles, all drawn from a 2013 conference on Mansfield held at Victoria University, include Aimee Gasston's witty 'Phenomenology Begins at Home' (*JNZL* 32:ii[2014] 31–51), a rumination on the 'material focus' of Mansfield's short fiction: 'sitting at the border between subject and object, the hand undergoes sensory experience before transcribing that experience from a liminal hinterland' (p. 31). Gasston is astute and adventurous in her account of the 'material sensibility' (p. 32) enlivening Mansfield's stories, sensitive as they are to the ways in which the associations of the domestic environment can work up 'the vivification of the insensate' (p. 37). Another highlight is Sarah Shieff's 'Katherine Mansfield's Fairytale Food' (*JNZL* 32:ii[2014] 68–84), a reading, by way of a stray comment by Frank Sargeson on the 'fairy tale passages' (p. 68) in Mansfield, of the strange, uncanny, and excessive qualities food is given in Mansfield's stories. Not all the essays collected are of this quality, although there are useful pieces on the process of rewriting: Davide Manenti, 'From the Store to the Story: Katherine Mansfield and the Process of Rewriting' (*JNZL* 32:ii[2014] 167–81), on the poetry of *Rhythm*; Richard Cappuccio, 'Katherine Mansfield's Russian Mask' (*JNZL* 32:ii[2014] 182–202); and on abjection, neurasthenia, and children. Erin Mercer's 'Manuka Bushes Covered with Thick Spider Webs: Katherine Mansfield and the Colonial Gothic Tradition' (*JNZL* 32:ii[2014] 85–105) continues Gothic literary studies' long colonizing march through the discipline, drawing together examples of something called 'the Gothic mode' (p. 107) to be found in Mansfield's work. Charles Ferrall's 'Katherine Mansfield and the Working Classes' (*JNZL* 32:ii[2014] 106–20) offers a very useful first survey of class positions and attitudes towards labour in Mansfield's fiction, only to undercut somewhat this work by leaving his central term—and its ambiguous plural form in his title—under-theorized and under-defined.

Colonial literature continues to provoke some of the most stimulating criticism. Clara Cheeseman's massive *A Rolling Stone* [1886], if discussed at all, is usually dismissed by critics as pointless melodrama, but Philip Steer's ingenious 'Antipodal Home Economics: International Debt and Settler Domesticity in Clara Cheeseman's *A Rolling Stone*' (in Wagner, ed., *Domestic Fiction in Colonial Australia and New Zealand*, pp. 145–59) suggests the enormous condescension of posterity may be misplaced. Arguing for an expansion of critical horizons beyond narrowly national boundaries, Steer argues that 'contextualising domestic settler fiction in light of shifting colonial and imperial economic conditions allows such texts...to be recognized as having much broader thematic and geographic horizons than has hitherto been assumed' (p. 145). Taking Edward Gibbon Wakefield's economic theories and settler plans as the novel's polemical silent partner, Steer follows the plots of 'economic downturn' (p. 152) through the novel to consider Cheeseman's achievement as a comment on mid-Victorian debates around investment, debt, and settlement. He extends this argument to the novel's bulky form itself, concluding that its formal qualities 'can be seen as final contributions to the novel's reflections on the colony's viability' (p. 158) as a form of dignifying aesthetic labour in 'solidity and length promising a profitable return on the reader's investment' (p. 159). Steer's is a rich and pleasing chapter on a little-read text. Also in *Domestic Fiction in Colonial Australia and New Zealand* (pp. 161–76), Kirstine Moffat's '"What Is in the Blood Will Come Out": Belonging, Expulsion and the New Zealand Settler Home in Jessie Weston's *Ko Méri*' connects ideological fantasies of Māori as a dying race with fictional 'expulsions' (p. 163) from the family home.

Lydia Wevers's important *Reading on the Farm* [2010] initiated a turn to book history and a concentration on material cultures in New Zealand literary studies. This continues unabated in 2014, with fine essays by Peter Simpson on 'The Odd Couple: Denis Glover, Leo Bensemann and the Caxton Press' (*JNZL* 32[2014] 31–68), and Kirstine Moffat on Alfred Nesbit Brown's book collection, '"A Habit of Walking with God": The Books of Alfred Nesbit Brown' (*JNZS* 17[2014] 73–92). Dougal McNeill's 'Reading Nowhere in Erewhon: Bellamy, Morris, and New Zealand' (*Kotare* [2014] 1–13) attempts similar work.

Articles of note on modern and contemporary authors covered a wider range of topics than in previous years. Daniel McKay's 'The Japanese Tourist Survival Guide: Undead Tropes of the Pacific War in Contemporary New Zealand Literature' (*JCL* 49:i[2014] 127–41) contains interesting discussions but, bafflingly, makes no mention of Carl Shuker's *The Method Actors* [2005], surely the signal example of its thesis. Marc Delrez's lively 'Fossil Capacities in the Work of Janet Frame' (*JNZPS* 2:i[2014] 69–81) riffs off suggestive lines from Wilson Harris in order to follow some of the 'lampooning of New Zealand parochialism and anti-intellectualism' (p. 74) at work in Frame's posthumously published *Towards Another Summer* [2007]. Delrez's Frame is a funnier and looser writer than criticism is used to presenting, alive to the clichés of national identity and making, in Delrez's case, space for 'decentrings' of the 'discourse of national identity' (p. 70). His is a stimulating, original, and thoughtful account. Cyrena Mazlin carries out a similar political or materialist turn, long overdue in Frame studies, in her 'Returned Soldiers in *Owls Do* Cry, *A State of Siege*, and *The Carpathians*: Janet Frame's Subversive Representations' (*Antipodes* 28:ii[2014] 327–38). Mazlin notes the presence of returned soldiers and victims of war in all of Frame's longer works, and considers what they might say about postwar masculine cultures. The 'border between the brave and noble soldier celebrated in public memory and the conflicted and haunted solider, represented as a harbinger of dis-ease in a domestic setting' is, Mazlin suggests, 'permeable' (p. 337), and Frame is the master-explorer of permeable boundaries.

I have had reason to complain in previous years that New Zealand literary studies can seem dominated by Frame and Mansfield. In a welcome shift, 2014 saw a cluster of worthwhile publications on contemporary poetry and poetics. Nicholas Wright's 'The Disenchanted Romanticism of James Brown' (*JNZL* 32[2014] 119–40) offers a first scholarly assessment of this writer, and places him as both an exemplary member of a generation of poets engaged in 'wary avoidance of... the tricky business of authority' in their writing of 'the poetry of not-writing-poetry' (pp. 130–1), and as an original explorer of the 'romantic sense of disenchantment' (p. 127). This sense, Wright suggests, has, in its mixture of laconic recognition that poetry 'makes nothing happen' and continuing commitment to produce, linked Brown both to long-standing trends in New Zealand verse and to international contemporary critical thought. Another writer only now finding critical attention is the late Leigh Davis, and Roger Horrocks's 'Leigh Davis: From *Willy's Gazette* to *Nameless*' (*JNZL* 32[2014] 69–106), a moving combination of biographical account from a friend and insightful critical acclamation of his work, is an excellent introduction to this complex poet's writings. Davis has been neglected, Horrocks suggests, because of local literary prejudice against his career in finance and critical hostility towards his anti-realist and openly intellectual poetics. But, after all, Eliot and Stevens were businessmen-poets, and there is something salutary in the challenge for writers to be 'worthy of their modernist ancestors' (p. 99). A loving and astute survey of this inheritor of the 'modern Symbolist tradition' (p. 99), Horrocks's essay ought to send readers to Davis's innovative collections. It's a particular pleasure to note a fine essay on Allen Curnow, a major poet still too little discussed in all his complexity. Tam Vosper, 'Reconnecting with Nature and Place: Place and Self-Construal in the Poetry of Allen Curnow' (*JNZL* 32[2014] 141–60), reads three canonical poems in order to consider the 'interdependent dynamic of place and self-construal' (p. 146) in Curnow's work. This 'conscious place-making' (p. 142) is not, thankfully, to do with yet another rehearsal of the old arguments about national identity and cultural nationalism but is, rather, a way of reading 'Steely, cold, apocalyptic, impersonal Curnow' (p. 157) as a poet of the 'local' and 'wild' (p. 144), newly approachable now in the light of ecocritical insights. Pairing extended close reading with environmental reflection, Vosper reminds us that ecocriticism need not be all vagueness and platitudes. Mark Williams's 'When You're Dead You Go on Television: Sex, Death and Household Objects in Some Recent New Zealand Poetry' (*Sport* 42[2014] 149–73) is in part an extended reading and appreciation of Bill Manhire's verse, and in part a consideration of the ways 'in our own post-religious culture the words of the older one in which religious ideas were widely shared still speaks to us, even if we have lost faith in or forgotten the meanings they once signified' (p. 163). Williams detects a 'new richness in the language of our poetry, even where it embraces a severe plainness of expression' (p. 167), and he makes generous use of extended quotation to demonstrate this richness and growth.

Finally, confusion, as much as clarity, has its scholarly uses, and Vincent O'Sullivan brings all his remarkable erudition to play in 'On the Beach at Stresa, in "The Whitesheaf" in Soho' (*JNZL* 32[2014] 11–30) to muddy and mess around some too-simple critical divisions and histories. Tracking Dan

Davin and Frank Sargeson's relationship and literary evaluations of each other and themselves, O'Sullivan then ponders each writer's response to Mansfield and Mulgan. If this 'had muddied the waters a little as we think about our writing forebears, then good. We are not part of a straightforward, consistent stream, although one might think at times that critical discourse would rather like us to be' (p. 27). O'Sullivan's own meandering journey through tributary and shoal, drawing on unpublished as well as published letters and talks, sends off its own insights for that very critical discourse he is at pains, a trifle disingenuously, to keep at a distance. The results are a pleasure to read and a spur to further critical thought.

7. Southeast Asia

(a) The Philippines

Scholarship about literature in English from the Philippines published in 2014 can be broadly divided into two strands: the first focuses on the effects of Spanish and American colonialism on national identity and the politics of language and literature, while the second examines specific writers, literary texts, and critical concepts in the context of transnational movements and globalizing currents, especially with regard to the Philippines' relationship with the United States.

Eugenio Matibag's book chapter 'Long-Distance Nationalism: The Filipino Ilustrados Abroad' (in Menon and Preziuso, eds., *Migrant Identities of 'Creole Cosmopolitans': Transcultural Narratives of Contemporary Postcoloniality*, pp. 95–106) examines the influence of nineteenth-century *ilustrados* (young male Filipinos studying in France and Spain) on the work of contemporary writers. Matibag interweaves an analysis of Miguel Syjuco's novel *Ilustrado* with a detailed discussion of the life and work of historical *ilustrados* such as José Rizal to show how Syjuco, as 'a modern-day ilustrado', is writing a new form of 'world literature with a decidedly Filipino imprimatur' (p. 105). José Rizal is also an important part of Maria Theresa Valenzuela's essay 'Constructing National Heroes: Postcolonial Philippine and Cuban Biographies of José Rizal and José Marti' (*Biography* 37:iii[2014] 745–61). Valenzuela uses 'a metacritical analysis' to discuss how Rizal's anti-colonial martyrdom was re-created and retold by different biographers and fiction writers for their 'particular nationalizing projects' (p. 746).

Moving from Spanish to American colonialism, in 'Colonial Management, Collaborative Dissent: English Readers in the Philippines and Camilo Osias, 1905–1932' (*JAAS* 17:ii[2014] 161–98), Malini Johar Schueller discusses the pivotal role played by English-language textbooks designed by American publishers in educating Filipino students to be good colonial subjects. Schueller focuses on Camilo Osias, the first Filipino superintendent of schools in the islands, and the series of readers he edited and published. Osias's textbooks, although written within the framework of American colonial hegemony, nonetheless contained visual and textual elements that subvert American authority and gesture towards Filipino independence. The effect of

English-language education on the Philippines and the varied responses by two different Filipino intellectuals during the 1960s are further examined by Vicente Rafael in his 'Mis-education, Translation and the Barkada of Languages: Reading Renato Constantino with Nick Joaquin' (*KK* 21/22[2013–2014] 40–68). Rafael points out that Constantino condemned English as a sign of American colonialism producing historical and cultural amnesia. Nick Joaquin, on the other hand, departs from a zero-sum view of language use and argues that Tagalog slang hybridizes the colonial linguistic legacies of Spanish and English into a vital and creative vernacular. The context of US colonialism is also key to Jonathan Chua's 'The Making of Jose Garcia Villa's *Footnote to Youth*' (*KK* 21/22[2013–2014] 9–39). Villa's only short-story collection faced a troubled publication process due to American perceptions of exoticism and otherness. Ironically, Chua observes, getting published by an American press actually consolidated Villa's position in the Philippines as an important man of letters, and his name was 'appropriated for extra-literary and arguably anti-colonial ends' (p. 30).

J. Neil C. Garcia's 'Translation and the Problem of Realism in Philippine Literature in English' (*KK* 23[2014] 99–127) warns against applying the conceptual binaries of realism/modernism and mimetic/non-mimetic representation to anglophone writing from the Philippines. Garcia sees realism as a fraught term because writers must translate different local languages and linguistic registers into English, thus the texts lack a degree of verisimilitude to begin with. He argues instead that the very translatedness of such writing in a language that bears the traces of American imperialism should compel critics to 'specify the postcolonial difference of the different aesthetic claims, posturings, and gestures of Filipino writers' (p. 121).

Garcia also published a book of essays, *Homeless in Unhomeliness: Postcolonial Critiques of Philippine Literature*, which contains a slightly different version of the piece discussed above. The essays in this collection dwell on the paradox signalled by the title, which refers to one of the key psychoanalytical concepts used in postcolonial theory: unhomeliness. Garcia examines topics such as transnational poetry/poetics, LGBT discourse, camp performativity, and city spaces from a perspective that engages with postcolonial theory but also with an eye on how the particular circumstances of the Philippines resist and reconfigure such theory. In Garcia's words, while it is possible to 'celebrate the instances of transcultural agency' and 'postcolonial performances' in Philippine letters, it is important to remember 'the historical determinations within which this agency precariously exists' (p. xviii). Garcia's collection shows that an attention to local or regional specificities can be in dialogue with and transform theoretical axioms.

The second strand of essays, which focuses on specific writers or concepts within a broadly transnational framework, is exemplified by Louie Jon A. Sanchez's 'Archipeligiality as a Southeast Asian Poetic in Cirilo F. Bautista's Sunlight on Broken Stones' (*Suvannabhumi* 6:i[2014] 193–221). Sanchez performs detailed close readings of Bautista's epic poem, *The Trilogy of Saint Lazarus*. Although the poems are focused on the history and sociopolitical situation of the Philippines, Sanchez argues for a broader, transnational relevance of what he calls Bautista's 'archipeligiality' (the creative positioning and writing of histories and memories through geographical places and metaphorical spaces) to other Southeast Asian literary cultures.

Myra Mendible highlights the work of Ninotchka Rosca in 'Literature as Activism: Ninotchka Rosca's Political Aesthetic' (*JPW* 50:iii[2014] 354–67). Emigrating to the USA in 1977 after being detained by Ferdinand Marcos's authoritarian regime, Rosca continues to write fiction about and advocate for social justice and political freedom in her home country. In Mendible's analysis, Rosca 'often assumes the ideological role of the historian' even as a writer, 'imagining and recording her nation's past in an effort to interpret its present conditions' (p. 357).

A special issue of *Kritika Kultura* on Carlos Bulosan brings together the anti-colonial and transnational strands of criticism. Although Bulosan moved to the United States in 1930 and never returned to the Philippines, his influence is still deeply felt in Filipino letters and contributes to anti-colonial and anti-imperial criticism and a growing conjunction between Asian and Asian American studies. E. San Juan's polemical piece, 'Excavating the Bulosan Ruins: What Is at Stake in Re-discovering the Anti-Imperialist Writer in the Age of US Global Terrorism?' (*KK* 23[2014] 154–67), argues against seeing Bulosan as an immigrant who assimilated into American society because he was a colonial subject and not just a migrant worker. San Juan thus highlights the anti-colonial aspects of Bulosan's life. Tim Libretti makes almost the same point in 'Beyond the Innocence of Globalization: The Abiding Necessity of Carlos Bulosan's Anti-Imperialist Imagination' (*KK* 23[2014] 236–54), but focuses more on Bulosan's use of literary aesthetics in his prose to challenge and interrogate imperialist ideology. Marilyn C. Alquizola and Lane Ryo Hirabayashi discuss newly discovered archival correspondence in 'Carlos Bulosan on Writing: The Role of Letters' (*KK* 23[2014] 168–88). They suggest that the set of letters sent and received in 1955 between Bulosan and his colleague Florentino B. Valeros (who was in the Philippines) shows that, even just before his death, Bulosan was unwavering in his political commitments. Monica Feria traces the connections between Bulosan and her mother in her essay 'Writers and Exile: Carlos Bulosan and Dolores Stephens Feria' (*KK* 23[2014] 189–209) and argues that even though Dolores, or Dee, was a white American woman who migrated to the Philippines, she encountered a similar experience of exile as Bulosan did after he moved to the United States. Exile, Feria suggests, becomes a defining characteristic of literature from the Philippines, even by writers who have not physically left the islands, because of decades of socio-political unrest and authoritarian government. Turning from Bulosan himself to the reception of his most famous work, *America Is in the Heart*, John Streamas shares his insights teaching this genre-blurring text to American undergraduates. In 'Organic and Multicultural Ways of Reading Bulosan' (*KK* 23[2014] 210–20) Streamas points out that first-year students who are not hampered by the need to fit Bulosan's text into a generic category (such as the immigrant novel or a multicultural coming-to-America autobiography) are more alive to the complex historical experiences and class conflicts depicted. Also taking issue with the incorporation of Bulosan's life and work under a depoliticized multicultural rubric is Amanda Solomon Amorao. 'The Manong's "Songs of

Love": Gendered and Sexualised Dimensions of Carlos Bulosan's Literature and Labor Activism' (*KK* 23[2014] 221–35) Amorao reads Bulosan's prose narratives, revealing 'how the Filipino immigrant's status as racialized labor is also gendered and sexualized', and that his writing also points towards the need for 'an intersectional liberatory praxis that is both anticolonial and anticapitalist' (p. 224). Bulosan's emphasis on the violence wrought by the divisions of race, class, and gender in the United States prevents his writing from being seamlessly included in a multicultural canon. Finally, Michael Viola, Valerie Francisco, and Amanda Solomon Amorao, who are scholar-activist members of the Critical Filipina and Filipino Studies Collective (CFFSC), discuss Bulosan's importance for their work in 'Carlos Bulosan and a Collective Outline for Critical Filipina and Filipino Studies' (*KK* 23[2014] 255–76). They focus on *America Is in the Heart* and on how Bulosan's insights in that text can advance 'a structural critique of neoliberal globalization in the Philippines and in the US' (p. 270).

(b) Malaysia

Perhaps the most notable publication regarding Malaysian literature in English this year is *Asiatic* 8:i[2014], devoted to the work of Shirley Geok-lin Lim. Lim, who was born and raised in Malaysia, lived and worked in Singapore for many years, now resides in the United States, and has become a renowned Asian American scholar and creative writer. Of the fourteen essays in the special issue, quite a number revisit topics in earlier scholarship, such as Lim's representations of migration, exile, and transnational subjectivity, her feminist interrogations of heroic and paternalistic national and cultural narratives, and her contributions to Asian American literature and scholarship. This entry will focus on the essays presenting fresh perspectives on Lim's work, such as Sneja Gunew's ' "A Multilingual Life": The Cosmopolitan and Globalectic Dimensions of Shirley Geok-lin Lim's Writings' (*Asiatic* 8:i[2014]12–24). Gunew interprets Lim's critical use of language in her memoir, poetry, and scholarship as evidence of a revised and renewed cosmopolitan stance. This stance is in line with recent scholarship conceptualizing cosmopolitanism as a subjectivity attentive to inequalities caused by economic globalization rather than one of detached privilege and transnational mobility. In ' "How Can I Prove That I Am Not Who I Am?"': Layered Identities and Genres in the Work of Shirley Geok-lin Lim' (*Asiatic* 8:i[2014] 25–39) Katrina M. Powell looks at how Lim's crossing of geographical borders is related to her intellectual crossing of generic borders as she moves between poetry, prose fiction, memoir, and criticism. Powell then focuses on Lim's memoir *Among the White Moon Faces* as an example of what she calls a 'performative autobiography' that mobilizes readers with 'a call to action' (p. 26). Silvia Schultermandl observes Lim's work making an aesthetic turn in ' "Imagination Is a Tricky Power": Transnationalism and Aesthetic Education in Shirley Geok-lin Lim's Work' (*Asiatic* 8:i[2014] 40–54). Schultermandl proposes that aesthetic education appears in Lim's work as a double-edged sword: the characters in Lim's first novel *Joss and Gold* 'gain agency precisely because of the tension between universal ideas of beauty and particular circumstances of lived experience' in Malaysia and Singapore (p. 49). Tracing a similar aesthetic thread in Lim's novel, Chitra Sankaran, 'Writing Back: Ethics and Aesthetics in *Joss and Gold*' (*Asiatic* 8:i[2014] 173–84), contends that Lim creates an intertwined ethical and aesthetic structure in order to interrogate Western stereotypes about Asians, especially Asian women. However, the novel refuses to simply generate alternative stereotypes; instead of inverting a binary opposition, Lim is actually 'showing the rift between autonomy and relational ethics' through her Malaysian, Singaporean, and American characters who are embedded in contested situations (p. 183). Moving from aesthetic to alimentary matters, Andrew Hock Soon Ng's essay ' "Eating Words": Alimentary Motifs in Shirley Geoklin Lim's Poetry' (*Asiatic* 8:i[2014] 55–71) relates Lim's use of food and eating to diaspora, gender, and nostalgia studies. Even though alimentary motifs are inextricable from a nostalgia that ambivalently connects diasporic subjects to the ancestral homeland, Ng argues that Lim is able to use them to illuminate and interrogate 'the status of women as valuable commodity within patriarchal economy' (p. 64).

The problems and possibilities of writing from a diasporic perspective are also a common thematic in three other essays. Guat Eng Chuah advances an intriguing argument in 'The Art of Fiction: Indian Diaspora's Gift to Malaysian Fiction-Writing Descendants of Other Diasporas' (*DiaS* 7:i[2014] 18–27), which reads three novels by Malaysian writers who are of non-Indian ancestry through the narrative logic of Indian (specifically Hindu) intellectual and spiritual thinking. Such an approach, Chuah proposes, departs from Eurocentric reading practices that interpret characteristics such as non-linear narrative and metafictional commentary as poststructuralist writing. Diasporic writers may be physically distanced but not emotionally estranged from their homeland, as Carol Leon and Gladys Koh reveal in their essay 'Retrieving Lost Histories: Spaces of Healing, Spaces of Liberation' (*Asiatic* 8:ii[2014] 110–24), which focuses on Twan Eng Tan's first novel *The Gift of Rain*. A work of historical fiction, Tan's novel 'reconstructs the narrative of [Tan's] homeland Malaysia' but develops its characters' 'sense of belonging and self in the spaces prised open by history and memory' rather than rewriting the historical record with new-found facts or verifiable events (p. 111). Tan's protagonist Philip Khoo's eventual reconciliation with his troubled past points towards the potential for healing and liberation for individuals who have suffered through colonial history. Similarly, although Preeta Samarasan writes from outside Malaysia, her novel is still an interrogation of class and racial discrimination in the country. In 'Class and the Time of the Nation in Preeta Samarasan's *Evening Is the Whole Day*' (*ArielE* 45:i–ii[2014] 195–220) Lee Erwin employs Homi Bhabha's distinction between the pedagogical and the performative aspects of nationalism to analyse the novels' doubled structure. Samarasan's novel not only takes issue with the patriarchal and racialized nature of the country's postcolonial nationalist discourse, but also highlights how the fate of Chellam the servant girl represents the class distinctions within an ethnic minority group such as the Indian community in Malaysia.

Connections between problems of race, class, and gender are highlighted in another three essays. Wai Chew Sim argues, in 'Beyond the Color Line: Intersectional Considerations in Chuah Guat Eng's Fiction' (*KK* 23[2014] 33–46), that Chuah's writing moves beyond identity politics in Malaysia to link ethnicity with the struggle for social justice and politico-economic equality. Sim claims that a reading practice attentive to national and regional contexts is needed to trace the intertwining of identity politics with problems of redistribution of power and wealth in the works of other Malaysian and Southeast Asian writers. Madiha Ramlan makes a similar point by showing how 'Malay Characters in Lloyd Fernando's *Green is the Colour*' (*Asiatic* 8:ii[2014] 125–36) occupy different subject positions, some of which are in conflict. Such a heterogeneous cast of Malay characters departs from a state-sponsored narrative stressing a national identity premised on a more or less homogeneous ethnic and cultural identity. Looking at Chinese rather than Malay subject formation, Fiona Lee, 'Epistemological Checkpoint: Reading Fiction as a Translation of History' (*PocoT* 9:i[2014] 21 pp.), discusses Han Suyin's *And the Rain My Drink* as a novel that shows how ethnic Chinese subjectivity was shaped and incorporated by British colonial authorities during the 1948–60 Malayan Emergency. Lee focuses on the crucial role that translation plays in shaping both communicative practices between characters and the racialized subject positions they are placed in or assume. Also, the novel's constant shifting between third- and first-person narration 'can be read as a strategy for coping with the consequences of critiquing colonial power' (p. 17), which was Han's intention as a doctor who witnessed at first hand the human cost of British anti-communist counterinsurgency efforts.

(c) Singapore

This year saw the publication of *Common Lines and City Spaces*, a set of essays edited by Weihsin Gui dedicated to the work of Arthur Yap. Yap, who died in 2006, was a poet, painter, and scholar of linguistics who taught for many years at the National University of Singapore. Although he is regarded as one of the pioneers of anglophone Singaporean literature, relatively little critical attention has been paid to him compared to contemporaries such as Edwin Thumboo and Robert Yeo. This collection offers diverse and provocative perspectives on Yap's poetry, fiction, and visual art. In 'The Transformation of Objects into Things in Arthur Yap's Poetry', Weihsin Gui shows how Yap's poetic language defamiliarizes commonplace objects and conceptual terms from their habitual usage, illuminating commodifying and disciplinary processes that subject Singaporeans' everyday experience. Kim Cheng Boey examines Yap's paintings in ' "The Same Tableau, Intrinsically Still": Arthur Yap, Poet-Painter', some of which appear as illustrations in his poetry collections. Boey discusses how his poetic and visual imaginations are intertwined; the abstract shapes and lines on his canvas work their way into the characteristic brevity and irony of his verse. Angus Whitehead's essay ' "Go to Bedok, You Bodoh": Arthur Yap's Mapping of Singaporean Space' focuses on Yap's poetic allusions to specific urban spaces and landmarks in Singapore. He suggests that Yap's attention to local details offers an alternative mapping of the country's social and cultural memory to those offered by official state narratives. Also highlighting the urban context in Yap's verse is Eddie Tay. In 'On Places and Spaces: The Possibilities of Teaching Arthur Yap', Tay uses Henri Lefebvre's analysis of the politics of urban spaces as a framework to discuss his own experiences teaching Yap's poetry to undergraduates in Hong Kong. From an ecocritical perspective, Xiaojing Zhou traces how Yap reconfigures the relationship between humans, their socio-cultural milieu and the natural environment in 'Arthur Yap's Ecological Poetics of the Daily'. Zhou points out how Yap's poems disrupt conventional hierarchies that position humans as agents who shape and control the cultural and natural worlds. Cyril Wong's detailed analysis of camp aesthetics in Yap's poems in ' "Except for a Word": Arthur Yap's Unspoken Homoeroticism' marks the first critical discussion of Yap's sexual identity. Although Yap never came out as a gay man, Wong's readings highlight the homoeroticism and emotional intimacy present in several poems, especially those dedicated to his long-time partner. In the closing co-authored essay, ' "A Long Way From What?": Folkways and Social Commentary in Arthur Yap's Short Stories', Angus Whitehead and Joel Gwynne discuss Yap's short fiction, which has hitherto been neglected due to his larger poetic output. Whitehead and Gwynne argue that Yap's short stories offer social commentary through an emphasis on local folkways that push back against state policies of racial and linguistic standardization in a rapidly modernizing Singapore.

Kim Cheng Boey, who wrote the chapter on Yap's paintings and poetry, is himself the focus of Bernadette Bernard's essay, 'Kim Cheng Boey's *Between Stations*: "The Architecture of Memory" ' (*LW* 11:i[2014] 39–54). Although Boey is the author of four poetry collections, *Between Stations* is his first collection of prose. It began as a travel-writing project but ended up becoming 'a layered memoir of loss and mourning' (p. 40). Bernard discusses how Boey's travels to cities such as Calcutta and Alexandria evoke memories of his childhood and time spent with his estranged and recently deceased father in the urban environment of Singapore. *Between Stations* is therefore Boey's meditation on both the loss of a parent and the role of writing as imaginative, geographical, and temporal border crossing.

The topic of loss is also central to Harry Aveling's essay '*1819*: Isa Kamari on the Foundation of Singapore' (*Asiatic* 8:ii[2014] 88–109). Isa's novel was originally written and published in Malay with the title *Duka Tuan Bertakha*, which means *Sadly You Rule*, but its English translation is worth noting. 1819 is commonly regarded as the year modern Singapore was established, when British East India Company official Thomas Stamford Raffles set up a trading port on the island. Aveling argues that Isa's *1819* is a subversive retelling of the events culminating in the British colonial takeover of Singapore that highlights how the Malay community on the island was socially and politically marginalized in ways that persisted even after Singapore achieved its independence.

Four essays published this year examine globalization and cosmopolitanism and their effects and possibilities for thinking about the politics of using language and reading literature in Singapore. Lionel Wee's 'Linguistic Chutzpah and the Speak Good Singlish Movement' (*WEn* 33:i[2014] 85–99) highlights how the state-sponsored Speak Good English Movement (SGEM) generated a resistant counterpart, the Speak Good Singlish Movement (SSGM), on social media. Whereas the former disciplines Singaporeans to speak grammatically correct standard English, the latter encourages the use of vernacular Singaporean English or Singlish. Wee coins the term 'linguistic chutzpah' to describe not only 'confidence in one's linguistic choices in the face of criticism' but also 'drawing upon linguistic knowledge to justify these choices' (p. 86). He argues that SSGM displays such chutzpah, which is salutary as language use in Singapore becomes ever more hybridized and fluid. As Wee points out in another essay, 'Language Politics and Global City' (*DSCP* 35:v[2014] 649–60), Singapore's self-presentation as a cosmopolitan city affects its long-standing bilingual policies that cast English as a language of business and administration and other languages as mother tongues or cultural anchors for the country's multiethnic population. Wee suggests that an 'open bilingual policy' (p. 655) based on individual choice is more suitable for developing more inclusive and diverse forms of citizenship in a globalized world.

In a similar vein, Suzanne S. Choo's 'Toward a Cosmopolitan Vision of English Education in Singapore' (*DSCP* 35:v[2014] 677–91) draws on Jürgen Habermas's tripartite distinction of cognitive, aesthetic, and moral domains in language to analyse how English language and English literature have been taught in Singapore's school system. Choo argues that splitting off the study of English language from literature has led to the former becoming associated with cognitive and instrumental usage while literature is studied aesthetically, separated from socio-political issues and Singapore's cultural context. Choo advocates an integrated approach to English studies driven by a 'communicative cosmopolitanism' to help Singaporeans develop 'responsiveness and responsibility toward the other' (p. 679) both within and beyond the nation-state. Choo's vision resonates with Philip Holden's argument in 'Cosmopolitan Pedagogies: Revisiting Shirley Geok-lin Lim's Short Fiction' (*Asiatic* 8:i[2014] 195–208; the special issue mentioned earlier). Drawing on his experiences teaching Lim's short stories to Singaporean undergraduates, Holden offers an intriguing argument: younger readers who are not familiar with the historical settings and contexts of Lim's short stories might actually gain more from them. Because Lim's stories have the 'potential to defamiliarise: to challenge normative assumptions regarding sexuality and race that students have learned' (p. 197), they compel readers to think in cosmopolitan terms, beyond their own experiences, and to consider other kinds of subject positions and relations.

Books Reviewed

Adams, Jenni, ed. *The Bloomsbury Companion to Holocaust Literature*. Bloomsbury. [2014] pp. 352. £200 ISBN 9 7814 4112 9086.
Ageteman-Duah, Ivor, and Ogochukwu Promise, eds. *Essays in Honour of Wole Soyinka at 80*. AC. [2014] pp. 243. £20 ISBN 9 7809 5693 0798.

Arua, Arua E., Taiwo Abioye, and Kehinde A. Ayoola, eds. *Language, Literature and Style in Africa*, CambridgeSP. [2014] pp. 185. £41.99 ISBN 9 7814 4387 0443.

Ascari, Maurizio. *Cinema and the Imagination in Katherine Mansfield's Writing*. Palgrave. [2014] pp. 108. £47 ISBN 9 7811 3740 0352.

Ayebia Clarke, Nana, and James Currey. *Chinua Achebe: Tributes and Reflections*. AC. [2014] pp. 340. pb £20 ISBN 9 7809 5693 0767.

Bailey, Carol. *A Poetics of Performance: The Oral-Scribal Aesthetic in Anglophone Caribbean Fiction*. UWIndiesP. [2014] pp. ix + 240. pb $37 ISBN 9 7897 6640 4956.

Baisnée, Valérie. '*Through the Long Corridor of Distance*': *Space and Self in Contemporary New Zealand Women's Autobiographies*. Rodopi. [2014] pp. 156. ?40 ISBN 9 7890 4203 8684.

Balaev, Michelle, ed. *Contemporary Approaches in Literary Trauma Theory*. PalMac. [2014] pp. 177. $95 ISBN 9 7813 7365 934.

Banerjee, Suparna. *Science, Gender and History: The Fantastic in Mary Shelley and Margaret Atwood*. CambridgeSP. [2014] pp. 160. £41.99 ISBN 9 7814 4386 2202.

Barrett, Ross, and Daniel Worden, eds. *Oil Culture*. UMinnP. [2014] pp. 456. $90 ISBN 9 7808 1668 9682.

Bayeh, Jumana. *The Literature of the Lebanese Diaspora: Representations of Place and National Identity*. Tauris. [2014] pp. 288. £62 ISBN 9 7817 8076 9987.

Blommaert, Jan. *State Ideology and Language in Tanzania*. 2nd edn. EdinUP. [2014] pp. 168. £70 ISBN 9 7807 4867 5791.

Bloom, Peter, Stephan Miescher, and Takyiwa Manuh, eds. *Modernisation as Spectacle in Africa*. IndUP. [2014] pp. 378. $85 ISBN 9 7802 5301 2258.

Blythe, Helen Lucy. *The Victorian Colonial Romance with the Antipodes*. Palgrave. [2014] pp. xii + 243. £57.50 ISBN 9 7811 3739 7829.

Bradley, Nicolas, ed. *We Go Far Back in Time: The Letters of Earle Birney and Al Purdy*. Harbour. [2014] pp. 480. C$39.95 ISBN 9 7815 5017 6100.

Brindle, Kym. *Epistolary Encounters in New-Victorian Fiction: Diaries and Letters*. PalMac. [2014] pp. 240. £55 ISBN 9 7811 3700 7155.

Bruhn, Mark J., and Donald R. Wehrs, eds. *Cognition, Literature, and History*. Routledge. [2014] pp. 284. £90 ISBN 9 7804 1572 2094.

Burnham, Karen. *Greg Egan*. UIllP. [2014] pp. 208. $95 ISBN 9 7802 5203 8419.

Burger, Jeff, ed. *Leonard Cohen on Leonard Cohen: Interviews and Encounters*. ChiR. [2014] pp. xix + 604. pb $29.95 ISBN 9 7816 1374 7582.

Butterss, Philip. *An Unsentimental Bloke: The Life and Work of C.J. Dennis*. Wakefield. [2014] pp. 296. pb A$34.95 ISBN 9 7817 4305 2877.

Campbell, Marion May. *Poetic Revolutionaries: Intertextuality and Subversion*. Rodopi. [2014] pp. 324. pb €70 ISBN 9 7890 4203 7861.

Canavan, Gerry, and Kim Stanley Robinson, eds. *Green Planets: Ecology and Science Fiction*. WesleyanUP. [2014] pp. 312. $85 ISBN 9 7808 1957 4268.

Castejon, Vanessa, Anna Cole, Oliver Haag, and Karen Hughes, eds. *Ngapartji Ngapartji: In Turn in Turn: Ego-Histoire, Europe and Indigenous Australia*. ANUP. [2014] pp. xvi + 296. pb A$33 ISBN 9 7819 2502 1721.

Ce, Chin, and Charles Smith, eds. *Counter Discourse in African Literature*. Handel. [2014] pp. 154. pb£18.95 ISBN 9 7897 8370 8563.

Ce, Chin, and Charles Smith, eds. *The Dark Edge of African Literature*. Hande. [2014] pp. 166. pb £18.95 ISBN 9 7897 8370 5556.

Ce, Chin, and Charles Smith, eds. *Gender Issues in African Literature*. Handel. [2014] pp. 200. pb £18.95 ISBN 9 7897 8370 8549.

Ceranowski, Karli June, and Megan Milks, eds. *Asexualities: Feminist and Queer Perspectives*. Routledge. [2014] pp. 396. £90 ISBN 9 7804 1571 4426.

Connor, Ralph [Charles William Gordon]. *The Foreigner: A Tale of Saskatchewan*. Early Canadian Literature. WLUP. [2014] pp. 312. pb C$24.99 ISBN 9 7815 5458 9449.

Conti, Christopher, and James Gourley, eds. *Literature as Translation/ Translation as Literature*. CambridgeSP. [2014] pp. xviii + 224. £44.99 ISBN 9 7814 4385 4948.

Crouch, David. *Colonial Psychosocial: Reading William Lane*. CambridgeSP. [2014] pp. 184. £41.99 ISBN 9 7814 4386 7559.

Coullie, Judith Lütge, and Andries Visagie, eds. *Antjie Krog: An Ethics of Body and Otherness*. UKNP. [2014] pp. xviii + 341. R385 ISBN 9 7818 6914 2537.

Cullhed, Anders, Lena Rydholm, and Janken Myrdal, eds. *True Lies Worldwide: Fictionality in Global Contexts*. Gruyter. [2014] pp. xi + 339. €99.95 ISBN 9 7831 1030 3124.

Dalley, Hamish. *The Postcolonial Historical Novel: Realism, Allegory, and the Representation of Contested Pasts*. PalMac. [2014] pp. 240. £55 ISBN 9 7811 3745 0081.

Däwes, Birgit, and Marc Beaufort, eds. *Enacting Nature: Ecocritical Perspectives on Indigenous Performance*. Lang. [2014] pp. 262. pb £38 ISBN 9 7828 7574 1462.

Deshmane, Chetan, ed. *Muses India: Essays on English-Language Writers from Mahomet to Rushdie*. McFarland. [2013] pp. 220. $55 ISBN 9 7807 8647 3083.

Dixon, Robert. *Alex Miller: The Ruin of Time*. SUP. [2014] pp. 229. pb A$30 ISBN 9 7817 4332 4073.

Dwivedi, Om Prakash, ed. *Tracing the New Indian Diaspora*. Rodopi. [2014] pp. xxvi + 303. €70 ISBN 9 7890 4203 8882.

Edmond, Murray. *Then It Was Now Again: Selected Critical Writing*. Atuanui. [2014] pp. x + 324. NZ$40 ISBN 9 7809 9224 5368.

Elkins, Caroline. *Britain's Gulag: The Brutal End of Empire in Kenya*. Bodley. [2014] pp. 496. pb £15.99 ISBN 9 7818 4792 2946.

Emberley, Julia V. *The Testimonial Uncanny: Indigenous Storytelling, Knowledge, and Reparative Practices*. SUNYP. [2014] pp. 352. $90 ISBN 9 7814 3845 3613.

Fink, Thomas, and Judith Haden-Sullivan, eds. *Reading the Difficulties: Dialogues with Contemporary American Innovative Poetry*. UAlaP. [2014] pp. 240. pb $34.95 ISBN 9 7808 1735 7528.

Francisco Fernández, José, and Alejandra Moreno Álvarez, eds. *A Rich Field Full of Pleasant Surprises: Essays in Honour of Professor Socorro Suárez Lafuente*. CambridgeSP. [2014] pp. x + 177. £39.99 ISBN 9 7814 4385 9493.

Frydman, Jason. *Sounding the Break: African American and Caribbean Routes of World Literature*. UPVirginia. [2014] pp. 192. $55 ISBN 9 7808 1393 5720.

Fumagalli, Maria Cristina, Bénédicte Ledent, and Roberto del Valle Alcalá, eds. *The Cross-Dressed Caribbean: Writing, Politics, Sexualities*. UPVirginia. [2014] pp. 320. $70 ISBN 9 7808 1393 5225.

Garcia, J.C. Neil *Homeless in Unhomeliness: Postcolonial Critiques of Philippine Literature*. DLSUP. [2014] pp. xx + 292. $24 ISBN 9 7897 1555 5982.

Gardner, Hunter, and Sheila Murnaghan, eds. *Odyssean Identities in Modern Cultures: The Journey Home*. OSUP. [2014] pp. 337. $79.95 ISBN 9 7808 1421 2486.

Gelder, Ken, and Rachael Weaver. *The Colonial Journals: The Emergence of Australian Literary Culture*. UWAP. [2014] pp. 440. pb A$45 ISBN 9 7817 4258 4973.

Gordon, Neta. *Catching the Torch: Contemporary Canadian Literary Responses to World War I*. WLUP. [2014] pp. viii + 214. C$65.99 ISBN 9 7815 5438 9869.

Grubisic, Brett Josef, Gisèle M. Baxter, and Tara Lee, eds. *Blast, Corrupt, Dismantle, Erase: Contemporary North American Dystopian Literature*. WLUP. [2014] pp. 486. C$48.99 ISBN 9 7815 5458 9890.

Gui, Weihsin, ed. *Common Lines and City Spaces: A Critical Anthology on Arthur Yap*. ISEAS. [2014] pp. x + 198. pb $26.90 ISBN 9 7898 1437 9908.

Hale, Elizabeth, ed. *Maurice Gee, a Literary Companion: The Fiction for Young Readers*. UOtagoP. [2014] pp. 208. NZ$35 ISBN 9 7818 7757 8847.

Hamam, Kinana. *Confining Spaces, Resistant Subjectivities: Towards a Metachronous Discourse of Literary Mapping and Transformation in Postcolonial Women's Writing*. CambridgeSP. [2014] pp. 223. £44.99 ISBN 9 7814 4385 9851.

Harrison, Chloe, Louise Nuttall, et al., eds. *Cognitive Grammar in Literature*. Benjamins. [2014] pp. xvii + 255. €99 ISBN 9 7890 2723 4049.

Hertz, Erich, and Jeffrey Roessner, eds. *Write in Tune: Contemporary Music in Fiction*. Bloomsbury. [2014] pp. xii + 264. $110 ISBN 9 7816 2356 4223.

Hubler, Angela E., ed. *Little Red Readings: Historical Materialist Perspectives on Children's Literature*. UPMissip. [2014] pp. 304. $60 ISBN 9 7816 1703 9874.

Jacobs, J.U., Derrick J. McLure, and Reiko Aiura, eds. *East Meets West*. CambridgeSP. [2014] pp. 231. £44.99 ISBN 9 7814 4385 3385.

Kaindl, Klaus, and Karlheinz Spitzl,eds. *Transfiction: Research into the Realities of Translation*. Benjamins. [2014] pp. ix + 373. €99 ISBN 9 7890 2725 8502.

Kaisary, Philip. *The Haitian Revolution in the Literary Imagination: Radical Horizons, Conservative Constraints*. UPVirginia. [2014] pp. 256. $59.50 ISBN 9 7808 1393 5461.

Kamboureli, Smaro, and Christl Verduyn, eds. *Critical Collaborations: Indigeneity, Diaspora, and Ecology in Canadian Literary Studies*. WLUP. [2014] pp. 296. C$42.99 ISBN 9 7815 5458 9111.

Kimber, Gerri, and Angela Smith, eds. *The Edinburgh Edition of the Collected Works of Katherine Mansfield: The Poetry and Critical Writings of Katherine Mansfield*, vol. 3. EdinUP. [2014] pp. xxvii + 754. £125 ISBN 9 7807 4868 5011.

Kimber, Gerri, W. Todd Martin, Delia da Sousa Correa, Alice Kelly, and Isobel Maddison. *Katherine Mansfield and World War One*. EdinUP. [2014] pp. i–viii, 224. £70 ISBN 9 7807 4869 5348.

King, Bruce. *Rewriting India: Eight Writers*. OUPI. [2014] pp. 280. Rs825 ISBN 9 7801 9809 9161.

Knutson, Susan, ed. *Rivering: The Poetry of Daphne Marlatt*. WLUP. [2014] pp. 96. pb C$16.99 ISBN 9 7817 7112 0388.

Korte, Barbara, and Frederic Regard, eds. *Narrating 'Precariousness': Modes, Media, Ethics*. Winter. [2014] pp. 138. €26 ISBN 9 7838 2536 2133.

Krishnan, Madhu. *Contemporary African Literature in English: Global Locations, Postcolonial Identifications*. PalMac. [2014] pp. 232. £58 ISBN 9 7811 3737 8323.

Lacey, Lauren J. *The Past That Might Have Been, the Future That May Come: Women Writing Fantastic Fiction, 1960s to the Present*. McFarland. [2014] pp. xii + 195. pb $40 ISBN 9 7807 8647 8262.

Lai, Larissa. *Slanting I, Imagining We: Asian Canadian Literary Production in the 1980s and 1990s*. WLUP. [2014] pp. xii + 260. pb C$42.99 ISBN 9 7817 7112 0418.

Lalla, Barbara, Jean D'Costa, and Velma Pollard. *Caribbean Literary Discourse: Voice and Cultural Identity in the Anglophone Caribbean*. UAlaP. [2014] pp. 296. $49.95 ISBN 9 7808 1731 8079.

Lederer, Mary. *Novels of Botswana in English, 1930–2006*. AfHP. [2014] pp. ix + 185. $24.95 ISBN 9 7819 4072 9152.

Lee, Rachel C. *The Exquisite Corpse of Asian America: Biopolitics, Biosociality and Posthuman Ecologies*. NYUP. [2014] pp. 325. pb $26 ISBN 9 7814 7980 9783.

Looser, Diana. *Remaking Pacific Pasts: History, Memory and Identity in Contemporary Theater from Oceania*. UHawaiiP. [2014] pp. vii + 305. $55 ISBN 9 7808 2483 9765.

Lorcin, Patricia M.E. *Historicizing Colonial Nostalgia: European Women's Narratives of Algeria and Kenya 1900–Present*. PalMac. [2012] pp. xii + 317. €89.99 ISBN 9 7802 3033 8654.

Löschnigg, Martin, and Marzena Sokołowska-Paryż, eds. *The Great War in Post-Memory Literature and Film*. Gruyter. [2014] pp. vii + 459. €89.95 ISBN 9 7831 1039 1527.

Maver, Igor. *Selected Essays on Canadian, Australian and New Zealand Literatures*. CambridgeSP. [2014] pp. 132. £39.99 ISBN 9 7814 4385 8977.

May, Brian T. *Extravagant Postcolonialism: Modernism and Modernity in Anglophone Fiction 1958–1988*. USCP. [2014] pp. 246. $49.95 ISBN 9 7816 1117 3796.

Mayer, Sylvia, and Alexa Weik von Mossner, eds. *The Anticipation of Catastrophe: Environmental Risk in North American Literature and Culture*. Winter. [2014] pp. 227. €35 ISBN 9 7838 2536 3345.

McClung, Nellie. *Painted Fires*. Early Canadian Literature. WLUP. [2014] pp. 334. pb C$24.99 ISBN 9 7815 5458 9791.

McCredden, Lyn, and Nathanael O'Reilly eds. *Tim Winton: Critical Essays*. UWAP. [2014] pp. 350. pb A$4.99 ISBN 9 7817 4258 6069.

McDonald-Rissanen, Mary. *In the Interval of the Wave: Prince Edward Island Women's Nineteenth- and Early Twentieth-Century Life Writing*. McG-QUP. [2014] pp. 292. C$34.95 ISBN 9 7807 7354 3898.

McLeod, Neal, ed. *Indigenous Poetics in Canada*. WLUP. [2014] pp. 416. C$36.99 ISBN 9 7815 5458 9821.

Mehta, Rini Bhattacharya, and Debali Mookerjea-Leonard, eds. *The Indian Partition in Literature and Films: History, Politics and Aesthetics*. Routledge. [2015] pp. 185. £90 ISBN 9 7811 3878 1801.

Menon, Nirmala, and Marika Preziuso, eds. *Migrant Identities of 'Creole Cosmopolitans': Transcultural Narratives of Contemporary Postcoloniality*. Lang. [2014] pp. 187. $82.95 ISBN 9 7814 3311 8128.

Meyrick, Julian. *The Retreat of Our National Drama*. Platform Papers 39. Currency. [2014] pp. 85. pb A$16.99 ISBN 9 7809 8721 1491.

Mirzeler, Mustafa K. *Remembering Nayeche and the Gray Bull Engiro: African Storytellers of the Karamoja Plateau and the Plains of Turkana*. UTorP. [2014] pp. 392. $80 ISBN 9 7814 4262 6317.

Misrahi-Barak, Judith, and Claudine Raynaud, eds. *Diasporas, Cultures of Mobilities, 'Race', 1. Diasporas and Cultures of Migrations*. PULM. [2014] pp. 376. pb €34 ISBN 9 8723 6781 0379.

Mordecai, Rachel L. *Citizenship Under Pressure: The 1970s in Jamaican Literature and Culture*. UWIndiesP. [2014] pp. 292. pb $45 ISBN 9 7897 6640 4581.

Morgan, Paula. *The Terror and the Time: Banal Violence and Trauma in Caribbean Discourse*. UWIndiesP. [2014] pp. ix + 247. pb $32 ISBN 9 7897 6640 4963.

Morris, Susana M. *Close Kin and Distant Relatives: The Paradox of Respectability in Black Women's Literature*. UPVirginia. [2014] pp. 192. $59.50 ISBN 9 7808 1393 5492.

Morton, Stephen. *States of Emergency. Colonialism, Literature and Law*. Postcolonialism Across the Disciplines 11. LiverUP. [2013] pp. 249. £75 ISBN 9 7818 4631 8498.

Moser, Christian, and Linda Simonis, eds. *Figuren des Globalen: Weltbezug und Welterzeugung in Literatur, Kunst und Medien*. V&R. [2014] pp. 743 €79.99 ISBN 9 7838 4710 1703.

Mukherjee, Ankhi. *What Is a Classic? Postcolonial Rewriting and Invention of the Canon*. StanfordUP. [2014] pp. 296. $65 ISBN 9 7808 0478 5211.

Murphet, Julian, Rónán McDonald, and Sascha Morrell, eds. *Flann O'Brien and Modernism*. Bloomsbury. [2014] pp. 248. pb $29.95 ISBN 9 7816 2356 8504.

Negash, Ghirmai, Andrea Frohne, and Samuel Zadi, eds. *At the Crossroads: Readings of the Postcolonial and the Global in African Literature and Visual Art*. AfWP. [2014] pp. 394. pb $39.95 ISBN 9 7815 9221 9636.

Neuman, Justin. *Fiction Beyond Secularism*. NorthwesternUP. [2014] pp. 242. $45 ISBN 9 7808 1012 9894.

Newell, Stephanie, and Onookome Okome, eds. *Popular Culture in Africa: The Episteme of the Everyday*. Routledge. [2013] pp. 324. £90 ISBN 9 7804 1553 2921.

Olubas, Brigitta, ed. *Shirley Hazzard*. SUP. [2014] pp. 164. pb A$30 ISBN 9 7817 4332 4103.

Owen, Percy, ed. *The Order in which We Do Things: The Poetry of Tom Wayman*. WLUP. [2014] pp. 112. pb C$18.99 ISBN 9 7815 5458 9951.

Panovsky, Ruth, ed. *The Collected Poems of Miriam Waddington: A Critical Edition*. UOttawaP. [2014] pp. 1,166. pb C$44.95 ISBN 9 7807 7662 1456.

Patterson, Annabel. *The International Novel*. YaleUP. [2014] pp. 261. pb $30 ISBN 9 7803 0019 8003.

Peebles, Stacey. *Violence in Literature*. Salem. [2014] pp. 300. $95 ISBN 9 7816 1925 4091.

Quayson, Ato. *Oxford Street, Accra*. DukeUP. [2014] pp. 312. $94.95 ISBN 9 7808 2235 7339.

Raducanu, Adriana. *Speaking the Language of the Night: Aspects of the Gothic in Selected Contemporary Novels*. Lang. [2014] pp. 206. £32 ISBN 9 7836 3162 8034.

Radović, Stanka. *Locating the Destitute: Space and Identity in Caribbean Fiction*. UPVirginia. [2014] pp. 240. $59.50 ISBN 9 7808 1393 6284.

Rampaul, Giselle, and Barbara Lalla, eds. *Postscripts: Caribbean Perspectives on the British Canon from Shakespeare to Dickens*. UWIndiesP. [2014] pp. 188. pb $40 ISBN 9 7897 6640 4628.

Richards, Cynthia, and Mary O'Donnell, eds. *Teaching Behn's Oroonoko*. MLA. [2013] pp. xv + 227. $37.50 ISBN 9 7816 0329 1297.

Sabiston, Elizabeth, and Robert Drummond, eds. *Pluri-culture et écrits migratoires / Pluri-Culture and Migrant Writings*. Human Sciences Monograph Series 17. LauU. [2014] pp. 559. C$30 ISBN 9 7808 8667 0887.

Sandwith, Corinne. *World of Letters: Reading Communities and Cultural Debates in Early Apartheid South Africa*. UKNZP. [2014] pp. ix + 309. R345 ISBN 9 7818 6914 2629.

Sedlmayr, Gerold, and Nicole Waller, eds. *Politics in Fantasy Media: Essays on Ideology and Gender in Fiction, Film, Television and Games*. McFarland. [2014] pp. 224. pb $40 ISBN 9 7807 8649 5108.

Sepsi, Enikö, Judit Nagy, Miklos Vassányi, and János Kenyeres, eds. *Indigenous Perspectives of North America: A Collection of Studies*. CambridgeSP. [2014] pp. xiii + 527. £59.99 ISBN 9 7814 4385 9158.

Shields, Tanya L. *Bodies and Bones: Feminist Rehearsal and Imagining Caribbean Belonging*. UPVirginia. [2014] pp. 248. $55 ISBN 9 7808 1393 5966.

Sloniowski, Jeannette, and Marilyn Rose, eds. *Detecting Canada: Essays on Canadian Crime Fiction, Television and Film*. WLUP. [2014] pp. 342. C$39.99 ISBN 9 7815 5458 9265.

Stanley, Liz, and Andrea Salter, eds. *The World's Great Question: Olive Schreiner's South African Letters 1889–1920*. Second Series 45. Van Riebeeck. [2014]. pp. xlviii + 423. R350 ISBN 9 7809 8142 6457.

Stępień, Justyna, ed. *Redefining Kitsch and Camp in Literature and Culture*. CambridgeSP. [2014] pp. 220. £47.99 ISBN 9 7814 4386 2219.

Sugars, Cynthia. *Canadian Gothic: Literature, History and the Spectre of Self-Invention.* UWalesP. [2014] pp. 325. £95 ISBN 9 7807 0832 7005.

Täuschel, Alexander. *World English(es): On the Examples of India and Nigeria.* epub. [2014] pp. 44. pb €13.99 ISBN 9 7837 3750 0692.

Teelucksingh, Jerome. *Caribbean Empire: The Impact of Culture, Literature and History.* Academica. [2014] pp. 236. $72.95 ISBN 9 7819 3632 0684.

Tonkin, Maggie, Mandy Treagus, Madeleine Seys, and Sharon Crozier-De Rosa, eds. *Changing the Victorian Subject.* UAdelaide. [2014] pp. 292. pb A$44 ISBN 9 7819 2206 4738.

Treagus, Mandy. *Empire Girls: The Colonial Heroine Comes of Age.* UAdelaide. [2014] pp. 280 pb A$44 ISBN 9 7819 2206 4547.

Tunca, Daria. *Stylistic Approaches to Nigerian Fiction.* PalMac. [2014] pp. 216. £55 ISBN 9 7811 3726 4404.

Upcher, Janet. *Changing Countries, Bridging Worlds: The Poetry and Prose of Margaret Scott.* Gininderra. [2014] pp. 122. pb A$22.50 ISBN 9 7817 4027 8539.

vanden Driesen, Cynthia, and Bill Ashcroft, eds. *Patrick White Centenary: The Legacy of a Prodigal Son.* CambridgeSP. [2014] pp. xii + 501. £57.99 ISBN 9 7814 4386 0406.

Wagner, Tamara S., ed. *Domestic Fiction in Colonial Australia and New Zealand.* P&C. [2014] pp. 240. £95 ISBN 9 7818 4893 5167.

Westling, Louise, ed. *The Cambridge Companion to Literature and the Environment.* CUP. [2014] pp. xiii + 266. £50 ISBN 9 7811 0702 9927.

Wilding, Michael. *Wild Bleak Bohemia: Marcus Clarke, Adam Lindsay Gordon and Henry Kendall.* ASP. [2014] pp. 580. pb A$39.95 ISBN 9 7819 2500 3802.

Wright, Laura, Jane Poyner, and Elleke Boehmer, eds. *Approaches to Teaching Coetzee's Disgrace and Other Works.* MLA. [2014] pp. 227 $40 ISBN 9 7816 0329 1385.

Yenika-Agbaw, Vivien, and Lindah Mhando, eds. *African Youth in Contemporary Literature and Popular Culture: Identity Quest.* Routledge. [2014] pp. 256. £90 ISBN 9 7804 1570 9057.

Zecchini, Laetitia. *Moving Lines: Arun Kolatkar and Literary Modernism in India.* Bloomsbury. [2014] pp. 229. £60 ISBN 9 7814 4116 7507.

XIX

Bibliography, Textual Criticism, and Reference Works

WILLIAM BAKER

This year witnessed much of interest to *YWES* readers in the area of bibliography, textual criticism, and reference works. This chapter also draws attention to selected items not noticed elsewhere in the present volume. To begin with journal publications, as stated in previous annual accounts of the year's work in bibliography and textual criticism, an invaluable journal that is regularly published on a quarterly basis is *The Book Collector*. The spring 2014 issue includes Nicolas Barker's editorial opening article 'Bond and the *Book Collector*' (*BC* 63:i[2014] 11–46). Barker discusses, amongst other matters, the importance of James Bond's creator Ian Fleming during the early years of *The Book Collector*. This is followed by an account by Stephen Clarke of 'Beckford and Nimby Pamby: William Beckford's Notes in Horace Walpole's *Works*' (*BC* 63:i[2014] 47–82), and Christopher de Hamel writes on 'J.R. Abbey as a Book Collector' (*BC* 63:i[2014] 83–92). Mirjam M. Foot describes, with illustrations, 'A Binding by Christopher Chapman for Lord Harley, 1724: English and Foreign Bookbindings 118' (*BC* 63:i[2014] 93–6). Sheila Markham continues her fascinating series of interview with contemporary booksellers in her 'William Ward: The Markham Interview (New Series) II' (*BC* 63:i[2014] 97–103). Other regular contributors include, John Saumarez Smith, who writes on 'Robertson Davies and the Introduction Fee' (*BC* 63:i[2014] 103–8); James Fergusson continues his incisive, informative reports in his 'The Corvine Society: Author Societies 21' (*BC* 63:i[2014] 109–13); Ann Baer on 'Unexpected Resemblances: Biblio-vignettes 13' (*BC* 63:i[2014] 113–14). Notable regular features of *The Book Collector* are its reviews, and informational features relating for instance to recent auctions, catalogues, and obituaries. The spring 2014 issue contains a reprint of Nicolas Barker's obituary, originally published in *The Independent*, of the lettering designer Michael Harvey (1931–2013)—(*BC* 63:i[2014] 151–2). The summer issue opens with David McKitterick's editorial 'Oxford University Press' (*BC* 63:ii[2014] 179–206). Other items of direct interest to *YWES* readers include: Germaine Warkentin, 'The Roof-Climber: W.W. Greg in His Time and Ours' (*BC* 63:ii[2014] 227–42); Pat Rogers, 'Speaking of the Unspeakable: The

The Year's Work in English Studies, Volume 95 (2016) © *The Author 2016. Published by Oxford University Press on behalf of the English Association. All rights reserved. For Permissions, please email: journals.permissions@oup.com*
doi:10.1093/ywes/maw011

Rehabilitation of Edmund Curll' (*BC* 63:ii[2014] 243–50); Ruth Lightbourne, 'A William Scott Binding in New Zealand' (*BC* 63:ii[2014] 251–7); Sheila Markham, 'David J. Hall: Contemporary Collectors LVIII' (*BC* 63:ii[2014] 263–70); John Saumarez Smith, 'Nancy Mitford and the Guerrilla War' (*BC* 63:ii[2014] 271–6); James Fergusson, 'The Kipling Society: Author Societies 22' (*BC* 63:ii[2014] 277–80); and Ann Baer, ' Stoning Charlotte Brontë: Biblio-vignettes 14' (*BC* 63:ii[2014] 281–2). In addition to the regular reviews and informational features, there are two obituaries of interest: Dorothy A. Harrop on Ivor Robinson (1924–2014)—(*BC* 63:ii[2014] 311–12), who was 'one of the greatest artistic bookbinders of the twentieth century' (p. 311); Ian Jackson on Russell Alvin Johanson (1941–2013)—(*BC* 63:ii[2014] 312–14), who was 'for over thirty years . . . one of the leading antiquarian bookmen in the Pacific Northwest' (p. 312). The autumn issue of *The Book Collector* opens with Nicolas Barker's 'The Leaf and the Printers' (*BC* 63:iii[2014] 347–68). Other contributions include: John Emmerson, 'The Early Education of a Book Collector' (*BC* 63:iii[2014] 369–82); Colin Franklin, 'Samuel Lysons, Antiquary' (*BC* 63:iii[2014] 383–96); Paul McGrane, 'The Pseudonymous Mr Bell' (*BC* 63:iii[2014] 397–416); Sheila Markham, 'Guardian of the Ganymeds: Ann Baer at 100' (*BC* 63:iii[2014] 417–26); John Saumarez Smith 'Hugh Trevor-Roper's Library' (*BC* 63:iii[2014] 427–34); Robert Harding, 'Lost and Found: Collector's Piece IX' (*BC* 63:iii[2014] 437–40); James Fergusson, 'The Angela Thirkell Society: Author Societies 23' (*BC* 63:iii[2014] 441–4); and Ann Baer, 'The Corpse in the Piano: Biblio-vignettes 15' (*BC* 63:iii[2014] 445–6). A regular feature, 'Bibliographical Notes & Queries', has an item pertinent to *YWES*: Terry I. Seymour is in the final stages of his 'reconstruction of the Boswell family library. In 'Query 526: Boswell's Books' (*BC* 63:iii[2014] 491) he requests assistance in locating the present whereabouts 'of books with the ownership signature of either James or Alexander Boswell or bearing the Auchinleck bookstamp'. There are also two obituaries, both penned by Nicolas Barker. The first is reprinted from *The Independent*: the subject is the eminent bibliographer, book historian, and book-binding authority Anthony Hobson (1921–2014)—(*BC* 63:iii[2014] 485–7). The subject of the second obituary is the eminent inheritor of a distinguished collection, Mary, duchess of Roxburghe (1915–2014). She 'was the last surviving grandchild of Richard Monckton Milnes (1809–1885)'. Her home 'became the repository of the major part of her grandfather's famous book collection. Monckton Milnes knew all the great men and women of his time, and had their books.' The collection 'has been left to Trinity College Cambridge, where her grandfather was a fellow-commoner' (*BC* 63:iii[2014] 487–8). The winter 2014 issue of *The Book Collector* also contains material of much interest. The editorial by Nicolas Barker is on 'The World of Popular Print' (*BC* 63:iv[2014] 519–40). Other contributions include: Ann M. Ridler, 'William Henry Ridler: Mapper of the "Minor Roads" of Modern Press Printing' (*BC* 63:iv[2014] 541–56); Nicholas D. Nace's intriguingly titled 'Some New Light on Sodom' (*BC* 63:iv[2014] 557–68); Sheila Markham, 'Toshiyuki Takamiya: Contemporary Collectors LIX' (*BC* 63:iv[2014] 569–76); Michael Treloar, 'The Cloud of All-Knowing: If the Day of the Scholar-Librarian is Gone, How Can the Rare Book Trade Help?' (*BC* 63:iv[2014] 579–92); John Saumarez

Smith, 'David Bacon, Proprietor' (*BC* 63:iv[2014] 593–8); and James Fergusson, 'The John Masefield Society: Author Societies 24' (*BC* 63:iv[2014] 599–602). In addition to the regular features such as information on recent sales, catalogues, and book reviews there are obituaries of considerable interest. Ian Jackson's subject is Eric Korn (1933–2014)—(*BC* 63:iv[2014] 633–9). As Jackson observes in the concluding paragraph of his lengthy and at times very witty obituary, 'Eric was short, squat and larger than life. His much-loved and endearingly scruffy presence will be profoundly missed by booksellers of all persuasions. There was no one like him' (p. 639). Korn's 'rambling discursive polymathic "remainders" column in the *TLS* throughout the 1980s was the delight of the truly bookish' (p. 637). Stella Butler writes on the very kind, generous, and knowledgeable Christopher Sheppard (1947–2014), who was really responsible for developing the Brotherton Collection at the University of Leeds to its prominence in the field of modern British letters. Butler's tribute (*BC* 63:iv[2014] 639–63) is followed by one from Joan Winterkorn of Quaritch, who like the present writer 'had the pleasure of working with Chris for more than thirty years' (p. 644). Nicolas Barker pens the obituary of John McLaren Emmerson (1938–2014), the Melbourne-based eminent book collector (*BC* 63:iv[2014] 644–6). Another distinguished collector is celebrated too by Barker in his obituary of Ladislaus Von Hoffman (1927–2014)—(*BC* 63:iv[2014] 646–8).

The March 2014 issue of *The Papers of the Bibliographical Society of America* contains two fascinating contributions featuring William Caxton. It opens with Maura Ives, 'The Place of Musical Settings in Author Bibliographies, with Examples from Christina Rossetti' (*PBSA* 108:i[2014] 5–41). Ives observes that 'scholarship on descriptive bibliography, including that devoted to the bibliography of music, has little to say about the treatment of musical settings of literary works within bibliographies of British and American authors, and author bibliographies rarely offer a rationale for their inclusion or treatment of musical works'. Ives's intention is 'to present an argument for musical settings' place in literary biography, and to offer suggestions about the content and format of sections devoted to musical settings' (pp. 5–6). This is undertaken through drawing upon examples from Christina Rossetti. Ives's pioneering article is organized into sections dealing with 'Musical Settings and Literary Research: The Case of Christiana Rossetti' (pp. 7–21) and 'Practical Matters' such as 'Scope and Definition', 'Structuring the Music Section', 'Composing Entries for Musical Settings', and so on (pp. 21–32). In addition there is a most helpful appendix of 'Selected Reference Sources for Music Biography'. This is alphabetically arranged and largely enumerative, although in instances also descriptive. It is divided into six sections: 'General Research and Reference Tools for Music'; 'Bibliographies and Other Scholarship on Musical Settings'; 'Musical Settings of Specific Authors'; 'Indexes to Songs in Collections'; 'Tools for Locating Collections of Musical Settings, Including Digital Collections'; and 'Significant Library Collections, Including Digital Archives' (pp. 33–9). An earlier period is the subject of Barbara Bordalejo's 'Caxton's Editing of the *Canterbury Tales*' (*PBSA* 108:i[2014] 41–60). William Caxton declared in his 'Preface to his second edition of the *Canterbury Tales* ... that a gentleman had told him that his first edition of the *Tales* was inaccurate and that he could provide a better manuscript, one truer to Chaucer's text. Caxton claimed that he corrected the book based on the manuscript with which he had been provided and printed a second edition.' Bordalejo 'shows that Caxton was accurate in his statement about the corrections introduced in his second edition of the *Tales*, and that he and his compositors were generally far more careful than some modern scholars have acknowledged'. She uses textual evidence 'from a direct comparison of the two editions' in order to 'demonstrate: that Caxton did more than add and remove lines; that besides those changes, he introduced more than 3000 alterations that originated in a different manuscript source'. Additionally Bordalejo reveals 'that this manuscript source, contained a text closer to the archetype of the tradition' (pp. 41–2). There are three appendices: 'Variants in the "Squire's Tale" '; 'Variants by Tale'; and 'Witness Sigils' of Manuscripts and 'Pre-1501 Printed Editions' (pp. 54–60). In the third article in the March 2014 *Papers of the Bibliographical Society of America*, Peter Robinson writes on 'Henry Delahay Symonds and James Ridgway's Conversion from Whig Pamphleteers to Doyens of the Radical Press, 1788–1793' (*PBSA* 108:i[2014] 61–90). Robinson examines Symonds and Ridgway, about whom personally little is known, 'both highly motivated publisher-booksellers, deeply politicized, and it is argued, politicizing men'. Further 'their political affiliations and orientation appear to have changed considerably between the years 1788 and 1793, a critical period that spanned the entirety of their publishing association with David Williams' and other radicals (p. 62). Indeed they were imprisoned and involved in 'three legal disputes' that reveal 'the long-term and decisive shift by Symonds and Ridgway—the latter perhaps more visibly—towards publishing independence and involvement with a burgeoning radical press, in the process casting off the Whig patronage and ideological identifications of the formative period of their businesses' (p. 89). There are following this article three 'Bibliographical Notes'. In the first of these, and the second contribution in this March issue concerning William Caxton, the prolific A.S.G. Edwards writes on 'Caxton's *Death-Bed Prayers* in Manuscript and Print' (*PBSA* 108:i[2014] 91–6). 'This single sheet broadside . . . was published by William Caxton' around 1484 and 'the only known copy is in the John Rylands Library of the University of Manchester' (p. 91). Edwards is concerned with the fact that the prayers 'enjoyed a quite extensive manuscript tradition' (p. 92) He 'offers . . . a transcription of the Kent State [University Library] version of the prayers' supplemented with a listing of 'Variants Between Kent State MS. And Caxton's Edition' (pp. 95–6). In the second note, Pervez Rizvi writes on 'Stemmata for Shakespeare Texts: A Suggested New Form' (*PBSA* 108:i[2014] 97–106). Supplemented with five diagrams, the article presents 'a small number of examples from current Shakespeare scholarship and [argues] that, at best, they miss the opportunity to combine information more usefully, and, at worst, they inadvertently risk confusing the reader'. The concern 'is solely to recommend to readers a better *form*'; Rizvi is 'not arguing for or against the *content* of the stemmata [he uses] as examples'. Moreover Rizvi concludes 'by suggesting a new design for early modern textual stemmata, one that enables them to be more rigorous, while remaining easy to both compose and comprehend' (pp. 97–8). In the third and final note, Nicholas A. Sparks writes on 'Finding Matthew Parker in Manuscripts of the *Anglo-Saxon Chronicle*' (*PBSA* 108:i[2014] 107–11). Sparks is concerned with identifying the hand of 'the antiquary Robert Talbot' known as 'the "Talbot annotator"' which is 'is not ... Robert Talbot himself' (p. 108). For Sparks 'To persist in referring to the scribe whose hand is found in books, mainly from Parker's collection at Cambridge as the "Talbot annotator" is misleading, and that name is best abandoned'. Ives argues that the 'volumes were either used or owned by Matthew Parker' (p. 109).

The June issue of *The Papers of the Bibliographical Society of America* similarly contains three contributions and in this instance a single 'Bibliographical Note' with one extensive book review (*PBSA* 108:ii[2014] 135)—there are in fact two reviews: in the March issue there were three. William Noblett draws upon contemporary documents in his 'Samuel Paterson and the London Auction Market for Second-Hand Books 1755–1802' (*PBSA* 108:ii[2014] pp. 139–90). For Noblett, Paterson 'had a significant impact on bibliography in its widest sense, and he made an important contribution to the practice of cataloguing'. Moreover 'he is known to have sold and catalogued many libraries including some of the grandest collections of the eighteenth century'. Consequently 'Paterson himself will be remembered as a pioneer-bibliographer and auctioneer whose catalogues can be regarded, and were regarded by his contemporaries, as very significant' (p. 157). Noblett's article concludes with a detailed appendix containing 'A Checklist of Libraries and Collections of Books Catalogued and Sold by Samuel Paterson, 1747–1802', arranged by individual years and accompanied by some descriptive detail (pp. 158–90). In the second article in the June issue, Christopher E. Garrett writes on 'How T.S. Became Known as Thomas Sherman: An Attribution Narrative' (*PBSA* 108:ii[2014] 191–216). Following a most thorough review of the evidence, Garrett concludes that 'it appears that a fictitious figure labeled as Thomas Sherman, a General Baptist preacher and author, was unknowingly but erroneously created to represent a writer who use the initials of T.S.' (p. 216). The third and final article in this June issue is by Kevin Byrne, who writes on '"Simple Devices are Always Best": An Examination of the Amateur Play Publishing Industry in the United States' (*PBSA* 108:ii[2014] 217–37), and draws upon the archives of, amongst others, the Denison company in order to demonstrate that: 'beginning as a collection of individual or family-run companies scattered across the country, the amateur play publishing industry grew and spread rapidly for over a century—acquiring more titles, more sophisticated methods of distribution, and eventually reaching a vast international clientele' (p. 235). A fascinating character whom Byrne discusses is Arthur Kaiser, who pretended to be a typist working at home, and all the while from '1920, and over the next thirty years sold 463 plays to thirteen different publishing houses, including 181 titles to Denison/Northwestern. [He] used sixty pseudonyms.' Moreover Arthur 'Kaiser rarely saw his work performed live' (pp. 232–3). Byrne concludes his interesting research with an appendix. This is a 'Transcription of Arthur Kaiser's hand-written logs, detailing the titles he sent to Denison publishing, if they purchased the work, and his payment' and covering the years 1933 to

1950. Thus, to give one instance on 1 March 1945, his *Riverboat Minstrels*, which was included in an *Amateur's Entertainment Book*—no publishing details are provided—consisted of seven pages; the postal charge isn't recorded and neither is the number of cast characters, features usually logged by Kaiser. He does record that he received $100 for this—that sum being the highest he received for his work (pp. 236–7). Byrne's article is accompanied by four illustrative figures. Anthony James West, an eminent authority on the history and subsequent distribution and locations of Shakespeare's First Folio of 1623, contributes a 'Bibliographical Note'. In his 'Correcting the First Folio's Table of Contents' (*PBSA* 108:ii[2014] 238–42), West provides, accompanied by three illustrative figures, an 'account of the "Troylus and Cressida" inscription in multiple copies [that] offers a tiny lens through which to witness Folio users' responses to the omission of the title in the CATALOGVE' (p. 241)—that is 'the First Folio's Table of Contents' (p. 237). West's contribution is followed by Ian Jackson's extensive review of Eric Rasmussen and Anthony James West's [and others], edited *The Shakespeare First Folio: A Descriptive Catalogue* published in 2012 (*PBSA* 108:ii[2014] 243–8). Jackson courageously doesn't his mince words: 'the exasperated reader might be forgiven for concluding that the *Catalogue* is no more scientific than Japanese whaling, but this would be unfair. Thousands of useful historical or philological needles are hidden somewhere in Rasmussen's tottering bibliographical haystack. All we need is a companion volume to tell us where they are' (p. 254). This June issue concludes with a shorter, largely most positive, review by Susan Hanson of Jeff Weber's *Annotated Dictionary of Fore-Edge Painting Artists & Binders...* [2010]—(*PBSA* 108:ii[2014] 255–8). The September issue follows a similar pattern to the June issue. There are more reviews included; on the other hand, the opening article, Goran Proot's 'Converging Design Paradigms: Long-Term Evolutions in the Layout of Title Pages of Latin and Vernacular Editions Published in the Southern Netherlands, 1541–1660' (*PBSA* 108:iii[2014] 269–305), is not really directly pertinent to *YWES* readers. The other two articles are. In the first Richard Wendorf writes on 'Declaring, Drafting, and Composing American Independence' (*PBSA* 108:iii[2014] 307–24). Accompanied by four black and white illustrative figures, the article pays close attention to Jefferson's 'idiosyncratic treatment of capitalization at the beginning of most sentences... Common nouns are not capitalized within the sentences themselves, and neither are most of the proper nouns' and so on (p. 311). When the Declaration 'left the press, its text was printed in an entirely traditional manner, employing typographical styling that was as conventional as it could be' (p. 315). It 'became public property and was subsequently printed, engrossed, authenticated disseminated throughout the colonies, and— of vital importance—dispatched to the foreign governments that might ally themselves with this fledgling nation'. Of these, 'twenty-five copies are known to survive' (p. 317). Wendorf's concern is with these and the variants within them and subsequent versions. The other article of relevance to *YWES* readers is J. Caitlin Finlayson's 'Thomas Heywood's *Londini Artium & Scientiarum Scaturigo* (1632)—Two Issues or Variant States?' (*PBSA* 108:iii[2014] 325–41). Finlayson examines the 'textual instability' found throughout 'the text of

Heywood's 1632 *Londini Artium & Scientiarum Scaturigo; or, Londons Fountaine of Arts and Sciences* (STC 13347) [that] shows substantial changes within the dedicatory material of the surviving copies, which raises questions about authorial revision, the relationship between the extant copies, and which text is most appropriate as the copy text for any future edition' (p. 327). She carefully examines the two extent copies: these are at the Huntington Library, San Marino, and Worcester College, Library, Oxford—black and white illustrations from both are provided (pp. 332–3). An appendix provides a 'List of Variants' (pp. 339–41) and Finlayson concludes that from the evidence 'that overall, the Huntington copy should be the copy text for any future edition of *Londini Artium*' (p. 338). A 'Bibliographical Note' by Dennis E. Rhodes is concerned with 'Sigieri? Or Ligieri? A Wandering Publisher in Sixteenth-Century Italy' (*PBSA* 108:iii[2014] 343–9). It is followed by Rhodes's 'Bibliographical Notes' on 'The Authorship of Wing F18' (*PBSA* 108:iii[2014] 350–1). Wing F18 refers to *England's Deplorable Condition...*, published in 1859, three copies of which 'are known to exist: [at] the British Library, National Trust, and University of Chicago'. According to Rhodes 'it is certain that Edward Furnise (or Fornis)'—born in 1612—'is the author of...Wing F18' (pp. 350–1). This note is followed by reviews. One of these, by the distinguished scholar of early Italian books and manuscripts and printing history curator at the Newberry Library, Paul F. Gehl, concerns sixteenth-century Italian books (*PBSA* 108:iii[2014] 353–5). The other reviews, two by Meaghan J. Brown, and one by Scott Gwara, relate to Renaissance literature, the library of the Sidney family at Penshurst Place, and a Festschrift for Christopher de Hamel (*PBSA* 108:iii[2014] 356–69). There is too a short review of three paragraphs by Roger E. Stoddard of Bernard M. Rosenthal, the eminent book-seller's, *Autobiography*, published in 2010 (*PBSA* 108:iii[2014] 370).

The final issue for 2014 of *The Papers of the Bibliographical Society of America* has four articles and the annual index to the volume (*PBSA* 108:iv[2014] 523–34). The opening article is a fascinating one. Matthew Kirschenbaum's subject is 'Operating Systems of the Mind: Bibliography After Word Processing (The Example of Updike)' (*PBSA* 108:iv[2014] 381–412). Accompanied by black and white largely photographic illustrations, taken from the Houghton Library at Harvard, John Updike holdings, he describes the problems encountered in working with late twentieth-century and early twenty-first-century writers' materials. Kirschenbaum writes, using at times some rather curious vocabulary, that the 'scholar working with born-digital materials must needs be conversant in the antiquarian cants of vanished operating systems, file systems, file formats, and data structures, as well as tools like hex viewers and emulators, just as we expect an early modernist doing book history to know something of formats, signatures, and collation formulae'. For Kirschenbaum 'the strange but ineluctably material world of digital storage once again instructs us that bibliography itself is not bound to particular media, methods, and tools: it is instead a habit of mind, one we consciously adopt so as to avoid conjuring the minds of printers—and now too, operating systems of the mind' (pp. 411–12). During the last decades of the previous century, various writers used word-processing as a means of composing their work, which was preserved—or so they thought—on disks as opposed to hard copy. These disks are now difficult to download and consequently, if they were not printed out at the time and preserved, then the content may indeed be lost. Although it is sometimes difficult to discern from Kirschenbaum's text, it does appear that what Updike placed on disk has been preserved in other forms. Whether the same is the case for others is no doubt the subject for future research. On a personal note, I was responsible for transferring much of the archive of the distinguished British writer Bernard Kops (b. 1927) to the Harry Ransom Research Center at the University of Texas at Austin in the early years of the present century. Kops used a word-processor and disks: it is to be hoped that the excellent librarians at the Ransom have found a way to download these diskettes and to preserve the creative work on them. In the second contribution to the December issue, Claire M.L. Bourne's concern is 'Dramatic Pilcrows' (*PBSA* 108:iv[2014] 413–52). None of the previous scholarship 'has ventured to account for why these particular pieces of type feature so prominently on the pages of the printed plays in the first place—beyond the suggestion that they represent the residue of scribal practice'. Moreover they are omitted in modern editions of early sixteenth-century plays. These opt rather 'for modern conventions of dramatic *mise-en-page*'. However, 'the type-facsimiles in the Malone Society Reprints series are obvious exceptions' (p. 413). Accompanied by twelve illustrative black and white figurative examples, the article concludes that 'pilcrows and other pieces of special type ... offered the early makers of English playbooks a material-textual means by which to organize the play reading experience around the peculiarities and conventions of dramatic form' (p. 452). Another century and country engage John J. Garcia in his 'The "Curious Affaire"' of Mason Locke Weems: Nationalism, the Book Trade, and Printed Lives in the Early United States' (*PBSA* 108:iv[2014] 435–75). Accompanied by three illustrative figures from Weems's (1759–1825) work, the article demonstrates the relationship between 'the bookseller, minister and popular writer' (p. 453), Weems, whose *The Life Of George Washington* was first published in 1813 and 'kept in standing type for nearly thirty years' (p. 466), and 'how the bookseller's cultivation of stimuli extended beyond the curiosity of public spectacle to the shape and feel of the book itself'. Garcia 'reconsiders the impact of American biographies on early US nationalism in light of a bibliographical analysis attuned to structural questions of production and distribution' (pp. 453–4). Interestingly, 'Weems's *Life of Washington* appears to progressively decay over the course of nearly thirty years of reprinting'. This 'should interest bibliographers and literary scholars alike, since this curious little book was popular, ideologically and culturally significant, and distributed by an itinerant bookseller whose correspondence ceaselessly reflects upon the place of the physical book, in all its aspects, in the production of a national literature' (p. 474). The final contribution to the 2014 issues of *The Papers of the Bibliographical Society of America*, Elizabeth Upper's 'Red Frisket Sheets, ca. 1490–1700: The Earliest Artifacts of Color Printing in the West' (*PBSA* 108:iv[2014] 477–522) is accompanied by eleven black and white illustrative figures and ten colour-plate illustrative examples. Upper's paper 'introduces a growing corpus of thirty fragments comprising twenty-three, other early modern frisket sheets for color printing' (p. 478). Upper's research adds to 'the increasing interest in early modern printers' working methods, continuing the material turn for the study of early modern printed material in fields including literature and art history'. Additionally Upper 'offers a case study that explains the significance of these fragments for the understanding of early modern books as material texts, in some cases physically linking manuscript culture to print culture' (p. 479). In an appendix, 'Early Modern Frisket Sheet Fragments' (pp. 518–22), Upper details 'the known early modern fragments of frisket sheets used for printing in red at the time [her] article went to press'. There are twenty-two of these (p. 518).

Yet again readers of *YWES* will find much to interest them in the articles published in *The Library: The Transactions of the Bibliographical Society*. The March issue contains the eminent Rochester scholar Nicholas Fisher's 'Rochester's Poems on Several Occasions, 1680: Some Further Light' (*Library* 15:i[2014] 45–62). Fisher's article, accompanied by four black and white illustrative figures 'represents a first step towards uncovering the full history surrounding the 1680 editions' (p. 61). Analytical bibliographical investigation is represented in Nicholas Pickwoad's 'Binders' Gatherings' (*Library* 15:i[2014] 63–78). Accompanied by a plethora of black and white illustrative figures, Pickwoad concludes by observing that 'In all the examples' he has discussed he has shown that binders have for one reason or another 'created new gatherings out of the material that they have been asked to bind'. For Pickwoad 'reasons for this may have been economic, practical or remedial, and the results pleasing and functional to a greater or lesser extent'. However, 'all show how binders can interfere with the original make-up of a book in the interests of placing a readable book in the hands of its readers'. Consequently Pickwoad writes 'that when discussing gatherings, the binders' gathering is a force to be reckoned with' (p. 78). Articles in the June issue include David Stoker's 'Another Look at the Dicey-Marshall Publications: 1736–1806' (*Library* 15:ii[2014] 111–57). As Stoker indicates in his abstract, 'the two London presses in Bow Churchyard and Aldermary Churchyard, which were founded by William and Cluer Dicey, are well known to have published a wide range of popular publications during the middle years of the eighteenth century'. The Dicey family operated the first from 1736 to 1763. They then in 1754 created the Aldermary-based business. This was run 'by their junior partner, Richard Marshall, who became an equal partner in 1764 and the proprietor in 1770'. His son John operated this business from 1779 until 1806 and then it moved to Fleet Street. However, Stoker observes 'many details concerning the dates of operation of the presses and the business relationship between the two families are not well understood and a number of misconceptions' have developed. Consequently he 'seeks to collate recently discovered evidence and survey the output of the presses, explaining how the Aldermary business came to be restructured at the turn of the nineteenth century'   (http://muse.jhu.edu/journals/lbt/summary/v015/15.2.stoker.htm). There are two appendices. The first lists the 'Dicey-Marshall Premises in London 1736–1806' (pp. 155–6). The second provides an account of the 'Dating [of] Dicey-Marshall Publications' (p. 157). In addition to these articles, there are two 'Bibliographical Notes' in this issue that will be of interest.

The first is Christopher D. Cook and Miriam M. Foot's 'An Additional Incunabulum in Westminster Abbey Library' (*Library* 15:ii[2014] 185–6). The second, by Alan Rogers, deals with 'The Ownership of *The Myrour of Recluses* (British Library, MS Harley 2372) in the Late Fifteenth Century' (*Library* 15:ii[2014] 187–92).

The September issue contains John D. Gordan III's 'John Nutt: Trade Publisher and Printer "In the Savoy"' (*Library* 15:iii[2014] 243–60). Gordan investigates the trade publishing activity of John Nutt during the years 1698 and 1706 and subsequently until his death in 1716. During his last decade he was the printer 'in the Savoy' (p. 243) of *The Tatler*. He also printed law books in his role as the royal law printing patent assignee. Gordan pays particular attention to Nutt's printing from 1708 and continued after his death by Elizabeth, his widow, and then in partnership with Richard their son, of multivolume serial publications and their championing of this specific type of publication format. In an appendix, 'Bibliographical Beginnings of "The Atlas Geographus"' (pp. 258–60), a specific time line is provided for this multivolume serial publication. Paul Davis, in his 'Popery and Publishing in the Restoration Crisis: A Whig Gentry Family's Credit Account with their London Bookseller, 1680–1683' (*Library* 15:iii[2014] 261–91), drawing upon primary materials from 'a collection of estate papers' (p. 261) now at the University of Nottingham Library, presents the bill of a London bookseller recording seventy-seven purchases made by a Nottinghamshire gentry family during the period from July 1680 to January 1683. There are three illustrations and a detailed listing of 'Identifications' of the purchases and descriptions with the appropriate Wing numbers and other bibliographical references (pp. 272–91). Jordan Howell's 'Eighteenth-Century Abridgements of *Robinson Crusoe*' (*Library* 15:iii[2014] 292–342) adds to our knowledge of 'bibliographical or historical scholarship on the *Robinson Crusoe* abridgements' that is lacking. The paucity of existing 'scholarship serves only to further marginalize and devalue hundreds of texts that played an important role in popularizing and canonizing *Robinson Crusoe*' (p. 293). Four appendices analytically compare in various statistical forms abridged and unabridged *Robinson Crusoe* publications in English published between 1719 and 1800 (pp. 319–42). The September issue also contains a 'Bibliographical Note' worthy of attention. Dennis E. Rhodes, in his 'Bernard Hampton and His Books' (*Library* 15:iii[2014] 343–6), identifies Barnard or Bernard Hampton as a clerk of the council and Queen Mary's Spanish secretary, who died in 1572. Rhodes lists and describes the books that have so far been identified as Hampton's. The December issue opens with Alison Walker's account of 'Sir Hans Sloane and the Library of Dr. Luke Rugeley' (*Library* 15:iv[2014] 383–409). Walker notes that 'Sir Hans Sloane (1660–1753) was one of the greatest collectors of his age, and books formed the largest single category of his collections.' Moreover, for him, books served a triple purpose as 'objects of value and curiosity in themselves, as well as aids for his successful practice as a physician, and tools for the study and management of his ever-expanding collections of specimens and objects'. Sloane used diverse channels to acquire his books and he obtained them especially through book auctions. Walker draws on information in specific copies assembled by the Sloane Printed Books Project at the

British Library, in order to examine 'Sloane's activities as a successful bidder at the auction of the library of another physician, Luke Rugeley, in early 1697' (p. 383). Walker's article is accompanied by eleven black and white figurative illustrations from sale catalogues and books. There are four appendices. The first contains 'Books from Rugeley's Library Acquired by Sloane in 1696' (pp. 399–405). The second lists 'Other Books in Sloane's Collection which Probably Derived from Rugeley's' (p. 406). The third concerns 'Other Books Priced in the Rugeley Sale Catalogue but which Cannot Be Firmly Identified with Sloane's Copies' (p. 407), and the final appendix details 'Other Books Annotated in the Hand Shown in Fig. 2 [copies of books Sloane acquired] but Not Located in Rugeley's Sale Catalogue' (pp. 408–9). In the article that follows, Alexandra da Costa, ' "Functional Ambiguity": Negotiating Censorship in the 1530s' (*Library* 15:iv[2014] 410–23), concludes that 'Censorship may have become theoretically more practicable with the arrival of print, but sophisticated ways of negotiating its restrictions developed remarkably fast. Such negotiations were not just a matter of disguising forbidden material, but a process of implicit accommodation between printers and the royal agenda' (p. 423). In her article she looks at the ways in which 'the strictures of censorship were negotiated in the early 1530s and uses the publication in London of the evangelical Patrick Hamilton's abbreviated theses by Thomas Godfray (RSTC 12731.6) as an illustrative case study' (p. 421). Additionally, the December issue has three 'Bibliographical Notes' of interest. In the first, E.A. Jones's '*A Mirror for Recluses*: A New Manuscript, New Information and Some New Hypotheses' (*Library* 15:iv[2014] 424–31), 'alerts the scholarly community to a newly-discovered manuscript of *A Mirror for Recluses*, a fifteenth-century English translation of the Latin rule for recluses, *Speculum Inclusorum*. The new manuscript includes substantial amounts of text that are missing from the only other extant copy, and it begins with a previously unknown translator's prologue. The latter (here transcribed in full) provides a date for the translation, and some substantial clues to provenance' (p. 424). In the second, Christopher D. Cook, ' "Mr Royston I Preye Send These Bookes": An Oxford Bookseller's Wife's Order of 1650' (*Library* 15:iv[2014] 432–8), 'publishes a 1650 book order written by Alice Curteyne—wife of the Oxford bookseller Henry Curteyne—and sent to Richard Royston in London. The order survived as binding waste and provides further evidence of the role of women in the seventeenth-century English book trade.' Accompanied by figurative illustrations, the article transcribes 'a book order from Alice Curteyne, wife of the Oxford bookseller Henry Curteyne, to the London bookseller Richard Royston' now at the University of Illinois, Urbana-Champaign. 'She requests at least eighty-three copies from seventeen contemporary editions.' The 'document provides further primary evidence of the role of women in the English book trade, the trade in books between London and the provinces, and the Oxford book market in the middle of the seventeenth century' (p. 432). The final note is by John McTague, whose subject is '*The New Atalantis* Arrests: A Reassessment' (*Library* 15:iv[2014] 439–46). Drawing upon arrest warrants issued on 28 September 1709, now at the National Archives in London, on the instructions of the earl of Sunderland acting in his capacity as a secretary of state,

McTague demonstrates that Delarivier Manley's biographers have been misled. The warrants (transcribed by McTague, p. 440) 'substantiate' the narrative 'related in Manley's *pseudo*-autobiographical *The Adventures of Rivella* (1709) as well as lending some insight into the processes of drafting and issuing warrants for arrest in Sunderland's office' (p. 439). All four issues of The *Library* contain excellent reviews of recent bibliographical and textual publications.

The *Eighteenth-Century Intelligencer*, edited by James E. May, offered several bibliographical and textual articles of note. The March issue begins with James Woolley's 'Editing Swift: Problems and Possibilities', the East-Central American Society for Eighteenth-Century Studies 2013 Presidential Address (*ECIntell* 28:i[2014] 1–6). Woolley, the editor of Swift and Thomas Sheridan's *The Intelligencer*, here also reflects on insights from co-editing with Stephen Karian Swift's poems for a projected four volumes of the Cambridge Edition of Swift. Woolley identifies various problems involving the editing of poems also widely circulated in manuscript. He also surveys various digital projects and editions, including the *Jonathan Swift Archive*, edited by James McLaverty et al. (http://jonathanswiftarchive.org.uk), and the *Online.Swift* edition, edited in Münster by Hermann J. Real, Kirsten Juhas, Dirk Passmann, and Sandra Simon (http://www.online-swift.de/), and announces plans for a 'complementary digitized edition [of the poems] that we expect to make freely available on the web' (p. 2). There is an erudite application of geographical literature, including books owned and not owned by Jonathan Swift, in Hermann J. Real's re-examination of a disputed incident late in Book III of *Gulliver's Travels*: 'The Trampling-upon-the-Crucifix Episode, Again' (*ECIntell* 28:i[2014] 12–22). The September issue contains James E. May's critique 'Are They Keeping Up? A Cursory Inspection' in September 2014 of the Modern Language Association's *International Bibliography* and MHRA's *Annual Bibliography of English Language and Literature* (*ECIntell* 28:ii[2014] 16–22). May's assessment of recent coverage on the two online bibliographies reveals that they often achieve very rapid postings for some journals, but that there are 'surprising gaps' in coverage, with 'important journals and books neglected, particularly in ... foreign-language publications overseas' (p. 16). The article compares the relative coverage of *MLAIB* and *ABELL*, and lists dozens of examples of recent journals, books, and scholarly websites missing from the bibliographies. In the March *Intelligencer*, one of the eleven book reviews is Robert D. Hume's examination of *Thomas Killigrew and the Seventeenth-Century English Stage: New Perspectives*, edited by Philip Major [2013], in which Hume corrects many scholarly errors and omissions, bringing much new detail to the bibliographical record (*ECIntell* 28:ii[2014] 32–41).

Script & Print (*BSANZB*) the quarterly bulletin of the Bibliographical Society of Australia and New Zealand, continues to appear regularly and produce articles of considerable interest. The 2014 issues continue in this tradition with each also having an arresting colour cover image. The front dust jacket of the 1965 first edition of G. M. Glaskin's *No End to the Way*, 'the novel for which he is most remembered today', graces the initial 2014 issue. The first article is an important one by Per Henningsgaard, Kristen Colgin, and Clyde Veleker. They write on 'A Pedagogical Tool for Studying the

History of the Book: Thirty-Five Years of Bibliographical Presses in Australia and New Zealand, 1977–2012' (*BSANZB* 38:i[2014] 5–25). Essentially this is an update of B.J. McMullin's survey of 'Bibliographical Presses in Australia and New Zealand' (*BSANZB* 3:ii[1977] 55–64). Henningsgaard, during the 2009 to 2012 period, 'conducted yet another survey (the results of which are published for the first time in this article) to determine the fate of the bibliographical press in Australia and New Zealand. A questionnaire was sent to all the universities of Australia and New Zealand.' The findings were 'that only two presses (University of Otago and Victoria University of Wellington) are functioning as bibliographical presses in Australia and New Zealand today' (p. 5). Various reasons are put forward for this, including the inappropriateness of the definition of a 'bibliographical press' (p. 6). Henningsgaard, Colgin, and Veleker write that, for instance, the 'University of Sydney's press never operated as a bibliographical press'; moreover, 'other presses that never actually operated as bibliographical presses include Australian national University, University of Canterbury (Underoak Press, School of Fine Arts), University of Melbourne and University of Canterbury (Department of English)' (p. 7). They write that the participants in the survey gave 'the most common explanation offered for the decline in bibliographical presses [as] the lack of staff to carry on the study of bibliography'. To cite one illustration 'Massey University's press folded in 2001 when its founder retired'—the eminent bibliographer John C. Ross, who was not replaced. Also the presses in their initial inception were associated in some way or other with 'the private press movement that first began in the 1960s' and subsequently declined (p. 11). Interestingly 'the work of a new set of scholars, especially in the 1970s and 1980s . . . sparked a new approach for studying the history of the book'. There was a notable 'shift from bibliography to book history'. Further 'the confluence of these two circumstances—the private press movement and new ideas about the influence of print—surrounding the foundation of bibliographical presses created a small explosion of interest in the printing press. This could explain why some universities began to acquire printing presses and look for ways to incorporate bibliography into their curriculum' (p. 12). Henningsgaard, Colgin, and Veleker write that 'since book history really only began to take shape as a discipline distinct from bibliography in the 1980s or even 1990s, it is possible we are in the middle of an analogous lag with regard to the pedagogical tools that will make this discipline appear more relevant to today's students' (p. 12). When the history of bibliography during the last decades of the twentieth century comes to be written, their article will serve as a valuable reference tool. It concludes with 'summary histories of each bibliographical press' post-McMullin (p. 14): fifteen are included, with responses from those individually involved with them in the past and to some extent in the present (pp. 15–25). As the authors comment in their concluding sentence: 'the history of bibliographical presses is full of people with good intentions that, for one reason or another, cannot be realized' (p. 25). This article is not only applicable to Australia and New Zealand but also to the situation in North America where in some state universities units producing bibliographical materials in the form of bibliographies or journals no longer exist or indeed have much interest for the university or the majority of its faculty or administration who previously supported such endeavours.

Stefanie Rudig, in her 'The Colonial Newspaper as a Stepping Stone for the Victorian New Zealand Writer: A Case Study of Louisa Alice Baker' (*BSANZB* 38:i[2014] 26–38), 'through a case study of the early writing career of Louisa Alice Baker (1856–1926), who came to New Zealand with her family through the assisted immigration scheme and settled near Christchurch in 1863 . . . analyzes what it meant to write and publish, or rather attempt to publish, in late Victorian New Zealand'. Rudig 'explores the importance of the colonial newspaper as the initial platform for the professional New Zealand writer as well as the tension between colonial authors and centres of power' (p. 26). Rudig concludes that 'even authors like Louisa Alice Baker, who successfully published both in England and America, complained bitterly that "a story with an English setting is of three times the value in London, commercially, of one with a colonial background." Yet, in her time Baker was hailed as "a colonial George Eliot," and managed to earn a living through her novels and freelance writing, prolifically contributing to the publishing landscape of her two "home countries"' (p. 38). Jeremy Fisher, in his 'A Professional Author—How G.M. Glaskin Earned a Living' (*BSANZB* 38:i[2014] 39–56), provides an account of the 'Western Australian author Gerald Marcus Glaskin [1923–2000; who] wrote from life, using his experiences to continually expand his creative repertoire'. As Fisher points out, 'in one sense, this was to be his downfall, as his life was unconventional for his time. Because he mined own experiences so much in his creative writing, his works eventually moved out of mainstream markets. However, [Fisher's] paper focuses on his financial success as a writer, details of which can be documented through study of the meticulous records kept by both [Glaskin] and his publisher, Barrie & Rockliff of London' (p. 39). Fisher concludes 'that being able to live off the proceeds of literary creation requires hard work, determination and considerable skills in business and time management. To have a talent for writing is certainly useful, especially', as is the case with Glaskin, 'it permits a writer to turn his or her hand to numerous forms and genres, but to achieve great success luck and serendipity probably play a greater role. This will not provide comfort to a would-be author, though it might offer some solace to one at the other end of his or her career' (p. 56).

The second issue of *Script & Print* contains five articles. In the first Lachy Paterson writes on 'Visual Identity in *Niupepa Māori* Nameplates and Title-Pages: From Traditional to Aspirational' (*BSANZB* 38:ii[2014] 67–79), which is accompanied by ten illustrative black and white figures and examines '*niupepa* (Māori-language newspaper[s]', their use of nameplates and title pages (p. 67). Paterson concludes that 'many [of them] did not use a pictorial design as a front cover page, or as part of their nameplate, but where they do appear they are clearly attempting to visually reinforce the textual messages of the newspaper, or to appeal to the readership in some way' (p. 79). The second article is J.E. Traue's 'Treasured Up on Purpose to a Life Beyond Life: A Public Lecture Delivered at the Opening of the 2013 Centre for the Book Symposium, Dunedin, 17 October 2013' (*BSANZB* 38:ii[2014] 80–93). It 'serves as a prologue to the . . . essays from that symposium that will be published as a special issue' in the September *Script & Print* (p. 80). Traue 'survey[s] the collecting tradition in New Zealand as it developed in the nineteenth and early twentieth centuries... look[s] at recent trends in overseas private and institutional collecting and the extent to which they are reflected in New Zealand, and... outline[s] the likely shape of private and institutional collecting in the future' (pp. 81–2). Overall, Traue is not over-optimistic regarding the present state or future of book collecting on most fronts. Shef Rogers, in 'Reflections on National Structures as a Basis for Print Culture Histories in the Twenty-First Century' (*BSANZB* 38:ii[2014] 94–109), demonstrates from various examples 'that literature disproportionately influences print culture, because an infrastructure of awards, advertising and reviews gives currency to the ideas in those books even if the books themselves have not been widely read' and further that 'books do not circulate as freely or widely as scholars might have imagined, and, as a consequence, book history does benefit from the structures of national boundaries' (p. 94). Rogers concludes, 'we still need much more research, from many different countries, to determine just how, when and why books move beyond their borders of production' (p. 103). Rogers provides an appendix listing availability of selected 2012 prize-winning books '(based on searches conducted in May-June 2013)' (pp. 104–9). B.J. McMullin continues to demonstrate that analytical bibliography is alive and well. His 'In 18s, signed $1, 5, 7, 9' (*BSANZB* 38:ii[2014] 110–14), examines 'the unusual practice of signing 45, 7, 9 (as $"2", "3", "4") in volumes gathered in eighteens, a practice exemplified by a handful of "chapbooks" in the Alexander Turnbull Library (ATL), National Library of New Zealand, but apparently not employed in the printing of any of the 761 items described' in John Meriton and Carlo Dumontet's *Small Books for the Common Man: A Descriptive Bibliography*, published in 2010 (p. 110). McMullin's contribution is followed by Patrick Spedding's description and discussion of 'Cancelled Errata in *John Buncle, Junior, Gentleman*' by Thomas Cogan, first published in 1776 (*BSANZB* 38:ii[2014] 115–21).

The September 2014 *Script & Print* is a special issue devoted to collectors and collecting, edited by Donald Kerr and Shef Rogers. In the opening essay Donald Kerr, 'Collectors: That Happy Band of Patriots' (*BSANZB* 38:iii[2014] 129–33), reflects on what motivates book collectors, and introduces the four papers that follow selected from those given at the one-day symposium held at the University of Otago Centre for the Book at Toitū Early Settlers Museum on 18 October 2013 (p. 131). The first, Rosi Crane's 'Stomachs and Serials in Nineteenth-Century Dunedin' (*BSANZB* 38:iii[2014] 134–43), is concerned with the collecting activities of 'Thomas Jeffery Parker (1850–97), first professor of biology at the University of Otago in 1880, and curator of the Otago Museum' (p. 132) and his obsession with collecting and preserving 'Stomachs and intestines' and 'zoological specimens' (p. 134). Crane concludes that 'for Parker and men like him the printed word was more than a useful adjunct: acquiring a working library was essential for tasks like researching the collections or experimenting with preservation techniques' (p. 143). In the second essay Merete Colding Smith is concerned with 'F.C. Morgan of Hereford (1878–1978): Collector and Benefactor' (*BSANZB* 38:iii[2014] 144–58. Illustrated by relevant and helpful black and white figures—as are many of the other contributions to *Script & Print*—Smith's concern is 'the collector, librarian and antiquarian F.C. Morgan . . . who lived in England all his life but donated his substantial collection of historical English children's books to the University of Melbourne in 1954'. Smith discusses 'why and how Morgan came to donate his collection to the University of Melbourne and his relationship with the University'. In addition by examining Morgan's life, Smith considers 'how he became a collector, what kind of collector he was, how he collected and the role of his daughter Penelope in his life as a collector' (p. 144). His reasons for choosing Melbourne were complex; however, 'the close political and emotional relationship between Australia and Britain at the time was a significant factor in both Morgan's decision to donate and the University's delight to receive the collection' (p. 147). David Bell, in the third essay from the symposium, writes on 'Japan in New Zealand: Collecting Art in Times of Conflict' (*BSANZB* 38:iii[2014] 159–76). Bell 'examines the print collections accumulated by four figures: Sir Joseph Kinsey (1852–1936), Ronald Stevens Munro (d. 1985), Major Keith Robert Mosheim (1919–87), and Francis Aubrey Shurrock (1919–2012)'. Bell 'describes the ways their different collecting agendas developed in relation to periods of international conflict and suggests their collecting interests reflected important trends in New Zealand's changing experiences of Japan and its place in the world during the twentieth century' (p. 159). The final essay, David Goodwin's 'Literary Cartography and the Collecting of Place and Experience, with Specific Reference to Collecting Arthur Ransome' (*BSANZB* 38:iii[2014] 177–90), describes the experience of a Ransome collector. Bell focuses on two particular areas of Ransome collecting: 'what [he terms] the "collecting of place," namely visiting and exploring places about which Ransome wrote. And second, what [he calls] the "collecting of experience," namely cultivating such skills as sailing and signalling, or engaging in pursuits such as camping, bird watching, and walking and exploring inspired by Ransome's work.' Bell consequently 'sets the context of a personal Ransome collection and then focuses on a question not adequately addressed by the literature, namely whether the use of cartography and the correspondence of literary territory with real places may influence collecting' (p. 177).

The December 2014 issue of *Script & Print* contains four contributions. In the first, Katherine Bode and Carol Hetherington describe 'Retrieving a World of Fiction: Building an Index—and an Archive—of Serialized Novels in Australian Newspapers, 1850–1914' (*BSANZB* 38:iv[2014] 197–211). The development of the archive is explained through their 'Methodology' (pp. 199–202), bibliography, and the issues raised (pp. 202–7), and 'Epistemology' (pp. 207–11). Bode and Hetherington conclude: 'In adding detail after detail to our picture of fiction serialized in Australian newspapers, this index and full-text archive, and the digital methods that enable its construction, provide the means by which to understand progressively more about the complexity, richness and cultural importance of this key aspect of print culture' (p. 211). In the second essay, Elizabeth Nichol's subject is explicitly stated in her title 'Bookseller, Circulating Library Owner, Printer, Publisher, Agent, Raconteur, Freemason, Volunteer Soldier and Cricket Enthusiast—John Varty's

Auckland Career, 1858–1868' (*BSANZB* 38:iv[2014] 212–28). The 'indefatigable' Varty, after contributing so much to Auckland in ten years, departed for Melbourne. However 'the financial bad luck (and/or naivety) which had beset him in Auckland followed him to Australia and he died aged fifty' in 1882 'in Adelaide leaving his wife and family' destitute. Nichol concludes that 'through examining his various enterprises we learn much of bookselling, printing and publishing activities in the growing Auckland metropolis and the manifold undertakings early practitioners had to turn their hands to in order to survive' (p. 228). The subject of Rachel Solomon's 'Two Studies: Henry Handel Richardson and the Great Extractor' (*BSANZB* 38:iv[2014] 229–48) is the relationship between Henry Handel Richardson (1870–1946), the Australian author, and 'Jacob Schwartz (b. 1899), of the Ulysses Bookshop' in London. Schwartz approached Richardson 'to publish some of his short stories in fine, limited edition booklets'. Solomon draws upon a plethora of previously unpublished manuscript archival material in her 'examination of the history of this fine print publication, and the relationship between the author and the publisher, within the context of the literary and publishing market of the late 1920s and early 1930s' (p. 229). The final contribution to the 2014 issues of *Script & Print* that contain so much of interest, are 'Responses to Patrick Spedding "Cancelled Errata in *John Buncle, Junior, Gentleman*" (*Script & Print* 38.2, 115–21)' (*BSANZB* 38:iv[2014] 249–52), from Carlo Dumontet, Brian McMullin, John Lancaster, Richard Nobel, and, last but by no means least, G. Thomas Tanselle, demonstrating that interest in the arcane areas of analytical bibliography is alive and well.

The second issue of *Textual Cultures*, published late in 2013 contains much of interest to *YWES* readers. Margaret Maurer and Dennis Flynn, in their 'The Text of *Goodf* and John Donne's Itinerary in April 1613' (*TC* 8:ii[2013] 50–94) are concerned with 'Two manuscript copies of John Donne's poem entitled in the first edition of his poems "Goodfriday, 1613. Riding Westward" [that] came to light in the 1970s, both in the hand of Nathaniel Rich, an acquaintance of Donne and a member of a family with whom Donne had other connections'. Maurer and Flynn amplify previous 'analysis of these manuscripts to argue for their importance. The versions of the poem they convey are coherent and substantially different from its received text, and geographical indications in their headings are compatible with a 1613 journey Donne may have made in the company of Rich himself or someone Rich knew. In relation to the canonical version of Donne's poem, these two manuscripts seem to record a revising mind at work, possibly Rich's, conceivably that of Donne himself' (p. 50). There are two illustrative figures for Donne's possible routes and four appendices. The first is a transcription of a manuscript in private hands of Donne's poem accompanied by a figurative copy of it (pp. 83–5). The second is a transcription of a manuscript of the poem in the Robert Taylor Collection at Princeton University Library (pp. 86–7). The third appendix lists variants against the Manuscript Groups, early editions, and Helen Gardner's 1978 text (pp. 88–90), and the fourth appendix provides manuscript headings for '*Goodf*' (p. 91). Activity in a slightly earlier decade engages I.R. Burrows in his ' "The peryod of my blisse" Commas, Ends and Utterance in *Solyman and Perseda*' (*TC* ii[2013] 95–120). Burrows is concerned with 'evidence that commas were used in the Edward Allde print shop to denote a particular kind of interruption', and draws out how 'an attention to those interruptions shapes a reading of the 1592 play *Solyman and Perseda*, often attributed to Thomas Kyd'. Burrows 'suggests that greater levels of literary interpretation are evinced in early modern compositors' work than is normally acknowledged, and that this should be brought to bear on the editing and discussion of the texts they produced' (p. 95). Burrows provides an appendix with diagrammatical representation on the subject of 'Compositorial Labour on *Solyman and Perseda* 1592' (pp. 114–19). A much more recent literary production preoccupies Ronald Bush and David Ten Eyck in their 'A Critical Edition of Ezra Pound's *Pisan Cantos*: Problems and Solutions' (*TC* ii[2013] 121–41). They argue that 'a critical edition of the *Pisan Cantos* will bring discussion about points such as these out of the realm of conjecture. It will not resolve the ambiguities of a supremely difficult poem, but it may make it possible to concentrate with new confidence on what Pound actually wrote'. Using six illustrative figures, the 'points' (p. 140) they raise are conveyed in their sections on 'The Textual History of the *Pisan Cantos*' (pp. 124–31), the need for 'A New Edition of the *Pisan Cantos*' (pp. 132–6), and 'The Importance of a New Critical Edition of the *Pisan Cantos*' (pp. 136–40).

A quarterly journal that contains much of interest is *Library & Information History*, formerly *Library History*. The 2014 issues continue this tradition. Hyder Abbas, in an essay accompanied by extensive footnote documentation, writes on ' "A Fund of Entertaining and Useful Information": Coffee Houses, Early Public Libraries and the Print Trade in Eighteenth-Century Dublin' (*LH* 30:i[2014] 41–61). In addition to extensive reviews of recent books, the February issue concludes with Katherine Birkwood and Edward Howard's useful enumerative, alphabetically arranged bibliography of recent publications in 'Library History' and 'Information History' (*LH* 30:i[2014] 64–72). In the May issue, Emma Jay's subject is 'Court Patronage Reconsidered: The English Literature in Queen Caroline's Library' (*LH* 30:ii[2014] 75–89). Jay 'examines the records of the library of Queen Caroline of Ansbach (1683–1737), wife of George II, focusing on the holdings of English poetry, drama, and prose fiction. [She] argues that Caroline's English literary patronage has been underestimated, and that several members of her court were also active literary patrons.' She believes that 'looking at Caroline's library can help us understand the nature and extent of early Hanoverian court patronage' (p. 75). Jay's article includes a colour illustration and 114 notes. Vivienne Dunstan, in her 'Professions, Their Private Libraries, and Wider Reading Habits in Late Eighteenth- and Early Nineteenth-Century Scotland' (*LH* 30:ii[2014] 110–28), using four tables and two illustrative figures 'studies professionals, a group particularly relevant to Scottish reading culture in the late eighteenth and early nineteenth centuries'. Dunstan uses 'a variety of case studies' and draws 'on evidence such as library borrowing records, evidence of book ownership, and readers' diaries and lists of books read. Issues explored include the private libraries that professionals built, the balance between work-related reading and their wider recreational reading interests, how professionals compared to other readers in Scotland and further afield, and change over time' (p. 110). Katherine Birkwood and Edward Howard continue their useful enumerative, alphabetically arranged bibliography of recent publications in 'Library History' and 'Information History' (*LH* 30:ii[2014] 143–50). Tracey Hill's research is found in the August issue. Her subject is 'Owners and Collectors of the Printed Books of the Early Modern Lord Mayor's Shows' (*LH* 30:iii[2014] 151–71) and is accompanied by seven illustrative figures. Hill writes that 'The annual London Lord Mayor's Show, which saw its heyday in the early modern period, exists in printed form from 1585. These books stand as permanent witnesses to an ephemeral event. Until quite recently they have not been subject to any thoroughgoing bibliographical study however.' She 'explores the evidence that remains of readers' ownership of and interactions with these works from the seventeenth century to the end of the eighteenth'. Moreover 'copies of these works were owned by collectors including Humphrey Dyson, Robert Burton, Anthony Wood, and John Philip Kemble'. Consequently, according to Hill, 'through an exploration of handlists and annotations, one can discover how these books were collected and categorized. Such an analysis reveals not just the original cultural meaning of these works but also the ways in which owners and collectors identified them in generic terms thus suggesting their changing value to readers' (p. 151). Of interest too are John C. Crawford's ' "The High State of Culture to which This Part of the Country Has Attained": Libraries, Reading, and Society in Paisley, 1760–1830' (*LH* 30:iii[2014] 172–94); Sterling Joseph Coleman, Jr., ' "Eminently Suited to Girls and Women": The Numerical Feminization of Public Librarianship in England 1914–31' (*LH* 30:iii[2014] 195–209); and also in this August issue Birkwood and Howard's bibliography (*LH* 30:iii[2014] 225–32). The November issue of *Library History* contains David J. Gary on 'Reading Roman History to Understand the French Revolution: Rufus King's Commonplacing of Edward Gibbon, 1799–1803' (*LH* 30:iv[2014] 233–53). Rufus King, who served as the American minister to Great Britain from 1799 to 1803, 'kept two commonplace books recording extracts on Roman history mostly culled from the works of Edward Gibbon. King adapted Gibbon's texts for his own means and used them in an attempt to understand the confusing events of the French Revolutionary period.' They 'show an anxious, yet hopeful, diplomat reading with three questions in mind: How could he be the best possible representative for his nation? How could he defend republican government from the challenges presented by the French Revolution? And, lastly, what was the nature of the new Atlantic-world revolutions and how could they be avoided or constrained?' (p. 233). In addition to the regular informative book reviews, appropriately the 2014 issues of *Library & Information History* conclude with Birkwood and Howard's bibliography (*LH* 30:iv[2014] 305–11).

Four issues of the *Journal of Scholarly Publishing* appeared in 2014. Of especial interest in the January issue are Rachel Soloveichik's 'Books as Capital Assets' (*JScholP* 45:ii[2014] 101–27). She 'finds that authors and publishers released book manuscripts with a value of $9.1 billion in 2007. The $9.1 billion covers the cost of authors writing the manuscript, and publishers editing the manuscript and completing other pre-publication work. Once publishers have a copyrighted book manuscript, they then print physical copies and sell those copies to the public.' Soloveichik 'only studies the intangible capital asset' known as 'book manuscripts'. She writes that 'physical books are a consumer good that is tracked elsewhere in the national accounts'. In her article she is 'referring to the intangible asset and not the physical copy' (pp. 101–2). In the article before the regular reviews Steven E. Gamp writes on 'Recovery the Covering Letter: Submitting the Mss to Scholarly Journals in the Twenty-First Century' (*JScholP* 45:ii[2014] 172–85): Gamp's article is North America-based. In the April issue, of particular interest is James Mulholland's 'What I've Learned about Publishing a Book' (*JScholP* 45:iii[2014] 211–36). His 'article seeks to inform authors—particularly first-time academic authors—about the overlooked details and unanticipated tasks that emerge during the production and publication of an academic book' (p. 211). It also contains acute advice relating to post-publication marketing and advertising, on the importance of continuous promotion of the book (pp. 231–4). The July issue contains tributes: 'Remembering Irving Louis Horowitz (1929–2012)' (*JScholP* 45:iv[2014] 353–408). Horowitz was, in the words of Tom Radko in his introduction to the tributes, 'a publisher, a rebel, a conservative, a teacher, a scholar, a writer, a husband, a herculean force, an incorruptible truth-teller' (p. 354). Of especial relevance to *YWES* readers in the initial issue of the next volume of the *Journal of Scholarly Publishing* is Elizabeth A. Jones and Paul N. Courant's 'Monographic Purchasing Trends in Academic Libraries: Did the "Serials Crisis" Really Destroy the University Press?' (*JScholP* 46:i[2014] 43–70). Accompanied by illustrative figures and statistical tables, this is an 'an exploratory study examining one contentious aspect of the relationship between university presses and academic libraries: the trends in purchases of university press books by academic libraries. The study provides an empirical basis for evaluating the frequent claim that the declining fortunes of university presses can be blamed primarily on declines in monographic purchasing by academic libraries.' They provide three reasons for being sceptical about this claim. In the first place, to 'the extent that purchasing reductions have occurred, they have occurred much more recently than many accounts have suggested'. Secondly, 'purchasing trends vary significantly between different sizes of libraries'. Thirdly, 'purchasing trends for university press books are very different from those for monographs in general'. Consequently such 'findings cast substantial doubt on the proposition that changes in university library purchasing behaviour dating to the 1990s "serials crisis" are principally responsible for the current economic malaise of university presses' (p. 43).

Contributions of interest found in other journals include Robert Adams and Thorlac Turville-Petre's 'The London Book-Trade and the Lost History of *Piers Plowman*' (*RES* 65[2014] 219–35). Adams and Turville-Petre 'examine the conflated text of *Piers Plowman*' in the manuscript at the National Library of Wales, Aberystwyth (MS 733B), 'tracing its relationships with other conflated texts of the poem, which we locate as products of the metropolitan book trade'. Other manuscripts located elsewhere are also considered in order to 'show that MS 733B, though of no value for determining Langland's text, illustrated different "lost history" from the one proposed by' recent scholarship (p. 219). MS 733B 'reveals a great deal about the activities and practices of *Piers Plowman* scribes in the London book trade and helps us to understand at least some aspects of this lost history of *Piers Plowman*' (p. 235). A different historical period and subject are found in Christopher Hilliard's 'The Twopenny Library: The Book Trade, Working-Class Readers, and "Middlebrow" Novels in Britain, 1930–42' (*TCBH* 25:ii[2014] 199–220). Hilliard explains that 'Twopenny libraries first appeared in North London in 1930 and quickly spread throughout urban Britain. Their innovation was to dispense with subscription fees and charge per loan. Unlike older commercial libraries such as Mudie's, twopenny libraries served a working-class clientele.' Moreover, as Hilliard indicates, 'Twopenny libraries carried a lot of so-called light fiction, but they also lent working-class readers the "middlebrow" bestsellers of the 1920s and 1930s. The wider significance of the twopenny library lies in the way it problematizes the distinction commonly made between a middle-class public for new hardcover novels and a working-class readership of fiction that appeared in cheap papers and magazines' (p. 199). Fred Inglis's biography *Richard Hoggart: Virtue and Reward* contains a mainly enumerative bibliography of Hoggart's works, chronologically arranged from the date of initial publication, and 'confined to books', discussed by Inglis (pp. 253–4). Two other articles that should not be ignored are found in the latest issue of *Publishing History* to come to our attention. The first, Maroussia Oakley's 'Alexander Stuart Strahan (c.1835–1918): "A Most Generous Publisher"' (*PubH* 73[2013] 7–56), contains the texts with extensive notation of twenty-eight hitherto unpublished letters held in the MacDonald Collection at the Yale University Beinecke Rare Book and Manuscript Library. These 'date from early September 1869 and the series concludes with a letter dated 13 December 1873' (p. 13). They are mostly from Strahan to Mrs George MacDonald but four were to George MacDonald (1824–1905), the novelist himself, and four were to their eldest daughter Lilia (Lily). The eminent publisher Strahan published MacDonald from 1864 until Strahan faced financial disaster in mid-1873. The letters 'vividly convey Strahan's character; they demonstrate how he interacted on a personal level with his authors and friends and show his witty and expressive nature, as well as his informality, impulsiveness, extravagance, and generosity' (p. 7). In the second article of interest, Anne Marie Hagen writes on 'Thomas Nelson & Sons and Their Publisher's Readers in the 1890s: Change and Continuity in Juvenile Publishing' (*PubH* 73[2013] 57–79). She draws upon the papers of Thomas Nelson & Sons at the University of Edinburgh Library Special Collections and 'examines the letters and reports sent by . . . two readers in the years 1893–7 to George Mackenzie Brown (1869–1946), the managing director' of the publishing firm 'and thereby aims to explore how the publisher balanced the changing literary tastes of the juvenile book market with the expectations of its established audiences'. The readers were Jane Borthwick (1813–97), who was 'mainly concerned with the religious lessons' a submitted manuscript 'promoted or . . . failed to promote'. The second reader was 'Jane McGregor (c.1860–?), [who] focused on literary cohesion within [a] manuscript' (p. 57).

The 2014 *Book History*, edited by Ezra Greenspan and Jonathan Rose, contains fascinating essays, some of which instructively reflect a non-Anglo-American focus: for instance the opening essay by Lianbin Dai, 'China's Bibliographic Tradition and the History of the Book' (*BoH* 17[2014] 1–50).

Augmented by over 200 notes following the text (pp. 39–50), Lianbin Dai writes that 'whereas Chinese bibliography focuses on intellectual and scholarly issues, the Anglo-American and European traditions highlight the book's physical features, a difference that results from the different roles of trade bibliography in traditional China and Europe'. The 'article concludes by discussing how Chinese bibliography has shaped traditional studies of the book, and proposes an archaeology of the Chinese book as a bridge from traditional Chinese bibliography to modern historical methods' (p. 1). Of more immediate interest to *YWES* readers is Meaghan J. Brown's ' "The Hearts of All Sorts of People were Enflamed": Manipulating Readers of Spanish Armada News' (*BoH* 17[2014] 94–116), which is concerned with the examination of the ways in which 'the attempts by the government to shape public reactions can help us to understand some of the ways the public-driven realm of discourse in late Tudor England was imagined by those in power' (p. 95). Scott McLaren writes on 'Brandishing Their Grey Goose Quills: The Struggle to Publish an Official Life of John Wesley, 1791–1805' (*BoH* 17[2014] 191–214), which is concerned to show Wesley's own engagement in the contemporary 'burgeoning market for books, pamphlets, and periodicals' (p. 214) and, by 'a close examination of the surviving evidence [to] show that the dispute over who would have the sanctioned right to interpret Wesley and his words to a wider reading public prepared the ground for many of the conflicts yet to come by providing a rhetorical framework through which the authority of Methodist preachers could be openly challenged' (p. 192). The yellow fever epidemic that struck Philadelphia in 1793 provides the background for Molly O'Hagan Hardy's 'Figures of Authorship in Mathew Carey's Transatlantic Yellow Fever Pamphlets' (*BoH* 17[2014] 221–49), in which she examines the London and Dublin reprints of Carey's *A Short Account of the Malignant Fever, Lately Prevalent in Philadelphia*. Initially published in 1793 and 1794, the pamphlet 'plays a central role in the formation of U.S. cultural history, and by examining the international iterations' of Carey's pamphlet 'we learn it was also engaged in a transatlantic radicalism permeating the 1790s, a radicalism that exceeded national designations'. Hardy traces the pamphlet across the Atlantic, first to London and then to Dublin. Hardy's intention is 'to define that radicalism and its relationship to the construction of authorship in the period' (p. 221). Her article is accompanied by five illustrative figures. The title of John L. Dwiggins's essay well conveys his subject, 'A Traveler's Guide to the American Military Establishment: The U.S. Military Academy at West Point as Viewed through Antebellum American Travel Literature, 1820–1860' (*BoH* 17[2014] 250–71). Shane Malhotra, in her ' "If She Escapes She Will Publish Everything": Lady Sale and the Media Frenzy of the First Anglo-Afghan War (1839–1842)' (*BoH* 17[2014] 272–97), examines 'the writings of Lady Florentia Sale (1790–1853), eyewitness and recorder of the First Anglo-Afghan War' (p. 272): Malhotra's article is accompanied by three poorly reproduced illustrations (pp. 278, 284, 291). Rachel Scarborough King's 'Letters from the Highlands: Scribal Publication and Media Shift in Victorian Scotland' (*BoH* 17[2014] 298–320) is concerned with Elizabeth Grant's memoirs 'composed between 1845 and 1854 but which were only published, under the title *Memoirs of a Highland*

Lady, in 1898 more than a decade after her death'. King analyses this 'little-known but plentiful and productive work in the light of the transformations in [the] British postal systems that took place during the nineteenth century, and their relationship to fluctuating concepts of manuscript and print as media of publication'. King argues that 'Grant chose to "publish" her work in a manuscript rather than print format, a choice that offers significant insights into the makeup of the early Victorian media environment' (pp. 298–9). Chris Louttit's ' "A Favour on the Million": The Household Edition, the Cheap Reprint, and the Posthumous Illustration and Reception of Charles Dickens' (*BoH* 17[2014] 321–64) is accompanied by thirteen illustrative figures. It provides 'a thorough analysis of the publication history of the Household Edition'. Such an analysis 'can provide further insight into' Dickens's posthumous reception (p. 321) and provide 'insight into how Dickens's work was understood by many late nineteenth-century readers' (p. 358). Simon Frost's object in his 'Economising in Public: Publishing History as a Challenge to Scientific Method' (*BoH* 17[2014] 365–79) 'is to suggest how economics as a discipline was, in part, constituted by the materiality of its production'. Frost 'outline[s] an economic theory known as marginalism; then focus[es] on some production details for one of its key works, [William Stanley] Jevons's *Theory of Political Economy* (1871)', and he concludes 'with some remarks on the socialization of science'. In doing so Frost demonstrates three key points: 'why the ability to use other than lexical semiotic modes, such as mathematical notation, was so important; [secondly] how the specifics of economics was incorporated into (and overwhelmed by) a professional publishing system that allowed important interpersonal networks to be built, chiefly thorough scholarly biography, that were constitutive of the discipline; [thirdly] how historic events coordinated to promote the new discipline via its imbrication in political and social conflict' (p. 365). In the penultimate contribution, Jose Bellido's concern is with 'The Editorial Quest for International Copyright (1886–1896)' (*BoH* 17[2014] 380–405). Bellido demonstrates the use of two editorial projects and 'how at the end of the nineteenth century, the internationalisation of copyright became an editorial quest' (p. 396). These projects based in Paris were Charles Lyon-Caen and Paul Delalain's *Lois françaises et étrangères sur la propriété littéraire et artistique* [1890], a collection of copyright laws over 1,000 pages in length, and 'a monthly journal exclusively devoted to international copyright starting with its first issue in 1888, *Le Droit d'Auteur* [that] quickly became the world's leading copyright journal' (p. 391). Both 'editorial projects were not just representing international copyright, but actually constituting it' (p. 396). The final contribution to this challenging issue of *Book History* is Matthew Kirschenbaum and Sarah Werner's 'Digital Scholarship and Digital Studies: The State of the Discipline' (*BoH* 17[2014] 406–58), accompanied by six illustrative figures. The authors acknowledge that their 'perspective is unavoidably parochial in that it is limited primarily to work not only in English but indeed originating in Anglophone nations' and they provide 'a list of resources at the end, which will be useful as a starting place for those seeking a hands-on introduction to the projects and resources' discussed (pp. 409–10). Kirschenbaum and Werner conclude that 'our scholarship will have to confront the reality that its largest challenges may not be technological but legalistic. Intellectual property, digital rights management, terms of service, end-user license agreements will govern access at least as much or more than media obsolescence, bit rot, or curatorial neglect' (p. 453).

The fifth volume in the Oxford History of the Novel in English is *The American Novel to 1870*. Edited by J. Gerald Kennedy and Leland S. Person, it is sparsely illustrated. Kennedy and Person write in their introduction that 'This volume reconstructs in thirty-four chapters the emergence and early cultivation of the novel in the United States of America' (p. 1). There is an absence of documentation, although there are detailed indexes, in addition to acknowledgements (p. ix) and a listing of contributors (pp. xi–xii) and the general editor's preface by Patrick Parrinder (pp. xiii–xiv). The contents include J. Gerald Kennedy and Leland S. Person's 'Introduction: The American Novel to 1870' (pp. 1–18). There are seven parts. The first, 'The Beginnings of the Novel in the United States', includes: chapter 1, 'Before the American Novel' (pp. 21–40) by Betsy Erkkilä; chapter 2, 'The Sentimental Novel and the Seductions of Postcolonial Imitation' (pp. 41–55) by Karen A. Weyler; chapter 3, 'Complementary Strangers: Charles Brockden Brown, Susanna Rowson, and the Early American Sentimental Gothic' (pp. 56–72) by Marion Rust; chapter 4, 'Trends and Patterns in the US Novel, 1800–1820' (pp. 73–88) by Ed White; and chapter 5, 'Unsettling Novels of the Early Republic' (pp. 89–104) by Leonard Tennenhouse'. Part II, 'The Novel and American Nation Building', contains: chapter 6, 'Walter Scott and the American Historical' (pp. 107–23) by Fiona Robertson; chapter 7, 'Revolutionary Novels and the Problem of Literary Nationalism' (pp. 124–41) by Joseph J. Letter; chapter 8, 'Frontier Novels, Border Wars, and Indian Removal' (pp. 142–58) by Dana D. Nelson; and chapter 9, 'America's Europe: Irving, Poe, and the Foreign Subject' (pp. 159–76) by J. Gerald Kennedy. The third part is devoted to 'The American Publishing World and the Novel' and contains: chapter 10, 'Publishers, Booksellers, and the Literary Market' (pp. 179–194) by Michael Winship; chapter 11, 'The Perils of Authorship: Literary Property and Nineteenth-Century American Fiction' (pp. 195–212) jointly authored by Lara Langer Cohen and Meredith L. McGill; chapter 12, 'Periodicals and the Novel' (pp. 213–28) by Patricia Okker; and chapter 13, 'Cheap Sensation: Pamphlet Potboilers and Beadle's Dime Novels' (pp. 229–43) by Shelley Streeby. The fourth part has five essays devoted to 'Leading Novelists of Antebellum America': chapter 14, 'James Fenimore Cooper: Beyond Leather-Stocking' (pp. 247–61) by Wayne Franklin; chapter 15, 'Catharine Maria Sedgwick: Domestic and National Narratives' (pp. 262–77) by James L. Machor; chapter 16, 'Hawthorne and the Historical Romance' (pp. 278–93) by Larry J. Reynolds; chapter 17, 'Herman Melville' (pp. 294–309) by Jonathan Arac. This section concludes with John Ernest writing on 'Harriet Beecher Stowe and the Antislavery Cause' (pp. 310–26). The fifth part has four essays on 'Major Novels' and consists of chapter 19, '*The Last of the Mohicans*: Race to Citizenship' (pp. 329–42) by Leland S. Person; chapter 20, '*The Scarlet Letter*' (pp. 343–54) by Monika Elbert; chapter 21, '*Moby-Dick* and Globalization' (pp. 355–67) by John Carlos Rowe; and concludes with chapter 22, 'Harriet Beecher Stowe's *Uncle Tom's Cabin*' (pp. 368–81) by

David S. Reynolds. The sixth part is devoted to 'Cultural Influences on the American Novel, 1820–1870' and has eight essays: chapter 23, 'Transatlantic Currents and Postcolonial Anxieties' (pp. 385–401) by Paul Giles; chapter 24, 'The Transamerican Novel' (pp. 402–18) by Anna Brickhouse; chapter 25, 'Slavery, Abolitionism, and the African American Novel' (pp. 419–34) by Ivy G. Wilson; chapter 26, 'Ethnic Novels and the Construction of the Multicultural Nation to 1870' (pp. 435–48) by John Lowe; chapter 27, 'Women's Novels and the Gendering of Genius' (pp. 449–65) by Renée Bergland; chapter 28, 'Male Hybrids in Classic American Fiction' (pp. 466–82) by David Leverenz; and chapter 29, 'Studying Nature in the Antebellum Novel' (pp. 483–99) by Timothy Sweet. In the last essay in this section Caroline Levander writes on 'Novels of Faith and Doubt in a Changing Culture' (pp. 500–14). The final section of *The American Novel to 1870* contains four contributions on the subject of 'Fictional Subgenres': chapter 31, 'Temperance Novels and Moral Reform' (pp. 517–31) by Debra J. Rosenthal; chapter 32, 'Novels of Travel and Exploration' (pp. 532–47) by Gretchen Murphy; and chapter 33, 'The City Mystery Novel' (pp. 548–63) by Scott Peeples. In the final essay Paul Christian Jones writes on 'Surviving National Disunion: Civil War Novels of the 1860s' (pp. 564–78). The volume concludes with a 'Composite Bibliography' (pp. 579–615) that is alphabetical and enumerative, combining primary and secondary works. This is followed by an 'Index of American Novelists to 1870' (pp. 617–25) that is also alphabetical and enumerative, but is double-columned, and contains authors and their work. Lastly there is an alphabetical, comprehensive, double-columned general index (pp. 626–40).

James H. Cox and Daniel Heath Justice are the editors of *The Oxford Handbook of Indigenous American Literature*. As they write in their acknowledgements to their volume, they believe it to be 'the most comprehensive handbook in Indigenous American literary studies to date' (p. xi). Furthermore it 'is a product of the transformation of Native American and Indigenous literary studies during the past twenty years' (p. 1). A strength of the forty-three contributions divided into four sections are the notes following most chapters and the alphabetical, enumeratively arranged listing of works cited also following the majority of the individual contributions—see for instance those by Malea Powell and Sarah Henzi. The contributions are uneven in length, and there are sixteen black and white illustrations scattered throughout the collection. The introduction—'Post-Renaissance Native American and Indigenous American Literary Studies' (pp. 1–11) by James H. Cox and Daniel H. Justice is followed by the first part, devoted to 'Histories'. There are eleven contributions: chapter 1, 'The Sovereign Obscurity of Inuit Literature' (pp. 15–30) by Keavy Martin; chapter 2, 'At the Crossroads of Red/Black Literature' (pp. 31–49) by Kiara Vigil and Tiya Miles; chapter 3, 'Ambivalence and Contradiction in Contemporary Maya Literature from Yucatan: Jorge Cocom Pech's *Muk'ult'an in Nool* [*Grandfather's Secrets*]' (pp. 50–64) by Emilio Del Valle Escalante; chapter 4, 'Early Native Literature as Social Practice' (pp. 65–80) by Phillip H. Round; chapter 5, 'Recovering Jane Schoolcraft's Cultural Activism in the Nineteenth Century' (pp. 81–101) by Maureen Konkle; chapter 6, 'Hawaiian Literature in

Hawaiian: An Overview' (pp. 102–17) by Noenoe K. Silvama; chapter 7, 'Metis Identity and Literature' (pp. 118–36) by Kristina Fagan Bidwell; chapter 8, 'Queering Indigenous Pasts, or Temporalities of Tradition and Settlement' (pp. 137–51) by Mark Rifkin; chapter 9, 'Singing Forwards and Backwards: Ancestral and Contemporary Chamorro Poetics' (pp. 152–66) by Craig Santos Perez; chapter 10, 'Indigenous Orality and Oral Literatures' (pp. 167–74) by Christopher B. Teuton, and chapter 11, '*Megwa Baabaamiiaayaayaang Dibaajomoyaang*: Anishinaabe Literature as Memory in Motion' by Margaret Noodin.

The second part has eleven essays on the subject of 'Genres'. These consist of: chapter 12, 'Native Nonfiction' (pp. 187–201) by Robert Warrior; chapter 13, 'Towards a Native American Women's Autobiographical Tradition: Genre as Political Practice' (pp. 202–14) by Crystal Kurzen; chapter 14, 'Ixtlamatiliztli/Knowledge with the Face: Intellectual Migrations and Colonial Dis-placements in Natalio Hernández's *Xochikoskatl*' (pp. 215–33) by Adam Coon; chapter 15, ' "our leaves of paper will be / dancing lightly": Indigenous Poetics' (pp. 234–49) by Sophie Mayer; chapter 16, 'The Story of Movement: Natives and Performance Culture' (pp. 250–65) by LeAnne Howe; chapter 17, 'Published Native American Drama, 1980–2011' (pp. 266–83) by Alexander Pettit; chapter 18, 'Indigenous American Cinema' (pp. 284–98) by Denise K. Cummings; chapter 19, 'Reading the Visual, Seeing the Verbal: Text and Image in Recent American Indian Literature and Art' (pp. 299–317) by Dean Rader, which has seven illustrative back and white examples accompanying the text; chapter 20, 'The Indigenous Novel' (pp. 318–32) by Sean Kicummah Teuton; chapter 21, 'Indigenous Children's Literature' (pp. 333–43) by Loriene Roy; and chapter 22, 'Red Dead Conventions: American Indian Transgeneric Fictions' (pp. 344–58) by Jodi Byrd. The third part has ten contributions devoted to the subject of 'Methods': chapter 23, 'Contested Images, Contested Lands: The Politics of Space in Louise Erdrich's *Tracks* and Leslie Marmon Silko's *Sacred Water*' (pp. 361–76) by Shari M. Huhndorf; chapter 24, 'Decolonizing Comparison: Towards a Trans-Indigenous Literary Studies' (pp. 377–94) by Chadwick Allen; chapter 25, 'Indigenous Trans/ Nationalism and the Ethics of Theory in Native Literary Studies' (pp. 395–408) by Joseph Bauerkemper; chapter 26, 'Beyond Continuance: Criticism of Indigenous Literatures in Canada' (pp. 409–26) by Sam McKegney; chapter 27, 'All that Is Native and Fine: Teaching Native American Literature' (pp. 427–32) by Frances Washburn; chapter 28, 'Teaching Native Literature Responsibly in a MultiEthnic Classroom' (pp. 433–40) by Channette Romero; chapter 29, 'Between "Colonizer-Perpetrator" and "Colonizer-Ally": Towards a Pedagogy of Redress' (pp. 441–54) by Renate Eigenbrod; chapter 30, 'Vine Deloria, Jr. and the Spacemen' (pp. 455–70) by Craig Womack; chapter 31, ' "A Basket Is a Basket Because...": Telling a Native Rhetorics Story' (pp. 471–88) by Malea Powell; and chapter 32, 'New Tribalism and Chicana/o Indigeneity in the Work of Gloria Anzaldúa' (pp. 489–502) by Domino Renee Perez. The fourth and final part has ten contributions devoted to the topic of 'Geographies': chapter 33, 'Literature and the Red Atlantic' (pp. 505–19) by Jace Weaver; chapter 34, 'The Re/Presentation of the Indigenous Caribbean in Literature' (pp. 520–35) by Shona N. Jackson; chapter 35, 'Writing and

Lasting: Native Northeastern Literary History' (pp. 536–58) by Lisa Brooks; chapter 36, 'Decolonizing Indigenous Oratures and Literatures of Northern British North America and Canada (Beginnings to 1960)' (pp. 559–76) by Margery Fee; chapter 37, 'Indigenous Literature and Other Verbal Arts, Canada (1960–2012)' (pp. 577–88) by Warren Cariou; chapter 38, 'Amerika Samoa: Writing Home' (pp. 589–607) by Caroline Sinavaiana Gabbard; chapter 39, 'Native Literatures of Alaska' (pp. 608–16) by James Ruppert; chapter 40, 'The *Popol Wuj* and the Birth of Mayan Literature' (pp. 617–37) by Thomas Ward; chapter 41, 'Keeping Oklahoma Indian Territory: Alice Callahan and John Oskison (Indian Enough)' (pp. 638–54) by Joshua B. Nelson; and chapter 42, 'Francophone Aboriginal Literature in Quebec' (pp. 655–72) by Sarah Henzi. This is followed by 'Afterwords': chapter 43, ' "I ka 'Olelo ke Ola": In Words Is Life: Imagining the Future of Indigenous Literatures' (pp. 675–82) by Ku'ualoha Ho'omanawanui, who reflects on the 'power of words' (p. 657) and on 'the direction of Indigenous literary studies' (p. 679). There is a detailed double-columned index (pp. 683–741) concluding this fascinating volume.

Reingard M. Nischik writes that her edited collection, *The Palgrave Handbook of Comparative North American Literature* is 'the very first of its kind in this research area' (p. vii) and 'is meant to chart relevant methodologies and major issues of Comparative North American Literature and to help this approach find its place in the ever-changing constellation of dealing with the United States and Canada and studying them across the disciplines' (p. 3). The *Handbook* is divided into five sections with often lengthy notation following the seventeen contributions. The first section, 'Charting the Territory', has two essays: 'Comparative North American Studies and Its Contexts: Introduction' (pp. 3–31) by Reingard M. Nischik; and 'Imagining North America' (pp. 33–45) by Rachel Adams. The second section is concerned with 'Perspectives on Multiculturalism' and contains four essays: 'Multiculturalism in the United States and Canada' (pp. 49–64) by Sabine Sielke; 'Comparative Race Studies: Black and White in Canada and the United States' (pp. 65–84) by Eva Gruber; 'Comparing Native Literatures in Canada and the United States' (pp. 85–102) by Katja Sarkowsky; and 'Naturalization and Citizenship in North America' (pp. 103–25) by Mita Banerjee. The third section focuses on 'French-Language and English-Language Cultures in North America' and contains three essays: 'Comparative Canadian/Québécois Literature Studies' (pp. 129–47) by Marie Vautier; 'Québécois Literature and American Literature' (pp. 149–63) by Jean Morency, translated by Jo-Anne Elder with brief notation; 'North America's Francophone Borderlands' (pp. 165–81) by Monika Giacoppe with no accompanying notation. The fourth section has four contributions on the subject of 'Regions and Symbolic Spaces': 'The Literatures of the Mexico–U.S. and Canada–U.S. Borders' (pp. 185–97) by Claudia Sadowski-Smith; 'Regionalism in American and Canadian Literature' (pp. 199–218) by Florian Freitag; 'The North in English Canada and Quebec' (pp. 219–35) by Christina Kannenberg; and 'North American Urban Fiction' (pp. 237–54) by Caroline Rosenthal. The fifth and final section focuses on 'National, Transnational, Global Perspectives' and also has four contributions:

'Modernism in the United States and Canada' (pp. 257–76) by Jutta Ernst; 'Postmodernism in the United States and Canada' (pp. 277–98) by Julia Breitbach; 'Literary Celebrity in the United States and Canada' (pp. 299–312) by Lorraine York; and finally 'North American Literature and Global Studies: Transnationalism at War' (pp. 313–36) by Georgiana Banita. A contributors listing (pp. 337–42), is followed by an alphabetically arranged enumerative listing of works cited (pp. 343–92). *The Palgrave Handbook of Comparative North American Literature* has some opaque contributions but contains much that is useful, including a detailed, double-columned index (pp. 393–417): the notations following most of the individual essays are produced in a smaller computer-generated typeface, making them at times difficult to read.

Paula Rabinowitz's concern in her *American Pulp: How Paperbacks Brought Modernism to Main Street* is with, as her title suggests, the ways in which cheap books opened the world of ideas to new readers. Rabinowitz's canvas is limited to the United States From the 1930s to the 1960s paperbacks were very popular and created a huge readership for various genres including detective stories and writers such as Henry James and D.H. Lawrence, amongst others. 'The mechanism of pulping a work', Rabinowitz writes, 'entailed a process of redistribution or, more precisely, remediation: writings often created for an educated and elite audience took on new lives by being repackaged as cheap paperbacks' (p. 23). Repackaging encompassed cover illustrations, which included sexually arresting depictions of violence and also modernist art. Pulp widened the panorama of the experience of Americans. Paperbacks were distributed to troops during the Second World War: they boosted morale and helped develop readers amongst those from a limited educational background and consequently created a subsequent postwar demand. The most popular paperbacks included crime novels, exploring the ways in which both psychological and economic forces come together in the individual. Particular attention is paid to the impact of the work of two black writers: Richard Wright and Ann Petry. The former's *12 Million Black Voices* [1941] was influenced by confessional magazines; Petry's *Country Place* [1947] concerns 'malice, calculation, infidelity, adultery, murder, sudden death, and a set of surprise bequests' (p. 131), with 'the geography of desire leading a returning vet to contemplate murdering his two-timing wife' (p. 34). Chapters include a fascinating one on 'Slips of the Tongue: Uncovering Lesbian Pulp' (pp. 184–208). Drawing upon a diversity of archival sources (see acknowledgements, pp. 301–5), Rabinowitz's study is enriched by twenty-four colour plates (between pp. 174 and 175) and accompanied by black and white illustrations throughout. Regrettably, no doubt the jacket, with its reproduction of Guy Pène Du Bois's *Portia in a Pink Blouse* [1942] at the Indianapolis Museum of Art will be thrown out when Rabinowitz's monograph is purchased by libraries. Useful and in some instances detailed notes (pp. 307–75; see for instance pp. 311–12, note 29, concerning the word 'pulp'), are followed by a double-columned index (pp. 377–90).

The thirty-seventh volume of *Resources for American Literary Studies*, edited by Jackson R. Bryer and Richard Kopley, contains much of interest. It opens with 'Prospects for the Study of Robert Frost' by Timothy D. O'Brien (*RALS* 37[2014] 3–28), that summarizes Frost criticism and scholarship and also suggests fresh directions it could take. Wayne Franklin's 'Six Early James Fenimore Cooper Letters' (*RALS* 37[2014] 29–59) presents six Fenimore Cooper letters 'dating from the years 1817 to 1820 [that] significantly expand our view of Cooper's concerns in that sparsely covered period' and 'are especially revealing because all arose from the ultimately unsuccessful efforts by Cooper and his brothers to resolve very serious issues linked to the estate of their father, Judge William Cooper 1854–1809' (pp. 29–30). David E.E. Sloane's '*The Herald of Glory and Adapted Citizen's Journal* of August 13, 1834: Early Advocacy for the Abolition of Slavery in an Urban Northeast Comic Newspaper' (*RALS* 37[2014] 61–5) contains the text of an article in *The Herald of Glory and Adapted Citizen's Journal*. The article 'satirized the predominant Southern defenses of slavery' (p. 61). Mary Lamb Sheldon's ' "Such a Great Light": Letters to Louisa and Abba Alcott from the Holley School for Freed People and the Story of Winnie Beale's Emancipation' (*RALS* 37[2014] 67–151) contains nineteen 'hitherto-unpublished...letters from Sallie Holley and Caroline Putnam, founders of the Holley School for the freed people of Lottsburgh on Virginia's Northern Neck, to the renowned author Louisa May Alcott and her mother Abigail May Alcott, who over many years solicited and sent contributions to the school' (p. 67): replete with extensive documentation and 145 notes, the article is accompanied by thirteen black and white illustrative figures. Some later authors engage Matt Miller in his 'Getting the Joke in "Of Being Numerous": George Oppen as Heir to Walt Whitman's Public Poetics' (*RALS* 37[2014] 153–80). Miller, 'using archival materials and recently published interviews...provides a comprehensive overview of Oppen's engagement with Whitman, highlighting the sophistication and complexity of his response and addressing what Oppen meant when he described the conclusion to "Of Being Numerous" as in part "a joke on Whitman" '. Consequently 'Oppen presents a version of Whitman at odds with both the critical responses of previous modernists and the more enthusiastic interpretations of Oppen's contemporaries in the 1950s and 1960s' (p. 153). The article is accompanied by two illustrative black and white figures. Robert W. Trogdon's ' "I Am Constructing a Legend": Ernest Hemingway in Guy Hickok's *Brooklyn Daily Eagle* Articles' (*RALS* 37[2014] 181–207) reprints six of the dispatches and interviews written by Hickok, the Paris correspondent of the *Brooklyn Daily Eagle*. They 'include an account of Hemingway's wounding during World War I, descriptions of Hemingway in Pamplona in 1929, and an extensive interview about Hemingway's 1933–4 African safari' (p. 181). In her 'A Forgotten Writer: Alice Beal Parsons and "Cross Purposes" ' (*RALS* 37[2014] 209–52), Sarah C. Holmes 'recovers a socialist and feminist writer previously overlooked by literary scholars', Alice Beal Parsons (1886–1962). In addition to an account of Parsons's life and activities, Holmes provides an annotated bibliographical listing of her published works (pp. 246–8). There is also a useful commentary on, and the text of, Parsons's short story 'Cross Purposes', which 'examines a wealthy woman's complicity in the oppression of working-class women' (pp. 225–46). Ralph Bauer, in his 'The Invention of Viking America' (*RALS* 37[2014] 253–60), provides 'an extended review of Annette Kolodny's *In Search of First Contact: The Vikings of Vinland, the Peoples of the Dawnland, and the Anglo-American Anxiety of Discovery*

(Durham, NC: Duke University Press, 2012)' (p. 253). Phyllis Cole in her review essay 'The New Emerson Canon' (*RALS* 37[2014] 261–73), 'salutes the completion of the final volume (*Uncollected Prose Writings*) in the fifty-year project of editing Ralph Waldo Emerson's *Collected Works* [Cambridge: HarvardUP, 1971–2013]' (p. 261). In the final two review essays in this volume of *RALS* Fritz Fleischmann, in his 'Reading Margaret Fuller' (*RALS* 37[2014] 275–88), discusses two biographies, John Matteson's *The Lives of Margaret Fuller: A Biography* (Norton [2012]) and Megan Marshall's *Margaret Fuller: A New American Life* (Houghton [2013]). Marilee Lindeman's 'Too Much of a Good Thing Is Wonderful: At Long Last, Cather's Letters' (*RALS* 37[2014] 289–97) 'explores the profound scholarly significance of the publication of *The Selected Letters of Willa Cather*, a nearly 700-page collection scrupulously edited by Andrew Jewell and Janis Stout (Knopf, 2013)' (p. 289). This is followed by seventeen shorter reviews of recent monographs (*RALS* 37[2014] 299–373). The volume concludes with Sharya De Silva's index to volume 37, divided into 'Index of Authors' (*RALS* 37[2014] 375–6), 'Index of Subjects' (*RALS* 37[2014] 376–83), and 'Index of Books Reviewed' (*RALS* 37[2014] 383–4). This is followed by 'Guidelines for Contributors to *Resources for American Literary Study*' (*RALS* 37[2014] 385).

Rob Latham, who edits *The Oxford Handbook of Science Fiction*, explains in his introduction that 'this is not a comprehensive work of reference designed to survey the field systematically or to summarize consensus views'. However 'the overall effect' of each of the forty-four chapters 'is to convey a strong sense of the heterogenous [*sic*] discourses and debates, histories and cultures, that have gone to make science fiction, broadly conceived, what it is today' (p. 6). Each chapter in the 'four broadly themed parts, each divided into eleven chapters' (p. 6) is followed by an enumerative, alphabetically arranged listing of works cited. Latham's introduction (pp. 1–19) is followed by Part I, 'Science Fiction as Genre', consisting of: chapter 1, 'Extrapolation and Speculation' (pp. 23–34) by Brooks Landon; chapter 2, 'Aesthetics' (pp. 35–46) by Peter Stockwell; chapter 3, 'Histories' (pp. 47–58) by Arthur B. Evans; chapter 4, 'Literary Movements' (pp. 59–70) by Gary K. Wolfe; chapter 5, 'Fandom' (pp. 71–80) by Farah Mendlesohn, who writes 'In this chapter, I will define fans as those who engage with others over their shared interest in science and fantasy' (p. 71). Perhaps not surprisingly only eight items are listed under works cited (p. 80). This is followed by chapter 6, 'The Marketplace' (pp. 81–92) by Gary Westfahl; chapter 7, 'Pulp Science Fiction' (pp. 93–103) by Jess Nevins; chapter 8, 'Literary Science Fiction' (pp. 104–14) by Joan Gordon; chapter 9, 'Slipstream' (pp. 115–26) by Victoria de Zwaan, who 'examine[s] the emergence of the term and its history inside SF discourse and writing' (p. 115); chapter 10, 'The Fantastic' (pp. 127–38) by Brian Attebery; the final essay in this first section is chapter 11, 'Genre vs. Mode' (pp. 139–51) by Veronica Hollinger. The second part is on 'Science Fiction as Medium' and consists of: chapter 12, 'Film' (pp. 155–68) by Mark Bould, which has two small black and white illustrations (pp. 161 and 165); chapter 13, 'Radio and Television' (pp. 169–83) by J.P. Telotte, also accompanied by black and white illustrations (pp. 174, 177, and 180); chapter 14, 'Animation' (pp. 184–95) by Paul Wells, somewhat surprisingly accompanied by one black and white illustration (p. 194); chapter 15, 'Art and Illustration' (pp. 196–211) by Jerome Winter with five accompanying black and white illustrations (pp. 198–9, 202, 205, 208); chapter 16, 'Comics' (pp. 212–25) by Corey Creekmur with two black and white illustrative examples (pp. 214, 222); chapter 17, 'Video Games' (pp. 226–38) by Paweł Frelik with two black and white figures of 'video games' (pp. 231, 234); chapter 18, 'Digital Arts and Hypertext' (pp. 239–51) by James Tobias; chapter 19, 'Music' (pp. 252–62) by John Cline, who notes that 'The definitional problem regarding what actually constitutes "science fiction music" presents a unique challenge for discussing the intersection of sound and SF' (p. 252); chapter 20, 'Performance Art' (pp. 263–76) by Steve Dixon, which has two black and white illustrations; chapter 21, 'Architecture' (pp. 277–90) by Nic Clear, which only contains three similar illustrations—rather a wasted opportunity on the part of the volume's publishers; chapter 22, 'Theme Parks' (pp. 291–301) by Leonie Cooper, which lacks any. Part III contains eleven essays devoted to the topic of 'Science Fiction as Culture': chapter 23, 'The Culture of Science' (pp. 305–16) by Sherryl Vint; chapter 24, 'Automation' (pp. 317–28) by Roger Luckhurst; chapter 25, 'Military Culture' (pp. 329–39) by Steffen Hantke; chapter 26, 'Atomic Culture and the Space Race' (pp. 340–51) by David Seed; chapter 27, 'UFOs, Scientology, and Other SF Religions' (pp. 352–63) by Gregory L. Reece; chapter 28, 'Advertising and Design' (pp. 364–82) by Jonathan M. Woodham, accompanied by eight black and white illustrations; chapter 29, 'Countercultures' (pp. 383–94) by Rob Latham; chapter 30, 'Sexuality' (pp. 395–407) by Patricia Melzer; chapter 31, 'Body Modification' (pp. 408–20) by Ross Farnell; chapter 32, 'Cyberculture' (pp. 421–33) by Thomas Foster, illustrated by a '1906 episode from Winsor McCay's comic strip Dream of the Rarebit Fiend' (p. 428); and the final contribution—the thirty-third—to this third section is on the subject of 'Retrofuturism and Steampunk' (pp. 434–47) by Elizabeth Guffey and Kate C. Lemay, containing two black and white illustrations with again an opportunity missed. The final section of the volume, Part IV, 'Science Fiction as Worldview', also contains eleven essays: chapter 34, 'The Enlightenment' (pp. 451–62) by Adam Roberts; chapter 35, 'The Gothic' (pp. 463–74) by William Hughes; chapter 36, 'Darwinism' (pp. 475–85) by Patrick B. Sharp; chapter 37, 'Colonialism and Postcolonialism' (pp. 486–97) by John Rieder; chapter 38, 'Pseudoscience' (pp. 498–512) by Anthony Enns, accompanied by three fascinating illustrative examples; chapter 39, 'Futurology' (pp. 513–23) by Andrew M. Butler; chapter 40, 'Posthumanism' (pp. 524–36) by Colin Milburn; chapter 41, 'Feminism' (pp. 537–48) by Lisa Yaszek; chapter 42, 'Libertarianism and Anarchism' (pp. 549–60) by Neil Easterbrook; chapter 43, 'Afrofuturism' (pp. 561–72) by De Witt Douglas Kilgore; and finally and somewhat appropriately a contribution on the subject of 'Utopianism' (pp. 573–83) by Phillip E. Wegner. The *Oxford Handbook of Science Fiction* concludes with a detailed, helpful double-columned index (pp. 585–620).

Arthur B. Evans has edited *Vintage Visions: Essays on Early Science Fiction*. This collection 'brings together some of the finest essays ever published on early science fiction (sf). These sixteen articles first appeared in the scholarly journal *Science Fiction Studies* from 1976 to 2010, and their collective focus spans nearly three centuries of sf, from Cyrano de Bergerac in 1657 to Olaf

Stapleton in 1937.' Further, 'each essay in this volume is also followed by a short afterword written by its author (or, in a few cases, by another scholar) that has been added expressly for *Vintage Visions*' (pp. vii–viii). The essays (pp. 1–351) are followed by a chronological listing, beginning 'circa 150' (p. 353) and concluding in 1938 (p. 356), of '150 Key Works of Early Science Fiction' compiled by the editor and Javier A. Martínez. They also include an enumerative, alphabetically arranged 'Bibliography of Criticism on Early Science Fiction' (pp. 357–432) divided into 'two major sections': general reference (pp. 357–70) and author studies (pp. 370–432). The general reference section is divided into three sub-sections: encyclopedias, research guides, companions, and critical bibliographies (pp. 357–9); collections and special issues whose essays are focused primarily on early science fiction (pp. 359–60); and historical and thematic studies (pp. 360–70). Additionally, 'The Author Section is arranged in (roughly) chronological order' (p. 357). The volume lacks an index.

Nicola Allen and David Simmons's collection, *Reassessing the Twentieth-Century Canon: From Joseph Conrad to Zadie Smith*, contains, in addition to the editors' introduction (pp. 1–12), twenty essays. Its aim is 'to deliver a critically informed "snapshot" of twentieth-century texts that are widely taught in the Anglophone University system. It cannot, and does not, claim to be exhaustive; however, one of the driving motivations behind this collection was to provide undergraduate students with a comprehensive section of essays that they might take forward with them as they explore and engage with what is an interesting and much contested body of writing' (p. 6). Contributions encompass: 'Snags in the Fairway: Reading *Heart of Darkness*' (pp. 13–26) by David Bradshaw; ' "Hasn't Got Any Name": Aesthetics, African Americans and Policemen in *The Great Gatsby*' (pp. 27–42) by Nicolas Tredell; 'Urban Spaces, Fragmented Consciousness, and Indecipherable Meaning in *Mrs Dalloway* ' (pp. 43–55) by Andrew Harrison; 'D.H. Lawrence's *Lady Chatterley's Lover* in the New Century: Literary Canon and Bodily Episteme' (pp. 56–74) by Richard Brown; '*A Handful of Dust*: Realism: Modernism/ Irony: Sympathy' (pp. 75–90) by Richard Jacobs; 'Studied Ambivalence: The Appalling Strangeness of Graham Greene's *Brighton Rock*' (pp. 91–108) by Susie Thomas; ' "Come Down from Your Thinkin' and Listen a Minute": The Multiple Voices of *The Grapes of Wrath*' by Jennifer Butler Keaton (pp. 109–21); 'Faulkner's *Go Down, Moses* Revisited' (pp. 122–33) by Linda Wagner Martin; 'Time, Space, and Resistance: Re-reading George Orwell's *Nineteen Eighty-Four*' (pp. 134–45) by Lawrence Phillips; '*Lucky Jim*: The Novel in Uncharted Times' (pp. 146–60) by Nicola Allen and Wasfi Shoqairat; 'Six Myths of *On the Road*, and Where These Might Lead Us' (pp. 161–74) by R. J. Ellis; ' "Hundred-per-Cent American Con Man": Character in Ken Kesey's *One Flew Over the Cuckoo's Nest*' (pp. 175–86) by David Simmons; '*Herzog*'s Masculine Dilemmas, and the Eclipse of the Transcendental "I" ' (pp. 187–205) by Gloria L. Cronin; 'Beyond Postmodernism in Alasdair Gray's *Lanark*' (pp. 206–20) by Claire Allen; 'Gender Vertigo: Queer Gothic and Angela Carter's *Nights at the Circus*' (pp. 221–34) by Sarah Gamble; 'Whole Families Paranoid at Night: Don DeLillo's *White Noise*' (pp. 235–49) by Martyn Colebrook; 'Hooked on Classics:

Oranges Are Not the Only Fruit 25 Years On' (pp. 250–265) by Sonya Andermahr; 'Remembering and Disremembering *Beloved*: Lacunae and Hauntings' (pp. 266–80) by Gina Wisker; 'Embracing Uncertainty: Hanif Kureishi's *Buddha of Suburbia* and *The Black Album*' (pp. 281–93) by Susan Alice Fischer; and 'Samad, Hancock, the Suburbs, and Englishness: Re-reading Zadie Smith's *White Teeth*' (pp. 294–309) by Philip Tew. There is an alphabetically arranged select bibliography (pp. 310–11), followed by a double-columned index (pp. 312–19), concluding this interesting, eclectic, but inevitably uneven collection in which some but not all of the essays would have benefited from stylistic pruning.

The non-attributed introduction to The *Bloomsbury Companion to Holocaust Literature*, edited by Jenni Adams, entitled 'Traces, Dis/ Continuities, Complicities: An Introduction to Holocaust Literature' (pp. 1– 24), is followed by accounts of 'current research' encompassing: 'A Genre of Rupture: The Literary Language of the Holocaust' (pp. 27–45) by Victoria Aarons; 'Questions of Truth in Holocaust Memory and Testimony' (pp. 47– 63) by Sue Vice; 'After Epic: Adorno's Scream and the Shadows of Lyric' (pp. 65–80) by David Miller; 'Relationships to Realism in Post-Holocaust Fiction: Conflicted Realism and the Counterfactual Historical Novel' (pp. 81–101) by Jenni Adams; 'Theory and the Ethics of Holocaust Representation' (pp. 103– 19) by Michael Bernard-Donals; '"Don't You Know Anything?": Childhood and the Holocaust' (pp. 121–38) by Adrienne Kertzer; 'Holocaust Postmemory: W.G. Sebald and Gerhard Richter' (pp. 139–57) by Brett Ashley Kaplan and Fernando Herrero-Matoses; 'Narrative Perspective and the Holocaust Perpetrator: Edgar Hilsenrath's *The Nazi and the Barber* and Jonathan Littell's *The Kindly Ones*' (pp. 159–77) by Erin McGlothlin; 'The Holocaust and the Taboo' (pp. 179–97) by Matthew Boswell; 'Holocaust Literature: Comparative Approaches' (pp. 199–218) by Stef Craps; and 'Depoliticizing and Repoliticizing Holocaust Memory' (pp. 219–36) by Richard Crownshaw. Each individual contribution begins with an abstract and concludes with notes and an alphabetically arranged, enumerative listing of works cited. There then follow three most useful non-attributed contributions that are probably the work of the editor Jenni Adams: 'New Directions in Holocaust Literary Studies' (pp. 237–63); an annotated bibliography (pp. 265–95), in an introductory paragraph to which its compiler writes that it 'aims not to provide an exhaustive list of materials in each of the subcategories listed, but instead to direct readers relatively new to the subject area towards key material and valuable starting points in research' and also that 'for reasons of accessibility and manageability, it is confined to material published in English or in English translation' (p. 265); and a highly useful 'Glossary of Major Terms and Concepts' (pp. 297–334), beginning with the concept of 'generation' (p. 297) and concluding with 'Yizker-bikher' or 'memorial books commemorating destroyed Jewish communities in Europe' (p. 330). The *Bloomsbury Companion to Holocaust Literature* is a highly important volume and appropriately concludes with a most useful double-columned index (pp. 335–7).

The first three volumes of Martin Wiggins, in association with Catherine Richardson's projected multi-volume *British Drama 1533–1642: A Catalogue* were assessed in *YWES* 93[2014] 247–8. Brief mention must be made of the fourth volume, covering the years 1598–1602. These are the years in which theatrical satire developed and the initial Globe Theatre opened. The format is as for the previous volumes with abbreviations (pp. vii–x) followed by 'List of Entries' (pp. xi–xiii), then a yearly annotated double-columned listing of 'British Drama, 1598–1602' (pp. 1–435). There are three indexes, of persons (pp. 455–66), places (pp. 467–8), and plays (pp. 469–74): the first two are double-columned and the third triple-columned. Yet again the computer-generated text is clear, as is the layout, and the binding is firm for this ongoing important reference work that should grace the shelves for a long time to come—Catharine Richardson is working on an online edition of the volumes.

Omitted from *YWES* 93[2014] coverage was Michael Calabrese and Stephen H.A. Shepherd, eds., *Yee? Baw for Bokes: Essays on Medieval Manuscripts and Poetics in Honor of Hoyt N. Duggan*. As the editors indicate in their introduction (pp. 1–7), Hoyt N. Duggan 'retired *emeritus* in 2007 after a 40-year career at the University of Virginia' and most of his scholarly engagement, but not all, had been with *Piers Plowman*. He is the 'master of medieval metrics and founder of the *Piers Plowman Electronic Archive* (*PPEA*)' (pp. 1–2). An enumerative bibliography of works by Hoyt N. Duggan (pp. 9–12) reveals six co-edited works, twenty-nine articles or review articles, and thirteen reviews. There are contributions from many eminent Anglo-American scholars too in this volume divided into two sections. The first focuses on 'Composition and Authorship' and contains: 'The **B** Archetype of *Piers Plowman* as a Corpus for Metrical Analysis' (pp. 17–30) by Thorlac Turville-Petre; '*The Bridges at Abingdon*: An Unnoticed Alliterative Poem' (pp. 31–44) by Ralph Hanna; 'Some Final -*e*'s in the Hoccleve Holographs' (pp. 45–53) by John Burrow; 'Final -*e* in the Middle English Translation of Palladius's *Opus Agricultura*' (pp. 55–66) by Judith Jefferson; 'John But and the Problem of Langlandian Authority' (pp. 67–85) by Thomas A. Prendergast; 'Filling the Gap in *Piers Plowman* **A**: Trinity College, Dublin, **MS 213**' (pp. 87–106) by Mícheál F. Vaughan. The second section is devoted to essays on 'Reception and Use' and contains: '"He is inwardly flayde": Inscription and the Wakefield *Buffeting*'s Self-Incriminating Jew' (pp. 111–26) by Regula Meyer Evitt; '**Hm 128** as a Medieval Book' (pp. 127–58) by Michael Calabrese, which is followed by an appendix: 'Ad Celebres Rex from **Hm 128**' (pp. 159–64); 'Text-Image Articulation in **MS Douce 104**' (pp. 165–201) by Stephen H.A. Shepherd; 'The Shadow of the Book: Piers Plowman, the Ilchester Prologue, and Inhumane Revision' (pp. 203–18) by D. Vance Smith; 'Intellect, Influence, and Evidence: the Elusive Allure of the **Ht** Scribe' (pp. 219–39), followed by three appendices—'Lines Unique to **Ht** Appearing within Runs of Lines Copied from a Single Version of Piers' (pp. 240–1), '**Ht**-Unique Lines at Points of Versional Shift' (p. 242), and 'Examples of Latin Emendations and Interpolations in **Ht**' (p. 243) by Patricia R. Bart; 'Langland as a Proto-Protestant: Was Thomas Fuller Right?' (pp. 245–66) by Robert Adams; and lastly 'Audience and Text: The Rylands Lydgate Manuscripts' (pp. 266–78) by A.S.G. Edwards, who observes that 'One of the distinctive aspects of Hoyt Duggan's scholarly achievement has been his early and creative grasp of the potential of computer technology, both in his studies of *Piers Plowman*'s metrics and his development of the *Piers Plowman Electronic Archive*' (p. 267). Following 'Notes on Contributors' (pp. 281–2) there are two indexes: of manuscripts cited (pp. 283–5) followed by a detailed general index (pp. 287–96). Notation, often detailed, is at the foot of the page, there is a listing of abbreviation' drawn upon in the collection (p. 13), although it is assumed that readers will know that for instance '**Ht**' (p. 219) refers to the Huntington Library. It is difficult at times to distinguish between bold lettering, and lower- and upper-case lettering owing to the design of this collection. Hoyt N. Duggan was a scholar who clearly influenced generations of scholars in his field.

'Skip Brack', as he was known, was 'an impressive figure in the academic world' according to Jerry Beasley in his 'Skip Brack: A Tribute from a Colleague and Friend' (p. ix), the introductory essay in Jesse G. Swan's *Editing Lives: Essays in Contemporary Textual and Biographical Studies in Honor of O.M. Brack, Jr.* Beasley's tribute (pp. ix–xiv) is followed by 'Print Borne and Born Digital: Considering Careers, My Father's and My Own' by Matthew Brack (pp. xv–xviii), a list of illustrations (p. xix)—there are three of them in black and white, in addition to the front jacket colour photo of O.M. Brack, Jr. standing in front of Sir Joshua Reynolds's (1775) portrait of 'Blinking Sam' (Samuel Johnson) now at the Huntington Library, San Marino, California. On the back jacket is a reproduction of a manuscript page from Dr Johnson's diary: the page deals with the subject of leading a useful life and is also at the Huntington. In his introduction (pp. xxiii–xxviii), Jesse G. Swan writes that 'Brack's scholarship concentrates on the transmission of early modern literature, especially of the British eighteenth century, notably of Samuel Johnson and Tobias Smollett. This collection reflects these interests, contributions, and accomplishments, by being organized into four parts: textual studies, biographical studies, an edition, and a brief coda on Brack's career.' There are also 'two personal reflections on Brack' (p. xxiii). There are four contributions to the first section, 'Textual Studies': 'Collecting Samuel Johnson and His Circle' (pp. 1–8) by Loren Rothschild; 'Some Notes on the Textual Fidelity of Eighteenth-Century Reprint Editions' (pp. 9–32) by James E. May; 'Learning from *Don Bilioso's Adventures*: Visualizing a Critical Edition of the Printed Works of John Arbuthnot' (pp. 33–44) by Walter H. Keithley; and '*The Solicitation* in Two Acts: James Robinson Planché's *Vampires* on Stage, in Color, and under Cover' (pp. 45–64) by Jennifer M. Santos. The second section is devoted to 'Biographical Studies' and consists of seven contributions: 'Samuel Parr's Epitaph for Johnson, His Library, and His Unwritten Biography' (pp. 67–92) by Robert DeMaria, Jr.; ' Samuel Johnson's Shakespearean Exit: Emendation and Amendment' (pp. 93–105) by Gordon Turnbull; 'Searching for the Invisible Man: The Images of Francis Barber' (pp. 107–22) by Michael Bundock; '*Alceste*: Tobias Smollett's Early Career' (pp. 123–30) by Leslie Chilton; 'Gender, State Power, and the Rhetoric of the Funeral Sermons for Queen Mary II' (pp. 131–49) by Marline W. Brownley; 'Swift's Politics Reconsidered' (pp. 151–76) by Thomas Kaminski; and 'The Work of a Professional Biographer: Oliver Goldsmith's *The Life of Richard Nash, Esq*' (pp. 177–94) by Christopher D. Johnson. The third part is devoted to the 'Edition' and contains a single contribution: 'Frances Burney on Hester

Thrale Piozzi: "Une Petite Histoire"' (pp. 197–218) by Peter Sabor. The 'contribution is dedicated to the memory of O M Brack, Jr.: Johnsonian, biographer, textual scholar, editor, and bibliophile extraordinaire' (p. 197). It is followed by a 'Coda "But when I come, let me have the benefit of your advice, and the consolation of your company": The Career, with a Listing of Publications, of O.M. Brack, Jr.' (pp. 219–41) by Jesse G. Swan. This, enumerative in order of its subject's most recent publications and then proceeding to his first, is divided into 'Editions and Books' (pp. 220–2), of which twenty-nine are listed, 'Collections' (p. 222) listing six, followed by well over a hundred 'Articles, Chapters, and Pamphlets' (pp. 222–5). An enumerative bibliography (pp. 227–41) is followed by a useful double-columned index (pp. 243–55). Individual contributions in the collection are followed by at times extensive note documentation in smaller computer-generated font than that of the larger essay texts, and this fascinating volume concludes with an 'About the Contributors' section (pp. 257–60).

L.W. Conolly, the general editor of the *Selected Correspondence of Bernard Shaw and Gilbert Murray*, in his 'General Editor's Note' (pp. vii–viii) to the volume dedicated to the correspondence of Shaw and the classicist and translator of classical Greek drama Gilbert Murray (1886–1957), who became the Regius Professor of Greek at Oxford, notes that it 'is the eighth in the series' (p. vii). As the editor of this volume, Charles A. Carpenter, observes in his introduction (pp. ix–xxxii), 'The present volume includes 171 letters, 86 from Murray, 85 from Shaw (only 30 of them in Dan H. Laurence's edition of Shaw's *Collected Letters* [published in four volumes between 1965 and 1988]' (p. ix). 'The friendship between Shaw and Murray began on 16 July 1895, at the drama critic William Archer's provocation... It ended in 1950, when 94-year-old Shaw died, seven years before Murray, who reached 91' (p. xi). In his 'Editor's Note' (pp. xxxiii–xxxv), Carpenter indicates that Shaw's idiosyncratic spelling has been retained 'except when the original letters were inaccessible or printed copies altered them', although 'typographical errors have generally been corrected' (p. xxxiv). Acknowledgements (pp. xxxvii–xl), and abbreviations (pp. xli–xlii) are followed by the text of the letters (pp. 3–255) with detailed explanatory annotation that not merely gives biographical details of people or plays mentioned but places each in its immediate historical context and that of Shaw's or Murray's other correspondence at the time of writing. The text of the letters is followed by a numbered 'Table of Correspondents' (pp. 257–61), an extensive, alphabetically arranged, enumerative list of references (pp. 263–74) arranged under 'Works by Bernard Shaw' (pp. 263–5), 'Works by Gilbert Murray' (pp. 265–6), and 'Other References' (pp. 266–74), and a very detailed double-columned index (pp. 275–96). My only caveat is that, with the exception of the jacket—that no doubt will be discarded once it reaches libraries—containing a facial drawing of the two correspondents—there are no photographs of either, or of the texts Carpenter has edited.

The fifth volume of the important Faber edition of *The Letters of T.S. Eliot* covers the years 1930–1. Eliot produced *Ash-Wednesday*, also in 1930 *Marina* was published, and in 1931 *Triumphal March*. As John Haffenden, observes in his preface (pp. xiii–xvii), 'Volume 5...documents a period of two years in which the poet, critic and editor endeavours, between the ages of forty-two and forty-four, to place his newly avowed faith in Christianity . . . At the centre of his life.' Additionally 'it is a tough time for Eliot, morally and socially. Several of his friends and associates, including Virginia Woolf, Herbert Reed and A.L. Rowse, are at odds with his religious commitment; some are even antagonistic or patronizing' (p. xiii). So there is much of interest personally, intellectually, and creatively for students of Eliot. Following Haffenden's 'Valerie Eliot Editing the Letters' (pp. xix–xxxvii), is a most useful 'Biographical Commentary 1930–1931' (pp. xxxix–lii) in the form of a lengthy paragraph narrating by month, and at times by the day of the month, its subject's activities. 'Abbreviations and Sources' (pp. liii–lviii) are then given: although these indicate some institutional and private Eliot holdings they are by no means comprehensive and do not indicate the extent of the holdings. Most of Eliot's letters or at least copies of them remain at the Faber Archive. There is a 'Chronology of *The Criterion*' (p. lix), the journal Eliot was editing during the period covered by this fifth volume, and 'Editorial Notes', stating for instance that 'the source of each letter is indicated at the top right. CC indicates a carbon copy. Where no other source is shown it may be assumed that the original or carbon copy is in the Valerie Eliot collection or at the Faber Archive' (p. lxi). The text of the letters with at times extensive footnote documentation (see for instance pp. 66–7 or 172) extends from pages 2 to 791. It is followed by a most helpful detailed 'Biographical Register' beginning with 'Conrad Aiken (1889–1973)' (p. 793) and concluding with 'Virginia Woolf (1882–1941)' (p. 827). The volume concludes with Douglas Matthews's, the doyen of indexers, splendid alphabetically arranged 'Index of Correspondents and Recipients' (pp. 829–34) and comprehensive double-columned general index (pp. 835–62). Mention too should be made of the twenty black and white well-reproduced illustrations inserted between pages 386 and 387 of the text, and the front wrapper photograph of Eliot 'by Elliott & Fry, c.1930' from the Faber Archive (p. vii). The binding is sturdy and the typesetting clear with the text of the letters in a slightly larger font than the footnotes that illuminate them.

Ian Hamilton Finlay (1925–2006), the Scottish poetic artist, has become something of a cult figure in the world of visual poetics with its focus on the ways in which written language communicates through letters, words, syllables, images, and so on. Indeed Finlay's artefacts have realized high prices in the rarefied collector's visual art market. *Midway: Letters from Ian Hamilton Finlay to Stephen Bann 1964–69*, as the distinguished academic recipient Bann indicates in his preface (pp. 7–10), constitutes 'the opening series of a total of well over six hundred letters that [he] received from Ian Hamilton Finlay in the period between 1964 and 2003'. Furthermore, 'the full interest lies . . . in the absorbing record of Finlay's life at a period when he was searching, quite often in a mood of desperation, for a fresh new direction in his work as a poet'. Bann's next claim is in dispute and only time will tell. He writes that 'Finlay later became one of the foremost artists of his generation, not just in Scotland but in the broader international context', and that this 'is now very widely accepted' (p. 7). Less controversial is Bann's observation that 'an overriding dilemma which cannot be ignored in these letters is his troubled and ambivalent relationship with Scotland; or to be more specific, with the

Scottish cultural institutions of the period and a wide section of the Scottish literary and artistic community' (p. 8). In a 'Note to the Reader', Bann writes that 'care has been taken to keep the spontaneity of the writing by retaining the frequent use of ellipses of different lengths ... to indicate variable breaks in continuity' (p. 9). As a measure of the high esteem in which Finlay is held his correspondence may be found at the University of Kansas and the Lilly Library at the University of Indiana, Bloomington, as well as in private hands. Bann's text is divided into four sections reflecting chronology and place; it is accompanied by helpful introductory commentary and footnote explication. Between pages 224 and 225 are twenty-four colour and black and white plates conveying place, individuals, and Finlay's work: some are especially evocative of time and place, especially the full-page plate of the 'banner made at the Chelsea College of Art ... exhibited at the Brighton Festival, April 1967' with three pensioners sitting on a municipal bench with the Dome and Royal Pavilion behind them and a van with the Bournemouth Symphony Orchestra's logo emblazoned on its side (see plate 10 and p. 227). This valuable collection concludes with a chronologically arranged, partly descriptive select bibliography, 1963–1970 (pp. 409–16) divided into two sections. The first is a listing of 'Critical Writings Relating to Ian Hamilton Finlay and Concrete Poetry 1963–1970' (pp. 409–11). The second part consists of 'Publications by Ian Hamilton Finlay 1963–1970' (pp. 411–16). In addition there is a helpful 'Biographical Index' (pp. 417–26). The book was 'Designed and typeset by Jane Havell Associates' (p. 4). Bann's volume is clearly an important contribution to the understanding of, amongst many things, a neglected poet and provides a perspective on a period of cultural activity in which the Beatles are not even mentioned. Unfortunately, when *Midway* enters libraries—as it should—its jacket will be thrown away: on the back is an evocative black and white photograph of Ian Hamilton Finlay sailing on a Scottish loch.

The third and penultimate volume of *The Letters of Samuel Beckett* opens with a list of illustrations (pp. x–xi); there are eighteen of these, largely photographs, scattered throughout the text followed by a general introduction (pp. xii–xxiv) that includes sections on the research for this particular third volume (p. xvii), 'Selection, Presentation, and Annotation' (pp. xvii–xxiii), and 'Lacunae' (pp. xxiii–xxiv). The introduction opens with a guide to the contents of volume 3. It 'reveals a Beckett who, astonished by the critical and commercial success of his plays, finds himself having recourse more than ever before to letters as a way of conveying thoughts, intentions, projects, even aspirations, to his friends and to his ever more numerous colleagues and collaborators—as well as his by now customary doubts and hesitations, about his own work above all' (p. xii). As George Craig indicates in his detailed 'French Translator's Preface' (pp. xxv–xxxiv), the third volume 'brings a Beckett who has had four major prose works in French published, and one play both published and staged'. For Craig the key questions are 'What effect does all this have on Beckett's language[?]' and 'how [am] I as translator ... to understand it[?]' (p. xxv). Craig concludes that 'Samuel Beckett is a great writer, and a part of his greatness is his sureness of linguistic touch. Whoever sets out to translate *him*: to catch the rhythms and sonorities of his prose, to represent the ebb and flow of his confidence, and to preserve his separateness (he is not *like* anybody)—well, any such venturer has to recognize that, quite simply, it cannot be done' (pp. xxxiii–xxxiv). Extensive and clear explanations of editorial procedure' are followed by acknowledgements (pp. xliv–li), an extensive listing of permissions (pp. lii–liv), abbreviations (lv–lix), and Dan Gunn's detailed introduction to the volume (pp. lxi–lxxxix). The text of 'Letters 1957–1965' (pp. 3–687) then follows with, before each individual year covered, a tabulated monthly and specific day chronology of important events, for instance for 1957: '15 March Grove Press publish *Murphy*' (p. 3). The text of individual letters is clearly set out and accompanied by notation in a slightly smaller computer-generated typeface, at the foot of the page and frequently extending to the following page, that is very detailed, helpful, and useful (see for instance pp. 8–10)—there are even, within parenthesis, English translations provided from the French (see for instance p. 9). 'Profiles' as an appendix (pp. 691–704), alphabetically organized, begins with details of 'Fernando Arrabel (b. 1932), his life and relationship with Beckett (pp. 691–2) and concludes with details of 'X. A Quarterly Review' that ran from 1959 to 1962 and 'owed its existence to the enthusiasm of [Beckett's] friend Mary Hutchinson' (p. 704). There is an extensive alphabetically arranged enumerative bibliography of works cited (pp. 705–20), an index of recipients (pp. 721–3), an index of first names (pp. 724–5), and a 'Summary Listing of Samuel Beckett's Works, Mentioned in Volume III' (pp. 726–9), and this splendid work of scholarship concludes with an extensive general index (pp. 730–71)— the work apparently of an anonymous but important contributor to the volume—that manages to indicate that the 'names of persons and publications with a profile in this volume are marked with an asterisk; those with a profile in a previous volume are noted with an asterisk and with that volume number' (p. 730).

The second of a projected six-volume edition of the *Letters of William Godwin*, edited by Pamela Clemit, covers the years 1798 to 1805.Clemit notes in her introduction (pp. xxvii–xl) that 'these were years of transition, in which Godwin had to meet the challenges of adversity: a decline in his public reputation, fewer readers for his political writings, and a fragmentation of his domestic and social milieu'. Furthermore, 'the turn in his fortunes was not reputational but also economic'. Clemit adds that 'the letters reveal him adapting to changes in public mood, seeking compromise in his philosophical commitments, rebuilding his social circles, and remaking himself as the author of novels, plays, biographies, and children's books' (p. xxvii). The second volume contains 242 letters: the first volume of covered the years 1778 to 1797 and consisted of 191 letters. Clemit as an editor is fortunate, as she indicates in her 'Note on Editorial Principles' (pp. xli–xliv), that 'Godwin's handwriting is nearly always clear and well-formed'. The letters in her edition 'are arranged in chronological sequence' (p. xli), and she clearly outlines the principles that she has adopted, including those dealing with drafts and explanatory notes. A 'Chronology of William Godwin, 1798–1805)' (pp. xlv–xlvii) is provided prior to the text of the letters (pp. 3–375). At times extensive notes are found at the foot of the page of the letters. These may be textual or explanatory or both, and also contain what the editor refers to as 'a rejected draft' (p. 23)—see for instance 'Godwin to [Harriet Lee], 2 June 1798' (pp. 22–6). There are four appendices: 'Undated Letters' (pp. 377–9); 'Receipts for Book Sales' (pp. 381–2); 'Promissory Notes' (pp. 383–90)—there are twelve of these 'used by Godwin to pay his household bills' (p. 383); and 'Letters in the Abinger Papers [at the Bodleian Library]: Old and New Shelfmarks' (pp. 391–9). The index (pp. 401–23) is very useful, utilizing bold print to indicate 'the names of Godwin's correspondents' (p. 401). This magisterial edition contains ten black and white illustrations (between pp. 242 and 243), a useful preliminary 'List of Letters' (pp. xiii–xix), and a helpful listing of 'Abbreviations and Symbols' (pp. xxiii–xxvi). There is something reassuring about the illusion of permanence of this volume, with the familiar publisher's shades of blue dust-jacket and gilt-decorated spine that are not to be found in the ephemerality of the electronic edition that may disappear somewhere into the ether. Long may such editions in print continue!

S.E. Gontarski has edited *The Edinburgh Companion to Samuel Beckett and the Arts*. This comprehensive reference work includes, in addition to the editor's introduction, 'Towards a Minoritarium Criticism: The Questions We Ask' (pp. 1–13), nine parts. In the first 'Art and Aesthetics' (pp. 17–63), there are four contributions: ' "Deux besoins": Samuel Beckett and the Aesthetic Dilemma' (pp. 17–24) by C. J. Ackerley; ' "Siege Laid Again": Arikha's Gaze, Beckett's Painted Stage' (pp. 25–43) by David Lloyd, who assesses Arikha's impact upon Beckett's work and which is prefaced by eight full-page colour plate illustrations from work by Beckett's close friend Avigdor Arikha (between pp. 24 and 25); 'Convulsive Aesthetics: Beckett, Chaplin and Charcot' (pp. 44–53) by Ulrika Maude, who places Beckett's development in the context of two other pioneers from different fields of human endeavour; and 'Pain Degree Zero' (pp. 54–63) by Sam Slote, who concludes in his consideration of Beckett and pain that 'The act of writing, of revising, of excavating one's works is a synaesthetic anaesthetic in that it translates pain into a different register until the faint, optative end' (pp. 61–2). The second part, 'Fictions' (pp. 67–99), has three contributions: 'Sexual Indifference in the Three Novels' (pp. 67–77) by Paul Stewart; 'A Neuropolitics of Subjectivity: Samuel Beckett's Three Novels' (pp. 78–88) by Andrew McFeaters; and 'Evening, Night, and other Shades of Dark: Beckett's Short Prose' (pp. 89–99) by Tomasz Wiśniewski. The third part is concerned with 'A European Context' (pp. 103–96) of Beckett's work and has seven contributions. First is 'French Beckett and French Literary Politics 1945–52' by Andrew Gibson, who writes that 'Beckett's French writings 1944–52 share with the dissidents and rightists a large measure of harsh disenchantment, even strains of populist brutality and cynicism. Yet they are also distinguished from them by a sophisticated, immensely demanding work of negation or "writing off" that is quite alien to and definitely exceeds them.' For Gibson, Beckett's 'ambivalence breeds what we now recognize as the specific mode of Beckett's gorgeous, bone-dry irony. It is an irony in some degree particular to the French texts and only quite comprehensible in a French context' (p. 113). 'Beckett/Sade: Texts for Nothing' (pp. 117–30), engages John Pilling, as does Beckett's relation to 'the art of André Masson' (p. 131) in 'Beckett's Masson: From Abstraction to Non-Relation' (pp. 131–45) by Jean-Michel Rabaté. Other contributions in this section include 'Beckett, Duthuit, and Ongoing Dialogue' (pp. 146–52) by Anthony Uhlmann; 'Gloria SMH and Beckett's Linguistic Encryptions' (pp. 153–60), by Laura Salisbury, a fascinating account that draws upon Beckett's wartime activities in the 'information network, known as GlorioSMH' (p. 153); '"I am writing a manifesto because I have nothing to say": Samuel Beckett and the Inter-War Avant-Garde' (pp. 170–84), is the concern of Peter Fifield; and the final contribution to this third part is 'Beckett and Contemporary French Literature' (pp. 185–96) by Sjef Houpermans.

The fourth part deals with 'An Irish Context' (pp. 199–234), and has three contributions: 'The "Irish" Translation of Samuel Beckett's *En Attendant Godot*' (pp. 199–208) by Anthony Roche, whose concern is 'to direct attention to the translation Beckett himself provided of his French original and to highlight the strong vein of Irish and Dublin idiom which Beckett introduced into the relatively neutral French' (p. 199); 'Odds, Ends, Beginnings: Samuel Beckett and Theatre Cultures in 1930s Dublin' (pp. 209–21) by Emilie Morin; and '"Bid Us Sigh On": Beckett and the Irish Big House"' (pp. 222–34) by Sean Kennedy, which is especially concerned with *Watt* and such questions as 'why would Beckett think to begin writing an Irish Big House novel in German occupied Paris in February 1941? And why would he continue to develop it into its final form while on the run from the Gestapo in the occupied zone?' (p. 222). The fifth part, 'Film, Radio and Television' (pp. 237–65), has, somewhat surprisingly, only two contributions. These are: 'A Womb with a View: *Film* as Regression Fantasy' (pp. 237–50) by Graley Herren, who writes that '*Film* investigates the nature of being by dramatising a figure's desperate attempt not to be' (p. 237), and '"The Sound Is Enough": Beckett's Radio Plays' (pp. 251–65) by Everett C. Frost, an all too brief account of an important area of Beckett's creative output. As Frost observes: 'the radio plays clarify and develop themes, concerns, strategies, sources and references that are of considerable interest in their own right and illuminate Beckett's prose fiction and plays for stage and television'. Unfortunately Frost limits his discussion to the area of 'Beckett's use in the radio plays of the philosophy of Arthur Schopenhauer, the Cartesian occasionalism of Arnold Geulincx, and the compulsion to tell stories and identify the voice in the head' (p. 251). The sixth part is on the subject of 'Language/Writing' (pp. 269–329), with four contributions. First, '"Was That a Point?": Beckett's Punctuation' (pp. 269–81) by Steven Connor, who in a fascinating contribution writes 'Beckett's prose takes much of its timbre and temper from its highly distinctive patterns of punctuation. Unusually, Beckett employed not one, but several systems of punctuation over the course of his writing life' (p. 269). Second, 'Beckett's Unpublished Canon' (pp. 282–305) by Mark Nixon, 'aims' with exceptions 'to give an overview of Beckett's unpublished creative writing, concentrating on texts that were developed beyond the stage of germination' (p. 283). Nixon's essay not only concludes, as is the case with other essays in the *Companion*, with, where appropriate, notes (in Nixon's case pp. 301–2), and an enumerative, alphabetically arranged, listing of works cited (pp. 304–5), but also contains a bibliography alphabetically arranged with brief description divided into 'Samuel Beckett—Archival Material' (pp. 302–3), 'Samuel Beckett—Correspondence' (pp. 303–4), and 'Samuel Beckett—Publications' (pp. 304). In his 'Textual Scars: Beckett, Genetic Criticism and Textual Scholarship' (pp. 306–19), Dirk Van Hulle 'explore[s] the possibilities of a bilingual edition of Samuel Beckett's works that combines the expertise of genetic criticism and scholarly editing, and that enables readers to explore both the *synchronic* structure of the texts as "finished products" and the *diachronic* structure of their writing processes, making use of both print and digital media' (p. 307)'. 'Beckett's *Ill Seen Ill Said*: Reading the Subject, Subject to Reading' (pp. 320–9) by Adam Piette contains his close reading of the 1981/1982 French/English Beckett text. The seventh part, 'Philosophies' (pp. 333–69), contains three contributions, opening with 'Beckett and Philosophy' (pp. 333–44), in which Matthew Feldman observes in his opening sentence that 'connections between Samuel Beckett and philosophy were varied and lively throughout his life, and are still kicking more than a generation of his death' (p. 333). In his brief ' "Ruse a by": *Watt*, the Rupture of the Everyday, and Transcendental Empiricism' (pp. 345–52), S.E. Gontarski considers some of the philosophical implications of Beckett's novel. 'Beckett, Modernism and Christianity' (pp. 353–69) is also short, although Erik Tonning accompanies it with 106 notes (pp. 364–7), and his opening sentence rather gives the game away when he writes 'Christianity is Samuel Beckett's fundamental antagonist: his thought, his aesthetics and his writing cannot be fully understood in isolation from his lifelong struggle with it' (p. 353). The penultimate part of the *Companion*, devoted to 'Theatre and Performance' (pp. 373–441), has six contributions. In ' "Oh Lovely Art": Beckett and Music' (pp. 373–85), David Tucker interestingly draws upon unpublished materials; 'Victimized Actors and Despotic Directors: Clichés of Theatre at Stake in Beckett's *Catastrophe*' (pp. 386–96) by Laura Peja centres upon Beckett's demands upon his actors; 'Beyond Eliot and Joyce: Restaging Solo Literary Performance in "A Piece of Monologue" ' (pp. 397–408) by John Paul Riquelme draw parallels between Beckett's monologues and his 'modernist precursors, especially James Joyce and T.S. Eliot' (p. 397); 'Designing Beckett: Jocelyn Herbert's Contribution to Samuel Beckett's Theatrical Aesthetics' (pp. 409–22) by Anna McMullan examines Beckett's work 'with particular designers, and [particularly] Jocelyn Herbert (1917–2003)...one of his closest collaborators' (p. 409); 'Dianoetic Laughter in Tragedy: Accepting Finitude—Beckett's *Endgame*' (pp. 423–32) by Annamaria Cascetta is translated from her Italian and is a close reading of Beckett's text; 'Performing the Formless' (pp. 433–41) is another brief contribution, in this instance by Geneviève Chevallier, who while focusing on Beckett's 'later works...[is] quite aware that all of Beckett's plays show a concern for the fabrication of an elaborate scenic image' (p. 433). The final part, the ninth of the *Companion*, on 'Global Beckett' (pp. 445–75), accompanied by black and white illustrations, has three contributions: ' "Facing other Windows": Beckett in Brazil' (pp. 445–52) by Fábio de Souza Andrade; 'Beckett in Belgrade' (pp. 453–464) by Predrag Todorovic; and ' "Struggling with a Dead Language": Language of Others in *All That Fall* and the Japanese Avant-Garde Theatre in the 1960s' (pp. 465–75) by Mariko Hori Tanaka. *The Edinburgh Companion to Samuel Beckett and the Arts* concludes with an alphabetically arranged detailed list of contributors (pp. 477–84), and a helpful index (pp. 485–504). Considerable attention has been paid in this comprehensive edition, well bound and 'typeset in 10/12 Goudy by Norman Tilley Graphics' (p. iv), to the bibliographical, textual, critical, and performative literature of a major writer.

Stephen Prickett's lavishly illustrated edited *The Edinburgh Companion to the Bible and the Arts* is divided into three sections: 'Inspiration and Theory' (pp. 11–127); 'Art and Architecture' (pp. 131–380); and 'Literature' (pp. 383–563). It is the contributions to this third and final section that are of immediate interest to *YWES* readers, although the other two sections are replete with fascinating contributions too. In 'Sacred Poetry: Watts and Wesley' (pp. 383–400), J.R. Watson considers the achievement of 'Isaac Watts ... born in 1674, the year of Milton's death. In his sacred poetry, he was exploring what it was like to inherit something of the great man's ambition to write inspired but human religious poetry' (p. 383). In his 'The Bible Interpreted by Hymns' (pp. 401–10), Robin Gill's 'focus ... is upon the way that the Bible is interpreted and, in turn, shapes modern hymn-books'. Gill examines 'examples of the way some of the most widely used British hymn-books in the Anglican and Presbyterian traditions have changed over the last half a century in their use of the Bible' (p. 401). 'Within the Hebrew and Christian scriptures, and even more on their fringes, are wild dreams and visions' (p. 411), writes Christopher Burdon in his 'The Art of Unveiling: Biblical, Apocalypse' (pp. 411–27). Whilst Dante's great poem is the focus of 'The *Divine Comedy* as the Word of God' (pp. 428–39), Patricia Erskine-Hill does also find room for treatment of Dante's poem in, for instance, C.S. Lewis's *The Great Divorce* [1946], which 'in particular is a paean to free will and almost a parody of the *Comedy*' (p. 436). 'The Mediaeval Bible as Literature' (pp. 440–58) by Alastair Minnis and A.B. Kraebel encompasses discussion of Alcuin of York, Nicholas Trevet, Henry Cossey, and others. 'Homer Writes Back: Rhetorical Art and Biblical Epic Justice in *Paradise Lost*, Book 1' (pp. 459–76) by Phillip Donnelly focuses upon a specific literary work. An author and his specific works are the subject of 'Biblical and Seventeenth-Century Poetry: The Case of the Psalms and George Herbert' (pp. 477–92) by Christopher Hodgkins. 'From Virtue to Goodness: Biblical Values in Victorian Literature' (pp. 493–506), is the subject of Jan-Melissa Schramm, whose focus is fiction, with particular attention to Dickens and others. Once again attention is directed to a specific author and work in 'The Mirror of the Law of Liberty: Reflecting the Hidden Christ in George MacDonald's *Lilith*' (pp. 507–20) by Bethany Bear. 'Figurative Literalism: the Image of the Creator/Creation from Frankenstein to Nietzsche' (pp. 521–33), is the subject of Norbert Lennartz's contribution. In 'From Satire to Sanctity: The Prophetic Books in T.S. Eliot's Poetry' (pp. 534–49), Jan Gorak illuminates the biblical indebtedness of Eliot especially in *The Waste Land* and the *Four Quartets*' (p. 549). Drama, especially '*Imitatio Pilati et Christi* in Modern Historical Drama' (pp. 550–63), absorbs James Alexander in the final essay in *The Edinburgh Companion to the Bible and the Arts*. According to Alexander, 'Modern historical drama reaches its climax when the *vicarious Christi* encounters the *vicarious Pilati*, and a decisions has to be made about what is to be done with truth' (p. 562). Some detailed notes are found at the foot of the page in the collection, and some contributions are also followed by an alphabetically arranged, enumerative bibliography, as in the case of Shirley Smith's essay on 'The Fresco Decoration in the Sistine Chapel: Biblical Authority and the Church of Rome' (pp. 254–71).

Jason McElligott and Eve Patten have edited *The Perils of Print Culture: Book, Print and Publishing History in Theory and Practice* in the Palgrave Macmillan New Directions in Book History series edited by Jonathan Rose and Shafquat Towheed. The prefatory material to *The Perils* contains a list of figures (p. vii; there are nine of these in black and white); a list of tables (p. viii; of which there are two); acknowledgements (p. ix); and 'Notes on the Contributors' (pp. x–xii). These are then followed by 'The Perils of Print Culture: An Introduction' (pp. 1–16) by Jason McElligott and Eve Patten; 'The Practice of Book and Print Culture: Sources, Methods, Readings' (pp. 17–34) by the eminent Leslie Howsam; ' "Pretious Treasures Made Cheap"? The Real Cost of Reading Roman History in Early Modern England' (pp. 35–50) by Freyja Cox Jensen; 'Early Printed Liturgical Books and the Modern Resources that Describe Them: The Case of the Hereford Breviary, 1505' (pp. 51–63) by Matthew Cheung Salisbury; ' "Lacking Ware, Withal": Finding Sir James Ware among the Many Incarnations of His Histories' (pp. 64–81) by Mark Williams; 'Balancing Theoretical Models and Local Studies: The Case of William St. Clair and Copyright in Ireland' (pp. 82–95) by Sarah Crider Arndt; 'The Impact of Print in Ireland, 1680–1800: Problems and Perils' (pp. 96–117) by T.C. Barnard, fluently written as ever by such an eminent contributor and accompanied by seventy-three erudite notes following the text; 'Signs of the Times? Reading Signatures in Two Late Seventeenth-Century Secret Histories' (pp. 118–33) by Rebecca Bullard; 'Dangerous Detours: The Perils of Victorian Periodicals in the Digitized Age' (pp. 134–49) by Margery Masterson; 'Nineteenth-Century Print on the Move: A Perilous Study of Trans-Local Migration and Print Skills Transfer' (pp. 150–66) by another eminent contributor, David Finkelstein; 'The Problem with Libraries: The Case of Thomas Marshall's Collection of English Civil War Printed Ephemera' (pp. 167–81) by Annette Walton; 'The "Lesser" Dürer? Text and Image in Early-Modern Broadsheets' (pp. 182–95) by Cristina Neagu—this contribution is accompanied by five illustrative black and white figures; and ' "Fair Forms" and "Withered Leaves": The *Rose Bud* and the Peculiarities of Periodical Print' (pp. 204–17) by Anna Luker Gilding. The final contribution is by yet another distinguished contributor, James Raven, who writes on ' "Print Culture" and the Perils of Practice' (pp. 218–37). This is followed by a rather brief enumerative, alphabetically arranged select bibliography (pp. 238–9). The volume, which contains some fascinating, well-written, and unpretentious contributions, concludes with a brief, name-orientated double-columned index (pp. 240–2). As McElligott and Patten indicate in their opening chapter 'The essays in this book are derived from a selection of the papers delivered at a conference entitled "The Perils of Print Culture" held at Trinity College Dublin in 2010' (p. 14). They 'put forward a working definition of print culture. A print culture can be said to exist when men and women from a range of backgrounds are used to seeing, reading, buying and borrowing print in a variety of social contexts. It exists when print is both commonplace and unexceptional, and when print is traded as a commodity within a market economy' (pp. 6–7).

An addition to Palgrave Macmillan's series New Directions in Book History is *Book Destruction from the Medieval to the Contemporary*, edited by Gill Partington and Adam Smyth. They indicate in their introduction that 'the five sections in this collection each present paradigmatic mechanisms of destruction: "Burning"; "Mutilating"; "Doctoring"; "Degrading"; and "Deforming/ Reshaping" ' (p. 9). A listing of the black and white figures accompanying the text (pp. vii–viii) is followed by 'Notes on the Contributors' (pp. ix–xi), and the editors' introduction (pp. 1–14). Each of the five parts each has two contributions. The first part consists of essays on: 'Burning Sexual Subjects: Books, Homophobia and the Nazi Destruction of the Institute of Sexual Sciences in Berlin' (pp. 17–33) by Heike Bauer; and 'Burning to Read: Ben Jonson's Library Fire of 1623' (pp. 33–55) by Adam Smyth. The second part, on 'Mutilating', has contributions on: 'From Books to Skoob; Or, Media Theory with a Circular Saw' (pp. 57–71) by Gill Partington, which 'examines the work of the radical British artist John Latham, whose career was a sustained attack on the book, astonishing in its range of methods, from burning to cutting and chewing' (p. 11). The text is accompanied by four black and white illustrations of Latham's work. This is followed by the editors' ' "Book Torture": An Interview with Ross Birrell' (pp. 74–86), 'an artist, writer and lecturer...[who] has a long-term interest in book destruction' (p. 74), which is accompanied by five examples of Birrell's work. The third part consists of: 'Belligerent Literacy, Bookplates, and Graffiti: Dorothy Helbarton's Book' (pp. 89–111), accompanied by three black and white illustrations, in which Anthony Bale focuses on a 'common kind of destructive impulse at work in a huge number of medieval books as they passed through time and changing audiences: the excised, cancelled or superseded ownership inscription, or bookplate' and specifically 'one medieval book that bears the marks of its history in the form of its bookplates' (p. 91). The second contribution is the editors' interview 'Doctoring Victorian Literature: *A Humument*: An Interview with Tom Phillips' (pp. 112–31): 'Phillips (b. 1937) is a painter, print maker and collagist, and the creator of *A Humument: A Treated Victorian Novel* (1970, 1980, 1986, 1998, 2004, and in 2010 as an IPhone and iPad app), a critically lauded blend of destruction and creativity' (p. 112), and the interview is accompanied by four black and white illustrations. The penultimate part, on 'Degrading', consists of: ' "Miss Cathy's riven th' back off 'Th' Helmet uh Salvation"': Representing Book Destruction in Mid-Victorian Print Culture' (pp. 135–51) by Stephen Colclough; and 'Waste Matters: Charles Dickens's *Our Mutual Friend* and Nineteenth-Century Book Recycling' (pp. 152–71) by Heather Tilley. In the fifth part Kate Flint writes on the 'Aesthetics of Book Destruction' (pp. 175–89). The final contribution is the editors' '*Kindle*: Recycling and the Future of the Book: An Interview with Nicola Dale ' (pp. 190–207), 'a visual artist specializing in paper' (p. 190) with five black and white illustrations of her work. Essays in *Book Destruction from the Medieval to the Contemporary* are accompanied by notation following the text, and the book concludes with an alphabetically arranged, enumerative select bibliography (pp. 208–12) and a brief index (pp. 213–16). Somewhat surprising is the omission of a contribution/s on the recent habit of digitalization leading to the destruction or throwing out (recycling?) of books and periodicals by institutional libraries.

In the introduction to Hinks and Gardner, eds., *The Book Trade in Early Modern England: Practices, Perceptions, Connections*, 'Practices, Perceptions and Connections' (pp. vii–xv), Victoria Gardner writes: 'this collection of essays, taken from the "Print Networks" series of conferences between 2008 and 2010, explores the ways in which early modern book-trade personnel interacted, understood themselves and networks within and beyond the trade'. Furthermore, 'each essay offers insights, specific to era and location, into the ways in which book-trade actors ultimately shaped the meaning of the texts that they produced' (p. vii). There is a listing of contributors (pp. xvii–xix). The essays are divided into two parts, with the first focusing on 'Practices and Perceptions'. Contributions include: ' "I maruell who the diuell is his Printer": Fictions of Book Production in Anthony Munday's and Henry Chettle's Paratexts' (pp. 1–17) by Louise Wilson; ' "Printer, that art the Midwife to my muse": Thomas Freeman and the Analogy between Printing and Midwifery in Renaissance England' (pp. 19–44) by Harry Newman; ' "I do more confidently presume to publish it in his absence": William Ponsonby's Print Network' (pp. 45–60) by Stacy Erickson; ' "To be unto them as the foundation of a library": The Books of Robert Ashley at the Middle Temple' (pp. 61–85) by Renae Satterley; 'Sir Thomas Smith: Elizabethan Author and Book Collector' (pp. 87–105) by Lucy Hughes; and 'Women and the Production of Texts: The Impact of the History of the Book ' (pp. 107–31) by Maureen Bell. The second part, on the subject of 'Connections', contains five contributions: 'Printing Protestant Texts under Mary Tudor: The Role of Antwerp' (pp. 135–60) by Charlotte Anne Panofre; 'Strange News: Translations of European Sensational News Pamphlets and Their Place in Early Modern English News Culture' (pp. 161–86) by S.K. Barker; 'Henry Neville and *The Isle of Pines*: Author, Translator and the Political Project of Print' (pp. 187–208) by Dan Mills; 'The Book Trade and the Distribution of Print in the 1650s' (pp. 209–28) by Bernard Carp; and 'The Eighteenth-Century Book Trade in Region and Nation: Newcastle and the North-East' (pp. 229–56) by Victoria Gardner, which has four diagrammatic illustrative figures. There is a name-based, double-columned index (pp. 257–67) to this volume, which has a pleasant computer-generated type face, in some instances detailed footnotes to the text of individual contributions, and accompanying black and white illustrations/figures throughout.

James Raven's *Bookscape: Geographies of Printing and Publishing in London before 1800. The Panizzi Lectures 2010* has been published by the British Library, superbly designed by John Trevitt, with excellent typesetting and print. Lavishly illustrated in colour and black and white figures, the volume is a delight to possess. Dedicated to memory of the late eminent bibliographer 'Giles Gaudard Barber 1930–2012' (p. v), the contents include a list of illustrations and tables (pp. ix–xii), Raven's preface (pp. xiii–xiv), and his list of abbreviations (p. xv). Raven writes that 'the aim of this book is to build on recent research to provide a more detailed picture of the transformation in the London book trades of the eighteenth century and to contextualise this by offering, where appropriate, an early modern perspective' (p. 2). The nine chapters focus on: 'Places and Transformations' (pp. 1–12); 'The Evidence' (pp. 13–38); 'Antient Sites and Reconstructions' (pp. 39–56); 'Versatility and the Gloomy Stories of Literature' (pp. 57–69); 'Conversible Men and Mighty Trade' (pp. 71–85); 'Unexpected Declines' (pp. 86–96); 'East and West in the City' (pp. 97–120); 'Publishing and Printing: The Fleet to the Strand' (pp. 121–35); and 'Industry, Fashion and Pettifogging Drivellers' (pp. 136–51). There are six appendices: 'Members of the Book Trades in Little Britain and Duck Lane, c.1640 to c.1666' (pp. 152–4); 'Members of the Book Trades in Little Britain and Duck Lane, c.1666 to c.1700' (pp. 154–9); 'Selected Publications Printed by Samuel Buckley, John Matthews and William Wilkins of Little Britain, c.1700–19' (pp. 159–61); 'Selected Publications Printed by Thomas Wood of Town Ditch, Little Britain, c.1719–39' (p. 169); 'Annotated Transcription of *A Catalogue of the Copies, and Remaining Part of the Quire-Stock of Mr. George Conyers, Deceas'd*, Sold by Auction at the Queen's Head, Paternoster Row, 14 February 1740' (pp. 163–4); and 'Extract from the Probate Inventory of John Bew [no. 28 Paternoster Row], St. Faith, London, 1794, NA PROB 31/849/388 (exhibit), ff. 18–20' (p. 165). These are followed by extensive notes (pp. 166–87), an alphabetically arranged, enumerative select bibliography (pp. 188–94), and a name- and place-focused double-columned index (pp. 195–208). The front jacket illustration is of a Thomas Colman Dibdin watercolour painting, and the back jacket's colour illustration is from a James Gillray etching. Essentially Raven's book is an important one for its wealth of data and information.

In his second book to be published in 2014, *Publishing Business in Eighteenth-Century England*, James Raven surveys the 'never complete supersession of the oral by the printed, of the changing impact of the printed within what was written and read, and, above all, the role of the printed in providing material items that served and affected the conduct of trade and finance' during that period (pp. 4–5). Of the ten chapters in his book, the earlier ones 'examine the practical and instructional role of print in administrative and commercial transactions' and Raven also 'considers the new business "knowledge" and behavior effected by printing and stationery, jobbing work, commercial information, advertising, and published guides and directories'. In 'the remaining chapters [he] examine[s] the contribution of print to the gathering and dissemination of "intelligence", the generation of popular, public debate and the development of an understanding of trade among different readerships'. In the final chapter, Raven 'approaches the relationship between print and trade from the perspective of the common reader, familiar with (if not always appreciative of) jobbing print, and seeking practical and general information about trading and monetary matters' (p. 16). Raven 'draws on an abundance of local archival material and an under-exploited wealth of evidence which demands further inspection' (p. 15). There is an extensive enumerative, alphabetically arranged 'Bibliography of Printed Sources' (pp. 276–310), followed by a comprehensive index (pp. 311–34) to this clearly written, well bound and clearly typeset, for ease of reading, paperback study.

Jeffrey D. Burson's edited, outrageously overpriced, *Eighteenth-Century Thought*, volume 5, contains three contributions of relevance to *YWES* readers. Burson observes in his preface (pp. vii–xiv) that some of the contributors have had to wait at least four years for their 'long overdue' pieces to see the light of day (p. xiii). Rowland Weston in his ' "The End of the Commandment": William Godwin and the Doctrine of Necessity' (pp. 67–98), 'traces Godwin's engagements with the doctrine of philosophical necessity across five decades and a generically diverse range of his writings, some of which have been mostly ignored by scholars. These latter include the novels *Cloudesley* (1830) and *Deloraine* (1833) and the collection of essays *Thoughts on Man* (1831)' (p. 67). Giovanni B. Grandi, in his 'Hume and Reid on Political Economy' (pp. 99–145), compares and contrasts the attitudes of the two. For Grandi, 'The contrast between David Hume and Thomas Reid, however, must not be taken too far. On some particular matters of economic policy, such as paper credit, Hume and Reid eventually came to similar views' (p. 99). J.R. Milton's 'Locke and the Perils of Anecdotal History' (pp. 147–77) analyses the 'stories about his views and activities [that] appeared in print...[b]etween Locke's death [1704] and the appearance of the first detailed account of Locke's life based on his own papers, published by Lord King in 1829. The conclusion is that even stories told within a few years of Locke's death are often of dubious reliability, and that for a few decades almost everything was discarded as reliable historical testimony' (p. 147). There are two items of particular relevance to bibliography and textual studies in Katherine Ellison, Kit Kincade, and Holly Faith Nelson, eds. *Topographies of the Imagination: New Approaches to Daniel Defoe*. Kit Kincade's 'Editing Defoe: *A System of Magick* as Case Study' (pp. 117–37) 'analyzes and explicates the editorial process involved in accurately representing a single text by Daniel Defoe' (p. 117). Kincaid is also concerned with opening 'up three levels of conversation'. In the first her 'focus [is] on the analytical and descriptive bibliographical issues of one particular text, Daniel Defoe's *A System of Magick* (1727). The second level addresses the larger question of how we can create a standard critical edition of Defoe. The final level broadens to the subject of how we create scholarly editions of eighteenth-century works' (p. 117). There are illuminating sections on 'Establishing a Copy-Text' (pp. 118–23), 'Deriving the Ideal Copy' (pp. 123–7), and 'Proving Authorship' (pp. 127–36). Andreas K.E. Mueller's ' "One of the Greatest Puzzles in Defoe Bibliography": John Toland, Daniel Defoe and Ennobling Foreigners' (pp. 271–97) is concerned with the 1717 pamphlet, *An Argument Proving that the Design of Employing and Enobling Foreigners, Is a Treasonable Conspiracy against the Constitution, Dangerous to the Kingdom, an Affront to the Nobility of Scotland in particular, and Dishonorable to the Peerage of Britain in general* (p. 271), which has only recently been allowed into the Defoe canon. Its attribution was questioned largely owing to 'the fact that the rhetorical stances he [Defoe] assumes stand in the starkest of contrasts to the ones evident in earlier publications' and 'caused considerable discomfort among Defoe scholars' (p. 272). Mueller 'seeks to address this troublesome attribution to Defoe by exploring it both in its immediate polemical context and in the light of Defoe's earlier publications' (p. 273). In doing so he demonstrates that the work is 'as much about party politics as it is about John Toland, and it is conceivable, and indeed likely, that the ironic stance that Defoe assumes in parts of it was shaped to a significant extent by his desire to expose his enemies' flaws' (p. 297). *Topographies of the Imagination* concludes with an alphabetically arranged, enumerative bibliography (pp. 299–325), and a detailed, helpful index (pp. 327–36).

A comparative Anglo-American study that shouldn't be overlooked is Barbara Alice Mann's *The Cooper Connection: The Influence of Jane Austen on James Fenimore Cooper*, the fifty-third volume in AMS Studies in the Nineteenth Century (p. ii). In essence Mann explores 'the intertextuality of Cooper and Austen' (p. 25) in chapters having titles reflecting their author's jaunty, lively style: 'Afloat in the Angelfish Aquarium: Twain, Cooper, and Austen' (pp. 27–54); 'The "Parade of Morals": Clergymen: Dogmatic, Daffy, and Prim' (pp. 55–91); '"A Most Beloved Sister": Sisterhood Is Powerful in Austen and Cooper' (pp. 93–124); 'Dirty Girls in Austen and Cooper' (pp. 125–66); and 'Dark Brows: Empire, Slavery, and Racial Slippage' (pp. 167–220). There is a detailed enumerative, alphabetically arranged bibliography (pp. 221–36), followed by an extensive index (pp. 237–51) to this challenging study.

In her introduction, 'A Writer's Apprenticeship' (pp. 5–14), to the first volume of a three-volume boxed set of reproductions of Jane Austen's early work, *Volume the First, Volume the Second, and Volume the Third In Her Own Hand*, Kathryn Sutherland notes that Austen 'was writing short sketches (fiction, drama, and poetry) from as early as 1786 or 1787, aged 11 or 12'. Moreover 'running through these pieces is a pronounced thread of comment on an exuberant misreading of the fiction of her day, showing how thoroughly and how early the activity of critical reading informed her character as a writer' (vol. 1, p. 5). As Sutherland indicates, 'this facsimile edition of *Volume the First* has been produced with care to match the size of the original notebook, the appearance of its paper and the brown black color of the iron gall ink that Jane Austen used' (vol. 1, p. 14). Interestingly, 'The transcription following the manuscript is that of the great twentieth-century Austen scholar Robert W Chapman. Chapman was the first to edit Jane Austen's manuscripts in full and his early editions now have classic status' (vol. 1, p. 14). This procedure has been followed in the other two volumes as well. Given Kathryn Sutherland's slightly negative critique of Chapman in her *Jane Austen's Textual Lives* [2005] (*passim*, especially pp. 26–54), perhaps her reliance upon his transcriptions reveals a revisionist stance on her part. Sutherland also refers in passing (vol. 2, p. 6) to the fascinating editions of Jane Austen's 'Juvenilia' issued in separate pamphlets with transcriptions and notes published in the Juvenile Press Editions under the general editorship of Christine Alexander at the University of Sydney, New South Wales (see www.arts.unsw.edu.au/juvenilia/). Whilst these three volumes do not pretend to be a full-fledged scholarly edition, with the exception of Sutherland's three introductions notation is remarkably absent. As Sutherland observes in her 'A Novelist of Ideas' (vol. 3, pp. 5–9), her introduction to *Volume the Third*, 'Facsimile publication extends the lives of these three notebooks to all her readers, allowing them to trace her hand across the page, to examine her corrections and revisions and to enjoy in all its aspects her playful apprenticeship in the art of bookmaking' (vol. 3, p. 9). It need hardly be added that the production of these volumes by the Abbeville Press is a delight. Another work on Jane Austen that should not be ignored in this section is Ingrid Tieken-Boon van Ostade's *In Search of Jane Austen: The Language of the Letters*. This may be conceived as a reference tool as it 'aims to throw light on Jane Austen's linguistic identity in as far as it can be reconstructed from her letters' (p. 5). In her preface (pp. ix–x), Tieken-Boon van Ostade writes that her study is concerned with Jane Austen's 'own spelling (rather than that of the printers in her published novels), her use of vocabulary (which proved to be rather less innovative than we might like to think) and her use of grammar' (p. ix). The eight chapters, in addition to an introductory section, encompass, in the opening chapter (pp. 1–25): 'The Language of the Letters' (pp. 5–10), 'A Sociolinguistic Analysis' (pp. 10–15), 'Jane Austen's Language' (pp. 15–21), 'A Single-Author Focused Corpus' (pp. 21–4), and 'The Wider Perspective' (pp. 24–5). In the second chapter, 'Letter-Writing' (pp. 26–50), there is material on 'The Surviving Letters and Those That Were Lost' (pp. 29–36), 'Letter-Writing Materials' (pp. 36–8), 'The Postal System' (pp. 39–43), 'Letter-Writing: A Social Activity' (pp. 43–9), and 'Being Dependent on the Post' (pp. 49–50). The third chapter, 'A Social Network of Letter-Writers' (pp. 51–78), includes: 'Jane Austen's Correspondents' (pp. 54–64), her 'Letter-Writing Formulas' (pp. 64–74), including 'An Index of Formality?' (pp. 64–5), subdivided into 'Opening Formulas' (pp. 65–8), 'Closing Formulas' (pp. 68–71), and 'Dating and Signing Letters' (pp. 71–4). These are followed by a section on 'The Correspondence Network and the Lost Letters' (pp. 74–8). Chapter 4 focuses on 'The Letters as a Corpus' (pp. 79–107), with sections on 'Types of Letters' (pp. 81–4), 'Self-Corrections' (pp. 84–93), 'Short Forms' (pp. 93–100), 'Dashes and Capitalisation' (pp. 100–6), followed by 'Two Corpora for Analysis' (pp. 106–7). The fifth chapter concentrates on 'The Language of the Letters: Spelling' (pp. 108–30), with discussion of 'A Dual Spelling System' (pp. 111–13), ' Epistolary Spelling' (pp. 113–14), 'Tho' and Thro'' (pp. 114–15), 'Older Spellings' (pp. 115–17), and 'Other Epistolary Spelling Features' (pp. 117–21), 'More Variable Spelling Features' (pp. 121–4), then 'Problems with the Apostrophe' (pp. 124–6), 'Spelling as Evidence of Pronunciation' (pp. 126–9), and 'A Consistent if Idiosyncratic Speller' (pp. 129–30). The sixth chapter is called 'The Language of the Letters: Words' (pp. 131–66), with sections on 'Jane Austen in the *Oxford English Dictionary*' (pp. 133–9), her 'Creative Language Use' (pp. 139–51), 'Vulgar Words and Intensifiers' (pp. 151–5)—what Tieken-Boon van Ostade tabulates as 'Vacuous Emphatics and Phrase Fillers' (p. 153)—'Linguistic Involvement' (pp. 155–7), 'Referring to Close Relatives' (pp. 157–60) and 'Jane Austen's Linguistic Fingerprint?' (pp. 160–6). This discussion contains a fascinating comparative table on the 'Relative size of Jane Austen's vocabulary' (p. 163). The seventh chapter is concerned with 'The Language of the Letters: Grammar' (pp. 167–207), with sections on 'Developing Grammatical Awareness' (pp. 170–9), 'Variable Grammar' in the letters, 'Verbal *-ing* Forms' (pp. 200–6) and 'Changing Grammar' (pp. 206–7). The subject of chapter 8 is Austen's 'Authorial Identity' (pp. 208–24), which turns its attention to the novels. There are discussions of 'The Discarded *Persuasion* Chapters' (pp. 211–14), 'Different House Styles for *Mansfield Park*?' (pp. 214–21), 'Dating *The Watsons*' (pp. 221–3), followed by 'Why Analysing Spelling Matters' (pp. 223–4). Tieken-Boon van Ostade writes: 'it is well worth our while to analyse an author's private spelling habits, as these along with their use of vocabulary and grammar, constitute their authorial identity'. Additionally 'In the light of the new circumstances [Jane Austen] found herself in as a result of her father's death in January 1805, we can . . . safely say that it was this event in [her] life that gave rise to the need to speed up her writing, rather than . . . the need to cut down on expenses by saving paper' (p. 224). Following Tieken-Boon van Ostade's 'Conclusion', in her ninth chapter (pp. 225–31), in which she stresses that she has 'taken a microlinguistics perspective' (p. 227), there are four appendices: 'Letters Referred to in the Text' (pp. 233–4), followed by in tabulated form details of 'Out-letters' (pp. 235–44) and five 'In-letters' of which three are from a single correspondent, James Stanier Clarke (p. 245); 'Letters (Sent and Received) Referred to by Jane Austen' (pp. 246–61), consisting of tables of 'Unattested Out-letters' (pp. 246–50) and 'Unattested In-letters' (pp. 250–61); there is a 'Transcription of Letter 139' (p. 262), reproduced in facsimile on page xiv and dated 'Chawton April 1| 1816'. The final appendix is a tabulated listing of 'Jane Austen's Epistolary Network' (pp. 263–6). These appendices are followed by an enumerative, alphabetically arranged listing of references (pp. 267–76). The double-columned index (pp. 277–82) to this important study pertinent to Jane Austen scholarship and one that may be used as a useful model for microlinguistic studies of other authors, indicates that 'the letter "n" following a page number refers to the footnote on the page in question' (p. 277). A caveat, however, must be made: while the author of *In Search of Jane Austen* is careful to indicate that her analysis is based upon highly reliable editions of her subject's letters and inspection of the originals where available in person or in facsimile form, there are instances where the editions of the letters of other authors may not be so reliable, especially in the case of the transmission of punctuation; also no doubt corpus analysis will become more sophisticated with time.

Kevin R. McNamara's *The Cambridge Companion to the City in Literature* is transnational and historical, exploring 'a rich literature devoted to the depiction of actual cities and the modes of life they support' (p. 5). Following 'Notes on Contributors ' (pp. xi–xiv), there is a detailed chronology (pp. xv–xxvii) and the editor's introduction (pp. 1–16). There then follow the essays: 'Celestial Cities and Rationalist Utopias' (pp. 17–29) by Antonis Balasopoulos, in which he attempts to respond to the question '*What is a city?*' (p. 17); 'The City in the Literature of Antiquity' (pp. 31–41) by Susan Stephens; 'The Medieval and Early Modern City in Literature' (pp. 42–56) by Karen Newman; 'The Spectator and the Rise of the Modern Metropole' (pp. 57–68) by Alison O'Byrne, which has for its focus 'eighteenth-century London' (p. 57); 'Memory, Desire, Lyric: The *Flâneur*' (pp. 69–84) by Catherine Nesci is largely concerned with 'a modern myth of lasting depth and melancholy' created by Charles Baudelaire in his 1859 poem 'To a Woman Passing By' (p. 69); 'Social Science and Urban Realist Narrative' (pp. 85–98) by Stuart Culver looks at 'both the urban realist narrative' and perceptions of 'social scientists' (p. 87); 'The Socioeconomic Outsider: Labor and the Poor' (pp. 99–113) by Bart Keunen and Luc De Droogh examines through literary, cinematic, and other artistic examples 'The Outsider as the Underdog' (pp. 101–3), 'The Outsider as Moral Problem' (pp. 103–7), 'The Sociology of the Outsider' (pp. 108–10), and 'The Tragic Outsider in the Modernist Discourse of Alienation' (pp. 110–12); 'The Urban Nightspace' (pp. 114–25) by James R. Giles, which looks at its literary depiction; 'Masses, Forces, and the Urban Sublime' (pp. 126–37) by Christophe Den Tandt; 'Fragment and Form in the City of Modernism' (pp. 138–52) by Arnold Weinstein, who observes that 'modernist texts, more than those of other period, ask us to ponder the plenitude of both time and space' (p. 151). The literary depiction of 'Cities of the Avant-Garde' (pp. 153–62) concern Malcolm Miles; 'Urban Dystopias' (pp. 163–74), concern Rob Latham and Jeff Hicks; however, Richard Jefferies's powerful *After London* [1885] was not written by 'Lionel Jeffries' as they state (p. 167); 'Postmodern Cities' (pp. 175–87) and their fictional representation by, amongst others, J.G. Ballard and Martin Amis, are discussed by Nick Bentley, as are 'Colonial Cities' (pp. 188–99) by Seth Graebner; 'Postcolonial Cities' (pp. 200–15) by Caroline Herbert; 'The Translated City: Immigrants, Minorities, Diasporans, and Cosmopolitans' (pp. 216–32) by Azade Seyhan; 'Gay and Lesbian Urbanity' (pp. 233–44) by Gregory Woods; and 'Some Versions of Urban Pastoral' (pp. 245–60) by Kevin R. McNamara and Timothy Gray, in which they draw upon various literary genres from diverse periods and cultures. Each essay is followed by notes. There is an alphabetically arranged, enumerative 'Guide to Further Reading' (pp. 261–71) and an index (pp. 273–86) to *The Cambridge Companion to the City in Literature*, a volume which mixes generalizations with insufficient exploration of individual texts and is uneven in the quality of its contributions.

An interesting reference work is *The Cambridge Companion to the Bloomsbury Group*, edited by Victoria Rosner. Following a listing of contributors (pp. xi–xiv), in her introduction (pp. 1–15), Rosner writes that 'the Bloomsbury Group was an intellectual and social coterie of British writers, painters, critics, and an economist who were at the height of their powers during the interwar period. The boundaries of the group were loose and flowing, though any membership roster would need to include'—and fourteen names are given, with the names of 'key associates' following (pp. 2–3). The names include Clive Bell, Vanessa Bell, E.M. Forster, Roger Fry, Duncan Grant, Maynard Keynes, and of course Leonard Woolf and Virginia Woolf, amongst others. Rosner's volume is divided into five parts. In the first part, 'Origins', there are two contributions: 'Victorian Bloomsbury' by Katherine Mullin (pp. 19–32) and 'Cambridge Bloomsbury' by Ann Banfield (pp. 33–53). The second part has two essays on the subject of 'Everyday Life': 'Domestic Bloomsbury' by Morag Shiach (pp. 57–70) and 'Bloomsbury as Queer Subculture' by Christopher Reed (pp. 71–89). The third part has two essays on the subject of 'Politics': 'War, Peace, and Internationalism' by Christine Froula (pp. 93–111) and 'Bloomsbury and Empire' by Gretchen Holbrook Gerzina (pp. 112–27). The fourth part is devoted to the 'Arts' and has three contributions: 'Pens and Paintbrushes' by

Mary Ann Caws—surprisingly without the black and white illustrations accompanying most of the other essays in the volume (pp. 131–43); 'The Bloomsbury Group and the Book Arts' by Helen Southworth (pp. 144–61); and 'Bloomsbury Aesthetics' by Laura Marcus (pp. 162–79). The fifth and final part in the *Companion* focuses on 'Reflections of Bloomsbury' and also has three contributions: 'The Bloomsbury Narcissus' by Vesna Goldsworthy (pp. 183–97), who writes that 'Life writing in its multiple forms was central to' the Bloomsbury Group (p. 183); 'Intellectual Crossings and Reception' by Brenda R. Silver (pp. 198–214); and 'Bloomsbury's Afterlife' by Regina Marler (pp. 215–30). The volume closes with two appendices: a chronology by Molly Pulda beginning in 1904 with the death of Leslie Stephen, amongst other events (p. 231), and concluding in 1945 with the ending of the Second World War (p. 235); and an alphabetically arranged, enumerative select further reading divided into four sections. These are 'Selected Works by Members, Associates, and Descendants of the Bloomsbury Group' (pp. 237–8), 'Letters and Life Writing' (p. 238), 'Biographies' (pp. 238–9), and 'Selected Criticism' (pp. 239–40). There is a largely name-orientated index too (pp. 241–6). Notation of varying length follows the individual essays, which are of a uniformly high quality.

Jean-Michel Rabaté, in *The Cambridge Introduction to Literature and Psychoanalysis*, wishes to overturn 'the bad press' that psychoanalysis has received 'in the field of literary studies' (p. 1). His 'contention is that one can and will learn directly from Freud and that the "lessons" he provides rebound and resound when reading literature' (p. 6). There are accordingly chapters on: 'Freud's Theater of the Unconscious: Oedipus, Hamlet, and "Hamlet"' (pp. 25–47); 'Literature and Fantasy, Toward a Grammar of the Subject' (pp. 48–70); 'From the Uncanny to the Unhomely' (pp. 71–92); 'Psychoanalysis and the Paranoid Critique of Pure Literature' (pp. 93–121); the intriguingly titled 'The Literary Phallus, from Poe to Gide' (pp. 122–49), that has as its main focus André Gide; 'A *Thing of Beauty* is a Freud *Forever*: Joyce with Jung and Freud, Lacan, and Borges' (pp. 150–73); and 'From the History of Perversion to the Trauma of History' (pp. 174–98). In his 'Conclusion: Ambassadors of the Unconscious' (pp. 199–214), Rabaté writes 'the knowledge provided by literature, when filtered through psychoanalysis, is not the knowledge about biographical facts, or just about emotions or feelings, or is it about the correlation between fact and theory, or even between affects and ideation'. Furthermore, 'it will not bring new insights about anger or guilt ... It does not consist in a more accurate evocation of passions. It is not a method, but it combines several features that we have observed in all these readings. First, it is a reading of the letter; a literalist approach that is not all that formalist' (p. 214). This informative and clever reference work concludes with a very useful alphabetically arranged 'Keywords and Index of Authors' (pp. 215–36), a helpful alphabetically arranged, enumerative bibliography (pp. 237–48), and an index (pp. 249–55).

In Laura Marcus's 'Introduction: Psychoanalysis at the Margins' (pp. 1–11), to the overpriced *A Concise Companion to Psychoanalysis, Literature, and Culture* which she has edited with Ankhi Mukherjee, she observes: 'The essays in this volume represents the variety of new ways of taking up the legacy of psychoanalytic thought and theory, reaching forward to us from the close of the nineteenth century.' Taking 'Maud Ellmann's excellent collection of essays, *Psychoanalytic Literary Criticism* (1994)' as an important signpost, Marcus adds that 'two decades later, our contributors continue to be preoccupied with questions of sexuality and psychic life, but their frameworks are substantially those of queer and postcolonial theory, cultural criticism, translation in its many senses, models of time and temporality, and the human–animal interface' (p. 1). There are four parts to Marcus and Mukerjee's *Companion*. The first, 'Histories' (pp. 13–101), contains the following essays: 'The Freudian Century' (pp. 15–33) by Stephen Frosh, which gives an 'account of the place of psychoanalysis in the twentieth century century–a long twentieth century, since the processes he describes seem to persist into the second decade of the current century' (pp. 1–2); 'The Case Study' (pp. 34–48), preoccupies Andrew Webber; 'Modernity, the Occult, and Psychoanalysis' (pp. 49–65), engage Carolyn Burdett; 'Back to Frankfurt School' (pp. 66–81), is the subject of Laurence A. Rickels essay; and in 'The Exception of Psychoanalysis: Adorno and Cavell as Readers of Freud' (pp. 82–101), Daniel Steuer is also preoccupied with the implications of the ideas of the Frankfurt school.

'The wish for [the] convergence of psychoanalysis and literary criticism was continuous across the twentieth century, though it was conceived in very different ways' and 'the latter decades of the century saw a shift of focus to texts and textual processes, including transference, narrative transmission, and the subversion of authority' (p. 4). The second part of the *Companion*, 'Literatures' (pp. 105–89), contains essays concerned with such issues. 'Freud's Textual Couch, or the Ambassador's Magic Carpet' (pp. 105–21) by Jean-Michel Rabaté opens with the questions 'should one apply psychoanalysis to literature? Can one do without having it unravel? Conversely, should one apply literature to psychoanalysis?' (p. 105). An explication of 'Freud's Double' (pp. 122–36) is the subject of Nicholas Royle's contribution. 'Medieval Dreams' (pp. 137–50), with a particular focus on Chaucer's *The House of Fame* (pp. 145–8), are the subject of Nicolette Zeeman's contribution. Large topics such as 'Queer Desire, Psychoanalytic Hermeneutics, and Love Lyric' (pp. 151–66), preoccupy Tim Dean; and 'Psychoanalysis, Literature, and the "Case" of Adolescence' (pp. 167–89) are the subjects of Pamela Thurschwell's contribution.

The third part engages with the subject of 'Visual Cultures' (pp. 193–286), and, using differing approaches, has five contributions exploring 'a wide range of contemporary images and visual narratives through the lens of psycho-analytic theory' (p. 7). In 'Intimate *Volver*' (pp. 193–215), Frances L. Restuccia writes on Pedro Almodóvar's 2006 film; in 'Psychoanalysis, Popular and Unpopular' (pp. 216–32), Catherine Liu's concern is with 'spectacle as commodity in late capitalism ... [she] addresses the rise and fall of psycho-analysis in US popular culture, with the initial enthusiasm in Hollywood and New York in the 1920s and 1930s waning in the 1970s and 1980s, just as it became more solidly established in the academy and notably in film studies, in North America as in Europe' (p. 7). The 'question of psychoanalysis as represented in popular culture, focusing on prime time TV and, in particular, the series *In Treatment* (2008)' is the subject of 'Primetime Psychoanalysis' (pp. 233–49) by Ankhi Mukherjee; 'The Art of the Symptom: Body, Writing, and Sex Change' (pp. 250–70) concerns Patricia Gherovici, paying particular attention to Joyce's *Stephen Dedalus* (p. 260) and Jan Morris's 1974 autobiographical *Conundrum* (pp. 263–5). In the final essay in this third part 'The Desert of the Real' (pp. 271–86), Todd McGowan contrasts 'the difference between imaginary and real enjoyment' in the contemporary cinema (p. 284).

There are seven essays in the final part 'Transformations' (pp. 289–424), of *A Concise Companion to Psychoanalysis, Literature, and Culture*. This final part 'addresses the ways in which psychoanalysis interacts with and transforms other discourses' (p. 9). In the opening essay '"One of the Most Obscure Regions of Psychoanalysis": Defamiliarizing Psychic Economy' (pp. 289–311), Anna Kornbluh is concerned with 'what Freud himself called his tortured relation to economic motifs' (p. 9). 'Chronolibido: From Socrates to Lacan and Beyond' (pp. 312–27) by Martin Hägglund pays particular attention to the work of Lacan, and in common with other essays in this final part of the *Companion*, the concern is with 'the issue of "resistance" to psychoanalysis"' (p. 10). This too is the subject of 'Psychoanalytic Animal' (pp. 328–50) by Maud Ellmann, although her attention is less to Lacan and more on Freud and thinkers such as Deleuze and Guattari. 'On the Right to Sleep, Perchance to Dream' (pp. 351–66), concerns Ranjana Khanna, who draws attention to 'Levinas' analysis of insomnia based initially on his work in a World War II prison camp' (p. 10), although Khanna fails to take the opportunity to broaden her canvas to encompass the work of Oliver Sacks for instance in his *Awakenings* [1973] and Harold Pinter's use of Sacks in his *A Kind of Alaska* [1982] and subsequent drama *Ashes to Ashes* [1996]. In 'Freud on Cultural Translation' (pp. 367–84), Robert J.C. Young looks 'at Freud's use of translation as a metaphor, or analogy' (p. 368). In the final two essays, 'Psychoanalysis and Pedagogy: Narratives of Teaching' (pp. 385–409), Isobel Armstrong draws upon her experiences of graduate teaching at Birkbeck College, University of London, and in 'Touching and Not Touching' (pp. 410–24), Naomi Segal 'takes up the topics of intersubjectivity and intrasubjectivity in its focus on those dimensions of the human sensorium which lie outside "the five senses" as they are conventionally understood' (p. 11). To conclude, each essay in Marcus and Mukherjee's *Companion* includes where relevant notation and an alphabetically arranged listing of references. There is too an index (pp. 425–36), that reveals far more references in the text to psychoanalytical thinkers such as Freud, Lacan, and Winnicott than for instance T.S. Eliot, Shakespeare, or other creative writers. So in a very real sense the title *A Concise Companion to Psychoanalysis, Literature, and Culture* is a misnomer.

Tim Hunt, in his *The Textuality of Soulwork: Jack Kerouac's Quest for Spontaneous Prose* draws upon unpublished Kerouac materials to focus 'on the nature of Kerouac's writing, particularly his interrogation of writing as a medium, first in *On the Road*, then in the posthumously published *Visions of Cody*'. Hunt's 'goal is to trace [Kerouac's] experiments in his formative period, 1950–2, in order to show that he was engaged in what might be termed a crisis of textuality—one with significant implications not only for understanding his

work but also for framing mid-century American literary experimentation'
(p. 1). There are chapters on 'Kerouac's 'experiment of drafting *On the Road*
by typing continuously onto a roll of paper in April 1951 and the subsequent
experiments that developed into *Visions of Cody*' (p. 9). In his 'Epilogue'
(pp. 172–92), Hunt 'considers the implications of Kerouac's approach to
writing for textual theory' (p. 9). The book concludes with extensive notes
(pp. 193–210), an alphabetically arranged, enumerative listing of works cited
(pp. 211–14), and a name-orientated index (pp. 215–18).

Sheila Markham's *Second Book of Booksellers* is a sequel to her *A Book of
Booksellers: Conversations with the Antiquarian Book Trade*, first published in
2004 and reprinted in 2007. This contained interviews with fifty booksellers
conducted between 1991 and 2003. The sequel has the texts of interviews with
thirty-one booksellers that took place between 2007 and 2013. The eminent
bibliographer, bookman, and editor of the *Book Collector* Nicolas Barker pens
the introduction to the second book, which appears in a limited edition of 500
copies. Each interview is prefaced by a black and white photograph of the
interviewee. Barker writes that '*A Second Book of Booksellers* is just as full of
the rich loam of character that made the first such capital reading' (p. 13). The
majority of the interviews in the first volume, and a few in the second volume,
appeared in the now defunct *Bookdealer*. The volume is dedicated to the
memory of the late Michael Silverman (1949–2011) with whose 'untimely
death . . . the world of literary and historical manuscripts has lost one of its
most respected dealers, and the antiquarian trade in general a much loved and
popular colleague' (p. 235). The great majority of booksellers interviewed in
the two books are English, with two Americans and at least one Canadian also
interviewed. Primarily, British-based, Markham's fascinating work throws
invaluable light upon bookselling, booksellers, the book business, the supply
of books, and so much else at the end of the twentieth century and the early
years of the new century. As such the volumes are a remarkable historical
document and glimpse into a world in which English graduates and scholars
plus their resources figure prominently. Well bound, designed, and 'typeset in
10pt Minion' (p. 4), with an attractive dark green jacket, there is an extensive
double-columned index (pp. 241–54), directing the reader for instance to
'poets, booksellers as, 12, 63, 99–100' (p. 251) and to take one other pertinent
example 'modern first editions, market for, 56, 59, 69, 142, 146, 156, 158, 176'
(p. 250).

The eminent librarian Marie Elana Korey, in her introduction to *A Long
Way from the Armstrong Beer Parlour. A Life in Rare Books: Essays by
Richard Landon*, observes that a love of books ran through the life and
activities of the great Canadian librarian Richard Landon (1942–2011). This
love took Landon from a distant British Columbia farmhouse to the Thomas
Fisher library at the University of Toronto. In 1977 Landon became Toronto's
head of rare books, soon after the department assumed the Fisher name that
Landon made famous. Korey's collection of Landon's publications—articles,
conference presentations, and introductions to Fisher exhibitions—reflects
these wide interests. The book has three sections, containing Landon on
'Autobiography' (pp. 25–60), 'Bibliography and Book History' (pp. 63–222),
and 'Collecting and the Antiquarian Book Trade' (pp. 225–410). Topics range

from 'Charles Darwin: Some Bibliographical Problems and Textual Implications' (pp. 85–104), 'Literary Forgery and Mystifications: Causes and Effects' (pp. 151–70), 'From Capell to Tanselle: Bibliography and Humanities Scholarship' (pp. 200–22), to 'Was William Morris Really a Pre-Raphaelite?' (pp. 323–38). Korey includes a 'Checklist of Publications' of Landon (pp. 411–28). This is chronological, enumerative, and is divided into articles, introductions to Fisher exhibitions, conference presentations, then Landon's extensive 'Reviews'. There is also an extensive index (pp. 429–40).

The second edition of Julia Miller's *Will Speak Plain: A Handbook for Identifying and Describing Historical Bindings* is a magnificent volume in terms of content and as a physical object. Replete with many full-page illustrative plates in black and white and colour, it also has an accompanying CD-ROM containing around 1,500 colour images. The second edition corrects the first, published four years earlier in 2010, and provides additional information, for instance on early canvas bindings and also images. Miller's aim, as she explains in her preface and acknowledgements (pp. ix–xiii), is to instruct on 'the conservation of books' and 'the history of bookbinding' (p. x). In her introduction (pp. 1–12), 'The Purpose of this Handbook' is summed up in two lines as Miller quotes from Emily Dickinson 'To meet an Antique Book— / in just the Dress his Century wore'—in this encounter 'we relate to how [the book] looks, how it feels, how it opens, even how it smells . . . We absorb much more than the information contained in the text. We record color, design, condition' (p. 1); but we must not ignore books that are not elaborately bound. Miller's concern is also with plain bindings: 'historical books carry the story of our intellectual development, artistic taste, and our reading habits; they testify to both our human condition and our connection to one another. For centuries, the book has been both a direct and indirect record of our intellectual achievement—direct because of content, indirect because of the evidence of interaction we leave in our books as we read them' (p. 12). There are richly illustrated chapters on 'The Early History of the Codex' (pp. 13–54), 'The Medieval Manuscript Book and Beyond' (pp. 55–91), '1450 to 1800: The Book Changes Radically' (pp. 92–144), and 'The Book from 1800–1900' (pp. 145–201), with a concluding section in this chapter on '*Is the End Near? Perhaps the End is Just the Beginning?*' (pp. 200–1), concluding: 'It is ironic that the invention [the Internet] that will replace the traditional book is also the invention that will aid us in finally understanding it' (p. 201). Miller's remaining chapters are on 'Identifying Binding Materials and Applications' (pp. 202–59), 'Describing Historical Bindings—a Template for Action' (pp. 260–309), and 'The Task Ahead and Conclusion' (pp. 310–17). Miller is too modest concerning her readership when she writes in this seventh chapter: 'This book was written with those in mind who may not already have made a study of historical bindings.' She is referring to 'anyone who has direct contact with the care and handling of an historical book collection, whether you are a collector, a curator, a librarian, a conservator, a bookdealer, or a volunteer who fills one of those roles' (p. 310). She ought to have added the student of the history of the book. There are three highly informative appendices (pp. 318–412), yet again richly illustrated with black and white and colour plate illustrative examples (see for instance pp. 339–93 in black and white).

The first appendix concerns 'Historical Bindings—Structure and Style Hierarchy' (pp. 318–93). The second consists of 'Sample Survey Suggestions and Descriptive Case Studies' (pp. 394–418) supplemented with (between pp. 400 and 401) colour plates of bindings, spines, and fore-edges. The third provides 'Stacks Maintenance and Physical Condition Assessment Guidelines' (pp. 419–32). *Will Speak Plain* concludes with an extensive, most useful alphabetically arranged glossary that 'offers definitions of bookbinding-related terms that have been used in this work, as well as other relevant terms that may be useful to the reader'. It begins with 'aberrant copy: A binding with binding and/or printing errors' (p. 433), and concludes with 'zoomorphic tools: Finishing rolls, stamps, all unit tools engraved with the figures of animals' (p. 500). There is an alphabetical, enumerative bibliography (pp. 501–22) that 'contains all the books of reference noted in *Books Will Speak Plain*, as well as additional works that have aided the author in her study of the history of the book and bookbinding' (p. 501). This bibliography is divided into books, articles, and websites on 'Early Printed Forms: Papyrus Rolls and Wood-Leaf Books' (pp. 501–3), 'The Early Coptic Codices: Nag Hammadi to Hamouli' (pp. 503–6), 'History, Structure, and Style in Hand Bookbinding: 400–1800' (pp. 506–17), 'The Nineteenth-Century Book: Britain and Beyond' (pp. 518–21), and 'Modern Times and the Historical Book: Bibliography and Modern Information Technology' (pp. 521–2). This erudite work concludes with a most comprehensive index (pp. 523–41). There is even a 'Colophon' with a small photograph of the author, her details, and the information that 'the text was set in Garamond Premier Pro, 11/14 and 10/12. Optima was 16/19.2 and 9/10.8. The paper [a delight to handle] is 70# SAPPI Flo Matte (10% PCR) FSC' (p. 542).

Published in 2013, Christopher D. Cook's *Incunabula in the Westminster Abbey and Westminster School Libraries: Bookbinding Descriptions by Mirjam M. Foot* 'is dedicated to the memory of Howard Nixon (1909–83) a much loved and esteemed figure in the bibliographical world [who] became a leading authority on the history of bookbinding' (p. 9). Accompanied by twenty-three colour illustrations, Cook's 'catalogue identifies and lists the incunabula in the Westminster Abbey and Westminster School libraries, and provides full descriptions of copy-specific features. Westminster Abbey Library contains examples of seventy-six editions of books printed before 1502, represented by fifty-six volumes and seventeen fragments' (p. 17). Cook's introduction (pp. 17–26) contains sections on 'A Note on the History of Incunabula in the Westminster Abbey and Westminster School Libraries' (pp. 17–21), 'A Brief Analysis of the Collections' (pp. 21–2), 'Earlier Inventories' (pp. 22–3), and 'Using the Catalogue' (pp. 23–6). It is followed by an alphabetically arranged, descriptive bibliography of 'Incunabula in the Westminster Abbey Library' (pp. 29–114). Descriptions begin with the title, followed by collation details, references in previous catalogues, binding literature references, notes, and binding description—the work of Mirjam M. Foot—signs of use such as marginalia, and the shelfmark. Similar organization is used for the description of 'Incunabula in Westminster School Library' (pp. 115–25), followed by the 'Fragments in Westminster Abbey Library' (pp. 127–42). There is an appendix: 'Copies Once Present in Westminster Abbey' (pp. 143–4); four are noted, two of which have associations with William Caxton (p. 144). There then follow a detailed descriptive alphabetical listing of abbreviations (pp. 145–52) used in the descriptive bibliography sections and an alphabetically arranged, enumerative bibliography (pp. 153–6), both of which provide a guide to fifteenth-century primary and critical materials. There are five 'Concordances' (pp. 157–61) arranged by the abbreviations used: for instance 'ISTC' to the *Incunabula Short-Title Catalogue* http://www.bl.uk/catalogues/istc/index.html (p. 161), and so on. There are four alphabetically arranged indexes (pp. 163–81): 'Printers and Publishers and their Locations' (pp. 163–6), 'Donors, Former Owners and Associated Names' (pp. 167–75), including, when known, basic biographical details such as date of birth and death, profession, for example 'Tripp [Trippe], Henry (1544/45–1612)... clergyman, author and translator' (p. 174). There is an 'Index of Copy-Specific Features' (pp. 177–8) and an 'Index of Binders and Binding Features' (pp. 179–81). Sturdily bound, 'designed and typeset by Paul W. Nash' (p. 4), Christopher D. Cook's *Incunabula in the Westminster Abbey and Westminster School Libraries* concludes with an alphabetically arranged listing of shelfmarks (pp. 183–5).

Sam Knowles's monograph *Travel Writing and the Transnational Author* is a 'cross-generic study [that] starts by analyzing the travelogues of [Michael] Ondaatje, [Vikram] Seth, [Amitav] Ghosh, and [Salman] Rushdie in their respective contexts, while also preparing for a consideration of the "postcolonial canonicity" of these four authors'. The focus is on their travel writing 'because of the important role that the authors' travelogues play within their later work' (p. 3). On the whole Knowles writes clearly, which is somewhat surprising given the dense literary styles of some of the works he is discussing. Notation follows his text (pp. 198–218). There is an alphabetically arranged, enumerative bibliography (pp. 219–34) followed by a helpful index (pp. 235–44). Bridget T. Chalk's *Modernism and Mobility: The Passport and Cosmopolitan Experience* argues 'that the broad, multifaceted European and American transformations in administering nationality in mobility shape the international character and themes of much experimental writing of the interwar period' (p. 3). The authors and texts chosen to amplify this range from D. H. Lawrence and his *Aaron's Rod* [1922], to Gertrude Stein, with especial emphasis given to her *The Autobiography of Alice B. Toklas* [1933], the more obscure Claude McKay's novel *Banjo* [1929], Jean Rhys's *Good Morning Midnight* [1938], Christopher Isherwood's short stories *Goodbye to Berlin* [1963], and W.H. Auden's poem 'Refugee Blues' [1939]. Extensive notes (pp. 179–215), follow the text, and there is an enumerative alphabetical listing of works cited (pp. 217–29) and a useful double-columned index (pp. 231–40).

Rivkah Zim, in her *The Consolations of Writing: Literary Strategies of Resistance from Boethius to Primo Levi*, 'offers close readings of... disparate texts related by their pragmatic functions as strategies of resistance to their authors' conditions of imprisonment, confinement, and persecution'. Further, her book 'juxtaposes a wide range of component subjects, including fiction, memoirs, letters, theology, poetry, and political philosophy, in pairing authors to propose hitherto unexplored similarities between their works, their ethical motives, intellectual lives, and responses to captivity and persecution'. Zim adds that 'the rationale for their selection here implies not only their differences from each other as writers from several different periods and language cultures but also comparative significance in their sites of textual production and recurrent themes' (p. 3). She draws upon Latin, French, Italian, German, and Russian texts in addition to English ones, with authors and readings ranging from pairings of Boethius and Dietrich Bonhoeffer, Thomas More and Antonio Gramsci, John Bunyan—a reading of his *Grace Abounding to the Chief of Sinners*—and Oscar Wilde's *De Profundis*, Marie-Jeanne Roland with Anne Frank, Jean Cassou with Irina Ratushinskaya, and texts by Primo Levi. Zim concludes her fine, sensitive study writing that 'These prisoners' vital self-impressions and the urgent clarity of their analyses of cultural values may inspire readers to build new lives and aspirations: the aims of life are also the politics of prison writing in action. The consolations of their writing can touch and teach us all' (p. 309). Footnotes are included, and there is an extensive select bibliography (pp. 311–17), and a short, author-orientated index (pp. 319–23).

Thomas A Bredehoft's *The Visible Text: Textual Production and Reproduction from Beowulf to Maus* is the initial text in a new series, Oxford Textual Perspectives, under the general editorship of Elaine Treharne and Greg Walker. As they say in their 'Series Editors' Preface', this 'is a new series of informative and provocative studies focused upon texts (conceived of in the broadest sense of that term) and the technologies, cultures, and communities that produce, inform, and receive them' (p. v). One of Bredehoft's 'central contentions in this book [is] that we must always see as well as read, whether the text in question is overtly cryptic or not. Further, the notion that the visible component of text is able to be discarded or ignored or bypassed must be understood as an ideological position' (p. 3). He states in the final paragraph of his introduction (pp. 1–22) that his 'central themes will involve the visible experience of texts, the ways in which textual production and reproduction configured themselves in relation to the available technologies, and the ways in which literature responds to the ideologies of its own production and reproduction' (p. 22). The four chapters that follow, concern themselves with 'Anglo-Saxon Textual Production' (pp. 23–57), followed by a bridging 'Interlude 1: Anglo-Saxon to Gothic' (pp. 58–60), leading into the second chapter and its concern with 'Gothic Textual Reproduction' (pp. 61–94), followed by 'Interlude 2: Gothic to Print' (pp. 95–6). In this second chapter Bredehoft pays particular attention to 'Producing *The Canterbury Tales*' (pp. 79–82). The third chapter discusses 'Typographic Print Reproduction' (pp. 97–125), with 'Interlude 3: Prints to Comics' (pp. 126–9), and the fourth chapter is devoted to the examination of 'Comics Textual Production' (pp. 130–56). There is an 'Epilogue' (pp. 157–68), that concludes 'we live at an exciting moment in the history of textual technologies and ideologies, as digital textuality evolves with startling rapidity, seemingly before our very eyes'. What Bredehoft in his 'little book attempts to do is merely to help us understand where we are, and where we've come from, in terms of our ever-evolving textual ideologies' (p. 168). There are six black and white illustrations in the book, and a bibliography that is enumerative, alphabetical, and divided into three sections: 'Manuscript References' (p. 169); 'Primary Sources:

Editions and Facsimiles' (pp. 169–72); and 'Secondary Sources' (pp. 172–5). This interesting short book concludes with a useful index (pp. 177–82).

George Koppelman and Daniel Wechsler, two New York-based antiquarian booksellers, are trumpeting their eBay acquisition for $4,050, made on 29 April 2008, of an annotated copy of John Baret's *Alvearie, or Quadruple Dictionarie* printed in London in 1580, in their *Shakespeare's Beehive: An Annotated Elizabethan Dictionary Comes to Light*. This is clothbound in red linen with a gilt-stamped 'Beehive' cover, printed in black and red with duotone illustrations, plus a folding plate containing a facsimile of annotations (pp. 221–2), 'set in Van Dijck and Caslon types, with Fell ornaments, and printed on Mohawk paper with design and typography by Jerry Kelly printed in a limited edition of 2,000 copies' (according to the colophon '26 lettered copies are bound in quarter leather & signed by the authors, and 100 are signed by the authors & numbered') (p. 340). Koppelman's book claims much: essentially that their copy of Baret is annotated by none other than William Shakespeare. If they could convince a buyer that this was indeed the case then their copy would be priceless, worth millions and millions. They have even constructed a fascinating website (http://shakespearesbeehive.com/) that contains the complete dictionary with its annotations online and other details and updates. Their work shows the importance they place upon annotations and their significance; it also tells us much about Elizabethan dictionaries and in particular John Baret's, and draws fascinating parallels between the annotations and Shakespeare's work. Koppelman and Wechsler admit that they 'are not Shakespeare scholars' and that theirs is 'speculation, the driving force behind our book, is that Baret's *Alvearie* is indeed part of the canon of source material' (p. 9), to repeat, *is* the copy used and annotated by Shakespeare. The annotations are well described. It is one thing to say that Baret's book is an important source for Shakespeare, another to believe that the copy Kopelman and Wechsler purchased *is the one* annotated by Shakespeare! *Shakespeare's Beehive* concludes with a useful, alphabetically arranged listing of sources cited (pp. 306–19) followed by notes to the text (pp. 320–38). In a prefatory 'Note to the Reader' Kopelman and Wechsler write 'we are, each of us that make up Axletree Press LLC, professional rare booksellers, and we view the effort printed here as a single-item catalogue' (p. ix). The review copy sent by the publisher's is unique—or is it? It is bound upside down with the binding label the wrong way up with the gilt-stamped beehive design on the back rather than the front cover. On the other hand it may not be the only copy bound and printed in such a fashion—only the publishers or binders, one assumes, know!

The subject of Steven W. May and Arthur F. Marotti's *Ink, Stink Bait, Revenge, and Queen Elizabeth: A Yorkshire Yeoman's Household Book* is the 2007 British Library acquisition of 'a fifty-folio manuscript that was among the muniments of the Spencer-Stanhope family of Cannon Hall, Yorkshire (now British Library Additional MS 82370)'. May and Marotti 'discover-ed . . . that the dominant hand throughout belonged to Stanhope's yeoman neighbor, John Hanson of Rastrick, Yorkshire (1517–99)' (p. 1). This 'compilation provides another window into the nature of scribal culture in the provinces as opposed to those centered in London and the universities that we associate, almost exclusively, with the transmission of literary manuscripts' (p. 7). May and Marotti observe in their conclusion that 'the document' they 'have examined has a striking but in many ways symptomatic heterogeneity that reveals some of the cultural complexities of the time' (p. 249). Ten black and white illustrations are included in this fascinating, clearly written study, and there is an enumerative, alphabetically arranged bibliography of primary and secondary sources (pp. 251–60), followed by a detailed, helpful index (pp. 261–72).

An expensively priced, at over a US dollar per page, but valuable addition to the Palgrave series of short research monographs is Samuel Larner's *Forensic Authorship Analysis and the World Wide Web*. Larner's analysis is not totally irrelevant to Koppelman and Wechsler's speculative *Shakespeare's Beehive* with its central belief that the annotations in the volume are Shakespeare's: this assumption might well have been assisted by 'forensic authorship analysis' (p. 3). Larner's concern is with material on the Internet that is susceptible to vocabulary and stylistic analysis, and the belief that 'idiolectal features' (p. 5) can be discerned in order to determine individual authorship. Such key elements as 'the frequency of function words...vocabulary richness' and so on may serve as 'a useful marker of authorship' (pp. 8–9). There is a chapter on 'The Web as Corpus and Authorship Attribution' (pp. 12–34). In the third chapter, 'Attributing Documents to Unknown Authors Using Idiolectical Co-selection and the Web' (pp. 35–48), empirical research is described especially from the Unabomber trial of Theodore Kaczynski, who blew up buildings and killed people during the period from May 1978 to April 1996. Kaczynski also sent a manifesto, the analysis of which was a major factor in his eventual identification. The fourth chapter, 'Attributing Documents to Candidate Authors Using Idiolectal Co-selection and the Web' (pp. 49–57), also describes empirical research, in this instance 'where a Questioned Document is compared to the known writings of three candidate authors, with the aim of establishing whether idiolectical co-selections are a useful marker of authorship and whether the web can be used to generate reliable evidence' (p. 49). The fifth and final chapter (pp. 58–69) assesses the previous empirical research, its positives and negatives, concluding that 'this research has demonstrated some of the limitations of using the web in cases of authorship attribution and has aimed to demonstrate the practicality of doing so' (p. 67). In his concluding sentences Larner observes: 'clearly far more research is required. But hopefully the debate about whether the web should be used as a corpus in forensic investigations can begin' (p. 69). There is a useful, alphabetically arranged, enumerative bibliography (pp. 70–5) and a disappointingly insufficient index limited to ten key terms (p. 76) concluding what is a thoughtful research monograph.

Stephen H. Grant's *Collecting Shakespeare: The Story of Henry and Emily Folger* is an account based on archival material at the Folger Library, Washington DC, of Henry (1857–1930) and Emily (1858–1936) Folger, their relationship, collecting passion, and creation of the library bearing their name and that of the great writer they loved. As Stephen H. Grant writes in the concluding paragraph of his well-written, black-and-white-illustrated book: 'as of 2013, the collection holds 275,000 books, with over half of these rare books.

The library holds the largest Shakespeare collection in the world, the largest collection of early British printed books in North America, and copies of half of what was published in England before 1640. It all started with one couple and their vision' (p. 205). Particular attention is paid to the sources for their collection and their trans-Atlantic transactions with booksellers and dealers. There is also mention of the acquisition of associated materials in the collection, such as artwork and annotated copies made by readers of Shakespeare. Somewhat curiously, perhaps owing to the fact that, as the notation following his text reveals (pp. 209–23), Grant has chiefly relied upon the Folger's own archives, other studies are ignored, for instance material in Joseph Rosenblum's edited *Dictionary of Literary Biography*, vol. 140: *American Book-Collectors and Bibliographers First Series* [1994]. There is, however, an impressive archives and periodicals listing (pp. 225–6), and also an enumerative, alphabetically arranged bibliography (pp. 226–33) of printed materials. This is followed by a useful index (pp. 235–44).

The aim of Francis X. Connor's *Literary Folios and Ideas of the Book in Early Modern England*, as he states in his introduction (pp. 1–21), which concludes with a tabulated listing of 'Literary Folios' chronologically listed from 1591 to 1650, 'is not to survey literary folios, but to identify the ones most engaged with thinking about ideas of the book in an age of print, and to this end chapters identify important folios that attempted to shape early modern understandings of the literary folio, and, more generally, printed English literary writing'. Furthermore, 'situating literary folio publication within its original commercial and textual contexts reveals a variety of ways that authors and publishers used folios to affirm or challenge particular developments in English literary culture' (p. 13). There are chapters on: '"Ungentle Hoarders": From Manuscript to Print in Sidney's *Arcadias*?' (pp. 23–59); 'Samuel Daniel's *Works* and the History and Theory of the Book' (pp. 61–92); 'Ben Jonson's *Workes* and Bibliographic Integrity' (pp. 93–120); and '"Whatever You Do, Buy": Literary Folios and the Marketplace in Shakespeare, Taylor, and Beaumont and Fletcher' (pp. 121–65). There is an 'Epilogue: Henry Herringman's Restoration Folios' (pp. 167–78), followed by extensive notes (pp. 179–227) and a useful index (pp. 229–36). Connor's is an intriguing study.

Another monograph of Shakespearian interest that has landed on my desk is Heather Hirschfeld's *The End of Satisfaction: Drama and Repentance in the Age of Shakespeare*. Not a bibliographical or textual study, it is sufficient to say that Hirschfeld 'explore[s] in detail what happens—first offstage and then on stage—when Christian understandings of repentance changed in ways that literally displaced the language and meaning of satisfaction' (p. 15). There are chapters on '"Adew, to All Popish Satisfactions": Reforming Repentance in Early Modern England' (pp. 16–38); 'The Satisfactions of Hell: Doctor Faustus and the *Descensus* Tradition' (pp. 39–64); 'Setting Things Right: The Satisfactions of Revenge' (pp. 65–93); 'As Good as a Feast? Playing (with) Enough on the Elizabethan Stage' (pp. 94–118); '"Wooing, Wedding, and Repenting": The Satisfactions of Marriage in *Othello* and *Love's Pilgrimage*' (pp. 119–46); and a 'Postscript: Where's the Stage at the End of Satisfaction?' (pp. 147–52). These are followed by extensive notes (pp. 153–203), an alphabetically arranged bibliographical listing of primary (pp. 205–12) and secondary (pp. 212–31), works, and an index (pp. 233–9).

Cedric Watts's discussion of twenty-five 'puzzles presented by Shakespeare's works' in his self-published paperback *Shakespeare Puzzles*, initially appeared in unrevised and non-augmented form in the magazine of Shakespeare's Globe theatre in London, *Around the Globe*—although Watts fails to include the date of first publication. Some of the puzzles discussed are textual, for instance 'A Vanishing Trick in *Midsummer Night's Dream*: Where Is the Wedding Song? And Why Is Recycling Apt?' (pp. 51–4), concerning the apparently missing 'words of the song that Oberon introduces—or of the songs, if Titania's promise is the cue for another' at the end of a *Midsummer Night's Dream* (p. 51). Or Watts's essay on 'What Is the Plot of *Love's Labour's Won*?' (pp. 17–20), 'an invisible play' (p. 17). Curiously this brief puzzle receives no endnotes, although some of the others tackled by Watts in his short, pithy, and entertaining book do. The computer print face of this paper-bound volume is easy on the eye. As Watts observes in his introduction (pp. 5–6), Shakespeare's 'plays and poems offer an abundance of mysteries and riddles' (p. 6).

In her important 1987 monograph *Shakespere's Verse. Iambic Pentameter and the Poet's Idiosyncrasies*, the eminent Russian American prosody scholar Marina Tarlinskaja analysed in considerable detail Shakespeare's versification. In the opening chapter of her *Shakespeare and the Versification of English Drama, 1561–1642* she observes that 'analysis of versification . . . is helpful in dating plays, in attribution of anonymous texts, and finding out how collaborators divided their task in co-authored texts'. Additionally, 'Dating and attribution of Elizabethan and Jacobean dramas are attracting scholars in various fields of linguistics and literary criticism.' Moreover, 'Shakespeare has been the central figure of the quests; but to identify Shakespeare's hand in doubtful texts we need to see what his predecessors, contemporaries, and followers were like. This is what this book is about: Shakespeare against the background of his literary setting'. Tarlinskaja's 'research material is iambic pentameter verse texts: poems and, particularly plays' (p. 1). A listing of tables—there are sixteen of them (p. vii)—is followed by a list of figures (pp. ix–x). The first chapter is concerned with 'Why Study Versification? Versification Verification Analysis; Tests' (pp. 1–32). The second chapter focuses upon 'How It All Began: From Surrey's *Aeneid* to Marlowe's *Tamburlaine*' (pp. 33–67). Three more chapters examine 'Early Elizabethan Playwrights: Kyd, Marlowe, Greene, Peele, Early Shakespeare, *2* and *3 Henry VI* and *Arden of Faversham*' (pp. 69–121), 'Shakespeare's Versification: Evolution. Co-authored Plays. The Poem *A Lover's Complaint*' (pp. 123–92), and 'Jacobean and Caroline Playwrights: From Shakespeare to Shirley' (pp. 193–255). The opening paragraph of her 'Conclusions: Shakespeare and Versification, 1540s–1640s' (pp. 257–66) clearly restates Tarlinskaja's central contention: 'the main aim of this book was to find out how English Renaissance playwrights used versification: why they started to compose plays in iambic pentameter, what did it add to the contents of the plays, how this verse form evolved, who were Shakespeare's predecessors, contemporaries, and followers. Thus the center of my attention was Shakespeare'. She adds, 'to understand an author, to find out his stylistic traits and his place in literature, to approach the chronology of his works and to establish his share in collaborative plays we need to know more about the poet's background. This is why the title of this book is *Shakespeare and the Versification of English Drama, 1561–1642*' (p. 257). There are two appendices: 'Verse-Form and Meaning: Rhythmical Italics' (pp. 267–86); and a lengthy second one consisting of 'General Tables' (pp. 287–375), indicating for instance the 'Frequency of Stresses' (pp. 288–9), although for some reason best known probably to the publishers of this work, these tables are not paginated! They are followed by a helpful, alphabetically arranged explanatory glossary (pp. 377–82), beginning with 'Accidental (Tonic) Verse' (p. 377), and concluding with the letters 'WS, WSW, SW [that] indicates adjacent syllabic positions of the iambic pentameter line that contains syllables whose stressing deviates from the expected' (p. 382). There is an alphabetically arranged, partially descriptive listing of references (pp. 383–99), notable for including studies written in languages other than English, such as Russian, and including those from periods such as the early twentieth century. This most comprehensive study will stand the test of time and concludes with a name-orientated index (pp. 401–11). Refreshingly it does not get bogged down in over-reliance on corpus or other software. To her credit, Tarlinskaja exercises caution, for instance when discussing 'Hands D and C...sometimes called Hand D+' (p. 186), in the text of *Sir Thomas More*. Following a very careful assessment of the evidence, she writes: 'Shakespeare seems to have added two scenes to the refurbished *Sir Thomas More*: a long monologue and lengthy exchanges with the upset citizens' (p. 189). The emphasis is on the word 'seems': 'most features of Hand D+ indicate Shakespeare: the location of strong syntactic breaks in the line, the stress profile, the types of line endings, both syllabic and syntactic, and almost complete absence of rhymes, and an extensive use of rhythmical figures for expressive purposes (cf. with *Othello*)'. She adds, however, that 'Hand D+ seems to belong to Shakespeare during the period of *Othello*, somewhere around 1603–4' (p. 192).

Alan Galey, in his *The Shakespearean Archive: Experiments in New Media from the Renaissance to Postmodernity*, 'offers a critical prehistory of digitization read through the textual afterlives of Shakespeare's complex and imperfect textual archive' (p. 5). His eight chapter headings somewhat clarify Galey's preoccupations: 'Introduction: Scenes from the Prehistory of Digitization' (pp. 1–40); 'Leaves of Brass: Shakespeare and the Idea of the Archive' (pp. 41–77); 'The Archive and the Book: Information Architectures from Folio to Variorum' (pp. 78–117); 'The Counterfeit Presentments of Victorian Photography' (pp. 118–57); 'Inventing Shakespeare's Voice: Early Sound Transmission and Recording' (pp. 158–99); 'Networks of Deep Impression: Shakespeare and the Modern Invention of Information' (pp. 200–35); 'Data and the Ghosts of Materiality' (pp. 236–70); 'Conclusion: Sites of Shakespearean Memory' (pp. 271–80). Galey's concluding words are helpful as to his intentions: 'our theories about the transmission of Shakespeare's texts are indivisible from deeply felt investments of desire and faith. What matters is how we respond to the gap between material records and the substantiation of what we desire to know about Shakespeare's texts. The Shakespearean archive is the substance of things hoped for, the evidence of things not seen' (p. 280). The text is accompanied by nineteen black and white illustrative figures. For instance '4.1 *Hamlet* quoted in a stereoscopic advertisement appearing in one of the first serial parts of Charles Dickens's *Little Dorrit* (1856)' (p. 123). Footnote documentation accompanies the text. There is an extensive, alphabetically arranged bibliography (pp. 281–307), and a detailed, helpful index (pp. 308–31). The front jacket contains an illustration of H.H. Furness's marginalia in his copy of *Romeo and Juliet* now at the Rare Book and Manuscript Library, University of Pennsylvania. Curiously there doesn't seem to be any discussion of these marginalia in Galey's book.

Susanna Fein and Michael Johnston have edited *Robert Thornton and His Books: Essays on the Lincoln and London Thornton Manuscripts*, eight essays devoted to the scholarly activities of a Yorkshire landowner, Robert Thornton (*c*.1397–*c*.1465). Thornton copied two key manuscripts, the 'Lincoln manuscript'—now Lincoln Cathedral, MS 91, and the 'London manuscript'—now British Library, MS Additional 31042 (p. 13), and their importance is the subject of the collection, which is accompanied by black and white illustrations throughout with, on the front cover in colour, an example from the Lincoln manuscript. A detailed listing of abbreviations (pp. x–xii), is followed by Michael Johnston's introduction, 'The Cheese and the Worms and Robert Thornton' (pp. 1–12), in which he sums up the contributions that follow and deals with the question 'why an entire essay collection on one manuscript compiler, who has left us but two manuscripts?' (p. 1). In the opening essay, 'The Contents of Robert Thornton's Manuscripts' (pp. 13–65), Susanna Fein offers a detailed 'overview of Robert Thornton of Yorkshire's surviving copies and an updated list of contents' (p. 13). In 'Robert Thornton: Gentleman, Reader and Scribe' (pp. 67–108), George R. Keiser reviews the evidence for Thornton's biography and attempts an 'explanation of the assembling of' (p. 106), what are today the Lincoln and London manuscripts. 'The Thornton Manuscripts and Book Production in York' (pp. 109–26) concerns Joel Fredell, who has as an appendix, 'The Structure and Decoration of the Thornton Manuscripts' (pp. 127–9). 'The Text of the Alliterative *Morte Arthure*: A Prolegomenon for a Future Edition' (pp. 131–55) is the subject of a joint contribution by Ralph Hanna and Thorlac Turville-Petre. They write, 'we have argued that Thornton's *Morte* is at least a third-generation copy with numerous erroneous accretions. Undoubtedly many authorial meanings cannot be recovered, but even so we believe it is possible, with critical scrutiny of the traditions, to establish a more satisfactory text of *Morte Arthure* than any so far published' (pp. 154–5). In her ' "The rosselde spere to his herte rynnes": Religious Violence in the Alliterative *Morte Arthure* and the Lincoln Thornton Manuscript' (pp. 157–75), Mary Michele Poellinger concludes that 'by portraying religious emotion through physical sacrifice, not just in Passion narratives but also in popular secular literature such as the alliterative *Morte Arthure*, violent images and the language of injuring become ways to borrow and share generic tropes, and, by their means, the secular protagonists of romance are both glorified and judged' (p. 175). In 'Constantinian Christianity in the London Thornton Manuscript: The Codicological and Linguistic Evidence of Thornton's Intentions' (pp. 177–201), Michael Johnston, after his consideration of the evidence, includes an appendix, 'Readings of the *Northern Passion*, Lines 1273–6, from All Surviving Manuscripts' (pp. 202–4). 'Apocryphal Romance in the London Thornton Manuscript' (pp. 205–32) by Julie Nelson Couch also concludes with an appendix, in this instance 'Comparative Chart of the Childhood of Christ in Two Versions' (pp. 233–4). 'Thornton's Remedies and Practices of Medical Reading' (pp. 235–55) by Julie Orlemanski demonstrates that John Lydgate's *Dietary* and the Lincoln manuscript 'realize some of the mercurial possibilities of Middle English medical writing during the period of its dissemination and help us today better to query the practices of medical reading in fifteenth-century England' (p. 255). In 'Afterword: Robert Thornton Country' (pp. 257–72), Rosalind Field with Dav Smith consider the importance of where he lived. Accompanied by informative footnote documentation, *Robert Thornton and His Books* concludes with an alphabetically arranged, enumerative bibliography divided into 'Published Primary Sources' (pp. 273–8) and 'Secondary Sources' (pp. 278–96). Additionally there is an 'Index of Manuscripts Cited' (pp. 297–300), and this fascinating collection concludes with a useful general index (pp. 301–10).

Bryan Fanning and Tom Garvin, both social scientists, write in their introduction, 'Irish Arguments' (pp. 1–7), to *The Books that Define Ireland* that 'each of us trawled through the historical and social literature of the island of the last three centuries to come up with books which seemed to have had an impact on Irish opinion, have defined or best exemplified long-running debates, or have been under-appreciated in terms of their significance'. As an illustration 'of the latter' they cite 'Brian Merriman's 1780 Irish-language poem *The Midnight Court*, which satirizes the reluctance of Irish men to get married early. This poem crops up over the centuries and several times in the book in discussions of social class, cultural revival and issues of sexuality' (p. 3). Merriman doesn't receive a separate entry: the authors and books chosen and discussed are: 'Geoffrey Keating, *Foras Feasa ar Eirinn/The History of Ireland* (1634)' (pp. 8–20); 'William Molyneux, *The Case of Ireland Being Bound by Acts of Parliament in England, Stated* (1698)' (pp. 21–7); 'Jonathan Swift, *A Modest Proposal* (1729)' (pp. 28–35); 'Andrew Dunleavy, *The Catechism on Christian Doctrine* (1742)' (pp. 36–43); 'William Theobald Wolfe Tone (ed.), *The Autobiography of Wolfe Tone* (1826)' (pp. 44–55); 'John Mitchel, *The Jail Journal* (1861)' (pp. 56–65); 'Horace Plunkett, *Ireland in the New Century* (1904) and Michael O'Riordan, *Catholicity and Progress in Ireland* (1905)' (pp. 66–76); 'James Connolly, *Labour in Irish History* (1910)' (pp. 77–85); 'Patrick A. Sheehan, *The Graves at Kilmorna* (1913)' (pp. 86–95); 'Desmond Ryan, *Collected Works of Padraic H. Pearse: Political Writings and Speeches* (1917)' (pp. 96–105); 'Daniel Corkery, *The Hidden Ireland: A Study of Gaelic Munster in the Eighteenth Century* (1924)' (pp. 106–13); 'P.S. O'Hegarty, *The Victory of Sinn Fein: How it Won It and How It Used It* (1924)' (pp. 114–20); 'Tomás O Criomhthain, *An tOileánach/The Islandman* (1929)' (pp. 121–30); 'Frank O'Connor, *Guests of the Nation* (1931)' (pp. 131–8); 'Sean O'Faolain, *King of the Beggars* (1938)' (pp. 139–47); 'Flann O'Brien, *At Swim-Two-Birds* (1939)' (pp. 148–57); 'James Kavanagh, *Manual of Social Ethics* (1954)' (pp. 158–63); 'Paul Blanshard, *The Irish and Catholic Power* (1954)' (pp. 164–72); 'Michael Sheehy, *Divided We Stand* (1955)' (pp. 173–9); 'Edna

O'Brien, *The Country Girls* (1960) and John McGahern, *The Dark* (1965)' (pp. 180–7); 'Cecil Woodham-Smith, *The Great Hunger* (1962)' (pp. 188–95); 'Conor Cruise O'Brien, *States of Ireland* (1972)' (pp. 196–203); 'A.T.Q. Stewart, *The Narrow Ground* (1977)' (pp. 204–10); 'C.S. Andrews, *Dublin Made Me* (1979)' (pp. 211–17); 'Nell McCafferty, *A Woman to Blame: The Kerry Babies Case* (1985)' (pp. 218–27); 'Noel Browne, *Against the Tide* (1985)' (pp. 228–37); 'Fintan O'Toole, *Meanwhile Back at the Ranch: The Politics of Irish Beef* (1995)' (pp. 238–45); 'Mary Raftery and Eoin O'Sullivan, *Suffer the Little Children: The Inside Story of Ireland's Industrial Schools* (1999)' (pp. 246–59); and 'Elaine A. Byrne, *Political Corruption in Ireland: A Crooked Harp?* (2012)' (pp. 260–6). Each chapter is followed by brief notation. There is also a listing of 'Publishing References' (pp. 267–9) arranged by chapter, and there is a useful index (pp. 270–4) to this interesting book that reveals much about perceptions of the history and literature of Ireland. Firmly bound and nicely printed, it is unfortunate that the arresting dust-jacket will probably be removed by libraries.

Richard Rankin Russell, in his introduction (pp. xix–xxvii), to *Peter Fallon: Poet, Publisher, Editor and Translator*, writes that the 'Irish poet Peter Fallon has run the Gallery Press since 1970, publishing hundreds of titles in Irish poetry, drama and fiction since then, mostly in poetry' and amongst his other accomplishments 'has also authored many volumes of his own poetry' (p. xix). Russell's volume 'redresses [Fallon's] critical neglect by collecting critical essays on the history of the Gallery Press, on Fallon's own poetry, on his translation of the Georgics, on his dramatic translation of Patrick Kavanagh's novel *Tarry Flynn*, on his relationship to other poets . . . and on Fallon's role as editor'. In addition, 'a number of poems by the poets he publishes are also included' (p. xx). There are five parts to this tribute. The first, 'Fallon and the Gallery Press' (pp. 1–47), contains four contributions: Thomas Dillon Redshaw, 'The Dublin Festival, Dublin, 1970: *Capella*, the Book of Invasions, and the Original Gallery Books' (pp. 1–22); Seamus Heaney, 'Gallery at the Abbey: An Introduction to the 40th Anniversary Reading' (pp. 23–6), a speech given on 7 June 2010 (p. 26); Dennis O'Driscoll, 'Peter Fallon Revisited' (pp. 27–44), which, following the text, has references (pp. 40–1), and sixty-eight notes (pp. 41–4); and Derek Mahon, 'Works and Days' (pp. 45–7). The second part focuses on 'The Contours of Fallon's Creative Work' (pp. 40–133). There are four contributions: Maurice Harmon, 'Peter Fallon's Profane Rituals' (pp. 49–78); John McAuliffe, 'Double Vision: Peter Fallon's Landscapes with Figures' (pp. 79–92); Thomas O'Grady, ' "This Blooming Place": Peter Fallon's *Tarry Flynn*' (pp. 93–106); and Ed Madden, 'Fellow Feeling; or, Mourning, Metonymy, Masculinity' (pp. 107–33), in Fallon's poetry. The third part concentrates on 'Fallon and the Natural World' (pp. 135–98), with four contributions. Shaun O'Connell, 'All That Lasts: Peter Fallon's Loughcrew' (pp. 135–8), recounts visits to Peter Fallon in north County Meath; the editor of the volume, Richard Rankin Russell, writes on 'Nature's News: The Place(s) of Peter Fallon's Poetry' (pp. 139–60); Justin Quinn's 'The Obscenities and Audiences of Peter Fallon' (pp. 161–71) discusses individual Fallon poems and also his use of voice, raising the issue of 'Who speaks?' in his poems. Joseph Heininger, in his 'Peter Fallon's

Georgics: Praises, Lessons, and Lamentations in Virgil's "Studies of the Arts of Peace"' (pp. 178–98), concentrates on 'Fallon's translation of the *Georgics* of Virgil' that was initially 'published in 2004 by the Gallery Press, [and] revised and republished in an Oxford World's Classics edition, with an introduction and notes by Elaine Fantham' (p. 178). The fourth part has contributors writing on the subject of 'Fallon and America' (pp. 200–33). Joyce Peseroff's 'Notes on Peter Fallon's *Deerfield Series: Strength of Heart*' (pp. 200–8) reflects on 'Fallon's *Deerfield Series: Strength of Heart*, first published by the Deerfield Press in 1997 and comprising a twenty-four-page section in his volume *News of the World: Selected and New Poems*...an occasional poem commemorating the bicentennial of Deerfield Academy in western Massachusetts where Fallon taught from 1976–7 and again from 1996–97' (p. 200). Bryan Giemza, in his 'The News of Poetry; or, What Love Does Life Require?' (pp. 209–26), writes upon 'the literary kinship and poetic affinities of Wendell Berry and Peter Fallon' after he had given a paper on the topic and then met Peter Fallon, who 'had something to say about [Giemza's] musings on Peter Fallon' and Wendell Berry (p. 209). Wendell Berry then contributes a foreword to '*Airs and Angels* by Peter Fallon', a chapbook published in 2007 (pp. 227–31). The section concludes with two recent poems by Richard Wilbur, 'Horsetail' and 'Sugar Maples, January' (pp. 232–3). The final section is devoted entirely to 'Poems in Honour of Peter Fallon' (pp. 235–60), and includes poems by Medbh McGuckian, Bernard O'Donoghue, Paul Muldoon, Conor O'Callaghan, Nuala Ní Dhomhnaill, Seamus Heaney, Michael Coady, Allan Gillis, John McAuliffe, Eamon Grennan, David Wheatley, Gerard Smyth, Vona Groarke, and Ciarán Carson. *Peter Fallon Poet, Publisher, Editor and Translator* concludes with an index (pp. 261–8). It is an important volume for its subject and content, that contains two of the very last writings by Seamus Heaney before his unexpected passing away on 30 August 2013 in Dublin (p. xiii): his 'Introduction to the 40th Anniversary Reading' dated 7 June 2010 (pp. 23.26), and his poem 'The Dapple-Grey Mare (Translated from the Italian of Giovanni Pascoli, 1855–1912)...For Peter Fallon, with his hands on the reins' (pp. 241–3).

Recent Irish writing engages Claire Lynch in her *Cyber Ireland: Text, Image, Culture*, in which she explores 'the intersections between cyberculture and Irish literature, including the ways in which Irish writers have started to engage with computer technology and the parallel impact that such technology has had on Irish writing' (pp. 1–2). In addition to the late great Seamus Heaney, Lynch's discussion encompasses writers as varied as Roddy Doyle, Anne Enright, Colum McCann, Paul Murray, and Élís Ní Dhuibhne amongst others. However, she makes no attempt 'to gather together every passing reference to Irish cyber culture. Instead, these curated examples of novels, poems, video games, apps and so on are suggestive of the variety of relevant sources already in circulation' (p. 12). Lynch provides an extensive, alphabetically arranged, enumerative bibliography (pp. 165–73) and there is a name-orientated index (pp. 174–8). It is worth noting that although there is discussion of works by James Joyce, Claire Lynch doesn't find room—if the index is a reliable guide—to mention even the name of Samuel Becket!

Coire Sois, The Cauldron of Knowledge: A Companion to Early Irish Saga is a collection of thirty-one previously published essays by Tomás Ó Cathasaigh. Edited by Matthieu Boyd, with a foreword by Declan Kiberd (pp. ix–xiv), it provides an account of early Irish narrative literature in the vernacular. As Boyd indicates, 'for thirty years, Tomás Ó Cathasaigh has been one of the foremost interpreters of early Irish narrative literature qua literature. His method combines a rare philological acuity with painstaking literary analysis' (p. xv). In his preface (pp. xv–xx), Boyd explains the organization of Ó Cathasaigh's essays into 'Themes', meaning 'studies on over-arching or recurrent issues in the field' (p. xviii) such as 'Curse and Satire' (pp. 95–100), and 'Texts', such as 'studies on individual literary works'. Further, with some exceptions, 'Articles are [arranged] in chronological order within each group' (p. xviii). In 'A Note on the Title', Boyd explains that 'the Cauldron of Knowledge, Coire Sois, is generated upside-down within a person, and knowledge is distributed out of it'. Also the subtitle of the collection, *A Companion to Early Irish Saga*, 'should not be construed as a claim of exhaustiveness. Not every early Irish saga extant is even mentioned in these pages, let alone comprehensively discussed. However, the book is a wise and dependable guide to the corpus' (pp. xix–xx). Following Ó Cathasaigh's essays the *Companion* concludes with a descriptive list of 'Further Reading Compiled by Matthieu Boyd with the Author's Input' (pp. 484–500), extensive notes to each essay (pp. 501–50), and an extensive enumerative 'Bibliography of Tomás Ó Cathasaigh' chronologically arranged by year of publication (pp. 551–4), followed by an alphabetically arranged enumerative listing of works cited (pp. 555–88) and an extensive index (pp. 589–618), that 'also serves as a glossary of Irish words introduced in the book, and as a reminder of the significance of people and places' (p. 589). *Coire Sois* is an important introduction to Celtic studies: perhaps an indication of the limited readership that its publishers, the University of Notre Dame Press expect is reflected in the high price of the paperback print compilation. The publishers' website, however, does indicate that an electronic version is available as an Adobe pdf e-book at a slightly lower price.

Augusta Rohrbach's 'fundamental goal' in her *Thinking Outside the Book* 'is to identify a shared purpose between print culture and new media and find a way to elaborate their commonalities without stifling either one' (p. 10). Rohrbach 'assemble[s] a cohort of literary figures—Jane Johnston Schoolcraft, Sojourner Truth, Hannah Crafts, Augusta Evans, and Mary Chesnut— who challenge the traditional vocabulary of book history'. She writes that 'collectively, their work constitutes an alternative to more familiar women writers, like Harriet Beecher Stowe' and others. Further, these less well-known figures 'are nonetheless representative of the various strategies authors, editors, and publishers developed in order to capture public interest and cultivate a sense of history-in-the-making'. Rohrbach is not afraid to make large claims: '*Thinking Outside the Book* overturns the primacy of print as the *sine qua non* of literary history to probe the question: What is literary in literary history?' Her case histories from Schoolcraft, Truth, Crafts, and others 'will show how the alternative terminology I present here up opens the contours of book history to a broader notion of text' (pp. 6–7). She proposes 'an alternate typology for . . . key concepts that better fits the needs of today—and also, not inconsequentially, of the past'. Consequently the terms 'Literacy, Authorship, Publication, Edition, Editor' would be replaced by '(re)mediation, memory, history, testimony, and loss as terms that better describe the energies now shared across media that we have previously associated with book culture' (p. 3). This is a challenging study that makes its readers rethink traditional vocabulary and what it means. Further, it makes us realize that authors such as Harriet Beecher Stowe, Emily Dickinson, Emerson, Hawthorne, and others did not work in isolation and were not the only authors around. Rohrbach's text is followed by extensive notation (pp. 129–54) and an index (pp. 155–61).

An interesting short narrative reference work is Shin Yamashiro's *American Sea Literature: Seascapes, Beach, Narratives, and Underwater Explorations*, in which 'sea literature is divided into three types: on the sea, by the sea, and beneath the sea'. There are chapters on each of these in order that 'we can better look at American sea literature from the colonial period to the twentieth century, appreciating its historical trends, multifaceted varieties, and ever-lasting imperatives' (p. 1). Following the introduction, 'On the Sea, By the Sea, Beneath the Sea' (pp. 1–11), there are three chapters on each of these (pp. 12–120), and 'Epilogue: Rooftop Water Tank' (pp. 121–3). In this 'is a sketch of the author's place, Okinawa, Japan, to reflect upon our general idea of the terrestrial and the oceanic'. Yamashiro adds that 'a sense of the extremely precious, even the miraculous nature of water . . . permeates reflections and expressions in sea literature' (p. 121). Each of the chapters is followed by notation, and there is a brief alphabetically arranged, name-orientated index (pp. 124–5).

An addition to the Palgrave Studies in the Enlightenment, Romanticism and Cultures of Print series is Yasmin Solomonescu's *John Thelwall and the Materialist Imagination*. Drawing upon 'new archival materials and spanning the four decades of Thelwall's career, this book examines the aesthetic and ideological ramifications of his heterodox "materialist" view that the properties and processes of living nature, from vitality and cognition to agency in imagination, could be explained with reference to certain immutable laws of organic matter'. Furthermore, Solomonescu 'brings a new perspective to bear on the rehabilitation of a long neglected figure' (p. 3) who lived between 1764 and 1834. Of particular interest are 'chapters 5 and 6' (pp. 95–119, 120–42), which 'take stock of the newly discovered manuscript poetry and prolific but uncollected elocutionary writings that span the period 1800 to 1830' (p. 12). There are three appendices: 'Peter Crompton, Letter to John Thelwall, 11 Sept. 1800. Source: The Morgan Library, New York, MA 77 (19)' (pp. 143–4); 'Thelwall, 'To Dr. Peter Crompton', Poems, Chiefly Written in Retirement (1801) Source: Cambridge University Library, Rare Books Y.19.43 (no. 1)' (pp. 145–6); and a poem, 'Thelwall, "The Star that Shone When Other Stars Were Dim: A Night-Walk in the Vicinity of Whitehall", *Monthly Magazine* 59 Supplement (1825), 661–3' (pp. 147–50). Following lengthy notes to the text and the appendices (pp. 151–91), there is an extensive alphabetically arranged, enumerative bibliography divided into 'Primary Works' (pp. 199–206), and 'Secondary Works' (pp. 206–18). This fascinating study concludes with a helpful index that is not restricted to names (pp. 219–26).

As José María Pérez Fernández and Edward Wilson-Lee explain in their introduction to the collection of essays *Translation and the Book Trade in Early Modern Europe*, the object of their book is to 'approach the material infrastructure' of the 'European mosaic... variegated, fragmentary, polyglot' that formed in the growth of 'national vernacular traditions... during the first century and a half of print'. Books were translated from classical Greek and Latin and 'new works produced within [the] vernacular canons were rendered into... other languages' (p. 1). Specific examples are discussed in the ten chapters that follow the introduction (pp. 1–21). Of particular pertinence are Rocío G. Sumillera on 'Language Manuals and the Book Trade in England' (pp. 61–80), and Guyda Armstrong on 'Translation Trajectories in Early Modern European Print Culture: The Case of Boccaccio' (pp. 126–44). Armstrong indicates that seven Boccaccio translations were printed in London during the 1567 to 1620 period (see pp. 126, 140). Edward Wilson-Lee, in his 'Glosses and Oracles: Guiding Readers in Early Modern Europe' (pp. 145–63), draws upon examples from glosses in English, for instance by Thomas Watson in his 'early English sonnet sequence... [the] Petrarchan *Hekatompathia* (1582)' (p. 145) and his printer John Wolfe, who was 'central to the history of translated books in England'. Wilson-Lee writes that in London 'Wolfe was, in effect, one center of a complex web of relations—material, social, and ideological—among England, northern Italy, and Basel'. Moreover 'in naturalizing Continental texts and print practices, and in preparing English and Continental works for (often clandestine) distribution on the Continent, Wolfe was cannily exploiting openings in the market and providing a crucial channel for intellectual and technical commerce between these locations' (pp. 146–7). Wilson-Lee also has interesting observations on Sidney in terms of such interconnections (see pp. 156–61). According to Stewart Mottram in his 'Spenser's Dutch Uncles: The Family of Love and the Four Translations of *A Theatre for Worldlings*' (pp. 164–84), the 'first printed verse of Edmund Spenser' may be found in '*A Theatre for Wordlings*... Commonly regarded as the first English emblem book'. Mottram's focus is not on the volume's 'seemingly eclectic collection of poems, prose commentary, and woodcut illustrations'. Mottram's intention is to restore 'Spenser's first translations to the commentary they were originally intended to illustrate, reading poems and prose together within the broader context of the community by whom, and for whom *A Theatre* was first produced'. The volume, published in 1569, was 'a product of London's Flemish community' and it was aimed at Flemish exiles. It 'was an English translation of a volume that had originally appeared in Dutch and French formats' the previous year (p. 164). English translations by Anthony Munday (pp. 209–14) are of interest to Louise Wilson in her 'The Publication of Iberian Romance in Early Modern Europe' (pp. 201–16), although her contribution also encompasses French, Castilian, and other non-English editions 'of the Iberian chivalric cycles, *Amadis de Gaula* and *Palmerin*' published 'in sixteenth-century Europe' (p. 201). Neil Rhodes, in his 'Afterword' (pp. 217–26), draws upon various databases to demonstrate 'how relatively marginal Britain was in the European book trade: in the process of transmission of both classical and modern authors, whether in the original language or in translation, London was pretty much the end of the line' (p. 224), with Antwerp at the centre—'mainly before 1550' (p. 225). With notation found at the end of individual contributions, this fascinating volume contains eight black and white illustrations, an alphabetically arranged enumerative list of works cited (pp. 227–62), and a name-orientated index (pp. 263–71).

Cécile Cottenet has edited *Race, Ethnicity and Publishing in America*, a collection divided into four sections. Following a list of figures (p. vii), of which there are six in black and white scattered throughout the text, a list of tables (p. viii), of which there are three, acknowledgements (pp. ix–x), 'Notes on the Contributors' (pp. xi–xiii), and a detailed, densely expressed, editors introduction (pp. 1–25), the first part focuses on 'Historiography' (pp. 29–76). It has two contributions: 'Early African American Historians: A Book History and Historiography Approach. The Case of William Cooper Nell (1816–1874)' (pp. 29–50) by Claire Parfait, and 'Publication and Reception of *The Southern Negro and the Public Library*' (pp. 51–76) by Cheryl Knott. The second part engages with the subject of 'Bilingualism and Ethic Identity' (pp. 79–119), with two contributions: 'Widening the Paradigm of American Literature: Small Presses in the Publishing and Creation of New Hispanic Texts' (pp. 79–94) by Manuel Brito, and 'Franco-American Writers: In-visible Authors in the Global Literary Market' (pp. 95–119), by Peggy Pacini. The third part, focusing on 'Challenging Stereotypes: A Gendered Perspective' (pp. 123–67), also has two contributions: 'Reacting to the White Publishing World: Zora Neale Hurston and Negro Stereotypes' (pp. 123–42) by Claudine Raynaud, and 'Beyond Mainstream Presses: Publishing Women of Color as Cultural and Political Critique' (pp. 143–67) by Matilde Martín González. The fourth and final part, 'Re-visiting the Canon' (pp. 171–230), has three rather than two contributions: 'The Roots of *Cane*: Jean Toomer in *The Double Dealer* and Modernist Networks' (pp. 171–92) by John K. Young; 'Popular Book Clubs and the Marketing of African American Best Sellers' (pp. 193–209) by Laurence Cossu-Beaumont; and 'The Poetry of Phillis Wheatley in Slavery's Recollective Economies, 1773 to the Present' (pp. 210–30) by Max Cavitch. In his 'Epilogue: An Experience in Literary Archaeology: Publishing a Black Lost Generation' (pp. 231–42), reflecting the French orientation of Cécile Cottenet's collection, Samuel Blumenfeld, a former reader for a French publisher, recalls his 'discovering parts of American culture that had been abandoned and [his] helping bringing them back into the limelight'. He adds: 'Such a story is that of many American writers, musicians or film-makers who obtained recognition in France, and of many French readers, critics or publishers who helped them become visible.' This is, he adds, 'a never-ending story' (p. 240). Each contribution is followed by extensive note documentation and an alphabetically arranged, enumerative select bibliography; there is an index, but there is no cumulative bibliography.

Kristie Macrakis writes in her preface (pp. ix–xiv) that '*Prisoners, Lovers, and Spies* is a biography of a special kind of secret communication, the invisible kind. It tells the story of the life and times of secret writing from the ancient Greeks to the present day in its social, political, scientific, and cultural context.' She adds that, 'unlike its big brother cryptography, the study of codes and ciphers, invisible secret writing didn't evolve in a progressive, linear fashion. It developed in fits and starts' (p. xii). In an appendix entitled 'Fun Kitchen Chemistry Experiments' (pp. 303–13), the author, with Jason Lye, 'describe some safe historical sympathetic ink experiments [they] undertook with household materials', including for instance the activities of 'Thomas Robins, imprisoned in Britain's Wandsworth prison, who developed invisible ink from oatmeal, or porridge, as it is called in Britain, in 1935' (p. 304). Informative notes (pp. 315–50) follow Macrakis's text. There is also an alphabetically arranged, enumerative listing of primary sources divided into 'Archival' (p. 351), 'Digital Primary Sources', and 'Printed Sources and Rare Book Libraries' (pp. 351–2). Black and white illustrative 'Credits' (p. 353) are followed by somewhat revealing acknowledgements (pp. 355–7) and a helpful index (pp. 359–77) to this eminently readable, fascinating study.

Of interest too is Michael Cook's *Detective Fiction and the Ghost Story: The Haunted Text*. This is a thematic rather than 'comprehensive history of the relationship between the two genres'. Cook's 'objective was not to apply the theory to the whole of detective fiction as being constructed entirely through its relationship with the ghost story, but to indicate that the latter had, nonetheless, been a considerable influence in its development'. Cook's 'preference has always been to analyze in some depth what the author actually wrote rather than sweeping historical contexts' (p. 11). Consequently there are close analyses of works by Conan Doyle, Agatha Christie, John Dickson Carr, Ian Rankin, Susan Hill, and Tony Hillerman. Interesting, informative notes (pp. 189–203) follow the text. There is also a useful, alphabetically arranged 'Select Bibliography and Suggested Reading' (pp. 204–18), and a helpful, name-orientated index (pp. 219–23).

The Author's Hand and the Printer's Mind contains twelve essays written by the eminent French book historian Roger Chartier since 2002. Translated by Lydia G. Cochrane, the essays are divided into three sections. In the first part, 'The Past in the Present' (pp. 1–55), the subjects are: 'Listen to the Dead with Your Eyes' (pp. 3–26); 'History: Reading Time' (pp. 27–43); and 'History and Social Science: A Return to [Fernand] Braudel' (pp. 44–55), who died in 1985 and was 'a student of global history, cast in the long term, which he practiced in all his great books' (p. 44). The second part, 'What Is a Book?' (pp. 57–119), consists of essays on 'The Powers of Print' (pp. 59–72); 'The Author's Hand' (pp. 73–86); 'Pauses and Pitches' (pp. 87–97); and 'Translation' (pp. 98–119). The third part is devoted to essays on 'Texts and Meanings' (pp. 121–80): ' Memory and Writing' (pp. 123–34); 'Paratext and Preliminaries' (pp. 135–49); 'Publishing Cervantes' (pp. 150–7); ''Publishing Shakespeare' (pp. 158–71); and 'The Time of the Work' (pp. 172–82), which discusses 'a copy of the 1676 edition of *Hamlet*' now 'owned by the John Work Garrett Library at the Johns Hopkins University in Baltimore'. This copy 'is particularly interesting...thanks to the manuscript annotations written in the margins and the corrections, deletions, or additions that one of its owners made in the printed text itself'. Furthermore, 'it enables us to enter into "the time of the work" because we can discern in this unique object different states of the text and successive forms of its performance' (p. 172). Such a commentary is not atypical of Chartier's work as reflected in the selection contained in this volume. Extensive notes (pp. 181–220) follow his text, and there is too a useful extensive index (pp. 221–31) to this well-produced collection—'typeset in 10.5 on 12 pt Sabon' (p. iv)—by an important book historian.

Daniel Robinson's *Myself and Some Other Being: Wordsworth and the Life of Writing* is a short mediation on Wordsworth's lifetime obsession with life-writing. In 1805 the poet, 'having settled on nearly 8500 lines of iambic pentameter for the story of his life . . . thought he had finished the project he began in the fall of 1798'. Robinson adds that 'the poem, however, would remain unread by anyone other than a handful of Wordsworth's closest friends and family for close to half a century. Wordsworth would edit, rewrite, delete, add, and otherwise tinker with those lines during most of that time' (p. 1). Robinson's concern is with this continuous life-writing, although his focus 'is roughly chronological, following [the poet] from when he begins his career in earnest through the completion of his first major draft of *The Prelude* in which he confirms his calling'. Robinson wishes 'to catch Wordsworth in the progress of becoming *Wordsworth*—not by writing his life so much as by reading his life-writing' (p. 3).

Ralph Hanna, in his extensive introduction (pp. 1–57) to his edition of Richard Holland's *The Buke of the Howlat*, comments that it 'is the oldest surviving alliterative poem in Scots, and probably the first Scots assay in what, from the later fifteenth century, appears a distinctive feature of Scots tradition, the thirteen-line stanza' (p. 45). The poem was written during the late 1440s for Elizabeth Douglas, the wife of Archibald Douglas, earl of Moray. It recounts the story of the borrowed feathers of an owl, the owl's pride and fall, and his fate decided by a bird parliament. Holland extols in his poem the virtues of the Douglas family and their service to Robert Bruce during the Scottish Independence Wars. Following 'References and Abbreviations' (pp. xi–xii), Hanna's introduction includes sections on 'The Sources of the Text' (pp. 1–10), 'Author and Date' (pp. 10–15), 'Holland's Language' (pp. 16–23), 'Literary Sources and Holland's Poem' (pp. 23–45), 'Holland's Verse' (pp. 45–50), and 'Editing the Text' (pp. 50–7). There then follows the text of the poem (pp. 59–85) with line numbering, 'Collation of the Witness' (pp. 87–91), or 'corpus of variants' (p. 87). There then follow the two most extensive parts of Hanna's edition: a most thorough line-based textual commentary (pp. 93–149) and a detailed, alphabetically arranged, explanatory glossary (pp. 151–206). This superb edition concludes with an enumerative, alphabetically arranged bibliography (pp. 207–12).

As John Flood writes in his 'Note on the Texts and Apparatus' (pp. 33–7) to *The Works of Walter Quin: An Irishman at the Stuart Courts*, 'the aim of this edition is to gather together the writings of Walter Quin and to present them in an accessible form' (p. 33). An addition to the Four Courts Press, Dublin, 'series of editions of English-language texts from seventeenth- and eighteenth-century Ireland' (p. 12), Flood's introduction, 'Walter Quin and His Work' (pp. 15–32), indicates that his subject, who was probably born around 1575 and who died in 1640, 'was born in Dublin and educated in Germany and Scotland'. It was 'in Edinburgh [that] his political poetry attracted the notice of King James VI, who had him appointed to the household of Henry, his eldest son. In 1603, when James ascended to the English throne as the first Stuart monarch, Quin also went to London, where he continued in royal service for the rest of his life.' Quin's 'literary output—in poetry and prose, written variously in English, Latin, French and Italian—includes works in praise of the Stuarts, along with historical and philosophical writing' (p. 15). Accompanied by seven black and white illustrations, the edition includes 'translations of texts written in languages other than English' (p. 33) and 'works on the basis of individual copy-texts' (p. 34). 'Editorial Principles', 'Typography, Scribal Features and Mise-en-Page' are clearly explained (pp. 34–5) as are the footnotes and headnotes (p. 36), although it is difficult to establish whether or not Flood has produced a complete edition of everything Quin wrote or not. He does observe that 'his extant output is not prodigious, although it is at once uniform and varied' (p. 30). The 'Works' (pp. 41–263) are followed by an appendix, 'Writings To and About Quin' (pp. 264–72), and a glossary (pp. 273–4). An extensive bibliography (pp. 275–85) includes 'Manuscripts and Special Collections' (p. 275), followed by an alphabetically arranged, enumerative bibliography of printed sources; there are indexes of titles, 'Works by Quin' (pp. 286–8), and 'Work by Other Authors' (p. 289), and a name-orientated general index (pp. 290–2).

In the acknowledgements to his and Declan Kiely's edition of W.B. Yeats, *On Baile's Strand: Manuscript Materials*, Jared Curtis observes 'with the publication of this volume the Cornell Yeats Editorial Board, completes the series of editions of the manuscripts of W.B. Yeats's poems and plays. Launched in 1982 with the appearance of Yeats's last play, *The Death of Cuchulain*, the series ends in 2013 with the completion of *On Baile's Strand*, the first of his plays based on the same heroic figure of Irish legend' (p. xi). An extensive listing of abbreviations (pp. xiii–xiv) is followed by an extensive 'Census of Manuscripts' (pp. xv–xvi) that includes measurements 'given as width by height in centimeters' (p. xv)— an illustration of the meticulous detail to be found in Curtis and Kiely's edition. In their extensive introduction they write 'On *Baile's Strand* is Yeats's finest play. It explores several powerful themes: vengeance, free will and fate, personal and dynastic survival, love and loyalty, betrayal and trust, the nature of heroism, filicide, remorse, and madness.' Initial drafts occurred in the summer of 1901 and the play 'was first published in August 1903', republished in March 1904, 'with some slightly revised dialogue... And it was first produced for the opening night of the Abbey Theatre, on December 27, 1904' (p. xxv). Following an account of their 'Transcription Principles and Procedures' (pp. lv–lvii) is the main body of the edition '*On Baile's Strand*: Transcriptions and Photographic Reproductions' (pp. 3–545). The text contains many black and white illustrations, and brief annotations are found at the foot of the page. The text is divided into two sections: 'I. Manuscripts and Typescripts, 1901–1904' (pp. 3–237); and 'II. Manuscripts, Typescripts, and Revised Proofs, 1905–1906' (pp. 241–545). Given the nature of Yeats's extensive revisions and erasures it is remarkable how Curtis and Kiely and their publishers have successfully been able to reproduce them. This splendid edition concludes with seven appendices, with much material drawn upon from the Berg Collection at the New York Public Library and the National Library of Ireland, Dublin ('NLI'): 'Text of *On*

Baile's Strand Published *in In the Seven Woods* (Dun Emer, 1903)' (pp. 549–72); 'List of Cast Members for *On Baile's Strand*, Berg F' (pp. 573–5); 'Program Notes for the 1906 Touring Production of *On Baile's Strand*, Berg G' (pp. 577–9); 'Stage Designs for the Abbey Theatre (c.1910), NLI, 30,588' (pp. 581–4); 'Edward Gordon Craig's Drawing of the Fool's Mask and Costume, 1911' (pp. 585–7); 'Note for *Plays in Prose and Verse*, 1922, NLI 13,571' (pp. 589–93); and 'Late Revisions (1906–1939)' (p. 595). Although this must have been a most expensive volume to produce it is a pity that an opportunity was not found to include one or two of the illustrations in colour rather than in black and white.

Mention too should be made of another work with Yeatsian associations that has been drawn to the present contributor's attention. Lucy McDiarmid's *The Literary History of the Meal: Poets and the Peacock Dinner* is a delightfully presented and written volume. The front jacket illustration is from Whistler's *The Peacock Room*, south-west mural, now at the Smithsonian in Washington DC. It is replete with illustrations, including reproductions of 'the first mention of the dinner in a letter from Yeats (in Pound's handwriting but signed by Yeats) to Lady Gregory, 24 November 1913' (p. xv) now at the Berg Collection, New York Public Library (pp. 32–3). In the opening sentence and paragraph of her prologue McDiarmid writes, 'On 18 January 1914, seven poets gathered to eat a peacock' (p. 1). The dinner honoured the poet Wilfred Scawen Blunt, and the others present at the meal were the poets Victor Plarr, Thomas Sturge Moore, W.B. Yeats, Ezra Pound, Richard Aldington, and F.S. Flint. Drawing upon unpublished letters, diaries, and memoirs, McDiarmid's book is about the meal, the circumstances that produced it, and the relationships between the participants, and especially about Pound, Yeats, his collaborator Lady Gregory, and Blunt who had secretly had an affair with Lady Gregory thirty years previously 'beginning in the summer of 1882' (p. 9). The dinner, with its 'friendships, romances, and rivalries' showed 'the way the profession of poetry, lacking systematic schools and licenses, lacking a single dominant institutional structure or any permanent institutions at all, functions through intimacies, visits, cohabitations, and provisional groupings like that of the seven men who assembled to eat the Peacock' and 'the network of women who connected the men' (p. 175). Moreover, there is in this narrative the foundation for a Pinter play that remained unwritten. There is a useful enumerative bibliography listing 'Manuscript Sources' (p. 195), 'Newspapers' (pp. 195–6), 'Unpublished Academic Work' (p. 196) and an alphabetically arranged listing of books and articles divided into 'Primary Sources' (pp. 196–9) and 'Secondary Sources' (pp. 199–204). There is too a most helpful double-columned index (pp. 205–12).

The University of Georgia Press's edition of the works of Tobias Smollett has added *The Adventures of Peregrine Pickle. In which are included Memoirs of a Lady of Quality*, with introduction and notes by John P. Zomchick and George S. Rousseau, the text is edited by the late O.M. Brack, Jr. and W.H. Keithley. This well-bound, thick volume contains black and white illustrations. John P. Zomchick's preface (pp. xv–xviii) has a judicious survey of previous editions. Acknowledgements (pp. xix–xxi), abbreviations (pp. xxiii–xxv), and an extensive introduction (pp. xxvii–lix) are followed by 160 accompanying notes (pp. lix–lxviii). The text of the novel (pp. 48–646) is similarly followed by 'Notes to the Text' (pp. 647–811), many of which are very detailed—see for instance the explanatory notes on the 'Duke of Marlborough' and 'madam de Maintenon...second wife to Louis XIV' (p. 713). There is then a 'Textual Commentary' (pp. 813–25) with 'Publication History' (pp. 813–14); 'Editorial Principles' (pp. 814–22) state that 'the spelling, punctuation, and capitalization of the 1751 first edition [have] been retained except when they are clearly in error or when they obscure meaning or distract the attention of the reader' (p. 822). 'Apparatus' (p. 822) is followed by 'Collation', explaining that 'the present edition has been reproduced from a photocopy of the 1751 first edition in the University of Iowa Library' collated with other early copies. The 'Textual Commentary' has notes too (pp. 823–5). There is an extensive 'List of Emendations' (pp. 827–36), 'Word-Division' (837–41), a 'Historical Collation' (pp. 843–909), and 'Bibliographical Descriptions' (pp. 911–14) of the first four editions of *Peregrine Pickle* (pp. 910–14). This definitive edition of the novel concludes with an index of 'Names, Places, and Topics in Introduction, Text, Notes to the Text, and Textual Commentary' (pp. 915–24): in the light of its depth of scholarship and reasonable pricing, the volume is not beyond the purchase reach of scholars as well as institutional libraries.

The ninth volume of the Florida Edition of the Works of Laurence Sterne, *The Miscellaneous Writings and Sterne's Subscribers, an Identification List*, edited by Melvyn New and W.B. Gerard, is the final volume in this magnificent edition to appear. As the editors observe in their introductory paragraph to their acknowledgements (pp. ix–xii), which appear in double-columned format with the senior editor, Melvyn New's, comments appearing on the left and W.B. Gerard's on the right, 'with it, one editor has come to the end of his forty-five-year career as a Sterne scholar, while the other editor is in mid-career' (p. ix). This is followed by a listing of 'Works Frequently Cited' (pp. xiii–xiv), and Melvyn New's introduction to 'The Miscellaneous Writings' (pp. xv–xxxi), 'Sterne's Subscription Lists' (pp. xxii–xxxi), and a 'Coda' (pp. xxxi–xxxiv), followed by twenty-seven at times detailed notes (pp. xxxiv–xxxix). New writes, 'a new scholarly edition of Sterne's works will perhaps not be undertaken for another decade or two, but if Sterne is to continue to be read, his work must be edited and annotated for different times and new readers'. He judiciously adds: 'scholarly editors cannot practice their trade for very long before they realize that their texts are only as valid as their present methodologies and the documents available to them, and that their annotations are only responses to questions their contemporaries ask' (p. xxxiv). The texts of 'Sterne's Miscellaneous Works' (pp. 3–273) are prefaced by an introduction that encompasses a manuscript description, details of its discovery, dating, text, and extensive notation to the text that on occasion is longer than the text itself—as for instance in the case of 'Sterne's Memoirs' with fifty-three notes (pp. 11–23) and the text covering just five pages (pp. 6–10). The second part of this edition is concerned with 'Sterne's Subscribers: An Identification List' (pp. 279–574). Following preliminary materials such as 'Works Cited by Short Titles' (pp. 279–81) and 'Contemporary Subscribers' Lists Frequently Cited' (pp. 281–3), there follows an extensive, alphabetically arranged, descriptive, biographically orientated listing of 'Sterne's Subscribers' beginning with 'Abdy... Sir Anthony Abdy, Bart., and Lady Abdy (1769)' (p. 283), and concluding with 'Young, Mr. R. (1768)' (p. 574). This splendid edition concludes with an 'Index to the Miscellaneous Writings' (pp. 575–91). It is appropriate in this final *YWES* notice of the Florida Sterne edition to cite its general editor Melvyn New's wisdom and awareness of the limitations of editing in the computer age: 'the growing tendency to equate Web sites to other bibliographical instruments, at least in terms of providing elaborated and elongated Internet addresses, seems to me an unexamined practice, equivalent perhaps to providing scholars with library maps indicating stacked locations for titles cited' (p. xxiv). An additional item of interest is Karen Harvey's 'The Manuscript History of Tristram Shandy' (*RES* 65[2014] 281–301). Instead of concentrating on the 'printed context that Sterne's satire and modernity are thought to derive' from, Harvey instead explores 'the manuscript hinterland of *Tristram Shandy*'. She 'reconstructs the quotidian context of domestic writing in which we might situate the novel [and] also undertakes a close examination of Laurence Sterne's own personal and parish manuscripts to demonstrate the way that he himself occupied—and struggled with—this everyday writing' (p. 281).

A valuable addition to the Four Courts Press series devoted to early Irish fiction is Daniel Sanjiv Roberts's edition of Charles Johnstone's *The History of Arsaces, Prince of Betlis*. First published anonymously in London in 1774, its author Charles Johnstone (c.1719–c.1800), 'an Irishman and a barrister, had already written one of the most successful satirical works of the age, *Chrysal; or, The Adventures of a Guinea*, whose first edition appeared in 1760' (p. 12). As Roberts explains in his introduction 'the eponymous hero of *The History of Arsaces, Prince of Betlis* [was] born a Muslim [who] learns through his adventures about Coptic Christians, Indian Brahmans, Parsis of Persia and other kinds of religious believers not to mention charlatans'. Roberts adds that 'the narrator's fulfillment of his destiny also functions as an Enlightenment narrative instructing the reader in theology, antiquity, geography, political science, civic virtue and morality' (p. 11). Amongst topics covered in the introduction are the novel's neglect 'over the course of the nineteenth century' (p. 17), and a 'comparison between Swift and Johnstone' (p. 19). Roberts writes that 'the wide-ranging historical and geographical scope of the work is entirely characteristic of an age notable for the production of encyclopedias and dictionaries of all kinds, works that gathered factual knowledge of the world and digested them for popular reference and consumption to meet the needs of a rapidly growing middle-class readership' (p. 20). Roberts concludes his introduction: 'the *History of Arsaces* is primarily a fictional work which seeks to apprehend its moment in time through the histories and geographies of other times and places. Its difficulty in keeping apart the boundaries between the fantasy of romance and the realism of the novel would, in the twentieth and twenty-first centuries, be renegotiated in the modes of postmodernist and magical realist fictions' (p. 27). A note on the choice of copy text (p. 29) is followed by the two-volume text (pp. 33–209), extensive, helpful notation (pp. 211–22), a list of emendations' (p. 223), then a biographical note on the author Charles Johnstone, correcting previous accounts (pp. 225–33).

There is an alphabetically arranged select bibliography that is partly descriptive, encompassing 'Primary Texts', 'Critical Editions', 'Translations', 'Primary Sources of Biographical Information', 'Archival Materials', 'Secondary Texts', and 'Bibliographies' (pp. 235–7).

Robert P. Irvine has produced an edition of a novel, *Prince Otto*, on which its author Robert Louis Stevenson 'spent a great deal of hope and time and effort'; the book 'received only lukewarm praise from reviewers and did little for his reputation as a writer'. Its editor believes it 'is a fascinating text, best understood as an experiment in genre' (p. xxii). In his introduction (pp. xxii–liv) to this edition, the first to appear in the New Edinburgh Edition of the Works of Robert Louis Stevenson, Irvine explains how the novel 'was written, published and received, and the literary sources and historical contexts on which it drew' (p. xxiii). There is commentary on the novel's 'Composition, Publication and Early Reception' (pp. xxiii–xxxv), 'Influences and Artistic Contexts' (pp. xxxv–xlvi), 'Historical and Political Contexts' (pp. xlvi–xlix), and 'Afterlife and Influence' (pp. xlix–li) followed by notes (pp. li–lii) and an alphabetically arranged enumerative listing of works cited (pp. liii–liv). Irvine concludes his introduction with the observation that 'the lesson Stevenson seems to have drawn' from writing *Prince Otto* and from its reception 'was to try less hard for the *magnum opus*, and instead to rely on his own genius for prose fiction ' (p. li). The introductory material to this edition contains, in addition to acknowledgements (pp. ix–x), a preface by the general editors (pp. xi–xiv), justifying the edition, which 'aims . . . to provide what cannot be found in his or any subsequent collected edition, namely accurate texts for all of Stevenson substantial oeuvre' (p. xi). There is too a list of abbreviations (p. xv), and a useful chronology of Robert Louis Stevenson (pp. xvi–xxii). There are two appendices following the text. The first consists of 'Magazine Passages Excised from the Book Edition' (pp. 163–5): 'one short passage of dialogue was removed in its entirety from Book 1 chapter 5, and this is reproduced . . . followed by the original ending of the last chapter of the novel, very extensively rewritten by Stevenson for the Chatto & Windus edition' (p. 163). The second appendix is concerned with 'Manuscript Fragments' (pp. 165–8): 'no manuscript version of *Prince Otto* has survived. The only manuscript materials relevant to this novel are lists of characters and chapters, and draft dedicatory matter, held in the Beinecke Collection of Yale University Library in New Haven Connecticut, and in the Huntington Library in San Marino, California' (p. 165). In a 'Note on the Text' (pp. 169–72) Irvine explains why the first book edition published by Chatto & Windus in 1885 rather than the serial version that appeared in the same year printed in *Longman's Magazine* is the chosen copy text (p. 169). There is a 'Bibliographical History' (pp. 169–72), an interesting 'Textual Essay' (pp. 173–84), followed by an 'Emendation List' (pp. 185–6), a short listing of 'End-of-Line Hyphens' (p. 189), and useful textual explanatory notes (pp. 189–213). Clearly this first publication in the New Edinburgh Edition of the Works of Robert Louis Stevenson represents much time, effort, and economic expenditure: indeed the collective edition constitutes a new academic endeavour that no doubt will engage many. Essentially Irvine's edition consists of fifty-four pages of exemplary prefatory material and thirty-four pages of supplementary material following a text that is not very difficult to find in institutional libraries. At the high price charged, unfortunately readership of Stevenson's *Prince Otto* will remain confined to those few with access to institutional libraries. Mention too should be made Ian Duncan's Oxford World's Classics edition of Stevenson's *Kidnapped*. In addition to a critical introduction (pp. ix–xxvi), the edition includes a 'Note on the Text' (pp. xxvii–xxx), select bibliography (pp. xxxi–xxxii), and a chronology of Robert Louis Stevenson (pp. xxxiii–xxxv). The text (pp. 1–196) is followed by useful explanatory notes (pp. 197–207) and a glossary (pp. 208–11). Duncan has 'chosen the 1895' edition published by Cassells 'as "Part One" of *The Adventures of David Balfour* as [his] copy text . . . on the supposition that it represents the closest version we have to the text if *Kidnapped* that Stevenson corrected before his death in December 1894 and before the interposition of further corrections by press intermediaries for the Edinburgh Edition' of October 1895 published by Longman, Cassells, and Scribner's (pp. xxviii–xxix). Duncan's unpretentious edition, cheaply priced, comes highly recommended and, given its light weight and portability, usefully slips into the pocket or hand luggage for a long-distance flight, providing an alternative to staring at a screen.

The London-based reprint house of Pickering & Chatto (part of Taylor & Francis post-March 2015) has in its Chawton House Library series, 'Women's Memoirs', reprinted all six volumes of Mary Hays's *Female Biography; or, Memoirs of Illustrations and Celebrated Women, of all Ages and Countries*, first published in 1803. The last three volumes, beginning with *Madame Dacier* (vol. 8, pp. 3–26 in the ten-volume series) and concluding in the final volume with *Zenobia* (vol. 10, pp. 476–8), have been made available for review purposes. In each of the three volumes the reprinted text is followed by extensive editorial notes (vol. 8, pp. 507–639; vol. 9, pp. 531–99; vol. 10, pp. 545–677). These are of a biographical rather than a textual nature. To cite one instance, Hays's entry on the poet 'Mrs. Thomas' in her final volume (vol. 10, pp. 427–36) refers to 'the death of Henry Cromwell Curl, the bookseller' (vol. 9, p. 436). Walker's explanatory note is found following the text and indicated by line number on the Hays page so the original reprint is not encumbered with notation—a publisher's expense-saving device rather than one directed at the reader's convenience. Gina Luria Walker, the editor, observes 'Edmund Curl (d.1747), [was] a successful London bookseller off the Strand who unscrupulously published literary works and ephemera without the formal permissions that were conventional in this pre-copyright age' (vol. 10, p. 652). The tenth volume contains, before the editorial notes, two appendices. The first is 'Memoirs of Mary Wollstonecraft' (pp. 479–80), an introduction to the text of '"Memories of Mary Wollstonecraft" published in *The Annual Necrology 1797–8*' (p. 479), a reprint of which then follows (pp. 481–534). The second appendix consists of a commentary by Mary Spongberg on 'The Sources of *Female Biography*' (pp. 535–44). There is also a listing of research contributors to the notes on the subjects in the three volumes (pp. 679–84) and a detailed, extensive index (pp. 685–733) to all six volumes. These reprint volumes are heavy, expensively priced, and clearly aimed at the university library market. An inexpensive lightweight reprint is to be found in the paperback *The Face in the Glass and Other Gothic Tales*. According to Greg Buzwell's all-too-brief introduction, its 'selection of stories... provides a taste of' its author Mary Elizabeth Braddon's (1835–1915) 'brilliance with the supernatural tale [and] gift for crafting haunting atmospheres' (pp. 8–9). Somewhat surprisingly for a selection published by the British Library and introduced by its 'Curator, Printed Literary Sources' (p. 9), the initial publication details of the fourteen short stories reprinted in it are not stated; there are no notations either, just the texts 'presented in chronological order' demonstrating 'Braddon's development as a writer' (p. 9).

However, attention should be drawn to two excellent editions of two texts from the second half of the nineteenth century that have appeared in the commendable Broadview Editions series. Shelley King and John B. Pierce's edition of George MacDonald's *The Princess and the Goblin and Other Fairy Tales* contains *The Princess and the Goblin*, initially published in serial form in *Good Words for the Young* 'between November 1870 and June 1871', and four short stories. As the editors explain in their 'Note on the Texts' (p. 43), which follows a substantial introduction (pp. 9–37), 'George MacDonald: A Brief Chronology' (pp. 39–40), and 'A Note on the Illustrations' (p. 41), 'a slightly modified version' of the novel 'appeared a year later in book form'. Their 'notes indicate substantive variations between the text of the serial publication and that of the 1872 single-volume edition' (p. 43). A strength of Broadview Editions is found in the appendices to the texts, and this edition is no exception, having four. The first consists of five contrasting 'Contemporary Reviews' of *the Princess and the Goblin* (pp. 309–17) and four reviews of the short stories (pp. 317–19). The second appendix, 'MacDonald on the Imagination' (pp. 321–55), contains the texts with annotations of two MacDonald 'essays, concerning the imagination as an essential faculty in human experience' (p. 321). The third appendix, 'Victorian Fairy Tales' (pp. 357–67), contains extracts from John Ruskin, William Makepeace Thackeray, and Norman Macleod. King and Pierce indicate in their introduction to this appendix that 'George MacDonald's fairy tales are best understood in the context of a Victorian approach to literary fairy tales that combined the supernatural elements associated with traditional fairy tales with either the comedy of social satire or a deep Christian mysticism' (p. 357). The final appendix, 'MacDonald's Composition and the Manuscript of *The Princess and the Goblin*' (pp. 369–75), accompanied by illustrative examples, usefully describes the manuscript held at the George MacDonald Collection of the Brander Library in Huntley Aberdeenshire (p. 369). This excellent edition concludes with an alphabetically arranged, enumerative select bibliography divided into 'Primary Sources' (pp. 377–8), 'Biography' (pp. 378–9), 'Bibliography' (p. 379), 'Selected Criticism Related to *The Princess and the Goblin*' (pp. 379–82), and 'Websites' (p. 382). Diana Maltz's Broadview edition of Arthur Morrison's *A Child of the Jago* first published in 1896 'is based on the third edition ... published by Methuen in 1897, which includes Morrison's Preface to the Third Edition' (p. 49). There are the usual informative elements expected of Broadview texts: an instructive introduction (pp. 9–43), 'Arthur Morrison: A Brief Chronology' (pp. 45–8), a brief textual note (p. 49), an extensively annotated text (pp. 55–238), a 'Glossary of Slang and Criminal

Terms' (pp. 239–42), and in this instance ten appendices (pp. 243–97), followed by a select bibliography (pp. 298–305). The ten appendices range from 'The Debate Over the Novel's Veracity' (pp. 243–52), the text of Lady Mary Jeune's—a 'prominent society hostess and social reformer [who] worked tirelessly to provide... children with clothing, boots, visits to the country, and free school dinners' (p. 253)—'essay "the Homes of the Poor" [that] offered a comprehensive diagnosis of the housing problem in East London' (pp. 253–9), and, to provide one other instance, 'Maps of the Area' (pp. 296–7) that provided the locational basis for Morrison's account. A select bibliography is alphabetically arranged and enumerative, consisting of 'Works by Arthur Morrison: Reviews of *A Child of the Jago*' (p. 300), 'Selected Late-Victorian and Edwardian Contextual Prose' (pp. 300–1), 'Literary Criticism on Morrison's Slum Fictions' (pp. 302–3), 'Social and Historical Contexts' (pp. 303–4), and finally a listing of 'Selected London Working-Class Autobiographies' (pp. 304–5).

A writer who also wrote about the impoverished, George Gissing, has a journal devoted to his life and work. The January issue of the *Gissing Journal* contains Pat Colling's 'Knowing Your Place: Place and Class in George Gissing's "Slum" Novels, Part 1' (*GissingJ* 50:i[2014] 3–18), followed by Robin Friedman's 'Gissing Reviewed on Amazon' (*GissingJ* 50:i[2014] 19–41) and 'Notes and News' (*GissingJ* 50:i[2014] 42–5). The April issue includes Rebecca Hutcheon's 'Mapping the City: The Problem with Mimesis in *The Nether World*' (*GissingJ* 50:ii[2014] 3–15); Pat Colling's 'Knowing Your Place: Place and Class in George Gissing's "Slum" Novels (concluded)' (*GissingJ* 50:ii[2014] 15–31); 'A New Gissing Ph.D.' (*GissingJ* 50:ii[2014] 31–3), an account of Rebecca Hutcheon's March 2014 University of Bristol thesis that 'examines place in the novels and writings of George Gissing' (p. 31); M.D. Allen's 'Gissing and the Victorian Web' (*GissingJ* 50:ii[2014] 33–8), accompanied by two colour illustrations, one of Gissing's grave, the other of La Maison Elgué (pp. 35, 37); 'Notes and News' (*GissingJ* 50:ii[2014] 39–40), and 'Recent Publications' (*GissingJ* 50:ii[2014] 41). The July issue includes the journal's editor M.D. Allen's 'J.J. Thomson's 1929 Letter Resurfaces' (*GissingJ* 50:iii[2014] 3–7), containing a letter dated 27 February 1929 from J.J. Thomson, an eminent physicist winning the Nobel Prize in Physics in 1906, who 'was privy to events immediately following Gissing's arrest' (p. 3), to Hamish Miles, who was working on a Gissing biography. Other contents include Una Forsyth's 'Marianne Helen Harrison: A Medical Diagnosis' (*GissingJ* 50:iii[2014] 7–13); an account of 'Another Gissing Dissertation' (*GissingJ* 50:iii[2014] 14–15), a 2013 doctoral thesis written by Ying Ying at Zhejiang University, Hangzhou, entitled 'The Writer's Crisis of Survival in George Gissing's Works' (p. 14); 'Book Reviews' (*GissingJ* 50:iii[2014] 15–30); 'Notes and News' (*GissingJ* 50:iii[2014] 30–4), accompanied by a colour illustration of a painting by 'Gissing's friend, the Barnsley-born John Wood Shortridge' (pp. 32–3); and an alphabetically arranged, briefly annotated listing of 'Recent Publications' (*GissingJ* 50:iii[2014] 34–5), concluding with a listing of translations of Gissing into Chinese and critical responses to him published in journals published in China (*GissingJ* 50:iii[2014] 36–8). The October issue opens with Petra Schenke's 'Sport and Leisure in Gissing's

Satirical Tales, Part 1' (*GissingJ* 50:iv[2014] 3–30). It is followed by Hélène Coustillas, 'In Memoriam: Anthony Curtis (1926–2014)' (*GissingJ* 50:iv[2014] 31–4), who contributed seven articles to the *Gissing Journal* and was a 'staunch and faithful Gissingite' (p. 31). A book review—one assumes by M.D. Allen— of Anthony Quinn's edition of *New Grub Street* published by Vintage Classics, Random House, in 2014 (*GissingJ* 50:iv[2014] 34–9) is followed by 'Notes and News' and a listing of 'Recent Publications' (*GissingJ* 50:iv[2014] 40). It is appropriate at this juncture to draw attention to Peter Keating's *Autobiographical Tales*. Keating, as regular *YWES* browsers will be aware, published on Gissing, produced editions of his novels, and wrote a biography of Arthur Morrison, and Keating's *The Working Classes in Victorian Fiction*, published by Routledge in 1971, has withstood the test of time. There is far too little on Keating's years as one of the early undergraduates and then a graduate student at the newly founded University of Sussex. There is more of an account of the period he spent in his first academic position at the University of Leicester, where he started in October 1968 at the Victorian Studies Centre, his encounter with the distinguished teacher Monica Jones, Philip Larkin's lover, and his subsequent move to the University of Edinburgh, from which he retired early. Chronologically the memoir ends in 1990, the year he 'took early retirement' (p. viii) to devote himself to full-time writing, and, although this isn't stated explicitly, to look after his unwell wife, Valerie Shaw, the fine critic of Tennyson. Keating's account of his south London background and obsession with jazz has its own intrinsic interest and may be compared and contrasted with two other accounts of a south London environment in the formation of literary critics, scholars, and creative writers found in the reminiscences of his near-contemporaries: John Sutherland in his *The Boy Who Loved Books: A Memoir* [2007] and David Lodge's *Quite a Good Time To Be Born: A Memoir: 1935–1975* [2015]. Lodge's work will be discussed in next year's *YWES*: Lodge's father was a professional musician who played saxophone and jazz. Notably, the three, amongst other elements they had in common, didn't attend Oxbridge!

Twentieth Century Vox (an imprint of Victorian Secrets Limited) has produced an edition of Elizabeth Robins's *The Convert*. Initially published in 1907, this suffrage novel, the work of the American-born advocate of women's militancy to obtain female suffrage Elizabeth Robins (1862–1952), is based upon her successful play *Votes for Women!* Edited with an introduction and notes by Emelyne Godfrey, there is an introduction with fascinating details of Robins's life (pp. 5–15), a 'Brief Chronology of Elizabeth Robins' (pp. 16–17), an alphabetically arranged, enumerative select bibliography (p. 18), a one-sentence 'Note on the Text' (p. 19), an annotated text (pp. 23–277), and four appendices. These contain contemporary documents ranging from 'Two Flyers from the Huddersfield By-Election (1906)' (pp. 278–80), to 'Contemporary Reviews' (pp. 284–91) of Robins novel. Not without interest is the concluding note of this edition pointing out that 'Elizabeth Robins's literary estate belongs to Independent Age, a charity providing advice service for older people, their families and carers...To find out more about their important work, or to make a donation, please visit: http://www.independen-tage.org' (p. 294).

Mike Webb writes, in his introduction (pp. v–x) to the Bodleian Library reprint of *If England Were Invaded*, initially published under the title *Invasion* in 1906, that its author William Tufnell Le Queux (1864–1927) 'became chiefly known for his contribution to the "invasion literature" genre' (p. vi). As Le Queux wrote in his preface to its 1910 republication, 'the object of this book is to illustrate our utter unpreparedness for war from a military standpoint; to show how, under certain conditions which may easily occur, England can be successfully invaded by Germany'. Webb observes that 'the book was to become' its author's 'best known work, and was promoted by many and satirized by others. It was translated into twenty-seven languages and sold over one million copies' (p. vii). The Bodleian Library reprint contains no annotation whatsoever, nor appendices. James Fitzjames Stephen, unlike Le Queux, was not a purveyor of exaggerated scaremongering fiction but a pre-eminent Victorian lawyer and authority on jurisprudence, whose selected writings are now the subject of a distinguished Oxford University Press edition. Stephen's *A General View of the Criminal Law of England* was first published in 1863. K.J.M. Smith's extensive 'Introduction and Commentary' (pp. 1–47) to Stephen's text (pp. 51–396), which contains Smith's annota-tions—although it is difficult to find where this is explicitly stated and the edition somewhat surprisingly lacks a textual note—as well as Stephen's original notation at the foot of the page, explains the 'Genesis and Writing of the General View' (pp. 1–4) and discusses reviews of its publication (pp. 4–7), followed by commentary and concluding with Smith's account of his subject's 'Principle Rules of Evidence and Advocacy's Ethics' (pp. 42–7). The text is followed by an alphabetically arranged, enumerative select bibliography that omits publishers (pp. 397–9), 'James Fitzjames Stephen: Original Index' (pp. 401–6), followed, also in double columns, by Smith's 'Supplemental Index' (pp. 407–8).

Lena Østermark-Johansen's *Walter Pater, 'Imaginary Portraits'* is the first volume of the Jewelled Tortoise, 'an MHRA series of critical editions of significant aesthetic and decadent texts, launched under the general editorship of Stefano Evangelista and Catherine Maxwell' (back cover). The edition includes an extensive introduction (pp. 1–66), an alphabetically arranged, descriptive select bibliography (pp. 67–70), 'A Pater Chronology' (pp. 71–3), and a 'Note on the Text' (pp. 75–6). Pater's text, with detailed annotation at the foot of the page and black and white illustrations (pp. 77–291), is followed by an English version of a Heine text *The Gods in Exile* [1853] (pp. 293–8) and the English version of another text that influenced Pater, 'From Edmond and Jules de Goncourt, "Watteau". *L'Art du XVIIIe siècle* (1873–75)' (pp. 299–304). The third and fourth appendices, also annotated, consist of the texts of two Pater journal articles pertinent to *Imaginary Portraits*: '"A Study of Dionysus: The Spiritual Form of Fire and Dew", *Fortnightly Review* No. CXX, vol. XX n.s. (1 December 1876), pp. 752–72' (pp. 305–13) and '"Lacedaemon", *Contemporary Review* LXI (June 1892), pp. 790–808' (pp. 315–21). The edition lacks an index, but for its price at just under £10 is remarkable value and puts the exorbitant prices charged by some other publishers of textual editions to shame.

Accompanied by black and white illustrations, Lori Emerson's *Reading Writing Interfaces: From the Digital to the Bookbound* is not only an 'account of the wonders of contemporary digital computing. From beginning to end, it is about the mystifying devices—especially *writerly* demystification . . . opening up how exactly interfaces limit and create certain creative possibilities' (p. ix). As she explains in her introduction, 'Opening Closings' (pp. ix–xxi), Emerson's four 'chapters move from the present moment and back to the present, each using a particular historical moment to understand the present' (p. xvi). Her first chapter, 'Indistinguishable from Magic: Invisible Interfaces and Digital Literature as Demystifier' (pp. 1–46), begins 'by describing, contemporary claims about ubiquitous computing (ubicomp) as the definitive technological innovation of this century' (p. xvii). She then describes 'a growing body of digital literature that embraces *visibility* by courting difficulty, defamiliariza-tion, and glitch and that stands as an antidote to ubicomp and this receding present' (p. xviii). The second chapter, 'From the Philosophy of the Open to the Ideology of the User-Friendly' (pp. 47–85), 'uncovers the shift from the late 1960s to the early 1980s that made way for the very interfaces touted as utterly invisible' (p. xviii) discussed in the initial chapter. The third chapter, 'Typewriter Concrete Poetry as Activist Media Poetics' (pp. 87–127), focuses on 'reading/writing interfaces [in] the era from the early 1960s to the mid-1970s in which poets, working heavily under the influence of Marshall McLuhan, sought to create (especially, so-called dirty) concrete poetry as a way to experiment with the limits and the possibilities of the typewriter' (p. 87). The fourth chapter, 'The Fascicle as Process and Product' (pp. 129–62), 'positions Emily Dickinson not only as a poet working equally with and against the limits and the possibilities of pen/pencil/paper as interface but also as one through which we can productively read twenty-first-century digital literary texts' (p. 129). In her 'Postscript: The Googlization of Literature' (pp. 163–84), Emerson writes that 'throughout this book I have attempted to create a friction between new and old writing interfaces while describing the media poetics of the writers themselves reading, through writing, writing interfaces'. She adds, 'now that we are all constantly connected to networks, driven by invisible, formidable algorithms, the role of the writer and the nature of writing itself is being significantly transformed' (p. 163). Extensive notes (pp. 185–218) follow the four chapters, and there is an index (pp. 219–22) to Emerson's book. Some may find her language pretentious and unclear, others may find it refreshing and challenging.

Amy Root Clements's fascinating, well-researched, and well-written *The Art of Prestige: The Formative Years at Knopf, 1915–1929* is a study of 'truly uncharted territory . . . the early history of Knopf' (p. xi), founded 'in June 1915' by the 'twenty-two-year-old Alfred Knopf' whose 'publishing firm . . . would come to be regarded by many as the pinnacle of America's book trade' (p. 1). Her study is based upon the publishing houses archive at the Harry Ransom Humanities Research Center, Austin, Texas. Her book, as she explains in her introduction, '*Books de Luxe*' (pp. 1–13), 'examines a branding effort that was conceived by a loquacious, flamboyantly dressed Columbia University graduate who, with his equally youthful fiancée, managed to forge a corporate identity exuding elderly gravitas before reaching the age of thirty' (p. 5). In her first chapter, 'Educating a Future Publisher' (pp. 14–32), Clements explains that 'three elements shaped Alfred's approach to book acquisition and ideals of literary prestige: the elegant home library of his childhood, paid for by his father's career as an advertising executive; his coursework at Columbia, which immersed him in scholarly firestorms over academia and literature; and his stints as an employee of other publishing houses' (p. 15). The second chapter, 'Apprenticeships and Partnerships' (pp. 33–51), focuses on his early attempts to find employment and his all-important meeting with Blanche Wolf, whom he would marry: 'he often claimed that his decision to abandon law school and pursue a publishing career was inspired in part by Blanche Wolf, a teenage girl he had met on Long Island' (p. 40). In her third chapter, 'The Borzoi [the firm's brand name] Abroad' (pp. 52–79), Clements considers the firm's reputation overseas and points out that 'in almost all of the company's first fifteen years, the majority of Borzoi Books were written by authors born in Europe' (p. 52). The fourth chapter, 'Producing American Literature' (pp. 80–99), examines 'key figures in the development of Borzoi's American list' (p. 80), Joseph Hergesheimer, the anti-Semitic H.L. Mencken, Carl Van Vechten, and Willa Cather. The physical nature of Knopf's imprints is the concern of chapter 5, 'Distinctive by Design' (pp. 100–19): 'the Knopfs' use of visual rhetoric shaped the company's identity as well as the cachet of their authors' (p. 100). The text of *The Art of Prestige* includes black and white illustrations, although the only image of the two leading protagonists, Alfred and Blanche Knopf, is found on the front cover of the paperback review copy. The sixth chapter, 'Bookselling and the Borzoi' (pp. 120–37), indicates that 'Blanche and Alfred Knopf produced catalogs, made sales calls, sent special keepsakes to booksellers, and ran trade advertisements—standard practices that didn't need genius to execute. What was special about the Knopfs' approach to bookselling was the Borzoi brand itself, a memorable, enticing identity that became ubiquitous among booksellers and their customers' (p. 120). The last chapter, 'A Majestic Brand' (pp. 138–61), continues the theme of the publishers' branding of their products. An afterword, 'The Legacies' (pp. 162–70), follows the 'prestigious' (p. 170) publishing house into the early years of the present century. Detailed notes (pp. 171–92), follow the text and there is a helpful index (pp. 193–206) to this valuable addition to the University of Massachusetts Press's Studies in Print Culture and the History of the Book series.

James Turner's mammoth monograph *Philology: The Forgotten Origins of the Modern Humanities* examines in depth the title word, its history and development. He also links it to 'humanistic studies'. In his prologue Turner writes: '*Studia humanitatis*—humanistic studies—in one guise or another have for many centuries dwelled at the heart of Western learning.' Drawing upon the fox and the hedgehog analogy, he adds, 'the many humanistic disciplines that today's fox knows date only from the nineteenth century. Trace their several origins, and (as the hedgehog realizes) the trail usually leads back to one big, old thing: philology—the multifaceted study of texts, languages, and the phenomenon of language itself' (p. ix). There are four parts to Turner's book: 'From the First Philologists to 1800' (pp. 1–121); 'On the Brink of the Modern Humanities, 1800 to the Mid-Nineteenth Century' (pp. 123–229). The final, and by far the most extensive, part deals with 'The Modern Humanities in the Modern University: The Mid-Nineteenth to the Twentieth Century' (pp. 231–386). Chapter 9 focuses upon ' "This Newly Opened Mine of Scientific Inquiry": Between History and Nature. Linguistics after 1850' (pp. 236–53), and the tenth chapter covers ' "Painstaking Research Quite Equal to Mathematical Physics": Literature, 1860–1920' (pp. 255–73), with sub-sections on 'Literature in Higher Education' (pp. 255–62), 'Literary Editing' (pp. 262–5)—which opens with the sentence 'Of all varieties of literary scholarship, editing most directly inherited methods from classical and biblical philology' (p. 262), 'Folklore as Literature' (pp. 265–7), 'Literary Criticism as Science and Art' (pp. 267–72), and 'Philology Becomes a Ghost' (pp. 272–3). In his 'Epilogue' (pp. 381–6), Turner astutely observes that 'Anglophone literary critics at certain periods have renounced history in favor of atemporal analysis, as in the New Criticism of the 1940s and 1950s' (p. 383). At the end of his penultimate paragraph Turner observes: ' today's multiple humanities collectively form the latest version of a millennia-long Western tradition of inquiry into language and its products—inquiry, that is, into worlds that human beings have created for themselves and expressed in words'. The concluding paragraph that follows is a five-word sentence that sums up his book and returns to its opening: 'Philology: the love of words' (p. 386). Extensive notes (pp. 387–452) follow the text. There is also an extensive, enumerative, alphabetically arranged listing of works cited (pp. 453–507), and a through index (pp. 509–50).

Teresa Michals, in her *Books for Children, Books for Adults: Age and the Novel from Defoe to James*, argues that 'eighteenth-century novels were written not for adults but rather for a popular mixed-age audience of women, children, and servants'. She 'traces this history of . . . reading from Daniel Defoe's *Robinson Crusoe* to Henry James's *The Awkward Age*'. Michals's study 'offers a series of case studies of key eighteenth- and nineteenth-century novels, popular in their day and canonical today. While the book examines ideas of adulthood within these novels, it also aims to raise questions about reception and the history of the book' (p. 2). Michals 'fundamentally . . . argues that in these novels and in the history of their marketing and reception, we can see how a world of masters and servants became a world of adults and children' (p. 3). Her chapters include 'Rewriting *Robinson Crusoe*: Age and the Island' (pp. 19–61), focusing upon the question why 'in the centuries that followed Robinson Crusoe's publication, Defoe's shipwreck plot dropped out of the mainstream of the novel to become instead a staple of children's literature' (p. 19). This is followed by one on 'Dating *Pamela*: Mr. B., *Goody Two-Shoes*, and the Age of Consent' (pp. 62–99), which also includes discussion of 'a successful children's book such as John Newberry's *Little Goody Two-Shoes* (1765)' (p. 62). Other chapters include 'Rational Moralists, Highland Barbarians, and the Taste for Adventures' (pp. 100–36), 'Educating Dickens: Old Boys, Little Mothers, and School Time' (pp. 137–75), and ' "The Time of Real Amusement": Henry James and the Cult of Adulthood' (pp. 176–208). These chapters are followed by extensive notes (pp. 209–43), an enumerative, alphabetically arranged bibliography (pp. 244–61), and an index (pp. 262–78).

Velma Bourgeois Richmond's quarto-size, black and white-illustrated, double-columned text, *Chivalric Stories as Children's Literature: Edwardian Retellings in Words and Pictures*, attempts 'to establish a bibliography of chivalric stories for children, discern ideals presented in such stories, assess the artistic worth of verbal and visual texts, and indicate the influence of chivalric stories for children as social commentary', notably in relation to World War I and upon the imaginations of significant writers of the twentieth century' (p. 4). These large aims are encompassed in twelve chapters divided into two parts. The first deals with 'Contexts and Criticisms' (pp. 5–76) and the second with 'Chivalric Stories Told to Edwardian Children' (pp. 77–344). These are followed by extensive, triple-columned notes that are bibliographically focused and provide a reference source in themselves (pp. 345–59), and an extensive select bibliography that is largely enumerative and alphabetically arranged, divided into 'Late Victorian and Edwardian Collections' (pp. 360–1) followed by details of illustrative books of four individual authors, Henry Wadsworth Longfellow, William Morris, Sir Walter Scott, and Alfred Lord Tennyson (p. 361). There is then a bibliography of 'Favored Medieval Stories', of 'Schoolbooks', 'Home Libraries', 'Pedagogy and Librarians Advice', and 'Literary Histories'. This most useful reference work concludes with a comprehensive author and title based index arranged in four columns (pp. 364–74). Twentieth-century writers referred to include C.S. Lewis, J.R.R. Tolkien, David Jones, and, somewhat surprisingly, Graham Greene, Ian Fleming, and John le Carré, although Richmond's discussion of them is far from extensive.

A book with much interest to *YWES* readers that otherwise might be ignored is James Anderson Winn's well-written full-scale biography *Queen Anne, Patroness of Arts*. Replete with black and white illustrations, eighteen colour plates (between pp. 394 and 395, and not 'after page 415' as stated in the illustrations listing at the beginning of the book (p. xii)), and a list of musical examples (pp. xiv–xvi). There are even details of a companion website to recordings of the musical examples that illuminate 'Queen Anne's keen interest in music'. The author, 'with the help of a group of Boston-based specialists in early music...[has] produced recordings of all twenty-eight examples, which [the reader] may hear by going to a companion website' (p. x). In his preface Winn observes that 'in order to provide a more comprehensive view of her life and reign, I have emphasized the dynamic and often competitive relations among the arts, as well as the interplay between all the arts and the religious, scientific, intellectual, and political developments of the period' (p. xix). Consequently, as a glance at the comprehensive index (pp. 771–92) demonstrates, there is much under individual writers, ranging from 'Addison, Joseph' to Wilmot, John' (p. 787). Indeed, to take three instances, there is much on Congreve (see p. 777), Dryden (see p. 778) and Swift (see p. 790). There is a bibliography of 'Manuscript Sources' (pp. 747–8) and 'Newspapers' (p. 748), and an extensive, alphabetically arranged enumerative listing of 'Printed Primary Sources' (pp. 748–60), followed by one of 'Secondary Scholarship' (pp. 760–9). James Anderson Winn's biography is superbly produced and reasonably priced by its publishers.

Firmly bound, on the front jacket is a striking colour image of Anne from the studio of Sir Godfrey Kneller.

Another biography of considerable interest is Jonathan Rose's *The Literary Churchill: Author, Reader, Actor*. Rose 'surveys all of Churchill's important writings, reconstructs (as far as [he] can) his reading and theatre-going experiences, and assesses their impact on his politics'. He writes that 'For Churchill, politics and literature were two sides of the same career, impossible to prise apart. His political goals and methods were shaped by what he read in books and saw on the stage. In turn, he recast his political experiences as literature, inevitable with some artistic license.' Additionally, Churchill 'made important policy decisions and composed memoranda with a view toward how they would appear on the page, in the grand story that he spent his life composing. He was an artist who used politics as his creative medium, as other writers used paper' (p. xi). There are chapters on Churchill's early obsession with the theatre, 'The Theatre Rage' (pp. 1–18), drawing especial attention to his being 'a fan of [Oscar] Wilde' (p. 15), and his schoolboy reading, 'An Uneducated Man' (pp. 20–33), as well as extensive discussion of his writing with especial emphasis upon his reading, which 'informed, refined and mobilized his instinctive libertarianism to political action' (pp. 95–6). Rose's study is accompanied by black and white illustrations (between pp. 244 and 245) including for instance Churchill's 'favourite Irish melodrama, *The English Rose* (*Penny Illustrated Paper*, 9 August 1890)' and an illustration from a scene from 'Jules Verne's spectacular melodrama *Michael Strogoff*, which portrayed an invasion of Russia a half-century before Operation Barbarossa' (figures 1 and 2 facing p. 244). 'In December 1891 [Churchill] saw [the play] a dramatization of Jules Verne's 1876 novel' (p. 12). There is a wealth of footnote documentation following Rose's text (pp. 451–94), although his use of abbreviations (explained on p. 451) is not always clear. There is also an extensive, useful index (pp. 495–516) that assists in tracking down Churchill's actual reading. So, for example, to see whether Churchill read Rider Haggard's *King Solomon's Mines*, an interested reader is referred to 'pp. 53, 57, 63, 178' (p. 504). Those bibliographically inclined might desire an appendix listing Churchill's fictional reading with additional appendices listing other reading with dates. But such an addition might not increase the sales of Rose's work or add to current academic kudos!

Peter Baldwin's *The Copyright Wars: Three Centuries of Trans-Atlantic Battle*, in addition to an introduction, 'The Agon of Author and Audience' (pp. 1–13), contains chapters on: 'The Battle between Anglo-American Copyright and European Authors' Rights' (pp. 14–52); ' From Royal Privilege to Literary Property: A Common Start to Copyright in the Eighteenth Century' (pp. 53–81); 'The Ways Part: Copyright and Authors' Rights in the Nineteenth Century' (pp. 82–125); 'Continental Drift: Europe Moves from Property to Personality at the Turn of the Century' (pp. 126–62); 'The Strange Birth of Moral Rights in Fascist Europe' (pp. 163–98); 'The Postwar Apotheosis of Authors' Rights' (pp. 199–261); 'America Turns European: The Battle of the Booksellers Redux in the 1990s' (pp. 262–317); 'The Rise of the Digital Public: The Copyright Wars Continue in the New Millennium' (pp. 318–82); and 'Conclusion: Reclaiming the Spirit of

Copyright' (pp. 383–9). Baldwin opens his first chapter, 'The Battle between Anglo-American Copyright and European Authors' Rights', by writing that 'Works are created by their authors, reproduced and distributed by their disseminators, and enjoyed by the audience. These three actors, each with their own concerns, negotiate a delicate dance. Most generally, all must be content: the author productive, the disseminator profitable, and the audience enlightened' (p. 14). Essentially his fascinating book is concerned with the history between these three interacting forces over the last three centuries and continuing to the present day, the age of 'digital technologies [that] threw up new problems in producing and disseminating works that required a response in law' (p. 382). Extensive notation (pp. 413–512) follows the text and there is also a detailed, helpful index (pp. 513–35) to a study that is not confined to literary work but ranges broadly over other art forms such as film and musical composition. Baldwin is only too aware of the political and ideological ramifications of his subject. His first two sentences in his introduction read: 'In 1948 several Soviet composers, including Dmitri Shostakovich, objected to the use of their music in an American spy film *The Iron Curtain* that was distinctly anticommunist. These Soviet composers understandably feared the gulag for appearing in Hollywood's first Cold War effort' (p. 1). His account of the differences in Anglo-American eighteenth- and nineteenth-century perceptions of literary property (pp. 53–125), and of twentieth-century transitions, is particularly instructive in spite of some at times dense prose (pp. 126–317). In short, Baldwin's book places current copyright issues in a historical perspective.

Enumerative bibliography as a discipline in the Internet age where quality control is difficult has sadly more or less disappeared. There are almost no refereed journal outlets for such work to appear and a publisher producing such work in book form would be bound to lose money. Further, the Internet provides the opportunity for continual updating and revision. Fortunately, analytic and descriptive bibliography is still being produced in a tangible form that will not disappear somewhere in a cloud or the ether. With this in mind, a revised and updated edition of an analytical and descriptive bibliography published in 2006 is doubly welcome. David J. Supino writes, in his preface to the second edition of his 'Catalogue of a collection of Henry James's editions and impressions published during the period 1875 to 1921 (and in a few cases later)', that it constitutes 'a significant expansion of the first edition of this Catalogue' (see *YWES* 89[2008] 1232]. In addition to 'covering many more volumes, this edition is in some ways a quite different work'. Most importantly, the second edition contains 'the inclusion of information on the printing and publishing history of James, as revealed by searches in publishers' archives'. Further, Supino adds, 'the aim of this collection, and the revised edition of this Catalogue which describes it, is to obtain all possible printings of James's works and to record them together with the publishers recordings of those printings'. For Supino, his 'revised edition of the Catalogue represents one of the few attempts to trace out in detail the publishing history of an author's texts in combination with a description of the books themselves' (p. xiii). Nearly 1,000 volumes, rather than the 775 volumes of the first edition, are found described in this revised edition, which comprehensively describes—as much as it is possible to do so—the extent of the reprinting of many of Henry James's works. An additional difference in this revised edition is to be found in its length: 650 pages of text compared with the 550 pages in the 2006 edition. In addition to the use of publishers' archives, there are eight appendices rather than the seven of the initial edition plus an additional index ('Index to Stories and Tales; First Magazine and Subsequent Book Publication 1875–1923', pp. 635–41), supplementing the extremely useful general index (pp. 642–50). Appendix G in the new edition is titled 'Documents Bearing on the Terms Relative to the New York Edition' (pp. 629–32). In the first edition this was titled 'Documents Bearing on the Terms Agreed between Scribners and Houghton, Mifflin Relative to the New York Edition' (pp. 504–7). The additional appendix consists of 'James titles listed for sale in the *Times Book Catalogue* of 1905' (p. 633). There is a plethora of valuable material in this volume of the highest production standards, with thirty-two colour plate illustrations of bindings (inserted between pages 318 and 319). Supino includes, as is expected of descriptive bibliography at its best, collations, contents, binding details and variants, information on inserted advertisements, bookplate data, information on binders' and booksellers' tickets, plus detailed description of dust-jackets where available. The opportunity has been missed to describe textual variants—admittedly this would be a massive task. In his Appendix E, 'A Note on the Text of *The Portrait of a Lady*' (pp. 624–5), Supino indicates that, while the three-volume first edition of the novel's first impression published by Macmillan in London in October 1881 'was chronologically the first published, it is actually the third book text, and arguably the most corrupt of the texts' (p. 625). In such an instance a description of specific textual differences would be of considerable interest not only for bibliographers and textual scholars but also for exponents of close critical reading.

There are two lavishly illustrated works in colour and black and white of typographical interest to *YWES* readers. Wolfgang Weingart (b. 1941), the eminent Swiss typesetter, has had an important impact upon typographical development since the 1970s on both sides of the Atlantic. His teaching at the Basle School of Design has been highly influential, and in the bilingual English and German *Typography*—a reprint of a work initially published in 2000—he gives a narrative with numerous illustrations of his career since his early days, and comprehensively surveys his work over a forty-year period. This book, measuring nearly 9 inches in width, nearly 11 inches in length and 1½ inches in thickness, firmly bound in stiff paper/card covers, is surprisingly heavy. Slightly less heavy or thick and also of a slightly smaller size is Steven Heller and Gail Anderson's *The Typographic Universe: Letterforms Found in Nature, the Built World and Human Imagination*, also profusely illustrated and cased. Essentially this is a celebration of the delights of typography, providing 'from the uncanny shapes formed by negative spaces between the city skyscrapers to contorted alphabets of torn underwear . . . extensive examples of typographic conjuring' (p. 7). Beginning with a dog's legs forming an 'M' and a setting sun 'making a lower-case "I"' (pp. 6–7), the illustrations conclude with an example of 'Respectable Gothic-style lettering' found in a rural building in Peru (p. 347). The volume ends with an enumerative alphabetical listing of

1480 BIBLIOGRAPHY, TEXTUAL CRITICISM, AND REFERENCE WORKS

further reading (p. 348), and an 'Index of Materials': 'the typographic forms in this book are made from an inventive variety of materials. Here is an inventory of the curious things we found.' These range from 'Dog/Sunset on Water' to 'Faded Signs, Paint on Wood, and Metal' (p. 349), and a listing of contributors who have provided examples with their Web information (pp. 350–1). Weingart's *Typography* and Heller and Anderson's *Typographical Universe*, both superbly produced, are remarkable value for money and highly instructive.

Another interesting volume well illustrated in colour and black and white, almost ¾ of an inch thick, 8½ inches in width, and just over 11¼ inches in length, thickly bound and heavy, is Nerida F. Ellerton and M.A. (Ken) Clements *Abraham Lincoln's Cyphering Book and Ten Other Extraordinary Cyphering Books*. V. Frederick Rickney, in his foreword, observes that the authors 'have amassed a personal collection of some 350 cyphering books and examined another 650 in various libraries. Out of this abundance of resources, eleven "exceptional" ciphering books have been selected for detailed examination in this volume. These eleven were selected for a variety of reasons: their age, the lovely handwriting, the beauty of the diagrams, their geographic origins, their mathematical content, and the context in which they were written' (p. xvii). The books are handwritten school mathematics manuscripts from the period from around 1630 to 1835: six were done in Britain, four in North America, and the other partly in the former and partly in the latter. One hundred and fifty, frequently full-page, figures accompany the explanatory text. The books described and analysed were prepared by: someone whose name is unknown living on a New England settlement during the 1660s (pp. 13–22); Thomas Prust, born in England in 1690, who went the New England in 1720 and whose cyphering book—in which 'the manuscript was dedicated to setting out rules, cases, model examples and exercises associated with the sequence of mathematical topics' (p. 1)—was passed on to a fellow New Englander in 1720, James Collings (pp. 23–8); a Martha and Elisabeth Ryan living in North Carolina, 1776–81 (pp. 49–96); a Mary Walters from Maryland in 1820 (pp. 97–121), in whose book are found eleven poems 'within the 18 pages dedicated to the rule of three' (p. 113; this 'was definitely the most famous rule in all of arithmetic during the period from 1200 through 1850. Known as the "golden rule"' it is summed up in a poem: 'The golden rule hath places three, / The first and third must so agree' and so on (p. 35)); the young Abraham Lincoln when in Indiana, 1819–26—a chapter written by Ellerton, Valeria Aguirre Holguin, and Ken Clements (pp. 123–86); the English Thomas Dixson in 1630 (pp. 187–204); the London-based George Bickham from around 1740 (pp. 205–32); an unknown British midshipman from around 1791 on his way to Botany Bay (pp. 233–54); Charles Page of the Royal Mathematical School, Christ's Hospital in London in 1825 (pp. 255–97); and two examples from the eminent Scottish physician who served King William IV of England, William Beattie, in 1835 and then a year later (pp. 299–316). Students at Christ's Hospital spent a 'vast amount of time...on preparing pages of exquisite writing... It seems that many of the pages in navigation ciphering books were copied from other written sources, or taken down in notes in dictation sessions' (p. 321). S.T. Coleridge and Charles Lamb were at Christ's Hospital during the waning years of the eighteenth century. Such issues raised by the analysis of mathematical education may well have had their impact upon them, and certainly raise questions concerning the layout and content of Coleridge's prolific marginalia and notations. Each chapter in Ellerton and Clements's book is accompanied by an enumerative alphabetical listing of references. These are found too in an enumerative alphabetically arranged listing of 'Combined References' following the text (pp. 341–54). This fascinating work with many bibliographical ramifications concludes with a helpful author index (pp. 357–60), and a subject index (pp. 361–7).

Replete with 289 illustrations in colour and black and white, firmly paperback bound with large illustrative inner flaps, Dan Mazur and Alexander Danner's intention in their *Comics: A Global History, 1968 to the Present* 'is to create an overview of comics... Over the past 50 years, from a global perspective.' While acknowledging that 'the entirety of comics history—150-plus years—deserves such a global approach, for this volume [they] have chosen to limit [their] chronological scope so as to be able to provide enough detail to make the narrative meaningful. Hence, after a brief introduction covering the post-Second World War decades [their] narrative begins around the year 1968, a watershed year in which a number of comics creators in Japan, America and Europe began to aggressively demonstrate that comics could be more than an ephemeral vehicle for children's entertainment' (pp. 7–8). Divided into three parts, the first covering the years 1968–1978 (pp. 23–128), the second the years 1978–1990 (pp. 129–12), and the final part the years 1990 onward (pp. 213–309), a succinct introduction (pp. 10–20) surveys on a regional basis the immediate post-Second World War situation. Source notation follows the text (pp. 310) and there is a detailed, alphabetically arranged enumerative bibliography (pp. 311–12) followed by a useful 'Index of Creatives' arranged in five columns per page (pp. 313–15), followed by a similarly arranged 'Index of Comics' (pp. 316–18), and, in even smaller type so as to be very difficult to read, 'Image Credits'—of which there are many (p. 319). Mazur and Danner's work is stronger on description, detail, and illustration than analysis. For instance, they write that 'children's genre comics thrived in post-war Great Britain... Popular magazines *The Beano* and *The Dandy* offered raucous comedy for youngsters from creators such as Leo Baxendale.' A listing of two of his works is given: *The Bash Street Kids*, *Minnie the Minx*. These titles are followed by 'British adventure and science-fiction comics, in weekly tabloid-sized titles, established a remarkably high level of graphic polish, including the painted pages of Frank Hampson and Frank Bellamy (who both worked on *Dan Dare, Pilot of the Future* in *Eagle*) and Ron Embleton (*Wulf the Briton* in *Express Weekly*)' (p. 12). Factually there is little to question here; however, it is unfortunate that no real analysis of content and effect follows. Although such a passage is from the introduction, it is not unrepresentative. There are exceptions, for instance in the comparison of Peter Miller's *The Dark Man Returns* with Alan Moore and Dave Gibbons's *Watchmen* [1986–7], a merciless deconstruction of superheroes steeped in Cold War-era nuclear paranoia (p. 175).

Jonathan Bate, the present provost, contributes an informative chapter on 'Literary Worcester' (pp. 142–9) to *Worcester College: Portrait of an Oxford College*, which he has edited with Jessica Goodman. With more than 250 colour and black and white illustrations, this is a heavy book, weighing 3.7 pounds, and in dimensions 9.8 by 0.9 by 11.3 inches not over-priced. As Bate writes in his preface, the book 'is a *portrait* of the college in the true sense of the word: not an academic history, but an *impression* of the place, its people and its customs' (p. 9). His chapter on 'Literary Worcester' begins with an account of 'the addiction that led to the publication of Thomas De Quincey's celebrated memoir *Confessions of an English Opium-Eater*'. We learn that De Quincey 'turned up in Oxford in December 1803, tried and failed to blag [interesting variant use perhaps of the word 'bluff'] his way into Christ Church, then fetched up at Worcester because he had heard it was less expensive than other colleges. This was an age when undergraduate life was dominated by gambling, boating, writing, private parties, coffee houses and taverns.' There is an account of 'the most illustrious poet to have been educated at Gloucester Hall'—part of Worcester College—'Richard Lovelace ... the celebrated Cavalier'. Another eminent poet to attend the college but many years later is 'the multi-award-winning Glynn Maxwell (born 1962) ... One of the most accomplished verse technicians of the late 20th and early 21st centuries' (pp. 142–3). Other notable literary figures with Worcester connections include the theatre critic and biographer John Lahr (b. 1941), the novelist and critic Toby Litt (b. 1968), Christopher Ricks (b. 1933) 'English Fellow at Worcester in the mid-1960s' (p. 145), and the provosts Sir John Masterman (1891–1977), who was deeply involved with the MI5, the double-cross system and novelist, and Bate himself (b. 1958). During the 1920s 'the two finest stylists among Worcester novelists' were undergraduates William Gerhardie (1895–1977) and Jocelyn Brooke (1908–66)—the latter only spend a year at Worcester (1927–8) but a paragraph is devoted to him (p. 147)! Quite a number of references are found throughout the volume to the celebrated English Fellow, the influential Canon Cyril Hackett Wilkinson (1888–1960), who served as the college librarian from 1919 to 1958 and 'who had T.J. Wise made an Honorary Fellow; he is said to have justified this after Wise's exposure as a forger and thief by remarking that he did stop Wise from stealing the [college's Library] collection!' (p. 98). In his preface Bate observes that 'A Shakespeare play by the Lake at the end of Trinity Term is a longstanding Worcester tradition' (p. 8), yet for an eminent Shakespearian critic and scholar the impact of a Worcester literary/theatrical production upon a significant modern writer appears to have eluded him. Tom Stoppard, in his1982 lecture to the International Shakespeare Association, published by the association in 1982, *Is It True What They Say About Shakespeare*, recalls the impact that a Worcester College garden production of *The Tempest* had upon him (pp. 3–4). In fairness Bate does refer to 'Neville Coghill's 1949 production of *The Tempest*, which ended with Ariel running to freedom across the lake'. This 'was a brilliant coup de théâtre that no one who saw it has ever forgotten'— although this was probably not the one Stoppard refers to as he would have been 12 years of age at the time. Bate does add that 'there was at least one re-staging in the 1950s' (p. 8). One other caveat: the dust-jacket, with its delightful photograph of one of the college garden's lush lawns (on a non-rainy Oxford day), will no doubt be thrown away when the volume enters an institutional library. There is little on the gardeners who have maintained one of the college's precious jewels; there is an all-too-brief mention of 'W.G. Ward, gardener from 1906 until 1968, who took great pride in the fact that he joined the College three years before Masterman came up as an under-graduate' (p. 140). The book concludes with a largely name-orientated index (pp. 219–22) and an alphabetically arranged enumerative select bibliography, divided into books and articles followed by a listing of 'Select Primary Documents' (p. 223). The final page (p. 225) contains acknowledgements and imprint details.

In 2014 David Graham and Michael Bath completed their stint as editor and review editor of *Emblematica: An Interdisciplinary Journal for Emblem Studies* with volume 21. This highly expensive collection of essays—priced at $164.50—includes some material of interest to *YWES* readers. The rest of the collection concerns material in Italian, French, and other languages. Chris Stamatakis's black and white-illustrated 'Image to Text: A Possible Visual Source for Sir Thomas Wyatt's Verse Epistles' (*Embl* 21[2014] 77–95) argues that 'in his translation of a verse epistle by Luigi Alamanni, Sir Thomas Wyatt supplies details not found in the text of his Italian source ... Wyatt drew ... on a visual source of inspiration—namely, a woodcut device used by the Sessa family of printer-publishers to preface their edition of Alamanni' (p. 77). Stamatakis's contribution concludes with an alphabetically arranged enu-merative listing of works cited (*Embl* 21[2014] 91–5). 'Research Reports, Notes, Queries, and Notices' (*Embl* 21[2014] 361–95) include Rubem Amaral, Jr., 'Does Strength to Wisdom Give Place? An Iconographic Critical Approach to Emblem 96 in Thomas Palmer's *Two Hundred Poosees*' (*Embl* 21[2014] 381–95). This black and white-illustrated report draws upon numismatics in order to illuminate a Palmer emblem 'now in the British Library (Sloane MS3794), the first known English emblem book' (*Embl* 21[2014] 382). This volume of *Emblematica* concludes with reviews of recent pertinent books (*Embl* 21[2014] 399–454), followed by a volume index alphabetically arranged by author (*Embl* 21[2014] 457–9).

Monika Fludernik and Miriam Nandi have compiled a useful collection of thirteen essays in their *Idleness, Indolence and Leisure in English Literature*. Their focus is, as they indicate in their joint introduction (pp. 1–16), 'the history of idleness in English literature. In English literary texts, idleness, indolence and leisure are synonyms for the practice or state of *otium*, the topic with which this volume is more particularly concerned.' Following a discussion of the 'Latin concept' (p. 3) in its various modes including 'idleness, indolence and leisure', they write that 'The essays which follow delineate a diachronic survey of notions of idleness in English literature and culture from the late Middle Ages to the present' (pp. 7–8). In the opening essay Gregory M. Sadlek writes on '*Otium*, *Negotium*, and the Fear of *Acedia* in the Writings of England's Late Medieval Ricardian Poets' (pp. 17–39), *Acedia* being one of the seven deadly sins. Miriam Nandi's subject is 'The Dangers and Pleasures of Filling Vacuous Time: Idleness in Early Modern Diaries' (pp. 40–59), and Abigail Scherer's 'The "Sweet Toyle" of Blissful Bowers: Arresting Idleness in the English Renaissance' (pp. 60–85). Emily Anglin tackles the work of two neglected writers in her 'Idleness, Apprentices and Machines in Deloney and Dekker' (pp. 86–128). Monika Fludernik is concerned with 'The Performativity of Idleness: Representations and Stagings of Idleness in the Context of Colonialism' (pp. 129–53). This is followed by Kerstin Fest's 'Dramas of Idleness: The Comedy of Manners in the Works of Richard Brinsley Sheridan and Oscar Wilde' (pp. 154–73) and Richard Adelman's 'Idleness and Creativity; Poetic Disquisitions on Idleness in the Eighteenth and Early Nineteenth Centuries' (pp. 174–94). The remaining contributions in their coverage extend into the present century and include Benjamin Kohlmann's 'Versions of Working-Class Idleness: Non-Productivity and the Critique of Victorian Workaholism' (pp. 195–214), Barbara Korte's 'Against Busyness: Idling in Victorian and Contemporary Travel Writing' (pp. 215–34), Simon Featherstone's 'Tramping: The Cult of the Vagabond in Early Twentieth-Century England' (pp. 235–51), and Leonie Wanitzek's 'Englishness, Summer and the Pastoral of Country Leisure in Twentieth-Century Literature' (pp. 252–72). Ken Roberts, in chapter 13, 'Sociology of Leisure and the Wars of the Lifestyle Gurus' (pp. 273–92), 'discusses how spare time has been treated in the sociology of leisure, principally in Britain, though he also suggests that the same issues have arisen in all Western countries' (p. 14). Hartmut Rosa, in 'Epilogue: *Remember that Time Is Knowledge, Health and Happiness*: On the Mysterious Disappearance of Leisure' (pp. 293–7), 'presents its own solution to the problems raised by Roberts, but also opens a perspective back on the historical and literary phenomena which figured in the previous essays' (p. 14). Individual contributions are followed by notes and alphabetically arranged listings of works cited. The volume concludes with an enumerative, alphabetically arranged 'Selected Bibliography on Idleness, Indolence and Leisure' divided into two sections: 'Texts Particularly Important for the Study of Idleness or *Otium*' (pp. 298–9) and 'Criticism and Theory' (pp. 299–303). There is an author index (pp. 304–6) and a subject index (pp. 307–9).

Notice should be made of a useful collection of essays that might otherwise be overlooked, edited by Marian Thérèse Keyes and Áine McGillicudy: *Politics and Ideology in Children's Literature*. The editors write in their introduction, 'Politics and Ideology in Children's Literature' (pp. 9–19), that their collection, 'through a variety of critical perspectives on historical and contemporary texts . . . Highlights conflicts between individualism and the desires and expectations of the community, extending to troubled visions of national identity and indeed global power.' Moreover, 'the essays in [their] book highlight how adult ideologies can imbue children with powerful philosophical mindsets' (p. 19). There are four parts. In the first, 'Ideology and Subversion' (pp. 20–71), essays encompass diverse subjects such as 'Little Tweaks and Fundamental Changes: Two Aspects of Socio-Political Transformation in Children's Literature' (pp. 20–30), in which Clémentine Beauvais 'explores new approaches to analyzing politically transformative children's literature' (p. 12). 'Ecocriticism, Ecopedagogy and the Life and Works of Beatrix Potter' concern Eithne O'Connell (pp. 31–44). The two other contributions to this first section are '"Creaturely Life": Biopolitical Intensity in Selected Children's Fables' by Victoria de Rijke (pp. 45–56) and '"That

Imprudent Old Person of Chili'": Individual and They in Edward Lear's Limericks' by Olga Springer (pp. 57–71). The second part focuses on 'Utopias and Dystopias' (pp. 72–103) and contains three contributions: 'Don't Let the Fire Go Out': Echoes of the Past, Aspirations for the Future in the Teenage Novels of Eilís Dillon' by Anne Marie Herron (pp. 72–82); 'Recovery of Origins: Identity and Ideology in the Work of O.R. Melling' (pp. 83–94), in which Ciara Ní Bhroin explores 'the interconnected themes of return, national identity and the tradition/modernity dialectic in the fantasy fiction of O.R. Melling, a writer of Irish birth and Canadian upbringing' (p. 84); and 'Distant Districts and Dark Days: National Identity in [Suzanne Collins's] *The Hunger Games*' by Susan Shau Ming Tan (pp. 95–103). The third part is concerned with 'Experiences of War and Exile' (pp. 104–41). There are three contributions: ' "You Are the Hope of the World!": The Figure of the Child in First World War Children's Literature' by Elizabeth A. Galway (pp. 104–14); ' "A Noi!": The Emergence of the Gallant Fascist in Italian Children's Literature of the Inter-War Period' by Jessica D'Eath (pp. 115–26), and 'Out of the Hitler Time: Growing Up in Exile' by Áine McGillicuddy (pp. 127–40), with a particular focus upon 'Judith Kerr, British children's author and illustrator, who was born in Berlin in 1923' (p. 127). The final part of *Politics and Ideology in Children's Literature* has three contributions on the subject of 'Gender Politics' (pp. 141–78): ' Paratexts and Gender Politics: A Study of Selected Works by Anna Maria Fielding Hall (1800–1889)' by Marian Thérèse Keyes (pp. 141–56); 'Young Women Dealing with Abuse: Catherine Breillat's Cinematic Perspective on *Bluebeard*' by Brigitte Le Juez *(pp. 157–67); and,* last but by no means least, 'Sexual Violence and Rape Myths in Contemporary Young Adult Fiction' by Marion Rana (pp. 168–78). Following details on the contributors (pp. 179–81), this interesting collection concludes with a useful index (pp. 183–91).

The Irish writer George Moore's (1852–1931) work spans the centuries and has been unfashionable for some time. An attempt to redress this is found in the collection of essays edited by María Elena Jaime de Pablos and Mary Pierse, *George Moore and the Quirks of Human Nature*, which focuses upon Moore's eclecticism in terms of style and subject matter. The collection of fourteen essays is divided into four sections. In the first, 'Hidden Links', there are five contributions following the editors' introduction (pp. 1–10): Adrian Frazier, 'Moore and Joyce: Confessions of a Young Man as an Influence on *A Portrait of the Artist as a Young Man*' (pp. 13–21); Stoddard Martin, 'Moore versus Wilde: The Vagaries of Spite' (pp. 13–38); Robert Becker, 'The Contrarian George Moore' (pp. 39–49); Mary Pierse, 'Moore and Fogazzaro, Body and Soul: Zeitgeister of the Fin de Siècle?' (pp. 51–67); and Conor Montague, 'Philosophical Dialogue between the Brothers Moore (1903–1905): A Capacity for Misunderstanding' (pp. 69–85). The second section is devoted to 'Terror and the Unconscious' and has three contributions: Elizabeth Grubgeld, 'George Moore's Autobiographies and the Vampiric Grasp of Home: To be Seduced, Transfixed, and Terrified' (pp. 89–102); Jayne Thomas 'George Moore and the Unconscious in *Evelyn Innes* and *Sister Teresa*: "Shapes from an Underworld" ' (pp. 103–21); and Melanie Grundmann, 'Diseased Human Natures and their Menace to Society' (pp. 123–40). The third part has three contributions on the subject of 'Paradox, Parody and Linguistic Significance': Fabienne Gaspari, 'George Moore's Sense of Paradox in *A Mere Accident*: "In Large and Serpentine Curves"' (pp. 143–61); Kathi R. Griffin, '*Esther Waters* as Parody: Naturalism, Victorian Morality, and the "Bulges" of Human Nature' (pp. 163–82); and José Antonio Hoyas Solís, 'Early Feminist or Mainstream Writer? A Linguistic Analysis of George Moore's Portrayal of Women in Three Novels' (pp. 183–203. The fourth and final part 'On Women' also has three contributions: María Elena Jaime de Pablos, 'Nora Glynn in *The Lake*: "A Natural Woman"' (pp. 207–21); Kathryn Laing '"On Women, on Art, on Life": George Moore (1852–1933) and Hannah Lynch (1859–1904)' (pp. 223–43); and last but by no means least in this most interesting and well-written collection, Catherine Smith, 'Listening to Héloïse in George Moore's *Héloïse and Abelard*: "A Barbarian Girl and a Great Sorceress"' (pp. 245–57). The essays are followed by a perfunctory 'George Moore Bibliography' restricted to two pages and simply listing titles with dates (pp. 259–60), 'Notes on Contributors' (pp. 261–4), and a reasonably detailed double-columned index (pp. 265–73). Expensively priced for a paperback, an irritating feature of the make-up of this book is the failure to indicate page numbers on the rectos at the start of chapters or sections.

A collection that should not be ignored is that edited by Hazel Mackenzie and Ben Winyard, *Charles Dickens and the Mid-Victorian Press, 1850–1870*, consisting of 'twenty-two of the thirty-six papers read at the Dickens Journals Online Conference held in March 2012 at the University of Buckingham (p. xi). There are four sections, the four contributions—by Joanne Shattock, Laurel Brake, Louis James, and Koenraad Claes—in the initial section group, as John Drew explains in his excellent introduction to the collection, in 'wide-ranging synoptic essays [examine] the publishing scene in the 1850s and 1860s, and the kinds of competition—commercial, aesthetic, ideological—encountered by *Household Words* and *All the Year Round*, the two weekly journals edited by Dickens during these decades'. In the second section five contributors—Laura Foster, Ignacio Ramos Gay, Clare Horrocks, John Tullock, and Hannah Lewis-Bill—consider 'the journal's handling of a number of central "Condition of England" questions' (p. xi). In the third section there are seven papers by Helen McKenzie, Jasper Schelstraete, Iain Crawford, Catherine Waters, Daragh Downes, David Parker, and Pete Orford, setting out 'to give some sense of how different contributors responded to the challenge of working for magazines so conspicuously "Conducted by" the most popular writers of their generation' (p. xv), and in the final fourth section six contributors, Judith Flanders, Holly Furneaux, Paul Schlicke, Robert L. Patten, David Paroissien, and Patrick Leary, 'tackle the "Chief" ... as a journalist and a man of letters who by 1850 was already difficult to "know" as anything other than a media creation' (p. xvii). Contributors have made distinguished contributions to the field and this fecund volume accompanied by black and white illustrations concludes with a rather perfunctory double-columned index (pp. 326–32).

Julie Anne Taddeo and Cynthia J. Miller's edited *Steaming into a Victorian Future: A Steampunk Anthology* is a collection of fourteen essays. Miller and Taddeo explain in their introduction that 'originally coined in the late 1980s, the term *steampunk* was applied to describe a group of nineteenth-century inspired technofantasies—darkly atmospheric novels of the time that never was'. These novels ranged 'from K.W. Jeter's *Morlock Night* (1979) and *Infernal Devices* (1987), James P. Blaycock's *Homonculus* (1986) to Tim Powers's *The Anubis Gates* (1983)'. Miller and Taddeo add that 'it is an uncommon hybrid of a term, describing even more uncommon tales of historical science fiction infused with Victorian visions of wildly anachronistic technologies' (p. xv). Their volume 'expands and extends existing scholarship on steampunk in order to explore previously unconsidered questions about cultural creativity, social networking, fandom, appropriation and the creation of meaning'. The chapters 'examine the many and varied manifestations of steampunk, both separately and in relation to each other, in order to better understand the steampunk subculture and its effect on—and interrelationship with—popular culture and the wider society' (p. xviii). Illustrated in black and white, there are three parts: 'Reimagining Characters/Reconfiguring Relationships', with five chapters (pp. 3–102); 'Refurbishing Time and Place', also with five chapters (pp. 105–210); and 'Retrofitting Things', with four chapters (pp. 213–301). In addition to Ken Dvorak's foreword (pp. ix–xi), this well-bound and well-designed volume, contains an afterword by Jeff Vander Meer, 'Steampunk: Looking at the Evidence' (pp. 299–301), followed by an extensive double-columned index (pp. 303–25) and a detailed 'About the Editors, Contributors and Artists' (pp. 327–34). Individual chapters written by different hands are followed by extensive notation and alphabetically arranged enumerative bibliographies.

Joep Leersen and Ann Rigney edit *Commemorating Writers in Nineteenth-Century Europe: Nation-Building and Centenary Fever*. This has fifteen chapters by various hands. Ann Rigney and Joep Leersen observe in their introduction, 'Fanning Out from Shakespeare' (pp. 1–23), that 'in the long century between Garrick's celebration of Shakespeare in 1769 and the outbreak of the First World War, a wave of writers' centenaries passed over Europe involving hyper-canonical writers like Shakespeare and Dante as well as writers ... who were less well known internationally but were important figures within their national canons'. The volume is 'the first to map the number and frequency of the centenaries, whose impact can still be seen today' (p. 4). Consequently there are chapters by Joep Leersen on 'Schiller 1859: Literary Historicism and Readership Mobilization' (pp. 24–39), Ann Rigney on 'Burns 1859: Embodied Communities and Transnational Federation' (pp. 40–64), the same writer on 'Scott 1871: Celebration as Cultural Diplomacy' (pp. 65–87), and Ronan Kelly on 'Moore 1879: Ireland, America, Australia' (pp. 88–101), Moore in this instance being 'Thomas Moore (1779–1852), known in the 1880s ... as "Ireland's national poet", the "bard of Erin"' (p. 88). Notation is found at the conclusion of the chapter followed by alphabetical enumerative listing of works cited in the chapter. The book is illustrated in black and white, and there is a double-columned name-orientated index (pp. 295–301).

LeRoy Lad Panek's *After Sherlock Holmes: The Evolution of British and American Detective Stories, 1891–1914* is an 'attempt to shed some light on the history of the detective story at the turn of the last century' (p. 3), that is, the period between 1891, the date on which Sherlock Holmes appeared in *The Strand Magazine*, and the outbreak of the First World War. Panek's is as much a reference source as a critical survey. There is a most useful alphabetically arranged, descriptive, double-columned appendix headed 'Biographical Notes', beginning with 'Samuel Hopkins Adams (1871–1958): American journalist, writer, instrumental in the passage of the U.S. Pure Food and Drug Act' of 1906 (p. 203) whose novel *Average Jones* [1911] is discussed (pp. 122–4). The appendix concludes with Israel Zangwill (p. 206). His *The Big Bow Mystery* [1892] is also discussed by Panek (pp. 51–2). There is also an alphabetically arranged listing of works cited (pp. 207–11), and a cumulative index (pp. 213–14).

In her comprehensive, clearly written *Victorian Reformations: Historical Fiction and Religious Controversy, 1820–1900* Miriam Burstein 'insists not only that controversial fiction played a crucial role in nineteenth-century popular religious and literary cultures, but that any study of religion and literature that dismisses them in favor of canonical works badly skewed our understanding of the Victorian religious landscape'. Consequently Burstein provides some of the initial detailed modern critical readings of 'some of the most successful religious novelists—figures like Deborah Alcock, Elizabeth Rundle Charles, A.D. Crake, Lady Georgiana Fullerton, Emily Sarah Holt, Emma Leslie, George E. Sargent and Francis Taylor' amongst others (p. 2). She also provides a detailed, enumerative, alphabetically arranged bibliography of both primary and secondary sources (pp. 263–91). Religion in the nineteenth-century novel is also the subject of Kelsey L. Bennett's *Principle and Propensity: Experience and Religion in the Nineteenth-Century British and American Bildungsroman*. As Bennett states in her preface, hers is a 'book both about the *Bildungsroman* and about the religious and intellectual traditions that inform it' (p. vii). Divided into two parts, the first part of the study is devoted 'to the foundational ideas of self-formation in...English, American, and German evangelical contexts' (p. 19): authors treated range from John Wesley and Jonathan Edwards to Goethe and his *Wilhelm Meister's Apprenticeship*. The second part consists of studies of *Jane Eyre*, *David Copperfield*, Melville's *Pierre*, and *The Portrait of a Lady*. Extensive notation follows the text (pp. 147–70), followed by an alphabetically enumerative listing of works cited (pp. 171–86) and a double-columned index (pp. 187–95). Bennett's study is Anglo-American-orientated, concerned with genre formation, and concentrates upon major writers, whereas Burstein's canvas is the Victorians, religion, and non-canonical authors. A different area is explored in Aaron Worth's short monograph, *Imperial Media: Colonial Networks and Information Technologies in the British Literary Imagination, 1857–1918*. Worth examines 'the media which so decisively shaped the world' during that period. 'It is about the role such media played in helping Britons to conceptualize Imperial systems' during those years (1857–1918), which 'witnessed firsthand the birth of the telephone, phonograph, and cinema as well as, of course, wireless telegraphy' (p. 2). There are chapters on 'Imperial Cybernetics' (pp. 9–35), 'Imperial Projections' (pp. 36–59), 'Imperial Transmissions' (pp. 60–79), and 'Imperial Informatics' (pp. 80–113), and a 'Coda' on 'Post-Imperial Media' (pp. 114–17). Authors and works treated include Kipling, Marie Corelli—*A Romance of Two Worlds*—H. Rider Haggard—*She*—H.G. Wells (the front-cover image is from his *The First Men in the Moon*), and John Buchan. Extensive notation follows the text (pp. 119–33), and there is an enumerative, alphabetically arranged bibliography (pp. 134–41) and an index (pp. 142–6).

In spite of rumours to the contrary, publishers are still publishing studies of individual authors. Brian Gibson's *Reading of Saki: The Fiction of H.H. Munro* constitutes the most detailed analytical, critical, and scholarly treatment, as opposed to a biography, of the late Victorian and Edwardian short-story writer to date. Munro (1870–1916) used the pen name Saki. Gibson attempts to 'illuminate the gap between Munro and Saki—the latter depending, though with dissidence, on the former's English society—while exploring many of the cross-currents and tensions in both Munro's England and Saki's tales' (p. 2). 'A Note on the Source Text and on Saki's Uncollected Writings' (pp. 3–4), and 'Introduction: Saki's Dependent Dissidence' (pp. 5–26) are followed by chapters intriguingly entitled '"A Furtive Sinister 'Something'": Saki's Camp' (pp. 27–90), '"The Threat": Saki's Anti-Auntness, Misogyny and Anti-Suffragettism' (pp. 91–149), and '"Cross Currents": Anti-Semitism, Slavic Europe and Britishness in Saki's Fiction' (pp. 150–96). Gibson's 'Conclusion' (pp. 197–215) is followed by three appendices that draw upon archival materials: the annotated 'H.H. Munro's Business Letters to John Lane The Bodley Head Publishing Company, 1911–15' (pp. 217–41); followed by two brief appendices, one containing the text of 'Munro's Letter to the Editor re: Enlistment, *Morning Post*, Wednesday, August 5, 1914' (p. 242), the other a 'Schematic of the Writing Personas of Hector Hugh Munro' (pp. 243–4). The study concludes with extensive double-columned chapter notes (pp. 245–66), an alphabetically arranged annotated bibliography (pp. 267–75), and a useful index (pp. 277–87). Gibson should be complimented on his research, his critical acumen, and his refusal to mitigate Munro's deep personal/creative paradoxes and prejudices. A very different personality is the subject of David M. Friedman's *Wilde in America: Oscar Wilde and the Invention of Celebrity*, a well-written account of Oscar Wilde's 1882, around 1,500-mile tour of North America and visit to 150 American cities. Friedman's study also involves tracing the growth of the celebrity cult, and the final sentence of his book appropriately reads 'The culture of celebrity he [Oscar Wilde] brought to life rose up to take *his*' (p. 258). Accompanied by black and white contemporary photographs and other illustrations (see for instance between pp. 128 and 129), and notes (pp. 261–94), there is also a useful index (pp. 295–316). Finally, mention should be made of two items. The first concerns William Beckford (1759–1844), bibliophile, chiefly remembered for his Gothic fantasy *Vathek* [1786]. The Beckford Society has published Jon Millington's edition of *Conversations with Beckford: Memoirs of William Beckford from the 'New Monthly Magazine' 1844*. These were the work of Beckford's first biographer Cyrus Redding (1785–1870), newspaper and journal editor who subsequently 'mainly devoted his energies to writing anecdotal books about the notable people he met during his journalistic career' (p. vi). Redding formed a close friendship with Beckford during Beckford's latter years. Millington's edition consists of an introduction (pp. v–x), followed by a reprint of the text of his *Conversations* and *Memoirs* without notation. Millington provides a useful index of names to this edition, that retains the original pagination found in the 1844 *New Monthly Magazine*. An excellent addition to textual scholarship and to our understanding of Henry James's working methodology is found in Nicola Bradbury's ' "Like a New Edition of an Old Book": Textual Variation in *The Ambassadors*' (*RES* 65[2014] 137–51). There is no better way of giving an account of Bradbury's article than to cite from her abstract. She writes that 'comparing the first edition of James's novel textually with subsequent versions, but also critically exploring the process of expression within the text, this article argues that editorial processes are central to the construction and experience of the novel, both within the fiction and in its production and reception'. Furthermore, 'textual variation highlights the principle of revision throughout *The Ambassadors* that refines impression and intuition into understanding' (p. 137).

Books Reviewed

Adams, Jenni, ed. *The Bloomsbury Companion to Holocaust Literature*. Bloomsbury. [2014]. pp. x + 337. $172 ISBN 9 7814 4112 9086.

Allen, Nicola, and David Simmons, eds. *Reassessing the Twentieth-Century Canon, from Joseph Conrad to Zadie Smith*. PalMac. [2014]. pp. xvi + 320. $90 ISBN 9 7811 3736 6016.

Austen, Jane. *Volume the First, Volume the Second, and Volume the Third In Her Own Hand series*. Introductions by Kathryn Sutherland. Abbeville. [2014] vol. 1 pp. 256; vol. 2 pp. 336; vol. 3 pp. 192. Boxed set, slipcase $75 ISBN 9 7807 8921 2108.

Baldwin, Peter. *The Copyright Wars: Three Centuries of Trans-Atlantic Battle*. PrincetonUP. [2014]. pp. 536. $35 ISBN 9 7806 9116 1822.

Bann, Stephen, ed. *Midway: Letters from Ian Hamilton Finlay to Stephen Bann 1964–69*. Wilmington. [2014]. pp. 426. £25 ISBN 9 7819 0852 4348.

Bate, Jonathan, and Emma Goodman, eds. *Worcester College: Portrait of an Oxford College*. Third Millennium. [2014]. pp. 224. £32.50 ISBN 9 7819 0650 7725.

Bennett, Kelsey L. *Principle and Propensity: Experience and Religion in the Nineteenth-Century British and American Bildungsroman*. USCP. [2014]. pp. x + 198. $49.95 ISBN 9 7816 1117 3642.

Boyd, Matthieu, ed. *Coire Sois, the Cauldron of Knowledge: A Companion to Early Irish Saga* by Tomás Ó Cathasaigh. UNDP. [2014]. pp. xxx + 618. $72 (e-book $50.40) ISBN 9 7802 6803 7369.

Brack, O.M. Jr., and W.H. Keithley, eds. *The Adventures of Peregrine Pickle. In which are included Memoirs of a Lady of Quality* by Tobias Smollett. Introduction and notes by John P. Zomchick, and George S. Rousseau. UGeoP. [2014] pp. lxviii + 924. $89.95 ISBN 9 7808 2034 5253.

Braddon, Mary Elizabeth. *The Face in the Glass and Other Gothic Tales*. BL. [2014]. pp. 272. £8.99 ISBN 9 7807 1235 7517.

Bredehoft, Thomas A. *The Visible Text: Textual Production and Reproduction from Beowulf to Maus.* OUP. [2014]. pp. x + 188. £18.99 ISBN 9 7801 9960 3152.

Burson, Jeffrey D., ed. *Eighteenth-Century Thought*, vol. 5. AMS [2014] pp. xiv + 266. $137.50 ISBN 9 7804 0463 7651.

Burstein, Miriam Elizabeth. *Victorian Reformations: Historical Fiction and Religious Controversy, 1820–1900.* UNDP. [2014]. pp. 312. $39 ISBN 9 7802 6802 2389.

Calabrese, Michael, and Stephen H.A. Shepherd, eds. *Yee? Baw for Bokes: Essays On Medieval Manuscripts and Poetics in Honor of Hoyt N. Duggan.* Marymount Institute Press/Tsehai. [2013]. pp. x + 296. $64.95 ISBN 9 7809 8396 1635.

Carpenter, Charles A., ed. *Selected Correspondence of Bernard Shaw: Bernard Shaw and Gilbert Murray.* UTorP. [2014]. pp. xlii + 298. $51.99 ISBN 9 7814 4264 3826.

Chalk, Bridget T. *Modernism and Mobility: The Passport and Cosmopolitan Experience.* PalMac. [2014]. pp. xii + 242. $90 ISBN 9 7811 3743 9826.

Chartier, Roger. *The Author's Hand and the Printer's Mind.* Polity. [2014]. pp. xiv + 232. $69.95 ISBN 9 7807 4565 6014.

Clements, Amy Root. *The Art of Prestige: The Formative Years at Knopf, 1915–1929.* UMassP. [2014]. pp. xiv + 208. $22.95 ISBN 9 7816 2534 0931.

Clemit, Pamela, ed. *The Letters of William Godwin*, vol 2: *1798–1805.* OUP. [2014] pp. xlviii + 424. $160 ISBN 9 7801 9956 2626.

Connor, Francis X. *Literary Folios and Ideas of the Book in Early Modern England.* PalMac. [2014]. pp. xii + 236. $95 ISBN 9 7811 3743 8348.

Cook, Christopher D. *Incunabula in the Westminster Abbey and Westminster School Libraries: Bookbinding Descriptions by Mirjam M. Foot.* BibS. [2013]. pp. 183. £45 ISBN 9 7809 4817 0239.

Cook, Michael. *Detective Fiction and the Ghost Story: The Haunted Text.* PalMac. [2014]. pp. viii + 224. $90 ISBN 9 7811 3729 4883.

Cottenet, Cécile, ed. *Race, Ethnicity and Publishing in America.* PalMac. [2014]. pp. xiv + 248. $85 ISBN 9 7811 3739 0516.

Cox, James H., and Daniel Heath Justice, eds. *The Oxford Handbook of Indigenous American Literature.* OUP. [2014]. pp. xxiv + 742. $150 ISBN 9 7801 9991 4036.

Craig, George, Martha Dow Fehsenfeld, Dan Gunn, and Lois More Overbeck, eds. *The Letters of Samuel Beckett*, vol 3: 1957–1965. CUP [2014] pp. xc + 772. $50 ISBN 9 7805 2186 7955.

Duncan, Ian, ed. *Kidnapped* by Robert Louis Stevenson. World's Classics. OUP. [2014]. pp. xxxviii + 218. £7.99 ISBN 9 7801 9967 4213.

Eliot, Valerie, and John Haffenden, eds. *The Letters of T.S. Eliot*, vol. 5: *1930–1931.* Faber. [2014] pp. lxii + 862. £50 ISBN 9 7805 7131 6328.

Ellerton, Nerida F., and M.A. (Ken) Clements. *Abraham Lincoln's Cyphering Book and Ten Other Extraordinary Cyphering Books.* Springer. [2014]. pp. xviii + 368. $179 ISBN 9 7833 1902 5018.

Ellison, Katherine, Kit Kincade, and Holly Faith Nelson, eds. *Topographies of the Imagination: New Approaches to Daniel Defoe.* AMS. [2014]. pp. xxxvi + 336. $115 ISBN 9 7804 0464 8695.

Emerson, Lori. *Reading Writing Interfaces: From the Digital to the Bookbound.* UMinnP. [2014]. pp. xxii + 222. $25 ISBN 9 7808 1669 1265.

Evans, Arthur B., ed. *Vintage Visions: Essays on Early Science Fiction.* WesleyanUP. [2014]. pp. xii + 434. $29.95. ISBN 9 7808 1957 4381.

Fanning, Bryan, and Tom Garvin, *The Books that Define Ireland.* Merrion/ IAP. [2014]. pp. vi + 274. $89.95 ISBN 9 7819 0892 8443.

Fein, Susanna, and Michael Johnston, eds. *Robert Thornton and His Books: Essays on the Lincoln and London Thornton Manuscripts.* YMP/B&B [2014] pp. xii + 314. $99 ISBN 9 7819 0315 3512.

Flood, John., ed. *The Works of Walter Quin: An Irishman at the Stuart Courts.* FCP. [2014]. pp. 292. $74.50 ISBN 9 7818 4682 5040.

Fludernik, Monika, and Miriam Nandi, eds. *Idleness, Indolence and Leisure in English Literature.* PalMac. [2014]. pp. xii + 310. $95 ISBN 9 7811 3740 3995.

Friedman, David M. *Wilde in America; Oscar Wilde and the Invention of Celebrity.* Norton. [2014]. pp. 320. $26.95 ISBN 9 7803 9306 3172.

Galey, Alan. *The Shakespearean Archive: Experiments in New Media from the Renaissance to Postmodernity.* CUP. [2014]. pp. xvi + 332. $95 ISBN 9 7811 0704 0649.

Gibson, Brian. *Reading Saki: The Fiction of H.H. Munro.* McFarland. [2014]. pp. viii + 288. $55 ISBN 9 7807 8647 9498.

Godfrey, Emelyne, ed. *The Convert* by Elizabeth Robins. Twentieth Century Vox. Victorian Secrets. [2014]. pp. 294. £10 ISBN 9 7819 0646 9498.

Gontarski, S.E., ed. *The Edinburgh Companion to Samuel Beckett and the Arts.* EdinUP . [2014]. pp. viii + 504. £150 ISBN 9 7807 4867 5685.

Grant, Stephen H. *Collecting Shakespeare: The Story of Henry and Emily Folger.* JHUP. [2014]. pp. xviii + 246. $29.95 ISBN 9 7814 2141 1873.

Hanna, Ralph, ed. *The Buke of the Howlat,* by Richard Holland. Scottish Text Society. Boydell. [2014]. pp. xiv + 212. $70 ISBN 9 7818 9797 6395.

Hays, Mary. *Female Biography; or, Memoirs of Illustrations and Celebrated Women, of All Ages and Countries* [1803]., in *Memoirs of Women Writers,* ed. Gina Luria Walker. Part III, vols. 8–10. P&C. [2014] pp. viii + 640; viii + 600; viii + 734. $495 ISBN 9 7818 4893 0534.

Heller, Steven, and Gail Anderson. *The Typographic Universe: Letterforms Found in Nature, the Built World and Human Imagination.* T&H. [2014]. pp. 352. $50 ISBN 9 7805 0024 1455.

Hinks, John, and Victoria Gardner, eds. *The Book Trade in Early Modern England: Practices, Perceptions, Connections.* OakK/BL. [2014]. pp. xix + 267. £35 ISBN 9 7807 1235 7111.

Hirschfeld, Heather. *The End of Satisfaction: Drama and Repentance in the Age of Shakespeare.* CornUP. [2014]. pp. xiv + 240. $55 ISBN 9 7808 0145 2741.

Hunt, Tim. *The Textuality of Soulwork: Jack Kerouac's Quest for Spontaneous Prose.* UMichP. [2014]. pp. x + 218. $27.95 ISBN 9 7804 7205 2165.

Inglis, Fred. *Richard Hoggart: Virtue and Reward.* Polity. [2014]. pp. xii + 260. $35 ISBN 9 7807 4565 1712.

Irvine, Robert P., ed. *Prince Otto* by Robert Louis Stevenson. EdinUP. [2014]. pp. liv + 214. £70 ISBN 9 7807 4864 5237.

Jaime de Pablos, María Elena, and Mary Pierse, eds. *George Moore and the Quirks of Human Nature*. Lang. [2014]. pp. x + 280. $64.95 ISBN 9 7830 3431 7528.

Keating, Peter. *Autobiographical Tales*. Priskus. [2013]. pp. xiv + 236. £12.50 ISBN 9 7809 9265 0704.

Kennedy, J. Gerald, and Leland S. Person, eds. *The American Novel to 1870*. Oxford History of the Novel in English 5. OUP. [2014]. pp. xiv + 640. $160 ISBN 9 7801 9538 5359.

Keyes, Thérèse, and Áine McGillicuddy, eds. *Politics and Ideology in Children's Literature*. FCP. [2014]. pp. 192. $70 ISBN 9 7818 4682 5262.

King, Shelley, and John B. Pierce, eds. *The Princess and the Goblin and Other Fairy Tales* by George MacDonald. Broadview. [2014]. pp. 384. $16.95 ISBN 9 7815 5481 0079.

Knowles, Sam. *Travel Writing and the Transnational Author*. PalMac. [2014]. pp. x + 244. $85 ISBN 9 7811 3733 2455.

Koppelman, George, and Daniel Wechsler. *Shakespeare's Beehive: An Annotated Elizabethan Dictionary Comes to Light*. Axletree. [2014]. pp. xii + 400. $75 ISBN 9 7809 9157 3004.

Korey, Marie Elena, ed. *A Long Way from the Armstrong Beer Parlour. A Life in Rare Books: Essays by Richard Landon*. OakK. [2014]. pp. 440. $49.95 ISBN 9 7815 8456 3303.

Larner, Samuel. *Forensic Authorship Analysis and the World Wide Web*. PalMac. [2014]. pp. x + 76. $67.50 ISBN 9 7811 3741 3741.

Latham, Rob, ed. *The Oxford Handbook of Science Fiction*. OUP. [2014]. pp. xviii + 620. $140.17 ISBN 9 7801 9983 8844.

Le Queux, William. *If England Were Invaded*. Bodleian. [2014]. pp. x + 274. £8.99 ISBN 9 7818 5124 4027.

Leersen, Joep, and Ann Rigney eds. *Commemorating Writers in Nineteenth-Century Europe: Nation-Building and Centenary Fever*. PalMac. [2014]. pp. xvi +302. $90 ISBN 9 7811 3741 2133.

Lynch, Claire. *Cyber Ireland: Text, Image, Culture*. PalMac. [2014]. pp. x +180. $95 ISBN 9 7802 3035 8171.

Mackenzie, Hazel, and Ben Winyard, eds. *Charles Dickens and the Mid-Victorian Press, 1850–1870*. UBuckP. [2013]. pp. xxi + 332. £25 ISBN 9 7819 0868 4202.

Macrakis, Kristie. *Prisoners, Lovers, & Spies: The Story of Invisible Ink from Herodotus to al-Qaeda*. YaleUP. [2014]. pp. xiv + 378. $27.50 ISBN 9 7803 0017 9255.

Maltz, Diana, ed. *A Child of the Jago* by Arthur Morrison. Broadview. [2014]. pp. 312. $15.95 ISBN 9 7815 5511 9854.

Mann, Barbara Alice. *The Cooper Connection: The Influence of Jane Austen on James Fenimore Cooper*. AMS. [2014]. pp. xiv + 252. $97.50 ISBN 9 7804 0464 4833.

Marcus, Laura, and Ankhi Mukherjee. *A Concise Companion to Psychoanalysis, Literature, and Culture*. Wiley. [2014]. pp. xiv + 436. $174.95 ISBN 9 7814 0518 8609.

Markham, Sheila. *A Second Book of Booksellers: Conversations with the Antiquarian Book Trade*. Introd. Nicolas Barker. Sheila Markham. [2014]. p. 254. £20 ISBN 9 7809 5479 9724.

May, Steven W., and Arthur E. Marotti. *Ink, Stink Bait, Revenge, and Queen Elizabeth: A Yorkshire Yeoman's Household Book*. CornUP. [2014]. pp. xiv + 274. $24.95 ISBN 9 7808 0145 6565.

Mazur, Dan, and Alexander Danner. *Comics: A Global History, 1968 to the Present*. T&H. [2014]. pp. 320. $39.95 ISBN 9 7805 0029 0965.

McDiarmid, Lucy. *The Literary History of the Meal: Poets and the Peacock Dinner*. OUP. [2014]. pp. xviii + 212. $45 ISBN 9 7801 9872 2786.

McElligott, Jason, and Eve Patten, eds. *The Perils of Print Culture: Book, Print and Publishing History in Theory and Practice*. PalMac. [2014]. pp. xii + 242. $90 ISBN 9 7811 3741 5318.

McNamara, Kevin R. , ed. *The Cambridge Companion to the City in Literature*. CUP. [2014]. pp. xxvii + 290. $29.99 ISBN 9 7811 0760 9150.

Michals, Teresa. *Books for Children, Books for Adults: Age and the Novel from Defoe to James*. CUP. [2014]. pp. x + 278. $95 ISBN 9 7811 0704 8546.

Miller, Julia. *Books Will Speak Plain: A Handbook for Identifying and Describing Historical Bindings*. . Legacy. [2014]. pp. xiii + 544 + CD-ROM. $80 ISBN 9 7809 7979 7477.

Millington, Jon, ed. *Conversations with Beckford: Memoirs of William Beckford from the 'New Monthly Magazine' 1844*. Beckford Society. [2014]. pp. x + 94. £6 ISBN 9 7809 5378 3663.

New, Melvyn, and W.B. Gerard, eds. *The Florida Edition of the Works of Laurence Sterne*, vol 9: *The Miscellaneous Writings and Sterne's Subscribers: An Identification List*. UPFlorida. [2014] pp. xl + 592. $100 ISBN 9 7808 1304 9472.

Nischik, Reingard M. , ed. *The Palgrave Handbook of Comparative North American Literature*. PalMac. [2014]. pp. x + 417. $185 ISBN 9 7811 3741 3895.

Østermark-Johansen, Lena, ed. *Walter Pater: Imaginary Portraits*. MHRA. [2014]. pp. xii + 324. £9.99 ISBN 9 7819 0732 2556.

Panek, LeRoy Lad. *After Sherlock Holmes: The Evolution of British and American Detective Stories, 1891–1914*. McFarland. [2014]. pp. viii + 214. $40 ISBN 9 7807 8647 7654.

Partington, Gill, and Adam Smyth, eds. *Book Destruction from the Medieval to the Contemporary*. PalMac. [2014]. pp. xii + 216. $90 ISBN 9 7811 3736 7655.

Pérez Fernández, José María, and Wilson-Lee Edward, eds. *Translation and the Book Trade in Early Modern Europe*. CUP. [2014]. pp. xii + 272. $99 ISBN 9 7811 0708 0041.

Prickett, Stephen ed. *The Edinburgh Companion to the Bible and the Arts*. EdinUP. [2014]. pp. xxxii + 576. £150 ISBN 9 7807 4863 9335.

Rabaté, Jean-Michel, *The Cambridge Introduction to Literature and Psychoanalysis*. CUP. [2014]. pp. viii + 258. $27.99 ISBN 9 7811 0742 3916.

Rabinowitz, Paula. *American Pulp: How Paperbacks Brought Modernism to Main Street*. PrincetonUP. [2014]. pp. xviii + 390. $29.95 ISBN 9 7806 9115 0604.

Raven, James. *Bookscape: Geographies of Printing and Publishing in London before 1800*. The Panizzi Lectures 2010. BL. [2014]. pp. xvi + 208. £50 ISBN 9 7807 1235 7333.

Raven, James. *Publishing Business in Eighteenth-Century England*. Boydell. [2014]. pp. xiv + 334. $29.95 ISBN 9 7818 4383 9101.

Richmond, Velma Bourgeois. *Chivalric Stories as Children's Literature: Edwardian Retellings in Words and Pictures*. McFarland. [2014]. pp. viii + 374. $55 ISBN 9 7807 8649 6228.

Roberts, Daniel Sanjiv, ed. *The History of Arsaces, Prince of Betlis* by Charles Johnstone. FCP. [2014]. pp. 238. $74.50 ISBN 9 7818 4682 3985.

Robinson, Daniel. *Myself and Some Other Being: Wordsworth and the Life of Writing*. UIowaP. [2014]. pp. xii + 122. $17 ISBN 9 7816 0938 2322.

Rohrbach, Augusta. *Thinking Outside the Book*. UMassP. [2014]. pp. xiv + 162. $24.95 ISBN 9 7816 2534 1266.

Rose, Jonathan. *The Literary Churchill: Author, Reader, Actor*. YaleUP. [2014]. pp. xii + 516. $35 ISBN 9 7803 0020 4070.

Rosner, Victoria, ed. *The Cambridge Companion to the Bloomsbury Group*. CUP. [2014]. pp. xiv + 246. $80 ISBN 9 7811 0701 8242.

Russell, Richard Rankin, ed. *Peter Fallon: Poet, Publisher, Editor and Translator*. IAP. [2014]. pp. xxviii + 268. $89.95 ISBN 9 7807 1653 1593.

Smith, K.J.M., ed. *Selected Writings of James Fitzjames Stephen: A General View of the Criminal Law of England*. OUP. [2014]. pp. 410. £110 ISBN 9 7801 9966 0834.

Solomonescu, Yasmin. *John Thelwall and the Materialist Imagination*. PalMac. [2014]. pp. xii + 226. $85 ISBN 9 7811 3742 6130.

Supino, David J. *Henry James: A Bibliographical Catalogue of a Collection of Editions to 1921*. 2nd edn. LiverUP. [2014]. pp. xxxiv + 650. £80 ISBN 9 7818 4631 8627.

Swan, Jesse G., ed. *Editing Lives: Essays in Contemporary Textual and Biographical Studies in Honor of O.M. Brack, Jr*. BuckUP. [2014]. pp. xxx + 262. $85 ISBN 9 7816 1148 5400.

Taddeo, Julie Ann, and Cynthia J. Miller, eds. *Steaming into a Victorian Future: A Steampunk Anthology*. Scarecrow. [2013]. pp. xxvi + 340. £49.95 ISBN 9 7808 1088 5868.

Tarlinskaja, Marina. *Shakespeare and the Versification of English Drama, 1561–1642*. Ashgate. [2014]. pp. xii + 412. £67.50 ISBN 9 7814 7243 0281.

Tieken-Boon van Ostade, Ingrid. *In Search of Jane Austen: The Language of the Letters*. OUP. [2014]. pp. xiv + 282. £41.99 ISBN 9 7801 9994 5115.

Turner, James. *Philology: The Forgotten Origins of the Modern Humanities*. PrincetonUP. [2014]. pp. xxiv + 550. $35 ISBN 9 7806 9114 5648.

Watts, Cedric. *Shakespeare Puzzles*. PublishNation. [2014]. pp. 128. $10.26 ISBN 9 7812 9166 4102.

Weingart, Wolfgang. *My Way to Typography: Retrospective in Ten Sections [2000]*. Lars Müller. [2014]. pp. 520. $37.84 ISBN 9 7830 3778 4266.

Wiggins, Martin, in association with Catherine Richardson. *British Drama 1533–1642: A Catalogue*, vol. 4: *1598–1602*. OUP. [2014] pp. xiv + 474. $160 ISBN 9 7801 9926 5749.

Winn, James Anderson. *Queen Anne, Patroness of Arts.* OUP. [2014]. pp. xxii + 792. $39.95 ISBN 9 7801 9937 2195.

Worth, Aaron. *Imperial Media: Colonial Networks and Information Technologies in the British Literary Imagination, 1857–1918.* OSUP. [2014]. pp. viii + 152. $49.95 ISBN 9 7808 1421 2516.

Yamashiro, Shin. *American Sea Literature: Seascapes, Beach Narratives, and Underwater Explorations.* PalMac. [2014]. pp. viii + 128. $67.50 ISBN 9 7822 3746 5665.

Yeats, W.B. *On Baile's Strand: Manuscript Materials,* ed. Jared Curtis and Declan Kiely. The Cornell Yeats. CornUP. [2014]. pp. lviii + 596. $140 ISBN 9 7808 0145 261.

Zim, Rivkah. *The Consolations of Writing: Literary Strategies of Resistance from Boethius to Primo Levi.* PrincetonUP. [2014]. pp. xii + 324. $35 ISBN 9 7806 9116 1808.

YWES Index of Critics

The Year's Work in English Studies, Volume 95 (2016) © The Author 2016. Published by Oxford University Press on behalf of the English Association. All rights reserved.
For Permissions, please email: journals.permissions@oup.com
doi:10.1093/ywes/maw022

YWES Index of Authors and Subjects

Notes

(1) Material which has not been seen by contributors is not indexed.

(2) Authors such as Don Paterson, who are both authors of criticism and subjects of discussion, are listed in whichever index is appropriate for each reference.

(3) Author entries have subdivisions listed in the following order:
    (a) author's relationship with other authors
    (b) author's relationship with other subjects
    (c) author's characteristics
    (d) author's works (listed alphabetically)

(5) A page reference in **bold** represents a main entry for that particular subject.